PEUGEOT GOLF GUIDE
1998

BELGIUM / BELGIQUE / BELGIË / BELGIEN / BÉLGICA

FRANCE / FRANKREICH / FRANCIA

GERMANY / DEUTSCHLAND / ALLEMAGNE / ALEMANIA

GREAT BRITAIN & IRELAND:

ENGLAND / SCOTLAND / WALES

IRELAND / NORTHERN IRELAND

LUXEMBOURG / LUXEMBURG / LUXEMBURGO

THE NETHERLANDS / NEDERLAND / HOLLANDE / HOLANDA

PORTUGAL

SPAIN / ESPAÑA / ESPAGNE / SPANIEN

SWITZERLAND / SUISSE / SCHWEIZ / SVIZZERA / SUIZA

EDITIONS D & G MOTTE

A longside all the other challenges that Automobiles Peugeot have taken on board in recent times, sport in general has always had the backing of a company that is keen to develop image and awareness in an active and prestigious style. Over the years, golf has become one of the major vectors for this development through our support for a whole range of amateur and professional events on five continents. The Peugeot Golf Guide was naturally bound to meet the wants and needs of players who are constantly on the look-out for new horizons. This year, besides the countries already featured, we have completed our study of courses in the British Isles, the historical home of golf and the last stage before completing our full tour of golf around Europe next year.

D abeisein, Mitwirken, Herausforderungen wahrnehmen - diese Ziehle möchte der Autohersteller Peugeot nicht nur erfolgreich im Autorennsport, sondern auch in anderen Bereichen und in anderen Sportarten verwirklichen und vor allem auch andere daran teilhaben lassen. So ist denn der Golfsport zu einem der wichtigsten Erfolgsfaktoren für das Image und die Bekanntheit unserer Gesellschaft weltweit geworden. Amateure und Pros haben uns dies auch immer wieder bestätigt, dass unser Unternehmen heute zu den massgebenden Förderern des Golfs zählt, insbesondere in Europa. Mit unserer Leidenschaft und unserem Verständnis für diesen Sport, die uns immer wieder von neuem inspirieren, möchten wir den Golfern in nichts nachstehen, die anhand des vorliegenden Peugeot Golf Guide immer wieder neue Orte und Plätze entdecken können. Dieser erste kritische Golf-Führer Europas, der Jahr für Jahr umfangreicher wird, findet aufgrund der sorgfältigen und strengen Kriterien, bereits bei allen Golfern grosse Beachtung.

A u delà des défis automobiles qu'Automobiles Peugeot a toujours relevés avec succès, le sport en général a toujours bénéficié du soutien de notre société, soucieuse de développer son image et sa notoriété de manière active et prestigieuse. Le golf est devenu au fil des années l'un des principaux vecteurs de ce développement, au travers du soutien de tout un ensemble d'épreuves amateurs et professionnelles sur les cinq continents. Le Peugeot Golf Guide devait naturellement répondre aux demandes des joueurs, sans cesse à la recherche de nouveaux espaces. Cette année, à côté des pays déjà étudiés, nous complétons l'examen des parcours des Iles Britanniques, foyer historique du golf, dernière étape avant d'achever l'an prochain le tour complet de l'Europe du golf.

A demás de los desafíos que los Automóviles Peugeot han abordado con éxito, el deporte en general se ha beneficiado siempre del apoyo de nuestra empresa, que ha cuidado el desarrollo de su imagen y notoriedad de manera activa y prestigiosa. El golf se ha convertido de año en año en uno de los motores de ese desarrollo, mediante el apoyo de todo un conjunto de competiciones tanto de aficionados como de profesionales en los cinco continentes. La Guía de Golf Peugeot debía corresponder a los deseos de los jugadores, siempre en busca de nuevos espacios. Este año, además de los países anteriormente presentados, hemos completado el estudio de los recorridos de las Islas Británicas, cuna histórica del golf y etapa última antes de finalizar el próximo año la vuelta completa de la Europa del golf.

Eric Peugeot

3

"Un swing, c'est comme une signature."

Fred Couples

Depuis qu'il a rejoint le circuit professionnel en 1980, Fred Couples a ébloui le monde du golf par son immense talent naturel. Avec son swing merveilleusement rythmé, qui semble n'être, pour beaucoup, qu'une simple frappe de balle, Couples offre au public une démonstration saisissante de puissance et de finesse.

Couples fait rêver le monde du golf en atteignant le plus haut niveau de performances tout en restant fidèle à un style personnel, fait d'aisance et de décontraction. Il n'est donc pas surprenant qu'il ait choisi une montre qui allie la performance et le style avec autant de succès. Une Rolex Day-Date.

Rolex Day-Date. Chronomètre en or 18 ct. Également disponible en or gris ou en platine.
Documentation sur demande à : Rolex France, 3 avenue Ruysdaël - 75008 Paris.

GOLFEUR

ARRIVER DÉTEN[
C'EST DÉJ[

EUROPCAR PROPOSE AUX PASSIONNÉS D[
POUR TOUTE INFORMAT[
POUR BÉNÉFICIER DU TARIF PRIVILÉG[

VOUS LOUEZ PLUS QU'UNE VO[

BATES

RS,
U SUR LE PARCOURS
À ÇA DE GAGNÉ.

If
you're going to take on
the world
you'd better be prepared.

If you have a business and would like more information
about accepting American Express call UK 0800 33 99 11.
Germany 0180 530 1133. France 01 47 77 75 75.

do more

CONTENTS

Page

SOMMAIRE

Page

HOW TO USE YOUR PEUGEOT GOLF GUIDE
COMMENT UTILISER LE PEUGEOT GOLF GUIDE

POSITION ON THE MAP

Situation sur la carte	Läge på kartan
Lage auf der Karte	Placering på kortet
Situación en el mapa	Kartta-sivu
Situatie op de kaart	Avmerket sted
Localização no mapa	på kartet
Posizione sulla carta	

PHONE NUMBER FOR BOOKING OFFICE

Numéro de téléphone pour réserver
Telefonnummer für Reservierung
Numero de teléfono para reservar
Tel No voor reserveringen
Numero de telefone para reservar
Numero telefonico per prenotare
Telefonnummer för reservation
Telefonnummer til reservation af starttid
Lähtöajan varaus
Telefonnummer forå bestille tee-time

FEES MAIN SEASON
Tarifs en haute saison
Preisliste hochsaison
Precios temporada alta
Hoogseizoen tarieve
Tarifas da época alta
Tariffe alta stagione
Tariff hög säsong
Priser i højsæson
Green-fees
Tariffer i høysesongen

POSITION ON THE MAP
Situation sur la carte
Lage auf der Karte
Situación en el mapa
Situatie op de kaart
Localização no mapa
Posizione sulla carta
Läge på kartan
Placering på kortet
Kartta-sivu
Avmerket sted på kartet

When calling from abroad, remember to omit the first digit (nearly always a 0) immediately after the international dialling code. E.g.: for (49) 09178 - 98 960, dial (49) 9178 98 960

ROYAL NORTH DEVON (Westward Ho!) | 18 | 6 | 6

This is the oldest links course in England. If you are disappointed when you set eyes on the flat-looking terrain, you certainly won't be once you are out on the course. It might look gentle, but it doesn't play that way. Take the difficulties for example: tight fairways, invisible ditches, small deep bunkers lined with railway sleepers, very well protected greens where the approach is sometimes blind and rough with sea-gorse where it is nigh on impossible to get the ball back onto the fairway. Sheep crop the grass and bleat at the top of your backswing, and then there is the wind. If you can keep the ball low, if you know your strengths and weaknesses, if you stay humble in your ambitions and if someone accompanies you around this huge open space, you can spend a great day and get the impression of having walked around a piece of golfing history.

Le plus vieux links d'Angleterre. L'arrivée à "Westward Ho!" peut paraître décevante tant le terrain est sans relief, mais votre partie ne va pas en manquer : c'est beaucoup moins tranquille qu'il n'y paraît. D'abord, les difficultés : fairways étroits, fossés invisibles, bunkers petits et profonds, parfois bordés de traverses, greens très défendus et dont l'entrée est parfois aveugle, dans les roughs et buissons de joncs marins d'où il est impossible de sortir. Des moutons broutent le gazon et bêlent quand vous êtes en haut du backswing. Il y a aussi du vent. Si vous savez jouer des balles basses, si vous connaissez bien vos forces et vos faiblesses, si vous envisagez humblement ce parcours, et si quelqu'un vous oriente dans cet immense espace, vous passerez une merveilleuse journée en ayant l'impression d'avoir fait vos pas dans l'histoire.

Royal North Devon Golf Club
Golf Links Road, Westward Ho!
ENG - BIDEFORD, Devon EX39 7HD

Office	Secrétariat	(44) 01237 - 473 817
Pro shop	Pro-shop	(44) 01237 - 477 598
Fax	Fax	(44) 01237 - 473 456
Situation	Situation	

4 km from Bideford (pop. 13 070)
12 km from Barnstaple (pop. 20 740)

Annual closure	Fermeture annuelle	no
Weekly closure	Fermeture hebdomadaire	no
Book for meals		

Fees main season	Tarifs haute saison	18 holes
	Week days	We/Bank holidays
	Semaine	We/Férié
Individual Individuel	£ 28	£ 34
Couple Couple	£ 56	£ 68
Full day: £ 34 - £ 36 (weekends)		

Caddy	Caddy	no
Electric Trolley	Chariot électrique	no
Buggy	Voiturette	no
Clubs	Clubs	£ 15/day

Credit cards Cartes de crédit
VISA - Eurocard - MasterCard

534

Access Accès : M5 Exit 27, A361 to Barnstaple, then A39 through Northam, take road down Bone Hill past Post Office, keep on left, Clubhouse ahead on hill.
Map 6 on page 416 Carte 6 page 416

GOLF COURSE PARCOURS | 18/20

Site	Site	
Maintenance	Entretien	
Architect	Architecte	Old Tom Morris
Type	Type	links
Relief	Relief	
Water in play	Eau en jeu	
Exp. to wind	Exposé au vent	
Trees in play	Arbres en jeu	

Scorecard	Chp.	Mens	Ladies
Carte de score	Chp.	Mess.	Da.
Length Long.	5930	5758	5137
Par	71	72	73

Advised golfing ability		0 12 24 36
Niveau de jeu recommandé		
Hcp required	Handicap exigé	certificate

CLUB HOUSE & AMENITIES CLUB HOUSE ET ANNEXES | 6/10

Pro shop	Pro-shop	
Driving range	Practice	
Sheltered	couvert	no
On grass	sur herbe	yes
Putting-green	putting-green	yes
Pitching-green	pitching green	yes

HOTEL FACILITIES ENVIRONNEMENT HOTELIER | 6/10

HOTELS HOTELS

Anchorage Hotel - 17 rooms, D £ 50 Tel (44) 01271 - 860 655 Fax (44) 01271 - 860 767	Instow 7 km
Newbridge - 10 rooms, D £ 65 Tel (44) 01237 - 474 989 Fax (44) 01237 - 474 989	Northam 1 km
Durrant House - 123 rooms, D £ 65 Tel (44) 01237 - 472 361 Fax (44) 01237 - 421 709	Northam 1 km

RESTAURANT RESTAURANT

The Beaver Inn Tel (44) 01237 - 474 822	Appledore 2 km

PEUGEOT GOLF GUIDE 1998

LITTLE	MUCH
Peu	Beaucoup
Wenig	Viel
Poco	Mucho
Weinig	Veel
Pouco	Muito
Poco	Molto
Få	Många
Lille	Meget
Vähän	Paljon
Lite	Mye

ADVISED GOLFING ABILITY (HCP)

```
0   12   24   36
0 ──► 24
```

Niveau de jeu recommandé
Empfohlene Spielstärke
Nivel de juego aconselado
Aanbevolen golfvaardigheid
Nivel de jogo recomendado
Livello di gioco consigliato
Rekommenderad spelnivå
Anbefalet golfkunnen
Tasoitusvaatimus
Anbefalt golfnivå

FAIR	EXCELLENT
Passable	Excellent
Mittelmässig	Hervorragend
Mediana	Excelente
Aanvaardboar	Uitstekend
Suficiente	Excelente
Passabile	Eccellente
Godkänd	Förträflig
Rimelig	Fantastik
Hyvä	Erinomainen
Godbra	Utmerket

WIE DER PEUGEOT GOLF GUIDE BENUTZT WIRD
COMO UTILIZAR SU PEUGEOT GOLF GUIDE

RECOMMENDED HOLIDAYS

Vacances recommandées
Empfohlener Ferienort
Sitio de vacaciones recomendado
Aanbevolen vacantie-oord
Local de férias recomendado

Località di vacanze raccomandata
Rekommenderad semesterort
Anbefalet som feriested
Suositellaan lomanviettopaikkana
Anbefalt feriested

RECOMMENDED GOLFING STAY

Séjour de golf recommandé
Empfohlener Golf Aufenthalt
Estancia de golf recomendada
Aanbevolen golf vacantie
Estadia de golf recomendada
Soggiorno golfitistico raccomandato
Rekommenderad golfvistelse
Anbefalet til golfophold
Suositellaan golfin pelaamisen
Anbefalt golfopphold

ROYAL ST GEORGE'S　　　　19　7　5

This is the sort of masterpiece that defies description. If a golf course is to be an adversary offering the toughest resistance to every shot, giving the player the opportunity to shine, sometimes forcing you to take the longer path to get a better shot at your goal, provoking the harder golfer before breaking him completely but respecting the wise and the knowledgeable, then Royal St. George is one of the very greatest of them all. If we had to find one fault with this regular venue for the British Open, it would be the fact that not all the hazards are clearly visible. You have to play the course every day to uncover its secrets but this is a privilege reserved for members only. Although the course is open during the week, we would advise visitors to play with a member, or at least with a caddie. You'll enjoy the experience even more.

C'est le genre de chef d'oeuvre qui échappe à toute description. Si un parcours de golf doit être un adversaire qui se défend contre tous les coups, offre des chances de briller à son adversaire, oblige parfois à contourner son objectif pour mieux y revenir ensuite, provoque les téméraires pour mieux les détruire, respecte les sages et les savants, Royal St George's est un des très grands parcours de golf. S'il est un seul défaut à ce links où le British Open revient régulièrement, c'est que tous les obstacles ne sont pas clairement visibles : il faudrait le jouer tous les jours pour en découvrir les secrets, et seuls les membres ont ce privilège. Bien que le parcours soit ouvert en semaine, on conseillera aux visiteurs de jouer avec eux, ou au moins de louer les services d'un caddie. Le plaisir n'en sera que plus grand encore.

17

Royal St George's Golf Club
ENG - SANDWICH, Kent CT13 9PB

Office	Secrétariat	(44) 01304 - 613090
Pro shop	Pro-shop	(44) 01304 - 615236
Fax	Fax	(44) 01304 - 611245
Situation	Situation	

2 km from Sandwich
7 km from Deal (pop. 28 504)

Annual closure	Fermeture annnuelle	no
Weekly closure	Fermeture hebdomadaire	
Fees main season	Tarifs haute saison	18 holes

	Week days Semaine	We/Bank holidays We/Férié
Individual Individuel	£ 60	no
Couple Couple	£ 120	no

No visitors during Weekends -
Permission required for Ladies to play

Caddy	Caddy	on request/£ 20
Electric Trolley	Chariot électrique	no
Buggy	Voiturette	no
Clubs	Clubs	no
Credit cards Cartes de crédit		no

GOLF
A 257 Canterbury
Ramsgate
Sandwich — Sandwich Bay
R. Stour
Hacklinge — A 258
A2 — Dover — Deal

Access Accès : Sandwich → "Golf Courses" x km along Sandown Road. Club drive on left after last houses
Map 7 on page 419 Carte 7 Page 419

PEUGEOT GOLF GUIDE 1998

GOLF COURSE
PARCOURS　　　　19/20

Site	Site	
Maintenance	Entretien	
Architect	Architecte	Dr W. Laidlaw Purves
Type	Type	seaside course, links
Relief	Relief	
Water in play	Eau en jeu	
Exp. to wind	Exposé au vent	
Trees in play	Arbres en jeu	

Scorecard Carte de score	Chp. Chp.	Mens Mess.	Ladies Da.
Length Long.	6174	5904	0
Par	70	70	0

Advised golfing ability Niveau de jeu recommandé	0 12 24 36
Hcp required	Handicap exigé	18 Men, 15 Ladies

CLUB HOUSE & AMENITIES
CLUB HOUSE ET ANNEXES　　　　7/10

Pro shop	Pro-shop	
Driving range	Practice	
Sheltered	couvert	no
On grass	sur herbe	yes
Putting-green	putting-green	yes
Pitching-green	pitching green	no

535

HOTEL FACILITIES
ENVIRONNEMENT HOTELIER　　　　5/10

HOTELS HOTELS

Bell Hotel - 29 rooms, D £ 100 Tel (44) 01304 - 613 388 Fax (44) 01304 - 615 308	Sandwich 2 km	
Jarvis Marina - 59 rooms, D £ 69 Tel (44) 01843 - 588 276 Fax (44) 01843 - 586 866	Ramsgate 12 km	
San Clu - 32 rooms, D £ 80 Tel (44) 01843 - 592 345 Fax (44) 01843 - 580 157	Ramsgate 12 km	

RESTAURANTS RESTAURANTS

Dunkerleys Restaurant Tel (44) 01304 - 375016	Deal 7 km
Griffins Head	Chillenden 10 km

SCORE FOR THE COURSE (1 TO 20)
Note du parcours (1 à 20)
Benotung des Platzes (1 bis 20)
Nota del campo (1 a 20)
Waardering van de baan (1 tot 20)
Nota do percurso (1 a 20)
Giudizio sul percorso (1 a 20)
Banans betyg (1 till 20)
Klassificering af banen (1 til 20)
Kentän laatuluokitus (1 to 20)
Rangering av golfbanen (1-20)

SCORE FOR THE CLUB HOUSE
AND ANNEXES (1 TO 10)
Note du Club House et annexes (1 à 10)
Benotung des Klubhauses (1 bis 10)
Nota del Club House (1 a 10)
Waardering van het Club House (1 tot 10)
Nota do Club House (1 a 10)
Giudizio sul Club House (1 a 10)
Klubhus betyg (1 till 10)
Klassificering af Klubhuset (1 til 10)
Klubitalon laatuluokitus (1 to 10)
Rangering av Klubhus (1-10)

SCORE FOR HOTEL FACILITIES (1 TO 10)
Note de l'environnement hôtelier (1 à 10)
Benotung des Hotelangebots (1 bis 10)
Nota del complejo hotelero (1 a 10)
Waardering van het Hotel
and ongeving (1 tot 10)
Nota das infraestructuras hoteleiras (1 a 10)
Giudizio su offerta alberghiera (1 a 10)
Hotellomgivningens betyg (1 till 10)
Klassificering af hotelfaciliteterne (1 til 10)
Hotellin laatuluokitus (1 to 10)
Rangering av Hotel (1-10)

7

6

D 1000 F: BEST ROOM PRICE FOR 2 PEOPLE (MAIN SEASON)

Premier prix chambre 2 personnes (haute saison)
Preis Hotelzimmer für 2 personen (Hauptsaison)
Primer precio habitación 2 personas (temporada alta)
1e Klas prijs 2 persoons kamer (hoog seizoen)
Primeiro preço quarto duplo (época alta)
Primo prezzo camera doppia (2 persone), alta stagione
Lägsta rumspris för 2 pers. under högsäsong
Lavere pris for dobbeltværelse (højsæson)
Alennus 2-hengen huoneesta
Lavere pris for et tommans rom (høysesong)

Bell Hotel
RECOMMENDED BY
THE PEUGEOT GOLF GUIDE

Recommandé par le Peugeot Golf Guide
Empfohlen durch Peugeot Golf Guide
Recomendado por el Peugeot Golf Guide
Aanbevolen door de Peugeot Golf Guide
Recomendado pelo Peugeot Golf Guide
Raccomandato da Peugeot Golf Guide
Rekommanderat av Peugeot Golf Guide
Anbefalet af Peugeot Golf Guide
Opaan suositettelema (Peugeot Golf Guide)
Anbefalt av Peugeot Golf Guide

Une jeune banque de 142 ans.

La Banque Piguet compte parmi les plus anciennes banques suisses. Les traditions d'excellence en matière de banque et de finance, profondément enracinées dans notre établissement, se sont alliées à la solidité de l'un des quatre plus grands groupes bancaires du pays, la Banque Cantonale Vaudoise.

Notre nouveau logo, la feuille de chêne, affirme ce changement tout comme les forces de la Banque Piguet: des notions telles que solidité, confidentialité, dynamisme et croissance. Avec ces atouts, nous nous sommes employés à définir une stratégie de croissance claire et solide, basée sur l'anticipation, pour aborder le 21e siècle en toute confiance.

Si notre banque a connu de profonds changements au cours de ces dernières années, il demeure un point immuable à la Banque Piguet: le temps que nous consacrons à échafauder des solutions taillées sur mesure, construites pour répondre aux besoins spécifiques de chacun de nos clients.

Banque Piguet. Après un siècle et demi d'existence, nous restons plus jeunes que jamais.

BANQUE PIGUET & CIE S.A.

DEPUIS 1856

GENÈVE
TÉLÉPHONE: (+41 22) 311 27 00
FAX: (+41 22) 311 26 80

LAUSANNE
TÉLÉPHONE: (+41 21) 310 10 10
FAX: (+41 21) 310 10 20

YVERDON-LES-BAINS
TÉLÉPHONE: (+41 24) 423 43 00
FAX: (+41 24) 423 43 05

PEUGEOT GOLF GUIDE FOREWORD

A REAL GUIDE

Was there a need for a new golf guide when there are already so many to choose from? We thought so, because as opposed to hotel or restaurant guides, there was no such thing as a qualitative guide to golf courses. It is the clubs themselves which supply existing guides with course information, which understandably always paint a positive picture. Yet as all golf-lovers know, every course is different and standards of excellence vary. Besides the unquestionable class of championship courses that everyone wants to play, there are all the others. «Remoter» courses, little gems in the depths of Europe, public courses with simple layouts whose sole ambition is to school new golfers, pretentiously labelled «international» courses where layouts often have no regard for common sense, and the small budget courses where the architect has worked wonders...

It was high time someone did some basic research work into European golf courses to draw up a sort of qualifying list of excellence, a ranking seen fairly and squarely from the point of view of users or «consumers», i.e. the people who pay to play and who look for service to match their expectations. It is, of course, impossible to erase all subjectivity when making a judgment, but it should be said that in most cases, the opinions of the contributors to this guide often tended to converge, despite a difference in traditions and levels of golfing proficiency. A sort of consensus was reached, over and above personal persuasions.

VISITS TO 1,100 COURSES

Over the past five years, we have visited and played 1,100 18-hole golf courses. We did so anonymously so we could see them in their usual condition, just like an ordinary golfer. While some clubs may not feel too happy about our sometimes ruthless verdicts, it is up to them and to them alone to make the improvements that are called for. We have nonetheless weighted our appreciation according to the time and season of our visits, the age of the course and periodical problems of maintenance. In other words we have attempted to be as objective as possible in our subjective views.

THREE SCORES FOR EACH COURSE

In our scoring system, the score for the course is explicitly given out of 20, while the score for the club-house/facilities and local hotel accommodation are clearly marked out of 10. So to our mind, the actual course score has a greater significance, while the other marks allows us to tone down the considerable differences seen in golfing and hotel accommodation from one country to the next.

On each page you will find the three scores in the top right-hand corner. The first concerns the actual course, the second is for the Club-House and facilities, and the third is for surrounding hotel accomodation. A little golfer indicates a few days golfing is recommended, a sun recommends a full holiday stay.

17

750 SELECTED COURSES

Of the 1,100 courses we played, we selected 750 which are open to the public, at least during weekdays. But we have also included a selection of private courses where you can always try your

Sentir bon. Se sentir bien.

EAU DYNAMISANTE CLARINS.

Le plaisir du parfum, l'efficacité des plantes.

Première Eau de Toilette de Beauté, l'Eau Dynamisante parfume, hydrate,* raffermit, vitalise. D'un seul geste, elle offre réunis, le parfum et l'action traitante des plantes.

* Les couches supérieures de l'épiderme.

Pour elle comme pour lui.

Eau Dynamisante, un regain de fraîcheur et de dynamisme, à tout moment de la journée, même sous le soleil.

Le plaisir décliné.

Lait Hydratant Parfumé, pour une peau souple, lisse et satinée. Gel Moussant Parfumé, d'une douceur extrême, pour la douche et le bain.

CLARINS
PARIS

L'expérience et l'efficacité du soin.

Une question-beauté? Demandez conseil à votre parfumeur ou écrivez à Clarins qui vous répondra personnellement.

Clarins Conseil. 4, rue Berteaux-Dumas 92203 Neuilly-sur-Seine Cedex.

luck. The Peugeot Golf Guide will be evolutive and updated each year thanks to visits from our «inspectors». The latter are not necessarily players of the highest level, but this is consistent with the fact that the majority of golfers have a handicap on the wrong side of 18 and that they are the ones of whom our «recommendations» are primarily directed. So some courses will be ruled out of future editions, others will be included. The scores for each course will also be liable to change.

STANDARD OF FACILITIES

We gave a general score to the course, but in the same way we also assessed the quality of the Club-House and related services: styling and comfort of buildings, practice and additional facilities such as tennis courts and swimming pool. We also took hospitality into consideration, an aspect, it should be said, that is not always very professional especially concerning the accuracy of informations.

SURROUNDING HOTEL ACCOMMODATION

Lastly, we assessed the regions's hotel facilities. Some highly reputed restaurants were thus selected, as were hotels and guest houses from different categories so that there would be something for every budget. As with the courses, we will in the future take account of any changes and of «nice little addresses» (not necessarily the best known) that might be recommended to us by specialists from the region in question. The score we have given is not confined solely to our assessment of hotel standards, because it indicates most importantly the numbers and diversity of hotel facilities within the immediate vicinity of the golf.

THE FUTURE EDITIONS

One last word to stress the fact that inaccuracies or errors are bound to creep in when working with such a mass of information. We are fully aware of this and consequently would very much like our readers, and the clubs themselves, to send us their remarks. Our aim is not systematically to criticise clubs, but to help them realise, whenever necessary, the shortcomings of their course and facilities, to help put things right when economically possible, improve standards of hospitality and adopt the customer service policy that is essential in a world of free enterprise and competition. Their prosperity depends on their reputation, their vigilance and their quality standards... rather as if each golfer were sent to play by this guide as an «inspector». After the third edition, in which we added the best courses in Germany, Ireland and the Netherlands to those already in the guide, this year we have completed our tour of the British Isles. In the next edition, we will have a full overview of the best golf courses in Europe.

PEUGEOT GOLF GUIDE AVANT-PROPOS ET PHILOSOPHIE

19

UN VÉRITABLE "GUIDE"

Contrairement aux guides des hôtels ou des restaurants, il n'existe aucun guide qualitatif des parcours à l'échelle européenne. Les guides existants se rapprochent souvent des annuaires, et reproduisent les informations fournies par les Clubs. Elles sont favorables, c'est normal. Mais, tous les amateurs de golf le savent, la qualité des parcours

Polo
Ralph Lauren

A Man's Fragrance in the Polo Tradition

est variable. A côté des parcours de championnat, que les meilleurs veulent affronter, il est des parcours ignorés qui sont de petits joyaux, des golfs publics au dessin très simple et aux ambitions réduites, des parcours prétentieux et décevants, des parcours à petit budget où l'architecte a fait des prodiges... Nous avons voulu entreprendre un travail de fond sur les golfs d'Europe, en se situant résolument du côté des utilisateurs, des "consommateurs", de ceux qui paient pour jouer et attendent un service à hauteur de leurs attentes. Bien sûr, tout jugement qualitatif est subjectif, nos critiques ne sauraient échapper à la critique, mais il faut reconnaître que les avis des différents collaborateurs de ce guide, de niveaux golfiques et de traditions différentes, ont convergé dans la plupart des cas. Après la troisième édition, où les meilleurs parcours d'Allemagne, d'Irlande et des Pays-Bas s'étaient ajoutés aux autres pays, nous terminons cette année le tour des Iles Britanniques. La prochaine édition complètera l'Europe.

1.100 PARCOURS VISITÉS

Nous avons visité et joué 1.100 parcours de 18 trous au cours des cinq dernières années. Et chaque fois de manière anonyme, ce qui permettait de les voir dans leur état habituel, comme n'importe quel golfeur. Certains clubs pourront s'estimer mécontents de nos jugements parfois cruels, mais nous avons pondéré nos appréciations en fonction de la période plus ou moins favorable des visites, de la jeunesse des parcours, des problèmes ponctuels d'entretien. Celui-ci étant sujet à variations, il n'entre que faiblement dans la note attribuée au parcours. Autrement dit, nous avons tenté d'introduire le maximum d'objectivité dans notre subjectivité.

UNE "TRIPLE NOTE"

La note du parcours est explicitement exprimée sur 20, les notes relatives au Club-house et à ses équipements, et à l'environnement hôtelier sont clairement indiquées sur 10. Pour nous, la note du parcours est ainsi prépondérante, les autres permettent d'atténuer les fortes différences des installations et de l'hôtellerie d'un pays à l'autre.
Sur chaque page, vous trouverez en haut et à droite les trois notes. La première concerne le parcours, la seconde le Club-House et ses équipements, la troisième l'environnement hôtelier. Un petit golfeur indique un séjour de golf recommandé, un soleil un séjour de vacances recommandé.

750 PARCOURS RETENUS

Parmi les 1.100 parcours joués, nous en avons retenu 750 ouverts au public, au moins en semaine, mais aussi certains parcours privés où vous pourrez essayer d'avoir accès.Le Peugeot Golf Guide est remis à jour chaque année, grâce aux informations fournies par nos lecteurs et amis golfeurs, grâce aux visites de nos "inspecteurs" : ce sont des joueurs de tous niveaux, compte tenu du fait que la majorité des golfeurs ont un handicap moyen, et que nos "conseils" s'adressent à eux en priorité. Certains parcours sont ainsi éliminés de la précédente édition du Guide, d'autres y entrent, et les notes relatives à chacun des parcours sont également susceptibles d'évoluer.

QUALITÉ DES INSTALLATIONS

Nous avons attribué une note globale aux parcours, et une autre pour la qualité du Club-House et de ses équipements : esthétique et confort des bâtiments, installations d'entraînement,

21

etc. Nous avons également pris en compte le professionnalisme de l'accueil.

ENVIRONNEMENT HOTELIER

Enfin, nous avons étudié l'environnement hôtelier dans la région. Certains restaurants de bonne réputation sont sélectionnés, de même que des hôtels et chambres d'hôte de différentes catégories. La note attribuée n'exprime pas seulement un jugement sur les hôtels, mais elle signale surtout la quantité et la diversité des équipements hôteliers à proximité du parcours.

LA PHILOSOPHIE DU PEUGEOT GOLF GUIDE

Un dernier mot pour souligner que nous sommes bien conscients de l'impossibilité d'échapper à certaines imprécisions ou erreurs, avec une telle masse d'informations. Notre but n'est pas de critiquer systématiquement mais d'aider les Clubs, quand c'est nécessaire, à prendre conscience des défauts de leur parcours ou de leurs installations, à y porter remède quand c'est économiquement possible, à améliorer la qualité de leur accueil et leur politique de services, obligatoire dans un monde de libre entreprise et de concurrence. Leur prospérité dépend de leur réputation, de leur vigilance, de leur exigence. Comme si chaque visiteur était envoyé par le Guide...

22

PEUGEOT GOLF GUIDE
EINLEITUNG UND PHILOSOPHIE

EIN ECHTER "FÜHRER"

Im Gegensatz zu den zahlreichen Hotel- und Restaurantführern gab es bis heute noch keinen bewertenden Golfplatzführer für Europa. Die bestehenden Führer gleichen oft eher Adressbüchern und geben die von den Clubs gelieferten Informationen wieder. Natürlich findet sich darin nur Positives.

Aber alle Golfspieler wissen, dass es zwischen den verschiedenen Plätzen qualitative Unterschiede gibt. Nebst den begehrten Plätzen, auf denen wichtige Meisterschaften ausgetragen werden, gibt es auch eigentliche Juwele unbekannter Plätze, öffentliche Golfplätze von einfacher Anlage und geringen Ansprüchen, begeisternde und enttäuschende Plätze, Plätze mit kleinem Budget aber erstaunlicher Architektur...

Unsere Absicht war es, ein Basiswerk über die europäischen Golfplätze zu schreiben und uns dabei mit aller Konsequenz auf die Seite des Benutzers, des "Konsumenten" zu stellen. Denn er bezahlt für das Spiel und erwartet auch eine dementsprechende Dienstleistung. Nun ist natürlich jede Beurteilung der Qualität subjektiv, und unsere Kritik wird ihrerseits neue Kritik hervorrufen. Dazu ist jedoch zu sagen, dass die verschiedenen Mitarbeiter dieses Führers in den meisten Fällen sehr ähnlicher Meinung waren, obwohl ihr spielerisches Niveau und ihre Herkunft sehr unterschiedlich sind.

Nach der ersten Ausgabe, die sich auf Frankreich beschränkte, kommen nun neu die besten Golfplätze in Belgien, Luxemburg, Portugal, Spanien und in der Schweiz hinzu. Für zukünftige Ausgaben sind auch noch andere Länder vorgesehen.

1 100 GOLFPLÄTZE BESUCHT

Wir haben in den vergangenen fünf Jahren 1100 18-Loch-Plätze besucht und darauf gespielt. Und zwar immer anonym, so dass wir einen Platz in seinem üblichen Zustand beurteilen konnten, wie ihn jeder Spieler antreffen kann. Gewisse Clubs werden nicht gerade glücklich sein mit unseren bisweilen harten Urteilen, aber wir haben bei unserer Beurteilung immer auch den Zeitpunkt des Besuchs, das Alter des Platzes sowie punktuelle Unterhaltsprobleme berücksichtigt. Da der Unterhalt Veränderungen unterliegt, fiel er für die Benotung der Plätze ohnehin nicht sehr stark ins Gewicht. Mit anderen Worten: Wir versuchten, möglichst viel Objektivität in unsere Subjektivität einfliessen zu lassen.

EINE DREIFACHE NOTE

In unserem Bewertungssystem ist die höchste Bewertungszahl für den Platz 20 Punkten, während für das Clubhaus, die sonstigen Einrichtungen und die regionale Hotelleriet bereits 10 Punkte die Höchsnoteist. Die Bewertung des Parcours ist für uns ausschlaggebend; die anderen Noten ermöglichen eine differenzierte Beurteilung der von Land zu Land recht unterschlieden Anlagen und Unterkunftsmöglich-keiten.
Auf jeder Seite finden Sie oben rechts drei Noten. Die erste für den Platz, die zweite für das Clubhaus und seine Einrichtungen, die dritte für das Hotelangebot der Umgebung. Ein kleiner Golfspieler zeigt an, dass Golfferien empfohlen werden können, eine Sonne, dass auch allgemein ein Ferienaufenthalt empfehlenswert ist.

750 GOLFPLÄTZE AUSGEWÄHLT

Von den 1100 bespielten Plätzen haben wir öffentlich zugängliche ausgewählt, darunter sind jedoch auch einige private Golfplätze, die nur beschränkt zugänglich sind. Der Peugeot Golf Guide wird jährlich mit Hilfe der Informationen, die wir von unseren Lesern und Freizeitspielern erhalten, aber auch aufgrund der Besuche unserer "Inspektoren" aktualisiert. Hinter unserem Führer stehen somit Spieler aller Stufen, da ja auch die meisten Golfspieler ein mittleres Handicap haben und sich unsere "Ratschläge" deshalb in erster Linie an sie richten. Gewisse Golfplätze, die in der letzten Ausgabe des Führers beschrieben wurden, sind herausgekippt, andere neu aufgenommen worden, und natürlich können sich auch die Noten für die verschiedenen Plätze im Laufe der Zeit verändern.

QUALITÄT DER EINRICHTUNGEN

Eine Gesamtnote haben wir dem Golfplatz erteilt, eine zweite der Qualität des Clubhauses und seinen Einrichtungen: Ästhetik und Komfort der Gebäude, Trainingsanlagen usw. Auch die Professionalität des Empfangs wurde bei der Bewertung berücksichtigt.

HOTELANGEBOT DER UMGEBUNG

Schliesslich haben wir das Hotelangebot der Umgebung untersucht. Es wurden einige gute Restaurants sowie Hotels und Gästezimmer verschiedener

23

Kategorien ausgewählt. Die erteilte Note ist nicht nur Ausdruck eines Urteils über die Hotels, sondern steht vor allem für die Grösse und Vielseitigkeit des Hotelangebots in der Umgebung des Golfplatzes.

DIE PHILOSOPHIE DES PEUGEOT GOLF GUIDE

Es ist uns sehr wohl bewusst, dass bei einer solchen Fülle von Informationen gewisse Ungenauigkeiten oder Fehler möglich sind. Wir wollen mit diesem Führer auch nicht die Clubs systematisch kritisieren, sondern ihnen wenn nötig helfen. Sie sollen so auf Mängel ihrer Golfplätze und Einrichtungen aufmerksam gemacht werden, um – soweit finanziell möglich – Abhilfe zu schaffen und die Qualität ihres Personals sowie ihre Dienstleistungspolitik zu verbessern. Denn in einer Welt des freien Wettbewerbs und der starken Konkurrenz ist dies unerlässlich. Ihr Gedeihen hängt ab von ihrem Ruf, ihrer Aufmerksamkeit, ihren Ansprüchen. Wie wenn jeder Besucher vom Guide geschickt worden wäre...

PEUGEOT GOLF GUIDE
INTRODUCCION Y FILOSOFIA

UNA AUTÉNTICA GUIA

Contrariamente a las guías de hoteles o de restaurantes, no existe ninguna guía cualitativa de campos de golf a nivel europeo. Las guías existentes son más bien anuarios que recogen las informaciones, favorables como es normal, facilitadas por los propios Clubs. Pero, como bien saben los

amateurs de golf, la calidad de los recorridos es muy diversa. Además de los recorridos de campeonato,que los mejores jugadores anhelan afrontar, existen recorridos desconocidos que son verdaderas joyas, golfs públicos con diseños sencillos y con pocas pretensiones, recorridos en los que con poca inversión el arquitecto ha realizado verdaderos prodigios.... Nosotros hemos llevado a cabo un estudio profundo de los golfs en Europa, situándonos en todo momento del lado de los "consumidores", de los que pagan para jugar y desean recibir un servicio a la altura de sus esperanzas. Por supuesto todo juicio cualitativo es subjetivo y nuestras críticas pueden a su vez ser criticadas, pero lo que es cierto es que la opinión de los colaboradores de esta guía, jugadores de todos los niveles y con experiencia de golf, ha coincidido en la mayoría de los casos. Después de la primera edición, dedicada exclusivamente a Francia, en la presente se añaden los mejores recorridos de Bélgica, Luxemburgo, Portugal, Suiza y España. En próximas ediciones se añadirán nuevos países.

1100 RECORRIDOS VISITADOS

Hemos visitado y jugado en 1100 recorridos de 18 hoyos durante los cinco últimos años. Siempre de manera anónima, lo que nos permitió apreciarlos en su estado habitual, como cualquier jugador de paso. Algunos Clubs tal vez no estén muy satisfechos con nuestros juicios a veces crueles, pero podemos afirmar que hemos ponderado nuestras apreciaciones en función del período más o menos favorable de nuestra visita, de la antigüedad de los recorridos y de los problemas esporádicos de los cuidados de mantenimiento. Estos factores, por supuesto variables, han tenido poca influencia en la nota. Dicho de otra manera, hemos intentado ser lo más objetivos posible dentro de nuestra subjetividad.

"TRIPLE NOTA"

La nota del recorrido se notifica sobre 20, las notas del Club-house y sus instalaciones, y la del entorno hotelero se indican sobre 10. Para nosotros, la nota del campo es preponderante, las otras sirven para atenuar las fuertes diferencias de instalaciones y de hosteleria que existen de un país a otro. Encontrará usted tres notas en la parte superior derecha de cada página. La primera se refiere al recorrido, la segunda al Club-house e instalaciones y la tercera a las prestaciones hoteleras. La silueta de un golfista diminuto indica que se recomienda como estancia de golf, y un sol lo recomienda como lugar de vacaciones.

750 RECORRIDOS SELECCIONADOS

Entre los 1100 campos jugados, nos hemos quedado con 750 abiertos al público, pero también con algunos privados donde podrán tener acceso mediante algunas condiciones.
La Guía de Golf Peugeot se actualiza cada año gracias a las informaciones facilitadas por nuestros lectores y amigos golfistas, y gracias a las visitas de nuestros "inspectores": jugadores de todos los niveles habida cuenta de que la mayoría de los golfistas tienen un handicap de tipo medio y nuestros "consejos" son precisamente para ellos. Se han eliminado algunos recorridos que figuraban en la edición anterior, se han añadido otros y las notas de cada uno de los recorridos podrá evolucionar.

CALIDAD DE LAS INSTALACIONES

Hemos atribuido una nota global al recorrido y otra a la calidad del club-house y sus servicios: estética y comodidad del edificio, instalaciones de entrenamiento, etc. También hemos tenido en cuenta el profesionalismo de la acogida.

INFRAESTRUCTURA HOTELERA

Finalmente hemos estudiado la infraestructura hotelera de la regón. Se han seleccionado algunos restaurantes con buena fama, así como hoteles de diferentes categorías. La nota atribuida no sólo conlleva un juicio sobre los hoteles, sino que indica sobre todo la disponibilidad hotelera a proximidad del golf.

FILOSOFIA DE LA GUIA DE GOLF PEUGEOT

Sólo unas palabras para subrayar que somos muy conscientes de lo difícil que es, con tal cantidad de datos, evitar ciertas imprecisiones o errores. Nuestro objetivo no es el de una crítica sistemática sino más bien ayudar a los Clubs a ser conscientes de los defectos de sus recorridos o instalaciones para poner remedio cuando sea económicamente posible, mejorar la calidad de su acogida y de sus servicios, cosa cada vez más imprescindible en un mundo de tanta competencia. Su prosperidad depende de su reputación, de su vigilancia, de su exigencia. Como si cada visitante fuese enviado por esta Guía...

25

Follow the course of events via the World's

Daily Newspaper

GLOSSARY	ORDLISTA	GLOSSAIRE	WORTSCHATZ	DICCIONARIO	WOORDENBOEK
Holes	Hål	Trous	Löcher	Hoyos	Holes
Office	Sekretariat	Secrétariat	Sekretariat	Secretaría	Secretariaat
Pro shop	Pro shop	Pro shop	Pro shop	Pro-shop	Pro shop
Restaurant	Restaurang	Restaurant	Restaurant	Restaurante	Restaurant
Fax	Fax	Fax	Fax	Fax	Fax
Situation	Läge	Situation	Lage	Situación	Situatie
N. (North)	N.	N.	N.	Norte	N.
N.E.	N.Ö.	N.E.	N.O.	Noreste	N.O.
E. (East)	Ö.	E.	O.	Este	O.
S.E.	S.Ö.	S.E.	S.O.	Sureste	Z.O.
S. (South)	S.	S.	S.	Sur	Z.
S.W	S.V.	S.O.	S.W.	Suroeste	Z.W.
W. (West)	V.	O.	W.	Oeste	W.
N.W	N.V.	N.O.	N.W.	Noroeste	N.W.
Residents	Invånare	Hab.	Bewohner	Habitantes	Inwoners
Temperature	Temperatur	Température	Temperatur	Temperatura	Temperatuur
January	Januari	Janvier	Januar	Enero	Januari
April	April	Avril	April	Abril	April
July	Juli	Juillet	Juli	Julio	Juli
October	Oktober	Octobre	Oktober	Octubre	Oktober
Altitude	Altitud	Altitude	Höhe	Altura	Hoogte
Airport	Flygplats	Aéroport	Flughafen	Aeropuerto	Luchthaven
Railway station	Station	Gare	Bahnhof	Estación	Station
Annual closure	Årlig stängning	Fermeture annuelle	Jährliche schliessung	Cierre anual	Jaarlijkse sluiting
Yes	Ja	Oui	Ja	Si	Ja
No	Nej	Non	Nein	No	Neen
Weekly closure	Daglig stängning	Fermeture hebdomadaire	Wöchentliche schliessung	Cierre semanal	Wekelijkse sluitingsdag
Monday	Måndag	Lundi	Montag	Lunes	Maandag
Tuesday	Tisdag	Mardi	Dienstag	Martes	Dinsdag
Wednesday	Onsdag	Mercredi	Mittwoch	Miércoles	Woensdag
Thursday	Torsdag	Jeudi	Donnerstag	Jueves	Donderdag
Friday	Fredag	Vendredi	Freitag	Viernes	Vrijdag
Saturday	Lördag	Samedi	Samstag	Sábado	Zaderdag
Sunday	Söndag	Dimanche	Sonntag	Domingo	Zondag
Golf schools	Träningsläger	Stages	Training	Cursillos	Cursus
Important competitions	Haft berömda tävlingar	Épreuves célèbres disputées	Berühmte wettbewerbe	Famosas competiciones jugadas	Beroemde wedstrijden
Fees Main Season	Tariff hög säsong	Tarifs haute saison	Preisliste hochsaison	Precios tempor. alta	Hoogseizoen tarieve
18 holes	Banan	Le parcours	18 löcher	El campo	18 holes
The day	Per dag	La journée	Den ganzen tag	Todo el día	De dag
Individual	Individuellt	Individuel	Individuell	Individual	Individueel
Couple	Par	Couple	Ehepaar	Pareja	Paar
Week days	Veckodag	Sem	Woche	Semana	Weekdagen
WE/Bank holidays	Lör/Söndag-helgdag	We/Férie	Wochenende/feiertag	Fin de semana/fiestas	We/Festdagen
Special offer	Förmånserbjudande	Formule Économique	Ermässigter eintrittspreis	Fórmula ecónomica	Prijsgunstige formule
Green fee	Green fee	Green fee	Green fee	Green fee	Green fee
Lunch	Lunch	Déjeuner	Mittagsessen	Almuerzo	Lunch
Caddy	Caddie	Caddy	Caddy	Caddy	Caddy

ORDLISTE	GLOSSAIRE	SANASTO	ORDLISTE	GLOSSARIO	
Huller	Buche	Reikiä	Huller	Buracos	ホール
Sekretariat	Segreteria	Toimisto	Kontor	Secretariado	受付
Pro-shop	Pro Shop	Pro shop	Pro shop	Pro-shop	プロショップ
Restaurant	Ristorante	Ravintola	Restaurant	Restaurante	レストラン
Fax	Fax	Fax	Fax	Fax	ファクス
Sted	Localita'	Sijainti	Beliggenhet	Localização	場所
N.	N.	Pohjoinen	N.	Norte	北
N.Ø.	N.E.	Koillinen	N.Ø.	Nordeste	北東
Ø	E.	Itä	Ø	Este	東
S.Ø.	S.E.	Kaakko	S.Ø.	Sudeste	南東
S.	S.	Etelä	S.	Sul	南
S.V.	S.W.	Lounas	S.V.	Sudoeste	南西
V.	W.	Länsi	V.	Oeste	西
N.V.	N.W.	Luode	N.V.	Noroeste	北西
Beboelse	Abitanti	Asukkaita	Fastboende	Habitantes	住民数
Temperatur	Temperatura	Lämpötila	Temperatur	Temperatura	温度
Januar	Gennaio	Tammikuu	Januar	Janeiro	一月
April	Aprile	Huhtikuu	April	Abril	四月
Juli	Luglio	Heinäkuu	Juli	Julho	七月
Oktober	Ottobre	Lokakuu	Oktober	Outubro	十月
Højde	Altitudine	Korkeus	Nivå over havet	Altitude	高度
Lufthavn	Aeroporto	Lentokenttä	Lufthavn	Aeroporto	空港
Jernbanestation	Stazione	Rautatieasema	Togstasjon	Estação	駅
Årlig lukkeperiode	Chiusura annuale	Kenttä suljetaan	Årlig stenging	Fecho anual	年次閉場
Ja	Si	Kyllä	Ja	Sim	はい
Nej	No	Ei	Nei	Não	いいえ
Ugentlig lukketid	Chiusura settimanale	Suljetan viikolla	Ukentlig stenging	Fecho semanal	週休
Mandag	Lunedi	Maanantai	Mandag	Segunda-feira	月曜日
Tirsdag	Martedi	Tiistai	Tirsdag	Terça-feira	火曜日
Onsdag	Mercoledi	Keskiviikko	Onsdag	Quarta-feira	水曜日
Torsdag	Giovedi	Torstai	Torsdag	Quinta-feira	木曜日
Fredag	Venerdi	Perjantai	Fredag	Sexta-feira	金曜日
Lørdag	Sabato	Lauantai	Lørdag	Sábado	土曜日
Søndag	Domenica	Sunnuntai	Søndag	Domingo	日曜日
Golfskoler	Corsi/Lezioni	Golf kurssit	Golfskole	Estágios	レェスン
Vigtige turneringer spillet	Tornei celebri disputati	Tärkeimmät kilpailut	Viktige turneringer	Provas célebres disputadas	有名トーナメント
Priser i højsæson	Tariffe alta stagione	Green fee	Tariffer i høysesongen	Tarifas da época alta	ハイシーズン料金
18 huller	Il percorso	18-reikää	18 hull	O percurso	コース
Dagen	La giornata	Päivä	Dagen	O dia	一日
Individuelt	Individuale	Henkilö	Individuell	Individual	個人
Par	Coppia	Pari	Par	Casal	カップル
Hverdage	Settimana	Arkipäivisin	Ukedager	Semana	平日
Helligdag	Feriale/Festivo	Pyhäpäivisin	Week-end / Fridag	Fim de semana/feriado	週末／休日
Særtilbud	Formula forfait	Erikoistarjous	Spesialtilbud	Fórmula económica	割引料金
Green fee	Green fee	Green fee	Green fee	Green fee	グリーン・フィ
Frokost	Pranzo	Lounas	Lunch	Almoço	昼食
Caddie	Caddy	Caddy	Caddy	Caddy	キャディ

Electric trolley	El vagn	Chariot électrique	Elecktrokarren	Carro eléctrico	Electrische trolley
Buggy	Golfbil	Voiturette	Elektrischer wagen	Coche	Buggy
Clubs	Klubbor	Clubs	Clubs	Palos	Clubs
Credit cards	Kredit kort	Cartes de crédit	Kreditkarten	Tarjetas de crédito	Creditkaarten
«EXTRA» facilities	«EXTRA» speciellt	Le « PLUS»	EXTRAS	EL «MAS»	ATTRACTIES
Access	Tillfart	Accès	Zufahrt	Acceso	Toegang
Map on page :	Se sid:	Carte page :	Karte seite:	Página plano :	Autokaart blz:

GOLF COURSE	BANA	PARCOURS	PLATZ	RECORRIDO	BAAN
Site	Läge	Site	Lage	Emplazamiento	Terrein
Maintenance	Underhåll	Entretien	Instandahltung	Mantenimiento	Onderhoud
First opened	Öppnad år	Année d'ouverture	Öffnungsjahr	Año de apertura	Jaar van opening
Redesigned	Omarbetad	Remanié	Umgebaut	Remodelado	Herzien
Architect	Arkitekt	Architecte	Architekt	Arquitecto	Architect
Type	Typ	Type	Typ	Tipo	Type
Copse	Skogsdungar	Bocage	Heckenlandschaft	Arboleda	Kreupelhont
Seaside course	Kustbana	Bord de mer	Am meer	Al borde del mar	Seaside baan
Country	Landsbygd	Campagne	Land	Campo	Baan inhet vrijeveild
Forest	Skog	Forêt	Wald	Bosque	Bos
Links	Links	Links	Links	Links	Links
Mountain	Berg	Montagne	Gebirge	Montaña	Berg
Parkland	Park	Parc	Park	Parque	Park
Open country	Slätt	Plaine	Fachland	Llanura	Een vlakke baan
Residential	Residensiellt	Résidentiel	Residenz	Urbano	Residentieel
Undulating	Dal	Vallon	Kleines tal	Vagüada	Heuvelachtig terrein
Relief	Relief	Relief	Relief	Relieve	Reliëf
Water in play	Vatten på spelfältet	Eau en jeu	Platz mit wasser	Aguá	Waterhazards
Trees in play	Träd på spelfältet	Arbres en jeu	Platz mit bäumen	Arboles	Bomen
Exposed to wind	Vindutsatt	Exposé au vent	Dem wind ausgesetzt	Expuesto al viento	Windgevoelig
Scorecard	Scorekort	Carte de score	Scorekarte	Tarjeta	Scorekaart
Length	Längd.	Long.	Länge	Longitud	Lengte
Par	Par	Par	Par	Par	Par
SSS	SSS	SSS	SSS	SSS	SSS
Champions' tees	Back tee	Chp.	Championship tees	Campeonato	Back tees
Mens' tees	Herrtee	Mess.	Herren	Caballeros	Heren
Ladies' tees	Damtee	Da.	Damen	Damas	Damen
Hcp required	Hcp erfordrad	Handicap exigé	Min. handicap	Handicap exigido	Vereiste handicap
Amateur record	Banrekord amatör	Record amateur	Platz rekord amateur	Record aficionados	Amateur record
Professional record	Banrekord pro.	Record pro	Platz rekord pro.	Record profesionales	Professional record
Dog on lead	Hund i koppel	Chien en laisse	Hund an der leihe	Perro con correa	Honden aan lijn

CLUB HOUSE & AMENITIES	KLUBBHUS OCH OMGIVNING	CLUB-HOUSE ET ANNEXES	KLUBHAUS UND NEBENGEBÄUDE	CLUB HOUSE Y DEPENDENCIAS	CLUB HOUSE EN ANNEXES
Architecture	Arkitektur	Architecture	Architektur	Arquitectura	Architectuur
Modern	Modern	Moderne	Modern	Moderno	Modern
Traditional	Klassisk	Classique	Klassisch	Clásico	Klassiek

🇩🇰	🇮🇹	🇫🇮	🇳🇴	🇵🇹	🇯🇵
Bagvogn	Carello elettrico	Sähkörattaat	Elektrisk vogn	Trolley eléctrico	電動カート
Golf car	Car	Golfauto	Golfbil	Buggy	カート
Køller	Bastoni	Mailat	Køller	Tacos	クラブ
Creditkort	Carte di credito	Luottokortit	Kredittkort	Cartão de crédito	クレジット・カード
«EXTRA»	IL «PLUS»	«TÄRKEÄÄ»	ET «MUST»	LE «MAIS»	特徴
Adgang	Itinerario	Pääsy	Adkomst	Acesso	道順
Kort på side	Carta, pagina :	Kartta sivulla :	Kort på side :	Mapa na página :	地図 / ページ

BAN	PERCORSO	GOLKENTTÄ	GOLFBANEN	PERCURSO	コース
Sted	Paesaggio	Sijainti	Område	Sitio	場所
Vedligeholdelse	Manutenzione	Hoito	Vedlikehold	Conversa	メインテナンス
Åbnet	Anno di apertura	Otettu käyttöön	Åpnet	Ano de abertura	開場時期
Gendesignet	Rimodellato	Uudistettu	Omtegnet	Remodelado	改造
Arkitekt	Architetto	Arkkitehti	Arkitekt	Arquitecto	デザイナー
Type	Tipologia	Kentän luonne	Type	Tipo	型
Krat	Boschetto	Pensaisto	Småskog / kratt	Mata	田園地帯
Seaside course	Sul mare	Merenrantakenttä	Bane ved sjøn	Beira-mar	海沿い
Landet	Campagna	Maa	Land	Campo	田舎
Skov	Foresta	Metsä	Skog	Floresta	森林
Links	Links	Links	Links	Links	リンクス
Bjerg	Montagna	Vuori	Fjell	Montanha	山岳
Parkområde	Parco	Puisto	Parklignende landskap	Parque	庭園
Åbent landområde	Pianura	Avomaisema	Åpent land	Planicie	平原
Bebygget	Urbano	Majoitusmandollisuus kentällä	Villastrøk	Urbano	都会風
Bakket	Valletta	Kumpuileva	Lave koller	Pequeno vale	起伏に富む
Lettelse	Rilievo terreno	Vapautuminen	Relief	Relevo	地形
Vand i spil	Acqua in gioco	Vesiesteitä	Vann-hinder	Lago	池
Træer i spil	Alberi in gioco	Puita	Tre-hinder	Arvores	林
Udsat vind	Esposto al vento	Tuulta	Utsatt for vind	Exposto ao vento	風
Scorekort	Carta-Score	Tuloskortti	Scorecard/poengkort	Cartão de resultados	スコア・カード
Længde	Lunghezza	Pituus	Lengde	Comprimento	距離
Par	Par	Par	Par	Par	パー
SSS	SSS	SSS	SSS	SSS	S. S. S.
Back tees	Campionato	Championship tees	Champion-tees	Campionato	Chp
Herre tee	Uomini	Miesten tii	Herre-tees	Homens	男性ティ
Dame tee	Donne	Naisten tii	Dame-tees	Senhoras	女性用ティ
Max. handicap	Handicap richiesto	Handicap-vaatimus	Obligatorisk handicap	Handicap exigido	必要ハンデ
Amatørekord	Record Am.	Kenttäennätys amatööri	Amatør-rekord	Record amador	アマチュア記録
Professionel rekord	Record Pro.	Kenttäennätys pro	Proff-rekord	Record profissional	プロ記録
Hund i snor	Cani al guinzaglio	Koiriepito sallittu kytkettynä	Hund i bånd	Cães com trela	犬（鎖付）

KLUBHUSET OG FACILITETER	CLUB HOUSE E SERVIZI	KLUBITALO	KLUBHUS OG OMGIVELSER	CLUB HOUSE E ANEXOS	クラブハウス他
Arkitektur	Architettura	Arkkitentuuri	Arkitektur	Arquitectura	建物
Moderne	Moderna	Nykyaikainen	Moderne	Moderno	近代的
Traditionel	Classica	Perinteinen	Tradisjonell	Clássico	伝統的

🇬🇧	🇩🇰	🇫🇷		🇪🇸	
Old	Gammal	Ancien	Alt	Antiguo	Vroegere
Old/Renovated	Gammal/ombygd	Ancien/rénové	Alt/renoviert	Antiguo/Renovado	Gerestaureerd
Creche	Barnpassning	Garderie d'enfants	Kindergarten	Guardería de niños	Kinderoppas
Driving range	Träningsbana	Practice	Übungsplatz	Campo de prácticas	Oefenbaan
Open air	Öppen	Découvert	Offen	Descubierto	Onoverdekt
Places	Platser	Places	Plätze	Puestos	Plaatsen
Sheltered	Täkt	Couvert	Überdacht	Cubierto	Overdekt
On grass	På gräs	Sur herbe	Auf rasen	Sobre hierba	Op gras
Putting-green	Putting-green	Putting-green	Putting-grün	Putting-green	Putting-green
Pitching-green	Pitching-green	Pitching-green	Pitching-grün	Pitching-green	Pitching-green
Tennis	Tennis	Tennis	Tennis	Tenis	Tennis
Clay	Grus	Terre battue	Sandplatz	Tierra batida	Graval
Hard surface	Hard court	Dur	Hart	Duro	Hard court
Grass	Gräs	Herbe	Grass	Hierba	Gras
Artificial grass	Matta	Moquette	Teppich	Moqueta	Moquette
Swimming pool	Simbassäng	Piscine	Schwimmbad	Piscina	Zwembad
Open air	Öppen	Découverte	Offen	Descubierta	Onoverdekt
Heated	Värmd	Chauffée	Geheitzt	Caliente	Verwarmd
Indoor	Täkt	Couverte	Überdacht	Cubierta	Overdekt
Relaxation centre	Fitness centrum	Centre de relaxation	Kuranlage	Centro de relajación	Ontspannings-centru
Balneotherapy	Vattenterapi	Balnéothérapie	Badekur	Balneoterapia	Balneotherapie
Sauna	Bastu	Sauna	Sauna	Sauna	Sauna
Jacuzzi	Jacuzzi	Jacuzzi	Jakusi	Jacuzzi	Jacuzzi
Residential seminar	Seminarium med pension	Séminaire résidentiel	Seminar	Seminario	Seminarie (e.v. met Hotel)
Capacity	Kapacitet	Capacité	Räume	Capacidad	Capaciteit

HOTEL FACILITIES	**HOTELL OMGIVNING**	**ENVIRONNEMENT HOTELIER**	**HOTEL BESCHREIBUNG**	**COMPLEJO HOTELERO**	**HOTELS IN OMGEVING**
HOTELS	HOTELL	HOTELS	HOTELS	HOTELES	HOTELS
Rooms	Rum	Chambres	Zimmer	Habitaciones	Kamers
GUEST ROOMS	GÄST RUM	CHAMBRE D'HOTE	PRIVATZIMMER	HABITACIONES HUÉSPEDES	OVERNACHTING FACILITEN
RESTAURANT	RESTAURANG	RESTAURANT	RESTAURANT	RESTAURANTE	RESTAURANT

TOURISM	**TURIST VÄSEN**	**TOURISME**	**FREMDENVERKEHR**	**TURISMO**	**TOERISME**
Tourist office	Turist byrå	Office du tourisme	Fremdenverkehrsbüro	Oficina de Turismo	V.V.V.
Town	Stad	Ville	Stadt	Ciudad	Stad
Castle	Slott	Château	Schloss	Castillo	Kasteel
Abbey/Cathedral	Kloster/Katedral	Abbaye/cathédrale	Kloster/Kathedrale	Abadía/ Catedral	Klooster/Kathedraa
Museum	Museum	Musée	Museum	Museo	Museum
Events	Evenemang	Evénement	Veranstaltungen	Acontecimientos	Evenementen
Environment	Omgivning	Environnement	Umgebung	Alrededores	Omgeving
Park and garden	Park och trädgård	Parc et jardin	Park und garten	Parque y jardín	Park en tuin
Celebrity Homes	Berömd mans hem	Maison d'homme célèbre	Berühmtes haus	Casa de personaje famoso	Beroemd herenhuis
Casino	Kasino	Casino	Spielbank	Casino	Casino

32

🇩🇰	🇮🇹	🇫🇮	🇳🇴	🇵🇹	🇯🇵
Gammel	Antica	Vanha	Gammel	Antigo	旧式
Gammel/renoveret	Antica Restaurata	Vanha / uudistettu	Gammel/modernisert	Antigo restaurado	旧式 / 改策
Børnepasning	**Club Bambini**	**Lasten päivähoito**	**Barnepass**	**Jardim de infância**	託児所
Driving range	**Campo pratica**	**Driving range**	**Treningsbane**	**Campo de prática**	練習場
Udendørs	Aperto	Ulkoilma	Friluft	Descoberto	室外
Steder	Posti	Paikat	Steder	Lugares	場所
Ly	**Coperto**	**Suoja**	**Ly**	**Coberto**	室内
På græs	**In erba**	**Ruoholla**	**På gress**	**Om relva**	芝 '
Putting-green	**Putting-green**	**Putting-green**	**Putting-green**	**Putting-green**	パッティンググリーン
Indspilsgreen	**Green-pratica**	**Pitching-green**	**Pitching-green**	**Pitching-green**	ピッチグリーン
Tennis	Tennis	Tennis	Tennis	Ténis	テニス
Grus	Terra battuta	Savi	Grusbane	Terra batida	アンツーカー
Kunstoverflade	Cemento	Kovapintainen	Asfaltbane	Piso rápido	ハードコート
Græs	Erba	Ruoho	Gress	Relva	ローンコート
Kunstigt græs	Moquette	Keinonurmi	Kunstig gress	Piso sintético	人工芝
Svimming pool	**Piscina**	**Uima-allas**	**Svømmebasseng**	**Piscina**	プール
Udendørs	Aperta	Ulkoilma	Friluft	Descoberta	室外
Opvarmed	Riscaldata	Lämitetty	Oppvarmet	Aquecida	温水
Indendørs	Coperta	Sisätila	Innendørs	Coberta	室内
Afslapsningsrum	**Centro-relax**	**Kuntosali**	**Senter for avslapping**	**Centro de Laser**	療養所
Badterapi	**Balneoterapia**	**Vesihoita**	**Sjøbadbehandling**	**Talasoterapia**	バルネオ
Sauna	**Sauna**	**Sauna**	**Badstu**	**Sauna**	サウナ
Jacuzzi	**Jacuzzi**	**Jacuzzi**	**Jacuzzi**	**Jacuzzi**	ジャクジー
Seminar med overnatning	**Sala Convegni**	**Seminaaritilat**	**Konferansested**	**Seminário Residencial**	セミナーハウス
Kapacitet	**Capienza**	**Kapasiteetti**	**Kapasitet**	**Capacidade**	人数

HOTELFACILI-TETERNE	**ALBERGHI**	**HOTELLI**	**HOTEL-FASILITETER**	**INFRAESTRUCTURAS HOTELEIRAS**	ホテル事情
HOTEL	**ALBERGHI**	**HOTELLI**	**HOTEL**	**HOTELS**	ホテル
Værelser	Camere	Huoneita	Hotelrom	Quartos	部屋
BED AND BREAKFAST	**PENSION**	**BED AND BREAKFAST**	**ROM TIL LEIE**	**QUARTO DE HOSPEDES**	民宿
RESTAURANT	**RISTORANTE**	**RAVINTOLA**	**RESTAURANT**	**RESTAURANTE**	レストラン

TURISME	**TURISMO**	**MATKAILU**	**TURISME**	**TURISMO**	観光
Turist bureau	**Ufficio del turismo**	**Matkailutoimisto**	**Turistkontor**	**Posto de Turismo**	観光局
By	**Citta'**	**Kaupunki**	**By**	**Cidade**	市
Slot	**Castello**	**Linna**	**Slott**	**Castelo**	城
Abbedi/Katedral	**Abbazia/Cattedrale**	**Luostari/Katetdraali**	**Kloster/Katedral**	**Abadia/ Catedral**	教会
Museum	**Museo**	**Museo**	**Museum**	**Museu**	美術館
Begivenheder	**Manifestazioni**	**Tapahtumia**	**Begivenheter**	**Evenementes**	
Miljø	**Dintorni**	**Ympäristö**	**Omgivelser**	**Ambiante**	郊外
Park og have	**Parco e giardino**	**Puisto ja puutarma**	**Park og hage**	**Parque e jardim**	公園
Berømthedshus	**Dimora celebre**	**Celebrity House**	**Huset til en berømthet**	**Casa de homem célebre**	名所、旧跡
Kasino	**Casino'**	**Kasino**	**Casino**	**Casino**	カジノ

33

CROSS CREEK. THE BRAND THAT WINS EVERY TIME.

From left to right: Jay Haas, Loren Roberts, Fred Funk, Tom Scherrer, Corey Pavin, Jeff Maggert, Jonathan Kaye

It's hardly a surprise that the toughest competitors in golf wear Cross Creek.

After all, our Pro Collection has the sure signs of a winner. The classic lines.

The generous cut. The 100% cotton comfort. The wealth of colours, patterns,

and textures. So whether you're competing for a national championship –

or deciding who buys lunch – you can count on Cross Creek's

winning style. Of course, what else you win is up to you.

THE EXCEPTIONAL SHIRT
Made in the USA

CLASSIFICATION OF COURSES
CLASSEMENT DES PARCOURS
CLASIFICACION DE LOS RECORRIDOS
CLASSIFICAÇÃO DOS PERCURSOS
EINTEILUNG DER GOLFPLÄTZE
RANGSCHIKKING VAN DE TERREINEN

This classification gives priority consideration to the score awarded to the actual course.
Ce classement donne priorité à la note attribuée au parcours.
Esta clasificación da prioridad a la nota atribuida al recorrido.
Esta classificação toma em linha de conta, em prioridade, a nota atribuida ao pércurso.
Deze rangschikking houdt eerst en vooral rekening met het cijfer,
dat aan het terrein werd toegekend.
Diese Einteilung berücksichtigt in erster Linie die dem Golfplatz erteilte Note.

B: Belgium/Belgique L: Luxembourg G: Germany/Deutschland Es: Spain/España F: France
I: Republic of Ireland U: Northern Ireland (Ulster) N: The Netherlands/Nederland
S: Suisse/Schweiz P: Portugal W: Wales Sc: Scotland Eng: England

Course score	Club-house and facilities	Hotel facility score	
Note du parcours	Note du Club-house et annexes	Note de l'environnement hôtelier	
Nota del recorrido	Nota del club-house y anejos	Nota de la infraestructura hotelera	
Nota do percurso	Nota do Club-House e anexos	Nota do envolvimento hoteleiro	
Note für den Golfplatz	Note für das Clubhaus und die Einrichtungen	Cijfer van hotelaccomodatie in de omgeving	
Cijfer van het terrein	Cijfer van het Club-House & dependances	Note für das Hotelangebot der Umgebung	
			Page
			Página
			Página
19 7 7	Ballybunion *Old Course*	I	707	Seite
				Bladzijde

19/20

19	7	7	Ballybunion *Old Course*	Ireland	707
19	8	8	Portmarnock	Ireland	752
19	6	7	Royal County Down	Ulster	790
19	7	7	Royal Portrush *Dunluce Links*	Ulster	791
19	3	4	Carnoustie *Championship*	Scotland	599
19	7	6	Muirfield	Scotland	640
19	7	8	Nairn	Scotland	643
19	7	7	Royal Dornoch	Scotland	656
19	7	7	Royal Troon Old Course	Scotland	658
19	9	8	Turnberry Ailsa Course	Scotland	670
19	8	5	Ganton	England	479
19	9	7	Royal Birkdale (The)	England	526
19	7	8	Royal Lytham & St Anne's	England	532
19	7	5	Royal St George's	England	535
19	7	5	Royal Porthcawl	Wales	688
19	8	6	Bordes (Les)	France	172
19	8	6	Valderrama	Spain	977

35

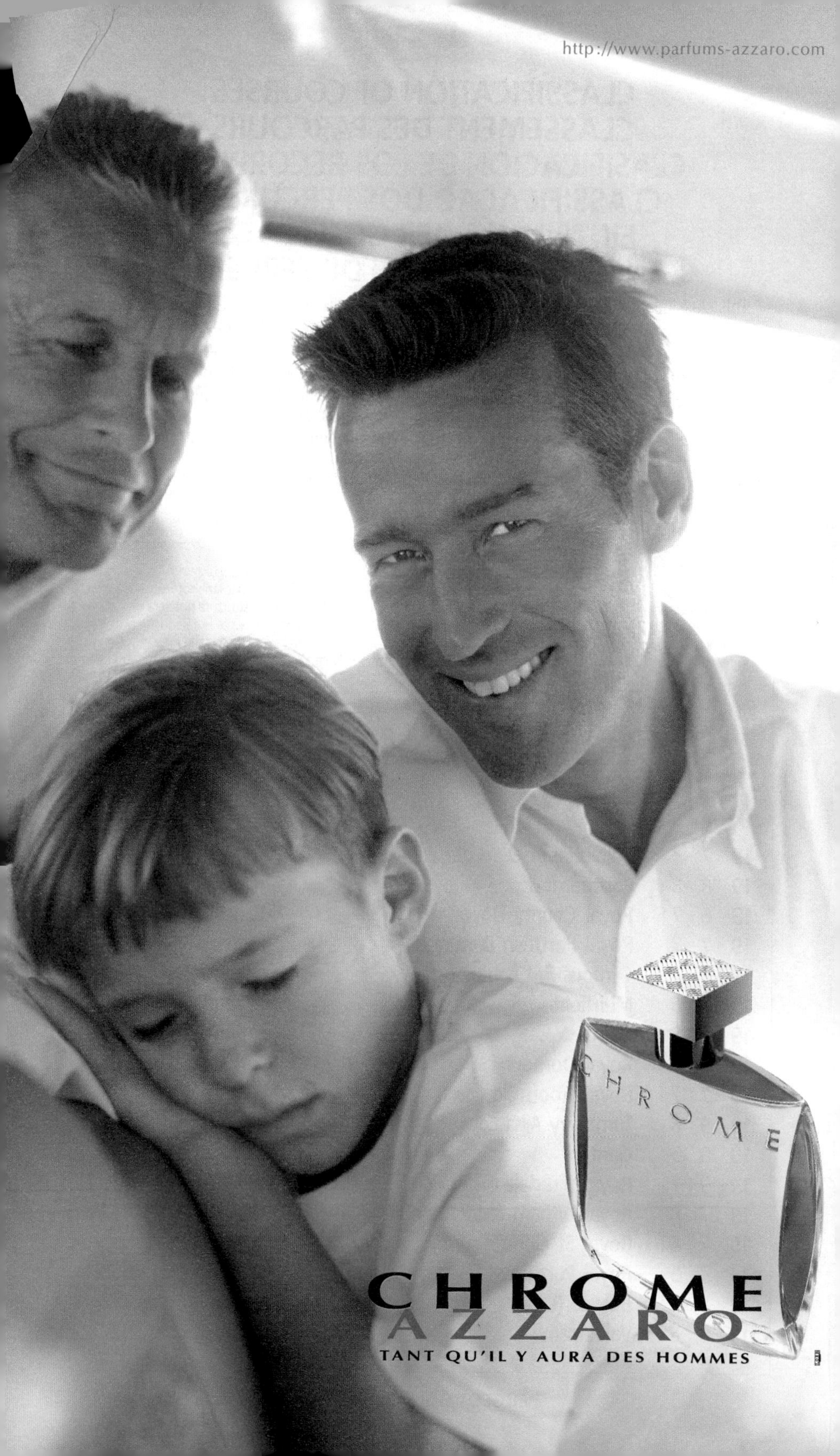
http://www.parfums-azzaro.com
CHROME
CHROME
AZZARO
TANT QU'IL Y AURA DES HOMMES

CLASSIFICATION OF COURSES

Score	Course	Country	Page
	18/20		
18 7 7	Alwoodley (The)	Eng	440
18 8 6	Blairgowrie *Rosemount*	Sc	593
18 7 6	Burnham & Berrow	Eng	457
18 6 8	Castletown	Eng	460
18 9 7	Celtic Manor*Roman Road*	W	679
18 7 6	Chantilly *Vineuil*	F	186
18 8 6	Chart Hills	Eng	461
18 6 5	Club zur Vahr (Garlstedt)	G	324
18 5 6	County Louth	I	719
18 7 6	Cruden Bay	Sc	602
18 8 6	Domaine Impérial	S	990
18 8 6	Eindhoven	N	807
18 7 6	El Saler	Es	913
18 6 6	European (The)	I	729
18 6 7	Falkenstein	G	329
18 7 6	Feldafing	G	330
18 6 5	Fontanals	Es	917
18 7 7	Formby	Eng	475
18 9 7	Gleneagles *King's*	Sc	618
18 7 8	Haagsche	N	813
18 7 7	Hillside	Eng	489
18 7 6	Ilkley	Eng	493
18 8 6	Kempferhof (Le)	F	225
18 8 8	Kennemer	N	817
18 6 6	Lahinch	I	742
18 7 7	Las Brisas	Es	937
18 6 4	Machrihanish	Sc	636
18 7 7	Moortown	Eng	509
18 8 6	Motzener See	G	364
18 9 8	Mount Juliet	I	747
18 6 6	National *L'Albatros*	F	237
18 7 8	Noordwijk	N	819
18 7 8	North Berwick	Sc	645
18 6 6	Notts (Hollinwell)	Eng	513
18 6 6	Pennard	W	685
18 6 7	Prestwick	Sc	651
18 7 6	R.S.H.E. Club de Campo	Es	965
18 7 8	Royal Aberdeen *Balgownie Links*	Sc	654
18 8 7	Royal Liverpool (Hoylake)	Eng	531
18 6 6	Royal North Devon (Westward Ho!)	Eng	534
18 6 5	Royal St David's	W	689
18 7 7	Royal Zoute	B	90
18 7 6	Saunton *East Course*	Eng	541
18 8 7	Scharmützelsee *Nick Faldo*	G	379

Score	Course	Country	Page
18 5 4	Seascale	Eng	543
18 7 4	Silloth-on-Solway	Eng	548
18 7 6	Sotogrande	Es	974
18 6 5	Southerness	Sc	661
18 7 7	Southport & Ainsdale	Eng	550
18 8 8	St Andrews *Old Course*	Sc	665
18 7 4	St Enodoc *Church Course*	Eng	551
18 8 8	Sunningdale *New Course*	Eng	556
18 8 8	Sunningdale *Old Course*	Eng	557
18 7 6	Tenby	W	691
18 7 6	Tralee	I	766
18 7 7	Walton Heath *Old Course*	Eng	566
18 8 7	Wentworth *West Course*	Eng	569
18 7 6	West Sussex	Eng	575
18 7 7	Woburn *Dukes Course*	Eng	578
18 7 8	Woodhall Spa	Eng	582
	17/20		
17 7 7	Aberdovey	W	677
17 7 7	Aloha	Es	895
17 6 5	Ashburnham	W	678
17 9 9	Bad Griesbach *Brunnwies*	G	314
17 6 5	Ballyliffin *Glashedy Links*	I	709
17 7 6	Barbaroux	F	163
17 8 7	Berkshire (The)*Blue Course*	Eng	446
17 8 7	Berkshire (The) *Red Course*	Eng	447
17 7 6	Beuerberg	G	320
17 6 5	Blackmoor	Eng	449
17 7 7	Bodensee-Weissensberg	G	321
17 6 6	Bowood G&CC	Eng	452
17 7 6	Brampton	Eng	453
17 6 7	Braunschweig	G	322
17 7 7	Broadstone	Eng	455
17 8 7	Buckinghamshire (The)	Eng	456
17 7 7	Carlisle	Eng	459
17 7 7	Castillo de Gorraiz	E	903
17 7 7	Clitheroe	Eng	462
17 7 8	Conwy	W	680
17 6 5	Côte d'Argent (La)	F	191
17 4 3	County Sligo	I	720
17 7 7	Cumberwell Park	Eng	465
17 8 8	Dalmahoy *East Course*	Sc	603
17 6 7	Downfield	Sc	604
17 8 7	East Sussex National *East Course*	Eng	469
17 7 6	El Prat *Verde*	E	912

37

C'est bien la première fois
que vos clients apprécieront un cadeau
où l'on n'a même pas enlevé le prix.

CLM/BBDO

Ce n'est pas parce que le prix apparaît sur les chèques carburants de TOTAL

que ce cadeau ne fera pas plaisir à vos équipes et à vos clients. Pratiques et

simples à gérer, ces chèques cadeaux sont disponibles en coupures de 20, 50

ou 100 francs et peuvent être personnalisés avec un texte choisi. De plus,

les bénéficiaires des chèques pourront très facilement les utiliser, puisque le

réseau TOTAL est très dense avec plus de 3 000 stations-service en France.

Pour toute information complémentaire ou pour obtenir

un bon de commande : Monique Lucas 01 41 35 80 43.

TOTAL

VOUS NE VIENDREZ PLUS CHEZ NOUS PAR HASARD.

CLASSIFICATION OF COURSES

Score	Course	Country	Page
17 7 6	Emporda	E	914
17 7 8	Fairhaven	Eng	470
17 7 7	Ferndown *Old Course*	Eng	472
17 7 7	Fontainebleau	F	205
17 6 7	Forest Pines *Forest + Pines*	Eng	474
17 7 8	Fulford	Eng	477
17 7 8	Genève	S	993
17 9 7	Gleneagles *Monarch's*	Sc	619
17 7 6	Grenoble Bresson	F	216
17 8 7	Gullane *No 1*	Sc	623
17 7 6	Gut Kaden		
	Platz B + Platz C	G	335
17 7 5	Gut Waldhof	G	339
17 8 7	Hamburg-Ahrensburg	G	340
17 8 6	Hubbelrath	G	349
17 7 6	Hunstanton	Eng	491
17 8 8	K Club	I	737
17 6 8	Kilmarnock (Barassie)	Sc	626
17 6 7	Köln	G	354
17 7 7	Krefelder	G	356
17 8 6	La Cala *Norte*	E	925
17 7 8	La Moye	Eng	497
17 7 5	Ladybank	Sc	628
17 7 4	Lerma	E	939
17 6 5	Limère	F	230
17 8 6	Linden Hall	Eng	498
17 6 6	Lindrick	Eng	499
17 7 5	Lüneburger Heide	G	359
17 7 7	Machrie	Sc	635
17 7 5	Médoc *Les Châteaux*	F	234
17 7 7	Monifieth	Sc	637
17 8 7	Montecastillo	E	950
17 5 6	Montrose	Sc	638
17 8 7	Moor Park *High Course*	Eng	508
17 5 5	Moray	Sc	639
17 7 7	Neguri	E	952
17 7 6	North Hants	Eng	512
17 6 5	Oberfranken	G	372
17 7 7	Orchardleigh	Eng	514
17 6 5	Panmure	Sc	646
17 7 5	Pléneuf-Val-André	F	245
17 7 8	Portmarnock Links	I	753
17 7 5	Praia d'El Rey	P	848
17 8 7	Prestbury	Eng	522
17 7 5	Pyle & Kenfig	W	686
17 8 7	Ravenstein	B	86
17 7 7	Reichswald-Nürnberg	G	377
17 6 5	Royal Cinque Ports	Eng	527
17 7 8	Royal Mougins	F	256

Score	Course	Country	Page
17 7 6	Royal West Norfolk		
	(Brancaster)	Eng	536
17 6 8	S. Lourenço	P	854
17 7 7	Saint-Germain	F	261
17 8 6	San Roque	E	967
17 5 7	Sandiway	Eng	540
17 7 6	Schloss Lüdersburg *Old/New*	G	386
17 6 4	Seacroft	Eng	542
17 7 7	Seignosse	F	270
17 7 8	Sevilla	E	971
17 7 6	Sherwood Forest	Eng	547
17 5 5	Shiskine (Blackwaterfoot)	Sc	660
17 8 7	Slaley Hall	Eng	549
17 7 7	Spa (Les Fagnes)	B	92
17 7 5	Spérone	F	273
17 8 8	St Andrews *New Course*	Sc	664
17 7 7	St George's Hill	Eng	552
17 9 7	St Mellion *Nicklaus Course*	Eng	553
17 7 6	St. Dionys	G	391
17 8 8	Stoke Poges	Eng	554
17 7 5	Stolper Heide	G	393
17 5 5	Stuttgarter Solitude	G	394
17 6 6	Tain	Sc	668
17 6 7	Touquet (Le) *La Mer*	F	278
17 7 7	Trevose *Championship*	Eng	563
17 6 4	Villette d'Anthon		
	Les Sangliers	F	283
17 7 7	Wallasey	Eng	564
17 6 7	Waterville	I	771
17 7 7	West Lancashire	Eng	573
17 5 7	Western Gailes	Sc	673
17 6 7	Whittington Heath	Eng	577

16 / 20

Score	Course	Country	Page
16 5 4	Aisses (Les) *Rouge/Blanc*	F	150
16 7 7	Antwerp	B	76
16 7 6	Ashridge	Eng	441
16 5 7	Ayr (Belleisle)	Sc	589
16 7 7	Ballybunion		
	Cashen (New Course)	I	706
16 6 9	Bath	Eng	443
16 7 7	Beau Desert	Eng	444
16 6 5	Belle-Dune	F	165
16 7 6	Berkhamsted	Eng	445
16 7 6	Bondues *Blanc*	F	170
16 7 6	Bonmont	E	899
16 7 6	Bowood (Cornwall)	Eng	451

Cartes et guides
Maps and guides
Michelin,
Michelin,
choisissez
choose
votre étape...
where to stay

CLASSIFICATION OF COURSES

Score			Course	Country	Page
16	6	6	Carlow	I	714
16	5	3	Carn	I	715
16	6	6	Castlerock	U	781
16	6	6	Charmeil	F	187
16	6	8	Chiberta	F	189
16	8	8	Club de Campo	E	906
16	7	3	Courson Vert/Noir	F	193
16	8	5	Cromstrijen	N	804
16	9	6	Dartmouth	Eng	466
16	8	7	De Pan	N	805
16	6	4	Dingle (Ceann Sibeal)	I	722
16	7	8	Disneyland Paris		
			Never Land + Wonderland	F	196
16	2	6	Donegal (Murvagh)	I	723
16	9	7	Druids Glen	I	726
16	7	8	Duke's Course St Andrews	Sc	607
16	5	6	Dunbar	Sc	609
16	8	5	Efteling	N	806
16	7	4	El Bosque	E	909
16	7	6	Enniscrone	I	728
16	6	7	Estérel Latitudes	F	200
16	6	5	Fortrose & Rosemarkie	Sc	616
16	7	8	Frankfurter GC	G	331
16	7	7	Glasson	I	734
16	7	6	Gouverneur (Le) Le Breuil	F	210
16	6	6	Grande Bastide (La)	F	212
16	6	4	Grande-Motte (La)		
			Les Flamants Roses	F	213
16	7	5	Gut Thailing	G	338
16	7	7	Hadley Wood	Eng	481
16	6	6	Hankley Common	Eng	482
16	7	7	Hannover	G	343
16	6	6	Hardelot Les Pins	F	219
16	7	7	Hayling	Eng	484
16	7	6	Herkenbosch	N	814
16	7	7	Hilversum	N	815
16	7	6	Hindhead	Eng	490
16	7	5	Hof Trages	G	346
16	7	5	Holyhead	W	681
16	6	6	Hossegor	F	221
16	7	6	Iffeldorf	G	350
16	7	7	Ipswich (Purdis Heath)	Eng	494
16	8	8	Islantilla	E	923
16	7	4	Isle Adam (L')	F	222
16	7	6	Isle of Purbeck	Eng	495
16	7	6	John O'Gaunt	Eng	496
16	8	7	Joyenval Marly	F	223
16	7	8	Killarney Killeen Course	I	739
16	8	6	La Cala Sur	E	926

Score			Course	Country	Page
16	7	8	La Moraleja La Moraleja 2	E	933
16	7	7	La Zagaleta	E	936
16	6	5	Lanark	Sc	629
16	7	7	Lausanne	S	996
16	6	6	Leven	Sc	631
16	7	4	Limburg	B	81
16	7	6	Liphook	Eng	500
16	7	7	Los Naranjos	E	941
16	5	6	Luffness New	Sc	633
16	6	7	Lundin	Sc	634
16	7	7	Manchester	Eng	503
16	8	7	Marriott St Pierre		
			Old Course	W	682
16	7	8	Maspalomas	E	945
16	7	6	Mediterraneo	E	946
16	6	7	Mijas Los Lagos	E	947
16	7	5	Montpellier-Massane	F	236
16	7	7	München-Riedhof	G	366
16	6	7	Neckartal	G	369
16	6	5	Nefyn & District	W	683
16	7	6	Nîmes-Campagne	F	239
16	7	7	Novo Sancti Petri	E	953
16	7	6	Pals	E	956
16	7	5	Paris International	F	243
16	7	8	Parkstone	Eng	517
16	6	5	Peralada	E	959
16	6	6	Perranporth	Eng	519
16	8	6	Pleasington	Eng	520
16	6	5	Pont Royal	F	247
16	5	5	Portsalon	I	754
16	7	7	Portstewart Strand Course	U	788
16	6	4	Powfoot	Sc	650
16	6	7	Prestwick St Nicholas	Sc	652
16	8	9	Puerta de Hierro	E	963
16	7	7	Purmerend	N	822
16	7	5	Quinta do Peru	P	853
16	6	4	Rebetz	F	251
16	7	6	Rosapenna	I	757
16	7	9	Royal Burgess	Sc	655
16	7	7	Royal Dublin	I	759
16	7	7	Royal Guernsey	Eng	529
16	7	8	Royal Jersey	Eng	530
16	8	7	Royal Musselburgh	Sc	657
16	7	4	Sablé-Solesmes		
			La Forêt/La Rivière	F	257
16	6	5	Saint-Jean-de-Monts	F	262
16	8	8	Saint-Nom-la-Bretèche		
			Rouge	F	265
16	7	7	Sart-Tilman	B	91

41

Score			Course	Country	Page
16	8	7	Scharmützelsee		
			Arnold Palmer	G	378
16	7	7	Schloss Braunfels	G	381
16	8	7	Schloss Langenstein	G	384
16	8	7	Schloss Liebenstein		
			Gelb + Blau	G	385
16	7	7	Schloss Myllendonk	G	387
16	6	6	Scotscraig	Sc	659
16	7	7	Sonnenalp	G	390
16	7	4	Soufflenheim	F	272
16	7	7	Southerndown	W	690
16	8	8	St Andrews *Jubilee Course*	Sc	663
16	7	7	St Margaret's	I	764
16	7	6	St. Eurach	G	392
16	6	4	Thurlestone	Eng	562
16	9	8	Turnberry *Arran Course*	Sc	671
16	6	6	Ulzama	E	976
16	7	7	Vilamoura *I (Old Course)*	P	859
16	7	6	Villamartin	E	978
16	7	6	Walton Heath *New Course*	Eng	565
16	6	6	Wantzenau (La)	F	285
16	8	7	Waterloo *La Marache*	B	94
16	7	6	Wendlohe *A-Kurs + B-Kurs*	G	399
16	7	6	Wentorf-Reinbeker	G	400
16	8	7	Wentworth *East Course*	Eng	568
16	7	6	West Cornwall	Eng	571
16	7	5	West Kilbride	Sc	672
16	6	7	Weston-Super-Mare	Eng	576
16	6	6	Woking	Eng	579
16	7	6	Woodenbridge	I	774
16	7	6	Worplesdon	Eng	583
16	7	6	Zaudin	E	979

42

15/20

Score			Course	Country	Page
15	6	4	Ableiges *Les Etangs*	F	148
15	6	7	Adare	I	704
15	6	5	Ailette (L')	F	149
15	6	6	Albi	F	152
15	7	6	Alloa	E	587
15	7	8	Amirauté (L')	F	153
15	7	7	Amsterdam	N	800
15	8	6	Apremont	F	157
15	6	6	Aroeira	P	840
15	7	7	Augsburg	G	313
15	9	9	Bad Griesbach-Sagmühle		
			Sagmühle	G	315

Score			Course	Country	Page
15	6	5	Baden	F	161
15	7	7	Bâle-Hagenthal	F	162
15	6	7	Ballater	Sc	591
15	6	5	Ballyliffin *Old Course*	I	710
15	7	7	Bamberg	G	318
15	7	3	Batouwe	N	802
15	7	8	Baule (La) *Rouge*	F	164
15	5	6	Belvoir Park	U	778
15	6	8	Berlin-Wannsee	G	319
15	6	5	Berwick-upon-Tweed	Eng	448
15	8	6	Blairgowrie *Lansdowne*	Sc	592
15	7	6	Blumisberg	S	987
15	5	7	Bolton Old Links	Eng	450
15	7	6	Bondues *Jaune*	F	171
15	6	4	Bresse (La)	F	173
15	7	7	Bretesche (La)	F	175
15	7	6	Broekpolder	N	803
15	7	7	Brora	Sc	595
15	8	9	Bruntsfield	Sc	596
15	7	6	Buxtehude	G	323
15	7	8	Cannes-Mougins	F	178
15	6	6	Canyamel	E	901
15	6	5	Cap d'Agde	F	179
15	7	6	Capdepera	E	902
15	6	5	Casteljaloux	F	180
15	7	6	Cély	F	181
15	6	7	Chamonix	F	183
15	6	6	Clandeboye *Dufferin Course*	U	782
15	7	7	Club d'Aro *(Mas Nou)*	E	905
15	3	5	Cork GC	I	718
15	7	5	County Tipperary	I	721
15	7	3	Courson *Lilas/Orange*	F	192
15	6	6	Coxmoor	Eng	464
15	6	6	Crail	Sc	600
15	7	7	Crieff *Ferntower Course*	Sc	601
15	6	7	Delamere Forest	Eng	467
15	7	7	Denham	Eng	468
15	5	5	Dooks	I	724
15	7	9	Duddingston	Sc	605
15	6	6	Duff House Royal	Sc	606
15	7	5	Dumfries & County	Sc	608
15	6	6	Dundalk	I	727
15	7	7	Dunfermline	Sc	610
15	6	8	East Renfrewshire	Sc	611
15	7	6	El Prat *Amarillo*	E	911
15	7	6	Elgin	Sc	613
15	6	6	Elie	Sc	614
15	6	6	Engadin	S	991
15	7	5	Esery	F	199

CLASSIFICATION OF COURSES

Score	Course	Country	Page
15 6 5	Etiolles *Les Cerfs*	F	201
15 7 9	Evian	F	203
15 6 6	Felixstowe Ferry		
	Martello Course	Eng	471
15 7 5	Feucherolles	F	204
15 7 6	Fota Island	I	731
15 7 7	Frégate	F	209
15 7 7	Gendersteyn	N	809
15 9 7	Gleneagles *Queen's*	Sc	620
15 3 6	Goes	N	810
15 7 8	Gog Magog *Old Course*	Eng	480
15 7 6	Graafschap	N	811
15 7 6	Gujan-Mestras	F	218
15 6 6	Gut Ludwigsberg	G	336
15 7 9	Haggs Castle	Sc	624
15 7 5	Hainaut *Bruyere-Quesnoy*	B	79
15 6 6	Hamburg-Holm	G	341
15 6 6	Hanau-Wilhelmsbad	G	342
15 8 7	Hawkstone Park *Hawkstone*	Eng	483
15 6 7	Hermitage	I	736
15 6 6	Herreria	E	922
15 7 7	Hertfordshire (The)	Eng	486
15 6 7	High Post	Eng	488
15 6 7	Hoge Kleij	N	816
15 7 6	Hohenpähl	G	347
15 7 6	Isernhagen	G	352
15 7 6	Jakobsberg	G	353
15 8 7	Joyenval *Retz*	F	224
15 7 8	Killarney *Mahony's Point*	I	740
15 4 5	Kingussie	Sc	627
15 6 5	Kirkistown Castle	U	783
15 7 6	Knock	U	784
15 7 8	La Boulie (R.C.F.) *La Vallée*	F	226
15 7 7	La Manga *Norte*	E	929
15 7 8	La Moraleja *La Moraleja 1*	E	932
15 8 7	La Quinta	E	934
15 6 5	La Sella	E	935
15 7 4	Largue (La)	F	228
15 7 5	Letham Grange *Old Course*	Sc	630
15 7 6	Lichtenau-Weickershof	G	357
15 7 6	Limerick County	I	744
15 7 6	Lisburn	U	785
15 7 8	Lugano	S	997
15 7 7	Luttrellstown	I	745
15 7 8	Lytham Green Drive	Eng	502
15 8 7	Manor House		
	(Castle Combe)	Eng	505
15 7 8	Marbella	E	943
15 7 6	Masia Bach	E	944
15 7 5	Médoc *Les Vignes*	F	235
15 5 7	Mendip	Eng	506
15 7 7	Mere	Eng	507
15 7 7	Mittelrheinischer	G	363
15 7 7	Montenmedio	E	951
15 6 6	Murcar	Sc	641
15 6 7	Nairn Dunbar	Sc	644
15 7 7	Neuhof	G	370
15 7 8	New Golf Deauville		
	Rouge/Blanc	F	238
15 6 7	Newbury & Crookham	Eng	510
15 6 7	Newport	W	684
15 5 3	Nunspeet *North/East*	N	820
15 6 6	Oberschwaben Bad Waldsee	G	373
15 7 7	Old Head	I	751
15 7 7	Oostende	B	83
15 7 7	Oosterhout	N	821
15 7 7	Öschberghof	G	374
15 6 7	Pannal	Eng	516
15 7 7	Patriziale Ascona	S	1002
15 7 8	Penha Longa	P	845
15 5 4	Peterhead	Sc	647
15 7 9	Pineda	E	960
15 7 6	Ploemeur Océan	F	246
15 6 6	Pornic	F	249
15 8 7	Portal *Championship*	Eng	521
15 6 7	Portpatrick (Dunskey)	Sc	649
15 7 7	Powerscourt	I	755
15 7 8	Quinta do Lago *B/C*	P	851
15 7 8	Quinta do Lago		
	Ria Formosa	P	852
15 7 6	Rathsallagh	I	756
15 6 6	Rolls of Monmouth (The)	W	687
15 7 4	Roncemay	F	255
15 7 7	Rosendael	N	824
15 5 6	Ross-on-Wye	Eng	524
15 7 7	Roxburghe (The)	Sc	653
15 7 7	Royal Belfast	U	789
15 7 6	Royal Cromer	Eng	528
15 8 6	Royal Latem	B	89
15 6 8	Royal Winchester	Eng	537
15 8 8	Rudding Park	Eng	538
15 7 8	Saint-Donat	F	259
15 7 4	Saint-Endréol	F	260
15 8 8	Saint-Nom-la-Bretèche *Bleu*	F	264
15 6 4	Savenay	F	269
15 7 7	Schloss Egmating	G	382
15 7 5	Schloss Wilkendorf	G	388
15 6 6	Seapoint	I	760

43

CLASSIFICATION OF COURSES

Score			Course	Country	Page	Score			Course	Country	Page
15	7	6	Shanklin & Sandown	Eng	544	14	6	6	Bangor	U	777
15	6	7	Sherborne	Eng	545	14	6	7	Beaufort	I	711
15	7	6	Sheringham	Eng	546	14	7	5	Béthemont	F	167
15	7	5	Sint Nicolaasga	N	825	14	6	8	Biarritz-le-Phare	F	168
15	8	6	Slieve Russell	I	762	14	6	5	Bitche	F	169
15	7	8	Stoneham	Eng	555	14	6	7	Boat of Garten	Sc	594
15	5	6	Strathaven	Sc	667	14	6	6	Bonalba	E	898
15	6	6	Sybrook	N	826	14	6	5	Brancepeth Castle	Eng	454
15	7	4	Taulane	F	275	14	7	6	Brest Iroise	F	174
15	7	8	Tegernseer Bad Wiessee	G	395	14	7	6	Brigode	F	176
15	7	7	The Island	I	765	14	6	6	Buchanan Castle	Sc	597
15	6	5	Thornhill	Sc	669	14	6	6	Campoamor	E	900
15	7	4	Toulouse Palmola	F	276	14	8	8	Carden Park	Eng	458
15	7	6	Toulouse-Seilh *Rouge*	F	277	14	3	4	Carnoustie *Burnside*	Sc	598
15	7	5	Troia	P	856	14	7	7	Cerdaña	E	904
15	6	5	Tullamore	I	768	14	8	6	Chailly (Château de)	F	182
15	7	6	Tutzing	G	397	14	6	3	Champ de Bataille	F	184
15	6	5	Val Queven	F	281	14	7	7	Chantaco	F	185
15	7	4	Vaucouleurs (La) *Les Vallons*	F	282	14	7	6	Cheverny	F	188
15	7	6	Walddörfer	G	398	14	8	7	Collingtree Park	Eng	463
15	7	8	Warwickshire (The)	Eng	567	14	6	6	Connemara	I	717
15	7	7	West Berkshire	Eng	570	14	7	8	Crans-sur-Sierre	S	989
15	6	6	West Hill	Eng	572	14	6	5	Dieppe-Pourville	F	194
15	7	7	West Surrey	Eng	574	14	6	7	Dinard	F	195
15	7	7	Westport	I	773	14	6	7	Divonne	F	197
15	7	7	Whitekirk	Sc	675	14	7	7	Dromoland Castle	I	725
15	4	5	Wimereux	F	286	14	6	3	Edzell	Sc	612
15	7	6	Wittelsbacher	Eng	401	14	7	7	Elfrather Mühle	G	327
15	9	6	Woodbury Park *The Oaks*	Eng	581	14	7	7	Eschenried	G	328
15	7	6	Wouwse Plantage	N	828	14	7	6	Estepona	E	916
15	7	6	Zumikon	S	1005	14	6	5	Etretat	F	202
						14	7	4	Falnuee	B	78
						14	6	6	Fontcaude	F	206
						14	7	6	Fontenailles *Blanc*	F	207
						14	7	4	Fontenelles (Les)	F	208
						14	8	8	Forest of Arden		
									Arden Course	Eng	473
14	7	6	Abenberg	G	312	14	6	6	Forfar	Sc	615
14	6	6	Aboyne	Sc	586	14	8	6	Formby Hall	Eng	476
14	6	5	Alcaidesa	E	892	14	7	6	Fränkische Schweiz	G	332
14	7	5	Alhaurin	E	893	14	7	6	Fürstliches Hofgut		
14	6	6	Almerimar	E	894				Kolnhausen	G	333
14	6	6	Alyth	Sc	588	14	8	6	Gainsborough-Karsten Lakes	Eng	478
14	7	6	Anderstein	N	801	14	7	6	Galway Bay	I	732
14	7	8	Arcangues	F	159	14	6	7	Garmisch-Partenkirchen	G	334
14	6	4	Ardglass	U	776	14	4	5	Gelpenberg	N	808
14	6	8	Baberton	Sc	590	14	7	7	Glen	Sc	617
14	7	7	Bad Liebenzell	G	316	14	7	6	Golf de la Gruyère	S	994
14	6	6	Bad Wörishofen	G	317	14	5	4	Golspie	Sc	621
14	7	7	Badgemore Park	Eng	442						
14	7	6	Ballykisteen	I	708						

44

CLASSIFICATION OF COURSES

Score			Course	Country	Page
14	7	6	Gouverneur (Le) *Montaplan*	F	211
14	6	5	Granada	E	919
14	6	7	Grantown on Spey	Sc	622
14	4	4	Granville *Les Dunes*	F	214
14	6	5	Greenore	I	735
14	7	4	Grevelingenhout	N	812
14	7	6	Guadalhorce	E	920
14	7	7	Guadalmina *Sur*	E	921
14	7	4	Guerville	F	217
14	7	6	Gut Rieden	G	337
14	6	4	Haut-Poitou	F	220
14	6	6	Hechingen-Hohenzollern	G	344
14	6	7	Henley	Eng	485
14	7	6	Hetzenhof	G	345
14	8	8	Hever	Eng	487
14	6	7	Huntercombe	Eng	492
14	6	6	Huntly	Sc	625
14	7	6	Im Chiemgau	G	351
14	6	6	Interlaken	S	995
14	7	6	Keerbergen	B	80
14	6	5	Killorglin	I	741
14	7	4	La Dehesa	E	927
14	7	7	La Manga *Oeste*	E	930
14	7	7	La Manga *Sur*	E	931
14	6	4	Lacanau	F	227
14	6	7	Lauswolt	N	818
14	7	5	Laval-Changé *La Chabossière*	F	229
14	7	8	Lindau-Bad Schachen	G	358
14	6	5	Littlestone	Eng	501
14	6	7	Los Arqueros	E	940
14	6	8	Lothianburn	Sc	632
14	7	5	Madeira	P	842
14	7	5	Maison Blanche	F	231
14	6	8	Makila Golf Club	F	232
14	8	6	Mannings Heath *Waterfall Course*	Eng	504
14	7	6	Märkischer Potsdam	G	361
14	5	6	Massereene	U	787
14	6	6	Memmingen Gut Westerhart	G	362
14	5	5	Mullingar	I	749
14	6	7	Münchner-Strasslach	G	367
14	7	8	Murrayshall	Sc	642
14	7	6	Nahetal	G	368
14	6	7	Neuchâtel	S	1000
14	7	7	Obere Alp	G	371
14	7	5	Omaha Beach *La Mer/Le Bocage*	F	240
14	6	4	Ormskirk	Eng	515
14	7	4	Osona Montana	E	955
14	6	6	Oudenaarde	B	84
14	6	4	Panoramica	E	957
14	6	5	Pedreña	E	958
14	7	8	Penina	P	846
14	8	8	Pinheiros Altos	P	847
14	6	6	Pinnau	G	375
14	6	7	Pitlochry	Sc	648
14	6	4	Porcelaine (La)	F	248
14	8	7	Quinta da Beloura	P	849
14	6	4	Raray (Château de) *La Licorne*	F	250
14	6	7	Reichsstadt Bad Windsheim	G	376
14	7	6	Rigenée	B	87
14	6	5	Rijk van Nijmegen *Nijmeegse Baan*	N	823
14	6	5	Rinkven *Red - White*	B	88
14	6	4	Rochefort-Chisan	F	254
14	7	6	Royal Ashdown Forest	Eng	525
14	7	8	Royal Mid-Surrey *Outer*	Eng	533
14	7	7	Saint-Cloud *Vert*	F	258
14	7	5	Saint-Laurent	F	263
14	7	5	Saint-Thomas	F	266
14	7	7	Salgados	P	855
14	6	6	San Sebastián	E	968
14	7	7	Sand Moor	Eng	539
14	6	6	Schloss Klingenburg	G	383
14	7	6	Schönenberg	S	1003
14	8	7	Semlin am See	G	389
14	7	6	Son Antem	E	972
14	6	7	Son Vida	E	973
14	7	8	Spiegelven	B	93
14	8	8	St Andrews *Eden Course*	Sc	662
14	6	6	St Helen's Bay	I	763
14	7	6	Tandridge	Eng	558
14	7	5	Thetford	Eng	559
14	7	6	Thorndon Park	Eng	560
14	7	7	Thorpeness	Eng	561
14	7	7	Torrequebrada	E	975
14	7	6	Toxandria	N	827
14	7	5	Val de Some	F	280
14	6	6	Vale da Pinta	P	857
14	7	7	Vila Sol	P	858
14	7	7	Vilamoura *III (Laguna)*	P	861
14	6	5	Volcans (Les)	F	284
14	6	6	Waterford	I	769
14	5	6	Waterford Castle	I	770
14	8	6	Westerwood	Sc	674
14	7	7	Woodbridge	Eng	580
14	7	7	Zuid Limburgse	N	829

45

CLASSIFICATION OF COURSES

Score	Course	Country	Page	Score	Course	Country	Page
				13 7 8	Malahide *R. + Bl. + Y.*	I	746
				13 6 6	Malone	U	786
				13 5 4	Mazamet-La Barouge	F	233
13 5 7	Aix-les-Bains	F	151	13 6 7	Mijas *Los Olivos*	E	948
13 6 7	Aldeburgh	Eng	439	13 7 6	Mont-Garni	B	82
13 6 5	Amnéville	F	154	13 7 6	Montado	P	843
13 6 6	Anjou-Champigné	F	155	13 5 5	Monte Mayor	E	949
13 6 5	Annonay-Gourdan	F	156	13 6 5	Montreux	S	999
13 6 6	Arcachon	F	158	13 6 5	Mount Wolsley	I	748
13 6 7	Atalaya *Old Course*	E	896	13 6 7	Mülheim	G	365
13 6 6	Athlone	I	705	13 7 5	Newcastle West	I	750
13 5 4	Augerville	F	160	13 7 7	Niederbüren	S	1001
13 7 6	Bad Ragaz	S	986	13 7 7	North Foreland	Eng	511
13 6 7	Bendinat	E	897	13 7 8	Olivar de la Hinojosa	E	954
13 7 7	Bercuit	B	77	13 6 7	Opio Valbonne	F	241
13 7 5	Besançon	F	166	13 7 5	Ozoir-la-Ferrière *Château/M*ᵀʸ	F	242
13 6 6	Blainroe	I	712	13 6 6	Palingbeek	B	85
13 7 6	Breitenloo	S	988	13 7 5	Palmares	P	844
13 6 7	Bundoran	I	713	13 8 8	Patshull Park Hotel	Eng	518
13 6 5	Cairndhu	U	779	13 7 7	Pessac	F	244
13 7 8	Cannes Mandelieu			13 6 4	Playa Serena	E	961
	Old Course	F	177	13 6 5	Poniente	E	962
13 7 6	Castle Hume	U	780	13 6 4	Prince's *Himalayas-Shore*	Eng	523
13 4 6	Charleville	I	716	13 6 5	Pula	E	964
13 7 5	Cognac	F	190	13 7 7	Quinta da Marinha	P	850
13 7 7	Costa Brava	E	907	13 7 6	Reims-Champagne	F	252
13 6 6	Costa Dorada	E	908	13 6 7	Rio Real	E	966
13 7 4	Domont-Montmorency	F	198	13 7 8	Riviéra Golf Club	F	253
13 6 6	Düsseldorf/Hösel	G	325	13 5 6	Rosslare	I	758
13 7 7	Düsseldorfer	G	326	13 7 7	Royal Portrush *Valley*	U	792
13 6 6	El Paraiso	E	910	13 7 6	Sainte-Baume (La)	F	267
13 7 6	Ennetsee-Holzhäusern	S	992	13 7 7	Sainte-Maxime	F	268
13 8 4	Escorpion	E	915	13 6 5	Sant Cugat	E	969
13 7 7	Estoril	P	841	13 6 7	Santa Ponsa	E	970
13 7 6	Faithlegg	I	730	13 7 7	Scheibenhardt	G	380
13 6 6	Galway GC	I	733	13 7 7	Servanes	F	271
13 7 5	Girona	E	918	13 6 6	Shannon	I	761
13 6 7	Grand Ducal de Luxembourg	L	95	13 5 5	Stonehaven	Sc	666
13 7 6	Grasse	F	215	13 7 6	Strasbourg Illkirch		
13 6 6	Hoisdorf	G	348		*Jaune + Rouge*	F	274
13 7 6	Jarama R.A.C.E.	E	924	13 7 6	Touraine	F	279
13 7 6	Kilkenny	I	738	13 7 6	Tramore	I	767
13 6 6	Königsfeld	G	355	13 8 7	Treudelberg	G	396
13 7 6	La Duquesa	E	928	13 7 7	Vilamoura *II (Pinhal)*	P	860
13 7 5	Lauro	E	938	13 6 5	Warrenpoint	U	793
13 7 6	Lee Valley	I	743	13 5 6	Woodstock	I	775
13 6 7	Luzern	S	998	13 6 6	Wylihof	S	1004
13 7 6	Main-Taunus	G	360	13 7 4	Yvelines *Les Chênes*	F	287
13 4 6	Malaga	E	942	12 7 6	West Waterford	I	772

46

ARCHITECTS AND COURSES
ARCHITECTES ET PARCOURS
ARQUITECTOS Y RECORRIDOS
ARQUITECTOS E PERCURSOS
ARCHITEKTEN UND GOLFPLÄTZE
ARCHITECTEN EN TERREINEN

Architect Golf course	Country	Score			Page
John Abercromby					
Worplesdon	Eng	16	7	6	583
Marc Adam					
Cély	F	15	7	6	181
Bitche	F	14	6	5	169
Peter Alliss					
Alcaidesa	Es	14	6	5	892
Cannes-Mougins	F	15	7	8	178
Manor House (Castle Combe)	Eng	15	8	7	505
Peter Alliss & Dave Thomas					
Baule (La) *Rouge*	F	15	7	8	164
Javier Arana					
El Saler	Es	18	7	6	913
Neguri	Es	17	7	7	952
Aloha	Es	17	7	7	895
El Prat *Verde*	Es	17	7	6	912
Club de Campo	Es	16	8	8	906
Ulzama	Es	16	6	6	976
Cerdaña	Es	14	7	7	904
Guadalmina *Sur*	Es	14	7	7	921
Jarama R.A.C.E.	Es	13	7	6	924
Rio Real	Es	13	6	7	966
Harold Bill Baker					
Amirauté (L')	F	15	7	8	153
Bretesche (La)	F	15	7	7	175
Brigode	F	14	7	6	176
Haut-Poitou	F	14	6	4	220
Yvelines *Les Chênes*	F	13	7	4	287
Oudenaarde	B	14	6	6	84
Palingbeek	B	13	6	6	85
Seve Ballesteros					
Novo Sancti Petri	Es	16	7	7	953
Pont Royal	F	16	6	5	247
Alhaurin	Es	14	7	5	893
Los Arqueros	Es	14	6	7	940
Westerwood	Sc	14	8	6	674
R.& F. M. Benjumea					
Pineda	Es	15	7	9	960
Bradford Benz					
La Zagaleta	Es	16	7	7	936

Architect Golf course	Country	Score			Page
Robert Berthet					
Sainte-Baume (La)	F	13	7	6	267
Nicholas Bielenberg					
Luttrellstown	I	15	7	7	745
Cecil R. Blandford					
Arcachon	F	13	6	6	158
Braid, Fowler, Colt					
Aberdovey	W	17	7	7	677
James Braid					
Gleneagles *King's*	Sc	18	9	7	618
Pennard	W	18	6	6	685
Southport & Ainsdale	Eng	18	7	7	550
St Enodoc *Church Course*	Eng	18	7	4	551
Tenby	W	18	7	6	691
Brampton	Eng	17	7	6	453
Clitheroe	Eng	17	7	7	462
Dalmahoy *East Course*	Sc	17	8	8	603
Fairhaven	Eng	17	7	8	470
Hunstanton	Eng	17	7	6	491
La Moye	Eng	17	7	8	497
North Hants	Eng	17	7	6	512
Ayr (Belleisle)	Sc	16	5	7	589
Fortrose & Rosemarkie	Sc	16	6	5	616
Holyhead	W	16	7	5	681
Ipswich (Purdis Heath)	Eng	16	7	7	494
Lundin	Sc	16	6	7	634
Nefyn & District	W	16	6	5	683
Perranporth	Eng	16	6	6	519
Powfoot	Sc	16	6	4	650
Royal Musselburgh	Sc	16	8	7	657
Alloa	Sc	15	7	6	587
Ballater	Sc	15	6	7	591
Berwick-upon-Tweed	Eng	15	6	5	448
Brora	Sc	15	7	7	595
East Renfrewshire	Sc	15	6	8	611
Gleneagles *Queen's*	Sc	15	9	7	620
Hawkstone Park *Hawkstone*	Eng	15	8	7	483
Kirkistown Castle	U	15	6	5	783
Mere	Eng	15	7	7	507
Shanklin & Sandown	Eng	15	7	6	544

47

Score	Course			Country	Page	Score	Course			Country	Page

James Braid

Tullamore	I	15 6 5	768
Bangor	U	14 6 6	777
Boat of Garten	Sc	14 6 7	594
Buchanan Castle	Sc	14 6 6	597
Henley	Eng	14 6 7	485
Lothianburn	Sc	14 6 8	632
Mullingar	I	14 5 5	749
Thorpeness	Eng	14 7 7	561
Scotscraig	Sc	16 6 6	659
Golspie	Sc	14 5 4	621
Sherborne	Eng	15 6 7	545

Olivier Brizon

Aisses (Les) *Rouge/Blanc*	F	16 5 4	150
Pessac	F	13 7 7	244

A.C. Brown/W. Park

Grantown on Spey	Sc	14 6 7	622

G. Bruns

Isernhagen	G	15 7 6	352

Yves Bureau

Saint-Jean-de-Monts	F	16 6 5	262
Baden	F	15 6 5	161
Val Queven	F	15 6 5	281
Fontenelles (Les)	F	14 7 4	208
Guerville	F	14 7 4	217
Omaha Beach			
La Mer/Le Bocage	F	14 7 5	240

Burrows

Hilversum	N	16 7 7	815

Sir Guy Campbell

West Sussex	Eng	18 7 6	575
Ashridge	Eng	16 7 6	441
Killarney *Mahony's Point*	I	15 7 8	740
Prince's *Himalayas-Shore*	Eng	13 6 4	523

Sir Guy Campbell & Hutchinson

Wimereux	F	15 4 5	286

Willie Campbell

Seascale	Eng	18 5 4	543
Machrie	Sc	17 7 7	635

Enrique Canales

Islantilla	Es	16 8 8	923

Tony Carroll

Castle Hume	U	13 7 6	780

M. Chantepie

Etretat	F	14 6 5	202

Hubert Chesneau

National *L'Albatros*	F	18 6 6	237

Neil Coles

Gainsborough-Karsten Lakes	Eng	14 8 6	478

Harry S. Colt

Chantaco	F	14 7 7	185
Cannes Mandelieu			
Old Course	F	13 7 8	177
Royal Portrush			
Dunluce Links	U	19 7 7	791
Alwoodley (The)	Eng	18 7 7	440
Eindhoven	N	18 8 6	807
Falkenstein	G	18 6 7	329
Haagsche	N	18 7 8	813
Ilkley	Eng	18 7 6	493
Kennemer	N	18 8 8	817
Sunningdale *New Course*	Eng	18 8 8	556
Wentworth *West Course*	Eng	18 8 7	569
Blackmoor	Eng	17 6 5	449
County Sligo	I	17 4 3	720
Moor Park *High Course*	Eng	17 8 7	508
Prestbury	Eng	17 8 7	522
Pyle & Kenfig	W	17 7 5	686
Saint-Germain	F	17 7 7	261
Sherwood Forest	Eng	17 7 6	547
St George's Hill	Eng	17 7 7	552
Stoke Poges	Eng	17 8 8	554
Trevose *Championship*	Eng	17 7 7	563
Whittington Heath	Eng	17 6 7	577
De Pan	N	16 8 7	805
Frankfurter GC	G	16 7 8	331
Isle of Purbeck	Eng	16 7 6	495
Manchester	Eng	16 7 7	503
Thurlestone	Eng	16 6 4	562
Wentworth *East Course*	Eng	16 8 7	568
Belvoir Park	U	15 5 6	778
Denham	Eng	15 7 7	468
Royal Belfast	U	15 7 7	789
Brancepeth Castle	Eng	14 6 5	454
Pedreña	Es	14 6 5	958
Saint-Cloud *Vert*	F	14 7 7	258
Tandridge	Eng	14 7 6	558
Thorndon Park	Eng	14 7 6	560
Bath	Eng	16 6 9	443
Royal Zoute	B	18 7 7	90
Royal Dublin	I	16 7 7	759
Malaga	Es	13 4 6	942

Harry S. Colt, MacKenzie

Knock	U	15 7 6	784

Harry S. Colt, Alison

Granville *Les Dunes*	F	14 4 4	214

E. Connaughton

Charleville	I	13 4 6	716

48

ARCHITECTS AND COURSES

Architect Golf course	Country	Score	Page	Architect Golf course	Country	Score	Page
Bill Coore				**Ramón Espinosa**			
Médoc *Les Châteaux*	F	17 7 5	234	Mediterraneo	Es	16 7 6	946
C.K. Cotton				Club d'Aro *(Mas Nou)*	Es	15 7 7	905
Downfield	Sc	17 6 7	604	Bonalba	Es	14 6 6	898
Marriott St Pierre *Old Course*	W	16 8 7	682	**Nick Faldo**			
Patriziale Ascona	S	15 7 7	1002	Chart Hills	Eng	18 8 6	461
Ross-on-Wye	Eng	15 5 6	524	Scharmützelsee *Nick Faldo*	G	18 8 7	379
(1960) West Lancashire	Eng	17 7 7	573	**Heinz Fehring**			
Henry Cotton				München-Riedhof	G	16 7'7	366
Penina	P	14 7 8	846	Fürstliches Hofgut Kolnhausen	G	14 7 6	333
Cotton, Penninck				**Michael Fenn**			
Keerbergen	B	14 7 6	80	Toulouse Palmola	F	15 7 4	276
Arthur Croome				Brest Iroise	F	14 7 6	174
Liphook	Eng	16 7 6	500	Saint-Laurent	F	14 7 5	263
Juan de la Cuadra				Besançon	F	13 7 5	166
La Sella	Es	15 6 5	935	Reims-Champagne	F	13 7 6	252
Robert E. Cupp				Touraine	F	13 7 6	279
East Sussex National				**Willie Fernie**			
East Course	Eng	17 8 7	469	Royal Troon *Old Course*	Sc	19 7 7	658
DeutscheGolf Consult				Shiskine (Blackwaterfoot)	Sc	17 5 5	660
Mülheim	G	13 6 7	365	Southerndown	W	16 7 7	690
Olivier Dongradi				Pitlochry	Sc	14 6 7	648
Augerville	F	13 5 4	160	Dumfries & County	Sc	15 7 5	608
George Duncan				Strathaven	Sc	15 5 6	667
Stonehaven	Sc	13 5 5	666	Thornhill	Sc	15 6 5	669
Tom Dunn				**Jean-Pascal Fourès**			
Broadstone	Eng	17 7 7	455	Rebetz	F	16 6 4	251
Royal Cinque Ports	Eng	17 6 5	527	Laval-Changé *La Chabossière*	F	14 7 5	229
Seacroft	Eng	17 6 4	542	Grasse	F	13 7 6	215
Weston-Super-Mare	Eng	16 6 7	576	**Herbert Fowler**			
Woking	Eng	16 6 6	579	Saunton *East Course*	Eng	18 7 6	541
Felixstowe Ferry				Walton Heath *Old Course*	Eng	18 7 7	566
Martello Course	Eng	15 6 6	471	Berkshire (The) *Blue Course*	Eng	17 8 7	446
Sheringham	Eng	15 7 6	546	Berkshire (The) *Red Course*	Eng	17 8 7	447
Tom Dunn, Harry Vardon				Beau Desert	Eng	16 7 7	444
Ganton	Eng	19 8 5	479	Delamere Forest	Eng	15 6 7	467
Tom Dunn, Willie Park				West Surrey	Eng	15 7 7	574
Lindrick	Eng	17 6 6	499	**Herbert Fowler, Harry S. Colt**			
Willie Dunn				Royal Lytham & St Anne's	Eng	19 7 8	532
Biarritz-le-Phare	F	14 6 8	168	**Herbert Fowler & Tom Simpson**			
Dinard	F	14 6 7	195	North Foreland	Eng	13 7 7	511
Pete & P.B. Dye				**Ronald Fream**			
Barbaroux	F	17 7 6	163	Disneyland Paris			
Pete Dye				*Never Land + Wonderland*	F	16 7 8	196
Domaine Impérial	S	18 8 6	990	Isle Adam (L')	F	16 7 4	222
Eschauzier & Thate				Montpellier-Massane	F	16 7 5	236
Graafschap	N	15 7 6	811	Cap d'Agde	F	15 6 5	179
Ramón Espinosa				Frégate	F	15 7 7	209
Fontanals	Es	18 6 5	917	Arcangues	F	14 7 8	159

49

ARCHITECTS AND COURSES

Architect Golf course	Country	Score			Page
Ronald Fream					
Pinheiros Altos	P	14	8	8	847
Vale da Pinta	P	14	6	6	857
Didier Fruchet/George Will					
Gouverneur (Le) *Le Breuil*	F	16	7	6	210
Gouverneur (Le) *Montaplan*	F	14	7	6	211
A. Gallardo, Peter Alliss					
Playa Serena	Es	13	6	4	961
José Gancedo					
Canyamel	Es	15	6	6	901
Torrequebrada	Es	14	7	7	975
Lerma	Es	17	7	4	939
Costa Dorada	Es	13	6	6	908
Monte Mayor	Es	13	5	5	949
Jean Garaïalde					
Porcelaine (La)	F	14	6	4	248
Cognac	F	13	7	5	190
Jonathan Gaunt					
Linden Hall	Eng	17	8	6	498
Michel Gayon					
Sablé-Solesmes					
La Forêt/La Rivière	F	16	7	4	257
Ailette (L')	F	15	6	5	149
Casteljaloux	F	15	6	5	180
Esery	F	15	7	5	199
Etiolles *Les Cerfs*	F	15	6	5	201
Pornic	F	15	6	6	249
Saint-Endréol	F	15	7	4	260
Savenay	F	15	6	4	269
Vaucouleurs (La) *Les Vallons*	F	15	7	4	282
Fontenailles *Blanc*	F	14	7	6	207
J. Hamilton Stutt					
Woodbury Park *The Oaks*	Eng	15	9	6	581
Charles Gibson					
Royal Porthcawl	W	19	7	5	688
Golden Bear Design					
La Moraleja *La Moraleja 2*	Es	16	7	8	933
G.H. Gowring					
Berkhamsted	Eng	16	7	6	445
Gratenau					
St. Dionys	G	17	7	6	391
Eddie Hackett					
Waterville	I	17	6	7	771
Carn	I	16	5	3	715
Dingle (Ceann Sibeal)	I	16	6	4	722
Donegal (Murvagh)	I	16	2	6	723
Enniscrone	I	16	7	6	728
Killarney *Killeen Course*	I	16	7	8	739
Dooks	I	15	5	5	724

Architect Golf course	Country	Score			Page
Eddie Hackett					
Connemara	I	14	6	6	717
Greenore	I	14	6	5	735
Killorglin	I	14	6	5	741
Malahide					
Red + Blue + Yellow	I	13	7	8	746
West Waterford	I	12	7	6	772
Donald Harradine					
Beuerberg	G	17	7	6	320
Schloss Myllendonk	G	16	7	7	387
Sonnenalp	G	16	7	7	390
Hamburg-Holm	G	15	6	6	341
Lugano	S	15	7	8	997
Tegernseer Bad Wiessee	G	15	7	8	395
Zumikon	S	15	7	6	1005
Bad Wörishofen	G	14	6	6	317
Grevelingenhout	N	14	7	4	812
Neuchâtel	S	14	6	7	1000
Schloss Klingenburg	G	14	6	6	383
Schönenberg	S	14	7	6	1003
Bad Ragaz	S	13	7	6	986
Breitenloo	S	13	7	6	988
Düsseldorfer	G	13	7	7	326
Niederbüren	S	13	7	7	1001
Opio Valbonne	F	13	6	7	241
Sainte-Maxime	F	13	7	7	268
Strasbourg Illkirch					
Jaune + Rouge	F	13	7	6	274
Peter Harradine					
Maison Blanche	F	14	7	5	231
FA Harris					
Berlin-Wannsee	G	15	6	8	319
John D. Harris					
Lacanau	F	14	6	4	227
Shannon	I	13	6	6	761
Poniente	Es	13	6	5	962
Hauser					
Neuhof	G	15	7	7	370
F.W. Hawtree					
Royal Birkdale (The)	Eng	19	9	7	526
Gog Magog *Old Course*	Eng	15	7	8	480
Son Vida	Es	14	6	7	973
Woodbridge	Eng	14	7	7	580
Fred Hawtree					
John O'Gaunt	Eng	16	7	6	496
Limburg	B	16	7	4	81
Saint-Nom-la-Bretèche *Rouge*	F	16	8	8	265
Lisburn	U	15	7	6	785
Royal Latem	B	15	8	6	89

50

ARCHITECTS AND COURSES

Architect Golf course	Country	Score			Page
Fred Hawtree					
Saint-Nom-la-Bretèche *Bleu*	F	15	8	8	264
The Island	I	15	7	7	765
Westport	I	15	7	7	773
Massereene	U	14	5	6	787
Rochefort-Chisan	F	14	6	4	254
Bendinat	Es	13	6	7	897
Domont-Montmorency	F	13	7	4	198
Malone	U	13	6	6	786
Hillside	Eng	18	7	7	489
Pals	Es	16	7	6	956
Bondues *Jaune*	F	15	7	6	171
Anjou-Champigné	F	13	6	6	155
Girona	Es	13	7	5	918
Zuid Limburgse	N	14	7	7	829
Waterloo *La Marache*	B	16	8	7	94
Hawtree & Sons					
Blainroe	I	13	6	6	712
Hawtree & Taylor					
High Post	Eng	15	6	7	488
Martin Hawtree					
Rudding Park	Eng	15	8	8	538
Oostende (remod. 1990)	B	15	7	7	83
Sandy Herd					
Lytham Green Drive	Eng	15	7	8	502
Pannal	Eng	15	6	7	516
E.D. Hess					
Wendlohe					
A-Kurs + B-Kurs	G	16	7	6	399
Wentorf-Reinbeker	G	16	7	6	400
L. Hewson					
Ballybunion *Old Course*	I	19	7	7	707
Alan Higgins					
Carden Park	Eng	14	8	8	458
Harold Hilton					
Ferndown *Old Course*	Eng	17	7	7	472
Ormskirk	Eng	14	6	4	515
Pierre Hirigoyen					
San Sebastián	Es	14	6	6	968
Karl-Heinz Hoffmann					
Mittelrheinischer	G	15	7	7	363
Col. S.V. Hotchkin					
Woodhall Spa	Eng	18	7	8	582
Brian Huggett					
Orchardleigh	Eng	17	7	7	514
Brian Huggett					
Bowood (Cornwall)	Eng	16	7	6	451
Charles Hunter					
Prestwick St Nicholas	Sc	16	6	7	652

Architect Golf course	Country	Score			Page
C.W. Hunter					
Portpatrick (Dunskey)	Sc	15	6	7	649
Ibergolf					
Granada	Es	14	6	5	919
Holcombe Ingleby					
Royal West Norfolk					
(Brancaster)	Eng	17	7	6	536
Tony Jacklin					
San Roque	Es	17	8	6	967
Wolfgang Jersombek					
Jakobsberg	G	15	7	6	353
John Jacobs					
Buckinghamshire (The)	Eng	17	8	7	456
Apremont	F	15	8	6	157
Patshull Park Hotel	Eng	13	8	8	518
R. Trent Jones Jr					
Grenoble Bresson	F	17	7	6	216
Bonmont	Es	16	7	6	899
Penha Longa	P	15	7	8	845
Saint-Donat	F	15	7	8	259
Robert Trent Jones Sr					
Valderrama	Es	19	8	6	977
Las Brisas	Es	18	7	7	937
Sotogrande	Es	18	7	6	974
Celtic Manor *Roman Road*	W	18	9	7	679
Bodensee-Weissensberg	G	17	7	7	321
Côte d'Argent (La)	F	17	6	5	191
Genève	S	17	7	8	993
Spérone	F	17	7	5	273
Ballybunion *(New Course)*	I	16	7	7	706
Bondues *Blanc*	F	16	7	6	170
El Bosque	Es	16	7	4	909
Estérel Latitudes	F	16	6	7	200
Grande-Motte (La)					
Les Flamants Roses	F	16	6	4	213
Joyenval *Marly*	F	16	8	7	223
Los Naranjos	Es	16	7	7	941
Mijas *Los Lagos*	Es	16	6	7	947
Adare	I	15	6	7	704
Chamonix	F	15	6	7	183
Joyenval *Retz*	F	15	8	7	224
Marbella	Es	15	7	8	943
Troia	P	15	7	5	856
Dromoland Castle	I	14	7	7	725
Madeira	P	14	7	5	842
Bercuit	B	13	7	7	77
La Duquesa	Es	13	7	6	928
Mijas *Los Olivos*	Es	13	6	7	948
Quinta da Marinha	P	13	7	7	850

51

Architect Golf course	Country	Score			Page	Architect Golf course	Country	Score			Page
Robert Trent Jones Sr						**Bernhard von Limburger**					
Riviéra Golf Club	F	13	7	8	253	Krefelder	G	17	7	7	356
E. Jonson-Sedibe						Oberfranken	G	17	6	5	372
Gut Waldhof	G	17	7	5	339	Stuttgarter Solitude	G	17	5	5	394
Jean Jottrand						Hannover	G	16	7	7	343
Falnuee	B	14	7	4	78	Neckartal	G	16	6	7	369
Armin Keller						Schloss Braunfels	G	16	7	7	381
Nahetal	G	14	7	6	368	Augsburg	G	15	7	7	313
Ron Kirby						Bâle-Hagenthal	F	15	7	7	162
Elfrather Mühle	G	14	7	7	327	Blumisberg	S	15	7	6	987
Spiegelven	B	14	7	8	93	Walddörfer	G	15	7	6	398
Escorpion	Es	13	8	4	915	Main-Taunus	G	13	7	6	360
J. Kirby, Carr, Merrigan, etc						**Karl Litten**					
Old Head	I	15	7	7	751	Warwickshire (The)	Eng	15	7	8	567
Kothe						**José Luis Lopez**					
Hanau-Wilhelmsbad	G	15	6	6	342	Estepona	Es	14	7	6	916
C. Kramer						**George Low**					
Tutzing	G	15	7	6	397	Pleasington	Eng	16	8	6	520
Kosti Kuronen						**Antonio Lucena Gomez**					
Guadalhorce	Es	14	7	6	920	Herreria	Es	15	6	6	922
Hugues Lambert						**Sandy Lyle**					
Villette d'Anthon						Schloss Wilkendorf	G	15	7	5	388
Les Sangliers	F	17	6	4	283	**Tom MacAuley**					
Val de Some	F	14	7	5	280	Cromstrijen	N	16	8	5	804
Patrice Lambert						Purmerend	N	16	7	7	822
Saint-Thomas	F	14	7	5	266	Mont-Garni	B	13	7	6	82
Bernhard Langer						**Alistair Mackenzie**					
Bad Griesbach *Brunnwies*	G	17	9	9	314	Cork GC	I	15	3	5	718
Portmarnock Links	I	17	7	8	753	Galway GC	I	13	6	6	733
Stolper Heide	G	17	7	5	393	Blairgowrie Rosemount	Sc	18	8	6	593
Soufflenheim	F	16	7	4	272	Moortown	Eng	18	7	7	509
Béthemont	F	14	7	5	167	Hadley Wood	Eng	16	7	7	481
Panoramica	Es	14	6	4	957	Bolton Old Links	Eng	15	5	7	450
Charles Lawrie						Duff House Royal	Sc	15	6	6	606
Woburn *Dukes Course*	Eng	18	7	7	578	Sand Moor	Eng	14	7	7	539
Hankley Common	Eng	16	6	6	482	**Cherles MacKenzie**					
Joseph Lee						Fulford	Eng	17	7	8	477
S. Lourenço	P	17	6	8	854	**John MacPherson**					
Vilamoura *III (Laguna)*	P	14	7	7	861	Elgin	Sc	15	7	6	613
Patrice Léglise						**Alejandro Maldonado**					
Raray (Château de)						Montenmedio	Es	15	7	7	951
La Licorne	F	14	6	4	250	**Dan Maples**					
Bernhard von Limburger						Capdepera	Es	15	7	6	902
Atalaya *Old Course*	Es	13	6	7	896	**C.H. Mayo**					
Club zur Vahr (Garlstedt)	G	18	6	5	324	Thetford	Eng	14	7	5	559
Feldafing	G	18	7	6	330	**J. McAllister**					
Hamburg-Ahrensburg	G	17	8	7	340	Athlone	I	13	6	6	705
Hubbelrath	G	17	8	6	349	**Peter McEvoy**					
Köln	G	17	6	7	354	Powerscourt	I	15	7	7	755

52

ARCHITECTS AND COURSES

Architect Golf course	Country	Score	Page	Architect Golf course	Country	Score	Page
Peter McEvoy				**Tim Morrison**			
Rathsallagh	I	15 7 6	756	Cairndhu	U	13 6 5	779
M. McKenna				Hossegor	F	16 6 6	221
Hermitage	I	15 6 7	736	**M. Nakowsky**			
Paddy Merrigan				Divonne	F	14 6 7	197
Slieve Russell	I	15 8 6	762	**Narbel**			
Woodenbridge	I	16 7 6	774	Lausanne	S	16 7 7	996
Patrick Merrigan				**Falco Nardi**			
Faithlegg	I	13 7 6	730	Lauro	Es	13 7 5	938
Johnny Miller				Santa Ponsa	Es	13 6 7	970
Collingtree Park	Eng	14 8 7	463	**Robin Nelson**			
William Mitchell				Champ de Bataille	F	14 6 3	184
Quinta do Lago *B/C*	P	15 7 8	851	**M. Nicholson**			
Quinta do Lago *Ria Formosa*	P	15 7 8	852	Crans-sur-Sierre	S	14 7 8	989
Theodore Moon				**Peter Nicholson**			
Kilmarnock (Barassie)	Sc	17 6 8	626	Hever	Eng	14 8 8	487
Léonard Morandi				**Jack Nicklaus**			
Nîmes-Campagne	F	16 7 6	239	Mount Juliet	I	18 9 8	747
John Morgan				Gleneagles *Monarch's*	Sc	17 9 7	619
Forest Pines *Forest + Pines*	Eng	17 6 7	474	Montecastillo	Es	17 8 7	950
Jack Morris				St Mellion *Nicklaus Course*	Eng	17 9 7	553
Royal Liverpool (Hoylake)	Eng	18 8 7	531	Paris International	F	16 7 5	243
Old Tom Morris				**Jack Nicklaus / Desmond Muirhead**			
Royal County Down	U	19 6 7	790	La Moraleja *La Moraleja 1*	Es	15 7 8	932
Lahinch	I	18 6 6	742	**Nicklaus Design**			
Royal North Devon				Hertfordshire (The)	Eng	15 7 7	486
(Westward Ho!)	Eng	18 6 6	534	**Christy O'Connor Jr**			
Rosapenna	I	16 7 6	757	Glasson	I	16 7 7	734
Carnoustie *Championship*	Sc	19 3 4	599	Fota Island	I	15 7 6	731
Muirfield	Sc	19 7 6	640	Galway Bay	I	14 7 6	732
Nairn	Sc	19 7 8	643	Lee Valley	I	13 7 6	743
Royal Dornoch	Sc	19 7 7	656	Mount Wolsley	I	13 6 5	748
Machrihanish	Sc	18 6 4	636	**José Maria Olazábal**			
Ladybank	Sc	17 7 5	628	Sevilla	Es	17 7 8	971
Moray	Sc	17 5 5	639	Masia Bach	Es	15 7 6	944
Tain	Sc	17 6 6	668	**Arnold Palmer**			
Dunbar	Sc	16 5 6	609	Tralee	I	18 7 6	766
Lanark	Sc	16 6 5	629	K Club	I	17 8 8	737
Luffness New	Sc	16 5 6	633	Scharmützelsee			
Royal Burgess	Sc	16 7 9	655	*Arnold Palmer*	G	16 8 7	378
West Kilbride	Sc	16 7 5	672	**Willie Park**			
Crail	Sc	15 6 6	600	Silloth-on-Solway	Eng	18 7 4	548
Alyth	Sc	14 6 6	588	Sunningdale *Old Course*	Eng	18 8 8	557
Forfar	Sc	14 6 6	615	Parkstone	Eng	16 7 8	517
Tom Morris/J. Braid				Bruntsfield	Sc	15 8 9	596
Wallasey	Eng	17 7 7	564	Duddingston	Sc	15 7 9	605
J. Morrison				Peterhead	Sc	15 5 4	647
Toxandria	N	14 7 6	827	Stoneham	Eng	15 7 8	555
Lüneburger Heide	G	17 7 5	359	West Hill	Eng	15 6 6	572

53

Architect Golf course	Country	Score	Page	Architect Golf course	Country	Score	Page
Willie Park				**Jean-Marie Poellot**			
Baberton	Sc	14 6 8	590	Feucherolles	F	15 7 5	204
Huntercombe	Eng	14 6 7	492	**P. Postel**			
Willie Park, Harry S. Colt				Iffeldorf	G	16 7 6	350
Formby	Eng	18 7 7	475	**Alain Prat**			
Willie Park Jr				Pléneuf-Val-André	F	17 7 5	245
Notts (Hollinwell)	Eng	18 6 6	513	Gujan-Mestras	F	15 7 6	218
Montrose	Sc	17 5 6	638	**P. Puttman**			
Antwerp	B	16 7 7	76	Villamartin	Es	16 7 6	978
Portstewart *Strand Course*	U	16 7 7	788	**Dr W. Laidlaw Purves**			
Dieppe-Pourville	F	14 6 5	194	Royal St George's	Eng	19 7 5	535
Waterford	I	14 6 6	769	Littlestone	Eng	14 6 5	501
Frank Pennink				**PSA Projects**			
Noordwijk	N	18 7 8	819	Formby Hall	Eng	14 8 6	476
Vilamoura *I (Old Course)*	P	16 7 7	859	**Quenouille**			
Aroeira	P	15 6 6	840	Ploemeur Océan	F	15 7 6	246
Broekpolder	N	15 7 6	803	**Ted Ray**			
Gelpenberg	N	14 4 5	808	Sandiway	Eng	17 5 7	540
Lauswolt	N	14 6 7	818	**Ruzzo Reuss**			
Palmares	P	13 7 5	844	Luzern	S	13 6 7	998
Vilamoura *II (Pinhal)*	P	13 7 7	860	Wylihof	S	13 6 6	1004
Gut Kaden				**J. Rivero**			
Platz B + Platz C	G	17 7 6	335	Son Antem	Es	14 7 6	972
Jeremy Pern				**Cabell B. Robinson**			
Charmeil	F	16 6 6	187	Castillo de Gorraiz	Es	17 7 7	903
Dartmouth	Eng	16 9 6	466	La Cala *Norte*	Es	17 8 6	925
Wantzenau (La)	F	16 6 6	285	Limère	F	17 6 5	230
Ableiges *Les Etangs*	F	15 6 4	148	Praia d'El Rey	P	17 7 5	848
Albi	F	15 6 6	152	Grande Bastide (La)	F	16 6 6	212
Bresse (La)	F	15 6 4	173	La Cala *Sur*	Es	16 8 6	926
Largue (La)	F	15 7 4	228	Evian	F	15 7 9	203
Roncemay	F	15 7 4	255	**W.R. Robinson**			
Toulouse-Seilh *Rouge*	F	15 7 6	277	Clandeboye *Dufferin Course*	U	15 6 6	782
Golf de la Gruyère				**Alan Rijks**			
(ancien Pont-la-Ville)	S	14 7 6	994	Batouwe	N	15 7 3	802
WG Pikeman				Gendersteyn	N	15 7 7	809
Portmarnock	I	19 8 8	752	Sybrook	N	15 6 6	826
Manuel Piñero				**José Rivero**			
La Quinta	Es	15 8 7	934	Olivar de la Hinojosa	Es	13 7 8	954
La Dehesa	Es	14 7 4	927	**Paul Rolin**			
H. Peters				Amsterdam	N	15 7 7	800
Hoisdorf	G	13 6 6	348	Nunspeet *North/East*	N	15 5 3	820
Chris Pittman				Sint Nicolaasga	N	15 7 5	825
Fontcaude	F	14 6 6	206	Rigenée	B	14 7 6	87
Gary Player				Rijk van Nijmegen			
Zaudin	Es	16 7 6	979	*Nijmeegse Baan*	N	14 6 5	823
Taulane	F	15 7 4	275	Rinkven *Red - White*	B	14 6 5	88
Almerimar	Es	14 6 6	894	**Rocky Roquemore**			
El Paraiso	Es	13 6 6	910	Quinta do Peru	P	16 7 5	853

54

ARCHITECTS AND COURSES

Architect Golf course	Country	Score	Page	Architect Golf course	Country	Score	Page
Rocky Roquemore				**Archie Simpson**			
Makila Golf Club	F	14 6 8	232	Murcar	Sc	15 6 6	641
Jean-Manuel Rossi				Aboyne	Sc	14 6 6	586
Belle-Dune	F	16 6 5	165	**Bob Simpson**			
Amnéville	F	13 6 5	154	Royal Aberdeen			
Mackenzie Ross				*Balgownie Links*	Sc	18 7 8	654
Castletown	Eng	18 6 8	460	Crieff *Ferntower Course*	Sc	15 7 7	601
Southerness	Sc	18 6 5	661	Edzell	Sc	14 6 3	612
Maspalomas	Es	16 7 8	945	**Tom Simpson**			
Glen	Sc	14 7 7	617	Chantilly *Vineuil*	F	18 7 6	186
Mackenzie Ross				Cruden Bay	Sc	18 7 6	602
Estoril	P	13 7 7	841	**Tom Simpson**			
Mazamet-La Barouge	F	13 5 4	233	Carlisle	Eng	17 7 7	459
Turnberry *Ailsa Course*	Sc	19 9 8	670	Fontainebleau	F	17 7 7	205
Turnberry *Arran Course*	Sc	16 9 8	671	Ravenstein	B	17 8 7	86
Kurt Rossknecht				Spa (Les Fagnes)	B	17 7 7	92
Motzener See	G	18 8 6	364	Carlow	I	16 6 6	714
Gut Thailing	G	16 7 5	338	Chiberta	F	16 6 8	189
Hof Trages	G	16 7 5	346	Hardelot *Les Pins*	F	16 6 6	219
Gut Ludwigsberg	G	15 6 6	336	Puerta de Hierro	Es	16 8 9	963
Hohenpähl	G	15 7 6	347	Sart-Tilman	B	16 7 7	91
Schloss Egmating	G	15 7 7	382	Hainaut			
Bad Griesbach-Sagmühle				*Bruyere-Quesnoy*	B	15 7 5	79
Sagmühle	G	15 9 9	315	New Golf Deauville			
Lucien Roux				*Rouge/Blanc*	F	15 7 8	238
Volcans (Les)	F	14 6 5	284	County Louth	I	18 5 6	719
W. Ruck				**Cameron Sinclair**			
Scheibenhardt	G	13 7 7	380	Whitekirk	Sc	15 7 7	675
Pat Ruddy				**Des Smyth**			
European (The)	I	18 6 6	729	Limerick County	I	15 7 6	744
Ballyliffin				Seapoint	I	15 6 6	760
Glashedy Links	I	17 6 5	709	Ballykisteen	I	14 7 6	708
Druids Glen	I	16 9 7	726	Waterford Castle	I	14 5 6	770
St Margaret's	I	16 7 7	764	**Jorge Soler**			
Bob Sandow				Peralada	Es	16 6 5	959
Badgemore Park	Eng	14 7 7	442	**Duarte Sottomayor**			
Gregorio Sanz				Quinta da Beloura	P	14 8 7	849
Campoamor	Es	14 6 6	900	Montado	P	13 7 6	843
Ben Sayers				**Thierry Sprecher**			
Castlerock	U	16 6 6	781	Chailly (Château de)	F	14 8 6	182
Archdeacon Scott				Annonay-Gourdan	F	13 6 5	156
Royal Ashdown Forest	Eng	14 7 6	525	Servanes	F	13 7 7	271
F.L. Segales				**Arthur Spring**			
Pula	Es	13 6 5	964	Beaufort	I	14 6 7	711
T. Shannon				Newcastle West	I	13 7 5	750
Dundalk	I	15 6 6	727	Woodstock	I	13 5 6	775
W. Siegmann				**Christoph Staedler**			
Schloss Lüdersburg *Old/New*	G	17 7 6	386	Märkischer Potsdam	G	14 7 6	361
Buxtehude	G	15 7 6	323	Semlin am See	G	14 8 7	389

55

ARCHITECTS AND COURSES

Architect Golf course	Country	Score	Page	Architect Golf course	Country	Score	Page
John Stagg				**J.H. Turner**			
West Berkshire	Eng	15 7 7	570	Newbury & Crookham	Eng	15 6 7	510
Donald Steel				**Reverend Tyack**			
Efteling	N	16 8 5	806	West Cornwall	Eng	16 7 6	571
Goes	N	15 3 6	810	**Urbis Planning**			
Hoge Kleij	N	15 6 7	816	Rolls of Monmouth (The)	W	15 6 6	687
Portal *Championship*	Eng	15 8 7	521	**O. van der Vynckt**			
Wouwse Plantage	N	15 7 6	828	Cheverny	F	14 7 6	188
Forest of Arden				**Joan Dudok van Heel**			
Arden Course	Eng	14 8 8	473	Herkenbosch	N	16 7 6	814
Vila Sol	P	14 7 7	858	Oosterhout	N	15 7 7	821
Treudelberg	G	13 8 7	396	Anderstein	N	14 7 6	801
Donald Steel/GK. Smith				**Joan Dudok van Heel**			
Letham Grange *Old Course*	Sc	15 7 5	630	Wittelsbacher	Eng	15 7 6	401
Adrian Stiff				Im Chiemgau	G	14 7 6	351
Cumberwell Park	Eng	17 7 7	465	**D.C. van Krimpen**			
Hamilton Stutt				Rosendael	N	15 7 7	824
Murrayshall	Sc	14 7 8	642	**Harry Vardon**			
Costa Brava	Es	13 7 7	907	Kingussie	Sc	15 4 5	627
Stutt & Co				Mendip	Eng	15 5 7	506
Dunfermline	Sc	15 7 7	610	Bundoran	I	13 6 7	713
Dieter Sziedat				**Pedro Vasconcelos**			
Hetzenhof	G	14 7 6	345	Salgados	P	14 7 7	855
J.H. Taylor				**Marco Verdieri**			
Hayling	Eng	16 7 7	484	Ennetsee-Holzhäusern	S	13 7 6	992
Hindhead	Eng	16 7 6	490	Engadin	S	15 6 6	991
Royal Cromer	Eng	15 7 6	528	**Robert von Hagge**			
Royal Winchester	Eng	15 6 8	537	Bordes (Les)	F	19 8 6	172
Royal Mid-Surrey *Outer*	Eng	14 7 8	533	Kempferhof (Le)	F	18 8 6	225
Touquet (Le) *La Mer*	F	17 6 7	278	R.S.H.E. Club de Campo	Es	18 7 6	965
David Thomas				Emporda	Es	17 7 6	914
Blairgowrie *Lansdowne*	Sc	15 8 6	592	Royal Mougins	F	17 7 8	256
Roxburghe (The)	Sc	15 7 7	653	Seignosse	F	17 7 7	270
La Manga *Oeste*	Es	14 7 7	930	Courson *Vert/Noir*	F	16 7 3	193
Bowood G&CC	Eng	17 6 6	452	Courson *Lilas/Orange*	F	15 7 3	192
Slaley Hall	Eng	17 8 7	549	National *Albatros(consultant)*	F	18 6 6	237
El Prat *Amarillo*	Es	15 7 6	911	**Philip Walton**			
Osona Montanya	Es	14 7 4	955	County Tipperary	I	15 7 5	721
David Thomas/Puttman				St Helen's Bay	I	14 6 6	763
La Manga *Norte*	Es	15 7 7	929	**Rod Whitman**			
La Manga *Sur*	Es	14 7 7	931	Médoc *Les Vignes*	F	15 7 5	235
John Thompson							
Aldeburgh	Eng	13 6 7	439				
Mr Thompson							
Portsalon	I	16 5 5	754				
Peter Thomson							
Duke's Course St Andrews	Sc	16 7 8	607				
Capt. Tippett							
Tramore	I	13 7 6	767				

56

Architect Golf course	Country	Score	Page		Architect Golf course	Country	Score	Page
Unknown / Inconnu / Unbekannt								
Burnham & Berrow	Eng	18 7 6	457		Abenberg	G	14 7 6	312
North Berwick	Sc	18 7 8	645		Ardglass	U	14 6 4	776
Prestwick	Sc	18 6 7	651		Bad Liebenzell	G	14 7 7	316
Royal St David's	W	18 6 5	689		Carnoustie Burnside	Sc	14 3 4	598
St Andrews *Old Course*	Sc	18 8 8	665		Eschenried	G	14 7 7	328
Ashburnham	W	17 6 5	678		Fränkische Schweiz	D	14 7 6	332
Braunschweig	G	17 6 7	322		Garmisch-Partenkirchen	G	14 6 7	334
Conwy	W	17 7 8	680		Gut Rieden	G	14 7 6	337
Gullane *No 1*	Sc	17 8 7	623		Hechingen-Hohenzollern	G	14 6 6	344
Monifieth	Sc	17 7 7	637		Huntly	Sc	14 6 6	625
Panmure	Sc	17 6 5	646		Interlaken	S	14 6 6	995
Reichswald-Nürnberg	G	17 7 7	377		Lindau-Bad Schachen	G	14 7 8	358
St Andrews *New Course*	Sc	17 8 8	664		Mannings Heath			
Leven	Sc	16 6 6	631		*Waterfall Course*	Eng	14 8 6	504
Royal Guernsey	Eng	16 7 7	529		Memmingen Gut Westerhart	G	14 6 6	362
Royal Jersey	Eng	16 7 8	530		Münchner-Strasslach	G	14 6 7	367
Schloss Langenstein	G	16 8 7	384		Obere Alp	G	14 7 7	371
Schloss Liebenstein					Pinnau	G	14 6 6	375
Gelb + Blau	G	16 8 7	385		Reichsstadt Bad Windsheim	G	14 6 7	376
St Andrews *Jubilee Course*	Sc	16 8 8	663		St Andrews *Eden Course*	Sc	14 8 8	662
St. Eurach	G	16 7 6	392		Aix-les-Bains	F	13 5 7	151
Walton Heath *New Course*	Eng	16 7 6	565		Düsseldorf/Hösel	G	13 6 6	325
Ballyliffin *Old Course*	I	15 6 5	710		Grand Ducal de Luxembourg	L	13 6 7	95
Bamberg	G	15 7 7	318		Kilkenny	I	13 7 6	738
Coxmoor	Eng	15 6 6	464		Königsfeld	G	13 6 6	355
Elie	Sc	15 6 6	614		Montreux	S	13 6 5	999
Haggs Castle	Sc	15 7 9	624		Ozoir-la-Ferrière			
La Boulie (R.C.F.) *La Vallée*	F	15 7 8	226		*Château/Monthéty*	F	13 7 5	242
Lichtenau-Weickershof	G	15 7 6	357		Rosslare	I	13 5 6	758
Nairn Dunbar	Sc	15 6 7	644		Royal Portrush *Valley*	U	13 7 7	792
Newport	W	15 6 7	684		Sant Cugat	Es	13 6 5	969
Oberschwaben Bad Waldsee	G	15 6 6	373		Warrenpoint	U	13 6 5	793
Öschberghof	G	15 7 7	374		Western Gailes	Sc	17 5 7	673

57

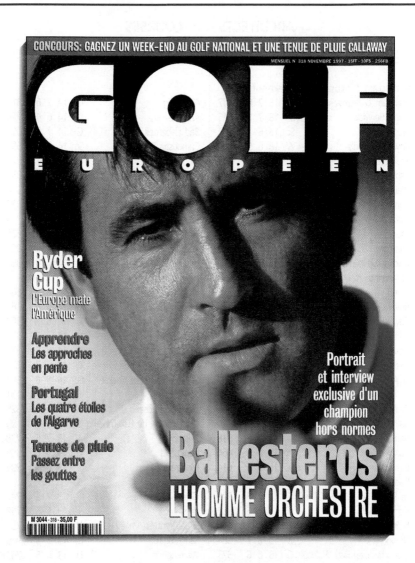

Retrouvez chaque mois :

l'actualité à travers les tournois et les stars du golf

la pratique vue par les champions, les conseils techniques, le matériel

les plus beaux parcours de golf...

RECOMMENDED SEASONS
SAISONS RECOMMANDEES
EPOCA DEL AÑO ACONSEJADA
ESTAÇOES DO ANOS RECOMENDADAS
EMPFOHLENE JAHRESZEITEN
AANBEVOLEN SEIZOENEN

Seasons: 1 2 3 4 5 6 7 8 9 10 11 12

Golf course	Country	Score			Page
Albi	F	15	6	6	152
Arcachon	F	13	6	6	158
Aroeira	P	15	6	6	840
Baule (La) *Rouge*	F	15	7	8	164
Bendinat	E	13	6	7	897
Biarritz-le-Phare	F	14	6	8	168
Bonalba	Es	14	6	6	898
Bretesche (La)	F	15	7	7	175
Campoamor	Es	14	6	6	900
Cannes Mandelieu *Old Course*	F	13	7	8	177
Cannes-Mougins	F	15	7	8	178
Canyamel	Es	15	6	6	901
Cap d'Agde	F	15	6	5	179
Capdepera	Es	15	7	6	902
Chiberta	F	16	6	8	189
Costa Dorada	Es	13	6	6	908
Côte d'Argent (La)	F	17	6	5	191
Dieppe-Pourville	F	14	6	5	194
El Bosque	Es	16	7	4	909
El Saler	Es	18	7	6	913
Escorpion	Es	13	8	4	915
Estérel Latitudes	F	16	6	7	200
Estoril	P	13	7	7	841
Etretat	F	14	6	5	202
Grande Bastide (La)	F	16	6	6	212
Granville *Les Dunes*	F	14	4	4	214
Hardelot *Les Pins*	F	16	6	6	219
Hossegor	F	16	6	6	221
La Manga *Norte*	Es	15	7	7	929
La Manga *Oeste*	Es	14	7	7	930
La Manga *Sur*	Es	14	7	7	931
La Sella	Es	15	6	5	935
Madeira	P	14	7	5	842
Maspalomas	Es	16	7	8	945
Mediterraneo	Es	16	7	6	946
Médoc *Les Châteaux*	F	17	7	5	234
Médoc *Les Vignes*	F	15	7	5	235
Montado	P	13	7	6	843
Montenmedio	Es	15	7	7	951
Montpellier-Massane	F	16	7	5	236
Palmares	P	13	7	5	844
Pals	Es	16	7	6	956
Penha Longa	P	15	7	8	845
Penina	P	14	7	8	846
Peralada	Es	16	6	5	959

Seasons: 1 2 3 4 5 6 7 8 9 10 11 12

Golf course	Country	Score			Page
Pineda	Es	15	7	9	960
Pinheiros Altos	P	14	8	8	847
Ploemeur Océan	F	15	7	6	246
Poniente	Es	13	6	5	962
Praia d'El Rey	P	17	7	5	848
Pula	Es	13	6	5	964
Quinta da Beloura	P	14	8	7	849
Quinta da Marinha	P	13	7	7	850
Quinta do Lago *B/C*	P	15	7	8	851
Quinta do Lago *Ria Formosa*	P	15	7	8	852
Quinta do Peru	P	16	7	5	853
Riviéra Golf Club	F	13	7	8	253
Royal Mougins	F	17	7	8	256
S. Lourenço	P	17	6	8	854
Saint-Donat	F	15	7	8	259
Saint-Jean-de-Monts	F	16	6	5	262
Saint-Laurent	F	14	7	5	263
Saint-Thomas	F	14	7	5	266
Salgados	P	14	7	7	855
San Roque	Es	17	8	6	967
Santa Ponsa	Es	13	6	7	970
Savenay	F	15	6	4	269
Seignosse	F	17	7	7	270
Son Antem	Es	14	7	6	972
Son Vida	Es	14	6	7	973
Sotogrande	Es	18	7	6	974
Touquet (Le) *La Mer*	F	17	6	7	278
Troia	P	15	7	5	856
Val Queven	F	15	6	5	281
Valderrama	Es	19	8	6	977
Vale da Pinta	P	14	6	6	857
Vila Sol	P	14	7	7	858
Vilamoura *I (Old Course)*	P	16	7	7	859
Vilamoura *II (Pinhal)*	P	13	7	7	860
Vilamoura *III (Laguna)*	P	14	7	7	861
Villamartin	Es	16	7	6	978
Wimereux	F	15	4	5	286

Seasons: 1 2 3 4 5 6 7 8 9 10 11 12

Golf course	Country	Score			Page
Alhaurin	Es	14	7	5	893
Almerimar	Es	14	6	6	894
Aloha	Es	17	7	7	895
Atalaya *Old Course*	Es	13	6	7	896
El Paraiso	Es	13	6	6	910

59

RECOMMENDED SEASONS

Seasons	Golf course	Country	Score	Page
1 2 3 4 5 6 7 8 9 10 11 12				
	Estepona	Es	14 7 6	916
	Guadalmina *Sur*	Es	14 7 7	921
	La Cala *Norte*	Es	17 8 6	925
	La Cala *Sur*	Es	16 8 6	926
	Malaga	Es	13 4 6	942
	Marbella	Es	15 7 8	943
	Mijas *Los Lagos*	Es	16 6 7	947
	Mijas *Los Olivos*	Es	13 6 7	948
	Rio Real	Es	13 6 7	966
1 2 3 4 5 6 7 8 9 10 11 12				
	Costa Brava	Es	13 7 7	907
	El Prat *Amarillo*	Es	15 7 6	911
	El Prat *Verde*	Es	17 7 6	912
	Girona	Es	13 7 5	918
	Nîmes-Campagne	F	16 7 6	239
	Novo Sancti Petri	Es	16 7 7	953
	Sant Cugat	Es	13 6 5	969
1 2 3 4 5 6 7 8 9 10 11 12				
	Aisses (Les) *Rouge/Blanc*	F	16 5 4	150
	Barbaroux	F	17 7 6	163
	Belle-Dune	F	16 6 5	165
	Bonmont	Es	16 7 6	899
	Chantaco	F	14 7 7	185
	Club de Campo	Es	16 8 8	906
	Emporda	Es	17 7 6	914
	Gujan-Mestras	F	15 7 6	218
	Hayling	Eng	16 7 7	484
	Lacanau	F	14 6 4	227
	Mazamet-La Barouge	F	13 5 4	233
	Opio Valbonne	F	13 6 7	241
	Royal Zoute	B	18 7 7	90
	Saint-Endréol	F	15 7 4	260
	Sainte-Maxime	F	13 7 7	268
	San Sebastián	Es	14 6 6	968
	Spérone	F	17 7 5	273
1 2 3 4 5 6 7 8 9 10 11 12				
	Alcaidesa	Es	14 6 5	892
	Aldeburgh	Eng	13 6 7	439
	Guadalhorce	Es	14 7 6	920
	Islantilla	Es	16 8 8	923
	La Duquesa	Es	13 7 6	928
	La Quinta	Es	15 8 7	934
	La Zagaleta	Es	16 7 7	936
	Las Brisas	Es	18 7 7	937
	Lauro	Es	13 7 5	938
	Los Arqueros	Es	14 6 7	940
	Los Naranjos	Es	16 7 7	941
	Monte Mayor	Es	13 5 5	949
	Montecastillo	Es	17 8 7	950
	Panoramica	Es	14 6 4	957
	Playa Serena	Es	13 6 4	961
	Sevilla	Es	17 7 8	971
	Torrequebrada	Es	14 7 7	975
	Zaudin	Es	16 7 6	979

Seasons	Golf course	Country	Score	Page
1 2 3 4 5 6 7 8 9 10 11 12				
	Arcangues	F	14 7 8	159
	Baden	F	15 6 5	161
	Berkshire (The) *Blue Course*	Eng	17 8 7	446
	Berkshire (The) *Red Course*	Eng	17 8 7	447
	Bordes (Les)	F	19 8 6	172
	Buckinghamshire (The)	Eng	17 8 7	456
	Casteljaloux	F	15 6 5	180
	Castillo de Gorraiz	Es	17 7 7	903
	Cély	F	15 7 6	181
	Champ de Bataille	F	14 6 3	184
	Chantilly *Vineuil*	F	18 7 6	186
	Charleville	I	13 4 6	716
	Chart Hills	Eng	18 8 6	461
	Club d'Aro (Mas Nou)	Es	15 7 7	905
	Cork GC	I	15 3 5	718
	County Louth	I	18 5 6	719
	County Sligo	I	17 4 3	720
	Denham	Eng	15 7 7	468
	Dinard	F	14 6 7	195
	East Sussex National				
	East Course	Eng	17 8 7	469
	Etiolles *Les Cerfs*	F	15 6 5	201
	European (The)	I	18 6 6	729
	Ferndown *Old Course*	Eng	17 7 7	472
	Fontainebleau	F	17 7 7	205
	Frégate	F	15 7 7	209
	Gog Magog *Old Course*	Eng	15 7 8	480
	Gouverneur (Le) *Le Breuil*	F	16 7 6	210
	Gouverneur (Le) *Montaplan*	F	14 7 6	211
	Grande-Motte (La)				
	Les Flamants Roses	F	16 6 4	213
	Henley	Eng	14 6 7	485
	Hermitage	I	15 6 7	736
	Hever	Eng	14 8 8	487
	Hubbelrath	G	17 8 6	349
	Jarama R.A.C.E.	Es	13 7 6	924
	La Dehesa	Es	14 7 4	927
	La Moraleja *La Moraleja 1*	Es	15 7 8	932
	La Moraleja *La Moraleja 2*	Es	16 7 8	933
	Limère	F	17 6 5	230
	Littlestone	Eng	14 6 5	501
	Makila Golf Club	F	14 6 8	232
	National *L'Albatros*	F	18 6 6	237
	Neguri	Es	17 7 7	952
	Newbury & Crookham	Eng	15 6 7	510
	North Foreland	Eng	13 7 7	511
	Olivar de la Hinojosa	Es	13 7 8	954
	Oostende	B	15 7 7	83
	Osona Montanya	Es	14 7 4	955
	Parkstone	Eng	16 7 8	517
	Pedreña	Es	14 6 5	958
	Perranporth	Eng	16 6 6	519
	Pont Royal	F	16 6 5	247
	Portmarnock	I	19 8 8	752
	Portmarnock Links	I	17 7 8	753
	Prince's *Himalayas-Shore*	Eng	13 6 4	523
	Puerta de Hierro	Es	16 8 9	963

60

Seasons (1 2 3 4 5 6 7 8 9 10 11 12)	Golf course	Country	Score			Page
	Ravenstein	B	17	8	7	86
	Rebetz	F	16	6	4	251
	Rochefort-Chisan	F	14	6	4	254
	Rosslare	I	13	5	6	758
	Royal County Down	U	19	6	7	790
	Royal Dublin	I	16	7	7	759
	Royal St George's	Eng	19	7	5	535
	Sainte-Baume (La)	F	13	7	6	267
	Servanes	F	13	7	7	271
	Stoke Poges	Eng	17	8	8	554
	Sunningdale *New Course*	Eng	18	8	8	556
	Sunningdale *Old Course*	Eng	18	8	8	557
	The Island	I	15	7	7	765
	Thorndon Park	Eng	14	7	6	560
	Thorpeness	Eng	14	7	7	561
	Toulouse Palmola	F	15	7	4	276
	Walton Heath *New Course*	Eng	16	7	6	565
	Walton Heath *Old Course*	Eng	18	7	7	566
	West Berkshire	Eng	15	7	7	570
	West Hill	Eng	15	6	6	572
	Woking	Eng	16	6	6	579
	Woodbridge	Eng	14	7	7	580
	Worplesdon	Eng	16	7	6	583

Seasons (1 2 3 4 5 6 7 8 9 10 11 12)	Golf course	Country	Score			Page
	Granada	Es	14	6	5	919

Seasons (1 2 3 4 5 6 7 8 9 10 11 12)	Golf course	Country	Score			Page
	Annonay-Gourdan	F	13	6	5	156
	Brigode	F	14	7	6	176
	Castlerock	U	16	6	6	781
	Cognac	F	13	7	5	190
	Dartmouth	Eng	16	9	6	466
	Dingle (Ceann Sibeal)	I	16	6	4	722
	Elie	E	15	6	6	614
	Goes	N	15	3	6	810
	Greenore	I	14	6	5	735
	Gullane *No 1*	Ec	17	8	7	623
	Haagsche	N	18	7	8	813
	Hainaut *Bruyere-Quesnoy*	B	15	7	5	79
	Isle of Purbeck	Eng	16	7	6	495
	Lisburn	U	15	7	6	785
	Luttrellstown	I	15	7	7	745
	Masia Bach	Es	15	7	6	944
	New Golf Deauville					
	Rouge/Blanc	F	15	7	8	238
	Noordwijk	N	18	7	8	819
	Nunspeet *North/East*	N	15	5	3	820
	Orchardleigh	Eng	17	7	7	514
	Pessac	F	15	7	4	244
	Portstewart *Strand Course*	U	16	7	7	788
	Royal Guernsey	Eng	16	7	7	529
	Royal Portrush *Dunluce Links*	U	19	7	7	791
	Royal Portrush *Valley*	U	13	7	7	792
	Saunton *East Course*	Eng	18	7	6	541
	Shannon	I	13	6	6	761
	Thurlestone	Eng	16	6	4	562

Seasons (1 2 3 4 5 6 7 8 9 10 11 12)	Golf course	Country	Score			Page
	Tullamore	I	15	6	5	768
	Turnberry *Ailsa Course*	Ec	19	9	8	670
	Turnberry *Arran Course*	Ec	16	9	8	671
	Waterford Castle	I	14	5	6	770
	Woodbury Park *The Oaks*	Eng	15	9	6	581

Seasons (1 2 3 4 5 6 7 8 9 10 11 12)	Golf course	Country	Score			Page
	Badgemore Park	Eng	14	7	7	442
	Ballybunion					
	Cashen (New Course)	I	16	7	7	706
	Ballybunion *Old Course*	I	19	7	7	707
	Ballyliffin *Glashedy Links*	I	17	6	5	709
	Ballyliffin *Old Course*	I	15	6	5	710
	Beaufort	I	14	6	7	711
	Blainroe	I	13	6	6	712
	Burnham & Berrow	Eng	18	7	6	457
	Delamere Forest	Eng	15	6	7	467
	Dooks	I	15	5	5	724
	Dromoland Castle	I	14	7	7	725
	Druids Glen	I	16	9	7	726
	Elfrather Mühle	G	14	7	7	327
	Enniscrone	I	16	7	6	728
	Felixstowe Ferry					
	Martello Course	Eng	15	6	6	471
	Fontanals	Es	18	6	5	917
	Forest Pines *Forest + Pines*	Eng	17	6	7	474
	Frankfurter GC	G	16	7	8	331
	Galway Bay	I	14	7	6	732
	Galway GC	I	13	6	6	733
	Grasse	F	13	7	6	215
	Gut Waldhof	G	17	7	5	339
	Hamburg-Ahrensburg	G	17	8	7	340
	Hanau-Wilhelmsbad	G	15	6	6	342
	Hankley Common	Eng	16	6	6	482
	Herreria	Es	15	6	6	922
	Hertfordshire (The)	Eng	15	7	7	486
	Hindhead	Eng	16	7	6	490
	Hof Trages	G	16	7	5	346
	Huntercombe	Eng	14	6	7	492
	Ipswich (Purdis Heath)	Eng	16	7	7	494
	Isle Adam (L')	F	16	7	4	222
	Jakobsberg	G	15	7	6	353
	La Moye	Eng	17	7	8	497
	Lahinch	I	18	6	6	742
	Lausanne	S	16	7	7	996
	Lerma	Es	17	7	4	939
	Lindrick	Eng	17	6	6	499
	Lugano	S	15	7	8	997
	Mere	Eng	15	7	7	507
	Moor Park *High Course*	Eng	17	8	7	508
	Muirfield	Ec	19	7	6	640
	Mülheim	G	13	6	7	365
	München-Riedhof	G	16	7	7	366
	Münchner-Strasslach	G	14	6	7	367
	Neuhof	G	15	7	7	370
	Newcastle West	I	13	7	5	750
	Ormskirk	Eng	14	6	4	515

61

Seasons Golf course	Country	Score	Page
1 2 3 4 5 6 7 8 9 10 11 12			
Portsalon	I	16 5 5	754
Rathsallagh	I	15 7 6	756
Roxburghe (The)	Ec	15 7 7	653
Royal Ashdown Forest	Eng	14 7 6	525
Royal Cinque Ports	Eng	17 6 5	527
Royal Latem	B	15 8 6	89
Royal Mid-Surrey *Outer*	Eng	14 7 8	533
Saint-Germain	F	17 7 7	261
Seacroft	Eng	17 6 4	542
Seapoint	I	15 6 6	760
Sherborne	Eng	15 6 7	545
Southerness	Ec	18 6 5	661
St George's Hill	Eng	17 7 7	552
St Helen's Bay	I	14 6 6	763
Stuttgarter Solitude	G	17 5 5	394
Tandridge	Eng	14 7 6	558
Toulouse-Seilh *Rouge*	F	15 7 6	277
Tralee	I	18 7 6	766
Tramore	I	13 7 6	767
Ulzama	Es	16 6 6	976
Villette d'Anthon *Les Sangliers*	F	17 6 4	283
Walddörfer	G	15 7 6	398
Waterloo *La Marache*	B	16 8 7	94
Waterville	I	17 6 7	771
Wentorf-Reinbeker	Eng	16 7 6	400
West Surrey	Eng	15 7 7	574
West Sussex	Eng	18 7 6	575
Weston-Super-Mare	Eng	16 6 7	576
Woburn *Dukes Course*	Eng	18 7 7	578
1 2 3 4 5 6 7 8 9 10 11 12			
Aberdovey	W	17 7 7	677
Ailette (L')	F	15 6 5	149
Aix-les-Bains	F	13 5 7	151
Alloa	Ec	15 7 6	587
Alwoodley (The)	Eng	18 7 7	440
Alyth	Ec	14 6 6	588
Amirauté (L')	F	15 7 8	153
Anderstein	N	14 7 6	801
Anjou-Champigné	F	13 6 6	155
Antwerp	B	16 7 7	76
Apremont	F	15 8 6	157
Ardglass	U	14 6 4	776
Ashburnham	W	17 6 5	678
Ashridge	Eng	16 7 6	441
Athlone	I	13 6 6	705
Augerville	F	13 5 4	160
Augsburg	G	15 7 7	313
Ayr (Belleisle)	Ec	16 5 7	589
Bad Ragaz	S	13 7 6	986
Ballykisteen	I	14 7 6	708
Bamberg	G	15 7 7	318
Bangor	U	14 6 6	777
Bath	Eng	16 6 9	443
Batouwe	N	15 7 3	802
Beau Desert	Eng	16 7 7	444
Bercuit	B	13 7 7	77

Seasons Golf course	Country	Score	Page
1 2 3 4 5 6 7 8 9 10 11 12			
Berkhamsted	Eng	16 7 6	445
Berlin-Wannsee	G	15 6 8	319
Béthemont	F	14 7 5	167
Beuerberg	G	17 7 6	320
Bitche	F	14 6 5	169
Blackmoor	Eng	17 6 5	449
Blairgowrie *Lansdowne*	Ec	15 8 6	592
Blairgowrie *Rosemount*	Ec	18 8 6	593
Bodensee-Weissensberg	G	17 7 7	321
Bolton Old Links	Eng	15 5 7	450
Bondues *Blanc*	F	16 7 6	170
Bondues *Jaune*	F	15 7 6	171
Bowood (Cornwall)	Eng	16 7 6	451
Bowood G&CC	Eng	17 6 6	452
Brampton	Eng	17 7 6	453
Brancepeth Castle	Eng	14 6 5	454
Brest Iroise	F	14 7 6	174
Broadstone	Eng	17 7 7	455
Broekpolder	N	15 7 6	803
Bruntsfield	Ec	15 8 9	596
Buchanan Castle	Ec	14 6 6	597
Bundoran	I	13 6 7	713
Buxtehude	G	15 7 6	323
Cairndhu	U	13 6 5	779
Carden Park	Eng	14 8 8	458
Carlow	I	16 6 6	714
Carn	I	16 5 3	715
Carnoustie *Burnside*	Ec	14 3 4	598
Carnoustie *Championship*	Ec	19 3 4	599
Castle Hume	U	13 7 6	780
Celtic Manor *Roman Road*	W	18 9 7	679
Charmeil	F	16 6 6	187
Clandeboye *Dufferin Course*	U	15 6 6	782
Clitheroe	Eng	17 7 7	462
Club zur Vahr (Garlstedt)	G	18 6 5	324
Collingtree Park	Eng	14 8 7	463
Connemara	I	14 6 6	717
Conwy	W	17 7 8	680
County Tipperary	I	15 7 5	721
Courson *Lilas/Orange*	F	15 7 3	192
Courson *Vert/Noir*	F	16 7 3	193
Coxmoor	Eng	15 6 6	464
Crail	Ec	15 6 6	600
Crieff *Ferntower Course*	Ec	15 7 7	601
Cromstrijen	N	16 8 5	804
Cruden Bay	Ec	18 7 6	602
Cumberwell Park	Eng	17 7 7	465
Dalmahoy *East Course*	Ec	17 8 8	603
De Pan	N	16 8 7	805
Disneyland Paris			
Never Land + Wonderland	F	16 7 8	196
Domaine Impérial	S	18 8 6	990
Domont-Montmorency	F	13 7 4	198
Donegal (Murvagh)	I	16 2 6	723
Duff House Royal	Ec	15 6 6	606
Duke's Course St Andrews	Ec	16 7 8	607
Dumfries & County	Ec	15 7 5	608

62

RECOMMENDED SEASONS

Seasons Golf course	Country	Score			Page
1 2 3 4 5 6 7 8 9 10 11 12					
Dunbar	Ec	16	5	6	609
Dundalk	I	15	6	6	727
Düsseldorf/Hösel	G	13	6	6	325
Düsseldorfer	G	13	7	7	326
Efteling	N	16	8	5	806
Eindhoven	N	18	8	6	807
Ennetsee-Holzhäusern	S	13	7	6	992
Eschenried	G	14	7	7	328
Esery	F	15	7	5	199
Fairhaven	Eng	17	7	8	470
Faithlegg	I	13	7	6	730
Falkenstein	G	18	6	7	329
Falnuee	B	14	7	4	78
Feucherolles	F	15	7	5	204
Fontcaude	F	14	6	6	206
Fontenailles *Blanc*	F	14	7	6	207
Fontenelles (Les)	F	14	7	4	208
Forest of Arden *Arden Course*	Eng	14	8	8	473
Formby	Eng	18	7	7	475
Formby Hall	Eng	14	8	6	476
Fortrose & Rosemarkie	Ec	16	6	5	616
Fota Island	I	15	7	6	731
Fulford	Eng	17	7	8	477
Fürstliches Hofgut Kolnhausen	G	14	7	6	333
Gainsborough-Karsten Lakes	Eng	14	8	6	478
Ganton	Eng	19	8	5	479
Gelpenberg	N	14	4	5	808
Gendersteyn	N	15	7	7	809
Genève	S	17	7	8	993
Glasson	I	16	7	7	734
Glen	Ec	14	7	7	617
Gleneagles *King's*	Ec	18	9	7	618
Gleneagles *Monarch's*	Ec	17	9	7	619
Gleneagles *Queen's*	Ec	15	9	7	620
Golspie	Ec	14	5	4	621
Graafschap	N	15	7	6	811
Grenoble Bresson	F	17	7	6	216
Grevelingenhout	N	14	7	4	812
Guerville	F	14	7	4	217
Gut Kaden *Platz B + Platz C*	G	17	7	6	335
Gut Thailing	G	16	7	5	338
Hadley Wood	Eng	16	7	7	481
Hamburg-Holm	G	15	6	6	341
Hannover	G	16	7	7	343
Haut-Poitou	F	14	6	4	220
Hawkstone Park *Hawkstone*	Eng	15	8	7	483
Hechingen-Hohenzollern	G	14	6	6	344
Hetzenhof	G	14	7	6	345
High Post	Eng	15	6	7	488
Hillside	Eng	18	7	7	489
Hilversum	N	16	7	7	815
Hoge Kleij	N	15	6	7	816
Hoisdorf	G	13	6	6	348
Holyhead	W	16	7	5	681
Hunstanton	Eng	17	7	6	491
Ilkley	Eng	18	7	6	493
John O'Gaunt	Eng	16	7	6	496

Seasons Golf course	Country	Score			Page
1 2 3 4 5 6 7 8 9 10 11 12					
K Club	I	17	8	8	737
Keerbergen	B	14	7	6	80
Kempferhof (Le)	F	18	8	6	225
Kennemer	N	18	8	8	817
Kilkenny	I	13	7	6	738
Killorglin	I	14	6	5	741
Kilmarnock (Barassie)	Ec	17	6	8	626
Kirkistown Castle	U	15	6	5	783
Knock	U	15	7	6	784
Köln	G	17	6	7	354
Krefelder	G	17	7	7	356
La Boulie (R.C.F.) *La Vallée*	F	15	7	8	226
Ladybank	Ec	17	7	5	628
Lanark	Ec	16	6	5	629
Lauswolt	N	14	6	7	818
Lee Valley	I	13	7	6	743
Letham Grange *Old Course*	Ec	15	7	5	630
Leven	Ec	16	6	6	631
Lichtenau-Weickershof	G	15	7	6	357
Limburg	B	16	7	4	81
Limerick County	I	15	7	6	744
Lindau-Bad Schachen	G	14	7	8	358
Liphook	Eng	16	7	6	500
Luffness New	Ec	16	5	6	633
Lundin	Ec	16	6	7	634
Lüneburger Heide	G	17	7	5	359
Lytham Green Drive	Eng	15	7	8	502
Machrie	Ec	17	7	7	635
Machrihanish	Ec	18	6	4	636
Main-Taunus	G	13	7	6	360
Malahide *Red + Blue + Yellow*	I	13	7	8	746
Malone	U	13	6	6	786
Manchester	Eng	16	7	7	503
Mannings Heath					
Waterfall Course	Eng	14	8	6	504
Manor House (Castle Combe)	Eng	15	8	7	505
Marriott St Pierre *Old Course*	W	16	8	7	682
Mendip	Eng	15	5	7	506
Mittelrheinischer	G	15	7	7	363
Monifieth	Ec	17	7	7	637
Mont-Garni	B	13	7	6	82
Montreux	S	13	6	5	999
Montrose	Ec	17	5	6	638
Moortown	Eng	18	7	7	509
Moray	Ec	17	5	5	639
Motzener See	G	18	8	6	364
Mount Juliet	I	18	9	8	747
Mount Wolsley	I	13	6	5	748
Mullingar	I	14	5	5	749
Murcar	Ec	15	6	6	641
Murrayshall	Ec	14	7	8	642
Nahetal	G	14	7	6	368
Nairn	Ec	19	7	8	643
Nairn Dunbar	Ec	15	6	7	644
Neckartal	G	16	6	7	369
Nefyn & District	W	16	6	5	683
Newport	W	15	6	7	684

Seasons Golf course	Country	Score	Page
North Berwick	Ec	18 7 8	645
North Hants	Eng	17 7 6	512
Notts (Hollinwell)	Eng	18 6 6	513
Oberschwaben Bad Waldsee	G	15 6 6	373
Omaha Beach La Mer/Le Bge	F	14 7 5	240
Oosterhout	N	15 7 7	821
Öschberghof	G	15 7 7	374
Oudenaarde	B	14 6 6	84
Ozoir-la-Ferrière			
Château/Monthéty	F	13 7 5	242
Palingbeek	B	13 6 6	85
Pannal	Eng	15 6 7	516
Paris International	F	16 7 5	243
Patriziale Ascona	S	15 7 7	1002
Patshull Park Hotel	Eng	13 8 8	518
Pennard	W	18 6 6	685
Peterhead	Ec	15 5 4	647
Pinnau	G	14 6 6	375
Pitlochry	Ec	14 6 7	648
Pleasington	Eng	16 8 6	520
Pléneuf-Val-André	F	17 7 5	245
Porcelaine (La)	F	14 6 4	248
Portal Championship	Eng	15 8 7	521
Portpatrick (Dunskey)	Ec	15 6 7	649
Powfoot	Ec	16 6 4	650
Prestbury	Eng	17 8 7	522
Prestwick	Ec	18 6 7	651
Prestwick St Nicholas	Ec	16 6 7	652
Purmerend	N	16 7 7	822
Pyle & Kenfig	W	17 7 5	686
R.S.H.E. Club de Campo	Es	18 7 6	965
Reichswald-Nürnberg	G	17 7 7	377
Reims-Champagne	F	13 7 6	252
Rigenée	B	14 7 6	87
Rijk van Nijmegen			
Nijmeegse Baan	N	14 6 5	823
Rinkven Red - White	B	14 6 5	88
Rolls of Monmouth (The)	W	15 6 6	687
Roncemay	F	15 7 4	255
Rosapenna	I	16 7 6	757
Rosendael	N	15 7 7	824
Royal Belfast	U	15 7 7	789
Royal Birkdale (The)	Eng	19 9 7	526
Royal Burgess	Ec	16 7 9	655
Royal Cromer	Eng	15 7 6	528
Royal Dornoch	Ec	19 7 7	656
Royal Jersey	Eng	16 7 8	530
Royal Liverpool (Hoylake)	Eng	18 8 7	531
Royal Lytham & St Anne's	Eng	19 7 8	532
Royal Musselburgh	Ec	16 8 7	657
Royal North Devon (Westward Ho!)	Eng	18 6 6	534
Royal Porthcawl	W	19 7 5	688
Royal St David's	W	18 6 5	689
Royal Troon Old Course	Ec	19 7 7	658
Royal West Norfolk (Brancaster)	Eng	17 7 6	536
Royal Winchester	Eng	15 6 8	537

Seasons Golf course	Country	Score	Page
Rudding Park	Eng	15 8 8	538
Sablé-Solesmes			
La Forêt/La Rivière	F	16 7 4	257
Saint-Cloud Vert	F	14 7 7	258
Saint-Nom-la-Bretèche Bleu	F	15 8 8	264
Saint-Nom-la-Bretèche Rouge	F	16 8 8	265
Sand Moor	Eng	14 7 7	539
Sandiway	Eng	17 5 7	540
Sart-Tilman	B	16 7 7	91
Scharmützelsee Arnold Palmer	G	16 8 7	378
Scharmützelsee Nick Faldo	G	18 8 7	379
Scheibenhardt	G	13 7 7	380
Schloss Braunfels	G	16 7 7	381
Schloss Egmating	G	15 7 7	382
Schloss Klingenburg	G	14 6 6	383
Schloss Liebenstein			
Gelb + Blau	G	16 8 7	385
Scotscraig	Ec	16 6 6	659
Seascale	Eng	18 5 4	543
Sheringham	Eng	15 7 6	546
Sherwood Forest	Eng	17 7 6	547
Slieve Russell	I	15 8 6	762
Soufflenheim	F	16 7 4	272
Southerndown	W	16 7 7	690
Southport & Ainsdale	Eng	18 7 7	550
Spa (Les Fagnes)	B	17 7 7	92
Spiegelven	B	14 7 8	93
St Andrews Eden Course	Ec	14 8 8	662
St Andrews Jubilee Course	Ec	16 8 8	663
St Andrews New Course	Ec	17 8 8	664
St Andrews Old Course	Ec	18 8 8	665
St Enodoc Church Course	Eng	18 7 4	551
St Margaret's	I	16 7 7	764
St Mellion Nicklaus Course	Eng	17 9 7	553
St. Dionys	G	17 7 6	391
Stolper Heide	G	17 7 5	393
Stoneham	Eng	15 7 8	555
Strasbourg Illkirch			
Jaune + Rouge	F	13 7 6	274
Sybrook	N	15 6 6	826
Tain	Ec	17 6 6	668
Tenby	W	18 7 6	691
Thetford	Eng	14 7 5	559
Thornhill	Ec	15 6 5	669
Touraine	F	13 7 6	279
Toxandria	N	14 7 6	827
Treudelberg	G	13 8 7	396
Trevose Championship	Eng	17 7 7	563
Vaucouleurs (La) Les Vallons	F	15 7 4	282
Volcans (Les)	F	14 6 5	284
Wallasey	Eng	17 7 7	564
Wantzenau (La)	F	16 6 6	285
Warrenpoint	U	13 6 5	793
Warwickshire (The)	Eng	15 7 8	567
Waterford	I	14 6 6	769
Wendlohe A-Kurs + B-Kurs	G	16 7 6	399
Wentworth East Course	Eng	16 8 7	568

64

RECOMMENDED SEASONS

Seasons Golf course	Country	Score	Page
1 2 3 4 5 6 7 8 9 10 11 12			
Wentworth *West Course*	Eng	18 8 7	569
West Cornwall	Eng	16 7 6	571
West Kilbride	Ec	16 7 5	672
West Lancashire	Eng	17 7 7	573
Western Gailes	Ec	17 5 7	673
Westport	I	15 7 7	773
Whitekirk	Ec	15 7 7	675
1 2 3 4 5 6 7 8 9 10 11 12			
Whittington Heath	Eng	17 6 7	577
Wittelsbacher	Eng	15 7 6	401
Woodenbridge	I	16 7 6	774
Woodhall Spa	Eng	18 7 8	582
Wouwse Plantage	N	15 7 6	828
Zuid Limburgse	N	14 7 7	829
1 2 3 4 5 6 7 8 9 10 11 12			
Abenberg	G	14 7 6	312
Ableiges *Les Etangs*	F	15 6 4	148
Aboyne	Ec	14 6 6	586
Adare	I	15 6 7	704
Amnéville	F	13 6 5	154
Amsterdam	N	15 7 7	800
Bad Griesbach *Brunnwies*	G	17 9 9	314
Bad Griesbach-Sagmühle			
Sagmühle	G	15 9 9	315
Bad Liebenzell	G	14 7 7	316
Bad Wörishofen	G	14 6 6	317
Belvoir Park	U	15 5 6	778
Bresse (La)	F	15 6 4	173
Brora	Ec	15 7 7	595
Cerdaña	Es	14 7 7	904
Chailly (Château de)	F	14 8 6	182
Cheverny	F	14 7 6	188
Divonne	F	14 6 7	197
Duddingston	Ec	15 7 9	605
East Renfrewshire	Ec	15 6 8	611
Edzell	Ec	14 6 3	612
Evian	F	15 7 9	203
Forfar	Ec	14 6 6	615
Garmisch-Partenkirchen	G	14 6 7	334
Grand Ducal de Luxembourg	L	13 6 7	95
Gut Ludwigsberg	G	15 6 6	336
Gut Rieden	G	14 7 6	337
Herkenbosch	N	16 7 6	814
Hohenpähl	G	15 7 6	347
Huntly	Ec	14 6 6	625
Iffeldorf	G	16 7 6	350
Im Chiemgau	G	14 7 6	351
Isernhagen	G	15 7 6	352
Joyenval *Marly*	F	16 8 7	223
Joyenval *Retz*	F	15 8 7	224
Killarney *Killeen Course*	I	16 7 8	739
Killarney *Mahony's Point*	I	15 7 8	740
Königsfeld	G	13 6 6	355
Linden Hall	Eng	17 8 6	498

Seasons Golf course	Country	Score	Page
Maison Blanche	F	14 7 5	231
Märkischer Potsdam	G	14 7 6	361
Memmingen Gut Westerhart	G	14 6 6	362
Obere Alp	G	14 7 7	371
Oberfranken	G	17 6 5	372
Powerscourt	I	15 7 7	755
Reichsstadt Bad Windsheim	G	14 6 7	376
Royal Aberdeen			
Balgownie Links	Ec	18 7 8	654
Schloss Langenstein	G	16 8 7	384
Schloss Myllendonk	G	16 7 7	387
Schloss Wilkendorf	G	15 7 5	388
Semlin am See	G	14 8 7	389
Shanklin & Sandown	15		
Val de Sorne	F	14 7 5	280
West Waterford	I	12 7 6	772
Woodstock	I	13 5 6	775
Wylihof	S	13 6 6	1004
1 2 3 4 5 6 7 8 9 10 11 12			
Blumisberg	S	15 7 6	987
Breitenloo	S	13 7 6	988
Elgin	Ec	15 7 6	613
Golf de la Gruyère			
(anc. Pont-la-Ville)	S	14 7 6	994
Haggs Castle	Ec	15 7 9	624
Neuchâtel	S	14 6 7	1000
Raray (Château de) *La Licorne*	F	14 6 4	250
Ross-on-Wye	Eng	15 5 6	524
Westerwood	Ec	14 8 6	674
Zumikon	S	15 7 6	1005
1 2 3 4 5 6 7 8 9 10 11 12			
Chamonix	F	15 6 7	183
Schloss Lüdersburg *Old/New*	G	17 7 6	386
1 2 3 4 5 6 7 8 9 10 11 12			
Baberton	Ec	14 6 8	590
Bâle-Hagenthal	F	15 7 7	162
Berwick-upon-Tweed	Eng	15 6 5	448
Besançon	F	13 7 5	166
Boat of Garten	Ec	14 6 7	594
Braunschweig	G	17 6 7	322
Carlisle	Eng	17 7 7	459
Castletown	Eng	18 6 8	460
Downfield	Ec	17 6 7	604
Dunfermline	Ec	15 7 7	610
Feldafing	G	18 7 6	330
Fränkische Schweiz	G	14 7 6	332
Grantown on Spey	Ec	14 6 7	622
Largue (La)	F	15 7 4	228
Laval-Changé *La Chabossière*	F	14 7 5	229
Lothianburn	Ec	14 6 8	632
Luzern	S	13 6 7	998
Massereene	U	14 5 6	787
Niederbüren	S	13 7 7	1001
Old Head	I	15 7 7	751
Panmure	Ec	17 6 5	646

65

Seasons Golf course	Country	Score		Page
1 2 3 4 **5 6 7 8 9** 10 11 12				
Schönenberg	S	14 7	6	1003
Shiskine (Blackwaterfoot)	Ec	17 5	5	660
Silloth-on-Solway	Eng	18 7	4	548
Sonnenalp	G	16 7	7	390
Strathaven	Ec	15 5	6	667
Tegernseer Bad Wiessee	G	15 7	8	395
Tutzing	G	15 7	6	397
Yvelines *Les Chênes*	F	13 7	4	287

Seasons Golf course	Country	Score		Page
1 2 3 **4** 5 6 7 **8** 9 **10** 11 12				
Interlaken	S	14 6	6	995
1 2 3 4 5 6 **7 8 9** 10 11 12				
Ballater	Ec	15 6	7	591
Crans-sur-Sierre	S	14 7	8	989
Engadin	S	15 6	6	991
Kingussie	Ec	15 4	5	627

RECOMMENDED GOLFING STAY
SEJOUR DE GOLF RECOMMANDÉ
ESTANCIA DE GOLF RECOMENDADA
ESTADIA DE GOLF RECOMENDADA
FÜR GOLFFERIEN EMPFOHLEN
AAN TE RADEN GOLFVERBLIJF

Golf course	Country	Score		Page	Golf course	Country	Score		Page
Almerimar	Es	14 6	6	894	Castletown	Eng	18 6	8	460
Aloha	Es	17 7	7	895	Celtic Manor Roman Road	W	18 9	7	679
Antwerp	B	16 7	7	76	Chart Hills	Eng	18 8	6	461
Bad Griesbach *Brunnwies*	G	17 9	9	314	Chiberta	F	16 6	8	189
Baden	F	15 6	5	161	Club de Campo	Es	16 8	8	906
Ballybunion *Old Course*	I	19 7	7	707	Club zur Vahr (Garlstedt)	G	18 6	5	324
Ballyliffin *Glashedy Links*	I	17 6	5	709	Côte d'Argent (La)	F	17 6	5	191
Ballyliffin *Old Course*	I	15 6	5	710	County Louth	I	18 5	6	719
Barbaroux	F	17 7	6	163	County Sligo	I	17 4	3	720
Belle-Dune	F	16 6	5	165	Courson *Lilas/Orange*	F	15 7	3	192
Berkshire (The) *Blue Course*	Eng	17 8	7	446	Courson *Vert/Noir*	F	16 7	3	193
Berkshire (The) *Red Course*	Eng	17 8	7	447	Cruden Bay	Ec	18 7	6	602
Beuerberg	G	17 7	6	320	Dalmahoy *East Course*	Ec	17 8	8	603
Blairgowrie *Lansdowne*	Ec	15 8	6	592	Dartmouth	Eng	16 9	6	466
Blairgowrie *Rosemount*	Ec	18 8	6	593	De Pan	N	16 8	7	805
Bondues *Blanc*	F	16 7	6	170	Domaine Impérial	S	18 8	6	990
Bondues *Jaune*	F	15 7	6	171	Druids Glen	I	16 9	7	726
Bordes (Les)	F	19 8	6	172	East Sussex National				
Brampton	Eng	17 7	6	453	*East Course*	Eng	17 8	7	469
Buckinghamshire (The)	Eng	17 8	7	456	Eindhoven	N	18 8	6	807
Burnham & Berrow	Eng	18 7	6	457	El Prat *Amarillo*	Es	15 7	6	911
Canyamel	Es	15 6	6	901	El Prat *Verde*	Es	17 7	6	912
Carlisle	Eng	17 7	7	459	El Saler	Es	18 7	6	913
Carnoustie *Burnside*	Ec	14 3	4	598	Emporda	Es	17 7	6	914
Carnoustie *Championship*	Ec	19 3	4	599	European (The)	I	18 6	6	729
Castillo de Gorraiz	Es	17 7	7	903	Evian	F	15 7	9	203

66

RECOMMENDED GOLFING STAY

Golf course	Country	Score			Page	Golf course	Country	Score			Page
Fairhaven	Eng	17	7	8	470	Madeira	P	14	7	5	842
Falkenstein	G	18	6	7	329	Marriott St Pierre *Old Course*	W	16	8	7	682
Felixstowe Ferry						Mediterraneo	Es	16	7	6	946
Martello Course	Eng	15	6	6	471	Médoc *Les Châteaux*	F	17	7	5	234
Ferndown *Old Course*	Eng	17	7	7	472	Médoc *Les Vignes*	F	15	7	5	235
Fontanals	Es	18	6	5	917	Mijas *Los Lagos*	Es	16	6	7	947
Forest Pines *Forest + Pines*	Eng	17	6	7	474	Mijas *Los Olivos*	Es	13	6	7	948
Formby	Eng	18	7	7	475	Montecastillo	Es	17	8	7	950
Ganton	Eng	19	8	5	479	Montpellier-Massane	F	16	7	5	236
Genève	S	17	7	8	993	Moor Park *High Course*	Eng	17	8	7	508
Gleneagles *King's*	Ec	18	9	7	618	Moray	Ec	17	5	5	639
Gleneagles *Monarch's*	Ec	17	9	7	619	Motzener See	G	18	8	6	364
Gleneagles *Queen's*	Ec	15	9	7	620	Mount Juliet	I	18	9	8	747
Gouverneur (Le) *Le Breuil*	F	16	7	6	210	Nairn	Ec	19	7	8	643
Gouverneur (Le) *Montaplan*	F	14	7	6	211	National *L'Albatros*	F	18	6	6	237
Grande Bastide (La)	F	16	6	6	212	Neguri	Es	17	7	7	952
Grande-Motte (La)						Nîmes-Campagne	F	16	7	6	239
Les Flamants Roses	F	16	6	4	213	Noordwijk	N	18	7	8	819
Grenoble Bresson	F	17	7	6	216	Oostende	B	15	7	7	83
Guadalmina *Sur*	Es	14	7	7	921	Pals	Es	16	7	6	956
Gujan-Mestras	F	15	7	6	218	Penha Longa	P	15	7	8	845
Gullane *No 1*	Ec	17	8	7	623	Portal *Championship*	Eng	15	8	7	521
Gut Kaden *Platz B + Platz C*	G	17	7	6	335	Portmarnock	I	19	8	8	752
Haagsche	N	18	7	8	813	Portmarnock Links	I	17	7	8	753
Hainaut *Bruyere-Quesnoy*	B	15	7	5	79	Portstewart *Strand Course*	U	16	7	7	788
Hanau-Wilhelmsbad	G	15	6	6	342	Praia d'El Rey	P	17	7	5	848
Hardelot *Les Pins*	F	16	6	6	219	Pyle & Kenfig	W	17	7	5	686
Hawkstone Park *Hawkstone*	Eng	15	8	7	483	Quinta do Lago *B/C*	P	15	7	8	851
Hayling	Eng	16	7	7	484	Quinta do Lago *Ria Formosa*	P	15	7	8	852
Hillside	Eng	18	7	7	489	Ravenstein	B	17	8	7	86
Hilversum	N	16	7	7	815	Reichswald-Nürnberg	G	17	7	7	377
Hunstanton	Eng	17	7	6	491	Royal Birkdale (The)	Eng	19	9	7	526
Islantilla	Es	16	8	8	923	Royal Cinque Ports	Eng	17	6	5	527
Isle of Purbeck	Eng	16	8	7	495	Royal County Down	U	19	6	7	790
John O'Gaunt	Eng	16	7	6	496	Royal Dornoch	Ec	19	7	7	656
K Club	I	17	8	8	737	Royal Dublin	I	16	7	7	759
Kempferhof (Le)	F	18	8	6	225	Royal Liverpool (Hoylake)	Eng	18	8	7	531
Kennemer	N	18	8	8	817	Royal Lytham & St Anne's	Eng	19	7	8	532
Killarney *Killeen Course*	I	16	7	8	739	Royal North Devon					
Killarney *Mahony's Point*	I	15	7	8	740	(Westward Ho!)	Eng	18	6	6	534
La Cala *Norte*	Es	17	8	6	925	Royal Porthcawl	W	19	7	5	688
La Cala *Sur*	Es	16	8	6	926	Royal Portrush *Dunluce Links*	U	19	7	7	791
La Dehesa	Es	14	7	4	927	Royal Portrush *Valley*	U	13	7	7	792
La Manga *Norte*	Es	15	7	7	929	Royal St David's	W	18	6	5	689
La Manga *Oeste*	Es	14	7	7	930	Royal St George's	Eng	19	7	5	535
La Manga *Sur*	Es	14	7	7	931	Royal Troon *Old Course*	Ec	19	7	7	658
La Moraleja *La Moraleja 1*	Es	15	7	8	932	Royal West Norfolk (Bter)	Eng	17	7	6	536
La Moraleja *La Moraleja 2*	Es	16	7	8	933	Royal Zoute	B	18	7	7	90
La Quinta	Es	15	8	7	934	S. Lourenço	P	17	6	8	854
Lahinch	I	18	6	6	742	Sablé-Solesmes					
Las Brisas	Es	18	7	7	937	*La Forêt/La Rivière*	F	16	7	4	257
Lausanne	S	16	7	7	996	Saint-Donat	F	15	7	8	259
Limère	F	17	6	5	230	Saint-Jean-de-Monts	F	16	6	5	262
Los Naranjos	Es	16	7	7	941	Saint-Nom-la-Bretèche *Bleu*	F	15	8	8	264
Machrihanish	Ec	18	6	4	636	Saint-Nom-la-Bretèche *Rouge*	F	16	8	8	265

67

PEUGEOT GOLF GUIDE 1998

RECOMMENDED GOLFING STAY

Golf course	Country	Score			Page	Golf course	Country	Score			Page
San Roque	Es	17	8	6	967	Touquet (Le) *La Mer*	F	17	6	7	278
San Sebastián	Es	14	6	6	968	Tralee	I	18	7	6	766
Saunton East Course	Eng	18	7	6	541	Trevose *Championship*	Eng	17	7	7	563
Scharmützelsee *Arnold Palmer*	G	16	8	7	378	Troia	P	15	7	5	856
Scharmützelsee *Nick Faldo*	G	18	8	7	379	Turnberry *Ailsa Course*	Ec	19	9	8	670
Seignosse	F	17	7	7	270	Turnberry *Arran Course*	Ec	16	9	8	671
Slaley Hall	Eng	17	8	7	549	Valderrama	Es	19	8	6	977
Sotogrande	Es	18	7	6	974	Vilamoura *I (Old Course)*	P	16	7	7	859
Southport & Ainsdale	Eng	18	7	7	550	Vilamoura *II (Pinhal)*	P	13	7	7	860
Spa (Les Fagnes)	B	17	7	7	92	Vilamoura *III (Laguna)*	P	14	7	7	861
Spérone	F	17	7	5	273	Villamartin	Es	16	7	6	978
Spiegelven	B	14	7	8	93	Villette d'Anthon *Les Sangliers*	F	17	6	4	283
St Andrews *Eden Course*	Ec	14	8	8	662	Wallasey	Eng	17	7	7	564
St Andrews *Jubilee Course*	Ec	16	8	8	663	Walton Heath *New Course*	A	16	7	6	565
St Andrews *New Course*	Ec	17	8	8	664	Walton Heath *Old Course*	Eng	18	7	7	566
St Andrews *Old Course*	Ec	18	8	8	665	Warwickshire (The)	A	15	7	8	567
St Enodoc *Church Course*	Eng	18	7	4	551	Waterloo *La Marache*	B	16	8	7	94
St Mellion *Nicklaus Course*	Eng	17	9	7	553	Waterville	I	17	6	7	771
Stoke Poges	Eng	17	8	8	554	Wentworth *East Course*	Eng	16	8	7	568
Sunningdale *New Course*	Eng	18	8	8	556	Wentworth *West Course*	Eng	18	8	7	569
Sunningdale *Old Course*	Eng	18	8	8	557	West Lancashire	Eng	17	7	7	573
Taulane	F	15	7	4	275	Woburn *Dukes Course*	Eng	18	7	7	578
Toulouse-Seilh *Rouge*	F	15	7	6	277	Woodhall Spa	Eng	18	7	8	582

RECOMMENDED GOLFING HOLIDAYS
VACANCES RECOMMANDEES
VACACIONES RECOMENDADAS
FÉRIAS RECOMENDADAS
FÜR EINEN FERIENAUFENTHALT EMPFOHLEN
AAN TE RADEN VAKANTIEVERBLIJF

Golf course	Country	Score			Page	Golf course	Country	Score			Page
Aix-les-Bains	F	13	5	7	151	Charleville	I	13	4	6	716
Aloha	Es	17	7	7	895	Costa Dorada	Es	13	6	6	908
Amirauté (L')	F	15	7	8	153	Crans-sur-Sierre	S	14	7	8	989
Arcachon	F	13	6	6	158	Dinard	F	14	6	7	195
Arcangues	F	14	7	8	159	Disneyland Paris					
Baule (La) *Rouge*	F	15	7	8	164	*Never Land + Wonderland*	F	16	7	8	196
Biarritz-le-Phare	F	14	6	8	168	El Bosque	Es	16	7	4	909
Bodensee-Weissensberg	G	17	7	7	321	El Saler	Es	18	7	6	913
Bonmont	Es	16	7	6	899	Emporda	Es	17	7	6	914
Cannes Mandelieu *Old Course*	F	13	7	8	177	Engadin	S	15	6	6	991
Cannes-Mougins	F	15	7	8	178	Estérel Latitudes	F	16	6	7	200
Cap d'Agde	F	15	6	5	179	Estoril	P	13	7	7	841
Capdepera	Es	15	7	6	902	Frégate	F	15	7	7	209
Casteljaloux	F	15	6	5	180	Garmisch-Partenkirchen	G	14	6	7	334
Chamonix	F	15	6	7	183	Gleneagles *King's*	Ec	18	9	7	618
Chantaco	F	14	7	7	185	Gleneagles *Monarch's*	Ec	17	9	7	619

RECOMMENDED GOLFING HOLIDAYS

Golf course	Country	Score			Page	Golf course	Country	Score			Page
Gleneagles *Queen's*	Ec	15	9	7	620	Patriziale Ascona	S	15	7	7	1002
Grande Bastide (La)	F	16	6	6	212	Penha Longa	P	15	7	8	845
Grande-Motte (La)						Penina	P	14	7	8	846
Les Flamants Roses	F	16	6	4	213	Pinheiros Altos	P	14	8	8	847
Hardelot Les Pins	F	16	6	6	219	Playa Serena	Es	13	6	4	961
Hossegor	F	16	6	6	221	Poniente	Es	13	6	5	962
Islantilla	Es	16	8	8	923	Pornic	F	15	6	6	249
La Cala *Norte*	Es	17	8	6	925	Praia d'El Rey	P	17	7	5	848
La Cala *Sur*	Es	16	8	6	926	Pula	Es	13	6	5	964
La Manga *Norte*	Es	15	7	7	929	Quinta da Marinha	P	13	7	7	850
La Manga *Oeste*	Es	14	7	7	930	Quinta do Lago *B/C*	P	15	7	8	851
La Manga *Sur*	Es	14	7	7	931	Quinta do Lago *Ria Formosa*	P	15	7	8	852
La Moye	Eng	17	7	8	497	Quinta do Peru	P	16	7	5	853
La Sella	Es	15	6	5	935	Royal Guernsey	Eng	16	7	7	529
Lacanau	F	14	6	4	227	Royal Jersey	Eng	16	7	8	530
Lindau-Bad Schachen	G	14	7	8	358	S. Lourenço	P	17	6	8	854
Lugano	S	15	7	8	997	Saint-Laurent	F	14	7	5	263
Madeira	P	14	7	5	842	Sainte-Maxime	F	13	7	7	268
Makila Golf Club	F	14	6	8	232	Salgados	P	14	7	7	855
Marbella	Es	15	7	8	943	Son Antem	Es	14	7	6	972
Maspalomas	Es	16	7	8	945	Spérone	F	17	7	5	273
Mediterraneo	Es	16	7	6	946	Torrequebrada	Es	14	7	7	975
Mijas *Los Lagos*	Es	16	6	7	947	Touquet (Le) *La Mer*	F	17	6	7	278
Mijas *Los Olivos*	Es	13	6	7	948	Vale da Pinta	P	14	6	6	857
New Golf Deauville						Vila Sol	P	14	7	7	858
Rouge/Blanc	F	15	7	8	238	Vilamoura *I (Old Course)*	P	16	7	7	859
Novo Sancti Petri	Es	16	7	7	953	Vilamoura *II (Pinhal)*	P	13	7	7	860
Öschberghof	G	15	7	7	374	Vilamoura *III (Laguna)*	P	14	7	7	861
Palmares	P	13	7	5	844						
Pals	Es	16	7	6	956						

69

Nouvelle Peugeot 406 Break.
Toute la sécurité qu'il faut pour faire durer le plaisir.

Nouvelle Peugeot 406 Break. Vous ne choisirez plus entre le plaisir et la sécurité. Peugeot vous invite à découvrir la nouvelle 406 Break sur le site Internet Peugeot à l'adresse suivante: http://www.PEUGEOT.COM

406
PEUGEOT

▌▌Belgium
Belgique België
Luxemburg
▬Luxembourg

L a Belgique compte plus de 30.000 joueurs de golf pour 45 parcours de 18 trous environ. Les golfs présentés ici sont ouverts au public. Certes, une partie d'entre eux peut être difficile d'accès en week-end, en raison de leur grand nombre de membres, mais les voyageurs ont souvent la possibilité d'y jouer en semaine. Pour les joueurs belges comme pour les étrangers, le fait d'être muni d'une lettre d'introduction de leur propre club peut cependant faciliter les choses.

België heeft meer dan 30.000 spelers op ongeveer 45 banen 18-holesbanen. De meeste golfclubs in Peugeot Golf Guide zijn vrij toegankelijk voor het publiek. In sommige raakt men wel moeilijker binnen tijdens het week-end, wegens hun groot aantal leden, maar 'reizigers' bevinden zich meestal gemakkelijker in de mogelijkheid om tijdens de week te spelen. Voor Belgische en buitenlandse spelers is een introductiebrief van de eigen club vaak een goed idee, om de zaken eenvoudiger te maken.

Belgium has more than 30,000 golfers playing on around 50 eighteen-hole courses. All golf courses presented in this Guide are open to the public. Some may be difficult to play on week-ends owing to the number of members, but travelling green-feers should often be able to play during the week. Carrying a letter of introduction from your club may be a help, both for Belgian and foreign players.

km
0   10   20

CLASSEMENT DES PARCOURS
RANGSCHIKKING VAN DE TERREINEN
CLASSIFICATION OF COURSES

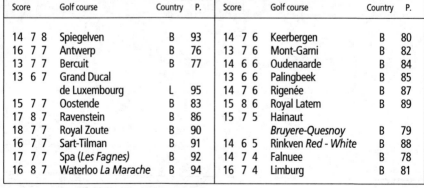

Note du Club-house et annexes
Cijfer van het Club-House & dependances
Club-house and facilities

Note du parcours
Cijfer van het terrein
(Course score)

Note de l'environnement hôtelier
Cijfer van hotelaccomodatie in de omgeving
Hotel facility score

Page
Bladzijde

18 7 7   Royal Zoute   B   90

Score			Golf course	Country	P.	Score			Golf course	Country	P.
18	7	7	Royal Zoute	B	90	14	7	4	Falnuee	B	78
17	8	7	Ravenstein	B	86	14	7	6	Keerbergen	B	80
17	7	7	Spa *(Les Fagnes)*	B	92	14	6	6	Oudenaarde	B	84
16	7	7	Antwerp	B	76	14	7	6	Rigenée	B	87
16	7	4	Limburg	B	81	14	6	5	Rinkven *Red - White*	B	88
16	7	7	Sart-Tilman	B	91	14	7	8	Spiegelven	B	93
16	8	7	Waterloo *La Marache*	B	94	13	7	7	Bercuit	B	77
15	7	5	Hainaut			13	6	7	Grand Ducal		
			Bruyere-Quesnoy	B	79				de Luxembourg	L	95
15	7	7	Oostende	B	83	13	7	6	Mont-Garni	B	82
15	8	6	Royal Latem	B	89	13	6	6	Palingbeek	B	85

CLASSEMENT DE L'ENVIRONNEMENT HOTELIER
RANGSCHIKKING VAN DE HOTELACCOMODATIE
CLASSIFICATION OF HOTELS FACILITIES

Score			Golf course	Country	P.	Score			Golf course	Country	P.
14	7	8	Spiegelven	B	93	14	7	6	Keerbergen	B	80
16	7	7	Antwerp	B	76	13	7	6	Mont-Garni	B	82
13	7	7	Bercuit	B	77	14	6	6	Oudenaarde	B	84
13	6	7	Grand Ducal			13	6	6	Palingbeek	B	85
			de Luxembourg	L	95	14	7	6	Rigenée	B	87
15	7	7	Oostende	B	83	15	8	6	Royal Latem	B	89
17	8	7	Ravenstein	B	86	15	7	5	Hainaut		
18	7	7	Royal Zoute	B	90				Bruyere-Quesnoy	B	79
16	7	7	Sart-Tilman	B	91	14	6	5	Rinkven *Red - White*	B	88
17	7	7	Spa *(Les Fagnes)*	B	92	14	7	4	Falnuee	B	78
16	8	7	Waterloo *La Marache*	B	94	16	7	4	Limburg	B	81

AAN TE RADEN VAKANTIEVERBLIJF
RECOMMENDED GOLFING STAY

Golf course	Country	Score	P.	Golf course	Country	Score	P.
Antwerp	16 7 7	76 B		Royal Zoute	18 7 7	90 B	
Hainaut *Bruyere-Quesnoy*	15 7 5	79 B		Spa *(Les Fagnes)*	17 7 7	92 B	
Oostende	15 7 7	83 B		Spiegelven	14 7 8	93 B	
Ravenstein	17 8 7	86 B		Waterloo *La Marache*	16 8 7	94 B	

SAISONS RECOMMANDÉES
AANBEVOLEN SEIZOENEN
RECOMMENDED SEASONS

Golf course	Country	Score	P.	Golf course	Country	Score	P.
1 2 **3** 4 5 6 7 8 9 **10** 11 12				Mont-Garni	B	13 7 6	82
Hainaut *Bruyere-Quesnoy*	B	15 7 5	79	Oudenaarde	B	14 6 6	84
1 2 **3** 4 5 6 **7 8 9 10** 11 12				Palingbeek	B	13 6 6	85
Oostende	B	15 7 7	83	Rigenée	B	14 7 6	87
Ravenstein	B	17 8 7	86	Rinkven *Red - White*	B	14 6 5	88
1 2 **3** 4 5 6 **7 8 9 10 11 12**				Sart-Tilman	B	16 7 7	91
Royal Zoute	B	18 7 7	90	Spa *(Les Fagnes)*	B	17 7 7	92
1 2 3 **4 5** 6 7 **8 9 10** 11 12				Spiegelven	B	14 7 8	93
Antwerp	B	16 7 7	76	1 2 3 **4 5** 6 7 **8 9 10** 11 12			
Bercuit	B	13 7 7	77	Royal Latem	B	15 8 6	89
Falnuee	B	14 7 4	78	Waterloo *La Marache*	B	16 8 7	94
Keerbergen	B	14 7 6	80	1 2 3 **4 5 6** 7 **8 9** 10 11 12			
Limburg	B	16 7 4	81	Grand Ducal de Luxembourg	L	13 6 7	95

RELIEF DES PARCOURS
RELIEF VAN DE TERREINEN
GEOGRAPHICAL RELIEF

Rather flat Peu de relief Weinig niveauverschil	Averagely hilly Moyennement accidenté Met gemiddelde hoogten en laagten	Very hilly Relief important Belangrijk niveauverschil

					Hainaut *Bruyere-Quesnoy*	B	15 7 5	79
Oostende	B	15 7 7	83	Limburg	B	16 7 4	81
					Ravenstein	B	17 8 7	86
Antwerp	B	16 7 7	76	Spiegelven	B	14 7 8	93
Keerbergen	B	14 7 6	80	Waterloo *La Marache*	B	16 8 7	94
Mont-Garni	B	13 7 6	82				
Rinkven *Red - White*	B	14 6 5	88	Rigenée	B	14 7 6	87
Royal Latem	B	15 8 6	89				
Royal Zoute	B	18 7 7	90	Spa (Les Fagnes)	B	17 7 7	92
Oudenaarde	B	14 6 6	84	Sart-Tilman	B	16 7 7	91
Palingbeek	B	13 6 6	85				
					Bercuit	B	13 7 7	77
Grand Ducal de Luxembourg	13 6 7	95		Falnuee	B	14 7 4	78

Dit parcours werd ontworpen in 1888, gewijzigd door Willie Park in 1913 en Tom Simpson in 1930, en is hiermee de oudste club in België, wat hem echter niet is aan te zien, eerder integendeel! Een voordeel van de ouderdom : de lengte verplicht u niet om te driven zoals John Daly, en de subtiele greens eisen niet dat u kunt putten zoals Corey Pavin, maar desondanks mogen de moeilijkheden niet onderschat worden : een harde hand in een fluwelen handschoen... Het terrein is een schoolvoorbeeld voor de moderne architecten, met zijn opvallend uitgekiende design, de strategische plaatsing van de bunkers, het bewuste aanwenden van bomen en heide in het ontwerp. Het was een wijze beslissing van de architecten om het grootste gedeelte van de moeilijkheden voor de beste spelers te bewaren, zodat het algemeen ontwerp voor iedereen inspirerend blijft. Hier spelen is een waar genoegen; spelen met een bijkomende competitiedruk is nog een groter genoegen. En deze prachtige plek voegt nog zijn visuele charme toe aan het speelplezier.

Created in 1888 then redesigned by Willie Park in 1913 and Tom Simpson in 1930, this is Belgium's oldest club, although it looks as young as ever. Having the privilege of being an old-style course, its length doesn't mean having to drive à la John Daly and the subtle greens hardly require the putting touch of a Corey Pavin. But the trouble in store should never be under-estimated, as this is an iron hand in a velvet glove. The remarkably intelligent layout, highly strategic bunkering and the presence and use of trees and heather are an example for all modern designers. Here, the main difficulties have cleverly been reserved for the better players, but the general layout is an inspiration for us all. Playing here is a real pleasure, and playing with the pressure of a tournament even more so. The site adds visual charm to the enjoyment of golfing.

Royal Antwerp Golf Club
G. Capiaulei, 2
B - 2950 KAPELLEN

Office	Secretariaat	(32) 03 - 666 61 90
Pro shop	Pro shop	(32) 03 - 666 46 87
Fax	Fax	(32) 03 - 666 44 37
Situation	Locatie	

15 km Antwerpen (Anvers), 403 072 inw.
48 km Brussel (Bruxelles), 667 825 inw.

Annual closure	Jaarlijkse sluiting	neen
Weekly closure	Wekelijkse sluitingsdag	neen
		maandag, pro shop

Fees main season
Hoogseizoen tarieven 18 holes

	Week days Weekdagen	We/Bank holidays We/Feestdagen
Individual Individueel	2 000 BF	neen
Couple Paar	4 000 BF	neen

Caddy	Caddy	neen
Electric Trolley	Electrische trolley	neen
Buggy	Buggy	1200 BF
Clubs	Clubs	neen

Credit cards Creditkaarten	VISA - Eurocard

Access Toegang : E19 Anvers → Breda, Exit 5 → N11
Map 1 on page 72 Auto kaart 1 Blz 72

GOLF COURSE
BAAN **16**/20

Site	Terrein	▮▮▮▮▮▮
Maintenance	Onderhoud	▮▮▮▮▮▮▮
Architect	Architect	Willie Park Jr Tom Simpson
Type	Type baan	park
Relief	Reliëf	▮▮
Water in play	Waterhazards	▮
Exp. to wind	Windgevoelig	▮▮▮▮
Trees in play	Bomen	▮▮▮▮▮▮

Scorecard Scorekaart	Chp. Back tees	Mens Heren	Ladies Damen
Length Lengte	6155	6155	5468
Par	73	73	73

Advised golfing ability Aanbevolen golfvaardigheid	0 12 24 36 ▮▮▮▮▮▮	
Hcp required Vereiste hcp	28	

CLUB HOUSE & AMENITIES
CLUB HOUSE EN ANNEXEN **7**/10

Pro shop	Pro shop	▮▮▮▮▮▮
Driving range	Oefenbaan	▮▮▮▮
Sheltered	overdekt	4 plaatsen
On grass	op gras	ja
Putting-green	putting-green	ja
Pitching-green	pitching-green	ja

HOTEL FACILITIES
HOTELS IN OMGEVING **7**/10

HOTELS HOTELS
Hilton **** · Antwerpen
199 kamers, D 10 900 BF · 15 km
tel. (32) 03 - 204 12 12, Fax (32) 03 - 204 12 13

Alfa Theater · Antwerpen
122 kamers, D 5 700 BF · 15 km
tel. (32) 03 - 231 17 20, Fax (32) 03 - 233 88 58

Rubens · Antwerpen
35 kamers, D 6 500 BF · 15 km
tel. (32) 03 - 222 48 48, Fax (32) 03 - 225 19 40

RESTAURANTS RESTAURANT
De Bellefleur · Kapellen
tel. (32) 03 - 664 67 19 · 1 km

't Fornuis · Antwerpen
tel. (32) 03 - 233 62 70 · 15 km

76

On ne retrouve pas ici le dessin de bunkers si caractéristique de Robert Trent Jones, et de son propre aveu, il n'a pas donné son meilleur. On s'en doute, tant les trous spectaculaires (5 et 11) alternent avec des trous "tricky", des trous tranquilles et des trous fatigants (voiturette conseillée), imposant un rythme heurté : on joue trop sur la défensive. Le relief très mouvementé interdit de quitter les fairways, et les frappeurs se sentiront privés de leur liberté d'expression, tant il faut souvent laisser le driver dans le sac. Les greens sont bien défendus, souvent pentus et ondulés : les négocier est problématique quand ils sont rapides ! Après l'avoir joué plusieurs fois, on comprend mieux les pièges de ce parcours, sans qu'il perde complètement son caractère hasardeux. C'est dommage, car le site est superbe et les maisons de belle qualité. Les joueurs droits aimeront davantage !

You won't find here the bunkers that have come to typify Robert Trent Jones, and he readily admits that this is not one of his best courses. You can guess it by the way some spectacular holes (the 5th and 11th) alternate with trickier, quieter and tiring holes (buggy recommended for the latter) which break up the rhythm. The golfer is always on the defensive. The steep slopes mean that staying in the fairway is a must, and big-hitters will feel a little restricted in their freedom of expression, given the number of holes where the driver should stay firmly in the bag. The greens are well defended with slopes and bumps, so when they are fast they can easily cause a few problems. After several rounds you start to understand the traps here a little better, but the course never loses its uncertain nature. And that's a pity because the site is superb and the villas attractive. Straight-hitters will enjoy Bercuit more than the others.

Golf de Bercuit

Domaine de Bercuit, Les Gottes, 3
B - 1390 GREZ-DOICEAU

Office	Secrétariat	(32) 010 - 84 15 01
Pro shop	Pro-shop	(32) 010 - 84 15 01
Fax	Fax	(32) 010 - 84 55 95
Situation	Situation	

5 km Wavre, 27162 hab. 30 km Bruxelles, 667825 hab.

Annual closure	Fermeture annnuelle	non
Weekly closure	Fermeture hebdomadaire	non
		lundi, pro-shop

Fees main season Tarifs haute saison le parcours

	Week days Semaine	We/Bank holidays We/Férié
Individual Individuel	1 450 BF	2 500 BF
Couple Couple	2 900 BF	5 000 BF

Caddy	Caddy	non
Electric Trolley	Chariot électrique	400 BF
Buggy	Voiturette	1 000 BF
Clubs	Clubs	350 BF

Credit cards Cartes de crédit
VISA - Eurocard - MasterCard

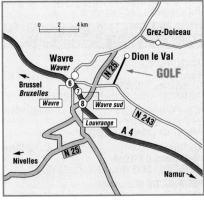

Access Accès : E411 Bruxelles → Namur, exit 8 → Grez Doiceau, N243 à droite, 2 km à gauche → Dion
Map 1 on page 73 Carte 1 Page 73

GOLF COURSE
PARCOURS

13/20

Site	Site	▬▬▬
Maintenance	Entretien	▬▬▬▬
Architect	Architecte	Robert Trent Jones
Type	Type	forêt
Relief	Relief	▬▬▬▬
Water in play	Eau en jeu	▬▬
Exp. to wind	Exposé au vent	▬▬▬
Trees in play	Arbres en jeu	▬▬▬▬▬

Scorecard Carte de score	Chp. Chp.	Mens Mess.	Ladies Da.
Length Long.	5931	5931	5208
Par	72	72	72

Advised golfing ability	0	12	24	36
Niveau de jeu recommandé		▬▬		
Hcp required Handicap exigé	32 Me, 36 Da.			

CLUB HOUSE & AMENITIES
CLUB HOUSE ET ANNEXES

7/10

Pro shop	Pro-shop	▬▬▬
Driving range	Practice	▬▬▬
Sheltered	couvert	10 places
On grass	sur herbe	non
Putting-green	putting-green	oui
Pitching-green	pitching green	oui

HOTEL FACILITIES
ENVIRONNEMENT HOTELIER

7/10

HOTELS HÔTELS

Le Domaine des Champs — Wavre, 5 km
18 chambres, D 2 800 BF
Tél (32) 010 - 22 75 25, Fax (32) 010 - 24 17 31

Novotel — Wavre, 5 km
102 chambres, D 3 200 BF
Tél (32) 010 - 41 13 63, Fax (32) 010 - 41 19 22

Comfort Inn — Wavre, 5 km
70 chambres, D 2 800 BF
Tél (32) 010 - 24 33 34, Fax (32) 010 - 24 36 80

RESTAURANTS RESTAURANT

Le Jardin Gourmand — Wavre, 5 km
Tél (32) 010 - 24 15 26

Le Vert Délice — Wavre, 5 km
Tél (32) 010 - 22 90 01

77

Un joli Club, avec son Club house dans les anciennes écuries voûtées remontant au Moyen-Age, le charme d'un paysage vallonné, la présence de deux rivières. Les puristes pourront relever une rupture avec la tradition, avec cinq par 3 (dont quatre au retour) et trois par 5, pour un par 70 et une longueur réduite. La grande difficulté consiste à tenir compte des dénivellations pour choisir les clubs, et aussi pour placer les drives : il suffit d'un peu d'inattention pour voir les obstacles très en jeu, et manquer quelques greens surélevés qu'il vaut mieux toucher directement. Jean Jottrand a produit un dessin agréable, bien qu'un peu rustique, mais si l'on regrette son imagination un peu timide, ce parcours reste accessible à tous niveaux. On conseillera plutôt de jouer ici entre amis, pour le plaisir, sans vouloir chercher d'émotions visuelles et golfiques très violentes.

A pretty golf club, with a club-house in former vaulted stables dating from the middle ages, rolling landscape and two rivers. The purists will point to the break from tradition, as this short course is a par 70 with five par 3s (four of which are on the back 9) and three par 5s. The major difficulty is assessing the slopes and hills before choosing your club, and positioning the tee-shot. A momentary lapse of concentration can take you straight into the hazards and result in missing some of the elevated greens, which you are well advised to pitch directly. Jean Jottrand has produced a pleasant layout, perhaps a little on the rustic side, but despite the regrettable lack of imagination, the course is playable by golfers of all levels. Your best bet here is a round with friends, just for fun, without looking for true visual or golfing excitement.

Golf de Falnuee

55, rue E. Pirson
B - 5032 MAZY

Office	Secrétariat	(32) 081 - 63 30 90
Pro shop	Pro-shop	(32) 081 - 63 30 90
Fax	Fax	(32) 081 - 63 37 64
Situation	Situation	

15 km Namur, 97845 hab.

Annual closure	Fermeture annnuelle	non
Weekly closure	Fermeture hebdomadaire	lundi

Fees main season
Tarifs haute saison le parcours

	Week days Semaine	We/Bank holidays We/Férié
Individual Individuel	850 BF	1 350 BF
Couple Couple	1 700 BF	2 700 BF

Caddy	Caddy	non
Electric Trolley	Chariot électrique	400 BF/18 tr.
Buggy	Voiturette	1 000 BF
Clubs	Clubs	400 BF

Credit cards	Cartes de crédit
VISA - Eurocard - AMEX

78

0   2   4 km

Gembloux-sur-Orneau

N 29
N 93
Mazy
A 15 - E 41
Namur
Temploux
Onoz
Mons
GOLF
N 98
Jemeppe
-sur-Sambre
Sambreville

Access Accès : E42 Mons → Liège, Exit 13 → Mazy N93
Map 1 on page 73 Carte 1 Page 73

GOLF COURSE / PARCOURS

14/20

Site	Site	
Maintenance	Entretien	
Architect	Architecte	Jean Jottrand
Type	Type	campagne, forêt
Relief	Relief	
Water in play	Eau en jeu	
Exp. to wind	Exposé au vent	
Trees in play	Arbres en jeu	

Scorecard	Chp.	Mens	Ladies
Carte de score	Chp.	Mess.	Da.
Length Long.	5590	5590	4750
Par	70	70	70

Advised golfing ability	0	12	24	36
Niveau de jeu recommandé				
Hcp required	Handicap exigé	36		

CLUB HOUSE & AMENITIES / CLUB HOUSE ET ANNEXES

7/10

Pro shop	Pro-shop	
Driving range	Practice	
Sheltered	couvert	6 places
On grass	sur herbe	non
Putting-green	putting-green	oui
Pitching-green	pitching green	oui

HOTEL FACILITIES / ENVIRONNEMENT HOTELIER

4/10

HOTELS HÔTELS
Beauregard   Namur 15 km
51 chambres, D 3250 BF
Tél (32) 081 - 23 00 28, Fax (32) 081 - 24 12 09

Grand Hôtel de Flandre   Namur 15 km
33 chambres, D 3 000 BF
Tél (32) 081 - 23 18 68, Fax (32) 081 - 22 80 60

Les Tanneurs   Namur 15 km
16 chambres, D 6 000 BF
Tél (32) 081 - 23 19 99, Fax (32) 081 - 22 97 03

RESTAURANTS RESTAURANT
La Bergerie   Lives-sur-Meuse 20 km
Tél (32) 081 - 58 06 13

Biétrumé Picar   Namur15 km
Tél(32) 081 - 23 07 39

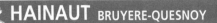
Pour le 18 trous traditionnel (Bruyères et Quesnoy), une architecture classique de Tom Simpson, sur un terrain sablonneux jouable pratiquement toute l'année. Les obstacles sont bien visibles, stratégiquement bien placés, notamment les bunkers de fairway, s'ajoutant aux nombreux arbres du parcours, qui donnent un sentiment de calme et de charme tout à fait plaisants. Mais c'est un aspect trompeur, car les greens sont dans l'axe de drives bien placés, laissant ensuite de petits clubs pour rejoindre des greens bien défendus. Pour bien scorer, il faut bien maîtriser les balles levées, avec assez d'effet quand les greens sont rapides. Ce parcours au caractère britannique réserve de grandes satisfactions, avec un petit parfum d'autrefois très agréable. "Les Etangs" (9 trous) complètent cet équipement, avec beaucoup de trous en dog-leg. Très scénique et plus "moderne", il exige un jeu très long et précis, au milieu des pins.

The traditional 18-hole course is a classic design from Tom Simpson on sandy soil that is playable virtually all year. The hazards are clearly visible and strategically well located, especially the fairway bunkers, adding to the many trees on the course which give a pleasing impression of tranquillity and charm. But appearances can be deceptive, and here the well-defended greens, always perfectly in line with well-placed drives, call for some pretty sharp short ironwork. Good scores need tight pitch and lob shots, and backspin too, when the greens are fast. The course has a pleasant British flavour and can give immense satisfaction with its very pleasant olde worlde charm. The 9-hole course ("Les Etangs") completes the picture and includes a lot of dog-legs. Very scenic and more "modern" (i.e. lots of water), it demands both length and precision through the pine-trees.

Royal Golf Club du Hainaut

2, rue de la Verrerie
B - 7050 ERBISOEUL

Office	Secrétariat	(32) 065 - 22 94 74
Pro shop	Pro-shop	(32) 065 - 22 96 10
Fax	Fax	(32) 065 - 22 51 54
Situation	Situation	

5 km N.E. Mons, 77021 hab.
60 km Bruxelles, 667825 hab.

Annual closure	Fermeture annnuelle	non
Weekly closure	Fermeture hebdomadaire	non

Fees main season
Tarifs haute saison le parcours

	Week days Semaine	We/Bank holidays We/Férié
Individual Individuel	1 400 FB	2 000 FB
Couple Couple	2 800 FB	4 000 FB

Caddy	Caddy	non
Electric Trolley	Chariot électrique	non
Buggy	Voiturette	1 000 BF
Clubs	Clubs	oui
Credit cards Cartes de crédit		non

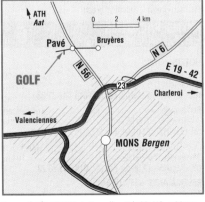

Access Accès : E42 Paris-Bruxelles, Exit 23, N6 → Mons,
N56 → Ath
Map 1 on page 72 Carte 1 Page 72

GOLF COURSE
PARCOURS   **15**/20

Site	Site	■■■■
Maintenance	Entretien	■■■■
Architect	Architecte	Tom Simpson
Type	Type	forêt, vallon
Relief	Relief	
Water in play	Eau en jeu	■
Exp. to wind	Exposé au vent	■■
Trees in play	Arbres en jeu	■■■■

Scorecard Carte de score	Chp. Chp.	Mens Mess.	Ladies Da.
Length Long.	6108	6108	5318
Par	72	72	72

Advised golfing ability		0 12 24 36		
Niveau de jeu recommandé		■■■■■		
Hcp required	Handicap exigé	36		

CLUB HOUSE & AMENITIES
CLUB HOUSE ET ANNEXES   **7**/10

Pro shop	Pro-shop	■■■■
Driving range	Practice	■■■
Sheltered	couvert	oui
On grass	sur herbe	non
Putting-green	putting-green	oui
Pitching-green	pitching green	oui

79

HOTEL FACILITIES
ENVIRONNEMENT HOTELIER   **5**/10

HOTELS HÔTELS
La Forêt   Masnuy St-Jean
51 chambres, D 3 900 BF   4 km
Tél (32) 065 - 72 36 85, Fax (32) 065 - 72 41 44

Lido   Mons
67 chambres, D 3 900 BF   6 km
Tél (32) 065 - 32 78 00, Fax (32) 065 - 84 37 22

Infotel   Mons
19 chambres, D 3 000 BF   6 km
Tél (32) 065 - 35 62 21, Fax (32) 065 - 35 62 24

RESTAURANTS RESTAURANT
La Forêt   Masnuy St-Jean
Tél (32) 065 - 72 36 85   4 km

Devos   Mons
Tél (32) 065 - 35 13 35   6 km

De namen van de architecten alleen al zijn een aanduiding voor een grondige kennis van de golfsport. Op 38 hectare zijn ze erin geslaagd een par 70 met 6 zeer afwisselende par 3 te herbergen. Dit is een klassiek parcours, zeer kort en vlak (het kan zeer vlug gespeeld worden), maar het is een echte "challenge" qua precisie en intelligent spel. Het is geschikt voor alle handicaps, en speciaal op prijs gesteld door de dames, waarvan de besten tee-offs hebben die quasi gelijk zijn aan die van de heren. Goed onderhouden met netjes opgeruimd onderhout : dit is de perfecte golf om zichzelf een pleziertje te gunnen, maar ook om het spel met de kleinere "irons" wat bij te schaven, dankzij zeer interessante approaches van de greens naargelang de positie van de vlaggen. Talrijke "out of bounds" zetten de slordige spelers wat onder druk, en verschillende strategisch aangelegde vijvers zorgen voor wat subtiliteit, vooral op de 2, 15 en 18, een par 4 langs de rand van een vijver, waarboven het Club-House uittoront.

The names of the architects obviously denote in-depth knowledge of the game of golf. They have successfully squeezed a par 70 into 38 hectares (95 acres), with 6 very different par 3s. This is a classical, very short and flat course (ideal for fast play), but also a challenge of precision and intelligence. Suitable for all levels, it is particularly popular with the ladies, the best of whom tee off very close to the men's tees. Well upkept with the rough and undergrowth also neatly cleared, this is a perfect course for enjoying yourself and honing your short irons; some of the approach shots are a real treat, depending on the pin positions. Wayward golfers will feel the pressure of a lot of out-of-bounds, and several strategic lakes call for subtle strategy, especially holes 2, 15 and 18, a par 4 edged by a lake and overlooked by the club-house.

Keerbergen Golf Club

Vlieghavenlaan, 50
B - 3140 KEERBERGEN

Office	Secretariaat	(32) 015 - 23 49 61
Pro shop	Pro shop	(32) 015 - 23 49 63
Fax	Fax	(32) 015 - 23 57 37
Situation	Locatie	

10 km Mechelen (Malines), 69430 inw.
25 km Brussel (Bruxelles), 667825 inw.

Annual closure	Jaarlijkse sluiting	neen
Weekly closure	Wekelijkse sluitingsdag	neen
		maandag, restaurant

Fees main season
Hoogseizoen tarieven 18 holes

	Week days Weekdagen	We/Bank holidays We/Feestdagen
Individual Individueel	1 000 BF	1 400 BF
Couple Paar	2 000 BF	2 800 BF

Caddy	Caddy	neen
Electric Trolley	Electrische trolley	neen
Buggy	Buggy	1 000 BF/18 holes
Clubs	Clubs	600 BF/18 holes

Credit cards Creditkaarten		neen

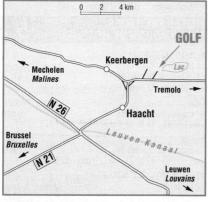

GOLF

Keerbergen
Lac
Mechelen
Malines
Tremolo
N 26
Haacht
Leuven Kanaal
Brussel
Bruxelles
N 21
Leuwen
Louvains

Access Toegang : N21 Bruxelles → Haacht, →
Keerbergen, → Tremolo, Golf
Map 1 on page 73 Auto kaart 1 Blz 73

GOLF COURSE / BAAN — 14/20

Site	Terrein	
Maintenance	Onderhoud	
Architect	Architect	Cotton, Penninck Lawree
Type	Type baan	park, residentieel
Relief	Reliëf	
Water in play	Waterhazards	
Exp. to wind	Windgevoelig	
Trees in play	Bomen	

Scorecard Scorekaart	Chp. Back tees	Mens Heren	Ladies Damen
Length Lengte	5600	5530	4867
Par	70	70	70

Advised golfing ability Aanbevolen golfvaardigheid		0 12 24 36
Hcp required Vereiste hcp		36

CLUB HOUSE & AMENITIES / CLUB HOUSE EN ANNEXEN — 7/10

Pro shop	Pro shop	
Driving range	Oefenbaan	
Sheltered	overdekt	3 plaatsen
On grass	op gras	neen
Putting-green	putting-green	ja
Pitching-green	pitching-green	ja

HOTEL FACILITIES / HOTELS IN OMGEVING — 6/10

HOTELS HOTELS
Alfa Alba — Mechelen
43 kamers, D 6 700 BF — 10 km
tel. (32) 015 - 42 03 03, Fax (32) 015 - 42 37 88

Berkenhof — Keerbergen
7 kamers, D 8 250 BF — 1 km
tel. (32) 015 - 73 01 01, Fax (32) 015 - 73 02 02

Den Grooten Wolsack — Mechelen
14 kamers, D 3 700 BF — 10 km
tel. (32) 015 - 21 86 03, Fax (32) 015 - 21 86 28

RESTAURANTS RESTAURANT
The Paddock — Keerbergen
tel. (32) 015 - 51 19 34 — 1 km

D'Hoogh — Mechelen
tel. (32) 015 - 21 75 53 — 10 km

80

Midden in een natuurreservaat en een landschap van sparren en berken, typerend voor de Kempen, wordt dit licht golvend terrein een ware streling voor het oog als de heide in bloei staat, op het einde van de zomer en in de herfst. Het is het stroke-play parcours bij uitstek, met een harmonisch speelritme, enkele moeilijke pieken die gespreksstof vormen voor achteraf (sommige par 4 zijn hardnekkig), zeer mooie par 5 en een juweeltje, de 8, een kleine technische par 4 zoals men er geen meer durft ontwerpen. Het design van FW Hawtree is van een op en top Brits classicisme, het ontwerp ziet eruit alsof de natuur zelf het zo gewild heeft, mooi gelegen tussen de heide en het bos, en het heeft een zeer "intelligente" bunkering. Daar het terrein zeer goed uitgebalanceerd is, met werkelijke verschillen tussen de champion tees en de andere, is het er zeer aangenaam spelen op elk niveau, en keert men met plezier nog eens terug. Eén enkel schoonheidsfoutje : de middelmatige staat van de greens en van sommige tee-offs.

Set in a nature reserve of pine and birch that are typical of the Campine region, this slightly rolling course is a beautiful sight when the heather is in full bloom in late summer and in autumn. This is an excellent course for stroke-play, neatly balanced with a few memorable tough moments on the back nine (some par 4s are really hard going), some fabulous par 5s and a gem of a hole, the 8th, which is a short but very technical 4-par, the likes of which are hardly ever found these days. F.W. Hawtree's layout is a pure British classic, winding its way almost naturally between heather and wood with particularly intelligent bunkering. Because it is so well balanced, with real differences between the tournament and hacker tees, it is pleasant to play, again and again, whatever your level. The only black spot is the average state of the greens and some tees.

Limburg Golf & Country Club

Golfstraat 1
B - 3530 HOUTHALEN

Office	Secretariaat	(32) 089 - 38 35 43
Pro shop	Pro shop	(32) 089 - 84 32 04
Fax	Fax	(32) 089 - 84 12 08
Situation	Locatie	

15 km Hasselt, 64 722 inw.

Annual closure	Jaarlijkse sluiting	neen
Weekly closure	Wekelijkse sluitingsdag	neen
		maandag, pro-shop

Fees main season
Hoogseizoen tarieven 18 holes

	Week days Weekdagen	We/Bank holidays We/Feestdagen
Individual Individueel	1 400 BF	1 800 BF
Couple Paar	2 800 BF	3 600 BF

Caddy	Caddy	neen
Electric Trolley	Electrische trolley	neen
Buggy	Buggy	1 200 BF/18 holes
Clubs	Clubs	neen

Credit cards Creditkaarten   neen

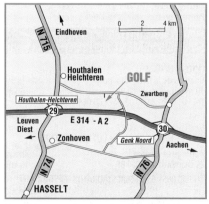

Access Toegang : E314 Brussel → Aix-la-Chapelle, Exit 29, N715 → Eindhoven, Houthalen, → Golf
Map 1 on page 73 Auto kaart 1 Blz 73

GOLF COURSE
BAAN
16/20

Site	Terrein	
Maintenance	Onderhoud	
Architect	Architect	Fred Hawtree
Type	Type baan	bos
Relief	Reliëf	
Water in play	Waterhazards	
Exp. to wind	Windgevoelig	
Trees in play	Bomen	

Scorecard Scorekaart	Chp. Back tees	Mens Heren	Ladies Damen
Length Lengte	6128	5750	5156
Par	72	72	72

Advised golfing ability Aanbevolen golfvaardigheid	0 12 24 36
Hcp required Vereiste hcp	36 weekdagen, 30/32 We

CLUB HOUSE & AMENITIES
CLUB HOUSE EN ANNEXEN
7/10

Pro shop	Pro shop	
Driving range	Oefenbaan	
Sheltered	overdekt	14 plaatsen
On grass	op gras	nee
Putting-green	putting-green	ja
Pitching-green	pitching-green	ja

HOTEL FACILITIES
HOTELS IN OMGEVING
4/10

HOTELS HOTELS

Scholteshof — Hasselt
11 kamers, D 12 000 BF — 15 km
tel. (32) 011 - 25 02 02, Fax (32) 011 - 25 43 28

Holiday Inn — Hasselt
106 kamers, D 6 900 BF — 15 km
tel. (32) 011 - 24 22 00, Fax (32) 011 - 22 39 35

Hassotel — Hasselt
30 kamers, D 3 820 BF — 15 km
tel. (32) 011 - 22 64 92, Fax (32) 011 - 22 94 77

Century - 17 kamers, D 2 500 BF — Hasselt
tel. (32) 011 - 22 47 99, Fax (32) 011 - 23 18 24 — 15 km

RESTAURANTS RESTAURANT

Savarin - tel. (32) 011 - 22 84 88 — Hasselt - 15 km

De Barrier - tel. (32) 011 - 52 55 25 — Houthalen - 3 km

81

MONT-GARNI

13	7	6

Avec quelques arbres en moins (2, 13, 14, 17) qui empiètent sur la bonne ligne de jeu, l'élagage de certaines branches (annoncé pour cet hiver) et un plus large nettoyage des sous-bois, Mont-Garni donnerait plus encore de plaisir aux golfeurs, rendrait plus évidente la stratégie de jeu et ne punirait vraiment que les coups lâchés. En revanche, le challenge est réel, beaucoup de trous sont intéressants, même si les pars 3 sont plus longs que vraiment subtils. Il faut constamment se méfier des arbres et des étangs, qui rendent cependant le site assez séduisant : sur ce parcours demandant de la précision, on ne conseillera les départs arrière qu'aux joueurs de très bon niveau, les autres s'y amuseront beaucoup en match-play, en famille ou entre amis de niveau équivalent. On suivra avec intérêt l'évolution de ce parcours, et les non-golfeurs peuvent préférer le centre équestre sur place que porter les sacs...

With fewer trees right in the line of fire (on the 2nd, 13th, 14 th and 17th holes), the trimming of a few branches and more extensive clearing of undergrowth, Mont-Garni would be even more enjoyable to play, would make game strategy more obvious and would punish only the really wayward shot. However, the challenge here hits you in the eye, with a lot of interesting holes, even though the par 3s are longer than they are subtle. You have to be constantly on the outlook to avoid the trees and lakes, which at the same time add to the course's appeal. On a course like this, which demands precision play, we would recommend the back-tees only for the better players ; the others can move forward and have fun with the family or friends with a round of match-play. It will be interesting to see how this course evolves. Rather than lug golf bags around, non-golfers may prefer the riding stables next door.

Golf du Mont-Garni

Rue du Mont-Garni, 3
B - 7331 BAUDOUR

Office	Secrétariat	(32) 065 - 62 27 19
Pro shop	Pro-shop	(32) 065 - 62 27 19
Fax	Fax	(32) 065 - 62 34 10
Situation	Situation	

7 km Mons, 77 021 hab.

Annual closure	Fermeture annnuelle	non
Weekly closure	Fermeture hebdomadaire	

Fees main season
Tarifs haute saison 18 trous

	Week days Semaine	We/Bank holidays We/Férié
Individual Individuel	1 000 BF	1 500 BF
Couple Couple	2 000 BF	3 000 BF

Caddy	Caddy	non
Electric Trolley	Chariot électrique	non
Buggy	Voiturette	1 000 BF
Clubs	Clubs le club	50 BF
Credit cards Cartes de crédit		VISA

82

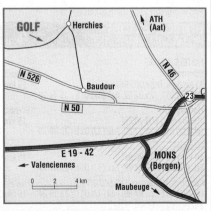

Access Accès : E19, sortie 25 → Baudour, → Golf
Map 1 on page 72 Carte 1 Page 72

GOLF COURSE
PARCOURS

13/20

Site	Site	
Maintenance	Entretien	
Architect	Architecte	Tom MacCauley
Type	Type	forêt, plaine
Relief	Relief	
Water in play	Eau en jeu	
Exp. to wind	Exposé au vent	
Trees in play	Arbres en jeu	

Scorecard Carte de score	Chp. Chp.	Mens Mess.	Ladies Da.
Length Long.	6353	6041	5615
Par	74	74	74

Advised golfing ability		0	12	24	36
Niveau de jeu recommandé					
Hcp required	Handicap exigé	28			

CLUB HOUSE & AMENITIES
CLUB HOUSE ET ANNEXES

7/10

Pro shop	Pro-shop	
Driving range	Practice	
Sheltered	couvert	8 places
On grass	sur herbe	oui
Putting-green	putting-green	oui
Pitching-green	pitching green	oui

HOTEL FACILITIES
ENVIRONNEMENT HOTELIER

6/10

HOTELS HÔTELS

Château de la Cense aux Bois	Nimy
10 chambres, D 4 900 BF	5 km
Tél (32) 065 - 31 60 00, Fax (32) 065 - 36 11 55	

Lido	Mons
67 chambres, D 3 900 BF	7 km
Tél (32) 065 - 32 78 00, Fax (32) 065 - 84 37 22	

Auberge Le 19 ème	Thulin
20 chambres, D 4 000 BF	10 km

Tél (32) 065 - 65 01 56 **RESTAURANTS** RESTAURANT

Fernez	Baudour
Tél (32) 065 - 64 44 67	1 km

Devos	Mons
Tél (32) 065 - 35 13 35	7 km

OOSTENDE

⟩ **15** | **7** | **7**

Spijtig genoeg moeten wij dikwijls vaststellen, dat moderne herstructureringen niet altijd geslaagd zijn. De "nieuwe" greens en het opofferen van enkele holes langs de kust hebben een schaduw geworpen op dit pracht-voorbeeld voor de perfecte links, en de overgang van zeer goed naar minder goed laat ons nog slechts 3/4 van het goede parcours over. Wat niet is verdwenen, is de lijn doorheen de duinen, die op een winderige dag een serieuze fysieke inspanning vergt en een test is voor de technische speler, die het lage balspel beheerst. Bij mooi weer kan men Oostende beschouwen als een parcours dat voor elk spelniveau geschikt is. De moeilijkheden op dit type ter-rein liggen vooral in de roughs en de vele bunkers. Eenmaal op de greens is het zwaarste wel achter de rug. Spijtig dat we de oorspronkelijke architect niet kennen!

As we have seen often enough, modern "updates" unfortunately don't always work. Here, the "new" greens and the disappearance of a few sea-board holes have spoilt this great example of a links course; moving from very good to not so good golf, you get three-quarters of a good course. The layout through the dunes, when the wind blows, is still good physical exercise and a great test for players of low shots. However in fine weather, Oostende can be considered to be a course for everyone. A few water hazards are never really much trouble, but the pro-blems on this type of layout are basically found in the rough and the numerous bunkers. Once on the green, you are as good as home, as they are flat and even. What a pity we don't know the name of the original architect.

Koninklijke Golf Club Oostende
Koninklijke baan 2
B - 8420 DE HAAN

Office	Secretariaat	(32) 059 - 23 32 83
Pro shop	Pro shop	(32) 059 - 23 32 83
Fax	Fax	(32) 059 - 23 37 49
Situation	Locatie	

Oostende, 67 257 Inw.

Annual closure	Jaarlijkse sluiting	neen
Weekly closure	Wekelijkse sluitingsdag	diensdag (winter)

Fees main season
Hoogseizoen tarieven 18 holes

	Week days Weekdagen	We/Bank holidays We/Feestdagen
Individual Individueel	1 500 BF	2 200 BF
Couple Paar	3 000 BF	4 400 BF

Caddy	Caddy	neen
Electric Trolley	Electrische trolley	neen
Buggy	Buggy	1200 BF/baan
Clubs	Clubs	neen
Credit cards Creditkaarten		VISA - Eurocard

Access Toegang : N34 De Haan-Oostende
Map 1 on page 72 Auto kaart 1 Blz 72

GOLF COURSE
BAAN **15**/20

Site	Terrein	
Maintenance	Onderhoud	
Architect	Architect	Unknown (1903) M. Hawtree (1990)
Type	Type baan	seaside baan, links
Relief	Reliëf	
Water in play	Waterhazards	
Exp. to wind	Windgevoelig	
Trees in play	Bomen	

Scorecard Scorekaart	Chp. Back tees	Mens Heren	Ladies Damen
Length Lengte	5517	5246	4648
Par	70	70	70

Advised golfing ability Aanbevolen golfvaardigheid	0	12	24	36
Hcp required Vereiste hcp	34			

CLUB HOUSE & AMENITIES
CLUB HOUSE EN ANNEXEN **7**/10

Pro shop	Pro shop	
Driving range	Oefenbaan	
Sheltered	overdekt	6 plaatsen
On grass	op gras	neen
Putting-green	putting-green	ja
Pitching-green	pitching-green	ja

HOTEL FACILITIES
HOTELS IN OMGEVING **7**/10

HOTELS HOTELS

Manoir Carpe Diem — De Haan (Le Coq)
15 kamers, D 4 500 BF — 2 km
tel. (32) 059 - 23 32 83, Fax (32) 059 - 23 33 96

Auberge des Rois-Beach — De Haan
23 kamers, D 4 500 BF — 2 km
tel. (32) 059 - 23 30 18, Fax (32) 059 - 23 60 78

Azur — De Haan
16 kamers, D 2 800 BF — 2 km
tel. (32) 059 - 23 83 16, Fax (32) 059 - 23 83 17

RESTAURANTS RESTAURANT

Villa Maritza — Oostende
tel. (32) 059 - 50 88 08

't Vistrapje — Oostende
tel. (32) 059 - 80 23 82

83

Vor een mooie wandeling te maken in een uitgestrekt park (prachtige beuken!) met nadien een drankje in een club-house, dat ingericht is in een kasteel van de XIXe eeuw, is men in Oudenaarde aan het juiste adres. Als men echter een golfparcours "van sterke emoties" zoekt, dat een grote sportieve uitdaging vormt, kan men al beter van de back tees vertrekken. Hier heeft men vooral aan het genoegen van de leden gedacht! Het parcours van Oudenaarde heeft onlangs enkele wijzigingen ondergaan, die niet al te gelukkig zijn uitgevallen, omdat er enkele "goeie ouwe holes" werden geïntegreerd in een nieuw circuit van 9 holes. De nieuwe holes, die de oude verdwenen holes op het bestaande parcours vervangen, vergen wel enige athletische vastberadenheid, maar missen de charme van echt leuke golf. Het oude parcours, als het vanaf de back tees wordt gespeeld, biedt mede dankzij de talrijke hindernissen een niet te onderschatten uitdaging, zowel qua lengte als qua precisie. De 18e hole is een meesterwerkje, dat u niet licht zal vergeten!

Personal assessment here depends on what you expect from a golf course. If you are looking primarily for a pleasant stroll through a large estate (with some beautiful beech trees) between Escaut and Vieil Escaut, before returning and relaxing in a club house converted from a mid-19th century castle, then Oudenaarde is for you. But if you are looking for exciting golf and a real sporting challenge, then start from the back tees. Emphasis here is on pleasing members, most of whom are only average golfers. The main course (18 holes) has some beautiful holes, like the stretch between the 5th and 12th holes. Some new holes are much too athletic, and the golfer will miss the pleasures of the holes we mentioned before. But the 18th hole is undoubtedly the one you won't forget.

Golf & Country-Club Oudenaarde

Kortrukstraat 52
B - 9790 WORTEGEM-PETEGEM

Office	Secretariaat	(32) 055 - 33 41 61
Pro shop	Pro shop	(32) 055 - 33 41 63
Fax	Fax	(32) 055 - 31 98 49
Situation	Locatie	

3 km Oudenaarde, 27 012 inw.
25 km Gent, 210 704 inw.

Annual closure	Jaarlijkse sluiting	neen

Weekly closure	Wekelijkse sluitingsdag	woensdag

Fees main season
Hoogseizoen tarieven 18 holes

	Week days Weekdagen	We/Bank holidays We/Feestdagen
Individual Individueel	1 200 BF	1 500 BF
Couple Paar	2 400 BF	3 000 BF

Caddy	Caddy	neen
Electric Trolley	Electrische trolley	neen
Buggy	Buggy	1000 BF
Clubs	Clubs	neen

Credit cards Creditkaarten	neen

Access Toegang : E17 Kortrijk-Gent, Exit 8 De Pinte, N60 → Ronse, N453 → Kortrijk
Map 1 on page 72 Auto kaart 1 Blz 72

GOLF COURSE
BAAN
14/20

Site	Terrein	
Maintenance	Onderhoud	
Architect	Architect	Harold Baker
Type	Type baan	park
Relief	Reliëf	
Water in play	Waterhazards	
Exp. to wind	Windgevoelig	
Trees in play	Bomen	

Scorecard Scorekaart	Chp. Back tees	Mens Heren	Ladies Damen
Length Lengte	6172	5740	4983
Par	72	72	72

Advised golfing ability Aanbevolen golfvaardigheid	0	12	24	36
Hcp required Vereiste hcp	36			

CLUB HOUSE & AMENITIES
CLUB HOUSE EN ANNEXEN
6/10

Pro shop	Pro shop	
Driving range	Oefenbaan	
Sheltered	overdekt	12 plaatsen
On grass	op gras	neen
Putting-green	putting-green	ja
Pitching-green	pitching-green	ja

HOTEL FACILITIES
HOTELS IN OMGEVING
6/10

HOTELS HOTELS
Le Shamrock — Ronse
5 kamers, D 3 250 BF — 12 km
tel. (32) 055 - 21 55 29, Fax (32) 055 - 21 56 83

La Pomme d'Or — Oudenaarde
8 kamers, D 1 600 BF — 3 km
tel. (32) 055 - 31 19 00, Fax (32) 055 - 30 08 44

De Rantere — Oudenaarde
20 kamers, D 1 700 BF — 3 km
tel. (32) 055 - 31 89 88, Fax (32) 055 - 33 01 11

RESTAURANTS RESTAURANT
't Craeneveldt — Oudenaarde
tel. (32) 055 - 31 72 91 — 3 km

Le Shamrock — Ronse
tel. (32) 055 - 21 55 29 — 12 km

PALINGBEEK

13	6	6

Gelegen langs de rand van het natuurdomein Palingbeek, doet dit parcours denken aan de esthetiek van de golf op z'n Amerikaans uit de jaren '70. Het betreft een terrein met weinig reliëf (helemaal niet vermoeiend), met enkele nogal ongevaarlijke waterhindernissen, waar de architect geen risico's heeft genomen om de stempel van zijn persoonlijkheid op het parcours te drukken (behalve op de 18). Zelfs de eerste keer staat de speler nooit voor verrassingen en verliest hij geen ballen. Deze ongedwongenheid kan veel spelers geruststellen, en indien ze al moeite hebben op de lange par 4, spelen ze toch meestal hun handicap. De greens zijn mooi ontworpen, en in goede staat, zoals trouwens het hele terrein. Er ontbreekt enkel wat beweging in het terrein zelf om het technisch gezien wat interessanter, en uit visueel oogpunt wat aangenamer te maken.

On the edge of the Palingbeek nature park, this course has all the look and appeal of american style courses at the beginning of the 1970s, and in particular the cachet of Trent Jones, minus his strategic genius. Over flattish terrain (easy on the legs), dotted with a few not too hostile water hazards, the architect backed away from the risks involved in asserting his personality on the course (except on the 18th). Players will meet with few surprises and lose few or no balls, even the first time out. In contrast, many will find such limpidity reassuring and probably play to their handicap, despite a few problems perhaps on the long par 4s. The greens are well shaped and in good condition, as is the course as a whole. The only thing missing is a little shifting of earth to make the course technically more appealing and visually more attractive.

Golf & Country Club de Palingbeek

Eekhofstraat 14
B - 8902 HOLLEBEKE

Office	Secretariaat	(32) 057 - 20 04 36
Pro shop	Pro shop	(32) 057 - 20 04 36
Fax	Fax	(32) 057 - 21 89 58
Situation	Locatie	

6 km Ieper, 34 874 inw.
30 km Kortrijk, 74 044 inw

Annual closure	Jaarlijkse sluiting	neen
Weekly closure	Wekelijkse sluitingsdag	neen

Fees main season
Hoogseizoen tarieven 18 holes

	Week days Weekdagen	We/Bank holidays We/Feestdagen
Individual Individueel	1 200 BF	1 500 BF
Couple Paar	2 400 BF	3 000 BF

Caddy	Caddy	nee
Electric Trolley	Electrische trolley	nee
Buggy	Buggy	ja
Clubs	Clubs	ja
Credit cards Creditkaarten		VISA - Eurocard

Access Toegang : A 19 Kortrijk-Veurne,
N8 → Ieper-Zuid, Zillebeke, Hollebeke, Palingbeek
Map 1 on page 72 Auto kaart 1 Blz 72

GOLF COURSE
BAAN
13/20

Site	Terrein	
Maintenance	Onderhoud	
Architect	Architect	Harold Baker
Type	Type baan	baan in open veld
Relief	Reliëf	
Water in play	Waterhazards	
Exp. to wind	Windgevoelig	
Trees in play	Bomen	

Scorecard Scorekaart	Chp. Back tees	Mens Heren	Ladies Damen
Length Lengte	6165	6165	5221
Par	72	72	72

Advised golfing ability Aanbevolen golfvaardigheid	0	12	24	36
Hcp required Vereiste hcp	36			

CLUB HOUSE & AMENITIES
CLUB HOUSE EN ANNEXEN
6/10

Pro shop	Pro shop	
Driving range	Oefenbaan	
Sheltered	overdekt	8 plaatsen
On grass	op gras	neen
Putting-green	putting-green	ja
Pitching-green	pitching-green	ja

HOTEL FACILITIES
CLUB HOUSE EN ANNEXEN
6/10

HOTELS HOTELS
Kemmelberg — Kemmel
16 kamers, D 3 250 BF — 8 km
tel. (32) 057 - 44 41 45, Fax (32) 057 - 44 40 89

Regina — Ieper
17 kamers, D 2 700 BF — 6 km
tel. (32) 057 - 21 88 88, Fax (32) 057 - 21 90 20

Rabbit Inn — Ieper
34 kamers, D 3 000 BF — 6 km
tel. (32) 057 - 21 70 00, Fax (32) 057 - 21 94 74

RESTAURANTS RESTAURANT
Kemmelberg — Kemmel
tel. (32) 057 - 44 41 45 — 8 km

Host. St Nicolas — Ieper
tel. (32) 057 - 20 06 22 — 6 km

85

Passionné par le golf, le Roi Léopold II a été notamment à l'origine d'Oostende et du Ravenstein. Il fit appel à un architecte "royal", le grand Tom Simpson, dont le dessin a été largement préservé, de même que la végétation, d'une beauté impressionnante. Chênes, bouleaux, cèdres bleus, ormes et saules offrent un spectacle qui ferait oublier le parcours, si celui-ci n'était d'une si évidente qualité. Il offre des drives sans gros problèmes (sauf aux 2, 4, 11 et 17), mais les attaques de green sont d'autant plus passionnantes que le putting ne sera pas ensuite évident. Les greens ne sont pas très ondulés, mais leurs surfaces sont plus difficiles à lire qu'il n'y paraît. Le Ravenstein peut être joué à tous les niveaux, mais les meilleurs y trouveront quelques défis de premier ordre, alors que sa longueur reste modérée, selon les exigences modernes en tout cas. Un "must".

A golf enthusiast, King Léopold II was the instigator of the courses at Oostende and Ravenstein. He called in a "royal" architect, the great Tom Simpson, whose design has remained largely unscathed. The same goes for the extremely beautiful vegetation. The impressive oak, birch, blue cedar, elm and willow trees could almost make you forget the course if it wasn't such an excellent layout. The tee shot is never too much of a problem (except on 2nd, 4th, 11th and 17th holes), but the approach shots are all the more exciting in that putting here is an equally challenging proposition. These are hardly what you would call undulating greens, but the putting surface is harder to read than you might think. Ravenstein can be played by golfers of all abilities, but the most proficient will find a number of challenges of the highest order, even though by modern standards the course posts only moderate yardage. Essential visiting.

Royal Golf Club de Belgique

Château de Ravenstein
B - 3080 TERVUREN

Office	Secrétariat	(32) 02 - 767 58 01
Pro shop	Pro-shop	(32) 02 - 767 55 60
Fax	Fax	(32) 02 - 767 28 41
Situation	Situation	

6 km Bruxelles, 667 825 hab.

Annual closure	Fermeture annnuelle	non
Weekly closure	Fermeture hebdomadaire	non

Fees main season
Tarifs haute saison le parcours

	Week days Semaine	We/Bank holidays We/Férié
Individual Individuel	2 000 BF	3 000 BF
Couple Couple	4 000 BF	6 000 BF

Caddy	Caddy	sur réservation
Electric Trolley	Chariot électrique	non
Buggy	Voiturette	non
Clubs	Clubs	non

Credit cards Cartes de crédit · non

86

Access Accès : Bruxelles, avenue de Tervuren
→ Tervuren, passer Les Quatre Bras, → Golf
Map 1 on page 72 Carte 1 Page 72

GOLF COURSE
PARCOURS · **17** /20

Site	Site	�▊▊▊
Maintenance	Entretien	▊▊▊
Architect	Architecte	Tom Simpson
Type	Type	parc, forêt
Relief	Relief	▊▊
Water in play	Eau en jeu	▊
Exp. to wind	Exposé au vent	▊▊
Trees in play	Arbres en jeu	▊▊▊

Scorecard Carte de score	Chp. Chp.	Mens Mess.	Ladies Da.
Length Long.	6082	5825	5361
Par	73	73	73

Advised golfing ability Niveau de jeu recommandé	0 12 24 36 ▊▊▊	
Hcp required Handicap exigé	20 Me, 24 Da.	

CLUB HOUSE & AMENITIES
CLUB HOUSE ET ANNEXES · **8** /10

Pro shop	Pro-shop	▊▊▊
Driving range	Practice	▊▊
Sheltered	couvert	10 places
On grass	sur herbe	non
Putting-green	putting-green	oui
Pitching-green	pitching green	oui

HOTEL FACILITIES
ENVIRONNEMENT HOTELIER · **7** /10

HOTELS HÔTELS

Montgomery — Woluwé-Saint-Pierre
61 chambres, D 10 000 BF — 5 km
Tél (32) 02 - 741 85 11, Fax (32) 02 - 741 85 00

Château du Lac — Genval
84 chambres, D 9 500 BF — 10 km
Tél (32) 02 - 655 71 11, Fax (32) 02 - 655 74 44

Lambeau — Woluwé-Saint-Lambert
24 chambres, D 3 000 BF — 6 km
Tél (32) 02 - 732 51 70, Fax (32) 02 - 732 54 90

RESTAURANTS RESTAURANT

Des Trois Couleurs — Woluwé-Saint-Pierre
Tél (32) 02 - 770 33 21 — 5 km

Le Vignoble de Margot — Woluwé-Saint-Pierre
Tél (32) 02 - 779 23 23 — 5 km

Très ouvert et peu arboré, c'est un parcours délicat quand le vent souffle. Les défauts originels du dessin ont été peu à peu gommés par Christophe Descampe, frère de la grande joueuse belge. De nouveaux plans d'eau et des plantations devraient faire progresser cette réalisation dont l'entretien est de très bonne qualité. Les trous sont assez bien équilibrés et imposent un rythme de jeu agréable, mais on notera surtout la qualité technique des par 5. Les roughs sont en jeu, les greens assez vastes et moyennement modelés sont bien défendus, ce qui impose un jeu précis. Assez naturel au départ, et sans prétendre au titre de chef-d'oeuvre, Rigenée progresse dans le bon sens. L'ambiance y est très familiale et sportive, c'est un point à souligner.

This very open and almost treeless course is a tricky proposition when the wind gets up. The original flaws have been gradually designed out by Christophe Descampe, the brother of the great Belgian player. New stretches of water and plantation programmes should keep the course moving in the right direction, helped by excellent upkeep. The holes are well balanced for a pleasant playing rhythm, but most notable is the technical excellence of the par 5s. The rough is very much in play, and the rather large and averagely contoured greens are well defended, thus calling for some precision play. A natural layout at the outset and with no pretence to the masterpiece label, Rigenée is improving all the time. The atmosphere is one of family entertainment and sport, an important point that deserves a special mention.

Golf de Rigenée

Rue du Châtelet, 62
B - 1495 VILLERS-LA-VILLE

Office	Secrétariat	(32) 071 - 87 77 65
Pro shop	Pro-shop	(32) 071 - 87 77 65
Fax	Fax	(32) 071 - 87 77 83
Situation	Situation	

35 km Bruxelles, 667 825 hab.
15 km Nivelles, 21 883 hab.

Annual closure	Fermeture annnuelle	non
Weekly closure	Fermeture hebdomadaire	lundi
		(restaurant)

Fees main season Tarifs haute saison le parcours

	Week days Semaine	We/Bank holidays We/Férié
Individual Individuel	1 000 BF	1 900 BF
Couple Couple	2 000 BF	3 800 BF

1600 BF avant 10 H (We)

Caddy	Caddy	non
Electric Trolley	Chariot électrique	non
Buggy	Voiturette	800 BF/18 trous
Clubs	Clubs	300 BF/18 trous
Credit cards Cartes de crédit		VISA - DC

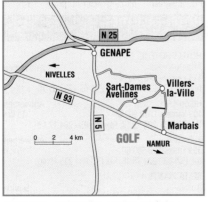

Access Accès : N93 Nivelles → Namur, Marbais →
Villers-la-Ville, Golf 2 km
Map 1 on page 73 Carte 1 Page 73

GOLF COURSE
PARCOURS
14/20

Site	Site	
Maintenance	Entretien	
Architect	Architecte	Paul Rolin C. Descampe
Type	Type	plaine
Relief	Relief	
Water in play	Eau en jeu	
Exp. to wind	Exposé au vent	
Trees in play	Arbres en jeu	

Scorecard Carte de score	Chp. Chp.	Mens Mess.	Ladies Da.
Length Long.	6354	6036	5111
Par	73	73	73

Advised golfing ability		0 12 24 36
Niveau de jeu recommandé		
Hcp required	Handicap exigé	30 Me, 36 Da.

CLUB HOUSE & AMENITIES
CLUB HOUSE ET ANNEXES
7/10

Pro shop	Pro-shop	
Driving range	Practice	
Sheltered	couvert	12 places
On grass	sur herbe	oui (été)
Putting-green	putting-green	oui
Pitching-green	pitching green	oui

HOTEL FACILITIES
ENVIRONNEMENT HOTELIER
6/10

HOTELS HÔTELS
Hostellerie La Falise — Baisy-Thy
6 chambres, D 3 000 BF
Tél (32) 067 - 77 35 11, Fax (32) 067 - 79 04 94

Nivelles-Sud — Nivelles
115 chambres, D 1 950 BF — 15 km
Tél (32) 067 - 21 87 21, Fax (32) 067 - 22 10 88

Ferme de Grambais — Nivelles
10 chambres, D 2 500 BF — 15 km
Tél (32) 067 - 22 01 18, Fax (32) 067 - 84 13 07

RESTAURANTS RESTAURANT
Hostellerie La Falise — Baisy-Thy
Tél (32) 067 - 77 35 11

Freddy Collette — Nivelles
Tél (32) 067 - 21 05 30 — 15 km

87

RINKVEN RED - WHITE

14	6	5

Na een mooie toegangsweg door de bossen, valt direct het professionalisme van de club op, door de kwaliteit van de installaties en het onderhoud van het terrein. Dit laatste bestaat uit 3 combineerbare 9-holes, van gelijke moeilijkheidsgraad (vooral de bomen en water) en met greens zonder enige variatie qua esthetiek, vaak verhoogd en smal. Men mist persoonlijkheid en stijl in de architectuur van dit parcours, en krijgt veeleer een indruk van eentonigheid, dermate dat men om het even welke combinatie van 18 holes kan spelen en toch een tamelijk duidelijk beeld van het geheel krijgt. Een voordeel is dat de moeilijkheidsgraad voor elk spelniveau min of meer gelijk is, maar de betere handicaps zullen zich wel ietwat gefrustreerd voelen wegens het gebrek aan grotere uitdagingen. Ze kunnen echter wel genieten van een mooie wandeling in een aangename omgeving van berken en sparren, met een rijke fauna.

After a pleasant drive through the woods, you can tell the club's professionalism by the standard of facilities and the upkeep of the course. There are three combinable 9-hole courses offering the same level of difficulty (basically trees and water) and similar-looking greens that are often narrow and elevated. It is a pity about the lack of personality and style, which creates a slight feeling of monotony, to the point where you can play any 18-hole combination and get exactly the same impression of the site. On the upside, we noticed the average difficulty for all players, although very low handicappers might feel frustrated at the lack of real challenge. At least they will enjoy a pretty stroll over a pleasant estate of birch and pine trees, and the extensive wildlife to keep them company.

Rinkven Golf Club

Sint-Jobsteenweg, 120
B - 2970 SCHILDE

Office	Secretariaat	(32) 03 - 385 04 83
Pro shop	Pro shop	(32) 03 - 384 07 78
Fax	Fax	(32) 03 - 384 29 33
Situation	Locatie	

15 km Antwerpen, 403 072 inw.

Annual closure	Jaarlijkse sluiting	neen
Weekly closure	Wekelijkse sluitingsdag	neen

Fees main season
Hoogseizoen tarieven 18 holes

	Week days Weekdagen	We/Bank holidays We/Feestdagen
Individual Individueel	1 400 BF	2 500 BF
Couple Paar	2 800 BF	5 000 BF

Caddy	Caddy	neen
Electric Trolley	Electrische trolley	400 BF/18 holes
Buggy	Buggy	900 BF/18 holes
Clubs	Clubs	neen

Credit cards Creditkaarten	neen

88

BREDA

N 117 (4) A 1 - E 19 N 115 naar Turnhout
ANTWERPEN
Kanaal van Antwerpen naar Turnhout
Sint-Job-in-'t-Goor

's. Gravenwezel

GOLF

0   2   4 km

Access Toegang : E19 Anvers → Breda, sortie St-Job-in-'t Goor → 's Gravenwesel → Golf
Map 1 on page 73 Auto kaart 1 Blz 73

GOLF COURSE
BAAN 14/20

Site	Terrein	
Maintenance	Onderhoud	
Architect	Architect	Paul Rolin
Type	Type baan	bos
Relief	Reliëf	
Water in play	Waterhazards	
Exp. to wind	Windgevoelig	
Trees in play	Bomen	

Scorecard Scorekaart	Chp. Back tees	Mens Heren	Ladies Damen
Length Lengte	6140	6046	5388
Par	72	72	72

Advised golfing ability Aanbevolen golfvaardigheid	0 12 24 36
Hcp required Vereiste hcp	28

CLUB HOUSE & AMENITIES
CLUB HOUSE EN ANNEXEN 6/10

Pro shop	Pro shop	
Driving range	Oefenbaan	
Sheltered	overdekt	6 plaatsen
On grass	op gras	neen
Putting-green	putting-green	ja
Pitching-green	pitching-green	ja

HOTEL FACILITIES
HOTELS IN OMGEVING 5/10

HOTELS HOTELS
Alfa De Keyser — Antwerpen
115 kamers, D 8 000 BF — 15 km
tel. (32) 03 - 234 01 35, Fax (32) 03 - 232 39 70

Hilton **** — Antwerpen
199 kamers, D 10 900 BF — 15 km
tel. (32) 03 - 204 12 12, Fax (32) 03 - 204 12 13

Rubens — Antwerpen
35 kamers, D 6 500 BF — 15 km
tel. (32) 03 - 222 48 48, Fax (32) 03 - 225 19 40

RESTAURANTS RESTAURANT
Apicius — Schilde
tel. (32) 03 - 383 45 65 — 5 km

't Fornuis — Antwerpen
tel. (32) 03 - 233 62 70 — 15 km

ROYAL LATEM

15	8	6

Het terrein werd geopend in 1909, maar de bunkers en de greens werden in de jaren '50 door Hawtree veranderd. Het gebrek aan ruimte brengt ook een beperking in afstand met zich mee, en "out of bounds" op de helft van de holes. Het grote park is aangeplant met prachtige bomen, eiken, dennen, en beuken van meer dan 200 jaar oud, wat voor een zeer aantrekkelijke omgeving zorgt. De hindernissen zijn hoofdzakelijk bunkers, maar ook enkele vijvers en grachten, niet echt moeilijk. Het design is tamelijk eenvoudig, en de strategie voor de hand liggend, behalve op de 6 en de 18, met blinde drives. De strategie om de greens te bereiken, is niet ingewikkeld te noemen, zelfs niet de keuze van de club, behalve voor de approach van vijf ervan, die verhoogd zijn. Dankzij een afwisselend design, een matig reliëf en een opvallende charme en volkomenheid, kan Latem een parcours bieden, dat voor elk spelersniveau een plezier betekent. De zanderige bodem en de volledige irrigatie maken het mogelijk in alle seizoenen te spelen.

Opened back in 1909, the greens and bunkers were redesigned by Hawtree in the 1950s. Lack of space has resulted in a shortish course and out-of-bounds on at least half of the holes. The estate is covered with some beautiful trees - oak, pine and beech - often more than 200 years old, and makes for a very attractive setting. The main hazards are the bunkers, but there are a number of ponds and ditches awaiting the mis-hit shot. The layout is clear and strategy obvious, except on the 6 and 18th holes, where the drive is blind. Approach shots are not too complex, either, and choice of club is more or less straightforward, except for the five elevated greens. A varied layout and averagely hilly, the course is not made for the very best players, but the rest will have fun. Sandy soil and comprehensive irrigation facilities make this a course that is playable virtually all year.

Royal Latem Golf Club
B - 9380 ST-MARTENS-LATEM

Office	Secretariaat	(32) 093 - 282 54 11
Pro shop	Pro shop	(32) 093 - 282 57 65
Fax	Fax	(32) 093 - 282 90 19
Situation	Locatie	
10 km Gent, 210 704 inw.		
Annual closure	Jaarlijkse sluiting	neen
Weekly closure	Wekelijkse sluitingsdag	

Fees main season
Hoogseizoen tarieven de dag

	Week days Weekdagen	We/Bank holidays We/Feestdagen
Individual Individueel	1 500 BF	2 000 BF
Couple Paar	3 000 BF	4 000 BF

Caddy	Caddy	neen
Electric Trolley	Electrische trolley	neen
Buggy	Buggy	1200 BF
Clubs	Clubs	neen

Credit cards Creditkaarten   neen

Access Toegang : E40 Brussel-Oostende, exit 14,
N43 → Kortrijk, → Golf
Map 1 on page 71 Auto kaart 1 Blz 71

GOLF COURSE
BAAN
15/20

Site	Terrein	
Maintenance	Onderhoud	
Architect	Architect	Fred Hawtree
Type	Type baan	bos, residentieel
Relief	Reliëf	
Water in play	Waterhazards	
Exp. to wind	Windgevoelig	
Trees in play	Bomen	

Scorecard Scorekaart	Chp. Back tees	Mens Heren	Ladies Damen
Length Lengte	5767	5767	5143
Par	72	72	72

Advised golfing ability	0	12	24	36
Aanbevolen golfvaardigheid				

Hcp required	Vereiste hcp	36 weekdagen, 28 We

CLUB HOUSE & AMENITIES
CLUB HOUSE EN ANNEXEN
8/10

Pro shop	Pro shop	
Driving range	Oefenbaan	
Sheltered	overdekt	3 plaatsen
On grass	op gras	neen
Putting-green	putting-green	ja
Pitching-green	pitching-green	ja

HOTEL FACILITIES
HOTELS IN OMGEVING
6/10

HOTELS HOTELS

Auberge du Pêcheur ***   Sint-Martens
26 kamers, D 3 200 BF   1,5 km
tel. (32) 09 - 282 31 44, Fax (32) 09 - 282 90 58

Alfa Flanders Hotel ****   Gent
50 kamers, D 6 000 BF   10 km
tel. (32) 09 - 222 60 65, Fax (32) 09 - 220 16 05

Holyday Inn Expo   Gent
137 kamers, D 5 700 BF   10 km
tel. (32) 09 - 220 24 24, Fax (32) 09 - 222 66 22

RESTAURANTS RESTAURANT

Auberge du Pêcheur   Sint-Martens
tel. (32) 09 - 282 31 44   1,5 km

Waterzooi   Gent
tel. (32) 09 - 225 05 63   8 km

Het terrein van het Zoute werd op maat gemaakt voor het genoegen van de speler, en behoort hiermee ook tot de beste links op het vasteland. De uitdaging is er een constante, vooral als de wind ook besloten heeft om die dag van de partij te zijn! Dit parcours is een maatstaf voor uw bekwaamheid om met uw tweede slag de green te bereiken. De par3, 3 en 16 zijn juweeltjes. Uiteraard is de hulde, die Nick Faldo dit parcours bracht, al een referentie op zich, net als de handtekening van een van de beste golfarchitecten uit de geschiedenis, nl. HS Colt. In ieder geval komt The Royal Zoute uit voor zijn moeilijkheden: het is onontbeerlijk, uw drive zodanig te plaatsen dat u in een gunstige positie verkeert om de greens te spelen, die snel, "welgevormd" en met een soort subtiele intelligentie verdedigd zijn. Tussen de duinen en de bomen ligt de juiste weg prachtig uitgestippeld; het is enkel zaak om die weg bescheiden aan te vatten, want de golvingen van de fairways hebben enkele interessante posities voor u in petto. Een echt klassiek ontwerp, dat zeker geen gat in uw golfcultuur mag blijven...

An easy-looking course, at least when the fairways eat into the rough, but a formidable challenge when the wind comes along. Its reputation has sometimes been questioned, but tributes from players such as Nick Faldo are a reference indeed, as is the label of H.S. Colt, one of greatest golf course designers in the history of golf. Anyway, Le Zoute never tries to hide any of its difficulties, notably placing the tee-shot for an easier approach shot to fast and well-contoured greens, that are cleverly and subtly defended. The "straight and narrow" is clearly laid out betwen dunes and trees, but don't feel too confident too soon. Some of the rolling fairways can provide unusual and unexpected positions. A very classic course and one that all golfers should know sooner or later.

Royal Zoute Golf Club
Caddiespad 14
B - 8300 KNOKKE-HEIST

Office	Secretariaat	(32) 050 - 60 12 27
Pro shop	Pro shop	(32) 050 - 60 19 60
Fax	Fax	(32) 050 - 62 30 29
Situation	Locatie	
Knokke-Heist, 31 237 Inw.		
Annual closure	Jaarlijkse sluiting	neen
Weekly closure	Wekelijkse sluitingsdag	neen

Fees main season
Hoogseizoen tarieven 18 holes

	Week days Weekdagen	We/Bank holidays We/Feestdagen
Individual Individueel	2 000 BF	3 000 BF
Couple Paar	4 000 BF	6 000 BF

Caddy	Caddy	ja
Electric Trolley	Electrische trolley	ja
Buggy	Buggy	ja
Clubs	Clubs	ja

Credit cards Creditkaarten | neen

GOLF COURSE
BAAN | 18/20

Site	Terrein	▬▬▬▬▬▬▬▯
Maintenance	Onderhoud	▬▬▬▬▬▬▬▯
Architect	Architect	Harry S. Colt
Type	Type baan	links
Relief	Reliëf	▬▬▯▯▯▯▯▯
Water in play	Waterhazards	▬▯▯▯▯▯▯▯
Exp. to wind	Windgevoelig	▬▬▬▬▬▬▯▯
Trees in play	Bomen	▬▬▬▯▯▯▯▯

Scorecard Scorekaart	Chp. Back tees	Mens Heren	Ladies Damen
Length Lengte	6172	6172	5416
Par	72	72	72

Advised golfing ability		0 12 24 36
Aanbevolen golfvaardigheid		▬▬▬▬▬▯
Hcp required	Vereiste hcp	20

CLUB HOUSE & AMENITIES
CLUB HOUSE EN ANNEXEN | 7/10

Pro shop	Pro shop	▬▬▬▬▬▬▯▯
Driving range	Oefenbaan	▬▬▬▬▬▬▬▯
Sheltered	overdekt	20 plaatsen
On grass	op gras	neen
Putting-green	putting-green	ja
Pitching-green	pitching-green	ja

HOTEL FACILITIES
HOTELS IN OMGEVING | 7/10

HOTELS HOTELS
Royal Zoute Golf Club — Golf
7 kamers, D 6 000 BF
tel. (32) 050 - 60 16 17, Fax (32) 050 - 62 24 26

Manoir du Dragon — Het Zoute
8 kamers, D 8 500 BF — 1 km
tel. (32) 050 - 62 35 36, Fax (32) 050 - 61 57 96

Villa Verdi — Het Zoute
8 kamers, D 4 950 BF — 1 km
tel. (32) 050 - 62 35 72, Fax (32) 050 - 62 11 46

RESTAURANTS RESTAURANT
Panier d'Or — Knokke-Heist
tel. (32) 050 - 60 31 89

Esmeralda — Albertstrand
tel. (32) 050 - 60 33 66

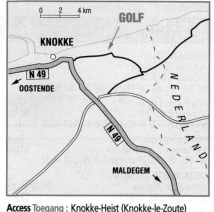

Access Toegang : Knokke-Heist (Knokke-le-Zoute)
Map 1 on page 72 Auto kaart 1 Blz 72

90

SART-TILMAN

C'est l'un des meilleurs parcours de match-play de Belgique. Sa longueur n'est pas démesurée, mais la longueur de certains trous, leur relief mesuré et naturel, la présence insistante des arbres, et des greens diaboliques le rendent difficile à scorer, notamment pour les joueurs de moins de 12 de handicap, qui pourront vraiment y tester leur jeu. Il faut établir sa stratégie dès le départ en fonction des positions de drapeau. Son relief mesuré, son excellent rythme, son honnêteté et la beauté du site traduisent bien le génie de son architecte Tom Simpson. Un seul point faible, le lac du 14, qui casse inutilement l'harmonie du dessin (il a été ajouté depuis la création). La qualité de l'entretien ajoute encore au plaisir : Le Sart-Tilman mérite un large détour pour sa franchise, son intérêt, son absence de "vices cachés", son confort général et son ambiance chaleureuse.

This is one of Belgium's finest match-play courses. The overall yardage is reasonable, but the length of some holes, the measured, natural relief, the looming presence of trees and devilishly tricky greens make scoring a tough business, especially for players with a handicap in the teens, who will find this a real test. Game strategy must be set before starting out, and be geared to the pin positions. The measured relief and excellent balance, plus the course's honesty and the beauty of the site are a good reflection on the genius of architect Tom Simpson. The one weak point is the double lake on the 14th, which needlessly breaks the harmony of the layout (it was added subsequently). The standard of upkeep only enhances the enjoyment of playing here. Royal Sart Tilman is well worth the time and journey for its openness, appeal, absence of hidden vices, general pleasantness and warm atmosphere.

Royal Golf Club du Sart-Tilman

Route de Condroz, 541
B - 4031 ANGLEUR

Office	Secrétariat	(32) 041 - 36 20 21
Pro shop	Pro-shop	(32) 041 - 36 20 21
Fax	Fax	(32) 041 - 37 20 26
Situation	Situation	

5 km Liège, 155 999 hab.

Annual closure	Fermeture annnuelle	non
Weekly closure	Fermeture hebdomadaire	non
		lundi, pro-shop

Fees main season
Tarifs haute saison le parcours

	Week days Semaine	We/Bank holidays We/Férié
Individual Individuel	1 250 BF	2 000 BF
Couple Couple	2 500 BF	4 000 BF

Caddy	Caddy	non
Electric Trolley	Chariot électrique	non
Buggy	Voiturette	1 300 BF/18 trous
Clubs	Clubs	non
Credit cards Cartes de crédit		non

Access Accès : N63 Liège - Marche
Map 1 on page 73 Carte 1 Page 73

GOLF COURSE
PARCOURS
16/20

Site	Site	
Maintenance	Entretien	
Architect	Architecte	Tom Simpson
Type	Type	forêt, vallon
Relief	Relief	
Water in play	Eau en jeu	
Exp. to wind	Exposé au vent	
Trees in play	Arbres en jeu	

Scorecard Carte de score	Chp. Chp.	Mens Mess.	Ladies Da.
Length Long.	6000	5624	5367
Par	72	72	72

Advised golfing ability Niveau de jeu recommandé	0	12	24	36
Hcp required Handicap exigé	36			

CLUB HOUSE & AMENITIES
CLUB HOUSE ET ANNEXES
7/10

Pro shop	Pro-shop	
Driving range	Practice	
Sheltered	couvert	10 places
On grass	sur herbe	non
Putting-green	putting-green	oui
Pitching-green	pitching green	oui

HOTEL FACILITIES
ENVIRONNEMENT HOTELIER
7/10

HOTELS HÔTELS
Ramada — Liège
105 chambres, D 6 600 BF — 5 km
Tél (32) 041 - 21 77 11, Fax (32) 041 - 21 77 01

Bedford — Liège
149 chambres, D 6 950 BF — 5 km
Tél (32) 041 - 28 81 11, Fax (32) 041 - 27 45 75

Holiday Inn — Liège
214 chambres, D 6 600 BF — 5 km
Tél (32) 041 - 42 60 20, Fax (32) 041 - 43 48 10

RESTAURANTS RESTAURANT
Michel Germeau — Liège
Tél (32) 041 - 43 72 42 — 5 km

Au Vieux Liège — Liège
Tél (32) 041 - 23 77 48 — 5 km

91

La signature de Tom Simpson est une garantie de parcours technique et stratégique. De relief modéré, c'est un des bons exemples d'architecture classique "inland", où il faut maîtriser l'ensemble de son jeu pour éviter les bois, les roughs et autres bunkers, admirablement disposés. Le placement du drive est essentiel, notamment sur quatre longs par 4, mais le travail ne s'arrête pas là, car les greens sont bien défendus, leurs surfaces assez subtiles à lire. Dans un site d'une parfaite tranquillité, on a l'impression de prendre une retraite pour méditer non seulement sur le golf, mais aussi sur l'intelligente sobriété de l'architecture, révélant une connaissance parfaite des joueurs de tous niveaux, mais sans jamais dissimuler les pièges. Exigeant, ce parcours donne un plaisir que l'on souhaite retrouver très souvent. Et l'arrosage automatique l'a encore amélioré.

The Tom Simpson label is the guarantee of a technical and strategic course. This moderately hilly layout is one of the classic examples of inland architecture, where every part of your game has to be in shape to avoid the woods, rough and admirably located bunkers. Placing the tee-shot is essential, especially on the four long par 4s, but the job doesn't stop there, because the greens are well defended and the putting surfaces tricky to read. On a site of perfect tranquillity, you get the impression of being in a sanctuary from where to meditate not only about the course, but also about the smart discretion of a layout, which reveals good insight into every golfing ability but never conceals the traps. It is a demanding course but an enjoyable one, too. The type you like to come back and play again and again. And the automatic watering system made it better still.

Royal Golf Club des Fagnes

Avenue de l'Hippodrome, 1
B - 4900 SPA

Office	Secrétariat	(32) 087 - 79 30 30
Pro shop	Pro-shop	(32) 087 - 79 30 32
Fax	Fax	(32) 087 - 79 30 39
Situation	Situation	

2 km Spa, 9 953 hab.

Annual closure	Fermeture annnuelle	non
Weekly closure	Fermeture hebdomadaire	

Fees main season
Tarifs haute saison le parcours

	Week days Semaine	We/Bank holidays We/Férié
Individual Individuel	1 600 BF	2 000 BF
Couple Couple	3 200 BF	4 000 BF

Caddy	Caddy	non
Electric Trolley	Chariot électrique	non
Buggy	Voiturette	1 200 BF/18 trous
Clubs	Clubs	non

Credit cards Cartes de crédit   non

92

Access Accès : Autoroute des Ardennes, sortie Spa → Golf
Map 2 on page 73 Carte 2 Page 73

GOLF COURSE
BAAN   17/20

Site	Site	■■■■■□□
Maintenance	Entretien	■■■■■■□
Architect	Architecte	Tom Simpson Simpson T.
Type	Type	forêt, vallon
Relief	Relief	■■■■□□□
Water in play	Eau en jeu	■■□□□□□
Exp. to wind	Exposé au vent	■■■■□□□
Trees in play	Arbres en jeu	■■■■■□□

Scorecard Carte de score	Chp. Chp.	Mens Mess.	Ladies Da.
Length Long.	6040	5671	5276
Par	72	72	72

Advised golfing ability Niveau de jeu recommandé	0	12	24	36

Hcp required   Handicap exigé   36

CLUB HOUSE & AMENITIES
CLUB HOUSE EN ANNEXEN   7/10

Pro shop	Pro-shop	■■■■□□□
Driving range	Practice	
Sheltered	couvert	2 places
On grass	sur herbe	non
Putting-green	putting-green	oui
Pitching-green	pitching green	oui

HOTEL FACILITIES
HOTELS IN OMGEVING   7/10

HOTELS HÔTELS

Dorint   Spa
97 chambres, D 5 000 BF   2 km
Tél (32) 087 - 77 25 81, Fax (32) 087 - 77 41 74

L'Auberge   Spa
21 chambres, D 4 500 BF   2 km
Tél (32) 087 - 77 44 10, Fax (32) 087 - 77 48 40

La Heid des Pairs   Spa
11 chambres, D 5 600 BF   4 km
Tél (32) 087 - 77 43 46, Fax (32) 087 - 77 06 44

RESTAURANTS RESTAURANT

Brasserie du Grand Maur   Spa
Tél (32) 087 - 77 36 16   2 km

Manoir de Lebiolles   Creppe
Tél (32) 087 - 77 04 20   6 km

Een terrein dat een juist uitgebalanceerd spel vraagt. De eerste 9 holes, in de bossen, eisen veel nauwkeurigheid en aandacht bij het plaatsen van de drives. De laatste 9 liggen temidden van de heide, en zijn ook langer, meer bepaald drie van de par 4. De moeilijkheden, fairway bunkers en waterhindernissen, zijn goed zichtbaar en op een slimme manier gesitueerd; de architect, Ron Kirby, had een goed inzicht in de mogelijkheden van de spelers, en dit op verschillende niveaus. Hij heeft tegelijk echter ook zoveel mogelijk het natuurlijke uitzicht van het terrein proberen te bewaren, en het prachtig geïntegreerd. De perfecte uitdunning van het onderhout is opmerkelijk. De greens zijn mooi ontworpen, niet te golvend, maar de speler moet, bij het bepalen van zijn strategie, rekening houden met de plaatsing van de vlaggen. Het terrein is tamelijk heuvelachtig, maar kan gemakkelijk te voet worden gespeeld. Geplaatst op een voormalige stortplaats, heeft dit terrein zeer vlug een plaats verworven onder de zeer goede, recente realisaties, die waar men herinneringen aan overhoudt.

This course demands a solid all-round game. The front nine, in the woods, call for precision in the extreme and a lot of care when placing the tee-shot. The back nine are in the heather and are longer, notably three of the par 4s. The difficulties, fairway bunkers and water hazards are clear to see and astutely located, revealing designer Ron Kirby's insight when it comes to understanding golfers of differing abilities. At the same time, he has preserved the course's natural look as far as possible, and the way it fits into the surroundings is exemplary. The undergrowth has been cleared to avoid penalising players too heavily, the greens are well designed and slope quite a bit, but the pin positions must be watched carefully if you want to establish an effective game strategy. The site is hilly but easily walkable.

Spiegelven Golf Club Genk

Wiemesmeerstraat 109
B - 3600 GENK

Office	Secretariaat	(32) 089 - 35 63 21
Pro shop	Pro shop	(32) 089 - 36 20 60
Fax	Fax	(32) 089 - 36 41 84
Situation	Locatie	

10 km Genk, 45 906 inw. - 20 km Hasselt, 64 722 inw.

Annual closure	Jaarlijkse sluiting	neen
Weekly closure	Wekelijkse sluitingsdag	

Fees main season
Hoogseizoen tarieven 18 holes

	Week days Weekdagen	We/Bank holidays We/Feestdagen
Individual Individueel	1 100 BF	1 600 BF
Couple Paar	2 200 BF	3 200 BF

Caddy	Caddy	neen
Electric Trolley	Electrische trolley	neen
Buggy	Buggy	1 200 BF
Clubs	Clubs	1 000 BF

Credit cards Creditkaarten — neen

Access Toegang : E314, Exit 32, N744 → Zutendal, Golf
Map 2 on page 73 Auto kaart 2 Blz 73

GOLF COURSE
BAAN
14/20

Site	Terrein	
Maintenance	Onderhoud	
Architect	Architect	Ron Kirby
Type	Type baan	bos
Relief	Reliëf	
Water in play	Waterhazards	
Exp. to wind	Windgevoelig	
Trees in play	Bomen	

Scorecard Scorekaart	Chp. Back tees	Mens Heren	Ladies Damen
Length Lengte	6198	6198	5436
Par	72	72	73

Advised golfing ability Aanbevolen golfvaardigheid	0 12 24 36	
Hcp required Vereiste hcp	36	

CLUB HOUSE & AMENITIES
CLUB HOUSE EN ANNEXEN
7/10

Pro shop	Pro shop	
Driving range	Oefenbaan	
Sheltered	overdekt	9 plaatsen
On grass	op gras	ja
Putting-green	putting-green	ja
Pitching-green	pitching-green	ja

HOTEL FACILITIES
HOTELS IN OMGEVING
8/10

HOTELS HOTELS

La Réserve — Golf
70 kamers, D 3 900 BF
tel. (32) 089 - 35 58 28, Fax (32) 089 - 35 58 03

Alfa Molenvijer — Genk
81 kamers, D 5 500 BF — 10 km
tel. (32) 089 - 36 41 50, Fax (32) 089 - 36 41 51

Arte — Genk
24 kamers, D 2 650 BF — 10 km
tel. (32) 089 - 35 20 06, Fax (32) 089 - 36 10 36

RESTAURANTS RESTAURANT

Da Vinci — Genk
tel. (32) 089 - 35 17 61 — 10 km

't Konintje — Genk
tel. (32) 089 - 35 26 45 — 10 km

93

Les Français ne trouveront guère que Waterloo soit une "morne plaine" (le retour est assez vallonné), et le parcours de "La Marache", plus ancien parcours du "Lion" voisin, doit être abordé avec prudence et sagesse. Très bon exemple de l'architecture de Hawtree, il se déroule dans un environnement boisé plaisant, et souvent dangereux. Les seconds coups sont ici très intéressants, même si beaucoup des très grands greens sont assez ouverts pour y parvenir en roulant. On aura compris la nécessité d'être droit, d'autant que la longueur de ce parcours reste modérée, permettant à chacun, selon son niveau, d'y prendre plaisir. Les drivers "sauvages" auront des problèmes, mais, dans le passé, Waterloo a été le cadre de tout autres tragédies ! Ce complexe s'étend au total sur 150 hectares, et ses équipements sont dignes de ces dimensions.

Even the French could hardly describe Waterloo as the "cheerless plain" it was once said to be (the back 9 are over rolling terrain), and "La Marache", older than the neighbouring "Lion" course, should be approached with caution and good sense. An excellent example of Hawtree architecture, the course unwinds in a pleasant but often hazardous woodland environment. The second shots are interesting propositions here, even though many of the very large greens have no frontal hazard and so can be reached with chipped or low approach shots. It is important to play straight at Waterloo, especially since the course is only moderate in length so that every one can enjoy playing here. Wild-hitters could be in trouble, but in the past Waterloo has seen worst disasters than wayward tee-shots! The full complex stretches over 150 hectares (370 acres) and facilities are of an equally high standard.

Royal Waterloo Golf Club
Vieux chemin de Wavre 50
B - 1380 LASNE

Office	Secrétariat	(32) 02 - 633 18 50
Pro shop	Pro-shop	(32) 02 - 633 43 16
Fax	Fax	(32) 02 - 633 28 66
Situation	Situation	

20 km Bruxelles, 667 825 hab.

Annual closure	Fermeture annnuelle	non
Weekly closure	Fermeture hebdomadaire	non

Fees main season
Tarifs haute saison la journée

	Week days Semaine	We/Bank holidays We/Férié
Individual Individuel	1 750 BF	2 500 BF
Couple Couple	3 500 BF	5 000 BF

Caddy	Caddy	non
Electric Trolley	Chariot électrique	400 BF/18 trous
Buggy	Voiturette	1200 BF/18 trous
Clubs	Clubs	non
Credit cards Cartes de crédit		non

BRUSSEL

WATERLOO
Waterloo - Lasne
23
GOLF

Ohain

La Marache

0   2   4 km

R 0
← BRUSSEL
CHARLEROI (A 7)

Access Accès : Bruxelles E, → Wavre, → Waterloo
Map 1 on page 73 Carte 1 Page 73

GOLF COURSE
PARCOURS   16/20

Site	Site	
Maintenance	Entretien	
Architect	Architecte	F. Hawtree
Type	Type	campagne, vallon
Relief	Relief	
Water in play	Eau en jeu	
Exp. to wind	Exposé au vent	
Trees in play	Arbres en jeu	

Scorecard Carte de score	Chp. Chp.	Mens Mess.	Ladies Da.
Length Long.	6271	5855	5517
Par	72	72	72

Advised golfing ability		0	12	24	36
Niveau de jeu recommandé					
Hcp required	Handicap exigé	28			

CLUB HOUSE & AMENITIES
CLUB HOUSE ET ANNEXES   8/10

Pro shop	Pro-shop	
Driving range	Practice	
Sheltered	couvert	16 places
On grass	sur herbe	oui
Putting-green	putting-green	oui
Pitching-green	pitching green	oui

HOTEL FACILITIES
ENVIRONNEMENT HOTELIER   7/10

HOTELS HÔTELS
Grand Hôtel   Waterloo
71 chambres, D 7 500 BF   6 km
Tél (32) 02 - 352 18 15, Fax (32) 02 - 352 18 88

Château du Lac   Genval
84 chambres, D 9 500 BF   5 km
Tél (32) 02 - 655 71 11, Fax (32) 02 - 655 74 44

Auberge de Waterloo   Rhode-Saint-Genèse
84 chambres, D 5 300 BF   12 km
Tél (32) 02 - 358 35 80, Fax (32) 02 - 358 38 06

RESTAURANTS RESTAURANT
Auberge d'Ohain   Ohain
Tél (32) 02 - 653 64 97   3 km

La Maison du Seigneur   Waterloo
Tél (32) 02 - 354 07 50   6 km

94

La faible longueur du "Grand Ducal" plaira à la majorité des joueurs de tous niveaux. Mais que les bons frappeurs se méfient, les arbres sont très beaux, mais les éviter constitue la difficulté essentielle d'un parcours dont l'esthétique très britannique (quelques "cross-bunkers") coïncide bien avec les traditions golfiques cultivées ici. Les bunkers sont assez nombreux, mais défendent les greens sans méchanceté. Ceux-ci sont de dimensions très raisonnables, mais leurs pentes exigent de l'attention. Le vallonnement du terrain reste modéré, sauf au 6, un long par 4 en montée, et seul trou vraiment difficile. En revanche, le 18, un par 5, laissera une bonne impression, car il présente une bonne occasion de birdie. En résumé, un parcours où le driver n'est pas indispensable, généralement en bon état, et très agréable quand on visite le pays. Cependant, les avions de l'aéroport tout proche manquent de respect au golf...

The short yardage of the "Grand Ducal" will appeal to the majority of golfers of all levels. Yet the big-hitters should beware, the trees might look a pretty picture, but avoiding them is one of the main difficulties on a course, whose very attractive and very British style (with a few cross-bunkers to boot) perfectly reflects the golfing traditions nurtured in this part of the world. There are a lot of bunkers, which defends the greens but are never unduly spiteful. The greens themselves are very reasonably sized, but their slopes call for careful reading. This is a moderately hilly course, but is especially steep on the 6th, a long uphill 4-par and the only really tough hole. In contrast, the 18th, a par 5, should leave you liking the course because the birdie here is a definite possibility. In a word or two, this is a course where the driver can easily stay in the bag. It is in good condition and very pleasant to play when you visit the "Grand Duché". Unfortunately, the planes from the neighbouring airport don't always respect the game of golf...

Golf Club Grand Ducal

Route de Trèves, 1
L - 2633 SENNINGERBERG

Office	Secrétariat	(352) 34 83 90
Pro shop	Pro-shop	(352) 34 83 94
Fax	Fax	(352) 34 83 91
Situation	Situation	

6 km Luxembourg, 75 377 hab.

Annual closure	Fermeture annnuelle	non
Weekly closure	Fermeture hebdomadaire	

Fees main season
Tarifs haute saison le parcours

	Week days Semaine	We/Bank holidays We/Férié
Individual Individuel	1 500 FLUX	2 000 FLUX
Couple Couple	3 000 FLUX	4 000 FLUX

Caddy	Caddy	non
Electric Trolley	Chariot électrique	non
Buggy	Voiturette	non
Clubs	Clubs	150 FLUX
Credit cards Cartes de crédit		non

GOLF Senningerberg | N 1
Senningerberg
A 1
Grevenmacher
N 2
LUXEMBOURG
Thionville
0   2   4 km

Access Accès : N1 Luxembourg → Aéroport
Map 1 on page 59 Carte 1 Page 59

GOLF COURSE
PARCOURS | 13/20

Site	Site	
Maintenance	Entretien	
Architect	Architecte	
Type	Type	parc
Relief	Relief	
Water in play	Eau en jeu	
Exp. to wind	Exposé au vent	
Trees in play	Arbres en jeu	

Scorecard Carte de score	Chp. Chp.	Mens Mess.	Ladies Da.
Length Long.	5782	5782	5179
Par	71	71	71

Advised golfing ability	0	12	24	36
Niveau de jeu recommandé				

Hcp required	Handicap exigé	36 Se, 28 We

CLUB HOUSE & AMENITIES
CLUB HOUSE ET ANNEXES | 6/10

Pro shop	Pro-shop	
Driving range	Practice	
Sheltered	couvert	9 places
On grass	sur herbe	oui
Putting-green	putting-green	oui
Pitching-green	pitching green	oui

95

HOTEL FACILITIES
ENVIRONNEMENT HOTELIER | 7/10

HOTELS HÔTELS

Sheraton Aérogolf		Aéroport
145 chambres, D 9 000 FLUX		1 km
Tél (352) 34 05 71, Fax (352) 34 02 17		
Le Royal		Luxembourg
165 chambres, D 10 500 FLUX		6 km
Tél (352) 416 16, Fax (352) 22 59 48		
Cravat		Luxembourg
59 chambres, D 7 200 FLUX		6 km
Tél (352) 22 19 75, Fax (352) 22 67 11		

RESTAURANTS RESTAURANT

Clairefontaine		Luxembourg
Tél (352) 46 22 11		6 km
Le Grimpereau		Senningerberg
Tél (352) 43 67 87		1 km

LA CAGE

L'ANIMAL

406
PEUGEOT

PEUGEOT 406 V6. VOUS NE CHOISIREZ PLUS ENTRE LE PLAISIR ET LA SÉCURITÉ.

France

L e golf en France ne s'est développé qu'à partir des années 80, et compte aujourd'hui plus de 260.000 golfeurs pour plus de 500 parcours, dont plus de 350 de 18 trous. Il reste de la place pour les visiteurs! Premier du monde pour le tourisme, le pays commence seulement à être considéré comme une destination golfique, et ses arguments ne manquent pas. Vous trouverez ici les meilleurs parcours ouverts au public, mais aussi les grands golfs privés traditionnels qui acceptent de plus en plus les visiteurs, en semaine notamment, et en été, mais sans toujours en faire la promotion. Avec une lettre d'introduction de votre club, vous pouvez tenter votre chance auprès des plus réputés: par exemple Chantilly, Saint-Germain, Fontainebleau, Saint-Nom-la-Bretèche, le Paris International, Joyenval, La Boulie. Tous figurent dans ce Guide...

97

Golf in France only really took off from the 1980s onward, and today there are more than 260,000 golfers for more than 500 courses, of which more than 350 are eighteen-hole layouts. So there is room enough for visitors. A world leader for tourism, France is now only starting to be considered as a golfing destination, and it has a lot going for it. We have included here the best courses open to the public, but also the great traditional private courses which admit more and more visitors, especially during the week and summer... without really promoting the idea. With a letter of introduction from your club, you can try your luck at some of the more highly-reputed courses such as Chantilly, Saint-Germain, Fontainebleau, Saint-Nom-la-Bretèche, Paris International, Joyenval and La Boulie in the greater Paris area. All are featured in this edition.

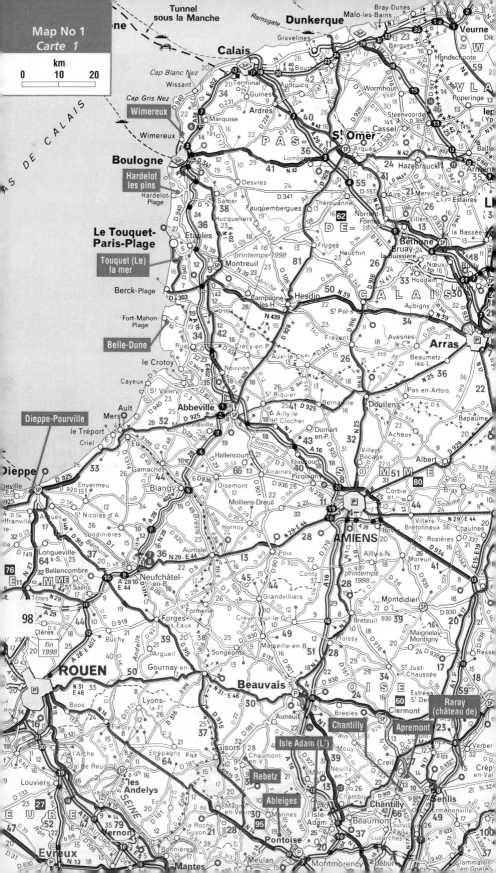

MICHELIN

d'après cartes n°237 - 18ème édition
et n°989 - 26ème édition - 1998. Autorisation n°9706332.

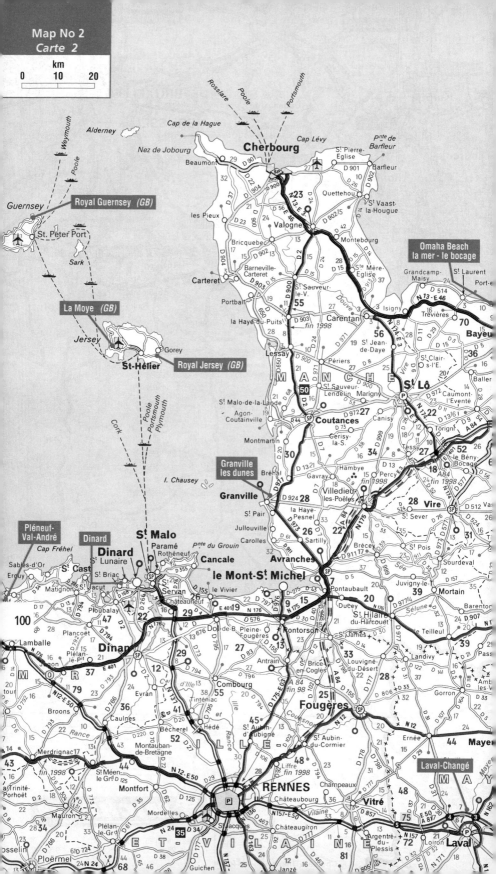

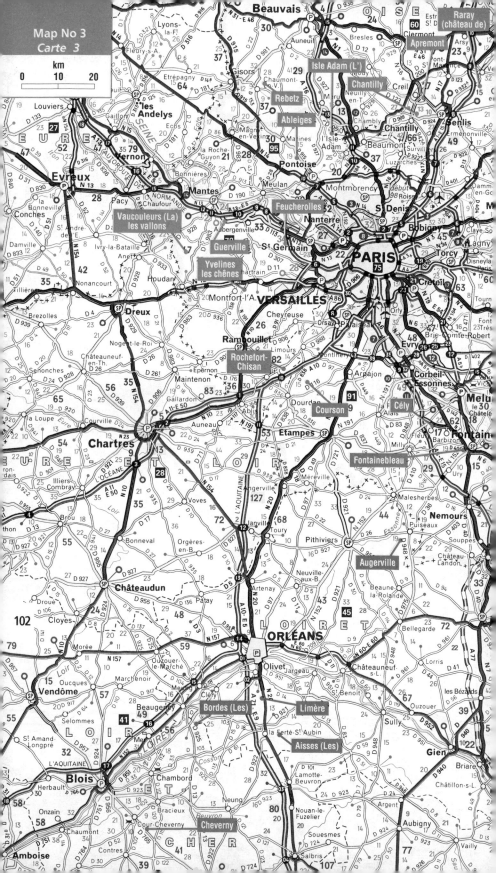

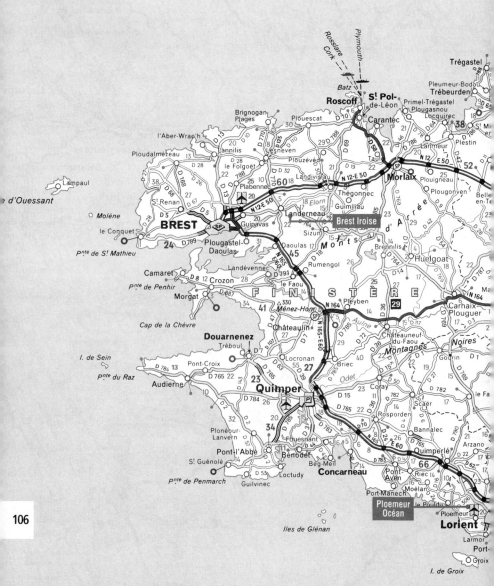

km
0   10   20

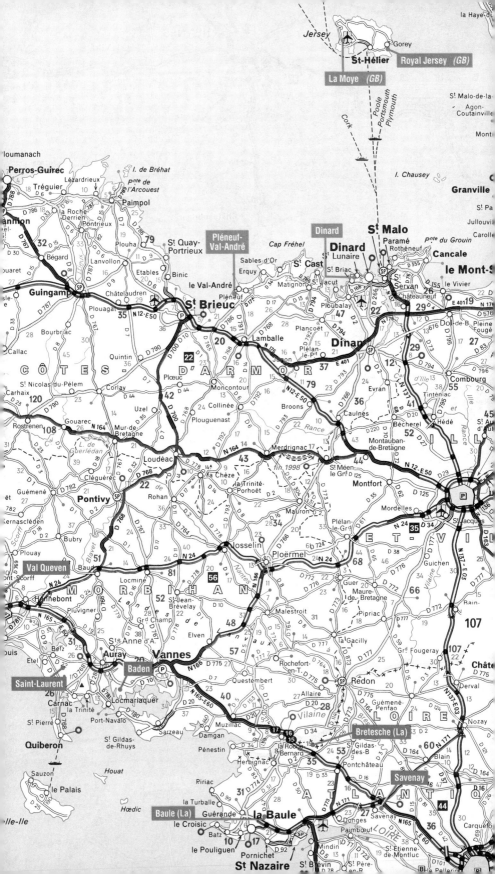

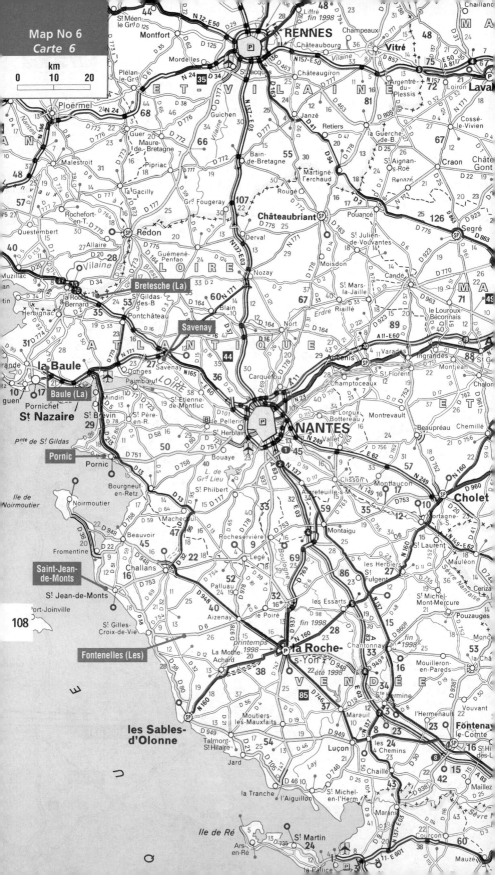

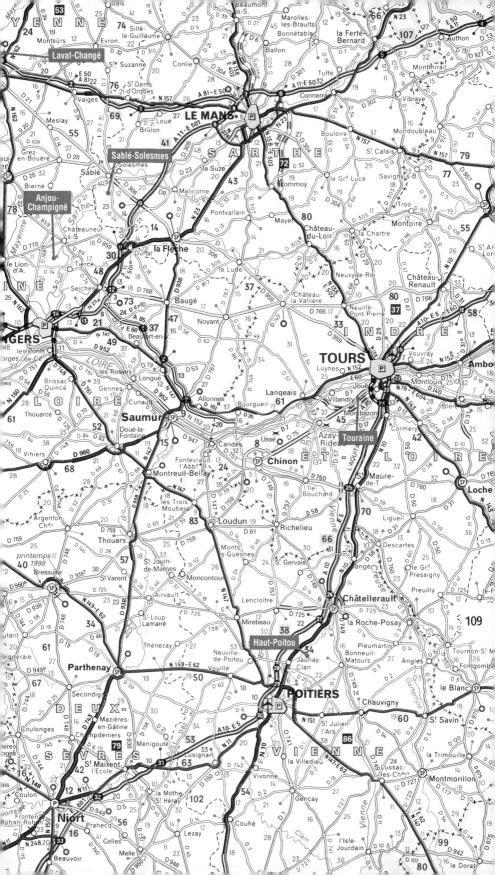

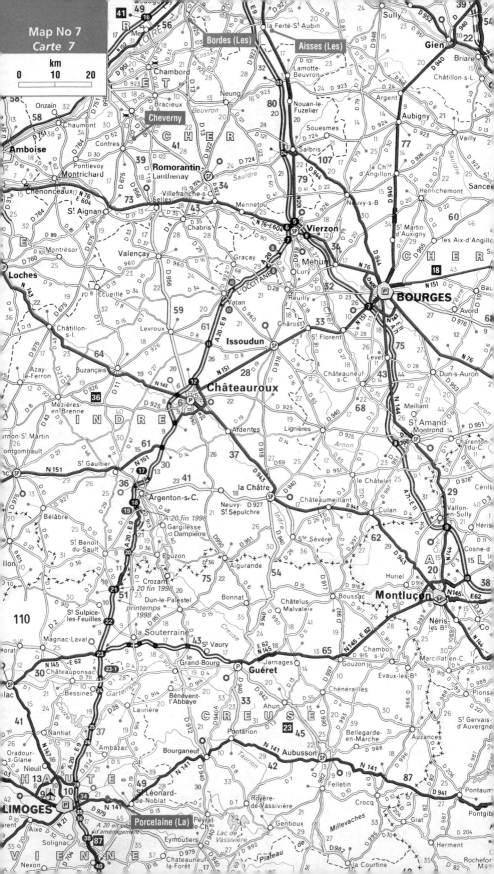

km
0   10   20

km
0   10   20

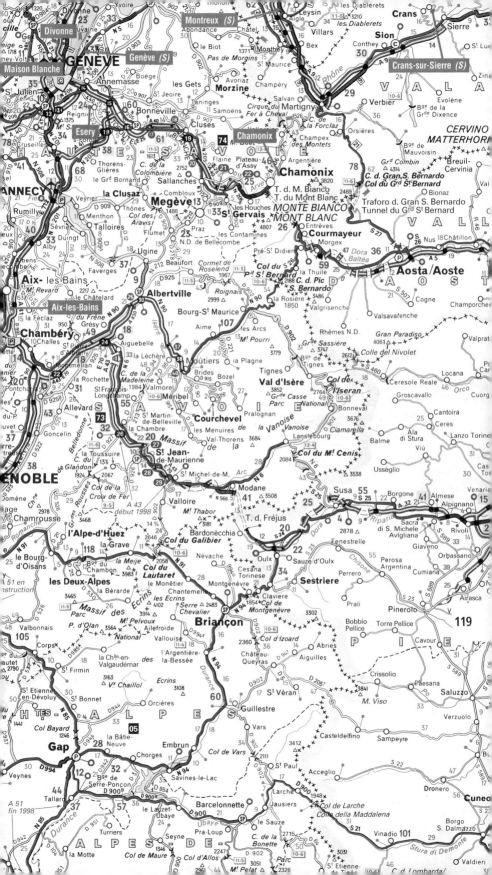

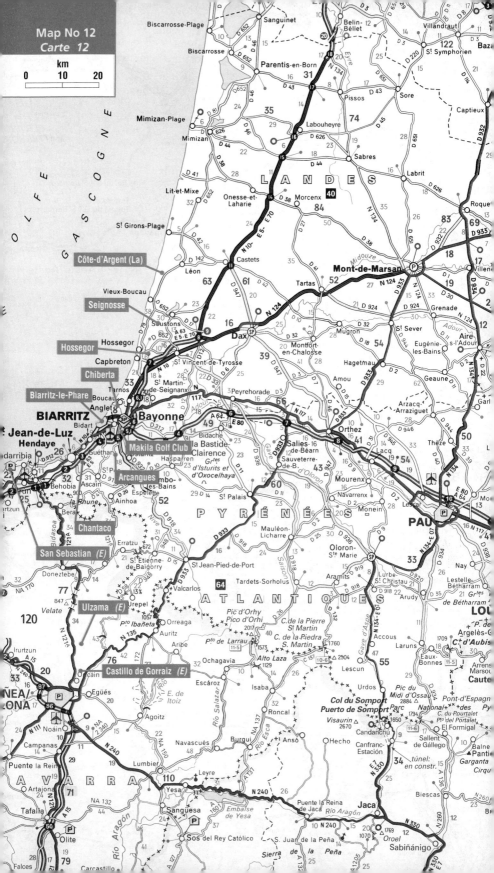

km
0 10 20

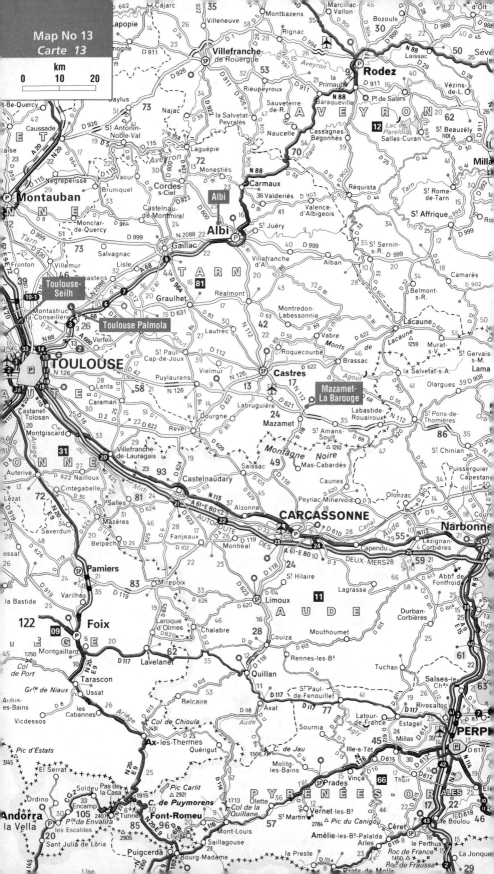

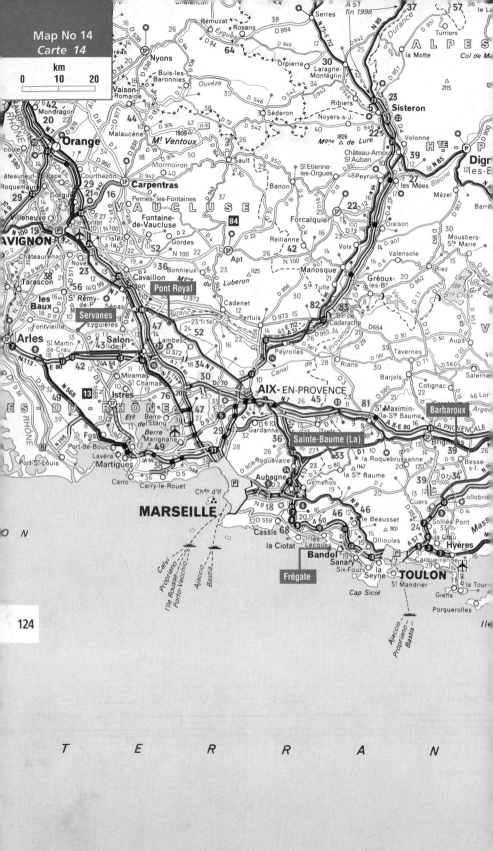

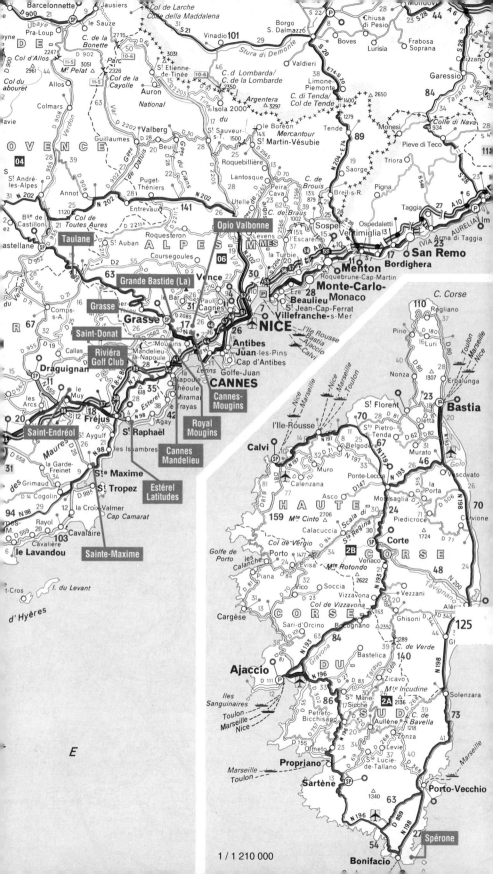

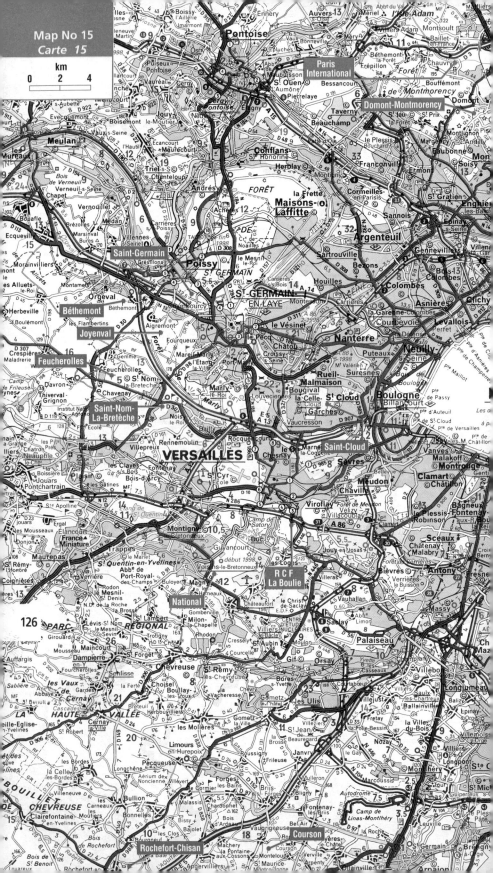

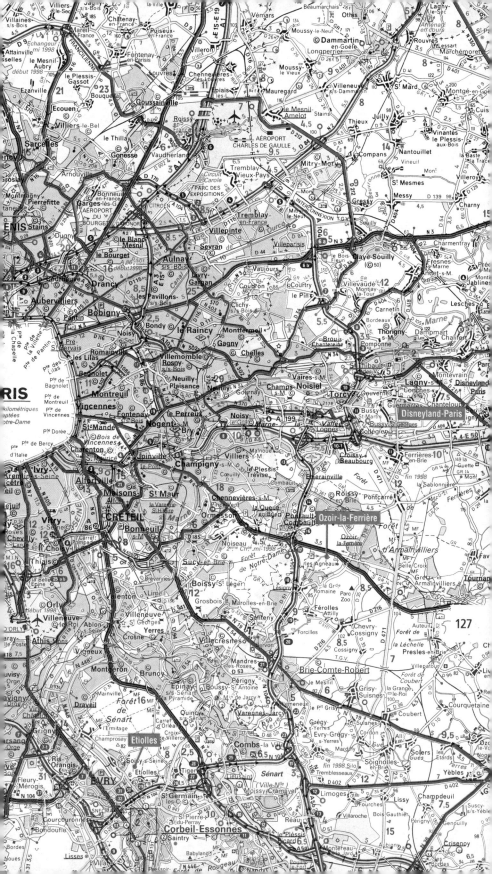

Aujourd'hui nous entreprenons la plus grande, la plus belle et la plus difficile conquête au monde, la vôtre.

Air France.
Gagner le cœur du monde.

AIR FRANCE

CLASSEMENT DES PARCOURS FRANÇAIS
CLASSIFICATION OF FRENCH COURSES

Ce classement donne priorité à la note attribuée au parcours .

This classification gives priority consideration
to the score awarded to the actual course.

Club-house and facilities
Note du Club-house et annexes

Course score
Note du parcours

Hotel facility score
Note de l'environnement hôtelier

Page

19 8 6   Bordes (Les)   172

Note			Parcours	Page	Note			Parcours	Page
19	8	6	Bordes (Les)	172	**16**	7	6	Nîmes-Campagne	239
18	7	6	Chantilly *Vineuil*	186	**16**	7	5	Paris International	243
18	8	6	Kempferhof (Le)	225	**16**	6	5	Pont Royal	247
18	6	6	National *L'Albatros*	237	**16**	6	4	Rebetz	251
17	7	6	Barbaroux	163	**16**	7	4	Sablé-Solesmes	
17	6	5	Côte d'Argent (La)	191				*La Forêt/La Rivière*	257
17	7	7	Fontainebleau	205	**16**	6	5	Saint-Jean-de-Monts	262
17	7	6	Grenoble Bresson	216	**16**	8	8	Saint-Nom-la-Bretèche *Rouge*	265
17	6	5	Limère	230	**16**	7	4	Soufflenheim	272
17	7	5	Médoc *Les Châteaux*	234	**16**	6	6	Wantzenau (La)	285
17	7	5	Pléneuf-Val-André	245	**15**	6	4	Ableiges *Les Etangs*	148
17	7	8	Royal Mougins	256	**15**	6	5	Ailette (L')	149
17	7	7	Saint-Germain	261	**15**	6	6	Albi	152
17	7	7	Seignosse	270	**15**	7	8	Amirauté (L')	153
17	7	5	Spérone	273	**15**	8	6	Apremont	157
17	6	7	Touquet (Le) *La Mer*	278	**15**	6	5	Baden	161
17	6	4	Villette d'Anthon *Les Sangliers*	283	**15**	7	7	Bâle-Hagenthal	162
16	5	4	Aisses (Les) *Rouge/Blanc*	150	**15**	7	8	Baule (La) *Rouge*	164
16	6	5	Belle-Dune	165	**15**	7	6	Bondues *Jaune*	171
16	7	6	Bondues *Blanc*	170	**15**	6	4	Bresse (La)	173
16	6	6	Charmeil	187	**15**	7	7	Bretesche (La)	175
16	6	8	Chiberta	189	**15**	7	8	Cannes-Mougins	178
16	7	3	Courson *Vert/Noir*	193	**15**	6	5	Cap d'Agde	179
16	7	8	Disneyland Paris		**15**	6	5	Casteljaloux	180
			Never Land + Wonderland	196	**15**	7	6	Cély	181
16	6	7	Estérel Latitudes	200	**15**	6	7	Chamonix	183
16	7	6	Gouverneur (Le) *Le Breuil*	210	**15**	7	3	Courson *Lilas/Orange*	192
16	6	6	Grande Bastide (La)	212	**15**	7	5	Esery	199
16	6	4	Grande-Motte (La)		**15**	6	5	Etiolles *Les Cerfs*	201
			Les Flamants Roses	213	**15**	7	9	Evian	203
16	6	6	Hardelot *Les Pins*	219	**15**	7	5	Feucherolles	204
16	6	6	Hossegor	221	**15**	7	7	Frégate	209
16	7	4	Isle Adam (L')	222	**15**	7	6	Gujan-Mestras	218
16	8	7	Joyenval *Marly*	223	**15**	8	7	Joyenval *Retz*	224
16	7	5	Montpellier-Massane	236	**15**	7	8	La Boulie (R.C.F.) *La Vallée*	226

129

Que la fête commence !

En 1998, Adshel a installé à Rennes une ligne complète de mobilier urbain d'avant-garde. En remportant à l'unanimité le premier appel d'offres d'une grande ville de France pour l'ensemble de son mobilier, Adshel a ainsi créé les conditions de la libre concurrence au profit des collectivités et des annonceurs.

ADSHEL
L'AUTRE GRAND DU MOBILIER URBAIN

191, avenue Charles De Gaulle 92200 Neuilly sur Seine Tél 01 41 43 88 91 - Fax 01 41 43 88 77

CLASSEMENT DES PARCOURS FRANÇAIS

131

Yamaha invente la voiture de Golf de demain : l'Ultima

Ecologie

Confort

Fiabilité

Silence

Economie

Electrique ou essence ; à vous de choisir...

La nouvelle référence des greens est désormais disponible en vert, rouge ou ivoire. Plus confortable (nouveaux amortisseurs et sièges plus larges), plus puissante (nouveaux moteurs : 4 temps ou électrique 48 volts), plus sûre (nouveau régulateur de vitesse et pare-chocs à absorption jusqu'à 8 km/h !) et encore plus fiable (carrosserie réalisée en thermoplastique ultra résistant), la nouvelle Ultima est aussi largement modulable avec ses nombreuses options (kit 4 places, benne, etc...). **Nouvelle Ultima de Yamaha :** le meilleur de la technologie d'avant-garde Yamaha, pour le respect de votre parcours et de votre drive.

YAMAHA

CLASSEMENT DE L'ENVIRONNEMENT HOTELIER
CLASSIFICATION OF HOTELS FACILITIES

This classification gives priority consideration
to the score awarded to the hotel facilities.

Ce classement donne priorité à la note attribuée à l'environnement hôtelier

Club-house and facilities
Note du Club-house et annexes

Course score
Note du parcours

Hotel facility score
Note de l'environnement hôtelier

Page

15　7　**9**　Evian　203

Note	Parcours	Page	Note	Parcours	Page
15 7 9	Evian	203	14 7 7	Saint-Cloud *Vert*	258
15 7 8	Amirauté (L')	153	17 7 7	Saint-Germain	261
14 7 8	Arcangues	159	13 7 7	Sainte-Maxime	268
15 7 8	Baule (La) Rouge	164	17 7 7	Seignosse	270
14 6 8	Biarritz-le-Phare	168	13 7 7	Servanes	271
13 7 8	Cannes Mandelieu *Old Course*	177	17 6 7	Touquet (Le) *La Mer*	278
15 7 8	Cannes-Mougins	178	15 6 6	Albi	152
16 6 8	Chiberta	189	13 6 6	Anjou-Champigné	155
16 7 8	Disneyland Paris		15 8 6	Apremont	157
	Never Land + Wonderland	196	13 6 6	Arcachon	158
15 7 8	La Boulie (R.C.F.) *La Vallée*	226	17 7 6	Barbaroux	163
14 6 8	Makila Golf Club	232	16 7 6	Bondues *Blanc*	170
15 7 8	New Golf Deauville		15 7 6	Bondues *Jaune*	171
	Rouge/Blanc	238	19 8 6	Bordes (Les)	172
13 7 8	Riviéra Golf Club	253	14 7 6	Brest Iroise	174
17 7 8	Royal Mougins	256	14 7 6	Brigode	176
15 7 8	Saint-Donat	259	15 7 6	Cély	181
15 8 8	Saint-Nom-la-Bretèche *Bleu*	264	14 8 6	Chailly (Château de)	182
16 8 8	Saint-Nom-la-Bretèche *Rouge*	265	18 7 6	Chantilly *Vineuil*	186
13 5 7	Aix-les-Bains	151	16 6 6	Charmeil	187
15 7 7	Bâle-Hagenthal	162	14 7 6	Cheverny	188
15 7 7	Breteche (La)	175	14 6 6	Fontcaude	206
15 6 7	Chamonix	183	14 7 6	Fontenailles *Blanc*	207
14 7 7	Chantaco	185	16 7 6	Gouverneur (Le) *Le Breuil*	210
14 6 7	Dinard	195	14 7 6	Gouverneur (Le) *Montaplan*	211
14 6 7	Divonne	197	16 6 6	Grande Bastide (La)	212
16 6 7	Estérel Latitudes	200	13 7 6	Grasse	215
17 7 7	Fontainebleau	205	17 7 6	Grenoble Bresson	216
15 7 7	Frégate	209	15 7 6	Gujan-Mestras	218
16 8 7	Joyenval *Marly*	223	16 6 6	Hardelot *Les Pins*	219
15 8 7	Joyenval *Retz*	224	16 6 6	Hossegor	221
13 6 7	Opio Valbonne	241	18 8 6	Kempferhof (Le)	225
13 7 7	Pessac	244	18 6 6	National *L'Albatros*	237

133

Esso

ESSO Lubrifiants

ESSO Uniflo

ESSO Ultra

ESSO Ultron Huile de synthèse 5W40

CLASSEMENT DE L'ENVIRONNEMENT HOTELIER

135

PHILIPS

INCREDIBLE HOME CINEMA

Ecran Large + Son Dolby Prologic **HOMECINEMA**

SEJOUR DE GOLF RECOMMANDÉ
RECOMMENDED GOLFING STAY

Exciting courses where a stay of a few days is to be recommended.
Les parcours dont les qualités permettent de conseiller un séjour de plusieurs jours.

Parours	Note			Page	Parours	Note			Page
Baden	15	6	5	161	Limère	17	6	5	230
Barbaroux	17	7	6	163	Médoc	17	7	5	234
Belle-Dune	16	6	5	165	Montpellier Massane	16	7	5	236
Bondues	16	7	6	170	National L'Albatros	18	6	6	237
Bordes (Les)	19	8	6	172	Nîmes-Campagne	16	7	6	239
Chiberta	16	6	8	189	Sablé-Solesmes	16	7	4	257
Côte d'Argent (La)	17	6	5	191	Saint-Donat	15	7	8	259
Courson	16	7	3	193	Saint-Jean-de-Monts	16	6	5	262
Evian	15	7	9	203	Saint-Nom-la-Bretèche	16	8	8	265
Gouverneur (Le)	16	7	6	210	Seignosse	17	7	7	270
Grande Bastide (La)	16	6	6	212	Spérone	17	7	5	273
Grande-Motte (La)	16	6	4	213	Taulane	15	7	4	275
Grenoble Bresson	17	7	6	216	Toulouse-Seilh	15	7	6	277
Gujan-Mestras	15	7	6	218	Touquet (Le)	17	6	7	278
Hardelot	16	6	6	219	Villette d'Anthon	17	6	4	283
Kempferhof (Le)	18	8	6	225					

VACANCES RECOMMANDEES
RECOMMENDED GOLFING HOLIDAYS

Vacances conseillées en famille, y compris pour les non-golfeurs.
Holiday on site with the family, including non-golfers.

Parours	Score			Page	Parours	Score			Page
Aix-les-Bains	13	5	7	151	Grande Bastide (La)	16	6	6	212
Amirauté (L')	15	7	8	153	Grande-Motte (La)	16	6	4	213
Arcachon	13	6	6	158	Hardelot	16	6	6	219
Arcangues	14	7	8	159	Hossegor	16	6	6	221
Baule (La)	15	7	8	164	Lacanau	14	6	4	227
Biarritz-le-Phare	14	6	8	168	Makila Golf Club	14	6	8	232
Cannes Mandelieu	13	7	8	177	New Golf Deauville	15	7	8	238
Cannes-Mougins	15	7	8	178	Pornic	15	6	6	249
Cap d'Agde	15	6	5	179	Saint-Laurent	14	7	5	263
Casteljaloux	15	6	5	180	Sainte-Maxime	13	7	7	268
Chamonix	15	6	7	183	Spérone	17	7	5	273
Chantaco	14	7	7	185	Touquet (Le)	17	6	7	278
Dinard	14	6	7	195					
Disneyland Paris	16	7	8	196					
Estérel Latitudes	16	6	7	200					
Frégate	15	7	7	209					

137

Quel Caddy préférez-vous ?

Le geste naturel est d'acheter son matériel chez un vrai spécialiste. Seul GOLF PLUS vous fait rencontrer des professionnels, des conseillers pour qui le golf est une seconde nature. Pas de têtes de gondole chez GOLF PLUS, uniquement des têtes de club.

Choix des marques, dernières nouveautés, essai avant l'achat, contrat prix, échange de la série sous 21 jours, un bon parcours commence toujours chez GOLF PLUS.

G O L F
P L U S

Catalogue gratuit sur simple demande

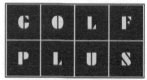

RELIEF DES PARCOURS
GEOGRAPHICAL RELIEF

Ce classement donne une indication sur la forme physique nécessaire pour jouer un parcours, et aussi sur la possibilité de jouer plusieurs fois le parcours dans une même journée. La possibilité de jouer en voiturette permet parfois de compenser les inconvénients du relief.

This list gives an idea of the fitness required for playing a course and also of the possibility of playing the same course several times in one day. The availability of golf carts sometimes makes up for the drawbacks of a hilly course.

Peu de relief	Moyennement accidenté	Relief important
Rather flat	*Averagely hilly*	*Very hilly*

Relief / Parcours	Note	Page	Relief / Parcours	Note	Page
Aisses (Les) Rouge/Blanc	16 5 4	150	Roncemay	15 7 4	255
Gouverneur (Le) Le Breuil	16 7 6	210	Sablé-Solesmes		
Grande-Motte (La)			*La Forêt/La Rivière*	16 7 4	257
Les Flamants Roses	16 6 4	213	Saint-Germain	17 7 7	261
Médoc *Les Châteaux*	17 7 5	234	Saint-Thomas	14 7 5	266
Médoc *Les Vignes*	15 7 5	235	Sainte-Baume (La)	13 7 6	267
			Soufflenheim	16 7 4	272
Montpellier-Massane	16 7 5	236	Strasbourg Illkirch		
Amirauté (L')	15 7 8	153	*Jaune + Rouge*	13 7 6	274
Anjou-Champigné	13 6 6	155	Touquet (Le) *La Mer*	17 6 7	278
Annonay-Gourdan	13 6 5	156	Wimereux	15 4 5	286
Apremont	15 8 6	157			
Biarritz-le-Phare	14 6 8	168	Ailette (L')	15 6 5	149
Bordes (Les)	19 8 6	172	Aix-les-Bains	13 5 7	151
Bresse (La)	15 6 4	173	Baule (La) *Rouge*	15 7 8	164
Bretesche (La)	15 7 7	175	Bondues *Blanc*	16 7 6	170
Brigode	14 7 6	176	Bondues *Jaune*	15 7 6	171
Cannes Mandelieu			Cannes-Mougins	15 7 8	178
Old Course	13 7 8	177	Charmeil	16 6 6	187
Cap d'Agde	15 6 5	179	Chiberta	16 6 8	189
Chailly (Château de)	14 8 6	182	Cognac	13 7 5	190
Cheverny	14 7 6	188	Dinard	14 6 7	195
Dieppe-Pourville	14 6 5	194	Fontainebleau	17 7 7	205
Disneyland Paris			Fontenelles (Les)	14 7 4	208
Never Land + Wonderland	16 7 8	196	Gouverneur (Le) *Montaplan*	14 7 6	211
Etiolles *Les Cerfs*	15 6 5	201	Hardelot *Les Pins*	16 6 6	219
Etretat	14 6 5	202	Kempferhof (Le)	18 8 6	225
Fontenailles *Blanc*	14 7 6	207	National *L'Albatros*	18 6 6	237
Grande Bastide (La)	16 6 6	212	New Golf Deauville		
Granville *Les Dunes*	14 4 4	214	*Rouge/Blanc*	15 7 8	238
Guerville	14 7 4	217	Nîmes-Campagne	16 7 6	239
Gujan-Mestras	15 7 6	218	Pessac	13 7 7	244
Hossegor	16 6 6	221	Ploemeur Océan	15 7 6	246
Limère	17 6 5	230	Porcelaine (La)	14 6 4	248
Ozoir-la-Ferrière			Saint-Jean-de-Monts	16 6 5	262
Château/Monthéty	13 7 5	242	Servanes	13 7 7	271
Raray (Château de)*La Licorne*	14 6 4	250	Taulane	15 7 4	275

139

RELIEF DES PARCOURS

Relief / Parcours	Note	Page	Relief / Parcours	Note	Page
Toulouse-Seilh *Rouge*	15 7 6	277	Pornic	15 6 6	249
Villette d'Anthon *Les Sangliers*	17 6 4	283	Royal Mougins	17 7 8	256
Wantzenau (La)	16 6 6	285	Saint-Cloud *Vert*	14 7 7	258
Yvelines *Les Chênes*	13 7 4	287	Saint-Donat	15 7 8	259
			Saint-Nom-la-Bretèche *Rouge*	16 8 8	265
			Savenay	15 6 4	269
Belle-Dune	16 6 5	165	Seignosse	17 7 7	270
Besançon	13 7 5	166	Spérone	17 7 5	273
Béthemont	14 7 5	167	Val de Sorne	14 7 5	280
Casteljaloux	15 6 5	180			
Cély	15 7 6	181	Baden	15 6 5	161
Chamonix	15 6 7	183	Barbaroux	17 7 6	163
Chantaco	14 7 7	185	Feucherolles	15 7 5	204
Chantilly *Vineuil*	18 7 6	186	Grasse	13 7 6	215
Courson *Lilas/Orange*	15 7 3	192	La Boulie (R.C.F.) *La Vallée*	15 7 8	226
Courson *Vert/Noir*	16 7 3	193	Largue (La)	15 7 4	228
Estérel Latitudes	16 6 7	200	Maison Blanche	14 7 5	231
Laval-Changé *La Chabossière*	14 7 5	2293	Pléneuf-Val-André	17 7 5	245
Mazamet-La Barouge	13 5 4	233	Pont Royal	16 6 5	247
Opio Valbonne	13 6 7	241	Rochefort-Chisan	14 6 4	254
Rebetz	16 6 4	251			
Reims-Champagne	13 7 6	252	Amnéville	13 6 5	154
Riviéra Golf Club	13 7 8	253	Arcangues	14 7 8	159
Saint-Laurent	14 7 5	263	Domont-Montmorency	13 7 4	198
Saint-Nom-la-Bretèche *Bleu*	15 8 8	264	Esery	15 7 5	199
Toulouse Palmola	15 7 4	276	Evian	15 7 9	203
Touraine	13 7 6	279	Frégate	15 7 7	209
Val Queven	15 6 5	281	Grenoble Bresson	17 7 6	216
Vaucouleurs (La) *Les Vallons*	15 7 4	282	Makila Golf Club	14 6 8	232
Volcans (Les)	14 6 5	284	Paris International	16 7 5	243
			Sainte-Maxime	13 7 7	268
Ableiges *Les Etangs*	15 6 4	148			
Albi	15 6 6	152	Bitche	14 6 5	169
Arcachon	13 6 6	158	Saint-Endréol	15 7 4	260
Augerville	13 5 4	160			
Bâle-Hagenthal	15 7 7	162			
Brest Iroise	14 7 6	174			
Champ de Bataille	14 6 3	184			
Côte d'Argent (La)	17 6 5	191			
Divonne	14 6 7	197			
Fontcaude	14 6 6	206			
Haut-Poitou	14 6 4	220			
Isle Adam (L')	16 7 4	222			
Joyenval *Marly*	16 8 7	223			
Joyenval *Retz*	15 8 7	224			
Lacanau	14 6 4	227			
Omaha Beach					
La Mer/Le Bocage	14 7 5	240			

	Altitude: more than 500 m (1 500 ft.) Golfs à plus de 500 mètres d'altitude		
509	Divonne	14 6 7	197
580	Esery	15 7 5	199
590	Maison Blanche	14 7 5	231
600	Grasse	13 7 6	215
650	Mazamet-La Barouge	13 5 4	233
836	Volcans (Les)	14 6 5	284
997	Taulane	15 7 4	275
1050	Chamonix	15 6 7	183

ESSO Vous Présente
sa Nouvelle Gamme
d'Huiles Moteur.

ESSO
Lubrifiants

SAISONS RECOMMANDEES
RECOMMENDED SEASONS

Depending on altitude, usual weather conditions, the type of soil
and the quality of drainage and maintenance.

En fonction de l'altitude, des conditions météorologiques habituelles, de la nature
du sol où est construit le parcours, de la qualité du drainage et de l'entretien.

Saison / Parcours	Note	Page
`1 2 3 4 5 6 7 8 9 10 11 12`		
Albi	15 6 6	152
Arcachon	13 6 6	158
Baule (La) *Rouge*	15 7 8	164
Biarritz-le-Phare	14 6 8	168
Bretesche (La)	15 7 7	175
Cannes Mandelieu *Old Course*	13 7 8	177
Cannes-Mougins	15 7 8	178
Cap d'Agde	15 6 5	179
Chiberta	16 6 8	189
Côte d'Argent (La)	17 6 5	191
Dieppe-Pourville	14 6 5	194
Estérel Latitudes	16 6 7	200
Etretat	14 6 5	202
Grande Bastide (La)	16 6 6	212
Granville *Les Dunes*	14 4 4	214
Hardelot *Les Pins*	16 6 6	219
Hossegor	16 6 6	221
Médoc *Les Châteaux*	17 7 5	234
Médoc *Les Vignes*	15 7 5	235
Montpellier-Massane	16 7 5	236
Ploemeur Océan	15 7 6	246
Riviéra Golf Club	13 7 8	253
Royal Mougins	17 7 8	256
Saint-Donat	15 7 8	259
Saint-Jean-de-Monts	16 6 5	262
Saint-Laurent	14 7 5	263
Saint-Thomas	14 7 5	266
Savenay	15 6 4	269
Seignosse	17 7 7	270
Touquet (Le) *La Mer*	17 6 7	278
Val Queven	15 6 5	281
Wimereux	15 4 5	286
`1 2 3 4 5 6 7 8 9 10 11 12`		
Nîmes-Campagne	16 7 6	239
`1 2 3 4 5 6 7 8 9 10 11 12`		
Pornic	15 6 6	249
`1 2 3 4 5 6 7 8 9 10 11 12`		
Barbaroux	17 7 6	163
Belle-Dune	16 6 5	165
Chantaco	14 7 7	185
Gujan-Mestras	15 7 6	218
Lacanau	14 6 4	227
Mazamet-La Barouge	13 5 4	233
Opio Valbonne	13 6 7	241
Saint-Endréol	15 7 4	260
Sainte-Maxime	13 7 7	268

Saison / Parcours	Note	Page
Spérone	17 7 5	273
`1 2 3 4 5 6 7 8 9 10 11 12`		
Arcangues	14 7 8	159
Baden	15 6 5	161
Bordes (Les)	19 8 6	172
Casteljaloux	15 6 5	180
Cély	15 7 6	181
Champ de Bataille	14 6 3	184
Chantilly *Vineuil*	18 7 6	186
Dinard	14 6 7	195
Etiolles *Les Cerfs*	15 6 5	201
Fontainebleau	17 7 7	205
Frégate	15 7 7	209
Gouverneur (Le)	16 7 6	210
Grande-Motte (La)		
Les Flamants Roses	16 6 4	213
Limère	17 6 5	230
Makila Golf Club	14 6 8	232
National *L'Albatros*	18 6 6	237
Pont Royal	16 6 5	247
Rebetz	16 6 4	251
Rochefort-Chisan	14 6 4	254
Sainte-Baume (La)	13 7 6	267
Servanes	13 7 7	271
Toulouse Palmola	15 7 4	276
`1 2 3 4 5 6 7 8 9 10 11 12`		
Aisses (Les) *Rouge/Blanc*	16 5 4	150
Grasse	13 7 6	215
Isle Adam (L')	16 7 4	222
Saint-Germain	17 7 7	261
Toulouse-Seilh *Rouge*	15 7 6	277
Villette d'Anthon *Les Sangliers*	17 6 4	283
`1 2 3 4 5 6 7 8 9 10 11 12`		
Annonay-Gourdan	13 6 5	156
Brigode	14 7 6	176
Cognac	13 7 5	190
New Golf Deauville *R^{ge}/Blanc*	15 7 8	238
Pessac	13 7 7	244
`1 2 3 4 5 6 7 8 9 10 11 12`		
Ailette (L')	15 6 5	149
Aix-les-Bains	13 5 7	151
Amirauté (L')	15 7 8	153
Anjou-Champigné	13 6 6	155
Apremont	15 8 6	157
Augerville	13 5 4	160
Béthemont	14 7 5	167

143

Cartes et guides Michelin,
le temps de vivre...

Michelin, Maps and guides for work, rest and play...

Saison / Parcours	Note	Page	Saison / Parcours	Note	Page
Bitche	14 6 5	169	Strasbourg Illkirch		
Bondues *Blanc*	16 7 6	170	*Jaune + Rouge*	13 7 6	274
Bondues *Jaune*	15 7 6	171	Touraine	13 7 6	279
Brest Iroise	14 7 6	174	Vaucouleurs (La) *Les Vallons*	15 7 4	282
Charmeil	16 6 6	187	Volcans (Les)	14 6 5	284
Courson *Lilas/Orange*	15 7 3	192	Wantzenau (La)	16 6 6	285
Courson *Vert/Noir*	16 7 3	193			
Disneyland Paris *Never Land*			1 2 3 **4 5 6 7 8 9** 10 11 12		
+ *Wonderland*	16 7 8	196	Raray (Château de)		
Domont-Montmorency	13 7 4	198	*La Licorne*	14 6 4	250
Esery	15 7 5	199			
Feucherolles	15 7 5	204	1 2 3 4 **5 6 7 8 9 10** 11 12		
Fontcaude	14 6 6	206	Ableiges *Les Etangs*	15 6 4	148
Fontenailles *Blanc*	14 7 6	207	Amnéville	13 6 5	154
Fontenelles (Les)	14 7 4	208	Bresse (La)	15 6 4	173
Grenoble Bresson	17 7 6	216	Chailly (Château de)	14 8 6	182
Guerville	14 7 4	217	Cheverny	14 7 6	188
Haut-Poitou	14 6 4	220	Divonne	14 6 7	197
Kempferhof (Le)	18 8 6	225	Evian	15 7 9	203
La Boulie (R.C.F.) *La Vallée*	15 7 8	226	Joyenval *Marly*	16 8 7	223
Omaha Beach			Joyenval *Retz*	15 8 7	224
La Mer/Le Bocage	14 7 5	240	Maison Blanche	14 7 5	231
Ozoir-la-Ferrière			Taulane	15 7 4	275
Château/Monthéty	13 7 5	242	Val de Sorne	14 7 5	280
Paris International	16 7 5	243			
Pléneuf-Val-André	17 7 5	245	1 2 3 4 **5 6 7 8 9** 10 11 12		
Porcelaine (La)	14 6 4	248	Bâle-Hagenthal	15 7 7	162
Reims-Champagne	13 7 6	252	Besançon	13 7 5	166
Roncemay	15 7 4	255	Largue (La)	15 7 4	228
Sablé-Solesmes			Laval-Changé	14 7 5	229
La Forêt/La Rivière	16 7 4	257	Yvelines *Les Chênes*	13 7 4	287
Saint-Cloud *Vert*	14 7 7	258			
Saint-Nom-la-Bretèche			1 2 3 4 5 **6 7 8 9 10** 11 12		
Rouge	16 8 8	265	Chamonix	15 6 7	183
Soufflenheim	16 7 4	272			

TYPE DE PARCOURS - TYPE OF COURSE

Type / Parcours	Note	Page	Type / Parcours	Note	Page
Bocage			**Campagne**		
Amirauté (L')	15 7 8	588	Anjou-Champigné	13 6 6	592
Cognac	13 7 5	666	Barbaroux	17 7 6	612
Fontenelles (Les)	14 7 4	708	Cap d'Agde	15 6 5	646
New Golf Deauville *Rouge/Blanc*	15 7 8	766	Gouverneur (Le) *Le Breuil*	16 7 6	712
Bord de mer			*Montaplan*	14 7 6	714
Arcachon	13 6 6	598	Laval-Changé *La Chabossière*	14 7 5	744
Baden	15 6 5	608	Maison Blanche	14 7 5	748
Cannes Mandelieu	13 7 8	642	Nîmes-Campagne	16 7 6	768
Dieppe-Pourville	14 6 5	678	Pont Royal	16 6 5	784
Dinard	13 5 7	680	Porcelaine (La)	14 6 4	786
Etretat	14 6 5	698	Rhin (Le)	12 6 5	796
Frégate	15 7 7	710	Saint-Malo	13 7 5	822
Grande-Motte (La)	16 6 4	718	Saint-Samson	13 7 6	824
Omaha Beach	14 7 5	772	Sainte-Baume (La)	13 7 6	828
Pléneuf-Val-André	17 6 5	780	Servanes	13 7 7	838
Ploemeur Océan	15 7 6	782	Strasbourg Illkirch	13 7 6	844
Saint-Cyprien	12 7 6	810	**Forêt**		
Spérone	17 7 5	842	Ailette (L')	15 6 5	580

145

GESTION ET DISTRIBUTION DES MATERIELS PUBLIPROMOTIONNELS, DES DOCUMENTS TECHNIQUES ET ADMINISTRATIFS

EURODISPATCH

Depuis de nombreuses années, EURODISPATCH assure la logistique des produits de communication d'AUTOMOBILE PEUGEOT.

EURODISPATCH
votre partenaire

Siège social :
8, avenue Albert Einstein
ZI du Coudray - BP 8
93152 Le Blanc-Mesnil
Cedex.
Tél. : **01 48 14 73 73**
Fax : **01 48 14 73 13**
http//www. eurodispatch.fr

Autres sites :
Z.I. de Gonesse
26 rue Gay Lussac
95500 Gonesse.

Service Commercial :
Tél. ; **01 48 14 73 15**
Fax : **01 48 14 72 02**

EURODISPATCH :

- Un engagement de tous les instants.
- Une grande implication dans l'action.
- Une disponibilité et une réactivité immédiates.
- Un prestataire intégrant la culture de ses clients.
- Et aussi, comme **AUTOMOBILES PEUGEOT** le souci constant de la qualité et la recherche de l'Excellence et du zéro défaut.

TYPE DE PARCOURS

Type / Parcours	Note			Page	Type / Parcours	Note			Page
Aisses (Les) *Rouge/Blanc*	16	5	4	582	**Parc**				
Amnéville	13	6	5	590	Aix-les-Bains	13	5	7	584
Apremont	15	8	6	596	Albi	15	6	6	586
Augerville	13	5	4	604	Annonay-Gourdan	13	6	5	594
Bâle-Hagenthal	15	7	7	610	Ardrée	12	7	6	602
Baule (La) *Rouge*	15	7	8	614	Avrillé	13	6	5	606
Belle-Dune	16	6	5	616	Brigode	14	7	6	640
Besançon	13	6	5	618	Cély	15	7	6	650
Béthemont	14	7	5	620	Coudray (Le)	13	7	5	670
Bitche	14	6	5	624	Domangère (La)	13	5	5	686
Bordes (Les)	19	8	6	632	Fontenailles *Blanc*	14	7	6	706
Bretesche (La)	15	7	7	638	Kempferhof (Le)	18	8	6	738
Cannes-Mougins	15	7	8	644	Makila Golf Club	14	6	8	750
Champ de Bataille	14	6	3	656	Ozoir-la-Ferrière	13	7	5	776
Chantaco	14	7	7	658	Rebetz	16	6	4	792
Cheverny	14	7	6	662	Reims-Champagne	13	7	6	794
Côte d'Argent (La)	17	6	5	668	Touraine	13	7	6	856
Domont-Montmorency	13	7	4	688	Vaudreuil (Le)	13	7	5	866
Estérel Latitudes	16	6	7	694	**Parc, vallon**				
Grasse	13	7	6	722	Savenay	15	6	4	834
Gujan-Mestras	15	7	6	728	**Plaine**				
Hardelot *Les Pins*	16	6	6	730	Bondoufle	14	7	4	626
Hossegor	16	6	6	734	Bondues *Jaune*	15	7	6	630
Isle Adam (L')	16	7	4	736	Bresse (La)	15	6	4	634
Lacanau	14	6	4	740	Chailly (Château de)	14	8	6	652
Limère	17	6	5	746	Charmeil	16	6	6	660
Médoc *Les Vignes*	15	7	5	756	Courson *Vert/Noir Lilas/Orange*	16	7	3	674
Opio Valbonne	13	6	7	774	Deauville-Saint-Gatien	12	7	4	676
Pessac	13	7	7	778	Disneyland Paris	16	7	8	682
Rochefort-Chisan	14	6	4	800	Etiolles *Les Cerfs*	15	6	5	696
Roncemay	15	7	4	802	Grande Bastide (La)	16	6	6	716
Royal Mougins	17	7	8	804	Guerville	14	7	4	726
Royan	13	6	6	806	Haut-Poitou	14	6	4	732
Saint-Endréol	15	7	4	814	Médoc *Les Châteaux*	17	7	5	754
Saint-Jean-de-Monts	16	6	5	816	Mont Griffon *Les Lacs*	12	8	3	760
Saint-Laurent	14	7	5	820	Montpellier-Massane	16	7	5	762
Seignosse	17	7	7	836	Raray (Château de)	14	6	4	790
Soufflenheim	16	7	4	840	Sablé-Solesmes	16	7	4	808
Taulane	15	7	4	846	Saint-Julien	13	7	6	818
Toulouse Palmola	15	7	4	848	Salvagny	13	6	6	832
Touquet (Le) *La Forêt*	14	6	7	852	Toulouse-Seilh *Rouge*	15	7	6	850
Villette d'Anthon	17	6	4	868	Wantzenau (La)	16	6	6	872
Yvelines *Les Chênes*	13	7	4	876	**Plaine, vallon**				
Forêt, plaine					Val Queven	15	6	5	860
Largue (La)	15	7	4	742	**Résidentiel**				
Vaucouleurs (La) *La Rivière*	13	7	4	862	Biarritz-le-Phare	14	6	8	622
Links					Bondues *Blanc*	16	7	6	628
Chiberta	16	6	8	664	Fontcaude	14	6	6	704
Granville *Les Dunes*	14	4	4	720	Sainte-Maxime	13	7	7	830
National *L'Albatros*	18	6	6	764	**Vallon**				
Pornic	15	6	6	788	Arcangues	14	7	8	600
Touquet (Le) *La Mer*	17	6	7	854	Brest Iroise	14	7	6	636
Vaucouleurs (La)	15	7	4	864	Casteljaloux	15	6	5	648
Wimereux	15	4	5	874	Divonne	14	6	7	684
Montagne					Dryades (Les)	13	7	5	690
Esery	15	7	5	692	Feucherolles	15	7	5	702
Mazamet-La Barouge	13	5	4	752	Nivelle (La)	12	6	7	770
Chamonix	15	6	7	654	Riviéra Golf Club	13	7	8	798
Evian	15	7	9	700	Saint-Donat	15	7	8	812
Grenoble Bresson	17	7	6	724	Saint-Thomas	14	7	5	826
Mont d'Arbois	13	7	6	758	Val de Sorne	14	7	5	858
Volcans (Les)	14	6	5	870	Ableiges *Les Etangs*	15	6	4	578

147

En plaine et dans les vallons du Vexin, l'architecture du 18 trous des "Etangs" présente des styles différents, sans rupture trop marquée. Le haut du domaine s'apparente aux links, avec de jolis mouvements de terrain, alors que la partie basse est plus "américaine". La plupart des drives, tout comme les approches, exigent une bonne technique et un placement attentif, en raison des nombreux obstacles très en jeu, qu'il s'agisse des bunkers, du rough ou de l'eau. L'architecte Jeremy Pern a généreusement modelé et défendu les greens, où les positions de drapeau peuvent changer radicalement le jeu. Les reliefs du terrain rendent assez physique ce parcours, à jouer des départs normaux au dessus de 10 de handicap. C'est un très bon test, mais l'entretien est à surveiller, certains trous pouvant être très humides.

On the plain and through the vales of Vexin, the architecture of the 18 hole "Etangs" course features a number of different styles stitched together in almost seamless fashion. The upper section is links territory, with attractive sandhills and dips, while the lower section is more American in its layout. Most tee-shots and approach-shots demand good technique and careful placing of the ball owing to the numerous hazards in play, ranging from unforgiving rough to water. Architect Jeremy Pern has generously contoured and defended the greens, where the pin-positions can radically change the course. Ableiges can be a tiring course on foot, and the back-tees should be for single-figure handicappers only. All in all, a great test of golf, but as some of the holes tend to be very wet, the course requires extra careful upkeep.

Golf Club d'Ableiges
Chaussée Jules César
F - 95450 ABLEIGES

Office	Secrétariat	(33) 01 30 27 97 00
Pro shop	Pro-shop	(33) 01 34 66 06 05
Fax	Fax	(33) 01 30 27 97 10
Situation	Situation	

9 km N.O Pontoise, 27 150 hab.
40 km N.O. Paris, 2 175 200 hab.

Annual closure	Fermeture annnuelle	non
Weekly closure	Fermeture hebdomadaire	

Fees main season
Tarifs haute saison le parcours

	Week days Semaine	We/Bank holidays We/Férié
Individual Individuel	150 F	250 F
Couple Couple	300 F	500 F

Jeudis d'Ableiges 150 F/compétition - Mardi :

Caddy	Caddy	non
Electric Trolley	Chariot électrique	70 F/jour
Buggy	Voiturette	non
Clubs	Clubs 1/2 série	50 F/jour

Credit cards Cartes de crédit
CB

148

Access Accès : A15 → Pontoise, N14 sortie Ableiges, → golf
Map 3 on page 102 Carte 3 Page 102

GOLF COURSE
PARCOURS | **15**/20

Site	Site	
Maintenance	Entretien	
Architect	Architecte	Jeremy Pern Jean Garaïalde
Type	Type	vallons, plaine
Relief	Relief	
Water in play	Eau en jeu	
Exp. to wind	Exposé au vent	
Trees in play	Arbres en jeu	

Scorecard Carte de score	Chp. Chp.	Mens Mess.	Ladies Da.
Length Long.	6261	5634	5274
Par	72	72	72

Advised golfing ability	0	12	24	36
Niveau de jeu recommandé				
Hcp required	Handicap exigé	35, 30 We		

CLUB HOUSE & AMENITIES
CLUB HOUSE ET ANNEXES | **6**/10

Pro shop	Pro-shop	
Driving range	Practice	
Sheltered	couvert	15 places
On grass	sur herbe	non
Putting-green	putting-green	oui
Pitching-green	pitching green	oui

HOTEL FACILITIES
ENVIRONNEMENT HOTELIER | **4**/10

HOTELS HÔTELS
Astrée ***   Pontoise 10 km
55 chambres, D 505 F
Tél (33) 01 34 24 94 94, Fax (33) 01 34 24 95 15

Campanile **   Pontoise 10 km
80 chambres, D 270 F
Tél (33) 01 30 38 55 44, Fax (33) 01 30 30 48 87

RESTAURANTS RESTAURANT
Gérard Cagna   Cormeilles-en-Vexin 4 km
Tél (33) 01 34 66 61 56

Le Chiquito   La Bonneville 5 km
Tél (33) 01 30 36 40 23

L'Ailette maintient son satut de très bon golf public. Bien que vallonné, il n'est pas difficile à marcher, mais quelques greens très surélevés peuvent déconcerter au premier abord, accentuant le côté technique et tactique du parcours. Ses difficultés augmentent à mesure que l'on joue les départs reculés, mais il reste à la portée des joueurs moyens, nombreux ici. On remarquera l'alternance de trous assez reposants et de trous plus difficiles, ce qui donne un bon rythme au jeu, et des possibilités de reprendre des forces quand il le faut. Les greens sont vastes et francs, et bien défendus par des bunkers dessinés avec soin. Le parcours propose des trous dans des bois généralement assez éloignés, et les obstacles d'eau sont dangereux sans être trop préoccupants. Le site du Chemin des Dames, témoin de la première Guerre Mondiale, n'est plus le théâtre que de pacifiques batailles...

Ailette has retained its status as an excellent public course. Although far from flat, the course is not too tiring to walk around. A number of elevated greens are a little disconcerting at first and emphasise the course's technical and tactical sides. The difficulties of playing here increase as you tee-off further back, but Ailette is playable by mid-to-high handicappers, of whom there are many here. This is a nicely balanced course, with pleasant alternation between tough and easier holes allowing players breathing space and the chance to recuperate. The greens are huge, forthright and well-defended by well-designed bunkers. Some holes run through woodland, although the trees are usually not too close, and the water hazards are dangerous but never over-bearing. The site of Chemin des Dames, a testimony to World War I, is now simply the theatre of more peaceful conflict with a little white ball.

Golf de l'Ailette
F - 02860 CERNY-EN LAONNOIS

Office	Secrétariat	(33) 03 23 24 83 99
Pro shop	Pro-shop	(33) 03 23 24 81 24
Fax	Fax	(33) 03 23 24 84 66
Situation	Situation	

17 km Laon, 26 490 hab.

Annual closure	Fermeture annnuelle	non
Weekly closure	Fermeture hebdomadaire	

mardi Club-house (01/09 → 31/03)

Fees main season
Tarifs haute saison la journée

	Week days Semaine	We/Bank holidays We/Férié
Individual Individuel	185 F	240 F
Couple Couple	370 F	480 F

Caddy	Caddy	non
Electric Trolley	Chariot électrique	non
Buggy	Voiturette	200 F/18 trous
Clubs	Clubs 1/2 série	30 F/jour

Credit cards Cartes de crédit
VISA - CB - Eurocard - MasterCard

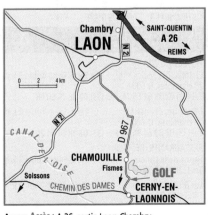

Access Accès : A 26, sortie Laon-Chambry.
D 967 → Fismes
Map 1 on page 99 Carte 1 Page 99

GOLF COURSE
PARCOURS

15/20

Site	Site	
Maintenance	Entretien	
Architect	Architecte	Michel Gayon
Type	Type	forêt, lac
Relief	Relief	
Water in play	Eau en jeu	
Exp. to wind	Exposé au vent	
Trees in play	Arbres en jeu	

Scorecard Carte de score	Chp. Chp.	Mens Mess.	Ladies Da.
Length Long.	6127	5759	5180
Par	72	72	72

Advised golfing ability		0 12 24 36
Niveau de jeu recommandé		
Hcp required	Handicap exigé	35

CLUB HOUSE & AMENITIES
CLUB HOUSE ET ANNEXES

6/10

Pro shop	Pro-shop	
Driving range	Practice	
Sheltered	couvert	5 places
On grass	sur herbe	oui
Putting-green	putting-green	oui
Pitching-green	pitching green	oui

HOTEL FACILITIES
ENVIRONNEMENT HOTELIER

5/10

HOTELS HÔTELS
Mercure Holigolf *** — Golf
58 chambres, D 490 FF
Tél (33) 03 23 24 84 85, Fax (33) 03 23 24 81 20

Campanile ** — Laon 17 km
47 chambres, D 270 F
Tél (33) 03 23 23 15 05, Fax (33) 03 23 23 04 25

RESTAURANTS RESTAURANT
La Petite Auberge — Laon 17 km
Tél (33) 03 23 23 02 38

Bannière de France — Laon17 km
Tél (33) 03 23 23 21 44

149

AISSES (LES) ROUGE/BLANC

| 16 | 5 | 4 |

Cet ensemble est composé de trois neuf trous combinables, le Rouge, le Blanc et le Bleu, dans un domaine de 250 hectares. Sur les deux premiers parcours, d'immenses bunkers sont à la fois des obstacles (mais ils ne sont pas trop profonds) et des éléments d'architecture pour mieux préciser les trous dans l'espace. Le paysage de Sologne est calme et séduisant, mais le relief est absent, et les architectes n'ont pas voulu modeler beaucoup le terrain. Sur le dernier 9 trous, les obstacles d'eau prennent le relais des bunkers. La végétation est assez naturelle, avec les bouleaux, hêtres, sapins et chênes de la région. Un ensemble plaisant, mais toujours inachevé (Club-House insuffisant), qui ne mérite pas à lui seul un long détour, mais complète bien l'équipement golfique remarquable de la région (Les Bordes, Limère).

This is a complex of three combinable 9-hole courses - Red, White and Blue - over an estate of some 250 hectares. The first two are marked by huge bunkers (although not too deep) which are at once the main hazards and the principal features of this lay-out. The Sologne landscape is calm and appealing, but the area is flat and the architects visibly avoided shaping the course. On the Blue course, bunkers are largely replaced by water. Vegetation is mostly natural, with birch, beech, pine and oak trees, typical of this area. A pleasant but still incomplete venue (the clubhouse is inadequate) which is hardly worth a long journey on its own, but which nicely completes some remarkable golfing facilities in this region (Les Bordes and Limère).

Golf des Aisses
Domaine des Aisses
F - 45240 LA FERTÉ-SAINT-AUBIN

Office	Secrétariat	(33) 02 38 64 80 87
Pro shop	Pro-shop	(33) 02 38 64 80 87
Fax	Fax	(33) 02 34 64 80 85
Situation	Situation	

24 km Orléans, 105 110 hab.
Annual closure Fermeture annnuelle
oui 1/01/99 → 10/01/99
Weekly closure Fermeture hebdomadaire
mercredi 1/11→28/02/99

Fees main season
Tarifs haute saison la journée

	Week days Semaine	We/Bank holidays We/Férié
Individual Individuel	180 F	250 F
Couple Couple	360 F	450 F
Caddy	Caddy	non
Electric Trolley	Chariot électrique	non
Buggy	Voiturette	180 F/18 trous
Clubs	Clubs 1/2 série	50 F/jour

Credit cards Cartes de crédit
VISA - CB - Eurocard - MasterCard - AMEX

150

Access Accès : A71 Orléans → Bourges, sortie Orléans
La Source. N20 → La Ferté-St-Aubin, 1 km. D17 →
Golf, à gauche. **Map 3 on page 102** Carte 3 Page 102

GOLF COURSE
PARCOURS
16/20

Site	Site	▬▬▬▬
Maintenance	Entretien	▬▬▬▬
Architect	Architecte	Olivier Brizon
		Groupe Taiyo
Type	Type	forêt, parc, lac
Relief	Relief	
Water in play	Eau en jeu	▬▬▬
Exp. to wind	Exposé au vent	▬▬
Trees in play	Arbres en jeu	▬▬▬

Scorecard Carte de score	Chp. Chp.	Mens Mess.	Ladies Da.
Length Long.	6438	6125	5202
Par	72	72	72

Advised golfing ability Niveau de jeu recommandé	0	12	24	36
		▬▬▬		

Hcp required Handicap exigé non

CLUB HOUSE & AMENITIES
CLUB HOUSE ET ANNEXES
5/10

Pro shop	Pro-shop	▬▬▬▬
Driving range	Practice	
Sheltered	couvert	non
On grass	sur herbe	oui
Putting-green	putting-green	oui
Pitching-green	pitching green	oui

HOTEL FACILITIES
ENVIRONNEMENT HOTELIER
4/10

HOTELS HÔTELS
Château des Muids *** La Ferté-Saint-Aubin 3 km
23 chambres, D 600 F
Tél (33) 02 38 64 65 14, Fax (33) 02 38 76 50 08

L'Orée des Chênes *** La Ferté-Saint-Aubin 3 km
21 chambres, D 600 F
Tél (33) 02 38 64 84 00, Fax (33) 02 38 64 84 20

RESTAURANTS RESTAURANT
Ferme de la Lande La Ferté-Saint-Aubin 3 km
Tél (33) 02 38 76 64 37

Les Brémailles La Ferté-Saint-Aubin3 km
Tél(33) 02 38 76 56 60

Ce parcours a été créé en 1936 pour répondre aux demandes de la clientèle étrangère de cette jolie ville d'eaux. Le terrain ne manque pas de charme, mais le rythme des trous est saccadé, donnant une sensation d'assemblage désordonné : du 6 au 12, on trouve cinq par 3 ! Avec des par 4 en général très courts et trois des cinq par 5 prenables en deux, un bon score est à la portée de tous les joueurs, par rapport à leur niveau bien sûr. S'ils évitent quelques horslimites dangereux, les joueurs du meilleur niveau seront vite frustrés par le manque de difficultés et de longueur de ce parcours, mais ils prendront du plaisir à jouer en famille ou avec des amis de plus faible niveau. Bien boisé, mais assez humide, surtout au retour, Aix-les-Bains est l'occasion d'une agréable promenade. On souhaite toujours un remodelage de ce tracé un peu désuet, notamment aux alentours des petits greens...

This course was opened in 1936 to cater to the numerous foreign visitors heading to this pretty spa town. It is a charming site, sure enough, but the general layout lacks any sort of pattern, rather as if the holes were just thrown together. For example, there are five par 3s between the 6th and 12th holes. With the par 4s generally pretty short and three of the five par 5s reachable in two, a good score is within the capability of most players, depending of course on their level of proficiency. If they avoid the few dangerous out-of-bounds, the better players will quickly feel a little frustrated at the lack of difficulty and yardage, but should have fun playing with the family or with friends of lesser ability. There are a lot of trees and the course is damp, especially on the back nine, but Aix-les-Bains is the opportunity to enjoy a pleasant round of golf, even though the slightly outdated layout could do with a little restyling, especially around the small greens.

Golf Club d'Aix-les-Bains

Avenue du Golf
F - 73100 AIX-LES-BAINS

Office	Secrétariat	(33) 04 79 61 23 35
Pro shop	Pro-shop	(33) 04 79 61 31 56
Fax	Fax	(33) 04 79 34 06 01
Situation	Situation	

Aix-les-Bains, 24 680 hab.

Annual closure	Fermeture annnuelle	non
Weekly closure	Fermeture hebdomadaire	

Fees main season
Tarifs haute saison la journée

	Week days Semaine	We/Bank holidays We/Férié
Individual Individuel	250 F	250 F
Couple Couple	500 F	500 F

Caddy	Caddy	sur réservation
Electric Trolley	Chariot électrique	70 F/18 trous
Buggy	Voiturette	non
Clubs	Clubs 1/2 série	40 F/jour

Credit cards Cartes de crédit
VISA - CB - Eurocard - MasterCard - AMEX - DC

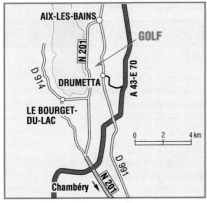

Access Accès : Grenoble, A43, sortie Aix Sud,
→ Aix-les-Bains, → Golf
Map 11 on page 119 Carte 11 Page 119

GOLF COURSE
PARCOURS   13/20

Site	Site	▬▬
Maintenance	Entretien	▬▬▬
Architect	Architecte	
Type	Type	parc
Relief	Relief	▬▬
Water in play	Eau en jeu	▬
Exp. to wind	Exposé au vent	▬
Trees in play	Arbres en jeu	▬▬

Scorecard Carte de score	Chp. Chp.	Mens Mess.	Ladies Da.
Length Long.	5627	5404	4966
Par	71	71	71

Advised golfing ability		0 12 24 36
Niveau de jeu recommandé		▭▬
Hcp required	Handicap exigé	35

CLUB HOUSE & AMENITIES
CLUB HOUSE ET ANNEXES   5/10

Pro shop	Pro-shop	▬▬▬
Driving range	Practice	▬▬
Sheltered	couvert	5 places
On grass	sur herbe	non
Putting-green	putting-green	oui
Pitching-green	pitching green	oui

151

HOTEL FACILITIES
ENVIRONNEMENT HOTELIER   7/10

HOTELS HÔTELS
Campanile **   sur place
60 chambres, D 270 F
Tél (33) 04 79 61 30 66

Ariana ****   Aix-les-Bains
60 chambres, D 610 F   1 km
Tél (33) 04 79 61 79 79, Fax (33) 04 79 61 79 00

Le Manoir ***   Aix-les-Bains
73 chambres, D 600 F   1 km
Tél (33) 04 79 61 44 00, Fax (33) 04 79 35 67 67

RESTAURANTS RESTAURANT
Le Manoir   Aix-les-Bains
Tél (33) 04 79 61 44 00

Park Hôtel   Aix-les-Bains
Tél(33) 04 79 34 19 19

Dans un très joli environnement à proximité du Tarn, ce parcours a été modelé dans un paysage de campagne par Jeremy Pern, architecte de nombreux parcours en France. On y retrouve sa mise en jeu traditionnelle de nombreux bunkers et d'obstacles d'eau, ici en jeu sur une demi-douzaine de trous, mais sans trop pénaliser les joueurs peu expérimentés. Une bonne alternance de trous techniques et de trous plus faciles offre un bon rythme de jeu, sans pression excessive. Lors de notre visite, l'entretien restait toujours honnête, médiocre sur les trous en bordure du Tarn, et les roughs mal travaillés, au point d'y perdre des balles. Sans tirer de conclusions permanentes à ce sujet, c'est encore un point à surveiller, il handicape un tracé au demeurant agréable.

Architect Jeremy Pern has designed many courses in France, including this one located in beautiful surroundings near the River Tarn. His traditional use of countless bunkers and water hazards is very much to the fore, coming into play on half a dozen holes but without penalising the less experienced players. The more difficult holes alternate agreeably with the easier ones to give a good playing pattern without too much pressure. During our visit, the greenkeeping and general upkeep were still fair only, and pretty poor alongside the river. The rough, too, was sufficiently overgrown for a number of balls to end up lost. Without wishing to draw any permanent conclusions on this subject, this is nonetheless a point that needs watching, as it mars what is otherwise a very pleasant golf course.

Golf Club d'Albi
Château de Lasbordes
F - 81000 ALBI

Office	Secrétariat	(33) 05 63 54 98 07
Pro shop	Pro-shop	(33) 05 63 54 98 07
Fax	Fax	(33) 05 63 47 21 55
Situation	Situation	

4 km Albi, 46 580 hab.

Annual closure	Fermeture annnuelle	non
Weekly closure	Fermeture hebdomadaire	non

club-house fermé le mardi

Fees main season
Tarifs haute saison la journée

	Week days Semaine	We/Bank holidays We/Férié
Individual Individuel	170 F	230 F
Couple Couple	340 F	460 F

Seniors: mercredi 100 F.

Caddy	Caddy	non
Electric Trolley	Chariot électrique	non
Buggy	Voiturette	170 F/18 trous
Clubs	Clubs 1/2 série	50 F/jour

Credit cards Cartes de crédit
VISA - CB - Eurocard - MasterCard

152

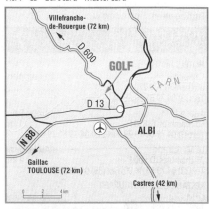

Villefranche-de-Rouergue (72 km)
D 600
GOLF
TARN
D 13
N 88
ALBI
Gaillac
TOULOUSE (72 km)
Castres (42 km)
0 2 4 km

Access Accès : Toulouse, A 68 et N 88 →Albi.
Albi → Villefranche-de-Rouergue, → Golf
Map 13 on page 122 Carte 13 Page 122

GOLF COURSE
PARCOURS **15**/20

Site	Site	
Maintenance	Entretien	
Architect	Architecte	Jeremy Pern
		Jean Garaïalde
Type	Type	parc, links
Relief	Relief	
Water in play	Eau en jeu	
Exp. to wind	Exposé au vent	
Trees in play	Arbres en jeu	

Scorecard Carte de score	Chp. Chp.	Mens Mess.	Ladies Da.
Length Long.	6199	5759	5226
Par	72	72	72

Advised golfing ability	0	12	24	36
Niveau de jeu recommandé				

Hcp required Handicap exigé 35

CLUB HOUSE & AMENITIES
CLUB HOUSE ET ANNEXES **6**/10

Pro shop	Pro-shop	
Driving range	Practice	
Sheltered	couvert	8 places
On grass	sur herbe	non
Putting-green	putting-green	oui
Pitching-green	pitching green	non

HOTEL FACILITIES
ENVIRONNEMENT HOTELIER **6**/10

HOTELS HÔTELS
La Réserve ★★★★ Fonvialane 3 km
24 chambres, D 800 F
Tél (33) 05 63 60 80 80, Fax (33) 05 63 47 63 60

Host. Saint-Antoine ★★★★ Albi 4 km
44 chambres, D 700 F
Tél (33) 05 63 54 04 04, Fax (33) 05 63 47 10 47

Host. du Vigan ★★★ Albi 4 km
40 chambres, D 350 F
Tél (33) 05 63 54 01 23, Fax (33) 05 63 47 05 42

RESTAURANTS RESTAURANT
Le Grand Ecuyer Cordes 20 km
Tél (33) 05 63 56 01 03

Le Goulu Albi 3 km
Tél (33) 05 63 54 16 56

Dominant un paysage normand de bocage et de marais, le Club house luxueux paraît annoncer un parcours exceptionnel. Ce n'est pas vraiment le cas. Avec ses larges boulevards, des obstacles de fairway peu dangereux, des greens sans grande personnalité et très peu défendus, la stratégie de jeu est évidente, et la motivation s'estompe si on joue souvent ici. Les obstacles d'eau constituent les seules véritables difficultés, les bunkers étant généralement peu profonds et éloignés des limites des greens. Si les joueurs expérimentés regretteront le manque de "souffle" du parcours, au demeurant bien entretenu, les joueurs de tous niveaux pourront y évoluer facilement, ce qui est bien la fonction de ce club "de vacances" et de week-end. Les installations d'entraînement sont de bonne qualité, et sept trous peuvent être éclairés (trois du 18 trous et quatre du parcours d'initiation).

Overlooking a Norman landscape of farmsteads and marshland, the luxurious club-house seems to suggest an exceptional course. This is not really so. With wide open fairways, a few benign fairway hazards, and greens with little character and even fewer bunkers to defend them, the course has no hidden dangers and can border on the monotonous if played often. The only real difficulties are the water hazards, as the bunkers are shallow and generally well away from the greens. While the more experienced player may regret the course's lack of gusto, (despite excellent upkeep, it should be said), players of all levels will find this an easy way to improve their game, which is exactly what this "holiday" and week-end course sets out to do. Practice facilities are good and seven holes can be lit up (three from the 18 hole course and four from the pitch 'n putt).

Golf Club de l'Amirauté
Tourgéville
F - 14800 DEAUVILLE

Office	Secrétariat	(33) 02 31 88 38 00
Pro shop	Pro-shop	(33) 02 31 88 38 00
Fax	Fax	(33) 02 31 88 32 00
Situation	Situation	

7 km Deauville, 4 260 hab.

Annual closure	Fermeture annnuelle	non
Weekly closure	Fermeture hebdomadaire	

Fees main season
Tarifs haute saison la journée

	Week days Semaine	We/Bank holidays We/Férié
Individual Individuel	250 F	350 F
Couple Couple	500 F	700 F

Caddy	Caddy	sur réservation
Electric Trolley	Chariot électrique	150 F/18 trous
Buggy	Voiturette	220 F/18 trous
Clubs	Clubs 1/2 série	100 F/jour

Credit cards Cartes de crédit
VISA - CB - Eurocard - MasterCard

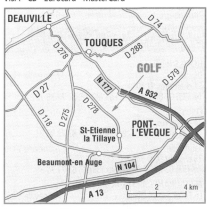

Access Accès : D27 → Saint-Arnoult,
D 275 → Beaumont-en-Auge, → Golf
Map 2 on page 101 Carte 2 Page 101

GOLF COURSE
PARCOURS   15/20

Site	Site	▬▬▬▬▬▭
Maintenance	Entretien	▬▬▬▬▬▭
Architect	Architecte	Bill Baker
Type	Type	bocage
Relief	Relief	▬▭
Water in play	Eau en jeu	▬▬▬▭
Exp. to wind	Exposé au vent	▬▬▭
Trees in play	Arbres en jeu	▬▭

Scorecard Carte de score	Chp. Chp.	Mens Mess.	Ladies Da.
Length Long.	6017	5806	5195
Par	73	73	73

Advised golfing ability		0	12	24	36
Niveau de jeu recommandé					
Hcp required	Handicap exigé	non			

CLUB HOUSE & AMENITIES
CLUB HOUSE ET ANNEXES   7/10

Pro shop	Pro-shop	▬▬▬▬▭
Driving range	Practice	▬▬▬▬▭
Sheltered	couvert	42 places
On grass	sur herbe	non
Putting-green	putting-green	oui
Pitching-green	pitching green	oui

153

HOTEL FACILITIES
ENVIRONNEMENT HOTELIER   8/10

HOTELS HÔTELS
L'Amirauté ***   Touques 6 km
121 chambres, D 825 F
Tél (33) 02 31 81 82 83, Fax (33) 02 31 81 82 93

Manoir de Roncheville   St-Martin-aux-Chartrains
6 chambres, D 450 F   4 km
Tél (33) 02 31 65 14 14, Fax (33) 02 31 65 20 44

Hôtel du Golf ****   Saint-Arnoult 6 km
178 chambres, D 1500 F
Tél (33) 02 31 88 19 01, Fax (33) 02 31 88 75 99

RESTAURANTS RESTAURANT
Le Ciro's   Deauville 7 km
Tél (33) 02 31 88 18 10

Le Spinnaker   Deauville 7 km
Tél(33) 02 31 88 24 40

AMNÉVILLE

13	6	5

Situé au coeur du centre touristique thermal d'Amnéville, ce parcours est accidenté et physique, mais bénéficie d'un environnement boisé très tranquille (chênes, hêtres, bouleaux) qui constitue l'essentiel des difficultés. Dans son dessin, l'architecte Jean-Manuel Rossi a conservé et suivi le caractère naturel du terrain. En revanche, il a beaucoup travaillé les greens, généralement de bonne taille. Les obstacles sont bien visibles, mais certains trous comme le 2, le 5, le 11 et le 17 sont délicats à négocier, et obligent à savoir jouer tous les coups. Amusant à jouer en famille, notamment en match-play, Amnéville est difficile à scorer pour tous les niveaux de jeu, mais plus encore pour les néophytes. En revanche, les situations de jeu sont assez variées pour que l'on revienne volontiers jouer ici. Dans une région pauvre en parcours de qualité, celui-ci s'impose comme le plus intéressant.

Located at the heart of the spa and tourist town of Amnéville, this is a hilly and physically testing course, laid out in a peaceful, woodland setting. Indeed, the oak, beech and birch trees are the main hazards on the course. In this lay-out, architect Jean-Manuel Rossi has preserved and espoused the natural features of the terrain. By contrast, he has done a lot of switchback work on the greens, which are generally quite large. The hazards are visible, but a number of holes, like the 2nd, 5th, 11th and 17th, are tricky little numbers and require the full range of shots. Fun to play with the family, particulary in match-play, Amnéville is a tough course for anyone to card low scores, especially beginners. Yet there so many different playing situations that can arise here that you always want to come back for more. In a region where golf courses are few and far between, this has to be the best.

Amnéville Cité Thermale

Boulevard de l'Europe
F - 57360 AMNEVILLE

Office	Secrétariat	(33) 03 87 71 30 13
Pro shop	Pro-shop	(33) 03 87 71 30 13
Fax	Fax	(33) 03 87 70 26 96
Situation	Situation	

15 km Metz, 119 590 hab. 15 km Thionville, 39 712 hab.

Annual closure	Fermeture annnuelle	oui
		25/12 → 1/01/99
Weekly closure	Fermeture hebdomadaire	
		lundi,1/11→28/02/99

Fees main season Tarifs haute saison la journée

	Week days Semaine	We/Bank holidays We/Férié
Individual Individuel	160 F	220 F
Couple Couple	320 F	440 F

Vendredi, GF + repas, 180 F

Caddy	Caddy	non
Electric Trolley	Chariot électrique	60 F/18 trous
Buggy	Voiturette	150 F/18 trous
Clubs	Clubs 1/2 série	40 F/jour

Credit cards Cartes de crédit
VISA - CB - Eurocard - MasterCard

154

Access Accès : A4 sortie Semecourt, Amnéville les Thermes → Centre touristique et thermal, → Golf
Map 4 on page 105 Carte 4 Page 105

GOLF COURSE
PARCOURS

13/20

Site	Site	▮▮▮▮▮▯▯
Maintenance	Entretien	▮▮▮▮▮▯▯
Architect	Architecte	Jean-Manuel Rossi
Type	Type	forêt
Relief	Relief	▮▮▮▮▯▯▯
Water in play	Eau en jeu	▮▮▯▯▯▯▯
Exp. to wind	Exposé au vent	▮▮▮▮▯▯▯
Trees in play	Arbres en jeu	▮▮▮▮▮▯▯

Scorecard Carte de score	Chp. Chp.	Mens Mess.	Ladies Da.
Length Long.	5985	5985	5618
Par	71	71	71

Advised golfing ability		0 12 24 36
Niveau de jeu recommandé		▮▮▮▮▮▮▯
Hcp required	Handicap exigé	carte verte

CLUB HOUSE & AMENITIES
CLUB HOUSE ET ANNEXES

6/10

Pro shop	Pro-shop	▮▮▮▮▯▯▯
Driving range	Practice	▮▮▮▮▯▯▯
Sheltered	couvert	10 places
On grass	sur herbe	non
Putting-green	putting-green	oui
Pitching-green	pitching green	oui

HOTEL FACILITIES
ENVIRONNEMENT HOTELIER

5/10

HOTELS HÔTELS

Diane	Amnéville 1 km
54 chambres, D 300 F	
Tél (33) 03 87 70 16 33, Fax (33) 03 87 72 36 72	
Orion	Amnéville 1 km
44 chambres, D 270 F	
Tél (33) 03 87 70 20 20, Fax (33) 03 87 72 36 21	
Saint-Eloi	Amnéville 1 km
36 chambres, D 300 F	
Tél (33) 03 87 70 32 62, Fax (33) 03 87 71 71 59	

RESTAURANTS RESTAURANT

La Forêt (Hôtel Diane)	Amnéville 1 km
Tél (33) 03 87 70 34 44	
Orion	Amnéville 1 km
Tél (33) 03 87 70 20 20	

Dessiné en 1988 par Frédéric Hawtree dans un domaine de 200 hectares, ce parcours est orné et défendu par de nombreux plans d'eau (pas trop en jeu) habités par une faune sauvage, ce qui amplifie l'aspect naturel voulu par l'architecte. Quelques grands arbres et des haies de bocage rythment le terrain et viennent parfois assez en jeu pour poser des problèmes aux joueurs peu précis. Les bunkers de fairway et de green ne sont pas très profonds, et disposés de manière classique : on aurait aimé un peu plus de variété de ce côté. Sans prétendre être exceptionnel, cet ensemble d'honorable facture convient à tous les niveaux, les meilleurs jouant résolument des départs arrière, où les trous proposent une belle montée en puissance jusqu'à la fin.

Designed in 1988 by Fred Hawtree in an estate of some 200 hectares, this course is enhanced and defended by countless stretches of water (which do not over-affect play) and is populated by wildlife which amplifies the natural aspect the architect was looking for. The course is dotted with a few large trees and hedges, which can cause problems for wayward hitters. The fairway bunkers are not particularly deep and are laid out in classic fashion. Indeed, a little variety would have been welcome here. Without claiming to be outstanding, this is a very decent golf course for players of all standards, the best of whom will move straight to the back-tees and enjoy the way the course gradually becomes more difficult from one hole to the next.

Anjou Golf & Country Club
Route de Cheffes
F - 49330 CHAMPIGNE

Office	Secrétariat	(33) 02 41 42 01 01
Pro shop	Pro-shop	(33) 02 41 42 01 01
Fax	Fax	(33) 02 41 42 04 37
Situation	Situation	

25 km Angers, 141 400 hab.

Annual closure	Fermeture annnuelle	non
Weekly closure	Fermeture hebdomadaire	

Fees main season
Tarifs haute saison la journée

	Week days Semaine	We/Bank holidays We/Férié
Individual Individuel	180 F	220 F
Couple Couple	360 F	440 F

Caddy	Caddy	non
Electric Trolley	Chariot électrique	non
Buggy	Voiturette	150 F/18 trous
Clubs	Clubs 1/2 série	80 F/jour

Credit cards Cartes de crédit
VISA - CB - Eurocard - MasterCard - AMEX

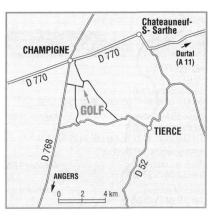

Access Accès : A11 → Angers, sortie 11 → Durtal.
D859 → Châteauneuf. D770 → Champigné, → Golf
Map 6 on page 107 Carte 6 Page 107

GOLF COURSE
PARCOURS 13/20

Site	Site	
Maintenance	Entretien	
Architect	Architecte	Frederic Hawtree
Type	Type	campagne
Relief	Relief	
Water in play	Eau en jeu	
Exp. to wind	Exposé au vent	
Trees in play	Arbres en jeu	

Scorecard Carte de score	Chp. Chp.	Mens Mess.	Ladies Da.
Length Long.	6227	5979	5241
Par	72	72	72

Advised golfing ability	0	12	24	36
Niveau de jeu recommandé				
Hcp required	Handicap exigé	35		

CLUB HOUSE & AMENITIES
CLUB HOUSE ET ANNEXES 6/10

Pro shop	Pro-shop	
Driving range	Practice	
Sheltered	couvert	6 places
On grass	sur herbe	non
Putting-green	putting-green	oui
Pitching-green	pitching green	non

155

HOTEL FACILITIES
ENVIRONNEMENT HOTELIER 6/10

HOTELS HÔTELS
Appartements du Golf   sur place
8 chambres, D 500 F
Tél (33) 02 41 42 01 01, Fax (33) 02 41 42 04 37

Hôtel des Voyageurs ***   Le Lion d'Angers 6 km
14 chambres, D 400 F
Tél (33) 02 41 95 81 81, Fax (33) 02 41 95 84 80

Château de Noirieux ****   Briollay 16 km
19 chambres, D 1 000 F
Tél (33) 02 41 42 50 05, Fax (33) 02 41 37 91 00

RESTAURANTS RESTAURANT
Château de Noirieux   Briollay 16 km
Tél (33) 02 41 42 50 05

13	6	5

A l'exception des trois premiers trous, ce parcours ouvert en 1988 est situé dans le parc d'un petit château, clos de hauts murs, ce qui garantit une atmosphère très calme. Sa longueur reste raisonnable et son relief modéré, ce qui permet de le jouer sans grande fatigue. L'eau vient en jeu sur une demi-douzaine de trous (étangs, ruisseau, fossés), mais essentiellement sur le 11 et le 15. Les greens ne sont pas très grands, ce qui exige un jeu de fers assez exact, mais permet de ne pas craindre les 3-putts toujours vexants, une fois que l'on y est en sécurité. Quelques beaux arbres (notamment des cyprès bleus) et un bon placement des bunkers amènent à recommander de faire attention pour préserver un bon score : les longs frappeurs se feront souvent dominer par les bons joueurs de fers. Mais tous les niveaux de jeu peuvent cohabiter ici.

With the exception of the first three holes, this 1988 course is laid out in the grounds of a small castle surrounded by high walls, so you couldn't hope for a more tranquil atmosphere. Length is reasonable and the course none too hilly, so you can walk it very easily. Water comes into play on half a dozen holes (lakes, a stream and ditches), but is basically dangerous on the 11th and 15th. The greens are not large, so accurate ironwork is a must. But once home on the green, you have less chance of recording those irksome 3-putts. A few beautiful trees (notably some fine blue cypress) and astutely-placed bunkers keep golfers on their toes if they want to hold their score down. Long-hitters will probably be outplayed here by good iron players, but all in all, this is a course for all types of player.

Golf Annonay-Gourdan

Saint-Clair
F - 07430 SAINT-CLAIR-ANNONAY

Office	Secrétariat	(33) 04 75 67 03 84
Pro shop	Pro-shop	(33) 04 75 67 03 84
Fax	Fax	(33) 04 75 67 79 50
Situation	Situation	

81 km Lyon, 413 090 hab.
40 km Saint-Etienne, 201 570 hab.

Annual closure	Fermeture annnuelle	non
Weekly closure	Fermeture hebdomadaire	

Fees main season
Tarifs haute saison le parcours

	Week days Semaine	We/Bank holidays We/Férié
Individual Individuel	180 F	230 F
Couple Couple	360 F	460 F

Caddy	Caddy	non
Electric Trolley	Chariot électrique	70 F/18 trous
Buggy	Voiturette	200 F/18 trous
Clubs	Clubs 1/2 série	70 F/18 trous

Credit cards Cartes de crédit
VISA - CB - Eurocard - MasterCard

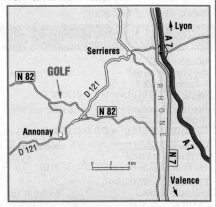

Access Accès : A7 Lyon - Valence, sortie Chanas,
→ Annonay, N82 → Saint-Etienne
Map 11 on page 118 Carte 11 Page 118

GOLF COURSE
PARCOURS

13/20

Site	Site			
Maintenance	Entretien			
Architect	Architecte	Thierry Sprecher Géry Watine		
Type	Type	parc		
Relief	Relief			
Water in play	Eau en jeu			
Exp. to wind	Exposé au vent			
Trees in play	Arbres en jeu			

Scorecard Carte de score	Chp. Chp.	Mens Mess.	Ladies Da.
Length Long.	5900	5557	5252
Par	72	72	72

Advised golfing ability Niveau de jeu recommandé	0	12	24	36
Hcp required Handicap exigé	non			

CLUB HOUSE & AMENITIES
CLUB HOUSE ET ANNEXES

6/10

Pro shop	Pro-shop	
Driving range	Practice	
Sheltered	couvert	6 places
On grass	sur herbe	oui
Putting-green	putting-green	oui
Pitching-green	pitching green	oui

HOTEL FACILITIES
ENVIRONNEMENT HOTELIER

5/10

HOTELS HÔTELS
Hôtel d'Ay ★★★   sur place
35 chambres, D 400 F
Tél (33) 04 75 67 01 00, Fax (33) 04 75 67 07 38

Hôtel du Midi ★★   Annonay 4 km
40 chambres, D 250 F
Tél (33) 04 75 33 23 77, Fax (33) 04 75 33 02 43

RESTAURANTS RESTAURANT
Marc et Christine   Annonay 4 km
Tél (33) 04 75 33 46 97

La Halle   Annonay 4 km
Tél (33) 04 75 32 04 62

156

APREMONT

15	8	6

Même si l'on pense toujours que le parcours aurait pu faire l'objet d'un investissement aussi important que le luxueux Club house, son entretien remarquable est un point fort. Conçu par John Jacobs, il reste très agréable à parcourir, avec 14 trous en forêt d'Halatte et les autres organisés autour de pièces d'eau. L'ensemble est plat, facile à marcher avec les départs très proches des greens. Certes, le dessin de John Jacobs ne propose pas de grands chocs visuels, la stratégie de jeu est assez évidente, mais faute d'affrontements épiques avec le parcours, on appréciera le silence des lieux et la majesté du cadre. Apremont n'a sans doute pas droit à l'appellation de chef-d'oeuvre, dans la mesure où les meilleurs golfeurs trouveront ses défis techniques un peu modestes, mais la majorité des joueurs y passeront une bonne journée, et pourront espérer "tourner" dans leur handicap.

Even though we still feel the course could have benefited from the same investment that was obviously given to the luxurious club-house, remarkable upkeep and green-keeping are definitely the club's forte. Designed by John Jacobs, this is a very pleasant course to play, with 14 holes in the forest of Halatte and the others laid out around lakes. The whole course is flat, with very little distance between green and next tee. There is nothing strikingly visual about this layout, and game strategy is pretty obvious, but in the absence of epic confrontation with the course, players will enjoy the silence and the majestic setting. Apremont could never really claim the label of golfing masterpiece in that the better player will find the technical challenge within easy reach, but most players spend a good day's golfing here and can hold out hopes of playing to their handicap.

Apremont Golf-Club
F - 60300 APREMONT

Office	Secrétariat	(33) 03 44 25 61 11
Pro shop	Pro-shop	(33) 03 44 25 61 11
Fax	Fax	(33) 03 44 25 11 72
Situation	Situation	

6 km Chantilly, 11 340 hab. 7 km Senlis, 14 430 hab.

Annual closure	Fermeture annnuelle	non
Weekly closure	Fermeture hebdomadaire	lundi
		1/10→31/03/99

Fees main season
Tarifs haute saison la journée

	Week days Semaine	We/Bank holidays We/Férié
Individual Individuel	250 F	480 F
Couple Couple	480 F	720 F

Lundi 200 F.

Caddy	Caddy	non
Electric Trolley	Chariot électrique	70 F/jour
Buggy	Voiturette	180 F/18 trous
Clubs	Clubs série	120 F/jour

Credit cards Cartes de crédit
VISA - CB - Eurocard - MasterCard - AMEX - JCB

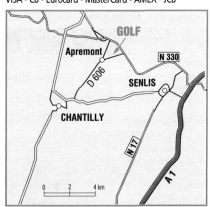

GOLF
Apremont
N 330
D 606
SENLIS
CHANTILLY
N 17
A 1
0   2   4 km

Access Accès : A1 Paris → Lille, sortie 8 Senlis-Creil.
N 330 → Creil. 7 km. de Senlis, → Apremont
à gauche. **Map 1 on page 98** Carte 1 Page 98

GOLF COURSE
PARCOURS   **15**/20

Site	Site	▬▬▬▬▬▬▭
Maintenance	Entretien	▬▬▬▬▬▬▬
Architect	Architecte	John Jacobs
Type	Type	forêt, parc
Relief	Relief	▬▭▭▭▭▭▭
Water in play	Eau en jeu	▬▬▭▭▭▭▭
Exp. to wind	Exposé au vent	▬▭▭▭▭▭▭
Trees in play	Arbres en jeu	▬▬▬▬▬▭▭

Scorecard Carte de score	Chp. Chp.	Mens Mess.	Ladies Da.
Length Long.	6436	5843	5395
Par	72	72	72

Advised golfing ability		0	12	24	36
Niveau de jeu recommandé			▬▬▬▬▬▬		
Hcp required	Handicap exigé	non			

CLUB HOUSE & AMENITIES
CLUB HOUSE ET ANNEXES   **8**/10

Pro shop	Pro-shop	▬▬▬▭▭▭▭
Driving range	Practice	▬▬▬▬▭▭▭
Sheltered	couvert	non
On grass	sur herbe	non
Putting-green	putting-green	oui
Pitching-green	pitching green	non

HOTEL FACILITIES
ENVIRONNEMENT HOTELIER   **6**/10

HOTELS HÔTELS
Golf Hôtel ★★★★   Domaine de Chantilly 4 km
111 chambres, D 820 F
Tél (33) 03 44 58 47 77, Fax (33) 03 44 58 50 11

Château Hôtel Mont-Royal ★★★★   La Chapelle-en-Serval
100 chambres, D 1 000 FF   15 km
Tél (33) 03 44 54 50 50, Fax (33) 03 44 54 50 20

Château de la Tour   Gouvieux 8 km
41 chambres, D 890 F
Tél (33) 03 44 57 07 39, Fax (33) 03 44 57 31 97

RESTAURANTS RESTAURANT
Restaurant du golf   Apremont
Tél (33) 03 44 25 61 11   sur place

Relais du Coq Chantant   Chantilly 6 km
Tél (33) 03 44 57 01 28

157

ARCACHON ✹ | 13 | 6 | 6

Depuis longtemps, c'est le golf des Bordelais en week-end, et des vacanciers du Pyla. Que l'on n'attende donc pas un parcours très moderne ni audacieux. En pays de vieille tradition britannique, les architectes Blandford et Pierre Hirigoyen ont dessiné un parcours sans grands éclats, épousant sans trop le bousculer un terrain accidenté à l'aller, et plus plat au retour. Avec le relief, l'approche de certains greens surélevés n'est pas toujours simple ; les fairways souvent étroits, bien défendus par les arbres, imposent de placer les coups de départ, quitte à laisser le driver dans le sac. Mais le parcours est assez court, et la précision plus souvent récompensée que la longueur. Avec les travaux de drainage sur la partie basse du parcours, il est jouable toute l'année. Les non-golfeurs de la famille trouveront de nombreuses activités dans la station balnéaire d'Arcachon, en haute saison. Le Club-House est placé au sommet de cet ensemble, l'ambiance est familiale et amicale.

This has long been the traditional week-end course for the good folk of Bordeaux and holiday-makers at Pylat, so don't expect a modern or bold layout here. In a region of British tradition, architects Blandford and Pierre Hirigoyen laid out a subdued course which embraces but never disrupts the hilly terrain on the front nine and the flatter holes around the back. The broken relief means that the second shot to a number of elevated greens is not always easy. And a few tight fairways, well-defended by trees, require a well-placed tee-shot, even if that means leaving the driver in the bag. But the course is short, and precision is more often better rewarded than length off the tee. With the lower section of the course now fitted with a drainage system, Arcachon is playable all year. Non-golfers in the family will find lots to do in the seaside resort of Arcachon in summer, while the club-house overlooking the course offers a friendly family atmosphere.

Golf d'Arcachon
35, boulevard d'Arcachon
F - 33260 LA TESTE

Office	Secrétariat	(33) 05 56 54 44 00
Pro shop	Pro-shop	(33) 05 57 52 62 83
Fax	Fax	(33) 05 56 66 86 32
Situation	Situation	
3 km Arcachon, 11 770 hab.		
Annual closure	Fermeture annnuelle	non
Weekly closure	Fermeture hebdomadaire	

Fees main season
Tarifs haute saison la journée

	Week days Semaine	We/Bank holidays We/Férié
Individual Individuel	270 F	270 F
Couple Couple	460 F	460 F

Caddy	Caddy	non
Electric Trolley	Chariot électrique	non
Buggy	Voiturette	160 F/18 trous
Clubs	Clubs 1/2 série	50 F/jour

Credit cards Cartes de crédit
VISA - CB- Eurocard - MasterCard - AMEX

Bassin d'Arcachon

ARCACHON

GOLF

Cap Ferret

Pyla-sur-mer

La Teste | N 250

Pilat-Plage

D 106

D 218

0   2   4 km

Access Accès : N250 → La Teste → Pyla-sur-Mer
Map 9 on page 115 Carte 9 Page 115

GOLF COURSE
PARCOURS   13/20

Site	Site	
Maintenance	Entretien	
Architect	Architecte	Cecil R. Blandford Pierre Hirigoyen
Type	Type	bord de mer, vallon
Relief	Relief	
Water in play	Eau en jeu	
Exp. to wind	Exposé au vent	
Trees in play	Arbres en jeu	

Scorecard Carte de score	Chp. Chp.	Mens Mess.	Ladies Da.
Length Long.	5953	5746	5065
Par	72	72	72

Advised golfing ability		0	12	24	36
Niveau de jeu recommandé					
Hcp required	Handicap exigé	35 (été)			

CLUB HOUSE & AMENITIES
CLUB HOUSE ET ANNEXES   6/10

Pro shop	Pro-shop	
Driving range	Practice	
Sheltered	couvert	6 places
On grass	sur herbe	non
Putting-green	putting-green	oui
Pitching-green	pitching green	oui

HOTEL FACILITIES
ENVIRONNEMENT HOTELIER   6/10

HOTELS HÔTELS
Séminaris ***   Arcachon 3 km
19 chambres, D 630 F
Tél (33) 05 56 83 25 87, Fax (33) 05 57 52 22 41

Deganne ***   Arcachon 3 km
57 chambres, D 900 F
Tél (33) 05 56 83 99 91, Fax (33) 05 56 83 87 92

Grand Hôtel Richelieu ***   Arcachon 3 km
43 chambres, D 700 F
Tél (33) 05 56 83 16 50, Fax (33) 05 56 83 47 78

Le Parc   Arcachon 3 km
30 chambres, D 570 F
Tél (33) 05 56 83 10 58, Fax (33) 05 56 54 05 30

RESTAURANTS RESTAURANT
L'Ombrière   Arcachon 3 km
Tél (33) 05 56 83 01 48

158

Le site offre de jolies vues sur la campagne basque et les Pyrénées, avec un bon rythme entre les trous dégagés et les trous boisés. Il a fallu beaucoup modifier le terrain accidenté pour le rendre jouable, mais de nombreux dévers et pentes étaient inévitables, et peuvent entraîner des coups délicats : il faut savoir jouer des balles à effets. Pour cela, on ne le conseillera pas aux débutants, ni aux seniors, à moins de jouer en voiturette. Comme souvent avec l'architecte Ronald Fream, les bunkers et les greens sont très travaillés et bien en jeu, mais c'est logique pour un parcours aassez court : vive la précision... Et aussi un peu la chance, car la franchise n'est pas le point fort de ce dessin. Ce golf très technique doit être reconnu avant d'espérer un bon score, il offre des caractéristiques bien différentes des autres parcours de la région.

The setting provides beautiful views over the Basque countryside and the Pyrenees, and there is a nice balance between woodland holes and holes through open country. A lot of earth was moved to make this once rugged landscape into a playable course, but inevitably slopes and hills still remain and can lead to some tricky shots. Being able to flight the ball is more of an advantage than usual. For this reason we would not recommend Arcangues to beginners or to seniors, unless on wheels. As is often the case with Ronald Fream, the bunkers and greens have been given a lot of careful thought, which is only logical for a course as short as this. The watchword here is precision play... with perhaps a bit of luck thrown in, as the layout is not as forthright as it might be. Arcangues is a very technical course that needs a little reconnaissance work before hoping to card a good score. And its features are very different from the other courses in the region.

Golf d'Arcangues
Club House
F - 64200 ARCANGUES

Office	Secrétariat	(33) 05 59 43 10 56
Pro shop	Pro-shop	(33) 05 59 43 10 56
Fax	Fax	(33) 05 59 43 12 60
Situation	Situation	

6 km Biarritz, 28 740 hab.
10 km Bayonne, 40 050 hab.

Annual closure	Fermeture annnuelle	non
Weekly closure	Fermeture hebdomadaire	lundi
		30/10→1/03/99

Fees main season
Tarifs haute saison le parcours

	Week days Semaine	We/Bank holidays We/Férié
Individual Individuel	300 F	300 F
Couple Couple	500 F	500 F

Caddy	Caddy	non
Electric Trolley	Chariot électrique	non
Buggy	Voiturette	150 F/18 trous
Clubs	Clubs 1/2 série	60 F

Credit cards Cartes de crédit
VISA - CB - Eurocard - MasterCard

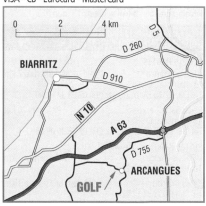

Access Accès : Biarritz, La Négresse → Arcangues
Map 12 on page 120 Carte 12 Page 120

GOLF COURSE
PARCOURS
14/20

Site	Site	▰▰▰▰▰▱
Maintenance	Entretien	▰▰▰▰▰▰
Architect	Architecte	Ronald Fream
Type	Type	vallon
Relief	Relief	▰▰▰▰▱▱
Water in play	Eau en jeu	▰▱▱▱▱▱
Exp. to wind	Exposé au vent	▰▰▱▱▱▱
Trees in play	Arbres en jeu	▰▰▰▱▱▱

Scorecard Carte de score	Chp. Chp.	Mens Mess.	Ladies Da.
Length Long.	6092	5687	5243
Par	72	72	72

Advised golfing ability		0	12	24	36
Niveau de jeu recommandé		▰▰▰▰▱			
Hcp required	Handicap exigé	35			

CLUB HOUSE & AMENITIES
CLUB HOUSE ET ANNEXES
7/10

Pro shop	Pro-shop	▰▰▰▰▰▱
Driving range	Practice	
Sheltered	couvert	5 places
On grass	sur herbe	oui
Putting-green	putting-green	oui
Pitching-green	pitching green	oui

159

HOTEL FACILITIES
ENVIRONNEMENT HOTELIER
8/10

HOTELS HÔTELS
Le Palais ★★★★ — Biarritz 6 km
156 chambres, D 1 800 F
Tél (33) 05 59 41 64 00, Fax (33) 05 59 41 67 99

Château de Brindos ★★★★ — Anglet 8 km
12 chambres, D 1300 F
Tél (33) 05 59 23 17 68, Fax (33) 05 59 23 48 47

Hôtel Laminak ★★★ — Arbonne 4 km
10 chambres, D 560 F
Tél (33) 05 59 41 95 40, Fax (33) 05 59 41 87 65

RESTAURANTS RESTAURANT
Auberge d'Achtal — Arcangues
Tél (33) 05 59 43 05 56

Les Platanes — Biarritz 6 km
Tél(33) 05 59 23 13 68

Pas très long, et bien accidenté, ce nouveau parcours bénéficie d'un bel environnement forestier, et de la présence d'un château du XVIIème siècle, qui devrait être aménagé bientôt en Club house. Pour l'instant, les installations sont très sommaires. A côté de très jolis trous, certains autres sont fort contestables, notamment un par 5 et quelques par 3 où des arbres empiètent fortement sur la ligne de jeu. On doit aussi signaler la présence de quelques greens aveugles, qui ne sont pas très "golfiques", obligent non seulement à bien connaître le parcours mais aussi la position des drapeaux. Un dernier regret : la difficulté excessive du 18, qui laisse sur une impression mitigée. La beauté du cadre et les promesses du lieu incitent à conseiller une visite, mais le manque de franchise du parcours et son entretien très moyen nous incitent à réserver notre jugement définitif.

Not very long and rather hilly, this new course lies in a beautiful setting of forest enhanced by a 17th century castle, shortly due to be refurbished to form the club-house. For the time being, facilities are pretty basic. Alongside some very pretty holes, others are very questionable, notably one par 5 and a few par 3s, where trees come right into the firing line. There are also a few blind greens, which do not make for good golf and which require prior knowledge of the course and the pin-position. Our last little regret is the excessively difficult 18th hole, which leaves the golfer with a mixed impression of the course as a whole. The beauty and promise of the setting and site make this a visit we would recommend, but with the course's lack of fairness and only very average upkeep, we feel we should reserve final judgment.

Golf du Château d'Augerville

Place du Château
F - 45330 AUGERVILLE-LA-RIVIERE

Office	Secrétariat	(33) 02 38 32 12 07
Pro shop	Pro-shop	(33) 02 38 32 12 07
Fax	Fax	(33) 02 38 32 12 15
Situation	Situation	

25 km Nemours, 12 075 hab.
20 km Pithiviers, 9 327 hab.

Annual closure	Fermeture annnuelle	non
Weekly closure	Fermeture hebdomadaire	

Fees main season
Tarifs haute saison la journée

	Week days Semaine	We/Bank holidays We/Férié
Individual Individuel	200 F	300 F
Couple Couple	400 F	600 F

Caddy	Caddy	non
Electric Trolley	Chariot électrique	non
Buggy	Voiturette	180 F/18 trous
Clubs	Clubs	gratuit

Credit cards Cartes de crédit
VISA - CB - Eurocard - MasterCard

160

```
        0    2    4 km        La Chapelle-
                              la-Reine
                              (A 6 à 16 km) →

                              N 152
    MALESHERBES
         ○
  N 152                   D 410
      Boulancourt
  Augerville-la-Rivière ○
                              Puiseaux
         GOLF
```

Access Accès : A6 sortie Ury, N152 → Malesherbes,
D958 → Puiseaux, → Golf
Map 3 on page 102 Carte 3 Page 102

GOLF COURSE
PARCOURS   13/20

Site	Site	▬
Maintenance	Entretien	▬
Architect	Architecte	Olivier Dongradi
Type	Type	forêt, vallon
Relief	Relief	▬
Water in play	Eau en jeu	▬
Exp. to wind	Exposé au vent	▬
Trees in play	Arbres en jeu	▬

Scorecard Carte de score	Chp. Chp.	Mens Mess.	Ladies Da.
Length Long.	6268	5466	4699
Par	72	72	72

Advised golfing ability Niveau de jeu recommandé	0	12	24	36
Hcp required Handicap exigé	35 (We)			

CLUB HOUSE & AMENITIES
CLUB HOUSE ET ANNEXES   5/10

Pro shop	Pro-shop	▬
Driving range	Practice	▬
Sheltered	couvert	non
On grass	sur herbe	oui
Putting-green	putting-green	oui
Pitching-green	pitching green	non

HOTEL FACILITIES
ENVIRONNEMENT HOTELIER   4/10

HOTELS HÔTELS
L'Ecu de France **   Malesherbes 7 km
13 chambres, D 250 F
Tél (33) 02 38 34 87 25, Fax (33) 02 38 34 68 99

Relais Saint Georges   Pithiviers 20 km
42 chambres, D 350 F
Tél (33) 02 38 30 40 25, Fax (33) 02 38 30 09 05

RESTAURANTS RESTAURANT
L'Ecu de France   Malesherbes 7 km
Tél (33) 02 38 34 87 25

Relais Briardis   Briarres-sur-Essonne 3 km
Tél (33) 02 38 32 11 22

BADEN

	15	6	5

Sans être un véritable links, Baden est un excellent parcours de bord de mer, dominant l'estuaire de la rivière d'Auray. Seuls quelques trous sont vraiment tracés dans les pins, mais on n'a jamais l'impression de monotonie, étant donnée la variété du tracé. Les reliefs du terrain, les arbustes, une végétation assez sauvage, quelques arbres isolés, et le dessin d'Yves Bureau en font un lieu de charme pour les yeux, et pour le jeu. Sans être d'une difficulté extrême, il offre aux meilleurs joueurs un défi constant, parfois rehaussé par le vent, tout en permettant aux joueurs moyens et même aux novices de passer une journée agréable. Un morceau de choix dans une région bien équipée en golfs. L'entretien y est correct, mais le Club house n'est pas vraiment à la hauteur.

While not a real links, Baden is an excellent seaside course overlooking the estuary of the river Auray. Only a few holes are laid out really amongst the pine-trees, but given the variety, the course is never boring. The sloping terrain, bushes, wild-growing vegetation, a few isolated trees and the layout of Yves Bureau make this a charming course both to look at and play. Although not over-difficult, the challenge to the better player never eases and is sometimes made tougher when the wind gets up. At the same time, high-handicappers and even beginners can enjoy a good day out. A choice venue in a region well-endowed with golf courses. Upkeep is good but the club-house not quite up to scratch.

Golf de Baden

Kernic
F - 56870 BADEN

Office	Secrétariat	(33) 02 97 57 18 96
Pro shop	Pro-shop	(33) 02 97 57 18 96
Fax	Fax	(33) 02 97 57 22 05
Situation	Situation	

8 km Auray, 10 320 hab.
13 km Vannes, 45 640 hab.

Annual closure	Fermeture annnuelle	non
Weekly closure	Fermeture hebdomadaire	

Fees main season
Tarifs haute saison la journée

	Week days Semaine	We/Bank holidays We/Férié
Individual Individuel	250 F	250 F
Couple Couple	500 F	500 F

Caddy	Caddy	non
Electric Trolley	Chariot électrique	60 F/18 trous
Buggy	Voiturette	150 F/18 trous
Clubs	Clubs 1/2 série	50 F/18 trous

Credit cards Cartes de crédit
VISA - CB - Eurocard - MasterCard

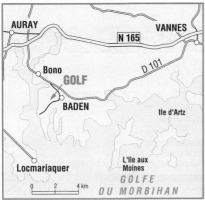

Access Accès : N165 → Le Bono, → Baden, Golf
Map 5 on page 107 Carte 5 Page 107

GOLF COURSE
PARCOURS
15 /20

Site	Site	
Maintenance	Entretien	
Architect	Architecte	Yves Bureau
Type	Type	bord de mer
Relief	Relief	
Water in play	Eau en jeu	
Exp. to wind	Exposé au vent	
Trees in play	Arbres en jeu	

Scorecard Carte de score	Chp. Chp.	Mens Mess.	Ladies Da.
Length Long.	6110	5761	5235
Par	72	72	72

Advised golfing ability Niveau de jeu recommandé	0	12	24	36
Hcp required Handicap exigé	35			

CLUB HOUSE & AMENITIES
CLUB HOUSE ET ANNEXES
6 /10

Pro shop	Pro-shop	
Driving range	Practice	
Sheltered	couvert	non
On grass	sur herbe	oui
Putting-green	putting-green	oui
Pitching-green	pitching green	oui

161

HOTEL FACILITIES
ENVIRONNEMENT HOTELIER
5 /10

HOTELS HÔTELS
Hostellerie Abbatiale *** — Le Bono 3 km
71 chambres, D 600 F
Tél (33) 02 97 57 84 00, Fax (33) 02 97 57 83 00

Le Gavrinis — Toulbroch 2 km
19 chambres, D 450 F
Tél (33) 02 97 57 00 82, Fax (33) 02 97 57 09 47

Auberge du Forban ** — Le Bono 3 km
21 chambres, D 300 F
Tél (33) 02 97 57 88 65, Fax (33) 02 97 57 92 76

RESTAURANTS RESTAURANT
Régis Mahé — Vannes 13 km
Tél (33) 02 97 42 61 41

Le Pressoir — Vannes13 km
Tél (33) 02 97 60 87 63

Dans un très beau site de campagne et de bois, ce parcours est une sorte d'enclave suisse en France. Dessiné par l'architecte allemand von Limburger, il est assez long, et quelques reliefs accentués obligent à réfléchir sur les choix de club. Sans présenter de caractère très original sur le plan visuel, c'est un parcours stratégique intelligent, avec des obstacles bien visibles, mais pas excessivement dangereux (sauf les arbres). Ces difficultés raisonnables amènent à le conseiller à tous les niveaux de joueurs classés, dans la mesure où ils pourront attaquer les greens, largement ouverts, en faisant rouler la balle. Mais pour jouer son handicap, il vaut mieux savoir faire des balles à effet. La deuxième partie du parcours, la plus boisée, est techniquement la plus intéressante. A connaître.

In a beautiful setting of countryside and woodland, this course is a sort of a Swiss enclave in France. Laid out by German architect von Limburger, it is longish and a few hilly mounds call for care when choosing the club to play. Although visually speaking the course is nothing to write home about, it is a strategically intelligent layout, with clearly visible but not excessively dangerous hazards (except the trees). We would therefore recommend it to high-handicappers and better, especially since the greens are wide open and reachable with easier chip shots. Being able to move the ball both ways (deliberately) will definitely be helpful for players looking to play to their handicap. The second part of the course, where the woods are thicker, is technically speaking the most interesting. Worth getting to know.

Golf & Country Club de Bâle

Route de Wentzwiller
F - 68220 HAGENTHAL-LE-BAS

Office	Secrétariat	(33) 03 89 68 50 91
Pro shop	Pro-shop	(33) 03 89 68 51 61
Fax	Fax	(33) 03 89 68 55 66
Situation	Situation	

9 km Bâle, 171 000 hab.

Annual closure	Fermeture annnuelle	non
Weekly closure	Fermeture hebdomadaire	

Fees main season
Tarifs haute saison la journée

	Week days Semaine	We/Bank holidays We/Férié
Individual Individuel	320 F	360 F
Couple Couple	640 F	720 F

Caddy	Caddy	non
Electric Trolley	Chariot électrique	60 F/18 trous
Buggy	Voiturette	non
Clubs	Clubs la série	80 F/jour

Credit cards   Cartes de crédit
VISA - CB - Eurocard - MasterCard

Access Accès : • Mulhouse A35 sortie Saint-Louis, → Aéroport, D473 → Hesingue, → Folgensbourg, D16 → Hagenthal. • Bâle → Hegenheim. • Belfort D419 → Bâle **Map 8 on page 113** Carte 8 Page 113

GOLF COURSE / PARCOURS   15/20

Site	Site	
Maintenance	Entretien	
Architect	Architecte	B. von Limburger
Type	Type	forêt, campagne
Relief	Relief	
Water in play	Eau en jeu	
Exp. to wind	Exposé au vent	
Trees in play	Arbres en jeu	

Scorecard Carte de score	Chp. Chp.	Mens Mess.	Ladies Da.
Length Long.	6255	5938	5497
Par	72	72	72

Advised golfing ability   0   12   24   36
Niveau de jeu recommandé
Hcp required   Handicap exigé   32

CLUB HOUSE & AMENITIES / CLUB HOUSE ET ANNEXES   7/10

Pro shop	Pro-shop	
Driving range	Practice	
Sheltered	couvert	5 places
On grass	sur herbe	non
Putting-green	putting-green	oui
Pitching-green	pitching green	oui

HOTEL FACILITIES / ENVIRONNEMENT HOTELIER   7/10

HOTELS HÔTELS
Jenny ***   Hagenthal 1 km
26 chambres, D 490 F
Tél (33) 03 89 68 50 09, Fax (33) 03 89 68 58 64
Trois Rois *****   Bâle 9 km
98 chambres, D 450 CHF
Tél (41) 061 - 261 52 52, Fax (41) 061 - 261 21 53
Merian *****   Bâle 9 km
65 chambres, D 290 CHF
Tél (41) 061 - 681 00 00, Fax (41) 061 - 681 11 01

RESTAURANTS RESTAURANT
Jenny   Hagenthal-le-Bas 1 km
Tél (33) 03 89 68 50 09
Ancienne Forge   Hagenthal-le-Haut 1 km
Tél (33) 03 89 68 56 10
Stucki   Bâle 9 km
Tél (41) 061 - 361 82 22

162

BARBAROUX

Un parcours controversé, notamment par son style composite, comme s'il s'agissait d'un catalogue : on a l'impression de se trouver successivement en Irlande, en Ecosse, aux Etats-Unis. Mais le paysage sauvage de Provence modère ce manque d'unité. Barbaroux est une succession de tests dont il serait vain de vouloir décrire tous les détails. Les mouvements de terrain créés par Pete et P.B. Dye, le dessin des bunkers et des greens constituent non seulement un spectacle permanent, mais aussi une série de difficultés que bien peu sauront maîtriser. Ici, la première qualité est de savoir accepter que l'on ne fait pas toujours un bon score avec du bon jeu, bref, savoir accepter d'être battu par un grand parcours, pas trop fréquenté. L'inversion pratique de l'aller et du retour a un peu diminué l'impact du finale originel. Quand l'entretien est à la hauteur, ce parcours est une expérience à vivre.

A controversial course, primarily because of its contrasting styles, the impression here is one of a mail-order catalogue for world golf-courses; one minute you feel you could be in Ireland, the next in Scotland and the next in the United States. Yet the wild Provence landscape tempers any lack of unity, making Barbaroux a succession of ordeals, all the details of which can hardly be described here. The contoured fariways, created by Pete and P.B. Dye, and the design of the greens and bunkers make not only for a never-ending spectacle but also for a series of difficulties that few golfers will find easy to master. Here, lesson number one is admitting that good play does not always end up as a good score, in other words accepting defeat at the hands of a great course that is never too crowded. The convenient reversal of the front and back nine has diminished somewhat the impact of the course's original "grand finale". When green-keeping is up to standard, this is an essential golfing experience.

Golf Club de Barbaroux
Route de Cabasse
F - 83170 BRIGNOLES

Office	Secrétariat	(33) 04 94 69 63 63
Pro shop	Pro-shop	(33) 04 94 69 63 63
Fax	Fax	(33) 04 94 59 00 93
Situation	Situation	

9 km Brignoles, 11 240 hab.

Annual closure	Fermeture annnuelle	non
Weekly closure	Fermeture hebdomadaire	

Fees main season
Tarifs haute saison le parcours

	Week days Semaine	We/Bank holidays We/Férié
Individual Individuel	260 F	260 F
Couple Couple	520 F	520 F

Seniors : mercredi, 2 GF + voiture: 500 F

Caddy	Caddy	sur réservation
Electric Trolley	Chariot électrique	non
Buggy	Voiturette	200 F/18 trous
Clubs	Clubs 1/2 série	60 F/jour

Credit cards Cartes de crédit
VISA - CB - Eurocard - MasterCard - AMEX

Access Accès : A8 Toulon-Cannes, sortie Brignoles, N7 → Flassans, Le Luc. 1,5 km, à gauche D79 → La Cabane
Map 14 on page 124 Carte 14 Page 124

GOLF COURSE
PARCOURS
17 /20

Site	Site	
Maintenance	Entretien	
Architect	Architecte	Pete & P.B. Dye
Type	Type	vallons, links
Relief	Relief	
Water in play	Eau en jeu	
Exp. to wind	Exposé au vent	
Trees in play	Arbres en jeu	

Scorecard Carte de score	Chp. Chp.	Mens Mess.	Ladies Da.
Length Long.	6124	5653	5168
Par	72	72	72

Advised golfing ability		0 12 24 36
Niveau de jeu recommandé		
Hcp required	Handicap exigé	non

CLUB HOUSE & AMENITIES
CLUB HOUSE ET ANNEXES
7 /10

Pro shop	Pro-shop	
Driving range	Practice	
Sheltered	couvert	non
On grass	sur herbe	oui
Putting-green	putting-green	oui
Pitching-green	pitching green	oui

HOTEL FACILITIES
ENVIRONNEMENT HOTELIER
6 /10

HOTELS HÔTELS
Golf de Barbaroux ***   sur place
24 chambres, D 460 F
Tél (33) 04 94 69 63 63, Fax (33) 04 94 59 00 93

La Grillade au feu de bois   Flassans-sur-Issole 8 km
16 chambres, D 800 F
Tél (33) 04 94 69 71 20, Fax (33) 04 94 59 66 11

RESTAURANTS RESTAURANT
Le Lingousto   Cuers 25 km
Tél (33) 04 94 28 69 10

163

Neuf des 18 trous originaux dessinés par Alliss et Thomas en 1978 ont été conservés, les neuf autres ont été séparés pour constituer un parcours de par 35. Pour compléter le "grand" parcours, Michel Gayon a tracé neuf trous supplémentaires, plus proches de la campagne que d'un parc, quant au paysage et même au jeu. Ils sont intercalés entre le 4 et le 14, ce qui rompt la monotonie des allers et retours d'autrefois (les anciens 10 à 16). Bien sûr, le manque d'unité de style est flagrant, mais le plaisir d'évoluer dans la campagne de La Baule reste intact. Tout aussi stratégiques que les autres, les "greens et bunkers Gayon" sont dessinés avec plus d'attention et de relief (à remarquer le double green des 5 et 12), et l'on pourrait souhaiter que l'architecte retravaille les neuf trous originaux afin de donner plus d'harmonie à cet ensemble bien organisé pour passer des vacances. La Baule passera bientôt à 36 trous.

Nine of the original 18 holes designed by Alliss and Thomas in 1978 have been retained, while the other nine now form a separate par 35 course. To complete the main course, Michel Gayon designed nine additional holes, which are more country than parkland in terms of landscape and the way they play. The new holes have been inserted between the 4th and the 14th, and so break up the monotony of the earlier up and down holes (formerly holes 10 to 16). Obviously, there is a clear lack of unity in style, but the pleasure of walking La Baule countryside is as great as ever. As strategic as on the other holes, the "Gayon" greens and bunkers have been more carefully designed, with sharper relief (note the double green shared by the 5th and 12th holes). Hopefully the architect will redesign the nine original holes to create a more harmonious feel to this course, which is nicely organised for holiday-makers. Nine more holes are under construction.

Golf de La Baule

Domaine de Saint-Denac
F - 44117 SAINT-ANDRE-DES-EAUX

Office	Secrétariat	(33) 02 40 60 46 18
Pro shop	Pro-shop	(33) 02 40 60 46 18
Fax	Fax	(33) 02 40 60 41 41
Situation	Situation	

12 km St-Nazaire, 64 810 hab.
7 km La Baule, 14 850 hab.

Annual closure	Fermeture annnuelle	non
Weekly closure	Fermeture hebdomadaire	mardi
		1/11→31/03/99

Fees main season
Tarifs haute saison la journée

	Week days Semaine	We/Bank holidays We/Férié
Individual Individuel	320 F	320 F
Couple Couple	640 F	640 F
Caddy	Caddy	non
Electric Trolley	Chariot électrique	non
Buggy	Voiturette	200 F/18 trous
Clubs	Clubs 1/2 série	100 F/jour

Credit cards Cartes de crédit
VISA - CB - Eurocard - MasterCard - AMEX

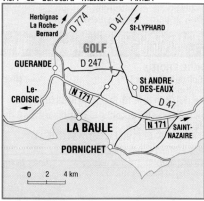

Herbignac
La Roche-Bernard
D 774
D 47
St-Lyphard
GOLF
GUERANDE
D 247
Le-CROISIC
N 171
St ANDRE-DES-EAUX
D 47
LA BAULE
N 171
SAINT-NAZAIRE
PORNICHET
0   2   4 km

Access Accès : La Baule → La Baule-Escoublac, traverser N 171. → Golf
Map 5 on page 107 Carte 5 Page 107

GOLF COURSE
PARCOURS
15/20

Site	Site	
Maintenance	Entretien	
Architect	Architecte	Alliss & Thomas Michel Gayon
Type	Type	forêt, plaine
Relief	Relief	
Water in play	Eau en jeu	
Exp. to wind	Exposé au vent	
Trees in play	Arbres en jeu	

Scorecard Carte de score	Chp. Chp.	Mens Mess.	Ladies Da.
Length Long.	6127	5769	5176
Par	72	72	72

Advised golfing ability   0   12   24   36
Niveau de jeu recommandé
Hcp required   Handicap exigé   30 (Haute saison)

CLUB HOUSE & AMENITIES
CLUB HOUSE ET ANNEXES
7/10

Pro shop	Pro-shop	
Driving range	Practice	
Sheltered	couvert	10 places
On grass	sur herbe	oui
Putting-green	putting-green	oui
Pitching-green	pitching green	oui

HOTEL FACILITIES
ENVIRONNEMENT HOTELIER
8/10

HOTELS HÔTELS
Castel Marie-Louise ****   La Baule 7 km
31 chambres, D 1 800 F
Tél (33) 02 40 11 48 38, Fax (33) 02 40 11 48 35

Hermitage ****   La Baule 7 km
217 chambres, D 1 600 F
Tél (33) 02 40 11 46 46, Fax (33) 02 40 11 46 45

Le Manoir du Parc ***   La Baule 7 km
18 chambres, D 550 F
Tél (33) 02 40 60 24 52, Fax (33) 02 40 60 55 96

RESTAURANTS RESTAURANT
La Marcandrerie   La Baule 7 km
Tél (33) 02 40 24 03 12

L'Hermitage   La Baule 7 km
Tél (33) 02 40 11 46 46

164

Constituant l'une des bonnes réalisations récentes, ce golf public a conservé ses qualités, mais on regrette que la plupart des bunkers n'aient toujours pas été "ensablés". Il le faut pour apporter quelques contrastes visuels dans une symphonie de verts, et accentuer le caractère de links, même si l'on trouve un environnement boisé sur un grand nombre de trous. Plusieurs greens sont presque aveugles, et leurs contours peuvent paraître parfois excessifs, mais on retrouve ces caractéristiques sur de nombreux links britanniques. Epousant les contours de dunes tourmentées (parfois de façon exagérée), ce golf est assez physique pour les golfeurs rouillés mais reste jouable à pied. Alors que les arbres protègent certains trous, d'autres plus dénudés deviennent très difficiles quand le vent est violent : il faudra alors davantage "limiter les dégâts" que rechercher les exploits. Le Club-House vient d'être enfin achevé, complétant un équipement à connaître.

One of several excellent achievements of late, this public course has retained a lot of its quality, although unfortunately most of the bunkers are still awaiting their sand. This is important to add a little visual contrast to a sea of green and to emphasise the links side to the course, even though a number of holes are more reminiscent of a woodland course. Several greens are almost blind and some of the slopes are a little excessive, but that is often the way it is on many British links. The course hugs the sometimes excessively twisting dunes, and although hilly, even the rustier golfers can play it without a buggy. While trees protect some of the holes, others are exposed and become a very tricky proposition once the wind gets up. The result is often an exercise in damage limitation rather than a quest for a good card. The club-house has recently been completed, adding the finishing touch to a course that is well worth getting to know.

Golf de Belle-Dune

Promenade du Marquenterre
F - 80790 FORT-MAHON-PLAGE

Office	Secrétariat	(33) 03 22 23 45 50
Pro shop	Pro-shop	(33) 03 22 23 45 50
Fax	Fax	(33) 03 22 23 93 41
Situation	Situation	

25 km Le Touquet, 5 590 hab.
20 km Berck-Plage, 14 160 hab.

Annual closure	Fermeture annnuelle	non
Weekly closure	Fermeture hebdomadaire	non
		Vendredi en hiver

Fees main season
Tarifs haute saison le parcours

	Week days Semaine	We/Bank holidays We/Férié
Individual Individuel	190 F	230 F
Couple Couple	345 F	415 F

Caddy	Caddy	non
Electric Trolley	Chariot électrique	75 F/18 trous
Buggy	Voiturette	200 F/jour
Clubs	Clubs la série	60 F/jour

Credit cards Cartes de crédit
VISA - CB - Eurocard

Access Accès : N1 Abbeville-Boulogne, → Rue,
→ Quend-Plage, D32 → Fort-Mahon-Plage, → Golf
Map 1 on page 98 Carte 1 Page 98

GOLF COURSE
PARCOURS

16/20

Site	Site	■■■■
Maintenance	Entretien	■■■■
Architect	Architecte	Jean-Manuel Rossi
Type	Type	forêt, bord de mer
Relief	Relief	■■
Water in play	Eau en jeu	■■
Exp. to wind	Exposé au vent	■■■
Trees in play	Arbres en jeu	■■■■

Scorecard Carte de score	Chp. Chp.	Mens Mess.	Ladies Da.
Length Long.	5909	5523	4972
Par	72	72	72

Advised golfing ability	0	12	24	36
Niveau de jeu recommandé				
Hcp required Handicap exigé	35			

CLUB HOUSE & AMENITIES
CLUB HOUSE ET ANNEXES

6/10

Pro shop	Pro-shop	■■■
Driving range	Practice	■■■
Sheltered	couvert	10 places
On grass	sur herbe	non
Putting-green	putting-green	oui
Pitching-green	pitching green	oui

165

HOTEL FACILITIES
ENVIRONNEMENT HOTELIER

5/10

HOTELS HÔTELS

La Terrasse ***	Fort-Mahon-Plage 1 km
56 chambres, D 450 F	
Tél (33) 03 22 23 37 77, Fax (33) 03 22 23 36 74	
Le Lion d'Or **	Rue 12 km
16 chambres, D 340 F	
Tél (33) 03 22 25 74 18, Fax (33) 03 22 25 66 63	
La Chipodière ***	Fort-Mahon-Plage 1 km
18 chambres, D 500 F	
Tél (33) 03 22 27 70 36, Fax (33) 03 22 23 38 16	

RESTAURANTS RESTAURANT

La Grenouillère	La Madelaine s. Montreuil 12 km
Tél (33) 03 21 06 07 22	
La Terrasse	Fort-Mahon-Plage 1 km
Tél(33) 03 22 23 37 77	
Auberge Le Fiacre	Routhiauville 2 km
Tél(33) 03 22 23 47 30	

Un golf très équilibré : le parcours se déroule dans un site agréable, entre plaine et forêt, il n'est pas trop plat, ni trop mouvementé, pas trop facile, ni trop difficile, avec très peu d'eau. Il offre ainsi un bon dosage des obstacles, une bonne alternance de trous faciles et plus délicats : de quoi satisfaire les débutants et les joueurs moyens, sans les effrayer par des difficultés hors de leurs compétences. Certes, les joueurs de haut niveau n'y trouveront alors pas leur compte, mais ce n'est pas la vocation de ce golf de les satisfaire exclusivement, il est essentiellement fréquenté par les joueurs de la région. Dessiné par Michael Fenn, il représente un style de parcours bien adapté à un usage "local", mais sans mériter vraiment le détour. Mais, d'avril à octobre, si vous êtes dans la région, vous y passerez une journée détendue. L'entretien a fait de bons progrès.

A nicely balanced course, pleasantly located between plain and forest, not too flat and not too hilly, not too easy yet none too difficult, with little in the way of water. Hazards are astutely dispensed here and there, with easier holes alternating pleasantly with harder numbers, giving enough to satisfy beginners and twenty-plus handicappers without scaring them off with hazards that might be beyond them. Better players will certainly feel a touch of frustration, but there again the course was not designed with only them in mind. It is basically played by local players. Designed by Michael Fenn, the course's style is well suited to local golfing but not really worth any long trip out of your way. But if you are in the region between April and October, drop by and enjoy a good day out.

Golf Club de Besançon

La Chevillotte
F - 25620 MAMIROLLE

Office	Secrétariat	(33) 03 81 55 73 54
Pro shop	Pro-shop	(33) 03 81 55 86 13
Fax	Fax	(33) 03 81 55 88 64
Situation	Situation	

12 km Besançon, 113 820 hab.

Annual closure	Fermeture annnuelle	non
Weekly closure	Fermeture hebdomadaire	non

Fees main season
Tarifs haute saison le parcours

	Week days Semaine	We/Bank holidays We/Férié
Individual Individuel	190 F	250 F
Couple Couple	380 F	500 F

Caddy	Caddy	non
Electric Trolley	Chariot électrique	non
Buggy	Voiturette	150 F/18 trous
Clubs	Clubs 1/2 série	50 F/jour

Credit cards	Cartes de crédit
VISA - CB - Eurocard - MasterCard

Access Accès : Besançon N57 → Pontarlier / Lausanne,
→ Saône, → Golf
Map 8 on page 113 Carte 8 Page 113

GOLF COURSE
PARCOURS
13/20

Site	Site	
Maintenance	Entretien	
Architect	Architecte	Michael Fenn
Type	Type	forêt, plaine
Relief	Relief	
Water in play	Eau en jeu	
Exp. to wind	Exposé au vent	
Trees in play	Arbres en jeu	

Scorecard Carte de score	Chp. Chp.	Mens Mess.	Ladies Da.
Length Long.	6070	5705	5117
Par	72	72	72

Advised golfing ability   0   12   24   36
Niveau de jeu recommandé

Hcp required Handicap exigé   35

CLUB HOUSE & AMENITIES
CLUB HOUSE ET ANNEXES
7/10

Pro shop	Pro-shop	
Driving range	Practice	
Sheltered	couvert	7 places
On grass	sur herbe	non
Putting-green	putting-green	oui
Pitching-green	pitching green	oui

HOTEL FACILITIES
ENVIRONNEMENT HOTELIER
5/10

HOTELS HÔTELS
Mercure-Parc Micaud ***   Besançon 12 km
95 chambres, D 500 F
Tél (33) 03 81 80 14 44, Fax (33) 03 81 53 29 83

Nord   Besançon 12 km
44 chambres, D 300 F
Tél (33) 03 81 81 34 56, Fax (33) 03 81 81 85 96

Ibis Centre **   Besançon 12 km
49 chambres, D 350 F
Tél (33) 03 81 81 02 02, Fax (33) 03 81 81 89 65

RESTAURANTS RESTAURANT
Mungo Park   Besançon 12 km
Tél (33) 03 81 81 28 01

Le Chaland   Besançon 12 km
Tél (33) 03 81 80 61 61

166

BÉTHEMONT

14	7	5

Les premiers et derniers trous donnent l'impression d'un parcours physique, mais la plupart des trous sont situés sur un plateau. Il est assez court, mais bordé d'arbres souvent bien en jeu, avec un grand nombre de bunkers, de beaux obstacles d'eau, et quelques doglegs assez diaboliques. La signature de Bernhard Langer est évidente en ce qu'elle réclame beaucoup de précision avec les fers, pas mal de réflexion avant de jouer, plus que de la longueur. Dans ces conditions, une seule visite ne suffit pas pour prétendre le maîtriser, et les joueurs moyens risquent de le trouver trop exigeant pour eux au premier abord, d'autant que les greens sont souvent très modelés. On ne saurait placer Béthemont parmi les grands parcours de la région parisienne, mais on peut y passer une bonne journée. Assez humide, il ne saurait être conseillé en dehors de la période de mai à octobre, où son entretien devient très correct.

The 1st and 18th at Béthemont give the impression of a physically demanding course, but in reality the majority of holes are laid out on a plateau. Rather short by today's standards, the course is edged by what sometimes seem to be unmissable trees and is generously dotted with bunkers, attractive water hazards and a few devilish dog-legs. This is a Bernhard Langer design, and it shows, calling for precision ironwork and a lot of thought before each stroke. Length off the tee is secondary. Under these conditions, a single round is hardly enough to get to grips with the course and the less experienced player may well find it too demanding first time out, especially with the undulating greens. Perhaps not one of the greatest courses around Paris, Béthemont does however make for an excellent day's golfing. Owing to the wet, we would not recommend the course outside the May to October period, when upkeep and green-keeping are very good.

Béthemont Chisan Club

12, rue du Parc de Béthemont
F - 78300 POISSY

Office	Secrétariat	(33) 01 39 75 51 13
Pro shop	Pro-shop	(33) 01 39 75 51 13
Fax	Fax	(33) 01 39 75 49 90
Situation	Situation	
25 km Paris, 2 175 200 hab.		
Annual closure	Fermeture annnuelle	non
Weekly closure	Fermeture hebdomadaire	mardi

Fees main season
Tarifs haute saison le parcours

	Week days Semaine	We/Bank holidays We/Férié
Individual Individuel	250 F	500 F
Couple Couple	500 F	1 000 F

Caddy	Caddy	sur réservation
Electric Trolley	Chariot électrique	non
Buggy	Voiturette	non
Clubs	Clubs série	100 F/jour

Credit cards Cartes de crédit
VISA - CB - Eurocard - MasterCard - AMEX - JCB

Mantes-la-Jolie
ROUEN
A 13
Orgeval
Bethemont
GOLF
Saint-Germain-en-Laye
0 2 4 km
A 13
PARIS

Access Accès : A13 Paris-Rouen, sortie Poissy →
Chambourcy, au rond-point → St-Germain, 1ère route
à droite. **Map 15 on page 126** Carte 15 Page 126

GOLF COURSE
PARCOURS
14/20

Site	Site	▬▬▬
Maintenance	Entretien	▬▬▬
Architect	Architecte	Bernhard Langer
Type	Type	forêt
Relief	Relief	▬▬
Water in play	Eau en jeu	▬▬▬
Exp. to wind	Exposé au vent	▬
Trees in play	Arbres en jeu	▬▬▬

Scorecard Carte de score	Chp. Chp.	Mens Mess.	Ladies Da.
Length Long.	6035	5550	5128
Par	72	72	72

Advised golfing ability		0	12	24	36
Niveau de jeu recommandé	▬▬▬▬				
Hcp required	Handicap exigé	35			

CLUB HOUSE & AMENITIES
CLUB HOUSE ET ANNEXES
7/10

Pro shop	Pro-shop	▬▬
Driving range	Practice	▬▬
Sheltered	couvert	5 places
On grass	sur herbe	non
Putting-green	putting-green	oui
Pitching-green	pitching green	non

HOTEL FACILITIES
ENVIRONNEMENT HOTELIER
5/10

HOTELS HÔTELS
Moulin d'Orgeval ****   Orgeval 5 km
14 chambres, D 720 F
Tél (33) 01 39 75 85 74, Fax (33) 01 39 75 48 52

Novotel ***   Orgeval 5 km
119 chambres, D 500 F
Tél (33) 01 39 22 35 11, Fax (33) 01 39 75 48 93

RESTAURANTS RESTAURANT
L'Esturgeon   Poissy 4 km
Tél (33) 01 39 65 00 04

167

Dessiné il y a plus de 100 ans par Willie Dunn, ce parcours a été tellement modifié qu'il n'a plus rien du quasi "links" des origines. Ayant perdu ses trous de bord de mer, c'est devenu un joli golf de parc, très court, ce qui ne veut pas dire facile à scorer. Les greens peuvent être rendus démoniaques, et même une attaque avec un petit fer peut alors s'avérer redoutable. Les fairways sont séparés par de minces rideaux d'arbres et arbustes, et si l'on n'est pas précis, il vaut mieux s'en écarter franchement que de rester entre deux fairways. Mais, sauf aux 1, 15 et 16, il est inutile de jouer le driver au départ, un bois 3 ou un long fer suffit largement. On peut considérer "Le Phare" comme un peu désuet, mais il porte la tradition irremplaçable du golf des origines en Pays Basque, et peut être joué à tous les niveaux.

Laid out more than 100 years ago by Willie Dunn, this course has seen so much change that there is virtually nothing left of the original links. Having lost its sea-side holes, it has become a pretty parkland course, very short but by no means easy. The greens can be devilishly tricky, and even short iron approach shots can prove to be a formidable ordeal. The fairways are separated by thin rows of trees and bushes, so if you are going to stray left or right, go the whole way to avoid being stuck in the middle ground. The 3-wood or a long iron will suffice here, except on the 1st, 15th and 16th holes where you can go for your driver. "Le Phare" could be considered a little antiquated, but it bears the irreplaceable tradition of the origins of golf in the Basque country and can be played by golfers of all levels.

Golf de Biarritz-Le-Phare

2, avenue Edith-Cavell
F - 64200 BIARRITZ

Office	Secrétariat	(33) 05 59 03 71 80
Pro shop	Pro-shop	(33) 05 59 03 71 80
Fax	Fax	(33) 05 59 03 26 74
Situation	Situation	

1 km Biarritz, 28 740 hab.

Annual closure	Fermeture annnuelle	non
Weekly closure	Fermeture hebdomadaire	mardi, hors saison

Fees main season
Tarifs haute saison le parcours

	Week days Semaine	We/Bank holidays We/Férié
Individual Individuel	320 F	320 F
Couple Couple	540 F	540 F

Caddy	Caddy	sur réservation
Electric Trolley	Chariot électrique	70 F/18 trous
Buggy	Voiturette	200 F/18 trous
Clubs	Clubs 1/2 série	50 F/jour

Credit cards Cartes de crédit
VISA - CB - Eurocard - MasterCard - AMEX

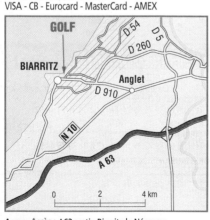

Access Accès : A63 sortie Biarritz la Négresse,
→ Biarritz, → Anglet
Map 12 on page 120 Carte 12 Page 120

168

GOLF COURSE
PARCOURS
14/20

Site	Site	▬▬
Maintenance	Entretien	▬▬
Architect	Architecte	Willie Dunn
Type	Type	résidentiel
Relief	Relief	
Water in play	Eau en jeu	▬
Exp. to wind	Exposé au vent	▬▬▬
Trees in play	Arbres en jeu	▬▬

Scorecard Carte de score	Chp. Chp.	Mens Mess.	Ladies Da.
Length Long.	5376	5059	4633
Par	69	69	69

Advised golfing ability	0	12	24	36
Niveau de jeu recommandé		▬▬▬▬		
Hcp required Handicap exigé	35			

CLUB HOUSE & AMENITIES
CLUB HOUSE ET ANNEXES
6/10

Pro shop	Pro-shop	▬▬
Driving range	Practice	▬▬
Sheltered	couvert	8 places
On grass	sur herbe	non
Putting-green	putting-green	oui
Pitching-green	pitching green	non

HOTEL FACILITIES
ENVIRONNEMENT HOTELIER
8/10

HOTELS HÔTELS
Le Palais ★★★★   Biarritz 1 km
156 chambres, D 1 800 F
Tél (33) 05 59 41 64 00, Fax (33) 05 59 41 67 99
Regina et Golf ★★★★   Biarritz 1 km
61 chambres, D 1200 F
Tél (33) 05 59 41 33 00, Fax (33) 05 59 41 33 99
Miramar ★★★★   Biarritz 1 km
126 chambres, D 2 000 F
Tél (33) 05 59 41 30 00, Fax (33) 05 59 24 77 20

RESTAURANTS RESTAURANT
Café de Paris   Biarritz 1 km
Tél (33) 05 59 24 19 53
La Rotonde   Biarritz1 km
Tél(33) 05 59 61 64 00
La Table des Frères Ibarboure   Bidart10 km
Tél(33) 05 59 54 81 64

Son excellent entretien distingue ce parcours, ainsi que son site pittoresque, entouré de forêt. Assez accidenté pour offrir de beaux points de vue sur la région, mais aussi demander une bonne forme physique, ses difficultés sont assez visibles pour être abordé sans complexes dès la première fois. L'architecture de Fromanger et Adam a conservé le caractère naturel du lieu, elle manque un peu de grandeur, mais la franchise de leur dessin est à souligner. Il n'a pas été possible d'éviter un green aveugle (le 14), mais s'il reste le seul, les autres sont assez bien défendus pour exiger souvent de porter la balle. Quelques obstacles d'eau ponctuent le paysage, mais ils sont assez peu en jeu. Assez facile des départs avancés, le parcours progresse en difficultés à mesure que l'on recule, et sa longueur est plus effective qu'au vu de la carte, en raison des importantes dénivellations.

A course that stands out for its excellent upkeep, plus a picturesque setting surrounded by a forest. Hilly enough to provide some fine views over the region and to require a good pair of legs, the course's difficulties are visible enough for players to cope first time out. The architecture, by Fromanger and Adam, has preserved the site's natural character, and although not a great layout, the course is open and fair, a point we would like to emphasise. They were unable to avoid one blind green (the 14th), while the others are defended enough to require lofted shots almost every time. The landscape is dotted with water hazards which don't really come into play. Easy enough from the front tees, it logically gets harder as you move back, and the overall yardage plays longer than you might guess from the card, owing to some steep slopes.

Golf de Bitche

Rue des Prés
F - 57230 BITCHE

Office	Secrétariat	(33) 03 87 96 15 30
Pro shop	Pro-shop	(33) 03 87 96 10 00
Fax	Fax	(33) 03 87 96 08 04
Situation	Situation	

33 km Sarreguemines, 23 117 hab.

Annual closure	Fermeture annnuelle	oui
		25/12 → 1/01/98
Weekly closure	Fermeture hebdomadaire	non

mardi, le restaurant - parcours, 1ᵉʳ mardi du mois

Fees main season
Tarifs haute saison le parcours

	Week days Semaine	We/Bank holidays We/Férié
Individual Individuel	210 F	320 F
Couple Couple	420 F	640 F
Caddy	Caddy	non
Electric Trolley	Chariot électrique	non
Buggy	Voiturette	250 F/18 trous
Clubs	Clubs 1/2 série	70 F/jour

Credit cards Cartes de crédit
VISA - CB - Eurocard - MasterCard

Access Accès : A32 → Metz, sortie Sarreguemines, N62 → Bitche
Map 4 on page 105 Carte 4 Page 105

GOLF COURSE
PARCOURS

14/20

Site	Site	▬▬▬▬▬□
Maintenance	Entretien	▬▬▬▬▬□
Architect	Architecte	Marc Adam Patrick Fromanger
Type	Type	forêt
Relief	Relief	
Water in play	Eau en jeu	▬□□□□
Exp. to wind	Exposé au vent	▬▬▬□□
Trees in play	Arbres en jeu	▬▬▬▬□

Scorecard Carte de score	Chp. Chp.	Mens Mess.	Ladies Da.
Length Long.	6074	5759	5127
Par	72	72	72

Advised golfing ability	0	12	24	36
Niveau de jeu recommandé				
Hcp required Handicap exigé	35			

CLUB HOUSE & AMENITIES
CLUB HOUSE ET ANNEXES

6/10

Pro shop	Pro-shop	▬▬▬▬□
Driving range	Practice	▬▬▬□□
Sheltered	couvert	6 places
On grass	sur herbe	oui
Putting-green	putting-green	oui
Pitching-green	pitching green	oui

HOTEL FACILITIES
ENVIRONNEMENT HOTELIER

5/10

HOTELS HÔTELS
Relais des Châteaux-Forts   Bitche 800 m
30 chambres, D 340 F
Tél (33) 03 87 96 14 14, Fax (33) 03 87 96 07 36

Auberge de Strasbourg   Bitche 1 km
11 chambres, D 290 F
Tél (33) 03 87 96 00 44, Fax (33) 03 87 06 10 60

RESTAURANTS RESTAURANT
Relais des Châteaux-Forts   Bitche 800 m
Tél (33) 03 87 96 14 14

Auberge de la Tour   Bitche 1 km
Tél (33) 03 87 96 29 25

Auberge de Strasbourg   Bitche 1 km
Tél (33) 03 87 96 00 44

169

	16	7	6

Le "Blanc" offre la particularité d'offrir neuf trous de Robert Trent Jones père et neuf trous du fils. L'architecture est évidemment très américaine, avec de multiples obstacles d'eau, en jeu sur près d'une douzaine de trous. Qaund ils le peuvent, les membres se réfugient sur le "Jaune", moins pénalisant de ce point de vue. Comme les arbres sont peu menaçants, marquant simplement les limites des trous, a panoplie des obstacles est complétée par de nombreux bunkers, protégeant à la fois les arrivées de drive et les greens. Cependant, le parcours n'est pas très long, et, une fois familiarisé avec l'eau, il n'est pas impossible de jouer son handicap. Certes, les joueurs de niveau moyen auront du mal à scorer, mais ce 18 trous amène une vraie rupture des habitudes tout à fait bienvenue. Les greens sont de bonne dimension, assez profonds pour poser des problèmes de choix de club.

The "Blanc" course has the peculiarity of featuring nine holes designed by Robert Trent Jones Sr et nine by his son Robert Trent Jones Jr. This is evidently a very American style course with countless water hazards in play on almost a dozen holes. Whenever they can, members seek solace on the "Jaune" course, a little easier a far as water is concerned. Since the trees offer very little threat and are there simply to demarcate the holes, the panoply of hazards is completed by numerous bunkers, protecting both the tee-shot landing site and the greens. With this said, the course is not too long, and once you have become acquainted with the water, playing to your handicap is not impossible. High handicappers might be hard put to card a good score, but this 18-hole layout makes a welcome break from your everyday course. The greens are nicely sized and deep enough to pose a few problems for club selection.

Golf de Bondues

Château de la Vigne
F - 59910 BONDUES

Office	Secrétariat	(33) 03 20 23 20 62
Pro shop	Pro-shop	(33) 03 20 23 20 62
Fax	Fax	(33) 03 20 23 24 11
Situation	Situation	

6 km Lille, 178 300 hab.
4 km Tourcoing, 93 760 hab.

Annual closure	Fermeture annnuelle	non
Weekly closure	Fermeture hebdomadaire	mardi

Fees main season
Tarifs haute saison la journée

	Week days Semaine	We/Bank holidays We/Férié
Individual Individuel	200 F	300 F
Couple Couple	300 F	450 F

Caddy	Caddy	non
Electric Trolley	Chariot électrique	non
Buggy	Voiturette	200 F/18 trous
Clubs	Clubs	non

Credit cards Cartes de crédit
VISA - CB

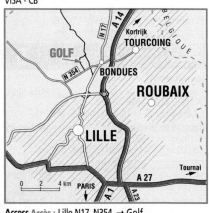

Access Accès : Lille N17, N354, → Golf
Map 1 on page 99 Carte 1 Page 99

GOLF COURSE
PARCOURS
16/20

Site	Site	
Maintenance	Entretien	
Architect	Architecte	R. Trent Jones Sr R. Trent Jones Jr
Type	Type	résidentiel
Relief	Relief	
Water in play	Eau en jeu	
Exp. to wind	Exposé au vent	
Trees in play	Arbres en jeu	

Scorecard Carte de score	Chp. Chp.	Mens Mess.	Ladies Da.
Length Long.	6012	5576	5072
Par	72	72	72

Advised golfing ability   0   12   24   36
Niveau de jeu recommandé
Hcp required   Handicap exigé   34

CLUB HOUSE & AMENITIES
CLUB HOUSE ET ANNEXES
7/10

Pro shop	Pro-shop	
Driving range	Practice	
Sheltered	couvert	8 places
On grass	sur herbe	non
Putting-green	putting-green	oui
Pitching-green	pitching green	oui

HOTEL FACILITIES
ENVIRONNEMENT HOTELIER
6/10

HOTELS HÔTELS
Sofitel ****   Marcq-en-Barœul 5 km
125 chambres, D 1 000 F
Tél (33) 03 20 72 17 30, Fax (33) 03 20 89 92 34
Alliance ****   Lille 6 km
83 chambres, D 670 F
Tél (33) 03 20 30 62 62, Fax (33) 03 20 42 94 25
Mercure ***   Roubaix 5 km
92 chambres, D 490 F
Tél (33) 03 20 73 40 00, Fax (33) 03 20 73 22 42

RESTAURANTS RESTAURANT
L'Huîtrière   Lille 6 km
Tél (33) 03 20 55 43 41
Auberge de la Garenne   Bondues 2 km
Tél(33) 03 20 46 20 20
Château Blanc   Verlinghem 6 km
Tél(33) 03 20 40 71 02

170

Bondues est l'un des grands clubs traditionnels de la région lilloise, et d'un accès parfois difficile en week-end. Le parcours "Jaune" est signé Fred Hawtree, dans la pure tradition britannique, avec assez peu d'obstacles d'eau, mais des arbres bien en jeu et des bunkers de dessin sans originalité particulière de forme, mais toujours bien placés. En revanche, il n'est pas très facile de mémoriser le parcours, sans grande personnalité ni recherche esthétique très affirmée. Il n'en est pas plus facile pour autant d'y scorer. Bondues "Jaune" fait partie de ces parcours classiques parfaitement adaptés à leur destination : il a été essentiellement conçu pour ses membres (qui trouvent facilement leurs marques et leurs habitudes) et non pour des voyageurs de passage. Certes, la région n'est pas vraiment une destination de vacances, mais la réouverture du parcours "Blanc" en a fait une halte très intéressante, avec deux parcours complémentaires.

Bondues is one of the great traditional clubs from the Lille region and is sometimes difficult to play on week-ends. The "Jaune" course was designed by Fred Hawtree in the pure British tradition, i.e. few water hazards but trees very much in play and bunkers that, although hardly original in shape and design, are always well placed. This is not a course that sticks in the memory ; it has no clear-cut personality or research into style, although that doesn't mean it is any easier to score on. Bondues "Jaune" is one of those classic courses that is perfectly suited to the people it was designed for, i.e. basically club members (who can easily find their landmarks and habits) and not for green-feers passing through. Sure, the region is not really a holiday destination, but the re-opening of the "Blanc" course has made it a very interesting stop-off, with two complementary layouts.

Golf de Bondues

Château de la Vigne
F - 59910 BONDUES

Office	Secrétariat	(33) 03 20 23 20 62
Pro shop	Pro-shop	(33) 03 20 23 20 62
Fax	Fax	(33) 03 20 23 24 11
Situation	Situation	

6 km Lille, 178 300 hab.
4 km Tourcoing, 93 760 hab.

Annual closure	Fermeture annnuelle	non
Weekly closure	Fermeture hebdomadaire	mardi

Fees main season
Tarifs haute saison la journée

	Week days Semaine	We/Bank holidays We/Férié
Individual Individuel	200 F	300 F
Couple Couple	300 F	450 F

Caddy	Caddy	non
Electric Trolley	Chariot électrique	non
Buggy	Voiturette	200 F/18 trous
Clubs	Clubs	non

Credit cards Cartes de crédit — VISA - CB

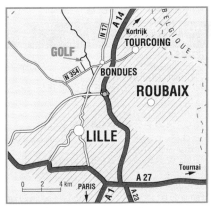

Access Accès : Lille N17, N354, → Golf
Map 1 on page 99 Carte 1 Page 99

GOLF COURSE
PARCOURS — 15/20

Site	Site	▬▬
Maintenance	Entretien	▬▬
Architect	Architecte	Frederic Hawtree
Type	Type	plaine
Relief	Relief	▬
Water in play	Eau en jeu	▬
Exp. to wind	Exposé au vent	▬▬
Trees in play	Arbres en jeu	▬▬

Scorecard Carte de score	Chp. Chp.	Mens Mess.	Ladies Da.
Length Long.	6260	5878	5150
Par	73	73	73

Advised golfing ability
Niveau de jeu recommandé — 0 12 24 36

Hcp required Handicap exigé — 34

CLUB HOUSE & AMENITIES
CLUB HOUSE ET ANNEXES — 7/10

Pro shop	Pro-shop	▬▬
Driving range	Practice	▬▬
Sheltered	couvert	8 places
On grass	sur herbe	non
Putting-green	putting-green	oui
Pitching-green	pitching green	oui

171

HOTEL FACILITIES
ENVIRONNEMENT HOTELIER — 6/10

HOTELS HÔTELS
Sofitel ****   Marcq-en-Barœul 5 km
125 chambres, D 1 000 F
Tél (33) 03 20 72 17 30, Fax (33) 03 20 89 92 34

Alliance ****   Lille 6 km
83 chambres, D 670 F
Tél (33) 03 20 30 62 62, Fax (33) 03 20 42 94 25

Mercure ***   Roubaix 5 km
92 chambres, D 490 F
Tél (33) 03 20 73 40 00, Fax (33) 03 20 73 22 42

RESTAURANTS RESTAURANT
L'Huîtrière   Lille 6 km
Tél (33) 03 20 55 43 41

Auberge de la Garenne   Bondues 2 km
Tél(33) 03 20 46 20 20

Château Blanc   Verlinghem 6 km
Tél(33) 03 20 40 71 02

Si ce parcours reste incontestablement au premier rang français, son entretien est devenu moins rigoureux depuis la disparition de son fondateur Marcel Bich. Mais il fait toujours partie de ces parcours impossibles à ignorer, pour son tracé d'une grande variété de jeu et de stratégie, et pour son environnement : Les Bordes est une initiation à la Sologne, le parcours un lieu de méditation sur la vérité de son propre jeu, où il est impossible de maquiller ses faiblesses. Notre jugement précédent reste entier : si vous l'abordez avec simplicité, intelligence et humilité, il pourra se montrer généreux. Le practice, le Club-House, les chambres rustiques sont exemplaires. Ici, l'argent investi ne s'étale pas, comme si cet ensemble récent avait des siècles d'existence. Désormais largement ouvert aux membres extérieurs, c'est un "incontournable" du golf, comme une grande adresse gastronomique où le prix du plaisir n'a pas d'importance.

While still undoubtedly one of France's top-rate courses, upkeep has fallen away somewhat since the death of its founder, Marcel Bich. But Les Bordes remains one of those courses you simply have to play for its variety in layout, its ever-changing game strategy and its setting. Les Bordes is an introduction to the Sologne and the course an arena of meditation for the truth about your golfing ability. Any chinks in your game are ruthlessly exposed. Our previous judgment is still valid. If you approach the course with simplicity, intelligence and humility, it can be rewarding in terms of score. The driving range, club-house and country-style rooms are excellent, with no ostentatious signs of new investment, rather as if this recently-designed course had been around for centuries. Now wide-open to green-feers, Les Bordes is an absolute must and a great address for excellent food. Here, the price of sheer pleasure matters little.

Golf International des Bordes
F - 41220 SAINT-LAURENT-NOUAN

Office	Secrétariat	(33) 02 54 87 72 13
Pro shop	Pro-shop	(33) 02 54 87 72 13
Fax	Fax	(33) 02 54 87 78 61
Situation	Situation	

11 km Beaugency, 6 910 hab. 30 km Orléans, 105 110 hab.

Annual closure	Fermeture annnuelle	non
Weekly closure	Fermeture hebdomadaire	

Fees main season
Tarifs haute saison le parcours

	Week days Semaine	We/Bank holidays We/Férié
Individual Individuel	350 F	550 F
Couple Couple	600 F	1 000 F

Seniors 175 F (semaine)

Caddy	Caddy	non
Electric Trolley	Chariot électrique	non
Buggy	Voiturette	250 F/18 trous
Clubs	Clubs série	150 F/jour

Credit cards Cartes de crédit
VISA - CB - Eurocard - MasterCard - AMEX - DC

172

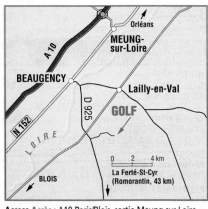

Access Accès : A10 Paris/Blois, sortie Meung-sur-Loire, N152 → Beaugency. A Beaugency → Lailly-en-Val. Après la Loire, → La Ferté Saint- Cyr (D925)
Map 3 on page 102 Carte 3 Page 102

GOLF COURSE
PARCOURS
19/20

Site	Site	
Maintenance	Entretien	
Architect	Architecte	Robert von Hagge
Type	Type	forêt, plaine
Relief	Relief	
Water in play	Eau en jeu	
Exp. to wind	Exposé au vent	
Trees in play	Arbres en jeu	

Scorecard Carte de score	Chp. Chp.	Mens Mess.	Ladies Da.
Length Long.	6412	6023	5317
Par	72	72	72

Advised golfing ability Niveau de jeu recommandé	0	12	24	36

Hcp required   Handicap exigé   non

CLUB HOUSE & AMENITIES
CLUB HOUSE ET ANNEXES
8/10

Pro shop	Pro-shop	
Driving range	Practice	
Sheltered	couvert	non
On grass	sur herbe	oui
Putting-green	putting-green	oui
Pitching-green	pitching green	oui

HOTEL FACILITIES
ENVIRONNEMENT HOTELIER
6/10

HOTELS HÔTELS
Dormy House ***   sur place
20 chambres, D 700 F
Tél (33) 02 54 87 72 13, Fax (33) 02 54 87 78 61

La Tonnellerie   Tavers 10 km
20 chambres, D 450 F
Tél (33) 02 38 44 68 15, Fax (33) 02 38 44 10 01

Les Chênes Rouges   Villeny 20 km
10 chambres, D 600 F
Tél (33) 02 54 98 23 94, Fax (33) 02 54 98 23 99

RESTAURANTS RESTAURANT
Ferme de la Lande   La Ferté-Saint-aubin 20 km
Tél (33) 02 38 76 64 37

Auberge Gourmande   Baule10 km
Tél(33) 02 38 45 03 08

15	6	4

Dans une région très calme, sur un terrain peu fatigant, Jeremy Pern a dessiné un parcours faisant appel à toutes les qualités : puissance, précision du grand jeu, subtilité du petit jeu, finesse du putting. Certes, il est difficile à jouer quand il est mouillé, mais il prend toute sa dimension aux beaux jours. Le rythme de jeu est excellent, avec une bonne alternance de trous de plaine et de trous tracés dans les bois, permettant à tous les goûts de trouver leur plaisir. Les golfeurs expérimentés auront l'occasion d'affronter des défis intéressants, notamment pour choisir leurs clubs, mais les joueurs de tous niveaux ne sont jamais vraiment découragés. Les greens, assez modelés, sont délicats à interpréter, et peuvent "charger la carte" quand on ne parvient pas à les lire. Seul regret : de nouveaux bunkers inutiles et laids. Le Club-House est sympathique, la restauration de bonne qualité est typique de la région.

In a calm region on flattish terrain, Jeremy Pern has designed a course which requires just about every golfing skill: power and precision off the tee, a sharp and clever short game and fine putting. It might be hard to play in damp conditions, but when the sun shines the course comes into its own. The tempo of play is good here, with a pleasant mixture of alternating open-field and woodland holes. In fact, there's something for all tastes. The more experienced golfer will enjoy the opportunity to get to grips with a number of interesting challenges, especially for club selection, but the lesser player will never really feel too despondent, either. The undulating greens are not always easy to read and can, as always, add a few unwelcome strokes to the card when mis-read. The club-house is very pleasant and the food is good... typical, you might suppose, of a region where they know what good food is all about. Upkeep is just average and some ugly bunkers have been built, we don't know why.

Golf-Club de la Bresse
Domaine de Mary
F - 01400 CONDEISSIAT

Office	Secrétariat	(33) 04 74 51 42 09
Pro shop	Pro-shop	(33) 04 74 51 42 09
Fax	Fax	(33) 04 74 51 40 09
Situation	Situation	

15 km Bourg-en-Bresse, 40 970 hab.

Annual closure	Fermeture annnuelle	non

Weekly closure	Fermeture hebdomadaire	

Fees main season
Tarifs haute saison la journée

	Week days Semaine	We/Bank holidays We/Férié
Individual Individuel	200 F	250 F
Couple Couple	350 F	450 F

Caddy	Caddy	sur réservation
Electric Trolley	Chariot électrique	non
Buggy	Voiturette	200 F/18 trous
Clubs	Clubs 1/2 série	50 F/jour

Credit cards Cartes de crédit
VISA - CB - Eurocard - MasterCard

Access Accès : • de Lyon, N83 → Bourg-en-Bresse.
Servas, → Condeissiat • Mâcon A40, sortie Bourg-en-Bresse Nord, D936 → Châtillon-sur-Chalaronne, à gauche Condeissiat → Servas
Map 11 on page 118 Carte 11 Page 118

GOLF COURSE
PARCOURS   **15**/20

Site	Site	▬▬
Maintenance	Entretien	▬▬
Architect	Architecte	Jeremy Pern
Type	Type	plaine, forêt
Relief	Relief	▬
Water in play	Eau en jeu	▬▬
Exp. to wind	Exposé au vent	▬▬
Trees in play	Arbres en jeu	▬▬

Scorecard	Chp.	Mens	Ladies
Carte de score	Chp.	Mess.	Da.
Length Long.	6217	5748	5190
Par	72	72	72

Advised golfing ability		0	12	24	36
Niveau de jeu recommandé					
Hcp required	Handicap exigé	non			

CLUB HOUSE & AMENITIES
CLUB HOUSE ET ANNEXES   **6**/10

Pro shop	Pro-shop	▬▬
Driving range	Practice	▬
Sheltered	couvert	7 places
On grass	sur herbe	oui
Putting-green	putting-green	oui
Pitching-green	pitching green	non

173

HOTEL FACILITIES
ENVIRONNEMENT HOTELIER   **4**/10

HOTELS HÔTELS
Georges Blanc ****   Vonnas 7 km
34 chambres, D 1000 F
Tél (33) 04 74 50 00 10, Fax (33) 04 74 50 08 80

La Résidence des Saules **   Vonnas 7 km
10 chambres, D 550 F
Tél (33) 04 74 50 90 51, Fax (33) 04 74 50 08 80

Hôtel de France ***   Bourg-en-Bresse 12 km
46 chambres, D 420 F
Tél (33) 04 74 23 30 24, Fax (33) 04 74 23 69 90

RESTAURANTS RESTAURANT
Jacques Guy   Bourg-en-Bresse 15 km
Tél (33) 04 74 45 29 11

Georges Blanc   Vonnas 7 km
Tél (33) 04 74 50 00 10

Tracé en paysage de landes, ce golf est le plus occidental de France. Michael Fenn y a dessiné un parcours épousant un terrain qui se prêtait bien à la construction d'un golf, avec un certain nombre de dénivellations pour rompre la monotonie. Elles permettent d'offrir de beaux points de vue sur la rade de Brest et les Monts d'Arée. Le paysage - sinon le jeu - est agrémenté d'une végétation rustique et dense, de genêts et de gros rochers. De longueur raisonnable, il est accessible à tous les niveaux, avec des greens généralement très fermes, et bien défendus par des bunkers au dessin cependant sans grande subtilité. L'entretien a beaucoup progressé, grâce à d'importants travaux de drainage. Le Club-House venant d'être transféré au Golf hôtel tout proche, totalement modernisé, Brest Iroise devient une véritable destination de week-end.

Laid out amidst heath and moorland, this is France's western-most course. Michael Fenn has designed a course that hugs terrain that was almost made for golf, with a number of slopes to break the monotony. This gives some fine views over the bay of Brest and the Monts d'Arée. The landscape, and the round, is enhanced with some thick country bush, gorse-bushes and rocks. Reasonable in length, golfers of all standards can play here and enjoy greens that are generally hard and well defended by some pretty ordinary bunkers. Upkeep has improved considerably thanks to some extensive drainage work, and now that the club-house has been transferred to the nearby and totally refurbished Golf hotel, Brest Iroise is now a real week-end destination.

Golf de Brest Iroise
Parc de Lann-Rohou, Saint-Urbain
F - 29800 LANDERNEAU

Office	Secrétariat	(33) 02 98 85 16 17
Pro shop	Pro-shop	(33) 02 98 85 16 17
Fax	Fax	(33) 02 98 85 19 39
Situation	Situation	

4 km Landerneau, 14 720 hab.
24 km Brest, 147 950 hab.

Annual closure	Fermeture annnuelle	non
Weekly closure	Fermeture hebdomadaire	

Fees main season
Tarifs haute saison la journée

	Week days Semaine	We/Bank holidays We/Férié
Individual Individuel	220 F	250 F
Couple Couple	440 F	500 F

Caddy	Caddy	non
Electric Trolley	Chariot électrique	non
Buggy	Voiturette	120 F/18 trous
Clubs	Clubs 1/2 série	50 F/jour

Credit cards Cartes de crédit
VISA - CB - Eurocard - MasterCard - AMEX

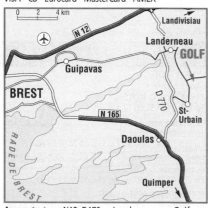

174

Access Accès : • N12, D170 → Landerneau, → Golf
• N165, Daoulas → Landerneau, → Golf
Map 5 on page 106 Carte 5 Page 106

GOLF COURSE
PARCOURS

14/20

Site	Site	■■■■■
Maintenance	Entretien	■■■■■
Architect	Architecte	Michael Fenn
Type	Type	vallon
Relief	Relief	■■■■
Water in play	Eau en jeu	■
Exp. to wind	Exposé au vent	■■■
Trees in play	Arbres en jeu	■■■

Scorecard Carte de score	Chp. Chp.	Mens Mess.	Ladies Da.
Length Long.	5672	5464	4873
Par	71	71	71

Advised golfing ability		0	12	24	36
Niveau de jeu recommandé	■■■■■■				
Hcp required	Handicap exigé	non

CLUB HOUSE & AMENITIES
CLUB HOUSE ET ANNEXES

7/10

Pro shop	Pro-shop	■■■
Driving range	Practice	■■■
Sheltered	couvert	11 places
On grass	sur herbe	non
Putting-green	putting-green	oui
Pitching-green	pitching green	oui

HOTEL FACILITIES
ENVIRONNEMENT HOTELIER

6/10

HOTELS HÔTELS
Golf Hôtel de l'Iroise ** — Golf
44 chambres, D 350 F — sur place
Tél (33) 02 98 85 16 17, Fax (33) 02 98 85 19 39

Le Clos du Pontic ** — Landerneau 3 km
32 chambres, D 350 F
Tél (33) 02 98 21 50 91, Fax (33) 02 98 21 34 33

RESTAURANTS RESTAURANT
Le Clos du Pontic — Landerneau 3 km
Tél (33) 02 98 21 50 91

La Mairie — Landerneau3 km
Tél(33) 02 98 85 01 83

D'un parcours sans grande longueur, on attendrait des greens très travaillés et bien défendus, dont l'approche soit d'autant plus compliquée qu'on les attaque avec des petits fers. Ce n'est pas la difficulté technique qui inspirera pour sublimer son jeu. Heureusement, l'environnement de parc est très joli, le château séduisant pour les étrangers : ce lieu typique d'une certaine idée de la France plaît beaucoup. S'il est difficile de souligner un quelconque aspect surprenant du parcours, sinon l'habituel trou en boomerang (le 16 ici) de l'architecte Bill Baker, le plaisir d'évoluer sur ce parcours bien entretenu est évident. Le dessin des trous est honorable, les greens et bunkers sans grosses difficultés, leurs défenses raisonnables. Cela fait donc un parcours sans danger et très plaisant en famille, et pour la majorité des joueurs, d'autant plus que cet ensemble est très soigné. Les meilleurs attendent sans doute des défis de plus grande ampleur.

Over a shortish course, you might expect carefully designed and well-defended greens, made even more complicated by the fact that the approach shot is more often than not a short iron. However here, it is certainly not the technical difficulty that will inspire golfers to better things. Fortunately, the park's surroundings are very pretty and the castle appealing to foreigners, who like the spot for the way it represents a typical picture thay have of France. While it is difficult to underline any one surprising aspect of the course, excepting the usual boomerang hole by designer Bill Baker (the 16th), the pleasure of playing here on a well-manicured course is obvious. The holes are pleasantly laid out, and the greens and bunkers are none too difficult and reasonably well-defended. All in all, this gives a course without too much danger which is agreeable to play with all the family and players of almost every ability, especially since the whole complex has been carefully designed. Perhaps the very best players could expect tougher challenges.

Golf de la Bretesche

Domaine de la Bretesche
F - 44780 MISSILLAC

Office	Secrétariat	(33) 02 51 76 86 86
Pro shop	Pro-shop	(33) 02 51 76 86 86
Fax	Fax	(33) 02 40 88 36 28
Situation	Situation	

24 km Redon, 9 260 hab.
30 km La Baule, 14 850 hab.

Annual closure	Fermeture annnuelle	non
Weekly closure	Fermeture hebdomadaire	

Fees main season
Tarifs haute saison la journée

	Week days Semaine	We/Bank holidays We/Férié
Individual Individuel	300 F	300 F
Couple Couple	600 F	600 F

Caddy	Caddy	sur réservation
Electric Trolley	Chariot électrique	non
Buggy	Voiturette	250 F/18 trous
Clubs	Clubs la série	100 F/jour

Credit cards Cartes de crédit
VISA - CB - Eurocard - MasterCard - AMEX

Access Accès : • Saint-Nazaire N171, D773 et N165 →
Golf • La Baule D774 et N165 → Golf
Map 6 on page 108 Carte 6 Page 108

GOLF COURSE
PARCOURS

15 /20

Site	Site	
Maintenance	Entretien	
Architect	Architecte	Bill Baker
Type	Type	forêt, parc
Relief	Relief	
Water in play	Eau en jeu	
Exp. to wind	Exposé au vent	
Trees in play	Arbres en jeu	

Scorecard Carte de score	Chp. Chp.	Mens Mess.	Ladies Da.
Length Long.	6080	5809	5136
Par	72	72	72

Advised golfing ability		0 12 24 36
Niveau de jeu recommandé		
Hcp required	Handicap exigé	35

CLUB HOUSE & AMENITIES
CLUB HOUSE ET ANNEXES

7 /10

Pro shop	Pro-shop	
Driving range	Practice	
Sheltered	couvert	10 places
On grass	sur herbe	oui
Putting-green	putting-green	oui
Pitching-green	pitching green	oui

HOTEL FACILITIES
ENVIRONNEMENT HOTELIER

7 /10

HOTELS HÔTELS
Golf de la Bretesche ***   sur place
27 chambres, D 640 F
Tél (33) 02 40 88 30 05, Fax (33) 02 40 66 99 47

Cottage de la Bretesche ***   sur place
30 chambres, 3890 F/sem.

Tél (33) 02 40 88 31 18 Domaine de Bodeuc *** Nivillac
8 chambres, D 500 F   12 km
Tél (33) 02 99 90 89 63, Fax (33) 02 99 90 90 32

Auberge de Kerhinet   Saint-Lyphard 14 km
7 chambres, D 270 F
Tél (33) 02 40 61 91 46, Fax (33) 02 40 61 97 57

RESTAURANTS RESTAURANT
Auberge Bretonne   La Roche-Bernard 11 km
Tél (33) 02 99 90 60 28

175

Ce parcours signé Harold Baker est l'un des grands clubs traditionnels des Lillois, dont beaucoup y ont élu résidence, mais l'impression d'un golf immobilier n'est pas trop pesante car les maisons sont de bonne qualité. Assez plat, quelques obstacles d'eau, un bon nombre de bunkers, et les arbres lui donnent des allures de grand parc à la britannique, d'allure assez harmonieuse et séduisante. A côté de cet environnement, c'est un parcours aussi agréable pour les joueurs de bon niveau que pour les joueurs moyens. Certes, ce n'est pas un test d'une énorme difficulté, l'architecture est restée sobre, peut-être même un peu timide, mais on a visiblement recherché à favoriser le plaisir du jeu en famille. Un vrai "golf de membres" où les golfeurs de passage seront mieux accueillis en semaine, les week-ends étant souvent chargés.

This Harold Baker course is one of the great traditional clubs of Lille and many people have bought homes here. The quality standard of houses fortunately rules out any great impression of this being a property development course. Being rather flat, with a few water hazards and a good number of bunkers, Brigode looks like a British park, at once harmonious and attractive. Alongside this setting, the course is pleasant for skilled and less skilful golfers alike. It is certainly not too tough a test for the better golfer, as the architecture is unobtrusive and even a little on the shy side, but the designers visibly were looking to promote the pleasure of family golfing. This is a real "members' club" where green-feers get a warmer welcome during the week. Week-ends are often heavily booked.

Golf de Brigode
36, avenue du Golf
F - 59650 VILLENEUVE-D'ASCQ

Office	Secrétariat	(33) 03 20 91 17 86
Pro shop	Pro-shop	(33) 03 20 91 17 86
Fax	Fax	(33) 03 20 05 96 36
Situation	Situation	

11 km Lille, 178 300 hab.

Annual closure	Fermeture annnuelle	non
Weekly closure	Fermeture hebdomadaire	mardi

Fees main season
Tarifs haute saison le parcours

	Week days Semaine	We/Bank holidays We/Férié
Individual Individuel	200 F	300 F
Couple Couple	400 F	600 F

Caddy	Caddy	non
Electric Trolley	Chariot électrique	non
Buggy	Voiturette	200 F/18 trous
Clubs	Clubs	non

Credit cards Cartes de crédit
VISA - CB - Eurocard - MasterCard

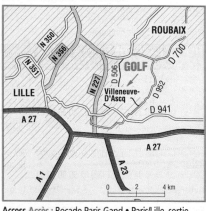

Access Accès : Rocade Paris-Gand • Paris/Lille, sortie Pont de Bois → Annappes-cousinerie • Gand-Tourcoing, sortie Roubaix-Est, à 1 km, à droite → Annappes, à 2 km, face au stade
Map 1 on page 99 Carte 1 Page 99

176

GOLF COURSE
PARCOURS
14/20

Site	Site	▮▮▮
Maintenance	Entretien	▮▮▮
Architect	Architecte	Bill Baker
Type	Type	parc
Relief	Relief	▮
Water in play	Eau en jeu	▮▮
Exp. to wind	Exposé au vent	▮
Trees in play	Arbres en jeu	▮▮

Scorecard Carte de score	**Chp.** Chp.	**Mens** Mess.	**Ladies** Da.
Length Long.	6106	6106	5152
Par	72	72	72

Advised golfing ability Niveau de jeu recommandé		0	12	24	36
Hcp required Handicap exigé	30				

CLUB HOUSE & AMENITIES
CLUB HOUSE ET ANNEXES
7/10

Pro shop	Pro-shop	▮▮
Driving range	Practice	▮▮▮
Sheltered	couvert	6 places
On grass	sur herbe	non
Putting-green	putting-green	oui
Pitching-green	pitching green	non

HOTEL FACILITIES
ENVIRONNEMENT HOTELIER
6/10

HOTELS HÔTELS
Alliance ****   Lille 11 km
83 chambres, D 670 F
Tél (33) 03 20 30 62 62, Fax (33) 03 20 42 94 25

Mercure Lille-Centre ***   Lille 11 km
102 chambres, D 480 F
Tél (33) 03 20 51 05 11, Fax (33) 03 20 74 01 65

Campanile **   Villeneuve-d'Ascq 1 km
50 chambres, D 270 F
Tél (33) 03 20 91 83 10, Fax (33) 03 20 67 21 18

RESTAURANTS RESTAURANT
L'Huitrière   Lille 11 km
Tél (33) 03 20 55 43 41

La Porte de Gand   Lille11 km
Tél(33) 03 20 74 28 66

Si personne ne sait qui a dessiné le 18 trous original de Mandelieu, on sait que le grand architecte Harry Colt a participé à son remaniement, comme en témoigne la forme des bunkers, parfois assez profonds pour poser problème aux joueurs moyens. Pourtant, ce sont les pins parasols qui constituent les principaux obstacles, leur envergure impressionnante rendant bien étroits les fairways. Les techniciens adorent ce parcours, car la plupart des coups de départ demandent des effets de fade ou de draw, un contrôle précis des trajectoires, un choix de club très subtil pour se retrouver en bonne position et signer les birdies que l'on peut espérer. Si sa longueur ne répond plus tout à fait aux exigences du jeu moderne, Cannes-Mandelieu reste un parcours de charme, malgré la proximité de la route du bord de mer et de la voie ferrée. Les par 3 (il y en a cinq) y sont d'une remarquable diversité. Les nouveaux propriétaires semblent décidés à améliorer un entretien longtemps délaissé.

While no-one knows exactly who laid out the original 18 holes at Mandelieu, we do know that the great Harry Colt had a hand in re-designing the course, as seen in the shape of the bunkers that are sometimes deep enough to cause high-handicappers a few headaches. Yet the main hazards here are the huge parasol pines, which stretch majestically upward and outward and make a number of fairways a little on the tight side. The more technically-minded golfers love this course, because the majority of tee-shots require draws or fades, precise flight control and very careful club selection to get into the right position to line up the birdies we all hope and pray for. While not as long as the modern game might require, Cannes-Mandelieu is nonetheless a charming course, despite being close to the coast road and a railway track. The five par 3s are remarkable for their variety.

Golf de Cannes Mandelieu Old Course

Route du Golf
F - 06210 MANDELIEU

Office	Secrétariat	(33) 04 93 49 55 39
Pro shop	Pro-shop	(33) 04 92 49 55 39
Fax	Fax	(33) 04 93 49 92 90
Situation	Situation	

5 km Cannes, 68 670 hab.

Annual closure	Fermeture annnuelle	non
Weekly closure	Fermeture hebdomadaire	

Fees main season
Tarifs haute saison la journée

	Week days Semaine	We/Bank holidays We/Férié
Individual Individuel	270 F	310 F
Couple Couple	540 F	620 F

Caddy	Caddy	non
Electric Trolley	Chariot électrique	non
Buggy	Voiturette	180 F/18 trous
Clubs	Clubs 1/2 série	100 F/jour

Credit cards Cartes de crédit
VISA - CB - Eurocard - MasterCard - AMEX

Access Accès : A8 sortie Mandelieu-La Napoule,
→ Mandelieu, → "Old Course"
Map 14 on page 125 Carte 14 Page 125

GOLF COURSE
PARCOURS   13 /20

Site	Site	▮▮▮▮▮
Maintenance	Entretien	▮▮▮▮
Architect	Architecte	Harry Colt
Type	Type	bord de mer
Relief	Relief	▮
Water in play	Eau en jeu	
Exp. to wind	Exposé au vent	▮▮▮
Trees in play	Arbres en jeu	▮▮▮▮

Scorecard Carte de score	Chp. Chp.	Mens Mess.	Ladies Da.
Length Long.	5676	5676	4973
Par	71	71	71

Advised golfing ability		0 12 24 36
Niveau de jeu recommandé		▮▮▮▮▮▮
Hcp required	Handicap exigé	28

CLUB HOUSE & AMENITIES
CLUB HOUSE ET ANNEXES   7 /10

Pro shop	Pro-shop	▮▮▮
Driving range	Practice	▮▮▮
Sheltered	couvert	non
On grass	sur herbe	oui
Putting-green	putting-green	oui
Pitching-green	pitching green	oui

HOTEL FACILITIES
ENVIRONNEMENT HOTELIER   8 /10

HOTELS HÔTELS
Hostellerie du golf ***   Mandelieu 1 km
39 chambres, D 640 F
Tél (33) 04 93 49 11 66, Fax (33) 04 92 97 04 01

Majestic ****   Cannes 5 km
263 chambres, D 2 200 F
Tél (33) 04 92 98 77 00, Fax (33) 04 93 38 97 90

Paris ***   Cannes 5 km
50 chambres, D 650 F
Tél (33) 04 93 38 30 89, Fax (33) 04 93 39 04 61

RESTAURANTS RESTAURANT
La Palme d'Or   Cannes 5 km
Tél (33) 04 92 98 74 14

Arcimboldo   Cannes 5 km
Tél(33) 04 93 94 14 15

Villa des Lys (Majestic)   Cannes 5 km
Tél(33) 04 92 98 77 00

177

Longtemps le club le plus prestigieux et le mieux entretenu de la région, il s'est un peu endormi face à la concurrence, mais paraît vouloir retrouver son prestige. Sa séduction apparente dissimule ses réelles difficultés. Les obstacles d'eau ne sont pas nombreux, mais ils sont placés de manière très stratégique. Si on peut avoir l'impression de pouvoir signer un bon score, le parcours résiste bien, notamment parce qu'il est difficile de récupérer le par quand on a manqué un green. Très divers dans son tracé, très bien paysagé, il ne récompense que les meilleurs, et surtout les techniciens du golf, les manieurs de balles. Pendant plus de dix ans, Cannes-Mougins a servi de cadre à un Open européen, ce qui a contribué à améliorer la qualité du terrain et à imposer des transformations. On souhaite que la grandeur passée puisse revivre ici.

For many a year the region's most prestigious and best-kept golf course, Cannes-Mougins has of late been caught napping by competitors. It only now seems to be striving to recover some of its prestige. The course's outer appeal tends to hide the real difficulties. There are not many water hazards, but what water there is is strategically placed. And while signing for a good score might look a possibility, the course always fights back, more notably because saving par can be so hard when you miss a green. Full of variety and nicely landscaped, this course rewards only the best, and especially the technicians who can flight the ball. Cannes-Mougins has hosted a top European Open event for more than 10 years, which has helped to improve the quality of the course and led to necessary changes. We all hope that Cannes Mougins soon recovers its past splendour.

Golf Country Club de Cannes Mougins
175, avenue du Golf
F - 06250 MOUGINS

Office	Secrétariat	(33) 04 93 75 79 13
Pro shop	Pro-shop	(33) 04 93 75 53 32
Fax	Fax	(33) 04 93 75 27 60
Situation	Situation	

9 km Cannes, 68 670 hab.

Annual closure	Fermeture annnuelle	non
Weekly closure	Fermeture hebdomadaire	

Fees main season
Tarifs haute saison la journée

	Week days Semaine	We/Bank holidays We/Férié
Individual Individuel	340 F	380 F
Couple Couple	680 F	760 F

Caddy	Caddy	sur réservation
Electric Trolley	Chariot électrique	non
Buggy	Voiturette	280 F/18 trous
Clubs	Clubs	non

Credit cards Cartes de crédit
VISA - CB - Eurocard - MasterCard - AMEX

Access Accès : A8 sortie Mougins, → Grasse,
sortie Antibes, → Golf
Map 14 on page 125 Carte 14 Page 125

GOLF COURSE
PARCOURS — 15/20

Site	Site	▬▬▬▬▬▬
Maintenance	Entretien	▬▬▬▬▬
Architect	Architecte	Peter Alliss Dave Thomas
Type	Type	forêt, campagne
Relief	Relief	▬▬▬
Water in play	Eau en jeu	▬▬▬
Exp. to wind	Exposé au vent	▬▬▬
Trees in play	Arbres en jeu	▬▬▬▬▬

Scorecard Carte de score	Chp. Chp.	Mens Mess.	Ladies Da.
Length Long.	6263	5889	5314
Par	72	72	72

Advised golfing ability
Niveau de jeu recommandé — 0 12 24 36

Hcp required Handicap exigé — 24 Mess. 28 Da.

CLUB HOUSE & AMENITIES
CLUB HOUSE ET ANNEXES — 7/10

Pro shop	Pro-shop	▬▬▬▬
Driving range	Practice	▬▬▬▬
Sheltered	couvert	5 places
On grass	sur herbe	oui
Putting-green	putting-green	oui
Pitching-green	pitching green	oui

HOTEL FACILITIES
ENVIRONNEMENT HOTELIER — 8/10

HOTELS HÔTELS
Hôtel de Mougins **** — Mougins 5
50 chambres, D 980 F
Tél (33) 04 92 92 17 07, Fax (33) 04 92 92 17 08
Les Muscadins **** — Mougins 5 km
8 chambres, D 900 F
Tél (33) 04 93 90 00 43, Fax (33) 04 92 92 88 23
Le Manoir de l'Etang *** — Mougins 5 km
15 chambres, D 900 F
Tél (33) 04 93 90 01 07, Fax (33) 04 92 92 20 70

RESTAURANTS RESTAURANT
Les Muscadins — Mougins 5 km
Tél (33) 04 93 90 00 43
Le Moulin de Mougins — Mougins 5 km
Tél (33) 04 93 75 78 24
L'Amandier de Mougins — Mougins 5 km
Tél (33) 04 93 90 00 91

178

Le dessin de Ronald Fream est de grande qualité, mais les abords immédiats des fairways restent trop rocailleux, ce qui pose toujours des problèmes quand on y envoie sa balle. Tous les trous demandent une bonne dose de réflexion avant de prendre les risques nécessaires pour espérer un bon score. Même si les obstacles sont bien visibles, leur nombre et leur placement stratégique poseront des problèmes aux débutants. Les joueurs moyens s'en sortiront mieux, et les frappeurs devront être d'une grande précision, surtout quand le vent souffle, ce qui arrive assez souvent ici. Une belle réussite architecturale, mais qui exigerait un entretien parfait. La station balnéaire de Cap d'Agde est très proche et pas bien belle, mais sa présence n'est pas trop envahissante, grâce aux modelages du parcours, et à une certaine végétation.

This layout, designed by Ronald Fream, is excellent, but the areas immediately skirting the fairways are still too rocky and so pose a few problems for wayward shots. All the holes here require careful thought before taking the risks required if you hope to card a good score. Even though most hazards are there to be seen, their number and strategic placement might be a little too much for beginners. Mid-handicappers should get by a little easier, although big-hitters should aim for precision, espcially when the wind gets up, as it does fairly often. In architectural terms this is an impressive site, but one which requires perfect upkeep. The seaside resort of Cap d'Agde is close by and hardly the most beautiful sight on earth, but the way the course is contoured and the vegetation keep most of it out of view.

Golf du Cap d'Agde
4, avenue des Alizés
F - 34300 CAP D'AGDE

Office	Secrétariat	(33) 04 67 26 54 40
Pro shop	Pro-shop	(33) 04 67 26 54 40
Fax	Fax	(33) 04 67 26 97 00
Situation	Situation	

22 km Béziers, 71 000 hab.

Annual closure	Fermeture annnuelle	non
Weekly closure	Fermeture hebdomadaire	

Fees main season
Tarifs haute saison la journée

	Week days Semaine	We/Bank holidays We/Férié
Individual Individuel	235 F	235 F
Couple Couple	470 F	470 F

Caddy	Caddy	non
Electric Trolley	Chariot électrique	non
Buggy	Voiturette	120 F/18 trous
Clubs	Clubs 1/2 série	60 F/jour

Credit cards Cartes de crédit
VISA - CB - Eurocard - MasterCard

Access Accès : A9 sortie 34 → Agde, → Ile des Loisirs, golf face à Aqualand
Map 13 on page 123 Carte 13 Page 123

GOLF COURSE
PARCOURS
15/20

Site	Site	▬
Maintenance	Entretien	▬
Architect	Architecte	Ronald Fream
Type	Type	campagne, bord de mer
Relief	Relief	▬
Water in play	Eau en jeu	▬
Exp. to wind	Exposé au vent	▬
Trees in play	Arbres en jeu	▬

Scorecard Carte de score	Chp. Chp.	Mens Mess.	Ladies Da.
Length Long.	6301	6160	5204
Par	72	72	72

Advised golfing ability		0 12 24 36
Niveau de jeu recommandé		▬▬▬▬▬
Hcp required	Handicap exigé	non

CLUB HOUSE & AMENITIES
CLUB HOUSE ET ANNEXES
6/10

Pro shop	Pro-shop	▬
Driving range	Practice	▬
Sheltered	couvert	non
On grass	sur herbe	oui
Putting-green	putting-green	oui
Pitching-green	pitching green	oui

HOTEL FACILITIES
ENVIRONNEMENT HOTELIER
5/10

HOTELS HÔTELS
Hôtel du Golf ***   Cap d'Agde 1,5 km
50 chambres, D 660 F
Tél (33) 04 67 26 87 03, Fax (33) 04 67 26 26 89

Capaô ***   Cap d'Agde 2 km
55 chambres, D 600 F
Tél (33) 04 67 26 99 44, Fax (33) 04 67 26 55 41

Azur **   200 m. du golf
34 chambres, D 400 F
Tél (33) 04 67 26 98 22, Fax (33) 04 67 26 48 14

RESTAURANTS RESTAURANT
La Tamarissière   Agde 2 km
Tél (33) 04 67 94 20 87

La Table d'Emilie   Marseillan 6 km
Tél (33) 04 67 77 63 59

179

L'une des belles réussites de l'architecte Michel Gayon dans une région assez à l'écart des grands circuits golfiques, mais très agréable pour de grands week-ends ou des vacances. Les cinq premiers trous du parcours se situent au milieu des pins et des chênes, avant qu'il s'élargisse dans un vaste espace autour d'un lac. Ses reliefs ne sont pas trop accentués, mais suffisants pour éviter l'écueil de la monotonie visuelle, permettant une grande variété de trous en montée ou en descente, avec cependant quelques coups aveugles. Les fairways et roughs ont été modelés avec goût. Très bien équilibré au plan du rythme de jeu, ce parcours n'offre pas de trous très longs, ce qui permet aux joueurs de tous niveaux d'y évoluer sans problèmes de cohabitation. Le golf fait partie d'un complexe sportif permettant aux non-golfeurs de décliner l'honneur de tirer le chariot : ils ont mieux à faire !

One of Michel Gayon's finest achievements in a region rather off the beaten track when it comes to golf courses, yet a pleasant spot for long week-ends or holidays. The first five holes run through pine-trees and oaks, before broadening out into a vast area around a lake. The course is not too hilly, but slopes enough to avoid visual monotony and to provide a good variety of uphill and downhill holes, plus, unfortunately, a few blind shots. The fairways and rough are tastefully designed. Nicely balanced for a brisk round of golf, the course has no really long holes, so is suitable for golfers of all handicaps to get along together. The golf course is part of a sports complex to tempt non-players away from pulling trolleys, and they certainly will have better things to do here.

Casteljaloux Golf Club

Avenue du Lac
F - 47700 CASTELJALOUX

Office	Secrétariat	(33) 05 53 93 51 60
Pro shop	Pro-shop	(33) 05 53 93 51 60
Fax	Fax	(33) 05 53 93 04 10
Situation	Situation	

60 km Agen, 30 550 hab. 90 km Bordeaux, 211 200 hab.

Annual closure	Fermeture annnuelle	non
Weekly closure	Fermeture hebdomadaire	

Fees main season
Tarifs haute saison la journée

	Week days Semaine	We/Bank holidays We/Férié
Individual Individuel	200 F	200 F
Couple Couple	390 F	390 F

Caddy	Caddy	non
Electric Trolley	Chariot électrique	non
Buggy	Voiturette	150 F/18 trous
Clubs	Clubs 1/2 série	60 F/jour

Credit cards Cartes de crédit
VISA - CB - Eurocard - MasterCard

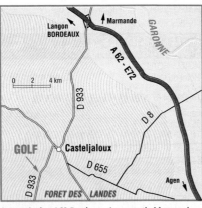

Access Accès : A62 Bordeaux-Agen, sortie Marmande, D933 → Casteljaloux, → Mont-de-Marsan, Golf à 3 km.
Map 12 on page 121 Carte 12 Page 121

GOLF COURSE
PARCOURS   15/20

Site	Site	▬▬
Maintenance	Entretien	▬
Architect	Architecte	Michel Gayon

Type	Type	vallon
Relief	Relief	▬▬
Water in play	Eau en jeu	▬▬▬
Exp. to wind	Exposé au vent	▬▬
Trees in play	Arbres en jeu	▬▬

Scorecard Carte de score	Chp. Chp.	Mens Mess.	Ladies Da.
Length Long.	5916	5484	4983
Par	72	72	72

Advised golfing ability		0 12 24 36
Niveau de jeu recommandé		▬▬▬▬▬
Hcp required	Handicap exigé	non

CLUB HOUSE & AMENITIES
CLUB HOUSE ET ANNEXES   6/10

Pro shop	Pro-shop	▬▬▬
Driving range	Practice	▬▬▬
Sheltered	couvert	6 places
On grass	sur herbe	non
Putting-green	putting-green	oui
Pitching-green	pitching green	oui

HOTEL FACILITIES
ENVIRONNEMENT HOTELIER   5/10

HOTELS HÔTELS
Village Hôtel   250 m. du golf
10 chambres, D 300 F
Tél (33) 05 53 93 51 60, Fax (33) 05 53 93 04 10

Château de Ruffiac ***   Route de Ruffiac
20 chambres, D 400 F   7 km
Tél (33) 05 53 93 18 63, Fax (33) 05 53 89 67 93

Les Cordeliers **   Casteljaloux
24 chambres, D 290 F   2 km
Tél (33) 05 53 93 02 19

RESTAURANTS RESTAURANT
Le Trianon   Marmande
Tél (33) 05 53 20 80 94   23 km

La Terrasse du Lac   Casteljaloux
Tél (33) 05 53 93 62 63   sur place

Dessiné par Fromanger et Adam, ce parcours a été remodelé à la suite de son achat par un groupe japonais, il est alors devenu un véritable jardin, très paysagé, où le moindre détail était soigné. Longtemps célèbre par un Club house luxueux et un entretien éblouissant, digne de véritables manucures, il a subi quelques revers financiers et ces avantages se sont aujourd'hui estompés, révélant les insuffisances du tracé. C'est un très agréable parcours, mais il manque de longueur et de difficultés stratégiques pour passionner les joueurs de bon niveau. Son tracé est agréable, les attaques de green sont très intéressantes, les trous sont de profils variés, mais il manque sans doute un zeste de génie et de "souffle" pour en faire un "grand" parcours. Jouer Cély est à recommander, le jouer souvent est une autre question. Un regret, le bruit de l'autoroute toute proche.

Originally designed by Fromanger and Adam, Cély has been restyled further to a buy-out by a Japanese group. It is now very much a landscaped garden in style, where no detail, no matter how small, has been overlooked. Famous for its luxurious club-house and manicured fairways and greens, the club has met with a few financial difficulties and these features have lost some of their shine, revealing in the process some of the layout's shortcomings. This is a very pleasant course, but it lacks the length and strategic complexity to excite the best players. The layout is pleasing with some interesting approach shots to the greens, and the holes offer variety enough, but it is almost certainly lacks that touch of genius and the staying power to be a truly great course. A round of golf at Cély is to be recommended, but playing it often is another matter. The one drawback is the noise from the adjacent A6 motorway.

Cély Golf Club

Château de Cély, route de Saint-Germain
F - 77930 CELY-EN-BIERE

Office	Secrétariat	(33) 01 64 38 03 07
Pro shop	Pro-shop	(33) 01 64 38 03 07
Fax	Fax	(33) 01 64 38 08 78
Situation	Situation	

14 km Fontainebleau, 15 710 hab.
12 km Melun, 35 320 hab.

Annual closure	Fermeture annnuelle	non
Weekly closure	Fermeture hebdomadaire	

Fees main season
Tarifs haute saison la journée

	Week days Semaine	We/Bank holidays We/Férié
Individual Individuel	300 F	400 F
Couple Couple	600 F	800 F

Dames le jeudi : GF + tea time: 250 F

Caddy	Caddy	non
Electric Trolley	Chariot électrique	100 F/18 trous
Buggy	Voiturette	non
Clubs	Clubs série	100 F/jour

Credit cards Cartes de crédit
VISA - CB - Eurocard - MasterCard - AMEX - DC - JCB

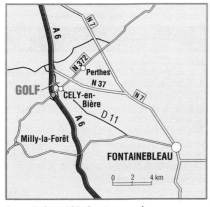

GOLF

N7
A 6
N 372
Perthes
N 37
CELY-en-Bière
N7
D 11
A 6
Milly-la-Forêt
FONTAINEBLEAU
0   2   4 km

Access Accès : • A6 Paris → Lyon, sortie Fontainebleau, Milly-la-Forêt • A 6 Lyon → Paris, sortie Cély **Map 3 on page 102** Carte 3 Page 102

GOLF COURSE
PARCOURS   15/20

Site	Site	▆▆▆▆▆
Maintenance	Entretien	▆▆▆▆▆
Architect	Architecte	Marc Adam Patrick Fromanger
Type	Type	parc
Relief	Relief	▆▆▆
Water in play	Eau en jeu	▆▆
Exp. to wind	Exposé au vent	▆
Trees in play	Arbres en jeu	▆▆▆

Scorecard Carte de score	Chp. Chp.	Mens Mess.	Ladies Da.
Length Long.	6026	5739	5118
Par	72	72	72

Advised golfing ability		0 12 24 36
Niveau de jeu recommandé		▆▆▆▆▆
Hcp required	Handicap exigé	30

CLUB HOUSE & AMENITIES
CLUB HOUSE ET ANNEXES   7/10

Pro shop	Pro-shop	▆▆▆▆
Driving range	Practice	▆▆▆
Sheltered	couvert	non
On grass	sur herbe	oui
Putting-green	putting-green	oui
Pitching-green	pitching green	oui

181

HOTEL FACILITIES
ENVIRONNEMENT HOTELIER   6/10

HOTELS HÔTELS

Bas Bréau ★★★★   Barbizon
12 chambres, D 1200 F   7 km
Tél (33) 01 60 66 40 08, Fax (33) 01 60 69 22 89

Les Pléiades ★★★   Barbizon
23 chambres, D 320 F   7 km
Tél (33) 01 60 66 40 25, Fax (33) 01 60 69 41 68

Aigle Noir ★★★★   Fontainebleau
51 chambres, D 1050 F   14 km
Tél (33) 01 64 22 32 65, Fax (33) 01 64 22 17 33

RESTAURANTS RESTAURANT

Le Bas Bréau   Barbizon
Tél (33) 01 60 66 40 05   7 km

Le Grand Veneur   Barbizon
Tél (33) 01 60 66 40 44   7 km

CHAILLY (CHÂTEAU DE)

14	8	6

Avec ce golf à proximité de Dijon et de l'autoroute A6 (sans bruits), le propriétaire souhaitait faire un "links" à l'intérieur des terres. Il n'a pas souhaité faire de plantations dans cet espace d'origine agricole parcouru par un ruisseau, et parsemé de quelques grandes pièces d'eau. L'architecture de Thierry Sprecher et Géry Watine est de bonne qualité et de bon goût, mais reste un peu timide et sans originalité frappante. Alors que les intentions originelles auraient demandé quelques modelages et davantage de violence visuelle, ils sont peu importants. Ce qui peut laisser une impression de platitude, avec pour avantage de permettre aux joueurs de tous niveaux de ne pas connaître trop de problèmes. Le château du domaine a été aménagé avec des chambres d'hôtel et un restaurant gastronomique, qui ont beaucoup contribué à la réputation du parcours.

The owner of this course, located near Dijon and the A6 motorway (no noise), set out to create an inland links. He also had no intention of planting trees or bushes on a site which was originally farming land crossed by a stream and dotted with a few stretches of water. The design by Thierry Sprecher and Géry Watine is high class and in good taste, but lacks boldness and originality. While original designs would have required a little shaping of ground and greater visual impact, neither one nor the other is very much in evidence. This gives an impression of flatness and a round of golf where players of all levels should stay out of trouble. The estate's castle has been refurbished with hotel rooms and a gourmet restaurant, which have done much to enhance the course's reputation.

Golf Club du Château de Chailly
F - 21320 CHAILLY-SUR-ARMENCON

Office	Secrétariat	(33) 03 80 90 30 40
Pro shop	Pro-shop	(33) 03 80 90 30 40
Fax	Fax	(33) 03 80 90 30 05
Situation	Situation	

55 km Dijon, 146 700 hab.
5 km Pouilly-en-Auxois, 1 370 hab.

Annual closure	Fermeture annnuelle	oui
		1/01/99 → 31/01/99
Weekly closure	Fermeture hebdomadaire	

Fees main season Tarifs haute saison la journée

	Week days Semaine	We/Bank holidays We/Férié
Individual Individuel	200 F	300 F
Couple Couple	400 F	600 F

Lundis (sauf fériés) 1 GF + 1 déj.-buffet : 200 F

Caddy	Caddy	non
Electric Trolley	Chariot électrique	60 F/18 trous
Buggy	Voiturette	250 F/18 trous
Clubs	Clubs série	100 F/jour

Credit cards Cartes de crédit
VISA - CB - Eurocard - MasterCard

182

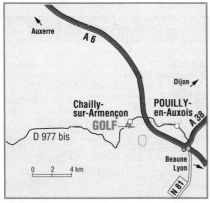

Access Accès : A6 sortie Pouilly-en-Auxois,
D977 bis → Saulieu
Map 7 on page 111 Carte 7 Page 111

GOLF COURSE
PARCOURS **14**/20

Site	Site	
Maintenance	Entretien	
Architect	Architecte	Thierry Sprecher
		Géry Watine
Type	Type	plaine, bocage
Relief	Relief	
Water in play	Eau en jeu	
Exp. to wind	Exposé au vent	
Trees in play	Arbres en jeu	

Scorecard Carte de score	Chp. Chp.	Mens Mess.	Ladies Da.
Length Long.	6146	5844	5224
Par	72	72	72

Advised golfing ability	0	12	24	36
Niveau de jeu recommandé				
Hcp required	Handicap exigé	non		

CLUB HOUSE & AMENITIES
CLUB HOUSE ET ANNEXES **8**/10

Pro shop	Pro-shop	
Driving range	Practice	
Sheltered	couvert	12 places
On grass	sur herbe	non
Putting-green	putting-green	oui
Pitching-green	pitching green	oui

HOTEL FACILITIES
ENVIRONNEMENT HOTELIER **6**/10

HOTELS HÔTELS
Château de Chailly **** — sur place
42 chambres, D 1900 F
Tél (33) 03 80 90 30 30, Fax (33) 03 80 90 30 00

Château de Sainte-Sabine *** — 14 km. S.E. du golf
18 chambres, D 590 F
Tél (33) 03 80 49 22 00, Fax (33) 03 80 49 20 01

Hostellerie du Château *** — Châteauneuf
18 chambres, D 430 F — 15 km
Tél (33) 03 80 49 22 00, Fax (33) 03 80 90 20 01

RESTAURANTS RESTAURANT
La Côte d'Or — Saulieu
Tél (33) 03 80 64 07 66 — 20 km

L'Armançon — Pouilly-en-Auxois
Tél(33) 03 80 90 30 30 — 5 km

CHAMONIX ✱ | 15 | 6 | 7

Dessiné par Robert Trent Jones, ce parcours souffrait d'un entretien très en deçà de son architecture, mais des travaux récents de drainage devraient y mettre bon ordre. Les greens demanderaient aussi une particulière attention. Dans un site exceptionnel dans la vallée de Chamonix, orné de sapins et de bouleaux, il n'a de golf de montagne que son paysage, car son relief est très modéré. Parcouru par de petits ruisseaux et par l'Arve, ses difficultés ne sont pas insurmontables pour un joueur de bon niveau capable de réfléchir sur la stratégie mais il peut être délicat pour un débutant, en raison de l'étroitesse de ses fairways. Conçu comme un golf de vacances, il peut être joué plusieurs fois sans ennui, mais ses difficultés assez subtiles apparaissent vite quand on chasse un bon score... C'est néanmoins l'un des tout meilleurs parcours de montagne.

Designed by Robert Trent Jones, this course has suffered from a standard of upkeep well below that of its layout, but recent drainage work should put things right. The greens, too, could do with some careful maintenance work. Laid out in an exceptional site in the valley of Chamonix, lined with fir and birch trees, the only thing mountaineous about this course is the landscape, because the actual terrain is flat. Crossed by a number of streams and the gushing Arve river, the difficulties here are not impossible for a player with good ability and a strategic brain, but it can pose a problem or two for beginners owing to a number of tight fairways. Designed as a holiday course, you can play it several times with the same fun and enthusiasm, although the subtle difficulties tend to emerge pretty quickly when you are after a good score. In the final reckoning, this is one of Europe's best Alpine golf courses.

Golf Club de Chamonix
35, route du Golf
F - 74400 CHAMONIX

Office	Secrétariat	(33) 04 50 53 06 28
Pro shop	Pro-shop	(33) 04 50 53 45 23
Fax	Fax	(33) 04 50 53 38 69
Situation	Situation	

3 km Chamonix, 9 700 hab.
85 km Genève, 167 200 hab.

Annual closure	Fermeture annnuelle	oui
		1/12/98 → 30/04/99
Weekly closure	Fermeture hebdomadaire	

Fees main season
Tarifs haute saison la journée

	Week days Semaine	We/Bank holidays We/Férié
Individual Individuel	300 F	300 F
Couple Couple	600 F	600 F

Caddy	Caddy	non
Electric Trolley	Chariot électrique	non
Buggy	Voiturette	200 F/18 trous
Clubs	Clubs 1/2 série	80 F/jour

Credit cards Cartes de crédit
VISA - CB - Eurocard - MasterCard

Access Accès : • Genève, A40 → Chamonix
• Megève, N212, D909, N205
Map 11 on page 119 Carte 11 Page 119

GOLF COURSE
PARCOURS 15/20

Site	Site	▰▰▰▰▰▱
Maintenance	Entretien	▰▰▰▱▱▱
Architect	Architecte	Robert Trent Jones
Type	Type	montagne , parc
Relief	Relief	▰▱▱▱▱▱
Water in play	Eau en jeu	▰▰▱▱▱▱
Exp. to wind	Exposé au vent	▰▱▱▱▱▱
Trees in play	Arbres en jeu	▰▰▱▱▱▱

Scorecard Carte de score	Chp. Chp.	Mens Mess.	Ladies Da.
Length Long.	6075	5735	5347
Par	72	72	72

Advised golfing ability		0 12 24 36
Niveau de jeu recommandé		▰▰▰▱
Hcp required	Handicap exigé	35

CLUB HOUSE & AMENITIES
CLUB HOUSE ET ANNEXES 6/10

Pro shop	Pro-shop	▰▰▰▱▱▱
Driving range	Practice	▰▰▱▱▱▱
Sheltered	couvert	6 places
On grass	sur herbe	non
Putting-green	putting-green	oui
Pitching-green	pitching green	oui

HOTEL FACILITIES
ENVIRONNEMENT HOTELIER 7/10

HOTELS HÔTELS
Le Labrador *** — sur place
32 chambres, D 830 F
Tél (33) 04 50 55 90 09, Fax (33) 04 50 53 15 85

Albert 1er **** — Chamonix
30 chambres, D 800 F — 2 km
Tél (33) 04 50 53 05 09, Fax (33) 04 50 53 95 48

Beausoleil ** — Le Lavancher
15 chambres, D 500 F — 2 km
Tél (33) 04 50 54 00 78, Fax (33) 04 50 54 17 34

RESTAURANTS RESTAURANT
Albert 1er — Chamonix
Tél (33) 04 50 53 05 09 — 2 km

Le Crochon — Chamonix
Tél (33) 04 50 53 41 78 — 2 km

183

En dehors du premier et du dernier trou, directement inspirés de l'architecture à la française, et assez insipides, ce parcours accidenté, dessiné par Nelson et Huau, est une jolie promenade dans les bois, avec quelques spécimens d'arbres magnifiques, mais des fairways généralement de bonne taille. De nombreux sapins font parfois imaginer être en montagne, alors que nous sommes au cœur de la Normandie. Chez les architectes, on sent les paysagistes sans doute plus que les golfeurs, mais si l'on peut regretter un certain manque de souffle, il n'y a pas de fautes graves, ce qui incite à le recommander davantage aux amoureux de belles balades en famille (ou avec des amis) qu'aux joueurs de haut niveau à la recherche de grands défis. Les écuries du château ont été aménagées pour recevoir le Club House.

Excepting the first and last holes, directly inspired by French style architecture but otherwise totally uninspired, this hilly course, designed by Nelson and Huau, is a beautiful stroll through the woods, where some magnificent trees leave enough room for some decently sized fairways. With some of the pine-trees, you'd think you were in the Alps, rather than in the heart of Normandy. Architecturally speaking, the course is the work of landscapers rather than golfers, but if we overlook a little lack of punch, there is nothing at all wrong with this course, which is to be recommended more for family outings (or rounds with friends) rather than for skilful players looking for a tough challenge. The castle's stables have been refurbished and converted into a club-house.

Golf du Champ de Bataille

Château du Champ-de-Bataille
F - 27110 LE NEUBOURG

Office	Secrétariat	(33) 02 32 35 03 72
Pro shop	Pro-shop	(33) 02 32 35 03 72
Fax	Fax	(33) 02 32 35 83 10
Situation	Situation	

27 km Evreux, 49 100 hab.

Annual closure	Fermeture annnuelle	non
Weekly closure	Fermeture hebdomadaire	

Fees main season
Tarifs haute saison le parcours

	Week days Semaine	We/Bank holidays We/Férié
Individual Individuel	220 F	350 F
Couple Couple	440 F	660 F

Après 17 h. : 200 F (We)

Caddy	Caddy	sur réservation
Electric Trolley	Chariot électrique	non
Buggy	Voiturette	220 F/18 trous
Clubs	Clubs	oui

Credit cards Cartes de crédit
VISA - CB - Eurocard - MasterCard - AMEX - DC

HARCOURT
Ste-Opportune-du-Bosc
Villez
LISIEUX
GOLF
Fibeuf
LE NEUBOURG
Louviers
Evreux

0   2   4 km

Access Accès : • Evreux, N13 → Lisieux → Le Neubourg
• Caen ou Lisieux, N13 → Evreux → Le Neubourg
Map 2 on page 101 Carte 2 Page 101

GOLF COURSE / PARCOURS — 14/20

Site	Site	
Maintenance	Entretien	
Architect	Architecte	Robin Nelson Thierry Huau
Type	Type	forêt
Relief	Relief	
Water in play	Eau en jeu	
Exp. to wind	Exposé au vent	
Trees in play	Arbres en jeu	

Scorecard Carte de score	Chp. Chp.	Mens Mess.	Ladies Da.
Length Long.	5983	5600	5130
Par	72	72	72

Advised golfing ability Niveau de jeu recommandé	0	12	24	36
Hcp required	Handicap exigé	non		

CLUB HOUSE & AMENITIES / CLUB HOUSE ET ANNEXES — 6/10

Pro shop	Pro-shop	
Driving range	Practice	
Sheltered	couvert	non
On grass	sur herbe	oui, été
Putting-green	putting-green	oui
Pitching-green	pitching green	oui

HOTEL FACILITIES / ENVIRONNEMENT HOTELIER — 3/10

HOTELS HÔTELS

Le Logis de Brionne ** — Brionne
12 chambres, D 350 F — 5 km
Tél (33) 02 32 44 81 73, Fax (33) 02 32 45 10 92

Pré Saint-Germain *** — Louviers
34 chambres, D 560 F — 20 km
Tél (33) 02 32 40 48 48, Fax (33) 02 32 50 75 60

RESTAURANTS RESTAURANT

Hôtel de France — Evreux
Tél (33) 02 32 39 09 25 — 27 km

Côté Jardin — Le Neubourg
Tél (33) 02 32 35 81 89 — 2 km

184

CHANTACO ✳ 14 7 7

Ce parcours, l'un des plus célèbres de la Côte Basque, reste incontournable par son charme, son ambiance et sa tradition sportive, cultivée par la famille Lacoste. Mais son manque de longueur ou l'espace commun au practice et au trou n°16 ne peuvent lui accorder le titre de grand golf. Relativement accidenté, il est cependant plus fatigant d'en déjouer les pièges que d'y marcher. Il donne l'impression de promettre une journée tranquille, mais résiste bien aux ambitieux : souvent étroit, avec quelques dévers redoutables et de petits greens, il demande plus de précision que de longueur. Si l'on ne cherche pas à défier un monstre pendant ses vacances, Chantaco reste par beau temps (il peut être humide) un parcours plaisant. L'architecte originel était Harry Colt, mais la diversité des styles rencontrés laisse à penser que son travail a été modifié...

Chantaco, one of the Basque Coast's most celebrated golf courses, is a must for its charm, atmosphere and sporting tradition, nurtured by the Lacoste family. But for the lack of space and the common area shared by the driving range and the 16th hole, it could be ranked as one of the greats in the area. Although rather a hilly lay-out, the most tiring thing about Chantaco is not so much the walking but trying to avoid the traps. It gives the impression of a quiet day's golfing, but even the most ambitious golfer will find it more than a handful. Often tight, with a few formidably sloping fairways and small greens, the course demands precision more than length off the tee. Avoid trying to defy this monster during your holidays and you will find Chantaco a very pleasant course when the weather is fine (it can get very wet). The original architect was Harry Colt, but with the variety of styles around the course, we suspect his design might have been altered here and there.

Golf de Chantaco
Route d'Ascain
F - 64500 SAINT-JEAN-DE-LUZ

Office	Secrétariat	(33) 05 59 26 14 22
Pro shop	Pro-shop	(33) 05 59 26 21 45
Fax	Fax	(33) 05 59 26 48 37
Situation	Situation	

2 km Saint-Jean-de-Luz, 13 030 hab.
15 km Biarritz, 28 740 hab.

Annual closure	Fermeture annnuelle	non
Weekly closure	Fermeture hebdomadaire	mardi
		haute saison

Fees main season
Tarifs haute saison le parcours

	Week days Semaine	We/Bank holidays We/Férié
Individual Individuel	340 F	340 F
Couple Couple	680 F	680 F

Caddy	Caddy	sur réservation
Electric Trolley	Chariot électrique	non
Buggy	Voiturette	200 F/18 trous
Clubs	Clubs série	80 F/jour

Credit cards Cartes de crédit
VISA - CB - Eurocard - MasterCard

ST-JEAN-DE-LUZ
Vers Biarritz
Vers Hendaye
A 63
N 10
0 2 4 km
CHANTACO
GOLF
D 918
ASCAIN

Access Accès : A63 Biarritz → Saint-Jean-de-Luz, sortie Saint-Jean-de-Luz Nord, D918 → Chantaco, Ascain
Map 12 on page 120 Carte 12 Page 120

GOLF COURSE
PARCOURS
14/20

Site	Site	▬▬▬
Maintenance	Entretien	▬▬▬
Architect	Architecte	Harry Colt
Type	Type	forêt, plaine
Relief	Relief	
Water in play	Eau en jeu	▬
Exp. to wind	Exposé au vent	▬▬
Trees in play	Arbres en jeu	▬▬▬

Scorecard Carte de score	Chp. Chp.	Mens Mess.	Ladies Da.
Length Long.	5722	5385	5224
Par	70	70	70

Advised golfing ability		0 12 24 36
Niveau de jeu recommandé		▬▬▬▬▬▬
Hcp required	Handicap exigé	non

CLUB HOUSE & AMENITIES
CLUB HOUSE ET ANNEXES
7/10

Pro shop	Pro-shop	▬▬▬
Driving range	Practice	▬▬▬
Sheltered	couvert	4 places
On grass	sur herbe	non
Putting-green	putting-green	oui
Pitching-green	pitching green	oui

HOTEL FACILITIES
ENVIRONNEMENT HOTELIER
7/10

HOTELS HÔTELS
Chantaco ★★★★ sur place
22 chambres, D 1500 F
Tél (33) 05 59 26 14 76, Fax (33) 05 59 26 35 97

La Devinière ★★★ Saint-Jean-de-Luz
8 chambres, D 650 F 2 km
Tél (33) 05 59 26 05 51, Fax (33) 05 59 51 26 38

Parc Victoria ★★★ Saint-Jean-de-Luz
10 chambres, D 1250 F 2 km
Tél (33) 05 59 26 78 78, Fax (33) 05 59 26 78 08

RESTAURANTS RESTAURANT
La Coupole Saint-Jean-de-Luz
Tél (33) 05 59 26 35 36 2 km

Chez Dominique Ciboure
Tél (33) 05 59 47 29 16 3 km

185

"Vineuil" reste l'incontournable grand classique en France, et si le passage du golf à 36 trous en a modifié le déroulement, notamment le finale de ce 18 trous, aucune blessure n'a été infligée aux trous "Simpson", une marque de respect dont bien des golfs auraient dû s'inspirer. Et bien des architectes aussi, qui devraient faire des stages prolongés ici, tant s'y exprime la grandeur dans la sobriété et la franchise, la subtilité technique dans la beauté esthétique. Hautement stratégique, diaboliquement intelligent, Vineuil exige une stratégie exactement adaptée à ses limites du moment, et se révèle un sérieux examen de passage des capacités à jouer au golf. Très difficile des départs les plus reculés, plus aimable des départs normaux, parfois un peu in-juste pour les dames de très bon niveau (de leurs départs), c'est simplement un très grand parcours (mais l'entretien est seulement moyen...).

The "Vineuil" course is still France's great classic contribution to golf, and while the upgrading to 36 holes has changed the way the course unwinds, particularly the finish of the former 18 holes, no harm has been done to Simpson's original layout, a mark of respect that many golf clubs might have done well to ponder. And many designers, as well, who should come here for extended training to see just how well greatness can spring from discretion and honesty, and technical subtlety from sheer beauty. Highly strategic and devilishly intelligent, Vineuil requires strategy tailored to your limitations on the day, and can prove to be a very serious examina-tion of your golfing ability. Very tough indeed from the back tees and sometimes a little unfair for the best la-dies players (from their own tees), this is simply a really great course (although green-keeping is fair only).

Golf de Chantilly
F - 60500 CHANTILLY

Office	Secrétariat	(33) 03 44 57 04 43
Pro shop	Pro-shop	(33) 03 44 58 26 72
Fax	Fax	(33) 03 44 57 26 54
Situation	Situation	

41 km N de Paris, 2 175 200 hab.
2 km de Chantilly, 11 341 hab.

Annual closure	Fermeture annnuelle	non
Weekly closure	Fermeture hebdomadaire	jeudi

Fees main season Tarifs haute saison 18 trous

	Week days Semaine	We/Bank holidays We/Férié
Individual Individuel	350 F	—
Couple Couple	700 F	—

We : membres et leurs invités (members and guests only)

Caddy	Caddy	réserver, F 250
Electric Trolley	Chariot électrique	50 F/18 trous
Buggy	Voiturette	non
Clubs	Clubs	non

Credit cards Cartes de crédit
VISA - CB - Eurocard - MasterCard

186

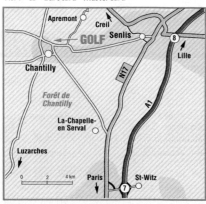

Access Accès : A1 sortie Survilliers, D922 → Fosses. N17 → La Chapelle en Serval. A La Chapelle, à gauche sur D924 → Chantilly. Après le Château, à droite → Vineuil, Golf. **Map 3 on page 102** Carte 3 Page 102

GOLF COURSE
PARCOURS   **18**/20

Site	Site	
Maintenance	Entretien	
Architect	Architecte	Tom Simpson
Type	Type	"inland", forêt
Relief	Relief	
Water in play	Eau en jeu	
Exp. to wind	Exposé au vent	
Trees in play	Arbres en jeu	

Scorecard Carte de score	Chp. Chp.	Mens Mess.	Ladies Da.
Length Long.	6396	5664	4809
Par	71	71	74

Advised golfing ability	0	12	24	36
Niveau de jeu recommandé				
Hcp required Handicap exigé	35			

CLUB HOUSE & AMENITIES
CLUB HOUSE ET ANNEXES   **7**/10

Pro shop	Pro-shop	
Driving range	Practice	
Sheltered	couvert	4 tapis
On grass	sur herbe	oui
Putting-green	putting-green	oui
Pitching-green	pitching green	oui

HOTEL FACILITIES
ENVIRONNEMENT HOTELIER   **6**/10

HOTELS HÔTELS
Le Parc   Chantilly
58 chambres, D 450 F   3 km
Tél (33) 03 44 58 20 00, Fax (33) 03 44 57 31 10

Château de la Tour   Gouvieux
41 chambres, D 890 F   6 km
Tél (33) 03 44 57 07 39, Fax (33) 03 44 57 31 97

Relais d'Aumale   Montgrésin
22 chambres, D 650 F   8 km
Tél (33) 03 44 54 61 31, Fax (33) 03 44 54 69 15

RESTAURANTS RESTAURANT
Relais Condé   Chantilly
Tél (33) 03 44 57 05 75   3 km

Le Verbois   St Maximin
Tél (33) 03 44 24 06 22   5 km

Avec une moitié de trous en forêt et l'autre en plaine, ce parcours est assez plat, mais jamais monotone. Jeremy Pern aime l'architecture de links, et le montre par son modelage de buttes et une grande utilisation de bunkers de toutes tailles, y compris des "pot-bunkers". Les obstacles d'eau sont pratiquement tous naturels, y compris un étang de trois hectares, ce qui apporte de jolis éléments paysagers. Un joueur réfléchi peut toujours jouer la sécurité, ce qui rend le parcours amusant pour tous les niveaux, les difficultés étant visibles. Franc et plaisant, il peut cependant être un peu long pour les joueurs de plus de 24 de handicap. Les greens sont assez faciles à lire, mais certaines attaques sont délicates à apprécier. Ce beau tracé bénéficie d'un entretien simplement moyen, ce qui le réserve aux périodes sèches : il supporte mal l'humidité.

With half the holes in the woods and the other half in open country, this is a fairly flat but never boring course. Architect Jeremy Pern is fond of links layouts and shows it here, with carefully shaped mounds and the widespread use of bunkers in all shapes and sizes, and a number of pot-bunkers. Nearly all the water is natural, including a lake of some 7 acres or more, which adds to the pretty landscape. A thoughtful player, as always, can play safe, thus making this an amusing course for all players of all abilities, as the difficulties are there to be seen. Honest and pleasant to play, it can however be a little long for high-handicappers. The greens are easy to read but some approach shots tend to be a little tricky to assess. The standard of green-keeping for this fine layout is average only. And as it doesn't like rain, this is a course for the drier days.

Golf du Charmeil
Saint-Quentin-sur-Isère
F - 38210 SAINT-QUENTIN-SUR-ISERE

Office	Secrétariat	(33) 04 76 93 67 28
Pro shop	Pro-shop	(33) 04 76 93 67 28
Fax	Fax	(33) 04 76 93 62 04
Situation	Situation	

24 km Grenoble, 150 750 hab.

Annual closure	Fermeture annnuelle	non

Weekly closure	Fermeture hebdomadaire	

Fees main season Tarifs haute saison la journée

	Week days Semaine	We/Bank holidays We/Férié
Individual Individuel	190 F	250 F
Couple Couple	380 F	500 F

Mardi (1/05 → 30/11) : GF+repas+compétition, 180 F.

Caddy	Caddy	non
Electric Trolley	Chariot électrique	non
Buggy	Voiturette	120 F/18 trous
Clubs	Clubs 1/2 série	50 F/jour

Credit cards Cartes de crédit
VISA - CB - Eurocard - MasterCard - AMEX - DC

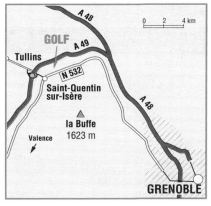

GOLF
A 48
A 49
Tullins
N 532
Saint-Quentin
sur-Isère
A 48
la Buffe
1623 m
Valence
GRENOBLE
0   2   4 km

Access Accès : • Grenoble A49 → Valence • Lyon A48 → Grenoble → A49 Valence, sortie Tullins → Saint-Quentin-sur-Isère
Map 11 on page 118 Carte 11 Page 118

GOLF COURSE
PARCOURS
16/20

Site	Site	
Maintenance	Entretien	
Architect	Architecte	Jeremy Pern Jean Garaïalde
Type	Type	plaine, forêt
Relief	Relief	
Water in play	Eau en jeu	
Exp. to wind	Exposé au vent	
Trees in play	Arbres en jeu	

Scorecard Carte de score	Chp. Chp.	Mens Mess.	Ladies Da.
Length Long.	6251	5852	5277
Par	73	73	73

Advised golfing ability		0 12 24 36
Niveau de jeu recommandé		
Hcp required	Handicap exigé	non

CLUB HOUSE & AMENITIES
CLUB HOUSE ET ANNEXES
6/10

Pro shop	Pro-shop	
Driving range	Practice	
Sheltered	couvert	8 places
On grass	sur herbe	non
Putting-green	putting-green	oui
Pitching-green	pitching green	non

HOTEL FACILITIES
ENVIRONNEMENT HOTELIER
6/10

HOTELS HÔTELS
Golf Hôtel du Charmeil ***   sur place
50 chambres, D 450 F
Tél (33) 04 76 93 67 28, Fax (33) 04 76 93 62 04

Auberge de Malatras **   Tullins
19 chambres, D 290 F   6 km
Tél (33) 04 76 07 02 30, Fax (33) 04 76 07 76 48

Campanile **   Saint-Egrène
39 chambres, D 270 F   10 km
Tél (33) 04 76 75 57 88, Fax (33) 04 76 75 06 49

RESTAURANTS RESTAURANT
Philippe Serratrice   Voiron
Tél (33) 04 76 05 29 88   16 km

La Table d'Ernest   Grenoble
Tél (33) 04 76 43 19 56   24 km

187

A proximité immédiate du château historique de Cheverny, ce parcours contribue au "parcours golfique" des Châteaux de la Loire. Il se déroule largement en forêt, mais aussi autour de l'étang de la Rousselière. De nombreux petits obstacles d'eau apportent des éléments de jeu bienvenus dans cet espace très plat, mais toujours humide en saison pluvieuse. L'architecte Olivier van der Vynckt a très peu bougé le terrain, recherché la subtilité des formes, notamment au niveau des alentours de green, mais on aurait souhaité que le terrain soit davantage modelé, ne serait-ce que pour mieux définir les trous dans cet espace, et donner de meilleurs points de repère. Le rythme de jeu est plaisant, les différents départs permettent de l'adapter à tous les niveaux. Une réalisation de bonne facture, avec un Club-House sympathique.

In the immediate vicinity of the historic Château de Cheverny, the course of the same name is one of a trail of golfing venues amidst the castles of the Loire valley. It is laid out mostly through a forest but also around a lake. Numerous minor water hazards add welcome spice to a very flat setting, which is always wet in autumn and winter. Architect Olivier van der Vinckt moved very little earth and preferred a more subtle touch, particularly around the greens. However, a little more shaping of terrain would have been welcome, if only to create greater definition for individual holes and clearer points of reference. Overall, the balance is pleasing and the difference in tee-off areas makes this a course for all abilities. A good quality course with a friendly club-house.

Golf de Cheverny
La Rousselière
F - 41700 CHEVERNY

Office	Secrétariat	(33) 02 54 79 24 70
Pro shop	Pro-shop	(33) 02 54 79 24 70
Fax	Fax	(33) 02 54 79 25 52
Situation	Situation	

15 km Blois, 49 310 hab.

Annual closure	Fermeture annnuelle	non
Weekly closure	Fermeture hebdomadaire	mardi
		1/11→1/03/99

Fees main season
Tarifs haute saison la journée

	Week days Semaine	We/Bank holidays We/Férié
Individual Individuel	190 F	260 F
Couple Couple	380 F	520 F

GF + déjeuner : Sem. 260 F, We 310 F

Caddy	Caddy	non
Electric Trolley	Chariot électrique	non
Buggy	Voiturette	150 F/18 trous
Clubs	Clubs 1/2 série	100 F/jour

Credit cards Cartes de crédit
VISA - CB - Eurocard - MasterCard - AMEX

188

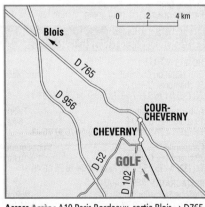

Access Accès : A10 Paris-Bordeaux, sortie Blois → D765
→ Romorantin → Cour-Cheverny, → Golf
Map 3 on page 102 Carte 3 Page 102

GOLF COURSE
PARCOURS
14/20

Site	Site	
Maintenance	Entretien	
Architect	Architecte	O. van der Vynckt
Type	Type	forêt, plaine
Relief	Relief	
Water in play	Eau en jeu	
Exp. to wind	Exposé au vent	
Trees in play	Arbres en jeu	

Scorecard Carte de score	Chp. Chp.	Mens Mess.	Ladies Da.
Length Long.	6276	5830	4933
Par	71	71	71

Advised golfing ability	0	12	24	36
Niveau de jeu recommandé				
Hcp required	Handicap exigé	non		

CLUB HOUSE & AMENITIES
CLUB HOUSE ET ANNEXES
7/10

Pro shop	Pro-shop	
Driving range	Practice	
Sheltered	couvert	5 places
On grass	sur herbe	non
Putting-green	putting-green	oui
Pitching-green	pitching green	oui

HOTEL FACILITIES
ENVIRONNEMENT HOTELIER
6/10

HOTELS HÔTELS

Château du Breuil ***		Cour-Cheverny
16 chambres, D 670 F		2 km
Tél (33) 02 54 44 20 20, Fax (33) 02 54 44 30 40		

Les Trois Marchands **		Cour-Cheverny
38 chambres, D 340 F		2 km
Tél (33) 02 54 79 96 44, Fax (33) 02 54 79 25 60		

Château de la Gondelaine **		Contres
15 chambres, D 800 F		10 km
Tél (33) 02 54 79 09 14, Fax (33) 02 54 79 64 92		

RESTAURANTS RESTAURANT

Les Trois Marchands		Cour-Cheverny
Tél (33) 02 54 79 96 44		2 km

Restaurant du Golf		Golf
Tél (33) 02 54 79 23 02		

Un des grands exemples français de links, signé par le légendaire Tom Simpson. L'essentiel de son dessin a été préservé, même si les aspects les plus sauvages ont été gommés par l'arrosage automatique et certaines "améliorations". La disparition de quelques difficultés a rendu le parcours plus accessible à tous les niveaux, surtout par beau temps comme sur tous ces types de golfs en bord de mer. Les greens sont de bonne qualité, les obstacles bien visibles, la stratégie assez évidente, l'absence de relief et le confort d'un sol sablonneux rendent la marche plaisante. Mais, quand le vent souffle, Chiberta devient un test où la maîtrise des trajectoires de balles est essentielle et les spécialistes du petit jeu s'en donneront à cœur joie. Les équipements du Club house restent spartiates, mais l'entretien a été très amélioré. A jouer sans réserve, y compris par mauvais temps !

One of the great French examples of a links course, designed by the legendary Tom Simpson. The original basic design has been preserved, although the wilder features have been smoothed away by automatic sprinklers and a number of "improvements". With fewer difficulties, the course is more accessible to all golfers, especially in fine weather (as always). The greens are good, the hazards clearly visible, strategy is pretty obvious, and the absence of any real relief with the comfort of sandy soil make for a pleasant walk. But once the wind gets up, Chiberta becomes a test where ball-control is essential and where players with a tight short game will come into their own. Club-house facilities are as Spartan as ever but upkeep has been much improved. A must, even in bad weather !

Golf de Chiberta
104, bd des Plages
F - 64600 ANGLET

Office	Secrétariat	(33) 05 59 63 83 20
Pro shop	Pro-shop	(33) 05 59 63 17 87
Fax	Fax	(33) 05 59 63 30 56
Situation	Situation	

3 km Biarritz, 28 740 hab.

Annual closure	Fermeture annnuelle	non
Weekly closure	Fermeture hebdomadaire	jeudi
		16/09 → 30/04/99

Fees main season Tarifs haute saison la journée

	Week days Semaine	We/Bank holidays We/Férié
Individual Individuel	320 F	320 F
Couple Couple	520 F	520 F

Eté : – 50% après 18 H

Caddy	Caddy	200 F/18 trous
Electric Trolley	Chariot électrique	70 F/18 trous
Buggy	Voiturette	non
Clubs	Clubs série	70 F/jour

Credit cards Cartes de crédit
VISA - CB - Eurocard - MasterCard

Access Accès : A63, sortie Biarritz. Biarritz → Anglet
Map 12 on page 120 Carte 12 Page 120

GOLF COURSE
PARCOURS
16/20

Site	Site	▆▆▆▆▆
Maintenance	Entretien	▆▆▆▆▆
Architect	Architecte	Tom Simpson
Type	Type	links, forêt
Relief	Relief	▆▆
Water in play	Eau en jeu	▆▆
Exp. to wind	Exposé au vent	▆▆▆▆
Trees in play	Arbres en jeu	▆▆▆

Scorecard Carte de score	Chp. Chp.	Mens Mess.	Ladies Da.
Length Long.	5650	5313	4882
Par	71	71	71

Advised golfing ability Niveau de jeu recommandé	0	12	24	36
Hcp required Handicap exigé	35			

CLUB HOUSE & AMENITIES
CLUB HOUSE ET ANNEXES
6/10

Pro shop	Pro-shop	▆▆▆▆
Driving range	Practice	▆▆▆
Sheltered	couvert	8 places
On grass	sur herbe	non
Putting-green	putting-green	oui
Pitching-green	pitching green	non

HOTEL FACILITIES
ENVIRONNEMENT HOTELIER
8/10

HOTELS HÔTELS

Chiberta et du Golf ***   sur place
98 chambres, D 750 F
Tél (33) 05 59 63 95 56, Fax (33) 05 59 63 57 84

La Résidence   sur place
50 chambres, 400 F
Tél (33) 05 59 52 87 65, Fax (33) 05 59 63 59 19

Hôtel Palais ****   Biarritz
156 chambres, D 1800 F   3 km
Tél (33) 05 59 41 64 00, Fax (33) 05 59 41 67 99

Château de Brindos ****   Anglet
12 chambres, D 1300 F   2 km
Tél (33) 05 59 23 17 68, Fax (33) 05 59 23 48 47

RESTAURANTS RESTAURANT
Château de Brindos   Anglet
Tél (33) 05 59 23 17 68

189

Dans une région très touristique en raison de ses vignobles (... et fameux alcools), la création de ce golf public était bienvenue, et on remarquera d'abord son Club-House sympathique, construit dans une ancienne ferme. Le paysage est un mélange plaisant de campagne et de bocages et le relief assez modéré. L'architecture du parcours est agréable visuellement et très honnête sur le plan du jeu, sans recherche excessive d'originalité. Les coups imprécis ne sont rarement pénalisés sévèrement car les fairways sont assez larges, les greens peu complexes et les bunkers rarement très dangereux. Seuls deux trous comportent des obstacles d'eau. Visiblement, ce parcours a été conçu pour les joueurs moyens, ce qui en fait un "produit" utile et de qualité estimable pour la majorité des golfeurs, de la région ou de passage. Les meilleurs joueurs ne s'y ennuieront pas.

The opening of a public course was most welcome in a region where vineyards (and the famous spirits they produce) attract tourists in their droves. Just as welcoming is the club-house built in an old farmhouse. The landscape is a pleasing "blend" (this is cognac country, after all) of open country and green pastures, and the course can be rather hilly in places. The design is visually attractive and very forthright in golfing terms, albeit not excessively original. Wayward shots are only rarely heavily penalised, as the fairways are rather wide, the greens comparatively straightforward and the bunkers seldom too dangerous. There are water hazards on two holes only. The course was visibly designed for the average golfer, thus making it a "useful" product of considerable class for the majority of golfers, whether local or passing through. But even the best players will enjoy their golf here.

Golf du Cognac

Saint-Brice
F - 16100 COGNAC

Office	Secrétariat	(33) 05 45 32 18 17
Pro shop	Pro-shop	(33) 05 45 32 37 60
Fax	Fax	(33) 05 45 35 10 76
Situation	Situation	

5 km Cognac, 19 520 hab.
32 km Angoulême, 42 880 hab.

Annual closure	Fermeture annnuelle	non
Weekly closure	Fermeture hebdomadaire	mardi
		30/09→30/04

Fees main season
Tarifs haute saison la journée

	Week days Semaine	We/Bank holidays We/Férié
Individual Individuel	240 F	240 F
Couple Couple	420 F	420 F

Caddy	Caddy	non
Electric Trolley	Chariot électrique	80 F/18 trous
Buggy	Voiturette	150 F/18 trous
Clubs	Clubs 1/2 série	50 F/jour

Credit cards Cartes de crédit
VISA - CB - Eurocard - MasterCard

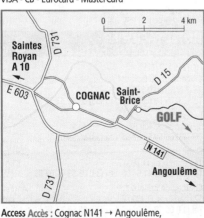

Access Accès : Cognac N141 → Angoulême,
D15 → Saint-Brice, → Golf
Map 9 on page 115 Carte 9 Page 115

GOLF COURSE
PARCOURS
13/20

Site	Site	■■■
Maintenance	Entretien	■■■
Architect	Architecte	Jean Garaïalde
Type	Type	bocage, plaine
Relief	Relief	■
Water in play	Eau en jeu	■
Exp. to wind	Exposé au vent	■■
Trees in play	Arbres en jeu	■■

Scorecard	Chp.	Mens	Ladies
Carte de score	Chp.	Mess.	Da.
Length Long.	6142	5665	5266
Par	72	72	72

Advised golfing ability	0	12	24	36
Niveau de jeu recommandé		■■■		
Hcp required	Handicap exigé	35		

CLUB HOUSE & AMENITIES
CLUB HOUSE ET ANNEXES
7/10

Pro shop	Pro-shop	■■■
Driving range	Practice	■■■
Sheltered	couvert	12 places
On grass	sur herbe	oui
Putting-green	putting-green	oui
Pitching-green	pitching green	oui

HOTEL FACILITIES
ENVIRONNEMENT HOTELIER
5/10

HOTELS HÔTELS
L'Echassier ***   Châteaubernard
21 chambres, D 450 F   5 km
Tél (33) 05 45 35 01 09, Fax (33) 05 45 32 22 43

Les Pigeons Blancs ***   Cognac
6 chambres, D 450 F/pers. 1/2 P.   5 km
Tél (33) 05 45 82 16 36, Fax (33) 05 45 82 29 29

Domaine du Breuil **   Cognac
24 chambres, D 350 F   5 km
Tél (33) 05 45 35 32 06, Fax (33) 05 45 35 48 06

RESTAURANTS RESTAURANT
Les Pigeons Blancs   Cognac
Tél (33) 05 45 82 16 36   5 km

L'Echassier   Cognac
Tél (33) 05 45 32 29 04   5 km

190

CÔTE D'ARGENT (LA) ⟩ | 17 | 6 | 5

Ce parcours remarquable a été réalisé dans la forêt de pins des Landes (treize trous), et en bord de mer (cinq trous). L'architecte Robert Trent Jones l'a incontestablement signé, avec des enjeux techniques et stratégiques dénotant une connaissance profonde du golf : si les joueurs de haut niveau y trouveront un "challenge" difficile, partir des départs avancés permet davantage d'erreurs. Visuellement, ses fameux bunkers dentelés défendent remarquablement les greens, dont trois sont pratiquement aveugles ; leurs surfaces sont modelées sans excès. Les fairways largement tondus favorisent le rythme de jeu, et la nature sablonneuse du sol permet de jouer facilement toute l'année. Il n'est pas trop fatigant, mais les distances entre greens et départs sont parfois importantes. Un bon 9 trous annexe permet d'occuper les débutants de la famille.

This remarkable course was laid out in the pine forests of Les Landes (for 13 holes) and along the coast (five holes). Welcome to a typical Robert Trent Jones design, where the technical and strategic challenges reflect an in-depth knowledge of golf. While the more proficient golfer will find this a tough challenge, playing from the forward tees is, funnily enough, often more conducive to error. The famous jagged bunkers are a remarkable form of defence for the greens, three of which are virtually blind, and the putting surfaces are neatly but never excessively contoured. The closely-cropped fairways help speed up the game and the sandy sub-soil keeps the course easily playable all year. This is not a tiring course, but distances between holes are sometimes a little on the long side. A good adjoining 9 hole course is ideal for beginners in the family.

Golf de la Côte d'Argent
Rue Mathieu Desbieys
F - 40660 MOLIETS

Office	Secrétariat	(33) 05 58 48 54 65
Pro shop	Pro-shop	(33) 05 58 48 55 55
Fax	Fax	(33) 05 58 48 54 88
Situation	Situation	

35 km Dax, 19 310 hab. 40 km Bayonne, 40 050 hab.

Annual closure	Fermeture annnuelle	non
Weekly closure	Fermeture hebdomadaire	

Fees main season
Tarifs haute saison le parcours

	Week days Semaine	We/Bank holidays We/Férié
Individual Individuel	300 F	300 F
Couple Couple	520 F	520 F

Caddy	Caddy	sur réservation
Electric Trolley	Chariot électrique	non
Buggy	Voiturette	150 F/18 trous
Clubs	Clubs 1/2 série	60 F/jour

Credit cards Cartes de crédit
VISA - CB - Eurocard - MasterCard

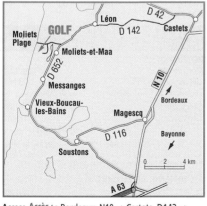

Access Accès : • Bordeaux, N10 → Castets. D142 → Léon, Moliets • Bayonne, N10 → Magescq, D116 → Soustons, D652 → Vieux-Boucau-les-Bains, Moliets
Map 12 on page 120 Carte 12 Page 120

GOLF COURSE
PARCOURS   **17**/20

Site	Site	▰▰▰▱▱
Maintenance	Entretien	▰▰▰▰▱
Architect	Architecte	Robert Trent Jones
Type	Type	forêt, links
Relief	Relief	▰▰▰▱▱
Water in play	Eau en jeu	▰▱▱▱▱
Exp. to wind	Exposé au vent	▰▰▰▱▱
Trees in play	Arbres en jeu	▰▰▰▱▱

Scorecard Carte de score	Chp. Chp.	Mens Mess.	Ladies Da.
Length Long.	6172	5823	5329
Par	72	72	72

Advised golfing ability   0   12   24   36
Niveau de jeu recommandé   ▰▰▰▰▰▰
Hcp required   Handicap exigé   non

CLUB HOUSE & AMENITIES
CLUB HOUSE ET ANNEXES   **6**/10

Pro shop	Pro-shop	▰▰▰▱▱
Driving range	Practice	▰▰▰▱▱
Sheltered	couvert	10 places
On grass	sur herbe	non
Putting-green	putting-green	oui
Pitching-green	pitching green	oui

HOTEL FACILITIES
ENVIRONNEMENT HOTELIER   **5**/10

HOTELS HÔTELS
Green Parc Ocean   sur place
340 chambres, D 450 F
Tél (33) 05 58 48 57 57, Fax (33) 05 58 48 57 58

Hôtel du Golf   Moliets
4 chambres, D 800 F   sur place
Tél (33) 05 58 49 16 00, Fax (33) 05 58 49 16 29

Côte d'Argent **   Vieux-Boucau
36 chambres, D 330 F   10 km
Tél (33) 05 58 48 13 17, Fax (33) 05 58 48 01 15

RESTAURANTS RESTAURANT
Restaurant du Golf   sur place
Tél (33) 05 58 48 44 55

191

Grand club omnisports, le Stade Français a créé un complexe golfique composé de quatre neuf trous combinables, dont la configuration idéale. est Vert-Noir et Lilas-Orange . Ce dernier 18 trous est un peu moins long, mais aussi exigeant techniquement. Dans un immense espace, Bob von Hagge a beaucoup modelé le terrain pour isoler les fairways., lui donnant un aspect un peu lunaire. L'esthétique est assez américaine, sans refuser pour autant certaines références aux links. Le "Orange" est assez accidenté, sans être vraiment fatigant : après quatre trous assez tranquilles, il en offre cinq de toute beauté, où les scores peuvent s'alourdir. Plus classique, le "Lilas" met en jeu quelques redoutables obstacles d'eau, généralement plus intimidants visuellement que dangereux. Ici, l'important est d'être précis, et de bien maîtriser le petit jeu quand on manque les greens.

Le Stade Français, one of the country's leading multi-sports clubs, has created a golf complex formed from four combinable 9-hole courses. The ideal combinations are Green and Black (see after) and Lilac and Orange (see here). The latter is a little less long but technically just as demanding. Over a huge area of land, Bob van Hagge has shifted a lot of earth to isolate the fairways and form a sort of lunar landscape. Although rather American in style, there is something of the links about all four courses. The "Orange" course is hilly but not too tiring. After four quietish holes, the next five are simply beautiful... and can ruin your card. The "Lilac" course, a little more classical if you will, involves some formidable water hazards, which are generally more intimidating to the eye than dangerous to the score. What matters here is straight-hitting and a sharp short game when you miss the greens.

Golf Courson-Monteloup

Stade Français
F - 91680 COURSON-MONTELOUP

Office	Secrétariat	(33) 01 64 58 80 80
Pro shop	Pro-shop	(33) 01 64 58 80 80
Fax	Fax	(33) 01 64 58 83 06
Situation	Situation	

15 km Les Ulis, 27 160 hab. 34 km Paris, 2 175 200 hab.

Annual closure	Fermeture annnuelle	non
Weekly closure	Fermeture hebdomadaire	mercredi

Fees main season
Tarifs haute saison la journée

	Week days Semaine	We/Bank holidays We/Férié
Individual Individuel	230 F	400 F
Couple Couple	460 F	800 F

110 F après 16 H (semaine)

Caddy	Caddy	sur réservation
Electric Trolley	Chariot électrique	80 F/18 trous
Buggy	Voiturette	200 F/18 trous
Clubs	Clubs 1/2 série	100 F/jour

Credit cards Cartes de crédit
VISA - CB - Eurocard - MasterCard

192

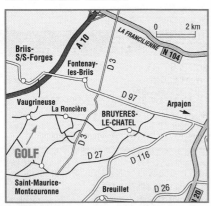

Access Accès : A10, sortie les Ulis, D3 → Dourdan, Château de Courson, La Roncière, → Golf
Map 15 on page 126 Carte 15 Page 126

GOLF COURSE
PARCOURS **15**/20

Site	Site	
Maintenance	Entretien	
Architect	Architecte	Robert von Hagge
Type	Type	plaine
Relief	Relief	
Water in play	Eau en jeu	
Exp. to wind	Exposé au vent	
Trees in play	Arbres en jeu	

Scorecard Carte de score	Chp. Chp.	Mens Mess.	Ladies Da.
Length Long.	6171	5746	4987
Par	72	72	72

Advised golfing ability Niveau de jeu recommandé	0 12 24 36		
Hcp required Handicap exigé	35/24-28 We		

CLUB HOUSE & AMENITIES
CLUB HOUSE ET ANNEXES **7**/10

Pro shop	Pro-shop	
Driving range	Practice	
Sheltered	couvert	15 places
On grass	sur herbe	non
Putting-green	putting-green	oui
Pitching-green	pitching green	oui

HOTEL FACILITIES
ENVIRONNEMENT HOTELIER **3**/10

HOTELS HÔTELS

Mercure *** — Les Ulis
108 chambres, D 560 F — 13 km
Tél (33) 01 69 07 63 96, Fax (33) 01 69 07 92 00

Campanile ** — Les Ulis
49 chambres, D 270 F — 13 km
Tél (33) 01 69 28 60 60, Fax (33) 01 69 28 06 35

Abbaye les Vaux de Cernay *** — Cernay-la-Ville
58 chambres, D 800 F — 11 km
Tél (33) 01 34 85 23 00, Fax (33) 01 34 85 11 60

RESTAURANTS RESTAURANT

Le Saint-Clément — Arpajon
Tél (33) 01 64 90 21 01 — 9 km

COURSON VERT/NOIR

Les quatre 9 trous de Courson constituent une véritable création en trois dimensions à partir d'un terrain sans grand relief naturel. Sur le "Vert", il vaut mieux partir des départs avancés, car sa longueur peut décourager les joueurs moyens (les pars 4 sont redoutables). Le "Noir" est moins brutal, parfois accidenté, mais les derniers trous mettent beaucoup d'eau en jeu. Le paysage ne manque pas de majesté, et les trous ont été bien isolés par la création de buttes spectaculaires, dont l'aspect visuel ne plaît pas à tous ! Très protégés par de beaux bunkers, les greens sont très vastes et souvent à multiples plateaux : il faut choisir celui où est le drapeau pour ne pas craindre les "trois-putts". Comme les par 5 sont difficilement prenables en deux coups, il est difficile d'y scorer très bien. Un parcours où il faut utiliser la tête autant que les clubs.

The four 9-hole courses at Courson form a genuine 3-dimensional creation built out of terrain with no great natural relief. On the "Green" course, swallow your pride and play from the forward tees; it is long enough to discourage any mid-handicapper (the par 4s are quite formidable). The "Black" course is a little kinder and sometimes hilly, and the last few holes involve a lot of water. There is something very majestic about the landscape here, and the holes are clearly separated by spectacular sand-hills and hillocks, which from a visual point of view are not to everyone's liking. The greens are huge, often multi-tiered and defended by magnificent bunkers, so wayward approach shots are often greeted with 3 putts. And as the par 5s are tough to reach in two, a good score is not always easy. A typical course where brains are almost as important as your clubs.

Golf Courson-Monteloup

Stade Français
F - 91680 COURSON-MONTELOUP

Office	Secrétariat	(33) 01 64 58 80 80
Pro shop	Pro-shop	(33) 01 64 58 80 80
Fax	Fax	(33) 01 64 58 83 06
Situation	Situation	

15 km Les Ulis, 27 160 hab. 34 km Paris, 2 175 200 hab.

Annual closure	Fermeture annnuelle	oui
		25/12 → 1/01/99
Weekly closure	Fermeture hebdomadaire	mercredi

Fees main season Tarifs haute saison la journée

	Week days Semaine	We/Bank holidays We/Férié
Individual Individuel	230 F	400 F
Couple Couple	460 F	800 F

110 F après 16 H (semaine)

Caddy	Caddy	sur réservation
Electric Trolley	Chariot électrique	80 F/18 trous
Buggy	Voiturette	200 F/18 trous
Clubs	Clubs 1/2 série	100 F/jour

Credit cards Cartes de crédit
VISA - CB - Eurocard - MasterCard

Access Accès : A10, sortie les Ulis, D3 → Dourdan, Château de Courson, La Roncière, → Golf
Map 15 on page 126 Carte 15 Page 126

GOLF COURSE PARCOURS 16/20

Site	Site	
Maintenance	Entretien	
Architect	Architecte	Robert von Hagge
Type	Type	plaine
Relief	Relief	
Water in play	Eau en jeu	
Exp. to wind	Exposé au vent	
Trees in play	Arbres en jeu	

Scorecard Carte de score	Chp. Chp.	Mens Mess.	Ladies Da.
Length Long.	6570	6043	5348
Par	72	72	72

Advised golfing ability	0 12 24 36
Niveau de jeu recommandé	
Hcp required Handicap exigé	35

CLUB HOUSE & AMENITIES CLUB HOUSE ET ANNEXES 7/10

Pro shop	Pro-shop	
Driving range	Practice	
Sheltered	couvert	15 places
On grass	sur herbe	non
Putting-green	putting-green	oui
Pitching-green	pitching green	oui

HOTEL FACILITIES ENVIRONNEMENT HOTELIER 3/10

HOTELS HÔTELS
Mercure *** — Les Ulis
108 chambres, D 560 F — 13 km
Tél (33) 01 69 07 63 96, Fax (33) 01 69 07 92 00

Campanile ** — Les Ulis
49 chambres, D 270 F — 13 km
Tél (33) 01 69 28 60 60, Fax (33) 01 69 28 06 35

Abbaye les Vaux de Cernay *** — Cernay-la-Ville
58 chambres, D 800 F — 11 km
Tél (33) 01 34 85 23 00, Fax (33) 01 34 85 11 60

RESTAURANTS RESTAURANT
Le Saint-Clément — Arpajon
Tél (33) 01 64 90 21 01 — 9 km

193

Un golf familial, dont le parcours tracé par le grand Willie Park en 1897, a été notablement modifié depuis, notamment après la dernière guerre et l'occupation. 9 des 27 trous d'avant-guerre n'ont alors pas été réouverts. Situé en bord de mer, ce n'est pas exactement un links, étant donné la nature du terrain mais les conditions de jeu en sont souvent proches (attention au vent !). Le style du parcours est très britannique, avec des greens bien protégés., mais souvent accessibles avec des "pitch and run". Sa longueur reste raisonnable, mais les scores ne sont pas toujours tels qu'on pourrait les espérer au vu de la carte. Le relief est modéré, ce qui convient bien aux joueurs de tous âges comme de tous niveaux. L'ambiance est sans prétention mais très plaisante, comme la simplicité des équipements. On ne perd certes pas sa journée à jouer ici, entre amis et en famille.

A family course designed by the great Willie Park in 1897 but considerably restyled, particularly since the end of last war and the occupation. Nine of the 27 pre-war holes have not been re-opened. Laid out along the sea-shore, this is not exactly a links course, given the nature of the terrain, but conditions of play are often very similar (watch out for the wind). Dieppe is a very British style course with well protected greens that can often be reached with bump and run shots. It is a reasonable length, but scores are not always as low as you might have hoped for when looking at the card. It is rather hilly but suitable for players of all ages and abilities. The atmosphere is unpretentious and pleasant, as is the simplicity of facilities. You certainly will not waste your time spending a day's golfing here, with friends or the family.

Dieppe-Pourville Golf Club

Route de Pourville
F - 76200 DIEPPE

Office	Secrétariat	(33) 02 35 84 25 05
Pro shop	Pro-shop	(33) 02 32 84 25 05
Fax	Fax	(33) 02 35 84 97 11
Situation	Situation	

2 km Dieppe, 35 890 hab.

Annual closure	Fermeture annnuelle	non
Weekly closure	Fermeture hebdomadaire	

Fees main season
Tarifs haute saison la journée

	Week days Semaine	We/Bank holidays We/Férié
Individual Individuel	190 F	240 F
Couple Couple	380 F	480 F

Caddy	Caddy	sur réservation
Electric Trolley	Chariot électrique	non
Buggy	Voiturette	100 F/18 trous
Clubs	Clubs 1/2 série	100 F/jour

Credit cards Cartes de crédit
VISA - CB - Eurocard - MasterCard

194

DIEPPE

D 925
Graincourt

GOLF

D 925

D 54   N 27

D 915

Offranville

Access Accès : Dieppe → Pourville
Map 1 on page 98 Carte 1 Page 98

GOLF COURSE
PARCOURS   14/20

Site	Site	▬▬▬▬▭▭
Maintenance	Entretien	▬▬▬▬▬▭
Architect	Architecte	Willie Park Jr
Type	Type	bord de mer, links
Relief	Relief	▬▭▭▭▭▭
Water in play	Eau en jeu	▭▭▭▭▭▭
Exp. to wind	Exposé au vent	▬▬▬▭▭▭
Trees in play	Arbres en jeu	▬▬▭▭▭▭

Scorecard Carte de score	Chp. Chp.	Mens Mess.	Ladies Da.
Length Long.	5763	5489	4866
Par	70	70	70

Advised golfing ability
Niveau de jeu recommandé   0   12   24   36

Hcp required   Handicap exigé   non

CLUB HOUSE & AMENITIES
CLUB HOUSE ET ANNEXES   6/10

Pro shop	Pro-shop	▬▬▬▬▭▭
Driving range	Practice	▬▬▬▭▭▭
Sheltered	couvert	10 places
On grass	sur herbe	oui
Putting-green	putting-green	oui
Pitching-green	pitching green	oui

HOTEL FACILITIES
ENVIRONNEMENT HOTELIER   5/10

HOTELS HÔTELS

La Présidence ***   Dieppe
89 chambres, D 540 F
Tél (33) 02 35 84 31 31, Fax (33) 02 35 84 86 70

Aguado ***   Dieppe
56 chambres, D 430 F
Tél (33) 02 35 84 27 00, Fax (33) 02 35 06 17 61

Auberge du Clos Normand **   Martin-Eglise
8 chambres, D 460 F   7 km
Tél (33) 02 35 04 40 34, Fax (33) 02 35 04 48 49

RESTAURANTS RESTAURANT

La Mélie   Dieppe
Tél (33) 02 35 84 21 19

Auberge du Trou Normand   Pourville
Tél (33) 02 35 84 59 84

Fondé en 1883, ce parcours a été, comme Biarritz, originellement dessiné par Willie Dunn, mais remanié à tel point, au cours des années, qu'il ne reste qu'une dizaine de trous d'une esthétique spécifiquement écossaise. Ils suffisent à faire de Dinard un golf à connaître. Sa longueur peut paraître dérisoire, même avec un par 69, mais elle devient démesurée quand le vent souffle un peu. Alors, il faut une tête de spécialiste en balistique pour calculer les dérives ! Et seuls deux par 5 offrent de franches occasions de birdies. Ailleurs, la difficulté vient du choix de club, et l'on se retrouve sans cesse "entre deux clubs" pour chercher les drapeaux. Les greens sont bien défendus, et souvent de petite taille, ce qui oblige à une extrême précision. Un golf très amusant, dont l'ambiance est très sportive, et à jouer avec les golfeurs de tous niveaux. L'arrosage des fairways va améliorer beaucoup l'entretien en été.

Opened in 1883, this course was originally designed, like Biarritz, by Willie Dunn, but it has been restyled so many times over the years that only about ten holes have preserved their special Scottish flavour. And they alone are enough to make Dinard a course worth knowing. The length may appear derisory by today's standards, even as a par 69, but when the wind howls, it feels and plays much longer. A specialist in ballistics can come in handy to calculate flight and deviation! Only two par 5s provide real birdie chances. Elsewhere, difficulties arise from club selection, and players are often stuck "between two clubs" for their approach shots. The greens are often small and well defended, thus calling for extreme precision. A very entertaining course with a great sporting atmosphere, to be played with golfers of all levels. The watering of fairways will improve upkeeping during summer months.

Golf de Dinard
Boulevard de la Houle
F - 35 800 SAINT-BRIAC-SUR-MER

Office	Secrétariat	(33) 02 99 88 32 07
Pro shop	Pro-shop	(33) 02 99 88 30 55
Fax	Fax	(33) 02 99 88 04 53
Situation	Situation	

5 km Dinard, 9 920 hab.

Annual closure	Fermeture annnuelle	non
Weekly closure	Fermeture hebdomadaire	

Fees main season
Tarifs haute saison la journée

	Week days Semaine	We/Bank holidays We/Férié
Individual Individuel	300 F	300 F
Couple Couple	600 F	600 F

Caddy	Caddy	non
Electric Trolley	Chariot électrique	non
Buggy	Voiturette	150 F/18 trous
Clubs	Clubs	oui

Credit cards Cartes de crédit
VISA - CB - Eurocard - MasterCard

Access Accès : Dinard → Saint-Lunaire, → Golf
Map 5 on page 107 Carte 5 Page 107

GOLF COURSE
PARCOURS 14/20

Site	Site	
Maintenance	Entretien	
Architect	Architecte	Willie Dunn
Type	Type	bord de mer, links
Relief	Relief	
Water in play	Eau en jeu	
Exp. to wind	Exposé au vent	
Trees in play	Arbres en jeu	

Scorecard Carte de score	Chp. Chp.	Mens Mess.	Ladies Da.
Length Long.	5137	4992	4651
Par	68	68	68

Advised golfing ability Niveau de jeu recommandé		0 12 24 36
Hcp required	Handicap exigé	35

CLUB HOUSE & AMENITIES
CLUB HOUSE ET ANNEXES 6/10

Pro shop	Pro-shop	
Driving range	Practice	
Sheltered	couvert	4 places
On grass	sur herbe	oui
Putting-green	putting-green	oui
Pitching-green	pitching green	oui

HOTEL FACILITIES
ENVIRONNEMENT HOTELIER 7/10

HOTELS HÔTELS
Golf Hôtel — St Briac
40 chambres, D 400 F
Tél (33) 02 99 88 30 30, Fax (33) 02 99 88 07 87

Grand-Hôtel **** — Dinard — 5 km
63 chambres, D 980 F
Tél (33) 02 99 88 26 26, Fax (33) 02 99 88 26 27

Reine Hortense *** — Dinard — 5 km
10 chambres, D 900 F
Tél (33) 02 99 46 54 31, Fax (33) 02 99 88 15 88

RESTAURANTS RESTAURANT
Altaïr — Dinard — 5 km
Tél (33) 02 99 46 13 58

Restaurant du Decolle — St Lunaire — 2 km
Tél (33) 02 99 46 01 70

195

Ce n'est pas encore un énorme complexe golfique comme Disneyworld à Orlando, mais Disneyland Paris offre un 18 trous et un 9 trous, construits par Ronald Fream sur un terrain plat, mais fortement modelé. Cet ensemble n'est pas d'une trop grande complexité technique, les pièges sont immédiatement visibles et les grands espaces favorisent les longs frappeurs. Cependant, les contours assez tourmentés des greens et quelques difficultés stratégiques permettent aux techniciens d'y exprimer leur virtuosité. L'ensemble présente un visage très américain, il ne faudra pas s'en étonner, avec bon nombre d'obstacles d'eau. Si les trois parcours affirment peu à peu leur personnalité, le Club House et les équipements sont fonctionnels, mais ils manquent de chaleur. C'est un complexe évidemment commercial, sans véritable vie de Club... On aime ou pas.

This is not yet your actual outsized golfing complex as in Disneyworld Orlando, but Disneyland Paris presently provides an 18-hole and a 9-hole course built by Ronald Fream over flat terrain bulldozed into shape. Technically speaking, the course is not too complex, as traps are immediately visible and wide open space is a gift for long-hitters. However, the twisting greens and a number of strategic difficulties also give the technicans a chance to practice their skills. Not surprisingly, the whole layout has a very American look to it with a good number of water hazards. While the three courses gradually forge a personality, the Club House and facilities are functional, but lack warmth or soul. This is obviously a business venture without any real club life, so not to everyone's liking.

Golf Disneyland Paris
Allée de la Mare-Houleuse
F - 77450 MAGNY-LE-HONGRE

Office	Secrétariat	(33) 01 60 45 68 04
Pro shop	Pro-shop	(33) 01 60 45 68 90
Fax	Fax	(33) 01 60 45 68 33
Situation	Situation	

38 km Paris, 2 175 200 hab.

Annual closure	Fermeture annnuelle	non
Weekly closure	Fermeture hebdomadaire	

Fees main season
Tarifs haute saison le parcours

	Week days Semaine	We/Bank holidays We/Férié
Individual Individuel	160 F	270 F
Couple Couple	320 F	540 F

Caddy	Caddy	non
Electric Trolley	Chariot électrique	non
Buggy	Voiturette	150 F/18 trous
Clubs	Clubs série	100 F/jour

Credit cards Cartes de crédit
VISA - CB - Eurocard - MasterCard - AMEX - DC - JCB

196

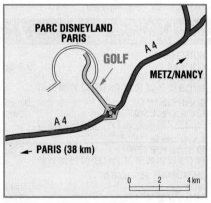

PARC DISNEYLAND PARIS
GOLF
A 4
METZ/NANCY
A 4
PARIS (38 km)

0   2   4 km

Access Accès : A4 Paris-Metz/Nancy,
→ Parc Disneyland Paris
Map 3 on page 103 Carte 3 Page 103

GOLF COURSE
PARCOURS   **16**/20

Site	Site	▬▬
Maintenance	Entretien	▬▬▬
Architect	Architecte	Ronald Fream
Type	Type	plaine, campagne
Relief	Relief	▬
Water in play	Eau en jeu	▬▬▬
Exp. to wind	Exposé au vent	▬▬▬
Trees in play	Arbres en jeu	▬▬

Scorecard Carte de score	Chp. Chp.	Mens Mess.	Ladies Da.
Length Long.	6032	5593	5172
Par	72	72	72

Advised golfing ability		0 12 24 36
Niveau de jeu recommandé		▬▬▬
Hcp required	Handicap exigé	35

CLUB HOUSE & AMENITIES
CLUB HOUSE ET ANNEXES   **7**/10

Pro shop	Pro-shop	▬▬▬
Driving range	Practice	▬▬▬
Sheltered	couvert	10 places
On grass	sur herbe	oui
Putting-green	putting-green	oui
Pitching-green	pitching green	oui

HOTEL FACILITIES
ENVIRONNEMENT HOTELIER   **8**/10

HOTELS HÔTELS
Centrale de réservation   sur place

Tél (33) 01 60 30 60 30 Disneyland ****   1 km. du golf
500 chambres, D 2500 F
Tél (33) 01 60 45 65 00, Fax (33) 01 60 45 65 33

Séquoia Lodge ***   1 km. du golf
1 011 chambres, D 900 F
Tél (33) 01 60 45 51 00, Fax (33) 01 60 45 51 33

Cheyenne **   1 km. du golf
1 000 chambres, D 695 F
Tél (33) 01 60 45 62 00, Fax (33) 01 60 45 62 33

RESTAURANTS RESTAURANT
Invention   Hôtel Disneyland
Tél (33) 01 60 45 65 00

Cape Cod et Yacht Club   Hôtel New-Port
Tél(33) 01 60 45 55 00

Avec six par 4, six par 5 et six par 3, le parcours de Divonne est original, mais le fait de commencer et de terminer par des par 3 n'est pas son point fort. Dominant le Lac Léman, ce parcours de moyenne montagne est assez bien rythmé pour ne pas être épuisant, quand il n'est pas trop humide. L'environnement boisé est très plaisant (en automne notamment), et permet au minimum de transformer une mauvaise partie en jolie promenade. Peut-être un peu difficile pour les joueurs non classés, Divonne permet cependant aux golfeurs de tous niveaux de jouer ensemble, et constitue un challenge appréciable pour les meilleurs frappeurs : ils auront de multiples occasions de prendre des risques, même si l'absence de subtilités stratégiques empêche de renouveler constamment le plaisir. C'est en tout cas une halte de qualité pendant un séjour à la belle saison.

With six par 4s, six par 5s and six par 3s, Divonne is an original course, but starting and finishing with par 3s is hardly its strong point. Overlooking lake Geneva, Divonne is a mid-mountain course which is not too tiring, when the weather is not too damp. The woody surroundings are very pleasant (especially in autumn) and at the very least can help change a rotten round into a pleasant walk. Divonne might be a little too tough for very high handicappers but it does allow golfers of all abilities to play together. It is certainly quite some challenge for the longer-hitters, who have countless opportunities to take risks, even though the course lacks strategic subtlety. At all events, this is a great stop-off over the summer months.

Golf de Divonne
F - 01220 DIVONNE-LES-BAINS

Office	Secrétariat	(33) 04 50 40 34 11
Pro shop	Pro-shop	(33) 04 50 40 34 11
Fax	Fax	(33) 04 50 40 34 25
Situation	Situation	

17 km Genève, 172 486 hab.

Annual closure	Fermeture annnuelle	non
Weekly closure	Fermeture hebdomadaire	non
	mardi, le restaurant 15/12 → 15/03	

Fees main season
Tarifs haute saison la journée

	Week days Semaine	We/Bank holidays We/Férié
Individual Individuel	300 F	500 F
Couple Couple	600 F	1 000 F

Caddy	Caddy	sur réservation
Electric Trolley	Chariot électrique	120 F/18 trous
Buggy	Voiturette	220 F/18 trous
Clubs	Clubs la série	150 F/jour

Credit cards Cartes de crédit
VISA - CB - Eurocard - MasterCard - AMEX - DC - JCB

Access Accès : • Genève → Nyon/Lausanne, sortie Divonne, → Golf • Gex (France) D 984 → Divonne
Map 8 on page 113 Carte 8 Page 113

GOLF COURSE
PARCOURS
14/20

Site	Site	▬▬▬▬
Maintenance	Entretien	▬▬▬▬
Architect	Architecte	M. Nakowsky Donald Harradine
Type	Type	vallon
Relief	Relief	
Water in play	Eau en jeu	▬▬
Exp. to wind	Exposé au vent	▬▬▬
Trees in play	Arbres en jeu	▬▬▬▬

Scorecard Carte de score	Chp. Chp.	Mens Mess.	Ladies Da.
Length Long.	6035	5607	5087
Par	72	72	72

Advised golfing ability Niveau de jeu recommandé	0	12	24	36

Hcp required Handicap exigé 35

CLUB HOUSE & AMENITIES
CLUB HOUSE ET ANNEXES
6/10

Pro shop	Pro-shop	▬▬▬
Driving range	Practice	▬▬▬
Sheltered	couvert	10 places
On grass	sur herbe	non
Putting-green	putting-green	oui
Pitching-green	pitching green	oui

197

HOTEL FACILITIES
ENVIRONNEMENT HOTELIER
7/10

HOTELS HÔTELS
Le Grand Hôtel ★★★★ 500 m. du golf
127 chambres, D 1200 F
Tél (33) 04 50 40 34 34, Fax (33) 04 50 40 34 24

Château de Divonne ★★★★ Divonne
22 chambres, D 950 F
Tél (33) 04 50 20 00 32, Fax (33) 04 50 20 03 73

Auberge des Chasseurs ★★★ Echenevex
15 chambres, D 650 F 9 km
Tél (33) 04 50 41 54 07, Fax (33) 04 50 41 90 61

RESTAURANTS RESTAURANT
Château de Divonne Divonne
Tél (33) 04 50 20 00 32

La Terrasse Divonne
Tél (33) 04 50 40 34 34

DOMONT-MONTMORENCY

| 13 | 7 | 4 |

Depuis 1966, Domont a conquis une réputation de club très familial, où l'accueil est toujours agréable. L'architecture manque un peu de style, mais l'architecte n'a visiblement pas souhaité bouleverser le terrain. Comme l'eau n'est en jeu que sur un seul trou, que les nombreux bunkers sont bien placés (ils ont tous été regarnis), mais rarement très profonds, les difficultés tiennent essentiellement à la présence imposante de beaux arbres souvent serrés les uns contre les autres. Ils donnent une impression trompeuse de parcours étroit : en fait, les arrivées de drive sont assez larges. Les accidents du terrain compliquent le choix de club, mais aussi l'exécution des coups quand on se trouve dans un dévers. Cependant, le parcours étant assez court, rien n'oblige à prendre des risques avec le driver, et les joueurs précis réussissent mieux ici que les frappeurs. Un parcours très plaisant.

Since 1966, Domont has built up the reputation of a very family club where visitors are always warmly welcomed. The layout lacks a wee bit of style, but the architect was clearly keen not to disrupt the natural terrain. With water in play on one hole only, and with numerous bunkers that, although cleverly placed, are never too deep, the main problems here come essentially from the beautiful trees that closely line nearly every fairway. They give the false impression of narrow fairways, but in fact the drive landing areas are wide enough. The undulating terrain makes club selection a little more difficult than usual, and stroke-making is never easy on some of the sloping fairways. On the upside, the course is comparatively short, so there's no need to risk the driver. All in all, a very pleasant golf course where the straight player will almost certainly card a better score than the long-hitters.

Golf de Domont-Montmorency

Route de Montmorency
F - 95330 DOMONT

Office	Secrétariat	(33) 01 39 91 07 50
Pro shop	Pro-shop	(33) 01 39 91 07 50
Fax	Fax	(33) 01 39 91 25 70
Situation	Situation	

10 km Enghien, 10 080 hab. 20 km Paris, 2 175 200 hab.

Annual closure	Fermeture annnuelle	non
Weekly closure	Fermeture hebdomadaire	mardi

Fees main season
Tarifs haute saison la journée

	Week days Semaine	We/Bank holidays We/Férié
Individual Individuel	250 F	480 F
Couple Couple	500 F	960 F

GF 200 F avant 9h30 (sem)

Caddy	Caddy	non
Electric Trolley	Chariot électrique	non
Buggy	Voiturette	non
Clubs	Clubs	non

Credit cards Cartes de crédit
non, sauf restaurant

198

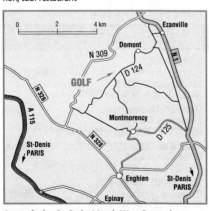

Access Accès : De Paris, A1 puis N1 → Beauvais, sortie Domont-Ezanville → Montmorency
Map 15 on page 126 Carte 15 Page 126

GOLF COURSE
PARCOURS
13/20

Site	Site	
Maintenance	Entretien	
Architect	Architecte	Fred Hawtree
Type	Type	forêt
Relief	Relief	
Water in play	Eau en jeu	
Exp. to wind	Exposé au vent	
Trees in play	Arbres en jeu	

Scorecard Carte de score	Chp. Chp.	Mens Mess.	Ladies Da.
Length Long.	5874	5569	5008
Par	71	71	71

Advised golfing ability
Niveau de jeu recommandé

| 0 | 12 | 24 | 36 |

Hcp required Handicap exigé 30

CLUB HOUSE & AMENITIES
CLUB HOUSE ET ANNEXES
7/10

Pro shop	Pro-shop	
Driving range	Practice	
Sheltered	couvert	15 places
On grass	sur herbe	non
Putting-green	putting-green	oui
Pitching-green	pitching green	non

HOTEL FACILITIES
ENVIRONNEMENT HOTELIER
4/10

HOTELS HÔTELS
Grand Hôtel ****   Enghien
45 chambres, D 720 F   10 km
Tél (33) 01 34 12 80 00, Fax (33) 01 34 12 73 81

Novotel Château de Maffliers ***   Maffliers
51 chambres, D 525 F   7 km
Tél (33) 01 34 73 93 05, Fax (33) 01 34 08 35 00

RESTAURANTS RESTAURANT
Au Cœur de la Forêt   Montmorency
Tél (33) 01 39 64 99 19   5 km

Auberge Landaise   Enghien
Tél (33) 02 34 12 78 36   10 km

Très fréquenté par les Suisses, ce parcours a été dessiné par Michel Gayon sur un terrain accidenté, avec très peu d'arbres. Ses difficultés viennent essentiellement des dévers, du relief, des rivières traversant les fairways et de quelques mares. Il serait sans doute plus délicat à négocier avec des roughs plus épais. Les greens sont dessinés avec beaucoup de soin, protégés par le relief naturel du terrain et par un grand nombre de bunkers, tout comme les arrivées de drive. Pour les joueurs à partir de 15 de handicap, il peut être très long, mais de nombreux départs différents permettent de se faire un parcours "à sa main", si l'on ne veut pas trop forcer son talent. Le rythme général est assez saccadé, avec des trous difficiles en succession, puis des moments de relâchement, mais la fin de parcours est technique, montant en puissance à partir du 13.

Very popular with Swiss golfers, Esery was designed by Michel Gayon over a hilly terrain with very few trees. The major difficulty comes from the sloping fairways, the relief, the rivers crossing the fairways and a few ponds. It would certainly be a tougher test with thicker rough. The greens have been very carefully designed and are very well defended, not only by the naturally hilly terrain but also by well-placed bunkers. The same goes for the fairways at driving distance. For players with handicaps in the upper teens, this could prove to be a very long course, but the large number of tees let you tailor the course to your own ability if you don't feel up to the test. The overall rhythm is a little disjointed with a series of difficult holes followed by a number of easier ones. The run-in is more technical, getting harder from the 13th hole onwards.

Golf Club d'Esery
Esery
F - 74930 REIGNIER

Office	Secrétariat	(33) 04 50 36 58 70
Pro shop	Pro-shop	(33) 04 50 31 20 15
Fax	Fax	(33) 04 50 36 57 62
Situation	Situation	

12 km S.E. de Genève, 172 486 hab.

Annual closure	Fermeture annnuelle	non
Weekly closure	Fermeture hebdomadaire	non
		lundi, club-house

Fees main season
Tarifs haute saison le parcours

	Week days Semaine	We/Bank holidays We/Férié
Individual Individuel	280 F	400 F
Couple Couple	560 F	800 F

Caddy	Caddy	sur réservation
Electric Trolley	Chariot électrique	100 F/18 trous
Buggy	Voiturette	200 F/18 trous
Clubs	Clubs série	100 F/jour

Credit cards Cartes de crédit
VISA - CB - Eurocard - MasterCard

Access Accès : • Genève, A40 sortie Annemasse →
Reignier • Annecy, A41 sortie 14, → Reignier
Map 11 on page 119 Carte 11 Page 119

GOLF COURSE
PARCOURS 15/20

Site	Site	
Maintenance	Entretien	
Architect	Architecte	Michel Gayon
Type	Type	montagne, vallon
Relief	Relief	
Water in play	Eau en jeu	
Exp. to wind	Exposé au vent	
Trees in play	Arbres en jeu	

Scorecard Carte de score	Chp. Chp.	Mens Mess.	Ladies Da.
Length Long.	6350	6044	5100
Par	72	72	72

Advised golfing ability	0	12	24	36
Niveau de jeu recommandé				
Hcp required Handicap exigé	35			

CLUB HOUSE & AMENITIES
CLUB HOUSE ET ANNEXES 7/10

Pro shop	Pro-shop	
Driving range	Practice	
Sheltered	couvert	10 places
On grass	sur herbe	non
Putting-green	putting-green	oui
Pitching-green	pitching green	non

199

HOTEL FACILITIES
ENVIRONNEMENT HOTELIER 5/10

HOTELS HÔTELS

Mercure ***	Annemasse
78 chambres, D 490 F	7 km
Tél (33) 04 50 92 05 25, Fax (33) 04 50 87 14 57	

Ibis ***	Archamps
84 chambres, D 300 F	12 km
Tél (33) 04 50 95 38 18, Fax (33) 04 50 95 38 95	

Hôtel des Bergues ****	Genève
123 chambres, D 320 CHF	12 km
Tél (41) 022 - 731 50 50, Fax (41) 022 - 732 19 8	

RESTAURANTS RESTAURANT

Le Béarn	Genève
Tél (41) 022 - 321 00 28	12 km

Le Chat Botté	Genève
Tél (41) 022 - 731 02 21	12 km

Dans un environnement de pins, et sur un terrain modérément accidenté, Robert Trent Jones a tracé un parcours techniquement très intéressant, d'une grande diversité de difficultés et souvent spectaculaire : notamment le 15, petit par 3 où il faut franchir un véritable gouffre. Il faut savoir bien travailler la balle pour y scorer convenablement, et choisir soigneusement son club à chaque coup, le driver n'étant certes pas obligatoire sur chaque départ. Des dizaines de bunkers et quelques obstacles d'eau très en jeu imposent de définir soigneusement sa stratégie. Les greens sont le point faible de ce parcours tactique, non par leur entretien, mais par leurs ondulations excessives (sur une demi-douzaine) qui laissent trop de place à la chance... Un parcours à connaître, malgré la présence des maisons qui enserrent ce golf de style "resort".

In a setting of pine forest and pretty hilly countryside, Robert Trent Jones has laid out what is technically a very interesting course with a number of varied and often spectacular hazards. This is particularly so on the 15th, a short 3-par, where a chasm separates tee from green. Careful club selection and ball-control are the key to a goodish score at Esterel, and the driver can certainly be banished on several holes. Dozens of bunkers and a few water hazards call for deliberate strategy. The weak point on this tactical course comes from the greens, not through their upkeep, but because of excessive slope and undulation (on half a dozen holes), which leave too much to chance. A course worth knowing, despite the presence of villas now all around this resort style complex.

Golf Estérel Latitudes

Avenue du Golf
F - 83700 SAINT-RAPHAEL

Office	Secrétariat	(33) 04 94 82 47 88
Pro shop	Pro-shop	(33) 04 94 82 47 88
Fax	Fax	(33) 04 94 44 64 61
Situation	Situation	

3 km N. Saint-Raphaël, 26 610 hab.

Annual closure	Fermeture annnuelle	non
Weekly closure	Fermeture hebdomadaire	

Fees main season
Tarifs haute saison la journée

	Week days Semaine	We/Bank holidays We/Férié
Individual Individuel	285 F	285 F
Couple Couple	570 F	570 F

Caddy	Caddy	sur réservation
Electric Trolley	Chariot électrique	70 F/18 trous
Buggy	Voiturette	200 F/18 trous
Clubs	Clubs la série	150 F/jour

Credit cards Cartes de crédit
VISA - CB - Eurocard - MasterCard - AMEX

La Napoule
A 8
Cannes
Toulon
Marseille
Aix-en
Provence 38
N 98
37
Valescure
GOLF Agay
Fréjus St-Raphaël
0   2   4 km

Access Accès : A 8, sortie Fréjus Saint-Raphaël, → Saint-Raphaël, puis Agay par Valescure
Map 14 on page 125 Carte 14 Page 125

GOLF COURSE
PARCOURS 16/20

Site	Site	
Maintenance	Entretien	
Architect	Architecte	R. Trent Jones Sr
Type	Type	forêt, résidentiel
Relief	Relief	
Water in play	Eau en jeu	
Exp. to wind	Exposé au vent	
Trees in play	Arbres en jeu	

Scorecard Carte de score	Chp. Chp.	Mens Mess.	Ladies Da.
Length Long.	5921	5533	5108
Par	71	71	71

Advised golfing ability   0   12   24   36
Niveau de jeu recommandé
Hcp required   Handicap exigé   35

CLUB HOUSE & AMENITIES
CLUB HOUSE ET ANNEXES 6/10

Pro shop	Pro-shop	
Driving range	Practice	
Sheltered	couvert	15 places
On grass	sur herbe	oui
Putting-green	putting-green	oui
Pitching-green	pitching green	non

HOTEL FACILITIES
ENVIRONNEMENT HOTELIER 7/10

HOTELS HÔTELS
Latitudes Valescure ***   sur place
95 chambres, D 900 F
Tél (33) 04 94 82 42 42, Fax (33) 04 94 44 61 37

San Pedro ***   Saint-Raphaël
28 chambres, D 850 F   800 m
Tél (33) 04 94 83 65 69, Fax (33) 04 94 40 57 20

RESTAURANTS RESTAURANT
L'arbousier   Saint-Raphaël
Tél (33) 04 94 95 25 00   4 km

San Pedro   Saint-Raphaël
Tél (33) 04 94 83 65 69   800 m

200

Construit dans une très vaste clairière (on souhaiterait plus d'arbres), avec quelques maisons assez séduisantes, Etiolles est un exemple de bon parcours commercial, indulgent aux coups décentrés, et donc accessible à tous. Dessiné par Michel Gayon, il permet à chacun de trouver son bonheur. Les fairways (de bonne dimension) sont bien isolés par des buttes importantes, qui non seulement ajoutent du relief à un terrain assez plat, mais ramènent volontiers les balles en jeu. Les greens sont vastes, mais pas trop difficiles à lire. Ils ne sont pas trop défendus quand l'approche se fait avec un long fer ou un bois. Parmi les trous remarquables, on distinguera le 18, de physionomie très américaine dans son dessin, ramenant vers le Club House de style colonial. L'entretien est très correct, et le neuf trous adjacent de bonne qualité.

Laid out over a huge clearing (a few more trees would be welcome), with some very attractive houses, Etiolles is a good example of a successful business golfing venture. Designed by Michel Gayon, there is something for everyone here. The wide fairways are neatly isolated by mounds, which not only add a little relief to a flat terrain but also obligingly bring the ball back into play. The greens are large but not too difficult to read, and are open to long approaches with a long iron or fairway wood. One of the most remarkable holes is the very American style 18th, leading the player back to the colonial style club-house. Upkeep is very good, and the same goes for the adjacent 9-hole course.

Golf d'Etiolles
Vieux Chemin de Paris
F - 91450 ETIOLLES

Office	Secrétariat	(33) 01 60 75 49 49
Pro shop	Pro-shop	(33) 01 60 75 49 49
Fax	Fax	(33) 01 60 75 64 20
Situation	Situation	

37 km S. Paris, 2 175 200 hab. 3 km Evry, 455 530 hab.

Annual closure	Fermeture annnuelle	non
Weekly closure	Fermeture hebdomadaire	

Fees main season
Tarifs haute saison la journée

	Week days Semaine	We/Bank holidays We/Férié
Individual Individuel	260 F	390 F
Couple Couple	400 F	600 F

Après 16 h, GF 100 F/sem, 130 F/We - Mardi 130 F :
Dames - Seniors : 180 F

Caddy	Caddy	non
Electric Trolley	Chariot électrique	65 F/18 trous
Buggy	Voiturette	200 F/18 trous
Clubs	Clubs 1/2 série	50 F/jour

Credit cards Cartes de crédit
VISA - CB - Eurocard - MasterCard - Amex

Access Accès : A6, sortie Melun Sénart/Marne-la-Vallée,
Francilienne (N104) 3 km, sortie Etiolles
Map 15 on page 127 Carte 15 Page 127

GOLF COURSE PARCOURS 15/20

Site	Site	
Maintenance	Entretien	
Architect	Architecte	Michel Gayon
Type	Type	plaine
Relief	Relief	
Water in play	Eau en jeu	
Exp. to wind	Exposé au vent	
Trees in play	Arbres en jeu	

Scorecard Carte de score	Chp. Chp.	Mens Mess.	Ladies Da.
Length Long.	6239	5710	5272
Par	73	73	73

Advised golfing ability Niveau de jeu recommandé	0 12 24 36
Hcp required Handicap exigé	non

CLUB HOUSE & AMENITIES CLUB HOUSE ET ANNEXES 6/10

Pro shop	Pro-shop	
Driving range	Practice	
Sheltered	couvert	9 places
On grass	sur herbe	non
Putting-green	putting-green	oui
Pitching-green	pitching green	oui

201

HOTEL FACILITIES ENVIRONNEMENT HOTELIER 5/10

HOTELS HÔTELS
Adagio *** Evry 3 km
114 chambres, D 490 F
Tél (33) 01 69 47 30 00, Fax (33) 01 69 47 30 10

Campanile ** Saint-Germain-lès-Corbeil
47 chambres, D 270 F 5 km
Tél (33) 01 69 89 12 13, Fax (33) 01 69 89 11 89

Auberge de l'Ile de Saussay *** Ile de Saussay
7 chambres, D 350 F 17 km
Tél (33) 01 64 93 20 12, Fax (33) 01 69 93 39 88

Climat ** Tigery
44 chambres, D 270 F 3 km
Tél (33) 01 69 89 19 00, Fax (33) 01 69 89 19 12

RESTAURANTS RESTAURANT
La Mare au Diable Moissy-Cramayel
Tél (33) 01 64 10 20 90 13 km

La vue sur la mer, les falaises et la ville est splendide. On ne se lassera pas du 10, plongeant au drive en bord de mer, pour remonter ensuite vers le green sur un plateau. Ouvert à tous les vents, ce parcours a fait l'objet de modifications depuis sa création en 1908. Pour le classer parmi les grands links, il faudrait reprendre pas mal de bunkers, quelques greens aux surfaces souvent sans intérêt, et déplacer plusieurs départs, mais ce golf familial ne dispose pas des moyens des clubs prestigieux et les améliorations ne peuvent être que progressives. Cela dit, on peut jouer ici plusieurs jours avec beaucoup de plaisir, par beau temps au moins. Quand le vent souffle, c'est une bataille contre le parcours, et il vaut mieux jouer en match-play ! L'atmosphère du club est sympathique, le profil général du parcours en fait un "challenge" attachant, ne serait ce que pour travailler les balles basses.

The view over the sea, cliffs and the town is magnificent, and the 10th hole, with a drive plunging seaward from the cliffs before sweeping back up to an elevated green, is a moment to cherish. Exposed to all winds, the course has been altered several times since its creation in 1908, but to be ranked among the truly great links, some tees need moving and a number of bunkers require attention, as do the putting surfaces on several greens. But this is a family club that lacks the resources of the more prestigious courses, and improvements can only come gradually. With this said, you can play here time and time again and enjoy every minute, at least if the weather holds. When the wind blows, it is a tough battle with the course and match-play is the obvious resort. The club has a friendly atmosphere and the general layout of the course makes it a pleasing challenge, if only for the opportunity to practice these low-trajectory shots.

Golf d'Etretat
Route du Havre
F - 76790 ETRETAT

Office	Secrétariat	(33) 02 35 27 04 89
Pro shop	Pro-shop	(33) 02 35 28 56 67
Fax	Fax	(33) 02 35 29 49 02
Situation	Situation	

16 km S.O. Fécamp, 20 800 hab.
30 km N. Le Havre, 197 210 hab.

Annual closure	Fermeture annnuelle	non
Weekly closure	Fermeture hebdomadaire	mardi
		mardi, le restaurant

Fees main season
Tarifs haute saison la journée

	Week days Semaine	We/Bank holidays We/Férié
Individual Individuel	200 F	330 F
Couple Couple	360 F	590 F

Caddy	Caddy	non
Electric Trolley	Chariot électrique	non
Buggy	Voiturette	180 F/18 trous
Clubs	Clubs	non

Credit cards Cartes de crédit
VISA - CB - Eurocard - MasterCard

GOLF COURSE
PARCOURS
14/20

Site	Site	
Maintenance	Entretien	
Architect	Architecte	M. Chantepie D. Fruchet (4 trous)
Type	Type	bord de mer
Relief	Relief	
Water in play	Eau en jeu	
Exp. to wind	Exposé au vent	
Trees in play	Arbres en jeu	

Scorecard Carte de score	Chp. Chp.	Mens Mess.	Ladies Da.
Length Long.	6072	5681	5137
Par	72	72	72

Advised golfing ability Niveau de jeu recommandé		0 12 24 36
Hcp required	Handicap exigé	35 - 28 We

CLUB HOUSE & AMENITIES
CLUB HOUSE ET ANNEXES
6/10

Pro shop	Pro-shop	
Driving range	Practice	
Sheltered	couvert	3 places
On grass	sur herbe	non
Putting-green	putting-green	oui
Pitching-green	pitching green	non

HOTEL FACILITIES
ENVIRONNEMENT HOTELIER
5/10

HOTELS HÔTELS
Dormy House Golf Hôtel ***   500 m. du golf
51 chambres, D 650 F
Tél (33) 02 35 27 07 88, Fax (33) 02 35 29 86 19

Le Donjon ***   Etretat
10 chambres, D 600 F   2 km
Tél (33) 02 35 27 08 23, Fax (33) 02 35 29 92 24

Les Falaises **   Etretat
24 chambres, D 380 F   2 km
Tél (33) 02 35 27 02 77**RESTAURANTS** RESTAURANT
Le Belvédère   Etretat
Tél (33) 02 35 20 13 76   2 km

Le Galion   Etretat
Tél (33) 02 35 29 48 74   2 km

202

Access Accès : D940 Etretat-Le Havre
Map 2 on page 101 Carte 2 Page 101

Le remodelage effectué par Cabell Robinson en 1990 a "réveillé" et beaucoup amélioré ce parcours et le remplacement récent du 3 (par 3) a fait disparaître son trou le plus contestable. Les greens sont maintenant très protégés, avec des jeux de buttes et de nombreux bunkers très en jeu, mettant beaucoup plus l'accent sur les aspects techniques du jeu. Si les joueurs très moyens ont parfois regretté ces nouvelles difficultés, le parcours a repris son rang parmi les meilleurs de la région lémanique. Assez accidenté (voiturette conseillée pour les seniors), quasiment comme un golf de montagne, Evian n'est pas très long, mais les dénivellations peuvent être trompeuses, notamment au 15, petit par 3 très spectaculaire dominant le lac Léman. Le plus joli point de vue du parcours, couronnant l'impression très agréable d'évoluer dans un beau parc.

The restyling carried out by Cabell Robinson in 1990 has revived and much improved this course, and the recent replacement of hole N° 3 (a par 3) has seen the end of one of the course's more controversial holes. The greens are now particularly well defended, with a series of sand-hills and easy-to-hit bunkers, thus placing much more emphasis on the technical side of the game. While high-handicappers may often come to regret these new difficulties, the course has recovered its status as one of the best courses in the region. Hilly enough to be virtually a mountain course (buggy recommended for seniors), Evian is not very long, but the steep slopes can be deceiving, especially on the 15th, a highly spectacular short par 3 overlooking Lake Geneva. This is the prettiest spot on the course and crowns the very pleasant impression of playing golf in a beautiful park.

Royal Golf Club Evian
B.P. No 8
F - 74502 EVIAN

Office	Secrétariat	(33) 04 50 75 46 66
Pro shop	Pro-shop	(33) 04 50 75 51 96
Fax	Fax	(33) 04 50 75 65 54
Situation	Situation	

2.5 km O. Evian, 8 900 hab.
46 km E. Genève, 172 486 hab.

Annual closure	Fermeture annnuelle	oui
		10/12 → 31/01/99

Weekly closure Fermeture hebdomadaire

Fees main season Tarifs haute saison Le parcours

	Week days Semaine	We/Bank holidays We/Férié
Individual Individuel	310 F	380 F
Couple Couple	620 F	760 F

GF après 17h00 : 1/2 tarif Sem. et We

Caddy	Caddy	160 F/18 trous
Electric Trolley	Chariot électrique	130 F/18 trous
Buggy	Voiturette	280 F/18 trous
Clubs	Clubs 1/2 série	100 F/18 trous

Credit cards Cartes de crédit
VISA - CB - Eurocard - MasterCard - AMEX - DC - JCB

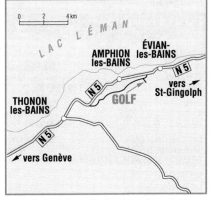

THONON les-BAINS
AMPHION les-BAINS
ÉVIAN-les-BAINS
LAC LÉMAN
N5
GOLF
vers St-Gingolph
vers Genève

Access Accès : Evian → Genève, à gauche → Golf
Map 8 on page 113 Carte 8 Page 113

GOLF COURSE
PARCOURS **15**/20

Site	Site	
Maintenance	Entretien	
Architect	Architecte	Cabell Robinson

Type	Type	montagne
Relief	Relief	
Water in play	Eau en jeu	
Exp. to wind	Exposé au vent	
Trees in play	Arbres en jeu	

Scorecard Carte de score	Chp. Chp.	Mens Mess.	Ladies Da.
Length Long.	6006	5651	5094
Par	72	72	72

Advised golfing ability	0	12	24	36
Niveau de jeu recommandé				
Hcp required	Handicap exigé	35		

CLUB HOUSE & AMENITIES
CLUB HOUSE ET ANNEXES **7**/10

Pro shop	Pro-shop	
Driving range	Practice	
Sheltered	couvert	10 places
On grass	sur herbe	oui
Putting-green	putting-green	oui
Pitching-green	pitching green	oui

203

HOTEL FACILITIES
ENVIRONNEMENT HOTELIER **9**/10

HOTELS HÔTELS
Le Royal ★★★★ Evian 3 km
156 chambres, D 1900 F
Tél (33) 04 50 26 85 00, Fax (33) 04 50 75 38 40

L'Ermitage ★★★★ Evian 2 km
90 chambres, D 1600 F
Tél (33) 04 50 26 85 00, Fax (33) 04 50 75 29 37

La Verniaz«Relais et Châteaux» ★★★★ Evian 2 km
35 chambres, D 750 F
Tél (33) 04 50 75 04 90, Fax (33) 04 50 70 78 92

Bourgogne et Ducs de Savoie ★★★ Evian 2 km
30 chambres, D 520 F
Tél (33) 04 50 75 01 05, Fax (33) 04 50 75 04 05

RESTAURANTS RESTAURANT
La Toque Royale Evian 2,5 km
Tél (33) 04 50 75 03 78

Un parcours assez vallonné, mais où la mise en oeuvre des reliefs a été faite avec intelligence, et le souci d'éviter les coups aveugles. Cette franchise a beaucoup contribué à sa réputation. Très varié, le dessin de l'américain Jean-Marie Poellot met en jeu tous les types d'obstacles et exige tous les coups de golf; il propose fréquemment des choix stratégiques intéressants, et des situations de petit jeu excitantes. La maturité du parcours et l'abondance des plantations contribuent au charme du jeu. Les trous sont de bonne longueur, à l'exception du 13, un par 3 démesuré, mais on ne recommandera les départs arrière qu'aux handicaps à un chiffre. Très travaillés, les greens demandent beaucoup de finesse et d'attention pour ne pas perdre trop de points au putting. Le fonctionnement du club est complètement commercial, mais l'ensemble reste accueillant. Le Club-House est à la hauteur.

A comparatively hilly course where relief has been employed intelligently to carefully avoid blind shots. This straight and honest side to the layout has done much to help the course's reputation. The very varied design of American architect Jean-Marie Poellot brings all types of hazard into play and demands every shot in the book. Interestingly, the layout often gives a choice of strategy and some exciting situations for short-play around the greens. The maturity of the course and the numerous plantations do much to add to the charm of playing here. All the holes are of a good length, except the outsized 13th hole, a par-3 of over 200 metres, but generally the back-tees are to be recommended for single-figure handicappers. A lot of work has gone into the greens, which require more than a touch of finesse if you want to avoid too many 3-putts (and who doesn't?). The club is a totally commercial affair, but the whole complex extends a warm welcome with a club-house worthy of the rest.

Golf de Feucherolles

Sainte-Gemme
F -78810 FEUCHEROLLES

Office	Secrétariat	(33) 01 30 54 94 94
Pro shop	Pro-shop	(33) 01 30 54 94 94
Fax	Fax	(33) 01 30 54 92 37
Situation	Situation	

12 km S.O. St-Germain-en-Laye, 39 920 hab.
39 km O. Paris, 2 175 200 hab.

Annual closure	Fermeture annnuelle	non
Weekly closure	Fermeture hebdomadaire	mardi
		1/11→28/02/99

Fees main season
Tarifs haute saison le parcours

	Week days Semaine	We/Bank holidays We/Férié
Individual Individuel	350 F	490 F
Couple Couple	700 F	980 F

Caddy	Caddy	sur réservation
Electric Trolley	Chariot électrique	non
Buggy	Voiturette	120 F/18 trous
Clubs	Clubs série	150 F/jour

Credit cards Cartes de crédit
VISA - CB - Eurocard - MasterCard - AMEX - DC - JCB

204

Access Accès : Paris A13 → Versailles, sortie Saint-Germain-en-Laye → Saint-Nom-la- Bretèche, → Feucherolles **Map 15 on page 127** Carte 15 Page 127

GOLF COURSE
PARCOURS

15/20

Site	Site	
Maintenance	Entretien	
Architect	Architecte	Jean-Marie Poellot
Type	Type	vallon, forêt
Relief	Relief	
Water in play	Eau en jeu	
Exp. to wind	Exposé au vent	
Trees in play	Arbres en jeu	

Scorecard Carte de score	Chp. Chp.	Mens Mess.	Ladies Da.
Length Long.	6358	5887	5486
Par	72	72	72

Advised golfing ability		0 12 24 36
Niveau de jeu recommandé		
Hcp required	Handicap exigé	non

CLUB HOUSE & AMENITIES
CLUB HOUSE ET ANNEXES

7/10

Pro shop	Pro-shop	
Driving range	Practice	
Sheltered	couvert	non
On grass	sur herbe	non
Putting-green	putting-green	oui
Pitching-green	pitching green	non

HOTEL FACILITIES
ENVIRONNEMENT HOTELIER

5/10

HOTELS HÔTELS

La Forestière — Saint-Germain
25 chambres, D 950 F — 12 km
Tél (33) 01 39 73 36 60, Fax (33) 01 39 73 93 88

Le Pavillon Henri IV — Saint-Germain
42 chambres, D 1 000 F — 12 km
Tél (33) 01 39 10 15 15, Fax (33) 01 39 93 73 93

Ermitage des Loges — Saint-Germain
57 chambres, D 550 F — 12 km
Tél (33) 01 34 51 88 86, Fax (33) 01 34 51 16 29

RESTAURANTS RESTAURANT

Les Trois Marches — Versailles
Tél (33) 01 39 50 13 21 — 10 km

Le Potager du Roy — Versailles
Tél (33) 01 39 50 35 34 — 10 km

Situé à l'orée de la superbe forêt de Fontainebleau, ce parcours est l'un des plus tranquilles de la région parisienne. Il fait partie de ces grands refuges d'une certaine tradition britannique, bien que l'on puisse regretter que certaines retouches aient été apportées au dessin de Simpson au cours des années, notamment sur quelques greens. Un regret mineur en regard des satisfactions visuelles et golfiques que l'on peut éprouver ici, au milieu des chênes, des pins et des hêtres, où l'on devine parfois les ombres des biches, où l'on dérange souvent lièvres et lapins. Grâce au terrain très sablonneux et au gazon très souple, on peut découvrir ici toute l'année un parcours plus que plaisant, pas trop difficile, bien que les greens soient souvent petits et parfois très torturés, mais où un bon score n'est jamais le fait du hasard. Un parcours complet.

This course, lying on the edge of the magnificent forest of Fontainebleau, is one of the quietest around Paris. It is one of those great bastions of British tradition, although some might regret the way Simpson's layout has been retouched here and there over the years, particularly on some of the greens. This is only a minor gripe given the visual and golfing pleasure to be had here amidst the oak, pine and beech trees, where you can sometimes make out the shape of deer or disturb hares and rabbits. With very sandy terrain and plush grass, you can play this more than pleasant and not too difficult course all year, although the greens are often small and very torturous. A complete course where a good score is never down to chance.

Golf de Fontainebleau

Route d'Orléans
F - 77300 FONTAINEBLEAU

Office	Secrétariat	(33) 01 64 22 22 95
Pro shop	Pro-shop	(33) 01 64 22 74 19
Fax	Fax	(33) 01 64 22 63 76
Situation	Situation	

1 km from Fontainebleau, 15 714 hab.

Annual closure	Fermeture annnuelle	non
Weekly closure	Fermeture hebdomadaire	mardi

Fees main season Tarifs haute saison la journée

	Week days Semaine	We/Bank holidays We/Férié
Individual Individuel	350 F	—
Couple Couple	700 F	—

Week-end : membres seulement (only members) -
07/08: We 500 F

Caddy	Caddy	oui, 190 F
Electric Trolley	Chariot électrique	non
Buggy	Voiturette	non
Clubs	Clubs	non

Credit cards Cartes de crédit
VISA - CB - MasterCard - AMEX - DC

Access Accès : A6 exit Fontainebleau. N7 →
Fontainebleau. Carrefour de l'Obélisque, N152 →
Malesherbes. Golf 500 m à droite.
Map 3 on page 102 Carte 3 Page 102

GOLF COURSE
PARCOURS

17 /20

Site	Site	
Maintenance	Entretien	
Architect	Architecte	Tom Simpson
Type	Type	forest
Relief	Relief	
Water in play	Eau en jeu	
Exp. to wind	Exposé au vent	
Trees in play	Arbres en jeu	

Scorecard Carte de score	Chp. Chp.	Mens Mess.	Ladies Da.
Length Long.	6074	5711	5168
Par	72	72	72

Advised golfing ability		0 12 24 36
Niveau de jeu recommandé		
Hcp required	Handicap exigé	24 Me, 28 Dames

CLUB HOUSE & AMENITIES
CLUB HOUSE ET ANNEXES

7 /10

Pro shop	Pro-shop	
Driving range	Practice	
Sheltered	couvert	6 places
On grass	sur herbe	oui
Putting-green	putting-green	oui
Pitching-green	pitching green	oui

205

HOTEL FACILITIES
ENVIRONNEMENT HOTELIER

7 /10

HOTELS HÔTELS
Aigle Noir ★★★★ — Fontainebleau
51 chambres, D 1050 F — 1 km
Tél (33) 01 64 22 32 65, Fax (33) 01 64 22 17 33

Mercure — Fontainebleau
97 chambres, D 800 F — 1 km
Tél (33) 01 64 69 34 34, Fax (33) 01 64 69 34 39

Ibis — Fontainebleau
80 chambres, D 360 F — 1 km
Tél (33) 01 64 23 45 25, Fax (33) 01 64 23 42 22

RESTAURANTS RESTAURANT
Bas- Bréau — Barbizon
Tél (33) 01 60 66 40 05 — 10 km

Le Vieux Logis — Thomery
Tél(33) 01 60 96 44 77 — 10 km

Grand Veneur — Barbizon
Tél(33) 01 60 66 40 44 — 9 km

FONTCAUDE

Dans un environnement immobilier manquant singulièrement de beauté, ce parcours a été dessiné par Chris Pittman sur un terrain relativement accidenté. Quelques accidents de terrain (ravin au 11), de petits arbustes, la garrigue et quelques grands arbres interviennent pour compliquer le jeu, ainsi que des dénivellations et dévers parfois préoccupants. Si l'on ajoute quelques trous en bordure de rivière, des greens bien modelés et des bunkers assez profonds pour inciter à s'entraîner avant de les affronter, les joueurs trouveront là un parcours varié et amusant, mais les meilleurs estimeront sans doute qu'il manque "un petit quelque chose" pour en faire un grand parcours. Néammoins, c'est un bon complément dans une région de bonne qualité golfique, notamment avec La Grande Motte, Massane, Cap d'Agde et Nîmes-Campagne.

Laid out in an environment of property development singularly lacking in appeal, this course was designed by Chris Pittman over comparatively hilly terrain. A few drastic features (a ravine on the 11th), small bushes, the "garrigue" and a few big trees actively complicate the course, as do some of the steep slopes and inclines, which can cause considerable concern. Add to this a few holes alongside a river, well-contoured greens and bunkers that are deep enough to prompt some sand practice before the round, and you have here a varied and amusing course, but one where the best players will doubtless feel that there is something missing for it to become a great course. Nevertheless, this is a good additional course in a great region for golf, with in particular La Grande Motte, Massane, Cap d'Agde and Nîmes-Campagne in the neighbourhood.

Golf de Fontcaude
Domaine de Fontcaude
F - 34990 JUVIGNAC

Office	Secrétariat	(33) 04 67 03 34 30
Pro shop	Pro-shop	(33) 04 67 03 34 30
Fax	Fax	(33) 04 67 03 34 51
Situation	Situation	

2 km N.O. Montpellier, 210 860 hab.

Annual closure	Fermeture annnuelle	non
Weekly closure	Fermeture hebdomadaire	

Fees main season
Tarifs haute saison la journée

	Week days Semaine	We/Bank holidays We/Férié
Individual Individuel	190 F	240 F
Couple Couple	380 F	480 F

Caddy	Caddy	non
Electric Trolley	Chariot électrique	non
Buggy	Voiturette	120 F/18 trous
Clubs	Clubs 1/2 série	65 F/jour

Credit cards Cartes de crédit
VISA - CB - Eurocard - MasterCard - AMEX - DC

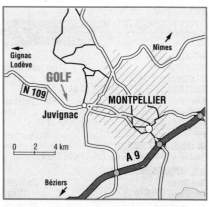

Access Accès : Montpellier, N109 → Lodève
Map 13 on page 123 Carte 13 Page 123

GOLF COURSE
PARCOURS   **14**/20

Site	Site	
Maintenance	Entretien	
Architect	Architecte	Chris Pittman
Type	Type	résidentiel, vallon
Relief	Relief	
Water in play	Eau en jeu	
Exp. to wind	Exposé au vent	
Trees in play	Arbres en jeu	

Scorecard Carte de score	Chp. Chp.	Mens Mess.	Ladies Da.
Length Long.	6292	5917	5056
Par	72	72	72

Advised golfing ability	0	12	24	36
Niveau de jeu recommandé				
Hcp required Handicap exigé	35			

CLUB HOUSE & AMENITIES
CLUB HOUSE ET ANNEXES   **6**/10

Pro shop	Pro-shop	
Driving range	Practice	
Sheltered	couvert	5 places
On grass	sur herbe	oui
Putting-green	putting-green	oui
Pitching-green	pitching green	oui

HOTEL FACILITIES
ENVIRONNEMENT HOTELIER   **6**/10

HOTELS HÔTELS
Golf de Fontcaude ***   sur place
46 chambres, D 530 F
Tél (33) 04 67 03 34 10, Fax (33) 04 67 03 34 51

New Hôtel du Midi ***   Montpellier
47 chambres, D 380 F   2 km
Tél (33) 04 67 92 69 61, Fax (33) 04 67 92 73 63

Demeure des Brousses ***   Montpellier
17 chambres, D 580 F   2 km
Tél (33) 04 67 65 77 66, Fax (33) 04 67 22 22 17

RESTAURANTS RESTAURANT
Jardin des Sens   Montpellier
Tél (33) 04 67 79 63 38   2 km

Le Chandelier   Montpellier
Tél (33) 04 67 92 61 62   2 km

206

FONTENAILLES BLANC

14	7	6

Dans cet ensemble de 27 trous, le 18 trous "Blanc" est considéré comme le pacours principal, même si le "Rouge" propose aussi quelques bons trous. L'architecte Michel Gayon a travaillé avec dextérité et imagination ce vaste espace plat et joliment boisé. Il faut profiter de quelques trous assez courts pour ne pas trop gâter une carte de score forcément mise à mal sur d'autres trous, exigeant beaucoup de puissance au drive. C'est en général un parcours mieux adapté aux frappeurs qu'aux techniciens. En tout cas, certains obstacles cachés impliquent de le jouer plusieurs fois pour bien le connaître avant d'espérer bien y scorer. L'entretien du parcours est généralement de bonne qualité, mais il est un peu humide en hiver, notamment dans les zones les plus boisées. Le complexe Club house-Hôtel est assez confortable et plaisant pour que l'on s'y attarde.

In this 27-hole complex, the 18-hole "White" course is considered to be the main layout, although the 9-hole "Red" alternative also features a few interesting holes. Architect Michel Gayon has employed a lot of skill and imagination in developing this enormous flat space, which has more than its fair share of woodland. Here, you take advantage of a few short holes in order to protect a card that will definitely be hard pushed to survive some of the others, which require power-play and length off the tee. Generally speaking, this is a course for long-hitters rather than for technicians. In any case, a number of hidden hazards call for several outings before hoping to card a good score. Upkeep is generally good, but the course is bit damp in winter, especially in the woodier areas. The club-house/hotel complex is comfortable and pleasant enough to warrant spending some time here.

Golf de Fontenailles
Domaine de Bois-Boudran
F - 77370 FONTENAILLES

Office	Secrétariat	(33) 01 64 60 51 52
Pro shop	Pro-shop	(33) 01 64 60 51 00
Fax	Fax	(33) 01 60 67 52 12
Situation	Situation	

25 km E. Melun, 35 320 hab.

Annual closure	Fermeture annnuelle	oui
		24/12 → 2/01/99

Weekly closure Fermeture hebdomadaire

Fees main season Tarifs haute saison la journée

	Week days Semaine	We/Bank holidays We/Férié
Individual Individuel	200 F	350 F
Couple Couple	350 F	600 F

après 16 H : 125 (sem) et 200 F (We)

Caddy	Caddy	non
Electric Trolley	Chariot électrique	60 F/18 trous
Buggy	Voiturette	200 F/18 trous
Clubs	Clubs 1/2 série	60 F/jour

Credit cards Cartes de crédit
VISA - CB - Eurocard - MasterCard - AMEX - DC - JCB

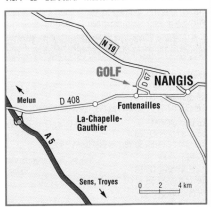

Access Accès : • A4 Paris-Nancy, N104 → Troyes, N19 → Provins • A5 → Melun, sortie 16 Châtillon-la-Borde, D408 → Nangis
Map 3 on page 103 Carte 3 Page 103

GOLF COURSE PARCOURS
14/20

Site	Site	
Maintenance	Entretien	
Architect	Architecte	Michel Gayon
Type	Type	parc
Relief	Relief	
Water in play	Eau en jeu	
Exp. to wind	Exposé au vent	
Trees in play	Arbres en jeu	

Scorecard Carte de score	**Chp.** Chp.	**Mens** Mess.	**Ladies** Da.
Length Long.	6256	5900	5299
Par	72	72	72

Advised golfing ability Niveau de jeu recommandé	0	12	24	36

Hcp required Handicap exigé 35, le We

CLUB HOUSE & AMENITIES
CLUB HOUSE ET ANNEXES
7/10

Pro shop	Pro-shop	
Driving range	Practice	
Sheltered	couvert	5 places
On grass	sur herbe	oui, l'été
Putting-green	putting-green	oui
Pitching-green	pitching green	oui

HOTEL FACILITIES
ENVIRONNEMENT HOTELIER
6/10

HOTELS HÔTELS
Domaine de Bois-Boudran ****   sur place
51 chambres, D 1200 F
Tél (33) 01 64 60 51 00, Fax (33) 01 60 67 52 12

Le Dauphin **   Nangis
17 chambres, D 300 F   6 km
Tél (33) 01 64 08 00 27, Fax (33) 01 64 08 12 97

RESTAURANTS RESTAURANT
Le Dauphin   Nangis
Tél (33) 01 64 08 00 27   6 km

La Forge   Fontenailles
Tél (33) 00 64 08 40 76   1 km

207

14	7	4

A proximité de Saint-Jean-de-Monts et de La Domangère, ce golf complète un bel itinéraire dans la province historique de Vendée. A proximité de la station balnéaire de Saint-Gilles-Croix-de-Vie, l'architecte Yves Bureau a conçu un parcours très propre (comme à son habitude) et pour tous niveaux, dans un site de campagne aux reliefs très doux, dans un paysage de chênes verts et de pins maritimes. Des plans d'eau pas trop en jeu agrémentent un dessin sans pièges, adapté à tous les types de joueurs, en harmonie visuelle avec les marais de la région. Ce parcours est de bonne longueur des départs arrière, ce qui permettra aux meilleurs de s'exprimer avec plaisir mais sans trop de soucis. Un joli golf de vacances, où le vent peut apporter un piment, et quelques surprises supplémentaires.

Close to Saint-Jean-de-Monts and La Domangère, this course is a fine addition to a great golfing itinerary through the historical province of La Vendée. Not far from the seaside resort of Saint-Gilles-Croix-de-Vie, architect Yves Bureau has, as usual, designed a very neat golf course for all golfers in gently undulating countryside, lined with oak trees and maritime pines. Stretches of water enhance a layout that is free of hidden traps and tailored to all types of golfer. Visually, the course also blends in well with the region's marshlands. This is a good length course from the back tees, thus giving the better players the chance to show their mettle without too much to worry about. All in all, a pretty holiday course where the wind can add a little spice and a few extra surprises.

Golf des Fontenelles
F - 85220 L'AIGUILLON-SUR-VIE

Office	Secrétariat	(33) 02 51 54 13 94
Pro shop	Pro-shop	(33) 02 51 54 13 94
Fax	Fax	(33) 02 51 55 45 77
Situation	Situation	

10 km S.E. St-Gilles-Croix-de-Vie, 6 290 hab.
65 km S.O. Nantes, 252 030 hab.

Annual closure	Fermeture annnuelle	non
Weekly closure	Fermeture hebdomadaire	lundi
	1/11 →	31/03/99

Fees main season Tarifs haute saison la journée

	Week days Semaine	We/Bank holidays We/Férié
Individual Individuel	245 F	245 F
Couple Couple	490 F	490 F

Caddy	Caddy	non
Electric Trolley	Chariot électrique	non
Buggy	Voiturette	200 F/18 trous
Clubs	Clubs 1/2 série	50 F/jour

Credit cards Cartes de crédit
VISA - CB - Eurocard - MasterCard

208

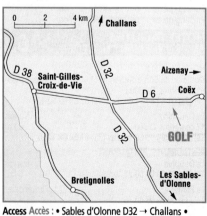

Access Accès : • Sables d'Olonne D32 → Challans •
La Roche-sur-Yon → Aizenay/Saint-Gilles-Croix-de-Vie
D6, Golf 2 km. après Coëx
Map 6 on page 108 Carte 6 Page 108

GOLF COURSE
PARCOURS **14**/20

Site	Site	
Maintenance	Entretien	
Architect	Architecte	Yves Bureau
Type	Type	bocage
Relief	Relief	
Water in play	Eau en jeu	
Exp. to wind	Exposé au vent	
Trees in play	Arbres en jeu	

Scorecard	Chp.	Mens	Ladies
Carte de score	Chp.	Mess.	Da.
Length Long.	6205	5824	5311
Par	72	72	72

Advised golfing ability		0 12 24 36
Niveau de jeu recommandé		
Hcp required	Handicap exigé	non

CLUB HOUSE & AMENITIES
CLUB HOUSE ET ANNEXES **7**/10

Pro shop	Pro-shop	
Driving range	Practice	
Sheltered	couvert	10 places
On grass	sur herbe	oui
Putting-green	putting-green	oui
Pitching-green	pitching green	oui

HOTEL FACILITIES
ENVIRONNEMENT HOTELIER **4**/10

HOTELS HÔTELS
Le Château de la Vérie ***   Challans 22 km
19 chambres, D 800 F
Tél (33) 02 51 35 33 44, Fax (33) 02 51 35 14 84

Le Lion d'Or **   Saint-Gilles-Croix-de-Vie
55 chambres, D 300 F   10 km
Tél (33) 02 51 55 50 39, Fax (33) 02 51 55 22 84

Embruns ***   Saint-Gilles-Croix-de-Vie
14 chambres, D 450 F   10 km
Tél (33) 02 51 55 11 40, Fax (33) 02 51 55 11 20

RESTAURANTS RESTAURANT
Les Embruns   Saint-Gilles-Croix-de-Vie
Tél (33) 02 51 55 11 40   10 km

La Grand Roche   Bretignolles-sur-Mer
Tél (33) 02 51 90 15 21   10 km

L'architecte Ronald Fream a tiré le meilleur parti d'un site très accidenté (en voie d'urbanisation), mais qui propose de belles vues sur la mer et des trous spectaculaires. Il faut payer le prix de ce décor tourmenté, dans une région où les reliefs sont très accentués : de nombreux dévers peuvent compliquer les trajectoires de balle, quelques coups sont aveugles (moins qu'on pourrait le croire), le rough est souvent très pénalisant, les fairways parfois étroits, et quelques rochers viennent dangereusement en jeu. Très bien paysagé, très technique, c'est un parcours que l'on prendra du plaisir à jouer en voiturette, ou au minimum avec un chariot électrique, pour conserver des forces physiques et mentales, non seulement pour choisir les bons clubs, mais aussi pour les utiliser. Si l'on connaît mal le parcours, il ne faut pas trop penser au score, mais commencer en match-play.

Architect Ronald Fream has made good use of a very hilly site (now being built upon more and more) which features fine views of the sea and some spectacular holes. But this twisted and winding scenery comes at a cost in a region of rolling hills and dales. A lot of slanting fairways make life a little difficult at times, a few shots are blind (but less so than you might imagine), the rough gives no quarter, the fairways are sometimes very tight indeed and a few rocks loom dangerously at strategic areas. Beautifully landscaped and a technically demanding course, Frégate is good fun to play in a buggy in order to preserve mental and physical strength, not only for choosing the right club but also for using them in the right way. If you don't know the course, don't worry too much about the score and go around in match-play.

Golf de Frégate
Route de Bandol RD 559
F - 83270 SAINT-CYR-SUR-MER

Office	Secrétariat	(33) 04 94 32 50 50
Pro shop	Pro-shop	(33) 04 94 32 50 50
Fax	Fax	(33) 04 94 29 96 94
Situation	Situation	

3 km O. Bandol, 7 430 hab.
25 km N.O. Toulon, 167 620 hab.

Annual closure	Fermeture annnuelle	non
Weekly closure	Fermeture hebdomadaire	

Fees main season
Tarifs haute saison la journée

	Week days Semaine	We/Bank holidays We/Férié
Individual Individuel	260 F	290 F
Couple Couple	520 F	580 F

Caddy	Caddy	sur réservation
Electric Trolley	Chariot électrique	90 F/18 trous
Buggy	Voiturette	170 F/18 trous
Clubs	Clubs 1/2 série	95 F/18 trous

Credit cards Cartes de crédit
VISA - CB - Eurocard - MasterCard - AMEX

Access Accès : • A50 Marseille → Toulon, sortie Saint-Cyr-sur-Mer
• A50 Toulon → Marseille, sortie Bandol, D559
Map 14 on page 124 Carte 14 Page 124

GOLF COURSE
PARCOURS
15/20

Site	Site	▇▇▇▇▇▇
Maintenance	Entretien	▇▇▇▇▇▇▇
Architect	Architecte	Ronald Fream
Type	Type	bord de mer, vignes
Relief	Relief	▇▇▇▇▇
Water in play	Eau en jeu	▇▇
Exp. to wind	Exposé au vent	▇▇▇▇
Trees in play	Arbres en jeu	▇▇▇

Scorecard Carte de score	Chp. Chp.	Mens Mess.	Ladies Da.
Length Long.	6209	5847	4950
Par	72	72	72

Advised golfing ability		0 12 24 36
Niveau de jeu recommandé		▇▇▇▇▇
Hcp required	Handicap exigé	35

CLUB HOUSE & AMENITIES
CLUB HOUSE ET ANNEXES
7/10

Pro shop	Pro-shop	▇▇▇▇▇
Driving range	Practice	▇▇▇▇
Sheltered	couvert	4 places
On grass	sur herbe	non
Putting-green	putting-green	oui
Pitching-green	pitching green	non

HOTEL FACILITIES
ENVIRONNEMENT HOTELIER
7/10

HOTELS HÔTELS
Frégate ****　　　　　　　　　　　　　　sur place
100 chambres, D 1350 F
Tél (33) 04 94 29 39 39, Fax (33) 04 94 29 39 40

L'Ile Rousse ****　　　　　　　　　　　　　Bandol
53 chambres, D 775 F　　　　　　　　　　　3 km
Tél (33) 04 94 29 46 86, Fax (33) 04 94 29 49 29

Bérard ***　　　　　　　　　La Cadière-d'Azur
40 chambres, D 650 F　　　　　　　　　　　7 km
Tél (33) 04 94 90 11 43, Fax (33) 04 94 90 01 94

RESTAURANTS RESTAURANT
L'Ile Rousse　　　　　　　　　　　　　　Bandol
Tél (33) 04 94 29 46 86　　　　　　　　　　3 km

Le Mas des Vignes　　　　　　　Saint-Cyr-sur-Mers
Tél (33) 04 94 29 39 39

209

Des deux 18 trous de ce complexe ambitieux, Le Breuil est le plus "héroïque" dans son déroulement, notamment avec neuf trous insinués entre les superbes étangs de la Dombe, dont l'aspect sauvage a été préservé. D'énormes travaux de drainage lui permettent d'être maintenant jouable en toutes saisons. Plat et long, c'est l'un des parcours les plus techniques et exigeants de la région lyonnaise, mais il affiche clairement ses difficultés stratégiques. On pourra seulement lui reprocher la longueur excessive de ses par 3, un manque de modelage des alentours de green et des bunkers. Délicat pour les joueurs peu expérimentés, il doit absolument être joué des départs normaux par les golfeurs moyens. Les greens sont peu complexes à lire, mais les difficultés étaient suffisantes pour ne pas en rajouter à ce niveau. Le Club-House établi dans de magnifiques bâtiments anciens est complété d'un hôtel sur le site.

"Le Breuil" is the boldest of the two 18-hole courses in this ambitious golfing resort, with nine holes winding their way through the superb lakes of La Dombe, which have lost nothing of their wild natural character. Very extensive draining work has now made this a course for all seasons. Flat and long, it is one of the most technical and most demanding courses in the Lyons region, but the strategic difficulties are clearly visible. The few criticisms that might be levelled are the very long par 3s and the lack of relief around the greens and bunkers. A tricky proposition for inexperienced players, this is a course that should be played from the normal tees for mid-handicappers. The greens are straightforward to read, but the course is already difficult enough without adding any more around the pin. In addition to the club-house, laid out in magnificent old buildings, there is an on-site hotel.

Golf du Gouverneur
Château du Breuil
F - 01390 MONTHIEUX

Office	Secrétariat	(33) 04 72 26 40 34
Pro shop	Pro-shop	(33) 04 72 26 40 34
Fax	Fax	(33) 04 72 26 41 61
Situation	Situation	

38 km S.O. Bourg-en-Bresse, 40 970 hab.
28 km N. Lyon, 413 090 hab.

Annual closure	Fermeture annnuelle	non
Weekly closure	Fermeture hebdomadaire	

Fees main season Tarifs haute saison le parcours

	Week days Semaine	We/Bank holidays We/Férié
Individual Individuel	200 F	280 F
Couple Couple	350 F	480 F
Mardi, 150 F		

Caddy	Caddy	non
Electric Trolley	Chariot électrique	50 F/18 trous
Buggy	Voiturette	180 F/18 trous
Clubs	Clubs 1/2 série	45 F/jour

Credit cards Cartes de crédit
VISA - CB - Eurocard - MasterCard - AMEX

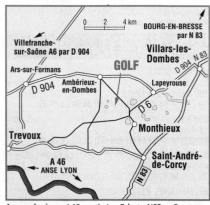

Access Accès : • A46, sortie Les Echets, N83 → Bourg-en- Bresse. St-André de Corcy → Monthieux • A6, sortie Villefranche, → Bourg, Ars, Ambérieux-en-Dombes → Monthieux
Map 11 on page 118 Carte 11 Page 118

GOLF COURSE
PARCOURS 16/20

Site	Site	▬▬▬▬▬□□
Maintenance	Entretien	▬▬▬▬▬□□
Architect	Architecte	Didier Fruchet George Will
Type	Type	campagne, plaine
Relief	Relief	▬□□□□□□
Water in play	Eau en jeu	▬▬▬▬□□□
Exp. to wind	Exposé au vent	▬▬□□□□□
Trees in play	Arbres en jeu	▬▬▬□□□□

Scorecard Carte de score	Chp. Chp.	Mens Mess.	Ladies Da.
Length Long.	6535	6165	4940
Par	72	72	72

Advised golfing ability		0 12 24 36
Niveau de jeu recommandé		▬▬▬▬▬□
Hcp required	Handicap exigé	non

CLUB HOUSE & AMENITIES
CLUB HOUSE ET ANNEXES 7/10

Pro shop	Pro-shop	▬▬▬▬▬□□
Driving range	Practice	▬▬▬▬▬□□
Sheltered	couvert	10 places
On grass	sur herbe	oui
Putting-green	putting-green	oui
Pitching-green	pitching green	oui

HOTEL FACILITIES
ENVIRONNEMENT HOTELIER 6/10

HOTELS HÔTELS
Hôtel Le Gouverneur **** — sur place
53 chambres, D 590 F
Tél (33) 04 72 26 42 00, Fax (33) 04 72 26 42 20

Auberge Les Bichonnières ** — Ambérieux-en-Dombes
9 chambres, D 320 F — 4 km
Tél (33) 04 74 00 82 07, Fax (33) 04 74 00 89 61

RESTAURANTS RESTAURANT
Le Gouverneur — sur place
Tél (33) 04 72 26 42 00

Alain Chapel — Mionnay
Tél(33) 04 78 91 82 02 — 8 km

Auberge des Chasseurs — Bouligneux
Tél(33) 04 74 98 10 02 — 8 km

210

Ce parcours plus "humain" que Le Breuil est accessible à tous les niveaux, même si quelques trous sont abondamment protégés par des obstacles d'eau. A peine plus accidenté, il n'est jamais fatigant, sa technicité comme sa franchise le rendent très plaisant, et si les bons joueurs auront plus d'émotions sur le parcours voisin, ils ne doivent pas se laisser abuser par l'apparente amabilité de Montaplan. Quelques trous boisés (surtout à l'aller) apportent une certaine variété à ce paysage typique de la Dombes, et un programme de plantations sur d'autres trous devrait mieux encore le "dessiner" visuellement. On remarquera la qualité et les reliefs subtils des greens, et les progrès de son entretien après l'achèvement des drainages. Les joueurs non classés auront ici l'occasion d'aborder un parcours de golf présentant pratiquement toutes les difficultés possibles sans se faire trop peur.

Slightly more "human" than "Breuil", the Montaplan course is within the reach of golfers of all levels, even though some holes are heavily protected by water hazards. Although slightly more hilly, the course's technical challenge and openness make it a very pleasant golfing experience. And while the better player will proably find its neighbour more exciting, no-one should be fooled by the apparent friendliness of Montaplan. A few holes amidst the trees (especially on the front nine) add a little variety to this typical landscape of La Dombes, and a plantation programme on other holes should eventually enhance the whole layout from a visual angle. We noted the excellence and subtle contours of the greens, and the progress achieved in upkeep further to drainage work. Here, beginners and high-handicappers have the opportunity to tackle a course which features just about every difficulty you can find on a golf course, without ever being too fearsome.

Golf du Gouverneur
Château du Breuil
F - 01390 MONTHIEUX

Office	Secrétariat	(33) 04 72 26 40 34
Pro shop	Pro-shop	(33) 04 72 26 40 34
Fax	Fax	(33) 04 72 26 41 61
Situation	Situation	

38 km S.O. Bourg-en-Bresse, 40 970 hab.
28 km N. Lyon, 413 090 hab.

Annual closure	Fermeture annnuelle		non
Weekly closure	Fermeture hebdomadaire		

Fees main season Tarifs haute saison Le parcours

	Week days Semaine	We/Bank holidays We/Férié
Individual Individuel	180 F	250 F
Couple Couple	300 F	430 F

Caddy	Caddy	non
Electric Trolley	Chariot électrique	50 F/18 trous
Buggy	Voiturette	180 F/18 trous
Clubs	Clubs 1/2 série	45 F/jour

Credit cards Cartes de crédit
VISA - CB - Eurocard - MasterCard - AMEX

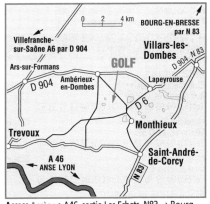

Villefranche-sur-Saône A6 par D 904
Ars-sur-Formans
BOURG-EN-BRESSE par N 83
Villars-les-Dombes
GOLF
D 904
Ambérieux-en-Dombes
Lapeyrouse
D 6
Monthieux
Trevoux
Saint-André-de-Corcy
A 46 ANSE LYON
N 83
0 2 4 km

Access Accès : • A46, sortie Les Echets, N83 → Bourg-en- Bresse. St-André de Corcy → Monthieux
• A6, sortie Villefranche, → Bourg, Ars, Ambérieux-en-Dombes → Monthieux
Map 11 on page 118 Carte 11 Page 118

GOLF COURSE
PARCOURS
14/20

Site	Site	
Maintenance	Entretien	
Architect	Architecte	Didier Fruchet George Will
Type	Type	campagne, plaine
Relief	Relief	
Water in play	Eau en jeu	
Exp. to wind	Exposé au vent	
Trees in play	Arbres en jeu	

Scorecard Carte de score	Chp. Chp.	Mens Mess.	Ladies Da.
Length Long.	5959	5678	5069
Par	72	72	72

Advised golfing ability Niveau de jeu recommandé	0	12	24	36
Hcp required Handicap exigé	non			

CLUB HOUSE & AMENITIES
CLUB HOUSE ET ANNEXES
7/10

Pro shop	Pro-shop	
Driving range	Practice	
Sheltered	couvert	10 places
On grass	sur herbe	oui
Putting-green	putting-green	oui
Pitching-green	pitching green	oui

211

HOTEL FACILITIES
ENVIRONNEMENT HOTELIER
6/10

HOTELS HÔTELS
Hôtel Le Gouverneur ★★★★   sur place
53 chambres, D 590 F
Tél (33) 04 72 26 42 00, Fax (33) 04 72 26 42 20

Auberge Les Bichonnières ★★   Ambérieux-en-Dombes
9 chambres, D 320 F   4 km
Tél (33) 04 74 00 82 07, Fax (33) 04 74 00 89 61

RESTAURANTS RESTAURANT
Le Gouverneur   sur place
Tél (33) 04 72 26 42 00

Alain Chapel   Mionnay
Tél(33) 04 78 91 82 02   8 km

Auberge des Chasseurs   Bouligneux
Tél(33) 04 74 98 10 02   8 km

Ce 18 trous créé par le Club Med a pris une place de choix parmi les bons parcours de la région. L'architecte Cabell Robinson a voulu faire un parcours "tous usages", jouable par tous, même si quelques obstacles d'eau peuvent effrayer les débutants. Les arrivées de drive sont assez larges, mais la densité des roughs incite à taper droit. Les obstacles tiennent essentiellement des mouvements de terrain et des vastes bunkers, souvent très en jeu, qui délimitent bien les fairways. Le programme de plantations devrait également atténuer une certaine imprécision des trous, dans un si vaste espace. Les greens sont assez modelés pour imposer une grande maîtrise du petit jeu et du putting. Amusant à jouer et très divers, ce parcours est facile à jouer à pied, ce n'est pas si fréquent sur la Côte d'Azur. Seul inconvénient : les joueurs sont nombreux ici, et pas toujours très rapides...

This 18-hole course, commissioned by the Club Med, now ranks among the best in the region. Architect Cabell Robinson set out to build an "all-purpose" course for all golfers, even though a number of water hazards might well scare the true beginner. At driving distance, the fairways are wide enough, but the thick rough is a good reason for hitting in the fairway. The basic hazards here are the graded fairways and huge bunkers, which are often fully in play and clearly demarcate the playing area. The new plantation programme should also give greater definition to some holes laid out over such a wide area. The greens are well-contoured and require a sharp short game and good putting. Fun to play with variety all round, this is an easily walkable course, which is seldom the case on courses on the French Riviera. The only drawback is the number of players and frequent slow play...

Golf de la Grande Bastide

Chemin des Picholines
F - 06740 CHATEAUNEUF-DE-GRASSE

Office	Secrétariat	(33) 04 93 77 70 08
Pro shop	Pro-shop	(33) 04 93 77 70 08
Fax	Fax	(33) 04 93 77 72 36
Situation	Situation	

27 km O. Nice, 345 670 hab.
17 km N. Cannes, 68 670 hab.

Annual closure	Fermeture annnuelle	non
Weekly closure	Fermeture hebdomadaire	

Fees main season
Tarifs haute saison la journée

	Week days Semaine	We/Bank holidays We/Férié
Individual Individuel	250 F	280 F
Couple Couple	500 F	560 F

GF soir 160 F/Sem., 200 F/We

Caddy	Caddy	non
Electric Trolley	Chariot électrique	non
Buggy	Voiturette	180 F/18 trous
Clubs	Clubs série	100 F/jour

Credit cards Cartes de crédit
VISA - CB - Eurocard - MasterCard - AMEX

Access Accès : • Cannes, N85 → Valbonne • Nice, A8 sortie Villeneuve-Loubet → Grasse, Roquefort-les-Pins, → Opio
Map 14 on page 125 Carte 14 Page 125

GOLF COURSE
PARCOURS

16/20

Site	Site	
Maintenance	Entretien	
Architect	Architecte	Cabell Robinson
Type	Type	plaine
Relief	Relief	
Water in play	Eau en jeu	
Exp. to wind	Exposé au vent	
Trees in play	Arbres en jeu	

Scorecard Carte de score	Chp. Chp.	Mens Mess.	Ladies Da.
Length Long.	6105	5610	5175
Par	72	72	72

Advised golfing ability		0	12	24	36
Niveau de jeu recommandé					
Hcp required	Handicap exigé	35			

CLUB HOUSE & AMENITIES
CLUB HOUSE ET ANNEXES

6/10

Pro shop	Pro-shop	
Driving range	Practice	
Sheltered	couvert	non
On grass	sur herbe	non
Putting-green	putting-green	oui
Pitching-green	pitching green	oui

HOTEL FACILITIES
ENVIRONNEMENT HOTELIER

6/10

HOTELS HÔTELS
Club Méditerranée ★★★★ — Opio
400 chambres, D 850 F — 2 km
Tél (33) 04 93 09 71 00, Fax (33) 04 93 77 33 57

Hôtel des Parfums ★★★ — Grasse
60 chambres, D 595 F — 4 km
Tél (33) 04 93 36 10 10, Fax (33) 04 93 36 35 48

Hôtel du Patti ★★ — Grasse
50 chambres, D 420 F — 4 km
Tél (33) 04 93 36 01 00, Fax (33) 04 93 36 36 40

RESTAURANTS RESTAURANT
L'Auberge Fleurie — Valbonne
Tél (33) 04 93 12 02 80 — 5 km

212

GRANDE-MOTTE (LA) ✳ 〉 | 16 | 6 | 4 |

En paysage d'étangs, à partir d'un terrain sans relief naturel, et très peu boisé Robert Trent Jones a signé un parcours de grande qualité, modelé avec une grande intelligence, sans jamais donner l'impression de monotonie. Certes, les longs frappeurs peuvent s'y déchaîner, mais les seconds coups, le petit jeu et le putting demandent beaucoup d'inspiration., et les joueurs précis pourront y réussir. L'eau joue un rôle important, mais sans sévérité excessive. Avec une bonne connaissance de ce parcours bien défini dans l'espace (notamment par la tonte du fairway et du petit rough) et un peu de réflexion, tous les joueurs peuvent y prendre plaisir, à l'exception des débutants, qui trouveront avec un joli parcours de 6 trous et un 18 trous de par 58 de quoi largement s'occuper et s'aguerrir. La Grande Motte est un golf commercial, mais le Club house manque de chaleur... et de distinction.

Set in a landscape of lakes with no natural relief and very few trees, Robert Trent Jones has cleverly shaped a high class course which never seems monotonous. Long-hitters can definitely open their shoulders, but approach shots, short play and putting call for a lot of inspiration which should suit the more accurate players. Water is a significant part of the course but is never too severe a test. When you know this neatly laid-out course well (especially the tidily-mown fairways and short rough) and with a little careful thought, every golfer will enjoy playing here, except beginners, who can learn the ropes and get to grips with the compact 6-holer and the par-58 18 hole course. La Grande Motte is a business venture course but the club-house lacks both warmth... and distinction.

Golf de La Grande-Motte

BP 16
F - 34280 LA GRANDE-MOTTE

Office	Secrétariat	(33) 04 67 56 05 00
Pro shop	Pro-shop	(33) 04 67 29 93 02
Fax	Fax	(33) 04 67 29 18 84
Situation	Situation	

22 km E. Montpellier, 210 860 hab.
La Grande-Motte, 5 010 hab.

Annual closure	Fermeture annnuelle	non
Weekly closure	Fermeture hebdomadaire	

Fees main season Tarifs haute saison la journée

	Week days Semaine	We/Bank holidays We/Férié
Individual Individuel	250 F	250 F
Couple Couple	500 F	500 F

Caddy	Caddy	non
Electric Trolley	Chariot électrique	non
Buggy	Voiturette	160 F/18 trous
Clubs	Clubs 1/2 série	80 F/18 trous

Credit cards Cartes de crédit
VISA - CB - Eurocard - MasterCard

Access Accès : • Nîmes, A9, sortie 26 Gallargues, N113
→ Lunel, D61 → La Grande-Motte • Montpellier A9
sortie Fréjorgues, D21 et D62 → La Grande-Motte
Map 13 on page 123 Carte 13 Page 123

GOLF COURSE
PARCOURS 16/20

Site	Site	
Maintenance	Entretien	
Architect	Architecte	R. Trent Jones Sr
Type	Type	bord de mer, résidentiel
Relief	Relief	
Water in play	Eau en jeu	
Exp. to wind	Exposé au vent	
Trees in play	Arbres en jeu	

Scorecard Carte de score	Chp. Chp.	Mens Mess.	Ladies Da.
Length Long.	6161	5768	5220
Par	72	72	72

Advised golfing ability		0	12	24	36
Niveau de jeu recommandé					
Hcp required	Handicap exigé	35			

CLUB HOUSE & AMENITIES
CLUB HOUSE ET ANNEXES 6/10

Pro shop	Pro-shop	
Driving range	Practice	
Sheltered	couvert	non
On grass	sur herbe	oui
Putting-green	putting-green	oui
Pitching-green	pitching green	oui

213

HOTEL FACILITIES
ENVIRONNEMENT HOTELIER 4/10

HOTELS HÔTELS
Frantour ***   sur place
80 chambres, D 475 F
Tél (33) 04 67 29 88 88, Fax (33) 04 67 29 17 01

Golf Hôtel **   300 m. du golf
43 chambres, D 500 F
Tél (33) 04 67 29 72 00, Fax (33) 04 67 29 12 44

RESTAURANTS RESTAURANT
Jardin des Sens   Montpellier
Tél (33) 04 67 79 63 38   22 km

Le Chandelier   Montpellier
Tél (33) 04 67 92 61 62   22 km

Originellement dessiné par Colt et Allison, Granville était un chef-d'oeuvre à l'écart des sentiers battus. Ce grand links était malheureusement traversé par une petite route, qui a obligé à modifier beaucoup de trous, alors qu'elle aurait sans doute pu être déviée. Hélas, ces trous n'ont pas été les seuls altérés, et une bonne partie du caractère a été perdue (les nouveaux bunkers n'ont rien à voir avec l'esthétique originelle). Il s'agissait là d'un véritable trésor caché, au niveau du Touquet et de Chiberta, mais il a suffi de quelques décisions hâtives pour détruire cinquante ans de tradition. S'il reste néammoins une bonne douzaine de bons trous, qui justifient à eux seuls une visite, on est bien obligé de passer par les autres. Granville est une bonne leçon de prudence et de respect pour les golfs qui veulent s'engager dans un remodelage.

Originally designed by Colt and Allison, Granville used to be a masterpiece off the beaten track. Unfortunately, this great links course has been crossed by a small road, which could have been re-routed, and a number of holes have had to be altered. Worse, other features of the course have also been tampered with, and a lot of its character has disappeared (the new bunkers have nothing common with the original style). This used to be a real gem of a course, pleasantly remote and on a par with Le Touquet or Chiberta, but a few hasty decisions were enough to destroy fifty years of tradition. While there are still a dozen excellent holes, which are worth the visit in themselves, there is no avoiding the others. Granville is a stern lesson in caution and respect for any golf course that might be considering a change in style and design.

Golf de Granville
Pavillon du Golf
F - 50290 BREVILLE

Office	Secrétariat	(33) 02 33 50 23 06
Pro shop	Pro-shop	(33) 02 33 50 23 06
Fax	Fax	(33) 02 33 61 91 87
Situation	Situation	

6 km N. Granville, 12 410 hab.

Annual closure	Fermeture annnuelle	non
Weekly closure	Fermeture hebdomadaire	mardi
	restaurant (basse saison)	

Fees main season
Tarifs haute saison la journée

	Week days Semaine	We/Bank holidays We/Férié
Individual Individuel	225 F	225 F
Couple Couple	390 F	390 F

Caddy	Caddy	non
Electric Trolley	Chariot électrique	non
Buggy	Voiturette	100 F/18 trous
Clubs	Clubs 1/2 série	60 F/jour

Credit cards Cartes de crédit
VISA - CB - Eurocard - MasterCard

214

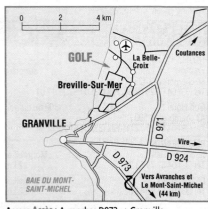

Access Accès : Avranches D973 → Granville, Bréville s/Mer
Map 2 on page 100 Carte 2 Page 100

GOLF COURSE
PARCOURS
14/20

Site	Site	■■■■■■□□
Maintenance	Entretien	■■■■■□□□
Architect	Architecte	Colt, Alison
Type	Type	links
Relief	Relief	■□□□□□□
Water in play	Eau en jeu	□□□□□□□
Exp. to wind	Exposé au vent	■■■■■□□
Trees in play	Arbres en jeu	□□□□□□□

Scorecard Carte de score	Chp. Chp.	Mens Mess.	Ladies Da.
Length Long.	5835	5835	4835
Par	71	71	71

Advised golfing ability   0   12   24   36
Niveau de jeu recommandé   ■■■■■■■□
Hcp required   Handicap exigé   35

CLUB HOUSE & AMENITIES
CLUB HOUSE ET ANNEXES
4/10

Pro shop	Pro-shop	■■■■□□□
Driving range	Practice	■■■□□□□
Sheltered	couvert	10 places
On grass	sur herbe	oui
Putting-green	putting-green	oui
Pitching-green	pitching green	oui

HOTEL FACILITIES
ENVIRONNEMENT HOTELIER
4/10

HOTELS HÔTELS
La Beaumonderie ***   Bréville-sur-Mer
12 chambres, D 550 F   1 km
Tél (33) 02 33 50 36 36, Fax (33) 02 33 50 36 45

Hôtel des Bains ***   Granville
45 chambres, D 800 F   6 km
Tél (33) 02 33 50 17 31, Fax (33) 02 33 50 89 22

RESTAURANTS RESTAURANT
Hôtel de la Mer   Granville
Tél (33) 02 33 50 01 86   6 km

Le Relais des Iles   Coudeville
Tél (33) 02 33 61 66 66   1 km

On a toujours le sentiment que ce parcours dessiné par Jean-Pascal Fourès n'a pas été achevé, ou pas par le même architecte, tant le style est inégal. A côté de très jolis trous (le 2 ou le 7), d'autres paraissent d'une étonnante banalité, certains greens dépourvus de défenses. La forêt de chênes est belle, mais réserve peu d'espace au parcours. Les fairways étroits sont bordés de roughs très cailouteux, obligeant à une grande prudence, ou une extrême précision. Mais, à 600 mètres d'altitude, les points de vue sur la région de Cannes et la mer sont magnifiques, et le climat contraste en été avec les chaleurs du littoral. Les joueurs assez droits prendront cependant du plaisir à faire une belle balade en moyenne montagne, plutôt que de vouloir batailler contre le parcours. Comme il est plutôt accidenté, on leur conseille la voiturette...

This layout, designed by Jean-Pascal Fourès, is so inconsistent in style as to leave the lasting impression of a course that has never really been completed, or at least not by the same architect. Next to some very pretty holes (the 2nd or 7th, for example), others seem amazingly ordinary and some greens are totally undefended. The oak-forest is a real beauty but leaves little space for the course. The tight fairways are edged with very stoney rough calling for great care or extreme precision (or both). But at 600 m above-sea level, the views over the Mediterranean and the region of Cannes are magnificent and the climate in summer is a pleasant contrast with the heat on the Riviera. Straight-hitters will have more fun roaming through this upland terrain than they will trying to take on the course. Being rather hilly, we recommend a buggy every time.

Grasse Country-Club

Lieu-dit «Claux Amic»
F - 06130 GRASSE

Office	Secrétariat	(33) 04 93 60 55 44
Pro shop	Pro-shop	(33) 04 93 60 55 44
Fax	Fax	(33) 04 93 60 55 19
Situation	Situation	

5 km O. Grasse, 41 380 hab.

Annual closure	Fermeture annnuelle	non
Weekly closure	Fermeture hebdomadaire	

Fees main season
Tarifs haute saison la journée

	Week days Semaine	We/Bank holidays We/Férié
Individual Individuel	250 F	280 F
Couple Couple	500 F	560 F

Mardi: GF 180 F.

Caddy	Caddy	non
Electric Trolley	Chariot électrique	non
Buggy	Voiturette	180 F/18 trous
Clubs	Clubs 1/2 série	50 F/jour

Credit cards Cartes de crédit
VISA - CB - Eurocard - MasterCard - AMEX - JCB

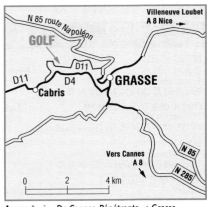

Access Accès : De Cannes, Pénétrante → Grasse.
Grasse → Golf
Map 14 on page 125 Carte 14 Page 125

GOLF COURSE
PARCOURS

13/20

Site	Site	▰▰▱
Maintenance	Entretien	▰▰▱
Architect	Architecte	Jean-Pascal Fourès
Type	Type	forêt, vallon
Relief	Relief	▰▰▱
Water in play	Eau en jeu	▰▱▱
Exp. to wind	Exposé au vent	▰▰▱
Trees in play	Arbres en jeu	▰▰▰

Scorecard Carte de score	Chp. Chp.	Mens Mess.	Ladies Da.
Length Long.	6021	5413	4662
Par	72	72	72

Advised golfing ability	0	12	24	36
Niveau de jeu recommandé		▰▰▱		
Hcp required	Handicap exigé	non		

CLUB HOUSE & AMENITIES
CLUB HOUSE ET ANNEXES

7/10

Pro shop	Pro-shop	▰▰▱
Driving range	Practice	▰▰▱
Sheltered	couvert	non
On grass	sur herbe	oui
Putting-green	putting-green	oui
Pitching-green	pitching green	non

215

HOTEL FACILITIES
ENVIRONNEMENT HOTELIER

6/10

HOTELS HÔTELS

Grasse Country-Club ****	sur place
15 chambres, D 1000 F	
Tél (33) 04 93 60 55 44, Fax (33) 04 93 60 55 19	
Hôtel des Parfums ***	Grasse
60 chambres, D 595 F	5 km
Tél (33) 04 93 36 10 10, Fax (33) 04 93 36 35 48	
Hôtel du Patti **	Grasse
50 chambres, D 420 F	5 km
Tél (33) 04 93 36 01 00, Fax (33) 04 93 36 36 40	

RESTAURANTS RESTAURANT

Pierre Baltus	Grasse
Tél (33) 04 93 36 32 90	5 km
Maître Boscq	Grasse
Tél (33) 04 93 36 45 76	5 km

Ce terrain reste très accidenté, parfois même épuisant (voiturette conseillée), mais Robert Trent Jones Jr a réussi l'exploit de ne pas imposer de coups aveugles. Cependant, il n'a pu éviter de faire trois ou quatre trous assez indifférents dans un ensemble autrement de belle qualité, et même excitant à parcourir. Souvent spectaculaire, ce parcours ne livre pas facilement ses secrets, et mérite d'être joué plusieurs fois, ne serait-ce que pour négocier les greens. Dans un paysage quasiment montagnard, des hêtres, des chênes et des genêts apportent des touches de végétation au modelage des fairways, à la sculpture des nombreux bunkers. Quelle que soit la beauté de la balade, la maîtrise du jeu que réclame Bresson incite à ne pas le recommander aux joueurs à haut handicap. Ce parcours exige un dessin précis des fairways et un entretien très attentif, ce n'est pas toujours facile.

This is a very hilly and sometimes exhausting course (buggy recommended) but Robert Trent Jones Jr has achieved the virtually impossible by avoiding blind shots. In contrast, there was no other way around three or four rather ordinary holes in an otherwise excellent setting, which makes for exciting golf. This sometimes spectacular course does not give up its secrets easily and deserves a number of rounds, if only to get to grips with the greens. In virtually mountainous landscape, oak-trees, beech and gorse add a touch of vegetation to the contoured fairways and numerous bunkers. But however beautiful the scenery, the skill required to play Bresson is perhaps beyond the abilities of high-handicappers. The course requires tightly-mown fairways and very careful upkeep, which is not always the case.

Golf International de Grenoble
Route de Montavie
F - 38320 BRESSON

Office	Secrétariat	(33) 04 76 73 65 00
Pro shop	Pro-shop	(33) 04 76 73 65 00
Fax	Fax	(33) 04 76 73 65 51
Situation	Situation	

5 km S. Grenoble, 150 750 hab.
8 km N. Vizille, 7 100 hab.

Annual closure	Fermeture annnuelle	non
Weekly closure	Fermeture hebdomadaire	

Fees main season
Tarifs haute saison la journée

	Week days Semaine	We/Bank holidays We/Férié
Individual Individuel	230 F	270 F
Couple Couple	460 F	540 F

Caddy	Caddy	non
Electric Trolley	Chariot électrique	non
Buggy	Voiturette	150 F/18 trous
Clubs	Clubs 1/2 série	70 F/jour

Credit cards Cartes de crédit
VISA - CB - Eurocard - MasterCard

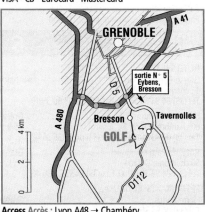

GRENOBLE

sortie N° 5
Eybens,
Bresson

Bresson   **Tavernolles**

GOLF

A 41
D 5
A 480
D112
4 km

Access Accès : Lyon A48 → Chambéry.
Péage prendre la rocade, sortie 5, Eybens,
Bresson → Tavernolles, → Golf
Map 11 on page 118 Carte 11 Page 118

GOLF COURSE PARCOURS — 17 /20

Site	Site	▰▰▰▰▱
Maintenance	Entretien	▰▰▰▰▱
Architect	Architecte	R. Trent Jones Jr
Type	Type	montagne
Relief	Relief	▰▰▰▰▱
Water in play	Eau en jeu	▰▱▱▱▱
Exp. to wind	Exposé au vent	▰▰▱▱▱
Trees in play	Arbres en jeu	▰▰▰▱▱

Scorecard Carte de score	Chp. Chp.	Mens Mess.	Ladies Da.
Length Long.	6345	5836	5356
Par	73	73	73

Advised golfing ability	0	12	24	36
Niveau de jeu recommandé				
Hcp required	Handicap exigé	non		

CLUB HOUSE & AMENITIES CLUB HOUSE ET ANNEXES — 7 /10

Pro shop	Pro-shop	▰▰▰▰▱
Driving range	Practice	▰▰▰▱▱
Sheltered	couvert	20 places
On grass	sur herbe	oui
Putting-green	putting-green	oui
Pitching-green	pitching green	oui

HOTEL FACILITIES ENVIRONNEMENT HOTELIER — 6 /10

HOTELS HÔTELS
Chavant ★★★★   Bresson
9 chambres, D 680 F   2 km
Tél (33) 04 76 25 15 14, Fax (33) 04 76 62 06 55

Château de la Commanderie ★★★   Eybens
25 chambres, D 650 F   2 km
Tél (33) 04 76 25 34 58, Fax (33) 04 76 46 49 88

Grand Hôtel ★★★   Uriage
44 chambres, D 545 F   7 km
Tél (33) 04 76 89 10 80, Fax (33) 04 76 89 04 62

RESTAURANTS RESTAURANT
Chavant   Bresson
Tél (33) 04 76 25 19 14   2 km

La Poularde Bressane   Grenoble
Tél(33) 04 76 87 08 90   5 km

216

Un parcours discret, mais très fréquenté en week-end par des joueurs souvent peu expérimentés. Destiné aux joueurs moyens, il les respecte, en leur offrant un équipement de très bon style, dessiné par Yves Bureau avec beaucoup de sensibilité, sans aucune prétention. Avec un placement d'obstacles intelligent, des greens bien modelés, ce parcours est l'un des plus sérieux équipements commerciaux de la région, et permet à tous de jouer sur un "vrai" terrain de golf, quel que soit leur niveau. Avec un bon nombre de trous dans les bois, et le reste en plaine sur un plateau exposé au vent, un entretien satisfaisant, ce parcours créé dans une ancienne carrière donne envie de jouer. Il n'est pas très long, mais comporte cinq par 3 et cinq par 5, ce qui n'est guère habituel. Le Club House est de bon goût, l'ambiance jeune et dynamique.

A discreet course which is often very busy at week-ends with inexperienced players. Intended for mid-handicappers, the course respects their ability with a very stylish layout designed by Yves Bureau. Thanks to sensibly located hazards and well-contoured greens, this course is one of the region's more serious commercial golfing facilities and gives all golfers access to a real course, whatever their level of proficiency. With a good number of holes in woodland and the rest in open country on a wind-swept plateau, plus satisfactory standards of upkeep, this course is a tempting proposition. Laid out in an old quarry, the course is by no means long but does offer 5 par 3s and five par 5s, an unusual format. The club-house is in very good taste with a young and exciting atmosphere.

Golf de Guerville

La Plagne
F - 78930 GUERVILLE

Office	Secrétariat	(33) 01 30 92 45 45
Pro shop	Pro-shop	(33) 01 30 92 45 45
Fax	Fax	(33) 01 30 98 43 39
Situation	Situation	

2 km S. Mantes-la-Jolie, 45 080 hab.
58 km O. Paris, 2 175 200 hab.

Annual closure	Fermeture annnuelle	non
Weekly closure	Fermeture hebdomadaire	

Fees main season Tarifs haute saison le parcours

	Week days Semaine	We/Bank holidays We/Férié
Individual Individuel	150 F	270 F
Couple Couple	300 F	540 F

GF + déjeuner: 185 F. le mardi

Caddy	Caddy	non
Electric Trolley	Chariot électrique	non
Buggy	Voiturette	120 F/18 trous
Clubs	Clubs 1/2 série	50 F/jour

Credit cards Cartes de crédit
VISA - CB - Eurocard - MasterCard

Access Accès : A13 Paris-Rouen, sortie Mantes-la-Jolie →
Houdan, D 983 → Guerville, D158 → La Plagne
Map 3 on page 102 Carte 3 Page 102

GOLF COURSE
PARCOURS
14/20

Site	Site	
Maintenance	Entretien	
Architect	Architecte	Yves Bureau
Type	Type	plaine, parc
Relief	Relief	
Water in play	Eau en jeu	
Exp. to wind	Exposé au vent	
Trees in play	Arbres en jeu	

Scorecard Carte de score	Chp. Chp.	Mens Mess.	Ladies Da.
Length Long.	5873	5375	4924
Par	72	72	72

Advised golfing ability   0   12   24   36
Niveau de jeu recommandé
Hcp required Handicap exigé   non

CLUB HOUSE & AMENITIES
CLUB HOUSE ET ANNEXES
7/10

Pro shop	Pro-shop	
Driving range	Practice	
Sheltered	couvert	12 places
On grass	sur herbe	oui
Putting-green	putting-green	oui
Pitching-green	pitching green	oui

HOTEL FACILITIES
ENVIRONNEMENT HOTELIER
4/10

HOTELS HÔTELS
Château de la Corniche ***   Rolleboise
3 chambres, D 450 F   15 km
Tél (33) 01 30 93 21 24, Fax (33) 01 30 42 27 44

Climat de France **   Mantes-la-Jolie
42 chambres, D 270 F   4 km
Tél (33) 01 30 33 03 70, Fax (33) 01 30 63 03 54

RESTAURANTS RESTAURANT
Château de la Corniche   Rolleboise
Tél (33) 01 30 93 21 24   15 km

Auberge de la Truite   Rosay
Tél(33) 01 34 76 30 52   6 km

217

15	7	6

Entre Arcachon et Bordeaux, ce 18 trous (complété par un petit 9 trous) a été dessiné par Alain Prat avec beaucoup de bon sens : il n'a pas voulu exagérer les difficultés et son tracé ne pénalise que ceux qui prennent des risques excessifs. Le terrain plat a été légèrement modelé pour les besoins de la cause, et le sol sablonneux est idéal pour le golf. Le déroulement dans les pins et la bruyère est agréable, avec des difficultés mesurées pour ne rebuter personne, les principaux dangers (en dehors de quelques obstacles d'eau) étant constitués par les bunkers et les arbres, qui laissent souvent libres les accès aux vastes greens. Mais les débutants auront sans doute du mal quand ils sont très défendus. On peut jouer facilement ici toute l'année : les hivers sont plutôt doux, le parcours supporte bien les intempéries et son entretien s'est considérablement amélioré.

Located between Arcachon and Bordeaux, this 18-hole course was designed by Alain Prat (with an adjoining 9 hole course). Using a lot of good sense, he has avoided any excessive difficulties and the layout only penalises the players who take one risk too many. The flat terrain has been slightly graded for greater relief and the sandy subsoil is ideal for a golf course. It winds its way pleasantly through pinetrees and heather, with playing difficulties carefully gauged to avoid scaring the lesser player. Aside from the few water hazards, the main problems are the bunkers and trees, which generally speaking afford easy access to the greens. Beginners will probably find the going a little harder when dealing with some of the better-defended holes. You can easily play here all year, as the winters are mild, the ground withstands all weathers and upkeep has considerably improved.

Golf de Gujan-Mestras
Route de Sanguinet
F - 33470 GUJAN-MESTRAS

Office	Secrétariat	(33) 05 57 52 73 73
Pro shop	Pro-shop	(33) 05 57 52 73 73
Fax	Fax	(33) 05 56 66 10 93
Situation	Situation	

6 km S.O. Gujan-Mestras, 11 430 hab.
12 km S.E. Arcachon, 11 770 hab.

Annual closure	Fermeture annnuelle	non
Weekly closure	Fermeture hebdomadaire	

Fees main season
Tarifs haute saison la journée

	Week days Semaine	We/Bank holidays We/Férié
Individual Individuel	260 F	260 F
Couple Couple	450 F	450 F

Caddy	Caddy	non
Electric Trolley	Chariot électrique	non
Buggy	Voiturette	120 F/18 trous
Clubs	Clubs 1/2 série	60 F/jour

Credit cards Cartes de crédit
VISA - CB - Eurocard - MasterCard - AMEX - DC

218

B A S S I N
D ' A R C A C H O N

ARCACHON

Gujan-Mestras

N 250

A 63 Bordeaux →

GOLF

D 652

Sanguinet

0   2   4 km

Access Accès : Bordeaux, A63, sortie Arcachon,
carrefour Aqua City, → Golf
Map 9 on page 115 Carte 9 Page 115

GOLF COURSE
PARCOURS
15/20

Site	Site	
Maintenance	Entretien	
Architect	Architecte	Alain Prat
Type	Type	forêt
Relief	Relief	
Water in play	Eau en jeu	
Exp. to wind	Exposé au vent	
Trees in play	Arbres en jeu	

Scorecard Carte de score	Chp. Chp.	Mens Mess.	Ladies Da.
Length Long.	6225	6005	5185
Par	72	72	72

Advised golfing ability		0 12 24 36
Niveau de jeu recommandé		
Hcp required	Handicap exigé	35

CLUB HOUSE & AMENITIES
CLUB HOUSE ET ANNEXES
7/10

Pro shop	Pro-shop	
Driving range	Practice	
Sheltered	couvert	8 places
On grass	sur herbe	oui
Putting-green	putting-green	oui
Pitching-green	pitching green	oui

HOTEL FACILITIES
ENVIRONNEMENT HOTELIER
6/10

HOTELS HÔTELS
La Guérinière ***   Gujan-Mestras
27 chambres, D 490 F   6 km
Tél (33) 05 56 66 08 78, Fax (33) 05 56 66 13 39

Séminaris ***   Arcachon
19 chambres, D 630 F   12 km
Tél (33) 05 56 83 25 87, Fax (33) 05 57 52 22 41

Deganne ***   Arcachon
57 chambres, D 900 F   12 km
Tél (33) 05 56 83 99 91, Fax (33) 05 56 83 87 92

RESTAURANTS RESTAURANT
L'Ombrière   Arcachon
Tél (33) 05 56 83 01 48   12 km

Depuis sa création en 1931, "Les Pins" est un des excellents exemples du style de Tom Simson et reste un parcours plus passionnant et plus franc que le récent parcours des "Dunes", bien qu'il soit beaucoup plus sec en été. Il constitue un témoignage de l'architecture classique britannique. Quelques coups sont aveugles, mais faussement trompeurs et sans véritable gêne pour le jeu. Avec des greens subtils, des bunkers diaboliquement placés, le parcours exige une grande précision, et de savoir profiter des occasions d'attaquer. On a ici l'impression de devoir simplement suivre les pas de l'architecte pour le négocier correctement, tant son dessin paraît empreint de bon sens. "Les Pins" est de ces parcours polis par le temps que l'on doit d'autant plus connaître si l'on joue surtout des golfs "modernes". Tout ici est empreint de tradition. Les Anglais ne s'y trompent pas, ils y viennent nombreux.

Designed in 1931 by Tom Simpson, "Les Pins" is still a more exciting and forthright course than the more recent "Les Dunes", although the latter is drier in summer. One of Simpson's finest works, "Les Pins" is testimony to classic British architecture. Some shots are blind but never really deceive the player or affect play. With subtle greens and devilishly well-placed bunkers, this course cries out for precision stroke-making and the ability to utilise opportunities for attacking play. The impression is one of simply following in the footsteps of the architect in order to play the course correctly. That is how sensible the layout is. "Les Pins" is one of those courses that becomes more polished with time and is a must for anyone raised exclusively on "modern" courses. Everything here smacks of tradition. The British know a good golf course when they see one, and a lot of Brits come and play here.

Golf d'Hardelot-les-Pins

3, avenue du Golf
F - 62152 HARDELOT

Office	Secrétariat	(33) 03 21 83 73 10
Pro shop	Pro-shop	(33) 03 21 83 73 10
Fax	Fax	(33) 03 21 83 24 33
Situation	Situation	

15 km S. Boulogne s/Mer, 43 670 hab.

Annual closure	Fermeture annnuelle	non
Weekly closure	Fermeture hebdomadaire	

Fees main season
Tarifs haute saison le parcours

	Week days Semaine	We/Bank holidays We/Férié
Individual Individuel	290 F	340 F
Couple Couple	580 F	680 F

Caddy	Caddy	non
Electric Trolley	Chariot électrique	non
Buggy	Voiturette	200 F/18 trous
Clubs	Clubs la série	100 F/18 trous

Credit cards Cartes de crédit
VISA - CB - Eurocard - MasterCard - AMEX

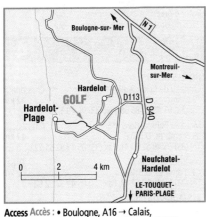

Access Accès : • Boulogne, A16 → Calais,
N1 → Montreuil, après Pont-de-Briques, D940
à droite → Hardelot • Montreuil, N1 → Boulogne-
sur-Mer, ou D940 depuis Le Touquet
Map 1 on page 98 Carte 1 Page 98

GOLF COURSE PARCOURS   16/20

Site	Site	▬▬▬▬
Maintenance	Entretien	▬▬▬
Architect	Architecte	Tom Simpson
Type	Type	forêt, links
Relief	Relief	▬▬
Water in play	Eau en jeu	▬▬▬
Exp. to wind	Exposé au vent	▬▬▬▬
Trees in play	Arbres en jeu	▬▬▬

Scorecard Carte de score	Chp. Chp.	Mens Mess.	Ladies Da.
Length Long.	5870	5870	5137
Par	72	72	72

Advised golfing ability   0   12   24   36
Niveau de jeu recommandé
Hcp required   Handicap exigé   35

CLUB HOUSE & AMENITIES CLUB HOUSE ET ANNEXES   6/10

Pro shop	Pro-shop	▬▬▬
Driving range	Practice	▬▬▬
Sheltered	couvert	6 places
On grass	sur herbe	non
Putting-green	putting-green	oui
Pitching-green	pitching green	oui

HOTEL FACILITIES ENVIRONNEMENT HOTELIER   6/10

HOTELS HÔTELS
Parc ***   Hardelot
80 chambres, D 620 F   1 km
Tél (33) 03 21 33 22 11, Fax (33) 03 21 83 29 71

Cléry ***   Hesdin-l'Abbé
19 chambres, D 325 F   7 km
Tél (33) 03 21 83 19 83, Fax (33) 03 21 87 52 59

Régina **   Hardelot
40 chambres, D 335 F   1 km
Tél (33) 03 21 83 81 88, Fax (33) 03 21 87 44 01

RESTAURANTS RESTAURANT
La Matelote   Boulogne-sur-Mer
Tél (33) 03 21 30 17 97   15 km

Host. de la Rivière   Pont-de-Briques
Tél (33) 03 21 32 22 81   7 km

219

14	6	4

Un parcours paradoxalement difficile pour une région où les néophytes sont nombreux, avec un relief qui rend assez fatigants les neuf derniers trous, tracés dans une zone agréable de pins et de bouleaux. A cause de sa longueur (même avec un par 73), on conseillera à tous de ne pas partir des départs les plus reculés, s'ils espèrent jouer leur handicap. Les neuf premiers trous sont plus plats, avec des obstacles d'eau pas trop pénalisants. L'architecture du parcours manque certes de charme et d'originalité (le 13 est joli), mais les greens sont en majorité bien dessinés. En résumé, un golf à jouer si l'on se trouve dans la région, notamment pour compléter un séjour en famille, un petit parcours de 9 trous permettant de loger les débutants. Une base de loisirs est toute proche, ainsi que le Futuroscope de Poitiers.

A paradoxically tough course in region where beginners abound. The sloping terrain makes the back 9 a tiring but pleasant walk through pines and birch trees. Haut Poitou is a long course, and even at a par 73 we would not recommend the back tees to anyone wishing to play to his handicap. The front 9 are flatter with water hazards that could be rated as avoidable and so not too heavy on the score. The overall architecture probably lacks originality and charm (although the 13th is a pretty hole), but the majority of greens are well-designed. In short, a course worth playing if you are in the region, especially if you are with the family, as a neighbouring 9 hole pitch 'n putt is ideal for beginners. The course is also close to a leisure centre and to the Futuroscope.

Golf Club du Haut-Poitou
F - 86130 SAINT-CYR

Office	Secrétariat	(33) 05 49 62 53 62
Pro shop	Pro-shop	(33) 05 49 62 53 62
Fax	Fax	(33) 05 49 88 77 14
Situation	Situation	

15 km S.O. Châtellerault, 34 670 hab.
20 km N.E. Poitiers, 78 890 hab.

Annual closure	Fermeture annnuelle	non
Weekly closure	Fermeture hebdomadaire	

Fees main season
Tarifs haute saison la journée

	Week days Semaine	We/Bank holidays We/Férié
Individual Individuel	170 F	200 F
Couple Couple	290 F	350 F

Caddy	Caddy	non
Electric Trolley	Chariot électrique	60 F/18 trous
Buggy	Voiturette	non
Clubs	Clubs le club	10 F/jour

Credit cards Cartes de crédit
VISA - CB - Eurocard - MasterCard

Access Accès : Poitiers ou Châtellerault, N10, sortie Beaumont, → Golf
Map 6 on page 109 Carte 6 Page 109

GOLF COURSE
PARCOURS
14/20

Site	Site	
Maintenance	Entretien	
Architect	Architecte	Bill Baker
Type	Type	plaine, forêt
Relief	Relief	
Water in play	Eau en jeu	
Exp. to wind	Exposé au vent	
Trees in play	Arbres en jeu	

Scorecard Carte de score	Chp. Chp.	Mens Mess.	Ladies Da.
Length Long.	6590	6124	5569
Par	73	73	73

Advised golfing ability
Niveau de jeu recommandé

0	12	24	36

Hcp required Handicap exigé   non

CLUB HOUSE & AMENITIES
CLUB HOUSE ET ANNEXES
6/10

Pro shop	Pro-shop	
Driving range	Practice	
Sheltered	couvert	18 places
On grass	sur herbe	oui
Putting-green	putting-green	oui
Pitching-green	pitching green	oui

HOTEL FACILITIES
ENVIRONNEMENT HOTELIER
4/10

HOTELS HÔTELS
Château de la Ribaudière ***   Chasseneuil
19 chambres, D 520 F   12 km
Tél (33) 05 49 52 86 66, Fax (33) 05 49 52 86 32

Mercure Poitiers Nord ***   Chasseneuil
89 chambres, D 530 F   12 km
Tél (33) 05 49 52 90 41, Fax (33) 05 49 52 51 72

Les Rives du Clain **   Dissay
43 chambres, D 310 F   2 km
Tél (33) 05 49 52 62 42, Fax (33) 05 49 52 62 62

RESTAURANTS RESTAURANT
Maxime   Poitiers
Tél (33) 05 49 41 09 55   20 km

Benjamin   Dissay
Tél (33) 05 49 52 42 37   2 km

220

HOSSEGOR ✴ 16 6 6

Un des grands classiques de la "Côte Basque", dont l'architecture rappelle les parcours intérieurs traditionnels de Grande-Bretagne, où les obstacles sont essentiellement les arbres et les bunkers. Dans un espace aussi évidemment fait pour le golf, il n'était guère utile de beaucoup modeler le terrain (pas de bulldozers à l'époque). Depuis les années 30, le dessin n'a pas pris une ride, sauf qu'il devrait être adapté au jeu actuel, en déplaçant (sans modifier leur forme) les bunkers de fairway des par 4, qui pénalisent surtout les joueurs moyens. Le parcours est plat, et de bonne qualité toute l'année, grâce au sol sablonneux. Les obstacles bien visibles, la variété des trous et le profil des greens en font un test de stratégie et de jeu, qui masque ses réelles difficultés sous un visage souriant. Un excellent parcours, qu'il s'agisse de jouer en compétition, ou en famille.

One of the great classics on the Basque coast with a layout reminiscent of traditional British inland courses, where the hazards are primarily trees and bunkers. On a site so obviously made for golf, there was hardly any need to shape the terrain (anyway there were no bulldozers around at the time). Since the 1930s, the course looks and feels as young as ever. But it might be better adjusted to the needs of modern play by shifting (without any change in shape) the fairway bunkers on the par 4s, which tend nowadays to penalise mid-handicappers more than anyone else. The course is flat and plays beautifully all year thanks to the sandy sub-soil. Clearly visible hazards, variety and the neat greens make this a fine test of golfing ability and strategy, and one that conceals its real difficulties beneath a cheerful exterior. An excellent course for tournaments or for all the family.

Golf Club d'Hossegor
Avenue du Golf
F - 40150 HOSSEGOR

Office	Secrétariat	(33) 05 58 43 56 99
Pro shop	Pro-shop	(33) 05 58 43 56 99
Fax	Fax	(33) 05 58 43 98 52
Situation	Situation	

32 km O. Dax, 19 310 hab.
20 km N. Bayonne, 40 050 hab.

Annual closure	Fermeture annnuelle	non
Weekly closure	Fermeture hebdomadaire	mardi
	basse saison (sauf vacances scolaires)	

Fees main season
Tarifs haute saison la journée

	Week days Semaine	We/Bank holidays We/Férié
Individual Individuel	350 F	350 F
Couple Couple	700 F	700 F

Caddy	Caddy	sur réservation
Electric Trolley	Chariot électrique	100 F/jour
Buggy	Voiturette	non
Clubs	Clubs 1/2 série	70 F / jour

Credit cards Cartes de crédit
VISA - CB - Eurocard - MasterCard

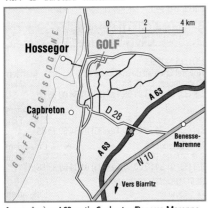

Access Accès : A63 sortie Capbreton/Benesse-Marenne
→ Hossegor, centre ville
Map 12 on page 120 Carte 12 Page 120

GOLF COURSE
PARCOURS — 16/20

Site	Site	
Maintenance	Entretien	
Architect	Architecte	Tim Morisson
Type	Type	forêt
Relief	Relief	
Water in play	Eau en jeu	
Exp. to wind	Exposé au vent	
Trees in play	Arbres en jeu	

Scorecard Carte de score	Chp. Chp.	Mens Mess.	Ladies Da.
Length Long.	6001	5867	5037
Par	71	71	71

Advised golfing ability
Niveau de jeu recommandé   0 12 24 36

Hcp required Handicap exigé 24 Mess.
28 Da. saison

CLUB HOUSE & AMENITIES
CLUB HOUSE ET ANNEXES — 6/10

Pro shop	Pro-shop	
Driving range	Practice	
Sheltered	couvert	20 places
On grass	sur herbe	non
Putting-green	putting-green	oui
Pitching-green	pitching green	non

HOTEL FACILITIES
ENVIRONNEMENT HOTELIER — 6/10

HOTELS HÔTELS
Beauséjour ***   Hossegor 2 km
45 chambres, D 700 F
Tél (33) 05 58 43 51 07, Fax (33) 05 58 43 70 13

Hôtel du Golf **   sur place
9 chambres, D 400 F
Tél (33) 05 58 43 50 59, Fax (33) 05 58 43 98 52

Les Hortensias du Lac   Hossegor 2 km
21 chambres, D 430 F
Tél (33) 05 58 43 99 00, Fax (33) 05 58 43 42 81

RESTAURANTS RESTAURANT
Les Huîtrières du Lac   Hossegor 2 km
Tél (33) 05 58 43 51 48

221

Ce parcours a vite conquis une belle réputation. Par sa franchise, par la très grande variété de dessin et d'environnement des trous, tracés en partie dans une forêt, en partie sur un beau plateau. Le seul inconvénient, c'est de passer de l'une à l'autre : il serait astucieux de prévoir des navettes, tant les montées sont épuisantes. La stratégie de jeu est évidente dès la première visite, les fairways sont larges, mais le placement de la balle est crucial pour pouvoir ensuite approcher les greens en bonne position, car leurs modelages et leurs dimensions exigent beaucoup d'attention. L'architecte Ronald Fream a beaucoup modelé le terrain, dans une synthèse heureuse des tendances britannique et américaine, permettant à tous les niveaux et tous les styles de jeu de s'exprimer. Les arbres et bunkers sont bien en jeu, et l'eau présente sur trois trous seulement. Une bonne réussite.

This course has rapidly gained a fine reputation for its fairness and for the great variety in the design and setting of holes, some of which are laid out through a forest, others on a pretty plateau. The only drawback is walking from one part of the course to the other. The climb is so exhausting that a shuttle service might be in order. Game strategy is clear from the very first visit; the fairways are wide, but it is essential to position the tee-shot accurately in order to get a good look at greens whose slopes and size require great care. Architect Ronald Fream has shaped the terrain a great deal and created a happy combination of British and American trends. The course is fun for golfers of all abilities and styles. The trees and bunkers are clearly in play and water threatens on just three holes. A good success.

Golf de l'Isle-Adam
1, ch. des Vanneaux
F - 95290 L'ISLE-ADAM

Office	Secrétariat	(33) 01 34 08 11 11
Pro shop	Pro-shop	(33) 01 34 08 11 11
Fax	Fax	(33) 01 34 08 11 19
Situation	Situation	

21 km. S.O. Chantilly, 11 340 hab. 35 km. N. Paris,.

Annual closure	Fermeture annnuelle	oui
		24/12→1/01/99
Weekly closure	Fermeture hebdomadaire	mardi

Fees main season Tarifs haute saison la journée

	Week days Semaine	We/Bank holidays We/Férié
Individual Individuel	250 F	375 F
Couple Couple	500 F	750 F

We (été) : membres seulement (members only)

Caddy	Caddy	non
Electric Trolley	Chariot électrique	50 F/jour
Buggy	Voiturette	non
Clubs	Clubs la série	150 F/jour

Credit cards Cartes de crédit
VISA - CB - Eurocard - MasterCard - AMEX - DC

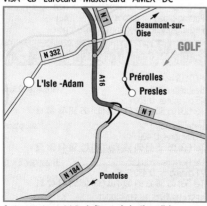

Access Accès : • A1 Paris (Porte de la Chapelle), sortie Beauvais, N1, sortie Beaumont-sur-Oise
• A15 Paris (Porte de Clignancourt), → Pontoise, → N184, sortie Beaumont-sur-Oise
Map 1 on page 99 Carte 1 Page 99

GOLF COURSE
PARCOURS
16/20

Site	Site	▨▨▨
Maintenance	Entretien	▨▨▨
Architect	Architecte	Ronald Fream
Type	Type	forêt, plaine
Relief	Relief	▨
Water in play	Eau en jeu	▨▨
Exp. to wind	Exposé au vent	▨
Trees in play	Arbres en jeu	▨▨▨

Scorecard	Chp.	Mens	Ladies
Carte de score	Chp.	Mess.	Da.
Length Long.	6230	5711	5152
Par	72	72	72

Advised golfing ability	0	12	24	36
Niveau de jeu recommandé		▨▨		
Hcp required	Handicap exigé	35		

CLUB HOUSE & AMENITIES
CLUB HOUSE ET ANNEXES
7/10

Pro shop	Pro-shop	▨▨
Driving range	Practice	▨▨
Sheltered	couvert	12 postes
On grass	sur herbe	oui (05-09)
Putting-green	putting-green	oui
Pitching-green	pitching green	oui

HOTEL FACILITIES
ENVIRONNEMENT HOTELIER
4/10

HOTELS HÔTELS
Novotel Château de Maffliers ***   Maffliers
51 chambres, D 525 F   7 km
Tél (33) 01 34 73 93 05, Fax (33) 01 34 08 35 00

Etap Hôtel   L'Isle-Adam
68 chambres, D 165 F   1 km
Tél (33) 01 34 69 09 85, Fax (33) 01 34 69 11 85

Le Cabouillet **   L'Isle-Adam
0 chambres, D 340 F   2 km
Tél (33) 01 34 69 00 90, Fax (33) 01 34 69 33 88

RESTAURANTS RESTAURANT
Le Cabouillet   L'Isle-Adam
Tél (33) 01 34 69 00 90   2 km

Gai Rivage   L'Isle Adam
Tél (33) 01 34 69 01 09   2 km

222

Après bien des péripéties, le Golf de Joyenval semble avoir trouvé sa vitesse de croisière, et sait parfois entr'ouvrir ses portes, bien qu'il soit très privé. L'avantage d'une fréquentation réduite, c'est que son entretien, notamment au niveau des greens, est généralement bon. Des deux parcours, Marly est celui qui a le moins souffert des contraintes administratives, souvent abusives, liées à la proximité du Désert de Retz (monument historique), mais on aimerait voir les trous souvent mieux définis par des plantations. Dans ces conditions, on ne voit souvent plus que les bunkers, aussi impressionnants à voir qu'à visiter. Très varié de paysage et de style, ce parcours est d'autant plus technique que les greens sont très difficiles à lire.

After a lot of starting and stopping, the Joyenval club now looks to be up and running and sometimes even opens its gate to outsiders, despite being a very private club. The upside of being under-played is that green-keeping and the greens in particular are generally good. Of the two courses, Marly is the one that suffered the least from often excessive administrative requirements related to the closeness of the Désert de Retz (an historical landmark), although we would like to see the holes better defined with a tree planting program. Under these conditions you often see only the bunkers, which are as impressive to see as they are to be in. Very varied in style and landscape, the course is made all the more technical by greens that are very difficult to read.

Golf de Joyenval

Chemin de la Tuilerie
F - 78240 CHAMBOURCY

Office	Secrétariat	(33) 01 39 22 27 61
Pro shop	Pro-shop	(33) 01 39 22 27 50
Fax	Fax	(33) 01 30 65 95 26
Situation	Situation	

28 km O. de Paris, 2 175 200 hab.

Annual closure	Fermeture annnuelle	non
Weekly closure	Fermeture hebdomadaire	lundi

Fees main season
Tarifs haute saison 18 trous

	Week days Semaine	We/Bank holidays We/Férié
Individual Individuel	*	*
Couple Couple	*	*

Accès limité : * sur demande (upon application)

Caddy	Caddy	réserver : 250 F
Electric Trolley	Chariot électrique	100 F/18 trous
Buggy	Voiturette	250 F/18 trous
Clubs	Clubs	100 F/18 trous

Credit cards Cartes de crédit
VISA - CB - Eurocard - MasterCard

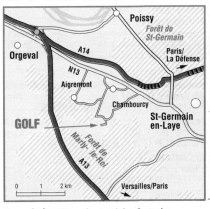

Access Accès : A13 sortie et → Saint-Germain.
N13 → Poissy, → Orgeval. Après Chambourcy,
à gauche → Désert de Retz, Golf de Joyenval.
Map 15 on page 126 Carte 15 Page 126

GOLF COURSE PARCOURS

16/20

Site	Site	
Maintenance	Entretien	
Architect	Architecte	R. Trent Jones Sr
Type	Type	plaine, forêt
Relief	Relief	
Water in play	Eau en jeu	
Exp. to wind	Exposé au vent	
Trees in play	Arbres en jeu	

Scorecard Carte de score	Chp. Chp.	Mens Mess.	Ladies Da.
Length Long.	6249	5776	5272
Par	72	72	72

Advised golfing ability Niveau de jeu recommandé	0	12	24	36
Hcp required	Handicap exigé	non		

CLUB HOUSE & AMENITIES CLUB HOUSE ET ANNEXES

8/10

Pro shop	Pro-shop	
Driving range	Practice	
Sheltered	couvert	5 places
On grass	sur herbe	oui
Putting-green	putting-green	oui
Pitching-green	pitching green	oui

223

HOTEL FACILITIES ENVIRONNEMENT HOTELIER

7/10

HOTELS HÔTELS
Pavillon Henri IV — Saint-Germain
42 chambres, D 1 000 F — 4 km
Tél (33) 01 39 10 15 15, Fax (33) 01 39 93 73 93

Novotel *** — Orgeval
119 chambres, D 500 F — 4 km
Tél (33) 01 39 22 35 11, Fax (33) 01 39 75 48 93

RESTAURANTS RESTAURANT
L'Esturgeon — Poissy
Tél (33) 01 39 65 00 04 — 5 km

Cazaudehore — Saint-Germain
Tél (33) 01 34 51 93 80 — 5 km

Le site est exceptionnel, entre la forêt de Marly et une vallée que les poètes n'aurait pas reniée, à proximité immédiate du Déser de Retz, folie architecturale dûe à l'imagination d'un gentilhomme du XVIII ème siècle. On aurait d'ailleurs aimé que le parcours soit vraiment une réponse moderne à cet esprit baroque, mais le crayon parfois austère de Trent Jones a permis de limiter au minimum les contraintes. Il reste quelques trous de haute volée, entre forêt et plaine, entre parc et jardin, avec des aspects évidemment américains dans leur franchise et leur brutalité, mais aussi britanniques quand les contours deviennent plus flous, plus subtils. Très scénique, moins stratégique que "Marly", ce parcours est aussi moins exigeant pour les joueurs moyens.

The site is outstanding, between the forest of Marly and a valley to make any poet wax lyrical, within the immediate vicinity of the Désert de Retz, a piece of architecture folly born from the imagination of an 18th century gentleman. We would have liked this course really to be a modern response to this baroque spirit, but the often austere design of Trent Jones helped keep restrictions to a minimum. There are a few top-notch holes between forest and plain, park-land and garden, obviously looking very American in their honesty and toughness, but also British when contours grow a little less sharp and more subtle. Very scenic and less strategic than Marly, Retz is also less demanding for the average golfer.

Golf de Joyenval
Chemin de la Tuilerie
F - 78240 CHAMBOURCY

Office	Secrétariat	(33) 01 39 22 27 61
Pro shop	Pro-shop	(33) 01 39 22 27 50
Fax	Fax	(33) 01 30 65 95 26
Situation	Situation	

28 km O. de Paris, 2 175 200 hab.

Annual closure	Fermeture annnuelle	non
Weekly closure	Fermeture hebdomadaire	lundi

Fees main season
Tarifs haute saison 18 trous

	Week days Semaine	We/Bank holidays We/Férié
Individual Individuel	*	*
Couple Couple	*	*

Accès limité : * sur demande (upon application)

Caddy	Caddy	réserver : 250 F
Electric Trolley	Chariot électrique	100 F/18 trous
Buggy	Voiturette	250 F/18 trous
Clubs	Clubs	100 F/18 trous

Credit cards Cartes de crédit
VISA - CB - Eurocard - MasterCard

224

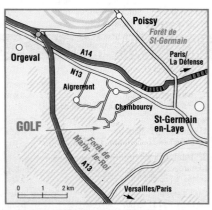

Access Accès : A13 sortie et → Saint-Germain.
N13 → Poissy, → Orgeval. Après Chambourcy,
à gauche → Désert de Retz, Golf de Joyenval.
Map 15 on page 126 Carte 15 Page 126

GOLF COURSE
PARCOURS   15/20

Site	Site	■■■■■■
Maintenance	Entretien	■■■■■■
Architect	Architecte	R. Trent Jones Sr
Type	Type	forêt, plaine
Relief	Relief	■■■■
Water in play	Eau en jeu	■■■
Exp. to wind	Exposé au vent	■■■
Trees in play	Arbres en jeu	■■■■

Scorecard Carte de score	Chp. Chp.	Mens Mess.	Ladies Da.
Length Long.	6211	5728	5248
Par	72	72	72

Advised golfing ability   0 12 24 36
Niveau de jeu recommandé   ■■■■■
Hcp required   Handicap exigé   non

CLUB HOUSE & AMENITIES
CLUB HOUSE ET ANNEXES   8/10

Pro shop	Pro-shop	■■■■
Driving range	Practice	■■■■
Sheltered	couvert	5 places
On grass	sur herbe	oui
Putting-green	putting-green	oui
Pitching-green	pitching green	oui

HOTEL FACILITIES
ENVIRONNEMENT HOTELIER   7/10

HOTELS HÔTELS

Pavillon Henri IV   Saint-Germain
42 chambres, D 1 000 F   4 km
Tél (33) 01 39 10 15 15, Fax (33) 01 39 93 73 93

Novotel ***   Orgeval
119 chambres, D 500 F   4 km
Tél (33) 01 39 22 35 11, Fax (33) 01 39 75 48 93

RESTAURANTS RESTAURANT

L'Esturgeon   Poissy
Tél (33) 01 39 65 00 04   5 km

Cazaudehore   Saint-Germain
Tél (33) 01 34 51 93 80   5 km

KEMPFERHOF (LE) ♪ | 18 | 8 | 6

Ce parcours signé Von Hagge donne d'abord une impression de finition et de soin du détail : le plaisir des yeux commence en arrivant sur le site. Dans un environnement de campagne, avec des sapins, des hêtres et des bouleaux, il est difficile de jouer son handicap mais ce parcours sans reliefs prononcés est jouable à tous les niveaux (les néophytes seront intimidés par quelques obstacles d'eau dangereux). Très sélectif, il demande souvent de travailler la balle et de démontrer sa maîtrise de tous les clubs, avec un accent aigu sur la précision, notamment pour approcher les vastes greens, très travaillés. Tous les obstacles étant visibles, ce parcours ne cache rien de ses exigences. Le terrain a été beaucoup modelé, mais la nature a repris ses droits, donnant au lieu une belle impression de calme. Une incontestable réussite, dans une région magnifique. L'hôtel sur place est très agréable.

This Von Hagge course gives the initial impression of careful grooming and attention to detail. The beauty of the site is apparent the moment you arrive. In a country setting of pine-trees, beech and birch, playing to your handicap might be too much to ask, but this flattish course can be played by all (although beginners may be unsettled by a few dangerous water hazards). We found this a very selective course, calling for skill in ball-control and stroke-making, and great emphasis on precision-play, especially for approaching the huge and carefully designed greens. As all the hazards are there to be seen, the course hides nothing of what it demands from golfers. The terrain has been contoured to a considerable extent, but mother nature has regained the upper hand to give an overall impression of tranquillity. A great course in a fabulous region. There is a very good hotel on site.

Kempferhof Golf Club

351, rue du Moulin
F - 67115 PLOBSHEIM

Office	Secrétariat	(33) 03 88 98 72 72
Pro shop	Pro-shop	(33) 03 88 98 72 72
Fax	Fax	(33) 03 88 98 74 76
Situation	Situation	

15 km S. Strasbourg, 252 260 hab.

Annual closure	Fermeture annnuelle	oui
		21/12→12/01/99
Weekly closure	Fermeture hebdomadaire	mardi
		1/11→31/03/99

Fees main season Tarifs haute saison le parcours

	Week days Semaine	We/Bank holidays We/Férié
Individual Individuel	330 F	450 F
Couple Couple	660 F	900 F

Caddy	Caddy	non
Electric Trolley	Chariot électrique	non
Buggy	Voiturette	200 F/18 trous
Clubs	Clubs 1/2 série	50 F/jour

Credit cards Cartes de crédit
VISA - CB - Eurocard - MasterCard - AMEX

Access Accès : Strasbourg A35,
sortie N°5 Baggersee → Eschau, → Plobsheim, → Golf
Map 4 on page 105 Carte 4 Page 105

GOLF COURSE / PARCOURS 18/20

Site	Site	▇▇▇▇▇▇
Maintenance	Entretien	▇▇▇▇▇▇
Architect	Architecte	Robert von Hagge
Type	Type	parc, plaine
Relief	Relief	▇▇▇
Water in play	Eau en jeu	▇▇▇▇
Exp. to wind	Exposé au vent	▇▇
Trees in play	Arbres en jèu	▇▇▇▇

Scorecard Carte de score	Chp. Chp.	Mens Mess.	Ladies Da.
Length Long.	5980	5583	4816
Par	72	72	72

Advised golfing ability		0	12	24	36
Niveau de jeu recommandé					
Hcp required Handicap exigé	35, le We				

CLUB HOUSE & AMENITIES / CLUB HOUSE ET ANNEXES 8/10

Pro shop	Pro-shop	▇▇▇▇▇
Driving range	Practice	▇▇▇▇▇
Sheltered	couvert	10 places
On grass	sur herbe	oui
Putting-green	putting-green	oui
Pitching-green	pitching green	oui

HOTEL FACILITIES / ENVIRONNEMENT HOTELIER 6/10

HOTELS HÔTELS

Kempferhof Hotel — Golf
13 chambres, D 600 à1100 F — sur place
Tél (33) 03 88 98 72 72, Fax (33) 03 88 98 74 76

Echiquier *** — Illkirch
68 chambres, D 565 F — 5 km
Tél (33) 03 88 40 84 84, Fax (33) 03 88 66 22 83

Alizés — Lipsheim
49 chambres, D 450 F — 3 km
Tél (33) 03 88 59 62 00, Fax (33) 03 88 64 21 61

RESTAURANTS RESTAURANT

Buerehiesel — Strasbourg
Tél (33) 03 88 61 62 24 — 13 km

Le Crocodile — Strasbourg
Tél (33) 03 88 32 13 02 — 13 km

225

Le seul véritable reproche que l'on puisse faire à ce parcours, c'est que les arbres ont pris une telle densité depuis les origines que s'ils constituent un bon écran contre l'autoroute voisine, on peut éprouver sinon une sensation de claustrophobie, du moins se trouver à l'étroit. Ce n'est pas fait pour ceux qui aiment les grands espaces. Parcours original du Golf de Paris, devenu Golf du Racing-Club de France (le plus grand club omnisports français), "La Vallée" réclame un jeu très complet, des drives puissants et droits, des fers très précis pour des greens souvent assez animés, et une grande maîtrise des coups de rattrapage (balles basses sous les arbres !). Sans oublier les sorties de bunker car ils protègent solidement les greens. Quelques coups aveugles sont ici inévitables en raison du relief général assez prononcé mais sans fatigue excessive (sauf au 9). A connaître.

The only real reproach you can level at this course is that the trees have grown so thick since its inception that, while now they form an effective sound barrier from the neighbouring motorway, they also create a feeling if not of claustrophobia then at least of having very little space to play in. This is not a course for golfers who love wide open expanses. The original Golf de Paris course and now one of the two courses of the Racing-Club de France (France's biggest all sports club), "La Vallée" requires a good all-round game, powerful and straight driving, accurate ironwork for greens that are often lively affairs, and mastery in the art of recovery (particularly hitting very low shots from under the trees). And that's not forgetting escaping from bunkers that offer a solid line of defence around the greens. A few blind shots were unavoidable here owing to the general relief of the terrain, which is hilly but not too tiring (except the 9th). Well worth knowing.

Golf de La Boulie - Racing Club de France
F - 78000 VERSAILLES

Office	Secrétariat	(33) 01 39 50 59 41
Pro shop	Pro-shop	(33) 01 39 49 92 77
Fax	Fax	(33) 01 39 49 04 16
Situation	Situation	
22 km SO de Paris, 2 175 200 hab.		
Annual closure	Fermeture annnuelle	non
Weekly closure	Fermeture hebdomadaire	mardi

Fees main season
Tarifs haute saison 18 trous

	Week days Semaine	We/Bank holidays We/Férié
Individual Individuel	400 F	500 F*
Couple Couple	800 F	1 000 F*

Week-end : * sur invitation d'un membre

Caddy	Caddy	sur réservation
Electric Trolley	Chariot électrique	80 F/18 trous
Buggy	Voiturette	non
Clubs	Clubs	150 F/18 trous
Credit cards Cartes de crédit		non

226

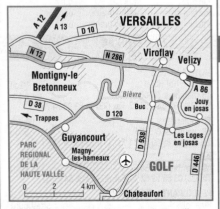

Access Accès : Paris A13 → Rouen, sortie Versailles-Vaucresson. D182 → Versailles, D185 → Château, → Versailles-Chantiers. N186 → Golf.
Map 15 on page 126 Carte 15 Page 126

GOLF COURSE
PARCOURS   15/20

Site	Site	▭▭▭▭
Maintenance	Entretien	▭▭▭▭
Architect	Architecte	
Type	Type	forêt
Relief	Relief	▭▭▭
Water in play	Eau en jeu	▭
Exp. to wind	Exposé au vent	▭▭▭
Trees in play	Arbres en jeu	▭▭▭▭

Scorecard Carte de score	**Chp.** Chp.	**Mens** Mess.	**Ladies** Da.
Length Long.	5995	5698	5062
Par	72	72	72

Advised golfing ability	0	12	24	36
Niveau de jeu recommandé				
Hcp required Handicap exigé	24 Me., 28 Dames			

CLUB HOUSE & AMENITIES
CLUB HOUSE ET ANNEXES   7/10

Pro shop	Pro-shop	▭▭▭▭
Driving range	Practice	▭▭▭
Sheltered	couvert	15 postes
On grass	sur herbe	non
Putting-green	putting-green	oui
Pitching-green	pitching green	oui

HOTEL FACILITIES
ENVIRONNEMENT HOTELIER   8/10

HOTELS HÔTELS
Trianon Palace   Versailles
94 chambres, D 1 800 F   3 km
Tél (33) 01 30 84 38 00, Fax (33) 01 39 49 00 77

Pavillon Trianon   Versailles
98 chambres, D 1 000 F   3 km
Tél (33) 01 30 84 38 00, Fax (33) 01 39 51 57 79

Résidence du Berry   Versailles
38 chambres, D 500 F   3 km
Tél (33) 01 39 49 07 07, Fax (33) 01 39 50 59 40

RESTAURANTS RESTAURANT
Les Trois Marches   Versailles
Tél (33) 01 39 50 13 21   3 km

La Rôtisserie   Versailles
Tél(33) 01 39 50 70 02   3 km

LACANAU ✳ | 14 | 6 | 4

Dans ce site magnifique et tranquille, modérément vallonné, et au milieu d'une forêt de pins, ce parcours aurait pu être un chef d'oeuvre. Mais le dessin de John Harris est simplement de bonne qualité, avec une demi-douzaine de trous sortant cependant de l'ordinaire. Des obstacles d'eau apportent un élément paysager intéressant, et quelques interrogations avant de jouer, mais ils ne sont pas effrayants. Certes, il faut jouer plusieurs fois pour bien comprendre la stratégie idéale en fonction des différents départs, mais seuls les mauvais coups sont vraiment punis. Même si les débutants auront des difficultés sur certains trous étroits, les golfeurs de tous niveaux peuvent passer un séjour vivifiant au grand air et à proximité de l'Atlantique, pratiquement toute l'année car le sol sablonneux du parcours absorbe bien la pluie.

Gently rolling through a pine forest in a balmy and magnificent setting, this course could have been a true masterpiece. As it is, the layout designed by John Harris is simply a good course, although half a dozen holes clearly emerge as out of the ordinary. Water hazards are an attractive addition to the general landscape and call for a little thought before shaping the shot, but they are less than awesome. Naturally, you need to play the course several times to grasp the ideal strategy depending on the tees you choose, but here, only the really bad shots are penalised. Although beginners (and even more proficient players) will find a number of holes a little on the tight side, golfers of all abilities can spend an invigorating holiday in the sea-air close to the Atlantic Ocean. And they can play virtually all year round, as the sandy soil quickly soaks up the rain.

Golf de Lacanau
Domaine de l'Ardilouse
F - 33680 LACANAU

Office	Secrétariat	(33) 05 56 03 92 98
Pro shop	Pro-shop	(33) 05 56 03 92 98
Fax	Fax	(33) 05 56 26 30 57
Situation	Situation	

50 km O. Bordeaux , 211 200 hab.

Annual closure	Fermeture annnuelle	non
Weekly closure	Fermeture hebdomadaire	

Fees main season
Tarifs haute saison la journée

	Week days Semaine	We/Bank holidays We/Férié
Individual Individuel	240 F	240 F
Couple Couple	420 F	420 F

Caddy	Caddy	non
Electric Trolley	Chariot électrique	non
Buggy	Voiturette	150 F/18 trous
Clubs	Clubs 1/2 série	45 F/jour

Credit cards Cartes de crédit
VISA - CB - Eurocard - MasterCard - AMEX - DC

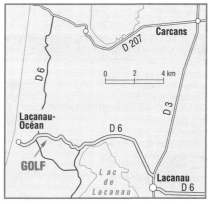

Access Accès : Rocade ouest de Bordeaux, sortie No 7,
N 215, D6 → Lacanau Océan
Map 9 on page 114 Carte 9 Page 114

GOLF COURSE
PARCOURS   14/20

Site	Site	▰▰▰▰▰
Maintenance	Entretien	
Architect	Architecte	John Harris
Type	Type	forêt, vallon
Relief	Relief	▰▰▰
Water in play	Eau en jeu	▰▰▰
Exp. to wind	Exposé au vent	▰▰
Trees in play	Arbres en jeu	▰▰▰▰

Scorecard	Chp.	Mens	Ladies
Carte de score	Chp.	Mess.	Da.
Length Long.	5932	5512	5065
Par	72	72	72

Advised golfing ability		0 12 24 36
Niveau de jeu recommandé		▰▰▰▰
Hcp required	Handicap exigé	35 (été/summer)

CLUB HOUSE & AMENITIES
CLUB HOUSE ET ANNEXES   6/10

Pro shop	Pro-shop	▰▰▰
Driving range	Practice	▰▰▰
Sheltered	couvert	10 places
On grass	sur herbe	oui
Putting-green	putting-green	oui
Pitching-green	pitching green	oui

HOTEL FACILITIES
ENVIRONNEMENT HOTELIER   4/10

HOTELS HÔTELS
Hôtel du Golf **   Domaine de l'Ardilouse
50 chambres, D 600 F   sur place
Tél (33) 05 56 03 23 15, Fax (33) 05 56 26 30 57

Les Maisons de l'Ardilouse   sur place
30 chambres, location, 3395 F/Sem
Tél (33) 05 56 03 23 15, Fax (33) 05 56 26 30 57

RESTAURANTS RESTAURANT
La Grange au Lierre   Lacanau
Tél (33) 05 56 26 50 39

La Vieille Auberge   Lacanau
Tél(33) 05 56 26 50 40

227

Dans une jolie propriété, traversée par la ligne Maginot, offrant alternativement un environnement de forêt et des trous de style links, ce parcours est accidenté mais plaisant, avec quelques pièces d'eau. Plus impressionnant visuellement que réellement, ses obstacles principaux sont les arbres et les nombreux bunkers. Les bunkers de green sont bien travaillés, mais parfois peu visibles. Ils constituent les principales difficultés, avec les arbres, mais La Largue est surtout délicat à négocier par le choix de clubs, étant donné sa topographie très vallonnée (voiturette recommandée pour les seniors). Les départs et fairways sont bien entretenus, les greens sont de bonne qualité et bien conçus : certains surélevés demandent de porter la balle. Un parcours d'entraînement de 9 trous permet de faire tranquillement progresser les enfants ou amis peu expérimentés encore.

This is a hilly and pleasant course with a few stretches of water, located on a pretty estate crossed by the Maginot line. Part woodland and part links, this is a visually impressive layout where the main hazards are the trees and numerous bunkers. The green-side bunkers in particular are well-designed, but sometimes hard to spot. The course is perhaps less impressive once you are on it, with the main difficulty coming from the trees, bunkers and club selection, owing to the hilly terrain (a buggy is recommended for senior players). The tees and fairways are in good condition and the greens are well laid-out and upkept. A number of elevated greens call for long high approaches. A 9-hole practice course is good news for children and friends still learning the game.

Golf de La Largue
Chemin du Largweg
F - 68580 MOOSLARGUE

Office	Secrétariat	(33) 03 89 07 67 67
Pro shop	Pro-shop	(33) 03 89 07 67 56
Fax	Fax	(33) 03 89 25 62 83
Situation	Situation	

30 km O. Bâle, 171 000 hab. 24 km S. Altkirch 5 090 hab.

Annual closure	Fermeture annnuelle	oui
		15/12→1/02/99
Weekly closure	Fermeture hebdomadaire	lundi, mardi, le restaurant (hiver)

Fees main season Tarifs haute saison le parcours

	Week days Semaine	We/Bank holidays We/Férié
Individual Individuel	220 F	320 F
Couple Couple	440 F	640 F
GF 140 F le soir		

Caddy	Caddy	sur réservation
Electric Trolley	Chariot électrique	70 F/jour
Buggy	Voiturette	220 F/18 trous
Clubs	Clubs série	70 F/jour

Credit cards Cartes de crédit
VISA - CB - Eurocard - MasterCard

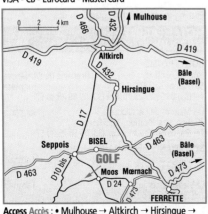

Access Accès : • Mulhouse → Altkirch → Hirsingue → Seppois • Bâle, autoroute → Delémont, sortie Reinach sud → Therwil → Leymen → Linsdorf → Ferrette → Moos **Map 8 on page 113** Carte 8 Page 113

GOLF COURSE
PARCOURS
15/20

Site	Site	
Maintenance	Entretien	
Architect	Architecte	Jeremy Pern
		Jean Garaïalde
Type	Type	forêt, plaine, parc
Relief	Relief	
Water in play	Eau en jeu	
Exp. to wind	Exposé au vent	
Trees in play	Arbres en jeu	

Scorecard Carte de score	Chp. Chp.	Mens Mess.	Ladies Da.
Length Long.	6200	5724	5415
Par	72	72	72

Advised golfing ability		0 12 24 36
Niveau de jeu recommandé		
Hcp required	Handicap exigé	35

CLUB HOUSE & AMENITIES
CLUB HOUSE ET ANNEXES
7/10

Pro shop	Pro-shop	
Driving range	Practice	
Sheltered	couvert	22 places
On grass	sur herbe	non
Putting-green	putting-green	oui
Pitching-green	pitching green	oui

HOTEL FACILITIES
ENVIRONNEMENT HOTELIER
4/10

HOTELS HÔTELS
Le Petit Kohlberg ** — Lucelle
35 chambres, D 295 F — 12 km
Tél (33) 03 89 40 85 30, Fax (33) 03 89 40 89 40

Aux Deux Clefs ** — Ferrette
7 chambres, D 240 F — 9 km
Tél (33) 03 89 40 80 56, Fax (33) 03 89 08 10 47

RESTAURANTS RESTAURANT
Ottié — Hirtzbach
Tél (33) 03 89 40 93 22 — 15 km

Au Raisin — Moernach
Tél (33) 03 89 40 80 73 — 5 km

228

14	7	5

Malheureusement à proximité immédiate de l'autoroute, ce parcours a été dessiné par Jean-Pascal Fourès dans un site dégagé et de relief assez prononcé. On souhaiterait une délimitation plus franche des fairways et des roughs (surtout entre le 1, le 9 et le 18) afin de mieux orienter le jeu du visiteur, d'autant que le manque d'arbres ne permet pas facilement de se repérer. Le tracé général, de longueur raisonnable, est de bonne qualité, avec quelques coups aveugles, mais inévitables en raison du terrain. Les greens sont raisonnablement modelés, et de très bonne qualité. Ce golf n'est pas vraiment un lieu traditionnel de vacances, mais il a visiblement été pensé pour des membres permanents, et pour tous les niveaux de jeu. Ses jolis points de vue sur la Mayenne et son ambiance plairont aux visiteurs de passage dans la région...

Unhappily located within the immediate vicinity of a motorway, this course was designed by Jean-Pascal Fourès in an open and rather hilly site. We would have preferred clearer demarcation between fairway and rough (especially between the 1st, 9th and 18th holes) for the visitor to get a clearer picture of the course. Bearings are already hard to find because there are no trees to speak of. The general layout is of reasonable length and good standard, although there are the few unavoidable blind holes on such sloping terrain. The greens are reasonably well contoured and excellent to play. This course is not really in traditional holiday country, but it has visibly been designed for permanent members and golfers of all playing skills. Pretty panoramas over the Mayenne river and the club's atmosphere will appeal to visitors passing through.

Golf de Laval-Changé
«La Chabossière»
F - 53810 CHANGE

Office	Secrétariat	(33) 02 43 53 16 03
Pro shop	Pro-shop	(33) 02 43 53 16 03
Fax	Fax	(33) 02 43 49 35 15
Situation	Situation	

5 km N. Laval, 50 470 hab.

Annual closure	Fermeture annnuelle	non
Weekly closure	Fermeture hebdomadaire	

Fees main season
Tarifs haute saison la journée

	Week days Semaine	We/Bank holidays We/Férié
Individual Individuel	180 F	220 F
Couple Couple	290 F	350 F

Caddy	Caddy	non
Electric Trolley	Chariot électrique	non
Buggy	Voiturette	150 F/18 trous
Clubs	Clubs 1/2 série	50 F/jour

Credit cards Cartes de crédit
VISA - CB - Eurocard - MasterCard

Access Accès : A81 Paris-Rennes, sortie Laval-Est
Map 2 on page 100 Carte 2 Page 100

GOLF COURSE
PARCOURS
14/20

Site	Site	
Maintenance	Entretien	
Architect	Architecte	Jean-Pascal Fourès
Type	Type	campagne, vallon
Relief	Relief	
Water in play	Eau en jeu	
Exp. to wind	Exposé au vent	
Trees in play	Arbres en jeu	

Scorecard Carte de score	Chp. Chp.	Mens Mess.	Ladies Da.
Length Long.	6068	5669	5132
Par	72	72	72

Advised golfing ability
Niveau de jeu recommandé

0	12	24	36

Hcp required Handicap exigé 35

CLUB HOUSE & AMENITIES
CLUB HOUSE ET ANNEXES
7/10

Pro shop	Pro-shop	
Driving range	Practice	
Sheltered	couvert	10 places
On grass	sur herbe	oui
Putting-green	putting-green	oui
Pitching-green	pitching green	oui

HOTEL FACILITIES
ENVIRONNEMENT HOTELIER
5/10

HOTELS HÔTELS

Les Blés d'Or ***	Laval
8 chambres, D 530 F	5 km
Tél (33) 02 43 53 14 10, Fax (33) 02 43 49 02 84	
Impérial Hôtel	Laval
34 chambres, D 440 F	5 km
Tél (33) 02 43 53 55 02, Fax (33) 02 43 49 16 74	

RESTAURANTS RESTAURANT

Bistro de Paris	Laval
Tél (33) 02 43 56 98 29	5 km
Table Ronde	Changé
Tél(33) 02 43 53 43 33	2 km
Le Capucin Gourmand	Laval
Tél (33) 02 43 66 02 02	5 km

229

L'un des meilleurs parcours français récents, et un quasi sans fautes sur le plan de l'architecture. Malgré un budget public limité, Cabell Robinson a réussi à faire un parcours réellement accessible à tous les niveaux, et passionnant pour tous les joueurs. Plat et peu fatigant, il est modérément modelé, mais toujours dans l'intérêt du jeu. Beaucoup d'arbres, de bunkers et quelques obstacles d'eau viennent menacer ceux qui manquent les fairways pourtant assez larges, les approches de green peuvent être délicates, et les placements de drapeau rendent plus intéressants encore les greens subtils et intelligemment construits. Sans excès esthétiques inutiles, le parcours se déroule avec un excellent rythme de difficultés. Dans un environnement agréable et absorbant bien l'eau, Limère mérite le détour, et un séjour, même si le Club house n'est pas tout à fait à la hauteur de l'ensemble.

One of the finest recent courses built in France and virtually faultless in terms of architecture. Despite limited public funds, Cabell Robinson has succeeded in producing a course that can be played by, and will excite, golfers of all levels. Flat and relaxing, the terrain has been given quite a bit of shape, but always in the right way. A lot of trees, bunkers and a few water hazards threaten balls that miss the fairways (although these are pleasantly wide), approach-shots to the greens can be tricky and pin-positions make the subtle and cleverly built greens even more enticing. Without any needless visual effects, the course unwinds with a nice balance of hazards and difficulties. In a pleasant setting which soaks up the rain as fast as it falls, Limère is well worth the trip and a few days stay, even though the club-house does not quite meet the standard of the actual course.

Golf de Limère

Allée de la Pomme-de-Pin
F - 45160 ARDON

Office	Secrétariat	(33) 02 38 63 89 40
Pro shop	Pro-shop	(33) 02 38 63 89 40
Fax	Fax	(33) 02 38 63 05 20
Situation	Situation	

13 km S. Orléans 105 110 hab.

Annual closure	Fermeture annnuelle	non
Weekly closure	Fermeture hebdomadaire	

Fees main season
Tarifs haute saison 18 trous

	Week days Semaine	We/Bank holidays We/Férié
Individual Individuel	210 F	310 F
Couple Couple	420 F	620 F

Caddy	Caddy	non
Electric Trolley	Chariot électrique	non
Buggy	Voiturette	100 F/18 trous
Clubs	Clubs 1/2 série	60 F/jour

Credit cards Cartes de crédit
VISA - CB - Eurocard - MasterCard - AMEX - DC

230

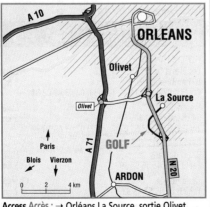

ORLÉANS

Olivet

La Source

Olivet

Paris

GOLF

Blois Vierzon

ARDON

0 2 4 km

A 10
A 71
N 20

Access Accès : → Orléans La Source, sortie Olivet,
RN20 → La Source, → Golf
Map 3 on page 102 Carte 3 Page 102

GOLF COURSE
PARCOURS
17/20

Site	Site	
Maintenance	Entretien	
Architect	Architecte	Cabell Robinson
Type	Type	forêt
Relief	Relief	
Water in play	Eau en jeu	
Exp. to wind	Exposé au vent	
Trees in play	Arbres en jeu	

Scorecard Carte de score	Chp. Chp.	Mens Mess.	Ladies Da.
Length Long.	6232	5769	5264
Par	72	72	72

Advised golfing ability	0	12	24	36
Niveau de jeu recommandé				
Hcp required	Handicap exigé	non		

CLUB HOUSE & AMENITIES
CLUB HOUSE ET ANNEXES
6/10

Pro shop	Pro-shop	
Driving range	Practice	
Sheltered	couvert	9 places
On grass	sur herbe	oui
Putting-green	putting-green	oui
Pitching-green	pitching green	oui

HOTEL FACILITIES
ENVIRONNEMENT HOTELIER
5/10

HOTELS HÔTELS
Domaine des Portes de Sologne ***   sur place
120 chambres, D 450 F
Tél (33) 02 38 49 99 99, Fax (33) 02 38 49 99 00
Les Quatre Saisons ***   Olivet
6 chambres, D 350 F   6 km
Tél (33) 02 38 66 14 30, Fax (33) 02 38 66 78 59
Novotel Orléans   La Source
107 chambres, D 470 F   3 km
Tél (33) 02 38 63 04 28, Fax (33) 02 38 69 24 04

RESTAURANTS RESTAURANT
Les Quatre Saisons   Olivet
Tél (33) 02 38 66 14 30   6 km
Les Antiquaires   Orléans
Tél(33) 02 38 53 52 35   13 km
La Poutrière   Orléans
Tél(33) 02 38 66 02 30   13 km

Avec des vues magnifiques sur les Alpes et un Club house luxueux, on attendait un parcours mieux entretenu en dehors des mois d'été : il faut être impeccable face à la concurrence des autres golfs de la région lémanique, devenue une destination de golf du printemps à l'automne. Et d'autant plus que le terrain supporte mal l'humidité. Dessiné par Peter Harradine et Olivier Dongradi, le parcours comprend de nombreux obstacles d'eau, des arbres très en jeu et des reliefs assez prononcés (surtout au retour). Ils peuvent poser des problèmes aux débutants, mais les autres joueurs prendront plaisir à un tracé intéressant, sinon inoubliable, et garderont au minimum l'impression d'une belle balade en montagne. On regrettera que les bunkers n'aient pas été davantage travaillés, ils ne gênent que les joueurs peu expérimentés.

With magnificent views over the Alps and a luxurious club-house, we were expecting a course in better condition than this outside the summer months. Upkeep has to be immaculate in the face of competition from other courses in the region of Geneva, which is nowadays a spring and autumn golf destination. What's more, the terrain here does not take too kindly to wet weather. Designed by Peter Harradine and Olivier Dongradi, the course features a number of water hazards and trees, both very much in play, plus some undulating fairways (especially on the back 9). These may pose a few problems for beginners, but other players will have fun on this interesting if not unforgettable layout, and at the very least will feel like having enjoyed a beautiful mountain stroll. The bunker locations might have been given a little more thought, as at present the sand bothers only the inexperienced player.

Golf de la Maison Blanche
Naz-Dessous
F - 01170 ECHENEVEX

Office	Secrétariat	(33) 04 50 42 44 42
Pro shop	Pro-shop	(33) 04 50 42 47 27
Fax	Fax	(33) 04 50 42 44 43
Situation	Situation	

15 km N.O. Genève, 172 486 hab.
2 km S. Gex, 6 620 hab.

Annual closure	Fermeture annnuelle	oui
		20/12→1/03/99
Weekly closure	Fermeture hebdomadaire	

Fees main season Tarifs haute saison	le parcours	
	Week days	We/Bank holidays
	Semaine	We/Férié
Individual Individuel	300 F	—
Couple Couple	600 F	—

We: membres seulement (members only)

Caddy	Caddy	sur réservation
Electric Trolley	Chariot électrique	100 F/18 trous
Buggy	Voiturette	non
Clubs	Clubs série	100 F/jour

Credit cards Cartes de crédit
VISA - CB - Eurocard - MasterCard

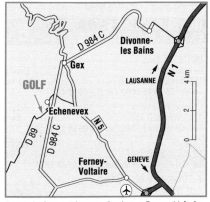

Access Accès : → Aéroport Genève → Ferney-Voltaire,
→ Gex, → Golf, à gauche
Map 8 on page 113 Carte 8 Page 113

GOLF COURSE / PARCOURS — 14/20

Site	Site	
Maintenance	Entretien	
Architect	Architecte	Peter Harradine
		Olivier Dongradi
Type	Type	campagne, montagne
Relief	Relief	
Water in play	Eau en jeu	
Exp. to wind	Exposé au vent	
Trees in play	Arbres en jeu	

Scorecard	Chp.	Mens	Ladies
Carte de score	Chp.	Mess.	Da.
Length Long.	6142	5775	5180
Par	72	72	72

Advised golfing ability	0	12	24	36
Niveau de jeu recommandé				
Hcp required Handicap exigé	30			

CLUB HOUSE & AMENITIES / CLUB HOUSE ET ANNEXES — 7/10

Pro shop	Pro-shop	
Driving range	Practice	
Sheltered	couvert	10 places
On grass	sur herbe	non
Putting-green	putting-green	oui
Pitching-green	pitching green	oui

231

HOTEL FACILITIES / ENVIRONNEMENT HOTELIER — 5/10

HOTELS HÔTELS
Auberge des Chasseurs *** — Echenevex
15 chambres, D 650 F — 2 km
Tél (33) 04 50 41 54 07, Fax (33) 04 50 41 90 61

La Mainaz *** — Mijoux
25 chambres, D 385 F — 8 km
Tél (33) 04 50 41 31 10, Fax (33) 04 50 41 31 77

Le Parc — Gex
17 chambres, D 330 F — 2 km
Tél (33) 04 50 41 50 18, Fax (33) 04 50 42 37 29

RESTAURANTS RESTAURANT
Le Champagne — Divonne
Tél (33) 04 50 20 13 13 — 8 km

La Marée — Divonne
Tél(33) 04 50 20 01 87 — 8 km

Peuplé de très beaux chênes, cet espace très vaste a permis de créer de larges fairways et de préserver l'isolement d'un trou à l'autre. Rocky Roquemore a dessiné un parcours de style américain sur fond de Pyrénées, avec des trous très variés, où l'on passe de la montagne aux plaines bordées d'obstacles d'eau. Les reliefs sont assez prononcés (sur trois trous), mais il était difficile de faire autrement dans cette superbe région et seuls les golfeurs en bonne condition physique pourront y évoluer sans voiturette. Avec près de 6200 mètres du fond, c'est un parcours solide pour les bons joueurs, mais les départs normaux permettent aux golfeurs de niveau moyen d'être à l'aise : les obstacles sont bien visibles, la stratégie assez évidente, les difficultés bien réparties. L'entretien est bon, mais le terrain est fragile par temps humide.

Lined with beautiful age-old oaks, this huge site gave the designer the possibility to lay out wide fairways and keep holes well apart. Rocky Roquemore has produced an American style layout set beneath the Pyrenees. Variety is the key word, ranging from mountain-side holes to lower-level holes edged with water hazards. It is pretty hilly (3 holes in particular) but it would have been difficult to do otherwise in this superb region. If you are not in top shape, take a buggy. This course plays 6,200 metres from the back tees, so is a good test for the better player, but the middle tees are perfect for the mid-handicapper. The hazards are visible, the strategy pretty obvious and difficulties are evenly spread around the course. Overall, the course is well looked after, but the terrain tends to suffer in wet conditions.

Makila Golf Club
Route de Cambo-Biarritz
F - 64200 BASSUSSARRY

Office	Secrétariat	(33) 05 59 58 42 42
Pro shop	Pro-shop	(33) 05 59 58 42 42
Fax	Fax	(33) 05 59 58 42 48
Situation	Situation	

5 km S.E. Biarritz, 28 740 hab.
6 km S.O. Bayonne, 40 050 hab.

Annual closure	Fermeture annnuelle	non
Weekly closure	Fermeture hebdomadaire	

Fees main season
Tarifs haute saison le parcours

	Week days Semaine	We/Bank holidays We/Férié
Individual Individuel	300 F	300 F
Couple Couple	480 F	480 F
Couple : GF + voiture, 640 F		

Caddy	Caddy	sur réservation
Electric Trolley	Chariot électrique	non
Buggy	Voiturette	160 F/18 trous
Clubs	Clubs série	100 F/18 trous

Credit cards Cartes de crédit
VISA - CB - Eurocard - MasterCard - AMEX

232

Access Accès : A63, sortie N° 5 Bayonne Sud → Cambo
D932. Golf à 800 m. après le rond-point
Map 12 on page 120 Carte 12 Page 120

GOLF COURSE
PARCOURS **14**/20

Site	Site	
Maintenance	Entretien	
Architect	Architecte	Rocky Roquemore
Type	Type	parc, vallon
Relief	Relief	
Water in play	Eau en jeu	
Exp. to wind	Exposé au vent	
Trees in play	Arbres en jeu	

Scorecard Carte de score	Chp. Chp.	Mens Mess.	Ladies Da.
Length Long.	6176	5790	5067
Par	72	72	72

Advised golfing ability		0 12 24 36
Niveau de jeu recommandé		
Hcp required	Handicap exigé	non

CLUB HOUSE & AMENITIES
CLUB HOUSE ET ANNEXES **6**/10

Pro shop	Pro-shop	
Driving range	Practice	
Sheltered	couvert	10 places
On grass	sur herbe	oui
Putting-green	putting-green	oui
Pitching-green	pitching green	non

HOTEL FACILITIES
ENVIRONNEMENT HOTELIER **8**/10

HOTELS HÔTELS
Le Palais ★★★★ — Biarritz — 5 km
156 chambres, D 1 800 F
Tél (33) 05 59 41 64 00, Fax (33) 05 59 41 67 99

Château de Brindos ★★★★ — Anglet — 8 km
12 chambres, D 1300 F
Tél (33) 05 59 23 17 68, Fax (33) 05 59 23 48 47

Chiberta — Anglet — 8 km
98 chambres, D 750 F
Tél (33) 05 59 63 95 56, Fax (33) 05 59 63 57 84

RESTAURANTS RESTAURANT
Café de Paris — Biarritz — 5 km
Tél (33) 05 59 24 19 53

Auberge d'Achtal — Arcangues — 2 km
Tél (33) 05 59 43 05 56

MAZAMET-LA BAROUGE   13 5 4

Les neuf premiers trous ont été conçus par Mackenzie Ross, puis remodelés et complétés par le cabinet Hawtree. Avec 5600 mètres, il peut paraître court, mais c'est un par 70. Les longs frappeurs pourront s'y déchaîner, sans trop craindre les arbres de ce grand parc (beaucoup de pins). Les joueurs moyens s'amuseront aussi, car les obstacles sont bien visibles, certains trous très courts, les roughs sont propres et les sous-bois bien nettoyés. Le terrain est assez plat pour être facilement marché, ce qui accentue la sensation générale de tranquillité et de golf reposant (à conseiller aux seniors). Les difficultés existent pourtant, mais elles sont aisément négociables si l'on possède un bon jeu de petits fers : les greens ne sont pas bien grands. L'environnement, l'ambiance amicale et l'utilisation rationnelle d'une surface réduite en font une halte agréable.

The first nine holes were designed by Mackenzie Ross, then completed and redesigned by Hawtree. It might appear short at just 5600 metres, but it is a par 70 where long hitters will be able to open their shoulders without worrying too much about the trees (there are a lot of pines). The average golfer can also have fun, because the hazards are clearly visible, a number of holes are short, the rough is trimmed and the undergrowth kept clear. The terrain is flat enough to make this an easily walkable course and add to the overall impression of a peaceful, relaxing golf course (recommended for seniors). But it is no push-over, and the difficulties are there to be negotiated - an easier proposition if your short irons are in good shape. Accuracy is at a premium because the greens are not enormous. The general setting, friendly atmosphere and rational utilisation of limited space make this a very pleasant stop-off.

Golf Club de Mazamet-La Barouge
F - 81660 PONT-DE-LARN

Office	Secrétariat	(33) 05 63 61 06 72
Pro shop	Pro-shop	(33) 05 63 61 79 79
Fax	Fax	(33) 05 63 61 13 03
Situation	Situation	

16 km S.E. Castres, 44 810 hab.
84 km E. Toulouse, 358 690 hab.

Annual closure	Fermeture annnuelle	non
Weekly closure	Fermeture hebdomadaire	

Fees main season
Tarifs haute saison la journée

	Week days Semaine	We/Bank holidays We/Férié
Individual Individuel	160 F	220 F
Couple Couple	300 F	400 F

Caddy	Caddy	non
Electric Trolley	Chariot électrique	non
Buggy	Voiturette	200 F/18 trous
Clubs	Clubs	non

Credit cards Cartes de crédit
VISA - CB - Eurocard - MasterCard

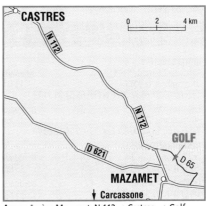

CASTRES

0   2   4 km

N 112
N 112
D 621
GOLF
D 65
MAZAMET
↓ Carcassone

Access Accès : Mazamet, N 112 → Castres, → Golf
Map 13 on page 122 Carte 13 Page 122

GOLF COURSE
PARCOURS   13/20

Site	Site	
Maintenance	Entretien	
Architect	Architecte	Mackenzie Ross Fred Hawtree
Type	Type	montagne, forêt
Relief	Relief	
Water in play	Eau en jeu	
Exp. to wind	Exposé au vent	
Trees in play	Arbres en jeu	

Scorecard Carte de score	Chp. Chp.	Mens Mess.	Ladies Da.
Length Long.	5635	5427	4898
Par	70	70	70

Advised golfing ability	0	12	24	36
Niveau de jeu recommandé				
Hcp required	Handicap exigé	non		

CLUB HOUSE & AMENITIES
CLUB HOUSE ET ANNEXES   5/10

Pro shop	Pro-shop	
Driving range	Practice	
Sheltered	couvert	6 places
On grass	sur herbe	non
Putting-green	putting-green	oui
Pitching-green	pitching green	non

233

HOTEL FACILITIES
ENVIRONNEMENT HOTELIER   4/10

HOTELS HÔTELS
La Métairie Neuve ***   Bout-du-Pont-de-Larn
11 chambres, D 460 F   1 km
Tél (33) 05 63 61 23 31, Fax (33) 05 63 61 94 75

Les Comtes d'Hautpoul   Mazamet Centre
40 chambres, D 260 F   1 km
Tél (33) 05 63 61 98 14, Fax (33) 05 63 98 95 76

Occitan   Castres
42 chambres, D 390 F   14 km
Tél (33) 05 63 35 34 20, Fax (33) 05 63 35 70 32

RESTAURANTS RESTAURANT
H. Jourdon   Mazamet
Tél (33) 05 63 61 56 93   1 km

Si le parcours des "Vignes" est une agréable promenade en plaine et dans une pinède, le parcours des "Châteaux" est de meilleur cru encore (nous sommes en plein Bordelais), et sa réputation est largement méritée. Dû au crayon habile de l'Américain Bill Coore, il se déroule dans un paysage de plaine dénudé, modelé comme un links, mais sans les dunes. Des obstacles d'eau et des "ditchs" viennent parfois perturber la quiétude du golfeur, mais les ondulations du fairway, le dessin des bunkers, la bonne densité des roughs et le profil des vastes greens en font l'un des parcours les plus remarquables de la région. Les amateurs de paysages boisés peuvent sans doute lui reprocher une légère monotonie visuelle, mais il s'avère de plus en plus intéressant, à mesure qu'on le joue. C'est sans aucun doute le parcours le plus technique de la région, et se joue avec tant de facilité qu'on peut jouer 36 trous dans la journée.

While "Les Vignes" course (The Vines) is a pleasant stroll through open country and a pine forest, the "Châteaux" course is an even better vintage (we are to the west of Bordeaux) and well worth its reputation. Designed by the American Bill Coore, the course unfolds over flat open country and is designed to play like a links course, but without the dunes. Some water hazards and ditches can be a little trying, but the rolling fairways, the well-designed bunkers, the thick rough and the profile of the huge greens make this one of the region's finest courses. People who prefer woodland courses will probably knock "Les Châteaux" as being visually boring, but this course gets better and better the more you play it. Without a doubt the most "technical" course in this part of the country, and easy enough on the feet to play 36 holes in the day.

Golf du Médoc
Chemin de Courmateau
F - 33290 LE PIAN-MEDOC

Office	Secrétariat	(33) 05 56 70 11 90
Pro shop	Pro-shop	(33) 05 56 70 11 90
Fax	Fax	(33) 05 56 70 11 99
Situation	Situation	

15 km N.O. Bordeaux, 211 200 hab.

Annual closure	Fermeture annnuelle	non
Weekly closure	Fermeture hebdomadaire	

Fees main season
Tarifs haute saison la journée

	Week days Semaine	We/Bank holidays We/Férié
Individual Individuel	210 F	280 F
Couple Couple	380 F	490 F

Caddy	Caddy	sur réservation
Electric Trolley	Chariot électrique	80 F/18 trous
Buggy	Voiturette	200 F/18 trous
Clubs	Clubs 1/2 série	80 F/jour

Credit cards Cartes de crédit
VISA - CB - Eurocard - MasterCard - AMEX

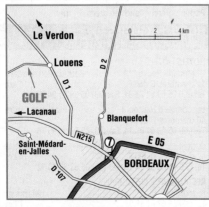

Access Accès : Bordeaux, Rocade,
sortie N° 7 → Lacanau, à droite D1 → Le Verdon
Map 9 on page 114 Carte 9 Page 114

234

GOLF COURSE
PARCOURS

17/20

Site	Site	▬▬▬▬▬
Maintenance	Entretien	▬▬▬▬
Architect	Architecte	Bill Coore
Type	Type	plaine, links
Relief	Relief	▬
Water in play	Eau en jeu	▬▬
Exp. to wind	Exposé au vent	▬▬▬
Trees in play	Arbres en jeu	▬

Scorecard Carte de score	Chp. Chp.	Mens Mess.	Ladies Da.
Length Long.	6316	5765	5120
Par	71	71	71

Advised golfing ability		0	12	24	36
Niveau de jeu recommandé				▬▬	
Hcp required	Handicap exigé	non			

CLUB HOUSE & AMENITIES
CLUB HOUSE ET ANNEXES

7/10

Pro shop	Pro-shop	▬▬▬▬
Driving range	Practice	▬▬▬
Sheltered	couvert	15 places
On grass	sur herbe	oui
Putting-green	putting-green	oui
Pitching-green	pitching green	oui

HOTEL FACILITIES
ENVIRONNEMENT HOTELIER

5/10

HOTELS HÔTELS
Relais de Margaux **** • Margaux
31 chambres, D 900 F 13 km
Tél (33) 05 57 88 38 30, Fax (33) 05 57 88 31 73

Bayonne *** Bordeaux
36 chambres, D 600 F 15 km
Tél (33) 05 56 48 00 88, Fax (33) 05 56 52 03 79

RESTAURANTS RESTAURANT
Le Chapon Fin Bordeaux
Tél (33) 05 56 79 10 10 15 km

Le Vieux Bordeaux Bordeaux
Tél (33) 05 56 52 94 36 15 km

Jean Ramet Bordeaux
Tél (33) 05 56 44 12 51 15 km

Sur un terrain généralement plat, l'ensemble des 36 trous du golf du Médoc peut être facilement joué dans la journée. Après le paysage très peu arboré du parcours des "Châteaux", le parcours des "Vignes" offre un contraste bienvenu, et des difficultés moins affirmées. Les amoureux des parcours dans les arbres seront comblés car un certain nombre de trous se situent dans une petite pinède, aux ombrages plaisants. Les autres trous offrent une végétation plus légère, mais néammoins souvent en jeu. Tout comme sur l'autre parcours, les greens sont de bonne qualité, et sans reliefs excessifs. Certes, "Les Châteaux" représente un défi plus constant, mais cet ensemble s'est incontestablement imposé comme l'un des tout meilleurs dans une région très touristique, et comme l'ensemble le plus intéressant à proximité immédiate de Bordeaux.

Laid out over what is generally flat terrain, the 36 holes at Le Pian Médoc can easily be played in one day. After the tree-less landscape of "Les Châteaux", "Les Vignes" provides a welcome contrast and plays a little more easily. Golfers who love playing woodland courses will be spoilt here, as a number of holes wind their way through a pretty and shady pine forest. The others provide a little lighter vegetation which nonetheless is very much in play. As with "Les Châteaux", the greens are excellent and not too undulating. Although a little less challenging, "Les Vignes" is still one of the best courses in a very busy tourist region, and the two courses together are the most attractive golfing proposition within the immediate vicinity of Bordeaux.

Golf du Médoc

Chemin de Courmateau
F - 33290 LE PIAN-MEDOC

Office	Secrétariat	(33) 05 56 70 11 90
Pro shop	Pro-shop	(33) 05 56 70 11 90
Fax	Fax	(33) 05 56 70 11 99
Situation	Situation	

15 km N.O. Bordeaux, 211 200 hab.

Annual closure	Fermeture annnuelle	non
Weekly closure	Fermeture hebdomadaire	

Fees main season
Tarifs haute saison la journée

	Week days Semaine	We/Bank holidays We/Férié
Individual Individuel	210 F	280 F
Couple Couple	380 F	490 F

Caddy	Caddy	sur réservation
Electric Trolley	Chariot électrique	80 F/18 trous
Buggy	Voiturette	200 F/18 trous
Clubs	Clubs 1/2 série	80 F/jour

Credit cards Cartes de crédit
VISA - CB - Eurocard - MasterCard - AMEX

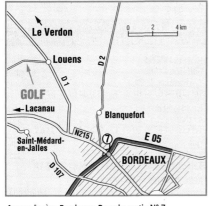

Access Accès : Bordeaux, Rocade, sortie N° 7
→ Lacanau, à droite D1 → Le Verdon
Map 9 on page 114 Carte 9 Page 114

GOLF COURSE PARCOURS 15/20

Site	Site	▰▰▰▰
Maintenance	Entretien	▰▰▰▱
Architect	Architecte	Rod Whitman
Type	Type	forêt, plaine
Relief	Relief	▱▱▱▱
Water in play	Eau en jeu	▰▱▱▱
Exp. to wind	Exposé au vent	▰▱▱▱
Trees in play	Arbres en jeu	▰▰▰▱

Scorecard Carte de score	Chp. Chp.	Mens Mess.	Ladies Da.
Length Long.	6220	5694	5136
Par	71	71	71

Advised golfing ability	0	12	24	36
Niveau de jeu recommandé				
Hcp required	Handicap exigé	non		

CLUB HOUSE & AMENITIES CLUB HOUSE ET ANNEXES 7/10

Pro shop	Pro-shop	▰▰▰▱
Driving range	Practice	▰▰▰▰
Sheltered	couvert	15 places
On grass	sur herbe	oui
Putting-green	putting-green	oui
Pitching-green	pitching green	oui

HOTEL FACILITIES ENVIRONNEMENT HOTELIER 5/10

HOTELS HÔTELS

Relais de Margaux **** — Margaux
31 chambres, D 900 F — 13 km
Tél (33) 05 57 88 38 30, Fax (33) 05 57 88 31 73

Bayonne *** — Bordeaux
36 chambres, D 600 F — 15 km
Tél (33) 05 56 48 00 88, Fax (33) 05 56 52 03 79

RESTAURANTS RESTAURANT

Le Chapon Fin — Bordeaux
Tél (33) 05 56 79 10 10 — 15 km

Le Vieux Bordeaux — Bordeaux
Tél (33) 05 56 52 94 36 — 15 km

Jean Ramet — Bordeaux
Tél (33) 05 56 44 12 51 — 15 km

235

Dessiné par Ronald Fream, le golf de Massane n'est certes pas à conseiller aux débutants. Et, pour vraiment s'amuser, les joueurs simplement moyens devront absolument choisir les départs avancés. En revanche, les golfeurs confirmés y trouveront de quoi tester l'ensemble de leur jeu. De nombreux obstacles d'eau, des bunkers frontaux, différentes alternatives d'attaque des trous obligent à savoir précisément quand décider de rester court ou de passer les obstacles, quelle tactique choisir : il faut parfois se résigner à la prudence pour ramener un bon score. Ce parcours se joue avec ses clubs, et vraiment avec sa tête. Les bunkers et les greens sont remarquablement dessinés, ce qui accentue encore la nécessité d'un petit jeu complet et bien aiguisé. Un parcours parfois controversé, mais à connaître, au moins pour pouvoir en parler.

Designed by Ronald Fream, the Massane course is definitely not for beginners, but if the average hacker wants to enjoy a good round of golf, he should make straight for the front tees. By contrast, skilled golfers will find this an excellent test for every aspect of their game. Numerous water hazards, front bunkers and different lines of approach to the green force players into tactical decisions and into choosing exactly when to lay up short or when to carry the hazard. A good score sometimes comes more from caution than from daring. This is another course where you really do play with your clubs and your brains. The bunkers and greens are remarkably well designed and only emphasise the need for an all-round and well-honed short game. A sometimes controversial course but one worth knowing, if only to be able to talk about it.

Golf de Montpellier-Massane

Mas de Massane
F - 34670 BAILLARGUES

Office	Secrétariat	(33) 04 67 87 87 89
Pro shop	Pro-shop	(33) 04 67 87 87 89
Fax	Fax	(33) 04 67 87 87 90
Situation	Situation	

13 km N.E. Montpellier, 210 860 hab.
34 km S.O. Nîmes, 128 470 hab.

Annual closure	Fermeture annnuelle	non
Weekly closure	Fermeture hebdomadaire	

Fees main season
Tarifs haute saison la journée

	Week days Semaine	We/Bank holidays We/Férié
Individual Individuel	250 F	250 F
Couple Couple	500 F	500 F

Caddy	Caddy	non
Electric Trolley	Chariot électrique	non
Buggy	Voiturette	180 F/18 trous
Clubs	Clubs 1/2 série	60 F/jour

Credit cards Cartes de crédit
VISA - CB - Eurocard - MasterCard - AMEX - DC

236

Access Accès : A9, sortie Vendargues- Baillargues,
N113 → Baillargues
Map 13 on page 123 Carte 13 Page 123

GOLF COURSE PARCOURS — 16/20

Site	Site	■
Maintenance	Entretien	■■■■■
Architect	Architecte	Ronald Fream
Type	Type	plaine, résidentiel
Relief	Relief	■
Water in play	Eau en jeu	■■■■
Exp. to wind	Exposé au vent	■■■■
Trees in play	Arbres en jeu	■

Scorecard Carte de score	Chp. Chp.	Mens Mess.	Ladies Da.
Length Long.	6550	6044	5098
Par	72	72	72

Advised golfing ability
Niveau de jeu recommandé   0   12   24   36

Hcp required Handicap exigé   non

CLUB HOUSE & AMENITIES CLUB HOUSE ET ANNEXES — 7/10

Pro shop	Pro-shop	■■■■
Driving range	Practice	■■■■
Sheltered	couvert	12 places
On grass	sur herbe	oui
Putting-green	putting-green	oui
Pitching-green	pitching green	oui

HOTEL FACILITIES ENVIRONNEMENT HOTELIER — 5/10

HOTELS HÔTELS
Golf-Hôtel ***   sur place
32 chambres, D 500 F
Tél (33) 04 67 87 87 87, Fax (33) 04 67 87 87 90

New Hôtel du Midi ***   Montpellier
47 chambres, D 380 F   13 km
Tél (33) 04 67 92 69 61, Fax (33) 04 67 92 73 63

Demeure des Brousses ***   Montpellier
17 chambres, D 580 F   13 km
Tél (33) 04 67 65 77 66, Fax (33) 04 67 22 22 17

RESTAURANTS RESTAURANT
Jardin des Sens   Montpellier
Tél (33) 04 67 79 63 38   13 km

Le Chandelier   Montpellier
Tél (33) 04 67 92 61 62   13 km

L'Albatros (site du Peugeot Open de France) est un parcours de championnat, réservé aux moins de 24 de handicap. Dessiné par Hubert Chesneau et Robert von Hagge, il alterne des trous à l'américaine et des trous typiques de bord de mer, insinués entre d'énormes dunes artificielles prévues pour accueillir les spectateurs. En contrebas sur le parcours, le dépaysement est total. La moindre erreur stratégique ou technique peut s'avérer catastrophique sur chacun des 18 trous, défendus par toutes sortes d'obstacles, mais aux difficultés bien réparties, où les quatre derniers trous sont toujours décisifs. Il vaut mieux jouer en match-play si l'on n'est pas dans sa meilleure forme. Pour atténuer cette exigence, le parcours est d'une parfaite franchise, et le résultat est à hauteur de la performance du joueur. A connaître absolument.

The "Albatros" (the venue for the Peugeot French Open) is a championship course reserved for players with a minimum handicap of 24. Designed by Hubert Chesneau and Robert von Hagge, this is a combination course where US style target golf alternates with typical links holes set amidst huge artificial dunes, designed with the spectators in mind. Down in the playing arena it's whole a different story. The slightest strategic or technical slip can lead to disaster on any one of the 18 holes, all of which are defended by every sort of hazard. And although difficulties are finely balanced over the whole course, the last 4 holes are decisive. If you are not on top of your game, try match-play. Although demanding, the course is forthright and the score on your card the reflection of just how well you played! An absolute must.

Le Golf National
2, avenue du Golf
F - 78280 GUYANCOURT

Office	Secrétariat	(33) 01 30 43 36 00
Pro shop	Pro-shop	(33) 01 30 43 36 00
Fax	Fax	(33) 01 30 43 85 58
Situation	Situation	

14 km S.E. Versailles, 87 790 hab. 30 km S.O. Paris.

Annual closure	Fermeture annnuelle	non
Weekly closure	Fermeture hebdomadaire	mercredi
	01/11 → 30/06 (Albatros)	

Fees main season Tarifs haute saison la journée

	Week days Semaine	We/Bank holidays We/Férié
Individual Individuel	240 F	360 F
Couple Couple	480 F	720 F

Seniors le mardi et Dames le jeudi: 18 trous + déj.200 F

Caddy	Caddy	non
Electric Trolley	Chariot électrique	60 F/18 trous
Buggy	Voiturette	non
Clubs	Clubs 1/2 série	40 F/jour

Credit cards Cartes de crédit
VISA - CB - Eurocard - MasterCard

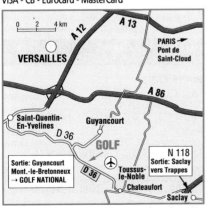

Access Accès : • De Paris A13, A12 → St-Quentin en Y., sortie Mont-le-Bretonneux • Paris N118 → Chartres (A10), sortie Saclay, D36 → Châteaufort, Trappes
Map 15 on page 126 Carte 15 Page 126

GOLF COURSE PARCOURS
18/20

Site	Site	
Maintenance	Entretien	
Architect	Architecte	Hubert Chesneau
		Robert von Hagge (Arch. consult.ant)
Type	Type	links
Relief	Relief	
Water in play	Eau en jeu	
Exp. to wind	Exposé au vent	
Trees in play	Arbres en jeu	

Scorecard Carte de score	Chp. Chp.	Mens Mess.	Ladies Da.
Length Long.	6515	6155	5200
Par	72	72	72

Advised golfing ability   0 12 24 36
Niveau de jeu recommandé
Hcp required   Handicap exigé   24 Mess. 28 Da.

CLUB HOUSE & AMENITIES CLUB HOUSE ET ANNEXES
6/10

Pro shop	Pro-shop	
Driving range	Practice	
Sheltered	couvert	30 places
On grass	sur herbe	oui
Putting-green	putting-green	oui
Pitching-green	pitching green	oui

HOTEL FACILITIES ENVIRONNEMENT HOTELIER
6/10

HOTELS HÔTELS
Novotel ***   Guyancourt
130 chambres, D 650 F   sur place
Tél (33) 01 30 57 65 65, Fax (33) 01 30 57 65 00

Trianon Palace *****   Versailles
94 chambres, D 1 800 F   14 km
Tél (33) 01 30 84 38 00, Fax (33) 01 39 49 00 77

Pavillon Trianon ****   Versailles
98 chambres, D 1 000 F   14 km
Tél (33) 01 30 84 38 00, Fax (33) 01 39 51 57 79

RESTAURANTS RESTAURANT
Les Trois Marches   Versailles
Tél (33) 01 39 50 13 21   14 km

La Belle Epoque   Châteaufort
Tél (33) 01 39 56 21 66   4 km

237

NEW GOLF DEAUVILLE ✳ 15 7 8

Un ensemble de 27 trous avec un bon 9 trous et un 18 trous de bon niveau, de style très britannique, assez vallonné sans être trop fatigant. Dessiné en 1929 par Tom Simpson, il a été agrandi et beaucoup remanié par Henry Cotton en 1964. Dans un agréable paysage normand, ce parcours avait tendance à se banaliser mais un dessin plus précis des limites de fairways et des roughs, la modification de certains bunkers, la décoration même lui ont donné une nouvelle jeunesse, et imposent maintenant de réfléchir sur la stratégie : les joueurs de bon niveau devraient y revenir. Il s'agit certes d'un golf commercial, pour les golfeurs en week-end et en vacances, et il convient d'assurer leur plaisir, mais les progrès réalisés incitent à le remonter notablement dans la hiérarchie. C'est de nouveau le meilleur parcours de la région, on souhaite que l'accueil y soit encore plus agréable.

A 27-hole complex with a good 9-hole course and an excellent British style 18-hole layout over rolling countryside. Designed in 1929 by Tom Simpson, it was enlarged and very much restyled by Henry Cotton in 1964. Set in pleasant Norman countryside, the course was beginning to look a bit ordinary, but clearer demarcation of the fairways and rough, plus changes to certain bunkers and to the general decor have given Deauville a new lease of life. Good players should and almost certainly do return for more of the same. This is a business venture, of course, for weekenders and holiday-makers, and their enjoyment is naturally important, but with what has been achieved here, we can only review the course's ranking upwards. This is once again the best course in the region, and we would like to see the hospitality a little warmer still.

New Golf de Deauville
Saint-Arnoult
F - 14800 DEAUVILLE

Office	Secrétariat	(33) 02 31 14 24 24
Pro shop	Pro-shop	(33) 02 31 14 24 24
Fax	Fax	(33) 02 31 14 24 25
Situation	Situation	

3 km S. Deauville, 4 260 hab.

Annual closure	Fermeture annnuelle	non
Weekly closure	Fermeture hebdomadaire	mardi
		sauf vacances

Fees main season
Tarifs haute saison la journée

	Week days Semaine	We/Bank holidays We/Férié
Individual Individuel	300 F	350 F
Couple Couple	600 F	700 F

Soir : – 50 %

Caddy	Caddy	160 F/18 trous
Electric Trolley	Chariot électrique	non
Buggy	Voiturette	200 F/18 trous
Clubs	Clubs 1/2 série	50 F/jour

Credit cards Cartes de crédit
VISA - CB - Eurocard - MasterCard - AMEX - DC

238

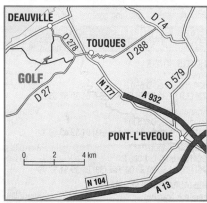

Access Accès : Paris A13, sortie Deauville, N177 →
Deauville. Touques, D27 → Golf
Map 2 on page 101 Carte 2 Page 101

GOLF COURSE
PARCOURS 15/20

Site	Site	
Maintenance	Entretien	
Architect	Architecte	Tom Simpson Henry Cotton
Type	Type	bocage
Relief	Relief	
Water in play	Eau en jeu	
Exp. to wind	Exposé au vent	
Trees in play	Arbres en jeu	

Scorecard Carte de score	Chp. Chp.	Mens Mess.	Ladies Da.
Length Long.	5951	5705	5035
Par	71	71	71

Advised golfing ability	0	12	24	36
Niveau de jeu recommandé				
Hcp required	Handicap exigé	24 Mess., 28 Da.		

CLUB HOUSE & AMENITIES
CLUB HOUSE ET ANNEXES 7/10

Pro shop	Pro-shop	
Driving range	Practice	
Sheltered	couvert	22 places
On grass	sur herbe	en été
Putting-green	putting-green	oui
Pitching-green	pitching green	oui

HOTEL FACILITIES
ENVIRONNEMENT HOTELIER 8/10

HOTELS HÔTELS

Hôtel du golf ★★★★ — sur place
121 chambres, D 825 F
Tél (33) 02 31 88 19 01, Fax (33) 02 31 88 75 99

Royal ★★★★ — Deauville
300 chambres, D 1 700 F — 3 km N
Tél (33) 02 31 98 66 33, Fax (33) 02 31 98 66 34

Normandy ★★★★ — Deauville
320 chambres, D 1 500 F — 3 km N
Tél (33) 02 31 98 66 22, Fax (33) 02 31 98 66 23

RESTAURANTS Restaurant

Le Spinnaker — Deauville
Tél (33) 02 31 88 24 40 — 3 km

Le Ciro's — Deauville
Tél(33) 02 31 88 18 10 — 3 km

NÎMES-CAMPAGNE

| 16 | 7 | 6 |

D'une année sur l'autre, on a plaisir à retrouver ce "classique" de la région, et de tradition sportive bien établie. Comme un ami d'enfance, il ne change pas. Dessiné par Morandi et Donald Harradine, il s'impose toujours comme un vrai parcours de championnat, surtout quand souffle le vent. Alors, les chênes et cyprès bleus deviennent redoutables, et les balles basses obligatoires, d'autant que quelques obstacles d'eau stratégiques viennent perturber le jugement comme la confiance. Les greens sont généralement bien dessinés, pas toujours très vastes. Pour les bons joueurs, la précision devra s'allier alors à la puissance, car les trous sont rarement courts des départs arrière : les joueurs lucides ne devront pas hésiter à choisir les départs normaux. Ce golf toujours bien entretenu est très fréquenté par ses nombreux membres, il est conseillé de réserver en toute saison.

Year in year out, it's always a pleasure to play this "classic" course which enjoys a well established sporting tradition. Like a life-long friend, Nîmes Campagne never changes. Designed by Morandi and Donald Harradine, this is a real championship course, especially when the wind blows. Then the oaks and the blue cypress trees are formidable foes, which make low-flighted balls a must, especially since a few strategic water hazards can affect both judgment and confidence. The greens are generally well-designed and not always that large. For the better player, the course demands both power and precision, as holes are seldom short from the back tees. Clear-headed average golfers should use the normal tees. The course is very well upkept and played by a large number of members, so whatever the season, always book a tee-off time.

Golf de Nîmes-Campagne
Route de Saint-Gilles
F - 30900 NIMES

Office	Secrétariat	(33) 04 66 70 17 37
Pro shop	Pro-shop	(33) 04 66 70 18 60
Fax	Fax	(33) 04 66 70 03 14
Situation	Situation	

10 km S. Nîmes, 128 470 hab.

Annual closure	Fermeture annnuelle	non
Weekly closure	Fermeture hebdomadaire	

Fees main season
Tarifs haute saison la journée

	Week days Semaine	We/Bank holidays We/Férié
Individual Individuel	220 F	220 F
Couple Couple	440 F	440 F

Après 17 H : - 50%

Caddy	Caddy	non
Electric Trolley	Chariot électrique	non
Buggy	Voiturette	150 F/18 trous
Clubs	Clubs 1/2 série	80 F/jour

Credit cards Cartes de crédit
VISA - CB - Eurocard - MasterCard

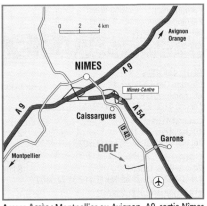

Access Accès : Montpellier ou Avignon, A9, sortie Nîmes
Centre, D42 → Saint-Gilles, route à droite
de l'aéroport, → Golf
Map 13 on page 123 Carte 13 Page 123

GOLF COURSE PARCOURS
16/20

Site	Site	
Maintenance	Entretien	
Architect	Architecte	Léonard Morandi Donald Harradine
Type	Type	campagne, parc
Relief	Relief	
Water in play	Eau en jeu	
Exp. to wind	Exposé au vent	
Trees in play	Arbres en jeu	

Scorecard Carte de score	Chp. Chp.	Mens Mess.	Ladies Da.
Length Long.	6135	5599	5045
Par	72	72	72

Advised golfing ability Niveau de jeu recommandé	0	12	24	36
Hcp required Handicap exigé	35			

CLUB HOUSE & AMENITIES CLUB HOUSE ET ANNEXES
7/10

Pro shop	Pro-shop	
Driving range	Practice	
Sheltered	couvert	2 places
On grass	sur herbe	non
Putting-green	putting-green	oui
Pitching-green	pitching green	oui

239

HOTEL FACILITIES ENVIRONNEMENT HOTELIER
6/10

HOTELS HÔTELS
Imperator Concorde ★★★★ — Nîmes
61 chambres, D 800 F — 10 km
Tél (33) 04 66 21 90 30, Fax (33) 04 66 67 70 25

Les Aubuns ★★★ — Caissargues
30 chambres, D 470 F — 6 km
Tél (33) 04 66 70 10 44, Fax (33) 04 66 70 14 97

New Hôtel La Baume — Nîmes
34 chambres, D 350 F — 10 km
Tél (33) 04 66 76 28 42, Fax (33) 04 66 76 28 45

RESTAURANTS RESTAURANT
Alexandre — Garons
Tél (33) 04 66 70 08 99 — 4 km

Les Alizés — Nîmes
Tél (33) 04 66 67 08 17 — 10 km

Les trois 9 trous sont combinables, mais "L'Etang", assez dénudé et accidenté, n'est pas aussi caractéristique que "Le Bocage" (dans un paysage typiquement normand) et "La Mer". Ces deux derniers parcours forment la combinaison la plus cohérente au plan du jeu et de l'unité esthétique, où l'architecte Yves Bureau a utilisé les reliefs naturels sans trop bouleverser le terrain, ponctuant la route des greens de quelques grands bunkers. "La Mer", assez vallonné, propose quelques trous sur un plateau dominant l'une des plages du Débarquement, avec de magnifiques points de vue sur la côte et la mer. Ces trous sur la mer n'ont pas vraiment le caractère de links, étant donné la nature du sol et l'absence de dunes (ils se rapprochent du style d'Etretat), mais le vent peut les rendre redoutables pour le jeu et surtout pour les scores. Une réalisation sympathique et de qualité.

The three nine hole courses can be played in any combination, but "L'Etang", a barren and hilly layout, does not have the character of "Le Bocage" (in typically Norman countryside) or "La Mer". The latter two form the most consistent combination in terms of golfing and visual unity, where architect Yves Bureau has employed the natural relief without too much excavation work, dotting the fairways with a few large bunkers. "La Mer", which unwinds over rolling landscape, includes a few holes on a plateau overlooking one of the D-Day beaches and providing magnificent views over the coastline and English channel. The seaboard holes are hardly your typical links holes, given the nature of the soil and the absence of dunes (they are more in the Etretat style), but the wind can play havoc with your game and your card. A very pleasant golf course of excellent standard.

Omaha Beach Golf Club

La Ferme Saint-Sauveur
F - 14520 PORT-EN-BESSIN

Office	Secrétariat	(33) 02 31 21 72 94
Pro shop	Pro-shop	(33) 02 31 22 76 45
Fax	Fax	(33) 02 33 51 79 61
Situation	Situation	

10 km N. Bayeux, 14 700 hab.

Annual closure	Fermeture annnuelle	non
Weekly closure	Fermeture hebdomadaire	mardi
	15/11 → 15/03	

Fees main season
Tarifs haute saison la journée

	Week days Semaine	We/Bank holidays We/Férié
Individual Individuel	260 F	260 F
Couple Couple	520 F	520 F

Caddy	Caddy	sur réservation
Electric Trolley	Chariot électrique	70 F/18 trous
Buggy	Voiturette	160 F/18 trous
Clubs	Clubs 1/2 série	60 F/jour

Credit cards Cartes de crédit
VISA - CB - Eurocard - MasterCard

240

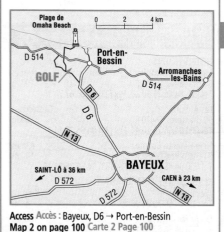

Access Accès : Bayeux, D6 → Port-en-Bessin
Map 2 on page 100 Carte 2 Page 100

GOLF COURSE
PARCOURS
14/20

Site	Site	
Maintenance	Entretien	
Architect	Architecte	Yves Bureau
Type	Type	bord de mer, bocage
Relief	Relief	
Water in play	Eau en jeu	
Exp. to wind	Exposé au vent	
Trees in play	Arbres en jeu	

Scorecard Carte de score	**Chp.** Chp.	**Mens** Mess.	**Ladies** Da.
Length Long.	6229	5867	5384
Par	72	72	72

Advised golfing ability
Niveau de jeu recommandé

0	12	24	36

Hcp required Handicap exigé non

CLUB HOUSE & AMENITIES
CLUB HOUSE ET ANNEXES
7/10

Pro shop	Pro-shop	
Driving range	Practice	
Sheltered	couvert	15 places
On grass	sur herbe	non
Putting-green	putting-green	oui
Pitching-green	pitching green	oui

HOTEL FACILITIES
ENVIRONNEMENT HOTELIER
5/10

HOTELS HÔTELS

Mercure Omaha Beach *** sur place
46 chambres, D 650 F
Tél (33) 02 31 22 44 44, Fax (33) 02 31 22 36 77

La Chenevière **** Commes
19 chambres, D 1 100 F 2 km
Tél (33) 02 31 21 47 96, Fax (33) 02 31 21 47 98

Château de Sully *** Bayeux
24 chambres, D 580 F 8 km
Tél (33) 02 31 22 29 48, Fax (33) 02 31 22 64 77

RESTAURANTS RESTAURANT

Marine Port-en-Bessin
Tél (33) 02 31 21 70 08 2 km

Château de Sully Bayeux
Tél (33) 02 31 22 29 48 6 km

Parcours traditionnel de la région de Cannes, Opio Valbonne vivait toujours sur sa réputation, mais les nouveaux parcours ont amené de nouvelles exigences, notamment par rapport à l'entretien, qui a été nettement amélioré. Dans un espace modérément accidenté, l'architecte Donald Harradine s'est appuyé sur la richesse de la végétation locale, sans bouleverser le paysage. On apprécie son aspect naturel , mais le dessin manque certainement de grandeur. Une petite rivière vient en jeu sur de nombreux trous, mais les obstacles principaux autour des petits greens sont des bunkers au dessin banal, dont le remodelage est en cours. Pas très long (surtout à l'aller), il se joue facilement, et la succession de deux par 5 pour terminer permet de sauver sa carte si besoin est. Le Club-House vient de bénéficier d'importants et bienvenus travaux de modernisation.

The traditional course in the region of Cannes, Opio Valbonne was still living on its reputation, but new courses in the neighbourhood have brought new requirements. This is particularly true for upkeep, which has much improved here. Set over rather hilly terrain, architect Donald Harradine focused on the wealth of the local vegetation without upsetting the landscape. You will enjoy the natural look to the course, but the layout definitely lacks ambition. A little river comes into play on many holes, but the main hazards around the small greens are the very ordinary bunkers, which happily are due to be redesigned shortly. This is not a very long course (especially the front nine) and it plays quite easily. The last two holes are easyish par 5s which can sometimes rescue your card if you are in trouble. The club-house has recently undergone significant modernisation work.

Golf Opio Valbonne

Château de la Bégude - Route de Roquefort-les-Pins
F - 06650 OPIO

Office	Secrétariat	(33) 04 93 12 00 08
Pro shop	Pro-shop	(33) 04 93 12 05 29
Fax	Fax	(33) 04 93 12 26 00
Situation	Situation	

10 km E. Grasse, 41 390 hab.

Annual closure	Fermeture annnuelle	non
Weekly closure	Fermeture hebdomadaire	

Fees main season
Tarifs haute saison le parcours

	Week days Semaine	We/Bank holidays We/Férié
Individual Individuel	320 F	350 F
Couple Couple	640 F	700 F

Caddy	Caddy	non
Electric Trolley	Chariot électrique	100 F/18 trous
Buggy	Voiturette	200 F/18 trous
Clubs	Clubs la série	100 F/18 trous

Credit cards Cartes de crédit
VISA - CB - Eurocard - MasterCard - AMEX - JCB

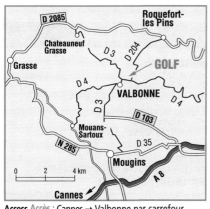

Access Accès : Cannes → Valbonne par carrefour
Saint-Basile puis Roquefort-les-Pins
Map 14 on page 125 Carte 14 Page 125

GOLF COURSE
PARCOURS
13 /20

Site	Site	
Maintenance	Entretien	
Architect	Architecte	Donald Harradine
Type	Type	forêt, parc
Relief	Relief	
Water in play	Eau en jeu	
Exp. to wind	Exposé au vent	
Trees in play	Arbres en jeu	

Scorecard Carte de score	Chp. Chp.	Mens Mess.	Ladies Da.
Length Long.	5931	5931	4963
Par	72	72	72

Advised golfing ability			0	12	24	36
Niveau de jeu recommandé						
Hcp required	Handicap exigé	35				

CLUB HOUSE & AMENITIES
CLUB HOUSE ET ANNEXES
6 /10

Pro shop	Pro-shop	
Driving range	Practice	
Sheltered	couvert	non
On grass	sur herbe	non
Putting-green	putting-green	oui
Pitching-green	pitching green	oui

241

HOTEL FACILITIES
ENVIRONNEMENT HOTELIER
7 /10

HOTELS HÔTELS

Hôtel du Golf *** — sur place
32 chambres, D 490 F
Tél (33) 04 93 12 21 05, Fax (33) 04 93 12 29 95

Pullman **** — Sophia-Antipolis
104 chambres, D 690 F — 4 km S.E.
Tél (33) 04 92 96 68 78, Fax (33) 04 92 96 68 96

RESTAURANTS Restaurant

Auberge du Colombier — Roquefort-les-Pins
Tél (33) 04 93 77 10 27 — 3 km

L'Auberge Fleurie — Valbonne
Tél (33) 04 93 12 02 80 — 2 km

Bistro de Valbonne — Valbonne
Tél (33) 04 93 12 05 59 — 2 km

Dans un superbe parc plat, mais avec un sol parfois humide, de larges avenues bordées de grands arbres offrent le sentiment d'espace que l'on attend d'un golf. Même si certains trous restent assez étroits pour exiger un jeu précis, les longs frappeurs trouveront aussi de quoi s'exprimer. On peut regretter que les fairways ne soient guère modelés, ce qui facilite le jeu, il est vrai, mais les meilleurs joueurs n'y trouveront pas tout à fait un test complet de leur jeu. Les bunkers sont avec les arbres les principaux obstacles, l'eau ne venant en jeu que sur deux trous. Golf de membres, c'est le parcours le plus "parisien" à l'est de Paris, comme en témoigne le très bourgeois Club-House, une vénérable maison de maître. Un très décent parcours de 9 trous, avec beaucoup d'obstacles d'eau, complète cet équipement de bon niveau, sinon exceptionnel.

In a beautiful, flat park which is sometimes a little damp underfoot, wide fairways lined by tall trees give the feeling of space you expect from a golf course. Although some holes are rather tight and demand precision play, long-hitters can let fly at Ozoir. We thought it a shame that no contouring has been done to the fairways. True, they are easier to play as they are, but they could be made more challenging for the better players. Bunkers and trees are the main hazards, as water enters the fray on only two holes. Very much a "members' club", Ozoir is the most "Parisian" course to the east of Paris, as seen with the classy clubhouse, a fine mansion. A very decent 9-holer with a lot of water hazards completes this excellent, if not to say exceptional, golfing complex.

Ozoir-la-Ferrière

Château des Agneaux
F - 77330 OZOIR-LA-FERRIERE

Office	Secrétariat	(33) 01 60 02 60 79
Pro shop	Pro-shop	(33) 01 64 40 18 51
Fax	Fax	(33) 01 64 40 28 20
Situation	Situation	

36 km E. Paris, 2 175 200 hab.
5 km S.E. Pontault-Combault, 26 800 hab.

Annual closure	Fermeture annnuelle	non
Weekly closure	Fermeture hebdomadaire	

Fees main season
Tarifs haute saison la journée

	Week days Semaine	We/Bank holidays We/Férié
Individual Individuel	200 F	400 F
Couple Couple	400 F	800 F

Caddy	Caddy	non
Electric Trolley	Chariot électrique	non
Buggy	Voiturette	200 F/18 trous
Clubs	Clubs 1/2 série	80 F/18 trous

Credit cards Cartes de crédit
VISA - CB - Eurocard - MasterCard

242

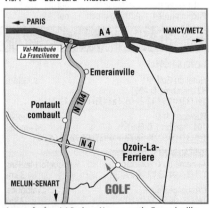

← PARIS

A 4   NANCY/METZ

Val-Maubuée
La Francilienne

Emerainville

N 104

Pontault
combault

N 4

Ozoir-La-
Ferrière

MELUN-SENART

GOLF

Access Accès : A4 Paris → Nancy, sortie Emerainville.
N104 (la Francilienne) → Pontault-Combault,
N4 → Ozoir-la-Ferrière
Map 15 on page 127 Carte 15 Page 127

GOLF COURSE
PARCOURS   13/20

Site	Site	
Maintenance	Entretien	
Architect	Architecte	
Type	Type	parc
Relief	Relief	
Water in play	Eau en jeu	
Exp. to wind	Exposé au vent	
Trees in play	Arbres en jeu	

Scorecard Carte de score	Chp. Chp.	Mens Mess.	Ladies Da.
Length Long.	6085	5720	5220
Par	71	71	71

Advised golfing ability		0 12 24 36
Niveau de jeu recommandé		
Hcp required	Handicap exigé	24 Mess. 28 Da.

CLUB HOUSE & AMENITIES
CLUB HOUSE ET ANNEXES   7/10

Pro shop	Pro-shop	
Driving range	Practice	
Sheltered	couvert	2 places
On grass	sur herbe	non
Putting-green	putting-green	oui
Pitching-green	pitching green	oui

HOTEL FACILITIES
ENVIRONNEMENT HOTELIER   5/10

HOTELS HÔTELS
Le Manoir ****   Fontenay-Trésigny
20 chambres, D 830 F   18 km
Tél (33) 01 64 25 91 17, Fax (33) 01 64 25 95 49

Château de la Grande Romaine ***   Lesigny
88 chambres, D 600 F   2 km
Tél (33) 01 60 02 26 01, Fax (33) 01 60 02 02 44

Le Pavillon Bleu **   Ozoir-la-Ferrière
38 chambres, D 300 F   2 km
Tél (33) 01 64 40 05 56, Fax (33) 01 64 40 29 74

RESTAURANTS RESTAURANT
Le Canadel   Pontault-Combault
Tél (33) 01 64 43 45 47   5 km

La Gueulardière   Ozoir-la-Ferrière
Tél (33) 01 60 02 94 56   2 km

PARIS INTERNATIONAL

16	7	5

Avec sa situation très favorable au nord de Paris et à proximité de l'aéroport Charles-de-Gaulle, ce parcours était d'autant plus espéré que son dessin a été confié à Jack Nicklaus. Mais autant on peut reconnaître sa patte sur une douzaine de trous, où un espace très ouvert lui permettait de donner sa pleine mesure, autant on a l'impression qu'il s'est trouvé moins à l'aise et à l'étroit dans les trous en forêt, où l'on a du mal à identifier sa signature, et où les très bons joueurs auront plus de mal à s'exprimer. Ces réserves viennent surtout du fait que l'on attendait beaucoup de Nicklaus, et pour garder le meilleur souvenir du parcours, on conseillera de commencer par le retour. A connaître néanmoins, mais on évitera les journées humides, que le terrain supporte mal (des travaux sont en cours pour y remédier).

Neatly located to the north of Paris close to Charles-de-Gaulle airport, this course was long awaited in that the designer was a one Jack Nicklaus. But as easily as you will recognize his style on a dozen or so holes, where wide open space gave him full scope od expression, as easily you will feel that the great man was not quite comfortable and a little cramped on the holes through the forest. Here, his style is not nearly as evident and even good players will have problems coming to terms with the course. These reservations are of course voiced because much was expected of Nicklaus. To get the best impression of this course, we would advise you to start from the 10th. Worth playing nonetheless, but avoid the wet days as the terrain does not take too well to water (a new drainage is planned).

Paris International Golf Club
18, route du Golf
F - 95560 BAILLET-en-FRANCE

Office	Secrétariat	(33) 01 34 69 90 00
Pro shop	Pro-shop	(33) 01 34 69 90 00
Fax	Fax	(33) 01 34 69 97 15
Situation	Situation	

30 km N de Paris, 2 175 200 hab.

Annual closure	Fermeture annnuelle	non
Weekly closure	Fermeture hebdomadaire	lundi

Fees main season
Tarifs haute saison 18 trous

	Week days Semaine	We/Bank holidays We/Férié
Individual Individuel	350 F	500 F
Couple Couple	700 F	1 000 F

Caddy	Caddy	sur réservation
Electric Trolley	Chariot électrique	80 F/18 trous
Buggy	Voiturette	200 F/18 trous
Clubs	Clubs	140 F/jour

Credit cards Cartes de crédit
VISA - CB - Eurocard - MasterCard - AMEX - DC - JCB

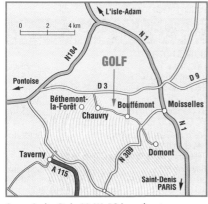

Access Accès : Paris, A1, N1. D3 à gauche →
Baillet-en-France
Map 15 on page 126 Carte 15 Page 126

GOLF COURSE PARCOURS

16/20

Site	Site	
Maintenance	Entretien	
Architect	Architecte	Jack Nicklaus
Type	Type	parc
Relief	Relief	
Water in play	Eau en jeu	
Exp. to wind	Exposé au vent	
Trees in play	Arbres en jeu	

Scorecard Carte de score	Chp. Chp.	Mens Mess.	Ladies Da.
Length Long.	6319	5905	4910
Par	72	72	72

Advised golfing ability		0 12 24 36
Niveau de jeu recommandé		
Hcp required	Handicap exigé	non

CLUB HOUSE & AMENITIES CLUB HOUSE ET ANNEXES

7/10

Pro shop	Pro-shop	
Driving range	Practice	
Sheltered	couvert	non
On grass	sur herbe	oui
Putting-green	putting-green	oui
Pitching-green	pitching green	oui

HOTEL FACILITIES ENVIRONNEMENT HOTELIER

5/10

HOTELS HÔTELS
Le Grand Hôtel — Enghien
45 chambres, D 750 F — 14 km
Tél (33) 01 34 12 80 00, Fax (33) 01 34 12 73 80

Campanile — Taverny
76 chambres, D 280 F — 10 km
Tél (33) 01 30 40 10 85, Fax (33) 01 30 40 10 87

Median — Goussainville
49 chambres, D 400 F — 10 km
Tél (33) 01 39 88 93 93, Fax (33) 01 39 88 75 65

RESTAURANTS RESTAURANT
Gai Rivage — L'Isle Adam
Tél (33) 01 34 69 01 09 — 9 km

Au Coeur de la Forêt — Montmorency
Tél (33) 01 39 64 99 19 — 11 km

243

PESSAC

Avec un 18 trous et un 9 trous, cet ensemble est principalement situé dans une pinède entourée de villas pas trop perturbantes. Le site était intéressant, mais l'architecte n'a malheureusement pas tiré la quintessence de ses possibilités. Beaucoup de trous se ressemblent, et donnent une impression de monotonie, même si l'environnement est agréable. Certaines difficultés sont peu gênantes pour les bons joueurs mais pénalisent inutilement les joueurs moyens, qui devront composer également avec la proximité de la forêt sur plusieurs trous. Les obstacles d'eau artificiels ont été joliment dessinés, et l'absence de relief permet de jouer plus de 18 trous dans la journée. Accessible aux joueurs de tous niveaux, ce parcours mérite une visite si l'on passe dans la région, d'autant que les travaux entrepris ont amélioré l'entretien du terrain de nature sablonneuse, en particulier les greens.

An 18-hole and 9-hole golf resort is sited primarily in a pine forest, surrounded by a number of unobtrusive villas. The site was an interesting one but the architect unfortunately failed to make the most of its potential. A lot of holes are similar and create an impression of monotony, even though the surroundings are very pleasant. Some hazards don't really bother the better players but do needlessly penalise the mid-handicappers, who also have to cope with an encroaching forest on several holes. The artificial water hazards have been prettily designed and the course's flatness makes 18 holes an easy proposition in one day. Accessible to players of all abilities, Pessac is well worth a visit if you are in the region, especially since maintenance work has considerably improved the state of the sandy terrain, particularly the greens.

Golf de Pessac
Rue de la Princesse
F - 33600 PESSAC

Office	Secrétariat	(33) 05 57 26 03 33
Pro shop	Pro-shop	(33) 05 57 26 03 33
Fax	Fax	(33) 05 56 36 52 89
Situation	Situation	

10 km S.O. Bordeaux, 211 200 hab.

Annual closure	Fermeture annnuelle	non
Weekly closure	Fermeture hebdomadaire	

Fees main season
Tarifs haute saison la journée

	Week days Semaine	We/Bank holidays We/Férié
Individual Individuel	200 F	260 F
Couple Couple	400 F	520 F

Mardi : Dames, 130 F - Jeudi : Seniors, 130 F

Caddy	Caddy	non
Electric Trolley	Chariot électrique	non
Buggy	Voiturette	120 F/18 trous
Clubs	Clubs 1/2 série	60 F/jour

Credit cards Cartes de crédit
VISA - CB - Eurocard - MasterCard - AMEX - DC

GOLF COURSE
PARCOURS
13/20

Site	Site	
Maintenance	Entretien	
Architect	Architecte	Olivier Brizon
Type	Type	forêt, résidentiel
Relief	Relief	
Water in play	Eau en jeu	
Exp. to wind	Exposé au vent	
Trees in play	Arbres en jeu	

Scorecard Carte de score	Chp. Chp.	Mens Mess.	Ladies Da.
Length Long.	6242	5848	5465
Par	72	72	72

Advised golfing ability		0 12 24 36
Niveau de jeu recommandé		
Hcp required	Handicap exigé	non

CLUB HOUSE & AMENITIES
CLUB HOUSE ET ANNEXES
7/10

Pro shop	Pro-shop	
Driving range	Practice	
Sheltered	couvert	10 places
On grass	sur herbe	oui
Putting-green	putting-green	oui
Pitching-green	pitching green	oui

HOTEL FACILITIES
ENVIRONNEMENT HOTELIER
7/10

HOTELS HÔTELS

La Réserve **** — Pessac — 5 km
22 chambres, D 600 F
Tél (33) 05 56 07 13 28, Fax (33) 05 56 36 31 02

Le Relais de Margaux **** — Margaux — 35 km
31 chambres, D 700 F
Tél (33) 05 57 88 38 30, Fax (33) 05 57 88 31 73

Mercure Château-Chartrons *** — Bordeaux — 10 km
144 chambres, D 570 F
Tél (33) 05 56 43 15 00, Fax (33) 05 56 69 15 21

Bayonne *** — Bordeaux — 10 km
36 chambres, D 600 F
Tél (33) 05 56 48 00 88, Fax (33) 05 56 52 03 79

RESTAURANTS RESTAURANT

Le Chapon Fin - Tél (33) 05 56 79 10 10 — Bordeaux

Jean Ramey - Tél(33) 05 56 44 12 51 — Bordeaux

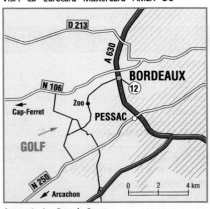

Access Accès : Rocade Ouest,
sortie No 12 → Zoo de Pessac
Map 9 on page 114 Carte 9 Page 114

Une jolie réussite signée par Alain Prat, en bordure de mer, sans pour autant se rattacher au style de links traditionnels. On remarquera une bonne montée en puissance des difficultés du parcours. De même que sur chacun des trous : les fairways sont généralement assez larges, ce qui facilite la plupart des tee-shots, mais les greens sont particulièrement défendus par de nombreux bunkers de sable et d'herbe, stratégiquement placés. Le trou le plus spectaculaire est le 11, un par 5 au départ arrière situé sur un éperon rocheux, dans la partie la plus accidentée du parcours. Mais ce n'est pas un golf trop fatiguant. On notera aussi la qualité particulière des installations d'entraînement, un bon entretien en toutes saisons, et de jolis points de vue, mais le Club house ne mérite sans doute pas les mêmes compliments.

A pretty layout by Alain Prat along the sea-shore, but without the traditional links style. Difficulties gradually increase as the day wears on, a good thing, and each hole has generally rather wide fairways for easier tee-shots. However, the greens are well defended by numerous bunkers and dips, all strategically located. The most spectacular hole is the 11th, a par 5 whose back-tee is placed on a rocky spur on the hilliest part of the course. But there is nothing too tiring about Pleneuf. Practice facilities are very good, as is upkeep in all seasons. There are also some pretty viewpoints, but unfortunately there is not too much that can be said in favour of the club-house.

Golf de Pléneuf-Val-André

Rue de la Plage des Vallées
F - 22370 PLENEUF-VAL-ANDRE

Office	Secrétariat	(33) 02 96 63 01 12
Pro shop	Pro-shop	(33) 02 96 63 01 12
Fax	Fax	(33) 02 96 63 01 06
Situation	Situation	

25 km N.O. Saint-Brieuc, 44 750 hab.

Annual closure	Fermeture annnuelle	non
Weekly closure	Fermeture hebdomadaire	

Fees main season
Tarifs haute saison le parcours

	Week days Semaine	We/Bank holidays We/Férié
Individual Individuel	250 F	250 F
Couple Couple	500 F	500 F

Caddy	Caddy	non
Electric Trolley	Chariot électrique	60 F/18 trous
Buggy	Voiturette	120 F/18 trous
Clubs	Clubs 1/2 série	50 F/jour

Credit cards Cartes de crédit
VISA - CB - Eurocard - MasterCard - AMEX - DC

GOLF
Le Val-Andre
D 786
Pleneuf-Val-André
D 17
Le Poirier
D 17A
Planguenoual
D 791
D 786

0   2   4 km

Access Accès : Saint-Brieuc, N12 → Lamballe, sortie Saint-René. D786 → Pléneuf- Val-André
Map 5 on page 107 Carte 5 Page 107

GOLF COURSE / PARCOURS — 17/20

Site	Site	
Maintenance	Entretien	
Architect	Architecte	Alain Prat
Type	Type	bord de mer
Relief	Relief	
Water in play	Eau en jeu	
Exp. to wind	Exposé au vent	
Trees in play	Arbres en jeu	

Scorecard Carte de score	Chp. Chp.	Mens Mess.	Ladies Da.
Length Long.	6052	5752	5125
Par	72	72	72

Advised golfing ability Niveau de jeu recommandé	0	12	24	36
Hcp required Handicap exigé	non			

CLUB HOUSE & AMENITIES / CLUB HOUSE ET ANNEXES — 7/10

Pro shop	Pro-shop	
Driving range	Practice	
Sheltered	couvert	10 places
On grass	sur herbe	oui
Putting-green	putting-green	oui
Pitching-green	pitching green	oui

245

HOTEL FACILITIES / ENVIRONNEMENT HOTELIER — 5/10

HOTELS HÔTELS
Grand Hôtel ** — Val-André
39 chambres, D 410 F — 1 km
Tél (33) 02 96 72 20 56, Fax (33) 02 96 63 00 24

Le Fanal ** — Fréhel
9 chambres, D 330 F — 17 km
Tél (33) 02 96 41 43 19

Manoir de Vaumadeuc **** — Pleven
14 chambres, D 850 F — 22 km
Tél (33) 02 96 84 46 17, Fax (33) 02 96 84 40 16

RESTAURANTS RESTAURANT
La Cotriade — Pléneuf-Val-André
Tél (33) 02 96 63 06 90 — 1 km

Le Haut Guen — Pléneuf-Val-André
Tél(33) 02 96 72 25 07

La Mer — Val-André
Tél(33) 02 96 72 20 44 — 1 km

A proximité de Lorient, un vaste espace de bord de mer et de campagne, sans guère plus de végétation que de bas buissons de lichens, mais dans le voisinage peu gracieux d'une grande carrière de sable et de gravier. Dommage, car ce parcours ouvert en 1990 et signé Quenouille est agréable, avec quelques jolis trous, des fairways bien fournis, des greens très corrects et de bons bunkers. Certains coups et approches sont assez techniques, mais les difficultés ne sont pas très accentuées, ce qui permet à tous les niveaux d'y évoluer simultanément. Quelques trous longent la mer, mais sans rendre vraiment un hommage évident aux parcours britanniques de situation analogue. Un plaisant parcours dans une région aujourd'hui bien fournie en golfs, mais il faut cependant en surveiller l'entretien. Le restaurant mérite une mention particulière.

Close to Lorient, a wide open space along the seaboard with hardly any more vegetation than a few low-cut lichen bushes, but set in a rather unsightly neighbourhood of a large sand and gravel quarry. This is a pity, because Ploemeur, designed by Quenouille and opened in 1990, is a pleasant course with a few pretty holes, well-grassed fairways, very decent greens and some good bunkers to boot. Some shots require a lot of technique but the difficulties are never excessive, so that players of all aspirations can enjoy a round together. A few holes run along the sea-shore, but there is nothing to obviously compare with British courses in a similar setting. A pleasant course in a region that today has more than its fair share of golfing facilities, but a tight rein needs to be kept on upkeep. The restaurant deserves a special mention.

Golf de Ploemeur Océan

Saint-Jude - Kerham
F - 56270 PLOEMEUR

Office	Secrétariat	(33) 02 97 32 81 82
Pro shop	Pro-shop	(33) 02 97 32 81 82
Fax	Fax	(33) 02 97 32 80 90
Situation	Situation	

10 km O. Lorient, 59 270 hab.

Annual closure	Fermeture annnuelle	non
Weekly closure	Fermeture hebdomadaire	

Fees main season
Tarifs haute saison le parcours

	Week days Semaine	We/Bank holidays We/Férié
Individual Individuel	250 F	250 F
Couple Couple	500 F	500 F

Caddy	Caddy	non
Electric Trolley	Chariot électrique	non
Buggy	Voiturette	150 F/18 trous
Clubs	Clubs 1/2 série	50 F/jour

Credit cards Cartes de crédit
VISA - CB - Eurocard - MasterCard

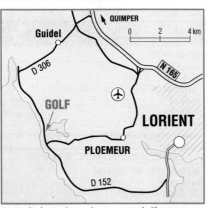

Access Accès : Lorient voie express sortie Ploemeur →
aéroport Lann-Bihoué → Fort Bloqué
Map 5 on page 106 Carte 5 Page 106

GOLF COURSE
PARCOURS

15/20

Site	Site	
Maintenance	Entretien	
Architect	Architecte	Quenouille & Macauley
Type	Type	bord de mer
Relief	Relief	
Water in play	Eau en jeu	
Exp. to wind	Exposé au vent	
Trees in play	Arbres en jeu	

Scorecard Carte de score	Chp. Chp.	Mens Mess.	Ladies Da.
Length Long.	5957	5495	4959
Par	72	72	72

Advised golfing ability	0 12 24 36	
Niveau de jeu recommandé		
Hcp required	Handicap exigé	non

CLUB HOUSE & AMENITIES
CLUB HOUSE ET ANNEXES

7/10

Pro shop	Pro-shop	
Driving range	Practice	
Sheltered	couvert	16 places
On grass	sur herbe	oui
Putting-green	putting-green	oui
Pitching-green	pitching green	non

HOTEL FACILITIES
ENVIRONNEMENT HOTELIER

6/10

HOTELS HÔTELS

Les Astéries ** 36 chambres, D 340 F Tél (33) 02 97 86 21 97, Fax (33) 02 97 86 34 33	Ploemeur 4 km
Le Vivier ** 14 chambres, D 400 F Tél (33) 02 97 82 99 60, Fax (33) 02 97 82 88 89	Lomener 6 km
Château de Locguénolé **** 22 chambres, D 1 200 F Tél (33) 02 97 76 29 04, Fax (33) 02 97 76 82 35	Hennebont 20 km

RESTAURANTS RESTAURANT

L'Amphitryon Tél (33) 02 97 83 34 04	Lorient 10 km
Le Poisson d'Or Tél(33) 02 97 21 57 06	Lorient 10 km
Château de Locguénolé Tél(33) 02 97 76 29 04	Hennebont 20 km

Premier parcours français signé par Ballesteros, Pont Royal bénéficie d'un excellent entretien. La dimension généreuse des bunkers peut réserver de longues sorties, spécialité du champion espagnol, et cauchemar des amateurs comme des professionnels. Avec de grands arbres, divers obstacles d'eau (rivière, étangs), quelques dangereux ravins, un relief assez accidenté (voiturette conseillée), Pont Royal réclame pas mal de technique, de sens tactique et une grande habileté dans le choix de clubs, ce qui le rendra difficile aux joueurs peu expérimentés. Les frappeurs auront de belles occasions de prendre des risques, avec émotions garanties. Plusieurs trous au dessin quelque peu torturé exigent d'être reconnus avant d'être négociés correctement, surtout quand souffle le mistral !

The first French course designed by Seve Ballesteros, Pont Royal is kept in excellent condition. The very large bunkers can lead to some very long escape shots from sand, one of the Spanish champion's specialities but often a nightmare for amateurs and pros alike. With large trees, various water hazards (a river and ponds), a few dangerous ravines and a hilly landscape (buggy recommended), Pont Royal requires a lot of technique, a good tactical mind and skill in choosing the right club. This makes it a difficult proposition for inexperienced players. Long-hitters have exciting opportunities to take risks, but several holes with a twisted layout need a little reconnaissance before hoping to make par, especially when the Mistral is blowing.

Pont Royal Golf Club
F - 13370 MALLEMORT

Office	Secrétariat	(33) 04 90 57 40 79
Pro shop	Pro-shop	(33) 04 90 57 40 79
Fax	Fax	(33) 04 90 59 45 83
Situation	Situation	

20 km N.E. Salon-de-Provence, 34 050 hab.

Annual closure	Fermeture annnuelle	non
Weekly closure	Fermeture hebdomadaire	

Fees main season
Tarifs haute saison le parcours

	Week days Semaine	We/Bank holidays We/Férié
Individual Individuel	300 F	300 F
Couple Couple	600 F	600 F

Caddy	Caddy	non
Electric Trolley	Chariot électrique	non
Buggy	Voiturette	200 F/18 trous
Clubs	Clubs série	100 F

Credit cards Cartes de crédit
VISA - CB - Eurocard - MasterCard

Access Accès : A7, sortie Sénas, N7 → Aix-en-Provence, golf à 10 km
Map 14 on page 124 Carte 14 Page 124

GOLF COURSE
PARCOURS

16/20

Site	Site	
Maintenance	Entretien	
Architect	Architecte	Seve Ballesteros
Type	Type	campagne, vallon
Relief	Relief	
Water in play	Eau en jeu	
Exp. to wind	Exposé au vent	
Trees in play	Arbres en jeu	

Scorecard Carte de score	Chp. Chp.	Mens Mess.	Ladies Da.
Length Long.	6307	6036	5356
Par	72	72	72

Advised golfing ability		0 12 24 36
Niveau de jeu recommandé		
Hcp required	Handicap exigé	35

CLUB HOUSE & AMENITIES
CLUB HOUSE ET ANNEXES

6/10

Pro shop	Pro-shop	
Driving range	Practice	
Sheltered	couvert	non
On grass	sur herbe	oui
Putting-green	putting-green	oui
Pitching-green	pitching green	non

HOTEL FACILITIES
ENVIRONNEMENT HOTELIER

5/10

HOTELS HÔTELS

Moulin de Vernègues ★★★★ — Vernègues
34 chambres, D 650 F — 1 km
Tél (33) 04 90 59 12 00, Fax (33) 04 90 59 15 90

Abbaye de Sainte-Croix ★★★ — Salon-de-Provence
24 chambres, D 900 F — 12 km
Tél (33) 04 90 56 24 55, Fax (33) 04 90 56 31 12

Angleterre — Salon-de-Provence
26 chambres, D 285 F — 20 km
Tél (33) 04 90 56 01 10, Fax (33) 04 90 56 71 75

RESTAURANTS RESTAURANT

Abbaye de Sainte-Croix — Salon-de-Provence
Tél (33) 04 90 56 24 55 — 12 km

Le Mas du Soleil — Salon-de-Provence
Tél(33) 04 90 56 06 53 — 12 km

247

14	6	4

Avec son relief accidenté et son sol, La Porcelaine est plus agréable à jouer aux beaux jours, du printemps à l'automne, quand la végétation prend des couleurs fort séduisantes. Ce parcours signé Jean Garaïalde a été conçu comme une alternative privée au golf de Limoges, le premier golf public en France. Des obstacles d'eau entrent en jeu sur la moitié des trous, et constituent, avec quelques arbres stratégiquement utilisés, les principales entraves à de bons scores. Ce parcours très "campagnard" a été destiné essentiellement à satisfaire l'ensemble des membres, résidents dans la région de Limoges, et reste jouable effectivement à tous niveaux. Cependant, les grands voyageurs de golf se livrent fatalement au jeu des comparaisons, et trouveront certainement son architecture sans éclat, et sans grandes surprises, mais son ambiance très agréable.

With its steep slopes and soil, La Porcelaine is most pleasant to play when the weather is at its best, from spring to autumn, and when the vegetation blooms into colour. This course, designed by French champion Jean Garaïalde, was designed as a private alternative to Limoges, France's first public course. Water hazards are in play on one half of the course and, along with some strategically located trees, are the main stumbling blocks to a good score. This is a very "country" style course, designed first and foremost to satisfy local members, and is effectively playable by golfers of all levels. However, hardened golf-trotters will make their usual and unavoidable comparisons and will certainly find that this design lacks sparkle and surprise. But a club with a very pleasant atmosphere.

Golf de la Porcelaine
Célicroux
F - 87350 PANAZOL

Office	Secrétariat	(33) 05 55 31 10 69
Pro shop	Pro-shop	(33) 05 55 31 10 69
Fax	Fax	(33) 05 55 31 10 69
Situation	Situation	

6 km N.E. Limoges, 133 460 hab.

Annual closure	Fermeture annnuelle	non
Weekly closure	Fermeture hebdomadaire	mardi
		du 01/10 → 31/03

Fees main season
Tarifs haute saison la journée

	Week days Semaine	We/Bank holidays We/Férié
Individual Individuel	200 F	200 F
Couple Couple	400 F	400 F

Caddy	Caddy	non
Electric Trolley	Chariot électrique	non
Buggy	Voiturette	150 F/18 trous
Clubs	Clubs	non

Credit cards Cartes de crédit
Visa - CB - Eurocard - MasterCard

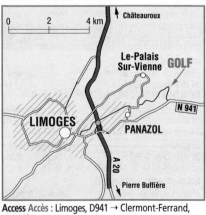

Access Accès : Limoges, D941 → Clermont-Ferrand, → Golf
Map 7 on page 110 Carte 7 Page 110

GOLF COURSE
PARCOURS **14**/20

Site	Site	
Maintenance	Entretien	
Architect	Architecte	Jean Garaïalde

Type	Type	campagne
Relief	Relief	
Water in play	Eau en jeu	
Exp. to wind	Exposé au vent	
Trees in play	Arbres en jeu	

Scorecard	Chp.	Mens	Ladies
Carte de score	Chp.	Mess.	Da.
Length Long.	6035	5562	5218
Par	72	72	72

Advised golfing ability		0	12	24	36
Niveau de jeu recommandé					
Hcp required	Handicap exigé	35			

CLUB HOUSE & AMENITIES
CLUB HOUSE ET ANNEXES **6**/10

Pro shop	Pro-shop	
Driving range	Practice	
Sheltered	couvert	4 places
On grass	sur herbe	oui
Putting-green	putting-green	oui
Pitching-green	pitching green	non

HOTEL FACILITIES
ENVIRONNEMENT HOTELIER **4**/10

HOTELS HÔTELS
Chapelle Saint-Martin ****   Saint-Martin-du-Fault
13 chambres, D 800 F   18 km
Tél (33) 05 55 75 80 17, Fax (33) 05 55 75 89 50

Royal Limousin ***   Limoges
77 chambres, D 680 F   6 km
Tél (33) 05 55 34 65 30, Fax (33) 05 55 34 55 21

Gd-Saint-Léonard **   Saint-Léonard-de-Noblat
14 chambres, D 300 F   13 km
Tél (33) 05 55 56 18 18, Fax (33) 05 55 56 98 32

RESTAURANTS RESTAURANT
Le Champlevé   Limoges
Tél (33) 05 55 34 43 34   6 km

Philippe Redon   Limoges
Tél (33) 05 55 34 66 22   6 km

PORNIC

A partir du neuf trous existant depuis 1929, Michel Gayon a reconstruit un 18 trous très intéressant en 1991, dans un espace assez accidenté. C'est une région traditionnelle de vacances, au sud de Nantes, mais il n'est jamais vraiment difficile d'y trouver un départ. De plus, le sol sablonneux permet de le recommander toute l'année. Cinq trous sont agrémentés de pins, les treize autres se trouvent dans une zone de bord de mer, où les fairways sont séparés par des buttes, créant ainsi un peu d'intimité. On regrettera qu'ils soient à peu près tous parallèles, mais cela permet aux frappeurs sauvages de s'écarter du droit chemin sans être trop pénalisés, ni menacer les joueurs de tous niveaux pouvant évoluer ici. Assez long des départs arrière, la disposition des départs permet cependant de se faire un parcours "à sa main".

Starting out with a 9-holer opened in 1929, Michel Gayon rebuilt a very interesting 18-hole course in 1991 over very hilly terrain. This is traditional holiday territory, to the south of Nantes, but getting a tee-off time poses no real problem. In addition, the sandy sub-soil is playable all year. Five holes are enhanced with pine-trees, the thirteen others run along the sea-shore, where the fairways are separated by sandhills and are sometimes a little too close together. It is a shame they all run more or less parallel, up and down, although this allows wild-hitters to wander off the straight and narrow without too much penalty and encourages players of all abilities to play here together. Rather long from the back, the number of different tees allows golfers to choose a course to suit their game.

Golf de Pornic
Avenue Sacalby-Newby
F - 44210 SAINTE-MARIE-SUR-MER

Office	Secrétariat	(33) 02 40 82 06 69
Pro shop	Pro-shop	(33) 02 40 82 06 69
Fax	Fax	(33) 02 40 82 80 65
Situation	Situation	

2 km O. Pornic, 9 810 hab.
52 km O. Nantes, 252 030 hab.

Annual closure	Fermeture annnuelle	non
Weekly closure	Fermeture hebdomadaire	mercredi
		en hiver (winter)

Fees main season Tarifs haute saison la journée

	Week days Semaine	We/Bank holidays We/Férié
Individual Individuel	240 F	240 F
Couple Couple	480 F	480 F

Caddy	Caddy	non
Electric Trolley	Chariot électrique	non
Buggy	Voiturette	150 F/18 trous
Clubs	Clubs 1/2 série	50 F/jour

Credit cards Cartes de crédit
VISA - CB - Eurocard - MasterCard

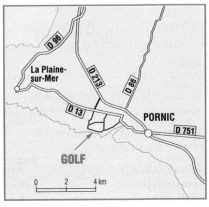

Access Accès : Nantes D751, sortie Pornic O.
→ Sainte-Marie-sur-Mer
Map 6 on page 108 Carte 6 Page 108

GOLF COURSE
PARCOURS **15**/20

Site	Site	
Maintenance	Entretien	
Architect	Architecte	Michel Gayon
		Jacques Lebreton
Type	Type	links, forêt
Relief	Relief	
Water in play	Eau en jeu	
Exp. to wind	Exposé au vent	
Trees in play	Arbres en jeu	

Scorecard	Chp.	Mens	Ladies
Carte de score	Chp.	Mess.	Da.
Length Long.	6112	5545	5017
Par	72	72	72

Advised golfing ability		0	12	24	36
Niveau de jeu recommandé					

Hcp required	Handicap exigé	non

CLUB HOUSE & AMENITIES
CLUB HOUSE ET ANNEXES **6**/10

Pro shop	Pro-shop	
Driving range	Practice	
Sheltered	couvert	6 places
On grass	sur herbe	oui
Putting-green	putting-green	oui
Pitching-green	pitching green	non

HOTEL FACILITIES
ENVIRONNEMENT HOTELIER **6**/10

HOTELS HÔTELS

Alliance ***
90 chambres, D 800 F
Tél (33) 02 40 82 21 21, Fax (33) 02 40 82 80 89
Pornic
2 km

Relais Saint-Giles **
28 chambres, D 350 F
Tél (33) 02 40 82 02 25Les Sablons **
30 chambres, D 420 F
Tél (33) 02 40 82 09 14, Fax (33) 02 40 82 04 26
Pornic
2 km
Sainte-Marie
1 km

RESTAURANTS RESTAURANT

Le Beau Rivage
Tél (33) 02 40 82 03 08
Pornic
2 km

Anne de Bretagne
Tél(33) 02 40 21 54 72
La Plaine-sur-Mer
10 km

249

Un entretien très moyen ne rend pas justice à ce parcours d'inspiration très britannique, tracé par le professionnel français Patrice Léglise. Plusieurs trous inspirés de l'architecture de links ont été tracés en plaine, et les autres dans la même esthétique dans une belle forêt, au terrain assez humide. Le dessin des bunkers est particulièrement réussi, de même que leur placement très stratégique. L'ensemble est d'une grande franchise, les difficultés techniques sont réelles mais raisonnables, avec quelques obstacles d'eau d'apparence naturelle. Le 18, dans une allée bordée de grands arbres, est d'une esthétique "à la française" très adéquate pour le retour vers le château, autrefois utilisé comme décor du film "La Belle et la Bête" de Jean Cocteau, et que l'on aimerait voir restauré. Le parcours étant plat, il permet aux joueurs de tous âges d'y évoluer. A jouer en "saison sèche".

Poorish upkeep does not do justice to this very British style course, laid out by the French professional Patrice Léglise. There are several holes in open countryside that are reminiscent of the best links courses, while the others, equally attractive, run through a beautiful forest over rather damp terrain. The bunkers are particularly well-designed, as is their strategic positioning. The whole course is an honest test of golf with real but reasonable technical difficulties and a few natural-looking water hazards. The 18th hole, laid out along a wide alley edged by large trees is very French in style and a suitable way to return to the castle which, may it be said, was used for filming "The Beauty and the Beast" by Jean Cocteau. A little restoration work here would be welcome. A flat course for golfers of all ages, but preferably in dry weather.

Château de Raray
4, rue Nicolas-de-Lancy
F - 60810 RARAY

Office	Secrétariat	(33) 03 44 54 70 61
Pro shop	Pro-shop	(33) 03 44 54 70 61
Fax	Fax	(33) 03 44 54 74 97
Situation	Situation	

6 km N.E. Senlis, 14 430 hab.
54 km N.E. Paris, 2 175 200 hab.

Annual closure	Fermeture annnuelle	non
Weekly closure	Fermeture hebdomadaire	mardi

Fees main season
Tarifs haute saison la journée

	Week days Semaine	We/Bank holidays We/Férié
Individual Individuel	220 F	400 F
Couple Couple	440 F	700 F

We après 15 H 30, GF 250 F

Caddy	Caddy	non
Electric Trolley	Chariot électrique	non
Buggy	Voiturette	150 F/18 trous
Clubs	Clubs série	100 F/jour

Credit cards Cartes de crédit
VISA - CB - Eurocard - MasterCard

250

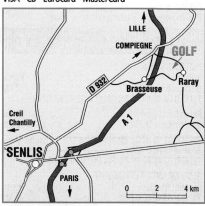

LILLE
COMPIEGNE
GOLF
D 932
Brasseuse
Raray
Creil
Chantilly
A1
SENLIS
PARIS
0   2   4 km

Access Accès : A1 Paris Lille, sortie No 8 Senlis → Creil Chantilly, D932 → Compiègne, → Château de Raray
Map 1 on page 98 Carte 1 Page 98

GOLF COURSE
PARCOURS   **14**/20

Site	Site	▮▮▭▭
Maintenance	Entretien	▮▮▭▭
Architect	Architecte	Patrice Léglise
Type	Type	plaine, forêt
Relief	Relief	▮▭▭▭
Water in play	Eau en jeu	▮▮▭▭
Exp. to wind	Exposé au vent	▮▮▮▭
Trees in play	Arbres en jeu	▮▮▮▭

Scorecard Carte de score	Chp. Chp.	Mens Mess.	Ladies Da.
Length Long.	6455	5915	5460
Par	72	72	72

Advised golfing ability		0 12 24 36
Niveau de jeu recommandé		
Hcp required	Handicap exigé	35 (We)

CLUB HOUSE & AMENITIES
CLUB HOUSE ET ANNEXES   **6**/10

Pro shop	Pro-shop	▮▮▮▭
Driving range	Practice	▮▮▭▭
Sheltered	couvert	8 places
On grass	sur herbe	oui
Putting-green	putting-green	oui
Pitching-green	pitching green	oui

HOTEL FACILITIES
ENVIRONNEMENT HOTELIER   **4**/10

HOTELS HÔTELS
Château de Raray ★★★★   sur place
10 chambres, D 1 200 F
Tél (33) 03 44 54 70 61, Fax (33) 03 44 54 74 97

Auberge de Fontaine   Fontaine-Chaalis
7 chambres, D 275 F   11 km
Tél (33) 03 44 54 20 22, Fax (33) 03 44 60 25 38

RESTAURANTS RESTAURANT
Le Vieux Logis   Fleurines
Tél (33) 03 44 54 10 13   10 km

La Maison du Gourmet   Le Meux
Tél (33) 03 44 91 10 10   12 km

16 6 4

Toujours avec ses excellents greens (notamment en hiver), ce parcours reconnu pour la qualité et la variété de son architecture (Jean-Pascal Fourès), a beaucoup profité de la pousse des nombreuses plantations. Les zones de plaine constituant la majorité du terrain sont ainsi bien mieux paysagées, et les différents trous mieux délimités. Relativement aisé par beau temps, il devient plus complexe avec le vent, souvent fréquent ici, comme sur un links, auxquels certains trous font référence. L'eau vient en jeu sur huit trous, complétant bien la diversité des obstacles rencontrés. Les greens sont souvent très modelés, et les placements de drapeau peuvent en modifier considérablement l'attaque. Sans être absolument exceptionnel, ce parcours a magnifiquement utilisé un budget limité. Le Club-House est une véritable maison de campagne où l'accueil est chaleureux.

With the greens as good as ever (especially in winter) and on a par with the quality and variety of architecture (designed by Jean-Pascal Fourès) which has helped to build the course's excellent reputation, Rebetz is all the better now the extensive plantation programme has started to take root. The areas of open countryside which form the largest part of the course are much better landscaped and the holes have gained in individuality. Relatively easy in fine weather, the frequent wind makes playing golf a trickier business, rather as if playing a links course. Indeed, a few holes could be taken as seaside holes. Water is in play on eight holes and completes the diversity of the course's hazards. The greens are often well-contoured and pin-positions can considerably change the configuration of approach shots. Without being really exceptional, the course has put restricted resources to magnificent use. The club-house is a genuine country-style manor and extends a warm welcome to all.

Golf Club de Rebetz

Route de Noailles
F - 60240 CHAUMONT-EN-VEXIN

Office	Secrétariat	(33) 03 44 49 15 54
Pro shop	Pro-shop	(33) 03 44 49 15 54
Fax	Fax	(33) 03 44 49 14 26
Situation	Situation	

67 km N.O. Paris,2 175 200 hab.
10 km E. Gisors, 9 480 hab.

Annual closure	Fermeture annnuelle	non
Weekly closure	Fermeture hebdomadaire	

Fees main season
Tarifs haute saison la journée

	Week days Semaine	We/Bank holidays We/Férié
Individual Individuel	150 F	350 F
Couple Couple	300 F	700 F

Vendredi : GF 100 F

Caddy	Caddy	non
Electric Trolley	Chariot électrique	non
Buggy	Voiturette	200 F/18 trous
Clubs	Clubs 1/2 série	60 F/jour

Credit cards Cartes de crédit
VISA - CB - Eurocard - MasterCard

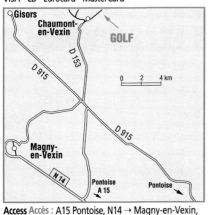

Access Accès : A15 Pontoise, N14 → Magny-en-Vexin,
D153 à droite → Chaumont-en-Vexin, → Golf à
Chaumont-en-Vexin
Map 1 on page 98 Carte 1 Page 98

GOLF COURSE
PARCOURS

16/20

Site	Site	
Maintenance	Entretien	
Architect	Architecte	Jean-Pascal Fourès
Type	Type	parc, plaine
Relief	Relief	
Water in play	Eau en jeu	
Exp. to wind	Exposé au vent	
Trees in play	Arbres en jeu	

Scorecard Carte de score	Chp. Chp.	Mens Mess.	Ladies Da.
Length Long.	6409	5885	5317
Par	73	73	73

Advised golfing ability	0	12	24	36
Niveau de jeu recommandé				
Hcp required Handicap exigé	35 We			

CLUB HOUSE & AMENITIES
CLUB HOUSE ET ANNEXES

6/10

Pro shop	Pro-shop	
Driving range	Practice	
Sheltered	couvert	14 places
On grass	sur herbe	oui
Putting-green	putting-green	oui
Pitching-green	pitching green	non

HOTEL FACILITIES
ENVIRONNEMENT HOTELIER

4/10

HOTELS HÔTELS

Château de la Rapée ***		Bazincourt-sur-Epte
12 chambres, D 550 F		13 km
Tél (33) 02 32 55 11 61, Fax (33) 02 32 55 95 65		
Moderne **		Gisors
30 chambres, D 300 F		10 km
Tél (33) 02 32 55 23 51, Fax (33) 02 32 55 08 75		

RESTAURANTS RESTAURANT

La Halte Henri II		Gisors
Tél (33) 02 32 27 37 37		10 km
Le Cygne		Gisors
Tél (33) 02 33 55 23 76		10 km

251

Relativement plat et dans un espace très agréablement boisé, c'est une sorte de grand domaine avec un joli château où tous les grands noms du Champagne ont laissé leur marque. Mais on peut aussi trouver de l'eau au bar du Club-house... Les 9 trous construits en 1927 ont été remodelés et portés à 18 trous par Michael Fenn en 1977. Leur dessin suit les contours du terrain sans imagination particulière et seuls les par 5 sortent un peu de l'ordinaire. Les arbres constituent les principaux obstacles, mais ils font plus de peur que de mal. En dépit d'un assez bon rythme de jeu, on ne fera certainement pas de long détour pour venir jouer ici, mais si l'on passe dans la région, la visite sera sympathique et amusante. Nous sommes peut-être difficiles, mais on imagine qu'il serait possible de remodeler le parcours sans lui retirer son caractère familial.

Relatively flat but in a pleasant woodland setting, this is a sort of large estate around a pretty castle where all the great names in champagne have left their mark. But it's also possible to order water at the bar... Originally a nine-hole course opened in 1927, it was upgraded to 18 holes by Michael Fenn in 1977. The layout follows the contours of the terrain without too much imagination, and only the par 5s really stand out. The main hazards here are the trees, but their bark (no pun intended) is worse than their bite. Despite a good playing tempo, it is hard to envisage making any long detour to come and play here, but if you are in the region, Reims-Champagne is a pleasant and amusing visit. Perhaps we are being a little too hard, but we believe this course could be redesigned for the better without detracting from its family-style character.

Reims-Champagne
Château des Dames de France
F - 51390 GUEUX

Office	Secrétariat	(33) 03 26 05 46 10
Pro shop	Pro-shop	(33) 03 26 03 49 82
Fax	Fax	(33) 03 26 05 46 19
Situation	Situation	

5 km O. Reims, 180 620 hab.

Annual closure	Fermeture annnuelle	non
Weekly closure	Fermeture hebdomadaire	lundi, restaurant (11→ 03)

Fees main season
Tarifs haute saison la journée

	Week days Semaine	We/Bank holidays We/Férié
Individual Individuel	200 F	250 F
Couple Couple	400 F	500 F

Caddy	Caddy	non
Electric Trolley	Chariot électrique	non
Buggy	Voiturette	100 F/18 trous
Clubs	Clubs 1/2 série	90 F/jour

Credit cards Cartes de crédit
VISA - CB

252

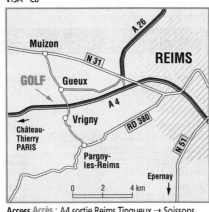

GOLF Gueux

Muizon

A 26

N 31

REIMS

A 4

Vrigny

RD 380

Château-Thierry
PARIS

Pargny-les-Reims

N 51

Epernay

0   2   4 km

Access Accès : A4 sortie Reims Tinqueux → Soissons,
→ Gueux
Map 3 on page 103 Carte 3 Page 103

GOLF COURSE PARCOURS 13/20

Site	Site	
Maintenance	Entretien	
Architect	Architecte	Michael Fenn
Type	Type	parc, forêt
Relief	Relief	
Water in play	Eau en jeu	
Exp. to wind	Exposé au vent	
Trees in play	Arbres en jeu	

Scorecard Carte de score	Chp. Chp.	Mens Mess.	Ladies Da.
Length Long.	6042	5902	5097
Par	72	72	72

Advised golfing ability Niveau de jeu recommandé	0	12	24	36

Hcp required   Handicap exigé   35

CLUB HOUSE & AMENITIES CLUB HOUSE ET ANNEXES 7/10

Pro shop	Pro-shop	
Driving range	Practice	
Sheltered	couvert	4 places
On grass	sur herbe	non
Putting-green	putting-green	oui
Pitching-green	pitching green	oui

HOTEL FACILITIES ENVIRONNEMENT HOTELIER 6/10

HOTELS HÔTELS
Les Crayères ****   Reims
16 chambres, D 1 300 F   5 km
Tél (33) 03 26 82 80 80, Fax (33) 03 26 82 65 52

Grand Hôtel des Templiers ****   Reims
19 chambres, D 1 200 F   5 km
Tél (33) 03 26 88 55 08, Fax (33) 03 26 47 80 60

La Paix ***   Reims
104 chambres, D 600 F   5 km
Tél (33) 03 26 40 04 08, Fax (33) 03 26 47 75 04

RESTAURANTS RESTAURANT
Les Crayères   Reims
Tél (33) 03 26 82 80 80   5 km

Royal Champagne   Epernay
Tél (33) 03 26 52 87 11   6 km

Non loin du parcours centenaire de Mandelieu, le Riviera s'inscrit dans un paysage totalement différent, démontrant la diversité des paysages français dans un espace pourtant réduit. Quelques trous assez plats et larges contrastent avec des trous "de montagne" souvent étroits et déconcertants par leur dessin. Les arbres, de nombreux bunkers et quelques obstacles d'eau créent de nombreuses difficultés, accentuées par des greens surélevés (parfois aveugles) et les dénivellations, qui amènent à conseiller de jouer en voiturette. Originalité : il n'y a que trois par 3, ce qui offre un par 72 malgré une longueur réduite, en raison de l'espace limité. Certains trous manquent singulièrement de franchise, et les visiteurs connaissant mal le parcours seront bien inspirés de jouer sans se soucier du score. Un golf parfois surprenant, au rythme heurté, où il faut garder la tête froide.

Not far from the centenary course of Cannes-Mandelieu, the Riviera course is located in a totally different setting, as if to demonstrate the variety of French landscapes over a relatively limited surface area. A few flat and wide holes are in stark contrast with the mountain-style holes, which are often tight and confusing in layout. The trees, countless bunkers and a few water hazards create a lot of problems, emphasised by elevated (and sometimes blind) greens and by steep slopes (buggy recommended). The course is original in having only 3 par 3s, still giving a par 72 despite the restricted yardage owing to shortage of space. Some holes are singularly lacking in openness and visitors who are not familiar with the course would be well advised to forget any idea of keeping score. A sometimes surprising course and a little unevenly balanced. A cool head can see you home safely.

Riviéra Golf Club

Avenue des Amazones
F - 06210 MANDELIEU-LA NAPOULE

Office	Secrétariat	(33) 04 92 97 67 67
Pro shop	Pro-shop	(33) 04 90 97 59 28
Fax	Fax	(33) 04 92 97 66 57
Situation	Situation	

8 km O. Cannes, 68 670 hab.

Annual closure	Fermeture annnuelle	non
Weekly closure	Fermeture hebdomadaire	non
		mercredi, le restaurant

Fees main season
Tarifs haute saison le parcours

	Week days Semaine	We/Bank holidays We/Férié
Individual Individuel	270 F	270 F
Couple Couple	540 F	540 F

Caddy	Caddy	non
Electric Trolley	Chariot électrique	non
Buggy	Voiturette	170 F/18 trous
Clubs	Clubs 1/2 série	50 F/jour

Credit cards Cartes de crédit
VISA - MasterCard

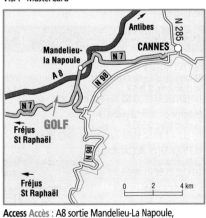

Access Accès : A8 sortie Mandelieu-La Napoule,
RN7 → Fréjus
Map 14 on page 125 Carte 14 Page 125

GOLF COURSE
PARCOURS

13/20

Site	Site	
Maintenance	Entretien	
Architect	Architecte	R. Trent Jones Sr
Type	Type	vallon, résidentiel
Relief	Relief	
Water in play	Eau en jeu	
Exp. to wind	Exposé au vent	
Trees in play	Arbres en jeu	

Scorecard Carte de score	Chp. Chp.	Mens Mess.	Ladies Da.
Length Long.	5736	5195	4830
Par	72	72	72

Advised golfing ability Niveau de jeu recommandé	0	12	24	36
Hcp required Handicap exigé	35			

CLUB HOUSE & AMENITIES
CLUB HOUSE ET ANNEXES

7/10

Pro shop	Pro-shop	
Driving range	Practice	
Sheltered	couvert	non
On grass	sur herbe	oui
Putting-green	putting-green	oui
Pitching-green	pitching green	oui

253

HOTEL FACILITIES
ENVIRONNEMENT HOTELIER

8/10

HOTELS HÔTELS

Hôtellerie du Golf ***		Mandelieu
55 chambres, D 640 F		2 km
Tél (33) 04 93 49 11 66, Fax (33) 04 92 97 04 01		

Majestic ****		Cannes
263 chambres, D 2 200 F		8 km
Tél (33) 04 92 98 77 00, Fax (33) 04 93 38 97 90		

Paris ***		Cannes
50 chambres, D 650 F		8 km
Tél (33) 04 93 38 30 89, Fax (33) 04 93 39 04 61		

RESTAURANTS RESTAURANT

La Palme d'Or		Cannes
Tél (33) 04 92 98 74 14		8 km

La Belle Otéro		Cannes
Tél (33) 04 93 39 69 69		8 km

ROCHEFORT-CHISAN 14 6 4

C'est toujours un plaisir de retrouver ce type de parcours en forêt, tel que l'on ne peut plus guère en construire aujourd'hui. Ce parcours classique, dessiné par Fred Hawtree, et ouvert en 1964, a été ensuite acquis par le groupe japonais Chisan. Ce parcours offre de magnifiques lumières au printemps et en automne, ajoutant à l'agrément du jeu sur un sol de sable et de terre de bruyère. On peut ainsi l'apparenter à des parcours " inland " tel que The Berkshire. Ce n'est sans doute pas un chef-d'Ïuvre absolu, mais il reste très plaisant à jouer, offrant une grande variété de coups, et nécessitant un bon travail des trajectoires de balle. Les obstacles sont essentiellement les arbres, souvent très dangereux car le parcours est assez étroit, mais aussi les bunkers de fairway et de green, et le relief, parfois assez accidenté pour troubler dans le choix de clubs.

It is always a pleasure to play this type of woodland course, which nowadays is virtually impossible to build. This classic layout, designed by Fred Hawtree, was opened in 1964 and subsequently purchased by the Japanese group Chisan. The light and reflections in spring and autumn are a joy to behold, adding to the pleasure of playing on sandy sub-soil and moor-land. This gives it much in common with inland courses such as The Berkshire. Rochefort is probably not an absolute masterpiece, but it is a very pleasant course to play, requiring a whole variety of shots and ball-control. The hazards are basically the trees, often dangerous as they lean over some pretty tight fairways. But don't forget the fairway and green-side bunkers, either, or the sharp relief which makes club selection harder than usual.

Rochefort-Chisan Country Club
Route de la Bâte
F - 78730 ROCHEFORT-EN-YVELINES

Office	Secrétariat	(33) 01 30 41 31 81
Pro shop	Pro-shop	(33) 01 30 41 31 81
Fax	Fax	(33) 01 30 41 94 01
Situation	Situation	

15 km S.E. Rambouillet, 24 340 hab.
45 km S.O. Paris, 2 175 200 hab.

Annual closure	Fermeture annnuelle	non
Weekly closure	Fermeture hebdomadaire	jeudi

Fees main season
Tarifs haute saison la journée

	Week days Semaine	We/Bank holidays We/Férié
Individual Individuel	250 F	450 F
Couple Couple	500 F	900 F

Dames : GF à 150 F le vendredi - Mercredi, 200 F

Caddy	Caddy	non
Electric Trolley	Chariot électrique	100 F/18 trous
Buggy	Voiturette	250 F/18 trous
Clubs	Clubs série	100 F/jour

Credit cards Cartes de crédit
VISA - CB - Eurocard - MasterCard - AMEX - DC - JCB

254

Access Accès : A10 Paris Chartres/Orléans,
sortie Dourdan
Map 15 on page 126 Carte 15 Page 126

GOLF COURSE
PARCOURS 14/20

Site	Site	
Maintenance	Entretien	
Architect	Architecte	Fred Hawtree
Type	Type	forêt
Relief	Relief	
Water in play	Eau en jeu	
Exp. to wind	Exposé au vent	
Trees in play	Arbres en jeu	

Scorecard Carte de score	Chp. Chp.	Mens Mess.	Ladies Da.
Length Long.	5735	5165	5165
Par	71	71	71

Advised golfing ability 0 12 24 36
Niveau de jeu recommandé
Hcp required Handicap exigé 24 Mess, 28 Da, le We

CLUB HOUSE & AMENITIES
CLUB HOUSE ET ANNEXES 6/10

Pro shop	Pro-shop	
Driving range	Practice	
Sheltered	couvert	8 places
On grass	sur herbe	non
Putting-green	putting-green	oui
Pitching-green	pitching green	oui

HOTEL FACILITIES
ENVIRONNEMENT HOTELIER 4/10

HOTELS HÔTELS
Abbaye les Vaux de Cernay *** Cernay-la-Ville
58 chambres, D 800 F 11 km
Tél (33) 01 34 85 23 00, Fax (33) 01 34 85 11 60

Auberge du Gros Marronnier Senlisse
16 chambres, D 375 F 13 km
Tél (33) 01 30 52 51 69, Fax (33) 01 30 52 55 91

RESTAURANTS RESTAURANT
La Brazoucade Rochefort-en-Yvelines
Tél (33) 01 30 41 49 09 2 km

L'Escu de Rohan Rochefort-en-Yvelines
Tél(33) 01 30 41 31 33 2 km

| 15 | 7 | 4 |

Tracé principalement en forêt de chênes, hêtres et bouleaux (avec une demi-douzaine de trous de style links), et sur un terrain peu accidenté, ce parcours porte sans aucun doute la signature de Jeremy Pern, pour le nombre et le dessin des bunkers, de fairways comme de défense des greens. Le dessin est assez varié pour exiger tous les types de coups, ou même offrir un choix entre les approches roulées à la britannique et le "jeu de cible" à l'américaine. Les obstacles d'eau sont peu nombreux et pas trop dangereux, tous les niveaux de jeu peuvent donc cohabiter sur ce golf plaisant, dans un décor très agréable. Les greens sont de bonne dimension, et généralement très modelés : attention aux trois putts...

This course is basically laid out through a forest of oak, beech and birch trees (plus half a dozen links holes) over flattish terrain. Looking at the number and design of bunkers, the fairways and greens, there is no doubt that this is a Jeremy Pern layout. The layout is varied enough to demand every shot in the book or even offer a choice between British "bump and run" shots and American-style target golf. Water hazards are few and far between and not too dangerous, so players of all abilities can play this pleasant course in a very attractive setting. The greens are large and slope a lot, so watch out for the 3 putts.

Domaine de Roncemay
F - 89110 CHASSY

Office	Secrétariat	(33) 03 86 73 50 50
Pro shop	Pro-shop	(33) 03 86 73 50 50
Fax	Fax	(33) 03 86 73 69 46
Situation	Situation	

19 km S. Joigny, 9 690 hab.
20 km N.O. Auxerre, 38 810 hab.

Annual closure	Fermeture annnuelle	non
Weekly closure	Fermeture hebdomadaire	

Fees main season
Tarifs haute saison la journée

	Week days Semaine	We/Bank holidays We/Férié
Individual Individuel	200 F	300 F
Couple Couple	400 F	600 F

Eté : 120 F après 17 H

Caddy	Caddy	non
Electric Trolley	Chariot électrique	85 F/18 trous
Buggy	Voiturette	200 F/18 trous
Clubs	Clubs 1/2 série	50 F/18 trous

Credit cards Cartes de crédit
VISA - CB - Eurocard - MasterCard

Access Accès : • Paris A6, sortie Joigny, → Golf • Lyon A6, sortie Auxerre Nord → Aillant-sur-Tholon par D 89, → Golf
Map 3 on page 103 Carte 3 Page 103

GOLF COURSE
PARCOURS
15/20

Site	Site	
Maintenance	Entretien	
Architect	Architecte	Jeremy Pern
Type	Type	forêt, plaine
Relief	Relief	
Water in play	Eau en jeu	
Exp. to wind	Exposé au vent	
Trees in play	Arbres en jeu	

Scorecard Carte de score	Chp. Chp.	Mens Mess.	Ladies Da.
Length Long.	6401	5808	5257
Par	72	72	72

Advised golfing ability Niveau de jeu recommandé	0	12	24	36
Hcp required Handicap exigé	35			

CLUB HOUSE & AMENITIES
CLUB HOUSE ET ANNEXES
7/10

Pro shop	Pro-shop	
Driving range	Practice	
Sheltered	couvert	12 places
On grass	sur herbe	oui, (04 → 10)
Putting-green	putting-green	oui
Pitching-green	pitching green	oui

HOTEL FACILITIES
ENVIRONNEMENT HOTELIER
4/10

HOTELS HÔTELS
A la Côte Saint-Jacques **** — Joigny — 19 km
29 chambres, D 1 000 F
Tél (33) 03 86 62 09 70, Fax (33) 03 86 91 49 70

Modern'Hôtel *** — Joigny — 19 km
21 chambres, D 400 F
Tél (33) 03 86 62 16 28, Fax (33) 03 86 62 44 33

Château de Prunoy — Prunoy — 24 km
11 chambres, D 600 F
Tél (33) 03 86 63 66 91, Fax (33) 03 86 63 77 79

RESTAURANTS RESTAURANT
La Côte Saint-Jacques — Joigny — 19 km
Tél (33) 03 86 62 09 70

Jean-Luc Barnabet — Auxerre — 20 km
Tél (33) 03 86 51 68 88

255

Robert von Hagge a intelligemment tiré profit d'un espace réduit, et créé un parcours excitant et spectacu-laire, qui ne laisse pas indifférent Au moins pour pouvoir en juger, Royal Mougins mérite une visite attentive. Certains joueurs discutent le "modernisme" du parcours comme son étroitesse, mais celle-ci est plus visuelle que réelle : certes, de nombreux mouvements de terrain animent de manière spectaculaire les limites de fair-way, mais ils ramènent volontiers la balle en jeu. Ici, il faut jouer avec sa tête, et rester précis, ne serait-ce que pour éviter les obstacles d'eau menaçants qui ponctuent le parcours. Mais comme sa longueur est raison-nable, les frappeurs peuvent facilement jouer leurs coups de départ avec un bois 3 ou un long fer. La plupart du temps, les seconds coups seront joués avec des petits et moyens fers, ce qui ne devrait pas poser de pro-blèmes aux joueurs expérimentés...

Robert von Hagge has made very intelligent use of limited space and created an exciting and spectacular course, with no room for indifference. Royal Mougins is well worth a close visit if only to judge for yourself. Some players question the course's modernism and tightness, but the latter is visual rather than real. We agree that the slanting terrain sometimes adds rather spectacular goings-on at the edges of the fairway, but it also helps bring the ball back into play. This is a course you play with your brains, where precision play is at a premium, if only to avoid the water hazards dotted around the 18 holes. But being of reasonable length, big-hitters can easily tee off with a 3-wood or long iron. Approach shots are played mostly with short or mid-irons, so experienced players should not find the going too tough...

Royal Mougins Golf Club
424, avenue du Roi
F - 06250 MOUGINS

Office	Secrétariat	(33) 04 92 92 49 69
Pro shop	Pro-shop	(33) 04 92 92 49 79
Fax	Fax	(33) 04 92 92 49 70
Situation	Situation	

10 km N. Cannes, 68 670 hab.
20 km S.E. Grasse, 41 390 hab.

Annual closure	Fermeture annnuelle	non
Weekly closure	Fermeture hebdomadaire	non
		mardi, le restaurant

Fees main season Tarifs haute saison la journée

	Week days Semaine	We/Bank holidays We/Férié
Individual Individuel	800 F	800 F
Couple Couple	1 600 F	1 600 F

800 F = GF journée (all-day) + practice + repas

Caddy	Caddy	sur réservation
Electric Trolley	Chariot électrique	70 F/18 trous
Buggy	Voiturette	100 F/18 trous
Clubs	Clubs série	100 F/jour

Credit cards Cartes de crédit
VISA - CB - Eurocard - MasterCard - AMEX

256

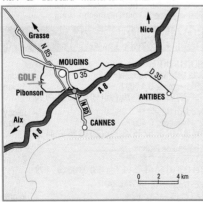
Grasse
Nice
MOUGINS
D 35
GOLF
D 35
Pibonson
ANTIBES
Aix
CANNES
N 85
A 8

0 2 4 km

Access Accès : A8 sortie Cannes-Grasse → Grasse, 3e sortie Mougins Pibonson, Saint-Martin
Map 14 on page 125 Carte 14 Page 125

GOLF COURSE
PARCOURS   17 /20

Site	Site	
Maintenance	Entretien	
Architect	Architecte	Robert von Hagge
Type	Type	forêt, vallon
Relief	Relief	
Water in play	Eau en jeu	
Exp. to wind	Exposé au vent	
Trees in play	Arbres en jeu	

Scorecard Carte de score	Chp. Chp.	Mens Mess.	Ladies Da.
Length Long.	6004	5697	4926
Par	71	71	71

Advised golfing ability	0	12	24	36
Niveau de jeu recommandé				
Hcp required Handicap exigé	30			

CLUB HOUSE & AMENITIES
CLUB HOUSE ET ANNEXES   7 /10

Pro shop	Pro-shop	
Driving range	Practice	
Sheltered	couvert	non
On grass	sur herbe	oui
Putting-green	putting-green	oui
Pitching-green	pitching green	oui

HOTEL FACILITIES
ENVIRONNEMENT HOTELIER   8 /10

HOTELS HÔTELS
Mas Candille ****	Mougins
23 chambres, D 900 F	3 km
Tél (33) 04 93 90 00 85, Fax (33) 04 92 92 85 56	
Hôtel de Mougins ****	Mougins
50 chambres, D 980 F	3 km
Tél (33) 04 92 92 17 07, Fax (33) 04 92 92 17 08	
Le Manoir de l'Etang ***	Mougins
15 chambres, D 900 F	3 km
Tél (33) 04 93 90 01 07, Fax (33) 04 92 92 20 70	

RESTAURANTS RESTAURANT
Les Muscadins	Mougins
Tél (33) 04 93 90 00 43	3 km
Le Feu Follet	Mougins
Tél(33) 04 93 90 15 78	3 km
La Ferme de Mougins	Mougins
Tél(33) 04 93 90 03 74	3 km

SABLÉ-SOLESMES FORÊT/RIVIÈRE 🏌 16 7 4

Entre les villes d'Angers et du Mans, cet ensemble de 27 trous s'est s'imposé dans le groupe de tête des parcours français, alors que l'on ne s'attendait pas à trouver des tracés d'une telle qualité en pleine campagne. Entre la Sarthe et la Forêt de Pincé, Michel Gayon a dessiné trois 9 trous combinables de longueur raisonnable et le terrain moyennement accidenté permet de les jouer tous en une seule journée. Sur la combinaison "La Forêt-La Rivière", l'eau intervient sur une dizaine de trous, sans être trop effrayant pour autant. "La Cascade" revendique un caractère plus écossais, avec beaucoup de bosses, de bunkers d'herbe et de sable, mais aussi un peu d'eau, comme au 8. On éprouve ici une très bonne impression d'espace et de calme, propice à la concentration que réclame ce golf à connaître, hors des circuits golfiques traditionnels.

Between Angers and Le Mans, this 27-hole complex has edged its way into the group of leading French courses at a time when no-one was expecting such a great layout right out in the country. Michel Gayon has designed three inter-combinable 9-hole courses of reasonable length, stretching between the river Sarthe and a large forest. On flattish terrain, all three can be played in one day. On the "Forêt-Rivière" combination, water is present on ten holes but is never too intimidating. "La Cascade" is more Scottish in nature, with lots of sandhills, grass- and sand-bunkers, and also a little water, like on the 8th. Here you get a great feeling of space and of tranquillity, suitable for the concentration required when playing a course like this. A club that is well worth discovering outside the traditional golfing circuits.

Golf de Sablé-Solesmes
Domaine de l'Outinière, route de Pincé
F - 72300 SABLE-SUR-SARTHE

Office	Secrétariat	(33) 02 43 95 28 78
Pro shop	Pro-shop	(33) 02 43 95 28 78
Fax	Fax	(33) 02 43 92 39 05
Situation	Situation	

26 km N.O. La Flèche, 14 950 hab.
59 km S.O. Le Mans, 145 500 hab.

Annual closure	Fermeture annnuelle	non
Weekly closure	Fermeture hebdomadaire	

Fees main season
Tarifs haute saison la journée

	Week days Semaine	We/Bank holidays We/Férié
Individual Individuel	220 F	280 F
Couple Couple	400 F	500 F

Caddy	Caddy	non
Electric Trolley	Chariot électrique	40 F/18 trous
Buggy	Voiturette	200 F/18 trous
Clubs	Clubs 1/2 série	60 F/jour

Credit cards Cartes de crédit
VISA - CB - Eurocard - MasterCard

Access Accès : Le Mans-Angers, A11 sortie La Flèche,
à droite D306 → Sablé-sur-Sarthe
Map 6 on page 109 Carte 6 Page 109

GOLF COURSE
PARCOURS
16/20

Site	Site	
Maintenance	Entretien	
Architect	Architecte	Michel Gayon
Type	Type	plaine, vallon
Relief	Relief	
Water in play	Eau en jeu	
Exp. to wind	Exposé au vent	
Trees in play	Arbres en jeu	

Scorecard Carte de score	Chp. Chp.	Mens Mess.	Ladies Da.
Length Long.	6207	5753	5250
Par	72	72	72

Advised golfing ability   0   12   24   36
Niveau de jeu recommandé
Hcp required   Handicap exigé   35

CLUB HOUSE & AMENITIES
CLUB HOUSE ET ANNEXES
7/10

Pro shop	Pro-shop	
Driving range	Practice	
Sheltered	couvert	7 places
On grass	sur herbe	oui
Putting-green	putting-green	oui
Pitching-green	pitching green	oui

257

HOTEL FACILITIES
ENVIRONNEMENT HOTELIER
4/10

HOTELS HÔTELS
Grand Hôtel ***   Solesmes
34 chambres, D 420 F   4 km
Tél (33) 02 43 95 45 10, Fax (33) 02 43 95 22 26

Haras de la Potardière ***   Crosnières
17 chambres, D 550 F   20 km
Tél (33) 02 43 45 83 47, Fax (33) 02 43 45 81 06

RESTAURANTS RESTAURANT
Escu du Roy   Sablé
Tél (33) 02 43 95 90 31   6 km

Hostellerie Saint-Martin   Sablé
Tél(33) 02 43 95 00 03   6 km

SAINT-CLOUD VERT

Etre le Club le plus proche de Paris a beaucoup contribué à sa réputation, mais aussi à la difficulté d'y venir jouer. A côté du petit parcours "Jaune," dont une bonne moitié des trous ne manquent pas d'intérêt, le "Vert" a reçu de nombreuses compétitions internationales, même si sa longueur peut paraître aujourd'hui insuffisante. Il a été dessiné par Harry S. Colt, mais a fait l'objet de divers aménagements qui peuvent parfois donner l'impression de styles différents, en particulier pour ceux des bunkers. Très agréable dans son déroulement, avec des vues superbes sur Paris, pas trop accidenté, ornementé d'une végétation somptueuse (à voir en automne !), c'est l'une des plus jolies oasis de la région, à déguster pendant les soirées d'été quand les membres sont en vacances ailleurs.

Being the closest club to Paris has done much for its reputation and for the difficulty encountered in being able to play here. Alongside the little "Jaune" course, where a good half of the holes offer much appeal, the "Vert" course has hosted many international tournaments even though its length, by today's standards, may appear a little on the short side. It was designed by Harry Colt but has been restyled in a variety of ways which can sometimes give the impression of different styles joined together, especially as far as the bunkers are concerned. The course unwinds very pleasantly with some superb views over Paris, is not too hilly and is cloaked with some lush vegetation (gorgeous in Autumn). This is one of the region's prettiest oases, a great "watering hole" to enjoy on Summer evenings when the members are on holiday elsewhere.

Golf de Saint-Cloud

60, rue du 19 Janvier
F - 92380 GARCHES

Office	Secrétariat	(33) 01 47 01 01 85
Pro shop	Pro-shop	(33) 01 47 41 01 45
Fax	Fax	(33) 01 47 01 19 57
Situation	Situation	

15 km O de Paris, 2 175 200 hab.

Annual closure	Fermeture annnuelle	non
Weekly closure	Fermeture hebdomadaire	lundi

Fees main season
Tarifs haute saison 18 trous

	Week days Semaine	We/Bank holidays We/Férié
Individual Individuel	450 F*	600 F**
Couple Couple	900 F	1 200 F

* introduction d'un membre - ** avec un membre

Caddy	Caddy	sur réservation
Electric Trolley	Chariot électrique	80 F/18 trous
Buggy	Voiturette	non
Clubs	Clubs	non

Credit cards Cartes de crédit
VISA - CB - Eurocard - MasterCard

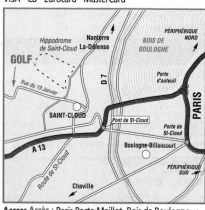

Access Accès : Paris Porte Maillot, Bois de Boulogne →
Suresnes. Pont de Suresnes, Bld H. Sellier, →
Hippodrome St Cloud. Tout droit.
Rue du 19 janvier à droite. → Golf St Cucufa.
Map 15 on page 126 Carte 15 Page 126

GOLF COURSE PARCOURS
14/20

Site	Site	
Maintenance	Entretien	
Architect	Architecte	Harry S. Colt
Type	Type	parc
Relief	Relief	
Water in play	Eau en jeu	
Exp. to wind	Exposé au vent	
Trees in play	Arbres en jeu	

Scorecard Carte de score	Chp. Chp.	Mens Mess.	Ladies Da.
Length Long.	5975	5975	4985
Par	72	72	72

Advised golfing ability		0 12 24 36
Niveau de jeu recommandé		
Hcp required	Handicap exigé	24 Me, 28 Dames

CLUB HOUSE & AMENITIES CLUB HOUSE ET ANNEXES
7/10

Pro shop	Pro-shop	
Driving range	Practice	
Sheltered	couvert	46 postes
On grass	sur herbe	non
Putting-green	putting-green	oui (2)
Pitching-green	pitching green	oui

HOTEL FACILITIES ENVIRONNEMENT HOTELIER
7/10

HOTELS HÔTELS
Villa Henri IV — Saint-Cloud
36 chambres, D 550 F — 4 km
Tél (33) 01 46 02 59 30, Fax (33) 01 49 11 11 02

Quorum — Saint-Cloud
58 chambres, D 500 F — 4 km
Tél (33) 01 47 71 22 33, Fax (33) 01 46 02 75 64

Concorde La Fayette — Paris Pte Maillot
950 chambres, D 1 500 F — 10 km
Tél (33) 01 40 68 50 68, Fax (33) 01 40 68 50 43

RESTAURANTS RESTAURANT
Guy Savoy — Paris 17e
Tél (33) 01 43 80 40 61 — 12 km

Le Petit Colombier — Paris 17e
Tél(33) 01 43 80 28 54 — 11 km

Michel Rostang — Paris 17e
Tél(33) 01 47 63 40 77 — 12 km

258

SAINT-DONAT

Saint Donat est un des premiers parcours de la région à présenter une architecture "moderne". Robert Trent Jones Jr lui a donné des contours très variés, utilisant avec intelligence la végétation existante, les reliefs (surtout au retour) et modelant sans excès les espaces plus plats. Ce qui donne un dessin très précis, où les méandres d'une petite rivière viennent en jeu sur une bonne demi-douzaine de trous. De nombreux bunkers et des bouquets d'arbres (notamment de très beaux vieux chênes) constituent des obstacles parfois préoccupants. Ici, il faut s'appuyer sur la technique, la sagesse dans le choix de club et pas sur la longueur, mais les joueurs de tous niveaux peuvent y évoluer, après une petite période d'adaptation. Alors que les dix premiers trous sont assez plats, le retour est accidenté, mais assez facile à marcher en condition physique normale. Le petit 9 trous annexe est de bonne qualité.

Saint Donat was one of the first courses in this region with so-called "modern" architecture. Robert Trent Jones Jr moulded the course into a variety of shapes, making intelligent use of existing vegetation and relief (especially on the back nine) and contouring the flatter areas without ever going over the top. The result is a very precise layout, where the meanders of a small river come into play on half a dozen or so holes. A good number of bunkers and groups of trees (including some beautiful oaks) form some pretty worrying hazards. Emphasis should be on technique and prudence in the choice of club, not on length. But after a period of adjustment, all players can enjoy a round of golf here. While the first ten holes are rather flat, the last eight are hilly encounters but easily walkable for the average able-bodied golfer. The compact 9-holer on the same site is also pretty good.

Golf de Saint-Donat
270, route de Cannes
F - 06130 PLAN-DE-GRASSE

Office	Secrétariat	(33) 04 93 09 76 60
Pro shop	Pro-shop	(33) 04 93 09 76 60
Fax	Fax	(33) 04 93 09 76 63
Situation	Situation	

2 km S.E. Grasse, 41 390 hab.
18 km N.O. Cannes, 68 670 hab.

Annual closure	Fermeture annnuelle	non
Weekly closure	Fermeture hebdomadaire	

Fees main season
Tarifs haute saison le parcours

	Week days Semaine	We/Bank holidays We/Férié
Individual Individuel	270 F	295 F
Couple Couple	540 F	590 F

GF 200 F le soir

Caddy	Caddy	non
Electric Trolley	Chariot électrique	90 F/18 trous
Buggy	Voiturette	200 F/18 trous
Clubs	Clubs 1/2 série	70 F/18 trous

Credit cards Cartes de crédit
VISA - CB - Eurocard - MasterCard - AMEX - DC

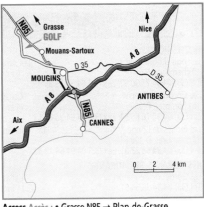

Access Accès : • Grasse N85 → Plan-de-Grasse
• de Cannes, pénétrante → Grasse, Mouans-Sartoux,
→ Golf **Map 14 on page 125** Carte 14 Page 125

GOLF COURSE
PARCOURS   16/20

Site	Site	▮▮▮▮
Maintenance	Entretien	▮▮▮▮▮
Architect	Architecte	R. Trent Jones Jr
Type	Type	vallon, campagne
Relief	Relief	▮▮▮
Water in play	Eau en jeu	▮▮
Exp. to wind	Exposé au vent	▮▮▮
Trees in play	Arbres en jeu	▮▮▮

Scorecard Carte de score	Chp. Chp.	Mens Mess.	Ladies Da.
Length Long.	6031	5558	5082
Par	71	71	71

Advised golfing ability Niveau de jeu recommandé	0	12	24	36
		▮▮▮▮▮▮		

Hcp required   Handicap exigé   non

CLUB HOUSE & AMENITIES
CLUB HOUSE ET ANNEXES   7/10

Pro shop	Pro-shop	▮▮▮▮
Driving range	Practice	▮▮▮
Sheltered	couvert	6 places
On grass	sur herbe	non
Putting-green	putting-green	oui
Pitching-green	pitching green	oui

HOTEL FACILITIES
ENVIRONNEMENT HOTELIER   8/10

HOTELS HÔTELS

Hôtel de Mougins **** — Mougins
50 chambres, D 980 F — 6 km
Tél (33) 04 92 92 17 07, Fax (33) 04 92 92 17 08

Le Manoir de l'Etang *** — Mougins
15 chambres, D 900 F — 6 km
Tél (33) 04 93 90 01 07, Fax (33) 04 92 92 20 70

Hôtel des Parfums *** — Grasse
60 chambres, D 595 F — 3 km
Tél (33) 04 93 36 10 10, Fax (33) 04 93 36 35 48

RESTAURANTS RESTAURANT

La Bastide Saint-Antoine — Grasse
Tél (33) 04 93 09 16 48 — 2 km

Amphytrion — Grasse
Tél(33) 04 93 36 58 73 — 2 km

Pierre Baltus — Grasse
Tél(33) 04 93 36 32 90 — 2 km

259

SAINT-ENDRÉOL

15 | 7 | 4

Dans un paysage typique de Provence, ce parcours de Michel Gayon en épouse les reliefs, d'où quelques greens aveugles, dont certains d'ailleurs auraient pu être évités. Certains coups forcément hasardeux atténuent le plaisir que l'on peut éprouver sur ce golf en pleine nature, dont le relief accentué invite à jouer en voiturette. Parce que la tactique de jeu n'est pas évidente à assimiler, parce qu'il faut connaître le parcours pour bien évaluer les distances, parce que que la chance joue ici un rôle important, on s'amusera beaucoup plus en match-play (où tout peut arriver) qu'en stroke play. Avec plusieurs trous spectaculaires et pour la beauté de son environnement, Saint-Endreol vaut incontestablement le détour. Le 17 a été conçu comme un par 5, mais reste bêtement inscrit en par 4. Ne tenez pas compte de la carte, jouez le en par 5, vous serez moins déçu par votre score.

Laid out in typical Provence style countryside, Michel Gayon's course hugs the contours of the landscape and in the process provides a number of blind greens, some of which could have been avoided. Certain hazardous shots tend to dampen the enjoyment of this course right out in the country, and whose hilly terrain make a buggy a wise decision. This is a match-play course (where anything can happen) rather than a course for stroke-play, simply because the tactics needed here are not always obvious, because you need to know the course to evaluate distances, and because luck plays perhaps a bigger role than usual. With several spectacular holes and a beautiful setting, Saint Endréol is most certainly well worth the visit. The 17th was designed like a par 5 but for some daft reason stays a par 4. Forget what's written on the card and play it in 5 to avoid disappointment.

Golf de Saint-Endréol
Route de Bagnols-en-Forêt
F - 83920 LA MOTTE-EN-PROVENCE

Office	Secrétariat	(33) 04 94 99 22 99
Pro shop	Pro-shop	(33) 04 94 99 22 99
Fax	Fax	(33) 04 94 99 23 99
Situation	Situation	

10 km S.E. Draguignan, 30 180 hab.
18 km N.O. Saint-Raphaël, 26 620 hab.

Annual closure	Fermeture annnuelle	non
Weekly closure	Fermeture hebdomadaire	

Fees main season
Tarifs haute saison le parcours

	Week days Semaine	We/Bank holidays We/Férié
Individual Individuel	300 F	300 F
Couple Couple	600 F	600 F

Caddy	Caddy	sur réservation
Electric Trolley	Chariot électrique	non
Buggy	Voiturette	150 F/18 trous
Clubs	Clubs 1/2 série	80 F/jour

Credit cards Cartes de crédit
VISA - CB - Eurocard - MasterCard - AMEX

260

Access Accès : Saint-Raphaël, N7, sortie Le Muy,
D54 → La Motte-en- Provence, → Golf
Map 14 on page 125 Carte 14 Page 125

GOLF COURSE
PARCOURS

15/20

Site	Site	
Maintenance	Entretien	
Architect	Architecte	Michel Gayon
Type	Type	forêt, vallon
Relief	Relief	
Water in play	Eau en jeu	
Exp. to wind	Exposé au vent	
Trees in play	Arbres en jeu	

Scorecard Carte de score	Chp. Chp.	Mens Mess.	Ladies Da.
Length Long.	6219	5940	5011
Par	72	72	72

Advised golfing ability		0	12	24	36
Niveau de jeu recommandé					
Hcp required	Handicap exigé	35			

CLUB HOUSE & AMENITIES
CLUB HOUSE ET ANNEXES

7/10

Pro shop	Pro-shop	
Driving range	Practice	
Sheltered	couvert	7 places
On grass	sur herbe	non
Putting-green	putting-green	oui
Pitching-green	pitching green	oui

HOTEL FACILITIES
ENVIRONNEMENT HOTELIER

4/10

HOTELS HÔTELS
Le Logis du Guetteur ★★★ — Les Arcs
10 chambres, D 450 F — 6 km
Tél (33) 04 94 73 30 82, Fax (33) 04 94 73 39 95

Les Gorges de Pennafort ★★★ — Callas
16 chambres, D 950 F — 11 km
Tél (33) 04 94 76 66 51, Fax (33) 04 94 76 67 23

Les Etoiles de l'Ange ★★★ — Draguignan
29 chambres, D 400 F — 15 km
Tél (33) 04 94 68 23 01, Fax (33) 04 94 68 13 30

RESTAURANTS RESTAURANT
Les Gorges de Pennafort — Callas
Tél (33) 04 94 76 66 51 — 11 km

Le Logis du Guetteur — Les Arcs
Tél (33) 04 94 73 30 82 — 6 km

Les Pignatelles — La Motte
Tél (33) 04 94 70 25 70 — 5 km

On le considère parfois comme trop court, c'est peut-être vrai pour les meilleurs professionnels, mais bien suffisant pour 99,99 % des golfeurs, qui ont souvent du mal à y jouer leur handicap ! On y verra plutôt la quintessence de l'architecture britannique sur un terrain très plat et très ramassé, avec un très bon rythme d'enchaînement des trous et des difficultés, quelques reliefs subtils, notamment en approche des greens et sur les greens, généralement très vastes. Les obstacles essentiels sont les arbres, majestueux mais pas oppressants, et surtout les bunkers, typiques des idées stratégiques de Colt, et souvent de formes très belles. Scorer ici demande un jeu très complet, et d'abord de ne pas se laisser endormir par la tranquille séduction du lieu. Un seul regret, le nouveau green du 2, sans rapport avec le style "d'époque."

Saint-Germain may well sometimes be considered too short for the top pros but it certainly is long enough for 99,99% of golfers who often find playing to their handicap here something of an exploit. We see it rather as the quintessence of British-style design over very flat and very squat landscape. There is a remarkable flow of continuity between holes and difficulties and some subtly-shaped terrain, particularly when approaching or actually on the generally very large greens. The basic hazards are trees, majestic enough but not too interfering, and especially bunkers, typical of designer Colt's ideas of strategy and often wonderfully shaped. You need an all-round game to score well here and don't let the balmy appeal of the site distract you from the task at hand. Our one regret is the new green on the 2nd hole, which has nothing in common with the course's "period" style.

Golf de Saint-Germain
Route de Poissy
F - 78100 SAINT-GERMAIN-EN-LAYE

Office	Secrétariat	(33) 01 39 10 30 30
Pro shop	Pro-shop	(33) 01 39 73 47 48
Fax	Fax	(33) 01 39 10 30 31
Situation	Situation	

26 km O de Paris, 2 175 200 hab.
4 km de Saint-Germain, 39 320 hab.

Annual closure	Fermeture annnuelle	non
Weekly closure	Fermeture hebdomadaire	lundi

Fees main season Tarifs haute saison 18 trous

	Week days Semaine	We/Bank holidays We/Férié
Individual Individuel	400 F	—
Couple Couple	800 F	—

We : Membres et leurs invités
(only member and guests)

Caddy	Caddy	réservation/200 F
Electric Trolley	Chariot électrique	non
Buggy	Voiturette	non
Clubs	Clubs 1/2 série	150 F/jour

Credit cards Cartes de crédit
VISA - Eurocard - MasterCard - AMEX

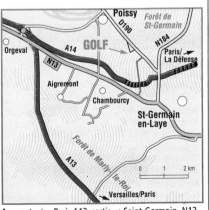

Access Accès : Paris A13, sortie → Saint-Germain. N13
→ Poissy, N184 et D190 → Poissy. Golf à gauche.
Map 15 on page 126 Carte 15 Page 126

GOLF COURSE
PARCOURS
17 /20

Site	Site	
Maintenance	Entretien	
Architect	Architecte	Harry S. Colt
Type	Type	forêt
Relief	Relief	
Water in play	Eau en jeu	
Exp. to wind	Exposé au vent	
Trees in play	Arbres en jeu	

Scorecard Carte de score	Chp. Chp.	Mens Mess.	Ladies Da.
Length Long.	6117	5805	5224
Par	72	72	72

Advised golfing ability		0	12	24	36
Niveau de jeu recommandé					

Hcp required	Handicap exigé	24 Mess., 28 Dames

CLUB HOUSE & AMENITIES
CLUB HOUSE ET ANNEXES
7 /10

Pro shop	Pro-shop	
Driving range	Practice	
Sheltered	couvert	17 tapis
On grass	sur herbe	non
Putting-green	putting-green	oui
Pitching-green	pitching green	oui

261

HOTEL FACILITIES
ENVIRONNEMENT HOTELIER
7 /10

HOTELS HÔTELS
La Forestière (Cazaudehore)   Saint-Germain
25 chambres, D 950 F   5 km
Tél (33) 01 39 73 36 60, Fax (33) 01 39 73 93 88

Pavillon Henri IV   Saint-Germain
42 chambres, D 1 000 F   4 km
Tél (33) 01 39 10 15 15, Fax (33) 01 39 93 73 93

Ermitage des Loges   Saint-Germain
57 chambres, D 550 F   5 km
Tél (33) 01 34 51 88 86, Fax (33) 01 34 51 16 29

RESTAURANTS RESTAURANT
Cazaudehore   Saint-Germain
Tél (33) 01 34 51 93 80   5 km

La Feuillantine   Saint-Germain
Tél (33) 01 34 51 04 24   4 km

SAINT-JEAN-DE-MONTS

16 6 5

Ce parcours s'est vite imposé parmi les meilleurs parcours de ces dernières années, et il maintient son standing. Il prouve que l'on peut faire de bons parcours même avec de petits budgets... Situé en bord de mer, son dessin est un hommage à l'architecture de links, même dans la dizaine de trous (parfois très étroits) situés dans une forêt de pins maritimes et de chênes verts. Les fairways très modelés, les greens souvent à double ou même triple plateau suivent les reliefs des dunes, dans un souci évident de préserver la nature. L'architecte Yves Bureau a joué davantage sur la nécessité de précision que sur la longueur, mais le vent peut rendre ce parcours démoniaque. Les Britanniques n'y seront certes pas dépaysés ! Le parcours est jouable sans problème toute l'année, et ses tarifs très raisonnables en font l'un des meilleurs rapports qualité/prix de France.

This course quickly became established as one of the best new layouts in recent years and has preserved its status. It also proves that good courses are possible even on low budgets. Laid out along the sea, this is a homage to links golf, even though ten or so holes (sometimes very tight indeed) wind their way through a forest of maritime pines and oak trees. The highly contoured fairways and two- or even three-tiered greens hug the relief of the dunes with obvious emphasis on preserving the natural landscape. Architect Yves Bureau has played more on the need for precision rather than length, but the wind can make this a devilishly hard course. The British will certainly feel at home here. Saint Jean de Monts is easily playable all year and green fees are very reasonable, thus making this one of the best values for money in France.

Golf de Saint-Jean-de-Monts

Avenue des Pays-de-la-Loire
F - 85160 SAINT-JEAN-DE-MONTS

Office	Secrétariat	(33) 02 51 58 82 73
Pro shop	Pro-shop	(33) 02 51 58 82 73
Fax	Fax	(33) 02 51 59 18 32
Situation	Situation	

17 k. O. Challans,14 200 hab.
70 km S.O. Nantes, 252 030 hab.

Annual closure	Fermeture annnuelle	non
Weekly closure	Fermeture hebdomadaire	non
	mardi, le club-house du 01/11 → 31/03	

Fees main season Tarifs haute saison la journée

	Week days Semaine	We/Bank holidays We/Férié
Individual Individuel	280 F	280 F
Couple Couple	560 F	560 F

GF + repas 320 F Sem. et We

Caddy	Caddy	non
Electric Trolley	Chariot électrique	non
Buggy	Voiturette	150 F/18 trous
Clubs	Clubs 1/2 série	70 F/jour

Credit cards Cartes de crédit
VISA - CB - Eurocard - MasterCard - AMEX

262

Access Accès : Challans → Saint-Jean-de-Monts,
→ Golf
Map 6 on page 108 Carte 6 Page 108

GOLF COURSE
PARCOURS **16**/20

Site	Site	
Maintenance	Entretien	
Architect	Architecte	Yves Bureau
Type	Type	forêt, links
Relief	Relief	
Water in play	Eau en jeu	
Exp. to wind	Exposé au vent	
Trees in play	Arbres en jeu	

Scorecard Carte de score	Chp. Chp.	Mens Mess.	Ladies Da.
Length Long.	5962	5620	5026
Par	72	72	72

Advised golfing ability		0 12 24 36
Niveau de jeu recommandé		
Hcp required	Handicap exigé	non

CLUB HOUSE & AMENITIES
CLUB HOUSE ET ANNEXES **6**/10

Pro shop	Pro-shop	
Driving range	Practice	
Sheltered	couvert	10 places
On grass	sur herbe	non
Putting-green	putting-green	oui
Pitching-green	pitching green	oui

HOTEL FACILITIES
ENVIRONNEMENT HOTELIER **5**/10

HOTELS HÔTELS

Mercure — 100 m
44 chambres, D 610 F
Tél (33) 02 51 59 15 15, Fax (33) 02 51 59 91 03

Hôtel de la Plage *** — N.-D.-de-Monts
49 chambres, D 350 F — 5 km
Tél (33) 02 51 58 83 09, Fax (33) 02 51 58 97 12

Château de la Vérie *** — Challans
19 chambres, D 800 F — 15 km
Tél (33) 02 51 35 33 44, Fax (33) 02 51 35 14 84

RESTAURANTS RESTAURANT

Le Pavillon Gourmand — Challans
Tél (33) 02 51 49 04 52 — 15 km

Hôtel de la Plage — N.-D.-de-Monts
Tél (33) 02 51 58 83 09 — 5 km

SAINT-LAURENT ✳ 14 7 5

Beaucoup de golfs prétendent convenir à tout le monde, mais ce n'est pas toujours vrai. Ici, oui : Saint-Laurent est un parcours réellement praticable par les joueurs de tous niveaux, même les joueurs de haut handicap, qui y perdront moins de balles que de points. Situé dans un bel espace vallonné et planté de pins ou de chênes, le 18 trous signé par Michael Fenn se déroule sans imagination particulière, mais il a été conçu et réalisé très sérieusement. Son entretien de bonne qualité incite à en recommander la visite, d'autant que cette belle région est une destination traditionnelle de vacances. Avec la mer et les activités balnéaires à proximité, un golfeur pourra sans trop mauvaise conscience abandonner sa famille quelques heures. Le 9 trous signé Yves Bureau est un lieu idéal pour initier les aspirants golfeurs.

A lot of courses claim to be suitable for all golfers, but are not. Saint Laurent is one of the exceptions, with a course that really is playable by golfers of all abilities, even high-handicappers, who will probably lose fewer balls than they drop strokes. Located in rolling landscape planted with pines and oak-trees, the 18-hole course, designed by Michael Fenn, unfolds with no great imagination, but it was designed and built with the most serious intentions. Excellent upkeep makes it well worth a visit, especially in this beautiful holiday region. With the sea and holiday resorts nearby, golfers can abandon the family for a few hourse without remorse. The 9-hole course designed by Yves Bureau is the ideal venue for beginners and new-comers to the game.

Golf de Saint-Laurent
Ploemel
F - 56400 AURAY

Office	Secrétariat	(33) 02 97 56 85 18
Pro shop	Pro-shop	(33) 02 97 56 85 18
Fax	Fax	(33) 02 97 56 89 99
Situation	Situation	

11 km O. Auray, 10 320 hab.
44 km O. Vannes, 45 640 hab.

Annual closure	Fermeture annnuelle	non
Weekly closure	Fermeture hebdomadaire	

Fees main season
Tarifs haute saison la journée

	Week days Semaine	We/Bank holidays We/Férié
Individual Individuel	250 F	250 F
Couple Couple	500 F	500 F

Caddy	Caddy	non
Electric Trolley	Chariot électrique	non
Buggy	Voiturette	150 F/18 trous
Clubs	Clubs 1/2 série	50 F/jour

Credit cards Cartes de crédit
VISA - CB - Eurocard - MasterCard

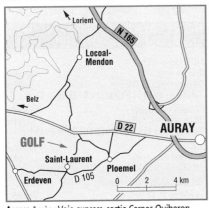

Access Accès : Voie express, sortie Carnac-Quiberon,
D22 → Belz-Etel pendant 6 km.
Map 5 on page 107 Carte 5 Page 107

GOLF COURSE
PARCOURS 14/20

Site	Site	▰▰▰▰▱
Maintenance	Entretien	▰▰▰▰▱
Architect	Architecte	Michael Fenn
Type	Type	forêt
Relief	Relief	
Water in play	Eau en jeu	▰▱▱▱▱
Exp. to wind	Exposé au vent	▰▰▱▱▱
Trees in play	Arbres en jeu	▰▰▰▱▱

Scorecard Carte de score	Chp. Chp.	Mens Mess.	Ladies Da.
Length Long.	6112	6112	5247
Par	72	72	72

Advised golfing ability		0 12 24 36
Niveau de jeu recommandé		▰▰▰▰▱
Hcp required	Handicap exigé	35

CLUB HOUSE & AMENITIES
CLUB HOUSE ET ANNEXES 7/10

Pro shop	Pro-shop	▰▰▰▰▱
Driving range	Practice	▰▰▰▱▱
Sheltered	couvert	10 places
On grass	sur herbe	oui
Putting-green	putting-green	oui
Pitching-green	pitching green	oui

HOTEL FACILITIES
ENVIRONNEMENT HOTELIER 5/10

HOTELS HÔTELS

Fairway	200 m
42 chambres, D 610 F	
Tél (33) 02 97 56 88 88, Fax (33) 02 97 56 88 28	
Best Western Celtique ***	Carnac
49 chambres, D 700 F	7 km
Tél (33) 02 97 52 11 49, Fax (33) 02 97 52 71 10	
Château de Locguénolé ****	Hennebont
22 chambres, D 1 200 F	23 km
Tél (33) 02 97 76 29 04, Fax (33) 02 97 76 82 35	

RESTAURANTS RESTAURANT

La Closerie du Kerdrain	Auray
Tél (33) 02 97 56 61 27	10 km

263

Saint-Nom fut à son ouverture un événement, un exemple aussi de golf résidentiel prestigieux, qui, après des efforts patients, a acquis aujourd'hui beaucoup de maturité, en même temps que les arbres en prenaient. Comme le "Rouge", celui-ci a été dessiné par Fred Hawtree, mais beaucoup de changements ont été apportés depuis, souvent avec bonheur, et de nombreux arbres plantés, ce qui constitue un bienfait visuel et technique. Un léger vallonnement le rend agréable à jouer, et ajoute de l'intérêt au choix de clubs. Mieux qu'un parent pauvre d'un parent prestigieux, ce parcours offre quelques parcs 4 très musclés, et peu de vraies occasions de birdies. L'entretien est de très bon niveau, le Club-house superbe.

When first opened, Saint Nom was an event and a fine example of a prestigious residential golf club which after much patient work has today grown to maturity in pace with the trees. Like the "Rouge" course, the "Bleu" layout was designed by Fred Hawtree, although a lot of changes have been made to it since, often to the better, with many new trees planted to add visual and technical appeal. The slightly rolling landscape makes it a pleasant course to play and adds to the importance of choosing the right club. Better than a poor relation to a prestigious neighbour, this layout contains a number of very demanding par 4s and few real birdie chances. Green-keeping is of very high standard and the Club-house simply superb.

Golf de Saint-Nom-la-Bretèche

Hameau de la Tuilerie Bignon
F - 78860 SAINT-NOM-LA-BRETECHE

Office	Secrétariat	(33) 01 30 80 04 40
Pro shop	Pro-shop	(33) 01 30 80 04 40
Fax	Fax	(33) 01 34 62 87 04
Situation	Situation	

22 km O de Paris, 2 175 200 hab.
9 km NO de Versailles, 87 789 hab.

Annual closure	Fermeture annnuelle	non
Weekly closure	Fermeture hebdomadaire	mardi

Fees main season
Tarifs haute saison 18 trous

	Week days Semaine	We/Bank holidays We/Férié
Individual Individuel	400 F	600 F*
Couple Couple	800 F	1 200 F*

* accompagné d'un membre (with a member)

Caddy	Caddy	250 F
Electric Trolley	Chariot électrique	100 F/18 trous
Buggy	Voiturette	certificat médical
Clubs	Clubs	non

Credit cards Cartes de crédit | VISA

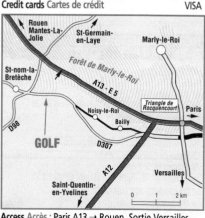

264

Access Accès : Paris A13 → Rouen. Sortie Versailles-Ouest. → Versailles. 500 m à droite sur D307 → Noisy-le-Roy, Saint-Nom-la-Bretèche
Map 15 on page 126 Carte 15 Page 126

GOLF COURSE
PARCOURS 15/20

Site	Site	
Maintenance	Entretien	
Architect	Architecte	Fred Hawtree
Type	Type	parc, résidentiel
Relief	Relief	
Water in play	Eau en jeu	
Exp. to wind	Exposé au vent	
Trees in play	Arbres en jeu	

Scorecard Carte de score	Chp. Chp.	Mens Mess.	Ladies Da.
Length Long.	6167	5674	4971
Par	72	72	72

Advised golfing ability Niveau de jeu recommandé		0 12 24 36
Hcp required	Handicap exigé	non

CLUB HOUSE & AMENITIES
CLUB HOUSE ET ANNEXES 8/10

Pro shop	Pro-shop	
Driving range	Practice	
Sheltered	couvert	5 tapis
On grass	sur herbe	non
Putting-green	putting-green	oui
Pitching-green	pitching green	oui

HOTEL FACILITIES
ENVIRONNEMENT HOTELIER 8/10

HOTELS HÔTELS
Trianon Palace   Versailles
94 chambres, D 1 800 F   9 km
Tél (33) 01 30 84 38 00, Fax (33) 01 39 49 00 77

Résidence du Berry   Versailles
38 chambres, D 500 F   9 km
Tél (33) 01 39 49 07 07, Fax (33) 01 39 50 59 40

Ibis   Versailles
85 chambres, D 480 F   9 km
Tél (33) 01 39 53 03 30, Fax (33) 01 39 50 06 31

RESTAURANTS RESTAURANT
La Marée de Versailles   Versailles
Tél (33) 01 30 21 73 73   9 km

Les Trois Marches   Versailles
Tél (33) 01 39 50 13 21   9 km

Ce parcours a été rendu célèbre par le Trophée Lancôme, qui se dispute maintenant sur un composite des deux parcours. On ne joue plus sept des derniers trous, venir ici est donc l'occasion de les redécouvrir. Le "Rouge" nécessite un driving très précis si l'on veut espérer scorer, et attaquer les greens en bonne posture. La stratégie de jeu est assez claire, la seule chose que l'on ne maîtrise pas immédiatement, c'est le putting, car les contours des greens sont peu visibles, mais souvent déconcertants. Assez vallonné, mais sans être trop fatiguant à marcher, ce parcours réclame de savoir faire (et bien faire) tous les coups de golf. La variété du dessin, la progression des difficultés permet de renouveler l'intérêt : jouer ici pour le plaisir ou en compétition n'est pas du tout la même chose !

This course owes its fame to the Trophée Lancôme, which these days is played on a combination of the two courses. Seven of the last "Rouge" holes are not used, so playing here yourself is the opportunity to get to know them. The "Rouge" course requires very straight driving if you want to card a good score and attack the greens from the ideal position. Game strategy is clear enough and the only thing you will immediately find anything but easy is your putting. The contours of these greens are not particularly visible and often disconcerting. rather hilly but not too tiring on the legs, this course demands every shot in the book (played accordingly to the book). The variety of the layout and the way difficulties slowly pile up make this an interesting course every time. But here, playing for fun and playing in a tournament are two very different propositions.

Golf de Saint-Nom-la-Bretèche
Hameau de la Tuilerie Bignon
F - 78860 SAINT-NOM-LA-BRETECHE

Office	Secrétariat	(33) 01 30 80 04 40
Pro shop	Pro-shop	(33) 01 30 80 04 40
Fax	Fax	(33) 01 34 62 87 04
Situation	Situation	

22 km O de Paris, 2 175 200 hab.
9 km NO de Versailles, 87 789 hab.

Annual closure	Fermeture annnuelle	non
Weekly closure	Fermeture hebdomadaire	mardi

Fees main season
Tarifs haute saison 18 trous

	Week days Semaine	We/Bank holidays We/Férié
Individual Individuel	400 F	600 F*
Couple Couple	800 F	1 200 F*

* accompagné d'un membre (with a member)

Caddy	Caddy	250 F
Electric Trolley	Chariot électrique	100 F/18 trous
Buggy	Voiturette	certificat médical
Clubs	Clubs	non

Credit cards Cartes de crédit — VISA

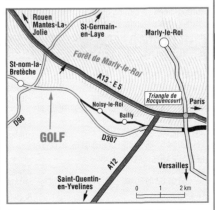

Access Accès : Paris A13 → Rouen. Sortie Versailles-Ouest. → Versailles. 500 m à droite sur D307 → Noisy-le-Roy, Saint-Nom-la-Bretèche
Map 15 on page 126 Carte 15 Page 126

GOLF COURSE
PARCOURS — 16/20

Site	Site	
Maintenance	Entretien	
Architect	Architecte	Fred Hawtree
Type	Type	parc, résidentiel
Relief	Relief	
Water in play	Eau en jeu	
Exp. to wind	Exposé au vent	
Trees in play	Arbres en jeu	

Scorecard Carte de score	Chp. Chp.	Mens Mess.	Ladies Da.
Length Long.	6252	5726	4920
Par	72	72	72

Advised golfing ability		0 12 24 36
Niveau de jeu recommandé		
Hcp required	Handicap exigé	non

CLUB HOUSE & AMENITIES
CLUB HOUSE ET ANNEXES — 8/10

Pro shop	Pro-shop	
Driving range	Practice	
Sheltered	couvert	5 tapis
On grass	sur herbe	non
Putting-green	putting-green	oui
Pitching-green	pitching green	oui

265
■ ■

HOTEL FACILITIES
ENVIRONNEMENT HOTELIER — 8/10

HOTELS HÔTELS
Trianon Palace — Versailles
94 chambres, D 1 800 F — 9 km
Tél (33) 01 30 84 38 00, Fax (33) 01 39 49 00 77

Résidence du Berry — Versailles
38 chambres, D 500 F — 9 km
Tél (33) 01 39 49 07 07, Fax (33) 01 39 50 59 40

Ibis — Versailles
85 chambres, D 480 F — 9 km
Tél (33) 01 39 53 03 30, Fax (33) 01 39 50 06 31

RESTAURANTS RESTAURANT
La Marée de Versailles — Versailles
Tél (33) 01 30 21 73 73 — 9 km

Les Trois Marches — Versailles
Tél (33) 01 39 50 13 21 — 9 km

SAINT-THOMAS

Près de Béziers, ce parcours offre un préjugé favorable, par son arrivée dans la garrigue, par l'environnement et les couleurs de la nature. Le tracé du parcours signé P. Lambert ne dément pas cette première impression. Sans apporter d'idées vraiment originales ni d'émotions de jeu exceptionnelles, les 18 trous sont généralement de bonne facture, peu fatigants à jouer, et le climat local comme la nature du sol permettent d'y jouer toute l'année, seul le vent pouvant augmenter les difficultés. L'architecte y a inclus quelques trous délicats (comme le 7 ou le 16 par exemple), mais aussi plusieurs trous assez reposants pour ne pas trop surcharger la carte, et permettre de le conseiller à tous les niveaux. Les équipements de ce club sympathique sont propres et de bonne qualité, sans prétention aucune, on se sent un peu en famille ici.

This course, close to Béziers, immediately gives a pleasing first impression as you drive along a track through the colourful garrigue (Mediterranean shrub). The actual layout, designed by P. Lambert, lives up to this impression. Without any really original ideas or excitement, the 18 holes make for good golfing over flattish terrain, and the local climate and the soil keep the course playable all year. Only the wind can come along and pose a few problems. There are a few very tricky holes (the 7th and 16th, for example), and also some more relaxing numbers to keep the score down and make this a course for everyone. The facilities in this very friendly club are good and stylish, and the visitor will very quickly feel one of the family.

Golf de Saint-Thomas
Route de Pézenas
F - 34500 BEZIERS

Office	Secrétariat	(33) 04 67 98 62 01
Pro shop	Pro-shop	(33) 04 67 98 55 71
Fax	Fax	(33) 04 67 98 61 01
Situation	Situation	
10 km N.E. Béziers, 71 000 hab.		
Annual closure	Fermeture annnuelle	non
Weekly closure	Fermeture hebdomadaire	

Fees main season
Tarifs haute saison le parcours

	Week days Semaine	We/Bank holidays We/Férié
Individual Individuel	250 F	250 F
Couple Couple	500 F	500 F

Caddy	Caddy	non
Electric Trolley	Chariot électrique	non
Buggy	Voiturette	180 F/18 trous
Clubs	Clubs 1/2 série	50 F/jour

Credit cards Cartes de crédit
VISA - CB - Eurocard - MasterCard - AMEX

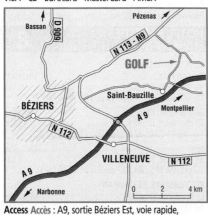

Access Accès : A9, sortie Béziers Est, voie rapide, au rond-point → Bassan, passer devant «le Rouge gorge», pont, → Golf
Map 13 on page 123 Carte 13 Page 123

GOLF COURSE
PARCOURS **14**/20

Site	Site	
Maintenance	Entretien	
Architect	Architecte	Patrice Lambert
Type	Type	vallon, garrigue
Relief	Relief	
Water in play	Eau en jeu	
Exp. to wind	Exposé au vent	
Trees in play	Arbres en jeu	

Scorecard	Chp.	Mens	Ladies
Carte de score	Chp.	Mess.	Da.
Length Long.	6130	5762	4996
Par	72	72	72

Advised golfing ability	0	12	24	36
Niveau de jeu recommandé				
Hcp required	Handicap exigé	non		

CLUB HOUSE & AMENITIES
CLUB HOUSE ET ANNEXES **7**/10

Pro shop	Pro-shop	
Driving range	Practice	
Sheltered	couvert	4 places
On grass	sur herbe	non
Putting-green	putting-green	oui
Pitching-green	pitching green	oui

HOTEL FACILITIES
ENVIRONNEMENT HOTELIER **5**/10

HOTELS HÔTELS
Impérator ***
45 chambres, D 410 F
Tél (33) 04 67 49 02 25, Fax (33) 04 67 28 92 30
Béziers
10 km

Du Nord ***
40 chambres, D 450 F
Tél (33) 04 67 28 34 09, Fax (33) 04 67 49 00 37
Béziers
10 km

RESTAURANTS RESTAURANT
Le Framboisier
Tél (33) 04 67 49 90 00
Béziers
10 km

Le Jardin
Tél (33) 04 67 36 41 31
Béziers
10 km

266

SAINTE-BAUME (LA)

13 7 6

Ce 18 trous aurait pu être une complète réussite si l'on ne trouvait çà et là quelques "idées d'architecte" plus paysagères que golfiques. Alors qu'un parcours commercial doit pouvoir être joué dès la première fois sans cacher ses obstacles, on peut penser que certains trous manquent de franchise, parallèlement à d'autres presque trop faciles. La stratégie n'est alors pas évidente. De fait, on a l'impression d'un ensemble de bonnes idées graphiques, mais pas toujours bien disposées sur le plan du jeu, d'où une impression de manque d'unité. Les joueurs moyens ou débutants seront sans doute moins exigeants que les joueurs qui attachent une grande importance à la logique des obstacles, au rythme d'un parcours. En dépit de ces appréciations, pour la beauté de l'environnement et la bonne qualité de son entretien, ce parcours mérite néammoins une visite.

This 18-hole course could have been a total success if it weren't for a few architectural ideas here and there, that have more to do with landscaping than with golf. And since a commercial course should be playable first time out without concealing its hazards, there is reason to believe that some holes are a little on the sneaky side, as opposed to others that are almost too easy. The overall impression is that of a whole series of good graphic ideas that are not always well translated into golfing language, hence the feeling of a disjointed layout. Mid-handicappers and beginners will probably be less demanding in this respect than players who attach considerable importance to the logic of hazards and the overall balance of a course. Despite these views, the course is well worth a visit for the beauty of the setting and the standard of upkeep.

Golf de la Sainte-Baume
F - 83860 NANS-LES-PINS

Office	Secrétariat	(33) 04 94 78 60 12
Pro shop	Pro-shop	(33) 04 94 78 60 12
Fax	Fax	(33) 04 94 78 63 52
Situation	Situation	

44 km N.E. Marseille, 800 550 hab.

Annual closure	Fermeture annnuelle	non
Weekly closure	Fermeture hebdomadaire	

Fees main season
Tarifs haute saison le parcours

	Week days Semaine	We/Bank holidays We/Férié
Individual Individuel	210 F	250 F
Couple Couple	420 F	500 F

Jeudi : Seniors, 160 F

Caddy	Caddy	non
Electric Trolley	Chariot électrique	80 F/18 trous
Buggy	Voiturette	200 F/18 trous
Clubs	Clubs 1/2 série	80 F/jour

Credit cards Cartes de crédit
VISA - CB - Eurocard - MasterCard - AMEX

SAINT-MAXIMIN-La-Sainte-Baume
N 7
GOLF   N 560
D 1
← Aix-en-Provence   A 8   Fréjus →
Nans-les-Pins   0   2   4 km
A 8
D 80

Access Accès : Aix-en-Provence/Saint-Maximin, sortie Saint-Maximin → La Sainte-Baume, Nans-les-Pins
Map 14 on page 124 Carte 14 Page 124

GOLF COURSE
PARCOURS   **13**/20

Site	Site	
Maintenance	Entretien	
Architect	Architecte	Robert Berthet
Type	Type	campagne
Relief	Relief	
Water in play	Eau en jeu	
Exp. to wind	Exposé au vent	
Trees in play	Arbres en jeu	

Scorecard Carte de score	Chp. Chp.	Mens Mess.	Ladies Da.
Length Long.	6167	5984	5205
Par	72	72	72

Advised golfing ability		0 12 24 36
Niveau de jeu recommandé		
Hcp required	Handicap exigé	35

CLUB HOUSE & AMENITIES
CLUB HOUSE ET ANNEXES   **7**/10

Pro shop	Pro-shop	
Driving range	Practice	
Sheltered	couvert	10 places
On grass	sur herbe	oui
Putting-green	putting-green	oui
Pitching-green	pitching green	.oui

267

HOTEL FACILITIES
ENVIRONNEMENT HOTELIER   **6**/10

HOTELS HÔTELS
Domaine de Châteauneuf ****   400 m. du golf
30 chambres, D 800 F
Tél (33) 04 94 78 90 06, Fax (33) 04 94 78 63 30
Plaisance **   Saint-Maximin
13 chambres, D 400 F   7 km
Tél (33) 04 94 78 16 74, Fax (33) 04 94 78 18 39
Hôtel de France   Saint-Maximin
26 chambres, D 350 F   7 km
Tél (33) 04 94 78 00 14, Fax (33) 04 94 59 83 80

RESTAURANTS RESTAURANT
Domaine de Châteauneuf   400 m
Tél (33) 04 94 78 90 06
Château de Nans   Nans-les-Pins
Tél(33) 04 94 78 92 06   2 km
Chez Nous   Saint-Maximin
Tél(33) 04 94 78 02 57   7 km

Il faut parfois grimper haut (il y a un téléphérique entre le 10 et le 11), et ce parcours est épuisant à pied, mais les vues sur la baie de Saint-Tropez et le massif des Maures récompensent les efforts. Taillé pour une bonne part dans la colline, il n'est pas d'une grande franchise, même si les travaux ont atténué les rebonds indésirables. On comprend que l'architecte Donald Harradine ait adapté son dessin au terrain, mais certains greens aveugles auraient pu être évités. Les fairways sont rarement larges, de nombreux pins empiètent sur les trajectoires de balle mais la longueur assez réduite du parcours permet de laisser souvent le driver de côté. Il faut soigneusement éviter de jouer en stroke-play, mais on peut s'amuser en match-play. Pour les joueurs peu expérimentés, ce parcours peut être décourageant. Qu'ils profitent du spectacle.

You sometimes have to scale considerable heights (a cable-car links the 10th and 11th holes) and the course is generally speaking exhausting to walk, but the views over the bay of Saint Tropez and the Maures uplands are more than worth the effort. Mostly cut out of a hill, this can be a deceitful course, even though recent work has reduced the unexpected and unwarranted kick. Architect Donald Harradine understandably adapted his layout to the terrain, but certain blind greens could have been avoided. The fairways are seldom wide and numerous pine-trees encroach upon the ball's flight-path, but on this short course, you can always leave the driver in the bag. Make a point of not playing stroke-play, have fun with match-play. A sometimes dispiriting course for inexperienced golfers, but they'll love the view.

Golf de Sainte-Maxime

Route du Débarquement
F - 83120 SAINTE-MAXIME

Office	Secrétariat	(33) 04 94 49 26 60
Pro shop	Pro-shop	(33) 04 94 49 26 60
Fax	Fax	(33) 04 93 49 00 39
Situation	Situation	

2 km N.E. Ste-Maxime, 10 010 hab.
24 km S. Draguignan, 30 180 hab.

Annual closure	Fermeture annnuelle	non
Weekly closure	Fermeture hebdomadaire	

Fees main season
Tarifs haute saison le parcours

	Week days Semaine	We/Bank holidays We/Férié
Individual Individuel	300 F	300 F
Couple Couple	520 F	520 F

Caddy	Caddy	non
Electric Trolley	Chariot électrique	non
Buggy	Voiturette	140 F/18 trous
Clubs	Clubs 1/2 série	80 F/jour

Credit cards Cartes de crédit
VISA - CB - Eurocard - MasterCard - AMEX - DC

268

GOLF
N 98
La Nartelle
Cap des Sardinaux
SAINTE-MAXIME
N 98
D 25
Beauvallon
SAINT-TROPEZ
D 98 A
D 559
0   2   4 km

Access Accès : A8 sortie 36, D25 →
Sainte-Maxime, → Golf
Map 14 on page 125 Carte 14 Page 125

GOLF COURSE
PARCOURS   **13**/20

Site	Site	▬▬▬▬▬▬▯▯
Maintenance	Entretien	▬▬▬▬▬▬▯▯
Architect	Architecte	Donald Harradine
		Peter Harradine
Type	Type	résidentiel, vallon
Relief	Relief	
Water in play	Eau en jeu	▬▯▯▯▯▯▯▯
Exp. to wind	Exposé au vent	
Trees in play	Arbres en jeu	▬▬▬▬▬▯▯▯

Scorecard Carte de score	Chp. Chp.	Mens Mess.	Ladies Da.
Length Long.	6155	5705	5143
Par	71	71	71

Advised golfing ability		0	12	24	36
Niveau de jeu recommandé			▬▬▬▬▬▬		
Hcp required	Handicap exigé	35			

CLUB HOUSE & AMENITIES
CLUB HOUSE ET ANNEXES   **7**/10

Pro shop	Pro-shop	▬▬▬▬▬▬▯▯
Driving range	Practice	▬▬▬▬▬▬▬▯
Sheltered	couvert	4 places
On grass	sur herbe	oui
Putting-green	putting-green	oui
Pitching-green	pitching green	oui

HOTEL FACILITIES
ENVIRONNEMENT HOTELIER   **7**/10

HOTELS HÔTELS·
Golf Plaza ****   sur place
111 chambres, D 1 350 F
Tél (33) 04 94 56 66 66, Fax (33) 04 94 56 66 00

Hostellerie de la Belle Aurore ****   Sainte-Maxime
16 chambres, D 1 000 F   2 km
Tél (33) 04 94 96 02 45, Fax (33) 04 94 96 63 87

Mas des Brugassières ** Plan de la Tour Sainte-Maxime
14 chambres, D 520 F   11 km
Tél (33) 04 94 43 72 42, Fax (33) 04 94 43 00 20

RESTAURANTS RESTAURANT
Hostellerie de la Belle Aurore   Sainte-Maxime
Tél (33) 04 94 96 02 45   2 km

L'Amiral   Sainte-Maxime
Tél (33) 04 94 43 99 36   2 km

SAVENAY

Entre Nantes et Saint-Nazaire, et dominant la Loire, Savenay est situé au coeur d'une région aujourd'hui très fournie en golfs de qualité. Un voyage de golf est ainsi agréable pour tous les niveaux, de la Vendée à la côte sud de Bretagne, dans des paysages très caractéristiques de ces régions. Ce parcours plutôt long (complété par un 9 trous d'entraînement) a été dessiné par Michel Gayon dans un site alternant les trous larges volontiers inspirés des "links" (par leur dessin et l'abondance des bunkers stratégiques), et des trous plus intimes, notamment les 7 et 8, le long d'une pièce d'eau. Les arbres (beaucoup de châtaigniers) sont assez nombreux, mais sans que l'on éprouve une impression d'étouffement. Un petit regret : le grand nombre de trous parallèles. Et une satisfaction : l'amélioration de l'entretien.

Between Nantes and Saint Nazaire, overlooking the Loire river, Savenay stands at the heart of a region which today boasts a number of excellent courses. This makes a golfing holiday to Brittany a pleasant proposition for all, from the Vendée to the southern Breton coastline, in typical settings. This is a rather long course (there is also a 9 hole pitch 'n putt) designed by Michel Gayon, on a site where deliberately wide holes, designed and strategically bunkered in true links style, alternate with more intimate holes, notably the 7th and 8th along a stretch of water. Trees abound (a lot of chestnut trees) but are never too imposing a presence. The one little regret is the number of holes running parallel. And the one pleasing factor is the improved upkeep.

Golf de Savenay
Le Chambeau
F - 44260 SAVENAY

Office	Secrétariat	(33) 02 40 56 88 05
Pro shop	Pro-shop	(33) 02 40 56 88 05
Fax	Fax	(33) 02 40 56 89 04
Situation	Situation	

26 km E. Saint-Nazaire, 64 810 hab.

Annual closure	Fermeture annnuelle	non
Weekly closure	Fermeture hebdomadaire	mardi
		1/11→1/03/99

Fees main season
Tarifs haute saison le parcours

	Week days Semaine	We/Bank holidays We/Férié
Individual Individuel	250 F	250 F
Couple Couple	500 F	500 F

Caddy	Caddy	non
Electric Trolley	Chariot électrique	non
Buggy	Voiturette	150 F/18 trous
Clubs	Clubs 1/2 série	50 F/jour

Credit cards Cartes de crédit
VISA - CB - Eurocard - MasterCard

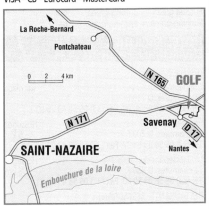

Access Accès : • Saint-Nazaire N171, sortie
Châteaubriand • Nantes N165, sortie Blain-Bouvron
Map 6 on page 108 Carte 6 Page 108

GOLF COURSE
PARCOURS
15/20

Site	Site	
Maintenance	Entretien	
Architect	Architecte	Michel Gayon
Type	Type	parc, vallon, bocage
Relief	Relief	
Water in play	Eau en jeu	
Exp. to wind	Exposé au vent	
Trees in play	Arbres en jeu	

Scorecard Carte de score	Chp. Chp.	Mens Mess.	Ladies Da.
Length Long.	6339	5778	5370
Par	73	73	73

Advised golfing ability		0	12	24	36
Niveau de jeu recommandé					
Hcp required	Handicap exigé	35			

CLUB HOUSE & AMENITIES
CLUB HOUSE ET ANNEXES
6/10

Pro shop	Pro-shop	
Driving range	Practice	
Sheltered	couvert	9 places
On grass	sur herbe	non
Putting-green	putting-green	oui
Pitching-green	pitching green	oui

269

HOTEL FACILITIES
ENVIRONNEMENT HOTELIER
4/10

HOTELS HÔTELS
Auberge du Chêne Vert ** — Savenay
20 chambres, D 300 F — 1 km
Tél (33) 02 40 56 90 16, Fax (33) 02 40 56 99 60

Manoir du Rodoir *** — La Roche-Bernard
26 chambres, D 490 F — 30 km
Tél (33) 02 99 90 82 68, Fax (33) 02 99 90 76 22

RESTAURANTS RESTAURANT
L'An II — Saint-Nazaire
Tél (33) 02 40 00 95 33 — 23 km

Au Bon Accueil — Saint-Nazaire
Tél (33) 02 40 22 07 05 — 23 km

Un parcours qui ne laisse personne indifférent. A proximité du parcours très plat d'Hossegor, il se déroule dans un paysage très accidenté, planté de pins et de chênes-liège. Les différences de dénivellation et l'étroitesse des fairways incitent à le conseiller aux joueurs en forme et golfiquement aguerris, qui devront bien étudier leur stratégie. En revanche, il n'est pas très long (notamment les par 3, sauf le 16), et demande un jeu de fers précis, en particulier pour attaquer les drapeaux, car les greens sont très modelés et de dimensions très variées. Les contours de fairway très travaillés et les abords des greens sont typiquement de von Hagge, de même que l'alternance de bunkers de sable et d'herbe et le dessin des pièces d'eau (sur cinq trous). Souvent spectaculaire et intimidant, il ne se maîtrise pas au premier abord. C'est un parcours follement amusant en match-play.

A course that leaves no-one indifferent. Close to the flat course of Hossegor, Seignosse unwinds over very hilly terrain planted with pine-trees and cork oaks. The steep slopes and narrow fairways mean this is a golf for seasoned players on top of their game, who will need to study their strategy. By contrast, the course is short (especially the par 3s, except the 16th) and requires precision ironwork, especially when attacking the contoured greens of all sizes. The rolling fairways and edges of the greens are typical of von Hagge, as are the alternating grass-bunkers and sand-traps and the design of the water hazards (on five holes). Often spectacular and intimidating, most golfers will have trouble first time out. A good course and great fun in match-play.

Golf de Seignosse
Avenue du Belvédère
F - 40510 SEIGNOSSE

Office	Secrétariat	(33) 05 58 41 68 30
Pro shop	Pro-shop	(33) 05 58 41 68 30
Fax	Fax	(33) 05 58 41 68 31
Situation	Situation	

28 km N. Bayonne, 40 050 hab.
37 km O. Dax, 19 310 hab.

Annual closure	Fermeture annnuelle	non
Weekly closure	Fermeture hebdomadaire	

Fees main season
Tarifs haute saison le parcours

	Week days Semaine	We/Bank holidays We/Férié
Individual Individuel	330 F	330 F
Couple Couple	620 F	620 F

Caddy	Caddy	non
Electric Trolley	Chariot électrique	non
Buggy	Voiturette	120 F/18 trous
Clubs	Clubs 1/2 série	60 F/jour

Credit cards Cartes de crédit
VISA - CB - Eurocard - MasterCard - AMEX - DC

270

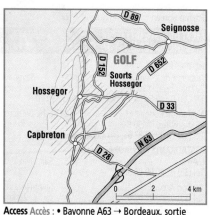

Access Accès : • Bayonne A63 → Bordeaux, sortie Capbreton → Capbreton/Hossegor • Bordeaux A63 → Bayonne, sortie Saint-Geours-de-Marenne → Seignosse **Map 12 on page 120** Carte 12 Page 120

GOLF COURSE
PARCOURS

17 /20

Site	Site	▰▰▰▱▱
Maintenance	Entretien	▰▰▰▰▱
Architect	Architecte	Robert von Hagge
Type	Type	forêt, bord de mer
Relief	Relief	▰▰▰▱▱
Water in play	Eau en jeu	▰▰▱▱▱
Exp. to wind	Exposé au vent	▰▰▱▱▱
Trees in play	Arbres en jeu	▰▰▰▰▱

Scorecard	Chp.	Mens	Ladies
Carte de score	Chp.	Mess.	Da.
Length Long.	6124	5774	5069
Par	72	72	72

Advised golfing ability		0 12 24 36
Niveau de jeu recommandé		▰▰▰▰▱
Hcp required	Handicap exigé	non

CLUB HOUSE & AMENITIES
CLUB HOUSE ET ANNEXES

7 /10

Pro shop	Pro-shop	▰▰▰▰▱
Driving range	Practice	▰▰▰▱▱
Sheltered	couvert	10 places
On grass	sur herbe	oui
Putting-green	putting-green	oui
Pitching-green	pitching green	oui

HOTEL FACILITIES
ENVIRONNEMENT HOTELIER

7 /10

HOTELS HÔTELS
Golf Hôtel Blue Green ***　　　　　　sur place
45 chambres, D 710 F
Tél (33) 05 58 43 30 00, Fax (33) 05 58 43 20 90

Beauséjour ***　　　　　　　　　　Hossegor
45 chambres, D 700 F　　　　　　　　　5 km
Tél (33) 05 58 43 51 07, Fax (33) 05 58 43 70 13

Les Hortensias du Lac　　　　　　　　Hossegor
21 chambres, D 430 F　　　　　　　　　5 km
Tél (33) 05 58 43 99 00, Fax (33) 05 58 43 42 81

RESTAURANTS RESTAURANT
Les Huîtrières du Lac　　　　　　　　Hossegor
Tél (33) 05 58 43 51 48　　　　　　　　5 km

Servanes ne peut renier sa Provence, avec les reliefs blancs et rocailleux des Alpilles, les oliviers, cyprès et platanes, et parfois un méchant coup de mistral, qui devrait empoisonner les golfeurs, mais ils en sont relativement protégés ici. Dans un site de campagne à peu près préservé d'immobilier, Sprecher et Watine ont dessiné un parcours bien paysagé, techniquement honnête, mais sans imagination excessive. Les contours de fairway auraient sans doute pu être mieux travaillés : en Provence, on préfère les sentiers aux boulevards. Autrement, il n'y a pas de grands commentaires à faire, sinon que, tout comme les joueurs de niveau moyen, les joueurs peu expérimentés trouveront ici le calme et de quoi assouvir leur passion naissante dans un cadre magnifique, à proximité du splendide village des Baux de Provence.

Servanes is Provence through and through, with the white rocky terrain of the Alpilles, cypress and plane trees, and sometimes a gust of mistral which can play havoc, although golfers are relatively sheltered on this course. On a country site more or less protected from property development, Sprecher and Watine have designed a nicely landscaped course which is technically fair but none too rich in imagination. The fairways could certainly have been better contoured, and in Provence they prefer pathways to boulevards. Otherwise, there is little else to say, except that high-handicappers and beginners alike will find the calm and the course they are looking for to satisfy their nascent enthusiasm for the game. All this in a magnificent setting close to the splendid village of Baux de Provence.

Golf Country-Club de Servanes

Domaine de Servanes
F - 13890 MOURIES

Office	Secrétariat	(33) 04 90 47 59 95
Pro shop	Pro-shop	(33) 04 90 47 59 95
Fax	Fax	(33) 04 90 47 52 58
Situation	Situation	

25 km E. Arles, 52 050 hab.

Annual closure	Fermeture annnuelle	non
Weekly closure	Fermeture hebdomadaire	

Fees main season
Tarifs haute saison la journée

	Week days Semaine	We/Bank holidays We/Férié
Individual Individuel	200 F	250 F
Couple Couple	400 F	500 F

2 GF + 2 déj. + voiturette: Sem 650 F, We 750 F

Caddy	Caddy	non
Electric Trolley	Chariot électrique	non
Buggy	Voiturette	200 F/18 trous
Clubs	Clubs 1/2 série	100 F/jour

Credit cards Cartes de crédit
VISA - CB - Eurocard - MasterCard - AMEX

Access Accès : A54/N113 Nîmes-Arles, → Marseille,
sortie Saint-Martin-de-Crau → Mouriès
Map 14 on page 124 Carte 14 Page 124

GOLF COURSE
PARCOURS
13/20

Site	Site	
Maintenance	Entretien	
Architect	Architecte	Thierry Sprecher Géry Watine
Type	Type	campagne
Relief	Relief	
Water in play	Eau en jeu	
Exp. to wind	Exposé au vent	
Trees in play	Arbres en jeu	

Scorecard Carte de score	Chp. Chp.	Mens Mess.	Ladies Da.
Length Long.	6101	5675	5150
Par	72	72	72

Advised golfing ability Niveau de jeu recommandé	0	12	24	36

Hcp required   Handicap exigé   35

CLUB HOUSE & AMENITIES
CLUB HOUSE ET ANNEXES
7/10

Pro shop	Pro-shop	
Driving range	Practice	
Sheltered	couvert	4 places
On grass	sur herbe	oui
Putting-green	putting-green	oui
Pitching-green	pitching green	oui

271

HOTEL FACILITIES
ENVIRONNEMENT HOTELIER
7/10

HOTELS HÔTELS
Oustau de Baumanière ★★★★   Les Baux-de-Provence
11 chambres, D 1 250 F   8 km
Tél (33) 04 90 54 33 07, Fax (33) 04 90 54 40 46
Cabro d'Or ★★★★   Les Baux-de-Provence
31 chambres, D 715 F   8 km
Tél (33) 04 90 54 33 21, Fax (33) 04 90 54 45 98
Valbaussenc ★★★   Maussane
21 chambres, D 650 F   7 km
Tél (33) 04 90 54 38 90, Fax (33) 04 90 54 33 36

RESTAURANTS RESTAURANT
Oustau de Baumanière   Les Baux-de-Provence
Tél (33) 04 90 54 33 07   8 km
Lou Pantaï   Maussane 7 km
Tél (33) 04 90 54 39 27
La Riboto de Taven   Les Baux-de-Provence
Tél (33) 04 90 54 34 23.   8 km

Avec ce très récent parcours, l'Alsace confirme son statut de région golfique de qualité. Bernhard Langer offre un dessin très technique, où les obstacles sont visuellement et réellement menaçants. La présence de nombreux bunkers de greens et de fairways (toujours un peu trop de sable) comme des obstacles d'eau (sur 14 trous) exige une attention constante et impose un rythme soutenu, mais les joueurs peu expérimentés pourront trouver des solutions et s'y amuser, en jouant des départs avancés. De nombreuses buttes séparent les fairways et entourent la plupart des greens, ajoutant du relief à cet espace naturellement plat, et entouré de forêts. Les greens sont de bonne dimension, souvent bien modelés, ajoutant à l'intérêt du jeu. Au moment de notre visite, l'entretien avait beaucoup progressé par rapport à l'an dernier.

With this new course, Alsace has confirmed its status as a great region for golf. Bernhard Langer has created a very technical layout where hazards are visually and truly threatening. The numerous green-side and fairway bunkers (still containing a little too much sand) and the water hazards (on 14 holes) demand constant care and establish a nice balance, but inexperienced golfers will find the answer and have fun by playing from the front tees. The fairways are separated by numerous sandhills, which also surround most of the greens, thus adding relief to a naturally flat terrain encircled by a forest. The greens are large and often well contoured, thus adding extra spice to the course. When we visited, the maintenance was better than last year.

Soufflenheim Baden Baden

Allée du Golf
F - 67620 SOUFFLENHEIM

Office	Secrétariat	(33) 03 88 05 77 00
Pro shop	Pro-shop	(33) 03 88 05 77 00
Fax	Fax	(33) 03 88 05 77 01
Situation	Situation	

40 km Strasbourg, 252 260 hab.
15 km Haguenau, 27 670 hab.

Annual closure	Fermeture annnuelle	non
Weekly closure	Fermeture hebdomadaire	non
		1/01/99→28/02/99

Fees main season Tarifs haute saison le parcours

	Week days Semaine	We/Bank holidays We/Férié
Individual Individuel	300 F	400 F
Couple Couple	600 F	800 F

Caddy	Caddy	sur réservation
Electric Trolley	Chariot électrique	non
Buggy	Voiturette	170 F/18 trous
Clubs	Clubs	100 F/18 trous

Credit cards Cartes de crédit
VISA - CB - Eurocard - MasterCard

Access Accès : Strasbourg, A4, sortie Karlsruhe-Lauterburg, D300 pendant 15 km, sortie Soufflenheim
→ Golf Map 4 on page 105 Carte 4 Page 105

GOLF COURSE
PARCOURS
16/20

Site	Site	
Maintenance	Entretien	
Architect	Architecte	Bernhard Langer
Type	Type	forêt, plaine
Relief	Relief	
Water in play	Eau en jeu	
Exp. to wind	Exposé au vent	
Trees in play	Arbres en jeu	

Scorecard Carte de score	Chp. Chp.	Mens Mess.	Ladies Da.
Length Long.	6208	5872	5459
Par	72	72	72

Advised golfing ability		0	12	24	36
Niveau de jeu recommandé				
Hcp required	Handicap exigé	35		

CLUB HOUSE & AMENITIES
CLUB HOUSE ET ANNEXES
7/10

Pro shop	Pro-shop	
Driving range	Practice	
Sheltered	couvert	35 postes
On grass	sur herbe	non
Putting-green	putting-green	oui
Pitching-green	pitching green	oui

HOTEL FACILITIES
ENVIRONNEMENT HOTELIER
4/10

HOTELS HÔTELS

Europe — Haguenau
81 chambres, D 355 F — 15 km
Tél (33) 03 88 93 58 11, Fax (33) 03 88 93 21 33

Kaiserhof — Haguenau
15 chambres, D 330 F — 15 km
Tél (33) 03 88 73 43 43, Fax (33) 03 88 73 28 91

Relais de la Tour Romaine — Schweighouse sur Moder
60 chambres, D 330 F — 15 km
Tél (33) 03 88 72 06 06, Fax (33) 03 88 72 05 36

RESTAURANTS RESTAURANT

Princesse Maria Leczinska — Marienthal
Tél (33) 03 88 93 70 39 — 15 km

A l'Agneau — Swenheim
Tél (33) 03 88 86 95 55 — 5 km

272

Dans un des sites les plus magnifiques d'Europe, Robert Trent Jones a tracé le parcours en plein maquis, à l'exception de six trous absolument splendides en bord de falaise, d'où l'on découvre la Méditerranée et la Sardaigne en arrière-plan. Pas très long, mais très technique et assez accidenté (voiturette conseillée), ce parcours spectaculaire ne peut laisser indifférent. Si on peut l'estimer difficile pour les joueurs peu expérimentés, on peut en revanche adorer son tracé parfois déconcertant, ses provocations, ses greens très modelés. Avec ses couleurs, ses lumières, les odeurs de la flore, c'est un parcours assez magique, mais parfois injuste quand le vent vient lui donner un air d'Ecosse en plein soleil. Alors, ceux qui maîtrisent mal les balles basses peuvent souffrir ! Une cinquantaine de maisons de belle architecture sont dissimulées dans ce vaste domaine.

On one of Europe's most fabulous sites, Robert Trent Jones designed this course amid gorse and heathland, with the exception of six absolutely splendid holes atop the cliffs, from where Sardinia can be viewed in the distance over the shimmering Mediterranean. Not particularly long but very much a course for the technician and hilly to boot (buggy recommended), this spectacular course leaves no-one indifferent. While it may be considered tough for inexperienced golfers, you have to love the sometimes disconcerting layout, the provocative nature of the course and the switchback greens. With its colours, light and fragrances, this is a magic course, but one which is sometimes unjust when the wind gets up and brings along a breath of Scottish air in the Corsican sun. In this case, low shots are a must to keep a decent score. Fifty or so villas are hidden on this vast estate.

Golf de Spérone
Domaine de Spérone
F - 20169 SPERONE

Office	Secrétariat	(33) 04 95 73 17 13
Pro shop	Pro-shop	(33) 04 95 73 17 13
Fax	Fax	(33) 04 95 73 17 85
Situation	Situation	

6 km S.E. Bonifacio, 2 680 hab.

Annual closure	Fermeture annnuelle	oui
		6/01/99→3/02/99
Weekly closure	Fermeture hebdomadaire	jeudi
	ap-m(01/05 → 30/09)	

Fees main season Tarifs haute saison la journée

	Week days Semaine	We/Bank holidays We/Férié
Individual Individuel	390 F	390 F
Couple Couple	780 F	780 F

Du 16/09 →15/06: GF 330 F

Caddy	Caddy	non
Electric Trolley	Chariot électrique	non
Buggy	Voiturette	220 F/18 trous
Clubs	Clubs 1/2 série	60 F/jour

Credit cards Cartes de crédit
VISA - CB - Eurocard - MasterCard - AMEX - DC

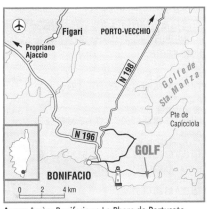

Access Accès : Bonifacio → Le Phare de Pertusato,
→ Golf
Map 14 on page 125 Carte 14 Page 125

GOLF COURSE / PARCOURS — 17 /20

Site	Site	
Maintenance	Entretien	
Architect	Architecte	R. Trent Jones Sr
Type	Type	bord de mer, vallons
Relief	Relief	
Water in play	Eau en jeu	
Exp. to wind	Exposé au vent	
Trees in play	Arbres en jeu	

Scorecard Carte de score	Chp. Chp.	Mens Mess.	Ladies Da.
Length Long.	6130	5603	5197
Par	72	72	72

Advised golfing ability Niveau de jeu recommandé	0 12 24 36
Hcp required Handicap exigé	28

CLUB HOUSE & AMENITIES / CLUB HOUSE ET ANNEXES — 7 /10

Pro shop	Pro-shop	
Driving range	Practice	
Sheltered	couvert	non
On grass	sur herbe	oui
Putting-green	putting-green	oui
Pitching-green	pitching green	oui

273

HOTEL FACILITIES / ENVIRONNEMENT HOTELIER — 5 /10

HOTELS HÔTELS
A Trama — Bonifacio
25 chambres, D 355 F — 6 km
Tél (33) 04 95 73 17 17, Fax (33) 04 95 73 17 79

Genovese *** — Bonifacio
14 chambres, D 1 700 F — 6 km
Tél (33) 04 95 73 12 34, Fax (33) 04 95 73 09 03

Roy d'Aragon — Bonifacio
31 chambres, D 700 F — 6 km
Tél (33) 04 95 73 03 99, Fax (33) 04 95 73 07 94

RESTAURANTS RESTAURANT
Stella d'Oro — Bonifacio
Tél (33) 04 95 73 03 63 — 6 km

Quatre Vents — Bonifacio
Tél (33) 04 95 73 07 50 — 6 km

Le golf des Strasbourgeois, avant la création de la Wantzenau et du Kempferhof. L'architecture semble en comparaison très traditionnelle, avec des bunkers peu pénalisants, quelques obstacles d'eau, surtout sur le Rouge, où les arbres ajoutent d'autres difficultés. Les trous les plus durs sont groupés au début du Jaune, mais cet ensemble reste rassurant, et ne suscite pas de grandes émotions visuelles ou techniques chez les meilleurs joueurs. En revanche, les nombreux membres y évoluent avec plaisir en famille, d'autant que les fairways sont excellents en toutes saisons. Les greens sont bien défendus, mais il est toujours possible d'y accéder en faisant rouler la balle. Mais les travaux entrepris pourraient modifier notre jugement. Il s'agit avant tout d'un club pour les locaux, cependant ouvert aux joueurs extérieurs (accès difficile en week-end). De passage à Strasbourg, ils y passeront une journée plaisante.

This was the traditional golf club of Strasbourg before Wantzenau and Kempferhof came along. By comparison, the architecture looks very traditional with flat bunkers and a few water hazards, notably on the Red course, where trees add further difficulties. The hardest holes are grouped at the start of the Yellow course, but the full layout is somewhat reassuring and will hardly cause much visual or technical stirrings among the best players. By contrast, the many members enjoy playing here with the family, especially since the fairways are in excellent condition all year round. The greens are well defended but not from the front, thus allowing the easier chipped (or topped!) shot onto the putting surface. Watch this space: remodeling is under progress... This is first and foremost a club for the locals, although the course is open to green-feers (not so easy on week-ends). When passing through Strasbourg, they can spend a pleasant day.

Golf de Strasbourg-Ilkirch
Route du Rhin
F - 67400 ILLKIRCH

Office	Secrétariat	(33) 03 88 66 17 22
Pro shop	Pro-shop	(33) 03 88 67 22 85
Fax	Fax	(33) 03 88 65 05 67
Situation	Situation	

12 km S. Strasbourg, 252 260 hab.

Annual closure	Fermeture annnuelle	oui
		22/12→3/01/99
Weekly closure	Fermeture hebdomadaire	non
		mercredi, le restaurant

Fees main season Tarifs haute saison le parcours

	Week days Semaine	We/Bank holidays We/Férié
Individual Individuel	230 F	300 F
Couple Couple	460 F	600 F

We haute saison, membres seulement (members only)

Caddy	Caddy	non
Electric Trolley	Chariot électrique	non
Buggy	Voiturette	200 F/18 trous
Clubs	Clubs	non

Credit cards Cartes de crédit
VISA - CB - Eurocard - MasterCard

274

Access Accès : • Strasbourg A35, sortie Baggersee,
1er rond-point → Markolsheim, 2e rond-point, voie express, → Golf • Colmar N83, traverser Fegersheim → Illkirch **Map 4 on page 105** Carte 4 Page 105

GOLF COURSE
PARCOURS   13/20

Site	Site	▰▰▰▱▱
Maintenance	Entretien	▰▰▰▱▱
Architect	Architecte	Donald Harradine
Type	Type	campagne
Relief	Relief	▰▱▱▱▱
Water in play	Eau en jeu	▰▰▱▱▱
Exp. to wind	Exposé au vent	▰▰▱▱▱
Trees in play	Arbres en jeu	▰▰▰▱▱

Scorecard Carte de score	Chp. Chp.	Mens Mess.	Ladies Da.
Length Long.	6105	5782	5194
Par	73	73	73

Advised golfing ability	0	12	24	36
Niveau de jeu recommandé		▱		
Hcp required Handicap exigé	35			

CLUB HOUSE & AMENITIES
CLUB HOUSE ET ANNEXES   7/10

Pro shop	Pro-shop	▰▰▰▱▱
Driving range	Practice	▰▰▰▱▱
Sheltered	couvert	15 places
On grass	sur herbe	oui (sauf hiver)
Putting-green	putting-green	oui
Pitching-green	pitching green	oui

HOTEL FACILITIES
ENVIRONNEMENT HOTELIER   6/10

HOTELS HÔTELS

Echiquier ***		Illkirch
68 chambres, D 565 F		3 km
Tél (33) 03 88 40 84 84, Fax (33) 03 88 66 22 83		
Alsace **		Illkirch
40 chambres, D 300 F		3 km
Tél (33) 03 88 66 41 60, Fax (33) 03 88 67 04 64		
Alizés		Lipsheim
49 chambres, D 450 F		6 km
Tél (33) 03 88 59 62 00, Fax (33) 03 88 64 21 61		

RESTAURANTS RESTAURANT

Buerehiesel	Strasbourg
Tél (33) 03 88 61 62 24	12 km
Le Crocodile	Strasbourg
Tél(33) 03 88 32 13 02	12 km
Maison Kammerzell et Baumann	Strasbourg
Tél(33) 03 88 32 42 14	12 km

A moyenne altitude (1.000 mètres), ce parcours n'est ouvert que huit mois par an, dans un site isolé et très naturel donnant une sensation de calme extrême. Gary Player a complètement remodelé un ancien tracé, avec beaucoup de goût et d'intelligence du jeu. On peut regretter un certain manque de souci de spectacle golfique, mais il a visiblement voulu préserver la beauté du lieu (l'automne y est splendide). Son tracé est très intéressant, sa difficulté globale raisonnable, il demande cependant une bonne technique pour être négocié avec succès. Les joueurs de tous niveaux peuvent y évoluer, de préférence en voiturette car les reliefs sont assez prononcés. Le plaisir ne sera certes pas éternellement renouvelé, car la stratégie sur chaque trou est pratiquement toujours la même, mais il sera toujours de grande qualité. Les amoureux de la nature vont adorer Taulane, d'autant que l'hôtel sur place est très agréable.

At mid-altitude (3,200 ft), Taulane is open just eight months a year in an isolated and very natural setting of extreme tranquillity. Gary Player completely restyled an old layout with considerable taste and golfing nous. Perhaps sadly there was a little lack of concern for the visual side of things, but he clearly set out to preserve the beauty of the site (magnificent in autumn). The layout is very interesting and overall difficulty quite reasonable, but a good round here requires a sound technique. Players of all levels will enjoy Taulane, preferably on 4-wheels since some of the slopes are on the steep side. But it is hard to imagine golfers enjoying playing here again and again, as game strategy is virtually the same for each hole. Yet this is good golfing. Nature-enthusiasts will love the site, which also boasts a very pleasant hotel.

Golf de Taulane
RN 85
F - 83840 LA MARTRE

Office	Secrétariat	(33) 04 93 60 31 30
Pro shop	Pro-shop	(33) 04 93 60 31 30
Fax	Fax	(33) 04 93 60 33 23
Situation	Situation	

50 km N.O. Grasse, 41 380 hab.

Annual closure	Fermeture annnuelle	non
Weekly closure	Fermeture hebdomadaire	

Fees main season
Tarifs haute saison le parcours

	Week days Semaine	We/Bank holidays We/Férié
Individual Individuel	350 F	350 F
Couple Couple	700 F	700 F

Caddy	Caddy	sur réservation
Electric Trolley	Chariot électrique	100 F/18 trous
Buggy	Voiturette	220 F/18 trous
Clubs	Clubs la série	150 F/jour

Credit cards Cartes de crédit
VISA - CB - Eurocard - MasterCard - AMEX - DC

Vers Castellane (17 km du golf)

GOLF

ROUTE NAPOLÉON

N 85

Le Castellas 1068 m

Vers Grasse (44 km)

La Bastide

0   2   4 km

Access Accès : Nice ou Cannes → Grasse Digne →
Le Logis du Pin, route Napoléon
Map 14 on page 125 Carte 14 Page 125

GOLF COURSE
PARCOURS   15/20

Site	Site	▬▬▬▬
Maintenance	Entretien	▬▬▬▬
Architect	Architecte	Gary Player
Type	Type	forêt
Relief	Relief	▬▬
Water in play	Eau en jeu	▬▬
Exp. to wind	Exposé au vent	▬▬
Trees in play	Arbres en jeu	▬▬▬

Scorecard Carte de score	Chp. Chp.	Mens Mess.	Ladies Da.
Length Long.	6269	5822	5341
Par	72	72	72

Advised golfing ability   0   12   24   36
Niveau de jeu recommandé
Hcp required   Handicap exigé   24 Mess. 28 Da.

CLUB HOUSE & AMENITIES
CLUB HOUSE ET ANNEXES   7/10

Pro shop	Pro-shop	▬▬▬
Driving range	Practice	▬▬▬
Sheltered	couvert	10 places
On grass	sur herbe	oui
Putting-green	putting-green	oui
Pitching-green	pitching green	oui

275

HOTEL FACILITIES
ENVIRONNEMENT HOTELIER   4/10

HOTELS HÔTELS
Château de Taulane ****   sur place
44 chambres, D 1 200 F
Tél (33) 04 93 40 60 80, Fax (33) 04 93 60 37 48

Château de Trigance ***   Trigance
10 chambres, D 900 F   20 km
Tél (33) 04 94 76 91 18, Fax (33) 04 94 85 68 99

RESTAURANTS RESTAURANT
Nouvel Hôtel du Commerce   Castellane
Tél (33) 04 92 83 61 00   15 km

L'Ancienne Station   La Martre
Tél (33) 04 93 60 38 48   1 km

Un club très vivant et professionnel, où il fait bon s'arrêter. Bien à l'abri du vent, avec de beaux chênes, quelques trouées offrant de jolies vues sur la vallée du Tarn, ce parcours a bien respecté l'environnement. Cette réussite générale rend certainement exigeant. Pour en faire un grand parcours, on souhaiterait par exemple que les bunkers soient un peu plus profonds, ce qui impliquerait une révision des avant-greens. Mais, en l'état, il faut déjà savoir jouer tous les coups, et utiliser tous les clubs du sac : les joueurs de bon handicap apprécieront particulièrement sa technicité. Assez varié pour ne jamais être ennuyeux, le tracé de Michael Fenn a évité les trous parallèles, et offre un rythme de jeu bien équilibré, alternant les trous difficiles et les trous plus reposants. Un golf très familial, avec une bonne politique sportive, qui mérite largement la visite.

A very lively, professional club where it is always a pleasure to stop-off. Nicely sheltered from the wind, this is a course that has espoused its environment and is laid out amidst some beautiful oaks. A few holes provide splendid views over the Tarn river. This initial very positive impression makes the visitor a little more demanding when it comes to the rest. For example, a great course would require slightly deeper bunkers and consequently a little re-design work around the greens. But as it is, it demands every shot in the book and probably every club in your bag. Low handicappers in particular will enjoy the course's technical aspect. With enough variety never to be boring, Michael Fenn's layout has avoided parallel holes and provides a nicely balanced course, alternating difficult holes with the not so difficult. A very family-style course, very well organised sports-wise and well worth the visit.

Golf de Toulouse Palmola
F - 31660 BUZET-SUR-TARN

Office	Secrétariat	(33) 05 61 84 20 50
Pro shop	Pro-shop	(33) 05 61 84 20 50
Fax	Fax	(33) 05 61 84 48 92
Situation	Situation	

20 km N.E. Toulouse, 358 680 hab.

Annual closure	Fermeture annnuelle	non
Weekly closure	Fermeture hebdomadaire	mardi

Fees main season
Tarifs haute saison la journée

	Week days Semaine	We/Bank holidays We/Férié
Individual Individuel	210 F	350 F
Couple Couple	420 F	600 F

Caddy	Caddy	non
Electric Trolley	Chariot électrique	non
Buggy	Voiturette	200 F/18 trous
Clubs	Clubs 1/2 série	80 F/jour

Credit cards Cartes de crédit
VISA - CB - Eurocard - MasterCard

276

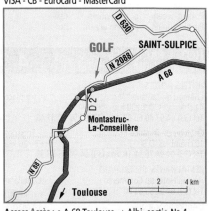

Access Accès : • A 68 Toulouse → Albi, sortie N° 4 Gémil-Buzet sur Tarn • Albi → Toulouse, sortie Montastruc la Conseillière, → Albi (N88), → Golf
Map 13 on page 122 Carte 13 Page 122

GOLF COURSE
PARCOURS

15/20

Site	Site	▬▬▬▬
Maintenance	Entretien	▬▬▬▬
Architect	Architecte	Michael Fenn
Type	Type	forêt, résidentiel
Relief	Relief	▬▬
Water in play	Eau en jeu	▬▬
Exp. to wind	Exposé au vent	▬
Trees in play	Arbres en jeu	▬▬

Scorecard Carte de score	Chp. Chp.	Mens Mess.	Ladies Da.
Length Long.	6156	5949	5292
Par	72	72	72

Advised golfing ability   0   12   24   36
Niveau de jeu recommandé
Hcp required   Handicap exigé   24-28 (We)

CLUB HOUSE & AMENITIES
CLUB HOUSE ET ANNEXES

7/10

Pro shop	Pro-shop	▬▬▬
Driving range	Practice	▬▬▬
Sheltered	couvert	4 places
On grass	sur herbe	oui
Putting-green	putting-green	oui
Pitching-green	pitching green	oui

HOTEL FACILITIES
ENVIRONNEMENT HOTELIER

4/10

HOTELS HÔTELS
Château de Saint-Lieux **   Saint-Lieux
12 chambres, D 350 F   13 km

Tél (33) 05 63 41 60 87A l'Hôtel **   L'Union
47 chambres, D 250 F   13 km
Tél (33) 05 61 09 06 06, Fax (33) 05 61 74 21 32

Campanile **   L'Union
72 chambres, D 270 F   13 km
Tél (33) 05 61 74 00 40, Fax (33) 05 61 09 53 38

RESTAURANTS RESTAURANT
Le Pastel   Toulouse
Tél (33) 05 61 40 59 01   20 km

Les Jardins de l'Opéra   Toulouse
Tél (33) 05 61 23 07 76   20 km

TOULOUSE-SEILH ROUGE

〉 15 | 7 | 6

Un Jeremy Pern typique. A partir d'un terrain plat, il a bien travaillé ses mouvements de terrain comme ses bunkers, de toutes formes et de toutes dimensions. Les greens sont vastes, avec des reliefs subtils, permettant de multiples positions de drapeaux. Les obstacles d'eau jouent aussi un grand rôle dans la stratégie, mais ils peuvent être dangereux s'il y a du vent. Autrement, les joueurs prudents peuvent jouer à l'écart. Peu boisé, il a fait l'objet de programmes immobiliers, mais pas trop agressifs visuellement. Ce parcours de style américain réclame un jeu très complet, et notamment un petit jeu bien affûté, il joue donc bien son rôle de "formation de golfeurs". Ici, la chance ne peut jouer aucun rôle dans un bon score. Les installations sont fonctionnelles, mais pas très chaleureuses : ce n'est pourtant pas hors de portée d'un golf commercial...

This is a typical Jeremy Pern layout, starting out with flat terrain and carefully designing-in sloping terrain and bunkers of all shapes and sizes. The greens are huge with subtle breaks, allowing numerous different pin positions. Water hazards play a major role in game strategy here and can be very dangerous if there is wind around. Otherwise, the cautious player will lay up or play around them. There are few trees but a number of property developments, which fortunately are not too hard on the eye. Toulouse-Seilh is an American style course requiring an all-round game and some slick short irons, thereby fulfilling its role as a course for "schooling golfers". A good score here owes little or nothing to luck. The facilities are functional but not over-welcoming, surely a feature that a business venture course like this should be able to afford.

Golf de Toulouse-Seilh Latitudes

Route de Grenade
F - 31860 SEILH

Office	Secrétariat	(33) 05 62 13 14 14
Pro shop	Pro-shop	(33) 05 62 13 14 14
Fax	Fax	(33) 05 61 42 34 17
Situation	Situation	

10 km N.O. Toulouse, 358 680 hab.

Annual closure	Fermeture annnuelle	non
Weekly closure	Fermeture hebdomadaire	

Fees main season
Tarifs haute saison la journée

	Week days Semaine	We/Bank holidays We/Férié
Individual Individuel	165 F	240 F
Couple Couple	330 F	480 F

Semaine : GF + déj. 200 F - Mardi : Dames et Seniors, GF 115 F - 100 F 07 → 08

Caddy	Caddy	non
Electric Trolley	Chariot électrique	non
Buggy	Voiturette	120 F/18 trous
Clubs	Clubs 1/2 série	50 F/jour

Credit cards Cartes de crédit
VISA - CB - Eurocard - MasterCard - AMEX

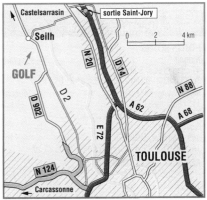

Access Accès : A62 ou A61 → Toulouse,
sortie Saint-Jory → Lespinasse → Blagnac, → Golf
Map 12 on page 121 Carte 12 Page 121

GOLF COURSE
PARCOURS

15/20

Site	Site	
Maintenance	Entretien	
Architect	Architecte	Jeremy Pern Jean Garaïalde
Type	Type	plaine, résidentiel
Relief	Relief	
Water in play	Eau en jeu	
Exp. to wind	Exposé au vent	
Trees in play	Arbres en jeu	

Scorecard Carte de score	Chp. Chp.	Mens Mess.	Ladies Da.
Length Long.	6330	5862	5018
Par	72	72	72

Advised golfing ability		0 12 24 36
Niveau de jeu recommandé		
Hcp required	Handicap exigé	28, le We

CLUB HOUSE & AMENITIES
CLUB HOUSE ET ANNEXES

7/10

Pro shop	Pro-shop	
Driving range	Practice	
Sheltered	couvert	30 places
On grass	sur herbe	oui
Putting-green	putting-green	oui
Pitching-green	pitching green	oui

277

HOTEL FACILITIES
ENVIRONNEMENT HOTELIER

6/10

HOTELS HÔTELS
Latitudes ***   sur place
115 chambres, D 600 F
Tél (33) 05 62 13 14 15, Fax (33) 05 61 59 77 97

Diane ***   Toulouse
35 chambres, D 520 F   10 km
Tél (33) 05 61 07 59 52, Fax (33) 05 61 86 38 94

Grand Hôtel de l'Opéra ****   Toulouse
49 chambres, D 700 F   10 km
Tél (33) 05 61 21 82 66, Fax (33) 05 61 23 41 04

RESTAURANTS RESTAURANT
Le Pastel   Toulouse
Tél (33) 05 61 40 59 01   10 km

Les Jardins de l'Opéra   Toulouse
Tél (33) 05 61 23 07 76   10 km

Ce 18 trous est le chef-d'oeuvre du Touquet, il vient d'être rétabli dans un tracé proche de celui d'avant-guerre, mais pas forcément avec la rigueur architecturale nécessaire à toute restauration d'un "monument historique" : on distingue nettement les différences de style. Il offre des reliefs modérés, des fairways très travaillés, quelques bunkers redoutables, et des greens parfois déconcertants, dans une végétation clairsemée, mais souvent en jeu. Une bonne partie des trous se déroulent dans des dunes spectaculaires : ici, il faut être humble avec son golf, car les punitions pour les coups manqués sont immédiates. Et quand le vent s'en mêle, la patience s'impose. Alors, les "manieurs de balles" et les tacticiens prennent le dessus sur les purs frappeurs. Difficile pour les débutants, c'est un parcours passionnant pour les joueurs aguerris. L'autre 18 trous, "La Forêt" n'est plus dans la même catégorie.

This 18-hole course is the unquestioned masterpiece of Le Touquet. The course has recently been remodelled back to a layout very close to the original pre-war design, but maybe not with the architectural thoroughness required by the restoration of an historical monument. The differences in style clearly stand out. "La Mer" is moderately hilly, boasts carefully designed fairways, a few formidable bunkers and sometimes disconcerting greens amidst sparse vegetation that nonetheless is often in play. A good number of holes are laid out among some spectacular dunes, where golfers need to be humble with their golf: mis-hit shots are punished immediately. And when the wind blows, patience, too, is a virtue. Flighters of the ball and the shrewd tactician will find the going easier than the long-hitter. A tough course for beginners, a good course for the seasoned golfer. "La Forêt", the other 18-holer is no more a in the same class.

Golf du Touquet

Avenue du Golf
F - 62520 LE TOUQUET

Office	Secrétariat	(33) 03 21 06 28 00
Pro shop	Pro-shop	(33) 03 21 06 28 03
Fax	Fax	(33) 03 21 06 28 01
Situation	Situation	

2,5 km Le Touquet, 5 590 hab.
18 km N.O. Montreuil, 2 450 hab.

Annual closure	Fermeture annnuelle	non
Weekly closure	Fermeture hebdomadaire	

Fees main season
Tarifs haute saison la journée

	Week days Semaine	We/Bank holidays We/Férié
Individual Individuel	250 F	320 F
Couple Couple	500 F	640 F

01/11 → 31/03 : GF Sem. 120 F, We 180 F

Caddy	Caddy	sur réservation
Electric Trolley	Chariot électrique	non
Buggy	Voiturette	240 F/18 trous
Clubs	Clubs 1/2 série	80 F/jour

Credit cards Cartes de crédit
VISA - CB - Eurocard - MasterCard

278

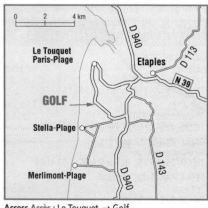

Access Accès : Le Touquet, → Golf
Map 1 on page 98 Carte 1 Page 98

GOLF COURSE
PARCOURS **17**/20

Site	Site	
Maintenance	Entretien	
Architect	Architecte	Taylor, Colt
Type	Type	links
Relief	Relief	
Water in play	Eau en jeu	
Exp. to wind	Exposé au vent	
Trees in play	Arbres en jeu	

Scorecard	Chp.	Mens	Ladies
Carte de score	Chp.	Mess.	Da.
Length Long.	6330	6330	5346
Par	72	72	72

Advised golfing ability	0	12	24	36
Niveau de jeu recommandé				
Hcp required	Handicap exigé	24 Mess., 28 Da.		

CLUB HOUSE & AMENITIES
CLUB HOUSE ET ANNEXES **6**/10

Pro shop	Pro-shop	
Driving range	Practice	
Sheltered	couvert	25 places
On grass	sur herbe	oui
Putting-green	putting-green	oui
Pitching-green	pitching green	oui

HOTEL FACILITIES
ENVIRONNEMENT HOTELIER **7**/10

HOTELS HÔTELS
Manoir *** — sur place
41 chambres, D 800 F
Tél (33) 03 21 05 20 22, Fax (33) 03 21 05 31 26
Westminster **** — Le Touquet
115 chambres, D 800 F — 2,5 km
Tél (33) 03 21 05 48 48, Fax (33) 03 21 05 45 45
Novotel *** — Le Touquet
149 chambres, D 800 F — 2,5 km
Tél (33) 03 21 09 85 00, Fax (33) 03 21 09 85 10

RESTAURANTS RESTAURANT
Flavio-Club de la Forêt — Le Touquet
Tél (33) 03 21 05 10 22 — 2,5 km
Le Café des Arts — Le Touquet
Tél (33) 03 21 05 21 55 — 2,5 km
L'Escale — Le Touquet
Tél (33) 03 21 05 23 22 — 5 km

13	7	6

Un vrai parc de Touraine, avec beaucoup de beaux arbres et une ambiance très familiale, où l'on se sent vite à l'aise. Michael Fenn y a tracé un parcours très varié, mais un peu conformiste, avec quelques trous délicats en raison de fairways étroits, compensés par de grandes "avenues" où les longs frappeurs pourront se déchaîner. L'ensemble n'est pas très long, le relief modérément accidenté, ce qui convient bien à une clientèle de joueurs moyens assez droits, mais les joueurs peu précis peuvent avoir quelques problèmes, car les greens ne sont pas non plus immenses. Pour agrémenter l'incertitude du jeu, quelques pièces d'eau et ruisseaux sont stratégiquement bien utilisés. Dans cette région très touristique des châteaux de la Loire, les visiteurs passeront une journée très agréable et éventuellement encourageante quant à leurs scores sur ce parcours (un peu humide en hiver).

A real Touraine park with many beautiful trees and a very family atmosphere where you soon feel at home. Michael Fenn has designed a course of great variety but a little conformist in nature. The few troublesome holes with tight fairways are offset somewhat by some wide "avenues" where big hitters can let fly. On the whole this is not a very long course, hilly in parts, and is particularly suitable for the average golfer who plays straight. Wayward hitters will have a few more problems, because the greens are also rather small. To add a little spice to uncertainty, a few stretches of water and streams are used to good strategic effect. In this holiday region of the Loire and castles, visitors will spend a very pleasant day's golfing on a course that can be a little wet in winter but which can be encouraging score-wise.

Golf de Touraine
Château de la Touche
F - 37510 BALLAN-MIRE

Office	Secrétariat	(33) 02 47 53 20 28
Pro shop	Pro-shop	(33) 02 47 53 20 28
Fax	Fax	(33) 02 47 53 31 54
Situation	Situation	

12 km S.O. Tours, 129 500 hab.

Annual closure	Fermeture annnuelle	non
Weekly closure	Fermeture hebdomadaire	non
		mardi, le restaurant

Fees main season
Tarifs haute saison la journée

	Week days Semaine	We/Bank holidays We/Férié
Individual Individuel	230 F	300 F
Couple Couple	460 F	600 F

Caddy	Caddy	sur réservation
Electric Trolley	Chariot électrique	non
Buggy	Voiturette	non
Clubs	Clubs série	100 F/jour

Credit cards Cartes de crédit
VISA - CB - Eurocard - MasterCard

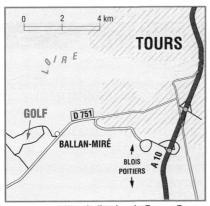

TOURS

LOIRE
GOLF   D 751
BALLAN-MIRÉ
BLOIS POITIERS
A 10

Access Accès : A10 sortie Chambray-les-Tours → Tours → Joué-les-Tours, Chinon → Ballan-Miré
Map 6 on page 109 Carte 6 Page 109

GOLF COURSE / PARCOURS   13/20

Site	Site	
Maintenance	Entretien	
Architect	Architecte	Michael Fenn
Type	Type	parc, vallon
Relief	Relief	
Water in play	Eau en jeu	
Exp. to wind	Exposé au vent	
Trees in play	Arbres en jeu	

Scorecard Carte de score	Chp. Chp.	Mens Mess.	Ladies Da.
Length Long.	5671	5424	4778
Par	71	71	71

Advised golfing ability Niveau de jeu recommandé	0	12	24	36
Hcp required Handicap exigé	35, We			

CLUB HOUSE & AMENITIES / CLUB HOUSE ET ANNEXES   7/10

Pro shop	Pro-shop	
Driving range	Practice	
Sheltered	couvert	8 places
On grass	sur herbe	non
Putting-green	putting-green	oui
Pitching-green	pitching green	oui

279

HOTEL FACILITIES / ENVIRONNEMENT HOTELIER   6/10

HOTELS HÔTELS

Mercure *** — Joué-les-Tours
75 chambres, D 450 F — 5 km
Tél (33) 02 47 53 16 16, Fax (33) 02 47 53 14 00

Château de Beaulieu *** — Joué-les-Tours
19 chambres, D 750 F — 5 km
Tél (33) 02 47 53 20 26, Fax (33) 02 47 53 84 20

Les Cèdres *** — Savonnières
37 chambres, D 500 F — 3 km
Tél (33) 02 47 53 00 28, Fax (33) 02 47 80 03 84

RESTAURANTS RESTAURANT

Jean Bardet — Tours
Tél (33) 02 47 41 41 11 — 12 km

VAL DE SORNE

Dans une région pas très riche en golfs, la création de ce golf était bienvenue. Dessiné par Hugues Lambert sur un terrain modérément accidenté dans un style plus américain que britannique, il comporte des obstacles d'eau sur une demi-douzaine de trous. En jouant des départs avancés et même si certains dévers obligent à jouer dans la pente, il est accessible à tous les niveaux, à l'exception du 16, un par 4 difficile dont le green est entouré d'eau. Le déroulement du parcours est assez agréable, sans être d'un tracé vraiment exceptionnel, les arbres sont souvent bien en jeu (comme au 13), mais il vaut mieux le visiter entre mai et octobre, même si des drainages ont été effectués. Les greens sont de dimensions et de difficultés moyenne : leur modelage un peu timide conviendra à tous les handicaps, et leurs défenses ne sont pas trop hermétiques.

This course was most welcome in a region where golf playing facilities are few and far between. Laid out over a moderately hilly terrain by Hugues Lambert in a rather more American style than British, it features water hazards on half a dozen or so holes. From the front-tees, and despite the sloping fairways, the course can be played by golfers of all abilities, with the possible exception of the 16th, a difficult par 4 where the green is surrounded by water. The course unfolds in a pleasant manner without ever being outstanding, and the trees are often very much in play (on the 13th, for example). And even though drainage work is now complete, the best time to play here is between May and October. The greens are of average size and difficulty, and are sufficiently flat and bunkerless to appeal to all handicaps.

Golf du Val de Sorne
Vernantois
F - 39570 LONS-LE-SAUNIER

Office	Secrétariat	(33) 03 84 43 04 80
Pro shop	Pro-shop	(33) 03 84 43 04 80
Fax	Fax	(33) 03 84 47 31 21
Situation	Situation	

6 km S.E. Lons-le-Saunier, 19 140 hab.

Annual closure	Fermeture annnuelle	non
Weekly closure	Fermeture hebdomadaire	non

Fees main season
Tarifs haute saison le parcours

	Week days Semaine	We/Bank holidays We/Férié
Individual Individuel	200 F	250 F
Couple Couple	400 F	500 F

Caddy	Caddy	non
Electric Trolley	Chariot électrique	60 F/18 trous
Buggy	Voiturette	200 F/18 trous
Clubs	Clubs 1/2 série	50 F/jour

Credit cards Cartes de crédit
VISA - CB - Eurocard - MasterCard

280

Access Accès : Lons-le-Saunier → Macornay
puis → Vernantois, → Golf
Map 8 on page 112 Carte 8 Page 112

GOLF COURSE
PARCOURS   14/20

Site	Site	▬▬▬▬▬▬□
Maintenance	Entretien	▬▬▬▬□□□
Architect	Architecte	Hugues Lambert
Type	Type	vallon
Relief	Relief	▬▬▬▬□□□
Water in play	Eau en jeu	▬▬▬□□□□
Exp. to wind	Exposé au vent	▬▬□□□□□
Trees in play	Arbres en jeu	▬▬▬□□□□

Scorecard Carte de score	Chp. Chp.	Mens Mess.	Ladies Da.
Length Long.	6270	6000	5056
Par	72	72	72

Advised golfing ability		0 12 24 36
Niveau de jeu recommandé		▬▬▬▬▬▬□
Hcp required	Handicap exigé	non

CLUB HOUSE & AMENITIES
CLUB HOUSE ET ANNEXES   7/10

Pro shop	Pro-shop	▬▬▬▬▬□□
Driving range	Practice	
Sheltered	couvert	5 places
On grass	sur herbe	non
Putting-green	putting-green	oui
Pitching-green	pitching green	non

HOTEL FACILITIES
ENVIRONNEMENT HOTELIER   5/10

HOTELS HÔTELS
Hôtel du Golf ★★★   Vernantois
36 chambres, D 460 F   sur place
Tél (33) 03 84 43 04 80, Fax (33) 03 84 47 31 21

Hostellerie des Monts-de-Vaux ★★★★   Poligny
10 chambres, D 700 F   29 km
Tél (33) 03 84 37 12 50, Fax (33) 03 84 37 09 07

Moulin de Bourgchâteau ★★   Louhans
18 chambres, D 300 F   26 km
Tél (33) 03 85 75 37 12, Fax (33) 03 85 75 45 11

RESTAURANTS RESTAURANT
La Comédie   Lons-le-Saunier
Tél (33) 03 84 24 20 66   6 km

Auberge de Chavannes   Courlans
Tél (33) 03 84 47 05 52   8 km

Un site vallonné dans la vallée du Scorff, et en pleine campagne bretonne, ponctuée de beaux arbres, notamment des chênes et châtaigniers, qui protègent bien du vent assez fréquent dans la région. Comme à son habitude, l'architecte Yves Bureau a dessiné un parcours très plaisant et diversifié, bien paysagé et assez large pour être rassurant, assez technique pour renouveler l'intérêt. Les bons scores ne sont pourtant pas si faciles car il faut tenir compte des dénivellations et de la présence de nombreux bunkers bien découpés. Les greens sont de bonne dimension, et bien construits, les obstacles d'eau peu nombreux. Tous les niveaux de jeu peuvent cohabiter ici, les joueurs moyens comme les meilleurs handicaps. Comme souvent en Bretagne, on peut y croiser de nombreux Britanniques. Une curiosité, la présence d'un tumulus antique.

This is a site of rolling landscape in the Scorff valley, at the heart of Breton countryside. It is dotted with some fine trees, particularly oak and horse-chestnut, which afford good protection from the frequent wind. As usual, architect Yves Bureau has laid out a very pleasant course, full of variety, well-landscaped and wide enough to reassure most of us, and technically difficult enough to keep it interesting. Yet good scores here are not always easy to come by, courtesy of some steep slopes and numerous nicely outlined bunkers. The greens are of a good size and well designed, and water hazards are rare. All golfers can play together here. And as is often the case in Brittany, the course is a favourite with British golfers. One little curiosity is the presence of a "tumulus", or sepulchral mound, on the course.

Golf de Val Queven
Kerruisseau
F - 56530 QUEVEN

Office	Secrétariat	(33) 02 97 05 17 96
Pro shop	Pro-shop	(33) 02 97 05 17 96
Fax	Fax	(33) 02 97 05 19 18
Situation	Situation	

8 km N.O. Lorient, 59 270 hab.

Annual closure	Fermeture annnuelle	non
Weekly closure	Fermeture hebdomadaire	

Fees main season
Tarifs haute saison le parcours

	Week days Semaine	We/Bank holidays We/Férié
Individual Individuel	255 F	255 F
Couple Couple	510 F	510 F

Caddy	Caddy	non
Electric Trolley	Chariot électrique	non
Buggy	Voiturette	150 F/18 trous
Clubs	Clubs 1/2 série	50 F/jour

Credit cards Cartes de crédit
VISA - CB - Eurocard - MasterCard

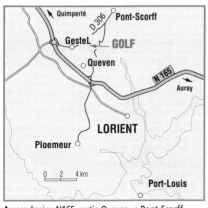

Access Accès : N165, sortie Queven → Pont-Scorff.
Queven, 1 km → Golf
Map 5 on page 107 Carte 5 Page 107

GOLF COURSE
PARCOURS
15/20

Site	Site	
Maintenance	Entretien	
Architect	Architecte	Yves Bureau
Type	Type	plaine, vallon, forêt
Relief	Relief	
Water in play	Eau en jeu	
Exp. to wind	Exposé au vent	
Trees in play	Arbres en jeu	

Scorecard Carte de score	Chp. Chp.	Mens Mess.	Ladies Da.
Length Long.	6140	5750	5200
Par	72	72	72

Advised golfing ability Niveau de jeu recommandé	0	12	24	36

Hcp required Handicap exigé 35

CLUB HOUSE & AMENITIES
CLUB HOUSE ET ANNEXES
6/10

Pro shop	Pro-shop	
Driving range	Practice	
Sheltered	couvert	10 places
On grass	sur herbe	oui
Putting-green	putting-green	oui
Pitching-green	pitching green	oui

HOTEL FACILITIES
ENVIRONNEMENT HOTELIER
5/10

HOTELS HÔTELS

Château de Locquénolé ****		Hennebont
22 chambres, D 1 200 F		11 km
Tél (33) 02 97 76 29 04, Fax (33) 02 97 76 82 35		

Les Moulins du Duc ****		Moëlan-sur-Mer
27 chambres, D 800 F		16 km
Tél (33) 02 98 39 60 73, Fax (33) 02 98 39 75 56		

RESTAURANTS RESTAURANT

L'Amphitryon		Lorient
Tél (33) 02 97 83 34 04		8 km
Le Jardin Gourmand		Lorient
Tél (33) 02 97 64 17 24		8 km

281

Beaucoup moins boisé que l'autre 18 trous, "La Rivière", "Les Vallons" est d'un style radicalement différent, où l'architecte Michel Gayon a rendu hommage aux links britanniques. Il s'agit d'une sorte de parcours de bord de mer, sans la mer bien sûr, avec de nombreuses buttes et roughs délimitant bien les fairways, et donnant du relief à un terrain originellement assez plat. Il n'est pas très long, et les longs frappeurs pourront se livrer, mais c'est un parcours plus dangereux et difficile à scorer qu'il n'y paraît, d'autant que le vent y est rarement absent, et que les greens peuvent être parfois complexes à lire. Alors, il faudra exprimer toutes les ressources de son petit jeu pour sauver le score. Bien entretenu, le complexe de La Vaucouleurs est un ensemble à connaître pour sa variété, à jouer plutôt quand les journées sont belles.

With little or no woodland, "Les Vallons" is radically different from the other 18-holer, "La Rivière" and is something of a tribute by architect Michel Gayon to British style links golfing. It is certainly a sort of seaside course, without the sea, of course, with a number of sandhills and rough clearly defining the fairways and giving considerable relief to terrain that was originally flat. It is not very long and big-hitters can let fly, but the course is more dangerous and harder to master than it looks, especially since the wind is never very far away and some of the greens are tricky to read. In this case, only a sharp short game will save your card. Well looked after with good green-keeping, the estate of La Vaucouleurs is a complex worth getting to know for its variety, but better played in dry weather.

Golf-Club de la Vaucouleurs
F - 78910 CIVRY-LA-FORET

Office	Secrétariat	(33) 01 34 87 62 29
Pro shop	Pro-shop	(33) 01 34 87 76 27
Fax	Fax	(33) 01 34 87 70 09
Situation	Situation	

20 km S.O. Mantes-la-Jolie, 45 080 hab. 61 km O. Paris.

Annual closure	Fermeture annnuelle	oui
		25/12 → 1/01/99
Weekly closure	Fermeture hebdomadaire	mercredi
		01/10 → 31/03

Fees main season Tarifs haute saison la journée

	Week days Semaine	We/Bank holidays We/Férié
Individual Individuel	200 F	350 F
Couple Couple	350 F	650 F

Mardi : GF 150 F. Vendredi : GF + déj. 250 F

Caddy	Caddy	sur réservation
Electric Trolley	Chariot électrique	non
Buggy	Voiturette	150 F/18 trous
Clubs	Clubs 1/2 série	50 F/jour

Credit cards Cartes de crédit
VISA - CB - Eurocard - MasterCard - AMEX

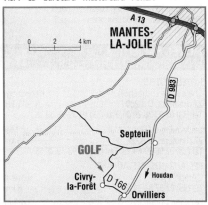

MANTES-LA-JOLIE

A 13

D 983

Septeuil

GOLF

Civry-la-Forêt

D 166

Houdan

Orvilliers

0   2   4 km

Access Accès : A13 Paris/Rouen, sortie Mantes-la-Jolie, D983 → Houdan. Orvilliers → Golf
Map 3 on page 102 Carte 3 Page 102

GOLF COURSE
PARCOURS
15/20

Site	Site	
Maintenance	Entretien	
Architect	Architecte	Michel Gayon
Type	Type	links, vallon
Relief	Relief	
Water in play	Eau en jeu	
Exp. to wind	Exposé au vent	
Trees in play	Arbres en jeu	

Scorecard Carte de score	Chp. Chp.	Mens Mess.	Ladies Da.
Length Long.	5638	5082	4833
Par	70	70	70

Advised golfing ability		0 12 24 36
Niveau de jeu recommandé		
Hcp required	Handicap exigé	

CLUB HOUSE & AMENITIES
CLUB HOUSE ET ANNEXES
7/10

Pro shop	Pro-shop	
Driving range	Practice	
Sheltered	couvert	6 places
On grass	sur herbe	oui (été)
Putting-green	putting-green	oui
Pitching-green	pitching green	oui

HOTEL FACILITIES
ENVIRONNEMENT HOTELIER
4/10

HOTELS HÔTELS
Dousseine ** — Anet
20 chambres, D 280 F — 16 km
Tél (33) 01 37 41 49 93, Fax (33) 01 37 41 90 54

Le Plat d'Etain ** — Houdan
8 chambres, D 280 F — 11 km
Tél (33) 01 30 59 60 28, Fax (33) 01 34 89 21 11

RESTAURANTS RESTAURANT
La Poularde — Houdan
Tél (33) 01 30 59 60 50 — 11 km

Le Donjon — Houdan
Tél (33) 01 30 59 79 14 — 11 km

282

Le très honnête 18 trous des "Brocards" signé par Michael Fenn n'est pas exaltant, mais il permet à tous les niveaux d'évoluer gentiment. L'autre 18 trous (Les Sangliers) signé par Hugues Lambert mérite largement le détour, mais les joueurs de moins de 24 de handicap l'apprécieront davantage. Très long (parfois à l'excès), avec de l'eau en jeu sur la moitié des trous, quelques buttes et pas mal de bunkers (sans sable !), il exige un jeu très complet, et beaucoup de puissance si l'on veut tenir son handicap, même des départs avancés. Ses nombreux obstacles impliquent de le jouer plusieurs fois avant d'en comprendre les aspects stratégiques. Si l'on manque les greens, bien travaillés, on peut parfois y rentrer en roulant, mais il vaut mieux savoir porter la balle. C'est l'un des tout meilleurs parcours de la région. Ce golf privé est difficile d'accès en week-end (sauf l'été).

"Les Brocards", is a fair and unpretentious 18-hole course, designed by Michael Fenn, and a pleasant round of golf for golfers of all levels. The other 18-hole course ("Les Sangliers"), laid out by Hugues Lambert, is a much more enticing proposition, although a 24 handicap would seem to be the minimum requirement for enjoying the course. Very long (sometimes excessively so) with water in play on half the holes, a few sandhills and a lot of bunkers (without sand !), the course demands an all-round game and power, even from the front tees. The countless hazards imply several exploratory rounds before fully understanding the strategic side to the course. Missed greens can sometimes be reached with chip shots, but controlled lob and pitch shots are important here. This is unquestionably one of the region's very best courses, and being private is difficult to play on week-ends (except in summer).

Golf Club de Lyon
F - 38280 VILLETTE-D'ANTHON

Office	Secrétariat	(33) 04 78 31 11 33
Pro shop	Pro-shop	(33) 04 72 02 28 76
Fax	Fax	(33) 04 72 02 48 27
Situation	Situation	

20 km E. Lyon, 413 090 hab.

Annual closure	Fermeture annnuelle	non
Weekly closure	Fermeture hebdomadaire	mardi, en basse saison

Fees main season Tarifs haute saison la journée

	Week days Semaine	We/Bank holidays We/Férié
Individual Individuel	200 F	280 F
Couple Couple	400 F	560 F

non membre de club : 230 F/350 F

Caddy	Caddy	sur réservation
Electric Trolley	Chariot électrique	non
Buggy	Voiturette	200 F/18 trous
Clubs	Clubs 1/2 série	100 F/jour

Credit cards Cartes de crédit
VISA - CB - Eurocard - MasterCard

Access Accès : • Lyon, rocade Est, sortie Meyzieu le Carreau → Villette d'Anthon • A42 Bourg-en-Bresse Lyon, sortie Péage de Balan, → Villette d'Anthon
Map 11 on page 118 Carte 11 Page 118

GOLF COURSE
PARCOURS

17 /20

Site	Site	
Maintenance	Entretien	
Architect	Architecte	Hugues Lambert
Type	Type	forêt, campagne
Relief	Relief	
Water in play	Eau en jeu	
Exp. to wind	Exposé au vent	
Trees in play	Arbres en jeu	

Scorecard Carte de score	Chp. Chp.	Mens Mess.	Ladies Da.
Length Long.	6727	6228	5395
Par	72	72	72

Advised golfing ability		0	12	24	36
Niveau de jeu recommandé					
Hcp required	Handicap exigé	35			

CLUB HOUSE & AMENITIES
CLUB HOUSE ET ANNEXES

6 /10

Pro shop	Pro-shop	
Driving range	Practice	
Sheltered	couvert	12 places
On grass	sur herbe	oui
Putting-green	putting-green	oui
Pitching-green	pitching green	oui

283

HOTEL FACILITIES
ENVIRONNEMENT HOTELIER

4 /10

HOTELS HÔTELS
Mont-Joyeux *** — Meyzieu
20 chambres, D 480 F — 12 km
Tél (33) 04 78 04 21 32, Fax (33) 04 72 02 85 72
Auberge de Jons *** — Jons
26 chambres, D 420 F — 3 km
Tél (33) 04 78 31 29 85, Fax (33) 04 72 02 48 24
Phénix Hôtel — Lyon (Vieux-Lyon)
36 chambres, D 1 000 F — 20 km
Tél (33) 04 78 28 24 24, Fax (33) 04 78 28 62 86

RESTAURANTS RESTAURANT
Paul Bocuse — Collonges-au-Mont-d'Or
Tél (33) 04 72 27 85 85 — 25 km
Léon de Lyon — Lyon
Tél(33) 04 78 28 11 33 — 20 km
Le Jura — Lyon
Tél(33) 04 78 42 20 57 — 20 km

Situé à près de 900 mètres d'altitude au pied du Puy de Dôme, ce parcours peut parfois être gelé le matin, sauf en été. Environné de bouleaux, de pins, de buissons sauvages et de bruyère, il présente une forte montée du 9 au 10, mais pas assez épuisante pour obliger à prendre une voiturette. Le dessin du professionnel local, Lucien Roux, ne prétend certes pas aux plus hautes distinctions, mais il reste plus que correct, avec une bonne utilisation des arbres et des bunkers, quelques greens délicats à double plateau, et un bon rythme de distribution des difficultés. Le parcours peut paraître un peu long du fond, mais les balles portent plus loin en altitude, et les départs avancés (notamment sur les longs par 3) permettent de prendre beaucoup de plaisir dans ce golf sympathique et très familial, situé dans un environnement magnifique et calme.

Lying 900 metres above sea level at the foot of the Puy de Dôme, this course is often frost-bound in the morning outside the summer months. Surrounded by birch trees, pines, wild bushes and heather, there is steep climb between the 9th and 10th, although not tiring enough to warrant a buggy. Designed by local pro Lucien Roux, the layout cannot and would not claim any of the higher accolades, but it is more than a decent course, with excellent use of trees and bunkers, a few tricky, two-tiered greens and nicely balanced hazards and headaches. The course looks a little long from the back-tees, but the thin air at altitude adds length to the drive. Playing from the front tees (especially the long par 3s) is great fun in this very friendly and family-style club, located in a magnificently calm setting.

Golf des Volcans
La Bruyère des Moines
F - 63870 ORCINES

Office	Secrétariat	(33) 04 73 62 15 51
Pro shop	Pro-shop	(33) 04 73 62 78 12
Fax	Fax	(33) 04 73 62 26 52
Situation	Situation	

8 km O. Clermont-Ferrand, 136 180 hab.

Annual closure	Fermeture annnuelle	non
Weekly closure	Fermeture hebdomadaire	mardi
	restaurant (01/12 → 01/04)	

Fees main season
Tarifs haute saison la journée

	Week days Semaine	We/Bank holidays We/Férié
Individual Individuel	250 F	250 F
Couple Couple	500 F	500 F

Caddy	Caddy	non
Electric Trolley	Chariot électrique	100 F/18 trous
Buggy	Voiturette	180 F/18 trous
Clubs	Clubs série	100 F/jour

Credit cards Cartes de crédit
VISA - CB - Eurocard - MasterCard

284

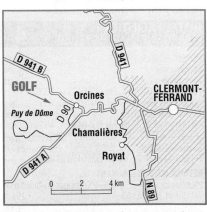

GOLF
Orcines
Puy de Dôme
Chamalières
Royat
CLERMONT-FERRAND
D 941 B
D 941
D 90
D 941 A
N 89
0   2   4 km

Access Accès : A71, Bourges → Clermont-Ferrand, sortie Clermont-Ferrand Centre → Le Puy-de-Dôme → Orcines **Map 7 on page 111** Carte 7 Page 111

GOLF COURSE / PARCOURS 14/20

Site	Site	▅▅▅
Maintenance	Entretien	▅▅▅
Architect	Architecte	Lucien Roux
Type	Type	montagne
Relief	Relief	▅▅
Water in play	Eau en jeu	▅
Exp. to wind	Exposé au vent	▅
Trees in play	Arbres en jeu	▅▅

Scorecard Carte de score	Chp. Chp.	Mens Mess.	Ladies Da.
Length Long.	6286	6106	5312
Par	72	72	72

Advised golfing ability				
Niveau de jeu recommandé	0	12	24	36
Hcp required Handicap exigé	35			

CLUB HOUSE & AMENITIES / CLUB HOUSE ET ANNEXES 6/10

Pro shop	Pro-shop	▅▅
Driving range	Practice	▅▅
Sheltered	couvert	20 places
On grass	sur herbe	non
Putting-green	putting-green	oui
Pitching-green	pitching green	oui

HOTEL FACILITIES / ENVIRONNEMENT HOTELIER 5/10

HOTELS HÔTELS
Radio ***   Chamalières
26 chambres, D 500 F   3 km
Tél (33) 04 73 30 87 83, Fax (33) 04 73 36 42 44

Galliéni **   Clermont-Ferrand
80 chambres, D 340 F   8 km
Tél (33) 04 73 93 59 69, Fax (33) 04 73 34 89 29

RESTAURANTS RESTAURANT
Hôtel Radio   Chamalières
Tél (33) 04 73 30 87 33   3 km

Bernard Andrieux   Durtol
Tél (33) 04 73 37 00 26   5 km

WANTZENAU (LA)

16	6	6

C'est un peu la Floride à l'alsacienne, avec un Club House de style résolument local et plutôt réussi. Le paysage est parsemé d'étangs venant en jeu sur neuf des 18 trous, essentiellement au retour, ce qui crée une forte pression sur les joueurs peu expérimentés. On signalera la grande qualité de dessin des par 5, très risqués à attaquer au deuxième coup, et l'habileté de Jeremy Pern à tirer parti d'un espace très plat. Les mouvements de terrain sont subtils, les greens assez vastes, mais leur entrée est généralement ouverte, ce qui permet de jouer la sécurité dans la plupart des cas, quitte à faire confiance à son petit jeu pour sauver le par. Même si l'on est bien loin de tout océan, le vent peut intervenir de manière importante sur ce parcours de très bonne facture, aux obstacles bien visibles, et technique quel que soit le départ choisi.

Welcome to Florida in Alsace, where US style golf combines with a rather attractive local-style club-house. The landscape is dotted with lakes in play on 9 of the 18 holes, basically on the back nine, and puts a lot of pressure on inexperienced players. The par 5s are particularly well-laid out, and going for the green in 2 is risky business. Architect Jeremy Pern has cleverly made the best of very flat terrain. There has been some clever grading work and the greens are huge and generally undefended up-front, thus allowing players to play safe, even if it means counting on their short game to save par. Although the course is far from any sea, the wind can get up and make a big difference on this excellent and skilful course, whatever tees you play from. All the hazards are clearly visible.

Golf de la Wantzenau
CD 302
F - 67610 LA WANTZENAU

Office	Secrétariat	(33) 03 88 96 37 73
Pro shop	Pro-shop	(33) 03 88 96 37 73
Fax	Fax	(33) 03 88 96 34 71
Situation	Situation	

12 km N. Strasbourg, 252 260 hab.

Annual closure	Fermeture annnuelle	non
Weekly closure	Fermeture hebdomadaire	mardi, le restaurant

Fees main season
Tarifs haute saison le parcours

	Week days Semaine	We/Bank holidays We/Férié
Individual Individuel	280 F	400 F
Couple Couple	560 F	800 F

We : membres de clubs seulement (Clubs members only)

Caddy	Caddy	non
Electric Trolley	Chariot électrique	non
Buggy	Voiturette	300 F/18 trous
Clubs	Clubs	le club 10 F/jour

Credit cards Cartes de crédit
VISA - CB - Eurocard - MasterCard

Access Accès : Strasbourg, D468 → La Wantzenau, → Golf
Map 4 on page 105 Carte 4 Page 105

GOLF COURSE
PARCOURS
16/20

Site	Site	
Maintenance	Entretien	
Architect	Architecte	Jeremy Pern
		Jean Garaïalde
Type	Type	plaine, résidentiel
Relief	Relief	
Water in play	Eau en jeu	
Exp. to wind	Exposé au vent	
Trees in play	Arbres en jeu	

Scorecard Carte de score	Chp. Chp.	Mens Mess.	Ladies Da.
Length Long.	6325	6142	5167
Par	72	72	72

Advised golfing ability Niveau de jeu recommandé	0	12	24	36

Hcp required	Handicap exigé	35

CLUB HOUSE & AMENITIES
CLUB HOUSE ET ANNEXES
6/10

Pro shop	Pro-shop	
Driving range	Practice	
Sheltered	couvert	8 places
On grass	sur herbe	oui
Putting-green	putting-green	oui
Pitching-green	pitching green	oui

285

HOTEL FACILITIES
ENVIRONNEMENT HOTELIER
6/10

HOTELS HÔTELS

Relais de la Poste ** — La Wantzenau
25 chambres, D 500 F — 3 km
Tél (33) 03 88 96 20 64, Fax (33) 03 88 96 36 84

Aigle d'Or *** — Reichstett
17 chambres, D 340 F — 2 km
Tél (33) 03 88 20 07 87, Fax (33) 03 88 81 83 75

Holiday Inn **** — Strasbourg
170 chambres, D 920 F — 10 km
Tél (33) 03 88 37 80 00, Fax (33) 03 88 37 07 04

RESTAURANTS RESTAURANT

A la Barrière — La Wantzenau
Tél (33) 03 88 96 20 23 — 3 km

Cour des Chasseurs — La Wantzenau
Tél (33) 03 88 96 24 83 — 3 km

Si l'on recherche seulement le confort et luxe, il faut passer son chemin, les installations étant spartiates. En revanche, cette simplicité contribue à en faire probablement le parcours français le plus proche des premiers links d'Ecosse, jusqu'aux trous de lapins dans le sol sablonneux. Généralement plat, avec une multitude de profonds bunkers, Wimereux peut présenter un visage aussi souriant et indulgent par beau temps (quand les balles roulent bien) qu'il peut se montrer brutal dès que souffle le vent. Créé en 1907, il a été remanié en 1958 sans trop perdre de son caractère ni de son charme un peu désuet. Ce refus de tout aspect sophistiqué, l'absence d'obstacles d'eau (la mer est à 200 mètres) et d'arbres en jeu peuvent rassurer les amateurs de tous niveaux, qui devront néanmoins éviter les écarts, le grand rough étant redoutable.

If you are looking for comfort and luxury and nothing else, drive on, as the facilities here are Spartan. In contrast, simplicity probably helps make this the closest French course to the original Scottish links, even as far as the rabbit-holes in the sandy soil. Generally flat with a number of deep bunkers, Wimereux can be as leisurely and forgiving in fine weather (when the ball rolls a long way) as it can be mean and unloving when the wind blows. Created in 1907, it was restyled in 1958 without sacrificing too much of the original character or olde worlde charm. This refusal of anything over-sophisticated, the absence of water hazards (the sea is 200 metres away) and trees in play is enough to reassure golfers of all playing abilities, as long as they keep on the straight and narrow. Be warned, the rough is wicked.

Golf de Wimereux
Route d'Ambleteuse
F - 62930 WIMEREUX

Office	Secrétariat	(33) 03 21 32 43 20
Pro shop	Pro-shop	(33) 03 21 32 43 20
Fax	Fax	(33) 03 21 33 62 21
Situation	Situation	

6 km N. Boulogne-sur-Mer, 43 670 hab.

Annual closure	Fermeture annnuelle	non
Weekly closure	Fermeture hebdomadaire	lundi
	restaurant (01/10 → 30/06)	

Fees main season
Tarifs haute saison la journée

	Week days Semaine	We/Bank holidays We/Férié
Individual Individuel	200 F	250 F
Couple Couple	400 F	500 F

Caddy	Caddy	non
Electric Trolley	Chariot électrique	non
Buggy	Voiturette	non
Clubs	Clubs	non

Credit cards Cartes de crédit
VISA - CB - Eurocard - MasterCard

GOLF
A 16
Wimereux
D 940
N 42
N 1
Boulogne-s-Mer

0   2   4 km

Access Accès : Boulogne s/Mer, D940 → Wimereux
Map 1 on page 98 Carte 1 Page 98

GOLF COURSE
PARCOURS
15/20

Site	Site	■■■■□□□□□□
Maintenance	Entretien	■■■■■■□□□□
Architect	Architecte	Campbell & Hutchinson
Type	Type	links
Relief	Relief	■□□□□□□□□□
Water in play	Eau en jeu	□□□□□□□□□□
Exp. to wind	Exposé au vent	■■■■■■□□□□
Trees in play	Arbres en jeu	■□□□□□□□□□

Scorecard Carte de score	Chp. Chp.	Mens Mess.	Ladies Da.
Length Long.	6150	5887	5184
Par	72	72	72

Advised golfing ability
Niveau de jeu recommandé

0	12	24	36

Hcp required Handicap exigé   35, le We

CLUB HOUSE & AMENITIES
CLUB HOUSE ET ANNEXES
4/10

Pro shop	Pro-shop	■■■■□□□□□□
Driving range	Practice	■■■■■□□□□□
Sheltered	couvert	20 places
On grass	sur herbe	oui
Putting-green	putting-green	oui
Pitching-green	pitching green	oui

HOTEL FACILITIES
ENVIRONNEMENT HOTELIER
5/10

HOTELS HÔTELS
Centre ** | Wimereux
25 chambres, D 360 F | 2 km
Tél (33) 03 21 32 41 08, Fax (33) 03 21 33 82 48

Paul et Virginie ** | Wimereux
15 chambres, D 400 F | 2 km
Tél (33) 03 21 32 42 12, Fax (33) 03 21 87 65 85

Atlantic *** | Wimereux
10 chambres, D 480 F | 2 km
Tél (33) 03 21 32 41 01, Fax (33) 03 21 87 46 17

RESTAURANTS RESTAURANT
Le Relais de la Brocante | Wimille
Tél (33) 03 21 83 19 31 | 3 km

La Matelote | Boulogne-sur-Mer
Tél (33) 03 21 30 17 97 | 6 km

286

Tracé en partie dans une belle forêt de chênes, c'est toujours un parcours très humide en dehors de la belle saison. La qualité du dessin de Bill Baker reste variable, mais le changement de numérotation a amélioré le rythme de jeu, les trous les plus contestables (notamment le 5, dog-leg à angle droit avec hors-limites en face du départ) étant désormais placés à l'aller. Le retour propose davantage de bons trous (sauf le 17), mais le manque fréquent de franchise donne "trop de chance à la chance" pour que l'on se sente totalement responsable de son score. Cela dit, l'ensemble des équipements (Club-House, practice, petit 9 trous) est de bonne qualité, convivial et sympathique. Pour jouer en famille, avec des niveaux différents, Les Yvelines est toujours une bonne adresse, mais les joueurs du meilleur niveau resteront certainement sur leur faim.

A number of holes run through a beautiful oak forest, which keeps the course very wet outside the summer months. The excellence of Bill Baker's lay-out is inconsistent, but a change in the numbering of holes has improved the overall balance and the most controversial holes (notably the 5th, a 90° dog-leg with out-of-bounds opposite the tee) is now on the front nine. The back nine now has more good holes (except the 17th), but a frequent lack of honesty leaves too much open to luck for a player to feel totally responsible for a good card. With that said, the full facilities (club-house, driving range and short 9 hole course) are excellent, friendly and enjoyable. For a round of golf with all the family or players of differing abilities, Les Yvelines is always a good address, but the more skilful players may want more than this.

Golf des Yvelines

Château de la Couharde
F - 78940 LA QUEUE-LES-YVELINES

Office	Secrétariat	(33) 01 34 86 48 89
Pro shop	Pro-shop	(33) 01 34 86 69 95
Fax	Fax	(33) 01 34 86 50 31
Situation	Situation	

29 km O. Versailles, 87 790 hab. 53 km O. Paris.

Annual closure	Fermeture annnuelle	oui
		22/12→10/01/99
Weekly closure	Fermeture hebdomadaire	non

Fees main season	Tarifs haute saison	le parcours	
		Week days Semaine	We/Bank holidays We/Férié
Individual Individuel		170 F	290 F
Couple Couple		340 F	580 F

Mardi après 15 h, GF 100 F

Caddy	Caddy	non
Electric Trolley	Chariot électrique	non
Buggy	Voiturette	non
Clubs	Clubs 1/2 série	60 F/jour

Credit cards Cartes de crédit
VISA - CB - Eurocard - MasterCard - AMEX

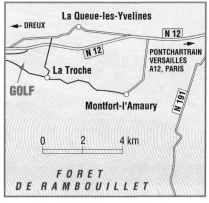

← DREUX

La Queue-les-Yvelines

N 12

PONTCHARTRAIN
VERSAILLES
A12, PARIS

La Troche

GOLF

Montfort-l'Amaury

N 191

0   2   4 km

FORET
DE RAMBOUILLET

Access Accès : Paris A13, A12 → Saint-Quentin,
N12 → Dreux, traverser Pontchartrain →
La Queue-les-Yvelines
Map 3 on page 102 Carte 3 Page 102

GOLF COURSE
PARCOURS   13 /20

Site	Site	
Maintenance	Entretien	
Architect	Architecte	Bill Baker
Type	Type	forêt, plaine
Relief	Relief	
Water in play	Eau en jeu	
Exp. to wind	Exposé au vent	
Trees in play	Arbres en jeu	

Scorecard	Chp.	Mens	Ladies
Carte de score	Chp.	Mess.	Da.
Length Long.	6344	5934	5640
Par	72	72	72

Advised golfing ability	0	12	24	36
Niveau de jeu recommandé				
Hcp required	Handicap exigé	30, We		

CLUB HOUSE & AMENITIES
CLUB HOUSE ET ANNEXES   7 /10

Pro shop	Pro-shop	
Driving range	Practice	
Sheltered	couvert	20 places
On grass	sur herbe	non
Putting-green	putting-green	oui
Pitching-green	pitching green	oui

HOTEL FACILITIES
ENVIRONNEMENT HOTELIER   4 /10

HOTELS HÔTELS
Domaine du Verbois ***   Neauphle-le-Château
20 chambres, D 800 F   13 km
Tél (33) 01 34 89 11 78, Fax (33) 01 34 89 57 33

Voyageurs **   Montfort-l'Amaury
7 chambres, D 300 F   6 km
Tél (33) 01 34 86 00 14, Fax (33) 01 34 86 14 56

RESTAURANTS RESTAURANT
La Toque Blanche   Les Mesnuls
Tél (33) 01 34 86 05 55   14 km

La Gentilhommière   Le Tremblay-sur-Mauldre
Tél (33) 01 34 87 80 96   6 km

Auberge de l'Arrivée   Montfort-l'Amaury
Tél (33) 01 34 86 00 28   6 km

287

Macht nichts.

Es gibt ja den 406.

Dank Servolenkung und aktivem Sicherheitsfahrwerk mit
Einzelradaufhängung und Mehrlenker-Hinterachse bringt er
Sie bequem nach oben; dank serienmäßigem 4-Sensoren-ABS
auch sicher wieder herunter: der PEUGEOT 406. Damit Sie
der nächsten Kurve stets gelassen entgegensehen können.

406
PEUGEOT

Mit Sicherheit mehr Vergnügen.

Germany
Deutschland

I n Deutschland, welches den stärksten Zuwachs ganz Europas aufweist, gibt es heute 275'000 Golfer und ungefähr 340 18-Loch-Plätze. Meist befinden sie sich in der Nähe grösserer Städte wie Düsseldorf, Hamburg, Stuttgart, München oder Berlin oder in stark touristisch erschlossenen Regionen wie Bayern. Viele davon sind Privatsclubs, welche jedoch für alle Besucher offen sind, zumindest unter der Woche. An den Wochenenden ist der Zutritt oft beschränkt, was wir denn auch beim jeweiligen Beschreibung vermerkt haben. Für Gruppen sind Reservierungen für das Wochenende daher schwierig, aber einzelne Spieler haben oft die Möglichkeit, mit Clubmitgliedern spielen zu gehen. Rufen Sie vorher an, und mit einem Empfehlungsschreiben Ihres Clubs werden Sie sicherlich eine Chance haben.

289

Germany today has 275,000 golfers, one of the highest growth rates in Europe, and about 340 eighteen-hole courses. They are mostly situated around the major cities such as Düsseldorf, Hamburg, Stuttgart, München or Berlin, or again in favourite tourist locations like Bavaria. The majority of clubs are private, but they all admit visitors, at least during the week, and may sometimes impose restrictions on week-ends. These are mentioned in the Guide. This makes it difficult for groups to book tee-off times at the week-end, but visitors playing alone will often be able to tee-off with members. Phone early and, with a letter of introduction from your club, try your luck.

Das ist der Fair Way,
um GOLF Journal zu testen.

Alles, was ein engagierter Golfspieler braucht:
Spieltechniken und Taktiken der Profis.
Berichte über die schönsten Plätze der Welt.
Reportagen aus der Turnierszene.
Fundierte Ausrüstungstips.
Und Unterhaltsames rund um das Golfspiel.
Testen Sie drei Ausgaben GOLF Journal
für nur 14,70 DM!
Einen Titleist Golfball gibt's gratis dazu.

Rufen Sie an!
0 83 82-9 63 10

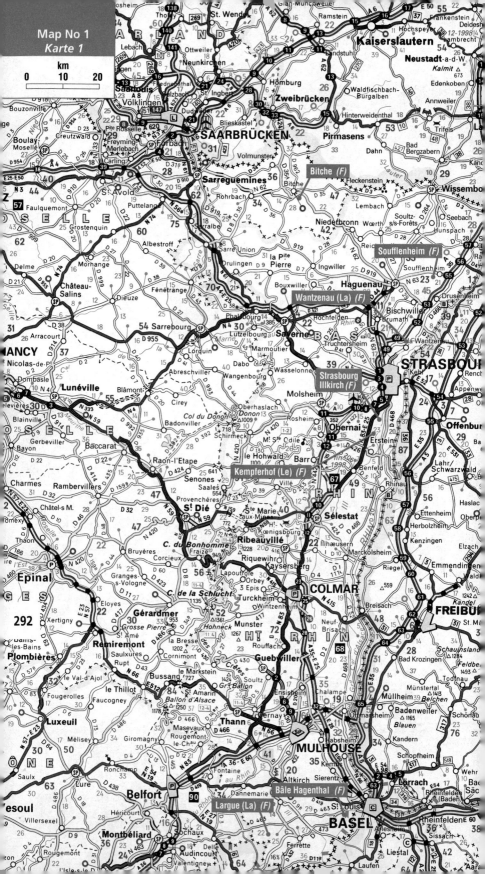

293

d'après carte n° 987 - 24ème édition - 1998.
Autorisation n°9706332.

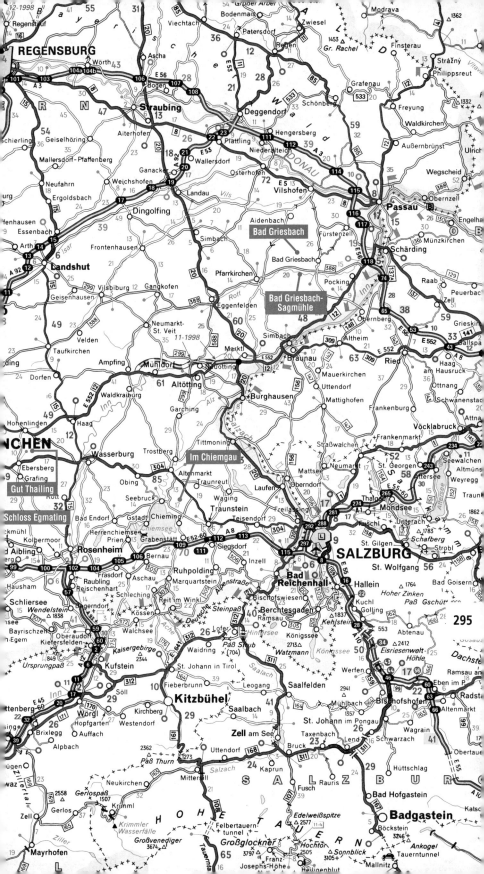

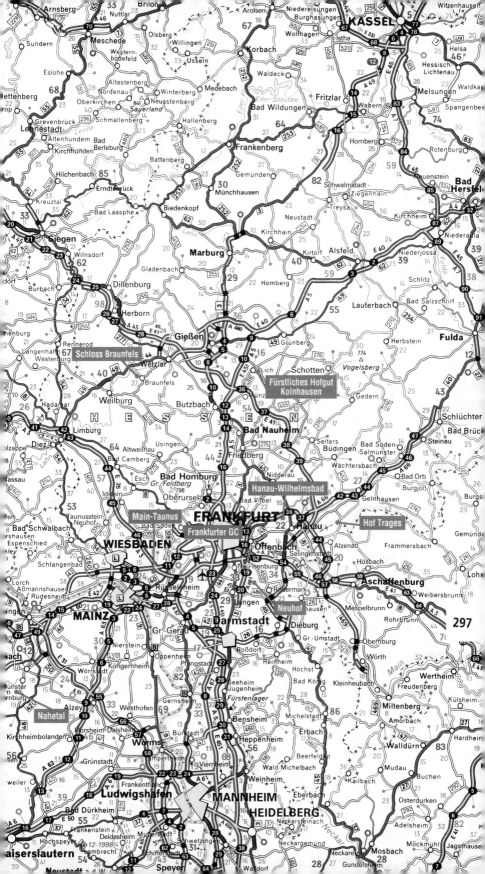

297

km
0   10   20

301

km
0   10   20

EINTEILUNG DER GOLFPLÄTZE

Diese Einteilung berücksichtigt in erster Linie die
dem Golfplatz erteilte Note
This classification gives priority consideration
to the score awarded to the actual course

Note für das Clubhaus und die Einrichtungen
Club-house and facilities

Note für den Golfplatz
Course score

Note für das Hotelangebot der Umgebung
Hotel facility score

| **18** | 6 | 5 | Club zur Vahr (Garlstedt) | 324 |

Seite
Page

Note			Golfplatz	Seite	Note			Golfplatz	Seite
18	6	5	Club zur Vahr (Garlstedt)	324	**16**	8	7	Schloss Langenstein	384
18	6	7	Falkenstein	329	**16**	8	7	Schloss Liebenstein	
18	7	6	Feldafing	330				*Gelb + Blau*	385
18	8	6	Motzener See	364	**16**	7	7	Schloss Myllendonk	387
18	8	7	Scharmützelsee *Nick Faldo*	379	**16**	7	7	Sonnenalp	390
17	9	9	Bad Griesbach *Brunnwies*	314	**16**	7	6	St. Eurach	392
17	7	6	Beuerberg	320	**16**	7	6	Wendlohe *A-Kurs + B-Kurs*	399
17	7	7	Bodensee-Weissensberg	321	**16**	7	6	Wentorf-Reinbeker	400
17	6	7	Braunschweig	322	**15**	7	7	Augsburg	313
17	7	6	Gut Kaden *Platz B + Platz C*	335	**15**	9	9	Bad Griesbach-Sagmühle	
17	7	5	Gut Waldhof	339				*Sagmühle*	315
17	8	7	Hamburg-Ahrensburg	340	**15**	7	7	Bamberg	318
17	8	6	Hubbelrath	349	**15**	6	8	Berlin-Wannsee	319
17	6	7	Köln	354	**15**	7	6	Buxtehude	323
17	7	7	Krefelder	356	**15**	6	6	Gut Ludwigsberg	336
17	7	5	Lüneburger Heide	359	**15**	6	6	Hamburg-Holm	341
17	6	5	Oberfranken	372	**15**	6	6	Hanau-Wilhelmsbad	342
17	7	7	Reichswald-Nürnberg	377	**15**	7	6	Hohenpähl	347
17	7	6	Schloss Lüdersburg		**15**	7	6	Isernhagen	352
			Old/New	386	**15**	7	6	Jakobsberg	353
17	7	6	St. Dionys	391	**15**	7	6	Lichtenau-Weickershof	357
17	7	5	Stolper Heide	393	**15**	7	7	Mittelrheinischer	363
17	5	5	Stuttgarter Solitude	394	**15**	7	7	Neuhof	370
16	7	8	Frankfurter GC	331	**15**	6	6	Oberschwaben	
16	7	5	Gut Thailing	338				Bad Waldsee	373
16	7	7	Hannover	343	**15**	7	7	Öschberghof	374
16	7	5	Hof Trages	346	**15**	7	7	Schloss Egmating	382
16	7	6	Iffeldorf	350	**15**	7	5	Schloss Wilkendorf	388
16	7	7	München-Riedhof	366	**15**	7	8	Tegernseer Bad Wiessee	395
16	6	7	Neckartal	369	**15**	7	6	Tutzing	397
16	8	7	Scharmützelsee		**15**	7	6	Walddörfer	398
			Arnold Palmer	378	**15**	7	6	Wittelsbacher	401
16	7	7	Schloss Braunfels	381	**14**	7	6	Abenberg	312

306

EINTEILUNG DER GOLFPLÄTZE

EINTEILUNG DES HOTELANGEBOTS DER UMGEBUNG

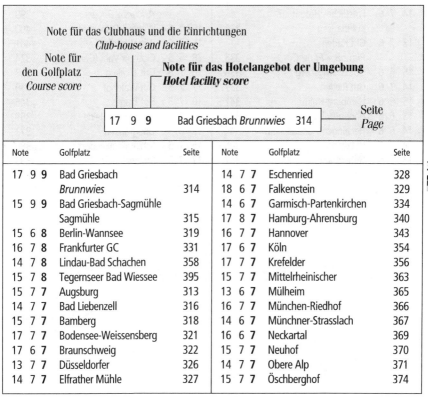

307

EINTEILUNG DES HOTELANGEBOTS DER UMGEBUNG

308

FÜR EINEN FERIENAUFENTHALT EMPFOHLEN

FÜR GOLFFERIEN EMPFOHLEN

Golfplatz	Note			Seite	Golfplatz	Note			Seite
Bad Griesbach *Brunnwies*	17	9	9	314	Motzener See	18	8	6	364
Beuerberg	17	7	6	320	Reichswald-Nürnberg	17	7	7	377
Club zur Vahr (Garlstedt)	18	6	5	324	Scharmützelsee				
Falkenstein	18	6	7	329	*Arnold Palmer*	16	8	7	378
Gut Kaden *Platz B + Platz C*	17	7	6	335	Scharmützelsee				
Hanau-Wilhelmsbad	15	6	6	342	*Nick Faldo*	18	8	7	379

GELÄNDEBESCHAFFENHEIT DER GOLFPLÄTZE

Geringe Höhenunterschiede	Mittlere Höhenunterschiede	Grosse Höhenunterschiede
Rather flat	Averagely hilly	Very hilly

Gelandebeschabbenheit der Golfplatze	Note			Page	Gelandebeschabbenheit der Golfplatze	Note			Page
Bad Wörishofen	14	6	6	317	Scharmützelsee *Nick Faldo*	18	8	7	379
Eschenried	14	7	7	328	Stolper Heide	17	7	5	393
Fürstliches Hofgut					Wendlohe *A-Kurs + B-Kurs*	16	7	6	399
Kolnhausen	14	7	6	333					
Hamburg-Ahrensburg	17	8	7	340	Abenberg	14	7	6	312
Hamburg-Holm	15	6	6	341	Bad Griesbach-Sagmühle				
Wittelsbacher	15	7	6	401	*Sagmühle*	15	9	9	315
					Frankfurter GC	16	7	8	331
Elfrather Mühle	14	7	7	327	Gut Ludwigsberg	15	6	6	336
Garmisch-Partenkirchen	14	6	7	334	Hanau-Wilhelmsbad	15	6	6	342
Gut Kaden *Platz B + Platz C*	17	7	6	335	Hof Trages	16	7	5	346
Hannover	16	7	7	343	Krefelder	17	7	7	356
Isernhagen	15	7	6	352	Lichtenau-Weickershof	15	7	6	357
Köln	17	6	7	354	Lindau-Bad Schachen	14	7	8	358
Main-Taunus	13	7	6	360	Memmingen Gut Westerhart	14	6	6	362
Mülheim	13	6	7	365	Neuhof	15	7	7	370
Neckartal	16	6	7	369	Scharmützelsee *Arnold Palmer*	16	8	7	378
Öschberghof	15	7	7	374	Schloss Braunfels	16	7	7	381
Pinnau	14	6	6	375	Schloss Lüdersburg Old/New	17	7	6	386
Reichswald-Nürnberg	17	7	7	377	Schloss Myllendonk	16	7	7	387

309

GELÄNDEBESCHAFFENHEIT DER GOLFPLÄTZE

Gelandebeschabbenheit der Golfplatze	Note	Page	Gelandebeschabbenheit der Golfplatze	Note	Page
▰▰▰			▰▰▰		
Semlin am See	14 8 7	389	Hechingen-Hohenzollern	14 6 6	344
Stuttgarter Solitude	17 5 5	394	Hetzenhof	14 7 6	345
Treudelberg	13 8 7	396	Hubbelrath	17 8 6	349
Wentorf-Reinbeker	16 7 6	400	Jakobsberg	15 7 6	353
▰▰▰			München-Riedhof	16 7 7	366
Beuerberg	17 7 6	320	Oberschwaben Bad Waldsee	15 6 6	373
Bodensee-Weissensberg	17 7 7	321	Schloss Liebenstein *Gelb + Blau*	16 8 7	385
Club zur Vahr (Garlstedt)	18 6 5	324	Schloss Wilkendorf	15 7 5	388
Düsseldorf/Hösel	13 6 6	325	St. Dionys	17 7 6	391
Gut Thailing	16 7 5	338	Tegernseer Bad Wiessee	15 7 8	395
Hohenpähl	15 7 6	347	Walddörfer	15 7 6	398
Im Chiemgau	14 7 6	351	▰▰▰		
Märkischer Potsdam	14 7 6	361	Braunschweig	17 6 7	322
Mittelrheinischer	15 7 7	363	Düsseldorfer	13 7 7	326
Motzener See	18 8 6	364	Feldafing	18 7 6	330
Münchner-Strasslach	14 6 7	367	Gut Waldhof	17 7 5	339
Nahetal	14 7 6	368	Schloss Langenstein	16 8 7	384
Obere Alp	14 7 7	371	▰▰▰		
Reichsstadt Bad Windsheim	14 6 7	376	Augsburg	15 7 7	313
Scheibenhardt	13 7 7	380	Bamberg	15 7 7	318
Schloss Egmating	15 7 7	382	Hoisdorf	13 6 6	348
Schloss Klingenburg	14 6 6	383	Lüneburger Heide	17 7 5	359
St. Eurach	16 7 6	392	Oberfranken	17 6 5	372
▰▰▰			Tutzing	15 7 6	397
Bad Liebenzell	14 7 7	316	▰▰▰		
Berlin-Wannsee	15 6 8	319	Bad Griesbach *Brunnwies*	17 9 9	314
Buxtehude	15 7 6	323	Iffeldorf	16 7 6	350
Falkenstein	18 6 7	329	Königsfeld	13 6 6	355
Fränkische Schweiz	14 7 6	332	Sonnenalp	16 7 7	390
Gut Rieden	14 7 6	337			

EMPFOHLENE JAHRESZEITEN

Jahreszeiten /Golfplatz	Note	Seite	Jahreszeiten /Golfplatz	Note	Seite
`1 2 3 4 5 6 7 8 9 10 11 12`			München-Riedhof	16 7 7	366
Hubbelrath	17 8 6	349	Münchner-Strasslach	14 6 7	367
			Neuhof	15 7 7	370
`1 2 3 4 5 6 7 8 9 10 11 12`			Stuttgarter Solitude	17 5 5	394
Elfrather Mühle	14 7 7	327	Walddörfer	15 7 6	398
Frankfurter GC	16 7 8	331	Wentorf-Reinbeker	16 7 6	400
Gut Waldhof	17 7 5	339			
Hamburg-Ahrensburg	17 8 7	340	`1 2 3 4 5 6 7 8 9 10 11 12`		
Hanau-Wilhelmsbad	15 6 6	342	Augsburg	15 7 7	313
Hof Trages	16 7 5	346	Bamberg	15 7 7	318
Jakobsberg	15 7 6	353	Berlin-Wannsee	15 6 8	319
Mülheim	13 6 7	365	Beuerberg	17 7 6	320

EMPFOHLENE JAHRESZEITEN

Jahreszeiten /Golfplatz	Note			Seite
1 2 3 **4** 5 **6 7 8 9 10** 11 12				
Bodensee-Weissensberg	17	7	7	321
Buxtehude	15	7	6	323
Club zur Vahr (Garlstedt)	18	6	5	324
Düsseldorf/Hösel	13	6	6	325
Düsseldorfer	13	7	7	326
Eschenried	14	7	7	328
Falkenstein	18	6	7	329
Fürstliches Hofgut				
Kolnhausen	14	7	6	333
Gut Kaden *Platz B + Platz C*	17	7	6	335
Gut Thailing	16	7	5	338
Hamburg-Holm	15	6	6	341
Hannover	16	7	7	343
Hechingen-Hohenzollern	14	6	6	344
Hetzenhof	14	7	6	345
Hoisdorf	13	6	6	348
Köln	17	6	7	354
Krefelder	17	7	7	356
Lichtenau-Weickershof	15	7	6	357
Lindau-Bad Schachen	14	7	8	358
Lüneburger Heide	17	7	5	359
Main-Taunus	13	7	6	360
Mittelrheinischer	15	7	7	363
Motzener See	18	8	6	364
Nahetal	14	7	6	368
Neckartal	16	6	7	369
Oberschwaben Bad Waldsee	15	6	6	373
Öschberghof	15	7	7	374
Pinnau	14	6	6	375
Reichswald-Nürnberg	17	7	7	377
Scharmützelsee *Arnold Palmer*	16	8	7	378
Scharmützelsee *Nick Faldo*	18	8	7	379
Scheibenhardt	13	7	7	380
Schloss Braunfels	16	7	7	381
Schloss Egmating	15	7	7	382
Schloss Klingenburg	14	6	6	383
Schloss Liebenstein *Gelb + Blau*	16	8	7	385
St. Dionys	17	7	6	391
Stolper Heide	17	7	5	393
Treudelberg	13	8	7	396

Jahreszeiten /Golfplatz	Note			Seite
1 2 3 **4** 5 **6 7** 8 **9 10** 11 12				
Wendlohe *A-Kurs + B-Kurs*	16	7	6	399
Wittelsbacher	15	7	6	401
1 2 3 **4 5 6 7 8 9 10** 11 12				
Abenberg	14	7	6	312
Bad Griesbach *Brunnwies*	17	9	9	314
Bad Griesbach-Sagmühle				
Sagmühle	15	9	9	315
Bad Liebenzell	14	7	7	316
Bad Wörishofen	14	6	6	317
Garmisch-Partenkirchen	14	6	7	334
Gut Ludwigsberg	15	6	6	336
Gut Rieden	14	7	6	337
Hohenpähl	15	7	6	347
Iffeldorf	16	7	6	350
Im Chiemgau	14	7	6	351
Isernhagen	15	7	6	352
Königsfeld	13	6	6	355
Märkischer Potsdam	14	7	6	361
Memmingen Gut Westerhart	14	6	6	362
Obere Alp	14	7	7	371
Oberfranken	17	6	5	372
Reichsstadt Bad Windsheim	14	6	7	376
Schloss Langenstein	16	8	7	384
Schloss Myllendonk	16	7	7	387
Schloss Wilkendorf	15	7	5	388
Semlin am See	14	8	7	389
St. Eurach	16	7	6	392
1 2 3 **4** 5 **6 7 8** 9 **10** 11 12				
Braunschweig	17	6	7	322
Feldafing	18	7	6	330
Fränkische Schweiz	14	7	6	332
Sonnenalp	16	7	7	390
Tegernseer Bad Wiessee	15	7	8	395
Tutzing	15	7	6	397
1 2 3 **4** 5 **6 7 8 9 10** 11 12				
Schloss Lüdersburg *Old/New*	17	7	6	386

311

Der Golfplatz liegt so nahe bei Nürnberg, dass man sich in dieser deutschen Hochburg des Mittelalters, in der Albrecht Dürer wohnte, gut einquartieren kann. Die Altstadt und das Germanische Nationalmuseum lohnen einen erholsamen Tag zwischen zwei Partien Golf! Die Spielbahn liegt in einem flachen Gelände mit vielen Bäumen. Die riesigen Bäume stellen einen wichtigen Teil der Schwierigkeiten dar, unter anderem verlangen auch die Fairways und die Länge von gewissen Par 4 bei bestimmten Abschlägen eine sehr sorgfältige Auswahl des Schlägers: Wenn man den Ball nicht lange und gerade schlagen kann, muss man einige Bogeys in Kauf nehmen. Die Bunker sind recht zahlreich, aber meist nur um die mittelgrossen, wenig welligen Greens angeordnet. Zwei Greens sind erhöht und zwei auf doppelten Stufen angelegt. Eine ehrliche, offene Anlage, auch wenn die Gestaltung und die Ausprägung der Erhebungen zu wünschen übrig lässt.

The Abenberg course is close enough to Nürnberg for you to establish base-camp in this high spot of Middle-Age Germany, where Albrecht Dürer once lived. The old town and the Germanisches Nationalmuseum are well worth a day's rest between two rounds of golf ! This course is laid out on generally flat terrain in very woody countryside, so big trees are not surprisingly a major factor in the difficulties awaiting you on either side of the fairways. On top of that, the length of some par 4s calls for very careful club selection from a number of tees. If you are not too sure of hitting it long and straight, there'll be a few bogeys in store. Bunkers abound but are basically placed around average-ly-sized greens with few contours. Two greens are elevated, two are two-tiered. A very decent course, but perhaps lacking a little contouring work to give the layout greater shape.

Golf Club Abenberg e.V.

Am Golfplatz 19
D - 91183 ABENBERG

Office	Sekretariat	(49) 09178 - 98 960
Pro shop	Pro shop	(49) 09178 - 98 960
Fax	Fax	(49) 09178 - 989 698
Situation	Lage	

25 km von Nürnberg, 498 000 Ew.

Annual closure	Jährliche Schliessung	ja 1/12→28/02
Weekly closure	Wöchentliche Schliessung	
		Montag,das Restaurant

Fees main season Preisliste hochsaison den ganzen Tag

	Week days Woche	We/Bank holidays We/Feiertag
Individual Individuell	DM 70,-	DM 90,-
Couple Ehepaar	DM 140,-	DM 180,-

- 22 Jahre, Studenten: – 50% Montag-Freitag (Week-days)

Caddy	Caddy	nein
Electric Trolley	Elektrokarren	nein
Buggy	Elektrischer Wagen	nein
Clubs	Clubs	ja

Credit cards Kreditkarten
VISA - Eurocard - MasterCard - AMEX

312

Access Zufahrt : A6 Nürnberg → Heilbronn. Ausf.
Schwabach West/ Abenberg. B466 → Abenberg
Map 4 on page 298 Karte 4 Seite 298

GOLF COURSE
PLATZ 14/20

Site	Lage	
Maintenance	Instandhaltung	
Architect	Architekt	

Type	Typ	Wald, Flachland
Relief	Relief	
Water in play	Platz mit Wasser	
Exp. to wind	Wind ausgesetzt	
Trees in play	Platz mit Bäumen	

Scorecard Scorekarte	Chp. Chp.	Mens Herren	Ladies Damen
Length Länge	6127	6127	5454
Par	72	72	72

Advised golfing ability		0	12	24	36
Empfohlene Spielstärke					
Hcp required	Min. Handicap	36			

CLUB HOUSE & AMENITIES
KLUBHAUS UND NEBENGEBÄUDE 7/10

Pro shop	Pro shop	
Driving range	Übungsplatz	
Sheltered	überdacht	6 Plätze
On grass	auf Rasen	ja
Putting-green	Putting-grün	ja
Pitching-green	Pitching-grün	ja

HOTEL FACILITIES
HOTEL BESCHREIBUNG 6/10

HOTELS HOTELS
Jägerhof   Roth-Pfaffenhofen
24 Zimmer, D DM 130,-   15 km
Tel (49) 09171 - 2038, Fax (49) 09171 - 2402

Raab-Inspektorsgarten   Schwabach
31 Zimmer, D DM 150,-   10 km
Tel (49) 09122 - 93 880, Fax (49) 09122 - 938 860

Löwenhof   Schwabach
20 Zimmer, D DM 160,-   10 km
Tel (49) 09122 -2047, Fax (49) 09122 -12 625

RESTAURANTS RESTAURANT
Goldener Stern   Schwabach
Tel (49) 09122 - 2335   10 km

Zirbelstube   Nürnberg-Worzeldorf
Tel(49) 0911 - 998 820   25 km

Dies ist ein gefährlicher Parcours. Die erste Runde wird man wohl damit beschäftigt sein, die Strategie für die zweite Runde zu analysieren, da die Hindernisse kaum sichtbar sind. Die Bäume dominieren und im Unterholz gehen die Bälle gerne verloren. Man wird schnell realisieren, dass man alle Schläge beherrschen muss und die Aufmerksamkeit nicht nachlassen darf, weil kein einziges Loch einfach anzuspielen ist. Gewöhnt man sich jedoch einmal daran, so muss man keine bösen Überraschungen befürchten: Es ist ein anspruchsvoller, interessanter Platz, die Schwierigkeiten sind gut verteilt und überfordern einen geübteren Spieler nicht. Zögern Sie jedoch nicht, die vorderen Abschläge zu wählen, wenn sie nicht in golferischer oder körperlicher Hochform sind, denn die Bahn ist zu Fuss recht anstrengend. Ob sie den Golfplatz nun mögen oder nicht, zumindest werden die Ruhe und der Charme dieses Ortes, ganz in der Nähe der schönen Stadt Augsburg, sie zu verführen wissen.

This is a dangerous course. First time out, you spend your time studying game strategy and how you might apply it for your next visit, as not all the hazards are visible. As the trees are very present and the undergrowth swallows up many a ball, you soon realise that for a good score here, you need flighted shots and constant concentration. Be warned : there is no one easy hole. But once acclimatised, there are no unpleasant surprises either. This is a demanding, competent and exciting course but the difficulties are well spread out and shouldn't be too much for even inexperienced players. Don't think twice about playing from the front tees if your game - and physical fitness - are not in tip-top condition, as Augsburg can be tough on the legs. Whether you like the course or not, you are bound to appreciate the tranquillity and charm of the spot, close to the pretty town of Augsburg.

Golf-Club Augsburg e.V.

Engelshofer Strasse 2
D - 86399 BOBINGEN-BURGWALDEN

Office	Sekretariat	(49) 08234 - 5621
Pro shop	Pro shop	(49) 08234 - 7311
Fax	Fax	(49) 08234 - 7855
Situation	Lage	

10 km von Augsburg, 265 000 Ew.
78 km von München, 1 300 000 Ew.

Annual closure	Jährliche Schliessung	nein
Weekly closure	Wöchentliche Schliessung	Montag
		das Restaurant

Fees main season Preisliste hochsaison den ganzen Tag

	Week days Woche	We/Bank holidays We/Feiertag
Individual Individuell	DM 60,-	DM 90,-
Couple Ehepaar	DM 120,-	DM 180,-

- 21 Jahre/Studenten: – 50%

Caddy	Caddy	nein
Electric Trolley	Elektrokarren	DM 25,-/ 18 Löcher
Buggy	Elektrischer Wagen	nein
Clubs	Clubs	DM 15,-
Credit cards Kreditkarten		nein

Access Zufahrt : A8 München-Augsburg. Ausf.
Augsburg-West. Ausf. Gersthofen Süd, B17 → Ausf.
Königsbrunn. Rechts → Bobingen, Strassberg.
Golfplatz → Burgwalden
Map 2 on page 294 Karte 2 Seite 294

GOLF COURSE
PLATZ

15/20

Site	Lage	
Maintenance	Instandhaltung	
Architect	Architekt	B. von Limburger
		Donald Harradine
Type	Typ	Wald, Gebirge
Relief	Relief	
Water in play	Platz mit Wasser	
Exp. to wind	Wind ausgesetzt	
Trees in play	Platz mit Bäumen	

Scorecard	Chp.	Mens	Ladies
Scorekarte	Chp.	Herren	Damen
Length Länge	6077	5833	5141
Par	72	72	72

Advised golfing ability	0	12	24	36
Empfohlene Spielstärke				
Hcp required	Min. Handicap	36		

CLUB HOUSE & AMENITIES
KLUBHAUS UND NEBENGEBÄUDE

7/10

Pro shop	Pro shop	
Driving range	Übungsplatz	
Sheltered	überdacht	3 Plätze
On grass	auf Rasen	ja
Putting-green	Putting-grün	ja
Pitching-green	Pitching-grün	ja

313

HOTEL FACILITIES
HOTEL BESCHREIBUNG

7/10

HOTELS HOTELS

Steigenberger Drei Mohren — Augsburg
107 Zimmer, D DM 300,- — 10 km
Tel (49) 0821 - 50 360, Fax (49) 0821 - 157 864

Schempp — Bobingen
46 Zimmer, D DM 130,- — 3 km
Tel (49) 08234 - 3046, Fax (49) 08234 - 4098

Dom Hotel — Augsburg
43 Zimmer, D DM 190,- — 12 km
Tel (49) 0821 - 153 031, Fax (49) 0821 - 510 126

RESTAURANTS RESTAURANT

Oblinger — Augsburg
Tel (49) 0821 - 345 8392 — 12 km

Fuggerei-Stube — Augsburg
Tel (49) 0821 - 30 870 — 12 km

Das Golf Resort Bad Griesbach umfasst vier 18-Loch Anlagen. Brunnwies sowie Sagmühle sind die beiden Top-Plätze des Resorts; Uttlau und Lederbach haben ebenfalls ihre Qualitäten, sind aber sehr hügelig (Golfwagen wird empfohlen). Brunnwies ist zwar auch auf unebenem Terrain angelegt, dieser Eindruck wird aber durch die hervorragende Platzgestaltung des Architekten Bernhard Langer weitgehend entschärft. Auffallend ist die sorgfältige Gestaltung des Geländes vom Abschlag zum Grün, wodurch die einzelnen Löchern eine deutliche Form und Definition erhalten. Grosse Beachtung wurde auch der Anlage breiter Fairways, sowie der Fairway- und Grünbunker geschenkt, die noch stärker ins Spiel kommen als die Bäume und das Wasser. Von den hinteren Abschlägen sind einige Löcher sehr lang, aber auch diese Bahnen sind von weiter vorne gespielt durchaus zu bewältigen. Gute Spieler tun sich auf Brunnwies schwerer als Durchschnittsgolfer, genau so soll es sein. Eine faszinierende Anlage mit einem sehr schönen Clubhaus im Stil der lokalen Bauernhöfe.

This enormous resort comprises four 18-hole courses. This and Sagmühle are the two gems, while Uttlau and Lederbach, despite their qualities, are very hilly (buggy recommended). Brunnwies is steep, too, but the excellence of architect Bernhard Langer tends to keep your mind off geographical considerations. The first thing you notice is the care taken over contouring the terrain, from tee to green, giving clear shape, form and physical definition to holes. There was also concern for wide fairways and fairway and green-side bunkers that are even more in play than the trees or water. From the back tees, some of the holes are long ; moving further forward, though, they are much more reasonable. It's tough for the good player but an easier proposition for the average golfer, so who could ask for more ?

Golf Resort Bad Griesbach

Holzhäuser 8
D - 94 086 BAD GRIESBACH

Office	Sekretariat	(49) 08535 - 96 010
Pro shop	Pro shop	(49) 08535 - 96 010
Fax	Fax	(49) 08535 - 960 115
Situation	Lage	

40 km von Passau, 50 000 Ew.
3 km von Griesbach, 8 200 Ew.

Annual closure	Jährliche Schliessung ja
	15/11→15/03
Weekly closure	Wöchentliche Schliessung nein

Fees main season
Preisliste hochsaison 18 Löcher

	Week days Woche	We/Bank holidays We/Feiertag
Individual Individuell	DM 80,-	DM 100,-
Couple Ehepaar	DM 160,-	DM 200,-

Caddy	Caddy	auf Reservierung
Electric Trolley	Elektrokarren	DM 15,-/ 18 Löcher
Buggy	Elektrischer Wagen	DM 40,-
Clubs	Clubs (1)	DM 2,-

Credit cards Kreditkarten Eurocard - MasterCard

314

Access Zufahrt : A3 Nürnberg-Regensburg-Passau. Ausf. Pocking. B12 und B388 → Bad Griesbach. → Golfplatz
Map 2 on page 295 Karte 2 Seite 295

GOLF COURSE
PLATZ **17**/20

Site	Lage	
Maintenance	Instandhaltung	
Architect	Architekt	Bernhard Langer
Type	Typ	Flachland, Gebirge
Relief	Relief	
Water in play	Platz mit Wasser	
Exp. to wind	Wind ausgesetzt	
Trees in play	Platz mit Bäumen	

Scorecard	Chp.	Mens	Ladies
Scorekarte	Chp.	Herren	Damen
Length Länge	6029	5701	5005
Par	70	70	71

Advised golfing ability	0 12 24 36
Empfohlene Spielstärke	
Hcp required Min. Handicap	nein

CLUB HOUSE & AMENITIES
KLUBHAUS UND NEBENGEBÄUDE **9**/10

Pro shop	Pro shop	
Driving range	Übungsplatz	
Sheltered	überdacht	12 Plätze
On grass	auf Rasen	nein
Putting-green	Putting-grün	ja
Pitching-green	Pitching-grün	ja

HOTEL FACILITIES
HOTEL BESCHREIBUNG **9**/10

HOTELS HOTELS
Golfhotel Maximilian — Golf Resort
232 Zimmer, D DM 300,-
Tel (49) 08532 - 79 50, Fax (49) 08532 - 795 150

Fürstenhof — Golf Resort
148 Zimmer, D DM 250,-
Tel (49) 08532 - 98 10, Fax (49) 08532 - 981 135

Parkhotel — Golf Resort
162 Zimmer, D DM 350,-
Tel (49) 08532 - 2 80, Fax (49) 08532 - 28 204

König Ludwig — Golf Resort
186 Zimmer, D DM 350,-
Tel (49) 08532 - 79 90, Fax (49) 08532 - 799 799

RESTAURANTS RESTAURANT
Fürstenstube — Golf Resort
Tel (49) 08532 - 98 10
Gutshof Uttlau - Tel (49) 08535 - 18 90 — Golf

Dies ist der älteste der vier Plätze in Deutschlands grösstem Golf-Resort. In etwas Enfernung zu den drei anderen Plätzen gelegen, verläuft Sagmühle auf wesentlich flacherem Gelände im Flusstal der Rott, deren Nebenarm immer wieder die Spielbahnen kreuzt. Wasser, ob als seitliches oder frontales Hindernis, ist die Hauptschwierigkeit auf diesem intelligent konzipierten Golfplatz, der leider häufig recht feucht ist. Um nicht allzuviele Bälle zu verlieren, sollte man daher seine eigenen Schlaglängen gut einschätzen können. Der Platz spielt sich insgesamt nicht allzu lang, sofern man nicht die hinteren Abschläge wählt. Bäume und Bunker sind so in das Platzdesign integriert, dass der Spieler auf der Runde mit allen möglichen Situationen und Hindernissen konfrontiert wird. Die gesamte Anlage, an der Grenze zwischen Bayern und Oberösterreich gelegen, umfasst ausserdem eine riesige Driving Range, eine Golfschule, zwei Kurz-Plätze und bietet zahlreiche weitere Aktivitäten für jeden Geschmack - egal ob Anfänger oder Könner.

This is the "oldest" of the four courses which grace Germany's largest golfing resort. A little out of the way from the three others, it is also much flatter and lies in the valley of the river Rott, a branch of which continually flows in and out of the course. As a frontal or lateral hazard, water is the main difficulty on this intelligently-designed (but often damp) layout, so it helps to know exactly what distance you can cover with each club to avoid losing too many balls. The overall yardage, though, is not excessive providing you steer clear of the back tees. With trees and bunkers, the course appears to be designed to put players in every imaginable situation with every possible hazard. The whole resort, located on the frontier between Bavaria and upper Austria, also features a huge driving range, a golfing school, two small courses and many other activities to keep everyone happy - the good, the not so good and the beginners.

Golf-Club Sagmühle

Schwaim 52
D - 94 086 BAD GRIESBACH

Office	Sekretariat	(49) 08532 - 2038
Pro shop	Pro shop	(49) 08532 - 7173
Fax	Fax	(49) 08532 - 3165
Situation	Lage	

40 km von Passau, 50 000 Ew.
3 km von Griesbach, 8 200 Ew.

Annual closure	Jährliche Schliessung	ja
		15/11 → 15/03
Weekly closure	Wöchentliche Schliessung	nein

Fees main season
Preisliste hochsaison 18 Löcher

	Week days Woche	We/Bank holidays We/Feiertag
Individual Individuell	DM 80,-	DM 100,-
Couple Ehepaar	DM 160,-	DM 200,-

Caddy	Caddy	auf Reservierung
Electric Trolley	Elektrokarren	DM 15,-/ 18 Löcher
Buggy	Elektrischer Wagen	DM 40,-
Clubs	Clubs (1)	DM 2,-

Credit cards Kreditkarten Eurocard - MasterCard

Access Zufahrt : A3 Nürnberg-Regensburg-Passau. Ausf. Pocking. B12 und B388 → Bad Griesbach. → Golfplatz
Map 2 on page 295 Karte 2 Seite 295

GOLF COURSE
PLATZ   15/20

Site	Lage	
Maintenance	Instandhaltung	
Architect	Architekt	K. Rossknecht
Type	Typ	Park
Relief	Relief	
Water in play	Platz mit Wasser	
Exp. to wind	Wind ausgesetzt	
Trees in play	Platz mit Bäumen	

Scorecard Scorekarte	Chp. Chp.	Mens Herren	Ladies Damen
Length Länge	6168	5916	5220
Par	72	72	72

Advised golfing ability		0 12 24 36
Empfohlene Spielstärke		
Hcp required	Min. Handicap	nein

CLUB HOUSE & AMENITIES
KLUBHAUS UND NEBENGEBÄUDE   9/10

Pro shop	Pro shop	
Driving range	Übungsplatz	
Sheltered	überdacht	ja
On grass	auf Rasen	nein
Putting-green	Putting-grün	ja
Pitching-green	Pitching-grün	ja

315

HOTEL FACILITIES
HOTEL BESCHREIBUNG   9/10

HOTELS HOTELS

Golfhotel Maximilian   Golf Resort
232 Zimmer, D DM 300,-
Tel (49) 08532 - 79 50, Fax (49) 08532 - 795 150
Fürstenhof   Golf Resort
148 Zimmer, D DM 250,-
Tel (49) 08532 - 98 10, Fax (49) 08532 - 981 135
Parkhotel   Golf Resort
162 Zimmer, D DM 350,-
Tel (49) 08532 - 2 80, Fax (49) 08532 - 28 204
König Ludwig   Golf Resort
186 Zimmer, D DM 350,-
Tel (49) 08532 - 79 90, Fax (49) 08532 - 799 799

RESTAURANTS RESTAURANT

Fürstenstube   Golf Resort
Tel (49) 08532 - 98 10
Gutshof Uttlau - Tel (49) 08535 - 18 90   Golf

BAD LIEBENZELL

Der Kurort Bad Liebenzell gilt als eines der nördlichen Tore zum Schwarzwald, der sich zwischen Karlsruhe und Basel erstreckt. Diese Landschaft ist geprägt von Weinbergen, Koniferen, Bauernhöfen, Kirchen und natürlich den berühmten Kuckucksuhren, die einem helfen die Startzeit nicht zu verschlafen. Auf gut 500 m Höhe, inmitten eines wunderschönen Waldgebietes gelegen, macht einem der hügelige Charakter des Platzes sofort klar, dass man sich hier im Mittelgebirge befindet. Der Parcours kann trotzdem gut zu Fuss bewältigt werden. Obwohl erst vor kurzem gebaut, strahlt der Platz bereits eine gewisse Reife aus, wobei spürbar wird, dass von Anfang an auf eine natürliche Einbettung der Anlage in die Umgebung Wert gelegt wurde. Man findet hier alle Arten von Hindernissen vor, von denen sicherlich der Wald und das Rough am gefährlichsten einzuschätzen sind, da es schwierig ist, Bälle von dort wieder herauszuspielen. Besonders wohl fühlen werden sich hier Spieler, die den Ball gerade schlagen, aber auch für alle anderen sollte ein guter Score möglich sein. Ein Platz für alle Spielklassen, der allerdings an die guten Spieler zu geringe Anforderungen stellt.

The spa town of Bad Liebenzell marks one of the northern gateways to the Black Forest (from Karlsruhe to Bâle), in a land of vineyards and conifers, farms and churches, and not forgetting the famous cuckoo clocks to help you make your tee-off time. Located some 500 metres up, this course nestles amid a beautiful part of the forest and is hilly enough to remind players that, although walkable, this is a mid-mountain course. Although recent, the course has already matured, although blending it into the surrounding landscape was obviously a clear priority from the outset. You will find all types of hazard here, the most dangerous unquestionably being the rough and woods, where escape shots are rarely easy. A course for all levels, but perhaps just lacking that little something for the best players.

Golfclub Bad Liebenzell e.V.
Golfplatz
D - 75378 BAD LIEBENZELL-MONAKAM

Office	Sekretariat	(49) 07052 - 1574
Pro shop	Pro shop	(49) 07052 - 1592
Fax	Fax	(49) 07052 - 5302
Situation	Lage	

15 km von Pforzheim, 115 000 Ew.

Annual closure	Jährliche Schliessung	ja
		1/11→28/02
Weekly closure	Wöchentliche Schliessung	nein

Fees main season
Preisliste hochsaison den ganzen Tag

	Week days Woche	We/Bank holidays We/Feiertag
Individual Individuell	DM 60,-	DM 80,-
Couple Ehepaar	DM 120,-	DM 160,-

Caddy	Caddy	auf Reservierung
Electric Trolley	Elektrokarren	DM 7,-
Buggy	Elektrischer Wagen	DM 60,-
Clubs	Clubs	DM 10,-

Credit cards Kreditkarten   nein

Access Zufahrt : A8 Stuttgart-Karlsruhe. Ausf.
Heimsheim. → Bad Liebenzell. Links →
Unterhaugstett. → Golfplatz
Map 1 on page 293 Karte 1 Seite 293

GOLF COURSE
PLATZ   **14**/20

Site	Lage	▰▰▰▰▱
Maintenance	Instandhaltung	▰▰▰▰▱
Architect	Architekt	
Type	Typ	Wald, Flachland
Relief	Relief	▰▰▰▰▱
Water in play	Platz mit Wasser	▰▰▱▱▱
Exp. to wind	Wind ausgesetzt	▰▰▱▱▱
Trees in play	Platz mit Bäumen	▰▰▰▰▱

Scorecard Scorekarte	Chp. Chp.	Mens Herren	Ladies Damen
Length Länge	6121	6121	5429
Par	72	72	72

Advised golfing ability	0	12	24	36
Empfohlene Spielstärke				

Hcp required Min. Handicap   We: 33

CLUB HOUSE & AMENITIES
KLUBHAUS UND NEBENGEBÄUDE   **7**/10

Pro shop	Pro shop	▰▰▰▰▱
Driving range	Übungsplatz	▰▰▰▱▱
Sheltered	überdacht	6 Plätze
On grass	auf Rasen	April-Nov.
Putting-green	Putting-grün	ja
Pitching-green	Pitching-grün	ja

HOTEL FACILITIES
HOTEL BESCHREIBUNG   **7**/10

HOTELS HOTELS
Kronen Hotel   Bad Liebenzell
43 Zimmer, D DM 250,-   3 km
Tel (49) 07052 - 4090, Fax (49) 07052 - 409 420

Ochsen   Bad Liebenzell
44 Zimmer, D DM 180,-   3 km
Tel (49) 07052 - 2074, Fax (49) 07052 - 2076

Schwarzwaldhotel Emendörfer   Bad Liebenzell
20 Zimmer, D DM 160,-   3 km
Tel (49) 07052 - 2323, Fax (49) 07052 - 2076

RESTAURANTS RESTAURANT
Adler   Calw-Stammheim
Tel (49) 07051 - 4287   10 km

Häckermühle   Tiefenbronn-Würmtal
Tel(49) 07234 - 6111   6 km

316

BAD WÖRISHOFEN

| 14 | 6 | 6 |

Dieser Platz hat einserseits weder schlechte Löcher, andererseits fehlt ihm aber auch ein wirklich herausragendes Loch, das einem im Gedächtnis bleibt. Dennoch ermöglichen das flache Terrain sowie andere Vorzüge dieser Anlage, dass man hier ohne zu ermüden 36 Löcher am Tag spielen, und sich dabei ganz auf das eigene Spiel konzentrieren kann. Die Spielstrategie ist offensichtlich. Der Golfplatz ist gut in die Natur integriert und bietet schöne Ausblicke auf den nahen Stausee und die bayerischen Alpen. Zahlreiche Bäume und Büsche grenzen die Löcher gut voneinander ab. Zwar sind einige der Par 4 Löcher recht lang, dafür sind deren Grüns relativ ungeschützt, so dass man trotzdem noch das Par retten kann. Geduldige, methodisch vorgehende Spieler werden hier belohnt. Breite Fairways und nur wenige Wasserhindernisse lassen diesen Golfplatz für alle Spielklassen geeignet erscheinen, jedoch sollte man vorzugsweise unter der Woche spielen, da es am Wochenende ziemlich voll wird.

There is no bad hole here, but there is no signature hole, either, to linger in your memory. Yet the flat terrain and other virtues can mean planning on 36 holes in one day without flagging and with no other worry than the state of your game. Game strategy is pretty obvious. Nicely hidden in its natural surroundings and offering pretty views over Stausee and the Bavarian Alps, this course is enhanced with the lush vegetation of trees and bushes which clearly separate holes. Granted, a number of par 4s are long, but the greens are relatively unguarded to help you save par. Patient and methodical players will feel at home here. Accessible to golfers of all abilities with widish fairways and little water to speak of, this is a course to be recommended during the week. Week-ends are crowded.

Golf Club Bad Wörishofen
Schlingener Strasse 27
D - 87668 RIEDEN

Office	Sekretariat	(49) 08346 - 777
Pro shop	Pro shop	(49) 08346 - 777-146
Fax	Fax	(49) 08346 - 1616
Situation	Lage	

58 km von Augsburg, 265 000 Ew.
88 km von München, 1 300 000 Ew.

Annual closure	Jährliche Schliessung	ja
		15/11→15/04
Weekly closure	Wöchentliche Schliessung	
	Montag, das Restaurant	

Fees main season Preisliste hochsaison den ganzen Tag		
	Week days Woche	**We/Bank holidays** We/Feiertag
Individual Individuell	DM 70,-	DM 90,-
Couple Ehepaar	DM 140,-	DM 180,-

-21 Jahre/Studenten: - 50%

Caddy	Caddy	nein
Electric Trolley	Elektrokarren	nein
Buggy	Elektrischer Wagen	ja
Clubs	Clubs	DM 10,-

Credit cards Kreditkarten nein

Access Zufahrt : A96 München-Memmingen. Ausf. Bad Wörishofen. → Kaufbeuren. In Schlingen, → Rieden → Golfplatz. **Map 2 on page 294** Karte 2 Seite 294

GOLF COURSE
PLATZ   **14**/20

Site	Lage	▭
Maintenance	Instandhaltung	▭
Architect	Architekt	Donald Harradine
Type	Typ	Park
Relief	Relief	▭
Water in play	Platz mit Wasser	▭
Exp. to wind	Wind ausgesetzt	▭
Trees in play	Platz mit Bäumen	▭

Scorecard Scorekarte	**Chp.** Chp.	**Mens** Herren	**Ladies** Damen
Length Länge	6348	5952	5294
Par	71	71	73

Advised golfing ability		0 12 24 36
Empfohlene Spielstärke		▭
Hcp required	Min. Handicap	36

CLUB HOUSE & AMENITIES
KLUBHAUS UND NEBENGEBÄUDE   **6**/10

Pro shop	Pro shop	▭
Driving range	Übungsplatz	▭
Sheltered	überdacht	ja
On grass	auf Rasen	ja
Putting-green	Putting-grün	ja
Pitching-green	Pitching-grün	ja

317

HOTEL FACILITIES
HOTEL BESCHREIBUNG   **6**/10

HOTELS HOTELS
Kneipp Kurhotel Fontenay   Bad Wörishofen
60 Zimmer, D DM 250,-   6 km
Tel (49) 08247 - 3060, Fax (49) 08247 - 306 185

Kurhotel Sonnengarten   Bad Wörishofen
78 Zimmer, D DM 300,-   6 km
Tel (49) 08247 - 3090, Fax (49) 08247 - 1068

Allgäuer Hof   Bad Wörishofen
36 Zimmer, D DM 150,-   6 km
Tel (49) 08247 - 96 990, Fax (49) 08247 - 969 960

RESTAURANTS RESTAURANT
Mühlbach   Bad Wörishofen
Tel (49) 08247 - 6039   6 km

Jagdhof   Schlingen
Tel (49) 08247 - 4879   4 km

Schöne Aussicht auf ein Schloss und das Dorf Altenhof, aber die erhöhte Lage hat auch Nachteile. Das Gelände ist extrem hügelig, so dass wir Senioren und konditionsschwachen Spielern diesen Platz nicht empfehlen können, es sei denn sie lassen sich von jemandem die Golftasche tragen. Darüberhinaus müssen vielfach Bälle aus ganz unterschiedlichen Schräglagen gespielt werden, was hohe Anforderungen an die Beherrschung solcher Schläge stellt. Am besten spielt man hier mitten in der Saison, wenn der Schwung gut funktioniert und man konditionell auf der Höhe ist, da einem der Platz wirklich alles abverlangt. Bamberg hat einen hohen technischen Standard, mit vielen Bäumen und einigen gefährlichen Wasserhindernissen. Hier sein Handicap zu spielen ist eine gute Leistung. Lohnt sich kennenzulernen, wenn man gerade in der Gegend ist.

You are greeted here by some pretty vistas over a castle and the village of Altenhof, but the elevated location does have its drawbacks. The terrain is very hilly so we would definitely not advise seniors and players short on physical fitness to come and play here, unless accompanied by someone to carry their bag. Besides, this configuration results in a good number of shots being played from all sorts of slopes, a good test for skill in this department of your game. The best time to play here is in mid-season, when there is less chance of your swing and legs throwing in the towel. You will need all the strength you can muster. With this said, Bamberg is a course of excellent technical standard with lots of trees and a few dangerous water hazards. Playing to your handicap is already a good performance. Well worth getting to know if you are in the region.

Golfclub Bamberg e.V. auf Gut Leimershof

Gut Leimershof
D - 96149 BREITENGÜSSBACH

Office	Sekretariat	(49) 09547 - 7109
Pro shop	Pro shop	(49) 09547 - 5202
Fax	Fax	(49) 09547 - 7817
Situation	Lage	

15 km von Bamberg, 70 000 Ew.

Annual closure	Jährliche Schliessung	ja
		1/12 → 28/02
Weekly closure	Wöchentliche Schliessung	Montag
		Das Restaurant

Fees main season Preisliste hochsaison 18 Löcher

	Week days Woche	We/Bank holidays We/Feiertag
Individual Individuell	DM 60,-	DM 80,-
Couple Ehepaar	DM 120,-	DM 160,-

-21 Jahre, Studenten: DM 35,- (Mo-Fr), DM 45,- (We)

Caddy	Caddy	auf Reservierung
Electric Trolley	Elektrokarren	nein
Buggy	Elektrischer Wagen	nein
Clubs	Clubs	ja

Credit cards Kreditkarten
VISA Eurocard - MasterCard - AMEX

318

Access Zufahrt : BAB Nürnberg-Bamberg. B173 →
Breitengüssbach. → Zückshut → Hohengüssbach
Map 4 on page 298 Karte 4 Seite 298

GOLF COURSE
PLATZ
15 /20

Site	Lage	▰▰▰▰
Maintenance	Instandhaltung	▰▰▰▰
Architect	Architekt	▰▰
Type	Typ	Flachland, Gebirge
Relief	Relief	▰▰▰
Water in play	Platz mit Wasser	▰▰
Exp. to wind	Wind ausgesetzt	▰▰
Trees in play	Platz mit Bäumen	▰▰▰

Scorecard Scorekarte	Chp. Chp.	Mens Herren	Ladies Damen
Length Länge	6175	6175	5470
Par	72	72	72

Advised golfing ability		0 12 24 36
Empfohlene Spielstärke		▰▰▰
Hcp required Min. Handicap	35	

CLUB HOUSE & AMENITIES
KLUBHAUS UND NEBENGEBÄUDE
7 /10

Pro shop	Pro shop	▰▰▰▰
Driving range	Übungsplatz	▰▰▰▰
Sheltered	überdacht	5 Plätze
On grass	auf Rasen	ja
Putting-green	Putting-grün	ja
Pitching-green	Pitching-grün	ja

HOTEL FACILITIES
HOTEL BESCHREIBUNG
7 /10

HOTELS HOTELS

Barock Hotel am Dom	Bamberg
19 Zimmer, D DM 160,-	15 km
Tel (49) 0951 - 54 031, Fax (49) 0951 - 54 021	

Residenzschloss Bamberg	Bamberg
184 Zimmer, D DM 250,-	15 km
Tel (49) 0951 - 60 910, Fax (49) 0951 - 609 1701	

Vierjahrszeiten	Breitengüssbach
35 Zimmer, D DM 160,-	6 km
Tel (49) 09544 - 861, Fax (49) 09544 - 864	

RESTAURANTS RESTAURANT

Schlencherla	Bamberg
Tel (49) 0951 - 56 060	15 km

Bassanese	Bamberg
Tel (49) 0951 - 57 551	15 km

BERLIN-WANNSEE

Der Mauerfall und die Wiedervereinigung Deutschlands haben dem Golfsport in der neuen Hauptstadt Auftrieb verliehen, wobei dieser Golfplatz der älteste ist. Auf halbem Weg zwischen Berlin und Potsdam ist er der ideale Ausgangspunkt für Besucher, die Sport und Kultur verbinden möchten. 1895 angelegt, wurde der Parcours in den 20er Jahren von Grund auf umgestaltet und weist für moderne Ansprüche eine ansehnliche Länge auf. Die grösste Schwierigkeit ist es, auf der Spielbahn zu bleiben und die Bäume entlang den Fairways zu vermeiden. Die Greens sind einfach zu lesen, gut, aber nicht übermässig geschützt, und das Fehlen von Wasserhindernissen wird diejenigen beruhigen (sie sind recht zahlreich), die das Wasser lieber trinken als es auf dem Golfplatz vorzufinden. Diese schöne und gut bespielbare Anlage ist eine erfreuliche Ergänzung zu den technisch anspruchsvolleren Golfplätzen der Region.

The collapse of the Berlin wall and the reunification of Germany have resulted in significant golfing boom in the new capital, where this is the oldest course. Located half-way between Berlin and Potsdam, this is the ideal base-camp for people looking to combine sport and culture. Designed back in 1895, the course was radically overhauled in the mid-1920s and now features a very decent length to today's standards. The basic problem is that of staying on the fairway and avoiding the trees on both sides. The greens are none too difficult to read and are well, but not excessively, guarded, and the absence of water will reassure those (very many) players who prefer to drink the stuff rather than find it on a golf course. A very pleasant course to see and play and an excellent companion for the other, more demanding courses in the region.

Golf- und Land-Club Berlin-Wannsee e.V;
Golfweg 22
D - 14109 BERLIN

Office	Sekretariat	(49) 030 - 806 7060
Pro shop	Pro shop	(49) 030 - 806 70619
Fax	Fax	(49) 030 - 806 70610
Situation	Lage	

12 km von Berlin, 3 500 000 Ew.

Annual closure	Jährliche Schliessung	ja
		1/11→31/03
Weekly closure	Wöchentliche Schliessung	
		Montag, das Restaurant

Fees main season Preisliste hochsaison 18 Löcher

	Week days Woche	We/Bank holidays We/Feiertag
Individual Individuell	DM 100,-	DM 120,-
Couple Ehepaar	DM 200,-	DM 240,-

– 21 Jahre/Studenten: – 50%

Caddy	Caddy	nein
Electric Trolley	Elektrokarren	nein
Buggy	Elektrischer Wagen	nein
Clubs	Clubs	nein
Credit cards Kreditkarten		nein

Access Zufahrt : Berlin-Zentrum → Wannsee.
Königstrasse, Chausseestrasse, → Kohlasenbruck
(Kohlasenbrücker Strasse), rechts, Stölpchenweg.
Map 6 on page 303 Karte 6 Seite 303

GOLF COURSE
PLATZ   **15**/20

Site	Lage	■■■■
Maintenance	Instandhaltung	■■■
Architect	Architekt	FA Harris
Type	Typ	Wald, Gebirge
Relief	Relief	
Water in play	Platz mit Wasser	■■
Exp. to wind	Wind ausgesetzt	■■■
Trees in play	Platz mit Bäumen	■■■■

Scorecard Scorekarte	**Chp.** Chp.	**Mens** Herren	**Ladies** Damen
Length Länge	6088	6088	5322
Par	72	72	72

Advised golfing ability		0 12 24 36	
Empfohlene Spielstärke		■■■	
Hcp required	Min. Handicap	34	

CLUB HOUSE & AMENITIES
KLUBHAUS UND NEBENGEBÄUDE   **6**/10

Pro shop	Pro shop	■■■
Driving range	Übungsplatz	■■■
Sheltered	überdacht	4 Plätze
On grass	auf Rasen	nein
Putting-green	Putting-grün	ja
Pitching-green	Pitching-grün	ja

HOTEL FACILITIES
HOTEL BESCHREIBUNG   **8**/10

HOTELS HOTELS
Villa Toscana   Berlin-Lichterfelde
16 Zimmer, D DM 260,-   10 km
Tel (49) 030 - 768 9270, Fax (49) 030 - 773 4488

Forsthaus ander Hubertusbrücke   Berlin- Wannsee
22 Zimmer, D DM 300,-   1 km
Tel (49) 030 - 805 3054, Fax (49) 030 - 805 3524

Forsthaus Paulborn   Berlin-Dahlem
10 Zimmer, D DM 240,-   9 km
Tel (49) 030 - 813 8010, Fax (49) 030 - 814 1156

RESTAURANTS RESTAURANT
Alter Krug   Berlin-Dahlem
Tel (49) 030 - 832 5089   9 km

Halali   Berlin-Wannsee
Tel (49) 030 - 805 3125   3 km

319

BEUERBERG

Der nationale und internationale Ruf dieses Golfplatzes ist hauptsächlich auf sein aussergewöhnliches Panorama der bayerischen Alpen zurückzuführen. Ihr Anblick tröstet über einen schlechten Score hinweg. Wem es gelingt, seine Aufmerksamkeit nicht der Lage und den herrlichen Ausblicken zu widmen, der wird auch vom Platz selbst - einem der besten Entwürfe Donald Harradines - nicht enttäuscht sein. Obwohl recht hoch gelegen, gibt es keine extremen Geländeerhebungen und trotz der vielen Bäume hat man nie den Eindruck, dass diese das Spiel einengen würden. Eher ungewöhnlich finden sich hier nur drei Par 3, aber fünf Par 5 Löcher. Dafür gibt es genügend kurze Par 4 Löcher, an denen das eine oder andere Birdie möglich ist. Während die Wasserhindernisse ziemlich bedrohlich wirken, sind die Grüns nur mittelmässig durch Bunker verteidigt. Nach modernen Designkriterien wäre sicherlich eine grössere Anzahl von Bunkern angelegt worden, um die besseren Spieler stärker zu fordern. In seinem jetzigen Zustand begünstigt der Platz Spieler mit mittleren und hohen Handicaps. Ein Besuch in Beuerberg lohnt sich in jedem Fall.

This course's national and international reputation stems widely from the exceptional view here over the Bavarian Alps. The sights can easily make up for a poor score. If you can put the sight and setting to the back of your mind, you won't be disappointed by the course, either, one of the best ever designed by Donald Harradine. Although high up, relief is never excessive, and while trees abound, they never give the impression of narrowness. Rather strangely, there are only three par 3s and five par 5s. The water hazards are rather threatening but the greens are only averagely guarded by bunkers: if modern-day criteria were followed, if they had wanted to upset the better players, they might have designed a few more: the game is made easier for mid- to high-handicappers. Beuerberg is well worth the journey.

Golfclub Beuerberg e.V.

Gut Sterz
D - 82547 BEUERBERG

Office	Sekretariat	(49) 08179 - 617 728
Pro shop	Pro shop	(49) 08179 - 1229
Fax	Fax	(49) 08179 - 5234
Situation	Lage	

45 km von München, 1 300 000 Ew.
15 km von Wolfratshausen, 16 000 Ew.

Annual closure	Jährliche Schliessung	ja
		15/11→15/03
Weekly closure	Wöchentliche Schliessung	nein

Fees main season
Preisliste hochsaison 18 Löcher

	Week days Woche	We/Bank holidays We/Feiertag
Individual Individuell	DM 90,-	DM 100,-
Couple Ehepaar	DM 180,-	DM 200,-

Caddy	Caddy	auf Reservierung
Electric Trolley	Elektrokarren	ja
Buggy	Elektrischer Wagen	nein
Clubs	Clubs	ja
Credit cards Kreditkarten		nein

Access Zufahrt : A95 München → Garmisch-Partenkirchen. Ausf. Seeshaupt, → Beuerberg
Map 2 on page 294 Karte 2 Seite 294

GOLF COURSE
PLATZ

17 /20

Site	Lage	▰▰▰▰▰
Maintenance	Instandhaltung	▰▰▰▰▰
Architect	Architekt	Donald Harradine
Type	Typ	Park
Relief	Relief	▰▰
Water in play	Platz mit Wasser	▰▰▰
Exp. to wind	Wind ausgesetzt	▰▰▰
Trees in play	Platz mit Bäumen	▰▰▰▰▰

Scorecard Scorekarte	Chp. Chp.	Mens Herren	Ladies Damen
Length Länge	6518	6036	5326
Par	74	74	74

Advised golfing ability Empfohlene Spielstärke	0	12	24	36
Hcp required Min. Handicap	36			

CLUB HOUSE & AMENITIES
KLUBHAUS UND NEBENGEBÄUDE

7 /10

Pro shop	Pro shop	▰▰▰▰
Driving range	Übungsplatz	▰▰▰
Sheltered	überdacht	6 Plätze
On grass	auf Rasen	ja
Putting-green	Putting-grün	ja
Pitching-green	Pitching-grün	ja

HOTEL FACILITIES
HOTEL BESCHREIBUNG

6 /10

HOTELS HOTELS

Gut Faistenberg — Eurasburg-Faistenberg
60 Zimmer, D DM 275,- — 7 km
Tel (49) 08179 - 1616, Fax (49) 08179 - 433

Posthotel Hofherr — Königsdorf
60 Zimmer, D DM 175,- — 5 km
Tel (49) 08179 - 5090, Fax (49) 08179 - 659

Stadthotel Berggeist — Penzberg
45 Zimmer, D DM 150,- — 13 km
Tel (49) 08856 - 80 10, Fax (49) 08856 - 81 913

RESTAURANTS RESTAURANT

Altes Fährhaus — Bad Tölz
Tel (49) 08041 - 60 30 — 15 km

Weinstube Schwaighofer — Bad Tölz
Tel (49) 08041 - 27 62 — 15 km

320

Die Handschrift von Trent Jones ist allein bereits ein Garant für Qualität. Dazu kommt in diesem Fall ein Gelände mit altem Mischwald-Bestand und natürlichen Wasserflächen. Angesichts dieser Vorzüge versteht man die Quelle seiner Inspiriration und das er keinerlei Zugeständnisse an die spielerischen Anforderungen des Platzes machen wollte. Der Platz ist sowohl visuell als auch technisch aussergewöhnlich gut gelungen und hat kaum ein Loch, an dem man sich entspannen könnte. Zu den natürlichen Hindernissen gesellen sich Fairway- und Grünbunker, von denen der Architekt grosszügig Gebrauch gemacht hat. Dennoch ist der Platz fair, da an jedem Loch die Spielstrategie deutlich vorgegeben ist. Spieler, die sich trotzdem an Schlägen versuchen, die ihre Tagesform übersteigen, müssen sich deshalb an der eigenen Nase fassen. Dieser Platz ist ein guter Test und scheint uns aufgrund der umfassenden Anforderungen, die er an die Spieler stellt, besonders geeignet für Wettspiele im Match-Play Format. Unbedingt spielen.

The Trent Jones label is already a token of quality. Add to that a site with naturally alternating forest and stretches of water and you will understand this source of inspiration here and his uncompromising refusal of facility. High-handicappers should be ready to lose a few balls without complaining. The course is visually and technically just magnificent, with hardly a hole to relax on. Needless to say, the natural hazards have been supplemented by fairway and green-side bunkers generously sprinkled around the course. But this is not a treacherous course, as from each tee game strategy is clear to see and players have only themselves to blame if they attempt to play beyond their current form. This comprehensive course is a tough examination and a marvellous invitation to the most suitable format for amateurs, namely match-play. A must.

Golfclub Bodensee Weissensberg e.V.
Lampertsweiler 51
D - 88138 WEISSENSBERG

Office	Sekretariat	(49) 08389 - 89190
Pro shop	Pro shop	(49) 08389 - 89192
Fax	Fax	(49) 08389 - 89 191
Situation	Lage	

7 km von Lindau, 25 000 Ew.
15 km von Bregenz (Österreich)

Annual closure	Jährliche Schliessung	nein
Weekly closure	Wöchentliche Schliessung Nov.-März, das Restaurant	

Fees main season
Preisliste hochsaison 18 Löcher

	Week days Woche	We/Bank holidays We/Feiertag
Individual Individuell	DM 70,-	DM 90,-
Couple Ehepaar	DM 140,-	DM 180,-

– 21 Jahre, Studenten: DM 40,-/60,-

Caddy	Caddy	auf Reservierung
Electric Trolley	Elektrokarren	nein
Buggy	Elektrischer Wagen	nein
Clubs	Clubs	ja
Credit cards Kreditkarten		MasterCard

Access Zufahrt : Lindau, → Golfplatz
Map 1 on page 293 Karte 1 Seite 293

GOLF COURSE
PLATZ   17 /20

Site	Lage	▬▬▬
Maintenance	Instandhaltung	▬▬▬
Architect	Architekt	R. Trent Jones Sr
Type	Typ	Wald, Park
Relief	Relief	▬
Water in play	Platz mit Wasser	▬▬
Exp. to wind	Wind ausgesetzt	▬▬
Trees in play	Platz mit Bäumen	▬▬▬

Scorecard Scorekarte	Chp. Chp.	Mens Herren	Ladies Damen
Length Länge	6112	5856	5189
Par	71	71	71

Advised golfing ability	0 12 24 36
Empfohlene Spielstärke	▬▬▬
Hcp required	Min. Handicap nein

CLUB HOUSE & AMENITIES
KLUBHAUS UND NEBENGEBÄUDE   7 /10

Pro shop	Pro shop	▬▬▬
Driving range	Übungsplatz	▬▬
Sheltered	überdacht	ja
On grass	auf Rasen	ja
Putting-green	Putting-grün	ja
Pitching-green	Pitching-grün	ja

321

HOTEL FACILITIES
HOTEL BESCHREIBUNG   7 /10

HOTELS HOTELS
Golfhotel Bodensee   Golf
21 Zimmer, D DM 300,-
Tel (49) 08389 - 8910, Fax (49) 08389 - 89 191

Bayerischer Hof   Lindau-Insel
104 Zimmer, D DM 400,-   7 km
Tel (49) 08382 - 91 50, Fax (49) 08382 - 915 591

Reutemann Seegarten   Lindau-Insel
64 Zimmer, D DM 300,-   7 km
Tel (49) 08382 - 91 50, Fax (49) 08382 - 915 591

RESTAURANTS RESTAURANT
Hoyerberg Schlössle   Lindau
Tel (49) 08382 - 25 295   7 km

Weinstube Frey   Lindau-Insel
Tel (49) 08382 - 52 78   7 km

Der Platz ist im typisch britischen Stil konzipiert und vermittelt das Flair eines alten Parks; zudem ist das Gelände für die Gegend recht hügelig. Auffallend sind die geschickt angelegten Fairway- und Grünbunker, welche nicht nur die Löcher optisch voneinander abgrenzen, sondern auch eine sehr wirksame Verteidigung darstellen. Am schwierigsten ist es jedoch seinen Drive gut zu plazieren, was durch eine Reihe sehr enger Fairways erschwert wird. Die dabei geforderte Präzison macht wett, was dem Platz an Länge fehlt. Eine Anzahl blinder Schläge, einige erhöht angelegte Grüns, Höhenunterschiede zwischen Abschlägen und Grüns, sowie relativ kleine Puttflächen erschweren die Schlägerwahl. Braunschweig ist ein spektakulär gestalteter Golfplatz, auf dessen strategisch angelegten Löchern das Spielen grossen Spass macht, wenngleich es Spielern mit mittleren und hohen Handicaps schwer fallen dürfte, hier einen guten Score zu erzielen. Letztere sind gut beraten sich einfach am Spiel zu erfreuen.

A rather hilly course for the region, Braunschweig gives the impression of an old park with a very obvious British style very much to the fore. We noted the clever placing of bunkers (fairway and green) which are as useful for demarcating the layout as they are for protecting it. But the prime difficulty here lies with placing the tee-shot, owing to a number of tight fairways which make up for the course's lack of length. A few blind shots, a number of elevated greens and differences in altitude between tee and green complicate the choice of club, especially since the putting surfaces are generally rather small. A spectacular and prettily landscaped course which is great fun to play and very strategic, although mid- and high-handicappers should not bank too much on carding a good score. They are better off just playing for the fun of it.

Golf-Klub Braunschweig e.V.

Scharzkopffstrasse 10
D - 38126 BRAUNSCHWEIG

Office	Sekretariat	(49) 0531 - 264 240
Pro shop	Pro shop	(49) 0531 - 695 797
Fax	Fax	(49) 0531 - 642 413
Situation	Lage	

3 km von Braunschweig, 260 000 Ew.
75 km von Hannover, 510 000 Ew.

Annual closure	Jährliche Schliessung	nein

Weekly closure	Wöchentliche Schliessung	
	Montag, das Restaurant	

Fees main season Preisliste hochsaison den ganzen Tag

	Week days Woche	We/Bank holidays We/Feiertag
Individual Individuell	DM 60,-	DM 70,-
Couple Ehepaar	DM 120,-	DM 140,-
– 21 Jahre/Studenten: – 50%		

Caddy	Caddy	nein
Electric Trolley	Elektrokarren	nein
Buggy	Elektrischer Wagen	nein
Clubs	Clubs	nein

Credit cards Kreditkarten	nein

nach A2 (Hannover)
BRAUNSCHWEIG
Helmstedt
Lindenberg
GOLF
Bahnhof
Zuckerberg Heidberg Mascherode
Salzgitter
Wolfenbüttel

Access Zufahrt : Hauptbahnhof, Salzdahlumer Strasse zum Krankenhaus
Map 6 on page 302 Karte 6 Seite 302

GOLF COURSE
PLATZ

17 /20

Site	Lage	▬▬▬▬▭
Maintenance	Instandhaltung	▬▬▬▬▭
Architect	Architekt	
Type	Typ	Land, Wald
Relief	Relief	▬▬▬▭▭
Water in play	Platz mit Wasser	▬▭▭▭▭
Exp. to wind	Wind ausgesetzt	▬▬▭▭▭
Trees in play	Platz mit Bäumen	▬▬▬▭▭

Scorecard Scorekarte	Chp. Chp.	Mens Herren	Ladies Damen
Length Länge	5893	5893	5219
Par	71	71	71

Advised golfing ability Empfohlene Spielstärke	0	12	24	36
Hcp required Min. Handicap	36			

CLUB HOUSE & AMENITIES
KLUBHAUS UND NEBENGEBÄUDE

6 /10

Pro shop	Pro shop	▬▬▬▬▭
Driving range	Übungsplatz	▬▬▬▭▭
Sheltered	überdacht	3 Plätze
On grass	auf Rasen	ja (Sommer)
Putting-green	Putting-grün	ja
Pitching-green	Pitching-grün	ja

HOTEL FACILITIES
HOTEL BESCHREIBUNG

7 /10

HOTELS HOTELS
Stadtpalais — Braunschweig
45 Zimmer, D DM 250,- — 3 km
Tel (49) 0531 - 241 024, Fax (49) 0531 - 241 025

An der Stadthalle — Braunschweig
24 Zimmer, D DM 170,- — 3 km
Tel (49) 0531 - 73 068, Fax (49) 0531 - 75 148

Fürstenhof — Braunschweig
52 Zimmer, D DM 160,- — 2 km
Tel (49) 0531 - 791 061, Fax (49) 0531 - 791 064

RESTAURANTS RESTAURANT
Gewandhaus — Braunschweig
Tel (49) 0531 - 242 077 — 3 km

Brabanter Hof — Braunschweig
Tel (49) 0531 - 43 090 — 3 km

322

Ein originelles Beispiel der sehr strengen Architektur Siegmanns, bei dem drei verschiedene Stile vorzufinden sind: Wald, offene Fläche und beinahe alpine Landschaft, wobei letztere körperlich die anstrengendste ist (bei drei Löchern). Der Architekt hat sich dem Gelände gefügt, ohne es stark umzugestalten, daher auch der etwas uneinheitliche Stil. Doch der Platz ist dadurch sehr abwechslungsreich und interessant und die Hindernisse sind von den Abschlägen aus gut sichtbar. Man muss jedoch sein Spiel schnell an die Gegebenheiten anpassen können. Spieler mit weniger guten Reflexen werden etwas Mühe haben. Buxtehude ist sehr lang, daher ergeben seine sechs Par 5 Löcher ein ansprechendes Par 74. Die Greens sind teils erhöht, teils auf Doppelstufen und recht klein, was äusserste Genauigkeit erfordert. Dafür sind ihre Verteidigungen durchaus zu durchbrechen. Geeignet für die ganze Familie, ohne sich allzusehr um den Score zu kümmern.

An original example of Siegmann's very serious style of architecture, where you find three different styles: one in the woods, another in more open countryside and the last virtually up in the hills and physically the most trying (over three holes). The designer has bowed to the landscape more than he has modelled it, hence the impression of a rather unassertive style. In contrast, the course is great fun to play with a lot of variety and clearly visible hazards from the tees. You have to adjust your game quickly, and players with slow reflexes will find it hard work. Buxtehude is very long, but the six par 5s make this a more reasonable par 74. The greens are sometimes elevated and two-tiered, and they are rather small, so extreme accuracy is essential. In contrast, their defences are not unbreachable. Play with all the family and don't worry too much about the score.

Golf-Club Buxtehude

Zum Lehmfeld 1
D - 21614 BUXTEHUDE

Office	Sekretariat	(49) 04161 - 81 333
Pro shop	Pro shop	(49) 04161 - 81 222
Fax	Fax	(49) 04161 - 87 268
Situation	Lage	

5 km von Buxtehude, 34 000 Ew.
50 km von Hamburg, 1 650 000 Ew.

Annual closure	Jährliche Schliessung	nein
Weekly closure	Wöchentliche Schliessung	
		Montag, das Restaurant

Fees main season
Preisliste hochsaison 18 Löcher

	Week days Woche	We/Bank holidays We/Feiertag
Individual Individuell	DM 60,-	DM 80,-
Couple Ehepaar	DM 120,-	DM 160,-

- 21 Jahre/Studenten: - 50%

Caddy	Caddy	auf Reservierung
Electric Trolley	Elektrokarren	nein
Buggy	Elektrischer Wagen	DM 50,-
Clubs	Clubs	nein
Credit cards Kreditkarten		nein

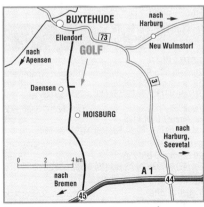

Access Zufahrt : A1 Hamburg-Bremen. Ausf.
Hollenstedt → Moisburg, Buxtehude. Daensen →
Golfplatz **Map 7 on page 304** Karte 7 Seite 304

GOLF COURSE
PLATZ   **15**/20

Site	Lage	■■■■■□□
Maintenance	Instandhaltung	■■■■■□□
Architect	Architekt	W. Siegmann
Type	Typ	Wald, Flachland
Relief	Relief	
Water in play	Platz mit Wasser	■□□□□□□
Exp. to wind	Wind ausgesetzt	■■□□□□□
Trees in play	Platz mit Bäumen	■■■■■■□

Scorecard Scorekarte	Chp. Chp.	Mens Herren	Ladies Damen
Length Länge	6480	6480	5710
Par	74	74	74

Advised golfing ability		0 12 24 36
Empfohlene Spielstärke		▭■■□
Hcp required	Min. Handicap	36

CLUB HOUSE & AMENITIES
KLUBHAUS UND NEBENGEBÄUDE   **7**/10

Pro shop	Pro shop	■■■■■□□
Driving range	Übungsplatz	■■■■■■□
Sheltered	überdacht	5 Plätze
On grass	auf Rasen	ja
Putting-green	Putting-grün	ja
Pitching-green	Pitching-grün	nein

HOTEL FACILITIES
HOTEL BESCHREIBUNG   **6**/10

HOTELS HOTELS

Seeburg   Buxtehude-Neukloster
14 Zimmer, D DM 170,-   5 km
Tel (49) 04161 - 74 100, Fax (49) 04161 - 741 074

Herzog Widukind   Buxtehude
45 Zimmer, D DM 195,-   7 km
Tel (49) 04161 - 6460, Fax (49) 04161 - 646 146

Zur Mühle   Buxtehude
36 Zimmer, D DM 250,-   7 km
Tel (49) 04161 - 50 650, Fax (49) 04161 - 506 530

RESTAURANTS RESTAURANT

Seeburg   Buxtehude-Neukloster
Tel (49) 04161 - 82 071   5 km

Herbstprinz   Jork
Tel (49) 04162- 7403   8 km

323

1905 erbaut, wurde der Platz Anfang der 60er Jahre neu gestaltet. An vier Löchern kommt Wasser ins Spiel; grosse Pinien dominieren den Platzcharakter. Es gibt insgesamt nur zwei Fairway-Bunker, da das Profil der Doglegs die Spielbahnen bereits sehr anspruchsvoll macht. Die Grüns sind bemerkenswert gut verteidigt, obschon die sie umgebenden Bunker weder besonders zahlreich noch allzu bedrohlich sind. Angesichts der Tatsache, dass die meisten Schwierigkeiten gut auszumachen sind und das Gelände nur wenige Unebenheiten aufweist, erkennt man, dass die Probleme, die einem dieser Platz bereitet, sehr subtiler Art sein müssen. Dazu gehören Länge, die Beherrschung einer Vielzahl von Schlagvarianten, die Fähigkeit den Ball vom Abschlag aus so zu plazieren, dass man das Grün mit dem zweiten Schlag gut anspielen kann, sowie die Allgegenwärtigkeit von Bäumen und Heidekraut, die alle verunglückten Schläge bestrafen. Nur die sehr guten Spieler werden sich für die hinteren Abschläge entscheiden, wenngleich die sechs Par 5 Löcher gute Gelegenheiten zu einem Birdie bieten. Es ist ein absolutes Vergnügen hier zu spielen.

Designed in 1905, it was re-modelled in the early 1960s. There is water on four holes and tall pine-trees virtually everywhere, but there are only two fairway bunkers. They must have thought that the tight dog-legs were already penalising enough. The greens are remarkably well guarded, even though the protective bunkers are neither too numerous nor too dangerous. If we add to this the fact that most difficulties are clearly visible and relief never more than a gentle roll, you will understand how subtle the problems are here. Length has a lot to do with this, as does the variety of shots to be played, the positioning of each shot to approach the greens from the best angle and the presence of trees and heather. Only the very good players will choose the back tees. A real treat to play.

Club zur Vahr e.V., Bremen, Platz Garlstedter Heide

Am Golfplatz 10
D - 27711 GARLSTEDT/OHZ

Office	Sekretariat	(49) 0421 - 204 480
Pro shop	Pro shop	(49) 0421 - 231 467
Fax	Fax	(49) 0421 - 244 9248
Situation	Lage	

26 km von Bremen, 552 000 Ew. 39 km von Bremerhaven

Annual closure	Jährliche Schliessung	ja
		1/01→1/03
Weekly closure	Wöchentliche Schliessung	Montag
		das Restaurant

Fees main season Preisliste hochsaison 18 Löcher

	Week days Woche	We/Bank holidays We/Feiertag
Individual Individuell	DM 70,-	DM 70,-
Couple Ehepaar	DM 140,-	DM 140,-

We: nur in Mitgliederbegleitung (with members)

Caddy	Caddy	nein
Electric Trolley	Elektrokarren	nein
Buggy	Elektrischer Wagen	nein
Clubs	Clubs	nein
Credit cards Kreditkarten		nein

Access Zufahrt : Bremen, A27 → Bremerhaven. Ausf. Ihlpol, B6 → Bremerhaven. 10 km zu Garlstedt. Links, → Golfplatz **Map 5 on page 301** Karte 5 Seite 301

GOLF COURSE
PLATZ   18/20

Site	Lage	▰▰▰▰▱
Maintenance	Instandhaltung	▰▰▰▰▱
Architect	Architekt	B. von Limburger
Type	Typ	Wald, Park
Relief	Relief	▰▰▰▱▱
Water in play	Platz mit Wasser	▰▰▰▱▱
Exp. to wind	Wind ausgesetzt	▰▰▱▱▱
Trees in play	Platz mit Bäumen	▰▰▰▰▱

Scorecard Scorekarte	Chp. Chp.	Mens Herren	Ladies Damen
Length Länge	6535	6340	5638
Par	74	74	74

Advised golfing ability Empfohlene Spielstärke	0	12	24	36

Hcp required   Min. Handicap   36

CLUB HOUSE & AMENITIES
KLUBHAUS UND NEBENGEBÄUDE   6/10

Pro shop	Pro shop	▰▰▰▱▱
Driving range	Übungsplatz	▰▰▰▰▱
Sheltered	überdacht	nein
On grass	auf Rasen	ja
Putting-green	Putting-grün	ja
Pitching-green	Pitching-grün	ja

HOTEL FACILITIES
HOTEL BESCHREIBUNG   5/10

HOTELS HOTELS

Zum alten Torfkahn   Osterholz-Scharmbeck
11 Zimmer, D DM 150,-   6 km
Tel (49) 04791 - 76 08, Fax (49) 04791 - 59 606

Tivoli   Osterholz-Scharmbeck
54 Zimmer, D DM 120,-   6 km
Tel (49) 04791 - 80 50, Fax (49) 04791 - 80 560

Eichenhof   Worpswede
20 Zimmer, D DM 250,-   18 km
Tel (49) 04792 - 26 76, Fax (49) 04792 - 44 27

RESTAURANTS RESTAURANT

Tietjen's Hütte   Osterholz-Scharmbeck
Tel (49) 04791 - 24 15   9 km

Zum alten Torfkahn   Osterholz-Scharmbeck
Tel (49) 04791 - 76 08   6 km

324

DÜSSELDORF/HÖSEL | 13 | 6 | 6 |

Ein Club in vollem Aufschwung, der Ende 1997 über weitere 18 Löcher verfügen wird. Dank dem sandigen Boden ist der nur leicht hügelige Platz der bestentwässerte in der Gegend - ein unschätzbarer Vorteil bei Regen. Der Architekt hatte beim Entwurf offenbar eher das Spielvergnügen der Clubmitgleider denn ein sportlich-anspruchsvolles Layout im Auge. Dieser Umstand muss, wenngleich gute Spieler dem widersprechen werden, nicht unbedingt von Nachteil sein. Optisch erinnert der Platz an einen gut gepflegten Park, von dem aus sich schöne Panoramablicke auf das Umland eröffnen. Im allgemeinen recht flach, eignet sich der Kurs für alle Spielstärken. Die Sicherheitszonen um die vorhandenen Hindernisse sind ausreichend grosszügig gestaltet, so dass man diese ohne allzu grosse Mühe unbeschadet umspielen kann. Ein angenehmer Platz, dessen strategische Konzeption den Golfern letztendlich ernsthafte Anstrengungen abverlangt.

Very much an up-and-coming club, with a new 18-holer due to open in late 1997. A none too hilly course, but the sandy sub-soil makes this the best-drained course in the region, an asset during the rainy season. The designer visibly thought more about club members than about creating a challenging course here, but although better players looking for something more demanding might disagree, this is not necessarily a shortcoming. The course's visual appeal is reminiscent of a well kept park, but there are a number of pretty panoramas across the region. Generally flat, this is a course for all levels, and while there is no shortage of hazards, the safety areas are wide enough to play around without too many scares and without having to work miracles. A pleasant and, at the final count, a rather strategic course, designed for some serious golfing.

Golfclub Düsseldorf/Hösel
In den Höfen 32
D - 40883 RATINGEN

Office	Sekretariat	(49) 02056 - 93 370
Pro shop	Pro shop	(49) 02056 - 93 370
Fax	Fax	(49) 02056 - 93 371
Situation	Lage	

7 km von Ratingen, 91 000 Ew.
15 km von Düsseldorf, 570 000 Ew.

Annual closure	Jährliche Schliessung	nein
Weekly closure	Wöchentliche Schliessung	Montag, das Restaurant

Fees main season Preisliste hochsaison 18 Löcher		
	Week days Woche	We/Bank holidays We/Feiertag
Individual Individuell	DM 80,-	DM 70,-
Couple Ehepaar	DM 160,-	DM 140,-

We: nur in Mitgliederbegleitung (with members),
- 21 Jahre/Studenten: – 50%

Caddy	Caddy	auf Reservierung
Electric Trolley	Elektrokarren	nein
Buggy	Elektrischer Wagen	nein
Clubs	Clubs	ja
Credit cards Kreditkarten		nein

Access Zufahrt : A3 Köln-Oberhausen. Ausf. Kreuz Breitscheid. B227 → Velbert. In Hösel, rechts. Erste Strasse links → Golfplatz
Map 3 on page 296 Karte 3 Seite 296

GOLF COURSE
PLATZ 13 /20

Site	Lage	▬▬▬▬▬□
Maintenance	Instandhaltung	▬▬▬▬□□
Architect	Architekt	

Type	Typ	Park
Relief	Relief	▬▬□□□□
Water in play	Platz mit Wasser	▬▬□□□□
Exp. to wind	Wind ausgesetzt	▬▬□□□□
Trees in play	Platz mit Bäumen	▬▬▬▬□□

Scorecard Scorekarte	Chp. Chp.	Mens Herren	Ladies Damen
Length Länge	6097	6097	5418
Par	72	72	72

Advised golfing ability	0	12	24	36
Empfohlene Spielstärke				
Hcp required Min. Handicap	36			

CLUB HOUSE & AMENITIES
KLUBHAUS UND NEBENGEBÄUDE 6 /10

Pro shop	Pro shop	▬▬▬□□□
Driving range	Übungsplatz	▬▬▬▬□□
Sheltered	überdacht	4 Plätze
On grass	auf Rasen	ja
Putting-green	Putting-grün	ja
Pitching-green	Pitching-grün	ja

HOTEL FACILITIES
HOTEL BESCHREIBUNG 6 /10

HOTELS HOTELS
Astoria   Ratingen
27 Zimmer, D DM 200,-   7 km
Tel (49) 02102 - 82 005, Fax (49) 02102 - 845 868

Altenkamp   Ratingen
25 Zimmer, D DM 200,-   7 km
Tel (49) 02102 - 99 020, Fax (49) 02102 - 21 217

Waldhotel   Heiligenhaus
69 Zimmer, D DM 250,-   6 km
Tel (49) 02056 - 5970, Fax (49) 02056 - 597 260

RESTAURANTS RESTAURANT
Kuhs-Deutscher Hof   Heiligenhaus
Tel (49) 02056 - 6528   6 km

San Marco   Ratingen
Tel (49) 02102 - 24 444   8 km

325

Wenn kein Golfwagen mehr verfügbar ist empfehlen wir die Benutzung eines Elektrotrolleys, da einige Anstiege in der Tat sehr steil sind. Dieser Umstand bietet den Vorzug einer Anzahl grossartiger Ausblicke auf die Stadt Düsseldorf. Der Architekt Donald Harradine hat zahlreiche Plätze in ganz Europa entworfen, und wenngleich dieser hier nicht zu seinen Besten zählt, ist er doch einer der interessantesten Kurse dieser Region. Es ist nicht Harradines Art spektakuläre Details einzubauen, wie dies einige seiner Kollegen tun. Dafür zwingt die überlegte Anordnung der gut erkennbaren Bunker, die Enge einiger Spielbahnen sowie die gute Verteidigung der meist erhöht angelegten Grüns die Golfer zu wohldurchdachter Schlägerwahl und kontrolliertem Spiel. Hier kann man sich mit der ganzen Familie wie auch im Freundeskreis prächtig amüsieren. Spieler mit hohem Handicap werden sicherlich für alle Ratschläge dankbar sein, die ihnen helfen, die Spieltaktik ihrem Können anzupassen.

If you can't lay your hands on a buggy, we would advice an electric trolley, as here some of the slopes are very steep indeed. The advantage of this is a number of marvellous views, especially over Düsseldorf. Designer Donald Harradine has produced many courses in Europe, and although this is by no means his best, it is nonetheless one of the most interest layouts in the region. You won't find those spectacular details that some designers use to stamp their authority, that's not his style, but the sensible layout of bunkers (clearly visible), the tightness of some fairways and the well-guarded greens (almost all elevated), oblige players to flight the ball and think long and hard about club selection. This is an amusing course to play with all the family or with friends, and the higher-handicappers will appreciate all the advice they can get about the tactics they will need to adopt in accordance with their playing ability.

Düsseldorfer Golf Club e.V.
Rittergut Rommeljansweg
D - 40882 RATINGEN

Office	Sekretariat	(49) 02102 - 81 092
Pro shop	Pro shop	(49) 02102 - 83 683
Fax	Fax	(49) 02102 - 81 782
Situation	Lage	

1 km von Ratingen, 91 000 Ew. 10 km von Düsseldorf.

Annual closure	Jährliche Schliessung	ja
		20/12→10/02
Weekly closure	Wöchentliche Schliessung	Montag
		das Restaurant

Fees main season Preisliste hochsaison den ganzen Tag

	Week days Woche	We/Bank holidays We/Feiertag
Individual Individuell	DM 100,-	DM 100,-
Couple Ehepaar	DM 200,-	DM 200,-

We: nur in Mitgliederbegleitung (with members) /
– 21 Jahre/Studenten: – 50 %

Caddy	Caddy	auf Reserv. DM 30,-
Electric Trolley	Elektrokarren	DM 20,-/ 18 Löcher
Buggy	Elektrischer Wagen	nein
Clubs	Clubs	DM 10,-
Credit cards Kreditkarten		nein

Access Zufahrt : A3, Ausf. Ratingen-Wülfrath, →
Ratingen. 400 m rechts → Golfplatz
Map 3 on page 296 Karte 3 Seite 296

GOLF COURSE
PLATZ   13 /20

Site	Lage	
Maintenance	Instandhaltung	
Architect	Architekt	Donald Harradine
Type	Typ	Wald
Relief	Relief	
Water in play	Platz mit Wasser	
Exp. to wind	Wind ausgesetzt	
Trees in play	Platz mit Bäumen	

Scorecard Scorekarte	Chp. Chp.	Mens Herren	Ladies Damen
Length Länge	5905	5905	5220
Par	71	71	71

Advised golfing ability			0	12	24	36
Empfohlene Spielstärke						
Hcp required	Min. Handicap	36				

CLUB HOUSE & AMENITIES
KLUBHAUS UND NEBENGEBÄUDE   7 /10

Pro shop	Pro shop	
Driving range	Übungsplatz	
Sheltered	überdacht	4 Plätze
On grass	auf Rasen	ja
Putting-green	Putting-grün	ja
Pitching-green	Pitching-grün	ja

HOTEL FACILITIES
HOTEL BESCHREIBUNG   7 /10

HOTELS HOTELS
Haus Kronenthal — Ratingen
30 Zimmer, D DM 230,- — 1 km
Tel (49) 02102 - 85 080, Fax (49) 02102 - 850 850

Allgäuer Hof — Ratingen
15 Zimmer, D DM 165,- — 3 km
Tel (49) 02102 - 95 410, Fax (49) 02102 - 954 123

Am Düsseldorfer Platz — Ratingen 2 km
49 Zimmer, D DM 200,-
Tel (49) 02102 - 20 180, Fax (49) 02102 - 201 850

RESTAURANTS RESTAURANT
Haus zum Haus — Ratingen
Tel (49) 02102 - 22 586 — 2 km

Auermühle — Ratingen
Tel (49) 02102 - 81 064 — 2 km

326

Eine alte, sorgfältig restaurierte Windmühle beeindruckt den Besucher gleich auf Anhieb. Der Eindruck von dem noch ziemlich jungen Platz ist dagegen weniger überwältigend. Trotzdem rechtfertigt sein allgemeiner Zustand, ihn mal zu spielen. Der Stil ist eher amerikanisch, mit einigen Wasserhindernissen, aber nur wenigen Bäumen, was den Platz sehr windanfällig macht. Es ist hier von Vorteil, den Ball flach schlagen zu können. Gleichzeitig wird es schwierig, die gut verteidigten Grüns anzuspielen, wenn man dem Ball nicht genügend Spin mitgibt. Durch den sandigen Untergrund ist der Platz auch bei nassem Wetter gut bespielbar. Das gesamte Layout wurde mit viel Sorgfalt angelegt, insbesondere die zum Teil in mehreren Stufen aufgebauten Grüns. Einige recht spektakuläre Löcher heben diesen Platz über das allgemeine Niveau hinaus, allerdings fehlt ihm zu einem wirklich grossartigen Kurs das gewisse Etwas. Dennoch eine gute Anlage, deren hügelige ersten neun Löcher zweifellos anspruchsvoller als die zweiten Neun sind.

An old but very carefully restored windmill gives an excellent first impression. The actual course is not quite as exceptional, but the overall standard makes it worth a round or two, even though the layout is still young. The style is a little on the American side, with a few water hazards in play but very few trees. This adds to the difficulties when the wind gets up. Hitting low balls is an asset here, and it is difficult to reach and stay on certain well-protected greens without enough spin on the ball. The sandy soil also makes this a playable course in wet weather. The whole layout has been carefully designed, especially the greens, always interesting to read. A number of rather spectacular holes lift the overall standard a little above average, but that little spark of genius, which makes a good course a great course, is missing. A competent course all the same with a hilly and doubtless more demanding front nine.

Golf Club Elfrather Mühle GmbH
An der Elfrather Mühle 145
D - 47802 KREFELD-TRAAR

Office	Sekretariat	(49) 02151 - 496 910
Pro shop	Pro shop	(49) 02151 - 496 922
Fax	Fax	(49) 02151 - 477 459
Situation	Lage	

5 km von Krefeld, 242 000 Ew. 30 km von Düsseldorf

Annual closure	Jährliche Schliessung	nein
Weekly closure	Wöchentliche Schliessung	Montag, das Restaurant

Fees main season
Preisliste hochsaison 18 Löcher

	Week days Woche	We/Bank holidays We/Feiertag
Individual Individuell	DM 80,-	DM 100,-
Couple Ehepaar	DM 160,-	DM 200,-

Caddy	Caddy	auf Reservierung
Electric Trolley	Elektrokarren	DM 20,-
Buggy	Elektrischer Wagen	DM 60,-
Clubs	Clubs	nein

Credit cards Kreditkarten
VISA - Eurocard - MasterCard - AMEX - DC

Access Zufahrt : A57 Ausf. Krefeld/Gartenstadt. →
Krefeld/Gartenstadt. Rechts auf Werner-Voss-Strasse
→ Traar/Elfrath. Links auf An der Elfrather Mühle.
Map 3 on page 296 Karte 3 Seite 296

GOLF COURSE
PLATZ
14/20

Site	Lage	▬▬
Maintenance	Instandhaltung	▬▬
Architect	Architekt	Ron Kirby Fritz Beindorf
Type	Typ	Flachland
Relief	Relief	▬▬
Water in play	Platz mit Wasser	▬▬
Exp. to wind	Wind ausgesetzt	▬▬▬
Trees in play	Platz mit Bäumen	▬

Scorecard Scorekarte	Chp. Chp.	Mens Herren	Ladies Damen
Length Länge	6544	6160	5370
Par	72	72	72

Advised golfing ability   0   12   24   36
Empfohlene Spielstärke
Hcp required   Min. Handicap   36/We 28

CLUB HOUSE & AMENITIES
KLUBHAUS UND NEBENGEBÄUDE
7/10

Pro shop	Pro shop	▬▬
Driving range	Übungsplatz	▬▬
Sheltered	überdacht	8 Plätze
On grass	auf Rasen	ja
Putting-green	Putting-grün	ja
Pitching-green	Pitching-grün	ja

HOTEL FACILITIES
HOTEL BESCHREIBUNG
7/10

HOTELS HOTELS
Dorint Hotel   Krefeld-Traar
158 Zimmer, D DM 250,-   5 km
Tel (49) 02151 - 9560, Fax (49) 02151 - 956 100

Parkhotel Krefelder Hof   Krefeld
150 Zimmer, D DM 300,-   5 km
Tel (49) 02151 - 5840, Fax (49) 02151 - 58 435

Garden Hotel   Krefeld
51 Zimmer, D DM 200,-   5 km
Tel (49) 02151 - 590 296, Fax (49) 02151 - 590 299

Zentral Hotel Poststuben   Krefeld
31 Zimmer, D DM 160,-   5 km
Tel (49) 02151 - 24 656, Fax (49) 02151 - 802 888

RESTAURANTS RESTAURANT
Koperpot, Tel (49) 02151 - 614 814   Krefeld 5 km
Et Bröckske, Tel (49) 02151 - 29 740   Krefeld 5 km

327

ESCHENRIED

| 14 | 7 | 7 |

Neues und Altes wurde hier vereint. Die "alten" neun baumgesäumten Spielbahnen wurden ergänzt durch weitere neun Löcher in eher offenem Gelände. Letztere bilden die ersten 9 der jetzigen 18-Loch-Anlage. Beim Bau der neuen Löcher wurde weniger Aufmerksamkeit einem einheitlichen Platzcharakter geschenkt, als vielmehr den Grüns, welche aufgrund ihres weitaus aufwendigeren Designs viel interessanter zu spielen sind als die Grüns der alten Bahnen. Die grössten Probleme bereiten den Spielern die Bäume, doch muss man sich ebenso vor den sehr natürlich wirkenden Wasserläufen und Teichen in acht nehmen. Leider ist das Wasser von den kaum erhöhten Abschlägen häufig nicht einsehbar. Insgesamt kommt Wasser aber eher selten ins Spiel und sollte daher auch unerfahrene Spieler nicht allzu sehr abschrecken. Eschenried ist ein gelungener Golfplatz, den zu spielen vor allem unter der Woche empfehlenswert ist, da er an Wochenenden viele Leute aus dem nahen München und Umgebung anzieht.

New and old. The "old" nine-holer through the trees has been supplemented by a second 9-hole course over more open space, which in fact forms the front nine. Nobody really bothered about respecting unity of character, a good job, too, as far as the greens are concerned, which are much better designed, contoured and amusing to play than those on the first nine-hole course. The main problems come from the trees and, just as importantly, the very natural looking streams and ponds. The only regret is that they could have been more visible from the tee, which have no height to speak of. However, water is hardly ever in play and crossing it should not discourage even inexperienced players. A very competent course that is fun to play during the week. Being close to Munich, it is not always easy playing on week-ends.

Golfclub Eschenried
Kurfürstenweg 10
D - 85232 ESCHENRIED

Office	Sekretariat	(49) 08131 - 87 238
Pro shop	Pro shop	(49) 08131 - 86 786
Fax	Fax	(49) 08131 - 567 418
Situation	Lage	

15 km von München, 1 300 000 Ew.

Annual closure	Jährliche Schliessung	ja
		1/12→28/02
Weekly closure	Wöchentliche Schliessung	Montag, das Restaurant

Fees main season
Preisliste hochsaison 18 Löcher

	Week days Woche	We/Bank holidays We/Feiertag
Individual Individuell	DM 70,-	DM 90,-
Couple Ehepaar	DM 140,-	DM 180,-

-21 Jahre/Studenten: - 50%

Caddy	Caddy	nein
Electric Trolley	Elektrokarren	nein
Buggy	Elektrischer Wagen	DM 30,-
Clubs	Clubs	DM 30,-
Credit cards Kreditkarten		nein

Access Zufahrt : A8 München-Stuttgart. Ausf.
Langwieder See → Eschenried, → Golfplatz
Map 2 on page 294 Karte 2 Seite 294

328

GOLF COURSE
PLATZ **14**/20

Site	Lage	
Maintenance	Instandhaltung	
Architect	Architekt	
Type	Typ	Flachland, Wald
Relief	Relief	
Water in play	Platz mit Wasser	
Exp. to wind	Wind ausgesetzt	
Trees in play	Platz mit Bäumen	

Scorecard Scorekarte	Chp. Chp.	Mens Herren	Ladies Damen
Length Länge	6046	5587	5020
Par	72	72	72

Advised golfing ability Empfohlene Spielstärke		0 12 24 36
Hcp required	Min. Handicap	nein

CLUB HOUSE & AMENITIES
KLUBHAUS UND NEBENGEBÄUDE **7**/10

Pro shop	Pro shop	
Driving range	Übungsplatz	
Sheltered	überdacht	ja
On grass	auf Rasen	ja
Putting-green	Putting-grün	ja
Pitching-green	Pitching-grün	ja

HOTEL FACILITIES
HOTEL BESCHREIBUNG **7**/10

HOTELS HOTELS
Kriemhild   München-Nymphenburg
18 Zimmer, D DM 180,-   10 km
Tel (49) 089 - 170 077, Fax (49) 089 - 177 478

Zur Post   München-Pasing
96 Zimmer, D DM 250,-   9 km
Tel (49) 089 - 896 950, Fax (49) 089 - 537 319

Arabella Westpark Hotel   München
258 Zimmer, D DM 350,-   15 km
Tel (49) 089 - 51 960, Fax (49) 089 - 519 6649

RESTAURANTS RESTAURANT
Schlosswirtschaft zur Schwaige München-Nymphenburg
Tel (49) 089 - 174 421   10 km

Zur Goldenen Gans   München-Pasing
Tel (49) 089 - 837 033   8 km

FALKENSTEIN) 18 6 7

Ein Klassiker traditioneller, englischer Landschaftsarchitektur, umgeben von Wald (Pinien und weisse Birken) und Heidekraut. Auf den ersten Blick fallen die gestalterischen Feinheiten nicht auf, doch wird der Golfplatz durch sie zunehmend interessanter. Die variantenreichen Löcher und die nüchterne Weite des Platzes auf diesem leicht hügeligen Terrain stellen eine echte Herausforderung dar. Die Hindernisse sind einfach und zugleich raffiniert angelegt. Jeder Schlag muss wohlüberlegt sein und alle spielerischen Aspekte müssen in die Überlegungen miteinbezogen werden. Die Greens, teils auf mehreren Stufen, teils erhöht, sind immer gut verteidigt und können die Scores ebenso zunichte machen wie unpräzise Schläge. Geradlinige Löcher wechseln mit spektakulären Doglegs ab. Falkenstein ist wohl einer der schönsten Golfplätze Europas und wird auch mit viel Liebe gepflegt – ein grossartiges Beispiel guter Golfarchitektur.

One of the great classics and a traditional British design, set in a forest of pine and silver birch, with heather thrown in for good measure. It is not easy to appreciate the subtlety of the course at first sight, but this serves to make the course more exciting every time. The variety of holes and the forbidding size of the layout on moderately hilly terrain produce a thoroughly good test of golf. Hazards are spread with an equal measure of simplicity and strategic intelligence, and each shot demands a lot of thought in every compartment of the game. Sometimes multi-tiered, often elevated but always well-protected, the greens can ruin your card as easily as fluffed shots. With alternating straight holes and spectacular dog-legs, all in a beautiful state of upkeep, Falkenstein remains one of Europe's greatest courses and a perfect showpiece for golf design.

Hamburger Golf Club
In De Bargen 59
D - 22587 HAMBURG

Office	Sekretariat	(49) 040 - 812 177
Pro shop	Pro shop	(49) 040 - 814 404
Fax	Fax	(49) 040 - 817 315
Situation	Lage	

10 km von Hamburg, 1 650 000 Ew.
Annual closure Jährliche Schliessung nein

Weekly closure Wöchentliche Schliessung Montag
das Restaurant

Fees main season Preisliste hochsaison 18 Löcher

	Week days Woche	We/Bank holidays We/Feiertag
Individual Individuell	DM 75,-	DM 80,-
Couple Ehepaar	DM 150,-	DM 160,-

Sa./So./Feiertage nur in Mitgliederbegleitung (with members)

Caddy	Caddy	auf Reserv. DM 30,-
Electric Trolley	Elektrokarren	nein
Buggy	Elektrischer Wagen	nein
Clubs	Clubs	nein
Credit cards Kreditkarten		nein

Access Zufahrt : A7. → Blankenese. Blankeneser Landtrasse. Risener Landstrasse. Links, In De Bargen.
Map 7 on page 304 Karte 7 Seite 304

GOLF COURSE
PLATZ   **18**/20

Site	Lage	▮▮▮▮▮▯
Maintenance	Instandhaltung	▮▮▮▮▮▯
Architect	Architekt	Harry S. Colt Alison, Morrison
Type	Typ	Wald, Park
Relief	Relief	
Water in play	Platz mit Wasser	▮▯▯▯▯▯
Exp. to wind	Wind ausgesetzt	▮▮▮▯▯▯
Trees in play	Platz mit Bäumen	▮▮▮▮▮▯

Scorecard Scorekarte	Chp. Chp.	Mens Herren	Ladies Damen
Length Länge	5964	5925	5276
Par	71	71	71

Advised golfing ability		0 12	24	36
Empfohlene Spielstärke				
Hcp required	Min. Handicap	36		

CLUB HOUSE & AMENITIES
KLUBHAUS UND NEBENGEBÄUDE   **6**/10

Pro shop	Pro shop	▮▮▮▮▯▯
Driving range	Übungsplatz	▮▮▮▮▯▯
Sheltered	überdacht	6 Plätze
On grass	auf Rasen	ja
Putting-green	Putting-grün	ja
Pitching-green	Pitching-grün	ja

329

HOTEL FACILITIES
HOTEL BESCHREIBUNG   **7**/10

HOTELS HOTELS
Stranhotel Blankenese   Hamburg
15 Zimmer, D DM 220,-   4 km
Tel (49) 040 - 861 344, Fax (49) 040 - 864 936

Hotel Senator   Wedel
46 Zimmer, D DM 178,-   5 km
Tel (49) 04103 - 80 870, Fax (49) 04103 - 8077250

Hotel Diamant   Wedel
39 Zimmer, D DM 168,-   5 km
Tel (49) 04103 - 702 600, Fax (49) 04103 - 702 700

RESTAURANTS RESTAURANT
Flic Flac Bistro   Hamburg
Tel (49) 040 - 865 345   2 km

König Pilsener Stuben   Hamburg
Tel (49) 040 - 860 931   3 km

Die grosse alte Lady des deutschen Golfsports (Feldafing ist der älteste Club des Landes) wurde nach erfolgreicher Ausführung Umbau- und Verjüngungsmassnahmen im letzten Jahr wiedereröffnet. Der Golfplatz liegt etwas erhöht direkt am Starnberger See, auf einem Gelände, das früher Maximilian II gehörte, dessen Schloss unmittelbar an den Parcours angrenzt. Trotz dieser Lage bletet sich nur selten ein freier Blick auf den See, da der Kurs von einer Vielzahl grosser alter Bäume umrahmt wird, die gleichzeitig einen Grossteil der Schwierigkeiten auf diesem Platz darstellen. Bernhard von Limburger hat das ziemlich hügelige Gelände hervorragend zu nutzen verstanden, so dass ein für ihn typisches Design entstanden ist, das sich durch eine nüchtern-eleganten und dabei immer seriösen Stil ausgezeichnet. Feldafing ist ein in vieler Hinsicht spektakulärer Golfplatz, der sich zudem wunderbar in die ihn umgebende Landschaft einfügt und den man allein schon aus diesem Grund unbedingt kennenlernen sollte.

This grand old Lady of German Golf (this is the country's oldest course) has re-opened after a welcome and successful rejuvenation scheme. Located on an estate formerly belonging to Maximilian II - his castle stands on the edge of the course - Feldafing overloooks the Starnberger See, although the view is not completely clear owing to the very many old trees which form the major share of hazards. Bernhard von Limburger made excellent use of rather hilly terrain (rather tiring when walking) and it is always a pleasure to see his elegant, sober and serious style again. An often spectacular course which blends wonderfully with its natural surroundings. Well worth getting to know.

Golf Club Feldafing e.V.
Tutzinger Strasse 15
D - 82340 TUTZING

Office	Sekretariat	(49) 08157 - 93 340
Pro shop	Pro shop	(49) 08157 - 93 340
Fax	Fax	(49) 08157 - 933 499
Situation	Lage	

40 km von München, 1 300 000 Ew.

Annual closure	Jährliche Schliessung	nein
Weekly closure	Wöchentliche Schliessung	Montag
		das Restaurant

Fees main season Preisliste hochsaison 18 Löcher

	Week days Woche	We/Bank holidays We/Feiertag
Individual Individuell	DM 100,-	DM 120,-
Couple Ehepaar	DM 200,-	DM 240,-

Caddy	Caddy	auf Reservierung
Electric Trolley	Elektrokarren	nein
Buggy	Elektrischer Wagen	nein
Clubs	Clubs	ja
Credit cards Kreditkarten		nein

Access Zufahrt : A95 München-Starnberg. Abfahrt Starnberg. Durch Starnberg. B2 → Pöcking. → Tutzing/Deldafing, rechts zur Tutzinger Strasse. 1 km links, Golfplatz. **Map 2 on page 294 Karte 2 Seite 294**

GOLF COURSE
PLATZ
18/20

Site	Lage	▰▰▰▰▱
Maintenance	Instandhaltung	▰▰▰▰▱
Architect	Architekt	B. von Limburger
Type	Typ	Gebirge
Relief	Relief	▰▰▰▱▱
Water in play	Platz mit Wasser	▰▰▱▱▱
Exp. to wind	Wind ausgesetzt	▰▰▰▰▱
Trees in play	Platz mit Bäumen	▰▰▰▰▰

Scorecard Scorekarte	Chp. Chp.	Mens Herren	Ladies Damen
Length Länge	5724	5442	4796
Par	71	69	69

Advised golfing ability	0	12	24	36
Empfohlene Spielstärke		▰▰▰▰▰▰▱		
Hcp required	Min. Handicap	34		

CLUB HOUSE & AMENITIES
KLUBHAUS UND NEBENGEBÄUDE
7/10

Pro shop	Pro shop	▰▰▰▰▱
Driving range	Übungsplatz	▰▰▰▰▱
Sheltered	überdacht	5 Plätze
On grass	auf Rasen	ja
Putting-green	Putting-grün	ja
Pitching-green	Pitching-grün	ja

HOTEL FACILITIES
HOTEL BESCHREIBUNG
6/10

HOTELS HOTELS

Forsthaus am See — Pöcking-Possenhofen
21 Zimmer, DM 270,- — 2 km
Tel (49) 08157 - 93 010, Fax (49) 08157 - 4292

Marina — Bernried
71 Zimmer, D DM 250,- — 7 km
Tel (49) 08158 - 9320, Fax (49) 08158 - 7117

Kefer — Pöcking
20 Zimmer, D DM 140,- — 3 km
Tel (49) 08157 - 1247

RESTAURANTS RESTAURANT

Forsthaus Ilkahöhe — Tutzing
Tel (49) 08158 - 8242 — 4 km

330

Viele Jahre zählte Frankfurt zu den Plätzen, die gut genug waren, die German Open auszutragen. Mittlerweile erscheinen jedoch modernere Anlagen besser geeignet, den heute höchsten Standards im Golfsport zu genügen. Nichtsdestoweniger ist das Spiel auf diesem wunderschön gelegenen Platz ein reines Vergnügen, auch wenn der nahe Flughafen etwas störend wirkt. Das Layout der leicht hügeligen Anlage ist typisch britisch. Kein Wunder, trägt der Platz doch die Handschrift von Colt und Morrison, die Qualität und hohes technisches Können garantiert, was auch in der im Spielverlauf allmählich spürbaren Steigerung der an den Golfer gestellten Anforderungen zum Ausdruck kommt. Durchschnittliche Spieler werden ihren Spass haben, während die besseren Spieler in guter Form sein müssen, um ein für sie gutes Ergebnis zu erzielen. Der Platz erfordert gerade Schläge ebenso wie die Beherrschung unterschiedlicher Ball-Flugkurven, um die vielen Bäumen vermeiden bzw. um diese herumspielen zu können. Die Grüns sind gut geformt, von mittlerer Grösse und gut verteidigt ohne unzugänglich zu sein.

For many a year this was one of the great courses used for the German Open, but now the more modern courses are better suited to today's highest golfing standards. Nevertheless, the Frankfurter is a real joy to play for the beauty of its setting, despite the airport being a shade too close for comfort. The layout is sometimes hilly, but never excessively so. It is plainly very British in style, and the Colt and Morrison label is a guarantee of quality and technical skill, with the course gradually getting harder geared to the golfer's ability. Average players will have fun, but the better players will need to be on their toes to card a good score. Here, of course, you have to play straight and sometimes flight the ball to avoid, or escape from, the many trees. The greens are well-contoured, medium-sized and reasonably well-protected.

Frankfurter Golf Club e.V.
Golfstrasse 41
D - 60528 FRANKFURT

Office	Sekretariat	(49) 069 - 666 2318
Pro shop	Pro shop	(49) 069 - 666 2441
Fax	Fax	(49) 069 - 666 7018
Situation	Lage	

3 km von Frankfurt, 660 000 Ew.

Annual closure	Jährliche Schliessung	nein
Weekly closure	Wöchentliche Schliessung	Montag, das Restaurant

Fees main season
Preisliste hochsaison 18 Löcher

	Week days Woche	We/Bank holidays We/Feiertag
Individual Individuell	DM 85,-	DM 100,-
Couple Ehepaar	DM 170,-	DM 200,-

- 21 Jahre/Studenten: - 50%

Caddy	Caddy	auf Reservierung
Electric Trolley	Elektrokarren	nein
Buggy	Elektrischer Wagen	nein
Clubs	Clubs	DM 40,-
Credit cards Kreditkarten		nein

Access Zufahrt : A3, Ausf. Frankfurt Süd → Niederrad, Flughafenstrasse, Golfstrasse
Map 3 on page 297 Karte 3 Seite 297

GOLF COURSE
PLATZ   16/20

Site	Lage	▰▰▰▰▰
Maintenance	Instandhaltung	▰▰▰▰▰
Architect	Architekt	Harry S. Colt
Type	Typ	Wald
Relief	Relief	▰▰
Water in play	Platz mit Wasser	▰
Exp. to wind	Wind ausgesetzt	▰▰
Trees in play	Platz mit Bäumen	▰▰▰▰

Scorecard Scorekarte	Chp. Chp.	Mens Herren	Ladies Damen
Length Länge	5869	5869	5205
Par	71	71	71

Advised golfing ability Empfohlene Spielstärke	0	12	24	36

Hcp required Min. Handicap 28

CLUB HOUSE & AMENITIES
KLUBHAUS UND NEBENGEBÄUDE   7/10

Pro shop	Pro shop	▰▰▰
Driving range	Übungsplatz	▰▰▰
Sheltered	überdacht	ja
On grass	auf Rasen	ja
Putting-green	Putting-grün	ja
Pitching-green	Pitching-grün	ja

HOTEL FACILITIES
HOTEL BESCHREIBUNG   8/10

HOTELS HOTELS
Arabella Congress Hotel   Frankfurt-Niederrad
393 Zimmer, D DM 450,-   1 km
Tel (49) 069 - 66 330, Fax (49) 069 - 663 3666

Hugenottenhof   Neu-Isenburg
86 Zimmer, D DM 180,-   8 km
Tel (49) 06102 - 17 053, Fax (49) 06102 - 25 212

Steigenberger Frankfurter Hof   Frankfurt
332 Zimmer, D DM 500,-   6 km
Tel (49) 069 - 21 502, Fax (49) 069 - 215 900

RESTAURANTS RESTAURANT
Weinhaus Brückenkeller   Frankfurt
Tel (49) 069 - 284 238   6 km

Weidemann   Frankfurt-Niederrad
Tel (49) 069 - 675 996   2 km

331

Die beste Zeit diesen Platz zu spielen ist Ende Frühling, wenn die Apfel- und Kirschbäume in voller Blüte stehen. Seit seiner Erweiterung zur 18-Loch-Anlage ist der GC Fränkische Schweiz, zwischen Nürnberg und Bamberg gelegen, zum beliebten Ziel für Golfer geworden. Die eine Hälfte der Löcher liegt im Wald, die andere in offenerem Gelände, wo auch die längsten Löcher zu finden sind und die Spieler mit langem Drive voll zum Zug kommen. Der Platz ist sehr natürlich angelegt. Wenngleich die Bunker besser modelliert sein könnten, bereiten sie doch auch so den meisten Spielern genug Kopfzerbrechen. Dasselbe gilt auch für die Grüns. Während Gestaltung und Formgebung der Grüns bei älteren Anlagen häufig nicht sehr ausgeprägt ist, hat man sich bei neueren Plätzen in dieser Hinsicht an ein aufwendigeres Design gewöhnt. Zusammenfassend können wir sagen, dass dieser Platz einen recht ausgewogenen Eindruck macht, angenehm zu spielen ist und Golfern aller Spielstärken entgegenkommt.

The best season to play here is in late spring, when the apple- and cherry-trees are in blossom. Between Nürnberg and Bamberg, this has been a traditional stop-off for golfers since it was enhanced to 18-hole status in 1989. Half the holes run through the woods, the other half in more open country, where the holes are longer and big-hitters can open their shoulders. The layout is very natural, and while we might have hoped for better contoured bunkers, there is no denying that they do pose a considerable problem for most players. The same observation applies to the greens; while older greens were often a little less elaborate, recent courses have accustomed us to a little more research. With that said, this is a very pleasant and friendly course for players of all levels, and it is well-balanced throughout. Fränkische Schweiz is also a very pretty region...

Golf-Club Fränkische Schweiz e.V.
Kanndorf 8
D - 91320 EBERMANNSTADT

Office	Sekretariat	(49) 09194 - 4827
Pro shop	Pro shop	(49) 09194 - 4827
Fax	Fax	(49) 09194 - 5410
Situation	Lage	

45 km von Nürnberg, 498 000 Ew.
35 km von Bamberg, 70 000 Ew.

Annual closure	Jährliche Schliessung	nein
Weekly closure	Wöchentliche Schliessung	nein

Fees main season
Preisliste hochsaison den ganzen Tag

	Week days Woche	We/Bank holidays We/Feiertag
Individual Individuell	DM 60,-	DM 80,-
Couple Ehepaar	DM 120,-	DM 160,-

– 21 Jahre, Studenten: – 50%

Caddy	Caddy	nein
Electric Trolley	Elektrokarren	nein
Buggy	Elektrischer Wagen	nein
Clubs	Clubs	ja
Credit cards Kreditkarten		nein

332

GdeWIESENTTAL
Muggendorf
nach PEGNITZ
(A9, Nürnberg/
Bayreuth)
EBERMANN
STADT
Kanndorf
GOLF
Moggast
470
Pretzfeld
nach
FORCHEIM
Wannbach
Veldensteiner Forst
(A73, Nürnberg/Bamberg)

0   2   4 km

Access Zufahrt : BAB-A73 Nürnberg-Bamberg. Ausf. Forchheim. B470 → Ebermannstadt. → Kanndorf, Golfplatz
Map 4 on page 298 Karte 4 Seite 298

GOLF COURSE
PLATZ   14/20

Site	Lage	
Maintenance	Instandhaltung	
Architect	Architekt	
Type	Typ	Land, Wald
Relief	Relief	
Water in play	Platz mit Wasser	
Exp. to wind	Wind ausgesetzt	
Trees in play	Platz mit Bäumen	

Scorecard	Chp.	Mens	Ladies
Scorekarte	Chp.	Herren	Damen
Length Länge	6050	6050	5388
Par	72	72	72

Advised golfing ability		0 12 24 36
Empfohlene Spielstärke		
Hcp required	Min. Handicap	35

CLUB HOUSE & AMENITIES
KLUBHAUS UND NEBENGEBÄUDE   7/10

Pro shop	Pro shop	
Driving range	Übungsplatz	
Sheltered	überdacht	3 Plätze
On grass	auf Rasen	nein
Putting-green	Putting-grün	ja
Pitching-green	Pitching-grün	ja

HOTEL FACILITIES
HOTEL BESCHREIBUNG   6/10

HOTELS HOTELS
Club Hotel   Golf-Club
15 Zimmer, D DM 100,-
Tel (49) 09194 - 9228, Fax (49) 09194 - 5410

Resengörg   Ebermannstadt
34 Zimmer, D DM 120,-   2 km
Tel (49) 09194 - 73 930, Fax (49) 09194 - 739 373

Schwanenbrau   Ebermannstadt
13 Zimmer, D DM 120,-   2 km
Tel (49) 09194 - 209, Fax (49) 09194 - 5836

RESTAURANTS RESTAURANT
Feiler   Muggendorf
Tel (49) 09196 - 322   4 km

Bierbrunnen   Ebermannstadt
Tel (49) 09194 - 5865   5 km

Der Architekt Heinz Fehring wurde offensichtlich stark vom amerikanischen Stil beeinflusst, obwohl die vier nahe beim Clubhaus gelegenen Löcher sich deutlich von den restlichen Spielbahnen unterscheiden. Dies war auch nicht anders zu erwarten, angesichts der Tatsache, dass Bäume kaum ins Spiel kommen und Wasserhindernisse, neben dem Wind natürlich, die Hauptschwierigkeiten dieses Platzes bilden. Daher kam ein "natürlicher" Platz von vornherein gar nicht in Frage. Um mit dem Kurs gleich beim ersten Mal zurechtzukommen, empfiehlt es sich, zur Orientierung eine Lochbeschreibung mitzunehmen, da weder die Spielstrategie deutlich vorgegeben, noch ein Grossteil der Hindernisse vom Abschlag aus erkennbar ist - es gibt sogar fünf blinde Löcher. Glücklicherweise sind die grösstenteils gut gestalteten Grüns wenigstens voll einsehbar. Auf diesem eher flachen Gelände ist die Länge kein ausschlaggebender Faktor, mit Ausnahme der Par 3 Löcher, bei denen Fehring dem neuzeitlichen Trend gefolgt ist, Länge den Vorzug zu geben gegenüber Präsision.

Designer Heinz Fehring was visibly influenced by the US style of course, even though the four holes close to the clubhouse are rather different from the rest. It could hardly be otherwise, when trees are hardly ever in play and when water hazards provide the main difficulties (with the wind, of course). There was no question of making this a natural course. First time out, you are best advised to take the course book with you to get your bearings. Nothing is obvious, not even the hazards are visible and there are, after all, five blind holes. Fortunately, the greens are in view (and by and large they are well designed). On this flattish terrain, length is not a key factor, except with the par 3s, where Fehring yielded to the current fashion of length in preference to accuracy in positioning the ball.

Golf- und Land-Club Fürstliches Hofgut Kolnhausen e.V.

D - 35423 LICH

Office	Sekretariat	(49) 06404 - 910 710
Pro shop	Pro shop	(49) 06404 - 910 753
Fax	Fax	(49) 06404 - 910 72
Situation	Lage	

15 km von Giessen - 55 km von Frankfurt, 660 000 Ew.

Annual closure	Jährliche Schliessung	nein
Weekly closure	Wöchentliche Schliessung	Montag
		das Restaurant

Fees main season Preisliste hochsaison 18 Löcher

	Week days Woche	We/Bank holidays We/Feiertag
Individual Individuell	DM 80,-	DM 100,-
Couple Ehepaar	DM 160,-	DM 200,-

Sonntag nur in Mitgliederbegleitung (Sunday with members) / - 21 Jahre/Studenten: - 50%

Caddy	Caddy	DM 50,-
Electric Trolley	Elektrokarren	DM 30,-
Buggy	Elektrischer Wagen	nein
Clubs	Clubs	DM 30,-
Credit cards Kreditkarten		nein

Access Zufahrt : A5 Frankfurt-Kassel. Kambacher Kreuz, A45 → Hanau. Ausf. Münzenberg/Lich. → Lich, Golfplatz 5 km. **Map 3 on page 297** Karte 3 Seite 297

GOLF COURSE
PLATZ   14/20

Site	Lage	▬▬▬
Maintenance	Instandhaltung	▬▬▬
Architect	Architekt	Heinz Fehring
Type	Typ	Flachland
Relief	Relief	▬
Water in play	Platz mit Wasser	▬▬▬
Exp. to wind	Wind ausgesetzt	▬▬▬
Trees in play	Platz mit Bäumen	▬

Scorecard Scorekarte	Chp. Chp.	Mens Herren	Ladies Damen
Length Länge	6065	5705	5039
Par	72	72	72

Advised golfing ability Empfohlene Spielstärke		0	12	24	36
Hcp required	Min. Handicap	36			

CLUB HOUSE & AMENITIES
KLUBHAUS UND NEBENGEBÄUDE   7/10

Pro shop	Pro shop	▬▬▬
Driving range	Übungsplatz	▬▬▬
Sheltered	überdacht	6 Plätze
On grass	auf Rasen	ja
Putting-green	Putting-grün	ja
Pitching-green	Pitching-grün	ja

HOTEL FACILITIES
HOTEL BESCHREIBUNG   6/10

HOTELS HOTELS

Landhaus Klosterwald	Lich
18 Zimmer, D DM 170,-	1 km
Tel (49) 06404 - 91 010, Fax (49) 06404 - 910 134	

Alte Klostermühle	Lich
26 Zimmer, D DM 230,-	1 km
Tel (49) 06404 - 91 900, Fax (49) 06404 - 4867	

Bergfried	Lich
24 Zimmer, D DM 150,-	3 km
Tel (49) 06404 - 91 170, Fax (49) 06404 - 911 755	

Steinsgarten	Giessen
129 Zimmer, D DM 250,-	15 km
Tel (49) 0641 - 38 990, Fax (49) 0641 - 389 9200	

RESTAURANTS RESTAURANT

Zum Stern	Butzbach
Tel (49) 06033 - 7977	20 km

333

In unmittelbarer Nähe zu einem der bekanntesten Winter- und Sommersportorte Europas gelegen, verläuft dieser Parcours auf so ebenem Terrain, dass man ihn als Flachland-Kurs inmitten einer Alpin-Region bezeichnen kann. Der Platz ist daher auch mühelos zu bewältigen. Trotz der schwierigen Witterungsbedingungen - lange kalte Winter, heisse Sommer - macht der Platz einen sehr gepflegten Eindruck. Den etwas "wilden" Spielern ist er nicht zu empfehlen, da die Fairways, eingegrenzt durch Bäume, Büsche und Felsen, recht schmal sind. Die Tücken dieses Platzes, der deutlich zu erkennende Hindernisse hat, sind eher psychologischer denn realer Natur. Spieler, die den Ball gerade schlagen, werden die Runde geniessen. Dasselbe gilt für Spieler mit mittlerem Handicap sowie jene, denen es an Länge fehlt, sofern sie die ihnen gewährten Schlagvorgaben richtig wahrzunehmen wissen. Einen zusätzlichen Anreiz dieses Ortes bietet das ausgezeichnete Restaurant im Clubhaus mit seiner typisch bayerischen Atmosphäre, wo sie einen schönen Golftag ausklingen lassen sollten.

Very close to one of Europe's most celebrated winter and summer resorts, this course is flat enough to be considered a lowland course transposed to the mountains. You can play it tirelessly. Green-keeping is very decent, given the length of the winters and the hot summers, but this is not a course we would recommend to wild hitters : the fairways are tight and guarded by trees, bushes and rocks. The dangers here are perhaps more psychological than real (hazards are clearly visible) and straight players will enjoy their round. The same might apply to mid-handicappers and players lacking length, if they use the strokes they receive intelligently. To enjoy your day to the full, pop inside the very country-style club-house and enjoy the excellent restaurant and typically Bavarian atmosphere. It is a great bonus for an excellent site.

Golf-Club Garmisch-Partenkirchen e.V.
Gut Buchwies
D - 82496 OBERAU

Office	Sekretariat	(49) 08824 - 8344
Pro shop	Pro shop	(49) 08824 - 1679
Fax	Fax	(49) 08824 - 325
Situation	Lage	

8 km von Garmisch-Partenkirchen, 26 500 Ew.
81 km von München, 1 300 000 Ew.

Annual closure	Jährliche Schliessung	ja
		1/12→31/03
Weekly closure	Wöchentliche Schliessung	Montag
		das Restaurant

Fees main season Preisliste hochsaison den ganzen Tag

	Week days Woche	We/Bank holidays We/Feiertag
Individual Individuell	DM 70,-	DM 90,-
Couple Ehepaar	DM 140,-	DM 180,-

– 21 Jahre/Studenten: – 50 %

Caddy	Caddy	auf Reservierung
Electric Trolley	Elektrokarren	nein
Buggy	Elektrischer Wagen	nein
Clubs	Clubs	DM 20,-
Credit cards Kreditkarten		AMEX

334

Access Zufahrt : A95 und B2 München → Garmisch-Partenkirchen. Ausf. Oberau. Links über die Loisach → Gut Buchwies, Golfplatz
Map 2 on page 294 Karte 2 Seite 294

GOLF COURSE
PLATZ   14/20

Site	Lage	▰▰▰▱▱
Maintenance	Instandhaltung	▰▰▰▱▱
Architect	Architekt	▰▰▱▱▱
Type	Typ	Park
Relief	Relief	▰▱▱▱▱
Water in play	Platz mit Wasser	▰▰▱▱▱
Exp. to wind	Wind ausgesetzt	▰▱▱▱▱
Trees in play	Platz mit Bäumen	▰▰▰▰▱

Scorecard Scorekarte	Chp. Chp.	Mens Herren	Ladies Damen
Length Länge	6190	6190	5505
Par	72	72	72

Advised golfing ability		0 12 24 36
Empfohlene Spielstärke		▰▰▰▰▱
Hcp required	Min. Handicap	nein

CLUB HOUSE & AMENITIES
KLUBHAUS UND NEBENGEBÄUDE   6/10

Pro shop	Pro shop	▰▰▰▱▱
Driving range	Übungsplatz	▰▰▰▱▱
Sheltered	überdacht	8 Plätze
On grass	auf Rasen	ja
Putting-green	Putting-grün	ja
Pitching-green	Pitching-grün	ja

HOTEL FACILITIES
HOTEL BESCHREIBUNG   7/10

HOTELS HOTELS
Grand Hotel Sonnenbichl   Garmisch-Partenkirchen
93 Zimmer, D DM 250,-   7 km
Tel (49) 08821 - 7020, Fax (49) 08821 - 702 131

Reindl's Partenkirchner Hof   Garmisch-Partenkirchen
65 Zimmer, D DM 200,-   8 km
Tel (49) 08821 - 58 025, Fax (49) 08821 - 73 401

Berggasthof Panorama   Garmisch-Partenkirchen
17 Zimmer, D DM 140,-   7 km
Tel (49) 08821 - 2515, Fax (49) 08821 - 4884

RESTAURANTS RESTAURANT
Husar   Garmisch-Partenkirchen
Tel (49) 08821 - 1713   8 km

Alpenhof   Garmisch-Partenkirchen
Tel (49) 08821 - 59 055   8 km

Der Turnierplatz (B + C) besteht aus 9 der 18 ursprünglichen Bahnen, sowie weiteren 9 Löchern, die 1993 fertiggestellt wurden. Der schöne A-Platz eignet sich für Spieler mit höherem Handicap. Dank der vorhandenen Übungseinrichtungen zählt Gut Kaden zu den Anlagen gehobener Klasse. Der Fluss Pinnau durchquert das bei Nässe sehr gut abtrocknende Golfgelände, auf dem es sich zudem sehr angenehm läuft. Der Platz liegt ziemlich offen und ist gespickt mit vielen Wasserhindernissen sowie einer beträchtlichen Anzahl geschickt positionierter Bunker. Diese vielfältigen Gefahren sind jedoch gut erkennbar, so dass ein einziger Besuch genügt, den klug angelegten Spielbahnverlauf schätzen zu lernen, was allerdings nicht als Garantie für einen guten Score misszuverstehen ist. Die richtige Schlägerwahl ist hier ausschlaggebend, besonders beim Anspiel der grossflächigen Grüns, die teilweise auf mehreren Stufen angelegt und sehr gut verteidigt sind. Gutes Putten ist gefragt auf diesem Platz, den man unbedingt kennenlernen sollte.

The championship course (B + C) is formed from 9 of the original 18 holes and from a further 9 holer completed in 1993. The pretty A course is more suitable for higher-handicappers. Gut Kaden as a whole is a class set-up, thanks in particular to the practice facilities. Crossed by the river Pinnau, this is an estate that drains well and is pleasant to walk. The course is rather open and brings a large number of water hazards into play (6 holes feature frontal water) plus a considerable number of very well-sited bunkers. But these manifold hazards are clearly visible and a single visit is enough for a player to appreciate the intelligent design, if not to guarantee a good score. Here, the choice of club is of key importance, especially when approaching the large greens that are sometimes multi-tiered and very well-guarded. Make sure your putting is in good shape. A course well worth getting to know.

Gut Kaden Golf und Land Club

Kadener Strasse 9
D - 25486 ALVESLOHE

Office	Sekretariat	(49) 04193 - 99 290
Pro shop	Pro shop	(49) 04193 - 99 290
Fax	Fax	(49) 04193 - 992 919
Situation	Lage	

5 km von Quickborn, 18 500 Ew.
10 km von Norderstedt, 70 500 Ew.

Annual closure	Jährliche Schliessung	nein
Weekly closure	Wöchentliche Schliessung	nein

Fees main season Preisliste hochsaison 18 Löcher

	Week days Woche	We/Bank holidays We/Feiertag
Individual Individuell	DM 60,-	DM 90,-
Couple Ehepaar	DM 120,-	DM 180,-

Montag: DM 40,-/- 21 Jahre: – 50%

Caddy	Caddy	nein
Electric Trolley	Elektrokarren	nein
Buggy	Elektrischer Wagen	nein
Clubs	Clubs	nein
Credit cards Kreditkarten		nein

Access Zufahrt : A7 Hamburg-Kiel. Ausfahrt Quickborn.
Links → Ellerau, Kaltenkirchen. Rechts → Alveslohe.
Map 7 on page 304 Karte 7 Seite 304

GOLF COURSE
PLATZ 17 /20

Site	Lage	
Maintenance	Instandhaltung	
Architect	Architekt	Frank Pennink (A+B)
		Karl F. Grohs (C)
Type	Typ	Land, Flachland
Relief	Relief	
Water in play	Platz mit Wasser	
Exp. to wind	Wind ausgesetzt	
Trees in play	Platz mit Bäumen	

Scorecard Scorekarte	Chp. Chp.	Mens Herren	Ladies Damen
Length Länge	6516	6063	5285
Par	72	72	72

Advised golfing ability Empfohlene Spielstärke	0	12	24	36
Hcp required	Min. Handicap	36		

CLUB HOUSE & AMENITIES
KLUBHAUS UND NEBENGEBÄUDE 7 /10

Pro shop	Pro shop	
Driving range	Übungsplatz	
Sheltered	überdacht	7 Plätze
On grass	auf Rasen	ja
Putting-green	Putting-grün	ja
Pitching-green	Pitching-grün	ja

HOTEL FACILITIES
HOTEL BESCHREIBUNG 6 /10

HOTELS HOTELS

Jagdhaus Waldfrieden	Quickborn
14 Zimmer, D DM 230,-	5 km
Tel (49) 04106 - 3771, Fax (49) 04106 - 69196	

Landhaus Quickborn-Heide	Quickborn
18 Zimmer, D DM 175,-	3 km
Tel (49) 04106 - 76 660, Fax (49) 04106 - 74 969	

Wiking Hotel	Henstedt-Ulzburg
36 Zimmer, D DM 140,-	3 km
Tel (49) 04193 - 9080, Fax (49) 04193 - 92 323	

RESTAURANTS RESTAURANT

Jagdhaus Waldfrieden	Quickborn
Tel (49) 04106 - 3771	5 km

Restaurant Scheelke	Henstedt-Ulzburg
Tel (49) 04193 - 2207	4 km

335

GUT LUDWIGSBERG

15 6 6

Ein Golfplatz für Sportliche, dessen Clubhaus und Einrichtungen bedauerlicherweise nicht den andernorts üblichen höheren Standards entsprechen. Da die Anlage noch relativ jung ist, bleibt zu hoffen, dass sich dies mit der Zeit ändern wird. Die Lage des Platzes ist eindrucksvoll: An klaren Tagen kann man bis zu 150 km weit sehen, insbesondere Richtung Deutsche Alpenstrasse im Süden, an deren Streckenverlauf von Lindau über Garmisch-Partenkirchen nach Salzburg die verrückten Schlösser Ludwigs II von Bayern einen Besuch lohnen. Architekt Rossknecht hat den weitgehend flachen Parcours mit einer enormen Vielfalt an Hindernissen versehen, wobei alle Arbeiten mit der für ihn üblichen Sorgfalt ausgeführt wurden. Obschon eine harte Nuss von den hinteren Abschlägen, ist der Platz von weiter vorne durchaus für alle Spielstärken geeignet. Zwischen dem 5. und 17. Loch ändert sich der Charakter des Platzes von Parkland hin zu einem eher amerikanischen Stil, wo "target Golf" vom Spieler gefordert wird.

The sporting man's golf course where you might wonder why the clubhouse does not have higher standard facilities. Perhaps they will come in time, as the course is still young. The location is rather remarkable: on a clear day you can see for 150 km, especially toward the Deutsche Alpenstrasse to the south, the road running from Lindau to Garmisch-Partenkirchen and Salzburg, where the crazy castles of Louis II of Bavaria are well worth a visit. The course has been designed on easily walkable terrain, with the usual care associated with a designer such as Rossknecht, who has included every hazard in the book. A tough number from the back tees, the course gets a little more human the further forward you go, making it suitable for all levels. From the 5th to the 17th holes, you leave a park style landscape to encounter a more American style of course, where target golf is more the order of the day.

Golfclub zu Gut Ludwigsberg
Augsburgerstrasse 51
D - 86842 TÜRKHEIM

Office	Sekretariat	(49) 08245 - 3322
Pro shop	Pro shop	(49) 08245 - 3934
Fax	Fax	(49) 08245 - 3789
Situation	Lage	

35 km von Augsburg, 265 000 Ew.
50 km von München,1 300 000 Ew.

Annual closure	Jährliche Schliessung	ja
		1/12→31/03
Weekly closure	Wöchentliche Schliessung	nein

Fees main season
Preisliste hochsaison 18 Löcher

	Week days Woche	We/Bank holidays We/Feiertag
Individual Individuell	DM 70,-	DM 90,-
Couple Ehepaar	DM 140,-	DM 180,-

Caddy	Caddy	nein
Electric Trolley	Elektrokarren	ja
Buggy	Elektrischer Wagen	ja
Clubs	Clubs	ja
Credit cards Kreditkarten		nein

Access Zufahrt : A96/B18 München-Lindau. B18 Ausf.
Türkheim-Bad Wörishofen. →
Ettringen/Schwabmünchen. → Golfplatz
Map 2 on page 294 Karte 2 Seite 294

GOLF COURSE
PLATZ **15**/20

Site	Lage	▬▬▬▬▬▬▢
Maintenance	Instandhaltung	▬▬▬▬▬▬▢
Architect	Architekt	Kurt Rossknecht
Type	Typ	Flachland, Park
Relief	Relief	▬▬▬▢▢
Water in play	Platz mit Wasser	▬▬▬▬▢
Exp. to wind	Wind ausgesetzt	▬▬▬▢▢
Trees in play	Platz mit Bäumen	▬▬▬▢▢

Scorecard Scorekarte	Chp. Chp.	Mens Herren	Ladies Damen
Length Länge	6159	5867	5395
Par	72	72	72

Advised golfing ability		0	12	24	36
Empfohlene Spielstärke			▬▬▬▬▬▬▬		
Hcp required	Min. Handicap	nein			

CLUB HOUSE & AMENITIES
KLUBHAUS UND NEBENGEBÄUDE **6**/10

Pro shop	Pro shop	▬▬▬▬▢
Driving range	Übungsplatz	▬▬▬▢▢
Sheltered	überdacht	5 Plätze
On grass	auf Rasen	ja
Putting-green	Putting-grün	ja
Pitching-green	Pitching-grün	ja

HOTEL FACILITIES
HOTEL BESCHREIBUNG **6**/10

HOTELS HOTELS
Kneipp Kurhotel Fontenay — Bad Wörishofen
60 Zimmer, D DM 250,- — 9 km
Tel (49) 08247 - 3060, Fax (49) 08247 - 306 185

Kurhotel Edelweiss — Bad Wörishofen
52 Zimmer, D DM 180,- — 9 km
Tel (49) 08247 - 35 010, Fax (49) 08247 - 350 175

Stadthotel — Buchloe
44 Zimmer, D DM 160,- — 6 km
Tel (49) 08241 - 5060, Fax (49) 08241 - 506 135

RESTAURANTS RESTAURANT
Mühlbach — Bad Wörishofen
Tel (49) 08247 - 6039 — 9 km

Jagdhof — Bad Wörishofen-Schlingen
Tel (49) 08247 - 4879 — 13 km

336

GUT RIEDEN

Aufgrund der unmittelbaren Nähe zu München und dem Starnberger See ist Gut Rieden an Wochenenden stark frequentiert, was gleichermassen auch für die meisten anderen Plätze der Gegend gilt. Greenfee-Spielern wird deshalb empfohlen, ihr Glück unter der Woche zu versuchen, insbesondere wenn sich der Flight aus einem oder mehreren Spielern mit hohem Handicap zusammensetzt. Angesichts des recht hügeligen Geländes empfehlen wir Senioren und weniger durchtrainierten Spielern die Benutzung eines Golfwagens. Die steilen Erhebungen erschweren naturgemäss die visuelle Einschätzung von Spielsituationen; dies gilt insbesondere beim Anspiel der sorgfältig gestalteten Grüns. Wald und Büsche erfordern gerade Schläge. Da der Platz nicht sonderlich lang ist, kann man häufig ein Holz 3 oder ein langes Eisen vom Abschlag benutzen. Trotz der zahlreichen Wasserhindernisse dürften selbst durchschnittliche Spieler keine allzu grossen Probleme haben. Gut Rieden ist ein durchaus bemerkenswerter, wenn auch nicht aussergewöhnlicher Platz.

The immediate closeness of Munich and the Starnberger See makes this a rather busy course on week-ends, as is the case with most other courses in the region. Green-fees are recommended to try their luck during the week, especially if some or all of the group or family are high-handicappers. Besides, as the terrain is rather hilly, it'll be easier to go round in a buggy if playing with seniors or people short on fitness. The steep slopes are naturally the reason for the many problems of visual appreciation, like for approaching some of the very carefully designed greens. The woods and bushes often demand straight shots, but the course is short enough to opt for a 3-wood or long iron off the tee. There are a lot of water hazards, but average golfers (them again) shouldn't have too many problems.

Golf- und Landclub Gut Rieden
Gut Rieden
D - 82319 STARNBERG

Office	Sekretariat	(49) 08151 - 90 770
Pro shop	Pro shop	(49) 08151 - 9077-40
Fax	Fax	(49) 08151 - 907 711
Situation	Lage	

4 km von Starnberg, 20 300 Ew.
25 km von München, 1 300 000 Ew.

Annual closure	Jährliche Schliessung	ja
		1/12→31/03
Weekly closure	Wöchentliche Schliessung	nein

Fees main season Preisliste hochsaison 18 Löcher

	Week days Woche	We/Bank holidays We/Feiertag
Individual Individuell	DM 80,-	DM 100,-
Couple Ehepaar	DM 160,-	DM 200,-

-21 Jahre/Studenten: - 50% (Wochentage)

Caddy	Caddy	auf Reservierung
Electric Trolley	Elektrokarren	DM 35,-
Buggy	Elektrischer Wagen	nein
Clubs	Clubs	DM 30,-
Credit cards Kreditkarten		nein

Access Zufahrt : A95 München → Garmisch Partenkichen. Ausf. Starnberg. Rechts → Gauting. 4 km → Bahnhof Mühltal. Links → Golfplatz
Map 2 on page 294 Karte 2 Seite 294

GOLF COURSE
PLATZ   **14**/20

Site	Lage	▬▬▬
Maintenance	Instandhaltung	▬▬▬
Architect	Architekt	▬▬
Type	Typ	Gebirge
Relief	Relief	▬▬▬
Water in play	Platz mit Wasser	▬▬▬
Exp. to wind	Wind ausgesetzt	▬▬▬
Trees in play	Platz mit Bäumen	▬▬

Scorecard Scorekarte	Chp. Chp.	Mens Herren	Ladies Damen
Length Länge	6075	6075	5442
Par	73	73	73

Advised golfing ability		0 12 24 36
Empfohlene Spielstärke		▬▭
Hcp required	Min. Handicap	36

CLUB HOUSE & AMENITIES
KLUBHAUS UND NEBENGEBÄUDE   **7**/10

Pro shop	Pro shop	▬▬▬
Driving range	Übungsplatz	▬▬▬
Sheltered	überdacht	4 Plätze
On grass	auf Rasen	ja
Putting-green	Putting-grün	ja
Pitching-green	Pitching-grün	ja

HOTEL FACILITIES
HOTEL BESCHREIBUNG   **6**/10

HOTELS HOTELS
Seehof   Starnberg
38 Zimmer, D DM 220,-   3 km
Tel (49) 08151 - 6001, Fax (49) 08151 - 28 136

La Villa   Pöcking
28 Zimmer, D DM 330,-   12 km
Tel (49) 08151 - 77 060, Fax (49) 08151 - 770 699

Park- und Strandhotel   Berg
50 Zimmer, D DM 250,-   6 km
Tel (49) 08151 - 50 101, Fax (49) 08151 - 50 105

RESTAURANTS RESTAURANT
Isola d'Elba   Starnberg
Tel (49) 08151 - 16 780   3 km

Illguth's Gasthaus   Starnberg
Tel (49) 08151 - 15 577   3 km

337

GUT THAILING

Thailing wirkt aufgrund seiner Nähe, demselben Architekten sowie dem Geländecharakter wie der zweieige Zwilling von Schloss Egmating. Nur das hier, insbesondere auf den zweiten 9 Löchern, weitaus öfter Wasser ins Spiel kommt, was diesem Platz einen ganz eigenständigen Charakter verleiht. Die Fairwaybunker sind aus genehmigungs-rechtlichen Gründen noch nicht mit Sand gefüllt, während die hervorragend geformten Grünbunker die sehr sorgfältig gestalteten Grüns (viele davon sind in mehreren Stufen angelegt) sehr wirkungsvoll verteidigen. Dies ist ein weitgehend offener Golfplatz, dessen umfangreiche Neuanpflanzungen noch einige Jahre brauchen werden, bevor sie eine wirkliche Gefahr darstellen. Man benötigt einige Runden, um mit dem leicht hügeligen Gelände vertraut zu werden. Charakter und Schwierigkeit der Löcher, von denen einige auf Spieler mit hohem Handicap ziemlich einschüchternd wirken können, lassen sich durch mehrere zur Auswahl stehende Abschlag-Boxen verändern. Dies ist eine der vielversprechendsten neuen Anlagen, die zudem bislang noch nicht überlaufen ist.

This is the false twin to Schloss Egmating through closeness, name of designer and character of terrain. Only here, there is much more water in play, emphatically so on one half of the course, thus giving it its own personality. For administrative reasons, the fairway bunkers are still awaiting their sand, but their green-side counterparts are well shaped and jealously guard the very carefully crafted putting surfaces (beware the multi-tiered greens). This is by and large an open space course with a lot of newly-planted saplings, which will need a number of years to grow into a real threat. While you need to play here several times to get to grips with a slightly hilly terrain (but never excessively so), the variety of tee-off areas also changes the character of holes, some of which are intimidating for high-handicappers.

Golfclub Gut Thailing e.V.
Thailing 4
D - 85643 STEINHÖRIG

Office	Sekretariat	(49) 08094 - 9210
Pro shop	Pro shop	(49) 08094 - 9210
Fax	Fax	(49) 08094 - 9220
Situation	Lage	

35 km von München, 1 300 000 Ew.
5 km von Ebersberg, 10 000 Ew.

Annual closure	Jährliche Schliessung	nein
Weekly closure	Wöchentliche Schliessung	nein

Fees main season
Preisliste hochsaison 18 Löcher

	Week days Woche	We/Bank holidays We/Feiertag
Individual Individuell	DM 80,-	DM 100,-
Couple Ehepaar	DM 160,-	DM 200,-

Caddy	Caddy	nein
Electric Trolley	Elektrokarren	nein
Buggy	Elektrischer Wagen	DM 50,-
Clubs	Clubs	ja

Credit cards Kreditkarten
Eurocard - Mastercard - AMEX

338

Access Zufahrt : München, A94 → Passau. Forstinning,
B12 → Passau. Hohenlinden → Ebersberg. 5,5 km,
links → Golfplatz
Map 2 on page 295 Karte 2 Seite 295

GOLF COURSE
PLATZ   **16**/20

Site	Lage	▬▬▬▬
Maintenance	Instandhaltung	▬▬▬▬
Architect	Architekt	Kurt Rossknecht
Type	Typ	Flachland
Relief	Relief	▬▬
Water in play	Platz mit Wasser	▬▬▬
Exp. to wind	Wind ausgesetzt	▬▬
Trees in play	Platz mit Bäumen	▬▬

Scorecard Scorekarte	Chp. Chp.	Mens Herren	Ladies Damen
Length Länge	6082	5788	5103
Par	72	72	72

Advised golfing ability			0	12	24	36
Empfohlene Spielstärke				▬▬▬▬▬		
Hcp required	Min. Handicap			36		

CLUB HOUSE & AMENITIES
KLUBHAUS UND NEBENGEBÄUDE   **7**/10

Pro shop	Pro shop	▬▬▬▬
Driving range	Übungsplatz	▬▬▬
Sheltered	überdacht	ja
On grass	auf Rasen	ja
Putting-green	Putting-grün	ja
Pitching-green	Pitching-grün	ja

HOTEL FACILITIES
HOTEL BESCHREIBUNG   **5**/10

HOTELS HOTELS
Hölzerbräu — Ebersberg
51 Zimmer, D DM 140,- — 5 km
Tel (49) 08092 - 24 020, Fax (49) 08092 - 24 031

Klostersee — Ebersberg
23 Zimmer, D DM 130,- — 5 km
Tel (49) 08092 - 82 850, Fax (49) 08092 - 828 550

Huber — Ebersberg-Oberndorf
50 Zimmer, D DM 190,- — 8 km
Tel (49) 08092 - 21 026, Fax (49) 08092 - 21 442

RESTAURANTS RESTAURANT
Hölzerbrau — Ebersberg
Tel (49) 08092 - 24 020 — 5 km

Klostersee — Ebersberg
Tel (49) 08092 - 82 850 — 5 km

GUT WALDHOF

| 17 | 7 | 5 |

In der Umgebung Hamburgs bietet Gut Waldhof eine vom Stil her eher amerikanische Alternative zu den bekannten Klassikern, da hier die Beherrschung von "target golf" sehr bedeutsam ist, insbesondere da man öfter mit der Aufgabe konfrontiert wird, erhöht und auf mehreren Stufen angelegte Grüns anzuspielen (das Gelände ist zum Teil recht hügelig). Spieler, die "bump an run" Schläge bevorzugen, werden es hier schwer haben, doch letztendlich hilft die geforderte Erweiterung des Schlagrepertoires diesen, bessere Golfer zu werden. Die Schwierigkeiten sind gut über den Platz verteilt, wo leichtere Löcher, die zum Entspannen einladen, sich mit solchen abwechseln, an denen hohe Präzision gefordert wird. Manche Hindernisse stellen tatsächlich Gefahren dar, während andere eher psychologischer Natur sind. Dadurch entsteht ein gut ausbalancierter und abwechslungsreicher Gesamteindruck, der sowohl gute als auch weniger gute Spieler zufriedenstellt. Weniger geübten Golfern dürfte es dennoch schwerfallen, allen Anforderungen, die der zum Teil doch sehr anspruchsvollen Platz stellt, gerecht zu werden.

Alongside some of the great classic numbers in the region of Hamburg, Gut Waldhof is a rather American-style alternative where skills in so-called target golf are essential, especially to reach certain elevated and multi-tiered greens (the terrain is sometimes a little on the hilly side). Players who like to bump and run the ball are at a disadvantage here, but a change of habit can only make you a better golfer. Problems are well spread around the course and leave a few lighter breathing spaces between trickier holes, where precision is at a premium. While some hazards are really dangerous, others are more psychological in their intimidation. This leaves an overall impression of variety and balance and will satisfy both the very good and not so good player. The lesser players will nonetheless be hard-pushed.

Golfclub Gut Waldhof
Am Waldhof
D - 24629 KISDORFERWOHLD

Office	Sekretariat	(49) 04194 - 99 740
Pro shop	Pro shop	(49) 04194 - 1005
Fax	Fax	(49) 04194 - 1251
Situation	Lage	

5 km von Henstedt-Ulzburg, 21 500 Ew.
25 km von Hamburg, 1 650 000 Ew.

Annual closure	Jährliche Schliessung	nein
Weekly closure	Wöchentliche Schliessung	Montag

Fees main season
Preisliste hochsaison 18 Löcher

	Week days Woche	We/Bank holidays We/Feiertag
Individual Individuell	DM 50,-	DM 70,-
Couple Ehepaar	DM 100,-	DM 140,-

We/Feiertage: nur in Mitgliederbegleitung (with members)

Caddy	Caddy	nein
Electric Trolley	Elektrokarren	nein
Buggy	Elektrischer Wagen	DM 50,-
Clubs	Clubs	nein

Credit cards Kreditkarten nein

Access Zufahrt : A7 Hamburg-Kiel. Ausf. Kaltenkirchen. B433 → Henstedt Ulzburg. Links → Kisdorferwohld. Rechts (B432) → Golfplatz
Map 7 on page 304 Karte 7 Seite 304

GOLF COURSE
PLATZ
17 /20

Site	Lage	▬▬▬▬
Maintenance	Instandhaltung	▬▬▬▬
Architect	Architekt	E. Jonson-Sedibe
Type	Typ	Wald, Park
Relief	Relief	▬▬▬▬
Water in play	Platz mit Wasser	▬▬
Exp. to wind	Wind ausgesetzt	▬▬
Trees in play	Platz mit Bäumen	▬▬▬▬▬

Scorecard Scorekarte	**Chp.** Chp.	**Mens** Herren	**Ladies** Damen
Length Länge	6044	6044	5318
Par	72	72	72

Advised golfing ability		0 12 24 36
Empfohlene Spielstärke		▬▬▬▬▬
Hcp required	Min. Handicap	36

CLUB HOUSE & AMENITIES
KLUBHAUS UND NEBENGEBÄUDE
7 /10

Pro shop	Pro shop	▬▬▬▬
Driving range	Übungsplatz	▬▬▬▬
Sheltered	überdacht	8 Plätze
On grass	auf Rasen	ja
Putting-green	Putting-grün	ja
Pitching-green	Pitching-grün	ja

HOTEL FACILITIES
HOTEL BESCHREIBUNG
5 /10

HOTELS HOTELS

Wiking Hotel — Henstedt-Ulzburg
36 Zimmer, D DM 140,- — 5 km
Tel (49) 04193 - 9080, Fax (49) 04193 - 92 323

Schmöker Hof — Norderstedt
80 Zimmer, D DM 200,- — 10 km
Tel (49) 040 - 526 170, Fax (49) 040 - 526 2231

Hotel Restaurant Scheelke — Henstedt-Ulzburg
5 Zimmer, D DM 120,- — 5 km
Tel (49) 04193 - 2207, Fax (49) 04193 - 95 590

RESTAURANTS RESTAURANT

Golf Club Restaurant — Gut Waldhof
Tel (49) 04194 - 1010

Hotel Restaurant Scheelke — Henstedt-Ulzburg
Tel (49) 04193 - 2207 — 5 km

339

Das Original-Platzdesign von Bernhard von Limburger wurde 1977 von Robert Trent Jones leicht verändert. Diese Änderungen haben den Platz für den Durchschnittsgolfer nicht schwerer gemacht, wenngleich jetzt gelegentlich Wasser zu überwinden ist. Kein Par 4 erreicht 400 Meter, einige sind sogar recht kurz, so dass praktisch alle Eisen zum Einsatz kommen. Trotz des eher flachen Geländes gibt es zwei praktisch blinde Grüns, deren Anspiel "target Golf" erfordert. Diese Anforderung gilt im Grunde generell, da die Grüns durchgehend gut verteidigt sind. Dieser im amerikanischen Stil gestaltete Platz, bei dem alle Schwierigkeiten deutlich sichtbar sind, ist eingebettet in eine parkartige Landschaft, in der sich eine Anzahl exotischer Bäume findet. Auffallend ist auch der Abwechslungsreichtum der Löcher, von denen praktisch jedes auf unterschiedliche Art verteidigt wird, sei es in Form von Büschen, Bäumen, Bunkern und/oder Wasserhindernissen. Man braucht einen kühlen Kopf und gute Ballkontrolle, wenn man hier sein Handicap spielen will.

The original design by Bernhard von Limburger was slightly altered in 1977 by Robert Trent Jones. This has not made it any tougher for average players, even though there is now some water to cross. No one par 4 reaches 400 metres, and some are even short, thus allowing a wide choice of irons. Despite rather flat terrain, two greens are virtually blind and call for some target play, but this is a general feature here owing to the well-guarded greens. In a parkland landscape (with a number of exotic varieties of tree), this is a US-style course with difficulties for all to see. Also noteworthy is the variety of holes, with each having practically its own style of defence: bushes, trees, bunkers and/or water hazards. With a cool head and good ball control, you can hope to play to your handicap.

Golf Club Hamburg-Ahrensburg

Am Haidschlag 39-45
D - 22926 AHRENSBURG

Office	Sekretariat	(49) 04102 - 51 309
Pro shop	Pro shop	(49) 04102 - 57 626
Fax	Fax	(49) 04102 - 81 410
Situation	Lage	

500 m von Ahrensburg, 27 000 Ew. 20 km von Hamburg.

Annual closure	Jährliche Schliessung	nein
Weekly closure	Wöchentliche Schliessung	Montag
		Das Restaurant

Fees main season Preisliste hochsaison 18 Löcher

	Week days Woche	We/Bank holidays We/Feiertag
Individual Individuell	DM 70,-	DM 80,-
Couple Ehepaar	DM 140,-	DM 160,-

We/Feiertage nur in Migliederbeleitung
(with members)

Caddy	Caddy	auf Reservierung
Electric Trolley	Elektrokarren	nein
Buggy	Elektrischer Wagen	DM 50,-
Clubs	Clubs	nein
Credit cards	Kreditkarten	nein

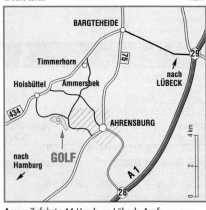

Access Zufahrt : A1 Hamburg-Lübeck, Ausf. Ahrensburg. B434 → Bargteheide. → Ammersbek. Im Bunningstedt, Franz-Kruse-Strasse → "Siedlung Daheim. Am Haidschlag → Golf
Map 7 on page 304 Karte 7 Seite 304

GOLF COURSE
PLATZ
17 /20

Site	Lage	▇▇▇▇▇▁
Maintenance	Instandhaltung	▇▇▇▇▇▁
Architect	Architekt	B. von Limburger
Type	Typ	Park
Relief	Relief	▇▁▁▁▁▁
Water in play	Platz mit Wasser	▇▇▁▁▁▁
Exp. to wind	Wind ausgesetzt	▇▇▁▁▁▁
Trees in play	Platz mit Bäumen	▇▇▇▇▁▁

Scorecard Scorekarte	Chp. Chp.	Mens Herren	Ladies Damen
Length Länge	5782	5782	5087
Par	71	71	71

Advised golfing ability		0	12	24	36
Empfohlene Spielstärke			▇▇▇▇▇▇		
Hcp required	Min. Handicap	36			

CLUB HOUSE & AMENITIES
KLUBHAUS UND NEBENGEBÄUDE
8 /10

Pro shop	Pro shop	▇▇▇▇▁▁
Driving range	Übungsplatz	▇▇▇▇▁▁
Sheltered	überdacht	6 Plätze
On grass	auf Rasen	nein
Putting-green	Putting-grün	ja
Pitching-green	Pitching-grün	ja

HOTEL FACILITIES
HOTEL BESCHREIBUNG
7 /10

HOTELS HOTELS
Park Hotel Ahrensburg — Ahrensburg
24 Zimmer, D DM 200,- — 1 km
Tel (49) 04102 - 2300, Fax (49) 04102 - 230 100

Ring Hotel Ahrensburg — Ahrensburg
11 Zimmer, D DM 160,- — 2 km
Tel (49) 04102 - 51 560, Fax (49) 04102 - 515 656

RESTAURANTS RESTAURANT
Golf Club Restaurant — Golf
Tel (49) 04102 - 57 522

Alte Schule — Siek
Tel (49) 04107 - 9114 — 6 km S

HAMBURG-HOLM

15 6 6

Dieser Golfplatz ist zwar einer der jüngsten Entwürfe von Donald Harradine, doch vermitteln Zustand und die etwas altmodische Platzarchitektur den Eindruck einer bereits viel älteren Anlage. Abgesehen von dem sehr dichten Rough sind die Hindernisse weder übermässig zahlreich noch sonderlich gefährlich. Der Platz wurde offensichtlich mehr mit Augenmerk auf die weniger erfahrenen Durchschnitts-Golfer entworfen, als für die besseren Spieler, denen es hier an Herausforderungen mangelt. Geübte Spieler können hier an ihrem Spiel arbeiten und dabei ohne grosse Anstrengung einen guten Score erzielen. Wir brauchen Plätze wie diesen. Sie bereiten deshalb soviel Vergnügen, weil man auf ihnen eine entspannte Runde Golf spielen kann, ohne das Spiel virtuos beherrschen zu müssen. Ein leicht begehbarer Parcours, auf dem man an seinem Spiel feilen kann, bevor man technisch anspruchsvollere Plätze in Angriff nimmt.

This is one of Donald Harradine's latest designs, although the way the course is prepared and the presently rather unfashionable style give the impression of a layout that has been around for some time. So if we forget the thick rough, hazards are neither too numerous nor really dangerous. The course has visibly been designed more for inexperienced mid-handicappers than for the better players, who might find this too easy a challenge. The skilled golfer can check his game here and card a good score without too much effort. We need courses like this; they always provide a great deal of pleasure and make for golf that is all the more relaxing in that you don't need to flight the ball like a virtuoso. It is also a pleasant course to walk. A course for everyone where you can hone your game without too much danger before moving on to more technically demanding layouts.

Golfclub Hamburg-Holm

Haverkamp 1
D - 25488 HOLM

Office	Sekretariat	(49) 04103 - 91 330
Pro shop	Pro shop	(49) 04103 - 91 330
Fax	Fax	(49) 04103 - 91 330
Situation	Lage	

12 km von Hamburg, 1 650 000 Ew.
6 km von Wedel, 34 000 Ew.

Annual closure	Jährliche Schliessung	nein
Weekly closure	Wöchentliche Schliessung	Montag
		Das Restaurant

Fees main season Preisliste hochsaison 18 Löcher

	Week days Woche	We/Bank holidays We/Feiertag
Individual Individuell	DM 65,-	DM 80,-
Couple Ehepaar	DM 130,-	DM 160,-

We/Feiertage: nur in Mitgliederbegleitung

Caddy	Caddy	nein
Electric Trolley	Elektrokarren	nein
Buggy	Elektrischer Wagen	nein
Clubs	Clubs	nein
Credit cards Kreditkarten		nein

Access Zufahrt : A23 Ausf. Pinneberg Süd → Wedel.
Rechts → Haseldorfer Marsch/Holm (Lehmweg).
2 km, links (Haverkamp)
Map 7 on page 304 Karte 7 Seite 304

GOLF COURSE
PLATZ
15/20

Site	Lage	
Maintenance	Instandhaltung	
Architect	Architekt	Donald Harradine
Type	Typ	Heckenlandschaft, Land
Relief	Relief	
Water in play	Platz mit Wasser	
Exp. to wind	Wind ausgesetzt	
Trees in play	Platz mit Bäumen	

Scorecard Scorekarte	Chp. Chp.	Mens Herren	Ladies Damen
Length Länge	6170	6170	5443
Par	72	72	72

Advised golfing ability   0   12   24   36
Empfohlene Spielstärke
Hcp required   Min. Handicap   36

CLUB HOUSE & AMENITIES
KLUBHAUS UND NEBENGEBÄUDE
6/10

Pro shop	Pro shop	
Driving range	Übungsplatz	
Sheltered	überdacht	3 Plätze
On grass	auf Rasen	ja
Putting-green	Putting-grün	ja
Pitching-green	Pitching-grün	ja

HOTEL FACILITIES
HOTEL BESCHREIBUNG
6/10

HOTELS HOTELS

Hotel Senator   Wedel
46 Zimmer, D DM 178,-   4 km
Tel (49) 04103 - 80 870, Fax (49) 04103 - 8077250

Hotel Diamant   Wedel
39 Zimmer, D DM 168,-   5 km
Tel (49) 04103 - 702 600, Fax (49) 04103 - 702 700

Strandhotel Blankenese   Hamburg
15 Zimmer, D DM 230,-   20 km
Tel (49) 040 - 861 344, Fax (49) 040 - 864 936

RESTAURANTS RESTAURANT

Flic Flac Bistro   Hamburg
Tel (49) 040 - 865 345   10 km

Dal Fabbro   Hamburg
Tel (49) 040 - 868 941   11 km

341

Der Golfplatz wurde 1939 auf der ehemaligen Fasanenzuchtfarm der Familie Hesse errichtet, ganz in der Nähe von Schloss Wilhelmsbad, einem der zahlreichen Mineral- und Thermalkurorte dieser Gegend. Dieser alte Besitz verfügt über einen grosszügigen alten Baumbestand. Daher rührt auch der Eindruck eines gemütlichen Spaziergangs inmitten eines grossen Parks, den man während der Runde auf dem völlig ebenen Platz gewinnt, dessen 18 Loch ganz mühelos zu Gehen sind. Dank ihres anspruchsvollen Layouts war die Anlage in der Vergangenheit mehrmals Austragungsort der Nationalen offenen Deutschen Golf-Meisterschaften. Die guten Spieler werden versuchen den Amateur-Rekord von 70 Schlägen zu brechen, während die weniger Ehrgeizigen unter uns, von den vorderen Abschlägen aus, einen grossartigen Golftag verbringen können. Da die Runde von Bäumen und einer kleinen Anzahl gefährlicher Wasserhindernisse gewürzt wird, sollten sie nicht zögern, von den vorderen Abschlägen zu spielen. Dies gilt speziell an Loch 7, einem Par 5 von 570 Metern Länge.

This course was designed in 1959 on the former pheasant farm of the Hesse family, close to the castle of Wilhelmsbad, one of the many spas and hydrotherapy centres found in this part of the world. The estate is lavishly lined with old trees, whence the very pleasant impression of a lovely walk in a huge park without any relief to speak of to stop you from walking the 18 holes. The layout is demanding enough for the National German Championships to have been held here several times, and while skilled players will relish the chance to attack the amateur record of 70, the less ambitious amongst us will play from the forward tees and spend a great day's golfing. The trees and a few dangerous water hazards tend to add a little spice to life, so don't shy away from playing the front tees.

Golf-Club Hanau-Wilhelmsbad e.V.
Wilhelmsbader Allee 32
D - 63454 HANAU-WILHELMSBAD

Office	Sekretariat	(49) 06181 - 82 071
Pro shop	Pro shop	(49) 06181 - 81 775
Fax	Fax	(49) 06181 - 86 967
Situation	Lage	

20 km von Frankfurt, 660 000 Ew.
3 km von Hanau, 90 000 Ew.

Annual closure	Jährliche Schliessung	nein
Weekly closure	Wöchentliche Schliessung	Montag
		das Restaurant

Fees main season Preisliste hochsaison 18 Löcher

	Week days Woche	We/Bank holidays We/Feiertag
Individual Individuell	DM 80,-	DM 100,-
Couple Ehepaar	DM 160,-	DM 200,-

We : nur in Mitgliederbegleitung (with members) -

Caddy	Caddy	nein
Electric Trolley	Elektrokarren	nein
Buggy	Elektrischer Wagen	nein
Clubs	Clubs	DM 30,-
Credit cards Kreditkarten		nein

342

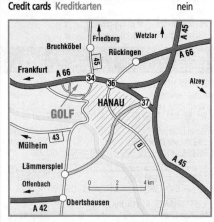

Access Zufahrt : Frankfurt, A66. Ausf. Hanau Nord.
Rechts auf B8/40 bis. Rechts → Wilhelmsbad. 20 m,
rechts (Wilhelmsbader Allee)
Map 3 on page 297 Karte 3 Seite 297

GOLF COURSE
PLATZ **15**/20

Site	Lage	▬▬▬
Maintenance	Instandhaltung	▬▬▬
Architect	Architekt	Kothe
Type	Typ	Park
Relief	Relief	▬
Water in play	Platz mit Wasser	▬
Exp. to wind	Wind ausgesetzt	▬
Trees in play	Platz mit Bäumen	▬▬

Scorecard Scorekarte	**Chp.** Chp.	**Mens** Herren	**Ladies** Damen
Length Länge	6227	6227	5497
Par	73	73	73

Advised golfing ability Empfohlene Spielstärke	0	12	24	36

Hcp required Min. Handicap 32, We: 28

CLUB HOUSE & AMENITIES
KLUBHAUS UND NEBENGEBÄUDE **6**/10

Pro shop	Pro shop	▬▬▬
Driving range	Übungsplatz	▬▬
Sheltered	überdacht	5 Plätze
On grass	auf Rasen	ja
Putting-green	Putting-grün	ja
Pitching-green	Pitching-grün	ja

HOTEL FACILITIES
HOTEL BESCHREIBUNG **6**/10

HOTELS HOTELS
Golfhotel — Golf
7 Zimmer, D DM 180,-
Tel (49) 06181 - 995 511

Brüder-Grimm Hotel — Hanau
95 Zimmer, D DM 200,- — 5 km
Tel (49) 06181 - 30 60, Fax (49) 06181 - 306 512

Zum Riesen — Hanau
28 Zimmer, D DM 200,- — 5 km
Tel (49) 06181 - 25 020, Fax (49) 06181 - 250 259

RESTAURANTS RESTAURANT
Brüder-Grimm Hotel — Hanau
Tel (49) 06181 - 33 838 — 5 km

Der 1923 gebaute Platz wurde später von Bernhard von Limburger umgestaltet, der seine klassische Handschrift hinterliess. Diese zeigt sich in einem klugen Platzdesign, das sich auszeichnet durch die ebenso angemessene wie geschickte Verwendung von Hindernissen, deren Plazierung gute Schläge nicht betraf. Die Lärmbelästigung durch die nahegelegene Autobahn Köln - Hannover wird von den vielen Bäumen etwas gedämpft, davon abgesehen lohnt sich der Besuch der insgesamt ausgezeichneten Anlage unbedingt. Die bereits erwähnten Bäume verlangen nach geraden Schlägen, um die engen Fairways zu treffen; vielfach ist man sogar gezwungen, einen Fade oder Draw zu spielen, um in die beste Position zu gelangen. Die ziemlich flachen, gut gestalteten Grüns werden von einer Reihe, teilweise sehr tiefer Bunker verteidigt. Die erforderliche Spielstrategie ist offensichtlich, so dass man schon auf der ersten Runde hoffen kann, einen guten Score zu erzielen. Hannover ist einer der besten Plätze der Region.

Designed in 1923, the course was reshaped by Bernhard von Limburger, who has left his own, very classical stamp with a sensible layout and reasonable use of hazards, always well placed but not too penalising for good shots. The one regret is the closeness of the Cologne-Hannover motorway, but the general excellence of the course makes it well worth visiting, and the very many trees do tend to dampen the noise somewhat. On the downside, these same trees leave the fairways rather narrow, hence the need to play straight or even flight the ball with fade and draw shots to get into the best position. The greens are well designed and relatively flat, but are protected by a host of bunkers, some of which are often very deep. Game strategy is pretty obvious to try and return a goodish card first time out, and the course is varied enough to keep it interesting. This is one of the region's best courses.

Golf-Club Hannover e.V.
Am Blauen See 120
D - 30823 GARBSEN

Office	Sekretariat	(49) 05137 - 73 068
Pro shop	Pro shop	(49) 05137 - 71 004
Fax	Fax	(49) 05137 - 75 851
Situation	Lage	

15 km von Hannover, 510 000 Ew.

Annual closure	Jährliche Schliessung	ja
		1/01→31/01
Weekly closure	Wöchentliche Schliessung	Montag

Fees main season
Preisliste hochsaison den ganzen Tag

	Week days Woche	We/Bank holidays We/Feiertag
Individual Individuell	DM 50,-	DM 70,-
Couple Ehepaar	DM 100,-	DM 140,-

– 21 Jahre, Studenten: – 50%

Caddy	Caddy	nein
Electric Trolley	Elektrokarren	nein
Buggy	Elektrischer Wagen	ja
Clubs	Clubs	ja
Credit cards Kreditkarten		nein

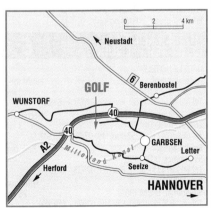

★ Neustadt

GOLF
6 Berenbostel
WUNSTORF
40
40
A2
Mittelland Kanal
Herford
GARBSEN
Letter
Seelze
HANNOVER →

Access Zufahrt : Hannover, Westschnellweg. Ausf.
Herrenhausen. A2 bis Rasthaus "Blauer See". 1,5 km,
Golfplatz südlich der A2
Map 5 on page 301 Karte 5 Seite 301

GOLF COURSE
PLATZ   16/20

Site	Lage	▬▬▬▬▬
Maintenance	Instandhaltung	▬▬▬▬▬
Architect	Architekt	B. von Limburger
Type	Typ	Land, Wald
Relief	Relief	▬▬
Water in play	Platz mit Wasser	▬
Exp. to wind	Wind ausgesetzt	▬▬
Trees in play	Platz mit Bäumen	▬▬▬▬▬

Scorecard Scorekarte	Chp. Chp.	Mens Herren	Ladies Damen
Length Länge	5846	5681	4994
Par	71	71	71

Advised golfing ability		0	12	24	36
Empfohlene Spielstärke			▬▬▬		

Hcp required	Min. Handicap	34

CLUB HOUSE & AMENITIES
KLUBHAUS UND NEBENGEBÄUDE   7/10

Pro shop	Pro shop	▬▬▬▬
Driving range	Übungsplatz	▬▬▬▬
Sheltered	überdacht	3 Plätze
On grass	auf Rasen	Juni → Sept.
Putting-green	Putting-grün	ja
Pitching-green	Pitching-grün	ja

HOTEL FACILITIES
HOTEL BESCHREIBUNG   7/10

HOTELS HOTELS
Maritim Grand Hotel Hannover   Hannover
285 Zimmer, D DM 400,-   15 km
Tel (49) 0511 - 97 370, Fax (49) 0511 - 325195

Landhaus am See   Garbsen-Berenbostel
37 Zimmer, D DM 200,-   3 km
Tel (49) 05131 - 46 860, Fax (49) 05131 - 468 666

Hotel Wildhage   Garbsen-Hevelse
30 Zimmer, D DM 200,-   2 km
Tel (49) 05137 - 75 033, Fax (49) 05137 - 75 401

RESTAURANTS RESTAURANT
Landhaus Ammann   Hannover
Tel (49) 0511 - 830 818   15 km

Gattopardo   Hannover
Tel (49) 0511 - 14 375   15 km

343

Die Nähe zum Schloss der Hohenzollern - dessen Lage weitaus beeindruckender ist als die nicht so alten Gebäude - haben viel zum Ruf und Bekannheitsgrad dieses Golfplatzes beigetragen. Seine idyllische Lage ist für viele, in dieser Hinsicht empfängliche Golfer, ein stichhaltiger Grund, hier zu spielen. Wer seine Aufmerksamkeit von der Umgebung dem Kurs zuwendet, entdeckt einen hübschen Platz mit engen, häufig baumbestandenen Fairways und einer Anzahl gefährlicher Büsche, welche die Hauptschwierigkeit dieser Anlage darstellen. Zwar gibt es auch Fairway- und Grünbunker, jedoch sind diese nicht wirklich gefährlich genug, um gute Spieler ernsthaft daran hindern zu können, die wohlproportionierten, leicht modellierten Grüns anzuspielen. Geeignet für alle Spielklassen, fehlt es diesem Platz ein wenig an Charakter, um den besseren Spielern auch langfristig Vergnügen zu bereiten. Beim Bau der Anlage stand sicherlich im Vordergrund, dass golfende Familien hier Spass haben sollen.

Being so close to the castle of Hohenzollern (even though the site is more impressive than the not-so-old buildings) has done much for the reputation and recognition of this course. Its idyllic setting is also a sound argument for players who are sensitive to this particular aspect of golf. If you can tear your eyes away from the surroundings, you are left facing a pretty course with narrow fairways often protected by trees and, above all, some dangerous bushes, which form the main hazard. The fairway and green-side bunkers are there all right, but are not really dangerous enough to worry good players unduly and prevent them from homing in on nicely-sized and discreetly contoured greens. Accessible to players of all abilities, this course is a little too short of personality to keep the better players happy for too long. Working for the enjoyment of family golf was certainly a major consideration when designing the course.

Golf Club Hechingen-Hohenzollern
Auf dem Hagelwasen, Postfach 1124
D - 72379 HECHINGEN

Office	Sekretariat	(49) 07471 - 2600
Pro shop	Pro shop	(49) 07471 - 62 272
Fax	Fax	(49) 07471 - 14 776
Situation	Lage	

2 km von Hechingen, 16 600 Ew.
25 km von Tübingen, 82 000 Ew.

Annual closure	Jährliche Schliessung	ja
		1/11→31/03

Weekly closure	Wöchentliche Schliessung	
	Montag,das Restaurant	

Fees main season Preisliste hochsaison den ganzen Tag

	Week days Woche	We/Bank holidays We/Feiertag
Individual Individuell	DM 60,-	DM 80,-
Couple Ehepaar	DM 120,-	DM 160,-

Studenten: – 50%

Caddy	Caddy	nein
Electric Trolley	Elektrokarren	ja
Buggy	Elektrischer Wagen	nein
Clubs	Clubs	DM 10,-

Credit cards Kreditkarten		nein

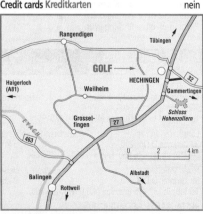

Access Zufahrt : Stuttgart, B27. Tübingen B27 →
Balingen. Hechingen → Burg Hohenzollern, →
Hechingen-Weilheim, → Golfplatz
Map 1 on page 293 Karte 1 Seite 293

GOLF COURSE
PLATZ 14/20

Site	Lage	
Maintenance	Instandhaltung	
Architect	Architekt	
Type	Typ	Flachland, Gebirge
Relief	Relief	
Water in play	Platz mit Wasser	
Exp. to wind	Wind ausgesetzt	
Trees in play	Platz mit Bäumen	

Scorecard Scorekarte	Chp. Chp.	Mens Herren	Ladies Damen
Length Länge	6064	6064	5346
Par	72	72	72

Advised golfing ability	0	12	24	36
Empfohlene Spielstärke				
Hcp required	Min. Handicap	36		

CLUB HOUSE & AMENITIES
KLUBHAUS UND NEBENGEBÄUDE 6/10

Pro shop	Pro shop	
Driving range	Übungsplatz	
Sheltered	überdacht	6 Plätze
On grass	auf Rasen	April-Oktober
Putting-green	Putting-grün	ja
Pitching-green	Pitching-grün	ja

HOTEL FACILITIES
HOTEL BESCHREIBUNG 6/10

HOTELS HOTELS
Hotel Brielhof — Hechingen
25 Zimmer, D DM 200,- — 5 km
Tel (49) 07471 - 4097, Fax (49) 07471 - 16 908

Café Klaiber — Hechingen
28 Zimmer, D DM 140,- — 3 km
Tel (49) 07471 - 2257, Fax (49) 07471 - 13 918

Stadt Balingen — Balingen
59 Zimmer, D DM 190,- — 10 km
Tel (49) 07433 - 8021, Fax (49) 07433 - 5119

Domizil — Tübingen
80 Zimmer, D DM 180,- — 25 km
Tel (49) 07071 - 1390, Fax (49) 07071 - 139 250

RESTAURANTS RESTAURANT
Waldhorn - Tel (49) 07071 - 61 270 — Tübingen 30 km
Rosenau - Tel (49) 07071 - 66 466 — Tübingen 25 km

344

Dieser erst kürzlich fertiggestellte Golfplatz wird noch ein paar Jahre benötigen, bis er sein volles Potential entfaltet hat, dennoch ist sein jetziger Zustand bereits recht vielversprechend. Angelegt auf leicht hügeligem Gelände, von dem man schöne Blicke auf den Höhenzug der Schwäbischen Alb hat, ist es dem Architekten gelungen, einen Platz zu bauen, dessen Schwierigkeiten gut erkennbar sind, so dass die Spieler sehr schnell die richtige Taktik herausfinden können, um hier einen guten Score zu erzielen. Alles in allem ist der Platz nicht sehr schwierig, so dass es jedem möglich sein sollte, sein Handicap zu spielen. Letzteres dürfte nur dann schwierig werden, wenn der Wind bläst, da in dem Fall die exponierte Lage des Platzes zum tragen kommt. Nur dann wird es wirklich nötig, auch die Flugkurve des Balles etwas zu steuern, da selbst die Roughzonen insgesamt eher harmlos sind. Das "Vorzeige-Loch" ist die 17, ein Par 3 von 117 Metern Länge, bei dem ein 70 Meter tiefer gelegenes Grün über ein Wasserhindernis anzuspielen ist.

This very recent course will need a few years to mellow before settling into its final physiognomy, but already it promises a great deal. Over a moderately hilly site, with pretty vistas over the "Schwäbische Alb" mountains, the designer has come up with a course where the main difficulties are clearly visible, so that players can quickly twig the ideal tactics and hope to card some good scores. After all, proportionally speaking this is not a tough course, and anyone can look forward to playing to his or her handicap. This might not be the case if the wind begins to blow, because there's nothing much here to stop it. This is the only time when you need to flight the ball a little, as elsewhere the rough is, on the whole, pretty friendly. The signature hole is the 17th, a 117-metre par 3 with a water hazard in front of the hole, 70 metres downhill. A pleasant and unpretentious course.

Golfclub Hetzenhof e.V.
Hetzenhof 7
D - 73547 LORCH

Office	Sekretariat	(49) 07172 - 9180-13
Pro shop	Pro shop	(49) 07172 - 91800
Fax	Fax	(49) 07172 - 9180-30
Situation	Lage	

10 km von Göppingen, 55 000 Ew. 40 km von Stuttgart.

Annual closure	Jährliche Schliessung	ja
		1/12→31/03
Weekly closure	Wöchentliche Schliessung	
	Montag,das Restaurant	

Fees main season Preisliste hochsaison 18 Löcher

	Week days Woche	We/Bank holidays We/Feiertag
Individual Individuell	DM 80,-	DM 80,-
Couple Ehepaar	DM 160,-	DM 160,-

We/Feiertage: nur in Mitgliederbegleitung (with members)

Caddy	Caddy	nein
Electric Trolley	Elektrokarren	nein
Buggy	Elektrischer Wagen	nein
Clubs	Clubs	DM 20,-
Credit cards Kreditkarten		nein

Access Zufahrt : Stuttgart, B29 → Aalen. Ausf. Loch.
B927 → Göppingen. → Golfplatz (5 km).
Map 1 on page 293 Karte 1 Seite 293

GOLF COURSE
PLATZ
14/20

Site	Lage	▮▮▮▮▮▯
Maintenance	Instandhaltung	▮▮▮▮▯▯
Architect	Architekt	Dieter Sziedat
Type	Typ	Flachland, Gebirge
Relief	Relief	▮▮▮▮▮▯
Water in play	Platz mit Wasser	▮▮▮▯▯▯
Exp. to wind	Wind ausgesetzt	▮▮▮▮▯▯
Trees in play	Platz mit Bäumen	▮▮▮▮▯▯

Scorecard Scorekarte	Chp. Chp.	Mens Herren	Ladies Damen
Length Länge	6135	6135	5407
Par	72	72	72

Advised golfing ability		0 12 24 36
Empfohlene Spielstärke		▮▮▮▮▮▯
Hcp required	Min. Handicap	nein

CLUB HOUSE & AMENITIES
KLUBHAUS UND NEBENGEBÄUDE
7/10

Pro shop	Pro shop	▮▮▮▮▯▯
Driving range	Übungsplatz	▮▮▮▮▯▯
Sheltered	überdacht	10 Plätze
On grass	auf Rasen	April-September
Putting-green	Putting-grün	ja
Pitching-green	Pitching-grün	ja

HOTEL FACILITIES
HOTEL BESCHREIBUNG
6/10

HOTELS HOTELS
Hohen Linde — Lorch
18 Zimmer, D DM 100,- — 500 m
Tel (49) 07172 - 7443Hotel Sonne — Lorch
25 Zimmer, D DM 110,- — 8 km
Tel (49) 07172 - 7373, Fax (49) 07172 - 8377
Hohenstaufen — Göppingen
50 Zimmer, D DM 180,- — 10 km
Tel (49) 07161 - 6700, Fax (49) 07161 - 70 070
Becher — Donzdorf
65 Zimmer, D DM 200,- — 23 km
Tel (49) 07162 - 20 050, Fax (49) 07162 - 200 555

RESTAURANTS RESTAURANT
Becher Restaurant de Balzac — Donzdorf
Tel (49) 07162 - 20 050 — 23 km
Burgrestaurant Staufeneck — Salach
Tel (49) 07162 - 5028 — 18 km

345

Erst kürzlich hat Kurt Rossknecht seinen Status als einer der kreativsten Golf-Architekten Europas mit dieser ausgezeichneten Anlage untermauert, die sich als perfekte Ergänzung zu einem der beeindruckendsten Clubhäuser Deutschlands erweist. Der leicht hügelige Platz leugnet nicht die amerikanischen Einflüsse, welche besonders an einer Vielzahl von Wasserhindernissen deutlich werden, die den Spielern, neben einigen durch den Wald verlaufenden Spielbahnen, die grössten Probleme bereiten. Obschon die Schwierigkeiten klar erkennbar sind, muss man doch einige Runden hier spielen, um die vorhandenen strategischen Fallen genau auszumachen. Der Platz ist nicht übermässig lang, so dass Spieler aller Kategorien hier einen schönen Golftag verleben können, sofern sie sich darauf konzentrieren ihr Handicap zu spielen, und keine Schläge unnötig verschenken. Die Grüns sind von guter Qualität, wie auch die gesamte Anlage bereits gut eingewachsen ist. Am 18 Loch, einem schwierigen Par 3, muss man acht geben in Hessen zu bleiben .... Wer hier sliced, findet seinen Ball wahrhaft "out of bounds" - nämlich im benachbarten Bayern.

Designer Kurt Rossknecht has recently asserted his status as one of the most creative course architects in Europe, and this good layout is the perfect complement to one of Germany's most impressive club-houses. Over averagely hilly terrain, the course doesn't try to hide its American influence, and water hazards abound as an obvious danger alongside the stretches through the forest. Even though the difficulties are clearly seen, you need to play the course several times to get a clear picture of the strategic traps. It is not excessively long and players of all levels can spend a good day's golfing if they don't throw strokes away and concentrate on keeping to their handicap. The greens are good. At the 18th, a tough par 3, be careful to stay in Hesse... if you slice, you will find your ball O.B. in neighbouring Bavaria!

Golfclub Hof Trages
Hofgut Trages
D - 65379 FREIGERICHT

Office	Sekretariat	(49) 06055 - 91 380
Pro shop	Pro shop	(49) 06055 - 993 818
Fax	Fax	(49) 06055 - 913 891
Situation	Lage	

25 km von Hanau, 90 000 Ew.
35 km von Frankfurt, 660 000 Ew.

Annual closure	Jährliche Schliessung	nein
Weekly closure	Wöchentliche Schliessung	nein

Fees main season Preisliste hochsaison 18 Löcher

	Week days Woche	We/Bank holidays We/Feiertag
Individual Individuell	DM 75,-	DM 90,-
Couple Ehepaar	DM 150,-	DM 180,-
Studenten: DM 35,-		

Caddy	Caddy	auf Reservierung
Electric Trolley	Elektrokarren	nein
Buggy	Elektrischer Wagen	DM 50,-
Clubs	Clubs	DM 40,-

Credit cards Kreditkarten
VISA - Eurocard - MasterCard - AMEX

Access Zufahrt : A66 Frankfurt → Gelnhausen. Ausf.
Erlensee → Rodenbach → Niederrodenbach,
Oberrodenbach. Golfplatz 3 km
Map 3 on page 297 Karte 3 Seite 297

GOLF COURSE
PLATZ   **16**/20

Site	Lage	
Maintenance	Instandhaltung	
Architect	Architekt	Kurt Rossknecht
Type	Typ	Park, Flachland
Relief	Relief	
Water in play	Platz mit Wasser	
Exp. to wind	Wind ausgesetzt	
Trees in play	Platz mit Bäumen	

Scorecard	Chp.	Mens	Ladies
Scorekarte	Chp.	Herren	Damen
Length Länge	5964	5964	5439
Par	71	71	71

Advised golfing ability		0	12	24	36
Empfohlene Spielstärke					
Hcp required	Min. Handicap	36, We: 28			

CLUB HOUSE & AMENITIES
KLUBHAUS UND NEBENGEBÄUDE   **7**/10

Pro shop	Pro shop	
Driving range	Übungsplatz	
Sheltered	überdacht	8 Plätze
On grass	auf Rasen	ja
Putting-green	Putting-grün	ja
Pitching-green	Pitching-grün	ja

HOTEL FACILITIES
HOTEL BESCHREIBUNG   **5**/10

HOTELS HOTELS

Herrenmühle   Michelbach
28 Zimmer, D DM 160,-   7 km
Tel (49) 06023 - 5080, Fax (49) 06023 - 3313

Schlossberg im Weinberg   Alzenau-Wasserlos
19 Zimmer, D DM 200,-   12 km
Tel (49) 06023 - 1058, Fax (49) 06023 - 30 253

Zeller   Kahl
60 Zimmer, D DM 170,-   25 km
Tel (49) 06188 - 9180, Fax (49) 06188 - 918 100

RESTAURANTS RESTAURANT

Hof Trages Restaurant   Golfplatz
Tel (49) 06055 - 91 380

Öhlmühle   Mömbris
Tel (49) 06029 - 9500   15 km

346

Clubmitglieder gewöhnen sich mit der Zeit an die blinden Grüns, nicht so die gelegentlichen Besucher. Angesichts der Lage von Hohenpähl inmitten einer Touristen-Region, müssen wir dem Architekten wohl ein Kompliment machen, dass er zumindest im stark hügeligen Teil des Geländes blinde Schläge zum Grün zu vermeiden wusste. Der Platz hat keine überflüssigen Hindernisse. Wo Bäume und Wasser bereits genug Gefahr darstellen, wird diese nicht noch etwa durch zusätzliche Bunker verstärkt. Ungeübten Spielern werden im Verlauf der Runde, die eine Vielzahl von Problemen für sie bereithält, deutlich ihre Schwächen aufgezeigt. Dieser meist recht enge Parcours verlangt vom Spieler sehr kontrolliertes Golf. Erwähnenswert ist auch die "Ehrlichkeit" des Layouts, abgesehen vom 4. Loch, wo ein vom Abschlag aus nicht sichtbarer Graben das Fairway in Höhe der Drive-Landezone kreuzt. Hohenpähl ist zwar anspruchsvoll, jedoch kein "Monsterplatz". Daher ist Loch 8, die schwerste Bahn des Platzes, an der Bogey ein gutes Ergebnis ist, eher die Ausnahme.

Visitors don't like blind greens. Given that Hohenpähl is located in a tourist region, we should compliment the designer for having avoided blind approaches on the hilly part of the course (9 holes). There are no needless traps here: when the trees and water present an obvious danger, this is never compounded by the addition of bunkers. Inexperienced players will certainly encounter a few problems on the way, but they will also get an insight into their weaknesses. This often narrow course demands control over your game and its honesty deserves a mention, except on the 4th hole where a concealed ditch crosses exactly where the drive should land. Although demanding, Hohenpähl is no monster and only the 8th is really tough going. It's a par 4 but the bogey will do nicely. Well worth knowing.

Golf Club Hohenpähl
D - 82396 PÄHL

Office	Sekretariat	(49) 08808 - 1330
Pro shop	Pro shop	(49) 08808 - 1308
Fax	Fax	(49) 08808 - 775
Situation	Lage	

44 km von München, 1 300 000 Ew.
9 km von Weilheim, 18 500 Ew.

Annual closure	Jährliche Schliessung	ja
		1/11→31/03
Weekly closure	Wöchentliche Schliessung	nein

Fees main season
Preisliste hochsaison 18 Löcher

	Week days Woche	We/Bank holidays We/Feiertag
Individual Individuell	DM 80,-	DM 100,-
Couple Ehepaar	DM 160,-	DM 200,-

We: nur in Mitgliederbegleitung (with members)
– 21 Jahre : – 50 %

Caddy	Caddy	auf Reservierung
Electric Trolley	Elektrokarren	DM 25,-
Buggy	Elektrischer Wagen	nein
Clubs	Clubs	DM 25,-
Credit cards Kreditkarten		nein

DIESSEN — Ammersee — nach Herrsching
nach Starnberg MÜNCHEN
Fischen
Kerschlach
Raisting
Pähl **GOLF**
Wielenbach
nach Schongau
WIELHEIM
nach Starnberg
0   2   4 km

Access Zufahrt : München, A99 → Garmisch-Partenkirchen. Ausf. Starnberg. Im Starnberg, B2 → Weilheim. Km 41, rechts → Pähl → Golfplatz
Map 2 on page 294 Karte 2 Seite 294

GOLF COURSE
PLATZ
15/20

Site	Lage	▰▰▰▱▱
Maintenance	Instandhaltung	▰▰▰▰▱
Architect	Architekt	Kurt Rossknecht
Type	Typ	Wald, Park
Relief	Relief	▰▰▰▰▱
Water in play	Platz mit Wasser	▰▰▱▱▱
Exp. to wind	Wind ausgesetzt	▰▰▱▱▱
Trees in play	Platz mit Bäumen	▰▰▰▰▱

Scorecard Scorekarte	Chp. Chp.	Mens Herren	Ladies Damen
Length Länge	6073	5765	5158
Par	71	71	71

Advised golfing ability	0	12	24	36
Empfohlene Spielstärke		▰▰▰▰▱		
Hcp required Min. Handicap	36			

CLUB HOUSE & AMENITIES
KLUBHAUS UND NEBENGEBÄUDE
7/10

Pro shop	Pro shop	▰▰▰▰▱
Driving range	Übungsplatz	▰▰▰▰▱
Sheltered	überdacht	ja
On grass	auf Rasen	ja
Putting-green	Putting-grün	ja
Pitching-green	Pitching-grün	ja

347

HOTEL FACILITIES
HOTEL BESCHREIBUNG
6/10

HOTELS HOTELS
Bräuwastl — Weilheim
50 Zimmer, D DM 150,- — 9 km
Tel (49) 0881 - 4547, Fax (49) 0881 - 69 485

Vollmann — Weilheim
38 Zimmer, D DM 120,- — 9 km
Tel (49) 0881 - 4255, Fax (49) 0881 - 63 332

Strand Hotel — Diessen
18 Zimmer, D DM 270,- — 8 km
Tel (49) 08807 - 92 220, Fax (49) 08807 - 8958

Seefelder Hof — Diessen
22 Zimmer, D DM 175,- — 8 km
Tel (49) 08807 - 1023, Fax (49) 08807 - 1024

RESTAURANTS RESTAURANT
Seehaus — Diessen-Riederau
Tel (49) 08807 - 7300 — 12 km

Forsthaus Ilkahöhe, Tel (49) 08158 - 8242 Tutzing 12 km

Jeder nach seinem Geschmack. Wer Doglegs, Schräglagen, Schläge bergauf und bergab oder erhöhte Grüns nicht mag, der wird sich von Hoisdorf bewusst fernhalten. Dasselbe gilt für Golfer, denen es an Ausdauer mangelt. Umgekehrt findet dieser Kurs seine Anhängerschaft unter Spielern, die ein ungewöhnliches Platzprofil (zumindest für die Region Hamburg), herzhafte Märsche durch das Gelände, hügelige Plätze, Doglegs, Bergauf-Schläge u.s.w., mit anderen Worten all das lieben, was für Überraschungen auf der Scorekarte sorgt. Solche Golfer werden wieder und wieder kommen, um, ähnlich Schachspielern, mit Geduld und gründlicher Überlegung, letztendlich ein Gespür für den Platz und dessen Anforderungen zu entwickeln. Die besseren Spieler können hier ihre Kenntnisse über den Ballflug testen, andere profitieren von den Erfahrungen, die sie hier machen werden. Wenn Sie in der Gegend sind, empfehlen wir Ihnen Sich selbst ein Bild von diesem umstrittenen Platz zu machen.

Each to his own taste, as they say. People who don't like dog-legs, uphill shots, downhill shots, sloping lies or elevated greens will keep well away from Hoisdorf. The same goes for golfers short on stamina. By contrast, players who like unusually shaped courses (at least in the region of Hamburg), hearty strolls through the countryside, hilly courses, dog-legs, uphill shots, and so forth, in a word everything that can cause a surprise a two on your scorecard, will love it. They'll come once and even several times, in order to understand the course and get to grips with it, rather like a game of chess, i.e. with patience and careful thought. The best players will test their understanding of ballistics, others will gain from the experience. If you are in the region, you can judge this controversial course for yourself.

Golf-Club Hoisdorf e.V.
Hof Bornbek-Hoisdorf
D - 22592 LÜTJENSEE

Office	Sekretariat	(49) 04107 - 7831
Pro shop	Pro shop	(49) 04107 - 7647
Fax	Fax	(49) 04107 - 9934
Situation	Lage	

10 km von Ahrensburg, 27 000 Ew.
20 km von Hamburg, 1 650 000 Ew.

Annual closure	Jährliche Schliessung	nein
Weekly closure	Wöchentliche Schliessung	
	Montag, das Restaurant	

Fees main season Preisliste hochsaison 18 Löcher

	Week days Woche	We/Bank holidays We/Feiertag
Individual Individuell	DM 70,-	DM 80,-
Couple Ehepaar	DM 140,-	DM 160,-

We/Feiertage: nur in Mitgliederbegleitung
(with members) / - 21 Jahre : – 50%

Caddy	Caddy	nein
Electric Trolley	Elektrokarren	nein
Buggy	Elektrischer Wagen	nein
Clubs	Clubs	nein
Credit cards Kreditkarten		nein

348

Access Zufahrt : A1 Hamburg-Lübeck. Ausf. Ahrensburg. → Siek, Lütjensee. "Sieker Berg", rechts in der Strasse "Lunken". → Golfplatz.
Map 7 on page 304 Karte 7 Seite 304

GOLF COURSE
PLATZ
13/20

Site	Lage	
Maintenance	Instandhaltung	
Architect	Architekt	H. Peters
Type	Typ	Park
Relief	Relief	
Water in play	Platz mit Wasser	
Exp. to wind	Wind ausgesetzt	
Trees in play	Platz mit Bäumen	

Scorecard	Chp.	Mens	Ladies
Scorekarte	Chp.	Herren	Damen
Length Länge	6010	6010	5300
Par	71	71	71

Advised golfing ability	0	12	24	36
Empfohlene Spielstärke				
Hcp required	Min. Handicap	36		

CLUB HOUSE & AMENITIES
KLUBHAUS UND NEBENGEBÄUDE
6/10

Pro shop	Pro shop	
Driving range	Übungsplatz	
Sheltered	überdacht	3 Plätze
On grass	auf Rasen	ja
Putting-green	Putting-grün	ja
Pitching-green	Pitching-grün	nein

HOTEL FACILITIES
HOTEL BESCHREIBUNG
6/10

HOTELS HOTELS
Forsthaus Seebergen   Lütjensee
12 Zimmer, D DM 160,-   4 km
Tel (49) 04154 - 7182, Fax (49) 04154 - 70 645

Ringhotel Ahrensburg   Ahrensburg
11 Zimmer, D DM 160,-   4 km
Tel (49) 04102 - 51 560, Fax (49) 04102 - 515 656

Seehof   Lütjensee
6 Zimmer, D DM 190,-   4 km
Tel (49) 04154 - 7100, Fax (49) 04154 - 7101

Fischerklause   Lütjensee
15 Zimmer, D DM 160,-   5 km
Tel (49) 04154 - 7165, Fax (49) 04154 - 75 185

RESTAURANTS RESTAURANT
Forsthaus Seebergen   Lütjensee
Tel (49) 04154 - 79 290   4 km

Seehof, Tel (49) 04154 - 7100   Lütjensee 5 km

Hubbelrath gehört zu den Plätzen in Deutschland, die jeder kennen sollte. Er ist gleichzeitig eines der besten Beispiele für das Können Bernhard von Limburgers, dessen Kunst, sich das hier ziemlich hügelige Gelände zunutze zu machen, von wirklich grosser Inspiration zeugt. Aufgrund teilweise nicht immer erkennbarer Schwierigkeiten ist dies ein Platz für erfahrene Spieler. Eine gute Ballkontrolle vorausgesetzt, werden diese mit den Hindernissen besser zurechtkommen als der Rest, auch deswegen, weil sie sich von den vielen blinden Schlägen und Grüns weniger einschüchtern lassen. Die Hindernisse sind ebenso zahlreich wie gefährlich und können den Eindruck eines tückischen Platzes vermitteln. Man braucht schon einige Runden, um den Kurs einigermassen in den Griff zu bekommen, was aber angesichts des Vergnügens hier zu spielen, leicht zu verschmerzen ist. Abgeschirmt von der Hektik des Ruhrgebiets, befindet sich der Platz in erhöhter Lage auf einem bewaldeten Hügel, von wo sich schöne Blicke auf Düsseldorf und Ratingen eröffnen.

This is one of Germany's courses that everyone should know, and one of the finest testimonies to the skill of Bernhard von Limburger, whose use of a rather hilly terrain can only be described as truly inspired. The sometimes concealed difficulties make this a layout reserved for experienced players; if they know how to control the ball, they will cope with the hazards better than the rest and, importantly, will be somewhat less intimidated by a number of blind shots and greens. The hazards are as numerous as they are truly dangerous and can give you the impression of playing a treacherous course. You certainly need to play several rounds to get to grips with it, but it is always a pleasure to come back here. Sheltered from the rumbling Ruhr region, its elevated location on a wood-covered hill provides some fine views over Düsseldorf and Ratingen. Hubbelrath is a lovely walk and an exciting challenge of the highest order.

Golf Club Hubbelrath e.V.

Bergische Landtrasse 700
D - 40629 DÜSSELDORF

Office	Sekretariat	(49) 02104 - 72 178
Pro shop	Pro shop	(49) 02104 - 72 178
Fax	Fax	(49) 02104 - 72 178
Situation	Lage	

15 km von Düsseldorf, 570 000 Ew.
2 km von Mettmann, 40 000 Ew.

Annual closure	Jährliche Schliessung	nein
Weekly closure	Wöchentliche Schliessung	
	Montag, das Restaurant	

Fees main season
Preisliste hochsaison 18 Löcher

	Week days Woche	We/Bank holidays We/Feiertag
Individual Individuell	DM 100,-	DM 120,-
Couple Ehepaar	DM 200,-	DM 240,-

We: nur in Mitgliederbegleitung (with members)

Caddy	Caddy	DM 40,-
Electric Trolley	Elektrokarren	nein
Buggy	Elektrischer Wagen	nein
Clubs	Clubs	DM 20,-
Credit cards Kreditkarten		nein

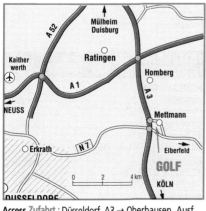

Access Zufahrt : Düsseldorf, A3 → Oberhausen. Ausf. Düsseldorf-Mettmann. B7 → Mettmann. 800 m, links → Golfplatz **Map 3 on page 296** Karte 3 Seite 296

GOLF COURSE
PLATZ
17 /20

Site	Lage	▰▰▰▱
Maintenance	Instandhaltung	▰▰▰▱
Architect	Architekt	B. von Limburger
Type	Typ	Wald, Gebirge
Relief	Relief	▰▰▰▰
Water in play	Platz mit Wasser	▰▱▱▱
Exp. to wind	Wind ausgesetzt	▰▰▱▱
Trees in play	Platz mit Bäumen	▰▰▰▱

Scorecard	Chp.	Mens	Ladies
Scorekarte	Chp.	Herren	Damen
Length Länge	6250	6053	5332
Par	72	72	72

Advised golfing ability		0 12 24 36
Empfohlene Spielstärke		▰▰▰▱
Hcp required	Min. Handicap	24

CLUB HOUSE & AMENITIES
KLUBHAUS UND NEBENGEBÄUDE
8 /10

Pro shop	Pro shop	▰▰▰▰
Driving range	Übungsplatz	▰▰▰▱
Sheltered	überdacht	11 Plätze
On grass	auf Rasen	nein
Putting-green	Putting-grün	ja
Pitching-green	Pitching-grün	ja

HOTEL FACILITIES
HOTEL BESCHREIBUNG
6 /10

HOTELS HOTELS

Hansa Hotel — Mettmann
178 Zimmer, D DM 250,- — 2 km
Tel (49) 02104 - 98 60, Fax (49) 02104 - 986 150

Alberga — Mettmann
47 Zimmer, D DM 200,- — 2 km
Tel (49) 02104 - 92 720, Fax (49) 02104 - 927 252

Gut Höhne — Mettmann
80 Zimmer, D DM 400,- — 1 km
Tel (49) 02104 - 77 80, Fax (49) 02104 - 75 625

RESTAURANTS RESTAURANT

Im Schiffchen — Düsseldorf
Tel (49) 0211 - 401 050 — 10 km

Am Weinberg — 400 m
Tel (49) 0211 - 289 333

349

Der zwischen Garmisch-Partenkirchen und München befindliche Teil Bayerns ist gesegnet mit zahlreichen Golfplätzen, von denen viele in die wunderschöne Voralpenlandschaft zwischen offenem Hügelland und Gebirgsszenerie eingebettet sind. Die meisten dieser Kurse sind naturgemäss ziemlich hügelig und damit ein echter Fitness-Test für die meist stadtverwöhnten Golfer. Iffeldorf ist in dieser Hinsicht ganz anders. Die Anlage ist ein ausgezeichnetes Beispiel für einen Golfplatz mit einem guten, wenn auch nicht herausragendem Design, das einerseits der ganzen Familie ungetrübtes Spielvergnügen bereitet, andererseits aber auch den guten Spielern genügend interessante Herausforderungen stellt. Das Layout ist sehr "ehrlich" und man findet die unterschiedlichsten Hindernisse vor, so dass der Kurs auch bei oftmaligem Spielen nicht langweilig wird. Das Sahnestück dieser qualitativ hochwertigen Anlage sind zweifellos die Grüns, die hervorragend gestaltet, von ausreichender Grösse und sorgfältig verteidigt sind.

From Garmisch-Partenkirchen to Munich, Bavaria is full of courses often set in wonderful landscapes between the open countryside and mountain scenery, doubtless a little hilly for town folk a great way to get fit again. The actual course is something else. It is a good example of an excellent golf course, well if not exceptionnally designed where all the family can play without any problem and where good players come face to face with interesting challenges. It is a very honest layout where difficulties are evenly spread around the course and varied enough to always enjoy coming back for more. The greens are of the same quality, well designed, reasonably sized and carefully protected.

Golfplatz Iffeldorf e.V.

Gut Rettenberg 3
D - 82393 IFFELDORF

Office	Sekretariat	(49) 08856 - 9255 55
Pro shop	Pro shop	(49) 08856 - 9255 20
Fax	Fax	(49) 08856 - 9255 59
Situation	Lage	

50 km von München, 1 300 000 Ew.
35 km von Garmisch-Partenkirchen, 26 500 Ew.

Annual closure	Jährliche Schliessung	nein
Weekly closure	Wöchentliche Schliessung	

Fees main season
Preisliste hochsaison 18 Löcher

	Week days Woche	We/Bank holidays We/Feiertag
Individual Individuell	DM 80,-	DM 100,-
Couple Ehepaar	DM 160,-	DM 200,-

Caddy	Caddy	DM 50,-
Electric Trolley	Elektrokarren	DM 25,-
Buggy	Elektrischer Wagen	DM 50,-
Clubs	Clubs	DM 20,-

Credit cards Kreditkarten
VISA - Eurocard - JCB

350

Access Zufahrt : A95 München → Garmisch. Ausf.
Iffeldorf-Penzberg. → Penzberg, Golf 200 m links
zum Gut Rettenberg.
Map 2 on page 294 Karte 2 Seite 294

GOLF COURSE
PLATZ 16/20

Site	Lage	
Maintenance	Instandhaltung	
Architect	Architekt	P. Postel
Type	Typ	Wald, Gebirge
Relief	Relief	
Water in play	Platz mit Wasser	
Exp. to wind	Wind ausgesetzt	
Trees in play	Platz mit Bäumen	

Scorecard Scorekarte	Chp. Chp.	Mens Herren	Ladies Damen
Length Länge	5904	5904	5234
Par	72	72	72

Advised golfing ability		0	12	24	36
Empfohlene Spielstärke					
Hcp required	Min. Handicap	nein			

CLUB HOUSE & AMENITIES
KLUBHAUS UND NEBENGEBÄUDE 7/10

Pro shop	Pro shop	
Driving range	Übungsplatz	
Sheltered	überdacht	3 Plätze
On grass	auf Rasen	ja
Putting-green	Putting-grün	ja
Pitching-green	Pitching-grün	ja

HOTEL FACILITIES
HOTEL BESCHREIBUNG 6/10

HOTELS HOTELS
Berggeist   Penzberg
46 Zimmer, D DM 175,-   4 km

Tel (49) 08856 - 8050Sterff   Seeshaupt
18 Zimmer, D DM 170,-   8 km
Tel (49) 08801 - 1711, Fax (49) 08856 - 2598

Gut Faistenberg   Faistenberg
10 Zimmer, D DM 200,-   10 km
Tel (49) 08179 - 1200

RESTAURANTS RESTAURANT
La Traviata   Golfplatz
Tel (49) 08856 - 9255 30

Der Golfplatz liegt oberhalb des "bayerischen Meers", wie der Chiemsee als grösster See des bayerischen Voralpenlandes auch häufig genannt wird. Auf einer seiner beiden Inseln findet man das Schloss "Herrenchiemsee", eine der Verrücktheiten König Ludwigs II, der hier eine Kopie von Versailles errichten wollte. Die Gegend ist touristisch stark erschlossen und bietet Nicht-Golfern zahlreiche Freizeitmöglichkeiten, unter denen ein Besuch, im weniger als eine Autostunde entfernten Salzburg, nicht fehlen darf. Der holländische Architekt Dudok van Heel hat hier einen Kurs entworfen, der, ohne grosse technische Schwierigkeiten, ganz auf die Bedürfnisse der Urlauber zugeschnitten ist. Trotzdem ist der Platz anspruchsvoll genug, um nicht uninteressant zu wirken. Nach einigen Runden hat man alle lauernden Gefahren entdeckt, und ist in der Lage, Bunkern und Wasser aus dem Weg zu gehen. Zudem kennt man dann die ideale Spiellinie auf den vielen, von grossen Bäumen gesäumten Fairways. Die Fairways sind von einladender Breite, so dass hier Spieler unterschiedlichen Niveaus problemlos zusammen in einem Flight spielen können.

A course over Chiemsee, or the lake of Bavaria, the region's largest facing the Alps with two pretty islands. One is the site of the "Herrenchiemsee", one of the whimsical notions of King Louis II (and in fact a carbon copy of the Château de Versailles). This is a busy tourist region with a lot to do and see for non-golfers, including a trip to Salzburg (less than an hour's drive). Dutch architect Dudok van Heel has designed a holiday course with no great technical difficulties, but tough enough to keep it interesting. Play it several times and you will discover the awaiting traps, perhaps be able to keep away from the bunkers and water and negotiate a way through the large trees that line many of the holes. With no steep contours, you can walk the course very easily, and players of all levels can play together.

Golfclub Im Chiemgau Chieming e.V.

Kötzing 1
D - 83339 CHIEMING

Office	Sekretariat	(49) 08669 - 7557
Pro shop	Pro shop	(49) 08669 - 7557
Fax	Fax	(49) 08669 - 78 153
Situation	Lage	

7 km von Chieming, 3 700 Ew.
18 km von Traunstein, 17 600 Ew.

Annual closure	Jährliche Schliessung	ja
		1/12→31/03
Weekly closure	Wöchentliche Schliessung	
		Montag, das Restaurant

Fees main season Preisliste hochsaison 18 Löcher

	Week days Woche	We/Bank holidays We/Feiertag
Individual Individuell	DM 70,-	DM 100,-
Couple Ehepaar	DM 140,-	DM 200,-

– 21 Jahre/Studenten: – 50%

Caddy	Caddy	nein
Electric Trolley	Elektrokarren	nein
Buggy	Elektrischer Wagen	nein
Clubs	Clubs	DM 35,-
Credit cards Kreditkarten		nein

Access Zufahrt : A8 München-Salzburg. Ausf. Grabenstätt. In Chieming → Laimgrub, Sondermoning. Links → Hart, Golfplatz → Knesing.
Map 2 on page 295 Karte 2 Seite 295

GOLF COURSE
PLATZ   14/20

Site	Lage	▰▰▰▱▱
Maintenance	Instandhaltung	▰▰▰▱▱
Architect	Architekt	Dudok van Heel
Type	Typ	Flachland
Relief	Relief	▰▰▱▱▱
Water in play	Platz mit Wasser	▰▰▱▱▱
Exp. to wind	Wind ausgesetzt	▰▰▱▱▱
Trees in play	Platz mit Bäumen	▰▰▰▱▱

Scorecard	Chp.	Mens	Ladies
Scorekarte	Chp.	Herren	Damen
Length Länge	6221	6069	5416
Par	72	72	72

Advised golfing ability		0	12	24	36
Empfohlene Spielstärke					
Hcp required	Min. Handicap	36			

CLUB HOUSE & AMENITIES
KLUBHAUS UND NEBENGEBÄUDE   7/10

Pro shop	Pro shop	▰▰▰▱▱
Driving range	Übungsplatz	▰▰▰▱▱
Sheltered	überdacht	5 Plätze
On grass	auf Rasen	ja
Putting-green	Putting-grün	ja
Pitching-green	Pitching-grün	ja (2)

HOTEL FACILITIES
HOTEL BESCHREIBUNG   6/10

HOTELS HOTELS
Unterwirt   Chieming
11 Zimmer, D DM 100,-   6 km
Tel (49) 08664 - 551, Fax (49) 08664 - 1649

Gut Ising   Chieming-Ising
105 Zimmer, D DM 300,-   3 km
Tel (49) 08667 - 790, Fax (49) 08667 - 79 432

Park-Hotel Traunsteiner Hof   Traunstein
59 Zimmer, D DM 180,-   20 km
Tel (49) 0861 - 69 041, Fax (49) 0861 - 8512

Eichenhof   Waging am See
34 Zimmer, D DM 240,-   30 km
Tel (49) 08681 - 4030, Fax (49) 08681 - 40 325

RESTAURANTS RESTAURANT
Gut Ising   Chieming-Ising
Tel (49) 08667 - 790   3 km

Malerwinkel, Tel (49) 08667 - 488   Seebruck, 7 km

351

Ein eher ländlicher Golfplatz, bei dem sich Wald- und Feldflächen abwechseln. Auf den ersten Neun spielt man durch teilweise enge, von alten Bäumen gesäumte Fairways, während die zweiten Neun in offenem Gelände liegen, wo sich hauptsächlich Junganpflanzungen finden. Dadurch gewinnt man den Eindruck, auf zwei unterschiedlichen Kursen zu spielen, auf die man sein Spiel anpassen muss. Während die ersten neun Löcher bei windigen Bedingungen guten Schutz bieten, halten die zweiten Neun für die Spieler einige Überraschungen bereit. Da die Hindernisse nicht immer deutlich erkennbar sind, bleibt wenig Hoffnung, den Platz auf Anhieb in den Griff zu bekommen. Die Anlage bietet in keiner Hinsicht Aussergewöhnliches, dennoch lohnt ein Besuch, wenn man eh in der Gegend ist. Von den hinteren Abschlägen ist der Platz relativ lang. Wenn man im Familien- oder Freundeskreis unterwegs ist, wo die Spielstärken häufig sehr unterschiedlich sind, empfiehlt es sich deshalb, von etwas weiter vorn zu spielen. Letzteres kommt sicher allen Mitspielern besonders an den wenigen, klug angelegten Wasserhindernissen, entgegen.

This is a country course with alternating woodland and farm landscapes. The course itself chops and changes, from narrow sections through already old trees (the front nine) to wider spaces with smaller saplings (the back nine), giving an impression of two rather different courses to which you need to adapt your game. When the wind blows, you are sheltered up to the 9th hole, but the back nine will have a few surprises in store. And since the hazards are not always clear to see, you can hardly hope to master the course first time around. This is a rather long course from the back tees, so move forward a touch to spend a good day's golfing, especially if you are playing with all the family or among friends of differing abilities. Then you can all cope together with the few very clever water hazards.

Golfclub Isernhagen e.V.

Gut Lohne
D - 30916 ISERNHAGEN

Office	Sekretariat	(49) 05139 - 89 3185
Pro shop	Pro shop	(49) 05139 - 2998
Fax	Fax	(49) 05139 - 27 033
Situation	Lage	

14 km von Hannover, 510 000 Ew.

Annual closure	Jährliche Schliessung	nein
Weekly closure	Wöchentliche Schliessung	Montag
		Das Restaurant

Fees main season
Preisliste hochsaison den ganzen Tag

	Week days Woche	We/Bank holidays We/Feiertag
Individual Individuell	DM 40,-	DM 60,-
Couple Ehepaar	DM 80,-	DM 120,-

Caddy	Caddy	nein
Electric Trolley	Elektrokarren	nein
Buggy	Elektrischer Wagen	ja
Clubs	Clubs	ja

Credit cards Kreditkarten	nein

GOLF COURSE
PLATZ
15/20

Site	Lage	▬▬▬▬▬▭
Maintenance	Instandhaltung	▬▬▬▬▭▭
Architect	Architekt	G. Bruns
Type	Typ	Wald, Flachland
Relief	Relief	
Water in play	Platz mit Wasser	▬▬▬▭▭▭
Exp. to wind	Wind ausgesetzt	▬▬▬▬▭▭
Trees in play	Platz mit Bäumen	▬▬▬▬▬▭

Scorecard Scorekarte	Chp. Chp.	Mens Herren	Ladies Damen
Length Länge	6379	6379	5631
Par	73	73	73

Advised golfing ability Empfohlene Spielstärke	0	12	24	36
Hcp required	Min. Handicap	34		

CLUB HOUSE & AMENITIES
KLUBHAUS UND NEBENGEBÄUDE
7/10

Pro shop	Pro shop	▬▬▭▭▭
Driving range	Übungsplatz	▬▬▬▭▭
Sheltered	überdacht	ja
On grass	auf Rasen	ja
Putting-green	Putting-grün	ja
Pitching-green	Pitching-grün	ja

HOTEL FACILITIES
HOTEL BESCHREIBUNG
6/10

HOTELS HOTELS

Queens Hotel — Hannover
176 Zimmer, D DM 260,- — 14 km
Tel (49) 0511 - 51 030, Fax (49) 0511 - 526 924

Sportpark Hotel — Hannover
40 Zimmer, D DM 160,- — 14 km
Tel (49) 0511 - 972 840, Fax (49) 0511 - 972 841

Parkhotel Welfenhof — Isernhagen
110 Zimmer, D DM 350,- — 2 km
Tel (49) 0511 - 65 406, Fax (49) 0511 - 651 050

RESTAURANTS RESTAURANT

Bakkarat im Kasino am Maschsee — Hannover
Tel (49) 0511 - 884 057 — 14 km

Maritim Seeterrassen — Hannover
Tel (49) 0511 - 884 057 — 14 km

Access Zufahrt : A7 Ausf. Kirchhorst. In Kirchhorst → Neuwarmbüchen. Links → Golfplatz Gut Lohne
Map 5 on page 301 Karte 5 Seite 301

JAKOBSBERG

Beheimatet in der Wiege der deutschen Romantik, liegt Jakobsberg auf einer Anhöhe, welche die schmalste Stelle des Rheintals überragt (tolle Ausblicke). Ganz in der Nähe befinden sich auch die Schlösser und der Fels der Lorelei. Der Platz selbst zählt zu den sehr guten Anlagen neueren Datums. Seine grossen Vorzüge liegen in der abwechslungsreichen Gestaltung der Löcher, sowie der klaren Erkennbarkeit der anzuwendenden Spieltaktik. Lediglich der Abschlag an Loch 5 und das Grünanspiel an Loch 17, wo man jeweils sehr auf der Hut sein muss, bilden in dieser Hinsicht eine Ausnahme. Loch 7 ist der einzige Schwachpunkt eines ansonsten sehr ausgewogenen Layouts, bei dem die Hindernisse (Bunker und Wasser) zwar immer im Spiel sind, aber niemals allzu bedrängend wirken. Dies wiederum ermöglicht ein reibungsloses Vorankommen bei Flights, die sich aus Spielern unterschiedlichen Niveaus zusammensetzen, sofern von den, dem Können Aller entsprechenden, Abschlägen gespielt wird.

Located in one of the cradles of German romanticism, overlooking the most boxed-in section of the Rhine valley (the views are superb) and close to the castles and the rock of Loreley, Jakobsberg is one of the very good recent courses. The variety of holes is an asset, as is the clarity of the tactics needed to play here, with the exception of the tee-shot on the 5th and the green on the 17th, which call for particular attention. The 7th is the only weak link on a course that is well-balanced overall, and where difficulties (bunkers and water) are in play but are never too oppressive. This means that players of all levels can get along well together, as long as they are wise enough to choose the right tees. In a region which such fascinating potential for tourists (landscapes, culture and vineyards), this course is a stop-off of considerable merit.

Golf-Club Jakobsberg
Im Tal der Loreley
D - 56154 BOPPARD-RHENS

Office	Sekretariat	(49) 06742 - 808 491
Pro shop	Pro shop	(49) 06742 - 808 496
Fax	Fax	(49) 06742 - 808 493
Situation	Lage	

10 km von Koblenz, 108 000 Ew.

Annual closure	Jährliche Schliessung	nein
Weekly closure	Wöchentliche Schliessung	nein

Fees main season
Preisliste hochsaison 18 Löcher

	Week days Woche	We/Bank holidays We/Feiertag
Individual Individuell	DM 70,-	DM 90,-
Couple Ehepaar	DM 140,-	DM 180,-
– 21 Jahre/Studenten: – 50%		
Caddy	Caddy	nein
Electric Trolley	Elektrokarren	DM 25,-
Buggy	Elektrischer Wagen	DM 50,-
Clubs	Clubs	DM 20,-

Credit cards Kreditkarten
VISA - Eurocard - MasterCard - AMEX - DC

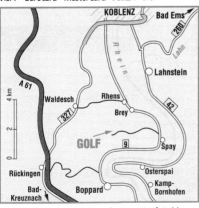

Access Zufahrt : A61 Mainz-Köln/Bonn. Ausf. Koblenz-Waldesch, → Rhens, B9 Brey. Rechts → Golfplatz.
Map 3 on page 296 Karte 3 Seite 296

GOLF COURSE
PLATZ **15**/20

Site	Lage	
Maintenance	Instandhaltung	
Architect	Architekt	Wolfgang Jersombek
Type	Typ	Flachland, Gebirge
Relief	Relief	
Water in play	Platz mit Wasser	
Exp. to wind	Wind ausgesetzt	
Trees in play	Platz mit Bäumen	

Scorecard Scorekarte	Chp. Chp.	Mens Herren	Ladies Damen
Length Länge	6351	6114	5363
Par	72	72	72

Advised golfing ability		0	12	24	36
Empfohlene Spielstärke					
Hcp required	Min. Handicap	nein			

CLUB HOUSE & AMENITIES
KLUBHAUS UND NEBENGEBÄUDE **7**/10

Pro shop	Pro shop	
Driving range	Übungsplatz	
Sheltered	überdacht	5 Plätze
On grass	auf Rasen	ja
Putting-green	Putting-grün	ja
Pitching-green	Pitching-grün	ja

353

HOTEL FACILITIES
HOTEL BESCHREIBUNG **6**/10

HOTELS HOTELS
Golfhotel Jakobsberg — Golfplatz
108 Zimmer, D DM 220,-
Tel (49) 06742 - 8080, Fax (49) 06742 - 3069
Bellevue — Boppard
94 Zimmer, D DM 300,- — 12 km
Tel (49) 06742 - 1020, Fax (49) 06742 - 102 602
Rebstock — Boppard
15 Zimmer, D DM 180,- — 12 km
Tel (49) 06742 - 4876, Fax (49) 06742 - 4877
Scandic Crown Hotel — Koblenz
168 Zimmer, D DM 320,- — 15 km
Tel (49) 0261 - 1360, Fax (49) 0261 - 136 1199

RESTAURANTS RESTAURANT
Königstuhl — Rhens
Tel (49) 02628 - 2244 — 3 km
Stresemann, Tel (49) 0261 - 15 464 — Koblenz, 15 km

Abgeschieden von der Aussenwelt, ist "Refrath" ein typischer Vertreter eines im traditionellen Stil erbauten Golfplatzes, bei dem der Waldcharakter dominiert, ohne das dabei der Eindruck von Weitläufigkeit verloren geht. Longhittern, die sich hier etwas beengt fühlen können, mag er ein wenig kurz erscheinen. Für Normalsterbliche hingegen ist er lang genug, nicht zuletzt weil der Weg zum Grün oft blockiert ist, wenn man die zahlreichen Doglegs nicht von der richtigen Seite anspielt. An Hindernissen gibt es neben einem kleinen Bach, der an einigen Löchern ins Spiel kommt, eine grosse Anzahl geschickt plazierter, teilweise tiefer Bunker, die bei ungenauen Schlägen eine Menge Probleme bereiten können. Spieler, die den Ball gerade schlagen, können zahlreiche Grüns auch mit der Variante "bump and run" anspielen, wenngleich grosses Können erforderlich ist, den Ball auf diese Weise nahe der Fahne zu plazieren. Immer makellos gepflegt, zeichnet sich das klare und ehrliche Layout von Köln besonders durch die abwechslungsreiche Gestaltung seiner Löcher - egal ob Par 5, Par 4 oder Par 3 -aus.

Withdrawn from the outside world, "Refrath" stands for the pure tradition of forest golf courses, without forasmuch being too narrow. It may certainly look a little short for the long-hitters, but it is long enough for the common mortal, who will see his or her path to the green irritatingly blocked if they take the dog-legs on the wrong side. Hazard-wise, there is just a little stream that comes into play on a few holes, but the very many bunkers, well located and sometimes very deep, will cause a lot of problems to wayward hitters. The straighter hitters can often bump and run their ball onto the greens, but getting close to the pin needs a lot of skill. Clear, honest and well up-kept, Köln stands out for the diversity of its holes, whether playing the par 5s, the par 4s or the three par 3s.

Golf- und Land Club Köln
Golfplatz 2, Bensberg-Refrath
D - 51429 BERGISCH-GLADBACH

Office	Sekretariat	(49) 02204 - 63 114
Pro shop	Pro shop	(49) 02204 - 69 192
Fax	Fax	(49) 02204 - 68 192
Situation	Lage	

20 km von Köln, 1 005 000 Ew.
3 km von Bergisch-Gladbach, 104 000 Ew.

Annual closure	Jährliche Schliessung	nein
Weekly closure	Wöchentliche Schliessung	Montag
		das Restaurant

Fees main season
Preisliste hochsaison 18 Löcher

	Week days Woche	We/Bank holidays We/Feiertag
Individual Individuell	DM 80,-	DM 100,-
Couple Ehepaar	DM 160,-	DM 200,-

Sonntag: nur in Mitgliederbegleitung (with members)

Caddy	Caddy	nein
Electric Trolley	Elektrokarren	ja
Buggy	Elektrischer Wagen	nein
Clubs	Clubs	ja
Credit cards Kreditkarten		nein

GOLF COURSE
PLATZ   **17** /20

Site	Lage	
Maintenance	Instandhaltung	
Architect	Architekt	B. von Limburger
Type	Typ	Wald
Relief	Relief	
Water in play	Platz mit Wasser	
Exp. to wind	Wind ausgesetzt	
Trees in play	Platz mit Bäumen	

Scorecard	Chp.	Mens	Ladies
Scorekarte	Chp.	Herren	Damen
Length Länge	6170	6170	5440
Par	72	72	72

Advised golfing ability	0	12	24	36
Empfohlene Spielstärke				

Hcp required	Min. Handicap	36. We : H.28, D. 35

CLUB HOUSE & AMENITIES
KLUBHAUS UND NEBENGEBÄUDE   **6** /10

Pro shop	Pro shop	
Driving range	Übungsplatz	
Sheltered	überdacht	6 Plätze
On grass	auf Rasen	ja
Putting-green	Putting-grün	ja
Pitching-green	Pitching-grün	ja

Access Zufahrt : A3 Frankfurt-Köln. Ausf. A4 → Olpe.
Ausf. Bergisch-Gladbach-Refrath. B55, 1.5 km.
→ Bensberg. Dolmanstr. rechts. Altrefratherstr.
Map 3 on page 294 Karte 3 Seite 294

HOTEL FACILITIES
HOTEL BESCHREIBUNG   **7** /10

HOTELS HOTELS
Waldhotel Mangold   Bensberg
21 Zimmer, D DM 250,-   3 km
Tel (49) 02204 - 95 550, Fax (49) 02204 - 955 560

Schlosshotel Lerbach   Bergisch-Gladbach
54 Zimmer, D DM 500,-   3 km
Tel (49) 02202 - 2040, Fax (49) 02202 - 204 940

Tannenhof Refrath   Refrath
34 Zimmer, D DM 250,-   2 km
Tel (49) 02204 - 67 085, Fax (49) 02204 - 21 773

RESTAURANTS RESTAURANT
Restaurant Dieter Müller   Bergisch-Gladbach
Tel (49) 02202 - 2040   3 km

Eggemans Bürgerhaus   Bergisch-Gladbach
Tel (49) 02202 - 36 134   3 km

Dieser Teil des Schwarzwaldes zwischen Schwenningen und Freiburg-im-Breisgau ist seit langem ein touristischer Anziehungspunkt und lohnt in der Zeit von Frühling (der hier meist früher kommt als im übrigen Deutschland) bis Herbst einen romantischen Kurzaufenthalt. Golf ist sicher nicht die Hauptattraktion dieser Gegend, deren hügeliges Landschaftsprofil sich für den diesen Sport auch nicht sonderlich eignet, dennoch hat dieser Platz einige Löcher die einen Besuch lohnen, sofern man dafür keinen grossen Umweg in Kauf nehmen muss. Der Platz ist eng und aufgrund einiger blinder oder erhöht angelegter Grüns auch ziemlich "tricky", und bereitet einem damit ständig Kopfzerbrechen bei der Schlägerwahl. Hindernisse gibt es genug, diese sind aber keineswegs unbezwingbar. Spieler, die mit dem Ball einigermassen umgehen können sollten hier gut zurechtkommen. Königsfeld - schön gelegen mit einem weniger schönen Clubhaus - ist etwas für Golfer mit guter Kondition, denen Entspannung wichtiger ist als ein guter Score.

This region of the Black Forest has long been a top spot for tourism and is well worth a short romantic visit between Schwennigen and Freiburg-im-Breisgau, from spring (generally earlier here than in the rest of Germany) to autumn (wunderbar!). Golf was not the prime concern here, as the rather hilly terrain is hardly ideal, but a few holes make a visit worthwhile if it means not going too far out of your way. The course is tight and rather tricky as a whole, with a few blind or elevated greens, and the choice of club is never obvious. There is no shortage of hazards, although these are not insurmountable. A goodish player who can (deliberately) flight the ball a little should come to terms with it. On a site that is much more pleasant than the clubhouse, Königsfeld is fine for players in good physical shape who are looking more for relaxation than a brilliant score.

Golf und Country Club Königsfeld e.V.
Angelmoos 20
D - 78126 KÖNIGSFELD-MARTINSWEILER

Office	Sekretariat	(49) 07725 - 93 960
Pro shop	Pro shop	(49) 07725 - 7459
Fax	Fax	(49) 07725 - 939 612
Situation	Lage	

10 km von Villingen-Schwenningen, 80 000 Ew.

Annual closure	Jährliche Schliessung	ja
		1/11→31/03
Weekly closure	Wöchentliche Schliessung	nein

Fees main season
Preisliste hochsaison den ganzen Tag

	Week days Woche	We/Bank holidays We/Feiertag
Individual Individuell	DM 60,-	DM 90,-
Couple Ehepaar	DM 120,-	DM 180,-

Caddy	Caddy	nein
Electric Trolley	Elektrokarren	nein
Buggy	Elektrischer Wagen	nein
Clubs	Clubs	DM 20,-
Credit cards Kreditkarten		nein

Access Zufahrt : A8 Stuttgart-Singen.
Ausf. Villingen-Schwenningen → St Georgen.
Mönchweiler, → Königsfeld, → Golfplatz.
Map 1 on page 293 Karte 1 Seite 293

GOLF COURSE
PLATZ   13/20

Site	Lage	■■■■■□
Maintenance	Instandhaltung	■■■■■□
Architect	Architekt	
Type	Typ	Gebirge, Flachland
Relief	Relief	■■■■□□
Water in play	Platz mit Wasser	■■□□□□
Exp. to wind	Wind ausgesetzt	■■■□□□
Trees in play	Platz mit Bäumen	■■■□□□

Scorecard Scorekarte	Chp. Chp.	Mens Herren	Ladies Damen
Length Länge	6167	6167	5427
Par	70	70	70

Advised golfing ability Empfohlene Spielstärke	0	12	24	36
Hcp required Min. Handicap	nein			

CLUB HOUSE & AMENITIES
KLUBHAUS UND NEBENGEBÄUDE   6/10

Pro shop	Pro shop	■■■■□□
Driving range	Übungsplatz	■■■□□□
Sheltered	überdacht	4 Plätze
On grass	auf Rasen	ja (Sommer)
Putting-green	Putting-grün	ja
Pitching-green	Pitching-grün	ja

355

HOTEL FACILITIES
HOTEL BESCHREIBUNG   6/10

HOTELS HOTELS
Fewotel Schwarzwaldtreff   Königsfeld
127 Zimmer, D DM 220,-   1 km
Tel (49) 07725 - 8080, Fax (49) 07725 - 808 808

Ochsen   Schönwald
37 Zimmer, D DM 200,-   2 km
Tel (49) 07722 - 1045, Fax (49) 07722 - 3018

Bosse   Villingen
36 Zimmer, D DM 160,-   8 km
Tel (49) 07721 - 58 011, Fax (49) 07721 - 58 013

Sonne   Obereschach
16 Zimmer, D DM 90,-   5 km
Tel (49) 07720 - 95 160, Fax (49) 07720 - 951 650

RESTAURANTS RESTAURANT
Rapp   Burgberg
Tel (49) 07725 - 7621   3 km

Ochsen ,Tel (49) 07722 - 1045   Schönwald 1 km

Der Platz ist typisch für eine Zeit, in der den Architekten weder die technischen noch die finanziellen Mittel zur Verfügung standen, das Gelände grundlegend zu verändern. So folgen die Spielbahnen den kleinen, natürlichen Unebenheiten des Geländes und führen durch teilweise sehr enge, baumgesäumte Fairwayschluchten, was den Spielern präzise Schläge abverlangt. Bei den zehn als Dogleg verlaufenden Bahnen erweist sich eine Draw vom Abschlag als sehr hilfreich. Strategische Überlegungen erfordert in erster Linie das Anspiel der Grüns, die mittelgross, leicht gewellt und halbwegs gut verteidigt sind. "Bump and run" Schläge empfehlen sich nur während der Sommermonate, wenn der Boden hart und trocken ist, ansonsten muss man versuchen die Grüns mit hohen Pitch- und Lobschlägen anzugreifen. Putten ist in den seltensten Fällen eine Formsache, doch wird einem dieser Platz in der Hinsicht wenig Ungemach bereiten. Wasser ist kaum im Spiel, so erkennt man schnell, dass dies die Art von Platz ist, an dem Schläge vorwiegend durch unpräzises Spiel eingebüsst werden.

This course is typical of an age when designers did not have the financial resources to change the lie of the land. It hugs the lightly rolling natural contours and winds its way (sometimes very tightly) through trees, which call for some straight hitting. A draw off the tee will come in handy as well to cope with the ten dog-legs. The basic strategy lies before you reach the greens, since these are mid-sized, moderately contoured and averagely well-guarded. Bump and run shots are recommended only in summer, when the ground is dry enough, otherwise this is a place for pitchers and lobbers. Actual putting is hardly a formality, but there are few nasty surprises in store. As water is only rarely in play, you will soon realise that this is the kind of course where you insidiously drop strokes through lack of accuracy.

Krefelder Golf Club e.V.

Eltweg 2
D - 47748 KREFELD-LINN

Office	Sekretariat	(49) 02151 - 570 071
Pro shop	Pro shop	(49) 02151 - 520 128
Fax	Fax	(49) 02151 - 572 486
Situation	Lage	

6 km von Krefeld, 242 000 Ew.

Annual closure	Jährliche Schliessung	nein

Weekly closure	Wöchentliche Schliessung	Montag, das Restaurant

Fees main season	Preisliste hochsaison	den ganzen Tag	
		Week days Woche	We/Bank holidays We/Feiertag
Individual Individuell		DM 70,-	DM 90,-
Couple Ehepaar		DM 140,-	DM 180,-

We: nur in Mitgliederbegleitung (with members)
- 21 Jahre/Studenten : – 50%

Caddy	Caddy	auf Reserv. DM 30,-
Electric Trolley	Elektrokarren	nein
Buggy	Elektrischer Wagen	nein
Clubs	Clubs	DM 15,-

Credit cards Kreditkarten	nein

Access Zufahrt : A57 Köln-Moers. Ausf. Krefeld-Oppum.
Erste Ampel rechts, nächste Ampel, rechts →
Autobahnbrücke. → Golfplatz.
Map 3 on page 296 Karte 3 Seite 296

GOLF COURSE
PLATZ
17 /20

Site	Lage	
Maintenance	Instandhaltung	
Architect	Architekt	B. von Limburger
Type	Typ	Wald
Relief	Relief	
Water in play	Platz mit Wasser	
Exp. to wind	Wind ausgesetzt	
Trees in play	Platz mit Bäumen	

Scorecard Scorekarte	Chp. Chp.	Mens Herren	Ladies Damen
Length Länge	6060	6060	5333
Par	72	72	72

Advised golfing ability Empfohlene Spielstärke	0 12 24 36
Hcp required	Min. Handicap	28

CLUB HOUSE & AMENITIES
KLUBHAUS UND NEBENGEBÄUDE
7 /10

Pro shop	Pro shop	
Driving range	Übungsplatz	
Sheltered	überdacht	6 Plätze
On grass	auf Rasen	ja
Putting-green	Putting-grün	ja
Pitching-green	Pitching-grün	ja

HOTEL FACILITIES
HOTEL BESCHREIBUNG
7 /10

HOTELS HOTELS

Parkhotel Krefelder Hof — Krefeld — 6 km
150 Zimmer, D DM 350,-
Tel (49) 02151 - 5840, Fax (49) 02151 - 58 435

Garden Hotel — Krefeld — 6 km
51 Zimmer, D DM 200,-
Tel (49) 02151 - 590 296, Fax (49) 02151 - 590 299

Hansa Hotel — Krefeld — 8 km
107 Zimmer, D DM 300,-
Tel (49) 02151 - 8290, Fax (49) 02151 - 829 150

Dorint Sport-und Country-Hotel — Krefeld-Traar — 15 km
158 Zimmer, D DM 250,-
Tel (49) 02151 - 9560, Fax (49) 02151 - 956 100

RESTAURANTS RESTAURANT

Koperpot — Krefeld — 8 km
Tel (49) 02151 - 614 814

Aquilon — Krefeld — 8 km
Tel (49) 02151 - 800 207

356

LICHTENAU-WEICKERSHOF 15 7 6

Der Golfplatz befindet sich in unmittelbarer Nachbarschaft der Kleinstadt Ansbach, deren Ortsbild mit seiner Mischung aus mittelalterlichen und barocken Elementen noch heute an die Familie der Hohenzollern erinnert, denen die Stadt einst Ruhm und höfisches Leben verdankte. Der Platz selbst ist eingebettet in eine typisch fränkische Landschaft. Die ersten neun Löcher führen durch hügeliges Gelände, während die zweiten Neun auf flachem, offenem Terrain liegen. Die Bemühungen um die Erhaltung des natürlichen Ökosystems der zum Golfgelände gehörenden Wälder und Wasserläufe haben dem Platz 1994 einen Sonderpreis für Umweltschutz-Massnahmen eingebracht. Eine respektable Länge sowie zahlreiche Hindernisse lassen den Kurs eher für gute Golfer geeignet erscheinen, doch selbst denen wird es nicht leicht fallen wird, hier ihr Handicap zu spielen. Dies liegt zum einen an den recht eigenwilligen, aber gut erkennbaren Hindernissen, wie auch an den enorm grossen, hervorragend gestalteten und gut verteidigten Grüns.

Here, we are next door to Ansbach, a small town mingling memories of the Middle Ages and the baroque era, which owed its fame and court life to a Hohenzollern lineage. The course is located in a typical Franconia landscape, with alternating rolling hills and flat open land. It cares enough for its appearance and for the balance of an ecosystem of woods and streams to have won a special award in 1994 for environmental protection. Very respectable yardage and the number of hazards make this a course more for the good golfer, who will be hard pushed to play to his or her handicap owing to the course's difficulties (well visible first time around) and the greens, which are huge, well-contoured and well-guarded. It doesn't have quite the personality to be rated amongst the best, but it does deserve a visit.

Golf- und Landclub Lichtenau-Weickershof e.V.

Weickershof 1
D - 91586 LICHTENAU

Office	Sekretariat	(49) 09827 - 920 40
Pro shop	Pro shop	(49) 09827 - 7288
Fax	Fax	(49) 09827 - 920 444
Situation	Lage	

40 km von Nürnberg, 498 000 Ew. 15 km von Ausbach
Annual closure Jährliche Schliessung ja
30/11→28/02
Weekly closure Wöchentliche Schliessung Montag
Das Restaurant
Fees main season Preisliste hochsaison den ganzen Tag

	Week days Woche	We/Bank holidays We/Feiertag
Individual Individuell	DM 60,-	DM 80,-
Couple Ehepaar	DM 120,-	DM 160,-

Caddy	Caddy	auf Reservierung
Electric Trolley	Elektrokarren	ja
Buggy	Elektrischer Wagen	ja
Clubs	Clubs	ja

Credit cards Kreditkarten
VISA - Eurocard - MasterCard - AMEX

Access Zufahrt : BAB A6 Nürnberg-Heilbronn. Ausf.
Lichtenau. → Golf
Map 4 on page 298 Karte 4 Seite 298

GOLF COURSE PLATZ 15/20

Site	Lage	
Maintenance	Instandhaltung	
Architect	Architekt	
Type	Typ	Park, Land
Relief	Relief	
Water in play	Platz mit Wasser	
Exp. to wind	Wind ausgesetzt	
Trees in play	Platz mit Bäumen	

Scorecard	Chp.	Mens	Ladies
Scorekarte	Chp.	Herren	Damen
Length Länge	6218	6218	5472
Par	72	72	72

Advised golfing ability		0 12 24 36
Empfohlene Spielstärke		
Hcp required	Min. Handicap	35

CLUB HOUSE & AMENITIES KLUBHAUS UND NEBENGEBÄUDE 7/10

Pro shop	Pro shop	
Driving range	Übungsplatz	
Sheltered	überdacht	6 PLätze
On grass	auf Rasen	ja
Putting-green	Putting-grün	ja
Pitching-green	Pitching-grün	ja

357

HOTEL FACILITIES HOTEL BESCHREIBUNG 6/10

HOTELS HOTELS
Am Drechselgarten — Ansbach
85 Zimmer, D DM 220,- — 15 km
Tel (49) 0981 - 89 020, Fax (49) 0981 - 890 2605

Gasthof Sonne — Neuendettelsau
37 Zimmer, D DM 150,- — 10 km
Tel (49) 09874 - 5080, Fax (49) 09874 - 50 818

Bürger-Palais — Ansbach
12 Zimmer, D DM 220,- — 15 km
Tel (49) 0981 - 95 131, Fax (49) 0981 - 95 600

RESTAURANTS RESTAURANT
Weinstube Leidl — Lichtenau
Tel (49) 09827 - 528 — 1 km

Gasthaus um Hochspessart — Lichtenau
Tel (49) 09352 - 1228 — 2 km

Der Golfplatz wurde rund um das Schloss Schönbühl angelegt, und verfügt über ein modernes, sehr komfortables Clubhaus mit einem hervorragenden Restaurant. Die Lage selbst ist beeindruckend, bietet sie doch schöne Ausblicke über den tiefer gelegenen Bodensee und auf die nahen Alpengipfel. In dieser Region grenzen drei Länder aneinander - Deutschland, Österreich und die Schweiz. Daher rührt die Vielfalt der touristischen Attraktionen, über denen man beinahe den Golfsport vergessen könnte. Dies wäre jedoch schade, denn obwohl der Platz weder in spieltechnischer noch ästhetischer Hinsicht Herausragendes bietet, zählt er doch zum besseren Durchschnitt. Mittelklasse-Spielern, deren Streben einem gemütlichen Golftag gilt, bereitet der Kurs keine grossen Schwierigkeiten. Aus demselben Grund werden ihn bessere Spieler nicht sonderlich aufregend finden. Letzteren sei empfohlen, sich auf der Runde um die schwächeren Golfer in der Familie zu kümmern, ohne Gefahr zu laufen, sich dadurch den eigenen Score zu ruinieren.

This course is laid out around the castle of Schönbühl, with a modern and very comfortable club-house which includes a very good restaurant. The site itself is quite remarkable, with some superb views over the Bodensee (with the Mainau Island down below) and the peaks of the Alps. This region lies at the crossroads between three countries - Germany, Austria and Switzerland - so there is much for tourists to see and do, perhaps almost enough to coax you off the golf-course. That would be a shame, because although not an exceptional layout in terms of golfing or style, this course rates well above average. It should hardly pose too many problems for average players whose first desire is to spend a relaxing day, but by the same token it will hardly excite the more proficient golfers. They can make up for it by helping the lesser golfers in the family without too much risk of spoiling their own card.

Golf-Club Lindau-Bad Schachen e.V.
Am Schönbühl 5
D - 88131 LINDAU

Office	Sekretariat	(49) 08382 - 78 090
Pro shop	Pro shop	(49) 08382 - 78 090
Fax	Fax	(49) 08382 - 78 998
Situation	Lage	

1,5 km von Lindau, 25 000 Ew.

Annual closure	Jährliche Schliessung	nein
Weekly closure	Wöchentliche Schliessung	Montag
		das Restaurant

Fees main season
Preisliste hochsaison 18 Löcher

	Week days Woche	We/Bank holidays We/Feiertag
Individual Individuell	DM 80,-	DM 100,-
Couple Ehepaar	DM 160,-	DM 200,-

– 21 Jahre/Studenten : – 50 %

Caddy	Caddy	nein
Electric Trolley	Elektrokarren	nein
Buggy	Elektrischer Wagen	nein
Clubs	Clubs	nein
Credit cards Kreditkarten		nein

Access Zufahrt : A96 München-Lindau. Ausf.
Sigmarszell. 3 km → Golfplatz
Map 1 on page 293 Karte 1 Seite 293

GOLF COURSE
PLATZ   14/20

Site	Lage	▬▬▬
Maintenance	Instandhaltung	▬▬▬
Architect	Architekt	
Type	Typ	Park
Relief	Relief	▬▬▬
Water in play	Platz mit Wasser	▬▬▬
Exp. to wind	Wind ausgesetzt	▬▬▬
Trees in play	Platz mit Bäumen	▬▬▬

Scorecard Scorekarte	Chp. Chp.	Mens Herren	Ladies Damen
Length Länge	5871	5677	5004
Par	71	71	71

Advised golfing ability Empfohlene Spielstärke		0 12 24 36
Hcp required	Min. Handicap	36

CLUB HOUSE & AMENITIES
KLUBHAUS UND NEBENGEBÄUDE   7/10

Pro shop	Pro shop	▬▬▬
Driving range	Übungsplatz	▬▬▬
Sheltered	überdacht	4 Plätze
On grass	auf Rasen	nein
Putting-green	Putting-grün	ja
Pitching-green	Pitching-grün	ja

HOTEL FACILITIES
HOTEL BESCHREIBUNG   8/10

HOTELS HOTELS
Bad Schachen   Lindau-Bad Schachen
110 Zimmer, D DM 300,-   1 km
Tel (49) 08382 - 29 80, Fax (49) 08382 - 25 390

Parkhotel Eden   Lindau-Bad Schachen
26 Zimmer, D DM 180,-   1 km
Tel (49) 08382 - 58 16, Fax (49) 08382 - 23 730

Bayerischer Hof   Lindau-Insel
104 Zimmer, D DM 400,-   2 km
Tel (49) 08382 - 91 50, Fax (49) 08382 - 915 591

RESTAURANTS RESTAURANT
Hoyerberg Schlössle   Lindau
Tel (49) 08382 - 25 295   1 km

Schachener Hof   Lindau-Bad Schachen 1 km
Tel (49) 08382 - 31 16

LÜNEBURGER HEIDE

17	7	5

Dieser nicht allzu lange, dafür hügelige und körperlich durchaus anstrengende Golfplatz, sollte von den Spielern in keinem Fall unterschätzt werden. Die geschickte Ausnutzung des Geländes spricht für die hervorragenden Golfkenntnisse der Architekten. Die ersten 11 Löcher sind recht eng von Wald begrenzt, so dass Genauigkeit vom Abschlag hier oberstes Gebot ist. Glücklicherweise reicht anstelle des Drivers häufig schon ein Holz 3 oder ein langes Eisen, um in eine Position zu gelangen, von der aus man die Grüns attackieren kann. Letzteres gilt insbesondere für Spieler, die den Ball gut kontrollieren können. Andererseits sind die Grüns in diesem Teil des Platzes nicht sonderlich gut verteidigt. Bei den restlichen Löchern findet man zwar breitere Fairways vor, dafür sind hier die Grüns teilweise erhöht und auch wesentlich besser geschützt. Ein "ehrlicher" Platz auf dem man, trotz leicht zu lesender Grüns, für einen guten Score hart arbeiten muss.

The very reasonable length of this course (pretty hilly and calling for a degree of physical fitness) should not result in golfers underestimating it before their round. The way the land has been used points to an excellent knowledge of the game by its designers. The first eleven holes are narrowish and laid out in a clearly demarcated forest, so accuracy off the tee is the order of the day. Fortunately, the driver can easily be left in the bag, especially since a 3-wood or a long iron is generally enough to find the right spot to attack the greens, particularly for players who can flight the ball. In contrast, the greens on this part of the course are not too heavily guarded. The fairways then grow wider, but, nothing is ever perfect, the greens are better protected and sometimes elevated, although reading them poses no particular problem. An honest course, but you have to work hard for a good score.

Hamburger Land- und Golf Club in der Lüneburger Heide

Am Golfplatz 24
D - 21218 SEEVETAL

Office	Sekretariat	(49) 04105 - 23 31
Pro shop	Pro shop	(49) 04105 - 23 51
Fax	Fax	(49) 04105 - 52 571
Situation	Lage	

2 km von Hittfeld
5 km von Buchholz, 33 000 Ew.

Annual closure	Jährliche Schliessung	nein

Weekly closure	Wöchentliche Schliessung	nein

Fees main season Preisliste hochsaison 18 Löcher

	Week days Woche	We/Bank holidays We/Feiertag
Individual Individuell	DM 60,-	DM 80,-
Couple Ehepaar	DM 120,-	DM 160,-

– 25 Jahre : – 50%

Caddy	Caddy	nein
Electric Trolley	Elektrokarren	nein
Buggy	Elektrischer Wagen	nein
Clubs	Clubs	nein
Credit cards Kreditkarten		nein

Access Zufahrt : A7/E45 Flensburg → Hannover.
Exit Fleestedt → Hittfeld. 2 km Rechts,
Natenbergweg. 1 km, Golfplatz.
Map 7 on page 304 Karte 7 Seite 304

GOLF COURSE PLATZ

17/20

Site	Lage	▬▬▬▬▬▬▬▭
Maintenance	Instandhaltung	▬▬▬▬▬▬▭▭
Architect	Architekt	J. Morrison Gärtner
Type	Typ	Wald
Relief	Relief	▬▬▬▬▬▬▬▭
Water in play	Platz mit Wasser	▬▭▭▭▭▭▭▭
Exp. to wind	Wind ausgesetzt	▬▬▬▭▭▭▭▭
Trees in play	Platz mit Bäumen	▬▬▬▬▬▬▬▭

Scorecard Scorekarte	Chp. Chp.	Mens Herren	Ladies Damen
Length Länge	5903	5903	5202
Par	71	71	71

Advised golfing ability		0	12	24	36
Empfohlene Spielstärke			▬▬▬▬▬▭▭		
Hcp required	Min. Handicap	nein			

CLUB HOUSE & AMENITIES KLUBHAUS UND NEBENGEBÄUDE

7/10

Pro shop	Pro shop	▬▬▬▬▬▬▭▭
Driving range	Übungsplatz	▬▬▬▬▬▭▭▭
Sheltered	überdacht	6 Plätze
On grass	auf Rasen	ja
Putting-green	Putting-grün	ja
Pitching-green	Pitching-grün	ja

359

HOTEL FACILITIES HOTEL BESCHREIBUNG

5/10

HOTELS HOTELS

Hotel Seppenser Mühle	Holm/Seppensen
21 Zimmer, D DM 140,-	14 km

Tel (49) 04187 - 69 50, Fax (49) 04187 - 69 09

Hotel Krohwinkel	Hittfeld
7 Zimmer, D DM 165	3 km

Tel (49) 04105 - 24 09, Fax (49) 04105 - 53 799

RESTAURANTS RESTAURANT

Hotel Krohwinkel	Hittfeld
Tel (49) 04105 - 24 09	3 km

Hotel Seppenser Mühle	Holm/Seppensen
Tel (49) 04187 - 69 50	14 km

MAIN-TAUNUS

13	7	6

Die Lage von Main-Taunus zwischen Wiesbaden und Frankfurt ist ein beachtlicher Vorzug, der zum Teil für die nahe Luftwaffenbasis und den häufigen Blick auf eine Zementfabrik entschädigt. Eine weitere Stärke liegt in der Handschrift Bernhard von Limburgers, auch wenn dieser Platz sicherlich nicht zu dessen besten Arbeiten zählt. Die Junganpflanzungen auf diesem offenen Gelände werden in absehbarer Zeit die intime Atmosphäre dieser Anlage noch verstärken. Als Hindernisse sind die Bäume jedoch keineswegs unüberwindlich. Im Gegensatz dazu kann das Wasser durchaus zum Problem werden. Es kommt bei etwa 10 Löchern ins Spiel und ist der Preis, der für einen Golfplatz mitten in einem Vogelschutzgebiet zu zahlen ist. Die nicht übermässig stark bebunkerten Grüns sind von guter Qualität, allerdings mangelt es ihnen nach heutigem Standard etwas an Form und Gestaltung. Dieser klassische Parcours hat ein höchst interessantes und schwieriges Finish, bei dem einem - zumindest auf der ersten Runde - eine Lochbeschreibung sehr gelegen kommt, um die lauernden Hindernisse auszumalen.

The position of Main-Taunus between Wiesbaden and Frankfurt is a considerable advantage, which in part makes up for the closeness of a neighbouring air-base and frequent views of a cement factory. Another strong point is the Bernhard von Limburger label, even though this is not one of his most inspired works. Over this open land, the saplings should eventually add to the intimate atmosphere, but the trees in general are not insurmountable hazards. By contrast, the water can be a problem, coming into play on ten or so holes, a fair price to pay for designing a course in a natural bird reserve. The greens are good but not over-guarded, and to modern standards lack a little surface relief. This rather classic design has an intriguing and tough finish, where a map of the course will come in handy.

Golf-Club Main-Taunus e.V.

Lange Seegewann 2
D - 65205 WIESBADEN-DELKENHEIM

Office	Sekretariat	(49) 06122 - 52 550
Pro shop	Pro shop	(49) 06122 - 935 078
Fax	Fax	(49) 06122 - 936 099
Situation	Lage	

12 km von Wiesbaden, 271 000 Ew.
19 km von Frankfurt, 660 000 Ew.

Annual closure	Jährliche Schliessung	nein
Weekly closure	Wöchentliche Schliessung	Montag
		Das Restaurant

Fees main season Preisliste hochsaison 18 Löcher

	Week days Woche	We/Bank holidays We/Feiertag
Individual Individuell	DM 80,-	DM 100,-
Couple Ehepaar	DM 160,-	DM 200,-
– 21 Jahre, Studenten: – 50 %		

Caddy	Caddy	nein
Electric Trolley	Elektrokarren	ja
Buggy	Elektrischer Wagen	ja
Clubs	Clubs	nein

Credit cards Kreditkarten VISA - CB - Eurocard -
MasterCard - AMEX - DC - JCB - Cofinoga

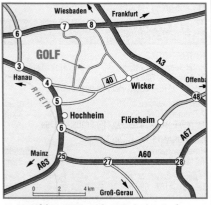

GOLF
Wiesbaden • Frankfurt
Hanau • Wicker • Offenba
RHEIN • Hochheim • Flörsheim
Mainz • A63 • Groß-Gerau

Access Zufahrt : A66 Frankfurt-Wiesbaden. Ausf.
Wiesbaden Nordenstadt. → Delkenheim, Hochheim.
Map 3 on page 297 Karte 3 Seite 297

360

GOLF COURSE
PLATZ
13/20

Site	Lage	▮▮
Maintenance	Instandhaltung	▮▮▮
Architect	Architekt	B. von Limburger
Type	Typ	Flachland
Relief	Relief	▮▮
Water in play	Platz mit Wasser	▮▮▮▮
Exp. to wind	Wind ausgesetzt	▮▮▮▮▮
Trees in play	Platz mit Bäumen	▮▮▮

Scorecard Scorekarte	Chp. Chp.	Mens Herren	Ladies Damen
Length Länge	6133	5925	5216
Par	72	72	72

Advised golfing ability		0	12	24	36
Empfohlene Spielstärke			▭		

Hcp required Min. Handicap 36

CLUB HOUSE & AMENITIES
KLUBHAUS UND NEBENGEBÄUDE
7/10

Pro shop	Pro shop	▮▮▮▮
Driving range	Übungsplatz	▮▮▮
Sheltered	überdacht	6 Plätze
On grass	auf Rasen	ja
Putting-green	Putting-grün	ja
Pitching-green	Pitching-grün	ja

HOTEL FACILITIES
HOTEL BESCHREIBUNG
6/10

HOTELS HOTELS

Nassauer Hof — Wiesbaden
202 Zimmer, D DM 500,- — 10 km
Tel (49) 0611 - 13 30, Fax (49) 0611 - 133 625

Treff Hotel Rhein-Main — Wiesbaden-Nordenstadt
150 Zimmer, D DM 215,- — 5 km
Tel (49) 06122 - 80 10, Fax (49) 06122 - 801 164

Burkartsmühle — Hofheim
28 Zimmer, D DM 260,- — 7 km
Tel (49) 06192 - 25 088, Fax (49) 06192 - 26 869

RESTAURANTS RESTAURANT

Die Ente vom Lehel — Wiesbaden
Tel (49) 0611 - 133 666 — 10 km

Estragon — Wiesbaden
Tel (49) 0611 - 303 906 — 10 km

PEUGEOT GOLF GUIDE 1998

Der Westen Berlins ist durchzogen von Kanälen und Seen und Potsdam gilt als historisches Zentrum mit dem wunderschönen Schloss Sanssouci und dem beeindruckenden Neuen Palais, die von Friedrich II von Preussen, einem aufgeklärten und kultivierten Herrscher sowie einem Freund Voltaires, erstellt wurden. Eine Besichtigung der Räumlichkeiten und des 300 Hektaren grossen Parks sollte man nicht verpassen. Etwa eine Viertelstunde von Potsdam ist der Golfplatz Märkischer Potsdam, der 1995 von Christian Staedler realisiert wurde. Ein welliges Gelände mit wenig Bäumen, die nie wirklich in die Spielbahn kommen, im Gegensatz zu den Fairway- und Greenbunkern sowie den Wasserhindernissen. Allerdings ist dies kein allzu schwieriger Platz, und die (zahlreichen) Mittelklasse-Spieler werden begeistert sein. Da die Schwierigkeiten gut sichtbar sind, ist es möglich (aber nicht sicher), sein Handicap zu spielen. Ein Platz von durchschnittlich-guter Qualität..

The west of Berlin is a region of canals and lakes, whose historical centre is Potsdam, a city with the extraordinary Schloss Sanssouci and Neues Palais. Both were creations of Frederick II of Prussia, an enlightened and cultured monarch, and friend of Voltaire. Visit both, and the 300 hectares of grounds that go with it. Twenty or so minutes away lies the Märkischer Potsdam course, created in 1995 by Christoph Staedler over relatively hilly terrain. The land is rather woody but trees never really come into play, as opposed to the fairway and green-side bunkers and the water hazards. However, this is not the world's toughest course and golfers of only average ability (and there are quite a few of those !) will love it. And as the difficulties are clearly visible, it is possible (but it is no give-away) to play to your handicap. A generally excellent course.

Märkischer Golfclub Potsdam e.V.

Schmiedeweg 1
D - 14542 KEMNITZ

Office	Sekretariat	(49) 03327 - 40 528
Pro shop	Pro shop	(49) 03327 - 40 528
Fax	Fax	(49) 03327 - 40 529
Situation	Lage	

20 km von Potsdam, 140 000 Ew.
45 km von Berlin, 3 500 000 Ew.

Annual closure	Jährliche Schliessung	nein
Weekly closure	Wöchentliche Schliessung	nein

Fees main season
Preisliste hochsaison 18 Löcher

	Week days Woche	We/Bank holidays We/Feiertag
Individual Individuell	DM 80,-	DM 100,-
Couple Ehepaar	DM 160,-	DM 200,-

Caddy	Caddy	nein
Electric Trolley	Elektrokarren	nein
Buggy	Elektrischer Wagen	DM 50,-
Clubs	Clubs	DM 25,-
Credit cards Kreditkarten		nein

Schmergow
Ketzin
GOLF
Krielow
Derwitz
nach
Brandeburg
A 10
nach
POTSDAM
Töplitz 5
Phöben
Kemnitz 6
Großer
Zernsee
7
Gd.
Plessower
See
nach
Leipzig (A9)
0 2 4 km

Access Zufahrt : Berlin A115 → Magdeburg.
Drewitz A10 → Hamburg (Berliner Ring).
Ausf. Phöben → Golfplatz
Map 6 on page 303 Karte 6 Seite 303

GOLF COURSE / PLATZ

14/20

Site	Lage	
Maintenance	Instandhaltung	
Architect	Architekt	Christoph Staedler
Type	Typ	Park
Relief	Relief	
Water in play	Platz mit Wasser	
Exp. to wind	Wind ausgesetzt	
Trees in play	Platz mit Bäumen	

Scorecard Scorekarte	Chp. Chp.	Mens Herren	Ladies Damen
Length Länge	6330	6120	5440
Par	72	72	74

Advised golfing ability Empfohlene Spielstärke	0	12	24	36
Hcp required	Min. Handicap	32		

CLUB HOUSE & AMENITIES / KLUBHAUS UND NEBENGEBÄUDE

7/10

Pro shop	Pro shop	
Driving range	Übungsplatz	
Sheltered	überdacht	6 Plätze
On grass	auf Rasen	ja
Putting-green	Putting-grün	ja
Pitching-green	Pitching-grün	ja

361

HOTEL FACILITIES / HOTEL BESCHREIBUNG

6/10

HOTELS HOTELS

Hotel Landgasthof am Golfplatz	Kemnitz
36 Zimmer, D DM 140,-	3 km
Tel (49) 03327 - 4646, Fax (49) 03327 - 464 747	

Schlosshotel Cecilienhof	Potsdam
43 Zimmer, D DM 350,-	20 km
Tel (49) 0331 - 37 050, Fax (49) 0331 - 292 498	

Residence Hotel	Potsdam
256 Zimmer, D DM 200,-	20 km
Tel (49) 0331 - 88 300, Fax (49) 0331 - 883 0511	

RESTAURANTS RESTAURANT

Pegasus	Potsdam
Tel (49) 0331 - 291 506	20 km

Börse	Potsdam
Tel (49) 0331 - 292 505	20 km

Dieser neue Platz wurde in einer Region eröffnet, der es an Golfanlagen nicht mangelt. Man findet ihn unweit von München, Augsburg und Ulm gelegen, in der Umgebung der alten Reichsstadt Memmingen, deren Stadtbild noch gut erhaltene Spuren des Mittelalters und der Renaissance trägt. Trotz seines jungen Alters präsentiert sich der Kurs bereits in ausgezeichnetem Zustand, der sich mit der Zeit weiter verbessern sollte. Die gut gearbeiteten Grüns, die schon dicht mit Gras bewachsen sind, spielen sich etwas weich. Zudem hätte es nicht geschadet, die Grünkörper stärker zu kontourieren, um das Putten, diesen für den Score so ausschlaggebenden Teil des Spiels etwas interssanter zu machen. Während freistehende Bäume nur vereinzelt eine Rolle spielen, kommt dem Wind als Gefahrenelement eine weitaus grössere Bedeutung zu, insbesondere da man auch noch mit dichtem Rough, Büschen, Fairway- und Grünbunkern, sowie einigen Wasserhindernissen fertigwerden muss. Von mittlerem Schwierigkeitsgrad, ohne nenneswerte Erhebungen, eignet sich der Platz für alle Spielstärken.

This new course was opened in a region where golfing facilities abound, within the immediate vicinity of Munich, Augsburg and Ulm and close to the former imperial city of Memmingen, which has preserved its vestiges of the past (Middle Ages and Renaissance). Despite this being early days, the course is already in excellent condition and should age still better. The well-built greens are already well covered and soft on top, but a little more contouring would not have gone amiss to add a little spice to this department of the game which is so important for scoring. Only a few isolated trees come into play and the wind can be a significant element to be considered, especially with thick rough, bushes, fairway and green-side bunkers and a few water hazards to contend with. This is a course for all levels.

Golfclub Memmingen Gut Westerhart e.V.

Westerhart 1b D - 87740 BUXHEIM

Office	Sekretariat	(49) 08331 - 71 016
Pro shop	Pro shop	(49) 08331 - 71 016
Fax	Fax	(49) 08331 - 71 018
Situation	Lage	

2 km von Memmingen, 40 000 Ew.
55 km von Ulm (Donau), 110 000 Ew.

Annual closure	Jährliche Schliessung	ja
		1/11→1/04
Weekly closure	Wöchentliche Schliessung	Montag,
		Das Restaurant

Fees main season Preisliste hochsaison 18 Löcher

	Week days Woche	We/Bank holidays We/Feiertag
Individual Individuell	DM 50,-	DM 70,-
Couple Ehepaar	DM 100,-	DM 140,-

– 21 Jahre/Studenten: – 50 %

Caddy	Caddy	nein
Electric Trolley	Elektrokarren	DM 5,-
Buggy	Elektrischer Wagen	DM 50,-
Clubs	Clubs	DM 10,-

Credit cards Kreditkarten · nein

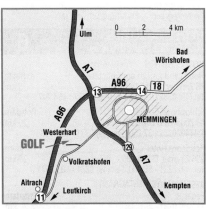

Access Zufahrt : A96 München-Lindau, Ausf. Aitrach, B12 → Memmingen, → Westerhart
Map 2 on page 294 Karte 2 Seite 294

GOLF COURSE
PLATZ **14**/20

Site	Lage	
Maintenance	Instandhaltung	
Architect	Architekt	
Type	Typ	Park, Flachland
Relief	Relief	
Water in play	Platz mit Wasser	
Exp. to wind	Wind ausgesetzt	
Trees in play	Platz mit Bäumen	

Scorecard Scorekarte	Chp. Chp.	Mens Herren	Ladies Damen
Length Länge	6331	6199	5507
Par	72	72	72

		0 12 24 36
Advised golfing ability Empfohlene Spielstärke		
Hcp required Min. Handicap	36	

CLUB HOUSE & AMENITIES
KLUBHAUS UND NEBENGEBÄUDE **6**/10

Pro shop	Pro shop	
Driving range	Übungsplatz	
Sheltered	überdacht	10 Plätze
On grass	auf Rasen	nein
Putting-green	Putting-grün	ja
Pitching-green	Pitching-grün	ja

HOTEL FACILITIES
HOTEL BESCHREIBUNG **6**/10

HOTELS HOTELS

Falken — Memmingen
39 Zimmer, D DM 180,- — 6 km
Tel (49) 08331 - 47 081, Fax (49) 08331 - 47 086

Park-Hotel an der Stadthalle — Memmingen
90 Zimmer, D DM 220,- — 6 km
Tel (49) 08331 - 9320, Fax (49) 08331 - 48 439

Adler — Memmingen
45 Zimmer, D DM 130,- — 6 km
Tel (49) 08331 - 87 015, Fax (49) 08331 - 48 540

RESTAURANTS RESTAURANT

Weinstube Weber am Bach — Memmingen
Tel (49) 08331 - 2414 — 6 km

Weinhaus Knöringer — Memmingen
Tel (49) 08331 - 2715 — 6 km

Der Mittelrheinische Golfclub liegt gleich neben dem Kurort Bad Ems, wo man sich auf die Behandlung von Hals- und Nasenkrankheiten spezialisiert hat. Der 1928 gebaute Platz ist eingebettet in dichte Vegetation und eröffnet immer wieder schöne Ausblicke auf die Höhenzüge von Eiffel und Taunus. Aufgrund des hügeligen Geländes wird man im Verlauf der Runde mit etwa einem halben Dutzend blinder Schläge konfrontiert. Die Grüns jedoch sind alle gut einsehbar. Leicht gewellt und von mittlerer Grösse bieten sie kaum Anlass für Desaster beim Putten. Golfer, die einen Fade spielen können, haben angesichts der engen Spielbahnen einen kleinen, wenn auch nicht entscheidenden Vorteil. Den Longhittern bieten sich an den fünf Par 5 Löchern gute Birdie-Chancen. Mit ausserdem fünf Par 3 Löchern hat der Platz eine eher ungewöhnliche Konfiguration. Die nicht übermässige Länge des Kurses (nur 9 Löcher verfügen über hintere Abschläge) erleichtert das Miteinander guter und weniger guter Golfer auf einer gemeinsamen Runde. Der Platz lohnt einen Besuch.

The Mittelrheinischer course is located next to the spa of Bad Ems, which specialises in nasal and throat affections. Designed in 1928, the course winds its way through thick vegetation while offering pretty vistas over the Eifel and Taunus uplands. Slightly hilly, the layout entails half a dozen blind shots but all the greens are clearly visible, moderately contoured and of average size (putting disasters are rare). Faders of the ball will enjoy a slight advantage in coping with the narrow fairways, but this is hardly a decisive factor. Long-hitters can look for birdies on the five par 5s; and with five par 3s as well, the course has a rather unusual feel to it. The overall length is very reasonable (there are back tees on 9 holes only) thus making it easier for experienced and inexperienced players to enjoy a round together. Worth knowing.

Mittelrheinischer Golf Club Bad Ems e.V.

Am Golfplatz
D - 55743 KIRSCHWEILER

Office	Sekretariat	(49) 02603 - 6541
Pro shop	Pro shop	(49) 02603 - 14 510
Fax	Fax	(49) 02603 - 13 995
Situation	Lage	

3 km von Bad Ems, 10 000 Ew.
10 km von Koblenz, 108 000 Ew.

Annual closure	Jährliche Schliessung	nein
Weekly closure	Wöchentliche Schliessung	Montag
		das Restaurant

Fees main season
Preisliste hochsaison 18 Löcher

	Week days Woche	We/Bank holidays We/Feiertag
Individual Individuell	DM 80,-	DM 110,-
Couple Ehepaar	DM 160,-	DM 220,-

– 21 Jahre : – 50 %

Caddy	Caddy	auf Reservierung
Electric Trolley	Elektrokarren	ja
Buggy	Elektrischer Wagen	nein
Clubs	Clubs	ja

Credit cards Kreditkarten　　　　　nein

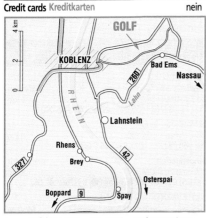

Access Zufahrt : A3 Frankfurt-Köln. Ausf. Montabaur.
B49 → Koblenz. → Bad Ems/Denzerheide.
Map 3 on page 296 Karte 3 Seite 296

GOLF COURSE
PLATZ   15/20

Site	Lage	▬▬▬
Maintenance	Instandhaltung	▬▬▬
Architect	Architekt	Karl-Heinz Hoffmann
		Park
Type	Typ	
Relief	Relief	
Water in play	Platz mit Wasser	▬
Exp. to wind	Wind ausgesetzt	▬
Trees in play	Platz mit Bäumen	▬▬▬

Scorecard Scorekarte	Chp. Chp.	Mens Herren	Ladies Damen
Length Länge	6050	6050	5330
Par	72	72	72

Advised golfing ability Empfohlene Spielstärke	0	12	24	36

Hcp required　Min. Handicap　36

CLUB HOUSE & AMENITIES
KLUBHAUS UND NEBENGEBÄUDE   7/10

Pro shop	Pro shop	▬▬
Driving range	Übungsplatz	▬▬
Sheltered	überdacht	6 Plätze
On grass	auf Rasen	ja
Putting-green	Putting-grün	ja
Pitching-green	Pitching-grün	ja

363

HOTEL FACILITIES
HOTEL BESCHREIBUNG   7/10

HOTELS HOTELS
Golf Hotel Denzerheide   Golfplatz
8 Zimmer, D DM 100,-
Tel (49) 02603 - 6159, Fax (49) 02603 - 13995

Atlantis Kurhotel   Bad Ems
107 Zimmer, D DM 250,-   3 km
Tel (49) 02603 - 7990, Fax (49) 02603 - 799 252

Kleiner Riesen   Koblenz
28 Zimmer, D DM 200,-   10 km
Tel (49) 0261 - 32 077, Fax (49) 0261 - 160 725

RESTAURANTS RESTAURANT
Schweizer Haus   Bad Ems
Tel (49) 02603 - 70 783   3 km

Histor. Wirtshaus an der Lahn   Lahnstein
Tel (49) 02621 - 7270   15 km

Dies ist einer der besten Plätze, die in jüngerer Zeit in Deutschland entstanden sind. Seine hohen technischen Qualitäten werden vor allem den besseren Golfern auffallen. Kurt Rossknecht liess sich beim Bau der Anlage sowohl von amerikanischen wie auch schottischen Stilelementen inspirieren. Entstanden ist dabei ein Platz, der mittels wellenförmiger Fairways und tiefer Bunkerprofile wie die moderne Version eines Linkskurses wirkt. Die gut erkennbaren Hindernisse geben die ideale Spiellinie vor. Zudem sind sie so klug positioniert, dass gute Golfschläge nicht bestraft werden. Diese Feststellung gilt im übrigen für das gesamte Layout des Platzes. Allrounder werden diesen Kurs ob seines abwechslungsreichen Lochdesigns - an 7 Löchern kommt Wasser ins Spiel - lieben. Je nach Charakter des Loches sind sowohl flache lang ausrollende, als auch hohe Schläge zum Grün gefordert, für deren Ausführung der komplette Schlägersatz herhalten muss. Die grosse Anzahl verschiedener Abschläge erlaubt jedem Golfer eine seiner Spielstärke entsprechende Wahl, aber auch die Möglichkeit je nach Tagesform und Lust zu variieren.

This is one of the best courses in Germany, with technical virtues that are more obvious to top level golfers. Kurt Rossknecht was inspired by both American and Scottish styles and has come up with a sort of modernised links (rolling fairways and shaped bunkers). The very clear view of hazards points to the ideal line of play, while their clever positioning and the honest layout never penalises good golf shots. Good all-round players will love this course, where they can chop and change between low rolled shots and high approaches required by the variety of holes (water is in play on seven holes). Here, you will play every club in the bag. The large number of tees makes this a course that caters to each level of proficiency, and to each player's form and mood... depending on the pin positions.

Berliner Golf- & Country Club am Motzener See e.V.

Am Golfplatz 5
D - 15741 MOTZEN

Office	Sekretariat	(49) 033769 - 50 130
Pro shop	Pro shop	(49) 033769 - 50 128
Fax	Fax	(49) 033769 - 50 134
Situation	Lage	

40 km von Berlin. 7 km von Teupitz, 1 700 Ew.

Annual closure	Jährliche Schliessung	ja
		1/01→1/02
Weekly closure	Wöchentliche Schliessung	Montag
		das Restaurant

Fees main season Preisliste hochsaison den ganzen Tag

	Week days Woche	We/Bank holidays We/Feiertag
Individual Individuell	DM 90,-	DM 90,-
Couple Ehepaar	DM 180,-	DM 180,-
– 21 Jahre/Studenten: – 50 %		
Caddy	Caddy	DM 35,-
Electric Trolley	Elektrokarren	nein
Buggy	Elektrischer Wagen	nein
Clubs	Clubs	DM 35,-
Credit cards Kreditkarten		nein

364

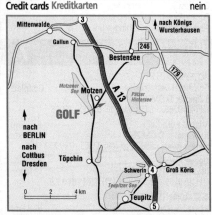

Access Zufahrt : Berlin, A13 → Dresden. Ausf.
Mittenwalde → Gallun-Bestensee → Golf
Map 6 on page 303 Karte 6 Seite 303

GOLF COURSE
PLATZ 18/20

Site	Lage	
Maintenance	Instandhaltung	
Architect	Architekt	Kurt Rossknecht
Type	Typ	Flachland
Relief	Relief	
Water in play	Platz mit Wasser	
Exp. to wind	Wind ausgesetzt	
Trees in play	Platz mit Bäumen	

Scorecard Scorekarte	Chp. Chp.	Mens Herren	Ladies Damen
Length Länge	6330	5915	5200
Par	73	72	72

Advised golfing ability	0 12 24 36
Empfohlene Spielstärke	
Hcp required Min. Handicap	36

CLUB HOUSE & AMENITIES
KLUBHAUS UND NEBENGEBÄUDE 8/10

Pro shop	Pro shop	
Driving range	Übungsplatz	
Sheltered	überdacht	10 Plätze
On grass	auf Rasen	ja
Putting-green	Putting-grün	ja
Pitching-green	Pitching-grün	ja

HOTEL FACILITIES
HOTEL BESCHREIBUNG 6/10

HOTELS HOTELS

Residenz am Motzener See — Motzen
63 Zimmer, D DM 245,- — 1 km
Tel (49) 033769 - 850, Fax (49) 033769 - 85 100

Schlosshotel Teupitz — Teupitz
38 Zimmer, D DM 200,- — 8 km
Tel (49) 033766 - 600, Fax (49) 033766 - 60 455

Lindengarten — Klein Koris
33 Zimmer, D DM 160,- — 5 km
Tel (49) 033766 - 42 063, Fax (49) 033766 - 42 062

RESTAURANTS RESTAURANT

Residenz am Motzener See — Motzen
Tel (49) 033769 - 850 — 1 km

Schlosshotel Teupitz — Teupitz
Tel (49) 033766 - 600 — 8 km

Die Anlage macht einen sehr kompletten Eindruck und verfügt über ausgezeichnete Übungseinrichtungen, der Golfplatz selbst befindet sich aber noch in einem sehr frühen Stadium. Es wird interessant sein zu beobachten wie er sich entwickelt. Er verfügt über weite offene Flächen, deutlich voneinander abgetrennte Spielbahnen und Roughzonen, die ebenso eine Gefahr darstellen wie die traditionellen Hindernisse Wasser, Bäume und Bunker. Mindestens bis Juli lässt man das Rough hier wachsen und verengt somit ganz beträchtlich die Fairway-Landezonen. Das flache Terrain lässt einen, auch wenn man mehr als 18 Loch am Tag spielt, nicht ermüden. Die Grüns sind gut einsehbar, ausgezeichnet geformt und ordentlich verteidigt. Bei der Planung des Platzes wurde offensichtlich auf die Bedürfnisse der Durchschnitts-Golfer Rücksicht genommen, so dass diese sich hier denn auch sehr wohl fühlen werden. Das liegt auch daran, dass es hier wenig gibt, was dem ohnehin geplagten Ego des Golfers zu schaffen macht. Wir brauchen Plätze wie diesen, wenngleich gute Spieler etwas anspruchsvolleren Anlagen den Vorzug geben werden.

A very comprehensive facility, with good practice installations, but the course is still in its infancy. It will be interesting to keep track of how it matures. There are wide open spaces here, clearly separated fairways and rough that is as much a hazard as the traditional dangers of water, trees and bunkers. Up until July, at least, it is kept long and thick and considerably narrows the fairways. The flattish terrain makes this an easily walkable course, even if you are out to play more than 18 holes in one day. The greens are clearly visible and properly designed with reasonable lines of defence. The designers obviously had the average golfer in mind, and he or she will find this very much to their liking. For once there is not too much here to inflict further suffering on the golfer's much-battered ego.

Golf Club Mülheim an der Ruhr e.V.
Am Golfplatz 1
D - 45481 MÜLHEIM

Office	Sekretariat	(49) 0208 - 483 607
Pro shop	Pro shop	(49) 0208 - 480 718
Fax	Fax	(49) 0208 - 481 153
Situation	Lage	

10 km von Mülheim, 177 000 Ew.
15 km von Düsseldorf, 570 000 Ew.

Annual closure	Jährliche Schliessung	nein
Weekly closure	Wöchentliche Schliessung	Montag
		das Restaurant

Fees main season Preisliste hochsaison 18 Löcher

	Week days Woche	We/Bank holidays We/Feiertag
Individual Individuell	DM 90,-	DM 90,-
Couple Ehepaar	DM 180,-	DM 180,-

We/Feiertage: nur in Mitgliederbegleitung
(with members) / - 21 Jahre/Studenten : - 50 %

Caddy	Caddy	nein
Electric Trolley	Elektrokarren	nein
Buggy	Elektrischer Wagen	nein
Clubs	Clubs	nein
Credit cards Kreditkarten		nein

Access Zufahrt : A3 Köln-Duisburg. Ausf.
"Autobahnkreuz Breitscheid" → Essen, → Mülheim.
2 km links → Golfplatz
Map 3 on page 296 Karte 3 Seite 296

GOLF COURSE
PLATZ   13/20

Site	Lage	▬▬▬
Maintenance	Instandhaltung	▬▬▬
Architect	Architekt	DeutscheGolf Consult
Type	Typ	Flachland, Wald
Relief	Relief	▬▬
Water in play	Platz mit Wasser	▬▬▬
Exp. to wind	Wind ausgesetzt	▬▬
Trees in play	Platz mit Bäumen	▬▬▬

Scorecard Scorekarte	Chp. Chp.	Mens Herren	Ladies Damen
Length Länge	6123	6123	5401
Par	72	72	72

Advised golfing ability		0	12	24	36
Empfohlene Spielstärke		▬▬▬▬▬▬			
Hcp required	Min. Handicap	36			

CLUB HOUSE & AMENITIES
KLUBHAUS UND NEBENGEBÄUDE   6/10

Pro shop	Pro shop	▬▬▬
Driving range	Übungsplatz	▬▬▬
Sheltered	überdacht	8 Plätze
On grass	auf Rasen	ja
Putting-green	Putting-grün	ja
Pitching-green	Pitching-grün	ja

365

HOTEL FACILITIES
HOTEL BESCHREIBUNG   7/10

HOTELS HOTELS
Dorint Budget Hotel   Ratingen
118 Zimmer, D DM 150,-   3 km
Tel (49) 02102 - 9185, Fax (49) 02102 - 918 900

Novotel Düsseldorf-Ratingen   Ratingen
118 Zimmer, D DM 280,-   3 km
Tel (49) 02102 - 1870, Fax (49) 02102 - 18 418

Allgäuer Hof   Ratingen
15 Zimmer, D DM 165,-   10 km
Tel (49) 02102 - 95 410, Fax (49) 02102 - 954 123

Steigenberger Parkhotel   Düsseldorf
160 Zimmer, D DM 450,- Tel (49) 0211 - 13 810   20 km

RESTAURANTS RESTAURANT
Ratinger Stube   Ratingen
Tel (49) 02102 - 24 800   10 km

Am Kamin, Tel (49) 0208 - 760 036   Mülheim, 8 km

Münchens Süden ist nicht nur aufgrund der vielen Touristenattraktionen eine bevorzugte Region, sondern auch wegen seiner zahlreichen Golfplätze unterschiedlicher Art. München-Riedhof liegt in unmittelbarer Nähe zum Starnberger See, einem der grössten bayerischen Seen, auf halbem Weg zwischen München und den bayerischen Alpen. Der von Heinz Fehring entworfene Kurs zählt allein schon aufgrund seiner Länge nicht zu den einfacheren Plätzen. Dieser Eindruck wird durch die Wasserhindernisse und einige recht steile Erhebungen im Gelände, die die Entfernungseinschätzung erheblich erschweren, bestätigt. Nichtsdestoweniger kann der Platz gut zu Fuss bewältigt werden. Die Schwierigkeiten sind gut erkennbar. Das gilt auch für die Wasserhindernisse, die für misratene Schläge allerdings weniger Gefahr darstellen, als dies Bäume und Bunker tun. Der grösstenteils spektakuläre, manchmal etwas trügerische Platz bleibt einem gut im Gedächtnis haften, was ein gutes Zeichen ist. Da die Grüns sehr gut verteidigt sind, ist eine gute Ballkontrolle unerlässlich; dennoch werden durchschnittliche Spieler hier ebenso auf ihre Kosten kommmen wie Fortgeschrittene.

Situated in a very privileged region, München-Riedhof is within immediate reach of the Starnberger See, one of Bavaria's largest lakes half-way between Munich and the Bavarian Alps. The course, designed by Heinz Fehring, is not the easiest in the world owing to yardage, water hazards and some steeply contoured terrain, which complicates appreciation of distance. The course is, though, very pleasant to walk around. The difficulties are there to be seen ; water is, too, but is not so dangerous for mis-hit shots as the trees and bunkers. Often spectacular and sometimes a wee treacherous, the course sticks in your memory, which is a good sign. As the greens are very well guarded, good ball control is, as always, important, but average players will have as much fun as the experts.

Golfclub München-Riedhof e.V.
Riedhof 16
D - 85244 EGLING-RIEDHOF

Office	Sekretariat	(49) 08171 - 7065
Pro shop	Pro shop	(49) 08171 - 7065
Fax	Fax	(49) 08171 - 72 452
Situation	Lage	

25 km von München, 1 300 000 Ew.
3 km von Wolfratshausen, 16 000 Ew.

Annual closure	Jährliche Schliessung	nein
Weekly closure	Wöchentliche Schliessung	Montag
		das Restaurant

Fees main season Preisliste hochsaison 18 Löcher

	Week days Woche	We/Bank holidays We/Feiertag
Individual Individuell	DM 140,-	DM 70,- *
Couple Ehepaar	DM 280,-	DM 140,- *

Gäste Montag-Freitag (weekdays only) -
* We: nur in Mitgliederbegleitung

Caddy	Caddy	nein
Electric Trolley	Elektrokarren	nein
Buggy	Elektrischer Wagen	nein
Clubs	Clubs	nein

Credit cards Kreditkarten   nein

Access Zufahrt : A95 München-Garmisch-Partenkirchen.
Ausf. Wolfratshausen, Richtung Autobahn Salzburg-
Wolfratshausen. → Egling
Map 2 on page 294 Karte 2 Seite 294

GOLF COURSE
PLATZ   16/20

Site	Lage	▬▬▬
Maintenance	Instandhaltung	▬▬▬
Architect	Architekt	Heinz Fehring
Type	Typ	Flachland, Gebirge
Relief	Relief	▬▬▬▬
Water in play	Platz mit Wasser	▬▬▬
Exp. to wind	Wind ausgesetzt	▬▬
Trees in play	Platz mit Bäumen	▬▬▬▬

Scorecard Scorekarte	Chp. Chp.	Mens Herren	Ladies Damen
Length Länge	6216	5778	5087
Par	72	70	70

Advised golfing ability   0   12   24   36
Empfohlene Spielstärke
Hcp required Min. Handicap   34

CLUB HOUSE & AMENITIES
KLUBHAUS UND NEBENGEBÄUDE   7/10

Pro shop	Pro shop	▬▬▬
Driving range	Übungsplatz	▬▬▬
Sheltered	überdacht	10 Plätze
On grass	auf Rasen	ja
Putting-green	Putting-grün	ja
Pitching-green	Pitching-grün	ja

HOTEL FACILITIES
HOTEL BESCHREIBUNG   7/10

HOTELS HOTELS
Thalhammer   Wolfratshausen
23 Zimmer, D DM 170,-   5 km
Tel (49) 08171 - 7149, Fax (49) 08171 - 76 185

Märchenwald   Wolfratshausen
14 Zimmer, D DM 130,-   5 km
Tel (49) 08171 - 29 096, Fax (49) 08171 - 22 236

Ritterhof   Grünwald
20 Zimmer, D DM 180,-   10 km
Tel (49) 089 - 649 0090, Fax (49) 089 - 649 3012

Tannenhof   Grünwald
21 Zimmer, D DM 200, Tel (49) 089 - 641 8960   10 km

RESTAURANTS RESTAURANT
Patrizierhof   Wolfratshausen
Tel (49) 08171 - 225 33   5 km

Vogelbauer, Tel (49) 08171 - 290 63   Neufahrn, 5 km

366

MÜNCHNER-STRASSLACH | 14 | 6 | 7 |

In der Umgebung der Metropole München ist dies wohl einer der meist bespielten Golfplätze, auf dem an Wochenenden kaum Greenfee-Spieler zugelassen werden. Golfer, die noch an ihrem Spiel arbeiten müssen (trifft das nicht auf uns alle zu ?) sollten sich daher möglichst wochentags auf die Anlage begeben, wenn es wesentlich ruhiger zugeht als am Wochenende. Der Platz wurde 1910 inmitten einer typisch bayerischen Landschaft auf leicht hügeligem Terrain angelegt. Auf dem Parcours findet sich eine Anzahl wunderschöner grosser Bäume, die an den Doglegs gefährlich ins Spiel kommen. Einige Seen und Wasserläufe sowie knapp 50 sehr sorgfältig platzierte Bunker komplettieren das Repertoire an Hindernissen. Auf den ersten Blick mag der Kurs nicht sonderlich schwierig erscheinen, dieser Eindruck wird sich allerdings im Verlauf der Runde revidieren, nicht zuletzt aufgrund einer Reihe schlecht erkennbarer Hindernisse. Auf der zweiten Runde fühlt man sich schon weitaus wohler, da man dann weiss, wie der Platz taktisch zu spielen ist. Der ausgezeichnete Hauptplatz wird ergänzt durch einen nicht minder guten 9-Loch-Kurzplatz.

This is one of the busiest courses around Munich, and playing here on week-ends can be very difficult for green-feers. It is much easier to enjoy the course during the week ; if players in your group or family are still trying to get to grips with the game (aren't we all ?), they'll feel easier on a quiet week-day than on a crowded week-end. Created in 1910 over averagely-hilly terrain, the course runs over typically Bavarian landscape, with some beautiful big trees (very dangerous on the dog-legs), a few lakes and streams and a little under 50 carefully-located bunkers. At first sight it doesn't look too difficult, but out on the course it can be quite a handful with a number of hazards hidden from view. Second time out, you feel more comfortable. A class course supplemented by a very good and shortish 9-holer.

Münchner Golf Club e.V., Strasslach
Tölzerstrasse 95
D - 82064 STRASSLACH

Office	Sekretariat	(49) 08170 - 450
Pro shop	Pro shop	(49) 08170 - 7254
Fax	Fax	(49) 08170 - 611
Situation	Lage	

25 km von München. 3 km von Strasslach, 2 700 Ew.

Annual closure	Jährliche Schliessung	nein
Weekly closure	Wöchentliche Schliessung	Montag
		das Restaurant

Fees main season
Preisliste hochsaison 18 Löcher

	Week days Woche	We/Bank holidays We/Feiertag
Individual Individuell	DM 100,-	DM 120,-
Couple Ehepaar	DM 200,-	DM 240,-

We: nur in Mitgliederbegleitung (with members)

Caddy	Caddy	nein
Electric Trolley	Elektrokarren	ja
Buggy	Elektrischer Wagen	ja
Clubs	Clubs	nein

Credit cards Kreditkarten   nein

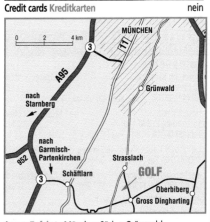

Access Zufahrt : München Süd → Grünwald.
Im Grünwald → Bad Tölz. Golfplatz links.
Map 2 on page 294 Karte 2 Seite 294

GOLF COURSE
PLATZ   14/20

Site	Lage	▬▬▬
Maintenance	Instandhaltung	▬▬▬
Architect	Architekt	
Type	Typ	Flachland
Relief	Relief	▬▬▬
Water in play	Platz mit Wasser	▬▬▬
Exp. to wind	Wind ausgesetzt	▬▬
Trees in play	Platz mit Bäumen	▬▬▬▬

Scorecard Scorekarte	**Chp.** Chp.	**Mens** Herren	**Ladies** Damen
Length Länge	6126	6126	5432
Par	72	72	72

Advised golfing ability		0 12 24 36
Empfohlene Spielstärke		▬▬
Hcp required	Min. Handicap	35

CLUB HOUSE & AMENITIES
KLUBHAUS UND NEBENGEBÄUDE   6/10

Pro shop	Pro shop	▬▬▬
Driving range	Übungsplatz	▬▬▬
Sheltered	überdacht	2 Plätze
On grass	auf Rasen	ja
Putting-green	Putting-grün	ja
Pitching-green	Pitching-grün	ja

367

HOTEL FACILITIES
HOTEL BESCHREIBUNG   7/10

HOTELS HOTELS

Ritterhof   Grünwald
20 Zimmer, D DM 180,-   4 km
Tel (49) 089 - 649 0090, Fax (49) 089 - 649 3012

Alter Wirt   Grünwald
50 Zimmer, D DM 170,-   4 km
Tel (49) 089 - 641 7855, Fax (49) 089 - 641 4266

Schloss Hotel   Grünwald
15 Zimmer, D DM 250,-   4 km
Tel (49) 089 - 641 8960, Fax (49) 089 - 641 930 3

RESTAURANTS RESTAURANT

Gasthof zum Wildpark   Strasslach
Tel (49) 08170 - 635   1 km

Hubertus   Schäfftlarn
Tel (49) 08178 - 4851   5 km

Golfplätze in der Nähe von Kurorten sind in Europa gang und gäbe, und Deutschland bildet in dieser Hinsicht keine Ausnahme. Nahetal, in der Nähe von Bad Münster und der alten Römerstadt Bad Kreuznach gelegen, besitzt denn auch genügend eigene Anziehungskraft. Der Platz wurde 1986 modernisiert, wobei aber die alten Schwierigkeiten erhalten blieben. Erste Notwendigkeit hier ist Präzision, da die Fairways meist nicht sehr breit und zudem von dichter Vegetation umwachsen sind, was dem Kurs den angenehmen Nebeneffekt von Ruhe und Abgeschiedenheit vermittelt. Obwohl nicht auf die leichte Schulter zu nehmen, ist Nahetal doch ein "ehrlicher" Platz, dessen Hindernisse gut erkennbar und nicht wirklich einschüchternd sind. Genauigkeit vorausgesetzt, sollte eine gute Runde jederzeit möglich sein. Wichtig dabei ist, ruhig und konzentriert zu Werke zu gehen. Etwas Abwechslung verspricht Loch 7, wo sich ein spektakulärer Blick auf Rotenfels und die zur Nahe abfallenden Klippen bietet.

Golf courses have naturally found a willing and suitable partner in European spas, and Germany is no exception to the rule. Nahetal, for example, is very close to Bad Munster and the old Roman town of Bad Kreuznach, and has its own appeal. Golf here, though, has become something of a younger sport than was once the case, but difficulties remain the same. The first is the need to play straight, as the fairways are not always wide and are lined with some pretty dense vegetation, a feature that adds to a pleasant impression of peace and quiet. But while this course is no walk-over, it is also very honest and proudly reveals its hazards, none of which are really too scary. If you are accurate, there's no reason why you shouldn't have a good round. What matters is keeping a cool head and your concentration, as always. You will find a little light entertainment on the 7th with the view over Rotenfels and the cliffs plunging over the Nahe.

Golfclub Nahetal e.V.
Drei Buchen
D - 55583 BAD MÜNSTER A. STEIN-EBERNBURG

Office	Sekretariat	(49) 06708 - 2145
Pro shop	Pro shop	(49) 06708 - 4399
Fax	Fax	(49) 06708 - 1731
Situation	Lage	

12 km von Bad Kreuznach, 43 000 Ew.
45 km von Mainz, 186 000 Ew.

Annual closure	Jährliche Schliessung	nein
Weekly closure	Wöchentliche Schliessung	Montag
		das Restaurant

Fees main season Preisliste hochsaison 18 Löcher

	Week days Woche	We/Bank holidays We/Feiertag
Individual Individuell	DM 60,-	DM 80,-
Couple Ehepaar	DM 120,-	DM 160,-

– 21 Jahre/Studenten : – 50 %

Caddy	Caddy	auf Reservierung
Electric Trolley	Elektrokarren	DM 20,-
Buggy Elektrischer Wagen		DM 50,- Krankenschein
Clubs	Clubs	DM 10,-

Credit cards Kreditkarten — nein

368

Access Zufahrt : Mainz A60 W, Kreuz Bingen A61 Süd.
Ausf. Bad Kreuznach. Bad Kreuznach B48
→ Bad Münster → Ebernburg. Rechts in die
Schlossgartenstrasse. Rechts Wanderweg
Dreibuchen. **Map 3 on page 297** Karte 3 Seite 297

GOLF COURSE
PLATZ   **14**/20

Site	Lage	▰▰▰▱▱
Maintenance	Instandhaltung	▰▰▰▰▱
Architect	Architekt	Armin Keller
Type	Typ	Wald
Relief	Relief	▰▰▱▱▱
Water in play	Platz mit Wasser	▰▰▱▱▱
Exp. to wind	Wind ausgesetzt	▰▰▱▱▱
Trees in play	Platz mit Bäumen	▰▰▰▰▱

Scorecard Scorekarte	Chp. Chp.	Mens Herren	Ladies Damen
Length Länge	6090	6090	5344
Par	72	72	72

Advised golfing ability		0	12	24	36
Empfohlene Spielstärke					
Hcp required	Min. Handicap	We: 36			

CLUB HOUSE & AMENITIES
KLUBHAUS UND NEBENGEBÄUDE   **7**/10

Pro shop	Pro shop	▰▰▰▰▱
Driving range	Übungsplatz	▰▰▰▱▱
Sheltered	überdacht	8 Plätze
On grass	auf Rasen	ja
Putting-green	Putting-grün	ja
Pitching-green	Pitching-grün	ja

HOTEL FACILITIES
HOTEL BESCHREIBUNG   **6**/10

HOTELS HOTELS

Hotel am Kurpark   Bad Münster a. Stein
30 Zimmer, D DM 180,-   2 km
Tel (49) 06708 - 1292, Fax (49) 06708 - 4648

Haus Lorenz   Bad Münster a. Stein
16 Zimmer, D DM 110,-   2 km
Tel (49) 06708 - 1841, Fax (49) 06708 - 1281

Landhotel Kauzenberg, 46 Zimmer   Bad Kreuznach
D DM 220,- Tel (49) 0671 - 38 000   12 km

Insel-Stuben, 22 Zimmer   Bad Kreuznach
D DM 180,- Tel (49) 0671 - 837 990   12 km

RESTAURANTS RESTAURANT

Metzlers Gasthof   Bad Kreuznach-Hackenheim
Tel (49) 0671 - 65 312   14 km

Die Kauzenburg,   Bad Kreuznach
Tel (49) 0671 - 380 0801   12 km

In unmittelbarer Nähe von Stuttgart gelegen ist der Platz leicht zu erreichen. Nicht-Golfer können sich die Zeit mit einem Besuch von Park, Märchengarten und dem stark von Versailles inspirierten Schloss Ludwigsburg vertreiben. Der nüchtern wirkende Golfplatz spiegelt in keiner Weise den "blühenden Barock" des Schlosses wider. Am Rand eines Waldes auf flachem Gelände angelegt, entwarf Bernhard von Limburger einen in Stil und Taktik eher amerikanisch anmutenden Kurs. Länge ist ein entscheidender Faktor um hier erfolgreich zu spielen. Daneben muss man noch mit Bäumen und Rough fertigwerden. Die Grüns sind ausgezeichnet verteidigt, so dass ein gutes Kurzes Spiel vonnöten ist, wenn man sein Handicap hier spielen will. Trotz ansprechender Gestaltung ist der Parcours ganz sicher kein Meisterwerk, ein Besuch lohnt sich dennoch allemal.

The course is next door to Stuttgart and so easy to reach. In addition, non-players will have all the time in the world to visit the park, the fairy-tale garden (Märchengarten) and Ludwigsburg castle, disproportionately inspired by Versailles. But there is no trace of the castle's "blossoming baroque style" on this very sober course. Designed by von Limburger along the edge of a forest over flattish terrain, it is rather American in style and in tactics. Length here is a key factor for a successful round and forms the major difficulty with the trees and rough. The greens are protected well enough to demand a very sharp short game if you wish to play to your handicap. Well landscaped, this course is by no means a masterpiece but playing here really is time well spent.

Golfclub Neckartal e.V.
Aldingerstrasse, 975
D - 71638 LUDWIGSBURG-PATTONVILLE

Office	Sekretariat	(49) 07141 - 871 319
Pro shop	Pro shop	(49) 07141 - 870 025
Fax	Fax	(49) 07141 - 81 716
Situation	Lage	

15 km von Stuttgart. 3 km von Ludwigsburg, 86 000 Ew.

Annual closure	Jährliche Schliessung	ja
		1/11→28/02
Weekly closure	Wöchentliche Schliessung	Montag
		das Restaurant

Fees main season
Preisliste hochsaison den ganzen Tag

	Week days Woche	We/Bank holidays We/Feiertag
Individual Individuell	DM 70,-	DM 75,-
Couple Ehepaar	DM 140,-	DM 150,-

Caddy	Caddy	nein
Electric Trolley	Elektrokarren	nein
Buggy	Elektrischer Wagen	nein
Clubs	Clubs	DM 10,-

Credit cards Kreditkarten   nein

Access Zufahrt : A8 Stuttgart-Heilbronn. Ausf. Stuttgart-Zuffenhausen. B27 → Kornwestheim. Ausf. Kornwestheim-Nord. → Remseck (Aldinger Strasse). 2 km links. **Map 1 on page 293** Karte 1 Seite 293

GOLF COURSE
PLATZ   16/20

Site	Lage	▰▰▰▰▰▱
Maintenance	Instandhaltung	▰▰▰▰▰▱
Architect	Architekt	B. von Limburger
Type	Typ	Wald, Flachland
Relief	Relief	▰▱▱▱▱▱
Water in play	Platz mit Wasser	▰▰▱▱▱▱
Exp. to wind	Wind ausgesetzt	▰▰▰▱▱▱
Trees in play	Platz mit Bäumen	▰▰▰▰▱▱

Scorecard	Chp.	Mens	Ladies
Scorekarte	Chp.	Herren	Damen
Length Länge	6278	6278	5496
Par	73	73	73

Advised golfing ability		0	12	24	36
Empfohlene Spielstärke			▰▰▰▰▱		
Hcp required	Min. Handicap	30/36 (Damen)			

CLUB HOUSE & AMENITIES
KLUBHAUS UND NEBENGEBÄUDE   6/10

Pro shop	Pro shop	▰▰▰▰▱▱
Driving range	Übungsplatz	▰▰▰▱▱▱
Sheltered	überdacht	6 Plätze
On grass	auf Rasen	April-Nov.
Putting-green	Putting-grün	ja
Pitching-green	Pitching-grün	ja

HOTEL FACILITIES
HOTEL BESCHREIBUNG   7/10

HOTELS HOTELS
Schlosshotel Monrepos   Ludwigsburg
81 Zimmer, D DM 280,-   7 km
Tel (49) 07141 - 3020, Fax (49) 07141 - 302 200

Kronen Stuben   Ludwigsburg
8 Zimmer, D DM 135,-   4 km
Tel (49) 07141 - 96250

Nestor Hotel   Ludwigsburg
60 Zimmer, D DM 180,-   4 km
Tel (49) 07141 - 9670, Fax (49) 07141 - 967 113

Adler   Asperg
65 Zimmer, D DM 250,-   8 km
Tel (49) 07141 - 26 600, Fax (49) 07141 - 266 060

RESTAURANTS RESTAURANT
Le Carat, Tel (49) 07141 - 47 600   Ludwigsburg, 5 km
Adler, Tel (49) 07141 - 26 600   Asperg, 8 km

369

Alles in allem sind die vorhandenen Schwierigkeiten durchaus dazu angetan, den durchschnittlichen "Hacker" permanent zu beunruhigen. Objektiv betrachtet ist der Platz aber gar nicht so schwierig, doch was heisst das schon in Anbetracht der Tatsache, dass Golf ebenso sehr mit dem Kopf wie mit dem Körper gespielt wird. Einige extrem lange Par 4 Löcher stellen eine anspruchsvolle Aufgabe selbst für bessere Spieler dar, die auch beim Anspiel einiger frontal von Gräben geschützter Grüns, eine harte Nuss zu knacken haben. Die intelligente Plazierung der Hindernisse spricht für den Sachverstand der Architekten. Die sehr amerikanische Platzarchitektur mit dem Merkmal gut erkennbarer Schwierigkeiten verlangt vom Golfer häufig die Entscheidung, entweder auf Angriff oder auf Sicherheit zu spielen. Bevor man daran geht, auf diesem technisch wie auch taktisch anspruchsvollen Layout, ein gutes Zählspiel-Ergebnis zu erreichen, empfiehlt es sich vorher einige Runden Matchplay zu spielen.

By and large there are quite a few difficulties around, enough to prevent the average hacker from ever really feeling confident, although objectively this is not the most difficult course in the world. But no-one needs telling that golf is as much a matter of mind as of body. Some very long par 4s will also be a handful for the better players, who will need to think long and hard before trying to hit several greens guarded by frontal ditches. The designers knew their golf and have laid out hazards intelligently. Rather American in style, Neuhof calls for serious debate over whether to "go for it" or lay up. In this sense the difficulties are clear to see, but before envisioning any idea of a good card from this technical and tactical examination of your golfing skills, you are better off trying a few rounds of matchplay.

Golf Club Neuhof e.V.
Hofgut Neuhof
D - 63303 DREIEICH

Office	Sekretariat	(49) 06102 - 327 010
Pro shop	Pro shop	(49) 06102 - 33 331
Fax	Fax	(49) 06102 - 327 012
Situation	Lage	

15 km von Frankfurt, 660 000 Ew. 6 km von Neu-Isenburg

Annual closure	Jährliche Schliessung	ja
		1/01→28/02
Weekly closure	Wöchentliche Schliessung	Montag
		das Restaurant

Fees main season Preisliste hochsaison 18 Löcher

	Week days Woche	We/Bank holidays We/Feiertag
Individual Individuell	DM 100,-	DM 100,-
Couple Ehepaar	DM 200,-	DM 200,-

We: nur in Mitgliederbegleitung (with members)
21 Jahre/Studenten: – 50 %

Caddy	Caddy	auf Reservierung
Electric Trolley	Elektrokarren	nein
Buggy	Elektrischer Wagen	nein
Clubs	Clubs	DM 10,-

Credit cards Kreditkarten   nein

Access Zufahrt : A3 Frankfurt-Würzburg. Ausf.
Offenbach-Kreuz? B661 → Langen/Darmstadt. Ausf.
Dreieich-Götzenhain. 3 km Golfplatz
Map 3 on page 297 Karte 3 Seite 297

GOLF COURSE
PLATZ   **15**/20

Site	Lage	
Maintenance	Instandhaltung	
Architect	Architekt	Hauser
		Patrick Merrigan
Type	Typ	Park
Relief	Relief	
Water in play	Platz mit Wasser	
Exp. to wind	Wind ausgesetzt	
Trees in play	Platz mit Bäumen	

Scorecard Scorekarte	Chp. Chp.	Mens Herren	Ladies Damen
Length Länge	6151	5995	5340
Par	72	72	72

Advised golfing ability	0	12	24	36
Empfohlene Spielstärke				

Hcp required	Min. Handicap	28/32 (Damen)

CLUB HOUSE & AMENITIES
KLUBHAUS UND NEBENGEBÄUDE   **7**/10

Pro shop	Pro shop	
Driving range	Übungsplatz	
Sheltered	überdacht	ja
On grass	auf Rasen	ja
Putting-green	Putting-grün	ja
Pitching-green	Pitching-grün	

HOTEL FACILITIES
HOTEL BESCHREIBUNG   **7**/10

HOTELS HOTELS
Kempinski Hotel Gravenbruch   Neu-Isenburg-
289 Zimmer, D DM 300,-   Gravenbruch 5 km
Tel (49) 06102 - 5050, Fax (49) 06102 - 505 445

Balance Hotel   Neu-Isenbuch
164 Zimmer, D DM 300,-   5 km
Tel (49) 06102 - 7460, Fax (49) 06102 - 746 746

Linde, 37 Zimmer - D DM 150,-   Neu-Isenburg
Tel (49) 06102 - 7020   5 km

Arabella Grand Hotel   Frankfurt
378 Zimmer, D DM 500,-   15 km
Tel (49) 069 - 29 810, Fax (49) 069 - 298 1810

RESTAURANTS RESTAURANT
Neuer Haferkasten   Neu-Isenburg 5 km
Tel (49) 06102 - 35 329

Grüner Baum Tel (49) 06102 - 38 318   Neu-Isenburg

Eine schöne Gegend für Ferien er etwas anderen Art. Mit dem Schwarzwald im Westen, der Schweiz im Süden und dem Bodensee im Osten herrscht hier kein Mangel an Golfgelegenheiten. Zumindest den Nicht-Golfern in der Familie bieten sich eine Vielzahl von Alternativen zur Freizeitgestaltung. Obere Alp ist zwar schon recht hoch gelegen und verläuft auch auf ziemlich hügeligem Gelände, kann deswegen aber noch nicht als "Gebirgsplatz" bezeichnet werden. Dafür spricht auch, dass von den erhöht angelegten Grüns keines wirklich "blind" ist. Obgleich die Platzarchitektur traditionell britisch wirkt, verlangen die gut geschützten Grüns eher nach "target Golf" denn nach für die Insel typischen "bump and run" Schlägen. Auf den ersten Blick erscheint der Platz recht lang. Dieser Eindruck wird aber durch die Ausgewogenheit des Layouts und den aufgrund der Höhenlage weiteren Ballflug, etwas gemildert. Die Trainingseinrichtungen sind hervorragend, insbesondere der Par 3 9-Loch-Platz.

A beautiful region for holidays "with a difference". With the Black Forest to the west, Switzerland to the south and Bodensee to the east, there is no shortage of opportunity to play golf. At least the family's non-golfers will have something to do to pass the time. Obere Alp is set pretty high up, and although rather hilly, it doesn't really qualify for the "mountain course" label. While some greens are elevated, none is really blind, so that's already a point in its favour. Yet they are well guarded enough to require a touch of target golf rather than the British style bump and run, even though the general design has a lot of British tradition about it. The course may seem long, but at altitude balls fly further, and the well balanced layout of the holes here tend to dampen this first impression. Practice facilities are excellent, especially the par 3 nine-hole course.

Golfclub Obere Alp e.V.
Am Golfplatz 1-3
D - 79780 STÜHLINGEN

Office	Sekretariat	(49) 07703 - 92 030
Pro shop	Pro shop	(49) 07703 - 920 330
Fax	Fax	(49) 07703 - 920 318
Situation	Lage	

25 km von Donaueschingen, 20 000 Ew.
8 km von Stühlingen, 5 000 Ew.

Annual closure	Jährliche Schliessung	ja
		1/12→31/03
Weekly closure	Wöchentliche Schliessung	nein

Fees main season Preisliste hochsaison 18 Löcher

	Week days Woche	We/Bank holidays We/Feiertag
Individual Individuell	DM 60,-	DM 90,-
Couple Ehepaar	DM 120,-	DM 180,-

Caddy	Caddy	nein
Electric Trolley	Elektrokarren	nein
Buggy	Elektrischer Wagen	nein
Clubs	Clubs	DM 20,-
Credit cards Kreditkarten		nein

Access Zufahrt : A8 Stuttgart-Singen →
Donaueschingen, Stühlingen.
Stühlingen, → Bonndorf.
Map 1 on page 293 Karte 1 Seite 293

GOLF COURSE
PLATZ — 14/20

Site	Lage	
Maintenance	Instandhaltung	
Architect	Architekt	
Type	Typ	Flachland, Gebirge
Relief	Relief	
Water in play	Platz mit Wasser	
Exp. to wind	Wind ausgesetzt	
Trees in play	Platz mit Bäumen	

Scorecard	Chp.	Mens	Ladies
Scorekarte	Chp.	Herren	Damen
Length Länge	6216	6047	5337
Par	72	72	72

Advised golfing ability	0	12	24	36
Empfohlene Spielstärke				
Hcp required	Min. Handicap	36		

CLUB HOUSE & AMENITIES
KLUBHAUS UND NEBENGEBÄUDE — 7/10

Pro shop	Pro shop	
Driving range	Übungsplatz	
Sheltered	überdacht	14 Plätzen
On grass	auf Rasen	April-Okt.
Putting-green	Putting-grün	ja
Pitching-green	Pitching-grün	ja

371

HOTEL FACILITIES
HOTEL BESCHREIBUNG — 7/10

HOTELS HOTELS
Obere Alp, 15 Zimmer, D DM 120,-   Golfplatz
Tel (49) 07703 - 7820, Fax (49) 07703 - 7053

Mittlere Alp, 10 Zimmer, D DM 100,-   Golfplatz
Tel (49) 07703 - 7395   500 m

Hetzel   Schluchsee
214 Zimmer, D DM 400,-   20 km
Tel (49) 07656 - 70 326, Fax (49) 07656 - 70 323

Hegers Parkhotel Flora   Schluchsee 20 km
34 Zimmer, D DM 200,-
Tel (49) 07656 - 452, Fax (49) 07656 - 1433

RESTAURANTS RESTAURANT
Hetzel, Tel (49) 07656 - 70 323   Schluchsee, 20 km

Schwarzwaldstube   Schluchsee, 20 km
Tel(49) 07656 - 1200

Diese ruhige Gegend Frankens wird in erster Linie von Liebhabern barocker Architektur, und mehr noch, von den Besuchern der Bayreuther Festspiele frequentiert. Von wagnerischem Pomp ist beim Golfplatz nichts zu spüren. Oberfranken ist eine klassisch konzipierte Anlage, die sich gut in das unebene Gelände einfügt, und daher vor allem Spielern mit guter Kondition zu empfehlen ist. Schöner, alter Baumbestand schmückt die Landschaft und stellt auf den ersten Blick die Hauptschwierigkeit dar, obschon auch Wasser und Bunker manchmal recht gefährlich werden können. Golfer mittlerer Spielstärke werden sich sicher schwer tun, hier ihr Handicap zu schaffen, obwohl das technische Niveau des Platzes eigentlich von allen Spielern zu meistern ist. Der diskret-elegante Kurs, der sich in der Zeit zwischen spätem Frühling und Frühherbst von seiner schönsten Seite zeigt, zählt zweifellos zu den besten Anlagen der Region.

This peaceful region of Franconia comes alive with visits from lovers of baroque architecture and, more particularly, from "pilgrims" to the Bayreuth Festival. But there's nothing grandiose or Wagnerian about this course, which is very classical in style and naturally hugs a terrain that is hilly enough to recommend it basically for golfers in good physical shape. Beautiful old trees enhance the landscape and at first sight form the main hazards, although water and sand are also sometimes a dangerous proposition. Mid-handicappers will certainly find it hard here to achieve a good score, even though the course is technically speaking within the grasp of most golfers. A discreet and elegant course, Oberfranken is at its best from late spring to early autumn and is one of the region's best golfing stop-offs.

Golf Club Oberfranken e.V., Thurnau

Petershof
D - 95349 THURNAU

Office	Sekretariat	(49) 09228 - 319
Pro shop	Pro shop	(49) 09228 - 1022
Fax	Fax	(49) 09228 - 7219
Situation	Lage	

25 km von Bayreuth, 72 000 Ew.
80 km von Nürnberg, 498 000 Ew.

Annual closure	Jährliche Schliessung	ja
		30/11→28/02
Weekly closure	Wöchentliche Schliessung	Montag
		das Restaurant

Fees main season Preisliste hochsaison den ganzen Tag

	Week days Woche	We/Bank holidays We/Feiertag
Individual Individuell	DM 60,-	DM 80,-
Couple Ehepaar	DM 120,-	DM 160,-

– 21 Jahre/Studenten : – 50%

Caddy	Caddy	nein
Electric Trolley	Elektrokarren	ja
Buggy	Elektrischer Wagen	ja
Clubs	Clubs	ja
Credit cards Kreditkarten		nein

Access Zufahrt : Nürnberg, A9 → Berlin. Ausf.
Kulmbach-Bayreuth. B505 Ausf. Thurnau.
Map 4 on page 298 Karte 4 Seite 298

GOLF COURSE
PLATZ   17 /20

Site	Lage	■■■■■□
Maintenance	Instandhaltung	■■■■■□
Architect	Architekt	B. von Limburger
		D. Harradine
Type	Typ	Wald, Park
Relief	Relief	■■■■□□
Water in play	Platz mit Wasser	■■■□□□
Exp. to wind	Wind ausgesetzt	■■□□□□
Trees in play	Platz mit Bäumen	■■■■■□

Scorecard	Chp.	Mens	Ladies
Scorekarte	Chp.	Herren	Damen
Length Länge	6152	6152	5433
Par	72	72	72

Advised golfing ability   0   12   24   36
Empfohlene Spielstärke   ■■■■■■■
Hcp required   Min. Handicap   36

CLUB HOUSE & AMENITIES
KLUBHAUS UND NEBENGEBÄUDE   6 /10

Pro shop	Pro shop	■■■■□□
Driving range	Übungsplatz	■■■■□□
Sheltered	überdacht	3 Plätze
On grass	auf Rasen	ja
Putting-green	Putting-grün	ja
Pitching-green	Pitching-grün	ja

HOTEL FACILITIES
HOTEL BESCHREIBUNG   5 /10

HOTELS HOTELS
Brauerei-Gasthof Schnupp   Neudrossenfeld
27 Zimmer, D DM 175,-   11 km
Tel (49) 09203 - 99 20, Fax (49) 09203 - 99 250

Bayerischer Hof   Bayreuth
49 Zimmer, D DM 250,-   20 km
Tel (49) 0921 - 78 600, Fax (49) 0921 - 22 085

Goldener Hirsch   Bayreuth
40 Zimmer, D DM 220,-   20 km
Tel (49) 0921 - 23 046, Fax (49) 0921 - 22 483

RESTAURANTS RESTAURANT
Schloss-Restaurant   Neudrossenfeld
Tel (49) 09203 - 68 368   10 km

Schlosshotel Thiergarten   Bayreuth
Tel (49) 09209 - 98 40   28 km

Der Platz liegt in einer traditionell bayerischen Umgebung, die einer dicht-bewaldeten Parkanlage ähnelt. Am Kurs werden in Kürze einige Änderungen vorgenommen, von denen wir hoffen, dass sie das Spielvergnügen noch weiter steigern werden. Es gibt hier jeweils fünf Par 3 und Par 5 Löcher, an denen kürzere Spieler genügend gute Chancen aufs Par haben, der Tatsache Rechnung tragend, dass sich der Durchchnitts-Golfer in dieser Hinsicht an Par 4 Löchern häufig am schwersten tut. Aus dem gleichen Grund sollte man die hinteren Abschläge meiden. Der schön gelegene Platz weist eine respektable Länge auf. Senioren empfehlen wir wegen des etwas hügeligen Geländes die Benutzung eines Golfwagens. Die heikelste Passage lauert zwischen Loch 10 und 12. Da der Boden oft feucht ist und ein halbes Dutzend Grüns erhöht liegen, sollte man einen hohen Pitch beherrschen. Insgesamt sind die einen erwartenden Schwierigkeiten keineswegs so bedrohlich, dass Mittelklasse-Spieler sich davon entmutigen lassen. Angenehm zu spielen und abwechslungsreich gestaltet, lohnt die Anlage einen Besuch sowohl der Lage als auch des Layouts wegen.

In a traditional Bavarian setting of densely wooded park-land, we can firstly only hope that the planned alterations will enhance the pleasure of playing here. With five par 5s and five par 3s, the course gives short-hitters the chance to sign for a few pars, knowing full well that the average hacker has the biggest problems with par 4s. In this case, don't opt for the back-tees. Set in a pretty region, the course is a little hilly for senior players (buggy recommended) and respectable in length; the trickiest section awaits you between the 10th and 12th. Since it is often wet and half a dozen greens are elevated, the high pitch shot is a must, but the hardships here are not threatening enough to discourage the average golfer. Pleasant and nicely varied, this course is worth the trip for both the layout and the site.

Golf-Club Oberschwaben Bad Waldsee

Fürstliches Hofgut Hopfenweiler
D - 88339 BAD WALDSEE

Office	Sekretariat	(49) 07524 - 5900
Pro shop	Pro shop	(49) 07524 - 48 778
Fax	Fax	(49) 07524 - 6106
Situation	Lage	

60 km von Ulm, 110 000 Ew.
20 km von Ravensburg, 46 000 Ew.

Annual closure	Jährliche Schliessung	ja
		1/11→31/03
Weekly closure	Wöchentliche Schliessung	Montag
		das Restaurant

Fees main season Preisliste hochsaison 18 Löcher

	Week days Woche	We/Bank holidays We/Feiertag
Individual Individuell	DM 65,-	DM 90,-
Couple Ehepaar	DM 130,-	DM 180,-

– 21 Jahre/Studenten: – 50%

Caddy	Caddy	nein
Electric Trolley	Elektrokarren	nein
Buggy	Elektrischer Wagen	nein
Clubs	Clubs	ja
Credit cards Kreditkarten		nein

Biberach ↑

0 — 2 — 4 km

Access Zufahrt : A8 München-Stuttgart. Ausf. Ulm-West. B30 → Bodensee. Bad Waldsee → Golfplatz
Map 1 on page 293 Karte 1 Seite 293

GOLF COURSE PLATZ   15/20

Site	Lage	▓▓▓▓░░
Maintenance	Instandhaltung	▓▓▓▓░░
Architect	Architekt	
Type	Typ	Wald, Park
Relief	Relief	
Water in play	Platz mit Wasser	▓▓░░░░
Exp. to wind	Wind ausgesetzt	▓▓░░░░
Trees in play	Platz mit Bäumen	▓▓▓▓▓░

Scorecard Scorekarte	Chp. Chp.	Mens Herren	Ladies Damen
Length Länge	6148	6148	5385
Par	72	72	72

Advised golfing ability		0 12 24 36
Empfohlene Spielstärke		▓▓▓▓▓░
Hcp required	Min. Handicap	34

CLUB HOUSE & AMENITIES KLUBHAUS UND NEBENGEBÄUDE   6/10

Pro shop	Pro shop	▓▓▓▓░░
Driving range	Übungsplatz	▓▓▓░░░
Sheltered	überdacht	ja
On grass	auf Rasen	ja
Putting-green	Putting-grün	ja
Pitching-green	Pitching-grün	ja

HOTEL FACILITIES HOTEL BESCHREIBUNG   6/10

HOTELS HOTELS
Kur-Parkhotel   Bad Waldsee
64 Zimmer, D DM 200,-   2 km
Tel (49) 07524 - 97 070, Fax (49) 07524 - 970 775

Altes Tor   Bad Waldsee
28 Zimmer, D DM 160,-   2 km
Tel (49) 07524 - 97 190, Fax (49) 07524 - 971 997

Kurpension Schwabenland   Bad Waldsee
17 Zimmer, D DM 130,-   2 km
Tel (49) 07524 - 5011

RESTAURANTS RESTAURANT
Waldhorn   Ravensburg
Tel (49) 0751 - 36 120   20 km

Krone   Schlier
Tel (49) 07529 - 1292   25 km

373

Der ideale Ort um ein paar Golftage zu verbringen und die herrlichen Umgebung von Schwarzwald und Donauquelle zu erkunden. Übernachten können Sie im gut ausgestatteten, komfortablen Hotel der Anlage. Der beachtlich lange Platz wird im Verlauf des Jahres um 9 Löcher erweitert. Er verläuft auf relativ ebenem Gelände und kann so leicht zu Fuss bewältigt werden. Obwohl die Hindernisse alle gut erkennbar sind, muss man mehrere Runden spielen um die strategischen Nuancen des Layouts zu begreifen. Ein Wasserlauf kreuzt acht Spielbahnen und bildet eine der Hauptschwierigkeiten, zu denen ebenfalls zahlreiche Bäume und Bunker zählen. Zum Glück sind die Grüns nicht ausgesprochen gut verteidigt, so dass auch der Durchschnitts-Golfer sie einigermassen gut anspielen kann. Der Kurs ist in der Tat so angelegt, dass er nervenschonendes Vergnügen bereitet und schmeichlerische Ergebnisse ermöglicht - ein typischer Urlaubsplatz eben.

An ideal site for a few days golfing, staying in a well-equipped, comfortable hotel (with pool, sauna and jacuzzi) or for exploring this superb region of the Black Forest and sources of the Danube. The course is flat enough for easy walking and during the year will be supplemented by a new 9 holer. It is very reasonable in terms of yardage, but although the hazards are generally visible on each hole, you need several rounds to appreciate the course's strategic "nuances". A stream winds it way across eight holes and forms a major, but not the only, difficulty, as trees and bunkers abound. Fortunately, the greens are not over-protected and approach shots are not too complicated for the average golfer. This is indeed a course designed for enjoyment, where you can card sometimes flattering scores without suffering from nervous exhaustion, so it's just the job the holidays.

Land- und Golf-Club Öschberghof

Golfplatz 1
D - 78166 DONAUESCHINGEN

Office	Sekretariat	(49) 0771 - 84 525
Pro shop	Pro shop	(49) 0771 - 84 530
Fax	Fax	(49) 0771 - 84 540
Situation	Lage	

5 km von Donaueschingen, 20 000 Ew.

Annual closure Jährliche Schliessung ja
1/11→31/03

Weekly closure Wöchentliche Schliessung Montag
Das Restaurant

Fees main season Preisliste hochsaison 18 Löcher

	Week days Woche	We/Bank holidays We/Feiertag
Individual Individuell	DM 80,-	DM 120,-
Couple Ehepaar	DM 160,-	DM 240,-

– 25 Jahre: – 50 %

Caddy	Caddy	DM 5,-
Electric Trolley	Elektrokarren	DM 30,-
Buggy	Elektrischer Wagen	DM 40,-
Clubs	Clubs	DM 25,-

Credit cards Kreditkarten
VISA - Eurocard - MasterCard - AMEX - DC

374

Access Zufahrt : A81 Stuttgart-Singen. Ausf. Bad Dürenheimer Kreuz, E70 → Donaueschingen. Ausf. Donaueschingen-Mitte. → Golfplatz
Map 1 on page 293 Karte 1 Seite 293

GOLF COURSE
PLATZ 15/20

Site	Lage	▰▰▰▰▱
Maintenance	Instandhaltung	▰▰▰▱▱
Architect	Architekt	
Type	Typ	Flachland, Park
Relief	Relief	▰▱▱▱▱
Water in play	Platz mit Wasser	▰▰▰▱▱
Exp. to wind	Wind ausgesetzt	▰▱▱▱▱
Trees in play	Platz mit Bäumen	▰▰▰▱▱

Scorecard Scorekarte	Chp. Chp.	Mens Herren	Ladies Damen
Length Länge	6155	6155	5413
Par	74	74	74

Advised golfing ability 0 12 24 36
Empfohlene Spielstärke ▰▰▰▰▱

Hcp required Min. Handicap 35

CLUB HOUSE & AMENITIES
KLUBHAUS UND NEBENGEBÄUDE 7/10

Pro shop	Pro shop	▰▰▰▰▱
Driving range	Übungsplatz	▰▰▰▱▱
Sheltered	überdacht	8 Plätze
On grass	auf Rasen	April → Sept.
Putting-green	Putting-grün	ja
Pitching-green	Pitching-grün	ja

HOTEL FACILITIES
HOTEL BESCHREIBUNG 7/10

HOTELS HOTELS
Hotel Öschberghof 500 m
93 Zimmer, D DM 290,-
Tel (49) 0771 - 840, Fax (49) 0771 - 84 260

Concord Donaueschingen
76 Zimmer, D DM 165,- 3 km
Tel (49) 0771 - 83 630, Fax (49) 0771 - 836 3120

Henzelhof Bad Dürrheim
61 Zimmer, D DM 192,- 10 km
Tel (49) 07726 - 6670, Fax (49) 07726 - 667 555

RESTAURANTS RESTAURANT
Hotel Öschberghof 500 m
Tel (49) 0771 - 84 610

Babitzle Donaueschingen
Tel (49) 0771 - 63 062 5 km

PINNAU

14 6 6

Der Platz verdankt seinen Namen dem Fluss Pinnau, der teilweise entlang des Golfgeländes verläuft. Obwohl der Fluss selbst nie ins Spiel kommt, gibt es andere Wasserhindernisse in bedrohlicher Lage vor den Grüns, um unerfahrene Spieler einzuschüchtern, die hier schnell einige Schläge verlieren können. Spielern mit hohen Handicaps machen auch die Grüns zu schaffen, die teilweise stark onduliert sind, aber in gestalterischer Hinsicht zu wünschen übrig lassen. Dieser Platz favorisiert technisch versierte Spieler, die es verstehen, mit den einzeln stehenden Bäumen fertigzuwerden, die vom Architekten geschickt mit ins strategische Kalkül einbezogen wurden. Der flache Platz ist einfach zu Gehen und trocknet gut ab. Golfer aller Spielstärken können sich hier entfalten, wenngleich methodische Spieler gegenüber Longhittern im Vorteil sind. Wenn möglich sollten Sie an der 10 beginnen, da die zweiten Neun etwas weniger interessant sind als der Rest. Wir empfehlen Matchplay, da auf diesem Kurs alles Mögliche passieren kann.

Pinnau takes its name from the river that partly skirts the course. And although this running water never really comes into play, other water hazards in front of the greens are threatening enough to intimidate the more inexperienced players, who can quickly suffer here. High-handicappers will also find the putting surfaces a handful, too, which are sometimes excessively contoured and lacking in inspiration design-wise. With that said, this is a course for the technicians, who will have to cope with strategically located isolated trees, the finest of which have been smartly used by the designer. Flattish and well-drained, the course is a pleasant one to walk, where golfers of all abilities can unfold their game, even though the thoughtful technician will have the upper hand over the long-hitter. If you can, tee off at the 10th, as the back nine are a little less exciting than the rest. And prefer match play, as well, because anything can happen here.

Golf Club An der Pinnau

Pinneberger Strasse 81a
D - 25451 QUICKBORN-RENZEL

Office	Sekretariat	(49) 04106 - 81 800
Pro shop	Pro shop	(49) 04106 - 60 876
Fax	Fax	(49) 04106 - 82 003
Situation	Lage	

1 km von Quickborn, 18 500 Ew.
25 km von Hamburg, 1 650 000 Ew.

Annual closure	Jährliche Schliessung	nein
Weekly closure	Wöchentliche Schliessung	nein

Fees main season
Preisliste hochsaison 18 Löcher

	Week days Woche	We/Bank holidays We/Feiertag
Individual Individuell	DM 60,-	DM 80,-
Couple Ehepaar	DM 120,-	DM 160,-

- 21 Jahre: – 50 %

Caddy	Caddy	auf Reservierung
Electric Trolley	Elektrokarren	nein
Buggy	Elektrischer Wagen	nein
Clubs	Clubs	nein

Credit cards Kreditkarten nein

Access Zufahrt : A7 Hamburg → Flensburg. Ausf.
Quickborn. → Quickborn, Renzel → Pinneberg.
Map 7 on page 304 Karte 7 Seite 304

GOLF COURSE
PLATZ

14/20

Site	Lage	
Maintenance	Instandhaltung	
Architect	Architekt	
Type	Typ	Land, Flachland
Relief	Relief	
Water in play	Platz mit Wasser	
Exp. to wind	Wind ausgesetzt	
Trees in play	Platz mit Bäumen	

Scorecard Scorekarte	Chp. Chp.	Mens Herren	Ladies Damen
Length Länge	6188	6188	5438
Par	72	72	72

Advised golfing ability Empfohlene Spielstärke		0 12 24 36
Hcp required	Min. Handicap	36

CLUB HOUSE & AMENITIES
KLUBHAUS UND NEBENGEBÄUDE

6/10

Pro shop	Pro shop	
Driving range	Übungsplatz	
Sheltered	überdacht	4 Plätze
On grass	auf Rasen	ja
Putting-green	Putting-grün	ja
Pitching-green	Pitching-grün	ja

HOTEL FACILITIES
HOTEL BESCHREIBUNG

6/10

HOTELS HOTELS
Jagdhaus Waldfrieden   Quickborn
14 Zimmer, D DM 230,-   3 km
Tel (49) 04106 - 3771, Fax (49) 04106 - 69196

Landhaus Quickborn-Heide   Quickborn-Heide
18 Zimmer, D DM 175,-
Tel (49) 04106 - 77 660, Fax (49) 04106 - 74 969

Wiking Hotel   Henstedt-Ulzburg
36 Zimmer, D DM 140,-   10 km
Tel (49) 04193 - 9080, Fax (49) 04193 - 92 323

RESTAURANTS RESTAURANT
Jagdhaus Waldfrieden   Quickborn
Tel (49) 04106 - 3771   3 km

375

REICHSSTADT BAD WINDSHEIM | 14 | 6 | 7 |

Nahe Würzburg und Nürnberg liegt der Golfplatz an der "Romantischen Strasse", die von Würzburg über Augsburg, durch die Schweiz nach Italien führt, und an deren Weg sich immer wieder Städte und Schlösser aus den Epochen des Mittelalters, der Renaissance und des Barock finden. Gleichermassen erwähnenswert sind die Weinberge (Frankenwein) des Maintals. Falls Sie sich von den kulturellen Attraktionen losreissen können, verpassen Sie auf keinen Fall die Golfplätze dieser Gegend, insbesondere nicht diesen, der ebenso handfest und bodenständig ist wie die regionale Küche. Ebene Flächen wechseln sich ab mit hügeligerem Terrain auf einem Parcours, der insgesamt einen sehr ausgewogenen Eindruck macht. Die Grüns sind enorm gross und sehr gut verteidigt. Es gibt praktisch keine Bäume, was den Platz sehr windanfällig macht. Einige Wasserhindernisse, gefährliche Bunker, Dickicht und Rough tragen dazu bei, dass der Score voraussichtlich ein paar Schläge über dem Handicap liegen wird.

Very close to Würzburg and Nürnberg, this course is on the route taken by the "Romantic Road", which started out from Würzburg and ran down to Augsburg then on to Switzerland and Italy, crossing towns and castles testifying to the Middle Ages, the Renaissance and the Baroque period. Equally important are the vineyards in the Main valley (Franconia wine). If you can tear yourself away from the cultural fascinations, don't miss the golf courses in this province, especially this one, as serious a layout as the regional cooking. With flat spaces alternating with hillier terrain and well-balanced overall, the course has huge, well-guarded greens, is virtually tree-less and can get very tough when the wind blows. A few water hazards and dangerous bunkers, the thickets and rough are all there to nudge your score a few strokes above your handicap. Inexperienced golfers will enjoy their round if they do not count their score.

Golf Club Reichsstadt Bad Windsheim e.V.

Am Weinturm 2
D - 91438 BAD WINDSHEIM

Office	Sekretariat	(49) 09841 - 5027
Pro shop	Pro shop	(49) 09841 - 2497
Fax	Fax	(49) 09841 - 3448
Situation	Lage	

40 km von Würzburg, 129 000 Ew. 50 km von Nürnberg.

Annual closure	Jährliche Schliessung	nein
Weekly closure	Wöchentliche Schliessung	Montag
		das Restaurant

Fees main season Preisliste hochsaison den ganzen Tag

	Week days Woche	We/Bank holidays We/Feiertag
Individual Individuell	DM 60,-	DM 80,-
Couple Ehepaar	DM 120,-	DM 160,-

– 21 Jahre/Studenten : – 50 %

Caddy	Caddy	auf Reservierung
Electric Trolley	Elektrokarren	nein
Buggy	Elektrischer Wagen	nein
Clubs	Clubs	ja
Credit cards Kreditkarten		nein

376

nach Uffenheim

GOLF

Neuherberg
Ergersheim
13
BAD WINDSHEIM

Illesheim
nach Neustadt a. d. Aisch

A7
470
107

nach Ansbach

0   2   4 km

Access Zufahrt : • A7 Ulm-Würzburg. Ausf. Bad Windsheim. B470 → Neustadt/Bad Windsheim. In Bad Windsheim → Oberntief. • Nürnberg → Fürth. B8 zu Neustadt. B470 → Bad Windsheim
Map 4 on page 298 Karte 4 Seite 298

GOLF COURSE
PLATZ 14/20

Site	Lage	■■■■■
Maintenance	Instandhaltung	■■■■■
Architect	Architekt	
Type	Typ	Flachland
Relief	Relief	■■■■
Water in play	Platz mit Wasser	■■■■
Exp. to wind	Wind ausgesetzt	■■■■■
Trees in play	Platz mit Bäumen	■

Scorecard Scorekarte	Chp. Chp.	Mens Herren	Ladies Damen
Length Länge	6265	6265	5524
Par	73	73	73

Advised golfing ability Empfohlene Spielstärke		0 12 24 36
		■■■■■
Hcp required Min. Handicap	36	

CLUB HOUSE & AMENITIES
KLUBHAUS UND NEBENGEBÄUDE 6/10

Pro shop	Pro shop	■■■■■
Driving range	Übungsplatz	■■■■
Sheltered	überdacht	4 Plätze
On grass	auf Rasen	ja
Putting-green	Putting-grün	ja
Pitching-green	Pitching-grün	ja

HOTEL FACILITIES
HOTEL BESCHREIBUNG 7/10

HOTELS HOTELS

Kurhotel Residenz   Bad Windsheim
128 Zimmer, D DM 200,-   5 km
Tel (49) 09841 - 910, Fax (49) 09841 - 912 663

Am Kurpark   Bad Windsheim
50 Zimmer, D DM 160,-   5 km
Tel (49) 09841 - 9020, Fax (49) 09841 - 90 243

Goldener Schwan   Bad Windsheim
22 Zimmer, D DM 120,-   5 km
Tel (49) 09841 - 5061, Fax (49) 09841 - 79 440

RESTAURANTS RESTAURANT

Neustadt Stuben   Neustadt an der Aisch
Tel (49) 09161 - 5622   20 km

Kurhotel Residenz   Bad Windsheim
Tel (49) 09841 - 910   5 km

REICHSWALD-NÜRNBERG ⟩ 17 7 7

Der Wald spiegelt wohl am besten den Geist der deutschen Romantik wider. Seine Erhaltung und sein Schutz sind zu einem wichtigen gesellschaftlichen Anliegen, insbesondere der Umweltschützer, geworden. Eine ganze Runde in einem solch mächtigen Wald zu spielen, vermittelt einem das Gefühl von Ruhe und Zufriedenheit - es ist, als wäre man ganz alleine auf der Welt. Hier muss man in Topform sein und den Ball kontrolliert schlagen, um den allgegenwärtigen Pinienbäumen aus dem Weg zu gehen und mit dem Drive in eine Position zu gelangen, die einem das Anspiel der gut durch Bunker verteidigten Grüns ermöglicht. Wenn man gut spielt, werden einen die Wasserläufe und Hindernisse, die ein - wenn auch nicht übermässiges - Gefahrenelement darstellen, weniger einschüchtern. Spieler, denen es an Übung und Genauigkeit fehlt, werden vermutlich einen Einbruch erleben, aber schliesslich zwingt sie ja niemand dazu, all ihre Schläge auch zu zählen. Reichswald ist ohne Zweifel einer der besten Plätze der Region.

Forests are one of the key constituents of the German romantic soul ; their conservation and protection are now one of society's major concerns, especially with the ecologists. Playing a whole course in a forest such as this procures a feeling of incomparable peace and contentment ; on the course, you feel as if you were alone in the world. Here, you will need to be on top of your game to keep out of the pine-trees and flight your ball to land the drive in the best position to approach the greens (which are well guarded by bunkers). If you're playing well, you won't be too scared of the streams and hazards that add an element of difficulty but never excessively so. Players with little experience and problems of direction will probably suffer, but they don't have to count every stroke, do they ? One of the region's top layouts, this is a spectacular course which is fun to play again and again.

Golf Club Am Reichswald e.V., Nürnberg
Schiestlstrasse 100
D - 90427 NÜRNBERG

Office	Sekretariat	(49) 0911 - 305 730
Pro shop	Pro shop	(49) 0911 - 305 959
Fax	Fax	(49) 0911 - 301 200
Situation	Lage	

5 km von Nürnberg, 498 000 Ew.

Annual closure	Jährliche Schliessung	nein
Weekly closure	Wöchentliche Schliessung	Montag
		Das Restaurant

Fees main season
Preisliste hochsaison den ganzen Tag

	Week days Woche	We/Bank holidays We/Feiertag
Individual Individuell	DM 70,-	DM 100,-
Couple Ehepaar	DM 140,-	DM 200,-

– 21 Jahre : – 50%

Caddy	Caddy	auf Reservierung
Electric Trolley	Elektrokarren	nein
Buggy	Elektrischer Wagen	nein
Clubs	Clubs	ja
Credit cards Kreditkarten		nein

Access Zufahrt : BAB A3 Nürnberg → Würzburg. Ausf.
Tennenlohe. B4 → Nürnberg. Kraftshof.
Rechts → Golfplatz
Map 4 on page 298 Karte 4 Seite 298

GOLF COURSE PLATZ   17/20

Site	Lage	
Maintenance	Instandhaltung	
Architect	Architekt	
Type	Typ	Wald
Relief	Relief	
Water in play	Platz mit Wasser	
Exp. to wind	Wind ausgesetzt	
Trees in play	Platz mit Bäumen	

Scorecard Scorekarte	Chp. Chp.	Mens Herren	Ladies Damen
Length Länge	6103	6103	5469
Par	72	72	72

Advised golfing ability   0   12   24   36
Empfohlene Spielstärke

Hcp required   Min. Handicap   36

CLUB HOUSE & AMENITIES KLUBHAUS UND NEBENGEBÄUDE   7/10

Pro shop	Pro shop	
Driving range	Übungsplatz	
Sheltered	überdacht	3 Plätze
On grass	auf Rasen	nein
Putting-green	Putting-grün	ja
Pitching-green	Pitching-grün	ja

HOTEL FACILITIES HOTEL BESCHREIBUNG   7/10

HOTELS HOTELS
Maritim   Nürnberg
316 Zimmer, D DM 350,-   7 km
Tel (49) 0911 - 23 630, Fax (49) 0911 - 236 3836

Intercity Hotel   Nürnberg
158 Zimmer, D DM 280,-   7 km
Tel (49) 0911 - 24 780, Fax (49) 0911 - 247 8999

Dürer-Hotel   Nürnberg
105 Zimmer, D DM 250,-   7 km
Tel (49) 0911 - 208 091, Fax (49) 0911 - 223 458

Tassilo 79 Zimmer, D DM 250,-   Nürnberg
Tel (49) 0911 - 32 666, Fax (49) 0911 - 326 6799   5 km

RESTAURANTS RESTAURANT
Schwarzer Adler   Kraftshof
Tel (49) 0911 - 305 858   2 km
Alte Post, Tel (49) 0911 - 396 215   Kraftshof, 2 km

377

Die deutsche Wiedervereinigung brachte dieser Region zwischen Berlin und Frankfurt an der Oder neuen Aufschwung, insbesondere dem Gebiet rund um den grossen Scharmützelsee. Der erst kürzlich erstellte Golfplatz ist Teil eines 36-Loch Resorts, zu dem auch ein von Nick Faldo entworfener 18-Loch Platz gehört. Die Betreiber zögerten nicht, für ihr Projekt die Mitarbeit der Besten in Anspruch zu nehmen, und beauftragten Arnold Palmer mit dem Bau seines in Deutschland bislang einzigen Kurses. Der amerikanische Stil des in leicht unebenem Gelände angelegten Parcours ist offensichtlich, und nur die Landschaft erinnert daran, dass wir uns im Norden Deutschlands befinden. Das Layout ist gut durchdacht und so machen es die vorhandenen Schwierigkeiten nötig, mehrere Runden hier zu spielen, bis man sich mit der Anlage vertraut fühlt. Natürlich ist der Platz, besonders von den hinteren Abschlägen, auch sehr anspruchsvoll. Mehrere Abschlag-Boxen pro Loch ermöglichen es aber jedem Spieler, eine seinem Niveau entsprechende Wahl zu treffen.

The reunification of Germany has opened up new development in this region close to Berlin and Frankfurt an der Oder, particularly close to the huge Scharmützelsee. The present course is part of a 36-hole resort which also includes a Nick Faldo offering. The promoters didn't hesitate to call on the best, and this is Germany's only course designed by Arnold Palmer. It is moderately hilly and there are no prizes for guessing that this is an American style course, with only the landscape there to remind us that we are in northern Germany. The design is very intelligent, but the difficulties call for several rounds before getting acclimatised. Obviously, it is also very demanding, especially from the back tees, but there are enough tee-boxes for everyone to play the course that suits them best.

Sporting Club Berlin Scharmützelsee e.V.
Parkallee 3
D - 15526 BAD SAAROW

Office	Sekretariat	(49) 033631 - 5628
Pro shop	Pro shop	(49) 033631 - 5628
Fax	Fax	(49) 033631 - 5270
Situation	Lage	

35 km von Frankfurt/Oder, 86 000 Ew.
75 km von Berlin, 3 500 000 Ew.

Annual closure   Jährliche Schliessung
   30/11→1/03/99
Weekly closure   Wöchentliche Schliessung   nein
Fees main season Preisliste hochsaison   18 Löcher

	Week days Woche	We/Bank holidays We/Feiertag
Individual Individuell	DM 80,-	DM 100,-
Couple Ehepaar	DM 160,-	DM 200,-

Caddy	Caddy	DM 30,-
Electric Trolley	Elektrokarren	DM 10,-
Buggy	Elektrischer Wagen	DM 60,-
Clubs	Clubs	DM 20,-

Credit cards Kreditkarten
VISA - Eurocard - MasterCard - AMEX - DC - JCB

378

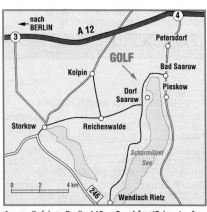

Access Zufahrt : Berlin A12 → Frankfurt/Oder. Ausf.
Fürstenwalde, → Bad Saarow → Golfplatz
Map 6 on page 303 Karte 6   Seite 303

GOLF COURSE
PLATZ   16/20

Site	Lage	▬▬▬▬▬▬
Maintenance	Instandhaltung	▬▬▬▬▬▬
Architect	Architekt	Arnold Palmer
Type	Typ	Wald, Park
Relief	Relief	▬▬▬▬
Water in play	Platz mit Wasser	▬▬
Exp. to wind	Wind ausgesetzt	▬▬▬
Trees in play	Platz mit Bäumen	▬▬▬▬

Scorecard Scorekarte	Chp. Chp.	Mens Herren	Ladies Damen
Length Länge	6582	6177	5466
Par	72	72	72

Advised golfing ability Empfohlene Spielstärke	0 12 24 36
	▬▬▬▬▬▬

Hcp required   Min. Handicap   nein

CLUB HOUSE & AMENITIES
KLUBHAUS UND NEBENGEBÄUDE   8/10

Pro shop	Pro shop	▬▬▬▬
Driving range	Übungsplatz	▬▬▬▬
Sheltered	überdacht	14 Plätze
On grass	auf Rasen	ja
Putting-green	Putting-grün	ja
Pitching-green	Pitching-grün	ja

HOTEL FACILITIES
HOTEL BESCHREIBUNG   7/10

HOTELS HOTELS
Hotel Kempinski   Golfplatz
160 Zimmer, D DM 290,-
   (49) 033631 - 60, (49) 033631 - 61 000

Palais Am See   Bad Saarow
12 Zimmer , D DM 180,-   4 km
Tel (49) 033631 - 8610, (49) 033631 - 86 186

Am Werl   Bad Saarow
13 , D DM 160,-   4 km
Tel (49) 033631 - 5231, (49) 033631 - 5233

RESTAURANTS RESTAURANT
Hotel Kempinski   Golfplatz
Tel (49) 033631 - 60

Am Werl   Bad Saarow
Tel (49) 033631 - 5231   4 km

Grosse Champions müssen sich oft den Vorwurf gefallen lassen, Plätze zu gestalten, ohne die dafür erforderliche Zeit und Mühe aufzuwenden. Auf Nick Faldo trifft dies nicht zu, da bei den leider nur wenigen von ihm bislang entworfenen Kursen seine ganz persönliche Handschrift deutlich erkennbar ist. Angesichts des herausragenden Designs dieses auf flachem, offenen Gelände erbauten Golfplatzes wünscht er sich, dass man bald eimal Gelegenheit bekommt, sein Können an einem Streifen "echten" Links-Terrains auszuprobieren. Die natürlichen und künstlichen Unebenheiten des häufig spektakulär und respekteinflössend anmutenden Geländes nutzt er geschickt für sein Spiel mit Links-typischen Elementen. Ungeachtet dessen eignet sich der Parcours für Golfer aller Spielstärken (die hinteren Abschläge sind für die Pros reserviert). Obwohl alle Schwierigkeiten gut erkennbar sind, benötigt man sicherlich einige Runden der Gewöhnung, bevor man hoffen darf, diesen Platz mit einem guten Ergebnis zu absolvieren. Der Kurs befindet sich bereits in einem ausgezeichneten Pflegezustand.

Great champions are often accused of signing courses without designing them too much. Not so for Nick Faldo, who visibly leaves his mark on the few (too few even) courses he designs. When you see the excellence of this course over a flat, open site, you can hardly wait to see him get to grips with a grand links site. He has toyed with the links idea here, using the natural and artificial undulations of often very spectacular and intimidating terrain. But golfers of all levels can play here easily enough (the back-tees are for the pros). Although the difficulties are clearly there to be seen, you will need to play this course several times (and in match-play) before even thinking about returning a good card at the end of the day. The course is already in good condition.

Sporting Club Berlin Scharmützelsee e.V.
Parkallee 3
D - 15526 BAD SAAROW

Office	Sekretariat	(49) 033631 - 5628
Pro shop	Pro shop	(49) 033631 - 5628
Fax	Fax	(49) 033631 - 5270
Situation	Lage	

35 km von Frankfurt/Oder, 86 000 Ew.
75 km von Berlin, 3 500 000 Ew.

Annual closure ährliche Schliessung
30/11→1/03/99

Weekly closure Wöchentliche Schliessung

Fees main season Preisliste hochsaison 18 Löcher

	Week days Woche	We/Bank holidays We/Feiertag
Individual Individuell	DM 80,-	DM 100,-
Couple Ehepaar	DM 160,-	DM 200,-

Caddy	Caddy	DM 30,-
Electric Trolley	Elektrokarren	DM 10,-
Buggy	Elektrischer Wagen	DM 60,-
Clubs	Clubs	DM 20,-

Credit cards Kreditkarten
VISA - Eurocard - MasterCard - AMEX - DC - JCB

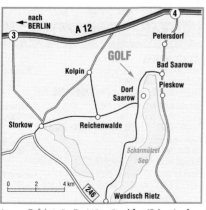

Access Zufahrt : Berlin A12 → Frankfurt/Oder. Ausf. Fürstenwalde, → Bad Saarow → Golfplatz
Map 6 on page 303 Karte 6 Seite 303

GOLF COURSE
PLATZ
18/20

Site	Lage	▬▬▬▬▭
Maintenance	Instandhaltung	▬▬▬▬▬
Architect	Architekt	Nick Faldo
Type	Typ	park
Relief	Relief	▬▬▬▭▭
Water in play	Platz mit Wasser	▬▬▭▭▭
Exp. to wind	Wind ausgesetzt	▬▬▬▭▭
Trees in play	Platz mit Bäumen	▬▬▭▭▭

Scorecard Scorekarte	Chp. Chp.	Mens Herren	Ladies Damen
Length Länge	6445	6054	5341
Par	72	72	72

Advised golfing ability
Empfohlene Spielstärke

0	12	24	36

Hcp required Min. Handicap 28

CLUB HOUSE & AMENITIES
KLUBHAUS UND NEBENGEBÄUDE
8/10

Pro shop	Pro shop	▬▬▬▬▬
Driving range	Übungsplatz	▬▬▬▬▭
Sheltered	überdacht	14 Plätze
On grass	auf Rasen	ja
Putting-green	Putting-grün	ja
Pitching-green	Pitching-grün	ja

HOTEL FACILITIES
HOTEL BESCHREIBUNG
7/10

HOTELS HOTELS
Hotel Kempinski · Golfplatz
160 Zimmer , D DM 290,-
Tel (49) 033631 - 60, (49) 033631 - 61 000

Palais Am See · Bad Saarow
12 Zimmer , D DM 180,- · 4 km
Tel (49) 033631 - 8610, (49) 033631 - 86 186

Am Werl · Bad Saarow
13 , D DM 160,- · 4 km
Tel (49) 033631 - 5231, (49) 033631 - 5233

RESTAURANTS RESTAURANT
Hotel Kempinski · Golfplatz
Tel (49) 033631 - 60

Am Werl · Bad Saarow
Tel (49) 033631 - 5231 · 4 km

379

Während das Golfgelände selbst keiner besonderen Erwähnung bedarf, ist die Lage in unmittelbarer Nachbarschaft zum Schwarzwald, Stuttgart und dem Elsass (Strassburg ist weniger als eine Autostunde entfernt) von weit grösserem Interesse. Dieser neue Platz hat in golferischer Hinsicht einiges zu bieten. Das Terrain ist weitgehend flach und sein "ehrliches" Design erlaubt, dass man ihn ohne Angst vor bösen Überraschungen spielen kann. Von den lauernden Hindernissen kann man sich relativ mühelos fernhalten. Richtig Würze bringen hier erst die Grüns ins Spiel. Zwei davon sind blind, was keiner so recht mag, acht sind erhöht angelegt und bringen den Spieler in eine schwierige Situation, wenn er sie verfehlt. Das Putten auf den stark kontourierten Grüns bereitet einiges Kopfzerbrechen und wird am Ende auf so mancher Scorekarte Schaden anrichten. Sollten Sie in der Gegend sein, lohnt Scheibenhardt den Besuch.

While the site here does not call for any special comment, the location is of some interest, being within the immediate vicinity of the Black Forest, Stuttgart and Alsace (Strasbourg is less than one hour's driver). This recent course has a lot going for it in golfing terms. The terrain is more or less flat and it is honest enough to be played without fear of unpleasant surprises. And while the hazards are definitely there lying in wait, they are not too difficult to avoid. The real difficulty here awaits you on the greens; two are blind, something no-one every really appreciates, eight are elevated and provide some delicate approach shots if you miss them, and they are generally severely contoured, enough for putting to cause more than a few headaches and terminal damage to any scorecard. If you are in the region, Scheibenhardt is well worth a visit.

Golfclub Hofgut Scheibenhardt

Gut Scheibenhardt
D - 76135 KARLSRUHE

Office	Sekretariat	(49) 0721 - 867 463
Pro shop	Pro shop	(49) 0721 - 867 560
Fax	Fax	(49) 0721 - 867 465
Situation	Lage	

10 km von Karlsruhe, 268 500 Ew.

Annual closure Jährliche Schliessung nein

Weekly closure Wöchentliche Schliessung Montag
das Restaurant

Fees main season
Preisliste hochsaison 18 Löcher

	Week days Woche	We/Bank holidays We/Feiertag
Individual Individuell	DM 70,-	DM 100,-
Couple Ehepaar	DM 140,-	DM 200,-
– 21 Jahre/Studenten: DM 50/70,-		
Caddy Caddy	auf Reservierung	
Electric Trolley Elektrokarren	nein	
Buggy Elektrischer Wagen	DM 50,-	
Clubs Clubs	DM 20,-	

Credit cards Kreditkarten nein

380

KARLSRUHE

GOLF

36 Bulach
Rüppur
45
A 8
48 47
A 5
3 Ettlingen

0 2 4 km

Access Zufahrt : A5 Frankfurt-Basel. Ausf. Karlsruhe-Süd, → Karlsruhe Mitte. 2 km → "Hofgut Scheibenhardt".
Map 1 on page 293 Karte 1 Seite 293

GOLF COURSE
PLATZ
13/20

Site	Lage	▬▬▬
Maintenance	Instandhaltung	▬▬
Architect	Architekt	W. Ruck
Type	Typ	Flachland
Relief	Relief	▬
Water in play	Platz mit Wasser	▬
Exp. to wind	Wind ausgesetzt	▬
Trees in play	Platz mit Bäumen	▬▬

Scorecard Scorekarte	Chp. Chp.	Mens Herren	Ladies Damen
Length Länge	6077	6077	5319
Par	72	72	72

Advised golfing ability Empfohlene Spielstärke	0	12	24	36

Hcp required Min. Handicap 36

CLUB HOUSE & AMENITIES
KLUBHAUS UND NEBENGEBÄUDE
7/10

Pro shop	Pro shop	▬▬▬
Driving range	Übungsplatz	▬▬▬
Sheltered	überdacht	6 Plätze
On grass	auf Rasen	April-Okt.
Putting-green	Putting-grün	ja
Pitching-green	Pitching-grün	ja

HOTEL FACILITIES
HOTEL BESCHREIBUNG
7/10

HOTELS HOTELS

Holiday Inn		Ettlingen
70 Zimmer, D DM 160,-		5 km
Tel (49) 07243 - 3800, Fax (49) 07243 - 380 666		
Renaissance Hotel Karlsruhe		Karlsruhe
215 Zimmer, D DM 400,-		10 km
Tel (49) 0721 - 37 170, Fax (49) 0721 - 377 156		
Blankenburg Hotel		Karlsruhe
49 Zimmer, D DM 220,-		10 km
Tel (49) 0721 - 60 950, Fax (49) 0721 - 609 560		
Berliner Hof, 55 Zimmer, D DM 160,-		Karlsruhe
Tel (49) 0721 - 23 981, Fax (49) 0721 - 27 218		10 km

RESTAURANTS RESTAURANT

Oberländer Weinstube	Karlsruhe 10 km
Tel (49) 0721 - 25 066	
Dudelsack, Tel (49) 0721 - 205 000	Karlsruhe, 10 km

Die alten Bauernhäuser, die einen willkommen heissen, sind gleichermassen beeindruckend wie die Aussicht auf Schloss Braunfels. Der Architekt hat das für einen Golfplatz gut geeignete Gelände absichtlich nur wenig verändert. Die Höhenunterschiede, die einen nicht davon abhalten sollten zu Fuss zu Gehen, spielen eine erheblich Rolle bei der Schlägerwahl, der wiederum eine Schlüsselrolle zukommt beim Anspiel einiger der zahlreichen, erhöht angelegten Grüns. Priorität hat auch die Vermeidung der Bäume und der Wasserhindernisse, letztere kommen an vier Löchern ins Spiel. Schloss Braunfels verlangt von den Spielern sicherlich kein überdurchschnittliches Können, dennoch kann die Fähigkeit den Ball sowohl mit Draw als auch Fade spielen zu können, bei der Endabrechnung von entscheidendem Vorteil sein. Sein Lage, die Umgebung, Vielseitigkeit und dazu ein komfortables Clubhaus, die für diesen Platz sprechen. Zudem liegt Wetzlar ganz in der Nähe, die Heimatstadt von Charlotte, der Heldin in Goethes "Werther".

The old farm buildings that welcome you are impressive, as are the views of Braunfels castle. The designer visibly did not want to upset terrain that is easily adaptable to golf. Although easy enough to play on foot, the slopes need to be reckoned with, at least when it comes to choosing the right club, a key factor here for attacking some of the many elevated greens. The first job is to avoid the trees and the water hazards in play on four holes. Schloss Braunfels certainly does not require above-average virtuosity, but being able to flight the ball both ways can be important in the final count. The location, the comfortable club-house, the setting and variety are major assets, as is the closeness to Wetzlar, the town of Charlotte, Goethe's heroine in "Werther".

Golf Club Schloss Braunfels
Homburger Hof
D - 35619 BRAUNFELS-LAHN

Office	Sekretariat	(49) 06442 - 4530
Pro shop	Pro shop	(49) 06442 - 5752
Fax	Fax	(49) 06442 - 6683
Situation	Lage	

15 km von Wetzlar, 53 000 Ew.
80 km von Frankfurt, 660 000 Ew.

Annual closure	Jährliche Schliessung	nein
Weekly closure	Wöchentliche Schliessung	Montag
		das Restaurant

Fees main season
Preisliste hochsaison 18 Löcher

	Week days Woche	We/Bank holidays We/Feiertag
Individual Individuell	DM 70,-	DM 90,-
Couple Ehepaar	DM 140,-	DM 180,-

– 21 Jahre/Studenten: – 50 %

Caddy	Caddy	auf Reservierung
Electric Trolley	Elektrokarren	nein
Buggy	Elektrischer Wagen	nein
Clubs	Clubs	ja

Credit cards Kreditkarten — nein

Access Zufahrt : Frankfurt A5 Nord, A45 → Wetzlar. Ausf. Wetzlar Ost, B49 → Limburg. Leun, → Braunfels. Restaurant Obermühle, → Golfplatz.
Map 3 on page 297 Karte 3 Seite 297

GOLF COURSE
PLATZ **16**/20

Site	Lage	▰▰▰▰▱
Maintenance	Instandhaltung	▰▰▰▰▱
Architect	Architekt	B. von Limburger
Type	Typ	Park
Relief	Relief	▰▰▰▰▱
Water in play	Platz mit Wasser	▰▰▱▱▱
Exp. to wind	Wind ausgesetzt	▰▰▱▱▱
Trees in play	Platz mit Bäumen	▰▰▰▰▱

Scorecard Scorekarte	Chp. Chp.	Mens Herren	Ladies Damen
Length Länge	6320	6220	5487
Par	73	73	73

Advised golfing ability Empfohlene Spielstärke	0 12 24 36	▰▰▰▰▱
Hcp required Min. Handicap	36	

CLUB HOUSE & AMENITIES
KLUBHAUS UND NEBENGEBÄUDE **7**/10

Pro shop	Pro shop	▰▰▰▰▱
Driving range	Übungsplatz	▰▰▰▱▱
Sheltered	überdacht	6 Plätze
On grass	auf Rasen	ja
Putting-green	Putting-grün	ja
Pitching-green	Pitching-grün	ja

HOTEL FACILITIES
HOTEL BESCHREIBUNG **7**/10

HOTELS HOTELS

Schloss-Hotel Braunfels	Braunfels
36 Zimmer, D DM 160,-	4 km
Tel (49) 06442 - 3050, Fax (49) 06442 - 305 222	

Zum Alten Amtsgericht	Braunfels
22 Zimmer, D DM 160,-	3 km
Tel (49) 06442 - 93 480, Fax (49) 06442 - 934 811	

Schloss-Hotel Weilburg	Weilburg
43 Zimmer, D DM 250,-	8 km
Tel (49) 06471 - 39 096, Fax (49) 06471 - 39 199	

RESTAURANTS RESTAURANT

La Lucia	Weilburg
Tel (49) 06471 - 2130	8 km

Zum Alten Amtsgericht	Braunfels
Tel (49) 06442 - 93 480	3 km

381

SCHLOSS EGMATING

| 15 | 7 | 7 |

Der Architekt Kurt Rossknecht versteht es, den von Ihm entworfenen Anlagen seinen ganz persönlichen Stempel aufzudrücken, was in erster Linie in der sorgfältigen Gestaltung und Positionierung von Bunkern und Grüns zum Ausdruck kommt. Da auf Schloss Egmating wenig Wasser und so gut wie keine Bäume ins Spiel kommen, bilden hier vor allem das hügelige Terrain sowie die Fairway-Bunker den Schwerpunkt der Verteidigung zwischen Abschlag und Grün. Wer glaubt, dass Longhitter hier im Vorteil sind, sollte nicht die Vorzüge eines guten kurzen Spiels sowie die Fähigkeit guter Techniker, den Ball in unterschiedlichen Flugkurven zu spielen, unterschätzen. Letzteres gilt umso mehr, als eine Mischung aus hohen Lob und "bump and run" Schlägen erforderlich ist, um die Grüns anzuspielen. Wenn der Wind weht, ist es recht hilfreich die Flugbahn des Balles richtig einschätzen zu können. Die grosse Anzahl von Abschlägen an jedem Loch macht den Platz für alle Spielstärken zugänglich, solange bei Spielern mit hohem Handicap der Score nicht zu sehr im Vordergrund steht. Den Platz sollte man auch in den nächsten Jahren im Auge behalten.

Designer Kurt Rossknecht likes to give courses his own personal stamp, if only through the careful attention he pays to the design of bunkers, to their positioning and to putting surfaces. At Schloss Egmating, water is not a major feature and trees hardly feature at all, so sloping terrain and fairway bunkers form the core of the difficulties en route to the green. You might think that long-hitters would have the upper hand here, but greater rewards often go to the technicians, the flighters of the ball, and even to the short game experts, who have to alternate between high lob and bump and run shots to get home and dry. The large number of tee-areas makes this a course for all skills, as long as high-handicappers don't worry unduly about a three-figure score. A course well worth watching in the years ahead.

Schloss Egmating

Schlosstrasse 15
D - 85658 EGMATING

Office	Sekretariat	(49) 08095 - 90 860
Pro shop	Pro shop	(49) 08095 - 908 610
Fax	Fax	(49) 08095 - 9086-66
Situation	Lage	

25 km von München, 1 300 000 Ew.
3 km von Aying, 3 000 Ew.

Annual closure	Jährliche Schliessung	ja
		1/12→31/03

Weekly closure Wöchentliche Schliessung

Fees main season
Preisliste hochsaison 18 Löcher

	Week days Woche	We/Bank holidays We/Feiertag
Individual Individuell	DM 80,-	DM 100,-
Couple Ehepaar	DM 160,-	DM 200,-

Caddy	Caddy	auf Reservierung
Electric Trolley	Elektrokarren	ja
Buggy	Elektrischer Wagen	ja
Clubs	Clubs	ja

Credit cards Kreditkarten   nein

Access Zufahrt : München, A99 Ost. Ausf.
Putzbrunn → Oberpframmen → Golfplatz
Map 2 on page 295 Karte 2 Seite 295

GOLF COURSE
PLATZ   15/20

Site	Lage	▬▬▬
Maintenance	Instandhaltung	▬▬▬
Architect	Architekt	Kurt Rossknecht
Type	Typ	Flachland
Relief	Relief	▬
Water in play	Platz mit Wasser	▬
Exp. to wind	Wind ausgesetzt	▬▬▬▬
Trees in play	Platz mit Bäumen	▬

Scorecard	Chp.	Mens	Ladies
Scorekarte	Chp.	Herren	Damen
Length Länge	6368	6116	5324
Par	72	72	72

Advised golfing ability	0	12	24	36
Empfohlene Spielstärke	▬▬▬▬			
Hcp required Min. Handicap	36			

CLUB HOUSE & AMENITIES
KLUBHAUS UND NEBENGEBÄUDE   7/10

Pro shop	Pro shop	▬▬▬
Driving range	Übungsplatz	▬▬▬
Sheltered	überdacht	ja
On grass	auf Rasen	ja
Putting-green	Putting-grün	ja
Pitching-green	Pitching-grün	ja

HOTEL FACILITIES
HOTEL BESCHREIBUNG   7/10

HOTELS HOTELS
Brauereigasthof Aying   Aying
27 Zimmer, D DM 300,-   3 km
Tel (49) 08095 - 705, Fax (49) 08095 - 2053

Aigner   Ottobrunn
73 Zimmer, D DM 250,-   13 km
Tel (49) 089 - 608 170, Fax (49) 089 -608 3213

Sauerlach Post, 51 Zimmer, D DM 250,-   Sauerlach
Tel (49) 08104 - 830, Fax (49) 08104 - 8383   10 km

Arabella   München-Bogenhausen
467 Zimmer, D DM 400,-   25 km
Tel (49) 089 - 92 320, Fax (49) 089 - 923 24449

RESTAURANTS RESTAURANT
Tantris   München-Schwabing 25 km
Tel (49) 089 - 362 061

Haflhof, Tel (49) 08093 - 5336   Egmating, 1 km

SCHLOSS KLINGENBURG

14 **6** **6**

In einem alten Schlosspark gelegen ist der Platz mit einer Vielzahl herrlicher Bäume unterschiedlicher Art bestanden. Der Ort strahlt, verstärkt durch den umliegenden Wald, eine Aura von Ruhe und Abgeschiedenheit aus. Obwohl der Kurs angenehm zu spielen ist, bleibt er angesichts der idealen Voraussetzungen, die den Architekten zu einem Meisterwerk hätten beflügeln sollen, etwas hinter den Erwartungen zurück. Dieser schien jedoch mehr darum besorgt einen spielbaren Parcours zu entwerfen als den Platz zu einer echten Herausforderung zu machen. Die wenigen Fairwaybunker haben ein sehr flaches Profil. Bäume, Grünbunker und Wasserhindernisse dagegen stellen eine angemessene Gefahr dar. Abgesehen von den Eröffnungs- und Schlusslöchern verläuft der Platz über relativ ebenes Terrain, auf dem alle Hindernisse gut erkennbar sind. Klingenburgs gut verteidigte Grüns (fünf davon sind blind) verlangen nach "target Golf", so dass Spieler die den Ball faden können einen gewissen Vorteil haben. Theoretisch für Jeden zu bezwingen, bedingt es doch einer guten Form, will man hier einen dem Handicap entsprechenden Score erzielen.

Laid out in old castle grounds, this course has retained some superb varieties of trees, and the impression of peace and tranquillity that exudes from the overall setting is enhanced by the surrounding forest. But while the course is very pleasant to play, it doesn't quite come up to expectations. The architect was probably more concerned with designing a pleasant course rather than looking for stiff challenges, so the rare fairway bunkers are virtually flat, and trees, green-side bunkers and water hazards were most likely thought to be too penalising. A flattish course (except at the beginning and end) without any hidden traps, Schloss Klingenburg is more of a target golf course with well-protected greens (five of which are blind) and will give greater help to people who fade the ball.

Golf-Club Schloss Klingenburg

Schloss Klingenburg
D - 89343 JETTINGEN-SCHEPPACH

Office	Sekretariat	(49) 08225 - 30 340
Pro shop	Pro shop	(49) 08225 - 30 320
Fax	Fax	(49) 08225 - 30 350
Situation	Lage	

50 km von Augsburg, 265 000 Ew.
45 km von Ulm, 110 000 Ew.

Annual closure	Jährliche Schliessung	nein
Weekly closure	Wöchentliche Schliessung	Montag
		das Restaurant

Fees main season
Preisliste hochsaison den ganzen Tag

	Week days Woche	We/Bank holidays We/Feiertag
Individual Individuell	DM 70,-	DM 90,-
Couple Ehepaar	DM 140,-	DM 180,-
–21 Jahre/Studenten: – 50 %		

Caddy	Caddy	nein
Electric Trolley	Elektrokarren	nein
Buggy	Elektrischer Wagen	ja
Clubs	Clubs	DM 10,-

Credit cards Kreditkarten · nein

← Günzburg A 8 Burgau Röfingen [10] A 8
Kammlach Wettenhausen Mindel Scheppach
Ettenbeuren Jettingen
Ichenhausen Schönenberg
Günz GOLF → Ried Burtenbach
Kemnat
Krumbach ↓ Thannhausen

Access Zufahrt : A8 Stuttgart-München. Ausf. Burgau.
→ Jettingen. Schöneberg. 8 km → Golfplatz.
Map 2 on page 294 Karte 2 Seite 294

GOLF COURSE / PLATZ

14/20

Site	Lage	▰▰▰▱▱
Maintenance	Instandhaltung	▰▰▰▱▱
Architect	Architekt	Donald Harradine
Type	Typ	Park
Relief	Relief	▰▰▰▱▱
Water in play	Platz mit Wasser	▰▰▱▱▱
Exp. to wind	Wind ausgesetzt	▰▰▱▱▱
Trees in play	Platz mit Bäumen	▰▰▰▰▱

Scorecard Scorekarte	Chp. Chp.	Mens Herren	Ladies Damen
Length Länge	6218	6067	5390
Par	72	72	72

Advised golfing ability Empfohlene Spielstärke		0 12 24 36 ▰▰▰▰▱
Hcp required	Min. Handicap	We: 36

CLUB HOUSE & AMENITIES / KLUBHAUS UND NEBENGEBÄUDE

6/10

Pro shop	Pro shop	▰▰▰▱▱
Driving range	Übungsplatz	▰▰▰▱▱
Sheltered	überdacht	ja
On grass	auf Rasen	ja
Putting-green	Putting-grün	ja
Pitching-green	Pitching-grün	ja

HOTEL FACILITIES / HOTEL BESCHREIBUNG

6/10

HOTELS HOTELS

Traubenbräu — Krumbach
10 Zimmer, D DM 100,- — 15 km
Tel (49) 08282 - 2093, Fax (49) 08282 - 5873

Zettler — Günzburg
49 Zimmer, D DM 190,- — 19 km
Tel (49) 08221 - 30 008, Fax (49) 08221 - 6714

Zum Hirsch — Ichenhausen
25 Zimmer, D DM 100,- — 10 km
Tel (49) 08223 - 2033, Fax (49) 08223 - 2034

RESTAURANTS RESTAURANT

Gasthof Traubenbräu — Krumbach
Tel (49) 08282 - 32093 — 15 km

Sonnenhof — Thannhausen
Tel (49) 08281 - 2014 — 9 km

383

Die Nähe zur Schweiz und der schönen Stadt Konstanz, sowie prächtige Ausblicke auf den Bodensee verleihen diesem noch recht neuen Golfplatz eine unbestreitbare Anziehungskraft. Der Föhn kann die Ankunft des Frühlings hier etwas beschleunigen, während der Rest von Deutschland noch vor Kälte bibbert. Das ziemlich hügelige Terrain verlangt vom Spieler eine gute Kondition. Trotz der Geländeunebenheiten sind die Hindernisse gut erkennbar und gibt es keine blinden Grüns. Das Schlüsselwort Kontrolle gilt sowohl für den Ball als auch das eigene Spiel, da die "wilderen" Golfer hier häufig ernsthaft in Schwierigkeiten geraten können. Ehrlich gesagt sollten Anfänger und "Hacker" ihre Schläger hier besser im Auto lassen und stattdessen den guten Spielern zuschauen, es sei denn, sie sind bereit die Runde als Teil des Lernprozesses zu betrachten. Gut ausgewogen und kompetent konzipiert ist Schloss Langenstein ein Muss für den der diese schöne Gegend erkundet.

Being very close to Switzerland and to the pretty town of Konstanz, and offering some fabulous views of the Bodensee, this recent course has unquestionable appeal. The foehn wind can bring spring a little early here, while the rest of Germany is still shivering, but you need to be in good shape, even early in the year, because the terrain is rather hilly. Despite the relief, difficulties are rarely hidden from view and no greens are blind. The key word here is control - of your ball and your game - as the wilder players can often end up in serious trouble. To be honest, even though the course makes for a superb walk, beginners and hackers are better off leaving their clubs in the car and watching the good players ply their trade... unless they consider a round here to be part of the learning process. Well-balanced and tastefully designed, Schloss Langenstein is a must if you are exploring this pretty region.

Country Club Schloss Langenstein

Schloss Langenstein
D - 78359 ORSINGEN-NENZINGEN

Office	Sekretariat	(49) 07774 - 50 651
Pro shop	Pro shop	(49) 07774 - 50 672
Fax	Fax	(49) 07774 - 50 699
Situation	Lage	

8 km von Singen, 44 000 Ew.
6 km von Stockach, 15 200 Ew.

Annual closure	Jährliche Schliessung	ja
		1/12→28/02
Weekly closure	Wöchentliche Schliessung	Montag
		das Restaurant

Fees main season Preisliste hochsaison 18 Löcher

	Week days Woche	We/Bank holidays We/Feiertag
Individual Individuell	DM 80,-	DM 100,-
Couple Ehepaar	DM 160,-	DM 200,-
– 21 Jahre/Studenten: – 50 %		
Caddy	Caddy	nein
Electric Trolley	Elektrokarren	DM 25,-
Buggy	Elektrischer Wagen	ja
Clubs	Clubs	DM 10,-

Credit cards Kreditkarten   nein

Access Zufahrt : A81 Stuttgart-Singen. Ausf. Engen.
B31 → Stockach. Eigeltingen, rechts → Schloss
Langenstein.
Map 1 on page 293 Karte 1 Seite 293

GOLF COURSE
PLATZ   16/20

Site	Lage	
Maintenance	Instandhaltung	
Architect	Architekt	
Type	Typ	Flachland, Gebirge
Relief	Relief	
Water in play	Platz mit Wasser	
Exp. to wind	Wind ausgesetzt	
Trees in play	Platz mit Bäumen	

Scorecard	Chp.	Mens	Ladies
Scorekarte	Chp.	Herren	Damen
Length Länge	6389	6062	5175
Par	72	72	72

Advised golfing ability		0	12	24	36
Empfohlene Spielstärke					
Hcp required	Min. Handicap	We: 32/35 (Damen)			

CLUB HOUSE & AMENITIES
KLUBHAUS UND NEBENGEBÄUDE   8/10

Pro shop	Pro shop	
Driving range	Übungsplatz	
Sheltered	überdacht	10 Plätze
On grass	auf Rasen	April-Okt.
Putting-green	Putting-grün	ja
Pitching-green	Pitching-grün	ja

HOTEL FACILITIES
HOTEL BESCHREIBUNG   7/10

HOTELS HOTELS
Haus Sättele   Steisslingen
16 Zimmer, D DM 150,-   5 km
Tel (49) 07738 - 92 200, Fax (49) 07738 - 929 059

Flohr's 8 Zimmer, D DM 195,-   Überlingen, 10 km
Tel (49) 07731 - 93 230, Fax (49) 07731 - 932 323

Zur Lochmühle   Eigeltingen
37 Zimmer, D DM 150,-   3 km
Tel (49) 07774 - 7086, Fax (49) 07774 - 6865

3 Stuben, 25 Zimmer, D DM 250,-   Meersburg
Tel (49) 07532 - 80 090, Fax (49) 07532 - 1367   20 km

RESTAURANTS RESTAURANT
Flohr's, Tel (49) 07731 - 93 230   Überlingen, 10 km

Salzburger Stub'n   Rielasingen-Worblingen
Tel (49) 07731 - 27 349   12 km

384

SCHLOSS LIEBENSTEIN GELB + BLAU

| 16 | 8 | 7 |

Der "noble" Golfsport scheint eine Vorliebe dafür zu haben, sich neben Schlössern anzusiedeln. Die äussere Erscheinung kann jedoch täuschen, und so entspricht die Qualität solcher Plätze nicht immer dem gediegenen Stil ihrer Umgebung. Das Schlosshotel ist ein denkmalgeschütztes Monument. Für diese Art von Ehre ist die 27-Loch Anlage sicher noch zu jung, dennoch zeugt die Gestaltung der drei vom Charakter her recht unterschiedlichen 9-Loch-Kurse von hinreichend Kompetenz. Longhitter werden sich auf dem "blauen" Kurs mit seinen drohenden Hindernissen und engen Fairways etwas beengt fühlen. Dagegen verzeihen der "gelbe" und der "rote" Kurs ungenaue Schläge schon eher. Gute Techniker und Golfer, die wissen wie man sein Handicap spielt, werden hier problemlos zurechtkommen. Trotz des ziemlich hügeligen Terrains kann man nur zwei der 27 Grüns als blind bezeichnen. Die richtige Strategie zu wählen ist relativ einfach, da alle Schwierigkeiten gut erkennbar sind. Fazit: ein sehr ansehnlicher Golfplatz.

As a noble sport, golf naturally likes to set up shop next to a castle. But as appearances can be deceptive, not all the courses that opt for the regal style can quite match the setting. Here, the castle hotel is a listed monument, and while its 27 holes are still too young for any form of listing, they have nonetheless been designed with a lot of skill and provide three different 9-holers. Big-hitters will feel the 'Blau' course a little tight, where hazards are threatening and fairways narrow. The 'Gelb' and 'Rot' courses on the other hand are little more lenient on wayward shots. For the technicians and golfers who know how to play to their handicap, the problem is not quite so bad. This is rather a hilly layout (buggies are not really necessary) but only two of the twenty-seven greens could be called blind. Finding the right strategy is easy, especially since all the difficulties are there to be seen. A very respectable course.

Golf- und Landclub Schloss Liebenstein

Schloss Liebenstein
D - 74382 NECKARWESTHEIM

Office	Sekretariat	(49) 07133 - 98 780
Pro shop	Pro shop	(49) 07133 - 12 445
Fax	Fax	(49) 07133 - 987 818
Situation	Lage	

15 km von Heilbronn, 126 000 Ew.

Annual closure	Jährliche Schliessung	nein

Weekly closure	Wöchentliche Schliessung	Montag
		Das Restaurant

Fees main season
Preisliste hochsaison 18 Löcher

	Week days Woche	We/Bank holidays We/Feiertag
Individual Individuell	DM 60,-	DM 80,-
Couple Ehepaar	DM 120,-	DM 160,-

Caddy	Caddy	DM 10,-
Electric Trolley	Elektrokarren	nein
Buggy	Elektrischer Wagen	nein
Clubs	Clubs	ja

Credit cards Kreditkarten	nein

Lauffen · Kirchheim · Gemmrigheim · Besigheim · Heilbronn · Ilsfeld · Neckarwestheim · **GOLF** · Mundelsheim · Stuttgart · Neckar · A 81

0 2 4 km

Access Zufahrt : A81 Stuttgart-Heilbronn. Ausf.
Mundelsheim → Kirchheim.
Neckarwestheim → Golfplatz
Map 1 on page 293 Karte 1 Seite 293

GOLF COURSE PLATZ

16/20

Site	Lage	▬▬▬▬▬▬□□
Maintenance	Instandhaltung	▬▬▬▬▬▬▬□
Architect	Architekt	
Type	Typ	Flachland
Relief	Relief	▬▬▬□□□□□
Water in play	Platz mit Wasser	▬▬□□□□□□
Exp. to wind	Wind ausgesetzt	▬▬□□□□□□
Trees in play	Platz mit Bäumen	▬▬▬▬▬▬▬□

Scorecard Scorekarte	Chp. Chp.	Mens Herren	Ladies Damen
Length Länge	6220	6220	5496
Par	73	73	73

Advised golfing ability Empfohlene Spielstärke	0	12	24	36

Hcp required	Min. Handicap	We 28

CLUB HOUSE & AMENITIES
KLUBHAUS UND NEBENGEBÄUDE

8/10

Pro shop	Pro shop	▬▬▬▬▬▬□□
Driving range	Übungsplatz	▬▬▬▬▬▬▬□
Sheltered	überdacht	6 Plätze
On grass	auf Rasen	April → Sept.
Putting-green	Putting-grün	ja
Pitching-green	Pitching-grün	ja

385

HOTEL FACILITIES
HOTEL BESCHREIBUNG

7/10

HOTELS HOTELS
Schloss Liebenstein   500 m
24 Zimmer, D DM
Tel (49) 07133 - 6041

Hofmann   Neckarwestheim
12 Zimmer, D DM 100,-   3 km
Tel (49) 07133 - 7876, Fax (49) 07133 - 4030

RESTAURANTS RESTAURANT
Hofstüble   Neckarwestheim
Tel (49) 07133 - 16 444   4 km

Schloss Liebenstein   500 m
Tel (49) 07133 - 6041

Die 18 von W. Siegmann entworfenen Löcher wurden vor kurzem um eine von Jack Nicklaus geplante 9-Loch-Anlage erweitert. Sämtliche Löcher können als technisch anspruchsvoll und optisch gelungen bezeichnet werden. Wer jedoch nicht alle 27 Löcher spielen kann, dem empfehlen wir - ohne damit den "Goldenen Bären" beleidigen zu wollen - dem einheitlichen Stil des ursprünglichen Platzes den Vorzug zu geben. Dieser Parcours mit seinen engen, von grossen Bäume gesäumten Spielbahnen wird von einem Wasserlauf durchschnitten, der an 6 Fairways als nur eines von vielen Wasserhindernissen ins Spiel kommt. Von diesen kleinen Boshaftigkeiten sollten sich auch durchschnittliche Spieler nicht abschrecken lassen. Wer die 27 Löcher erfolgreich bewältigen will, darf in seiner Aufmerksamkeit und Konzentration nie nachlassen. Dieser Platz passt gut in eine Region, der es an anspruchsvollen Golfplätzen nicht mangelt. Er wird einem selbst nach häufigem Spielen nie langweilig.

The 18 holes designed by Siegmann have recently been supplemented by a 9 holer laid out by Jack Nicklaus. They are all as technical as they are agreeable to the eye, but if you cannot play all 27, and without wishing to offend the Golden Bear, you are best advised going for the unity of style offered by the original layout. It is rather narrow, lined with large trees and cut by a stream that crosses the fairways six times as one of the many water hazards. However, Schloss Lüdersburg is not spiteful enough to put off the average player. They may not return a fabulous card, but the fun of golf does not depend solely on performance. The 27 holes call for some hard work if they are to be successfully negotiated, enough to keep the player constantly on his toes. In a region where there is no shortage of challenging golf courses, this one is well placed. What's more, you can play it again and again without a minute's boredom.

Golf- und Landclub Schloss Lüderburg

Lüdersburger Strasse 21
D - 21379 LÜDERSBURG/LÜNEBURG

Office	Sekretariat	(49) 04139 - 69 700
Pro shop	Pro shop	(49) 04139 - 69 700
Fax	Fax	(49) 04139 - 697 070
Situation	Lage	

15 km von Lüneburg, 65 000 Ew.
50 km von Hamburg, 1 650 000 Ew.

Annual closure	Jährliche Schliessung	nein
Weekly closure	Wöchentliche Schliessung	

Fees main season
Preisliste hochsaison 18 Löcher

	Week days Woche	We/Bank holidays We/Feiertag
Individual Individuell	DM 60,-	DM 80,-
Couple Ehepaar	DM 120,-	DM 160,-

Montag-Dienstag (Monday-Tuesday): DM 30,-

Caddy	Caddy	nein
Electric Trolley	Elektrokarren	nein
Buggy	Elektrischer Wagen	ja
Clubs	Clubs	ja

Credit cards Kreditkarten   Eurocard - MasterCard

nach Hamburg
Brietlingen
Lüdersburg
Bardowick
Adendorf
Scharnebeck
GOLF
Erbstrof
LÜNEBURG
0   2   4 km
nach Uelzen
nach Dahlenburg

Access Zufahrt : A250 Hamburg-Lüneburg. Ausf. Lüneburg/Ebersberg. Scranebeck. Lüdersburg.
Map 7 on page 304 Karte 7 Seite 304

GOLF COURSE
PLATZ   17 /20

Site	Lage	
Maintenance	Instandhaltung	
Architect	Architekt	W. Siegmann Jack Nicklaus
Type	Typ	Park
Relief	Relief	
Water in play	Platz mit Wasser	
Exp. to wind	Wind ausgesetzt	
Trees in play	Platz mit Bäumen	

Scorecard Scorekarte	Chp. Chp.	Mens Herren	Ladies Damen
Length Länge	6711	6091	5344
Par	73	73	73

Advised golfing ability Empfohlene Spielstärke	0 12 24 36	
Hcp required	Min. Handicap	36

CLUB HOUSE & AMENITIES
KLUBHAUS UND NEBENGEBÄUDE   7 /10

Pro shop	Pro shop	
Driving range	Übungsplatz	
Sheltered	überdacht	ja
On grass	auf Rasen	ja
Putting-green	Putting-grün	ja
Pitching-green	Pitching-grün	ja

HOTEL FACILITIES
HOTEL BESCHREIBUNG   6 /10

HOTELS HOTELS
Seminaris   Lüneburg
185 Zimmer, D DM 200,-   16 km
Tel (49) 04131 - 7130, Fax (49) 04131 - 713 128

Hof Reinstorf   Reinstorf
81 Zimmer, D DM 200,-   15 km
Tel (49) 04137 - 8090, Fax (49) 04137 - 809 100

Heiderose, 21 Zimmer, D DM 140,-   Lüneburg, 16 km
Tel (49) 04131 - 44 410, Fax (49) 04131 - 48 357

Lauenburger Mühle   Lauenburg
34 Zimmer, D DM 170,-   9 km
Tel (49) 04153 - 5890, Fax (49) 04153 - 55 555

RESTAURANTS RESTAURANT
Hof Reinstorf, Tel (49) 04137 - 8090   Reinstorf, 15 km
Zum Heidkrug, Tel (49) 04131 - 31 249Lüneburg, 16 km

386

SCHLOSS MYLLENDONK

Das im Mittelalter erbaute Schloss Myllendonk dient nicht nur als Clubhaus, sondern gibt dem Golfplatz, der im ürigen einen ausgezeichneten Ruf hat, auch seinen Namen. Die schöne Lage täuscht in vielen Fällen über schwerwiegende Schwächen beim Platzdesign hinweg. So enttäuscht uns eine Anzahl sehr nahe beieinander liegender Spielbahnen, trotz der sie begrenzenden schönen Bäume, die das Spiel erschweren. Genaue Drives und kontrolliert geschlagene Bälle sind Voraussetzung, um die Grüns von der besten Position aus angreifen zu können. Aufgrund des sehr ebenen Geländes sind die meisten Hindernisse gut erkennbar. Dies verleiht denen, die hier zum ersten mal spielen, eine gewisse Zuversicht, wenngleich einen das berechtigte Gefühl beschleicht, dass die Wasserläufe und Seen nur darauf lauern, einem das Leben schwer zu machen. Ungeübte Golfer, denen der Platz möglicherweise etwas schwierig erscheint, seien daran erinnert, dass der Score nicht alles ist worum es beim Golf geht.

The castle of Myllendonk, which dates from the Middle Ages, gives this course of excellent repute both its name and its clubhouse. The beauty of the setting can often conceal some glaring errors in design, and while we might regret a number of fairways which are too close to each other, the trees between them are magnificent and really add to the playing difficulty. Accurate driving and flighted shots are vital if you want to have any hope of hitting the greens from the easiest position. As the terrain is very flat, most hazards are clearly visible. This gives the new-comer a certain degree of confidence first time out, even though you can feel that streams and lakes are lying in wait to make life more difficult (a feeling that proves to be true!). Inexperienced golfers might find the layout a little tough, but just tell them that the score is not the only thing in golf...

Golf Club Schloss Myllendonk e.V. Korschenbroich

Myllendonker Strasse 113
D - 41352 KORSCHENBROICH

Office	Sekretariat	(49) 02161 - 641 049
Pro shop	Pro shop	(49) 02161 - 644 955
Fax	Fax	(49) 02161 - 648 806
Situation	Lage	

5 km von Mönchengladbach, 260 000 Ew.
25 km von Düsseldorf, 570 000 Ew.

Annual closure	Jährliche Schliessung	nein
Weekly closure	Wöchentliche Schliessung	Montag
		das Restaurant

Fees main season Preisliste hochsaison 18 Löcher

	Week days Woche	We/Bank holidays We/Feiertag
Individual Individuell	DM 80,-	DM 100,-
Couple Ehepaar	DM 160,-	DM 200,-

Caddy	Caddy	nein
Electric Trolley	Elektrokarren	nein
Buggy	Elektrischer Wagen	nein
Clubs	Clubs	ja

Credit cards Kreditkarten nein

Access Zufahrt : A44 Ausf. Mönchengladbach-Ost →
"Gewerbegebiet Üdding". 1 km links, Jakobshöhe
Strasse. 600 m, links, Myllendonker Strasse. →
Schlosshof-Parkplatz.
Map 3 on page 296 Karte 3 Seite 296

GOLF COURSE PLATZ 16/20

Site	Lage	▰▰▰▰
Maintenance	Instandhaltung	▰▰▰▰
Architect	Architekt	Donald Harradine
Type	Typ	Park, Wald
Relief	Relief	▰▰
Water in play	Platz mit Wasser	▰▰▰
Exp. to wind	Wind ausgesetzt	▰▰
Trees in play	Platz mit Bäumen	▰▰▰▰

Scorecard Scorekarte	Chp. Chp.	Mens Herren	Ladies Damen
Length Länge	6120	5856	5176
Par	72	72	72

Advised golfing ability Empfohlene Spielstärke	0	12	24	36
Hcp required Min. Handicap	36			

CLUB HOUSE & AMENITIES KLUBHAUS UND NEBENGEBÄUDE 7/10

Pro shop	Pro shop	▰▰▰
Driving range	Übungsplatz	▰▰▰
Sheltered	überdacht	
On grass	auf Rasen	ja (Sommer)
Putting-green	Putting-grün	ja
Pitching-green	Pitching-grün	ja

387

HOTEL FACILITIES HOTEL BESCHREIBUNG 7/10

HOTELS HOTELS

Queens Hotel Mönchengladbach-Rheydt
127 Zimmer, D DM 280,- 5 km
Tel (49) 02161 - 93 80, Fax (49) 02161 - 938 807

Dorint Hotel Mönchengladbach
162 Zimmer, D DM 350,- 5 km
Tel (49) 02161 - 89 30, Fax (49) 02161 - 87 231

Palazzo Mönchengladbach
50 Zimmer, D DM 170,- 5 km
Tel (49) 02161 - 244 600, Fax (49) 02161 - 244 888

RESTAURANTS RESTAURANT

Tho Penningshof Mönchengladbach
Tel (49) 02161 - 818 900 5 km

Alt Herrenshoff Korschenbroich
Tel (49) 02161 - 641 080 1 km

Mit Sandy Lyle wurde hier ein weiterer Top-Designer für den Entwurf eines Golfplatzes im Berliner Raum enga-
giert. Dies ist Lyles erstes Projekt in Kontinental-Europa. Wie in Scharmützelsee handelt es sich dabei um ein
Resort mit öffentlichem 18-Loch-Golfplatz. Der aufwendig gebaute Parcours erfüllt trotz seines jungen Alters die
in ihn gesetzten Erwartungen. Der schottische Champion kennt sich offenbar mit den Feinheiten der
Platzarchitektur aus und folgt der Tradition seiner heimatlichen Vorbilder, bei der die Schwierigkeiten meist sehr
subtiler Natur sind. Auf ziemlich hügeligem Terrain erbaut, finden sich auf diesem Kurs - typisch für die Region -
Wasserhindernisse, deren Charakter jedoch nicht so aggressiv ist wie etwa bei amerikanischen Plätzen üblich.
Neben vielen Bäumen kommen selbstverständlich auch zahlreiche Bunker ins Spiel, welche die mittelgrossen,
gut wenn auch relativ flach gestalteten Grüns verteidigen. Mehrere Runden sind notwendig um sich hier die pas-
sende Strategie zu erarbeiten, für deren Umsetzung man alle Schläger benötigen wird.

*Another top designer name for a Berlin course is Sandy Lyle, who here designed his first course on the continent of
Europe. As at Scharmützelsee, this is a whole resort with an 18-hole public course. It was, of course, given every
consideration and despite its early age has come up to expectations. The Scottish champion is a fine connoisseur of
architecture and remains very attached to his national tradition, where difficulties are often more on the subtle side.
Over rather hilly, but easily walkable, terrain, there are naturally the water hazards inherent in this region, but they
are less aggressive than on more American courses. A lot of trees come into play, and many bunkers too, naturally,
protecting well-designed greens without excessive slopes. You need to play here several times to establish a strategy.*

Golfclub Schloss Wilkendorf e.V.
Wilkendorfer Strasse 19
D - 15345 WILKENDORF

Office	Sekretariat	(49) 03341 - 23 933
Pro shop	Pro shop	(49) 03341 - 330 910
Fax	Fax	(49) 03341 - 330 911
Situation	Lage	

40 km von Berlin, 3 500 000 Ew.
5 km von Strausberg

Annual closure	Jährliche Schliessung	nein
Weekly closure	Wöchentliche Schliessung	nein

Fees main season Preisliste hochsaison 18 Löcher

	Week days Woche	We/Bank holidays We/Feiertag
Individual Individuell	DM 70,-	DM 90,-
Couple Ehepaar	DM 140,-	DM 180,-

Caddy	Caddy	auf Reserv./DM 40,-
Electric Trolley	Elektrokarren	nein
Buggy	Elektrischer Wagen	nein
Clubs	Clubs	DM 15,-
Credit cards Kreditkarte		nein

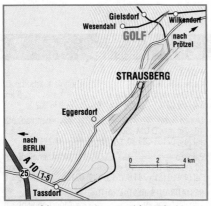

Access Zufahrt : B1-5 Berlin → Frankfurt/Oder bis
Berliner Ring (A10). 1 km links → Strausberg. →
Golfplatz Map 6 on page 303 Karte 6 Seite 303

GOLF COURSE
PLATZ 15/20

Site	Lage	
Maintenance	Instandhaltung	
Architect	Architekt	Sandy Lyle
Type	Typ	Park
Relief	Relief	
Water in play	Platz mit Wasser	
Exp. to wind	Wind ausgesetzt	
Trees in play	Platz mit Bäumen	

Scorecard Scorekarte	Chp. Chp.	Mens Herren	Ladies Damen
Length Länge	6536	6049	5373
Par	72	72	72

Advised golfing ability	0	12	24	36
Empfohlene Spielstärke				
Hcp required	Min. Handicap	nein		

CLUB HOUSE & AMENITIES
KLUBHAUS UND NEBENGEBÄUDE 7/10

Pro shop	Pro shop	
Driving range	Übungsplatz	
Sheltered	überdacht	16 Plätze
On grass	auf Rasen	ja
Putting-green	Putting-grün	ja
Pitching-green	Pitching-grün	ja

HOTEL FACILITIES
HOTEL BESCHREIBUNG 5/10

HOTELS HOTELS

Lakeside Hotel Strausberg		Strausberg
50 Zimmer, D DM 160,-		2 km
Tel (49) 03341 - 34 690, Fax (49) 03341 - 346 915		

Abacus Tierpark Hotel		Berlin-Lichtenberg
278 Zimmer, D DM 300,-		35 km
Tel (49) 030 - 51 620, Fax (49) 030 - 516 2400		

Kempinski Hotel Bristol Berlin		Berlin
315 Zimmer, D DM 500,-		40 km
Tel (49) 030 - 884 340, Fax (49) 030 - 883 6075		

RESTAURANTS RESTAURANT

Bamberger Reiter		Berlin
Tel (49) 030 - 218 4282		40 km

Alt Luxemburg		Berlin
Tel (49) 030 - 323 8730		40 km

388

SEMLIN AM SEE

14 **8** **7**

Semlin wurde wie auch der Märkische Golfclub Potsdam von Christian Staedler entworfen. Mit ihrem dazugehörigen Hotel entspricht die Anlage einem Resort, und eignet sich somit ausgezeichnet als Wochenend-Ziel für Golfgruppen - auch solche deren Handicaps weit auseinanderklaffen, wenngleich "Hacker" den Platz als etwas zu schwer empfinden mögen. Die Schwierigkeiten sind recht gut erkennbar, so dass man durchaus gleich die erste Runde in Zählspiel absolvieren kann, obschon Matchplay sicherlich genauso viel Spass macht. Das Fehlen gefahrbringender Bäume, die Gestaltung der Grüns und Bunker, sowie das fast völlig ebene Gelände erinnern stark an Florida, damit ist aber nicht eine simple Kopie der dortigen Plätze gemeint. Die Schwierigkeiten sind gut verteilt, so wechseln sich im Verlauf der Runde schwierige und leichtere Löcher miteinander ab. Als sehr hilfreich erweist sich die Fähigkeit den Ball sowohl mit Draw als auch Fade spielen zu können. Die Grüns sind ausgezeichnet und der sandige Boden gewährleistet eine gute Entwässerung.

Like Märkischer Potsdam, Semmlin am See chose Christian Staedler as course architect. This is a sort of resort, with a hotel on site, and can be a very decent week-end destination for a group of golfers, even playing to very different handicaps, although the hackers might find it a little too tough for their liking. The difficulties are visible enough to consider stroke-play first time out, although match-play will be at least just as much fun. The absence of dangerous trees, the design of the greens and bunkers and the very slight physical relief are reminiscent of Florida, but this is no carbon copy. The difficulties are well spread around, with tough holes alternating nicely with easier numbers. Moving the ball (deliberately) both ways will be a great help. The greens are excellent and the sandy soil gives good drainage.

Golf- und Landclub Semlin am See
Ferchesarerstrasse
D - 14715 SEMLIN

Office	Sekretariat	(49) 03385 - 5540
Pro shop	Pro shop	(49) 03385 - 554 410
Fax	Fax	(49) 03385 - 554 400
Situation	Lage	

5 km von Rathenow, 28 000 Ew. 70 km von Berlin.

Annual closure	Jährliche Schliessung	nein
Weekly closure	Wöchentliche Schliessung	nein

Fees main season
Preisliste hochsaison 18 Löcher

	Week days Woche	We/Bank holidays We/Feiertag
Individual Individuell	DM 60,-	DM 80,-
Couple Ehepaar	DM 120,-	DM 160,-
– 21 Jahre/Studenten: – 50 %		

Caddy	Caddy	auf Reserv. DM 35,-
Electric Trolley	Elektrokarren	nein
Buggy	Elektrischer Wagen	DM 50,-
Clubs	Clubs	DM 25,-

Credit cards Kreditkarten
VISA - Eurocard - MasterCard - AMEX - DC

Access Zufahrt : Berlin, B5. Brisen, B188 → Rathenow.
Stechow → Ferchesar. → Golfplatz
Map 6 on page 303 Karte 6 Seite 303

GOLF COURSE
PLATZ
14/20

Site	Lage	▮▮▮▮▯▯
Maintenance	Instandhaltung	▮▮▮▮▯▯
Architect	Architekt	Christoph Staedler
Type	Typ	Wald, Park
Relief	Relief	▮▮▯▯▯▯
Water in play	Platz mit Wasser	▮▮▮▯▯▯
Exp. to wind	Wind ausgesetzt	▮▮▮▯▯▯
Trees in play	Platz mit Bäumen	▮▮▯▯▯▯

Scorecard Scorekarte	Chp. Chp.	Mens Herren	Ladies Damen
Length Länge	6386	6094	5435
Par	72	72	72

Advised golfing ability		0 12 24 36
Empfohlene Spielstärke		▮▮▮▮▯▯
Hcp required	Min. Handicap	36

CLUB HOUSE & AMENITIES
KLUBHAUS UND NEBENGEBÄUDE
8/10

Pro shop	Pro shop	▮▮▮▮▯▯
Driving range	Übungsplatz	▮▮▮▮▮▯
Sheltered	überdacht	5 Plätze
On grass	auf Rasen	ja
Putting-green	Putting-grün	ja
Pitching-green	Pitching-grün	ja

HOTEL FACILITIES
HOTEL BESCHREIBUNG
7/10

HOTELS HOTELS
Golf- und Landhotel — Golfplatz
72 Zimmer, D DM 185,-
Tel (49) 03385 - 5540, Fax (49) 03385 - 554 400

Hotel Probst — Rathenow
24 Zimmer, D DM 150,- — 5 km
Tel (49) 03385 - 545 300, Fax (49) 03385 - 545 332

Sorat — Brandenburg
88 Zimmer, D DM 240,- — 37 km
Tel (49) 03381 - 5970, Fax (49) 03381 - 597 444

RESTAURANTS RESTAURANT
Golf- und Landhotel — Golfplatz
Tel (49) 03385 - 554 412

389

Grundsätzlich empfehlen wir nur ungern die Benutzung eines Golfwagens, da das Begehen eines Golfplatzes - insbesondere auf der ersten Runde - unseres Erachtens einen wesentlichen Teil des Spielvergnügens ausmacht. Es erfordert allerdings schon die Fitness und das Können eines Bergsteigers, die Anstiege von Sonnenalp zu bewältigen und dabei noch zwischendurch einen kleinen weissen Ball zu schlagen. Dies ist allerdings der einzige Schwachpunkt eines ansonsten angenehmen Platzes, dessen herrliche Lage einen so manchen Fehler vergessen lässt. Natürlich kann man nicht erwarten, mit den Problemen die das Gelände, die vielen Bäume sowie Hindernisse aller Art und Grösse bereiten, auf Anhieb fertig zu werden. Bevor man diesen Kurs zähmen kann, muss man ihn erstmal gründlich kennenlernen. Mit etwas Überlegung vor dem Schlag können hier aber durchaus Golfer aller Spielstärken zurechtkommen. Auch wer kein grosser Champion ist kann hier Spass haben, da die Schläge zum Grün nicht allzu anspruchsvoll sind. Ein Wort noch zu der aussergewöhnlichen Zusammenstellung des Parcours, es gibt sechs Par 5, sechs Par 4 und sechs Par 3 Löcher.

We never like to recommend a buggy, because walking a course is an integral part of the enjoyment of golf, especially on your first time out. But to scale the heights of Sonnenalp while intermittently hitting a little white ball, you need the fitness and skills of a mountaineer. This is the only weak point of an otherwise pleasant course, where contemplation of a superb site will help you to forget many a mistake. Quite clearly, you cannot hope to master immediately the problems caused by the slopes and hills and the very many trees and hazards that come in all shapes and sizes. To tame this course, you need to get to know it. But players of all abilities can play here, with a little thought before each stroke. One last word on the very special configuration here at Sonnenalp: there are six par 5s, six par 3s and six par 4s.

Golfclub Sonnenalp

Sonnenalp
D - 87527 OFTERSCHWANG

Office	Sekretariat	(49) 08321 - 27 276
Pro shop	Pro shop	(49) 08321 - 27 297
Fax	Fax	(49) 08321 - 272 238
Situation	Lage	

8 km von Oberstdorf, 11 000 Ew.
5 km von Sonthofen, 20 500 Ew.

Annual closure	Jährliche Schliessung	ja
		1/12→31/03
Weekly closure	Wöchentliche Schliessung	nein

Fees main season Preisliste hochsaison 18 Löcher

	Week days Woche	We/Bank holidays We/Feiertag
Individual Individuell	DM 100,-	DM 100,-
Couple Ehepaar	DM 200,-	DM 200,-

Caddy	Caddy	auf Reserv. DM 50,-
Electric Trolley	Elektrokarren	DM 30,-
Buggy	Elektrischer Wagen	nein
Clubs	Clubs set	DM 30,-
Credit cards Kreditkarten		nein

Access Zufahrt : München A96/B18 → Memmingen.
A7 → Kempten. Ausf. Oberstdorf. B19. Sonthofen.
2 km → Sonnenalp
Map 2 on page 294 Karte 2 Seite 294

GOLF COURSE
PLATZ   16/20

Site	Lage	■■■■
Maintenance	Instandhaltung	■■■■
Architect	Architekt	Donald Harradine
Type	Typ	Wald, Gebirge
Relief	Relief	■■■■■
Water in play	Platz mit Wasser	■■
Exp. to wind	Wind ausgesetzt	■■
Trees in play	Platz mit Bäumen	■■■■

Scorecard Scorekarte	Chp. Chp.	Mens Herren	Ladies Damen
Length Länge	5938	5433	4713
Par	71	71	71

Advised golfing ability		0 12 24 36
Empfohlene Spielstärke		■■■■■
Hcp required	Min. Handicap	34

CLUB HOUSE & AMENITIES
KLUBHAUS UND NEBENGEBÄUDE   7/10

Pro shop	Pro shop	■■■■
Driving range	Übungsplatz	■■■
Sheltered	überdacht	15 Plätze
On grass	auf Rasen	nein
Putting-green	Putting-grün	ja
Pitching-green	Pitching-grün	ja

HOTEL FACILITIES
HOTEL BESCHREIBUNG   7/10

HOTELS HOTELS

Sonnenalp Hotel & Resort — Golf
225 Zimmer, D DM 500,- (1/2 P) — 400 m
Tel (49) 08321 - 2720, Fax (49) 08321 - 272 242

Dora, 18 Zimmer, D DM 160,- — Ofterschwang
Tel (49) 08321 - 3509, Fax (49) 08321 - 84 244 — 1,5 km

Parkhotel Frank — Obertsdorf
68 Zimmer, D DM 350,- — 10 km
Tel (49) 08322 - 7060, Fax (49) 08322 - 706 286

Kurhotel Filser 91 Zimmer, D DM 200,- — Obertsdorf
Tel (49) 08322 - 7080, Fax (49) 08322 - 708 530 — 10 km

RESTAURANTS RESTAURANT

Alte Post, Tel (49) 08321 - 2508 — Sonthofen, 3 km

Grüns Restaurant — Obertsdorf
Tel (49) 08322 - 2424 — 10 km

St. Dionys, in einiger Entfernung zu Hamburg gelegen, bietet einen guten Vorwand zur Erkundung der Lüneburger Heide, einer Moorlandschaft, deren Bild geprägt wird von Pinien, Birken und Heidekraut. Gerade Letzteres taucht diese ansonsten karge Gegend im August und September in üppige Farben. Der Platz selbst weist nur leichte Unebenheiten auf und kann so jedermann empfohlen werden. Die Vegetation ist teilweise sehr dominant, dennoch gibt es auch für Longhitter genügend offene Flächen. Obwohl die gut gestalteten Grüns meist ausgezeichnet verteidigt sind, ist es doch in vielen Fällen möglich, sie flach anzuspielen. Ärgerlich ist die Position einiger Fairwaybunker, durch die gute Schläge bestraft werden können. Es ist nichts Neues, dass für ein gutes Ergebnis lange und gerade Schläge von Bedeutung sind. Diese Feststellung ist hier jedoch - vor allem von den hinteren Abschlägen - ganz besonders zutreffend. Das Vergnügen St. Dionys zu spielen geht weit über den landschaftlichen Reiz der Umgebung hinaus.

St Dionys is some distance from Hamburg, but is a good excuse for discovering the "Lüneburger Heide", moorland dotted with pine-trees and birch, and covered with heather. Both add sumptuous colour to rather austere landscape in August and September. The course itself is only moderately hilly and so can be recommended for everyone. The vegetation is sometimes very much to the fore but there is no lack of open space to attract the big-hitters, and while the greens are generally well-designed and frequently well-guarded, you can often run the ball in. One regret is the layout of some fairway bunkers, which can penalise good shots. Saying you have to play long and straight for a good round is stating the obvious, but here it really is very true, especially from the back tees. The fun of playing St Dionys is more than simply admiring the surroundings.

Golf Club St. Dionys
Widukindweg
D - 21357 ST. DYONIS

Office	Sekretariat	(49) 04133 - 6277
Pro shop	Pro shop	(49) 04133 - 7736
Fax	Fax	(49) 04133 - 6218
Situation	Lage	

8 km von Winsen, 27 000 Ew.
10 km von Lüneburg, 65 000 Ew.

Annual closure	Jährliche Schliessung	nein
Weekly closure	Wöchentliche Schliessung	nein

Fees main season Preisliste hochsaison 18 Löcher

	Week days Woche	We/Bank holidays We/Feiertag
Individual Individuell	DM 60,-	DM 80,-
Couple Ehepaar	DM 120,-	DM 160,-

– 25 Jahre: – 50% - We: Gäste nur bis 10 Uhr
(only before 10 am)

Caddy	Caddy	nein
Electric Trolley	Elektrokarren	nein
Buggy	Elektrischer Wagen	nein
Clubs	Clubs	nein

Credit cards Kreditkarten   nein

Access Zufahrt : A7 Hamburg → Hannover. Ausf. Maschen. A250 → Lüneburg. Ausf. Winsen Ost. B4 → Lüneburg. Wittorf, links nach Barum. → St. Dionys.
Map 7 on page 304 Karte 7 Seite 304

GOLF COURSE
PLATZ   17/20

Site	Lage	
Maintenance	Instandhaltung	
Architect	Architekt	Gratenau
Type	Typ	Heckenlandschaft
Relief	Relief	
Water in play	Platz mit Wasser	
Exp. to wind	Wind ausgesetzt	
Trees in play	Platz mit Bäumen	

Scorecard Scorekarte	Chp. Chp.	Mens Herren	Ladies Damen
Length Länge	6225	6225	5479
Par	72	72	72

Advised golfing ability	0	12	24	36
Empfohlene Spielstärke				
Hcp required Min. Handicap	36			

CLUB HOUSE & AMENITIES
KLUBHAUS UND NEBENGEBÄUDE   7/10

Pro shop	Pro shop	
Driving range	Übungsplatz	
Sheltered	überdacht	4 Plätze
On grass	auf Rasen	ja
Putting-green	Putting-grün	ja
Pitching-green	Pitching-grün	ja

HOTEL FACILITIES
HOTEL BESCHREIBUNG   6/10

HOTELS HOTELS

Hotel Bergström   Lüneburg
52 Zimmer, D DM 250,-   11 km
Tel (49) 04131 - 3080, Fax (49) 04131 - 308 499

Hotel Zum Heidkrug   Lüneburg
10 Zimmer, D DM 160,-   11 km
Tel (49) 04131 - 31 249

RESTAURANTS RESTAURANT

Restaurant Hotel Zum Heidkrug   Lüneburg
Tel (49) 04131 - 31 249   11 km

Jagdschänke   Lüdersburg
Tel (49) 04153 - 68 422   10 km

391

ST. EURACH

Mit seinem dominierenden Clubhaus, dem Platz, dessen Spielbahnen sich durch Bäume und Wälder winden, und dem Blick auf die Alpen im Hintergrund vermittelt St. Eurach den Eindruck von Exclusivität, der durch das Greenfee (Wochenenden vermeiden) bestätigt wird. Genaugenommen hinterlässt der Reiz der umgebenden Natur einen stärkeren Eindruck als der Platz selbst, dem es etwas an Persönlichkeit mangelt. Wir wollen niemand vergraulen, aber Spielern mit hohem Handicap wird es hier schwerfallen, ihre Runde wirklich zu geniessen. Der lange und enge Platz wurde durch die von Bernhard Langer vorgenommenen Veränderungen an den Bunkern zusätzlich erschwert, so dass völlige Kontrolle über das eigene Spiel vonnöten ist, will man hier erfolgreich sein. Entscheidend ist der gekonnte Umgang mit allen Schlägern sowie die Beherrschung von Schlägen aus Notsituationen. Ein anspruchsvoller Kurs, den man am besten in guter Form spielen sollte.

With the estate dominated by the clubhouse, a course winding its way through trees and the Alps visible in the background on a clear day, St Eurach gives the impression of an exclusive site... an impression confirmed by the green fee (so avoid week-ends). When thinking about it, the natural environment leaves a greater impression than the actual course, and it certainly has the glamour to offset a rather bland personality. When it comes to playing, and we hate to put visitors off, high-handicappers will be hard pushed to have enjoy their golf here. The layout is long and narrow, and the alterations made to bunkers by Bernhard Langer have added a little spice, but all this implies complete control of your game if you want to excel. You have to feel easy with all your clubs, including those you need for recovery shots. A demanding course to play when on top of your game.

St. Eurach Land- und Golf Club e.V.

Eurach 8
D - 82393 IFFELDORF

Office	Sekretariat	(49) 08801 - 1332
Pro shop	Pro shop	(49) 08801 - 1532
Fax	Fax	(49) 08801 - 2523
Situation	Lage	

35 km von München, 1 300 000 Ew.
5 km von Penzberg, 14 000 Ew.

Annual closure	Jährliche Schliessung	ja
		15/11→15/04
Weekly closure	Wöchentliche Schliessung	nein

Fees main season Preisliste hochsaison 18 Löcher

	Week days Woche	We/Bank holidays We/Feiertag
Individual Individuell	DM 100,-	DM 100,-
Couple Ehepaar	DM 200,-	DM 200,-

We/Feiertage: nur in Mitgliederbegleitung
(with members)

Caddy	Caddy	auf Reservierung
Electric Trolley	Elektrokarren	nein
Buggy	Elektrischer Wagen	ja
Clubs	Clubs	ja
Credit cards Kreditkarten		nein

Access Zufahrt : München, A95 → Garmisch-Partenkirchen. Ausf. Penzberg → Iffeldorf-Seeshaupt. 1,5 km rechts → Golfplatz
Map 2 on page 294 Karte 2 Seite 294

392

GOLF COURSE
PLATZ   16/20

Site	Lage	▰▰▰▰▱
Maintenance	Instandhaltung	▰▰▰▰▱
Architect	Architekt	▰▰▰▱▱
Type	Typ	Wald
Relief	Relief	▰▰▱▱▱
Water in play	Platz mit Wasser	▰▱▱▱▱
Exp. to wind	Wind ausgesetzt	▰▰▱▱▱
Trees in play	Platz mit Bäumen	▰▰▰▰▱

Scorecard Scorekarte	**Chp.** Chp.	**Mens** Herren	**Ladies** Damen
Length Länge	6505	5888	5261
Par	71	71	74

Advised golfing ability			0	12	24	36
Empfohlene Spielstärke		▰▰▰▱				
Hcp required	Min. Handicap	28				

CLUB HOUSE & AMENITIES
KLUBHAUS UND NEBENGEBÄUDE   7/10

Pro shop	Pro shop	▰▰▰▰▱
Driving range	Übungsplatz	▰▰▰▱▱
Sheltered	überdacht	
On grass	auf Rasen	ja
Putting-green	Putting-grün	ja
Pitching-green	Pitching-grün	ja

HOTEL FACILITIES
HOTEL BESCHREIBUNG   6/10

HOTELS HOTELS
Landgasthof Osterseen   Iffeldorf
24 Zimmer, D DM 200,-   2 km
Tel (49) 08856 - 10 11, Fax (49) 08856 - 96 06

Stadthotel Berggeist   Penzberg
45 Zimmer, D DM 150,-   6 km
Tel (49) 08856 - 80 10, Fax (49) 08856 - 81 913

Gut Faistenberg   Eurasburg-Faistenberg
60 Zimmer, D DM 275,-   10 km
Tel (49) 08179 - 1616, Fax (49) 08179 - 433

RESTAURANTS RESTAURANT
Landgasthof Osterseen   Iffeldorf
Tel (49) 08856 - 1011   2 km

Stadthotel Berggeist   Penzberg
Tel (49) 08856 - 78 99   6 km

Stolper Heide ist Bestandteil einer schnell-wachsenden Wohnanlage und ist zweifellos einer der vielversprechendsten Golfplätze in ganz Deutschland. Die Namen Bernhard Langer und Kurt Rossknecht bürgen für ehrlichen Charakter und den Abwechslungsreichtum des Designs, das sich hervorragend an die unterschiedlichen Spielstärken der Golfer anpasst, wenngleich insbesondere die besseren Spieler ihren Spass daran haben werden, die strategischen Herausforderungen des Kurses zu meistern. Auf dem ausgezeichnet und intelligent gestalteten Gelände brauchen die Bäume sicherlich noch Zeit ihr Wachstum zu entfalten, aber bereits jetzt weisen die sorgfältig gearbeiteten Abgrenzungen zwischen Fairway und Rough dem Golfer deutlich die Spiellinie für den nächsten Schlag. Die Schlusslöcher stellen die Spieler vor allem im Match-Play vor eine interessante Aufgabe. Die Pflegezustand des Platzes, besonders im Bereich der sorgfältig gestalteten Grüns, ist bereits ausgezeichnet..

In a fast-growing residential area, Stolper Heide is one of Germany's most promising courses. The names of Bernhard Langer and Rossknecht were sure-fire guarantees for the honesty and variety of this layout and for the way it adapts to different levels of proficiency, although the better players will have the most fun here solving questions of strategy. Well-landscaped and intelligent, the course needs the trees to grow but the careful way in which the fairways and roughs are demarcated means you are never in any doubt as to where the next shot should go. The finishing holes are particularly interesting here if competing in match-play. The green-keeping is already very good, particularly the carefully designed greens.

Stolper Heide Golf Club
Frihnauer Weg 3
D - 16540 STOLPE

Office	Sekretariat	(49) 03303 - 5490
Pro shop	Pro shop	(49) 03303 - 549 214
Fax	Fax	(49) 03303 - 549 222
Situation	Lage	

20 km von Berlin, 3 500 000 Ew.

Annual closure	Jährliche Schliessung	ja
		1/01/99→31/01/99
Weekly closure	Wöchentliche Schliessung	

Fees main season
Preisliste hochsaison 18 Löcher

	Week days Woche	We/Bank holidays We/Feiertag
Individual Individuell	DM 80,-	DM 100,-
Couple Ehepaar	DM 160,-	DM 200,-

Caddy	Caddy	nein
Electric Trolley	Elektrokarren	nein
Buggy	Elektrischer Wagen	nein
Clubs	Clubs	DM 20,-
Credit cards	Kreditkarten	nein

Access Zufahrt : Berlin A111 → Hamburg. Ausfahrt Henningsdorf-Stolpe. Links → Stolpe.
Map 6 on page 303 Karte 6 Seite 303

GOLF COURSE
PLATZ
17/20

Site	Lage	
Maintenance	Instandhaltung	
Architect	Architekt	Bernhard Langer Kurt Rossknecht
Type	Typ	Park
Relief	Relief	
Water in play	Platz mit Wasser	
Exp. to wind	Wind ausgesetzt	
Trees in play	Platz mit Bäumen	

Scorecard Scorekarte	Chp. Chp.	Mens Herren	Ladies Damen
Length Länge	6245	5853	5151
Par	72	71	71

Advised golfing ability Empfohlene Spielstärke	0	12	24	36

Hcp required   Min. Handicap   36 (We)

CLUB HOUSE & AMENITIES
KLUBHAUS UND NEBENGEBÄUDE
7/10

Pro shop	Pro shop	
Driving range	Übungsplatz	
Sheltered	überdacht	15 Plätze
On grass	auf Rasen	April → Oktober
Putting-green	Putting-grün	ja
Pitching-green	Pitching-grün	ja

393

HOTEL FACILITIES
HOTEL BESCHREIBUNG
5/10

HOTELS HOTELS

Solitude erweist sich als echter Gütetest für das Können eines Golfers, insbesondere dessen Fähigkeit gerade Drives zu schlagen. Kraftvollen Spielern werden die Fairways - Genauigkeit vorausgesetzt - vergleichsweise breit erscheinen, aber auch das Anspiel der mittelgrossen, erst kürzlich umgebauten Grüns erfordert in vielen Fällen nochmals höchste Präzision. Kürzere Spieler müssen sich vor allem auf gute lange Eisen und ihr kurzes Spiel verlassen können. Dies gilt im besonderen an den langen Par 4 Löchern, die regulär nur schwer zu erreichen sind, sowie den ausgezeichneten Par 3 Löchern. Wasser kommt nur selten ins Spiel, so ist es primär der Wald, der nicht nur den optischen sondern auch den spieltechnischen Charakter dieses Platzes prägt. Dank eines sehr durchdachten Layouts macht der leicht begehbare Kurs einen ausgewogenen Eindruck. Solitude ist eine Anlage, die man kaum ignorieren kann, eignet sich aber eher für die etwas besseren Golfer.

A good example of a von Limburger design and of his concern for the demands of golf. While golf is the examination of a player's abilities, Solitude is a test of value with emphasis on straight driving. If they play straight, powerful hitters will find the fairways comparatively wide, but they will need extreme accuracy to reach a number of mid-sized elevated greens that have been recently reshaped. The shorter-hitters will have to sharpen up their long irons and even their short game on some of the long par 4s, that are tough to hit in regulation, and the very good par 3s. As there is little water to speak of, the course's visual appeal is primarily the forest. The forest is, in fact, the whole point of the course, which is well-balanced, easy on the legs, and a thoroughly well designed affair. It is difficult to overlook Solitude, but it is a course reserved for golfers who can play a bit.

Stuttgarter Golf-Club Solitude
Am Golfplatz
D - 71297 MÖNSHEIM

Office	Sekretariat	(49) 07044 - 920 578
Pro shop	Pro shop	(49) 07044 - 5171
Fax	Fax	(49) 07044 - 920 579
Situation	Lage	

20 km von Stuttgart, 560 000 Ew.

Annual closure	Jährliche Schliessung	ja
		1/12→31/03
Weekly closure	Wöchentliche Schliessung	nein

Fees main season Preisliste hochsaison den ganzen Tag

	Week days Woche	We/Bank holidays We/Feiertag
Individual Individuell	DM 80,-	DM 100,-
Couple Ehepaar	DM 160,-	DM 200,-

We/Feiertage: nur in Mitgliederbegleitung
(with members)

Caddy	Caddy	auf Reserv./DM 10,-
Electric Trolley	Elektrokarren	nein
Buggy	Elektrischer Wagen	nein
Clubs	Clubs	nein
Credit cards Kreditkarten		nein

394

Access Zufahrt : A8 Stuttgart-Karlsruhe. Ausf. Heimsheim-Mönsheim. Golf → Mönsheim
Map 1 on page 293 Karte 1 Seite 293

GOLF COURSE
PLATZ 17 /20

Site	Lage	
Maintenance	Instandhaltung	
Architect	Architekt	B. von Limburger
Type	Typ	Flachland, Wald
Relief	Relief	
Water in play	Platz mit Wasser	
Exp. to wind	Wind ausgesetzt	
Trees in play	Platz mit Bäumen	

Scorecard	Chp.	Mens	Ladies
Scorekarte	Chp.	Herren	Damen
Length Länge	6045	6045	5365
Par	72	72	72

Advised golfing ability	0	12	24	36
Empfohlene Spielstärke				
Hcp required	Min. Handicap	36		

CLUB HOUSE & AMENITIES
KLUBHAUS UND NEBENGEBÄUDE 5 /10

Pro shop	Pro shop	
Driving range	Übungsplatz	
Sheltered	überdacht	6 Plätze
On grass	auf Rasen	ja
Putting-green	Putting-grün	ja
Pitching-green	Pitching-grün	ja

HOTEL FACILITIES
HOTEL BESCHREIBUNG 5 /10

HOTELS HOTELS
Parkhotel — Pforzheim
144 Zimmer, D 200,- — 12 km
Tel (49 7231) 1610, Fax (49 7044) 1616 90

Hotel Eiss — Leonburg
32 Zimmer, D DM 170,- — 15 km
Tel (49) 07152 - 9440, Fax (49) 07152 - 42 134

RESTAURANTS RESTAURANT
Häckermühle — Tiefenbronn
Tel (49) 07234 - 6111 — 10 km

Ochsenpost — Tiefenbronn
Tel (49) 07234 - 920 578 — 10 km

Mit dem Auto braucht man eine gute Stunde nach Österreich und nicht viel mehr nach Innsbruck. Aber zunächst sollte man den Charme des Tegernsees erkunden, der zu Füssen des Golfplatzes liegt. Auch wenn der Kurs sicher kein Überflieger ist, profitiert er doch, wie seine Nachbarn auch, von der einzigartigen Umgebung. In dieser Hinsicht ist Bayern eine absolute Golf-Hochburg. Der vielbeschäftigte Donald Harradine entwarf den Platz 1960, aber komplett fertiggestellt wurde er erst im Jahr 1984. Der Kurs zeigt viele typische Merkmale seines Architekten, der zweifellos nicht wie viele seiner Kollegen daran interessiert war, sich selbst ein Denkmal zu setzen. Das sehr britisch anmutende Design zeugt vielmehr von einer ausgezeichneten Kenntnis des Spiels in all seinen Facetten. Manchmal hätten wir uns gewünscht, dass er den Fairways und Bunkern etwas mehr Form verliehen hätte, aber andererseits blieb durch diese Nüchternheit der natürliche Aspekt des Geländes gewahrt. Der Platz ist recht hügelig.

It is hardly more than an hour's drive to the Austrian border and not much more to visit Innsbrück once you have discovered all the charms of the lake lying at the foot of the course here. While this layout is hardly a world-beater, it does, like its neighbours, have the advantage of an exceptional natural setting. In this sense, Bavaria is a real golfing destination. Designed in 1960 by Donald Harradine, a decidedly prolific architect, it was only really completed in 1984. It shows all the typical features of its designer, who was undoubtedly less concerned with marking his period than many of his colleagues, but it is very British in style as far as understanding the game at all levels is concerned. We sometimes felt he might have contoured the fairways and bunkers a little more, but this sobriety has the advantage of preserving the terrain's natural aspect. The course is rather hilly but only for the very unfit golfers.

Tegernseer Golf-Club Bad Wiessee e.V.
Robognerhof
D - 83707 BAD WIESSEE

Office	Sekretariat	(49) 08022 - 8769
Pro shop	Pro shop	(49) 08022 - 83 350
Fax	Fax	(49) 08022 - 82 747
Situation	Lage	

1 km von Bad Wiessee, 5 000 Ew.
18 km von Bad Tölz, 16 000 Ew.

Annual closure	Jährliche Schliessung	ja
		1/12→31/03
Weekly closure	Wöchentliche Schliessung	Montag
		das Restaurant

Fees main season Preisliste hochsaison 18 Löcher

	Week days Woche	We/Bank holidays We/Feiertag
Individual Individuell	DM 90,-	DM 90,-
Couple Ehepaar	DM 180,-	DM 180,-

We: nur in Mitgliederbegleitung / –21
Jahre/Studenten : – 50%

Caddy	Caddy	auf Reserv. DM 50,-
Electric Trolley	Elektrokarren	DM 30,-
Buggy	Elektrischer Wagen	nein
Clubs	Clubs	DM 35,-
Credit cards Kreditkarten		nein

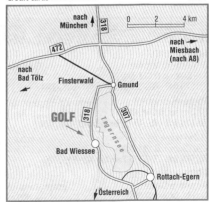

Access Zufahrt : A8 München → Salzburg. Ausf. Holzkirchen. 318 → Gmund. In Gmund 318 → Bad Wiessee. **Map 2 on page 294** Karte 2 Seite 294

GOLF COURSE
PLATZ
15/20

Site	Lage	
Maintenance	Instandhaltung	
Architect	Architekt	Donald Harradine
Type	Typ	Gebirge, Park
Relief	Relief	
Water in play	Platz mit Wasser	
Exp. to wind	Wind ausgesetzt	
Trees in play	Platz mit Bäumen	

Scorecard	Chp.	Mens	Ladies
Scorekarte	Chp.	Herren	Damen
Length Länge	5501	5501	4869
Par	70	70	70

Advised golfing ability		0	12	24	36
Empfohlene Spielstärke					
Hcp required	Min. Handicap	36			

CLUB HOUSE & AMENITIES
KLUBHAUS UND NEBENGEBÄUDE
7/10

Pro shop	Pro shop	
Driving range	Übungsplatz	
Sheltered	überdacht	nein
On grass	auf Rasen	ja
Putting-green	Putting-grün	ja
Pitching-green	Pitching-grün	ja

395

HOTEL FACILITIES
HOTEL BESCHREIBUNG
8/10

HOTELS HOTELS
Lederer am See, 90 Zimmer, D DM 300,-   Bad Wiessee
Tel (49) 08022 - 8290, Fax (49) 08022 - 829 261   1 km

Terrassenhof   Bad Wiessee
102 Zimmer, D DM 350,-   1 km
Tel (49) 08022 - 8630, Fax (49) 08022 - 81 794

Wilhelmy, 22 Zimmer, D DM 240,-   Bad Wiessee
Tel (49) 08022 - 98 680, Fax (49) 08022 - 84 074   1 km

Park-Hotel Egerner-Hof   Rottach-Egern
86 Zimmer, D DM 395,-   6 km
Tel (49) 08022 - 6660, Fax (49) 08022 - 666 200

RESTAURANTS RESTAURANT
Freihaus Brenner   Bad Wiessee, 1 km
Tel (49) 08022 - 82 004

Altes Fährhaus, Tel (49) 08041 - 60 30   Bad Tölz, 18 km

Beim Bau dieses Golfplatzes inmitten eines Naturschutzgebietes standen die ökologischen Gesichtspunkte eindeutig im Vordergrund, was zeigt, dass sich Golf und Umwelt durchaus gut vertragen. Treudelberg ist seiner Konzeption nach ein echter Sportclub im Stil amerikanischer Resorts, der aufgrund der angebotenen Palette an Möglichkeiten sicherlich der grösste seiner Art in dieser Region ist. Etwas mehr Charakter würde dem sehr zurückhaltend gestalteten Platz gut zu Gesicht stehen. Da die Anlage sehr stark dem Wind ausgesetzt ist, wären grössere Erdbewegungen wie man sie auch auf flachen Linksplätzen vorfindet, wünschenswert gewesen. Es gibt nur wenig Bäume, dieser Mangel wird aber durch Bunker, zahlreiche Wasserhindernisse sowie, je nach Saison, auch Rough wettgemacht. Ein ganz brauchbarer Platz, auf dem Spieler mit mittleren und hohen Handicaps lernen können, wie man mit Wasserhindernissen zurechtkommt.

This course was laid out in a nature reserve where ecological considerations were top priority. This just goes to show that golf and ecology can get along together. Treudelberg is a real sports club (in the style of US resorts) which is doubtless the largest of its kind in the region, judging by facilities. The course is very discreetly designed, and a little more personality would have been welcome. As exposure to the wind is a dominant factor, we would have liked to see more earth moving and grading, like on links courses, even when flat. Trees are not in great supply, but the bunkers and many water hazards largely make up for that, as does the rough at certain times of year. A useful course where mid- and high-handicappers will learn how to handle water hazards.

Golf & Country Club Treudelberg

Lehmsaler Landstrasse 45
D - 22397 HAMBURG

Office	Sekretariat	(49) 040 - 60822 500
Pro shop	Pro shop	(49) 040 - 60822 535
Fax	Fax	(49) 040 - 60822 444
Situation	Lage	

15 km von Hamburg (Zentrum), 1 650 000 Ew.
3 km von Hamburg-Poppenbüttel

Annual closure	Jährliche Schliessung	nein
Weekly closure	Wöchentliche Schliessung	nein

Fees main season
Preisliste hochsaison 18 Löcher

	Week days Woche	We/Bank holidays We/Feiertag
Individual Individuell	DM 70,-	DM 90,-
Couple Ehepaar	DM 140,-	DM 180,-

Caddy	Caddy	nein
Electric Trolley	Elektrokarren	nein
Buggy	Elektrischer Wagen	DM 50,-
Clubs	Clubs	DM 30,-

Credit cards Kreditkarten
VISA - Eurocard - MasterCard - AMEX - DC

Access Zufahrt : A7 Hamburg-Flesburg. Ausf. Schnelsen Nord. Rechts → Flughafen. → Poppenbüttel. Links → Lemsahl-Duvenstedt (Ulzburger Strasse), Lemsahl Landstrasse. **Map 7 on page 304** Karte 7 Seite 304

GOLF COURSE
PLATZ   13/20

Site	Lage	▬▬▬
Maintenance	Instandhaltung	▬▬▬▬
Architect	Architekt	Donald Steel
Type	Typ	Flachland
Relief	Relief	
Water in play	Platz mit Wasser	▬▬▬
Exp. to wind	Wind ausgesetzt	▬▬▬▬▬
Trees in play	Platz mit Bäumen	▬▬

Scorecard Scorekarte	Chp. Chp.	Mens Herren	Ladies Damen
Length Länge	6182	6182	5338
Par	72	72	72

Advised golfing ability		0 12 24 36
Empfohlene Spielstärke		▬▬▬▬
Hcp required	Min. Handicap	nein

CLUB HOUSE & AMENITIES
KLUBHAUS UND NEBENGEBÄUDE   8/10

Pro shop	Pro shop	▬▬▬▬
Driving range	Übungsplatz	▬▬▬
Sheltered	überdacht	16 Plätze
On grass	auf Rasen	ja
Putting-green	Putting-grün	ja
Pitching-green	Pitching-grün	ja

HOTEL FACILITIES
HOTEL BESCHREIBUNG   7/10

HOTELS HOTELS

Treudelberg Marriott · Golfplatz
135 Zimmer, D DM 300,-
Tel (49) 040 - 608 220, Fax (49) 040 - 608 22 44

Poppenbütteler Hof · Hamburg-Poppenbüttel
32 Zimmer, D DM 300,- · 3 km
Tel (49) 040 - 602 1072, Fax (49) 040 - 602 3130

Hafen Hamburg · Hamburg
250 Zimmer, D DM 210,- · 15 km
Tel (49) 040 - 311 130, Fax (49) 040 - 319 2736

RESTAURANTS RESTAURANT

Ristorante Dante · Hamburg-Lemsahl
Tel (49) 040 - 602 0043 · 500 m

Treudelberg Marriott · Golfplatz
Tel (49) 040 - 608 220

396

Der auf 700 Meter Höhe gelegene Golfplatz ist wie viele andere Kurse dieser Region besonders bei Touristen sehr beliebt. Am schönsten spielt sich Tutzing entweder im Herbst oder aber im Frühling, wenn die Vegetation nach dem Winter wieder voll erblüht ist. Die bayerischen Alpen bilden einen malerischen Hintergrund und verstärken so das Spielvergnügen auf dieser ausgezeichneten Anlage mit zahlreichen Bäumen und einigen hübschen Wasserläufen, welche die Spielbahnen - nicht selten zum Verdruss der Golfer - kreuzen. Der Kurs verfügt über keinerlei aussergewöhnliche aufregende Designelemente, sondern spiegelt vielmehr die Absicht des Architekten wider, in erster Linie einen Platz zu bauen, bei dem das Golfvergnügen im Vordergrund steht. Wenn Sie sich in dieser herrlichen Gegend aufhalten, sollten Sie diesen schön gelegenen Golfplatz und das dazugehörige Clubhaus im Stil eines Chalets keinesfalls links liegen lassen.

At an altitude of 700 metres and like most courses in this region very popular with tourists, Tutzing is particularly pleasant to play from the middle of Spring - when the vegetation is filling out after Winter - to the middle of Autumn. The backdrop of the Bavarian Alps adds to the pleasure of this excellent course with its numerous trees and pretty streams which cross the course, sometimes to the distress of the golfer. Don't look for anything outstandingly exciting design-wise here; this is the work of a serious artist who was thinking first and foremost of golfing pleasure. When you are in this superb region, Tutzing is a course not to be missed and a charming site enhanced by the chalet-style clubhouse.

Golf-Club Tutzing e.V.
Deixlfurt
D - 82327 TUTZING

Office	Sekretariat	(49) 08158 - 3600
Pro shop	Pro shop	(49) 08158 - 1761
Fax	Fax	(49) 08158 - 7234
Situation	Lage	

40 km von Munchen, 1 300 000 Ew.

Annual closure Jährliche Schliessung ja
15/11→15/02/99

Weekly closure Wöchentliche Schliessung

Fees main season
Preisliste hochsaison 18 Löcher

	Week days Woche	We/Bank holidays We/Feiertag
Individual Individuell	DM 80,-	DM 100,-
Couple Ehepaar	DM 160,-	DM 200,-

Caddy	Caddy	nein
Electric Trolley	Elektrokarren	DM 50,-
Buggy	Elektrischer Wagen	DM 70,-
Clubs	Clubs	DM 50,-

Credit cards Kreditkarten nein

Access Zufahrt : A95 München → Starnberg.
Von Starnberg, B2 (Olympiastr.) → Weilheim.
Nach Traubing, 1km links → Deixlfurt.
Map 2 on page 294 Karte 2 Seite 294

GOLF COURSE
PLATZ 15/20

Site	Lage	
Maintenance	Instandhaltung	
Architect	Architekt	C. Kramer
Type	Typ	Gebirge
Relief	Relief	
Water in play	Platz mit Wasser	
Exp. to wind	Wind ausgesetzt	
Trees in play	Platz mit Bäumen	

Scorecard Scorekarte	Chp. Chp.	Mens Herren	Ladies Damen
Length Länge	6159	6159	5438
Par	72	72	72

Advised golfing ability 0 12 24 36
Empfohlene Spielstärke
Hcp required Min. Handicap 35

CLUB HOUSE & AMENITIES
KLUBHAUS UND NEBENGEBÄUDE 7/10

Pro shop	Pro shop	
Driving range	Übungsplatz	
Sheltered	überdacht	3 Plätze
On grass	auf Rasen	ja
Putting-green	Putting-grün	ja
Pitching-green	Pitching-grün	ja

397

HOTEL FACILITIES
HOTEL BESCHREIBUNG 6/10

HOTELS HOTELS
Forsthaus am See — Pöcking-Possenhofen
21 Zimmer, DM 270,- — 10 km
Tel (49) 08157 - 93 010, Fax (49) 08157 - 4292

Marina — Bernried
71 Zimmer, D DM 250,- — 10 km
Tel (49) 08158 - 9320, Fax (49) 08158 - 7117

Kefer — Pöcking
20 Zimmer, D DM 140,- — 12 km
Tel (49) 08157 - 1247

RESTAURANTS RESTAURANT
Forsthaus Ilkahöhe — Tutzing
Tel (49) 08158 - 8242 — 4 km

WALDDÖRFER

Wie Ahrensburg ist auch Walddörfer am Ufer des Bredenbeker Sees gelegen, inmitten einer Parklandschaft mit für diese Region typischen Hecken und Bäumen. Dutzende unterschiedlicher Baumarten verleihen vielen Spielbahnen ihren ganz eigenen Charakter. Die hügeligen ersten neun Löcher mit ihren durchgehend engen Fairways zwingen speziell beim Abschlag zur Vorsicht. Die Spielbahnen sind zudem noch recht lang; es gibt vier Par 5, drei Par 3 und zwei Par 4 Löcher. Auf den zweiten Neun wird das Gelände flacher und offener. Besonders bei aufkommendem Wind werden sich selbst Longhitter schwer tun ihr Ergebnis zu reparieren, wenn sie auf den ersten Neun zu sehr gestreut haben. Bemerkenswert am Layout von Walddörfer ist, dass es nur sieben Par 4 Löcher gibt. Die gut erkennbaren Schwierigkeiten kommen stark ins Spiel. Das letzte Wort gebührt der ausgezeichneten 18. Bahn, die den würdigen Abschluss einer grossartigen Golfrunde bildet.

Like Ahrensburg, Walddörfer is located on the banks of lake Bredenbeker, in a setting of parkland, hedgerows and trees that are typical of the region. The trees are magnificent, with dozens of varieties giving a distinctive flavour to different holes. The front nine are hilly, with generally narrow fairways calling for care, especially off the tee. The holes are pretty long, too, and there are four par 5s, two par 3s and two par 4s. The landscape then becomes flatter and wider, although big-hitters will still be hard-pushed to repair their card if they were too wayward over the front 9, especially if the unstoppable wind gets up. In all, there are only seven par 4s here, a feature that adds to the originality of Walddörfer. Difficulties are very much in play and generally very visible. One last word should go to the 18th, an excellent hole with which to complete a great round of golf.

Golfclub Hamburg-Walddörfer
Schevenbarg
D - 22949 AMMERSBEK

Office	Sekretariat	(49) 040 - 605 1337
Pro shop	Pro shop	(49) 040 - 605 2725
Fax	Fax	(49) 040 - 605 4879
Situation	Lage	

2 km von Ahrensburg, 27 000 Ew.
20 km von Hamburg, 1 650 000 Ew.

Annual closure	Jährliche Schliessung	nein
Weekly closure	Wöchentliche Schliessung	Montag
	Das Restaurant	

Fees main season Preisliste hochsaison 18 Löcher

	Week days Woche	We/Bank holidays We/Feiertag
Individual Individuell	DM 70,-	DM 85,-
Couple Ehepaar	DM 140,-	DM 170,-

We/Feiertage: nur in Mitgliederbeleitung
(with members)

Caddy	Caddy	nein
Electric Trolley	Elektrokarren	nein
Buggy	Elektrischer Wagen	nein
Clubs	Clubs	nein
Credit cards Kreditkarten		nein

Access Zufahrt : A1 Hamburg-Lübeck. Ausf. Ahrenburg.
B434 → Ammersbek. Im Ortsteil Hoisbüttel, rechts:
Wulfsdorfer Weg → Golf
Map 7 on page 304 Karte 7 Seite 304

GOLF COURSE
PLATZ 15/20

Site	Lage	▬▬▬
Maintenance	Instandhaltung	▬▬▬
Architect	Architekt	B. von Limburger
Type	Typ	Wald, Park
Relief	Relief	
Water in play	Platz mit Wasser	▬▬
Exp. to wind	Wind ausgesetzt	▬▬▬▬
Trees in play	Platz mit Bäumen	▬▬▬▬

Scorecard Scorekarte	Chp. Chp.	Mens Herren	Ladies Damen
Length Länge	6154	6154	5416
Par	73	73	73

Advised golfing ability   0   12   24   36
Empfohlene Spielstärke   ▬▬▬▬
Hcp required   Min. Handicap   36

CLUB HOUSE & AMENITIES
KLUBHAUS UND NEBENGEBÄUDE 7/10

Pro shop	Pro shop	▬▬▬
Driving range	Übungsplatz	▬▬▬
Sheltered	überdacht	8 Plätze
On grass	auf Rasen	ja
Putting-green	Putting-grün	ja
Pitching-green	Pitching-grün	nein

HOTEL FACILITIES
HOTEL BESCHREIBUNG 6/10

HOTELS HOTELS
Park Hotel Ahrensburg   Ahrensburg
24 Zimmer, D DM 200,-   6 km
Tel (49) 04102 - 2300, Fax (49) 04102 - 230 100

Ring Hotel Ahrensburg   Ahrensburg
11 Zimmer, D DM 160,-   6 km
Tel (49) 04102 - 51 560, Fax (49) 04102 - 515 656

RESTAURANTS RESTAURANT
Golfclub Restaurant   Golf
Tel (49) 040 - 605 4211

398

Die grosszügige Weite Schleswig-Holsteins bildet die ruhige und beschauliche Umgebung für Wendlohe, wo die zahlreichen Bäume kaum beunruhigen, da man seinen Ball auch unter den Bäumen immer in einer guten Lage vorfindet. Wenig Wasser und nur vereinzelte Fairway-Bunker weisen darauf hin, dass die Hauptschwierigkeit im Anspiel der Grüns liegt. Unterschiedlich gross, mit starken Kontouren versehen und teilweise auf mehreren Stufen angelegt, sind diese ohne Frage die interessantesten Grüns weit und breit. Sie sind durchgängig gut verteidigt, sehr schnell aber nie unspielbar. Um sie von der richtigen Position aus anzuspielen, bedarf es sehr präziser Eisenschläge. Deswegen wird es einem auch zumindest auf der ersten Runde schwerfallen, ein seinem Handicap entsprechendes Ergebnis zu spielen. Im Winter ist der Platz etwas feucht. Das Clubhaus erfreut sich einer schönen Terrasse, von der aus man das 18. Loch einsehen kann.

The wide open spaces of Schleswig-Holstein provide a calm and pastoral setting at "Auf der Wendlohe", where trees are hardly a worry. There are enough of them, but you always find your ball well-placed when you meet them. With only a little water and few fairway bunkers, you will guess that the main problem is the approach to the greens. These are unquestionably some of the most interesting putting surfaces to contend with in this part of the world, with different sizes, serious contours and multi-tiering. They are generally fast, well-protected but never unplayable. To approach them from the right position, you need a sharp and accurate iron game. This is why returning a card to reflect your handicap is hardly likely, at least not the first time out. A wee damp in winter, the course boasts a pretty terrace overlooking the 18th hole.

Golf Club auf der Wendlohe

Oldesloher Strasse 251
D - 22457 HAMBURG

Office	Sekretariat	(49) 040 - 550 5014
Pro shop	Pro shop	(49) 040 - 550 6151
Fax	Fax	(49) 040 - 550 3668
Situation	Lage	

3 km von Norderstedt, 70 500 Ew.
15 km von Hamburg, 1 650 000 Ew.

Annual closure	Jährliche Schliessung	nein
Weekly closure	Wöchentliche Schliessung	nein

Fees main season Preisliste hochsaison 18 Löcher

	Week days Woche	We/Bank holidays We/Feiertag
Individual Individuell	DM 70,-	DM 90,-
Couple Ehepaar	DM 140,-	DM 160,-

We/Feiertage: nur in Mitgliederbegleitung
(with members)

Caddy	Caddy	auf Reservierung
Electric Trolley	Elektrokarren	nein
Buggy	Elektrischer Wagen	nein
Clubs	Clubs	nein
Credit cards Kreditkarten		nein

Access Zufahrt : A7 Hamburg-Kiel. Ausf. Hamburg-.
Schnelsen-Nord. 432 → Norderstedt (Oldesloher-
Strasse). Links (Wendloher Weg) → Golf
Map 7 on page 304 Karte 7 Seite 304

GOLF COURSE
PLATZ

16/20

Site	Lage	■■■■■
Maintenance	Instandhaltung	■■■■
Architect	Architekt	E.D. Hess
Type	Typ	Land, Flachland
Relief	Relief	
Water in play	Platz mit Wasser	■■
Exp. to wind	Wind ausgesetzt	■■■
Trees in play	Platz mit Bäumen	■■■■

Scorecard Scorekarte	Chp. Chp.	Mens Herren	Ladies Damen
Length Länge	6050	6050	5325
Par	72	72	72

Advised golfing ability		0 12 24 36
Empfohlene Spielstärke		■■■■
Hcp required	Min. Handicap	36

CLUB HOUSE & AMENITIES
KLUBHAUS UND NEBENGEBÄUDE

7/10

Pro shop	Pro shop	■■■■
Driving range	Übungsplatz	■■■
Sheltered	überdacht	4 Plätze
On grass	auf Rasen	ja
Putting-green	Putting-grün	ja
Pitching-green	Pitching-grün	ja

HOTEL FACILITIES
HOTEL BESCHREIBUNG

6/10

HOTELS HOTELS
Hotel Heuberg — Norderstedt
15 Zimmer, D DM 150,- — 3 km
Tel (49) 040 - 523 1197, Fax (49) 040 - 523 8067

Hotel Ausspann — Schnelsen
12 Zimmer, D DM 165,- — 6 km
Tel (49) 040 - 559 8700, Fax (49) 040 - 559 87060

RESTAURANTS RESTAURANT
Golf Club Restaurant — GC Wendlohe
Tel (49) 040 - 550 8583

Champs — Schnelsen
Tel (49) 040 - 559 791-0 — 6 km

399

Dies ist der älteste Golfplatz der Region. Fehlende Länge könnte ihm unter Beurteilung moderner Gesichtspunkte negativ ausgelegt werden, aber dennoch ist er nicht leicht zu spielen. Der Platz entpuppt sich als wahrer Widersacher des Golfers und entspricht so der Philosophie derer, die Golf in erster Linie als Spiel verstehen. Enge Fairways, Doglegs, kleine, oftmals auf mehreren Stufen angelegte Grüns, der ständig ins Spiel kommende Wald, ein Par 3 über eine Schlucht, mehrere Gräben sowie sehr gefährliche Bunker zwingen den Golfer dazu, den Ball permanent kontrolliert zu spielen. Die Schläge zum Grün sind hier häufig dem Angriff auf eine Festung vergleichbar, daher muss man versuchen die Grüns eher hoch denn flach anzuspielen. Leicht zu Gehen, eignet sich der Platz für eine Runde mit der Familie, unabhängig vom Können der Einzelnen, da er auch für Spieler mit hohem Handicap eine interessante Erfahrung darstellt. Der Kurs wird etwas einfacher, sobald man einmal alle nicht immer deutlich erkennbaren Hindernisse identifiziert hat.

The lack of length of this course might count against it when judged to modern-day criteria, but it is still not that easy to master. If golf is just a game, then Wentorf-Reinbeker well reflects that image: it is a real adversary for players. Narrow fairways, dog-legs, small greens that are often multi-tiered, a forest that is always in the picture, a par 3 across a gorge, a few ditches and very relevant bunkers constantly oblige players to flight their ball. And to pitch the greens rather than roll their shots, since attacking the greens here is often comparable to taking a fortress! Easily walkable, this is a course for a family outing, whatever the ability of players (a good experience for high-handicappers), but it gets easier to play once you have clearly identified the hazards, which are not always clear to see from the tee.

Wentorf-Reinbeker Golf-Club

Golfstrasse 2
D - 21465 WENTORF/HAMBURG

Office	Sekretariat	(49) 040 - 729 78066
Pro shop	Pro shop	(49) 040 - 720 2141
Fax	Fax	(49) 040 - 720 2141
Situation	Lage	

2 km von Reinbek, 24 600 Ew.
1 km von Weintorf

Annual closure	Jährliche Schliessung
Weekly closure	Wöchentliche Schliessung Montag
	Das Restaurant

Fees main season Preisliste hochsaison 18 Löcher

	Week days Woche	We/Bank holidays We/Feiertag
Individual Individuell	DM 60,-	DM 70,-
Couple Ehepaar	DM 120,-	DM 140,-

We/Feiertage: nur in Mitgliederbegleitung

Caddy	Caddy	nein
Electric Trolley	Elektrokarren	nein
Buggy	Elektrischer Wagen	nein
Clubs	Clubs	nein
Credit cards Kreditkarten		nein

400

Access Zufahrt : A24 Hamburg → Berlin. Ausf. Reinbek. Im Reinbek, → Wentorf (Hamburger Strasse). Am Mühlenteich, Golfstrasse.
Map 7 on page 304 Karte 7 Seite 304

GOLF COURSE
PLATZ   16 /20

Site	Lage	■■■■■
Maintenance	Instandhaltung	■■■■
Architect	Architekt	E.D. Hess (1991)
Type	Typ	Wald, Park
Relief	Relief	■
Water in play	Platz mit Wasser	■■
Exp. to wind	Wind ausgesetzt	■■■
Trees in play	Platz mit Bäumen	■■■■

Scorecard	Chp.	Mens	Ladies
Scorekarte	Chp.	Herren	Damen
Length Länge	5698	5698	5029
Par	70	70	70

Advised golfing ability		0	12	24	36
Empfohlene Spielstärke			■■■■		

Hcp required   Min. Handicap   36

CLUB HOUSE & AMENITIES
KLUBHAUS UND NEBENGEBÄUDE   7 /10

Pro shop	Pro shop	■■■
Driving range	Übungsplatz	■■■
Sheltered	überdacht	4 Plätze
On grass	auf Rasen	ja
Putting-green	Putting-grün	ja
Pitching-green	Pitching-grün	ja

HOTEL FACILITIES
HOTEL BESCHREIBUNG   6 /10

HOTELS HOTELS

Fürst-Bismarck-Mühle   Aumühle
6 Zimmer, D DM 190,-   6 km
Tel (49) 04104 - 2028, (49) 04104 - 1200

Waldhaus Reinbek   Reinbek
12 Zimmer, D DM 265,-   2 km
Tel (49) 040 - 727 520, (49) 040 - 727 52 10

RESTAURANTS RESTAURANT

Fürst Bismarck Mühle   Aumühle
Tel (49) 04104 - 2028   6 km

Waldhaus Reinbek   Reinbek
Tel (49) 040 - 727 520   2 km

Unweit der Donau liegt dieser flache Platz in einer parkähnlichen Landschaft mit wunderschönen alten Bäumen, meist Eichen. Der Kurs ist nicht wirklich schwierig, solange es einem gelingt den erwähnten Bäumen und dem extrem dicken Rough aus dem Weg zu gehen. Die wenigen Wasserhindernisse und spärlichen Fairway-Bunker stellen keine echte Gefahr dar. Wer deshalb lang genug vom Abschlag ist, kann in eine günstige Position gelangen, um von dort die Grüns zu attackieren, welche, von herausragender Qualität, die grosse Stärke des Platzes sind. Die Grünkörper sind hervorragend positioniert und sehr sorgfältig gestaltet. Sie sind zudem ausgezeichnet verteidigt und von teilweise immenser Grösse, was das Putten zu einem absoluten Vergnügen macht, auch wenn man den einen oder anderen 3-Putt einkalkulieren muss. Bedauerlich ist nur, dass nicht mehr Mittel in eine aufwendigere Gestaltung der Fairways geflossen sind, selbst wenn dies den Bau eines etwas weniger imposanten Clubhauses bedeutet hätte.

In countryside along the Danube, this is a flat course surrounded by some really beautiful trees, mainly oak, which give the impression of a large English-style park. There is no really great difficulty with this course, as long as you avoid those trees and the very thick rough. There is a little water and a few fairway bunkers, but they are no real threat. As a result, if you are long enough off the tee, you can get into a good position to attack the greens, which are the course's forte. Their surroundings have been carefully designed, so they are well positioned. They are large and well guarded with widely varying contours, thus adding to the fun of playing and the problem of scoring. It is a shame perhaps that more money was not spent on manicuring the fairways in the same way, even if it meant building a slightly less impressive clubhouse.

Wittelsbacher Golfclub Rohrenfeld-Neuburg

Gut Rohrenfeld
D - 86633 NEUBURG/DONAU

Office	Sekretariat	(49) 08431 - 44 118
Pro shop	Pro shop	(49) 08431 - 44 118
Fax	Fax	(49) 08431 - 41 301
Situation	Lage	

20 km von Ingolstadt, 108 000 Ew.
45 km von Augsburg, 265 000 Ew.

Annual closure	Jährliche Schliessung	nein
Weekly closure	Wöchentliche Schliessung	nein

Fees main season	Preisliste hochsaison 18 Löcher	
	Week days Woche	We/Bank holidays We/Feiertag
Individual Individuell	DM 70,-	DM 90,-
Couple Ehepaar	DM 140,-	DM 180,-

Ermässigung für Jugendliche und Studenten

Caddy	Caddy	nein
Electric Trolley	Elektrokarren	ja
Buggy	Elektrischer Wagen	ja
Clubs	Clubs	ja
Credit cards Kreditkarten		MasterCard

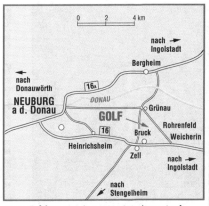

Access Zufahrt : München, A9 → Nürnberg. Ausf. Manching B16 → Neuburg. Ausf. Rohrenfeld → Golfplatz.
Map 2 on page 294 Karte 2 Seite 294

GOLF COURSE
PLATZ
15/20

Site	Lage	■■■■■□
Maintenance	Instandhaltung	■■■■■□
Architect	Architekt	Dudok van Heel
Type	Typ	Park
Relief	Relief	■□□□□□
Water in play	Platz mit Wasser	■■□□□□
Exp. to wind	Wind ausgesetzt	■■□□□□
Trees in play	Platz mit Bäumen	■■■■□□

Scorecard Scorekarte	Chp. Chp.	Mens Herren	Ladies Damen
Length Länge	6317	6065	5156
Par	72	72	72

Advised golfing ability Empfohlene Spielstärke	0	12	24	36
Hcp required Min. Handicap	36			

CLUB HOUSE & AMENITIES
KLUBHAUS UND NEBENGEBÄUDE
7/10

Pro shop	Pro shop	■■■■□□
Driving range	Übungsplatz	■■■■□□
Sheltered	überdacht	ja
On grass	auf Rasen	ja
Putting-green	Putting-grün	ja
Pitching-green	Pitching-grün	ja

HOTEL FACILITIES
HOTEL BESCHREIBUNG
6/10

HOTELS HOTELS
Wittelsbacher Gästehaus — Golfplatz
26 Zimmer, D DM 150,-
Tel (49) 08431 - 49 616, Fax (49) 08431 - 41 301

Bergbauer — Neuburg
22 Zimmer, D DM 155,- 6 km
Tel (49) 08431 - 47 095, Fax (49) 08431 - 47 090

Gasthof Vogelsang — Weichering
12 Zimmer, D DM 78,- 3 km
Tel (49) 08454 - 20 79, Fax (49) 08454 - 81 71

RESTAURANTS RESTAURANT
Arco Schlösschen — Neuburg
Tel (49) 08431 - 22 85 6 km

Im Stadttheater — Ingolstadt
Tel (49) 0841 - 93 5150 20 km

401

THE NEW PEUGEOT 406 COUPÉ. THE DRIVE OF YOUR LIFE.

Great Britain and Ireland

A s far as travel is concerned there are no frontiers. From a golfing point of view, the term "Great Britain and Ireland" covers three criteria, namely geography, language and sport. The best players from both islands were selected for the Ryder Cup team in years gone by, and still are for the Walker Cup and Curtis Cup against the United States. A fourth criterion might be unity of style in terms of golf courses, imposed, despite the variety of landscapes, by the pounding seas around each and every coastline. Seas which, miraculously, have left ample space for the great links courses of England, Scotland, Wales, Northern Ireland and the Republic of Ireland.

When you make choices you necessarily leave yourself open to criticism, and amongst the some 2,500 eighteen-hole courses to be found in this home of golf, we will certainly be accused of having forgotten a number of excellent layouts in Britain and Ireland. Some of them asked not to be included here because they are totally private. But we won't deny the fact that we have also given preference to the more specifically British style course, even though they may appear a little outdated in terms of yardage. In the same way, the scores given to clubhouses were awarded in relation to the general standard of clubhouse found in the British Isles. Some may be considered very low compared to their counterparts in the United States, Japan and even continental Europe. We have considered warmth of atmosphere, respect for tradition and the "golfing" excellence of the site to be of greater importance than marble hallways, thick-pile carpets and gym rooms.

As a general rule, visitors need to be aware of certain local customs. First of all, driving ranges are few and far between. Here people learnt to play out on the course. If you want a few practice swings, bring a bag of balls with you in the boot of your car. Hit them and pick them up yourself on the area provided for practice.

Next, we have done all we can to point out the restrictions on admission to →

Essential reading from the best in the game

12 reasons you need to buy the six issues of *Golf International* in 1998

1. Its panel of exclusively contracted golf professionals includes: SEVE BALLESTEROS, Europe's victorious Ryder Cup captain and one of the most charismatic figures in sport
2. NICK FALDO, the finest British golfer born this century and the winner of a European-record six major championships
3. DAVID LEADBETTER, the world's leading golf teacher – for the stars of the game, for the club golfer and for the beginner
4. NICK PRICE, one of the most popular players in golf, winner of three majors and twice PGA Tour leading money-winner
5. Golf International also brings you the best writing about the game. JOHN UPDIKE and HUGH MCILVANNEY were among its contributors in its first year, and each month you can enjoy the musings, opinions and expertise of our matchless array of top-class columnists:
6. PETER ALLISS, the Voice of Golf
7. IAN WOOLDRIDGE, ace sportswriter on the Daily Mail
8. JEREMY CHAPMAN of The Sporting Life on betting
9. JEFF RANDALL of Sunday Business on financial matters
10. DAVID SPITTLES of The Observer on property

Add to all this the regular appearances of:

11. The photographs of DAVID CANNON
12. The art of HAROLD RILEY

and you have a magazine that you want to miss about as much as a one-foot putt

Golf International will be published bi-monthly in 1998: in February, April, June, August, October and December. All subscribers are eligible to receive discounts of 10% or more off David Leadbetter game-improvement teaching products.

each club, but these may change, as may the minimum handicap required to play the course. We advise you to call in advance every time.

Out on the course, players from Europe will often be surprised at the speed of the game in the UK. Never hesitating to let people play through is one thing, but more importantly they should learn to speed up their own game.

Last but by no means least, always pack a shirt, tie and jacket in your car. Most clubs impose the tie and jacket rule in the bar or restaurant or both, often in the evening but also during the day. So don't get caught out on that one.

E n matière de voyage, il n'y a plus de frontières. L'appellation "Grande-Bretagne et Irlande" a trois justifications. D'abord géographique, ensuite linguistique, et enfin sportive : en golf, on unit les meilleurs joueurs des deux îles, autrefois pour disputer la Ryder Cup, aujourd'hui encore pour jouer la Walker Cup et la Curtis Cup contre les Etats-Unis. On pourrait ajouter en dernier lieu une unité de style de parcours, imposée en dépit des diversités des paysages par les assauts de l'océan, de tous côtés, qui ont par miracle laissé de grands espaces vierges pour y tracer les grands links d'Angleterre, d'Ecosse, du Pays de Galles, d'Irlande et d'Irlande du Nord.

Quand on fait des choix, on est forcément vulnérable aux critiques, et on nous reprochera probablement d'avoir "oublié" certains parcours de grande valeur, en Grande-Bretagne et Irlande, parmi les quelques 2.500 parcours de 18 trous que comptent ces berceaux du golf. Certains ont demandé à ne pas figurer ici, car ils sont totalement privés. Mais nous ne cacherons pas avoir aussi privilégié les parcours les plus spécifiquement britanniques de style, même s'ils peuvent parfois paraître désuets par leur manque de longueur. De la même façon, les notes attribuées aux Clubhouses ont été attribuées en relation avec leur niveau général dans les îles britanniques : certains d'entre eux seraient jugés très modestes en comparaison avec leurs équivalents les plus luxueux aux Etats-Unis, au Japon, ou même sur le continent. Pour nous, la chaleur de l'ambiance, le respect de la tradition, la qualité "golfique" du lieu a plus d'importance que le marbre, les moquettes et les salles de mise en forme.

En règle générale, les visiteurs doivent être informés de certaines coutumes locales. D'abord, les practices ou driving ranges sont rares. Ici, on apprenait à jouer sur le parcours. Si vous souhaitez vous entraîner, ayez un sac de balles dans votre coffre, que vous ramasserez vous-même sur les zones prévues à cet effet.

Ensuite, nous avons signalé au maximum les restrictions d'accès dans chaque club, mais elles peuvent changer, tout comme les limites de handicap, nous vous conseillons donc de toujours téléphoner à l'avance.

Sur le parcours, les joueurs du continent seront souvent surpris par la rapidité de jeu sur les parcours. Qu'ils n'hésitent jamais à laisser passer est une chose, mais qu'ils apprennent surtout à accélérer leur propre rythme.

Enfin, ayez toujours dans votre voiture un petit sac avec une chemise de ville, une cravate et une veste. La plupart des clubs imposent "tie and jacket," au bar, au restaurant, ou les deux, souvent le soir, mais aussi dans la journée. Vous ne serez pas pris au dépourvu.

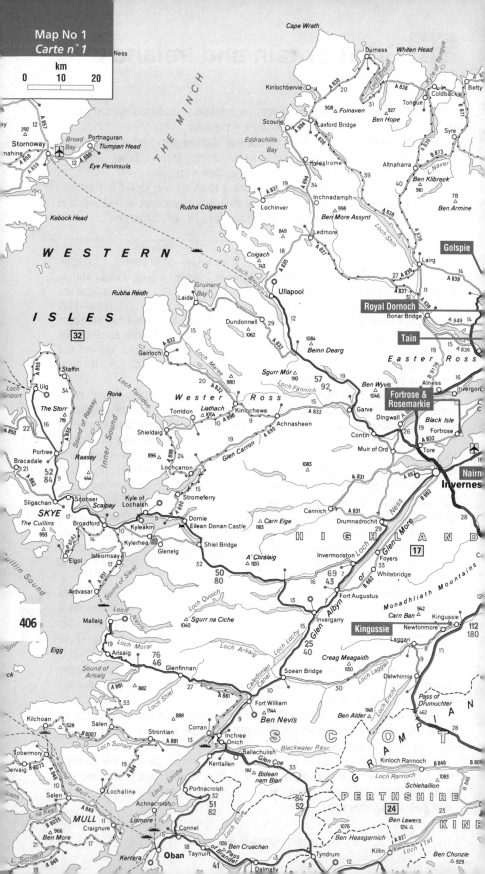

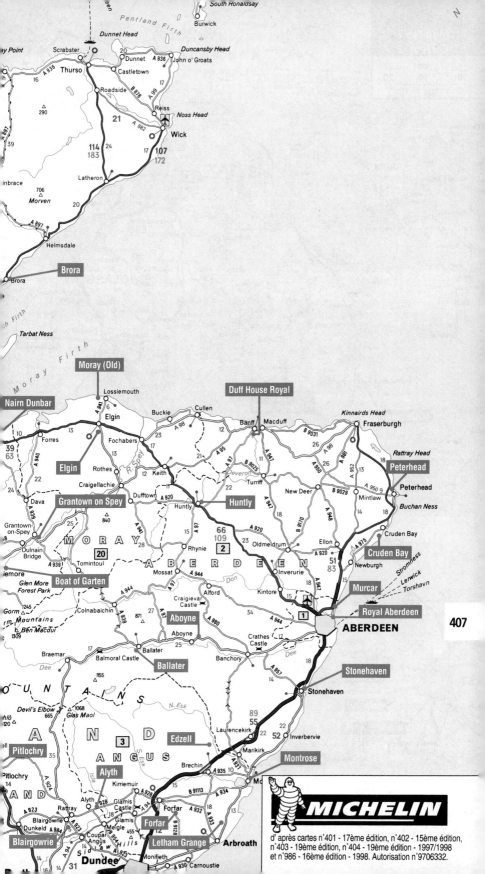

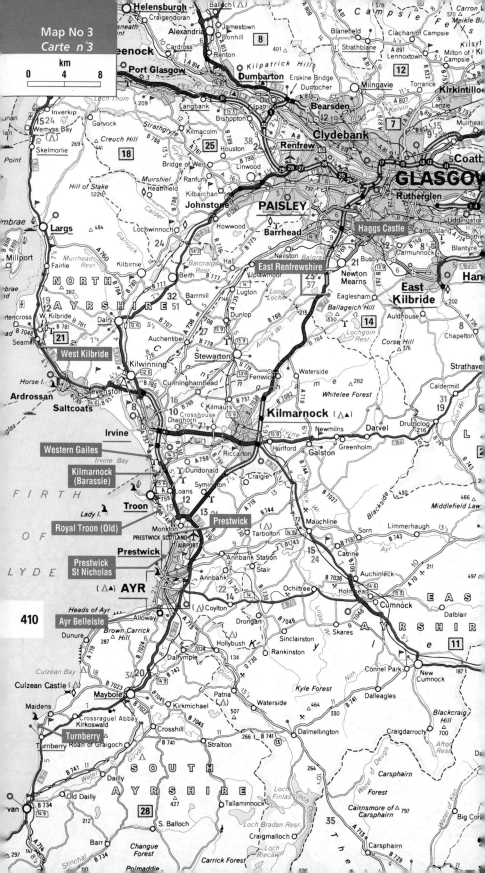

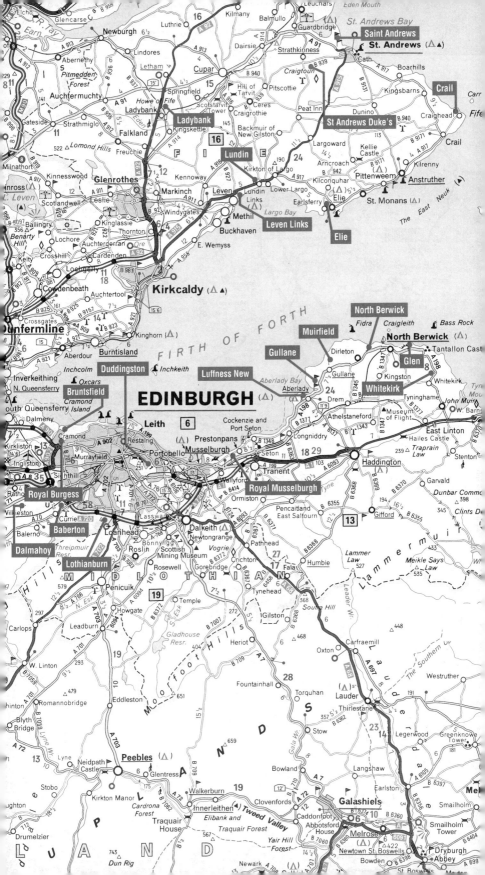

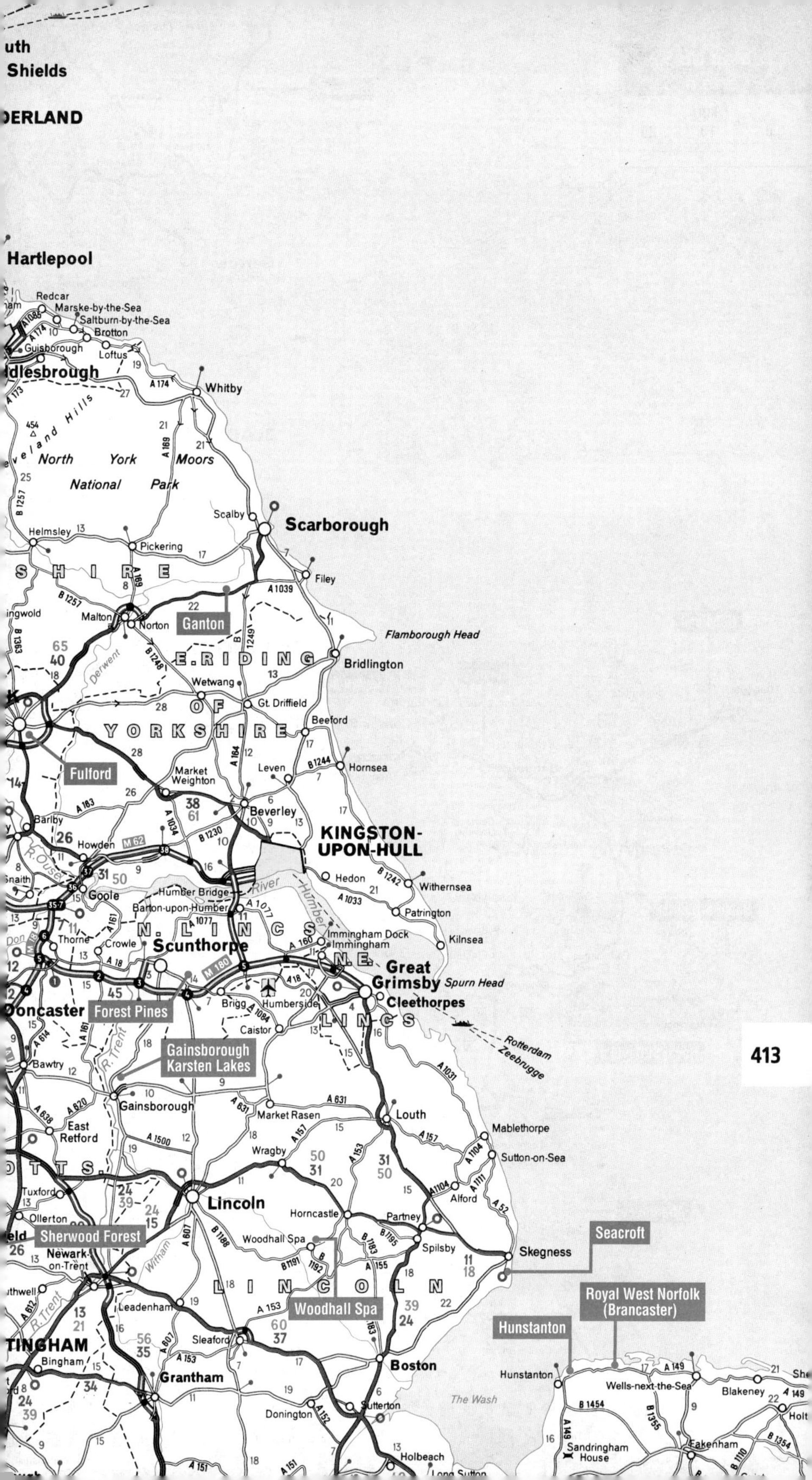

Hartlepool

Redcar
Marske-by-the-Sea
Saltburn-by-the-Sea
A 174
Brotton
Guisborough
Loftus
ddlesbrough
A 173
A 174
Whitby

454
North   York   Moors
eland Hills
National   Park
B 1257
Helmsley 13
Pickering
Scalby
Scarborough
ngwold
Malton
Norton
Ganton
Filey
A 1039

B 1257
E. RIDING
Flamborough Head
Wetwang
Gt. Driffield
Bridlington

OF   YORKSHIRE
Beeford
Fulford
Market
Weighton
Leven
B 1244
Hornsea
A 164
A 183
Bariby
Beverley
KINGSTON-
Howden
M 62
A 1034
B 1230
UPON-HULL
A 26
Goole
Humber Bridge
Hedon
B 1242
Withernsea
Snaith
Barton-upon-Humber
A 1033
Patrington
Thorne
1077
Kilnsea
Crowle
Scunthorpe
Immingham Dock
A 18
M 180
Immingham
N. E.
Great
Doncaster
Forest Pines
Brigg
A 1084
Humberside
Grimsby
Spurn Head
Bawtry
Caistor
Cleethorpes
Rotterdam
Gainsborough
Zeebrugge
Karsten Lakes
Tuxford
A 1500
Market Rasen
A 631
Louth
Mablethorpe
Ollerton
Gainsborough
A 631
A 157
Sutton-on-Sea
East
Retford
Wragby
50
A 1104
Sherwood Forest
31
A 153
50
Alford
A 52
Newark-
Tuxford
24
Lincoln
Horncastle
Partney
on-Trent
39
Woodhall Spa
Spilsby
Skegness
Seacroft
Leadenham
B 1191
B 1195
A 153
Woodhall Spa
Royal West Norfolk
TINGHAM
56
39
(Brancaster)
Bingham
35
Sleaford
24
Hunstanton
Grantham
Boston
A 149
Hunstanton
Wells-next-the-Sea
Blakeney
A 149
Donington
The Wash
A 1454
Holt
Sandringham
B 1355
House
Fakenham
B 1354
Holbeach
A 151

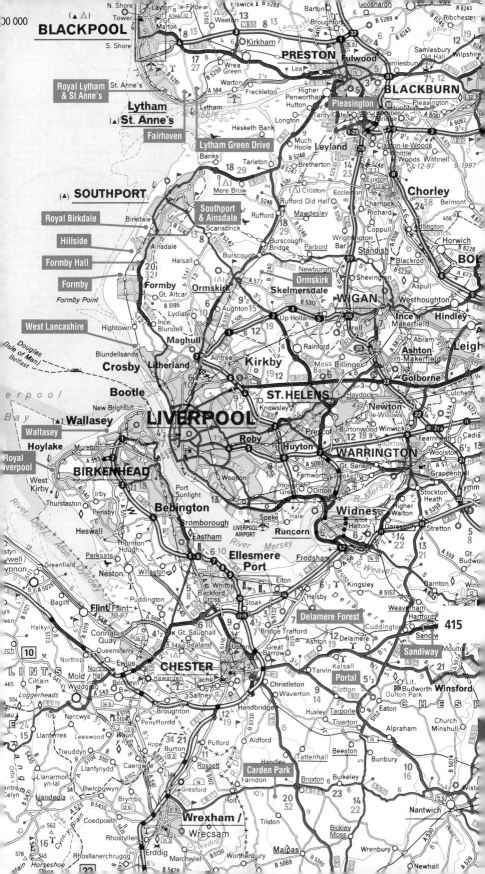

Map No 6
Carte n° 6

km
0   10   20

GEORGE'S

Strumble Head
Pembrokeshire Coast National Park
St. David's Head
St. David's
PEMBROKESHIRE
St. Bride's Bay
Haverfordwest/
Hwlffordd
Milford Haven/
Aberdaugleddau
Pembroke Dock/
Doc Penfro
Pembroke
St. Govan's Head

Aberaeron
New Quay
Aberporth
Cardigan/
Aberteifi
Newport
Fishguard/
Abergwaun

Tenby

Ashburnham

Rosslare
Cork

Newcastle Emlyn
Crymmych
CARMARTHENSH
Whitland
Narberth
Neyland
Saundersfoot
Tenby/
Dinbych-y-pysgod
Carmarthen Bay

Synod Inn
Lampeter
Landysul

Carmarthen
Caerfyrddin

St. Clears/
Sanclêr
Pendine
Kidwelly
Burry Port

7

Cross Hands
Llanelli
Swansea /
Abertawe
Rhossili
Worms Head
Port-Eynon
The Mumb

Pennard

Cork

B R I S T O L

Lundy

Ilfracombe
Combe Martin
Saunton
Croyde
Braunton
Royal North Devon
(Westward Ho)
Northam
Bar
Hartland Point
Clovelly
Bideford

Great Torrington

Kilkhampton
Bude
Stratton
Holsworthy
Winkleig
Hatherleig

Bowood (Cornwall)
Tintagel
Launceston
D **E**
Oke
High Moreton
Dartmoo

St Enodoc
Padstow
Camelford
182   113
St Mellion

Trevose
Wadebridge
Tavistock
Princetown
Park
Buckfa

Perranporth
Newquay
Fraddon
Bodmin
Callington

West Cornwall
Lostwithiel
Liskeard
Saltash
Plympton

Truro
Fowey
Looe
Torpoint
Plymstock
Modbury

St. Ives
Hayle
Redruth
St. Austell
Polperro
PLYMOUTH
Newton Ferrers
Salco

Penzance
Camborne
Penryn
St. Mawes
Mevagissey

St. Just
St. Michael's Mount
Falmouth
Thurlestone

Sennen
Land's End
Helston
St. Keverne

Mount's Bay
Lizard
Lizard Point

416

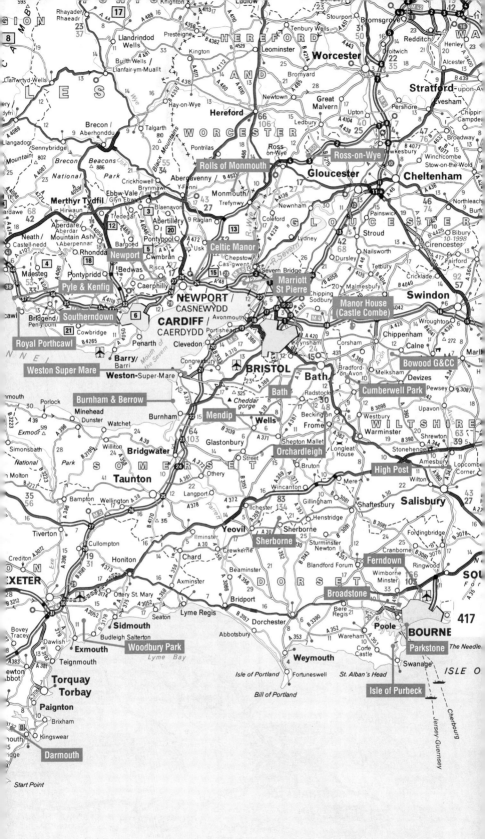

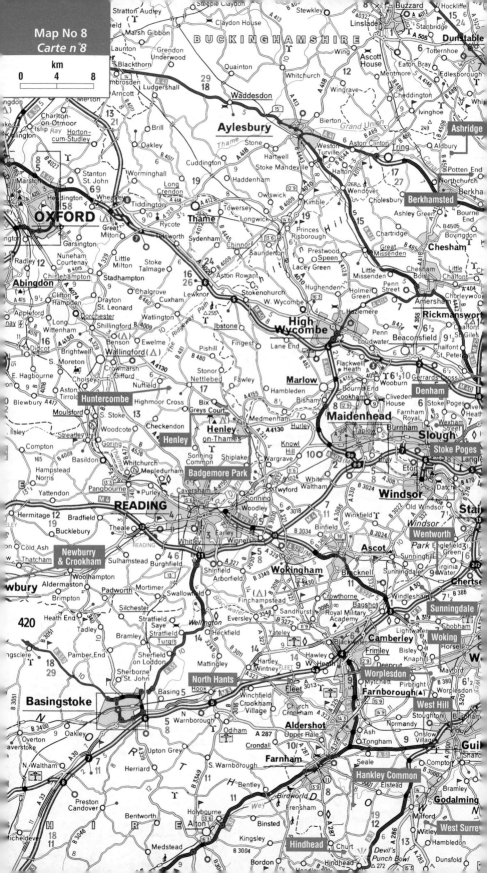

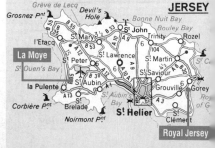

CLASSIFICATION OF COURSES
CLASSEMENT DES PARCOURS

This classification gives priority consideration
to the score awarded to the actual course.

Ce classement donne priorité à la note attribuée au parcours.

Eng: England   Sc: Scotland   W: Walles

Club-house and facilities
Note du Club-house et annexes

Course score   Hotel facility score
Note du parcours ⌐   ⌐ *Note de l'environnement hôtelier*   Page

19 3 4 Carnoustie *Championship* Sc   599

Score	Course	Country	Page	Score	Course	Country	Page
19 3 4	Carnoustie *Championship*	Sc	599	**18** 7 6	Saunton *East Course*	Eng	541
19 8 5	Ganton	Eng	479	**18** 5 4	Seascale	Eng	543
19 7 6	Muirfield	Sc	640	**18** 7 4	Silloth-on-Solway	Eng	548
19 7 8	Nairn	Sc	643	**18** 6 5	Southerness	Sc	661
19 9 7	Royal Birkdale (The)	Eng	526	**18** 7 7	Southport & Ainsdale	Eng	550
19 7 7	Royal Dornoch	Sc	656	**18** 7 4	St Enodoc *Church Course*	Eng	551
19 7 8	Royal Lytham & St Anne's	Eng	532	**18** 8 8	Sunningdale *New Course*	Eng	556
19 7 5	Royal Porthcawl	W	688	**18** 8 8	Sunningdale *Old Course*	Eng	557
19 7 5	Royal St George's	Eng	535	**18** 7 6	Tenby	W	691
19 7 7	Royal Troon *Old Course*	Sc	658	**18** 7 7	Walton Heath *Old Course*	Eng	566
19 9 8	Turnberry *Ailsa Course*	Sc	670	**18** 8 7	Wentworth *West Course*	Eng	569
18 8 8	St Andrews *Old Course*	Sc	665	**18** 7 6	West Sussex	Eng	575
18 7 7	Alwoodley (The)	Eng	440	**18** 7 7	Woburn *Dukes Course*	Eng	578
18 8 6	Blairgowrie *Rosemount*	Sc	593	**18** 7 8	Woodhall Spa	Eng	582
18 7 6	Burnham & Berrow	Eng	457	**17** 7 7	Aberdovey	W	677
18 6 8	Castletown	Eng	460	**17** 6 5	Ashburnham	W	678
18 9 7	Celtic Manor *Roman Road*	W	679	**17** 8 7	Berkshire (The)		
18 8 6	Chart Hills	Eng	461		*Blue Course*	Eng	446
18 7 6	Cruden Bay	Sc	602	**17** 8 7	Berkshire (The) *Red C*se	Eng	447
18 7 7	Formby	Eng	475	**17** 6 5	Blackmoor	Eng	449
18 9 7	Gleneagles *King's*	Sc	618	**17** 6 6	Bowood G&CC	Eng	452
18 7 7	Hillside	Eng	489	**17** 7 6	Brampton	Eng	453
18 7 6	Ilkley	Eng	493	**17** 7 7	Broadstone	Eng	455
18 6 4	Machrihanish	Sc	636	**17** 8 7	Buckinghamshire (The)	Eng	456
18 7 7	Moortown	Eng	509	**17** 7 7	Carlisle	Eng	459
18 7 8	North Berwick	Sc	645	**17** 7 7	Clitheroe	Eng	462
18 6 6	Notts (Hollinwell)	Eng	513	**17** 7 8	Conwy	W	680
18 6 6	Pennard	W	685	**17** 7 7	Cumberwell Park	Eng	465
18 6 7	Prestwick	Sc	651	**17** 8 8	Dalmahoy *East Course*	Sc	603
18 7 8	Royal Aberdeen			**17** 6 7	Downfield	Sc	604
	Balgownie Links	Sc	654	**17** 8 7	East Sussex National		
18 8 7	Royal Liverpool (Hoylake)	Eng	531		*East Course*	Eng	469
18 6 6	Royal North Devon			**17** 7 8	Fairhaven	Eng	470
	(Westward Ho!)	Eng	534	**17** 7 7	Ferndown *Old Course*	Eng	472
18 6 5	Royal St David's	W	689	**17** 6 7	Forest Pines *Forest + Pines*	Eng	474

423

PEUGEOT GOLF GUIDE 1998

CLASSIFICATION OF COURSES

Score	Course	Country	Page	Score	Course	Country	Page
17 7 8	Fulford	Eng	477	16 7 6	Hindhead	Eng	490
17 9 7	Gleneagles *Monarch's*	Sc	619	16 7 5	Holyhead	W	681
17 8 7	Gullane *No 1*	Sc	623	16 7 7	Ipswich (Purdis Heath)	Eng	494
17 7 6	Hunstanton	Eng	491	16 7 6	Isle of Purbeck	Eng	495
17 6 8	Kilmarnock (Barassie)	Sc	626	16 7 6	John O'Gaunt	Eng	496
17 7 8	La Moye	Eng	497	16 6 5	Lanark	Sc	629
17 7 5	Ladybank	Sc	628	16 6 6	Leven	Sc	631
17 8 6	Linden Hall	Eng	498	16 7 6	Liphook	Eng	500
17 6 6	Lindrick	Eng	499	16 5 6	Luffness New	Sc	633
17 7 7	Machrie	Sc	635	16 6 7	Lundin	Sc	634
17 7 7	Monifieth	Sc	637	16 7 7	Manchester	Eng	503
17 5 6	Montrose	Sc	638	16 8 7	Marriott St Pierre		
17 8 7	Moor Park *High Course*	Eng	508		*Old Course*	W	682
17 5 5	Moray	Sc	639	16 6 5	Nefyn & District	W	683
17 7 6	North Hants	Eng	512	16 7 8	Parkstone	Eng	517
17 7 7	Orchardleigh	Eng	514	16 6 6	Perranporth	Eng	519
17 6 5	Panmure	Sc	646	16 8 6	Pleasington	Eng	520
17 8 7	Prestbury	Eng	522	16 6 4	Powfoot	Sc	650
17 7 5	Pyle & Kenfig	W	686	16 6 7	Prestwick St Nicholas	Sc	652
17 6 5	Royal Cinque Ports	Eng	527	16 7 9	Royal Burgess	Sc	655
17 7 6	Royal West Norfolk			16 7 7	Royal Guernsey	Eng	529
	(Brancaster)	Eng	536	16 7 8	Royal Jersey	Eng	530
17 5 7	Sandiway	Eng	540	16 8 7	Royal Musselburgh	Sc	657
17 6 4	Seacroft	Eng	542	16 6 6	Scotscraig	Sc	659
17 7 6	Sherwood Forest	Eng	547	16 7 7	Southerndown	W	690
17 5 5	Shiskine (Blackwaterfoot)	Sc	660	16 8 8	St Andrews *Jubilee Course*	Sc	663
17 8 7	Slaley Hall	Eng	549	16 6 4	Thurlestone	Eng	562
17 8 8	St Andrews *New Course*	Sc	664	16 9 8	Turnberry *Arran Course*	Sc	671
17 7 7	St George's Hill	Eng	552	16 7 6	Walton Heath *New Course*	Eng	565
17 9 7	St Mellion *Nicklaus Course*	Eng	553	16 8 7	Wentworth *East Course*	Eng	568
17 8 8	Stoke Poges	Eng	554	16 7 6	West Cornwall	Eng	571
17 6 6	Tain	Sc	668	16 7 5	West Kilbride	Sc	672
17 7 7	Trevose *Championship*	Eng	563	16 6 7	Weston-Super-Mare	Eng	576
17 7 7	Wallasey	Eng	564	16 6 6	Woking	Eng	579
17 7 7	West Lancashire	Eng	573	16 7 6	Worplesdon	Eng	583
17 5 7	Western Gailes	Sc	673	15 7 6	Alloa	Sc	587
17 6 7	Whittington Heath	Eng	577	15 6 7	Ballater	Sc	591
16 7 6	Ashridge	Eng	441	15 6 5	Berwick-upon-Tweed	Eng	448
16 5 7	Ayr (Belleisle)	Sc	589	15 8 6	Blairgowrie *Lansdowne*	Sc	592
16 6 9	Bath	Eng	443	15 5 7	Bolton Old Links	Eng	450
16 7 7	Beau Desert	Eng	444	15 7 7	Brora	Sc	595
16 7 6	Berkhamsted	Eng	445	15 8 9	Bruntsfield	Sc	596
16 7 6	Bowood (Cornwall)	Eng	451	15 6 6	Coxmoor	Eng	464
16 9 6	Dartmouth	Eng	466	15 6 6	Crail	Sc	600
16 7 8	Duke's Course St Andrews	Sc	607	15 7 7	Crieff *Ferntower Course*	Sc	601
16 5 6	Dunbar	Sc	609	15 6 7	Delamere Forest	Eng	467
16 6 5	Fortrose & Rosemarkie	Sc	616	15 7 7	Denham	Eng	468
16 7 7	Hadley Wood	Eng	481	15 7 9	Duddingston	Sc	605
16 6 6	Hankley Common	Eng	482	15 6 6	Duff House Royal	Sc	606
16 7 7	Hayling	Eng	484	15 7 5	Dumfries & County	Sc	608

424

CLASSIFICATION OF COURSES

Score	Course	Country	Page
15 7 7	Dunfermline	Sc	610
15 6 8	East Renfrewshire	Sc	611
15 7 6	Elgin	Sc	613
15 6 6	Elie	Sc	614
15 6 6	Felixstowe Ferry Martello Course	Eng	471
15 9 7	Gleneagles Queen's	Sc	620
15 7 8	Gog Magog Old Course	Eng	480
15 7 9	Haggs Castle	Sc	624
15 8 7	Hawkstone Park Hawkstone	Eng	483
15 7 7	Hertfordshire (The)	Eng	486
15 6 7	High Post	Eng	488
15 4 5	Kingussie	Sc	627
15 7 5	Letham Grange Old Cse	Sc	630
15 7 8	Lytham Green Drive	Eng	502
15 8 7	Manor House (Castle Combe)	Eng	505
15 5 7	Mendip	Eng	506
15 7 7	Mere	Eng	507
15 6 6	Murcar	Sc	641
15 6 7	Nairn Dunbar	Sc	644
15 6 7	Newbury & Crookham	Eng	510
15 6 7	Newport	W	684
15 6 7	Pannal	Eng	516
15 5 4	Peterhead	Sc	647
15 8 7	Portal Championship	Eng	521
15 6 7	Portpatrick (Dunskey)	Sc	649
15 6 6	Rolls of Monmouth (The)	W	687
15 5 6	Ross-on-Wye	Eng	524
15 7 7	Roxburghe (The)	Sc	653
15 7 6	Royal Cromer	Eng	528
15 6 8	Royal Winchester	Eng	537
15 8 8	Rudding Park	Eng	538
15 7 6	Shanklin & Sandown	Eng	544
15 6 7	Sherborne	Eng	545
15 7 6	Sheringham	Eng	546
15 7 8	Stoneham	Eng	555
15 5 6	Strathaven	Sc	667
15 6 5	Thornhill	Sc	669
15 7 8	Warwickshire (The)	Eng	567
15 7 7	West Berkshire	Eng	570
15 6 6	West Hill	Eng	572
15 7 7	West Surrey	Eng	574
15 7 7	Whitekirk	Sc	675
15 9 6	Woodbury Park The Oaks	Eng	581
14 6 6	Aboyne	Sc	586
14 6 6	Alyth	Sc	588
14 6 8	Baberton	Sc	590
14 7 7	Badgemore Park	Eng	442

Score	Course	Country	Page
14 6 7	Boat of Garten	Sc	594
14 6 5	Brancepeth Castle	Eng	454
14 6 6	Buchanan Castle	Sc	597
14 8 8	Carden Park	Eng	458
14 3 4	Carnoustie Burnside	Sc	598
14 8 7	Collingtree Park	Eng	463
14 6 3	Edzell	Sc	612
14 8 8	Forest of Arden Arden Course	Eng	473
14 6 6	Forfar	Sc	615
14 8 6	Formby Hall	Eng	476
14 8 6	Gainsborough- Karsten Lakes	Eng	478
14 7 7	Glen	Sc	617
14 5 4	Golspie	Sc	621
14 6 7	Grantown on Spey	Sc	622
14 6 7	Henley	Eng	485
14 8 8	Hever	Eng	487
14 6 7	Huntercombe	Eng	492
14 6 6	Huntly	Sc	625
14 6 5	Littlestone	Eng	501
14 6 8	Lothianburn	Sc	632
14 8 6	Mannings Heath Waterfall Course	Eng	504
14 7 8	Murrayshall	Sc	642
14 6 4	Ormskirk	Eng	515
14 6 7	Pitlochry	Sc	648
14 7 6	Royal Ashdown Forest	Eng	525
14 7 8	Royal Mid-Surrey Outer	Eng	533
14 7 7	Sand Moor	Eng	539
14 8 8	St Andrews Eden Course	Sc	662
14 7 6	Tandridge	Eng	558
14 7 5	Thetford	Eng	559
14 7 6	Thorndon Park	Eng	560
14 7 7	Thorpeness	Eng	561
14 8 6	Westerwood	Sc	674
14 7 7	Woodbridge	Eng	580
13 6 7	Aldeburgh	Eng	439
14 7 7	North Foreland	Eng	511
14 8 8	Patshull Park Hotel	Eng	518
14 6 4	Prince's Himalayas-Shore	Eng	523
14 5 5	Stonehaven	Sc	666

425

CLASSEMENT DE L'ENVIRONNEMENT HOTELIER
CLASSIFICATION OF HOTELS FACILITIES

This classification gives priority consideration
to the score awarded to the hotel facilities.

Ce classement donne priorité à la note attribuée à l'environnement hôtelier

		Club-house and facilities *Note du Club-house et annexes*		
Course score *Note du parcours*		**Hotel facility score** ***Note de l'environnement hôtelier***		Page
16	6 **9**	Bath	Eng	443

Score			Course	Country Page	Score			Course	Country Page
16	6	9	Bath	Eng 443	15	8	8	Rudding Park	Eng 538
15	8	9	Bruntsfield	Sc 596	14	8	8	St Andrews *Eden Course*	Sc 662
15	7	9	Duddingston	Sc 605	16	8	8	St Andrews *Jubilee Course*	Sc 663
15	7	9	Haggs Castle	Sc 624	17	8	8	St Andrews *New Course*	Sc 664
16	7	9	Royal Burgess	Sc 655	18	8	8	St Andrews *Old Course*	Sc 665
14	6	8	Baberton	Sc 590	17	8	8	Stoke Poges	Eng 554
14	8	8	Carden Park	Eng 458	15	7	8	Stoneham	Eng 555
18	6	8	Castletown	Eng 460	18	8	8	Sunningdale *New Course*	Eng 556
17	7	8	Conwy	W 680	18	8	8	Sunningdale *Old Course*	Eng 557
17	8	8	Dalmahoy *East Course*	Sc 603	19	9	8	Turnberry *Ailsa Course*	Sc 670
16	7	8	Duke's Course St Andrews	Sc 607	16	9	8	Turnberry *Arran Course*	Sc 671
15	6	8	East Renfrewshire	Sc 611	15	7	8	Warwickshire (The)	Eng 567
17	7	8	Fairhaven	Eng 470	18	7	8	Woodhall Spa	Eng 582
14	8	8	Forest of Arden		17	7	7	Aberdovey	W 677
			Arden Course	Eng 473	13	6	7	Aldeburgh	Eng 439
17	7	8	Fulford	Eng 477	18	7	7	Alwoodley (The)	Eng 440
15	7	8	Gog Magog *Old Course*	Eng 480	16	5	7	Ayr (Belleisle)	Sc 589
14	8	8	Hever	Eng 487	14	7	7	Badgemore Park	Eng 442
17	6	8	Kilmarnock (Barassie)	Sc 626	15	6	7	Ballater	Sc 591
17	7	8	La Moye	Eng 497	16	7	7	Beau Desert	Eng 444
14	6	8	Lothianburn	Sc 632	17	8	7	Berkshire (The) *Blue Course*Eng446
15	7	8	Lytham Green Drive	Eng 502	17	8	7	Berkshire (The) *Red Course*Eng447
14	7	8	Murrayshall	Sc 642	14	6	7	Boat of Garten	Sc 594
19	7	8	Nairn	Sc 643	15	5	7	Bolton Old Links	Eng 450
18	7	8	North Berwick	Sc 645	17	7	7	Broadstone	Eng 455
16	7	8	Parkstone	Eng 517	15	7	7	Brora	Sc 595
13	8	8	Patshull Park Hotel	Eng 518	17	8	7	Buckinghamshire (The)	Eng 456
18	7	8	Royal Aberdeen		17	7	7	Carlisle	Eng 459
			Balgownie Links	Sc 654	18	9	7	Celtic Manor *Roman Road*	W 679
16	7	8	Royal Jersey	Eng 530	17	7	7	Clitheroe	Eng 462
19	7	8	Royal Lytham & St Anne's	Eng 532	14	8	7	Collingtree Park	Eng 463
14	7	8	Royal Mid-Surrey *Outer*	Eng 533	15	7	7	Crieff *Ferntower Course*	Sc 601
15	6	8	Royal Winchester	Eng 537	17	7	7	Cumberwell Park	Eng 465

426

CLASSIFICATION OF HOTELS FACILITIES

Score	Course	Country Page	Score	Course	Country Page
15 6 7	Delamere Forest	Eng 467	19 7 7	Royal Dornoch	Sc 656
15 7 7	Denham	Eng 468	16 7 7	Royal Guernsey	Eng 529
17 6 7	Downfield	Sc 604	18 8 7	Royal Liverpool (Hoylake)	Eng 531
15 7 7	Dunfermline	Sc 610	16 8 7	Royal Musselburgh	Sc 657
17 8 7	East Sussex National		19 7 7	Royal Troon *Old Course*	Sc 658
	East Course	Eng 469	14 7 7	Sand Moor	Eng 539
17 7 7	Ferndown *Old Course*	Eng 472	17 5 7	Sandiway	Eng 540
17 6 7	Forest Pines *Forest + Pines*	Eng 474	15 6 7	Sherborne	Eng 545
18 7 7	Formby	Eng 475	17 8 7	Slaley Hall	Eng 549
14 7 7	Glen	Sc 617	16 7 7	Southerndown	W 690
18 9 7	Gleneagles *King's*	Sc 618	18 7 7	Southport & Ainsdale	Eng 550
17 9 7	Gleneagles *Monarch's*	Sc 619	17 7 7	St George's Hill	Eng 552
15 9 7	Gleneagles *Queen's*	Sc 620	17 9 7	St Mellion *Nicklaus Course*	Eng 553
14 6 7	Grantown on Spey	Sc 622	14 7 7	Thorpeness	Eng 561
17 8 7	Gullane *No 1*	Sc 623	17 7 7	Trevose *Championship*	Eng 563
16 7 7	Hadley Wood	Eng 481	17 7 7	Wallasey	Eng 564
15 8 7	Hawkstone Park *Hawkstone*	Eng 483	18 7 7	Walton Heath *Old Course*	Eng 566
16 7 7	Hayling	Eng 484	16 8 7	Wentworth *East Course*	Eng 568
14 6 7	Henley	Eng 485	18 8 7	Wentworth *West Course*	Eng 569
15 7 7	Hertfordshire (The)	Eng 486	15 7 7	West Berkshire	Eng 570
15 6 7	High Post	Eng 488	17 7 7	West Lancashire	Eng 573
18 7 7	Hillside	Eng 489	15 7 7	West Surrey	Eng 574
14 6 7	Huntercombe	Eng 492	17 5 7	Western Gailes	Sc 673
16 7 7	Ipswich (Purdis Heath)	Eng 494	16 6 7	Weston-Super-Mare	Eng 576
16 6 7	Lundin	Sc 634	15 7 7	Whitekirk	Sc 675
17 7 7	Machrie	Sc 635	17 6 7	Whittington Heath	Eng 577
16 7 7	Manchester	Eng 503	18 7 7	Woburn *Dukes Course*	Eng 578
15 8 7	Manor House		14 7 7	Woodbridge	Eng 580
	(Castle Combe)	Eng 505	14 6 6	Aboyne	Sc 586
16 8 7	Marriott St Pierre		15 7 6	Alloa	Sc 587
	Old Course	W 682	14 6 6	Alyth	Sc 588
15 5 7	Mendip	Eng 506	16 7 6	Ashridge	Eng 441
15 7 7	Mere	Eng 507	16 7 6	Berkhamsted	Eng 445
17 7 7	Monifieth	Sc 637	15 8 6	Blairgowrie *Lansdowne*	Sc 592
17 8 7	Moor Park *High Course*	Eng 508	18 8 6	Blairgowrie *Rosemount*	Sc 593
18 7 7	Moortown	Eng 509	16 7 6	Bowood (Cornwall)	Eng 451
15 6 7	Nairn Dunbar	Sc 644	17 6 6	Bowood G&CC	Eng 452
15 6 7	Newbury & Crookham	Eng 510	17 7 6	Brampton	Eng 453
15 6 7	Newport	W 684	14 6 6	Buchanan Castle	Sc 597
13 7 7	North Foreland	Eng 511	18 7 6	Burnham & Berrow	Eng 457
17 7 7	Orchardleigh	Eng 514	18 8 6	Chart Hills	Eng 461
15 6 7	Pannal	Eng 516	15 6 6	Coxmoor	Eng 464
14 6 7	Pitlochry	Sc 648	15 6 6	Crail	Sc 600
15 8 7	Portal *Championship*	Eng 521	18 7 6	Cruden Bay	Sc 602
15 6 7	Portpatrick (Dunskey)	Sc 649	16 9 6	Dartmouth	Eng 466
17 8 7	Prestbury	Eng 522	15 6 6	Duff House Royal	Sc 606
18 6 7	Prestwick	Sc 651	16 5 6	Dunbar	Sc 609
16 6 7	Prestwick St Nicholas	Sc 652	15 7 6	Elgin	Sc 613
15 7 7	Roxburghe (The)	Sc 653	15 6 6	Elie	Sc 614
19 9 7	Royal Birkdale (The)	Eng 526	15 6 6	Felixstowe Ferry *Martello C.*	Eng 471

427

CLASSIFICATION OF HOTELS FACILITIES

Score			Course	Country Page		Score			Course	Country Page
14	6	6	Forfar	Sc 615		15	9	6	Woodbury Park *The Oaks*	Eng 581
14	8	6	Formby Hall	Eng 476		16	7	6	Worplesdon	Eng 583
14	8	6	Gainsborough-Karsten Lakes	Eng 478		17	6	5	Ashburnham	W 678
16	6	6	Hankley Common	Eng 482		15	6	5	Berwick-upon-Tweed	Eng 448
17	7	6	Hindhead	Eng 490		17	6	5	Blackmoor	Eng 449
17	7	6	Hunstanton	Eng 491		14	6	5	Brancepeth Castle	Eng 454
14	6	6	Huntly	Sc 625		15	7	5	Dumfries & County	Sc 608
18	7	6	Ilkley	Eng 493		16	6	5	Fortrose & Rosemarkie	Sc 616
16	7	6	Isle of Purbeck	Eng 495		19	8	5	Ganton	Eng 479
16	7	6	John O'Gaunt	Eng 496		16	7	5	Holyhead	W 681
16	6	6	Leven	Sc 631		15	4	5	Kingussie	Sc 627
17	8	6	Linden Hall	Eng 498		17	7	5	Ladybank	Sc 628
17	6	6	Lindrick	Eng 499		16	6	5	Lanark	Sc 629
16	7	6	Liphook	Eng 500		15	7	5	Letham Grange *Old Course*	Sc 630
16	5	6	Luffness New	Sc 633		14	6	5	Littlestone	Eng 501
14	8	6	Mannings Heath *Waterfall Course*	Eng 504		17	5	5	Moray	Sc 639
17	5	6	Montrose	Sc 638		16	6	5	Nefyn & District	W 683
19	7	6	Muirfield	Sc 640		17	6	5	Panmure	Sc 646
15	6	6	Murcar	Sc 641		17	7	5	Pyle & Kenfig	W 686
17	7	6	North Hants	Eng 512		17	6	5	Royal Cinque Ports	Eng 527
18	6	6	Notts (Hollinwell)	Eng 513		19	7	5	Royal Porthcawl	W 688
18	6	6	Pennard	W 685		18	6	5	Royal St David's	W 689
16	6	6	Perranporth	Eng 519		19	7	5	Royal St George's	Eng 535
16	8	6	Pleasington	Eng 520		17	5	5	Shiskine (Blackwaterfoot)	Sc 660
15	6	6	Rolls of Monmouth (The)	W 687		18	6	5	Southerness	Sc 661
15	5	6	Ross-on-Wye	Eng 524		13	5	5	Stonehaven	Sc 666
14	7	6	Royal Ashdown Forest	Eng 525		14	7	5	Thetford	Eng 559
15	7	6	Royal Cromer	Eng 528		15	6	5	Thornhill	Sc 669
18	6	6	Royal North Devon (Westward Ho!)	Eng 534		16	7	5	West Kilbride	Sc 672
17	7	6	Royal West Norfolk (Brancaster)	Eng 536		14	3	4	Carnoustie *Burnside*	Sc 598
18	7	6	Saunton *East Course*	Eng 541		19	3	4	Carnoustie *Championship*	Sc 599
16	6	6	Scotscraig	Sc 659		14	5	4	Golspie	Sc 621
15	7	6	Shanklin & Sandown	Eng 544		18	6	4	Machrihanish	Sc 636
15	7	6	Sheringham	Eng 546		14	6	4	Ormskirk	Eng 515
17	7	6	Sherwood Forest	Eng 547		15	5	4	Peterhead	Sc 647
15	5	6	Strathaven	Sc 667		16	6	4	Powfoot	Sc 650
17	6	6	Tain	Sc 668		13	6	4	Prince's *Himalayas-Shore*	Eng 523
14	7	6	Tandridge	Eng 558		17	6	4	Seacroft	Eng 542
18	7	6	Tenby	W 691		18	5	4	Seascale	Eng 543
14	7	6	Thorndon Park	Eng 560		18	7	4	Silloth-on-Solway	Eng 548
16	7	6	Walton Heath *New Course*	Eng 565		18	7	4	St Enodoc *Church Course*	Eng 551
16	7	6	West Cornwall	Eng 571		16	6	4	Thurlestone	Eng 562
15	6	6	West Hill	Eng 572		14	6	3	Edzell	Sc 612
18	7	6	West Sussex	Eng 575						
14	8	6	Westerwood	Sc 674						
16	6	6	Woking	Eng 579						

428

SEJOUR DE GOLF RECOMMANDÉ
RECOMMENDED GOLFING STAY

Exciting courses where a stay of a few days is to be recommended.
Les parcours dont les qualités permettent de conseiller un séjour de plusieurs jours.

Score	Course	Country				Page
Berkshire (The)						
Blue Course	Eng	17	8	7	446
Berkshire (The) *Red Course*	Eng	17	8	7	447
Blairgowrie *Lansdowne*	Sc	15	8	6	592
Blairgowrie *Rosemount*	Sc	18	8	6	593
Brampton	Eng	17	7	6	453
Buckinghamshire (The)	Eng	17	8	7	456
Burnham & Berrow	Eng	18	7	6	457
Carlisle	Eng	17	7	7	459
Carnoustie *Burnside*	Sc	14	3	4	598
Carnoustie *Championship*	Sc	19	3	4	599
Castletown	Eng	18	6	8	460
Celtic Manor *Roman Road*	W	18	9	7	679
Chart Hills	Eng	18	8	6	461
Cruden Bay	Sc	18	7	6	602
Dalmahoy *East Course*	Sc	17	8	8	603
Dartmouth	Eng	16	9	6	466
East Sussex National					
East Course	Eng	17	8	7	469
Fairhaven	Eng	17	7	8	470
Felixstowe Ferry					
Martello Course	Eng	15	6	6	471
Ferndown *Old Course*	Eng	17	7	7	472
Forest Pines *Forest + Pines*	Eng	17	6	7	474
Formby	Eng	18	7	7	475
Ganton	Eng	19	8	5	479
Gleneagles *King's*	Sc	18	9	7	618
Gleneagles *Monarch's*	Sc	17	9	7	619
Gleneagles *Queen's*	Sc	15	9	7	620
Gullane *No 1*	Sc	17	8	7	623
Hawkstone Park					
Hawkstone	Eng	15	8	7	483
Hayling	Eng	16	7	7	484
Hillside	Eng	18	7	7	489
Hunstanton	Eng	17	7	6	491
Isle of Purbeck	Eng	16	7	6	495
John O'Gaunt	Eng	16	7	6	496
Machrihanish	Sc	18	6	4	636
Marriott St Pierre					
Old Course	W	16	8	7	682
Moor Park *High Course*	Eng	17	8	7	508

Score	Course	Country				Page
Moray	Sc	17	5	5	639
Nairn	Sc	19	7	8	643
Portal *Championship*	Eng	15	8	7	521
Pyle & Kenfig	W	17	7	5	686
Royal Birkdale (The)	Eng	19	9	7	526
Royal Cinque Ports	Eng	17	6	5	527
Royal Dornoch	Sc	19	7	7	656
Royal Liverpool (Hoylake)	Eng	18	8	7	531
Royal Lytham & St Anne's	Eng	19	7	8	532
Royal North Devon					
(Westward Ho!)	Eng	18	6	6	534
Royal Porthcawl	W	19	7	5	688
Royal St David's	W	18	6	5	689
Royal St George's	Eng	19	7	5	535
Royal Troon *Old Course*	Sc	19	7	7	658
Royal West Norfolk					
(Brancaster)	Eng	17	7	6	536
Saunton *East Course*	Eng	18	7	6	541
Slaley Hall	Eng	17	8	7	549
Southport & Ainsdale	Eng	18	7	7	550
St Andrews *Eden Course*	Sc	14	8	8	662
St Andrews *Jubilee Course*	Sc	16	8	8	663
St Andrews *New Course*	Sc	17	8	8	664
St Andrews *Old Course*	Sc	18	8	8	665
St Enodoc *Church Course*	Eng	18	7	4	551
St Mellion *Nicklaus Course*	Eng	17	9	7	553
Stoke Poges	Eng	17	8	8	554
Sunningdale *New Course*	Eng	18	8	8	556
Sunningdale *Old Course*	Eng	18	8	8	557
Trevose *Championship*	Eng	17	7	7	563
Turnberry *Ailsa Course*	Sc	19	9	8	670
Turnberry *Arran Course*	Sc	16	9	8	671
Wallasey	Eng	17	7	7	564
Walton Heath *New Course*	Eng	16	7	6	565
Walton Heath *Old Course*	Eng	18	7	7	566
Warwickshire (The)	Eng	15	7	8	567
Wentworth *East Course*	Eng	16	8	7	568
Wentworth *West Course*	Eng	18	8	7	569
West Lancashire	Eng	17	7	7	573
Woburn *Dukes Course*	Eng	18	7	7	578
Woodhall Spa	Eng	18	7	8	582

429

RECOMMENDED GOLFING HOLIDAYS
VACANCES RECOMMANDEES

Vacances conseillées en famille, y compris pour les non-golfeurs.
Holiday on site with the family, including non-golfers.

Score	Course				Country Page	Score	Course			Country Page
	Gleneagles *King's*	Sc	18 9 7	618			La Moye	17	7 8497	A
	Gleneagles *Monarch's*	17	9	7619	E		Royal Guernsey	16	7 7529	A
	Gleneagles Queen's	15	9	7620	E		Royal Jersey	16	7 8530	A

RECOMMENDED SEASONS
SAISONS RECOMMANDEES

Depending on altitude, usual weather conditions, the type of soil
and the quality of drainage and maintenance.

En fonction de l'altitude, des conditions météorologiques habituelles, de la nature
du sol où est construit le parcours, de la qualité du drainage et de l'entretien.

Seasons/Golf course		Score	Page	Seasons/Golf course		Score	Page
1 2 3 4 5 6 7 8 9 10 11 12				Walton Heath			
Hayling	Eng	16 7 7	484	*Old Course*	*Eng* 18 7 7		566
				West Berkshire	Eng 15 7 7		570
1 2 3 4 5 6 7 8 9 10 11 12				West Hill	Eng 15 6 6		572
Berkshire (The) *Blue Course*	A17	8	7446	Woking	Eng 16 6 6		579
Berkshire (The) *Red Course*	A17	8	7447	Woodbridge	Eng 14 7 7		580
Buckinghamshire (The)	Eng	17 8 7	456	Worplesdon	Eng 16 7 6		583
Chart Hills	Eng	18 8 6	461				
Denham	Eng	15 7 7	468	**1 2 3 4 5 6 7 8 9 10 11 12**			
East Sussex National				Dartmouth	Eng 16 9 6		466
East Course	Eng	17 8 7	469	Elie	Sc 15 6 6		614
Ferndown *Old Course*	Eng	17 7 7	472	Gullane *No 1*	Sc 17 8 7		623
Gog Magog *Old Course*	Eng	15 7 8	480	Isle of Purbeck	Eng 16 7 6		495
Henley	Eng	14 6 7	485	Orchardleigh	Eng 17 7 7		514
Hever	Eng	14 8 8	487	Royal Guernsey	Eng 16 7 7		529
Littlestone	Eng	14 6 5	501	Saunton *East Course*	Eng 18 7 6		541
Newbury & Crookham	Eng	15 6 7	510	Thurlestone	Eng 16 6 4		562
North Foreland	Eng	13 7 7	511	Turnberry *Ailsa Course*	Sc 19 9 8		670
Parkstone	Eng	16 7 8	517	Turnberry *Arran Course*	Sc 16 9 8		671
Perranporth	Eng	16 6 6	519	Woodbury Park *The Oaks*	Eng 15 9 6		581
Prince's							
Himalayas-Shore	Eng	13 6 4	523	**1 2 3 4 5 6 7 8 9 10 11 12**			
Royal St George's	Eng	19 7 5	535	Badgemore Park	Eng 14 7 7		442
Stoke Poges	Eng	17 8 8	554	Burnham & Berrow	Eng 18 7 6		457
Sunningdale *New Course*	Eng	18 8 8	556	Delamere Forest	Eng 15 6 7		467
Sunningdale *Old Course*	Eng	18 8 8	557	Felixstowe Ferry			
Thorndon Park	Eng	14 7 6	560	*Martello Course*	*Eng* 15 6 6		471
Thorpeness	Eng	14 7 7	561	Forest Pines *Forest + Pines*	Eng 17 6 7		474
Walton Heath				Hankley Common	Eng 16 6 6		482
New Course	Eng	16 7 6	565	Hertfordshire (The)	Eng 15 7 7		486

430

RECOMMENDED SEASONS

Seasons/Golf course	Score	Page	Seasons/Golf course	Score	Page

1 2 3 `4` `5` `6` 7 `8` `9` `10` 11 12 | **1 2 3 `4` `5` `6` 7 `8` `9` `10` 11 12**

Seasons/Golf course	Score	Page	Seasons/Golf course	Score	Page
Hindhead	Eng 16 7 6	490	Conwy	W 17 7 8	680
Huntercombe	Eng 14 6 7	492	Coxmoor	Eng 15 6 6	464
Ipswich (Purdis Heath)	Eng 16 7 7	494	Crail	Sc 15 6 6	600
La Moye	Eng 17 7 8	497	Crieff *Ferntower Course*	Sc 15 7 7	601
Lindrick	Eng 17 6 6	499	Cruden Bay	Sc 18 7 6	602
Mere	Eng 15 7 7	507	Cumberwell Park	Eng 17 7 7	465
Moor Park *High Course*	Eng 17 8 7	508	Dalmahoy *East Course*	Sc 17 8 8	603
Muirfield	Sc 19 7 6	640	Duff House Royal	Sc 15 6 6	606
Ormskirk	Eng 14 6 4	515	Duke's Course *St Andrews*	Sc 16 7 8	607
Roxburghe (The)	Sc 15 7 7	653	Dumfries & County	Sc 15 7 5	608
Royal Ashdown Forest	Eng 14 7 6	525	Dunbar	Sc 16 5 6	609
Royal Cinque Ports	Eng 17 6 5	527	Fairhaven	Eng 17 7 8	470
Royal Mid-Surrey *Outer*	Eng 14 7 8	533	Forest of Arden		
Seacroft	Eng 17 6 4	542	*Arden Course*	Eng 14 8 8	473
Sherborne	Eng 15 6 7	545	Formby	Eng 18 7 7	475
Southerness	Sc 18 6 5	661	Formby Hall	Eng 14 8 6	476
St George's Hill	Eng 17 7 7	552	Fortrose & Rosemarkie	Sc 16 6 5	616
Tandridge	Eng 14 7 6	558	Fulford	Eng 17 7 8	477
West Surrey	Eng 15 7 7	574	Gainsborough-		
West Sussex	Eng 18 7 6	575	Karsten Lakes	Eng 14 8 6	478
Weston-Super-Mare	Eng 16 6 7	576	Ganton	Eng 19 8 5	479
Woburn *Dukes Course*	Eng 18 7 7	578	Glen	Sc 14 7 7	617
			Gleneagles *King's*	Sc 18 9 7	618

1 2 3 `4` `5` `6` 7 `8` `9` `10` 11 12

Seasons/Golf course	Score	Page	Seasons/Golf course	Score	Page
Aberdovey	W 17 7 7	677	Gleneagles *Monarch's*	Sc 17 9 7	619
Alloa	Sc 15 7 6	587	Gleneagles *Queen's*	Sc 15 9 7	620
Alwoodley (The)	Eng 18 7 7	440	Golspie	Sc 14 5 4	621
Alyth	Sc 14 6 6	588	Hadley Wood	Eng 16 7 7	481
Ashburnham	W 17 6 5	678	Hawkstone Park *Hawkstone*	Eng 15 8 7	483
Ashridge	Eng 16 7 6	441	High Post	Eng 15 6 7	488
Ayr (Belleisle)	Sc 16 5 7	589	Hillside	Eng 18 7 7	489
Bath	Eng 16 6 9	443	Holyhead	W 16 7 5	681
Beau Desert	Eng 16 7 7	444	Hunstanton	Eng 17 7 6	491
Berkhamsted	Eng 16 7 6	445	Ilkley	Eng 18 7 6	493
Blackmoor	Eng 17 6 5	449	John O'Gaunt	Eng 16 7 6	496
Blairgowrie *Lansdowne*	Sc 15 8 6	592	Kilmarnock (Barassie)	Sc 17 6 8	626
Blairgowrie *Rosemount*	Sc 18 8 6	593	Ladybank	Sc 17 7 5	628
Bolton *Old Links*	Eng 15 5 7	450	Lanark	Sc 16 6 5	629
Bowood (Cornwall)	Eng 16 7 6	451	Letham Grange *Old Cse*	Sc 15 7 5	630
Bowood G&CC	Eng 17 6 6	452	Leven	Sc 16 6 6	631
Brampton	Eng 17 7 6	453	Liphook	Eng 16 7 6	500
Brancepeth Castle	Eng 14 6 5	454	Luffness New	Sc 16 5 6	633
Broadstone	Eng 17 7 7	455	Lundin	Sc 16 6 7	634
Bruntsfield	Sc 15 8 9	596	Lytham Green Drive	Eng 15 7 8	502
Buchanan Castle	Sc 14 6 6	597	Machrie	Sc 17 7 7	635
Carden Park	Eng 14 8 8	458	Machrihanish	Sc 18 6 4	636
Carnoustie *Burnside*	Sc 14 3 4	598	Manchester	Eng 16 7 7	503
Carnoustie *Championship*	Sc 19 3 4	599	Mannings Heath		
Celtic Manor *Roman Road*	W 18 9 7	679	*Waterfall Course*	*Eng* 14 8 6	504
Clitheroe	Eng 17 7 7	462	Manor House		
Collingtree Park	Eng 14 8 7	463	(Castle Combe)	Eng 15 8 7	505
			Marriott St Pierre *Old Cse*	W 16 8 7	682

431

Seasons/Golf course	Score	Page	Seasons/Golf course	Score	Page

1 2 3 4 5 6 7 8 9 10 11 12 / **1 2 3 4 5 6 7 8 9 10 11 12**

Seasons/Golf course	Score	Page	Seasons/Golf course	Score	Page
Mendip	Eng 15 5 7	506	Southerndown	W 16 7 7	690
Monifieth	Sc 17 7 7	637	Southport & Ainsdale	Eng 18 7 7	550
Montrose	Sc 17 5 6	638	St Andrews *Eden Course*	Sc 14 8 8	662
Moortown	Eng 18 7 7	509	St Andrews *Jubilee Cse*	Sc 16 8 8	663
Moray	Sc 17 5 5	639	St Andrews *New Course*	Sc 17 8 8	664
Murcar	Sc 15 6 6	641	St Andrews *Old Course*	Sc 18 8 8	665
Murrayshall	Sc 14 7 8	642	St Enodoc *Church Course*	Eng 18 7 4	551
Nairn	Sc 19 7 8	643	St Mellion *Nicklaus Cse*	Eng 17 9 7	553
Nairn Dunbar	Sc 15 6 7	644	Stoneham	Eng 15 7 8	555
Nefyn & District	W 16 6 5	683	Tain	Sc 17 6 6	668
Newport	W 15 6 7	684	Tenby	W 18 7 6	691
North Berwick	Sc 18 7 8	645	Thetford	Eng 14 7 5	559
North Hants	Eng 17 7 6	512	Thornhill	Sc 15 6 5	669
Notts (Hollinwell)	Eng 18 6 6	513	Trevose *Championship*	Eng 17 7 7	563
Pannal	Eng 15 6 7	516	Wallasey	Eng 17 7 7	564
Patshull Park Hotel	Eng 13 8 8	518	Warwickshire (The)	Eng 15 7 8	567
Pennard	W 18 6 6	685	Wentworth *East Course*	Eng 16 8 7	568
Peterhead	Sc 15 5 4	647	Wentworth *West Course*	Eng 18 8 7	569
Pitlochry	Sc 14 6 7	648	West Cornwall	Eng 16 7 6	571
Pleasington	Eng 16 8 6	520	West Kilbride	Sc 16 7 5	672
Portal *Championship*	Eng 15 8 7	521	West Lancashire	Eng 17 7 7	573
Portpatrick (Dunskey)	Sc 15 6 7	649	Western Gailes	Sc 17 5 7	673
Powfoot	Sc 16 6 4	650	Whitekirk	Sc 15 7 7	675
Prestbury	Eng 17 8 7	522	Whittington Heath	Eng 17 6 7	577
Prestwick	Sc 18 6 7	651	Woodhall Spa	Eng 18 7 8	582
Prestwick St Nicholas	Sc 16 6 7	652			

1 2 3 4 5 6 7 8 9 10 11 12

Seasons/Golf course	Score	Page
Elgin	Sc 15 7 6	613
Haggs Castle	Sc 15 7 9	624
Ross-on-Wye	Eng 15 5 6	524
Westerwood	Sc 14 8 6	674

Seasons/Golf course	Score	Page
Pyle & Kenfig	W 17 7 5	686
Rolls of Monmouth (The)	W 15 6 6	687
Royal Birkdale (The)	Eng 19 9 7	526
Royal Burgess	Sc 16 7 9	655
Royal Cromer	Eng 15 7 6	528
Royal Dornoch	Sc 19 7 7	656
Royal Jersey	Eng 16 7 8	530
Royal Liverpool (Hoylake)	Eng 18 8 7	531
Royal Lytham & St Anne's	Eng 19 7 8	532
Royal Musselburgh	Sc 16 8 7	657
Royal North Devon (Westward Ho!)	Eng 18 6 6	534
Royal Porthcawl	W 19 7 5	688
Royal St David's	W 18 6 5	689
Royal Troon *Old Course*	Sc 19 7 7	658
Royal West Norfolk (Brancaster)	Eng 17 7 6	536
Royal Winchester	Eng 15 6 8	537
Rudding Park	Eng 15 8 8	538
Sand Moor	Eng 14 7 7	539
Sandiway	Eng 17 5 7	540
Scotscraig	Sc 16 6 6	659
Seascale	Eng 18 5 4	543
Sheringham	Eng 15 7 6	546
Sherwood Forest	Eng 17 7 6	547

1 2 3 4 5 6 7 8 9 10 11 12

Seasons/Golf course	Score	Page
Aboyne	Sc 14 6 6	586
Brora	Sc 15 7 7	595
Duddingston	Sc 15 7 9	605
East Renfrewshire	Sc 15 6 8	611
Edzell	Sc 14 6 3	612
Forfar	Sc 14 6 6	615
Huntly	Sc 14 6 6	625
Linden Hall	Eng 17 8 6	498
Royal Aberdeen *Balgownie Links*	Sc 18 7 8	654
Shanklin & Sandown	Eng 15 7 6	544
Slaley Hall	Eng 17 8 7	549
Stonehaven	Sc 13 5 5	666

1 2 3 4 5 6 7 8 9 10 11 12

Seasons/Golf course	Score	Page
Baberton	Sc 14 6 8	590
Berwick-upon-Tweed	Eng 15 6 5	448
Boat of Garten	Sc 14 6 7	594

432

RECOMMENDED SEASONS

Seasons/Golf course		Score			Page
`1 2 3 4 5 6 7 8 9 10 11 12`					
Carlisle	Eng	17	7	7	459
Castletown	Eng	18	6	8	460
Downfield	Sc	17	6	7	604
Dunfermline	Sc	15	7	7	610
Grantown on Spey	Sc	14	6	7	622
Lothianburn	Sc	14	6	8	632
Panmure	Sc	17	6	5	646
Shiskine (Blackwaterfoot)	Sc	17	5	5	660

Seasons/Golf course		Score			Page
`1 2 3 4 5 6 7 8 9 10 11 12`					
Silloth-on-Solway	Eng	18	7	4	548
Strathaven	Sc	15	5	6	667
`1 2 3 4 5 6 7 8 9 10 11 12`					
Ballater	Sc	15	6	7	591
Kingussie	Sc	15	4	5	627
Aldeburgh	Eng	13	6	7	439

GEOGRAPHICAL RELIEF
RELIEF DES PARCOURS

Ce classement donne une indication sur la forme physique nécessaire pour jouer un parcours, et aussi sur la possibilité de jouer plusieurs fois le parcours dans une même journée. La possibilité de jouer en voiturette permet parfois de compenser les inconvénients du relief.
This list gives an idea of the fitness required for playing a course and also of the possibility of playing the same course several times in oe day. The availability of golf carts sometimes makes up for the drawbacks of a hilly course.

Rather flat / **Peu de relief**   **Averagely hilly** / **Moyennement accidenté**   **Very hilly** / **Relief important**

Geographical relief/Golf course		Score			Page
Alwoodley (The)	Eng	18	7	7	440
Ashburnham	W	17	6	5	678
Berkhamsted	Eng	16	7	6	445
Clitheroe	Eng	17	7	7	462
Duff House Royal	Sc	15	6	6	606
Fairhaven	Eng	17	7	8	470
Felixstowe Ferry *Martello Cse*	Eng	15	6	6	471
Formby	Eng	18	7	7	475
Fulford	Eng	17	7	8	477
Hayling	Eng	16	7	7	484
Ilkley	Eng	18	7	6	493
La Moye	Eng	17	7	8	497
Lytham Green Drive	Eng	15	7	8	502
North Berwick	Sc	18	7	8	645
Ormskirk	Eng	14	6	4	515
Prestwick St Nicholas	Sc	16	6	7	652
Prince's Himalayas-Shore	Eng	13	6	4	523
Royal Cinque Ports	Eng	17	6	5	527
Royal Jersey	Eng	16	7	8	530
Royal Lytham & St Anne's	A	19	7	8	532
Royal Mid-Surrey *Outer*	Eng	14	7	8	533
Royal North Devon (Westward Ho!)	Eng	18	6	6	534
Rudding Park	Eng	15	8	8	538
St Andrews *Old Course*	Sc	18	8	8	665
Thorpeness	Eng	14	7	7	561
Walton Heath *New Course*	Eng	16	7	6	565

Geographical relief/Golf course		Score			Page
Walton Heath *Old Course*	Eng	18	7	7	566
West Berkshire	Eng	15	7	7	570
West Cornwall	Eng	16	7	6	571
West Kilbride	Sc	16	7	5	672
West Lancashire	Eng	17	7	7	573
Aberdovey	W	17	7	7	677
Badgemore Park	Eng	14	7	7	442
Blackmoor	Eng	17	6	5	449
Blairgowrie Lansdowne	Sc	15	8	6	592
Buchanan Castle	Sc	14	6	6	597
Buckinghamshire (The)	Eng	17	8	7	456
Carnoustie *Burnside*	Sc	14	3	4	598
Carnoustie *Championship*	Sc	19	3	4	599
Conwy	W	17	7	8	680
Dumfries & County	Sc	15	7	5	608
Dunbar	Sc	16	5	6	609
East Sussex National *East Cse*	Eng	17	8	7	469
Formby Hall	Eng	14	8	6	476
Golspie	Sc	14	5	4	621
Hankley Common	Eng	16	6	6	482
Hillside	Eng	18	7	7	489
Holyhead	W	16	7	5	681
Ipswich (Purdis Heath)	Eng	16	7	7	494
Ladybank	Sc	17	7	5	628
Leven	Sc	16	6	6	631
Liphook	Eng	16	7	6	500

433

Geogrphical relief/Golf course		Score			Page	Geogrphical relief/Golf course		Score			Page
▆▆▬▬▬						▆▆▬▬▬					
Machrie	Sc	17	7	7	635	Lindrick	Eng	17	6	6	499
Monifieth	Sc	17	7	7	637	Littlestone	Eng	14	6	5	501
Moray	Sc	17	5	5	639	Luffness *New*	Sc	16	5	6	633
Nairn Dunbar	Sc	15	6	7	644	Lundin	Sc	16	6	7	634
North Hants	Eng	17	7	6	512	Mere	Eng	15	7	7	507
Pannal	Eng	15	6	7	516	Montrose	Sc	17	5	6	638
Royal Birkdale (The)	Eng	19	9	7	526	Muirfield	Sc	19	7	6	640
Royal Burgess	Sc	16	7	9	655	Murcar	Sc	15	6	6	641
Royal Guernsey	Eng	16	7	7	529	Murrayshall	Sc	14	7	8	642
Royal Liverpool (Hoylake)	Eng	18	8	7	531	Nairn	Sc	19	7	8	643
Royal West Norfolk						North Foreland	Eng	13	7	7	511
(Brancaster)	Eng	17	7	6	536	Notts (Hollinwell)	Eng	18	6	6	513
Saunton *East Course*	Eng	18	7	6	541	Peterhead	Sc	15	5	4	647
Scotscraig	Sc	16	6	6	659	Portpatrick (Dunskey)	Sc	15	6	7	649
Silloth-on-Solway	Eng	18	7	4	548	Prestwick	Sc	18	6	7	651
St Andrews *Eden Course*	Sc	14	8	8	662	Royal Aberdeen					
St Andrews *Jubilee Course*	Sc	16	8	8	663	*Balgownie Links*	Sc	18	7	8	654
St Andrews *New Course*	Sc	17	8	8	664	Royal Musselburgh	Sc	16	8	7	657
Thetford	Eng	14	7	5	559	Royal St George's	Eng	19	7	5	535
Trevose *Championship*	Eng	17	7	7	563	Royal Troon *Old Course*	Sc	19	7	7	658
West Hill	Eng	15	6	6	572	Sand Moor	Eng	14	7	7	539
Western Gailes	Sc	17	5	7	673	Seacroft	Eng	17	6	4	542
Whittington Heath	Eng	17	6	7	577	Shanklin & Sandown	Eng	15	7	6	544
Woodhall Spa	Eng	18	7	8	582	Southerness	Sc	18	6	5	661
▆▆▆▬▬						Southport & Ainsdale	Eng	18	7	7	550
Aldeburgh	Eng	13	6	7	439	Strathaven	Sc	15	5	6	667
Ayr (Belleisle)	Sc	16	5	7	589	Sunningdale *New Course*	Eng	18	8	8	556
Baberton	Sc	14	6	8	590	Sunningdale *Old Course*	*Eng*	18	8	8	557
Berkshire (The) *Blue Course*	Eng	17	8	7	446	Tenby	W	18	7	6	691
Berkshire (The) *Red Course*	*Eng*	17	8	7	447	Thorndon Park	Eng	14	7	6	560
Blairgowrie *Rosemount*	Sc	18	8	6	593	Turnberry *Ailsa Course*	Sc	19	9	8	670
Bowood G&CC	Eng	17	6	6	452	Turnberry *Arran Course*	Sc	16	9	8	671
Brora	Sc	15	7	7	595	Wallasey	Eng	17	7	7	564
Burnham & Berrow	Eng	18	7	6	457	Wentworth *West Course*	Eng	18	8	7	569
Castletown	Eng	18	6	8	460	West Surrey	Eng	15	7	7	574
Collingtree Park	Eng	14	8	7	463	West Sussex	Eng	18	7	6	575
Denham	Eng	15	7	7	468	Weston-Super-Mare	Eng	16	6	7	576
Duddingston	Sc	15	7	9	605	Woburn *Dukes Course*	Eng	18	7	7	578
Elie	Sc	15	6	6	614	Woking	Eng	16	6	6	579
Ferndown *Old Course*	Eng	17	7	7	472	Woodbridge	Eng	14	7	7	580
Forest of Arden *Arden Cse*	Eng	14	8	8	473	▆▆▆▆▬					
Forest Pines *Forest + Pines*	Eng	17	6	7	474	Ashridge	Eng	16	7	6	441
Fortrose & Rosemarkie	Sc	16	6	5	616	Ballater	Sc	15	6	7	591
Ganton	Eng	19	8	7	479	Bath	Eng	16	6	9	443
Haggs Castle	Sc	15	7	9	624	Beau Desert	Eng	16	7	7	444
Hertfordshire (The)	Eng	15	7	7	486	Berwick-upon-Tweed	Eng	15	6	5	448
Hever	Eng	14	8	8	487	Brancepeth Castle	Eng	14	6	5	454
Hunstanton	Eng	17	7	6	491	Bruntsfield	Sc	15	8	9	596
Huntly	Sc	14	6	6	625	Carlisle	Eng	17	7	7	459
John O'Gaunt	Eng	16	7	6	496	Chart Hills	Eng	18	8	6	461
Kilmarnock (Barassie)	Sc	17	6	8	626	Crail	Sc	15	6	6	600
Lanark	Sc	16	6	5	629	Cruden Bay	Sc	18	7	6	602
Linden Hall	Eng	17	8	6	498	Cumberwell Park	Eng	17	7	7	465

434

GEOGRAPHICAL RELIEF

Geographical relief/Golf course	Score	Page
▰▱		
Dalmahoy *East Course*	Sc 17 8 8	603
Downfield	Sc 17 6 7	604
East Renfrewshire	Sc 15 6 8	611
Elgin	Sc 15 7 6	613
Gainsborough-Karsten Lakes	Eng 14 8 6	478
Grantown on Spey	Sc 14 6 7	622
Hadley Wood	Eng 16 7 7	481
Hawkstone Park Hawkstone	Eng 15 8 7	483
Henley	Eng 14 6 7	485
Huntercombe	Eng 14 6 7	492
Marriott St Pierre *Old Course*	W 16 8 7	682
Moor Park *High Course*	Eng 17 8 7	508
Moortown	Eng 18 7 7	509
Nefyn & District	W 16 6 5	683
Newbury & Crookham	Eng 15 6 7	510
Newport	W 15 6 7	684
Orchardleigh	Eng 17 7 7	514
Parkstone	Eng 16 7 8	517
Perranporth	Eng 16 6 6	519
Powfoot	Sc 16 6 4	650
Pyle & Kenfig	W 17 7 5	686
Royal Porthcawl	W 19 7 5	688
Royal St David's	W 18 6 5	689
Royal Winchester	Eng 15 6 8	537
Seascale	Eng 18 5 4	543
Sherborne	Eng 15 6 7	545
Sheringham	Eng 15 7 6	546
Slaley Hall	Eng 17 8 7	549
Stoke Poges	Eng 17 8 8	554
Tain	Sc 17 6 6	668
Thornhill	Sc 15 6 5	669
Thurlestone	Eng 16 6 4	562
Wentworth *East Course*	Eng 16 8 7	568
Woodbury Park *The Oaks*	Eng 15 9 6	581
Worplesdon	Eng 16 7 6	583
▰▱		
Aboyne	Sc 14 6 6	586
Alyth	Sc 14 6 6	588
Bowood (Cornwall)	Eng 16 7 6	451
Brampton	Eng 17 7 6	453
Carden Park	Eng 14 8 8	458
Dunfermline	Sc 15 7 7	610
Edzell	Sc 14 6 3	612
Forfar	Sc 14 6 6	615
Gleneagles *King's*	Sc 18 9 7	618
Gleneagles *Queen's*	Sc 15 9 7	620
Gog Magog *Old Course*	Eng 15 7 8	480
High Post	Eng 15 6 7	488
Hindhead	Eng 16 7 6	490
Isle of Purbeck	Eng 16 7 6	495

Geographical relief/Golf course	Score	Page
▰▱		
Machrihanish	Sc 18 6 4	636
Mendip	Eng 15 5 7	506
Panmure	Sc 17 6 5	646
Patshull Park Hotel	Eng 13 8 8	518
Pleasington	Eng 16 8 6	520
Ross-on-Wye	Eng 15 5 6	524
Royal Cromer	Eng 15 7 6	528
Royal Dornoch	Sc 19 7 7	656
Southerndown	W 16 7 7	690
St Enodoc *Church Course*	Eng 18 7 4	551
Tandridge	Eng 14 7 6	558
Whitekirk	Sc 15 7 7	675
▰▱		
Alloa	Sc 15 7 6	587
Boat of Garten	Sc 14 6 7	594
Broadstone	Eng 17 7 7	455
Celtic Manor *Roman Road*	W 18 9 7	679
Dartmouth	Eng 16 9 6	466
Delamere Forest	Eng 15 6 7	467
Glen	Sc 14 7 7	617
Gleneagles *Monarch's*	Sc 17 9 7	619
Gullane *No 1*	Sc 17 8 7	623
Letham Grange *Old Course*	Sc 15 7 5	630
Pennard	W 18 6 6	685
Portal *Championship*	Eng 15 8 7	521
Prestbury	Eng 17 8 7	522
Rolls of Monmouth (The)	W 15 6 6	687
Royal Ashdown Forest	Eng 14 7 6	525
Sandiway	Eng 17 5 7	540
Sherwood Forest	Eng 17 7 6	547
Shiskine (Blackwaterfoot)	Sc 17 5 5	660
Warwickshire (The)	Eng 15 7 8	567
▰▱		
Bolton Old Links	Eng 15 5 7	450
Coxmoor	Eng 15 6 6	464
Crieff *Ferntower Course*	Sc 15 7 7	601
Duke's Course *St Andrews*	Sc 16 7 8	607
Kingussie	Sc 15 4 5	627
Lothianburn	Sc 14 6 8	632
Manchester	Eng 16 7 7	503
Mannings Heath *Waterfall Course*	Eng 14 8 6	504
St George's Hill	Eng 17 7 7	552
St Mellion *Nicklaus Course*	Eng 17 9 7	553
Stoneham	Eng 15 7 8	555
Stonehaven	Sc 13 5 5	666
▰▱		
Manor House (Castle Combe)	Eng 15 8 7	505
Pitlochry	Sc 14 6 7	648
Roxburghe (The)	Sc 15 7 7	653

435

TYPE OF COURSE
TYPE DE PARCOURS

Type of course / Golf course	Page	Type of course / Golf course	Page	Type of course / Golf course	Page
copse		**inland**		**links**	
Bath - Eng	443	Liphook Eng	500	Machrie Sc	635
Bowood (C^{wall}) Eng	451	Mannings Heath *Waterfall* C^{se}		Machrihanish Sc	636
High Post Eng	488	Eng	504	Monifieth Sc	637
Manor House		Moortown Eng	509	Montrose Sc	638
(Cast. Combe) Eng	505	North Hants Eng	512	Moray Sc	639
		Notts (Hollinwell) Eng	513	Muirfield Sc	640
downland		Orchardleigh Eng	514	Murcar Sc	641
Southerndown W	690	Prestbury Eng	522	Nairn Sc	643
		Royal Ashdown Forest Eng	525	Nairn Dunbar Sc	644
forest		Royal Winchester Eng	537	North Berwick Sc	645
Beau Desert Eng	444	St George's Hill Eng	552	Panmure Sc	646
Forest Pines Eng	474	Stoneham Eng	555	Pennard W	685
Parkstone Eng	517	Thetford Eng	559	Powfoot Sc	650
Sherwood Forest Eng	547	Walton Heath Eng	565	Prestwick Sc	651
Sunningdale Eng	556	*New Course*		Prestwick St Nicholas Sc	652
New Course/Old Course		Walton Heath Eng	566	Pyle & Kenfig W	686
		Old Course		Royal Aberdeen Sc	654
heathland		Wentworth *East Course* Eng	568	*Balgownie Links*	
Alwoodley (The) Eng	440	Wentworth *West Course* Eng	569	Royal Birkdale (The) Eng	526
Alyth Sc	588	West Hill Eng	572	Royal Dornoch Sc	656
Blairgowrie *Lansdowne* Sc	592	West Sussex Eng	575	Royal Liverpool Eng	531
Blairgowrie *Rosemount* Sc	593	Whittington Heath Eng	577	(Hoylake)	
Boat of Garten Sc	594	Woburn *Dukes Course* Eng	578	Royal Lytham & St Anne's	
Broadstone Eng	455	Woking Eng	579	Eng	532
Edzell Sc	612	Woodbridge Eng	580	Royal North Devon	
Forfar Sc	615	Woodbury Park		(Westward Ho!) Eng	534
Holyhead W	681	*The Oaks* Eng	581	Royal Porthcawl W	688
Huntercombe Eng	492	Woodhall Spa Eng	582	Royal St David's W	689
Ladybank Sc	628	Worplesdon Eng	583	Royal Troon *Old Course* Sc	658
Thornhill Sc	669			Scotscraig Sc	659
		links		Seascale Eng	543
hilly		Ashburnham W	678	Shanklin & Sandown Eng	544
Lothianburn Sc	632	Berwick-upon-Tweed Eng	448	Shiskine (Blackwaterfoot) Sc	660
		Brora Sc	595	Silloth-on-Solway Eng	548
inland		Carnoustie Burnside Sc	598	Southerness Sc	661
Berkhamsted Eng	445	Carnoustie *Championship* Sc	599	Southport & Ainsdale Eng	550
Berkshire (The) *Blue Course*		Conwy W	680	St Andrews *Eden Course* Sc	662
Red Course Eng	446	Crail Sc	600	St Andrews *Jubilee Course*	
Blackmoor Eng	449	Cruden Bay Sc	602	Sc	663
Bolton *Old Links* Eng	450	Elie Sc	614	St Andrews *New Course* Sc	664
East Renfrewshire Sc	611	Fairhaven Eng	470	St Andrews *Old Course* Sc	665
Ferndown *Old Course* Eng	472	Formby Eng	475	Tain Sc	668
Gainsborough-Karsten Lakes		Fortrose & Rosemarkie Sc	616	Tenby W	691
Eng	478	Golspie Sc	621	Turnberry *Ailsa Course* Sc	670
Gog Magog *Old Course* Eng	480	Hillside Eng	489	Turnberry *Arran Course* Sc	671
Hankley Common Eng	482	Kilmarnock (Barassie) Sc	626	West Kilbride Sc	672
Hindhead Eng	490	Leven Sc	631	West Lancashire Eng	573
Ipswich (Purdis Heath) Eng	494	Luffness New Sc	633	Western Gailes Sc	673
Lindrick Eng	499	Lundin Sc	634		

436

TYPE OF COURSE

437

PEUGEOT GOLF GUIDE 1998

🇬🇧 England ✠

No, we didn't forget to visit Rye, we simply did not want to get you too excited about a course you will never be able to play, unless accompanied by a member. We haven't included the London Club, either, or Swinley Forest or a number of other very private clubs, who didn't want to have to reply to inquiries from Peugeot Guide readers. Other clubs do not figure in this year's edition because their course or clubhouse is closed for extensive improvement work; these include Royal Worlington, Rochester & Cobham and Meon Valley. Rest assured, they will be reviewed for next year's edition. Lastly, other courses were visited but did not deign to reply to requests for practical information: we can only suppose that the Belfry or Old Thorns have the same attitude to precious income from green-fees. With this said, our choice is neither final nor categorical. Other courses will be added to the guide next year, but all the courses included this year are, to coin a wine phrase, good vintages. You will find the greatest links, the top parkland courses, courses which are ranked amongst the best and also those little "gems" which we hope you will be proud to talk about to your friends.

438
✠

Non, nous n'avons pas oublié de visiter Rye. Mais nous ne voulions pas vous faire saliver alors que vous ne pourrez jamais y jouer à moins d'être accompagné par un membre. Nous n'avons pas non plus inclus le London Club, ou Swinley Forest, ou quelques autres clubs très privés, qui ne souhaitaient pas devoir répondre non aux demandes des lecteurs du Guide. Certains clubs ne figurent pas non plus dans cette édition, parce qu'ils ont entrepris des travaux importants sur le parcours ou au Clubhouse: c'est le cas de Royal Worlington, Rochester & Cobham, Meon Valley. Ils seront revus pour la prochaine édition. D'autres enfin ont été visités, mais n'ont pas daigné répondre aux demandes d'informations pratiques : The Belfry ou Old Thorns considéreront sans doute de la même manière la manne des green-fees... Cela dit, notre choix n'est ni définitif, ni catégorique. D'autres parcours entreront dans ce Guide l'an prochain. Mais tous les parcours présentés sont, comme on dit en gastronomie, de "bonnes tables." On y trouve les plus grands links, les meilleurs "parkland," les parcours qui figurent dans les grands classements, mais aussi quelques petits joyaux dont nous espérons que vous serez fier de parler ensuite à vos amis.

ALDEBURGH

Music lovers might like to know that the English composer Benjamin Britten lived alongside this course for many years. They can also take advantage of their visit here to attend the music festival (in June) in Aldeburgh's superb Snape Maltings. This course is not a grand tournament layout but it is a pleasant holiday course to be included in any golfing tour around this area. Just avoid coming here after any prolonged dry period because the fairways are not watered and get very hard. With gorse and heather in the wings, the holes don't look all that wide and the wind will probably prompt you to play this as you would a links course. But don't let the benevolence of the site make you lower your concentration, either, as there is no shortage of difficulties waiting to make life really complicated. Luckily, inexperienced players can try the 9-hole "River" course to test their progress without getting lost in the heather.

Les amateurs de musique auront une pensée pour le compositeur Benjamin Britten, qui vécut longtemps à côté du golf. Ils en profiteront pour venir au festival de musique (en juin) dans les superbes Snape Maltings d'Aldeburgh. Le présent parcours n'est pas un très grand tracé de championnat, mais il reste un parcours de vacances agréable à intégrer dans un festival de golf dans la région, en évitant toutefois les longues périodes de sécheresse car les fairways ne sont pas arrosés. Avec la présence de bruyère et d'ajoncs, les trous ne paraissent pas bien larges, et le vent incite à jouer comme sur des links. Et l'amabilité apparente du site ne doit pas inciter à baisser sa garde, car les difficultés ne manquent pas de compliquer la quiétude du golfeur. Heureusement pour les joueurs peu expérimentés, le 9 trous supplémentaire ("River Course") permet de s'aguerrir sans craindre de se perdre dans la bruyère.

Aldeburgh Golf Club

Saxmundham Road
ENG - ALDEBURGH, Suffolk IP15 5PE

Office	Secrétariat	(44) 01728 - 452890
Pro shop	Pro-shop	(44) 01728 - 453309
Fax	Fax	
Situation	Situation	

38 km from Ipswich (pop. 130 157)
2 km from Aldeburgh (pop. 2 654)

Annual closure	Fermeture annnuelle	no
Weekly closure	Fermeture hebdomadaire	no

Fees main season	Tarifs haute saison	18 holes
	Week days Semaine	**We/Bank holidays** We/Férié
Individual Individuel	£ 35	£ 42
Couple Couple	£ 70	£ 84

£ 24 after 12.00 pm (weekdays)

Caddy	Caddy	on request/£ 15
Electric Trolley	Chariot électrique	£ 5/18 holes
Buggy	Voiturette	no
Clubs	Clubs	£ 7.50/18 holes

Credit cards Cartes de crédit no

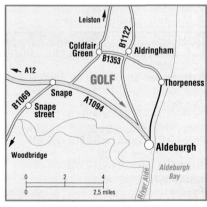

Access Accès : London A12. Ipswich → Felixstowe.
Right unto A1094. Course on left
of the road before entering Aldeburgh
Map 7 on page 419 Carte 7 Page 419

GOLF COURSE
PARCOURS 13/20

Site	Site	▬▬▬▬▬
Maintenance	Entretien	▬▬▬▬▬
Architect	Architecte	John Thompson Willie Fernie
Type	Type	open country, heathland
Relief	Relief	▬▬
Water in play	Eau en jeu	▬▬
Exp. to wind	Exposé au vent	▬▬
Trees in play	Arbres en jeu	▬▬▬

Scorecard	Chp.	Mens	Ladies
Carte de score	Chp.	Mess.	Da.
Length Long.	5698	5238	5238
Par	72	72	74

Advised golfing ability	0	12	24	36
Niveau de jeu recommandé		▬▬▬▬		
Hcp required	Handicap exigé	24		

CLUB HOUSE & AMENITIES
CLUB HOUSE ET ANNEXES 6/10

Pro shop	Pro-shop	▬▬▬
Driving range	Practice	▬▬
Sheltered	couvert	no
On grass	sur herbe	yes
Putting-green	putting-green	yes
Pitching-green	pitching green	yes

HOTEL FACILITIES
ENVIRONNEMENT HOTELIER 7/10

HOTELS HÔTELS

Wentworth Hotel Aldeburgh
38 rooms, D £ 70 2 km
Tel (44) 01728 - 452 312, Fax (44) 01728 - 454 343

Uplands Hotel Aldeburgh
20 rooms, D £ 65 2 km
Tel (44) 01728 - 452 420, Fax (44) 01728 - 454 872

White Lion Aldeburgh
38 rooms, D £ 60 2 km
Tel (44) 01728 - 452 720, Fax (44) 01728 - 452 986

RESTAURANTS RESTAURANTS

New Regatta Aldeburgh
Tel (44) 01728 - 452011 2 km

Lighthouse Aldeburgh
Tel (44) 01728 - 453377 2 km

439

ALWOODLEY (THE)

| 18 | 7 | 7 |

A recently-built clubhouse has only added to the comfort of this remarkable course, which is a revelation for anyone who has never played here before. You have to admit that the partnership between Harry Colt and Alistair Mackenzie will always appeal to connoisseurs. The greens were relaid along the lines of the original layouts, but to modern American specifications. Likewise, several new tee-boxes have helped to restyle the course without changing any of the strategy involved in coping with hazards. Besides the trees, which come into play only for the really bad shot, heather (always impossible to get out of) and especially the bunkers create most of the trouble. On the fairways, finding sand can cost you half a shot. Around the greens, where access is tight, it can cost even more. A demanding course but the fairest adversary you could hope for. You won't forget it in a long, long while.

Un récent Clubhouse n'a fait qu'ajouter du confort à un parcours remarquable qui sera une révélation pour ceux qui ne le connaissent pas encore. Il faut dire que l'association de Harry Colt et Alister MacKenzie ne peut laisser indifférent les connaisseurs. Les greens ont été refaits suivant les dessins originaux, mais avec les spécifications américaines modernes. De même, quelques nouveaux départs ont permis d'adapter le parcours, sans rien changer à la stratégie par rapport aux obstacles. A côté des bois qui ne sont vraiment en jeu que pour les mauvais coups, la bruyère (il est toujours impossible de s'en extraire) et surtout les bunkers constituent l'essentiel des obstacles. Sur les fairways, ils coûtent un demi-coup. Près des greens, dont les ouvertures sont rendues assez étroites, ils peuvent en coûter plus encore. Ce parcours est exigeant, mais il constitue l'adversaire le plus loyal qui soit. On s'en souviendra longtemps.

The Alwoodley Golf Club
Wigton Lane
ENG - LEEDS, Yorkshire LS17 8SA

Office	Secrétariat	(44) 0113-268 1680
Pro shop	Pro-shop	(44) 0113-268 9603
Fax	Fax	(44) 0113-293 9458
Situation	Situation	

8 km N of Leeds (pop. 680 725)

Annual closure	Fermeture annnuelle	no
Weekly closure	Fermeture hebdomadaire	no

Fees main season
Tarifs haute saison — full day

	Week days Semaine	We/Bank holidays We/Férié
Individual Individuel	£ 50	£ 60
Couple Couple	£ 100	£ 120

Caddy	Caddy	on request/£ 20+tip
Electric Trolley	Chariot électrique	£ 5/18 holes
Buggy	Voiturette	no
Clubs	Clubs	£ 10/18 holes

Credit cards Cartes de crédit
VISA - Eurocard - MasterCard - AMEX - DC - JCB

440

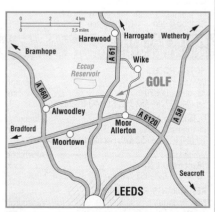

Access Accès : Turn off A61 (→ Harrogate) at traffic lights at Wigton Lane X-roads 8 km N of Leeds.
Map 4 on page 412 Carte 4 Page 412

GOLF COURSE
PARCOURS

18/20

Site	Site	
Maintenance	Entretien	
Architect	Architecte	Harry S. Colt Alister MacKenzie
Type	Type	heathland
Relief	Relief	
Water in play	Eau en jeu	
Exp. to wind	Exposé au vent	
Trees in play	Arbres en jeu	

Scorecard Carte de score	Chp. Chp.	Mens Mess.	Ladies Da.
Length Long.	6017	5671	5097
Par	72	70	73

Advised golfing ability		0 12 24 36
Niveau de jeu recommandé		
Hcp required	Handicap exigé	no

CLUB HOUSE & AMENITIES
CLUB HOUSE ET ANNEXES

7/10

Pro shop	Pro-shop	
Driving range	Practice	
Sheltered	couvert	no
On grass	sur herbe	practice range only
Putting-green	putting-green	yes
Pitching-green	pitching green	yes

HOTEL FACILITIES
ENVIRONNEMENT HOTELIER

7/10

HOTELS HÔTELS

Forte Posthouse - 123 rooms, D £ 70   Bramhope, 6 km
Tel (44) 0113 - 284 2911, Fax (44) 0113 - 284 3451

Jarvis Parkway - 105 rooms, D £ 98   Bramhope, 5 km
Tel (44) 0113 - 267 2551, Fax (44) 0113 - 267 4410

Stakis Leeds - 100 rooms, D £ 85   Leeds, 8 km
Tel (44) 0113 - 273 2323, Fax (44) 0113 - 232 3018

The Calls - 41 rooms, D £ 120   Leeds, 8 km
Tel (44) 0113 - 244 0099, Fax (44) 0113 - 234 4100

RESTAURANTS RESTAURANTS

Pool Court at 42   Leeds, 8 km
Tel (44) 0113 - 244 4242

Hereford Beefstouw   Leeds, 8 km
Tel(44) 0113 - 245 3870

Rascasse   Leeds, 8 km
Tel (44) 0113 - 244 6611

ASHRIDGE

Not far from the Thames valley, the Chiltern Hills and Whipsnade zoo, the largest wildlife reserve in Europe, Ashridge sits right in the middle of this peaceful, wonderful countryside where the aristocrats of yesteryear built superb castles. The course was opened in 1932 and has undergone only minor changes since, even though Henry Cotton was the club professional for many a year. In a superb parkland setting, the course is pleasantly classical in style with each hole having a distinctly individual character. The designers obviously had the pleasure of week-end golfers in mind, and only the sometimes high rough represents any sort of difficulty. Yardage is very reasonable but some of the par 4s are designed to set a very serious challenge. A very good course for all players, male and female.

Non loin de la vallée de la Tamise, des Chiltern Hills, ou de la réserve d'animaux sauvages de Whipsnade, la plus vaste d'Europe, Ashridge est situé au calme dans cette adorable campagne où les familles aristocrates ont bâti de superbes châteaux. Ce parcours date de 1932, et n'a fait l'objet que de minimes modifications, pas même d'Henry Cotton, qui fut longtemps le professionnel du club. Dans un superbe environnement de parc, le dessin est d'un classicisme satisfaisant, chaque trou ayant pourtant un cacatère individuel bien marqué. Les architectes ont visiblement pensé surtout au plaisir des amateurs en week-end, seul le rough, souvent haut et épais, représentant une difficulté importante. La longueur reste très raisonnable, quelques par 4 pouvant présenter de sérieux challenges par leur dessin. Un très bon parcours adapté à tous les joueurs... et joueuses !

Ashridge Golf Club
Little Gaddesden
ENG - BERKHAMSTED, Herts HP4 1LY

Office	Secrétariat	(44) 01442 - 842244
Pro shop	Pro-shop	(44) 01442 - 842307
Fax	Fax	(44) 01442 - 843770
Situation	Situation	

10 km from Hemel Hemstead (pop. 79 235)
11 km from Aylesbury (pop. 145 935)

Annual closure	Fermeture annnuelle	no
Weekly closure	Fermeture hebdomadaire	no

Fees main season	Tarifs haute saison	18 holes
	Week days Semaine	**We/Bank holidays** We/Férié
Individual Individuel	£ 36	—
Couple Couple	£ 72	—

Weekends: no visitors -
No Ladies in spike bar before 2 pm...

Caddy	Caddy	on request/£ 20
Electric Trolley	Chariot électrique	£ 5/18 holes
Buggy	Voiturette	no
Clubs	Clubs	£ 15/18 holes
Credit cards Cartes de crédit		not for greenfees

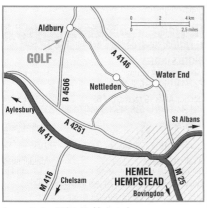

Aldbury
GOLF
A 4146
Water End
Nettleden
B 4506
Aylesbury
A 4251
St Albans
M 41
M 416
Chelsam
HEMEL HEMPSTEAD
M 25
Bovingdon

0 2 4 km
0 2.5 miles

Access Accès : A41 to Berkhamsted.
At Northchurch, turn right onto B4506.
Map 8 on page 420 Carte 8 Page 420

GOLF COURSE
PARCOURS
16/20

Site	Site	
Maintenance	Entretien	
Architect	Architecte	Sir Guy Campbell Hutchinson, Hotchkin
Type	Type	parkland
Relief	Relief	
Water in play	Eau en jeu	
Exp. to wind	Exposé au vent	
Trees in play	Arbres en jeu	

Scorecard Carte de score	Chp. Chp.	Mens Mess.	Ladies Da.
Length Long.	5892	5595	5100
Par	72	72	73

Advised golfing ability		0 12 24 36
Niveau de jeu recommandé		
Hcp required	Handicap exigé	certificate

CLUB HOUSE & AMENITIES
CLUB HOUSE ET ANNEXES
7/10

Pro shop	Pro-shop	
Driving range	Practice	
Sheltered	couvert	no
On grass	sur herbe	yes
Putting-green	putting-green	yes
Pitching-green	pitching green	yes

HOTEL FACILITIES
ENVIRONNEMENT HOTELIER
6/10

HOTELS HÔTELS
Pendley Manor - 69 rooms, D £ 90   Tring, 5 km
Tel (44) 01442 - 891 891, Fax (44) 01442 - 890 687

Hartwell House   Aylesbury
34 rooms, D £ 150   12 km
Tel (44) 01296 - 747 444, Fax (44) 01296 - 747 450

Forte Posthouse   Hemel Hempstead
146 rooms, D £ 69   10 km
Tel (44) 01442 - 251 122, Fax (44) 01442 - 211 812

Bell Inn   Aston Clinton
15 rooms, D £ 65   8 km
Tel (44) 01296 - 630 252, Fax (44) 01296 - 631 250

RESTAURANTS RESTAURANTS
Hartwell House   Aylesbury
Tel (44) 01296 - 747 444   12 km

441

BADGEMORE PARK

14 7 7

Come here in July and dress up for the royal regattas on the Thames. They are held just after Royal Ascot and just before the international polo tournament at Windsor. All three events could be combined and easily be called the "Hat Festival". Here we are in the magnificent Thames valley that would be fun to discover by boat, but only after a good round of golf here for example, where this recent layout designed by Bob Sandow has quickly forged a fine reputation for itself. The one regret is that there is no driving range, but maybe this reflects a desire not to break with a tradition that has also shaped the style of the course: squat, rather tight and with trees looming skyward. Well-balanced, imaginative and very natural in style, Badgemore Park is presently undergoing improvement work to build new tee-boxes. Watch this space.

Il faut venir en juillet pour les régates royales sur la Tamise, où l'on sort les mêmes toilettes qu'au Royal Ascot, quelques jours plus tôt. Pour faire bon poids, on ajoutera l'International Polo à Windsor. L'ensemble pourrait être dénommé "Festival des Chapeaux." Nous sommes ici dans l'adorable vallée de la Tamise, que l'on aimera parcourir en bateau. Après une bonne partie de golf, ici par exemple, où ce récent parcours de Bob Sandow s'est vite fait une bonne réputation. On regrette seulement l'absence de practice, mais c'est peut-être un souci de rester dans la tradition, comme en témoigne le style du parcours, bien ramassé, assez étroit, avec des arbres prenant pas mal de place dans le ciel ! Bien équilibré, imaginatif et très naturel, il fait actuellement l'objet de travaux avec de nouveaux départs. A suivre.

Badgemore Park Golf Club

Badgemore Park
ENG - HENLEY-ON-THAMES, Oxon RG9 4NR

Office	Secrétariat	(44) 01491 - 572206
Pro shop	Pro-shop	(44) 01491 - 574175
Fax	Fax	
Situation	Situation	

1.2 km from Henley (pop. 10 058)
11 km from Maidenhead (pop. 59 605)

Annual closure	Fermeture annnuelle	no
Weekly closure	Fermeture hebdomadaire	no

Christmas Day only

Fees main season
Tarifs haute saison · 18 holes

	Week days Semaine	We/Bank holidays We/Férié
Individual Individuel	£ 15	£ 25
Couple Couple	£ 30	£ 50

Caddy	Caddy	no
Electric Trolley	Chariot électrique	£ 5/18 holes
Buggy	Voiturette	£ 15/18 holes
Clubs	Clubs	no

Credit cards Cartes de crédit · not for greenfees

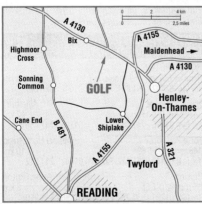

Access Accès : Leave M4 at Jct 8/9, A404, A4130 through Henley-on-Thames. Club house 1.2 km (3/4 m.) after Henley. Map 8 on page 420 Carte 8 Page 420

GOLF COURSE / PARCOURS · **14**/20

Site	Site	
Maintenance	Entretien	
Architect	Architecte	Bob Sandow
Type	Type	parkland
Relief	Relief	
Water in play	Eau en jeu	
Exp. to wind	Exposé au vent	
Trees in play	Arbres en jeu	

Scorecard Carte de score	Chp. Chp.	Mens Mess.	Ladies Da.
Length Long.	5500	5082	5036
Par	69	69	72

Advised golfing ability · 0 12 24 36
Niveau de jeu recommandé
Hcp required · Handicap exigé · no

CLUB HOUSE & AMENITIES / CLUB HOUSE ET ANNEXES · **7**/10

Pro shop	Pro-shop	
Driving range	Practice	
Sheltered	couvert	no
On grass	sur herbe	no
Putting-green	putting-green	yes
Pitching-green	pitching green	yes

HOTEL FACILITIES / ENVIRONNEMENT HOTELIER · **7**/10

HOTELS HÔTELS

Shepherds - 4 rooms, D £ 48 · Henley, 4 km
Tel (44) 01491 - 628 413

Stonor Arms - 9 rooms, D £ 85 · Stonor, 4 km
Tel (44) 01491 - 638 345, Fax (44) 01491 - 638 863

Holiday Inn · Maidenhead
187 rooms, D £ 120 · 11 km
Tel (44) 01628 - 23 444, Fax (44) 01628 - 770 035

Walton Cottage · Maidenhead
64 rooms, D £ 100 · 11 km
Tel (44) 01628 - 24 394, Fax (44) 01628 - 773 851

RESTAURANTS RESTAURANTS

Stonor Arms - Tel (44) 01491 - 638 345 · Stonor, 4 km
Villa Marina - Tel (44) 01491 - 575 262 · Henley, 4 km
Fredrick's - Tel(44) 01628 - 35 934 · Maidenhead, 11 km

442

A highly reputed spa city for more than two centuries, Bath is essential visiting particularly during the music festival held here in May-June, one of the best times to visit England anyway. Very busy on weekends, Bath has several good courses including this one, located on high ground (and providing some splendid views) and laid out over a former stone quarry. Tips from the locals will help you negotiate a number of blind shots and some sloping fairways, avoid some disconcerting kicks and make allowance for wind that can blow your game away. Their help will only increase your enjoyment on what is a rather forgiving course for hackers and beginners, but where better players will need to keep their wits about them if they want to score as well as they hope to. Hardly a major championship course but one with real personality that is well worth getting to know. After your round, go visit the impressive Roman baths in the city centre.

Ville d'eau de grande réputation depuis deux siècles, Bath est aussi à visiter, au moment du festival de musique en mai-juin, l'une des plus belles périodes pour venir en Angleterre. Très fréquenté en week-end, Bath a plusieurs bons golfs, dont celui-ci, situé sur les hauteurs (avec de très belles vues), et dessiné sur le site d'anciennes carrières de pierre. L'aide des joueurs locaux vous aidera à bien négocier quelques coups aveugles et certains fairways en pente, éviter certains rebonds déconcertants, et tenir compte d'un vent qui peut être assez prononcé. Vous n'en apprécierez que mieux ce tracé assez indulgent pour les joueurs moyens ou peu expérimentés, mais où les bons joueurs devront maintenir leur attention en éveil pour faire des scores à hauteur de leurs espérances. Sans être un parcours de championnat, il présente une personnalité à connaître. Ensuite, allez piquer une tête dans les Bains Romains de la ville.

Bath Golf Club

Sham Castle, North Road
ENG - BATH, Somerset BA2 6JG

Office	Secrétariat	(44) 01225 - 463 834
Pro shop	Pro-shop	(44) 01225 - 466 953
Fax	Fax	(44) 01225 - 331 027
Situation	Situation	

2 km from Bath (pop. 78 689)
20 km from Bristol (pop. 376 146)

Annual closure	Fermeture annnuelle	no
Weekly closure	Fermeture hebdomadaire	no

Christmas Day

Fees main season	Tarifs haute saison	18 holes
	Week days Semaine	We/Bank holidays We/Férié
Individual Individuel	£ 25	£ 30
Couple Couple	£ 50	£ 60

Full day: £ 30 - £ 40 (weekends)

Caddy	Caddy	no
Electric Trolley	Chariot électrique	£ 10/day
Buggy	Voiturette	no
Clubs	Clubs	£ 12/day
Credit cards Cartes de crédit		no

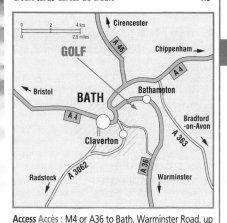

Access Accès : M4 or A36 to Bath. Warminster Road, up North Road, 0,7 km (800 yds) on left up hill.
Map 6 on page 417 Carte 6 Page 417

GOLF COURSE
PARCOURS

16/20

Site	Site	
Maintenance	Entretien	
Architect	Architecte	Harry S. Colt (1937)
Type	Type	copse, open country
Relief	Relief	
Water in play	Eau en jeu	
Exp. to wind	Exposé au vent	
Trees in play	Arbres en jeu	

Scorecard Carte de score	Chp. Chp.	Mens Mess.	Ladies Da.
Length Long.	5795	5422	5243
Par	71	71	74

Advised golfing ability		0 12	24 36
Niveau de jeu recommandé			
Hcp required	Handicap exigé	28 Men, 36 Ladies	

CLUB HOUSE & AMENITIES
CLUB HOUSE ET ANNEXES

6/10

Pro shop	Pro-shop	
Driving range	Practice	
Sheltered	couvert	no
On grass	sur herbe	yes
Putting-green	putting-green	yes
Pitching-green	pitching green	yes

HOTEL FACILITIES
ENVIRONNEMENT HOTELIER

9/10

HOTELS HÔTELS

Bath Spa — Bath
91 rooms, D £ 150 — 2 km
Tel (44) 01225 - 444 424, Fax (44) 01225 - 444 006

Homewood Park — Hinton Charterhouse
15 rooms, D £ 130 — 8 km
Tel (44) 01225 - 723 731, Fax (44) 01225 - 723 820

Hunstrete House — Hunstrete
22 rooms, D £ 150 — 8 km
Tel (44) 01761 - 490 490, Fax (44) 01225 - 490 732

RESTAURANTS RESTAURANTS

Vellore (Bath Spa Hotel) — Bath
Tel (44) 01225 - 444 424 — 2 km

Garlands — Bath
Tel (44) 01225 - 442 283 — 2 km

443

Opened in 1921, Beau Desert is aptly named, not because of any similarity with the Sahara but because this is an idyllic golfing retreat. For French readers, the word "Beau" could very easily be replaced by "Elégant". This Fowler layout has of course easily embraced a magnificent setting, using the many trees and often digging bunkers (a little in the Harry Colt style) rather than flanking them with sand-hills. This is not a long course but it is narrow, so the choice of club off the tee is important. Most of the time a 3-wood or a long iron will do to get your ball into the right spot for approaching the greens. The rough is generously lined with heather and gorse, as is often the case on a classic style of course such as this which easily soaks up the rain (rainfalls have been known to occur in this part of the world, even in a Desert). An amusing and little known course.

Ouvert en 1921, Beau Desert porte bien son nom. Sauf qu'il ne s'agit pas d'un quelconque Sahara mais plutôt d'un lieu de retraite idyllique. Et si l'on veut traduire "Beau" en français, ce sera aussi le terme d'élégant que l'on utilisera. Le dessin de Fowler s'est bien sûr adapté à un environnement magnifique, utilisant les nombreux arbres, et creusant souvent les bunkers (un peu dans le style de Colt) au lieu de les flanquer de buttes au-dessus du sol. Ce parcours n'est pas bien long, mais il est étroit, ce qui oblige à bien réfléchir sur le club à jouer au départ. La plupart du temps, un bois 3 ou un long fer suffisent pour se placer en bonne position par rapport aux greens. La bruyère et les ajoncs garnissent généreusement les roughs, comme sur ces types de parcours classiques supportant bien la pluie, ce qui semble se produire de temps à autre dans ce pays, même dans un "Desert". Un parcours amusant et méconnu.

Beau Desert Golf Club

Hazel Slade
ENG - CANNOCK, Staffs. WS12 5PJ

Office	Secrétariat	(44) 01543 - 422626
Pro shop	Pro-shop	(44) 01543 - 422492
Fax	Fax	(44) 01543 - 451137
Situation	Situation	

5 km from Cannock (pop. 88 833)
25 km from Birmingham (pop. 961 041)

Annual closure	Fermeture annnuelle	no
Weekly closure	Fermeture hebdomadaire	no

Fees main season
Tarifs haute saison — full day

	Week days Semaine	We/Bank holidays We/Férié
Individual Individuel	£ 35	—
Couple Couple	£ 70	—

No visitors at w/ends

Caddy	Caddy	no
Electric Trolley	Chariot électrique	£ 5/18 holes
Buggy	Voiturette	no
Clubs	Clubs	no

Credit cards Cartes de crédit	no

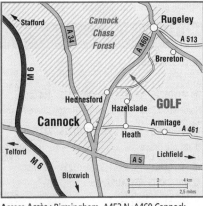

Access Accès : Birmingham, A452 N. A460 Cannock through Hednesford, right at signpost to Hazel Slade, and next left. **Map 7 on page 418** Carte 7 Page 418

GOLF COURSE
PARCOURS

16/20

Site	Site	
Maintenance	Entretien	
Architect	Architecte	Herbert Fowler
Type	Type	forest, heathland
Relief	Relief	
Water in play	Eau en jeu	
Exp. to wind	Exposé au vent	
Trees in play	Arbres en jeu	

Scorecard Carte de score	Chp. Chp.	Mens Mess.	Ladies Da.
Length Long.	5679	5365	4850
Par	71	70	71

Advised golfing ability Niveau de jeu recommandé	0 12 24 36
Hcp required Handicap exigé	certificate

CLUB HOUSE & AMENITIES
CLUB HOUSE ET ANNEXES

7/10

Pro shop	Pro-shop	
Driving range	Practice	
Sheltered	couvert	no
On grass	sur herbe	practice ground only
Putting-green	putting-green	yes
Pitching-green	pitching green	yes

HOTEL FACILITIES
ENVIRONNEMENT HOTELIER

7/10

HOTELS HÔTELS
Roman Way - 56 rooms, D £ 65 — Cannock 5 km
Tel (44) 01543 - 572 121, Fax (44) 01543 - 502 742

Uxbridge Arms - 21 rooms, D £ 32 — Hednesford 3 km
Tel (44) 01543 - 426 211

Asquith House - 10 rooms, D £ 67 — Birmingham 25 km
Tel (44) 0121 - 454 5282, Fax (44) 0121 - 456 4668

Jonathan's - 30 rooms, D £ 100 — Birmingham 25 km
Tél (44) 0121 - 429 3757, Fax (44) 0121 - 434 3107

RESTAURANTS RESTAURANTS
Thrales - Tel (44) 01543 - 255 091 — Lichfield 10 km

Old Farmhouse — Armitage 5 km
Tel (44) 01543 - 490 353

Number 282 (Hyatt Regency) — Birmingham 25 km
Tel (44) 0121 - 643 1234

444

BERKHAMSTED

16	7	6

Berkhamsted is one of those courses that is close enough to London to be within easy reach and far enough away so as not to be over-crowded. Even so, you still need to call to book a tee-off time. The new clubhouse is just perfect in terms of comfort but you leave your shoes in the hallway. The landscape here is similar to that at Ashridge, a few miles down the road, and is just as respectable and pleasant. The one big difference is that there are no bunkers. This is logical enough in that bunkers are created by sheep and here there are no sheep, just horses in the woods and lots of people out walking. Fortunately they do not come into play. The absence of sand is largely made good by the bushes and heather and by the dips that you might call grass bunkers. Getting out of them with the desired results is never easy, either. The greens are small and so emphasise the need for accuracy. Worth knowing.

Berkhamsted fait partie de ces clubs assez proches de Londres pour en faciliter l'accès, et assez éloignés pour ne pas être trop surchargés, bien qu'il soit toujours nécessaire de téléphoner à l'avance. Le nouveau Clubhouse est tout à fait confortable, mais on laisse ses clous à la porte. On trouve ici un paysage assez proche de celui d'Ashridge,à quelques kilomètres, et un parcours tout aussi respectable et plaisant. Mais avec une grande différence : ici, aucun bunker ! C'est bien logique, les bunkers ont été créés par des moutons, on ne trouve ici que des chevaux dans les bois, et beaucoup de promeneurs, mais rarement en jeu. Ce manque de sable est largement compensé par les buissons et la bruyère, et par des dépressions que l'on peut appeler "bunkers d'herbe," dont il n'est guère facile de s'extraire avec des résultats garantis. Les greens sont petits, ce qui accentue la nécessité d'être précis. A connaître.

Berkhamsted Golf Club

The Common
ENG - BERKHAMSTED, Herts HP4 2QB

Office	Secrétariat	(44) 01442 - 865832
Pro shop	Pro-shop	(44) 01442 - 865851
Fax	Fax	
Situation	Situation	

1.5 km from Berkhamsted
8 km from Hemel Hempstead (pop. 79 235)

Annual closure	Fermeture annnuelle	no
Weekly closure	Fermeture hebdomadaire	no

Fees main season	Tarifs haute saison	18 holes
	Week days Semaine	**We/Bank holidays** We/Férié
Individual Individuel	£ 22.50	£ 35
Couple Couple	£ 45	£ 70

Book in advance - Weekends: visitors after 11.30 am

Caddy	Caddy	no
Electric Trolley	Chariot électrique	no
Buggy	Voiturette	no
Clubs	Clubs	£ 10/18 holes
Credit cards Cartes de crédit		not for greenfees

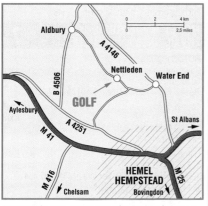

Access Accès : M1, Jct 8 to Hemel Hempstead. At roundabout, take Leighton Buzzard Road. After 4.5 km (3 m.) take Potten End. Turn on left. Golf 4.5 km on left. **Map 8 on page 420** Carte 8 Page 420

GOLF COURSE
PARCOURS

16/20

Site	Site	
Maintenance	Entretien	
Architect	Architecte	G.H. Gowring
Type	Type	inland, heathland
Relief	Relief	
Water in play	Eau en jeu	
Exp. to wind	Exposé au vent	
Trees in play	Arbres en jeu	

Scorecard Carte de score	**Chp.** Chp.	**Mens** Mess.	**Ladies** Da.
Length Long.	5945	5580	5161
Par	71	71	73

Advised golfing ability Niveau de jeu recommandé		0 12 24 36	
Hcp required	Handicap exigé	certificate	

CLUB HOUSE & AMENITIES
CLUB HOUSE ET ANNEXES

7/10

Pro shop	Pro-shop	
Driving range	Practice	
Sheltered	couvert	no
On grass	sur herbe	yes
Putting-green	putting-green	yes
Pitching-green	pitching green	no

445

HOTEL FACILITIES
ENVIRONNEMENT HOTELIER

6/10

HOTELS HÔTELS

Pendley Manor - 69 rooms, D £ 90 — Tring
Tel (44) 01442 - 891 891
Fax (44) 01442 - 890 687

Hartwell House - 34 rooms, D £ 150 — Aylesbury
Tel (44) 01296 - 747 444
Fax (44) 01296 - 747 450

Forte Posthouse -146 rooms, D £ 69 — Hemel Hempstead
Tel (44) 01442 - 251 122
Fax (44) 01442 - 211 812

Bell Inn - 15 rooms, D £ 65 — Aston Clinton
Tel (44) 01296 - 630 252
Fax (44) 01296 - 631 250

RESTAURANT RESTAURANT

Hartwell House — Aylesbury
Tel (44) 01296 - 747 444

As it is not always easy to choose between the Red and the Blue courses, play both on either side of lunch. The clubhouse, although renovated, has lost nothing of its charm worthy of characters from P.G. Wodehouse. The trees, not so old but already venerable, are the main setting for this discreet course designed by Herbet Fowler, an equally discreet designer but a real connoisseur of golf (see also Saunton and Walton Heath). The other hazards are fewer in number but just as daunting, for example the bunkers or the stream which crosses several fairways. Here you need every club in your bag, a sign of excellence if ever there was one. Green-keeping is always of the highest standard although without reaching the virtually fanatical levels of preparation that you see all too often these days. Berkshire may not have the "royal" tag but "princely" will do just nicely.

Comme il n'est pas possible de choisir vraiment entre les deux parcours du Berkshire, il faudra jouer les deux, avec une petite visite pour déjeuner à la mi-temps au Clubhouse dont l'intérieur rénové n'a pas perdu son atmosphère digne des héros de P.G. Wodehouse. Les arbres (pas si anciens, mais déjà très vénérables) constituent le décor entourant ce parcours sobrement dessiné par Herbert Fowler, architecte discret, mais toujours aussi connaisseur du jeu de golf (voir aussi Saunton ou Walton Heath). Les autres obstacles ne sont pas très nombreux, mais sont toujours efficaces, comme les bunkers ou le ruisseau traversant plusieurs fairways. Ici, on utilise tous les clubs du sac, c'est un signe de qualité. L'entretien y est de grande qualité, sans les excès de préparation quasi maniaque que l'on voit trop souvent aujourd'hui. Berkshire n'est peut-être pas (ou plus) "Royal," mais il vous offre un plaisir princier.

The Berkshire Golf Club

Swinley Road
ENG - ASCOT, Berks SL5 8AY

Office	Secrétariat	(44) 01344 - 21 495
Pro shop	Pro-shop	(44) 01344 - 22 351
Fax	Fax	
Situation	Situation	

3 km from Ascot (pop. 150 244)
5 km from Bracknell (pop. 50 325)

Annual closure	Fermeture annnuelle	no
Weekly closure	Fermeture hebdomadaire	no
Fees main season	Tarifs haute saison	18 holes

	Week days Semaine	We/Bank holidays We/Férié
Individual Individuel	£ 50	—
Couple Couple	£ 100	—

Booking essential - Full weekday: £ 65 -
No visitors at weekends

Caddy	Caddy	on request/£ 20
Electric Trolley	Chariot électrique	no
Buggy	Voiturette	£ 20/18 holes
Clubs	Clubs	£ 20/18 holes

Credit cards Cartes de crédit — no

446

Access Accès : M3 Jct 3. A322 → Bracknell.
A332 on right → Ascot. Club house 750 m on left.
Map 8 on page 420 Carte 8 Page 420

GOLF COURSE
PARCOURS

17/20

Site	Site	
Maintenance	Entretien	
Architect	Architecte	Herbert Fowler
Type	Type	inland, forest
Relief	Relief	
Water in play	Eau en jeu	
Exp. to wind	Exposé au vent	
Trees in play	Arbres en jeu	

Scorecard Carte de score	Chp. Chp.	Mens Mess.	Ladies Da.
Length Long.	5635	5420	5077
Par	71	71	73

Advised golfing ability	0	12	24	36
Niveau de jeu recommandé				
Hcp required Handicap exigé	introduction from home club			

CLUB HOUSE & AMENITIES
CLUB HOUSE ET ANNEXES

8/10

Pro shop	Pro-shop	
Driving range	Practice	
Sheltered	couvert	no
On grass	sur herbe	yes
Putting-green	putting-green	yes
Pitching-green	pitching green	yes

HOTEL FACILITIES
ENVIRONNEMENT HOTELIER

7/10

HOTELS HÔTELS

Royal Berkshire — Sunninghill 3 km
60 rooms, D £ 140
Tel (44) 01344 - 23 322, Fax (44) 01344 - 27 100

Coppid Beech — Bracknell
205 rooms, D £ 175 — 8 km
Tel (44) 01344 - 303 333
Fax (44) 01344 - 301 200

Hilton — Bracknell
167 rooms, D £ 120 — 5 km
Tel (44) 01344 - 424 801, Fax (44) 01344 - 487 454

RESTAURANTS RESTAURANTS

Stateroom (Royal Berkshire) — Sunninghill
Tel (44) 01344 - 23 322 — 3 km

Jade Fountain — Sunninghill
Tel (44) 01344 - 27 070 — 3 km

If you have only ever played here once, you will probably be hard pushed to remember whether it was the Blue course or the Red. They are not quite twins but the similarities of landscape and in length can be confusing. Here is some valuable help: if you played six par 5s, six par 3s and six par 4s, then you played the Red course. You will need at least all those par 5s (some are trimmed to par 4s for certain top tournaments) to bag some birdies and recover what you will have certainly lost on the par 3s. They are all dangerous and making par can be a real problem should you miss the green. You need a steady game and some straight hitting to do well here, particularly with your longer irons. The pines, chestnut trees and birch trees certainly make for a pretty country setting, but you probably won't find them so appealing when you come to add up your score. And even if you do keep out of the trees, there is still the heather to contend with.

Si vous n'avez joué ici qu'une seule fois, vous avez peu de chances de vous souvenir si c'était le "Blue" ou le "Red." L'un ou l'autre ne sont sans doute pas aussi semblables que des jumeaux, mais même leurs similitudes de longueur peut ajouter à la confusion. Une indication précieuse : si vous avez joué six par 5, six par 3 et six par 4, c'était le "Red." Il faut au moins tous ces par 5 (certains sont ramenés en par 4 dans les grands tournois) pour attraper quelques birdies et récupérer ce que les par 3 vont vous coûter : ils sont tous dangereux et il est très problématique d'y faire le par si vous manquez le green. Il faut ici un jeu solide et bien droit, savoir bien taper les longs fers, car les-pins, les châtaigniers et les bouleaux offrent peut-être un cadre bucolique, mais on ne les aime pas toujours autant quand on totalise les scores. Et les éviter ne signifie pas que l'on évitera la bruyère.

The Berkshire Golf Club

Swinley Road
ENG - ASCOT, Berks SL5 8AY

Office	Secrétariat	(44) 01344 - 21 495
Pro shop	Pro-shop	(44) 01344 - 22 351
Fax	Fax	
Situation	Situation	

3 km from Ascot (pop. 150 244)
5 km from Bracknell (pop. 50 325)

Annual closure	Fermeture annnuelle	no
Weekly closure	Fermeture hebdomadaire	no
Fees main season	Tarifs haute saison	18 holes

	Week days Semaine	We/Bank holidays We/Férié
Individual Individuel	£ 50	—
Couple Couple	£ 100	—

Booking essential - Full weekdays: £ 65 -
No visitors at weekends

Caddy	Caddy	on request/£ 20
Electric Trolley	Chariot électrique	no
Buggy	Voiturette	£ 20/18 holes
Clubs	Clubs	£ 20/18 holes

Credit cards Cartes de crédit — no

Access Accès : M3 Jct 3. A322 → Bracknell. A332
on right → Ascot. Club house 750 m on left.
Map 8 on page 420 Carte 8 Page 420

GOLF COURSE PARCOURS

17/20

Site	Site	
Maintenance	Entretien	
Architect	Architecte	Herbert Fowler
Type	Type	inland, forest
Relief	Relief	
Water in play	Eau en jeu	
Exp. to wind	Exposé au vent	
Trees in play	Arbres en jeu	

Scorecard Carte de score	Chp. Chp.	Mens Mess.	Ladies Da.
Length Long.	5741	5525	5160
Par	72	72	73

Advised golfing ability		0 12 24 36
Niveau de jeu recommandé		
Hcp required	Handicap exigé	introduction from home club

CLUB HOUSE & AMENITIES
CLUB HOUSE ET ANNEXES

8/10

Pro shop	Pro-shop	
Driving range	Practice	
Sheltered	couvert	no
On grass	sur herbe	yes
Putting-green	putting-green	yes
Pitching-green	pitching green	yes

447

HOTEL FACILITIES
ENVIRONNEMENT HOTELIER

7/10

HOTELS HÔTELS
Royal Berkshire — Sunninghill
60 rooms, D £ 140 — 3 km
Tél (44) 01344 - 23 322, Fax (44) 01344 - 27 100

Coppid Beech — Bracknell
205 rooms, D £ 175 — 8 km
Tél (44) 01344 - 303 333, Fax (44) 01344 - 301 200

Cricketers — Bagshot
27 rooms, D £ 40 — 4 km
Tél (44) 01276 - 473 196, Fax (44) 01276 - 451 357

RESTAURANTS RESTAURANTS
Stateroom (Royal Berkshire) — Sunninghill
Tel (44) 01344 - 23 322 — 3 km

The Cottage — Winkfield Row
Tel (44) 01344 - 882 242 — 6 km

BERWICK-UPON-TWEED

| 15 | 6 | 5 |

A site of endless warring between the English and the Scots, Berwick-upon-Tweed brought peace between both sides and called in designers from both banks of the river Tweed to build a golf course. As you approach, the site looks nothing to write home about, an impression that lasts even as far as the clubhouse, which is simple but functional. The course follows the same style over two wide circles and terrain that is generally on the flat side, with the exception of a few incursions into the sand dunes. This is certainly a less memorable course than others, but its somewhat outdated simplicity, a site between the sea and countryside and the peaceful surroundings combine to create an appealing layout. It would be unthinkable not to play here when in the region, but this slumbering "old lady" is due for some restyling work. In what is an up-and-running project, Dave Thomas has plans to cut out the blind shots and improve the bunkers. Come and play soon, if only to be able to say afterwards how it used to be before.

Eternel théâtre des guerres entre Ecossais et Anglais, Berwick-upon-Tweed a fait la paix pour appeler des architectes des deux bords de la Tweed pour s'occuper du parcours. L'arrivée est sans prétention jusqu'au Clubhouse simple, fonctionnel. Le parcours est dans le même style, en deux boucles sur terrain généralement plat, quelques incursions dans les dunes mises à part. Il n'est sans doute pas aussi mémorable que d'autres, mais sa simplicité un peu surannée, une situation entre campagne et mer, la tranquillité de la région lui donnent un charme certain. Il est impensable de ne pas le jouer quand on passe à proximité, mais on attend un réveil de cette "vieille dame." Il semble que ce soit en projet, avec des plans de Dave Thomas pour éliminer les coups aveugles et améliorer les bunkers. A jouer vite, rien que pour raconter après comme c'était "avant."

Berwick-upon-Tweed Golf Club

Goswick, Beal
ENG - BERWICK-UPON-TWEED, Northumb. TD15 2RW

Office	Secrétariat	(44) 01289 - 387256
Pro shop	Pro-shop	(44) 01289 - 387380
Fax	Fax	(44) 01289 - 387256
Situation	Situation	

7 km S of Berwick-upon-Tweed (pop. 26 731)

Annual closure	Fermeture annnuelle	no
Weekly closure	Fermeture hebdomadaire	no

Fees main season
Tarifs haute saison 18 holes

	Week days Semaine	We/Bank holidays We/Férié
Individual Individuel	£ 20	£ 25
Couple Couple	£ 40	£ 50

Full day: £ 25/£ 32

Caddy	Caddy	no
Electric Trolley	Chariot électrique	no
Buggy	Voiturette	no
Clubs	Clubs	£ 10/18 holes

Credit cards Cartes de crédit no

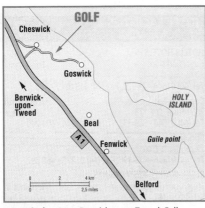

GOLF
Cheswick
Goswick
Berwick-upon-Tweed
Beal
HOLY ISLAND
Fenwick
Guile point
Belford

| 0 | 2 | 4 km |
| 0 | 2,5 miles | |

Access Accès : A1 → Berwick-upon-Tweed. Follow signs after Fenwick village.
Map 2 on page 409 Carte 2 Page 409

448

GOLF COURSE
PARCOURS

15/20

Site	Site	
Maintenance	Entretien	
Architect	Architecte	James Braid
		F. Pennink, D. Steel
Type	Type	links
Relief	Relief	
Water in play	Eau en jeu	
Exp. to wind	Exposé au vent	
Trees in play	Arbres en jeu	

Scorecard Carte de score	Chp. Chp.	Mens Mess.	Ladies Da.
Length Long.	5816	5665	5018
Par	72	72	74

Advised golfing ability 0 12 24 36
Niveau de jeu recommandé
Hcp required Handicap exigé no

CLUB HOUSE & AMENITIES
CLUB HOUSE ET ANNEXES

6/10

Pro shop	Pro-shop	
Driving range	Practice	
Sheltered	couvert	no
On grass	sur herbe	yes
Putting-green	putting-green	yes
Pitching-green	pitching green	yes

HOTEL FACILITIES
ENVIRONNEMENT HOTELIER

5/10

HOTELS HÔTELS

Marshall Meadows Country House — Berwick — 10 km
17 rooms, D £ 75
Tel (44) 01289 - 331 133
Fax (44) 01289 - 331 438

Blue Bell Hotel — Belford — 10 km
17 rooms, D £ 80
Tel (44) 01668 - 213 543
Fax (44) 01668 - 213 787

Purdy Lodge - 20 rooms, D £ 40 — Belford — 10 km
Tel (44) 01668 - 213 000
Fax (44) 01289 - 213 111

Tillmouth Park — Cornhill-on-Tweed — 25 km
14 rooms, D £ 110
Tel (44) 01890 - 882 255
Fax (44) 01890 - 882 540

BLACKMOOR

Golf is not really about preferring such and such a style of course design, as each has its great side and each its shortcomings. What makes golf such a rich game is the diversity of challenge thrown down to the player. Blackmoor is the perfect example of this, being a very carefully thought out course without the visual gimmickry. Harry Colt placed the hazards, with emphasis as usual on fairness so you see exactly what needs to be done. Given the amount of land available, he preferred a good par 69 to a tricky par 72 and came up with a layout that you will want to play twice in the same day to savour every detail. There are a lot of ditches and especially wonderfully classical bunkers, heather and ubiquitous trees. That sort of description could apply to many other courses, we agree, but Blackmoor has real personality that you meet and feel out on the course.

Il n'est pas question de préférer tel ou tel style d'architecture de golf, chacun a sa grandeur et ses défauts. La richesse du golf vient de cette diversité des défis offerts aux joueurs. Blackmoor est un parfait exemple d'une architecture mûrement pensée, mais sans gadgets visuels. Harry Colt était le maître du placement des obstacles, mais toujours dans un souci de franchise du parcours : on voit ce que l'on doit accomplir. Ici, compte tenu du terrain disponible, il a préféré un bon par 69 à un par 72 "tricky," et l'on aimera le jouer deux fois dans la journée pour mieux en savourer chaque détail. On trouve ici de nombreux fossés, mais surtout, de manière terriblement classique, les bunkers, la bruyère, les arbres omniprésents : c'est une description que l'on pourrait trouver ailleurs... La personnalité de Blackmoor, vous la trouverez avec votre jeu et votre sensibilité.

Blackmoor Golf Club

Firgrove Road
ENG - WHITEHILL, Hants GU35 9EH

Office	Secrétariat	(44) 01420 - 472775
Pro shop	Pro-shop	(44) 01420 - 472345
Fax	Fax	(44) 01420 - 487666
Situation	Situation	

10 km from Alton (pop. 16 356)
10 km from Liphook

Annual closure	Fermeture annnuelle	no
Weekly closure	Fermeture hebdomadaire	no
Fees main season	Tarifs haute saison	18 holes

	Week days Semaine	We/Bank holidays We/Férié
Individual Individuel	£ 30	£ 15*
Couple Couple	£ 60	£ 30*

Weekends: * only with member

Caddy	Caddy	no
Electric Trolley	Chariot électrique	£ 5/18 holes
Buggy	Voiturette	no
Clubs	Clubs	no

Credit cards Cartes de crédit   VISA - MasterCard

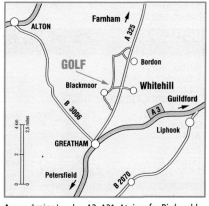

Access Accès : London A3, A31. At signs for Birdworld, A325. Pass Birdworld through Bordon. About 0.75 km out of Bordon, turn right to Blackmoor.
Map 7 on page 418 Carte 7 Page 418

GOLF COURSE
PARCOURS   17 /20

Site	Site	
Maintenance	Entretien	
Architect	Architecte	Harry S. Colt
Type	Type	inland, heathland
Relief	Relief	
Water in play	Eau en jeu	
Exp. to wind	Exposé au vent	
Trees in play	Arbres en jeu	

Scorecard Carte de score	Chp. Chp.	Mens Mess.	Ladies Da.
Length Long.	5547	5350	5095
Par	69	69	72

Advised golfing ability		0 12 24 36
Niveau de jeu recommandé		
Hcp required	Handicap exigé	30

CLUB HOUSE & AMENITIES
CLUB HOUSE ET ANNEXES   6 /10

Pro shop	Pro-shop	
Driving range	Practice	
Sheltered	couvert	no
On grass	sur herbe	no
Putting-green	putting-green	yes
Pitching-green	pitching green	yes

HOTEL FACILITIES
ENVIRONNEMENT HOTELIER   5 /10

HOTELS HÔTELS

Swan - 36 rooms, D £ 70 Tel (44) 01420 - 83 777 Fax (44) 01420 - 87 975	Alton 10 km
Grange - 30 rooms, D £ 75 Tel (44) 01420 - 86 565 Fax (44) 01420 - 541 346	Alton 10 km
Alton House - 39 rooms, D £ 60 Tel (44) 01420 - 80 033 Fax (44) 01420 - 89 222	Alton 10 km
Forte Travelodge - 31 rooms, D £ 45 Tel (44) 01420 - 562 659	Four Marks 11 km

RESTAURANTS RESTAURANTS

White Hart Tel (44) 01420 - 87 654	Alton (Holybourne) 11 km
Grange - Tel (44) 01420 - 86 565	Alton 10 km

449

BOLTON OLD LINKS

15	5	7

Despite the name, this course has neither the sub-soil nor the physical relief of a real links (it is laid out on the side of a hill). Very close to Manchester, it is still a real change of surroundings for local players, except for the few old factory chimneys you can see in the distance. Bolton Old Links actually lies in some pretty English countryside, full of trees, bushes and a few old flint walls, particularly on the 12th hole where there is also a ravine waiting to ruin your card. Note, too, the small and sloping greens on the short par 4s, and the overall difficulty of the putting surfaces in general (the 17th, for instance). Here lie the origins of some of the greens at Augusta, in which Alister Mackenzie had an active hand. This is one of the region's finest tests of golf where, at least for the first time out and especially if it is windy, you shouldn't bother counting your score. Just have a lot of fun.

Ni par le sol, ni par le relief (il est à flanc de colline), ce n'est un vrai "links," mais on donna longtemps aux parcours cette dénomination, par extension. Situé à proximité immédiate de Manchester, il n'en est pas moins dépaysant, n'étaient quelques hautes cheminées d'usine au loin. Bolton Old Links est dans une jolie campagne anglaise, avec plein d'arbres et de buissons, quelques vieux murs de pierre, entre autres au 12, qui comprend également un ravin où votre score peut se perdre. A noter encore, la petite taille et les pentes des greens sur les par 4 courts, mais aussi leur difficulté générale (le 17...). On peut retrouver là l'origine de quelques greens d'Augusta, auxquels Alister Mackenzie a si efficacement participé. C'est un des meilleurs tests de golf de la région. La première fois, et surtout s'il y a du vent, on ne compte pas son score, et on s'amuse beaucoup.

Bolton Old Links Golf Club

Chorley Old Road
ENG - BOLTON, Gtr Manchester BL1 5SU

Office	Secrétariat	(44) 01204 - 842 307
Pro shop	Pro-shop	(44) 01204 - 843 089
Fax	Fax	
Situation	Situation	

5 km NW of Bolton (pop. 258 584)

Annual closure	Fermeture annnuelle	no
Weekly closure	Fermeture hebdomadaire	no

Fees main season
Tarifs haute saison

		full day
	Week days Semaine	We/Bank holidays We/Férié
Individual Individuel	£ 27	£ 40
Couple Couple	£ 54	£ 80

Caddy	Caddy	no
Electric Trolley	Chariot électrique	no
Buggy	Voiturette	no
Clubs	Clubs	no

Credit cards Cartes de crédit — no

450

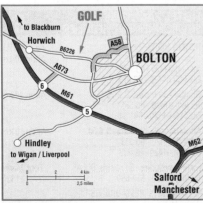

Access Accès : M61 Jct 5, A58 North, then B6226
Map 4 on page 412 Carte 4 Page 412

GOLF COURSE
PARCOURS

15/20

Site	Site	▰▰▰▰▰
Maintenance	Entretien	▰▰▰▰▰
Architect	Architecte	Alister MacKenzie
Type	Type	inland, open country
Relief	Relief	▰▰▰
Water in play	Eau en jeu	▰▰
Exp. to wind	Exposé au vent	▰▰
Trees in play	Arbres en jeu	▰▰▰

Scorecard Carte de score	Chp. Chp.	Mens Mess.	Ladies Da.
Length Long.	5830	5490	4995
Par	72	71	73

Advised golfing ability	0	12	24	36
Niveau de jeu recommandé		▰▰▰		

Hcp required Handicap exigé — certificate

CLUB HOUSE & AMENITIES
CLUB HOUSE ET ANNEXES

5/10

Pro shop	Pro-shop	▰▰▰▰
Driving range	Practice	▰▰
Sheltered	couvert	2 indoor nets
On grass	sur herbe	yes
Putting-green	putting-green	yes
Pitching-green	pitching green	no

HOTEL FACILITIES
ENVIRONNEMENT HOTELIER

7/10

HOTELS HÔTELS

Bolton Moat House — Bolton
126 rooms, D £ 100 — 5 km
Tel (44) 01204 - 383 338, Fax (44) 01204 - 380 777

Last Drop Village — Bromley Cross
80 rooms, D £ 95 — 5 km
Tel (44) 01204 - 591 131, Fax (44) 01204 - 304 122

Broomfield — Bolton
15 rooms, D £ 42 — 6 km
Tel (44) 01204 - 61 570, Fax (44) 01204 - 650 932

RESTAURANTS RESTAURANTS

Bolton Moat House — Bolton
Tel (44) 01204 - 383 338 — 5 km

Last Drop Village — Bromley Cross
Tel (44) 01204 - 591 131 — 5 km

Cornwall is traditionally associated with great links courses, but recent additions such as St Mellion have been designed in rather different landscapes. The same goes for Bowood (not to be confused with the Bowood in Wiltshire), a recent course opened in 1992. Laid out in what was once the Black Prince's hunting estate, there are a lot of trees, an unusual feature in Cornwall, many of which the designers have generously brought into play. The style is generally rather British (there is nothing aggressive about this course) although there is a multitude of water hazards in play that most beginners will find rather intimidating. With that said the difficulties are not insurmountable, as long as you can get the ball cleanly up in the air, especially on the 5th hole, a long par 4 with an island green. The clubhouse is huge with pretty views over a country landscape and is to be given 29 rooms to accommodate visitors. Land is also available for housing projects.

On associe la Cornouailles avec les grands links, mais de récentes réalisations comme St Mellion se sont inscrites dans des paysages tout différents. C'est le cas de ce Bowood (ne pas confondre avec celui du Wiltshire) ouvert en 1992. Situé dans un ancien domaine de chasse du Prince Noir, on y trouve beaucoup d'arbres (c'est inhabituel dans la région), généreusement mis en jeu par les architectes. Le style est resté assez britannique (le dessin n'est jamais agressif) bien qu'il y ait une multitude d'obstacles d'eau en jeu, que les débutants trouveront intimidants. Cela dit, les difficultés ne sont pas insurmontables... si l'on sait porter la balle, en particulier au 5, un long par 4 avec un green en île. Le Clubhouse est immense, avec de jolies vues sur un paysage rural, et devrait être aménagé avec 29 chambres pour recevoir les visiteurs. Des terrains sont aussi disponibles pour des maisons individuelles.

Bowood Golf Club

Valley Truckle, Lanteglos
ENG - CAMELFORD, Cornwall PL32 9RF

Office	Secrétariat	(44) 01840 - 213 017
Pro shop	Pro-shop	(44) 01840 - 213 017
Fax	Fax	(44) 01840 - 212 622
Situation	Situation	

65 km NW of Plymouth (pop. 243 373)
40 km N of Newquay (pop. 17 390)

Annual closure	Fermeture annnuelle	no
Weekly closure	Fermeture hebdomadaire	no
Fees main season	Tarifs haute saison	18 holes

	Week days Semaine	We/Bank holidays We/Férié
Individual Individuel	£ 25	£ 25
Couple Couple	£ 50	£ 50

Full day (any): £ 35

Caddy	Caddy	no
Electric Trolley	Chariot électrique	no
Buggy	Voiturette	£ 15/18 holes
Clubs	Clubs	£ 5/18 holes

Credit cards Cartes de crédit
VISA - Eurocard - MasterCard

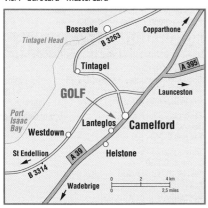

Access Accès : M5, Jct 31 (Exeter), then A30. After Launceston, A395, then A39 South through Camelford. 2 km (1 1/4 m.), turn right on B3266 → Tintagel. First left after garage. **Map 6 on page 416** Carte 6 Page 416

GOLF COURSE
PARCOURS

16/20

Site	Site	▬▬▬▬▬▬
Maintenance	Entretien	▬▬▬▬▬
Architect	Architecte	Brian Huggett Knott/Bridge
Type	Type	copse, parkland
Relief	Relief	▬▬▬
Water in play	Eau en jeu	▬▬▬▬
Exp. to wind	Exposé au vent	▬▬▬
Trees in play	Arbres en jeu	▬▬▬▬

Scorecard Carte de score	Chp. Chp.	Mens Mess.	Ladies Da.
Length Long.	6090	5731	5188
Par	72	72	72

Advised golfing ability Niveau de jeu recommandé	0	12	24	36
Hcp required Handicap exigé	certificate			

CLUB HOUSE & AMENITIES
CLUB HOUSE ET ANNEXES

7/10

Pro shop	Pro-shop	▬▬▬▬
Driving range	Practice	▬▬▬
Sheltered	couvert	9 bays
On grass	sur herbe	no
Putting-green	putting-green	yes
Pitching-green	pitching green	yes

451

HOTEL FACILITIES
ENVIRONNEMENT HOTELIER

6/10

HOTELS HÔTELS

Tintagel Arms Hotel 7 rooms, D £ 50 Tel (44) 01840 - 770 780	Tintagel 9 km
Trebrea Lodge 7 rooms, D £ 80 Tel (44) 01840 - 770 410 Fax (44) 01840 - 770 092	Tintagel 9 km
Tolcarne House 8 rooms, D £ 60 Tel (44) 01840 - 250 654	Boscastle 12 km

RESTAURANT RESTAURANT

Port William Tel (44) 01840 - 770 230	Tintagel 8 km

Question: are today's course designers incapable of producing approaches to greens that call for the good old "bump 'n run" shot? Or do they go for the easier option of placing hazards that force players to pitch the greens? We're sorry that Dave Thomas didn't choose to preserve this very British feature here, but his style blends well with the modernity probably required for this sort of course. Bowood is an ambitious resort of a high standard overall where the par 5s are very good, the greens remarkably well defended and where you need to play several rounds before understanding the ins and outs of a very imaginative layout. One word of advice, however: unless you drive straight and long, keep away from the back tees, play further forward and have fun. An impressive resort which is exciting to play, but perhaps not for those continental Europeans who are looking for the traditional English touch of worn tweed and pantaloons.

Les architectes d'aujourd'hui ne sauraient-ils plus dessiner des approches de greens permettant de faire les "bump 'n run" ? C'est plus difficile que de mettre des obstacles obligeant à faire des coups levés. On regrette que Dave Thomas n'ait pu conserver cet art très britannique, même si son style s'adapte bien à la modernité probablement souhaitée dans ce genre de réalisation. Bowood est un domaine ambitieux, de haute qualité générale, où les par 5 sont très réussis, où les greens sont remarquablement défendus, et où il faut jouer plusieurs fois avant de comprendre les subtilités d'un dessin très imaginatif. Un conseil cependant, ne partez pas des départs reculés, à moins de driver fort et droit. Choisissez de vous amuser, avant tout. Un ensemble impressionnant, passionnant à jouer, mais les continentaux aiment aussi le côté old fashioned et tweed râpé.

Bowood Golf & Country Club
Derry Hill
ENG - CALNE, Wiltshire SN11 9PQ

Office	Secrétariat	(44) 01249 - 822 228
Pro shop	Pro-shop	(44) 01249 - 822 228
Fax	Fax	(44) 01249 - 822 218
Situation	Situation	

8 km from Calne (pop. 13 894)
5 km from Chippenham (pop. 25 794)

Annual closure	Fermeture annnuelle	no
Weekly closure	Fermeture hebdomadaire	no

Fees main season	Tarifs haute saison	18 holes
	Week days Semaine	We/Bank holidays We/Férié
Individual Individuel	£ 32	£ 32
Couple Couple	£ 64	£ 64

Full day: £ 42

Caddy	Caddy	no
Electric Trolley	Chariot électrique	£ 6/18 holes
Buggy	Voiturette	£ 20/18 holes
Clubs	Clubs	£ 12.50/18 holes

Credit cards Cartes de crédit
VISA - Eurocard - MasterCard - AMEX - DC

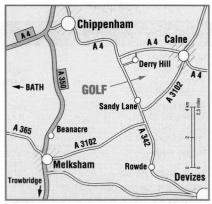

Access Accès : M4 Exit 16, then A420, A3102 to Calne, then A4. At T-junction, turn left → Derry Hill, Golf on left side. **Map 6 on page 417** Carte 6 Page 417

GOLF COURSE
PARCOURS

17 /20

Site	Site	
Maintenance	Entretien	
Architect	Architecte	David Thomas
Type	Type	parkland
Relief	Relief	
Water in play	Eau en jeu	
Exp. to wind	Exposé au vent	
Trees in play	Arbres en jeu	

Scorecard Carte de score	Chp. Chp.	Mens Mess.	Ladies Da.
Length Long.	6659	6270	5669
Par	72	72	77

Advised golfing ability Niveau de jeu recommandé	0	12	24	36

Hcp required	Handicap exigé	no

CLUB HOUSE & AMENITIES
CLUB HOUSE ET ANNEXES

6 /10

Pro shop	Pro-shop	
Driving range	Practice	
Sheltered	couvert	no
On grass	sur herbe	yes
Putting-green	putting-green	yes
Pitching-green	pitching green	yes

HOTEL FACILITIES
ENVIRONNEMENT HOTELIER

6 /10

HOTELS HÔTELS

Chilvester Hill house - 3 rooms, D £ 75	Calne
Tél (44) 01249 - 813 981	8 km
Fax (44) 01249 - 814 217	
Fenwicks - 3 rooms, D £ 45	Lower Goanacre
Tél (44) 01249 - 760 645	12 km
Fax (44) 01249 - 821 329	
At the Sign of the Angel	Lacock
6 rooms, D £ 50	6 km
Tel (44) 01249 - 730 230	
Fax (44) 01249 - 730 527	

RESTAURANTS RESTAURANTS

George & Dragon	Rowde
Tel (44) 01380 - 723 053	9 km
At the Sign of the Angel	Lacock
Tel (44) 01249 - 730 230	6 km

452

With Carlisle, this is another little known "gem of a course." The only thing is finding the opportunity to drive as far as this region and the intuition to stop off here. At 1,000 ft. above sea level, it provides some splendid views over the Lake District peaks which soon soothe your sorely tested golfer's nerves. In fact the whole course gives an impression of peace and tranquillity. This is a typical James Braid layout, where the purity of style - there is nothing superfluous on this course - is plain to see: few fairway bunkers, careful thought required for each shot, punishment in keeping with the errors of your ways and rewards for the good shot. You can pitch high balls into the greens but the wisest decision will always be to roll the ball up to the pin (or thereabouts). Fair (despite a few blind shots), direct and clear, the course is rather hilly and at least looks tiring to play. We say "looks" because the senior members walk it several times a week. So maybe you can too.

Non loin de Carlisle, voici encore un petit joyau méconnu. Mais il faut avoir l'occasion de venir dans cette région, et de l'intuition pour s'y arrêter. A 300 mètres d'altitude, il offre des vues superbes sur les montagnes du Lake District, qui vous calmeront vite si vous êtes arrivé sur les nerfs. Tout comme le parcours vous donnera une sensation de paix. C'est un des plus typiques de James Braid. La pureté de son style, où rien n'est inutile, transparaît ici : peu de bunkers de fairway, une exigence de réflexion avant chaque coup, des punitions à la hauteur des fautes, et des récompenses pour les bons coups. Arrivés à proximité des greens, vous aurez la possibilité de faire des balles levées, mais la bonne décison consiste à la faire rouler. Franc (malgré des coups aveugles), direct et clair, ce parcours est assez accidenté et paraît fatigant, mais les membres seniors le jouent à pied plusieurs fois par semaine. Alors...

Brampton Golf Club

Tarn Road
ENG - BRAMPTON, Cumbria CA8 1HN

Office	Secrétariat	(44) 016977 - 2255
Pro shop	Pro-shop	(44) 016977 - 2255
Fax	Fax	
Situation	Situation	

15 km from Carlisle (pop. 100 562)

Annual closure	Fermeture annnuelle	no
Weekly closure	Fermeture hebdomadaire	no

Fees main season
Tarifs haute saison full day

	Week days Semaine	We/Bank holidays We/Férié
Individual Individuel	£ 20	£ 25
Couple Couple	£ 40	£ 50

Caddy	Caddy	no
Electric Trolley	Chariot électrique	£ 5/18 holes
Buggy	Voiturette	no
Clubs	Clubs	£ 7/18 holes

Credit cards Cartes de crédit — no

Access Accès : M6 to Carlisle. Jct 43, then A69.
At Brampton, B6413 → Castle Carrock.
Golf on right side.
Map 2 on page 409 Carte 2 Page 409

GOLF COURSE / PARCOURS

17/20

Site	Site	▰▰▰▰▰
Maintenance	Entretien	▰▰▰▰▰
Architect	Architecte	James Braid
Type	Type	parkland
Relief	Relief	▰▰▰
Water in play	Eau en jeu	▰
Exp. to wind	Exposé au vent	▰▰
Trees in play	Arbres en jeu	▰▰

Scorecard Carte de score	Chp. Chp.	Mens Mess.	Ladies Da.
Length Long.	5766	5475	4930
Par	72	72	74

Advised golfing ability		0 12 24 36
Niveau de jeu recommandé		▰▰▰▰▰
Hcp required	Handicap exigé	no

CLUB HOUSE & AMENITIES / CLUB HOUSE ET ANNEXES

7/10

Pro shop	Pro-shop	▰▰▰▰
Driving range	Practice	▰▰▰
Sheltered	couvert	no
On grass	sur herbe	yes
Putting-green	putting-green	yes
Pitching-green	pitching green	yes

HOTEL FACILITIES / ENVIRONNEMENT HOTELIER

6/10

HOTELS HÔTELS

Farlam Hall — Brampton
12 rooms, D £ 140 (with dinner) — 3 km
Tel (44) 016977 - 46 234, Fax (44) 016977 - 46 683

Kirby Moor Country House — Brampton 5 km
6 rooms, D £ 48
Tel (44) 016977 - 3893, Fax (44) 016977 - 41 847

Crown Hotel — Wetheral
50 rooms, D £ 116 — 13 km
Tel (44) 01228 - 561 888, Fax (44) 01228 - 561 637

Crown + Mitre - 97 rooms, D £ 99 — Carlisle 15 km
Tel (44) 01228 - 25 491, Fax (44) 01228 - 514 553

RESTAURANTS RESTAURANTS

The Weary Sportsman (Pub) — Castle Carrock 5 km
Tél (44) 016977 - 70 230

No 10 - Tel (44) 01228 - 24 183 — Carlisle 15 km

453

You come here first and foremost to visit Durham, which has retained many vestiges of the Norman conquest, including a castle and an amazing cathedral which in many ways is quite unique. But this course is not to be outshone, as it is laid out around a castle flanked by a church, which both add to the majesty of what is a fine Harry Colt design. A good number of isolated trees are very much in play and seem to detach themselves from the woods like fairway sentinels. A large ravine is another hazard which has to be crossed three times over a wobbling bridge which can only take six players at a time. A very interesting and sometimes surprising course, where the finishing holes should be handled with the utmost care. The whole site is quite superb, so what more could you ask for?

On vient d'abord ici pour visiter Durham, qui conserve de multiples traces de la conquête normande, dont le château et surtout une cathédrale étonnante, dont certains aspects décoratifs sont uniques. Ce parcours n'est pas en reste, car il a trouvé place auprès d'un château flanqué de son église, ce qui apporte plus encore de majesté au beau dessin de Harry Colt. De nombreux arbres isolés sont bien en jeu, et se détachent comme les gardes des bois environnants. Un grand ravin vient également en jeu, et doit être traversé trois fois sur un pont chancelant qui ne peut supporter plus de six personnes à la fois. Un parcours très intéressant, parfois surprenant, et dont les derniers trous doivent être considérés avec attention. L'endroit est superbe, que demander de plus ?

Brancepeth Castle Golf Club

Brancepeth Village
ENG - DURHAM, Durham DH7 8EA

Office	Secrétariat	(44) 0191 - 378 0075
Pro shop	Pro-shop	(44) 0191 - 378 0183
Fax	Fax	(44) 0191 - 378 3835
Situation	Situation	

6 km W of Durham (pop. 36 937)

Annual closure	Fermeture annnuelle	no
Weekly closure	Fermeture hebdomadaire	no

Fees main season
Tarifs haute saison

	Week days Semaine	We/Bank holidays We/Férié
		full day
Individual Individuel	£ 29	£ 34
Couple Couple	£ 58	£ 68

Caddy	Caddy	no
Electric Trolley	Chariot électrique	no
Buggy	Voiturette	no
Clubs	Clubs	no

Credit cards Cartes de crédit
VISA - Eurocard - MasterCard

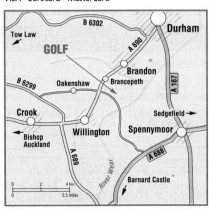

Access Accès : A1 (M) to Durham, then A690 → Crook.
Turn left at crossroads in Brancepeth village. Take slip road left immediately before Castle gates.
Map 2 on page 409 Carte 2 Page 409

GOLF COURSE
PARCOURS

14/20

Site	Site	
Maintenance	Entretien	
Architect	Architecte	Harry S. Colt
Type	Type	parkland
Relief	Relief	
Water in play	Eau en jeu	
Exp. to wind	Exposé au vent	
Trees in play	Arbres en jeu	

Scorecard Carte de score	Chp. Chp.	Mens Mess.	Ladies Da.
Length Long.	5720	5720	5312
Par	70	70	75

Advised golfing ability Niveau de jeu recommandé	0	12	24	36

Hcp required	Handicap exigé	no

CLUB HOUSE & AMENITIES
CLUB HOUSE ET ANNEXES

6/10

Pro shop	Pro-shop	
Driving range	Practice	
Sheltered	couvert	no
On grass	sur herbe	yes
Putting-green	putting-green	yes
Pitching-green	pitching green	yes

HOTEL FACILITIES
ENVIRONNEMENT HOTELIER

5/10

HOTELS HÔTELS

Bridge Toby
46 rooms, D £ 62
Tel (44) 0191 - 378 0524
Fax (44) 0191 - 378 9981
Croxdale
4 km

Royal County
149 rooms, D £ 110
Tel (44) 0191 - 386 6821
Fax (44) 0191 - 386 0704
Durham
6 km

RESTAURANT RESTAURANT

County (Royal County)
Tel (44) 0191 - 386 6821
Durham
6 km

454

Some golfers have called Broadstone the Gleneagles of the south. This heather-clad terrain enhanced with pine, birch, oak, chestnut trees and rhododendrons, has kept all the natural appearance of Tom Dunn's original layout, which was later perfected by Harry Colt. Although the holes are often flat, some of the hills are steep and tiring. Never easy to play, the course is a good test for every compartment of your game: length when you need it, accurate ironwork to the rather large but well defended greens, strategy for judging the right distance and flight to avoid the traps, including several dangerous water hazards. If that were not enough, you will also need an excellent short game to make up for mistakes, with lofted or bump 'n roll approach shots, and an acute sense of observation to make the most of the extremely useful experience of local players. Not forgetting your putting and a stop-off at the fountain on the 10th hole, one of the excellent features of a very likeable course.

Certains l'ont appelé le Gleneagles du sud. En terrain de bruyère, orné de pins, bouleaux, chênes, marronniers et rhododendrons, ce terrain a gardé l'aspect naturel du tracé de Tom Dunn, perfectionné et affiné par Harry Colt. Bien que les trous y soient très souvent plats, certaines montées peuvent être assez fatigantes. Peu facile à jouer, c'est un bon test de tous les secteurs de son jeu : la longueur quand il faut porter assez loin la balle, la précision du jeu de fers vers des greens assez grands mais bien protégés, la stratégie quand il faut bien juger des distances et effets pour éviter les obstacles, dont quelques dangereux obstacles d'eau, le petit jeu pour rattraper toutes les fautes, avec des approches levées ou roulées suivant la situation, et l'observation pour tirer profit de l'expérience fort utile des joueurs locaux. Sans oublier le putting ni de s'arrêter à la fontaine du 10, un des attraits d'une très attachante réalisation.

Broadstone Dorset Golf Club

Wentworth Drive, Off Station Approach
ENG - BROADSTONE, Dorset BH18 8DQ

Office	Secrétariat	(44) 01202 - 692 595
Pro shop	Pro-shop	(44) 01202 - 692 835
Fax	Fax	(44) 01202 - 692 595
Situation	Situation	

7 km from Poole (pop. 133 050)
12 km from Bournemouth (pop. 151 300)

Annual closure	Fermeture annnuelle	no
Weekly closure	Fermeture hebdomadaire	no

Fees main season	Tarifs haute saison		18 holes
		Week days	We/Bank holidays
		Semaine	We/Férié
Individual Individuel		£ 28	£ 40
Couple Couple		£ 56	£ 80

Full weekday: £ 37 - Book in advance

Caddy	Caddy	no
Electric Trolley	Chariot électrique	£ 5/18 holes
Buggy	Voiturette	no
Clubs	Clubs	yes (ask Pro)
Credit cards Cartes de crédit		no (only Pro Shop)

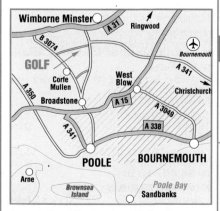

Access Accès : • M3, M27, A31, A349, then Dunyeats Road on the right. • From Poole, B3074, Broadstone Links Road → Blandford, Golf on the right.
Map 6 on page 417 Carte 6 Page 417

GOLF COURSE
PARCOURS **17** /20

Site	Site	
Maintenance	Entretien	
Architect	Architecte	Tom Dunn
		Harry S. Colt (1925)
Type	Type	heathland, hilly
Relief	Relief	
Water in play	Eau en jeu	
Exp. to wind	Exposé au vent	
Trees in play	Arbres en jeu	

Scorecard	Chp.	Mens	Ladies
Carte de score	Chp.	Mess.	Da.
Length Long.	5746	5547	4975
Par	70	70	72

Advised golfing ability	0	12	24	36
Niveau de jeu recommandé				
Hcp required Handicap exigé	certificate			

CLUB HOUSE & AMENITIES
CLUB HOUSE ET ANNEXES **7** /10

Pro shop	Pro-shop	
Driving range	Practice	
Sheltered	couvert	no
On grass	sur herbe	• yes
Putting-green	putting-green	yes
Pitching-green	pitching green	yes

455

HOTEL FACILITIES
ENVIRONNEMENT HOTELIER **7** /10

HOTELS HÔTELS

Mansion House - 28 rooms, D £ 90	Poole
Tel (44) 01202 - 685 666	6 km
Fax (44) 01202 - 665 709	
Royal Bath - 124 rooms, D £ 130	Bournemouth
Tel (44) 01202 - 555 555	8 km
Fax (44) 01202 - 554 158	
The Dormy - 123 rooms, D £ 100	Ferndown
Tel (44) 01202 - 872 121	7 km
Fax (44) 01202 - 895 388	

RESTAURANTS RESTAURANTS

La Roche	Poole
Tel (44) 01202 - 707 333	6 km
Fisherman's Haunt	Christchurch
Tel (44) 01202 - 484 071	10 km

This is one of those resorts that you find either very pretentious or very cosy. All that's missing is the obligatory fitness centre, but that will come. With this said, you would never judge this John Jacobs course to this sort of criteria. The layout was created with much thought given to today's trends in professional and amateur golfing, forcing the player to take decisions as to the line of fire, the type of shot, whether to attack or whether to play safe. Choosing the right tee-boxes for your game is also an important decision. The woods, isolated trees, lakes and bunkers have been used, created or laid out as if geared to all these technical requirements. Dare we say it, here you get the impression of sitting an examination to ascertain your golf playing skills. As a wily craftsman himself, John Jacobs would not necessarily disagree. We will wait until this course mellows a little and acquires the indulgence of some of the more benign "older" courses.

C'est un de ces complexes que l'on trouvera soit très prétentieux, soit très confortable. Il n'y manque que l'inévitable unité de remise en forme, mais cela ne saurait tarder. Cela dit, le parcours dessiné par John Jacobs ne saurait être jugé sur des critères de goût de ce genre ! Le tracé en a été fait avec beaucoup de réflexion sur les tendances des professionnels et des amateurs, il force à prendre des décisions sur la ligne de jeu, le type de coup, l'attaque ou la sécurité, il force même à choisir les départs adaptés à sa force du jour. Les bois, les arbres isolés, les lacs et les bunkers ont été utilisés ou créés, ou disposés en fonction de ces exigences techniques. Dirons-nous que l'on a un peu l'impression de passer un examen d'aptitude à jouer au golf ? Le fin technicien qu'est Jacobs ne dirait pas forcément non. Nous attendrons que ce parcours vieillisse un peu pour prendre un peu de cette indulgence des bons vieux golfs.

The Buckinghamshire Golf Club

Denham Court, Denham Court Drive
ENG - DENHAM, Bucks UB9 5BG

Office	Secrétariat	(44) 01895 - 835 777
Pro shop	Pro-shop	(44) 01895 - 835 777
Fax	Fax	(44) 01895 - 835 210
Situation	Situation	

3 km from Denham
25 km from Central London (pop. 6 679 700)

Annual closure	Fermeture annnuelle	no
Weekly closure	Fermeture hebdomadaire	no

Fees main season	Tarifs haute saison	18 holes

	Week days Semaine	We/Bank holidays We/Férié
Individual Individuel	£ 60	£ 70
Couple Couple	£ 120	£ 140

Booking 48 hrs in advance

Caddy	Caddy	on request/£ 35
Electric Trolley	Chariot électrique	£ 10/18 holes
Buggy	Voiturette	no
Clubs	Clubs	yes

Credit cards Cartes de crédit
VISA - Eurocard - MasterCard - AMEX - DC

456

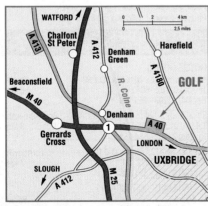

Access Accès : M40 Jct 1. Roundabout on A40, turn into Denham Court Drive, follow signs to the club.
Map 8 on page 420 Carte 8 Page 420

GOLF COURSE
PARCOURS

17 /20

Site	Site	
Maintenance	Entretien	
Architect	Architecte	John Jacobs
Type	Type	parkland
Relief	Relief	
Water in play	Eau en jeu	
Exp. to wind	Exposé au vent	
Trees in play	Arbres en jeu	

Scorecard Carte de score	Chp. Chp.	Mens Mess.	Ladies Da.
Length Long.	6192	5761	5123
Par	72	72	74

Advised golfing ability		0	12	24	36
Niveau de jeu recommandé					
Hcp required	Handicap exigé	no			

CLUB HOUSE & AMENITIES
CLUB HOUSE ET ANNEXES

8 /10

Pro shop	Pro-shop	
Driving range	Practice	
Sheltered	couvert	no
On grass	sur herbe	yes
Putting-green	putting-green	yes
Pitching-green	pitching green	yes

HOTEL FACILITIES
ENVIRONNEMENT HOTELIER

7 /10

HOTELS HÔTELS
De Vere Bull - 93 rooms, D £ 140   Gerrards Cross
Tél (44) 01753 - 885 995   7 km
Fax (44) 01753 - 885 504

Copthorne - 217 rooms, D £ 120   Slough
Tél (44) 01753 - 516 222   12 km
Fax (44) 01753 - 516 237

Courtyard - 148 rooms, D £ 85   Slough
Tél (44) 01753 - 551 551   12 km
Fax (44) 01753 - 553 333

RESTAURANTS RESTAURANTS
Water Hall   Chalfont St Peter
Tel (44) 01494 - 873 430   5 km

Roberto's - Tel(44) 01895 - 632 519   Ickenham 4 km

Waterfront Brasserie   Yiewsley
Tel (44) 0181 - 899 1733   8 km

Played for many a year by J.H. Taylor, this classic course has been profoundly altered throughout the 20th century, in particular to avoid hitting worshippers as they leave the church set in the middle of the course. The changes also cut out many of the blind shots, thereby reducing a little the glorious uncertainty of golf but giving the layout a more forthright feel as it winds its way between majestic sand-dunes. The plant-life here is superb, especially the orchids, and as on many links courses there are very few water hazards (here on the 6th and behind the 13th holes). Dare we say it, these should only bother the higher handicappers. Generally speaking you have to hit the ball straight, as bushes, rough and bunkers await wayward drives, while hilly slopes and pot-bunkers snap up mis-hit approach shots. As the greens are small and steeply contoured, this is a great course for getting your short game together.

Longtemps arpenté par J.H. Taylor, ce classique a été profondément modifié tout au long de ce siècle, en particulier pour éviter de frapper les fidèles de l'église au milieu du parcours. Les modifications ont aussi permis d'éliminer beaucoup de coups aveugles, retirant un peu de la glorieuse incertitude du golf, mais offrant plus de franchise au tracé, à présent mieux insinué entre des dunes majestueuses. On trouve ici une flore sauvage superbe, notamment des orchidées. Comme sur la plupart des links, il y a peu d'obstacles d'eau (au 6 et derrière le 13), mais ils ne concernent que les handicaps élevés. En général, il faut placer la balle, car les buissons, le rough et les bunkers attendent les drives égarés, les mouvements de terrain et les pot bunkers happent les approches imprécises. Comme les greens sont petits et très mouvementés, on travaille son petit jeu sur ce grand parcours...

Burnham & Berrow Golf Club

St Christophers Way
ENG - BURNHAM-ON-SEA, Somerset TA8 2PE

Office	Secrétariat	(44) 01278 - 785 760
Pro shop	Pro-shop	(44) 01278 - 785 545
Fax	Fax	(44) 01278 - 795 440
Situation	Situation	

50 km SW of Bristol (pop. 376 146)
8 km S of Weston-Super-Mare (pop. 64 935)

Annual closure	Fermeture annnuelle	no
Weekly closure	Fermeture hebdomadaire	no

Fees main season	Tarifs haute saison		full day
		Week days Semaine	**We/Bank holidays** We/Férié
Individual Individuel		£ 36	£ 50
Couple Couple		£ 72	£ 100

Caddy	Caddy	on request
Electric Trolley	Chariot électrique	yes
Buggy	Voiturette	no
Clubs	Clubs	yes
Credit cards Cartes de crédit		no

Access Accès : M5 Jct 22, 1,5 km (1 m.)
N. of Burnham-on-Sea. Follow signs to Golf.
Map 6 on page 417 Carte 6 Page 417

GOLF COURSE
PARCOURS
18/20

Site	Site	
Maintenance	Entretien	
Architect	Architecte	Unknown
Type	Type	seaside course, links
Relief	Relief	
Water in play	Eau en jeu	
Exp. to wind	Exposé au vent	
Trees in play	Arbres en jeu	

Scorecard Carte de score	Chp. Chp.	Mens Mess.	Ladies Da.
Length Long.	6151	6012	5227
Par	71	71	74

Advised golfing ability	0	12	24	36
Niveau de jeu recommandé				
Hcp required	Handicap exigé	22 Men, 30 Ladies		

CLUB HOUSE & AMENITIES
CLUB HOUSE ET ANNEXES
7/10

Pro shop	Pro-shop	
Driving range	Practice	
Sheltered	couvert	no
On grass	sur herbe	yes
Putting-green	putting-green	yes
Pitching-green	pitching green	yes

HOTEL FACILITIES
ENVIRONNEMENT HOTELIER
6/10

HOTELS HÔTELS
Dormy House — Golf on site
4 rooms, D £ 65
Tel (44) 01278 - 785 760
Fax (44) 01278 - 795 440

Grand Atlantic — Weston-Super-Mare 8 km
76 rooms, D £ 75
Tel (44) 01934 - 626 543
Fax (44) 01934 - 415 048

Royal Pier — Weston-Super-Mare 8 km
36 rooms, D £ 75
Tel (44) 01934 - 626 644
Fax (44) 01934 - 624 169

RESTAURANT RESTAURANT
Duets — Weston-Super-Mare 8 km
Tel (44) 01934 - 413 428

457

Another luxury golfing programme with a 125-room hotel. The first course has been open since 1993, the second should be up and running by the summer of 1998, designed by Jack Nicklaus and looking promising indeed. The present course, laid out by Alan Higgins, will eventually be the second course but is already good enough to warrant a closer examination. It is wide enough to forgive a few errors of direction (except on the 6th and 8th holes) and can prove to be rather an instructive experience because six holes unwind through a forest, six have water and six are very open and so exposed to the wind. This is certainly no tournament course but it is very pleasant to play for all the family, even though you'll need a little patience with beginners (don't you always?) Wet in Winter and very dry in Summer, this is a site to visit in the Spring or Autumn. Practice facilities are excellent.

Encore un programme golfique de luxe, avec hôtel de 125 chambres. Le premier parcours est ouvert depuis 1993, le second devrait ouvrir au début de cet été 1998, et son dessin de Jack Nicklaus paraît prometteur. Le présent tracé de Alan Higgins deviendra ainsi le complément, mais sa qualité mérite que l'on s'y attarde. Sa largeur permet de pardonner quelques erreurs de direction, sauf aux 6 et 8. En fait, ce parcours sest assez éducatif car six trous se déroulent dans les arbres, six avec de l'eau et six très ouverts, en particulier au vent. Ce n'est certes pas un parcours de grands championnats, mais un bon parcours très agréable, où toute la famille peut évoluer, même s'il faut un peu de patience avec les plus faibles (n'en faut-il pas toujours ?). Humide en hiver, très sec en été, c'est un site à visiter au printemps et en automne, où les installations d'entraînement sont excellentes.

Carden Park Hotel, Golf Resort & Spa
ENG - CHESTER, Ches. CH3 9DQ

Office	Secrétariat	(44) 01829 - 731630
Pro shop	Pro-shop	(44) 01829 - 731500
Fax	Fax	(44) 01829 - 731625
Situation	Situation	

25 km S of Chester (pop. 115 971)
15 km W of Nantwich (pop. 11 695)

Annual closure	Fermeture annnuelle	no
Weekly closure	Fermeture hebdomadaire	no

Fees main season	Tarifs haute saison	18 holes
	Week days Semaine	We/Bank holidays We/Férié
Individual Individuel	£ 30	£ 30
Couple Couple	£ 60	£ 60

Caddy	Caddy	no
Electric Trolley	Chariot électrique	no
Buggy	Voiturette	£ 15/18 holes
Clubs	Clubs	£ 10/18 holes

Credit cards Cartes de crédit
VISA - Eurocard - MasterCard - AMEX - DC

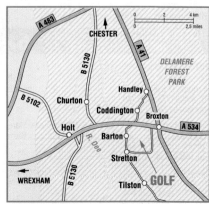

Access Accès : Chester, A41 → Whitchurch. Broxton roundabout, turn right onto A534 → Wrexham.
Golf approx. 2.5 km (1.5 m) on left side.
Map 4 on page 412 Carte 4 Page 412

GOLF COURSE
PARCOURS
14/20

Site	Site	
Maintenance	Entretien	
Architect	Architecte	Alan Higgins
Type	Type	parkland
Relief	Relief	
Water in play	Eau en jeu	
Exp. to wind	Exposé au vent	
Trees in play	Arbres en jeu	

Scorecard Carte de score	Chp. Chp.	Mens Mess.	Ladies Da.
Length Long.	5907	5661	5100
Par	72	72	73

Advised golfing ability	0	12	24	36
Niveau de jeu recommandé				
Hcp required	Handicap exigé	no		

CLUB HOUSE & AMENITIES
CLUB HOUSE ET ANNEXES
8/10

Pro shop	Pro-shop	
Driving range	Practice	
Sheltered	couvert	13 bays
On grass	sur herbe	oppos. end of range
Putting-green	putting-green	yes
Pitching-green	pitching green	yes

HOTEL FACILITIES
ENVIRONNEMENT HOTELIER
8/10

HOTELS HÔTELS
Carden Park Hotel — on site
125 rooms, D £ 150 (all incl.)
Tel (44) 01829 - 731 000
Fax (44) 01829 - 731 032

Rowton Hall - 42 rooms, D £ 90 — Chester
Tel (44) 01244 - 335 262 — 10 km
Fax (44) 01244 - 335 464

Broxton Hall - 12 rooms, D £ 70 — near Chester
Tél (44) 01829 - 782 321 — 5 km
Fax (44) 01829 - 782 330

RESTAURANTS RESTAURANTS
Arkle - Tel (44) 01244 - 324 024 — Chester 15 km
Crabwall Manor — Chester 15 km
Tel (44) 01244 - 851 666
Garden House - Tel (44) 01244 - 320 004 — Chester 15 km

458

	17	7	7

As you drive up past the great links courses from Ayrshire to Carlisle and Scotland, forget the M6 motorway and keep to the A6, which crosses the breath-taking scenery of the Lake District and Hadrian's Wall. If it inspires you the way it inspired Keats, Wordsworth or Beatrix Potter, you could be in for a good day's golfing. Carlisle leaves no-one indifferent, and as this a Tom Simpson design, no-one will be too surprised about that. You will find his trade-mark cross-bunkers (Simpson hated topped shots), greens protected by bunkers on the one side, by bumps and hollows on the other, which offer their own particular brand of difficulty. Plus the never-ending need to think with a clear head on the length and direction of the ideal shot before choosing your club. The par 3s here are outstanding and the par 5s no less memorable. The only shortcoming might be the course's overall length, but hopefully would-be designers will think long and hard before making any alterations.

En remontant des grands links de l'Ayrshire vers Carlisle et l'Ecosse, renoncez à la M6 au profit de l'A6, qui traverse les paysages sublimes du Lake District puis le Mur d'Hadrien. Vous y trouverez peut-être l'inspiration, comme Keats, Wordsworth ou Beatrix Potter. Au moins pour le golf, car Carlisle n'est pas un parcours qui laisse indifférent. La signature de Tom Simpson est une garantie. Vous y trouverez ses cross-bunkers car il haïssait les balles toppées, les greens souvent défendus d'un côté par les bunkers, et de l'autre par des creux et des bosses d'où il n'est guère plus facile de jouer, plus la nécessité de réfléchir sur la longueur et la direction du coup idéal avant de choisir un club. Les par 3 sont ici exceptionnels, les par 5 non moins mémorables. Seul défaut, un certain manque de longueur, mais que l'on réfléchisse bien avant de toucher quoi que ce soit...

Carlisle Golf Club

Aglionby
ENG - CARLISLE, Cumbria CA4 8AG

Office	Secrétariat	(44) 01228 - 513029
Pro shop	Pro-shop	(44) 01228 - 513241
Fax	Fax	(44) 01228 - 513303
Situation	Situation	

3 km from Carlisle (pop. 100 562)

Annual closure	Fermeture annnuelle	no
Weekly closure	Fermeture hebdomadaire	no

Fees main season
Tarifs haute saison 18 holes

	Week days Semaine	We/Bank holidays We/Férié
Individual Individuel	£ 22	£ 30
Couple Couple	£ 44	£ 60

Full days: £ 33/£ 40 - No visitors on Saturdays

Caddy	Caddy	no
Electric Trolley	Chariot électrique	£ 5/18 holes
Buggy	Voiturette	£ 15/18 holes
Clubs	Clubs	no
Credit cards Cartes de crédit		no

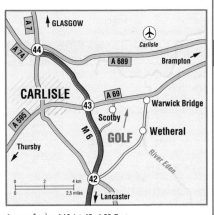

Access Accès : M6 Jct 43, A69 East,
Golf 1 km on the right.
Map 2 on page 409 Carte 2 Page 409

GOLF COURSE
PARCOURS
17 /20

Site	Site	
Maintenance	Entretien	
Architect	Architecte	Tom Simpson Mackenzie Ross
Type	Type	parkland
Relief	Relief	
Water in play	Eau en jeu	
Exp. to wind	Exposé au vent	
Trees in play	Arbres en jeu	

Scorecard Carte de score	Chp. Chp.	Mens Mess.	Ladies Da.
Length Long.	5601	5408	4945
Par	71	71	73

Advised golfing ability Niveau de jeu recommandé		0 12 24 36
Hcp required	Handicap exigé	certificate

CLUB HOUSE & AMENITIES
CLUB HOUSE ET ANNEXES
7 /10

Pro shop	Pro-shop	
Driving range	Practice	
Sheltered	couvert	no
On grass	sur herbe	practice area
Putting-green	putting-green	yes
Pitching-green	pitching green	yes

HOTEL FACILITIES
ENVIRONNEMENT HOTELIER
7 /10

HOTELS HÔTELS

Crown Hotel - 50 rooms, D £ 116   Wetheral 4 km
Tél (44) 01228 - 561 888, Fax (44) 01228 - 561 637

Cumbrian - 70 rooms, D £ 95   Carlisle 5 km
Tél (44) 01228 - 31 951, Fax (44) 01228 - 47 799

Cumbria Park - 49 rooms, D £ 82   Carlisle 5 km
Tél (44) 01228 - 22 887, Fax (44) 01228 - 514 796

Crown + Mitre - 97 rooms, D £ 99   Carlisle 5 km
Tél (44) 01228 - 25 491, Fax (44) 01228 - 514 553

RESTAURANTS RESTAURANTS

No 10   Carlisle
Tel (44) 01228 - 24 183   5 km

Crown Hotel   Wetheral
Tel (44) 01228 - 561 888   4 km

459

In the middle of the Irish Sea, the Isle of Man is reached by ferry or by air from Blackpool. Castledown is located on a sort of triangular-shaped peninsula surrounded by the sea. They say that on the 17th hole, you are driving in Ireland, Scotland, England or Wales. Whatever, this course is exposed to all winds and only the bunkers give any real shelter. Only a few small dunes and rocks give any relief to this flat, superbly-turfed landscape. After the war, Mackenzie Ross brought Castledown back to life with all the talent he showed at Turnberry and even a touch of genius. This is a golfer's paradise on the edge of a rock, but it can be hell if ever a storm sets in and sends players scampering to seek refuge in the hotel on the course. We would recommend a visit here on a fine summer's day.

En plein milieu de la mer d'Irlande, l'Ile de Man est accessible par ferry ou par avion depuis Blackpool. Castletown est situé sur une sorte de presqu'île en forme de triangle cerné par la mer : on dit que du 17, on peut driver en Irlande, en Ecosse, en Angleterre ou au Pays de Galles. En tout cas, ce parcours est ouvert à tous les vents, et seuls les bunkers forment vraiment des abris. Quelques petites dunes et quelques rochers donnent un semblant de relief à ce paysage plat, mais au gazon superbe. Après la guerre, Mackenzie Ross a rendu Castletown à la vie, avec autant de talent qu'à Turnberry, parfois même une forme de génie. C'est un paradis de golfeur sur un bout de rocher, que seule la tempête peut transformer en enfer, mais il ne reste plus alors qu'à se réfugier à l'hôtel sur le site. On conseillera plutôt de venir par une belle journée d'été.

Castletown Golf Club
Fort Island
ENG - CASTLETOWN, Isle of Man

Office	Secrétariat	(44) 01624 - 822201
Pro shop	Pro-shop	(44) 01624 - 822211
Fax	Fax	(44) 01624 - 824633
Situation	Situation	

4.5 km E of Castletown (pop. 3 152)
15 km SW of Douglas (pop. 22 214)

Annual closure	Fermeture annnuelle	no
Weekly closure	Fermeture hebdomadaire	no
Fees main season	Tarifs haute saison	18 holes

	Week days Semaine	We/Bank holidays We/Férié
Individual Individuel	£ 22.50	£ 27.50
Couple Couple	£ 45	£ 55

£ 13 after 4.00 pm

Caddy	Caddy	on request
Electric Trolley	Chariot électrique	£ 9/18 holes
Buggy	Voiturette	£ 20/18 holes
Clubs	Clubs	£ 8/18 holes

Credit cards Cartes de crédit
VISA - Eurocard - MasterCard - AMEX - DC

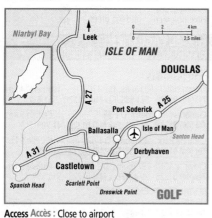

ISLE OF MAN

Niarbyl Bay
Leek
0 — 2 — 4 km
0 — 2,5 miles
DOUGLAS
A 27
Port Soderick — A 25
Ballasalla — Isle of Man
Santon Head
Derbyhaven
A 31
Castletown
Spanish Head — Scarlett Point
Dreswick Point — **GOLF**

Access Accès : Close to airport
Map 9 on page 422 Carte 9 Page 422

GOLF COURSE PARCOURS — 18/20

Site	Site	▬▬▬▬
Maintenance	Entretien	▬▬▬▬▬
Architect	Architecte	Mackenzie Ross
Type	Type	seaside course, links
Relief	Relief	▬▬
Water in play	Eau en jeu	▬
Exp. to wind	Exposé au vent	▬▬▬▬▬▬
Trees in play	Arbres en jeu	▬

Scorecard Carte de score	Chp. Chp.	Mens Mess.	Ladies Da.
Length Long.	6040	5880	5072
Par	72	72	73

Advised golfing ability   0   12   24   36
Niveau de jeu recommandé

Hcp required   Handicap exigé   no

CLUB HOUSE & AMENITIES CLUB HOUSE ET ANNEXES — 6/10

Pro shop	Pro-shop	▬▬▬▬
Driving range	Practice	▬▬
Sheltered	couvert	no
On grass	sur herbe	practice ground only
Putting-green	putting-green	yes
Pitching-green	pitching green	yes

HOTEL FACILITIES ENVIRONNEMENT HOTELIER — 8/10

HOTELS HÔTELS
Links Hotel — Castletown
55 rooms, D £ 60 — on site
Tel (44) 01624 - 822 201, Fax (44) 01624 - 824 633

Empress — Douglas, 15 km
99 rooms, D £ 65
Tél (44) 01624 - 661 155, Fax (44) 01624 - 673 554

Castle Mona - — Douglas, 15 km
66 rooms, D £ 48
Tél (44) 01624 - 624 540, Fax (44) 01624 - 675 360

RESTAURANTS RESTAURANTS
Chablis Cellar — Castletown
Tel (44) 01624 - 823 527 — 3 km

Swiss Chalet — Glen Helen
Tel (44) 01624 - 801 657 — 20 km

Links Hotel - Tel (44) 01624 - 822 201   Castletown, on site

460

They say you shouldn't always expect champions to be great course designers. Well here, Nick Faldo, backed by the top American specialist Steve Smyers, has produced a masterly layout. We admit that our very high score is intended more for experienced players, and many golfers find this course a little over-elaborate with a touch too much sand and water. Those who are afraid that their game might not be up to such a challenge should head shamelessly straight for the front tees. Only there will they learn how to tame a layout which is psychologically rather than really difficult. It was designed with brilliant, bold and uncompromising intelligence. Upholders of the British tradition for discreet courses will be a little surprised here, that's for sure, but you need visual and technical shocks such as this to keep your game moving. The overall excellence of this place is outstanding.

On ne doit pas toujours espérer des champions qu'ils soient de grands architectes. Epaulé par l'excellent spécialiste américain Steve Smyers, Nick Faldo a réussi un coup de maître. Certes, notre note très favorable est plutôt destinée aux joueurs expérimentés, car beaucoup trouvent ce parcours "trop dessiné," avec un rien trop de sable et un peu trop d'eau. Ceux qui ont peur que leur jeu ne soit pas à la hauteur des défis présentés choisiront sans honte les départs avancés, ils apprendront à apprivoiser ce tracé plus difficile psychologiquement que réellement, conçu avec une brillante intelligence, avec hardiesse, sans concessions. Certes, les tenants de la tradition britannique d'une architecture discrète seront ici surpris, mais il faut des chocs visuels et techniques de ce genre pour progresser. La qualité générale de ce complexe est exceptionnelle.

Chart Hills Golf Club

Weeks Lane
ENG - BIDDENDEN, Kent TN27 8JX

Office	Secrétariat	(44) 01580 - 292 222
Pro shop	Pro-shop	(44) 01580 - 292 148
Fax	Fax	(44) 01580 - 292 233
Situation	Situation	

14 km from Ashford (pop. 52 002)
20 km from Maidstone (pop. 136 209)

Annual closure	Fermeture annnuelle	no
Weekly closure	Fermeture hebdomadaire	no

Fees main season	Tarifs haute saison		18 holes
		Week days	We/Bank holidays
		Semaine	We/Férié
Individual Individuel		£ 60	£ 65
Couple Couple		£ 120	£ 130

Monday & Saturday: members only

Caddy	Caddy	on request/£ 15
Electric Trolley	Chariot électrique	no
Buggy	Voiturette	£ 20/18 holes
Clubs	Clubs	£ 10/18 holes

Credit cards Cartes de crédit VISA - MasterCard - AMEX

Access Accès : • M20, Jct 6 to Maidstone. A274 →
Biddenden. After Headcorn, left at Petrol Station,
signpost to Smarden • Ashford, A28 to Tenderden,
A262 to Biddenden, A274 → Headcorn.
Map 7 on page 419 Carte 7 Page 419

GOLF COURSE / PARCOURS — 18/20

Site	Site	
Maintenance	Entretien	
Architect	Architecte	Nick Faldo
		Steven Smyers
Type	Type	parkland,
		open country
Relief	Relief	
Water in play	Eau en jeu	
Exp. to wind	Exposé au vent	
Trees in play	Arbres en jeu	

Scorecard	Chp.	Mens	Ladies
Carte de score	Chp.	Mess.	Da.
Length Long.	6375	5780	4980
Par	72	72	72

Advised golfing ability		0 12 24 36
Niveau de jeu recommandé		
Hcp required	Handicap exigé	no

CLUB HOUSE & AMENITIES / CLUB HOUSE ET ANNEXES — 8/10

Pro shop	Pro-shop	
Driving range	Practice	
Sheltered	couvert	no
On grass	sur herbe	yes
Putting-green	putting-green	yes
Pitching-green	pitching green	yes (2)

HOTEL FACILITIES / ENVIRONNEMENT HOTELIER — 6/10

HOTELS HÔTELS
Eastwell Manor - 23 rooms, D £ 120   Ashford, 20 km
Tel (44) 01233 - 219 955, Fax (44) 01233 - 635 530

Ashford International   Ashford, 14 km
200 rooms, D £ 100
Tel (44) 01233 - 219 988, Fax (44) 01233 - 627 708

Forte Posthouse - 60 rooms, D £ 60   Ashford, 14 km
Tel (44) 01233 - 625 790, Fax (44) 01233 - 643 176

RESTAURANTS RESTAURANTS
West House   Biddenden
Tel (44) 01580 - 291 341   2 km

Star & Eagle   Goudhurst
Tel (44) 01580 - 211 512   20 km

Eastwell Manor   Ashford
Tel (44) 01233 - 219 955   14 km

461

The fairways are carpeted with thick turf which prevents balls from ever rolling too far, trees abound but the fairways are wide and the rough not too severe. A few water hazards threaten and readily swallow up any miscued shots, but they are there to be seen and so won't cause any unpleasant surprises. As on many of James Braid's courses, a sharp short game is of the essence, as is skill in rolling the ball. This is another course that deserves rehabilitation, even if its short yardage may not always be to the liking of golfers who hit the ball a long way. But as long-hitters sometimes tend to hook the ball, the out-of-bounds areas down the left on the front 9 will teach them a little respect. The course's location on the edge of the forest of Bowland in the Ribble Valley makes this an ideal site for a few days off the beaten track exploring rivers, old villages, a Roman camp and an abbey or two.

Ce parcours bénéficie d'un gazon dense, ce qui évite aux balles de trop rouler. Les arbres sont très nombreux, mais les fairways sont larges et les roughs peu pénalisants. Quelques obstacles d'eau menacent ou retiennent quelques mauvais coups, mais ils sont bien visibles et ne sauraient causer de mauvaises surprises. De fait, comme sur de nombreux parcours de James Braid, il est essentiel d'avoir un bon petit jeu, en particulier savoir jouer les balles roulées. Encore un parcours à réhabiliter, même si sa longueur le fait regarder avec indifférence par les frappeurs. Comme ce sont souvent des "hookers," les hors-limites à gauche à l'aller leur apprendront le respect. Sa situation en bordure de la forêt de Bowland, au coeur de la Ribble Valley, en fait un site idéal pour quelques jours hors des sentiers battus, à la découverte des rivières et vieux villages, d'un camp romain ou d'une abbaye.

Clitheroe Golf Club
Whalley Road
ENG - PENDLETON, Lancs BB7 1PP

Office	Secrétariat	(44) 01200 - 422292
Pro shop	Pro-shop	(44) 01943 - 424242
Fax	Fax	(44) 01943 - 422292
Situation	Situation	

3 km S of Clitheroe (pop. 13 548)
15 km NE of Blackburn (pop. 136 612)

Annual closure	Fermeture annnuelle	no
Weekly closure	Fermeture hebdomadaire	no

Fees main season	Tarifs haute saison	full day
	Week days Semaine	We/Bank holidays We/Férié
Individual Individuel	£ 33	£ 39
Couple Couple	£ 66	£ 78

Caddy	Caddy	no
Electric Trolley	Chariot électrique	no
Buggy	Voiturette	no
Clubs	Clubs	no

Credit cards Cartes de crédit
VISA - Eurocard - MasterCard - AMEX - DC - JCB

462

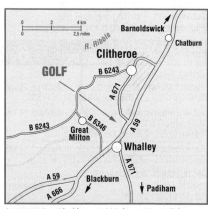

Access Accès : Blackburn, A666 then A59 → Clitheroe.
Golf 3 km on Whalley Road.
Map 4 on page 412 Carte 4 Page 412

GOLF COURSE
PARCOURS

17/20

Site	Site	
Maintenance	Entretien	
Architect	Architecte	James Braid
Type	Type	parkland
Relief	Relief	
Water in play	Eau en jeu	
Exp. to wind	Exposé au vent	
Trees in play	Arbres en jeu	

Scorecard	Chp.	Mens	Ladies
Carte de score	Chp.	Mess.	Da.
Length Long.	5693	5490	4586
Par	71	71	74

Advised golfing ability		0 12 24 36
Niveau de jeu recommandé		
Hcp required	Handicap exigé	no

CLUB HOUSE & AMENITIES
CLUB HOUSE ET ANNEXES

7/10

Pro shop	Pro-shop	
Driving range	Practice	
Sheltered	couvert	no
On grass	sur herbe	yes (3 areas)
Putting-green	putting-green	yes
Pitching-green	pitching green	yes

HOTEL FACILITIES
ENVIRONNEMENT HOTELIER

7/10

HOTELS HÔTELS
Foxfields - 44 rooms, D £ 85   Whalley 5 km
Tel (44) 01254 - 822 556, Fax (44) 01254 - 824 613

Mytton Old Farm - 27 rooms, D £ 70   Whalley 5 km
Tel (44) 01254 - 240 662, Fax (44) 01254 - 248 119

Spread Eagle - 10 rooms, D £ 55   Sawley 6 km
Tel (44) 01200 - 441 202, Fax (44) 01200 - 441 973

RESTAURANTS RESTAURANTS
Northcote Manor   Blackburn 8 km
Tel (44) 01254 - 240 555

Paul Heathcote's   Longridge 18 km
Tel (44) 01772 - 784 969

Auctioner - Tel (44) 01200 - 427 153   Clitheroe 3 km

Foxfields - Tel (44) 01254 - 822 556   Whalley 5 km

COLLINGTREE PARK

14 | **8** | **7**

A corner of the United States in England, a nice change of style for the English but continental Europeans might prefer a little more local colour. With water in play on eight of the 18 holes, numerous well-placed bunkers which lack the "feeling" of what a Simpson, a Colt or a Braid might have produced, and well-balanced difficulties geared to the very many different tee-boxes, Collingtree Park is a good, very pleasant and often very interesting American course but without the often acclaimed visual shocks. It doesn't always blend into the surrounding landscape as well as one might have wished. Johnny Miller was a great player but maybe we expected more of him as a course designer. Problems with the greens probably also weighed in our judgment. At all events, there is no disputing the excellence of practice facilities and services on offer.

Un coin d'Etats-Unis en Angleterre, c'est dépaysant pour les Anglais, mais les continentaux attendent plus de couleur locale. Avec de l'eau en jeu sur huit des 18 trous, des bunkers nombreux, et bien placés, mais aux formes moins "sensuelles" que les créations de Simpson, Braid ou Colt, des difficultés bien balancées suivant les différents (et nombreux) départs, Collingtree Park est un bon parcours à l'américaine, très agréable et souvent très intéressant, mais sans les chocs visuels qui emportent totalement l'adhésion. Son intégration à la nature environnante n'est pas toujours aussi complète qu'on le souhaiterait. Johnny Miller a été un très grand joueur de golf, mais on attendait peut-être davantage de lui comme architecte... Et les problèmes des greens influencent sans doute notre jugement. En tout cas, la qualité remarquable des installations d'entraînement et des services offerts est incontestable.

Collingtree Park Golf Club

Windingbrook Lane
ENG - NORTHAMPTON NN4 0XN

Office	Secrétariat	(44) 01604 - 700000
Pro shop	Pro-shop	(44) 01604 - 700000
Fax	Fax	(44) 01604 - 700000
Situation	Situation	

10 km from Northampton (pop. 180 567)

Annual closure	Fermeture annnuelle	no
Weekly closure	Fermeture hebdomadaire	no
Fees main season	Tarifs haute saison	18 holes

	Week days Semaine	We/Bank holidays We/Férié
Individual Individuel	£ 30	£ 40
Couple Couple	£ 60	£ 80

Booking necessary

Caddy	Caddy	no
Electric Trolley	Chariot électrique	no
Buggy	Voiturette	£ 20/18 holes
Clubs	Clubs	£ 15/18 holes

Credit cards Cartes de crédit
VISA - Eurocard - MasterCard - AMEX - DC

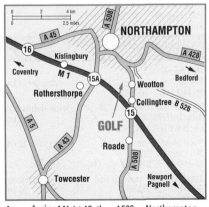

NORTHAMPTON

Access Accès : M1 Jct 15, then A508 → Northampton.
10 mins drive, golf on left.
Map 7 on page 418 Carte 7 Page 418

GOLF COURSE
PARCOURS

14/20

Site	Site	
Maintenance	Entretien	
Architect	Architecte	Johnny Miller
Type	Type	parkland
Relief	Relief	
Water in play	Eau en jeu	
Exp. to wind	Exposé au vent	
Trees in play	Arbres en jeu	

Scorecard Carte de score	Chp. Chp.	Mens Mess.	Ladies Da.
Length Long.	6217	5598	4860
Par	72	72	73

Advised golfing ability Niveau de jeu recommandé	0	12	24	36

Hcp required Handicap exigé no

CLUB HOUSE & AMENITIES
CLUB HOUSE ET ANNEXES

8/10

Pro shop	Pro-shop	
Driving range	Practice	
Sheltered	couvert	16 bays (floodlit)
On grass	sur herbe	yes
Putting-green	putting-green	yes
Pitching-green	pitching green	yes

HOTEL FACILITIES
ENVIRONNEMENT HOTELIER

7/10

HOTELS HÔTELS
Stakis Hotel - 139 rooms, D £ 101   Northampton
Tel (44) 01604 - 700 666   1 km
Fax (44) 01604 - 702 850

Swallow - 120 rooms, D £ 115   Northampton 10 km
Tel (44) 01604 - 768 700, Fax (44) 01604 - 769 011

Courtyard (Marriott)   Northampton 10 km
104 chambres, D £ 80
Tél (44) 01604 - 22 777, Fax (44) 01604 - 35 454

Lime Trees - 25 rooms, D £ 60   Northampton 10 km
Tél (44) 01604 - 32 188, Fax (44) 01604 - 233 012

RESTAURANTS RESTAURANTS
La Fontana (Swallow)   Northampton 10 km
Tel (44) 01604 - 768 700

Roadhouse - Tel (44) 01604 - 863 372   Roade 6 km

French Partridge - Tel (44) 01604 - 870 033 Horton 7 km

463

With Notts, Sherwood Forest and Coxmoor, this region has three no-nonsense courses, of which the latter lies over moorland and is hilly enough to test your fitness as well as your golfing skills. A good score is there for the taking as long as you avoid the traps on some of the dog-leg holes or carry a number of dangerous hazards, but there could be some nasty surprises in store when you come to add up your score. Strategy here is even more important than the standard of your game and the hazards are generally in clear view from the many elevated tee-boxes. Very pleasant to play with the family or friends, there is an obvious parallel to be drawn with the many similar courses found in Surrey, the one reservation being the sameness of several holes.

Entre Notts, Sherwood Forest et Coxmoor, cette région dispose de trois parcours peu contestables. Celui-ci est dans un espace de landes, et assez accidenté pour tester la forme physique autant que golfique. Un bon score est à votre portée du moment que vous savez déjouer les pièges de certains doglegs ou survoler quelques obstacles dangereux, mais on peut avoir des surprises au moment de l'addition. La stratégie est ici encore plus importante que la qualité du jeu, et les obstacles sont généralement visibles car beaucoup de départs sont en hauteur. Très agréable à jouer avec des amis ou en famille, que ce soit en stroke play ou en match-play, ce parcours est à mettre en parallèle avec de nombreux parcours similaires du Surrey, avec une petite restriction sur la similarité de plusieurs trous, qui gêne la précision des souvenirs.

Coxmoor Golf Club
Coxmoor Road
ENG - SUTTON-IN- ASHFIELD, Notts. NG17 5LF

Office	Secrétariat	(44) 01623 - 557359
Pro shop	Pro-shop	(44) 01623 - 559906
Fax	Fax	(44) 01623 - 559854
Situation	Situation	

Annual closure	Fermeture annnuelle	no
Weekly closure	Fermeture hebdomadaire	no

Fees main season
Tarifs haute saison — 18 holes

	Week days Semaine	We/Bank holidays We/Férié
Individual Individuel	£ 28	—
Couple Couple	£ 56	—

27 holes: £ 36 - Full weekday: £ 40
No visitors Tuesdays & weekends

Caddy	Caddy	on request/£ 25
Electric Trolley	Chariot électrique	no
Buggy	Voiturette	no
Clubs	Clubs	no
Credit cards Cartes de crédit		Pro shop only

464

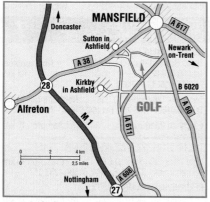

Access Accès : M1 Jct 27. A608 then A611 → Coxmoor
Map 4 on page 412 Carte 4 Page 412

GOLF COURSE
PARCOURS
15/20

Site	Site	■■■■□
Maintenance	Entretien	■■■■□
Architect	Architecte	Unknown
Type	Type	parkland
Relief	Relief	■■□□□
Water in play	Eau en jeu	■□□□□
Exp. to wind	Exposé au vent	■■■□□
Trees in play	Arbres en jeu	■■■□□

Scorecard Carte de score	Chp. Chp.	Mens Mess.	Ladies Da.
Length Long.	5914	5626	4936
Par	73	73	74

Advised golfing ability Niveau de jeu recommandé	0	12	24	36
Hcp required Handicap exigé	no			

CLUB HOUSE & AMENITIES
CLUB HOUSE ET ANNEXES
6/10

Pro shop	Pro-shop	■■■■□
Driving range	Practice	■■■□□
Sheltered	couvert	no
On grass	sur herbe	yes
Putting-green	putting-green	yes
Pitching-green	pitching green	yes

HOTEL FACILITIES
ENVIRONNEMENT HOTELIER
6/10

HOTELS HÔTELS
Pine Lodge - 20 rooms, D £ 60 — Mansfield 4 km
Tel (44) 01623 - 622 308

Swallow -157 rooms, D £ 120 — South Normanton 10 km
Tel (44) 01773 - 812 000
Fax (44) 01773 - 580 032

Royal Moat House — Nottingham 20 km
200 rooms, D £ 100
Tel (44) 0115 - 936 9988, Fax (44) 0115 - 475 667

Stage Hotel - 52 rooms, D £ 53 — Nottingham 20 km
Tel (44) 0115 - 960 3261
Fax (44) 0115 - 969 1040

RESTAURANTS RESTAURANTS
Swallow — South Normanton 10 km
Tel (44) 01773 - 812 000

Sonny's - Tel (44) 0115 - 947 3041 — Nottingham 20 km

CUMBERWELL PARK

From the back tees, this is a tough course with at least two par 5s that are definitely unreachable in two. The designer made up for this, though, by refusing those huge par 3s and preferring shorter but more technical holes. With four short par 4s, you'll find a good number of opportunities to scent some of those evasive birdies. Adrian Stiff has cleverly combined stress and relaxation. In doing so, he has made Cumberwell Park a very pleasant course to play over gently rolling landscape, dotted with ash and oak trees and crossed by a stream that is very much a part of your game. The terrain has been carefully contoured, without overdoing the visual side but with extra concern for enhancing the course within its environment. For the time being, this promising layout is good value for money and its success has prompted the promoters to begin building a second course. The clubhouse extends a warm welcome and the practice facilities are well above the norm for the UK.

Des départs arrière, c'est un parcours solide, avec au moins deux par 5 pratiquement intouchables en deux, mais l'architecte a compensé en renonçant à ces par 3 interminables, au profit de petits trous plus techniques. Avec quatre par 4 courts, les occasions de birdie ne manqueront pas. Adrian Stiff a bien alterné la tension et la détente, ce qui rend Cumberwell Park très agréable à jouer, dans ce paysage gentiment vallonné et orné de chênes et de pins, où circule un cours d'eau bien mis en jeu. Le modelage du terrain a été fait avec soin, sans excès visuels, mais avec un bon souci de mettre en valeur le parcours dans son environnement. Cette réalisation prometteuse présente pour l'instant un bon rapport qualité/prix, et son succès a incité les promoteurs à entreprendre la construction d'un second parcours. Le Clubhouse est accueillant, les installations de practice très au-dessus des normes britanniques.

Cumberwell Park Golf Club
ENG - BRADFORD-ON-AVON, Wiltshire, BA15 2PQ

Office	Secrétariat	(44) 01225 - 863 322
Pro shop	Pro-shop	(44) 01225 - 862 332
Fax	Fax	(44) 01225 - 868 160
Situation	Situation	

8 km E of Bath (pop. 78 689)

Annual closure	Fermeture annnuelle	no
Weekly closure	Fermeture hebdomadaire	no
Fees main season	Tarifs haute saison	18 holes

	Week days Semaine	We/Bank holidays We/Férié
Individual Individuel	£ 18	£ 25
Couple Couple	£ 36	£ 50

Full day: £ 25 - £ 40 (weekends)

Caddy	Caddy	no
Electric Trolley	Chariot électrique	no
Buggy	Voiturette	£ 15/18 holes
Clubs	Clubs	£ 10/18 holes

Credit cards Cartes de crédit
VISA - MasterCard - AMEX - DC

Access Accès : On A363 between Bathford and Bradford-on-Avon
Map 6 on page 417 Carte 6 Page 417

GOLF COURSE
PARCOURS
17 /20

Site	Site	
Maintenance	Entretien	
Architect	Architecte	Adrian Stiff
Type	Type	parkland
Relief	Relief	
Water in play	Eau en jeu	
Exp. to wind	Exposé au vent	
Trees in play	Arbres en jeu	

Scorecard Carte de score	Chp. Chp.	Mens Mess.	Ladies Da.
Length Long.	6218	5902	5070
Par	72	72	72

Advised golfing ability		0 12 24 36
Niveau de jeu recommandé		
Hcp required	Handicap exigé	certificate

CLUB HOUSE & AMENITIES
CLUB HOUSE ET ANNEXES
7 /10

Pro shop	Pro-shop	
Driving range	Practice	
Sheltered	couvert	no
On grass	sur herbe	yes
Putting-green	putting-green	yes
Pitching-green	pitching green	yes

HOTEL FACILITIES
ENVIRONNEMENT HOTELIER
7 /10

465

HOTELS HÔTELS
Widbrook Grange — Bradford-on-Avon
19 rooms, D £ 90 — 3 km
Tel (44) 01225 - 863 173
Fax (44) 01225 - 862 890

The Lodge — Bathford
11 rooms, from D £ 70 — 8 km
Tel (44) 01225 - 858 467
Fax (44) 01225 - 858 172

Old School House — Bathford
4 rooms, D £ 70 — 8 km
Tel (44) 01225 - 859 593
Fax (44) 01225 - 859 590

RESTAURANTS RESTAURANTS
Hole in the Wall — Bath
Tel (44) 01225 - 425 242 — 12 km

Olive Tree - Tel (44) 01225 - 447 928 — Bath 12 km

Together with Bowood, this is one of the most promising new courses in this very romantic region of moor-land and heathland. It is also as surprising as the gardens of neighbouring Torquay might appear to foreign visitors... they would do the French Riviera proud. This new course is an inland and rather hilly layout (buggy highly recommended, and the club has 30 for hire). Designer Jeremy Pern has created many very good courses on the continent of Europe (particularly in France) but this is probably one of his very best. He has used land very cleverly indeed, forcing players from the back-tees to carry the ball a long way, particularly to clear the many water hazards. First time out, this is your typical match-play course. The clubhouse (with cottages) is remarkably well equipped with a pool, sauna, jacuzzi and gymnasium.

Avec Bowood, c'est l'une des réalisations prometteuses dans cette région très romantique aux paysages de landes, mais souvent aussi surprenante que les jardins de Torquay, dignes de la Rivièra française, à quelques kilomètres de Dartmouth, d'où partirent les navires des croisades. Ce nouveau parcours est à l'intérieur des terres, et assez accidenté pour ne pas avoir honte d'emprunter une voiturette (il y en a ici plus de 30). L'architecte Jeremy Pern a fait de nombreux très bons parcours sur le continent (en France notamment), et celui-ci est sans doute l'un de ses tout meilleurs, notamment par l'utilisation très intelligente du terrain, obligeant à porter loin la balle des départs arrière, en particulier au-dessus des nombreux obstacles d'eau. La première fois, c'est le parcours de match-play typique. Le Clubhouse (avec cottages) est remarquablement équipé, avec piscine, sauna, jaccuzzi et gymnase.

Dartmouth Golf & Country Club

Blackawton
ENG - TOTNES, Devon TQ9 7 DE

Office	Secrétariat	(44) 01803 - 712 686
Pro shop	Pro-shop	(44) 01803 - 712 650
Fax	Fax	(44) 01803 - 712 628
Situation	Situation	

12 km S of Totnes (pop. 7 018)
4 km W of Dartmouth (pop. 5 712)

Annual closure	Fermeture annnuelle	no
Weekly closure	Fermeture hebdomadaire	no

Fees main season
Tarifs haute saison — full day

	Week days Semaine	We/Bank holidays We/Férié
Individual Individuel	£ 25	£ 40
Couple Couple	£ 50	£ 80

Caddy	Caddy	£ 20/18 holes
Electric Trolley	Chariot électrique	no
Buggy	Voiturette	£ 15/18 holes
Clubs	Clubs	£ 10/18 holes

Credit cards Cartes de crédit
VISA - Eurocard - MasterCard - AMEX

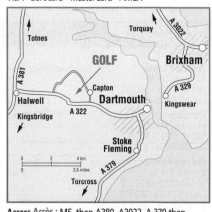

Access Accès : M5, then A380, A3022, A 379 then A3122. Golf on right hand side.
Map 6 on page 417 Carte 6 Page 417

GOLF COURSE
PARCOURS

16/20

Site	Site	
Maintenance	Entretien	
Architect	Architecte	Jeremy Pern
Type	Type	parkland, hilly
Relief	Relief	
Water in play	Eau en jeu	
Exp. to wind	Exposé au vent	
Trees in play	Arbres en jeu	

Scorecard Carte de score	Chp. Chp.	Mens Mess.	Ladies Da.
Length Long.	6544	6064	5169
Par	72	72	73

Advised golfing ability	0 12 24 36	
Niveau de jeu recommandé		
Hcp required	Handicap exigé	certificate

CLUB HOUSE & AMENITIES
CLUB HOUSE ET ANNEXES

9/10

Pro shop	Pro-shop	
Driving range	Practice	
Sheltered	couvert	4 bays
On grass	sur herbe	no
Putting-green	putting-green	yes
Pitching-green	pitching green	yes

HOTEL FACILITIES
ENVIRONNEMENT HOTELIER

6/10

HOTELS HÔTELS
Fingals (Old Coombe Farm)   Dittisham
9 rooms, D £ 75   6 km
Tel (44) 01803 - 722 398
Fax (44) 01803 - 722 401

Royal Castle - 25 rooms, D £ 100   Dartmouth
Tel (44) 01803 - 833 033   8 km
Fax (44) 01803 - 835 445

Dart Marina - 35 rooms, D £ 75   Dartmouth
Tel (44) 01803 - 832 580   8 km
Fax (44) 01803 - 835 040

RESTAURANTS RESTAURANTS
Carved Angel   Dartmouth
Tel (44) 01803 - 832 465   8 km

Billy Budd's   Dartmouth
Tel(44) 01803 - 834 842   8 km

466

Here we are at the traditional heart of England and this layout seems to be so symbolic of old English golf that even the card still uses the old term "bogey" instead of "par". It is rather as if the course were gently reminding you that you shouldn't expect miracles on the tougher holes. Let's forget that this should be a par 69 and be proud of playing to our handicap. Designed by Herbert Fowler, this is the perfect heathland course with just the right amount of trees, bunkers (sometimes very deep), heather, a splattering of water and the contours to test your legs and pose a few problems of kicks left and right. There is nothing easy about it, but nothing impossible, either. You can pitch your approach or, preferably, roll it onto the green. Golf here is built into nature and the two lie very comfortably together.

C'est ici le cœur traditionnel de l'Angleterre, et ce parcours est comme le symbole des parcours de golf anglais, au point que la carte de score porte le terme "bogey" au lieu de par, comme pour souligner avec indulgence que l'on n'attend pas de miracles sur les trous difficiles. Oublions donc que ce devrait être un par 69, et soyons fier de jouer notre handicap. Dessiné par Herbert Fowler, c'est le parfait parcours de bruyère, avec les arbres qu'il faut, les bunkers qu'il faut (parfois très profonds), la bruyère bien sûr, quelques soupçons d'eau, des reliefs pour tester les jambes et poser quelques problèmes de rebonds. Rien de facile mais rien d'impossible. On peut y jouer des coups levés, mais plutôt des balles roulées. Le golf est ici logé dans la nature, et il s'y trouve bien à l'aise.

Delamere Forest Golf Club
Station Road, Delamere
ENG - NORTHWICH, Cheshire CW8 2JE

Office	Secrétariat	(44) 01606 - 883264
Pro shop	Pro-shop	(44) 01606 - 883307
Fax	Fax	
Situation	Situation	

23 km E of Chester (pop.115 971)

Annual closure	Fermeture annnuelle	no
Weekly closure	Fermeture hebdomadaire	no

Fees main season	Tarifs haute saison	18 holes
	Week days Semaine	We/Bank holidays We/Férié
Individual Individuel	£ 30	£ 35
Couple Couple	£ 60	£ 70

Full weekdays: £ 40 - No 3 or 4-balls on weekends
No visitors on medal day (ask before coming).

Caddy	Caddy	no
Electric Trolley	Chariot électrique	no
Buggy	Voiturette	no
Clubs	Clubs	£ 10/18 holes

Credit cards Cartes de crédit   no

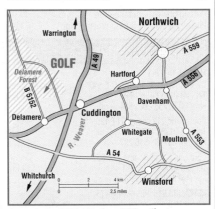

Access Accès : M6 Jct 19, then A556 → Chester.
Golf on right side.
Map 4 on page 412 Carte 4 Page 412

GOLF COURSE
PARCOURS   15/20

Site	Site	▰▰▰▰▱
Maintenance	Entretien	▰▰▰▱▱
Architect	Architecte	Herbert Fowler
Type	Type	parkland, heathland
Relief	Relief	▰▰▰▱▱
Water in play	Eau en jeu	▰▱▱▱▱
Exp. to wind	Exposé au vent	▰▰▰▱▱
Trees in play	Arbres en jeu	▰▰▰▱▱

Scorecard Carte de score	Chp. Chp.	Mens Mess.	Ladies Da.
Length Long.	5463	5463	4972
Par	72	72	72

Advised golfing ability	0	12	24	36
Niveau de jeu recommandé		▰▰▰▰▰▰		

Hcp required   Handicap exigé   no

CLUB HOUSE & AMENITIES
CLUB HOUSE ET ANNEXES   6/10

Pro shop	Pro-shop	▰▰▰▱▱
Driving range	Practice	▰▰▱▱▱
Sheltered	couvert	no
On grass	sur herbe	yes
Putting-green	putting-green	yes
Pitching-green	pitching green	no

467

HOTEL FACILITIES
ENVIRONNEMENT HOTELIER   7/10

HOTELS HÔTELS
Nunsmere Hall   Sandiway 2 km
31 rooms, D £ 120
Tel (44) 01606 - 543 000, Fax (44) 01606 - 889 055

Hartford Hall   Northwich 5 km
20 rooms, D £ 65
Tel (44) 01606 - 75 711, Fax (44) 01606 - 782 285

Rookery Hall   Nantwich 20 km
45 rooms, D £ 95
Tel (44) 01270 - 610 016, Fax (44) 01270 - 626 027

Oaklands -11 rooms, D £ 55   Weaverham 5 km
Tel (44) 01606 - 853 249, Fax (44) 01606 - 852 419

RESTAURANTS RESTAURANTS
Arkle - Tel (44) 01244 - 324 024   Chester 22 km

Garden House   Chester
Tel(44) 01244 - 320 004   22 km

Along with Aberdovey, this is one of the few golf courses to have its own railway station. It also has the type of Clubhouse architecture that reminds you very much of a country residence, and, last but not least, is the type of course that makes you want to take up golf and continue playing for ever. There is nothing particularly spectacular about it, but no Harry Colt course is ever bland. It also has its share of *clichés* that are typical of other courses he has designed. Here, there are some cleverly placed bunkers but which never bar the entrance to greens (except on the 11th hole), trees but no forest, no hidden terrors, no heather to bury your ball in and no water hazards. It is also a nice length for players who will never hit it as far as Tiger Woods even if they do use high-tech drivers. A course is always an adversary, but this one is fair and most likeable.

C'est un des seuls golfs, avec Aberdovey, qui dispose de sa propre station de chemin de fer. Il a aussi ce genre de Clubhouse dont l'architecture vous donne des idées de maison de campagne. Et c'est enfin le genre de parcours qui donne envie de commencer le golf, et de continuer à l'aimer au point de devenir un jour "oldest member" quelque part. Il n'a rien de très spectaculaire, mais un tracé de Harry Colt n'est jamais banal, même s'il existe des "clichés," typiques d'autres parcours qu'il a dessiné. Ici, il y a des bunkers bien placés mais pas en travers de la route du green (sauf au 11), des arbres mais pas de forêt, rien d'horrible n'est caché, il n'y a pas de bruyère pour happer les balles, pas d'obstacles d'eau, et la longueur est très favorable aux joueurs qui n'auront jamais la puissance de Tiger Woods, même avec un driver high-tech. Si le parcours est l'adversaire du golfeur, Denham est un "jolly good fellow."

Denham Golf Club

Tilehouse Lane
ENG - DENHAM, Bucks UB9 5DE

Office	Secrétariat	(44) 01895 - 832022
Pro shop	Pro-shop	(44) 01895 - 832801
Fax	Fax	(44) 01895 - 835340
Situation	Situation	

8 km from Slough (pop. 101 066)
25 km from Central London (pop. 6 679 700)

Annual closure	Fermeture annnuelle	no
Weekly closure	Fermeture hebdomadaire	no
Christmas Day only		

Fees main season	Tarifs haute saison		18 holes
		Week days Semaine	We/Bank holidays We/Férié
Individual Individuel		£ 35	—
Couple Couple		£ 70	—

Full weekday: £ 50 each - No visitors at weekends

Caddy	Caddy	on request/£ 25
Electric Trolley	Chariot électrique	no
Buggy	Voiturette	no
Clubs	Clubs	£ 10/18 holes
Credit cards Cartes de crédit		not for greenfees

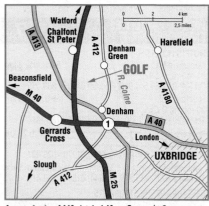

Access Accès : M40, Jct 1, A40 → Gerrards Cross, then A412 → Watford. 2nd left to Club house.
Map 8 on page 420 Carte 8 Page 420

GOLF COURSE
PARCOURS

15/20

Site	Site	
Maintenance	Entretien	
Architect	Architecte	Harry S. Colt
Type	Type	parkland
Relief	Relief	
Water in play	Eau en jeu	
Exp. to wind	Exposé au vent	
Trees in play	Arbres en jeu	

Scorecard	Chp.	Mens	Ladies
Carte de score	Chp.	Mess.	Da.
Length Long.	5806	5543	5014
Par	70	70	72

Advised golfing ability	0	12	24	36
Niveau de jeu recommandé				
Hcp required	Handicap exigé		28 Men, 36 Ladies	

CLUB HOUSE & AMENITIES
CLUB HOUSE ET ANNEXES

7/10

Pro shop	Pro-shop	
Driving range	Practice	
Sheltered	couvert	no
On grass	sur herbe	yes
Putting-green	putting-green	yes
Pitching-green	pitching green	no

HOTEL FACILITIES
ENVIRONNEMENT HOTELIER

7/10

HOTELS HÔTELS
De Vere Bull - 93 rooms, D £ 140 — Gerrards Cross
Tel (44) 01753 - 885 995 — 5 km
Fax (44) 01753 - 885 504

Copthorne 217 rooms, D £ 120 — Slough
Tel (44) 01753 - 516 222 — 11 km
Fax (44) 01753 - 516 237

Courtyard - 148 Rooms, D £ 85 — Slough
Tel (44) 01753 - 551 551 — 11 km
Fax (44) 01753 - 553 333

RESTAURANTS RESTAURANTS
Water Hall — Chalfont St Peter
Tel (44) 01494 - 873 430 — 3 km

Roberto's - Tel (44) 01895 - 632 519 — Ickenham 6 km

Waterfront Brasserie — Yiewsley 10 km
Tel (44) 0181 - 899 1733

468

This is a 36-hole complex, although the more intimate "West" course is reserved more for members. The "East" course is more like a tournament layout with mounds designed for spectators. Designed by the very talented Robert Cupp, the American style is never too loud and you can even sometimes roll your ball onto the green. The many different tee-boxes add to the variety and allow you to approach the course with the caution it deserves first time out, as some of the hazards are hard to spot and game strategy requires some careful thought. Start with a round of match-play, an excellent idea especially since the finishing holes are very impressive. The appeal of the site is supplemented by the hotel on site, a superb driving range and a huge clubhouse.

Cet ensemble comprend 36 trous, mais le parcours "Ouest," plus intime, est à priori réservé aux membres. Celui-ci ressemble davantage à un parcours de tournoi, avec des buttes prévues pour accueillir des spectateurs. Dessiné par le très talentueux Robert Cupp, le style américain n'est pourtant pas trop agressif, il est parfois même possible d'arriver en roulant sur les greens. La multiplicité des départs permet de renouveler chaque fois les plaisirs, mais aussi, la première fois, de reconnaître prudemment le parcours, car certains obstacles sont peu visibles, et la stratégie du jeu réclame aussi quelque réflexion. Commencer par jouer en match-play sera d'autant plus agréable que le "finish" est excellent. Pour situer la séduction du lieu, ajoutons l'hôtel sur place, un practice superbe et un vaste Clubhouse.

East Sussex National
Little Horsted
ENG - UCKFIELD, East Sussex TN22 5ES

Office	Secrétariat	(44) 01825 - 880 088
Pro shop	Pro-shop	(44) 01825 - 880 256
Fax	Fax	(44) 01825 - 880 012
Situation	Situation	

3 km S of Uckfield (pop. 12 090)
10 km N of Lewes (pop. 15 376)

Annual closure	Fermeture annnuelle	no
Weekly closure	Fermeture hebdomadaire	no
Fees main season	Tarifs haute saison	18 holes

	Week days Semaine	We/Bank holidays We/Férié
Individual Individuel	£ 55	£ 55*
Couple Couple	£ 110	£ 110

* Sunday only - Weekdays: £ 80 for 36 holes & meal

Caddy	Caddy	on request/£ 10/15
Electric Trolley	Chariot électrique	no
Buggy	Voiturette	£ 20/18 holes
Clubs	Clubs	£ 15/18 holes

Credit cards Cartes de crédit
VISA - Eurocard - MasterCard - AMEX - DC - JCB

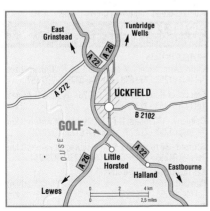

Access Accès : London, A23 then A22 through East Grinstead, Uckfield. Golf 4.5 km South of Uckfield on A22. **Map 7 on page 419** Carte 7 Page 419

GOLF COURSE
PARCOURS   17 /20

Site	Site	
Maintenance	Entretien	
Architect	Architecte	Robert E. Cupp
Type	Type	open country
Relief	Relief	
Water in play	Eau en jeu	
Exp. to wind	Exposé au vent	
Trees in play	Arbres en jeu	

Scorecard Carte de score	Chp. Chp.	Mens Mess.	Ladies Da.
Length Long.	6424	6084	4764
Par	72	72	72

Advised golfing ability		0 12 24 36
Niveau de jeu recommandé		
Hcp required	Handicap exigé	certificate

CLUB HOUSE & AMENITIES
CLUB HOUSE ET ANNEXES   8 /10

Pro shop	Pro-shop	
Driving range	Practice	
Sheltered	couvert	no
On grass	sur herbe	yes
Putting-green	putting-green	yes
Pitching-green	pitching green	yes

469

HOTEL FACILITIES
ENVIRONNEMENT HOTELIER   7 /10

HOTELS HÔTELS

Horsted Place Hotel	Uckfield
20 rooms, D £ 130	adjacent
Tel (44) 01825 - 750 581	
Fax (44) 01825 - 750 459	

Hooke Hall	Uckfield
9 rooms, D £ 65	3 km
Tel (44) 01825 - 761 578	
Fax (44) 01825 - 768 025	

RESTAURANTS RESTAURANTS

Horsted Place Hotel	Uckfield
Tel (44) 01825 - 750 581	adjacent

Pailin	Lewes
Tel (44) 01273 - 473 906	10 km

La Scaletta (Hooke Hall)	Uckfield
Tel (44) 01825 - 761 578	3 km

Golfers who love lush green courses, neatly mown rough, soft greens and trees which shelter from the wind, and who like to get a tan in the process should avoid all the courses on this side of England. On this coast you play golf with all the clubs in your bag, with your head, your technical know-how, all the inspiration you can muster and with locals who will explain where you should hit the ball and where the greens and pins actually are. Fairhaven is simply a great course, not really beautiful from the style point of view, but honest, absorbing, exciting and very well maintained. There are others that have all these attributes but they don't have the pureness of style. To play well here, it's always the same thing: hit it straight, hard and clean. Otherwise don't bother too much counting your strokes, take the gimmies or make full use of the strokes you are given.

Ceux qui aiment les parcours bien verts, les roughs bien tondus, les greens bien mous, les arbres qui abritent du vent, et bronzer en plus, doivent éviter tous les golfs de cette côte d'Angleterre. Ici, on joue au golf avec tous ses clubs et sa tête, avec son bagage technique, avec l'inspiration du moment et avec les joueurs du coin qui vont vous expliquer où sont les points cardinaux, s'il y a des drapeaux au bout des fairways, et où. Fairhaven est simplement un grand parcours pas très très beau (au sens esthétique du terme), mais franc, absorbant, passionnant, très bien entretenu. Il en est d'autres qui ont toutes ces qualités, mais pas la pureté du style. Pour bien le jouer, il faut la même chose, taper droit, fort, nettement. Ou alors ne pas trop s'occuper de compter les coups, ceux que l'on donne et ceux que l'on reçoit.

Fairhaven Golf Club

Lytham Hall Park, Ansdell
ENG - LYTHAM ST ANNE'S, Lancs FY8 4JU

Office	Secrétariat	(44) 01253 - 736741
Pro shop	Pro-shop	(44) 01253 - 736976
Fax	Fax	(44) 01253 - 731461
Situation	Situation	

close to Lytham St Anne's (pop. 40 866)
9 km from Blackpool (pop. 146 069)

Annual closure	Fermeture annnuelle	no
Weekly closure	Fermeture hebdomadaire	no
Fees main season	Tarifs haute saison	18 holes

	Week days Semaine	We/Bank holidays We/Férié
Individual Individuel	£ 35	—
Couple Couple	£ 70	—

Full weekdays: £ 45
Weekends: limited access (upon request)

Caddy	Caddy	no
Electric Trolley	Chariot électrique	no
Buggy	Voiturette	no
Clubs	Clubs	no

Credit cards Cartes de crédit
VISA - MasterCard (Pro shop only)

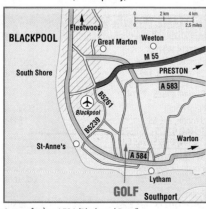

Access Accès : A584 (Blackpool Road).
B5261 Next to rugby ground
Map 5 on page 415 Carte 5 Page 415

GOLF COURSE
PARCOURS

17/20

Site	Site	▰▰▰▱
Maintenance	Entretien	▰▰▰▱
Architect	Architecte	James Braid Jim Steer
Type	Type	links
Relief	Relief	▰▱▱▱
Water in play	Eau en jeu	▱▱▱▱
Exp. to wind	Exposé au vent	▰▰▰▱
Trees in play	Arbres en jeu	▰▱▱▱

Scorecard Carte de score	Chp. Chp.	Mens Mess.	Ladies Da.
Length Long.	6195	5847	5386
Par	74	72	75

Advised golfing ability Niveau de jeu recommandé	0	12	24	36
Hcp required	Handicap exigé	28 Men, 36 Ladies		

CLUB HOUSE & AMENITIES
CLUB HOUSE ET ANNEXES

7/10

Pro shop	Pro-shop	▰▰▰▱
Driving range	Practice	▰▱▱▱
Sheltered	couvert	no
On grass	sur herbe	(pract.ground only)
Putting-green	putting-green	yes
Pitching-green	pitching green	yes

HOTEL FACILITIES
ENVIRONNEMENT HOTELIER

8/10

HOTELS HÔTELS
Clifton Arms Hotel - 44 rooms, D £ 86   Lytham 2 km
Tel (44) 01253 - 739 898 - Fax (44) 01253 - 730 657

Glendover Hotel - 63 rooms, D £ 76   Lytham St Anne's
Tél (44) 01253 - 723 241   3 km

Dalmeny - 130 rooms, D £ 75   Lytham St Anne's 3 km
Tel (44) 01253 - 712 236 - Fax (44) 01253 - 724 447

Bedford - 36 rooms, D £ 59   Lytham St Anne's 3 km
Tel (44) 01253 - 724 636, Fax (44) 01253 - 729 244

RESTAURANTS RESTAURANTS
Pleasant Street	Lytham
Tel (44) 01253 - 788 786	2 km
Tiggy's Italian	Lytham
Tel (44) 01253 - 714 714	2 km
Grand Hotel	Lytham
Tel (44) 01253 - 721 288	3 km

470

This is the fifth oldest club in the history of English golf and a course little known to the majority of golfers on the continent. Yet this is a top notch links course, without the spectacular dunes of the west coast but slightly reminiscent of the courses in Scotland's East Lothian. Re-designed by Henry Cotton after the second world war which left the site in ruins, Tom Dunn's original layout is now a challenge of the highest order despite being rather on the short side. Cut in two by a road, the course's most interesting holes run along the sea-shore. These are the last six holes which make for a highly interesting finish, especially when the wind blows a little (it does happen). A course to bravely go out and pitch into, in the same way as Julie Hall and Jo Hockley, who both learnt their trade here, the hard way.

C'est le cinquième club de l'histoire du golf en Angleterre, et un parcours dont bien peu de continentaux ont entendu parler. C'est pourtant un links de première qualité, sans les dunes spectaculaires de la côte ouest, mais qui n'est pas sans rappeler les parcours de l'East Lothian en Ecosse. Remodelé par Henry Cotton, après la Seconde Guerre Mondiale qui l'avait laissé en ruines, le dessin de Tom Dunn est aujourd'hui redevenu un challenge de premier ordre, même avec sa longueur réduite. Séparé en deux par une route, il offre ses trous les plus intéressants le long de la mer, et ce sont justement les six derniers, ce qui permet un finale des plus intéressants, quand le vent daigne souffler un peu (ce qui arrive). Un parcours à attaquer avec bravoure, comme savent le faire Julie Hall et Jo Hockley, formées ici, à la dure !

Felixstowe Ferry Golf Club
Ferry Road
ENG - FELIXSTOWE, Suffolk IP11 9RY

Office	Secrétariat	(44) 01394 - 286834
Pro shop	Pro-shop	(44) 01394 - 286834
Fax	Fax	
Situation	Situation	

18 km from Ipswich (pop. 130 157)
1 km from Felixstowe (pop. 23 189)

Annual closure	Fermeture annnuelle	no
Weekly closure	Fermeture hebdomadaire	no

Fees main season	Tarifs haute saison		18 holes
		Week days Semaine	**We/Bank holidays** We/Férié
Individual Individuel		£ 22	—
Couple Couple		£ 44	—

No visitors at weekends.

Caddy	Caddy	no
Electric Trolley	Chariot électrique	£ 5/18 holes
Buggy	Voiturette	no
Clubs	Clubs	no
Credit cards Cartes de crédit		no

IPSWICH
A 14
Trimley Heath
Trimley
B1083
A12
Alderton
Bawdsey
River Deben
Felixstowe Ferry
Old Felixstowe
GOLF
FELIXSTOWE
Harwich Harbour
0 ... 2 ... 4
0 ... 2,5 miles

Access Accès : Ipswich, A14 → North Felixstowe.
At beach, continue on the left.
Course entrance on the right.
Map 7 on page 419 Carte 7 Page 419

GOLF COURSE / PARCOURS — 15/20

Site	Site	
Maintenance	Entretien	
Architect	Architecte	Tom Dunn Henry Cotton
Type	Type	seaside course, links
Relief	Relief	
Water in play	Eau en jeu	
Exp. to wind	Exposé au vent	
Trees in play	Arbres en jeu	

Scorecard Carte de score	**Chp.** Chp.	**Mens** Mess.	**Ladies** Da.
Length Long.	5645	5562	4935
Par	72	72	72

Advised golfing ability — 0 12 24 36
Niveau de jeu recommandé
Hcp required Handicap exigé — certificate

CLUB HOUSE & AMENITIES / CLUB HOUSE ET ANNEXES — 6/10

Pro shop	Pro-shop	
Driving range	Practice	
Sheltered	couvert	no
On grass	sur herbe	yes
Putting-green	putting-green	yes
Pitching-green	pitching green	yes

HOTEL FACILITIES / ENVIRONNEMENT HOTELIER — 6/10

HOTELS HÔTELS
Orwell Hotel - 58 rooms, D £ 78 — Felixstowe 2 km
Tel (44) 01394 - 309 955
Fax (44) 01394 - 670 687

Waverley - 19 rooms, D £ 75 — Felixstowe 2 km
Tel (44) 01394 - 282 811
Fax (44) 01394 - 670 185

Fludyer Arms Hotel - 8 rooms, D £ 40 — Felixstowe 2 km
Tél (44) 01394 - 283 279
Fax (44) 01394 - 670 754

RESTAURANTS RESTAURANTS
Orwell Hotel Tel (44) 01394 - 309955 — Felixstowe 2 km
St Peter's - Tel (44) 01473 - 210810 — Ipswich 18 km
Mortimer's on the Quay — Ipswich 18 km
Tel (44) 01473 - 230225

471

With sand, heather, pine-trees and conifers, Ferndown is first and foremost a beautiful site with a simple but very functional clubhouse. Once a very dry course during rain-free summers, the course is now watered automatically so that you no longer get those infuriatingly unfair kicks left and right down the fairway, especially on the dog-legs. Be careful with Ferndown, because despite the impression of dealing with a fair and open course, some of the trees are more in play than you think and a number of ditches lie hidden in the rough. Good scores depend a lot on your driving, not only to avoid the dangerous fairway bunkers but also to get the ball in the right spot and have a good shot at the green. Although close to Bournemouth, this is not just a simple holiday course but one that has staged some top tournaments: a little short for the big boys, but ideal for the top ladies.

De sable et de bruyère, orné de pins et de sapins, Ferndown est d'abord un bel endroit, avec un Clubhouse sans prétentions architecturales, mais très fonctionnel. Autrefois très sec lors des étés sans pluie, il bénéficie maintenant d'un arrosage qui a retiré certains rebonds imprévus et souvent injustes, en particulier sur les nombreux do-glegs. Il faut se méfier de Ferndown, car on a l'impression d'un parcours très franc, alors que certains arbres sont plus en jeu qu'ils ne paraissent, et des fossés se dissimulent dans les roughs. Les bons scores dépendent beaucoup du driving, pour non seulement éviter les dangereux bunkers de fairway, mais aussi placer la balle en bonne position pour attaquer les greens. Bien que proche de Bournemouth, il vaut bien mieux qu'un simple parcours de vacances. Il fut le théâtre de grandes compétitions : un peu court pour les machos, il était idéal pour les proettes.

Ferndown Golf Club

119, Golf Links Road
ENG - FERNDOWN, Dorset BH22 8BU

Office	Secrétariat	(44) 01202 - 874 602
Pro shop	Pro-shop	(44) 01202 - 873 825
Fax	Fax	(44) 01202 - 873 926
Situation	Situation	

8 km from Bournemouth (pop. 151 300)
5 km from Poole (pop. 133 050)

Annual closure	Fermeture annnuelle	no
Weekly closure	Fermeture hebdomadaire	no
Christmas Day		

Fees main season	Tarifs haute saison	18 holes
	Week days Semaine	We/Bank holidays We/Férié
Individual Individuel	£ 40	£ 45
Couple Couple	£ 80	£ 90

Full day: £ 45 - £ 50 (weekends)

Caddy	Caddy	no
Electric Trolley	Chariot électrique	no
Buggy	Voiturette	£ 20/18 holes
Clubs	Clubs	£ 15/18 holes

Credit cards Cartes de crédit   no

472

Access Accès : M3 last exit, then A31 to Trickett's Cross, then A348 to Ferndown, follow signs → Golf.
Map 6 on page 417 Carte 6 Page 417

GOLF COURSE
PARCOURS   17 /20

Site	Site	
Maintenance	Entretien	
Architect	Architecte	Harold Hilton
Type	Type	inland, heathland
Relief	Relief	
Water in play	Eau en jeu	
Exp. to wind	Exposé au vent	
Trees in play	Arbres en jeu	

Scorecard Carte de score	Chp. Chp.	Mens Mess.	Ladies Da.
Length Long.	5895	5651	5176
Par	71	71	72

Advised golfing ability		0 12 24 36
Niveau de jeu recommandé		
Hcp required	Handicap exigé	28 Men, 30 Ladies

CLUB HOUSE & AMENITIES
CLUB HOUSE ET ANNEXES   7 /10

Pro shop	Pro-shop	
Driving range	Practice	
Sheltered	couvert	no
On grass	sur herbe	yes
Putting-green	putting-green	yes
Pitching-green	pitching green	no

HOTEL FACILITIES
ENVIRONNEMENT HOTELIER   7 /10

HOTELS HÔTELS
Mansion House - 28 rooms, D £ 90   Poole
Tel (44) 01202 - 685 666   8 km
Fax (44) 01202 - 665 709

Royal Bath - 124 rooms, D £ 130   Bournemouth
Tel (44) 01202 - 555 555   5 km
Fax (44) 01202 - 554 158

The Dormy - 123 rooms, D £ 100   Ferndown
Tel (44) 01202 - 872 121   0,5 km
Fax (44) 01202 - 895 388

RESTAURANTS RESTAURANTS
La Roche   Poole
Tel (44) 01202 - 707 333   5 km

Fisherman's Haunt   Christchurch
Tel (44) 01202 - 484 071   10 km

The very fine hotel today belongs to the Marriott Group, as does the course. The "Aylesford" hotel is very respectable and perfectly complements this "Arden" course, which is technically a very interesting layout, especially for the better player. All in all, it is a very pleasant spot for a few days golfing with a group or with the family, even if you are playing with golfers of very different abilities. We would simply recommend avoiding the wetter months as the soil takes a long time to soak up surface water. "Arden" was designed by Donald Steel and features many different tee-boxes, of which we would advise the yellow tees, at least for your first round, unless you are a good player of long irons. A tricky course overall with quite a few water hazards, trees which neatly outline the fairways and thick rough, Arden can only get better and better in what is a very professional golfing resort.

Le très bel hôtel appartient aujourd'hui au groupe Marriott, tout comme les parcours. Le "Aylesford" est fort honorable, et complète agréablement le "Arden," plus intéressant techniquement, en particulier pour les meilleurs joueurs. C'est ainsi un lieu très agréable pour passer quelques jours en groupe ou en famille, même si les niveaux de golf sont très différents. On recommandera simplement d'éviter les mois très humides, car le sol a du mal à évacuer les excès d'eau. Le "Arden" a été dessiné par Donald Steel, qui a fait un tracé avec de multiples départs, dont nous conseillerons les "jaunes," au moins la première fois, à moins d'être un solide joueur de longs fers et de savoir lever la balle. Assez "tricky" en général, avec pas mal d'obstacles d'eau, des arbres sculptant bien les trous, un rough épais, c'est un parcours qui peut nettement progresser, dans un complexe très professionnel.

Marriott Forest of Arden Golf Club

Maxstoke Lane
ENG - MERIDEN, Warwicks. CV7 7HR

Office	Secrétariat	(44) 01676 - 522335
Pro shop	Pro-shop	(44) 01676 - 522335
Fax	Fax	(44) 01676 - 523711
Situation	Situation	

16 km NW of Coventry (pop. 294 387)
24 km W of Birmingham (pop. 961 041)

Annual closure	Fermeture annnuelle	no
Weekly closure	Fermeture hebdomadaire	no
Fees main season	Tarifs haute saison	18 holes

	Week days Semaine	We/Bank holidays We/Férié
Individual Individuel	£ 60	£ 70
Couple Couple	£ 120	£ 140

Caddy	Caddy	on request/£ 30
Electric Trolley	Chariot électrique	no
Buggy	Voiturette	£ 25/18 holes
Clubs	Clubs	£ 20/18 holes

Credit cards Cartes de crédit
VISA - Eurocard - MasterCard - AMEX - DC

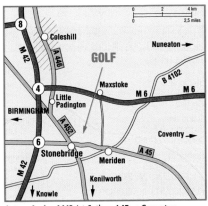

Access Accès : M42 Jct 6, then A45 → Coventry.
After 1.5 km (1 m), left into Shepherds Lane, by "Little Chef". Golf 2 km on the left.
Map 7 on page 418 Carte 7 Page 418

GOLF COURSE / PARCOURS — 14/20

Site	Site	
Maintenance	Entretien	
Architect	Architecte	Donald Steel
Type	Type	parkland
Relief	Relief	
Water in play	Eau en jeu	
Exp. to wind	Exposé au vent	
Trees in play	Arbres en jeu	

Scorecard Carte de score	Chp. Chp.	Mens Mess.	Ladies Da.
Length Long.	6420	5867	5106
Par	72	72	72

Advised golfing ability   0   12   24   36
Niveau de jeu recommandé
Hcp required   Handicap exigé   no

CLUB HOUSE & AMENITIES / CLUB HOUSE ET ANNEXES — 8/10

Pro shop	Pro-shop	
Driving range	Practice	
Sheltered	couvert	6 bays
On grass	sur herbe	no
Putting-green	putting-green	yes
Pitching-green	pitching green	yes

473

HOTEL FACILITIES / ENVIRONNEMENT HOTELIER — 8/10

HOTELS HÔTELS

Marriott Forest of Arden Hotel — Meriden
215 rooms, D £ 115 — on site
Tel (44) 01676 - 522 335, Fax (44) 01676 - 523 711

Manor (De Vere) - 74 rooms, D £ 95 — Meriden 3 km
Tel (44) 01676 - 522 735, Fax (44) 01676 - 522 186

Haigs - 13 rooms, D £ 68 — Balsall Common 6 km
Tel (44) 01676 - 533 004, Fax (44) 01676 - 535 132

Arden - 146 rooms, D £ 79 Nat. Ex. Centre, Birmingham
Tel (44) 01675 - 443 221 — 6 km

Hyatt Regency - 315 rooms, D £ 100 — Birmingham
Tel (44) 0121 - 643 1234
Fax (44) 0121 - 616 2323

RESTAURANT RESTAURANT
Sir Edward Elgar's — Birmingham 24 km
Tel (44) 0121 - 452 1144

It is easier than you might think to get a course all wrong when the terrain is not up to standard. Not so here, where the impression is one of a site blessed by Mother Nature and given the able help of John Morgan. He had to know how to trace the right path through a forest, how to define an intelligent layout, adapt the course to players of different levels, individualise the holes while respecting overall harmony, bring hazards into play without penalising the good shots, and keep a few surprises in store so that it's fun to play again and again. There are courses with which you have an affair and courses which you embrace for life. Forest Pines would be in the latter category, but we will wait a while to see whether it stays as good as it is right now as it comes of age. Opened in 1996 and also featuring a good standard 9 hole course ("The Beeches"), this is a resort you cannot afford to miss.

Il est plus facile qu'on ne le croit de rater un parcours alors que le terrain s'y prête. Ici, on peut avoir l'impression que Mère Nature a béni les lieux, mais John Morgan lui a donné un coup de main. Il fallait savoir tracer la route dans la forêt, définir un itinéraire intelligent, adapter son parcours aux différents niveaux de jeu, individualiser les trous tout en conservant une harmonie générale, mettre en jeu les obstacles sans pénaliser les bons coups de golf, et réserver des surprises pour que le plaisir ne soit pas émoussé après la première fois. Il est des parcours avec lesquels on a une liaison et d'autres que l'on épouse. Celui-ci pourrait bien faire partie de la seconde catégorie, même si l'on attend encore un peu pour voir s'il garde sa qualité actuelle en prenant quelques rides. Ouvert en 1996, et proposant également un 9 trous de bonne facture ("Beeches"), c'est un ensemble à connaître sans faute.

Forest Pines

Ermine Street, Broughton
ENG - BRIGG, Lincs DN20 04Q

Office	Secrétariat	(44) 01652 - 650 756
Pro shop	Pro-shop	(44) 01652 - 650 756
Fax	Fax	(44) 01652 - 650 495
Situation	Situation	

8 km E of Scunthorpe (pop. 61 550)

Annual closure	Fermeture annnuelle	no
Weekly closure	Fermeture hebdomadaire	no

Fees main season
Tarifs haute saison 18 holes

	Week days Semaine	We/Bank holidays We/Férié
Individual Individuel	£ 30	£ 30
Couple Couple	£ 60	£ 60

Full day: £ 35

Caddy	Caddy	on request
Electric Trolley	Chariot électrique	no
Buggy	Voiturette	£ 15/18 holes
Clubs	Clubs	£ 5/18 holes

Credit cards Cartes de crédit
VISA - Eurocard - MasterCard - AMEX - DC - Switch

474

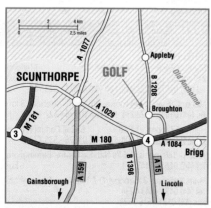

Access Accès : M1, M18 at Jct 32, then M180. At Jct 4, Golf 2 km North
Map 4 on page 413 Carte 4 Page 413

GOLF COURSE
PARCOURS
17 /20

Site	Site	
Maintenance	Entretien	
Architect	Architecte	John Morgan
Type	Type	forest
Relief	Relief	
Water in play	Eau en jeu	
Exp. to wind	Exposé au vent	
Trees in play	Arbres en jeu	

Scorecard Carte de score	Chp. Chp.	Mens Mess.	Ladies Da.
Length Long.	6262	5920	5295
Par	73	73	74

Advised golfing ability	0	12	24	36
Niveau de jeu recommandé				

Hcp required Handicap exigé certificate

CLUB HOUSE & AMENITIES
CLUB HOUSE ET ANNEXES
6 /10

Pro shop	Pro-shop	
Driving range	Practice	
Sheltered	couvert	17 bays
On grass	sur herbe	yes
Putting-green	putting-green	yes
Pitching-green	pitching green	yes

HOTEL FACILITIES
ENVIRONNEMENT HOTELIER
7 /10

HOTELS HÔTELS
Briggate Lodge — Golf / on site
86 rooms, D £ 78
Tel (44) 01652 - 650 770
Fax (44) 01652 - 650 495

Scunthorpe — Scunthorpe / 10 km
86 rooms, D £ 60
Tel (44) 01724 - 842 223

Royal Hotel — Scunthorpe / 10 km
42 rooms, D £ 65
Tel (44) 01724 - 282 233

RESTAURANTS RESTAURANTS
Brigg Hotel + Restaurant — Brigg / 7 km
Tel (44) 01652 - 657 633

Briggate Lodge — Golf / on site
Tel (44) 01652 - 650 770

It is easier to play here as a green-feer (the course is often deserted on weekdays) than to become a member. In this sort of golfing paradise, the latter is perfectly understandable. The layout, soil and dunes bear the hallmark of a links course, but there are trees on a good number of holes, meaning that the wind is not such an important factor as it can be on the region's other links courses. Donald Steel has recently lengthened the course but has taken nothing away from the highly strategic and penalising placing of bunkers, laid out initially by Willie Park then improved upon by Harry Colt. Seen overall, this is a unique and exciting course which offers a permanent challenge. Playing here is a blissful experience, except perhaps for the ladies, who have their own course (a gem) and their own clubhouse. No comment.

Il est plus facile de jouer ici en visiteur (en semaine, c'est souvent désert) que d'y devenir membre. On comprend que ce soit difficile, car Formby est une sorte de paradis. Le dessin, le sol, les dunes sont ceux des links, mais les arbres y sont assez présents sur une bonne partie des trous pour que le vent ne soit pas un facteur aussi terriblement important que sur les autres links de la région. Donald Steel a récemment allongé le parcours, mais sans rien ôter du placement très stratégique et pénalisant des bunkers, établi par Willie Park d'abord, mais surtout par Harry Colt. Au total, le caractère de ce parcours est unique, le jeu passionnant, le challenge permanent. On éprouve ici une impression de bonheur... sauf les Dames, qui ont un parcours à elles (un petit bijou) et leur propre Clubhouse. Sans commentaires.

Formby Golf Club
Freshfields
ENG - FORMBY, Lancs L37 1LQ

Office	Secrétariat	(44) 01704 - 872 164
Pro shop	Pro-shop	(44) 01704 - 873 090
Fax	Fax	
Situation	Situation	

8 km S of Southport (pop. 90 959)
23 km N of Liverpool (pop. 452 450)

Annual closure	Fermeture annnuelle	no
Weekly closure	Fermeture hebdomadaire	no
Fees main season	Tarifs haute saison	full day

	Week days Semaine	We/Bank holidays We/Férié
Individual Individuel	£ 50	£ 50
Couple Couple	£ 100	£ 100

Caddy	Caddy	on request
Electric Trolley	Chariot électrique	no
Buggy	Voiturette	no
Clubs	Clubs	no

Credit cards Cartes de crédit
VISA - Eurocard - MasterCard - AMEX - DC - JCB
(Pro shop only)

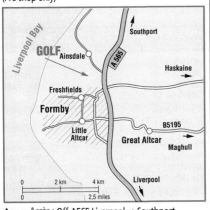

Access Accès : Off A565 Liverpool → Southport.
Formby, green lane to Victoria Road (signposted),
near Freshfields Rail Station.
Map 5 on page 415 Carte 5 Page 415

GOLF COURSE
PARCOURS
18/20

Site	Site	▰▰▰▰▰▱
Maintenance	Entretien	▰▰▰▰▰▱
Architect	Architecte	W. Park, H.S. Colt F. Pennink, D. Steel
Type	Type	links
Relief	Relief	▰▱▱▱▱▱
Water in play	Eau en jeu	▰▰▱▱▱▱
Exp. to wind	Exposé au vent	▰▰▰▱▱▱
Trees in play	Arbres en jeu	▰▰▰▰▱▱

Scorecard Carte de score	Chp. Chp.	Mens Mess.	Ladies Da.
Length Long.	6293	6030	0
Par	72	72	0

Advised golfing ability Niveau de jeu recommandé	0	12	24	36
			▰▰▰	

Hcp required   Handicap exigé   24 (Males only)!

CLUB HOUSE & AMENITIES
CLUB HOUSE ET ANNEXES
7/10

Pro shop	Pro-shop	▰▰▰▰▱▱
Driving range	Practice	▰▱▱▱▱▱
Sheltered	couvert	no
On grass	sur herbe	yes
Putting-green	putting-green	yes
Pitching-green	pitching green	yes

475

HOTEL FACILITIES
ENVIRONNEMENT HOTELIER
7/10

HOTELS HÔTELS
Dormy House (Males only!!!)   Formby Golf Club
7 rooms, £ 60 (twin & single)   on site
Tél (44) 01704 - 872 164, Fax (44) 01704 - 833 028

Blundellsands 41 rooms, D £ 70   Crosby 10 km
Tel (44) 0151 - 924 6515, Fax (44) 0151 - 931 5364

Park - 62 rooms, D £ 34   Netherton 10 km
Tel (44) 0151 - 525 7555, Fax (44) 0151 - 525 2481

RESTAURANTS RESTAURANTS
Ristorante del Secolo   Liverpool
Tel (44) 0151 - 236 4004   18 km

Est, Est, Est!   Liverpool
Tel (44) 0151 - 708 6969   18 km

Tree Tops Hotel   Formby
Tel (44) 01704 - 879 651   1 km

Very close to Birkdale, Hillside, Formby and Southport & Ainsdale, this new country course is anything but a links. So players who don't like the sometimes lunar and often brutal type of landscape found on your typical links course will find a more "human" alternative waiting for them here. There are not too many trees for the moment but a lot have been planted, so the course can only get better over the years. There are a whole lot of hazards but the only really surprising traps are the ditches that cross about a dozen fairways. On the flat side and exposed to the wind, Formby Hall seems to call for low shots, but your approach work to the well-defended greens will need some high iron shots as well. Fortunately, the greens are big enough for the balls that run rather than pitch. At all events the members seem to like it here, which augurs well for the future of this still young course.

Si près de Birkdale, Hillside, Formby ou Southport & Ainsdale, ce nouveau parcours en campagne n'a rien d'un links, mais certains joueurs n'aiment pas trop l'esthétique parfois lunaire, austère, ou même violente de ce type de parcours, ils trouveront ici une alternative plus "humaine." Les arbres n'y sont pas encore nombreux, mais beaucoup ont été plantés, et ce parcours ne saurait qu'évoluer dans le bon sens avec les années. Les obstacles sont nombreux, mais les seuls vraiment surprenants sont les fossés traversant une douzaine de fairways. Assez plat, exposé au vent, Formby Hall semble appeler des balles basses, mais les coups vers les greens bien protégés obligent souvent à les lever, à moins de savoir vite les arrêter. Heureusement, ces greens sont assez vastes. En tout cas, les membres semblent apprécier, ce qui rend optimiste quant à la progression de ce parcours encore bien jeune.

Formby Hall Golf Club

Southport Old Road
ENG - FORMBY, Lancs

Office	Secrétariat	(44) 01704 - 875699
Pro shop	Pro-shop	(44) 01704 - 875699
Fax	Fax	(44) 01704 - 832134
Situation	Situation	

12 km from Southport (pop. 90 959)
21 km from Liverpool (pop. 452 450)

Annual closure	Fermeture annnuelle	no
Weekly closure	Fermeture hebdomadaire	no
Fees main season	Tarifs haute saison	18 holes

	Week days Semaine	We/Bank holidays We/Férié
Individual Individuel	£ 25	£ 30
Couple Couple	£ 50	£ 60

Full weekdays: £ 45

Caddy	Caddy	on request
Electric Trolley	Chariot électrique	no
Buggy	Voiturette	£ 15/18 holes
Clubs	Clubs	no

Credit cards Cartes de crédit
VISA - Eurocard - MasterCard - AMEX - DC - JCB

476

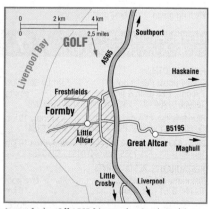

Access Accès : Off A565 (Liverpool → Southport) just beyond Formby turn-off, close to Coast Road traffic lights. Opposite RAF Station at Woodvale.
Map 5 on page 415 Carte 5 Page 415

GOLF COURSE / PARCOURS — 14/20

Site	Site	
Maintenance	Entretien	
Architect	Architecte	PSA Projects
Type	Type	parkland
Relief	Relief	
Water in play	Eau en jeu	
Exp. to wind	Exposé au vent	
Trees in play	Arbres en jeu	

Scorecard Carte de score	Chp. Chp.	Mens Mess.	Ladies Da.
Length Long.	6203	5791	5143
Par	72	72	72

Advised golfing ability Niveau de jeu recommandé	0	12	24	36

Hcp required	Handicap exigé	28 Men, 36 Ladies

CLUB HOUSE & AMENITIES / CLUB HOUSE ET ANNEXES — 8/10

Pro shop	Pro-shop	
Driving range	Practice	
Sheltered	couvert	24 mats
On grass	sur herbe	no
Putting-green	putting-green	yes
Pitching-green	pitching green	yes

HOTEL FACILITIES / ENVIRONNEMENT HOTELIER — 6/10

HOTELS HÔTELS

Treetops Hotel D £ 78 Tel (44) 01704 - 879 651		Formby 5 km
Blundellsands 41 rooms, D £ 70 Tel (44) 0151 - 924 6515 Fax (44) 0151 - 931 5364		Crosby 10 km
Park - 62 rooms, D £ 34 Tel (44) 0151 - 525 7555 Fax (44) 0151 - 525 2481		Netherton 10 km

RESTAURANTS RESTAURANTS

Formby Hall Golf Club Tel (44) 01704 - 872 164		Formby on site
Ristorante del Secolo Tel (44) 0151 - 236 4004		Liverpool

FULFORD

Even before the excellence of the course, Fulford has always been famed for its standard of green-keeping, a reputation enhanced further by the staging here of the English Open and Benson & Hedges International tournaments. Sure, the very low scores carded by the pros have shown that the course might now be a little short for them, but they also holed any number of putts. The greens have always been fast and true, adding to the pleasure of playing here, and the course is definitely long enough for most of us. This is a driver course, not power-wise but in terms of accuracy off the tee, as approach shots must be played from the right spot (bunkers are often on one side of the green only) and will vary according to pin positions. A tactical, technical and fair course for all levels, Fulford has retained its dominant position in York, a superb city to visit with a pedestrians-only centre.

Avant même la qualité de son parcours, Fulford a toujours été renommé pour la qualité de son entretien en général. Et la venue de l'English Open comme celle du Benson & Hedges International ont ensuite accentué cette réputation. Certes, les scores très bas des professionnels ont montré que le parcours était maintenant un peu "court" pour eux, mais ils rentraient aussi beaucoup de putts... Les greens sont toujours rapides et fermes, ce qui n'ajoute qu'un peu plus de plaisir, et le parcours est bien assez "long" pour la majorité d'entre nous. C'est un parcours de driver, pas en termes de puissance, mais de précision, car il faut aborder les greens dans un bon angle (bunkers souvent d'un seul côté), et qui peut varier selon les placements de drapeaux. Tactique et technique, franc et pour tous niveaux, Fulford conserve sa situation dominante à York, qui reste une superbe ville à visiter, avec son centre ville piétonnier.

Fulford Golf Club

Hessington Lane
ENG - YORK, Yorkshire Y01 5DY

Office	Secrétariat	(44) 01904 - 413579
Pro shop	Pro-shop	(44) 01904 - 412882
Fax	Fax	(44) 01904 - 416918
Situation	Situation	

3 km from York (pop. 98 745)

Annual closure	Fermeture annnuelle	no
Weekly closure	Fermeture hebdomadaire	no

Fees main season	Tarifs haute saison	18 holes
	Week days Semaine	We/Bank holidays We/Férié
Individual Individuel	£ 30	—
Couple Couple	£ 60	—
Full weekday: £ 40 - Limited access at weekends		

Caddy	Caddy	no
Electric Trolley	Chariot électrique	£ 5/18 holes
Buggy	Voiturette	no
Clubs	Clubs	£ 7.50/18 holes

Credit cards Cartes de crédit
VISA - Eurocard - MasterCard - AMEX - DC - JCB

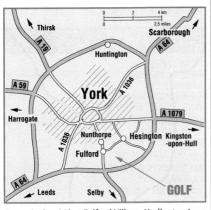

Access Accès : A19 → Fulford Village. Heslington Lane on left. Follow signs for University.
Map 4 on page 413 Carte 4 Page 413

GOLF COURSE
PARCOURS

17/20

Site	Site	
Maintenance	Entretien	
Architect	Architecte	Charles MacKenzie
Type	Type	parkland
Relief	Relief	
Water in play	Eau en jeu	
Exp. to wind	Exposé au vent	
Trees in play	Arbres en jeu	

Scorecard	Chp.	Mens	Ladies
Carte de score	Chp.	Mess.	Da.
Length Long.	6100	5698	4875
Par	72	72	74

Advised golfing ability	0 12 24 36
Niveau de jeu recommandé	
Hcp required	Handicap exigé	28 Men, 36 Ladies

CLUB HOUSE & AMENITIES
CLUB HOUSE ET ANNEXES

7/10

Pro shop	Pro-shop	
Driving range	Practice	
Sheltered	couvert	no
On grass	sur herbe	practice ground only
Putting-green	putting-green	yes
Pitching-green	pitching green	yes

HOTEL FACILITIES
ENVIRONNEMENT HOTELIER

8/10

HOTELS HÔTELS

Middlethorpe Hall - 30 rooms, D £ 120 Tel (44) 01904 - 641 241 Fax (44) 01904 - 620 176	York 2 km	
Forte Posthouse - 139 rooms, D £ 70 Tel (44) 01904 - 707 921 Fax (44) 01904 - 702 804	York 3 km	
Novotel - 124 rooms, D £ 76 Tel (44) 01904 - 611 660 Fax (44) 01904 - 610 925	York 3 km	
Arndale Hotel - 10 rooms, D £ 65 Tél (44) 01904 - 702 424	York 3 km	

RESTAURANTS RESTAURANTS

Melton's Tel (44) 01904 - 634 341	York 3 km
19 Grape Lane Tel (44) 01904 - 636 366	York 3 km

477

This club was purchased in 1985 by Ping, who run a golf equipment factory nearby, so don't be surprised by the manufacturer's dominant presence, particularly in the Pro Shop. The original course, played at a time when the club was called Thonock, has been restyled by Brian Waites and goes very well with this one, a more ambitious affair with a lot of water in play and few trees as yet. A lot have been planted, though, so visually the course can only get better. For the moment, the contours of the land and the bunkers do not always give you a clear idea of what you have to do. From the back tees this is a tough proposition which is probably too hard to handle for many average golfers. Further forward, the course is a fair and much more accessible test. A very serious course in a comparatively deserted region golf-wise with an impressive clubhouse (there is an excellent coffee-house for snacks).

Ce club a été acheté en 1985 par Ping, dont l'usine de matériel de golf est située à Gainsborough, on ne sera pas étonné de sentir cette présence, en particulier au Pro-shop ! Le parcours de l'époque où le club s'appelait Thonock avait été remodelé par Brian Waites et complète bien celui-ci, plus ambitieux, avec beaucoup d'eau en jeu, peu d'arbres encore mais certaines plantations vont le faire visuellement évoluer. Pour l'instant, les mouvements de terrain et les bunkers ne précisent pas toujours parfaitement ce qu'il faut faire, le "yardage book" (carnet de parcours) sera utile. Des départs arrière, c'est un solide parcours où beaucoup souffriront, mais les départs avancés proposent un test très franc et accessible à beaucoup. Une réalisation très sérieuse dans une région un peu déserte, avec un Clubhouse impressionnant (excellent Coffee shop pour une petite faim).

Gainsborough Golf Club-Karsten Lakes
Thonock
ENG - GAINSBOROUGH, Lincs DN21 1PZ

Office	Secrétariat	(44) 01427 - 613 088
Pro shop	Pro-shop	(44) 01427 - 612 278
Fax	Fax	(44) 01427 - 810 172
Situation	Situation	

1.5 km N of Gainsborough
30 km NW of Lincoln (pop. 80 218)

Annual closure	Fermeture annnuelle	no
Weekly closure	Fermeture hebdomadaire	no
Fees main season	Tarifs haute saison	18 holes

	Week days Semaine	We/Bank holidays We/Férié
Individual Individuel	£ 25	£ 25
Couple Couple	£ 50	£ 50
Full day: £ 35		

Caddy	Caddy	no
Electric Trolley	Chariot électrique	no
Buggy	Voiturette	£ 18/18 holes
Clubs	Clubs	£ 12/18 holes

Credit cards Cartes de crédit
VISA - MasterCard - AMEX - Switch

GOLF COURSE
PARCOURS `14`/20

Site	Site	
Maintenance	Entretien	
Architect	Architecte	Neil Coles
Type	Type	inland, parkland
Relief	Relief	
Water in play	Eau en jeu	
Exp. to wind	Exposé au vent	
Trees in play	Arbres en jeu	

Scorecard Carte de score	Chp. Chp.	Mens Mess.	Ladies Da.
Length Long.	6279	5901	5310
Par	72	72	72

Advised golfing ability   0 12 24 36
Niveau de jeu recommandé
Hcp required   Handicap exigé   certificate

CLUB HOUSE & AMENITIES
CLUB HOUSE ET ANNEXES `8`/10

Pro shop	Pro-shop	
Driving range	Practice	
Sheltered	couvert	20 bays
On grass	sur herbe	no
Putting-green	putting-green	yes
Pitching-green	pitching green	yes

HOTEL FACILITIES
ENVIRONNEMENT HOTELIER `6`/10

HOTELS HÔTELS
Hickmont Hill Hotel   Gainsborough
8 rooms, D £ 50   2 km
Tel (44) 01427 - 613 639
Fax (44) 01427 - 677 591

White Swan Hotel   Gainsborough
12 rooms, D £ 52   20 km
Tel (44) 01724 - 762 342
Fax (44) 01724 - 764 268

RESTAURANTS RESTAURANTS
Cross Keys   Gainsborough
Tel (44) 01427 - 788 314   5 km

White Heather   Gainsborough
Tel (44) 01427 - 878 604   5 km

478

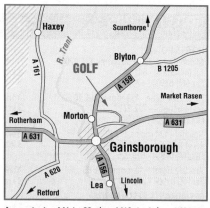

Access Accès : M1 Jct 32, then M18, Jct 1 then A631 to Gainsborough. A 159 golf 1.5 km N.
Map 4 on page 413 Carte 4 Page 413

This is one of the very few inland courses to find favour with links enthusiasts. The sea must have stretched this far in times gone by because you can still find sea-shells in the sand and the soil is of the kind found on every links course. Located between the resort of Scarborough and the superb city of York (a former Viking stronghold), this is a sheer masterpiece of a course where Dunn, Vardon, Harry Colt and C.K. Cotton all had a hand in its design. The links style is all the more obvious in that trees come into play only on a very few holes. Elsewhere, the fairways are bordered by bushes, tall grass and rough, while deep hungry bunkers snap up anything within reach. But all the hazards are there to be seen and the course is not responsible for your shortcomings (or is it?). The slick greens are well-protected but leave the way open for bump 'n roll shots. As we were saying, all that is missing is the sea.

C'est l'un des seuls "inland" à trouver grâce auprès des amoureux des links. La mer devait autrefois venir ici, car on a retrouvé des coquillages dans le sable et le sol est celui des links. Entre la station balnéaire de Scarborough et la ville superbe d'York (ancienne place forte viking), il y a ce chef d'oeuvre absolu où Tom Dunn, Harry Vardon, Harry Colt et C.K. Cotton ont apporté leur contribution. Le style de links est d'autant plus flagrant que les arbres ne sont en jeu que sur quelques trous. Ailleurs, les buissons, les hautes herbes du rough délimitent les fairways, de profonds bunkers pleins d'appétit attrapent tout ce qui passe à portée. Mais tous les obstacles sont bien en vue, et le parcours n'est pas responsable de vos fautes. Les greens subtils et bien défendus laissent néanmoins la porte ouverte aux approches roulées. Il ne manque que la mer, on vous le disait.

Ganton Golf Club

Ganton
ENG - SCARBOROUGH, Yorkshire YO12 4PA

Office	Secrétariat	(44) 01944 - 710329
Pro shop	Pro-shop	(44) 01944 - 710260
Fax	Fax	
Situation	Situation	

15 km SW of Scarborough (pop. 38 809)

Annual closure	Fermeture annnuelle	no
Weekly closure	Fermeture hebdomadaire	no

Fees main season
Tarifs haute saison — full day

	Week days Semaine	We/Bank holidays We/Férié
Individual Individuel	£ 43	£ 48
Couple Couple	£ 86	£ 96

Caddy	Caddy	on request/£ 15
Electric Trolley	Chariot électrique	£ 5/18 holes
Buggy	Voiturette	£ 20/18 holes
Clubs	Clubs	£ 10/18 holes

Credit cards Cartes de crédit
VISA - Eurocard - MasterCard - AMEX - DC - JCB

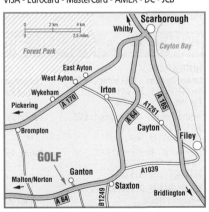

Access Accès : On A64 Leeds-York-Scarborough,
15 km before Scarborough
Map 4 on page 413 Carte 4 Page 413

GOLF COURSE / PARCOURS 19/20

Site	Site	▮▮▮▮▯
Maintenance	Entretien	▮▮▮▮▮
Architect	Architecte	Tom Dunn, H. Vardon, H.S. Colt, CK Cotton
Type	Type	open country, heathland
Relief	Relief	▮▯▯▯▯
Water in play	Eau en jeu	▯▯▯▯▯
Exp. to wind	Exposé au vent	▮▮▮▯▯
Trees in play	Arbres en jeu	▮▮▯▯▯

Scorecard Carte de score	Chp. Chp.	Mens Mess.	Ladies Da.
Length Long.	6061	5827	5447
Par	73	73	75

Advised golfing ability Niveau de jeu recommandé		0 12 24 36
Hcp required	Handicap exigé	24 Men, 36 Ladies

CLUB HOUSE & AMENITIES / CLUB HOUSE ET ANNEXES 8/10

Pro shop	Pro-shop	▮▮▮▮▮
Driving range	Practice	
Sheltered	couvert	no
On grass only	sur herbe	practice ground
Putting-green	putting-green	yes
Pitching-green	pitching green	yes

479

HOTEL FACILITIES / ENVIRONNEMENT HOTELIER 5/10

HOTELS HÔTELS

Crescent Hotel — Scarborough 15 km
20 rooms, D £ 60
Tel (44) 01723 - 360 929, Fax (44) 01723 - 354 126

Crown (Forte) — Scarborough 15 km
77 rooms, D £ 65
Tel (44) 01723 - 373 491, Fax (44) 01723 - 362 271

Bradley Court — Scarborough 15 km
40 rooms, D £ 75
Tel (44) 01723 - 360 476, Fax (44) 01723 - 376 661

RESTAURANTS RESTAURANTS
Jade Garden (Chinese) — Scarborough 15 km
Tel (44) 01723 - 369 099

Lanterna Tel (44) 01723 - 363 616 — Scarborough15 km

The landscape in this part of the country is generally so flat that it could hardly have inspired early course designers who probably had little more than ploughs and wheelbarrows to move earth. If you don't play much golf here, you will enjoy visiting Cambridge, Ely, Bury St. Edmonds or the Fens with their windmills. Gog Magog, though, is the exception to the rule and is laid out over some small hills which are easy to walk. The club has a long tradition of hospitality (but is closed to green-feers on weekends) and also a second course, Wandlesbury, which has everything perhaps except the charm of this Old Course. There are not too many trees but they are sometimes placed to block your second shot if the drive is not perfect. A fair and shortish course which rewards good shots, Gog Magog is pleasant to play with friends or with the family, whatever their level.

La paysage de cette région est en général d'une platitude qui ne pouvait guère inspirer les architectes de golf des origines, qui ne disposaient guère que de charrues et de brouettes pour modeler le terrain. Faute de beaucoup jouer, la visite de Cambridge, d'Ely, de Bury St Edmunds ou les marais des Fens avec leurs moulins à vent sont déjà un dépaysement. Gog Magog est l'exception à la règle, et a trouvé place sur de petites collines assez aimables pour les jambes. Ce club a la longue tradition d'accueil (mais fermé aux visiteurs en week-end) offre un second parcours, Wandlesbury, mais le Old Course garde tout son charme. Les arbres n'y sont pas trop nombreux, mais parfois placés pour bloquer les seconds coups si les drives n'ont pas été parfaits. Honnête, récompensant les bons coups de golf, pas très long, c'est un parcours agréable pour jouer en famille ou avec des amis, quel que soit leur niveau.

The Gog Magog Golf Club
ENG - SHELFORD BOTTOM, Cambridgeshire CB2 4AB

Office	Secrétariat	(44) 01223 - 247 626
Pro shop	Pro-shop	(44) 01223 - 246 058
Fax	Fax	(44) 01223 - 414 990
Situation	Situation	

4 km from Cambridge (pop. 91 535)

Annual closure	Fermeture annnuelle	no
Weekly closure	Fermeture hebdomadaire	no

Fees main season
Tarifs haute saison 18 holes

	Week days Semaine	We/Bank holidays We/Férié
Individual Individuel	£ 30	—
Couple Couple	£ 60	—

Full day: £ 37.50 - No visitors at weekends
Booking advisable

Caddy	Caddy	no
Electric Trolley	Chariot électrique	£ 6/18 holes
Buggy	Voiturette	no
Clubs	Clubs	£ 7.50/18 holes
Credit cards Cartes de crédit		no

480

Access Accès : Cambridge A1307 SE. Second roundabout turn left → Fulbourn. Entrance 200 m on the right. **Map 7 on page 419** Carte 7 Page 419

GOLF COURSE PARCOURS
15/20

Site	Site	
Maintenance	Entretien	
Architect	Architecte	F.W. Hawtree
Type	Type	inland, copse
Relief	Relief	
Water in play	Eau en jeu	
Exp. to wind	Exposé au vent	
Trees in play	Arbres en jeu	

Scorecard Carte de score	Chp. Chp.	Mens Mess.	Ladies Da.
Length Long.	5760	5565	5010
Par	70	70	71

Advised golfing ability
Niveau de jeu recommandé 0 12 24 36
Hcp required Handicap exigé 22

CLUB HOUSE & AMENITIES
CLUB HOUSE ET ANNEXES
7/10

Pro shop	Pro-shop	
Driving range	Practice	
Sheltered	couvert	no
On grass	sur herbe	yes
Putting-green	putting-green	yes
Pitching-green	pitching green	yes

HOTEL FACILITIES
ENVIRONNEMENT HOTELIER
8/10

HOTELS HÔTELS

University Arms - 114 rooms, D £ 80 — Cambridge 4 km
Tel (44) 01223 - 351 241
Fax (44) 01223 - 315 256

Arundel House - 105 rooms, D £ 65 — Cambridge 4 km
Tel (44) 01223 - 367 701
Fax (44) 01223 - 367 721

Centennial - 39 rooms, D £ 65 — Cambridge 4 km
Tel (44) 01223 - 314 652
Fax (44) 01223 - 315 443

RESTAURANTS RESTAURANTS

Sycamore House — Little Shelford 3 km
Tel (44) 01223 - 843396

Midsummer House — Cambridge 4 km
Tel (44) 01223 - 69299

HADLEY WOOD

16 | 7 | 7

Whichever direction you're travelling, London just seems never-ending. The strangest thing is that you start finding golf courses where you would never expect them and, what's more, in calm secluded spots. Less than a mile from Cockfosters tube station, Hadley Wood is one such course, where a very smart clubhouse is surrounded by flowers and bushes whose colours contrast sharply with the grey (or blue) skies. The same elegance and eye for detail are found in what is a very distinguished layout by Alister Mackenzie, landscaped like a garden and whose bunkers, streams and lakes look like items of decoration straight out of a magazine. But deceptive as ever, even the sweetest looking courses can prove deadly and easily end any hope of a good score.

Que l'on aille dans n'importe quelle direction, Londres semble ne jamais finir. Le plus étrange est de parvenir à trouver beaucoup de golfs là où on ne penserait pas en chercher, et à les trouver dans des endroits calmes. Hadley Wood fait partie de ces sites privilégiés, à moins d'un mile du métro Cockfosters. Autour du très beau Clubhouse, fleurs et arbustes témoignent une fois de plus d'un amour des végétaux coloriés qui tranchent avec le ciel gris (et d'ailleurs parfois bleu !). On retrouve cette élégance, ce souci du détail dans le tracé très distingué d'Alister Mackenzie, paysagé comme un jardin, où les bunkers, les petits cours d'eau et les lacs paraissent des éléments d'un décor pour magazine. Mais il faut se méfier des apparences, les dessins les plus évidents peuvent être meurtriers, du moins si l'on tente de faire un bon score.

Hadley Wood Golf Club

Beech Hill
ENG - BARNET, Herts EN4 0JJ

Office	Secrétariat	(44) 0181 - 4494328
Pro shop	Pro-shop	(44) 0181 - 4493285
Fax	Fax	(44) 0181 - 3648633
Situation	Situation	

16 km N of Central London (pop. 6 679 700)

Annual closure	Fermeture annnuelle	no
Weekly closure	Fermeture hebdomadaire	no

Fees main season
Tarifs haute saison — 18 holes

	Week days Semaine	We/Bank holidays We/Férié
Individual Individuel	£ 33	—
Couple Couple	£ 66	—

Full weekday: £ 44 - No visitors at weekends

Caddy	Caddy	on request/£ 40
Electric Trolley	Chariot électrique	£ 6/18 holes
Buggy	Voiturette	no
Clubs	Clubs	£ 7.50/18 holes

Credit cards Cartes de crédit
VISA - MasterCard - AMEX - DC

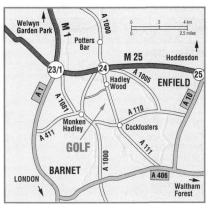

Access Accès : M25 Jct 24. A111 → Cockfosters.
3rd right into Beech Hill. Golf 400 m on left.
Map 8 on page 421 Carte 8 Page 421

GOLF COURSE
PARCOURS

16 /20

Site	Site	
Maintenance	Entretien	
Architect	Architecte	Alister MacKenzie
Type	Type	parkland
Relief	Relief	
Water in play	Eau en jeu	
Exp. to wind	Exposé au vent	
Trees in play	Arbres en jeu	

Scorecard Carte de score	Chp. Chp.	Mens Mess.	Ladies Da.
Length Long.	5811	5612	4710
Par	72	70	73

Advised golfing ability		0 12 24 36
Niveau de jeu recommandé		
Hcp required	Handicap exigé	certificate

CLUB HOUSE & AMENITIES
CLUB HOUSE ET ANNEXES

7 /10

Pro shop	Pro-shop	
Driving range	Practice	
Sheltered	couvert	no
On grass	sur herbe	yes
Putting-green	putting-green	yes
Pitching-green	pitching green	yes

HOTEL FACILITIES
ENVIRONNEMENT HOTELIER

7 /10

HOTELS HÔTELS

West Lodge Park — Hadley Wood
45 rooms, D £ 120 — 1 km
Tel (44) 0181 - 440 8311, Fax (44) 0181 - 449 3698

Royal Chace — Enfield
92 rooms, D £ 85 — 3 km
Tel (44) 0181 - 366 6500, Fax (44) 0181 - 367 7191

Holiday Inn Garden Court — Brent Cross
152 rooms, D £ 85 — 9 km
Tel (44) 0181 - 201 8686, Fax (44) 0181 - 455 4660

Forte Posthouse — South Mimms
120 rooms, D £ 70 — 8 km
Tel (44) 01707 - 643 311, Fax (44) 01707 - 646 728

RESTAURANT RESTAURANT

West Lodge Park — Hadley Wood
Tel (44) 0181 - 440 8311 — 1 km

481

First of all a word of praise for the slick, very fast greens and the flawless green-keeping. Might this be a tribute to Bobby Locke, one of the greatest putters of all time who for years lived right beside this course? Hankley Common used to be very dry in Summer but now has automatic sprinklers which tend to lengthen the course and stress the need for long-hitting. Keep it straight, too, because the fairway bunkers snap up anything remotely off-line, and even if you miss the sand, there's enough heather to keep you busy for longer than you would like, finding ways of getting your ball back into play. The felling of a number of trees has exposed the course to the wind and sometimes gives a part of the course an unexpected links character, with all the technical challenge that that entails. A final word for the beautiful finishing holes, especially the 18th, where our advice is always to take one club more than you think you need to hit the green.

D'abord un mot pour les greens subtils, très rapides et d'un entretien irréprochable, comme en hommage à l'un des meilleurs putters de tous les temps, Bobby Locke, qui habita longtemps à côté d'ici. Longtemps très sec en été, ce parcours bénéficie maintenant de l'arrosage automatique, qui l'a en quelque sorte "allongé," renforçant la nécessité d'être long, et droit car les nombreux bunkers de fairway accueillent avec le sourire les balles incertaines. Et quand on réussit à les passer, la bruyère est volontaire pour les retenir un certain temps. L'abattage de nombreux arbres a exposé davantage les joueurs au vent, ce qui donne parfois un caractère de links inattendu à certains trous, avec l'exigence technique que cela représente. A signaler enfin, la beauté du finale, en particulier du 18ème trou : prenez toujours un club de plus pour jouer le green.

Hankley Common Golf Club

Tilford Road, Tilford
ENG - FARNHAM, Surrey GU10 2DD

Office	Secrétariat	(44) 01252 - 792493
Pro shop	Pro-shop	(44) 01252 - 792761
Fax	Fax	(44) 01252 - 792493
Situation	Situation	

6 km from Farnham (pop. 30 430)

Annual closure	Fermeture annnuelle	no
Weekly closure	Fermeture hebdomadaire	no

Fees main season
Tarifs haute saison — full day

	Week days Semaine	We/Bank holidays We/Férié
Individual Individuel	£ 50	£ 50*
Couple Couple	£ 100	£ 100*

* For 18 holes and after 2.00 pm

Caddy	Caddy	no
Electric Trolley	Chariot électrique	no
Buggy	Voiturette	no
Clubs	Clubs	no

Credit cards Cartes de crédit — no

GOLF COURSE PARCOURS — 16/20

Site	Site	▉▉▉▉▉▉
Maintenance	Entretien	▉▉▉▉▉▉▉
Architect	Architecte	Charles Lawrie
Type	Type	inland, heathland
Relief	Relief	
Water in play	Eau en jeu	▉▉
Exp. to wind	Exposé au vent	▉▉▉▉▉▉▉▉
Trees in play	Arbres en jeu	▉▉▉▉▉▉

Scorecard Carte de score	Chp. Chp.	Mens Mess.	Ladies Da.
Length Long.	5795	5503	5002
Par	71	71	72

Advised golfing ability Niveau de jeu recommandé	0	12	24	36

Hcp required — Handicap exigé — certificate

CLUB HOUSE & AMENITIES CLUB HOUSE ET ANNEXES — 6/10

Pro shop	Pro-shop	▉▉▉▉
Driving range	Practice	▉▉▉▉▉
Sheltered	couvert	no
On grass	sur herbe	yes
Putting-green	putting-green	yes
Pitching-green	pitching green	yes

HOTEL FACILITIES ENVIRONNEMENT HOTELIER — 6/10

HOTELS HÔTELS

Bush (Forte Heritage) - 66 rooms, D £ 85 — Farnham
Tel (44) 01252 - 715 237 — 5 km
Fax (44) 01252 - 733 530

Bishop's Table - 16 rooms, D £ 85 — Farnham
Tel (44) 01252 - 710 222 — 5 km
Fax (44) 01252 - 733 494

Pride of the Valley - 11 rooms, D £ 70 — Churt
Tel (44) 01428 - 605 799 — 5 km
Fax (44) 01428 - 605 875

RESTAURANTS RESTAURANTS

Wings Cottage — Farnborough
Tel (44) 01252 - 544 141 — 10 km

Fleur de Sel — Haslemere
Tel (44) 01428 - 651 462 — 10 km

Banaras (Indian) — Farnham
Tel (44) 01252 - 734 081 — 5 km

482

Access Accès : A3 (→ Portsmouth). After Devils Punch Bowl, turn right onto Tilford Road. Golf Club is approx; 6 km (4 m) on the right.
Map 7 on page 418 Carte 7 Page 418

A strange place where the "Follies" of Hawkstone Park could be a setting for a video game with caves, secret passages or little monuments, all hidden in lush vegetation. They also say that King Arthur is buried somewhere on this estate. What is certain is that Sandy Lyle learnt how to play here. Today, this is a real resort with a hotel and two courses, including "Hawkstone", which was designed by James Braid, with some of the greens in the style of Alister Mackenzie. The course was restored and adapted to the modern game by Brian Huggett, who also laid out the resort's other 18-hole course. Imaginative, sometimes spectacular, very well landscaped and blending perfectly with its environment, this is a course whose subtleties will probably appeal more to the better golfer. Non-golfers can always visit the pretty town of Shrewsbury in the footsteps of Cadfael, the hero of the medieval murder novels by Ellis Peters.

Etrange endroit où les "Follies" de Hawkstone Park pourraient servir de cadre à un jeu vidéo avec grottes, passages secrets ou petits monuments, tous cachés dans une végétation très riche. On murmure que le Roi Arthur aurait été enterré sur ce domaine, mais la seule chose certaine, c'est que Sandy Lyle a appris le golf ici. C'est aujourd'hui un resort, avec hôtel et deux parcours, dont le "Hawkstone" est un James Braid avec certains greens à la Alister Mackenzie, restauré et adapté au jeu moderne par Brian Huggett, qui a également signé l'autre 18 trous du domaine. Imaginatif, parfois spectaculaire, bien paysagé mais en même temps magnifiquement intégré à son environnement, c'est un parcours dont les joueurs d'un bon niveau apprécieront le plus les subtilités. Les autres pourront chercher dans la jolie ville de Shrewsbury les traces de Frère Cadfael, héros des romans policiers médiévaux d'Ellis Peters.

Hawkstone Park Hotel

Weston-under-Redcastle
ENG - SHREWSBURY, Shropshire SY4 5UY

Office	Secrétariat	(44) 01939 - 200611
Pro shop	Pro-shop	(44) 01939 - 200611
Fax	Fax	(44) 01939 - 200311
Situation	Situation	

19 km N of Shrewsbury (pop. 91 749)

Annual closure	Fermeture annnuelle	no
Weekly closure	Fermeture hebdomadaire	no

Fees main season
Tarifs haute saison 18 holes

	Week days Semaine	We/Bank holidays We/Férié
Individual Individuel	£ 27	£ 34.50
Couple Couple	£ 54	£ 69

Full day: £ 40/£ 48 (weekends)

Caddy	Caddy	on request/£ 20
Electric Trolley	Chariot électrique	£ 7.50/18 holes
Buggy	Voiturette	£ 25/18 holes
Clubs	Clubs	£ 15/18 holes

Credit cards Cartes de crédit
VISA - Eurocard - MasterCard - AMEX

Access Accès : M6 Birmingham → Liverpool. Jct 10A through Telford, A5 → Shrewsbury. A49 North. Follow signs for Hawkstone Historic Park
Map 5 on page 414 Carte 5 Page 414

GOLF COURSE / PARCOURS · 15/20

Site	Site	
Maintenance	Entretien	
Architect	Architecte	James Braid
Type	Type	parkland
Relief	Relief	
Water in play	Eau en jeu	
Exp. to wind	Exposé au vent	
Trees in play	Arbres en jeu	

Scorecard Carte de score	Chp. Chp.	Mens Mess.	Ladies Da.
Length Long.	5842	5519	5153
Par	72	72	72

Advised golfing ability		0 12 24 36
Niveau de jeu recommandé		
Hcp required	Handicap exigé	certificate

CLUB HOUSE & AMENITIES / CLUB HOUSE ET ANNEXES · 8/10

Pro shop	Pro-shop	
Driving range	Practice	
Sheltered	couvert	no
On grass	sur herbe	yes
Putting-green	putting-green	yes
Pitching-green	pitching green	yes

HOTEL FACILITIES / ENVIRONNEMENT HOTELIER · 7/10

HOTELS HÔTELS

Hawkstone Park Hotel — Weston on site
65 rooms, D £ 120
Tel (44) 01939 - 200 611
Fax (44) 01939 - 200 311

Albrighton Hall — Albrighton 12 km
39 rooms, D £ 95
Tel (44) 01939 - 291 000
Fax (44) 01939 - 291 123

Prince Rupert — Shrewsbury 19 km
62 rooms, D £ 68
Tel (44) 01939 - 499 955
Fax (44) 01939 - 357 306

RESTAURANT RESTAURANT

Hawkstone Park Hotel — Weston on site
Tel (44) 01939 - 200 611

483

The southern coast of England has very few genuine links courses. Rye (totally private) can claim the label, and so can Hayling, whose reputation has never gone beyond England despite being designed by Tom Simpson, a hallmark of quality. As usual, the hazards are remarkably well located with the best route to the green always being the most dangerous (as with Donald Ross). At the same time visibility is 90% perfect so you can get to grips with the course from the first time out. Here you are adapting your game all the time, but that is one of the pleasures of golf. This easy-walking course is ideal for the holidays if you are not too concerned about your card. Close to the beach and a very rich nature reserve, Hayling deserves a good visit.

Cette côte sud de l'Angleterre propose bien peu de sites de vrais links, seul Rye (totalement privé) pouvant prétendre en être un. Ainsi que Hayling, dont la notoriété n'a pas dépassé les frontières, en dépit de la signature de Tom Simpson, une garantie de qualité. Comme d'habitude avec lui, le placement des obstacles est remarquable, la meilleure route étant toujours la plus dangereuse (comme avec Donald Ross), et la visibilité est à 90 % parfaite, de manière à pouvoir entrer dans le vif du sujet dès la première visite. Les problèmes posés diffèrent d'un trou à l'autre, et d'un vent à l'autre, ce qui oblige à s'adapter sans cesse, mais c'est un des plaisirs du golf. Peu fatigant à marcher, c'est un parcours idéal pour les vacances, si l'on n'est pas trop soucieux de son score. Proche de la plage et d'une très riche réserve naturelle, Hayling mérite une visite attentive.

Hayling Golf Club

Links Lane
ENG- HAYLING ISLAND, Hampshire PO11 0BX

Office	Secrétariat	(44) 01705 - 464446
Pro shop	Pro-shop	(44) 01705 - 464491
Fax	Fax	(44) 01705 - 46446
Situation	Situation	

15 km from Portsmouth (pop. 243 373)
8 km from Havant (pop. 46 510)

Annual closure	Fermeture annnuelle	no
Weekly closure	Fermeture hebdomadaire	no

Fees main season	Tarifs haute saison	18 holes
	Week days Semaine	We/Bank holidays We/Férié
Individual Individuel	£ 25	£ 30
Couple Couple	£ 50	£ 60

Full day: £ 30/40
Weekends: no green-fees before 10.00 am

Caddy	Caddy	no
Electric Trolley	Chariot électrique	£ 7.50/18 holes
Buggy	Voiturette	no
Clubs	Clubs	no

Credit cards Cartes de crédit
VISA - MasterCard (Pro-shop only)

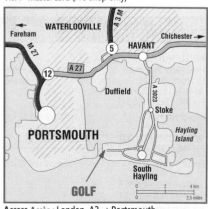

Access Accès : London, A3 → Portsmouth, A27 → Havant. A 3023 to Hayling Island. Seafront, turn right **Map 7 on page 418** Carte 7 Page 418

GOLF COURSE / PARCOURS — 16/20

Site	Site	
Maintenance	Entretien	
Architect	Architecte	J.H. Taylor Tom Simpson
Type	Type	seaside course, links
Relief	Relief	
Water in play	Eau en jeu	
Exp. to wind	Exposé au vent	
Trees in play	Arbres en jeu	

Scorecard Carte de score	Chp. Chp.	Mens Mess.	Ladies Da.
Length Long.	5870	5675	5220
Par	71	71	74

Advised golfing ability Niveau de jeu recommandé		0 12 24 36
Hcp required	Handicap exigé	certificate

CLUB HOUSE & AMENITIES / CLUB HOUSE ET ANNEXES — 7/10

Pro shop	Pro-shop	
Driving range	Practice	
Sheltered	couvert	2 mats
On grass	sur herbe	no
Putting-green	putting-green	yes
Pitching-green	pitching green	no

HOTEL FACILITIES / ENVIRONNEMENT HOTELIER — 7/10

HOTELS HÔTELS

Bear - 42 rooms, D £ 70
Tel (44) 01705 - 486 501
Fax (44) 01705 - 470 551
Havant
8 km

Forte Posthouse - 163 rooms, D £ 59
Tel (44) 01705 - 827 651
Fax (44) 01705 - 756 715
Portsmouth
15 km

Hospitality Inn
113 rooms, D £ 75
Tel (44) 01705 - 731 281
Fax (44) 01705 - 817 572
Portsmouth
15 km

RESTAURANTS RESTAURANTS

Cockle Warren Cottage
Tel (44) 01705 - 463226
Hayling Island
1 km

MA Bakers
Tel (44) 01705 - 463226
Hayling Island
1 km

484

We have already talked about this very popular region of Henley (see Badgemore) and the Thames Valley with its pretty villages and timbered houses: the Tudor style is gradually replaced by flint as you move towards the Cotswolds. Another landmark to visit is the Uffington White Horse, carved out of chalk on the hillside. While you are here, play this pretty little Henley course with unpretentious facilities and clubhouse but a well-thought out design by James Braid. There is nothing really distinctive about this course but it makes for a good day's golfing with friends of all different playing levels. You will have a good round relaxing between two more difficult courses in the region, have fun at very little cost and might almost believe you play golf better than you ever thought possible. With that said, proceed with care, as even the most benign course can turn spiteful at times.

Avec Badgemore Park, nous avons évoqué cette région très courue d'Henley et de la vallée de la Tamise, avec les petits villages aux maisons à colombages, qui deviennent peu à peu maisons de pierre à mesure que l'on va vers les Costwolds. Il faudra aussi voir le "Cheval Blanc" d'Uffington, gigantesque figure de craie préhistorique. Et aussi penser à jouer ce joli parcours d'Henley, au Clubhouse et aux installations assez modestes, au dessin bien pensé de James Braid. Certes, il n'offre pas de caractère particulier très notable, mais il permet de passer une bonne journée avec des joueurs de tous niveaux, en guise de détente entre deux parcours plus difficiles, de se faire plaisir à peu de frais, et presque de croire que l'on joue mieux qu'on ne l'imaginait. Il faut cependant faire attention, les parcours les plus souriants ont aussi des dents.

Henley Golf Club

Harpsden
ENG - HENLEY-ON-THAMES, Oxon RG9 4HG

Office	Secrétariat	(44) 01491 - 575742
Pro shop	Pro-shop	(44) 01491 - 575710
Fax	Fax	(44) 01491 - 412179
Situation	Situation	

3 km from Henley (pop. 10 058)
10 km from Reading (pop. 128 877)

Annual closure	Fermeture annnuelle	no
Weekly closure	Fermeture hebdomadaire	no
Christmas Day only		

Fees main season	Tarifs haute saison		full day
		Week days Semaine	We/Bank holidays We/Férié
Individual Individuel		£ 30	—
Couple Couple		£ 60	—

No visitors at weekends

Caddy	Caddy	no
Electric Trolley	Chariot électrique	yes
Buggy	Voiturette	no
Clubs	Clubs	£ 15/18 holes
Credit cards Cartes de crédit		no

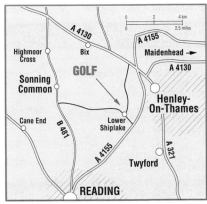

Access Accès : Leave M4 at Jct 8/9, A404, A4130 to Henley-on-Thames, then A4155 → Reading, turn right through Harpsden Village, Golf on the right.
Map 8 on page 420 Carte 8 Page 420

GOLF COURSE
PARCOURS

14/20

Site	Site	
Maintenance	Entretien	
Architect	Architecte	James Braid
Type	Type	parkland
Relief	Relief	
Water in play	Eau en jeu	
Exp. to wind	Exposé au vent	
Trees in play	Arbres en jeu	

Scorecard Carte de score	Chp. Chp.	Mens Mess.	Ladies Da.
Length Long.	5696	5517	4931
Par	70	70	73

Advised golfing ability		0	12	24	36
Niveau de jeu recommandé					
Hcp required	Handicap exigé	certificate			

CLUB HOUSE & AMENITIES
CLUB HOUSE ET ANNEXES

6/10

Pro shop	Pro-shop	
Driving range	Practice	
Sheltered	couvert	no
On grass	sur herbe	yes
Putting-green	putting-green	yes
Pitching-green	pitching green	yes

HOTEL FACILITIES
ENVIRONNEMENT HOTELIER

7/10

HOTELS HÔTELS

Shepherds - 4 rooms, D £ 48 — Henley
Tel (44) 01491 - 628 413 — 3 km

Holiday Inn - 107 rooms, D £ 105 — Reading 10 km
Tel (44) 01734 - 259 988, Fax (44) 01734 - 391 665

Forte Posthouse - 138 rooms, D £ 69 — Reading 10 km
Tel (44) 01734 - 875 485, Fax (44) 01734 - 311 958

Great House — Sonning-on-Thames
34 rooms, D £ 85 — 5 km
Tel (44) 01734 - 692 277, Fax (44) 01734 - 441 296

RESTAURANTS RESTAURANTS

Villa Marina - Tel (44) 01491 - 575 262 — Henley 3 km

French Horn — Sonning-on-Thames
Tel (44) 01734 - 692 204 — 5 km

L'Ortolan - Tel (44) 01734 - 883 783 — Shinfield 18 km

485

HERTFORDSHIRE (THE)

| | 15 | 7 | 7 |

The Tudor style architecture of this listed clubhouse gives an excellent first impression when you arrive here. You might expect a traditional course, but in fact you are met with excellent practice facilities and a very modern layout by Nicklaus Design, the company that Jack built. Nicklaus did not actually design this course in person, but over a rather limited area you find the same strategic approach with well designed and often large bunkers, water which comes very much into play but which can be avoided, and huge, well-contoured greens. The front nine are very interesting, the back nine a little less so. The whole layout doubtless needs to mature a little. Being so close to London, this very tranquil course deserves more than one visit.

L'architecture Tudor d'un Clubhouse classé donne d'emblée une impression de majesté. On attendrait un parcours très traditionnel. En fait, il y a ici de remarquables installations d'entraînement, et un parcours de dessin très moderne, créé par Nicklaus Design, la société du grand joueur et architecte américain, qui n'a pas vraiment signé lui-même le parcours. On y trouve cependant, sur un espace assez réduit, la même approche stratégique, avec des bunkers très dessinés et souvent grands, des obstacles d'eau bien en jeu, mais dont il est possible (et conseillé) de ne pas trop s'approcher, des greens vastes et très travaillés. L'aller est très intéressant, le retour un peu moins. L'ensemble a besoin de mûrir, sans aucun doute. Si proche de Londres, ce parcours très tranquille mérite plus qu'une visite.

The Hertfordshire Golf & Country Club

Broxbournebury Mansion, White Stubbs Lane
ENG - BROXBOURNE, Herts EN10 7 PY

Office	Secrétariat	(44) 01992 - 466666
Pro shop	Pro-shop	(44) 01992 - 466666
Fax	Fax	(44) 01992 - 470326
Situation	Situation	

8 km S of Hertford (pop. 22 176)
5 km N of Cheshunt (pop. 57 980)

Annual closure	Fermeture annuelle	no
Weekly closure	Fermeture hebdomadaire	no
Fees main season	Tarifs haute saison	18 holes

	Week days Semaine	We/Bank holidays We/Férié
Individual Individuel	£ 21	£ 25
Couple Couple	£ 42	£ 50

Full day: £ 33 / 39 (weekends)

Caddy	Caddy	on request/£ 25
Electric Trolley	Chariot électrique	no
Buggy	Voiturette	£ 18/18 holes
Clubs	Clubs	£ 8.50/18 holes

Credit cards Cartes de crédit
VISA - MasterCard - AMEX - DC - JCB

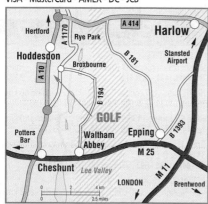

Access Accès : M25. At Jct 25 take A10 → Cambridge. Exit for Turnford, take A1170 to Bell Lane. Turn left, Bell Lane becomes White Stubbs Lane. Course on right. **Map 8 on page 421** Carte 8 Page 421

GOLF COURSE
PARCOURS
15/20

Site	Site	
Maintenance	Entretien	
Architect	Architecte	Nicklaus Design
Type	Type	parkland
Relief	Relief	
Water in play	Eau en jeu	
Exp. to wind	Exposé au vent	
Trees in play	Arbres en jeu	

Scorecard Carte de score	Chp. Chp.	Mens Mess.	Ladies Da.
Length Long.	5750	5403	4390
Par	70	70	70

| Advised golfing ability Niveau de jeu recommandé | 0 | 12 | 24 | 36 |
| Hcp required | Handicap exigé | 28 Men, 36 Ladies |

CLUB HOUSE & AMENITIES
CLUB HOUSE ET ANNEXES
7/10

Pro shop	Pro-shop	
Driving range	Practice	
Sheltered	couvert	30 bays
On grass	sur herbe	yes (May → Oct)
Putting-green	putting-green	yes
Pitching-green	pitching green	yes

HOTEL FACILITIES
ENVIRONNEMENT HOTELIER
7/10

HOTELS HÔTELS
Cheshunt Marriott - 133 rooms, D £ 110   Cheshunt
Tel (44) 01992 - 451 245   4 km
Fax (44) 01992 - 440 120

Churchgate Manor - 82 rooms, D £ 80   Old Harlow
Tel (44) 01279 - 420 246   12 km
Fax (44) 01279 - 437 720

Harlow Moat House - 118 rooms, D £ 65   Harlow
Tel (44) 01279 - 829 988   10 km
Fax (44) 01279 - 635 094

White Horse - 42 rooms, D £ 90   Hertingfordbury
Tel (44) 01992 - 586 791   9 km
Fax (44) 01992 - 550 809

RESTAURANT RESTAURANT
Cheshunt Marriott   Cheshunt
Tel (44) 01992 - 451 245   4 km

486

HEVER

An impressive site and one of the great new clubs you need to know in the South-West of England which is now so easy to reach courtesy of Eurotunnel. The course, clubhouse and hotel have been laid out in the estate of a castle where Ann Boleyn spent her childhood before briefly becoming Henry VIII's second wife. A stream is in play on almost one half of the course before running into the castle lake, but the hazard is psychologically rather than really dangerous. The trees are much more of a problem and those already on the estate have been supplemented by young plantations which will gradually make their presence felt on the fairways and alter the course as the years go by. As a general rule, Nicholson has made good use of existing features, particularly on the dog-legs, and has created enough variety for the course to be constantly enjoyable. Good work and a pretty place to spend a fine day's golfing.

Un site impressionnant, et l'un des grands nouveaux clubs à connaître dans le sud-ouest de l'Angleterre, si facilement accessible maintenant par Eurotunnel. Le golf, le Clubhouse et l'hôtel ont été créés dans le domaine d'un château où Ann Boleyn passa son enfance, avant d'être la seconde et passagère épouse d'Henry VIII. Le parcours met en jeu sur près de la moitié des trous un cours d'eau se jetant dans le lac du château, mais cet obstacle est plus psychologique que vraiment dangereux. Les arbres le sont bien davantage, et ceux existant dans le parc ont été complétés par de jeunes plantations, qui viendront empiéter sur les fairways et modifier le parcours avec les années. En règle générale, Nicholson a fait bon usage des éléments existant, en particulier sur les doglegs, et donné assez de diversité pour que le plaisir soit constamment renouvelé. Du bon travail et un joli endroit pour passer une bonne journée de golf.

Hever Golf Club
ENG - HEVER, Kent TN8 7NG

Office	Secrétariat	(44) 01732 - 700771
Pro shop	Pro-shop	(44) 01732 - 700785
Fax	Fax	(44) 01732 - 700775
Situation	Situation	

3 km from Edenbridge (pop. 7 581)
10 km from Tonbridge (pop. 101 765)

Annual closure	Fermeture annnuelle	no
Weekly closure	Fermeture hebdomadaire	no

Fees main season	Tarifs haute saison	18 holes
	Week days Semaine	We/Bank holidays We/Férié
Individual Individuel	£ 29	£ 45
Couple Couple	£ 58	£ 90

Visitors after 11.00 pm on weekends

Caddy	Caddy	no
Electric Trolley	Chariot électrique	no
Buggy	Voiturette	£ 20/18 holes
Clubs	Clubs	£ 25/18 holes

Credit cards Cartes de crédit
VISA - MasterCard - AMEX

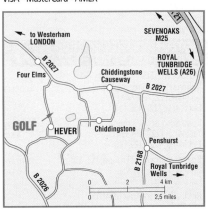

Access Accès : M25 Jct 6, A22, A25 → Sevenoaks.
Limpsfield B269 to Crockam Hill, Four Elms, Bough
Beech → Hever Castle
Map 7 on page 419 Carte 7 Page 419

GOLF COURSE
PARCOURS
14/20

Site	Site	
Maintenance	Entretien	
Architect	Architecte	Peter Nicholson
Type	Type	parkland
Relief	Relief	
Water in play	Eau en jeu	
Exp. to wind	Exposé au vent	
Trees in play	Arbres en jeu	

Scorecard Carte de score	Chp. Chp.	Mens Mess.	Ladies Da.
Length Long.	6302	6085	5144
Par	72	72	73

Advised golfing ability Niveau de jeu recommandé	0 12 24 36
Hcp required Handicap exigé	certificate

CLUB HOUSE & AMENITIES
CLUB HOUSE ET ANNEXES
8/10

Pro shop	Pro-shop	
Driving range	Practice	
Sheltered	couvert	no
On grass	sur herbe	yes
Putting-green	putting-green	yes
Pitching-green	pitching green	yes

HOTEL FACILITIES
ENVIRONNEMENT HOTELIER
8/10

HOTELS HÔTELS
Hever Golf Hotel — on site
64 rooms, D £ 80
Tel (44) 01732 - 700 136
Fax (44) 01732 - 700 138

Rose & Crown — Tonbridge
48 rooms, D £ 65 — 10 km
Tel (44) 01732 - 357 966
Fax (44) 01732 - 357 194

RESTAURANTS RESTAURANTS
Honours Mill — Edenbridge
Tel (44) 01732 - 866757 — 4 km

The Office — Tonbridge
Tel (44) 01732 - 353660 — 10 km

487

Here we are out in the country, with wild peacocks strutting around the clubhouse, jet fighters and trainers flying overhead to disturb your putting stroke, and an obligatory stop at tea-time to taste the delicious cakes. High Post is a hilly course which can be tough on the legs and on your score, but the chalky terrain drains well and doesn't get heavy after rain. The fairways are wide and the rough not too exacting, except when you get too close to the hawthorn bushes. High Post might easily have led a quiet life out of the headlines, except that Peter Alliss drew attention to the course by rating the 9th hole as one of the best 18 holes in England. It is certainly the best without a single grain of sand, and the hollows and grassy sand-hills are often a tougher proposition than bunkers.

Ici, on est à la campagne. Des paons sauvages se promènent autour du Clubhouse, des avions de chasse et d'entraînement vous dérangent quand vous puttez, il faut s'arrêter à l'heure du thé pour déguster quelques fameux Cakes. On monte et on descend, ce qui tire sur les jambes comme sur les scores, mais le terrain crayeux est bien draînant, ce qui évite un sol trop lourd par temps de pluie. Les fairways sont larges, les roughs pas trop pénalisants, sauf auprès des nombreux buissons d'aubépine. On pouvait croire que High Post poursuivra sa vie tranquille à l'écart des grandes histoires, quand Peter Alliss attira l'attention sur ce parcours, en classant son 9 parmi les 18 meilleurs trous d'Angleterre. C'est en tout cas le meilleur où il n'y ait pas un grain de sable, et les dépressions ou buttes d'herbe sont souvent moins faciles à négocier que les bunkers.

High Post Golf Club
Great Durnford
ENG - SALISBURY, Wiltshire SP4 6AT

Office	Secrétariat	(44) 01722 - 782 356
Pro shop	Pro-shop	(44) 01722 - 782 219
Fax	Fax	(44) 01722 - 782 356
Situation	Situation	

6 km N of Salisbury (pop. 105 318)

Annual closure	Fermeture annnuelle	no
Weekly closure	Fermeture hebdomadaire	no

Restaurant: limited service on Mondays

Fees main season	Tarifs haute saison		18 holes
		Week days Semaine	**We/Bank holidays** We/Férié
Individual Individuel		£ 23	£ 28
Couple Couple		£ 46	£ 56

Full day: £ 30 - £ 35 (weekends)

Caddy	Caddy	no
Electric Trolley	Chariot électrique	no
Buggy	Voiturette	no
Clubs	Clubs	no
Credit cards Cartes de crédit		no

Access Accès : M3 to Southampton, then M27. Jct 2, A36 to Salisbury, then A345 → Amesbury. Golf on right side.
Map 6 on page 417 Carte 6 Page 417

GOLF COURSE
PARCOURS
15/20

Site	Site	▮▮▮▮▮▯
Maintenance	Entretien	▮▮▮▮▮▮
Architect	Architecte	Hawtree & Taylor
Type	Type	copse, open country
Relief	Relief	▮▮▮▮▮▮
Water in play	Eau en jeu	▮▯▯▯▯▯
Exp. to wind	Exposé au vent	▮▮▮▮▮▯
Trees in play	Arbres en jeu	▮▮▯▯▯▯

Scorecard Carte de score	Chp. Chp.	Mens Mess.	Ladies Da.
Length Long.	5738	5490	5172
Par	70	69	73

Advised golfing ability		0	12	24	36
Niveau de jeu recommandé				▮▮▮▯	

Hcp required Handicap exigé certificate (weekends)

CLUB HOUSE & AMENITIES
CLUB HOUSE ET ANNEXES
6/10

Pro shop	Pro-shop	▮▮▮▮▯▯
Driving range	Practice	▮▮▮▯▯▯
Sheltered	couvert	no
On grass	sur herbe	yes
Putting-green	putting-green	yes
Pitching-green	pitching green	yes

HOTEL FACILITIES
ENVIRONNEMENT HOTELIER
7/10

HOTELS HÔTELS
Milford Hall - 35 rooms, D £ 70 — Salisbury 6 km
Tel (44) 01722 - 417 411
Fax (44) 01722 - 419 444

Byways House - 23 rooms, D £ 50 — Salisbury 6 km
Tel (44) 01722 - 328 364
Fax (44) 01722 - 322 146

Rose and Crown - 28 rooms, D £ 130 — Harnham 8 km
Tel (44) 01722 - 399 955
Fax (44) 01722 - 339 816

RESTAURANTS RESTAURANTS
Just Brahms' — Salisbury 6 km
Tel (44) 01722 - 328 402

Rose and Crown — Harnham 8 km
Tel (44) 01722 - 399 955

488

A quiet course up until 1962, Hillside took on a new dimension with the acquisition of dune-land which Fred Hawtree set to work on. A part of the course is lined by pine-trees, forming an unusual setting rather as if the trees had been plucked and placed on a real links. The first holes run along the railway line and set a "down-the-middle" tone from the very beginning. The dunes and tall rough are more concentrated on the back nine (which won the admiration of Jack Nicklaus) and the fairways run down the dune valleys. In such a motley landscape where the wind can have such a diverse influence on the ball, it is not a bad idea to know how it blows in order to stay on track. Highly manicured but still looking very natural, always pleasant to play and walk on with this links-type soil, Hillside is certainly not the best known links course outside England but it is a must to play.

Parcours tranquille jusqu'en 1962, Hillside a pris une dimension nouvelle avec l'acquisition de terrains travaillés par Fred Hawtree en zone dunaire. De grands pins ornent une partie du parcours, formant un cadre inhabituel, comme un décor posé sur un links authentique. Les premiers trous longent la voie ferrée et annoncent qu'il sera impossible de se relâcher. Les dunes et les haut roughs sont davantage concentrés sur le retour (qui faisait l'admiration de Nicklaus), les fairways glissant dans les vallées. Dans un paysage aussi divers où le vent peut influer de manière différente sur la balle, il n'est pas mauvais de connaître les effets pour rester en piste. Très soigné, tout en conservant un aspect naturel, toujours agréable avec ce genre de sol de links si agréable à marcher et à jouer, Hillside n'est sans doute pas le plus connu des links hors des frontières, mais il est inévitable.

Hillside Golf Club

Hastings Road, Hillside
ENG - SOUTHPORT, Lancs PR8 2 LU

Office	Secrétariat	(44) 01704 - 567169
Pro shop	Pro-shop	(44) 01704 - 568360
Fax	Fax	(44) 01704 - 563192
Situation	Situation	

3 km S of Southport (pop. 90 959)
28 km N of Liverpool (pop. 452 450)

Annual closure	Fermeture annnuelle	no
Weekly closure	Fermeture hebdomadaire	no
Fees main season	Tarifs haute saison	18 holes

	Week days Semaine	We/Bank holidays We/Férié
Individual Individuel	£ 40	£ 50
Couple Couple	£ 80	£ 100

Full weekdays: £ 50

Caddy	Caddy	on request/£ 25+tip
Electric Trolley	Chariot électrique	no
Buggy	Voiturette	yes
Clubs	Clubs	£ 2 each/18 holes

Credit cards Cartes de crédit
VISA - Eurocard - MasterCard - AMEX - DC - JCB

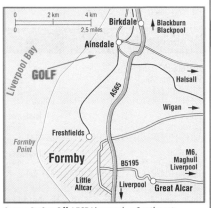

Access Accès : Off A565 Liverpool → Southport, between Hillside railway station and Royal Birkdale gates. Map 5 on page 415 Carte 5 Page 415

GOLF COURSE
PARCOURS — 18/20

Site	Site	
Maintenance	Entretien	
Architect	Architecte	Fred Hawtree, 1962
Type	Type	links
Relief	Relief	
Water in play	Eau en jeu	
Exp. to wind	Exposé au vent	
Trees in play	Arbres en jeu	

Scorecard Carte de score	Chp. Chp.	Mens Mess.	Ladies Da.
Length Long.	6165	5920	5345
Par	72	72	75

Advised golfing ability		0 12 24 36
Niveau de jeu recommandé		
Hcp required	Handicap exigé	certificate

CLUB HOUSE & AMENITIES
CLUB HOUSE ET ANNEXES — 7/10

Pro shop	Pro-shop	
Driving range	Practice	
Sheltered	couvert	no
On grass	sur herbe	yes
Putting-green	putting-green	yes
Pitching-green	pitching green	yes

489

HOTEL FACILITIES
ENVIRONNEMENT HOTELIER — 7/10

HOTELS HOTELS

Cambridge House Hotel — Southport
18 rooms, D £ 51 — 5 km
Tel (44) 01704 - 538 372, Fax (44) 01704 - 547 183

Scarisbrick — Southport
77 rooms, D £ 90 — 3 km
Tel (44) 01704 - 543 000, Fax (44) 01704 - 533 335

Stutelea — Southport
24 rooms, D £ 80 — 3 km
Tel (44) 01704 - 544 220, Fax (44) 01704 - 500 232

RESTAURANTS RESTAURANTS

The Warehouse — Southport
Tel (44) 01704 - 544 662 — 3 km

Valentino's — Southport
Tel (44) 01704 - 538 401 — 3 km

The Jasmin Tree — Southport
Tel (44) 01704 - 530 141 — 3 km

For a few days golfing in this region of Surrey, on the border with Hampshire and Sussex, Hindhead is one of a threesome which includes Hankley Common and West Surrey. This is very country landscape and a little tiring if you are pulling your own cart. The two parts of the course are very different, with the first 9 holes played in a valley (rather unusual in Surrey) and the back 9 at the top of a hill. From a visual point of view the front 9 are more memorable, especially the 6th, a 3-par looking down steeply onto a well-protected green. Before your round, go and have a drink at the bar, enjoy the magnificent view over the 18th hole and listen to the locals explaining how to play the course. It all comes down to one pint of best bitter and two ideas: keep it straight and keep out of the heather. They could also tell you to avoid the trees and bushes as well, but one look is enough for that to go without saying.

Pour quelques jours de golf dans cette région du Surrey à la limite du Hampshire et du Sussex, Hindhead apporte sa contribution à Hankley Common et West Surrey, dans un paysage très campagnard, mais un peu fatigant s'il faut aussi tirer son chariot. Les deux parties du parcours sont très différentes, les neuf premiers étant joués dans une vallée (c'est peu habituel dans le Surrey) et les neuf derniers au sommet d'une colline. Visuellement, l'aller est plus mémorable, on se souviendra en particulier du 6, un par 3 au green en contrebas et très défendu. Avant de jouer, allez donc faire un tour au bar où les vues sur le 18 sont magnifiques, et où les locaux vous expliqueront la stratégie du parcours. Elle tient en une pinte et deux idées : restez droit et évitez la bruyère. On ne vous dira pas d'éviter aussi les bois et buissons, cela va sans dire en jetant un seul coup d'oeil.

Hindhead Golf Club

Churt Road
ENG - HINDHEAD, Surrey GU26 6HX

Office	Secrétariat	(44) 01428 - 604614
Pro shop	Pro-shop	(44) 01428 - 604458
Fax	Fax	(44) 01428 - 608508
Situation	Situation	

4 km from Haslemere (pop. 7 326)

Annual closure	Fermeture annnuelle	no
Weekly closure	Fermeture hebdomadaire	no

Fees main season
Tarifs haute saison · 18 holes

	Week days Semaine	We/Bank holidays We/Férié
Individual Individuel	£ 36	£ 44
Couple Couple	£ 72	£ 88

Caddy	Caddy	no
Electric Trolley	Chariot électrique	no
Buggy	Voiturette	no
Clubs	Clubs	no

Credit cards Cartes de crédit
VISA - MasterCard (not for greenfees)

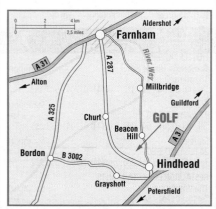

Access Accès : London, A3 (→ Portsmouth). Approx. 9 km (5 m) after Milford, turn right onto A287 → Hindhead, Farnham. After Beacon Hill, golf on right side. **Map 7 on page 418** Carte 7 Page 418

GOLF COURSE / PARCOURS · 16/20

Site	Site	▰▰▰▱▱
Maintenance	Entretien	▰▰▰▱▱
Architect	Architecte	J.H. Taylor
Type	Type	inland, heathland
Relief	Relief	▰▰▰▱▱
Water in play	Eau en jeu	▰▱▱▱▱
Exp. to wind	Exposé au vent	▰▱▱▱▱
Trees in play	Arbres en jeu	▰▰▰▰▱

Scorecard Carte de score	Chp. Chp.	Mens Mess.	Ladies Da.
Length Long.	5735	5520	4992
Par	70	69	72

Advised golfing ability
Niveau de jeu recommandé · 0 12 24 36
Hcp required · Handicap exigé · certificate

CLUB HOUSE & AMENITIES / CLUB HOUSE ET ANNEXES · 7/10

Pro shop	Pro-shop	▰▰▰▱▱
Driving range	Practice	▰▰▰▱▱
Sheltered	couvert	2 nets
On grass	sur herbe	yes
Putting-green	putting-green	yes
Pitching-green	pitching green	yes

HOTEL FACILITIES / ENVIRONNEMENT HOTELIER · 6/10

HOTELS HÔTELS
Pride of the Valley · Churt
11 rooms, D £ 70 · 2 km
Tel (44) 01428 - 605 799, Fax (44) 01428 - 605 875

Lythe Hill · Haslemere
28 rooms, D £ 85 · 6 km
Tel (44) 01428 - 651 251, Fax (44) 01428 - 644 131

Georgian · Haslemere
24 rooms, D £ 75 · 4 km
Tel (44) 01428 - 651 555, Fax (44) 01428 - 661 304

RESTAURANTS RESTAURANTS
Undershaw - Tel (44) 01428 - 604 039 · Hindhead 1 km
Fleur de Sel - Tel (44) 01428 - 651 462 · Haslemere 4 km
Auberge de France · Haslemere 4 km
Tel(44) 01428 - 651 251

490

If you mentioned East Anglia to the majority of continental golfers who are unfamiliar with England, they'd probably think you were talking about a make of car. In fact it is a region and home to some of the country's finest links including Hunstanton, nestling in a superb landscape of dunes, wild grass and scrubby bushes. From the 4th to the 15th holes, after a comparatively placid start, the course winds in every direction and makes that all-important judgment for each shot even more complicated. And just to prove once and for all that golf is an unfair game, this course boasts a famous par 3 hole with a blind green. In contrast, neither the sea nor the beach is out of bounds. Hunstanton plays host to major amateur tournaments, which is only fair dues for this often unorthodox and uplifting course. You might find it more enjoyable if you lose your scoring pencil.

On peut parier que pour les continentaux (qui ne connaissent guère l'Angleterre), East Anglia est le nom d'une voiture. Dans cette région, on trouve quelques-uns des plus beaux links du pays, dont Hunstanton, blotti dans un superbe paysage de dunes couronnées d'herbes folles et de buissons touffus. Du 4 au 15, après un départ assez calme, les trous ne cessent de tourner dans toutes les directions, ce qui n'est pas fait pour faciliter le jugement, pourtant plus que nécessaire ici. Pour faire définitivement comprendre que le golf n'est pas un jeu juste, on trouve ici un fameux par 3 avec green aveugle. En revanche, ni la mer ni la plage ne sont hors limites. Hunstanton reçoit de grandes compétitions amateur, c'est justice, avec ce tracé souvent peu orthodoxe, exaltant et d'autant plus amusant que l'on a perdu son crayon pour noter le score.

Hunstanton Golf Club

Golf Course Road
ENG - OLD HUNSTANTON, Norfolk PE36 6JQ

Office	Secrétariat	(44) 01485 - 532811
Pro shop	Pro-shop	(44) 01485 - 532751
Fax	Fax	(44) 01485 - 532319
Situation	Situation	

1 km from Hunstanton (pop. 4 736)
27 km from King's Lynn (pop. 41 281)

Annual closure	Fermeture annnuelle	no
Weekly closure	Fermeture hebdomadaire	no

Fees main season
Tarifs haute saison — 18 holes

	Week days Semaine	We/Bank holidays We/Férié
Individual Individuel	£ 42	£ 53
Couple Couple	£ 84	£ 106

Caddy	Caddy	no
Electric Trolley	Chariot électrique	no
Buggy	Voiturette	no
Clubs	Clubs	no

Credit cards Cartes de crédit — no

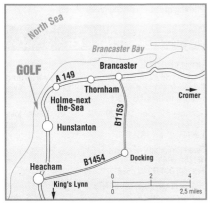

Access Accès : London M11. Cambridge A10 to King's Lynn. A149 North through Hunstanton to Old Hunstanton. Turn left → Golf course.
Map 4 on page 413 Carte 4 Page 413

GOLF COURSE
PARCOURS
17/20

Site	Site	▰▰▰▰▱
Maintenance	Entretien	▰▰▰▰▱
Architect	Architecte	James Braid George Fernie
Type	Type	seaside course, links
Relief	Relief	▰▱▱▱▱
Water in play	Eau en jeu	▰▱▱▱▱
Exp. to wind	Exposé au vent	▰▰▰▰▱
Trees in play	Arbres en jeu	▰▱▱▱▱

Scorecard Carte de score	Chp. Chp.	Mens Mess.	Ladies Da.
Length Long.	6061	5700	5375
Par	72	72	75

Advised golfing ability Niveau de jeu recommandé	0	12	24	36

Hcp required — Handicap exigé — certificate

CLUB HOUSE & AMENITIES
CLUB HOUSE ET ANNEXES
7/10

Pro shop	Pro-shop	▰▰▰▱▱
Driving range	Practice	▰▰▰▱▱
Sheltered	couvert	no
On grass	sur herbe	yes
Putting-green	putting-green	yes
Pitching-green	pitching green	no

HOTEL FACILITIES
ENVIRONNEMENT HOTELIER
6/10

HOTELS HÔTELS

Le Strange Arms - 36 rooms, D £ 70 — Hunstanton 200 m
Tel (44) 01485 - 534 411
Fax (44) 01485 - 534 724

Congham Hall -12 rooms, D £ 100 — Grimston 28 km
Tel (44) 01485 - 600 250
Fax (44) 01485 - 601 191

Duke's Head - 71 rooms, D £ 70 — King's Lynn 27 km
Tel (44) 01553 - 774 996
Fax (44) 01553 - 763 556

RESTAURANTS RESTAURANTS

The Hoste Arms — Burnham Market 15 km
Tel (44) 01328 - 738777

Rococo — King's Lynn 27 km
Tel (44) 01553 - 771483

491

14	6	7

At the beginning of the century, Daimlers and then a bus would ferry players to and from Henley railway station. Those were the good old days when service and hospitality meant more than they do today. Huntercombe has become a members' course where green-fees are tolerated on week-days only, although from our experience with no great enthusiasm. This is a pity because here is a layout, designed by Willie Park Jr. over heather and gorse, which is an excellent course, demanding an accurate and serious game. On this very classical and so very British course, keep your head down and don't let yourself be distracted by the pretty view over the plain of Oxford. While in the region, spend a good day out in Oxford and visit Blenheim Palace, the castle of the Dukes of Marlborough whose gardens were designed by Capability Brown.

Au début du siècle, des Daimler puis un autobus du club faisaient l'aller-retour jusqu'à la gare d'Henley pour en ramener les joueurs. C'était l'époque héroïque où le service et l'accueil voulaient dire davantage qu'aujourd'hui. Huntercombe est devenu un golf de membres où l'accès en semaine est toléré, mais pas forcément enthousiaste d'après notre expérience. C'est dommage car le tracé de Willie Park Jr en terrain de bruyère est d'excellente qualité, il exige un jeu précis et sérieux, où on ne lèvera la tête que pour admirer de jolis panoramas sur la plaine d'Oxford. Un parcours très classique et terriblement britannique. Dans la région, il ne faudra pas oublier de passer une bonne journée à Oxford et au Blenheim Palace, château des ducs de Marlborough, où les jardins créés par le grand paysagiste Capability Brown vous donneront des idées.

Huntercombe Golf Club

Nuffield
ENG - HENLEY-ON-THAMES, Oxon RG9 5SL

Office	Secrétariat	(44) 01491 - 641207
Pro shop	Pro-shop	(44) 01491 - 641241
Fax	Fax	(44) 01491 - 642060
Situation	Situation	

10 km from Henley (pop. 10 058)
5 km from Wallingford (pop. 6 616)

Annual closure	Fermeture annnuelle	no
Weekly closure	Fermeture hebdomadaire	no
Fees main season	Tarifs haute saison	18 holes

	Week days Semaine	We/Bank holidays We/Férié
Individual Individuel	—	—
Couple Couple	—	—

Greenfees on request

Caddy	Caddy	no
Electric Trolley	Chariot électrique	no
Buggy	Voiturette	no
Clubs	Clubs	no

Credit cards Cartes de crédit	no

Access Accès : Leave M4 at Jct 8/9, A404, A4130 through Henley, → Oxford. Clubhouse on the left after 10 km (6 m.)
Map 8 on page 420 Carte 8 Page 420

492

GOLF COURSE
PARCOURS

14/20

Site	Site	
Maintenance	Entretien	
Architect	Architecte	Willie Park
Type	Type	heathland
Relief	Relief	
Water in play	Eau en jeu	
Exp. to wind	Exposé au vent	
Trees in play	Arbres en jeu	

Scorecard Carte de score	Chp. Chp.	Mens Mess.	Ladies Da.
Length Long.	5671	5498	5115
Par	70	70	72

Advised golfing ability Niveau de jeu recommandé	0	12	24	36
Hcp required	Handicap exigé	certificate		

CLUB HOUSE & AMENITIES
CLUB HOUSE ET ANNEXES

6/10

Pro shop	Pro-shop	
Driving range	Practice	
Sheltered	couvert	no
On grass	sur herbe	yes
Putting-green	putting-green	yes
Pitching-green	pitching green	no

HOTEL FACILITIES
ENVIRONNEMENT HOTELIER

7/10

HOTELS HÔTELS
George - 39 rooms, D £ 72 — Wallingford 5 km
Tel (44) 01491 - 836 665
Fax (44) 01491 - 835 359

Springs - 34 rooms, D £ 120 — North Stoke 5 km
Tel (44) 01491 - 836 687
Fax (44) 01491 - 836 877

Swan Diplomat - 46 rooms, D £ 120 — Streatley 9 km
Tel (44) 01491 - 873 737
Fax (44) 01491 - 872 554

RESTAURANTS RESTAURANTS
Leatherne Bottel — Goring 8 km
Tel (44) 01491 - 872 667

Beetle and Wedge — Moulsford 7 km
Tel (44) 01491 - 651 381

Welcome to the beautiful region of the Yorkshire Dales, where you can visit the Wharfe valley and Ilkley, Fountains Abbey and the town of Haworth, home to the Brontë sisters. While you are here, don't forget to play this superb course designed by Colt and Mackenzie, where the river Wharfe threatens your card on seven holes. Flat and laid out in picturesque landscape, Ilkley is a charming course where nothing is easy but where nothing is impossible, either. Just avoid the trees, the fairway bunkers and the traps beside the greens. Nothing could be simpler. The green-side bunkers also tend to obstruct the obvious approach route to what are generally excellent putting surfaces. A good score is by no means a certainty here, as there are only two par 5s for the chance of a birdie, five par 3s and a few long par 4s where you can easily waste precious strokes. Mark James, Gordon Brand and Colin Montgomerie are members here, and this course is good enough to make you feel almost envious.

De cette région très belle, on retiendra le Parc National des Vallées du Yorkshire, dont celle de la Wharfe qui irrigue Ilkley, le très bel et très curieux ensemble religieux et aristocratique de Fountains Abbey, et la ville d'Haworth, foyer des soeurs Brontë. Et l'on n'oubliera pas de jouer ce superbe parcours, dessiné par Colt et Mackenzie, où la Wharfe vient en jeu sur sept trous. Plat et dans un paysage pittoresque, c'est un parcours de charme, où rien n'est facile, mais rien impossible. Il suffit d'éviter les arbres, les bunkers de fairway, les bunkers de greens qui ferment l'entrée de greens généralement en condition parfaite. Un bon score n'est pas donné d'avance car il n'y a que deux par 5 pour espérer des birdies, cinq par 3 et quelques longs par 4 pour gaspiller toute ses réserves. Mark James, Gordon Brand et Colin Montgomerie sont membres ici, on n'est pas loin de les envier.

Ilkley Golf Club
Myddleton
ENG - ILKLEY, Yorkshire LS29 0BE

Office	Secrétariat	(44) 01943 - 600214
Pro shop	Pro-shop	(44) 01943 - 607463
Fax	Fax	
Situation	Situation	

1.5 km from Ilkley (pop. 13 530)
25 km from Leeds (pop. 680 725)

Annual closure	Fermeture annnuelle	no
Weekly closure	Fermeture hebdomadaire	no

Fees main season	Tarifs haute saison	full day
	Week days Semaine	We/Bank holidays We/Férié
Individual Individuel	£ 35	£ 40
Couple Couple	£ 70	£ 80

Weekdays: £ 15 after 5.00 pm

Caddy	Caddy	no
Electric Trolley	Chariot électrique	£ 4/18 holes
Buggy	Voiturette	no
Clubs	Clubs	£ 5/18 holes

Credit cards Cartes de crédit
VISA - Eurocard - MasterCard - AMEX - DC

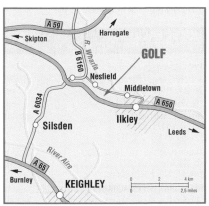

Access Accès : From Leeds, A660, then A65 W → Ilkley, Skipton. In Ilkley, turn right at town centre traffic lights and then second left.
Map 4 on page 412 Carte 4 Page 412

GOLF COURSE
PARCOURS
18/20

Site	Site	
Maintenance	Entretien	
Architect	Architecte	Harry S. Colt
		Alister MacKenzie
Type	Type	parkland
Relief	Relief	
Water in play	Eau en jeu	
Exp. to wind	Exposé au vent	
Trees in play	Arbres en jeu	

Scorecard	Chp.	Mens	Ladies
Carte de score	Chp.	Mess.	Da.
Length Long.	5636	5357	5120
Par	69	69	73

Advised golfing ability	0	12	24	36
Niveau de jeu recommandé				
Hcp required	Handicap exigé	no		

CLUB HOUSE & AMENITIES
CLUB HOUSE ET ANNEXES
7/10

Pro shop	Pro-shop	
Driving range	Practice	
Sheltered	couvert	no
On grass	sur herbe	yes
Putting-green	putting-green	yes (3)
Pitching-green	pitching green	yes (2)

493

HOTEL FACILITIES
ENVIRONNEMENT HOTELIER
6/10

HOTELS HÔTELS
Rombalds - 13 rooms, D £ 85	Ilkley
Tel (44) 01943 - 603 201	1 km
Fax (44) 01943 - 600 298	
Grove - 6 rooms, D £ 54	Ilkley
Tel (44) 01943 - 600 298	1 km
Randell's - 76 rooms, D £ 100	Skipton
Tel (44) 01756 - 700 100	12 km
Fax (44) 01756 - 700 107	

RESTAURANTS RESTAURANTS
Box Tree	Ilkley
Tel (44) 01943 - 608 484	1 km
Cow and Calf	Ilkley
Tel (44) 01943 - 607 335	1 km
David Woolley's	Burley-in-Wharfedale
Tel (44) 01943 - 864 602	5 km

This is exactly the hide-out you dream of when the wind is too strong to attempt the links course on the coast. It is also the opportunity to discover what is much more than an understudy course, an unthinkable notion for a course designed by James Braid. Even though the great man designed more than a hundred courses, he always succeeded in squeezing the very best out of the land or in creating an extraordinary challenge. Like on the 17th, a par 5 which would be quite harmless if he hadn't placed a few pot bunkers to make you wonder about the length of your second shot. If you decide to lay up, you have a tough third shot on your hands. Then there is the 4th hole where the green is hidden in a vale; if your drive is not just perfect, you have a blind second shot to contend with. Just a few examples to prove that nothing is given away here, and that "old" courses and "old" architects can still teach today's over-confident youngsters a thing or two.

C'est exactement le refuge dont on rêve quand le vent souffle trop pour aller sur les links de la côte. Et c'est l'occasion de découvrir ce qui est bien mieux qu'une doublure. Dire qu'il a été dessiné par James Braid devrait être une signature suffisante. Même s'il a fait des centaines de parcours, il a toujours su tirer du terrain la quintessence, ou alors créer des défis inédits. Comme au 17, un par 5 qui serait anodin s'il n'avait placé quelques pot bunkers pour que l'on s'interroge sur la longueur du second coup : si on décide de rester court, le troisième coup ne sera pas facile ! Prenons le 4, un énorme par 4 où le green est ici caché dans un vallon : si le drive n'est pas exceptionnel, le second coup est aveugle. De rares exemples pour dire que rien n'est ici donné, que les "vieux" architectes et les "vieux" parcours peuvent encore donner des leçons aux jeunes stars trop sûres d'elles.

Ipswich Golf Club

Purdis Heath, Bucklesham Road
ENG - IPSWICH, Suffolk IP 3 88VQ

Office	Secrétariat	(44) 01473 - 727 474
Pro shop	Pro-shop	(44) 01473 - 724 017
Fax	Fax	(44) 01473 - 715 236
Situation	Situation	

5 km from Ipswich (pop. 130 157)

Annual closure	Fermeture annnuelle	no
Weekly closure	Fermeture hebdomadaire	no

Fees main season	Tarifs haute saison	18 holes
	Week days Semaine	We/Bank holidays We/Férié
Individual Individuel	£ 30	—
Couple Couple	£ 60	—

Full day: £ 45 - No visitors at weekends
Booking essential

Caddy	Caddy	no
Electric Trolley	Chariot électrique	no
Buggy	Voiturette	no
Clubs	Clubs	no

Credit cards Cartes de crédit — no

494

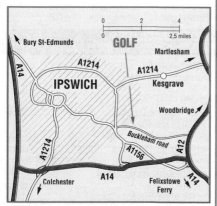

Access Accès : Ipswich A14 E. Left at roundabout
by St Augustine's Church. Golf into Bucklesham Road
Map 7 on page 419 Carte 7 Page 419

GOLF COURSE
PARCOURS   16/20

Site	Site	
Maintenance	Entretien	
Architect	Architecte	James Braid
Type	Type	inland, heathland
Relief	Relief	
Water in play	Eau en jeu	
Exp. to wind	Exposé au vent	
Trees in play	Arbres en jeu	

Scorecard Carte de score	Chp. Chp.	Mens Mess.	Ladies Da.
Length Long.	5792	5792	5172
Par	71	71	73

Advised golfing ability		0	12	24	36
Niveau de jeu recommandé					
Hcp required	Handicap exigé	certificate			

CLUB HOUSE & AMENITIES
CLUB HOUSE ET ANNEXES   7/10

Pro shop	Pro-shop	
Driving range	Practice	
Sheltered	couvert	no
On grass	sur herbe	yes
Putting-green	putting-green	yes
Pitching-green	pitching green	no

HOTEL FACILITIES
ENVIRONNEMENT HOTELIER   7/10

HOTELS HÔTELS

Suffolk Grange - 60 rooms, D £ 75 Tel (44) 01473 - 272 244 Fax (44) 01473 - 272 484	Ipswich 2 km
Novotel - 100 rooms, D £ 55 Tel (44) 01473 - 232 400 Fax (44) 01473 - 232 414	Ipswich 5 km
Marlborough - 21 rooms, D £ 70 Tel (44) 01473 - 257 677 Fax (44) 01473 - 226 927	Ipswich 5 km

RESTAURANTS RESTAURANTS

St Peter's Tel (44) 01473 - 210810	Ipswich 5 km
Galley Tel (44) 01473 - 281131	Ipswich 5 km

This is the kind of course where the superb views add a point or two to the artistic score. In the distance are the busy south-coast resorts of Poole and Bournemouth, and the Solent. Here you have all the peace and quiet of superb country landscape on the edge of a natural reserve for plant and bird-lovers. The broom and heather add to the decoration and to the problems awaiting players who are wayward or blown off line by the wind. Design-wise this is not exactly a links course but it does require the same skills of flighting and rolling the ball, of trying to outwit and outfox the course. A pretty site for a long weekend with a very pleasant clubhouse, warm welcome, excellent food and a classy additional 9 hole course where you can leave the less gifted members of the family to discover the joys of golf.

C'est le genre de parcours où la qualité des vues donne un petit point de "note artistique" en plus. Au loin, les stations très fréquentées de Poole, Bournemouth, le Solent. Ici, c'est le calme dans un superbe paysage de campagne, en bordure d'une réserve naturelle pour amoureux de plantes et d'oiseaux. Les genêts et la bruyère apportent un élément de décor, mais pas mal aussi d'empoisonnement aux joueurs peu précis, ou emportés par le vent. Ce parcours n'est pas exactement un links dans son style d'architecture, mais il demande les mêmes qualités, savoir travailler la balle, la faire rouler comme il faut, avoir aussi un peu de ruse, être en quelque sorte plus intelligent que le parcours. Un joli lieu de long week-end, avec un Clubhouse très agréable, un accueil chaleureux, une bonne cuisine et un 9 trous supplémentaire de bonne facture pour poser les joueurs les moins compétents de la famille.

Isle of Purbeck Golf Club
ENG - SWANAGE, Dorset BH19 3AB

Office	Secrétariat	(44) 01929 - 450 354
Pro shop	Pro-shop	(44) 01929 - 450 354
Fax	Fax	(44) 01929 - 450 501
Situation	Situation	

12 km S of Poole (pop. 133 050)
5 km from Swanage (pop. 9 037)

Annual closure	Fermeture annnuelle	no
Weekly closure	Fermeture hebdomadaire	no

Fees main season	Tarifs haute saison	18 holes
	Week days Semaine	We/Bank holidays We/Férié
Individual Individuel	£ 26	£ 32
Couple Couple	£ 52	£ 64
Full day: £ 35 - £ 40 (weekends) - £ 18 after 4.00 pm		

Caddy	Caddy	no
Electric Trolley	Chariot électrique	no
Buggy	Voiturette	£ 40/day
Clubs	Clubs	£ 10/18 holes

Credit cards Cartes de crédit
VISA - Eurocard - MasterCard

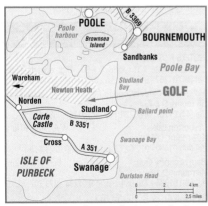

Access Accès : • Ferry from Sandbanks to Studland
• Poole, A351 through Wareham and
B3351 → Studland
Map 6 on page 417 Carte 6 Page 417

GOLF COURSE
PARCOURS
16/20

Site	Site	
Maintenance	Entretien	
Architect	Architecte	Harry S. Colt
Type	Type	seaside course, heathland
Relief	Relief	
Water in play	Eau en jeu	
Exp. to wind	Exposé au vent	
Trees in play	Arbres en jeu	

Scorecard Carte de score	Chp. Chp.	Mens Mess.	Ladies Da.
Length Long.	5730	5450	5080
Par	70	70	73

Advised golfing ability	0	12	24	36
Niveau de jeu recommandé				

Hcp required	Handicap exigé	28 Men, 36 Ladies

CLUB HOUSE & AMENITIES
CLUB HOUSE ET ANNEXES
7/10

Pro shop	Pro-shop	
Driving range	Practice	
Sheltered	couvert	no
On grass	sur herbe	yes
Putting-green	putting-green	yes
Pitching-green	pitching green	yes

HOTEL FACILITIES
ENVIRONNEMENT HOTELIER
6/10

HOTELS HÔTELS

Havenhurst	Swanage
17 rooms, D £ 50	5 km
Tel (44) 01929 - 424 224	

Mortons House - 16 rooms, D £ 80	Corfe Castle
Tel (44) 01929 - 480 988	5 km
Fax (44) 01929 - 480 280	

Crowthorne - 8 rooms, D £ 44	Swanage
Tel (44) 01929 - 422 108	5 km

RESTAURANTS RESTAURANTS

Cauldron Bistro	Swanage
Tel (44) 01929 - 422 671	5 km

The Galley	Swanage
Tel (44) 01929 - 427 299	5 km

495

) 16 | 7 | 6

A great club, as British as you could ever imagine, with two 18-hole courses and a huge and very comfortable clubhouse with wonderful old-style architecture. John O'Gaunt is close enough to London to be within easy reach but far enough not to be too busy, at least during the week. The trees are magnificent and give the course a very park-like appearance, adding style to what is a very discreet layout from Hawtree, at least for the main course. A classic layout which calls for no particular comment but which gives an impression of balance and fulfilment when you play it, especially for lovers of traditional courses that seem to have been around for ever. The other course, Carthagena, opened in 1981, is more of a heather-land course.

Un grand club bien britannique comme on l'imagine, avec deux parcours de 18 trous et un vaste Clubhouse à l'architecture ancienne digne d'une bonne série policière télévisée, et parfaitement confortable. John O'Gaunt est assez proche de Londres pour être facilement accessible, mais assez loin pour ne pas être trop encombré, en tout cas en semaine. Les arbres y sont magnifiques, donnant une allure de parc, qui convient bien à l'esthétique assez sobre de Hawtree, pour le parcours principal en tout cas. Très classique, c'est le genre de réalisation qui n'appelle pas de commentaires particuliers, mais donne une impression d'équilibre et de plénitude quand on le joue. Pour amoureux des bons parcours traditionnels, qui donnent l'impression d'être là depuis toujours. L'autre parcours, Carthagena, inauguré en 1981, est plus proche d'un style de terre de bruyère.

John O'Gaunt Golf Club

Sutton Park
ENG - SANDY, Bedshire SG19 2LY

Office	Secrétariat	(44) 01767 - 260360
Pro shop	Pro-shop	(44) 01767 - 260094
Fax	Fax	(44) 01767 - 261381
Situation	Situation	

18 km from Bedford (pop. 13 066)
35 km from Cambridge (pop. 91 933)

Annual closure	Fermeture annnuelle	no
Weekly closure	Fermeture hebdomadaire	no
Fees main season	Tarifs haute saison	full day

	Week days Semaine	We/Bank holidays We/Férié
Individual Individuel	£ 45	£ 50
Couple Couple	£ 90	£ 100

Caddy	Caddy	no
Electric Trolley	Chariot électrique	no
Buggy	Voiturette	£ 18/18 holes
Clubs	Clubs	no

Credit cards Cartes de crédit
not for greenfees

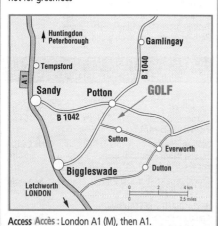

Access Accès : London A1 (M), then A1.
At Biggleswade, turn on B1040 → Potton.
Golf on right side before Potton.
Map 7 on page 418 Carte 7 Page 418

496

GOLF COURSE PARCOURS

16/20

Site	Site	
Maintenance	Entretien	
Architect	Architecte	Fred Hawtree
Type	Type	parkland
Relief	Relief	
Water in play	Eau en jeu	
Exp. to wind	Exposé au vent	
Trees in play	Arbres en jeu	

Scorecard Carte de score	Chp. Chp.	Mens Mess.	Ladies Da.
Length Long.	5861	5593	5112
Par	71	71	75

Advised golfing ability		0 12 24 36
Niveau de jeu recommandé		
Hcp required Handicap exigé		28 Men, 36 Ladies

CLUB HOUSE & AMENITIES CLUB HOUSE ET ANNEXES

7/10

Pro shop	Pro-shop	
Driving range	Practice	
Sheltered	couvert	no
On grass	sur herbe	yes
Putting-green	putting-green	yes
Pitching-green	pitching green	yes

HOTEL FACILITIES ENVIRONNEMENT HOTELIER

6/10

HOTELS HÔTELS
Stratton House - 31 rooms, D £ 38   Biggleswade 3 km
Tel (44) 01767 - 312 442, Fax (44) 01767 - 600 416

Holiday Inn Garden Court   Sandy 3 km
56 rooms, D £ 45
Tel (44) 01767 - 692 220, Fax (44) 01767 - 680 452

Wyboston Lakes   Wyboston 10 km
102 rooms, D £ 50
Tel (44) 01480 - 212 625, Fax (44) 01480 - 223 000

Barns Country Club   Bedford 18 km
48 rooms, D £ 67
Tel (44) 01234 - 270 044, Fax (44) 01234 - 273 102

RESTAURANTS RESTAURANTS
St Helena   Elstow (Bedford) 20 km
Tel (44) 01234 - 344 848

Barns Country Club   Bedford 16 km
Tel (44) 01767 - 270 044

Designed by James Braid, La Moye has been considerably lengthened and altered to become the great tournament course of the Channel Islands and long-time home to the Jersey Open. Laid out over the dunes and rolling mounds on the promontory overlooking St Ouen's Bay, it provides an outstanding view and a constantly entertaining challenge. Length and wind together don't make reaching the greens any easier, some of which are blind, all of which are well protected by bunkers or sand-hills. In this setting, only a sharp short game can help save a normal score. If you don't understand how to roll the ball up to the pin ask the pro or some of the local players. During the long evenings of May and early Summer, there are few places on earth where you can get so much pleasure out of playing golf.... no matter how well or badly you are playing.

Dessiné par James Braid, La Moye a été considérablement allongé et modifié, et représente le grand parcours de championnat des îles anglo-normandes, où s'est longtemps disputé le Jersey Open. Tracé sur les dunes et ondulations du promontoire dominant St Ouen's Bay, il offre un panorama exceptionnel et constitue un défi constamment intéressant. Cette longueur combinée au vent ne facilite pas l'accès aux greens, dont certains sont presque aveugles, et tous bien protégés par des bunkers ou les ondulations du terrain. Dans ces conditions, la qualité du petit jeu peut seule garantir un score correct, mais si on n'arrive pas à comprendre comment faire rouler la balle jusqu'au drapeau, il faut demander au pro ou aux joueurs locaux ! Au cours des longues fins de journée du mois de mai au début de l'été, il y a peu d'endroits où l'on puisse éprouver autant de plaisir à jouer au golf. Bien ou mal, peu importe.

La Moye Golf Club

La Moye
ENG - ST BRELADE, Jersey JE3 8GQ

Office	Secrétariat	(44) 01534 - 43 401
Pro shop	Pro-shop	(44) 01534 - 43 130
Fax	Fax	(44) 01534 - 47 289
Situation	Situation	

10 km W of St Helier (pop. 28 123)
4 km W of St Aubin

Annual closure	Fermeture annnuelle	no
Weekly closure	Fermeture hebdomadaire	no
Fees main season	Tarifs haute saison	18 holes

	Week days Semaine	We/Bank holidays We/Férié
Individual Individuel	£ 40	£ 45*
Couple Couple	£ 80	£ 90*

* only after 2.30 pm at weekends - Full weekday: £55

Caddy	Caddy	no
Electric Trolley	Chariot électrique	£ 5/18 holes
Buggy	Voiturette	£ 18/18 holes
Clubs	Clubs	£ 10/18 holes

Credit cards Cartes de crédit
VISA - MasterCard

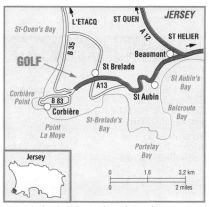

Access Accès : St Helier A1 through St Aubin,
then A13 → St Brelade.
Map 9 on page 422 Carte 9 Page 422

GOLF COURSE
PARCOURS
17 /20

Site	Site	▬▬▬▬
Maintenance	Entretien	▬▬▬▬
Architect	Architecte	James Braid
Type	Type	seaside course, links
Relief	Relief	▬
Water in play	Eau en jeu	
Exp. to wind	Exposé au vent	▬▬▬▬
Trees in play	Arbres en jeu	▬

Scorecard Carte de score	Chp. Chp.	Mens Mess.	Ladies Da.
Length Long.	5998	5775	5320
Par	72	72	74

Advised golfing ability	0	12	24	36
Niveau de jeu recommandé				

Hcp required Handicap exigé   24 Men, 30 Ladies

CLUB HOUSE & AMENITIES
CLUB HOUSE ET ANNEXES
7 /10

Pro shop	Pro-shop	▬▬▬▬
Driving range	Practice	▬▬▬
Sheltered	couvert	10 mats
On grass	sur herbe	no
Putting-green	putting-green	yes
Pitching-green	pitching green	yes

HOTEL FACILITIES
ENVIRONNEMENT HOTELIER
8 /10

HOTELS HÔTELS

L'Horizon - 107 rooms, D £ 150	St Brelade's Bay
Tel (44) 01534 - 43 101	2 km
Fax (44) 01534 - 46 269	
St Brelade's Bay - 80 rooms, D £ 120	St Brelade's Bay
Tel (44) 01534 - 46 141	2 km
Fax (44) 01534 - 47 278	
Sea Crest - 7 rooms, D £ 80	Corbière
Tel (44) 01534 - 46 353	2 km
Fax (44) 01534 - 47 316	

RESTAURANTS RESTAURANTSB

Broome's	St Aubin
Tel (44) 01534 - 42 760	4 km
Star Grill (L'Horizon)	St Brelade's Bay
Tel (44) 01534 - 43 101	2 km

497

It was the superb hotel of the same name that added this new 18-hole course to its estate, which includes a semi-detached pub transformed, quite logically, into a clubhouse. The owners love the end result, and quite rightly so. They wanted a course that was playable by all, an extremely difficult task but one that Jonathan Gaunt managed to achieve. This is a fair course that you can get to grips with right away, as the thick rough and rather frequent hazards (ditches and lakes) only penalise the truly wayward shot. Only two holes really call for high pitching shots, and even then the distances involved are short. Despite the course's tender age, green-keeping is excellent on a site where everything has been done so very professionally. Pleasant to play, challenging from the back tees and set in a very peaceful part of the country where there is a lot to do and see, Linden Hall is one of the excellent surprises to have emerged in recent years.

C'est le superbe hôtel du même nom qui a ajouté ce tout nouveau 18 trous à son domaine, comprenant un pub mitoyen transformé (c'était logique) en Clubhouse. Les propriétaires aiment leur réalisation, ils n'ont pas tort. Ils voulaient un parcours jouable par tous, ce qui reste bien le plus difficile, mais Jonathan Gaunt a bien rempli sa tâche. D'abord, c'est un parcours franc, jouable directement, mais le rough épais, comme les assez nombreux obstacles d'eau (fossés et lacs) ne pénalisent que les coups lâchés. Seuls deux trous obligent vraiment à porter la balle, mais ce sont alors de petits coups. L'entretien est excellent en dépit de la jeunesse du parcours, mais les choses ont été faites très professionnellement. Plaisant à jouer, exigeant des départs arrière, situé dans une région très calme avec beaucoup de choses à faire et à voir, c'est une des très bonnes surprises de ces dernières années.

Linden Hall Hotel & Golf Club
ENG - LONGHORSLEY, Northumberland

Office	Secrétariat	(44) 01670 - 516611
Pro shop	Pro-shop	(44) 01670 - 788050
Fax	Fax	(44) 01670 - 788544
Situation	Situation	

10 km from Morpeth (pop. 14 394)
40 km from Newcastle (pop. 259 541)

Annual closure	Fermeture annnuelle	no
Weekly closure	Fermeture hebdomadaire	no

Fees main season	Tarifs haute saison	18 holes
	Week days Semaine	We/Bank holidays We/Férié
Individual Individuel	£ 22.50	£ 30
Couple Couple	£ 45	£ 60

Caddy	Caddy	no
Electric Trolley	Chariot électrique	no
Buggy	Voiturette	no
Clubs	Clubs	yes

Credit cards Cartes de crédit
VISA - Eurocard - MasterCard - AMEX - DC

498

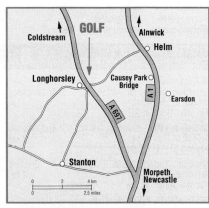

Access Accès : A1. After Morpeth, A697.
Golf at Longhorsley Village.
Map 2 on page 409 Carte 2 Page 409

GOLF COURSE
PARCOURS
17 /20

Site	Site	▬▬▬▬▬▬□
Maintenance	Entretien	▬▬▬▬▬▬□
Architect	Architecte	Jonathan Gaunt
Type	Type	parkland
Relief	Relief	▬▬□□□
Water in play	Eau en jeu	▬▬▬▬□
Exp. to wind	Exposé au vent	▬▬▬□□
Trees in play	Arbres en jeu	▬▬▬□□

Scorecard	Chp.	Mens	Ladies
Carte de score	Chp.	Mess.	Da.
Length Long.	6128	5857	4977
Par	72	72	72

Advised golfing ability		0	12	24	36
Niveau de jeu recommandé		▬▬▬▬▬▬			
Hcp required	Handicap exigé	24 Men, 36 Ladies			

CLUB HOUSE & AMENITIES
CLUB HOUSE ET ANNEXES
8 /10

Pro shop	Pro-shop	▬▬▬▬▬□
Driving range	Practice	▬▬▬□□
Sheltered	couvert	no
On grass	sur herbe	yes (not in winter)
Putting-green	putting-green	yes
Pitching-green	pitching green	yes

HOTEL FACILITIES
ENVIRONNEMENT HOTELIER
6 /10

HOTELS HÔTELS

Linden Hall Hotel — Longhorsley
50 rooms, D £ 120 — on site
Tel (44) 01670 - 516 611
Fax (44) 01670 - 788 544

Bondgate House Hotel — Alnwick
8 rooms, D £ 45 — 20 km
Tel (44) 01665 - 602 025
Fax (44) 01665 - 602 554

Orchard — Rothbury
6 rooms, D £ 70 — 15 km
Tel (44) 01669 - 620 684

RESTAURANT RESTAURANT
Linden Hall Hotel — Longhorsley
Tel (44) 01670 - 516 611 — on site

Lindrick was for a long while the last course where the American Ryder Cup team actually lost. And while it can be considered to be a very short course for the most powerful pros, it was once the venue for the British Ladies Open and showed itself to be most suitable for that event. For amateurs, men or women, this is a magnificent test of golf in heather-land shorn of any trees to speak of. It demands a style of play similar to when playing on a links course. Driving is very important, if only to avoid the well-placed bunkers and especially the very tough and highly penalising rough with ball-eating bushes. But the fairways are so wonderfully groomed that you won't want to miss them. Original for its landscape, intelligent for its strategic layout, natural-looking, fun to play and never all that busy, Lindrick is a must.

Lindrick fut longtemps le dernier parcours à avoir vu défaite l'équipe américaine de Ryder Cup. Et s'il peut être considéré comme un parcours très court pour les pros les plus puissants, il fut une fois le théâtre d'un British Open féminin qui le montrait bien adapté aux "proettes". Pour les amateurs, hommes ou femmes, ce magnifique test de golf en pleine terre de bruyère, avec assez peu d'arbres, demande un style de jeu assez analogue à celui des links. Le driving est très important, ne serait-ce que pour éviter les bunkers bien placés, mais surtout un rough très sévère, très pénalisant, avec en supplément des buissons mangeurs de balles. Mais les fairways sont d'une telle qualité que l'on serait assez stupide de les manquer ! Original par son paysage, intelligent par ses aspects stratégiques, naturel dans son aspect, amusant à apprivoiser, et assez peu fréquenté, Lindrick est un "Must."

Lindrick Golf Club

Lindrick
ENG - WORKSOP, Notts S81 8BH

Office	Secrétariat	(44) 01909 - 475282
Pro shop	Pro-shop	(44) 01909 - 475820
Fax	Fax	(44) 01909 - 488685
Situation	Situation	

5 km W of Worksop (pop. 38 222)
20 km E of Sheffield (pop. 501 202)

Annual closure	Fermeture annnuelle	no
Weekly closure	Fermeture hebdomadaire	no

Fees main season
Tarifs haute saison — full day

	Week days Semaine	We/Bank holidays We/Férié
Individual Individuel	£ 45	—
Couple Couple	£ 90	—

No visitors: Tuesdays and Weekends

Caddy	Caddy	on request/£ 15+tip
Electric Trolley	Chariot électrique	no
Buggy	Voiturette	no
Clubs	Clubs	no
Credit cards Cartes de crédit		Pro shop only

Access Accès : M1 Jct 31. A 57 East → Worksop.
Golf on right side after South Anston.
Map 4 on page 412 Carte 4 Page 412

GOLF COURSE / PARCOURS — 18 /20

Site	Site	
Maintenance	Entretien	
Architect	Architecte	Tom Dunn, W. Park Herbert Fowler
Type	Type	inland, heathland
Relief	Relief	
Water in play	Eau en jeu	
Exp. to wind	Exposé au vent	
Trees in play	Arbres en jeu	

Scorecard Carte de score	Chp. Chp.	Mens Mess.	Ladies Da.
Length Long.	5945	5643	5195
Par	74	71	74

Advised golfing ability		0	12	24	36

Niveau de jeu recommandé

Hcp required Handicap exigé certificate

CLUB HOUSE & AMENITIES / CLUB HOUSE ET ANNEXES — 6 /10

Pro shop	Pro-shop	
Driving range	Practice	
Sheltered	couvert	no
On grass	sur herbe	yes (2 grounds)
Putting-green	putting-green	yes
Pitching-green	pitching green	yes

499

HOTEL FACILITIES / ENVIRONNEMENT HOTELIER — 6 /10

HOTELS HÔTELS
Red Lion - 30 rooms, D £ 56 — Todwick 5 km
Tel (44) 01909 - 771 654, Fax (44) 01909 - 773 704

Aston Hall Hotel - 21 rooms, D £ 96 — Aston 6 km
Tel (44) 01142 - 872 309, Fax (44) 01142 - 873 228

Van Dyk - 16 rooms, D £ 55 — Clowne 8 km
Tel (44) 01246 - 810 219, Fax (44) 01246 - 819 566

Forte Travelodge - 40 rooms, D £ 35 — Worksop 4 km
Tel (44) 01909 - 501 528

Hunter House - 23 rooms, D £ 48 — Sheffield 20 km
Tel (44) 0114 - 266 2709, Fax (44) 0114 - 268 6370

RESTAURANTS RESTAURANTS
Old Vicarage - Tel (44) 0114 - 247 5814 Ridgeway 15 km
Le Neptune - Tel (44) 0114 - 279 6677 Sheffield 20 km

LIPHOOK

16	7	6

Hampshire is one of those counties whose villages, landscape and greenery seem to symbolise the English countryside as seen in films. The drive to Liphook and the hospitality awaiting visitors in the clubhouse are this and more. The designer has bent the course to match the landscape instead of the opposite, maybe because the excavators in service in the 1920s were not up to moving much earth. Liphook is a gem of a course and the hazards penalise absolutely every mis-hit shot. As they are clearly visible, the sanction comes as no surprise. The charming landscape might make you think this to be a kindly course, but nothing could be further from the truth. You need to flight the ball and play with care or else resign yourself to trying to hack your ball out of the heather. Add to this slick subtle greens and you have the full picture: Liphook is an exciting course whose visual discretion cleverly hides the difficulties in store.

Le Hampshire est l'une de ces régions qui symbolisent par leurs villages, leur paysage, leur végétation ce qu'est la campagne anglaise, comme dans les films. L'arrivée au golf de Liphook, comme l'hospitalité du Clubhouse vont dans le même sens. L'architecte a plié le parcours au paysage au lieu du contraire, mais il faut bien dire que, dans les années 20, les engins de terrassement ne permettaient pas de bouger beaucoup de terre. Liphook est un petit joyau, et les obstacles pénalisent absolument tous les coups manqués. Comme ils sont bien visibles, on ne saurait en être surpris. Le charme du paysage peut faire penser à un parcours aimable. Ce n'est pas le cas, il faut savoir travailler la balle, jouer avec prudence, ou alors accepter de devoir sortir ses balles de la bruyère. Si l'on ajoute la subtilité des greens, on aura compris : c'est un parcours passionnant, dont la discrétion visuelle cache bien les difficultés.

Liphook Golf Club
Wheatsheaf Enclosure
ENG - LIPHOOK, Hants GU30 7EH

Office	Secrétariat	(44) 01428 - 723271
Pro shop	Pro-shop	(44) 01428 - 723271
Fax	Fax	(44) 01428 - 724853
Situation	Situation	

2 km from Liphook
8 km from Petersfield (pop. 12 618)

Annual closure	Fermeture annnuelle	no
Weekly closure	Fermeture hebdomadaire	no

Fees main season	Tarifs haute saison	18 holes
	Week days Semaine	We/Bank holidays We/Férié
Individual Individuel	£ 37	£ 37
Couple Couple	£ 74	£ 74

Full day: £ 47 - Sunday: only after 12.00 pm
Saturday : booking in advance

Caddy	Caddy	no
Electric Trolley	Chariot électrique	£ 5/18 holes
Buggy	Voiturette	no
Clubs	Clubs	£ 7.50/18 holes
Credit cards Cartes de crédit		no

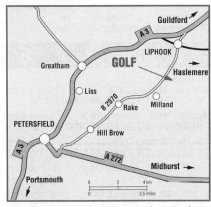

Access Accès : A3 London to Portsmouth. B2131, then B2070 (old A3). Golf on the right after Railway line
Map 7 on page 418 Carte 7 Page 418

GOLF COURSE
PARCOURS
16/20

Site	Site	■■■■■
Maintenance	Entretien	■■■■■
Architect	Architecte	Arthur Croome
Type	Type	inland, heathland
Relief	Relief	■
Water in play	Eau en jeu	■
Exp. to wind	Exposé au vent	■■
Trees in play	Arbres en jeu	■■■■

Scorecard Carte de score	Chp. Chp.	Mens Mess.	Ladies Da.
Length Long.	5550	5270	4975
Par	70	70	72

Advised golfing ability		0	12	24	36
Niveau de jeu recommandé					
Hcp required	Handicap exigé	certificate			

CLUB HOUSE & AMENITIES
CLUB HOUSE ET ANNEXES
7/10

Pro shop	Pro-shop	■■■■
Driving range	Practice	■■■
Sheltered	couvert	2 mats
On grass	sur herbe	no
Putting-green	putting-green	yes
Pitching-green	pitching green	yes

HOTEL FACILITIES
ENVIRONNEMENT HOTELIER
6/10

HOTELS HÔTELS
Lythe Hill — Haslemere
28 rooms, D £ 85 — 10 km
Tel (44) 01428 - 651 251, Fax (44) 01428 - 644 131

Georgian — Haslemere
24 rooms, D £ 75 — 10 km
Tel (44) 01428 - 651 555, Fax (44) 01428 - 661 304

Langrish House — Langrish
18 rooms, D £ 65 — 11 km
Tel (44) 01730 - 266 941, Fax (44) 01730 - 260 543

RESTAURANTS RESTAURANTS
Fleur de Sel — Haslemere
Tel (44) 01428 - 651 462 — 10 km

Lythe Hill — Haslemere
Tel (44) 01428 - 651 251 — 10 km

500

Having failed to get on the very private Rye course, make it along to Littlestone. It is not in the same league, but not to be sniffed at, either. Without ever being boring, the first seven holes are pretty ordinary, at least from a visual viewpoint. It is only after the 8th hole that the landscape really comes to life. And while you won't see any really impressive dunes, you are rarely on the flat with your feet level with your ball. Naturally the wind plays a very important role, especially since it is virtually never blowing in the same direction from the 7th to the 15th holes. The same goes for the last three holes, but here you have other things to worry about. This is a devilishly tough finish to the course, starting with a par 4 and a horrendous second shot, followed by a par 3 where you are likely to need more than one tee shot, and finally a par 5 dotted with bunkers. This is an excellent holiday course in summer. For the rest of the year you will need to shape all kinds of different shots.

Faute de pouvoir aller jouer Rye, aux portes fermement closes, Littlestone est loin d'être négligeable, même s'il n'est pas dans la même catégorie. Les sept premiers trous commencent de manière assez banale, du moins visuel-lement, même si les architectes ont réussi à ne jamais faire ennuyeux, mais le paysage s'anime à partir du 8. Et si l'on ne verra pas de dunes très impressionnantes, on se retrouve rarement les pieds au même niveau que la balle. Le vent joue un rôle très important, d'autant plus qu'il n'est jamais dans le même sens du 7 au 15. Il sera le même dans les trois derniers trous, mais ce finale est assez diabolique avec un par 4 où le second coup est terrible, puis un par 3 où le coup de départ risque d'être suivi de bien d'autres, et enfin un par 5 constellé de bunkers. En été, c'est un excellent parcours de vacances. Le reste de l'année, il faut savoir fabriquer tous les coups de golf.

Littlestone Golf Club

St Andrews Road, Littlestone
ENG - NEW ROMNEY, Kent TN28 8RB

Office	Secrétariat	(44) 01797 - 363355
Pro shop	Pro-shop	(44) 01797 - 362231
Fax	Fax	
Situation	Situation	

adjacent to New Romney
30 km from Ashford (pop. 52 000)

Annual closure	Fermeture annnuelle	no
Weekly closure	Fermeture hebdomadaire	no
Fees main season	Tarifs haute saison	18 holes

	Week days Semaine	We/Bank holidays We/Férié
Individual Individuel	£ 30	£ 45
Couple Couple	£ 60	£ 90

Full day: £ 42/50 - Some restrictions during weekends

Caddy	Caddy	no
Electric Trolley	Chariot électrique	no
Buggy	Voiturette	no
Clubs	Clubs	no

Credit cards Cartes de crédit
VISA - MasterCard

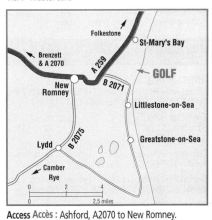

Access Accès : Ashford, A2070 to New Romney.
Follow signs to Littlestone. Turn left at seafront
Map 7 on page 419 Carte 7 Page 419

GOLF COURSE
PARCOURS

14/20

Site	Site	
Maintenance	Entretien	
Architect	Architecte	W. Laidlaw Purves Alistair Mackenzie
Type	Type	seaside course, links
Relief	Relief	
Water in play	Eau en jeu	
Exp. to wind	Exposé au vent	
Trees in play	Arbres en jeu	

Scorecard Carte de score	Chp. Chp.	Mens Mess.	Ladies Da.
Length Long.	5823	5497	5140
Par	71	71	73

Advised golfing ability Niveau de jeu recommandé	0	12	24	36
Hcp required Handicap exigé	24			

CLUB HOUSE & AMENITIES
CLUB HOUSE ET ANNEXES

6/10

Pro shop	Pro-shop	
Driving range	Practice	
Sheltered	couvert	no
On grass	sur herbe	yes
Putting-green	putting-green	yes (2)
Pitching-green	pitching green	yes (2)

HOTEL FACILITIES
ENVIRONNEMENT HOTELIER

5/10

HOTELS HÔTELS
Hythe Imperial - 98 rooms, D £ 100 — Hythe 10 km
Tel (44) 01303 - 267 441, Fax (44) 01303 - 264 610

Romney Bay House — Littlestone
11 rooms, D £ 90 — adjacent
Tel (44) 01797 - 364 747, Fax (44) 01797 - 367 156

Stade Court - 42 rooms, D £ 75 — Hythe 10 km
Tel (44) 01303 - 268 263, Fax (44) 01303 - 261 803

Broadacre Hotel - 10 rooms, D £ 50 — New Romney
Tel (44) 01797 - 362 381 — 1 km

RESTAURANTS RESTAURANTS
Romney Bay House — Littlestone
Tel (44) 01797 - 364747 — adjacent

Hythe Imperial - Tel (44) 01303 - 267441 — Hythe 10 km

501

Being close to the popular seaside resort of Blackpool, all the courses in the region are always busy on week-ends and in the Summer. And Summer is the only season when Lytham Green Drive, although not a links course, can be played like one. The rest of the year it plays much longer than the card would suggest as the fairways are heavily grassed. This was, in fact, one of the most immaculately prepared courses we encountered, hence our enthusiasm for the very advanced plans to extend and enlarge a very pretty and very elegant layout. Enjoy the course while it is still playing short, when it looks just great but probably plays a little more easily than you think. Walking the fairways in this sort of manicured park is recreation indeed after the thrills and spills of the coastal links courses.

La proximité de Blackpool, station balnéaire de grand renom et paradis du jeu, assure une importante fréquentation des golfs de la région en week-end et en été. Cette dernière saison est la seule époque où, sans être un links, Lytham Green Drive peut se jouer comme tel. Le reste de l'année, il paraît plus long que la carte ne l'indique, car le gazon est très fourni. C'était d'ailleurs cette année l'un des parcours les plus impeccablement préparés que nous ayions vus, et l'on ne peut qu'accueillir avec faveur les projets très avancés d'extension et d'agrandissement de ce très joli et très élégant parcours. Profitez des moments où il est encore court, où il est aussi plus séduisant que vraiment difficile : jouer dans un parc aussi manucuré représente une sorte de récréation après avoir connu l'exaltation sur les grands links de la côte.

Lytham Green Drive Golf Club
Ballam Road
ENG - LYTHAM, Lancs FY8 4 LE

Office	Secrétariat	(44) 01253 - 737390
Pro shop	Pro-shop	(44) 01253 - 737379
Fax	Fax	(44) 01253 - 731350
Situation	Situation	

1 km from Lytham St Anne's (pop. 40 866)
10 km from Blackpool (pop. 146 069)

Annual closure	Fermeture annnuelle	no
Weekly closure	Fermeture hebdomadaire	no

Fees main season	Tarifs haute saison	18 holes
	Week days Semaine	We/Bank holidays We/Férié
Individual Individuel	£ 25	£ 30
Couple Couple	£ 50	£ 60
Full weekday: £ 30		

Caddy	Caddy	no
Electric Trolley	Chariot électrique	no
Buggy	Voiturette	no
Clubs	Clubs	£ 10/18 holes

Credit cards Cartes de crédit
VISA - Eurocard - MasterCard - AMEX - DC - JCB
(Pro shop only)

502

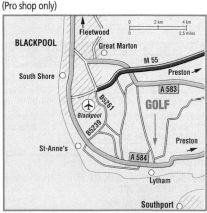

BLACKPOOL
Fleetwood
Great Marton
South Shore
M 55
Preston
A 583
B5261
Blackpool
GOLF
B5239
Preston
St-Anne's
A 584
Lytham
Southport

0 — 2 km — 4 km
0 — 2,5 miles

Access Accès : M6, Jct 32, M55 → Blackpool. Peel Corner lights to Ballam Road. Club on the left.
Map 5 on page 415 Carte 5 Page 415

GOLF COURSE
PARCOURS   **15**/20

Site	Site	
Maintenance	Entretien	
Architect	Architecte	Sandy Herd Jim Steer
Type	Type	parkland
Relief	Relief	
Water in play	Eau en jeu	
Exp. to wind	Exposé au vent	
Trees in play	Arbres en jeu	

Scorecard	Chp.	Mens	Ladies
Carte de score	Chp.	Mess.	Da.
Length Long.	5543	5390	5057
Par	70	70	73

Advised golfing ability		0 12 24 36
Niveau de jeu recommandé		
Hcp required	Handicap exigé	28 Men, 36 Ladies

CLUB HOUSE & AMENITIES
CLUB HOUSE ET ANNEXES   **7**/10

Pro shop	Pro-shop	
Driving range	Practice	
Sheltered	couvert	no
On grass	sur herbe	yes
Putting-green	putting-green	yes
Pitching-green	pitching green	yes

HOTEL FACILITIES
ENVIRONNEMENT HOTELIER   **8**/10

HOTELS HÔTELS
Clifton Arms Hotel - 44 rooms, D £ 86   Lytham 2 km
Tel (44) 01253 - 739 898, Fax (44) 01253 - 730 657

Glendover Hotel   Lytham St Anne's
63 rooms, D £ 76   3 km
Tel (44) 01253 - 723 241

Dalmeny - 130 rooms, D £ 75   Lytham St Anne's 3 km
Tel (44) 01253 - 712 236, Fax (44) 01253 - 724 447

Bedford - 36 rooms, D £ 59   Lytham St Anne's 3 km
Tel (44) 01253 - 724 636, Fax (44) 01253 - 729 244

RESTAURANTS RESTAURANTS
Pleasant Street - Tel (44) 01253 - 788 786   Lytham 2 km
Tiggy's Italian - Tel (44) 01253 - 714 714   Lytham 2 km
Grand Hotel - Tel (44) 01253 - 721 288   Lytham 3 km

Very close to the city of Manchester, this fine course is easy to play during the week, particularly for meetings where business and extreme pleasure mix very well indeed. Practice facilities are excellent, which is not always the case in Britain. The layout is not very long but the tee-boxes are well placed to provide each category of player with a good challenge. On an open moorland landscape, the course is very exposed to the wind which can become a major obstacle, particularly on the dog-leg holes, where, as on all Harry Colt courses, you need to think long and hard about where to put your drive to get the right approach to the greens, which are protected by bushes, trees and bunkers. Strategy is to the fore again at the 12th, where hitting the driver will leave you a short approach shot but on a sloping lie, while a 2 iron will leave you on a flat part of the fairway but with a longer approach to the green. A rather hilly course (buggy recommended), Manchester offers some fine views to make up for the difficulty of club selection.

Proche de Manchester, ce beau parcours est très accessible en semaine, notamment pour des réunions d'affaires joignant l'utile au très agréable. Il offre aussi, c'est rare, de bons équipements d'entraînement. Le tracé n'est pas très long, et les départs assez bien placés pour offrir un bon "challenge" à toutes les catégories de joueurs. Dans son paysage de lande, il est très exposé au vent, qui peut devenir l'obstacle essentiel, notamment sur les doglegs où il faut réfléchir sur sa ligne pour avoir les greens ouverts, comme sur beaucoup de dessins d'Harry Colt. Ils sont protégés par des buissons, arbres et bunkers. Stratégie encore au 12, où jouer le drive vous fera jouer un second coup court, mais dans une pente, alors que jouer un fer du départ vous permettra d'avoir les pieds à plat, mais un coup plus long. Assez accidenté, Manchester offre de très belles vues, comme pour compenser la difficulté de sélection de clubs.

Manchester Golf Club

Hopwood Cottage, Middleton
ENG - MANCHESTER M24 2QP

Office	Secrétariat	(44) 0161 - 643 3202
Pro shop	Pro-shop	(44) 0161 - 643 2638
Fax	Fax	(44) 0161 - 643 9174
Situation	Situation	

10km N of Manchester (pop. 404 861)
6 km S of Rochdale (pop. 202 164)

Annual closure	Fermeture annnuelle	no
Weekly closure	Fermeture hebdomadaire	no

Fees main season	Tarifs haute saison		18 holes
		Week days Semaine	We/Bank holidays We/Férié
Individual Individuel		£ 30	—
Couple Couple		£ 60	—

Full weekday: £ 40 - No visitors at weekends

Caddy	Caddy	no
Electric Trolley	Chariot électrique	£ 5/18 holes
Buggy	Voiturette	no
Clubs	Clubs	no

Credit cards Cartes de crédit
VISA - Eurocard - MasterCard

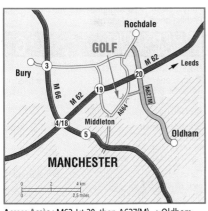

Access Accès : M62 Jct 20, then A627(M) → Oldham.
First exit, follow A664 signs.
Club on the right over humped back bridge.
Map 4 on page 412 Carte 4 Page 412

GOLF COURSE
PARCOURS

16/20

Site	Site	
Maintenance	Entretien	
Architect	Architecte	Harry S. Colt
Type	Type	parkland, moorland
Relief	Relief	
Water in play	Eau en jeu	
Exp. to wind	Exposé au vent	
Trees in play	Arbres en jeu	

Scorecard	Chp.	Mens	Ladies
Carte de score	Chp.	Mess.	Da.
Length Long.	5873	5660	5198
Par	72	72	74

Advised golfing ability		0	12	24	36
Niveau de jeu recommandé					
Hcp required	Handicap exigé	certificate			

CLUB HOUSE & AMENITIES
CLUB HOUSE ET ANNEXES

7/10

Pro shop	Pro-shop	
Driving range	Practice	
Sheltered	couvert	no
On grass	sur herbe	yes
Putting-green	putting-green	yes
Pitching-green	pitching green	yes

503

HOTEL FACILITIES
ENVIRONNEMENT HOTELIER

7/10

HOTELS HÔTELS

Norton Grange - 51 rooms, D £ 120 — Castleton
Tel (44) 01706 - 630 788 — 5 km
Fax (44) 01706 - 649 313

Midway Park Hotel - 24 rooms, D £ 90 — Castleton
Tel (44) 01706 - 632 881 — 5 km
Fax (44) 01706 - 653 522

Victoria and Albert - 128 rooms, D £ 132 — Manchester
Tel (44) 0161 - 832 1188 — 10 km
Fax (44) 0161 - 834 2484

RESTAURANTS RESTAURANTS

French Connection — Norden
Tel (44) 01706 - 50 167 — 6 km

After Eight — Rochdale
Tel (44) 01706 - 46 432 — 7 km

If we were to give golf course clubhouses a score for artistic content, Mannings Heath would be up there with the front-runners. And a good thing too, because after the 18th hole here you have the one idea of relaxing and putting your feet up. This is a steeply sloping course in a charming corner of Sussex, where golf can be a strenuous exercise (but you knew that already). So buggy and caddie are recommended. Between the woods, the sections of heather and the parkland, find time to admire the landscape and many squirrels, they might give you some valuable inspiration. Although not a long course, you need a good golfing brain to score well. Some drives have to be long enough to be able to see the green for the approach shot (2nd, 4th or 8th holes), while tee-shots on the par 3s need careful thought and execution to avoid the meanders of the Horkins. The 10th hole, with its cascade, is a particularly memorable experience, as is the par 4 11th hole. The second "Kingfisher" course is very pleasant but less testing.

Si l'on devait décerner une note artistique aux Clubhouses, Mannings Heath serait dans le peloton de tête. Tant mieux, car on a l'unique idée de se re-poser dans ce manoir après le 18, tant les ondulations de ce charmant coin de campagne du Sussex font du golf un sport (pour ceux qui en douteraient). Chariot électrique ou caddie conseillé. Entre les bois, les parties de bruyère ou de parc, on doit se donner le temps d'admirer le paysage, et le jeu des écureuils : c'est un bon prétexte pour reprendre ses esprits car, en dépit de sa faible longueur, il ne s'agit pas de jouer sans cervelle. Certains drives doivent être assez longs pour pouvoir ensuite apercevoir le green (2, 4 ou 8), et les coups de départ bien calculés sur les par 3 pour éviter la présence fréquente des méandres du Horkins : on retiendra en particulier le 10 avec sa cascade. Ou encore un par 4, le 11. Le second parcours, Kingfisher, est très plaisant, mais moins décisif.

Mannings Heath Golf Club

Fullers, Hammerspond Road, Manning Heath
ENG - HORSHAM, W. Sussex RH13 6PG

Office	Secrétariat	(44) 01403 - 210 228
Pro shop	Pro-shop	(44) 01403 - 210 228
Fax	Fax	(44) 01403 - 270 974
Situation	Situation	

3.5 km SE of Horsham (pop. 42 552)
12 km SW of Crawley (pop. 87 644)

Annual closure	Fermeture annnuelle	no
Weekly closure	Fermeture hebdomadaire	no
Fees main season	Tarifs haute saison	full day

	Week days Semaine	We/Bank holidays We/Férié
Individual Individuel	£ 42	£ 55
Couple Couple	£ 84	£ 110

Caddy	Caddy	on request
Electric Trolley	Chariot électrique	£ 10/18 holes
Buggy	Voiturette	no
Clubs	Clubs	£ 20/18 holes

Credit cards Cartes de crédit
VISA - Eurocard - MasterCard - AMEX - DC

504

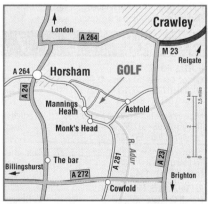

Access Accès : M23 Jct 11, through Pease Pottage
to Grouse Lane (left hand side). 5 km (3.5 m.)
to T junction, right and first left to Golf.
Map 7 on page 418 Carte 7 Page 418

GOLF COURSE PARCOURS | 14/20

Site	Site	▰▰▰▱▱
Maintenance	Entretien	▰▰▰▱▱
Architect	Architecte	Unknown
Type	Type	inland, heathland
Relief	Relief	▰▰▰▰▱
Water in play	Eau en jeu	▰▰▱▱▱
Exp. to wind	Exposé au vent	▰▱▱▱▱
Trees in play	Arbres en jeu	▰▰▰▰▱

Scorecard Carte de score	Chp. Chp.	Mens Mess.	Ladies Da.
Length Long.	5805	5460	4920
Par	73	71	73

Advised golfing ability Niveau de jeu recommandé		0 12 24 36
Hcp required	Handicap exigé	certificate

CLUB HOUSE & AMENITIES CLUB HOUSE ET ANNEXES | 8/10

Pro shop	Pro-shop	▰▰▰▰▱
Driving range	Practice	▰▰▰▱▱
Sheltered	couvert	no
On grass	sur herbe	yes (balls provided)
Putting-green	putting-green	yes
Pitching-green	pitching green	no

HOTEL FACILITIES ENVIRONNEMENT HOTELIER | 6/10

HOTELS HÔTELS

South Lodge — Lower Beeding
37 rooms, D £ 130 — 4 km
Tel (44) 01403 - 891 711
Fax (44) 01403 - 891 766

Ockenden Manor — Cuckfield
20 rooms, D £ 120 — 15 km
Tel (44) 01444 - 416 111
Fax (44) 01444 - 415 549

Cisswood House — Lower Beeding
30 chambres, D £ 85
Tel (44) 01403 - 891 216
Fax (44) 01403 - 891 621

RESTAURANT RESTAURANT

Jeremy's — Lower Beeding
Tel (44) 01403 - 891 257 — 4 km

It is no coincidence if there are so many buggies here. The superb views from the tee or green come courtesy of some roller-coaster landscape which makes this course something of an ordeal to walk. Designers Alliss and Clark followed the natural lie of the land and evidently had a lot of fun here, alternating pot bunkers or sprawling "sand-traps" and making extensive use of water hazards. All these difficulties are really dangerous because they are so strategic. And the relatively short yardage doesn't mean much when you are constantly shooting uphill or downhill. A spectacular, exciting and, first time out, often a surprising course in a category of its own. You come here for a few days of leisure, staying if you can at Manor House, a pretty piece of architecture with all the most modern amenities. You can also play as a green-feer.

S'il y a autant de voiturettes ici, ce n'est pas par hasard. Les vues superbes du haut des départs ou des greens, c'est au prix de montagnes russes qui rendent le jeu à pied très éprouvant. Les architectes Alliss et Clark ont suivi les contours naturels et se sont bien amusés dans un tel espace, alternant les "pot" bunkers ou de longues étendues de sable, et faisant usage généreux des obstacles d'eau. Toutes ces difficultés sont réellement dangereuses, car très stratégiques, et la longueur relativement faible ne veut pas dire grand chose avec ces changements incessants de niveau. Un parcours spectaculaire, souvent surprenant la première fois, parfois passionnant, et à classer à part. On vient ici passer quelques jours de plaisir, si l'on peut en logeant au Manor House, jolie pièce d'architecture, avec le confort le plus moderne, mais on peut aussi jouer au green-fee.

Manor House (at Castle Combe)
ENG - CASTLE COMBE, Wiltshire SN14 7 PL

Office	Secrétariat	(44) 01249 - 782 982
Pro shop	Pro-shop	(44) 01249 - 783 101
Fax	Fax	(44) 01249 - 782 992
Situation	Situation	

37 km E of Bristol (pop. 376 146)
18 km NE of Bath (pop. 78 689)

Annual closure	Fermeture annnuelle	no
Weekly closure	Fermeture hebdomadaire	no

Fees main season	Tarifs haute saison	18 holes
	Week days Semaine	We/Bank holidays We/Férié
Individual Individuel	£ 35	£ 45
Couple Couple	£ 70	£ 90
Full day: £ 55 - £ 70 (weekends)		

Caddy	Caddy	no
Electric Trolley	Chariot électrique	no
Buggy	Voiturette	£ 20/18 holes
Clubs	Clubs	£ 10/18 holes

Credit cards Cartes de crédit
VISA - Eurocard - MasterCard - AMEX - DC - JCB

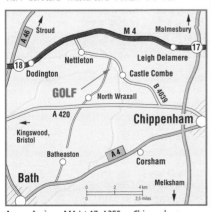

Access Accès : • M4 Jct 17, A350 → Chippenham, A420 on the right, then B4039 N of Castle Combe. • Bath: A46, A420 to Ford, then turn left to Castle Combe. **Map 6 on page 417** Carte 6 Page 417

GOLF COURSE
PARCOURS   **15**/20

Site	Site	
Maintenance	Entretien	
Architect	Architecte	Peter Alliss Clive Clark
Type	Type	copse, parkland
Relief	Relief	
Water in play	Eau en jeu	
Exp. to wind	Exposé au vent	
Trees in play	Arbres en jeu	

Scorecard Carte de score	Chp. Chp.	Mens Mess.	Ladies Da.
Length Long.	5496	5298	4659
Par	73	71	72

Advised golfing ability	0	12	24	36
Niveau de jeu recommandé				
Hcp required	Handicap exigé		28 Men, 36 Ladies	

CLUB HOUSE & AMENITIES
CLUB HOUSE ET ANNEXES   **8**/10

Pro shop	Pro-shop	
Driving range	Practice	
Sheltered	couvert	
On grass	sur herbe	yes
Putting-green	putting-green	yes
Pitching-green	pitching green	yes

505

HOTEL FACILITIES
ENVIRONNEMENT HOTELIER   **7**/10

HOTELS HÔTELS

Manor House Hotel 44 rooms, D £ 130 Tel (44) 01249 - 782 206 Fax (44) 01249 - 782 159	Golf on site
Castle Inn 7 rooms, D £ 95 Tel (44) 01249 - 783 030 Fax (44) 01249 - 782 315	Castle Combe 1 km
White Hart Inn 11 rooms, D £ 60 Tel (44) 01249 - 782 213 Fax (44) 01249 - 783 075	Ford 3 km

RESTAURANT RESTAURANT

Manor House Hotel Tel (44) 01249 - 782 206	Golf on site

The highest point of this course is more than 1,000 ft. above sea-level from where you can see as far as Glastonbury and the abbey (you need good eyes), Exmoor (you need binoculars) and Wales. If they add America to the list, then you must be at the bar. Despite the altitude, this is not too hilly a course and the turf is wonderfully springy underfoot. This adds comfort to the pleasure of playing a course where you are rarely on the flat, where you need to think, and where you need some good ironwork and razor-sharp putting: the greens come in all shapes, sizes, slopes and contours and rarely forgive poor reading. Although minor details are always being shuffled around, the original 9 hole course by Vardon, later completed by Frank Pennink, remained unchanged until 1988, when the purchase of new land took the par up to 71. The clubhouse is perhaps not the world's prettiest but the atmosphere inside is very friendly, which is better than the other way around.

Le point le plus haut du parcours est à plus de 300 mètres, d'où l'on voit jusqu'à Glastonbury et son abbaye (il faut de bons yeux), Exmoor (il faut des jumelles) et le Pays de Galles. Mais si l'on vous parle de l'Amérique, c'est que vous êtes au bar. Pourtant, le parcours n'est pas trop accidenté, et le gazon est d'une rare souplesse, ce qui ne fait qu'ajouter le confort au plaisir d'un parcours où l'on n'a pas toujours les pieds à plat, où il faut un peu de tête, un très bon jeu de fers et un putting affûté comme un rasoir, car les greens sont de formes, de tailles, et de reliefs variés, ils ne pardonnent pas une lecture négligente. Tout en remaniant en permanence les détails, le dessin de 9 trous par Vardon, complété par Frank Pennink, est resté inchangé jusqu'en 1988, où l'achat de terrains a permis de porter le par à 71. Le Clubhouse n'est peut-être pas le plus joli du monde mais l'atmosphère y est très amicale. C'est mieux que l'inverse.

Mendip Golf Club

Gurney Slade
ENG - BATH, Somerset BA3 4UT

Office	Secrétariat	(44) 01749 - 840 570
Pro shop	Pro-shop	(44) 01749 - 840 793
Fax	Fax	(44) 01749 - 841 439
Situation	Situation	

28 km SW of Bath (pop. 78 689)
38 km S of Bristol (pop. 376 146)

Annual closure	Fermeture annuelle	no
Weekly closure	Fermeture hebdomadaire	no
Fees main season	Tarifs haute saison	18 holes

	Week days Semaine	We/Bank holidays We/Férié
Individual Individuel	£ 20	£ 30
Couple Couple	£ 40	£ 60

Full weekday: £ 25

Caddy	Caddy	no
Electric Trolley	Chariot électrique	no
Buggy	Voiturette	£ 10/18 holes
Clubs	Clubs	£ 5/18 holes
Credit cards Cartes de crédit		no

Map

4 km
2,5 miles
B 3135
Midsomer Norton
Weston-super-Mare, Cheddar
Green Ore
A 39
B 3139
B 3135
A 37
Wells
A 371
East Horrington
Oakhill
GOLF
A 371
Cokley
A 39
Shepton Mallet
Glastonbury
A 361

Access Accès : Bristol, A37 → Shepton Mallet, Golf 4.5 km (3 m.) before Shepton Mallet. From Bath, A367.
Map 6 on page 417 Carte 6 Page 417

GOLF COURSE
PARCOURS
15/20

Site	Site	■■■■
Maintenance	Entretien	■■■■■
Architect	Architecte	Harry Vardon Frank Pennink 1965
Type	Type	open country
Relief	Relief	■■■■
Water in play	Eau en jeu	■
Exp. to wind	Exposé au vent	■■
Trees in play	Arbres en jeu	■■

Scorecard Carte de score	Chp. Chp.	Mens Mess.	Ladies Da.
Length Long.	5833	5653	5452
Par	71	71	75

Advised golfing ability Niveau de jeu recommandé	0 12 24 36	
Hcp required Handicap exigé	no	

CLUB HOUSE & AMENITIES
CLUB HOUSE ET ANNEXES
5/10

Pro shop	Pro-shop	■■■
Driving range	Practice	■■■
Sheltered	couvert	no
On grass	sur herbe	yes
Putting-green	putting-green	yes
Pitching-green	pitching green	yes

HOTEL FACILITIES
ENVIRONNEMENT HOTELIER
7/10

HOTELS HÔTELS

Shrubbery - 7 rooms, D £ 70 Tel (44) 01749 - 346 671 Fax (44) 01749 - 346 581	Shepton Mallet 5 km
Ston Easton Park - 19 rooms, D £ 150 Tel (44) 01761 - 241 671 Fax (44) 01749 - 241 377	Ston Easton 6 km
Thatched Cottage Inn 8 rooms, D £ 70 Tel (44) 01749 - 342 058 Fax (44) 01749 - 343 265	Shepton Mallet 5 km

RESTAURANTS RESTAURANTS

Bowlish House (book first) Tel (44) 01749 - 342 022	Shepton Mallet 6 km
Brottens Lodge Tel (44) 01749 - 880 352	Shepton Mallet 8 km

Mere was revived in 1985 when the clubhouse was completely overhauled (adding swimming pools, sauna, tennis courts, etc.), an extensive tree-planting program was begun and the course was given new tee-boxes and a new 18th green. The face-lift has "modernised" the original design by Braid and Duncan - you don't have to love the water hazards on the 7th and 8th holes - and generally enhanced the site with a more challenging finish to the course. Some rolling landscape adds a little variety to the layout where there is a pleasant mix of tight and wider holes. Putting and approach shots can be a tricky business on some of the tiered greens. And your best bet here is to pitch the greens rather than roll the ball. This is one of the most accomplished courses in the region of Manchester, a fair test and always a pleasure to play but only on week-days for visitors. Pity about the rather dubious pink scorecard for the ladies.

Mere a été réveillé en 1985 avec une refonte totale du Clubhouse (avec piscines, sauna, tennis, etc), la plantation de nombreux arbres, de nouveaux départs, un nouveau green au 18. Ce rajeunissement a un peu "modernisé" le dessin de Braid et de Duncan - on peut ne pas adorer les obstacles d'eau du 7 et du 8 - mais au profit de l'embellissement général du site, et du renforcement d'un finale très exigeant. Quelques ondulations apportent de la variété au terrain, où le tracé alterne agréablement les trous étroits et les espaces plus larges. Le putting et les approches sont intéressants et délicats à apprécier sur certains greens à plateaux : en général, on devra ici privilégier les coups levés. Dans la région de Manchester, c'est une des réalisations les plus achevées, et le parcours d'une grande franchise reste un plaisir à jouer. En semaine pour les visiteurs. Les dames ont une carte de score rose d'un parfait mauvais goût !

Mere Golf & Country Club

Chester Road, Mere
ENG - KNUTSFORD, Cheshire WA16 6LJ

Office	Secrétariat	(44) 01565 - 830155
Pro shop	Pro-shop	(44) 01565 - 830155
Fax	Fax	(44) 01565 - 830518
Situation	Situation	

20 km SW of Manchester (pop. 404 861)
3 km NW of Knutsford (pop. 13 352)

Annual closure	Fermeture annnuelle	no
Weekly closure	Fermeture hebdomadaire	no

Fees main season	Tarifs haute saison	full day

	Week days Semaine	We/Bank holidays We/Férié
Individual Individuel	£ 60	£ 60
Couple Couple	£ 120	£ 120

Visitors: Mondays, Tuesdays and Thursdays only

Caddy	Caddy	on request/£ 20
Electric Trolley	Chariot électrique	no
Buggy	Voiturette	£ 20/18 holes
Clubs	Clubs	£ 15/18 holes

Credit cards Cartes de crédit
VISA - Eurocard - MasterCard - AMEX - DC

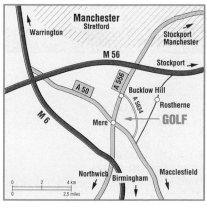

Access Accès : Manchester, M56 Jct 7. A556 S →
Northwich. Golf on left side before A50.
Map 4 on page 412 Carte 4 Page 412

GOLF COURSE
PARCOURS

15/20

Site	Site	▰▰▰▰▱▱
Maintenance	Entretien	▰▰▰▰▰▱
Architect	Architecte	James Braid George Duncan
Type	Type	parkland
Relief	Relief	▰▰▱▱▱▱
Water in play	Eau en jeu	▰▰▰▱▱▱
Exp. to wind	Exposé au vent	▰▰▱▱▱▱
Trees in play	Arbres en jeu	▰▰▰▰▱▱

Scorecard Carte de score	Chp. Chp.	Mens Mess.	Ladies Da.
Length Long.	6135	5910	5192
Par	71	71	74

Advised golfing ability Niveau de jeu recommandé	0	12	24	36

Hcp required   Handicap exigé   certificate

CLUB HOUSE & AMENITIES
CLUB HOUSE ET ANNEXES

7/10

Pro shop	Pro-shop	▰▰▰▰▱▱
Driving range	Practice	▰▰▰▰▱▱
Sheltered	couvert	no
On grass	sur herbe	no
Putting-green	putting-green	yes
Pitching-green	pitching green	yes

507

HOTEL FACILITIES
ENVIRONNEMENT HOTELIER

7/10

HOTELS HÔTELS
Kilton Inn - 28 rooms, D £ 49   Mere
Tel (44) 01565 - 830 420   1 km
Fax (44) 01565 - 830 411

The Cottons - 73 rooms, D £ 124   Knutsford 3 km
Tel (44) 01565 - 650 333, Fax (44) 01565 - 755 351

Victoria and Albert   Manchester 20 km
128 rooms, D £ 132
Tel (44) 0161 - 832 1188, Fax (44) 0161 - 834 2484

RESTAURANTS RESTAURANTS
Belle Epoque Brasserie   Knutsford
Tel (44) 01565 - 633 060   4 km
Sherlock Holmes   Manchester
Tel (44) 0161 - 832 1188   20 km
Magnolia (The Cottons)   Knutsford
Tel (44) 01565 - 650 333   3 km

Originally there were three courses here, two of which have survived beneath the impressive and even intimidating shadows of the clubhouse. The shirt and tie rule is so obvious here that you're surprised to see people actually dressed in casual wear on the course. The "West Course" is on the short side but goes very well with the "High" course, where from the 2nd hole onward you realise you'll need some sort of bearings or benchmarks if you are ever going to card a good score. The yardage book will come in handy for knowing where you should put your drive and for identifying the gardens where your ball should not go (especially on the front 9). A Harry Colt course is never a bland affair and this is no exception to the rule. The last nine holes are particularly memorable with three par 3s more than worthy of the designer's reputation. This is most definitely not the place where you could ever imagine golf becoming a sport for all and sundry, but it is one hell of a good course.

Au départ, il y avait trois parcours, dont deux sont restés sous l'ombre impressionnante, et même intimidante d'un Clubhouse où le port d'une cravate paraît tellement évident qu'on la gardera pour jouer (au cas où). Le "West Course" est assez court, mais constitue un bon complément au "High," où dès le 2, on comprend qu'il va falloir trouver ses marques pour espérer un score décent. Le "yardage book" ne sera pas inutile pour savoir où poser le drive, et pour identifier (surtout à l'aller) les jardins où il ne faut pas envoyer sa balle. Un parcours dessiné par Harry Colt n'est jamais indifférent, et celui-ci ne fait pas exception à la règle. on gardera un souvenir particulier des neuf derniers trous, avec trois par 3 à la hauteur de la réputation de l'architecte. Certes, ce n'est pas vraiment le lieu où l'on imagine que le golf puisse devenir un sport démocratique, mais c'est un bon parcours !

Moor Park Golf Club
ENG - RICKMANSWORTH, Herts WD31QN

Office	Secrétariat	(44) 01923 - 773146
Pro shop	Pro-shop	(44) 01923 - 774113
Fax	Fax	(44) 01923 - 777109
Situation	Situation	

35 km from Central London (pop. 6 679 700)
8 km from Watford (pop. 74 566)

Annual closure	Fermeture annnuelle	no
Weekly closure	Fermeture hebdomadaire	no

Fees main season	Tarifs haute saison		18 holes
		Week days Semaine	We/Bank holidays We/Férié
Individual Individuel		£ 50	—
Couple Couple		£ 100	—

Full day: £ 75 - Booking essential
No visitors at weekends

Caddy	Caddy	on request/£ 25
Electric Trolley	Chariot électrique	£ 7.50/18 holes
Buggy	Voiturette	£ 20/18 holes
Clubs	Clubs	£ 15/18 holes

Credit cards Cartes de crédit
not for greenfees

508

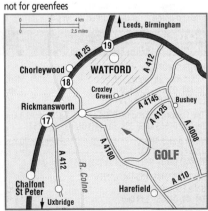

Access Accès : London, M4 Jct 3, A312, A4180, A404 →
Rickmansworth, Golf on the right.
Map 8 on page 420 Carte 8 Page 420

GOLF COURSE
PARCOURS

17 /20

Site	Site	
Maintenance	Entretien	
Architect	Architecte	Harry S. Colt
Type	Type	parkland
Relief	Relief	
Water in play	Eau en jeu	
Exp. to wind	Exposé au vent	
Trees in play	Arbres en jeu	

Scorecard Carte de score	Chp. Chp.	Mens Mess.	Ladies Da.
Length Long.	6045	5735	5130
Par	72	72	73

Advised golfing ability Niveau de jeu recommandé		0 12 24 36
Hcp required	Handicap exigé	certificate

CLUB HOUSE & AMENITIES
CLUB HOUSE ET ANNEXES

8 /10

Pro shop	Pro-shop	
Driving range	Practice	
Sheltered	couvert	no
On grass	sur herbe	yes
Putting-green	putting-green	yes
Pitching-green	pitching green	yes

HOTEL FACILITIES
ENVIRONNEMENT HOTELIER

7 /10

HOTELS HÔTELS
Hilton National   Watford
194 rooms, D £ 94   8 km
Tel (44) 01923 - 235 881
Fax (44) 01923 - 220 836

Cumberland   Harrow
81 rooms, D £ 80   8 km
Tel (44) 0181 - 863 4111
Fax (44) 0181 - 861 5668

RESTAURANTS RESTAURANTS
Percy's   North Harrow
Tel (44) 0181 - 427 2021   6 km

Friends   Pinner
Tel (44) 0181 - 866 0286   5 km

Trattoria Sorrentina   Harrow
Tel (44) 0181 - 427 9411   8 km

With Alwoodley and Sand Moor, here you have a great threesome of courses close to Leeds, certainly not the prettiest city in England one whose region has a lot to be said for it, especially the city of York. The present course, or at least 16 holes of the present course, were designed by Alister Mackenzie while the last two were added in 1989, giving the whole layout more than respectable yardage and leaving the original style untouched. Classic, well-landscaped and with huge greens in excellent condition, the course gives nothing away. By the same token it doesn't steal strokes, either. Here, you score what you deserved to score. The Ryder Cup was held here for the first time in England, as was a particular English Amateur championship where one player had to hit his third shot on the 18th from inside the bar. A good place to go, but only after you have sunk that final putt.

Avec The Alwoodley et Sand Moor, voici un fameux trio de parcours voisins, à proximité de Leeds, qui n'est sans doute pas la plus belle ville d'Angleterre, mais la région ne manque pas de séductions, en particulier avec York. Le présent parcours a été dessiné par Alister Mackenzie. Du moins 16 trous, car deux nouveaux trous ont été ajoutés en 1989, permettant d'afficher maintenant une longueur fort respectable. Le style original n'en a pas été modifié. Classique, bien paysagé, avec de vastes greens généralement excellents, ce parcours ne fait certes pas de cadeaux, mais il ne vole non plus personne : on y fait le score que l'on mérite. La Ryder Cup 1929 s'y est disputée pour la première fois en Grande-Bretagne, tout comme un English Amateur où un joueur dut taper son troisième coup du 18 depuis l'intérieur du bar. On comprend qu'il y soit allé.

Moortown Golf Club

Harrogate Road
ENG - LEEDS, W. Yorkshire LS17 7DB

Office	Secrétariat	(44) 0113 - 268 6521
Pro shop	Pro-shop	(44) 0113 - 268 3636
Fax	Fax	(44) 0113 - 268 6521
Situation	Situation	

8 km N of Leeds (pop. 680 722)

Annual closure	Fermeture annnuelle	no
Weekly closure	Fermeture hebdomadaire	no

Fees main season	Tarifs haute saison	18 holes
	Week days Semaine	We/Bank holidays We/Férié
Individual Individuel	£ 42	£ 47
Couple Couple	£ 84	£ 94

Full day: £ 47 (weekdays) - £ 55 (weekends)

Caddy	Caddy	no
Electric Trolley	Chariot électrique	£ 5/18 holes
Buggy	Voiturette	£ 25/18 holes
Clubs	Clubs	no

Credit cards Cartes de crédit
VISA - Eurocard - MasterCard - AMEX - JCB - Switch
(not in Club house)

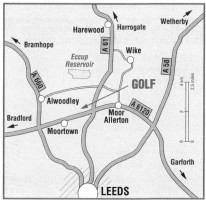

Access Accès : On A61 approx. 8 km (5 m.) N of Leeds
Map 4 on page 412 Carte 4 Page 412

GOLF COURSE
PARCOURS

18/20

Site	Site	▬▬▬▬▬▭
Maintenance	Entretien	▬▬▬▬▬▭
Architect	Architecte	Alister MacKenzie
Type	Type	inland, moorland
Relief	Relief	▬▬▬▭▭
Water in play	Eau en jeu	▬▬▭▭▭
Exp. to wind	Exposé au vent	▬▬▬▭▭
Trees in play	Arbres en jeu	▬▬▬▬▭

Scorecard Carte de score	Chp. Chp.	Mens Mess.	Ladies Da.
Length Long.	6390	5883	5398
Par	72	72	75

Advised golfing ability		0 12 24 36
Niveau de jeu recommandé		▬▬▬▬▬▬▭
Hcp required	Handicap exigé	certificate

CLUB HOUSE & AMENITIES
CLUB HOUSE ET ANNEXES

7/10

Pro shop	Pro-shop	▬▬▬▬▭
Driving range	Practice	▬▬▬▭▭
Sheltered	couvert	no
On grass	sur herbe	yes
Putting-green	putting-green	yes
Pitching-green	pitching green	yes

HOTEL FACILITIES
ENVIRONNEMENT HOTELIER

7/10

HOTELS HÔTELS
Forte Posthouse - 123 rooms, D £ 70 — Bramhope
Tel (44) 0113 - 284 2911
Fax (44) 0113 - 284 3451

Jarvis Parkway - 105 rooms, D £ 98 — Bramhope
Tel (44) 0113 - 267 2551
Fax (44) 0113 - 267 4410

Stakis Leeds - 100 rooms, D £ 85 — Leeds
Tel (44) 0113 - 273 2323, Fax (44) 0113 - 232 3018

The Calls - 41 rooms, D £ 120 — Leeds
Tel (44) 0113 - 244 0099, Fax (44) 0113 - 234 4100

RESTAURANTS RESTAURANTS
Pool Court at 42 - Tel (44) 0113 - 244 4242 — Leeds
Hereford Beefstouw - Tel (44) 0113 - 245 3870 — Leeds
Rascasse - Tel (44) 0113 - 244 6611 — Leeds

509

Horse-racing enthusiasts will already have heard of Newbury, whose racecourse is visible from the 17th hole. But despite being so close, the ground here is far from flat although easy enough to walk. The course was built in 1873, making it one of the oldest in England, and is still popular and busy enough to be closed to non-members on week-ends. Like many of the courses from that period, Newbury & Crookham has a lot of trees and the design has hardly got any younger, but this is not a course to be taken lightly, despite a lack of yardage. It is a very pretty challenge with several holes of the highest order defended by some very well-placed bunkers. There is an obvious need to put your drive in the right place and we would recommend this as a "disciplinary" course for "sprayers". The trees and thick rough will soon get them back on the straight and narrow. The clubhouse is small and not the most cheerful place in the world, but the food is good.

Les amateurs de chevaux connaissent Newbury par son hippodrome, que l'on aperçoit du 17. Malgré ce voisinage, le terrain n'est pas plat, même s'il est facile à jouer à pied. Le parcours a été construit en 1873, ce qui en fait l'un des clubs de golf les plus anciens d'Angleterre, et qui reste très fréquenté car il n'est pas possible d'y jouer en week-end. Comme beaucoup de parcours de cette époque, il est abondamment pourvu d'arbres, et son dessin n'a guère été que rajeuni, mais son manque de longueur ne doit pas le faire sous-estimer. C'est un très joli challenge, avec plusieurs trous de premier ordre, défendus par des bunkers très bien placés, et la nécessité de placer correctement les drives est évidente : on recommande un petit séjour "disciplinaire" pour les "arroseurs." Les arbres, mais aussi un rough épais sauront redresser leurs trajectoires. Le Clubhouse est petit et pas très gai, mais la table est très correcte.

Newbury & Crookham Golf Club

Burysbank Road, Greenham
ENG - NEWBURY, Berks RG19 8BZ

Office	Secrétariat	(44) 01635 - 40 035
Pro shop	Pro-shop	(44) 01635 - 31 201
Fax	Fax	(44) 01635 - 40 045
Situation	Situation	

3 km from Newbury (pop. 136 700)
25 km from Reading (pop. 128 877)

Annual closure	Fermeture annnuelle	no
Weekly closure	Fermeture hebdomadaire	no
Fees main season	Tarifs haute saison	18 holes

	Week days Semaine	We/Bank holidays We/Férié
Individual Individuel	£ 20	—
Couple Couple	£ 40	—

Full day: £ 30 each - No visitors at weekends

Caddy	Caddy	no
Electric Trolley	Chariot électrique	no
Buggy	Voiturette	no
Clubs	Clubs	on request
Credit cards Cartes de crédit		not for greenfees

510

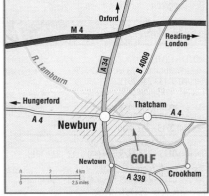

Access Accès : London, M4. Jct 13, A34 South through Newbury. Turn into Newbury Retall Park, 2.5 km SE of Newbury. Golf on left.
Map 7 on page 418 Carte 7 Page 418

GOLF COURSE
PARCOURS — 15/20

Site	Site	
Maintenance	Entretien	
Architect	Architecte	J.H. Turner
Type	Type	parkland
Relief	Relief	
Water in play	Eau en jeu	
Exp. to wind	Exposé au vent	
Trees in play	Arbres en jeu	

Scorecard Carte de score	Chp. Chp.	Mens Mess.	Ladies Da.
Length Long.	5346	5141	4745
Par	69	69	70

Advised golfing ability Niveau de jeu recommandé	0	12	24	36
Hcp required	Handicap exigé	no		

CLUB HOUSE & AMENITIES
CLUB HOUSE ET ANNEXES — 6/10

Pro shop	Pro-shop	
Driving range	Practice	
Sheltered	couvert	no
On grass	sur herbe	yes
Putting-green	putting-green	yes
Pitching-green	pitching green	yes

HOTEL FACILITIES
ENVIRONNEMENT HOTELIER — 7/10

HOTELS HÔTELS

Hollington House - 19 rooms, D £ 160 — Woolton Hill
Tel (44) 01635 - 255 100 — 4 km
Fax (44) 01635 - 255 075

Foley Lodge - 68 rooms, D £ 115 — Newbury
Tel (44) 01635 - 528 770 — 3 km
Fax (44) 01635 - 528 398

Hilton - 109 rooms, D £ 105 — Newbury
Tel (44) 01635 - 529 000 — 3 km
Fax (44) 01635 - 529 337

Holiday Inn - 107 rooms, D £ 105 — Reading
Tel (44) 01734 - 259 988 — 25 km
Fax (44) 01734 - 391 665

RESTAURANT RESTAURANT
L'Ortolan — Shinfield-Reading
Tel (44) 01734 - 883 783 — 30 km

This virtually tree-less course was designed by Fowler and Simpson at the top of some cliffs, which naturally exposes it to all winds and weathers. Winds in the plural, because there are hardly ever two holes running in the same direction, so keep a cool head and control your shots. Beginners will hardly ever be penalised by the rough because it rarely comes into play for their kind of shots. The same applies to the bunker fairways which more often punish the mistakes made by longer and better players. So you might call this a logical course. At all events it is an excellent venue for playing with all the family because you will also find a real 18-hole course for children (holes measuring between 70 and 140 yards). And this region is the sunniest and driest in all England. Although many of you may know Margate's reputation as a seaside resort, only the really knowledgeable will know that Charles Dickens used to come on holiday here, in Broadstairs, where he wrote *David Copperfield*.

Pratiquement sans arbres, ce parcours a été dessiné par Fowler et Simpson au sommet de la falaise, ce qui l'expose bien sûr au vent. Aux vents, car on ne trouve pratiquement pas deux trous de suite dans le même sens : il faut garder la tête froide et contrôler ses coups. Les joueurs sans expérience seront peu pénalisés car le rough est rarement en jeu pour eux, tout comme les bunkers de fairway, ce qui pénalise surtout les fautes des meilleurs joueurs : voilà un parcours très logique. Et venir en famille est très agréable car l'on trouve ici un parcours de 18 trous de moins de 130 mètres, à l'échelle des enfants. Et la région est la plus ensoleillée et la moins arrosée d'Angleterre. Si l'on connaît, de réputation, la station balnéaire de Margate, seuls les fanatiques de Charles Dickens savent qu'il prenait ses vacances ici, à Broadstairs, où il écrivit "David Copperfield."

North Foreland Golf Club

Convent Road
ENG - BROADSTAIRS, Kent CT10 3PU

Office	Secrétariat	(44) 01843 - 862140
Pro shop	Pro-shop	(44) 01843 - 869628
Fax	Fax	(44) 01843 - 862140
Situation	Situation	

1 km from Broadstairs (pop. 23 695)
3 km from Margate

Annual closure	Fermeture annnuelle	no
Weekly closure	Fermeture hebdomadaire	no

Fees main season	Tarifs haute saison	18 holes	
		Week days Semaine	**We/Bank holidays** We/Férié
Individual Individuel		£ 26	£ 26
Couple Couple		£ 52	£ 52

No visitors Sunday & Monday mornings.
Short course: £ 3 for juniors,

Caddy	Caddy	no
Electric Trolley	Chariot électrique	£ 4/18 holes
Buggy	Voiturette	£ 15/18 holes
Clubs	Clubs	no
Credit cards Cartes de crédit		no

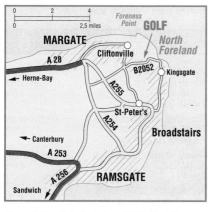

MARGATE · Cliftonville · Foreness Point · GOLF · North Foreland · Kingsgate · B2052 · A 28 · Herne-Bay · A255 · St-Peter's · A254 · Canterbury · A 253 · Broadstairs · A 256 · RAMSGATE · Sandwich

Access Accès : A2 to Canterbury. A28 to Margate,
A299 to Kingsgate (past St Peter's Church), B2052
Map 7 on page 419 Carte 7 Page 419

GOLF COURSE
PARCOURS

13 /20

Site	Site	▰▰▰▱
Maintenance	Entretien	▰▰▰▱
Architect	Architecte	Fowler & Simpson
Type	Type	seaside course
Relief	Relief	▰▰▱▱
Water in play	Eau en jeu	▱▱▱▱
Exp. to wind	Exposé au vent	▰▰▰▰
Trees in play	Arbres en jeu	▰▱▱▱

Scorecard Carte de score	Chp. Chp.	Mens Mess.	Ladies Da.
Length Long.	5790	5564	5185
Par	71	70	75

Advised golfing ability
Niveau de jeu recommandé

0	12	24	36

Hcp required Handicap exigé — certificate or letter

CLUB HOUSE & AMENITIES
CLUB HOUSE ET ANNEXES

7 /10

Pro shop	Pro-shop	▰▰▰▱
Driving range	Practice	▰▰▱▱
Sheltered	couvert	no
On grass	sur herbe	yes
Putting-green	putting-green	yes
Pitching-green	pitching green	no

HOTEL FACILITIES
ENVIRONNEMENT HOTELIER

7 /10

HOTELS HÔTELS

Castlemere - 36 rooms, D £ 70 Tel (44) 01843 - 861 566 Fax (44) 01843 - 866 379		Broadstairs 1 km
Bay Tree Hotel - 11 rooms, D £ 44 Tel (44) 01843 - 862 502 Fax (44) 01843 - 860 589		Broadstairs 1 km
East Horndon - 10 rooms, D £ 40 Tel (44) 01843 - 868 306		Broadstairs 1 km
Greswolde Hotel - 6 rooms, D £ 36 Tél (44) 01843 - 223 956		Cliftonville 2 km

RESTAURANTS RESTAURANTS

Marchesi Tel (44) 01843 - 862481		Broadstairs 1 km
Castlemere Tel (44) 01843 - 861566		Broadstairs 1 km

511

17	7	6

With Blackmoor and Liphook, North Hants completes an excellent clan of courses in a very beautiful part of Hampshire where Harry Colt, Arthur Croome and here James Braid have left their mark. This is a sort of exercise in style with rather similar spaces hewn out of the heather and woods. With Braid, a very great champion in his time, there is always serious emphasis on making each hole different so that the whole course forms a comprehensive examination of a player's ability. If you want to score well, you will need to flight the ball both ways, and while there are few dog-legs here, there is always a right side and a wrong side of the fairway, depending on pin positions. As the greens are very large and protected in proportion to the theoretical length of the approach shot, you will need to be accurate and self-assured. High-handicappers might not feel all that comfortable here but the majority of amateurs will have a lot of fun. North Hants looks great and plays great.

Il forme avec Blackmoor et Liphook une excellente famille de parcours dans cette très belle région du Hampshire, où Harry Colt, Arthur Croome et (ici) James Braid ont apposé leur sceau. C'est une sorte d'exercice de style avec des espaces assez similaires, où la bruyère et les bois constituent la matière à travailler. Avec Braid, qui était un très grand champion, on a toujours un grand souci de différencier chaque trou, afin que l'ensemble constitue un examen complet du joueur. Si l'on veut très bien scorer, il faut travailler la balle dans tous les sens. Et s'il y a très peu de doglegs, il y a toujours un "bon" côté du fairway suivant la position du drapeau. Comme les greens sont très grands et protégés en proportion de la longueur théorique du deuxième coup, il faudra être précis et sûr de soi. Les handicaps élevés ne seront pas très à l'aise, mais la majorité des amateurs prendra beaucoup de plaisir. North Hants est beau et bon.

North Hants Golf Club

Minley Road
ENG - FLEET, Hants GU13 8BR

Office	Secrétariat	(44) 01252 - 616443
Pro shop	Pro-shop	(44) 01252 - 616655
Fax	Fax	(44) 01252 - 811627
Situation	Situation	

1 km from Fleet
4 km from Camberley (pop. 46 120)

Annual closure	Fermeture annnuelle	no
Weekly closure	Fermeture hebdomadaire	no
Fees main season	Tarifs haute saison	18 holes

	Week days Semaine	We/Bank holidays We/Férié
Individual Individuel	£ 27	—
Couple Couple	£ 54	—

Full day: £ 34 - Weekends: only as a guest of member

Caddy	Caddy	no
Electric Trolley	Chariot électrique	no
Buggy	Voiturette	no
Clubs	Clubs	

Credit cards Cartes de crédit
VISA - Eurocard - MasterCard - DC

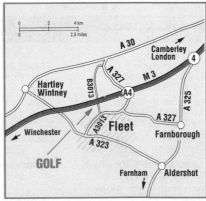

Access Accès : London M3 Jct 4A → Fleet
Map 8 on page 420 Carte 8 Page 420

GOLF COURSE
PARCOURS

17 /20

Site	Site	▰▰▰▰▰▰▱
Maintenance	Entretien	▰▰▰▰▰▰▱
Architect	Architecte	James Braid
Type	Type	inland, heathland
Relief	Relief	▰▱▱
Water in play	Eau en jeu	▰▰▱
Exp. to wind	Exposé au vent	▰▰▰▱
Trees in play	Arbres en jeu	▰▰▰▰▰▱

Scorecard Carte de score	Chp. Chp.	Mens Mess.	Ladies Da.
Length Long.	5631	5480	4905
Par	69	69	71

Advised golfing ability		0 12 24 36
Niveau de jeu recommandé		▰▰▰▰▰▱
Hcp required	Handicap exigé	24

CLUB HOUSE & AMENITIES
CLUB HOUSE ET ANNEXES

7 /10

Pro shop	Pro-shop	▰▰▰▰▱
Driving range	Practice	▰▱
Sheltered	couvert	no
On grass	sur herbe	yes
Putting-green	putting-green	yes
Pitching-green	pitching green	no

HOTEL FACILITIES
ENVIRONNEMENT HOTELIER

6 /10

HOTELS HÔTELS

Frimley Hall - 66 rooms, D £ 105 — Camberley
Tel (44) 01276 - 283 21 — 6 km
Fax (44) 01276 - 691 253

Forte Crest - 110 rooms, D £ 125 — Farnborough
Tel (44) 01252 - 545 051 — 6 km
Fax (44) 01252 - 377 210

Falcon - 30 rooms, D £ 75 — Farnborough
Tel (44) 01252 - 545 378 — 6 km
Fax (44) 01252 - 522 539

RESTAURANTS RESTAURANTS

Wings Cottage — Farnborough
Tel (44) 01252 - 544 141 — 6 km

Chesa — Crondall
Tel (44) 01252 - 850 328 — 4 km

512

NOTTS (HOLLINWELL)

18	6	6

In a superb setting with a good old clubhouse the way we all like them, this is one inland course to put up there with the very best. Designed by Willie Park Jr. then given bunkers by J.H. Taylor, this is a nicely modelled course typical of a heathland layout which winds it way amidst silver birch and oak trees. There is little water to speak of, but when there is, watch out. Try the 8th hole from the back tees and you will see what we mean. By and large this is a sort of monster where the back-tees are reserved for very good players who know how to flight a ball. It is a little meeker from the front tees, which for the ladies are even too far forward. Notts is also a great course for the rhythm it strikes up, because it has no time for poor shots (except on hole N° 1, the most forgiving). And because you never play the same two shots twice in a row. The members must love it here.

Dans un environnement superbe, avec un bon vieux Clubhouse tel qu'on les aime, c'est l'un des parcours "inland" à placer parmi les plus grands. Dessiné par Willie Park Jr, le bunkering ayant ensuite été fait par J.H. Taylor, c'est un parcours bien modelé et typique de terre de bruyère, insinué entre les bouleaux blancs et les chênes. L'eau y est peu abondante, mais de quelle manière au 8, des départs arrière ! En règle générale, c'est une sorte de monstre, et jouer du fond est réservé aux joueurs de très bon niveau, et qui savent manoeuvrer la balle. Le parcours est plus doux des départs avancés, qui le sont d'ailleurs un peu trop pour les dames. Notts est aussi un très grand parcours par le rythme qu'il impose, parce qu'il ne supporte pas les coups médiocres (sauf au 1, le trou le plus indulgent), et parce que l'on ne joue jamais deux fois le même coup deux fois de suite. Les membres doivent s'y régaler...

Notts Golf Club Hollinwell

Hollinwell, Derby Road
ENG - KIRBY-IN-ASHFIELD, Notts NG17 7QR

Office	Secrétariat	(44) 01623 - 753 225
Pro shop	Pro-shop	(44) 01623 - 753 225
Fax	Fax	(44) 01623 - 753 655
Situation	Situation	

20 km N of Nottingham (pop. 270 222)

Annual closure	Fermeture annnuelle	no
Weekly closure	Fermeture hebdomadaire	no

Fees main season
Tarifs haute saison — 18 holes

	Week days Semaine	We/Bank holidays We/Férié
Individual Individuel	£ 40	—
Couple Couple	£ 80	—

Full weekdays: £ 50 -
No visitors at weekends & Bank holidays

Caddy	Caddy	on request/£ 15
Electric Trolley	Chariot électrique	£ 5/18 holes
Buggy	Voiturette	no
Clubs	Clubs	no
Credit cards Cartes de crédit		Pro Shop only

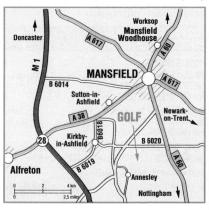

Access Accès : M1 Jct 27. A608 then A611 → Kirby, Mansfield. Golf 3 km on the right.
Map 4 on page 412 Carte 4 Page 412

GOLF COURSE
PARCOURS
18/20

Site	Site	■■■■■■■
Maintenance	Entretien	■■■■■■
Architect	Architecte	Willie Park Jr
Type	Type	inland
Relief	Relief	■■
Water in play	Eau en jeu	■■
Exp. to wind	Exposé au vent	■■■
Trees in play	Arbres en jeu	■■■■

Scorecard Carte de score	Chp. Chp.	Mens Mess.	Ladies Da.
Length Long.	6398	6250	5187
Par	72	72	74

Advised golfing ability Niveau de jeu recommandé	0 12 24 36
	■■■
Hcp required Handicap exigé	certificate

CLUB HOUSE & AMENITIES
CLUB HOUSE ET ANNEXES
6/10

Pro shop	Pro-shop	■■■■
Driving range	Practice	■■■■
Sheltered	couvert	no
On grass	sur herbe	yes
Putting-green	putting-green	yes
Pitching-green	pitching green	yes

HOTEL FACILITIES
ENVIRONNEMENT HOTELIER
6/10

HOTELS HÔTELS
Pine Lodge - 20 rooms, D £ 60 — Mansfield
Tel (44) 01623 - 622 308 — 8 km

Swallow - 157 rooms, D £ 120 — South Normanton
Tel (44) 01773 - 812 000 — 8 km
Fax (44) 01773 - 580 032

Royal Moat House - 200 rooms, D £ 100 — Nottingham
Tel (44) 0115 - 936 9988 — 20 km
Fax (44) 0115 - 475 667

Stage Hotel - 52 rooms, D £ 53 — Nottingham 20 km
Tel (44) 0115 - 960 3261
Fax (44) 0115 - 969 1040

RESTAURANTS RESTAURANTS
Swallow — South Normanton 8 km
Tel (44) 01773 - 812 000

Sonny's - Tel (44) 0115 - 947 3041 — Nottingham 20 km

513

ORCHARDLEIGH

Designed by Brian Huggett with the help of Peter McEvoy, this is a very ambitious resort with a second course already planned, an hotel, swimming pool and tennis courts. Close to Bath, this is already a course you will want to get to know. A little on the hilly side with a lot of water in play on six holes, Orchardleigh is an American style course calling for some "target golf" to hit the greens. We are a far cry from the traditional "down to earth" game, but the demands of present-day golfers and the nature of available sites mean that is the way golf seems to be moving. So there are few trees in play but a lot of fairway bunkers, as dangerous as water for high-handicappers (which is a bit of shame). On a peaceful site rich in wildlife and neatly landscaped, this is a sound layout which from a technical angle is very interesting to discover and play.

Dessiné par Brian Huggett avec l'aide de Peter McEvoy, c'est un complexe très ambitieux, avec en projet un second parcours, un hôtel, une piscine et des tennis. A proximité de Bath, c'est déjà un parcours à connaître. Assez vallonné, mais sans excès, il présente beaucoup d'obstacles d'eau (en jeu sur un tiers des trous), ce qui donne à l'évidence un style américain que la nécessité de jouer du "jeu de cibles" vers les greens accentue encore. Nous sommes loin du "jeu à terre" de la tradition, mais l'exigence des golfeurs d'aujourd'hui, comme la nature des terrains disponibles imposent cette tendance : on trouve ainsi peu d'arbres en jeu, mais de nombreux bunkers de fairway, aussi dangereux que l'eau pour les hauts handicaps (c'est un peu dommage). Dans un site tranquille, riche en vie sauvage et bien paysagé, c'est une solide réalisation, techniquement très intéressante à découvrir et jouer.

Orchardleigh Golf Club

Near Frome
ENG - BATH, Somerset BA11 2PH

Office	Secrétariat	(44) 01373 - 454 200
Pro shop	Pro-shop	(44) 01373 - 454 200
Fax	Fax	(44) 01373 - 454 202
Situation	Situation	

18 km S of Bath (pop. 78 689) - 3.5 km NW of Frome

Annual closure	Fermeture annnuelle	no
Weekly closure	Fermeture hebdomadaire	no

Fees main season	Tarifs haute saison	18 holes
	Week days Semaine	We/Bank holidays We/Férié
Individual Individuel	£ 30	£ 40
Couple Couple	£ 60	£ 80

Weekends: Visitors after 11.00 am

Caddy	Caddy	on request/£ 15
Electric Trolley	Chariot électrique	no
Buggy	Voiturette	£ 20/18 holes
Clubs	Clubs	£ 15/18 holes

Credit cards Cartes de crédit
VISA - Eurocard - MasterCard

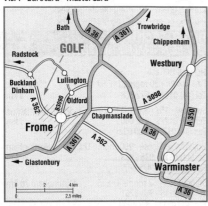

Access Accès : M4 Jct 18, A46 to Bath,
then A36 to Frome then A362 → Radstock.
3.5 km NW of Frome, main entrance on right side,
before village of Buckland Dinham.
Map 6 on page 417 Carte 6 Page 417

514

GOLF COURSE
PARCOURS   **17** /20

Site	Site	▬▬▬▬▬▬
Maintenance	Entretien	▬▬▬▬▬
Architect	Architecte	Brian Huggett
Type	Type	inland, parkland
Relief	Relief	▬▬▬
Water in play	Eau en jeu	▬▬▬
Exp. to wind	Exposé au vent	▬▬▬
Trees in play	Arbres en jeu	▬▬▬

Scorecard	Chp.	Mens	Ladies
Carte de score	Chp.	Mess.	Da.
Length Long.	6198	5691	5026
Par	72	72	73

Advised golfing ability	0	12	24	36
Niveau de jeu recommandé				

Hcp required   Handicap exigé   28 Men, 36 Ladies

CLUB HOUSE & AMENITIES
CLUB HOUSE ET ANNEXES   **7** /10

Pro shop	Pro-shop	▬▬▬▬
Driving range	Practice	▬▬▬
Sheltered	couvert	no
On grass	sur herbe	yes
Putting-green	putting-green	yes
Pitching-green	pitching green	yes

HOTEL FACILITIES
ENVIRONNEMENT HOTELIER   **7** /10

HOTELS HÔTELS

Woolpack Inn - 10 rooms, D £ 80   Beckington
Tel (44) 01373 - 831 244   3 km
Fax (44) 01373 - 831 223

Royal Crescent - 38 rooms, D £ 150   Bath
Tel (44) 01373 - 739 955   18 km
Fax (44) 01373 - 339 401

Bloomfield House - 6 rooms, D £ 90   Bath 18 km
Tel (44) 01225 - 420 105, Fax (44) 01225 - 481 958

RESTAURANTS RESTAURANTS

Woolpack Inn   Beckington
Tel (44) 01373 - 831 244   3 km

Brottens Lodge   Doulting
Tel (44) 01749 - 880 352   9 km

Bowlish House   Shepton Mallet
Tel (44) 01749 - 342 022   12 km

ORMSKIRK

Admittedly we are close to the cities of Manchester, Liverpool and Blackburn, but it is still exceptional to see such a concentration of good golf courses in one area. Those on the coast have always attracted the most publicity, but the inland courses have a lot going for them, as well. Take Ormskirk for example, right out in the sticks, far from the hurly-burly of today's modern world. In contrast with links courses, everything here is as green as in those glossy magazines, with birch trees and heather which is a pretty sight indeed... from afar. There is only a single water hazard, on the 3rd hole, but the rough is thick and eats into several fairways. Accurate driving is of the essence, especially on the very many doglegs on which you will have to make a whole range of second shots to reach the greens. The par 3s here are excellent, especially the 14th and 17th holes. Intelligent, natural and very fair, Ormskirk will be a real eye-opener for many golfers.

Certes, nous sommes tout près de Manchester, Liverpool et Blackburn, mais il est exceptionnel de voir une telle concentration de golfs, et de bons golfs. Bien sûr, les parcours de la côte ont bénéficié du maximum de publicité, mais ceux de l'intérieur ne manquent pas d'attraits. Témoin Ormskirk, situé en pleine campagne, très à l'écart des bruits de ce monde. Ici, en contraste avec les links, tout est bien vert comme sur les photos de magazines, avec des bouleaux et la bruyère, si jolie à voir... de loin. Un seul obstacle d'eau, au 3, mais le rough est épais, empiète sur plusieurs fairways, ce qui oblige à la précision des drives, notamment avec les nombreux doglegs qui imposent une très grande variété de seconds coups. On remarquera encore la qualité des par 3, notamment les 14 et 17. Intelligent, naturel et très franc, Ormskirk sera pour beaucoup une découverte.

Ormskirk Golf Club
Cranes Lane, Lathom
ENG - ORMSKIRK, Lancs L40 5UJ

Office	Secrétariat	(44) 01695 - 572 112
Pro shop	Pro-shop	(44) 01695 - 572 074
Fax	Fax	(44) 01695 - 572 112
Situation	Situation	

22 km N of Liverpool (pop. 452 450)
2 km E of Ormskirk (pop. 23 425)

Annual closure	Fermeture annnuelle	no
Weekly closure	Fermeture hebdomadaire	no
Fees main season	Tarifs haute saison	full day

	Week days Semaine	We/Bank holidays We/Férié
Individual Individuel	£ 40	£ 45
Couple Couple	£ 80	£ 90
£ 45 also on Wednesdays		

Caddy	Caddy	no
Electric Trolley	Chariot électrique	£ 5/18 holes
Buggy	Voiturette	no
Clubs	Clubs	£ 3/18 holes

Credit cards Cartes de crédit
VISA - Eurocard - MasterCard - AMEX - DC - JCB
(not for greenfees)

Access Accès : M58 Jct 3. Follow signs to Burscough.
First left at T-junction. Right at Hulton Castle Pub.
Right at next T-junction. Golf on right.
Map 5 on page 415 Carte 5 Page 415

GOLF COURSE
PARCOURS **14**/20

Site	Site	
Maintenance	Entretien	
Architect	Architecte	Harold Hilton
Type	Type	parkland, seaside course
Relief	Relief	
Water in play	Eau en jeu	
Exp. to wind	Exposé au vent	
Trees in play	Arbres en jeu	

Scorecard Carte de score	Chp. Chp.	Mens Mess.	Ladies Da.
Length Long.	5898	5786	5107
Par	70	70	73

Advised golfing ability		0 12 24 36
Niveau de jeu recommandé		
Hcp required	Handicap exigé	certificate

CLUB HOUSE & AMENITIES
CLUB HOUSE ET ANNEXES **6**/10

Pro shop	Pro-shop	
Driving range	Practice	
Sheltered	couvert	no
On grass	sur herbe	yes
Putting-green	putting-green	yes
Pitching-green	pitching green	yes

HOTEL FACILITIES
ENVIRONNEMENT HOTELIER **4**/10

HOTELS HÔTELS
Beaufort   Burscough
21 rooms, D £ 70   2 km
Tel (44) 01695 - 892 655
Fax (44) 01695 - 895 135

Red Lion   Newburgh
13 rooms, D £ 35   3 km
Tel (44) 01257 - 462 336
Fax (44) 01695 - 462 827

RESTAURANT RESTAURANT
Pubs in Ormskirk   Ormskirk 2 km

515

Yorkshire has more specialities than just Yorkshire pudding (which for non-English readers is a sort of batter pastry served with roast-beef, especially on a Sunday). There are also excellent golf courses and the hot springs of Harrogate, which were particularly popular before the first world war. But before trying out the city's superb Turkish baths, spend a day on this very fine course, laid out on a plateau which dominates the surrounding region. This is a typical Yorkshire moorland course, very exposed to the wind but with a lot of trees. The difficulties lie with the thickness of the rough, and your score will depend on how well you drive. Despite the slopes, the course is not tiring to walk, only one green and one drive are blind and only a few elevated greens call for high approach shots. Otherwise you can practice your newly acquired art of rolling the ball onto the green. Green-keeping is remarkable, the clubhouse elegant and cosy.

Qu'on le sache, le Yorkshire Pudding n'est pas un dessert, mais une pâte à choux servie avec le rôti du dimanche. Le Yorkshire a d'autre spécialités, dont les bons golfs et les sources thermales à Harrogate, très en activité avant la Grande Guerre. Avant de vous remettre au superbe Sauna Turc de la ville, vous pourrez vous dépenser sur ce très beau parcours, qui vous amène sur un plateau dominant la région. C'est un parcours typique des landes du Comté, très exposé au vent, mais bien arboré. Les difficultés principales tiennent à la densité du rough, et la qualité du drive commande celle du score. En dépit du relief, le parcours n'est pas épuisant, on ne trouve qu'un seul drive et un seul green aveugles, et seules quelques greens surélevés qui appellent des balles levées. Autrement, on peut se livrer à l'amour des balles tendues et des approches roulées. L'entretien est remarquable, le Clubhouse élégant et chaleureux.

Pannal Golf Club

Follifoot Road
ENG - HARROGATE, Yorkshire HG3 1ES

Office	Secrétariat	(44) 01423 - 872628
Pro shop	Pro-shop	(44) 01423 - 872620
Fax	Fax	(44) 01423 - 870043
Situation	Situation	

4 km from Harrogate (pop. 143 530)
21 km from Leeds (pop. 680 725)

Annual closure	Fermeture annnuelle	no
Weekly closure	Fermeture hebdomadaire	no

Fees main season	Tarifs haute saison	18 holes
	Week days Semaine	**We/Bank holidays** We/Férié
Individual Individuel	£ 35	£ 40
Couple Couple	£ 70	£ 80
Full weekdays: £ 40		

Caddy	Caddy	no
Electric Trolley	Chariot électrique	£ 5.50/18 holes
Buggy	Voiturette	no
Clubs	Clubs	£ 15/18 holes

Credit cards Cartes de crédit
VISA - Eurocard - MasterCard - AMEX - DC - JCB

Access Accès : A61 Leeds → Harrogate.
Map 4 on page 412 Carte 4 Page 412

GOLF COURSE
PARCOURS

15/20

Site	Site	
Maintenance	Entretien	
Architect	Architecte	Sandy Herd Charles MacKenzie
Type	Type	open country, moorland
Relief	Relief	
Water in play	Eau en jeu	
Exp. to wind	Exposé au vent	
Trees in play	Arbres en jeu	

Scorecard Carte de score	Chp. Chp.	Mens Mess.	Ladies Da.
Length Long.	5960	5808	5237
Par	72	72	74

Advised golfing ability		0	12	24	36
Niveau de jeu recommandé					
Hcp required	Handicap exigé	24 Men, 28 Ladies			

CLUB HOUSE & AMENITIES
CLUB HOUSE ET ANNEXES

6/10

Pro shop	Pro-shop	
Driving range	Practice	
Sheltered	couvert	no
On grass	sur herbe	practice range only
Putting-green	putting-green	yes
Pitching-green	pitching green	yes

HOTEL FACILITIES
ENVIRONNEMENT HOTELIER

7/10

HOTELS HÔTELS
Rudding Park House Hotel   Rudding Park 3 km
50 rooms, D £ 129
Tel (44) 01423 - 871 350, Fax (44) 01423 - 872 286

Sandringham - 6 rooms, D £ 90   Beckwithshaw 5 km
Tel (44) 01423 - 500 722, Fax (44) 01423 - 530 509

Crown - 116 rooms, D £ 80   Harrogate 5 km
Tel (44) 01423 - 567 755, Fax (44) 01423 - 502 284

Ruskin Hotel - 7 rooms, D £ 89   Harrogate 5 km
Tel (44) 01423 - 502 045, Fax (44) 01423 - 506 131

RESTAURANTS RESTAURANTS
Drum & Monkey - Tel (44) 01423 - 502 650   Harrogate

Clocktower Brasserie   Rudding Park 3 km
Tel (44) 01423 - 872 100

The Bistro - Tel (44) 01423 - 530 708   Harrogate 5 km

516

The best time to come here is in Spring, to see how the rhododendrons add colour to the picturesque landscape of heather and pine, or to listen to the ducks quacking as your ball splashes into its watery grave. Parkstone is virtually in town, between Poole and Bournemouth, one of England's most popular seaside resorts. But everything is peace and quiet in a pretty setting where you feel so privileged to be walking the fairways that it is almost unthinkable not to play well. Yet Willie Park and Harry Colt used their combined talents to set traps and decorate their work of art with heather from where a decent recovery is nigh on impossible. High-handicappers will certainly not consider this to be a holiday course, but after all there is something to be said for being thrown in at the deep end. They'll learn that this is a good course and if they make it to the 18th (a big par 3) they will do the same as everyone else, take one shot more than they expected.

Ici, il faut venir au printemps quand les rhododendrons ajoutent leurs couleurs de fête du printemps au paysage de bruyères et de pins, et les canards lecuni cris de joie quand les balles de golf font des ronds dans l'eau. Parkstone est pratiquement en ville, entre Poole et Bournemouth, une des stations balnéaires les plus fréquentées d'Angleterre. Mais on est ici au calme, dans un joli paysage où il est impossible de mal jouer tant on a le sentiment d'être privilégié. Pourtant, Willie Park et Harry Colt se sont ingéniés à tendre des pièges, à décorer leur oeuvre de bruyère dont il est impossible de sortir dignement. Les handicaps un peu élevés ne vont pas trouver qu'il s'agisse d'un parcours de vacances, mais après tout, il faut d'abord apprendre à nager, même au golf. Qu'ils apprennent seulement ce qu'est un bon parcours. Au 18 (un gros par 3), ils feront comme tout le monde, un coup de plus qu'ils n'espérent.

Parkstone Golf Club

Links Road, Parkstone
ENG - POOLE, Dorset BH14 9QS

Office	Secrétariat	(44) 01202 - 707 138
Pro shop	Pro-shop	(44) 01202 - 708 092
Fax	Fax	(44) 01202 - 706 027
Situation	Situation	

2 km E of Poole (pop. 133 050)
3 km W of Bournemouth (pop. 151 302)

Annual closure	Fermeture annnuelle	no
Weekly closure	Fermeture hebdomadaire	no
Fees main season	Tarifs haute saison	18 holes

	Week days Semaine	We/Bank holidays We/Férié
Individual Individuel	£ 30	£ 40
Couple Couple	£ 60	£ 80

Caddy	Caddy	no
Electric Trolley	Chariot électrique	£ 7/18 holes
Buggy	Voiturette	no
Clubs	Clubs	£ 8/day

Credit cards Cartes de crédit
VISA - CB - Eurocard - MasterCard - AMEX - DC - JCB - Cofinoga

Access Accès : A35 Bournemouth → Poole.
Turn left on St Osmunds Road
Map 6 on page 417 Carte 6 Page 417

GOLF COURSE
PARCOURS

16/20

Site	Site	▰▰▱
Maintenance	Entretien	▰▰▱
Architect	Architecte	Willie Park James Braid
Type	Type	forest, heathland
Relief	Relief	▰▰▱
Water in play	Eau en jeu	▰▰▱
Exp. to wind	Exposé au vent	▰▱▱
Trees in play	Arbres en jeu	▰▰▰

Scorecard Carte de score	Chp. Chp.	Mens Mess.	Ladies Da.
Length Long.	5690	5405	4952
Par	72	71	71

Advised golfing ability
Niveau de jeu recommandé

0	12	24	36

Hcp required   Handicap exigé   28 Men, 30 Ladies

CLUB HOUSE & AMENITIES
CLUB HOUSE ET ANNEXES

7/10

Pro shop	Pro-shop	▰▰▱
Driving range	Practice	▰▰▱
Sheltered	couvert	no
On grass	sur herbe	yes
Putting-green	putting-green	yes
Pitching-green	pitching green	yes

HOTEL FACILITIES
ENVIRONNEMENT HOTELIER

8/10

HOTELS HÔTELS
Haven - 90 rooms, D £ 130   Sandbanks 2 km
Tel (44) 01202 - 707 333, Fax (44) 01202 - 708 796

Mansion House - 28 rooms, D £ 90   Poole 2 km
Tel (44) 01202 - 685 666, Fax (44) 01202 - 665 709

East Cliff Court - 70 rooms, D £ 60   Bournemouth 2 km
Tel (44) 01202 - 554 545, Fax (44) 01202 - 557 456

Wood Lodge - 15 rooms, D £ 60   Bournemouth
Tel (44) 01202 - 290 891   2 km

RESTAURANTS RESTAURANTS
La Roche   Sandbanks
Tel (44) 01202 - 707 333   2 km

Bankes Bistro   Parkstone
Tel (44) 01202 - 736 735   0.5 km

517

Nature specialists will often talk to you about Capability Brown, no relation to Calamity Jane, but the father-figure of English landscape gardening in the 18th century in reaction to the more austere French-style gardens. Patshull was laid out in an estate planted by the great man and it gives considerable visual appeal to this very discreet and classical course by John Jacobs. The water hazards certainly add a little extra spice. Some of the trees are dangerously in play because they transform a number of straight holes into dog-legs, so you have to play around them. Not too long, Patshull is a pleasant family course to play on foot, although hiring a buggy is not a bad idea, either, at least for carrying your bags. You don't come here to play top tournaments but to spend a day or two's pleasant golfing. The hotel on site is very well appointed with sauna, pool and jacuzzi, and you can also fish here.

Les spécialistes de la nature vous parleront de Capability Brown, qui n'était pas le cousin de Calamity Jane, mais le père du paysage à l'anglaise au XVIIIème siècle, en réaction contre les austères jardins à la française. C'est dans un domaine qu'il a créé que ce parcours a pris place. Il ajoute un attrait visuel indéniable au tracé très sobre et classique de John Jacobs, où les obstacles d'eau apportent un certain piment. Quelques arbres ont été dangereusement mis en jeu, car ils transforment certains trous droits en doglegs. Il faut savoir tourner autour. Pas trop long, Patshull est très agréable à jouer en famille, à pied éventuellement, mais jouer en voiturette n'est pas mal non plus, au moins pour mettre les sacs de golf. Ici, on ne vient pas jouer de grands championnats, mais passer une ou deux bonnes journées. L'hôtel sur place est très bien équipé, avec sauna, piscine, jacuzzi. Il est aussi possible de pêcher.

Patshull Park Golf & Country Club
ENG - PATTINGHAM, Shropshire WV6 7HR

Office	Secrétariat	(44) 01902 - 700 100
Pro shop	Pro-shop	(44) 01902 - 700 342
Fax	Fax	(44) 01902 - 700 874
Situation	Situation	

13 km W of Wolverhampton (pop. 242 190)
16 km E of Telford (pop. 119 340)

Annual closure	Fermeture annnuelle	no
Weekly closure	Fermeture hebdomadaire	no
Fees main season	Tarifs haute saison	18 holes

	Week days Semaine	We/Bank holidays We/Férié
Individual Individuel	£ 22.50	£ 27.50
Couple Couple	£ 45	£ 55

Caddy	Caddy	on request
Electric Trolley	Chariot électrique	no
Buggy	Voiturette	£ 19.50/18 holes
Clubs	Clubs	£ 15/18 holes

Credit cards Cartes de crédit
VISA - Eurocard - MasterCard - AMEX - DC

518

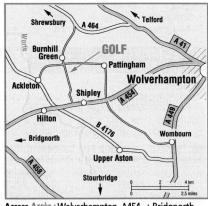

Access Accès : Wolverhampton, A454 → Bridgnorth. Nearly 4 km (2 1/2 m.) until The Mermaid Inn. Turn right after lights (Tinacre Hill) through Pattingham. Turn right at the Church. Golf 2 km on the right.
Map 7 on page 418 Carte 7 Page 418

GOLF COURSE
PARCOURS 13/20

Site	Site	
Maintenance	Entretien	
Architect	Architecte	John Jacobs
Type	Type	parkland
Relief	Relief	
Water in play	Eau en jeu	
Exp. to wind	Exposé au vent	
Trees in play	Arbres en jeu	

Scorecard Carte de score	Chp. Chp.	Mens Mess.	Ladies Da.
Length Long.	5834	5601	5157
Par	72	72	74

Advised golfing ability	0	12	24	36
Niveau de jeu recommandé				
Hcp required	Handicap exigé	27		

CLUB HOUSE & AMENITIES
CLUB HOUSE ET ANNEXES 8/10

Pro shop	Pro-shop	
Driving range	Practice	
Sheltered	couvert	
On grass	sur herbe	yes
Putting-green	putting-green	yes
Pitching-green	pitching green	no

HOTEL FACILITIES
ENVIRONNEMENT HOTELIER 8/10

HOTELS HÔTELS
Patshull Park Hotel - 49 rooms, D £ 70 Golf
Tél (44) 01902 - 700 100 on site
Fax (44) 01902 - 700 874

Hundred House - 10 rooms, D £ 80 Norton
Tel (44) 01952 - 730 353 7 km
Fax (44) 01952 - 730 355

Mount (Jarvis) - 55 rooms, D £ 85 Tettenhall Wood
Tel (44) 01902 - 752 055 10 km
Fax (44) 01902 - 745 263

RESTAURANTS RESTAURANTS
Old Vicarage Worfield
Tel (44) 01746 - 716 497 6 km

Lakeside Restaurant Golf
Tel (44) 01902 - 700 100 on site

PERRANPORTH

16 | 6 | 6

The cliffs and reefs of the west coast of Cornwall sometimes give way to little bays and fine beaches, such as here and the neighbouring holiday resort of Newquay, a surfer's paradise. It's also pretty good for golfers, too, who should make it along here in the same breath as St Enodoc and Trevose. You are in for a relatively easy round if you don't stray from the fairways, but it's a big "if". The "short stuff" is very tight, hilly (with dips, bumps, mounds and hillocks) and difficult to hit. After climbing up the dunes, you can find yourself in long grass, from where good scoring can pose something of a problem. At first glance you might think this an easy course, as there are very few bunkers. Paradoxically it is easier for mid-handicappers than it is for better players, who often prefer to play their approach shots out of sand rather than in thick grass.

Les falaises et les écueils de la côte ouest de Cornouailles laissent parfois place à de petites criques et même des plages, où ont trouvé place des stations de vacances comme Newquay, un paradis des surfeurs. Mais aussi des golfeurs, qui se doivent de venir ici en même temps qu'à St Enodoc et Trevose. Si l'on ne quitte pas les fairways, le jeu y sera relativement aisé. Mais ils sont très étroits, assez mouvementés (des creux et des bosses, des petites buttes et monticules), et on en sort un peu trop facilement. Après avoir grimpé dans les dunes, on peut alors se retrouver dans des herbes bien hautes, d'où un bon score devient problématique. On peut avoir l'illusion qu'il s'agit d'un parcours facile en jetant un premier coup d'oeil, car les bunkers sont peu nombreux : il est paradoxalement plus facile pour les handicaps moyens que pour les bons, qui préfèrent souvent jouer leurs balles dans le sable que dans l'herbe haute...

Perranporth Golf Club
The Clubhouse, Budnic Hill
ENG - PERRANPOTH, Cornwall TR6 0AB

Office	Secrétariat	(44) 01872 - 573 701
Pro shop	Pro-shop	(44) 01872 - 572 317
Fax	Fax	(44) 01872 - 573 701
Situation	Situation	

10 km S of Newquay (pop. 17 390)
15 km NW of Truro (pop. 16 522)

Annual closure	Fermeture annnuelle	no
Weekly closure	Fermeture hebdomadaire	no

Fees main season	Tarifs haute saison		18 holes
		Week days Semaine	**We/Bank holidays** We/Férié
Individual Individuel		£ 20	£ 25
Couple Couple		£ 40	£ 50

Caddy	Caddy	no
Electric Trolley	Chariot électrique	no
Buggy	Voiturette	no
Clubs	Clubs	£ 8/day

Credit cards Cartes de crédit
VISA - MasterCard

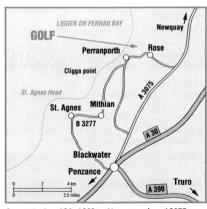

GOLF
LIGGER OR PERRAN BAY
Newquay
Perranporth — Rose
Cligga point
St. Agnes Head
St. Agnes — Mithian
B 3277
A 3075
A 30
Blackwater
Penzance
Truro
A 390
0   2   4 km
0   2,5 miles

Access Accès : A30, A392 to Newquay, then A3075.
At Goonhavern, B3285. Golf on edge of Perranporth,
next to beach
Map 6 on page 416 Carte 6 Page 416

GOLF COURSE
PARCOURS   **16**/20

Site	Site	
Maintenance	Entretien	
Architect	Architecte	James Braid
Type	Type	seaside course, links
Relief	Relief	
Water in play	Eau en jeu	
Exp. to wind	Exposé au vent	
Trees in play	Arbres en jeu	

Scorecard Carte de score	Chp. Chp.	Mens Mess.	Ladies Da.
Length Long.	5722	5460	4880
Par	72	72	72

Advised golfing ability		0	12	24	36
Niveau de jeu recommandé					
Hcp required	Handicap exigé	certificate			

CLUB HOUSE & AMENITIES
CLUB HOUSE ET ANNEXES   **6**/10

Pro shop	Pro-shop	
Driving range	Practice	
Sheltered	couvert	no
On grass	sur herbe	yes
Putting-green	putting-green	yes
Pitching-green	pitching green	no

HOTEL FACILITIES
ENVIRONNEMENT HOTELIER   **6**/10

HOTELS HÔTELS
Rose-in-Vale - 19 rooms, D £ 70   St Agnes
Tel (44) 01872 - 552 202   5 km
Fax (44) 01872 - 552 700

Bristol - 73 rooms, D £ 75   Newquay
Tel (44) 01637 - 875 181   10 km
Fax (44) 01637 - 879 347

Crantock Bay - 34 rooms, D £ 80 (w. dinner)   Crantock
Tel (44) 01637 - 830 229   5 km
Fax (44) 01637 - 831 111

RESTAURANT RESTAURANT
Pennypots   Truro 15 km
Tel (44) 01209 - 820 347

519

This is one the region's great parkland courses and has just treated itself to an impressively sized brand new clubhouse. There are a lot of trees, particularly on the 16th (a par 3) which you have to hit over in order to reach the green, but elsewhere they are rarely in play, except for slicers. The other hazards are the heather and the many large bunkers. Once again, a good score here means you really did play well. You may be lucky once, but rarely twice. Because of the technical challenge here, inexperienced players can expect to sweat a little, so stableford, match-play or a Texas scramble might be a more enjoyable option. This is indeed an excellent course for match-play golf, almost a testimony to the not too distant day and age when match-play was the formula used by all amateur golfers. The general excellence of green-keeping makes a visit here something we would eagerly recommend, despite the proximity of some pretty good links courses.

C'est un des grands parcours "de parc" de cette région, et vient de s'offrir un nouveau Clubhouse de taille impressionnante. On trouve ici beaucoup d'arbres, notamment au 16 (par 3), qu'il faut survoler pour atteindre le green, mais ils sont rarement très en jeu... sauf pour les sliceurs. Les autres auront plutôt de la bruyère, de grands et nombreux bunkers. Un bon score est forcément la preuve d'un bon jeu. Ici, on peut avoir de la chance une fois, mais rarement deux. En raison de ses exigences techniques, les joueurs peu expérimentés doivent s'attendre à souffrir, on leur conseillera donc le stableford, le match-play ou le scramble ! Car c'est un excellent parcours de match-play, témoin d'un époque pas si lointaine où il s'agissait de la formule de jeu des amateurs. La qualité générale de l'entretien permet de recommander une visite, même si les grands links sont à proximité.

Pleasington Golf Club
Pleasington
ENG - BLACKBURN, Lancs BB2 5JF

Office	Secrétariat	(44) 01254 - 202177
Pro shop	Pro-shop	(44) 01254 - 201630
Fax	Fax	(44) 01254 - 201028
Situation	Situation	

5 km from Blackburn (pop. 136 612)
10 km from Preston (pop. 126 080)

Annual closure	Fermeture annnuelle	no
Weekly closure	Fermeture hebdomadaire	no
Fees main season	Tarifs haute saison	full day

	Week days Semaine	We/Bank holidays We/Férié
Individual Individuel	£ 30	£ 35
Couple Couple	£ 60	£ 70

Caddy	Caddy	no
Electric Trolley	Chariot électrique	no
Buggy	Voiturette	no
Clubs	Clubs	£ 7.50/18 holes

Credit cards Cartes de crédit
VISA - Eurocard - MasterCard - AMEX - DC - JCB

520

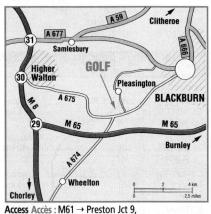

Access Accès : M61 → Preston Jct 9,
then M65 → Blackburn. Jct 3, then A674 →
Blackburn, to Pleasington Lane.
Golf 200 m from Pleasington Station.
Map 5 on page 415 Carte 5 Page 415

GOLF COURSE
PARCOURS

16/20

Site	Site	
Maintenance	Entretien	
Architect	Architecte	George Low Sandy Herd
Type	Type	parkland, heathland
Relief	Relief	
Water in play	Eau en jeu	
Exp. to wind	Exposé au vent	
Trees in play	Arbres en play	

Scorecard Carte de score	Chp. Chp.	Mens Mess.	Ladies Da.
Length Long.	5816	5816	5217
Par	71	71	74

Advised golfing ability		0 12 24 36
Niveau de jeu recommandé		
Hcp required	Handicap exigé	no

CLUB HOUSE & AMENITIES
CLUB HOUSE ET ANNEXES

8/10

Pro shop	Pro-shop	
Driving range	Practice	
Sheltered	couvert	no
On grass	sur herbe	practice range only
Putting-green	putting-green	yes
Pitching-green	pitching green	yes

HOTEL FACILITIES
ENVIRONNEMENT HOTELIER

6/10

HOTELS HÔTELS
Swallow Trafalgar Hotel — Samlesbury 6 km
78 rooms, D £ 95
Tel (44) 01772 - 877 351, Fax (44) 01772 - 877 424

Forte Posthouse - 121 rooms, D £ 60 — Preston 10 km
Tel (44) 01772 - 259 411, Fax (44) 01772 - 201 923

Millstone - 17 rooms, D £ 85 — Mellor 6 km
Tel (44) 01254 - 813 333, Fax (44) 01254 - 812 628

RESTAURANTS RESTAURANTS
Heathcotes Brasserie — Preston 10 km
Tel (44) 01772 - 252 732

Birch House - Tel (44) 01772 - 251 366 — Preston 10 km

Golf Club — Pleasington
Tel (44) 01254 - 202 177 — on site

They needed a big clubhouse here to cater to the number of players on the two 18 hole courses (the second course is the old Oaklands Golf Club). The Championship Course (1989), probably one of Donald Steel's best, is hilly enough for us to recommend a buggy to keep all your strength for playing golf (you will need it). The existing lie of the land was used and enhanced to great effect, completed by some shifting of earth that never clashes with landscape where the impression is more that of a park than open countryside. A little decoration never does any harm, like the little waterfalls on the 15th hole or the plants on the 6th. Owing to the length of this course, you will be hard pushed to play it twice in one day, so you will be pleased to learn that all the hazards are clearly visible, although to avoid them you will have to pitch the ball in high, sometimes flighting it both ways. A fine course.

Il fallait un Clubhouse imposant pour s'accommoder de la fréquentation sur deux 18 trous (le second parcours est l'ancien Oaklands Golf Club). Le Championship Course (1989) est probablement une des meilleures réalisations de Donald Steel, mais on conseillera l'usage d'une voiturette afin de garder assez de forces pour jouer au golf. Le terrain existant a été très bien utilisé et mis en valeur, et complété de mouvements qui ne heurtent jamais un paysage quand même plus proche du parc que de la campagne. Un peu de décoration ne nuit pas, comme les petites cascades du 15 ou les plantations du 6. Comme on jouera difficilement deux fois dans la journée en raison de la longueur du parcours, il faut savoir que tous les obstacles sont bien visibles, mais qu'il vaut mieux savoir bien lever la balle, et parfois la travailler pour réussir. Une belle réalisation.

Portal Golf Club
Cobblers Cross
ENG - TARPORLEY, Cheshire CW6 0DJ

Office	Secrétariat	(44) 01829 - 733933
Pro shop	Pro-shop	(44) 01829 - 733933
Fax	Fax	(44) 01829 - 733928
Situation	Situation	

16 km E of Chester (pop. 115 971)

Annual closure	Fermeture annnuelle	no
Weekly closure	Fermeture hebdomadaire	no

Fees main season
Tarifs haute saison   18 holes

	Week days Semaine	We/Bank holidays We/Férié
Individual Individuel	£ 40	£ 40
Couple Couple	£ 80	£ 80

Caddy	Caddy	no
Electric Trolley	Chariot électrique	no
Buggy	Voiturette	£ 20/18 holes
Clubs	Clubs	on request

Credit cards Cartes de crédit
VISA - Eurocard - MasterCard - AMEX - DC

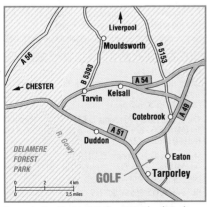

Access Accès : Chester A51, then A49. 1 km (0.5 m) north of Tarporley.
Map 4 on page 412 Carte 4 Page 412

GOLF COURSE PARCOURS   15/20

Site	Site	
Maintenance	Entretien	
Architect	Architecte	Donald Steel
Type	Type	parkland
Relief	Relief	
Water in play	Eau en jeu	
Exp. to wind	Exposé au vent	
Trees in play	Arbres en jeu	

Scorecard Carte de score	Chp. Chp.	Mens Mess.	Ladies Da.
Length Long.	6333	5854	5362
Par	73	73	73

Advised golfing ability	0	12	24	36
Niveau de jeu recommandé				
Hcp required	Handicap exigé	no		

CLUB HOUSE & AMENITIES
CLUB HOUSE ET ANNEXES   8/10

Pro shop	Pro-shop	
Driving range	Practice	
Sheltered	couvert	6 mats
On grass	sur herbe	yes
Putting-green	putting-green	yes
Pitching-green	pitching green	yes

HOTEL FACILITIES
ENVIRONNEMENT HOTELIER   7/10

HOTELS HÔTELS
Swan Hotel - 20 rooms, D £ 68.50   Tarporley
Tel (44) 01829 - 733 838   5 km
Fax (44) 01829 - 732 932

Rookery Hall Hotel - 45 rooms, D £ 95   Nantwich
Tel (44) 01270 - 610 016   10 km
Fax (44) 01270 - 626 027

Wild Boar - 37 rooms, D £ 85   Beeston
Tel (44) 01829 - 260 309   6 km
Fax (44) 01829 - 261 081

Nunsmere Hall - 31 rooms, D £ 120   Sandiway
Tel (44) 01606 - 543 000   5 km
Fax (44) 01606 - 889 055

RESTAURANTS RESTAURANTS
Swan Hotel - Tel (44) 01829 - 733 838   Tarporley 5 km
Blue Bell - Tel (44) 01244 - 317 759   Chester 15 km

521

The green-keeper is one of the five "masters" of Britain and his sterling efforts only add to the pleasure of playing one of the very few moorland courses designed by Harry Colt. A huge planting programme has enhanced the course both visually and in terms of giving each hole clearer definition over wide open space. Colt didn't do much to the terrain, he just used it with his usual brilliance, and you might be surprised by some of the sloping fairways. You need an accurate driver here, but the basic work consists in hitting some very-well defended greens which are sometimes tiered, sometimes terraced owing to the lie of the land. You need to play every shot in the book, in every direction. Basically you will want at least one good shot per hole (and some good putts), so you don't have much breathing space. A very sound course that makes an impression on all who play it, although visitors can only tee-off during the week. The ideal time would be a fine Autumn afternoon.

Le greenkeeper est l'un des cinq «Masters» de Grande-Bretagne, son travail ne fait qu'ajouter au plaisir d'un des seuls dessins de Harry Colt en paysage de lande, auquel un énorme programme de plantations a donné à la fois beauté visuelle et définition des trous dans l'espace. Colt n'a pas beaucoup touché au terrain, il l'a utilisé avec son génie habituel, et certaines inclinaisons des fairways pourront surprendre. Il faut être précis au drive, mais le travail essentiel est dans les approches de greens très protégés, parfois en plateau ou en balcons en raison des mouvements du terrain. Il faut alors savoir jouer tous les coups, et dans tous les sens : il faut au minimum un bon coup de golf par trou (et de bons putts), ce qui ne laisse guère respirer. Un solide parcours qui ne laissera pas indifférent, mais on ne peut le jouer qu'en semaine. A voir par un bel après-midi d'automne.

Prestbury Golf Club
Macclesfield Road
ENG - PRESTBURY, Cheshire SK10 4BJ

Office	Secrétariat	(44) 01625 - 828241
Pro shop	Pro-shop	(44) 01625 - 828242
Fax	Fax	
Situation	Situation	

3 km NW of Macclesfield (pop. 49 024)
25 km from Manchester (pop. 404 861)

Annual closure	Fermeture annnuelle	no
Weekly closure	Fermeture hebdomadaire	no

Fees main season Tarifs haute saison		full day
	Week days	We/Bank holidays
	Semaine	We/Férié
Individual Individuel	£ 37.50	—
Couple Couple	£ 75	—

No visitors at weekends

Caddy	Caddy	on request/£ 8.50
Electric Trolley	Chariot électrique	£ 5/18 holes
Buggy	Voiturette	no
Clubs	Clubs	£ 5/18 holes

Credit cards Cartes de crédit
VISA - Eurocard - MasterCard - AMEX - DC

522

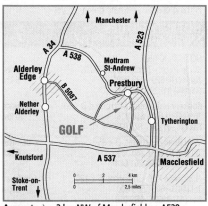

Access Accès : 3 km NW of Macclesfield on A538 off A523.
Map 4 on page 412 Carte 4 Page 412

GOLF COURSE / PARCOURS — 17/20

Site	Site	▰▰▰▰▰▱▱
Maintenance	Entretien	▰▰▰▰▰▰▱
Architect	Architecte	Harry S. Colt J. Morrison
Type **Relief**	Type Relief	inland, open country
Water in play	Eau en jeu	▰▱▱▱▱▱▱
Exp. to wind	Exposé au vent	▰▰▰▱▱▱▱
Trees in play	Arbres en jeu	▰▰▰▰▱▱▱

Scorecard	Chp.	Mens	Ladies
Carte de score	Chp.	Mess.	Da.
Length Long.	5723	5528	4917
Par	71	71	74

Advised golfing ability		0 12 24 36
Niveau de jeu recommandé		▰▰▰▰▰▰▱
Hcp required	Handicap exigé	no

CLUB HOUSE & AMENITIES / CLUB HOUSE ET ANNEXES — 8/10

Pro shop	Pro-shop	▰▰▰▰▰▰▱
Driving range	Practice	▰▰▰▰▰▱▱
Sheltered	couvert	no
On grass	sur herbe	yes (own balls)
Putting-green	putting-green	yes
Pitching-green	pitching green	yes

HOTEL FACILITIES / ENVIRONNEMENT HOTELIER — 7/10

HOTELS HÔTELS

White House Manor - 9 rooms, D £ 95 — Prestbury 1 km
Tel (44) 01625 - 829 376
Fax (44) 01625 - 828 627

The Bridge Hotel - 23 rooms, D £ 56 — Prestbury 1 km
Tel (44) 01625 - 829 326
Fax (44) 01625 - 827 557

Shrigley Hall - 156 rooms, D £ 120 — Adlington 5 km
Tel (44) 01625 - 575 757
Fax (44) 01625 - 573 323

RESTAURANTS RESTAURANTS

White House - Tel (44) 01625 - 829 376 — Prestbury 1 km

The Bridge Hotel - — Prestbury 1 km
Tel (44) 01625 - 829 326

Mauro's - Tel (44) 01625 - 573 898 — Bollington 2 km

Restoration work and alterations since the war, the arranging of the course into 3 nine-hole loops and a commitment to making this a course more for your average golfer have somewhat unseated the original layout by Campbell and Morrison and probably detracted from its overall standard as well. The fairways are wider than they used to be and the bunkers and greens are smaller, thereby reducing the risk of 3-putts. The only really interesting combination is almost certainly "Shore-Himalayas" which, and this is no coincidence, embraces most of the original layout. Of course, alongside Royal St. George and Royal Cinque Ports, a number of less experienced golfers will enjoy their first taste of links golfing with getting too much of a bloody nose. And of course if the wind blows (often a cross-wind here) Prince's can be long and tough. But all the same, the better players will still find the challenge here a little less demanding than it might be. The clubhouse is modern and facilities very respectable.

Les restaurations de l'après-guerre, la disposition en trois boucles de neuf trous, l'adaptation de Prince's aux handi-caps moyens ont quelque peu bouleversé le dessin original de Campbell et Morrison. Et l'ont affaibli, il faut bien le dire. Les fairways sont plus larges qu'autrefois, les bunkers souvent plus petits, tout comme les greens : on n'y risque plus trois putts. Et la seule combinaison réellement intéressante est incontestablement "Shore-Himalayas", où l'on trouve, ce n'est pas un hasard, la majorité du tracé d'origine. Certes, à côté de Royal St George's et de Royal Cinque Ports, certains golfeurs peu aguerris aimeront faire leur expérience des links sans trop se casser les dents. Certes, si le vent souffle (souvent en travers), Prince's peut être être long et difficile. Il n'empêche que les meilleurs joueurs trouveront le défi un peu moins agressif qu'il pourrait l'être. Le Clubhouse est moderne, les équipements convenables.

Prince's Golf Club
ENG - SANDWICH BAY, Kent CT13 9QB

Office	Secrétariat	(44) 01304 - 611 118
Pro shop	Pro-shop	(44) 01304 - 613 797
Fax	Fax	(44) 01304 - 612 000
Situation	Situation	

4 km from Sandwich (pop. 4 729)
10 km from Deal (pop. 28 504)

Annual closure	Fermeture annnuelle	no
Weekly closure	Fermeture hebdomadaire	no

Fees main season	Tarifs haute saison	18 holes
	Week days	We/Bank holidays
	Semaine	We/Férié
Individual Individuel	£ 40	£ 42
Couple Couple	£ 80	£ 84

£ 45/51 for 36 holes (Weekdays/Week-ends)

Caddy	Caddy	no
Electric Trolley	Chariot électrique	no
Buggy	Voiturette	£ 20/18 holes
Clubs	Clubs	£ 20

Credit cards Cartes de crédit
VISA - MasterCard - DC

Access Accès : Sandwich, → "The Golf Courses".
3 km Toll gate into Sandwich Bay Estate, left 1 km and left again. Continue 2 km along seafront.
Map 7 on page 419 Carte 7 Page 419

GOLF COURSE
PARCOURS
13/20

Site	Site	
Maintenance	Entretien	
Architect	Architecte	Sir Guy Campbell
		John Morrison
Type	Type	seaside course, links
Relief	Relief	
Water in play	Eau en jeu	
Exp. to wind	Exposé au vent	
Trees in play	Arbres en jeu	

Scorecard	Chp.	Mens	Ladies
Carte de score	Chp.	Mess.	Da.
Length Long.	5860	5614	5260
Par	71	71	73

Advised golfing ability		0	12	24	36
Niveau de jeu recommandé					
Hcp required	Handicap exigé	no			

CLUB HOUSE & AMENITIES
CLUB HOUSE ET ANNEXES
6/10

Pro shop	Pro-shop	
Driving range	Practice	
Sheltered	couvert	3 mats
On grass	sur herbe	yes
Putting-green	putting-green	yes
Pitching-green	pitching green	yes

HOTEL FACILITIES
ENVIRONNEMENT HOTELIER
4/10

HOTELS HÔTELS

Bell Hotel - 29 rooms, D £ 100 — Sandwich
Tel (44) 01304 - 613 388 — 4 km
Fax (44) 01304 - 615 308

Jarvis Marina - 59 rooms, D £ 69 — Ramsgate
Tel (44) 01843 - 588 276 — 12 km
Fax (44) 01843 - 586 866

San Clu - 32 rooms, D £ 80 — Ramsgate
Tel (44) 01843 - 592 345 — 12 km
Fax (44) 01843 - 580 157

RESTAURANTS RESTAURANTS

Blazing Donkey — Ham, Sandwich
Tel (44) 01304 - 617362 — 7 km

Dunkerleys Restaurant — Deal
Tel (44) 01304 - 375016 — 10 km

Hare & Hounds - Tel (44) 01304 - 365 429 — Deal 10 km

523

Driving up from London, you will have stopped off at Stratford-upon-Avon (the birthplace of Shakespeare) and then at Gloucester to visit the cathedral and the docks that have now been transformed into a museum. As you pursue your cultural trek on to Hereford, home of the world's first map (in the cathedral), you drive along the very beautiful Wye valley and stop off in the pretty town that has given its name to this golf course. It was laid out in 1964 in a forest with literally thousands of trees, especially birch, which make this pleasant course such a beautiful site with its small, exciting and very well protected greens. There are a few blind shots but overall this is a very fair course with clearly identifiable hazards. Free of traps, well maintained and very pleasant to play, Ross-on-Wye extends a simple but very friendly welcome to green-feers.

Venant de Londres, vous vous serez arrêté à Stratford-upon-Avon (ville natale de Shakespeare), puis à Gloucester pour visiter la cathédrale et les docks transformés en musée. Avant de poursuivre votre quête culturelle à Hereford où l'on trouve la première carte du monde (à la cathédrale), vous devez passer par la très belle vallée de la Wye et vous arrêter dans la jolie ville qui a donné son nom au parcours. Il date de 1964, a été tracé dans une forêt composée de millions d'arbres, en particulier de bouleaux, qui donnent une grande beauté à ce plaisant parcours, avec de petits greens très animés et bien défendus. On trouve quelques coups aveugles, mais l'ensemble est néanmoins très franc, avec des obstacles clairement identifiables. Sans pièges, bien entretenu, très agréable à jouer, Ross-on-Wye bénéficie également d'un accueil simple, mais très amical.

Ross-on-Wye Golf Club

Two Park, Gorsley
ENG - ROSS-ON-WYE, Hereford HR9 7UT

Office	Secrétariat	(44) 01989 - 720 267
Pro shop	Pro-shop	(44) 01989 - 720 439
Fax	Fax	(44) 01989 - 720 212
Situation	Situation	

20 km W of Gloucester (pop. 101 608)
5 km E of Ross-on-Wye (pop. 9 606)

Annual closure	Fermeture annnuelle	no
Weekly closure	Fermeture hebdomadaire	no
Fees main season	Tarifs haute saison	18 holes

	Week days Semaine	We/Bank holidays We/Férié
Individual Individuel	£ 30	£ 30
Couple Couple	£ 60	£ 60

Full day: £ 35

Caddy	Caddy	no
Electric Trolley	Chariot électrique	£ 6/18 holes
Buggy	Voiturette	no
Clubs	Clubs	£ 5/18 holes

Credit cards Cartes de crédit
VISA - MasterCard (only Pro shop)

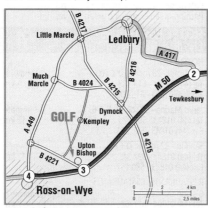

Little Marcle · Ledbury · B 4211 · A 417 · Much Marcle · B 4024 · B 4216 · B 4215 · M 50 · 2 · Tewkesbury · Dymock · GOLF · Kempley · A 449 · B 4215 · Upton Bishop · B 4221 · 4 · 3 · Ross-on-Wye

Access Accès : Adjacent Jct 3 of M50.
Map 6 on page 417 Carte 6 Page 417

GOLF COURSE
PARCOURS

15/20

Site	Site	▰▰▰▰▱
Maintenance	Entretien	▰▰▰▰▱
Architect	Architecte	C.K. Cotton
Type	Type	parkland
Relief	Relief	▰▰▰▱▱
Water in play	Eau en jeu	▰▱▱▱▱
Exp. to wind	Exposé au vent	▰▰▱▱▱
Trees in play	Arbres en jeu	▰▰▰▰▱

Scorecard Carte de score	Chp. Chp.	Mens Mess.	Ladies Da.
Length Long.	5897	5443	5130
Par	72	72	73

Advised golfing ability Niveau de jeu recommandé	0	12	24	36
Hcp required	Handicap exigé	certificate		

CLUB HOUSE & AMENITIES
CLUB HOUSE ET ANNEXES

5/10

Pro shop	Pro-shop	▰▰▰▱▱
Driving range	Practice	▰▰▱▱▱
Sheltered	couvert	no
On grass	sur herbe	yes
Putting-green	putting-green	yes
Pitching-green	pitching green	yes

HOTEL FACILITIES
ENVIRONNEMENT HOTELIER

6/10

HOTELS HÔTELS

Chase - 39 rooms, D £ 80 Tel (44) 01989 - 763 161 Fax (44) 01989 - 768 330	Ross-on-Wye 6 km
Sunnymount - 6 rooms, D £ 50 Tel (44) 01989 - 563 880	Ross-on-Wye 6 km
Forte Posthouse - 122 rooms, D £ 65 Tel (44) 01452 - 613 311 Fax (44) 01452 - 371 036	Gloucester 20 km

RESTAURANTS RESTAURANTS

Pheasants Tel (44) 01989 - 565 751	Ross-on-Wye 6 km
Epicurean Tel (44) 01242 - 222 466	Cheltenham 30 Km

524

14	7	6

Players who can't handle sand breathe an almost audible sigh of relief here, where there is not a single bunker in sight. So it could claim to be the most natural course around, as no-one has ever seen a bunker on wholly natural terrain except perhaps on links courses where grazing sheep keep the place in shape. This was the result of an administrative ban but has now become a sort of coquetry. But don't be too relieved, as there is no shortage of difficulties elsewhere: there are pine and birch trees, a stream on several holes, heather, which is even more dangerous than water that often has to be carried with your drive or even your second shot (on the 12th). As a general rule, and with a couple of exceptions, members will tell you to hit the ball high into the greens, which are rather large, very quick in summer and which slope in all directions. A pretty course and a superb clubhouse.

Alleluia, disent les golfeurs qui restent sur le sable. Il n'y a pas ici un seul bunker, c'est donc le parcours le plus naturel qui soit, car qui a vu des bunkers à l'état naturel, sinon dans les jardins d'enfant et sur les links authentiques où paissent les moutons ? C'était le résultat d'une interdiction administrative, c'est devenu une sorte de coquetterie. Que l'on ne soit pas trop vite soulagé, les difficultés ne manquent pas : les pins et les bouleaux d'abord, un cours d'eau sur plusieurs trous, la bruyère encore, bien plus pénalisante que l'eau, dont il faut souvent franchir des étendues au drive ou même au second coup (au 12). En règle générale, les membres vous souffleront qu'il faut ici lever la balle, sauf pour approcher un ou deux greens. Ceux-ci sont assez grands, avec des pentes dans tous les sens, et très rapides en été. Un joli parcours, avec un superbe Clubhouse.

Royal Ashdown Forest Golf Club

Chapel Lane, Forest Row
ENG - EAST GRINSTEAD, East Sussex RH18 5LR

Office	Secrétariat	(44) 01342 - 822 018
Pro shop	Pro-shop	(44) 01342 - 822 247
Fax	Fax	(44) 01342 - 825 211
Situation	Situation	

8 km SE of East Grinstead (pop. 24 383)

Annual closure	Fermeture annnuelle	no
Weekly closure	Fermeture hebdomadaire	no

Fees main season
Tarifs haute saison — full day

	Week days Semaine	We/Bank holidays We/Férié
Individual Individuel	£ 36	£ 40
Couple Couple	£ 72	£ 80

Caddy	Caddy	£ 15
Electric Trolley	Chariot électrique	no
Buggy	Voiturette	no
Clubs	Clubs	£ 10/18 holes

Credit cards Cartes de crédit
VISA - Eurocard - MasterCard - AMEX - DC
(not for green fees)

Access Accès : M25 Jct 6 then A22 South through East Grinstead. At Forest Row, turn left into B2110. 0.8 km (1/2 m.) right into Chapel Lane. Top of hill turn left.
Map 7 on page 419 Carte 7 Page 419

GOLF COURSE / PARCOURS — 14/20

Site	Site	
Maintenance	Entretien	
Architect	Architecte	Archdeacon Scott
Type	Type	inland, heathland
Relief	Relief	
Water in play	Eau en jeu	
Exp. to wind	Exposé au vent	
Trees in play	Arbres en jeu	

Scorecard Carte de score	Chp. Chp.	Mens Mess.	Ladies Da.
Length Long.	5712	5675	5032
Par	72	72	73

Advised golfing ability Niveau de jeu recommandé	0	12	24	36

Hcp required	Handicap exigé	certificate

CLUB HOUSE & AMENITIES / CLUB HOUSE ET ANNEXES — 7/10

Pro shop	Pro-shop	
Driving range	Practice	
Sheltered	couvert	no
On grass	sur herbe	yes
Putting-green	putting-green	yes
Pitching-green	pitching green	yes

525

HOTEL FACILITIES / ENVIRONNEMENT HOTELIER — 6/10

HOTELS HÔTELS
Ashdown Park - 89 rooms, D £ 100 — Wych Cross 3 km
Tel (44) 01342 - 824 988
Fax (44) 01342 - 826 206

Brambletye - 22 rooms, D £ 60 — Forest Row 2 km
Tel (44) 01342 - 824 144
Fax (44) 01342 - 824 833

Woodbury House — East Grinstead 5 km
14 rooms, D £ 85
Tel (44) 01342 - 313 657
Fax (44) 01342 - 314 801

RESTAURANTS RESTAURANTS
Brambletye — Forest Row 2 km
Tel (44) 01342 - 824 144

Chequers Inn — Forest Row 2 km
Tel (44) 01342 - 823 333

Royal Birkdale has hosted each and every top tournament: the Open, the Ryder, Walker and Curtis Cups, and the Ladies Open. It has done so more than others probably because this is an open and honest course where you can draw up your strategy according to the wind and not to the imponderables that create the "rough justice" charm of other links. Here, if you stay on the fairway you will avoid any blind shots. If you stray onto the surrounding dunes, you can end up in some very nasty situations indeed. This is a course for the technician and artist, not the big-hitter. Thomson, Watson, Trevino and Miller have all won here, as did Arnold Palmer, a more refined golfer than some might believe. There is no point in describing what could easily fill a whole book. Suffice it to say that Birkdale is unforgettable and that, like a dinner in a top hotel, this immense pleasure comes at a price. So make it a full day's golfing.

Royal Birkdale a reçu toutes les grandes compétitions : l'Open, la Ryder Cup, la Walker Cup, la Curtis Cup, le Ladies Open... Plus que d'autres sans doute, parce que sa franchise permet d'établir la stratégie en fonction du vent, et non des impondérables qui font le charme d'autres links, mais pas toujours dans la justice ! Pas de coups aveugles ici, du moins si l'on reste sur le fairway, car les dunes alentour peuvent vous imposer des situations peu confortables. Ce n'est pas un parcours de frappeur, mais de technicien, d'artiste du travail de la balle : Thomson, Watson, Trevino, Miller ont gagné ici, mais aussi Arnold Palmer, plus fin golfeur qu'on ne le croit. Inutile de décrire ce qui prendrait un livre entier, disons seulement que Birkdale est inoubliable, que cet immense plaisir se paie cher, comme un dîner dans un trois étoiles. Alors, prenez la journée.

The Royal Birkdale Golf Club

Waterloo Road
ENG - SOUTHPORT, Lancs PR8 2LX

Office	Secrétariat	(44) 01704 - 567 920
Pro shop	Pro-shop	(44) 01704 - 568 857
Fax	Fax	
Situation	Situation	

1.5 km S of Southport (pop. 90 959)
30 km N of Liverpool (pop. 452 450)

Annual closure	Fermeture annnuelle	no
Weekly closure	Fermeture hebdomadaire	no

Fees main season	Tarifs haute saison		18 holes
		Week days Semaine	We/Bank holidays We/Férié
Individual Individuel		£ 75	£ 95*
Couple Couple		£ 150	£ 190*

* Not Saturdays - Full weekdays: £ 95

Caddy	Caddy	on request/£ 23+tip
Electric Trolley	Chariot électrique	£ 6.50/18 holes
Buggy	Voiturette	no
Clubs	Clubs	£ 10/18 holes

Credit cards Cartes de crédit
VISA - Eurocard - MasterCard - AMEX - DC - JCB
(Pro-shop only)

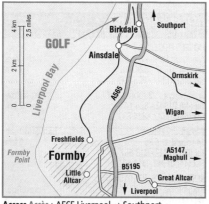

Access Accès : A565 Liverpool → Southport, 1.5 km (1 m.) before Southport.
Map 5 on page 415 Carte 5 Page 415

GOLF COURSE
PARCOURS   19/20

Site	Site	▬▬▬▬
Maintenance	Entretien	▬▬▬▬
Architect	Architecte	F.W. Hawtree
		J.H. Taylor
Type	Type	links
Relief	Relief	▬▬
Water in play	Eau en jeu	
Exp. to wind	Exposé au vent	▬▬▬
Trees in play	Arbres en jeu	

Scorecard	Chp.	Mens	Ladies
Carte de score	Chp.	Mess.	Da.
Length Long.	6290	6021	5195
Par	70	72	75

Advised golfing ability	0	12	24	36
Niveau de jeu recommandé				

Hcp required   Handicap exigé   28 Men, 36 Ladies

CLUB HOUSE & AMENITIES
CLUB HOUSE ET ANNEXES   9/10

Pro shop	Pro-shop	▬▬▬▬
Driving range	Practice	▬▬▬
Sheltered	couvert	no
On grass	sur herbe	yes
Putting-green	putting-green	yes
Pitching-green	pitching green	yes

HOTEL FACILITIES
ENVIRONNEMENT HOTELIER   7/10

HOTELS HÔTELS

Cambridge House Hotel - 18 rooms, D £ 51   Southport
Tel (44) 01704 - 538 372   6 km
Fax (44) 01704 - 547 181

Scarisbrick - 77 rooms, D £ 90   Southport
Tel (44) 01704 - 543 000   3 km
Fax (44) 01704 - 533 335

Stutelea - 24 rooms, D £ 80   Southport 3 km
Tel (44) 01704 - 544 220
Fax (44) 01704 - 500 232

RESTAURANTS RESTAURANTS

The Warehouse   Southport
Tel (44) 01704 - 544 662   3 km

Valentino's   Southport
Tel (44) 01704 - 538 401   3 km

The Jasmin Tree   Southport
Tel (44) 01704 - 530 141   3 km

Here you are a sliced drive away from the sea but you hardly ever see it. Deal (the course's other name) needs this barrier of dunes to protect the course from the sea-water which is deadly for turf. On a narrow strip of land, dotted with a few dunes and flanked by a little road and houses, you'd think it almost impossible to lay-out such a marvellous course. Less majestic than Royal St. George but more constantly demanding than Prince's, Deal requires the intuition that comes from long years of golfing. For example, knowing that on a particular day a particular shot will need three or even four clubs more. Highly strategic and full of small pot bunkers, this is a lively, clever and smart course which should make you a more intelligent golfer, or else leave you feeling a real fool.

Ici, on est à deux pas de la mer, mais on ne la voit pratiquement jamais. Il faut ce cordon de dunes pour protéger "Deal" (comme on le nomme aussi) des assauts d'eau salée, mortelle pour les gazons. Sur cette étroite langue de terre à peine animée par quelques dunes, longée par une petite route et des maisons, on aurait peine à imaginer pouvoir loger un aussi merveilleux parcours. Moins majestueux que St George's, plus constamment exigeant que Prince's, Deal réclame l'intuition que donne une longue pratique, pour savoir par exemple qu'il faut aujourd'hui trois ou quatre clubs de plus à cause du vent. Hautement stratégique, plein de petits bunkers où seul un mouton peut tenir, c'est un parcours vivant, astucieux et malin, d'où on sort intelligent, ou définitivement stupide.

Royal Cinque Ports Golf Club

Golf Road
ENG - DEAL, Kent

Office	Secrétariat	(44) 01304 - 374007
Pro shop	Pro-shop	(44) 01304 - 374170
Fax	Fax	
Situation	Situation	

adjacent to Deal (pop.28 504)
8 km from Sandwich (pop. 4 729)

Annual closure	Fermeture annnuelle	no
Weekly closure	Fermeture hebdomadaire	no
Fees main season	Tarifs haute saison	18 holes

	Week days Semaine	We/Bank holidays We/Férié
Individual Individuel	£ 50	£ 50
Couple Couple	£ 100	£ 100

Visitors strictly by arrangement on weekends -
Weekdays after 1.00 pm, £ 40

Caddy	Caddy	on request/£ 20
Electric Trolley	Chariot électrique	no
Buggy	Voiturette	no
Clubs	Clubs	no
Credit cards Cartes de crédit		VISA - MasterCard

Access Accès : A2, A258 to Deal. Seafront to the end.
Turn left and right into Golf Road
Map 7 on page 419 Carte 7 Page 419

GOLF COURSE
PARCOURS
17/20

Site	Site	
Maintenance	Entretien	
Architect	Architecte	Tom Dunn Guy Campbell
Type	Type	seaside course, links
Relief	Relief	
Water in play	Eau en jeu	
Exp. to wind	Exposé au vent	
Trees in play	Arbres en jeu	

Scorecard Carte de score	Chp. Chp.	Mens Mess.	Ladies Da.
Length Long.	6080	5835	5105
Par	72	70	74

Advised golfing ability
Niveau de jeu recommandé

0	12	24	36

Hcp required Handicap exigé certificate

CLUB HOUSE & AMENITIES
CLUB HOUSE ET ANNEXES
6/10

Pro shop	Pro-shop	
Driving range	Practice	
Sheltered	couvert	no
On grass	sur herbe	yes
Putting-green	putting-green	yes
Pitching-green	pitching green	yes

527

HOTEL FACILITIES
ENVIRONNEMENT HOTELIER
5/10

HOTELS HÔTELS
Royal — Deal
Tel (44) 01304 - 375 555 — 1 km

Bell Hotel - 29 rooms, D £ 100 — Sandwich
Tel (44) 01304 - 613 388 — 7 km
Fax (44) 01304 - 615 308

RESTAURANTS RESTAURANTS
Dunkerleys Restaurant — Deal
Tel (44) 01304 - 375016 — 1 km

Griffins Head — Chillenden
— 5 km

Chequers Inn — Deal
Tel (44) 01304 - 636296 — on site

Royal Cromer is a select location between Yarmouth and Brancaster. Select firstly for its site atop cliffs which alternate with sandy dunes right down the coastline and afford some superb views. Secondly in historical terms, because this is where they thought up the idea of the Curtis Cup between the top British and American amateur ladies. And last but by no means least for the course, which although not a links has the same sort of difficulties including gorse bushes, wind and beautiful bunkering, for which Harry Colt is largely responsible. Although not quite of the same standard as its illustrious neighbours in this region, and without the typical contours of a links course, this layout is well worth a good visit. While you are here, make the most of your time and see the very pretty old town of Norwich.

Entre Yarmouth et Brancaster, Royal Cromer s'est fait une place de choix. Par sa situation d'abord, au sommet des falaises qui alternent sur toute la côte avec les sites dunaires, et qui offrent des vues superbes. Par l'histoire aussi, car c'est là qu'est née l'idée de la future Curtis Cup, entre les meilleures dames amateur de Grande-Bretagne et des USA. Par le parcours enfin, qui n'est pas un links, mais dont les difficultés en sont bien proches, avec les buissons d'ajoncs, le vent, un "bunkering" de toute beauté, dont Harry Colt est sans doute largement responsable. Sans être tout à fait au niveau de ses illustres voisins de la région, sans avoir ces mouvements de terrain typiques des links, ce parcours mérite une visite approfondie. Et tant que vous êtes là, profitez-en pour visiter la très jolie vieille ville de Norwich.

Royal Cromer Golf Club

Overstrand Road
ENG - CROMER, Norfolk NR27 0JH

Office	Secrétariat	(44) 01263 - 512884
Pro shop	Pro-shop	(44) 01263 - 512267
Fax	Fax	(44) 01263 - 512884
Situation	Situation	

1.5 km from Cromer (pop. 5 025)
32 km from Norwich (pop. 120 895)

Annual closure	Fermeture annnuelle	no
Weekly closure	Fermeture hebdomadaire	no

Fees main season	Tarifs haute saison	18 holes
	Week days Semaine	We/Bank holidays We/Férié
Individual Individuel	£ 39	£ 43
Couple Couple	£ 78	£ 86

Caddy	Caddy	no
Electric Trolley	Chariot électrique	no
Buggy	Voiturette	no
Clubs	Clubs	no

Credit cards Cartes de crédit — no

GOLF COURSE PARCOURS — 15/20

Site	Site	
Maintenance	Entretien	
Architect	Architecte	J.H. Taylor Harry S. Colt
Type	Type	seaside course, open country
Relief	Relief	
Water in play	Eau en jeu	
Exp. to wind	Exposé au vent	
Trees in play	Arbres en jeu	

Scorecard	Chp.	Mens	Ladies
Carte de score	Chp.	Mess.	Da.
Length Long.	5802	5652	5233
Par	72	72	74

Advised golfing ability	0 12 24 36	
Niveau de jeu recommandé		
Hcp required	Handicap exigé	certificate

CLUB HOUSE & AMENITIES CLUB HOUSE ET ANNEXES — 7/10

Pro shop	Pro-shop	
Driving range	Practice	
Sheltered	couvert	no
On grass	sur herbe	yes
Putting-green	putting-green	yes
Pitching-green	pitching green	no

HOTEL FACILITIES ENVIRONNEMENT HOTELIER — 6/10

HOTELS HÔTELS

Cliftonville Hotel - 30 rooms, D £ 90 — Cromer 1.5 km
Tel (44) 01263 - 512 543

Links Country Park - 40 rooms, D £ 120 — West Runton 3 km
Tel (44) 01263 - 838 383
Fax (44) 01263 - 838 264

Dormy House - 14 rooms, D £ 90 — West Runton 3 km
Tel (44) 01263 - 835 537
Fax (44) 01263 - 837 537

RESTAURANTS RESTAURANTS

Westgate Lodge — Cromer 1.5 km
Tel (44) 01263 - 512840

Links Country Park — West Runton 3 km
Tel(44) 01263 - 838383

528

NORTH SEA

West Runton — East Runton — Cromer — GOLF
A 149 Sheringham
Holt KING'S LYNN A 148
A 149
Overstrand
A 140
A 149
NORWICH
North Walsham

0 — 2 — 4
0 — 2,5 miles

Access Accès : Norwich, A149. In Cromer, turn right on Coast Road past lighthouse.
Map 7 on page 419 Carte 7 Page 419

ROYAL GUERNSEY ✳ 16 | 7 | 7

The Channel Islands are a curious blend of things English and French, with food coming under the latter influence (happily for the French). But golfing here is very British, as seen with this course. Firstly, given the incredible number of players who walks these fairways, Royal Guernsey is very well maintained (but often very dry in Summer). Then it requires good golfing skills and experience of playing in the wind, a capricious element here, often changing directions several times in one round. Under these conditions you don't often damage (pitch) the little greens, at least not as much as one would like. This traditional links course looks as natural as ever despite a number of restyling operations, particularly from Mackenzie Ross and Fred Hawtree. As a bonus, you get splendid views over the sea, the gardens close to the clubhouse... and the cows.

Les îles anglo-normandes (Channel Islands) présentent un curieux mélange d'anglais et de français, cette dernière influence étant aussi sensible (heureusement) sur la cuisine locale. Mais le golf est bien britannique, ce parcours en est l'illustration. D'abord, compte-tenu du nombre incroyable de joueurs qui y passent, il est bien entretenu (mais souvent très sec en été), ensuite, il réclame un jeu très aguerri et une bonne expérience du vent, car celui-ci est capricieux et peut changer plusieurs fois de sens pendant une partie. Dans ces conditions, on n'abîme pas beaucoup les petits greens, du moins aussi vite qu'on le voudrait. Parcours de links traditionnel, il continue à paraître naturel, malgré de nombreuses révisions, surtout de Mackenzie Ross et Fred Hawtree. En prime, les vues sont magnifiques, sur la mer, sur les jardins près du Clubhouse... et sur les vaches.

Royal Guernsey Golf Club
L'Ancresse
ENG - VALE, Guernsey, Channel Islands

Office	Secrétariat	(44) 01481 - 46 523
Pro shop	Pro-shop	(44) 01481 - 45 070
Fax	Fax	(44) 01481 - 43 960
Situation	Situation	

4.5 km N of St Peter Port

Annual closure	Fermeture annnuelle	no
Weekly closure	Fermeture hebdomadaire	no

Fees main season	Tarifs haute saison		18 holes
		Week days Semaine	We/Bank holidays We/Férié
Individual Individuel		£ 30	—
Couple Couple		£ 60	—

Thursdays, Saturdays afternoon & Sundays only with a member

Caddy	Caddy	no
Electric Trolley	Chariot électrique	no
Buggy	Voiturette	no
Clubs	Clubs	on request

Credit cards Cartes de crédit
VISA - MasterCard

GOLF
L'Ancresse Bay
Grand Havre
L'Ancresse
Vale
St Sampson
GUERNSEY
Belle Grève Bay
Castel
St Peter Port

0 — 1,6 — 3,2 km
0 — 2 miles

Access Accès : Near Pembroke Bay, north of the island
Map 9 on page 422 Carte 9 Page 422

GOLF COURSE
PARCOURS   16/20

Site	Site	▮▮▮▯▯
Maintenance	Entretien	▮▮▮▮▯
Architect	Architecte	Unknown
Type	Type	seaside course, links
Relief	Relief	▮▯▯▯▯
Water in play	Eau en jeu	▮▯▯▯▯
Exp. to wind	Exposé au vent	▮▮▮▯▯
Trees in play	Arbres en jeu	▮▯▯▯▯

Scorecard Carte de score	Chp. Chp.	Mens Mess.	Ladies Da.
Length Long.	5585	5585	5005
Par	70	70	72

Advised golfing ability Niveau de jeu recommandé	0	12	24	36

Hcp required	Handicap exigé	no

CLUB HOUSE & AMENITIES
CLUB HOUSE ET ANNEXES   7/10

Pro shop	Pro-shop	▮▮▮▯▯
Driving range	Practice	▮▮▮▯▯
Sheltered	couvert	no
On grass	sur herbe	no
Putting-green	putting-green	yes
Pitching-green	pitching green	yes

529

HOTEL FACILITIES
ENVIRONNEMENT HOTELIER   7/10

HOTELS HÔTELS
Symphony House Hotel - 15 rooms, D £ 84 L'Ancresse
Tel (44) 01481 - 45 418   1 km
Fax (44) 01481 - 43 581

Pembroke Bay - 12 rooms, D £ 84   L'Ancresse 100 m
Tel (44) 01481 - 47 573, Fax (44) 01481 - 48 838

De Havelet - 34 rooms, D £ 80   St Peter Port 5 km
Tel (44) 01481 - 722 199, Fax (44) 01481 - 714 057

St Pierre Park - 132 rooms, D £ 130   St Peter Port 5 km
Tel (44) 01481 - 782 282, Fax (44) 01481 - 712 041

RESTAURANTS RESTAURANTS
Victor Hugo - Tel (44) 01481 - 782 282   St Peter Port
The Absolute End - Tel (44) 01481 - 723 822 St Peter Port
Wellington Boot - Tél (44) 01481 - 722 199 St Peter Port

Harry Vardon was born next door, just before Ted Ray. Add to that the fact that more recently Tommy Horton learnt how to play here and that makes a lot of champions for one club. The views from the impressive clubhouse are simply magnificent on a course which is a real paradise for golfers, especially players who can produce shots while interpreting every change in land level and get their distances right. In this respect, you are almost better off trusting your eyes than the yardage book. There is no par 4 longer than 400 yards (360 metres), there are five par 3s and only two par 5s at the beginning. Hazards abound and are very well positioned, the deadliest being the sea, at least for slicers. Royal Jersey is very busy in Summer but playable all year because of the warm climate. Spring and Autumn are wonderful times to play here.

Harry Vardon est né à côté, précédant Ted Ray. Si on ajoute que, plus récemment, Tommy Horton a appris le golf ici, cela fait beaucoup de champions pour un seul club. Les vues sont magnifiques depuis l'impressionnant Clubhouse sur ce parcours qui est un véritable paradis pour ceux qui savent fabriquer des coups de golf, en interprétant tous les changements de niveau du terrain, notamment pour les distances. A ce propos, il est presque plus sûr de se fier à ses yeux qu'au carnet de parcours. Aucun par 4 ne dépasse 360 mètres (400 yards), il y a cinq par 3 et seulement deux par 5 placés dès le début, sans doute pour commencer avec le sourire. Les obstacles sont nombreux, très bien placés, le plus redoutable étant la mer, en tout cas pour les sliceurs. Très fréquenté en été, Royal Jersey est jouable toute l'année à cause de la douceur du climat, mais le printemps et l'automne sont sublimes.

Royal Jersey Golf Club
ENG - GROUVILLE, Jersey JE3 9BD

Office	Secrétariat	(44) 01534 - 854416
Pro shop	Pro-shop	(44) 01534 - 852234
Fax	Fax	(44) 01534 - 854684
Situation	Situation	

7 km E of St Helier (pop. 28 123)
1 km S of Gorey

Annual closure	Fermeture annnuelle	no
Weekly closure	Fermeture hebdomadaire	no

Fees main season	Tarifs haute saison		18 holes
		Week days Semaine	We/Bank holidays We/Férié
Individual Individuel		£ 35	£ 40*
Couple Couple		£ 70	£ 80*

* Visitors after 2.30 pm at weekends -
Very busy during summer

Caddy	Caddy	no
Electric Trolley	Chariot électrique	no
Buggy	Voiturette	£ 10/18 holes
Clubs	Clubs	£ 10/18 holes

Credit cards Cartes de crédit
VISA - Eurocard - MasterCard - DC

530

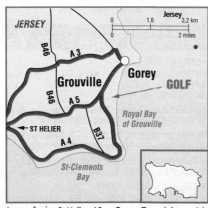

JERSEY

Grouville Gorey GOLF

ST HELIER

Royal Bay of Grouville

St-Clements Bay

Access Accès : St Helier, A3 → Gorey. Turn right on A4.
Map 9 on page 422 Carte 9 Page 422

GOLF COURSE
PARCOURS
16/20

Site	Site	
Maintenance	Entretien	
Architect	Architecte	Unknown
Type	Type	seaside course, links
Relief	Relief	
Water in play	Eau en jeu	
Exp. to wind	Exposé au vent	
Trees in play	Arbres en jeu	

Scorecard Carte de score	Chp. Chp.	Mens Mess.	Ladies Da.
Length Long.	5480	5480	4890
Par	70	70	71

Advised golfing ability Niveau de jeu recommandé	0 12 24 36
Hcp required Handicap exigé	28 Men, 36 Ladies

CLUB HOUSE & AMENITIES
CLUB HOUSE ET ANNEXES
7/10

Pro shop	Pro-shop	
Driving range	Practice	
Sheltered	couvert	no
On grass	sur herbe	no
Putting-green	putting-green	yes
Pitching-green	pitching green	no

HOTEL FACILITIES
ENVIRONNEMENT HOTELIER
8/10

HOTELS HÔTELS
Longueville Manor   St Saviour/St Helier 6 km
30 rooms, D £ 200
Tel (44) 01534 - 25 501, Fax (44) 01534 - 31 613

Old Court House - 58 rooms, D £ 70   Gorey 1 km
Tel (44) 01534 - 854 444, Fax (44) 01534 - 853 587

De Vere Grand - 110 rooms, D £ 120   St Helier 7 km
Tel (44) 01534 - 22 301, Fax (44) 01534 - 37 815

Hotel De La Plage - 78 rooms, D £ 70   St Helier 7 km
Tel (44) 01534 - 23 474, Fax (44) 01534 - 68 642

RESTAURANTS RESTAURANTS
Longueville Manor   St Saviour/St Helier 6 km
Tel (44) 01534 - 25 501

Jersey Pottery - Tel (44) 01534 - 851119   Gorey 1 km

La Petite Pomme - Tel (44) 01534 - 66 608 St Helier7 km

Whenever you can, always play a links you don't know with a caddie. With the wind and out-of-bounds (some of which are inside the course), this is particularly true at Hoylake in order to identify certain hazards (the ground is flat) and draw up your game strategy. They say that Hoylake is a match for Carnoustie in terms of difficulty, and they're not wrong, even in fine weather. Here, you need patience, imagination and skill to improvise and invent shots you won't find in golf text-books, particularly on the less spectacular holes where you might be tempted to relax your concentration. There certainly are more spectacular and more baroque-looking courses in the world, but this one is less austere than it looks. Somehow, Hoylake is all a part of English humour; you need wit - a golfing wit - to understand what it's all about.

Quand c'est possible sur les links que vous ne connaissez pas, prenez un caddie. C'est encore plus vrai ici, avec le vent et les hors-limites (certains sont intérieurs), pour identifier certains obstacles car le terrain est plat, et pour établir une stratégie. On dit que Hoylake tient tête à Carnoustie en matière de difficulté. Ce n'est pas faux, même par beau temps : il faut ici de la patience et de l'imagination, savoir improviser, inventer des coups qui ne sont pas dans les livres. Et surtout sur les trous les moins spectaculaires, où l'on aurait tendance à baisser sa garde. Certes, il est des parcours plus impressionnants, visuellement plus baroques, mais celui-ci est moins sévère qu'il n'y paraît. Quelque part, Hoylake participe de l'humour anglais : il faut un certain esprit pour comprendre. Un esprit de joueur.

Royal Liverpool Golf Club
Meols Drive, Hoylake
ENG - WIRRAL, Cheshire L47 4AL

Office	Secrétariat	(44) 0151 - 632 6757
Pro shop	Pro-shop	(44) 0151 - 632 5868
Fax	Fax	(44) 0151 - 632 3739
Situation	Situation	

5 km from Wallasey
16 km from Liverpool (pop. 452 450)

Annual closure	Fermeture annnuelle	no
Weekly closure	Fermeture hebdomadaire	no
Fees main season	Tarifs haute saison	18 holes

	Week days Semaine	We/Bank holidays We/Férié
Individual Individuel	£ 50	£ 75
Couple Couple	£ 100	£ 150

Full weekdays: £ 65

Caddy	Caddy	£ 20 + tip
Electric Trolley	Chariot électrique	£ 5/18 holes
Buggy	Voiturette	no
Clubs	Clubs	£ 15/18 holes

Credit cards Cartes de crédit
VISA - Eurocard - MasterCard - AMEX - DC - JCB

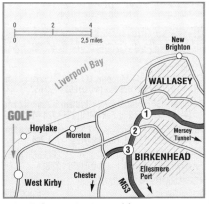

Access Accès : A551/A553 to Hoylake.
Map 5 on page 415 Carte 5 Page 415

GOLF COURSE
PARCOURS — 18/20

Site	Site	
Maintenance	Entretien	
Architect	Architecte	Jack Morris
Type	Type	links
Relief	Relief	
Water in play	Eau en jeu	
Exp. to wind	Exposé au vent	
Trees in play	Arbres en jeu	

Scorecard Carte de score	Chp. Chp.	Mens Mess.	Ladies Da.
Length Long.	6345	6139	5180
Par	72	72	74

Advised golfing ability		0 12 24 36
Niveau de jeu recommandé		
Hcp required	Handicap exigé	24

CLUB HOUSE & AMENITIES
CLUB HOUSE ET ANNEXES — 8/10

Pro shop	Pro-shop	
Driving range	Practice	
Sheltered	couvert	no
On grass	sur herbe	practice fairway
Putting-green	putting-green	yes
Pitching-green	pitching green	yes

HOTEL FACILITIES
ENVIRONNEMENT HOTELIER — 7/10

HOTELS HÔTELS

Grove Hotel - 14 rooms, D £ 50 — Wallasey
Tel (44) 0151 - 630 4558 — 6 km
Fax (44) 0151 - 639 0028

Leasowe Castle Hotel - 22 rooms, D £ 66 — Moreton
Tel (44) 0151 - 606 9191 — 4 km
Fax (44) 0151 - 678 5551

Bowler Hat - 32 rooms, D £ 85 — Birkenhead
Tel (44) 0151 - 652 4931 — 8 km
Fax (44) 0151 - 653 8127

Twelfth Man Lodge - 30 rooms, D £ 39 — Greasby
Tel (44) 0151 - 677 5445 — 5 km
Fax (44) 0151 - 678 5085

RESTAURANTS RESTAURANTS
Grove Hotel - Tel (44) 0151 - 630 4558 — Wallasey 6 km
Lee Ho - Tel (44) 0151 - 677 6440 — Moreton 4 km

531

Like Fairhaven, Royal Lytham doesn't look the most spectacular of courses at first sight, nor the most isolated. It is surrounded by houses and a railway line and has no sea-views. In fact you might think it has done everything to avoid any superfluous cosmetic appearance. But this is a golfer's course, and when the wind blows, it is a monster, almost on a par with Carnoustie, the most brutal of all courses in Britain. Fowler, Colt and Simpson joined forces to make this the ultimate test, the obligatory final examination which was later to be fine-tuned by C.K. Cotton. Pure and tough, it reveals all its hazards but you need to play here fifty times or more to take them all in. Green-keeping is excellent and the greens are slick but prone to push balls towards the deep bunkers. At the end of the day, this style of austerity does have its appeal.

Comme Fairhaven, Royal Lytham ne donne pas au premier abord la plus spectaculaire des impressions, ni celle de l'isolement que proposent souvent les golfs. Entouré par les maisons, la voie ferrée et sans aucune vue sur la mer, c'est un parcours dont on pourrait croire qu'il a évité tout aspect décoratif superflu. C'est un parcours pour golfeurs. Avec le vent, c'est un monstre, l'égal presque de Carnoustie, le plus brutal des parcours de Grande-Bretagne. Fowler, Colt et Simpson se sont alliés pour en faire un test absolu, un examen de passage inévitable, C.K. Cotton l'a enfin peaufiné. Pur, dur, il dévoile tous ses obstacles, mais il faut jouer cinquante fois pour bien assimiler. L'entretien est excellent, les greens subtils, mais ils rejettent volontiers la balle vers de profonds bunkers. Finalement, une telle austérité ne manque pas de charme.

Royal Lytham & St Anne's Golf Club
St Patrick's Road South
ENG - LYTHAM, Lancs FY8 3LQ

Office	Secrétariat	(44) 01253 - 724 206
Pro shop	Pro-shop	(44) 01253 - 720 094
Fax	Fax	(44) 01253 - 780 946
Situation	Situation	

Centre of Lytham St Anne's (pop. 40 866)
8 km from Blackpool (pop. 146 069)

Annual closure	Fermeture annnuelle	no
Weekly closure	Fermeture hebdomadaire	no
Fees main season	Tarifs haute saison	18 holes

	Week days Semaine	We/Bank holidays We/Férié
Individual Individuel	£ 75	—
Couple Couple	£ 150	—
No visitors at weekends		

Caddy	Caddy	on request/£ 25
Electric Trolley	Chariot électrique	no
Buggy	Voiturette	no
Clubs	Clubs	on request

Credit cards Cartes de crédit
VISA - Eurocard - MasterCard - AMEX - DC - JCB

532

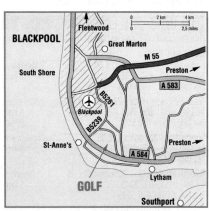

BLACKPOOL
Fleetwood
Great Marton
M 55
South Shore
Preston
A 583
B5261
Blackpool
B5259
St-Anne's
Preston
A 584
Lytham
GOLF
Southport
0 2 km 4 km
0 2,5 miles

Access Accès : 1 km from centre of St Anne's
Map 5 on page 415 Carte 5 Page 415

GOLF COURSE
PARCOURS 19/20

Site	Site	
Maintenance	Entretien	
Architect	Architecte	H. Fowler, H.S. Colt T.Simpson/C.K.Cotton
Type	Type	links
Relief	Relief	
Water in play	Eau en jeu	
Exp. to wind	Exposé au vent	
Trees in play	Arbres en jeu	

Scorecard Carte de score	Chp. Chp.	Mens Mess.	Ladies Da.
Length Long.	6202	6011	5232
Par	71	71	75

Advised golfing ability		0 12 24 36
Niveau de jeu recommandé		
Hcp required	Handicap exigé	18 maximum

CLUB HOUSE & AMENITIES
CLUB HOUSE ET ANNEXES 7/10

Pro shop	Pro-shop	
Driving range	Practice	
Sheltered	couvert	no
On grass	sur herbe	practice ground only
Putting-green	putting-green	yes
Pitching-green	pitching green	yes

HOTEL FACILITIES
ENVIRONNEMENT HOTELIER 8/10

HOTELS HÔTELS
Clifton Arms Hotel - 44 rooms, D £ 86   Lytham 2 km
Tel (44) 01253 - 739 898 Fax (44) 01253 - 730 657

Dalmeny - 130 rooms, D £ 75   Lytham St Anne's 2 km
Tel (44) 01253 - 712 236, Fax (44) 01253 - 724 447

Imperial (Forte) - 173 rooms, D £ 120   Blackpool 8 km
Tel (44) 01253 - 23 971, Fax (44) 01253 - 751 784

Pembroke - 268 rooms, D £ 120   Blackpool 8 km
Tel (44) 01253 - 23 434, Fax (44) 01253 - 27 864

RESTAURANTS RESTAURANTS
September Brasserie   Blackpool
Tel (44) 01253 - 23 282   8 km

Cromwellian   Kirkham
Tel (44) 01772 - 685 680   13 km

With two courses (including the "Inner" course which is not quite as good), this is one of the great clubs close to London. Unfortunately it lies beneath a flight route in and out of London airport and so, even though located in a residential area, is less tranquil than it might have been. There is a warm welcome for visitors during the week, a none too frequent occurrence in this part of the country. The clubhouse is magnificent with enough golfing mementoes for a small museum. This generally flat course, designed by J.H. Taylor, has no outstanding difficulty, except perhaps some very tough rough that might test a few weak wrists. Except holes 1 (a long par 3) and 17, this is a very decent course for enjoying your golf even when your swing is not quite in tune. The recent automatic watering system has considerably improved the standard of green-keeping after several years of drought.

Avec deux parcours, dont le "Inner" (intérieur) est moins intéressant, c'est un des grands clubs proches de Londres, mais aussi sur le passage des avions de ligne, ce qui perturbe un endroit autrement très calme, bien qu'il soit situé dans une zone résidentielle. L'accueil est agréable en semaine, ce n'est pas forcément si fréquent dans la région. Le Clubhouse est magnifique, avec des souvenirs de golf qui en font un petit musée. Généralement plat, le parcours de JH Taylor n'offre pas de difficultés particulières, bien que quelques zones de rough puissent inquiéter les poignets fragiles. Mis à part le 1 (long par 3) et le 17, c'est un très honorable parcours pour se faire plaisir même quand on n'est pas dans son meilleur swing. Le récent arrosage automatique a permis d'améliorer considérablement son entretien après plusieurs années de sécheresse.

Royal Mid-Surrey Golf Club
Old Deer Park
ENG - RICHMOND, Surrey TW9 2SB

Office	Secrétariat	(44) 0181 - 9401894
Pro shop	Pro-shop	(44) 0181 - 9400459
Fax	Fax	(44) 0181 - 3322957
Situation	Situation	

1 km from Richmond
15 km from Central London (pop. 6 679 700)

Annual closure	Fermeture annnuelle	no
Weekly closure	Fermeture hebdomadaire	no
Fees main season	Tarifs haute saison	full day

	Week days Semaine	We/Bank holidays We/Férié
Individual Individuel	£ 55	—
Couple Couple	£ 110	—

Summer: £ 35 full day after 1.00 pm
Weekends: with member only

Caddy	Caddy	no
Electric Trolley	Chariot électrique	£ 6/18 holes
Buggy	Voiturette	no
Clubs	Clubs	£ 7.50/18 holes
Credit cards Cartes de crédit		not for greenfees

Access Accès : A316, 300 m before Richmond roundabout → London (close to Royal Botanic Gardens).
Map 8 on page 421 Carte 8 Page 421

GOLF COURSE / PARCOURS

14/20

Site	Site	
Maintenance	Entretien	
Architect	Architecte	J.H. Taylor
Type	Type	parkland
Relief	Relief	
Water in play	Eau en jeu	
Exp. to wind	Exposé au vent	
Trees in play	Arbres en jeu	

Scorecard Carte de score	Chp. Chp.	Mens Mess.	Ladies Da.
Length Long.	5747	5450	5231
Par	69	69	73

Advised golfing ability Niveau de jeu recommandé		0 12 24 36
Hcp required	Handicap exigé	certificate

CLUB HOUSE & AMENITIES / CLUB HOUSE ET ANNEXES

7/10

Pro shop	Pro-shop	
Driving range	Practice	
Sheltered	couvert	4 indoor nets
On grass	sur herbe	yes
Putting-green	putting-green	yes
Pitching-green	pitching green	yes

HOTEL FACILITIES / ENVIRONNEMENT HOTELIER

8/10

HOTELS HÔTELS
Petersham - 54 rooms, D £ 130   Richmond 2 km
Tel (44) 0181 - 940 7471
Fax (44) 0181 - 940 9998

Richmond Gate - 64 rooms, D £ 130   Richmond 2 km
Tel (44) 0181 - 940 0061
Fax (44) 0181 - 332 0354

Bingham - 23 rooms, D £ 85   Richmond 2 km
Tel (44) 0181 - 940 0902
Fax (44) 0181 - 948 8737

RESTAURANTS RESTAURANTS
Nightingales (Petersham Hotel)   Richmond 2 km
Tel (44) 0181 - 940 7471

Chez Lindsay - Tel (44) 0181 - 948 7473 Richmond 1 km

McClements   Twickenham
Tel (44) 0181 - 744 9598   1 km

533

This is the oldest links course in England. If you are disappointed when you set eyes on the flat-looking terrain, you certainly won't be once you are out on the course. It might look gentle, but it doesn't play that way. Take the difficulties for example: tight fairways, invisible ditches, small deep bunkers sometimes lined with railway sleepers, very well protected greens where the approach is sometimes blind and rough with sea-gorse where it is nigh on impossible to get the ball back onto the fairway. Sheep crop the grass and bleat at the top of your backswing, and then there is the wind. If you can keep the ball low, if you know your strengths and weaknesses, if you stay humble in your ambitions and if someone accompanies you around this huge open space, you can spend a great day and get the impression of having walked around a piece of golfing history.

Le plus vieux links d'Angleterre. L'arrivée à "Westward Ho!" peut paraître décevante tant le terrain est sans relief, mais votre partie ne va pas en manquer : c'est beaucoup moins tranquille qu'il n'y paraît. D'abord, les difficultés : fairways étroits, fossés invisibles, bunkers petits et profonds, parfois bordés de traverses, greens très défendus et dont l'entrée est parfois aveugle, dans les roughs et buissons de joncs marins d'où il est impossible de sortir. Des moutons broutent le gazon et bêlent quand vous êtes en haut du backswing. Il y a aussi du vent. Si vous savez jouer des balles basses, si vous connaissez bien vos forces et vos faiblesses, si vous envisagez humblement ce parcours, et si quelqu'un vous oriente dans cet immense espace, vous passerez une merveilleuse journée en ayant l'impression d'avoir mis vos pas dans l'histoire.

Royal North Devon Golf Club
Golf Links Road, Westward Ho!
ENG - BIDEFORD, Devon EX39 7HD

Office	Secrétariat	(44) 01237 - 473 817
Pro shop	Pro-shop	(44) 01237 - 477 598
Fax	Fax	(44) 01237 - 473 456
Situation	Situation	

4 km from Bideford (pop. 13 070)
12 km from Barnstaple (pop. 20 740)

Annual closure	Fermeture annnuelle	no
Weekly closure	Fermeture hebdomadaire	no
Book for meals		

Fees main season	Tarifs haute saison	18 holes
	Week days Semaine	**We/Bank holidays** We/Férié
Individual Individuel	£ 28	£ 34
Couple Couple	£ 56	£ 68

Full day: £ 34 - £ 36 (weekends)

Caddy	Caddy	no
Electric Trolley	Chariot électrique	no
Buggy	Voiturette	no
Clubs	Clubs	£ 15/day

Credit cards Cartes de crédit
VISA - Eurocard - MasterCard

534

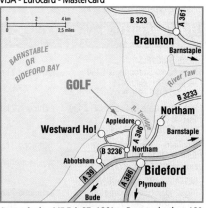

Access Accès : M5 Exit 27, A361 to Barnstaple, then A39 through Northam, take road down Bone Hill past Post Office, keep on left, Clubhouse ahead on hill.
Map 6 on page 416 Carte 6 Page 416

GOLF COURSE
PARCOURS **18**/20

Site	Site	
Maintenance	Entretien	
Architect	Architecte	Old Tom Morris
Type	Type	links
Relief	Relief	
Water in play	Eau en jeu	
Exp. to wind	Exposé au vent	
Trees in play	Arbres en jeu	

Scorecard	Chp.	Mens	Ladies
Carte de score	Chp.	Mess.	Da.
Length Long.	5990	5758	5137
Par	71	72	73

Advised golfing ability	0	12	24	36
Niveau de jeu recommandé				
Hcp required	Handicap exigé	certificate		

CLUB HOUSE & AMENITIES
CLUB HOUSE ET ANNEXES **6**/10

Pro shop	Pro-shop	
Driving range	Practice	
Sheltered	couvert	no
On grass	sur herbe	yes
Putting-green	putting-green	yes
Pitching-green	pitching green	yes

HOTEL FACILITIES
ENVIRONNEMENT HOTELIER **6**/10

HOTELS HÔTELS
Anchorage Hotel - 17 rooms, D £ 50 — Instow
Tel (44) 01271 - 860 655 — 7 km
Fax (44) 01271 - 860 767

Newbridge - 10 rooms, D £ 65 — Northam
Tel (44) 01237 - 474 989 — 1 km
Fax (44) 01237 - 474 989

Durrant House - 123 rooms, D £ 65 — Northam
Tel (44) 01237 - 472 361 — 1 km
Fax (44) 01237 - 421 709

RESTAURANT RESTAURANT
The Beaver Inn — Appledore
Tel (44) 01237 - 474 822 — 2 km

This is the sort of masterpiece that defies description. If a golf course is to be an adversary offering the toughest resistance to every shot, giving the player the opportunity to shine, sometimes forcing you to take the longer path to get a better shot at your goal, provoking the hardier golfer before breaking him completely but respecting the wise and the knowledgeable, then Royal St. George is one of the very greatest of them all. If we had to find one fault with this regular venue for the British Open, it would be the fact that not all the hazards are clearly visible. You have to play the course every day to uncover its secrets but this is a privilege reserved for members only. Although the course is open during the week, we would advise visitors to play with a member, or at least with a caddie. You'll enjoy the experience even more.

C'est le genre de chef d'oeuvre qui échappe à toute description. Si un parcours de golf doit être un adversaire qui se défende contre tous les coups, offre des chances de briller à son adversaire, oblige parfois à contourner son objectif pour mieux y revenir ensuite, provoque les téméraires pour mieux les détruire, respecte les sages et les savants, Royal St George's est un des très grands parcours de golf. S'il est un seul défaut à ce links où le British Open revient régulièrement, c'est que tous les obstacles ne sont pas clairement visibles : il faudrait le jouer tous les jours pour en découvrir les secrets, et seuls les membres ont ce privilège. Bien que le parcours soit ouvert en semaine, on conseillera aux visiteurs de jouer avec eux, ou au moins de louer les services d'un caddie. Le plaisir n'en sera que plus grand encore.

Royal St George's Golf Club
ENG - SANDWICH, Kent CT13 9PB

Office	Secrétariat	(44) 01304 - 613090
Pro shop	Pro-shop	(44) 01304 - 615236
Fax	Fax	(44) 01304 - 611245
Situation	Situation	

2 km from Sandwich
7 km from Deal (pop. 28 504)

Annual closure	Fermeture annnuelle	no
Weekly closure	Fermeture hebdomadaire	

Fees main season	Tarifs haute saison	18 holes
	Week days Semaine	**We/Bank holidays** We/Férié
Individual Individuel	£ 60	no
Couple Couple	£ 120	no

No visitors during Weekends -
Permission required for Ladies to play

Caddy	Caddy	on request/£ 20
Electric Trolley	Chariot électrique	no
Buggy	Voiturette	no
Clubs	Clubs	no
Credit cards Cartes de crédit		no

Access Accès : Sandwich → "Golf Courses". 1 km along Sandown Road. Club drive on left after last houses **Map 7 on page 419** Carte 7 Page 419

GOLF COURSE
PARCOURS
19/20

Site	Site	▰▰▰▰
Maintenance	Entretien	▰▰▰
Architect	Architecte	Dr W. Laidlaw Purves
Type	Type	seaside course, links
Relief	Relief	▰▰
Water in play	Eau en jeu	▰
Exp. to wind	Exposé au vent	▰▰▰
Trees in play	Arbres en jeu	▰

Scorecard	Chp.	Mens	Ladies
Carte de score	Chp.	Mess.	Da.
Length Long.	6174	5904	0
Par	70	70	0

Advised golfing ability	0	12	24	36
Niveau de jeu recommandé			▰▰▰▰	
Hcp required Handicap exigé	18 Men, 15 Ladies			

CLUB HOUSE & AMENITIES
CLUB HOUSE ET ANNEXES
7/10

Pro shop	Pro-shop	▰▰▰▰
Driving range	Practice	▰▰▰
Sheltered	couvert	no
On grass	sur herbe	yes
Putting-green	putting-green	yes
Pitching-green	pitching green	no

HOTEL FACILITIES
ENVIRONNEMENT HOTELIER
5/10

HOTELS HÔTELS

Bell Hotel - 29 rooms, D £ 100		Sandwich
Tel (44) 01304 - 613 388		2 km
Fax (44) 01304 - 615 308		
Jarvis Marina - 59 rooms, D £ 69		Ramsgate
Tel (44) 01843 - 588 276		12 km
Fax (44) 01843 - 586 866		
San Clu - 32 rooms, D £ 80		Ramsgate
Tel (44) 01843 - 592 345		12 km
Fax (44) 01843 - 580 157		

RESTAURANTS RESTAURANTS

Dunkerleys Restaurant		Deal
Tel (44) 01304 - 375016		7 km
Griffins Head		Chillenden
		10 km

535

If you are one of those golfers who go for nature, wildlife and vegetation, this course is for you, set in a landscape of dunes and salt-marshes that flood at every high tide and which are home to a host of wild animals. Brancaster is famous for its railway sleeper bunkers and its devilish greens, which are tough to putt on and tough to reach because they are small and often hit with long irons. If it's windy, you can forget it. Get out on the course, by all means, and enjoy what is an uplifting experience for any golfer, but go around in matchplay and play to see who pays for the drink at the bar. You won't want to leave the clubhouse, which has never been anything else but old and smells of wood woods and balatas. Time has stood still at Brancaster, which is why you feel so privileged to be here. A little on the short side, did you say? What the hell.

Si vous êtes de ces golfeurs qui sont aussi amoureux de la nature, de la flore et de la faune, ce parcours est pour vous, dans un paysage de dunes et de marais salés inondés lors des grandes marées, qui abritent une vie sauvage très riche. Brancaster est célèbre pour ses bunkers renforcés par des traverses de chemin de fer, mais aussi pour des greens diaboliques, difficiles à toucher car ils sont petits et souvent attaqués avec des longs fers, et difficiles à putter. Les jours de vent, n'insistez pas : jouez car l'expérience est exaltante, mais en match-play, avec un enjeu à consommer au Clubhouse. Il est vieux depuis toujours, il y règne une odeur de bois en bois et de balatas, il fait bon y rester. Ici, le temps s'est arrêté, c'est pourquoi on s'y sent autant privilégié. Le parcours est un peu court ? Et alors...

Royal West Norfolk Golf Club
ENG - BRANCASTER, Norfolk PE31 8 AY

Office	Secrétariat	(44) 01485 - 210223
Pro shop	Pro-shop	(44) 01485 - 210616
Fax	Fax	(44) 01485 - 210087
Situation	Situation	

12 km from Hunstanton (pop. 4 736)
30 km from King's Lynn (pop. 41 281)

Annual closure	Fermeture annnuelle	no
Weekly closure	Fermeture hebdomadaire	no

Fees main season	Tarifs haute saison		18 holes
		Week days Semaine	**We/Bank holidays** We/Férié
Individual Individuel		£ 39	£ 49
Couple Couple		£ 78	£ 98

In August, visitors only with a member

Caddy	Caddy	on request
Electric Trolley	Chariot électrique	no
Buggy	Voiturette	no
Clubs	Clubs	no
Credit cards Cartes de crédit		no

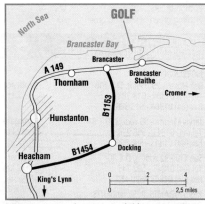

GOLF
North Sea
Brancaster Bay
Brancaster
A 149
Brancaster Staithe
Thornham
Cromer →
B1153
Hunstanton
B1454 Docking
Heacham
King's Lynn

0	2	4
0		2,5 miles

Access Accès : London M11. Cambridge A10 to King's Lynn. A149 North through Hunstanton to Brancaster. Turn left into Beach Road, continue across marsh.
Map 4 on page 413 Carte 4 Page 413

GOLF COURSE
PARCOURS | **17**/20

Site	Site	
Maintenance	Entretien	
Architect	Architecte	Holcombe Ingleby
Type	Type	seaside course, links
Relief	Relief	
Water in play	Eau en jeu	
Exp. to wind	Exposé au vent	
Trees in play	Arbres en jeu	

Scorecard Carte de score	**Chp.** Chp.	**Mens** Mess.	**Ladies** Da.
Length Long.	5785	5785	5334
Par	71	71	75

Advised golfing ability		0	12	24	36
Niveau de jeu recommandé					
Hcp required	Handicap exigé	certificate			

CLUB HOUSE & AMENITIES
CLUB HOUSE ET ANNEXES | **7**/10

Pro shop	Pro-shop	
Driving range	Practice	
Sheltered	couvert	no
On grass	sur herbe	yes
Putting-green	putting-green	yes
Pitching-green	pitching green	no

HOTEL FACILITIES
ENVIRONNEMENT HOTELIER | **6**/10

HOTELS HÔTELS
Le Strange Arms — Hunstanton
36 rooms, D £ 70 — 12 km
Tel (44) 01485 - 534 411
Fax (44) 01485 - 534 724

Congham Hall — Grimston
12 rooms, D £ 100 — 25 km
Tel (44) 01485 - 600 250
Fax (44) 01485 - 601 191

RESTAURANTS RESTAURANTS
Gurney's — Burnham Market
Tel (44) 01328 - 738937 — 7 km

The Hoste Arms — Burnham Market
Tel (44) 01328 - 738777 — 7 km

536

The famous Winchester cathedral has the longest nave in Europe and bears vestiges of Norman architecture. It is one of the treasures to be found in this city, others including the legendary Round Table, which was actually built several centuries late! This J.H. Taylor course is also a piece of history, dating from the last century, where you might get the impression you can play a bit until it comes to counting your score. On each tee you will need to think long and hard about the direction of your shot and the club you should play in order to avoid the bunkers. Here the finer technicians of the game are probably better rewarded than thoughtless big-hitters. At least the trees are not too much in play, but there is wind to contend with. A pleasant course to walk (except the 10th), this excellent layout has hardly aged at all, except in yardage, but none of us will lose much sleep about that. Well worth getting to know.

La célèbre cathédrale de Winchester aurait la plus longue nef d'Europe. Elle porte de nombreuses traces de l'architecture normande, mais elle n'est qu'un des trésors d'une très belle ville, dont la Table Ronde de la légende, mais qui fut fabriquée des siècles après ! Le parcours de JH Taylor est aussi une pièce d'histoire plus que centenaire, où l'on aura l'illusion de pouvoir bien jouer jusqu'au moment de compter le score. Sur chaque départ, il faut bien réfléchir à la fois à la trajectoire et au club à utiliser pour ne pas risquer les bunkers. Ici, ce sont les fins techniciens qui seront récompensés, et pas les frappeurs sans cervelle ! Au moins, les arbres ne sont guère en jeu, ce qui laisse d'ailleurs le champ libre aux caprices du vent. Agréable à marcher (sauf le 10), cette excellente réalisation n'a guère pris de l'âge que pour sa longueur, mais cela ne gênera pas grand-monde. A connaître.

Royal Winchester Golf Club

Sarum Road
ENG - WINCHESTER, Hants SO22 5QE

Office	Secrétariat	(44) 01962 - 852462
Pro shop	Pro-shop	(44) 01962 - 852473
Fax	Fax	(44) 01962 - 865048
Situation	Situation	

2.5 km from Winchester (pop. 96 390)

Annual closure	Fermeture annnuelle	no
Weekly closure	Fermeture hebdomadaire	no
Fees main season	Tarifs haute saison	full day

	Week days Semaine	We/Bank holidays We/Férié
Individual Individuel	£ 28	—
Couple Couple	£ 56	—

Weekends: only with a member

Caddy	Caddy	no
Electric Trolley	Chariot électrique	no
Buggy	Voiturette	no
Clubs	Clubs	£ 5/18 holes

Credit cards Cartes de crédit
VISA - MasterCard

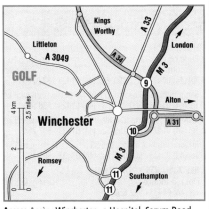

GOLF

Kings Worthy
A 33
London
M 3
Littleton
A 3049
A 34
Alton →
9
Winchester
10
A 31
M 3
Romsey
11 Southampton
11

4 km 2.5 miles

Access Accès : Winchester, → Hospital, Sarum Road, Golf on the right
Map 7 on page 418 Carte 7 Page 418

GOLF COURSE
PARCOURS

15/20

Site	Site	
Maintenance	Entretien	
Architect	Architecte	J.H. Taylor
Type	Type	inland
Relief	Relief	
Water in play	Eau en jeu	
Exp. to wind	Exposé au vent	
Trees in play	Arbres en jeu	

Scorecard Carte de score	Chp. Chp.	Mens Mess.	Ladies Da.
Length Long.	5585	5416	4950
Par	71	71	72

Advised golfing ability Niveau de jeu recommandé	0	12	24	36

Hcp required   Handicap exigé   certificate

CLUB HOUSE & AMENITIES
CLUB HOUSE ET ANNEXES

6/10

Pro shop	Pro-shop	
Driving range	Practice	
Sheltered	couvert	no
On grass	sur herbe	yes
Putting-green	putting-green	yes
Pitching-green	pitching green	yes

HOTEL FACILITIES
ENVIRONNEMENT HOTELIER

8/10

HOTELS HÔTELS
Royal Hotel - 75 rooms, D £ 100   Winchester
Tel (44) 01962 - 840 840   2.5 km
Fax (44) 01962 - 841 582

Lainston House - 37 rooms, D £ 130   Winchester
Tel (44) 01962 - 863 588   3 km
Fax (44) 01962 - 776 672

Hotel du Vin - 19 rooms, D £ 80   Winchester
Tel (44) 01962 - 841 414   3 km
Fax (44) 01962 - 842 458

RESTAURANTS RESTAURANTS
Nine the Square   Winchester
Tel (44) 01962 - 864 004   3 km

Bistro (Hotel du Vin)   Winchester
Tel (44) 01962 - 841 414   3 km

Old Chesil Rectory   Winchester
Tel (44) 01962 - 851 555   3 km

537

Faced with administrative restrictions, there was the choice between giving up the ghost or simple ingenuity. Designer Martin Hawtree chose the second option and here has produced one of his best courses. As no bunkers were allowed except in woody areas, there are only 6 greenside bunkers but the edges of the putting surfaces are well contoured with slopes and hollows and the trees are brought into play to be more strategic than decorative. As far as your game is concerned, approach shots are tricky and putting calls for some inspired play. Water has also been cleverly brought into the frame, although on several holes the ladies may have problems carrying it. It will be interesting to see how this interesting project matures, particularly with such a pleasant hotel on site.

Devant les restrictions administratives, on a le choix entre l'abandon et l'ingéniosité. L'architecte Martin Hawtree a choisi la deuxième solution et produit là un de ses meilleurs ouvrages. Comme il était interdit de mettre des bunkers sauf dans les zones boisées, on ne trouve ici que six bunkers de greens, mais les alentours des surfaces de putting sont modelés en reliefs et en creux, et les arbres mis en jeu de manière encore plus stratégique que décorative. Sur le plan du jeu, les approches sont beaucoup plus délicates, et les greens très modelés demandent de l'inspiration. Les obstacles d'eau ont aussi été mis en jeu avec intelligence, mais certaines dames auront peut-être du mal à les franchir sur certains trous en portant la balle. On suivra avec intérêt la maturation de ce projet intéressant, d'autant que l'hôtel sur place est tout à fait agréable.

Rudding Park Golf Club

Rudding Park, Follifoot
ENG - HARROGATE, Yorkshire HG3 1DJ

Office	Secrétariat	(44) 01423 - 872100
Pro shop	Pro-shop	(44) 01254 - 872100
Fax	Fax	(44) 01254 - 873011
Situation	Situation	

5 km from Harrogate (pop. 143 530)
22 km from Leeds (pop. 680 725)

Annual closure	Fermeture annnuelle	no
Weekly closure	Fermeture hebdomadaire	no
Fees main season	Tarifs haute saison	18 holes

	Week days Semaine	We/Bank holidays We/Férié
Individual Individuel	£ 18.50	£ 20
Couple Couple	£ 37	£ 40
Full day: £ 30/£ 32.50		

Caddy	Caddy	on request/£ 20+tip
Electric Trolley	Chariot électrique	£ 7.50/18 holes
Buggy	Voiturette	£ 15/18 holes
Clubs	Clubs	£ 7.50/18 holes

Credit cards Cartes de crédit
VISA - Eurocard - MasterCard - AMEX - DC

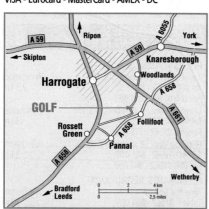

Access Accès : Leeds → Harrogate on A61,
then A658 (Harrogate by-pass), follow brown tourist
signs for Rudding Park.
Map 4 on page 412 Carte 4 Page 412

538

GOLF COURSE
PARCOURS

15/20

Site	Site	
Maintenance	Entretien	
Architect	Architecte	Martin Hawtree
Type	Type	parkland
Relief	Relief	
Water in play	Eau en jeu	
Exp. to wind	Exposé au vent	
Trees in play	Arbres en jeu	

Scorecard Carte de score	Chp. Chp.	Mens Mess.	Ladies Da.
Length Long.	6184	5873	5167
Par	72	72	72

Advised golfing ability		0 12 24 36
Niveau de jeu recommandé		
Hcp required	Handicap exigé	28 Men, 36 Ladies

CLUB HOUSE & AMENITIES
CLUB HOUSE ET ANNEXES

8/10

Pro shop	Pro-shop	
Driving range	Practice	
Sheltered	couvert	18 bays
On grass	sur herbe	yes
Putting-green	putting-green	yes
Pitching-green	pitching green	yes

HOTEL FACILITIES
ENVIRONNEMENT HOTELIER

8/10

HOTELS HÔTELS
Rudding Park House Hotel — Rudding Park
50 rooms, D £ 129 — adjacent
Tel (44) 01423 - 871 350, Fax (44) 01423 - 872 286

Sandringham - 6 rooms, D £ 90 — Beckwithshaw 5 km
Tel (44) 01423 - 500 722, Fax (44) 01423 - 530 509

Crown - 116 rooms, D £ 80 — Harrogate 5 km
Tel (44) 01423 - 567 755, Fax (44) 01423 - 502 284

Ruskin Hotel - 7 rooms, D £ 89 — Harrogate 5 km
Tel (44) 01423 - 502 045, Fax (44) 01423 - 506 131

RESTAURANTS RESTAURANTS
Drum & Monkey — Harrogate 5 km
Tel (44) 01423 - 502 650

Clocktower Brasserie — Rudding Park
Tel (44) 01423 - 872 100 — adjacent

The Bistro - Tel (44) 01423 - 530 708 — Harrogate 5 km

Modern clubhouses unquestionably lack the charm of their older counterparts but they are more comfortable. Following this same modern trend, many clubs have also laid out practice areas, if only to cater to the ever greater number of players. In 1961, Sand Moor was given a face-lift and at the same time re-styled, adhering most respectfully to the layout of Alister MacKenzie on one side of Alwoodley Lane. The land is rather hilly, but as the use of buggies requires a medical certificate we will simply recommend an electric trolley. Laid out over moorland, the feeling of space here is very pleasant and the rough not too hard on your game, but some of the bunches of trees and carefully placed fairway bunkers do their job very well. We noted the excellence of the par 3s on what is a very good test of golf, albeit a little on the short side for the better players.

Les Clubhouses modernes manquent sans doute un peu du charme des anciens, mais ils ont gagné en confort. De même, bien des clubs ont aménagé des espaces d'entraînement, ne serait-ce que pour répondre à l'élargissement du public. En 1961, Sand Moor s'est ainsi rajeuni et en a profité pour réaménager - avec beaucoup de respect d'ailleurs - le tracé d'Alister Mackenzie d'un seul côté d'Alwoodley Lane. Le terrain est assez accidenté, mais seul un certificat médical permettant de jouer en voiturette, on conseillera le chariot électrique. En terre de lande, la sensation d'espace est ici très agréable, le rough n'est pas trop pénalisant, mais certains bouquets d'arbres et des bunkers de fairway judicieusement placés ne manquent pas de jouer leur rôle. A remarquer enfin, la qualité des pars 3. Un très bon test de golf, un peu court pour les meilleurs joueurs.

Sand Moor Golf Club
Alwwodley Lane
ENG - LEEDS, W. Yorkshire LS17 7DJ

Office	Secrétariat	(44) 0113 - 268 5180
Pro shop	Pro-shop	(44) 0113 - 268 3925
Fax	Fax	(44) 0113 - 268 5180
Situation	Situation	

8 km N of Leeds (pop. 680 722)

Annual closure	Fermeture annnuelle	no
Weekly closure	Fermeture hebdomadaire	no
Fees main season	Tarifs haute saison	18 holes

	Week days Semaine	We/Bank holidays We/Férié
Individual Individuel	£ 30	£ 40
Couple Couple	£ 60	£ 80

Full weekdays:£ 38 - No visitors on Saturdays

Caddy	Caddy	no
Electric Trolley	Chariot électrique	£ 5/18 holes
Buggy	Voiturette	no
Clubs	Clubs	£ 10/18 holes

Credit cards Cartes de crédit
VISA - Eurocard - MasterCard (not in Club house)

Access Accès : Leeds, A61 North, left into Alwoodley
Lane, Golf 0.8 km (1/2 m.) on right hand side.
Map 4 on page 412 Carte 4 Page 412

GOLF COURSE
PARCOURS

14/20

Site	Site	▬▬▬▬▬▬□
Maintenance	Entretien	▬▬▬▬▬▬□
Architect	Architecte	Alister MacKenzie
Type	Type	parkland
Relief	Relief	▬▬□
Water in play	Eau en jeu	▬□
Exp. to wind	Exposé au vent	▬▬▬▬□
Trees in play	Arbres en jeu	▬▬▬□

Scorecard Carte de score	Chp. Chp.	Mens Mess.	Ladies Da.
Length Long.	5851	5464	5092
Par	71	71	73

Advised golfing ability	0	12	24	36
Niveau de jeu recommandé		▬▬▬▬		
Hcp required	Handicap exigé	certificate		

CLUB HOUSE & AMENITIES
CLUB HOUSE ET ANNEXES

7/10

Pro shop	Pro-shop	▬▬▬▬□
Driving range	Practice	▬▬▬▬□
Sheltered	couvert	no
On grass	sur herbe	yes
Putting-green	putting-green	yes
Pitching-green	pitching green	yes

HOTEL FACILITIES
ENVIRONNEMENT HOTELIER

7/10

HOTELS HÔTELS
Forte Posthouse - 123 rooms, D £ 70   Bramhope
Tel (44) 0113 - 284 2911
Fax (44) 0113 - 284 3451

Jarvis Parkway - 105 rooms, D £ 98   Bramhope
Tel (44) 0113 - 267 2551
Fax (44) 0113 - 267 4410

Stakis Leeds - 100 rooms, D £ 85   Leeds
Tel (44) 0113 - 273 2323
Fax (44) 0113 - 232 3018

The Calls - 41 rooms, D £ 120   Leeds
Tel (44) 0113 - 244 0099
Fax (44) 0113 - 234 4100

RESTAURANTS RESTAURANTS
Pool Court at 42 - Tel (44) 0113 - 244 4242   Leeds
Hereford Beefstouw - Tel (44) 0113 - 245 3870   Leeds
Rascasse - Tel (44) 0113 - 244 6611   Leeds

539

Sandiway stands in a little compact group of courses to the east of Chester, the others being Mere and the similarly styled Delamere Forest. If Sandiway was in the western suburbs of London it would surely be better known than it is, but there again for a golfer there is something gratifying about being able to talk about little gems that no-one else has ever set eyes upon. With lots of trees lining sloping fairways, keeping your ball in play is anything but easy, so think twice before taking the driver out of the bag. This very varied course demands good tactics and skill in flighting the ball... at least when it comes to getting out of trouble. A very pretty course and a very intelligent one, too, which demands the same quality from the people who play it.

Sandiway tient bien sa place dans un petit groupe compact à l'est de Chester, qui comprend également Mere et Delamere Forest, le second nommé lui étant le plus comparable par son paysage et son style. Sans nul doute, s'il était dans la banlieue ouest de Londres, ce parcours serait bien plus connu, mais, pour un golfeur, c'est très gratifiant de pouvoir parler des trésors que les autres n'ont jamais vu ! Avec beaucoup d'arbres délimitant les trous, et des fairways souvent en pente, il n'est pas évident d'y garder sa balle en sécurité, il faudra donc réfléchir avant d'empoigner son driver. Très varié, ce parcours exige une tactique solide et souvent de savoir travailler la balle... au moins pour s'extraire des problèmes. Ce très joli parcours est d'une grande intelligence, il en demande aussi aux joueurs.

Sandiway Golf Club

Chester Road, Sandiway
ENG - NORTHWICH, Cheshire CW8 20 J

Office	Secrétariat	(44) 01606 - 883247
Pro shop	Pro-shop	(44) 01606 - 883180
Fax	Fax	(44) 01606 - 883548
Situation	Situation	

6 km SW of Northwich
25 km E of Chester (pop. 115 971)

Annual closure	Fermeture annnuelle	no
Weekly closure	Fermeture hebdomadaire	no
Fees main season	Tarifs haute saison	18 holes

	Week days Semaine	We/Bank holidays We/Férié
Individual Individuel	£ 30	£ 35
Couple Couple	£ 60	£ 70

Full day: £ 35/£ 40

Caddy	Caddy	no
Electric Trolley	Chariot électrique	£ 5/18 holes
Buggy	Voiturette	no
Clubs	Clubs	no

Credit cards Cartes de crédit
VISA - Eurocard - MasterCard - AMEX - DC

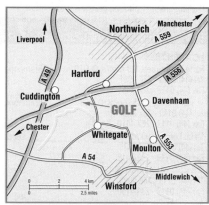

540

Access Accès : Manchester M56. Jct 7,
A556 → Northwich, Chester.
Golf on left side after Northwich.
Map 4 on page 412 Carte 4 Page 412

GOLF COURSE
PARCOURS

17 /20

Site	Site	■■■■■■■□□
Maintenance	Entretien	■■■■■■■□□
Architect	Architecte	Ted Ray
Type	Type	parkland
Relief	Relief	■■■■■□□□□
Water in play	Eau en jeu	■□□□□□□□□
Exp. to wind	Exposé au vent	■□□□□□□□□
Trees in play	Arbres en jeu	■■■■■■■□□

Scorecard Carte de score	Chp. Chp.	Mens Mess.	Ladies Da.
Length Long.	5791	5438	5071
Par	70	70	73

Advised golfing ability		0 12 24 36
Niveau de jeu recommandé		■■■■■■■■
Hcp required	Handicap exigé	certificate

CLUB HOUSE & AMENITIES
CLUB HOUSE ET ANNEXES

5 /10

Pro shop	Pro-shop	■■■■■■□□□
Driving range	Practice	■■■□□□□□□
Sheltered	couvert	no
On grass ground	sur herbe	only practice
Putting-green	putting-green	yes
Pitching-green	pitching green	yes

HOTEL FACILITIES
ENVIRONNEMENT HOTELIER

7 /10

HOTELS HÔTELS
Nunsmere Hall - 31 rooms, D £ 120   Sandiway 2 km
Tel (44) 01606 - 543 000, Fax (44) 01606 - 889 055

Rookery Hall - 45 rooms, D £ 95   Nantwich 20 km
Tél (44) 01270 - 610 016, Fax (44) 01270 - 626 027

Hartford Hall - 20 rooms, D £ 65   Northwich 4 km
Tel (44) 01606 - 75 711, Fax (44) 01606 - 782 285

Tall Trees Lodge - 20 rooms, D £ 38   Weaverham 3 km
Tel (44) 01606 - 790 824, Fax (44) 01606 - 791 330

RESTAURANTS RESTAURANTS
Nunsmere Hall   Sandiway 2 km
Tel (44) 01606 - 889 100

Churche's Mansion   Nantwich
Tel (44) 01270 - 625 933   20 km

Saunton does not carry the Royal Seal but if it did it would be well deserved. Harry Vardon dreamed of retiring here, but he was just a professional wasn't he? As such he must have appreciated the amazing balance of the East course, the more fluent of the two. If you play from the back tees, the first four holes will most likely cause irreparable damage to your card. Likewise, if you don't watch out, the last five will finish it off completely. The other holes are not quite so devastating, but the worst danger here is being caught off-guard. Winding between magnificent dunes with sheltered greens, all 18 holes at Saunton make for fantastic golf if you play from the tees that suit your level. The humbler you are, the more fun you will have. Especially since the greens are real beauties.

Si Saunton n'a pas eu droit à l'annoblissement, il ne le mérite pas moins : Harry Vardon rêvait de s'y retirer, mais peut-être n'était-il qu'un professionnel ? Comme tel, il dut apprécier le rythme étonnant de ce parcours Est, le plus éloquent des deux. Quand vous jouez des départs arrière, les quatre premiers trous vont dévorer votre carte, comme les cinq derniers la détruiront définitivement si vous n'y restez pas attentif. Les autres trous sont moins brutaux, mais le pire danger est de baisser la garde. Insinués entre des dunes magnifiques, les greens bien à l'abri, les trous de Saunton apportent un plaisir fou, si l'on joue des départs correspondant à son niveau : plus vous serez humble, plus vous prendrez du plaisir. Et d'autant plus que les greens sont un véritable régal.

Saunton Golf Club

Saunton
ENG - BRAUNTON EX33 1LG

Office	Secrétariat	(44) 01271 - 812 436
Pro shop	Pro-shop	(44) 01271 - 812 013
Fax	Fax	(44) 01271 - 814 241
Situation	Situation	

3 km W of Braunton
8 km W of Barnstaple (pop. 20 740)

Annual closure	Fermeture annnuelle	no
Weekly closure	Fermeture hebdomadaire	no
Fees main season	Tarifs haute saison	full day

	Week days Semaine	We/Bank holidays We/Férié
Individual Individuel	£ 37	£ 42
Couple Couple	£ 74	£ 84

Weekends: booking essential

Caddy	Caddy	no
Electric Trolley	Chariot électrique	£ 5/18 holes
Buggy	Voiturette	no
Clubs	Clubs	£ 7.50/18 holes

Credit cards Cartes de crédit
VISA - Eurocard - MasterCard - DC - JCB

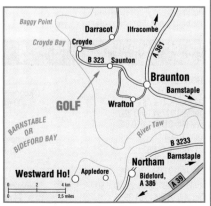

Access Accès : M5 Jct 27, then A361 to Barnstaple, then A361 to Braunton. Follow signs to Saunton, golf on the left. **Map 6 on page 416** Carte 6 Page 416

GOLF COURSE / PARCOURS — 18/20

Site	Site	■■■■■
Maintenance	Entretien	■■■■■
Architect	Architecte	Herbert Fowler
Type	Type	seaside course, links
Relief	Relief	
Water in play	Eau en jeu	■
Exp. to wind	Exposé au vent	■■
Trees in play	Arbres en jeu	□

Scorecard Carte de score	Chp. Chp.	Mens Mess.	Ladies Da.
Length Long.	6123	5800	4555
Par	73	71	74

Advised golfing ability Niveau de jeu recommandé	0	12	24	36
Hcp required	Handicap exigé	certificate		

CLUB HOUSE & AMENITIES / CLUB HOUSE ET ANNEXES — 7/10

Pro shop	Pro-shop	■■■■
Driving range	Practice	■■■
Sheltered	couvert	no
On grass	sur herbe	yes (own balls)
Putting-green	putting-green	yes
Pitching-green	pitching green	yes

HOTEL FACILITIES / ENVIRONNEMENT HOTELIER — 6/10

HOTELS HÔTELS

Preston House 15 rooms, D £ 80 Tel (44) 01271 - 890 472 Fax (44) 01271 - 890 555		Saunton close
Kittiwell House 12 rooms, D £ 108 (dinner inc) Tel (44) 01271 - 890 247 Fax (44) 01271 - 890 469		Croyde 3 km

RESTAURANTS RESTAURANTS

Lynwood House Tel (44) 01271 - 43 695		Barnstaple 8 km
Whiteleaf at Croyde Tel (44) 01271 - 890 266		Croyde 3 km

541

Moving up the coast, this is the only real links course after Hunstanton. The one further on is Seaton Carew which unfortunately lies in such surroundings that only local golfers really enjoy playing there. The landscape at Seacroft will hardly have you gasping with admiration but it is agreeable enough to give this course a pleasant setting. All the holes are neatly laid out in single file, out and in, except the disorderly 6th hole. This makes club selection a little easier when the wind is howling and forces you to hit low shots. In fine weather, you can hit any shot, which makes life easier for those of you who like to hit the ball high. Whatever, the very strategic bunkering here requires a clear-cut tactical approach to every round, but the hazards are visible enough for you to do so. Varied, very authentic and traditional, this is a course you should try.

En remontant la côte, c'est le seul vrai links après Hunstanton, et le suivant sera Seaton Carew, hélas situé dans un tel environnement que seuls les golfeurs locaux y trouveront du plaisir. Les paysages de Seacroft ne vous arracheront pas des cris d'admiration, mais il sont assez plaisants pour offrir un décor agréable au parcours. Tous les trous sont sagement rangés en file indienne, en aller et retour, mis à part un indiscipliné, le 6. Cet ordre facilite le choix de clubs quand il y a du vent, qui seul vous obligera aux balles basses. Par beau temps, tous les coups sont permis, ce qui peut faciliter le travail de ceux qui savent surtout lever la balle. En tous les cas, le placement très stratégique des bunkers implique de bien définir la tactique de jeu, mais les obstacles sont assez visibles pour ce faire. Varié, très authentique et traditionnel, c'est un parcours à découvrir.

Seacroft Golf Club

Drummond Road
ENG - SKEGNESS, Lincolnshire PE25 3AU

Office	Secrétariat	(44) 01754 - 763020
Pro shop	Pro-shop	(44) 01754 - 769624
Fax	Fax	(44) 01754 - 769624
Situation	Situation	

1.5 km S of Skegness - 30 km NE of Boston (pop. 53 226)

Annual closure	Fermeture annnuelle	no
Weekly closure	Fermeture hebdomadaire	

Christmas Day only

Fees main season	Tarifs haute saison	18 holes
	Week days Semaine	We/Bank holidays We/Férié
Individual Individuel	£ 25	£ 30
Couple Couple	£ 50	£ 60

Full day: £ 35/£ 40

Caddy	Caddy	no
Electric Trolley	Chariot électrique	no
Buggy	Voiturette	no
Clubs	Clubs	no

Credit cards Cartes de crédit
VISA - Eurocard - MasterCard - AMEX - DC
(Pro shop only)

542

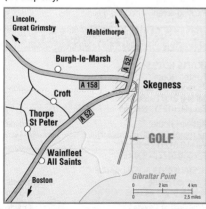

Access Accès : A52 to Skegness. 1.5 km S of Skegness alongside Gibraltar Road Bird Sanctuary.
Map 4 on page 413 Carte 4 Page 413

GOLF COURSE
PARCOURS

17 /20

Site	Site	
Maintenance	Entretien	
Architect	Architecte	Tom Dunn
Type	Type	seaside course, links
Relief	Relief	
Water in play	Eau en jeu	
Exp. to wind	Exposé au vent	
Trees in play	Arbres en jeu	

Scorecard Carte de score	Chp. Chp.	Mens Mess.	Ladies Da.
Length Long.	5831	5421	5275
Par	71	71	73

Advised golfing ability Niveau de jeu recommandé	0	12	24	36
Hcp required	Handicap exigé	certificate		

CLUB HOUSE & AMENITIES
CLUB HOUSE ET ANNEXES

6 /10

Pro shop	Pro-shop	
Driving range	Practice	
Sheltered	couvert	no
On grass	sur herbe	practice ground
only		
Putting-green	putting-green	yes
Pitching-green	pitching green	yes

HOTEL FACILITIES
ENVIRONNEMENT HOTELIER

4 /10

HOTELS HÔTELS

Crown Hotel — Skegness
28 rooms, D £ 65 — 400 m
Tel (44) 01754 - 610 760
Fax (44) 01754 - 610 847

Vine Hotel — Skegness
21 rooms, D £ 65 — 1 km
Tel (44) 01754 - 610 611
Fax (44) 01754 - 769 845

Links Hotel - 10 rooms, D £ 50 — Skegness
Tel (44) 01754 - 761 255 — 1 km

SEASCALE

18 5 4

A strange place where the Sellafield power station ought to give golfers at least the energy to turn their backs on the cooling towers. When you think of how much flak golf courses get from some environmentalists, it makes you wonder why they don't protect courses from this sort of eyesore. Seascale is a hidden gem, away from the world and off the beaten track. You can talk about this course in glowing terms, no-one will ever argue. An imposing but subtle layout, and odd in that the railway line runs between the course and the sea, Seascale is anything but a fashionable course, just one to severely test any player's capacity for invention and adaptability. As on every links course, you either act positively or suffer the consequences, depending on the state of your game. If you do not know Seascale, then enter it now into your list of best little-known courses.

Etrange endroit où la centrale électrique de Sellafield devrait surtout donner l'énergie aux golfeurs de lui tourner le dos. Quand on sait à quel point on peut ennuyer les golfs avec les problèmes d'environnement, pourquoi ne pas préserver aussi les golfs des pollutions visuelles ? Seascale est un joyau caché, à l'écart du monde et des sentiers battus et, quand vous en parlerez avec émotion, personne ne viendra vous contredire. Puissant et subtil, assez curieux dans la mesure où le chemin de fer passe entre le golf et la mer, Seascale est tout sauf un parcours "fashionable." Il met en oeuvre la capacité d'invention et d'adaptation des joueurs. Comme sur les links, on agit ou on subit, suivant sa forme du moment. Si vous ne le connaissez pas, c'est un parcours à inscrire à votre tableau de chasse des meilleurs parcours méconnus.

Seascale Golf Club

The Banks
ENG - SEASCALE, Cumbria CA20 1QL

Office	Secrétariat	(44) 01946 - 728 202
Pro shop	Pro-shop	(44) 01946 - 728 202
Fax	Fax	
Situation	Situation	

15 km S of Whitehaven (pop. 9 358)
45 km N of Barrow-in-Furness (pop. 73 125)

Annual closure	Fermeture annnuelle	no
Weekly closure	Fermeture hebdomadaire	no
Fees main season	Tarifs haute saison	18 holes

	Week days Semaine	We/Bank holidays We/Férié
Individual Individuel	£ 20	£ 25
Couple Couple	£ 40	£ 50

Full day: £ 25 - £ 30 (Weekends)

Caddy	Caddy	no
Electric Trolley	Chariot électrique	no
Buggy	Voiturette	no
Clubs	Clubs	£ 5/18 holes
Credit cards Cartes de crédit		no

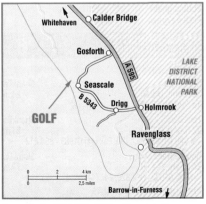

Access Accès : M6 Jct 36, A590 → Barrow-in-Furness.
At Greenodd, A5092, then A595 to Seascale.
Golf N. of village (can't miss it!)
Map 4 on page 412 Carte 4 Page 412

GOLF COURSE
PARCOURS
18/20

Site	Site	
Maintenance	Entretien	
Architect	Architecte	Willie Campbell
Type	Type	links
Relief	Relief	
Water in play	Eau en jeu	
Exp. to wind	Exposé au vent	
Trees in play	Arbres en jeu	

Scorecard Carte de score	Chp. Chp.	Mens Mess.	Ladies Da.
Length Long.	5840	5554	5226
Par	71	71	74

Advised golfing ability	0	12	24	36
Niveau de jeu recommandé				
Hcp required Handicap exigé	no			

CLUB HOUSE & AMENITIES
CLUB HOUSE ET ANNEXES
5/10

Pro shop	Pro-shop	
Driving range	Practice	
Sheltered	couvert	no
On grass	sur herbe	yes
Putting-green	putting-green	yes
Pitching-green	pitching green	yes

543

HOTEL FACILITIES
ENVIRONNEMENT HOTELIER
4/10

HOTELS HÔTELS
Westlakes
9 rooms, D £ 55
Tel (44) 019467 - 25 221
Fax (44) 019467 - 25 099
Gosforth
4 km

Howgate
20 rooms, D £ 60
Tel (44) 01946 - 66 286
Fax (44) 01946 - 66 286
Whitehaven
15 km

RESTAURANT RESTAURANT
Westlakes
Tel (44) 019467 - 25 221
Gosforth
4 km

Shanklin & Sandown is the best of the seven courses on the Isle of Wight. It is short, naturally, as designers at the turn of the century were wiser than they are today. They weren't unaware of the fact that big-hitters make up only a minority of golfers and that wind can really bother simply anyone, whether blowing with or against the ball. A part of this layout is similar to links golfing, another part is more inland in style with some impressive heather and broom. Despite a distinctly hilly character, there are only three blind drives, otherwise playing strategy is clear. The sole element of chance is the stance and lie, sometimes difficult to negotiate for players who are used to flat courses. With tight fairways and well placed bunkers, we would recommend this course to players who have some control over their ball. Beginners here could easily spend all day looking for theirs.

Shanklin & Sandown se détache parmi les sept parcours de l'île de Wight. Il est bien sûr assez court, mais les architectes du début du siècle étaient des sages. Ils n'ignoraient pas que les bons frappeurs ne sont pas les plus nombreux, et que le vent avait tendance à gêner tout le monde, qu'il soit contre ou avec. Ce parcours comporte une partie apparentée aux links et une partie "inland" avec une très belle végétation de bruyère et de genêts. On ne trouve ici, en dépit d'un certain relief, que trois drives aveugles. Autrement, la stratégie à mettre en oeuvre est assez claire, la part de hasard étant préservée par des stances parfois difficiles pour ceux qui jouent habituellement les pieds à plat. Avec ses fairways étroits et ses bunkers bien placés, on le recommendera à ceux qui savent déjà contrôler la balle car les débutants peuvent passer la journée à chercher la leur !

Shanklin & Sandown Golf Club

The Fairway Lake
ENG - SANDOWN, Isle of Wight PO36 9 PR

Office	Secrétariat	(44) 01983 - 403217
Pro shop	Pro-shop	(44) 01983 - 404424
Fax	Fax	(44) 01983 - 403217
Situation	Situation	

Isle of Wight (pop. 124 580)

Annual closure	Fermeture annnuelle	no
Weekly closure	Fermeture hebdomadaire	no

Fees main season
Tarifs haute saison · 18 holes

	Week days Semaine	We/Bank holidays We/Férié
Individual Individuel	£ 22	£ 25
Couple Couple	£ 44	£ 50

Saturday: only after 1.00 pm - Sunday: after 9.00 am

Caddy	Caddy	no
Electric Trolley	Chariot électrique	no
Buggy	Voiturette	no
Clubs	Clubs	no

Credit cards Cartes de crédit
VISA - MasterCard (Pro shop only)

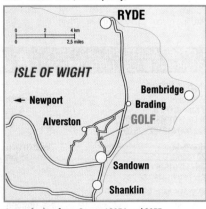

ISLE OF WIGHT

RYDE

← Newport
Alverston
Bembridge
Brading
GOLF
Sandown
Shanklin

0 2 4 km
0 2,5 miles

Access Accès : from Cowes A3054 and 3055 to Sandown. Avenue Road on left, then Broadway, Lake Hill on the right, The Fairway on the right.
Map 9 on page 422 Carte 9 Page 422

GOLF COURSE
PARCOURS

15/20

Site	Site	
Maintenance	Entretien	
Architect	Architecte	James Braid M. Cowper
Type	Type	links, parkland
Relief	Relief	
Water in play	Eau en jeu	
Exp. to wind	Exposé au vent	
Trees in play	Arbres en jeu	

Scorecard Carte de score	Chp. Chp.	Mens Mess.	Ladies Da.
Length Long.	5456	5223	4960
Par	70	70	72

Advised golfing ability
Niveau de jeu recommandé · 0 12 24 36

Hcp required Handicap exigé · certificate

CLUB HOUSE & AMENITIES
CLUB HOUSE ET ANNEXES

7/10

Pro shop	Pro-shop	
Driving range	Practice	
Sheltered	couvert	no
On grass	sur herbe	yes
Putting-green	putting-green	yes
Pitching-green	pitching green	yes

HOTEL FACILITIES
ENVIRONNEMENT HOTELIER

6/10

HOTELS HÔTELS

Brunswick · Shanklin
32 rooms, D £ 60 · 2 km
Tel (44) 01983 - 863 245

Fern Bank · Shanklin
22 rooms, D £ 80 · 2 km
Tél (44) 01983 - 862 790, Fax (44) 01983 - 864 412

Bourne Hall Country · Shanklin
30 rooms, D £ 80 · 2 km
Tel (44) 01983 - 862 820, Fax (44) 01983 - 865 138

RESTAURANTS RESTAURANTS

Bourne Hall Country · Shanklin
Tel (44) 01983 - 862820 · 2 km

Luccombe Chine · Shanklin
Tel (44) 01983 - 862037 · 2 km

544

This course, about a mile from the city of Sherborne, is testimony to the design skills of James Braid over a country landscape. It was completed in 1936 on a layout dating from 1894. The course is not too hilly but the slopes do pose a few questions, particularly on the sloping fairways of holes 6 and 13. The five par 3s are all excellent holes. The greens are average in size, never blind but do have some stiff slopes at the front on half a dozen holes. This is a fair test and a good family course. For a little culture after your round, drive into town. In the 16th century, the transformation of Sherborne Abbey into a school led to the building being saved at a time when Henry VIII's break with Rome was resulting in the dissolution of monasteries and often the destruction of some of Britain's finest landmarks.

Ce parcours à deux kilomètres de Sherborne reste un bon témoignage de l'architecture de James Braid en paysage de campagne, réalisé en 1936 à partir d'un tracé de 1894. Les reliefs ne sont pas assez importants mais ils permettent d'apporter quelques éléments d'interrogation, en particulier avec les fairways en pente au 6 et au 13. A remarquer aussi, la qualité des cinq par 3. Les greens sont de taille moyenne, jamais aveugles mais avec des pentes sévères en début de surface, sur une demi-douzaine de trous. Aucun green n'est aveugle, ce qui confirme la franchise de ce bon parcours familial. Pour la culture, on ira en ville : au XVIè siècle la transformation de l'abbaye de Sherborne en école a permis de la préserver, après que la rupture d'Henry VIII avec Rome ait eu pour conséquence la dissolution des monastères, leur abandon et souvent la destruction de monuments magnifiques dans toute la Grande-Bretagne.

Sherborne Golf Club

Higher Clatcombe
ENG - SHERBORNE, Dorset DT9 4RN

Office	Secrétariat	(44) 01935 - 814 431
Pro shop	Pro-shop	(44) 01935 - 812 274
Fax	Fax	(44) 01935 - 814 218
Situation	Situation	

2 km N of Sherborne (pop. 7 606)
10 km E of Yeovil (pop. 28 317)

Annual closure	Fermeture annnuelle	no
Weekly closure	Fermeture hebdomadaire	no
Fees main season	Tarifs haute saison	full day

	Week days Semaine	We/Bank holidays We/Férié
Individual Individuel	£ 25	£ 30
Couple Couple	£ 50	£ 60

Caddy	Caddy	no
Electric Trolley	Chariot électrique	no
Buggy	Voiturette	no
Clubs	Clubs	ask Pro

Credit cards Cartes de crédit
VISA - MasterCard

Access Accès : • London M3, Jct 8, A303 to Wincanter, A357 then B3145 → Sherborne. • Bristol A37 to Yeovil, A30 to Sherborne, then B3145 → Wincanton.
Map 6 on page 417 Carte 6 Page 417

GOLF COURSE
PARCOURS
15/20

Site	Site	■■■■■■
Maintenance	Entretien	■■■■■
Architect	Architecte	James Braid (1936)
Type	Type	parkland
Relief	Relief	■■■■
Water in play	Eau en jeu	■
Exp. to wind	Exposé au vent	■■■■■
Trees in play	Arbres en jeu	■■■

Scorecard Carte de score	Chp. Chp.	Mens Mess.	Ladies Da.
Length Long.	5377	5220	5018
Par	70	70	73

Advised golfing ability Niveau de jeu recommandé	0	12	24	36
Hcp required	Handicap exigé	certificate		

CLUB HOUSE & AMENITIES
CLUB HOUSE ET ANNEXES
6/10

Pro shop	Pro-shop	■■■■
Driving range	Practice	■■■
Sheltered	couvert	no
On grass	sur herbe	yes
Putting-green	putting-green	yes
Pitching-green	pitching green	no

545

HOTEL FACILITIES
ENVIRONNEMENT HOTELIER
7/10

HOTELS HÔTELS

Eastbury - 14 rooms, D £ 100
Tel (44) 01935 - 813 131
Fax (44) 01935 - 817 296
Sherborne 2 km

Antelope - 19 rooms, D £ 65
Tel (44) 01935 - 812 077
Fax (44) 01935 - 816 473
Sherborne 2 km

Summer Lodge
17 chambres, D £ 100
Tel (44) 01935 - 83 424
Fax (44) 01935 - 83 005
Evershot 16 km

RESTAURANTS RESTAURANTS

Pheasants
Tel (44) 01935 - 815 252
Sherborne 2 km

Grange
Tel (44) 01935 - 813 463
Oborne 4 km

Less well known than Royal West Norfolk and Hunstanton, Sheringham (together with Royal Cromer) is one of the excellent courses along this magnificent northern coast of East Anglia. Once you have actually found the entrance to the course, some of the views from atop chalk cliffs are quite magnificent. This is not a links course but the wind plays an even more important role in that there are no dunes to offer any shelter. The professionals find Sheringham a little on the short side but the course is looked upon with the greatest respect by the best amateur golfers, for whom the need to improvise and shape shots is an even more essential factor than length. Bunkers play a key role in the definition of each hole and in strategy, but so do the heather and gorse. At least there are no hidden traps on this Tom Dunn layout (created in 1891), and it is perhaps this fairness which deserves our greatest respect.

Moins connu que Royal West Norfolk et Hunstanton, Sheringham est avec Royal Cromer l'un des excellents parcours de cette magnifique côte nord de l'East Anglia, et offre des vues exceptionnelles, du haut de ses falaises de craie... une fois que l'on a trouvé l'entrée du golf. Bien sûr, ce n'est pas un links, mais le vent y joue un rôle encore plus important : il n'y a pas de dunes pour s'en abriter ! Les professionnels le trouvent un peu court, mais c'est un tracé hautement respecté par les meilleurs amateurs, pour qui la nécessité de savoir créer des coups de golf est un facteur plus essentiel que la distance. Les bunkers jouent un rôle important dans la définition des trous et la stratégie, mais peut-être plus encore les buissons d'ajoncs et de fougère. Au moins n'y a t-il aucun piège caché sur ce dessin de Tom Dunn (en 1891), et cette honnêteté mérite le plus grand respect.

Sheringham Golf Club

Weybourne Road
ENG - SHERINGHAM, Norfolk NR26 8HG

Office	Secrétariat	(44) 01263 - 822038
Pro shop	Pro-shop	(44) 01263 - 822980
Fax	Fax	(44) 01263 - 825189
Situation	Situation	

8 km from Cromer (pop. 5 025)
35 km from Norwich (pop. 120 895)

Annual closure	Fermeture annnuelle	no
Weekly closure	Fermeture hebdomadaire	no

Fees main season
Tarifs haute saison · 18 holes

	Week days Semaine	We/Bank holidays We/Férié
Individual Individuel	£ 38	£ 43
Couple Couple	£ 76	£ 86

Booking advised

Caddy	Caddy	no
Electric Trolley	Chariot électrique	no
Buggy	Voiturette	no
Clubs	Clubs	no

Credit cards Cartes de crédit · no

546

GOLF COURSE
PARCOURS · 15/20

Site	Site	
Maintenance	Entretien	
Architect	Architecte	Tom Dunn
Type	Type	seaside course, open country
Relief	Relief	
Water in play	Eau en jeu	
Exp. to wind	Exposé au vent	
Trees in play	Arbres en jeu	

Scorecard	Chp.	Mens	Ladies
Carte de score	Chp.	Mess.	Da.
Length Long.	5817	5485	5256
Par	70	70	73

Advised golfing ability	0	12	24	36
Niveau de jeu recommandé				

Hcp required · Handicap exigé · certificate

CLUB HOUSE & AMENITIES
CLUB HOUSE ET ANNEXES · 7/10

Pro shop	Pro-shop	
Driving range	Practice	
Sheltered	couvert	no
On grass	sur herbe	yes
Putting-green	putting-green	yes
Pitching-green	pitching green	yes

HOTEL FACILITIES
ENVIRONNEMENT HOTELIER · 6/10

HOTELS HÔTELS

Beaumaris Hotel · Sheringham
22 rooms, D £ 76 · 500 m
Tel (44) 01263 - 822 370
Fax (44) 01263 - 821 421

Links Country Park · West Runton
40 chambres, D £ 120 · 6 km
Tel (44) 01263 - 838 383
Fax (44) 01263 - 838 264

Sandcliff Private Hotel · Cromer
23 rooms, D £ 50 · 5 km
Tel (44) 01263 - 512 888

RESTAURANT RESTAURANT

Adlard's · Norwich
Tel (44) 01603 -633522 · 35 km

NORTH SEA

GOLF

Sheringham · East Runton · Cromer
Weybourne · West Runton · A 149
Holt
KING'S LYNN · A 148 · A 149
NORWICH

0 · 2 · 4
0 · 2,5 miles

Access Accès : Norwich, A140 N to Cromer.
A149 W through Sheringham,
Golf on the right opposite Mobil Garage
Map 7 on page 419 Carte 7 Page 419

Here we are in Robin Hood country where you can visit the cities of Nottingham and Lincoln and what is left of Sherwood Forest. As you might expect, trees are the main feature on this course and they play a major role throughout. It will be surprising if you don't have to play at least one swirling recovery to get back onto the fairway (the undergrowth is cut back short). Otherwise Harry Colt and James Braid have laid out bunkers as effectively as usual, including around the greens which can be approached in different ways, according to their line of defence. A rather traditional course but with a back 9 that can upset your score. Having spent many years in the shadow of Notts Hollinwell, this hilly course deserves a little limelight of its own.

Nous voici dans le monde de Robin des Bois. Entre une visite à Nottingham et une excursion vers Lincoln, la forêt de Sherwood n'est plus inquiétante que pour les imaginations d'enfants. Comme on pouvait s'y attendre, les arbres constituent l'essentiel du décor de ce parcours, mais un décor qui joue les rôles principaux. Il serait étonnant que vous n'ayez jamais à jouer de balles à effet pour vous en extraire (les sous-bois sont bien dégagés). Autrement, Harry Colt et James Braid ont développé leur jeu de bunkers toujours aussi efficace, y compris autour des greens. Ceux-ci peuvent cependant être attaqués de différentes manières, selon les lignes de défense. Un parcours assez traditionnel, mais la difficulté du retour peut perturber le score. Longtemps à l'ombre de Notts (Hollinwell), ce parcours très vallonné mérite d'être placé en pleine lumière.

Sherwood Forest Golf Club

Eakring Road
ENG - MANSFIELD, Notts. NG18 3EW

Office	Secrétariat	(44) 01623 - 626 689
Pro shop	Pro-shop	(44) 01623 - 627 403
Fax	Fax	(44) 01623 - 626 689
Situation	Situation	

25 km N of Nottingham (pop. 270 222)
3 km E of Mansfield

Annual closure	Fermeture annnuelle	no
Weekly closure	Fermeture hebdomadaire	no
Fees main season	Tarifs haute saison	18 holes

	Week days Semaine	We/Bank holidays We/Férié
Individual Individuel	£ 35	—
Couple Couple	£ 70	—

Full weekday: £. 45 - No visitors at weekends

Caddy	Caddy	no
Electric Trolley	Chariot électrique	yes
Buggy	oiturette	no
Clubs	Clubs	on request

Credit cards Cartes de crédit VISA - MasterCard - AMEX

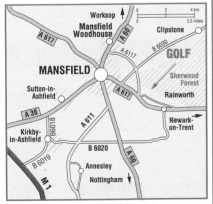

Access Accès : M1 Jct 27. Mansfield exit from roundabout. Left at T-junction, left again at next T-junction (8 km or 5 m.). Right at next lights, right again at next T-junction. Left at lights. Right at 3rd mini-roundabout. Golf 1 km on left. **Map 4 on page 413** Carte 4 Page 413

GOLF COURSE
PARCOURS

17/20

Site	Site	▰▰▰▰▰▱
Maintenance	Entretien	▰▰▰▰▰▱
Architect	Architecte	Harry S. Colt remod. by J. Braid
Type	Type	forest, heathland
Relief	Relief	▰▰▰▰▱▱
Water in play	Eau en jeu	▰▰▱▱▱▱
Exp. to wind	Exposé au vent	▰▰▱▱▱▱
Trees in play	Arbres en jeu	▰▰▰▰▱▱

Scorecard Carte de score	Chp. Chp.	Mens Mess.	Ladies Da.
Length Long.	6028	5654	5082
Par	71	71	73

Advised golfing ability Niveau de jeu recommandé		0 12 24 36
Hcp required	Handicap exigé	certificate

CLUB HOUSE & AMENITIES
CLUB HOUSE ET ANNEXES

7/10

Pro shop	Pro-shop	▰▰▰▰▱▱
Driving range	Practice	▰▰▰▰▱▱
Sheltered	couvert	no
On grass	sur herbe	yes
Putting-green	putting-green	yes
Pitching-green	pitching green	yes

HOTEL FACILITIES
ENVIRONNEMENT HOTELIER

6/10

HOTELS HÔTELS

Pine Lodge - 20 rooms, D £ 60   Mansfield
Tel (44) 01623 - 622 308   3 km

Swallow - 157 rooms, D £ 120   South Normanton
Tel (44) 01773 - 812 000, Fax (44) 01773 - 580 032 18 km

Royal Moat House   Nottingham
200 rooms, D £ 100   25 km
Tel (44) 0115 - 936 9988, Fax (44) 0115 - 475 667

Stage Hotel - 52 rooms, D £ 53   Nottingham 25 km
Tel (44) 0115 - 960 3261, Fax (44) 0115 - 969 1040

RESTAURANTS RESTAURANTS

Swallow   South Normanton 18 km
Tel (44) 01773 - 812 000

Sonny's - Tel (44) 0115 - 947 3041   Nottingham 25 km

547

A course to take in on your way from Liverpool to Scotland, or from Glasgow to England, together with Southerness just opposite on the other side of Solway Firth. Keep looking in this direction, too, because the industrial complex nearby is something of an eyesore. The course's location in the middle of nowhere has kept Silloth from staging any top tournaments, but this does have it advantages: being a quiet course and frequented mostly only by the inhabitants of Carlisle, its overall condition is simply marvellous. It has its enthusiasts, who rate this amongst their top-five links courses, and understandably so. The well-contoured fairways rarely have you standing on flat ground, fairway bunkers have been replaced by heather and gorse, the approaches to greens are tight and putting surfaces are tricky. Bring your best game here and a suitcase because you won't want to leave. Play Silloth before it becomes too fashionable.

Un parcours à inclure dans un voyage de Liverpool vers l'Ecosse, ou de Glasgow vers l'Angleterre, avec celui de Southerness, juste en face, de l'autre côté du Solway Firth. Regardez plutôt de ce côté, car le complexe industriel à proximité n'est pas beau du tout. Sa situation à l'écart de tout a empêché Silloth d'avoir beaucoup de grands championnats, mais il y a un avantage : peu fréquenté, sinon par les habitants de Carlisle, il est dans un état généralement merveilleux. Il a ses amoureux, qui le classent dans leur "Top 5" des links, et on les comprend. Les fairways bien modelés vous mettent rarement à plat, les bunkers de fairway sont remplacés par la bruyère et les ajoncs, les entrées de greens sont étroites, leurs surfaces subtiles. A Silloth-on-Solway, il faut amener son meilleur jeu, et sa valise, car on aura envie de rester... A jouer avant qu'il ne devienne trop à la mode.

Silloth-on-Solway Golf Club
ENG - SILLOTH-ON-SOLWAY, Cumbria CA5 4AT

Office	Secrétariat	(44) 016973 - 31304
Pro shop	Pro-shop	(44) 016973 - 32404
Fax	Fax	(44) 016973 - 31782
Situation	Situation	

40 km from Carlisle (pop. 100 562)

Annual closure	Fermeture annnuelle	no
Weekly closure	Fermeture hebdomadaire	no

Fees main season
Tarifs haute saison — full day

	Week days Semaine	We/Bank holidays We/Férié
Individual Individuel	£ 25	£ 30
Couple Couple	£ 50	£ 60

Caddy	Caddy	no
Electric Trolley	Chariot électrique	no
Buggy	Voiturette	no
Clubs	Clubs	£ 10/18 holes

Credit cards Cartes de crédit
VISA - Eurocard - MasterCard - AMEX - DC

548

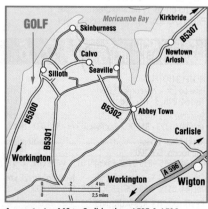

GOLF
Moricambe Bay   Kirkbride
Skinburness
Calvo   Newtown Arlosh
Silloth   Seaville
B5300   B5302   Abbey Town
B5301   Carlisle
Workington
Workington   Wigton

0   2   4 km
0   2.5 miles

Access Accès : M6 to Carlisle, then A595 & A596.
At Wigton, B5302 to Silloth Promenade.
Go right 200 m.
Map 2 on page 409 Carte 2 Page 409

GOLF COURSE
PARCOURS

18/20

Site	Site	
Maintenance	Entretien	
Architect	Architecte	Willie Park
Type	Type	links
Relief	Relief	
Water in play	Eau en jeu	
Exp. to wind	Exposé au vent	
Trees in play	Arbres en jeu	

Scorecard Carte de score	Chp. Chp.	Mens Mess.	Ladies Da.
Length Long.	5952	5721	5203
Par	72	72	75

Advised golfing ability		0	12	24	36
Niveau de jeu recommandé					
Hcp required	Handicap exigé	certificate			

CLUB HOUSE & AMENITIES
CLUB HOUSE ET ANNEXES

7/10

Pro shop	Pro-shop	
Driving range	Practice	
Sheltered	couvert	no
On grass	sur herbe	yes
Putting-green	putting-green	yes
Pitching-green	pitching green	yes

HOTEL FACILITIES
ENVIRONNEMENT HOTELIER

4/10

HOTELS HÔTELS
Silloth Golf Hotel   Silloth
21 rooms, D £ 52   200 m
Tel (44) 016973 - 31 438
Fax (44) 016973 - 32 582

Crown + Mitre   Carlisle
97 rooms, D £ 99   40 km
Tel (44) 01228 - 25 491
Fax (44) 01228 - 514 553

RESTAURANT RESTAURANT
Silloth Golf Hotel   Silloth
Tel (44) 016973 - 31 438   200 m

SLALEY HALL

17 | 8 | 7

The Woburn of the north or the Gleneagles of the south, it doesn't matter either way. Slaley Hall is one of those courses that has brought life to a region where good courses were comparatively few and far between. The vegetation is typical of the north, with a good number of pine-trees lining the fairways or adding dark colour to contrast with the lighter greens of the fairways and putting surfaces, the sand in the bunkers and the lakes. Familiar colours to golfers, certainly, but here they just look smarter than anywhere else. The many different playing options add variety to the fun of playing here; you can change the complexion of the course by switching tee-boxes but still keep the same panoply of hazards, including fairway bunkers whose shape (Dave Thomas style) gives this magnificent English style park a little American touch. If you are feeling tired after the very challenging finishing holes, the clubhouse and hotel offer all the facilities of a major golfing resort, due to be enhanced still further in 1999 with a second course.

Woburn du nord ou Gleneagles du sud, peu importe, Slaley Hall fait partie, des golfs qui ont un peu réveillé une région assez pauvre en grands parcours. La végétation est néanmoins plus typique du nord, avec les nombreux sapins bordant les fairways ou fournissant des couleurs sombres harmonisées à celles des greens et des fairways, au sable des bunkers et aux lacs. Ce sont des couleurs familières aux golfeurs, mais ici plus soignées que partout ailleurs. De multiples options de jeu permettent de varier les plaisirs : d'un jour à l'autre, changez de difficultés en changeant de tees, tout en conservant une panoplie d'obstacles, les formes des bunkers de fairway (à la Dave Thomas !) apportant une touche américaine à ce beau parc à l'anglaise. Si vous êtes un peu fatigué après un finale exigeant, le Clubhouse et l'hôtel offrent tous les services d'un grand "resort", qui sera encore amélioré avec un second parcours, en 1999.

Slaley Hall Hotel & Golf Club

Slaley
ENG - HEXHAM, Northumberland NE47 0BY

Office	Secrétariat	(44) 01434 - 673350
Pro shop	Pro-shop	(44) 01434 - 673154
Fax	Fax	(44) 01434 - 673152
Situation	Situation	

30 km from Newcastle (pop. 259 541)
15 km from Hexham (pop. 11 342)

Annual closure	Fermeture annuelle	no
Weekly closure	Fermeture hebdomadaire	no

Fees main season Tarifs haute saison 18 holes

	Week days Semaine	We/Bank holidays We/Férié
Individual Individuel	£ 40	—
Couple Couple	£ 80	—

Weekends: members and Hotel guests only

Caddy	Caddy	no
Electric Trolley	Chariot électrique	no
Buggy	Voiturette	£ 20/18 holes
Clubs	Clubs	£ 20/18 holes

Credit cards Cartes de crédit
VISA - Eurocard - MasterCard - AMEX - DC

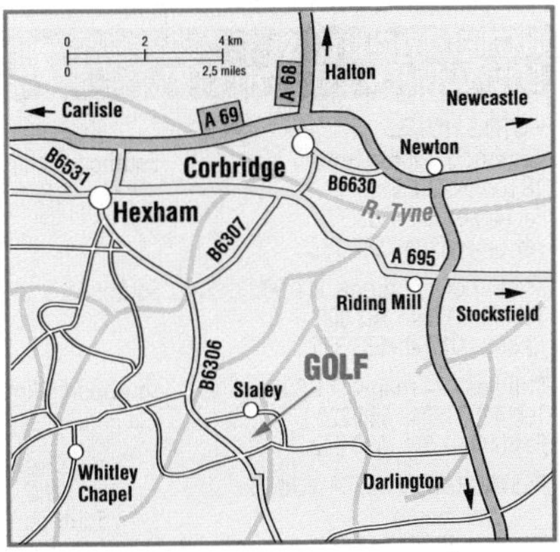

Access Accès : Newcastle, A69 W, turn to Hexham, then B6306 to Slaley.
Map 2 on page 409 Carte 2 Page 409

GOLF COURSE PARCOURS 17/20

Site	Site	
Maintenance	Entretien	
Architect	Architecte	David Thomas
Type	Type	parkland
Relief	Relief	
Water in play	Eau en jeu	
Exp. to wind	Exposé au vent	
Trees in play	Arbres en jeu	

Scorecard Carte de score	Chp. Chp.	Mens Mess.	Ladies Da.
Length Long.	6320	6085	5255
Par	72	72	75

Advised golfing ability 0 12 24 36
Niveau de jeu recommandé
Hcp required Handicap exigé 24 Men, 36 Ladies

CLUB HOUSE & AMENITIES CLUB HOUSE ET ANNEXES 8/10

Pro shop	Pro-shop	
Driving range	Practice	
Sheltered	couvert	8 bays
On grass	sur herbe	yes
Putting-green	putting-green	yes
Pitching-green	pitching green	yes

HOTEL FACILITIES ENVIRONNEMENT HOTELIER 7/10

HOTELS HÔTELS
Slaley Hall Hotel - 139 rooms, D £ 220 — Slaley, on site
Tel (44) 01434 - 673 350, Fax (44) 01434 - 673 152

Beaumont - 23 rooms, D £ 70 — Hexham
Tel (44) 01434 - 602 331 — 12 km

County - 9 rooms, D £ 58 — Hexham
Tel (44) 01434 - 602 030 — 12 km

Forte Crest - 165 rooms, D £ 80 — Newcastle 30 km
Tel (44) 0191 - 232 6191, Fax (44) 0191 - 261 8529

RESTAURANTS RESTAURANTS
2 restaurants at the Hotel — Slaley, on site
Tel (44) 01434 - 673 350

Black House - Tel (44) 01434 - 604 744 — Hexham 10 km

Queen Street - Tel (44) 0191 - 222 0755 — Newcastle 30 km

SOUTHPORT & AINSDALE

Although it has staged the Ryder Cup and the British Ladies Open, this course has suffered from being overshadowed by its towering neighbours Birkdale and Hillside, although actually there is little to choose between them. It may look short, but only to the better players. For the rest of us it has yardage enough, especially since driving these tight fairways is never easy. The paths to the greens are never very wide, either, and call for bump 'n run shots which can make the job even tougher. In contrast, game strategy will vary with the wind and always be clear: you see exactly what needs to be done. Whether you play here twice or a hundred times, it is always as exciting as that very first day in an elegant, traditional and warm atmosphere.

Bien qu'il ait reçu la Ryder Cup et le British Ladies Open, ce parcours a souffert de l'ombre de ses puissants voisins, Birkdale et Hillside, mais sans vraiment devoir leur envier grand'chose. Il peut paraître court, mais seulement aux meilleurs joueurs : il est bien assez long pour la plupart d'entre nous, en particulier par ce que driver sur ces fairways étroits n'est guère facile. Les entrées de greens ne sont pas toujours très larges, mais on doit les approcher en roulant, ce qui ne facilite pas non plus la tâche. En revanche, la stratégie peut varier en fonction du vent, mais elle apparaît toujours clairement : on voit exactement ce que l'on doit faire. Que l'on joue deux fois ou cent fois, le plaisir est comme au premier jour dans ce club à l'ambiance élégante, traditionnelle et chaleureuse.

Southport & Ainsdale Golf Club

Bradshaws Lane, Ainsdale
ENG - SOUTHPORT, Lancs PR8 3LG

Office	Secrétariat	(44) 01704 - 578092
Pro shop	Pro-shop	(44) 01704 - 577316
Fax	Fax	(44) 01704 - 570896
Situation	Situation	

5 km S of Southport (pop. 90 959)
26 km N of Liverpool (pop. 452 450)

Annual closure	Fermeture annnuelle	no
Weekly closure	Fermeture hebdomadaire	no
Fees main season	Tarifs haute saison	18 holes

	Week days Semaine	We/Bank holidays We/Férié
Individual Individuel	£ 35	£ 45*
Couple Couple	£ 70	£ 90*

* Limited access at weekends - Full weekdays: £ 45

Caddy	Caddy	on request
Electric Trolley	Chariot électrique	£ 5/18 holes
Buggy	Voiturette	no
Clubs	Clubs	yes

Credit cards Cartes de crédit
VISA - Eurocard - MasterCard - AMEX - DC - JCB
(Pro-shop only)

550

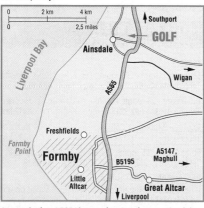

Access Accès : A565 Liverpool → Southport. Ainsdale Village centre, turn left on Bradshaws Lane
Map 5 on page 415 Carte 5 Page 415

GOLF COURSE
PARCOURS

18/20

Site	Site	
Maintenance	Entretien	
Architect	Architecte	James Braid
Type	Type	links
Relief	Relief	
Water in play	Eau en jeu	
Exp. to wind	Exposé au vent	
Trees in play	Arbres en jeu	

Scorecard Carte de score	Chp. Chp.	Mens Mess.	Ladies Da.
Length Long.	5950	5924	5052
Par	72	72	74

Advised golfing ability   0   12   24   36
Niveau de jeu recommandé
Hcp required   Handicap exigé   28 Men, 36 Ladies

CLUB HOUSE & AMENITIES
CLUB HOUSE ET ANNEXES

7/10

Pro shop	Pro-shop	
Driving range	Practice	
Sheltered	couvert	no
On grass	sur herbe	yes
Putting-green	putting-green	yes
Pitching-green	pitching green	yes

HOTEL FACILITIES
ENVIRONNEMENT HOTELIER

7/10

HOTELS HÔTELS
Cambridge House Hotel   Southport 6 km
18 rooms, D £ 51
Tel (44) 01704 - 538 372
Fax (44) 01704 - 547 183

Scarisbrick - 77 rooms, D £ 90   Southport 5 km
Tel (44) 01704 - 543 000
Fax (44) 01704 - 533 335

Stutelea - 24 rooms, D £ 80   Southport 5 km
Tel (44) 01704 - 544 220
Fax (44) 01704 - 500 232

RESTAURANTS RESTAURANTS
The Warehouse   Southport
Tel (44) 01704 - 544 662   5 km

Valentino's - Tel (44) 01704 - 538 401   Southport 5 km

The Jasmin Tree (44) 01704 - 530 141   Southport 5 km

You will remember three things about this course: the wonderful views over the Cornish coast and the Camel estuary, the little church on the 10th hole, dug out of the sand 60 years ago, and Himalaya, a giant hill-shaped bunker standing some 80 feet high where you watch golfers walk up and down in a vain attempt to get their ball back in the fairway. But this is not the only hill over steeply undulating terrain, which can be tiring for the fainter-hearted. Some greens are difficult to reach other than with lofted shots, meaning that good scores go to good players. Beginners will spend their time in the dunes and the very thick rough. St. Enodoc is a superb golfing arena, with special mention going to the final holes where you play for the match and an excellent meal in the clubhouse.

Vous vous souviendrez au moins de trois choses : les vues magnifiques sur la côte de Cornouailles et le Camel Estuary, la petite église au 10, tirée du sable il y a 60 ans, et l'Himalaya, gigantesque bunker en forme de colline de 25 mètres de haut, d'où il est distrayant de regarder les joueurs monter et descendre sans parvenir à sortir leur balle. Mais ce n'est pas la seule colline d'un terrain très mouvementé, parfois assez fatigant pour les plus faibles. Certains greens sont difficiles à atteindre autrement qu'avec des balles levées, ce qui réserve les bons scores aux bons joueurs. Les débutants passeront leur vie dans les dunes et dans les roughs très épais. St Enodoc est une superbe arène pour jouer, avec une mention particulière pour les derniers trous quand on y joue le match et un très bon repas au Clubhouse.

St Enodoc Golf Club

Rock
ENG - WADEBRIDGE, Cornwall PL2T 6LD

Office	Secrétariat	(44) 01208 - 863216
Pro shop	Pro-shop	(44) 01208 - 862402
Fax	Fax	(44) 01208 - 862976
Situation	Situation	

10 km from Wadebridge - 32 km from Bodmin

Annual closure	Fermeture annnuelle	no
Weekly closure	Fermeture hebdomadaire	no

Fees main season	Tarifs haute saison	18 holes
	Week days Semaine	We/Bank holidays We/Férié
Individual Individuel	£ 35	£ 40
Couple Couple	£ 70	£ 80

Full day: £ 50 - £ 55 (weekends)

Caddy	Caddy	no
Electric Trolley	Chariot électrique	£ 9/day
Buggy	Voiturette	no
Clubs	Clubs	£ 10/18 holes
Credit cards Cartes de crédit		no

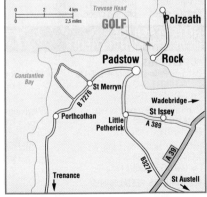

Constantine Bay, Trevose Head, GOLF, Polzeath, Padstow, Rock, St Merryn, B 7276, Porthcothan, Little Petherick, Wadebridge, St Issey, A 389, Trenance, B3274, A39, St Austell

Access Accès : A30 Exeter to Bodmin, then A389 to Wadebridge, follow signs to Rock, drive through Rock, past Boat Club and Matiner's pub, sharp right uphill to Clubhouse (signposted)
Map 6 on page 416 Carte 6 Page 416

GOLF COURSE PARCOURS — 18/20

Site	Site	
Maintenance	Entretien	
Architect	Architecte	James Braid
Type	Type	seaside course, links
Relief	Relief	
Water in play	Eau en jeu	
Exp. to wind	Exposé au vent	
Trees in play	Arbres en jeu	

Scorecard Carte de score	Chp. Chp.	Mens Mess.	Ladies Da.
Length Long.	5619	5450	5115
Par	69	69	73

Advised golfing ability	0	12	24	36
Niveau de jeu recommandé				

Hcp required Handicap exigé certificate

CLUB HOUSE & AMENITIES CLUB HOUSE ET ANNEXES — 7/10

Pro shop	Pro-shop	
Driving range	Practice	
Sheltered	couvert	no
On grass	sur herbe	no
Putting-green	putting-green	yes (2)
Pitching-green	pitching green	yes

551

HOTEL FACILITIES ENVIRONNEMENT HOTELIER — 4/10

HOTELS HÔTELS

Pentire Rocks - 15 rooms, D £ 55 — New Polzeath
Tel (44) 01208 - 862 213 — 5 km
Fax (44) 01208 - 862 259

Port Gaverne - 19 rooms, D £ 85 — Port Isaac
Tel (44) 01208 - 880 244 — 10 km
Fax (44) 01208 - 880 151

Roskarnon House Hotel - 12 rooms, D £ 40 — Rock
Tel (44) 01208 - 862 329 — 3 km
Fax (44) 01208 - 862 785

RESTAURANTS RESTAURANTS

St Kew Inn — St Kew
Tel (44) 01208 - 841 259 — 12 km

Maltsters Arms — Chapel Amble
Tel (44) 01208 - 812 473 — 8 km

Come and play here in May. If you're game lets you down, you'll probably find some consolation in the rhododendrons in full bloom, whose colours contrast with the purple heather, silver birch and pines to produce a wonderful setting for a superb course designed by Harry Colt. For those of you who are not as fit as you were, this is a very hilly course. If you run out of puff, make it back to the clubhouse and admire the superb views. Actually on the course, the changes of gradient and the slopes call for a little reconnoitring before hoping to card a good score, especially since the greens are very quick, full of breaks and sometimes multi-tiered. A few blind drives or tee-shots to steeply sloping fairways also require extreme accuracy. St George's Hill is not only picturesque, it is also one of the country's very good inland courses.

Venez donc au mois de mai. Si votre jeu vous a déçu, vous vous consolerez à la vue des rhododendrons en pleine floraison, dont les couleurs s'ajoutent aux bruyères pourpres, aux bouleaux blancs, aux pins et aux sapins pour offrir un cadre somptueux au superbe dessin de Harry Colt. Hélas pour ceux qui n'ont pas une excellente forme, ce parcours est très physique. Ils pourront toujours rester au Clubhouse, qui offre des vues superbes. Quant au parcours, ses changements de niveaux et ses pentes exigent une petite reconnaissance préalable avant d'espérer un bon score, d'autant plus que les greens sont rapides, très mouvementés, parfois à plusieurs plateaux. Quelques drives aveugles ou vers des fairways en dévers demandent aussi beaucoup de précision. St George's Hill n'est pas seulement pittoresque, c'est aussi un des très bons parcours "inland" du pays.

St George's Hill Golf Club

Golf Club Road, St George's Hill
ENG - WEYBRIDGE, Surrey KT13 0NL

Office	Secrétariat	(44) 01932 - 847758
Pro shop	Pro-shop	(44) 01932 - 847523
Fax	Fax	(44) 01932 - 821564
Situation	Situation	

1 km from Weybridge (pop. 7 919)
37 km from Central London (pop. 6 679 700)

| Annual closure | Fermeture annnuelle | no |
| Weekly closure | Fermeture hebdomadaire | no |

Fees main season	Tarifs haute saison	18 holes
	Week days Semaine	We/Bank holidays We/Férié
Individual Individuel	£ 50	—
Couple Couple	£ 100	—

Full weekday: £ 65 - Weekends: only with a member

Caddy	Caddy	on request/£ 20+tip
Electric Trolley	Chariot électrique	no
Buggy	Voiturette	no
Clubs	Clubs	£ 15/18 holes

Credit cards Cartes de crédit
VISA - Eurocard - MasterCard - AMEX - JCB

552

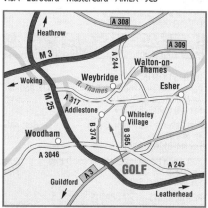

Access Accès : London A3. Cobham Bridge A245 (Byfleet Road). After 2 km (1.2 m.), B374 (Brooklands Road) on right. Golf on right (Golf Club Road).
Map 8 on page 421 Carte 8 Page 421

GOLF COURSE
PARCOURS
17/20

Site	Site	
Maintenance	Entretien	
Architect	Architecte	Harry S. Colt
Type	Type	inland, parkland
Relief	Relief	
Water in play	Eau en jeu	
Exp. to wind	Exposé au vent	
Trees in play	Arbres en jeu	

| Scorecard | Chp. | Mens | Ladies |
Carte de score	Chp.	Mess.	Da.
Length Long.	5910	5960	5020
Par	70	70	72

Advised golfing ability		0 12 24 36
Niveau de jeu recommandé		
Hcp required	Handicap exigé	certificate

CLUB HOUSE & AMENITIES
CLUB HOUSE ET ANNEXES
7/10

Pro shop	Pro-shop	
Driving range	Practice	
Sheltered	couvert	no
On grass	sur herbe	yes
Putting-green	putting-green	yes
Pitching-green	pitching green	no

HOTEL FACILITIES
ENVIRONNEMENT HOTELIER
7/10

HOTELS HÔTELS
Oatlands Park - 112 rooms, D £ 120   Weybridge
Tel (44) 01932 - 847 242   3 km
Fax (44) 01932 - 842 252

Ship Thistle - 39 rooms, D 110   Weybridge
Tel (44) 01932 - 848 364   1 km
Fax (44) 01932 - 857 153

Hilton National - 146 rooms, D £ 120   Cobham
Tel (44) 01932 - 864 471   3 km
Fax (44) 01932 - 868 017

RESTAURANTS RESTAURANTS
Casa Romana   Weybridge 1 km
Tel (44) 01932 - 843 470

Les Alouettes   Esher-Claygate 6 km
Tel (44) 01372 - 464 882

Good Earth - Tel (44) 01932 - 462 489   Esher 4 km

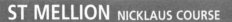

ST MELLION NICKLAUS COURSE

17	9	7

This is a Jack Nicklaus course and golfers who know his style in the United States will recognise the way in which he has bent and twisted the Cornish countryside to fit his requirements. Turning around a hill which is the setting for another 18 hole course, St. Mellion is exposed to all winds and weathers which will make the course even more difficult than usual. Let's be honest here: even from the front tees this course will be beyond most average players. The bunkers, water and lakes are impressive enough to put off any visitor. Equally true though is the fact that it mellows a little more each time you play it. Maybe because you pay less attention to features such as the many tiny, multi-tiered greens. This is a course you cannot pass by, especially given the club's outstanding facilities, but it is not exactly what you would call a holiday course and there is little local colour to talk of. A must to play to form your own opinion. And test the state of your game.

D'accord, St Mellion est signé Jack Nicklaus. Ceux qui connaissent ses parcours aux USA reconnaîtront qu'il a su plier le paysage de Cornouailles à ses volontés. Tournant autour d'une colline où est logé un autre 18 trous, celui-ci est exposé à tous les vents, ce qui renforce encore sa difficulté. Disons-le franchement, même des départs avancés, ce parcours n'est pas à la portée des joueurs moyens. Les bunkers, les cours d'eau, les lacs impressionnent assez pour refroidir le visiteur. Il est vrai que ce parcours s'adoucit à mesure qu'on le joue, on remarque moins que certains greens sont minuscules, beaucoup à plateaux. Il est impossible d'ignorer ce golf, d'autant que les équipements sont remarquables, mais ce n'est pas exactement un parcours de vacances, et l'on cherchera vainement une couleur vraiment locale. A connaître absolument, pour se faire une opinion. Et tester son jeu.

St Mellion International

St Mellion
ENG - SALTASH, Cornwall PL12 6 SD

Office	Secrétariat	(44) 01579 - 351 351
Pro shop	Pro-shop	(44) 01579 - 350 724
Fax	Fax	(44) 01579 - 350 116
Situation	Situation	

16 km NW of Plymouth (pop. 243 373)

Annual closure	Fermeture annnuelle	no
Weekly closure	Fermeture hebdomadaire	no

Fees main season	Tarifs haute saison	18 holes
	Week days Semaine	We/Bank holidays We/Férié
Individual Individuel	£ 35	£ 35
Couple Couple	£ 70	£ 70

Caddy	Caddy	no
Electric Trolley	Chariot électrique	no
Buggy	Voiturette	£ 18/18 holes
Clubs	Clubs	£ 12.50/18 holes

Credit cards Cartes de crédit
VISA - MasterCard - AMEX - DC - JCB

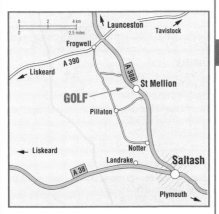

Access Accès : M5 then A38 to Saltash,
then A388 to St Mellion. Golf signposted.
Map 6 on page 416 Carte 6 Page 416

GOLF COURSE
PARCOURS

17/20

Site	Site	▮▮▮▮▮▯
Maintenance	Entretien	▮▮▮▮▮▯
Architect	Architecte	Jack Nicklaus
Type	Type	parkland, open country
Relief	Relief	▮▮▮▮▯▯
Water in play	Eau en jeu	▮▮▮▮▯▯
Exp. to wind	Exposé au vent	▮▮▮▮▯▯
Trees in play	Arbres en jeu	▮▮▮▯▯▯

Scorecard Carte de score	Chp. Chp.	Mens Mess.	Ladies Da.
Length Long.	6080	5846	5146
Par	72	72	73

Advised golfing ability		0 12 24 36
Niveau de jeu recommandé		▮▮▮▮▯
Hcp required	Handicap exigé	no

CLUB HOUSE & AMENITIES
CLUB HOUSE ET ANNEXES

9/10

Pro shop	Pro-shop	▮▮▮▮▮▯
Driving range	Practice	▮▮▮▮▮▯
Sheltered	couvert	6 mats
On grass	sur herbe	yes
Putting-green	putting-green	yes
Pitching-green	pitching green	yes

553

HOTEL FACILITIES
ENVIRONNEMENT HOTELIER

7/10

HOTELS HÔTELS

St Mellion Hotel — Golf on site
24 rooms, D £ 90
Tel (44) 01579 - 351 351

Bowling Green — Plymouth 16 km
12 rooms, D £ 45
Tel (44) 01752 - 209 090
Fax (44) 01752 - 209 092

Forte Posthouse — Plymouth 16 km
106 rooms, D £ 60
Tel (44) 01752 - 662 828
Fax (44) 01752 - 660 974

RESTAURANTS RESTAURANTS

Chez Nous - Tel (44) 01752 - 266 793   Plymouth 16 km

Danescombe - Tel (44) 01822 - 832 414   Calstock 16 km

Agreed, at this price the week-end green-fee is a little high, but we suppose they have to find some sort of deterrent. The most surprising thing here is not the price nor the Clubhouse, presently being re-designed to cater to the addition of a new 9-hole course, hotel rooms and a swimming pool. No, what really surprises the visitor is the absence of heather, found on every other course in the region virtually without exception. We are in the purest "parkland" style, where fairways lined with splendid trees cover space that only Harry Colt could have turned into such a clever course. Everyone talks about the 7th hole, an exemplary par 3, but the rest are no less exciting. With Colt you always have to weigh up the pros and cons of each shot, look twice and watch out for illusions such as hazards that are too visible. If you want to talk about the course, there are some excellent restaurants in the clubhouse.

D'accord, à ce prix en week-end, c'est un peu cher, mais le tarif doit être surtout dissuasif ! Ce qui est le plus surprenant ici, ce n'est pas cela, ni le Clubhouse, actuellement en refonte, car un nouveau 9 trous, des chambres d'hôtel, une piscine vont être ajoutés. Ce qui est le plus surprenant, c'est qu'il n'y a pas ici de bruyère, comme dans tous les parcours de la région, pratiquement sans exception. Nous sommes dans le style "parkland" le plus pur, avec des fairways décorés d'arbres splendides, dans un espace dont seul un Harry Colt pouvait tirer un parcours d'une telle intelligence. On parle toujours du 7, un par 3 exemplaire, mais les autres ne sont pas moins passionnants à envisager. Avec Colt, il faut toujours regarder à deux fois, se méfier des illusions comme des obstacles trop visibles, il faut toujours peser le pour et le contre de chaque coup. Pour en parler, il y a les excellents restaurants du Clubhouse...

Stoke Poges Golf Club
North Drive, Park Road, Stoke Poges
ENG - SLOUGH, Bucks SL2 4PG

Office	Secrétariat	(44) 01753 - 717 171
Pro shop	Pro-shop	(44) 01753 - 717 172
Fax	Fax	(44) 01753 - 717 181
Situation	Situation	

3 km from Slough (pop. 101 066)
8 km from Windsor (pop. 30 136)

Annual closure	Fermeture annnuelle	no
Weekly closure	Fermeture hebdomadaire	no
Fees main season	Tarifs haute saison	18 holes

	Week days Semaine	We/Bank holidays We/Férié
Individual Individuel	£ 50	£ 100
Couple Couple	£ 100	£ 200

Caddy	Caddy	on request/£ 25
Electric Trolley	Chariot électrique	£ 7.50/18 holes
Buggy	Voiturette	£ 25/18 holes
Clubs	Clubs	£ 20/18 holes

Credit cards Cartes de crédit
VISA - MasterCard - AMEX - DC - JCB

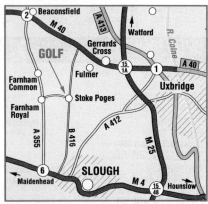

Access Accès : M4 Jct 6 at Slough,
A355 → Beaconsfield. At double mini roundabout in Farnham Royal turn right into Park Road.
Map 8 on page 420 Carte 8 Page 420

GOLF COURSE
PARCOURS

17 /20

Site	Site	■■■■■
Maintenance	Entretien	■■■■■
Architect	Architecte	Harry S. Colt
Type	Type	parkland
Relief	Relief	■■■
Water in play	Eau en jeu	■■
Exp. to wind	Exposé au vent	■■■■
Trees in play	Arbres en jeu	■■■■

Scorecard Carte de score	Chp. Chp.	Mens Mess.	Ladies Da.
Length Long.	6003	5682	5280
Par	71	71	74

Advised golfing ability		0 12 24 36
Niveau de jeu recommandé		■■■■■■
Hcp required	Handicap exigé	28 Men, 36 Ladies

CLUB HOUSE & AMENITIES
CLUB HOUSE ET ANNEXES

8 /10

Pro shop	Pro-shop	■■■■■
Driving range	Practice	■■■■
Sheltered	couvert	no
On grass	sur herbe	yes
Putting-green	putting-green	yes
Pitching-green	pitching green	yes

HOTEL FACILITIES
ENVIRONNEMENT HOTELIER

8 /10

HOTELS HÔTELS

Stoke Park - 20 rooms, D £ 275 Tel (44) 01753 - 717171 Fax (44) 01753 - 717181	Stoke Poges, on site
Copthorne - 217 rooms, D £ 120 Tel (44) 01753 - 516 222 Fax (44) 01753 - 516 237	Slough 5 km
Courtyard - 148 rooms, D £ 85 Tel (44) 01753 - 551 551 Fax (44) 01753 - 553 333	Slough 5 km
Burnham Beeches - 73 rooms, D £ 120 Tel (44) 01628 - 429 955 Fax (44) 01628 - 603 994	Burnham 4 km

RESTAURANTS RESTAURANTS

Club house (3 restaurants) Tel (44) 01753 - 717171	Stoke Poges, on site
Waldo's - Tel (44) 01628 - 668 561	Taplow 6 km

554

A lack of yardage did not prevent Stoneham from staging the first British Masters in 1946 or the Brabazon Trophy in 1993. We'll simply say that this is a good par 70 for golfers who know the course well and pay more attention to their overall score, rather than concentrating on playing to par on each individual hole. At all events, the fairway bunkers should not bother too many players and should ideally be moved to restore their original purpose. The main hazards are now the heather and gorse-bushes, together with the slopes and hills on a site that can be tiring to walk on a number of holes (the 3rd and 18th). This course poses enough problems for us to recommend it first and foremost to experienced players, who will appreciate the uncompromising severity of the challenge. Last but not least, although so close to the port of Southampton, the course is a haven of peace and quiet.

Son manque de longueur n'a pas empêché Stoneham de recevoir le premier British Masters en 1946, ainsi que le Brabazon Trophy en 1993. Nous dirons simplement que c'est un bon par 70 pour ceux qui le connaissent bien et font plus attention au par total qu'au par de chaque trou. En tout cas, les bunkers de fairway ne gêneront pas grand-monde, il faudrait les déplacer pour leur restituer leur fonction originelle. Ce sont la bruyère et les buissons d'ajoncs qui sont maintenant les obstacles principaux, avec les changements de niveau ou même les ondulations d'un terrain assez fatigant sur quelques trous (3 et 18). Ce parcours pose assez de problèmes pour qu'on le conseille d'abord aux joueurs expérimentés, qui apprécieront la rigueur sans concession du défi présenté. Enfin, si près du port de Southampton, on est ici parfaitement au calme.

Stoneham Golf Club

Monks Wood Close
ENG - SOUTHAMPTON, Hampshire SO16 3TT

Office	Secrétariat	(44) 01703 - 769272
Pro shop	Pro-shop	(44) 01703 - 768399
Fax	Fax	(44) 01703 - 766320
Situation	Situation	

Southampton (pop. 196 865)

Annual closure	Fermeture annnuelle	no
Weekly closure	Fermeture hebdomadaire	no
Fees main season	Tarifs haute saison	full day

	Week days Semaine	We/Bank holidays We/Férié
Individual Individuel	£ 36	£ 40
Couple Couple	£ 72	£ 80

18 holes weekdays: £ 29
Under 18 with member, £ 10 any time

Caddy	Caddy	no
Electric Trolley	Chariot électrique	£ 8/18 holes
Buggy	Voiturette	no
Clubs	Clubs	no
Credit cards Cartes de crédit		no

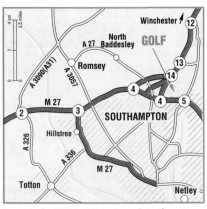

Access Accès : M27 Jct 5. Drive towards Southampton. Turn right at first traffic lights on A27 (Bassett Green Road). 1.2 km, turn right into Golf Club.
Map 7 on page 418 Carte 7 Page 418

GOLF COURSE
PARCOURS

15/20

Site	Site	
Maintenance	Entretien	
Architect	Architecte	Willie Park
Type	Type	inland, heathland
Relief	Relief	
Water in play	Eau en jeu	
Exp. to wind	Exposé au vent	
Trees in play	Arbres en jeu	

Scorecard Carte de score	Chp. Chp.	Mens Mess.	Ladies Da.
Length Long.	5680	5360	4809
Par	72	72	71

Advised golfing ability Niveau de jeu recommandé	0	12	24	36
Hcp required Handicap exigé	certificate			

CLUB HOUSE & AMENITIES
CLUB HOUSE ET ANNEXES

7/10

Pro shop	Pro-shop	
Driving range	Practice	
Sheltered	couvert	2 mats
On grass	sur herbe	no
Putting-green	putting-green	yes
Pitching-green	pitching green	yes

555

HOTEL FACILITIES
ENVIRONNEMENT HOTELIER

8/10

HOTELS HÔTELS

Hilton National - 133 rooms, D £ 90 Tel (44) 01703 - 702 700 Fax (44) 01703 - 767 233		Southampton 4 km
De Vere Grand Harbour 169 rooms, D £ 130 Tel (44) 01703 - 633 033 Fax (44) 01703 - 633 066		Southampton 4 km
County - 66 rooms, D £ 65 Tel (44) 01703 - 359 955 Fax (44) 01703 - 583 910		Southampton 4 km

RESTAURANTS RESTAURANTS

Kuti's Brasserie Tel (44) 01703 - 221585		Southampton 4 km
Old Manor House Tel (44) 01794 - 517353		Romsey 12 km

When you find two great courses at the same Club, you always have a slight preference. But don't be disappointed if you cannot play the "Old" course, its "New" counterpart is just as good and some excellent players even prefer it. If you forget the less enchanting and more "manly" landscape, the "New" course has a lot to be said for it. It allows more aggressive driving, although placing the ball is still crucially important. You need to avoid the fairway bunkers (the edges of which are very high), a very dangerous pond on the 15th, and a few wicked ditches. Your ironwork will have to be up to scratch, too, to hit the right spot on greens which readily cast off any mis-hit approach shots. Technical and tactical, lovely to walk but not so easy to score on, this is one of Harry Colt's vintage courses. Make it a whole day here at this very chic Club so you can play both courses.

Quand on trouve deux grands parcours dans le même golf, on a toujours une légère inclination. Que ceux qui ne pourraient jouer le "Old" ne soient pas déçus, le "New" est d'une qualité très comparable, certains excellents joueurs le préférant même. Si l'on fait abstraction d'un paysage moins charmeur, plus "viril," le New ne manque pas d'arguments. Il autorise des drives plus agressifs, mais le placement de la balle reste crucial : il faut éviter les bunkers de fairway (leurs rebords sont très hauts), une mare très dangereuse au 15, quelques fossés pernicieux, et avoir un excellent jeu de fers pour placer la balle en bonne position sur les greens, qui rejettent sans hésiter les balles un peu approximatives. Technique, tactique, très agréable à marcher, pas facile à scorer, c'est un des bons crus de son architecte Harry Colt. Prenez donc la journée pour jouer les deux parcours de ce club très chic.

Sunningdale Golf Club

Ridgemount Road
ENG - SUNNINGDALE, Berks SL5 9RW

Office	Secrétariat	(44) 01344 - 21 681
Pro shop	Pro-shop	(44) 01344 - 20 128
Fax	Fax	(44) 01344 - 24 154
Situation	Situation	

10 km from Windsor (pop. 30 136)
5 km from Ascot (pop. 150 244)

Annual closure	Fermeture annnuelle	no
Weekly closure	Fermeture hebdomadaire	no
Fees main season	Tarifs haute saison	full day

	Week days Semaine	We/Bank holidays We/Férié
Individual Individuel	£ 100	—
Couple Couple	£ 200	—

Visitors from Monday to Thursday -
Prior booking essential

Caddy	Caddy	on request/£ 25
Electric Trolley	Chariot électrique	no
Buggy	Voiturette	no
Clubs	Clubs	no
Credit cards Cartes de crédit		VISA - MasterCard

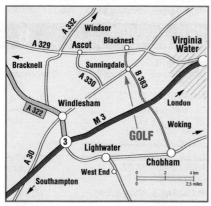

Access Accès : London, A30. 1st left after Sunningdale level crossing. Club 300 m on left.
Map 8 on page 420 Carte 8 Page 420

GOLF COURSE
PARCOURS
18/20

Site	Site	
Maintenance	Entretien	
Architect	Architecte	Harry S. Colt
Type	Type	forest, heathland
Relief	Relief	
Water in play	Eau en jeu	
Exp. to wind	Exposé au vent	
Trees in play	Arbres en jeu	

Scorecard Carte de score	Chp. Chp.	Mens Mess.	Ladies Da.
Length Long.	5955	5798	5256
Par	71	71	74

Advised golfing ability Niveau de jeu recommandé		0 12 24 36
Hcp required	Handicap exigé	18 Men, 24 Ladies

CLUB HOUSE & AMENITIES
CLUB HOUSE ET ANNEXES
8/10

Pro shop	Pro-shop	
Driving range	Practice	
Sheltered	couvert	no
On grass	sur herbe	yes
Putting-green	putting-green	yes
Pitching-green	pitching green	yes

HOTEL FACILITIES
ENVIRONNEMENT HOTELIER
8/10

HOTELS HÔTELS
Berystede - 90 rooms, D £ 120 — Sunninghill
Tel (44) 01344 - 23 311 — 1 km
Fax (44) 01344 - 872 301

Cricketers - 27 rooms, D £ 40 — Bagshot
Tel (44) 01276 - 473 196 — 3 km
Fax (44) 01276 - 451 357

Oakley Court - 91 rooms, D £ 150 — Windsor
Tel (44) 01753 - 609 988 — 12 km
Fax (44) 01628 - 37 011

RESTAURANTS RESTAURANTS
Stateroom (Royal Berkshire Hotel) — Sunninghill
Tel (44) 01344 - 23 322 — 1 km

Ciao Ninety - Tel (44) 01344 - 22 285 — Ascot 3 km

Jade Fountain — Sunninghill
Tel (44) 01344 - 27 070 — 1 km

556

This is one of those courses where the impression of space unfolding before you is as inviting as it is deceptive. In a magnificent setting, the trees are a sight to behold and are enhanced by heather which has invaded all the rough. When in flower it all looks wonderful, although you might wish you'd never set eyes on it when trying to hack your ball back onto the fairway. Laid out on ideal sandy soil, Sunningdale may lack yardage but is still a model of course design. This is one of Willie Park's masterpieces, such is the need for accuracy and inspiration, for a constant choice of tactics and for control over the full panoply of shots, particularly near the greens. But on a fine day when the ball rolls and rolls and when the greens are at their sublime best, scores can be flattering. This "Old Lady" has boundless charm and appeal.

C'est l'un des parcours où l'impression d'espace devant soi invite au jeu, mais elle peut être aussi trompeuse que la séduction du lieu. Les arbres sont un spectacle, mis en valeur par la bruyère qui envahit tous les roughs, magnifique quand elle prend ses couleurs, impossible quand il faut en déloger sa balle. Construit sur cette terre sablonneuse qui fait de si bons golfs, Sunningdale manque peut-être de longueur, mais reste un modèle d'architecture, et l'un des chefs-d'oeuvre de Willie Park, tant il réclame de précision et d'inspiration, tant il offre constamment des choix tactiques, tant il oblige à disposer de la gamme complète des coups de golf, notamment au petit jeu. Mais en un beau jour d'été où les balles n'en finissent pas de rouler, et où les greens sont à leur sommet, les scores peuvent être flatteurs. Cette "Old Lady" sait toujours se laisser séduire.

Sunningdale Golf Club

Ridgemount Road
ENG - SUNNINGDALE, Berks SL5 9RW

Office	Secrétariat	(44) 01344 - 21 681
Pro shop	Pro-shop	(44) 01344 - 20 128
Fax	Fax	(44) 01344 - 24 154
Situation	Situation	

10 km from Windsor (pop. 30 136)
5 km from Ascot (pop. 150 244)

Annual closure	Fermeture annnuelle	no
Weekly closure	Fermeture hebdomadaire	no
Fees main season	Tarifs haute saison	full day

	Week days Semaine	We/Bank holidays We/Férié
Individual Individuel	£ 100	—
Couple Couple	£ 200	—

Visitors: Monday-Thursday only -
Prior booking essential

Caddy	Caddy	on request/£ 25
Electric Trolley	Chariot électrique	no
Buggy	Voiturette	no
Clubs	Clubs	no
Credit cards Cartes de crédit		VISA - MasterCard

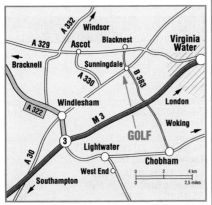

Access Accès : London, A30. 1st left after Sunningdale level crossing. Club 300 m on left.
Map 8 on page 420 Carte 8 Page 420

GOLF COURSE / PARCOURS

18/20

Site	Site	
Maintenance	Entretien	
Architect	Architecte	Willie Park
Type	Type	forest, heathland
Relief	Relief	
Water in play	Eau en jeu	
Exp. to wind	Exposé au vent	
Trees in play	Arbres en jeu	

Scorecard Carte de score	Chp. Chp.	Mens Mess.	Ladies Da.
Length Long.	5948	5707	5242
Par	72	70	74

Advised golfing ability	0 12 24 36	
Niveau de jeu recommandé		
Hcp required Handicap exigé	18 Men, 24 Ladies	

CLUB HOUSE & AMENITIES / CLUB HOUSE ET ANNEXES

8/10

Pro shop	Pro-shop	
Driving range	Practice	
Sheltered	couvert	no
On grass	sur herbe	yes
Putting-green	putting-green	yes
Pitching-green	pitching green	yes

557

HOTEL FACILITIES / ENVIRONNEMENT HOTELIER

8/10

HOTELS HÔTELS

Berystede - 90 rooms, D £ 120 Tel (44) 01344 - 23 311 Fax (44) 01344 - 872 301	Sunninghill 1 km
Cricketers - 27 rooms, D £ 40 Tel (44) 01276 - 473 196 Fax (44) 01276 - 451 357	Bagshot 3 km
Oakley Court - 91 rooms, D £ 150 Tel (44) 01753 - 609 988 Fax (44) 01628 - 37 011	Windsor 12 km

RESTAURANTS RESTAURANTS

Stateroom (Royal Berkshire Hotel) Tel (44) 01344 - 23 322	Sunninghill 1 km
Ciao Ninety - Tel (44) 01344 - 22 285	Ascot 3 km
Jade Fountain Tel (44) 01344 - 27 070	Sunninghill 1 km

A little road leads you one of England's prettiest clubhouses in pure Tudor style. The actual course offers not only some wonderful views over Surrey, Sussex and Kent, but also an exhilarating sensation of open space where most of the tee-boxes are elevated and give a very clear idea of the strategy required. The downside to this hilly landscape is that the course is tiring to walk over the last 9 holes. Tandridge is a rather short course and the wide fairways are an invitation to use your driver, but a few bushes, trees and sometimes very thick rough severely penalise wayward hitting. When approaching the greens, watch out for the bunkers, which are placed well forward. The result is an optical illusion which makes club selection more difficult than usual. The members' favourite hole here is the 14th, where you drive into a valley before hitting your approach shot up the hill towards a very well protected green. Tandridge is a model of simplicity and intelligence, Harry Colt style.

Une petite route vous mène à l'un des plus jolis Clubhouses d'Angleterre, en style Tudor. Le parcours offre non seulement des vues imprenables sur le Surrey, le Sussex et le Kent, mais aussi un sentiment d'espace tout à fait exaltant, car la plupart des départs sont ici en hauteur, donnant une idée très claire de la stratégie. Mais ce relief a l'inconvénient d'être un peu fatigant sur les neuf derniers trous. Tandridge est assez court, et la largeur des fairways permet de sortir souvent le driver, mais quelques buissons, les arbres et un rough parfois dense peuvent punir sévèrement les coups lâchés. A l'approche des greens, il faut remarquer les bunkers placés très en avant, rendant la sélection des clubs difficile en raison des illusions d'optique. Le trou favori des membres est ici le 14, où l'on drive dans une vallée pour remonter ensuite vers un green très défendu : c'est un modèle de simplicité et d'intelligence "à la Colt."

Tandridge Golf Club
ENG - OXTED, Surrey RH8 9NQ

Office	Secrétariat	(44) 01883 - 712274
Pro shop	Pro-shop	(44) 01883 - 713701
Fax	Fax	(44) 01883 - 730537
Situation	Situation	

10 km E of Reigate (pop. 52 007)
30 km from Central London (pop. 6 679 700)

Annual closure	Fermeture annnuelle	no
Weekly closure	Fermeture hebdomadaire	no
Fees main season	Tarifs haute saison	18 holes

	Week days Semaine	We/Bank holidays We/Férié
Individual Individuel	£ 45*	—
Couple Couple	£ 90*	—

* Restricted to Monday, Wednesday and Thursday (please call in advance)

Caddy	Caddy	no
Electric Trolley	Chariot électrique	no
Buggy	Voiturette	no
Clubs	Clubs	£ 5/18 holes

Credit cards Cartes de crédit
VISA - Eurocard - MasterCard - AMEX - DC (Pro-shop only)

558

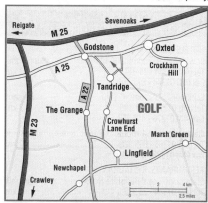

Access Accès : M 25 Jct 7. A22 South → East Grinstead. Left on A25 → Oxted. Golf Club 1.5 km (1 m) on the right. Map 8 on page 421 Carte 8 Page 421

GOLF COURSE
PARCOURS 14/20

Site	Site	
Maintenance	Entretien	
Architect	Architecte	Harry S. Colt
Type	Type	parkland
Relief	Relief	
Water in play	Eau en jeu	
Exp. to wind	Exposé au vent	
Trees in play	Arbres en jeu	

Scorecard Carte de score	Chp. Chp.	Mens Mess.	Ladies Da.
Length Long.	5625	5270	4877
Par	70	68	71

Advised golfing ability	0	12	24	36
Niveau de jeu recommandé				
Hcp required Handicap exigé	certificate			

CLUB HOUSE & AMENITIES
CLUB HOUSE ET ANNEXES 7/10

Pro shop	Pro-shop	
Driving range	Practice	
Sheltered	couvert	2 nets
On grass	sur herbe	yes
Putting-green	putting-green	yes
Pitching-green	pitching green	yes

HOTEL FACILITIES
ENVIRONNEMENT HOTELIER 6/10

HOTELS HÔTELS
Kings Arms - 16 rooms, D £ 75 — Westerham, 8 km
Tel (44) 01959 - 562 990
Fax (44) 01959 - 561 240

Bridge House - 37 rooms, D £ 75 — Reigate, 10 km
Tel (44) 01737 - 246 801
Fax (44) 01737 - 223 756

Cranleigh - 9 rooms, D £ 75 — Reigate, 10 km
Tel (44) 01737 - 223 417
Fax (44) 01737 - 223 734

RESTAURANTS RESTAURANTS
The Dining Room — Reigate, 10 km
Tel (44) 01737 - 226 650

The George Inn — Oxted, 2 km

THETFORD

| 14 | 7 | 5 |

Between the pretty Georgian town of Swaffham, the national stud-farm of Newmarket, the Neolithic site of Grimes Graves and the beautiful medieval town of Norwich, you might find the time to play this 1912 course which was restyled and lengthened by Donald Steel in 1985. A pity perhaps that the fairways are so wide, but they do prompt the bigger-hitters to open their shoulders and dispatch their ball into the waiting fairway bunkers. There are trees, of course, but not all that close to the fairways. When they do come close, it is to complicate your second shot. Very pretty, calm, well-balanced and with pleasant springy turf over sandy sub-soil, Thetford is not the course of the century but it does enable golfers of all levels to play together very easily. For the less experienced player, however, we would shamelessly recommend the front tees.

Entre les visites de la jolie ville georgienne de Swaffham, du haras national de Newmarket, du site néolithique de Grimes Graves et de la belle ville médiévale de Norwich, il vous restera probablement quelques heures pour jouer ce parcours de 1912, mais remodelé et allongé par Donald Steel en 1985. On regrette que les fairways soient très larges, mais ils incitent les frappeurs à se déchaîner... et à expédier leurs balles dans les bunkers de fairway ! Certes, on trouve aussi des arbres, mais ils ne sont pas très proches des fairways, et quand ils le sont, c'est plutôt pour gêner les seconds coups. Très joli, très calme, bien équilibré, avec un gazon très agréable sur un sol de sable et de tourbe, Thetford n'est pas le parcours du siècle, mais il permet au moins à tous les niveaux d'évoluer en bonne harmonie. On conseillera cependant aux joueurs peu expérimentés de choisir sans honte les départs avancés.

Thetford Golf Club

Brandon Road
ENG - THETFORD, Norfolk IP24 3NE

Office	Secrétariat	(44) 01842 - 752258
Pro shop	Pro-shop	(44) 01842 - 752662
Fax	Fax	
Situation	Situation	

2 km from Thetford (pop. 19 900)
50 km from Cambridge (pop. 91 935)

Annual closure	Fermeture annnuelle	no
Weekly closure	Fermeture hebdomadaire	no
Fees main season	Tarifs haute saison	full day

	Week days Semaine	We/Bank holidays We/Férié
Individual Individuel	£ 32	—
Couple Couple	£ 64	—

No visitors during weekends & public holidays
Booking essential

Caddy	Caddy	no
Electric Trolley	Chariot électrique	no
Buggy	Voiturette	no
Clubs	Clubs	no

Credit cards Cartes de crédit — no

KING'S LYNN

NORWICH

Brandon

THETFORD
FOREST PARK

GOLF

THETFORD

Bury
St-Edmunds

Access Accès : London M11. Jct 9, A11 → Norwich.
Thetford Bypass B1107 → Brandon, Golf 500 m
on the left. **Map 7 on page 419** Carte 7 Page 419

GOLF COURSE
PARCOURS

14/20

Site	Site	■■■■□
Maintenance	Entretien	■■■■□
Architect	Architecte	C.H. Mayo Donald Steel,1985
Type	Type	inland, forest
Relief	Relief	□□□□□
Water in play	Eau en jeu	□□□□□
Exp. to wind	Exposé au vent	■■■□□
Trees in play	Arbres en jeu	■■■□□

Scorecard Carte de score	Chp. Chp.	Mens Mess.	Ladies Da.
Length Long.	6190	5970	5405
Par	72	72	74

Advised golfing ability		0	12	24	36
Niveau de jeu recommandé				■■■	
Hcp required	Handicap exigé	no			

CLUB HOUSE & AMENITIES
CLUB HOUSE ET ANNEXES

7/10

Pro shop	Pro-shop	■■■■□
Driving range	Practice	■■■□□
Sheltered	couvert	no
On grass	sur herbe	yes
Putting-green	putting-green	yes

HOTEL FACILITIES
ENVIRONNEMENT HOTELIER

5/10

HOTELS HÔTELS
Bell Hotel - 46 rooms, D £ 70 — Thetford / 2 km
Tel (44) 01842 - 754 455
Fax (44) 01842 - 755 552

Strattons - 7 rooms, D £ 78 — Swaffham / 25 km
Tel (44) 01760 - 723 845
Fax (44) 01760 - 720 458

Angel - 41 rooms, D £ 90 — Bury St Edmunds / 20 km
Tel (44) 01284 - 753 926
Fax (44) 01284 - 750 092

RESTAURANTS RESTAURANTS
Mortimer's — Bury St Edmunds / 20 km
Tél (44) 01284 - 760623

Strattons - Tel (44) 01760 - 723845 — Swaffham 25 km

Theobalds — Ixworth / 17 km
Tel (44) 01359 - 231707

559

Essex is not really a golfing county like Surrey, for example, on the other side of London. But some of the courses here do stand out, like this one, laid out in 1920 over a former hunting estate which sports a gigantic neo-classical mansion where everyone seems to speak in whispered tones. The clubhouse is more modern and less imposing, but jacket and tie are required. This is one course of the hundreds designed by Harry Colt, as intelligent in its layout, as imaginative in its use of the land and as fair and open as the others. When you realise how few technical resources they had at the time (1920), it makes you think how much many modern designers could learn from this style of layout. Of course, like many British courses from another age, this one lacks length but the vast majority of players won't complain. A course for everyone, even the best.

L'Essex n'est pas vraiment une région à golf comme peut l'être le Surrey par exemple, de l'autre côté de Londres. Mais quelques parcours se distinguent comme celui-ci, créé en 1920 dans un ancien domaine de chasse orné d'une gigantesque bâtisse néo-classique que l'on dénomme "mansion," et dans laquelle on doit parler à voix basse. Le Clubhouse est plus moderne, moins imposant, mais on y porte veste et cravate. C'est un parcours parmi les centaines créés par Harry Colt, aussi intelligent dans son déroulement, imaginatif dans son utilisation du terrain, aussi franc et honnête que les autres. Quand on imagine le manque de moyens techniques à l'époque (1920), bien des architectes modernes devraient y prendre des leçons. Bien sûr, comme la plupart des parcours britanniques d'autrefois, il manque de longueur, mais l'immense majorité des joueurs ne s'en plaindra pas. Pour tous, même les meilleurs.

Thorndon Park Golf Club

Ingrave
ENG - BRENTWOOD, Essex CM13 3RH

Office	Secrétariat	(44) 01277 - 811666
Pro shop	Pro-shop	(44) 01277 - 810736
Fax	Fax	
Situation	Situation	

3 km from Brentwood (pop. 70 600)
35 km from Central London (pop. 6 679 700)

Annual closure	Fermeture annnuelle	no
Weekly closure	Fermeture hebdomadaire	no
Fees main season	Tarifs haute saison	18 holes

	Week days Semaine	We/Bank holidays We/Férié
Individual Individuel	£ 30	—
Couple Couple	£ 60	—

Booking essential - No visitors at weekends

Caddy	Caddy	no
Electric Trolley	Chariot électrique	no
Buggy	Voiturette	no
Clubs	Clubs	no

Credit cards Cartes de crédit	no

560

Access Accès : London E, A11 then A12 to Brentwood.
A 128 SE → East Horndon. Golf on the right.
Map 7 on page 419 Carte 7 Page 419

GOLF COURSE
PARCOURS
14/20

Site	Site	■■■■■□□□□□
Maintenance	Entretien	■■■■■■□□□□
Architect	Architecte	Harry S. Colt
Type	Type	parkland, inland
Relief	Relief	■■■□□□□□□□
Water in play	Eau en jeu	■■□□□□□□□□
Exp. to wind	Exposé au vent	■■□□□□□□□□
Trees in play	Arbres en jeu	■■■■■■□□□□

Scorecard Carte de score	Chp. Chp.	Mens Mess.	Ladies Da.
Length Long.	5845	5620	4580
Par	71	71	72

Advised golfing ability Niveau de jeu recommandé	0	12	24	36
		■■■■■□□		

Hcp required	Handicap exigé	certificate

CLUB HOUSE & AMENITIES
CLUB HOUSE ET ANNEXES
7/10

Pro shop	Pro-shop	■■■■■■■□□□
Driving range	Practice	■■■■■□□□□□
Sheltered	couvert	no
On grass	sur herbe	yes
Putting-green	putting-green	yes
Pitching-green	pitching green	no

HOTEL FACILITIES
ENVIRONNEMENT HOTELIER
6/10

HOTELS HÔTELS

Forte Posthouse - 113 rooms, D £ 69   Brentwood
Tel (44) 01277 - 260 260   5 km
Fax (44) 01277 - 264 264

Marygreen Manor - 32 rooms, D £ 110   Brentwood
Tel (44) 01277 - 225 252   6 km
Fax (44) 01277 - 262 809

Forte Travelodge - 22 rooms, D £ 35   East Horndon
Tél (44) 01277 - 810 819   4 km

Ivy Hill - 34 rooms, D £ 85   Ingatestone
Tel (44) 01277 - 353 040   12 km
Fax (44) 01277 - 355 038

RESTAURANTS RESTAURANTS

Marygreen Manor   Brentwood 6 km
Tel (44) 01277 - 225 252

Forte Posthouse - Tel (44) 01277 - 260 260   Brentwood

Thorpeness is just outside Aldeburgh, not far from Minsmere nature reserve in Dunwich, where you can watch an incredible variety of birds. The hotel-clubhouse is excellent and makes this a fine destination, especially since there is an abundance of good courses round and about (Ipswich, Aldeburgh, Woodbridge, Felixstowe Ferry, etc.). This one was initially designed in 1923 by James Braid and slightly re-shaped in 1965. Here, you keep out of the heather and avoid the lupins, very pretty when in flower but not the ideal place to put your ball. An uncomplicated layout, prepared to make life easier for the average golfer, but one which requires good placing of the ball, so don't think twice about playing an iron off the tee (except perhaps for the half a dozen long par 4s). Other landmarks to cap a very pleasant day's golfing are a wind-mill, a curious "house in the clouds" and an unsightly nuclear power station in the distance.

Thorpeness est juste à l'extérieur d'Aldeburgh, non loin de la réserve naturelle de Minsmere à Dunwich, d'où l'on peut observer une incroyable variété d'oiseaux. L'Hôtel-Clubhouse est de grande qualité, ce qui en fait une destination tout à fait agréable, d'autant que les bons parcours alentour ne manquent pas (Ipswich, Aldeburgh, Woodbridge, Felixstowe Ferry...). Celui-ci a été dessiné par James Braid en 1923, et légèrement retouché vers 1965. On veillera à éviter les bruyères et les buissons de lupin, très jolis en fleur, mais dont il vaut mieux ne pas s'approcher avec une balle de golf. Ce tracé sans histoires, préparé pour faciliter les choses, nécessite avant tout un bon placement : il ne faut pas hésiter à jouer des fers au départ, sauf sur la demi-douzaine de longs par 4. Pour décorer une très agréable journée, un moulin à vent, un curieuse "maison dans les nuages," et une centrale nucléaire au loin, pas bien belle.

Thorpeness Golf Club
ENG - THORPENESS, Suffolk IP16 4NH

Office	Secrétariat	(44) 01728 - 452176
Pro shop	Pro-shop	(44) 01728 - 454926
Fax	Fax	(44) 01728 - 453869
Situation	Situation	

3 km from Aldeburgh (pop. 2 654)
39 km from Ipswich (pop. 130 157)

Annual closure	Fermeture annnuelle	no
Weekly closure	Fermeture hebdomadaire	no
Fees main season	Tarifs haute saison	18 holes

	Week days Semaine	We/Bank holidays We/Férié
Individual Individuel	£ 25	£ 30
Couple Couple	£ 50	£ 60

Under 18: £ 15 (full day) - After 3.00 pm £ 15/£ 18

Caddy	Caddy	no
Electric Trolley	Chariot électrique	£ 5/18 holes
Buggy	Voiturette	£ 30/18 holes
Clubs	Clubs	no

Credit cards Cartes de crédit
VISA - MasterCard

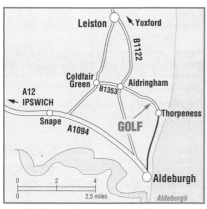

Access Accès : Ipswich A12 → Saxmundham.
Turn right on B119 → Leiston. At Leiston, turn right on B1353 **Map 7 on page 419** Carte 7 Page 419

GOLF COURSE
PARCOURS

14/20

Site	Site	▬▬▬▬
Maintenance	Entretien	▬▬▬▬
Architect	Architecte	James Braid
Type	Type	seaside course, open country
Relief	Relief	▬
Water in play	Eau en jeu	▬▬▬
Exp. to wind	Exposé au vent	▬▬▬▬
Trees in play	Arbres en jeu	▬▬▬

Scorecard Carte de score	Chp. Chp.	Mens Mess.	Ladies Da.
Length Long.	5645	5674	4922
Par	69	69	74

Advised golfing ability Niveau de jeu recommandé	0	12	24	36

Hcp required   Handicap exigé   certificate

CLUB HOUSE & AMENITIES
CLUB HOUSE ET ANNEXES

7/10

Pro shop	Pro-shop	▬▬▬
Driving range	Practice	▬▬
Sheltered	couvert	no
On grass	sur herbe	yes
Putting-green	putting-green	yes
Pitching-green	pitching green	yes

HOTEL FACILITIES
ENVIRONNEMENT HOTELIER

7/10

HOTELS HÔTELS

Thorpeness GC Hotel — Thorpeness
20 rooms, D £ 15 (GF incl.) — on site
Tel (44) 01728 - 452 176, Fax (44) 01728 - 453 868

Wentworth Hotel — Aldeburgh
38 rooms, D £ 70 — 4 km
Tel (44) 01728 - 452 312, Fax (44) 01728 - 454 343

Brudenell — Aldeburgh
47 rooms, D £ 90 — 4 km
Tel (44) 01728 - 452 071, Fax (44) 01728 - 454 082

RESTAURANTS RESTAURANTS

Thorpeness GC Hotel — Thorpeness
Tel (44) 01728 - 452176 — on site

New Regatta — Aldeburgh
Tel (44) 01728 - 452011 — 4 km

561

This is a magnificent spot where you savour every moment along a rugged coastline with rocky cliffs and pounding waves. This course is beside the sea, but most of the holes are pretty high up. Only the dunes are missing to make this a text-book links course, although the sandy soil is just right and the layout well worthy of the label. After much hesitation, the original short 9 hole course was happily extended and altered by Harry Colt; the back 9 are 1,000 yards longer than the front 9 and have added a good deal of zip to the course. The first seven holes are short, rather treacherous and very technical in style, while the remainder are longer and more open but still to be played with care and caution when the wind blows. In windy weather, punchers of the ball will have fun while the others can always divide their score by two or else admire the landscape and visit the region.

C'est un magnifique endroit à savourer chaque instant le long d'une côte tourmentée, avec d'impressionnantes fa-laises où la mer livre ses assauts. Ce parcours est situé en bordure de mer, mais la plupart des trous sont bien en hauteur. Il ne manque que les dunes pour en faire un links comme dans les livres, mais le sol sablonneux a la qua-lité requise, et le dessin est à la hauteur. Après bien des hésitations, le petit 9 trous initial fut heureusement modi-fié et agrandi par Harry Colt : le retour est près de 1000 mètres plus long que l'aller et a donné de la vigueur au tracé. Les sept premiers trous sont courts, assez traîtres et très techniques, les suivants plus longs et ouverts, à négocier avec attention et prudence quand le vent souffle. Les "puncheurs" de balles pourront alors s'y régaler, les autres diviseront leur score par deux, à moins de se contenter d'admirer le paysage ou de visiter la région.

Thurlestone Golf Club

Thurlestone
ENG - KINGSBRIDGE, S. Devon TQ7 3NZ

Office	Secrétariat	(44) 01548 - 560 405
Pro shop	Pro-shop	(44) 01548 - 560 715
Fax	Fax	(44) 01548 - 560 405
Situation	Situation	

6 km W of Kingsbridge (pop. 5 081)
8 km W of Salcombe (pop. 2 189)

Annual closure	Fermeture annnuelle	no
Weekly closure	Fermeture hebdomadaire	no
Fees main season	Tarifs haute saison	full day

	Week days Semaine	We/Bank holidays We/Férié
Individual Individuel	£ 26	£ 26
Couple Couple	£ 52	£ 52
£ 13 under 17 years		

Caddy	Caddy	no
Electric Trolley	Chariot électrique	£ 10/day
Buggy	Voiturette	no
Clubs	Clubs	£ 10/day
Credit cards Cartes de crédit		no

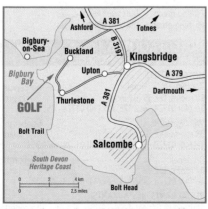

Access Accès : M5, then A38, A382 to Newton Abbott, then A381 through Totens and Kingsbridge. In Sutton, → South Milton and Thurlestone. Follow signs.
Map 6 on page 416 Carte 6 Page 416

GOLF COURSE
PARCOURS

16/20

Site	Site	
Maintenance	Entretien	
Architect	Architecte	Harry S. Colt
Type	Type	seaside course, open country
Relief	Relief	
Water in play	Eau en jeu	
Exp. to wind	Exposé au vent	
Trees in play	Arbres en jeu	

Scorecard Carte de score	Chp. Chp.	Mens Mess.	Ladies Da.
Length Long.	5770	5626	5086
Par	71	71	73

Advised golfing ability		0 12 24 36
Niveau de jeu recommandé		
Hcp required	Handicap exigé	28 Men, 36 Ladies

CLUB HOUSE & AMENITIES
CLUB HOUSE ET ANNEXES

6/10

Pro shop	Pro-shop	
Driving range	Practice	
Sheltered	couvert	no
On grass	sur herbe	yes
Putting-green	putting-green	yes
Pitching-green	pitching green	yes

HOTEL FACILITIES
ENVIRONNEMENT HOTELIER

4/10

HOTELS HÔTELS
Thurlestone Hotel · Thurlestone
68 rooms, D £ 90 · close
Tel (44) 01548 - 560 382
Fax (44) 01548 - 561 069

Henley · Bigbury-on-Sea
7 rooms, D £ 80 (dinner inc.)
Tel (44) 01548 - 810 240
Fax (44) 01548 - 810 020

RESTAURANT RESTAURANT
Church House · Churchstow
Tel (44) 01548 - 852 237 · 6 km

With tighter fairways and rough as wild as the tops of the dunes, Trevose would be much more difficult. But this is first and foremost a holiday location, where regular golfers return each year with their children. The kids eventually get to play the "big»"18-hole course after cutting their teeth on the two 9-holers. Spectacular, charming and technical, Trevose is a course for golfers of all levels where the best players will never grow tired. This Harry Colt layout is highly strategic and very honest, even though not all the hazards are visible, but there are seldom any really unpleasant surprises. They say that a friendly atmosphere adds to the pleasure of playing golf, and that is certainly true here, even with the wind. And that King Arthur met Merlin the Wizard nearby. It might even have been over a meal in the clubhouse, because the food is excellent.

Avec des fairways plus étroits, un rough aussi sauvage que les sommets des dunes, Trevose serait bien plus diffi-cile encore. Mais c'est d'abord un lieu de vacances, où les habitués reviennent chaque année, avec les enfants qui finissent un jour par passer au "grand" 18 trous après avoir débuté et pris de l'expérience sur les deux 9 trous. Spectaculaire, plein de charme, technique, Trevose est un parcours pour tous les niveaux, où les meilleurs ne s'ennuient jamais. Le dessin de Harry Colt est très stratégique et très franc, même si les obstacles ne sont pas tous bien visibles, mais on a rarement de mauvaises surprises. On dit qu'une atmosphère amicale contribue au plaisir du jeu, c'est bien le cas ici, même avec le vent. Le Roi Arthur aurait rencontré l'Enchanteur Merlin dans les environs, c'était peut-être ici au Clubhouse, car les repas sont excellents.

Trevose Golf & Country Club
Constantine Bay
ENG - PADSTOW, Cornwall PL28 8J13

Office	Secrétariat	(44) 01841 - 520 208
Pro shop	Pro-shop	(44) 01841 - 520 261
Fax	Fax	(44) 01841 - 521 057
Situation	Situation	

6 km from Padstow (pop. 4 250)

Annual closure	Fermeture annnuelle	no
Weekly closure	Fermeture hebdomadaire	no

Fees main season
Tarifs haute saison

	Week days Semaine	We/Bank holidays We/Férié
Individual Individuel	£ 33	£ 33
Couple Couple	£ 66	£ 66

low season, £ 22 / mid-season, £ 28

Caddy	Caddy	no
Electric Trolley	Chariot électrique	£ 5/18 holes
Buggy	Voiturette	£ 17/18 holes
Clubs	Clubs	no

Credit cards Cartes de crédit
VISA - Eurocard - MasterCard

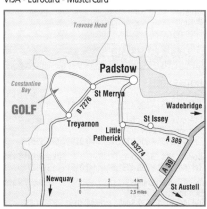

Trevose Head

GOLF

Padstow

Constantine Bay

St Merryn

B 3276

Treyarnon

Little Petherick

B3274

Wadebridge

St Issey

A 389

A 39

Newquay

0 — 2 — 4 km
0 — 2,5 miles

St Austell

Access Accès : M5 Exit 31, then A30 (→ Exeter) through Bodwin, then B3274 on right after Victoria → Padstow. → St Merryn. Follow signs to golf.
Map 6 on page 416 Carte 6 Page 416

GOLF COURSE / PARCOURS — 17/20

Site	Site	■■■■■■
Maintenance	Entretien	■■■■■■
Architect	Architecte	Harry S. Colt
Type	Type	seaside course, links
Relief	Relief	■■■
Water in play	Eau en jeu	■■■■
Exp. to wind	Exposé au vent	■■■■■■
Trees in play	Arbres en jeu	■

Scorecard Carte de score	Chp. Chp.	Mens Mess.	Ladies Da.
Length Long.	5947	5792	5142
Par	71	71	73

Advised golfing ability Niveau de jeu recommandé	0	12	24	36

Hcp required Handicap exigé   28 Men, 36 Ladies

CLUB HOUSE & AMENITIES / CLUB HOUSE ET ANNEXES — 7/10

Pro shop	Pro-shop	■■■■
Driving range	Practice	■■■
Sheltered	couvert	no
On grass	sur herbe	yes
Putting-green	putting-green	yes
Pitching-green	pitching green	yes

563

HOTEL FACILITIES / ENVIRONNEMENT HOTELIER — 7/10

HOTELS HÔTELS

Treglos   Constantine Bay
41 rooms, D £ 65   1 km
Tel (44) 01841 - 520 727
Fax (44) 01841 - 521 163

Metropole   Padstow
44 rooms, D £ 100   5 km
Tel (44) 01841 - 532 486
Fax (44) 01841 - 532 867

RESTAURANTS RESTAURANTS

Seafood   Padstow
Tel (44) 01841 - 532 485   5 km

St Petroc's Bistro   Padstow
Tel (44) 01841 - 532 700   5 km

What with coastal erosion having washed away three of the original holes and the problems of ownership which caused some bad blood and the need to borrow less favourable terrain, the course has evolved considerably since its creation. Today, everything seems to have settled down. Laid out on more hilly landscape than its (near) neighbour Royal Liverpool, Wallasey requires a lot of serious thought as to where to place your drive in order to attack the greens from the best position and keep well away from the dunes, bushes and fairway bunkers (few in number but the penalty is always high). With that said, the pleasure you get from hitting good recovery shots on this sort of course is such that you might almost stray off the straight and narrow deliberately in order to add to your fond memories. So try match-play, or even the stableford points system, whose homonymous inventor came from Wallasey and certainly knew a thing or two about the problems of counting a score once you reach a certain number.

L'érosion de la côte ayant supprimé trois des trous originaux, des problèmes de propriété ayant empoisonné le club, le parcours a évolué depuis sa création, devant emprunter des terrains moins favorables, mais tout cela semble résolu. Dans un paysage plus mouvementé que celui de son (presque) voisin Royal Liverpool, Wallasey demande quelque réflexion sur le placement des drives afin d'attaquer les greens en bonne position, et ne pas se retrouver dans les dunes, les buissons, les bunkers de fairway - peu nombreux mais pénalisants. Cela dit, le plaisir de réussir les recoveries sur ce genre de parcours est tel que l'on pourrait presque faire exprès de s'égarer pour se fabriquer des souvenirs ! Alors, jouez en match-play, ou en stableford, l'inventeur de la formule qui porte son nom venait d'ici, il savait donc à quoi s'en tenir sur la difficulté de compter à partir d'un certain chiffre.

Wallasey Golf Club
Bayswater Road
ENG - WALLASEY, Cheshire L45 8LA

Office	Secrétariat	(44) 0151 - 6911024
Pro shop	Pro-shop	(44) 0151 - 6383888
Fax	Fax	(44) 0151 - 6911024
Situation	Situation	

5 km from Liverpool (pop. 452 450)

Annual closure	Fermeture annnuelle	no
Weekly closure	Fermeture hebdomadaire	no
Fees main season	Tarifs haute saison	18 holes

	Week days Semaine	We/Bank holidays We/Férié
Individual Individuel	£ 27	£ 32
Couple Couple	£ 54	£ 64

Full weekdays: £ 32/full weekend days: £ 37

Caddy	Caddy	on request/£ 25
Electric Trolley	Chariot électrique	no
Buggy	Voiturette	no
Clubs	Clubs	no

Credit cards Cartes de crédit
VISA - Eurocard - MasterCard - AMEX - DC

Access Accès : Liverpool, Wallasey tunnel to Jct 1.
Follow signs to New Brighton. Golf on A 551.
Map 5 on page 415 Carte 5 Page 415

GOLF COURSE
PARCOURS
17/20

Site	Site	
Maintenance	Entretien	
Architect	Architecte	Tom Morris/J. Braid Taylor/Hawtree...
Type	Type	seaside course, links
Relief	Relief	
Water in play	Eau en jeu	
Exp. to wind	Exposé au vent	
Trees in play	Arbres en jeu	

Scorecard	Chp.	Mens	Ladies
Carte de score	Chp.	Mess.	Da.
Length Long.	5946	5710	5241
Par	72	72	74

Advised golfing ability		0 12 24 36
Niveau de jeu recommandé		
Hcp required	Handicap exigé	certificate

CLUB HOUSE & AMENITIES
CLUB HOUSE ET ANNEXES
7/10

Pro shop	Pro-shop	
Driving range	Practice	
Sheltered	couvert	no
On grass	sur herbe	no
Putting-green	putting-green	yes
Pitching-green	pitching green	yes

HOTEL FACILITIES
ENVIRONNEMENT HOTELIER
7/10

HOTELS HOTELS
Grove Hotel - 14 rooms, D £ 50   Wallasey 2 km
Tel (44) 0151 - 630 4558, Fax (44) 0151 - 639 0028

Leasowe Castle Hotel   Moreton 2 km
22 rooms, D £ 66
Tel (44) 0151 - 606 9191, Fax (44) 0151 - 678 5551

Bowler Hat - 32 rooms, D £ 85   Birkenhead 3 km
Tel (44) 0151 - 652 4931, Fax (44) 0151 - 653 8127

Twelfth Man Lodge   Greasby 4 km
30 rooms, D £ 39
Tel (44) 0151 - 677 5445 , Fax (44) 0151 - 678 5085

RESTAURANTS RESTAURANTS
Grove Hotel - Tel (44) 0151 - 630 4558   Wallasey 2 km
Lee Ho - Tel (44) 0151 - 677 6440   Moreton 2 km

The history of Walton Heath is closely tied to politics, with many members being Ministers (including Winston Churchill in his younger days) or Peers. The Prince of Wales was club captain in 1935, but apparently that was not enough for the club to receive the royal seal. Soil and space are both ideal here, despite being so close to London, but sand and heather land were of no use to farmers in those days. The wind can be an important factor here, as the course is high up. There are trees, but they don't detract from a great feeling of open space, or relieve the anxiety as you eye the ubiquitous heather and wonder how on earth anyone could ever get out of there. It is especially dangerous on the 12th hole, where you need a long drive to have any hope of reaching a very well-protected green. Although this "New" course is not easy, the members will tell you that it is two shots easier than its "Old" neighbour. We suggest you check that out for yourself.

L' histoire de Walton Heath est étroitement liée à la politique, avec quantité de membres ministres, dont Winston Churchill, ou appartenant à la Chambre des Lords. Le Prince de Galles en a été capitaine en 1935, sans que le club en soit annobli pour autant. Les parcours ont eu un sol idéal, et de l'espace, même à proximité de Londres car les terres de sable et de bruyère étaient inutilisées pour l'agriculture. Le vent y est un facteur important, car nous sommes ici en hauteur. Malgré la présence des arbres, on éprouve une grande sensation d'espace, avec un soupçon d'inquiétude devant l'omniprésence de la bruyère, dont aucun traité ne vous enseigne comment en sortir. Elle est spécialement dangereuse au 12, où il faut un long drive pour espérer toucher le green très défendu. Bien que ce "New" ne soit pas facile, les membres vous diront qu'il est de deux coups plus facile que le "Old." A vérifier par vous-même !

Walton Heath Golf Club

Deans Lane, Walton-on-the-Hill
ENG - TADWORTH, Surrey, KT20 7TP

Office	Secrétariat	(44) 01737 - 812 380
Pro shop	Pro-shop	(44) 01737 - 812 152
Fax	Fax	(44) 01737 - 814 225
Situation	Situation	

7 km from Reigate (pop. 52 010)
5 km from Epsom (pop. 67007)

Annual closure	Fermeture annnuelle	no
Weekly closure	Fermeture hebdomadaire	no
Fees main season	Tarifs haute saison	full day

	Week days Semaine	We/Bank holidays We/Férié
Individual Individuel	£ 67	—
Couple Couple	£ 134	—

Weekends: visitors only with a member

Caddy	Caddy	on request/£ 20+tip
Electric Trolley	Chariot électrique	no
Buggy	Voiturette	no
Clubs	Clubs	£ 7.50/18 holes

Credit cards Cartes de crédit
VISA - Eurocard - MasterCard - AMEX - JCB

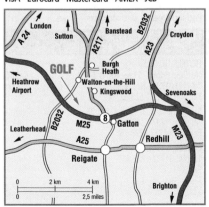

Access Accès : M25 Jct 8. A217 → Sutton. After 3 km (2 m.) B270 into Mill Lane, then left along B2032. Deans Lane on the right after 1.5 km (1 m.).
Map 8 on page 421 Carte 8 Page 421

GOLF COURSE PARCOURS 16/20

Site	Site	███████░░
Maintenance	Entretien	███████░░
Architect	Architecte	
Type	Type	inland, heathland
Relief	Relief	██░░░░░░░
Water in play	Eau en jeu	█░░░░░░░░
Exp. to wind	Exposé au vent	███████░░
Trees in play	Arbres en jeu	████░░░░░

Scorecard Carte de score	Chp. Chp.	Mens Mess.	Ladies Da.
Length Long.	5948	5643	5328
Par	72	72	74

Advised golfing ability		0 12 24 36
Niveau de jeu recommandé		████████░
Hcp required	Handicap exigé	certificate

CLUB HOUSE & AMENITIES CLUB HOUSE ET ANNEXES 7/10

Pro shop	Pro-shop	██████░░░
Driving range	Practice	██████░░░
Sheltered	couvert	2 indoor nets
On grass	sur herbe	yes
Putting-green	putting-green	yes
Pitching-green	pitching green	yes

565

HOTEL FACILITIES ENVIRONNEMENT HOTELIER 6/10

HOTELS HOTELS

Nutfield Priory - 52 rooms, D £ 120 Tel (44) 01737 - 822 066 Fax (44) 01737 - 823 321	Redhill 7 km
Bridge House - 37 rooms, D £ 75 Tel (44) 01737 - 246 801 Fax (44) 01737 - 223 756	Reigate 4 km
Cranleigh - 9 rooms, D £ 75 Tel (44) 01737 - 223 417 Fax (44) 01737 - 223 734	Reigate 7 km

RESTAURANTS RESTAURANTS

Gemini - Tel (44) 01737 - 812179	Tadworth 2 km
The Dining Room Tel (44) 01737 - 226 650	Reigate 7 km
La Barbe - Tel (44) 01737 - 241 966	Reigate 7 km

Herbert Fowler designed the courses for this club where James Braid was the first professional. He was here for 50 years and although his name does not figure anywhere, it would be hard to imagine him never having retouched the original layout here and there, or never having given others the benefit of his invaluable advice. With the soft turf, the layout and even the sensation of space, you might think yourself on a links course, if it weren't for the pine, birch and oak trees, and the heather. And when the wind blows (this is the highest spot in Surrey), the illusion is complete. The wide, deep bunkers are a feature you'll remember for many a month, as they outline the holes to perfection and attract any ball sailing slightly off course. The greens are well grassed, fast, fair and particularly well defended. A difficult course with its very own character, but every golfer will improve his game here as long as he remembers the one basic rule of golf... humility.

Herbert Fowler a dessiné les parcours de ce club dont James Braid a été le premier professionnel. Il y est resté pendant plus de 50 ans, et si son nom n'apparaît pas, on imagine mal qu'il n'ait jamais eu à retoucher çà et là le dessin original, ou à donner quelques précieux conseils. Par la qualité du gazon comme par le dessin ou même la sensation d'espace, on pourrait se croire sur un links, n'était la présence de pins, de bouleaux, de chênes et de bruyère. Et quand le vent souffle (c'est le plus haut point du Surrey), l'illusion est complète. Les bunkers larges et profonds sont un élément dont on se souvient, tant ils dessinent les trous à la perfection, tout en attirant les balles un peu trop écartées. Les greens sont bien fournis, rapides et francs, et surtout très défendus. C'est un parcours difficile, au caractère bien marqué, mais tous les joueurs y feront des progrès s'ils l'abordent avec modestie.

Walton Heath Golf Club

Deans Lane, Walton-on-the-Hill
ENG - TADWORTH, Surrey, KT20 7TP

Office	Secrétariat	(44) 01737 - 812 380
Pro shop	Pro-shop	(44) 01737 - 812 152
Fax	Fax	(44) 01737 - 814 225
Situation	Situation	

7 km from Reigate (pop. 52 010)
5 km from Epsom (pop. 67007)

Annual closure	Fermeture annnuelle	no
Weekly closure	Fermeture hebdomadaire	no
Fees main season	Tarifs haute saison	full day

	Week days Semaine	We/Bank holidays We/Férié
Individual Individuel	£ 67	—
Couple Couple	£ 134	—

Weekends: only with a member

Caddy	Caddy	on request/£ 20+tip
Electric Trolley	Chariot électrique	no
Buggy	Voiturette	no
Clubs	Clubs	£ 7.50/18 holes

Credit cards Cartes de crédit
VISA - Eurocard - MasterCard - AMEX - JCB

Access Accès : M25 Jct 8. A217 → Sutton. After 3 km (2 m.) B270 into Mill Lane, then left along B2032. Deans Lane on the right after 1.5 km (1 m.).
Map 8 on page 421 Carte 8 Page 421

GOLF COURSE PARCOURS

18/20

Site	Site	▬▬▬
Maintenance	Entretien	▬▬▬
Architect	Architecte	Herbert Fowler
Type	Type	inland, heathland
Relief	Relief	▬
Water in play	Eau en jeu	▬
Exp. to wind	Exposé au vent	▬▬
Trees in play	Arbres en jeu	▬▬

Scorecard Carte de score	Chp. Chp.	Mens Mess.	Ladies Da.
Length Long.	6121	5705	5346
Par	72	71	74

Advised golfing ability		0 12 24 36
Niveau de jeu recommandé		▬▬▬▬▬
Hcp required	Handicap exigé	certificate

CLUB HOUSE & AMENITIES CLUB HOUSE ET ANNEXES

7/10

Pro shop	Pro-shop	▬▬▬
Driving range	Practice	▬▬▬
Sheltered	couvert	2 indoor nets
On grass	sur herbe	yes
Putting-green	putting-green	yes
Pitching-green	pitching green	yes

HOTEL FACILITIES ENVIRONNEMENT HOTELIER

7/10

HOTELS HÔTELS

Nutfield Priory - 52 rooms, D £ 120 Tel (44) 01737 - 822 066 Fax (44) 01737 - 823 321		Redhill 7 km
Bridge House - 37 rooms, D £ 75 Tel (44) 01737 - 246 801 Fax (44) 01737 - 223 756		Reigate 4 km
Cranleigh - 9 rooms, D £ 75 Tel (44) 01737 - 223 417 Fax (44) 01737 - 223 734		Reigate 7 km

RESTAURANTS RESTAURANTS

Gemini Tel (44) 01737 - 812179	Tadworth 2 km
The Dining Room Tel (44) 01737 - 226 650	Reigate 7 km
La Barbe - Tel (44) 01737 - 241 966	Reigate 7 km

566

15	7	8

This is a complex of four inter-combinable nine-hole courses. The East and North courses are rather hilly, the South and West courses are simply sloping. Karl Litten's design is unashamedly American with a lot of dangerous water hazards (except on the North where there are more trees). Carefully placing your shots is important, and if you are an attacking player you should follow your instinct, as any hesitation can cost you dearly. The greens must be attacked with high shots, but when we visited they were very firm and so will surely cause problems for average-players. The length of each hole is such that we would suggest the forward tees for all except the very good player, and would recommend beginners to head for the pitch 'n putt course. With a very flexible combination of courses, spectacular golf and very modern facilities, this is a very well designed resort but not quite as hospitable as it could be. Our advice: rent a buggy and shoot 36 holes.

C'est un ensemble de quatre fois neuf trous combinables, l'Est et le Nord étant assez accidentés, le Sud et l'Ouest simplement ondulés. L'architecture de Karl Litten est américaine sans honte, avec beaucoup d'obstacles d'eau dangereux (sauf le Nord, plus arboré). Il est partout nécessaire de bien placer la balle, mais aussi d'attaquer sans réserves si on a ce caractère, car les hésitations ne pardonnent pas. Les greens doivent être attaqués comme des cibles, mais ils étaient très fermes lors de notre visite, ce qui ne facilitait pas la tâche des joueurs moyens. La longueur de chacun des neuf trous incite à ne recommander les départs arrière qu'aux très bons amateurs, et à conseiller aux presque débutants d'aller sur le parcours de par 3. Flexible dans ses combinaisons, spectaculaire, avec des équipements très modernes, c'est un ensemble très bien conçu, mais pas vraiment chaleureux. Notre conseil : 36 trous en voiturette.

The Warwickshire

Leek Wootton
ENG - WARWICK, Warwickshire CV35 7QT

Office	Secrétariat	(44) 01926 - 409409
Pro shop	Pro-shop	(44) 01926 - 409409
Fax	Fax	(44) 01926 - 408409
Situation	Situation	

5 km N of Warwick (pop. 22 709)
13 km S of Coventry (pop. 294 387)

Annual closure	Fermeture annnuelle	no
Weekly closure	Fermeture hebdomadaire	no
Fees main season	Tarifs haute saison	18 holes

	Week days Semaine	We/Bank holidays We/Férié
Individual Individuel	£ 40	£ 40
Couple Couple	£ 80	£ 80

Many golf packages for 36 holes, different fees in winter and summer

Caddy	Caddy	on request/£ 30
Electric Trolley	Chariot électrique	no
Buggy	Voiturette	£ 20/18 holes
Clubs	Clubs	£ 12.50/18 holes

Credit cards Cartes de crédit
VISA - Eurocard - MasterCard - AMEX

Access Accès : M40 Jct 15, then A46 → Coventry.
Follow signs to Leek Wootton (B4115).
Map 7 on page 418 Carte 7 Page 418

GOLF COURSE
PARCOURS

15/20

Site	Site	
Maintenance	Entretien	
Architect	Architecte	Karl Litten
Type	Type	parkland
Relief	Relief	
Water in play	Eau en jeu	
Exp. to wind	Exposé au vent	
Trees in play	Arbres en jeu	

Scorecard Carte de score	Chp. Chp.	Mens Mess.	Ladies Da.
Length Long.	6500	6000	5000
Par	72	72	72

Advised golfing ability Niveau de jeu recommandé	0	12	24	36

Hcp required	Handicap exigé	certificate

CLUB HOUSE & AMENITIES
CLUB HOUSE ET ANNEXES

7/10

Pro shop	Pro-shop	
Driving range	Practice	
Sheltered	couvert	10 bays
On grass	sur herbe	no
Putting-green	putting-green	yes
Pitching-green	pitching green	yes

HOTEL FACILITIES
ENVIRONNEMENT HOTELIER

8/10

HOTELS HÔTELS
Chesford Grange - 150 rooms, D £ 90   Kenilworth
Tel (44) 01926 - 859 331   3 km
Fax (44) 01926 - 859 075

De Montfort - 96 rooms, D £ 95   Kenilworth 4 km
Tel (44) 01926 - 855 944, Fax (44) 01926 - 857 830

Mallory Court   Royal Leamington Spa
10 chambres, D £ 200+   4 km
Tel (44) 01926 - 330 214, Fax (44) 01926 - 451 714

RESTAURANTS RESTAURANTS
Simpson's - Tel (44) 01926 - 864 567   Kenilworth 4 km
Bosquet - Tel (44) 01926 - 852 463   Kenilworth 4 km
Les Plantagenets   Royal Leamington Spa
Tel (44) 01926 - 453 171   4 km

567

If you don't get lost in the very comfortable and totally gigantic clubhouse at Wentworth (a little over the top, maybe?), try to forget the West course and go for the East. This was the first course laid out at Wentworth by Harry Colt and many prefer it to its illustrious neighbour. It simply has not had the benefit of the same rejuvenation programmes nor maybe the same standard of green-keeping, but the soil is more pleasant (sand) and drier, and the heather adds a touch of colour. It is difficult to explain other than that we felt this a more "cheerful" layout, without the same severity that you find on the West course. Very fair and with some very amusing greens, this course has been under-estimated for too long. The full Wentworth complex has been supplemented with a third course, "Edinburgh", which despite everything it has to offer is not necessarily worth a green-fee of some £85!

Si vous ne vous êtes pas perdu dans le Clubhouse très confortable et totalement gigantesque (un peu "too much ?") de Wentworth, tournez un jour le dos au "West" et dirigez-vous vers "l'East." Ce fut le premier des parcours dessinés par Harry Colt à Wentworth, et beaucoup le préfèrent à son illustre voisin. Il n'a simplement pas bénéficié des mêmes programmes de rajeunissement, ni peut-être du même entretien, mais le sol y est plus agréable (c'est du sable), plus sec, et la bruyère ajoute une touche de couleur. Il est difficile d'expliquer autrement qu'en disant qu'il est plus "souriant," dénué de cette sévérité que l'on peut trouver au parcours West. Franc, avec des greens souvent amusants, ce parcours a été trop longtemps sous-estimé. Cet ensemble de Wentworth a été complété par un troisième parcours, "Edinburgh" qui, en dépit de ses qualités, ne vaut certainement pas un green-fee de 85 Livres...

Wentworth Golf Club

Wentworth Drive
ENG - VIRGINIA WATER, Surrey GU25 4 LS

Office	Secrétariat	(44) 01344 - 842201
Pro shop	Pro-shop	(44) 01344 - 843353
Fax	Fax	(44) 01344 - 842804
Situation	Situation	

7 km from Ascot (pop. 150 244)
10 km from Staines (pop. 51 167)

Annual closure	Fermeture annnuelle	no
Weekly closure	Fermeture hebdomadaire	no
Fees main season	Tarifs haute saison	18 holes

	Week days Semaine	We/Bank holidays We/Férié
Individual Individuel	£ 85	—
Couple Couple	£ 170	—

No visitors at weekends

Caddy	Caddy	on request/£ 25+tip
Electric Trolley	Chariot électrique	no
Buggy	Voiturette	£ 30/18 holes
Clubs	Clubs	£ 30/18 holes

Credit cards Cartes de crédit
VISA - MasterCard

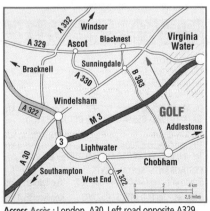

Access Accès : London, A30. Left road opposite A329 turning to Ascot.
Map 8 on page 420 Carte 8 Page 420

GOLF COURSE
PARCOURS

16/20

Site	Site	
Maintenance	Entretien	
Architect	Architecte	Harry S. Colt
Type	Type	inland, forest
Relief	Relief	
Water in play	Eau en jeu	
Exp. to wind	Exposé au vent	
Trees in play	Arbres en jeu	

Scorecard	Chp.	Mens	Ladies
Carte de score	Chp.	Mess.	Da.
Length Long.	5558	5354	4855
Par	68	68	72

Advised golfing ability		0	12	24	36
Niveau de jeu recommandé					
Hcp required	Handicap exigé	28 Men, 36 Ladies			

CLUB HOUSE & AMENITIES
CLUB HOUSE ET ANNEXES

8/10

Pro shop	Pro-shop	
Driving range	Practice	
Sheltered	couvert	10 mats
On grass	sur herbe	yes
Putting-green	putting-green	yes
Pitching-green	pitching green	yes

HOTEL FACILITIES
ENVIRONNEMENT HOTELIER

7/10

HOTELS HÔTELS

Royal Berkshire - 60 rooms, D £ 140   Sunninghill
Tél (44) 01344 - 23 322   3 km
Fax (44) 01344 - 27 100

Berystede - 90 rooms, D £ 120   Sunninghill
Tel (44) 01344 - 23 311   5 km
Fax (44) 01344 - 872 301

Great Fosters - 42 rooms, D £ 140   Egham
Tel (44) 01784 - 433 822   5 km
Fax (44) 01784 - 472 455

Thames Lodge - 44 rooms, D £ 95   Staines 10 km
Tel (44) 01784 - 464 433
Fax (44) 01784 - 454 858

RESTAURANTS RESTAURANTS
Stateroom (Royal Berkshire)   Sunninghill 3 km
Tel (44) 01344 - 23 322

Royal Forresters - Tel (44) 01344 - 884 747   Ascot 5 km

This is one of those courses that has become familiar to many through the staging here every year of the PGA and the World Match-Play Championships. The price of the green-fee is such that you'd better get here in good shape if you really want to enjoy your day. Another solution is to take advantage of the special rates and play between October and March, although the landscape is not always very pretty at that time of year. You just get a clearer view of some of the superb houses on this very exclusive site. The "West" course is a great test of golf, where the yardage book will prove most handy to get a clearer idea of the position of difficulties, particularly some not very visible ditches. The positioning of hazards here is subtlety itself and nothing is left to chance. Your game must be absolutely tip-top, with a lot of inspiration to boot in the tricky run from the 13th to the 15th holes. Our judgment is a little more reserved for the two par 5s at the end of a course which is unquestionably one of the best inland layouts in England.

Ce parcours est de ceux que la télévision a rendus familiers, grâce au PGA Championship et au World Match-Play qui s'y disputent tous les ans. Et le prix du green-fee est tel qu'il faut y arriver en forme pour vraiment savourer sa journée, ou alors profiter de tarifs spéciaux d'octobre à mars, mais le paysage n'est pas très gai à cette période, sauf que les vues sont plus dégagées sur les superbes maisons de ce domaine très exclusif. Le parcours "Ouest" est un grand test de golf, où le carnet de parcours sera fort utile pour identifier les difficultés, notamment des fossés pas très visibles. Le placement des obstacles est d'une subtilité exceptionnelle, et rien de bon ici n'est dû au hasard. Il faut un jeu absolument complet, et beaucoup d'inspiration dans le très délicat passage du 13 au 15. On sera plus réservé sur les deux par 5 clôturant ce parcours, qui reste incontestablement l'un des meilleurs "inland" du pays.

Wentworth Golf Club

Wentworth Drive
ENG - VIRGINIA WATER, Surrey GU25 4 LS

Office	Secrétariat	(44) 01344 - 842201
Pro shop	Pro-shop	(44) 01344 - 843353
Fax	Fax	(44) 01344 - 842804
Situation	Situation	

7 km from Ascot (pop. 150 244)
10 km from Staines (pop. 51 167)

Annual closure	Fermeture annnuelle	no
Weekly closure	Fermeture hebdomadaire	no
Fees main season	Tarifs haute saison	18 holes

	Week days Semaine	We/Bank holidays We/Férié
Individual Individuel	£ 140	—
Couple Couple	£ 280	—

No visitors at weekends
Reduced greenfees October to March

Caddy	Caddy	on request/£ 25+tip
Electric Trolley	Chariot électrique	no
Buggy	Voiturette	£ 30/18 holes
Clubs	Clubs	£ 30/18 holes

Credit cards Cartes de crédit
VISA - MasterCard

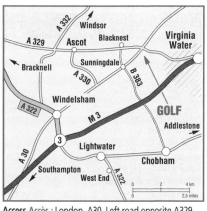

Access Accès : London, A30. Left road opposite A329 turning to Ascot.
Map 8 on page 420 Carte 8 Page 420

GOLF COURSE
PARCOURS 18/20

Site	Site	▬▬▬▬▭
Maintenance	Entretien	▬▬▬▬▭
Architect	Architecte	Harry S. Colt
Type	Type	inland, forest
Relief	Relief	▬▬▭▭▭
Water in play	Eau en jeu	▬▬▬▭▭
Exp. to wind	Exposé au vent	▬▬▬▭▭
Trees in play	Arbres en jeu	▬▬▬▬▭

Scorecard Carte de score	Chp. Chp.	Mens Mess.	Ladies Da.
Length Long.	6261	6008	5440
Par	73	73	75

Advised golfing ability   0   12   24   36
Niveau de jeu recommandé
Hcp required   Handicap exigé   24 Men, 32 Ladies

CLUB HOUSE & AMENITIES
CLUB HOUSE ET ANNEXES 8/10

Pro shop	Pro-shop	▬▬▬▬▭
Driving range	Practice	▬▬▬▭▭
Sheltered	couvert	10 mats
On grass	sur herbe	yes
Putting-green	putting-green	yes
Pitching-green	pitching green	yes

HOTEL FACILITIES
ENVIRONNEMENT HOTELIER 7/10

HOTELS HÔTELS

Royal Berkshire - 60 rooms, D £ 140   Sunninghill
Tel (44) 01344 - 23 322   3 km
Fax (44) 01344 - 27 100

Berystede - 90 rooms, D £ 120   Sunninghill
Tel (44) 01344 - 23 311   5 km
Fax (44) 01344 - 872 301

Great Fosters - 42 rooms, D £ 140   Egham
Tel (44) 01784 - 433 822   5 km
Fax (44) 01784 - 472 455

Thames Lodge - 44 rooms, D £ 95   Staines
Tel (44) 01784 - 464 433   10 km
Fax (44) 01784 - 454 858

RESTAURANTS RESTAURANTS

Stateroom (Royal Berkshire)   Sunninghill
Tel (44) 01344 - 23 322   3 km

Royal Forresters - Tel (44) 01344 - 884 747   Ascot 5 km

569

Without wishing to appear "reactionary", there are a number of trends in modern course design which don't always go down very well. Take the length of the par 5s here, for example, and particularly hole N°5, which is a full 635 yards. Admittedly professional golfers hit the ball further than they used to, but this can be a windy course, the ground can often be wet and while the normal tee-boxes bring everything down to more human proportions, there must be a happy medium somewhere for good golfers who don't have to be huge-hitters. It is a pity that such an ambitious facility, with some magnificent views, seems to have forgotten somewhat that playing golf is about enjoyment, that the aim of the game is not for a golfer to end up on his knees with his swing in tatters. Even though the course is flat, you will appreciate this very interesting and often captivating layout much more in a buggy, competing with friends more than with the course.

Sans être un vieux réactionnaire, on peut ne pas apprécier certaines tendances des architectes modernes. Ici, tous les par 5 le sont vraiment, le trou n°5 atteignant 570 mètres (635 yards). Il est vrai que les pros tapent plus fort qu'avant, mais le vent n'est pas rare ici, le sol peut être humide (non ?), et si les départs "normaux" ramènent les trous à des proportions normales, il y a sans doute un juste milieu pour les golfeurs d'un bon niveau sans carrure d'athlètes. Il est dommage qu'un équipement aussi ambitieux, offrant des vues magnifiques, ait un peu oublié la dimension de plaisir du joueur, ou, en tout cas, qu'il ne doit pas finir à genoux et le swing en compote. Même si le terrain est très plat, on appréciera beaucoup plus en voiturette ce tracé intéressant et souvent captivant, en dehors de tout esprit de compétition, sauf bien sûr avec les amis.

570

West Berkshire Golf Club

Chaddleworth
ENG - NEWBURY, Berks RG16 0HS

Office	Secrétariat	(44) 01488 - 638574
Pro shop	Pro-shop	(44) 01488 - 638851
Fax	Fax	(44) 01488 - 638781
Situation	Situation	

8 km NW from Newbury (pop. 136 700)
7 km NE of Hungerford (pop. 6 174)

Annual closure	Fermeture annnuelle	no
Weekly closure	Fermeture hebdomadaire	no

Christmas Day only

Fees main season	Tarifs haute saison		18 holes
	Week days Semaine	**We/Bank holidays** We/Férié

	Week days	We/Bank holidays
Individual Individuel	£ 18	£ 22
Couple Couple	£ 36	£ 44

Full weekday: £ 26
Visitors after 12.30 pm at weekends

Caddy	Caddy	no
Electric Trolley	Chariot électrique	no
Buggy	Voiturette	£ 10/18 holes
Clubs	Clubs	£ 10/18 holes

Credit cards Cartes de crédit
VISA - Eurocard - MasterCard - AMEX - DC

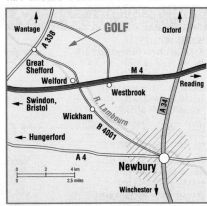

Access Accès : London M4. Jct 14 A338, → RAF Welford, Club house on right.
Map 7 on page 418 Carte 7 Page 418

GOLF COURSE
PARCOURS
15/20

Site	Site	
Maintenance	Entretien	
Architect	Architecte	John Stagg
Type	Type	open country
Relief	Relief	
Water in play	Eau en jeu	
Exp. to wind	Exposé au vent	
Trees in play	Arbres en jeu	

Scorecard Carte de score	Chp. Chp.	Mens Mess.	Ladies Da.
Length Long.	6353	5618	5200
Par	73	73	74

Advised golfing ability	0	12	24	36
Niveau de jeu recommandé				
Hcp required	Handicap exigé	no		

CLUB HOUSE & AMENITIES
CLUB HOUSE ET ANNEXES
7/10

Pro shop	Pro-shop	
Driving range	Practice	
Sheltered	couvert	no
On grass	sur herbe	yes
Putting-green	putting-green	yes
Pitching-green	pitching green	yes

HOTEL FACILITIES
ENVIRONNEMENT HOTELIER
7/10

HOTELS HÔTELS

Bear at Hungerford — Hungerford
41 rooms, D £ 85 — 7 km
Tel (44) 01488 - 682 512
Fax (44) 01488 - 684 357

Three Swans - 15 rooms, D £ 70 — Hungerford
Tel (44) 01488 - 682 721 — 7 km
Fax (44) 01488 - 681 708

Stakis Newbury - 109 rooms, D £ 90 — Newbury
Tel (44) 01635 - 247 010 — 8 km
Fax (44) 01635 - 247 077

RESTAURANTS RESTAURANTS

Just William's — Hungerford
Tel (44) 01488 - 681 199 — 7 km

Blue Boar Inn — Newbury
Tel (44) 01635 - 248 236 — 4 km

On the first hole at West Cornwall, you understand the religious and sporting nature of the game of golf, as you line up your drive on the steeple of the village church, the birthplace of Jim Barnes, one of the few British golfers to have won both the British and the US Opens. The course has not changed much since his time. It is rather short and a little devious in that the sloping terrain can easily draw your ball off the fairway. At the same time the railway line exerts a strange attraction on slicers over four holes. Once you are out of "Calamity Corner," where two par 3s and a short par 4 (holes 5 to 7) have ruined many a card, you will need a cool head for the remaining 11 holes in the dunes, up until the 18th, where you are in for a gentle landing downhill. A very natural and imaginative course, West Cornwall is excellent golfing before visiting the pretty fishing village and the artists of Saint Ives.

Le premier trou de West Cornwall permet de comprendre la nature religieuse et sportive du golf, il faut s'aligner sur le clocher de l'église du village où est né Jim Barnes, l'un des rares Britanniques à avoir remporté le British et l'US Open. Et le parcours n'a pas dû changer beaucoup. Assez court, il n'est pas d'une parfaite franchise, car les pentes peuvent sortir la balle du fairway, et la voie ferrée attire étrangement les sliceurs sur quatre trous. Une fois sorti indemne de "Calamity Corner," où deux par 3 et un minuscule par 4 (du 5 au 7) ont détruit bien des cartes, il faut garder son sang-froid pour les onze trous restant, toujours dans les dunes, et jusqu'au 18, un atterrissage en douceur et en descente. Très naturel et imaginatif, West Cornwall est à connaître, avant de visiter St Ives, joli village de pêcheurs et d'artistes.

West Cornwall Golf Club

Church Lane, Lelant
ENG - ST IVES, Cornwall TR26 3D2

Office	Secrétariat	(44) 01736 - 753 401
Pro shop	Pro-shop	(44) 01736 - 753 177
Fax	Fax	
Situation	Situation	

3 km SE of St Ives (pop. 7 254)
16 km NE of Penzance (pop. 20 284)

Annual closure	Fermeture annnuelle	no
Weekly closure	Fermeture hebdomadaire	no

Fees main season	Tarifs haute saison		full day
		Week days Semaine	We/Bank holidays We/Férié
Individual Individuel		£ 20	£ 25
Couple Couple		£ 40	£ 50

half price when playing with a member

Caddy	Caddy	no
Electric Trolley	Chariot électrique	no
Buggy	Voiturette	no
Clubs	Clubs	£ 10/day

Credit cards Cartes de crédit   no

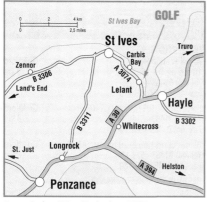

St Ives Bay — **GOLF**

St Ives — Carbis Bay — Truro
Zennor — B 3306 — A 3074
Land's End — Lelant
B 3311 — A 30 — **Hayle** — B 3302
St. Just — Whitecross — Helston
Longrock — A 394
Penzance

Access Accès : A30 to Hayle, then A3074
(Golf signposted)
Map 6 on page 416 Carte 6 Page 416

GOLF COURSE
PARCOURS
16/20

Site	Site	
Maintenance	Entretien	
Architect	Architecte	Reverend Tyack, vicar of Lelant...
Type	Type	seaside course, links
Relief	Relief	
Water in play	Eau en jeu	
Exp. to wind	Exposé au vent	
Trees in play	Arbres en jeu	

Scorecard Carte de score	Chp. Chp.	Mens Mess.	Ladies Da.
Length Long.	5354	5180	4890
Par	69	69	73

Advised golfing ability Niveau de jeu recommandé	0	12	24	36

Hcp required   Handicap exigé   28 Men, 36 Ladies

CLUB HOUSE & AMENITIES
CLUB HOUSE ET ANNEXES
7/10

Pro shop	Pro-shop	
Driving range	Practice	
Sheltered	couvert	no
On grass	sur herbe	yes
Putting-green	putting-green	yes
Pitching-green	pitching green	yes

HOTEL FACILITIES
ENVIRONNEMENT HOTELIER
6/10

HOTELS HÔTELS

Boskerris - 19 rooms, D £ 60	Carbis Bay
Tel (44) 01736 - 795 295	2 km
Fax (44) 01736 - 798 632	

Porthminster - 46 rooms, D £ 90	St Ives
Tel (44) 01736 - 795 221	4 km
Fax (44) 01736 - 797 043	

Ped'n Olva - 35 rooms, D £ 50	St Ives
Tel (44) 01736 - 796 222	4 km
Fax (44) 01736 - 797 710	

RESTAURANT RESTAURANT

Pig'n'Fish	St Ives
Tel (44) 01736 - 794 204	4 km

571

This is the third of a compact threesome of courses, the other two being virtual neighbours Woking and Worplesdon. In fact these are three courses belonging to the same club, and each has its own personality. We suppose you are bound to prefer one of the three, but each to his own, as they say. West Hill is very short and only moderately contoured over land strewn with pines, birch and conifers. The heather narrows the fairways and even cuts them in two on the 5th and 17th holes, two par 5s where that age-old decision arises once again: do I carry the hazard or lay up short? In fact the whole course calls for constant thought on the best way of driving, hitting the second shot and approaching the greens. This is why it is always such fun to play. A natural and well-landscaped course whose sandy soil drains easily, West Hill has inimitable charm, matched only perhaps by the other two "Ws"...

C'est le troisième d'un trio compact, avec Woking et Worplesdon, pratiquement voisins. Comme s'il s'agissait de trois parcours d'un même club, alors que chacun a préservé sa personnalité. Que l'on préfère l'un à l'autre est inévitable, mais "chacun a son goût." West Hill est très court, avec un relief très modéré, et un espace arboré de pins, de bouleaux et de sapins. La bruyère rétrécit les fairways, et vient parfois même les interrompre comme au 5 et au 17, deux par 5 où il faut prendre la décision de risquer de passer ou de rester court. L'ensemble du parcours demande une réflexion constante sur la meilleure façon de driver, de jouer le second coup, d'approcher, c'est pourquoi il reste aussi amusant. Naturel et bien paysagé, bien drainant avec son sol sablonneux, West Hill a un charme inimitable, sauf par les deux autres "W," peut-être...

West Hill Golf Club

Bagshot Road
ENG - BROOKWOOD, Surrey GU24 0BH

Office	Secrétariat	(44) 01483 - 474365
Pro shop	Pro-shop	(44) 01483 - 473172
Fax	Fax	(44) 01483 - 474252
Situation	Situation	

8 km from Guildford (pop. 122 378)
6 km from Woking

Annual closure	Fermeture annnuelle	no
Weekly closure	Fermeture hebdomadaire	no
Fees main season	Tarifs haute saison	full day

	Week days Semaine	We/Bank holidays We/Férié
Individual Individuel	£ 45	—
Couple Couple	£ 90	—

Weekends: only with a member

Caddy	Caddy	on request/£ 20+tip
Electric Trolley	Chariot électrique	no
Buggy	Voiturette	no
Clubs	Clubs	£ 30/18 holes

Credit cards Cartes de crédit
VISA - Eurocard - AMEX (not for greenfees)

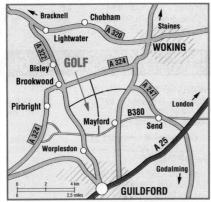

Access Accès : London A3 → Guildford. At Cobham, A245 on right. Through Woking. At Brookwood, turn left on A322 → Guildford. Entrance on left next to railway bridge. **Map 8 on page 420** Carte 8 Page 420

GOLF COURSE / PARCOURS — 15/20

Site	Site	
Maintenance	Entretien	
Architect	Architecte	Willie Park Jack White
Type	Type	inland, heathland
Relief	Relief	
Water in play	Eau en jeu	
Exp. to wind	Exposé au vent	
Trees in play	Arbres en jeu	

Scorecard Carte de score	Chp. Chp.	Mens Mess.	Ladies Da.
Length Long.	5731	5731	0
Par	69	69	0

Advised golfing ability Niveau de jeu recommandé		0 12 24 36
Hcp required	Handicap exigé	certificate

CLUB HOUSE & AMENITIES / CLUB HOUSE ET ANNEXES — 6/10

Pro shop	Pro-shop	
Driving range	Practice	
Sheltered	couvert	2 mats
On grass	sur herbe	yes
Putting-green	putting-green	yes
Pitching-green	pitching green	no

HOTEL FACILITIES / ENVIRONNEMENT HOTELIER — 6/10

HOTELS HÔTELS

Angel Posting House 18 rooms, D £ 105 Tel (44) 01483 - 64 555 Fax (44) 01483 - 33 770	Guildford	8 km
Forte Crest - 109 rooms, D £ 109 Tel (44) 01483 - 574 444 Fax (44) 01483 - 302 960	Guildford	8 km
Blanes Court Hotel - 29 rooms, D £ 70 Tel (44) 01483 - 573 171 Fax (44) 01483 - 32 780	Guildford	8 km

RESTAURANTS RESTAURANTS

Michel's Tel (44) 01483 - 224 777	Ripley	10 km
Café de Paris Tel (44) 01483 - 34 896	Guildford	8 km

572

The string of great courses running from Liverpool to Southport is unmatched anywhere in the world. And although West Lancashire is undoubtedly one of them, it has seldom staged top tournaments. The views over the Mersey estuary and the Welsh mountains are superb from the clubhouse, yet are less visible from the actual course, which lies sheltered behind a line of dunes. This is not a very hilly course, a fact that tends to give it an air of austerity but also its very own personality. What's more, this impression of infinity makes it very difficult to judge distances. It is already a tough task choosing the right club for the wind, avoiding bunkers, many of which just swallow up your ball, and getting to grips with firm, subtle and very slick greens. But despite everything, game strategy is pretty obvious, even though a few hazards are hard to spot from the tee-boxes.

Nulle part au monde on ne trouve une telle succession de grands parcours que de Liverpool à Southport. West Lancashire y figure sans conteste, alors qu'il a rarement reçu de grandes épreuves. Du Clubhouse, les vues sont superbes sur l'estuaire de la Mersey et les montagnes du Pays de Galles, mais on les voit peu du parcours, à l'abri derrière un cordon de dunes. Le relief n'est pas ici très prononcé, ce qui lui donne un caractère d'austérité, mais aussi sa personnalité. De plus, cette impression d'infinité rend très difficile le jugement des distances : il est déjà délicat de choisir les bons clubs en fonction du vent, d'éviter les bunkers, dont beaucoup sont d'une grande voracité, de négocier des greens fermes, subtils et très rapides. La stratégie est malgré tout assez évidente, alors que certains obstacles sont peu visibles des départs.

West Lancashire Golf Club

Hall Road West, Blundellsands
ENG - LIVERPOOL, Lancs L23 8SZ

Office	Secrétariat	(44) 0151 - 9241076
Pro shop	Pro-shop	(44) 0151 - 9245662
Fax	Fax	
Situation	Situation	

1.5 km from Crosby (pop. 22 000)
14 km from Liverpool (pop. 452 450)

Annual closure	Fermeture annnuelle	no
Weekly closure	Fermeture hebdomadaire	no

Fees main season	Tarifs haute saison	18 holes
	Week days	We/Bank holidays
	Semaine	We/Férié
Individual Individuel	£ 28	£ 50
Couple Couple	£ 56	£ 100

Full weekdays: £ 40

Caddy	Caddy	on request
Electric Trolley	Chariot électrique	no
Buggy	Voiturette	no
Clubs	Clubs	£ 5/18 holes

Credit cards Cartes de crédit
VISA - Eurocard - MasterCard - AMEX - DC - JCB
(Pro shop only)

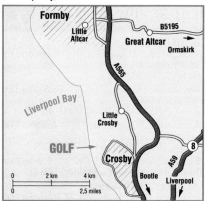

Access Accès : Liverpool, A565 to Crosby. +Follow signs to club by Hall Road Rail Station
Map 5 on page 415 Carte 5 Page 415

GOLF COURSE
PARCOURS

17/20

Site	Site	
Maintenance	Entretien	
Architect	Architecte	Unknown until 1960
		C.K. Cotton (1960)
Type	Type	links
Relief	Relief	
Water in play	Eau en jeu	
Exp. to wind	Exposé au vent	
Trees in play	Arbres en jeu	

Scorecard	Chp.	Mens	Ladies
Carte de score	Chp.	Mess.	Da.
Length Long.	6086	5594	5135
Par	72	70	73

Advised golfing ability		0	12	24	36
Niveau de jeu recommandé					
Hcp required	Handicap exigé	28 Men, 36 Ladies			

CLUB HOUSE & AMENITIES
CLUB HOUSE ET ANNEXES

7/10

Pro shop	Pro-shop	
Driving range	Practice	
Sheltered	couvert	no
On grass	sur herbe	yes
Putting-green	putting-green	yes
Pitching-green	pitching green	yes

HOTEL FACILITIES
ENVIRONNEMENT HOTELIER

7/10

HOTELS HÔTELS
Blundellsands - 41 rooms, D £ 70   Crosby 3 km
Tel (44) 0151 - 924 6515, Fax (44) 0151 - 931 5364

Atlantic Tower Thistle   Liverpool 15 km
223 rooms, D £ 90
Tel (44) 0151 - 227 4444, Fax (44) 0151 - 236 3973

Liverpool Moat House   Liverpool 15 km
244 rooms, D £ 98
Tel (44) 0151 - 471 9988, Fax (44) 0151 - 709 2706

Park - 62 rooms, D £ 34   Netherton 3 km
Tel (44) 0151 - 525 7555, Fax (44) 0151 - 525 2481

RESTAURANTS RESTAURANTS
Ristorante del Secolo   Liverpool
Tel (44) 0151 - 236 4004   15 km

Blundellsands - Tel (44) 0151 - 924 6515   Crosby 3 km

573

West Surrey is one of those courses where you soon start feeling excited about your game as all the hazards and the tactics you need to overcome them are crystal clear. This is important, because placing the drive is of prime importance if you want a relatively simple approach shot. So players who are playing to form should card their handicap and perhaps even better if they excel on the greens. In Summer the course gets a little harder because the fairways are not watered and the ball will roll on easily into the long thick rough from where only a wedge can be of any use. With this said, there are not many other hazards to contend with. With a longer outward 9 and tight back 9, there is something for every kind of player, and the long-hitters who keep out of the trees will enjoy a number of birdie opportunities on the par 5s.

West Surrey est de ces parcours où l'on éprouve vite de bonnes sensations, parce que l'on voit aussi clairement les obstacles que la tactique à mettre en oeuvre. C'est important car le placement du drive est essentiel pour garantir un second coup assez facile. Ainsi, les joueurs qui sont à leur bon niveau joueront normalement leur handicap, et mieux même s'ils sont inspirés sur les greens. En été, le parcours est plus difficile car les fairways ne sont pas arrosés, et l'on roule assez facilement dans des roughs longs et épais, d'où on ne peut souvent sortir qu'avec un wedge. Cela dit, il n'y a pas beaucoup d'autres obstacles. Avec un aller plus long, mais un retour plus étroit, tous les types de joueurs sont bien servis, et les longs frappeurs sachant éviter les arbres trouveront de belles occsions de birdies sur les par 5.

West Surrey Golf Club

Enton Green
ENG - GODALMING, Surrey GU8 5AF

Office	Secrétariat	(44) 01483 - 421275
Pro shop	Pro-shop	(44) 01483 - 417278
Fax	Fax	(44) 01483 - 415419
Situation	Situation	

6 km from Guildford (pop. 122 378)- next to Godalming

Annual closure	Fermeture annnuelle	no
Weekly closure	Fermeture hebdomadaire	no

Tuesday 08 → 12

Fees main season	Tarifs haute saison		18 holes
		Week days Semaine	We/Bank holidays We/Férié
Individual Individuel		£ 38.50	£ 50*
Couple Couple		£ 77	£ 100*

Restrictions at weekends (please call)

Caddy	Caddy	no
Electric Trolley	Chariot électrique	£ 6/18 holes
Buggy	Voiturette	no
Clubs	Clubs	£ 10/18 holes

Credit cards Cartes de crédit
VISA - Eurocard - MasterCard - AMEX - DC - JCB
(not for green fees)

574

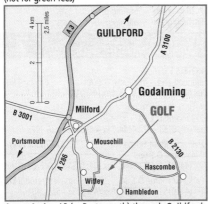

Access Accès : A3 (→ Portsmouth) through Guildford. Turn left to Milford. At traffic lights turn left onto A 3100 (→Portsmouth). Right onto Station Lane. Golf 3 km down (2 m.) on right side.
Map 7 on page 418 Carte 7 Page 418

GOLF COURSE
PARCOURS
15/20

Site	Site	
Maintenance	Entretien	
Architect	Architecte	Herbert Fowler
Type	Type	parkland
Relief	Relief	
Water in play	Eau en jeu	
Exp. to wind	Exposé au vent	
Trees in play	Arbres en jeu	

Scorecard Carte de score	Chp. Chp.	Mens Mess.	Ladies Da.
Length Long.	5633	5842	4970
Par	71	71	72

Advised golfing ability		0	12	24	36
Niveau de jeu recommandé					
Hcp required	Handicap exigé	certificate			

CLUB HOUSE & AMENITIES
CLUB HOUSE ET ANNEXES
7/10

Pro shop	Pro-shop	
Driving range	Practice	
Sheltered	couvert	no
On grass	sur herbe	yes (summer)
Putting-green	putting-green	yes
Pitching-green	pitching green	yes

HOTEL FACILITIES
ENVIRONNEMENT HOTELIER
7/10

HOTELS HÔTELS

Inn on the Lake - 17 rooms, D £ 80   Godalming 3 km
Tel (44) 01483 - 415 575
Fax (44) 01483 - 860 445

Kings Arms and Royal   Godalming 3 km
16 rooms, D £ 60
Tel (44) 01483 - 421 545, Fax (44) 01483 - 415 403

Angel Posting House and Livery   Guildford 7 km
18 rooms, D £ 105
Tel (44) 01483 - 64 555, Fax (44) 01483 - 33 770

Bramley Grange - 45 rooms, D £ 90   Bramley 3 km
Tel (44) 01483 - 893 434, Fax (44) 01483 - 893 835

RESTAURANTS RESTAURANTS

White Horse - Tel (44) 01483 - 208 258 Hascombe 3 km

Café de Paris - Tel (44) 01483 - 34 896   Guildford 7 km

Squirrel at Hurtmore   Hurtmore
Tel (44) 01483 - 860 223   5 km

The good news for most amateurs is that West Sussex is not a long course. The bad news is that there is only one par 5, hole N°1, where your swing might not quite be in the right groove to hit the green in two. There are also a number of holes where you will hope to get by unscathed, for example the 6th and 15th, two tough par 3s where you need to carry water, and the 16th, a beautiful par 4 whose green looks depressingly tiny beyond a wide ravine. Here, you have every opportunity to shoot a good round as long as your game is in tip-top condition, and although the greens are very well protected, there is often an easy way in. You need to play every shot there is, one at a time, firstly in your mind, then with your club. This absolute gem of a course does not have the recognition it deserves, but the people here seem to have opted for the sweet life, preferring to leave the limelight for others.

La bonne nouvelle pour la plupart des amateurs, c'est que West Sussex n'est pas bien long ! La mauvaise, c'est qu'il y a un seul par 5, et c'est le 1, où l'on n'est généralement pas assez assoupli pour vraiment attaquer le green en deux. Il y a aussi quelques trous dont il faut sortir indemne, comme le 6 et le 15, deux solides par 3 où il faut passer l'eau, ou le 16, très beau par 4 dont le green paraît minuscule au delà d'un large ravin. Autrement, il est ici beaucoup d'occasions de réussir si l'on a amené son meilleur jeu, d'autant que les greens sont bien protégés, mais qu'ils laissent très souvent une ouverture. Il faut ici savoir jouer tous les coups, et un seul à la fois, d'abord avec sa tête puis avec son club. Ce merveilleux petit bijou n'a pas la notoriété qu'il mérite, mais, ici, on a choisi de vivre heureux, sans souci des projecteurs trop violents.

West Sussex Golf Club
ENG - PULBOROUGH, West Sussex RH20 2EN

Office	Secrétariat	(44) 01798 - 875563
Pro shop	Pro-shop	(44) 01798 - 872426
Fax	Fax	(44) 01798 - 875563
Situation	Situation	

2.5 km from Pulborough (pop. 4 309)
25 km from Brighton (pop. 228 946)

Annual closure	Fermeture annnuelle	no
Weekly closure	Fermeture hebdomadaire	no
Fees main season	Tarifs haute saison	18 holes

	Week days Semaine	We/Bank holidays We/Férié
Individual Individuel	£ 35	£ 40
Couple Couple	£ 70	£ 80

Full weekdays: £ 45 - No visitors on Friday

Caddy	Caddy	no
Electric Trolley	Chariot électrique	£ 5/18 holes
Buggy	Voiturette	no
Clubs	Clubs	£ 5/18 holes

Credit cards Cartes de crédit
VISA - MasterCard (Pro shop only)

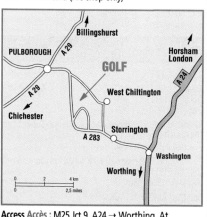

Access Accès : M25 Jct 9, A24 → Worthing. At Washington, A283 on the right through Storrington → Pulborough. Golf course on the right.
Map 7 on page 418 Carte 7 Page 418

GOLF COURSE
PARCOURS

18/20

Site	Site	
Maintenance	Entretien	
Architect	Architecte	Sir Guy Campbell C.K. Hutchinson
Type	Type	inland, heathland
Relief	Relief	
Water in play	Eau en jeu	
Exp. to wind	Exposé au vent	
Trees in play	Arbres en jeu	

Scorecard Carte de score	Chp. Chp.	Mens Mess.	Ladies Da.
Length Long.	5600	5320	5020
Par	68	68	73

Advised golfing ability	0	12	24	36
Niveau de jeu recommandé				

Hcp required Handicap exigé   certificate

CLUB HOUSE & AMENITIES
CLUB HOUSE ET ANNEXES

7/10

Pro shop	Pro-shop	
Driving range	Practice	
Sheltered	couvert	1 mat
On grass	sur herbe	yes
Putting-green	putting-green	yes
Pitching-green	pitching green	yes

575

HOTEL FACILITIES
ENVIRONNEMENT HOTELIER

6/10

HOTELS HÔTELS

Chequers - 11 rooms, D £ 75 Tel (44) 01798 - 872 486 Fax (44) 01798 - 872 715	Pulborough 3 km
Little Thakeham - 7 rooms, D £ 130 Tel (44) 01903 - 744 416 Fax (44) 01903 - 745 022	Storrington 4 km
Mill House - 12 rooms, D £ 80 Tel (44) 01670 - 892 426 Fax (44) 01670 - 892 855	Ashington 10 km

RESTAURANTS RESTAURANTS

Stane Street Hollow Tel (44) 01798 - 872819	Pulborough 5 km
Manley's Tel (44) 01903 - 742331	Storrington 4 km

The beginning of the course is not so simple, between the sand-dunes and out-of-bounds. If the wind is blowing, don't go for the pin, you will be asking for trouble. The 15th is also surprising, because you have to cut the ball over an out-of-bounds area. Try and get a round with some local players so they can tell you about the traps that are not always clearly in view. For example, the rough is never the same from one season to the next and even disappears altogether in the Winter (hardly the best time to come here anyway). Facing the Welsh coast, Weston-Super-Mare provides some spectacular views over the Bristol Channel and the general flatness of the course means you can easily play 36 holes in a day when on holiday. Similar to Saunton in style but without offering quite the same challenge, this is a course in the grand links tradition.

Le début du parcours n'est pas si simple, entre les dunes et le hors-limites. S'il y a du vent, ne jouez pas directement les drapeaux, vous risquez des problèmes. Le 15 est aussi surprenant, où il faut couper au-dessus du hors-limites. Essayez donc de faire une partie avec des joueurs locaux, ils vous en apprendront les pièges pas toujours bien visibles, notamment que le rough n'est jamais le même suivant la saison, et qu'il est absent en hiver. Mais il est vari que l'on vient rarement ici en cette période de l'année. En face du Pays de Galles, Weston-super-Mare offre des vues spectaculaires sur le Bristol Channel. Son absence de relief en fait un parcours idéal pour jouer 36 trous en vacances. Assez proche par son style de Saunton, sans prétendre à son exigence, c'est un parcours de grande tradition de links.

Weston-Super-Mare Golf Club

Uphill Road North
ENG - WESTON-SUPER-MARE, Bristol BS23 4NQ

Office	Secrétariat	(44) 01934 - 626 968
Pro shop	Pro-shop	(44) 01934 - 633 360
Fax	Fax	(44) 01934 - 626 968
Situation	Situation	

2 km S of Weston-Super-Mare (pop. 64 935)
23 km SW of Bristol (pop. 376 146)

Annual closure	Fermeture annnuelle	no
Weekly closure	Fermeture hebdomadaire	no

Fees main season	Tarifs haute saison		full day
		Week days	We/Bank holidays
		Semaine	We/Férié
Individual Individuel		£ 24	£ 35
Couple Couple		£ 48	£ 70

Caddy	Caddy	no
Electric Trolley	Chariot électrique	no (batteries)
Buggy	Voiturette	no
Clubs	Clubs	yes (ask pro)

Credit cards Cartes de crédit	no

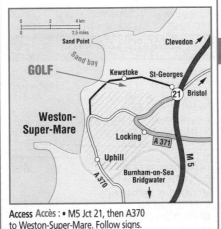

Access Accès : • M5 Jct 21, then A370
to Weston-Super-Mare. Follow signs.
• From Bristol centre, A370.
Map 6 on page 417 Carte 6 Page 417

GOLF COURSE
PARCOURS
16/20

Site	Site	
Maintenance	Entretien	
Architect	Architecte	Tom Dunn
Type	Type	seaside course, links
Relief	Relief	
Water in play	Eau en jeu	
Exp. to wind	Exposé au vent	
Trees in play	Arbres en jeu	

Scorecard	Chp.	Mens	Ladies
Carte de score	Chp.	Mess.	Da.
Length Long.	5651	5540	5006
Par	70	70	72

Advised golfing ability	0	12	24	36
Niveau de jeu recommandé				

Hcp required	Handicap exigé	certificate

CLUB HOUSE & AMENITIES
CLUB HOUSE ET ANNEXES
6/10

Pro shop	Pro-shop	
Driving range	Practice	
Sheltered	couvert	no
On grass	sur herbe	yes
Putting-green	putting-green	yes
Pitching-green	pitching green	yes

HOTEL FACILITIES
ENVIRONNEMENT HOTELIER
7/10

HOTELS HÔTELS

Beachlands - 17 rooms, D £ 80   Weston-Super-Mare
Tel (44) 01934 - 621 401   on site
Fax (44) 01934 -621 966

Grand Atlantic - 76 rooms, D £ 75 Weston-Super-Mare
Tel (44) 01934 - 626 543   2 km
Fax (44) 01934 - 415 048

Commodore - 18 rooms, D £ 70   Weston-Super-Mare
Tel (44) 01934 - 415 778   2 km
Fax (44) 01934 - 636 483

RESTAURANTS RESTAURANTS

Duets   Weston-Super-Mare
Tel (44) 01934 - 413 428   3 km

Claremont Vaults   Weston-Super-Mare 2 km

576

This is the kind of course you would like to keep to yourself. Very much underrated and often completely unknown, it is a sort of delectable gem that long-hitters will look down upon until they reach the 14th tee. In a none too impressive site of heathland and on the springy turf that comes with peat, the layout was designed by Harry Colt, who knew a thing or two about teasing dog-legs. Missing the open side of the fairway calls for some acrobatics through or over the trees, or some sheepish save-shots back into play. If you score well it's because you thought it out well. The greens are well defended, distinctly well contoured, pretty huge and a pleasure to putt on. What lingers here is an impression of happiness, of having discovered something personal, but which you have to share with others...

C'est le genre de parcours que l'on aimerait garder pour soi. Très sous-estimé, souvent complètement ignoré, c'est une sorte de délicieux petit bijou que les longs frappeurs regarderont de haut jusqu'au moment où ils parviendront au départ du 14. Dans un site de terre de bruyère pas spécialement impressionnant, sur ce gazon élastique que donne un sol de tourbe, le tracé est signé Harry Colt, qui savait notamment faire des doglegs provoquants, où manquer l'ouverture oblige à des coups d'acrobate, ou encore à des retours penauds en sécurité sur le fairway. Et si l'on a bien scoré, c'est que l'on a bien pensé. Bien défendus, très travaillés, et plutôt vastes, les greens sont un plaisir à négocier. C'est cette impression de bonheur qui reste ici, d'avoir découvert quelque chose, même si on est loin d'être le seul...

Whittington Heath Golf Club

Tamworth Road
ENG - LICHFIELD, Staffs WS14 9PW

Office	Secrétariat	(44) 01543 - 432317
Pro shop	Pro-shop	(44) 01543 - 432261
Fax	Fax	(44) 01543 - 432317
Situation	Situation	

6 km from Lichfield (pop. 28 666)
20 km from Birmingham (pop. 961 041)

Annual closure	Fermeture annnuelle	no
Weekly closure	Fermeture hebdomadaire	no

Fees main season	Tarifs haute saison	18 holes
	Week days	We/Bank holidays
	Semaine	We/Férié
Individual Individuel	£ 24	—
Couple Couple	£ 48	—

Full weekdays: £ 32 - No visitors at weekends

Caddy	Caddy	no
Electric Trolley	Chariot électrique	no
Buggy	Voiturette	no
Clubs	Clubs	no
Credit cards Cartes de crédit		no

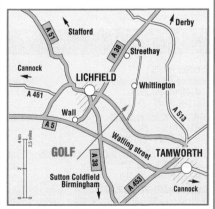

Access Accès : On A51, 4 km from Lichfield Station
Map 7 on page 418 Carte 7 Page 418

GOLF COURSE
PARCOURS | 17/20

Site	Site	▰▰▰▰▰▱
Maintenance	Entretien	▰▰▰▰▰▱
Architect	Architecte	Harry S. Colt
Type	Type	inland, heathland
Relief	Relief	▰▰▱▱▱▱
Water in play	Eau en jeu	▰▱▱▱▱▱
Exp. to wind	Exposé au vent	▰▰▰▰▱▱
Trees in play	Arbres en jeu	▰▰▰▰▰▱

Scorecard	Chp.	Mens	Ladies
Carte de score	Chp.	Mess.	Da.
Length Long.	5841	5542	5117
Par	70	70	72

Advised golfing ability		0	12	24	36
Niveau de jeu recommandé		▰▰▰▰▰▰			
Hcp required	Handicap exigé	certificate			

CLUB HOUSE & AMENITIES
CLUB HOUSE ET ANNEXES | 6/10

Pro shop	Pro-shop	▰▰▰▰▱▱
Driving range	Practice	▰▰▰▱▱▱
Sheltered	couvert	no
On grass	sur herbe	no
Putting-green	putting-green	yes
Pitching-green	pitching green	yes

577

HOTEL FACILITIES
ENVIRONNEMENT HOTELIER | 7/10

HOTELS HÔTELS
Little Barrow - 24 rooms, D £ 60   Lichfield 6 km
Tel (44) 01543 - 414 500, Fax (44) 01543 - 415 734

Travel Inn - 40 rooms, D £ 35   Tamworth 5 km
Tel (44) 01827 - 54 414, Fax (44) 01827 - 310 420

New Hall - 62 rooms, D £ 125   Sutton Coldfield 15 km
Tel (44) 0121 - 378 2442, Fax (44) 0121 - 378 4637

Parson and Clerk - 36 rooms, D £ 40   Sutton Coldfield
Tel (44) 0121 - 353 1747   13 km
Fax (44) 0121 - 352 1340

RESTAURANTS RESTAURANTS
Thrales - Tel (44) 01543 - 255 091   Lichfield 6 km

La Truffe   Sutton Coldfield
Tel (44) 0121 - 355 5836   13 km

In a very elegant setting with an equally comfortable clubhouse, both the courses at Woburn are pleasantly sited well away from the noise of the outside world. The Duchess course is more than honourable but is not in the same league as the Duke, made famous by the British Masters and the Women's British Open. Except for the first few holes, this is a rather flat layout which winds its way through a beautiful old forest of pine and chestnut trees, sufficiently in play for the rough not to be too difficult. The sandy soil makes for pleasant golfing all the year round, enhanced by the excellence of the greens, which are never easy to read. The holes all have a distinct individual character but without detracting from a pleasant unity of style. The back-tees are for very good players only, especially from the 13th onward, where some of the par-4s are quite formidable. In such a serious layout, the only regret might be a slight lack of fantasy (maybe a touch of British humour might help).

D'une grande élégance générale, l'ensemble des deux parcours de Woburn bénéficie d'une situation bien à l'écart du monde. Le parcours "Duchess" est plus qu'honorable, mais ne saurait lutter avec le "Dukes," rendu célèbre par le British Masters et le Women's British Open. Assez plat, sauf dans ses premiers trous, il est insinué dans une belle et ancienne forêt, où dominent les pins et les châtaigniers, assez présents dans le jeu pour que les roughs ne soient pas trop difficiles. Le sol sablonneux le rend très agréable à jouer toute l'année, et la qualité des greens, pas faciles à lire, augmente encore ce plaisir. Les trous sont bien individualisés, tout en offrant une bonne unité de style. On ne conseillera les départs arrière qu'aux très bons joueurs, surtout à partir du 13, où quelques par 4 sont redoutables. Sur un tracé aussi sérieux, on regrettera peut-être un léger manque de fantaisie (d'humour anglais?).

Woburn Golf & Country Club

Bow Brickhill
ENG - MILTON KEYNES, Bucks MK17 9 LJ

Office	Secrétariat	(44) 01332 - 378 436
Pro shop	Pro-shop	(44) 01332 - 647 987
Fax	Fax	(44) 01332 - 370 756
Situation	Situation	

10 km from Milton Keynes (pop. 176 330)
35 km from Bedford (pop. 73 917)

Annual closure	Fermeture annnuelle	no
Weekly closure	Fermeture hebdomadaire	no

(Christmas Day only)

Fees main season	Tarifs haute saison	18 holes

	Week days Semaine	We/Bank holidays We/Férié
Individual Individuel	*	*
Couple Couple	*	*

On request: depends on number, time of the year, availability. Visitors must call before coming.

Caddy	Caddy	on request
Electric Trolley	Chariot électrique	no
Buggy	Voiturette	£ 40/18 holes
Clubs	Clubs	yes

Credit cards Cartes de crédit
VISA - MasterCard - AMEX - DC

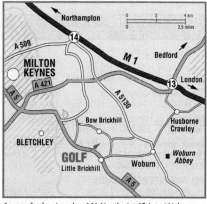

Access Accès : London M1 North. Jct 13 into Woburn Sands. Left to Woburn. After 0.75 km (1/2 m), right at sign. **Map 7 on page 418** Carte 7 Page 418

GOLF COURSE
PARCOURS

18/20

Site	Site	
Maintenance	Entretien	
Architect	Architecte	Charles Lawrie
Type	Type	inland, forest
Relief	Relief	
Water in play	Eau en jeu	
Exp. to wind	Exposé au vent	
Trees in play	Arbres en jeu	

Scorecard	Chp.	Mens	Ladies
Carte de score	Chp.	Mess.	Da.
Length Long.	6264	5898	5454
Par	72	72	75

Advised golfing ability	0	12	24	36
Niveau de jeu recommandé				

Hcp required	Handicap exigé	28 Men, 36 Ladies

CLUB HOUSE & AMENITIES
CLUB HOUSE ET ANNEXES

7/10

Pro shop	Pro-shop	
Driving range	Practice	
Sheltered	couvert	no
On grass	sur herbe	no
Putting-green	putting-green	yes
Pitching-green	pitching green	yes

HOTEL FACILITIES
ENVIRONNEMENT HOTELIER

7/10

HOTELS HOTELS

Bedford Arms - 51 rooms, D £ 80   Woburn
Tel (44) 01525 - 290 441   5 km
Fax (44) 01525 - 290 432

Bell Inn - 27 rooms, D £ 82   Woburn
Tel (44) 01525 - 290 280   5 km
Fax (44) 01525 - 290 017

Moore Place - 53 rooms, D £ 85   Aspley Guise
Tel (44) 01908 - 282 000   6 km
Fax (44) 01908 - 281 888

RESTAURANTS RESTAURANTS

Paris House - Tel (44) 01525 - 290 692   Woburn 5 km

Shenley Church Inn   Milton Keynes
Tel (44) 01908 - 505 467   12 km

Bell Inn   Woburn
Tel (44) 01525 - 290 280   5 km

578

16	6	6

The second of the threesome of "Ws", we could almost write the same report for each one, although each does have its own personality. Here it all starts with the clubhouse, as British as a cricket pavilion where you drink tea after your round. Otherwise the landscape is the same as on the other two courses, with heather just about everywhere you look. Isn't it about time someone invented a special "heather wedge" to help get balls back onto the fairway? And heather it is that puts the most pressure on your tee-shot here, where apprehension will always be your worst enemy. Add to this first class bunkering and very subtle, medium-sized greens that need time and patience to figure out and you realise that although a very fair proposition, Woking is a difficult course for carding a good score. A charming site, but watch out for its bite...

Avec West Hill et Worplesdon, ce sont de faux triplés. On pourrait d'ailleurs imaginer le même texte, avec trois copies. Chacun a son caractère. Celui-ci commence par son Clubhouse, à ce point British que l'on imagine un pavillon de cricket, où l'on boit le thé à la fin de la partie. Sinon, le paysage est analogue, avec une omniprésente bruyère dont il faudra bien que quelqu'un dessine un jour un "heather wedge" pour en sortir. C'est d'ailleurs cette possibilité qui met tant de pression sur les coups de départ : en golf aussi, la peur est mauvaise conseillère. Et si l'on ajoute un bunkering de premier ordre, ainsi que des greens de taille moyenne, mais d'une telle subtilité qu'il faut du temps et de la patience pour les comprendre, on se doute que, en dépit de sa franchise, Woking n'est pas un parcours évident à scorer. Derrière le charme du lieu, il y a de solides mâchoires.

Woking Golf Club
Pond Road, Hook Heath
ENG - WOKING, Surrey GU22 0JZ

Office	Secrétariat	(44) 01483 - 760053
Pro shop	Pro-shop	(44) 01483 - 769582
Fax	Fax	(44) 01483 - 772441
Situation	Situation	

6 km from Guildford (pop. 122 378)
48 km from Central London (pop. 6 679 700)

Annual closure	Fermeture annnuelle	no
Weekly closure	Fermeture hebdomadaire	no

Fees main season
Tarifs haute saison | | full day

	Week days Semaine	We/Bank holidays We/Férié
Individual Individuel	£ 45	—
Couple Couple	£ 90	—

Weekends: only with a member

Caddy	Caddy	on request
Electric Trolley	Chariot électrique	£ 10/18 holes
Buggy	Voiturette	no
Clubs	Clubs	£ 10/18 holes
Credit cards Cartes de crédit		no

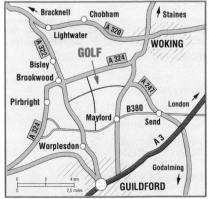

Access Accès : London A3 → Guildford. At Cobham, A245 on right. Through Woking. → St Johns Village.
Map 8 on page 420 Carte 8 Page 420

GOLF COURSE
PARCOURS
16/20

Site	Site	▬▬▬▬▬▬
Maintenance	Entretien	▬▬▬▬▬▬
Architect	Architecte	Tom Dunn
Type	Type	inland, heathland
Relief	Relief	▬▬▬
Water in play	Eau en jeu	▬▬
Exp. to wind	Exposé au vent	▬▬▬
Trees in play	Arbres en jeu	▬▬▬▬

Scorecard Carte de score	Chp. Chp.	Mens Mess.	Ladies Da.
Length Long.	5706	5361	5055
Par	70	70	73

Advised golfing ability	0	12	24	36
Niveau de jeu recommandé			▬▬▬	
Hcp required Handicap exigé	certificate			

CLUB HOUSE & AMENITIES
CLUB HOUSE ET ANNEXES
6/10

Pro shop	Pro-shop	▬▬▬
Driving range	Practice	
Sheltered	couvert	no
On grass	sur herbe	yes
Putting-green	putting-green	yes
Pitching-green	pitching green	yes

HOTEL FACILITIES
ENVIRONNEMENT HOTELIER
6/10

HOTELS HOTELS

Angel Posting House - 18 rooms, D £ 105 — Guildford
Tel (44) 01483 - 64 555 — 6 km
Fax (44) 01483 - 33 770

Forte Crest - 109 rooms, D £ 109 — Guildford
Tel (44) 01483 - 574 444 — 6 km
Fax (44) 01483 - 302 960

Blanes Court Hotel - 29 rooms, D £ 70 — Guildford
Tel (44) 01483 - 573 171 — 6 km
Fax (44) 01483 - 32 780

RESTAURANTS RESTAURANT

Michel's — Ripley 6 km
Tel (44) 01483 - 224 777

Café de Paris — Guildford 6 km
Tel (44) 01483 - 34 896

579

Since 1893, Woodbridge has moved with the times and got equipped with a modern clubhouse in the early 1970s. Once much wider, the course has become much tighter as the trees have grown, a factor rarely given full consideration but one which can and will significantly change the designer's original intentions. A lot of courses should be studying the question right now. As it happens, the trees at Woodbridge hardly make it the ideal course for wayward hitters or beginners, unless they can master a 1 iron off the tee, which for the latter at least is hardly likely. This is a pity because here you have a very good test of golf where many holes widen out after the driving area and things get a little easier if you stay out of the heather. Those of you who can flight the ball either way will enjoy Woodbridge, a fine course and an excellent test, but never an ordeal. Very pleasant to play with the family, for fun.

Depuis 1893, Woodbridge a évolué avec le temps, et s'est doté d'un Clubhouse moderne vers 1970. Autrefois large, le parcours est devenu beaucoup plus étroit avec la croissance des arbres : c'est un élément rarement pris en compte, alors qu'il peut beaucoup modifier les intentions des architectes. Cette question doit en tout cas se poser pour beaucoup de parcours. En l'occurrence, ce détail empêche de conseiller Woodbridge aux frappeurs pas trop précis et aux débutants, à moins qu'ils ne soient des maîtres du fer 1, ce qui serait étonnant, du moins chez les débutants. C'est dommage car c'est un très bon test de golf, beaucoup de trous s'élargissent après la zone de drive, et les choses vont mieux si l'on a évité la bruyère. Les travailleurs de balle s'amuseront beaucoup sur ce beau parcours, un bon test sans être une bataille, et très agréable à jouer en famille, pour le plaisir.

Woodbridge Golf Club
Bromeswell Heath
ENG - WOODBRIDGE, Suffolk IP12 2PF

Office	Secrétariat	(44) 01394 - 382038
Pro shop	Pro-shop	(44) 01394 - 382394
Fax	Fax	(44) 01394 - 382392
Situation	Situation	

13 km from Ipswich (pop. 2 654)
15 km from Aldeburgh (pop. 130 157)

Annual closure	Fermeture annnuelle	no
Weekly closure	Fermeture hebdomadaire	no

Fees main season	Tarifs haute saison	18 holes
	Week days Semaine	We/Bank holidays We/Férié
Individual Individuel	£ 30	—
Couple Couple	£ 60	—

Full day: £ 35/70
No visitors on main course at weekends

Caddy	Caddy	no
Electric Trolley	Chariot électrique	no
Buggy	Voiturette	no
Clubs	Clubs	no

Credit cards Cartes de crédit	no

GOLF COURSE
PARCOURS   **14**/20

Site	Site	
Maintenance	Entretien	
Architect	Architecte	F.W. Hawtree
Type	Type	inland, heathland
Relief	Relief	
Water in play	Eau en jeu	
Exp. to wind	Exposé au vent	
Trees in play	Arbres en jeu	

Scorecard Carte de score	Chp. Chp.	Mens Mess.	Ladies Da.
Length Long.	5670	5456	5137
Par	70	70	73

Advised golfing ability	0	12	24	36
Niveau de jeu recommandé				
Hcp required	Handicap exigé	certificate		

CLUB HOUSE & AMENITIES
CLUB HOUSE ET ANNEXES   **7**/10

Pro shop	Pro-shop	
Driving range	Practice	
Sheltered	couvert	no
On grass	sur herbe	yes
Putting-green	putting-green	yes
Pitching-green	pitching green	yes

HOTEL FACILITIES
ENVIRONNEMENT HOTELIER   **7**/10

HOTELS HÔTELS
Seckford Hall - 32 rooms, D £ 90 — Woodbridge 3 km
Tel (44) 01394 - 385 678
Fax (44) 01394 - 380 610

Wood Hall Hotel - 14 rooms, D £ 100 — Shottisham 6 km
Tel (44) 01394 - 411 283
Fax (44) 01394 - 410 007

Ufford Park - 37 rooms, D £ 80 — Woodbridge 3 km
Tel (44) 01394 - 383 555
Fax (44) 01394 - 383 582

RESTAURANTS RESTAURANTS
Seckford Hall — Woodbridge 3 km
Tel (44) 01394 - 385678

Ufford Park - Tel (44) 01394 - 383555 Woodbridge 3 km

Woodhall Hotel — Shottisham 6 km
Tel (44) 01394 - 411283

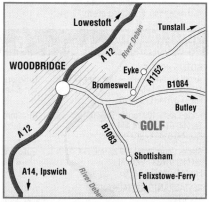

Access Accès : Ipswich A12. At Woodbridge, B1084 through Melton. Over bridge. Left at roundabout. Golf course 200 m on the right.
Map 7 on page 419 Carte 7 Page 419

580

As this course belongs to Nigel Mansell, it is only logical to drive around it rather than walk. It is actually pretty hilly but it won't wear you out, at least not physically. Mentally, chronic hookers might find their ball in deep trouble on at least one half of the holes. Opened in 1992, this 18-hole course is still maturing, although the well-wooded countryside has retained its typical Devonshire landscape. Holes through the woods alternate with holes over open space where water hazards beckon (on 7 holes). Add to this some pretty huge and deep bunkers with high lips and you can feel a very distinct American influence where target golf is the order of the day. There is no way you can roll your ball onto the greens. This is a very interesting test where you should play from the tee-boxes designed for your level of ability. Beginners will certainly feel more comfortable on the neighbouring 9-holer, unless they prefer a little fishing, the swimming pool, tennis courts or aerobics available in this very well equipped resort.

Comme ce golf appartient à Nigel Mansell, il est assez logique de le jouer en voiture ! Il est effectivement assez accidenté mais pas épuisant, sauf mentalement pour les spécialistes du hook, qui risquent la sortie de route sur une bonne moitié des trous. Ouvert en 1992, le 18 trous n'a pas encore atteint sa maturité, même si le paysage bien boisé a gardé son style de campagne typique du Devon. Il alterne les trous très boisés et les espaces plus ouverts, où les obstacles d'eau sont dangereux (sur sept trous). Si l'on ajoute les bunkers plutôt vastes, profonds avec des faces très relevées, on a ici une sensation très nette d'influence américaine, et il n'est pas question de faire rouler la balle. C'est un test très intéressant, si l'on joue les départs à son niveau. Les débutants seront plus à l'aise sur le 9 trous voisin, à moins de se livrer aux plaisirs de la pêche, de la piscine, du tennis ou de l'aérobic que propose ce club très bien équipé.

Woodbury Park Golf & Country Club

Woodbury Castle, Woodbury
ENG - EXETER EX5 1JJ

Office	Secrétariat	(44) 01395 - 233 382
Pro shop	Pro-shop	(44) 01395 - 233 382
Fax	Fax	(44) 01395 - 233 384
Situation	Situation	

9 km SE of Exeter (pop. 98 125)

Annual closure	Fermeture annnuelle	no
Weekly closure	Fermeture hebdomadaire	no

Fees main season
Tarifs haute saison — full day

	Week days Semaine	We/Bank holidays We/Férié
Individual Individuel	£ 35	£ 45
Couple Couple	£ 70	£ 90

Caddy	Caddy	£ 20/18 holes
Electric Trolley	Chariot électrique	£ 5/18 holes
Buggy	Voiturette	£ 20/18 holes
Clubs	Clubs	£ 12.50/18 holes

Credit cards Cartes de crédit
VISA - Eurocard - MasterCard

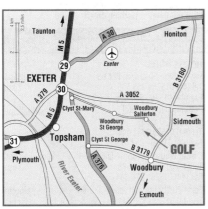

Access Accès : M5 Jct 30. A376 to Sidmouth/Exmouth. Take A3052 to Sidmouth. Turn right at Half Way House Inn. **Map 6 on page 417 Carte 6 Page 417**

GOLF COURSE PARCOURS — 15/20

Site	Site	
Maintenance	Entretien	
Architect	Architecte	J. Hamilton Stutt
Type	Type	inland, parkland
Relief	Relief	
Water in play	Eau en jeu	
Exp. to wind	Exposé au vent	
Trees in play	Arbres en jeu	

Scorecard Carte de score	Chp. Chp.	Mens Mess.	Ladies Da.
Length Long.	6252	6030	5201
Par	72	72	73

Advised golfing ability		0 12 24 36
Niveau de jeu recommandé		
Hcp required	Handicap exigé	certificate

CLUB HOUSE & AMENITIES CLUB HOUSE ET ANNEXES — 9/10

Pro shop	Pro-shop	
Driving range	Practice	
Sheltered	couvert	18 bays
On grass	sur herbe	yes
Putting-green	putting-green	yes (3)
Pitching-green	pitching green	yes

581

HOTEL FACILITIES ENVIRONNEMENT HOTELIER — 6/10

HOTELS HÔTELS

Rougemont Thistle — Exeter 9 km
88 rooms, D £ 75
Tel (44) 01392 - 54 982
Fax (44) 01392 - 420 928

Exeter Arms Toby — Exeter 9 km
37 rooms, D £ 60
Tel (44) 01392 - 435 353
Fax (44) 01392 - 420 826

RESTAURANTS RESTAURANTS

Golsworthy's — Exeter 9 km
Tel (44) 01392 - 217 736

Lamb's — Exeter 9 km
Tel (44) 01392 - 54 269

Woodhall Spa is still a very important leisure and holiday centre, like a sort of wood-strewn oasis in the middle of the Lincolnshire countryside. It is similar to Pinehurst in the United States but with only one course (a second is opening shortly). And what a course this is, regularly ranked amongst the best in Britain. Originally laid out by Vardon and Colt amidst pines, birch-trees and heather on ideal sandy soil, it was re-designed by the owner, Hotchkin. The number one requirement is to keep your drive in play and the ball alive in order to square up to some of the toughest second (and third) shots you could imagine. You then avoid the bunkers: you can spend quite some time there, especially on the par 3s. Might we add that to avoid putting beginners off the game altogether, here they will be better off watching or carrying someone's bag. Hiring a caddie is also money well spent.

Ancienne ville d'eau, Woodhall Spa est resté un centre de loisirs et de vacances important, comme une sorte d'oasis boisée au milieu de la campagne du Lincolnshire, à l'instar de Pinehurst aux USA, mais avec un seul parcours (un second ouvre bientôt). Quel parcours aussi, régulièrement classé parmi les meilleurs de Grande-Bretagne. Tracé par Vardon et Colt dans les pins, les bouleaux et la bruyère, sur un sol sablonneux idéal, il a été redessiné par le propriétaire, Hotchkin. Il exige d'abord de garder la balle en jeu du départ, afin d'être encore vivant pour affronter quelques-uns des deuxièmes coups les plus difficiles qui soient (comme les troisièmes !), où il importe d'éviter des bunkers où l'on peut rester longtemps, notamment sur les par 3. On ajoutera seulement que les débutants doivent porter le sac des autres joueurs s'ils ne veulent pas se décourager, et que prendre un caddie est un bon investissement.

Woodhall Spa Golf Club

The Broadway
ENG - WOODHALL SPA, Lincolnshire LN10 6PU

Office	Secrétariat	(44) 01526 - 352 511
Pro shop	Pro-shop	(44) 01526 - 352 511
Fax	Fax	(44) 01526 - 352 778
Situation	Situation	

28 km SE of Lincoln (pop. 80 218)
10 km SW of Horncastle (pop. 4 994)

Annual closure	Fermeture annnuelle		no
Weekly closure	Fermeture hebdomadaire		no
Fees main season	Tarifs haute saison		18 holes

	Week days Semaine	We/Bank holidays We/Férié
Individual Individuel	£ 40	£ 40
Couple Couple	£ 80	£ 80

Full day £ 65 - Prior arrangement with the Secretary

Caddy	Caddy	on request/£ 20
Electric Trolley	Chariot électrique	no
Buggy	Voiturette	no
Clubs	Clubs	no

Credit cards Cartes de crédit
VISA - Eurocard - MasterCard - AMEX - DC
(Pro Shop only)

Access Accès : On B1191 10 km SW of Horncastle
Map 4 on page 413 Carte 4 Page 413

GOLF COURSE
PARCOURS

18/20

Site	Site	
Maintenance	Entretien	
Architect	Architecte	Col. S.V. Hotchkin
Type	Type	inland, heathland
Relief	Relief	
Water in play	Eau en jeu	
Exp. to wind	Exposé au vent	
Trees in play	Arbres en jeu	

Scorecard Carte de score	Chp. Chp.	Mens Mess.	Ladies Da.
Length Long.	6250	5897	5203
Par	73	71	73

Advised golfing ability		0	12	24	36
Niveau de jeu recommandé					
Hcp required	Handicap exigé	20 Men, 30 Ladies			

CLUB HOUSE & AMENITIES
CLUB HOUSE ET ANNEXES

7/10

Pro shop	Pro-shop	
Driving range	Practice	
Sheltered	couvert	yes (floodlit)
On grass	sur herbe	no
Putting-green	putting-green	yes
Pitching-green	pitching green	yes

HOTEL FACILITIES
ENVIRONNEMENT HOTELIER

8/10

HOTELS HÔTELS

Golf Hotel - 50 rooms, D £ 65   Woodhall Spa
Tel (44) 01526 - 353 535   2 km
Fax (44) 01526 - 353 096

Petwood House Hotel   Woodhall Spa
47 rooms, D £ 90   2 km
Tel (44) 01526 - 352 411
Fax (44) 01526 - 353 473

Dower House - 7 rooms, D £ 60   Woodhall Spa
Tel (44) 01526 - 352 588   1 km
Fax (44) 01526 - 354 045

Forte Posthouse - 70 rooms, D £ 60   Lincoln
Tel (44) 01522 - 520 341   25 km
Fax (44) 01522 - 510 780

RESTAURANTS RESTAURANTS

Hornblowers - Tel (44) 01526 - 342 124 Coningsby 4 km
Jew's House - Tel (44) 01522 - 524 851   Lincoln 25 km

This is the third of the three "Ws" around Woking, designed by John Abercromby, who worked with, amongst others, the inimitable Tom Simpson. On arriving you notice the winding first hole and the beautiful houses around the course. You never grow tired of that sensation of privilege you get from playing golf over wide open spaces. A watering system has further enhanced green-keeping, and the greens are very quick, so you'd better stay on the right side of the slopes and the right tier of the multi-tiered greens. If you are looking for a brilliant score, the pin placements here will dictate game strategy. While West Hill and Woking are, in a way, courses where the tee-shot is all-important, Worplesdon calls for excellence on your second shot. Choosing between the three would be like having to refuse the starter, main course or dessert in a good restaurant.

C'est le troisième de la trinité de Woking, cette fois dessiné par John Abercromby, qui a travaillé notamment avec l'inimitable Tom Simpson. En arrivant, on remarque d'une part les méandres du premier trou, et la beauté des maisons environnantes. On ne saurait être insensible à cette sensation de privilège que donne le golf dans de beaux espaces. Et l'arrosage a fait encore progresser l'entretien. Les greens sont souvent très rapides, ce qui implique d'être du bon côté des pentes, et sur le bon plateau quand il y en a plusieurs. Le placement des drapeaux va en fait dicter toute la stratégie si l'on veut faire un score brillant. Si West Hill et Woking sont, un peu, des parcours de mise en jeu, Worplesdon est un parcours de seconds coups. On ne choisira pas plus qu'on ne refuse l'entrée, le plat ou le dessert dans un bon restaurant...

Worplesdon Golf Club

Heath House Road
ENG - WOKING, Surrey GU22 0RA

Office	Secrétariat	(44) 01483 - 472277
Pro shop	Pro-shop	(44) 01483 - 473287
Fax	Fax	(44) 01483 - 473303
Situation	Situation	

6 km from Guildford (pop. 122 378)
49 km from Central London (pop. 6 679 700)

Annual closure	Fermeture annnuelle	no
Weekly closure	Fermeture hebdomadaire	no
Fees main season	Tarifs haute saison	full day

	Week days Semaine	We/Bank holidays We/Férié
Individual Individuel	£ 55	—
Couple Couple	£ 110	—

Weekends: only with a member

Caddy	Caddy	on request/£ 25
Electric Trolley	Chariot électrique	no
Buggy	Voiturette	no
Clubs	Clubs	£ 10/18 holes

Credit cards Cartes de crédit
VISA - Eurocard - AMEX - DC

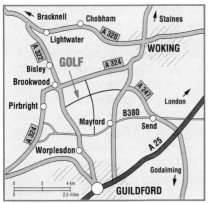

Access Accès : London A3 → Guildford. At Cobham, A245 on right. At Woking, A320 → Guildford, At Mayford, right into Heath House Road (B380).
Map 8 on page 420 Carte 8 Page 420

GOLF COURSE / PARCOURS — 16/20

Site	Site	
Maintenance	Entretien	
Architect	Architecte	John Abercromby
Type	Type	inland, heathland
Relief	Relief	
Water in play	Eau en jeu	
Exp. to wind	Exposé au vent	
Trees in play	Arbres en jeu	

Scorecard Carte de score	Chp. Chp.	Mens Mess.	Ladies Da.
Length Long.	5760	5760	5040
Par	71	71	73

Advised golfing ability
Niveau de jeu recommandé — 0 12 24 36

Hcp required Handicap exigé 20 Men, 30 Ladies

CLUB HOUSE & AMENITIES / CLUB HOUSE ET ANNEXES — 7/10

Pro shop	Pro-shop	
Driving range	Practice	
Sheltered	couvert	no
On grass	sur herbe	yes
Putting-green	putting-green	yes
Pitching-green	pitching green	no

583

HOTEL FACILITIES / ENVIRONNEMENT HOTELIER — 6/10

HOTELS HÔTELS

Angel Posting House - 18 rooms, D £ 105 Guildford
Tel (44) 01483 - 64 555 6 km
Fax (44) 01483 - 33 770

Forte Crest - 109 rooms, D £ 109 Guildford
Tel (44) 01483 - 574 444 6 km
Fax (44) 01483 - 302 960

Blanes Court Hotel - 29 rooms, D £ 70 Guildford
Tel (44) 01483 - 573 171 6 km
Fax (44) 01483 - 32 780

RESTAURANTS RESTAURANTS

Michel's Ripley
Tél (44) 01483 - 224 777 10 km

Café de Paris Guildford
Tel (44) 01483 - 34 896 6 km

❖ Scotland
Ecosse ❖

A s a country, Scotland is a small in terms of land surface but quite exceptional when it comes to golf, with courses sometimes laid out one after the other in an uninterrupted sequence on either side of the country. There are huge clusters of links course on both the east coast and the west coast of Ayrshire. Here we have included the great links courses but also some lesser known gems around Glasgow and Edinburgh, or between Aberdeen and Inverness (the latter course was omitted this year owing to improvement work). But besides the links courses - the glory of Scotland - we have also elected to present a number of inland clubs, some of which have been laid out over areas of immense beauty, for example in the Highlands. Of course some might consider their yardage to be bordering on the "ridiculous" by today's standards, but they are certainly more than a match for your average long-hitter.

As here we are at the very heart of golf, we could quite easily have included "North Inch" in Perth, a course that was played by King James VI in 1603, or again Askernish on the isle of South Uist, but rather than opt for history or unusual surroundings, we preferred Shiskine in Blackwaterfoot which, although only having twelve holes, remains an amazing reference in course design and for the game of golf. This is particularly relevant at a time when the temptation from America or influence from south of the border has pushed green-fees upward, and when golf in Scotland has always been and fortunately always will be a game for everyone.

With money to spare you can build courses like the now highly reputed Loch Lomond, which would have deserved inclusion here despite its very "un-Scottish" design, but no visitors are allowed. With money to spare you can →

shift mountains, dig lakes, model and sometimes even massacre natural landscape, but you won't change the sun's path across the sky or the rhythm of the seasons. In Scotland, golf courses were created by Mother Nature helped by the genius of a few brilliant designers, and golf is a shining light for all. Some courses are snow-bound in Winter, it sometimes rains and the wind can play havoc. But while the best time to play is from April to September, you can tee-off virtually all year... just don't forget to pack a few thick sweaters. You don't come to Scotland the way you would fly to the Caribbean. You come here to play, breathe and live golf.

L'Ecosse est un petit pays en superficie mais un exceptionnel pays de golf, où les parcours peuvent se succéder de manière pratiquement ininterrompue sur les grandes concentrations de links des côtes Est comme de la côte de l'Ayrshire à l'Ouest. Nous avons inclus ici les plus grands links, mais aussi de petites merveilles moins connues, rassemblés autour de Glasgow et d'Edimbourg, mais aussi d'Aberdeen à Inverness (dont le parcours a été écarté cette année en raison de travaux). En dehors des links qui ont fait la gloire de l'Ecosse, nous avons aussi choisi de vous présenter des parcours «inland», dont la plupart ont été comme posés sur des espaces d'une intense beauté, comme dans les Highlands. Bien sûr, on pourra estimer leur longueur parfois «ridicule,» mais en ramener un bon score n'est pas à la portée du premier cogneur venu.

Sans aucun doute, comme nous sommes au coeur du golf, nous aurions presque pu inclure le "North Inch" de Perth, sur un terrain où a joué le roi James VI en 1603, ou encore Askernish dans l'île de South Uist, mais, quitte à être historique ou dépaysant, nous avons préféré Shiskine à Blackwaterfoot, qui compte peut-être douze trous, mais constitue une étonnante référence d'architecture et de jeu. Il n'est pas inutile de rappeler les fondamentaux du dessin de parcours, ou tout au moins les garnds témoignages du passé, à l'heure où la tentation américaine ou l'exemple des grands clubs modernes anglais ont poussé les green-fees vers le haut, alors même que le golf en Ecosse a toujours été un jeu pour tous, et le reste fort heureusement.

Avec beaucoup d'argent, on peut créer des parcours comme Loch Lomond, de fameuse réputation, qui aurait évidemment mérite de figurer ici en dépit de son caractère architectural peu « écossais », mais il n'accepte aucun visiteur. Avec beaucoup d'argent, on peut déplacer des montagnes, creuser des lacs, modeler la nature, la torturer parfois, mais on ne changera pas la course du soleil ni le rythme des saisons. En Ecosse, les golfs ont été fait par la nature et quelques architectes de génie, le soleil du golf brille pour tous, certains parcours sont enneigés en hiver, la pluie tombe parfois, le vent souffle aussi, et si la meilleure saison va d'avril à septembre, on peut jouer pratiquement toute l'année... avec de gros pulls dans la valise. On ne vient pas en Ecosse comme dans les Caraïbes. On vient ici pour jouer au golf, pour respirer le golf, vivre le golf.

14	6	6

There is no shortage of golf courses in the region of Deeside, each one having its own character often shaped by the setting. Aboyne is a real park and is by and large flat, except on the edge of the course where the holes run around a small hill and the slopes from the 11th to the 14th holes take us into more rocky countryside. Reassuringly, particularly for your game strategy, the course is free of hidden hazards as no-one likes to fall into that sort of trap the first time they play a new course. There are though just a few elevated or tiered greens that might cause you trouble. Generally speaking, Aboyne is a little similar to Ballater, only with a little more variety in hole layout.

Cette région du Deeside ne manque pas de parcours de golf, chacun avec son propre caractère, souvent fonction de l'environnement. Aboyne est un véritable parc, généralement plat. Sauf à l'extrémité du parcours où les trous tournent autour d'une petite colline et ces quelques reliefs du 11 au 14 qui nous amènent dans un paysage de lande rocailleuse. Quand on joue un parcours pour la première fois, il n'est pas toujours agréable d'être piégé par des obstacles cachés, mais ici, ce n'est pas le cas, ce qui peut rassurer sur la stratégie à mettre en oeuvre. Seuls quelques greens surélevés, ou à plateau peuvent causer quelques surprises, pas forcément désagréables d'ailleurs. En règle général, Aboyne est un peu similaire de caractère avec Ballater, mais avec un peu plus de variété de dessin des trous.

Aboyne Golf Club

Formaston Park
SCO - ABOYNE, Aberdeenshire AB34 5 HE

Office	Secrétariat	(44) 01339 - 886 328
Pro shop	Pro-shop	(44) 01339 - 886 469
Fax	Fax	(44) 01339 - 887 078
Situation	Situation	

48 km W of Aberdeen (pop. 204 885)
19 km W of Banchory (pop. 6 230)

Annual closure	Fermeture annnuelle	no
Weekly closure	Fermeture hebdomadaire	no

Fees main season
Tarifs haute saison 18 holes

	Week days Semaine	We/Bank holidays We/Férié
Individual Individuel	£ 17	£ 21
Couple Couple	£ 34	£ 42

Full days: £ 21 - £ 26 (Weekends)

Caddy	Caddy	on request
Electric Trolley	Chariot électrique	no
Buggy	Voiturette	no
Clubs	Clubs	yes

Credit cards Cartes de crédit
Eurocard - MasterCard

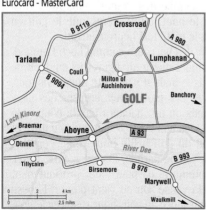

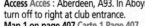

Access Accès : Aberdeen, A93. In Aboyne,
turn off to right at club entrance.
Map 1 on page 407 Carte 1 Page 407

GOLF COURSE
PARCOURS

14/20

Site	Site	
Maintenance	Entretien	
Architect	Architecte	Archie Simpson
Type	Type	parkland
Relief	Relief	
Water in play	Eau en jeu	
Exp. to wind	Exposé au vent	
Trees in play	Arbres en jeu	

Scorecard Carte de score	Chp. Chp.	Mens Mess.	Ladies Da.
Length Long.	5447	5112	4906
Par	68	67	72

Advised golfing ability		0	12	24	36
Niveau de jeu recommandé					
Hcp required	Handicap exigé	no			

CLUB HOUSE & AMENITIES
CLUB HOUSE ET ANNEXES

6/10

Pro shop	Pro-shop	
Driving range	Practice	
Sheltered	couvert	no
On grass	sur herbe	no
Putting-green	putting-green	yes
Pitching-green	pitching green	yes

HOTEL FACILITIES
ENVIRONNEMENT HOTELIER

6/10

HOTELS HÔTELS
Birse Lodge — Aboyne, close
12 rooms, D £ 70
Tel (44) 01339 - 886 253

Tullich Lodge — Ballater, 14 km
10 rooms, D £ 200 (w. dinner)
10 (44) 013397 - 55 406, Fax (44) 013397 - 55 397

RESTAURANTS RESTAURANT
The Boat Inn (Pub) — Aboyne, close
10 (44) 01339 - 886 137

Alloa is one of a bunch of very good inland courses in Scotland, in a region little known by golfing tourists. You shouldn't pass through here without stopping off and playing this fine course, once again restyled by James Braid. Where hasn't the man left his mark in Scotland? If you are a "collector" of James Braid courses, you will recognise his strategic placing of bunkers denoting an astute knowledge of both the game at the highest level and of average players' abilities, a rare feature from a former champion such as he. While there are courses for driving and courses for approach shots, this one demands both to reach greens which are sometimes elevated and even blind and call for special care. This is a hilly course so physical fitness will help.

Alloa fait partie du petit peloton des très bons parcours "inland" d'Ecosse, dans une région assez peu connue des touristes golfiques. Il ne faudrait pas passer par là sans connaître cette belle réalisation, une fois de plus remaniée par James Braid, mais où n'est-il pas intervenu ? Si vous "collectionnez" ses réalisations, vous retrouverez ici un placement stratégique des obstacles, dénotant une connaissance aiguë du jeu au plus haut niveau mais aussi des joueurs moyens, ce qui est plus rare de la part d'un ancien champion comme lui. S'il est des parcours de drivers et des parcours de "seconds coups," celui-ci exige autant des départs aux greens, avec une attention particulière pour ces derniers, parfois surélevés, voire aveugles. Le relief est ici bien marqué, attention à venir en bonne forme physique.

Alloa Golf Club

Schawpark
SCO - SAUCHIE, Clackmannanshire FK10 3AX

Office	Secrétariat	(44) 01259 - 722 745
Pro shop	Pro-shop	(44) 01259 - 724 476
Fax	Fax	
Situation	Situation	

24 km W of Dunfermline (pop. 29 436)

Annual closure	Fermeture annnuelle	no
Weekly closure	Fermeture hebdomadaire	no

Fees main season
Tarifs haute saison 18 holes

	Week days Semaine	We/Bank holidays We/Férié
Individual Individuel	£ 16	£ 20
Couple Couple	£ 32	£ 40

Full days: £ 25 - £ 30 (weekends)

Caddy	Caddy	no
Electric Trolley	Chariot électrique	no
Buggy	Voiturette	no
Clubs	Clubs	yes

Credit cards Cartes de crédit
VISA - Eurocard - MasterCard - AMEX - DC

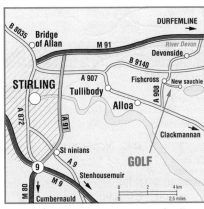

Access Accès : Edinburgh, A90, A907 to Dunfermline and Alloa. Turn right onto A908.
course on the right in the village of Sauchie.
Map 2 on page 409 Carte 2 Page 409

GOLF COURSE
PARCOURS

15/20

Site	Site	▬▬▬▬▬
Maintenance	Entretien	
Architect	Architecte	James Braid
Type	Type	parkland
Relief	Relief	▬▬▬▬
Water in play	Eau en jeu	▬
Exp. to wind	Exposé au vent	▬
Trees in play	Arbres en jeu	▬▬▬▬

Scorecard Carte de score	Chp. Chp.	Mens Mess.	Ladies Da.
Length Long.	5570	5460	4895
Par	70	69	73

Advised golfing ability Niveau de jeu recommandé	0	12	24	36

Hcp required   Handicap exigé   no

CLUB HOUSE & AMENITIES
CLUB HOUSE ET ANNEXES

7/10

Pro shop	Pro-shop	▬▬▬▬
Driving range	Practice	▬▬▬
Sheltered	couvert	no
On grass	sur herbe	yes
Putting-green	putting-green	yes
Pitching-green	pitching green	yes

587

HOTEL FACILITIES
ENVIRONNEMENT HOTELIER

6/10

HOTELS HÔTELS

Gean House   Alloa
7 rooms, D £ 140   5 km
Tel (44) 01259 - 219 275, Fax (44) 01259 - 213 827

Stirling Highland   Stirling
70 rooms, D £ 90   14 km
Tel (44) 01786 - 475 444, Fax (44) 01786 - 462 929

RESTAURANTS RESTAURANT

Farriers   Alva
Tel (44) 01259 - 762 702   5 km

Unicorn Inn   Kincardine
Tel (44) 01259 - 730 704   6 km

Within the immediate vicinity of Blairgowrie, Dundee and Perth, the Alyth course does not have the fame it deserves, partly because fame today comes through hosting top tournaments. This course now is too short for the best professionals, but is way above average in terms of appeal. With good, well protected greens, endless trees and heather edging the fairways and dangerous bunkers, Alyth requires great accuracy and is ideal for getting your ironwork into good shape. A few very good holes and some superb views over the Perthshire countryside add extra appeal to a guaranteed good day's golfing. The region of Angus also offers a variety facilities for leisure and excursions.

A proximité immédiate de Blairgowrie, Dundee et Perth, le parcours d'Alyth n'a pas connu la notoriété qu'il mérite, en partie parce qu'elle se fait aujourd'hui en recevant de grands tournois. Ce parcours est aujourd'hui trop court pour les meilleurs professionnels, mais son intérêt est nettement au-dessus de la moyenne. Avec de bons greens correctement défendus contre les assauts, des arbres nombreux et la bruyère bordant les fairways, des bunkers dangereux, il demande une grande précision, et c'est idéal pour travailler son jeu de fers. Quelques très bons trous et des vues superbes sur la campagne du Perthshire ajoutent un intérêt supplémentaire à une bonne journée de golf garanti sans souffrances. Et cette région de l'Angus offre de multiples opportunités de loisirs et d'excursions.

Alyth Golf Club
Pitcrocknie
SCO - ALYTH, Perthshire PH10 7AB

Office	Secrétariat	(44) 01828 - 632 268
Pro shop	Pro-shop	(44) 01828 - 633 411
Fax	Fax	(44) 01828 - 633 491
Situation	Situation	

8 km E of Blairgowrie (pop. 5 208)
24 km NW of Dundee (pop. 165 873)

Annual closure	Fermeture annnuelle	no
Weekly closure	Fermeture hebdomadaire	no

Fees main season Tarifs haute saison 18 holes

	Week days Semaine	We/Bank holidays We/Férié
Individual Individuel	£ 18	£ 23
Couple Couple	£ 36	£ 46

Full day: £ 27 - £ 32 (weekends)

Caddy	Caddy	on request
Electric Trolley	Chariot électrique	£ 4/18 holes
Buggy	Voiturette	no
Clubs	Clubs	no

Credit cards Cartes de crédit
VISA - Eurocard - MasterCard - JCB

588

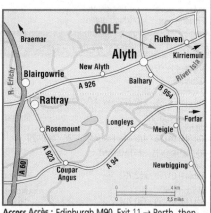

Access Accès : Edinburgh M90, Exit 11 → Perth, then A94 through Coupar to Meigle. Turn right on B954. Golf 1.5 km (1 m.) before Alyth.
Map 1 on page 407 Carte 1 Page 407

GOLF COURSE
PARCOURS
14/20

Site	Site	
Maintenance	Entretien	
Architect	Architecte	Tom Morris James Braid
Type	Type	heathland
Relief	Relief	
Water in play	Eau en jeu	
Exp. to wind	Exposé au vent	
Trees in play	Arbres en jeu	

Scorecard Carte de score	Chp. Chp.	Mens Mess.	Ladies Da.
Length Long.	5646	5409	4770
Par	70	70	71

Advised golfing ability Niveau de jeu recommandé	0	12	24	36

Hcp required	Handicap exigé	certificate

CLUB HOUSE & AMENITIES
CLUB HOUSE ET ANNEXES
6/10

Pro shop	Pro-shop	
Driving range	Practice	
Sheltered	couvert	not yet
On grass	sur herbe	yes
Putting-green	putting-green	yes
Pitching-green	pitching green	no

HOTEL FACILITIES
ENVIRONNEMENT HOTELIER
6/10

HOTELS HÔTELS

Lands of Loyal 14 rooms, D £ 79 Tel (44) 01828 - 633 151, Fax (44) 01828 - 633 313		Alyth 1 km
Alyth Hotel 8 rooms, D £ 70 Tel (44) 01828 - 632 447, Fax (44) 01828 - 632 355		Alyth 1 km
Drumnacree House. 6 rooms, D £ 80 Tel (44) 01828 - 632 194		Alyth 1 km

RESTAURANTS RESTAURANT

Lands of Loyal Tel (44) 01828 - 633 151		Alyth 1 km

AYR (BELLEISLE) | 16 | 5 | 7

Most of the visitors to this region head for Prestwick, Royal Troon and Turnberry and might easily neglect a number of little gems of which this is a typical example. Designed by James Braid (who else?) in 1927 to meet the huge demand for new courses, Belleisle was laid out in a public park close to the sea but without the features of a links. This is nonetheless a challenging course with a lot of character where there is something almost odd about the views over the sea in the setting of trees. With no hidden dangers, golfing can be enjoyed without fear as long as you choose the right clubs and the right way of playing them. The weather will decide whether you aim high or low. An ideal course for week-end golfing when the "big" courses are crowded.

La plupart des visiteurs de la région se concentrent sur Prestwick, Royal Troon et Turnberry, et risquent de négliger quelques petits joyaux. En voici un exemple typique. Dessiné par James Braid en 1927 pour satisfaire une demande galopante de nouveaux parcours, Belleisle a été créé dans un parc public proche de la mer, mais sans les caractéristiques des links. Il n'empêche qu'il s'agit d'un parcours exigeant, avec beaucoup de caractère, où certains points de vue sur l'eau ont quelque chose d'étrange dans cet environnement d'arbres. Sans aucun danger caché, ce parcours peut être immédiatement dégusté sans crainte, du moment que l'on y choisit les bons clubs et la bonne manière de s'en servir. Suivant le temps, on pourra y jouer balles roulées ou balles levées. Idéal pour jouer en week-end quand les "grands" sont très difficiles d'accès.

Belleisle Golf Course

Belleisle Park, Doonfoot Road
SCO - AYR, Ayrshire KA7 4DU

Office	Secrétariat	(44) 01292 - 441 258
Pro shop	Pro-shop	(44) 01292 - 441 314
Fax	Fax	(44) 01292 - 442 632
Situation	Situation	

1 km from Ayr (pop. 47 872)

Annual closure	Fermeture annnuelle	no
Weekly closure	Fermeture hebdomadaire	no

Fees main season
Tarifs haute saison 18 holes

	Week days Semaine	We/Bank holidays We/Férié
Individual Individuel	£ 18.50	£ 20
Couple Couple	£ 37	£ 40

Full days: £ 26 - £ 30 (weekends)

Caddy	Caddy	on request
Electric Trolley	Chariot électrique	no
Buggy	Voiturette	no
Clubs	Clubs	£ 10/18 holes

Credit cards   Cartes de crédit
VISA - Eurocard - MasterCard

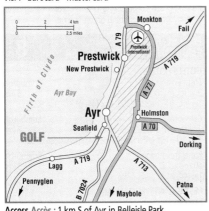

Access Accès : 1 km S of Ayr in Belleisle Park
Map 3 on page 410 Carte 3 Page 410

GOLF COURSE PARCOURS — 16/20

Site	Site	▬▬▬▬
Maintenance	Entretien	▬▬▬▬
Architect	Architecte	James Braid
Type	Type	parkland
Relief	Relief	▬▬
Water in play	Eau en jeu	▬
Exp. to wind	Exposé au vent	▬▬▬▬
Trees in play	Arbres en jeu	▬▬▬

Scorecard Carte de score	Chp. Chp.	Mens Mess.	Ladies Da.
Length Long.	5855	5509	5150
Par	71	71	74

Advised golfing ability		0 12 24 36
Niveau de jeu recommandé		▬▬▬▬▭
Hcp required	Handicap exigé	no

CLUB HOUSE & AMENITIES CLUB HOUSE ET ANNEXES — 5/10

Pro shop	Pro-shop	▬▬
Driving range	Practice	▬▬
Sheltered	couvert	no
On grass	sur herbe	yes
Putting-green	putting-green	yes
Pitching-green	pitching green	no

589

HOTEL FACILITIES ENVIRONNEMENT HOTELIER — 7/10

HOTELS HÔTELS

Fairfield House — Ayr
33 rooms, D £ 120 — 3 km
Tel (44) 01292 - 267 461, Fax (44) 01292 - 261 456

Kylestrome — Ayr
12 rooms, D £ 80 — 3 km
Tel (44) 01292 - 262 474, Fax (44) 01292 - 260 863

Pickwick — Ayr
15 rooms, D £ 70 — 2 km
Tel (44) 01292 - 260 111, Fax (44) 01292 - 285 348

Northpark House — Alloway
5 rooms, D £ 85 — 2 km
Tel (44) 01292 - 442 336, Fax (44) 01292 - 445 572

RESTAURANTS RESTAURANT

Fouters — Ayr
Tel (44) 01292 - 261 391 — 3 km

While the family is visiting Edinburgh or doing some shopping, you'll have the time to play 18 holes at Baberton to the south-west of the city. Created in 1893 and designed by the great Wille Park Jnr, this is no longer a tournament course but some of the par 4s and par 3s are anything but easy. Without being really dangerous, the trees, bunkers and ditches are in play just enough to bother average players, who make up the major share of green-feers here during the week. The trees are particularly beautiful especially in their Autumn colours, when we visited. Don't be surprised if you're late getting back, as the Clubhouse reserves a warm welcome to all. The best idea would be for the family to come and meet you there.

Pendant que la famille visite Edimbourg ou fait du shopping, vous avez le temps de faire 18 trous à Baberton, au sud-ouest de la ville. Fondé en 1893 et dessiné par le grand Willie Park Jr, ce n'est plus au-jourd'hui un parcours de championnat, bien que certains de ses par 4 et ses cinq par 3 ne soient pas des plus faciles. Sans être vaiment dangereux, les arbres, les bunkers et les fossés sont assez en jeu pour in-quiéter le joueur moyen, qui fournit l'essentiel de la clientèle extérieure en semaine. Les arbres sont ici particulièrement beaux, spécialement dans leurs teintes d'automne. Et si vous êtes en retard pour rejoindre les vôtres, rien d'étonnant à ce que vous ayiez oublié de repartir, le Clubhouse est accueillant. La bonne idée, c'est qu'ils vous rejoignent ici.

Baberton Golf Club
50 Baberton Avenue, Juniper Green
SCO - EDINBURGH EH14 5DU

Office	Secrétariat	(44) 0131 - 453 3555
Pro shop	Pro-shop	(44) 0131 - 453 3555
Fax	Fax	
Situation	Situation	

9 km SW of Edinburgh centre (pop. 418 914)

Annual closure	Fermeture annnuelle	no
Weekly closure	Fermeture hebdomadaire	no

Fees main season
Tarifs haute saison 18 holes

	Week days Semaine	We/Bank holidays We/Férié
Individual Individuel	£ 18.50	—
Couple Couple	£ 37	—

Full weekday: £ 28.50 - Weekends: members only

Caddy	Caddy	no
Electric Trolley	Chariot électrique	no
Buggy	Voiturette	no
Clubs	Clubs	yes
Credit cards Cartes de crédit		no

590

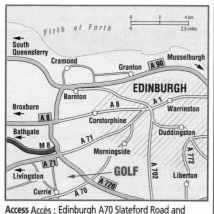

Access Accès : Edinburgh A70 Slateford Road and Lanark Road until by-pass (A720), Juniper Green and Baberton Junction.
Map 3 on page 411 Carte 3 Page 411

GOLF COURSE
PARCOURS
14/20

Site	Site	
Maintenance	Entretien	
Architect	Architecte	Willie Park
Type	Type	parkland
Relief	Relief	
Water in play	Eau en jeu	
Exp. to wind	Exposé au vent	
Trees in play	Arbres en jeu	

Scorecard Carte de score	Chp. Chp.	Mens Mess.	Ladies Da.
Length Long.	5571	5571	4985
Par	69	69	72

Advised golfing ability		0 12 24 36
Niveau de jeu recommandé		
Hcp required	Handicap exigé	no

CLUB HOUSE & AMENITIES
CLUB HOUSE ET ANNEXES
6/10

Pro shop	Pro-shop	
Driving range	Practice	
Sheltered	couvert	no
On grass	sur herbe	no
Putting-green	putting-green	yes
Pitching-green	pitching green	no

HOTEL FACILITIES
ENVIRONNEMENT HOTELIER
8/10

HOTELS HÔTELS

Forte Posthouse — Edinburgh
204 rooms, D £ 70 — 5 km
Tel (44) 0131 - 334 0390, Fax (44) 0131 - 334 9237

Caledonian — Edinburgh
223 rooms, D £ 200 — 7 km
Tel (44) 0131 - 459 9988, Fax (44) 0131 - 225 6632

Forte Travelodge — Edinburgh
40 rooms, D £ 35 — 3 km
Tel (44) 0131 - 441 4296

RESTAURANTS RESTAURANT

Mackenzies — Edinburgh
Tel (44) 0131 - 441 2587 — 2 km

Indian Cavalry Club — Edinburgh
Tel (44) 0131 - 228 3282 — 5 km

Here we are just a few miles from Balmoral Castle, the Royal Family's summer residence, in a beautiful region of the Highlands along the banks of the river Dee, which borders the course. The area is more popular for tourism than golf, or even for fishing or hunting from Spring to late Autumn only (at 2,000 ft. above sea level, the winter weather always has the final say). The course, rather hilly although never too exhausting to walk on a soft carpet of grass, winds its way through heather, broom and trees. James Braid and Harry Vardon added their personal touch to a very pleasant layout, where the land has been used very intelligently. This may not be the world's most difficult course but playing here certainly is time well spent.

Nous ne sommes qu'à quelques kilomètres du château de Balmoral, résidence d'été de la famille royale, dans une très belle région des Highlands, en bordure de la rivière Dee servant de limite au parcours. On vient plus ici pour le tourisme que pour le golf, ou encore pour la pêche et la chasse, du printemps à la fin de l'automne, car nous sommes à 600 mètres d'altitude. Les reliefs du parcours sont assez prononcés, bien que l'ensemble ne soit pas épuisant, grâce à un gazon très fourni, insinué dans la bruyère, les genêts et les arbres. James Braid et Harry Vardon ont apporté leur touche personnelle à un dessin très agréable, où le terrain a été utilisé avec beaucoup d'à-propos. Ce n'est peut-être pas le parcours le plus difficile du monde, mais on n'y perdra jamais son temps.

Ballater Golf Club
Victoria Road
SCO - BALLATER, Aberdeenshire AB35 5QX

Office	Secrétariat	(44) 013397 - 55 567
Pro shop	Pro-shop	(44) 013397 - 55 658
Fax	Fax	(44) 013397 - 55 057
Situation	Situation	

67 km W of Aberdeen (pop. 204 885)

Annual closure	Fermeture annnuelle	no
Weekly closure	Fermeture hebdomadaire	no

Chances of snow in winter months

Fees main season
Tarifs haute saison 18 holes

	Week days Semaine	We/Bank holidays We/Férié
Individual Individuel	£ 17	£ 20
Couple Couple	£ 34	£ 40

Full day: £ 26 - £ 30 (weekends)

Caddy	Caddy	on request
Electric Trolley	Chariot électrique	no
Buggy	Voiturette	no
Clubs	Clubs	yes

Credit cards Cartes de crédit
VISA - MasterCard - Switch

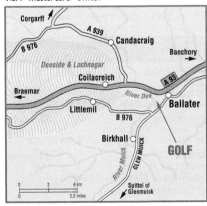

Access Accès : Aberdeen, A93 West → Ballater, Balmoral Castle
Map 1 on page 407 Carte 1 Page 407

GOLF COURSE
PARCOURS
15/20

Site	Site	
Maintenance	Entretien	
Architect	Architecte	James Braid
Type	Type	parkland
Relief	Relief	
Water in play	Eau en jeu	
Exp. to wind	Exposé au vent	
Trees in play	Arbres en jeu	

Scorecard Carte de score	Chp. Chp.	Mens Mess.	Ladies Da.
Length Long.	5545	5638	5278
Par	70	67	71

Advised golfing ability		0 12 24 36
Niveau de jeu recommandé		
Hcp required	Handicap exigé	no

CLUB HOUSE & AMENITIES
CLUB HOUSE ET ANNEXES
6/10

Pro shop	Pro-shop	
Driving range	Practice	
Sheltered	couvert	no
On grass	sur herbe	no
Putting-green	putting-green	no
Pitching-green	pitching green	no

591

HOTEL FACILITIES
ENVIRONNEMENT HOTELIER
7/10

HOTELS HÔTELS
Glen Lui — Ballater
19 rooms, D £ 60 — very close
Tel (44) 013397 - 55 402, Fax (44) 013397 - 55 545

Alexandra Hotel — Ballater
7 rooms, D £ 60 — 0,5 km
Tel (44) 013397 - 55 376, Fax (44) 013397 - 55 416

Darroch Learg — Ballater
18 rooms, D £ 90 — close
Tel (44) 013397 - 55 443, Fax (44) 013397 - 55 252

RESTAURANTS RESTAURANT
Highlander — Ballater, 0,5 km

Oaks — Ballater
Tel (44) 013397 - 55 858 — 2 km

In a magnificent resort located in some of Scotland's finest countryside, this course designed by Thomas and Alliss in 1974 brought a welcome alternative to the famous Rosemount course. There is of course a definite American influence in this layout over a thickly treed landscape (pine-trees especially). The fairways are narrow and then the heather makes things a little more complicated, but the designers have often left a few open corridors to the greens to make things easier for Scottish golfers who are not always experts at lofting the ball. We would have liked a little more breathing space for the tee-shot, as players who are neither too long nor too straight will have a tough time if they choose to play from the back tees. The course has aged well even though some might find this still just a touch artificial.

Dans ce magnifique ensemble situé dans un des très beaux paysages d'Ecosse, ce parcours de Thomas et Alliss a apporté en 1974 une alternative bienvenue au fameux Rosemount Course. Bien sûr, on trouve une certaine influence américaine dans leur dessin tracé dans un paysage très boisé (surtout de pins). Les fairways sont étroits, la bruyère complique ensuite les choses, mais les architectes ont souvent laissé quelques passages en ouverture des greens pour faciliter le travail des joueurs écossais pas toujours virtuoses des balles levées. On aimerait parfois une plus grande sensation d'espace au moment de driver, car les joueurs ni très longs, ni très droits souffriront s'ils choisissent les départs reculés. Le parcours a bien vieilli, bien qu'on puisse toujours le trouver un rien artificiel.

Blairgowrie Golf Club

Rosemount
SCO - BLAIRGOWRIE, Perthshire PH10 6LG

Office	Secrétariat	(44) 01250 - 872 622
Pro shop	Pro-shop	(44) 01250 - 872 594
Fax	Fax	(44) 01250 - 875 451
Situation	Situation	

35 km from Perth (pop. 123 495)

Annual closure	Fermeture annnuelle	no
Weekly closure	Fermeture hebdomadaire	no

Fees main season
Tarifs haute saison 18 holes

	Week days Semaine	We/Bank holidays We/Férié
Individual Individuel	£ 40	£ 45
Couple Couple	£ 80	£ 90

Day ticket for a round on both courses:
£ 60- £ 75 (Weekends)

Caddy	Caddy	on request
Electric Trolley	Chariot électrique	
Buggy	Voiturette	£ 17/18 holes
Clubs	Clubs	£ 5-20/18 holes

Credit cards Cartes de crédit
VISA - Eurocard - MasterCard - AMEX - DC - JCB

592

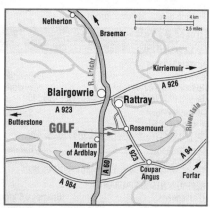

Access Accès : Edinburgh M90 to Perth, then A93 →
Blairgowrie (golf 2 km South of Blairgowrie)
Map 1 on page 407 Carte 1 Page 407

GOLF COURSE
PARCOURS

15/20

Site	Site	
Maintenance	Entretien	
Architect	Architecte	Dave Thomas Peter Alliss
Type	Type	heathland, inland
Relief	Relief	
Water in play	Eau en jeu	
Exp. to wind	Exposé au vent	
Trees in play	Arbres en jeu	

Scorecard Carte de score	Chp. Chp.	Mens Mess.	Ladies Da.
Length Long.	6290	5805	5420
Par	72	71	73

Advised golfing ability Niveau de jeu recommandé	0 12 24 36
Hcp required Handicap exigé	certificate

CLUB HOUSE & AMENITIES
CLUB HOUSE ET ANNEXES

8/10

Pro shop	Pro-shop	
Driving range	Practice	
Sheltered	couvert	no
On grass	sur herbe	yes
Putting-green	putting-green	yes
Pitching-green	pitching green	no

HOTEL FACILITIES
ENVIRONNEMENT HOTELIER

6/10

HOTELS HÔTELS
Rosemount   Golf
12 rooms, D £ 55   on site
Tel (44) 01250 - 872 604, Fax (44) 01250 - 874 496

Kinloch House   Blairgowrie
21 rooms, D £ 165 (w. dinner)   3 km
Tel (44) 01250 - 884 237, Fax (44) 01250 - 884 333

Altamount House   Blairgowrie
7 rooms, D £ 75   2 km
Tel (44) 01250 - 873 512, Fax (44) 01250 - 876 200

RESTAURANTS RESTAURANT
Rosemount   Golf
Tel (44) 01250 - 872 604   on site

For many golfers this is one of the best British inland courses. It's a pity they had to sacrifice two or three holes to cater to the building of the Lansdowne course but James Braid had already altered the original layout by Alister MacKenzie. Despite this, Rosemount has lost nothing of its charm and of the marvellous feeling of tranquillity you get when playing here, as each hole is clearly separated from the others by a thick row of trees. The wildlife and flora add to the beauty of the spot, particularly in Autumn, and to this excellent course where you need to play in every direction. Beneath its kindly exterior, Rosemount cleverly conceals perhaps not the hazards but at least its difficulties. And as it is never tiring to play, it is worth more than the one visit.

C'est pour beaucoup l'un des meilleurs parcours intérieurs de Grande-Bretagne. On regrette un peu le sacrifice de deux ou trois trous au moment de la construction du Lansdowne Course, mais James Braid avait déjà retouché le travail original d'Alister MacKenzie. Rosemount n'a rien perdu pour autant de son charme, et de la merveilleuse sensation de paix qu'on y éprouve, chaque trou étant nettement séparé des autres par d'épais rideaux d'arbres. La vie sauvage et le flore ajoutent encore à la beauté du lieu, notamment en automne. En plus, c'est un excellent parcours où il faut savoir jouer dans tous les sens, et qui cache bien, sinon ses obstacles, du moins ses difficultés sous des dehors souriants. Comme il n'est pas non plus fatigant à jouer, il mérite cent fois mieux qu'une simple visite.

Blairgowrie Golf Club
Rosemount
SCO - BLAIRGOWRIE, Perthshire PH10 6LG

Office	Secrétariat	(44) 01250 - 872 622
Pro shop	Pro-shop	(44) 01250 - 872 594
Fax	Fax	(44) 01250 - 875 451
Situation	Situation	

35 km from Perth (pop. 123 495)

Annual closure	Fermeture annnuelle	no
Weekly closure	Fermeture hebdomadaire	no

Fees main season Tarifs haute saison 18 holes

	Week days Semaine	We/Bank holidays We/Férié
Individual Individuel	£ 50	£ 55
Couple Couple	£ 100	£ 110

Day ticket for a round on both courses:
£ 60- £ 75 (Weekends)

Caddy	Caddy	on request
Electric Trolley	Chariot électrique	
Buggy	Voiturette	£ 17/18 holes
Clubs	Clubs	£ 5-20/18 holes

Credit cards Cartes de crédit
VISA - Eurocard - MasterCard - AMEX - DC - JCB

Access Accès : Edinburgh M90 to Perth, then A93 →
Blairgowrie (golf 2 km South of Blairgowrie)
Map 1 on page 407 Carte 1 Page 407

GOLF COURSE
PARCOURS
18/20

Site	Site	■■■■■■■
Maintenance	Entretien	■■■■■■
Architect	Architecte	Alister MacKenzie James Braid
Type	Type	heathland, inland
Relief	Relief	■■■
Water in play	Eau en jeu	■■
Exp. to wind	Exposé au vent	■■■
Trees in play	Arbres en jeu	■■■■■

Scorecard Carte de score	Chp. Chp.	Mens Mess.	Ladies Da.
Length Long.	6014	5693	5445
Par	72	70	74

Advised golfing ability Niveau de jeu recommandé	0	12	24	36
Hcp required Handicap exigé	certificate			

CLUB HOUSE & AMENITIES
CLUB HOUSE ET ANNEXES
8/10

Pro shop	Pro-shop	■■■■■
Driving range	Practice	■■■
Sheltered	couvert	no
On grass	sur herbe	yes
Putting-green	putting-green	yes
Pitching-green	pitching green	no

593

HOTEL FACILITIES
ENVIRONNEMENT HOTELIER
6/10

HOTELS HÔTELS
Rosemount — Golf
12 rooms, D £ 55 — on site
Tel (44) 01250 - 872 604, Fax (44) 01250 - 874 496

Kinloch House — Blairgowrie
21 rooms, D £ 165 (w. dinner) — 3 km
Tel (44) 01250 - 884 237, Fax (44) 01250 - 884 333

Altamount House — Blairgowrie
7 rooms, D £ 75 — 2 km
Tel (44) 01250 - 873 512, Fax (44) 01250 - 876 200

RESTAURANTS RESTAURANT
Rosemount — Golf
Tel (44) 01250 - 872 604 — on site

Boat of Garten is the gateway to the Cairngorms, the highest peaks in the UK, and lies within the immediate vicinity of a natural reserve created to protect wildlife, a few miles from the mountain resort of Aviemore to which it is linked by a charming steam train. The flora and fauna (bison, wolves and bears) in this region are worth the visit as much as the distilleries. And there is also a golf course, a little but not too hilly over the first few holes, whose general excellence makes this more than just an added distraction or a site for spectacular panoramas. James Braid's layout is top notch and features a par 6, one of the best holes in Scotland, which is saying something. A holiday course, but what a holiday !

A proximité immédiate d'une réserve naturelle créée pour protéger les orfraies, à quelques kilomètres de la station de montagne d'Aviemore, reliée par un charmant train à vapeur, Boat of Garten marque l'entrée dans les Cairngorns, les plus hautes montagnes de Grande-Bretagne. La flore et la faune (bisons, loups, ours) de cette région valent le déplacement autant que les distilleries. Mais il y a aussi un parcours de golf. Il est un peu accidenté dans les premiers trous, mais sans excès, et sa qualité générale en fait plus qu'une distraction annexe ou le prétexte à aller voir des panoramas spectaculaires. Le dessin de James Braid est de première qualité, notamment au 6, l'un des meilleurs trous de toute l'Ecosse. C'est un parcours de vacances, mais de bonnes vacances.

Boat of Garten Golf Club
SCO - BOAT OF GARTEN, Inverness-shire PH24 3BQ

Office	Secrétariat	(44) 01479 - 831 282
Pro shop	Pro-shop	(44) 01479 - 831 282
Fax	Fax	(44) 01479 - 831 523
Situation	Situation	

8 km from Aviemore (pop. 2 214)
48 km SE of Inverness (pop. 62 186)

Annual closure	Fermeture annnuelle	yes
		1/11→1/04/99
Weekly closure	Fermeture hebdomadaire	no

Fees main season
Tarifs haute saison 18 holes

	Week days Semaine	We/Bank holidays We/Férié
Individual Individuel	£ 21	£ 26
Couple Couple	£ 42	£ 52

Full day: £ 26 - £ 31 (weekends)

Caddy	Caddy	on request/£ 20
Electric Trolley	Chariot électrique	no
Buggy	Voiturette	no
Clubs	Clubs	£ 5/18 holes

Credit cards Cartes de crédit   VISA - MasterCard

594

Access Accès : Inverness, A9. A938 to Carrbridge. Then B9153 and A95 on the left. First right on B970 to Boat of Garten. **Map 1 on page 407** Carte 1 Page 407

GOLF COURSE
PARCOURS   **14**/20

Site	Site	
Maintenance	Entretien	
Architect	Architecte	James Braid
Type	Type	heathland
Relief	Relief	
Water in play	Eau en jeu	
Exp. to wind	Exposé au vent	
Trees in play	Arbres en jeu	

Scorecard Carte de score	Chp. Chp.	Mens Mess.	Ladies Da.
Length Long.	5340	5340	4640
Par	69	69	71

Advised golfing ability Niveau de jeu recommandé	0	12	24	36
Hcp required	Handicap exigé	certificate		

CLUB HOUSE & AMENITIES
CLUB HOUSE ET ANNEXES   **6**/10

Pro shop	Pro-shop	
Driving range	Practice	
Sheltered	couvert	no
On grass	sur herbe	no
Putting-green	putting-green	yes
Pitching-green	pitching green	yes

HOTEL FACILITIES
ENVIRONNEMENT HOTELIER   **7**/10

HOTELS HÔTELS
The Boat Hotel   Boat of Garten
35 rooms, D £ 50   1 km
Tel (44) 01479 - 831 258, Fax (44) 01479 - 831 414

The Craigard Hotel   Boat of Garten
18 rooms, D £ 70   1 km
Tel (44) 01479 - 831 206, Fax (44) 01479 - 831 423

Heathbank House   Boat of Garten
7 rooms, D £ 70   1 km
Tel (44) 01479 - 831 234

RESTAURANTS RESTAURANT
Heathbank House   Boat of Garten
Tel (44) 01479 - 831 234   1 km

Craggan Mill   Grantown on Spey
Tel (44) 01479 - 872 288   5 km

This course is found no further than the end of the world, a little after Dornoch and Golspie, where the length of the days in summer could almost let you play all three in the same day. Brora is one of the great traditional links, fine-tuned in 1924 after a design by James Braid. Electric fences protect all the greens from the sheep employed to keep the grass cropped. The tee-boxes and greens are often elevated, built between dunes of between 5 and 12 metres high, and the texture of the turf is particularly pleasant, especially for putting. Although rather short, Brora is not an easy course, even though sometimes you might prefer slightly more penalising rough (especially for the guys you're playing with). This is a club of perfect hospitality, where the 19th hole is both reward and consolation. More should be said about this side of Brora to people who are not curious enough to come and discover the course.

Ce n'est pas plus loin que le bout du monde, un peu après Dornoch et Golspie, là où la longueur des journées de début d'été vous permettraient presque de jouer les trois le même jour. Brora est un des grands links traditionnels, peaufiné en 1924 d'après un dessin de James Braid. Des clôtures électriques préservent chaque green des moutons chargés de tondre. Les départs et greens sont souvent surélevés, construits entre des dunes de 5 à 12 mètres de haut, la texture du gazon particulièrement agréable, notamment au putting. Bien qu'assez court, Brora n'est pas un parcours facile, même si l'on souhaiterait parfois (pour ses adversaires !) un rough plus pénalisant. Un club à la parfaite hospitalité, où le 19ème trou est à la fois récompense et consolation, dont on aimera parler à ceux qui ne sont pas assez curieux pour le connaître.

Brora Golf Club
Golf Road
SCO - BRORA, Highland KW9 6QS

Office	Secrétariat	(44) 01408 - 621 417
Pro shop	Pro-shop	(44) 01408 - 621 423
Fax	Fax	(44) 01408 - 622 157
Situation	Situation	

85 km N of Inverness (pop. 62 186)

Annual closure	Fermeture annnuelle	no
Weekly closure	Fermeture hebdomadaire	no

Fees main season
Tarifs haute saison 18 holes

	Week days Semaine	We/Bank holidays We/Férié
Individual Individuel	£ 18	£ 18
Couple Couple	£ 36	£ 36

Caddy	Caddy	on request/£ 20
Electric Trolley	Chariot électrique	no
Buggy	Voiturette	no
Clubs	Clubs	£ 7/18 holes
Credit cards Cartes de crédit		no

Access Accès : Inverness, A9 to the North
Map 1 on page 407 Carte 1 Page 407

GOLF COURSE
PARCOURS
15/20

Site	Site	▬▬▬▬▬
Maintenance	Entretien	▬▬▬▬▬
Architect	Architecte	James Braid
Type	Type	links
Relief	Relief	▬▬▬
Water in play	Eau en jeu	▬▬
Exp. to wind	Exposé au vent	▬▬▬▬▬
Trees in play	Arbres en jeu	▬

Scorecard Carte de score	Chp. Chp.	Mens Mess.	Ladies Da.
Length Long.	5560	5328	4800
Par	69	69	70

Advised golfing ability Niveau de jeu recommandé	0	12	24	36
Hcp required	Handicap exigé	no	

CLUB HOUSE & AMENITIES
CLUB HOUSE ET ANNEXES
7/10

Pro shop	Pro-shop	▬▬▬▬
Driving range	Practice	▬▬▬
Sheltered	couvert	no
On grass	sur herbe	yes
Putting-green	putting-green	yes
Pitching-green	pitching green	yes

HOTEL FACILITIES
ENVIRONNEMENT HOTELIER
7/10

HOTELS HÔTELS

Royal Marine Hotel — Brora
22 rooms, D £ 90 — on site
Tel (44) 01408 - 621 252, Fax (44) 01408 - 621 181

Links Hotel — Brora
24 rooms, D £ 90 — on site
Tel (44) 01408 - 621 225, Fax (44) 01408 - 621 383

RESTAURANTS RESTAURANT

Garden Room — Brora
Tel (44) 01408 - 621 252 — 1 km

Brora Golf Club — Brora
Tel (44) 01408 - 621 417 — on site

595

For many continental Europeans, playing golf virtually in town is a unique experience. This club used to be right in the middle of Edinburgh but has since moved to the outskirts where space is a little less cramped. Willie Park and the great Alistair Mackenzie are responsible for a very pleasant layout at the edge of some hills but where steep slopes have been avoided. This park-style course is generally in excellent condition with immaculate fairways and not over-sized greens. In addition to traditional bunkers, trees are often a dangerous hazard if you play without thinking. This course is a good test for everyone before they square up to more formidable tests on either side of the Forth. Enjoy the excellent restaurant.

Pour bien des continentaux, jouer au golf quasiment en ville est une expérience unique. Ce club était autrefois en plein milieu d'Edimbourg, mais il a émigré à la périphérie, moins à l'étroit. Willie Park et le grand Alister Mackenzie sont responsables d'un tracé très plaisant, en bordure de collines, mais où les fortes pentes ont été évitées. Ce véritable parc est généralement en excellente condition, avec des fairways impeccables et des greens pas très vastes. En plus des bunkers traditionnels, les arbres constituent souvent des obstacles dangereux, si l'on ne réfléchit pas assez. C'est un bon test pour tous, avant d'affronter des adversaires plus redoutables, d'un côté ou de l'autre du Forth. A signaler enfin, l'excellent restaurant.

Bruntsfield Links Golfing Society

32 Barton Avenue
SCO - EDINBURGH EH4 6JH

Office	Secrétariat	(44) 0131 - 336 1479
Pro shop	Pro-shop	(44) 0131 - 336 4050
Fax	Fax	(44) 0131 - 336 5538
Situation	Situation	

5 km of Edinburgh City Centre

Annual closure	Fermeture annnuelle	no
Weekly closure	Fermeture hebdomadaire	no

Fees main season
Tarifs haute saison 18 holes

	Week days Semaine	We/Bank holidays We/Férié
Individual Individuel	£ 36	£ 42
Couple Couple	£ 72	£ 84

Full day: £ 50 - £ 55 (weekends)

Caddy	Caddy	no
Electric Trolley	Chariot électrique	no
Buggy	Voiturette	£ 10/18 holes
Clubs	Clubs	no

Credit cards Cartes de crédit
VISA - MasterCard (Pro Shop only)

596

Access Accès : Edinburgh centre, A90 West (Queenferry Road) Right into Quality St and Crammond Road, then left into Barnton Avenue.
Map 3 on page 411 Carte 3 Page 411

GOLF COURSE
PARCOURS
15/20

Site	Site	
Maintenance	Entretien	
Architect	Architecte	Willie Park Alister MacKenzie
Type Relief	Type Relief	parkland
Water in play	Eau en jeu	
Exp. to wind	Exposé au vent	
Trees in play	Arbres en jeu	

Scorecard Carte de score	Chp. Chp.	Mens Mess.	Ladies Da.
Length Long.	5830	5560	5007
Par	71	70	70

Advised golfing ability		0 12 24 36	
Niveau de jeu recommandé			
Hcp required	Handicap exigé	36	

CLUB HOUSE & AMENITIES
CLUB HOUSE ET ANNEXES
8/10

Pro shop	Pro-shop	
Driving range	Practice	
Sheltered	couvert	members only
On grass	sur herbe	members only
Putting-green	putting-green	yes
Pitching-green	pitching green	yes

HOTEL FACILITIES
ENVIRONNEMENT HOTELIER
9/10

HOTELS HÔTELS
Edinburgh Capital — Edinburgh
111 rooms, D £ 100 — 3 km
Tel (44) 0131 - 535 9988, Fax (44) 0131 - 334 9712

Forte Posthouse — Edinburgh
204 rooms, D £ 70 — 3 km
Tel (44) 0131 - 334 0390, Fax (44) 0131 - 334 9237

Lodge — Edinburgh
12 rooms, D £ 80 — 5 km
Tel (44) 0131 - 337 3682, Fax (44) 0131 - 313 1700

RESTAURANTS RESTAURANT
Pompadour — Edinburgh
Tel (44) 0131 - 459 9988 — 6 km

Martins — Edinburgh
Tel (44) 0131 - 225 3106 — 6 km

BUCHANAN CASTLE

<table>
<tr><td>14</td><td>6</td><td>6</td></tr>
</table>

While Donald Ross or Tom Simpson might define their designer art as the straight hole, James Braid prefers the dog-leg. Here on the former training grounds for the horses of the Dukes of Montrose, Braid designed a good dozen holes, which were shortened somewhat to cater to members who found the layout a little too difficult. The site is almost flat and so easy on the legs, but keep away from the thick rough which can be really sticky in wet weather. The river Endrick, although theoretically out of reach for normal shots, seems to attract balls like a magnet and it is true that your average hacker is pretty good at going where he never wanted to. Since this course is close to Loch Lomond, Scotland's most private course, come and dream here. You will be made most welcome.

Si l'aboutissement de l'art de Donald Ross ou de Tom Simpson en tant qu'architectes, c'est le trou rectiligne, celui de James Braid, c'est le dog-leg. Ici, sur les anciennes pistes d'entraînement des chevaux des Ducs de Montrose, il en a dessiné une bonne dizaine. Un peu raccourcis depuis, car on estimait que son tracé était trop difficile pour les membres. Le terrain est pratiquement plat, ce qui le rend facile à marcher, mais il vaut mieux échapper aux roughs, très épais quand le temps est à la pluie. Mais rien n'oblige à y aller ! La rivière Endrick est théoriquement hors de portée des coups normaux, mais elle semble avoir un effet magnétique, tant il est vrai que les golfeurs moyens réussissent surtout à aller là où ils ne veulent pas aller. Comme ce parcours est proche de Loch Lomond, le club le plus fermé d'Ecosse, venez rêver ici, vous serez les bienvenus.

Buchanan Castle Golf Club
SCO - DRYMEN, Glasgow G63 0HY

Office	Secrétariat	(44) 01360 - 660 369
Pro shop	Pro-shop	(44) 01360 - 660 330
Fax	Fax	
Situation	Situation	

29 km N of Glasgow (pop. 662 853)

Annual closure	Fermeture annnuelle	no
Weekly closure	Fermeture hebdomadaire	no

Fees main season
Tarifs haute saison 18 holes

	Week days Semaine	We/Bank holidays We/Férié
Individual Individuel	£ 30	—
Couple Couple	£ 60	—

No visitors on Saturdays - Some visitors allowed on Sundays (ask)

Caddy	Caddy	no
Electric Trolley	Chariot électrique	on request
Buggy	Voiturette	no
Clubs	Clubs	yes
Credit cards Cartes de crédit		no

Access Accès : Glasgow, A81 to Milngavie, then A809, A811, off the A811 → Drymen, Golf just South of Drymen.
Map 2 on page 408 Carte 2 Page 408

GOLF COURSE
PARCOURS

14/20

Site	Site	▬▬▬▬
Maintenance	Entretien	▬▬▬▬
Architect	Architecte	James Braid
Type	Type	parkland
Relief	Relief	▬▬
Water in play	Eau en jeu	▬▬▬
Exp. to wind	Exposé au vent	▬▬▬
Trees in play	Arbres en jeu	▬▬▬

Scorecard Carte de score	Chp. Chp.	Mens Mess.	Ladies Da.
Length Long.	5538	5180	4795
Par	70	68	71

Advised golfing ability Niveau de jeu recommandé		0 12 24 36
Hcp required	Handicap exigé	26 Men, 36 Ladies

CLUB HOUSE & AMENITIES
CLUB HOUSE ET ANNEXES

6/10

Pro shop	Pro-shop	▬▬▬▬
Driving range	Practice	▬▬▬
Sheltered	couvert	no
On grass	sur herbe	yes
Putting-green	putting-green	yes
Pitching-green	pitching green	yes

597

HOTEL FACILITIES
ENVIRONNEMENT HOTELIER

6/10

HOTELS HÔTELS
Buchanan Arms — Drymen
52 rooms, D £ 115 — 1 km
Tel (44) 01360 - 660 588, Fax (44) 01360 - 660 943

Cameron House (De Vere) — Balloch
68 rooms, D £ 130 — 5 km
Tel (44) 01389 - 755 565, Fax (44) 01389 - 759 522

RESTAURANTS RESTAURANT
Georgian Room (Cameron House) — Balloch
Tel (44) 01389 - 755 565 — 5 km

CARNOUSTIE BURNSIDE

Of course you don't come here only to play this "Burnside Course", but if you consider this simply as a warm-up round before playing the Championship course, then watch out: this is not a layout for beginners. It is certainly much shorter than its prestigious older companion but does have enough difficulties for it to hold its head high. It is laid out in a similar setting, the only blemish being that it runs alongside the railway track. Bunkers form the main line of defence, but there is also a number of trees which accentuate the countryside appearance found here and there on the Championship course. On a site that could contain in all almost a dozen courses, this layout more than does itself justice. And the uncertain appeal of the environment could only benefit from the building, at last, of a clubhouse with an eye to the British Open in 1999.

Certes, on ne vient pas ici uniquement pour jouer ce "Burnside Course", mais s'il s'agit simplement de s'échauffer avant de jouer le "Championship", méfiance car ce n'est pas un parcours pour débutants. Il est certes beaucoup plus court que son prestigieux aîné, mais présente assez de difficultés pour garder la tête haute. Il est d'ailleurs situé dans un environnement similaire, son seul défaut étant de longer davantage la voie ferrée. Les bunkers constituent la défense essentielle, avec aussi pas mal d'arbres, ce qui accentue un aspect campagne que l'on retrouve çà et là sur le "Championship." Dans un site qui pourrait au total contenir une bonne dizaine de parcours, celui-ci est plus qu'honorable. Et la séduction incertaine de l'environnement ne pourra que bénéficier de la construction (enfin) d'un Club-house en perspective du British Open 1999.

Carnoustie Golf Links

Links Parade
SCO- CARNOUSTIE, Angus, DD7 7JE

Office	Secrétariat	(44) 01241 - 853 789
Pro shop	Pro-shop	
Fax	Fax	(44) 01241 - 853 789
Situation	Situation	

17 km NE of Dundee (pop. 165 873)
9 km SW of Abroath

Annual closure	Fermeture annnuelle	no
Weekly closure	Fermeture hebdomadaire	no

Fees main season
Tarifs haute saison 18 holes

	Week days Semaine	We/Bank holidays We/Férié
Individual Individuel	£ 19	£ 19
Couple Couple	£ 38	£ 38

Burnside + Championship (same day): £ 62

Caddy	Caddy	£ 25
Electric Trolley	Chariot électrique	no
Buggy	Voiturette	no
Clubs	Clubs	nearby Pro shop

Credit cards Cartes de crédit
VISA - Eurocard - MasterCard - AMEX

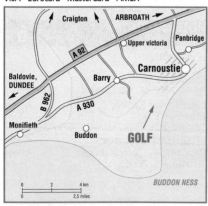

Access Accès : Dundee, A92 and A930
Map 2 on page 409 Carte 2 Page 409

598

GOLF COURSE PARCOURS 14/20

Site	Site	■■■■■■
Maintenance	Entretien	■■■■
Architect	Architecte	Unknown
Type	Type	links
Relief	Relief	■■■
Water in play	Eau en jeu	■■■■
Exp. to wind	Exposé au vent	■■■■■
Trees in play	Arbres en jeu	■■

Scorecard Carte de score	Chp. Chp.	Mens Mess.	Ladies Da.
Length Long.	5478	5478	5478
Par	68	68	72

Advised golfing ability Niveau de jeu recommandé	0 12 24 36
Hcp required	Handicap exigé	no

CLUB HOUSE & AMENITIES CLUB HOUSE ET ANNEXES 3/10

Pro shop	Pro-shop	▭
Driving range	Practice	▭
Sheltered	couvert	no
On grass	sur herbe	no
Putting-green	putting-green	no
Pitching-green	pitching green	no

HOTEL FACILITIES ENVIRONNEMENT HOTELIER 4/10

HOTELS HÔTELS

Stakis Dundee — Dundee
104 rooms, D £ 90 — 18 km
Tel (44) 01382 - 22 9271, Fax (44) 01382 - 200 072

Tayview — Broughty Ferry
11 rooms, D £ 65 — 12 km
Tel (44) 01382 - 779 438

Kingsley — Arbroath
16 rooms, D £ 35 — 9 km
Tél (44) 01241 - 879 933

RESTAURANTS RESTAURANT

11 Park Avenue — Carnoustie
Tel (44) 01241 - 853 336 — 3 km

When the British Open comes back here in 1999, it will take a truly great champion to follow in the footsteps of Armour, Cotton, Ben Hogan, Gary Player and Tom Watson. Because contrary to many links courses, this one is very difficult without the wind. When the wind does blow, it can be a real brute. There are no large dunes, just a sort of space where the sea has apparently withdrawn to leave room for a few streams, bushes, a little scrub and long grass. Designers have successively added a few very nasty bunkers, very tricky greens and optical illusions that make club choice very difficult. If you survive the first 15 holes, the last 3 can easily finish you off. For this inhuman greatness, some prefer Carnoustie to the Old Course at St Andrews. There is little to choose...

Quand le British Open reviendra en 1999 à Carnoustie, il faudra un très grand champion pour succéder à Armour, Cotton, Ben Hogan, Player et Watson. Car, au contraire de beaucoup de links, celui-ci est très diffi-cile quand il n'y a pas de vent. Et s'il souffle, c'est carrément une brute. Pas de grandes dunes ici, mais une sorte d'espace d'où la mer se serait retirée doucement pour laisser place à quelques ruisseaux, aux buis-sons, à de rares arbustes, aux longues herbes. Les architectes y ont successivement ajouté quelques bun-kers très méchants, des greens d'une grande subtilité, et des illusions d'optique qui rendent très difficile le choix de clubs. Et si l'on a survécu à quinze trous, les trois derniers peuvent vous achever. Pour cette gran-deur inhumaine, certains préfèrent Carnoustie au "Old Course" de St Andrews... Il n'est pas inférieur.

Carnoustie Golf Links
Links Parade
SCO- CARNOUSTIE, Angus, DD7 7JE

Office	Secrétariat	(44) 01241 - 853 789
Pro shop	Pro-shop	
Fax	Fax	(44) 01241 - 853 789
Situation	Situation	

17 km NE of Dundee (pop. 165 873)
9 km SW of Abroath

Annual closure	Fermeture annnuelle	no
Weekly closure	Fermeture hebdomadaire	no

Fees main season Tarifs haute saison 18 holes

	Week days Semaine	We/Bank holidays We/Férié
Individual Individuel	£ 52	£ 52
Couple Couple	£ 104	£ 104

Championship + Burnside (same day): £ 62

Caddy	Caddy	£ 25
Electric Trolley	Chariot électrique	no
Buggy	Voiturette	no
Clubs	Clubs	nearby Pro shop

Credit cards Cartes de crédit
VISA - Eurocard - MasterCard - AMEX

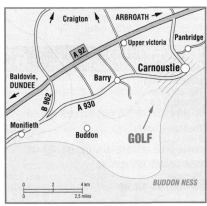

Access Accès : Dundee, A92 and A930
Map 2 on page 409 Carte 2 Page 409

GOLF COURSE PARCOURS 19/20

Site	Site	▬▬▬
Maintenance	Entretien	▬▬▬▬
Architect	Architecte	Tom Morris James Braid
Type	Type	links, seaside course
Relief	Relief	▬▬
Water in play	Eau en jeu	▬▬▬
Exp. to wind	Exposé au vent	▬▬▬▬
Trees in play	Arbres en jeu	▬

Scorecard Carte de score	Chp. Chp.	Mens Mess.	Ladies Da.
Length Long.	6643	6246	6127
Par	72	72	73

Advised golfing ability Niveau de jeu recommandé	0 12 24 36	
Hcp required Handicap exigé	28 Men, 36 Ladies	

CLUB HOUSE & AMENITIES CLUB HOUSE ET ANNEXES 3/10

Pro shop	Pro-shop	▭
Driving range	Practice	▭
Sheltered	couvert	no
On grass	sur herbe	no
Putting-green	putting-green	no
Pitching-green	pitching green	no

HOTEL FACILITIES ENVIRONNEMENT HOTELIER 4/10

HOTELS HÔTELS
Stakis Dundee — Dundee
104 rooms, D £ 90 — 18 km
Tel (44) 01382 - 22 9271, Fax (44) 01382 - 200 072

Tayview — Broughty Ferry
11 rooms, D £ 65 — 12 km
Tél (44) 01382 - 779 438

Kingsley — Arbroath
16 rooms, D £ 35 — 9 km
Tel (44) 01241 - 879 933

RESTAURANTS RESTAURANT
11 Park Avenue — Carnoustie
Tel (44) 01241 - 853 336 — 3 km

599

Don't expect impressive dunes here. In fact, the east coast of Scotland is less undulating than the west side, which feels the full brunt of Atlantic storms. Crail is the 7th oldest club in the history of golf and its course goes by the name of Balcomie Links. This is reputed to be one of the most hospitable clubs in the whole country and its closeness to St Andrews has in no way gone to its head. The best golf here is to be found with the opening and closing holes, where the sea is very much in play (more than anywhere else in this region), but the rest of the course, more inland in style, is still exposed to the wind and interesting enough for players to keep "focused" right to the end. Less manicured and more natural than other layouts, Crail is a club with ambition, as witnessed by the future opening of Craighead, a second 18-hole course.

Que l'on n'attende pas ici de dunes impressionnantes. Le relief de la côte Est de l'Ecosse est d'ailleurs moins mouvementé que celui de la côte Ouest, soumise à toutes les tempêtes. Crail est le 7ème plus ancien club de l'histoire du golf, et son parcours porte le nom de Balcomie Links. C'est un des clubs les plus accueillants de tout le pays, selon sa réputation, et sa proximité de St Andrews ne l'a pas rendu plus prétentieux. Le meilleur est ici contenu dans les premiers et derniers trous, ceux qui mettent la mer en jeu (plus que partout ailleurs dans cette région), mais le reste du parcours, plus "inland," n'est pas moins exposé au vent, et assez intéressant pour que l'on reste concentré jusqu'à la fin. Moins manucuré que d'autres, plus naturel aussi, Crail a de l'ambition, dont témoigne la prochaine ouverture d'un second 18 trous, Craighead.

Crail Golfing Society

Balcomie Clubhouse, Fifeness
SCO - CRAIL, Fife KY10 3XN

Office	Secrétariat	(44) 01333 - 450 686
Pro shop	Pro-shop	(44) 01333 - 450 960
Fax	Fax	(44) 01333 - 450 416
Situation	Situation	

14 km S of St Andrews (pop. 11 136)

Annual closure	Fermeture annnuelle	no
Weekly closure	Fermeture hebdomadaire	no

Fees main season
Tarifs haute saison 18 holes

	Week days Semaine	We/Bank holidays We/Férié
Individual Individuel	£ 20	£ 25
Couple Couple	£ 40	£ 50

Caddy	Caddy	on request
Electric Trolley	Chariot électrique	no
Buggy	Voiturette	no
Clubs	Clubs	£ 10/18 holes

Credit cards Cartes de crédit
VISA - Eurocard - MasterCard - JCB

GOLF COURSE
PARCOURS

15/20

Site	Site	
Maintenance	Entretien	
Architect	Architecte	Tom Morris
Type	Type	links
Relief	Relief	
Water in play	Eau en jeu	
Exp. to wind	Exposé au vent	
Trees in play	Arbres en jeu	

Scorecard Carte de score	Chp. Chp.	Mens Mess.	Ladies Da.
Length Long.	5390	4945	4760
Par	69	67	70

Advised golfing ability
Niveau de jeu recommandé

0   12   24   36

Hcp required   Handicap exigé   no

CLUB HOUSE & AMENITIES
CLUB HOUSE ET ANNEXES

6/10

Pro shop	Pro-shop	
Driving range	Practice	
Sheltered	couvert	no
On grass	sur herbe	no
Putting-green	putting-green	yes
Pitching-green	pitching green	no

HOTEL FACILITIES
ENVIRONNEMENT HOTELIER

6/10

HOTELS HÔTELS

The Golf Hotel		Crail
5 rooms, D £ 44		1 km
Tel (44) 01333 - 450 206, Fax (44) 01333 - 450 795		
The Marine Hotel		Crail
8 rooms, D £ 60		1 km
Tel (44) 01333 - 450 207, Fax (44) 01333 - 451 145		

RESTAURANTS RESTAURANT

The Cellar		Ansruther
Tel (44) 01333 - 477 540		6 km

600

Access Accès : Edinburgh A92 to Kirkcaldy, then A915 through Leven, B942 and A 917 through Crail until Golf Hotel, turn right → Golf.
Map 3 on page 411 Carte 3 Page 411

For a start, we would not recommend Crieff to any one without sturdy legs, as the course is largely laid out on the side of a hill. Most golfers though get used to the climbing but not always to shaping their shots or choosing the right strategy with due consideration given to the slopes. This Ferntower course follows a part of the layout created by Archie Simpson then re-designed by James Braid (the remaining section is on the Dornock course), but the final work, completed in 1980, was made in a way to avoid any excessive disparity in style. Of course you need to play here several times to understand the full layout, but it's fun every time because the enjoyment of playing here is more than enhanced by the warm reception and hospitality. The people from Crieff really do make you feel at home.

Déjà, on ne saurait conseiller Crieff à ceux dont les jambes sont faibles, car il a été construit largement à flanc de colline, mais la plupart des golfeurs s'en accommoderont. Les pentes doivent d'ailleurs souvent être prises en considération pour établir une stratégie efficace, comme pour choisir les meilleures trajectoires. Ce Ferntower Course a repris une partie du tracé créé par Archie Simpson puis remanié par James Braid (les autres sont sur le Dornock Course), mais les travaux définitifs achevés en 1980 ont été assez bien menés pour que l'on n'ait pas trop de disparités de style. Certes, il est utile de jouer plusieurs fois pour bien comprendre ce tracé, mais on le fera avec plaisir quand on ajoute au plaisir du jeu celui de la réception et de l'accueil : on se sent ici en famille.

Crieff Golf Club

Perth Road
SCO - CRIEFF, Perthshire PH7 3LR

Office	Secrétariat	(44) 01764 - 652 909
Pro shop	Pro-shop	(44) 01764 - 652 397
Fax	Fax	(44) 01764 - 655 096
Situation	Situation	

27 km W of Perth (pop. 123 495)

Annual closure	Fermeture annnuelle	no
Weekly closure	Fermeture hebdomadaire	no

Fees main season
Tarifs haute saison 18 holes

	Week days Semaine	We/Bank holidays We/Férié
Individual Individuel	£ 20	£ 27
Couple Couple	£ 40	£ 54

Full days: £ 27 - £ 35 (weekends)

Caddy	Caddy	on request
Electric Trolley	Chariot électrique	no
Buggy	Voiturette	no
Clubs	Clubs	yes
Credit cards Cartes de crédit		no

Access Accès : Edinburgh M90 to Perth, then A85 →
Crieff. Golf on right at the edge of town.
Map 2 on page 409 Carte 2 Page 409

GOLF COURSE PARCOURS 15/20

Site	Site	
Maintenance	Entretien	
Architect	Architecte	Bob Simpson James Braid
Type	Type	parkland
Relief	Relief	
Water in play	Eau en jeu	
Exp. to wind	Exposé au vent	
Trees in play	Arbres en jeu	

Scorecard Carte de score	Chp. Chp.	Mens Mess.	Ladies Da.
Length Long.	5830	5830	5830
Par	71	71	76

Advised golfing ability   0   12   24   36
Niveau de jeu recommandé
Hcp required   Handicap exigé   certificate

CLUB HOUSE & AMENITIES CLUB HOUSE ET ANNEXES 7/10

Pro shop	Pro-shop	
Driving range	Practice	
Sheltered	couvert	no
On grass	sur herbe	yes
Putting-green	putting-green	yes
Pitching-green	pitching green	yes

HOTEL FACILITIES ENVIRONNEMENT HOTELIER 7/10

HOTELS HÔTELS
Crieff Hydro   Golf
225 rooms, D £ 120   adjacent
Tel (44) 01764 - 655 555, Fax (44) 01764 - 653 087

Murraypark Hotel   Crieff
19 rooms, D £ 70   close
Tel (44) 01764 - 653 731, Fax (44) 01764 - 655 311

RESTAURANTS RESTAURANT
Murraypark   Crieff
Tel (44) 01764 - 653 731   close

601

This is one of the very few Tom Simpson courses in Scotland, a masterpiece on a par with County Louth, another hidden gem but this time in Ireland. They say that Slain Castle in the background inspired Bram Stoker for his Dracula. Well you'll find drama enough here and maybe blood on your card too when the wind starts to blow and the designer, as if in a game of chess, takes your pieces one by one as the course unwinds. You will find every challenge to test your game: subtle, well-protected greens, strategic fairway bunkers, deep green-side bunkers, burns, blind shots, majestic long holes or teasing shorter ones. There was once a grand hotel on the site but it was demolished, a fact that might explain the relative anonymity from which Cruden Bay deserves to emerge... but don't tell anybody.

C'est un des seuls parcours de Tom Simpson en Ecosse, un chef-d'oeuvre à mettre à côté de County Louth, lui aussi un des joyaux cachés, mais d'Irlande cette fois. On dit que Slain Castle, en arrière plan du lieu, a inspiré Bram Stoker pour son "Dracula." Nul doute qu'il y aura aussi des drames et du sang sur les cartes de score quand le vent souffle un peu, et que la patiente partie d'échec de l'architecte enlève les joueurs tourne à la déconfiture des seconds. Greens subtils et bien défendus, bunkers de fairway stratégiques, profonds bunkers de green, petits "burns" piégeux, coups aveugles, longs trous majestueux ou petits trous provocants : on a ici tous les défis pour mettre son jeu à l'épreuve. Il y avait autrefois un grand hôtel sur place, il a été détruit, ce qui explique le relatif anonymat dont Cruden Bay mérite de sortir. Mais ne le dites à personne...

Cruden Bay Golf Club

Aulton Road, Cruden Bay
SCO - PETERHEAD, Aberdeenshire AB42 0NN

Office	Secrétariat	(44) 01779 - 812 285
Pro shop	Pro-shop	(44) 01779 - 812 414
Fax	Fax	(44) 01779 - 812 945
Situation	Situation	

40 km N of Aberdeen (pop. 204 885)
12 km S of Peterhead (pop. 20 789)

Annual closure	Fermeture annnuelle	no
Weekly closure	Fermeture hebdomadaire	no

Fees main season
Tarifs haute saison 18 holes

	Week days Semaine	We/Bank holidays We/Férié
Individual Individuel	£ 35	£ 45
Couple Couple	£ 70	£ 90

Some weekend restrictions: ask before

Caddy	Caddy	on request/£ 17+tip
Electric Trolley	Chariot électrique	no
Buggy	Voiturette	no
Clubs	Clubs	£ 7.50/18 holes

Credit cards Cartes de crédit
VISA - MasterCard

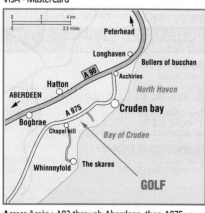

Access Accès : A92 through Aberdeen, then A975 →
Peterhead to Cruden Bay.
Map 1 on page 407 Carte 1 Page 407

GOLF COURSE
PARCOURS 18/20

Site	Site	
Maintenance	Entretien	
Architect	Architecte	Tom Simpson
Type	Type	links
Relief	Relief	
Water in play	Eau en jeu	
Exp. to wind	Exposé au vent	
Trees in play	Arbres en jeu	

Scorecard Carte de score	Chp. Chp.	Mens Mess.	Ladies Da.
Length Long.	5820	5480	5243
Par	70	70	74

Advised golfing ability		0	12	24	36
Niveau de jeu recommandé					
Hcp required	Handicap exigé	certificate			

CLUB HOUSE & AMENITIES
CLUB HOUSE ET ANNEXES 7/10

Pro shop	Pro-shop	
Driving range	Practice	
Sheltered	couvert	no
On grass	sur herbe	yes
Putting-green	putting-green	yes
Pitching-green	pitching green	no

HOTEL FACILITIES
ENVIRONNEMENT HOTELIER 6/10

HOTELS HÔTELS
Waterside Inn — Peterhead
109 rooms, D £ 95 — 13 km
Tel (44) 01779 - 471 121, Fax (44) 01779 - 470 670

Udny Arms — Newburgh
24 rooms, D £ 60 — 10 km
Tel (44) 01358 - 789 444, Fax (44) 01779 - 789 012

Queens Hotel — Aberdeeen
26 rooms, D £ 90 — 35 km
Tel (44) 01224 - 206 999, Fax (44) 01224 - 584 352

RESTAURANTS RESTAURANT
Udny Arms — Newburgh
Tel (44) 01358 - 789 444 — 10 km

Waterside Inn — Peterhead
Tel (44) 01779 - 471 121 — 13 km

With two courses, one of which is in the international league, this golfing complex controlled by Marriott is now a very high class resort with a full-facility hotel, particularly for non-golfers (tennis, swimming pool, fitness, etc.). The East Course, designed by James Braid, has played host to some major tournaments, including the Solheim Cup in 1992. Although some aspects of the course are reminiscent of a links, here we are in a beautiful park where trees are important not so much as dangerous hazards but for outlining the holes. Water comes into play but only on two holes. So really if you drive straight you're half-way there, but only half-way. You need some accurate ironwork to hit the well-protected greens, so a few rudiments of target golf will more than come in handy. A good test of golf.

Avec deux parcours, dont un de classe internationale, cet ensemble contrôlé par Marriott est devenu un complexe de tout premier ordre avec un hôtel très bien équipé, notamment pour les non-golfeurs (tennis, piscine, mise en forme, etc). Dessiné par James Braid, l'East Course a accueilli de grandes épreuves, dont la Solheim Cup en 1992. Bien que certains aspects puissent rappeler les links, nous sommes ici dans un parc de toute beauté, où les arbres jouent un certain rôle, mais ils définissent plus les trous qu'ils ne constituent des obstacles dangereux. L'eau n'est en jeu que sur deux trous. De fait, si l'on drive bien, on aura fait une bonne partie du chemin, mais c'est loin d'être suffisant : il faut être d'autant plus précis que les greens sont bien défendus, ce qui exige parfois de connaître les secrets du "target golf." Un bon test de golf.

Marriott Dalmahoy Golf & Country Club

Kirknewton
SCO - EDINBURGH EH27 8EB

Office	Secrétariat	(44) 0131 - 333 1845
Pro shop	Pro-shop	(44) 0131 - 333 1845
Fax	Fax	(44) 0131 - 333 1433
Situation	Situation	

12 km SW of Edinburgh (pop. 418 914)

Annual closure	Fermeture annnuelle	no
Weekly closure	Fermeture hebdomadaire	no

Fees main season
Tarifs haute saison 18 holes

	Week days Semaine	We/Bank holidays We/Férié
Individual Individuel	£ 48	£ 65
Couple Couple	£ 96	£ 130

Hotel residents: £ 39 - £ 48

Caddy	Caddy	on request/£ 25
Electric Trolley	Chariot électrique	no
Buggy	Voiturette	£ 24/18 holes
Clubs	Clubs	£ 19/18 holes

Credit cards Cartes de crédit
VISA - Eurocard - MasterCard - AMEX - DC

South Queensferry
EDINBURGH
Barnton
Broxburn
Corstorphine
Bathgate
Morningside
Duddingston
Livingston
GOLF
Herminston
Currie

Access Accès : From Edinburgh, on A 71 → Livingston
Map 3 on page 411 Carte 3 Page 411

GOLF COURSE PARCOURS 17/20

Site	Site	
Maintenance	Entretien	
Architect	Architecte	James Braid
Type	Type	parkland
Relief	Relief	
Water in play	Eau en jeu	
Exp. to wind	Exposé au vent	
Trees in play	Arbres en jeu	

Scorecard Carte de score	Chp. Chp.	Mens Mess.	Ladies Da.
Length Long.	6030	5836	5356
Par	72	71	75

Advised golfing ability
Niveau de jeu recommandé　　　0　12　24　36

Hcp required Handicap exigé　certificate

CLUB HOUSE & AMENITIES CLUB HOUSE ET ANNEXES 8/10

Pro shop	Pro-shop	
Driving range	Practice	
Sheltered	couvert	10 bays
On grass	sur herbe	no
Putting-green	putting-green	yes
Pitching-green	pitching green	yes

HOTEL FACILITIES ENVIRONNEMENT HOTELIER 8/10

HOTELS HÔTELS
Marriott Dalmahoy　　　　　　　Golf
151 rooms, from D £ 110　　　　　on site
Tel (44) 0131 - 333 1845, Fax (44) 0131 - 333 1433

Malmaison　　　　　　　　　Edinburgh
25 rooms, D £ 85　　　　　　　12 km
Tel (44) 0131 - 555 6868, Fax (44) 0131 - 555 6989

RESTAURANTS RESTAURANT
L'Auberge　　　　　　　　　Edinburgh
Tel (44) 0131 - 556 5888　　　　12 km

Aye (Japanese)　　　　　　　Edinburgh
Tel (44) 0131 - 320 1238　　　　12 km

603

Located in the north-west confines of Dundee, Downfield is without a doubt one of the very great British inland courses, even though it is still little known outside of Scotland and even less so to players from continental Europe. If you are in the region it would be a great pity to miss it. C.K. Cotton has designed an uncompromising challenge in an already very heavily wooded area. The course's park style means that the ball doesn't roll much so each yard of the course really counts on your card. Only good drivers can hope to get a good score, as long they keep on the straight and narrow. But short-game experts will feel very welcome here, as well. At an equal distance from St Andrews and Carnoustie, this is an excellent stop-over and a serious test of golf, more sheltered from the wind.

Situé aux limites nord-ouest de Dundee, Downfield est sans conteste un des très bons parcours "inland" de Grande-Bretagne, bien qu'il reste peu connu en dehors des limites de l'Ecosse, et ne parlons même pas des joueurs du continent. Il serait fort dommage de le négliger si l'on passe dans les environs. C.K. Cotton a créé un défi sans compromis dans un espace déjà très boisé. La nature de parc implique que la balle roule peu sur les fairways, et chaque mètre de ce parcours compte sur la carte. Seuls les bons drivers peuvent espérer un score honorable, du moment qu'ils ne s'égarent pas trop. Mais les maîtres du petit jeu y sont aussi les bienvenus. A égale distance de Carnoustie et de St Andrews, voici une halte de qualité, et un sérieux test... plus à l'abri du vent.

Downfield Golf Club
Turnberry Avenue
SCO - DUNDEE DD2 3QP

Office	Secrétariat	(44) 01382 - 825 595
Pro shop	Pro-shop	(44) 01382 - 889 246
Fax	Fax	(44) 01382 - 813 111
Situation	Situation	

3 km from Dundee (pop. 165 873)

Annual closure Fermeture annnuelle   no

Weekly closure Fermeture hebdomadaire

Fees main season
Tarifs haute saison 18 holes

	Week days Semaine	We/Bank holidays We/Férié
Individual Individuel	£ 30	£ 35
Couple Couple	£ 60	£ 70

Caddy	Caddy	£ 15
Electric Trolley	Chariot électrique	£ 6/18 holes
Buggy	Voiturette	no
Clubs	Clubs	£ 6/18 holes

Credit cards Cartes de crédit   no

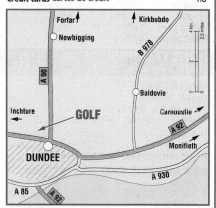

Access Accès : In Dundee, A90 Kingsway (Ring Road). A923 Coupar Angus Road. 50 m, right Faraday St, 1st left on Harrison Rd. 200 m, T junction, lezft onto Dalamhoy Dr. 400 m, left.
Map 1 on page 407 Carte 1 Page 407

GOLF COURSE PARCOURS   17/20

Site	Site	
Maintenance	Entretien	
Architect	Architecte	C.K. Cotton
Type	Type	parkland
Relief	Relief	
Water in play	Eau en jeu	
Exp. to wind	Exposé au vent	
Trees in play	Arbres en jeu	

Scorecard Carte de score	Chp. Chp.	Mens Mess.	Ladies Da.
Length Long.	6208	5702	5330
Par	73	70	74

Advised golfing ability   0   12   24   36
Niveau de jeu recommandé
Hcp required   Handicap exigé   no

CLUB HOUSE & AMENITIES CLUB HOUSE ET ANNEXES   6/10

Pro shop	Pro-shop	
Driving range	Practice	
Sheltered	couvert	no
On grass	sur herbe	yes
Putting-green	putting-green	yes
Pitching-green	pitching green	yes

HOTEL FACILITIES ENVIRONNEMENT HOTELIER   7/10

HOTELS HÔTELS
Swallow Hotel   Dundee
107 rooms, D £ 100   3 km
Tel (44) 01382 - 641 122, Fax (44) 01382 - 568 340

Stakis Hotel   Dundee
104 rooms, D £ 90   5 km
Tel (44) 01382 - 22 9271, Fax (44) 01382 - 200 072

Travel Inn   Dundee
40 rooms, D £ 40   5 km
Tel (44) 01382 - 20 3240, Fax (44) 01382 - 568 431

RESTAURANTS RESTAURANT
Birkhill Inn   Dundee
Tel (44) 01382 - 581 297   2 km

Beefeater   Dundee
Tel (44) 01382 - 561 115   5 km

Raffles - Tel (44) 01382 - 226 344   Dundee, 4 km

604

DUDDINGSTON

One of the good Edinburgh courses, of which there are several dozen. The club has a good sporting reputation with an encouraging policy for young golfers that is none too common in the often crowded big city clubs. Located immediately behind Arthur's Seat to the east of the famous castle, this is a park course with the meanders of Braid's burn to make life a misery for golfers who like a round without hazards. The trees are also dangerously in play when there are no fairway bunkers. This moderately hilly course is well worth playing, especially since the designers always kept the cohorts of average players very much in mind. In the olden days it was often thus. A very pleasant course and a hospitable club, but only on weekdays.

L'un des bons parcours d'Edimbourg, qui en compte plusieurs dizaines. Celui-ci s'est fait une bonne réputation sportive, avec une politique de jeunes pas toujours si évidente dans les grands clubs citadins, souvent très fréquentés. Situé immédiatement derrière Arthur's Seat, à l'est du célèbre château, c'est un golf de parc, avec les méandres du Braid's burn pour empoisonner la vie de ceux qui aiment la vie (au golf) sans obstacles. Et les arbres viennent aussi dangereusement en jeu quand les bunkers de fairway manquent à l'appel. D'un relief modéré, c'est un parcours à connaître, d'autant que les architectes n'ont jamais perdu de vue les armées de joueurs moyens. Mais il est vrai que l'on y pensait davantage autrefois... Un parcours très plaisant, et un club accueillant, mais seulement en semaine.

Duddingston Golf Club

Duddingston Road West
SCO - EDINBURGH EH15 3QD

Office	Secrétariat	(44) 0131 - 661 1005
Pro shop	Pro-shop	(44) 0131 - 661 4301
Fax	Fax	(44) 0131 - 661 4301
Situation	Situation	

3 km E of Edinburgh centre (pop. 418 914)

Annual closure	Fermeture annnuelle	no
Weekly closure	Fermeture hebdomadaire	no

Fees main season
Tarifs haute saison 18 holes

	Week days Semaine	We/Bank holidays We/Férié
Individual Individuel	£ 27	—
Couple Couple	£ 54	—

No visitors at weekends

Caddy	Caddy	no
Electric Trolley	Chariot électrique	no
Buggy	Voiturette	yes
Clubs	Clubs	yes
Credit cards Cartes de crédit		no

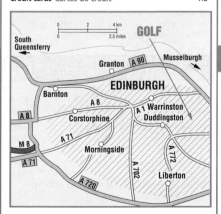

Access Accès : Edinburgh Princes Street, Regent Road, London Road, turn off right to Willowbrae Road, right to Duddingston Road West (near Duddingston Loch).
Map 3 on page 411 Carte 3 Page 411

GOLF COURSE
PARCOURS

15/20

Site	Site	▰▰▰▱▱
Maintenance	Entretien	▰▰▰▰▱
Architect	Architecte	Willie Park
Type	Type	parkland
Relief	Relief	▰▰▱▱▱
Water in play	Eau en jeu	▰▰▰▱▱
Exp. to wind	Exposé au vent	▰▰▱▱▱
Trees in play	Arbres en jeu	▰▰▰▰▱

Scorecard Carte de score	Chp. Chp.	Mens Mess.	Ladies Da.
Length Long.	5845	5556	5091
Par	71	71	69

Advised golfing ability Niveau de jeu recommandé	0	12	24	36

Hcp required Handicap exigé no

CLUB HOUSE & AMENITIES
CLUB HOUSE ET ANNEXES

7/10

Pro shop	Pro-shop	▰▰▰▱▱
Driving range	Practice	▰▰▱▱▱
Sheltered	couvert	no
On grass	sur herbe	no
Putting-green	putting-green	yes
Pitching-green	pitching green	yes

HOTEL FACILITIES
ENVIRONNEMENT HOTELIER

9/10

HOTELS HÔTELS

King James Thistle
147 rooms, D £ 110
Tel (44) 0131 - 556 0111, Fax (44) 0131 - 557 5333
Edinburgh
3 km

17 Abercromby Place
6 rooms, D £ 70
Tel (44) 0131 - 557 8036, Fax (44) 0131 - 558 3453
Edinburgh
5 km

Balmoral Forte
189 rooms, D £ 130
Tel (44) 0131 - 556 2414, Fax (44) 0131 - 557 8740
Edinburgh
5 km

RESTAURANTS RESTAURANT

Merchants
Tel (44) 0131 - 225 4009
Edinburgh
3 km

Raffaelli (Italian)
Tel (44) 0131 - 225 6060
Edinburgh
6 km

605

DUFF HOUSE ROYAL

15	6	6

There are courses you play in tournaments and courses you prefer for a bright stroll. This is one of the latter, where enjoyment comes first. Although designer Alister MacKenzie also laid out Augusta and Cypress Point, here he was looking above all else to satisfy golfers of all levels. The difficulties are there, certainly (clever bunkering, trees or the estuary of the river Deveron) but they are never insurmountable or unavoidable. So you can hope to reach the green without too much to-do, keeping to your handicap on rather flat terrain, but be careful not to waste those precious handicap strokes: the greens are often two-tiered with tricky slopes and are well protected.

Il y a des parcours pour s'affronter en compétition et d'autres pour faire une intelligente balade. Celui-ci fait évidemment partie de la seconde catégorie, celle du plaisir avant tout. Certes, l'architecte Alister MacKenzie a aussi créé Augusta et Cypress Point, mais il a surtout cherché ici à satisfaire tous les niveaux. Les difficultés sont présentes (bunkering intelligent, arbres, ou l'embouchure de la rivière Deveron) mais jamais insurmontables ou impossibles à éviter. On peut ainsi espérer arriver paisiblement sur le green en utilisant sagement ses points de handicap sur le terrain assez plat, mais il faut rester attentif à ne pas les gâcher : les greens sont souvent ici à double plateau, avec des pentes subtiles. Ils sont aussi bien protégés.

Duff House Royal
The Barnyards
SCO - BANFF, AB45 3SX

Office	Secrétariat	(44) 01261 - 812 062
Pro shop	Pro-shop	(44) 01261 - 812 075
Fax	Fax	(44) 01261 - 812 224
Situation	Situation	

1 km from Banff (pop. 4 402)

Annual closure	Fermeture annnuelle	no
Weekly closure	Fermeture hebdomadaire	no

Fees main season
Tarifs haute saison 18 holes

	Week days Semaine	We/Bank holidays We/Férié
Individual Individuel	£ 16	£ 20
Couple Couple	£ 32	£ 40

Full days: £ 23 - £ 28 (weekends)

Caddy	Caddy	no
Electric Trolley	Chariot électrique	no
Buggy	Voiturette	no
Clubs	Clubs	yes

Credit cards Cartes de crédit — no

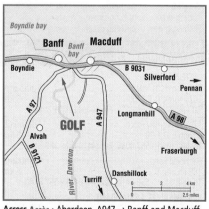

606

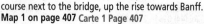

Access Accès : Aberdeen, A947 → Banff and Macduff.
In Macduff, cross the river Deveron,
course next to the bridge, up the rise towards Banff.
Map 1 on page 407 Carte 1 Page 407

GOLF COURSE / PARCOURS — 15/20

Site	Site	
Maintenance	Entretien	
Architect	Architecte	Alister MacKenzie
Type	Type	parkland
Relief	Relief	
Water in play	Eau en jeu	
Exp. to wind	Exposé au vent	
Trees in play	Arbres en jeu	

Scorecard Carte de score	Chp. Chp.	Mens Mess.	Ladies Da.
Length Long.	5665	5665	5665
Par	69	69	69

Advised golfing ability Niveau de jeu recommandé	0	12	24	36

Hcp required — Handicap exigé — no

CLUB HOUSE & AMENITIES / CLUB HOUSE ET ANNEXES — 6/10

Pro shop	Pro-shop	
Driving range	Practice	
Sheltered	couvert	no
On grass	sur herbe	no
Putting-green	putting-green	yes
Pitching-green	pitching green	no

HOTEL FACILITIES / ENVIRONNEMENT HOTELIER — 6/10

HOTELS HÔTELS
Eden House — Banff
5 rooms, D £ 68 — 8 km

Tél (44) 01261 - 821 282Fife Lodge — Banff
7 rooms, D £ 50 — 1 km
Tel (44) 01261 - 812 436, Fax (44) 01261 - 812 636

Banff Springs Hotel — Banff
30 rooms, D £ 80 — 1.5 km
Tel (44) 01261 - 812 881, Fax (44) 01261 - 815 546

RESTAURANTS RESTAURANT
Banff Springs Hotel — Banff
Tel (44) 01261 - 812 881 — 1.5 km

Five times British Open winner Peter Thompson designed this course at the request of the Old Course Hotel. It was intended for hotel patrons owing to the problem of getting firm guaranteed tee-off times on the adjacent Old Course. Contrary to its illustrious neighbour, the Duke's Course is 3 miles inland and very different in character. It is situated on high land offering magnificent views over the old town of St Andrews and the mountains to the north beyond the bay of St Andrews. Owing to the steep slopes and distances between green and next tee, we would advise a buggy, something that would certainly be seen as sacrilege on the "real" St Andrews. Difficult, intelligent and well landscaped, the Duke's is a solid test of golf, best played from the front tees.

Cinq fois vainqueur du British Open, Peter Thomson a dessiné ce parcours à la demande du Old Course Hotel et à l'intention de ses clients, en raison de la difficulté d'obtenir des départs garantis sur le "Old Course" jouxtant cet hôtel. Contrairement à son illustre voisin, le "Duke's" est un parcours intérieur à 5 km de la mer, et d'un caractère très différent. Il se situe sur un terrain élevé, propose des vues magnifiques sur la vieille ville de St Andrews, et sur les montagnes au nord au delà de la baie de St Andrews. A cause du relief et des distances entre greens et départs, on conseillera l'usage de la voiturette, qui serait une hérésie sur le "vrai" St Andrews. Difficile, intelligent, bien paysagé, le "Duke's" propose un solide test de golf, où l'on conseillera les départs avancés.

The Duke's Golf Club
Craigton
SCO - ST ANDREWS, Fife KY16 8NS

Office	Secrétariat	(44) 01334 - 479 947
Pro shop	Pro-shop	(44) 01334 - 479 947
Fax	Fax	(44) 01334 - 479 456
Situation	Situation	

5 km SE of St Andrews (pop. 11 136)

Annual closure	Fermeture annnuelle	no
Weekly closure	Fermeture hebdomadaire	no

Fees main season Tarifs haute saison 18 holes

	Week days Semaine	We/Bank holidays We/Férié
Individual Individuel	£ 50	£ 55
Couple Couple	£ 100	£ 110

Caddy	Caddy	no
Electric Trolley	Chariot électrique	no
Buggy	Voiturette	£ 28/18 holes
Clubs	Clubs	£ 25/18 holes

Credit cards Cartes de crédit
VISA - Eurocard - MasterCard - AMEX - DC - JCB

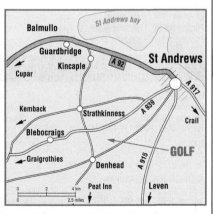

Access Accès : A91 → St Andrews through Guardbridge, then right to Strathkinness, go through towards Craigtoun (on left). Follow signs to Craigtoun Country Park).
Map 3 on page 411 Carte 3 Page 411

GOLF COURSE
PARCOURS

16/20

Site	Site	
Maintenance	Entretien	
Architect	Architecte	Peter Thomson
Type	Type	parkland
Relief	Relief	
Water in play	Eau en jeu	
Exp. to wind	Exposé au vent	
Trees in play	Arbres en jeu	

Scorecard Carte de score	Chp. Chp.	Mens Mess.	Ladies Da.
Length Long.	6616	6145	5528
Par	72	72	72

Advised golfing ability Niveau de jeu recommandé	0	12	24	36
Hcp required Handicap exigé	36			

CLUB HOUSE & AMENITIES
CLUB HOUSE ET ANNEXES

7/10

Pro shop	Pro-shop	
Driving range	Practice	
Sheltered	couvert	no
On grass	sur herbe	yes (05 → 09)
Putting-green	putting-green	yes
Pitching-green	pitching green	yes

HOTEL FACILITIES
ENVIRONNEMENT HOTELIER

8/10

HOTELS HÔTELS
Old Course Hotel — St Andrews
125 rooms, D £ 224 — 5 km
Tel (44) 01334 - 474 371, Fax (44) 01334 - 477 668

Russell Hotel — St Andrews
10 rooms, from D £ 65 — 5 km
Tel (44) 01334 - 473 447, Fax (44) 01334 - 478 279

St Andrews Golf Hotel — St Andrews
22 rooms, D £ 130 — 5 km
Tel (44) 01334 - 472 611, Fax (44) 01334 - 472 188

RESTAURANTS RESTAURANT
The Cellar — Ansruther
Tel (44) 01333 - 477 540 — 12 km

The Peat Inn — Peat Inn
Tel (44) 01334 - 840 206 — 8 km

607

This is one of the best courses in south-west Scotland, a region too often neglected by foreign tourists. Off the beaten track, Dumfries & County is generally in excellent condition and very pleasant on the eye with the river Nith alongside the course. This adds a pastoral note to a very tree-bound landscape. Designed by Willie Fernie, this is one of those collection of courses which will probably never mark the history of golf design but which you are glad to have played. An unpretentious layout, it is happy to be just a rather difficult course to test the average player, kind enough not to put off the rather less experienced golfer and clever enough to tease the experts. The one hole no-one will forget is the tiny 14th, a par-3.

C'est un des meilleurs parcours du sud-ouest de l'Ecosse, une région trop souvent négligée par les touristes étrangers. Hors des sentiers battus, Dumfries & County est généralement en excellente condition, et très plaisant visuellement, avec la rivière Nith le long du terrain, qui ajoute une note pastorale à un paysage très arboré. Dessiné par Willie Fernie, il fait partie de cet ensemble de golfs qui ne marqueront sans doute pas l'histoire de l'architecture de golf, mais que l'on est heureux de connaître. Sans prétention aucune, il se contente d'être un parcours assez difficile pour tester les joueurs moyens, assez aimable pour ne pas rebuter les joueurs peu expérimentés, assez astucieux pour provoquer les experts. Ils garderont au moins le souvenir du minuscule 14, un par 3.

Dumfries & County Golf Club
Nunfields, Edinburgh Road
SCO - DUMFRIES DG1 1JX

Office	Secrétariat	(44) 01387 - 253 585
Pro shop	Pro-shop	(44) 01387 - 268 918
Fax	Fax	
Situation	Situation	

1.5 km N of Dumfries (pop. 21 164)

Annual closure	Fermeture annnuelle	no
Weekly closure	Fermeture hebdomadaire	no

Fees main season
Tarifs haute saison full day

	Week days Semaine	We/Bank holidays We/Férié
Individual Individuel	£ 22	£ 25
Couple Couple	£ 44	£ 50

Restrictions at weekends during summer months

Caddy	Caddy	no
Electric Trolley	Chariot électrique	yes
Buggy	Voiturette	no
Clubs	Clubs	yes

Credit cards Cartes de crédit
no (Pro Shop only)

GOLF COURSE
PARCOURS
15/20

Site	Site	
Maintenance	Entretien	
Architect	Architecte	Willie Fernie
Type	Type	parkland
Relief	Relief	
Water in play	Eau en jeu	
Exp. to wind	Exposé au vent	
Trees in play	Arbres en jeu	

Scorecard Carte de score	Chp. Chp.	Mens Mess.	Ladies Da.
Length Long.	5418	5418	4954
Par	68	68	72

Advised golfing ability		0 12 24 36
Niveau de jeu recommandé		
Hcp required	Handicap exigé	no

CLUB HOUSE & AMENITIES
CLUB HOUSE ET ANNEXES
7/10

Pro shop	Pro-shop	
Driving range	Practice	
Sheltered	couvert	no
On grass	sur herbe	yes
Putting-green	putting-green	yes
Pitching-green	pitching green	no

HOTEL FACILITIES
ENVIRONNEMENT HOTELIER
5/10

HOTELS HÔTELS

Cairndale		Dumfries
76 rooms, D £ 105		2 km
Tel (44) 01387 - 254 111, Fax (44) 01387 - 250 155		
Station		Dumfries
32 rooms, D £ 80		1.5 km
Tel (44) 01387 - 254 316, Fax (44) 01387 - 250 388		

RESTAURANTS RESTAURANT

Golf restaurant		Dumfries
Tel (44) 01387 - 253 585		on site
Cairndale		Dumfries
Tel (44) 01387 - 254 111		2 km

608

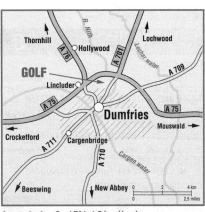

Access Accès : On A701, 1.5 km (1 m.)
North of Dumfries
Map 2 on page 409 Carte 2 Page 409

One of the classic courses of East Lothian, nestling on a narrow strip of land along a rocky seashore hardly big enough for two fairways. This means that you have not only the sea but also a wall and out-of-bounds to contend with, so when the wind blows you just might feel you haven't a friend on earth. In this case do what all amateurs used to do and go around in match-play, a very exciting format on this type of course. The most memorable part of the course is from the 7th to the 16th holes, as the holes close to the clubhouse are rather squeezed together. This is where the Firth of Forth becomes the North Sea and the view of this mass of water adds to the pleasure of playing golf in the bracing sea-air.

C'est un des classiques de l'East Lothian, blotti sur une étroite bande le long d'un rivage rocheux, avec à peine assez de place pour deux fairways. Ce qui implique que non seulement la mer est en jeu, mais aussi un mur et des hors-limites. Autrement dit, les jours de vent, les joueurs peuvent avoir l'impression de n'avoir que des adversaires. Alors, qu'ils se réfugient dans la formule de tous les amateurs d'autrefois, le match-play, toujours très excitant sur des parcours de ce style. Ici, on retiendra particulièrement le passage du 7 au 16, les trous proches du Clubhouse étant plus resserrés. C'est ici que le Firth of Forth devient vraiment la Mer du Nord, et la vue de cette immensité ajoute encore au plaisir du jeu de golf dans un air vivifiant.

Dunbar Golf Club

East Links
SCO - DUNBAR, East Lothian, EH42 1LT

Office	Secrétariat	(44) 01368 - 862 317
Pro shop	Pro-shop	(44) 01368 - 862 086
Fax	Fax	(44) 01368 - 865 202
Situation	Situation	

48 km E of Edinburgh (pop. 418 914)

Annual closure	Fermeture annnuelle	no
Weekly closure	Fermeture hebdomadaire	no

Fees main season
Tarifs haute saison full day

	Week days Semaine	We/Bank holidays We/Férié
Individual Individuel	£ 30	£ 40
Couple Couple	£ 60	£ 80

Caddy	Caddy	£ 20 + tip
Electric Trolley	Chariot électrique	£ 6/18 holes
Buggy	Voiturette	no
Clubs	Clubs	£ 10/18 holes

Credit cards Cartes de crédit
VISA - MasterCard

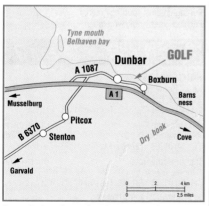

Tyne mouth
Belhaven bay

Dunbar **GOLF**
A 1087
Boxburn
A1
Barns ness
Musselburg
Pitcox
B 6370
Stenton
Dry book
Cove
Garvald

0 ____ 2 ____ 4 km
0 ____ 2,5 miles

Access Accès : 1 km E of Dunbar on A1 and A1087
Map 2 on page 409 Carte 2 Page 409

GOLF COURSE
PARCOURS
16/20

Site	Site	■■■■■■■
Maintenance	Entretien	■■■■■
Architect	Architecte	Tom Morris
Type	Type	seaside course
Relief	Relief	
Water in play	Eau en jeu	■
Exp. to wind	Exposé au vent	■■■■■■
Trees in play	Arbres en jeu	■

Scorecard Carte de score	Chp. Chp.	Mens Mess.	Ladies Da.
Length Long.	5848	5848	5848
Par	71	71	74

Advised golfing ability		0	12	24	36
Niveau de jeu recommandé				■■	
Hcp required	Handicap exigé	certificate			

CLUB HOUSE & AMENITIES
CLUB HOUSE ET ANNEXES
5/10

Pro shop	Pro-shop	■■■■■
Driving range	Practice	
Sheltered	couvert	no
On grass	sur herbe	no
Putting-green	putting-green	no
Pitching-green	pitching green	no

HOTEL FACILITIES
ENVIRONNEMENT HOTELIER
6/10

HOTELS HÔTELS
Marine
9 rooms, D £ 32
Tel (44) 01368 - 863 315
Dunbar
close

Marine Hotel
74 rooms, D £ 80
Tel (44) 01620 - 892 406, Fax (44) 01620 - 894 480
North Berwick
15 km

Courtyard
6 rooms, D £ 50
Tel (44) 01368 - 864 169
Dunbar
close

RESTAURANTS RESTAURANT
Courtyard
Tel (44) 01368 - 864 169
Dunbar
close

609

This city was the capital of Scotland up until 1603 and still carries the vestiges of its prestigious past. Now while the kingdom of Fife is famous for its links, shaped by nature over several hundred years, this particular course is an inland layout which has much to be said for it but without quite the same nobility. Tradition here goes back more than 110 years, and although the course was simply modernised at the beginning of the 1950s, no great change was made to the 600 year-old clubhouse. Trees and bunkers form the traditional hazards of a well-balanced course which is moderately hilly and fun for all. In short, this is your standard middle-of-the-road course that will sometimes have you raring to go. The watchword here is always fun.

La ville fut la capitale de l'Ecosse jusqu'en 1603, et porte les vestiges d'un prestigieux passé. Mais si le royaume de Fife est célèbre par ses links patinés depuis des siècles par la nature, le présent parcours "inland" ne manque pas de qualités, sans prétendre à tant de noblesse. Sa tradition remonte à plus de 110 ans, il a simplement été modernisé au début des années 50, sans que l'on touche beaucoup au Clubhouse, datant de plus de six siècles. Les arbres et les bunkers forment les obstacles traditionnels d'un parcours bien équilibré dans ses difficultés, modérément mouvementé, amusant pour tous les niveaux. Bref, un modèle de golf "middle-of-the-road," que l'on pourrait parfois avoir envie de violenter un peu, mais le maître mot est ici le plaisir...

Dunfermline Golf Club
Pitfirrane, Crossford
SCO - DUNFERMLINE, Fife KY12 7QW

Office	Secrétariat	(44) 01383 - 723 534
Pro shop	Pro-shop	(44) 01383 - 729 061
Fax	Fax	
Situation	Situation	

3 km W of Dunfermline (pop.29 436)
27 km NW of Edinburgh (pop. 418 914)

Annual closure	Fermeture annnuelle	no
Weekly closure	Fermeture hebdomadaire	no

Fees main season
Tarifs haute saison 18 holes

	Week days Semaine	We/Bank holidays We/Férié
Individual Individuel	£ 20	£ 25
Couple Couple	£ 40	£ 50

Full day: £ 28 - £ 35 (weekends)

Caddy	Caddy	no
Electric Trolley	Chariot électrique	no
Buggy	Voiturette	no
Clubs	Clubs	no

Credit cards Cartes de crédit   no

GOLF COURSE
PARCOURS   **15**/20

Site	Site	■■■■■□□
Maintenance	Entretien	■■■■■□□
Architect	Architecte	Stutt & Co
Type	Type	parkland
Relief	Relief	■■■■□□□
Water in play	Eau en jeu	■□□□□□□
Exp. to wind	Exposé au vent	■■■■□□□
Trees in play	Arbres en jeu	■■■■■□□

Scorecard Carte de score	Chp. Chp.	Mens Mess.	Ladies Da.
Length Long.	5575	5263	4917
Par	72	70	72

Advised golfing ability   0   12   24   36
Niveau de jeu recommandé
Hcp required   Handicap exigé   certificate

CLUB HOUSE & AMENITIES
CLUB HOUSE ET ANNEXES   **7**/10

Pro shop	Pro-shop	■■■■■□□
Driving range	Practice	■■■□□□□
Sheltered	couvert	no
On grass	sur herbe	no
Putting-green	putting-green	yes
Pitching-green	pitching green	yes

HOTEL FACILITIES
ENVIRONNEMENT HOTELIER   **7**/10

HOTELS HÔTELS
Keavil House Hotel   Crossford
33 rooms, D £ 75   5 km
Tel (44) 01383 - 736 258, Fax (44) 01383 - 621 600

King Malcolm Thistle Hotel   Dunfermline
48 rooms, from D £ 64   4 km
Tél (44) 01383 - 722 611, Fax (44) 01383 - 730 865

Davaar House Hotel   Dunfermline
8 rooms, D £ 56   4 km
Tel (44) 01383 - 721 886, Fax (44) 01383 - 623 633

RESTAURANTS RESTAURANT
Noble Cuisine   Dunfermline
Tel (44) 01383 - 620 555   4 km

King Malcolm   Dunfermline
Tel (44) 01383 - 722 611   4 km

610

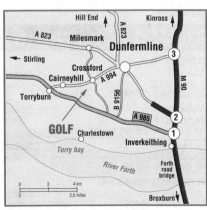

Access Accès : On A994, West of Dunfermline
Map 2 on page 409 Carte 2 Page 409

Although close to Glasgow, this course is located away from any residential area. We are out in the country on Scottish moorland with its typical covering of whin (gorse) and heather, very many trees and a stream that crosses the course, running down the side of the fairways and sometimes cutting across them at strategic distances. This was only to be expected from James Braid. It is very easy to see your ball end up there if you don't give enough thought to flight and roll. Mid-handicappers, though, can always choose a line of flight without too many risks, although the experts will be keen to flex their muscles. In a word, a good score here is not as easy as all that. The clubhouse is spacious but the course crowded enough for us to advise you to book your tee-off time in advance.

Bien qu'il soit proche de Glasgow, ce parcours est situé en dehors de toute zone résidentielle. Nous sommes à la campagne, dans la lande écossaise, avec sa végétation typique d'ajoncs et de bruyère, de nombreux arbres, mais aussi un ruisseau qui parcourt l'espace, longeant les fairways ou venant les interrompre, de manière stratégique, ce qu'il fallait attendre de James Braid. Il est très facile d'y voir les balles y terminer sa course si l'on n'a pas réfléchi un peu sur leur portée et leur roulement. Cependant, les handicaps moyens peuvent toujours choisir des lignes de jeu sans grands risques, alors que les experts voudront montrer leurs muscles. Bref, il n'est pas si facile de scorer ici. Le Clubhouse est spacieux, mais le parcours assez fréquenté pour que l'on conseille de réserver les départs à l'avance.

East Renfrewshire Golf Course
Pilmuir, Newton Mearns
SCO - GLASGOW G77 6RT

Office	Secrétariat	(44) 01355 - 500 256
Pro shop	Pro-shop	(44) 01355 - 500 206
Fax	Fax	
Situation	Situation	

15 km S of centre of Glasgow (pop. 622 853)

Annual closure	Fermeture annnuelle	no
Weekly closure	Fermeture hebdomadaire	no

Fees main season
Tarifs haute saison 18 holes

	Week days Semaine	We/Bank holidays We/Férié
Individual Individuel	£ 30	£ 30
Couple Couple	£ 60	£ 60

Full day: £ 35

Caddy	Caddy	no
Electric Trolley	Chariot électrique	no
Buggy	Voiturette	no
Clubs	Clubs	yes

Credit cards Cartes de crédit
VISA - Eurocard - MasterCard - AMEX - DC

Access Accès : Glasgow M8 and A77 → Kilmarnoch.
Club on the right shortly after Eastwood Toll.
Map 3 on page 410 Carte 3 Page 410

GOLF COURSE PARCOURS   15/20

Site	Site	▆▆▆▆
Maintenance	Entretien	▆▆▆▆
Architect	Architecte	James Braid
Type	Type	inland, moorland
Relief	Relief	▆▆
Water in play	Eau en jeu	▆▆
Exp. to wind	Exposé au vent	▆▆▆▆▆
Trees in play	Arbres en jeu	▆▆▆

Scorecard Carte de score	Chp. Chp.	Mens Mess.	Ladies Da.
Length Long.	5577	5577	4668
Par	70	70	71

Advised golfing ability Niveau de jeu recommandé	0	12	24	36

Hcp required   Handicap exigé   certificate

CLUB HOUSE & AMENITIES CLUB HOUSE ET ANNEXES   6/10

Pro shop	Pro-shop	▆▆▆
Driving range	Practice	▆▆
Sheltered	couvert	no
On grass	sur herbe	yes
Putting-green	putting-green	yes
Pitching-green	pitching green	yes

HOTEL FACILITIES ENVIRONNEMENT HOTELIER   8/10

HOTELS HÔTELS

Glasgow Hilton
315 rooms, D £ 120
Tel (44) 0141 - 204 5555, Fax (44) 0141 - 204 5004
Glasgow
15 km

One Devonshire Gardens
25 rooms, D £ 135
Tel (44) 0141 - 339 2001, Fax (44) 0141 - 337 1663
Glasgow
15 km

Carrick
121 rooms, D £ 65
Tel (44) 0141 - 248 2355, Fax (44) 0141 - 221 1014
Glasgow
15 km

RESTAURANTS RESTAURANT

One Devonshire Gardens
Tel (44) 0141 - 339 2001
Glasgow
15 km

Buttery
Tel (44) 0141 - 221 8188
Glasgow
15 km

611

14	6	3

This course is located virtually in town, or should we say village, as Edzell has often been voted "the best preserved village in Scotland". It was certainly one of the most stylishly frequented for many a year, as princes and maharajahs would come here for the fishing and hunting at the edge of the Highlands, and certainly to play this course designed in 1895 by Bob Simpson of Carnoustie. Laid out over gorse-land, this is a gem of a course, with a wide variety of holes, small, well-kept greens, soft fairways and hazards of all shapes and sizes, including bunkers, a steep-banked river and trees. This is one of the places in Scotland where you can still feel "out of time", as you are so far away from the main roads. Don't expect a Japanese-style clubhouse on this kind of course; what really matters here is hospitality, and here you will find that aplenty.

Ce parcours est pratiquement en ville. Ou en village, car Edzell a été souvent élu comme "le village le mieux préservé d'Ecosse." Il fut longtemps aussi le "mieux" fréquenté, car princes et maharadjahs venaient ici pêcher, chasser en bordure des Highlands, et sans doute aussi jouer sur ce parcours créé en 1895 par Bob Simpson de Carnoustie. Tracé en terre de bruyère, c'est un petit bijou, avec des trous très variés, de petits greens bien entretenus, des fairways souples et des obstacles en tous genres, depuis les bunkers jusqu'à la rivière et ses rives abruptes en passant par les bois. C'est un des endroits d'Ecosse où l'on peut le plus se croire hors du temps, parce qu'on se trouve aussi à l'écart des grandes routes. Dans ce genre de golf, que l'on n'attende pas un Clubhouse à la japonaise : l'essentiel est dans la chaleur de l'accueil.

The Edzell Golf Club

High Street
SCO - EDZELL, by Brechin, Tayside DD9 7TF

Office	Secrétariat	(44) 01356 - 647 283
Pro shop	Pro-shop	(44) 01356 - 648 462
Fax	Fax	(44) 01356 - 648 094
Situation	Situation	

8 km N of Brechin
20 km NW of Montrose (pop. 8 473)

Annual closure	Fermeture annnuelle	no
Weekly closure	Fermeture hebdomadaire	no

Fees main season
Tarifs haute saison 18 holes

	Week days Semaine	We/Bank holidays We/Férié
Individual Individuel	£ 20	£ 26
Couple Couple	£ 40	£ 39

Full weekdays: £ 30

Caddy	Caddy	no
Electric Trolley	Chariot électrique	no
Buggy	Voiturette	£ 12/18 holes
Clubs	Clubs	yes
Credit cards Cartes de crédit		no

612

Access Accès : Dundee A90. After Brechin, B966 to Edzell. Golf alongside main entrance to village.
Map 1 on page 407 Carte 1 Page 407

GOLF COURSE
PARCOURS

14/20

Site	Site	
Maintenance	Entretien	
Architect	Architecte	Bob Simpson
Type	Type	heathland, parkland
Relief	Relief	
Water in play	Eau en jeu	
Exp. to wind	Exposé au vent	
Trees in play	Arbres en jeu	

Scorecard Carte de score	Chp. Chp.	Mens Mess.	Ladies Da.
Length Long.	5776	5498	5040
Par	71	71	74

Advised golfing ability
Niveau de jeu recommandé
0   12   24   36

Hcp required Handicap exigé no

CLUB HOUSE & AMENITIES
CLUB HOUSE ET ANNEXES

6/10

Pro shop	Pro-shop	
Driving range	Practice	
Sheltered	couvert	9 mats
On grass	sur herbe	yes
Putting-green	putting-green	yes
Pitching-green	pitching green	no

HOTEL FACILITIES
ENVIRONNEMENT HOTELIER

3/10

HOTELS HÔTELS
Glenesk Hotel   Edzell
25 rooms, D £ 82   adjacent
Tel (44) 01356 - 648 319, Fax (44) 01356 - 647 333

ELGIN

This course has the enviable reputation of being one of the best inland courses in northern Scotland. At all events it is a very good test of golf, and although its length may seem a little outdated, there is only the one par 5 and this can often dash any hope of carding a good score. Precision is at a premium here, but hazards are in good view and so can help you recover an efficient game strategy. Eight of the par-4s are longer than 390 yards, so you can understand Elgin's reputation for being a serious examination of every green-feer's talent. For want of beating any records, you can always enjoy the view over the old city of Elgin to the north (well worth a visit) and to the south the superb Cairngorm Mountains (well worth exploring).

Ce parcours a la réputation enviable d'être l'un des meilleurs parcours "intérieurs" du nord de l'Ecosse. C'est en tout cas un très bon test de golf, et si sa longueur peut le faire paraître désuet, il y a un seul par 5, ce qui complique bien souvent l'espérance d'un bon score. Il faut être ici très précis, mais les obstacles sont assez en vue pour établir une stratégie efficace. Huit des par 4 mesurant plus de 360 mètres, on comprend que la réputation de Elgin soit aussi d'être un sérieux examen du talent des visiteurs. A défaut de battre tous les records, ceux-ci pourront se livrer à la contemplation du panorama sur la vieille cité d'Elgin au nord (à visiter) et, au sud, sur les superbes Cairngorm Mountains (à explorer).

Elgin Golf Club

Birnie Road
SCO - ELGIN, Moray IV30 3SX

Office	Secrétariat	(44) 01343 - 542 338
Pro shop	Pro-shop	(44) 01343 - 542 884
Fax	Fax	(44) 01343 - 542 341
Situation	Situation	

1 km from Elgin (pop. 11 855)
62 km E of Inverness (pop. 62 186)

Annual closure	Fermeture annnuelle	no
Weekly closure	Fermeture hebdomadaire	no

Fees main season
Tarifs haute saison 18 holes

	Week days Semaine	We/Bank holidays We/Férié
Individual Individuel	£ 21	£ 27
Couple Couple	£ 42	£ 54

Caddy	Caddy	£10
Electric Trolley	Chariot électrique	no
Buggy	Voiturette	no
Clubs	Clubs	£ 10/18 holes
Credit cards Cartes de crédit		no

Access Accès : Aberdeen or Inverness A96 to Elgin.
Golf on A941 just South of town limits
Map 1 on page 407 Carte 1 Page 407

GOLF COURSE
PARCOURS

15 /20

Site	Site	
Maintenance	Entretien	
Architect	Architecte	John MacPherson
Type	Type	parkland
Relief	Relief	
Water in play	Eau en jeu	
Exp. to wind	Exposé au vent	
Trees in play	Arbres en jeu	

Scorecard Carte de score	Chp. Chp.	Mens Mess.	Ladies Da.
Length Long.	5834	5608	5290
Par	69	69	74

Advised golfing ability
Niveau de jeu recommandé   0   12   24   36

Hcp required   Handicap exigé   no

CLUB HOUSE & AMENITIES
CLUB HOUSE ET ANNEXES

7 /10

Pro shop	Pro-shop	
Driving range	Practice	
Sheltered	couvert	16 mats
On grass	sur herbe	no
Putting-green	putting-green	yes
Pitching-green	pitching green	no

HOTEL FACILITIES
ENVIRONNEMENT HOTELIER

6 /10

HOTELS HÔTELS

Mansion House		Elgin
23 rooms, D £ 120		1 km
Tel (44) 01343 - 548 811		
Fax (44) 01343 - 547 916		
Mansfield House		Elgin
16 rooms, D £ 80		1 km
Tel (44) 01343 - 540 883		
Fax (44) 01343 - 552 491		

RESTAURANTS RESTAURANT

Mansion House		Elgin
Tel (44) 01343 - 548 811		1 km

613

This is where James Braid learnt his golf, and you can understand why he became such a great champion and such a good course designer. Elie is a delightful course, as picturesque as they come with a number of rural features that will stay for ever, notably its location virtually in the middle of the village. But if you get the impression you are in for a pleasure cruise, watch out. The traps here are as frequent as the number of shots that, although not completely blind, do raise a few questions and eyebrows. Exposure to the wind is so fierce that there is no point in worrying about the theoretical par for each hole. It changes from one day to the next. Likewise you'll learn how to bump and run the ball by asking the locals who are always willing to give advice. One of the region's most amusing courses.

C'est ici que James Braid a appris le golf, l'on comprend qu'il soit devenu à la fois un si grand champion et un architecte aussi remarquable. Elie est un délicieux parcours, aussi pittoresque que possible, avec certains aspects rustiques à préserver, notamment sa situation quasiment au milieu du village. Mais si l'on a l'impression de s'y livrer à une partie de plaisir, il faut méfiance garder. Les pièges sont ici aussi nombreux que les coups sinon aveugles, du moins bien soulignés de points d'interrogation. L'exposition au vent est si importante qu'il ne faut pas se soucier du par théorique de chaque trou, il change d'un jour à l'autre. De même on y apprendra à faire rouler la balle, en demandant leur avis aux joueurs locaux, qui n'hésitent jamais à livrer leurs bons conseils... avec l'accent. L'un des plus amusants parcours de la région.

Golf House Club Elie
SCO - ELIE, LEVEN, Fife, KY9 1AS

Office	Secrétariat	(44) 01333 - 330 327
Pro shop	Pro-shop	(44) 01333 - 320 955
Fax	Fax	(44) 01333 - 330 895
Situation	Situation	.

19 km S of St Andrews (pop. 11 136)
65 km E of Edinburgh (pop. 418 914)

Annual closure	Fermeture annnuelle	no
Weekly closure	Fermeture hebdomadaire	no

Fees main season
Tarifs haute saison 18 holes

	Week days Semaine	We/Bank holidays We/Férié
Individual Individuel	£ 32	£ 40
Couple Couple	£ 64	£ 80

Full days: £ 45 - £ 55 (weekends)

Caddy	Caddy	£ 15
Electric Trolley	Chariot électrique	yes
Buggy	Voiturette	no
Clubs	Clubs	yes
Credit cards Cartes de crédit		no

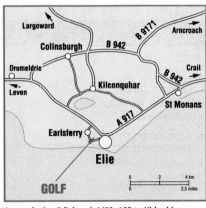

Largoward		
Colinsburgh	B 942	B 9171 Arncroach
Drumeldrie		Crail
Leven	Kilconquhar	B 942
	A 917	St Monans
Earlsferry		

Elie

GOLF

| 0 | 2 | 4 km |
| 0 | | 2.5 miles |

Access Accès : Edinburgh M90, A92 to Kirkcaldy, then A917. Golf 8 km in the centre of village.
Map 3 on page 410 Carte 3 Page 410

GOLF COURSE
PARCOURS
15/20

Site	Site	▬▬▬▬
Maintenance	Entretien	▬▬▬▬
Architect	Architecte	Unknown
Type	Type	links
Relief	Relief	▬▬▬
Water in play	Eau en jeu	▬
Exp. to wind	Exposé au vent	▬▬▬▬▬
Trees in play	Arbres en jeu	

Scorecard Carte de score	Chp. Chp.	Mens Mess.	Ladies Da.
Length Long.	5697	5697	5697
Par	70	70	75

Advised golfing ability Niveau de jeu recommandé	0	12	24	36
		▬▬▬▬▬		

Hcp required Handicap exigé   no

CLUB HOUSE & AMENITIES
CLUB HOUSE ET ANNEXES
6/10

Pro shop	Pro-shop	▬▬▬▬
Driving range	Practice	▬▬▬
Sheltered	couvert	no
On grass	sur herbe	no
Putting-green	putting-green	yes
Pitching-green	pitching green	no

HOTEL FACILITIES
ENVIRONNEMENT HOTELIER
6/10

HOTELS HÔTELS
Old Manor   Leven
20 rooms, D £ 100   5 km
Tel (44) 01333 - 320 368
Fax (44) 01333 - 320 911

Balbirnie House   Glenrothes
28 rooms, D £ 150   8 km
Tel (44) 01592 - 610 066
Fax (44) 01592 - 610 529

RESTAURANTS RESTAURANT
Bouquet Garni   Elie
Tel (44) 01333 - 330 374   close

Cellar   Ansruther
Tel (44) 01333 - 310 378   4 km

614

FORFAR

Old Tom Morris came from Forfar to lay out the first nine holes of this course in beautiful landscape dotted with heather. In 1925, the Club asked James Braid to come and complete the course, which he did for the princely sum of £10. At that rate you can understand why the man travelled Scotland far and wide, designing hundreds of courses and managing to earn his living as a golf-course designer. Today, the course has been enhanced by some tall pine-trees, but you can still feel Tom Morris' beloved springy turf underfoot. Not a long course - although it is only a par 69 with just the one par 5 - it is still exciting to play, especially the par 3s and a number of blind shots for a few extra thrills. If you are in the region, Forfar is well worth a visit.

Old Tom Morris vint de Saint Andrews pour tracer les neuf premiers trous de ce parcours dans un beau paysage parsemé de bruyère. En 1925, le Club demanda à James Braid de le compléter, ce qu'il fit pour la somme de 10 Livres. A ce tarif, on comprend qu'il ait sillonné l'Ecosse pour dessiner une multitude de parcours et parvenir à gagner sa vie d'architecte de golf ! Aujourd'hui, de grands pins viennent agrémenter le tracé, mais on y trouve toujours ce sol élastique que Tom Morris aimait tant. De longueur assez modeste - mais c'est un par 69 avec un seul par 5 - il n'en est pas moins passionnant à jouer, en particulier avec ses très beaux par 3, et quelques coups aveugles pour donner un peu d'émotions. Si vous êtes dans la région, Forfar mérite une halte.

Forfar Golf Club
Cunning Hill, Arbroath Road
SCO - FORFAR, Angus DD8 2RL

Office	Secrétariat	(44) 01307 - 463 773
Pro shop	Pro-shop	(44) 01307 - 465 683
Fax	Fax	(44) 01307 - 468 495
Situation	Situation	

2.5 km E of Forfar (pop. 14 159)
27 km N of Dundee (pop. 165 873)

Annual closure	Fermeture annnuelle	no
Weekly closure	Fermeture hebdomadaire	no

Fees main season
Tarifs haute saison 18 holes

	Week days Semaine	We/Bank holidays We/Férié
Individual Individuel	£ 16	£ 20
Couple Couple	£ 32	£ 40

Full day: £ 24 - £ 32 (weekends)

Caddy	Caddy	no
Electric Trolley	Chariot électrique	£ 5/18 holes
Buggy	Voiturette	no
Clubs	Clubs	no
Credit cards Cartes de crédit		no

Access Accès : Dundee A929 to Forfar, then A932 East
Map 1 on page 407 Carte 1 Page 407

GOLF COURSE
PARCOURS
14/20

Site	Site	
Maintenance	Entretien	
Architect	Architecte	Tom Morris
		James Braid
Type	Type	heathland
Relief	Relief	
Water in play	Eau en jeu	
Exp. to wind	Exposé au vent	
Trees in play	Arbres en jeu	

Scorecard Carte de score	Chp. Chp.	Mens Mess.	Ladies Da.
Length Long.	5507	5236	4945
Par	69	69	72

Advised golfing ability		0 12 24 36
Niveau de jeu recommandé		
Hcp required	Handicap exigé	certificate

CLUB HOUSE & AMENITIES
CLUB HOUSE ET ANNEXES
6/10

Pro shop	Pro-shop	
Driving range	Practice	
Sheltered	couvert	no
On grass	sur herbe	no
Putting-green	putting-green	yes
Pitching-green	pitching green	no

HOTEL FACILITIES
ENVIRONNEMENT HOTELIER
6/10

HOTELS HÔTELS

Chapelbank House		Forfar
4 rooms, D £ 70		2 km
Tel (44) 01307 - 463 151		
Fax (44) 01307 - 461 922		
Royal Hotel		Forfar
19 rooms, D £ 70		2 km
Tel (44) 01307 - 462 691		

RESTAURANTS RESTAURANT

Chapelbank House		Forfar
Tel (44) 01307 - 463 151		2 km
August Moon		Forfar
Tel (44) 01307 - 468 688		2 km

615

This delightful course is sited on a promontory on Black Isle and gives a magnificent view over Cromarty Firth. It's shortish length might make you feel that only accuracy is of any importance here, and that's true if the wind keeps low, which is rare. Twice restyled by James Braid, it uses the land in remarkable fashion and is extremely dangerous in the way the sea comes into play. You will need a broad pair of shoulders to keep your score down on an off-day, but you don't have to keep score. Doubtless a little kinder than its neighbours Royal Dornoch and Nairn, this gently rolling course is magic for everyone, and remarkable value for money. On the 17th, watch out for the stone marking the tomb of the "last" Scottish witch. Was she really the last?

Ce délicieux parcours est situé sur un promontoire sur la Black Isle et offre un spectacle magnifique sur le Cromarty Firth. Sa longueur très modérée pourrait faire croire que seule va compter la précision. C'est vrai si le vent ne souffle pas, ce qui est bien rare. Révisé à deux reprises par James Braid, il utilise le terrain de manière remarquable, et met en jeu la mer de manière fort dangereuse. Il faut certes avoir les épaules larges pour serrer le score quand le jeu n'est pas au rendez-vous... mais on n'est pas obligé de compter les coups. Moins brutal sans doute que ses voisins Royal Dornoch et Nairn, ce parcours gentiment ondulé est un régal pour tous, avec un rapport qualité/prix remarquable. A remarquer au 17, la pierre marquant la tombe de la "dernière" sorcière d'Ecosse. La dernière, vraiment ?

Fortrose & Rosemarkie
Ness Road East, Fortrose
SCO - BLACK ISLE, Ross-shire IV10 8SE

Office	Secrétariat	(44) 01381 - 620 529
Pro shop	Pro-shop	(44) 01381 - 620 733
Fax	Fax	
Situation	Situation	.

21 km NE of Inverness (pop. 62 186)

Annual closure	Fermeture annnuelle	no
Weekly closure	Fermeture hebdomadaire	no

Fees main season
Tarifs haute saison 18 holes

	Week days Semaine	We/Bank holidays We/Férié
Individual Individuel	£ 16	£ 22
Couple Couple	£ 32	£ 44

Caddy	Caddy	no
Electric Trolley	Chariot électrique	no
Buggy	Voiturette	no
Clubs	Clubs	on request

Credit cards Cartes de crédit
VISA - MasterCard

616

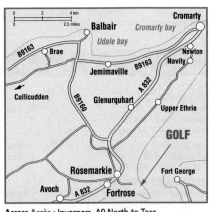

Access Accès : Inverness, A9 North to Tore.
At roundabout, A382 to Fortrose
Map 1 on page 406 Carte 1 Page 406

GOLF COURSE
PARCOURS   16/20

Site	Site	▬▬▬▬▬▬
Maintenance	Entretien	▬▬▬▬▬
Architect	Architecte	James Braid
Type	Type	links
Relief	Relief	▬▬
Water in play	Eau en jeu	▬▬▬▬
Exp. to wind	Exposé au vent	▬▬▬▬▬▬
Trees in play	Arbres en jeu	▬

Scorecard Carte de score	Chp. Chp.	Mens Mess.	Ladies Da.
Length Long.	5331	5095	4876
Par	71	71	71

Advised golfing ability		0 12 24 36
Niveau de jeu recommandé		
Hcp required	Handicap exigé	28 Men, 36 Ladies

CLUB HOUSE & AMENITIES
CLUB HOUSE ET ANNEXES   6/10

Pro shop	Pro-shop	▬▬▬▬
Driving range	Practice	▬
Sheltered	couvert	no
On grass	sur herbe	no
Putting-green	putting-green	yes
Pitching-green	pitching green	no

HOTEL FACILITIES
ENVIRONNEMENT HOTELIER   5/10

HOTELS HÔTELS
Royal   Cromarty
10 rooms, D £ 55   15 km
Tel (44) 01381 - 600 217

Ballyfeary House   Inverness
8 rooms, D £ 68   25 km
Tel (44) 01463 - 235 572, Fax (44) 01463 - 717 583

Craigmonie Hotel   Inverness
35 rooms, D £ 96   25 km
Tel (44) 01463 - 231 649, Fax (44) 01463 - 233 720

RESTAURANTS RESTAURANT
Dunain Park   Inverness
Tel (44) 01463 - 230 512   25 km

Culloden House   Inverness
Tel (44) 01463 - 790 461   25 km

GLEN

This is the "East Links" of North Berwick, less well known than its neighbour doubtless because it is less of a complete links and has several inland holes. It is laid out over two levels but is still easy on the legs. Designed at the turn of the century and tastefully restyled by MacKenzie Ross with a considerate thought for all players, it offers some splendid views over the Firth of Forth and over the famous bird reserve of Bass Rock in the open sea. It is not over-long (compared as always with today's standards) but is still a stiff test of golf, especially with the wind which although not too blustery is never far away. Green-feers will at least remember the drive from the 18th tee, from a severely elevated tee, and the excitement of a number of blind shots.

C'est le "East Links" de North Berwick, moins connu que son voisin, sans doute parce qu'il a un caractère moins totalement "links", avec plusieurs trous nettement "inland." Construit sur deux niveaux, il n'est pas fatigant à jouer. Créé au début du siècle, remanié par Mackenzie Ross avec beaucoup de goût et de souci d'adaptation à tous les joueurs, il propose de superbes vues sur le Firth of Forth et sur la fameuse réserve d'oiseaux du Bass Rock, au large. Bien qu'il ne soit pas très long (toujours en regard des célèbres critères modernes), c'est néanmoins un solide test de jeu, spécialement avec le vent, pas toujours violent, mais toujours présent. Les visiteurs garderont d'ici au moins le souvenir du drive du 18, depuis un départ très en hauteur, et celui de quelques émotions sur certains coups aveugles.

Glen Golf Club

Tantallon Terrace
SCO - NORTH BERWICK, East Lothian EH39 4LE

Office	Secrétariat	(44) 01620 - 892 726
Pro shop	Pro-shop	(44) 01620 - 894 596
Fax	Fax	(44) 01620 - 895 288
Situation	Situation	

25 km E of Edinburgh (pop. 418 914)

Annual closure	Fermeture annnuelle	no
Weekly closure	Fermeture hebdomadaire	no

Fees main season
Tarifs haute saison 18 holes

	Week days Semaine	We/Bank holidays We/Férié
Individual Individuel	£ 16	£ 20
Couple Couple	£ 32	£ 40

Caddy	Caddy	on request
Electric Trolley	Chariot électrique	£ 5/18 holes
Buggy	Voiturette	no
Clubs	Clubs	£ 10/18 holes
Credit cards Cartes de crédit		no

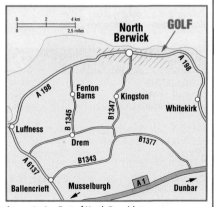

Access Accès : East of North Berwick town.
Follow seafront road from harbour. Course signposted.
Map 3 on page 411 Carte 3 Page 411

GOLF COURSE
PARCOURS
14/20

Site	Site	▇▇▇▇▇□□
Maintenance	Entretien	▇▇▇▇▇□□
Architect	Architecte	Mackenzie Ross
Type	Type	seaside course
Relief	Relief	▇▇▇□□□□
Water in play	Eau en jeu	▇□□□□□□
Exp. to wind	Exposé au vent	▇▇▇▇▇□□
Trees in play	Arbres en jeu	▇▇▇□□□□

Scorecard Carte de score	Chp. Chp.	Mens Mess.	Ladies Da.
Length Long.	5523	5293	5116
Par	69	69	72

Advised golfing ability		0 12 24 36
Niveau de jeu recommandé		▇▇▇▇▇▇□
Hcp required	Handicap exigé	no

CLUB HOUSE & AMENITIES
CLUB HOUSE ET ANNEXES
7/10

Pro shop	Pro-shop	▇▇▇▇▇□□
Driving range	Practice	▇▇▇▇□□□
Sheltered	couvert	no
On grass	sur herbe	yes
Putting-green	putting-green	yes
Pitching-green	pitching green	yes

HOTEL FACILITIES
ENVIRONNEMENT HOTELIER
7/10

HOTELS HÔTELS

Marine Hotel — North Berwick
74 rooms, D £ 80 — 3 km
Tel (44) 01620 - 892 406, Fax (44) 01620 - 894 480

Belhaven — North Berwick
12 rooms, D £ 45 — 2 km
Tel (44) 01620 - 893 009

Nether Abbey — North Berwick
16 rooms, D £ 55 — 3 km
Tel (44) 01620 - 892 802

RESTAURANTS RESTAURANT

Tantallon Inn — North Berwick
Tel (44) 01620 - 892 238 — 0.5 km

The Grange — North Berwick
Tel (44) 01620 - 895 894 — 1 km

617

You come here as a true golfing fanatic, and to hell with the cost. The Gleneagles hotel, an absolute must, is a genuine palace hotel in an idyllic region of the Highlands. At the end of the first world war, James Braid designed the first two 18-hole courses - the King's and Queen's - while the third, the Monarch, was laid out by Jack Nicklaus. The King's Course is without a doubt the finest of the three, magnificently crafted from the surrounding landscape, winding its way through trees, bushes and hills and teeming with wildlife. The course has one essential quality, namely the variety of holes and a sort of indefinable logic in its balance. The artistry in the shapes of greens and bunkers only adds to the visual and technical pleasure of playing this challenging, very technical and remarkably well-groomed course. Exposure to the wind may vary considerably, depending on how protected the fairways are.

On vient ici en passionné du golf, en décidant de ne pas compter ses sous. Le Gleneagles Hotel, point de passage obligatoire, est un véritable palace, dans une région idyllique des Highlands. A la fin de la première Guerre Mondiale, James Braid dessina les deux premiers 18 trous, le King's et le Queen's, le troisième le Monarch's, ayant été créé par Jack Nicklaus. Le premier nommé reste sans doute le plus savoureux des trois. Magnifiquement sculpté dans la campagne environnante, insinué au milieu des arbres, des buissons, des collines, parcourus d'une vie animale intense, il a une qualité essentielle, la variété des trous et une sorte de logique de rythme indéfinissable. Et la sensualité des formes des greens ou des bunkers ne fait qu'ajouter au plaisir visuel et technique de ce parcours exigeant, très technique, remarquablement entretenu. L'exposition au vent peut varier considérablement, suivant la protection ou non des fairways.

Gleneagles Hotel & Golf Courses

Gleneagles Hotel
SCO - AUCHTERARDER, Perthshire PH3 1NF

Office	Secrétariat	(44) 01764 - 663 543
Pro shop	Pro-shop	(44) 01764 - 694 362
Fax	Fax	(44) 01764 - 694 383
Situation	Situation	

30 km SW of Perth (pop. 123 495)
85 km NW of Edinburgh (pop. 418 914)

Annual closure	Fermeture annnuelle	no
Weekly closure	Fermeture hebdomadaire	no
Fees main season	Tarifs haute saison	full day

	Week days Semaine	We/Bank holidays We/Férié
Individual Individuel	£ 80	£ 80
Couple Couple	£ 160	£ 160
For residents only		

Caddy	Caddy	£ 28
Electric Trolley	Chariot électrique	no
Buggy	Voiturette	£ 28/18 holes
Clubs	Clubs	£ 28/18 holes

Credit cards Cartes de crédit
VISA - Eurocard - MasterCard - AMEX - DC - JCB

618

Access Accès : • Glasgow A80, M9, A9. Turn left at junction with A823 signed Crieff & Gleneagles • Edinburgh M90. Jct 2, then A823 through Dunfermline, → Crieff.
Map 2 on page 408 Carte 2 Page 408

GOLF COURSE
PARCOURS **18**/20

Site	Site	▬▬▬▬▬
Maintenance	Entretien	▬▬▬▬▬
Architect	Architecte	James Braid
Type	Type	moorland
Relief	Relief	▬
Water in play	Eau en jeu	▬▬
Exp. to wind	Exposé au vent	▬▬▬
Trees in play	Arbres en jeu	▬▬▬

Scorecard Carte de score	Chp. Chp.	Mens Mess.	Ladies Da.
Length Long.	5888	5574	5345
Par	70	68	75

Advised golfing ability		0 12 24 36
Niveau de jeu recommandé		▬▬▬▬
Hcp required	Handicap exigé	no

CLUB HOUSE & AMENITIES
CLUB HOUSE ET ANNEXES **9**/10

Pro shop	Pro-shop	▬▬▬▬
Driving range	Practice	▬▬▬▬
Sheltered	couvert	10 mats
On grass	sur herbe	yes (04 → 10)
Putting-green	putting-green	yes
Pitching-green	pitching green	yes

HOTEL FACILITIES
ENVIRONNEMENT HOTELIER **7**/10

HOTELS HÔTELS
Gleneagles Hotel — Golf on site
234 rooms, from D £ 130 (ask)
Tel (44) 01764 - 662 231
Fax (44) 01764 - 662 134

RESTAURANTS RESTAURANT
Strathearn — Gleneagles Hotel on site
Tel (44) 01764 - 662 231

Dormy Grill — Gleneagles Hotel on site
Tel (44) 01764 - 662 231

Auchterarder House — Auchterarder 6 km N
Tel (44) 01764 - 663 646

We could talk for ever about the suitability of Jack Nicklaus' design for the Monarch's course at Gleneagles, but so much earth was shifted that not all the scars have healed and mother nature has yet to regain the upper hand. Despite certain reverences to the artistry of James Braid, the design can look distinctly American and often artificial in this landscape. With this said, the course is of an excellent strategic standard, as might be expected, even though Nicklaus was visibly thinking more of the proficient golfer than the less experienced hacker. The superb setting will silence even those people who feel that the difference in style with the other two courses is over the top. No-one, though, can fault the imagination employed here.

On pourrait éternellement discuter de l'adéquation du dessin de Jack Nicklaus pour le "Monarch's" à Gleneagles, mais tant de terre a été remuée que toutes les cicatrices ne sont pas encore refermées, que la nature n'a pas encore repris tous ses droits. En dépit de certaines révérences aux modelages de James Braid, le dessin peut apparaître nettement américain, souvent artificiel dans le paysage. Cela dit, le parcours est d'une excellente qualité stratégique, comme on pouvait s'y attendre, même si Nicklaus a visiblement plus pensé aux bons joueurs qu'aux joueurs peu expérimentés. L'environnement superbe fera taire même ceux qui estiment la différence esthétique excessive par rapport aux deux autres parcours. Tous devront s'incliner au moins devant l'imagination déployée ici.

Gleneagles Hotel & Golf Courses

Gleneagles Hotel
SCO - AUCHTERARDER, Perthshire PH3 1NF

Office	Secrétariat	(44) 01764 - 663 543
Pro shop	Pro-shop	(44) 01764 - 694 362
Fax	Fax	(44) 01764 - 694 383
Situation	Situation	

30 km SW of Perth (pop. 123 495)
85 km NW of Edinburgh (pop. 418 914)

Annual closure	Fermeture annnuelle	no
Weekly closure	Fermeture hebdomadaire	no
Fees main season	Tarifs haute saison	full day

	Week days Semaine	We/Bank holidays We/Férié
Individual Individuel	£ 80	£ 80
Couple Couple	£ 160	£ 160

For residents only

Caddy	Caddy	£ 28
Electric Trolley	Chariot électrique	no
Buggy	Voiturette	£ 28/18 holes
Clubs	Clubs	£ 28/18 holes

Credit cards Cartes de crédit
VISA - Eurocard - MasterCard - AMEX - DC - JCB

Access Accès : • Glasgow A80, M9, A9. Turn left at junction with A823 signed Crieff & Gleneagles • Edinburgh M90. Jct 2, then A823 through Dunfermline, → Crieff.
Map 2 on page 408 Carte 2 Page 408

GOLF COURSE
PARCOURS
17 /20

Site	Site	▬▬▬▬▬▬▭
Maintenance	Entretien	▬▬▬▬▬▬▭
Architect	Architecte	Jack Nicklaus
Type	Type	moorland
Relief	Relief	▬▬▬▬▭▭▭
Water in play	Eau en jeu	▬▬▬▬▭▭▭
Exp. to wind	Exposé au vent	▬▬▬▬▬▭▭
Trees in play	Arbres en jeu	▬▬▬▬▬▭▭

Scorecard Carte de score	Chp. Chp.	Mens Mess.	Ladies Da.
Length Long.	6444	5581	4610
Par	72	72	72

Advised golfing ability	0	12	24	36
Niveau de jeu recommandé		▬▬▬▬▬▭		
Hcp required	Handicap exigé	no		

CLUB HOUSE & AMENITIES
CLUB HOUSE ET ANNEXES
9 /10

Pro shop	Pro-shop	▬▬▬▬▬▬▭
Driving range	Practice	▬▬▬▬▬▬▭
Sheltered	couvert	10 mats
On grass	sur herbe	yes (04 → 10)
Putting-green	putting-green	yes
Pitching-green	pitching green	yes

HOTEL FACILITIES
ENVIRONNEMENT HOTELIER
7 /10

HOTELS HÔTELS
Gleneagles Hotel — Golf / on site
234 rooms, from D £ 130 (ask)
Tel (44) 01764 - 662 231
Fax (44) 01764 - 662 134

RESTAURANTS RESTAURANT
Strathearn — Gleneagles Hotel / on site
Tel (44) 01764 - 662 231

Dormy Grill — Gleneagles Hotel / on site
Tel (44) 01764 - 662 231

Duchally House — Auchterarder / 4 km N
Tel (44) 01764 - 663 071

619

In a series of courses like these, there is often an ugly duckling that is reserved for the lesser players or which you play to take a break from the others. Queen's is certainly not as long, as difficult or as exposed as its fellow courses, but it is not really much more than a foil for the other two. Elsewhere it would be a very good course. Kinder, gentler and might we say more feminine and enhanced with pretty stretches of water, this is in fact a more ornamental course. And while it is more reassuring because it offers less resistance to good golfers, it is still essential playing when you are here. From Spring to late Autumn, Gleneagles is one of the finest places in the world to stay and play golf, even though there are perhaps more thrilling masterpieces elsewhere.

Dans un tel ensemble de parcours, il y a souvent un "vilain petit canard," un parcours que l'on réserve aux moins bons joueurs, ou qui figure là comme un repos pour le guerrier. Certes, le "Queen's" n'est pas aussi long, aussi difficile, aussi exposé que ses deux compagnons, mais il n'en est pas moins bien mieux qu'un faire-valoir. Ailleurs, ce serait un très bon parcours. Plus aimable, plus doux (faut-il dire plus féminin ?), orné de jolies pièces d'eau, il est finalement plus ornemental. Et s'il doit rassurer par une moindre résistance, il n'en est pas moins inévitable quand on se trouve ici. Du printemps à la fin de l'automne, Gleneagles est un des plus beaux endroits au monde pour séjourner, et aussi pour jouer au golf, même si l'on trouve ailleurs des chef-d'oeuvres plus émouvants.

Gleneagles Hotel & Golf Courses

Gleneagles Hotel
SCO - AUCHTERARDER, Perthshire PH3 1NF

Office	Secrétariat	(44) 01764 - 663 543
Pro shop	Pro-shop	(44) 01764 - 694 362
Fax	Fax	(44) 01764 - 694 383
Situation	Situation	

30 km SW of Perth (pop. 123 495)
85 km NW of Edinburgh (pop. 418 914)

Annual closure	Fermeture annnuelle	no
Weekly closure	Fermeture hebdomadaire	no

Fees main season	Tarifs haute saison	full day
	Week days Semaine	**We/Bank holidays** We/Férié
Individual Individuel	£ 80	£ 80
Couple Couple	£ 160	£ 160
For residents only		
Caddy	Caddy	£ 28
Electric Trolley	Chariot électrique	no
Buggy	Voiturette	£ 28/18 holes
Clubs	Clubs	£ 28/18 holes

Credit cards Cartes de crédit
VISA - Eurocard - MasterCard - AMEX - DC - JCB

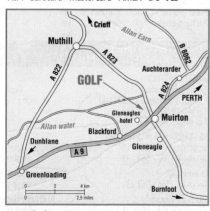

Access Accès : • Glasgow A80, M9, A9. Turn left at junction with A823 signed Crieff & Gleneagles • Edinburgh M90. Jct 2, then A823 through Dunfermline, → Crieff.
Map 2 on page 408 Carte 2 Page 408

GOLF COURSE
PARCOURS 15/20

Site	Site	▰▰▰▱
Maintenance	Entretien	▰▰▰▱
Architect	Architecte	James Braid
Type	Type	moorland
Relief	Relief	▰▱
Water in play	Eau en jeu	▰▱
Exp. to wind	Exposé au vent	▰▰▱
Trees in play	Arbres en jeu	▰▰▰▱

Scorecard Carte de score	Chp. Chp.	Mens Mess.	Ladies Da.
Length Long.	5428	5150	5001
Par	68	68	74

Advised golfing ability Niveau de jeu recommandé	0	12	24	36
Hcp required Handicap exigé	no			

CLUB HOUSE & AMENITIES
CLUB HOUSE ET ANNEXES 9/10

Pro shop	Pro-shop	▰▰▰▱
Driving range	Practice	▰▰▰▱
Sheltered	couvert	10 mats
On grass	sur herbe	yes (04 → 10)
Putting-green	putting-green	yes
Pitching-green	pitching green	yes

HOTEL FACILITIES
ENVIRONNEMENT HOTELIER 7/10

HOTELS HÔTELS
Gleneagles Hotel — Golf
234 rooms, from D £ 130 (ask) — on site
Tel (44) 01764 - 662 231
Fax (44) 01764 - 662 134

RESTAURANTS RESTAURANT
Strathearn — Gleneagles Hotel
Tel (44) 01764 - 662 231 — on site

Dormy Grill — Gleneagles Hotel
Tel (44) 01764 - 662 231 — on site

Auchterarder House — Auchterarder
Tel (44) 01764 - 663 646 — 6 km N

620

GOLSPIE

Golspie is particularly interesting for the shape and layout of the course. Over limited space, you start off virtually in a park before moving on to pure links holes (not necessarily the best), then into woods and heather before returning to park landscape. There is no shortage of interesting holes of all shapes and sizes, with some very long and very short par 4s, five par 3s and just the one par 5. A very pleasant course to play on holiday, far from the crowds who flock to more fashionable and less remote venues, Golspie also offers some beautiful views over the coast, north and south. A word should go the excellent green-keeping despite only very few staff working on the course. Play here in Summer, when the wind keeps away, before playing Brora and Dornoch.

Golspie est particulièrement intéressant en raison de sa conformation. Sur un espace restreint, on part quasiment d'un parc pour passer ensuite par des trous de pur links (ce ne sont pas forcément les meilleurs), puis dans les bois, la bruyère et enfin revenir au parc. Les trous intéressants ne manquent pas ici, de tous genres car on trouve des longs par 4 mais aussi de très courts, cinq par 3 et un seul par 5. Très agréable à jouer en vacances, loin de la foule qui choisit des endroits plus à la mode, ou moins lointains, Golspie offre en outre des vues très belles sur la côte, au nord comme au sud. On signalera enfin l'excellente qualité de l'entretien, malgré un personnel très restreint. A jouer en été, quand le vent est amical, et avant de jouer Brora et Dornoch.

Golspie Golf Club
Ferry Road
SCO - GOLSPIE, Sutherland KW10 6ST

Office	Secrétariat	(44) 01408 - 633 266
Pro shop	Pro-shop	(44) 01408 - 633 266
Fax	Fax	(44) 01408 - 633 393
Situation	Situation	

18 km N of Dornoch (pop. 2 042)
80 km N of Inverness (pop. 62 186)

Annual closure	Fermeture annnuelle	no
Weekly closure	Fermeture hebdomadaire	no

Fees main season
Tarifs haute saison 18 holes

	Week days Semaine	We/Bank holidays We/Férié
Individual Individuel	£ 18	£ 18
Couple Couple	£ 36	£ 36

Full days: £ 20 - £ 25 (weekends)

Caddy	Caddy	on request
Electric Trolley	Chariot électrique	yes
Buggy	Voiturette	no
Clubs	Clubs	yes

Credit cards Cartes de crédit
VISA - MasterCard

Access Accès : Off the main A9. Turn right after railway crossing. Golf on the sea side.
Map 1 on page 407 Carte 1 Page 407

GOLF COURSE
PARCOURS — 14/20

Site	Site	▬▬▬▭▭
Maintenance	Entretien	▬▬▬▬▭
Architect	Architecte	James Braid (1926)
Type	Type	links, parkland
Relief	Relief	▬▬▭▭▭
Water in play	Eau en jeu	▬▭▭▭▭
Exp. to wind	Exposé au vent	▬▬▬▬▭
Trees in play	Arbres en jeu	▬▬▭▭▭

Scorecard	Chp.	Mens	Ladies
Carte de score	Chp.	Mess.	Da.
Length Long.	5360	5167	4766
Par	68	68	71

Advised golfing ability		0 12 24 36
Niveau de jeu recommandé		▬▬▬▬▬▬
Hcp required	Handicap exigé	no

CLUB HOUSE & AMENITIES
CLUB HOUSE ET ANNEXES — 5/10

Pro shop	Pro-shop	▬▬▬▭▭
Driving range	Practice	▬▬▭▭▭
Sheltered	couvert	n,o
On grass	sur herbe	yes
Putting-green	putting-green	yes
Pitching-green	pitching green	no

HOTEL FACILITIES
ENVIRONNEMENT HOTELIER — 4/10

HOTELS HÔTELS

Royal Marine — Brora
24 rooms, D £ 90 — 10 km
Tel (44) 01408 - 621 252
Fax (44) 01408 - 621 181

Morangie House — Tain
26 rooms, D £ 80 — 24 km
Tel (44) 01862 - 892 281
Fax (44) 01862 - 892 872

Golf Links — Golspie
9 rooms, D £ 40 — c
Tel (44) 01408 - 633 408

RESTAURANTS RESTAURANT
Morangie House — Tain
Tel (44) 01862 - 892 281 — 24 km

621

This is the kind of course you want to show those golfers who know only the links courses in Scotland. But why go and play mountain courses, you may ask? Firstly because they are located in superb, untamed regions and then because they are flat enough not to tire the legs of people who spend the rest of the year behind a desk. And perhaps you'll find more things to do outside golf (for non-golfers) in the Highlands than beside the sea. Close to Boat of Garten and Aviemore, this course was designed by Willie Park and James Braid. It has no needless complications, is very short (even for a par 68), is quick to play and is playable by golfers of all levels. The best players might find it a little on the easy side, but there is nothing to stop them from trying to beat the course record (60)!

Le genre de parcours à mettre sous les yeux de ceux qui ne connaissent de l'Ecosse que le pays des links. Pourquoi aller jouer ses parcours de montagne ? D'abord parce qu'ils se trouvent dans des régions superbes et sauvages, ensuite parce qu'ils sont souvent assez plats pour ne pas effrayer ceux qui passent leur vie dans un bureau. Enfin parce que l'on trouve peut-être plus d'activités annexes (pour ceux qui ne jouent pas) dans les Highlands qu'en bord de mer. A proximité de Boat of Garten et d'Aviemore, des réserves des Cairngorms, ce parcours de Willie Park et Braid est sans complications inutiles, très court (même pour un par 68), rapide à jouer et bien adapté à tous les niveaux. Les meilleurs le trouveront un peu limité pour eux, mais rien ne les empêche d'essayer de battre le record (60) !

Grantown on Spey Golf Club
Golf Course Road
SCO - GRANTOWN ON SPEY, Morayshire PH26 3HY

Office	Secrétariat	(44) 01479 - 872 079
Pro shop	Pro-shop	(44) 01479 - 872 079
Fax	Fax	(44) 01479 - 873 725
Situation	Situation	

56 km SE of Inverness (pop. 62 186)

Annual closure	Fermeture annnuelle	no

Weekly closure	Fermeture hebdomadaire	no

Clubhouse closed 11 → 03 inclusive

Fees main season
Tarifs haute saison full day

	Week days Semaine	We/Bank holidays We/Férié
Individual Individuel	£ 18	£ 23
Couple Couple	£ 36	£ 46

Caddy	Caddy	no
Electric Trolley	Chariot électrique	no
Buggy	Voiturette	no
Clubs	Clubs	£ 5/18 holes

Credit cards Cartes de crédit
VISA - Eurocard - MasterCard

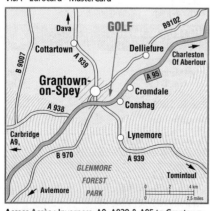

Access Accès : Inverness, A9, A938 & A95 to Grantown. Course lies off the road to Nairn and Forres, on NE side of Grantown **Map 1 on page 407** Carte 1 Page 407

GOLF COURSE
PARCOURS
14/20

Site	Site	▰▰▰▰▱
Maintenance	Entretien	▰▰▰▰▱
Architect	Architecte	A.C. Brown/W. Park/ James Braid
Type	Type	parkland
Relief	Relief	▰▰▰▱▱
Water in play	Eau en jeu	▰▱▱▱▱
Exp. to wind	Exposé au vent	▰▰▱▱▱
Trees in play	Arbres en jeu	▰▰▰▱▱

Scorecard Carte de score	Chp. Chp.	Mens Mess.	Ladies Da.
Length Long.	5198	4930	4801
Par	70	69	72

Advised golfing ability   0   12   24   36
Niveau de jeu recommandé
Hcp required   Handicap exigé   no

CLUB HOUSE & AMENITIES
CLUB HOUSE ET ANNEXES
6/10

Pro shop	Pro-shop	▰▰▰▰▱
Driving range	Practice	▰▰▱▱▱
Sheltered	couvert	no
On grass	sur herbe	no
Putting-green	putting-green	yes
Pitching-green	pitching green	no

HOTEL FACILITIES
ENVIRONNEMENT HOTELIER
7/10

HOTELS HÔTELS

Muckrach Lodge — Dulnain Bridge
9 rooms, from D£ 90 — 5 km
Tel (44) 01479 - 851 257, Fax (44) 01479 - 851 325

Culdearn House — Grantown
9 rooms, D £ 100 (w. dinner) — 0.5 km
Tel (44) 01479 - 872 106, Fax (44) 01479 - 873 641

Ravenscourt House — Grantown
6 rooms, D £ 55 — 0.5 km
Tel (44) 01479 - 872 286, Fax (44) 01479 - 873 260

RESTAURANTS RESTAURANT

Craggan Mill — Grantown
Tel (44) 01479 - 872 288 — 0.5 km

La Taverna — Aviemore
Tel (44) 01479 - 810 636 — 22 km

622

Of the three courses at Gullane, the N° 1 is unquestionably the most spectacular and the most challenging in golfing terms, although its two neighbours are a pleasant alternative on holiday or for less experienced golfers in the family. The slow climb along an impressive hill takes you gradually up above the Firth of Forth until you can make out the famous Muirfield links not far away. But Gullane is much more than an observatory. Wide open spaces, where only the tall rough can break the feeling of immensity, accommodate a high class course where the work of anonymous designers consisted primarily in laying out the greens, digging the bunkers (often deep) and leaving time do the rest. If you want to enjoy rather than endure this often austere course, give it everything you've got.

Des trois parcours de Gullane, le 1 est sans conteste le plus spectaculaire et le plus exigeant au plan golfique, bien que ses deux voisins apportent une alternative heureuse en vacances, ou pour les golfeurs les moins expérimentés de la famille. La lente montée le long d'une imposante colline permet de s'élever peu à peu au-dessus du Firth of Forth, jusqu'à distinguer non loin les fameux links de Muirfield. Mais Gullane est bien plus qu'un observatoire des parcours d'à côté. Les vastes espaces, où seul le haut rough peut rompre le sentiment d'immensité, accueillent un parcours de haute volée, où le travail anonyme des architectes a surtout consisté à aménager les greens, creuser les bunkers (souvent profonds) et laisser faire le temps. Ici, sur ce tracé souvent austère, on exprime tout son golf, ou on le subit...

Gullane Golf Club

West Links Road
SCO - GULLANE, East Lothian EH31 2BB

Office	Secrétariat	(44) 01620 - 842 255
Pro shop	Pro-shop	(44) 01620 - 842 255
Fax	Fax	(44) 01620 - 842 327
Situation	Situation	

29 km E of Edinburgh (pop. 418 914)

Annual closure	Fermeture annnuelle	no
Weekly closure	Fermeture hebdomadaire	no

Fees main season
Tarifs haute saison 18 holes

	Week days Semaine	We/Bank holidays We/Férié
Individual Individuel	£ 54	£ 67
Couple Couple	£ 108	£ 134

Full Weekdays: £ 80

Caddy	Caddy	£ 20
Electric Trolley	Chariot électrique	£ 5/18 holes
Buggy	Voiturette	£ 20/18 holes
Clubs	Clubs	£ 15/18 holes

Credit cards Cartes de crédit
VISA - Eurocard - MasterCard - AMEX

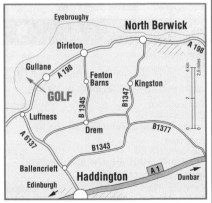

Access Accès : Edinburgh A198 to Gullane
Map 3 on page 411 Carte 3 Page 411

GOLF COURSE PARCOURS 17/20

Site	Site	▓▓▓▓▓▓░░
Maintenance	Entretien	▓▓▓▓▓▓░░
Architect	Architecte	Unknown
Type	Type	seaside course, links
Relief	Relief	▓▓▓░░░░░
Water in play	Eau en jeu	▓▓░░░░░░
Exp. to wind	Exposé au vent	▓▓▓▓▓░░░
Trees in play	Arbres en jeu	▓░░░░░░░

Scorecard Carte de score	Chp. Chp.	Mens Mess.	Ladies Da.
Length Long.	5884	5530	5530
Par	71	71	75

Advised golfing ability Niveau de jeu recommandé	0	12	24	36
Hcp required	Handicap exigé	24 Men, 30 Ladies		

CLUB HOUSE & AMENITIES CLUB HOUSE ET ANNEXES 8/10

Pro shop	Pro-shop	▓▓▓▓░░░░
Driving range	Practice	▓▓▓░░░░░
Sheltered	couvert	no
On grass	sur herbe	yes
Putting-green	putting-green	yes
Pitching-green	pitching green	yes

HOTEL FACILITIES ENVIRONNEMENT HOTELIER 7/10

HOTELS HÔTELS

Mallard Hotel — Gullane
18 rooms, D £ 76 — 2 km
Tel (44) 01620 - 843 288

Brown's Hotel — Haddington
5 rooms, D £ 78 — 3 km
Tel (44) 01620 - 822 254

Maitlandfield House — Haddington
22 rooms, D £ 90 — 3 km
Tel (44) 01620 - 826 513, Fax (44) 01620 - 826 713

RESTAURANTS RESTAURANT

Brown's — Haddington
Tel (44) 01620 - 822 254 — 3 km

La Potinière — Gullane
Tel (44) 01620 - 843 214 — 2 km

623

The fine layout of this well-known Glaswegian club unwinds between rows of fully grown trees a few miles to the south-west of the city centre. It is one of the easiest-to-reach courses around Glasgow, useful to know in that although a private club, it willingly welcomes visitors during the week. Of course it doesn't offer the array of technical challenges found on the great championship courses but it has often been used for some very high level tournaments which testify to its status. The Scottish Open was one such before it moved on to Gleneagles and then Carnoustie. Good drivers will feel easy here, the others will need all their expertise to reach the well-protected greens which pitch well. There are very few bump 'n run shots to be played here, rather more in the American target golf style, despite the very British nature of the course overall.

Le beau tracé de ce club bien connu de Glasgow s'étire entre des rangées d'arbres à maturité, à quelques kilomètres au sud-ouest du centre ville. C'est un des golfs de Glasgow les plus faciles d'accès. Et d'autant plus que, bien qu'il soit privé, il accueille volontiers les visiteurs en semaine. Certes, le parcours ne présente pas la variété des défis techniques des plus grands parcours de championnat, mais il a souvent été utilisé pour de très bonnes épreuves, ce qui témoigne de son rang : nous ne citerons que le Scottish Open, qui émigra ensuite à Gleneagles puis Carnoustie. Les bons drivers y seront ici à l'aise. Les autres devront témoigner de virtuosité pour rejoindre des greens bien protégés, mais qui tiennent bien la balle. Ici, peu de "bump 'n run," mais plutôt un jeu de cible à l'américaine, malgré le caractère général très britannique de l'ensemble.

Haggs Castle Golf Club

70 Dumbreck Road
SCO - GLASGOW G41 4SN

Office	Secrétariat	(44) 0141 - 427 0480
Pro shop	Pro-shop	(44) 0141 - 427 3355
Fax	Fax	(44) 0141 - 427 1157
Situation	Situation	

5 km SW of Glasgow centre (pop. 662 853)

Annual closure	Fermeture annnuelle	no
Weekly closure	Fermeture hebdomadaire	no

Fees main season
Tarifs haute saison 18 holes

	Week days Semaine	We/Bank holidays We/Férié
Individual Individuel	£ 27	—
Couple Couple	£ 54	—

No visitors at weekends

Caddy	Caddy	on request
Electric Trolley	Chariot électrique	no
Buggy	Voiturette	no
Clubs	Clubs	on request

Credit cards Cartes de crédit — no

GOLF COURSE
PARCOURS

15/20

Site	Site	▆▆
Maintenance	Entretien	▆▆
Architect	Architecte	Unknown
Type	Type	parkland
Relief	Relief	
Water in play	Eau en jeu	▆
Exp. to wind	Exposé au vent	▆
Trees in play	Arbres en jeu	▆▆▆

Scorecard Carte de score	Chp. Chp.	Mens Mess.	Ladies Da.
Length Long.	5908	5441	5070
Par	72	69	73

Advised golfing ability Niveau de jeu recommandé	0	12	24	36

Hcp required Handicap exigé — certificate

CLUB HOUSE & AMENITIES
CLUB HOUSE ET ANNEXES

7/10

Pro shop	Pro-shop	▆▆
Driving range	Practice	▆
Sheltered	couvert	no
On grass	sur herbe	no
Putting-green	putting-green	yes
Pitching-green	pitching green	no

HOTEL FACILITIES
ENVIRONNEMENT HOTELIER

9/10

HOTELS HÔTELS

Swallow Glasgow — Glasgow
117 rooms, D £ 130 — 3 km
Tel (44) 0141 - 427 3146, Fax (44) 0141 - 427 4059

Glasgow Hilton — Glasgow
315 rooms, D £ 120 — 5 km
Tel (44) 0141 - 204 5555, Fax (44) 0141 - 204 5004

Forte Crest — Glasgow
248 rooms, D £ 100 — 5 km
Tel (44) 0141 - 248 2656, Fax (44) 0141 - 221 8986

RESTAURANTS RESTAURANT

Camerons (Hilton) — Glasgow
Tel (44) 0141 - 204 5511 — 5 km

One Devonshire Gardens — Glasgow
Tel (44) 0141 - 339 2001 — 7 km

Rogano - Tel (44) 0141 - 248 4055 — Glasgow, 5 km

624

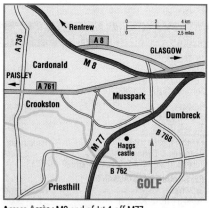

Access Accès : M8 end of Jct 1 off M77.
SW of Glasgow city centre.
Map 3 on page 410 Carte 3 Page 410

HUNTLY

14 | **6** | **6**

This may not be the masterpiece of the century when it comes to course design, and as a course off the beaten track, you wouldn't expect it to be. But if you want to know what everyday golf is like in Scotland, come along to Huntly. You'll easily find a playing partner and learn things about the country that you will never find in any book. Flattish and running alongside the river Deveron (in play on a few holes), this is an excellent course for playing with the family or on holiday, and one where you can card a flattering score without deceiving yourself. But be careful, the trees and often very thick rough can humble anyone who takes this course too lightly. You might not want to travel 500 km just to play a round of golf here, but if you did you would spend a great day, somewhere between Aberdeen and Nairn.

D'accord, ce n'est pas le chef-d'oeuvre du siècle en matière d'architecture de golf, mais on ne saurait en rechercher un, autant à l'écart des chemins très fréquentés du golf. Mais pour quelqu'un qui veut connaître le golf des Ecossais au quotidien, Huntly est un des parcours à connaître, où il trouvera facilement des partenaires de jeu, et apprendra à découvrir le pays en dehors des livres. Peu accidenté, le long de la rivière Deveron qui joue son rôle sur quelques-uns des trous, c'est un excellent parcours pour jouer en famille et en vacances, où il est possible de faire un score flatteur sans se faire d'illusions sur sa propre valeur. Mais il faut faire attention, les arbres et un rough souvent épais peuvent étrangler celui qui prendrait ce parcours à la légère. Certes, on ne fait pas 500 kilomètres pour venir ici, mais il n'empêche que vous passerez une bonne journée ici, disons entre Aberdeen et Nairn.

Huntly Golf Club

Cooper Park
SCO - HUNTLY, Aberdeenshire AB54 4SH

Office	Secrétariat	(44) 01466 - 792 643
Pro shop	Pro-shop	(44) 01466 - 794 181
Fax	Fax	
Situation	Situation	

62 km NW of Aberdeen (pop. 204 885)

Annual closure	Fermeture annnuelle	no
Weekly closure	Fermeture hebdomadaire	no

Fees main season
Tarifs haute saison 18 holes

	Week days Semaine	We/Bank holidays We/Férié
Individual Individuel	£ 13	£ 20
Couple Couple	£ 26	£ 40

Caddy	Caddy	no
Electric Trolley	Chariot électrique	no
Buggy	Voiturette	no
Clubs	Clubs	yes
Credit cards Cartes de crédit		no

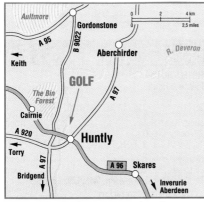

Access Accès : Aberdeen A96 to Huntly. Golf approx. 1 km from town centre, adjacent to the Gordon School and Huntly Castle.
Map 1 on page 407 Carte 1 Page 407

GOLF COURSE
PARCOURS

14/20

Site	Site	
Maintenance	Entretien	
Architect	Architecte	Unknown
Type	Type	parkland
Relief	Relief	
Water in play	Eau en jeu	
Exp. to wind	Exposé au vent	
Trees in play	Arbres en jeu	

Scorecard Carte de score	Chp. Chp.	Mens Mess.	Ladies Da.
Length Long.	4913	7764	4187
Par	66	64	67

Advised golfing ability   0   12   24   36
Niveau de jeu recommandé

Hcp required   Handicap exigé   no

CLUB HOUSE & AMENITIES
CLUB HOUSE ET ANNEXES

6/10

Pro shop	Pro-shop	
Driving range	Practice	
Sheltered	couvert	no
On grass	sur herbe	yes
Putting-green	putting-green	yes
Pitching-green	pitching green	no

HOTEL FACILITIES
ENVIRONNEMENT HOTELIER

6/10

HOTELS HÔTELS
Castle Hotel   Huntly
20 rooms, D £ 60   1 km
Tel (44) 01466 - 792 696
Fax (44) 01466 - 792 641

Huntly Hotel   Huntly
9 rooms, D £ 50   1 km
Tel (44) 01466 - 792 703

RESTAURANTS RESTAURANT
Tandoorie   Huntly
Tel (44) 01466 - 792 667   1 km

625

Much closer to the holiday resort of Troon than to Kilmarnock, Barassie is also much more than a friendly leisure course. Although near the sea it often feels like an inland course, but don't let that fool you. This is an impressive challenge even for the best players and each visit is the opportunity to discover new surprises and enjoy it again and again. A few blind shots add a little spice to the fun and the difficulties are evenly spread around the course. You'll need the full range of shots to see you home, but then again you do on virtually every course of this type. Testimony to the excellence of this layout is the fact that this is one of the courses for the final qualification rounds when the British Open is played at Troon. It has also hosted some of the greatest amateur tournaments. Essential visiting when in this region that is spoilt for great courses.

Bien plus près de la station de vacances de Troon que de Kilmarnock, Barassie est beaucoup plus qu'un aimable parcours de loisirs. Bien qu'il soit proche de la mer, il offre parfois la sensation d'être un parcours "inland," mais il ne faut pas se laisser piéger : il présente un imposant défi, même aux meilleurs, et chaque visite est l'occasion de surprises, et d'un plaisir renouvelé. Quelques coups aveugles ajoutent un peu de piment, les difficultés sont très bien équilibrées, et il faudra toute la panoplie de coups du sac pour en sortir, mais c'est pratiquement le cas sur tous les parcours de ce type. Témoin de sa qualité, c'est l'un des parcours des ultimes qualifications quand le British Open se joue à Royal Troon, il a aussi été le site de grandes compétitions amateur. A ne pas manquer dans cette région richissime en grands golfs.

Kilmarnock (Barassie) Golf Club

29, Hillhouse Road, Barassie
SCO - TROON, Ayrshire KA10 6SY

Office	Secrétariat	(44) 01292 - 313 920
Pro shop	Pro-shop	(44) 01292 - 311 322
Fax	Fax	(44) 01292 - 313 920
Situation	Situation	

3 km N of Troon (pop. 15 116)
45 km SW of Glasgow (pop. 662 853)

Annual closure	Fermeture annnuelle	no
Weekly closure	Fermeture hebdomadaire	no

Fees main season	Tarifs haute saison	18 holes
	Week days Semaine	We/Bank holidays We/Férié
Individual Individuel	£ 32.50	—
Couple Couple	£ 65	—

Full weekday: £ 50
No visitors: wednesday & weekends

Caddy	Caddy	on request
Electric Trolley	Chariot électrique	no
Buggy	Voiturette	no
Clubs	Clubs	£ 15/18 holes

Credit cards Cartes de crédit	no

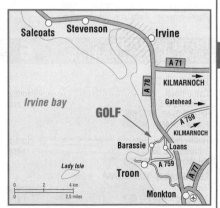

Access Accès : On A78 3 km N of Troon,
opposite Barassie railway station
Map 3 on page 410 Carte 3 Page 410

626

GOLF COURSE
PARCOURS

17 /20

Site	Site	■■■■■■□
Maintenance	Entretien	■■■■■■□
Architect	Architecte	Theodore Moon

Type	Type	links
Relief	Relief	■■■□□
Water in play	Eau en jeu	■■□□□
Exp. to wind	Exposé au vent	■■■■□
Trees in play	Arbres en jeu	■■□□□

Scorecard Carte de score	Chp. Chp.	Mens Mess.	Ladies Da.
Length Long.	6203	5902	5511
Par	72	72	74

Advised golfing ability Niveau de jeu recommandé	0	12	24	36
Hcp required	Handicap exigé	no		

CLUB HOUSE & AMENITIES
CLUB HOUSE ET ANNEXES

6 /10

Pro shop	Pro-shop	■■■■□
Driving range	Practice	■■■□□
Sheltered	couvert	no
On grass	sur herbe	yes
Putting-green	putting-green	yes
Pitching-green	pitching green	yes

HOTEL FACILITIES
ENVIRONNEMENT HOTELIER

8 /10

HOTELS HÔTELS

Piersland House	Troon
19 rooms, D £ 95	3 km
Tel (44) 01292 - 314 747, Fax (44) 01292 - 315 613	

South Beach Hotel	Troon
29 rooms, D £ 90	3 km
Tel (44) 01292 - 312 033, Fax (44) 01292 - 318 438	

Marine Highland	Troon
66 rooms, D £ 120	3 km
Tel (44) 01292 - 314 444, Fax (44) 01292 - 316 922	

RESTAURANTS RESTAURANT

Piersland House	Troon
Tel (44) 01292 - 314 747	3 km

Hospitality Inn	Irvine
Tel (44) 01294 - 274 272	3 km

This highlands course, located at 1,000 ft. above sea level, provides some breath-taking views over Speyside and the Cairngorms. The river Gynack crosses the course and comes into play on several occasions. Kingussie was originally designed on farmland, and Harry Vardon has made so much out of it that you'd willingly believe he had shifted tons of earth. He was unable to avoid a few blind shots over rather hilly terrain, but they are few and far between. The course is not really too tiring, either; the designer was a great champion and knew what can be asked of an amateur golfer. On this terrain of peat and moor-land, the ball never rolls much so the course plays every yard of its length. With a charming setting and warm welcome, Kingussie is a good holiday course.

Situé à environ 300 mètres d'altitude, ce parcours des Highlands offre de vastes panoramas sur le Speyside et les montagnes des Cairngorns. La rivière Gynack parcourt le site, venant en jeu sur quelques trous. À l'origine, ce parcours a été dessiné sur un terrain d'élevage, et Harry Vardon en a tiré un tel parti que l'on croirait qu'il a déplacé des tonnes de terre. Avec cet espace assez accidenté, il n'a pu éviter quelques coups aveugles, mais ils sont bien rares. De plus, on ne peut pas dire que ce parcours soit épuisant : l'architecte était un grand champion, il savait ce qu'on peut demander à un amateur. Sur ce terrain de tourbe et de lande, la balle ne roule jamais beaucoup, ce qui rend à peine plus long ce parcours. Le charme de l'environnement, comme l'accueil font de Kingussie un bon golf de vacances.

Kingussie Golf Club
Gynack Road
SCO - KINGUSSIE, Inverness-shire PH21 1LR

Office	Secrétariat	(44) 01540 - 661 600
Pro shop	Pro-shop	(44) 01540 - 661 600
Fax	Fax	(44) 01540 - 662 066
Situation	Situation	

20 km from Aviemore (pop. 2 214)

Annual closure	Fermeture annnuelle	no
Weekly closure	Fermeture hebdomadaire	no

Chances of snow during winter months

Fees main season
Tarifs haute saison full day

	Week days Semaine	We/Bank holidays We/Férié
Individual Individuel	£ 16.50	£ 20.50
Couple Couple	£ 33	£ 41

Caddy	Caddy	no
Electric Trolley	Chariot électrique	no
Buggy	Voiturette	no
Clubs	Clubs	£ 4/18 holes

Credit cards Cartes de crédit   no

Access Accès : Just off main A9
Map 1 on page 406 Carte 1 Page 406

GOLF COURSE
PARCOURS   **15** /20

Site	Site	▬▬▬▬▬
Maintenance	Entretien	▬▬▬▬▬
Architect	Architecte	Harry Vardon
Type	Type	mountain
Relief	Relief	▬▬▬▬
Water in play	Eau en jeu	▬▬▬
Exp. to wind	Exposé au vent	▬▬▬
Trees in play	Arbres en jeu	▬▬▬▬

Scorecard Carte de score	Chp. Chp.	Mens Mess.	Ladies Da.
Length Long.	5813	4813	4575
Par	66	66	73

Advised golfing ability	0	12	24	36
Niveau de jeu recommandé		▬▬▬▬▬▬		

Hcp required	Handicap exigé	no

CLUB HOUSE & AMENITIES
CLUB HOUSE ET ANNEXES   **4** /10

Pro shop	Pro-shop	▬▬▬
Driving range	Practice	▬▬
Sheltered	couvert	no
On grass	sur herbe	yes
Putting-green	putting-green	yes
Pitching-green	pitching green	yes

HOTEL FACILITIES
ENVIRONNEMENT HOTELIER   **5** /10

HOTELS HÔTELS

Scot House
9 rooms, D £ 95 (dinner included)   Kingussie
Tel (44) 01540 - 661 351   close
Fax (44) 01540 - 661 111

Columba House
7 rooms, D £ 45   Kingussie
Tel (44) 01540 - 661 402   close

RESTAURANTS RESTAURANT
The Cross (booking essential)   Kingussie
Tél (44) 01540 - 661 166   close

627

Although not a links, Ladybank is used as a qualifying course for the British Open when held at St Andrews. In other words it is held in high esteem by the game's governing bodies, and deserves to be. Amidst pine-trees, heather and gorse, this is a technical challenge of the highest order where accuracy is at a premium. You are best advised to keep well away from the formidable rough here where you can lose balls, clubs and perhaps even players too! But while good players may suffer, the humbler hacker can get by with a minimum of careful thought. With superb use of the land, pleasantly contoured fairways and well-defended greens where there is always one safe way in, Ladybank really is worth the trip.

Bien qu'il ne s'agisse pas d'un links, Ladybank est utilisé comme parcours de qualification pour le British Open quand il a lieu à St Andrews. C'est dire qu'il est tenu en haute estime par les pouvoirs sportifs. Il le mérite. Au milieu des pins, de la bruyère et des ajoncs, c'est un défi technique de première grandeur, où la précision est d'abord essentielle, car il vaut mieux ne pas s'égarer dans les roughs redoutables où l'on perd les balles, les clubs et sans doute aussi les joueurs ! Mais si les bons joueurs peuvent souffrir, les joueurs plus humbles et modestes tireront leur épingle du jeu avec un minimum de réflexion. Par sa superbe utilisation du terrain, son relief agréable, ses greens bien défendus mais qui laissent toujours une porte ouverte, Ladybank mérite vraiment le détour.

Ladybank Golf Club
Annsmuir
SCO - LADYBANK, Fife KY7 7RA

Office	Secrétariat	(44) 01337 - 830 814
Pro shop	Pro-shop	(44) 01337 - 830 725
Fax	Fax	(44) 01337 - 831 505
Situation	Situation	

9 km from Cupar (pop. 8 174)

Annual closure	Fermeture annnuelle	no
Weekly closure	Fermeture hebdomadaire	no

Fees main season
Tarifs haute saison 18 holes

	Week days Semaine	We/Bank holidays We/Férié
Individual Individuel	£ 28	£ 28
Couple Couple	£ 56	£ 56

Full day: £ 38

Caddy	Caddy	no
Electric Trolley	Chariot électrique	no
Buggy	Voiturette	no
Clubs	Clubs	on request

Credit cards Cartes de crédit
VISA - MasterCard

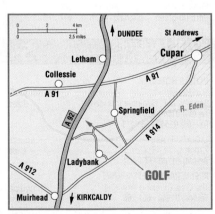

Access Accès : Just off the A914, between Glenrothes and Dundee
Map 3 on page 411 Carte 3 Page 411

GOLF COURSE
PARCOURS

17/20

Site	Site	
Maintenance	Entretien	
Architect	Architecte	Tom Morris
Type	Type	heathland
Relief	Relief	
Water in play	Eau en jeu	
Exp. to wind	Exposé au vent	
Trees in play	Arbres en jeu	

Scorecard Carte de score	Chp. Chp.	Mens Mess.	Ladies Da.
Length Long.	6043	5707	5707
Par	71	71	73

Advised golfing ability	0	12	24	36
Niveau de jeu recommandé				
Hcp required	Handicap exigé	certificate		

CLUB HOUSE & AMENITIES
CLUB HOUSE ET ANNEXES

7/10

Pro shop	Pro-shop	
Driving range	Practice	
Sheltered	couvert	no
On grass	sur herbe	yes
Putting-green	putting-green	yes
Pitching-green	pitching green	yes

HOTEL FACILITIES
ENVIRONNEMENT HOTELIER

5/10

HOTELS HÔTELS
Crusoe Hotel — Lower Largo
13 rooms, D £ 92 — 15 km
Tel (44) 01333 - 320 759, Fax (44) 01333 - 320 865

Laurel Bank — Markinch, Leven
11 rooms, D £ 55 — 10 km
Tel (44) 01592 - 611 205

Old Manor — Leven
20 rooms, D £ 100 — 15 km
Tel (44) 01333 - 320 368, Fax (44) 01333 - 320 911

RESTAURANTS RESTAURANT
Ostler's Close — Cupar
Tel (44) 01334 - 655 574 — 9 km

Crusoe Hotel — Lower Largo
Tel (44) 01333 - 320 759 — 15 km

628

LANARK

They say that the total length of courses designed by James Braid exceeds the combined length and width of Great Britain. That's probably true inasmuch as he basically retouched a lot of existing courses. This layout was designed by Old Tom Morris, another prolific designer, but at the time "designing" was primarily a question of laying out the route of the course and the position of bunkers and greens. The course was then completed by the work of nature. Lanark is one of those courses where golf seems always to have been a part of the scene on land of heather and moorland which make such excellent playing surfaces. Rather short, moderately hilly and with only one or two blind shots, this is a no-nonsense course and a serious test for all levels. Quality golf.

On dit que la longueur totale des parcours dessinés par James Braid totalise plus de la longueur et de la largeur cumulés de la Grande-Bretagne. C'est probablement vrai, dans la mesure où s'il en a conçu beaucoup, il a essentiellement retouché beaucoup de parcours existants. Celui-ci avait été dessiné par Old Tom Morris, lui aussi architecte très prolifique : mais, à l'époque, l'architecture consistait avant tout à définir l'itinéraire du parcours, l'emplacement des greens et bunkers. Un parcours devait s'accommoder de la nature. Lanark est l'un de ces sites où le golf paraît avoir toujours été présent, en terre de bruyère et de lande qui fait de bons tapis de jeu. Assez court, avec un relief modéré, et seulement un ou deux coups aveugles, c'est un parcours sans autres histoires que celles que l'on y fait, un test sérieux pour tous niveaux. La qualité.

Lanark Golf Club
The Moor, Whiteless Road
SCO - LANARK, ML11 7RX

Office	Secrétariat	(44) 01555 - 663 219
Pro shop	Pro-shop	(44) 01555 - 661 456
Fax	Fax	
Situation	Situation	

1 km from Lanark town centre

Annual closure	Fermeture annnuelle	no
Weekly closure	Fermeture hebdomadaire	no

Fees main season
Tarifs haute saison 18 holes

	Week days Semaine	We/Bank holidays We/Férié
Individual Individuel	£ 24	—
Couple Couple	£ 48	—

Full Weekdays: £ 36 - No visitors at weekends

Caddy	Caddy	no
Electric Trolley	Chariot électrique	no
Buggy	Voiturette	£ 12/18 holes
Clubs	Clubs	no
Credit cards Cartes de crédit		no

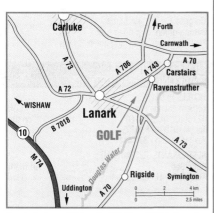

Access Accès : • Edinburgh, A71, then A706 to Lanark
• Glasgow, M74 and A72 to Lanark
Map 2 on page 409 Carte 2 Page 409

GOLF COURSE
PARCOURS
16/20

Site	Site	
Maintenance	Entretien	
Architect	Architecte	Tom Morris James Braid
Type	Type	moorland
Relief	Relief	
Water in play	Eau en jeu	
Exp. to wind	Exposé au vent	
Trees in play	Arbres en jeu	

Scorecard Carte de score	Chp. Chp.	Mens Mess.	Ladies Da.
Length Long.	5845	5570	5330
Par	70	70	74

Advised golfing ability Niveau de jeu recommandé	0	12	24	36
Hcp required	Handicap exigé	certificate		

CLUB HOUSE & AMENITIES
CLUB HOUSE ET ANNEXES
6/10

Pro shop	Pro-shop	
Driving range	Practice	
Sheltered	couvert	no
On grass	sur herbe	no
Putting-green	putting-green	yes
Pitching-green	pitching green	no

HOTEL FACILITIES
ENVIRONNEMENT HOTELIER
5/10

HOTELS HÔTELS
Abington Hotel   Abington, by Biggar
28 rooms, D £ 74   15 km
Tel (44) 01864 - 502 467
Fax (44) 01864 - 502 223

Cartland Bridge   Lanark
17 rooms, D £ 58-68   2 km
Tel (44) 01555 - 664 426

RESTAURANTS RESTAURANT
La Vigna   Lanark
Tel (44) 01555 - 664 320   2 km

Crown Tavern   Lanark
Tel(44) 01555 - 662 465   2 km

629

LETHAM GRANGE OLD COURSE

15	7	5

This course was opened in 1987 at the foot of the splendid Letham Grange Hotel and was designed by gentleman farmer Ken Smith who drew his inspiration from the Augusta National course, hoping that one day this might become known as the Scottish Augusta. In actual fact there are very few similarities but this is nonetheless a pretty and rather challenging layout with tree-lined fairways and a few rather dangerous water hazards. The course is rather hilly in places, which means a few blind shots. Target golf is virtually an obligation here, and this is why you don't always get the impression of playing in Scotland. But despite everything, it is fun playing here with friends of all levels, of whom the least experienced will probably enjoy more the second, shorter course.

Ce parcours a été créé en 1987 au pied du splendide Letham Grange Hotel, et dessiné par Ken Smith, un gentleman farmer qui s'inspira d'Augusta National en espérant que ce parcours pourrait un jour être appelé le "Augusta d'Ecosse." En fait, on trouve peu de ressemblances, mais c'est malgré tout un joli tracé, assez exigeant, aux fairways bordés d'arbres, avec quelques obstacles d'eau assez dangereux. Le relief est parfois assez prononcé, ce qui implique quelques coups aveugles. Ici, le target golf est quasiment une obligation, c'est pourquoi on n'a pas forcément l'impression de se trouver en Ecosse. Malgré tout, on aura plaisir à évoluer ici avec des amis de tous niveaux, dont les moins expérimentés aimeront jouer le second parcours, plus court.

Letham Grange Golf Club
Letham Grange Hotel
SCO - COLLISTON, by Arbroath, Angus DD11 4 RL

Office	Secrétariat	(44) 01241 - 890 373
Pro shop	Pro-shop	(44) 01241 - 890 377
Fax	Fax	(44) 01241 - 890 414
Situation	Situation	.

8 km N of Arbroath (pop. 24 002)
32 km E of Dundee (pop. 165 873)

Annual closure	Fermeture annnuelle	yes
		1/01/99→31/01/99
Weekly closure	Fermeture hebdomadaire	no

Fees main season
Tarifs haute saison 18 holes

	Week days Semaine	We/Bank holidays We/Férié
Individual Individuel	£ 24	£ 36
Couple Couple	£ 48	£ 72

Caddy	Caddy	no
Electric Trolley	Chariot électrique	no
Buggy	Voiturette	yes
Clubs	Clubs	yes

Credit cards Cartes de crédit
VISA - Eurocard - MasterCard - AMEX - DC - JCB

630

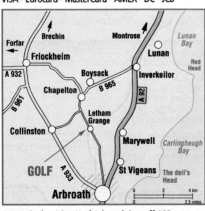

Access Accès : 8 km N of Arbroath just off A92.
Well signposted.
Map 1 on page 407 Carte 1 Page 407

GOLF COURSE
PARCOURS

15/20

Site	Site	
Maintenance	Entretien	
Architect	Architecte	D. Steel/GK. Smith
Type	Type	parkland
Relief	Relief	
Water in play	Eau en jeu	
Exp. to wind	Exposé au vent	
Trees in play	Arbres en jeu	

Scorecard Carte de score	Chp. Chp.	Mens Mess.	Ladies Da.
Length Long.	6341	5777	5254
Par	73	73	75

Advised golfing ability Niveau de jeu recommandé	0	12	24	36

Hcp required	Handicap exigé	no

CLUB HOUSE & AMENITIES
CLUB HOUSE ET ANNEXES

7/10

Pro shop	Pro-shop	
Driving range	Practice	
Sheltered	couvert	no
On grass	sur herbe	yes
Putting-green	putting-green	yes
Pitching-green	pitching green	yes

HOTEL FACILITIES
ENVIRONNEMENT HOTELIER

5/10

HOTELS HÔTELS
Letham Grange Hotel — Golf
42 rooms, from D £ 60 — on site
Tel (44) 01241 - 890 373
Fax (44) 01241 - 890 414

RESTAURANTS RESTAURANT
But'n'Ben — Arbroath
Tél (44) 01241 - 877 233 — 5 km

LEVEN

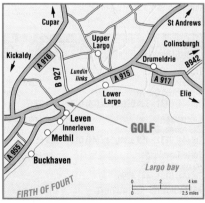

16	6	6

The original course was shared with the Lundin Golf Club. But when the railways arrived in the region, the course was split nine holes on one side and nine on the other, with each club creating an extra nine holes. So instead of one good course, here we have two, as adjacent now as they were in the past. Most of the holes at Leven are pure links style, but two or three are close to the heather-bound inland courses that are so common in both Scotland and England. Here again the wind has a say in things, because Leven is distinctly vulnerable when played by long-hitters and skilled technicians in fine weather. In this case even the least experienced players will have fun, although the last few holes can easily upset their card. The least they should do is avoid the deep fairway bunkers and the traps around the green.

Le parcours original a été partagé avec le Lundin Golf Club, à l'arrivée du chemin de fer dans la région. Chacun étant reparti de son côté avec neuf trous a créé neuf autres trous. Au lieu d'un seul bon parcours, en voilà deux, toujours mitoyens. La plupart de trous de Leven ont un caractère de pur link, mais deux ou trois sont assez proches des parcours inland de bruyère, que l'on trouve souvent en Écosse comme en Angleterre. Là encore, le vent fait la différence, car Leven s'avère assez fragile face aux solides frappeurs et aux bons techniciens quand le temps est beau. Alors, même les moins expérimentés y trouveront leur plaisir, mais les derniers trous peuvent leur créer des problèmes. Qu'ils évitent en tous cas les profonds bunkers de fairway comme de défense de green.

Leven Golfing Society

P.O. Box 14609, Links Road
SCO - LEVEN, Fife KY9 1LG

Office	Secrétariat	(44) 01333 - 42 096
Pro shop	Pro-shop	(44) 01333 - 421 390
Fax	Fax	(44) 01333 - 424 229
Situation	Situation	

20 km SW of St Andrews (pop. 11 136)

Annual closure	Fermeture annnuelle	no
Weekly closure	Fermeture hebdomadaire	no

Fees main season
Tarifs haute saison 18 holes

	Week days Semaine	We/Bank holidays We/Férié
Individual Individuel	£ 24	£ 28
Couple Couple	£ 48	£ 56

Caddy	Caddy	no
Electric Trolley	Chariot électrique	no
Buggy	Voiturette	no
Clubs	Clubs	no

Credit cards Cartes de crédit   no

Access Accès : Edinburgh, M90 then A92 (Jct3), A955.
Golf East of Leven, on Promenade.
Map 3 on page 411 Carte 3 Page 411

GOLF COURSE
PARCOURS   16/20

Site	Site	
Maintenance	Entretien	
Architect	Architecte	Unknown
Type	Type	links, seaside course
Relief	Relief	
Water in play	Eau en jeu	
Exp. to wind	Exposé au vent	
Trees in play	Arbres en jeu	

Scorecard Carte de score	Chp. Chp.	Mens Mess.	Ladies Da.
Length Long.	5882	5475	5217
Par	71	69	73

Advised golfing ability Niveau de jeu recommandé	0	12	24	36
Hcp required	Handicap exigé	no		

CLUB HOUSE & AMENITIES
CLUB HOUSE ET ANNEXES   6/10

Pro shop	Pro-shop	
Driving range	Practice	
Sheltered	couvert	no
On grass	sur herbe	no
Putting-green	putting-green	no
Pitching-green	pitching green	no

HOTEL FACILITIES
ENVIRONNEMENT HOTELIER   6/10

HOTELS HÔTELS

Old Manor Hotel   Lundin Links
24 rooms, D £ 115   3 km
Tel (44) 01333 - 320 368, Fax (44) 01333 - 320 911

Lundin Links Hotel   Lundin Links
21 rooms, D £ 122   3 km
Tel (44) 01333 - 320 201, Fax (44) 01333 - 320 930

Crusoe Hotel   Lundin Links
16 rooms, D £ 95   3 km
Tel (44) 01333 - 320 759, Fax (44) 01333 - 320 865

RESTAURANTS RESTAURANT

Old Manor Hotel   Lundin Links
Tel (44) 01333 - 320 368   3 km

Lundin Links Hotel   Lundin Links
Tel (44) 01333 - 320 207   3 km

631

LOTHIANBURN

14	6	8

Lying to the south of Edinburgh at the boundary with the Pentland Hills, this course has undergone many a change since its inception in 1893. Four such major alterations were made by James Braid and the last change in 1993 seems to have given the course its final complexion (but who knows?). The terrain is full of slopes, some of which are really steep (especially out in the middle section), so we would recommend this to fit players only. The reward is the beauty of vistas over the Firth of Forth from atop the hill. The course has a number of excellent holes, whose contours seem to follow those of the natural terrain. The downside is that you need to play here several times to establish any sort of game strategy. As on any unknown course, give matchplay a shot first time around.

Au sud d'Edinburgh et à la limite des Pentland Hills, ce parcours créé en 1893 a connu bien des modifications, dont au moins quatre majeures sous la direction de James Braid, et une dernière en 1993 qui semble lui avoir donné son caractère définitif (mais sait-on jamais ?). Le terrain est très vallonné, parfois de façon assez brutale (surtout dans la partie centrale) et l'on ne conseillera qu'aux joueurs en forme de s'y mesurer. La récompense, c'est la beauté des points de vue sur le Firth of Forth, au sommet de la colline. On trouve ici bon nombre d'excellents trous de golf, dont le tracé a suivi les contours des reliefs. Mais le revers de la médaille, c'est qu'il faut avoir joué plusieurs fois pour bien établir une stratégie. Comme sur tous les parcours inconnus, jouez au début en match-play...

Lothianburn Golf Club

106A Biggar Road
SCO - EDINBURGH EH10 7DU

Office	Secrétariat	(44) 0131 - 445 2206
Pro shop	Pro-shop	(44) 0131 - 445 2288
Fax	Fax	
Situation	Situation	.

limits of Edinburgh city (pop. 418 914)

Annual closure	Fermeture annnuelle	no
Weekly closure	Fermeture hebdomadaire	no

Fees main season
Tarifs haute saison 18 holes

	Week days Semaine	We/Bank holidays We/Férié
Individual Individuel	£ 15	£ 21
Couple Couple	£ 30	£ 42

Full days: £ 21 - £ 26 (Weekends)

Caddy	Caddy	no
Electric Trolley	Chariot électrique	no
Buggy	Voiturette	yes
Clubs	Clubs	yes

Credit cards Cartes de crédit   no

632

GOLF COURSE
PARCOURS   14/20

Site	Site	
Maintenance	Entretien	
Architect	Architecte	James Braid
Type	Type	hilly
Relief	Relief	
Water in play	Eau en jeu	
Exp. to wind	Exposé au vent	
Trees in play	Arbres en jeu	

Scorecard Carte de score	Chp. Chp.	Mens Mess.	Ladies Da.
Length Long.	5090	5090	4438
Par	71	71	70

Advised golfing ability		0 12 24 36
Niveau de jeu recommandé		
Hcp required	Handicap exigé	28 Men/Ladies

CLUB HOUSE & AMENITIES
CLUB HOUSE ET ANNEXES   6/10

Pro shop	Pro-shop	
Driving range	Practice	
Sheltered	couvert	no
On grass	sur herbe	no
Putting-green	putting-green	yes
Pitching-green	pitching green	no

HOTEL FACILITIES
ENVIRONNEMENT HOTELIER   8/10

HOTELS HÔTELS

Forte Posthouse   Edinburgh
204 rooms, D £ 70   6 km
Tel (44) 0131 - 334 0390, Fax (44) 0131 - 334 9237

Caledonian   Edinburgh
223 rooms, D £ 200   8 km
Tel (44) 0131 - 459 9988, Fax (44) 0131 - 225 6632

Forte Travelodge   Edinburgh
40 rooms, D £ 35   1 km
Tel (44) 0131 - 441 4296

RESTAURANTS RESTAURANT

Mackenzies   Edinburgh
Tel (44) 0131 - 441 2587   2 km

Indian Cavalry Club   Edinburgh
Tel (44) 0131 - 228 3282   5 km

Access Accès : City by-pass. Lothianburn exit.
Map 3 on page 411 Carte 3 Page 411

LUFFNESS NEW

16 5 6

Arriving here, you seem to be carrying on from Gullane in a whole cluster of courses the equivalent of which is to be found only at St Andrews or Pinehurst. Although Luffness New is not as well known as its neighbours or even nearby Muirfield, it is a course of great character which is always in perfect condition (the greens are famous for this). It rewards the good shots and punishes the bad ones, the way it should be not always is. The wind is an important factor but the direction changes at almost every hole. With a network of bunkers and formidable, omnipresent rough, carding a good score here is the sign of a talented player. Even if you are short of talent, you'll still have fun.

En arrivant ici, on se retrouve dans la continuité des parcours de Gullane, et dans une véritable galaxie dont on ne retrouve l'équivalent qu'à St Andrews ou, plus encore, Pinehurst. Bien que Luffness New n'ait pas la notoriété de ses voisins ou, plus encore, de Muirfield tout proche, c'est un parcours de caractère fort, toujours en bon état (ses greens sont célèbres), qui récompense les bons coups et punit les mauvais, ce qui devrait toujours être le cas, mais n'est pas si fréquent. Le vent y est un facteur important, mais l'orientation change pratiquement à chaque trou. Avec le réseau de bunkers et un rough aussi redoutable qu'omniprésent, signer un bon score ici est une preuve de talent. Si l'on en manque, on s'y amusera aussi beaucoup.

Luffness New Golf Club
SCO - ABERLADY EH32 0QA

Office	Secrétariat	(44) 01620 - 843 114
Pro shop	Pro-shop	(44) 01620 - 843 114
Fax	Fax	(44) 01620 - 842 933
Situation	Situation	

27 km E of Edinburgh (pop. 418 914)

Annual closure	Fermeture annnuelle	no
Weekly closure	Fermeture hebdomadaire	no

Fees main season
Tarifs haute saison 18 holes

	Week days Semaine	We/Bank holidays We/Férié
Individual Individuel	£ 29	—
Couple Couple	£ 58	—

Full weekday: £ 40 - No visitors at weekends - Drestrictions for Ladies (ask)

Caddy	Caddy	on request
Electric Trolley	Chariot électrique	no
Buggy	Voiturette	no
Clubs	Clubs	no

Credit cards Cartes de crédit — no

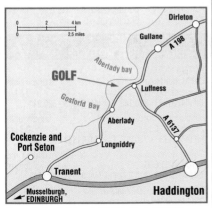

Access Accès : Edinburgh A1. Near Tranent, A198 through Longniddry and Aberlady. Turn off right to Luffness Clubhouse.
Map 3 on page 411 Carte 3 Page 411

GOLF COURSE
PARCOURS

16/20

Site	Site	
Maintenance	Entretien	
Architect	Architecte	Tom Morris
Type	Type	links
Relief	Relief	
Water in play	Eau en jeu	
Exp. to wind	Exposé au vent	
Trees in play	Arbres en jeu	

Scorecard Carte de score	Chp. Chp.	Mens Mess.	Ladies Da.
Length Long.	5576	5576	5576
Par	69	69	73

Advised golfing ability Niveau de jeu recommandé	0 12 24 36	
Hcp required	Handicap exigé	certificate

CLUB HOUSE & AMENITIES
CLUB HOUSE ET ANNEXES

5/10

Pro shop	Pro-shop	
Driving range	Practice	
Sheltered	couvert	no
On grass	sur herbe	no
Putting-green	putting-green	yes
Pitching-green	pitching green	no

HOTEL FACILITIES
ENVIRONNEMENT HOTELIER

6/10

HOTELS HÔTELS

Mallard Hotel 18 rooms, D £ 76 Tél (44) 01620 - 843 288	Gullane 4 km
Brown's Hotel 5 rooms, D £ 78 Tel (44) 01620 - 822 254	Haddington 5 km
Maitlandfield House 22 rooms, D £ 90 Tel (44) 01620 - 826 513, Fax (44) 01620 - 826 713	Haddington 5 km

RESTAURANTS RESTAURANT

Brown's Tel (44) 01620 - 822 254	Haddington 5 km
La Potinière Tel (44) 01620 - 843 214	Gullane 4 km

633

The twin brother to Leven Links, Lundin was born from a split in 1868, where each course took 9 holes and went their own way up to 18. Don't wait for the annual tournament that bring both courses together, just try and play this course which originated beside the sea. Restyled like so many other courses by James Braid, this is a good old links - there is even an old railway track running through the middle - used for the qualifying rounds when the British Open is held at Saint Andrews. You'll find some holes in heathland, particularly the 12th and 13th holes, where the view over the Forth is impressive, from the confines of Edinburg to Muirfield, just opposite. On the course the major hazard is the wind, and let's hope that the watering system is not over-used. Soft terrain kills a little of the subtlety of playing a links course and requires less creativity from the golfer.

Frère jumeau de Leven Links, Lundin est né d'une scission en 1868, chacun gardant neuf trous et complétant son parcours. N'attendez pas la compétition annuelle qui les réunit, essayez aussi de jouer ce parcours des origines le long de la mer. Remodelé comme bien d'autres par James Braid, c'est un vrai bon links (avec même une ancienne voie ferrée au milieu) utilisé pour les qualifications du British Open quand il est à Saint Andrews. Mais on y trouve aussi des trous en terrain de bruyère, en particulier au 12 et au 13, d'où la vue est impressionnante sur le Forth, des confins d'Edimbourg à Muirfield, en face. Sur le parcours, le vent est le principal obstacle, mais on peut souhaiter que l'arrosage ne soit pas trop utilisé, un terrain mou retire un peu de leur subtilité aux links, et exige moins de créativité.

Lundin Golf Club

Golf Road
SCO - LUNDIN LINKS, Fife KY8 6BA

Office	Secrétariat	(44) 01333 - 320 202
Pro shop	Pro-shop	(44) 01333 - 320 051
Fax	Fax	(44) 01333 - 329 743
Situation	Situation	

20 km SW of St Andrews (pop. 11 136)
17 km E of Kirkcaldy

Annual closure	Fermeture annnuelle	no
Weekly closure	Fermeture hebdomadaire	no

Fees main season	Tarifs haute saison	18 holes
	Week days Semaine	**We/Bank holidays** We/Férié
Individual Individuel	£ 27	£ 36
Couple Couple	£ 54	£ 72

Full weekdays: £ 36 - Saturday: after 2.30 pm - Not on Sundays.

Caddy	Caddy	on request
Electric Trolley	Chariot électrique	no
Buggy	Voiturette	no
Clubs	Clubs	no
Credit cards Cartes de crédit		no

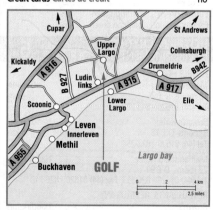

Access Accès : Edinburgh A92 and A915. In the village of Lundin Links on the sea front, turn right at the Bank of Scotland, thereafter first right and second left.
Map 3 on page 411 Carte 3 Page 411

GOLF COURSE
PARCOURS
16/20

Site	Site	
Maintenance	Entretien	
Architect	Architecte	James Braid
Type	Type	links
Relief	Relief	
Water in play	Eau en jeu	
Exp. to wind	Exposé au vent	
Trees in play	Arbres en jeu	

Scorecard Carte de score	Chp. Chp.	Mens Mess.	Ladies Da.
Length Long.	5818	5818	5818
Par	71	71	75

Advised golfing ability Niveau de jeu recommandé		0 12 24 36
Hcp required	Handicap exigé	certificate

CLUB HOUSE & AMENITIES
CLUB HOUSE ET ANNEXES
6/10

Pro shop	Pro-shop	
Driving range	Practice	
Sheltered	couvert	no
On grass	sur herbe	yes
Putting-green	putting-green	yes
Pitching-green	pitching green	no

HOTEL FACILITIES
ENVIRONNEMENT HOTELIER
7/10

HOTELS HÔTELS

Old Manor Hotel — Lundin Links 0.4 km
24 rooms, D £ 115
Tel (44) 01333 - 320 368, Fax (44) 01333 - 320 911

Lundin Links Hotel — Lundin Links 0.3 km
21 rooms, D £ 122
Tel (44) 01333 - 320 201, Fax (44) 01333 - 320 930

Crusoe Hotel — Lundin Links 0.4 km
16 rooms, D £ 95
Tel (44) 01333 - 320 759, Fax (44) 01333 - 320 865

RESTAURANTS RESTAURANT

Old Manor Hotel — Lundin Links 0.4 km
Tel (44) 01333 - 320 368

Lundin Links Hotel — Lundin Links 0.3 km
Tel (44) 01333 - 320 207

634

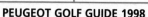

MACHRIE

17 | 7 | 7

So far away from the "civilised" world, this course, where designer Willie Campbell worked wonders, could but adapt to existing terrain. With a 100-year-old hotel or small cottages, there is no shortage of accommodation or pleasure facilities, aided by some exceptional pure malt whiskies smoked over a peat fire, even tastier when drunk after some wholesome sporting activities. The beaches are superb and the views equally magnificent and romantic. The fairways lie like a carpet and form nothing less than a good, pure and authentic golf course. There are few places in the world that feel so different to what you know already as Machrie. You can get here by boat, but it's a long haul, or by plane in a quick hop from Glasgow.

Autant à l'écart du monde "civilisé", ce parcours ne pouvait que s'adapter au terrain existant, et l'architecte Willie Campbell en a tiré des merveilles. Avec un hôtel plus que centenaire ou de petits cottages, le lieu ne manque pas de possibilités d'accueil, ni de plaisirs : on y distille alentour d'exceptionnels whiskies pur malt fumé à la tourbe, on s'y livre à de saines activités sportives avant de les déguster. Les plages sont superbes, les vues magnifiques, romantiques. Le parcours est posé comme un tapis sur le sol, c'est un pur, vrai et bon parcours de golf. Il est peu d'endroits au monde qui soient si "différents" de tout ce que l'on connaît. On peut y aller en bateau, mais c'est long, ou en avion : c'est un saut de puce depuis Glasgow.

Machrie Hotel & Golf Links

Western Cottage, Port Ellen
SCO - ISLE OF ISLAY, PA42 7AT

Office	Secrétariat	(44) 01496 - 302 310
Pro shop	Pro-shop	(44) 01496 - 302 310
Fax	Fax	(44) 01496 - 302 404
Situation	Situation	

5 km from Port Ellen (Isle of Islay)

Annual closure	Fermeture annnuelle	no
Weekly closure	Fermeture hebdomadaire	no

Fees main season
Tarifs haute saison 18 holes

	Week days Semaine	We/Bank holidays We/Férié
Individual Individuel	£ 17.50	£ 17.50
Couple Couple	£ 35	£ 35

Caddy	Caddy	on request
Electric Trolley	Chariot électrique	no
Buggy	Voiturette	no
Clubs	Clubs	yes

Credit cards Cartes de crédit
VISA - Eurocard - MasterCard

Access Accès : • By Plane, 25 mn from Glasgow
(twice daily flights)
• Road & Ferry, 5 hrs from Glasgow
Map 2 on page 408 Carte 2 Page 408

GOLF COURSE / PARCOURS — **17** /20

Site	Site	
Maintenance	Entretien	
Architect	Architecte	Willie Campbell Donald Steel
Type	Type	links
Relief	Relief	
Water in play	Eau en jeu	
Exp. to wind	Exposé au vent	
Trees in play	Arbres en jeu	

Scorecard Carte de score	Chp. Chp.	Mens Mess.	Ladies Da.
Length Long.	5665	5331	4741
Par	71	71	69

Advised golfing ability Niveau de jeu recommandé	0	12	24	36
Hcp required Handicap exigé	no			

CLUB HOUSE & AMENITIES / CLUB HOUSE ET ANNEXES — **7** /10

Pro shop	Pro-shop	
Driving range	Practice	
Sheltered	couvert	no
On grass	sur herbe	yes
Putting-green	putting-green	yes
Pitching-green	pitching green	yes

HOTEL FACILITIES / ENVIRONNEMENT HOTELIER — **7** /10

HOTELS HÔTELS
The Machrie Hotel — Golf on site
27 rooms, from £ 65
Tel (44) 01496 - 302 310
Fax (44) 01496 - 302 404

RESTAURANTS RESTAURANT
Byre Restaurant — Golf on site
Tél (44) 01496 - 302 310

635

The road you take to reach here is as long as it is picturesque, the only problem being that you can't stay for ever. The course is superb, as are the distilleries and the hospitality of the inhabitants of Kintyre here at the ends of the world. So step into this wide open space "created by the Almighty to play golf", as Old Tom Morris would say, who knew a good sales pitch when he saw one and could design a course or two. He obviously lent our Good Lord a hand here to make this marvellous test of golf between the dunes and the foot of the hills. With a simply beautiful first hole, a par 4 over the sea, where the men will envy the ladies. For the fairer sex this is a par 5, for many male players too. You won't regret a single second of your visit here.

La route pour arriver ici est aussi longue que splendide. Le seul problème est qu'il faut ensuite repartir. S'arracher à Machrihanish est d'autant plus dur que si le parcours est superbe, les distilleries ne le sont pas moins, et l'accueil des habitants du Kintyre d'autant plus agréable que l'on est au bout de l'ancien monde, et du monde tout court. Alors, immergez-vous dans un espace "créé par le Tout-Puissant pour jouer au golf" comme disait Old Tom Morris qui avait le sens du commerce, et du dessin de golf aussi. Car il est évidemment venu en aide au Seigneur pour en faire un merveilleux test de golf entre les dunes et le pied des collines. Avec un premier trou de toute beauté, un par 4 à jouer au-dessus de la mer où les hommes jalouseront les dames : c'est pour elles un par 5... pour beaucoup d'hommes aussi ! Vous ne regretterez rien du voyage.

Machrihanish Golf Club

Machrihanish
SCO - CAMPBELTOWN, Argyll PA28 6PT

Office	Secrétariat	(44) 01586 - 810 213
Pro shop	Pro-shop	(44) 01586 - 810 277
Fax	Fax	(44) 01586 - 810 221
Situation	Situation	

8 km S of Campbeltown

Annual closure	Fermeture annnuelle	no
Weekly closure	Fermeture hebdomadaire	no

Fees main season
Tarifs haute saison full day

	Week days Semaine	We/Bank holidays We/Férié
Individual Individuel	£ 30	£ 36
Couple Couple	£ 60	£ 72

18 holes, weekdays only: £ 21

Caddy	Caddy	on request
Electric Trolley	Chariot électrique	no
Buggy	Voiturette	no
Clubs	Clubs	yes

Credit cards Cartes de crédit
VISA - MasterCard

636

Access Accès : • By air: from Glasgow, 15 mn flight to Machrihanish Airport. • By car: 3 hrs drive by A82, A83, via Tarbet, Inverraray... or Ferry to Isle of Arran, and to Claonaig. **Map 2 on page 408** Carte 2 Page 408

GOLF COURSE
PARCOURS

18/20

Site	Site	
Maintenance	Entretien	
Architect	Architecte	Tom Morris
Type	Type	links
Relief	Relief	
Water in play	Eau en jeu	
Exp. to wind	Exposé au vent	
Trees in play	Arbres en jeu	

Scorecard Carte de score	Chp. Chp.	Mens Mess.	Ladies Da.
Length Long.	5670	5425	5025
Par	70	70	72

Advised golfing ability Niveau de jeu recommandé	0	12	24	36
Hcp required	Handicap exigé	no		

CLUB HOUSE & AMENITIES
CLUB HOUSE ET ANNEXES

6/10

Pro shop	Pro-shop	
Driving range	Practice	
Sheltered	couvert	no
On grass	sur herbe	yes
Putting-green	putting-green	yes
Pitching-green	pitching green	yes

HOTEL FACILITIES
ENVIRONNEMENT HOTELIER

4/10

HOTELS HÔTELS

Balegreggan Country House
4 chambres, from D £ 70
Campbeltown
8 km

Tél (44) 01586 - 552 062Westbank
8 chambres, D £ 34
Tél (44) 01586 - 553 660
Campbeltown
8 km

MONIFIETH

We know that golf was played here in the first half of the 17th century but the first signs of a real course really date from 1850. Like nearby Carnoustie, the course is shared by five different clubs, as is the Ashludie Course, a little more modest and restful but nonetheless interesting. The wide open spaces of the "great" course naturally leaves it exposed to the wind, but anything else would come as a great surprise. Classic and discreet in design with no hidden traps, Monifieth is respectable in length and deserves to be better known outside Scotland. This is one of the best surprises that any visitor could hope to find on the east coast. A course for connoisseurs but pleasant for players of all levels.

On sait que le golf a été pratiqué ici dès la première moitié du XVIIème siècle, mais les premiers signes d'un véritable parcours datent vraiment de 1850. Comme le tout proche Carnoustie, le parcours est partagé par cinq clubs différents, de même que le "Ashludie Course", plus modeste et reposant, mais néanmoins intéressant. Les vastes espaces où s'épanouit le "grand" parcours l'exposent bien sûr au vent, mais c'est le contraire qui serait étonnant. D'une architecture classique et sobre, sans pièges dissimulés, et d'une longueur très respectable, Monifieth devrait connaître une meilleure notoriété hors des frontières, et c'est l'une des meilleures surprises que les visiteurs pourront trouver de ce côté de l'Ecosse. Un parcours pour connaisseurs, mais agréable à tous niveaux de jeu.

Monifieth Golf Club

Medal Starter's Box, Princes Street
SCO - MONIFIETH, Dundee DD5 4AW

Office	Secrétariat	(44) 01382 - 535 553
Pro shop	Pro-shop	(44) 01382 - 532 945
Fax	Fax	(44) 01382 - 535 553
Situation	Situation	

8 km E of Dundee (pop. 165 873)

Annual closure	Fermeture annnuelle	no
Weekly closure	Fermeture hebdomadaire	no

Fees main season
Tarifs haute saison 18 holes

	Week days Semaine	We/Bank holidays We/Férié
Individual Individuel	£ 24	£ 28
Couple Couple	£ 48	£ 56

Full day: £ 34 - £ 40 (weekends)

Caddy	Caddy	on request/£ 25
Electric Trolley	Chariot électrique	no
Buggy	Voiturette	no
Clubs	Clubs	yes
Credit cards Cartes de crédit		no

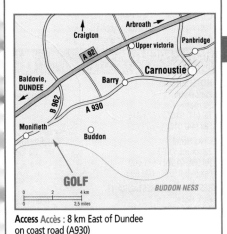

Access Accès : 8 km East of Dundee
on coast road (A930)
Map 2 on page 409 Carte 2 Page 409

GOLF COURSE
PARCOURS
17/20

Site	Site	
Maintenance	Entretien	
Architect	Architecte	Unknown
Type	Type	links
Relief	Relief	
Water in play	Eau en jeu	
Exp. to wind	Exposé au vent	
Trees in play	Arbres en jeu	

Scorecard Carte de score	Chp. Chp.	Mens Mess.	Ladies Da.
Length Long.	6056	5877	5361
Par	71	71	73

Advised golfing ability	0	12	24	36
Niveau de jeu recommandé				
Hcp required	Handicap exigé	certificate		

CLUB HOUSE & AMENITIES
CLUB HOUSE ET ANNEXES
7/10

Pro shop	Pro-shop	
Driving range	Practice	
Sheltered	couvert	no
On grass	sur herbe	yes
Putting-green	putting-green	yes
Pitching-green	pitching green	no

HOTEL FACILITIES
ENVIRONNEMENT HOTELIER
7/10

HOTELS HÔTELS
Panmure Hotel — Monifieth
13 rooms, from D £ 64 — adjacent
Tel (44) 01382 - 532 911, Fax (44) 01382 - 535 859

Woodlands Hotel — Broughty Ferry
18 rooms, from D £ 64 — 2.5 km
Tel (44) 01382 - 480 033, Fax (44) 01382 - 480 126

Queen's Hotel — Dundee
47 rooms, from D £ 52 — 8 km
Tel (44) 01382 - 322 515, Fax (44) 01382 - 202 668

RESTAURANTS RESTAURANT
Panmure Hotel — Monifieth
Tel (44) 01382 - 532 911 — adjacent

L'Auberge — Broughty Ferry
Tel (44) 01382 - 730 890 — 5 km

637

17	5	6

A great classic shared by three golf clubs, as is Carnoustie a few miles down the coast. If the history books are right, then this is the 5th oldest club in the world and golf has been played on the grounds of the Earl of Montrose since the 16th century. It is true that there is tradition in the air here, with a tinge of austerity as well. Here you'll find all the finest components that go to make up a great links course: deep bunkers, wonderfully soft soil, bushes and towering dunes covered by wild grass that shape the winding fairways and greens. Very reasonable in length, although this can change in a matter of minutes when the wind blows, this excellent course (complemented by the little Broomfield Course) has been a little neglected for the benefit of more powerful neighbours, but the course is so steeped in history that it should be a part of your own experience.

Un grand classique partagé par trois clubs de golf, comme Carnoustie, quelques kilomètres plus bas sur la côte. L'histoire voudrait que ce soit le 5ème club du monde, et que l'on ait joué sur ces terres du Marquis de Montrose depuis le XVIè siècle. Il est vrai que l'on respire ici la tradition, non sans une certaine austérité. On trouve ici à l'état pur ce qui fait la grandeur des links, de profonds bunkers, un sol merveilleusement souple, des buissons, de hautes dunes envahies d'herbes folles entre lesquelles s'insinuent les fairways et les greens. De longueur très raisonnable, mais que le vent peut bien sûr métamorphoser d'un instant à l'autre, cet excellent parcours (complété par le petit Broomfield Course) a été un peu négligé au profit de puissants voisins, mais il témoigne de toute une histoire, et doit faire partie de la vôtre.

Montrose Links Trust
Traill Drive
SCO - MONTROSE, Angus DD10 8SW

Office	Secrétariat	(44) 01674 - 672 932
Pro shop	Pro-shop	(44) 01674 - 672 634
Fax	Fax	(44) 01674 - 671 800
Situation	Situation	

in Montrose (pop. 8 473)
35 km E of Dundee (pop. 165 873)

Annual closure	Fermeture annnuelle	no
Weekly closure	Fermeture hebdomadaire	

Fees main season	Tarifs haute saison		18 holes
		Week days Semaine	We/Bank holidays We/Férié
Individual Individuel		£ 20	£ 28
Couple Couple		£ 40	£ 56

Saturday: members only. "Special deals"
with catering.

Caddy	Caddy	no
Electric Trolley	Chariot électrique	£ 5/18 holes
Buggy	Voiturette	no
Clubs	Clubs	£ 8/18 holes

Credit cards Cartes de crédit
VISA - MasterCard - JCB

638

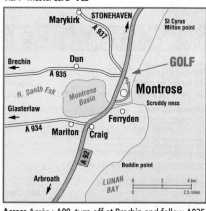

Access Accès : A90, turn off at Brechin and follow A935 to Montrose. Golf 0.8 km (1/2 m) from town centre.
Map 1 on page 407 Carte 1 Page 407

GOLF COURSE
PARCOURS
17/20

Site	Site	■■■■
Maintenance	Entretien	■■■■
Architect	Architecte	Willie Park Jr

Type	Type	links
Relief	Relief	■
Water in play	Eau en jeu	■
Exp. to wind	Exposé au vent	■■■
Trees in play	Arbres en jeu	■

Scorecard Carte de score	Chp. Chp.	Mens Mess.	Ladies Da.
Length Long.	5887	5670	5134
Par	71	71	73

Advised golfing ability		0	12	24	36
Niveau de jeu recommandé			■■■		
Hcp required	Handicap exigé	certificate			

CLUB HOUSE & AMENITIES
CLUB HOUSE ET ANNEXES
5/10

Pro shop	Pro-shop	■■■■
Driving range	Practice	■■■
Sheltered	couvert	no
On grass	sur herbe	no
Putting-green	putting-green	yes
Pitching-green	pitching green	yes

HOTEL FACILITIES
ENVIRONNEMENT HOTELIER
6/10

HOTELS HÔTELS
Park Hotel
59 rooms, D £ 90
Tel (44) 01674 - 673 415
Fax (44) 01674 - 677 091
Montrose
1 km

Links Hotel
22 rooms, D £ 74
Tel (44) 01674 - 671 000
Fax (44) 01674 - 672 698
Montrose
1 km

RESTAURANTS RESTAURANT
Park Hotel
Tel (44) 01674 - 673 415
Montrose
1 km

This is not the best known links in Scotland but it is a good one. Firstly for its antiquated charm, because like the Old Course at St Andrews, it starts and ends in town, in Lossiemouth, the name by which the course is also sometimes known. A large part of this "old" course was designed by Old Tom Morris, although patient changes have given the layout its present-day look, custom-made for the requirements of modern golf. Players of all levels will enjoy this course, and the less experienced golfers can get acquainted with the subtle side of links golf without too much to worry about. Moray is also home to the "New Course" designed by Henry Cotton, a very pleasant layout but without the cachet of its "old" stable-mate. We would also emphasise the mildness of the climate here and the superb views over the Moray Firth. Highly recommended.

Ce n'est pas le plus connu des links d'Ecosse, mais ce n'est pas le moindre. Par son charme désuet d'abord : comme le Old Course de St Andrews, il commence et s'achève en ville, à Lossiemouth, qui lui a donné parfois son nom. Ce "Old" a en grande partie été conçu par Old Tom Morris, mais de patientes modifications lui ont donné son visage actuel, parfaitement adapté aux exigences du golf moderne. Cependant, les joueurs de tous niveaux y prendront plaisir, et les moins expérimentés pourront s'y familiariser avec les subtilités du golf de links sans être trop intimidés. De plus, on trouve également à Moray le "New Course" dessiné par Henry Cotton, très agréable mais moins empreint de la grandeur du "Old." On soulignera enfin la douceur du climat local, et les vues superbes sur le Moray Firth. Visite conseillée !

Moray Golf Club

Stotfield Road
SCO - LOSSIEMOUTH, Moray JV31 6QS

Office	Secrétariat	(44) 01343 - 812 018
Pro shop	Pro-shop	(44) 01343 - 813 330
Fax	Fax	(44) 01343 - 815 102
Situation	Situation	

9 km N of Elgin (pop. 11 855)

Annual closure   Fermeture annnuelle   no

Weekly closure   Fermeture hebdomadaire
end of september/beginning of october

Fees main season
Tarifs haute saison 18 holes

	Week days Semaine	We/Bank holidays We/Férié
Individual Individuel	£ 30	£ 40
Couple Couple	£ 60	£ 80

Full days: £ 40 - £ 50 (weekends)

Caddy	Caddy	on request
Electric Trolley	Chariot électrique	no
Buggy	Voiturette	no
Clubs	Clubs	yes

Credit cards Cartes de crédit   only Pro-shop

GOLF
Lossiemouth
B 9040
Burnside
spey bay
Duffus
A 941
B 9012
Bishopmill   Elgin
B 9103
Linkwood

Access Accès : Inverness, A96 to Elgin, then A941 North.
Map 1 on page 407 Carte 1 Page 407

GOLF COURSE / PARCOURS   17/20

Site	Site	
Maintenance	Entretien	
Architect	Architecte	Tom Morris
Type	Type	links
Relief	Relief	
Water in play	Eau en jeu	
Exp. to wind	Exposé au vent	
Trees in play	Arbres en jeu	

Scorecard Carte de score	Chp. Chp.	Mens Mess.	Ladies Da.
Length Long.	6066	5735	5580
Par	71	70	75

Advised golfing ability Niveau de jeu recommandé	0	12	24	36
Hcp required Handicap exigé	24			

CLUB HOUSE & AMENITIES / CLUB HOUSE ET ANNEXES   5/10

Pro shop	Pro-shop	
Driving range	Practice	
Sheltered	couvert	no
On grass	sur herbe	no
Putting-green	putting-green	no
Pitching-green	pitching green	no

HOTEL FACILITIES / ENVIRONNEMENT HOTELIER   5/10

HOTELS HÔTELS
Stotfield   Lossiemouth
45 rooms, D £ 70   adjacent
Tel (44) 01343 - 812 011
Fax (44) 01343 - 814 820

Skerry Brae Hotel   Lossiemouth
10 rooms,   adjacent
Tel (44) 01343 - 812 040

RESTAURANTS RESTAURANT
1629 Restaurant   Lossiemouth
Tel (44) 01343 - 813 743   1 km

Skerry Brae   lossiemouth
Tel (44) 01343 - 812 040   adjacent

639

The course of the Honourable Company of Edinburg Golfers, who drew up the first collection of the rules of golf, is first and foremost one of the great courses used for the British Open. Winners here include Nicklaus, Trevino and Faldo, three players of very different talent, suggesting that great courses adapt to all styles of play. While there are no spectacular dunes and no sea in the immediate vicinity for this to be labelled a reference links course, the thick and very tall rough, deep bunkering that reflects a shrewd golfing mind, narrow (but welcoming) fairways and tricky greens where you need magic fingers, make it a reference course, full stop. The course asks a lot of players when it comes to shaping the right shot. A good shot is rewarded but any flaw is a shortcut to disaster. This is a great test of golf. The clubhouse is superb, historically very instructive and a great place to eat.

Le parcours de l'Honourable Company of Edinburgh Golfers, qui a établi le premier recueil de règles de golf est surtout l'un des grands parcours du British Open, où l'on triomphé notamment Nicklaus, Trevino et Faldo, trois hommes aux talents dissemblables, comme quoi les grands golfs s'adaptent à tous les types de jeu. S'il manque de dunes spectaculaires et de proximité immédiate de la mer pour être un links de référence, les roughs épais et très hauts, de profonds bunkers placés avec une très grande connaissance du jeu, des fairways étroits (mais accueillants), des greens subtils où il faut avoir des doigts de fée en font une référence. Ici, on exige beaucoup du joueur afin qu'il fasse le coup qui convient. Un bon coup est récompensé, mais toute défaillance amène un désastre. Un grand test de golf. Le Club house est superbe, historiquement très instructif, et la table excellente.

Honourable Company of Edinburgh Golfers

Muirfield
SCO - GULLANE, E. Lothian, EH31 2EG

Office	Secrétariat	(44) 01620 - 842 123
Pro shop	Pro-shop	(44) 01620 - 842 123
Fax	Fax	(44) 01620 - 842 977
Situation	Situation	

30 km E of Edinburgh (pop. 418 914)

Annual closure	Fermeture annnuelle	no
Weekly closure	Fermeture hebdomadaire	no
Fees main season	Tarifs haute saison	full day

	Week days Semaine	We/Bank holidays We/Férié
Individual Individuel	£ 80	—
Couple Couple	£ 160	—

Ask for availability - No visitors at weekends

Caddy	Caddy	on request
Electric Trolley	Chariot électrique	yes
Buggy	Voiturette	limited use
Clubs	Clubs	no

Credit cards Cartes de crédit
VISA - CB - Eurocard - MasterCard - AMEX - DC - JCB - Cofinoga

640

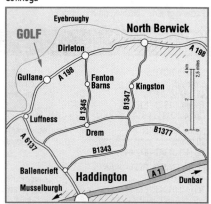

Access Accès : Edinburgh A198 along Firth of Forth. Turn left at the end of Gullane, follow signs to Greywalls Hotel. Map 3 on page 411 Carte 3 Page 411

GOLF COURSE / PARCOURS — 19/20

Site	Site	
Maintenance	Entretien	
Architect	Architecte	Tom Morris Harry S. Colt
Type	Type	links
Relief	Relief	
Water in play	Eau en jeu	
Exp. to wind	Exposé au vent	
Trees in play	Arbres en jeu	

Scorecard Carte de score	Chp. Chp.	Mens Mess.	Ladies Da.
Length Long.	6336	6007	0
Par	73	73	0

Advised golfing ability Niveau de jeu recommandé		0 12 24 36
Hcp required	Handicap exigé	certificate

CLUB HOUSE & AMENITIES / CLUB HOUSE ET ANNEXES — 7/10

Pro shop	Pro-shop	
Driving range	Practice	
Sheltered	couvert	no
On grass	sur herbe	yes
Putting-green	putting-green	yes
Pitching-green	pitching green	yes

HOTEL FACILITIES / ENVIRONNEMENT HOTELIER — 6/10

HOTELS HÔTELS

Greywalls — Gullane
22 rooms, D £ 95 — next to golf
Tel (44) 01620 - 842 144
Fax (44) 01620 - 842 241

Green Craigs — Aberlady
6 rooms, D £ 90 — 3 km
Tel (44) 01875 - 870 301
Fax (44) 01875 - 870 440

RESTAURANTS RESTAURANT

La Potinière — Gullane
Tel (44) 01620 - 843 214 — 0.5 km

Greywalls — Gullane
Tél(44) 01620 - 842 144 — next to golf

MURCAR

Murcar lies alongside Royal Aberdeen but has never been awarded the royal seal. But if they say that mongrels are a tougher species than pedigrees, then Murcar is definitely a course not to be missed. Only just a little shorter than its neighbour, the course is a permanent challenge which should never be taken lightly even when there's no wind. And that's about as rare as the layout of holes here, where there are three par 3s, three par 5s and twelve par 4s. The latter include those devilishly tricky short par 4s that you think you can drive in one, only to end up on your knees praying for a bogey. Naturally you won't find the tremendous challenges that await you on the monster courses in Scotland, but Murcar deserves much more than just a quick look. We had seen it in better condition than when we visited this time, but this is certainly only a temporary fault.

Il jouxte le parcours de Royal Aberdeen et n'a pas eu droit à l'annoblissement. Mais si on dit que les bâtards sont les plus vigoureux, Murcar est effectivement un parcours à ne pas manquer. A peine plus court que son voisin, il présente un défi permanent, à ne jamais prendre à la légère, même quand le vent ne souffle pas, ce qui est tout aussi rare que la distribution avec trois par 3, trois par 5 et douze par 4, dont ces démoniaques petits trous techniques que l'on croit pouvoir driver et qui vous mettent à genoux. Certes, l'on n'attendra pas ici d'aussi formidables défis que dans le groupe des grands monstres d'Ecosse, mais Murcar mérite beaucoup mieux qu'un simple regard. Certes, nous l'avons vu en meilleure condition qu'au moment de notre visite, mais c'était sans doute provisoire...

Murcar Golf Club

Bridge of Don
SCO - ABERDEEN, Aberdeenshire AB23 8BD

Office	Secrétariat	(44) 01224 - 704 345
Pro shop	Pro-shop	(44) 01224 - 704 370
Fax	Fax	(44) 01224 - 704 354
Situation	Situation	

8 km N of Aberdeen (pop. 204 885)

Annual closure	Fermeture annnuelle	no
Weekly closure	Fermeture hebdomadaire	no

Fees main season
Tarifs haute saison 18 holes

	Week days Semaine	We/Bank holidays We/Férié
Individual Individuel	£ 28	£ 43
Couple Couple	£ 56	£ 86

Full Weekdays: £ 38

Caddy	Caddy	on request
Electric Trolley	Chariot électrique	no
Buggy	Voiturette	no
Clubs	Clubs	yes
Credit cards Cartes de crédit		no

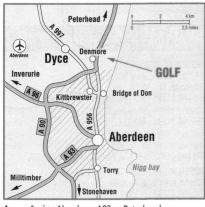

Access Accès : Aberdeen, A92 → Peterhead.
Signposted to right.
Map 1 on page 407 Carte 1 Page 407

GOLF COURSE
PARCOURS
15/20

Site	Site	
Maintenance	Entretien	
Architect	Architecte	Archie Simpson James Braid
Type	Type	links
Relief	Relief	
Water in play	Eau en jeu	
Exp. to wind	Exposé au vent	
Trees in play	Arbres en jeu	

Scorecard Carte de score	Chp. Chp.	Mens Mess.	Ladies Da.
Length Long.	5679	5287	5036
Par	70	68	73

Advised golfing ability Niveau de jeu recommandé	0	12	24	36
Hcp required Handicap exigé	certificate			

CLUB HOUSE & AMENITIES
CLUB HOUSE ET ANNEXES
6/10

Pro shop	Pro-shop	
Driving range	Practice	
Sheltered	couvert	no
On grass	sur herbe	yes
Putting-green	putting-green	yes
Pitching-green	pitching green	no

HOTEL FACILITIES
ENVIRONNEMENT HOTELIER
6/10

HOTELS HÔTELS

Marcliffe at Piffodels — Aberdeen
42 rooms, D £ 150 — 9 km
Tel (44) 01224 - 861 000, Fax (44) 01224 - 868 860

Quality — Bridge of Don
123 rooms, D £ 120 — 4 km
Tel (44) 01224 - 706 707, Fax (44) 01224 - 823 923

Corner House — Aberdeen
17 rooms, D £ 58 — 8 km
Tél (44) 01224 - 313 063

RESTAURANTS RESTAURANT

Courtyard on the Lane — Aberdeen
Tel (44) 01224 - 213 795 — 8 km

Silver Darling — Aberdeen
Tel (44) 01224 - 576 229 — 8 km

641

Located in a well-forested setting not far from Perth, this country course was opened in 1981 and has quickly built up an excellent reputation among local players for its pleasant site, the hazards and the challenge of playing here. This is by no means an easy course but is one of those layouts which quickly help you forget a bad score. If your card is bad, there's no blaming the course. Game strategy is obvious from the first time out, difficulties are evenly spread around the course with just the right balance of stress and relaxation, and the greens are well designed and protected. This is one of the best-equipped golf clubs you can find, with a real driving range and a very comfortable hotel.

Situé dans un environnement bien boisé non loin de Perth, ce parcours campagnard né en 1981 s'est vite bâti une excellente réputation parmi les joueurs de la région, en raison de l'agrément du site, mais aussi des difficultés présentées et du "challenge" offert. Ce n'est certes pas un parcours facile, mais il fait partie de ceux qui vous font vite oublier un mauvais score. En tout cas, on ne pourra pas en accuser le parcours. La stratégie de jeu y est assez évidente dès la première visite, les difficultés sont bien réparties, avec ce qu'il faut de tension et de détente, les greens bien dessinés et bien défendus. Le Club est l'un des mieux équipés que l'on puisse trouver, notamment avec un vrai practice et un hôtel très confortable.

Murrayshall Golf Club

Murrayshall Country House Hotel
SCO - SCONE, Perthshire PH2 7PH

Office	Secrétariat	(44) 01738 - 551 171
Pro shop	Pro-shop	(44) 01738 - 552 784
Fax	Fax	(44) 01738 - 552 595
Situation	Situation	

8 km NE of Perth (pop. 123 495)

| Annual closure | Fermeture annnuelle | no |
| Weekly closure | Fermeture hebdomadaire | no |

Fees main season
Tarifs haute saison 18 holes

	Week days Semaine	We/Bank holidays We/Férié
Individual Individuel	£ 22	£ 27
Couple Couple	£ 44	£ 54

Full days: £ 30 - £ 45 (weekends)

Caddy	Caddy	on request/£ 15
Electric Trolley	Chariot électrique	£ 7.50/18 holes
Buggy	Voiturette	£ 20/18 holes
Clubs	Clubs	£ 15/18 holes

Credit cards Cartes de crédit
VISA - Eurocard - MasterCard - AMEX

642

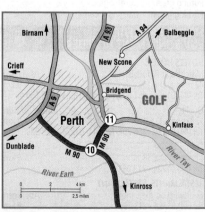

Access Accès : Edinburgh M90 to Perth,
then A94 → Coupar Angus, Golf at Scone.
Map 2 on page 409 Carte 2 Page 409

GOLF COURSE
PARCOURS   14/20

Site	Site	
Maintenance	Entretien	
Architect	Architecte	Hamilton Stutt
Type	Type	parkland
Relief	Relief	
Water in play	Eau en jeu	
Exp. to wind	Exposé au vent	
Trees in play	Arbres en play	

Scorecard Carte de score	Chp. Chp.	Mens Mess.	Ladies Da.
Length Long.	5862	5502	4842
Par	73	72	74

Advised golfing ability		0	12	24	36
Niveau de jeu recommandé					
Hcp required	Handicap exigé	no			

CLUB HOUSE & AMENITIES
CLUB HOUSE ET ANNEXES   7/10

Pro shop	Pro-shop	
Driving range	Practice	
Sheltered	couvert	11 mats
On grass	sur herbe	no
Putting-green	putting-green	yes
Pitching-green	pitching green	yes

HOTEL FACILITIES
ENVIRONNEMENT HOTELIER   8/10

HOTELS HÔTELS
Murrayshall Country House	Golf
30 rooms, D £ 100	on site
Tel (44) 01738 - 551 171, Fax (44) 01738 - 552 595	

| Queens Hotel - 51 rooms, D £ 100 | Perth |
| Tel (44) 01738 - 442 222 | 8 km |

Salutation Hotel	Perth
84 rooms, D £ 80	8 km
Tel (44) 01738 - 630 066, Fax (44) 01738 - 633 598	

RESTAURANTS RESTAURANT
| Old Masters (Murrayshall) | Golf |
| Tel (44) 01738 - 551 171 | on site |

| Patrick's - | Perth |
| Tel (44) 01738 - 624 114 | 8 km |

| Number Thirty Three | Perth |
| Tel (44) 01738 - 633 771 | 8 km |

This is one of the great Scottish links and for many a year was one of the country's best guarded secrets. The heather, broom and gorse complete a fine collection of hazards preying on your ball once you have avoided the traps along the Moray Firth. But on the whole Nairn is a remarkable challenge, notably with greens that are often firm and very quick. If you add James Braid's high class bunkering, you'll understand that you don't drive past without stopping off a day or three to test your game on the long golfing road that leads the visitor from Aberdeen to Inverness then to Dornoch and beyond. The landscape is maybe plainer than on other courses in the region, but it is also a little more sheltered, if that is the right word.

C'est l'un des grands links d'Ecosse et ce fut longtemps l'un de ses secrets les mieux gardés. La bruyère, les genêts et les ajoncs complètent une belle collection d'entraves à la liberté des balles, une fois que l'on a déjoué les pièges le long du Moray Firth. Mais Nairn est dans l'ensemble un défi remarquable, avec notamment des greens souvent fermes et très rapides. Si l'on ajoute la contribution majeure de James Braid, un "bunkering" de haute volée, on aura compris que l'on ne saurait passer devant la porte sans s'arrêter un bon moment pour tester sa forme, sur la longue route golfique menant d'Aberdeen à Inverness puis Dornoch et au-delà. Le paysage est moins mouvementé que sur d'autres parcours de la région, mais il est aussi un peu plus abrité... si l'on peut dire.

Nairn Golf Club

Seabank Road
SCO - NAIRN, IV12 4HB

Office	Secrétariat	(44) 01667 - 453 208
Pro shop	Pro-shop	(44) 01667 - 452 787
Fax	Fax	(44) 01667 - 456 328
Situation	Situation	

24 km E of Inverness (pop. 62 186)

Annual closure	Fermeture annnuelle	no
Weekly closure	Fermeture hebdomadaire	no

Full catering: only 04 → 10 inclusive

Fees main season	Tarifs haute saison	18 holes
	Week days Semaine	We/Bank holidays We/Férié
Individual Individuel	£ 50	£ 50
Couple Couple	£ 100	£ 100

Caddy	Caddy	on request/£ 20
Electric Trolley	Chariot électrique	£ 6/18 holes
Buggy	Voiturette	no
Clubs	Clubs	£ 12/18 holes

Credit cards Cartes de crédit
VISA - MasterCard

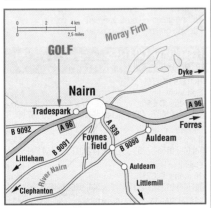

GOLF

Moray Firth

Nairn

Dyke →

Tradespark

A 96

Forres

B 9092

A 96

A 939

Foynes
field

B 9090

Auldeam

Littleham

B 9091

River Nairn

Auldeam

Littlemill

Clephanton

Access Accès : Off A96 Inverness to Nairn road.
Golf to the West of town centre.
Map 1 on page 407 Carte 1 Page 407

GOLF COURSE
PARCOURS

19/20

Site	Site	■■■■■■□
Maintenance	Entretien	■■■■■■□
Architect	Architecte	Tom Morris James Braid
Type	Type	links
Relief	Relief	■■■■□□□
Water in play	Eau en jeu	■■□□□□□
Exp. to wind	Exposé au vent	■■■□□□□
Trees in play	Arbres en jeu	■■□□□□□

Scorecard Carte de score	Chp. Chp.	Mens Mess.	Ladies Da.
Length Long.	6138	5890	5562
Par	72	71	75

Advised golfing ability		0	12	24	36
Niveau de jeu recommandé			■■■■		
Hcp required	Handicap exigé	certificate			

CLUB HOUSE & AMENITIES
CLUB HOUSE ET ANNEXES

7/10

Pro shop	Pro-shop	■■■■■□□
Driving range	Practice	■■■■□□□
Sheltered	couvert	no
On grass	sur herbe	yes
Putting-green	putting-green	yes
Pitching-green	pitching green	no

HOTEL FACILITIES
ENVIRONNEMENT HOTELIER

8/10

HOTELS HÔTELS

Golf View — Nairn close
48 rooms, D £ 90
Tel (44) 01667 - 452 301, Fax (44) 01667 - 455 267

Lochloy House — Nairn 4 km
8 rooms, D £ 130
Tel (44) 01667 - 455 355, Fax (44) 01667 - 454 809

Windsor Hotel — Nairn close
40 rooms, D £ 75
Tel (44) 01667 - 453 108, Fax (44) 01667 - 456 108

RESTAURANTS RESTAURANT

Longhouse — Nairn close
Tel (44) 01667 - 455 532

Golf View Hotel — Nairn close
Tel (44) 01667 - 452 301

643

NAIRN DUNBAR

<table>
<tr><td>15</td><td>6</td><td>7</td></tr>
</table>

This course is located to the east of the town, as opposed to its famous cousin. It was originally created for the Craftsmen's Guild, as is often the case in Great Britain. Remodelled and changed on many different occasions, it now seems to have found its final form. Close to the sea and the estuary, it has been intelligently tailored to the site with a lot of inventive flair which gives the course variety. There aren't many bunkers, but the bushes, gorse and a few trees are all there to get in the way and give this a rather unusual appearance for a course so close to the sea, although the soil is very much that of a links. Even though this is not really in the top drawer of Scottish courses, it is very pleasant (the 10th hole if excellent) and the atmosphere very friendly.

Ce parcours est situé à l'est de la ville, à l'opposé de son célèbre cousin. Il fut originellement créé pour le club des artisans, comme on en trouvait beaucoup en Grande-Bretagne. Remodelé et modifié à de multiples reprises, il semble avoir trouvé sa forme définitive. Près de la mer et de l'embouchure de la rivière, il a été intelligemment adapté au site, avec beaucoup d'esprit d'invention, qui lui donne une grande variété. Les bunkers sont peu nombreux, mais buissons, ajoncs et quelques arbres viennent contrarier les joueurs, et donnent un aspect un peu inhabituel à un parcours si proche de la mer, mais avec un sol de links pour nous le rappeler. Même s'il n'appartient pas totalement à l'élite, c'est un golf très plaisant (le 10 est de premier ordre), et l'atmosphère y est très amicale.

Nairn Dunbar Golf Club
Lochloy Road
SCO - NAIRN, IV12 5AE

Office	Secrétariat	(44) 01667 - 452 741
Pro shop	Pro-shop	(44) 01667 - 453 964
Fax	Fax	(44) 01667 - 456 897
Situation	Situation	

25 km E of Inverness (pop. 62 186)

Annual closure	Fermeture annnuelle	no
Weekly closure	Fermeture hebdomadaire	no

Fees main season
Tarifs haute saison full day

	Week days Semaine	We/Bank holidays We/Férié
Individual Individuel	£ 30	£ 35
Couple Couple	£ 60	£ 70

Caddy	Caddy	on request
Electric Trolley	Chariot électrique	yes
Buggy	Voiturette	£ 15/18 holes
Clubs	Clubs	£ 10/18 holes

Credit cards Cartes de crédit
VISA - Access

644

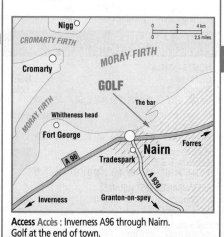

Access Accès : Inverness A96 through Nairn.
Golf at the end of town.
Map 1 on page 407 Carte 1 Page 407

GOLF COURSE
PARCOURS
15/20

Site	Site	
Maintenance	Entretien	
Architect	Architecte	Unknown
Type	Type	links
Relief	Relief	
Water in play	Eau en jeu	
Exp. to wind	Exposé au vent	
Trees in play	Arbres en jeu	

Scorecard Carte de score	Chp. Chp.	Mens Mess.	Ladies Da.
Length Long.	6108	5726	5196
Par	72	72	75

Advised golfing ability
Niveau de jeu recommandé   0   12   24   36

Hcp required   Handicap exigé   no

CLUB HOUSE & AMENITIES
CLUB HOUSE ET ANNEXES
6/10

Pro shop	Pro-shop	
Driving range	Practice	
Sheltered	couvert	no
On grass	sur herbe	no
Putting-green	putting-green	yes
Pitching-green	pitching green	no

HOTEL FACILITIES
ENVIRONNEMENT HOTELIER
7/10

HOTELS HÔTELS
Golf View   Nairn
48 rooms, D £ 90   close
Tel (44) 01667 - 452 301, Fax (44) 01667 - 455 267

Lochloy House   Lochloy
8 rooms, D £ 120   4 km
Tel (44) 01667 - 455 355, Fax (44) 01667 - 454 809

Claymore House   Nairn
16 rooms, D £ 75   close
Tel (44) 01667 - 453 731, Fax (44) 01667 - 455 290

RESTAURANTS RESTAURANT
Longhouse   Nairn
Tel (44) 01667 - 455 532   close

Golf View   Nairn
Tel (44) 01667 - 452 301   close

18	7	8

This is probably one of the courses that is closest to the origins of the game, where you start off along the beach trying to avoid passers-by who watch without a smile. It's then onto a wide strip of land with a few, reasonably high dunes, and a wall you'll have to get over one day to reach the green. Although this is flattish terrain, there are a few blind holes. North Berwick was modelled by mother nature and the sands of time, although they did need an architect (unknown) to build "Perfection (a par 4) and the famous "Redan", a diabolical and often imitated par 3. At once archaic and very modern, seemingly friendly but ferocious when the wind blows (any high ball can be disastrous), North Berwick slowly unveils its secrets which you can only discover with a good measure of patience and humility.

C'est probablement l'un des parcours les plus proches des origines, où l'on commence le long de la plage en essayant d'éviter les promeneurs qui vous regardent sans rire. On se promène ensuite dans une large bande de terrain avec quelques dunes pas trop hautes. Il y a un mur au-dessus duquel il faudra passer un jour pour atteindre le green. Il y a quelques coups aveugles bien que le terrain soit assez plat. C'est la nature et les siècles qui ont modelé North Berwick, mais il a bien fallu un architecte (inconnu) pour faire le "Perfection" (par 4) et le célèbre "Redan", par 3 diabolique souvent copié. A la fois archaïque et très moderne, apparemment aimable et sauvage quand le vent le balaie (toute balle haute provoque un désastre), North Berwick révèle lentement ses secrets. Il faut savoir les découvrir avec patience et humilité.

North Berwick Golf Club
New Club House, Beach Road
SCO - NORTH BERWICK, East Lothian, EH39 4BB

Office	Secrétariat	(44) 01620 - 892 135
Pro shop	Pro-shop	(44) 01620 - 893 233
Fax	Fax	(44) 01620 - 893 274
Situation	Situation	

37 km E of Edinburgh (pop. 418 914)

Annual closure	Fermeture annnuelle	no
Weekly closure	Fermeture hebdomadaire	no

Fees main season
Tarifs haute saison 18 holes

	Week days Semaine	We/Bank holidays We/Férié
Individual Individuel	£ 30	£ 45
Couple Couple	£ 60	£ 90

Full days: £ 45 - £ 60 (weekends)

Caddy	Caddy	on request/£ 18.50
Electric Trolley	Chariot électrique	no
Buggy	Voiturette	no
Clubs	Clubs	£ 10/18 holes

Credit cards Cartes de crédit
VISA - MasterCard

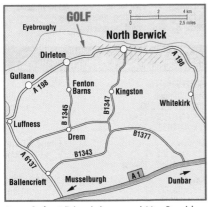

GOLF

Eyebroughy

North Berwick

Dirleton

Gullane

Fenton Barns — Kingston

Whitekirk

Luffness

Drem

B1377

B1343

Ballencrieff — Musselburgh — Dunbar

A198, A1347, B1345, B1343, B1377, A6137, A1

0 — 2 — 4 km
0 — 2,5 miles

Access Accès : Edinburgh, by-pass and A1 → Berwick upon Tweed. Exit for A198, follow to North Berwick.
Map 3 on page 411 Carte 3 Page 411

GOLF COURSE / PARCOURS
18/20

Site	Site	■■■■■■□
Maintenance	Entretien	■■■■■■□
Architect	Architecte	Unknown
Type	Type	links
Relief	Relief	■□□□□□
Water in play	Eau en jeu	■■□□□□
Exp. to wind	Exposé au vent	■■■■□□
Trees in play	Arbres en jeu	■□□□□□

Scorecard Carte de score	Chp. Chp.	Mens Mess.	Ladies Da.
Length Long.	5842	5490	5233
Par	71	70	74

Advised golfing ability Niveau de jeu recommandé	0 12 24 36
Hcp required Handicap exigé	25 Men, 35 Ladies

CLUB HOUSE & AMENITIES / CLUB HOUSE ET ANNEXES
7/10

Pro shop	Pro-shop	■■■■□□
Driving range	Practice	■□□□□□
Sheltered	couvert	no
On grass	sur herbe	yes
Putting-green	putting-green	yes
Pitching-green	pitching green	no

645

HOTEL FACILITIES / ENVIRONNEMENT HOTELIER
8/10

HOTELS HÔTELS

Marine Hotel — North Berwick adjacent
74 rooms, D £ 80
Tel (44) 01620 - 892 406, Fax (44) 01620 - 894 480

Point Garry Hotel — North Berwick close
15 rooms, D from £ 70
Tel (44) 01620 - 892 380, Fax (44) 01620 - 892 848

Blenheim House Hotel — North Berwick close
11 rooms, D £ 68
Tel (44) 01620 - 892 385, Fax (44) 01620 - 894 010

RESTAURANTS RESTAURANT

Marine Hotel — North Berwick adjacent
Tel (44) 01620 - 892 406

The Grange — North Berwick close
Tel (44) 01620 - 895 894

Although this course has paled somewhat in the shadow of neighbouring Carnoustie, Panmure (like the other neighbour Monifieth) does not fall far short from featuring in the same class. Anywhere else it would be very highly rated, so take advantage of your stay in the region to play it. In a rather hilly landscape, sometimes even dotted with oddly-shaped dunes, you'll have to be pretty hot with your bump and run shots, regardless of wind direction, in order to control the flight of your shots even though from first reading the card you might think that the course has nothing over-difficult to offer. The greens are extremely well protected and the putting surface is always tricky but never impossible. A classic and very forthright links to which access is restricted on weekends but where a warm welcome awaits the visitor on weekdays.

Bien qu'il ait un peu pâli du puissant voisinage de Carnoustie, il manque peu de chose à Panmure (tout comme à Monifieth, son autre voisin) pour figurer dans la même classe. Partout ailleurs, il serait hautement considéré : profitez d'être dans la région pour le découvrir. Dans un paysage assez mouvementé, parfois même orné de petites dunes de formes curieuses, il vous faudra savoir jouer les balles roulées, que le vent soit dans n'importe quel sens, afin de parvenir à bien contrôler vos trajectoires de balles, même si la lecture de la carte peut faire penser de prime abord que les difficultés ne sont pas immenses. Les greens sont très bien défendus, leurs surfaces subtiles mais sans exagérations. Un links classique d'une grande franchise, où l'accès est limité en week-end, mais l'accueil chaleureux en semaine.

Panmure Golf Club
Barry
SCO- CARNOUSTIE, Angus DD7 7RT

Office	Secrétariat	(44) 01241 - 855 120
Pro shop	Pro-shop	(44) 01241 - 852 460
Fax	Fax	(44) 01241 - 859 737
Situation	Situation	

16 km E of Dundee (pop. 165 873)

Annual closure	Fermeture annnuelle	no
Weekly closure	Fermeture hebdomadaire	no

Fees main season
Tarifs haute saison 18 holes

	Week days Semaine	We/Bank holidays We/Férié
Individual Individuel	£ 30	£ 30*
Couple Couple	£ 60	£ 60*

* Not Saturdays - Full Weekday: £ 45

Caddy	Caddy	on request
Electric Trolley	Chariot électrique	no
Buggy	Voiturette	£ 20/18 holes
Clubs	Clubs	yes

Credit cards Cartes de crédit
VISA - Eurocard - MasterCard - JCB

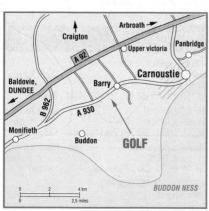

Access Accès : Dundee A930 to Barry Village. Golf 1 km
Map 2 on page 409 Carte 2 Page 409

GOLF COURSE
PARCOURS
17/20

Site	Site	▬▬▬▬▬□
Maintenance	Entretien	▬▬▬▬□□
Architect	Architecte	Unknown
Type	Type	links
Relief	Relief	▬▬▬□□□
Water in play	Eau en jeu	▬▬□□□□
Exp. to wind	Exposé au vent	▬▬▬▬□□
Trees in play	Arbres en jeu	▬▬▬□□□

Scorecard Carte de score	Chp. Chp.	Mens Mess.	Ladies Da.
Length Long.	5925	5538	5215
Par	70	70	73

Advised golfing ability		0 12 24 36
Niveau de jeu recommandé		▬▬▬▬□
Hcp required	Handicap exigé	no

CLUB HOUSE & AMENITIES
CLUB HOUSE ET ANNEXES
6/10

Pro shop	Pro-shop	▬▬▬▬□□
Driving range	Practice	▬▬▬▬□□
Sheltered	couvert	1 mat
On grass	sur herbe	yes (own balls)
Putting-green	putting-green	yes
Pitching-green	pitching green	yes

HOTEL FACILITIES
ENVIRONNEMENT HOTELIER
5/10

HOTELS HÔTELS

Stakis Dundee 104 rooms, D £ 90 Tél (44) 01382 - 22 9271 Fax (44) 01382 - 200 072	Dundee 16 km
Tayview 11 rooms, D £ 65 Tél (44) 01382 - 779 438	Broughty Ferry 6 km
Kingsley 16 rooms, D £ 35 Tel (44) 01241 - 879 933	Arbroath 10 km

RESTAURANTS RESTAURANT

11 Park Avenue Tél (44) 01241 - 853 336	Carnoustie 3 km

646

PETERHEAD

After the more famous Cruden Bay, you are strongly recommended to drive on a few more miles. The curiosity here is firstly that you have to cross a car-park bridge up to the rather Spartan clubhouse, where there is no locker-room for visitors. This very interesting course often looks like a links but is more like a park course when it ventures inland. It doesn't appear to have been altered a great deal since the various retouching operations firstly by Willie Park then by Braid and Auchterlonie. Bushes, rough, bunkers and ditches are the basic hazards on this layout where very little sand has ever been moved. But the terrain was made for an interesting course and there was enough space to lay-out another excellent 9-hole course, where the lesser golfer can get to grips with the game.

Après le plus célèbre Cruden Bay, il est fortement conseillé de pousser quelques kilomètres plus loin. La curiosité, c'est d'abord de devoir traverser un pont, du parking jusqu'au Clubhouse assez spartiate, où les visiteurs n'ont pas de vestiaire. Ce très intéressant parcours aux allures de links le plus souvent, parfois de parc dans les parties les plus intérieures, ne paraît pas avoir été beaucoup modifié depuis les différentes interventions de Willie Park d'abord, Braid et Auchterlonie ensuite. Buissons, roughs, bunkers et fossés constituent l'essentiel des obstacles sur ce dessin où peu de sable a été bougé. Mais le terrain se prêtait à un parcours intéressant, et l'espace était assez vaste pour que l'on trouve également ici un 9 trous de bonne facture où les moins compétents pourront s'aguerrir.

Peterhead Golf Club

Craigewan Links, Riverside Drive
SCO - PETERHEAD, Aberdeenshire AB42 1LT

Office	Secrétariat	(44) 01779 - 472 149
Pro shop	Pro-shop	(44) 01779 - 472 149
Fax	Fax	(44) 01779 - 480 785
Situation	Situation	

56 km N of Aberdeen (pop. 204 885)

Annual closure	Fermeture annnuelle	no
Weekly closure	Fermeture hebdomadaire	no

Fees main season
Tarifs haute saison full day

	Week days Semaine	We/Bank holidays We/Férié
Individual Individuel	£ 20	£ 27
Couple Couple	£ 40	£ 54

Caddy	Caddy	no
Electric Trolley	Chariot électrique	no
Buggy	Voiturette	no
Clubs	Clubs	no

Credit cards Cartes de crédit no

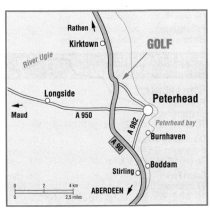

Access Accès : Aberdeen, A92 North, turn right on A952 → Peterhead. Go for north edge of town. Park on south of river Ugie. Walk across bridge to Clubhouse. **Map 1 on page 407** Carte 1 Page 407

GOLF COURSE / PARCOURS **15**/20

Site	Site	
Maintenance	Entretien	
Architect	Architecte	Willie Park James Braid
Type	Type	seaside course, links
Relief	Relief	
Water in play	Eau en jeu	
Exp. to wind	Exposé au vent	
Trees in play	Arbres en jeu	

Scorecard Carte de score	Chp. Chp.	Mens Mess.	Ladies Da.
Length Long.	5642	5263	4930
Par	70	69	72

Advised golfing ability Niveau de jeu recommandé	0	12	24	36

Hcp required Handicap exigé certificate

CLUB HOUSE & AMENITIES / CLUB HOUSE ET ANNEXES **5**/10

Pro shop	Pro-shop	
Driving range	Practice	
Sheltered	couvert	no
On grass	sur herbe	no
Putting-green	putting-green	no
Pitching-green	pitching green	no

HOTEL FACILITIES / ENVIRONNEMENT HOTELIER **4**/10

HOTELS HÔTELS

Waterside Inn Peterhead
109 rooms, D £ 95 1 km
Tel (44) 01779 - 471 121, Fax (44) 01779 - 470 670

Meldrum House Oldmeldrum
9 rooms, D £ 120 28 km
Tel (44) 01651 - 872 294, Fax (44) 01651 - 872 464

Udny Arms Newburgh
24 rooms, D £ 60 30 km
Tel (44) 01358 - 789 444, Fax (44) 01779 - 789 012

RESTAURANTS RESTAURANT

Udny Arms Newburgh
Tel (44) 01358 - 789 444 30 km

647

A visit here in Winter would probably come as something as a surprise, as even at a moderate altitude, snow is not rare. This little town, one of Queen Victoria's favourite destinations, is surrounded by hills edged with pine-trees and looks it best in Summer, when nature and the course are in full bloom and the salmon are on their way up to Loch Faskally. Accommodation here is both extensive and good standard and there is even a theatre. The actual course lies on a hill above Pitlochry, and although the first few holes are something of a climb, the layout soon levels out and the view from the top of the course really is worth the effort. Slopes have been used so intelligently that you don't always notice them, and while tee-boxes and greens are frequently at the same level, you'll find a few surprises in store as you progress from one to the other. Interestingly, the bunkers here contain quartz sand.

Venir par ici en hiver pourrait bien vous surprendre. Même à une altitude modérée, il n'est pas rare d'y voir de la neige. Les collines bordées de pins entourent la petite ville, que la reine Victoria adorait. Il faut venir ici en été, quand la végétation est à sa plénitude, et que les saumons remontent le Loch Faskally. L'hébergement est ici aussi abondant que de qualité, on trouve même un théâtre. Le parcours est situé sur une colline au-dessus de Pitlochry, le début est physiquement assez difficile, mais les choses s'arrangent rapidement, et la vue du haut du parcours valait cet effort. On ne remarque pas toujours les pentes, car elles sont intelligemment utilisées, les départs et les greens sont fréquemment au même niveau, mais on peut avoir entre les deux quelques surprises. A remarquer, le sable de quartz dans les bunkers.

Pitlochry Golf Club

Golf Course Road
SCO - PITLOCHRY, TH16 5QY

Office	Secrétariat	(44) 01796 - 472 792
Pro shop	Pro-shop	(44) 01796 - 472 792
Fax	Fax	(44) 01796 - 473 599
Situation	Situation	

45 km N of Perth (pop. 123 495)
close to Pitlochry (Pop. 3 126)

Annual closure	Fermeture annnuelle	no
Weekly closure	Fermeture hebdomadaire	

Chances of snow during winter months

Fees main season
Tarifs haute saison 18 holes

	Week days Semaine	We/Bank holidays We/Férié
Individual Individuel	£ 25	£ 25
Couple Couple	£ 50	£ 50

Caddy	Caddy	on request
Electric Trolley	Chariot électrique	yes
Buggy	Voiturette	no
Clubs	Clubs	yes
Credit cards Cartes de crédit		no

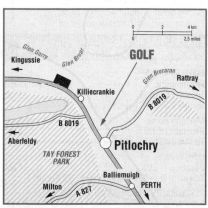

GOLF
Kingussie — Glen Garry — Glen Bruar
Rattray
Glen Breraran
Killiecrankie — B 8019
B 8019
Aberfeldy
Pitlochry
TAY FOREST PARK
Balliemuigh
Milton — A 827 — PERTH

0 ... 2 ... 4 km
0 ... 2,5 miles

Access Accès : Edinburgh M90 then A9 to Pitlochry.
Turn uphill at sign in middle of town.
Map 1 on page 407 Carte 1 Page 407

GOLF COURSE
PARCOURS

14/20

Site	Site	▰▰▰▰▰▱
Maintenance	Entretien	▰▰▰▰▱▱
Architect	Architecte	W. Fernie
Type	Type	mountain
Relief	Relief	▰▰▰▰▱▱
Water in play	Eau en jeu	▱▱▱▱▱▱
Exp. to wind	Exposé au vent	▰▱▱▱▱▱
Trees in play	Arbres en jeu	▰▰▰▱▱▱

Scorecard Carte de score	Chp. Chp.	Mens Mess.	Ladies Da.
Length Long.	5290	5290	5290
Par	69	69	72

Advised golfing ability
Niveau de jeu recommandé

0	12	24	36

Hcp required Handicap exigé   certificate

CLUB HOUSE & AMENITIES
CLUB HOUSE ET ANNEXES

6/10

Pro shop	Pro-shop	▰▰▰▱▱▱
Driving range	Practice	▰▰▱▱▱▱
Sheltered	couvert	no
On grass	sur herbe	yes
Putting-green	putting-green	yes
Pitching-green	pitching green	no

HOTEL FACILITIES
ENVIRONNEMENT HOTELIER

7/10

HOTELS HÔTELS

Pine Trees   Pitlochry
20 chambres, D £ 95   close
Tél (44) 01796 - 472 121, Fax (44) 01796 - 472 460

Dunfallandy House   Pitlochry
8 chambres, D £ 64   close
Tél (44) 01796 - 472 648, Fax (44) 01796 - 472 017

Green Park   Pitlochry
37 chambres, D £ 95   close
Tél (44) 01796 - 473 248, Fax (44) 01796 - 473 520

RESTAURANTS RESTAURANT

East Haugh House   Pitlochry
Tél (44) 01796 - 473 121   4 km

648

This course dominates the little village of Portpatrick from atop the cliffs overlooking the Irish sea, with views stretching to the distant Isle of Man, the Irish coast and the Mull of Kintyre. Although close to the ocean, this is not a dunes links, although the scrub and bushes are just as dangerous. Because of its location it is very exposed to the prevailing south-westerlies, and of course overcoming, or at least accepting, this element is essential, particularly when it comes to club selection. Make full allowance for side-winds or head-winds or any possible combination of the two. This is a pretty spot to spend a holiday, especially as the little 9-holer is ideal for beginners to cut their teeth or even for non-golfers in the family to hit a ball or two. It is also the opportunity to discover a little known region of Scotland.

Ce parcours domine le petit village de Portpatrick du haut des falaises dominant la mer d'Irlande, avec des vues dans le lointain sur l'Ile de Man, la côte irlandaise et le Mull of Kintyre. Il est proche de l'océan, mais ce n'est pas un links de dunes, bien que les bosquets et arbustes y jouent un rôle identique. A cause de sa situation, il est très exposé aux vents dominants de sud-ouest. Bien sûr, savoir maîtriser - ou au moins accepter - cet élément est ici une nécessité, notamment au moment du choix des clubs : il faut prévoir large par vent contre ou latéral, ou toutes combinaisons imaginables des deux. C'est un joli endroit où passer pendant les vacances, d'autant que le petit 9-trous est idéal pour aguerrir les débutants, voire initier les non-golfeurs de la famille. C'est aussi l'occasion de découvrir une région peu connue d'Ecosse...

Portpatrick Golf Club

Golf Course Road,
SCO - PORTPATRICK, STRANRAER, Wigtownshire DG9 8TB

Office	Secrétariat	(44) 01776 - 810 273
Pro shop	Pro-shop	(44) 01776 - 810 273
Fax	Fax	(44) 01776 - 810 811
Situation	Situation	

10 km from Stranraer (pop. 11 348)

Annual closure	Fermeture annnuelle	no
Weekly closure	Fermeture hebdomadaire	no

Fees main season	Tarifs haute saison	18 holes
	Week days Semaine	**We/Bank holidays** We/Férié
Individual Individuel	£ 18	£ 31
Couple Couple	£ 36	£ 62

Full days: £ 27 - £ 32 (weekends)

Caddy	Caddy	on request
Electric Trolley	Chariot électrique	no
Buggy	Voiturette	medical certificate
Clubs	Clubs	£ 6/18 holes

Credit cards Cartes de crédit
VISA - Eurocard - MasterCard - AMEX - DC

Access Accès : Glasgow, A77 through Ayr, Turnberry, to Stranraer, then A716 and A77 to Portpatrick.
Map 2 on page 408 Carte 2 Page 408

GOLF COURSE PARCOURS 15/20

Site	Site	
Maintenance	Entretien	
Architect	Architecte	C.W. Hunter
Type	Type	seaside course, parkland
Relief	Relief	
Water in play	Eau en jeu	
Exp. to wind	Exposé au vent	
Trees in play	Arbres en jeu	

Scorecard	Chp.	Mens	Ladies
Carte de score	Chp.	Mess.	Da.
Length Long.	5401	5061	4707
Par	70	70	70

Advised golfing ability	0	12	24	36
Niveau de jeu recommandé				

Hcp required Handicap exigé 24 Men, 36 Ladies

CLUB HOUSE & AMENITIES
CLUB HOUSE ET ANNEXES 6/10

Pro shop	Pro-shop	
Driving range	Practice	
Sheltered	couvert	no
On grass	sur herbe	yes
Putting-green	putting-green	yes
Pitching-green	pitching green	yes

HOTEL FACILITIES
ENVIRONNEMENT HOTELIER 7/10

HOTELS HÔTELS

Knockinaam Lodge — Portpatrick
10 rooms, D £ 150 — 8 km
Tel (44) 01776 - 810 471
Fax (44) 01776 - 810 435

Fernhill — Portpatrick
20 rooms, D £ 100 — 2 km
Tel (44) 01776 - 810 220
Fax (44) 01776 - 810 596

North West Castle — Stranraer
67 rooms, D £ 70 — 10 km
Tel (44) 01776 - 704 413, Fax (44) 01776 - 702 646

RESTAURANTS RESTAURANT

Knockinaam Lodge — Portpatrick
Tel (44) 01776 - 810 471 — 8 km

649

It has often been said that the finest turf in the world is to be found close to Solway Firth. Whatever, the grass at Powfoot does nothing to undermine that claim. And although the course is not specifically a links, the type of soil here means you play it as if it were. There is a lot of gorse to worry wayward hitters, although the fairways are wide enough for players to open their shoulders, as long as the wind behaves itself. Mid- and high-handicappers can rest assured: this is a friendly layout and they shouldn't be over-awed by the one or two blind shots. The surprises in store from off-target shots are more often pleasant than unpleasant. The better players will need to think harder to keep the ball straight and avoid the very many bunkers, which were laid out by James Braid. Need we say more? Excellent golfing.

On a souvent dit que l'on trouvait les meilleurs gazons du monde près du Solway Firth. Celui de Powfoot prouve en tout cas que ce n'est pas faux. Et bien que le parcours ne soit pas spécifiquement un links, la nature du sol fait qu'on le joue comme tel. Les ajoncs sont ici abondants pour inquiéter les joueurs imprécis, mais les fairways sont assez larges pour qu'ils oublient leurs craintes, tant que le vent ne souffle pas trop... Que les joueurs de handicap moyen ou élevé se rassurent, c'est un tracé des plus amicaux, et les quelques coups aveugles ne devraient pas trop les préoccuper : ils auront plus de bonnes surprises que de mauvaises avec leurs écarts imprévus ! Les meilleurs joueurs devront réfléchir davantage à garder la balle assez droite, à éviter les nombreux bunkers : James Braid les a disposés, il n'est pas nécessaire d'en dire plus. Une halte de qualité.

Powfoot Golf Club
Cummertrees
SCO - ANNAN, Dumfriesshire DG12 5QE

Office	Secrétariat	(44) 01461 - 700 276
Pro shop	Pro-shop	(44) 01461 - 700 327
Fax	Fax	(44) 01461 - 700 276
Situation	Situation	

19 km SE of Dumfries (pop. 21 164)

Annual closure	Fermeture annnuelle	no
Weekly closure	Fermeture hebdomadaire	no

Fees main season
Tarifs haute saison 18 holes

	Week days Semaine	We/Bank holidays We/Férié
Individual Individuel	£ 23	£ 23
Couple Couple	£ 46	£ 46
Full day: £ 30		

Caddy	Caddy	no
Electric Trolley	Chariot électrique	no
Buggy	Voiturette	no
Clubs	Clubs	no
Credit cards Cartes de crédit		VISA - JCB - Switch

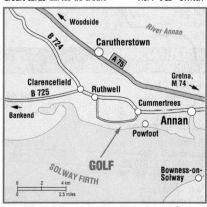

Access Accès : Glasgow, M74 and A74. Exit 18 after Lockerbie, B723 → Annan. B724 on right before Annan → Cummertrees. After 5 km (3 m.), pass under railway bridge, turn sharp left → Golf.
Map 2 on page 409 Carte 2 Page 409

650

GOLF COURSE
PARCOURS

16/20

Site	Site	
Maintenance	Entretien	
Architect	Architecte	James Braid
Type	Type	links
Relief	Relief	
Water in play	Eau en jeu	
Exp. to wind	Exposé au vent	
Trees in play	Arbres en jeu	

Scorecard Carte de score	Chp. Chp.	Mens Mess.	Ladies Da.
Length Long.	5710	5475	5010
Par	70	70	74

Advised golfing ability   0   12   24   36
Niveau de jeu recommandé
Hcp required   Handicap exigé   no

CLUB HOUSE & AMENITIES
CLUB HOUSE ET ANNEXES

6/10

Pro shop	Pro-shop	
Driving range	Practice	
Sheltered	couvert	
On grass	sur herbe	yes
Putting-green	putting-green	yes
Pitching-green	pitching green	yes

HOTEL FACILITIES
ENVIRONNEMENT HOTELIER

4/10

HOTELS HÔTELS
Cairndale   Dumfries
76 rooms, D £ 105   15 km
Tel (44) 01387 - 254 111
Fax (44) 01387 - 250 155

Station   Dumfries
32 rooms, D £ 80   15 km
Tél (44) 01387 - 254 316
Fax (44) 01387 - 250 388

RESTAURANTS RESTAURANT
Cairndale   Dumfries
Tel (44) 01387 - 254 111   15 km

PRESTWICK

This was the first course used for the British Open but was withdrawn from the course rotation in 1925 for being too short and perhaps, too, for a number of eccentric features such as the blind par-3 fifth hole or the second shot on the 17th, where the green is nowhere to be seen. But no lover of authentic golf will miss playing this delightful and one-of-a-kind links course which is kept in excellent condition. Like many courses in Scotland, it unwinds between a railway track and the sea. It has been lengthened since the days when there were only twelve holes but this has added to the course's variety if not its unity. The bunkers here are particularly tough, especially the famous Cardinal, which cuts hole N°3 in two. Prestwick thrives on hospitality (on week-days) and memories of the past that you can't and won't miss in the clubhouse.

Ce fut le premier parcours du British Open, mais il fut retiré de la rotation des parcours en 1925, pour sa longueur insuffisante, mais peut-être aussi quelques aspects excentriques comme le 5, un par 3 aveugle, ou le second coup du 17, où le green n'est pas plus visible. Mais aucun amoureux de golfeur authentique ne manquera de jouer ce links savoureux et unique en son genre, où l'entretien est d'excellente qualité. Comme beaucoup de parcours en Ecosse, il se déroule entre la voie ferrée et la mer. Il a été allongé depuis l'époque où il ne comptait que 12 trous, mais cela a contribué à ajouter à sa variété, sinon à son unité. Les bunkers ici sont particulièrement féroces, notamment le fameux Cardinal, qui coupe le 3 en deux parties. Prestwick cultive l'hospitalité (en semaine) et les souvenirs des temps passés, que vous ne manquerez pas au Club house.

Prestwick Golf Club

2 Links Road
SCO - PRESTWICK, Ayrshire KA9 1QG

Office	Secrétariat	(44) 01292 - 477 404
Pro shop	Pro-shop	(44) 01292 - 479 483
Fax	Fax	(44) 01292 - 477 255
Situation	Situation	

4 km N of Ayr (pop. 47 872)
50 km SW of Glasgow (pop. 662 853)

Annual closure	Fermeture annnuelle	no
Weekly closure	Fermeture hebdomadaire	no
Fees main season	Tarifs haute saison	18 holes

	Week days Semaine	We/Bank holidays We/Férié
Individual Individuel	—	—
Couple Couple	—	—

Restrictions for visitors (weekdays only):
ask for details

Caddy	Caddy	on request
Electric Trolley	Chariot électrique	yes
Buggy	Voiturette	no
Clubs	Clubs	yes

Credit cards Cartes de crédit
VISA - MasterCard - AMEX (Pro shop)

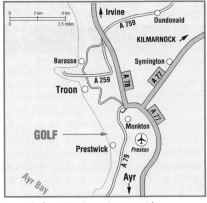

Access Accès : A77, take road to Prestwick,
Golf adjacent to railway station
Map 3 on page 410 Carte 3 Page 410

GOLF COURSE
PARCOURS

18/20

Site	Site	
Maintenance	Entretien	
Architect	Architecte	Unknown
Type	Type	links
Relief	Relief	
Water in play	Eau en jeu	
Exp. to wind	Exposé au vent	
Trees in play	Arbres en jeu	

Scorecard Carte de score	Chp. Chp.	Mens Mess.	Ladies Da.
Length Long.	6068	6068	0
Par	72	72	0

Advised golfing ability	0 12 24 36
Niveau de jeu recommandé	
Hcp required Handicap exigé	certificate

CLUB HOUSE & AMENITIES
CLUB HOUSE ET ANNEXES

6/10

Pro shop	Pro-shop	
Driving range	Practice	
Sheltered	couvert	no
On grass	sur herbe	yes
Putting-green	putting-green	yes
Pitching-green	pitching green	yes

HOTEL FACILITIES
ENVIRONNEMENT HOTELIER

7/10

HOTELS HÔTELS
Carlton Toby — Prestwick / close
37 rooms, D £ 80
Tel (44) 01292 - 476 811
Fax (44) 01292 - 474 845

Fairfield House — Ayr / 4 km
33 rooms, D £ 120
Tel (44) 01292 - 267 461
Fax (44) 01292 - 261 456

Pickwick — Ayr / 3 km
15 rooms, D £ 70
Tel (44) 01292 - 260 111
Fax (44) 01292 - 285 348

RESTAURANTS RESTAURANT
Fouters — Ayr / 4 km
Tel (44) 01292 - 261 391

651

The reputation of the other Prestwick course has doubtless helped keep this course out of the limelight. That might be so with non-Scots, but the local players know that this is not just another course but one that should be included when making an intelligent and exhaustive survey of good courses in Ayrshire. This is a genuine typical Scottish links laid out between the sea and a railway line, both of which come into play depending on where the wind is blowing from. While some of the natural bunkers can keep you out of the wind, you'll have to get out of them sooner or later to affront the tricky slopes of the huge greens, which are often firm and slick. With difficulties spread evenly over the 18 holes, don't put too much faith in the lengths written on the card. You can certainly play to your handicap here, but it's no walk-over either.

La réputation de l'autre Prestwick a sans doute maintenu celui-ci dans une certaine obscurité, au moins auprès des étrangers car les joueurs de la région savent qu'il ne s'agit pas là d'un parcours indifférent, et qu'il faut l'inclure dans une exploration intelligente et exhaustive des bons parcours de l'Ayrshire. Il s'agit là d'un vrai et typique "Scottish links," situé entre la mer et le chemin de fer, qui viennent tous deux en jeu selon que le vent souffle d'un côté ou de l'autre : émotions garanties. Et si certains bunkers naturels vous fourniront un abri, il faudra pourtant bien en sortir un jour pour affronter les subtils reliefs de greens vastes, souvent fermes et bien roulants. Avec des difficultés bien réparties tout au long des 18 trous, il ne faut pas se fier aux longueurs inscrites sur la carte. Certes, on peut jouer ici son handicap, mais ce n'est pas donné d'avance.

Prestwick St Nicholas Golf Club
Grangemuir Road
SCO - PRESTWICK, Ayrshire KA9 1SN

Office	Secrétariat	(44) 01292 - 477 608
Pro shop	Pro-shop	(44) 01292 - 477 608
Fax	Fax	(44) 01292 - 678 570
Situation	Situation	

3 km N of Ayr (pop. 47 872)
51 km SW of Glasgow (pop. 662 853)

Annual closure	Fermeture annnuelle	no
Weekly closure	Fermeture hebdomadaire	no

Fees main season	Tarifs haute saison	18 holes
	Week days Semaine	**We/Bank holidays** We/Férié
Individual Individuel	£ 30	£ 35
Couple Couple	£ 60	£ 70

Full weekdays: £ 45 - Visitors at weekends:
Sunday p.m. only

Caddy	Caddy	on request
Electric Trolley	Chariot électrique	no
Buggy	Voiturette	no
Clubs	Clubs	yes
Credit cards Cartes de crédit		no

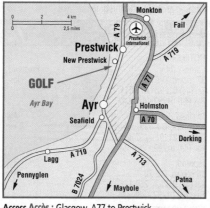

Access Accès : Glasgow, A77 to Prestwick
Map 3 on page 410 Carte 3 Page 410

GOLF COURSE
PARCOURS
16/20

Site	Site	
Maintenance	Entretien	
Architect	Architecte	Charles Hunter James Allan
Type	Type	links
Relief	Relief	
Water in play	Eau en jeu	
Exp. to wind	Exposé au vent	
Trees in play	Arbres en jeu	

Scorecard Carte de score	Chp. Chp.	Mens Mess.	Ladies Da.
Length Long.	5416	5416	4836
Par	69	69	70

Advised golfing ability
Niveau de jeu recommandé   0   12   24   36

Hcp required Handicap exigé   no

CLUB HOUSE & AMENITIES
CLUB HOUSE ET ANNEXES
6/10

Pro shop	Pro-shop	
Driving range	Practice	
Sheltered	couvert	no
On grass	sur herbe	no
Putting-green	putting-green	yes
Pitching-green	pitching green	no

HOTEL FACILITIES
ENVIRONNEMENT HOTELIER
7/10

HOTELS HÔTELS

Carlton Toby   Prestwick
37 rooms, D £ 80   close
Tel (44) 01292 - 476 811
Fax (44) 01292 - 474 845

Fairfield House   Ayr
33 rooms, D £ 120   4 km
Tel (44) 01292 - 267 461
Fax (44) 01292 - 261 456

Pickwick   Ayr
15 rooms, D £ 70   3 km
Tel (44) 01292 - 260 111
Fax (44) 01292 - 285 348

RESTAURANTS RESTAURANT

Fouters   Ayr
Tel (44) 01292 - 261 391   4 km

The Duke and Duchess of Roxburghe were personally involved in the decoration and style of the Sunlaws Hotel and everyone should visit their "home sweet home", i.e. the hundreds of rooms in the Floors Castle. Fishing, pigeon-shooting, riding and tennis are some of the activities on offer on this estate located very close to the English border, plus an 18-hole course designed by Dave Thomas alongside a river, following the natural relief of the estate and alternating stretches in the forest and the attractive park (the course is not always easy to walk). Modern in style with many different hazards, it demands target golf more than your usual bump and run shots. A high-class location for a sporting holiday in very pretty countryside. Excellent practice for your game.

Le Duc et la Duchesse de Roxburghe ont mis eux-même la main à la décoration et au style de l'hôtel Sunlaws, et l'on ne manquera pas de visiter leur "sweet home", c'est-à-dire les centaines de pièces du Floors Castle. Pêche, tir au pigeon, équitation et tennis sont quelques-unes des activités proposées dans ce domaine tout proche de la frontière avec l'Angleterre, auxquelles s'ajoute un 18 trous dessiné par Dave Thomas en bordure de rivière. Il suit les reliefs naturels du domaine et alterne passages en forêt et esthétique de parc (le parcours n'est pas toujours facile à marcher). De style moderne, avec de multiples obstacles, exigeant un jeu de cible plus que des coups roulés, c'est un lieu de vacances sportives de très bonne facture, dans un très joli paysage. Très beau practice !

The Roxburghe Golf Course

Sunlaws House Hotel
SCO - KELSO, Roxburghshire TD5 8JZ

Office	Secrétariat	(44) 01573 - 450 331
Pro shop	Pro-shop	(44) 01573 - 450 331
Fax	Fax	(44) 01573 - 450 611
Situation	Situation	

5 km SW of Kelso (pop. 6 167)

Annual closure	Fermeture annnuelle	no
Weekly closure	Fermeture hebdomadaire	no

Fees main season
Tarifs haute saison 18 holes

	Week days Semaine	We/Bank holidays We/Férié
Individual Individuel	£ 30	£ 40
Couple Couple	£ 60	£ 80

Caddy	Caddy	on request/£ 20
Electric Trolley	Chariot électrique	no
Buggy	Voiturette	£ 20/18 holes
Clubs	Clubs	£ 20/18 holes

Credit cards Cartes de crédit
VISA - MasterCard - AMEX - DC

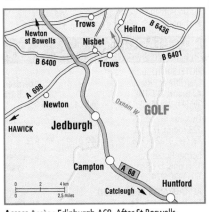

Access Accès : Edinburgh A68. After St Boswells and before Jedburgh, turn left on A698, Golf approx.10 km (6 m.).
Map 2 on page 409 Carte 2 Page 409

GOLF COURSE
PARCOURS 15/20

Site	Site	
Maintenance	Entretien	
Architect	Architecte	Dave Thomas
Type	Type	parkland
Relief	Relief	
Water in play	Eau en jeu	
Exp. to wind	Exposé au vent	
Trees in play	Arbres en jeu	

Scorecard	Chp.	Mens	Ladies
Carte de score	Chp.	Mess.	Da.
Length Long.	6471	5943	5167
Par	72	72	72

Advised golfing ability	0	12	24	36
Niveau de jeu recommandé				
Hcp required	Handicap exigé	24		

CLUB HOUSE & AMENITIES
CLUB HOUSE ET ANNEXES 7/10

Pro shop	Pro-shop	
Driving range	Practice	
Sheltered	couvert	no
On grass	sur herbe	yes
Putting-green	putting-green	yes
Pitching-green	pitching green	yes

653

HOTEL FACILITIES
ENVIRONNEMENT HOTELIER 7/10

HOTELS HÔTELS
Sunlaws House — Golf on site
22 rooms, D £ 145
Tel (44) 01573 - 450 331
Fax (44) 01573 - 450 611

Ednam House — Kelso 5 km
32 rooms, D £ 93
Tel (44) 01573 - 224 168
Fax (44) 01573 - 226 319

Dryburgh Abbey — St Boswells 10 km
24 rooms, D £ 110
Tel (44) 01835 - 822 261
Fax (44) 01835 - 823 945

RESTAURANTS RESTAURANT
Sunlaws House — Golf on site
Tel (44) 01573 - 450 331

A page of golf was written here, less than 2 miles from the "city of granite". Royal Aberdeen originated in 1780, was the world's sixth golf club and the first to adopt the 5-minute rule when looking for your ball. You probably won't lose yours as long as you play "Balgownie" (its more familiar name) carefully, avoid the bushes and tall grass and, in a word, stay in the fairway. You'll probably have a tougher time distinguishing the fairways amongst the dunes, keeping a solid swing when the wind blows a little too hard, or remembering to turn around at the 9th, as the holes that continue belong to Murcar. A little off the beaten golf-trotter track, this is one of the great classics for every links-collector, fun to play every time.

A seulement 3 km de la "ville de granit" s'est tournée une page du golf : le Royal Aberdeen trouve ses origines en 1780, c'est le sixième club du monde et le premier à avoir adopté la règle de cinq minutes pour chercher une balle. Mais on ne risque pas trop d'en perdre si l'on joue sagement "Balgownie" (comme on le connaît mieux), en évitant les buissons et les hautes herbes. Bref si l'on ne quitte pas le fairway. On perdra davantage la tête à repérer certains fairways parmi les dunes, à garder un swing solide quand le vent souffle un peu trop fort, ou si l'on oublie de revenir en arrière au 9 : les trous qui suivent appartiennent à Murcar. Un peu en dehors des sentiers touristiques du golf, c'est un des grands classiques quand on fait collection de links. Et c'est toujours un plaisir d'y revenir.

Royal Aberdeen Golf Club

Balgownie, Links Road, Bridge of Don
SCO- ABERDEEN AB23 8AT

Office	Secrétariat	(44) 01224 - 702 571
Pro shop	Pro-shop	(44) 01224 - 702 221
Fax	Fax	(44) 01224 - 826 591
Situation	Situation	

3 km from Aberdeen (pop. 204 885)

Annual closure	Fermeture annnuelle	no
Weekly closure	Fermeture hebdomadaire	no

Fees main season
Tarifs haute saison

		18 holes
	Week days Semaine	We/Bank holidays We/Férié
Individual Individuel	£ 45	£ 60
Couple Couple	£ 90	£ 120

Caddy	Caddy	on request
Electric Trolley	Chariot électrique	£ 6/18 holes
Buggy	Voiturette	no
Clubs	Clubs	£ 10/18 holes

Credit cards Cartes de crédit
VISA - Eurocard - MasterCard - JCB

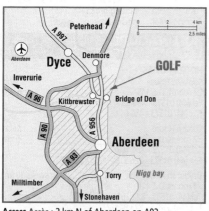

Access Accès : 3 km N of Aberdeen on A92.
Cross River Don, on right at first traffic lights,
on Links Road to golf course.
Map 1 on page 407 Carte 1 Page 407

GOLF COURSE
PARCOURS
18 /20

Site	Site	▬▬▬▬▬
Maintenance	Entretien	▬▬▬▬▬
Architect	Architecte	Bob Simpson
		James Braid
Type	Type	links
Relief	Relief	
Water in play	Eau en jeu	▬▬□□□
Exp. to wind	Exposé au vent	▬▬▬▬□
Trees in play	Arbres en jeu	▬□□□□

Scorecard	Chp.	Mens	Ladies
Carte de score	Chp.	Mess.	Da.
Length Long.	5915	5915	0
Par	70	70	0

Advised golfing ability	0	12	24	36
Niveau de jeu recommandé			▬▬▬	
Hcp required	Handicap exigé	24		

CLUB HOUSE & AMENITIES
CLUB HOUSE ET ANNEXES
7 /10

Pro shop	Pro-shop	▬▬▬▬▬
Driving range	Practice	▬□□□□
Sheltered	couvert	no
On grass	sur herbe	no
Putting-green	putting-green	yes
Pitching-green	pitching green	yes

HOTEL FACILITIES
ENVIRONNEMENT HOTELIER
8 /10

HOTELS HÔTELS
Marcliffe at Piffodels   Aberdeen
42 rooms, D £ 150   6 km
Tel (44) 01224 - 861 000, Fax (44) 01224 - 868 860

Quality   Bridge of Don
123 rooms, D £ 120   2 km
Tel (44) 01224 - 706 707, Fax (44) 01224 - 823 923

Corner House   Aberdeen
17 rooms, D £ 58   5 km
Tel (44) 01224 - 313 063

RESTAURANTS RESTAURANT
Courtyard on the Lane   Aberdeen
Tel (44) 01224 - 213 795   5 km

Silver Darling   Aberdeen
Tel(44) 01224 - 576 229   5 km

654

This club was apparently formed in 1735 and played the Brunstfield Links behind Edinburgh Castle. Today it lies adjoined to the Brunstfield Club (whose history runs parallel to this club) in the north-west of the city in magnificently laid out park landscape. The work of Old Tom Morris and then James Braid, this course has its own very personal character with alternating old trees and young saplings standing alone or in clumps. Accuracy is recommended, needless to say, as for many golfers this is a "second-shot" course where you have to be so efficient to hit the greens or save your score when you miss them. The putting surfaces are such a pleasure to play that sometimes you would like to putt a little more often. Well worth knowing, but not easy to reach.

Ce club aurait été formé en 1735, et aurait eu comme parcours les Bruntsfield Links derrière le Château d'Edinburgh. Toujours est-il qu'il est aujourd'hui mitoyen au Club de Bruntsfield (dont l'histoire est parallèle), au nord-ouest de la ville, et dans un paysage de parc magnifiquement sculpté. Dû aux crayons bien connus de Old Tom Morris, puis de James Braid, ce parcours possède un caractère très personnel, avec son alternance d'arbres anciens et de jeunes pousses, solitaires ou en bosquets. Inutile de dire que la précision est recommandée, car c'est pour beaucoup un parcours "de seconds coups," tant il faut être efficace pour rejoindre les greens, et pour sauver le score quand on les a manqués. Les surfaces de putting sont d'ailleurs un tel régal que l'on aimerait devoir faire plein de putts ! A connaître, mais l'accès n'y est pas facile.

Royal Burgess Golfing Society of Edinburgh

181 Whitehouse Road, Barnton
SCO - EDINBURGH EH4 6BY

Office	Secrétariat	(44) 0131 - 339 2075
Pro shop	Pro-shop	(44) 0131 - 339 6474
Fax	Fax	(44) 0131 - 339 3712
Situation	Situation	

5 km NW of Edinburgh centre (pop. 418 914)

Annual closure	Fermeture annnuelle	no
Weekly closure	Fermeture hebdomadaire	no
Fees main season	Tarifs haute saison	18 holes

	Week days Semaine	We/Bank holidays We/Férié
Individual Individuel	£ 30	—
Couple Couple	£ 60	—

Weekends: members only -
Restrictions for Ladies (ask before)

Caddy	Caddy	on request
Electric Trolley	Chariot électrique	yes
Buggy	Voiturette	no
Clubs	Clubs	yes
Credit cards Cartes de crédit		no

Access Accès : On Queensferry Road (A90). Turn right at Barnton roundabout on Whitehouse Road.
Map 3 on page 411 Carte 3 Page 411

GOLF COURSE
PARCOURS   16/20

Site	Site	▬▬▬
Maintenance	Entretien	▬▬
Architect	Architecte	Tom Morris James Braid
Type	Type	parkland
Relief	Relief	
Water in play	Eau en jeu	▬
Exp. to wind	Exposé au vent	▬▬
Trees in play	Arbres en jeu	▬▬▬

Scorecard Carte de score	Chp. Chp.	Mens Mess.	Ladies Da.
Length Long.	5910	5910	0
Par	71	71	0

Advised golfing ability Niveau de jeu recommandé	0	12	24	36
Hcp required Handicap exigé	24			

CLUB HOUSE & AMENITIES
CLUB HOUSE ET ANNEXES   7/10

Pro shop	Pro-shop	▬▬▬
Driving range	Practice	
Sheltered	couvert	no
On grass	sur herbe	yes
Putting-green	putting-green	yes
Pitching-green	pitching green	no

HOTEL FACILITIES
ENVIRONNEMENT HOTELIER   9/10

HOTELS HÔTELS
Edinburgh Capital   Edinburgh
111 rooms, D £ 100
Tel (44) 0131 - 535 9988, Fax (44) 0131 - 334 9712

Forte Posthouse   Edinburgh
204 rooms, D £ 70
Tel (44) 0131 - 334 0390, Fax (44) 0131 - 334 9237

Lodge   Edinburgh
12 rooms, D £ 80
Tel (44) 0131 - 337 3682, Fax (44) 0131 - 313 1700

RESTAURANTS RESTAURANT
Pompadour   Edinburgh
Tel (44) 0131 - 459 9988

Martins   Edinburgh
Tel(44) 0131 - 225 3106

655

Golf has been played here since about 1616, but it was Old Tom Morris and particularly the admirable Donald Ross who had the honour of really designing the course before John Sutherland added the final gloss. For untamed natural beauty and the challenge it offers any player, Royal Dornoch is one of the world's greatest courses. Located away from any large towns, this is a haven of peace and tranquillity in a unique atmosphere where you can chew long and hard over your technical flaws and the philosophy of golf. In fact it is only this isolation that has kept this gem of a course from being on the British Open rotation. In July you might often see some of the top champions who come here to re-acclimatise themselves to links golfing, the beginning and the end for every true golfer. Two of the greatest fans of Dornoch and none other than Tom Watson and Ben Crenshaw.

Le golf a été pratiqué sur le site depuis 1616 environ, mais ce fut à Old Tom Morris et surtout à l'admirable Donald Ross que revinrent l'honneur de dessiner vraiment le parcours, plus tard peaufiné par John Sutherland. Pour sa beauté sauvage et naturelle, pour les défis qu'il présente aux joueurs, Royal Dornoch est un des plus grands parcours au monde. Situé à l'écart des grandes villes, c'est un havre de paix à l'atmosphère unique où l'on peut méditer sur ses faiblesses techniques et la philosophie du jeu, et seul cet isolement a pu empêcher cette merveille d'être l'un des parcours du British Open. En juillet, il n'est pas rare d'y croiser de grands champions, venus se réacclimater au jeu sur les links, l'alpha et l'oméga du vrai golfeur. Tom Watson et Ben Crenshaw notamment n'ont pas été les moins élogieux sur "Dornoch."

Royal Dornoch Golf Club

Golf Road
SCO - DORNOCH, Sutherland IV25 3LW

Office	Secrétariat	(44) 01862 - 810 219
Pro shop	Pro-shop	(44) 01862 - 810 902
Fax	Fax	(44) 01862 - 810 792
Situation	Situation	

72 km N of Inverness (pop. 62 186)

Annual closure	Fermeture annnuelle	no
Weekly closure	Fermeture hebdomadaire	no

Fees main season
Tarifs haute saison 18 holes

	Week days Semaine	We/Bank holidays We/Férié
Individual Individuel	£ 40	£ 50
Couple Couple	£ 80	£ 100

Caddy	Caddy	on request/£ 20
Electric Trolley	Chariot électrique	£ 5/18 holes
Buggy	Voiturette	£ 20/18 holes
Clubs	Clubs	£ 10/18 holes

Credit cards Cartes de crédit
VISA - MasterCard

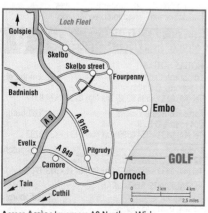

656

Access Accès : Inverness A9 North → Wick.
Golf on A949 to the east of the town.
Map 1 on page 406 Carte 1 Page 406

GOLF COURSE
PARCOURS

19/20

Site	Site	
Maintenance	Entretien	
Architect	Architecte	Tom Morris Donald Ross
Type	Type	links
Relief	Relief	
Water in play	Eau en jeu	
Exp. to wind	Exposé au vent	
Trees in play	Arbres en jeu	

Scorecard Carte de score	Chp. Chp.	Mens Mess.	Ladies Da.
Length Long.	5927	5630	5420
Par	70	70	76

Advised golfing ability		0	12	24	36
Niveau de jeu recommandé					
Hcp required	Handicap exigé	24 Men, 35 Ladies			

CLUB HOUSE & AMENITIES
CLUB HOUSE ET ANNEXES

7/10

Pro shop	Pro-shop	
Driving range	Practice	
Sheltered	couvert	no
On grass	sur herbe	yes
Putting-green	putting-green	yes
Pitching-green	pitching green	yes

HOTEL FACILITIES
ENVIRONNEMENT HOTELIER

7/10

HOTELS HÔTELS

Burghfield House 30 rooms, D £ 62 Tel (44) 01862 - 810 212 Fax (44) 01862 - 810 404	Dornoch
Dornoch Castle 17 rooms, D £ 66 Tel (44) 01862 - 810 216 Fax (44) 01862 - 810 981	Dornoch
Mallin House 10 rooms, D £ 52 Tel (44) 01862 - 810 335 Fax (44) 01862 - 810 810	Dornoch

RESTAURANTS RESTAURANT

Morangie House Hotel Tél (44) 01862 - 892 281	Tain, 10 km

ROYAL MUSSELBURGH

The club was founded in 1774 but we imagine that golf was played at the Old Musselburgh long before that. That course still exists but its original tenants left on one side to form the Muirfield club and on the other to open this course in 1925. This is not a links but a park course laid out around a majestic barony used as the clubhouse. James Braid designed the first layout, but in 1939 the Club asked Mungo park to give it a thorough overhaul. The very many trees form impressive lines of defence completed by some very effective bunkering to swallow any wayward shot. This is not a long course but there is only one par 5, something that generally speaking bothers the long-hitters on the look-out for "easy" birdies. This well-balanced course is a pleasant alternative when you have had enough of wind howling over the dunes.

Le Club a été fondé en 1774, mais on présume que le "Old Musselburgh" avait vu jouer au golf bien avant. Il existe toujours mais ses premiers locataires sont partis d'un côté créer Muirfield, et de l'autre celui-ci, en 1925. Il ne s'agit pas d'un links, mais d'un golf de parc, autour d'une majestueuse baronnie utilisée comme Club-house. James Braid créa le premier tracé, mais le Club demanda en 1939 à Mungo Park de le réviser sérieusement. Les nombreux arbres forment des défenses imposantes, complétées par un bunkering très efficace pour recueillir les coups un peu égarés. Ce n'est pas un parcours bien long, mais il n'a qu'un seul par 5, ce qui gêne en général beaucoup les frappeurs en quête de birdies faciles. Bien équilibré, c'est une bonne alternative quand on est un peu saoûlé par le vent dans les dunes.

Royal Musselburgh Golf Club

Prestongrange House
SCO - PRESTONPANS, East Lothian EH32 9RP

Office	Secrétariat	(44) 01875 - 810 276
Pro shop	Pro-shop	(44) 01875 - 810 139
Fax	Fax	(44) 01875 - 810 276
Situation	Situation	

13 km E of Edinburgh (pop. 418 914)

Annual closure	Fermeture annnuelle	no
Weekly closure	Fermeture hebdomadaire	no

Fees main season
Tarifs haute saison 18 holes

	Week days Semaine	We/Bank holidays We/Férié
Individual Individuel	£ 20	£ 20
Couple Couple	£ 40	£ 40

Full days: £ 35 (any)

Caddy	Caddy	on request/£ 25
Electric Trolley	Chariot électrique	£ 4/18 holes
Buggy	Voiturette	no
Clubs	Clubs	£ 6/18 holes
Credit cards Cartes de crédit		no

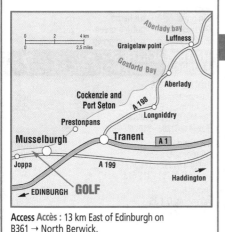

Access Accès : 13 km East of Edinburgh on
B361 → North Berwick.
Map 3 on page 411 Carte 3 Page 411

GOLF COURSE / PARCOURS — 16/20

Site	Site	
Maintenance	Entretien	
Architect	Architecte	James Braid Mungo Park
Type	Type	parkland
Relief	Relief	
Water in play	Eau en jeu	
Exp. to wind	Exposé au vent	
Trees in play	Arbres en jeu	

Scorecard Carte de score	Chp. Chp.	Mens Mess.	Ladies Da.
Length Long.	5701	5346	5048
Par	70	70	72

Advised golfing ability	0	12	24	36
Niveau de jeu recommandé				
Hcp required	Handicap exigé	certificate		

CLUB HOUSE & AMENITIES / CLUB HOUSE ET ANNEXES — 8/10

Pro shop	Pro-shop	
Driving range	Practice	
Sheltered	couvert	no
On grass	sur herbe	no
Putting-green	putting-green	yes
Pitching-green	pitching green	no

HOTEL FACILITIES / ENVIRONNEMENT HOTELIER — 7/10

HOTELS HÔTELS

Woodside Hotel — Musselburgh
11 rooms, D £ 74 — 2 km
Tel (44) 0131 - 665 0404

Granada Lodge — Musselburgh
44 rooms, D £ 45 — 5 km
Tel (44) 0131 - 653 6070
Fax (44) 0131 - 653 6106

RESTAURANTS RESTAURANT

Woodside Hotel — Musselburgh
Tel (44) 0131 - 665 0404 — 2 km

Caprice — Musselburgh
Tel (44) 0131 - 665 2991 — 2 km

657

The "Championship" course is the most remarkable of the five courses around Troon and has staged many a British Open. It also offers magnificent views of the Firth of Clyde towards the Isle of Arran and the Mull of Kintyre, lulling you into a false sense of tranquillity. On this tremendous links course, the outward 9 may seem comparatively easy, but the back 9 is one of the most horrendous in the world of golf. It is the wind that makes all the difference, especially as here it is often a side wind adding even more spice to the course. At the famous "postage-stamp" hole, the green can seem more like a pin-head when the wind is playing tricks. All those golfers who love Castles in Spain, huge trees bathed in sunlight and flattering scores can be on their way. Sure there's the Gulf Stream nearby, and sure you'll see more impressive dunes elsewhere, but this is no place for the mild or meek-hearted.

Le "Championship" est le plus remarquable des cinq parcours autour de Troon, il a été le théâtre de nombreux British Open. Il offre des vues magnifiques au-delà du Firth of Clyde vers l'Ile d'Arran et le Mull of Kintyre, dans une trompeuse tranquillité. Sur ce formidable links, l'aller peut paraître assez facile et le retour un des plus féroces au monde. Mais le vent fera la différence, d'autant qu'il est souvent en travers, et ajoute encore à l'intérêt du parcours : au fameux "Postage Stamp", le green est encore plus petit qu'un timbre-poste quand il souffle ! Que ceux qui aiment les châteaux en Espagne, les grands arbres baignés de soleil et les scores flatteurs passent leur chemin. Certes, le Gulf Stream passe par ici, certes, les dunes peuvent être encore plus impressionnantes ailleurs, mais on n'est jamais ici au royaume de la douceur.

Royal Troon Golf Club
SCO - TROON, Ayrshire KA10 6EP

Office	Secrétariat	(44) 01292 - 311 555
Pro shop	Pro-shop	(44) 01292 - 313 281
Fax	Fax	(44) 01292 - 318 204
Situation	Situation	

8 km N of Prestwick (pop. 13 705)
20 km N of Ayr (pop. 47 872)

Annual closure	Fermeture annnuelle	no
Weekly closure	Fermeture hebdomadaire	no

Fees main season
Tarifs haute saison — full day

	Week days Semaine	We/Bank holidays We/Férié
Individual Individuel	£ 110	—
Couple Couple	£ 220	—

Visitors: Monday, Tuesday, Thursday only.
Ladies on other course only !!!

Caddy	Caddy	on request/£ 15-25
Electric Trolley	Chariot électrique	no
Buggy	Voiturette	no
Clubs	Clubs	£ 25/18 holes
Credit cards Cartes de crédit		no

658

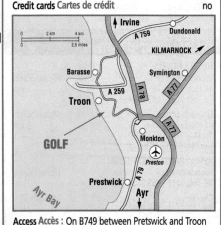

Access Accès : On B749 between Prestwick and Troon
Map 3 on page 410 Carte 3 Page 410

GOLF COURSE / PARCOURS — **19**/20

Site	Site	
Maintenance	Entretien	
Architect	Architecte	Willie Fernie
Type	Type	links
Relief	Relief	
Water in play	Eau en jeu	
Exp. to wind	Exposé au vent	
Trees in play	Arbres en jeu	

Scorecard Carte de score	Chp. Chp.	Mens Mess.	Ladies Da.
Length Long.	6458	6042	0
Par	71	71	74

Advised golfing ability Niveau de jeu recommandé	0	12	24	36
Hcp required	Handicap exigé	20		

CLUB HOUSE & AMENITIES / CLUB HOUSE ET ANNEXES — **7**/10

Pro shop	Pro-shop	
Driving range	Practice	
Sheltered	couvert	no
On grass	sur herbe	no
Putting-green	putting-green	yes
Pitching-green	pitching green	no

HOTEL FACILITIES / ENVIRONNEMENT HOTELIER — **7**/10

HOTELS HÔTELS

Marine Highland — Troon, close
66 rooms, D £ 120
Tel (44) 01292 - 314 444
Fax (44) 01292 - 316 922

Piersland House — Troon, close
19 rooms, D £ 95
Tel (44) 01292 - 314 747
Fax (44) 01292 - 315 613

Travel Inn — Prestwick, 4 km
40 rooms, D £ 35
Tel (44) 01292 - 678 262

RESTAURANTS RESTAURANT

Highgrove House — Troon, 3 km
Tel (44) 01292 - 312 511

SCOTSCRAIG

This is one of Scotland's oldest courses, whose reputation has not really benefited from the closeness of St Andrews, at least not with outsiders. The road that gets you here is nothing special, but when you reach the course, all that changes. A little links and a little inland with heather, this is a course that is none too tiring to play but one which requires a lot of concentration to play well. The wind plays a vital role, it must be said, but so do the deep bunkers and the well-contoured greens which, like the course as a whole, are in good condition. Scotscraig has been used as a qualifying course for the British Open, which speaks volumes for its quality as a test of golf, but this doesn't stop less experienced players from having a go themselves.

C'est un des plus anciens golfs d'Ecosse, dont la réputation n'a pas vraiment bénéficié de la proximité de ceux de St Andrews, en tout cas auprès des étrangers à la région. La route d'arrivée n'est pas merveilleuse, mais tout change dès que l'on arrive. Un peu links, un peu inland avec de la bruyère, c'est un parcours peu fatigant à jouer mais qui demande beaucoup d'attention pour être maîtrisé. Le vent y joue un rôle essentiel, faut-il le dire, mais aussi les profonds bunkers, les greens bien modelés et généralement bien préparés, comme du reste le parcours. Scotscraig a été utilisé comme parcours qualificatif pour le British Open, c'est le signe de sa qualité de test, mais que cela n'empêche pas les joueurs moins expérimentés de l'affronter.

Scotscraig Golf Club

Golf Road
SCO - TAYPORT, Fife DD6 9DZ

Office	Secrétariat	(44) 01382 - 552 515
Pro shop	Pro-shop	(44) 01382 - 552 855
Fax	Fax	(44) 01382 - 553 130
Situation	Situation	

16 km N of St Andrews (pop. 11 136)

Annual closure	Fermeture annnuelle	no
Weekly closure	Fermeture hebdomadaire	no

Fees main season
Tarifs haute saison 18 holes

	Week days Semaine	We/Bank holidays We/Férié
Individual Individuel	£ 27	£ 32
Couple Couple	£ 54	£ 64

Full weekday: £ 36

Caddy	Caddy	on request
Electric Trolley	Chariot électrique	no
Buggy	Voiturette	no
Clubs	Clubs	yes
Credit cards Cartes de crédit		no

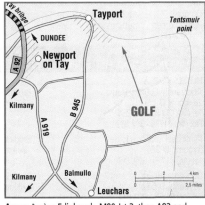

Access Accès : Edinburgh, M90 Jct 3, then A92 and A914 → Dundee. Before Tay Bridge, turn right to Tayport on B945. Golf signposted to left in Tayport.
Map 2 on page 409 Carte 2 Page 409

GOLF COURSE
PARCOURS

16/20

Site	Site	
Maintenance	Entretien	
Architect	Architecte	James Braid (1920s)
Type	Type	links, heathland
Relief	Relief	
Water in play	Eau en jeu	
Exp. to wind	Exposé au vent	
Trees in play	Arbres en jeu	

Scorecard Carte de score	Chp. Chp.	Mens Mess.	Ladies Da.
Length Long.	5960	5960	5960
Par	69	69	74

Advised golfing ability	0	12	24	36
Niveau de jeu recommandé				

Hcp required Handicap exigé certificate

CLUB HOUSE & AMENITIES
CLUB HOUSE ET ANNEXES

6/10

Pro shop	Pro-shop	
Driving range	Practice	
Sheltered	couvert	no
On grass	sur herbe	yes
Putting-green	putting-green	yes
Pitching-green	pitching green	no

HOTEL FACILITIES
ENVIRONNEMENT HOTELIER

6/10

HOTELS HÔTELS

Stakis Dundee		Dundee
104 rooms, D £ 90		7 km
Tel (44) 01382 - 22 9271		
Fax (44) 01382 - 200 072		
Shaftesbury		Dundee
12 rooms, D £ 70		7 km
Tel (44) 01382 - 669 216		
Fax (44) 01382 - 641 598		
Travel Inn		Dundee
40 rooms, D £ 40		7 km
Tel (44) 01382 - 20 3240		
Fax (44) 01382 - 568 431		

RESTAURANTS RESTAURANT

Stakis Dundee		Dundee
Tel (44) 01382 - 229 271		7 km

659

This is the one exception to our rule of featuring only 18-hole courses. Shiskine has only twelve but it is one of the most frequently visited courses by the world's golf designers. There is one blind shot on virtually each hole and signals in every direction telling players when it is safe to play. This is golf in its original pure style and enjoyment (but also with its own idiosyncrasies). The sheep are there to crop the sprinkler-free fairways, which haven't changed at all since the course first opened. That was when Willie Fernie brought the very best out of a space of land without even the most primitive excavator to call on. The greens are amazingly good, when you finally reach them. You need to play here a hundred times in order to fully understand the ins and outs of the course, but who's objecting...

C'est la seule exception à notre règle de ne signaler que des parcours de 18 trous. Le Shiskine n'a que douze trous, mais c'est un des parcours les plus visités par les architectes du monde entier. On trouve un coup aveugle sur pratiquement chaque trou, et des signaux dans tous les sens pour préciser aux joueurs quand ils peuvent jouer en toute sécurité. C'est ici le golf dans sa pureté et son plaisir originels (mais aussi ses excès baroques), avec des moutons pour tondre des fairways sans arrosage, qui n'ont pas bougé depuis la création. Alors, Willie Fernie avait tiré la quintessence d'un espace où il ne disposait pas du moindre engin de terrassement. Les greens y sont d'une surprenante qualité... quand on y parvient enfin. Il faut jouer ici cent fois pour comprendre toutes les astuces, mais on ne demande que çà...

Shiskine Golf & Tennis Club
Shiskine
SCO - BLACKWATERFOOT, Isle of Arran KA27 8 HA

Office	Secrétariat	(44) 01770 - 860 226
Pro shop	Pro-shop	(44) 01770 - 860 226
Fax	Fax	(44) 01770 - 860 205
Situation	Situation	

Isle of Arran (pop. 4 474)

Annual closure	Fermeture annnuelle	no
Weekly closure	Fermeture hebdomadaire	no

Fees main season
Tarifs haute saison 12 holes round

	Week days Semaine	We/Bank holidays We/Férié
Individual Individuel	£ 13	£ 18
Couple Couple	£ 26	£ 36

Caddy	Caddy	no
Electric Trolley	Chariot électrique	no
Buggy	Voiturette	no
Clubs	Clubs	no

Credit cards Cartes de crédit		no

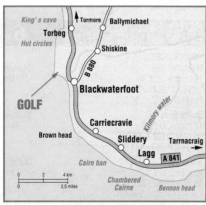

Access Accès : Ferry from Ardrossan to Brodick. Cross island via String Road (20 km) to village of Blackwaterfoot. **Map 2 on page 408** Carte 2 Page 408

GOLF COURSE / PARCOURS 17/20

Site	Site	
Maintenance	Entretien	
Architect	Architecte	Willie Fernie
Type	Type	links
Relief	Relief	
Water in play	Eau en jeu	
Exp. to wind	Exposé au vent	
Trees in play	Arbres en jeu	

Scorecard Carte de score	Chp. Chp.	Mens Mess.	Ladies Da.
Length Long.	2745	2745	2561
Par	42	42	44

Advised golfing ability
Niveau de jeu recommandé   0   12   24   36

Hcp required   Handicap exigé   no

CLUB HOUSE & AMENITIES / CLUB HOUSE ET ANNEXES 5/10

Pro shop	Pro-shop	
Driving range	Practice	
Sheltered	couvert	no
On grass	sur herbe	no
Putting-green	putting-green	yes
Pitching-green	pitching green	no

HOTEL FACILITIES / ENVIRONNEMENT HOTELIER 5/10

HOTELS HÔTELS

Auchrannie Country House — Brodick
26 rooms, D £ 80 — 20 km
Tel (44) 01770 - 302 234
Fax (44) 01770 - 302 812

Kilmichael Country House — Brodick
5 rooms, D £ 80 — 20 km
Tel (44) 01770 - 302 219

Dunvegan House — Brodick
10 rooms, D £ 52 — 20 km
Tel (44) 01770 - 302 811

RESTAURANTS RESTAURANT

Carraigh Mhor — Lamlash
Tel (44) 01770 - 600 453 — 22 km

660

SOUTHERNESS

18 6 5

A course for connoisseurs off the traditional golfing trail but your journey will be more than rewarded by a superb day out. This is one of the most recent links to date in Scotland, designed by Mackenzie Ross while he was working on Turnberry. The excellence of the design, very elaborate despite the course's natural look, quickly caught the attention of the better players, who appreciate the distinctive layout and the variety of challenge, with a special mention for the 12th, one of the finest par 4s in Scotland. Golfing here can be very enjoyable when the weather is fine, but that doesn't happen all that often. What's more, the holes are always running in different directions, thus calling for constant improvisation. Generally flat with only a few welcome slopes and difficulties that are always visible, this course is well worth the trip.

Un golf de connaisseurs, à l'écart des sentiers traditionnels, mais le déplacement sera récompensé par une superbe journée. C'est l'un des derniers en date des links d'Ecosse, dessiné par Mackenzie Ross alors qu'il ressuscitait Turnberry. La qualité du dessin, très travaillé malgré son apparence naturelle, a vite attiré l'attention des bons joueurs. Ils apprécient la distinction du tracé, la diversité des défis proposés, avec une mention particulière pour le 12, un des plus beaux par 4 d'Ecosse. Le golf peut ici être très plaisant quand le temps est calme, mais ce n'est pas si fréquent. De plus, les trous vont dans des directions toujours différentes, ce qui oblige à un sens constant de l'improvisation. Généralement plat, avec quelques ondulations bienvenues, mais des difficultés toujours visibles, ce parcours vaut le voyage.

Southerness Golf Club

Clubhouse
SCO - SOUTHERNESS, Dumfries, DG2 8AZ

Office	Secrétariat	(44) 01387 - 880 677
Pro shop	Pro-shop	(44) 01387 - 880 677
Fax	Fax	(44) 01387 - 880 644
Situation	Situation	

24 km S of Dumfries (pop. 21 164)

Annual closure	Fermeture annnuelle	no
Weekly closure	Fermeture hebdomadaire	no

Fees main season
Tarifs haute saison full day

	Week days Semaine	We/Bank holidays We/Férié
Individual Individuel	£ 28	£ 40
Couple Couple	£ 56	£ 80

Caddy	Caddy	on request
Electric Trolley	Chariot électrique	no
Buggy	Voiturette	no
Clubs	Clubs	yes

Credit cards Cartes de crédit
VISA - Eurocard - MasterCard

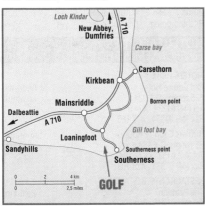

Loch Kindar
New Abbey, Dumfries
Carse bay
Carsethorn
Kirkbean
Mainsriddle
Borron point
Dalbeattie
A 710
Loaningfoot
Gill foot bay
Sandyhills
Southerness point
Southerness
GOLF

0   2   4 km
0   2,5 miles

Access Accès : Glasgow M74 to Abbington. Edinburgh A702 to Abington. Then A74 to Beattock and A701 to Dumfries. Then A710. After Kirkbean, left to Southerness. **Map 2 on page 409 Carte 2 Page 409**

GOLF COURSE / PARCOURS

18/20

Site	Site	
Maintenance	Entretien	
Architect	Architecte	Mackenzie Ross
Type	Type	links
Relief	Relief	
Water in play	Eau en jeu	
Exp. to wind	Exposé au vent	
Trees in play	Arbres en jeu	

Scorecard Carte de score	Chp. Chp.	Mens Mess.	Ladies Da.
Length Long.	5975	5556	5116
Par	69	69	73

Advised golfing ability Niveau de jeu recommandé	0 12 24 36
Hcp required Handicap exigé	28

CLUB HOUSE & AMENITIES / CLUB HOUSE ET ANNEXES

6/10

Pro shop	Pro-shop	
Driving range	Practice	
Sheltered	couvert	no
On grass	sur herbe	yes
Putting-green	putting-green	yes
Pitching-green	pitching green	no

HOTEL FACILITIES / ENVIRONNEMENT HOTELIER

5/10

HOTELS HÔTELS

Cairngill House — Sandyhills
7 rooms, D £ 50 — 5 km
Tel (44) 01387 - 780 681

Cairndale Hotel — Dumfries
76 rooms, D £ 80 — 24 km
Tel (44) 01387 - 254 111
Fax (44) 01387 - 250 555

Cavens House — Kirkbean
6 rooms, D £ 56 — 2 km
Tel (44) 01387 - 880 234

661

Notably shorter than its three most prestigious neighbours, the Eden Course is a very respectful course and probably, if not the most forthright then at least the least difficult of the three to figure out first time around, even though the wind will always be there to make things a little harder. This is a more conventional course, laid out in two loops of 9 holes, but the hazards are intelligently placed with a good number of bunkers from which average players will find escaping a little easier than on the other courses around here. Don't underestimate the Eden course, it can be fun playing here when everyone is swarming over the other courses of the golf factory that St Andrews has now become.

Notablement plus court que ses trois voisins les plus prestigieux, l'Eden Course est cependant un parcours plus qu'honorable, et probablement, sinon le plus franc des trois, du moins le moins difficile à déchiffrer au premier abord, même si le vent vient tout autant y compliquer les choses. De fait, c'est un parcours plus conventionnel, au point même d'avoir deux boucles de 9 trous, mais les obstacles sont intelligemment placés, les bunkers sont assez nombreux, mais les joueurs moyens pourront en sortir un jour (ce n'est pas toujours facile sur les autres parcours du site !). Il ne faut pas sous-estimer ce parcours, et le plaisir de jouer ici n'est pas négligeable quand tout le monde s'agite dans les autres ateliers de cette véritable usine à golf qu'est devenu St Andrews.

St Andrews Links

Pilmour Cottage
SCO - ST ANDREWS, Fife, KY16 9SF

Office	Secrétariat	(44) 01334 - 466 666
Pro shop	Pro-shop	
Fax	Fax	(44) 01334 - 477 036
Situation	Situation	

St Andrews (pop. 11 136)
30 km SE of Dundee (pop. 165 873)

Annual closure	Fermeture annnuelle	no
Weekly closure	Fermeture hebdomadaire	no

Fees main season
Tarifs haute saison 18 holes

	Week days Semaine	We/Bank holidays We/Férié
Individual Individuel	£ 16	£ 16
Couple Couple	£ 32	£ 32

Caddy	Caddy	£ 27
Electric Trolley	Chariot électrique	no
Buggy	Voiturette	no
Clubs	Clubs	£ 20/18 holes

Credit cards Cartes de crédit
VISA - Eurocard - MasterCard

662

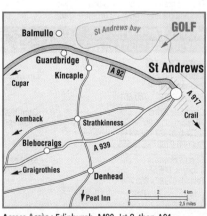

Access Accès : Edinburgh, M90, Jct 8, then A91 to St Andrews.
Map 3 on page 411 Carte 3 Page 411

GOLF COURSE PARCOURS 　 14/20

Site	Site	■■■■■□
Maintenance	Entretien	■■■■■
Architect	Architecte	Unknown
Type	Type	links
Relief	Relief	■■■
Water in play	Eau en jeu	■■
Exp. to wind	Exposé au vent	■■■■
Trees in play	Arbres en jeu	□

Scorecard Carte de score	Chp. Chp.	Mens Mess.	Ladies Da.
Length Long.	5588	5588	4987
Par	70	70	73

Advised golfing ability		0　12　24　36
Niveau de jeu recommandé		■■■■■
Hcp required	Handicap exigé	certificate

CLUB HOUSE & AMENITIES CLUB HOUSE ET ANNEXES 　 8/10

Pro shop	Pro-shop	■■■■■
Driving range	Practice	■■■■
Sheltered	couvert	14 mats
On grass	sur herbe	yes
Putting-green	putting-green	yes
Pitching-green	pitching green	yes

HOTEL FACILITIES ENVIRONNEMENT HOTELIER 　 8/10

HOTELS HÔTELS
Old Course Hotel 　 St Andrews
125 rooms, D £ 224 　 adjacent
Tel (44) 01334 - 474 371
Fax (44) 01334 - 477 668

Rufflets Country House 　 St Andrews
25 rooms, D £ 138 　 2 km
Tel (44) 01334 - 472 594
Fax (44) 01334 - 478 703

RESTAURANTS RESTAURANT
The Peat Inn 　 Peat Inn
Tel (44) 01334 - 840 206 　 8 km

Grange Inn 　 St Andrews
Tel (44) 01334 - 472 670 　 2 km

Cellar 　 Ansruther
Tel (44) 01333 - 310 378 　 17 km

Having celebrated its centenary in 1997, the Jubilee Course has been given a recent face-lift and is now the longest course at St Andrews. Although laid out in a single stretch with no return to the Club House at the 9th, there are no double fairways. The course is a little more hilly and gives some pretty viewpoints in a region which is rather flat. There is little in the way of vegetation on the holes close to the sea if you except tall grass, but this layout requires accurate driving and a lot of concentration. Like the others, the course is run by St Andrews Links Management and the Links Trust which built a very well equipped clubhouse reserved for visitors. Needless to say any trip should be organised in advance, especially between April and September.

Centenaire en 1997, le "Jubilee" a bénéficié d'une récente cure de rajeunissement qui en a fait le plus long de St Andrews. On ne trouve pas ici les fameux double fairways, bien que le parcours se déroule aussi d'un seul trait, sans retour au Club-house au 9. On trouve aussi davantage de relief, et donc quelques jolis points de vue dans une région somme toute peu accidentée. Les trous proches de la mer ont une végétation assez limitée, les hautes herbes mises à part, mais l'ensemble demande des drives précis, et généralement beaucoup d'attention. Comme les autres, ce parcours est géré par le St Andrews Links Management, et le Links Trust, qui a construit un Club-house de très bien équipé, et réservé aux visiteurs. Inutile de dire qu'il est nécessaire d'organiser son voyage à l'avance, surtout d'avril à septembre.

St Andrews Links

Pilmour Cottage
SCO - ST ANDREWS, Fife, KY16 9SF

Office	Secrétariat	(44) 01334 - 466 666
Pro shop	Pro-shop	
Fax	Fax	(44) 01334 - 477 036
Situation	Situation	

St Andrews (pop. 11 136)
30 km SE of Dundee (pop. 165 873)

Annual closure	Fermeture annnuelle	no
Weekly closure	Fermeture hebdomadaire	no

Fees main season
Tarifs haute saison 18 holes

	Week days Semaine	We/Bank holidays We/Férié
Individual Individuel	£ 20	£ 20
Couple Couple	£ 40	£ 40

Caddy	Caddy	£ 27
Electric Trolley	Chariot électrique	no
Buggy	Voiturette	no
Clubs	Clubs	£ 20/18 holes

Credit cards Cartes de crédit
VISA - Eurocard - MasterCard

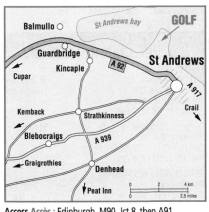

Access Accès : Edinburgh, M90, Jct 8, then A91 to St Andrews.
Map 3 on page 411 Carte 3 Page 411

GOLF COURSE
PARCOURS

16/20

Site	Site	■■■■■■□
Maintenance	Entretien	■■■■■■□
Architect	Architecte	Unknown
		Donald Steel
Type	Type	links
Relief	Relief	■■□□□□
Water in play	Eau en jeu	□□□□□□
Exp. to wind	Exposé au vent	■■■■■□
Trees in play	Arbres en jeu	□□□□□□

Scorecard Carte de score	Chp. Chp.	Mens Mess.	Ladies Da.
Length Long.	6218	5150	5525
Par	72	69	75

Advised golfing ability		0 12 24 36
Niveau de jeu recommandé		■■■■■□
Hcp required	Handicap exigé	certificate

CLUB HOUSE & AMENITIES
CLUB HOUSE ET ANNEXES

8/10

Pro shop	Pro-shop	■■■■■■□
Driving range	Practice	■■■■■□
Sheltered	couvert	14 mats
On grass	sur herbe	yes
Putting-green	putting-green	yes
Pitching-green	pitching green	yes

HOTEL FACILITIES
ENVIRONNEMENT HOTELIER

8/10

HOTELS HÔTELS
Old Course Hotel — St Andrews adjacent
125 rooms, D £ 224
Tel (44) 01334 - 474 371
Fax (44) 01334 - 477 668

Rufflets Country House — St Andrews 2 km
25 rooms, D £ 138
Tel (44) 01334 - 472 594
Fax (44) 01334 - 478 703

RESTAURANTS RESTAURANT
The Peat Inn — Peat Inn 8 km
Tel (44) 01334 - 840 206

Grange Inn — St Andrews 2 km
Tel (44) 01334 - 472 670

Cellar — Ansruther 17 km
Tel (44) 01333 - 310 378

663

Fortunately, there are several other excellent golf courses at St Andrews when it is impossible to play the Old Course. The New Course is one of them and does not settle for playing second fiddle to its illustrious neighbour. Some local players even consider this their favourite course. At all events it is a very demanding layout, rather similar to the Old Course in its general physiognomy and the way it demands technical skill and powers of invention. Here you don't play the club you need for such and such a distance, rather the club that will roll the ball up to the pin. Hazard-wise there are no trees, naturally, only threatening thick gorse and bunkers like those on the Old Course which collect any ball coming their way. The greens are huge and undulating and the turf a pleasure to walk and play on.

Heureusement, quand il est impossible de jouer le "Old Course", il reste plusieurs excellents autres parcours à St Andrews. Le "New" est de ceux-là, et c'est bien plus que le second violon de son voisin géographique immédiat. On trouve même des joueurs locaux pour en faire leur favori ! C'est en tout cas un parcours très exigeant, assez proche de son aîné pour sa physionomie générale et pour ce qu'il réclame de qualités techniques et de capacités d'invention. Ici, on ne joue pas le club qu'il faut pour telle distance, mais celui qui fera arriver la balle en roulant jusqu'au drapeau. Côté obstacles, pas d'arbres bien sûr, mais des ajoncs menaçants et denses, et aussi des bunkers comme ceux du "Old", qui recueillent toutes les balles qui passent aux alentours. Les greens sont très vastes et ondulés, et le gazon un plaisir à fouler et à jouer.

St Andrews Links

Pilmour Cottage
SCO - ST ANDREWS, Fife, KY16 9SF

Office	Secrétariat	(44) 01334 - 466 666
Pro shop	Pro-shop	
Fax	Fax	(44) 01334 - 477 036
Situation	Situation	

St Andrews (pop. 11 136)
30 km SE of Dundee (pop. 165 873)

Annual closure	Fermeture annnuelle	no
Weekly closure	Fermeture hebdomadaire	no

Fees main season
Tarifs haute saison 18 holes

	Week days Semaine	We/Bank holidays We/Férié
Individual Individuel	£ 24	£ 24
Couple Couple	£ 48	£ 48

Caddy	Caddy	£ 27
Electric Trolley	Chariot électrique	no
Buggy	Voiturette	no
Clubs	Clubs	£ 20/18 holes

Credit cards Cartes de crédit
VISA - Eurocard - MasterCard

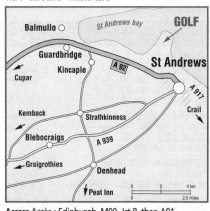

Access Accès : Edinburgh, M90, Jct 8, then A91 to St Andrews.
Map 3 on page 411 Carte 3 Page 411

GOLF COURSE PARCOURS 17/20

Site	Site	
Maintenance	Entretien	
Architect	Architecte	Unknown
Type	Type	links
Relief	Relief	
Water in play	Eau en jeu	
Exp. to wind	Exposé au vent	
Trees in play	Arbres en jeu	

Scorecard Carte de score	Chp. Chp.	Mens Mess.	Ladies Da.
Length Long.	6038	6038	5479
Par	71	71	76

Advised golfing ability   0   12   24   36
Niveau de jeu recommandé
Hcp required   Handicap exigé   no

CLUB HOUSE & AMENITIES
CLUB HOUSE ET ANNEXES 8/10

Pro shop	Pro-shop	
Driving range	Practice	
Sheltered	couvert	14 mats
On grass	sur herbe	yes
Putting-green	putting-green	yes
Pitching-green	pitching green	yes

HOTEL FACILITIES
ENVIRONNEMENT HOTELIER 8/10

HOTELS HÔTELS
Old Course Hotel
125 rooms, D £ 224
Tel (44) 01334 - 474 371
Fax (44) 01334 - 477 668
St Andrews
adjacent

Rufflets Country House
25 rooms, D £ 138
Tel (44) 01334 - 472 594
Fax (44) 01334 - 478 703
St Andrews
2 km

RESTAURANTS RESTAURANT
The Peat Inn
Tel (44) 01334 - 840 206
Peat Inn
8 km

Grange Inn
Tel (44) 01334 - 472 670
St Andrews
2 km

Cellar
Tel (44) 01333 - 310 378
Ansruther
17 km

664

ST ANDREWS OLD COURSE

	18	8	8

Is there anything left to write about the Old Course? The world's most famous venue is a public course even though you do need to be patient if you want to play here. It is well thought of to say that this is the greatest course in the British Isles, so often in the public eye that when you come here for the first time you get the impression you have already played it. Be wise and take a caddy, as the devilish subtleties, traps, double fairways and double greens make every decision a tough one. The work of no real designer, the Old Course has been shaped by the passing centuries, the wind, champions and green-keepers. The atmosphere alone is enough to intimidate or even terrorise amateurs stepping onto the first tee. But if you disregard the "religiousness" of this hallowed site there are, dare we say it, many more challenging links courses when the weather is calm (may the gods of golf forgive us). You cannot not play the Old Course.

Est-il encore possible d'écrire sur l'Old Course ? Le plus célèbre parcours du monde est un golf public, même s'il faut de la patience pour pouvoir le jouer. Il est bien vu de dire que c'est le plus grand parcours des Iles Britanniques, tellement montré qu'on a l'impression de l'avoir déjà joué quand on vient pour la première fois. Mais il reste prudent de prendre un caddie car ses diaboliques subtilités, ses pièges, ses double fairways et double greens rendent difficiles toutes les décisions. Sans véritable architecte, le "Old" a été admirablement façonné par les siècles, le vent, les champions, les green-keepers, et rien que son atmosphère rend les amateurs sinon terrorisés, du moins intimidés au départ du 1. Si l'on fait abstraction de la "religiosité du lieu", il est des links bien plus exigeants, quand le temps est calme. Mais a t-on le droit de le dire sans aller en enfer ? L'Old Course est inévitable.

St Andrews Links
Pilmour Cottage
SCO - ST ANDREWS, Fife, KY16 9SF

Office	Secrétariat	(44) 01334 - 466 666
Pro shop	Pro-shop	
Fax	Fax	(44) 01334 - 477 036
Situation	Situation	

St Andrews (pop. 11 136)
30 km SE of Dundee (pop. 165 873)

Annual closure	Fermeture annnuelle	no
Weekly closure	Fermeture hebdomadaire	Sunday

Fees main season
Tarifs haute saison 18 holes

	Week days Semaine	We/Bank holidays We/Férié
Individual Individuel	£ 72	£ 72
Couple Couple	£ 144	£ 144

Caddy	Caddy	£ 27
Electric Trolley	Chariot électrique	no
Buggy	Voiturette	no
Clubs	Clubs	£ 20/18 holes

Credit cards Cartes de crédit
VISA - Eurocard - MasterCard

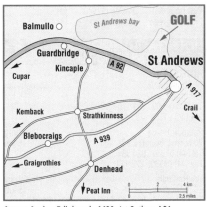

Access Accès : Edinburgh, M90, Jct 8, then A91 to St Andrews.
Map 3 on page 411 Carte 3 Page 411

GOLF COURSE
PARCOURS
18/20

Site	Site	
Maintenance	Entretien	
Architect	Architecte	Unknown
Type	Type	links
Relief	Relief	
Water in play	Eau en jeu	
Exp. to wind	Exposé au vent	
Trees in play	Arbres en jeu	

Scorecard Carte de score	Chp. Chp.	Mens Mess.	Ladies Da.
Length Long.	6300	6004	5512
Par	72	72	76

Advised golfing ability   0 12 24 36
Niveau de jeu recommandé
Hcp required   Handicap exigé   certificate

CLUB HOUSE & AMENITIES
CLUB HOUSE ET ANNEXES
8/10

Pro shop	Pro-shop	
Driving range	Practice	
Sheltered	couvert	14 mats
On grass	sur herbe	yes
Putting-green	putting-green	yes
Pitching-green	pitching green	yes

665

HOTEL FACILITIES
ENVIRONNEMENT HOTELIER
8/10

HOTELS HÔTELS
Old Course Hotel   St Andrews
125 rooms, D £ 224   adjacent
Tel (44) 01334 - 474 371
Fax (44) 01334 - 477 668

Rufflets Country House   St Andrews
25 rooms, D £ 138   2 km
Tel (44) 01334 - 472 594
Fax (44) 01334 - 478 703

RESTAURANTS RESTAURANT
The Peat Inn   Peat Inn
Tel (44) 01334 - 840 206   8 km

Grange Inn   St Andrews
Tel (44) 01334 - 472 670   2 km

Cellar   Ansruther
Tel (44) 01333 - 310 378   17 km

The clubhouse is not as comfortable and facilities not as comprehensive as continental golfers prefer, but this course is so far off the beaten track that you don't really mind. It lies on a sort of platform atop some often wind-swept cliffs. When it is stormy, just settle for the view. By contrast when the sun shines, you'll see that the difficulties are more psychological than real and there are enough of them for the designer not to have added any more. This is evidently not a course for beginners, who would be best advised to take the day off, pull someone's cart or take a lesson or two. Basically, this has to be one of the courses where playing to your handicap is the toughest, even though the course is not long. There are seven par 3s, each one a real handful.

Le Clubhouse n'est pas aussi confortable et les services pas aussi complets que les golfeurs continentaux le souhaitent, mais ce parcours semble tellement à l'écart du monde qu'on ne se pose pas ces questions. Il est situé sur une sorte de plate-forme au sommet des falaises, souvent très ventée : les jours de tempête, il faut se contenter de regarder. En revanche, par beau temps, on peut apprécier que les difficultés sont encore plus psychologiques que réelles. D'ailleurs, elles sont assez nombreuses au naturel pour que l'architecte n'en ait pas rajouté. Evidemment, ce n'est pas un parcours pour débutants : ce jour-là, ils tireront le chariot et prendront une leçon. En fin de compte, c'est sans doute un des parcours où il est le plus difficile de jouer son handicap, bien qu'il ne soit pas long... Il y a sept par 3, pas faciles.

Stonehaven Golf Club

Cowie
SCO - STONEHAVEN, Aberdeenshire AB39 3RH

Office	Secrétariat	(44) 01569 - 762 124
Pro shop	Pro-shop	
Fax	Fax	(44) 01569 - 765 973
Situation	Situation	

25 km S of Aberdeen (pop. 204 885)

Annual closure	Fermeture annnuelle	no
Weekly closure	Fermeture hebdomadaire	no

Fees main season
Tarifs haute saison — full day

	Week days Semaine	We/Bank holidays We/Férié
Individual Individuel	£ 29	£ 29
Couple Couple	£ 58	£ 58

£ 18 after 1.30 pm - No visitors on Saturdays

Caddy	Caddy	no
Electric Trolley	Chariot électrique	no
Buggy	Voiturette	no
Clubs	Clubs	no
Credit cards Cartes de crédit		no

666

Access Accès : A92 S of Aberdeen, Golf 1.5 km (1 m.) before Stonehaven.
Map 1 on page 407 Carte 1 Page 407

GOLF COURSE
PARCOURS — **13**/20

Site	Site	▬▬▬▬
Maintenance	Entretien	▬▬▬▬
Architect	Architecte	George Duncan
Type	Type	seaside course
Relief	Relief	▬▬▬
Water in play	Eau en jeu	▬
Exp. to wind	Exposé au vent	▬▬▬▬▬
Trees in play	Arbres en jeu	▬▬

Scorecard Carte de score	Chp. Chp.	Mens Mess.	Ladies Da.
Length Long.	4664	4390	4103
Par	66	64	68

Advised golfing ability Niveau de jeu recommandé	0	12	24	36
Hcp required Handicap exigé	certificate			

CLUB HOUSE & AMENITIES
CLUB HOUSE ET ANNEXES — **5**/10

Pro shop	Pro-shop	▬
Driving range	Practice	▬▬▬
Sheltered	couvert	no
On grass	sur herbe	no
Putting-green	putting-green	yes
Pitching-green	pitching green	yes

HOTEL FACILITIES
ENVIRONNEMENT HOTELIER — **5**/10

HOTELS HÔTELS

Muchalls Castle — Stonehaven
8 rooms, D £ 120 — 5 km
Tel (44) 01569 - 731 170
Fax (44) 01569 - 731 480

Raemoir House — Banchory
20 rooms, from D £ 85 — 15 km
Tel (44) 01330 - 824 884
Fax (44) 01330 - 822 171

Tor-Na-Coille — Banchory
24 rooms, from D £ 76 — 15 km
Tel (44) 01330 - 822 242, Fax (44) 01330 - 824 012

RESTAURANTS RESTAURANT

Lairhillock — Netherley
Tel (44) 01569 - 730 001 — 10 km

STRATHAVEN

15	5	6

Located some 30 miles from Glasgow, this is one of those gems tucked away in the west of Scotland. It is an inland course, often with a lot of heather, which winds around the very many trees here. The layout was extended to 18 holes in 1965 in a style that is very much in keeping with the original course. Bunkers are strategically located and the rough very penalising, both of which call for careful game strategy. For many, this is a course for accurate drivers, sometimes a little treacherous, which needs to be played several times over before getting to grips with the traps and appreciating its many qualities. Even when you reach the very tricky greens, you are still not through because you need a magic putter here to pick up strokes. Many high-level tournaments have been played here, a token of the course's overall excellence.

A quelques 45 km de Glasgow, c'est un des petits bijoux cachés à l'ouest de l'Ecosse. Parcours "inland," souvent en terre de bruyère, il est insinué entre les nombreux arbres du site. Le tracé a été porté à 18 trous en 1965, dans un style qui reste très cohérent avec l'original. Les bunkers sont stratégiquement placés et le rough très pénalisant, ce qui oblige à bien réfléchir sur la tactique à mettre en oeuvre. C'est pour beaucoup un parcours de drivers précis, parfois un peu traître, et il faut jouer plusieurs fois pour en comprendre à la fois les pièges et en savourer toutes les qualités. Et une fois arrivé sur des greens très subtils, le travail n'est pas fini, il faut un toucher d'orfèvre pour y gagner des points. De nombreux bons tournois ont été disputés ici, c'est une marque de qualité.

Strathaven Golf Club
Overton Avenue, Glasgow Road
SCO - STRATHAVEN, Strathclyde, ML10 6NL

Office	Secrétariat	(44) 01357 - 520 421
Pro shop	Pro-shop	(44) 01357 - 521 812
Fax	Fax	(44) 01357 - 520 421
Situation	Situation	

12 km SE of East Kilbride (pop. 73 378)

Annual closure	Fermeture annnuelle	no
Weekly closure	Fermeture hebdomadaire	no

Fees main season
Tarifs haute saison — full day

	Week days Semaine	We/Bank holidays We/Férié
Individual Individuel	£ 32	—
Couple Couple	£ 64	—

Weekends: members only

Caddy	Caddy	no
Electric Trolley	Chariot électrique	no
Buggy	Voiturette	no
Clubs	Clubs	no

Credit cards Cartes de crédit — no

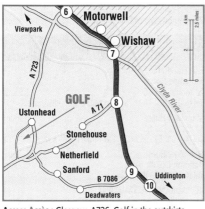

Access Accès : Glasgow, A726. Golf in the outskirts of Strathaven city.
Map 3 on page 410 Carte 3 Page 410

GOLF COURSE
PARCOURS
15/20

Site	Site	▬▬▬
Maintenance	Entretien	▬▬▬
Architect	Architecte	Willie Fernie J.R. Stutt
Type	Type	parkland
Relief	Relief	▬
Water in play	Eau en jeu	▬
Exp. to wind	Exposé au vent	▬▬
Trees in play	Arbres en jeu	▬▬▬

Scorecard Carte de score	Chp. Chp.	Mens Mess.	Ladies Da.
Length Long.	5665	5665	5066
Par	71	71	73

Advised golfing ability — 0   12   24   36
Niveau de jeu recommandé
Hcp required Handicap exigé — 28 Men, 36 Ladies

CLUB HOUSE & AMENITIES
CLUB HOUSE ET ANNEXES
5/10

Pro shop	Pro-shop	▬▬▬
Driving range	Practice	▬
Sheltered	couvert	no
On grass	sur herbe	no
Putting-green	putting-green	yes
Pitching-green	pitching green	no

667

HOTEL FACILITIES
ENVIRONNEMENT HOTELIER
6/10

HOTELS HÔTELS
Strathaven Hotel — Strathaven
22 rooms, D £ 75 — 2 km
Tel (44) 01357 - 521 778

Stakis East Kilbride — East Kilbride
73 rooms, D £ 90 — 5 km
Tel (44) 01357 - 36 300, Fax (44) 01357 - 33 552

Stuart — East Kilbride
38 rooms, D £ 75 — 2 km
Tel (44) 01357 - 21 161, Fax (44) 01357 - 64 410

RESTAURANTS RESTAURANT
Simpsons (Stakis) — East Kilbride
Tel (44) 01357 - 36 300 — 5 km

Waterside Inn — Strathaven

TAIN

17	6	6

Although it doesn't have the aura of Dornoch, Tain is worth much more than just a casual visit. All the more so in that green-keeping here is on a par with that found at "posher" courses. The site is superb and very quiet and the alternating heather and seaside holes produce a variety of landscapes, but playing here always requires a shrewd brain. Nothing is given away and players constantly have to adapt to new problems. The greens are never very large and the tricky breaks can be disastrous if you're not really careful. Ongoing work in the clubhouse should enhance still further the enjoyment of playing here, especially considering the value for money and warm welcome.

Sans avoir l'aura de Dornoch, Tain mérite néanmoins bien plus qu'un regard distrait. Et d'autant plus que l'entretien rivalise généralement avec celui de parcours plus huppés. Le site en est superbe et très tranquille, l'alternance de trous de links et de trous dans la bruyère apporte une variété de paysages, mais le jeu doit constamment être réfléchi. Rien n'est donné, et le joueur doit sans cesse s'adapter à de nouveaux problèmes. Les greens ne sont jamais très grands, et leurs subtiles ondulations peuvent provoquer des désastres si l'on n'y prête pas attention. Les travaux en cours au Club house devraient augmenter encore le plaisir que l'on éprouve ici, d'autant que le rapport qualité-prix-accueil est très favorable !

Tain Golf Club

Chapel Road
SCO - TAIN, Ross-shire, IV19 1PA

Office	Secrétariat	(44) 01862 - 892 314
Pro shop	Pro-shop	(44) 01862 - 893 313
Fax	Fax	
Situation	Situation	

56 km N of Inverness (pop. 62 186)
1 km of Tain (pop. 4 540)

Annual closure	Fermeture annnuelle	no
Weekly closure	Fermeture hebdomadaire	no

Fees main season
Tarifs haute saison 18 holes

	Week days Semaine	We/Bank holidays We/Férié
Individual Individuel	£ 20	£ 24
Couple Couple	£ 40	£ 48

Caddy	Caddy	on request
Electric Trolley	Chariot électrique	no
Buggy	Voiturette	£ 15/18 holes
Clubs	Clubs	no

Credit cards Cartes de crédit
VISA - MasterCard

668

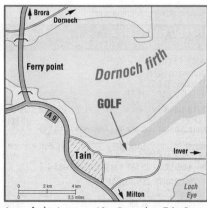

Access Accès : Inverness, A9 → Dornoch to Tain. From Tain town centre, down Castle Brae over railway, past cemetery **Map 1 on page 406** Carte 1 Page 406

GOLF COURSE
PARCOURS

17/20

Site	Site	
Maintenance	Entretien	
Architect	Architecte	Tom Morris
Type	Type	links, heathland
Relief	Relief	
Water in play	Eau en jeu	
Exp. to wind	Exposé au vent	
Trees in play	Arbres en jeu	

Scorecard Carte de score	Chp. Chp.	Mens Mess.	Ladies Da.
Length Long.	5743	5471	5142
Par	70	70	73

Advised golfing ability
Niveau de jeu recommandé 0 12 24 36

Hcp required Handicap exigé no

CLUB HOUSE & AMENITIES
CLUB HOUSE ET ANNEXES

6/10

Pro shop	Pro-shop	
Driving range	Practice	
Sheltered	couvert	no
On grass	sur herbe	no
Putting-green	putting-green	yes
Pitching-green	pitching green	yes

HOTEL FACILITIES
ENVIRONNEMENT HOTELIER

6/10

HOTELS HÔTELS

Morangie House		Tain
26 rooms, D £ 80		0.5 km
Tel (44) 01862 - 892 281, Fax (44) 01862 - 892 872		

Mansfield House		Tain
17 rooms, D £ 80		0.5 km
Tel (44) 01862 - 892 052, Fax (44) 01862 - 892 260		

Golf View House		Tain
5 rooms, D £ 40		0.5 km
Tel (44) 01862 - 892 856		

RESTAURANTS RESTAURANT

Morangie Hotel		Tain
Tel (44) 01862 - 892 281		0.5 km

Mansfield House		Tain
Tel (44) 01862 - 892 052		0.5 km

THORNHILL

15	6	5

After the city, seaside and sometimes upland courses, here we are out in the country with some pretty views over the surrounding hills. Created by Willie Fernie and then restyled in 1979, this is a very short but rather technical layout designed more for families or friendly rounds but also completed with remarkable concern for quality. You need to be accurate because the greens are small and often treacherous and multi-tiered. Although rather hilly, it is still very much a rural park and its difficulties shouldn't be taken lightly. Judging by the success of the club's prodigal son Andrew Coltart, this is a good course to learn on. The clubhouse of this "village course" is unpretentious but warm. Close by, art enthusiasts will visit Drumlanrig Castle which houses a fine collection of paintings and mementoes of Bonnie Prince Charlie.

Après les golfs des villes, du bord de mer, des montagnes parfois aussi, nous voici à la campagne, avec de jolies vues sur les collines alentour. Créé par Willie Fernie, remanié en 1979, c'est un tracé très court, assez technique, très orienté vers le jeu en famille ou entre amis, mais avec un souci de qualité à remarquer. Il faut être précis, car les greens sont petits, souvent assez traîtres, parfois à plateaux. Assez accidenté, il conserve néanmoins un caractère de parc rural, et il ne faut pas prendre à la légère ses difficultés. Si l'on en juge par la réussite de l'enfant du club, Andrew Coltart, c'est un parcours formateur. Le Clubhouse de ce "golf de village" est modeste, mais chaleureux. A proximité, les amateurs d'art visiteront le Drumlanrig Castle, avec une riche collection de peinture et des souvenirs du Bonnie Prince Charlie.

Thornhill Golf Club
Blacknest
SCO - THORNHILL, Dumfries-shire DG3 5DW

Office	Secrétariat	(44) 01848 - 330 546
Pro shop	Pro-shop	
Fax	Fax	
Situation	Situation	

22 km NW of Dumfries (pop. 21 164)

Annual closure	Fermeture annnuelle	no
Weekly closure	Fermeture hebdomadaire	no

Fees main season
Tarifs haute saison — full day

	Week days Semaine	We/Bank holidays We/Férié
Individual Individuel	£ 21	£ 26
Couple Couple	£ 42	£ 52

Caddy	Caddy	no
Electric Trolley	Chariot électrique	no
Buggy	Voiturette	no
Clubs	Clubs	on request

Credit cards Cartes de crédit — no

GOLF COURSE
PARCOURS **15**/20

Site	Site	
Maintenance	Entretien	
Architect	Architecte	Willie Fernie
Type	Type	heathland, parkland
Relief	Relief	
Water in play	Eau en jeu	
Exp. to wind	Exposé au vent	
Trees in play	Arbres en jeu	

Scorecard Carte de score	Chp. Chp.	Mens Mess.	Ladies Da.
Length Long.	5562	5562	4925
Par	71	71	74

Advised golfing ability Niveau de jeu recommandé		0 12 24 36
Hcp required Handicap exigé		28 Men, 36 Ladies

CLUB HOUSE & AMENITIES
CLUB HOUSE ET ANNEXES **6**/10

Pro shop	Pro-shop	
Driving range	Practice	
Sheltered	couvert	no
On grass	sur herbe	yes
Putting-green	putting-green	yes
Pitching-green	pitching green	no

669

HOTEL FACILITIES
ENVIRONNEMENT HOTELIER **5**/10

HOTELS HÔTELS
Blackaddie House — Sanquhar
10 rooms, D £ 60 — 19 km
Tel (44) 01659 - 50 270
Fax (44) 01659 - 50 270

Cairndale — Dumfries
76 rooms, D £ 105 — 22 km
Tel (44) 01387 - 254 111
Fax (44) 01387 - 250 155

Station — Dumfries
32 rooms, D £ 80 — 22 km
Tel (44) 01387 - 254 316
Fax (44) 01387 - 250 388

Access Accès : Glasgow, M74 - Edinburgh A702. In Abington, A74, then A702 to Thornhill. Golf on A76 (turn East in middle of village).
Map 2 on page 409 Carte 2 Page 409

Regularly playing host to the British Open has forged this course's reputation as one of the world's greatest championship venues. The course is located at the southernmost end of a majestic series of links in Ayrshire and offers a splendid view over the Isle of Arran, the dark and mysterious Mull of Kintyre and the rock of Ailsa. Try and play here in fine weather (it happens more often than you might imagine) as the wind can make this a hellish course to handle. After an almost innocent first few holes, you soon find the sea down the left for the 8 most spectacular holes with the famous lighthouse, but the finish is no less gripping. Brought back to life after the war thanks to the work of MacKenzie Ross, the Ailsa course is challenging, untamed and beguiling. It simply has to be experienced at least once in a lifetime, at any price (and here it is not just any price). A course to savour from end to end, without worrying too much about your card.

La venue régulière du British Open a fait sa réputation parmi les plus grands parcours de championnat au monde. Situé dans la partie la plus au sud d'une série majestueuse de links de l'Ayrshire, il offre un spectacle splendide sur l'île d'Arran, le sombre et mystérieux Mull of Kintyre et le rocher d'Ailsa. A savourer par beau temps (plus fréquent qu'on ne le croit !), car le vent peut transformer le parcours en enfer du jeu. Après un départ presque innocent, on trouve vite la mer à main gauche, pour les huit trous les plus spectaculaires, avec le célèbre phare, mais la conclusion n'est pas moins prenante. Ressuscité après la guerre grâce au travail de Mackenzie Ross, l'Ailsa est exigeant, sauvage, enchanteur, il constitue une expérience à connaître au moins une fois dans sa vie, à n'importe quel prix (c'est effectivement le cas...). Un parcours à savourer de bout en bout, sans trop penser au score.

Turnberry Hotel Golf Courses
SCO - TURNBERRY, Ayrshire, KA26 9LT

Office	Secrétariat	(44) 01655 - 331 000
Pro shop	Pro-shop	(44) 01655 - 331 000
Fax	Fax	(44) 01655 - 331 706
Situation	Situation	

24 km S of Ayr (pop. 47 872)

Annual closure	Fermeture annnuelle	no
Weekly closure	Fermeture hebdomadaire	no
Fees main season	Tarifs haute saison	18 holes

	Week days Semaine	We/Bank holidays We/Férié
Individual Individuel	—	—
Couple Couple	—	—

Principally for Hotel residents (ask for details). Others must write before.

Caddy	Caddy	£ 22
Electric Trolley	Chariot électrique	no
Buggy	Voiturette	no
Clubs	Clubs	£ 35/day

Credit cards Cartes de crédit
VISA - CB - Eurocard - MasterCard - AMEX - DC - JCB - Cofinoga

670

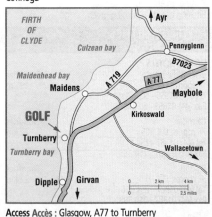

FIRTH OF CLYDE
Culzean bay
Ayr
Pennyglenn
B7023
Maidenhead bay
A 719
A 77
Maidens
Maybole
GOLF
Kirkoswald
Turnberry
Wallacetown
Turnberry bay
Dipple Girvan

0   2 km   4 km
0   2,5 miles

Access Accès : Glasgow, A77 to Turnberry
Map 3 on page 410 Carte 3 Page 410

GOLF COURSE PARCOURS 19/20

Site	Site	■■■■■■■■
Maintenance	Entretien	■■■■■■■
Architect	Architecte	Mackenzie Ross, 1945
Type	Type	links
Relief	Relief	
Water in play	Eau en jeu	■
Exp. to wind	Exposé au vent	■■■■■■
Trees in play	Arbres en jeu	□

Scorecard Carte de score	Chp. Chp.	Mens Mess.	Ladies Da.
Length Long.	6348	5860	5239
Par	70	69	75

Advised golfing ability Niveau de jeu recommandé	0	12	24	36
Hcp required Handicap exigé	no			

CLUB HOUSE & AMENITIES CLUB HOUSE ET ANNEXES 9/10

Pro shop	Pro-shop	■■■■■■■■
Driving range	Practice	■■■■■
Sheltered	couvert	no
On grass	sur herbe	yes
Putting-green	putting-green	yes
Pitching-green	pitching green	yes

HOTEL FACILITIES ENVIRONNEMENT HOTELIER 8/10

HOTELS HÔTELS
Turnberry Hotel   on site
132 rooms, from D £ 200
Tel (44) 01655 - 331 000
Fax (44) 01655 - 331 706

RESTAURANTS RESTAURANT
3 restaurants   at the Hotel
Tel (44) 01655 - 331 000

If it were located anywhere else than beside one of the world's greatest courses, Arran would be considered to be a course of very considerable merit. Shorter than Ailsa and better protected from the sea but not the wind, there is no shortage of charm or technical challenge. Golfers who take it only as a warm-up round before playing the Ailsa course are in for a shock, as this is a worthy adversary for any player. And an ideal companion to Ailsa for a bit of a breather before turning into one of the world's most delightful grand hotels with white walls and red tiled roof. Okay, so you have to dig into your savings to play and stay here, but if there are places in this world where pecuniary considerations come last, this has to be one of them.

S'il était situé ailleurs qu'à côté d'un des plus grands parcours du monde, l'Arran serait considéré comme un parcours de très grand mérite. Plus court que l'Ailsa Course, plus protégé de la mer, mais pas vraiment du vent, il ne manque ni de charme, ni surtout de propositions techniques à résoudre. Ceux qui croient y trouver seulement une occasion de s'échauffer avant de jouer l'Ailsa risquent les désillusions : c'est un adversaire de valeur pour n'importe quel joueur. Et un complément idéal pour reprendre son souffle, avant de rejoindre l'un des grands hôtels les plus attachants au monde, avec ses murs blanchis et ses toits de tuiles rousses. Certes, il faut casser sa tirelire pour séjourner et jouer ici, mais s'il y a des endroits sans prix, celui-ci en fait partie.

Turnberry Hotel Golf Courses
SCO - TURNBERRY, Ayrshire, KA26 9LT

Office	Secrétariat	(44) 01655 - 331 000
Pro shop	Pro-shop	(44) 01655 - 331 000
Fax	Fax	(44) 01655 - 331 706
Situation	Situation	

24 km S of Ayr (pop. 47 872)

Annual closure	Fermeture annnuelle	no
Weekly closure	Fermeture hebdomadaire	no

Fees main season	Tarifs haute saison		18 holes
		Week days Semaine	We/Bank holidays We/Férié
Individual Individuel		—	—
Couple Couple		—	—

Principally for Hotel residents (ask for details).
Others must write before.

Caddy	Caddy	£ 22
Electric Trolley	Chariot électrique	no
Buggy	Voiturette	no
Clubs	Clubs	£ 35/day

Credit cards Cartes de crédit
VISA - CB - Eurocard - MasterCard - AMEX - DC - JCB - Cofinoga

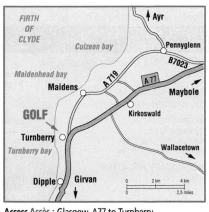

Access Accès : Glasgow, A77 to Turnberry
Map 3 on page 410 Carte 3 Page 410

GOLF COURSE / PARCOURS — 16/20

Site	Site	
Maintenance	Entretien	
Architect	Architecte	Mackenzie Ross, 1945
Type	Type	links
Relief	Relief	
Water in play	Eau en jeu	
Exp. to wind	Exposé au vent	
Trees in play	Arbres en jeu	

Scorecard Carte de score	Chp. Chp.	Mens Mess.	Ladies Da.
Length Long.	5475	5475	5020
Par	68	68	72

Advised golfing ability		0	12	24	36
Niveau de jeu recommandé					
Hcp required	Handicap exigé	no			

CLUB HOUSE & AMENITIES / CLUB HOUSE ET ANNEXES — 9/10

Pro shop	Pro-shop	
Driving range	Practice	
Sheltered	couvert	no
On grass	sur herbe	yes
Putting-green	putting-green	yes
Pitching-green	pitching green	yes

HOTEL FACILITIES / ENVIRONNEMENT HOTELIER — 8/10

HOTELS HÔTELS
Turnberry Hotel — on site
132 rooms, from D £ 200
Tel (44) 01655 - 331 000
Fax (44) 01655 - 331 706

RESTAURANTS RESTAURANT
3 restaurants — at the Hotel
Tel (44) 01655 - 331 000

671

A very pretty course on the Ayrshire coast, without the claim to fame of its prestigious neighbours but always very welcoming on weekdays. The site is as magnificent as it is peaceful, with superb views over the Isle of Arran, Ailsa Craig and the north-west hills. But this 18-hole course is worth much more than its scenery. A very reasonable length makes this interesting prey for good golfers and the best players will find more than one opportunity to shine. The spread of difficulties makes for a well-balanced round of golf with only a single burn to interrupt the links landscape: bunkers that look to have been here since time began, thick bushes and the few trees that the wind has left standing. And of course the sea, whose incursions often tend to complicate the job of club officials.

Un très joli parcours de la côte de l'Ayrshire, sans prétendre aux grands titres de gloire de ses prestigieux voisins, mais toujours accueillant en semaine. Le site est aussi magnifique et très tranquille, avec des vues superbes sur l'Ile d'Arran, Ailsa Craig et les collines du nord-ouest. Mais ce 18 trous vaut mieux que son panorama. Sa longueur très raisonnable en fait une proie intéressante pour les golfeurs de niveau honorable, et les meilleurs y trouveront plus d'une occasion de s'y casser les dents. Le répartition des difficultés offre un bon rythme de jeu, un "burn" venant seul rompre leur nature propre aux links : des bunkers qui paraissent là depuis l'éternité, des buissons bien épais, quelques arbres ayant résisté au vent. Et à la mer, dont l'action vient parfois compliquer la tâche des responsables du Club.

The West Kilbride Golf Club

33-35 Fullerton Drive, Seamill
SCO - WEST KILBRIDE, Ayrshire KA23 9HT

Office	Secrétariat	(44) 01294 - 823 911
Pro shop	Pro-shop	(44) 01294 - 823 042
Fax	Fax	(44) 01294 - 823 911
Situation	Situation	

56 km SW of Glasgow (pop. 662 853)

Annual closure	Fermeture annnuelle	no
Weekly closure	Fermeture hebdomadaire	no

Fees main season	Tarifs haute saison	18 holes

	Week days Semaine	We/Bank holidays We/Férié
Individual Individuel	£ 21	—
Couple Couple	£ 42	—

Full weekday: £ 35 - No visitors at weekends

Caddy	Caddy	no
Electric Trolley	Chariot électrique	yes
Buggy	Voiturette	no
Clubs	Clubs	£ 5/18 holes

Credit cards   Cartes de crédit
VISA - Eurocard - MasterCard - AMEX - DC - JCB

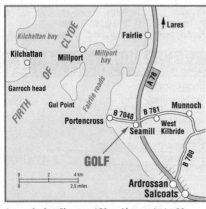

Access Accès : Glasgow, A80 → Airport. At Jct 29, A737 through Paisley, Beith. After Dalry turn right on B781. In West Kilbride, turn right towards the sea. **Map 3 on page 410** Carte 3 Page 410

672

GOLF COURSE PARCOURS

16/20

Site	Site	
Maintenance	Entretien	
Architect	Architecte	Tom Morris James Braid
Type	Type	links
Relief	Relief	
Water in play	Eau en jeu	
Exp. to wind	Exposé au vent	
Trees in play	Arbres en jeu	

Scorecard	Chp.	Mens	Ladies
Carte de score	Chp.	Mess.	Da.
Length Long.	5898	5898	5292
Par	71	71	72

Advised golfing ability		0	12	24	36
Niveau de jeu recommandé					
Hcp required	Handicap exigé	certificate			

CLUB HOUSE & AMENITIES CLUB HOUSE ET ANNEXES

7/10

Pro shop	Pro-shop	
Driving range	Practice	
Sheltered	couvert	no
On grass	sur herbe	no
Putting-green	putting-green	yes
Pitching-green	pitching green	yes

HOTEL FACILITIES ENVIRONNEMENT HOTELIER

5/10

HOTELS HÔTELS
Hospitality Inn — Irvine
126 rooms, D £ 100 — 6 km
Tel (44) 01294 - 274 272
Fax (44) 01294 - 277 287

Brisbane House — Largs
23 rooms, D £ 80 — 5 km
Tel (44) 01475 - 687 200
Fax (44) 01475 - 676 295

RESTAURANTS RESTAURANT
Braidwoods — Dalry
Tel (44) 01294 - 833 544 — 6 km

WESTERN GAILES

17 5 7

Between the seaside dunes and the railway lines, Western Gailes is one of the best links down the whole coast of Scotland. Totally exposed to the prevailing south-west wind, it subtly changes its nature even if the wind varies just a few degrees. There are only three par 3s, every one more difficult than it looks. Rather strangely for a course that is hardly much wider than two fairways, the clubhouse is almost in the middle. This means you play one half of the front 9 and one half of the back 9 with the wind behind you, and holes 5 to 13 with the wind in your face. This calls for some careful thinking over the line of play and attack. This private club welcomes visitors, even of the female variety, although there are no ladies tees. We'll just say that for them, this is an excellent par 74.

Entre les dunes de bord de mer et la voie ferrée, Western Gailes est un des meilleurs links de toute cette côte de l'Ecosse. Totalement exposé aux vents dominants de sud-ouest, il change subtilement de caractère selon que l'orientation se modifie de quelques degrés seulement. Il n'y a que trois par 3 ici, mais tous plus difficiles qu'ils ne paraissent. Assez curieusement pour un parcours guère plus large que deux fairways, le Club-house est presqu'au milieu : on joue ainsi la moitié de l'aller et la moitié du retour vent avec, et toute la partie du 5 au 13 vent contre, ce qui exige pas mal de réflexion sur la ligne de jeu... et la façon de négocier. Ce club privé est accueillant aux visiteurs, même féminins, bien qu'elles n'aient pas ici de départs spécifiques : disons que c'est pour elles un excellent par 74.

Western Gailes Golf Club
Gailes
SCO - IRVINE, Ayrshire KA11 5AE

Office	Secrétariat	(44) 01294 - 311 649
Pro shop	Pro-shop	(44) 01294 - 311 649
Fax	Fax	(44) 01294 - 312 312
Situation	Situation	

5 km N of Troon (pop. 15 116)

Annual closure	Fermeture annnuelle	no
Weekly closure	Fermeture hebdomadaire	no

Restaurant closed 10 → 04 inclusive

Fees main season	Tarifs haute saison	18 holes
	Week days	We/Bank holidays
	Semaine	We/Férié
Individual Individuel	£ 52	—
Couple Couple	£ 104	—

Visitors: only Monday, Tuesday (except Ladies), Wednesday and Friday.

Caddy	Caddy	on request/£ 25
Electric Trolley	Chariot électrique	no
Buggy	Voiturette	no
Clubs	Clubs	no
Credit cards Cartes de crédit		no

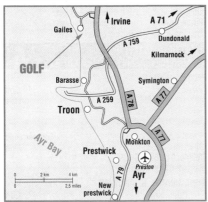

Access Accès : On A78, 3 km S of junction with A 71.
Map 3 on page 410 Carte 3 Page 410

GOLF COURSE
PARCOURS
17/20

Site	Site	
Maintenance	Entretien	
Architect	Architecte	Original greenkeeper links
Type	Type	
Relief	Relief	
Water in play	Eau en jeu	
Exp. to wind	Exposé au vent	
Trees in play	Arbres en jeu	0

Scorecard	Chp.	Mens	Ladies
Carte de score	Chp.	Mess.	Da.
Length Long.	6110	6040	5622
Par	71	71	75

Advised golfing ability		0 12 24 36
Niveau de jeu recommandé		
Hcp required	Handicap exigé	24

CLUB HOUSE & AMENITIES
CLUB HOUSE ET ANNEXES
5/10

Pro shop	Pro-shop	
Driving range	Practice	
Sheltered	couvert	no
On grass	sur herbe	no
Putting-green	putting-green	yes
Pitching-green	pitching green	no

HOTEL FACILITIES
ENVIRONNEMENT HOTELIER
7/10

HOTELS HÔTELS
Hospitality Inn — Irvine
126 rooms, D £ 100 — 2 km
Tel (44) 01294 - 274 272
Fax (44) 01294 - 277 287

Marine Highland — Troon
66 rooms, D £ 120 — 5 km
Tel (44) 01292 - 314 444
Fax (44) 01292 - 316 922

RESTAURANTS RESTAURANT
Highgrove House — Troon
Tel (44) 01292 - 312 511 — 5 km

673

This is one of the very ambitious projects of recent years, designed by Dave Thomas and Seve Ballesteros in search of commercial success. The site is beautiful with an excellent hotel atop a hill, guaranteeing a scenic view and exposure to the wind. The course unwinds around the hotel but is never very hilly. The only real regret is that the course gets very wet when it rains and stays very dry for the rest of the time, which doesn't make playing very easy either way. You have to play long and straight, the greens are very well protected and the wind can make life complicated even in the middle of the trees. An often interesting and sometimes even spectacular course which is well worth playing in fine weather. Still in its infancy, Westerwood can only get better.

C'est l'un des projets très ambitieux de ces dernières années, avec les signatures de Dave Thomas et Seve Ballesteros pour rechercher le succès commercial. Le site est très beau, avec un excellent hôtel au sommet d'une colline, ce qui garantit le panorama, mais aussi l'exposition au vent. Le parcours se déroule à son pied, mais les reliefs ne sont pas très importants. Le seul vrai regret que l'on puisse avoir est qu'il soit très humide quand il a plu, et très sec par ailleurs, ce qui ne facilite pas le jeu dans un cas comme dans l'autre. Car il faut être long, précis, les greens sont très bien défendus et le vent peut compliquer les choses, même au milieu des arbres. Un parcours souvent intéressant, parfois même spectaculaire et qui vaut la peine d'être découvert par beau temps. Mais il est encore jeune et ne peut que progresser.

The Westerwood Hotel, Golf & Country Club

St Andrews Drive
SCO - WESTERWOOD, Cumbernauld G68 0EW

Office	Secrétariat	(44) 01236 - 452 772
Pro shop	Pro-shop	(44) 01236 - 725 181
Fax	Fax	(44) 01236 - 738 478
Situation	Situation	

23 km NE of Glasgow (pop. 662 853)

Annual closure	Fermeture annnuelle	no
Weekly closure	Fermeture hebdomadaire	no

Fees main season
Tarifs haute saison — 18 holes

	Week days Semaine	We/Bank holidays We/Férié
Individual Individuel	£ 22.50	£ 27.50
Couple Couple	£ 45	£ 55

Caddy	Caddy	on request/£ 15
Electric Trolley	Chariot électrique	no
Buggy	Voiturette	yes
Clubs	Clubs	yes

Credit cards Cartes de crédit
VISA - Eurocard - MasterCard - AMEX - DC - JCB

674

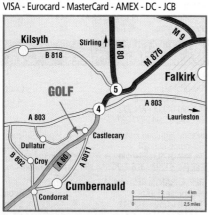

Access Accès : Glasgow, A80. turn off at Cumbernauld on the road labelled to Dullatur. At first roundabout, look for Westerwood sign (not obvious!).
Map 2 on page 408 Carte 2 Page 408

GOLF COURSE
PARCOURS
14/20

Site	Site	
Maintenance	Entretien	
Architect	Architecte	Seve Ballesteros Dave Thomas
Type	Type	parkland
Relief	Relief	
Water in play	Eau en jeu	
Exp. to wind	Exposé au vent	
Trees in play	Arbres en jeu	

Scorecard Carte de score	Chp. Chp.	Mens Mess.	Ladies Da.
Length Long.	6030	5560	4965
Par	72	72	75

Advised golfing ability		0 12 24 36
Niveau de jeu recommandé		
Hcp required	Handicap exigé	no

CLUB HOUSE & AMENITIES
CLUB HOUSE ET ANNEXES
8/10

Pro shop	Pro-shop	
Driving range	Practice	
Sheltered	couvert	no
On grass	sur herbe	yes
Putting-green	putting-green	yes
Pitching-green	pitching green	yes

HOTEL FACILITIES
ENVIRONNEMENT HOTELIER
6/10

HOTELS HÔTELS
Westerwood — Golf
49 rooms, D £ 85 — on site
Tel (44) 01236 - 457 171
Fax (44) 01236 - 738 478

Travel Inn — Cumbernauld
37 rooms, D £ 35 — 3 km
Tel (44) 01236 - 725 339
Fax (44) 01236 - 736 380

RESTAURANTS RESTAURANT
The Tipsy Laird — Golf
Tél (44) 01236 - 457 171 — on site

In a region where there are many high quality courses, the Whitekirk promoters scored a significant victory over those who thought there wouldn't be enough space for another one. This course is a fine example of what can still be done with a restricted budget but with the determination to offer visitors excellent value for money. Practice facilities are of a standard seldom found in the UK, the greens are excellent, the layout very varied and the views (free of charge) over the Firth of Forth are magnificent. Naturally this layout cannot really match the genuine links courses found in the vicinity here, but it is a very serious design and strategy is immediately obvious without any hidden traps. This is essential for a "pay-as-you-play" course.

Dans une région présentant des parcours d'une telle qualité, les promoteurs de Whitekirk ont remporté une belle victoire sur ceux qui estimaient qu'il n'y avait plus de place disponible. Ce parcours est un bon exemple de ce que l'on peut encore faire avec un budget limité, mais avec la détermination d'offrir un bon rapport qualité-prix aux visiteurs de passage. Ils y trouveront des installations d'entraînement d'une rare qualité en Grande-Bretagne, des greens excellents, un tracé très varié et (gratuitement) de très belles vues sur le Firth of Forth. Certes, ce parcours ne peut tout à fait lutter avec les véritables links que l'on peut trouver alentour, mais son dessin a été sérieusement réalisé, la stratégie est immédiatement évidente, sans pièges dissimulés, ce qui est essentiel pour un parcours "pay-as-you-play."

Whitekirk Golf Course
Whitekirk
SCO - Nr NORTH BERWICK, E. Lothian EH39 5PR

Office	Secrétariat	(44) 01620 - 870 300
Pro shop	Pro-shop	(44) 01620 - 870 300
Fax	Fax	(44) 01620 - 870 330
Situation	Situation	

5 km SE of North Berwick (pop. 5 871)

Annual closure	Fermeture annnuelle	no
Weekly closure	Fermeture hebdomadaire	no

Fees main season
Tarifs haute saison — 18 holes

	Week days Semaine	We/Bank holidays We/Férié
Individual Individuel	£ 18	£ 25
Couple Couple	£ 36	£ 50

Full days: £ 30 - £ 35 (weekends)

Caddy	Caddy	on request
Electric Trolley	Chariot électrique	yes
Buggy	Voiturette	£ 12/18 holes
Clubs	Clubs	£ 5/18 holes

Credit cards Cartes de crédit
VISA - Eurocard - MasterCard

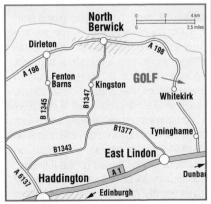

Access Accès : Edinburgh A1 → Berwick-upon-Tweed.
After East Linton, A198 on the left. Golf on left side after Whitekirk village.
Map 3 on page 411 Carte 3 Page 411

GOLF COURSE
PARCOURS
15/20

Site	Site	
Maintenance	Entretien	
Architect	Architecte	Cameron Sinclair
Type	Type	open country
Relief	Relief	
Water in play	Eau en jeu	
Exp. to wind	Exposé au vent	
Trees in play	Arbres en jeu	

Scorecard Carte de score	Chp. Chp.	Mens Mess.	Ladies Da.
Length Long.	5842	5645	4835
Par	71	71	71

Advised golfing ability		0	12	24	36
Niveau de jeu recommandé					
Hcp required Handicap exigé	no				

CLUB HOUSE & AMENITIES
CLUB HOUSE ET ANNEXES
7/10

Pro shop	Pro-shop	
Driving range	Practice	
Sheltered	couvert	no
On grass	sur herbe	yes
Putting-green	putting-green	yes
Pitching-green	pitching green	yes

HOTEL FACILITIES
ENVIRONNEMENT HOTELIER
7/10

HOTELS HÔTELS
Marine Hotel — North Berwick 5 km
74 rooms, D £ 80
Tel (44) 01620 - 892 406
Fax (44) 01620 - 894 480

Point Garry — North Berwick 5 km
15 rooms, D £ 80
Tel (44) 01620 - 892 380
Fax (44) 01620 - 892 848

Courtyard — Dunbar 12 km
6 rooms, D £ 50
Tel (44) 01368 - 864 169

RESTAURANTS RESTAURANT
Marine — North Berwick 5 km
Tel (44) 01620 - 892 406

675

🇬🇧 Wales 🏴󠁧󠁢󠁷󠁬󠁳󠁿

I n the British Isles, Wales is not the best known country for golf, at least to players on the continent, who are often only familiar with those courses seen on the television during the British Open or other top tournaments. Yet Wales has one of the highest concentrations of great courses seen anywhere in the world. The problem is that they are sometimes so far away from any major city that it is virtually impossible for them to organise any of the world's top tournaments. You won't find the sunny climes of Spain here, but the Gulf Stream does bring a lot of mild weather and a few spots of rain are always good for the skin. So there are very few tourists, which can only be good news for golf-trotters, who often have hundreds of acres of forest, miles of rugged coastline or sandy beaches, and splendid landscapes all to themselves. And these are courses where you will have more than one opportunity to find playing partners and to discover the Welsh people, who are the very picture of their country: sometimes a little rough on the edges, discreet, always proud and deeply hospitable. All they need do now is tell the rest of the world that their golf courses are first-rate, but do they really want to get involved in big publicity and promotion campaigns? If a happy life means a hidden life out-of-the-way, then real happiness is right here.

676

D ans les Iles Britanniques, le Pays de Galles n'est pas le pays le plus connu pour le golf, en tout cas par les continentaux, qui ne connaissent souvent que les parcours vus à la télévision au moment de championnats comme le British Open. Pourtant, le Pays de Galles réunit l'une des plus fortes concentrations de grands parcours par rapport au nombre total, mais ils sont parfois tellement à l'écart des grandes métropoles qu'il est presque impossible d'y organiser les plus grandes compétitions. Ici, on ne trouve pas la chaleur de l'Espagne, mais le Gulf Stream adoucit le climat, et les quelques gouttes de pluie attendrissent la peau. S'il y a peu de touristes, tant mieux : on a souvent pour soi tout seul des centaines d'hectares de forêt, des kilomètres de côtes sauvages ou de plages, des paysages splendides, et des parcours de golf où l'on aura l'occasion de trouver des compagnons de jeu, de découvrir des Gallois à l'image de leur pays, rudes parfois, discrets , chaleureux et fiers. Il leur reste à faire savoir que leurs parcours sont de première grandeur, mais ont-ils vraiment envie de se lancer dans de grandes campagnes de promotion ? S'il faut être bien caché pour vivre heureux, le bonheur est ici.

You can get here by train, bringing your clubs with you, a throw-back to the times when courses were always close to railway tracks. The line here does indeed run alongside the course but not enough to make a nuisance of itself. And that's probably good news, because this layout, which has benefited from the flair of designers Fowler, Colt and Braid, is one of the best in Wales. Located in the Dovey estuary at the foot of some hills, this is a flat course lying alongside the pretty resort of Aberdovey, hence the rather crowded fairways in Summer. As the Old Course at St. Andrews, the holes are in a straight line out and in, thus making play a little easier in the wind. Yet the shifting landscape and dunes bring variety and sometimes even surprises like at the 3rd, a par 3 where the green is totally out of view. Aberdovey is Ian Woosnam's retreat between tournaments. So if it suits him, it'll probably suit you, too.

On peut venir en train avec ses clubs, ce qui rappelle le temps où les golfs étaient près du chemin de fer. Certes, il longe tout le parcours, mais pas assez souvent pour être une nuisance. Heureusement, car ce tracé, où des gloires comme Fowler, Colt et Braid ont laissé leur «patte» est un des meilleurs du pays. Dans l'embouchure de la Dovey, au pied des collines, c'est un parcours plat, à côté de la jolie station balnéaire d'Aberdovey, d'où une forte fréquentation en été. A l'instar du Old Course de St Andrews, les trous sont pratiquement alignés en aller et retour, ce qui facilite le jeu quand il y a du vent, mais les mouvements du terrain et les dunes apportent de la variété, parfois même la surprise comme au 3, un par 3 où le green est totalement dissimulé. Pour Ian Woosnam, Aberdovey est une retraite entre les tournois. Si c'est bien pour lui...

Aberdovey Golf Club
WAL - ABERDOVEY, Gwynedd LL35 0RT

Office	Secrétariat	(44) 01654 - 767 493
Pro shop	Pro-shop	(44) 01654 - 767 602
Fax	Fax	
Situation	Situation	

5 km NW of Aberdovey (Aberdyfi)
140 km from Cardiff (pop. 279 055)

Annual closure	Fermeture annnuelle	no
Weekly closure	Fermeture hebdomadaire	no
Fees main season	Tarifs haute saison	full day

	Week days Semaine	We/Bank holidays We/Férié
Individual Individuel	£ 32	£ 38
Couple Couple	£ 64	£ 46

Caddy	Caddy	no
Electric Trolley	Chariot électrique	yes
Buggy	Voiturette	yes
Clubs	Clubs	no

Credit cards Cartes de crédit
VISA - Eurocard - MasterCard - AMEX

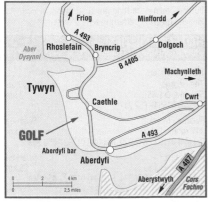

Access Accès : Cardiff A470 to Glantwymyn, then A489 to Machynlleth, A493 through Aberdyfi.
Golf course NW near Railway Station.
Map 5 on page 414 Carte 5 Page 414

GOLF COURSE
PARCOURS
17 /20

Site	Site	
Maintenance	Entretien	
Architect	Architecte	Braid, Fowler, Colt
Type	Type	seaside course, links
Relief	Relief	
Water in play	Eau en jeu	
Exp. to wind	Exposé au vent	
Trees in play	Arbres en jeu	

Scorecard Carte de score	Chp. Chp.	Mens Mess.	Ladies Da.
Length Long.	5865	5551	5314
Par	71	71	74

Advised golfing ability		0 12 24 36
Niveau de jeu recommandé		
Hcp required	Handicap exigé	certificate

CLUB HOUSE & AMENITIES
CLUB HOUSE ET ANNEXES
7 /10

Pro shop	Pro-shop	
Driving range	Practice	
Sheltered	couvert	no
On grass	sur herbe	yes
Putting-green	putting-green	yes
Pitching-green	pitching green	yes

677

HOTEL FACILITIES
ENVIRONNEMENT HOTELIER
7 /10

HOTELS HÔTELS
Plas Penhelig Country House — Aberdovey
11 rooms, D £ 80 — 6 km
Tel (44) 01654 - 767 676
Fax (44) 01654 - 767 783

Trefeddian — Aberdovey
46 rooms, D £ 80 — 3 km
Tel (44) 01654 - 767 213
Fax (44) 01654 - 767 777

Penhelig Arms — Aberdovey
10 rooms, D £ 75 — 5 km
Tel (44) 01654 - 767 215
Fax (44) 01654 - 767 690

RESTAURANTS RESTAURANTS
Plas Penhelig Country House — Aberdovey
Tel (44) 01654 - 767 676 — 6 km

Located to the west of Llanelli and not so far from Swansea, this is one of the oldest courses in Wales, overlooking Camarthen Bay. The fairways are very busy in Summer, so be warned. The first and last two holes have a rather marked inland character, but for the rest of the course you have the prevailing south-westerlies to contend with. Holes 3 to 8 run parallel to the sea with a head-wind, holes 9 to 15 are played with the wind behind you. With tight fairways, dangerous rough and other unwelcome but easily identifiable hazards, you play here with your clubs and your brains. The greens are on the large side and equally difficult to read, which would explain why the course record here is only 70. Even though players of all levels can measure up to this test, the least experienced should not hold out too much hope when the wind roars (except perhaps for learning how to play with it).

Situé à l'ouest de Llanelli, et pas si loin de Swansea, ce parcours très fréquenté en été, et l'un des plus anciens du Pays de Galles, domine la baie de Carmarthen. Les deux premiers et deux derniers trous ont un caractère inland assez marqué. Ensuite, il faut jouer avec le vent dominant, car si les trous du 3 ou 8 sont joués parallèlement à la mer et vent contre, par contre les trous 9 à 15 se jouent vent avec... Avec les fairways étroits, un rough et des obstacles bien dangereux, mais aussi bien identifiables, il faut jouer avec ses clubs, mais aussi sa tête. Les greens sont assez grands, mais aussi très difficiles à lire, ce qui explique que le record ne soit ici que de 70. Et même si les joueurs de tous niveaux trouveront le test à leur mesure, les moins expérimentés ne doivent pas trop espérer quand le vent souffle (sinon apprendre à en jouer...)

Ashburnham Golf Club

Cliff Terrace
WAL - BURRY PORT, Dyfed SA16 0HN

Office	Secrétariat	(44) 01554 - 832 269
Pro shop	Pro-shop	(44) 01554 - 833 846
Fax	Fax	
Situation	Situation	

8 km W of Llanelli
25 km W of Swansea (pop. 181 906)

Annual closure	Fermeture annnuelle	no
Weekly closure	Fermeture hebdomadaire	no

Fees main season
Tarifs haute saison full day

	Week days Semaine	We/Bank holidays We/Férié
Individual Individuel	£ 30	£ 30
Couple Couple	£ 60	£ 60

Restrictions at weekends: ask before coming

Caddy	Caddy	no
Electric Trolley	Chariot électrique	yes
Buggy	Voiturette	no
Clubs	Clubs	yes

Credit cards Cartes de crédit
VISA - MasterCard - AMEX

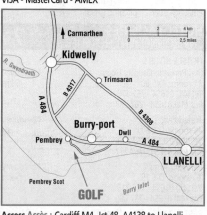

Access Accès : Cardiff M4. Jct 48, A4138 to Llanelli, then A484 to Burry Port.
Map 6 on page 416 Carte 6 Page 416

GOLF COURSE
PARCOURS
17 /20

Site	Site	
Maintenance	Entretien	
Architect	Architecte	Unknown
Type	Type	links
Relief	Relief	
Water in play	Eau en jeu	
Exp. to wind	Exposé au vent	
Trees in play	Arbres en jeu	

Scorecard Carte de score	**Chp.** Chp.	**Mens** Mess.	**Ladies** Da.
Length Long.	6312	5652	5007
Par	72	72	75

Advised golfing ability		0	12	24	36
Niveau de jeu recommandé					
Hcp required	Handicap exigé	certificate			

CLUB HOUSE & AMENITIES
CLUB HOUSE ET ANNEXES
6 /10

Pro shop	Pro-shop	
Driving range	Practice	
Sheltered	couvert	no
On grass	sur herbe	yes
Putting-green	putting-green	yes
Pitching-green	pitching green	yes

HOTEL FACILITIES
ENVIRONNEMENT HOTELIER
5 /10

HOTELS HÔTELS
The George
5 rooms, D £ 45
Tel (44) 01554 - 832 211
Burry Port
2 km

Swansea Marriott
117 rooms, D £ 76
Tel (44) 01792 - 642 020, Fax (44) 01792 - 650 345
Swansea
25 km

Forte Crest
99 rooms, D £ 69
Tel (44) 01792 - 651 074, Fax (44) 01792 - 456 044
Swansea
25 km

RESTAURANTS RESTAURANTS
Four Seasons
Tel (44) 01267 - 290 238
Carmarthen
20 km

Annie's
Tel (44) 01792 - 655 603
Swansea
25 km

678

Alongside a remarkable hotel, you find here a real driving range, two-stories high, and a very well-appointed clubhouse. This ambitious golfing resort is organised around two courses (a third is presently under construction) designed by Robert Trent Jones, who thus returned to the land of his ancestors. You'll find the remains of a Roman Way here, and also of a Roman gladiator school, although the battles waged here nowadays are of a more pacific nature, fought over a little white ball. In this hilly landscape (a buggy is a good idea for the less athletic players), the designer has laid out a very American style course calling for accurate play to get the ball onto huge, well-contoured greens. On the way you'll be negotiating lakes, ravines, woods, other stretches of water and huge sand-traps. No effort was spared to make Celtic Manor a highly impressive and successful venture.

A côté d'un hôtel remarquable, on trouve ici un vrai driving-range à deux étages et un Clubhouse remarquablement équipé. Cet ambitieux complexe a été organisé autour de deux parcours (un troisième est en travaux), dûs au crayon de Robert Trent Jones, revenu ainsi sur la terre de ses ancêtres. On trouve ici les restes d'une voie romaine, et même d'une école de gladiateurs, mais on aura à batailler de manière plus pacifique. Dans ce paysage vallonné (voiturette conseillée pour les moins en forme), l'architecte a placé un parcours très américain de style, avec la nécessité, en passant au large des lacs, des ravins, des bois, des cours d'eau, des immenses bunkers, de poser sa balle sur de vastes greens très travaillés. Rien n'a été épargné pour faire de Celtic Manor une impressionnante réussite.

Celtic Manor
Coldra Woods
WAL - NEWPORT NP6 2YA

Office	Secrétariat	(44) 01633 - 413 000
Pro shop	Pro-shop	(44) 01633 - 410 268
Fax	Fax	(44) 01633 - 412 910
Situation	Situation	

25 km E of Cardiff (pop. 279 055)
5 km NE of Newport (pop. 133 318)

Annual closure	Fermeture annnuelle	no
Weekly closure	Fermeture hebdomadaire	no

Fees main season	Tarifs haute saison	18 holes
	Week days Semaine	We/Bank holidays We/Férié
Individual Individuel	£ 30	£ 35
Couple Couple	£ 60	£ 70

Caddy	Caddy	on request
Electric Trolley	Chariot électrique	yes
Buggy	Voiturette	yes
Clubs	Clubs	yes

Credit cards Cartes de crédit
VISA - MasterCard - AMEX

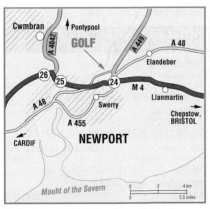

Cwmbran — Pontypool — A 4042 — A 4051 — GOLF — A 48 — Elandeber — 26 — 25 — 24 — M 4 — Llanmartin — A 48 — Swerry — Chepstow, BRISTOL — A 455 — CARDIF — NEWPORT — Mouht of the Severn — 0 — 2 — 4 km — 0 — 2,5 miles

Access Accès : M4 Jct 24, then A48 → Newport.
First right at Royal Oak Public House. Turn right at top of the hill. Golf on right hand side.
Map 6 on page 417 Carte 6 Page 417

GOLF COURSE
PARCOURS

18/20

Site	Site	
Maintenance	Entretien	
Architect	Architecte	R. Trent Jones Sr
Type	Type	parkland
Relief	Relief	
Water in play	Eau en jeu	
Exp. to wind	Exposé au vent	
Trees in play	Arbres en jeu	

Scorecard Carte de score	Chp. Chp.	Mens Mess.	Ladies Da.
Length Long.	6371	5998	4430
Par	70	70	70

Advised golfing ability		0	12	24	36
Niveau de jeu recommandé					
Hcp required	Handicap exigé	certificate			

CLUB HOUSE & AMENITIES
CLUB HOUSE ET ANNEXES

9/10

Pro shop	Pro-shop	
Driving range	Practice	
Sheltered	couvert	10 bays
On grass	sur herbe	yes
Putting-green	putting-green	yes
Pitching-green	pitching green	yes

679

HOTEL FACILITIES
ENVIRONNEMENT HOTELIER

7/10

HOTELS HÔTELS
Celtic Manor Hotel — Golf
75 rooms, D £ 100 — on site
Tel (44) 01633 - 413 000
Fax (44) 01633 - 412 910

Newport Lodge — Newport
27 rooms, D £ 67 — 5 km
Tel (44) 01633 - 821 818
Fax (44) 01633 - 856 360

Knoll — Newport
11 rooms, D £ 40 — 5 km
Tel (44) 01633 - 263 557
Fax (44) 01633 - 212 168

RESTAURANTS RESTAURANTS
Hedley's (Celtic Manor) — on site
Tel (44) 01633 - 413 000

Sections of the artificial port for the 1944 Normandy landings were built behind the green on the 2nd hole. This is only one page of history amongst many others, as the city has even held onto its medieval ramparts. The course is much flatter than its counterparts on the western and southern coasts, but there is never any question of tedium thanks to subtle shifts in landscape and the ubiquitous gorse. Naturally, you can add to this the course's own specific headaches, including length from the back tees. Playing further forward can put it within easier reach. In every case this is a perfectly honest layout, where the penalty to pay matches the gravity of your mis-hit. Very natural and with obvious personality, Conwy deserves a prolonged and respectful visit.

Derrière le green du 2 ont été construites, en 1943, des portions du port artificiel du débarquement de 1944. Ce n'est qu'une page d'histoire parmi d'autres, car la ville a conservé jusqu'à ses remparts médiévaux. Le parcours est beaucoup plus plat que ceux des côtes ouest et sud, mais il échappe à la monotonie grâce à de subtils mouvements de terrain, et aussi à l'omniprésence de buissons d'ajoncs. Il faut encore y ajouter les difficultés propres du parcours, très long des départs les plus reculés, mais plus accessible des départs avancés. En tous les cas, il est d'une parfaite franchise, les punitions étant à la hauteur de la gravité des fautes commises. Très naturel, avec son évidente personnalité, Conwy mérite une visite aussi prolongée que respectueuse.

Conwy (Caernarvonshire) Golf Club
Morfa
WAL - CONWY, Gwynedd LL32 8 ER

Office	Secrétariat	(44) 01492 - 592 423
Pro shop	Pro-shop	(44) 01492 - 593 225
Fax	Fax	
Situation	Situation	

8 km W of Colwyn Bay (pop. 9 471)
4 km S of Llandudno (pop. 18 647)

Annual closure	Fermeture annnuelle	no
Weekly closure	Fermeture hebdomadaire	no

Fees main season
Tarifs haute saison 18 holes

	Week days Semaine	We/Bank holidays We/Férié
Individual Individuel	£ 24	£ 28
Couple Couple	£ 48	£ 56

Caddy	Caddy	no
Electric Trolley	Chariot électrique	yes
Buggy	Voiturette	yes
Clubs	Clubs	yes

Credit cards Cartes de crédit
VISA - MasterCard - AMEX

680

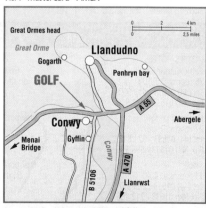

Access Accès : A55 to Conwy and follow signs to Conwy Marina.
Map 5 on page 414 Carte 5 Page 414

GOLF COURSE
PARCOURS **17**/20

Site	Site	▬▬▬▬
Maintenance	Entretien	▬▬▬▬
Architect	Architecte	Unknown
Type	Type	links
Relief	Relief	▬▬
Water in play	Eau en jeu	▬
Exp. to wind	Exposé au vent	▬▬▬
Trees in play	Arbres en jeu	▬▬

Scorecard Carte de score	Chp. Chp.	Mens Mess.	Ladies Da.
Length Long.	6049	5819	5299
Par	72	72	74

Advised golfing ability		0	12	24	36
Niveau de jeu recommandé		▬▬▬▬▬▬			
Hcp required	Handicap exigé	certificate			

CLUB HOUSE & AMENITIES
CLUB HOUSE ET ANNEXES **7**/10

Pro shop	Pro-shop	▬▬▬
Driving range	Practice	▬▬▬
Sheltered	couvert	no
On grass	sur herbe	yes
Putting-green	putting-green	yes
Pitching-green	pitching green	yes

HOTEL FACILITIES
ENVIRONNEMENT HOTELIER **8**/10

HOTELS HÔTELS
Bodysgallen Hall — Llandudno
34 rooms, D £ 120 — 6 km
Tél (44) 01492 - 584 466, Fax (44) 01492 - 582 519

Berthlwyd Hall — Conwy
9 rooms, D £ 65 — 3 km
Tél (44) 01492 - 592 409, Fax (44) 01492 - 572 290

Old Rectory — Llansanffraid Glan Conwy
6 rooms, D £ 100 — 6 km
Tel (44) 01492 - 580 611, Fax (44) 01492 - 584 555

RESTAURANTS RESTAURANTS
Martin's — Llandudno
Tel (44) 01492 - 870 070 — 6 km

Old Rectory — Llansanffraid Glan Conwy
Tel (44) 01492 - 580 611 — 6 km

Paysanne - Tel (44) 01492 - 582 079 — Deganwy, 5 km

A bridge has made Anglesey a peninsula and Trearddur Bay (as Holyhead is properly known) a better known course. Local players will tell you some horrible stories about lost golfers and terrifying scores, but Wales is also known as a land of tall stories. This course is difficult in the wind, but that is true for all links courses. It is short enough not to stage very many prestigious tournaments, and rather hilly with tight, neatly contoured fairways. The natural rough is often dotted with thick heather, broom, gorse and even ferns, so it is an honest test for players of all levels (it was designed by James Braid, which says it all) with some of the best greens in the country. Exciting to play, intelligent and imaginative, Holyhead is well worth going out of your way for and in Summer is quite superb.

Le pont a fait d'Anglesey une presqu'île, et de «Trearddur Bay» (comme on appelle Holyhead) une oeuvre mieux connue. Les joueurs locaux vous raconteront quelques horribles histoires sur des golfeurs perdus et des scores terrifiants, mais le Pays de Galles est aussi celui des contes de fées. Ce parcours est difficile par grand vent, mais c'est le cas de tous les links. Assez court, ce qui explique qu'il n'ait pas reçu beaucoup de championnats très prestigieux, pas trop accidenté, il a des fairways étroits, bien modelés, des roughs naturels souvent parsemés d'une dense végétation de bruyère, de genêts, d'ajoncs et même de fougères. C'est un test d'une grande franchise pour tous les niveaux (il est signé James Braid, une référence), avec des greens parmi les meilleurs du pays. Superbe au printemps, excitant à jouer, intelligent et imaginatif, Holyhead mérite le détour.

Holyhead (Caergybi) Golf Club
Lon Carreg Fawr, Trearddur Bay
WAL - HOLYHEAD, Gwynedd LL65 2YG

Office	Secrétariat	(44) 01407 - 763 279
Pro shop	Pro-shop	(44) 01407 - 762 022
Fax	Fax	
Situation	Situation	
3 km S of Holyhead (pop. 11 796)		
Annual closure	Fermeture annnuelle	no
Weekly closure	Fermeture hebdomadaire	no

Fees main season
Tarifs haute saison 18 holes

	Week days Semaine	We/Bank holidays We/Férié
Individual Individuel	£ 20	£ 25
Couple Couple	£ 40	£ 50

Caddy	Caddy	no
Electric Trolley	Chariot électrique	no
Buggy	Voiturette	no
Clubs	Clubs	yes

Credit cards Cartes de crédit
VISA - AMEX

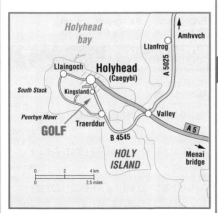

Access Accès : A55 then A5. In Valley, turn left on B4545.
Map 5 on page 414 Carte 5 Page 414

GOLF COURSE / PARCOURS — 16/20

Site	Site	■■■■
Maintenance	Entretien	■■■■
Architect	Architecte	James Braid
Type	Type	heathland
Relief	Relief	■■
Water in play	Eau en jeu	
Exp. to wind	Exposé au vent	■■■■■
Trees in play	Arbres en jeu	

Scorecard Carte de score	Chp. Chp.	Mens Mess.	Ladies Da.
Length Long.	5922	5180	4825
Par	71	68	72

Advised golfing ability Niveau de jeu recommandé	0	12	24	36

Hcp required Handicap exigé certificate

CLUB HOUSE & AMENITIES / CLUB HOUSE ET ANNEXES — 7/10

Pro shop	Pro-shop	■■■■
Driving range	Practice	■
Sheltered	couvert	no
On grass	sur herbe	no
Putting-green	putting-green	yes
Pitching-green	pitching green	yes

HOTEL FACILITIES / ENVIRONNEMENT HOTELIER — 5/10

HOTELS HÔTELS
Trearddur Bay Hotel — Holyhead
32 rooms, D £ 60 — 3 km
Tel (44) 01407 - 860 301
Fax (44) 01407 - 861 181

Moranedd — Trearddur Bay
6 rooms, D £ 49 — 3 km
Tel (44) 01407 - 860 324

RESTAURANTS RESTAURANTS
Trearddur Bay Hotel — Holyhead
Tel (44) 01407 - 860 301 — 3 km

681

MARRIOTT ST PIERRE OLD COURSE 〉 16 8 7

Purchasing this course allowed the Marriott group to rejuvenate and put the whole site centre-stage, with notably the arrival of the Solheim Cup in 1996. With a hotel now set up in the little 14th century manor here, the venue has become a leading resort which comprises two courses, the best known and most demanding of which is the «Old Course», named thus because it dates from only 1961. Designed by Ken Cotton, this has all the style of a typical park-land course where the finishing holes bring a lot of water into play. It is certainly not the world's most subtle course, but this honesty has the advantage of letting the golfer feel immediately at home and of carding the score he or she really deserves. We would advise green-feers not to go for the back-tees, especially on the 18th, a huge par 3.

L'achat de ce golf par le groupe Marriott a permis un rajeunissement notable, mais lui a aussi donné un coup de projecteur accentué par la venue de la Solheim Cup 1996. Avec son hôtel installé dans un petit manoir du XIVème siècle, c'est devenu un «resort» important, qui comprend deux parcours dont le plus connu et le plus exigeant est le «Old Course,» dénommé ainsi bien qu'il ne date que de 1961. Dessiné par Ken Cotton, c'est un parcours typique de l'esthétique des parcs, avec un finale où l'eau est très en jeu. Ce n'est sans doute pas le parcours le plus subtil du monde, mais cette franchise a l'avantage de permettre immédiatement de s'y sentir à l'aise, et de faire le score que l'on mérite vraiment. On conseillera aux visiteurs de ne pas choisir les départs arrière, surtout au 18, énorme par 3.

Marriott St Pierre Hotel & Country Club
St Pierre Park
WAL - CHEPSTOW, Gwent NP6 6YA

Office	Secrétariat	(44) 01291 - 625 261
Pro shop	Pro-shop	(44) 01291 - 621 400
Fax	Fax	(44) 01291 - 629 975
Situation	Situation	

20 km E of Newport (pop. 133 318)

Annual closure	Fermeture annnuelle	no
Weekly closure	Fermeture hebdomadaire	no

Fees main season
Tarifs haute saison full day

	Week days Semaine	We/Bank holidays We/Férié
Individual Individuel	£ 50	—
Couple Couple	£ 100	—

Weekends: members and hotel guests only

Caddy	Caddy	on request
Electric Trolley	Chariot électrique	yes
Buggy	Voiturette	yes
Clubs	Clubs	yes

Credit cards Cartes de crédit
VISA - Eurocard - AMEX - DC

682

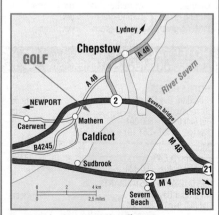

Access Accès : Newport A48 → Chepstow.
Golf 3 km (2 m. before Chepstow).
Map 6 on page 417 Carte 6 Page 417

GOLF COURSE
PARCOURS
16/20

Site	Site	
Maintenance	Entretien	
Architect	Architecte	C.K. Cotton
Type	Type	parkland
Relief	Relief	
Water in play	Eau en jeu	
Exp. to wind	Exposé au vent	
Trees in play	Arbres en jeu	

Scorecard Carte de score	Chp. Chp.	Mens Mess.	Ladies Da.
Length Long.	6280	5920	5337
Par	71	71	75

Advised golfing ability		0 12 24 36
Niveau de jeu recommandé		
Hcp required	Handicap exigé	certificate

CLUB HOUSE & AMENITIES
CLUB HOUSE ET ANNEXES
8/10

Pro shop	Pro-shop	
Driving range	Practice	
Sheltered	couvert	no
On grass	sur herbe	yes
Putting-green	putting-green	yes
Pitching-green	pitching green	yes

HOTEL FACILITIES
ENVIRONNEMENT HOTELIER
7/10

HOTELS HÔTELS
Marriott Hotel — Golf
148 rooms, D £ 110 — on site
Tel (44) 01291 - 625 261, Fax (44) 01291 - 629 975

George — Chepstow
14 rooms, D £ 95 — 3 km
Tel (44) 01291 - 625 363, Fax (44) 01291 - 627 418

Beaufort — Chepstow
18 rooms, D £ 50 — 3 km
Tel (44) 01291 - 622 497, Fax (44) 01291 - 627 389

RESTAURANTS RESTAURANTS
Marriott Hotel — Golf
Tel (44) 01291 - 625 261 — on site

Parva Farmhouse — Tintern
Tel (44) 01291 - 689 411 — 8 km

NEFYN & DISTRICT

This course is hardly close to the major tourist routes, but the site at least deserves a visit. Perched atop cliffs, it is very similar to a links course although some holes prefer heather to dunes. The course was founded in 1907, re-styled by J.H. Taylor and James Braid and completed in 1993. The site also houses a 9-holer between two sea inlets. The 18 hole course is no walk-over but never too tough or unfair. You also have to play every shot in the book, compounded by the fact that you often have a choice between playing safe or «going for it». The latter option can turn out to be foolhardy indeed on certain blind-shots. Never mind, you can stop off at the pub close to the 12th hole to boost your sagging spirits before squaring up to a wonderful finish, of which for us the 15th is the crowning moment. Maintenance is excellent and the clubhouse extends a warm welcome.

Ce n'est pas exactement sur les autoroutes de touristes, mais le site au moins mérite une visite. Perché sur les falaises, il est apparenté à un links, bien que certains trous soient assez proches des terrains de bruyère. Ce golf a été fondé en 1907, remanié par J.H. Taylor et James Braid, et achevé en 1993. On y trouve aussi un petit 9 trous entre deux bras de mer. Le 18 trous n'est pas facile, mais n'est jamais trop sévère ni injuste. On doit d'autant plus y jouer toute la gamme des coups de golf que l'on a souvent le choix entre la sécurité et l'héroïsme, qui peut s'avérer folie sur certains coups aveugles. Mais on peut faire une halte pour reprendre ses esprits au pub non loin du green du 12, afin d'affronter un très beau finish, dont le 15 est pour nous le sommet. L'entretien est de très bonne qualité, et le Clubhouse très chaleureux.

Nefyn & District Golf Club

Morfa Nefyn
WAL - PWLLHELI, Gwynedd LL53 6DA

Office	Secrétariat	(44) 01758 - 720 966
Pro shop	Pro-shop	(44) 01758 - 720 102
Fax	Fax	
Situation	Situation	

3 km W of Nefyn (pop. 2 548)
32 km W of Caernarfon (pop. 9 695)

Annual closure	Fermeture annnuelle	no
Weekly closure	Fermeture hebdomadaire	no

Fees main season	Tarifs haute saison		18 holes
		Week days Semaine	We/Bank holidays We/Férié
Individual Individuel		£ 22	£ 37
Couple Couple		£ 44	£ 74

Caddy	Caddy	on request
Electric Trolley	Chariot électrique	yes
Buggy	Voiturette	£ 15/18 holes
Clubs	Clubs	yes

Credit cards Cartes de crédit
VISA - MasterCard - AMEX

GOLF

Gyrn-Fawr
Porth-Dinllaen · Llithraen · B 4417
Morfa Nefyn · **Nefyn** · B 4354
Groesflordd · Edern
· Criccieth
B 4417 · Bodluan · A 497
Carn Fadryn
Tudweiliog · B 4415 · **Pwllhei**
Aberdaron · A 499
B 4413
Abersoch · Y Gamlas

0 2 4 km
0 2,5 miles

Access Accès : North coast Lleyn Peninsula, on B4417
Map 5 on page 414 Carte 5 Page 414

GOLF COURSE
PARCOURS

16/20

Site	Site	
Maintenance	Entretien	
Architect	Architecte	James Braid J.H. Taylor
Type	Type	seaside course, links
Relief	Relief	
Water in play	Eau en jeu	
Exp. to wind	Exposé au vent	
Trees in play	Arbres en jeu	

Scorecard Carte de score	Chp. Chp.	Mens Mess.	Ladies Da.
Length Long.	5958	5750	5420
Par	71	71	75

Advised golfing ability Niveau de jeu recommandé		0 12 24 36
Hcp required	Handicap exigé	certificate

CLUB HOUSE & AMENITIES
CLUB HOUSE ET ANNEXES

6/10

Pro shop	Pro-shop	
Driving range	Practice	
Sheltered	couvert	no
On grass	sur herbe	yes
Putting-green	putting-green	yes
Pitching-green	pitching green	yes

HOTEL FACILITIES
ENVIRONNEMENT HOTELIER

5/10

HOTELS HÔTELS
Caeau Capel Hotel — Nefyn, 2 km
18 rooms, D £ 37
Tel (44) 01758 - 720 240

Plas Bodegroes — Pwllheli, 12 km
8 rooms, D £ 100 (with dinner)
Tél (44) 01758 - 612 363
Fax (44) 01758 - 701 247

Abersoch Harbour - 14 rooms, D £ 60 — Abersoch, 25 km
Tel (44) 01758 - 712 406

RESTAURANTS RESTAURANTS
Plas Bodegroes — Pwllheli, 12 km
Tel (44) 01758 - 612 363

Caeau Capel — Nefyn, 2 km
Tel (44) 01758 - 720 240

683

A week's golfing in the Cardiff and Swansea region can be a week of playing a different course every day and of getting to know some superb and visually very contrasting layouts. Between St. Pierre and Porthcawl, close to Celtic Manor, the Newport course is one of the best examples of a park-land golf course you could ever hope to find. What's more, green-keeping is excellent and the welcome from both the clubhouse and members is warm and friendly. They are rightly extremely proud of a varied layout with very reasonable yardage, spread over rolling landscape which is very pleasant to walk. You won't find any breath-taking designer ploys or excesses, just a sort of sobriety in a pretty country landscape. A quality course, quite simply.

Une semaine de golf dans la région de Cardiff et Swansea peut permettre de ne jamais jouer deux fois le même parcours, et d'en jouer de superbes, d'esthétiques très différentes, voire opposées. Entre St Pierre et Porthcawl, près de Celtic Manor, le parcours de Newport est l'un des meilleurs exemples de golfs de parcs que l'on puisse trouver. Ce qui ne gâte rien, l'entretien y est toujours très soigné, et l'accueil, du club comme des membres, très amical et chaleureux. Ils sont fiers à juste raison d'un tracé très varié, et de longueur très raisonnable sur un terrain vallonné, mais où il est agréable de jouer à pied. On ne trouvera pas ici de trouvailles architecturales à couper le souffle, ni d'excès, mais une sorte de sobriété élégante dans un joli paysage de campagne. La qualité, tout simplement.

Newport Golf Club

Great Oak, Rogerstone
WAL - NEWPORT, Gwent NP1 9FX

Office	Secrétariat	(44) 01633 - 892 643
Pro shop	Pro-shop	(44) 01633 - 893 271
Fax	Fax	(44) 01633 - 896 676
Situation	Situation	

6 km W of Newport (pop.133 318)

Annual closure	Fermeture annnuelle	no
Weekly closure	Fermeture hebdomadaire	no

Fees main season
Tarifs haute saison 18 holes

	Week days Semaine	We/Bank holidays We/Férié
Individual Individuel	£ 30	—
Couple Couple	£ 60	—

Weekends: members only

Caddy	Caddy	no
Electric Trolley	Chariot électrique	yes
Buggy	Voiturette	no
Clubs	Clubs	yes

Credit cards Cartes de crédit
VISA - MasterCard - AMEX - DC

684

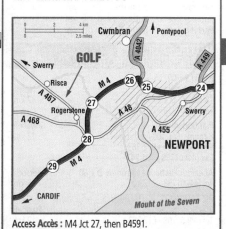

Access Accès : M4 Jct 27, then B4591.
Golf 1 km (1/2 m) W of exit.
Map 6 on page 417 Carte 6 Page 417

GOLF COURSE
PARCOURS

15/20

Site	Site	
Maintenance	Entretien	
Architect	Architecte	Unknown
Type	Type	parkland
Relief	Relief	
Water in play	Eau en jeu	
Exp. to wind	Exposé au vent	
Trees in play	Arbres en jeu	

Scorecard	Chp.	Mens	Ladies
Carte de score	Chp.	Mess.	Da.
Length Long.	5852	5632	5195
Par	72	72	74

Advised golfing ability	0	12	24	36
Niveau de jeu recommandé				

Hcp required   Handicap exigé   certificate

CLUB HOUSE & AMENITIES
CLUB HOUSE ET ANNEXES

6/10

Pro shop	Pro-shop	
Driving range	Practice	
Sheltered	couvert	no
On grass	sur herbe	yes
Putting-green	putting-green	yes
Pitching-green	pitching green	yes

HOTEL FACILITIES
ENVIRONNEMENT HOTELIER

7/10

HOTELS HÔTELS

Westgate - 69 rooms, D £ 75   Newport, 3 km
Tél (44) 01633 - 244 444
Fax (44) 01633 - 246 616

Newport Lodge - 27 rooms, D £ 67   Newport, 3 km
Tel (44) 01633 - 821 818, Fax (44) 01633 - 856 360

Parkway   Cwmbran
70 rooms, D £ 82.50   6 km
Tel (44) 01633 - 871 199, Fax (44) 01633 - 869 160

Celtic Manor Hotel   Newport
73 rooms, D £ 99   5 km
Tel (44) 01633 - 413 000, Fax (44) 01633 - 412 910

RESTAURANTS RESTAURANTS

Hedley's (Celtic Manor)   Newport
Tel (44) 01633 - 413 000   5 km

PENNARD

Firstly there are the superb views over a rugged coastline, the sea, smugglers' beaches and dunes, then the countryside with remains of castles. In a highly romantic setting, don't ever let this course catch you napping. At first sight it can be intimidating with steep hills that make club selection a delicate business (there are a few blind shots to contend with) but the difficulties are not insurmountable even for a mid-handicapper, unless the wind begins to blow a little too hard. In calm weather, Pennard certainly could not claim to be a major championship course, but it is incredibly enjoyable both visually and technically. And when you do finally get to grips with it, you feel that you could be a good player. Green-keeping is of a very high standard, and the greens are slick and firm all year round (Winters are very mild here). Discovery recommended.

D'abord il y a des vues superbes sur les côtes découpées, la mer, des plages de contrebandiers, les dunes, la campagne, des châteaux en ruines. Dans un site aussi hautement romantique, il ne faut pas rêver pour jouer ce parcours. Il peut intimider au premier abord avec ses reliefs qui compliquent notamment la sélection des clubs (quelques coups aveugles), mais ses difficultés ne sont pas insurmontables, même pour un joueur moyen, sauf si le vent se met à souffler un peu fort. Certes, par temps calme, Pennard ne saurait prétendre être un parcours de grands championnats, mais il procure un plaisir fou, visuellement et techniquement. Et quand vous parvenez à l'apprivoiser, vous avez l'impression d'être un grand joueur. L'entretien est ici très soigné, les greens rapides et fermes toute l'année (les hivers sont assez doux). A découvrir !

Pennard Golf Club

2, Southgate Road, Southgate
WAL - SWANSEA SA3 2BT

Office	Secrétariat	(44) 01792 - 233 131
Pro shop	Pro-shop	(44) 01792 - 233 451
Fax	Fax	
Situation	Situation	

12 km W of Swansea (pop. 181 906)

Annual closure	Fermeture annnuelle	no
Weekly closure	Fermeture hebdomadaire	no

Fees main season
Tarifs haute saison full day

	Week days Semaine	We/Bank holidays We/Férié
Individual Individuel	£ 24	£ 30
Couple Couple	£ 48	£ 60

Caddy	Caddy	no
Electric Trolley	Chariot électrique	no
Buggy	Voiturette	no
Clubs	Clubs	yes

Credit cards Cartes de crédit
VISA

GOLF

SWANSEA
Dunvant
Swansea
A 4118
A 4067
Swansea bay
Bishopston
Penamen
Pennard
The mumbles
B4422
Mumbles head
Southgate
Pwlldu head
Okswich bay

0   2   4 km
0   2.5 miles

Access Accès : Cardiff, M4, A4067, B4436 to Pennard Church, → Golf
Map 6 on page 416 Carte 6 Page 416

GOLF COURSE PARCOURS 18/20

Site	Site	████████
Maintenance	Entretien	████████
Architect	Architecte	James Braid C.K. Cotton
Type	Type	links
Relief	Relief	███
Water in play	Eau en jeu	██
Exp. to wind	Exposé au vent	███████
Trees in play	Arbres en jeu	███

Scorecard Carte de score	Chp. Chp.	Mens Mess.	Ladies Da.
Length Long.	5701	5508	4880
Par	71	71	73

Advised golfing ability		0	12	24	36
Niveau de jeu recommandé				████	
Hcp required	Handicap exigé	no			

CLUB HOUSE & AMENITIES CLUB HOUSE ET ANNEXES 6/10

Pro shop	Pro-shop	██████
Driving range	Practice	████
Sheltered	couvert	no
On grass	sur herbe	yes
Putting-green	putting-green	yes
Pitching-green	pitching green	yes

HOTEL FACILITIES ENVIRONNEMENT HOTELIER 6/10

HOTELS HÔTELS

Hilton National
120 rooms, D £ 75
Tel (44) 01792 - 310 330
Fax (44) 01792 - 797 535
Swansea
12 km

Forte Crest
99 rooms, D £ 69
Tel (44) 01792 - 651 074
Fax (44) 01792 - 456 044
Swansea
15 km

Windsor Lodge
18 rooms, D £ 60
Tel (44) 01792 - 642 158
Fax (44) 01792 - 648 996
Swansea
15 km

RESTAURANTS RESTAURANTS

Annie's
Tel (44) 01792 - 655 603
Swansea
15 km

685

There is not much missing at Pyle & Kenfig for this to rank amongst the very great courses. For once, a course of this type returns to the clubhouse at the 9th and in doing so emphasises the difference between the front and back nines, separated by a road. Although the outward half is not to be sniffed at, it doesn't have the dune landscape of the epic back nine, which has a single par 5 but some beefy par 3s and huge par 4s (from hole 16 to 18 with a head-wind to boot). The greatest difficulties are the rough, the positions you can get yourself into when straying off the fairway and the cleverly placed pot bunkers. The greens are on the flat side and generally reachable with bump and run shots, luckily for the players, because they are of course often very exposed to the wind. Not an easy course, but very forthright.

Il ne manque pas grand-chose à Pyle & Kenfig pour être dans la cour des très grands parcours. Pour une fois, un parcours de ce type revient au Clubhouse au 9, cela ne fait que souligner la différence entre l'aller et le retour, séparés par une route. Bien que l'aller ne soit pas négligeable, il lui manque le caractère dunaire marquant un retour héroïque, où l'on trouve un seul par 5, mais des par 3 très musclés et d'énormes par 4 (du 16 au 18, contre les vents dominants). Les plus grandes difficultés sont les roughs, les positions où l'on se trouve par rapport à la balle quand on s'égare hors des fairways, et de profonds bunkers (trop) bien placés. Les greens sont assez plats, leur accès généralement possible en roulant, ce qui est fort heureux car l'exposition au vent est bien sûr importante. Un parcours pas facile, mais franc.

Pyle & Kznfig Golf Club
Waun-y-Mer
WAL - KENFIG, Mid Glamorgan CF33 4PU

Office	Secrétariat	(44) 01656 - 783 093
Pro shop	Pro-shop	(44) 01656 - 772 446
Fax	Fax	
Situation	Situation	

40 km W of Cardiff (pop. 279 055)
10 km E of Port Talbot (pop. 51 023)

Annual closure	Fermeture annnuelle	no
Weekly closure	Fermeture hebdomadaire	no

Fees main season
Tarifs haute saison 18 holes

	Week days Semaine	We/Bank holidays We/Férié
Individual Individuel	£ 30	—
Couple Couple	£ 60	—

Weekends: with members only

Caddy	Caddy	no
Electric Trolley	Chariot électrique	yes
Buggy	Voiturette	no
Clubs	Clubs	yes

Credit cards Cartes de crédit
VISA - AMEX

686

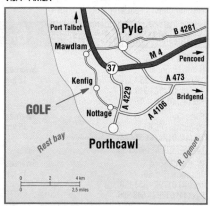

Port Talbot
Pyle B 4281
Mawdlam
M 4
Pencoed
37
Kenfig A 473
A 4229 Bridgend
GOLF Nottage A 4106
Rest bay **Porthcawl**
R. Ogmore

0 — 2 — 4 km
0 — 2,5 miles

Access Accès : M4, Jct 37, → Porthcawl,
at 3rd roundabout, 1st right
Map 6 on page 417 Carte 6 Page 417

GOLF COURSE
PARCOURS 17 /20

Site	Site	▬▬▬▬▬▬
Maintenance	Entretien	▬▬▬▬▬▬
Architect	Architecte	Harry S. Colt
Type	Type	links, open country
Relief	Relief	▬▬▬
Water in play	Eau en jeu	▬▬▬
Exp. to wind	Exposé au vent	▬▬▬▬
Trees in play	Arbres en jeu	▬▬

Scorecard Carte de score	Chp. Chp.	Mens Mess.	Ladies Da.
Length Long.	6086	5571	4941
Par	71	71	74

Advised golfing ability 0 12 24 36
Niveau de jeu recommandé ▬▬▬▬▬▬
Hcp required Handicap exigé certificate

CLUB HOUSE & AMENITIES
CLUB HOUSE ET ANNEXES 7 /10

Pro shop	Pro-shop	▬▬▬▬
Driving range	Practice	▬▬▬
Sheltered	couvert	no
On grass	sur herbe	yes
Putting-green	putting-green	yes
Pitching-green	pitching green	yes

HOTEL FACILITIES
ENVIRONNEMENT HOTELIER 5 /10

HOTELS HÔTELS
Fairways Hotel Porthcawl
25 rooms, D £ 65 2 km
Tel (44) 01656 - 782 085 - Fax (44) 01656 - 785 351

The Porthcawl Hotel Porthcawl
28 rooms, D £ 44 2 km
Tel (44) 01656 - 783 544

Heritage Hotel Porthcawl
8 rooms, D £ 50 2 km
Tel (44) 01656 - 771 881

RESTAURANTS RESTAURANTS
Heritage Hotel Porthcawl
Tel (44) 01656 - 771 881 2 km

You sometimes wonder why some good courses never reach the sort of stardom they might deserve. Here, despite the excellent road from Birmingham to Cardiff running close by, the reason might be the absence of any top tournament. From another angle, this tranquillity is a blessing for players who love to feel alone in the world. Although laid out over «rolling» landscape, the course's name comes from the Rolls family (as in Royce), whose estate overlooks the course. It is sited around a forest-covered hill in a park-land landscape lined with some superb trees. Walking can be a little hard on the legs but there are buggies to give you the time to admire the landscape and wild-life or to drive on and reconnoitre some of the blind shots that await you. As far as the course's very own personality is concerned, you'll remember best of all the magnificent par 3s.

On se demande pourquoi de bons parcours restent à l'écart de la célébrité. Dans le cas présent, l'excellente route de Birmingham à Cardiff passant pourtant à côté, il manque peut-être un grand tournoi. D'un autre côté, cette tranquillité est une bénédiction pour les joueurs, qui adorent être seuls au monde, c'est bien connu. Certes le terrain est «rolling,» mais le nom vient de la famille Rolls (comme Royce) dont la propriété domine le parcours, dessiné autour d'une grande colline boisée, dans un paysage de parc et de bois superbes. Marcher peut-être ici fatigant, mais il y a des voiturettes pour se donner le temps d'admirer le paysage et la vie sauvage, ou d'aller repérer les lieux sur les quelques coups aveugles. Pour ce qui est de la personnalité du parcours, on se souviendra notamment des très beaux par 3.

The Rolls of Monmouth

The Hendre
WAL - MONMOUTH, Gwent NP5 4HG

Office	Secrétariat	(44) 01600 - 715 353
Pro shop	Pro-shop	(44) 01600 - 715 353
Fax	Fax	(44) 01600 - 713 115
Situation	Situation	

7 km W of Monmouth (pop. 8 204)
58 km NE of Cardiff (pop. 279 055)

Annual closure	Fermeture annnuelle	no
Weekly closure	Fermeture hebdomadaire	no

Fees main season
Tarifs haute saison full day

	Week days Semaine	We/Bank holidays We/Férié
Individual Individuel	£ 30	£ 35
Couple Couple	£ 60	£ 70

Caddy	Caddy	no
Electric Trolley	Chariot électrique	yes
Buggy	Voiturette	£ 25/18 holes
Clubs	Clubs	no
Credit cards Cartes de crédit		VISA - AMEX - DC

Access Accès : Cardiff, M4 East, Jct 24, then A449
to Monmouth. Golf on B4233 (Abergavenny Road),
5 km W of Monmouth.
Map 6 on page 417 Carte 6 Page 417

GOLF COURSE PARCOURS   15/20

Site	Site	■■■■■
Maintenance	Entretien	■■■■■
Architect	Architecte	Urbis Planning
Type	Type	parkland, hilly
Relief	Relief	■■■■■■
Water in play	Eau en jeu	■■■
Exp. to wind	Exposé au vent	■■
Trees in play	Arbres en jeu	■■■■

Scorecard Carte de score	Chp. Chp.	Mens Mess.	Ladies Da.
Length Long.	6127	5718	5215
Par	72	72	75

Advised golfing ability		0 12 24 36
Niveau de jeu recommandé		■■■■■
Hcp required	Handicap exigé	no

CLUB HOUSE & AMENITIES CLUB HOUSE ET ANNEXES   6/10

Pro shop	Pro-shop	▭
Driving range	Practice	▭
Sheltered	couvert	no
On grass	sur herbe	no
Putting-green	putting-green	yes
Pitching-green	pitching green	yes

687

HOTEL FACILITIES ENVIRONNEMENT HOTELIER   6/10

HOTELS HÔTELS
Riverside   Monmouth
17 rooms, D £ 70   6 km
Tel (44) 01600 - 715 577

Penyclawdd Court   Llanfihangel Crucorney
3 rooms, D £ 60   10 km
Tel (44) 01873 - 890 719
Fax (44) 01873 - 890 848

Llansantffraed Court   Abergavenny
21 rooms, D £ 120   10 km
Tel (44) 01873 - 840 678
Fax (44) 01873 - 840 674

RESTAURANTS RESTAURANTS
Clytha Arms   Raglan
Tel (44) 01873 - 840 206   8 km

ROYAL PORTHCAWL

This the most famous course in Wales and does full honour to its reputation. Royal Porthcawl is an absolute must for great course "trophy-hunters". It is, of course, a links, although half a dozen very distinctive holes are more heather-land in style and are played on a sort of high plateau overlooking the Bristol Channel. Contrary to many links, where holes are often laid out in line, the holes here shoot out in all directions and make club selection a real headache, depending on the wind. This is a part of what goes to make up the greatness and test value of this layout, where the slightest technical shortcoming will cost you dearly, and where the uninterrupted view over the sea might make you wish you had gone to the beach instead. A true masterpiece, beautifully maintained, which has staged some memorable Curtis Cup and Walker Cup matches and five British Amateur Championships.

C'est le plus fameux parcours du Pays de Galles, il honore dignement sa réputation, et doit figurer dans le "tableau" des chasseurs de grands golfs. C'est évidemment un links, bien qu'une demi-douzaine de trous de caractère un peu plus "terre de bruyère" trouvent place sur une sorte de haut plateau dominant le Canal de Bristol. Au contraire de nombreux links, dont les trous sont souvent alignés, ceux-ci tournent dans toutes les directions, à vous donner le vertige quant au choix de clubs suivant le vent. C'est une part de ce qui fait la grandeur et la valeur de test de ce parcours, où la moindre faiblesse technique se paie cher, où la vue constante de la mer peut vous faire regretter de ne pas avoir choisi d'aller à la plage. Un vrai chef-d'oeuvre merveilleusement entretenu, où se sont déroulées de mémorables Curtis Cup et Walker Cup, ainsi que cinq British Amateur.

Royal Porthcawl Golf Club
WAL - PORTHCAWL, Mid Glamorgan CF36 3VW

Office	Secrétariat	(44) 01656 - 782 251
Pro shop	Pro-shop	(44) 01656 - 773 702
Fax	Fax	
Situation	Situation	

40 km W of Cardiff (pop. 279 055)
10 km E of Port Talbot (pop. 51 023)

Annual closure	Fermeture annnuelle	no
Weekly closure	Fermeture hebdomadaire	no
Fees main season	Tarifs haute saison	full day

	Week days Semaine	We/Bank holidays We/Férié
Individual Individuel	£ 45	—
Couple Couple	£ 90	—

Weekends: with members only

Caddy	Caddy	on request
Electric Trolley	Chariot électrique	yes
Buggy	Voiturette	no
Clubs	Clubs	yes

Credit cards Cartes de crédit
VISA - MasterCard - AMEX - DC

688

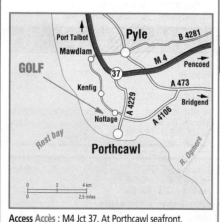

Access Accès : M4 Jct 37. At Porthcawl seafront, right → Locks Common, then left.
Map 6 on page 417 Carte 6 Page 417

GOLF COURSE
PARCOURS

19/20

Site	Site	
Maintenance	Entretien	
Architect	Architecte	Charles Gibson
Type	Type	links
Relief	Relief	
Water in play	Eau en jeu	
Exp. to wind	Exposé au vent	
Trees in play	Arbres en jeu	

Scorecard Carte de score	Chp. Chp.	Mens Mess.	Ladies Da.
Length Long.	6083	5608	5231
Par	72	72	75

Advised golfing ability
Niveau de jeu recommandé

0 12 24 36

Hcp required   Handicap exigé   certificate

CLUB HOUSE & AMENITIES
CLUB HOUSE ET ANNEXES

7/10

Pro shop	Pro-shop	
Driving range	Practice	
Sheltered	couvert	no
On grass	sur herbe	yes
Putting-green	putting-green	yes
Pitching-green	pitching green	yes

HOTEL FACILITIES
ENVIRONNEMENT HOTELIER

5/10

HOTELS HÔTELS
Fairways Hotel   Porthcawl
25 rooms, D £ 65   2 km
Tel (44) 01656 - 782 085 - Fax (44) 01656 - 785 351

The Porthcawl Hotel   Porthcawl
28 rooms, D £ 44   2 km
Tel (44) 01656 - 783 544

Heritage Hotel   Porthcawl
8 rooms, D £ 50   2 km
Tel (44) 01656 - 771 881

RESTAURANTS RESTAURANTS
Heritage Hotel   Porthcawl
Tel (44) 01656 - 771 881   2 km

ROYAL ST DAVID'S) 18 6 5

Overlooked by the extraordinary medieval Harlech castle with a fortified stairway running down to the sea, this course (named after the patron saint of Wales) is more majestic than ever. The pros say this is the toughest par 69 in the world, but one thing is sure: for the ordinary mortal, playing 3 strokes over your handicap is already a right "royal" exploit. The constant changes in hole direction are a further disruptive factor for golfers who already have to contend with the optical illusions created by the dune environment and the sensation of space. The shot you need to master here is of course the low ball and you need a good measure of flair to place your bump 'n run shots close to the pin. High shots will more often than not end up in spots where your recovery can be "most amusing". A great course.

Dominé par l'extraordinaire château médiéval d'Harlech, avec son escalier fortifié allant jusqu'à la mer, ce parcours (portant le nom du patron du Pays de Galles) acquiert une majesté supplémentaire. Les professionnels disent qu'il s'agit du par 69 le plus difficile du monde. Une chose est sûre, pour le commun des mortels, jouer trois au-dessus de son handicap est déjà «royal». Les changements constants d'orientation des trous perturbent les joueurs, déjà aux prises avec les illusions de distance que donnent l'environnement de dunes, mais aussi la sensation d'espace. Le coup à maîtriser est bien sûr la balle basse, et il faut beaucoup de flair pour placer les obligatoires "bump 'n run" à proximité du trou. Quant aux balles hautes, elles terminent leur course dans des endroits d'où il est amusant de s'extraire. Un grand parcours.

Royal St David's Golf Club
WAL - HARLECH, Gwynedd LL46 2UB

Office	Secrétariat	(44) 01766 - 780 361
Pro shop	Pro-shop	(44) 01766 - 780 851
Fax	Fax	
Situation	Situation	

3 km from Harlech (pop. 1 880)

Annual closure	Fermeture annnuelle	no
Weekly closure	Fermeture hebdomadaire	no

Fees main season
Tarifs haute saison 18 holes

	Week days Semaine	We/Bank holidays We/Férié
Individual Individuel	£ 27	£ 32
Couple Couple	£ 54	£ 64

Booking essential at weekends

Caddy	Caddy	no
Electric Trolley	Chariot électrique	yes
Buggy	Voiturette	yes
Clubs	Clubs	yes

Credit cards Cartes de crédit
VISA - AMEX

Access Accès : Manchester M56, A55 to Bangor, then A487 South to Porthmadog, A470 and A496 → Harlech. Golf on right side before Harlech.
Map 5 on page 414 Carte 5 Page 414

GOLF COURSE
PARCOURS   18/20

Site	Site	
Maintenance	Entretien	
Architect	Architecte	Unknown
Type	Type	links
Relief	Relief	
Water in play	Eau en jeu	
Exp. to wind	Exposé au vent	
Trees in play	Arbres en jeu	

Scorecard Carte de score	Chp. Chp.	Mens Mess.	Ladies Da.
Length Long.	5848	5713	5266
Par	69	69	74

Advised golfing ability Niveau de jeu recommandé		0 12 24 36
Hcp required	Handicap exigé	certificate

CLUB HOUSE & AMENITIES
CLUB HOUSE ET ANNEXES   6/10

Pro shop	Pro-shop	
Driving range	Practice	
Sheltered	couvert	no
On grass	sur herbe	yes
Putting-green	putting-green	yes
Pitching-green	pitching green	yes

HOTEL FACILITIES
ENVIRONNEMENT HOTELIER   5/10

HOTELS HÔTELS
St David's Hotel Harlech
60 rooms, D £ 40 adjacent
Tel (44) 01766 - 780 366
Fax (44) 01766 - 780 820

Castle Cottage Harlech
6 rooms, D £ 52 3 km
Tel (44) 01766 - 780 479

RESTAURANTS RESTAURANTS
Castle Cottage Harlech
Tel (44) 01766 - 780 479 close

689

A good number of specialists lent a hand in laying out this course, including Fernie, Vardon, Braid, Fowler, Willie Park, H.S. Colt and, more recently Donald Steel. Perched high up overlooking Porthcawl, Southerndown has resisted any attempts at serious human interference and stayed very natural in style. And it is true that the land was ideal for the building of a golf course. The fairways are cropped by sheep, who never go on strike and work most methodically. Very British in its sloping and hilly design but never over-tiring on the legs, this is not a links because the terrain is clay (well drained) but there are more bushes than trees in play. Still, you are playing links-style golf here, hitting boring low shots. A tough test from the back tees, a little easier from the front and all in all, well worth getting to know.

Bien des spécialistes se sont penchés sur ce parcours : Fernie, Vardon, Braid, Fowler, Willie Park, H.S. Colt et dernièrement Donald Steel. Perché haut et dominant Porthcawl, Southerndown a pourtant réussi à se préserver des atteintes et rester très naturel : il est vrai que le terrain se prêtait idéalement à la construction d'un golf. Les fairways sont d'ailleurs tondus par les moutons, qui ne font jamais grève et travaillent avec méthode ! Très britannique dans son dessin typique des terrains en pente, mais sans fatigue excessive, ce n'est pas un links, parce que le terrain est argileux (bien drainé) et bien que l'on y trouve plus de buissons que d'arbres en jeu, mais il faut utiliser le même type de jeu, avec des balles pénétrantes et basses. Difficile des départs arrière, il s'adoucit quand on avance un peu. A connaître.

Southerndown Golf Club

Ewenny
WAL - BRIDGEND, Mid. Glam. CF32 0QP

Office	Secrétariat	(44) 01656 - 880 476
Pro shop	Pro-shop	(44) 01656 - 880 476
Fax	Fax	
Situation	Situation	

5 km SW of Bridgend (pop. 14 311)

Annual closure	Fermeture annnuelle	no
Weekly closure	Fermeture hebdomadaire	no

Fees main season
Tarifs haute saison 18 holes

	Week days Semaine	We/Bank holidays We/Férié
Individual Individuel	£ 25	£ 35
Couple Couple	£ 50	£ 70

Weekends: only with a member

Caddy	Caddy	no
Electric Trolley	Chariot électrique	no
Buggy	Voiturette	no
Clubs	Clubs	yes

Credit cards Cartes de crédit
VISA

690

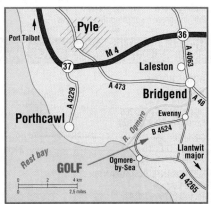

Access Accès : On the coast road Bridgend to Ogmore-by-Sea. Turn off at Pelican Inn (opp. Ogmore Castle)
Map 6 on page 417 Carte 6 Page 417

GOLF COURSE
PARCOURS

16/20

Site	Site	▬▬▬▬
Maintenance	Entretien	▬▬▬▬
Architect	Architecte	Willie Fernie
Type	Type	downland
Relief	Relief	▬▬▬
Water in play	Eau en jeu	▬▬
Exp. to wind	Exposé au vent	▬▬▬▬▬
Trees in play	Arbres en jeu	▬▬

Scorecard Carte de score	Chp. Chp.	Mens Mess.	Ladies Da.
Length Long.	5840	5395	5049
Par	70	69	74

Advised golfing ability		0	12	24	36
Niveau de jeu recommandé			▬▬▬▬		
Hcp required	Handicap exigé	certificate			

CLUB HOUSE & AMENITIES
CLUB HOUSE ET ANNEXES

7/10

Pro shop	Pro-shop	▬▬▬▬
Driving range	Practice	▬▬▬
Sheltered	couvert	no
On grass	sur herbe	yes
Putting-green	putting-green	yes
Pitching-green	pitching green	yes

HOTEL FACILITIES
ENVIRONNEMENT HOTELIER

7/10

HOTELS HÔTELS

Heronston	Bridgend
76 rooms, D £ 80	3 km
Tel (44) 01656 - 668 811	
Fax (44) 01656 - 667 391	
Coed-y-Mwstwr	Coychurch
22 rooms, D £ 100	6 km
Tel (44) 01656 - 860 261	
Fax (44) 01656 - 863 122	

RESTAURANTS RESTAURANTS

Frolics	Southerndown
Tel (44) 01656 - 880 127	3 km
Great House	Laleston
Tel (44) 01656 - 657 644	7 km

Firstly there is a landscape of pot-holed dunes, looking as if they have been stirred by the wind for years on end. And then comes the course, fashioned by men and nature for centuries with the sporadic help of James Braid, as witnessed by the contours of some of the greens and the location of the many bunkers. There are very few continental golfers who have heard much about Welsh courses. This one is a must as you travel around the magnificent coastline of this very likeable country. Depending on the weather, the course can turn into a major championship test or a superb walk in the bracing sea-air. This is the time to test your creativity and invent special shots, because you will often end up in situations that are completely new to you. Tenby is a surprising, honest and charming course to play.

D'abord, il y a un paysage de dunes agitées comme par des années de caprices du vent, un parcours façonné par les hommes et la nature pendant plus d'un siècle, avec l'aide sporadique de James Braid, visible par les contours de certains greens, et le placement de nombreux bunkers. Rares sont les golfeurs du continent qui ont entendu parler des parcours du Pays de Galles. Celui-ci est incontournable dans un circuit des côtes magnifiques de ce pays attachant. Suivant le temps, il prendra des allures de grand test de championnat, ou de superbe promenade dans un air vivifiant. C'est alors le moment de tester votre créativité, d'inventer des coups de golf, parce que vous serez souvent dans des situations inconnues. Surprenant et franc, Tenby est aussi un parcours de charme.

Tenby Golf Club

The Burrows
WAL - TENBY, Dyfed SA70 7NP

Office	Secrétariat	(44) 01834 - 842 978
Pro shop	Pro-shop	(44) 01834 - 842 978
Fax	Fax	
Situation	Situation	

W of Tenby (pop. 4 809)

Annual closure	Fermeture annnuelle	no
Weekly closure	Fermeture hebdomadaire	no

Fees main season
Tarifs haute saison — 18 holes

	Week days Semaine	We/Bank holidays We/Férié
Individual Individuel	£ 20	£ 24
Couple Couple	£ 40	£ 48

Caddy	Caddy	no
Electric Trolley	Chariot électrique	no
Buggy	Voiturette	no
Clubs	Clubs	yes

Credit cards Cartes de crédit
VISA - MasterCard - AMEX - DC

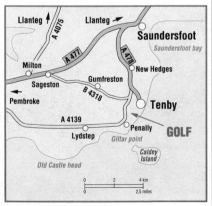

Access Accès : Cardiff, M4 West, A48, A477, A478 to Tenby. Golf near railway station.
Map 6 on page 416 Carte 6 Page 416

GOLF COURSE / PARCOURS — 18/20

Site	Site	
Maintenance	Entretien	
Architect	Architecte	James Braid
Type	Type	links
Relief	Relief	
Water in play	Eau en jeu	
Exp. to wind	Exposé au vent	
Trees in play	Arbres en jeu	

Scorecard Carte de score	Chp. Chp.	Mens Mess.	Ladies Da.
Length Long.	5767	5120	4943
Par	69	68	73

Advised golfing ability	0	12	24	36
Niveau de jeu recommandé				

Hcp required Handicap exigé — certificate

CLUB HOUSE & AMENITIES / CLUB HOUSE ET ANNEXES — 7/10

Pro shop	Pro-shop	
Driving range	Practice	
Sheltered	couvert	no
On grass	sur herbe	yes
Putting-green	putting-green	yes
Pitching-green	pitching green	yes

691

HOTEL FACILITIES / ENVIRONNEMENT HOTELIER — 6/10

HOTELS HÔTELS

Waterwynch House — Tenby
14 rooms, D £ 65 — 3 km
Tel (44) 01834 - 842 464
Fax (44) 01834 - 845 076

Penally Abbey — Penally
12 rooms, D £ 100 — 2 km
Tel (44) 01834 - 843 033
Fax (44) 01834 - 844 714

Heywood Mount Hotel — Tenby
21 rooms, D £ 52 — 1.5 km
Tel (44) 01834 - 842 087

St Brides Hotel — Saundersfoot
43 rooms, D £ 62.50 — 6 km
Tel (44) 01834 - 812 304
Fax (44) 01834 - 813 303

JAMESON
IRISH WHISKEY

L'IRLÁNDE en 70 cl.

Ireland
Northern Ireland

V ous trouverez ici, successivement, les parcours de la République d'Irlande et d'Irlande du Nord. Pour choisir les 90 meilleurs d'entre eux, nous avons volontairement mis l'accent sur les plus représentatifs, en particulier les links, que les golfeurs continentaux ont rarement l'habitude de trouver chez eux. Avec près de 250 parcours de 18 trous et 113 de 9 trous pour 200.000 joueurs licenciés, la place ne manque pas pour les visiteurs, et le territoire de l'Irlande est une destination touristique connue du monde entier. Vous y serez toujours le bienvenu, mais ne vous attendez pas à trouver des practices magnifiques (on trouve souvent de simples zones où l'on tape ses propres balles), ni toujours des Club-house somptueux). Ici, le modernisme et le luxe passent après la qualité du parcours et la chaleur de l'accueil. Une lettre d'introduction de votre club n'est jamais inutile. Pensez aussi à réserver vos départs.

693

Here, we have included in succession courses from the Republic of Ireland and Northern Ireland. When trimming the list down to 90, we deliberately focused on the most representative courses, especially the links courses, which continental golfers seldom have the chance to play locally. With nearly 250 eighteen-hole and 113 nine-hole courses or 200,000 registered players, there is no shortage of space for visitors, and Ireland is a golfing destination renowned the world over. You will always be made most welcome, but don't expect to find any magnificent driving ranges (you often find just rough practice areas where you can hit your own balls), or sumptuous club-houses. Here, modern facilities and luxury come second to the excellence of the course and warm hospitality. A letter of introduction from your own club is never a bad idea, and also remember to book your tee-off times.

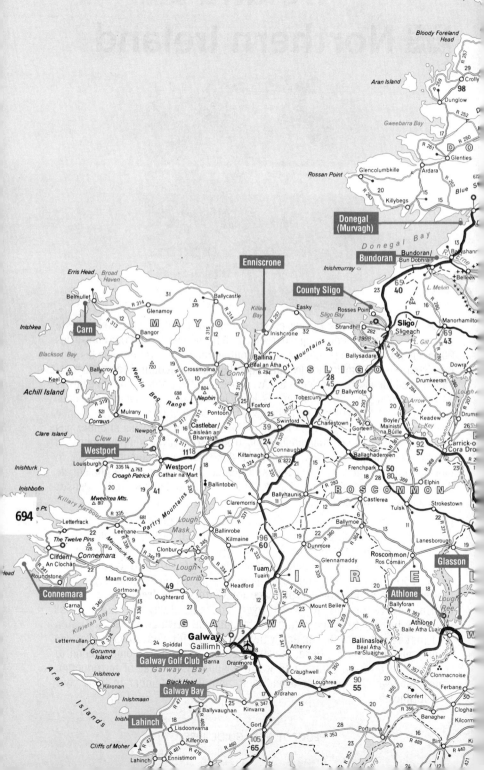

Map No 1
Carte n°1

km
0 10 20

694

695

d'après cartes n°405 - 13ème édition - 1997/1998
et n°986 - 16ème édition - 1998. Autorisation n°9607332.

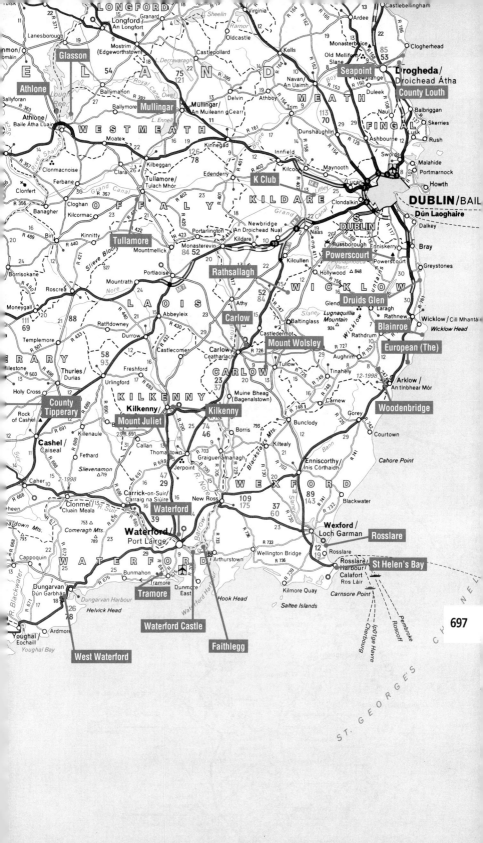

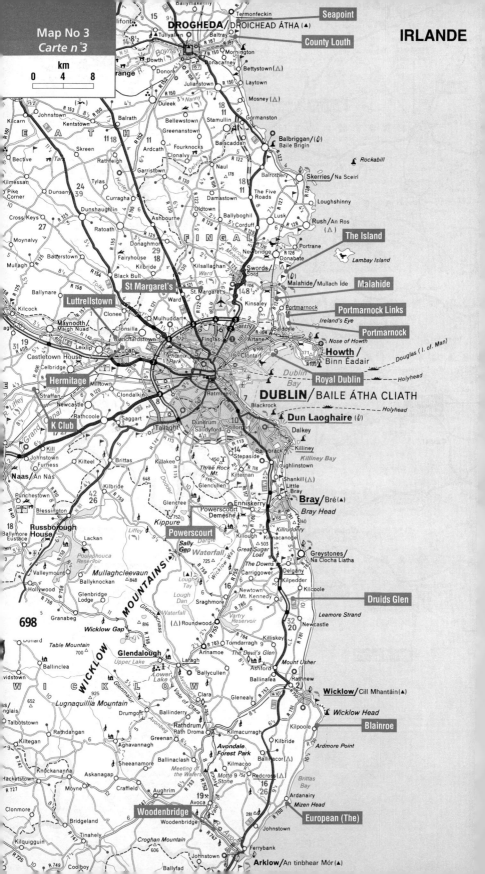

CLASSIFICATION OF IRISH COURSES
CLASSEMENT DES PARCOURS IRLANDAIS

This classification gives priority consideration
to the score awarded to the actual course.

Ce classement donne priorité à la note attribuée au parcours.

I: Republic of Ireland   U: Northern Ireland (Ulster)

Club-house and facilities
Note du Club-house et annexes

Course score
Note du parcours

Hotel facility score
Note de l'environnement hôtelier

Country
Pays

Page

| 19 | 7 | 7 | Ballybunion *Old Course* | I | 707 |

Score			Course	Country	Page	Score			Course	Country	Page
19	7	7	Ballybunion Old Course	I	707	15	6	5	Ballyliffin *Old Course*	I	710
19	8	8	Portmarnock	I	752	15	5	6	Belvoir Park	U	778
19	6	7	Royal County Down	U	790	15	6	6	Clandeboye		
19	7	7	Royal Portrush						*Dufferin Course*	U	782
			Dunluce Links	U	791	15	3	5	Cork GC	I	718
18	5	6	County Louth	I	719	15	7	5	County Tipperary	I	721
18	6	6	European (The)	I	729	15	5	5	Dooks	I	724
18	6	6	Lahinch	I	742	15	6	6	Dundalk	I	727
18	9	8	Mount Juliet	I	747	15	7	6	Fota Island	I	731
18	7	6	Tralee	I	766	15	6	7	Hermitage	I	736
17	6	5	Ballyliffin *Glashedy Links*	I	709	15	7	8	Killarney *Mahony's Point*	I	740
17	4	3	County Sligo	I	720	15	6	5	Kirkistown Castle	U	783
17	8	8	K Club	I	737	15	7	6	Knock	U	784
17	7	8	Portmarnock Links	I	753	15	7	6	Limerick County	I	744
17	6	7	Waterville	I	771	15	7	6	Lisburn	U	785
16	7	7	Ballybunion			15	7	7	Luttrellstown	I	745
			Cashen (New Course)	I	706	15	7	7	Old Head	I	751
16	6	6	Carlow	I	714	15	7	6	Powerscourt	I	755
16	5	3	Carn	I	715	15	7	6	Rathsallagh	I	756
16	6	6	Castlerock	U	781	15	7	7	Royal Belfast	U	789
16	6	4	Dingle (Ceann Sibeal)	I	722	15	6	6	Seapoint	I	760
16	2	6	Donegal (Murvagh)	I	723	15	8	6	Slieve Russell	I	762
16	9	7	Druids Glen	I	726	15	7	7	The Island	I	765
16	7	6	Enniscrone	I	728	15	6	5	Tullamore	I	768
16	7	7	Glasson	I	734	15	7	7	Westport	I	773
16	7	8	Killarney *Killeen Course*	I	739	14	6	4	Ardglass	U	776
16	5	5	Portsalon	I	754	14	7	6	Ballykisteen	I	708
16	7	7	Portstewart *Strand Course*	U	788	14	6	6	Bangor	U	777
16	7	6	Rosapenna	I	757	14	6	7	Beaufort	I	711
16	7	7	Royal Dublin	I	759	14	6	6	Connemara	I	717
16	7	7	St Margaret's	I	764	14	7	7	Dromoland Castle	I	725
16	7	6	Woodenbridge	I	774	14	7	6	Galway Bay	I	732
15	6	7	Adare	I	704	14	6	5	Greenore	I	735

699

CLASSIFICATION OF IRISH COURSES

Score	Course	Country	Page	Score	Course	Country	Page
14 6 5	Killorglin	I	741	13 7 6	Kilkenny	I	738
14 5 6	Massereene	U	787	13 7 6	Lee Valley	I	743
14 5 5	Mullingar	I	749	13 7 8	Malahide		
14 6 6	St Helen's Bay	I	763		Red + Blue + Yellow	I	746
14 6 6	Waterford	I	769	13 6 6	Malone	U	786
14 5 6	Waterford Castle	I	770	13 6 5	Mount Wolsley	I	748
13 6 6	Athlone	I	705	13 7 5	Newcastle West	I	750
13 6 6	Blainroe	I	712	13 5 6	Rosslare	I	758
13 6 7	Bundoran	I	713	13 7 7	Royal Portrush *Valley*	U	792
13 6 5	Cairndhu	U	779	13 6 6	Shannon	I	761
13 7 6	Castle Hume	U	780	13 7 6	Tramore	I	767
13 4 6	Charleville	I	716	13 6 5	Warrenpoint	U	793
13 7 6	Faithlegg	I	730	13 5 6	Woodstock	I	775
13 6 6	Galway GC	I	733	12 7 6	West Waterford	I	772

CLASSIFICATION OF HOTELS FACILITIES
CLASSEMENT DE L'ENVIRONNEMENT HOTELIER

This classification gives priority consideration
to the score awarded to the hotel facilities.

Ce classement donne priorité à la note attribuée à l'environnement hôtelier

I: Republic of Ireland   U: Northern Ireland (Ulster)

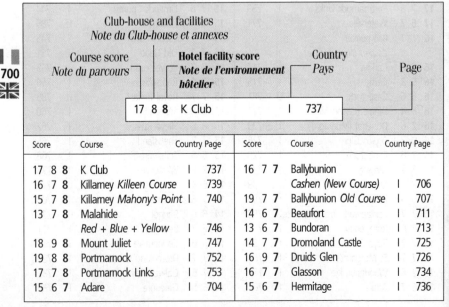

Club-house and facilities
Note du Club-house et annexes

Course score — *Note du parcours* ⌐ **Hotel facility score** *Note de l'environnement hôtelier* ⌐ Country *Pays* ⌐ Page

17 8 8   K Club   I   737

Score	Course	Country	Page	Score	Course	Country	Page
17 8 8	K Club	I	737	16 7 7	Ballybunion		
16 7 8	Killarney *Killeen Course*	I	739		Cashen *(New Course)*	I	706
15 7 8	Killarney *Mahony's Point*	I	740	19 7 7	Ballybunion *Old Course*	I	707
13 7 8	Malahide			14 6 7	Beaufort	I	711
	Red + Blue + Yellow	I	746	13 6 7	Bundoran	I	713
18 9 8	Mount Juliet	I	747	14 7 7	Dromoland Castle	I	725
19 8 8	Portmarnock	I	752	16 9 7	Druids Glen	I	726
17 7 8	Portmarnock Links	I	753	16 7 7	Glasson	I	734
15 6 7	Adare	I	704	15 6 7	Hermitage	I	736

700

CLASSIFICATION OF HOTELS FACILITIES

Score			Course	Country	Page	Score			Course	Country	Page
15	7	7	Luttrellstown	I	745	13	7	6	Lee Valley	I	743
15	7	7	Old Head	I	751	15	7	6	Limerick County	I	744
16	7	7	Portstewart *Strand Course*	U	788	15	7	6	Lisburn	U	785
15	7	7	Powerscourt	I	755	13	6	6	Malone	U	786
15	7	7	Royal Belfast	U	789	14	5	6	Massereene	U	787
19	6	7	Royal County Down	U	790	15	7	6	Rathsallagh	I	756
16	7	7	Royal Dublin	I	759	16	7	6	Rosapenna	I	757
19	7	7	Royal Portrush			13	5	6	Rosslare	I	758
			Dunluce Links	U	791	15	6	6	Seapoint	I	760
13	7	7	Royal Portrush Valley	U	792	13	6	6	Shannon	I	761
16	7	7	St Margaret's	I	764	15	8	6	Slieve Russell	I	762
15	7	7	The Island	I	765	14	6	6	St Helen's Bay	I	763
17	6	7	Waterville	I	771	18	7	6	Tralee	I	766
15	7	7	Westport	I	773	13	7	6	Tramore	I	767
13	6	6	Athlone	I	705	14	6	6	Waterford	I	769
14	7	6	Ballykisteen	I	708	14	5	6	Waterford Castle	I	770
14	6	6	Bangor	U	777	12	7	6	West Waterford	I	772
15	5	6	Belvoir Park	U	778	16	7	6	Woodenbridge	I	774
13	6	6	Blainroe	I	712	13	5	6	Woodstock	I	775
16	6	6	Carlow	I	714	17	6	5	Ballyliffin *Glashedy Links*	I	709
13	7	6	Castle Hume	U	780	15	6	5	Ballyliffin *Old Course*	I	710
16	6	6	Castlerock	U	781	13	6	5	Cairndhu	U	779
13	4	6	Charleville	I	716	15	3	5	Cork GC	I	718
15	6	6	Clandeboye			15	7	5	County Tipperary	I	721
			Dufferin Course	U	782	15	5	5	Dooks	I	724
14	6	6	Connemara	I	717	14	6	5	Greenore	I	735
18	5	6	County Louth	I	719	14	6	5	Killorglin	I	741
16	2	6	Donegal (Murvagh)	I	723	15	6	5	Kirkistown Castle	U	783
15	6	6	Dundalk	I	727	13	6	5	Mount Wolsley	I	748
16	7	6	Enniscrone	I	728	14	5	5	Mullingar	I	749
18	6	6	European (The)	I	729	13	7	5	Newcastle West	I	750
13	7	6	Faithlegg	I	730	16	5	5	Portsalon	I	754
15	7	6	Fota Island	I	731	15	6	5	Tullamore	I	768
14	7	6	Galway Bay	I	732	13	6	5	Warrenpoint	U	793
13	6	6	Galway GC	I	733	14	6	4	Ardglass	U	776
13	7	6	Kilkenny	I	738	16	6	4	Dingle (Ceann Sibeal)	I	722
15	7	6	Knock	U	784	16	5	3	Carn	I	715
18	6	6	Lahinch	I	742	17	4	3	County Sligo	I	720

701

RECOMMENDED SEASONS
SAISONS RECOMMANDEES

Depending on altitude, usual weather conditions, the type of soil
and the quality of drainage and maintenance.

En fonction de l'altitude, des conditions météorologiques habituelles, de la nature
du sol où est construit le parcours, de la qualité du drainage et de l'entretien.

Seasons / Golf Course	Country	Score			Page
1 2 3 4 5 6 7 8 9 10 11 12					
Charleville	I	13	4	6	716
Cork GC	I	15	3	5	718
County Louth	I	18	5	6	719
County Sligo	I	17	4	3	720
European (The)	I	18	6	6	729
Hermitage	I	15	6	7	736
Portmarnock	I	19	8	8	752
Portmarnock Links	I	17	7	8	753
Rosslare	I	13	5	6	758
Royal County Down	U	19	6	7	790
Royal Dublin	I	16	7	7	759
The Island	I	15	7	7	765
1 2 3 4 5 6 7 8 9 10 11 12					
Castlerock	U	16	6	6	781
Dingle (Ceann Sibeal)	I	16	6	4	722
Greenore	I	14	6	5	735
Lisburn	U	15	7	6	785
Luttrellstown	I	15	7	7	745
Portstewart *Strand Course*	U	16	7	7	788
Royal Portrush					
Dunluce Links	U	19	7	7	791
Royal Portrush *Valley*	U	13	7	7	792
Shannon	I	13	6	6	761
Tullamore	I	15	6	5	768
Waterford Castle	I	14	5	6	770
1 2 3 4 5 6 7 8 9 10 11 12					
Ballybunion *Cashen*					
(New Course)	I	16	7	7	706
Ballybunion *Old Course*	I	19	7	7	707
Ballyliffin *Glashedy Links*	I	17	6	5	709
Ballyliffin *Old Course*	I	15	6	5	710
Beaufort	I	14	6	7	711
Blainroe	I	13	6	6	712
Dooks	I	15	5	5	724
Dromoland Castle	I	14	7	7	725
Druids Glen	I	16	9	7	726
Enniscrone	I	16	7	6	728
Galway Bay	I	14	7	6	732

Seasons / Golf Course	Country	Score			Page
1 2 3 4 5 6 7 8 9 10 11 12					
Galway GC	I	13	6	6	733
Lahinch	I	18	6	6	742
Newcastle West	I	13	7	5	750
Portsalon	I	16	5	5	754
Rathsallagh	I	15	7	6	756
Seapoint	I	15	6	6	760
St Helen's Bay	I	14	6	6	763
Tralee	I	18	7	6	766
Tramore	I	13	7	6	767
Waterville	I	17	6	7	771
1 2 3 4 5 6 7 8 9 10 11 12					
Ardglass	U	14	6	4	776
Athlone	I	13	6	6	705
Ballykisteen	I	14	7	6	708
Bangor	U	14	6	6	777
Bundoran	I	13	6	7	713
Cairndhu	U	13	6	5	779
Carlow	I	16	6	6	714
Carn	I	16	5	3	715
Castle Hume	U	13	7	6	780
Clandeboye					
Dufferin Course	U	15	6	6	782
Connemara	I	14	6	6	717
County Tipperary	I	15	7	5	721
Donegal (Murvagh)	I	16	2	6	723
Dundalk	I	15	6	6	727
Faithlegg	I	13	7	6	730
Fota Island	I	15	7	6	731
Glasson	I	16	7	7	734
K Club	I	17	8	8	737
Kilkenny	I	13	7	6	738
Killorglin	I	14	6	5	741
Kirkistown Castle	U	15	6	5	783
Knock	U	15	7	6	784
Lee Valley	I	13	7	6	743
Limerick County	I	15	7	6	744
Malahide					
Red + Blue + Yellow	I	13	7	8	746
Malone	U	13	6	6	786

702

RECOMMENDED SEASONS

Seasons / Golf Course	Country	Score			Page
`1 2 3 [4 5 6] 7 [8 9 10] 11 12`					
Mount Juliet	I	18	9	8	747
Mount Wolsley	I	13	6	5	748
Mullingar	I	14	5	5	749
Rosapenna	I	16	7	6	757
Royal Belfast	U	15	7	7	789
Slieve Russell	I	15	8	6	762
St Margaret's	I	16	7	7	764
Warrenpoint	U	13	6	5	793
Waterford	I	14	6	6	769
Westport	I	15	7	7	773
Woodenbridge	I	16	7	6	774

Seasons / Golf Course	Country	Score			Page
`1 2 3 4 [5 6] 7 [8] 9 10 11 12`					
Massereene	U	14	5	6	787
Old Head	I	15	7	7	751
`1 2 3 4 [5 6] 7 [8 9 10] 11 12`					
Adare	I	15	6	7	704
Belvoir Park	U	15	5	6	778
Killarney *Killeen Course*	I	16	7	8	739
Killarney *Mahony's Point*	I	15	7	8	740
Powerscourt	I	15	7	7	755
West Waterford	I	12	7	6	772
Woodstock	I	13	5	6	775

RECOMMENDED GOLFING STAY
SEJOUR DE GOLF RECOMMANDÉ

Exciting courses where a stay of a few days is to be recommended.
Les parcours dont les qualités permettent de conseiller un séjour de plusieurs jours.

Course	Country	Score			Page
Ballybunion *Old Course*	I	19	7	7	707
Ballyliffin *Glashedy Links*	I	17	6	5	709
Ballyliffin *Old Course*	I	15	6	5	710
County Louth	I	18	5	6	719
County Sligo	I	17	4	3	720
Druids Glen	I	16	9	7	726
European (The)	I	18	6	6	729
K Club	I	17	8	8	737
Killarney *Killeen Course*	I	16	7	8	739
Killarney *Mahony's Point*	I	15	7	8	740
Lahinch	I	18	6	6	742
Mount Juliet	I	18	9	8	747
Portmarnock	I	19	8	8	752
Portmarnock Links	I	17	7	8	753
Portstewart *Strand Course*	U	16	7	7	788
Royal County Down	U	19	6	7	790
Royal Dublin	I	16	7	7	759
Royal Portrush					
Dunluce Links	U	19	7	7	791
Royal Portrush Valley	U	13	7	7	792
Tralee	I	18	7	6	766
Waterville	I	17	6	7	771

703

ADARE

15	6	7

From time to time, being iconoclastic can make a pleasant change. There could be no doubting that Adare was designed by Robert Trent Jones, because this could just as easily be a course on the Costa del Sol. In other words, there is no real "feeling" with the Irish landscape, probably on account of the over-extensive earthworks and grading used to shape the course, the give-away bunker designs and the huge water hazard on the front 9, which cost a fortune to build. But this is still a great course once you forget its artificial side, which anyway is less apparent on the way in. Here, golfers have to cope with the river Maigue and indigenous trees such as oak, beech, pine and cedar. There is no hidden trap, which only emphasises the psychological fear factor. Long and challenging, the course is almost certainly too tough for high-handicappers on account of the very many hazards. Even the better players will find it hard going.

De temps à autre, il n'est pas désagréable d'être iconoclaste : Adare a certes été dessiné par Robert Trent Jones, mais pourrait tout aussi bien se trouver sur la Costa del Sol. Autrement dit, on ne trouvera pas ici de véritable "sympathie" avec le paysage irlandais, en raison sans doute de mouvements de terrain trop importants, de dessin de bunkers trop révélateurs de leur auteur, de l'immense obstacle d'eau de l'aller, dont l'aménagement a coûté une fortune. Mais il reste un grand parcours de golf, dont on oubliera le côté parfois artificiel, d'ailleurs moins sensible au retour : il met essentiellement en jeu la rivière Maigue, et les arbres natifs du lieu : chênes, hêtres, pins ou cèdres. Aucun piège n'est caché, ce qui accentue le facteur psychologique de crainte. Long et exigeant, ce parcours est sans doute très difficile pour les handicaps élevés, en raison de la multiplicité des obstacles, les autres n'y connaîtront guère de repos...

Adare Golf Club

Adare Manor
IRL - ADARE, Co Limerick

Office	Secrétariat	(353) 061 - 395 044
Pro shop	Pro-shop	(353) 061 - 395 044
Fax	Fax	(353) 061 - 396 987
Situation	Situation	

10 km S. of Limerick (pop. 52 083)

Annual closure	Fermeture annnuelle	no
Weekly closure	Fermeture hebdomadaire	no

Fees main season
Tarifs haute saison 18 holes

	Week days Semaine	We/Bank holidays We/Férié
Individual Individuel	IR£ 45	IR£ 45
Couple Couple	IR£ 90	IR£ 90

Special fees for early tee-times

Caddy	Caddy	IR£ 16/18 holes
Electric Trolley	Chariot électrique	no
Buggy	Voiturette	IR£ 30/18 holes
Clubs	Clubs	IR£ 12/18 holes

Credit cards Cartes de crédit
VISA - Eurocard - MasterCard - AMEX

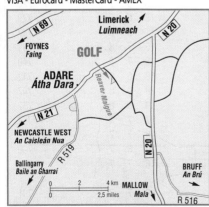

Access Accès : Limerick, N7 → Adare. Patrick's Well, straight through the fork in road, first left in village at gates, right to proshop
Map 2 on page 696 Carte 2 Page 696

GOLF COURSE
PARCOURS
15/20

Site	Site	
Maintenance	Entretien	
Architect	Architecte	R. Trent Jones Sr
Type	Type	inland, parkland
Relief	Relief	
Water in play	Eau en jeu	
Exp. to wind	Exposé au vent	
Trees in play	Arbres en jeu	

Scorecard Carte de score	Chp. Chp.	Mens Mess.	Ladies Da.
Length Long.	6489	5993	4925
Par	72	72	72

Advised golfing ability
Niveau de jeu recommandé — 0 12 24 36

Hcp required Handicap exigé — 28 Men, 36 Ladies

CLUB HOUSE & AMENITIES
CLUB HOUSE ET ANNEXES
6/10

Pro shop	Pro-shop	
Driving range	Practice	
Sheltered	couvert	no
On grass	sur herbe	yes
Putting-green	putting-green	yes
Pitching-green	pitching green	yes

HOTEL FACILITIES
ENVIRONNEMENT HOTELIER
7/10

HOTELS HÔTELS

Adare Manor Hotel — on site
64 rooms, D IR£ 190
Tel (353) 061 - 396 566, Fax (353) 061 - 396 124

Woodlands Hotel — Adare
57 rooms, D IR£ 70 — 2 km
Tel (353) 061 - 396 118, Fax (353) 061 - 396 073

Dunraven Arms Hotel — Adare
66 rooms, D IR£ 104 — 0.5 km
Tel (353) 061 - 396 633, Fax (353) 061 - 396 541

RESTAURANTS RESTAURANT

Wild Geese — Adare
Tel (353) 061 - 396 451 — 1 km

Dunraven Arms, Tel (353) 061 - 396 633   Adare, 0.5 km

704

ATHLONE

13 6 6

The gently rolling course of Athlone is magnificently sited on a peninsula overlooking Lough Ree. An old course that was remodelled in the late 1930s, the lack of yardage might lead to the better players under-estimating its difficulty and will invite them to play from the back-tees. It demands a wide variety of shots, especially when the wind blows from the lake, and skills in flighting the ball will help. The woods are on the outskirts of the course, as are most of the water hazards, although some isolated trees can come into play. Otherwise, you just avoid the bunkers, whose only criticism is the bland uniformity in design and shape. The greens are generally in good condition and moderately contoured, but they do tend to be soft in winter. Long-hitters will have fun on the three rather short par 5s, but accuracy is always important. Watch out for some tight fairways.

Doucement vallonné, le parcours d'Athlone dispose d'une situation magnifique sur une péninsule dominant le Lough Ree. Déjà ancien, bien que révisé à la fin des années 30, son manque de longueur ne doit pas le faire sous estimer par les joueurs de bon niveau, à qui on conseillera bien sûr les départs arrière. Il demande une grande variété de coups, surtout quand le vent vient du lac, il faut alors savoir travailler la balle. Les bois sont à la périphérie du parcours, de même que la plupart des obstacles d'eau, mais certains arbres isolés peuvent venir en jeu. Autrement, il suffit d'éviter les bunkers, auxquels on peut simplement reprocher une certaine uniformité de dessin et de forme. Les greens sont généralement en bonne condition et de relief modéré, mais ils peuvent être assez mous en hiver. Les longs frappeurs s'amuseront sur trois par 5 assez courts, mais ne devront pas oublier la précision, les fairways peuvent être étroits.

Athlone Golf Club
Hodson Bay
IRL - ATHLONE, Co. Westmeath

Office	Secrétariat	(353) 0902 - 92 073
Pro shop	Pro-shop	(353) 0902 - 94 285
Fax	Fax	(353) 0902 - 94 080
Situation	Situation	

5 km from Athlone (pop. 8 170)
120 km from Dublin (pop. 859 976)

Annual closure	Fermeture annnuelle	no
Weekly closure	Fermeture hebdomadaire	no

Fees main season
Tarifs haute saison 18 holes

	Week days Semaine	We/Bank holidays We/Férié
Individual Individuel	IR£ 15	IR£ 18
Couple Couple	IR£ 30	IR£ 36

Caddy	Caddy	on request/IR£ 10
Electric Trolley	Chariot électrique	no
Buggy	Voiturette	IR£ 15
Clubs	Clubs	IR£ 10

Credit cards Cartes de crédit
VISA - MasterCard

ROSCOMMON
Ros Comáin
LOUGH REE
BALLYMAHON
Baile Uí Mhatháin
Kiltoom
Glassan
GOLF
Killinure Lake
N 61
N 55
ATHLONE
Baile Átha Luain
N 6
N 6
BALLINASLOE
Béal Atha-na Sluaighe
MOATE
An Móta
0   2   4 km
0   2,5 miles

Access Accès : Athlone, N61 → Roscommon.
Golf beside Hodson Bay Hotel
Map 2 on page 697 Carte 2 Page 697

GOLF COURSE
PARCOURS

13/20

Site	Site	▰▰▰▰▰▱▱
Maintenance	Entretien	▰▰▰▰▱▱▱
Architect	Architecte	J. McAllister Fred Hawtree
Type	Type	parkland
Relief	Relief	
Water in play	Eau en jeu	▰▱▱▱▱▱▱
Exp. to wind	Exposé au vent	▰▰▱▱▱▱▱
Trees in play	Arbres en jeu	▰▰▰▰▰▱▱

Scorecard Carte de score	**Chp.** Chp.	**Mens** Mess.	**Ladies** Da.
Length Long.	5922	5773	5104
Par	71	71	75

Advised golfing ability		0	12	24	36
Niveau de jeu recommandé				▰▰▱	
Hcp required	Handicap exigé	no			

CLUB HOUSE & AMENITIES
CLUB HOUSE ET ANNEXES

6/10

Pro shop	Pro-shop	▰▰▰▰▱▱▱
Driving range	Practice	▰▰▰▱▱▱▱
Sheltered	couvert	no
On grass	sur herbe	yes
Putting-green	putting-green	yes
Pitching-green	pitching green	yes

705

HOTEL FACILITIES
ENVIRONNEMENT HOTELIER

6/10

HOTELS HÔTELS
Hodson Bay Hotel — Athlone
100 rooms, D IR£ 100 — beside golf
Tel (353) 0902 - 92 404, Fax (353) 0902 - 92 688

Prince of Wales Hotel — Athlone
73 rooms, D IR£ 60 — 6 km
Tel (353) 0902 - 72 626, Fax (353) 0902 - 75 658

Shamrock Lodge — Athlone
25 rooms, D IR£ 60 — 5 km
Tel (353) 0902 - 92 601

RESTAURANTS RESTAURANT
Cornloft — on road 362
Tel (353) 0902 - 94 753 — 6 km

Le Chateau — Athlone
Tel (353) 0902 - 94 517 — 5 km

Designing a new course in a mythical site such as this can be fatal to any course architect. But Robert Trent Jones has already designed enough great courses of his own to shrug off any mention of comparison, and his personality told him not to ape the old course, even though the dune-peppered landscape is similar (and sometimes even more impressive). The result here is a course that is slightly harder to decipher, where there is less room for intuition and more knowledge of distance when choosing your clubs. A little American touch, even though approach shots can still be played "British" style. However, he has made maximum use of the terrain's natural contours and limited earth-works, while giving each hole its own individual character. The course's forceful personality (it is not everyone's cup of tea) would make this a must anywhere else, but here it lives in the shadow of the "Old Course".

Pour un architecte, signer un nouveau parcours dans un site aussi mythique peut être meurtrier. Robert Trent Jones avait déjà créé assez de grands parcours pour ne pas craindre la comparaison, et sa personnalité ne l'incitait pas à essayer de singer le "Old", bien que le paysage dunaire soit similaire (parfois plus impressionnant encore). De fait, il a créé un parcours plus complexe à déchiffrer, où la place de l'intuition est moins importante que la connaissance des distances pour choisir les clubs. Une petite touche américaine... même si les petites approches peuvent être souvent jouées "à la britannique". Cependant, il a su utiliser au maximum les contours naturels du terrain et limiter les terras-sements, tout en donnant la touche de caractère individuel à chaque trou. La forte personnalité de ce parcours (qui ne fait pas toujours l'unanimité) en ferait n'importe où ailleurs un "must", mais le "Old" lui fait forcément ombrage.

Ballybunion Golf Club
Sandhill Road
IRL - BALLYBUNION, Co Kerry

Office	Secrétariat	(353) 068 - 27 146
Pro shop	Pro-shop	(353) 068 - 27 146
Fax	Fax	(353) 068 - 27 387
Situation	Situation	

1 km from Ballybunion Town (pop. 1 346)

Annual closure	Fermeture annnuelle	no
Weekly closure	Fermeture hebdomadaire	no

Fees main season
Tarifs haute saison 18 holes

	Week days Semaine	We/Bank holidays We/Férié
Individual Individuel	IR£ 30	IR£ 30
Couple Couple	IR£ 60	IR£ 60

IR£ 72 for both courses (same day)

Caddy	Caddy	IR£ 15/18 holes
Electric Trolley	Chariot électrique	no
Buggy	Voiturette	no
Clubs	Clubs	IR£ 20/18 holes

Credit cards Cartes de crédit
VISA - MasterCard

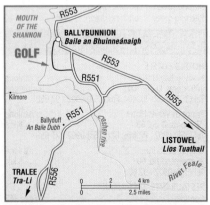

MOUTH OF THE SHANNON
R553
BALLYBUNNION
Baile an Bhuinneánaigh
GOLF
R553
R551
Kilmore
Ballyduff
An Baile Dubh
R551
Cashen river
R553
LISTOWEL
Lios Tuathail
River Feale
TRALEE
Tra-Li
R556
0   2   4 km
0   2,5 miles

Access Accès : Limerick, N21 → Newcastle West,
→ Listowel, → Ballybunion
Map 2 on page 696 Carte 2 Page 696

GOLF COURSE / PARCOURS 16 /20

Site	Site	▬▬▬
Maintenance	Entretien	▬▬▬
Architect	Architecte	R. Trent Jones Sr
Type	Type	links
Relief	Relief	▬▬
Water in play	Eau en jeu	▬
Exp. to wind	Exposé au vent	▬▬▬
Trees in play	Arbres en jeu	▬▬

Scorecard Carte de score	Chp. Chp.	Mens Mess.	Ladies Da.
Length Long.	5830	5350	5160
Par	72	72	72

Advised golfing ability   0   12   24   36
Niveau de jeu recommandé   ▬▬▬▬▬
Hcp required   Handicap exigé   24 Men, 36 Ladies

CLUB HOUSE & AMENITIES / CLUB HOUSE ET ANNEXES 7 /10

Pro shop	Pro-shop	▬▬▬
Driving range	Practice	▬▬
Sheltered	couvert	
On grass	sur herbe	yes
Putting-green	putting-green	yes
Pitching-green	pitching green	no

HOTEL FACILITIES / ENVIRONNEMENT HOTELIER 7 /10

HOTELS HÔTELS
Golf Hotel   Ballybunion
96 rooms, D IR£ 60   2 km
Tel (353) 068 - 27 111, Fax (353) 068 - 27 166

Cliff House Hotel   Ballybunion
51 rooms, D IR£ 70   2 km
Tel (353) 068 - 27 398, Fax (353) 068 - 27 783

RESTAURANTS RESTAURANT
Three Mermaids   Listowel
Tel (353) 068 - 21 184   15 km

Harty-Costello   Ballybunion
Tel (353) 068 - 27 129   1 km

706

There are some courses you could write a book about, where anything less you know will fail to do them justice. The old course at Ballybunion is one such course. On a windless day (a rare occurrence), it's not easy playing here. In a strong wind, it can be hell. But losing out to a living masterpiece such as this is sheer bliss. The numbers on your card lose all their significance: there are no such things as par 3s, par 4s or par 5s, all that matters is survival. After a few almost ordinary holes (relatively speaking), the pulse starts to quicken on the 6th. The rest is one long epic adventure where you need ball control in every direction, skills with every club in the bag and technique for high and low shots alike. At the same time you'll admire the layout. Lost between huge sand dunes, the fairway looks so narrow, the greens tiny and the bunkers absolutely ruthless. Tom Watson considers this ultimate test of technique and inspiration to be the greatest course in the world. Suffice it to say, every golfer will have to check it out for himself or herself, one day or another.

Faute de pouvoir écrire un livre sur certains parcours, il faudrait ne rien en dire. Le "Old Course" de Ballybunion est de ceux-là. Sans vent (c'est rare), il n'est pas facile. Il devient infernal par vent fort, mais quel bonheur d'être battu par un chef-d'oeuvre aussi vivant : alors, les chiffres inscrits sur la carte ne signifient plus rien. Plus de par 3, 4 ou 5, il s'agit de survivre. Après quelques trous presque anodins (c'est relatif !), le pouls s'accélère à partir du 6, la suite n'est plus qu'une longue épopée, où il faut travailler la balle dans tous les sens, jouer tous les clubs et tous les coups, maîtriser les balles hautes comme les balles au ras du sol. Et admirer le génie du dessin. Perdus dans d'immenses dunes, le fairway paraît bien étroit, les greens minuscules, les bunkers sans pitié. Tom Watson considère cet examen suprême de la technique et de l'inspiration comme le plus grand parcours du monde, tout golfeur doit le vérifier un jour.

Ballybunion Golf Club
Sandhill Road
IRL - BALLYBUNION, Co Kerry

Office	Secrétariat	(353) 068 - 27 146
Pro shop	Pro-shop	(353) 068 - 27 146
Fax	Fax	(353) 068 - 27 387
Situation	Situation	

1 km from Ballybunion Town (pop. 1 346)

Annual closure	Fermeture annnuelle	no
Weekly closure	Fermeture hebdomadaire	no

Fees main season
Tarifs haute saison 18 holes

	Week days Semaine	We/Bank holidays We/Férié
Individual Individuel	IR£ 55	IR£ 55
Couple Couple	IR£ 110	IR£ 110

IR£ 72 for both courses (same day)

Caddy	Caddy	IR£ 15/18 holes
Electric Trolley	Chariot électrique	no
Buggy	Voiturette	no
Clubs	Clubs	IR£ 20/18 holes

Credit cards Cartes de crédit
VISA - MasterCard

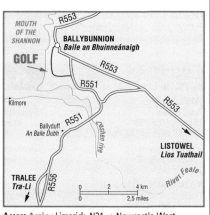

MOUTH OF THE SHANNON
BALLYBUNNION *Baile an Bhuinneánaigh*
GOLF
R553
R551
Kilmore
Ballyduff *An Baile Dubh* R551
R553
LISTOWEL *Lios Tuathail*
Cashen rive
River Feale
TRALEE *Tra-Li* R556
0   2   4 km
0   2,5 miles

Access Accès : Limerick, N21 → Newcastle West,
→ Listowel, → Ballybunion
Map 2 on page 696 Carte 2 Page 696

GOLF COURSE / PARCOURS — 19/20

Site	Site	▰▰▰▰▰▱
Maintenance	Entretien	▰▰▰▰▰▱
Architect	Architecte	L. Hewson T. Simpson
Type	Type	links
Relief	Relief	▰▰▰▱▱▱
Water in play	Eau en jeu	▰▱▱▱▱▱
Exp. to wind	Exposé au vent	▰▰▰▰▱▱
Trees in play	Arbres en play	▰▱▱▱▱▱

Scorecard Carte de score	Chp. Chp.	Mens Mess.	Ladies Da.
Length Long.	6241	6201	5004
Par	71	71	74

Advised golfing ability Niveau de jeu recommandé	0	12	24	36

Hcp required Handicap exigé   28 Men, 36 Ladies

CLUB HOUSE & AMENITIES / CLUB HOUSE ET ANNEXES — 7/10

Pro shop	Pro-shop	▰▰▰▰▱▱
Driving range	Practice	▰▰▰▱▱▱
Sheltered	couvert	
On grass	sur herbe	yes
Putting-green	putting-green	yes
Pitching-green	pitching green	no

HOTEL FACILITIES / ENVIRONNEMENT HOTELIER — 7/10

HOTELS HÔTELS
Golf Hotel — Ballybunion
96 rooms, D IR£ 60 — 2 km
Tel (353) 068 - 27 111, Fax (353) 068 - 27 166

Cliff House Hotel — Ballybunion
51 rooms, D IR£ 70 — 2 km
Tel (353) 068 - 27 398, Fax (353) 068 - 27 783

RESTAURANTS RESTAURANT
Three Mermaids — Listowel
Tel (353) 068 - 21 184 — 15 km

Harty-Costello — Ballybunion
Tel (353) 068 - 27 129 — 1 km

707

BALLYKISTEEN

Laid out over a former horse farm and riding stables, Ballykisteen looks like a large park where trees and water form the main hazards. But the designers (Des Smyth and Declan Branigan) spared a thought for everyone. The further back you tee off, the narrower the fairways become, and the great number of tees means you can adapt each round to your ability. The course calls for every shot in the book: here a fade, there a draw. The greens are guarded to allow either the good old bump and run shots, or the new-style target shot approaches. Water is in play on ten holes, but with varying degrees of difficulty. It is at its worst on the 15th (with out-of-bounds to the left), one of Ireland's most demanding par 3s - the bogey should be gratefully accepted. Forthright and well-balanced, Ballykisteen perhaps lacks in yardage, but who's complaining?

Réalisé dans un ancien élevage de chevaux, Ballykisteen présente un caractère de grand parc, où les arbres et l'eau constituent les dangers. Mais les architectes (le champion irlandais Des Smyth et Declan Branigan) ont pensé à tout le monde. Plus on recule de départ, plus le parcours est étroit, et la multiplicité des départs permet de se faire un parcours "à sa main". Le dessin exige tous les coups de golf : certains trous demandent une balle en fade, un nombre égal réclame le draw. Et les défenses de green autorisent soit des balles roulées (bump and run), soit des balles levées (target golf). L'eau vient en jeu sur dix trous, mais avec différents niveaux de difficulté. Elle est au maximum sur le 15 (avec hors-limites à gauche), un des plus exigeants par 3 d'Irlande : le bogey y est très acceptable ! Honnête et bien équilibré, Ballykisteen manque peut-être un peu de longueur, mais qui s'en plaindra ?

Ballykisteen Golf Club
IRL - MONARD, Co Tipperary

Office	Secrétariat	(353) 062 - 33 333
Pro shop	Pro-shop	(353) 062 - 33 333
Fax	Fax	(353) 062 - 33 668
Situation	Situation	

5 km from Tipperary
32 km from Limerick (pop. 52 083)

Annual closure	Fermeture annnuelle	no
Weekly closure	Fermeture hebdomadaire	no

Fees main season
Tarifs haute saison 18 holes

	Week days Semaine	We/Bank holidays We/Férié
Individual Individuel	IR£ 22	IR£ 22
Couple Couple	IR£ 44	IR£ 44

Caddy	Caddy	on request/IR£ 15
Electric Trolley	Chariot électrique	no
Buggy	Voiturette	IR£ 20/18 holes
Clubs	Clubs	IR£ 8/18 holes

Credit cards Cartes de crédit
VISA - MasterCard - DC

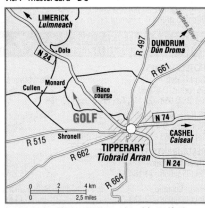

Access Accès : Tipperary N24 → Limerick. Golf 5 km, opposite Tipperary Racecourse
Map 2 on page 696 Carte 2 Page 696

GOLF COURSE PARCOURS 14/20

Site	Site	
Maintenance	Entretien	
Architect	Architecte	Des Smyth D. Branigan
Type	Type	parkland
Relief	Relief	
Water in play	Eau en jeu	
Exp. to wind	Exposé au vent	
Trees in play	Arbres en jeu	

Scorecard Carte de score	Chp. Chp.	Mens Mess.	Ladies Da.
Length Long.	6150	5713	5110
Par	72	72	74

Advised golfing ability
Niveau de jeu recommandé   0 12 24 36
Hcp required Handicap exigé 28 Men, 36 Ladies

CLUB HOUSE & AMENITIES CLUB HOUSE ET ANNEXES 7/10

Pro shop	Pro-shop	
Driving range	Practice	
Sheltered	couvert	no
On grass	sur herbe	yes
Putting-green	putting-green	yes
Pitching-green	pitching green	yes

HOTEL FACILITIES ENVIRONNEMENT HOTELIER 6/10

HOTELS HÔTELS
Royal Hotel — Tipperary
16 rooms, D IR£ 50 — 4 km
Tel (353) 062 - 33 244, Fax (353) 062 - 33 596

Aherlow House — Glen of Aherlow
30 rooms, D IR£ 70 — 10 km
Tel (353) 062 - 56 153, Fax (353) 062 - 56 212

RESTAURANTS RESTAURANT
Cranleys — Tipperary
Tel (353) 062 - 33 917 — 5 km

The Brown Trout — Tipperary
Tel (353) 062 - 51 912 — 5 km

708

This very recent course outstrips its neighbour in terms of technical play. The landscape is even more moon-like, with massive dunes, but a little grading work has resulted in levelling out a number of drive landing areas and in creating a collection of fairway and green-side bunkers that you are sure to encounter every now and then. This course grabs you by the throat from the word go and doesn't let you go. You need to hit low shots into the wind and with the wind, otherwise your ball will float upwards like a feather. You need to know how to fade and draw the ball to get around the dog-legs, you need brains and nerves to approach the greens, to stay on the putting surface and make the putt. You need a cool head to go fetch your ball instead of admiring the landscape (especially Glashedy Rock, off the coast). You need to play here and spend some time on the course to measure what you are capable of. And then wait a little longer to judge the course for its real worth.

Ce très récent parcours dépasse son voisin en matière de technicité. Le paysage est encore plus lunaire, avec des dunes massives, où quelques terrassements ont permis d'adoucir certaines zones d'arrivée de drive, mais aussi de creuser une collection de bunkers de fairway et de green que l'on ne manquera pas d'expérimenter. Ce parcours vous prend à la gorge dès les premiers trous, et ne vous lâchera plus. Il faudra faire des balles basses, contre le vent, mais aussi avec, pour ne pas les voir voler comme des plumes. Il faudra maîtriser les effets de fade et de draw pour négocier les dog-legs, il faudra de la science et des nerfs pour attaquer les greens, pour y rester, et pour putter. Il faudra du sang-froid pour revenir à sa balle au lieu d'admirer le paysage (notamment sur le Glashedy Rock, au large). Il faudra jouer ici, y faire une retraite de golf pour mesurer vos capacités. Et attendre encore un peu pour situer ce parcours à sa vraie place.

Ballyliffin Golf Club
IRL - BALLYLIFFIN, Co Donegal

Office	Secrétariat	(353) 077 - 76 119
Pro shop	Pro-shop	(353) 077 - 76 119
Fax	Fax	(353) 077 - 76 672
Situation	Situation	

40 km from Derry (72 334)
160 km from Belfast (279 237)

Annual closure	Fermeture annnuelle	no
Weekly closure	Fermeture hebdomadaire	no

Fees main season
Tarifs haute saison 18 holes

	Week days Semaine	We/Bank holidays We/Férié
Individual Individuel	IR£ 20	IR£ 30
Couple Couple	IR£ 40	IR£ 60

Caddy	Caddy	on request/IR£ 10
Electric Trolley	Chariot électrique	no
Buggy	Voiturette	IR£ 20/18 holes
Clubs	Clubs	IR£ 10

Credit cards Cartes de crédit
VISA - Eurocard - MasterCard - Access

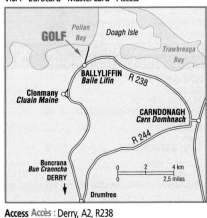

GOLF
Pollan Bay
Doagh Isle
Trawbreaga Bay
BALLYLIFFIN Baile Lifín R 238
Clonmany Cluain Maine
CARNDONAGH Carn Domhnach
R 244
Buncrana Bun Cranncha
DERRY
Drumfree
0   2   4 km
0   2,5 miles

Access Accès : Derry, A2, R238
→ Buncrana, Dumfree, Ballyliffin
Map 1 on page 695 Carte 1 Page 695

GOLF COURSE
PARCOURS **17** /20

Site	Site	▨▨▨
Maintenance	Entretien	▨▨▨
Architect	Architecte	Pat Ruddy Tom Craddock
Type	Type	links, seaside course
Relief	Relief	▨▨▨
Water in play	Eau en jeu	▨▨
Exp. to wind	Exposé au vent	▨▨▨▨
Trees in play	Arbres en jeu	▨

Scorecard Carte de score	Chp. Chp.	Mens Mess.	Ladies Da.
Length Long.	6456	6154	5328
Par	72	73	72

Advised golfing ability
Niveau de jeu recommandé   0   12   24   36

Hcp required   Handicap exigé   28 Men, 36 Ladies

CLUB HOUSE & AMENITIES
CLUB HOUSE ET ANNEXES **6** /10

Pro shop	Pro-shop	▨▨
Driving range	Practice	▨▨
Sheltered	couvert	no
On grass	sur herbe	yes
Putting-green	putting-green	yes
Pitching-green	pitching green	yes

709

HOTEL FACILITIES
ENVIRONNEMENT HOTELIER **5** /10

HOTELS HÔTELS

The Strand   Ballyliffin
20 rooms, D IR£ 108   2 km
Tel (353) 077 - 76 107, Fax (353) 077 - 76 486

Ballyliffin Hotel   Ballyliffin
13 rooms, D IR£ 90   2 km
Tel (353) 077 - 76 106, Fax (353) 077 - 76 658

Lake of Shadows   Buncrana
23 rooms, D IR£ 50   17 km
Tel (353) 077 - 61 005, Fax (353) 077 - 62 131

RESTAURANTS RESTAURANT

Corncrake   Carndonagh
Tel (353) 077 - 74 534   12 km

Ubiquitous Chip   Burcrana
Tel (353) 077 - 62 530   16 km

15	6	5

The trip to the northern tip of Ireland is not the easiest in the world, but the recent addition of another 18 holes has made this one of the country's finest golfing destinations. Summer days are very long here, enough to give anyone more than their fill of golf, no matter how tempting a proposition these courses may be. Nick Faldo called the Old Links here "the most natural course ever" when making a surprise visit that did much for the site's recognition. Here, you play the ball where it lies, on rolling fairways between the rough, sometimes with no visible limits, and rarely on the flat. The landscape has an amazing austere beauty to it, between the ocean, hills and endless stretches of dunes, tall grass and bushes, dotted with the odd white house in the distance. In this huge sanctuary of tranquillity, every player cuts his own path, as if he were the first to play here. A bit short, did you say? That's just the way it is, and no more.

Le voyage à l'extrême nord de l'Irlande n'est pas des plus faciles, mais la récente addition d'un autre 18 trous à celui-ci en fait une des plus belles destinations du pays. Les journées d'été y sont très longues, assez pour se donner une... indigestion de golf, alors que ces parcours sont bien digestes ! Le "Old Links" a été qualifié par Nick Faldo de "Golf le plus naturel qui soit" lors d'une visite surprise qui a beaucoup fait pour la notoriété du lieu. Ici, on joue la balle où elle est, sur des fairways ondulant entre les roughs, parfois sans limite visible, où l'on joue rarement la balle à plat. Le paysage est stupéfiant d'austère beauté, entre les flots de l'océan, les collines et des étendues infinies de dunes, de buissons, d'herbes hautes, ponctuées de rares maisons blanches dans le lointain. Dans cet espace immense de paix, chacun trace son chemin, comme s'il était le premier à jouer ici. Le parcours est un peu court ? Il est ce qu'il est, c'est tout.

Ballyliffin Golf Club
IRL - BALLYLIFFIN, Co Donegal

Office	Secrétariat	(353) 077 - 76 119
Pro shop	Pro-shop	(353) 077 - 76 119
Fax	Fax	(353) 077 - 76 672
Situation	Situation	

40 km from Derry (72 334)
160 km from Belfast (279 237)

Annual closure	Fermeture annnuelle	no
Weekly closure	Fermeture hebdomadaire	no

Fees main season
Tarifs haute saison 18 holes

	Week days Semaine	We/Bank holidays We/Férié
Individual Individuel	IR£ 15	IR£ 20
Couple Couple	IR£ 30	IR£ 40

Caddy	Caddy	on request/IR£ 10
Electric Trolley	Chariot électrique	no
Buggy	Voiturette	IR£ 20/18 holes
Clubs	Clubs	IR£ 10

Credit cards Cartes de crédit
VISA - Eurocard - MasterCard - Access

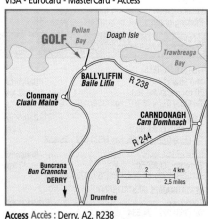

Access Accès : Derry, A2, R238
→ Buncrana, Dumfree, Ballyliffin
Map 1 on page 695 Carte 1 Page 695

GOLF COURSE
PARCOURS
15/20

Site	Site	■■■■
Maintenance	Entretien	■■■■
Architect	Architecte	Unknown
Type	Type	links
Relief	Relief	■■
Water in play	Eau en jeu	■
Exp. to wind	Exposé au vent	■■■■
Trees in play	Arbres en jeu	■

Scorecard Carte de score	Chp. Chp.	Mens Mess.	Ladies Da.
Length Long.	5750	0	0
Par	72	0	0

Advised golfing ability		0	12	24	36
Niveau de jeu recommandé				■■■	
Hcp required	Handicap exigé	Men 28, Ladies 36			

CLUB HOUSE & AMENITIES
CLUB HOUSE ET ANNEXES
6/10

Pro shop	Pro-shop	■■■
Driving range	Practice	■■■
Sheltered	couvert	no
On grass	sur herbe	yes
Putting-green	putting-green	yes
Pitching-green	pitching green	yes

HOTEL FACILITIES
ENVIRONNEMENT HOTELIER
5/10

HOTELS HÔTELS
The Strand   Ballyliffin
20 rooms, D IR£ 108   2 km
Tel (353) 077 - 76 107, Fax (353) 077 - 76 486

Ballyliffin Hotel   Ballyliffin
13 rooms, D IR£ 90   2 km
Tel (353) 077 - 76 106, Fax (353) 077 - 76 658

Lake of Shadows   Buncrana
23 rooms, D IR£ 50   17 km
Tel (353) 077 - 61 005, Fax (353) 077 - 62 131

RESTAURANTS RESTAURANT
Corncrake   Carndonagh
Tel (353) 077 - 74 534   12 km

Ubiquitous Chip   Burcrana
Tel (353) 077 - 62 530   16 km

It was not so easy to create a new course within the immediate vicinity of Killarney, but with such a superb setting (the Mcgillicuddy Reeks form an impressive backdrop) and even the ruins of castle Gore to add a touch of history to the back nine, the appeal of the site could only enhance the actual course. Designed by Arthur Springs over pleasantly rolling and woody terrain, this recent course needs time to mellow, although it is already in very good condition. Of special note are the excellence of the par 3s (especially the 8th), the care taken over the placement of hazards, especially the bunkers, the use of trees and the variety of greens, sometimes elevated or multi-tiered and requiring some accurate ironwork. You can seldom roll the ball here. A few blind shots call for a careful choice of line, but things are generally rather obvious. A pleasant course for all.

Il n'était pas si facile de créer un nouveau golf à proximité immédiate de celui de Killarney, mais sa séduction du lieu ne pouvait que profiter au parcours lui-même avec une situation aussi favorable (les Mcgillicuddy Reeks sont en toile de fond), et même les ruines du Castle Core pour donner une touche d'histoire aux neuf derniers trous. Dessiné par Arthur Springs sur un terrain agréablement vallonné et boisé, ce récent parcours a besoin de gagner en maturité, mais sa condition est déjà très bonne. On y remarquera en particulier la qualité des pars 3 (notamment le 8), le soin apporté au placement des obstacles, des bunkers en particulier, la mise en jeu des arbres et la diversité des greens, parfois surélevés ou à plateaux, obligeant à un jeu de fers précis : il est rarement possible de faire rouler la balle. Certains coups aveugles obligent à bien choisir la ligne de jeu, mais elle reste assez évidente. Un parcours agréable pour tous.

Beaufort Golf Club
IRL - BEAUFORT, Co. Kerry

Office	Secrétariat	(353) 064 - 44 440
Pro shop	Pro-shop	(353) 064 - 44 440
Fax	Fax	(353) 064 - 44 752
Situation	Situation	

11 km W of Killarney (pop. 7 275)
10 km E of Killorglin (pop. 1 229)

Annual closure	Fermeture annnuelle	no
Weekly closure	Fermeture hebdomadaire	no

Fees main season
Tarifs haute saison 18 holes

	Week days Semaine	We/Bank holidays We/Férié
Individual Individuel	IR£ 25	IR£ 28
Couple Couple	IR£ 50	IR£ 56

Caddy	Caddy	on request/IR£ 10
Electric Trolley	Chariot électrique	no
Buggy	Voiturette	no
Clubs	Clubs	IR£ 10

Credit cards Cartes de crédit
VISA

KILLORGLIN Cill Orglan
R 563
R 562 GOLF
Beaufort
CORK Corcaigh
KILLARNEY Cill Airne
Lough Leane
Kate Kearney's Cottage
Nature Reserve
KENMARE Neidin
N 71
0   2   4 km
0   2,5 miles

Access Accès : Killarney, R562 to Beaufort.
Golf signposted
Map 2 on page 696 Carte 2 Page 696

GOLF COURSE
PARCOURS
14/20

Site	Site	
Maintenance	Entretien	
Architect	Architecte	Arthur Spring
Type	Type	parkland
Relief	Relief	
Water in play	Eau en jeu	
Exp. to wind	Exposé au vent	
Trees in play	Arbres en jeu	

Scorecard Carte de score	Chp. Chp.	Mens Mess.	Ladies Da.
Length Long.	6005	5535	4803
Par	71	71	71

Advised golfing ability			0	12	24	36
Niveau de jeu recommandé						
Hcp required	Handicap exigé	no				

CLUB HOUSE & AMENITIES
CLUB HOUSE ET ANNEXES
6/10

Pro shop	Pro-shop	
Driving range	Practice	
Sheltered	couvert	no
On grass	sur herbe	no
Putting-green	putting-green	yes
Pitching-green	pitching green	no

711

HOTEL FACILITIES
ENVIRONNEMENT HOTELIER
7/10

HOTELS HÔTELS

Dunloe Castle — Beaufort
120 rooms, D IR£ 100 — 2 km
Tel (353) 064 - 44 111, Fax (353) 064 - 44 583

Hotel Europe — Killarney
205 rooms, D IR£ 120 — 6 km
Tel (353) 064 - 31 900, Fax (353) 064 - 32 118

Aghadoe Heights — Killarney
60 rooms, D IR£ 165 — 7 km
Tel (353) 064 - 31 766, Fax (353) 064 - 31 345

RESTAURANTS RESTAURANT

Fredrick's at the Heights — Killarney
Tel (353) 064 - 31 766 — 7 km

Gaby's — Killarney
Tel(353) 064 - 32 519 — 11 km

BLAINROE

13	6	6

A seaside course but not a links, with pronounced hilly relief between the 2nd and 8th holes before becoming a little easier. The architects have made good use of difficult terrain for golf but were unable to prevent the 6th, 7th and 14th from being rather tricky little numbers. The 4 closing holes more than make up for this minor shortcoming. In a region where there is no shortage of very good courses, Blainroe compares well. Water is in play on two holes only, news that will delight those players who have been playing with the same ball all season, and the basic difficulties, excluding the wind, are the 58 bunkers, all more strategic than really penalising. When the ground is dry, the greens are open enough to allow rolled shots. Players of all abilities can enjoy their golf here, but single-figure handicappers might prefer to wait for the wind to make this a tougher challenge.

Un parcours de bord de mer, mais sans être un links, avec des reliefs prononcés entre le 2 et le 8, mais ensuite nettement assagis. Les architectes ont fait bon usage d'un terrain difficile à adapter au golf, et n'ont pu éviter de rendre le 6, le 7 et le 14 assez "tricky", mais les quatre derniers trous rachètent ces faiblesses ponctuelles. Dans une région où les très bons parcours ne manquent pas, Blainroe s'est taillé une place très honorable. L'eau n'y vient en jeu que sur deux trous, ce qui ne manquera pas de plaire à ceux qui jouent avec la même balle depuis des années, et les difficultés essentielles (en dehors du vent) sont les 58 bunkers, tous plus stratégiques que vraiment pénalisants. Quand le terrain est sec, les greens sont assez ouverts pour permettre de faire rouler la balle. Tous les niveaux de jeu peuvent s'exprimer ici, mais les meilleurs attendront le vent pour trouver un challenge encore plus décisif.

Blainroe Golf Club
IRL - BLAINROE, Co. Wicklow

Office	Secrétariat	(353) 0404 - 68 168
Pro shop	Pro-shop	(353) 0404 - 68 168
Fax	Fax	(353) 0404 - 69 369
Situation	Situation	

6 km S of Wicklow (pop. 5 847)
51 km from Dublin (pop. 859 976)

Annual closure	Fermeture annnuelle	no
Weekly closure	Fermeture hebdomadaire	no

Fees main season
Tarifs haute saison 18 holes

	Week days Semaine	We/Bank holidays We/Férié
Individual Individuel	IR£ 25	IR£ 35
Couple Couple	IR£ 50	IR£ 70

Caddy	Caddy	IR£ 10/18 holes
Electric Trolley	Chariot électrique	no
Buggy	Voiturette	no
Clubs	Clubs	IR£ 10

Credit cards Cartes de crédit
VISA - MasterCard - AMEX

712

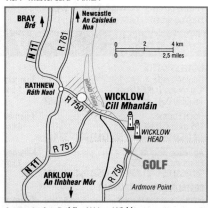

Access Accès : Dublin, N11 to Wicklow.
R750 (Coast Road) to Golf.
Map 3 on page 698 Carte 3 Page 698

GOLF COURSE / PARCOURS

13/20

Site	Site	
Maintenance	Entretien	
Architect	Architecte	Hawtree & Sons
Type	Type	seaside course, parkland
Relief	Relief	
Water in play	Eau en jeu	
Exp. to wind	Exposé au vent	
Trees in play	Arbres en jeu	

Scorecard Carte de score	Chp. Chp.	Mens Mess.	Ladies Da.
Length Long.	6175	6070	5365
Par	72	72	74

Advised golfing ability Niveau de jeu recommandé	0	12	24	36
Hcp required	Handicap exigé	no		

CLUB HOUSE & AMENITIES / CLUB HOUSE ET ANNEXES

6/10

Pro shop	Pro-shop	
Driving range	Practice	
Sheltered	couvert	no
On grass	sur herbe	yes
Putting-green	putting-green	yes
Pitching-green	pitching green	yes

HOTEL FACILITIES / ENVIRONNEMENT HOTELIER

6/10

HOTELS HÔTELS

Tinakilly House Hotel — Rathnew
29 rooms, D IR£ 130 — 10 km
Tel (353) 0404 - 69 274, Fax (353) 0404 - 67 806

Blainroe Golf Hotel — adjacent
10 rooms, D IR£ 70
Tel (353) 0404 - 67 500, Fax (353) 0404 - 69 737

Grand Hotel — Wicklow
32 rooms, D IR£ 70 — 6 km
Tel (353) 0404 - 67 337, Fax (353) 0404 - 69 607

RESTAURANTS RESTAURANT

The Old Rectory — Wicklow
Tel (353) 0404 - 67 048 — 6 km

The Bakery — Wicklow
Tel(353) 0404 - 66 770 — 6 km

The shortest courses are not always the easiest, often lacking par 5s to make those coveted birdies. Bundoran is one such number, and is also a part of history, being over 100 years old. Between the wars, the course was re-shaped and toughened up by the grand champion Harry Vardon (the designer of Little Aston and the first designer of Woodhall Spa in England). Alternating park-land country with links holes, this is a good quality test that is ideal for a few rounds with friends or the family. Of course, with the wind, which can blow very hard indeed, things may get tough. Visitors enjoy a picturesque setting with several holes running alongside the ocean (you can even see people surfing) and some superb beaches. When exploring for golf in the north-west of Ireland - which is making itself a nice little international reputation - Bundoran is a highly recommendable stop-off.

Les parcours les plus courts ne sont pas toujours les plus faciles : il y a peu de pars 5 pour faire des birdies ! Bundoran en fait partie. Comme il fait partie de l'histoire, car il a plus d'un siècle d'existence. Entre les deux guerres, il a été remodelé et durci par le grand champion Harry Vardon (l'auteur de Little Aston et le premier architecte de Woodhall Spa, en Angleterre). Alternant les paysages de parc et les vrais trous de links, c'est un test de bonne qualité, idéal pour quelques bonnes parties de golf entre amis ou en famille, mais qui (bien sûr) prend de la puissance avec le vent, parfois très fort ici. Il fait profiter ses visiteurs d'une situation pittoresque, avec plusieurs trous le long de l'océan (on y voit souvent des surfeurs) et de superbes plages. Dans une exploration golfique du Nord-Ouest de l'Irlande, qui commence à acquérir une réputation internationale, Bundoran est une halte très recommandable.

Bundoran Golf Club
IRL - BUNDORAN, Co Donegal

Office	Secrétariat	(353) 072 - 41 302
Pro shop	Pro-shop	(353) 072 - 41 302
Fax	Fax	(353) 072 - 42 014
Situation	Situation	

1 km from Bundoran
40 km from Sligo (pop. 17 302)

Annual closure	Fermeture annnuelle	no
Weekly closure	Fermeture hebdomadaire	no

Fees main season
Tarifs haute saison 18 holes

	Week days Semaine	We/Bank holidays We/Férié
Individual Individuel	IR£ 16	IR£ 18
Couple Couple	IR£ 28	IR£ 32

Caddy	Caddy	on request/IR£ 10
Electric Trolley	Chariot électrique	no
Buggy	Voiturette	IR£ 20/18 holes
Clubs	Clubs	IR£ 10

Credit cards Cartes de crédit
no

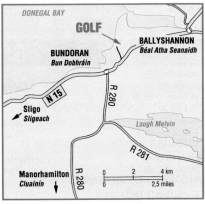

DONEGAL BAY
GOLF
BALLYSHANNON
Béal Atha Seanaidh
BUNDORAN
Bun Dobhráin
N 15
R 280
Sligo
Sligeach
Lough Melvin
R 281
Manorhamilton
Cluainín
R 280
0 — 2 — 4 km
0 — 2,5 miles

Access Accès : On N15 Sligo to Donegal
Map 1 on page 694 Carte 1 Page 694

GOLF COURSE
PARCOURS
13/20

Site	Site	
Maintenance	Entretien	
Architect	Architecte	Harry Vardon
Type	Type	links, parkland
Relief	Relief	
Water in play	Eau en jeu	
Exp. to wind	Exposé au vent	
Trees in play	Arbres en jeu	

Scorecard Carte de score	Chp. Chp.	Mens Mess.	Ladies Da.
Length Long.	5599	5234	5178
Par	69	69	75

Advised golfing ability   0   12   24   36
Niveau de jeu recommandé
Hcp required   Handicap exigé   no

CLUB HOUSE & AMENITIES
CLUB HOUSE ET ANNEXES
6/10

Pro shop	Pro-shop	
Driving range	Practice	
Sheltered	couvert	no
On grass	sur herbe	yes
Putting-green	putting-green	yes
Pitching-green	pitching green	yes

713

HOTEL FACILITIES
ENVIRONNEMENT HOTELIER
7/10

HOTELS HÔTELS
Great Northern Hotel   Bundoran
98 rooms, D IR£ 90   on site
Tel (353) 072 - 41 204, Fax (353) 072 - 41 114

Holyrood   Bundoran
85 rooms, D IR£ 60   1 km
Tel (353) 072 - 41 232, Fax (353) 072 - 41 100

Allingham Arms   Bundoran
88 rooms, D IR£ 50   1 km
Tel (353) 072 - 41 075, Fax (353) 072 - 41 171

RESTAURANTS RESTAURANT
Le Chateaubrianne   Bundoran
Tel (353) 072 - 42 160   2 km

Fitzgerald's Bistro   Bundoran
Tel (353) 072 - 41 336   2 km

There are some designers that always arouse our curiosity. Alongside Braid, Colt or Mackenzie, one such is Tom Simpson, whose philosophy has been taken up by numerous modern course architects, but not always so successfully. For Simpson, a course must be demanding for champions, less and less difficult the further forward the tee, and the most dangerous hazards should be designed to worry the very best players. This spirit abounds at Carlow, where virtually nothing has changed since the earliest days. It could be lengthened, that's for sure, but this par 70 stands up well to every assault. All the difficulties are visible, but the strategic and aesthetic subtleties appear only gradually: the bunkering, the shaping of the fairways and the use of a little elevated land and rare water hazards reveal an in-depth knowledge of the game of golf. A engaging course, off the beaten track.

Il est des signatures qui éveillent la curiosité. A côté de Braid, Colt ou Mackenzie, Tom Simpson est de celles-là. Sa philosophie a été reprise par de nombreux architectes modernes, pas toujours avec un tel succès : un parcours doit être exigeant pour les champions, de moins en moins difficile à mesure que l'on avance de départ, et les obstacles les plus dangereux doivent inquiéter avant tout les premiers nommés. On retrouve cet esprit à Carlow, où pratiquement rien n'a changé depuis les origines. Certes, on pourrait l'allonger un peu, mais ce par 70 résiste aux assauts. Toutes les difficultés sont visibles, mais les subtilités stratégiques et esthétiques n'apparaissent que progressivement : le placement des bunkers, le travail de modelage des fairways, l'utilisation des quelques élévations de terrain et des rares obstacles d'eau révèlent une connaissance profonde du jeu. Un parcours attachant, hors des sentiers battus.

Carlow Golf Club
Deerpark, Dublin Road
IRL - CARLOW, Co Carlow

Office	Secrétariat	(353) 0503 - 31 695
Pro shop	Pro-shop	(353) 0503 - 41 745
Fax	Fax	(353) 0503 - 40 065
Situation	Situation	

5 km from Carlow

Annual closure	Fermeture annnuelle	no
Weekly closure	Fermeture hebdomadaire	no

Fees main season
Tarifs haute saison 18 holes

	Week days Semaine	We/Bank holidays We/Férié
Individual Individuel	IR£ 20	IR£ 25
Couple Couple	IR£ 40	IR£ 50

Caddy	Caddy	on request
Electric Trolley	Chariot électrique	no
Buggy	Voiturette	IR£ 20/18 holes
Clubs	Clubs	IR£ 10

Credit cards Cartes de crédit
VISA - MasterCard

714

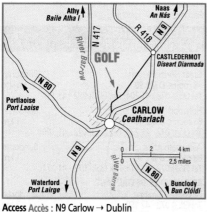

Access Accès : N9 Carlow → Dublin
Map 2 on page 697 Carte 2 Page 697

GOLF COURSE
PARCOURS   16/20

Site	Site	
Maintenance	Entretien	
Architect	Architecte	Tom Simpson
Type	Type	parkland
Relief	Relief	
Water in play	Eau en jeu	
Exp. to wind	Exposé au vent	
Trees in play	Arbres en jeu	

Scorecard Carte de score	Chp. Chp.	Mens Mess.	Ladies Da.
Length Long.	5844	5731	5218
Par	70	70	75

Advised golfing ability   0   12   24   36
Niveau de jeu recommandé

Hcp required Handicap exigé   no

CLUB HOUSE & AMENITIES
CLUB HOUSE ET ANNEXES   6/10

Pro shop	Pro-shop	
Driving range	Practice	
Sheltered	couvert	no
On grass	sur herbe	yes
Putting-green	putting-green	yes
Pitching-green	pitching green	no

HOTEL FACILITIES
ENVIRONNEMENT HOTELIER   6/10

HOTELS HÔTELS
Royal Hotel   Carlow
34 rooms, D IR£ 48   5 km
Tel (353) 0503 - 31 621, Fax (353) 0503 - 31 621

Seven Oaks Hotel   Carlow
32 rooms, D IR£ 80   5 km
Tel (353) 0503 - 31 308, Fax (353) 0503 - 32 155

Kilkea Castle   Castledermot
38 rooms, D IR£ 120   8 km
Tel (353) 0503 - 45 156, Fax (353) 0503 - 45 187

RESTAURANTS RESTAURANT
Kilkea Castle   Castledermot
Tel (353) 0503 - 45 156   8 km

Tonlegee House   Athy
Tel (353) 0507 - 31 473   15 km

CARN

Also known by the name of Belmullet, this is yet another world's end course, with impressive views over the rocky coast to the north of Mayo and Blacksod Bay. It is also one of the most recent designs by Eddie Hackett (over 80 years old). The course is very hilly, so we would advise a buggy for all seniors if they want to keep a cool head. Everyone else would be well advised to study the course closely (without counting their score first time out), because a lot of shots and greens turn blind if you are too far off the fairway, and the eight dog-legs are difficult to cope with if you don't get the right distance and angle for the green. Carn is an exciting prospect in match-play, because miracles are as frequent as disasters. However, this course is not to everyone's liking, especially to players who like parks with a pretty castle in the middle, but it is an essential experience in a site very exposed to the wind. But then, which links is not?

Egalement connu sous le nom de Belmullet, avec d'impressionnants panoramas sur la côte sauvage au nord du Mayo et Blacksod Bay, c'est encore un parcours au bout du monde, et l'un des plus récents de Eddie Hackett (à plus de 80 ans). Comme il est très accidenté, on conseillera aux seniors de prendre une voiturette, s'ils veulent garder la tête froide. Et à tout le monde de bien l'étudier (sans compter leur score la première fois) car beaucoup de coups et de greens seront aveugles s'ils s'écartent trop du fairway, et les huit doglegs seront difficiles à négocier si l'on évalue mal les distances pour avoir l'ouverture. En match-play, Carn est passionnant, car les miracles sont aussi fréquents que les désastres. Ce parcours excitant ne plaira pas à tout le monde, notamment à ceux qui aiment les parcs avec joli château, mais c'est une expérience à vivre, dans un site très exposé au vent, mais que serait un links sans lui ?

Carn Golf Links
IRL - BELMULLET, Co Mayo

Office	Secrétariat	(353) 097 - 82 292
Pro shop	Pro-shop	(353) 097 - 82 292
Fax	Fax	(353) 097 - 81477
Situation	Situation	

1 km from Belmullet
60 km from Ballina (pop. 6 563)

Annual closure	Fermeture annnuelle	no
Weekly closure	Fermeture hebdomadaire	no

Fees main season
Tarifs haute saison 18 holes

	Week days Semaine	We/Bank holidays We/Férié
Individual Individuel	IR£ 17	IR£ 17
Couple Couple	IR£ 27	IR£ 27

Caddy	Caddy	IR£ 10/18 holes
Electric Trolley	Chariot électrique	no
Buggy	Voiturette	IR£ 20/18 holes
Clubs	Clubs	IR£ 8

Credit cards Cartes de crédit
VISA - Eurocard - MasterCard

Eagle Island
Termancarragh lake
GOLF
Inishglora
Belmullet
Béal an Mhuirthead
R 313
R 313
BLASTOCK B
N 59

Access Accès : Ballina, N59 to Bangor.
R313 to Belmullet. → Airport. Golf on the right
Map 1 on page 694 Carte 1 Page 694

GOLF COURSE
PARCOURS   **16**/20

Site	Site	
Maintenance	Entretien	
Architect	Architecte	Eddie Hackett
Type	Type	links
Relief	Relief	
Water in play	Eau en jeu	
Exp. to wind	Exposé au vent	
Trees in play	Arbres en jeu	

Scorecard Carte de score	Chp. Chp.	Mens Mess.	Ladies Da.
Length Long.	6090	5804	4704
Par	72	72	73

Advised golfing ability	0	12	24	36
Niveau de jeu recommandé				
Hcp required	Handicap exigé	no		

CLUB HOUSE & AMENITIES
CLUB HOUSE ET ANNEXES   **5**/10

Pro shop	Pro-shop	
Driving range	Practice	
Sheltered	couvert	no
On grass	sur herbe	yes
Putting-green	putting-green	yes
Pitching-green	pitching green	no

HOTEL FACILITIES
ENVIRONNEMENT HOTELIER   **3**/10

HOTELS HÔTELS

Western Strand Hotel		Belmullet
15 rooms, D IR£ 25		1 km

Tel (353) 097 - 81 096, Fax (353) 097 - 81 096

Downhill Hotel		Ballina
50 rooms, D IR£ 93		60 km

Tel (353) 096 - 21 033, Fax (353) 096 - 21 338

RESTAURANTS RESTAURANT

Club House Restaurant		on site

Tel (353) 097 - 82 292

The River Boat Inn		Ballina

Tel (353) 096 - 22 183   60 km

715

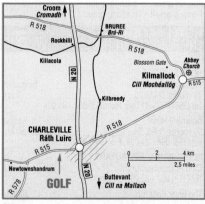

CHARLEVILLE

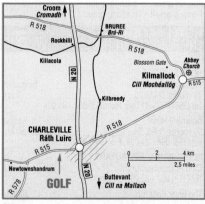

13	4	6

One of the best courses to the north of Cork has just been supplemented by an extra 9 holes, to make it even more pleasant to play. At the heart of the Golden Vale at the foot of the Ballyhoura Mountains, this is one of Ireland's best known farming regions and a good opportunity to note that the Irish are not just a people of sailors and fishermen. On this subject, the nearby Blackwater river is one of the finest sites in Ireland for tickling trout. This very busy course is in excellent condition (greens and fairways) but the bunkers are average only and rainy days are not ideal for playing here. The very many trees are often dangerous and clearly suggest a 3-wood rather than the driver. As the course is relatively short, this is not too much of a problem. It was designed more for club members than for over-demanding green-feers, but if you are in the region, you won't be disappointed.

L'un des meilleurs parcours au nord de Cork vient d'être complété par un 9 trous supplémentaire, qui en augmente encore l'agrément. Au coeur de la "Golden Vale", au pied des Ballyhoura Mountains, c'est l'une des régions agricoles les plus connues d'Irlande, une bonne occasion de vérifier que les Irlandais ne sont pas seulement un peuple de marins et de pêcheurs. A ce propos, la proche rivière Blackwater est l'un des meilleurs sites d'Irlande pour taquiner le poisson. Ce parcours très fréquenté est en excellente condition (greens et fairways), mais les bunkers sont simplement moyens, et les périodes pluvieuses ne sont pas idéales. Les arbres abondants sont souvent dangereux, ils incitent à laisser le driver dans le sac : comme le parcours n'est pas long, ce n'est pas un problème. Il a été conçu davantage pour les membres d'un club que pour des visiteurs trop exigeants. Si vous passez dans la région, vous ne serez pas déçu.

Charleville Golf Club

Smiths Road
IRL - CHARLEVILLE (RATH LUIRC), Co Cork

Office	Secrétariat	(353) 063 - 81 257
Pro shop	Pro-shop	(353) 063 - 81 274
Fax	Fax	(353) 063 - 81 274
Situation	Situation	

45 km from Limerick (pop. 52 083)
58 km from Cork (pop. 174 400)

Annual closure	Fermeture annnuelle	no
Weekly closure	Fermeture hebdomadaire	no

Fees main season
Tarifs haute saison 18 holes

	Week days Semaine	We/Bank holidays We/Férié
Individual Individuel	IR£ 13.50	IR£ 15
Couple Couple	IR£ 27	IR£ 30
Students, IR£ 7		
Caddy	Caddy	IR£ 10/18 holes
Electric Trolley	Chariot électrique	no
Buggy	Voiturette	no
Clubs	Clubs	no

Credit cards Cartes de crédit
VISA - MasterCard - AMEX

Access Accès : On main road Cork-Limerick
Map 2 on page 696 Carte 2 Page 696

GOLF COURSE
PARCOURS

13/20

Site	Site	▮▮▮▮▮
Maintenance	Entretien	▮▮▮▮▮▮
Architect	Architecte	E. Connaughton
Type	Type	inland, parkland
Relief	Relief	▮▮
Water in play	Eau en jeu	▮
Exp. to wind	Exposé au vent	▮
Trees in play	Arbres en jeu	▮▮▮▮

Scorecard Carte de score	Chp. Chp.	Mens Mess.	Ladies Da.
Length Long.	5845	5647	4585
Par	71	71	72

Advised golfing ability		0 12 24 36
Niveau de jeu recommandé		▮▮▮▮▮▮▮▮
Hcp required	Handicap exigé	28 Men, 36 Ladies

CLUB HOUSE & AMENITIES
CLUB HOUSE ET ANNEXES

4/10

Pro shop	Pro-shop	▮▮
Driving range	Practice	▮▮▮
Sheltered	couvert	4 mats
On grass	sur herbe	yes
Putting-green	putting-green	yes
Pitching-green	pitching green	yes

HOTEL FACILITIES
ENVIRONNEMENT HOTELIER

6/10

HOTELS HÔTELS

Deerpark — Charleville
20 rooms, D IR£ 45 — 1.5 km
Tel (353) 063 - 81 581, Fax (353) 063 - 81 581

Hibernian Hotel — Mallow
49 rooms, D IR£ 70 — 40 km
Tel (353) 022 - 21 588, Fax (353) 022 - 22 632

Duhallow Hotel — 6 km Kenturk
22 rooms, D IR£ 50 — 40 km
Tel (353) 029 - 56 042, Fax (353) 029 - 56 152

RESTAURANTS RESTAURANT

Longueville — Mallow
Tel (353) 027 - 47 156 — 24 km

The Coffee Pot — Charlevillea
Tel (353) 063 - 81 203 — adjacent

716

When setting eyes on a site as exceptional, as romantic and as captivating as this, set between the ocean and national park mountains, one imagines nothing less than boundless enthusiasm. Here, you are transported hundreds of years back in history, and the actual course looks as if it has always been a part of the picture. But as with Waterville, the total absence of any relief over the first few holes is disappointing, and the serious business only starts at the 8th. Then come a number of gems (the 8th, 9th and 13th) and all the closing holes from the 15th onward. If you started out playing some slack golf, the course will soon very roughly remind you of the real state of your game, and inexperienced players can easily suffer. The fairway bunkers are more or less dangerous, depending on the wind, and the same goes for the rough and some formidable thickets (often around the greens). The original budget was restricted, but we'd be willing to pay a little more to finance a few improvements to the front 9.

On aimerait bien être complètement enthousiaste quand on voit un site aussi exceptionnel, romantique et attachant, entre l'Océan et les montagnes du Parc National. On est transporté des milliers d'années en arrière, et le golf lui-même donne l'impression d'avoir toujours été là. Un peu comme à Waterville, on peut regretter le manque total de relief des premiers trous, les choses sérieuses ne commençant vraiment qu'à partir du 8. Alors, on trouve quelques joyaux (8, 9, 13) et toute la fin, à partir du 15. Si vous avez commencé avec un jeu négligent, le parcours vous rappelle brutalement à la réalité de votre golf, et les joueurs peu expérimentés risquent de souffrir. Selon le vent, les bunkers de fairway peuvent être dangereux ou non, de même que le rough et quelques redoutables buissons (souvent autour des greens). Le budget initial était limité, on serait prêt à payer plus cher pour financer quelques travaux sur l'aller.

Connemara Golf Club
Ballyconneely
IRL - CLIFDEN, Co Galway

Office	Secrétariat	(353) 095 - 23 602
Pro shop	Pro-shop	(353) 095 - 23 502
Fax	Fax	(353) 095 - 23 662
Situation	Situation	

16 km from Clifden (pop. 808)

Annual closure	Fermeture annnuelle	no
Weekly closure	Fermeture hebdomadaire	no

Fees main season
Tarifs haute saison 18 holes

	Week days Semaine	We/Bank holidays We/Férié
Individual Individuel	IR£ 25	IR£ 25
Couple Couple	IR£ 50	IR£ 50

Caddy	Caddy	on request/IR£ 15
Electric Trolley	Chariot électrique	no
Buggy	Voiturette	IR£ 20/18 holes
Clubs	Clubs	IR£ 12/18 holes

Credit cards Cartes de crédit
VISA - Eurocard - MasterCard

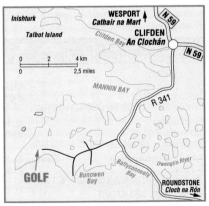

Access Accès : Galway N59 → Clifden. 16 km S of Clifden, golf in seaside village of Ballyconneely
Map 1 on page 694 Carte 1 Page 694

GOLF COURSE
PARCOURS
14/20

Site	Site	
Maintenance	Entretien	
Architect	Architecte	Eddie Hackett
Type	Type	links
Relief	Relief	
Water in play	Eau en jeu	
Exp. to wind	Exposé au vent	
Trees in play	Arbres en jeu	

Scorecard Carte de score	Chp. Chp.	Mens Mess.	Ladies Da.
Length Long.	6611	6263	5055
Par	72	72	72

Advised golfing ability Niveau de jeu recommandé	0	12	24	36
Hcp required Handicap exigé	28 Men, 36 Ladies			

CLUB HOUSE & AMENITIES
CLUB HOUSE ET ANNEXES
6/10

Pro shop	Pro-shop	
Driving range	Practice	
Sheltered	couvert	no
On grass	sur herbe	yes
Putting-green	putting-green	yes
Pitching-green	pitching green	no

717

HOTEL FACILITIES
ENVIRONNEMENT HOTELIER
6/10

HOTELS HÔTELS
Abbey Glen		Clifden
32 rooms, D IR£ 69		16 km
Tel (353) 095 - 21 201, Fax (353) 095 - 21 797		

Rock Glen		Clifden
29 rooms, D IR£ 90		16 km
Tel (353) 095 - 21 035, Fax (353) 095 - 21 737		

Erriseask Hotel		Ballyconneely
13 rooms, D IR£ 80		5 km
Tel (353) 095 - 23 553, Fax (353) 095 - 23 639		

RESTAURANTS RESTAURANT
O'Grady's Seafood		Clifden
Tel (353) 095 - 21 450		16 km

High Moors		Clifden
Tel (353) 095 - 21 342		16 km

CORK GC

This course, which is more than 100 years old, was remodelled by Alister Mackenzie, one of the great names from the classical era (he was the joint designer of Augusta, no less). Although well off the beaten golfer's track, Cork G.C. is well worth the visit. Located in a park on an island opposite the port of Cork, this is a marvellously technical course and you are constantly amazed at how easy it can be to drop so many strokes on such an honest and apparently benign course. But here, placing the drive is crucial, hazards are magnificently well placed and the putting surfaces are not easy to read. Water comes into play on only a few holes (ditches), but the rough can be as formidable as a huge lake. This very prettily landscaped and very well kept course has victoriously weathered the passing of time. Discover or return to Cork G.C. before setting out to explore the very many sights to see in this pretty region.

Ce parcours plus que centenaire a été remodelé par Alister Mackenzie, l'un des grands architectes de l'ère classique (c'est le co-auteur d'Augusta). Bien qu'il figure à l'écart des grands circuits golfiques, il mérite largement la visite. Dans un paysage de parc et situé dans une petite île face au port de Cork, c'est une petite merveille de technicité, et l'on s'étonne constamment de perdre autant de points sur un tracé aussi franc et apparemment aimable. Mais le placement des drives y est crucial, les obstacles sont magnifiquement placés, les surfaces de green sont peu faciles à lire. L'eau ne vient en jeu que sur quelques trous (fossés), mais le rough peut être tout aussi redoutable que l'immense lac. Ce parcours très joliment paysagé et très bien entretenu a victorieusement subi les atteintes du temps. A découvrir, ou redécouvrir, avant d'explorer les richesses touristiques de cette jolie région.

Cork Golf Club
IRL - LITTLE ISLAND, Co Cork

Office	Secrétariat	(353) 021 - 353 451
Pro shop	Pro-shop	(353) 021 - 353 451
Fax	Fax	(353) 021 - 353 410
Situation	Situation	

8 km from Cork (pop. 174 400)
30 km from Cobh (pop. 6 227)

Annual closure	Fermeture annnuelle	no
Weekly closure	Fermeture hebdomadaire	no

Fees main season
Tarifs haute saison 18 holes

	Week days Semaine	We/Bank holidays We/Férié
Individual Individuel	IR£ 35	IR£ 40
Couple Couple	IR£ 70	IR£ 80

Caddy	Caddy	IR£ 15/18 holes
Electric Trolley	Chariot électrique	no
Buggy	Voiturette	no
Clubs	Clubs	IR£ 12/18 holes

Credit cards Cartes de crédit
VISA - MasterCard - AMEX

Access Accès : Cork East, N25, Golf 8 km.
Map 2 on page 696 Carte 2 Page 696

GOLF COURSE
PARCOURS
15/20

Site	Site	
Maintenance	Entretien	
Architect	Architecte	Alister Mackenzie
Type	Type	parkland
Relief	Relief	
Water in play	Eau en jeu	
Exp. to wind	Exposé au vent	
Trees in play	Arbres en jeu	

Scorecard Carte de score	Chp. Chp.	Mens Mess.	Ladies Da.
Length Long.	6115	5910	5262
Par	72	72	74

Advised golfing ability
Niveau de jeu recommandé   0   12   24   36

Hcp required   Handicap exigé   no

CLUB HOUSE & AMENITIES
CLUB HOUSE ET ANNEXES
3/10

Pro shop	Pro-shop	
Driving range	Practice	
Sheltered	couvert	no
On grass	sur herbe	yes
Putting-green	putting-green	yes
Pitching-green	pitching green	yes

HOTEL FACILITIES
ENVIRONNEMENT HOTELIER
5/10

HOTELS HÔTELS
Silver Springs Hotel — Cork
109 rooms, D IR£ 90 — 6 km
Tel (353) 021 - 507 533, Fax (353) 021 - 507 641

Jurys Cork Inn — Cork
133 rooms, D IR£ 50 — 8 km
Tel (353) 021 - 276 444, Fax (353) 021 - 276 144

John Barleycorn Inn Hotel — Glanmire, Cork
D IR£ 50 — 4 km
Tel (353) 021 - 821 499, Fax (353) 021 - 821 221

RESTAURANTS RESTAURANT
Oyster Tavern — Cork
Tel (353) 021 - 272 716 — 8 km

Flemings — Cork
Tel (353) 021 - 821 621 — 8 km

718

How do you explain the fame of a golf course? County Louth (or Baltray) has never hosted major international tournaments, is not one of the star courses in the south-west of Ireland and is an hour's drive from Dublin, where there is no shortage of top courses. But recognition comes from being known by the connoisseurs. While some courses may be controversial, this one is acclaimed by all. The dunes may not be as Dantesque as elsewhere and all the difficulties are there to be seen, but this course needs a humble and clear-headed approach and close observation of each detail to appreciate the aristocratic grandeur of the whole layout. Designer Tom Simpson was perhaps the greatest strategist of all for the placing and design of bunkers, and here you recognise his cachet from hole 1 to 18. Whichever direction the wind blows, it is always in play. The fairways are comparatively wide but the rough and thickets are deadly. This sheer gem deserves both respect and glory.

A quoi tient la célébrité d'un parcours ? County Louth (ou Baltray) n'a pas reçu de grandes compétitions internationales, ne fait pas partie des vedettes du Sud-Ouest, est à une heure de Dublin, où les grands parcours ne manquent pas. Mais on reconnaît un connaisseur s'il le connaît. S'il est des parcours controversés, celui-ci fait l'unanimité. Certes, les dunes n'y sont pas aussi dantesques qu'ailleurs, on distingue toutes les difficultés, mais il faut l'aborder avec humilité et lucidité, en observer chaque détail pour apprécier la grandeur aristocratique de l'ensemble. L'architecte Tom Simpson était peut-être le plus grand stratège du placement et du dessin même des bunkers : on reconnaît sa signature du premier au dernier trou. Quelle que soit la direction du vent, il s'en trouve toujours en jeu. Les fairways sont relativement larges, mais les roughs et les buissons sont redoutables. Ce pur joyau mérite le respect, et la gloire.

County Louth Golf Club

Baltray
IRL - DROGHEDA, Co Louth

Office	Secrétariat	(353) 041 - 22 329
Pro shop	Pro-shop	(353) 041 - 22 444
Fax	Fax	(353) 041 - 22 969
Situation	Situation	

5 km from Drogheda (pop. 23 848)

| Annual closure | Fermeture annnuelle | no |
| Weekly closure | Fermeture hebdomadaire | no |

Fees main season
Tarifs haute saison 18 holes

	Week days Semaine	We/Bank holidays We/Férié
Individual Individuel	IR£ 40	IR£ 50
Couple Couple	IR£ 80	IR£ 100

Caddy	Caddy	IR£ 20/18 holes
Electric Trolley	Chariot électrique	no
Buggy	Voiturette	IR£ 20/18 holes
Clubs	Clubs	IR£ 12/18 holes

Credit cards Cartes de crédit
VISA - MasterCard

CASTLEBELLINGHAM
Baile an Ghearlánaigh
R 166
CLOGERHEAD
Ceann Chlochair
GOLF
Baltray *Baile Trá*
SLANE
Baile Shláine
R 166
R 167
N 51
DROGHEDA
Droichead Atha
BALBRIGGAN
Baile Brigín
0   2   4 km
0   2,5 miles

Access Accès : Dublin, M1 North → Drogheda.
7 km NE of Drogheda on R167
Map 3 on page 698 Carte 3 Page 698

GOLF COURSE
PARCOURS

18/20

Site	Site	
Maintenance	Entretien	
Architect	Architecte	Tom Simpson
Type	Type	links
Relief	Relief	
Water in play	Eau en jeu	
Exp. to wind	Exposé au vent	
Trees in play	Arbres en jeu	

Scorecard Carte de score	Chp. Chp.	Mens Mess.	Ladies Da.
Length Long.	6113	5952	5740
Par	73	73	75

Advised golfing ability	0	12	24	36
Niveau de jeu recommandé				
Hcp required	Handicap exigé	no		

CLUB HOUSE & AMENITIES
CLUB HOUSE ET ANNEXES

5/10

Pro shop	Pro-shop	
Driving range	Practice	
Sheltered	couvert	no
On grass	sur herbe	yes
Putting-green	putting-green	yes
Pitching-green	pitching green	yes

719

HOTEL FACILITIES
ENVIRONNEMENT HOTELIER

6/10

HOTELS HÔTELS
Boyne Valley Hotel — Drogheda
35 rooms, D IR£ 60 — 5 km
Tel (353) 041 - 37 737, Fax (353) 041 - 39 188

Neptune — Bettystown
25 rooms, D IR£ 45 — 10 km
Tel (353) 041 - 27 107, Fax (353) 041 - 27 243

Westcourt — Drogheda
20 rooms, D IR£ 60 — 5 km
Tel (353) 041 - 30 965, Fax (353) 041 - 30 970

RESTAURANTS RESTAURANT
Buttergate — Drogheda
Tel (353) 041 - 34 759 — 6 km

Triple House — Termonfeckin
Tel (353) 041 - 22 616 — 3 km

From the fairways, magnificent views over the Atlantic, the bay of Drumcliff and Ben Bulben warrant a trip to Rosses Point. But this is also home to one of Ireland's greatest golf courses. As windless days are few and far between, the elements are an overriding factor: the fairways are wide enough, but balls too far left or right are snapped up by the bunkers and rough, both equally penalising. With this said, and if we exclude two or three blind shots, all the hazards are clearly visible and the player knows perfectly well what needs to be done to avoid them. It is simply a question of doing it! Golfers with little experience or even less nerve can choose their own tees, they are all well placed to vary the shape of the course. With 9 holes overlooking the site and the other half in a valley, you can look forward to a few climbs (nothing too exhausting) and elevated greens, but none are blind. A great links to savour, yard by yard. At the time of our visit, some greens were under repair.

Depuis le parcours, les vues magnifiques sur l'Atlantique et le mont Ben Bulben justifieraient le voyage à Rosses Point. Mais c'est aussi l'un des plus grands parcours d'Irlande. Comme les jours sans vent sont rares, c'est un facteur dominant : les fairways sont larges, mais un petit écart amène vite la balle dans les roughs et les bunkers. Cela dit, à l'exception de deux ou trois coups aveugles, tous les obstacles sont visibles, et l'on sait parfaitement ce qu'il faut éviter ! Les golfeurs peu expérimentés ou pas trop courageux pourront choisir leurs tees de départ, ils sont tous bien placés pour varier le parcours. Avec une moitié des trous dominant le site et l'autre moitié dans une vallée, on peut s'attendre à quelques greens montées (elles ne sont pas épuisantes), et à quelques greens surélevés, mais aucun n'est aveugle. Un grand links à savourer. Quelques greens étaient en réparation au moment de notre visite.

County Sligo Golf Club
IRL - ROSSES POINT, Co Sligo

Office	Secrétariat	(353) 071 - 77 134
Pro shop	Pro-shop	(353) 071 - 77 171
Fax	Fax	(353) 071 - 77 460
Situation	Situation	

8 km from Sligo (pop. 17 332)

| Annual closure | Fermeture annnuelle | no |
| Weekly closure | Fermeture hebdomadaire | no |

Fees main season
Tarifs haute saison 18 holes

	Week days Semaine	We/Bank holidays We/Férié
Individual Individuel	IR£ 27	IR£ 35
Couple Couple	IR£ 54	IR£ 60

Caddy	Caddy	IR£ 15-20/18 holes
Electric Trolley	Chariot électrique	no
Buggy	Voiturette	IR£ 20/18 holes
Clubs	Clubs	IR£ 10/18 holes

Credit cards Cartes de crédit
no

Access Accès : N15, 8 km NW of Sligo.
Map 1 on page 694 Carte 1 Page 694

GOLF COURSE PARCOURS — 17/20

Site	Site	
Maintenance	Entretien	
Architect	Architecte	Harry S. Colt Alison
Type	Type	links
Relief	Relief	
Water in play	Eau en jeu	
Exp. to wind	Exposé au vent	
Trees in play	Arbres en jeu	

Scorecard Carte de score	Chp. Chp.	Mens Mess.	Ladies Da.
Length Long.	6043	5840	5280
Par	71	71	75

Advised golfing ability
Niveau de jeu recommandé   0   12   24   36

Hcp required Handicap exigé   28 Men, 36 Ladies

CLUB HOUSE & AMENITIES CLUB HOUSE ET ANNEXES — 4/10

Pro shop	Pro-shop	
Driving range	Practice	
Sheltered	couvert	no
On grass	sur herbe	yes
Putting-green	putting-green	yes
Pitching-green	pitching green	no

HOTEL FACILITIES ENVIRONNEMENT HOTELIER — 3/10

HOTELS HÔTELS

Yeats Country Hotel — Rosses Point
79 rooms, D IR£ 70 — on site
Tel (353) 071 - 77 221, Fax (353) 071 - 77 203

Ballincar House Hotel — Rosses Point
30 rooms, D IR£ 110 — 4 km
Tel (353) 071 - 45 361, Fax (353) 071 - 44 198

Sligo Park Hotel — Sligo
89 rooms, D IR£ 80 — 8 km
Tel (353) 071 - 60 291, Fax (353) 071 - 69 556

RESTAURANTS RESTAURANT

The Moorings — Rosses Point
Tel (353) 071 - 77 112 — 1 km

Austies — Rosses Point
Tel (353) 071 - 77 111 — 2 km

720

A long way to Tipperary? Not from Shannon, Cork or Dublin at any rate, although this course is rather off the traditional golfing track and it's a pity, because professional golfer Philip Walton has also shown himself to be a good course architect. He has used the natural contours well, along with the lakes and the river that cross the course rather dangerously on the 4th, and there are visible signs of the so-called American influence, particularly around the greens. These have been carefully designed and call more for lofted approaches rather than the traditional British style run shots. Designed for all levels of play, this rather, but never excessively, long course (even from the back) was designed on rolling terrain (easily walkable) around an 18th century manor, now converted into a hotel.. As a result, this is now a very agreeable week-end destination in the peaceful Irish countryside.

De Shannon, de Cork ou de Dublin, ce n'est pas une longue route pour aller à Tipperary... Pourtant, ce parcours reste en dehors des circuits golfiques traditionnels, et c'est dommage, car l'excellent professionnel Philip Walton s'y révèle également bon architecte. Il a ainsi très bien utilisé les contours naturels, les lacs et la rivière qui traverse de manière dangereuse le 4, avec une influence de l'architecture dite américaine que l'on retrouve dans le dessin des greens, très travaillés, et qui appellent davantage un jeu de balles levées que des "bump 'n run" à la britannique. Conçu pour tous les niveaux de jeu, ce parcours assez long, mais sans excès (même du fond) a été construit sur un terrain assez ondulé (facile à marcher) autour d'un manoir du XVIIIème siècle transformé en hôtel, ce qui en fait une destination de week-end tout à fait acceptable, dans le calme de la campagne irlandaise.

County Tipperary Golf & Country Club

Dundrum House Hotel
IRL - DUNDRUM, Co Tipperary

Office	Secrétariat	(353) 062 - 71 116
Pro shop	Pro-shop	(353) 062 - 71 116
Fax	Fax	(353) 062 - 71 366
Situation	Situation	

8 km N of Tipperary
9 km W of Cashel (pop. 2 473)

Annual closure	Fermeture annnuelle	no
Weekly closure	Fermeture hebdomadaire	no

Fees main season
Tarifs haute saison 18 holes

	Week days Semaine	We/Bank holidays We/Férié
Individual Individuel	IR£ 20	IR£ 24
Couple Couple	IR£ 40	IR£ 48

Caddy	Caddy	no
Electric Trolley	Chariot électrique	IR£ 5
Buggy	Voiturette	IR£ 20/18 holes
Clubs	Clubs	IR£ 8/18 holes

Credit cards Cartes de crédit
VISA - MasterCard - AMEX

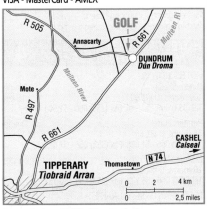

Access Accès : • Dublin N7 to Portlaoise.
N8 to Cashel. R505 to Dundrum
• Cork N8 to Cashel. R505 to Dundrum
Map 2 on page 697 Carte 2 Page 697

GOLF COURSE
PARCOURS
15/20

Site	Site	
Maintenance	Entretien	
Architect	Architecte	Philip Walton
Type	Type	parkland
Relief	Relief	
Water in play	Eau en jeu	
Exp. to wind	Exposé au vent	
Trees in play	Arbres en jeu	

Scorecard Carte de score	Chp. Chp.	Mens Mess.	Ladies Da.
Length Long.	6150	5700	5100
Par	72	72	72

Advised golfing ability		0	12	24	36
Niveau de jeu recommandé					
Hcp required	Handicap exigé	no			

CLUB HOUSE & AMENITIES
CLUB HOUSE ET ANNEXES
7/10

Pro shop	Pro-shop	
Driving range	Practice	
Sheltered	couvert	no
On grass	sur herbe	no
Putting-green	putting-green	yes
Pitching-green	pitching green	no

721

HOTEL FACILITIES
ENVIRONNEMENT HOTELIER
5/10

HOTELS HÔTELS
Dundrum House Hotel — Dundrum
60 rooms, D IR£ 90 — on site
Tel (353) 062 - 71 116, Fax (353) 062 - 71 366

Royal Hotel — Tipperary
16 rooms, D IR£ 50 — 8 km
Tel (353) 062 - 33 244, Fax (353) 062 - 33 596

Rectory House Hotel — Dundrum
10 rooms, D IR£ 55 — 2 km
Tel (353) 062 - 71 266, Fax (353) 062 - 71 115

RESTAURANTS RESTAURANT
Rosemore — Dundrum House Hotel
Tel (353) 062 - 71 116

Cashel Palace — Cashel
Tel (353) 062 - 61 411 — 5 km

The first thing here is the magic of an outstanding site, overlooking Dingle Bay, the Blasket Islands and Mount Brandon, on a peninsula where you can find the vestiges of the stone age or the beginnings of Christianity. The many panels in Gaelic only add to the impression of a journey back in time. Designed by Eddie Hackett and Christy O'Connor Jnr., this course looks as if it has always been here, and is a real pleasure to play on long summer days, even if the wind blows or if it rains a little (this may sometimes occur in Ireland). Without pretending to be in the same league as Ballybunion or Waterville, this is an interesting course for everyone, where emphasis should be laid on trying to play low shots. The main difficulty is making clean contact with the ball on sandy soil, escaping from bunkers and avoiding a meandering stream which comes into play on about ten holes. A delightful experience.

D'abord, il y a la magie d'une situation exceptionnelle sur la baie de Dingle, les Blasket Islands et le Mount Brandon, dans une péninsule où l'on trouve des vestiges de l'Age de pierre ou des débuts du christianisme. La présence de nombreux panneaux en gaélique accentue encore cette impression de voyage en remontant le temps. Créé par Eddie Hackett et Christy O'Connor Jr, ce parcours paraît avoir toujours été là, et c'est un plaisir d'y jouer pendant les longues journées d'été, même si le vent souffle, ou s'il pleut un peu (ce qui arrive parfois en Irlande). Sans prétendre appartenir à la même division que Ballybunion ou Waterville, c'est un parcours intéressant pour tous, où l'on jouera de préférence des balles basses, où la principale difficulté consiste à bien contacter la balle sur le sol sablonneux, à s'échapper des bunkers, et à éviter les méandres d'un cours d'eau, en jeu sur une dizaine de trous. Avec le charme en plus.

Golf Chumann Cean Sibeal

Ballyoughteragh
IRL - BALLYFERRITER, Co Kerry

Office	Secrétariat	(353) 066 - 56 408
Pro shop	Pro-shop	(353) 066 - 56 255
Fax	Fax	(353) 066 - 56 409
Situation	Situation	

2 km from Ballyferriter
16 km from Dingle

Annual closure	Fermeture annnuelle	no
Weekly closure	Fermeture hebdomadaire	no

Fees main season
Tarifs haute saison 18 holes

	Week days Semaine	We/Bank holidays We/Férié
Individual Individuel	IR£ 22	IR£ 22
Couple Couple	IR£ 44	IR£ 44

Cad,dy	Caddy	on request/IR£ 10
Electric Trolley	Chariot électrique	no
Buggy	Voiturette	no
Clubs	Clubs	IR£ 10

Credit cards Cartes de crédit
VISA - MasterCard

Access Accès : Tralee N86 → Derrymore, Camp, Anascaul, Dingle. R559 → Ballynana, Ballyferriter (Dingle Peninsula)
Map 2 on page 696 Carte 2 Page 696

GOLF COURSE PARCOURS 16/20

Site	Site	
Maintenance	Entretien	
Architect	Architecte	Eddie Hackett Christy O'Connor Jr
Type	Type	seaside course, links
Relief	Relief	
Water in play	Eau en jeu	
Exp. to wind	Exposé au vent	
Trees in play	Arbres en jeu	

Scorecard Carte de score	Chp. Chp.	Mens Mess.	Ladies Da.
Length Long.	6030	5870	4700
Par	72	72	73

Advised golfing ability
Niveau de jeu recommandé | 0 12 24 36

Hcp required Handicap exigé no

CLUB HOUSE & AMENITIES CLUB HOUSE ET ANNEXES 6/10

Pro shop	Pro-shop	
Driving range	Practice	
Sheltered	couvert	no
On grass	sur herbe	yes
Putting-green	putting-green	yes
Pitching-green	pitching green	no

HOTEL FACILITIES ENVIRONNEMENT HOTELIER 4/10

HOTELS HÔTELS
Dingle Skellig — Dingle 16 km
100 rooms, D IR£ 90
Tel (353) 066 - 51 144, Fax (353) 066 - 51 501

Benners Hotel — Dingle 16 km
24 rooms, D IR£ 60
Tel (353) 066 - 51 638, Fax (353) 066 - 51 412

Dun an Oir Golf Hotel — on site
20 rooms, D IR£ 50
Tel (353) 066 - 56 133, Fax (353) 066 - 56 153

RESTAURANTS RESTAURANT
Doyle's Seafood Bar — Dingle 16 km
Tel (353) 066 - 51 174

Beginish — Dingle 16 km
Tel (353) 066 - 51 588

722

16	2	6

Be warned, this is not a course for the faint-hearted. A word of advice: if your driving is not in tip-top condition, and unless you couldn't give the proverbial two hoots about playing 10 strokes over your handicap, avoid the back tees. The tiger tees are definitely no-go, except if you have the wind behind you all the way (and St Patrick to watch over you). You guessed it, this is the longest course in all of Ireland. Some of the par 4s are real monsters, not to mention the 16th, a par 3, that is inaccessible to the common run of people. From the front tees, however, it is a little easier, and the effort of walking over hilly terrain will be rewarded by a great day's golfing. The greens are often open to bump and runs, and the short game experts can have a whale of a time. The surrounding dunes and general layout make this a very good, spectacular and exciting links course, but emphasis is more on the roughness of the course than on the finesse you find with the really great courses of this type. The Clubhouse has been burnt and is not yet rebuilt.

Un bon conseil : à moins d'avoir réglé votre driving à la perfection, de vous moquer éperdument de jouer dix coups au-dessus de votre handicap, évitez les départs arrière. A moins d'avoir vent avec sur tous les trous (il faut St Patrick pour veiller sur vous), évitez les départs de championnat, c'est le plus long parcours d'Irlande. Quelques par 4 sont de véritables monstres, sans même parler du 16, un par 3 inaccessible au commun des mortels. Cela dit, il s'adoucit un peu des départs avancés, et les efforts de la marche sur ce terrain accidenté seront récompensés par une belle journée de golf. Les greens sont souvent accessibles en roulant, et les virtuoses du petit jeu pourront s'y régaler. L'environnement de dunes, et le tracé général en font un très bon links, spectaculaire et excitant, mais l'accent a été mis davantage sur la rudesse que sur la finesse des plus grands parcours du genre. Le Clubhouse a brûlé, et n'est pas encore reconstruit.

Donegal Golf Club
IRL - LAGHY, Co Donegal

Office	Secrétariat	(353) 073 - 34 054
Pro shop	Pro-shop	(353) 073 - 34 054
Fax	Fax	(353) 073 - 34 377
Situation	Situation	

7 km from Donegal Town (pop. 2 193)

Annual closure	Fermeture annnuelle	no
Weekly closure	Fermeture hebdomadaire	no

Fees main season
Tarifs haute saison 18 holes

	Week days / Semaine	We/Bank holidays / We/Férié
Individual Individuel	IR£ 18	IR£ 25
Couple Couple	IR£ 36	IR£ 50

Caddy	Caddy	on request/IR£ 12
Electric Trolley	Chariot électrique	no
Buggy	Voiturette	IR£ 20/18 holes
Clubs	Clubs	no
Credit cards Cartes de crédit		no

Access Accès : • Sligo, N15 → Donegal. 3 km before Donegal, turn left to Mullinasole/Murvagh peninsula • Donegal N15 South →Ballyshannon. Laghy, turn right to Mullinasole/Murvagh peninsula
Map 1 on page 694 Carte 1 Page 694

GOLF COURSE
PARCOURS
16/20

Site	Site	
Maintenance	Entretien	
Architect	Architecte	Eddie Hackett
Type	Type	links
Relief	Relief	
Water in play	Eau en jeu	
Exp. to wind	Exposé au vent	
Trees in play	Arbres en jeu	

Scorecard / Carte de score	Chp. / Chp.	Mens / Mess.	Ladies / Da.
Length Long.	6574	6249	5253
Par	73	73	75

Advised golfing ability		0 12 24 36
Niveau de jeu recommandé		
Hcp required	Handicap exigé	28 Men, 36 Ladies

CLUB HOUSE & AMENITIES
CLUB HOUSE ET ANNEXES
2/10

Pro shop	Pro-shop	
Driving range	Practice	
Sheltered	couvert	no
On grass	sur herbe	yes
Putting-green	putting-green	yes
Pitching-green	pitching green	yes

HOTEL FACILITIES
ENVIRONNEMENT HOTELIER
6/10

HOTELS HÔTELS

Sand House — Rossnowlagh
40 rooms, D IR£ 100 — 7 km
Tel (353) 072 - 51 777, Fax (353) 072 - 52 100

Harvey's Point Country — Donegal
20 rooms, D IR£ 90 — 12 km
Tel (353) 073 - 22 208, Fax (353) 073 - 22 352

Highland Central — Donegal
90 rooms, D IR£ 93 — 7 km
Tel (353) 073 - 21 027, Fax (353) 073 - 22 295

RESTAURANTS RESTAURANT

Belshade — Donegal
Tel (353) 073 - 22 660 — 7 km

The Castle Bar — Donegal
Tel (353) 073 - 21 062 — 7 km

Harvey's Point Country — Donegal
Tel (353) 073 - 22 208 — 12 km

723

A very good links course, whose international fame has been eclipsed somewhat by its prestigious neighbours. While this course alone may not warrant a long journey, it would be a shame not to include Dooks in any golfing itinerary to south-west Ireland. It is an excellent practice outing before getting to grips with some even more difficult courses nearby. Opened in the 19th century, it was completed in 1973 by Eddie Hackett, with praiseworthy concern for preserving unity of style. There are no gigantic dunes here, just endless mounds and dales which add to the course's character and complicate the round just enough to keep everyone happy. Not very long but often narrow, Dooks gets tougher with the wind. The greens are not huge but are well-guarded, so accuracy and a sharp short game are the order of the day, with excellent scope for bump and run approach shots. The one or two blind shots merely add to the excitement.

Un très bon parcours de links, dont la notoriété internationale a été éclipsée par de prestigieux voisins. S'il ne justifie pas à lui seul un long voyage, il serait fort dommage de ne pas l'intégrer à un séjour golfique dans le Sud-Ouest de l'Irlande. C'est même un très bon galop d'entraînement avant d'affronter des adversaires encore plus difficiles. Créé au siècle dernier, il a été complété en 1973 par Eddie Hackett, avec un louable souci de lui conserver son unité. On ne trouve pas ici de dunes gigantesques, mais les nombreuses buttes et dépressions ajoutent à son caractère, et compliquent assez le jeu pour plaire à tous. Pas très long, mais souvent étroit, il prend de la force avec le vent. Les greens ne sont pas immenses, et bien protégés, il convient alors d'être très exact, ou de sortir son meilleur petit jeu, en favorisant ces approches roulées qui sont un des plaisirs des links, avec quelques coups aveugles pour donner des émotions.

Dooks Golf Club
IRL - GLENBEIGH, Co Kerry

Office	Secrétariat	(353) 066 - 68 205
Pro shop	Pro-shop	(353) 066 - 68 205
Fax	Fax	(353) 066 - 68 476
Situation	Situation	

24 km from Killarney (pop. 7 275)
8 km from Killorglin (pop. 1 229)

Annual closure	Fermeture annnuelle	no
Weekly closure	Fermeture hebdomadaire	no

Fees main season
Tarifs haute saison 18 holes

	Week days Semaine	We/Bank holidays We/Férié
Individual Individuel	IR£ 20	IR£ 20
Couple Couple	IR£ 40	IR£ 40

Caddy	Caddy	on request/IR£ 15
Electric Trolley	Chariot électrique	IR£ 8/18 holes
Buggy	Voiturette	no
Clubs	Clubs	no

Credit cards Cartes de crédit
VISA - Eurocard - MasterCard - AMEX

Access Accès : Killarney N72 → Killorglin.
N70 → Glenbeigh (Ring of Kerry).
Golf 3 km from Glenbeigh
Map 2 on page 696 Carte 2 Page 696

GOLF COURSE
PARCOURS

15/20

Site	Site	
Maintenance	Entretien	
Architect	Architecte	Eddie Hackett
Type	Type	links, seaside course
Relief	Relief	
Water in play	Eau en jeu	
Exp. to wind	Exposé au vent	
Trees in play	Arbres en jeu	

Scorecard Carte de score	Chp. Chp.	Mens Mess.	Ladies Da.
Length Long.	6010	5702	4848
Par	70	70	70

Advised golfing ability		0 12 24 36
Niveau de jeu recommandé		
Hcp required	Handicap exigé	24 Men, 36 Ladies

CLUB HOUSE & AMENITIES
CLUB HOUSE ET ANNEXES

5/10

Pro shop	Pro-shop	
Driving range	Practice	
Sheltered	couvert	no
On grass	sur herbe	no
Putting-green	putting-green	yes
Pitching-green	pitching green	no

HOTEL FACILITIES
ENVIRONNEMENT HOTELIER

5/10

HOTELS HÔTELS
Ard Na Sidhe — Caragh Lake, Killorglin
20 rooms, D IR£ 100 — 5 km
Tel (353) 066 - 69 105, Fax (353) 066 - 69 282

Glenbeigh Hotel — Glenbeigh
16 rooms, D IR£ 50 — 3 km
Tel (353) 066 - 68 333, Fax (353) 066 - 68 404

Falcon Inn Hotel — Glenbeigh
13 rooms, D IR£ 36 — 3 km
Tel (353) 066 - 68 215, Fax (353) 066 - 68 411

RESTAURANTS RESTAURANT
Nicks — Killorglin
Tel (353) 066 - 61 219 — 7 km

Red Fox Inn — Glenbeigh
Tel (353) 066 - 69 184 — 2 km

724

DROMOLAND CASTLE

14	7	7

Give Robert Trent Jones Snr. a big lake (in play on many of the holes) and a reasonably sized parkland estate, and he will produce a course that is well above average. He probably lacked a bit of space here to create the length he usually gives his courses, so he laid more emphasis on the technical side. Being able to flight the ball is a decisive advantage here. Although only very slightly hilly, certain rolling fairways have resulted in blind tee shots, but the greens and traps along the way are clearly visible for the second shot (or at least they should be). People who are used to Trent Jones courses will recognise his strategic style for locating bunkers and the work made on and around the greens, which are always fascinating to putt on. Dromoland Castle has earned itself a very handy reputation, particularly thanks to the work made on the course in recent years.

Donnez un grand lac (en jeu sur de nombreux trous) et un parc de taille raisonnable à Robert Trent Jones Sr, il saura vous faire un parcours nettement au dessus de la moyenne. Il a sans doute manqué un peu d'espace pour lui donner la longueur habituelle de ses parcours, il a donc mis davantage l'accent sur la technicité. Ainsi, savoir travailler la balle est un avantage décisif. Bien que le relief soit limité, certaines ondulations du terrain ont imposé des départs aveugles, mais les greens et leurs défenses sont bien visibles au second coup. Les habitués des golfs de Trent Jones reconnaîtront son style stratégique de placement de bunkers, ainsi que le travail efffectué sur les greens, toujours intéressants à putter. Dromoland Castle a acquis une très bonne réputation, en particulier grâce au travail effectué sur le parcours depuis quelques années.

Dromoland Castle Golf Club
IRL - NEWMARKET-ON-FERGUS, Co Clare

Office	Secrétariat	(353) 061 - 368 444
Pro shop	Pro-shop	(353) 061 - 368 444
Fax	Fax	(353) 061 - 363 355
Situation	Situation	

28 km from Limerick (pop. 52 083)
11 km from Ennis (pop. 13 730)

Annual closure	Fermeture annnuelle	no
Weekly closure	Fermeture hebdomadaire	no

Fees main season
Tarifs haute saison 18 holes

	Week days Semaine	We/Bank holidays We/Férié
Individual Individuel	IR£ 22	IR£ 27
Couple Couple	IR£ 44	IR£ 54

Caddy	Caddy	IR£ 15/18 holes
Electric Trolley	Chariot électrique	no
Buggy	Voiturette	IR£ 30/18 holes
Clubs	Clubs	IR£ 10

Credit cards Cartes de crédit
VISA - Eurocard - MasterCard - AMEX - DC

Access Accès : Limerick, N18 → Ennis. Outside Newmarket-on-Fergus, right → Dromoland Castle.
Map 2 on page 696 Carte 2 Page 696

GOLF COURSE / PARCOURS — 14/20

Site	Site	
Maintenance	Entretien	
Architect	Architecte	R. Trent Jones Sr
Type	Type	parkland
Relief	Relief	
Water in play	Eau en jeu	
Exp. to wind	Exposé au vent	
Trees in play	Arbres en jeu	

Scorecard Carte de score	Chp. Chp.	Mens Mess.	Ladies Da.
Length Long.	5719	5646	5542
Par	71	71	71

Advised golfing ability
Niveau de jeu recommandé   0   12   24   36

Hcp required   Handicap exigé   no

CLUB HOUSE & AMENITIES / CLUB HOUSE ET ANNEXES — 7/10

Pro shop	Pro-shop	
Driving range	Practice	
Sheltered	couvert	no
On grass	sur herbe	yes
Putting-green	putting-green	yes
Pitching-green	pitching green	yes

HOTEL FACILITIES / ENVIRONNEMENT HOTELIER — 7/10

HOTELS HÔTELS
Dromoland Castle Hotel — on site
73 rooms, D IR£ 202
Tel (353) 061 - 368 144, Fax (353) 061 - 363 355

Clare Inn — Newmarket-on-Fergus
121 rooms, D IR£ 70 — 1,5 km
Tel (353) 061 - 368 161, Fax (353) 061 - 368 622

Bunratty Shamrock Hotel — Bunratty
115 rooms, D IR£ 115 — 12 km
Tel (353) 061 - 361 177, Fax (353) 061 - 471 252

RESTAURANTS RESTAURANT
Earl of Thomond — on site
Tel (353) 061 - 368 144

Weavers Inn — Newmarket-on-Fergus
Tel (353) 061 - 368 482 — 1,5 km

725

You might easily imagine the club-house here in a chic suburb of London. It is certainly impressive for comfort, but it lacks Irish warmth. Likewise, you might find this course just about anywhere in the United States, and the very American style is compounded by the necessity to be practised in the art of target golf. These remarks come to mind only because of the course's stated cultural identity, as the problem for any foreign visitor is to decipher the sign-posts showing the way here - they are all written in Gaelic. With this said, we are talking about an excellent and often intimidating course, notably the 12th, 13th and 14th (another Amen corner), the only holes that are really hilly and often less challenging than they look, at least if you avoid playing the "tiger-tees" and stick more or less to the fairway. Very spectacular and extremely well kept, this luxury course is well worth a close inspection.

On imaginerait bien le Club-house dans la banlieue chic de Londres. Il est certes impressionnant de confort, mais il manque la chaleur irlandaise. De même, on pourrait trouver le parcours n'importe où aux USA, son style très américain étant accentué par la nécessité de jouer un "target golf". Ces remarques ne viennent à l'esprit qu'en raison de l'identité culturelle affichée : le problème pour un étranger est de déchiffrer les panneaux pour y parvenir, ceux-ci étant exclusivement rédigés en gaëlique. Cela dit, il reste un excellent parcours, souvent très intimidant, notamment aux 12, 13 et 14 (l'Amen Corner), seuls trous au relief vraiment accidenté, mais souvent moins exigeant qu'il n'y paraît, si l'on évite du moins les départs de championnat, et si l'on ne s'écarte pas trop de la piste. Très spectaculaire, remarquablement entretenu, ce parcours de grand luxe mérite une visite attentive.

Druids Glen Golf Club
IRL - NEWTOWN MOUNT KENNEDY, Co Wicklow

Office	Secrétariat	(353) 01 - 287 3600
Pro shop	Pro-shop	(353) 01 - 287 3600
Fax	Fax	(353) 01 - 287 3699
Situation	Situation	

2 km from Kilcoole
35 km from Dublin (pop. 859 976)

Annual closure	Fermeture annnuelle	no
Weekly closure	Fermeture hebdomadaire	no

Fees main season
Tarifs haute saison 18 holes

	Week days Semaine	We/Bank holidays We/Férié
Individual Individuel	IR£ 75	IR£ 75
Couple Couple	IR£ 150	IR£ 150

Caddy	Caddy	on request/IR£ 20
Electric Trolley	Chariot électrique	no
Buggy	Voiturette	no
Clubs	Clubs	IR£ 15/18 holes

Credit cards Cartes de crédit
VISA - Eurocard - AMEX - DC

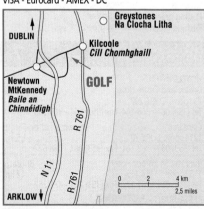

GREYSTONES
Na Clocha Litha
DUBLIN
Kilcoole
Cill Chomhghaill
GOLF
Newtown MtKennedy
Baile an Chinnéidigh
R 761
N 11
R 761
ARKLOW
0 2 4 km
0 2,5 miles

Access Accès : Dublin, N11 South.
Turn left at Newtown Mt Kennedy (signpost). Golf 2 km
Map 3 on page 698 Carte 3 Page 698

GOLF COURSE
PARCOURS   16/20

Site	Site	
Maintenance	Entretien	
Architect	Architecte	Pat Ruddy M. Craddock
Type	Type	parkland
Relief	Relief	
Water in play	Eau en jeu	
Exp. to wind	Exposé au vent	
Trees in play	Arbres en jeu	

Scorecard Carte de score	Chp. Chp.	Mens Mess.	Ladies Da.
Length Long.	6416	5997	4773
Par	72	72	72

Advised golfing ability   0 12 24 36
Niveau de jeu recommandé
Hcp required   Handicap exigé   no

CLUB HOUSE & AMENITIES
CLUB HOUSE ET ANNEXES   9/10

Pro shop	Pro-shop	
Driving range	Practice	
Sheltered	couvert	no
On grass	sur herbe	yes
Putting-green	putting-green	yes
Pitching-green	pitching green	yes

HOTEL FACILITIES
ENVIRONNEMENT HOTELIER   7/10

HOTELS HÔTELS
Glenview Hotel   Glen of the Downs
40 rooms, D IR£ 130   8 km
Tel (353) 01 - 287 3399, Fax (353) 01 - 287 7511

Tinakilly House Hotel   Rathnew
29 rooms, D IR£ 130   18 km
Tel (353) 0404 - 69 274, Fax (353) 0404 - 67 806

Grand Hotel   Wicklow
32 rooms, D IR£ 70   20 km
Tel (353) 0404 - 67 337, Fax (353) 0404 - 69 607

RESTAURANTS RESTAURANT
Wicklow Arms   Delgany
Tel (353) 01 - 287 46 11   6 km

Cooper's   Greystones
Tel (353) 01 - 287 3914   6 km

726

On a road linking some of the very greatest Irish courses, Dundalk is located between County Louth and Royal County Down. You certainly won't be wasting your time stopping off here, in the shadow of the Cooley Mountains and with the Mountains of Mourne in the background. Rejuvenated by Alliss and Thomas, this is one of the country's most under-rated inland courses. Firstly, it is a course to test your driver, with a few long and very tough par 4s and strategically located fairway bunkers. The architects have also tightened the entrances to many of the greens, thus attaching greater importance to spot-on second shots, which are, nonetheless, made easier by the elimination of blind approaches. A generally very open course, you need to get into your stride right away, as many of the difficulties are concentrated over the first seven holes. With little difference between the white and yellow tees, there's every chance that inexperienced golfers will find this tough going score-wise.

Sur une route des très grands parcours d'Irlande, Dundalk se situe entre County Louth et Royal County Down, mais l'on ne perdra pas son temps en marquant une halte ici, à l'ombre des Cooley Mountains, avec au loin les Mountains of Mourne. Rajeuni par Alliss et Thomas, c'est l'un des "inland" les plus sous-estimés du pays. C'est d'abord un parcours pour tester les drivers, avec quelques longs par 4 très difficiles, et des bunkers de fairway très stratégiques. Les architectes ont aussi rétréci les entrées de beaucoup de greens, ce qui accentue la nécessité de seconds coups précis, mais facilités par l'élimination des coups aveugles. Généralement très ouvert, il oblige à prendre vite le rythme, avec une forte concentration des difficultés sur les sept premiers trous. Il y a peu de différences entre les départs arrière et les départs hommes normaux : les golfeurs peu expérimentés auront du mal à y scorer...

Dundalk Golf Club

Blackrock

IRL - DUNDALK, Co Louth

Office	Secrétariat	(353) 042 - 21 731
Pro shop	Pro-shop	(353) 042 - 22 022
Fax	Fax	(353) 042 - 22 022
Situation	Situation	

5 km S. of Dundalk (pop. 25 843)

Annual closure	Fermeture annnuelle	no
Weekly closure	Fermeture hebdomadaire	no

Fees main season

Tarifs haute saison full day

	Week days Semaine	We/Bank holidays We/Férié
Individual Individuel	IR£ 20	IR£ 25
Couple Couple	IR£ 40	IR£ 50

Caddy	Caddy	IR£ 10/18 holes
Electric Trolley	Chariot électrique	IR£ 2/18 holes
Buggy	Voiturette	no
Clubs	Clubs	no

Credit cards Cartes de crédit
VISA - Eurocard - MasterCard

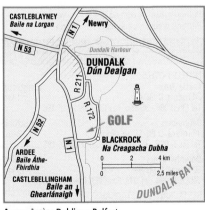

Access Accès : Dublin → Belfast,
1 km N. of Blackrock Village
Map 1 on page 695 Carte 1 Page 695

GOLF COURSE / PARCOURS

15/20

Site	Site	
Maintenance	Entretien	
Architect	Architecte	T. Shannon Alliss & Thomas
Type	Type	inland, parkland
Relief	Relief	
Water in play	Eau en jeu	
Exp. to wind	Exposé au vent	
Trees in play	Arbres en jeu	

Scorecard Carte de score	Chp. Chp.	Mens Mess.	Ladies Da.
Length Long.	6160	6028	5134
Par	72	72	73

Advised golfing ability
Niveau de jeu recommandé   0 12 24 36

Hcp required   Handicap exigé   28 Men, 36 Ladies

CLUB HOUSE & AMENITIES / CLUB HOUSE ET ANNEXES

6/10

Pro shop	Pro-shop	
Driving range	Practice	
Sheltered	couvert	no
On grass	sur herbe	yes
Putting-green	putting-green	yes
Pitching-green	pitching green	yes

HOTEL FACILITIES / ENVIRONNEMENT HOTELIER

6/10

HOTELS HÔTELS

Fairways Hotel   Dundalk
48 rooms, D IR£ 75   1 km
Tel (353) 042 - 21 500, Fax (353) 042 - 21 511

Derryhill Hotel   Dundalk
23 rooms, D IR£ 60   8 km
Tel (353) 042 - 35 471, Fax (353) 042 - 35 471

RESTAURANTS RESTAURANT

Mashie + Spoon   on site
Tel (353) 042 - 22 255

Jade Garden   Dundalk
Tel (353) 042 - 30 378   5 km

727

16	7	6

For many a year, Enniscrone was the most underrated links in Ireland, or at least one of the least known. The rediscovery of this region has pulled it out of the shadows, and although lacking the subtle features associated with the greatest links courses, it is well worth the trip. Weaker souls would be well advised to hire a buggy or, even better, take a caddie, so they don't have to carry their bag. The front 9 never really venture into the coastal dunes and emphasis is primarily on length off the tee, with difficulties caused by a number of ditches. From the 9th hole onward, excursions into moon landscape are much more frequent, with a number of holes calling for some pretty accurate ironwork. You only see the sea from the 17th tee, but you can feel it close by. The frequent wind can easily make Enniscrone doubly challenging and only the better player can hope to make any impression on the course.

Enniscrone a longtemps été l'un des links les plus sous-estimés d'Irlande, ou du moins les plus méconnus. La redécouverte de cette région l'a tiré de l'ombre. Bien qu'il manque des subtilités associées aux plus grands parcours de links, il mérite largement le détour, même si l'on conseillera aux constitutions fragiles de le jouer en voiturette ou (mieux) de prendre un caddie, pour ne pas avoir de sac à porter. L'aller ne pénètre pas vraiment dans les dunes côtières, et l'accent est porté essentiellement sur la longueur au drive, avec les difficultés dûes à la présence de fossés. A partir du 9, les voyages dans un paysage lunaire sont bien plus effectifs, avec quelques trous où les coups de fer devront être exacts. On n'aperçoit l'océan qu'au départ du 17, mais on la sent toujours très proche. Le vent fréquent peut facilement doubler l'exigence d'Enniscrone, et seuls les joueurs de niveau honorable pourront espérer s'imposer !

Enniscrone Golf Club
IRL - ENNISCRONE, Co Sligo

Office	Secrétariat	(353) 096 - 36 297
Pro shop	Pro-shop	(353) 096 - 36 297
Fax	Fax	(353) 096 - 36 657
Situation	Situation	
13 km N of Ballina (pop. 6 563)		
Annual closure	Fermeture annnuelle	no
Weekly closure	Fermeture hebdomadaire	no

Fees main season
Tarifs haute saison 18 holes

	Week days Semaine	We/Bank holidays We/Férié
Individual Individuel	IR£ 18	IR£ 24
Couple Couple	IR£ 25	IR£ 32

Caddy	Caddy	IR£ 10/18 holes
Electric Trolley	Chariot électrique	no
Buggy	Voiturette	IR£ 20/18 holes
Clubs	Clubs	IR£ 12

Credit cards Cartes de crédit
VISA - Eurocard - Mastercard

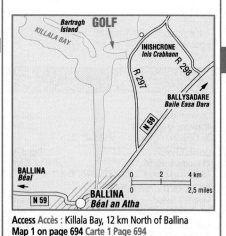

Access Accès : Killala Bay, 12 km North of Ballina
Map 1 on page 694 Carte 1 Page 694

GOLF COURSE
PARCOURS

16/20

Site	Site	
Maintenance	Entretien	
Architect	Architecte	Eddie Hackett
Type	Type	seaside course, links
Relief	Relief	
Water in play	Eau en jeu	
Exp. to wind	Exposé au vent	
Trees in play	Arbres en jeu	

Scorecard Carte de score	Chp. Chp.	Mens Mess.	Ladies Da.
Length Long.	6044	5958	5076
Par	72	72	73

Advised golfing ability
Niveau de jeu recommandé

0	12	24	36

Hcp required Handicap exigé — 28 Men, 36 Ladies

CLUB HOUSE & AMENITIES
CLUB HOUSE ET ANNEXES

7/10

Pro shop	Pro-shop	
Driving range	Practice	
Sheltered	couvert	6 mats
On grass	sur herbe	yes
Putting-green	putting-green	yes
Pitching-green	pitching green	no

HOTEL FACILITIES
ENVIRONNEMENT HOTELIER

6/10

HOTELS HÔTELS

Castle Arms	Enniscrone	1 km
24 rooms, D IR£ 40		
Tel (353) 096 - 36 156, Fax (353) 096 - 36 156		
Benbulben	Enniscrone	3 km
16 rooms, D IR£ 55 (w. dinner)		
Tel (353) 096 - 36 185, Fax (353) 096 - 36 185		
Downhill Hotel	Ballina	13 km
50 rooms, D IR£ 93		
Tel (353) 096 - 21 033, Fax (353) 096 - 21 338		

RESTAURANTS RESTAURANT

Clark's	Enniscrone	adjacent
Tel (353) 096 - 36 405		
Alpine Hotel	Enniscrone	adjacent
Tel (353) 096 - 36 252		

728

How a site like this remained unknown until the late 1980s will always be a mystery. The creation of "The European" was the work of Pat Ruddy, a professional, enthusiast, journalist and course designer. This is his masterpiece, and looks almost hand-made. Between the dunes, the beach, the fairways, the greens and the bunkers bolstered by railway line sleepers (the sand-wedge is the only way out), there was just enough room for a little marsh and a water hazard that is as worrying as it is unexpected. This course is a great trip to the land of golf where each round is so varied, so demanding and so exciting that no-one would care to mention the layout's one or two weaknesses. It takes time to appreciate the course's finer points, but the only thing on your mind when leaving is knowing when you can come back. The atmosphere of freshness and golfing purism that reigns here is the icing on the cake, as opposed to clubs where personal wealth seems to be the only criterion for playing.

Comment un site comme celui-ci est resté ignoré jusqu'à la fin des années 1980 restera un éternel mystère. La création de "The European" est dûe à Pat Ruddy, enthousiaste professionnel, journaliste et architecte. C'est son chef-d'oeuvre, donnant l'impression d'avoir été fait à la main. Entre les dunes, la plage, les fairways, les greens et des bunkers renforcés de traverses de chemin de fer (sandwedge obligatoire), il restait à peine place pour un petit marais, et pour un obstacle d'eau aussi préoccupant qu'inattendu. Ce parcours est un grand voyage au pays du golf, où l'on n'a pas le courage de relever des faiblesses de dessin tant le jeu y est varié, exigeant, excitant. Il faut du temps pour en apprécier toutes les nuances, mais on a une seule idée en le quittant, c'est d'y revenir. L'atmosphère de fraîcheur et de purisme golfique qui règne ici est la cerise sur un gâteau, à l'opposé de clubs où la fortune paraît le seul critère pour jouer.

The European Club
IRL - BRITTAS BAY, Co Wicklow

Office	Secrétariat	(353) 0404 - 47 415
Pro shop	Pro-shop	(353) 0404 - 47 415
Fax	Fax	(353) 0404 - 47 449
Situation	Situation	

12 km from Wicklow (pop. 5 847)
10 km from Arklow

Annual closure	Fermeture annnuelle	no
Weekly closure	Fermeture hebdomadaire	no

Fees main season
Tarifs haute saison 18 holes

	Week days Semaine	We/Bank holidays We/Férié
Individual Individuel	IR£ 35	IR£ 35
Couple Couple	IR£ 70	IR£ 70

Caddy	Caddy	IR£ 15-20/18 holes
Electric Trolley	Chariot électrique	no
Buggy	Voiturette	IR£ 25/18 holes
Clubs	Clubs	IR£ 20/18 holes

Credit cards Cartes de crédit
VISA - Eurocard - MasterCard

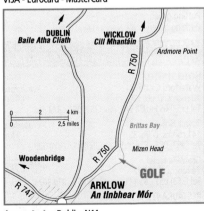

DUBLIN
Baile Atha Cliath

WICKLOW
Cill Mhantáin

Ardmore Point

R 750

0   2   4 km
0   2,5 miles

Brittas Bay

R 750

Mizen Head

Woodenbridge

R 750

GOLF

R 747

ARKLOW
An tInbhear Mór

Access Accès : Dublin, N11.
56 km turn left at Jack White's Inn.
Turn right at T Junction → Brittas Bay. 2 km
Map 3 on page 698 Carte 3 Page 698

GOLF COURSE / PARCOURS   18/20

Site	Site	
Maintenance	Entretien	
Architect	Architecte	Pat Ruddy
Type	Type	links
Relief	Relief	
Water in play	Eau en jeu	
Exp. to wind	Exposé au vent	
Trees in play	Arbres en jeu	

Scorecard Carte de score	Chp. Chp.	Mens Mess.	Ladies Da.
Length Long.	6187	5922	5153
Par	71	71	71

Advised golfing ability	0	12	24	36
Niveau de jeu recommandé				
Hcp required	Handicap exigé	no		

CLUB HOUSE & AMENITIES / CLUB HOUSE ET ANNEXES   6/10

Pro shop	Pro-shop	
Driving range	Practice	
Sheltered	couvert	under construction
On grass	sur herbe	yes
Putting-green	putting-green	yes
Pitching-green	pitching green	yes

729

HOTEL FACILITIES / ENVIRONNEMENT HOTELIER   6/10

HOTELS HÔTELS

Grand Hotel — Wicklow
32 rooms, D IR£ 70 — 11 km
Tel (353) 0404 - 67 337, Fax (353) 0404 - 69 607

Tinakilly House Hotel — Rathnew
29 rooms, D IR£ 130 — 14 km
Tel (353) 0404 - 69 274, Fax (353) 0404 - 67 806

Glenview Hotel — Glen of the Downs
40 rooms, D IR£ 130 — 27 km
Tel (353) 01 - 287 3399, Fax (353) 01 - 287 7511

RESTAURANTS RESTAURANT

Old Rectory — Wicklow
Tel (353) 0404 - 67 048 — 12 km

Tinakilly House — Rathnew
Tel (353) 0404 - 69 274 — 14 km

The south-eastern coast is not the most popular with golftrotters, and that's a good reason for discovering the region once you have visited the rest. A recent course, Faithlegg was laid out over a former estate, as you can see with the old trees, which outline the fairways, the enclosure wall and the gardens. They add extra style and difficulties to the course as a whole. The architect has designed a very varied layout with no excessively steep hills, although some hazards are hardly visible and so complicate matters slightly in terms of strategy. With this said, they only await the really wayward shot. This is an averagely difficult and very competent course, the one criticism being the very ordinary bunkers with sand a little on the coarse side. However, you can get round the course quickly, as the rough is lenient and the undergrowth kept neatly trimmed.

La côte Sud-Est n'est pas la plus fréquentée par les touristes golfiques, c'est une bonne raison de l'explorer quand vous aurez parcouru les régions plus classiques. Ouvert depuis peu, Faithlegg a été construit dans une ancienne propriété, comme on le remarque avec les arbres très adultes qui définissent les trous, le mur d'enceinte et les jardins : ils apportent une beauté supplémentaire et quelques difficultés au parcours. L'architecte a conçu un tracé très varié, sans reliefs excessifs, certains obstacles d'eau par exemple ne sont guère visibles, ce qui complique légèrement la stratégie, mais ils ne recueillent que les balles très écartées du bon chemin. De difficulté moyenne, c'est une réalisation sérieuse. On peut cependant estimer que la forme des bunkers ne sort pas de l'ordinaire, et que le sable pourrait être plus fin. En revanche, la vitesse de jeu est garantie par la clémence des roughs et le bon entretien des sous-bois.

Faithlegg Golf Club
IRL - FAITHLEGG, Co. Waterford

Office	Secrétariat	(353) 051 - 382 241
Pro shop	Pro-shop	(353) 051 - 382 241
Fax	Fax	(353) 051 - 382 664
Situation	Situation	

7 km from Waterford (pop. 40 328)

Annual closure	Fermeture annnuelle	no
Weekly closure	Fermeture hebdomadaire	no

Fees main season
Tarifs haute saison 18 holes

	Week days Semaine	We/Bank holidays We/Férié
Individual Individuel	IR£ 22	IR£ 25
Couple Couple	IR£ 44	IR£ 50

Caddy	Caddy	on request/IR£ 10/15
Electric Trolley	Chariot électrique	no
Buggy	Voiturette	IR£ 20/18 holes
Clubs	Clubs	IR£ 10

Credit cards Cartes de crédit
VISA - MasterCard

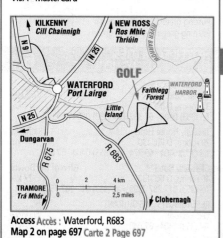

Access Accès : Waterford, R683
Map 2 on page 697 Carte 2 Page 697

GOLF COURSE
PARCOURS **13**/20

Site	Site	
Maintenance	Entretien	
Architect	Architecte	Patrick Merrigan
Type	Type	parkland
Relief	Relief	
Water in play	Eau en jeu	
Exp. to wind	Exposé au vent	
Trees in play	Arbres en jeu	

Scorecard Carte de score	Chp. Chp.	Mens Mess.	Ladies Da.
Length Long.	6057	5712	5160
Par	72	72	73

Advised golfing ability		0 12 24 36
Niveau de jeu recommandé		
Hcp required	Handicap exigé	no

CLUB HOUSE & AMENITIES
CLUB HOUSE ET ANNEXES **7**/10

Pro shop	Pro-shop	
Driving range	Practice	
Sheltered	couvert	no
On grass	sur herbe	yes
Putting-green	putting-green	yes
Pitching-green	pitching green	no

HOTEL FACILITIES
ENVIRONNEMENT HOTELIER **6**/10

HOTELS HÔTELS
Waterford Castle
19 rooms, D IR£ 170 — Waterford 3,5 km
Tel (353) 051 - 878 203, Fax (353) 051 - 879 316

Tower Hotel
141 rooms, D IR£ 85 — Waterford 7 km
Tel (353) 051 - 875 801, Fax (353) 051 - 870 129

Granville Hotel
74 rooms, D IR£ 72 — Waterford 7 km
Tel (353) 051 - 55 111, Fax (353) 051 - 870 307

RESTAURANTS RESTAURANT
Dwyer's — Waterford 7 km
Tel (353) 051 - 77 478

Prendiville's — Waterford 7 km
Tel (353) 051 - 78 851

730

This is the brainchild of Kevin Mulcahy, the son of the founder of Waterville. It is not a links, but it makes no difference, and the designers McEvoy and O'Connor Jnr. have made a point of including some seaside features like pot bunkers and a double green, amongst the many other difficulties. These start with the greens, moderately contoured, but only the short putts are more or less straight. You often see water (as far as the port of Cork) but it only comes into play on half a dozen holes, dangerously so on the 12th, 14th and 18th. The other hazards are primarily trees, green-side bunkers and a few stone walls here and there. This course is suitable for all players, who often have the choice between lofted and ground shots. Here, you hone your short game and play with your brains. You will also see a few ostriches, monkeys or llamas roaming in the adjacent natural park.

C'est l'enfant de Kevin Mulcahy, fils du fondateur de Waterville. Que ce ne soit pas un links n'enlève rien à ses qualités, et les architectes McEvoy et O'Connor Jr n'ont pas manqué d'en citer quelques traits, comme quelques pot-bunkers et un double-green, parmi bien d'autres difficultés. A commencer par les greens, de relief modéré, mais où seuls les petits putts seront quasiment droits. On voit souvent l'eau (jusqu'au port de Cork), elle ne vient réellement en jeu que sur une demi-douzaine de trous, et de manière dangereuse au 12, au 14 et au 18. Les autres obstacles sont principalement de grands arbres, les bunkers de green et un petit mur çà et là. Ce parcours convient à tous les joueurs, qui auront souvent le choix entre les balles portées (target golf) et les approches roulées. Ici, on travaille son petit jeu, on joue avec sa tête et on peut apercevoir quelques autruches, singes ou lamas en balade hors du parc naturel adjacent.

Fota Island Golf Club
IRL - CARRIGTWOHILL, Co Cork

Office	Secrétariat	(353) 021 - 883 700
Pro shop	Pro-shop	(353) 021 - 883 710
Fax	Fax	(353) 021 - 883 713
Situation	Situation	

14 km from Cork (pop. 174 400)
10 km from Cobh (pop. 6 227)

Annual closure	Fermeture annuelle	no
Weekly closure	Fermeture hebdomadaire	no

Fees main season
Tarifs haute saison 18 holes

	Week days Semaine	We/Bank holidays We/Férié
Individual Individuel	IR£ 27	IR£ 30
Couple Couple	IR£ 54	IR£ 60

Caddy	Caddy	on request/IR£ 12
Electric Trolley	Chariot électrique	no
Buggy	Voiturette	IR£ 25/18 holes
Clubs	Clubs	IR£ 12/18 holes

Credit cards Cartes de crédit
VISA - MasterCard - AMEX

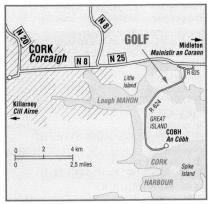

Access Accès : Cork N8 East → Cobh. R624
→ Fota Island
Map 2 on page 696 Carte 2 Page 696

GOLF COURSE
PARCOURS
15/20

Site	Site	
Maintenance	Entretien	
Architect	Architecte	Christy O'Connor Jr Peter McEvoy
Type	Type	parkland
Relief	Relief	
Water in play	Eau en jeu	
Exp. to wind	Exposé au vent	
Trees in play	Arbres en jeu	

Scorecard Carte de score	Chp. Chp.	Mens Mess.	Ladies Da.
Length Long.	6197	5788	4967
Par	72	72	72

Advised golfing ability   0   12   24   36
Niveau de jeu recommandé
Hcp required   Handicap exigé   24 Men, 36 Ladies

CLUB HOUSE & AMENITIES
CLUB HOUSE ET ANNEXES
7/10

Pro shop	Pro-shop	
Driving range	Practice	
Sheltered	couvert	no
On grass	sur herbe	yes
Putting-green	putting-green	yes
Pitching-green	pitching green	no

731

HOTEL FACILITIES
ENVIRONNEMENT HOTELIER
6/10

HOTELS HÔTELS

Jurys Cork Inn		Cork
133 rooms, D IR£ 50		7 km
Tel (353) 021 - 276 444, Fax (353) 021 - 276 144		
Rochestown Hotel		Cork
63 rooms, D IR£ 85		12 km
Tel (353) 021 - 892 233, Fax (353) 021 - 892 178		
Silver Springs Hotel		Cork
109 rooms, D IR£ 90		12 km
Tel (353) 021 - 507 533, Fax (353) 021 - 507 641		

RESTAURANTS RESTAURANT

Ballymaloe House	Midleton
Tel (353) 021 - 352 531	33 km
Crawford Gallery	Cork
Tel (353) 021 - 274 415	15 km

Overlooking the Atlantic and the town of Galway, this recent course provides some outstanding viewpoints, but don't let them blur your judgment. The terrain given to Christy O'Connor Jnr. was naturally nothing more than ordinary, but he has made a great job of it and designed in a lot of appeal at the expense of some highly appropriate earthworks. As usual, the bunkers are very well placed and ready to collect any ball that doesn't quite manage to short-cut the dog-legs. There are also three lakes, but there are in play on three holes only. The many tee-off areas spread the range of difficulties, but only the back tees make this a severe test. The general difficulties are clearly visible and game strategy is obvious; this is important because the wind can turn nasty and make it even more essential to know how to play with it and against it. Welcome to a course designed with considerable talent, lacking only that intangible touch of greatness that separates the excellent from the exceptional.

Dominant l'océan et la ville de Galway, ce récent parcours offre des points de vue exceptionnels. Mais ils ne doivent pas influencer le jugement ! Le terrain mis à la disposition de Christy O'Connor Jr était naturellement assez ordinaire, il en a tiré un très bon parti, et l'a même rendu séduisant, au prix de travaux de terrassement très adéquats. Ses bunkers sont comme d'habitude très bien placés, et prêts à accueillir ceux qui ne parviennent pas à couper les dog-legs. De même, trois lacs sont mis en jeu, mais sur trois trous seulement. Les nombreux départs proposent un éventail de difficultés, seuls les départs arrière rendent ce parcours sévère. Les difficultés générales sont bien visibles, et la stratégie de jeu évidente : c'est important car le vent peut devenir méchant, et renforcer encore la nécessité de savoir jouer avec et contre lui. Un parcours réalisé avec talent, auquel ne manque que l'indéfinissable grandeur qui fait les exceptions.

Galway Bay Golf & Country Club

Renville
IRL - ORANMORE, Co Galway

Office	Secrétariat	(353) 091 - 790 500
Pro shop	Pro-shop	(353) 091 - 790 503
Fax	Fax	(353) 091 - 790 510
Situation	Situation	

5 km from Oranmore Village
13 km from Galway (pop. 50 855)

Annual closure	Fermeture annnuelle	no
Weekly closure	Fermeture hebdomadaire	no

Fees main season
Tarifs haute saison 18 holes

	Week days Semaine	We/Bank holidays We/Férié
Individual Individuel	IR£ 30	IR£ 35
Couple Couple	IR£ 60	IR£ 70

Weekdays: IR£ 45 for 2 rounds - Week-ends: IR£ 53 for 2 rounds

Caddy	Caddy	on request/IR£ 20
Electric Trolley	Chariot électrique	no
Buggy	Voiturette	IR£ 20/18 holes
Clubs	Clubs	IR£ 10

Credit cards Cartes de crédit
VISA - Eurocard - MasterCard

732

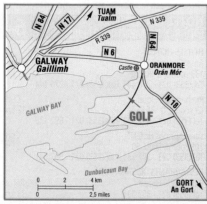

Access Accès : Galway N6 → Oranmore, → Renville
Map 1 on page 694 Carte 1 Page 694

GOLF COURSE
PARCOURS
14/20

Site	Site	
Maintenance	Entretien	
Architect	Architecte	Christy O'Connor Jr
Type	Type	seaside course
Relief	Relief	
Water in play	Eau en jeu	
Exp. to wind	Exposé au vent	
Trees in play	Arbres en jeu	

Scorecard Carte de score	Chp. Chp.	Mens Mess.	Ladies Da.
Length Long.	6533	6091	5205
Par	72	72	74

Advised golfing ability
Niveau de jeu recommandé

| 0 | 12 | 24 | 36 |

Hcp required	Handicap exigé	28 Men, 36 Ladies

CLUB HOUSE & AMENITIES
CLUB HOUSE ET ANNEXES
7/10

Pro shop	Pro-shop	
Driving range	Practice	
Sheltered	couvert	no
On grass	sur herbe	yes
Putting-green	putting-green	yes
Pitching-green	pitching green	yes

HOTEL FACILITIES
ENVIRONNEMENT HOTELIER
6/10

HOTELS HÔTELS

Corrib Great Southern — Galway
179 rooms, D IR£ 117 — 8 km
Tel (353) 091 - 755 281, Fax (353) 091 - 751 390

Galway Ryan — Galway
96 rooms, D IR£ 120 — 9 km
Tel (353) 091 - 753 181, Fax (353) 091 - 753 187

Oranmore Lodge Hotel — Oranmore
40 rooms, D IR£ 80 — 5 km
Tel (353) 091 - 794 400, Fax (353) 091 - 790 227

RESTAURANTS RESTAURANT

Paddy Burkes — Clarinbridge
Tel (353) 091 - 796 226 — 7 km

Galway Bay Golf Club — on site
Tel (353) 091 - 790 500

We expect a lot from a great designer such as Alistair Mackenzie, but there's no denying the fact that Galway GC is now in need of a little careful remodelling from a modern designer who can preserve the course's style and spirit. The trees have obviously grown considerably since 1923, compounding the course's general tightness, the only real difficulty for the modern player. Precision play and flighting the ball take precedence over length, to the extent that long-hitters can leave the driver firmly in the bag and card a better score in return. On the other hand, average players will doubtless find the course long enough as it is. The space available was used to good effect and there are a lot of bunkers which are never excessively penalising. If we add to all this the superb views over Galway Bay, Burren and the Aran islands, plus the very busy city of Galway, then there is a welcome for you here.

On attend beaucoup de la signature d'un très grand architecte tel que Alister Mackenzie, mais il faut bien reconnaître que ce parcours mériterait un "lifting" attentif de la part d'un architecte moderne soucieux de lui conserver son esthétique et son esprit. Les arbres ont dû beaucoup pousser depuis 1923, accentuant l'étroitesse du parcours, seule véritable difficulté pour un joueur d'aujourd'hui. La précision et le travail de balle prennent nettement le pas sur la longueur, au point que les longs joueurs pourront laisser le driver dans le sac, avec une incidence favorable sur leur score. En revanche, les joueurs moyens trouveront sans doute la longueur du parcours suffisante ! L'espace disponible a été bien utilisé, le bunkering est important, mais rarement de manière trop pénalisante. Si l'on ajoute les points de vue superbes sur la baie de Galway, le Burren et les Iles d'Arran, et la proximité de la ville très animée de Galway... bienvenue ici.

Galway Golf Club
Blackrock
IRL - SALTHILL, GALWAY, Co Galway

Office	Secrétariat	(353) 091 - 522 033
Pro shop	Pro-shop	(353) 091 - 523 038
Fax	Fax	(353) 091 - 522 033
Situation	Situation	

2 km from Galway (pop. 50 855)

Annual closure	Fermeture annnuelle	no
Weekly closure	Fermeture hebdomadaire	no

Fees main season
Tarifs haute saison 18 holes

	Week days Semaine	We/Bank holidays We/Férié
Individual Individuel	IR£ 18	IR£ 23
Couple Couple	IR£ 36	IR£ 46

Caddy	Caddy	on request/IR£ 15
Electric Trolley	Chariot électrique	IR£ 5/18 holes
Buggy	Voiturette	IR£ 25/18 holes
Clubs	Clubs	IR£ 8/18 holes

Credit cards Cartes de crédit
VISA - MasterCard

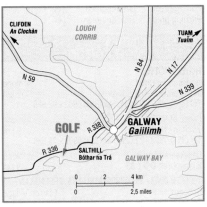

Access Accès : Galway R336 West. Golf at the end of the Promenade at Salthill.
Map 1 on page 694 Carte 1 Page 694

GOLF COURSE
PARCOURS
13/20

Site	Site	▬▬▬▬
Maintenance	Entretien	▬▬▬▬
Architect	Architecte	Alistair Mackenzie
seaside course,		**Type** Type
Relief	Relief	parkland
Water in play	Eau en jeu	▬
Exp. to wind	Exposé au vent	▬▬▬▬
Trees in play	Arbres en jeu	▬▬▬▬

Scorecard Carte de score	Chp. Chp.	Mens Mess.	Ladies Da.
Length Long.	5832	5598	4752
Par	70	71	73

Advised golfing ability Niveau de jeu recommandé	0	12	24	36

Hcp required   Handicap exigé   28 Men, 36 Ladies

CLUB HOUSE & AMENITIES
CLUB HOUSE ET ANNEXES
6/10

Pro shop	Pro-shop	▬▬▬▬
Driving range	Practice	▬▬▬
Sheltered	couvert	no
On grass	sur herbe	yes
Putting-green	putting-green	yes
Pitching-green	pitching green	no

HOTEL FACILITIES
ENVIRONNEMENT HOTELIER
6/10

HOTELS HÔTELS
Corrib Great Southern   Galway
179 rooms, D IR£ 117   1 km
Tel (353) 091 - 755 281, Fax (353) 091 - 751 390

Spinnaker Hotel   Galway
20 rooms, D IR£ 60   adjacent
Tel (353) 091 - 526 788, Fax (353) 091 - 526 650

Glenlo Abbey   Galway
45 rooms, D IR£ 150   2 km
Tel (353) 091 - 526 666, Fax (353) 091 - 527 800

RESTAURANTS RESTAURANT
Moran's Oyster Cottage   Kilcolgan
Tel (353) 091 - 796 113   10 km

Cavey's Westwood   Galway
Tel (353) 091 - 21 442   3 km

733

Very positively adapting a course to players of all abilities is something you would expect from a fine connoisseur of amateur and professional golf such as Christy O'Connor Jnr. Given a remarkable site, long a favourite haunt of hikers and cyclists, he visibly rose to the occasion, and the views over Lough Ree are as magnificent as his deployment of the course on several holes. Other lakes add to both the course's scenic beauty and difficulty. And if we add to this a lot of very careful design on and around the greens, intelligently placed bunkers and the general balance of the layout, you will understand that this is one of the finest recent additions to the collection of Irish courses and one that will leave nobody indifferent. A little hilly but not excessively so, Glasson calls for a very precise game strategy and a cool head at all times. One further detail: you can reach the 18th tee by boat from Athlone.

On peut attendre d'un fin connaisseur du golf amateur et professionnel comme Christy O'Connor Jr une adaptation très sûre à tous les niveaux de jeu. Disposant d'un site remarquable, depuis longtemps connu des amateurs de randonnées cyclistes et pédestres, il en a visiblement été exalté, les vues sur le Lough Ree sont aussi magnifiques que sa mise en jeu sur quelques trous. D'autres lacs contribuent aussi bien à la beauté scénique du parcours qu'à sa difficulté. Et si l'on ajoute le travail très soigné des greens, le placement intelligent des bunkers et l'équilibre général du tracé, on aura compris qu'il s'agit d'une des meilleures additions récentes à la collection des golfs irlandais, et qui ne peut laisser indifférent. Un peu accidenté, mais sans excès, Glasson demande une stratégie de jeu très précise et de garder la tête froide. Pour l'anecdote, on peut parvenir en bateau au départ du 18, depuis Athlone.

Glasson Golf Club

Glasson
IRL - ATHLONE, Co West Meath

Office	Secrétariat	(353) 0902 - 85 120
Pro shop	Pro-shop	(353) 0902 - 85 120
Fax	Fax	(353) 0902 - 85 444
Situation	Situation	

9 km from Athlone (pop. 8 170)

Annual closure	Fermeture annnuelle	non
Weekly closure	Fermeture hebdomadaire	no

Fees main season
Tarifs haute saison 18 holes

	Week days Semaine	We/Bank holidays We/Férié
Individual Individuel	IR£ 25	IR£ 30
Couple Couple	IR£ 50	IR£ 60

Caddy	Caddy	on request/IR£ 15
Electric Trolley	Chariot électrique	no
Buggy	Voiturette	IR£ 20/18 holes
Clubs	Clubs	IR£ 12/18 holes

Credit cards Cartes de crédit
VISA - MasterCard

GOLF COURSE
PARCOURS 16/20

Site	Site	
Maintenance	Entretien	
Architect	Architecte	Christy O'Connor Jr
Type	Type	parkland
Relief	Relief	
Water in play	Eau en jeu	
Exp. to wind	Exposé au vent	
Trees in play	Arbres en jeu	

Scorecard Carte de score	Chp. Chp.	Mens Mess.	Ladies Da.
Length Long.	6510	6083	5100
Par	72	72	73

Advised golfing ability Niveau de jeu recommandé	0	12	24	36

Hcp required Handicap exigé 24 Men, 36 Ladies

CLUB HOUSE & AMENITIES
CLUB HOUSE ET ANNEXES 7/10

Pro shop	Pro-shop	
Driving range	Practice	
Sheltered	couvert	no
On grass	sur herbe	yes
Putting-green	putting-green	yes
Pitching-green	pitching green	yes

HOTEL FACILITIES
ENVIRONNEMENT HOTELIER 7/10

HOTELS HÔTELS
Hodson Bay Hotel — Athlone
100 chambres, D IR£ 100 — 12 km
Tél (353) 0902 - 92 404, Fax (353) 0902 - 92 688

Prince of Wales — Athlone
75 chambres, D IR£ 70 — 9 km
Tél (353) 0902 - 72 626, Fax (353) 0902 - 75 658

Ballykeeran Lodge — Athlone
8 chambres, D IR£ 32 — 5 km
Tél (353) 0902 - 85 063

RESTAURANTS RESTAURANT
Grogans — Glasson Village
Tél (353) 0902 - 85 158 — 2 km

Glasson Village — Glasson/Athlone
Tél (353) 0902 - 85 001 — 2 km

Access Accès : 10 km N.E. of Athlone on N55.
Cavan road
Map 2 on page 697 Carte 2 Page 697

734

This age-old course, completed and overhauled by Eddie Hackett, is a mixture of wooded inland course and links, resulting in a lot of variety and an original appearance. There are even surprises in store, with the presence of the old disused railway line, whose infrastructure offers protection from the Irish sea and serves as a platform (no pun intended) for four elevated tees. If you like surprises, this course harbours a number of traps and is no walk-over first time out. Six greens are blind, there is a double green (2 and 10), a few hazards are invisible on several holes, a ditch makes its presence felt on four holes and there are ponds for a watery grave on three others. Fortunately, if you miss the fairway, the rough is perfectly playable. Laid out along Carlingford Lough, close to the pretty fishing village of Carlingford (an oyster centre), this is a very amusing, far from easy and rather uncommon course.

Ce parcours centenaire complété et révisé par Eddie Hackett est un mélange de parcours inland boisé et de links, ce qui lui donne beaucoup de variété, mais aussi un visage assez original. Il est même surprenant à cause de la présence d'une ancienne ligne de chemin de fer, aujourd'hui désaffectée, dont l'infrastructure protège de la mer d'Irlande, et sert de base pour quatre départs surélevés. Si vous aimez les surprises, ce parcours recèle pas mal de pièges, et n'est pas évident à première vue : six greens sont aveugles, on trouve un double green (2 et 10), quelques obstacles sont invisibles sur plusieurs trous, un fossé vient en jeu sur quatre trous, et des mares sur trois trous. Heureusement, si l'on manque les fairways, le rough reste tout à fait jouable. Le long du Carlingford Lough, près du joli village de pêcheurs de Carlingford (la capitale des huîtres), c'est un parcours très amusant, pas facile et dépaysant.

Grenore Golf Club
IRL - GRENORE, Co Louth

Office	Secrétariat	(353) 042 - 73 678
Pro shop	Pro-shop	(353) 042 - 73 678
Fax	Fax	(353) 042 - 73 678
Situation	Situation	

12 km from Dundalk (pop. 25 843)
16 km from Newry

Annual closure	Fermeture annnuelle	non
Weekly closure	Fermeture hebdomadaire	no

Fees main season
Tarifs haute saison 18 holes

	Week days Semaine	We/Bank holidays We/Férié
Individual Individuel	IR£ 14	IR£ 20
Couple Couple	IR£ 28	IR£ 40

Caddy	Caddy	no
Electric Trolley	Chariot électrique	no
Buggy	Voiturette	no
Clubs	Clubs	no

Credit cards Cartes de crédit
no

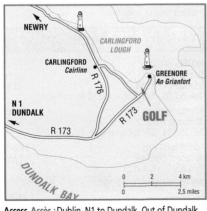

NEWRY

CARLINGFORD LOUGH

CARLINGFORD Cairlinn

R 176

N 1 DUNDALK

R 173

R 173 GOLF

GREENORE An Grianfort

DUNDALK BAY

| 0 | 2 | 4 km |
| 0 | | 2,5 miles |

Access Accès : Dublin, N1 to Dundalk. Out of Dundalk, turn right on R173 to Greenore. Golf 12 km
Map 1 on page 695 Carte 1 Page 695

GOLF COURSE
PARCOURS

14/20

Site	Site	
Maintenance	Entretien	
Architect	Architecte	Eddie Hackett
Type	Type	seaside course
Relief	Relief	
Water in play	Eau en jeu	
Exp. to wind	Exposé au vent	
Trees in play	Arbres en jeu	

Scorecard Carte de score	Chp. Chp.	Mens Mess.	Ladies Da.
Length Long.	5954	5700	5198
Par	71	71	74

Advised golfing ability		0	12	24	36
Niveau de jeu recommandé					

Hcp required	Handicap exigé	24 Men, 36 Ladies

CLUB HOUSE & AMENITIES
CLUB HOUSE ET ANNEXES

6/10

Pro shop	Pro-shop	
Driving range	Practice	
Sheltered	couvert	no
On grass	sur herbe	yes
Putting-green	putting-green	yes
Pitching-green	pitching green	no

HOTEL FACILITIES
ENVIRONNEMENT HOTELIER

5/10

HOTELS HÔTELS
Ballymascanlon Hotel — Dundalk
36 chambres, D IR£ — 12 km

Tél (353) 042 - 71 124Village Hotel — Carlingford
13 chambres, D IR£ 45 — 2 km

Tél (353) 042 - 73 116

RESTAURANTS RESTAURANT
Jordans Townhouse — Carlingford
Tél (353) 042 - 73 223 — 3 km

McKevitts Village — Carlingford
Tél (353) 042 - 73 116 — 3 km

735

This course has led a quiet existence since the turn of the century and continues to figure regularly amongst the better Irish golf courses. There is nothing of the links about it, sure, but its park-landscape configuration (the trees are superb) on the banks of the Liffey, the moderately hilly relief (two or three steep climbs) and the closeness to Dublin make this a very interesting stop-off. It is not very long (especially from the normal tees) but it does require a lot of precision play and probably every club in your bag. A few blind shots and greens add a little uncertainty to it all, and the 10th (a par 3 along the Liffey river) is an exciting prospect with the green way down below you. You shouldn't under-estimate Hermitage, it is capable of baring its teeth to anyone who is not permanently on his or her toes. This is a very fine example of an inland course and has hosted a number of top tournaments. It may not always stand up to the best player, but it has lost none of its charm.

Ce golf vit paisiblement depuis le début du siècle, et continuer à figurer régulièrement parmi les bons parcours d'Irlande. Certes, il n'a rien d'un links, mais sa configuration de grand parc (les arbres sont superbes) en bordure de la Liffey, son relief modéré (deux ou trois fortes montées) et sa proximité de Dublin en font une étape fort intéressante. Il n'est pas très long (surtout des départs normaux), mais il demande pas mal de précision, et l'utilisation probable de tous les clubs du sac. Quelques coups et un green aveugles ajoutent un peu d'incertitude, et le 10 (un par 3 le long de la Liffey) amène quelque émotion, avec son green très en contrebas du départ. On ne doit pas sous-estimer Hermitage, il est capable de montrer les dents à ceux qui négligeraient de conserver en permanence leur concentration. Ce très bel exemple de parcours "inland" a reçu de grandes compétitions, il conserve son charme, sinon sa résistance aux meilleurs joueurs.

Hermitage Golf Club
Ballydowd
IRL - LUCAN, Co Dublin

Office	Secrétariat	(353) 01 - 626 4781
Pro shop	Pro-shop	(353) 01 - 626 8072
Fax	Fax	(353) 01 - 626 4781
Situation	Situation	

12 km from Dublin (pop. 859 976)
4 km from Maynooth (pop. 6 027)

Annual closure	Fermeture annnuelle	no
Weekly closure	Fermeture hebdomadaire	no

Fees main season
Tarifs haute saison 18 holes

	Week days Semaine	We/Bank holidays We/Férié
Individual Individuel	IR£ 32	IR£ 45
Couple Couple	IR£ 64	IR£ 90

Weekdays: IR£ 21 before 9.00 am

Caddy	Caddy	on request/IR£ 15
Electric Trolley	Chariot électrique	IR£ 5
Buggy	Voiturette	no
Clubs	Clubs	IR£ 10/18 holes

Credit cards Cartes de crédit
VISA - MasterCard

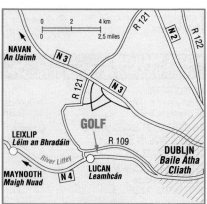

Access Accès : Dublin, N4 West.
Map 3 on page 698 Carte 3 Page 698

GOLF COURSE
PARCOURS
15/20

Site	Site	
Maintenance	Entretien	
Architect	Architecte	M. McKenna
Type	Type	parkland
Relief	Relief	
Water in play	Eau en jeu	
Exp. to wind	Exposé au vent	
Trees in play	Arbres en jeu	

Scorecard Carte de score	Chp. Chp.	Mens Mess.	Ladies Da.
Length Long.	6051	5833	5215
Par	71	71	75

Advised golfing ability Niveau de jeu recommandé	0	12	24	36

Hcp required Handicap exigé   24 Men, 36 Ladies

CLUB HOUSE & AMENITIES
CLUB HOUSE ET ANNEXES
6/10

Pro shop	Pro-shop	
Driving range	Practice	
Sheltered	couvert	no
On grass	sur herbe	yes
Putting-green	putting-green	yes
Pitching-green	pitching green	yes

HOTEL FACILITIES
ENVIRONNEMENT HOTELIER
7/10

HOTELS HÔTELS
Spa Hotel — Lucan
53 rooms, D IR£ 64 — 4 km
Tel (353) 01 - 628 0494, Fax (353) 01 - 628 0841

Finnstown House Hotel — Lucan
45 rooms, D IR£ 70 — 6 km
Tel (353) 01 - 628 0644, Fax (353) 01 - 628 1088

Springfield Hotel — Leixlip
40 rooms, D IR£ 44 — 2 km
Tel (353) 01 - 624 4925

RESTAURANTS RESTAURANT
Finnstown — Lucan
Tel (353) 01 - 628 0644 — 6 km

Ryans — Dublin
Tel (353) 01 - 820 8210 — 6 km

This is one of the most ambitious projects ever carried out in Ireland. Straffan House has been converted into a top luxury hotel and a course built without counting the cost, the whole piece co-ordinated by the Jefferson Smurfit group, one of the country's most dynamic entrepreneurs. Arnold Palmer pitched and won the official tender to design the course and has come up with one of his most exacting layouts. In length and tactical difficulty, it is reminiscent of Bay Hill in Florida. Only the most accomplished golfers can hope to cope without feeling too disillusioned about their game. Even from the front tees, this is an uncompromising challenge, so don't waste time counting your strokes, or even your balls if you start flirting too boldly with the water, especially over the closing holes. What with the closeness of the river Liffey, we would suggest you play here in summer, despite the excellent drainage.

C'est l'une des plus ambitieuses réalisations jamais effectuées en Irlande, avec la transformation de la Straffan House en hôtel de grand luxe, et la construction d'un parcours où l'argent n'a pas été compté, sous la houlette du Jefferson Smurfit Group, l'une des entreprises les plus dynamiques du pays. Arnold Palmer est sorti vainqueur du concours d'architectes, il a livré l'un des ses parcours les plus exigeants : par sa longueur et ses difficultés tactiques, il n'est pas sans rappeler Bay Hill en Floride. Et seul les golfeurs accomplis pourront prétendre le négocier sans trop perdre d'illusions sur leur golf. Même des départs avancés, il reste un challenge sans concessions, on évitera donc de compter ses coups, et parfois même ses balles, si l'on flirte trop audacieusement avec l'eau, notamment dans les derniers trous. En dépit d'importants drainages, la proximité de la rivière Liffey incite à le recommander en été.

The K Club
IRL - STRAFFAN, Co Kildare

Office	Secrétariat	(353) 01 - 601 7300
Pro shop	Pro-shop	(353) 01 - 601 7321
Fax	Fax	(353) 01 - 601 7399
Situation	Situation	

34 km W of Dublin (pop. 859 976)

Annual closure	Fermeture annnuelle	no
Weekly closure	Fermeture hebdomadaire	no

Fees main season
Tarifs haute saison 18 holes

	Week days Semaine	We/Bank holidays We/Férié
Individual Individuel	IR£ 120	IR£ 120
Couple Couple	IR£ 240	IR£ 240

Caddy	Caddy	on request/IR£ 25
Electric Trolley	Chariot électrique	IR£ 10
Buggy	Voiturette	IR£ 30/18 holes
Clubs	Clubs	IR£ 30/18 holes

Credit cards Cartes de crédit
VISA - Eurocard - MasterCard - AMEX - DC

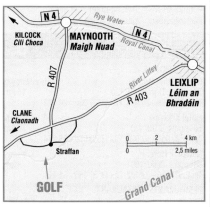

Access Accès : N7 → Kill, → Straffan
Map 3 on page 698 Carte 3 Page 698

GOLF COURSE
PARCOURS   17/20

Site	Site	▬▬▬▬▬
Maintenance	Entretien	▬▬▬▬▬
Architect	Architecte	Arnold Palmer
Type	Type	inland, parkland
Relief	Relief	▬▬
Water in play	Eau en jeu	▬▬▬▬
Exp. to wind	Exposé au vent	▬▬▬
Trees in play	Arbres en jeu	▬▬▬

Scorecard Carte de score	**Chp.** Chp.	**Mens** Mess.	**Ladies** Da.
Length Long.	6519	6063	4990
Par	72	72	73

Advised golfing ability		0	12	24	36
Niveau de jeu recommandé				▬▬▬	
Hcp required	Handicap exigé		28 Men, 36 Ladies		

CLUB HOUSE & AMENITIES
CLUB HOUSE ET ANNEXES   8/10

Pro shop	Pro-shop	▬▬▬▬
Driving range	Practice	▬▬▬
Sheltered	couvert	no
On grass	sur herbe	yes
Putting-green	putting-green	yes
Pitching-green	pitching green	yes

HOTEL FACILITIES
ENVIRONNEMENT HOTELIER   8/10

HOTELS HÔTELS

Kildare Hotel and Country Club	on site
45 rooms, D IR£ 260	
Tel (353) 01 - 627 3333, Fax (353) 01 - 627 3312	
Leixlip House Hotel	Leixlip
16 rooms, D IR£ 100	10 km
Tel (353) 01 - 624 2268, Fax (353) 01 - 624 4177	
Moyglare Manor	Maynooth
16 rooms, D IR£ 130	10 km
Tel (353) 01 - 628 63 51, Fax (353) 01 - 628 5405	

RESTAURANTS RESTAURANT

The Legends	K Club
Tel (353) 01 - 627 3111	on site
The Burly Turk	K Club
Tel (353) 01 - 627 3111	on site

737

The thousands of trees planted in the 1960s and 1970s have grown and compounded the difficulty of this course. But being on the short side, it is within the grasp of most golfers, although the best will see this more as a good practice course rather than a top-level test of skill. Here, then, is the opportunity to look after the rest of the family or the lesser players in the group. They will, though, need to be careful on the par 3s, on the 11th, a long par 4, and on the closing holes, which can spoil a good card. The main hazards are generally speaking the trees, which neatly outline the holes, the fairway bunkers (they can be punishing at times) and the sand around the greens. The greens themselves are forthright, medium-sized and not bumpy enough to be really difficult to read. This is a pleasant day's golfing over terrain where holes alternate over flat and rolling landscape.

La croissance des milliers d'arbres plantés dans les années 60 et 70 a accru la difficulté de ce parcours. Cependant, sa faible longueur le place à la portée de tous les niveaux de jeu, mais les meilleurs doivent le considérer comme un bon parcours d'entraînement, et non comme un test de première grandeur : ce sera l'occasion pour eux de s'occuper des autres joueurs de la famille ou du groupe ! Mais ils devront être vigilants sur les pars 3, sur le 11(un long par 4) et sur les derniers trous, qui peuvent endommager un bon score. Les principaux obstacles sont en général les arbres, qui définissent bien les trous, les bunkers de fairway (ils pourraient être plus punitifs), et les bunkers défendant les greens. Ces derniers sont francs, de taille moyenne, ne sont pas assez accidentés pour être vraiment difficiles à lire. Et comme le relief du terrain alterne les trous plats et les trous plus vallonnés, c'est une agréable promenade.

Kilkenny Golf Club
IRL - GLENDINE, Co Kilkenny

Office	Secrétariat	(353) 056 - 22 125
Pro shop	Pro-shop	(353) 056 - 61 730
Fax	Fax	(353) 056 - 22 125
Situation	Situation	

1.5 km from Kilkenny (pop. 8 515)

Annual closure	Fermeture annnuelle	no
Weekly closure	Fermeture hebdomadaire	no

Fees main season
Tarifs haute saison 18 holes

	Week days Semaine	We/Bank holidays We/Férié
Individual Individuel	IR£ 20	IR£ 22
Couple Couple	IR£ 40	IR£ 44

Caddy	Caddy	IR£ 10/15
Electric Trolley	Chariot électrique	no
Buggy	Voiturette	IR£ 20/18 holes
Clubs	Clubs	IR£ 6

Credit cards Cartes de crédit
VISA - MasterCard

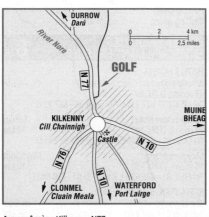

```
                    DURROW
                    Darú
River Nore          0      2      4 km
                    0        2,5 miles
              GOLF
         N77
                                    MUINE
                                    BHEAG
    KILKENNY
    Cill Chainnigh
              Castle   N10
    N76
         N10
       CLONMEL      WATERFORD
       Cluain Meala  Port Lairge
```

Access Accès : Kilkenny, N77
→ Castlecomer. Golf 1.5 km
Map 2 on page 697 Carte 2 Page 697

GOLF COURSE
PARCOURS

13/20

Site	Site	
Maintenance	Entretien	
Architect	Architecte	
Type	Type	parkland
Relief	Relief	
Water in play	Eau en jeu	
Exp. to wind	Exposé au vent	
Trees in play	Arbres en jeu	

Scorecard Carte de score	Chp. Chp.	Mens Mess.	Ladies Da.
Length Long.	5857	5600	5112
Par	71	71	73

Advised golfing ability	0 12 24 36
Niveau de jeu recommandé	
Hcp required	Handicap exigé	no

CLUB HOUSE & AMENITIES
CLUB HOUSE ET ANNEXES

7/10

Pro shop	Pro-shop	
Driving range	Practice	
Sheltered	couvert	no
On grass	sur herbe	yes
Putting-green	putting-green	yes
Pitching-green	pitching green	no

HOTEL FACILITIES
ENVIRONNEMENT HOTELIER

6/10

HOTELS HÔTELS

Mount Juliet House — Thomastown
32 rooms, D from IR£ 120 — 16 km
Tel (353) 056 - 24 455, Fax (353) 056 - 24 522

Hotel Kilkenny — Kilkenny
60 rooms, D IR£ 100 — 3 km
Tel (353) 056 - 62 000, Fax (353) 056 - 65 984

Newpark Hotel — Kilkenny
84 rooms, D IR£ 100 — 3 km
Tel (353) 056 - 22 122, Fax (353) 056 - 61 111

RESTAURANTS RESTAURANT

Lacken House — Kilkenny
Tel (353) 056 - 61 085 — 3 km

Kytlers Inn — Kilkenny
Tel (353) 056 - 21 064 — 3 km

738

Although the closing holes here are not quite as spectacular as those on its illustrious neighbour, Killeen is generally considered to be the most challenging course of this remarkable complex. It staged the Irish Open in 1991 and 1992, when Nick Faldo triumphed. Some of the original holes designed by Sir Guy Campbell are included here, but the basic layout is the work of Eddie Hackett and Billy O'Sullivan. The landscape is that of a huge park with every imaginable hazard. Let's start with the trees: from the back tees, the fairways look and are narrow, and demand very accurate driving. As you move forward, they obligingly become a little wider. The path to the green is dotted with strategically placed bunkers, and water hazards also play a significant role. While it is difficult to prefer one or the other of the Killarney courses (everyone to his own), the purists say that Killeen just has the edge.

Bien qu'il ne produise pas un finish aussi spectaculaire que son voisin, Killeen est généralement considéré comme le plus exigeant de ce remarquable complexe. C'est d'ailleurs celui qui a reçu l'Irish Open, notamment en 1991 et 1992 quand Nick Faldo s'y imposa. Quelques-uns des trous du tracé original de Sir Guy Campbell ont été repris ici, mais l'essentiel en est dû à Eddie Hackett et Billy O'Sullivan. Le paysage est celui d'un vaste parc, avec tous les obstacles imaginables. A commencer par les arbres : des départs arrière, les fairways paraissent étroits et imposent un driving très précis, mais ils s'élargissent amicalement pour les départs plus avancés. Le chemin des greens est alors très fourni en bunkers stratégiques, et les obstacles d'eau jouent également un rôle important. S'il est difficile de préférer l'un ou l'autre parcours de Killarney (chacun son goût), celui-ci est un soupçon supérieur selon les puristes.

Killarney Golf Club
O'Mahoney's Point
IRL - KILLARNEY, Co Kerry

Office	Secrétariat	(353) 064 - 31 034
Pro shop	Pro-shop	(353) 064 - 31 165
Fax	Fax	(353) 064 - 33 065
Situation	Situation	

3 km from Killarney (pop. 7 275)

| Annual closure | Fermeture annnuelle | no |
| Weekly closure | Fermeture hebdomadaire | no |

Fees main season
Tarifs haute saison 18 holes

	Week days Semaine	We/Bank holidays We/Férié
Individual Individuel	IR£ 38	IR£ 38
Couple Couple	IR£ 76	IR£ 76

Caddy	Caddy	IR£ 15/18 holes
Electric Trolley	Chariot électrique	no
Buggy	Voiturette	no
Clubs	Clubs	IR£ 11/18 holes

Credit cards Cartes de crédit
VISA - Eurocard - MasterCard - AMEX - DC

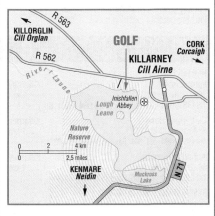

Access Accès : Killarney W, 3 km on R562 → Killorglin
Map 2 on page 696 Carte 2 Page 696

GOLF COURSE / PARCOURS — 16/20

Site	Site	
Maintenance	Entretien	
Architect	Architecte	Eddie Hackett Billy O'Sullivan
Type	Type	parkland
Relief	Relief	
Water in play	Eau en jeu	
Exp. to wind	Exposé au vent	
Trees in play	Arbres en jeu	

Scorecard Carte de score	Chp. Chp.	Mens Mess.	Ladies Da.
Length Long.	6474	5993	4928
Par	72	72	74

Advised golfing ability
Niveau de jeu recommandé: 0 12 24 36

Hcp required Handicap exigé 28 Men, 36 Ladies

CLUB HOUSE & AMENITIES / CLUB HOUSE ET ANNEXES — 7/10

Pro shop	Pro-shop	
Driving range	Practice	
Sheltered	couvert	no
On grass	sur herbe	yes
Putting-green	putting-green	yes
Pitching-green	pitching green	no

HOTEL FACILITIES / ENVIRONNEMENT HOTELIER — 8/10

HOTELS HÔTELS

Europe Hotel
205 rooms, D IR£ 132
Tel (353) 064 - 31 900, Fax (353) 064 - 32 118
Killarney
1 km

Castlerosse Hotel
114 rooms, D IR£ 110
Tel (353) 064 - 31 144, Fax (353) 064 - 31 031
Killarney
1 km

Aghadoe Heights
60 rooms, D IR£ 165
Tel (353) 064 - 31 766, Fax (353) 064 - 31 345
Killarney
1 km

RESTAURANTS RESTAURANT

Dingle's
Tel (353) 064 - 31 079
Killarney
4 km

Failte Restaurant
Tel (353) 064 - 33 404
Killarney
4 km

739

A lively place to be at night, this charming little town is a major tourist centre and an ideal holiday stop-off to explore the lakes in the National Park, the Kerry mountains... and the prestigious golf courses of south-west Ireland. The two 18-hole courses at Killarney are a part of these, and golfers often tend to show a slight sentimental preference for this one, especially the 3 closing holes, which include the 18th, a tough par 3 magnificently set alongside Lough Leane. Try and arrange to play here in the early evening to watch the sun set, when the surrounding forests blossom in the colours of autumn (play Killeen in the morning). A rather short course, it is less of a handful than it looks at first sight, but it does require a careful short game around very well-guarded greens. The beauty of the environment, the trees and the layout add to the pleasure of your day spent here, and the best players in your group will enjoy a good round without having to dig too deeply into their reserves.

Très animée le soir, cette charmante petite ville est un grand centre touristique, un lieu de séjour idéal pour explorer les lacs du National Park, les monts du Kerry... et pour aller jouer les prestigieux parcours du Sud-Ouest. Les deux 18 trous de Killarney en font partie, et les joueurs ont souvent une petite préférence sentimentale pour celui-ci, notamment pour les trois derniers trous, dont le magnifique 18, un par 3 difficile et magnifiquement situé le long du Lough Leane : il faut s'arranger pour le jouer au coucher du soleil, quand les forêts environnantes prennent leurs couleurs d'automne (jouer Killeen le matin). Assez court, ce parcours est moins difficile à négocier qu'il n'y paraît à première vue, mais il réclame un petit jeu attentif, car les greens sont bien défendus. La beauté de l'environnement, des arbres et du dessin ajoute au plaisir de la journée, et les meilleurs joueurs du groupe auront plaisir à briller sans trop puiser dans leurs réserves.

Killarney Golf Club

O'Mahoney's Point
IRL - KILLARNEY, Co Kerry

Office	Secrétariat	(353) 064 - 31 034
Pro shop	Pro-shop	(353) 064 - 31 165
Fax	Fax	(353) 064 - 33 065
Situation	Situation	

3 km from Killarney (pop. 7 275)

Annual closure	Fermeture annnuelle	no
Weekly closure	Fermeture hebdomadaire	no

Fees main season
Tarifs haute saison 18 holes

	Week days Semaine	We/Bank holidays We/Férié
Individual Individuel	IR£ 38	IR£ 38
Couple Couple	IR£ 76	IR£ 76

Caddy	Caddy	IR£ 15/18 holes
Electric Trolley	Chariot électrique	no
Buggy	Voiturette	no
Clubs	Clubs	IR£ 11/18 holes

Credit cards Cartes de crédit
VISA - Eurocard - MasterCard - AMEX - DC

Access Accès : Killarney W, 3 km on R562 → Killorglin
Map 2 on page 696 Carte 2 Page 696

GOLF COURSE
PARCOURS

15/20

Site	Site	
Maintenance	Entretien	
Architect	Architecte	Sir Guy Campbell
Type	Type	parkland
Relief	Relief	
Water in play	Eau en jeu	
Exp. to wind	Exposé au vent	
Trees in play	Arbres en jeu	

Scorecard Carte de score	Chp. Chp.	Mens Mess.	Ladies Da.
Length Long.	6164	5826	4932
Par	72	72	74

Advised golfing ability
Niveau de jeu recommandé

0   12   24   36

Hcp required Handicap exigé   28 Men, 36 Ladies

CLUB HOUSE & AMENITIES
CLUB HOUSE ET ANNEXES

7/10

Pro shop	Pro-shop	
Driving range	Practice	
Sheltered	couvert	no
On grass	sur herbe	yes
Putting-green	putting-green	yes
Pitching-green	pitching green	no

HOTEL FACILITIES
ENVIRONNEMENT HOTELIER

8/10

HOTELS HÔTELS

Europe Hotel   Killarney
205 rooms, D IR£ 132   1 km
Tel (353) 064 - 31 900, Fax (353) 064 - 32 118

Castlerosse Hotel   Killarney
114 rooms, D IR£ 110   1 km
Tel (353) 064 - 31 144, Fax (353) 064 - 31 031

Aghadoe Heights   Killarney
60 rooms, D IR£ 165   1 km
Tel (353) 064 - 31 766, Fax (353) 064 - 31 345

RESTAURANTS RESTAURANT

Dingle's   Killarney
Tel (353) 064 - 31 079   4 km

Failte Restaurant   Killarney
Tel (353) 064 - 33 404   4 km

As the courses in this region are very busy, catering to not only tourists but also the locals, this recent course was more than welcome. It was designed by the busiest of all Irish designers, Eddie Hackett. Running on the side of hill, the terrain overlooks Dingle Bay (the weaker souls will find the course tiring to walk) and gives golfers some pretty viewpoints over the estuary, the Slieve Mish Mountains opposite and Macgillicuddy's Reeks to the west. Although not outstanding, Killorglin is well worth a visit, especially for a round with friends or the family, without undue suffering (except, of course, when the wind gets up). The difficulties are easily seen but are more psychological than real. You can even play to your handicap first time round, providing you don't misjudge your approach shots - some greens are elevated, others multi-tiered.

Les parcours de la région étant très fréquentés, non seulement par les touristes, mais aussi par la clientèle locale, ce récent parcours était plus que bienvenu. C'est le plus occupé des architectes irlandais, Eddie Hackett, qui en est l'auteur. A flanc de colline, le terrain domine la baie de Dingle (les plus fatigués souffriront à pied), ce qui offre aux joueurs quelques jolis points de vue sur cet estuaire, comme sur les Slieve Mish Mountains en face et, à l'ouest, sur les Macgilliguddy Reeks. Sans être exceptionnel, le parcours de Killorglin mérite la visite, notamment pour y faire une partie amicale ou en famille, sans trop souffrir, sauf quand le vent souffle fort, bien sûr. Les difficultés sont aisément identifiables, mais sont plus psychologiques que réelles. Dès la première fois, on peut y jouer son handicap, à condition de bien juger ses approches : certains greens sont surélevés et quelques-uns à plateaux.

Killorglin Golf Club
Stealroe
IRL - KILLORGLIN, Co. Kerry

Office	Secrétariat	(353) 066 - 61 979
Pro shop	Pro-shop	(353) 066 - 61 979
Fax	Fax	(353) 066 - 61 437
Situation	Situation	

21 km from Killarney (pop. 7 275)
24 km from Tralee (pop. 17 225)

Annual closure	Fermeture annnuelle	no
Weekly closure	Fermeture hebdomadaire	no

Fees main season
Tarifs haute saison 18 holes

	Week days Semaine	We/Bank holidays We/Férié
Individual Individuel	IR£ 14	IR£ 16
Couple Couple	IR£ 28	IR£ 32

Caddy	Caddy	on request/IR£ 10
Electric Trolley	Chariot électrique	no
Buggy	Voiturette	no
Clubs	Clubs	IR£ 10

Credit cards Cartes de crédit
VISA - Eurocard - MasterCard - AMEX

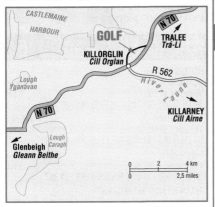

Access Accès : Killarney, N72 W to Killorglin.
Killorglin bridge, turn right on N70. Golf, 1.6 km.
Map 2 on page 696 Carte 2 Page 696

GOLF COURSE
PARCOURS 14/20

Site	Site	
Maintenance	Entretien	
Architect	Architecte	Eddie Hackett
Type	Type	parkland
Relief	Relief	
Water in play	Eau en jeu	
Exp. to wind	Exposé au vent	
Trees in play	Arbres en jeu	

Scorecard	Chp.	Mens	Ladies
Carte de score	Chp.	Mess.	Da.
Length Long.	5821	5358	4678
Par	72	72	74

Advised golfing ability		0 12 24 36
Niveau de jeu recommandé		
Hcp required	Handicap exigé	no

CLUB HOUSE & AMENITIES
CLUB HOUSE ET ANNEXES 6/10

Pro shop	Pro-shop	
Driving range	Practice	
Sheltered	couvert	no
On grass	sur herbe	no
Putting-green	putting-green	no
Pitching-green	pitching green	yes

HOTEL FACILITIES
ENVIRONNEMENT HOTELIER 5/10

HOTELS HÔTELS
Bianconi — Killorglin
15 rooms, D IR£ 50 — 1.6 km
Tel (353) 066 - 61 146, Fax (353) 066 - 61 950

Dunloe Castle — Killarney
120 rooms, D IR£ 120 — 14 km
Tel (353) 064 - 44 111, Fax (353) 064 - 44 583

Europe — Killarney
205 rooms, D IR£ 125 — 17 km
Tel (353) 064 - 31 900, Fax (353) 064 - 32 118

RESTAURANTS RESTAURANT
Bianconi — Killorglin
Tel (353) 066 - 61 146 — 1.6 km

The Fishery — Killorglin
Tel (353) 066 - 61 670 — 1.6 km

741

Lahinch has long held pride of place in the collection of great courses in south-west Ireland. The surrounding dunes invite visual comparison with Ballybunion, although it is not quite as challenging. For example, if you can keep on the straight and narrow here, approach shots to the greens are altogether an easier matter, with bump and run shots a distinct possibility. But you need to know the course to cope, to appreciate the effects of the wind, to identify where hazards are placed and to come to terms with the sand-dunes, where balls can end up in some unusual positions. Care is rewarded on this spectacular layout, where high variety is the watchword and where flighters of the ball will have fun (beginners probably much less so). Look out for the extraordinary 5th and 6th holes, the first a par 5, where the second shot has to fly over a huge dune, the latter a par 3 with a blind green. A must.

Dans la collection des grands parcours du sud-ouest de l'Irlande, Lahinch tient depuis longtemps une belle place. Son environnement de grandes dunes le rapproche visuellement de Ballybunion, bien qu'il ne soit pas aussi exigeant. Par exemple, si l'on parvient à rester droit, les approches des greens y sont moins complexes, ceux-ci étant directement accessibles avec des coups roulés. Mais il faut bien connaître ce parcours pour le négocier, apprécier les effets du vent, identifier la place des obstacles, composer avec les dunes, où la balle peut se trouver dans des situations "intéressantes". La prudence sera récompensée sur ce tracé spectaculaire et d'une très grande variété, où les virtuoses des effets de balle s'amuseront beaucoup (les débutants beaucoup moins). A signaler, les extraordinaires trous 5 et 6, un par 5 où le second coup doit survoler une énorme dune, et un par 3 avec un green aveugle. A connaître sans faute.

Lahinch Golf Club

IRL - LAHINCH, Co Clare

Office	Secrétariat	(353) 065 - 81 003
Pro shop	Pro-shop	(353) 065 - 81 408
Fax	Fax	(353) 065 - 81 592
Situation	Situation	

0.5 km from Lahinch (pop. 550)
32 km from Ennis (pop. 13 730)

Annual closure	Fermeture annnuelle	no
Weekly closure	Fermeture hebdomadaire	no

Fees main season
Tarifs haute saison 18 holes

	Week days Semaine	We/Bank holidays We/Férié
Individual Individuel	IR£ 45	IR£ 45
Couple Couple	IR£ 90	IR£ 90

Green-fees on Castle Course: IR£ 25

Caddy	Caddy	IR£ 15/18 holes
Electric Trolley	Chariot électrique	IR£ 7,50
Buggy	Voiturette	no
Clubs	Clubs	IR£ 12/18 holes

Credit cards Cartes de crédit
VISA - Eurocard - MasterCard

Access Accès : N18 Limerick → Ennis, N85 Ennis
→ Ennistymon, → Lahinch, 3 km
Map 2 on page 696 Carte 2 Page 696

GOLF COURSE
PARCOURS

18/20

Site	Site	▬▬▬▬
Maintenance	Entretien	▬▬▬▬
Architect	Architecte	Old Tom Morris Alistair MacKenzie
Type	Type	links
Relief	Relief	▬▬
Water in play	Eau en jeu	▬
Exp. to wind	Exposé au vent	▬▬▬
Trees in play	Arbres en jeu	▬

Scorecard Carte de score	Chp. Chp.	Mens Mess.	Ladies Da.
Length Long.	6123	5890	4997
Par	72	72	74

Advised golfing ability
Niveau de jeu recommandé

0   12   24   36

Hcp required Handicap exigé   28 Men, 36 Ladies

CLUB HOUSE & AMENITIES
CLUB HOUSE ET ANNEXES

6/10

Pro shop	Pro-shop	▬▬▬▬
Driving range	Practice	▬▬▬
Sheltered	couvert	no
On grass	sur herbe	yes
Putting-green	putting-green	yes
Pitching-green	pitching green	no

HOTEL FACILITIES
ENVIRONNEMENT HOTELIER

6/10

HOTELS HÔTELS

Aberdeen Arms	Lahinch
55 rooms, D IR£	5 km
Tel (353) 065 - 81 100, Fax (353) 065 - 81 228	
Atlantic Hotel	Lahinch
14 rooms, D IR£ 50	5 km
Tel (353) 065 - 81 049, Fax (353) 065 - 81 029	
Falls Hotel	Ennistymon
100 rooms, D IR£ 50	3 km
Tel (353) 065 - 71 004, Fax (353) 065 - 71 367	

RESTAURANTS RESTAURANT

Mr Eamons	Lahinch
Tel (353) 065 - 81 050	2 km
Aberdeen Arms	Lahinch
Tel (353) 065 - 81 100	5 km

A rather hilly site for players out of condition or those who have taken a little too kindly to delicious Irish food and drink. Over this pleasantly landscaped and country style terrain, Christy O'Connor Jnr has produced a perfectly honest layout, where good shots are rewarded. It still needs getting to know to cope with some tricky holes, like the 10th or the tough 18th, to keep away from the numerous water hazards (on the 8th and 15th especially), and to read the greens, which are sometimes a real handful. There are many different tee-off areas, so the course adjusts easily to players of all abilities and to how you might be feeling on any one particular day. Lee Valley will present its final face once the trees have grown, but it is already one of the busiest courses in the region, which goes to prove that players like to come back here.

Un site parfois bien accidenté pour les joueurs en forme physique moyenne... ou qui auront un peu trop goûté les spécialités irlandaises. Sur ce terrain au paysage très agréable et campagnard, mais pas idéal pour un golf, Christy O'Connor Jr a produit un dessin d'une parfaite honnêteté, où les bons coups de golf sont récompensés, même si une bonne connaissance du terrain permet de mieux négocier quelques trous, comme le 10 ou le difficile 18, d'échapper aux nombreux obstacles d'eau, au 8 et au 15 notamment, et enfin de bien interpréter les greens, parfois d'une grande subtilité. La multiplicité des départs permet d'adapter facilement le parcours à tous les niveaux de jeu, ou à l'inspiration du jour. Lee Valley prendra son véritable visage quand tous les arbres auront poussé, mais c'est déjà l'un des parcours les plus fréquentés de la région, ce qui prouve que les joueurs aiment y revenir.

Lee Valley Golf & Country Club
Clashanure
IRL - OVENS, Co Cork

Office	Secrétariat	(353) 021 - 331 721
Pro shop	Pro-shop	(353) 021 - 331 758
Fax	Fax	(353) 021 - 331 695
Situation	Situation	

14 km from Cork (pop. 174 400)
10 km from Blarney (pop. 2 043)

Annual closure	Fermeture annnuelle	no
Weekly closure	Fermeture hebdomadaire	no

Fees main season
Tarifs haute saison 18 holes

	Week days Semaine	We/Bank holidays We/Férié
Individual Individuel	IR£ 25	IR£ 27
Couple Couple	IR£ 50	IR£ 54

IR£ 15 before 10.30 am

Caddy	Caddy	on request/IR£ 12
Electric Trolley	Chariot électrique	IR£ 6
Buggy	Voiturette	IR£ 25/18 holes
Clubs	Clubs	IR£ 10/18 holes

Credit cards Cartes de crédit
VISA - MasterCard - AMEX

Access Accès : Cork, N22 → Killarney. At Ballincolig → Ovens
Map 2 on page 696 Carte 2 Page 696

GOLF COURSE
PARCOURS
13/20

Site	Site	
Maintenance	Entretien	
Architect	Architecte	Christy O'Connor Jr
Type	Type	parkland, hilly
Relief	Relief	
Water in play	Eau en jeu	
Exp. to wind	Exposé au vent	
Trees in play	Arbres en jeu	

Scorecard Carte de score	Chp. Chp.	Mens Mess.	Ladies Da.
Length Long.	6050	5795	4900
Par	72	72	72

Advised golfing ability Niveau de jeu recommandé		0 12 24 36
Hcp required	Handicap exigé	24 Men, 36 Ladies

CLUB HOUSE & AMENITIES
CLUB HOUSE ET ANNEXES
7/10

Pro shop	Pro-shop	
Driving range	Practice	
Sheltered	couvert	15 mats
On grass	sur herbe	yes
Putting-green	putting-green	yes
Pitching-green	pitching green	yes

743

HOTEL FACILITIES
ENVIRONNEMENT HOTELIER
6/10

HOTELS HÔTELS

Blarney Park Hotel — Blarney
65 rooms, D IR£ 60 — 10 km
Tel (353) 021 - 385 281, Fax (353) 021 - 381 506

Oriel House Hotel — Ballincollig
10 rooms, D IR£ 40 — 6 km
Tel (353) 021 - 870 888, Fax (353) 021 - 397 760

RESTAURANTS RESTAURANT

Clashanure — Lee Valley GC
Tel (353) 021 - 331 721 — on site

Christys — Blarney
Tel (353) 021 - 385 01 — 12 km

The cottages on site are an excellent base camp for exploring the courses in this region, especially this one. Des Smyth has used the terrain to good effect, but we will have to wait until the trees grow to see how it will look in the end. For the moment, the saplings are obviously not a problem, but the same cannot be said for the collection of bunkers and obligatory water hazards found on modern courses. Very difficult from the back tees, it is a little kinder further forward, from where we recommend you play unless you are a long driver. A few tees and greens are played blind, which requires good knowledge of the course to fix any definite strategy, especially on the back 9, which happens to be much flatter than the first half of the course. The greens are hospitable but certain pin positions can make them a tricky proposition. This very competent layout is already rated amongst the country's top twenty or thirty inland courses.

Les cottages sur place en font une bonne base pour explorer les golfs de la région, et notamment celui-ci. Des Smyth a bien utilisé le terrain, mais il faudra attendre qu'il prenne son visage définitif, le temps que grandissent les nombreux arbres plantés. Pour l'instant, ils ne sont pas un facteur de difficulté, au contraire de la collection de bunkers et d'obstacles d'eau incontournables dans les parcours modernes. Très difficile des départs arrière, il est plus amical des autres, on les conseillera, à moins d'avoir affaire à de bons frappeurs. Quelques départs et greens sont aveugles, imposant une bonne connaissance du parcours pour avoir une stratégie précise, notamment au retour, qui est en revanche plus plat que l'aller. Les greens sont accueillants, mais certaines positions de drapeau peuvent les rendre très délicats. Cette très solide réalisation figure déjà parmi les vingt ou trente meilleurs parcours inland du pays.

Limerick County Golf & Country Club
IRL - BALLYNEETY, Co Limerick

Office	Secrétariat	(353) 061 - 351 881
Pro shop	Pro-shop	(353) 061 - 351 881
Fax	Fax	(353) 061 - 351 384
Situation	Situation	.

11 km from Limerick (pop. 52 083)

Annual closure	Fermeture annnuelle	no
Weekly closure	Fermeture hebdomadaire	no

Fees main season
Tarifs haute saison 18 holes

	Week days Semaine	We/Bank holidays We/Férié
Individual Individuel	IR£ 20	IR£ 25
Couple Couple	IR£ 40	IR£ 50

Weekdays: IR£ 12.50 before 9.30 am

Caddy	Caddy	on request/IR£ 12
Electric Trolley	Chariot électrique	no
Buggy	Voiturette	IR£ 20/18 holes
Clubs	Clubs	IR£ 10/18 holes

Credit cards Cartes de crédit
VISA - MasterCard

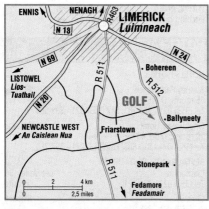

Access Accès : Limerick, R512.
Map 2 on page 696 Carte 2 Page 696

GOLF COURSE
PARCOURS
15/20

Site	Site	▬▬▬▬▬
Maintenance	Entretien	▬▬▬▬▬
Architect	Architecte	Des Smyth
Type	Type	parkland
Relief	Relief	▬▬
Water in play	Eau en jeu	▬▬▬▬
Exp. to wind	Exposé au vent	▬▬▬▬
Trees in play	Arbres en jeu	▬▬▬

Scorecard Carte de score	Chp. Chp.	Mens Mess.	Ladies Da.
Length Long.	6194	5784	5050
Par	72	72	73

Advised golfing ability	0	12	24	36
Niveau de jeu recommandé				

Hcp required Handicap exigé 28 Men, 36 Ladies

CLUB HOUSE & AMENITIES
CLUB HOUSE ET ANNEXES
7/10

Pro shop	Pro-shop	▬▬▬▬
Driving range	Practice	▬▬▬▬
Sheltered	couvert	20 mats
On grass	sur herbe	yes
Putting-green	putting-green	yes
Pitching-green	pitching green	yes

HOTEL FACILITIES
ENVIRONNEMENT HOTELIER
6/10

HOTELS HÔTELS

Castletroy Park Hotel — Limerick
107 rooms, D IR£ 120 — 8 km
Tel (353) 061 - 335 566, Fax (353) 061 - 335 117

Jurys Hotel — Limerick
95 rooms, D IR£ 90 — 11 km
Tel (353) 061 - 327 77, Fax (353) 061 - 326 400

Limerick Ryan Hotel — Limerick
180 rooms, D IR£ 70 — 11 km
Tel (353) 061 - 453 922, Fax (353) 061 - 326 333

RESTAURANTS RESTAURANT

Moll Darby's — Limerick
Tel (353) 061 - 411 511 — 11 km

Freddy's Bistro — Limerick
Tel (353) 061 - 418 749 — 11 km

744

LUTTRELLSTOWN

| 15 | 7 | 7 |

In the grounds of a famous castle hotel, whose illustrious guests have included Queen Victoria, Fred Astaire, Ronald Reagan and Rainiers of Monaco, this recent course was designed by Nicholas Bielenberg. It is laid out in a huge park, where age-old trees add beauty and majesty to a matchless atmosphere of tranquility. The few straight up and down holes are rather a pity, although the fairways are clearly separated by trees and water. These two elements are the main hazards here, especially the many lakes and ponds, which call for long, lofted shots (on about half a dozen holes). This might not be too much to the liking of high-handicappers, but target golf buffs will have fun. The geographical relief is only very slight and enough to give each hole clear definition. Very long from the tiger-tees, this is a stiff challenge for any golfer, although much more approachable from the front tees.

Dans le domaine d'un célèbre Château-hôtel, qui a reçu des gloires telles que la Reine Victoria, Fred Astaire, Ronald Reagan ou Rainier de Monaco, ce récent parcours a été dessiné par Nicholas Bielenberg, dans un immense parc avec des arbres centenaires, qui ajoutent leur beauté et leur majesté à une atmosphère incomparable de tranquillité. On peut regretter certains allers et retours du tracé, malgré que les fairways soient bien séparés par les bois et l'eau. Ces deux éléments constituent des difficultés évidentes, notamment les nombreux lacs et mares, qui obligent souvent à porter la balle (sur une demi-douzaine de trous environ). Si cela ne plaira guère aux handicaps élevés, les habitués du "target golf" auront de quoi s'amuser. Le relief est très modéré, et suffisant pour assurer une bonne définition des trous. Très long des départs de championnat, ce parcours reste un "challenge", mais plus abordable, des départs avancés.

Luttrellstown Golf & Country Club
IRL - CLONSILLA, Co Dublin

Office	Secrétariat	(353) 01 - 808 9988
Pro shop	Pro-shop	(353) 01 - 808 9988
Fax	Fax	(353) 01 - 820 5218
Situation	Situation	

10 km from Dublin (pop. 859 976)

Annual closure	Fermeture annnuelle	no
Weekly closure	Fermeture hebdomadaire	no

Fees main season
Tarifs haute saison 18 holes

	Week days Semaine	We/Bank holidays We/Férié
Individual Individuel	IR£ 40	IR£ 45
Couple Couple	IR£ 80	IR£ 90

Caddy	Caddy	on request/IR£ 20
Electric Trolley	Chariot électrique	no
Buggy	Voiturette	IR£ 25/18 holes
Clubs	Clubs	IR£ 10/18 holes

Credit cards Cartes de crédit
VISA - MasterCard - AMEX - DC

Access Accès : 10 km NW from Dublin on N3
→ Clonsilla
Map 3 on page 698 Carte 3 Page 698

GOLF COURSE
PARCOURS
15/20

Site	Site	
Maintenance	Entretien	
Architect	Architecte	Nicholas Bielenberg
Type	Type	parkland
Relief	Relief	
Water in play	Eau en jeu	
Exp. to wind	Exposé au vent	
Trees in play	Arbres en jeu	

Scorecard Carte de score	Chp. Chp.	Mens Mess.	Ladies Da.
Length Long.	6384	6032	5246
Par	72	72	72

Advised golfing ability Niveau de jeu recommandé	0	12	24	36
Hcp required	Handicap exigé	24 Men, 36 Ladies		

CLUB HOUSE & AMENITIES
CLUB HOUSE ET ANNEXES
7/10

Pro shop	Pro-shop	
Driving range	Practice	
Sheltered	couvert	no
On grass	sur herbe	yes
Putting-green	putting-green	yes
Pitching-green	pitching green	no

HOTEL FACILITIES
ENVIRONNEMENT HOTELIER
7/10

HOTELS HÔTELS
Burlington Hotel — Dublin
451 rooms, D IR£ 160 — 10 km
Tel (353) 01 - 660 5222, Fax (353) 01 - 660 3172

Jurys Christchurch Inn — Dublin
182 rooms, D IR£ 64 — 10 km
Tel (353) 01 - 475 0111, Fax (353) 01 - 475 0488

West County Hotel — Lucan
50 rooms, D IR£ 74 — 5 km
Tel (353) 01 - 626 4011, Fax (353) 01 - 623 1378

RESTAURANTS RESTAURANT
Annadale — Lucan
Tel (353) 01 - 628 0622 — 4 km

Scott's — Castleknock
Tel (353) 01 - 821 3482 — 3 km

745

MALAHIDE RED + BLUE + YELLOW

| 13 | 7 | 8 |

If you want to play every Eddie Hackett course in Ireland, you sure have a lot of golfing to do. With the experience of age, he was very kind here with the average week-enders, who return the compliment and come to play here in droves on 27 holes combinable in every different way. In addition to the actual layout, the wind and wetness of the terrain can seriously dent any hopes of a good card. First time around, a number of blinds shots should require some reconnaissance work, but the course is by no means hilly. Bunkering is high quality, as is the use of water hazards, especially on the par 3s. Another side to the course's resistance is the elevation of certain greens, calling for some accurate ironwork. Once on the green, the surfaces are easy to read (perhaps too easy ?). A recent course, Malahide needs time to mature but is already good fun in amongst the region's great links courses.

Si vous voulez jouer tous les parcours d'Eddie Hackett en Irlande, vous n'avez pas fini... Avec l'expérience de l'âge, il a été ici très amical avec les golfeurs moyens : ils le lui rendent bien et viennent nombreux sur les 27 trous, combinables à volonté. En dehors du tracé lui-même, le vent et l'humidité du terrain peuvent perturber les prétentions à bien scorer. La première fois, certains coups aveugles nécessitent une certaine reconnaissance, mais le parcours est facilement jouable à pied. Le "bunkering" est de grande qualité, de même que l'utilisation des obstacles d'eau, notamment sur les pars 3. Autre facteur de résistance du parcours, l'élévation de certains greens, qui oblige à des coups de fer très exacts, mais les surfaces de putting ne sont guère complexes à lire (pas assez ?). De construction récente, Malahide a besoin de prendre de la maturité, c'est déjà une bonne récréation entre les grands links de la région.

Malahide Golf Club

Beechwood, The Grange
IRL - MALAHIDE, Co Dublin

Office	Secrétariat	(353) 01 - 846 1611
Pro shop	Pro-shop	(353) 01 - 846 0002
Fax	Fax	(353) 01 - 846 1270
Situation	Situation	

18 km from Dublin (pop 859 976)

Annual closure	Fermeture annnuelle	no
Weekly closure	Fermeture hebdomadaire	no

Fees main season
Tarifs haute saison 18 holes

	Week days Semaine	We/Bank holidays We/Férié
Individual Individuel	IR£ 30	IR£ 40
Couple Couple	IR£ 55	IR£ 75

Caddy	Caddy	on request/IR£ 25
Electric Trolley	Chariot électrique	no
Buggy	Voiturette	no
Clubs	Clubs	IR£ 15

Credit cards Cartes de crédit
VISA - Eurocard - MasterCard - AMEX

746

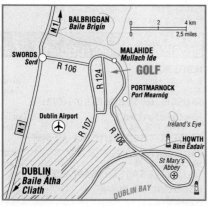

Access Accès : Dublin to Portmarnock Village. Left turn at traffic lights beside Church. Golf 3 km from there.
Map 3 on page 698 Carte 3 Page 698

GOLF COURSE
PARCOURS

13/20

Site	Site	
Maintenance	Entretien	
Architect	Architecte	Eddie Hackett
Type	Type	parkland
Relief	Relief	
Water in play	Eau en jeu	
Exp. to wind	Exposé au vent	
Trees in play	Arbres en jeu	

Scorecard Carte de score	Chp. Chp.	Mens Mess.	Ladies Da.
Length Long.	6066	5742	5146
Par	71	70	74

Advised golfing ability		0	12	24	36
Niveau de jeu recommandé					
Hcp required	Handicap exigé	Men 28, Ladies 36			

CLUB HOUSE & AMENITIES
CLUB HOUSE ET ANNEXES

7/10

Pro shop	Pro-shop	
Driving range	Practice	
Sheltered	couvert	no
On grass	sur herbe	yes
Putting-green	putting-green	yes
Pitching-green	pitching green	no

HOTEL FACILITIES
ENVIRONNEMENT HOTELIER

8/10

HOTELS HÔTELS
Grand Hotel — Malahide
100 rooms, D IR£ 95 — 1 km
Tel (353) 01 - 845 0000, Fax (353) 01 - 845 0987

Portmarnock Links Hotel **** — Portmarnock
110 rooms, D IR£ 190 — 4 km
Tel (353) 01 - 846 0611, Fax (353) 01 - 846 2442

Sands Hotel — Portmarnock
10 rooms, D IR£ 70 — 2 km
Tel (353) 01 - 846 0003, Fax (353) 01 - 846 0420

RESTAURANTS RESTAURANT
Bon Appetit — Malahide
Tel (353) 01 - 845 0314 — 1 km

Colonnade — Malahide
Tel (353) 01 - 845 0000 — 1 km

There is hardly a country in the world where Jack Nicklaus has not left his mark as a course designer, with, it should be said, mixed success. If he claims to be the greatest course designer, our reply is that there are probably many better than he around the world. It all depends on what a designer can squeeze out of a given space. At Mount Juliet, Nicklaus was presented with a magnificent estate, profusely covered with oak, lime and beech trees. A lot of use has been found for water (there is even a waterfall) and very US-style bunkers, or sand-traps, as they say. The greens, vast and well-designed, only add to the difficulties of a course which demands a complete game from start to finish and, in particular an aptitude for target golf. The many different tee-off areas cater to players of differing abilities, but given the overall length the back-tees should most definitely be reserved for single-figure handicappers. Spectacular and remarkable intelligent, this is an excellent Nicklaus vintage.

Il n'est guère de pays au monde où Jack Nicklaus n'ait laissé sa trace en tant qu'architecte, avec - il faut bien le dire - des bonheurs divers. Et s'il annonce vouloir être le plus grand architecte, on répondra qu'il y a beaucoup de meilleurs architectes du monde ! Tout dépend du parti qu'ils tirent d'un espace. A Mount Juliet, il a trouvé une magnifique propriété, généreusement occupée par les chênes, les tilleuls, les hêtres. Un généreux usage a été fait de l'eau (il y a même une cascade), et de bunkers au profil très américain. Et les greens eux-mêmes, vastes et bien travaillés, ajoutent aux difficultés : ce parcours exige un jeu complet, du départ au dernier trou, et singulièrement un jeu de "target golf". La diversité des départs permet de l'adapter aux possibilités des joueurs, mais sa longueur réserve les départs arrière aux handicaps à un chiffre. Spectaculaire et remarquablement intelligent, c'est un excellent Nicklaus...

Mount Juliet Golf Club
IRL - THOMASTOWN, Co Kilkenny

Office	Secrétariat	(353) 056 - 24 455
Pro shop	Pro-shop	(353) 056 - 24 455
Fax	Fax	(353) 056 - 24 522
Situation	Situation	

16 km from Kilkenny (pop. 8 515)

Annual closure	Fermeture annnuelle	no
Weekly closure	Fermeture hebdomadaire	no

Fees main season
Tarifs haute saison 18 holes

	Week days Semaine	We/Bank holidays We/Férié
Individual Individuel	IR£ 70	IR£ 75
Couple Couple	IR£ 140	IR£ 150

Early or late tee-times (off peak hours): IR£ 40

Caddy	Caddy	on request/IR£ 16
Electric Trolley	Chariot électrique	no
Buggy	Voiturette	no
Clubs	Clubs	IR£ 15/18 holes

Credit cards Cartes de crédit
VISA - MasterCard - AMEX - DC

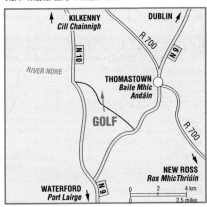

KILKENNY
Cill Chainnigh
DUBLIN
R 700
N 10
N 9
RIVER NORE
THOMASTOWN
Baile Mhic Andáin
GOLF
R 700
NEW ROSS
Ros MhicThriúin
WATERFORD
Port Lairge
N 9
0   2   4 km
0   2.5 miles

Access Accès : N10 S. of Kilkenny
N 9 S. of Carlow
Map 2 on page 697 Carte 2 Page 697

GOLF COURSE
PARCOURS
18/20

Site	Site	▬▬▬▬▭
Maintenance	Entretien	▬▬▬▬▭
Architect	Architecte	Jack Nicklaus
Type	Type	parkland
Relief	Relief	▬▬▭▭▭
Water in play	Eau en jeu	▬▬▬▭▭
Exp. to wind	Exposé au vent	▬▬▬▭▭
Trees in play	Arbres en jeu	▬▬▬▭▭

Scorecard Carte de score	Chp. Chp.	Mens Mess.	Ladies Da.
Length Long.	7111	6705	5554
Par	72	72	73

Advised golfing ability Niveau de jeu recommandé	0	12	24	36
Hcp required Handicap exigé	28 Men, 36 Ladies			

CLUB HOUSE & AMENITIES
CLUB HOUSE ET ANNEXES
9/10

Pro shop	Pro-shop	▬▬▬▬▭
Driving range	Practice	▬▬▬▬▭
Sheltered	couvert	5 bays
On grass	sur herbe	yes
Putting-green	putting-green	yes
Pitching-green	pitching green	yes

747 ▮▮

HOTEL FACILITIES
ENVIRONNEMENT HOTELIER
8/10

HOTELS HÔTELS

Mount Juliet House — Thomastown
32 rooms, D from IR£ 120 — on site
Tel (353) 056 - 24 455, Fax (353) 056 - 24 522

Hunters Yard — Thomastown
13 rooms, D IR£ 120 — on site
Tel (353) 056 - 24 455, Fax (353) 056 - 24 522

Newpark Hotel — Kilkenny
84 rooms, D IR£ 100 — 17 km
Tel (353) 056 - 22 122, Fax (353) 056 - 61 111

RESTAURANTS RESTAURANT

Parliament House — Kilkenny
Tel (353) 056 - 63 666 — 16 km

Langtons — Kilkenny
Tel (353) 056 - 65 133 — 16 km

This new course is quite typical of the style of Christy O'Connor Jr., with water hazards (especially on the outward nine) and fairway bunkers which some might feel often unfairly penalise good shots. High-level lady players will also feel frustrated as their tee-boxes are often too far forward (a frequent feature these days). However this very likeable course is most welcome in a lovely region and the overall honesty of the layout is conducive to attacking golf without the fear of too many unpleasant surprises. We noted the variety of design and protection for the greens, thus allowing all sorts of approach shots. The course is already in very respectable condition.

Ce nouveau parcours est tout à fait typique du style architectural de Christy O'Connor Jr, avec ses obstacles d'eau (surtout à l'aller) et ses bunkers de fairway, mais on peut trouver que ces derniers pénalisent souvent les bons coups. Les femmes de bon niveau seront aussi frustrées, car leurs départs sont souvent trop avancés (c'est aujourd'hui fréquent). Cependant, cette sympathique réalisation est bienvenue dans une région très agréable, et la franchise générale du tracé permet de l'attaquer sans trop de crainte des mauvaises surprises. Il faut enfin remarquer la variété de dessin et de défense des greens, ce qui permet toutes sortes d'approches. L'état du parcours est déjà très honorable.

Mount Wolsley Golf Club
IRL - TULLOW, Co. Carlow

Office	Secrétariat	(353) 0503 - 51 674
Pro shop	Pro-shop	(353) 0503 - 51 674
Fax	Fax	(353) 0503 - 52 123
Situation	Situation	

80 km S of Dublin, 14 km E of Carlow on N. 81

Annual closure	Fermeture annnuelle	no
Weekly closure	Fermeture hebdomadaire	

Fees main season
Tarifs haute saison 18 holes

	Week days Semaine	We/Bank holidays We/Férié
Individual Individuel	IR£ 25	IR£ 30
Couple Couple	IR£ 50	IR£ 60

Caddy	Caddy	no
Electric Trolley	Chariot électrique	no
Buggy	Voiturette	IR£ 20/18 holes
Clubs	Clubs	IR£ 10/18 holes

Credit cards Cartes de crédit
VISA - MasterCard - AMEX - DC

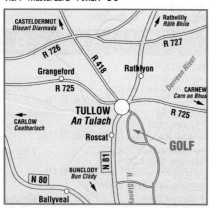

Access Accès : Dublin, N9 → Carlow. In Castledermot, R418 to Tullow
Map 2 on page 697 Carte 2 Page 697

GOLF COURSE
PARCOURS **13**/20

Site	Site	
Maintenance	Entretien	
Architect	Architecte	Christy O'Connor Jr
Type	Type	parkland
Relief	Relief	
Water in play	Eau en jeu	
Exp. to wind	Exposé au vent	
Trees in play	Arbres en jeu	

Scorecard Carte de score	Chp. Chp.	Mens Mess.	Ladies Da.
Length Long.	6497	6140	4963
Par	72	72	74

Advised golfing ability Niveau de jeu recommandé	0	12	24	36
Hcp required	Handicap exigé	no		

CLUB HOUSE & AMENITIES
CLUB HOUSE ET ANNEXES **6**/10

Pro shop	Pro-shop	
Driving range	Practice	
Sheltered	couvert	
On grass	sur herbe	yes
Putting-green	putting-green	yes
Pitching-green	pitching green	yes

HOTEL FACILITIES
ENVIRONNEMENT HOTELIER **5**/10

HOTELS HÔTELS

Mount Wolsley Hotel — Tullow on site
20 rooms, D IR£ 80
Tel (353) 0503 - 51 674, Fax (353) 0503 - 52 123

Royal Hotel — Carlow 14 km
34 rooms, D IR£ 48
Tel (353) 0503 - 31 621, Fax (353) 0503 - 31 621

Kilkea Castle — Castledermot 8 km
38 rooms, D IR£ 120
Tel (353) 0503 - 45 156, Fax (353) 0503 - 45 187

RESTAURANTS RESTAURANT

Mount Wolsley Hotel — Tullow on site
Tel (353) 0503 - 51 674

Kilkea Castle — Castledermot 8 km
Tel (353) 0503 - 45 156

748

MULLINGAR

James Braid, who reshaped this course in 1937, considered Mullingar to be one of his best designs. A little on the short side today (there was little space available at the time), this is still a very popular course with Irish players, although it has still to gain an international reputation. It shouldn't leave foreigners feeling too lost, as you can find similar courses in the UK and on the continent, which only show how typical an inland design this is. The one slight difference would be the need to go for target golf, as the greens are very well guarded up front. The hazards are dangerous and call for precision play (the par 3s are excellent). Skills in working the ball both ways, although not decisive, do give an advantage here. A pleasant course for all levels (the ladies tees are nicely well forward) and one you won't be sorry to discover.

James Braid, qui remodela ce parcours en 1937, le considérait comme un de ses meilleurs dessins. Aujourd'hui un peu court (l'espace disponible était réduit), c'est malgré tout un golf très populaire auprès des joueurs irlandais, mais sa réputation internationale reste à établir. Il ne devrait pas trop dépayser les étrangers, car on pourrait trouver aussi bien en Grande-Bretagne que sur le continent des parcours similaires, tant il est typique de l'esthétique et de l'architecture des "inland". Une seule nuance dans cette appréciation : il vaut mieux jouer des balles de "target golf", car les greens sont bien défendus frontalement. Les obstacles sont dangereux, obligeant à un jeu précis (les pars 3 sont excellents), et si l'on sait travailler la balle, l'avantage sera sinon décisif, du moins important. Un parcours plaisant, pour tous niveaux (les départs dames sont gentiment avancés) et que l'on ne sera pas déçu de découvrir.

Mullingar Golf Club
Mullingar
IRL - BELVEDERE, Co West Meath

Office	Secrétariat	(353) 044 - 48 366
Pro shop	Pro-shop	(353) 044 - 40 088
Fax	Fax	(353) 044 - 41 499
Situation	Situation	

5 km from Mullingar (pop. 8 003)

Annual closure	Fermeture annnuelle	no
Weekly closure	Fermeture hebdomadaire	no

Fees main season
Tarifs haute saison 18 holes

	Week days Semaine	We/Bank holidays We/Férié
Individual Individuel	IR£ 20	IR£ 25
Couple Couple	IR£ 40	IR£ 50

Caddy	Caddy	no
Electric Trolley	Chariot électrique	no
Buggy	Voiturette	IR£ 20/18 holes
Clubs	Clubs	IR£ 7/18 holes

Credit cards Cartes de crédit — no

EDGEWORTHSTOWN
Meathas Troim
N4

DELVIN
Dealbhna
N 52

MULLINGAR
An Muileann
gCear
N 4

N 52

KINNEGAD
Clonn Atha Gad

LOUGH
ENNELL

GOLF

0   2   4 km
0   2,5 miles

KILBEGGAN
Cill Bheagáin

Access Accès : Dublin, M4 / N4 → Mullingar.
In Mullingar, R52 to Belvedere
Map 2 on page 697 Carte 2 Page 697

GOLF COURSE
PARCOURS
14/20

Site	Site	
Maintenance	Entretien	
Architect	Architecte	James Braid
Type	Type	parkland
Relief	Relief	
Water in play	Eau en jeu	
Exp. to wind	Exposé au vent	
Trees in play	Arbres en jeu	

Scorecard Carte de score	Chp. Chp.	Mens Mess.	Ladies Da.
Length Long.	5913	5721	4991
Par	72	72	74

Advised golfing ability Niveau de jeu recommandé	0	12	24	36

Hcp required   Handicap exigé   28 Men, 36 Ladies

CLUB HOUSE & AMENITIES
CLUB HOUSE ET ANNEXES
5/10

Pro shop	Pro-shop	
Driving range	Practice	
Sheltered	couvert	no
On grass	sur herbe	yes
Putting-green	putting-green	yes
Pitching-green	pitching green	no

HOTEL FACILITIES
ENVIRONNEMENT HOTELIER
5/10

HOTELS HÔTELS
Bloomfield House — Mullingar
33 rooms, D IR£ 74 — 500 m
Tel (353) 044 - 40 894, Fax (353) 044 - 43 767

Greville Arms — Mullingar
40 rooms, D IR£ 70 — 5 km
Tel (353) 044 - 48 563, Fax (353) 044 - 48 052

RESTAURANTS RESTAURANT
Hacketts — Mullingar
Tel (353) 044 - 49 755 — 5 km

Oscars — Mullingar
Tel (353) 044 - 44 909 — 5 km

749

This is a rather hilly course out in the country, running alongside the village of Ardagh with its pretty stone houses. The averagely fit player, though, shouldn't have too much trouble walking the course. Plant-lovers will admire the fine varieties of fully-grown trees, which have been designed into the layout to clearly define the fairways and make life a little more sticky for players. However, water is the main difficulty, with dangerous lakes and streams, but they are clearly visible and there is nothing to force you into them... if you choose the right clubs. The greens are very generously designed and are easier to reach with lofted shots than with bump and rolls. They are all visible on the second shot, even when the tee shot is blind. Despite being a young course, this layout is already showing signs of healthy maturity and should develop well over the coming years.

Tout à côté du village d'Ardagh, avec ses jolis maisons de pierre, ce parcours en pleine campagne est assez accidenté, mais les joueurs en bonne santé ne devraient pas avoir trop de mal à marcher à pied. Les amateurs de plantes y admireront quelques belles espèces d'arbres en pleine maturité, incorporés au tracé de manière à bien définir les trous, mais aussi à compliquer le travail des joueurs. L'eau constitue cependant la difficulté essentielle, avec des lacs et cours d'eau dangereux. Mais ils sont bien visibles, et rien n'oblige à y envoyer ses balles... si l'on choisit les bons clubs. Les greens ont été généreusement dessinés, ils sont plus facilement accessibles en portant la balle qu'en la faisant rouler. Ils sont tous visibles au second coup, même quand les drives sont aveugles. Malgré sa jeunesse, ce parcours montre beaucoup de maturité, et devrait favorablement évoluer avec le temps.

Newcastle West Golf Club
IRL - ARDAGH, Co. Limerick

Office	Secrétariat	(353) 069 - 76 500
Pro shop	Pro-shop	(353) 069 - 76 500
Fax	Fax	(353) 069 - 76 511
Situation	Situation	

40 km from Limerick (pop. 52 083)
10 km from Newcastle West

Annual closure	Fermeture annnuelle	no
Weekly closure	Fermeture hebdomadaire	no

Fees main season
Tarifs haute saison full day

	Week days Semaine	We/Bank holidays We/Férié
Individual Individuel	IR£ 18	IR£ 18
Couple Couple	IR£ 36	IR£ 36

Caddy	Caddy	on request
Electric Trolley	Chariot électrique	no
Buggy	Voiturette	IR£ 20/18 holes
Clubs	Clubs	IR£ 7

Credit cards Cartes de crédit
VISA - Eurocard - MasterCard

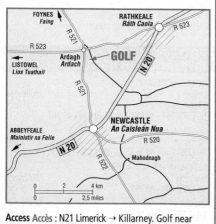

Access Accès : N21 Limerick → Killarney. Golf near Armagh. Follow signposts
Map 2 on page 696 Carte 2 Page 696

GOLF COURSE
PARCOURS

13/20

Site	Site	
Maintenance	Entretien	
Architect	Architecte	Arthur Spring
Type	Type	parkland, open country
Relief	Relief	
Water in play	Eau en jeu	
Exp. to wind	Exposé au vent	
Trees in play	Arbres en jeu	

Scorecard Carte de score	Chp. Chp.	Mens Mess.	Ladies Da.
Length Long.	5773	5381	4834
Par	71	71	72

Advised golfing ability
Niveau de jeu recommandé

0   12   24   36

Hcp required   Handicap exigé   no

CLUB HOUSE & AMENITIES
CLUB HOUSE ET ANNEXES

7/10

Pro shop	Pro-shop	
Driving range	Practice	
Sheltered	couvert	no
On grass	sur herbe	yes
Putting-green	putting-green	yes
Pitching-green	pitching green	yes

HOTEL FACILITIES
ENVIRONNEMENT HOTELIER

5/10

HOTELS HÔTELS

River Room Hotel   Newcastle West
15 rooms, D IR£ 39   9 km
Tel (353) 069 - 62 244, Fax (353) 069 - 62 244

Dunraven Arms Hotel   Adare
66 rooms, D IR£ 104   16 km
Tel (353) 061 - 396 633, Fax (353) 061 - 396 541

Devon Inn Hotel   Templeglantine
37 rooms, D IR£ 50   20 km
Tel (353) 069 - 84 122, Fax (353) 069 - 84 255

RESTAURANTS RESTAURANT

Mustard Seed   Ballingarry
Tel (353) 069 - 68 508   8 km

The Arches   Adare
Tel (353) 061 - 396 246   14 km

750

Like a boat leaving its harbour, this new course is exposed to all winds. So there was really little point in adding an array of difficulties to those already inherent in an excellent and virtually sea-bound setting. Perched atop cliffs but not really a links course in the strict sense of the term, this is still one of the most exciting courses to play at the present time. The number of tee-boxes helps adapt the course to its strengths and the forces of nature, but you are best advised to opt for match-play rather than aim to score to your handicap. The pretty town of Kinsale deserved a class course, and here it is, laid out by a host of designers (Kirby, Carr, Merrigan, Hackett and Higgins). Not surprisingly, the purist may point of a little lack of unity in style.

Comme un navire sortant du port, ce nouveau parcours est exposé à tous les vents. Il n'était alors pas utile d'ajouter une profusion de difficultés à celles imposées par un site exceptionnel, pratiquement encerclé par la mer. Situé au sommet des falaises, sans être un links à proprement parler, il n'en est pas moins l'un des plus excitants à jouer actuellement. Le nombre de tees permet d'adapter le parcours à ses forces et celles de la nature, mais il vaudra mieux y jouer en match-play que de faire la course derrière son handicap. La jolie ville de Kinsale méritait un parcours de grande classe. Dessiné par une armée d'architectes (Ron Kirby, Joe Carr, Pat Merrigan, EddieHackett et Higgins), il manquera cependant un peu d'unité de style aux yeux des puristes...

Old Head of Kinsale Golf Links
IRL - KINSALE, Co. Cork

Office	Secrétariat	(353) 021 - 778 444
Pro shop	Pro-shop	(353) 021 - 778 444
Fax	Fax	(353) 021 - 778 022
Situation	Situation	

10 km S of Kinsale (pop. 1800)
48 km from Cork (pop. 174 400)

Annual closure	Fermeture annnuelle	yes
		1/12→28/02/99
Weekly closure	Fermeture hebdomadaire	

Fees main season
Tarifs haute saison 18 holes

	Week days Semaine	We/Bank holidays We/Férié
Individual Individuel	IR£ 50	IR£ 60
Couple Couple	IR£ 100	IR£ 120

Caddy	Caddy	IR£ 15
Electric Trolley	Chariot électrique	no
Buggy	Voiturette	IR£ 30/18 holes
Clubs	Clubs	IR£ 20/18 holes

Credit cards Cartes de crédit
VISA - MasterCard - AMEX - DC

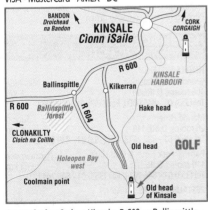

Access Accès : Cork → Kinsale, R 600 → Ballinspittle
Map 2 on page 696 Carte 2 Page 696

GOLF COURSE
PARCOURS
15/20

Site	Site	
Maintenance	Entretien	
Architect	Architecte	Ron Kirby, Joe Carr P. Merrigan...
Type	Type	seaside course
Relief	Relief	
Water in play	Eau en jeu	
Exp. to wind	Exposé au vent	
Trees in play	Arbres en jeu	

Scorecard	Chp.	Mens	Ladies
Carte de score	Chp.	Mess.	Da.
Length Long.	6080	5657	4827
Par	72	72	72

Advised golfing ability	0	12	24	36
Niveau de jeu recommandé				

Hcp required	Handicap exigé	no

CLUB HOUSE & AMENITIES
CLUB HOUSE ET ANNEXES
7/10

Pro shop	Pro-shop	
Driving range	Practice	
Sheltered	couvert	no
On grass	sur herbe	yes (03 → 10)
Putting-green	putting-green	yes
Pitching-green	pitching green	no

HOTEL FACILITIES
ENVIRONNEMENT HOTELIER
7/10

HOTELS HÔTELS
Actons Hotel, 56 rooms, D IR£ 70 — Kinsale
Tel (353) 021 - 772 135, Fax (353) 021 - 772 231 — 10 km

Trident Hotel — Kinsale
58 rooms, D IR£ 70 — 10 km
Tel (353) 021 - 772 301, Fax (353) 021 - 774 173

Innishannon House Hotel — Innishannon
14 rooms, D IR£ 90 — 20 km
Tel (353) 021 - 775 121, Fax (353) 021 - 775 609

RESTAURANTS RESTAURANT
The Vintage, Tel (353) 021 - 772 502 — Kinsale, 10 km

Blue Haven Hotel — Kinsale
Tel (353) 021 - 774 075 — 10 km

The White House, — Kinsale
Tel (353) 021 - 772 125 — 10 km

751

A masterpiece. Straight to the point, honest, blunt and diabolical when the wind blows. While Ballybunion can sometimes appear a little baroque, Portmarnock posts an almost austere classicism. There is not one hazard too many, and not one too few to collect wayward shots, not to mention the rough, which is knee-high in places. The greens are huge, subtly contoured and formidably well-guarded. Every shot has to be perfect, from tee to final putt, otherwise stick your tail between your legs and accept that what you get is no more than what you give, with no chance of blaming a single hidden difficulty. If there is one course in this world to be admired for its power, visual amazement, intelligence and variety within unity of style, then it has to be Portmarnock. It is also a great lesson in sobriety for all the world's golf-course designers. You haven't lived if you haven't played Portmarnock at least once. There again, you could also spend your whole life playing here.

Un chef-d'oeuvre. Direct, franc, brutal, et diabolique quand le vent souffle. Si Ballybunion peut paraître parfois baroque, Portmarnock est d'un classicisme presque austère. Il n'y a pas un obstacle superflu, mais il n'en manque pas un pour recevoir les coups égarés, sans même parler d'un rough qui peut monter jusqu'aux genoux. Les greens sont vastes, leurs contours subtils, leurs défenses redoutables. Tous les coups doivent être parfaits, du départ au dernier putt, sinon, il faut faire preuve d'humilité, accepter de ne recevoir que ce que vous donnez, sans pouvoir accuser une seule difficulté cachée. S'il est un parcours admirable par sa puissance, sa grandeur visuelle, son intelligence, sa diversité à l'intérieur même d'une unité de style, c'est Portmarnock. C'est aussi une grande leçon de sobriété pour tous les architectes du monde. On ne saurait vivre sans avoir joué ici une fois, on pourrait aussi y passer sa vie.

Portmarnock Golf Club
IRL - PORTMARNOCK, Co. Dublin

Office	Secrétariat	(353) 01 - 846 2968
Pro shop	Pro-shop	(353) 01 - 846 2634
Fax	Fax	(353) 01 - 846 2601
Situation	Situation	

16 km NE of Dublin (pop. 859 976)

Annual closure	Fermeture annnuelle	no
Weekly closure	Fermeture hebdomadaire	Wednesday
	Restaurant open all days	

Fees main season
Tarifs haute saison 18 holes

	Week days Semaine	We/Bank holidays We/Férié
Individual Individuel	IR£ 60	IR£ 75
Couple Couple	IR£ 120	IR£ 150

No women at weekend or public holidays!!!

Caddy	Caddy	on request/IR£ 20
Electric Trolley	Chariot électrique	no
Buggy	Voiturette	no
Clubs	Clubs	IR£ 15.50/full day

Credit cards Cartes de crédit
VISA - Eurocard - MasterCard - AMEX - DC

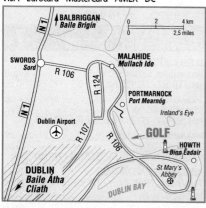

Access Accès : Baldoyle, Portmarnock Village. Golf Links bar, turn right. Golf 1,5 km
Map 3 on page 698 Carte 3 Page 698

GOLF COURSE
PARCOURS
19/20

Site	Site	▬▬▬▬
Maintenance	Entretien	▬▬▬▬
Architect	Architecte	WG Pikeman George Ross
Type	Type	links
Relief	Relief	
Water in play	Eau en jeu	▬
Exp. to wind	Exposé au vent	▬▬
Trees in play	Arbres en jeu	▬▬

Scorecard Carte de score	Chp. Chp.	Mens Mess.	Ladies Da.
Length Long.	6497	6251	5304
Par	72	72	72

Advised golfing ability		0 12 24 36
Niveau de jeu recommandé		▬▬▬▬
Hcp required	Handicap exigé	28 Men, 36 Ladies

CLUB HOUSE & AMENITIES
CLUB HOUSE ET ANNEXES
8/10

Pro shop	Pro-shop	▬▬▬▬
Driving range	Practice	▬▬▬
Sheltered	couvert	no
On grass	sur herbe	yes
Putting-green	putting-green	yes
Pitching-green	pitching green	yes

HOTEL FACILITIES
ENVIRONNEMENT HOTELIER
8/10

HOTELS HÔTELS
Grand Hotel Malahide   Malahide
100 rooms, D IR£ 90   5 km
Tel (353) 01 - 845 0000, Fax (353) 01 - 845 0987

Marine Hotel   Sutton
26 rooms, D IR£ 110   5 km
Tel (353) 01 - 832 2613, Fax (353) 01 - 839 04 42

Portmarnock Hotel & Golf Links   Portmarnock
110 rooms, D IR£ 115   1 km
Tel (353) 01 - 846 0611, Fax (353) 01 - 846 2442

RESTAURANTS RESTAURANT
Colonnade   Grand Hotel, Malahide
Tel (353) 01 - 845 0000   5 km

Meridian Restaurant   Marine Hotel, Sutton
Tel (353) 01 - 839 0000   5 km

752

PORTMARNOCK LINKS

Assuming such a prestigious name was a stiff task, but Bernhard Langer and Stan Eby accepted the challenge and came up with a great course. Only history will tell how great, but their initial achievement was to approach the site with a degree of modesty, and to learn from others - including its illustrious neighbour and other gems such as Carnoustie and Muirfield - without copying a single thing. There is nothing visually excessive and no signature hole, just a natural layout in unforgiving, changing landscape. While the first holes are visually unimpressive, their technical challenge is something else. From the 8th hole onward, the terrain becomes a little more lively and the choice of club a little tougher in a spectacular landscape of dunes. There is no water (to speak of) and no trees, either, nothing but bushes, dangerous rough, magnificently designed and located bunkers and greens that are really exciting to play. The result is more than anyone could ever have hoped for.

Il était difficile de porter un nom aussi prestigieux. Bernhard Langer et Stan Eby ont relevé le défi, et réussi un grand parcours. L'histoire dira sa place exacte, mais la réussite première est d'avoir abordé modestement ce site, de n'avoir rien copié tout en retenant les leçons de l'illustre voisin, mais aussi de merveilles telles que Carnoustie ou Muirfield. Rien ici d'excessif visuellement, pas de trou-signature, rien que le déroulement naturel dans un paysage rude et changeant. Si les premiers trous ne sont pas visuellement impressionnés, quels challenges techniques ils présentent ! A partir du 8, le terrain devient plus animé, le choix de club plus difficile dans un paysage spectaculaire de dunes. Ici, pas d'eau (ou presque), pas d'arbres, rien que des buissons, un rough dangereux, des bunkers magnifiquement dessinés et placés, des greens passionnants à jouer. Le résultat dépasse les espérances.

Portmarnock Hotel & Golf Links
IRL - PORTMARNOCK, Co Dublin

Office	Secrétariat	(353) 01 - 846 1800
Pro shop	Pro-shop	(353) 01 - 846 1800
Fax	Fax	(353) 01 - 846 1077
Situation	Situation	

8 km from Dublin (pop. 859 976)

Annual closure	Fermeture annnuelle	no
Weekly closure	Fermeture hebdomadaire	no

Fees main season
Tarifs haute saison 18 holes

	Week days Semaine	We/Bank holidays We/Férié
Individual Individuel	IR£ 50	IR£ 50
Couple Couple	IR£ 100	IR£ 100

Hotel guests: IR£ 30

Caddy	Caddy	on request/IR£ 20
Electric Trolley	Chariot électrique	no
Buggy	Voiturette	no
Clubs	Clubs	IR£ 15/18 holes

Credit cards Cartes de crédit
VISA - MasterCard - AMEX

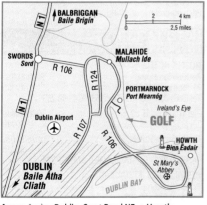

Access Accès : Dublin, Coast Road NE → Howth.
Map 3 on page 698 Carte 3 Page 698

GOLF COURSE
PARCOURS
17 /20

Site	Site	
Maintenance	Entretien	
Architect	Architecte	Bernhard Langer
Type	Type	links
Relief	Relief	
Water in play	Eau en jeu	
Exp. to wind	Exposé au vent	
Trees in play	Arbres en jeu	

Scorecard Carte de score	Chp. Chp.	Mens Mess.	Ladies Da.
Length Long.	6195	5909	4987
Par	71	71	71

Advised golfing ability		0 12 24 36
Niveau de jeu recommandé		
Hcp required	Handicap exigé	24 Men, 36 Ladies

CLUB HOUSE & AMENITIES
CLUB HOUSE ET ANNEXES
7 /10

Pro shop	Pro-shop	
Driving range	Practice	
Sheltered	couvert	yes
On grass	sur herbe	yes
Putting-green	putting-green	yes
Pitching-green	pitching green	yes

HOTEL FACILITIES
ENVIRONNEMENT HOTELIER
8 /10

HOTELS HÔTELS
Portmarnock Links Hotel ****   Portmarnock
110 rooms, D IR£ 190   on site
Tel (353) 01 - 846 0611, Fax (353) 01 - 846 2442

Grand Hotel   Malahide
100 rooms, D IR£ 95   4 km
Tel (353) 01 - 845 0000, Fax (353) 01 - 845 0987

Sands Hotel, 10 rooms, D IR£ 70   Portmarnock
Tel (353) 01 - 846 0003, Fax (353) 01 - 846 0420   1 km

RESTAURANTS RESTAURANT
Bon Appetit   Malahide
Tel (353) 01 - 845 0314   4 km

Old Street Wine Bar   Malahide
Tel (353) 01 - 845 1882   4 km

Ostborne (at Hotel), Tel (353) 01 846 0611   on site

753

PORTSALON

16	5	5

Portsalon is an outstanding site, between the beach of Ballymostocker bay, one of the world's finest, and the Knockalla mountains. This age-old course is today run by local Irishmen, which means a friendly welcome guaranteed every time. The course is a shortish links with no real geographical relief, and so is ideal for a romantic stroll, even for the non-golfers in the family. The terrain has stayed very natural, with unpredictable kicks that are all part of the fun of golf, when they bounce and rebound in the right direction. The rough is not too severe and the bunkers are nicely, but not excessively, in play. Golfers who are new to the game will enjoy the opportunity here to learn about the architecture of a links course, without undue suffering, especially continental Europeans, who have little contact with this style of golf. The water on the 3rd and 15th shouldn't bother them too much, either. The wind is, of course, an element to be reckoned with, but it puts colour into your cheeks and gives you a hearty appetite for after the round.

Portsalon bénéficie d'une situation exceptionnelle, entre la plage de Ballymostocker Bay, l'une des plus belles du monde, et les Knockalla Mountains. Ce golf centenaire est aujourd'hui géré par des Irlandais locaux, c'est une garantie d'accueil amical. Le parcours est un links de longueur réduite, sans relief trop prononcé, ce qui permet une promenade romantique, même pour les non-golfeurs de la famille. Le terrain est resté très naturel, avec les rebonds imprévisibles qui font le plaisir du jeu... quand ils sont favorables. Le rough n'est pas trop sévère, les bunkers bien en jeu, mais sans excès. Les golfeurs peu expérimentés auront ici une belle occasion d'apprendre à aimer sans douleur l'architecture de links, notamment les Européens du continent, peu familiarisés avec elle. Et la présence de l'eau, au 3 et au 15, ne devrait pas trop les gêner. Bien sûr, le vent est un élément important, mais il donne bonne mine et ouvre l'appétit.

Portsalon Golf Club

Portsalon
IRL - FANAD, Co Donegal

Office	Secrétariat	(353) 074 - 59 459
Pro shop	Pro-shop	(353) 074 - 59 459
Fax	Fax	(353) 074 - 59 459
Situation	Situation	

50 km from Derry (pop. 72 334)
32 km from Letterkenny (pop. 7 166)

Annual closure	Fermeture annnuelle	no
Weekly closure	Fermeture hebdomadaire	no

Fees main season
Tarifs haute saison 18 holes

	Week days Semaine	We/Bank holidays We/Férié
Individual Individuel	IR£ 10	IR£ 12
Couple Couple	IR£ 20	IR£ 24

Caddy	Caddy	IR£ 10/18 holes
Electric Trolley	Chariot électrique	no
Buggy	Voiturette	no
Clubs	Clubs	no
Credit cards Cartes de crédit		no

754

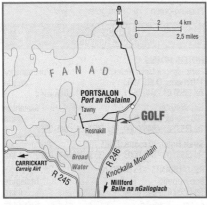

		0 __ 2 __ 4 km
		0 __ 2,5 miles

F A N A D

PORTSALON
Port an tSalainn
Tawny
GOLF
Rosnakill

CARRICKART
Carraig Airt
Broad Water
R 246
Knockalla Mountain
R 245
Millford
Baile na nGalloglach

Access Accès : Derry, A2, N13 to Letterkenny.
R245 to Rathmelton, Milford. R246 to Portsalon (Fanad Peninsula) Map 1 on page 695 Carte 1 Page 695

GOLF COURSE PARCOURS

16/20

Site	Site	▬▬▬
Maintenance	Entretien	▬▬▬
Architect	Architecte	Mr Thompson
Type	Type	links
Relief	Relief	▬
Water in play	Eau en jeu	▬▬
Exp. to wind	Exposé au vent	▬▬▬
Trees in play	Arbres en jeu	▬▬

Scorecard Carte de score	Chp. Chp.	Mens Mess.	Ladies Da.
Length Long.	5354	5354	4499
Par	69	69	70

Advised golfing ability
Niveau de jeu recommandé

0	12	24	36

Hcp required Handicap exigé no

CLUB HOUSE & AMENITIES CLUB HOUSE ET ANNEXES

5/10

Pro shop	Pro-shop	▭
Driving range	Practice	▭
Sheltered	couvert	no
On grass	sur herbe	no
Putting-green	putting-green	yes
Pitching-green	pitching green	no

HOTEL FACILITIES ENVIRONNEMENT HOTELIER

5/10

HOTELS HÔTELS

Rathmullan House | Rathmullan
21 rooms, D IR£ 100 | 10 km
Tel (353) 074 - 59 115, Fax (353) 074 - 58 200

Pier Hotel, D IR£ 60 | Rathmullan
Tel (353) 074 - 59 115 | 10 km

Castle Grove Hotel | Letterkenny
8 rooms, D IR£ 65 | 30 km
Tel (353) 074 - 51 118, Fax (353) 074 - 51 384

RESTAURANTS RESTAURANT

Portsalon Store | Portsalon
Tel (353) 074 - 59 107 | 1 km

Rosapenna Hotel | Downings
Tel (353) 074 - 55 301

This is a magnificent site alongside the little town of Enniskerry, the gateway to the "Military Road" that crosses the wild landscape of the Wicklow Mountains in the immediate vicinity of Powerscourt Castle (hence the name of the course). The course winds it way around a majestic estate over some sharp slopes that might make a buggy advisable for senior players. Amateur champion Peter McEvoy has produced a championship course that is as honest as it is technically demanding, where water comes into play on only two holes (including the superb 16th hole, a par 3 and obvious tribute to the 12th at Augusta). The main hazards are the large trees and very strategically placed bunkers. Powerscourt is still a very young course but the sand-based greens are already in excellent condition ; for the moment, the fairways still need to gain a little firmness and the back-tees are best left alone...

C'est un site magnifique, à côté de la petite ville d'Enniskerry, porte d'entrée de la "Military Road" traversant les paysages sauvages des Wicklow Mountains, à proximité immédiate du Château de Powerscourt, dont le golf a emprunté le nom. Le parcours a été insinué dans cet espace majestueux, au prix de quelques reliefs incitant à conseiller une voiturette aux seniors. Le grand champion amateur Peter McEvoy en a fait un parcours de championnat aussi franc qu'exigeant techniquement, où l'eau n'est en jeu que sur deux trous (dont le superbe 16, un par 3 en référence évidente au 12 d'Augusta). Les grands arbres constituent les principaux obstacles, avec des bunkers très stratégiques. Powerscourt est très jeune encore, mais les greens en sable sont déjà en excellente condition, alors que les fairways ont besoin d'acquérir un peu de fermeté : il vaut mieux ne pas jouer des départs arrière pour l'instant...

Powerscourt Golf Club
Powerscourt Estate
IRL - ENNISKERRY, Co Wicklow

Office	Secrétariat	(353) 01 - 204 6033
Pro shop	Pro-shop	(353) 01 - 204 6033
Fax	Fax	(353) 01 - 286 3561
Situation	Situation	

19 km S of Dublin (pop. 859 976)
1 km from Enniskerry

Annual closure	Fermeture annnuelle	no
Weekly closure	Fermeture hebdomadaire	no

Fees main season
Tarifs haute saison 18 holes

	Week days Semaine	We/Bank holidays We/Férié
Individual Individuel	IR£ 50	IR£ 60
Couple Couple	IR£ 100	IR£ 120

Caddy	Caddy	on request
Electric Trolley	Chariot électrique	no
Buggy	Voiturette	IR£ 30/18 holes
Clubs	Clubs	IR£ 15/18 holes

Credit cards Cartes de crédit
VISA - MasterCard - AMEX - Laser

Access Accès : N11, South of Bray
Map 3 on page 698 Carte 3 Page 698

GOLF COURSE / PARCOURS — 15/20

Site	Site	
Maintenance	Entretien	
Architect	Architecte	Peter McEvoy
Type	Type	inland, parkland
Relief	Relief	
Water in play	Eau en jeu	
Exp. to wind	Exposé au vent	
Trees in play	Arbres en jeu	

Scorecard Carte de score	Chp. Chp.	Mens Mess.	Ladies Da.
Length Long.	6410	5858	5322
Par	72	72	75

Advised golfing ability Niveau de jeu recommandé		0	12	24	36
Hcp required	Handicap exigé	no			

CLUB HOUSE & AMENITIES / CLUB HOUSE ET ANNEXES — 7/10

Pro shop	Pro-shop	
Driving range	Practice	
Sheltered	couvert	no
On grass	sur herbe	yes
Putting-green	putting-green	yes
Pitching-green	pitching green	yes

HOTEL FACILITIES / ENVIRONNEMENT HOTELIER — 7/10

HOTELS HÔTELS

Summerhill Hotel — Enniskerry
30 rooms, D IR£ 50
Tel (353) 01 - 286 7928, Fax (353) 01 - 286 79 29

Glenview Hotel — Delgany
43 rooms, D IR£ 125 — 13 km
Tel (353) 01 - 287 3399, Fax (353) 01 - 287 7511

Charlesland Golf & Country C. — Greystones
12 rooms, D IR£ 66 — 16 km
Tel (353) 01 - 287 6764, Fax (353) 01 - 287 3882

RESTAURANTS RESTAURANT

Roly's Bistro, Tel (353) 01 - 668 2611 — Dublin, 15 km

Cooper's, Tel (353) 01 - 287 3914 — Greystones, 13 km

Hungry Monk, — Greystones
Tel (353) 01 - 287 5759 — 13 km

755

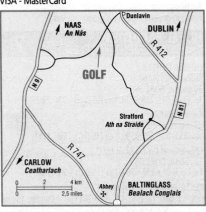

Welcome to a huge park, where the age-old trees provide a sumptuous splash of colour come Autumn. Away from the madding crowd, the trees here are in fact a real factor to complicate the course and your game. The slopes are sometimes steep and might hinder some senior players, but they also add to the problem of club selection. This is compounded by well-guarded and cleverly designed greens, where you can rarely get home without lofting the ball. A noticeable feature is the variety of the holes, with more than a few slight dog-legs that ideally call for some flighted shots (when the ground is damp the course plays very long). There is water on seven holes, and it is often dangerous. Although generally honest and open, the course nonetheless harbours a few traps, including the 6th, a par 5 peppered with bunkers, ponds and ditches and a tricky hole to master. Other features are the difficulty of the closing holes and the very family atmosphere that reigns throughout the club.

Un immense parc avec des arbres centenaires, dont les couleurs automnales sont somptueuses. A l'écart des bruits du monde, leur présence est un facteur de difficulté effective dans le jeu. Les dénivellées sont parfois importantes, et peuvent poser des problèmes aux seniors, mais aussi pour bien choisir son club, et d'autant plus que les greens sont très défendus, très travaillés : on peut rarement y entrer en faisant rouler la balle. On remarquera aussi la variété des trous, avec pas mal de légers dog-legs obligeant à travailler ses effets (le parcours est très long quand le sol est humide). L'eau est présente sur sept trous, souvent de manière dangereuse. Généralement assez franc, ce parcours recèle néanmoins quelques pièges, dont le 6, un par 5 truffé de bunkers, de mares et de fossés, et bien délicat à décrypter. A signaler aussi, la difficulté des derniers trous, et l'atmosphère très familiale qui règne ici.

Rathsallagh Golf Club
IRL - DUNLAVIN, Co Wicklow

Office	Secrétariat	(353) 045 - 403 316
Pro shop	Pro-shop	(353) 045 - 403 316
Fax	Fax	(353) 045 - 403 295
Situation	Situation	

4 km from Dunlavin (pop. 720)

Annual closure	Fermeture annnuelle	no
Weekly closure	Fermeture hebdomadaire	no

Fees main season
Tarifs haute saison 18 holes

	Week days Semaine	We/Bank holidays We/Férié
Individual Individuel	IR£ 30	IR£ 40
Couple Couple	IR£ 60	IR£ 80

Weekdays: IR£ 20 before 9.30 am

Caddy	Caddy	on request
Electric Trolley	Chariot électrique	IR£ 8
Buggy	Voiturette	IR£ 25/18 holes
Clubs	Clubs	IR£ 25/18 holes

Credit cards Cartes de crédit
VISA - MasterCard

Access Accès : Dublin, N7 West. N9 → Waterford.
→ Dunlavin
Map 2 on page 697 Carte 2 Page 697

GOLF COURSE
PARCOURS
15/20

Site	Site	
Maintenance	Entretien	
Architect	Architecte	Peter McEvoy Ch. O'Connor Jr
Type	Type	inland, parkland
Relief	Relief	
Water in play	Eau en jeu	
Exp. to wind	Exposé au vent	
Trees in play	Arbres en jeu	

Scorecard Carte de score	Chp. Chp.	Mens Mess.	Ladies Da.
Length Long.	6321	5940	5033
Par	72	72	73

Advised golfing ability Niveau de jeu recommandé	0	12	24	36

Hcp required Handicap exigé   28 Men, 36 Ladies

CLUB HOUSE & AMENITIES
CLUB HOUSE ET ANNEXES
7/10

Pro shop	Pro-shop	
Driving range	Practice	
Sheltered	couvert	2 mats
On grass	sur herbe	yes
Putting-green	putting-green	yes
Pitching-green	pitching green	no

HOTEL FACILITIES
ENVIRONNEMENT HOTELIER
6/10

HOTELS HÔTELS
Rathsallagh House   on site
17 rooms, D IR£ 160
Tel (353) 045 - 403 112, Fax (353) 045 - 403 343

Kilkee Castle   Castledermot
36 rooms, D IR£ 120   20 km
Tel (353) 0503 - 45 156, Fax (353) 0503 - 45 187

RESTAURANTS RESTAURANT
Rathsallagh House   on site
Tel (353) 045 - 403 112

Priory Inn   Carlow-Kilkenny Road
Tel (353) 045 - 403 355   4 km

ROSAPENNA

Originally designed by Old Tom Morris in 1893, Rosapenna was reshaped by James Braid and Harry Vardon in 1906 before Eddie Hackett added the final touches in 1993. With names like these, the course should, on the face of it, be quite something, and it is. This is one of the obligatory stop-offs in the long trek of exploring golfing treasures in the north-west of Ireland, often unknown to foreign tourists but not so to the Irish themselves. Playing on a links is like going back to the origins of the game, when intuition and inspiration held the upper hand over pure technique, when the size of your score was merely relative because match-play was the formula that reigned supreme with amateur golfers. Exposure to the wind makes Rosapenna a tricky number to play, and even if the traps are seldom hidden, playing here several times makes it easier to choose tactics. Lack of experience could be a serious setback for high-handicappers.

D'abord dessiné par Old Tom Morris en 1893, Rosapenna a bénéficié des aménagements de James Braid et Harry Vardon en 1906, avant que Eddie Hackett lui donne la dernière touche en 1993. Avec de tels signataires, ce parcours ne peut laisser indifférent, à priori ! Il constitue effectivement l'un des étapes obligées dans une longue exploration des trésors golfiques du Nord-Ouest, souvent ignorés par les touristes étrangers, alors que les Irlandais en ont pris souvent le chemin. Jouer sur un links, c'est retrouver les origines du jeu, où l'intuition et l'inspiration prenaient le pas sur la technique pure, où l'importance du score était toute relative quand le match-play était la formule reine des amateurs. L'exposition au vent rend forcément Rosapenna délicat à jouer, et même si les pièges sont rarement dissimulés, jouer plusieurs fois améliore les choix tactiques. Le manque d'expérience peut gêner les golfeurs très moyens.

Rosapenna Hotel & Golf Links
IRL - DOWNINGS, Co Donegal

Office	Secrétariat	(353) 074 - 55 301
Pro shop	Pro-shop	(353) 074 - 55 301
Fax	Fax	(353) 074 - 55 128
Situation	Situation	

40 km from Letterkenny (pop. 7 166)

Annual closure	Fermeture annnuelle	no
Weekly closure	Fermeture hebdomadaire	no

Fees main season
Tarifs haute saison 18 holes

	Week days Semaine	We/Bank holidays We/Férié
Individual Individuel	IR£ 20	IR£ 25
Couple Couple	IR£ 40	IR£ 50

Caddy	Caddy	on request
Electric Trolley	Chariot électrique	no
Buggy	Voiturette	IR£ 20/18 holes
Clubs	Clubs	IR£ 10

Credit cards Cartes de crédit
VISA - Eurocard - MasterCard - DC

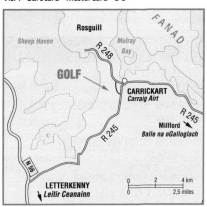

Access Accès : Letterkenny: R245 to Rathmelton, Millford, Cranford, Carrigart. Golf 2 km → Rosapenna
Map 1 on page 695 Carte 1 Page 695

GOLF COURSE
PARCOURS   **16**/20

Site	Site	
Maintenance	Entretien	
Architect	Architecte	Old Tom Morris Braid, Vardon links
Type	Type	
Relief	Relief	
Water in play	Eau en jeu	
Exp. to wind	Exposé au vent	
Trees in play	Arbres en jeu	

Scorecard Carte de score	Chp. Chp.	Mens Mess.	Ladies Da.
Length Long.	5950	5644	4555
Par	71	70	74

Advised golfing ability		0 12 24 36
Niveau de jeu recommandé		
Hcp required	Handicap exigé	Men 24, Ladies 36

CLUB HOUSE & AMENITIES
CLUB HOUSE ET ANNEXES   **7**/10

Pro shop	Pro-shop	
Driving range	Practice	
Sheltered	couvert	6 mats
On grass	sur herbe	yes
Putting-green	putting-green	yes
Pitching-green	pitching green	yes

757

HOTEL FACILITIES
ENVIRONNEMENT HOTELIER   **6**/10

HOTELS HÔTELS
Rosapenna Hotel   on site
46 rooms, D IR£ 95
Tel (353) 074 - 55 301, Fax (353) 074 - 55 128

Shandon Hotel   Marble Hill
55 rooms, D IR£ 80   13 km
Tel (353) 074 - 36 137, Fax (353) 074 - 36 430

Arnold's Hotel   Dunfanaghy
34 rooms, D IR£ 60   25 km
Tel (353) 074 - 36 208, Fax (353) 074 - 36 352

RESTAURANTS RESTAURANT
Rosapenna Hotel   on site
Tel (353) 074 - 55 301

The Cove   Dunfanaghy
Tel (353) 074 - 36 300   25 km

This course is located on a peninsula, and what with there being no trees to protect it, is clearly exposed to the wind. This element makes any links course an exciting proposition and adds to the pleasure when you can keep control. It can, though, easily upset the more inexperienced player. This is the main difficulty at Rosslare, which otherwise can appear a little dated to top level players. The bunkers are more strategic than really penalising and the well-watered greens will still hold slightly miscued shots, but before reaching them you need an accurate tee-shot to avoid the unforgiving rough. One particular feature here is the excellence of the par 3s and the closing holes along the sea, which are superb fun in matchplay. Today better suited to holiday golf than tournaments, Rosslare is a good course on which to become acclimatised with links golf.

La situation de ce parcours sur une péninsule et l'absence d'arbres protecteurs impliquent une forte exposition au vent. Cet élément rend très excitants les parcours de links, et renforce le plaisir quand on réussit à en maîtriser les effets. Mais il tourne la tête des joueurs peu expérimentés ! C'est la principale difficulté de Rosslare, autrement un peu désuet au regard des joueurs du meilleur niveau. Les bunkers sont plus stratégiques que vraiment pénalisants, l'arrosage des greens a facilité la réception des coups imparfaits, mais il faut encore de la précision au drive pour pouvoir les attaquer, car le rough peut être méchant. On distinguera particulièrement ici la qualité des pars 3, et celle des derniers trous le long de la mer, qui offrent un espace superbe en matchplay. Aujourd'hui mieux adapté à un golf de vacances que de championnat, Rosslare est un bon parcours pour se familiariser avec l'architecture de links.

Rosslare Golf Club
IRL - ROSSLARE STRAND, Co Wicklow

Office	Secrétariat	(353) 053 - 32 113
Pro shop	Pro-shop	(353) 053 - 32 238
Fax	Fax	(353) 053 - 32 203
Situation	Situation	.

18 km from Wexford (pop. 15 393)

Annual closure	Fermeture annnuelle	no
Weekly closure	Fermeture hebdomadaire	no

Fees main season
Tarifs haute saison 18 holes

	Week days Semaine	We/Bank holidays We/Férié
Individual Individuel	IR£ 20	IR£ 25
Couple Couple	IR£ 40	IR£ 50

Caddy	Caddy	no
Electric Trolley	Chariot électrique	no
Buggy	Voiturette	IR£ 20/18 holes
Clubs	Clubs	IR£ 6

Credit cards Cartes de crédit no

Map 2 on page 697 Carte 2 Page 697

Access Accès : Wexford, N25 → Rosslare Harbour.
1 km after Killinick, left on R740 to Rosslare.
Golf → Rosslare Point/Burrow

758

GOLF COURSE
PARCOURS
13/20

Site	Site	
Maintenance	Entretien	
Architect	Architecte	
Type	Type	seaside course, links
Relief	Relief	
Water in play	Eau en jeu	
Exp. to wind	Exposé au vent	
Trees in play	Arbres en jeu	

Scorecard Carte de score	Chp. Chp.	Mens Mess.	Ladies Da.
Length Long.	5920	5650	5075
Par	72	72	73

Advised golfing ability
Niveau de jeu recommandé 0 12 24 36

Hcp required Handicap exigé no

CLUB HOUSE & AMENITIES
CLUB HOUSE ET ANNEXES
5/10

Pro shop	Pro-shop	
Driving range	Practice	
Sheltered	couvert	no
On grass	sur herbe	yes
Putting-green	putting-green	yes
Pitching-green	pitching green	yes

HOTEL FACILITIES
ENVIRONNEMENT HOTELIER
6/10

HOTELS HÔTELS

Kelly's Resort — Rosslare Strand
99 rooms, D IR£ 85 — 1 km
Tel (353) 053 - 32 114, Fax (353) 053 - 32 222

Cedars Hotel — Rosslare Strand
34 rooms, D IR£ 58 — 1 km
Tel (353) 053 - 32 124, Fax (353) 053 - 32 243

Great Southern — Rosslare Harbour
100 rooms, D IR£ 70 — 4 km
Tel (353) 053 - 33 233, Fax (353) 053 - 33 543

RESTAURANTS RESTAURANT

Ocean Bed Seafood Restaurant — Wexford
Tel (353) 053 - 23 935 — 20 km

Kelly's Resort — Rosslare Strand
Tel (353) 053 - 32 114 — 1 km

Although not inside the very closed club of exceptional golf courses, Royal Dublin is an excellent example of a classic links, peppered with deep fairway and green-side bunkers (sometimes very penalising indeed) and a number of bushes, but these are often more decorative or useful for gauging distance than really dangerous. Although the terrain is none too hilly, there are a couple of blind drives but nothing blind when approaching the greens. You could almost call this a kind course if the prevailing wind wasn't blowing in your face on the way in. This makes the back 9 an even trickier proposition, which demands certain skills in drawing the ball, a feat that many will find harder than others. A very natural looking course and very busy, being so close to Dublin, this layout has started to show its age and probably needs a little restyling (especially in terms of yardage) if it is to recover its championship course status.

Bien qu'il n'appartienne pas au club très fermé des parcours exceptionnels, Royal Dublin est un excellent exemple de links classique, avec ses profonds bunkers de fairway et de greens (parfois très pénalisants), des buissons, mais souvent plus décoratifs ou utiles comme points de repère que vraiment dangereux. Bien que le terrain soit peu accidenté, on trouve ici quelques drives aveugles, mais aucun green de la sorte. On pourrait presque le qualifier d'aimable si le vent dominant n'était contraire au retour, ce qui rend cette partie du parcours encore plus délicate, exigeant notamment une bonne maîtrise des effets de draw, ce qui n'est pas donné à tout le monde ! Très naturel d'aspect, très fréquenté aussi en raison de sa proximité de Dublin, ce parcours porte un peu son âge, mais aurait sans doute besoin d'un petit lifting (notamment au niveau de la longueur), s'il souhaite du moins retrouver un statut de parcours de championnat.

Royal Dublin Golf Club
Bull Island
IRL - DUBLIN 3

Office	Secrétariat	(353) 01 - 833 6346
Pro shop	Pro-shop	(353) 01 - 833 6477
Fax	Fax	(353) 01 - 833 6504
Situation	Situation	

7 km E of Dublin (pop. 859 976)

Annual closure	Fermeture annnuelle	no
Weekly closure	Fermeture hebdomadaire	no

Fees main season
Tarifs haute saison 18 holes

	Week days Semaine	We/Bank holidays We/Férié
Individual Individuel	IR£ 45	IR£ 55
Couple Couple	IR£ 90	IR£ 110

No Ladies on Week-ends and Public Holidays!!!

Caddy	Caddy	IR£ 15 (+ Tip)
Electric Trolley	Chariot électrique	no
Buggy	Voiturette	no
Clubs	Clubs	IR£ 15

Credit cards Cartes de crédit
VISA - MasterCard - AMEX - DC

Access Accès : Dublin City, Coast road → Howth.
Bull Island Bridge, turn right
Map 3 on page 698 Carte 3 Page 698

GOLF COURSE
PARCOURS
16/20

Site	Site	
Maintenance	Entretien	
Architect	Architecte	H.S. Colt
Type	Type	links
Relief	Relief	
Water in play	Eau en jeu	
Exp. to wind	Exposé au vent	
Trees in play	Arbres en jeu	

Scorecard	Chp.	Mens	Ladies
Carte de score	Chp.	Mess.	Da.
Length Long.	6281	6030	5439
Par	72	72	74

Advised golfing ability		0	12	24	36
Niveau de jeu recommandé					
Hcp required	Handicap exigé	28 Men, 36 Ladies			

CLUB HOUSE & AMENITIES
CLUB HOUSE ET ANNEXES
7/10

Pro shop	Pro-shop	
Driving range	Practice	
Sheltered	couvert	no
On grass	sur herbe	yes
Putting-green	putting-green	yes
Pitching-green	pitching green	yes

759

HOTEL FACILITIES
ENVIRONNEMENT HOTELIER
7/10

HOTELS HÔTELS
Marine Hotel, 26 rooms, D IR£ 110 — Sutton
Tel (353) 01 - 832 2613, Fax (353) 01 - 839 04 42 — 7 km

Grand Hotel Malahide — Malahide
100 rooms, D IR£ 90 — 10 km
Tel (353) 01 - 845 0000, Fax (353) 01 - 845 0987

Portmarnock Hotel & Golf Links — Portmarnock
110 rooms, D IR£ 115 — 7 km
Tel (353) 01 - 846 0611, Fax (353) 01 - 846 2442

RESTAURANTS RESTAURANT
Colonnade — Grand Hotel, Malahide
Tel (353) 01 - 845 0000 — 10 km

King Sitric Fish — East Pier, Howth
Tel (353) 01 - 832 5235 — 8 km

Roly's Bistro, Tel (353) 01 - 668 2611 — Dublin, 13 km

SEAPOINT

From the 14th at County Louth, you can see practically all the neighbouring course of Seapoint, opened only recently. Here, it is a return to similar moonscape scenery, but with a large section of the course winding through heather and a more rural landscape. This is rather an attractive contrast, and gives the impression of a course gradually building up speed through to the closing holes, all very spectacular and exciting when using the matchplay format. The wind often has a word or two to say, and good ball control is required, especially with the tee shot, in order to avoid the fairway bunkers and get a good view of the greens to keep out of the often dangerous green-side traps. These greens are large and distinguished more by general slopes than by individual contouring. By and large, the difficulties are clearly visible (water comes into play on the 4th and 9th holes), so at least you can start out here with a degree of confidence. Well worth knowing.

Depuis le 14 de County Louth, on aperçoit pratiquement tout le parcours voisin de Seapoint, ouvert récemment. On y retrouve au retour un paysage dunaire analogue, alors qu'une grande partie se déroule dans la bruyère et un paysage plus rural. Ce contraste est d'ailleurs assez séduisant, et donne une impression de montée en puissance progressive, jusqu'aux derniers trous, très spectaculaires et excitants en match-play. Le vent joue souvent un rôle et il faut un bon contrôle de balle, en particulier depuis les départs, pour éviter les bunkers de fairway et avoir une ouverture suffisante sur les greens pour échapper à leurs bunkers, souvent dangereux. Ces greens sont largement dimensionnés, et caractérisés davantage par des pentes générales que par des ondulations ponctuelles. En règle générale, les difficultés sont bien visibles (eau en jeu au 4 et au 9), ce qui permet d'aborder Seapoint avec un minimum de confiance. A connaître.

Seapoint Golf Club

IRL - TERMONFECKIN, Co Louth

Office	Secrétariat	(353) 041 - 22 333
Pro shop	Pro-shop	(353) 041 - 22 333
Fax	Fax	(353) 041 - 22 331
Situation	Situation	.

8 km from Drogheda (pop. 23 848)

Annual closure	Fermeture annnuelle	no
Weekly closure	Fermeture hebdomadaire	no

Fees main season
Tarifs haute saison 18 holes

	Week days Semaine	We/Bank holidays We/Férié
Individual Individuel	IR£ 25	IR£ 30
Couple Couple	IR£ 45	IR£ 54

Caddy	Caddy	on request/IR£ 15
Electric Trolley	Chariot électrique	no
Buggy	Voiturette	no
Clubs	Clubs	no

Credit cards Cartes de crédit
VISA - MasterCard

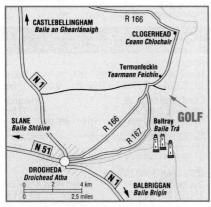

Access Accès : Drogheda, Termonfeckin Road
Map 3 on page 698 Carte 3 Page 698

GOLF COURSE
PARCOURS

15/20

Site	Site	
Maintenance	Entretien	
Architect	Architecte	Des Smyth Declan Branigan
Type	Type	links
Relief	Relief	
Water in play	Eau en jeu	
Exp. to wind	Exposé au vent	
Trees in play	Arbres en jeu	

Scorecard Carte de score	Chp. Chp.	Mens Mess.	Ladies Da.
Length Long.	6339	5904	4999
Par	72	72	73

Advised golfing ability
Niveau de jeu recommandé

0 12 24 36

Hcp required   Handicap exigé   28 Men, 36 Ladies

CLUB HOUSE & AMENITIES
CLUB HOUSE ET ANNEXES

6/10

Pro shop	Pro-shop	
Driving range	Practice	
Sheltered	couvert	no
On grass	sur herbe	yes
Putting-green	putting-green	yes
Pitching-green	pitching green	no

HOTEL FACILITIES
ENVIRONNEMENT HOTELIER

6/10

HOTELS HÔTELS

Boyne Valley — Drogheda
37 rooms, D IR£ 82 — 8 km
Tel (353) 041 - 37 737, Fax (353) 041 - 39188

West Court House — Drogheda
27 rooms, D IR£ 75 — 15 km
Tel (353) 041 - 30 965, Fax (353) 041 - 30 970

Ross Naree — Drogheda
19 rooms, D IR£ 46 — 9 km
Tel (353) 041 - 37 673, Fax (353) 041 - 33 116

RESTAURANTS RESTAURANT

Triple House — Termonfeckin
Tel (353) 041 - 22 616 — 1 km

Donegans — Monasterboice
Tel (353) 041 - 37 383 — 5 km

760

Located close to Shannon airport, this is a good starting point for a golfing holiday in the region, with enough difficulties to get you into your stride. High handicappers, though, might not feel so confident about it. In a park landscape, the trees are always in play, but there are not enough of them to trouble even the most claustrophobic player, despite the tightness of some fairways. The essential difficulties are the bunkers and many water hazards, which call for some straight driving and good club selection for the second shot. Most holes give you the choice of lofted approaches or rolled shots. But just following the layout is not enough here, you need to take the initiative. With well-spread hazards and a pleasant variety of holes, this complete course requires some powerful hitting when playing from the back-tees. A very competent course in its style.

Situé près de l'aéroport de Shannon, c'est un bon point de départ pour un séjour golfique dans la région, avec assez de difficultés pour prendre le bon rythme, mais les handicaps élevés auront du mal à se mettre en confiance. Dans un paysage de parc, les arbres entrent en jeu, et si certains trous sont étroits, ils ne sont pas assez nombreux pour gêner les claustrophobes. Les difficultés essentielles sont les bunkers et les nombreux obstacles d'eau, qui imposent pas mal de précision au drive, et un choix de club précis aux seconds coups. Sur la plupart des trous, on peut avoir les options de porter la balle ou de jouer des balles roulées. Il ne suffit pas ici de se laisser porter par le tracé, encore faut-il prendre des initiatives. Avec ses obstacles bien répartis et une bonne variété des trous, ce parcours complet demande aussi quelque puissance si l'on choisit les départs arrière. Une solide réalisation dans son genre.

Shannon Golf Club

IRL - SHANNON, Co. Clare

Office	Secrétariat	(353) 061 - 471 849
Pro shop	Pro-shop	(353) 061 - 471 551
Fax	Fax	(353) 061 - 471 507
Situation	Situation	

2 km from Shannon (pop. 7 920)
23 km from Limerick (pop. 52 083)

Annual closure	Fermeture annnuelle	no
Weekly closure	Fermeture hebdomadaire	no

Fees main season
Tarifs haute saison 18 holes

	Week days Semaine	We/Bank holidays We/Férié
Individual Individuel	IR£ 22	IR£ 27
Couple Couple	IR£ 44	IR£ 54

Caddy	Caddy	on request/IR£ 25
Electric Trolley	Chariot électrique	IR£ 15
Buggy	Voiturette	IR£ 25/18 holes
Clubs	Clubs	IR£ 15

Credit cards Cartes de crédit
VISA - MasterCard

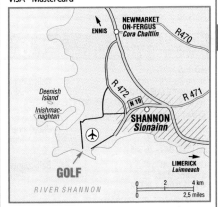

Access Accès : Limerick, N18 → Ennis. N19 to Shannon.
Golf 800 m from Shannon Airport.
Map 2 on page 696 Carte 2 Page 696

GOLF COURSE
PARCOURS
13/20

Site	Site	
Maintenance	Entretien	
Architect	Architecte	John D. Harris
Type	Type	parkland
Relief	Relief	
Water in play	Eau en jeu	
Exp. to wind	Exposé au vent	
Trees in play	Arbres en jeu	

Scorecard Carte de score	Chp. Chp.	Mens Mess.	Ladies Da.
Length Long.	6186	5863	5209
Par	72	72	74

Advised golfing ability   0   12   24   36
Niveau de jeu recommandé
Hcp required   Handicap exigé   Men 24, Ladies 36

CLUB HOUSE & AMENITIES
CLUB HOUSE ET ANNEXES
6/10

Pro shop	Pro-shop	
Driving range	Practice	
Sheltered	couvert	no
On grass	sur herbe	yes
Putting-green	putting-green	yes
Pitching-green	pitching green	yes

HOTEL FACILITIES
ENVIRONNEMENT HOTELIER
6/10

HOTELS HÔTELS

Great Southern Hotel   Shannon Airport
115 rooms, D IR£ 90   1 km
Tel (353) 061 - 471 122, Fax (353) 061 - 471 982

Fitzpatrick Shamrock Hotel   Bunratty
115 rooms, D IR£ 100   9 km
Tel (353) 061 - 361 177, Fax (353) 061 - 471 252

West County Inn   Ennis
110 rooms, D IR£ 66   20 km
Tel (353) 065 - 28 421, Fax (353) 065 - 28 801

RESTAURANTS RESTAURANT

MacCloskey's   Bunratty
Tel (353) 061 - 364 082   9 km

Mr Pickwick's   Shannon
Tel (353) 061 - 364 290   2 km

761

The early 1990s saw the advent of a fine group of excellent new courses in Ireland, often tied in with hotels. Slieve Russell is one such project in a region that hitherto had earned a reputation as being a paradise for anglers, and whose isolation should appeal to golfers who want to get away from the world for a few days spent in the heart of nature. The landscape is park-land in style, but certain geographical features are reminiscent of a links course. Two large lakes come into play, joined by a stretch of water which lurks just as threateningly, and complete a full barrage of difficulties: sometimes very thick rough, thickets, fairway and green-side bunkers and greens with sometimes very pronounced contours. Of the more memorable holes, we noted the excellence of the par 3s (especially the 16th), the 2nd, where the water is already upon you, and the 13th, a magnificent par 5 alongside Lough Rud. This course has very quickly forged itself a pretty fine reputation, and understandably so.

Le début des années 90 a vu naître en Irlande un bon groupe d'excellents nouveaux parcours, souvent associés à des hôtels. Slieve Russell est de ceux-ci, dans une région jusqu'ici réputée comme un paradis des pêcheurs, et dont l'isolement devrait séduire les golfeurs qui veulent se retirer du monde, du moins en pleine nature et au moins quelques jours. Il se trouve dans un paysage de parc, mais certains reliefs font parfois penser aux links. Deux grands lacs viennent en jeu, réunis par un cours d'eau tout aussi menaçant, et complètent un arsenal de difficultés : rough parfois épais, buissons, bunkers de fairway et de greens, ceux-ci protégeant des greens au relief parfois prononcé. Parmi quelques trous mémorables, on soulignera la qualité des par 3 (notamment le 16), du 2, où l'eau est déjà présente, et du 13, un magnifique par 5 le long du Lough Rud. Ce parcours s'est vite fait une jolie réputation, on comprend pourquoi.

Slieve Russell Golf Club
IRL - BALLYCONNELL, Co Cavan

Office	Secrétariat	(353) 049 - 26 458
Pro shop	Pro-shop	(353) 049 - 26 444
Fax	Fax	(353) 049 - 26 474
Situation	Situation	

11 km from Belturbet
25 km from Cavan (pop. 3 332)

Annual closure	Fermeture annnuelle	no
Weekly closure	Fermeture hebdomadaire	no

Fees main season
Tarifs haute saison 18 holes

	Week days Semaine	We/Bank holidays We/Férié
Individual Individuel	IR£ 28	IR£ 36
Couple Couple	IR£ 56	IR£ 72

Hotel residents : IR£ 19 (W/D) and IR£ 26 (W/E)

Caddy	Caddy	on request/IR£ 20
Electric Trolley	Chariot électrique	no
Buggy	Voiturette	IR£ 25/18 holes
Clubs	Clubs	IR£ 10/18 holes

Credit cards Cartes de crédit
VISA - Eurocard - MasterCard - AMEX

Access Accès : Dublin, N3 → Cavan. Belturbet,
R200 → Ballyconnell
Map 1 on page 695 Carte 1 Page 695

GOLF COURSE
PARCOURS
15/20

Site	Site	
Maintenance	Entretien	
Architect	Architecte	Paddy Merrigan
Type	Type	parkland
Relief	Relief	
Water in play	Eau en jeu	
Exp. to wind	Exposé au vent	
Trees in play	Arbres en jeu	

Scorecard Carte de score	**Chp.** Chp.	**Mens** Mess.	**Ladies** Da.
Length Long.	6449	6018	4849
Par	72	72	72

Advised golfing ability Niveau de jeu recommandé	0	12	24	36

Hcp required	Handicap exigé	no

CLUB HOUSE & AMENITIES
CLUB HOUSE ET ANNEXES
8/10

Pro shop	Pro-shop	
Driving range	Practice	
Sheltered	couvert	no
On grass	sur herbe	yes
Putting-green	putting-green	yes
Pitching-green	pitching green	yes

HOTEL FACILITIES
ENVIRONNEMENT HOTELIER
6/10

HOTELS HÔTELS
Slieve Russell Hotel — Ballyconnell
150 rooms, D IR£ 150 — on site
Tel (353) 049 - 26 442, Fax (353) 049 - 26 474

GUEST ROOMS CHAMBRES D'HÔTE
An Crannog — Ballyconnell
5 rooms, D IR£ 32 — 1 km
Tel (353) 049 - 26 545

Greenmount — Ballyconnell
5 rooms, D IR£ 32 — 2 km
Tel (353) 049 - 26 628

RESTAURANTS RESTAURANT
Summit — Golf Club
Tel (353) 049 - 26 444 — on site

Erin Bistro — Belturbet, 11 km

762

ST HELEN'S BAY

| 14 | 6 | 6 |

Some 6,000 trees have been planted at St Helen's Bay, and they will of course underline the park landscape of a part of this course. Philip Walton, who made his golf-designer debut here, visibly had the amateur golfer in mind. Sure, there is water on six holes, but it is more psychologically scaring than terribly dangerous, the fairway bunkers are on the lenient side and the greens (moderately sized) are well defended but leave a way open for rolled approach shots, if preferred to lofted pitches. From the 14th hole onward, you are in links country, and the going gets tougher as you progress. The coup de grâce awaits you at the 17th and 18th holes, where your card can end in tatters... or maybe not, since you have had 16 holes to hone your swing. One of the major assets of this course is its versatility, and it gives a lot of pleasure to players of all levels. We should mention, in closing, that the "wall of famine", dating from 1846, comes into play on three holes.

6.000 arbres ont été plantés à St Helen's Bay, qui vont accentuer le paysage de parc d'une partie du parcours. Philip Walton, dont c'est le premier dessin, a visiblement pensé aux amateurs. Certes, l'eau vient en jeu sur six trous, mais de manière plus psychologique que terriblement dangereuse, les bunkers de fairway ne sont pas trop pénalisants, les greens (de dimension confortable) sont bien défendus, mais on peut en aborder la plupart en faisant rouler la balle, ou en la portant, au choix. A partir du 14, nous voici dans un paysage de links, dont la difficulté va croissant, pour culminer au 17 et au 18, deux trous pour détruire sa carte, ou pour la soigner : vous avez 16 trous pour vous y préparer ! La versatilité du parcours est l'un de ses arguments majeurs, il donne beaucoup de plaisir aux joueurs de tous niveaux. Pour l'anecdote, soulignons la mise en jeu sur trois trous du "mur de la famine", qui remonte à 1846.

St Helen's Bay Golf & Country Club

Kilrane
IRL - ROSSLARE HARBOUR, Co. Wexford

Office	Secrétariat	(353) 053 - 33 234
Pro shop	Pro-shop	(353) 053 - 33 669
Fax	Fax	(353) 053 - 33 803
Situation	Situation	

13 km from Wexford (pop. 15 393)
2 km from Rosslare Harbour

Annual closure	Fermeture annnuelle	no
Weekly closure	Fermeture hebdomadaire	no

Fees main season
Tarifs haute saison 18 holes

	Week days Semaine	We/Bank holidays We/Férié
Individual Individuel	IR£ 20	IR£ 20
Couple Couple	IR£ 40	IR£ 40

Caddy	Caddy	IR£ 10/18 holes
Electric Trolley	Chariot électrique	IR£ 6
Buggy	Voiturette	IR£ 20/18 holes
Clubs	Clubs	IR£ 8

Credit cards Cartes de crédit
VISA - Eurocard - MasterCard - AMEX

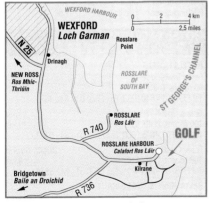

Access Accès : Dublin, N11 to Wexford.
N25 to Rosslare Harbour
Map 2 on page 697 Carte 2 Page 697

GOLF COURSE
PARCOURS
14/20

Site	Site	■■■■
Maintenance	Entretien	■■■■
Architect	Architecte	Philip Walton
Type	Type	links, parkland
Relief	Relief	■■
Water in play	Eau en jeu	■■■
Exp. to wind	Exposé au vent	■■■
Trees in play	Arbres en jeu	■■

Scorecard	Chp.	Mens	Ladies
Carte de score	Chp.	Mess.	Da.
Length Long.	6091	5813	4967
Par	72	72	72

Advised golfing ability		0	12	24	36
Niveau de jeu recommandé			■■■■■		
Hcp required	Handicap exigé	no			

CLUB HOUSE & AMENITIES
CLUB HOUSE ET ANNEXES
6/10

Pro shop	Pro-shop	■■■
Driving range	Practice	■■■
Sheltered	couvert	no
On grass	sur herbe	yes
Putting-green	putting-green	yes
Pitching-green	pitching green	no

HOTEL FACILITIES
ENVIRONNEMENT HOTELIER
6/10

HOTELS HÔTELS
Kelly's Resort — Rosslare Strand
99 rooms, D IR£ 85 — 5 km
Tel (353) 053 - 32 114, Fax (353) 053 - 32 222

Great Southern — Rosslare Harbour
100 rooms D IR£ 70 — 4 km
Tel (353) 053 - 33 233, Fax (353) 053 - 33 543

Cedars Hotel — Rosslare Strand
34 rooms, D IR£ 58 — 5 km
Tel (353) 053 - 32 124, Fax (353) 053 - 32 243

RESTAURANTS RESTAURANT
Coopers — Killinick
Tel (353) 053 - 58 942 — 6 km

Lobster Pot — Carne
Tel (353) 053 - 31 110 — 3 km

763

Before designing Druid's Glen, Pat Ruddy and Tom Craddock gave Dublin one of its best inland courses, at the expense of significant earthwork, as the former farming land was singularly lacking in geographical relief. They evidently had champion golfers in mind, but didn't forget the average amateur player either. Yet despite the many different tee-off areas, they haven't really managed to make it easy. Many of the greens are very well-guarded, and the style of golf is more American than British, meaning a lot of lofted iron shots, long and short. There are a few memorable holes, like the 8th or 12th, two real par 5s reachable only in three, and the 7th and 18th, two grand par 4s. These are all holes where water lurks dangerously. Elsewhere, the bunkers are comparatively flat and so don't set too many problems, even for players who have an aversion to sand. A course well worth getting to know.

Avant de produire Druids Glen, Pat Ruddy et Tom Craddock ont donné à Dublin l'un de ses meilleurs parcours intérieurs, au prix de terrassements importants, car ces anciens terrains agricoles manquaient singulièrement de relief. S'ils ont pensé aux champions, ils n'ont pas oublié les amateurs moyens, mais ils n'ont pas vraiment réussi, malgré le nombre de départs, à le rendre facile. Il faut dire que de nombreux greens sont très défendus, et que l'on joue plus un golf à l'américaine qu'à la "britannique", avec l'obligation de porter haut les coups de fer, y compris les petites approches. Quelques trous sont mémorables, comme le 8 et le 12, deux véritables par 5 à trois coups, le 7 et surtout le 18, deux par 4 de grand style. Ce sont tous des trous où l'eau est dangereuse. Ailleurs, les bunkers sont relativement plats, ce qui ne pose pas trop de problèmes, même à ceux qui n'adorent pas le sable. Un parcours à connaître.

St Margaret's Golf & Country Club
IRL - ST MARGARET'S, Co Dublin

Office	Secrétariat	(353) 01 - 864 0400
Pro shop	Pro-shop	(353) 01 - 864 0400
Fax	Fax	(353) 01 - 864 0289
Situation	Situation	

20 km from Dublin (pop. 859 976)
10 km from Malahide (pop. 12 088)

Annual closure	Fermeture annnuelle	no
Weekly closure	Fermeture hebdomadaire	no

Fees main season
Tarifs haute saison 18 holes

	Week days Semaine	We/Bank holidays We/Férié
Individual Individuel	IR£ 40	IR£ 40
Couple Couple	IR£ 80	IR£ 80

Caddy	Caddy	IR£ 25/18 holes
Electric Trolley	Chariot électrique	no
Buggy	Voiturette	IR£ 25/18 holes
Clubs	Clubs	IR£ 15/18 holes

Credit cards Cartes de crédit
VISA - MasterCard - AMEX

GOLF COURSE
PARCOURS   **16**/20

Site	Site	
Maintenance	Entretien	
Architect	Architecte	Pat Ruddy Tom Craddock
Type	Type	parkland, inland
Relief	Relief	
Water in play	Eau en jeu	
Exp. to wind	Exposé au vent	
Trees in play	Arbres en jeu	

Scorecard Carte de score	Chp. Chp.	Mens Mess.	Ladies Da.
Length Long.	6226	5967	5195
Par	73	73	75

Advised golfing ability Niveau de jeu recommandé	0	12	24	36

Hcp required Handicap exigé   24 Men, 36 Ladies

CLUB HOUSE & AMENITIES
CLUB HOUSE ET ANNEXES   **7**/10

Pro shop	Pro-shop	
Driving range	Practice	
Sheltered	couvert	no
On grass	sur herbe	yes
Putting-green	putting-green	yes
Pitching-green	pitching green	no

HOTEL FACILITIES
ENVIRONNEMENT HOTELIER   **7**/10

HOTELS HÔTELS
Forte Travelodge   Swords
40 rooms, D IR£ 32   6 km
Tel (353) 01 - 840 9233, Fax (353) 01 - 832 4476

Grand Hotel   Malahide
100 rooms, D IR£ 95   10 km
Tel (353) 01 - 845 0000, Fax (353) 01 - 845 0987

Forte Crest   Dublin Airport
188 rooms, D IR£ 110   6 km
Tel (353) 01 - 844 4211, Fax (353) 01 - 842 5874

RESTAURANTS RESTAURANT
Red Bank   Skerries
Tel (353) 01 - 849 1005   15 km

Old School House   Swords
Tel (353) 01 - 840 2846   8 km

764

Access Accès : 6 km W. of Dublin Airport
Map 3 on page 698 Carte 3 Page 698

A hundred years after it was first created, the original design here was drastically remodelled by Fred Hawtree and Eddie Hackett. In the past, you could only reach the course by boat. Now, they have made it meaner but removed some of its beauty in the process. In contrast, there are no more blind greens, even though the terrain is hilly (but not too punishing). A kind course when there is little or no wind, The Island can turn nasty when the wind blows, especially on the holes close to the sea. This is when you need the deliberate low shot and, if that were not enough, the ability to stop the ball on the greens at the same time. Here you learn how to fashion every shot in the book, so much so that this club has schooled an impressive list of top men and lady players, which goes to show that power play on its own is not enough. The Island is an ideal venue for the region's golfing technicians.

Cent ans après sa naissance, Fred Hawtree et Eddie Hackett ont révisé de manière drastique le dessin original d'un parcours auquel on ne pouvait autrefois accéder qu'en barque. Ils lui ont donné de la rudesse, mais retiré un peu de la beauté. En revanche, il n'y a plus de greens aveugles, même si le terrain est un peu accidenté (pas de manière punitive). Assez aimable par vent faible ou nul, The Island peut devenir très méchant par vent fort, en particulier sur les trous proches de la mer, il faut alors maîtriser les balles basses, mais ce n'est pas suffisant, il faut en même temps arrêter la balle sur les greens. Ici, on apprend à fabriquer tous les coups de golf. Tellement bien que ce club a formé une liste impressionnante de joueurs et surtout de bonnes joueuses, comme quoi la puissance ne suffit pas. The Island est un des excellents lieux de rendez-vous pour les "techniciens" de la région.

The Island Golf Club
IRL - DONABATE, Co Dublin

Office	Secrétariat	(353) 01 - 843 6205
Pro shop	Pro-shop	(353) 01 - 843 5002
Fax	Fax	(353) 01 - 843 6860
Situation	Situation	

20 km from Dublin (pop. 859 976)

Annual closure	Fermeture annnuelle	no
Weekly closure	Fermeture hebdomadaire	no

Fees main season
Tarifs haute saison 18 holes

	Week days Semaine	We/Bank holidays We/Férié
Individual Individuel	IR£ 35	IR£ 45
Couple Couple	IR£ 70	IR£ 90

Caddy	Caddy	on request/IR£ 25
Electric Trolley	Chariot électrique	no
Buggy	Voiturette	no
Clubs	Clubs	IR£ 25/18 holes

Credit cards Cartes de crédit
VISA - MasterCard

Access Accès : Dublin, N1 → Belfast. Turn right to Donabate. Side road to The Island signposted.
Map 3 on page 698 Carte 3 Page 698

GOLF COURSE
PARCOURS
15/20

Site	Site	
Maintenance	Entretien	
Architect	Architecte	Fred Hawtree Eddie Hackett
Type	Type	links
Relief	Relief	
Water in play	Eau en jeu	
Exp. to wind	Exposé au vent	
Trees in play	Arbres en jeu	

Scorecard Carte de score	Chp. Chp.	Mens Mess.	Ladies Da.
Length Long.	6078	5791	5447
Par	71	71	70

Advised golfing ability		0 12 24 36
Niveau de jeu recommandé		
Hcp required	Handicap exigé	28 Men, 36 Ladies

CLUB HOUSE & AMENITIES
CLUB HOUSE ET ANNEXES
7/10

Pro shop	Pro-shop	
Driving range	Practice	
Sheltered	couvert	no
On grass	sur herbe	yes
Putting-green	putting-green	yes
Pitching-green	pitching green	yes

765

HOTEL FACILITIES
ENVIRONNEMENT HOTELIER
7/10

HOTELS HÔTELS
Forte Crest — Dublin Airport
188 rooms, D IR£ 110 — 8 km
Tel (353) 01 - 844 4211, Fax (353) 01 - 842 5874

Dunes Hotel — Donabate
16 rooms, D IR£ 50 — 5 km
Tel (353) 01 - 843 6153, Fax (353) 01 - 843 6111

Pier Hotel — Skerries
10 rooms, D IR£ 35 — 10 km
Tel (353) 01 - 849 1708, Fax (353) 01 - 849 1708

RESTAURANTS RESTAURANT
The Food Fare — Dublin Airport
Tel (353) 01 - 844 4085 — 8 km

Giovanni's — Malahide
Tel (353) 01 - 845 1733 — 8 km

Give a golfer terrain like this and he will give you a course to match his designer skills, imagination and audacity. Arnold Palmer had no shortage of the latter and he learnt the former; Tralee (with the complicity of mother nature) is one of his greatest courses. The front 9 unwind partly atop a cliff overhanging the ocean, which comes dangerously into play if direction and accuracy are wayward. The back 9 are even more impressive, amidst huge dunes in their natural state. Here, you often need to carry the ball a long way and you will be best advised to play from the front tees if your drive and long ironwork are not quite up to scratch. A heroic course, not always as refined in diabolical details as say Ballybunion, Portrush or County Down, but essential visiting for every true golfing enthusiast.

Donnez un terrain comme celui-ci à un golfeur, il vous fera un parcours à la hauteur de ses connaissances d'architecte, de son imagination et de son audace. Le champion Arnold Palmer ne manquait pas de ces dernières qualités, il a appris les premières et Tralee (avec la complicité de la nature) est l'une de ses plus grandes réussites. L'aller se déroule partiellement au sommet d'une falaise longeant l'océan, qui vient dangereusement en jeu si l'on manque de direction et de précision. Le retour est plus impressionnant encore, au milieu d'énormes dunes à l'état sauvage. Là, il faut souvent porter loin la balle, et l'on aura intérêt à choisir les départs avancés si la qualité du drive et des longs fers n'est pas à la hauteur des défis. Un parcours héroïque, pas toujours aussi raffiné dans les détails diaboliques que Ballybunion, Portrush ou County Down, mais incontournable pour tout véritable amoureux du golf.

Tralee Golf Club

West Barron
IRL - ARDFERT, Co Kerry

Office	Secrétariat	(353) 066 - 36 379
Pro shop	Pro-shop	(353) 066 - 36 379
Fax	Fax	(353) 066 - 36 008
Situation	Situation	

12 km from Tralee (pop. 17 225)

Annual closure	Fermeture annnuelle	no
Weekly closure	Fermeture hebdomadaire	no

Fees main season
Tarifs haute saison 18 holes

	Week days Semaine	We/Bank holidays We/Férié
Individual Individuel	IR£ 45	IR£ 45
Couple Couple	IR£ 90	IR£ 90

No green-fees on Sunday
Early tee times: IR£ 35 (→ 9.30 am)

Caddy	Caddy	on request/IR£ 15
Electric Trolley	Chariot électrique	no
Buggy	Voiturette	no
Clubs	Clubs	no

Credit cards Cartes de crédit
VISA - Mastercard

GOLF COURSE
PARCOURS
18/20

Site	Site	
Maintenance	Entretien	
Architect	Architecte	Arnold Palmer
Type	Type	links
Relief	Relief	
Water in play	Eau en jeu	
Exp. to wind	Exposé au vent	
Trees in play	Arbres en jeu	

Scorecard Carte de score	Chp. Chp.	Mens Mess.	Ladies Da.
Length Long.	6252	5961	4792
Par	71	71	72

Advised golfing ability		0	12	24	36
Niveau de jeu recommandé					
Hcp required	Handicap exigé		24 Men, 36 Ladies		

CLUB HOUSE & AMENITIES
CLUB HOUSE ET ANNEXES
7/10

Pro shop	Pro-shop	
Driving range	Practice	
Sheltered	couvert	no
On grass	sur herbe	yes
Putting-green	putting-green	yes
Pitching-green	pitching green	yes

HOTEL FACILITIES
ENVIRONNEMENT HOTELIER
6/10

HOTELS HÔTELS

Brandon Hotel	Tralee
160 rooms, D IR£ 70	12 km
Tel (353) 066 - 23 333, Fax (353) 066 - 25 019	
Grand Hotel	Tralee
44 rooms, D IR£ 70	12 km
Tel (353) 066 - 21 499, Fax (353) 066 - 22 877	
Imperial	Tralee
29 rooms, D IR£ 44	12 km
Tel (353) 066 - 27 755, Fax (353) 066 - 27 800	

RESTAURANTS RESTAURANT

Tankard	Tralee
Tel (353) 066 - 36 349	2 km
Oyster Tavern	Tralee
Tel (353) 066 - 36 102	3 km

GOLF
Carrallane /Strand
ARDFERT
Ard Fhearta
R551
Barrow
Barrow harbour
Drehidasillagh
FENIT
An Fhlanait
L
R558
Nature reserve
TRALEE
Tra-Li
N 21
TRALEE
BAY
Blennerville
Derrymore
N 86
0 — 2 — 4 km
0 — 2,5 miles

Access Accès : Fenit Road, 12 km NW of Tralee
Map 2 on page 696 Carte 2 Page 696

766

Tramore is first and foremost an impressive site by the sea, which in the past caused more than a few problems in stormy weather. The present course has no links holes and is much better protected. The clay soil and heathery terrain drain the course well owing to its elevated position, and the sloping terrain makes an easy walk. This is a driver's course, where long-hitters have an obvious advantage. However, while they can open their shoulders on the first few holes, they will need to keep on the straight and narrow coming home, where the course gets much narrower. Generally speaking, the hazards (especially trees) are placed to catch wayward shots, and players lacking power should avoid the back-tees. Tramore is suitable for players of all levels, but there is just a touch of extra difficulty on the last four holes, especially on the 16th, where a little stream comes into play rather dangerously.

Tramore, c'est d'abord une situation impressionnante en bord de mer, qui a posé autrefois bien des problèmes lors de grandes tempêtes. Le parcours actuel n'a pas de trous de links, il est beaucoup mieux protégé. Le sol d'argile et de terre de bruyère est bien drainant en raison de sa situation surélevée, et les pentes du terrain sont assez favorables à la marche. C'est un parcours de driver où les joueurs longs seront évidemment avantagés, mais s'ils pourront se déchaîner dans les premiers trous, ils devront aussi être droits vers la fin, bien plus étroite. En règle générale, les obstacles (surtout les arbres) sont placés pour recevoir les coups écartés, les joueurs pas trop puissants auront intérêt à ne pas jouer des départs arrière. Tramore convient à tous les niveaux de jeu, avec une nuance de difficulté supplémentaire sur les quatre derniers trous, particulièrement au 16, où un ruisseau vient en jeu de manière dangereuse.

Tramore Golf Club

Newtown Hill
IRL - TRAMORE, Co Waterford

Office	Secrétariat	(353) 051 - 386 170
Pro shop	Pro-shop	(353) 051 - 381 706
Fax	Fax	(353) 051 - 390 961
Situation	Situation	

10 km from Waterford City (pop. 40 328)

Annual closure	Fermeture annnuelle	no
Weekly closure	Fermeture hebdomadaire	no

Fees main season
Tarifs haute saison 18 holes

	Week days Semaine	We/Bank holidays We/Férié
Individual Individuel	IR£ 25	IR£ 30
Couple Couple	IR£ 50	IR£ 60

Caddy	Caddy	IR£ 10/18 holes
Electric Trolley	Chariot électrique	no
Buggy	Voiturette	IR£ 20/18 holes
Clubs	Clubs	IR£ 8/18 holes

Credit cards Cartes de crédit
VISA - MasterCard

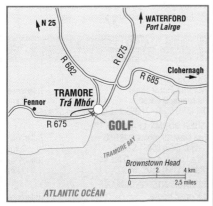

Access Accès : Cork → Tramore. Left junction,
outcoast road to top of the hill
Map 2 on page 697 Carte 2 Page 697

GOLF COURSE PARCOURS
13/20

Site	Site	
Maintenance	Entretien	
Architect	Architecte	Capt. Tippett
Type	Type	seaside course, parkland
Relief	Relief	
Water in play	Eau en jeu	
Exp. to wind	Exposé au vent	
Trees in play	Arbres en jeu	

Scorecard Carte de score	Chp. Chp.	Mens Mess.	Ladies Da.
Length Long.	6055	5871	5146
Par	72	72	75

Advised golfing ability	0	12	24	36
Niveau de jeu recommandé				

Hcp required Handicap exigé no

CLUB HOUSE & AMENITIES
CLUB HOUSE ET ANNEXES
7/10

Pro shop	Pro-shop	
Driving range	Practice	
Sheltered	couvert	no
On grass	sur herbe	yes
Putting-green	putting-green	yes
Pitching-green	pitching green	no

HOTEL FACILITIES
ENVIRONNEMENT HOTELIER
6/10

HOTELS HÔTELS

O'Sheds Hotel — Tramore
14 rooms, D IR£ 55 — 1.5 km
Tel (353) 051 - 381 246, Fax (353) 051 - 390 144

Grand Hotel — Tramore
80 rooms, D IR£ 68 — 1.5 km
Tel (353) 051 - 381 414, Fax (353) 051 - 386 428

The Majestic Hotel — Tramore
57 rooms, D IR£ 33 — 1.5 km
Tel (353) 051 - 381 761, Fax (353) 051 - 381 766

RESTAURANTS RESTAURANT

Pine Rooms — Tramore
Tel (353) 051 - 381 683 — 2 km

Esquire — Tramore
Tel (353) 051 - 386 237 — 2 km

767

This has long been one of Ireland's very good inland courses (it is over 100 years old). Reviewed by James Braid in 1926, it has been rejuvenated by Paddy Merrigan and given a planting programme involving 5,000 trees to add to the surrounding forest (oak and beech trees). So trees should become an even more significant factor here, alongside the classic bunkers and a meandering stream. The shape of the fairways brings the rough into play in a very honest way, only really penalising the truly wayward shot. The clearly visible hazards clearly show the best way forward, a friendly gesture which is repeated right around this very open and forthright course. And even though yardage is low, this is still a course where scoring can be difficult; you need to be very accurate to get to a good position on averagely sized greens, which pitch and bite nicely. This is a flat course, and an interesting day's golf.

C'est depuis longtemps (il est centenaire) l'un des très bons parcours inland. Revu par James Braid en 1926, il fait l'objet d'un rajeunissement par Paddy Merrigan, et d'un programme de plantations de 5.000 arbres, alors que la forêt l'entoure (chênes et hêtres). Les arbres devraient donc devenir un facteur encore plus important, à côté des bunkers classiques et des méandres d'un ruisseau. Le dessin des fairways met en jeu le rough, mais de façon très honnête, ne pénalisant vraiment que les coups très écartés. Les obstacles bien visibles indiquent clairement la ligne de jeu, cet aspect amical se confirme sur ce parcours d'une grande franchise. Il reste cependant difficile d'y réaliser un très bon score, même si la longueur est réduite : il faut beaucoup de précision pour être en bonne position sur des greens de taille moyenne, mais assez réceptifs. Si l'on ajoute que ce parcours est plat, le détour est intéressant.

Tullamore Golf Club
Brookfield
IRL - TULLAMORE, Co Offaly

Office	Secrétariat	(353) 0506 - 21 439
Pro shop	Pro-shop	(353) 0506 - 51 757
Fax	Fax	(353) 0506 - 51 757
Situation	Situation	

90 km from Dublin (pop. 859 976)
2 km from Tullamore(pop. 8 622)

Annual closure	Fermeture annnuelle	no
Weekly closure	Fermeture hebdomadaire	no

Fees main season
Tarifs haute saison 18 holes

	Week days Semaine	We/Bank holidays We/Férié
Individual Individuel	IR£ 11	IR£ 13
Couple Couple	IR£ 22	IR£ 26

Caddy	Caddy	on request/IR£ 15
Electric Trolley	Chariot électrique	no
Buggy	Voiturette	no
Clubs	Clubs	IR£ 10/18 holes
Credit cards Cartes de crédit		no

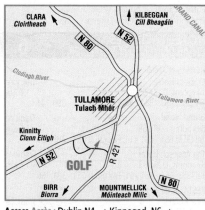

Access Accès : Dublin N4 → Kinnegad. N6 → Kilbeggan. N52 → Tullamore. R421 → Kinnitty, 2 km from Tullamore
Map 2 on page 697 Carte 2 Page 697

GOLF COURSE
PARCOURS
15/20

Site	Site	
Maintenance	Entretien	
Architect	Architecte	James Braid Paddy Merrigan
Type	Type	parkland
Relief	Relief	
Water in play	Eau en jeu	
Exp. to wind	Exposé au vent	
Trees in play	Arbres en jeu	

Scorecard Carte de score	Chp. Chp.	Mens Mess.	Ladies Da.
Length Long.	5779	5555	5070
Par	71	71	74

Advised golfing ability		0	12	24	36
Niveau de jeu recommandé					
Hcp required	Handicap exigé	no			

CLUB HOUSE & AMENITIES
CLUB HOUSE ET ANNEXES
6/10

Pro shop	Pro-shop	
Driving range	Practice	
Sheltered	couvert	no
On grass	sur herbe	yes
Putting-green	putting-green	yes
Pitching-green	pitching green	yes

HOTEL FACILITIES
ENVIRONNEMENT HOTELIER
5/10

HOTELS HÔTELS
Moorhill House Hotel — Tullamore
12 rooms, D IR£ 50 — 3 km
Tel (353) 0506 - 21 395, Fax (353) 0506 - 52 424

GUEST ROOMS CHAMBRES D'HÔTE
Sea Dew, 10 rooms, D IR£ 50 — Tullamore
Tel/fax (353) 0506 - 52 054 — 2 km
Pine Lodge, 4 rooms, D IR£ 44 — Tullamore
Tel/fax (353) 0506 - 51 927 — 2 km

RESTAURANTS RESTAURANT
Moorhill House — Tullamore
Tel (353) 0506 - 21 395 — 2 km
Sli Dala — Kinnitty
Tel (353) 0509 - 37 318 — 20 km

768

The first nine holes, designed by the great Willie Park Jnr., were completed by the no less great James Braid. From these two we would have expected a course to resist the skilled player and show a kinder face to the less experienced golfer. This is indeed the case, but today its yardage might seem a little on the short side. Likewise, although the fairway bunkers are strategically well placed, their design has faded over the years. This is perfect on a day when you want golf to be fun. In contrast, the green-side bunkers are well-placed to gather the wayward shot, and you will need to play some sharp short and medium irons. The greens are medium-sized, slightly contoured and are virtually all elevated above ground level, thus emphasising the need for accuracy. This pleasant course leaves a pleasant memory thanks to the 18th hole, a downhill par 4 with a splendid scenic view from the tee.

Les neuf premiers trous conçus par le grand Willie Park Jr ont été complétés par le non moins grand James Braid. On pouvait attendre d'eux un parcours résistant aux efforts des joueurs de haut niveau, et plus amical pour les moins expérimentés. C'est effectivement le cas, mais on peut trouver aujourd'hui sa longueur insuffisante, de même que, si le placement des bunkers de fairway est très stratégique, leur dessin s'est affadi au cours des années. Le jour où l'on a envie que le golf soit amusant, c'est parfait ! En revanche, les bunkers de green sont bien placés pour accueillir les coups insuffisants de précision, et l'on devra bien toucher ses petits et moyens fers. Les greens sont de surface moyenne, faiblement ondulés, mais ils sont pratiquement tous au-dessus du niveau du sol, ce qui accentue la nécessité d'être précis. De ce plaisant parcours, on retiendra le 18, un par 4 en descente avec une vue panoramique splendide depuis le départ.

Waterford Golf Club
IRL - NEWRATH, Co Waterford

Office	Secrétariat	(353) 051 - 876 748
Pro shop	Pro-shop	(353) 051 - 854 256
Fax	Fax	(353) 051 - 853 405
Situation	Situation	

3 km from Waterford (pop. 40 328)

Annual closure	Fermeture annnuelle	no
Weekly closure	Fermeture hebdomadaire	no

Fees main season
Tarifs haute saison 18 holes

	Week days Semaine	We/Bank holidays We/Férié
Individual Individuel	IR£ 22	IR£ 25
Couple Couple	IR£ 44	IR£ 50

Caddy	Caddy	on request/IR£ 10
Electric Trolley	Chariot électrique	IR£ 7
Buggy	Voiturette	IR£ 20/18 holes
Clubs	Clubs	IR£ 10

Credit cards Cartes de crédit		no

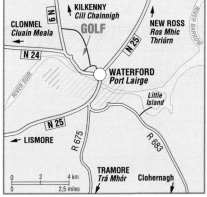

Access Accès : Waterford, N9 → Dublin. Golf 3 km
Map 2 on page 697 Carte 2 Page 697

GOLF COURSE
PARCOURS

14/20

Site	Site	■■■■■
Maintenance	Entretien	■■■■■
Architect	Architecte	Willie Park Jr James Braid
Type	Type	parkland
Relief	Relief	
Water in play	Eau en jeu	■
Exp. to wind	Exposé au vent	■
Trees in play	Arbres en jeu	■■■■

Scorecard Carte de score	Chp. Chp.	Mens Mess.	Ladies Da.
Length Long.	5722	5491	5168
Par	71	71	74

Advised golfing ability	0	12	24	36
Niveau de jeu recommandé				
Hcp required	Handicap exigé	no		

CLUB HOUSE & AMENITIES
CLUB HOUSE ET ANNEXES

6/10

Pro shop	Pro-shop	■■■■
Driving range	Practice	■■
Sheltered	couvert	no
On grass	sur herbe	yes
Putting-green	putting-green	yes
Pitching-green	pitching green	no

HOTEL FACILITIES
ENVIRONNEMENT HOTELIER

6/10

HOTELS HÔTELS

Tower Hotel — Waterford
141 rooms, D IR£ 85 — 5 km
Tel (353) 051 - 875 801, Fax (353) 051 - 870 129

Granville Hotel — Waterford
74 rooms, D IR£ 72 — 5 km
Tel (353) 051 - 55 111, Fax (353) 051 - 870 307

Jurys Hotel — Waterford
98 rooms, D IR£ 90 — 4 km
Tel (353) 051 - 832 111, Fax (353) 051 - 832 863

RESTAURANTS RESTAURANT

Granville Hotel — Waterford
Tel (353) 051 - 855 111 — 5 km

Prendiville's — Waterford
Tel (353) 051 - 78 851 — 7 km

A few minutes on a ferry to cross the Suir river, and there you are in a sanctuary of peace and quiet where, if you break into your piggy bank, you can enjoy a dream stay at the on-site hotel and admire some of the walls, which date back to the middle ages. This is perhaps not the course where you would spend the rest of your golfing days, but despite its young age it is in excellent condition and shouldn't be overlooked when in the region. The architects have worked wonders with the physical relief (none too hilly) and the trees which neatly demarcate the holes. This is not really a championship course, but the hazards have been placed to worry the very good players more than the average week-end golfer, who will, or should, have fun here. The large greens make it essential to choose the right club to get close to the pin. A number of water hazards add to the course's appeal.

Quelques minutes de ferry pour traverser la rivière Suir, et vous voilà dans une enclave de tranquillité où vous pourrez faire un séjour de rêve à l'hôtel sur place (certains des murs remontent au Moyen-Age) si vous cassez un peu la tirelire... Le parcours n'est peut-être pas celui que l'on choisirait pour passer le reste de sa vie, mais il est en très bon état malgré sa jeunesse, et ne saurait être ignoré quand on visite la région. Les architectes ont tiré un excellent parti des reliefs (peu importants) du terrain, et des nombreux arbres pour définir les trous dans l'espace. Il ne s'agit pas vraiment d'un parcours de championnat, mais les obstacles ont été placés pour perturber plutôt les très bons joueurs que les joueurs moyens, qui s'y amuseront beaucoup. Les greens, de grande dimension, obligent à faire les bons choix de clubs pour se trouver près des drapeaux. Les obstacles d'eau ajoutent à l'intérêt de ce parcours.

Waterford Castle Golf Club

The Island
IRL - BALLYNAKILL, Co Waterford

Office	Secrétariat	(353) 051 - 871 633
Pro shop	Pro-shop	(353) 051 - 841 569
Fax	Fax	(353) 051 - 871 634
Situation	Situation	

1,5 km from Waterford (pop. 40 328)

Annual closure	Fermeture annnuelle	no
Weekly closure	Fermeture hebdomadaire	no

Fees main season
Tarifs haute saison 18 holes

	Week days Semaine	We/Bank holidays We/Férié
Individual Individuel	IR£ 24	IR£ 27
Couple Couple	IR£ 48	IRL 54

IR£ 16.50 before 10 a.m.

Caddy	Caddy	on request/IR£ 15
Electric Trolley	Chariot électrique	no
Buggy	Voiturette	IR£ 20
Clubs	Clubs	IR£ 10

Credit cards Cartes de crédit
VISA - MasterCard - AMEX

GOLF COURSE
PARCOURS   **14**/20

Site	Site	■■■■■
Maintenance	Entretien	■■■■
Architect	Architecte	Des Smyth Declan Brannigan
Type	Type	parkland
Relief	Relief	■■■
Water in play	Eau en jeu	■■■
Exp. to wind	Exposé au vent	■■■
Trees in play	Arbres en jeu	■■■■

Scorecard Carte de score	Chp. Chp.	Mens Mess.	Ladies Da.
Length Long.	6209	5810	5073
Par	72	72	72

Advised golfing ability Niveau de jeu recommandé	0	12	24	36

Hcp required   Handicap exigé   no

CLUB HOUSE & AMENITIES
CLUB HOUSE ET ANNEXES   **5**/10

Pro shop	Pro-shop	■■■■
Driving range	Practice	■■■
Sheltered	couvert	no
On grass	sur herbe	yes
Putting-green	putting-green	yes
Pitching-green	pitching green	yes

HOTEL FACILITIES
ENVIRONNEMENT HOTELIER   **6**/10

HOTELS HÔTELS
Waterford Castle Hotel   on site
19 rooms, D IR£ 200
Tel (353) 051 - 878 203, Fax (353) 051 - 879 316

Tower Hotel   Waterford
141 rooms, D IR£ 85   4 km
Tel (353) 051 - 875 801, Fax (353) 051 - 870 129

Granville Hotel   Waterford
74 rooms, D IR£ 72   4 km
Tel (353) 051 - 55 111, Fax (353) 051 - 870 307

RESTAURANTS RESTAURANT
Dwyer's   Waterford
Tel (353) 051 - 77 478   4 km

Waterford Castle   on site
Tel (353) 051 - 878 203

Access Accès : Waterford, R683. 4 km Ballinakill Road, private ferry to the island
Map 2 on page 697 Carte 2 Page 697

770

The pleasure of playing Waterville starts on the road, the "Ring of Kerry", which you first take from the south, from Killarney. The first nine holes unwind over very flat countryside, but the remainder, snaking their way through sand dunes, are impressive to say the least. The design work, no matter how natural it might look today, was considerable: there are no blind holes, virtually flat fairways and almost no dog-legs (except the 16th). But with sometimes blustery side-winds, you need to know how to flight the ball to keep it in play. If we add to this the fact that the putting surfaces are a little less enigmatic than those at Ballybunion, for example, the overall problem here stems from its length (a "man's course", as they say), plus the technical side to the second shot once the drive has avoided the rough and a number of fairway bunkers. A great course, to be played off the front tees.

Le plaisir de jouer Waterville commence sur la route, le "Ring of Kerry" qu'il faut prendre d'abord par le sud, depuis Killarney. Les neuf premiers trous se déroulent dans un paysage de campagne très plat, mais la suite, insinuée dans les dunes, est impressionnante. Le travail architectural, pour naturel qu'il paraisse aujourd'hui, a été important : pas de trous aveugles, des fairways quasiment plats, quasiment aucun dog-leg (sauf le 16). Mais il faudra savoir travailler la balle pour la garder en jeu, avec des vents latéraux souvent violents. Si l'on ajoute que les surfaces de greens ne sont pas aussi énigmatiques qu'elles peuvent l'être à Ballybunion par exemple, la difficulté générale de Waterville tient certes beaucoup à sa longueur, comme on l'a dit ("un parcours d'hommes" !), on peut aussi parler de la technicité des seconds coups, une fois que le drive a évité les roughs et certains bunkers de fairway. Un grand parcours, à jouer des départs avancés.

Waterville
IRL - WATERVILLE, Co Kerry

Office	Secrétariat	(353) 066 - 74 102
Pro shop	Pro-shop	(353) 066 - 74 102
Fax	Fax	(353) 066 - 74 482
Situation	Situation	

4 km from Waterville (pop. 463)

Annual closure	Fermeture annnuelle	no
Weekly closure	Fermeture hebdomadaire	no

Fees main season
Tarifs haute saison 18 holes

	Week days Semaine	We/Bank holidays We/Férié
Individual Individuel	IR£ 40	IR£ 40
Couple Couple	IR£ 80	IR£ 80

Caddy	Caddy	IR£ 15/18 holes
Electric Trolley	Chariot électrique	no
Buggy	Voiturette	IR£ 35/18 holes
Clubs	Clubs	IR£ 10/18 holes

Credit cards Cartes de crédit
VISA - Eurocard - MasterCard - AMEX - DC

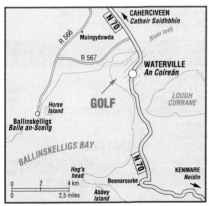

Access Accès : • Killarney N71 → Kenmate. N70 → Parknasilla, Waterville • Killarney → Killorglin. N70 → Glenbeigh, Cahirciveen, Waterville
Map 2 on page 696 Carte 2 Page 696

GOLF COURSE
PARCOURS
17 /20

Site	Site	▬▬▬▬▭
Maintenance	Entretien	▬▬▬▬▭
Architect	Architecte	Eddie Hackett John A. Mulcahy
Type	Type	links
Relief	Relief	
Water in play	Eau en jeu	▬▬▭▭▭
Exp. to wind	Exposé au vent	▬▬▬▬▭
Trees in play	Arbres en jeu	▬▭▭▭▭

Scorecard Carte de score	Chp. Chp.	Mens Mess.	Ladies Da.
Length Long.	6430	5954	4789
Par	72	73	73

Advised golfing ability		0 12 24 36
Niveau de jeu recommandé		▬▬▬▬▬▭
Hcp required	Handicap exigé	28 Men, 36 Ladies

CLUB HOUSE & AMENITIES
CLUB HOUSE ET ANNEXES
6 /10

Pro shop	Pro-shop	▬▬▬▭▭
Driving range	Practice	▬▬▬▭▭
Sheltered	couvert	no
On grass	sur herbe	yes
Putting-green	putting-green	yes
Pitching-green	pitching green	yes

HOTEL FACILITIES
ENVIRONNEMENT HOTELIER
7 /10

HOTELS HÔTELS

Club Med — Waterville
88 rooms, D IR£ 110 — 3 km
Tel (353) 066 - 74 133, Fax (353) 066 - 74 483

Butler Arms — Waterville
35 rooms, D IR£ 110 — 2 km
Tel (353) 066 - 74 144, Fax (353) 066 - 74 520

Bayview Hotel — Waterville
10 rooms, D IR£ 48 — 2 km
Tel (353) 066 - 74 122, Fax (353) 066 - 74 680

RESTAURANTS RESTAURANT

Sheilin Seafood — Waterville
Tel (353) 066 - 74 231 — nearby

Villa Maria — Watervillen
Tel (353) 066 - 74 635 — nearby

771

The Pratt family, all fanatical golfers, made their dream come true by building this course, which they continue to run today. This sort of initiative would bring a smile to anyone's face, and the choice of Eddie Hackett as architect has led to a course nicely tailored to the pleasantly rolling landscape without any extravagant earth-works, and a thought spared for golfers of all levels. The setting is calm indeed, on the banks of the Brickey River, which sometimes comes into play rather dangerously. But it really is difficult to design a course for all golfers, and while mid-handicappers will love this, the 24+ hacker will probably suffer (they shouldn't bother counting their score). To score, you need to cope well with holes 12 to 16 where water, trees and bushes play a crucial part. The splendid environment of small mountains also plays a significant role in the charm of this site.

Fanatique de golf, la famille Pratt a transformé son rêve en réalité en construisant ce parcours qu'elle continue à diriger. On regarde avec sympathie ce genre d'initiative, et le choix d'Eddie Hackett comme architecte signi-fiait qu'il allait s'adapter à un terrain agréablement vallonné sans y faire de gigantesques terrassements, et qu'il penserait à tous les niveaux. La situation du golf est très tranquille, sur les rives de la Brickey River, qui vient parfois en jeu de manière menaçante. Il est très difficile de faire un parcours pour tous les joueurs et si les golfeurs moyens trouveront leur bonheur, les handicaps les plus élevés souffriront un peu (qu'ils ne comp-tent pas leur score). Pour y faire une bonne carte, il faudra en particulier bien négocier les trous 12 à 16, où l'eau, les arbres et les buissons jouent un rôle crucial. L'environnement splendide de petites montagnes joue un rôle important dans la séduction du lieu.

West Waterford Golf Club

Coolcormack
IRL - DUNGARVAN, Co. Waterford

Office	Secrétariat	(353) 058 - 43 216
Pro shop	Pro-shop	(353) 058 - 43 216
Fax	Fax	(353) 058 - 44 343
Situation	Situation	

5 km of Dungarvan (pop. 6920)

Annual closure	Fermeture annnuelle	no
Weekly closure	Fermeture hebdomadaire	no

Fees main season
Tarifs haute saison 18 holes

	Week days Semaine	We/Bank holidays We/Férié
Individual Individuel	IR£ 18	IR£ 22
Couple Couple	IR£ 36	IR£ 40

Caddy	Caddy	IR£ 10/18 holes
Electric Trolley	Chariot électrique	IR£ 5
Buggy	Voiturette	IR£ 20/18 holes
Clubs	Clubs	IR£ 8

Credit cards Cartes de crédit	no

772

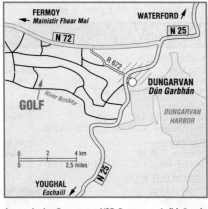

FERMOY ← Mainistir Fhear Maí	WATERFORD ↗

N 72
N 25
R 672
River Brickey
GOLF
DUNGARVAN
Dún Garbhán
DUNGARVAN
HARBOR

0   2   4 km
0   2,5 miles

N 25

YOUGHAL
Eochaill ↙

Access Accès : Dungarvan N25. By-pass on Aglish Road.
Map 2 on page 697 Carte 2 Page 697

GOLF COURSE / PARCOURS

12/20

Site	Site	
Maintenance	Entretien	
Architect	Architecte	Eddie Hackett
Type	Type	parkland
Relief	Relief	
Water in play	Eau en jeu	
Exp. to wind	Exposé au vent	
Trees in play	Arbres en jeu	

Scorecard Carte de score	Chp. Chp.	Mens Mess.	Ladies Da.
Length Long.	6162	5902	4773
Par	72	72	72

Advised golfing ability Niveau de jeu recommandé	0	12	24	36

Hcp required	Handicap exigé	Men 28, Ladies 36

CLUB HOUSE & AMENITIES / CLUB HOUSE ET ANNEXES

7/10

Pro shop	Pro-shop	
Driving range	Practice	
Sheltered	couvert	no
On grass	sur herbe	yes
Putting-green	putting-green	yes
Pitching-green	pitching green	yes

HOTEL FACILITIES / ENVIRONNEMENT HOTELIER

6/10

HOTELS HÔTELS

Park Hotel Dungarvan — Dungarvan
40 rooms, D IR£ 80 — 5 km
Tel (353) 058 - 42 899, Fax (353) 058 - 42 899

Lawlors — Dungarvan
89 rooms, D IR£ 60 — 5 km
Tel (353) 058 - 41 122, Fax (353) 058 - 41 000

Gold Coast Golf Hotel — Ballynacourty-Dungarvan
37 rooms, D IR£ 80 — 7 km
Tel (353) 058 - 42 249, Fax (353) 058 - 43 378

RESTAURANTS RESTAURANT

Mary's Restaurant — Dungarvan
Tel (353) 058 - 41 974 — 5 km

Richmond House — Cappoquin
Tel (353) 058 - 54 278 — 9 km

WESTPORT

15 | 7 | 7

Although located on the edge of Clew Bay, this is essentially a parkland course. For many players, it will be the opportunity to catch their breath between Connemara and Carn or Enniscrone, and to find a little shelter when the wind is playing havoc elsewhere. The views here are just magnificent, between the bay and the blessed mountain of Croagh Patrick, where Ireland's patron saint spent 40 days of fasting and prayer. We wouldn't ask golfers to do the same, as they'll need all their strength to cope with this top-class course. The only slight shortcoming is the relative blandness of the first few holes, but the challenge grows stronger on the way in, with a special mention going to the very pretty 14th, a par 3, and especially the 15th, a splendid and very long par 5 along the bay. The hazards are visibly in play and clear enough to make strategy pretty obvious on your first visit.

Bien qu'il soit situé en bordure de la Clew Bay, ce parcours présente un caractère de parc. Ce sera pour beaucoup de joueurs l'occasion de reprendre leur souffle entre Connemara et Carn ou Enniscrone, et de trouver quelque abri, quand le vent joue un rôle important. Les vues sont ici magnifiques, entre la baie et la "montagne sacrée", le Croagh Patrick, où le saint patron de l'Irlande aurait passé 40 jours de jeûne et de prières. On n'en demandera pas autant aux golfeurs, qui ont besoin de toutes leurs forces sur ce parcours de qualité. La seule nuance dans ce jugement, c'est la relative faiblesse des premiers trous, mais le challenge devient plus exigeant au retour, avec une mention particulière pour le 14, très joli par 3, et surtout le 15, un splendide par 5 très long en bordure de la baie. Les obstacles sont honnêtement en jeu, et assez visibles pour que la stratégie soit évidente dès la première visite.

Westport Golf Club
Carrowholly
IRL - WESTPORT, Co Mayo

Office	Secrétariat	(353) 098 - 28 262
Pro shop	Pro-shop	(353) 098 - 27 481
Fax	Fax	(353) 098 - 27 217
Situation	Situation	

16 km from Castlebar
32 km from Ballinrobe

Annual closure	Fermeture annnuelle	no
Weekly closure	Fermeture hebdomadaire	no

Fees main season
Tarifs haute saison 18 holes

	Week days Semaine	We/Bank holidays We/Férié
Individual Individuel	IR£ 18	IR£ 22.50
Couple Couple	IR£ 36	IR£ 45

Caddy	Caddy	on request / IR£ 12
Electric Trolley	Chariot électrique	IR£ 7/18 holes
Buggy	Voiturette	IR£ 20/18 holes
Clubs	Clubs	IR£ 12/18 holes

Credit cards Cartes de crédit	no

Access Accès : 4 km from Westport on Newport Road
Map 1 on page 694 Carte 1 Page 694

GOLF COURSE
PARCOURS
15/20

Site	Site	
Maintenance	Entretien	
Architect	Architecte	Fred Hawtree
Type	Type	seaside course, parkland
Relief	Relief	
Water in play	Eau en jeu	
Exp. to wind	Exposé au vent	
Trees in play	Arbres en jeu	

Scorecard Carte de score	Chp. Chp.	Mens Mess.	Ladies Da.
Length Long.	6355	6095	5233
Par	73	73	74

Advised golfing ability
Niveau de jeu recommandé   0   12   24   36

Hcp required	Handicap exigé	no

CLUB HOUSE & AMENITIES
CLUB HOUSE ET ANNEXES
7/10

Pro shop	Pro-shop	
Driving range	Practice	
Sheltered	couvert	no
On grass	sur herbe	yes
Putting-green	putting-green	yes
Pitching-green	pitching green	no

773

HOTEL FACILITIES
ENVIRONNEMENT HOTELIER
7/10

HOTELS HÔTELS
Hotel Westport   Westport
49 rooms, D IR£ 60   4 km
Tel (353) 098 - 25 122, Fax (353) 098 - 26 739

Railway Hotel   Westport
27 rooms, D IR£ 60   4 km
Tel (353) 098 - 25 166, Fax (353) 098 - 25 090

Westport Woods   Westport
57 rooms, D IR£ 90   3 km
Tel (353) 098 - 25 811, Fax (353) 098 - 26 224

RESTAURANTS RESTAURANT
Ardmore House   Westport
Tel (353) 098 - 25 994   4 km

The Moorings   Westport
Tel (353) 098 - 25 874   4 km

Woodenbrige is located in the very pretty Vale of Avoca, famous for its tweeds, and essential visiting in the spring when the cherry trees are in full blossom. You will be following in the footsteps of the poet Thomas Moore. Created 100 years ago, this fine course became very popular when Paddy Merrigan upgraded it to 18 holes in 1993. The only vegetation are the few trees, here and there (woods outline the course's boundaries), which come very much into play from time to time, but the main hazards are the bunkers (none too penalising) and water, notably the river Avoca, which naturally abounds in this region. There are no unpleasant surprises for visitors, as the difficulties are clearly visible from each tee and add to the course's overall honesty. There is no great need to flight your shots, and only the variety of approach shots (lofted or run) call for real talent.

Woodenbridge est situé dans la très jolie Vallée d'Avoca, célèbre pour ses tweeds, et qu'il faut voir au printemps, quand les cerisiers sont en fleurs : vous y suivrez les traces du poète Thomas Moore. Créé il y a cent ans, ce bon parcours est devenu très populaire quand Paddy Merrigan l'a porté à 18 trous en 1993. La seule végétation est ici constituée par des arbres çà et là (les bois marquant les limites du golf), ils sont parfois très en jeu, mais les obstacles principaux sont les bunkers (pas trop pénalisants quand on s'y retrouve) et des obstacles d'eau - notamment la rivière Avoca - naturellement abondants dans cette région. Les visiteurs ne risquent pas de mauvaises surprises, les difficultés sont bien visibles de chaque départ, ajoutant à la franchise générale du tracé. Il n'est pas utile de beaucoup travailler la balle, seule la variété des approches (balles levées ou balles roulées) exigeant un certain talent.

Woodenbridge Golf Club

Woodenbridge
IRL - ARKLOW, Co Wicklow

Office	Secrétariat	(353) 0402 - 35 202
Pro shop	Pro-shop	(353) 0402 - 35 202
Fax	Fax	(353) 0402 - 31 402
Situation	Situation	

74 km from Dublin (pop. 859 976)
7 km from Arklow

Annual closure	Fermeture annnuelle	no
Weekly closure	Fermeture hebdomadaire	no

Fees main season
Tarifs haute saison 18 holes

	Week days Semaine	We/Bank holidays We/Férié
Individual Individuel	IR£ 25	IR£ 30
Couple Couple	IR£ 50	IR£ 60

Caddy	Caddy	on request/IR£ 20
Electric Trolley	Chariot électrique	no
Buggy	Voiturette	no
Clubs	Clubs	no

Credit cards Cartes de crédit   no

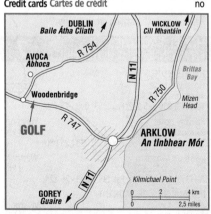

Access Accès : Dublin N11 South → Arklow. 7 km NW of Arklow on R747
Map 3 on page 698 Carte 3 Page 698

GOLF COURSE
PARCOURS

16/20

Site	Site	
Maintenance	Entretien	
Architect	Architecte	Paddy Merrigan, 1993
Type	Type	forest, parkland
Relief	Relief	
Water in play	Eau en jeu	
Exp. to wind	Exposé au vent	
Trees in play	Arbres en jeu	

Scorecard Carte de score	Chp. Chp.	Mens Mess.	Ladies Da.
Length Long.	6350	6074	5490
Par	71	71	72

Advised golfing ability	0	12	24	36
Niveau de jeu recommandé				

Hcp required   Handicap exigé   24 Men, 36 Ladies

CLUB HOUSE & AMENITIES
CLUB HOUSE ET ANNEXES

7/10

Pro shop	Pro-shop	
Driving range	Practice	
Sheltered	couvert	no
On grass	sur herbe	yes
Putting-green	putting-green	yes
Pitching-green	pitching green	no

HOTEL FACILITIES
ENVIRONNEMENT HOTELIER

6/10

HOTELS HÔTELS

Woodenbridge Hotel   Arklow
12 rooms, D IR£ 60   1 km
Tel (353) 0402 - 35 146, Fax (353) 0402 - 35 573

Valley Hotel   Woodenbridge
10 rooms, D IR£ 40   1 km
Tel (353) 0402 - 35 200, Fax (353) 0402 - 35 542

Arklow Bay Hotel   Arklow
38 rooms, D IR£ 50   7 km
Tel (353) 0402 - 32 309, Fax (353) 0402 - 32 300

RESTAURANTS RESTAURANT

Sheepwalk House   Avoca
Tel (353) 0402 - 35 189   8 km

Mitchell's   Laragh, Glendalough
Tel (353) 0404 - 45 302   28 km

774

If you have a whole day to spare, stop off on the Lahinch road for a great round of golf in a huge and moderately hilly park, full of country charm. This course is a typical product of modern architecture, with a few water hazards, including a big lake that is fully in play on the 7th, present on the 6th and 7th holes and extending onward to the 12th. There are only a few fairway bunkers, but their role of dissuasion is assumed more often by the trees here. The shape of the dog-legs calls ideally for flighted shots in both directions so as to be in a better position for the second shot and reach the well-designed greens without too much trouble. Here, you need a complete and consistent game, and are helped by the clearly staggered tee-boxes which allow everyone to play a round according to the shape of his or game. There is nothing exceptionally difficult on this pleasant and welcoming course, which is a good address.

Si vous disposez d'une grande journée, arrêtez vous sur la route de Lahinch pour une bonne partie de golf, dans un vaste parc au relief modéré, au charme très campagnard. Ce parcours est typique des architectures modernes, avec quelques obstacles d'eau, dont un grand lac venant fortement en jeu au 7, mais aussi au 6 et au 8, avant d'en retrouver la prolongation au 12. On trouve assez peu de bunkers de fairway, mais leur rôle de dissuasion est bien occupé par les arbres. La forme des dog-legs amène à travailler la balle dans les deux sens pour mieux négocier les coups suivants, et parvenir sans encombre sur des greens bien dessinés et bien construits. Il faut ici un jeu complet et cohérent, avec l'avantage de départs très bien étagés, permettant à chacun de se faire un parcours selon ses capacités du moment. Sans difficultés exceptionnelles, cette réalisation plaisante et très accueillante est une bonne adresse.

Woodstock Golf & Country Club

Shanaway Road
IRL - ENNIS, Co Clare

Office	Secrétariat	(353) 065 - 42 406
Pro shop	Pro-shop	(353) 065 - 42 463
Fax	Fax	(353) 065 - 20 304
Situation	Situation	

4 km from Ennis (pop. 13 730)

Annual closure	Fermeture annnuelle	no
Weekly closure	Fermeture hebdomadaire	no

Fees main season
Tarifs haute saison 18 holes

	Week days Semaine	We/Bank holidays We/Férié
Individual Individuel	IR£ 20	IR£ 20
Couple Couple	IR£ 40	IR£ 40

Caddy	Caddy	IR£ 12/18 holes
Electric Trolley	Chariot électrique	no
Buggy	Voiturette	IR£ 20/18 holes
Clubs	Clubs	IR£ 10/18 holes

Credit cards Cartes de crédit
VISA - MasterCard

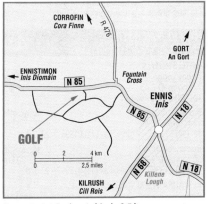

Access Accès : Ennis → Lahinch. 2.5 km, signposted left at pub.
Map 2 on page 696 Carte 2 Page 696

GOLF COURSE
PARCOURS

13/20

Site	Site	
Maintenance	Entretien	
Architect	Architecte	Arthur Spring
Type	Type	inland, parkland
Relief	Relief	
Water in play	Eau en jeu	
Exp. to wind	Exposé au vent	
Trees in play	Arbres en jeu	

Scorecard Carte de score	Chp. Chp.	Mens Mess.	Ladies Da.
Length Long.	5879	5513	5062
Par	71	71	73

Advised golfing ability		0 12 24 36
Niveau de jeu recommandé		
Hcp required	Handicap exigé	no

CLUB HOUSE & AMENITIES
CLUB HOUSE ET ANNEXES

5/10

Pro shop	Pro-shop	
Driving range	Practice	
Sheltered	couvert	no
On grass	sur herbe	yes
Putting-green	putting-green	yes
Pitching-green	pitching green	no

775

HOTEL FACILITIES
ENVIRONNEMENT HOTELIER

6/10

HOTELS HÔTELS

Templegate Hotel	Ennis
34 rooms, D IR£ 65	2 km
Tel (353) 065 - 23 300, Fax (353) 065 - 23 322	
Auburn Lodge	Ennis
100 rooms, D IR£ 76	2 km
Tel (353) 065 - 21 247, Fax (353) 065 - 21 202	
Old Grand Hotel	Ennis
58 rooms, D IR£ 100	2 km
Tel (353) 065 - 28 127, Fax (353) 065 - 28 112	

RESTAURANTS RESTAURANT

The Four Seasons	Ennis
Tel (353) 065 - 42 406	on site
Branigans	Ennis
Tel (353) 065 - 20 211	2 km

In this region, occupied by the Vikings, pirates and smugglers, you will also find the vestiges of a castle built by the Normans alongside the club-house. Other good news for non-golfers is the nearby Strangford Lough, a real sanctuary for birds. But back to golf. As the course runs impressively atop coastal cliffs, this is one of the country's finest sites, with a view as far as the Isle of Man (on a clear day). Worth seeing, and worth playing, too. An age-old course from an unknown architect, this is a good layout and links course with no steep relief and none of those enormous dunes that can have such an effect on easily influenced players. You need to play several rounds to grasp the subtleties of the course, because there are quite a few blind drives and so a high risk of ending up in the rough or bushes, that do your card no good at all. And that's no to mention the exposure to the wind, which hardly helps matters. The bunkers are rather small, as are the greens. First time out, have fun with a match-play round.

Dans ce pays occupé par les Vikings, les pirates et les contrebandiers, on trouve aussi, à côté du Club-house, les vestiges d'un château bâti par les Normands. A proximité, le Strangford Lough est un véritable sanctuaire d'oiseaux. Et comme la situation du parcours sur de hautes falaises est impressionnante, c'est un des grands sites du pays, avec une vue jusqu'à l'Ile de Man (quand il fait beau). A voir mais aussi à jouer. Centenaire, et d'architecte inconnu, c'est un bon tracé, un links au relief très modéré, mais sans les dunes énormes qui peuvent ailleurs effrayer les joueurs influençables. Il faut plusieurs visites pour en comprendre les subtilités, on trouve pas mal de départs aveugles, avec le risque de se retrouver dans un rough ou des buissons dangereux pour le score. Et l'exposition au vent n'arrange rien en ce domaine. Les bunkers sont assez petits, mais les greens aussi... La première fois, amusez-vous en match-play.

Ardglass Golf Club
Castle Place
NIR - ARDGLASS, Co Down BT30 7 TP

Office	Secrétariat	(44) 01396 - 841 219
Pro shop	Pro-shop	(44) 01396 - 841 022
Fax	Fax	(44) 01396 - 841 841
Situation	Situation	

11 km from Downpatrick
48 km from Belfast (pop. 279 237)

Annual closure	Fermeture annnuelle	no
Weekly closure	Fermeture hebdomadaire	Monday Restaurant

Fees main season
Tarifs haute saison 18 holes

	Week days Semaine	We/Bank holidays We/Férié
Individual Individuel	£ 17	£ 22
Couple Couple	£ 34	£ 44

Caddy	Caddy	on request/£ 12
Electric Trolley	Chariot électrique	no
Buggy	Voiturette	no
Clubs	Clubs	£ 6

Credit cards Cartes de crédit   no

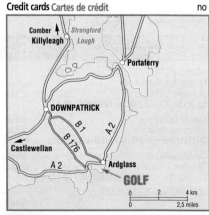

Access Accès : Belfast, A24, A7 to Downpatrick.
B1 to Ardglass. → Golf
Map 1 on page 695 Carte 1 Page 695

GOLF COURSE
PARCOURS   14/20

Site	Site	
Maintenance	Entretien	
Architect	Architecte	
Type	Type	seaside course
Relief	Relief	
Water in play	Eau en jeu	
Exp. to wind	Exposé au vent	
Trees in play	Arbres en jeu	

Scorecard Carte de score	Chp. Chp.	Mens Mess.	Ladies Da.
Length Long.	5500	5500	4765
Par	70	70	70

Advised golfing ability Niveau de jeu recommandé	0 12 24 36
Hcp required Handicap exigé	Men 24, Ladies 36

CLUB HOUSE & AMENITIES
CLUB HOUSE ET ANNEXES   6/10

Pro shop	Pro-shop	
Driving range	Practice	
Sheltered	couvert	no
On grass	sur herbe	yes
Putting-green	putting-green	yes
Pitching-green	pitching green	no

HOTEL FACILITIES
ENVIRONNEMENT HOTELIER   4/10

HOTELS HÔTELS
Abbey Lodge   Downpatrick
22 rooms, D £ 45   11 km
Tél (44) 01396 - 614 511

Brook Cottage   Newcastle
12 rooms, D £ 46   30 km
Tel (44) 013967 - 22 204, Fax (44) 013967 - 22 193

Burrendale Hotel   Newcastle
50 rooms, D £ 80   30 km
Tel (44) 013967 - 22 599, Fax (44) 013967 - 22 328

RESTAURANTS RESTAURANT
Aldo's   Ardglass
Tel (44) 01396 - 841 315   1 km

Seaford Inn   Seaford
Tel (44) 01396 - 812 232   22 km

776

BANGOR

The course is located virtually in the city of Bangor, David Feherty's home town, where, so they say, you'll see the finest landscapes in the whole of Northern Ireland. Bird-watching enthusiasts are just a few minutes away from the boat that takes them to the Copeland Islands, inhabited only by birds, and you are not far from the pretty town of Newtownards. Inveterate golfers, on the other hand, will enjoy playing on this course, rather off the beaten track, a little dated in terms of yardage but great fun to play all the same. James Braid laid out a few elevated greens, others being multi-tiered, plus a few fairway bunkers that are both strategic and punishing. Some of the dog-legs (the 5th, 13th, 14th and 15th holes) call for very accurate driving. In all, a course where you would probably not spend the rest of your life playing, but a good addition to the region's other courses.

Le golf est situé pratiquement dans la ville de Bangor, ville natale du champion David Feherty, où l'on trouve paraît-il les plus beaux paysages d'Irlande du Nord. Les amateurs d'ornithologie n'auront que quelques minutes à faire pour embarquer à destination des Copeland Islands, où ne vivent plus que des oiseaux, ou pour découvrir la jolie ville de Newtownards. Quant aux golfeurs invétérés, ils pourront s'exprimer sur ce parcours hors des sentiers battus, un peu daté en ce qui concerne la longueur, mais très amusant au demeurant. James Braid y a disposé quelques greens surélevés, d'autres à double plateau, et quelques bunkers de fairway à la fois stratégiques et punitifs. Certains dog-legs (5, 13, 14 et 15) demandent un driving très précis pour être maîtrisés. Au total, un parcours sur lequel on ne jouerait peut-être pas toute sa vie, mais un bon complément aux autres parcours de la région.

Bangor Golf Club
Broadway
NIR - BANGOR, Co. Down BT20 4RH

Office	Secrétariat	(44) 01247 - 270 922
Pro shop	Pro-shop	(44) 01247 - 462 164
Fax	Fax	(44) 01247 - 453 394
Situation	Situation	

10 km from Newtownards
20 km from Belfast (pop. 279 237)

Annual closure	Fermeture annnuelle	no
Weekly closure	Fermeture hebdomadaire	no

Fees main season
Tarifs haute saison 18 holes

	Week days Semaine	We/Bank holidays We/Férié
Individual Individuel	£ 17.50	£ 25
Couple Couple	£ 35	£ 50

Saturday: members only

Caddy	Caddy	no
Electric Trolley	Chariot électrique	no
Buggy	Voiturette	no
Clubs	Clubs	£ 10/18 holes

Credit cards Cartes de crédit	VISA - Access

Access Accès : Belfast, A2 → Bangor
Map 1 on page 695 Carte 1 Page 695

GOLF COURSE
PARCOURS 14/20

Site	Site	▬▬▬▬
Maintenance	Entretien	▬▬▬
Architect	Architecte	James Braid
Type	Type	inland
Relief	Relief	▬▬
Water in play	Eau en jeu	▬
Exp. to wind	Exposé au vent	▬▬▬▬
Trees in play	Arbres en jeu	▬▬

Scorecard Carte de score	Chp. Chp.	Mens Mess.	Ladies Da.
Length Long.	5781	5577	5113
Par	71	71	72

Advised golfing ability	0	12	24	36
Niveau de jeu recommandé		▬▬▬▬▬		
Hcp required Handicap exigé	no			

CLUB HOUSE & AMENITIES
CLUB HOUSE ET ANNEXES 6/10

Pro shop	Pro-shop	▬▬▬
Driving range	Practice	▬▬
Sheltered	couvert	no
On grass	sur herbe	yes
Putting-green	putting-green	yes
Pitching-green	pitching green	yes

777

HOTEL FACILITIES
ENVIRONNEMENT HOTELIER 6/10

HOTELS HÔTELS

Royal Hotel	Bangor
50 rooms, D £ 72	1.5 km
Tel (44) 01247 - 271 866, Fax (44) 01247 - 467 810	
Crawfordsburn Inn	Crawfordsburn
33 rooms, D £ 90	5 km
Tel (44) 01247 - 853 255, Fax (44) 01247 - 852 775	
Sands Hotel	Bangor
12 rooms, D £ 75	1.5 km
Tel (44) 01247 - 270 696, Fax (44) 01247 - 271 678	

RESTAURANTS RESTAURANT

Shanks	Bangor
Tel (44) 01247 - 853 313	8 km
Jenny Watts	Bangor
Tel (44) 01247 - 270 401	2.5 km

The energetic rejuvenation of this course has turned it into one of the region's hidden gems in the region of Belfast, without ever affecting the intelligence of Harry Colt's original layout. Very reasonable in length, it is a real pleasure to play in this lush green park, well protected from the city noise by woods and thick curtains of trees, which also separate the fairways and call for unfailing accuracy. Despite everything, the fairways are of a fair width, and while there are fairway bunkers, their design rarely makes them dangerous. Ditches on the 10th and 12th are the only water hazards, but they play a key role. The course is generally not too hilly, except on the 3rd and 17th, the latter being a part of a very difficult finish, where many a card can fall apart. Fun to play and very prettily landscaped, Belvoir Park is rated amongst the country's finest inland courses.

Le rajeunissement énergique de ce parcours en a fait l'un des petits bijoux cachés de la région de Belfast, sans pour autant altérer l'intelligence du tracé original de Harry Colt, d'une longueur très raisonnable. C'est un plaisir d'évoluer dans ce grand parc en pleine verdure, bien protégé des bruits de la ville par de petits bois et d'épais rideaux d'arbres, séparant bien les fairways, tout en impliquant une certaine précision. Malgré tout, les fairways restent d'une largeur très acceptable, et si les bunkers y sont présents, leur dessin les rend rarement très dangereux. Les fossés au 10 et au 12 sont les seuls obstacles d'eau, mais ils y jouent un rôle fondamental. Le parcours est généralement de relief très modéré, sauf au 3 et au 17, ce dernier trou faisant partie d'un "finish" très difficile, où bien des cartes vont s'alourdir. Amusant à jouer, très joliment paysagé, Belvoir Park figure parmi les très bons parcours "inland" du pays.

Belvoir Park Golf Club

Church Road, Newtownbreda
NIR - BELFAST BT8 4AN

Office	Secrétariat	(44) 01232 - 491 693
Pro shop	Pro-shop	(44) 01232 - 646 714
Fax	Fax	(44) 01232 - 646 113
Situation	Situation	

5 km S from Belfast (pop. 279 237)

Annual closure	Fermeture annnuelle	no
Weekly closure	Fermeture hebdomadaire	no

Fees main season
Tarifs haute saison full day

	Week days Semaine	We/Bank holidays We/Férié
Individual Individuel	£ 30	£ 35
Couple Couple	£ 60	£ 70

Caddy	Caddy	on request / £ 10
Electric Trolley	Chariot électrique	no
Buggy	Voiturette	£ 20/18 holes
Clubs	Clubs	£ 10/18 holes

Credit cards Cartes de crédit
VISA - Eurocard - AMEX

778

Access Accès : Belfast A24 → Saintfield. Turn off Ormeau Road (Newtownbreda)
Map 1 on page 695 Carte 1 Page 695

GOLF COURSE
PARCOURS

15/20

Site	Site	▣▣▣□□
Maintenance	Entretien	▣▣▣▣□
Architect	Architecte	Harry S. Colt
Type	Type	parkland
Relief	Relief	▣▣□□□
Water in play	Eau en jeu	▣▣□□□
Exp. to wind	Exposé au vent	▣▣□□□
Trees in play	Arbres en jeu	▣▣▣▣□

Scorecard Carte de score	Chp. Chp.	Mens Mess.	Ladies Da.
Length Long.	5958	5739	5152
Par	71	70	73

Advised golfing ability	0	12	24	36
Niveau de jeu recommandé		▣▣▣▣		
Hcp required	Handicap exigé	24 Men, 36 Ladies		

CLUB HOUSE & AMENITIES
CLUB HOUSE ET ANNEXES

5/10

Pro shop	Pro-shop	▣▣▣□□
Driving range	Practice	▣▣▣□□
Sheltered	couvert	no
On grass	sur herbe	yes
Putting-green	putting-green	yes
Pitching-green	pitching green	no

HOTEL FACILITIES
ENVIRONNEMENT HOTELIER

6/10

HOTELS HÔTELS

Stormont Hotel — Belfast
109 rooms, D £ 115 — 5 km
Tel (44) 01232 - 658 621, Fax (44) 01232 - 480 240

La Mon House Hotel — Belfast
46 rooms, D £ 20 — 5 km
Tel (44) 01232 - 448 631, Fax (44) 01232 - 448 026

RESTAURANTS RESTAURANT

Antica Roma — Belfast
Tel (44) 01232 - 311 121 — 2 km

La Belle Epoque — Belfast
Tel (44) 01232 - 323 244 — 3 km

There are trees here, but if you hit your ball into the woods, you are almost certainly out of bounds. Cairndhu is a seaside course (not really a links) along the Antrim coast road. This is the beginner's road leading from Belfast to the great links courses in the north, and the views are often quite spectacular. Excellence of setting and environment are, though, virtually a constant factor throughout Ireland. Don't be too put out when setting eyes on the contours and relief of the first few holes, things calm down a little after the 4th hole and the terrain gently rolls, nothing more. The course demands some straight driving and accurate approach shots, especially when homing in on a number of small greens, although "average" hitters will basically be playing mid to short irons. Don't place too much faith in your own instinct for gauging distances, because here they can be misleading. The architect has made the most of the terrain and it would be a pity not to get to known a course like this.

Il y a des arbres, mais si vous envoyez votre balle dans les bois, elle est sans doute hors limites. Cairndhu est un parcours de bord de mer (pas vraiment un links), le long de l'Antrim Coast Road. C'est le chemin des écoliers pour aller de Belfast aux grands links du nord, et les vues y sont parfois spectaculaires, mais cette qualité d'environnement est quasiment une constante dans toute l'Irlande. A moins d'être cardiaque, ne vous affolez pas trop à la vue du relief des premiers trous, il s'adoucit après le 4 pour laisser place à de sobres ondulations. Ce parcours réclame de la précision au drive et aux approches, particulièrement pour attaquer certains greens de petite taille, mais les frappeurs "normaux" auront alors essentiellement à jouer des moyens et petits fers. Ne vous fiez pas trop à votre instinct pour les distances, il peut vous tromper. L'architecte a tiré un bon parti du terrain, il serait dommage de ne pas le connaître.

Cairndhu Golf Club

192 Coast Road, Ballygally
NIR - LARNE, Co Antrim

Office	Secrétariat	(44) 01574 - 583 324
Pro shop	Pro-shop	(44) 01574 - 583 324
Fax	Fax	(44) 01574 - 583 477
Situation	Situation	

6 km from Larne (pop. 17 575)

Annual closure	Fermeture annnuelle	no
Weekly closure	Fermeture hebdomadaire	no

Fees main season
Tarifs haute saison 18 holes

	Week days Semaine	We/Bank holidays We/Férié
Individual Individuel	£ 15	£ 25
Couple Couple	£ 30	£ 32

Caddy	Caddy	on request
Electric Trolley	Chariot électrique	no
Buggy	Voiturette	no
Clubs	Clubs	£ 10/18 holes
Credit cards Cartes de crédit		VISA - MasterCard

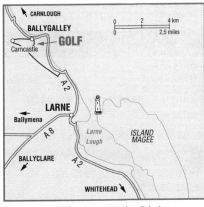

Map 1 on page 695 Carte 1 Page 695

Access Accès : Belfast, M2 → Antrim. Exit 4.
A8 to Larne. A2 to Ballygally

GOLF COURSE
PARCOURS

13/20

Site	Site	
Maintenance	Entretien	
Architect	Architecte	T. Morrison
Type	Type	seaside course, parkland
Relief	Relief	
Water in play	Eau en jeu	
Exp. to wind	Exposé au vent	
Trees in play	Arbres en jeu	

Scorecard Carte de score	Chp. Chp.	Mens Mess.	Ladies Da.
Length Long.	5500	5436	4861
Par	70	70	73

Advised golfing ability		0 12 24 36
Niveau de jeu recommandé		
Hcp required	Handicap exigé	no

CLUB HOUSE & AMENITIES
CLUB HOUSE ET ANNEXES

6/10

Pro shop	Pro-shop	
Driving range	Practice	
Sheltered	couvert	no
On grass	sur herbe	yes
Putting-green	putting-green	yes
Pitching-green	pitching green	no

HOTEL FACILITIES
ENVIRONNEMENT HOTELIER

5/10

HOTELS HÔTELS

Ballygally Castle Hotel — Ballygally
30 rooms, D £ 69 — 3 km
Tel (44) 01574 - 583 212, Fax (44) 01574 - 583 681

Magheramorne House — Larne
22 rooms, D £ 80 — 6 km
Tel (44) 01574 - 279 444, Fax (44) 01574 - 260 138

Londonderry Arms Hotel — Carnlough
21 rooms, D £ 65 — 18 km
Tel (44) 01574 - 885 255, Fax (44) 01574 - 885 263

RESTAURANTS RESTAURANT

Lynden Heights — Ballygally
Tel (44) 01574 - 583 560 — 3 km

779

CASTLE HUME

13	7	6

Golf in Northern Ireland has developed more particularly in County Down, around Belfast and along the northern coast. There are, of course, pleasant courses in other areas, but they could hardly be rated as unforgettable playing experiences and anyway, tourists don't have time enough to play them all. Located on the banks of Lower Lough Erne, a paradise for anglers, nature and history-lovers, Castle Hume is an exception to the above. A recent course, it will need a few years for the several thousand saplings to grow to see how the course will eventually look, and the club-house is still on the drawing board. But the course itself is worth the visit. The architect has visibly been influenced by the American style, and accurate target golf is called for to cope with a course where water hazards have enhanced what is already a stiff challenge. Castle Hume is already an address to be recommended.

Le golf en Irlande du Nord a surtout été développé dans le County Down, autour de Belfast et sur la côte Nord. Bien sûr, on trouve aussi des parcours sympathiques dans les autres régions, mais ils ne sauraient vraiment prendre place parmi les réalisations mémorables, et les touristes ne disposent pas d'assez de temps pour les visiter tous. Situé en bordure du Lower Lough Erne, un paradis des pêcheurs et des amateurs de nature comme d'histoire, Castle Hume fait exception. Récemment construit, il faudra attendre que les milliers d'arbres plantés aient poussé pour qu'il prenne son allure définitive, et le Club-house reste à l'état de projet, mais le parcours vaut la visite. L'architecte a visiblement été influencé par le style américain, et il faudra jouer des approches levées précises pour bien le négocier, d'autant que les obstacles d'eau relèvent le niveau du défi, mais Castle Hume est déjà une adresse recommandable.

Castle Hume Golf Club
Belleek Road
NIR - ENNISKILLEN, Co. Fermanagh BT93 7ED

Office	Secrétariat	(44) 01365 - 327 077
Pro shop	Pro-shop	(44) 01365 - 327 075
Fax	Fax	(44) 01365 - 327 076
Situation	Situation	

6 km from Enniskillen (pop. 11 436)

Annual closure	Fermeture annnuelle	no
Weekly closure	Fermeture hebdomadaire	no

Fees main season
Tarifs haute saison 18 holes

	Week days Semaine	We/Bank holidays We/Férié
Individual Individuel	£ 12	£ 18
Couple Couple	£ 24	£ 36

Caddy	Caddy	on request/£ 12
Electric Trolley	Chariot électrique	no
Buggy	Voiturette	£ 15/18 holes
Clubs	Clubs	£ 5

Credit cards Cartes de crédit VISA - MasterCard

Access Accès : Belfast M1 exit 15 (Dungannon).
A4 to Enniskillen, A46 → Belleek.
Map 1 on page 695 Carte 1 Page 695

GOLF COURSE
PARCOURS

13/20

Site	Site	
Maintenance	Entretien	
Architect	Architecte	Tony Carroll
Type	Type	parkland
Relief	Relief	
Water in play	Eau en jeu	
Exp. to wind	Exposé au vent	
Trees in play	Arbres en jeu	

Scorecard Carte de score	Chp. Chp.	Mens Mess.	Ladies Da.
Length Long.	5941	5685	4980
Par	72	72	72

Advised golfing ability 0 12 24 36
Niveau de jeu recommandé

Hcp required Handicap exigé no

CLUB HOUSE & AMENITIES
CLUB HOUSE ET ANNEXES

7/10

Pro shop	Pro-shop	
Driving range	Practice	
Sheltered	couvert	no
On grass	sur herbe	yes
Putting-green	putting-green	yes
Pitching-green	pitching green	yes

HOTEL FACILITIES
ENVIRONNEMENT HOTELIER

6/10

HOTELS HÔTELS

Killyhevlin Hotel — Enniskillen
45 rooms, D £ 80 — 6 km
Tel (44) 01365 - 323 481, Fax (44) 01365 - 324 726

Fort Lodge — Enniskillen
35 rooms, D £ 70 — 6 km
Tel (44) 01365 - 323 275, Fax (44) 01365 - 323 275

Manor House — Killadeas, Enniskillen
46 rooms, D £ 80 — 15 km
Tel (44) 01365 6- 21 561, Fax (44) 01365 6- 21 545

RESTAURANTS RESTAURANT

Franco's — Enniskillen
Tel (44) 01365 - 324 424 — 6 km

Mulligan's — Enniskillen
Tel (44) 01365 - 322 059 — 6 km

Already at a venerable age, Castlerock is certainly not one of the best known links courses, but it would be shame to overlook it. It certainly won't disappoint the better players, and it is also more within the reach of mid- to high-handicappers than its prestigious neighbours. This is a great introduction for people who have never played links golf ; it has a very natural look to it, is in a beautifully wild setting and has the traditional difficulties found on this type of course. The bunkers, though, are appreciably less severe than elsewhere. To maintain the suspense, you will find a few blind drives, but the hazards everywhere are visible enough for you to forget, temporarily at least, that golf is a sport where there's no justice. Smallish greens call for great precision, and if you miss them you will have the opportunity to put your newly-honed short game to the test. Another important factor here is the warm welcome in the clubhouse.

Ayant déjà atteint un âge vénérable, Castlerock ne figure sans doute pas parmi les links les plus connus, mais il serait bien regrettable de le négliger. Il ne décevra en rien les meilleurs joueurs, mais il est aussi davantage à la portée du golfeur de handicap moyen ou élevé que ses voisins prestigieux. Pour ceux qui n'ont jamais joué un links, c'est une bonne initiation, par son aspect très naturel, la beauté sauvage de son environnement de dunes, et les difficultés traditionnelles de ce type de parcours : les bunkers sont notamment moins sévères qu'ailleurs. Pour maintenir le suspense, on trouve quelques drives aveugles, mais les obstacles sont partout assez visibles pour ne pas trop s'apercevoir que le golf est un sport sans justice. Des greens de surface assez réduite obligent à une certaine précision. Si on les manque, ce sera l'occasion de mettre en valeur sa virtuosité au petit jeu. La qualité de l'accueil est aussi à souligner.

Castlerock Golf Club
Circular Road
NIR - CASTLEROCK, Co Derry

Office	Secrétariat	(44) 01265 - 848 314
Pro shop	Pro-shop	(44) 01265 - 848 314
Fax	Fax	(44) 01265 - 848 714
Situation	Situation	

90 km from Belfast (pop. 279 237)
9 km from Coleraine (pop. 20 721)

Annual closure	Fermeture annnuelle	no
Weekly closure	Fermeture hebdomadaire	no

Fees main season
Tarifs haute saison 18 holes

	Week days Semaine	We/Bank holidays We/Férié
Individual Individuel	£ 25	£ 35
Couple Couple	£ 40	£ 70

Caddy	Caddy	on request/£ 20
Electric Trolley	Chariot électrique	no
Buggy	Voiturette	no
Clubs	Clubs	on request/£ 10
Credit cards Cartes de crédit		no

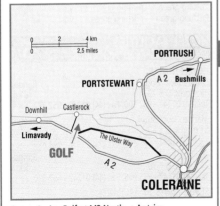

	0 2 4 km	
	0 2,5 miles	PORTRUSH

PORTSTEWART   A 2 Bushmills

Downhill   Castlerock

Limavady   *The Ulster Way*

GOLF   A 2

COLERAINE

Access Accès : Belfast M2 North → Antrim.
Turn right to A26 → Ballymena/Coleraine.
Coleraine A2 → Castlerock
Map 1 on page 695 Carte 1 Page 695

GOLF COURSE
PARCOURS
16/20

Site	Site	▬▬▬▬
Maintenance	Entretien	▬▬▬▬
Architect	Architecte	Ben Sayers
Type	Type	links, seaside course
Relief	Relief	▬▬▬
Water in play	Eau en jeu	▬▬
Exp. to wind	Exposé au vent	▬▬▬▬
Trees in play	Arbres en jeu	▬

Scorecard Carte de score	Chp. Chp.	Mens Mess.	Ladies Da.
Length Long.	6115	5850	5299
Par	73	73	75

Advised golfing ability Niveau de jeu recommandé	0	12	24	36
Hcp required	Handicap exigé	28 Men, 36 Ladies		

CLUB HOUSE & AMENITIES
CLUB HOUSE ET ANNEXES
6/10

Pro shop	Pro-shop	▬▬
Driving range	Practice	▬▬
Sheltered	couvert	no
On grass	sur herbe	yes
Putting-green	putting-green	yes
Pitching-green	pitching green	no

781

HOTEL FACILITIES
ENVIRONNEMENT HOTELIER
6/10

HOTELS HÔTELS
Golf Hotel   Castlerock
16 rooms, D £ 50   1 km
Tel (44) 01265 - 848 204, Fax (44) 01265 - 848 295

Lodge, 20 rooms, D £ 70   Coleraine
Tel (44) 01265 - 44 848   8 km

Marine Hotel   Castlerock
9 rooms, D £ 40   2 km
Tel (44) 01265 - 848 456

RESTAURANTS RESTAURANT
Bushtown House   Coleraine
Tel (44) 01265 - 58 367   8 km

The Lodge   Coleraine
Tel (44) 01265 - 44 848   8 km

Standing alongside the short and amusing "Ava Course", Clandeboye is a layout of greater calibre in its variety and technical demands on players. Yardage is definitely no difficulty, especially for the long-hitters (they will enjoy the wide fairways), but players who are too short might have problems in carrying the ball. What's more, the uneven soil can also create some interesting lies. Game strategy is pretty obvious, as the difficulties are easily identifiable from the tee, albeit in a sometimes intimidating way. There is just the one blind green here, and the few elevated greens call for accurately and cleanly hit approach shots, especially since the putting surfaces are rather firm. Add to this the water, stream and ditches and you will realise that playing to your handicap here requires careful thought and attention.

A côté du "Ava Course", court et assez amusant, Clandeboye propose ici un parcours de plus grand calibre, par sa diversité et ses exigences techniques. Sa longueur n'est certes pas un facteur de difficulté particulière, en particulier pour les longs frappeurs (ils pourront se déchaîner sur des fairways larges), mais certains joueurs courts risquent d'avoir des problèmes quand il faut porter la balle. Par ailleurs, le sol irrégulier provoque quelques positions de balle intéressantes. La stratégie est assez évidente, les difficultés étant facilement identifiables de chaque départ, mais elles peuvent intimider. On trouve ici un seul green aveugle, quelques greens surélevés, les approches devront y être d'autant plus précises et les coups bien touchés que les surfaces de putting sont souvent assez fermes. Ajoutons la présence de cours d'eau et de fossés, et vous aurez compris que jouer son handicap demande de la réflexion et de l'attention.

Clandeboye Golf Club

Tower Road, Conlig
NIR - NEWTOWNARDS, Co Down BT23 3PN

Office	Secrétariat	(44) 01247 - 271 767
Pro shop	Pro-shop	(44) 01247 - 271 750
Fax	Fax	(44) 01247 - 473 711
Situation	Situation	

4 km from Newtownwards and Bangor
15 km from Belfast (pop. 279 237)

Annual closure	Fermeture annnuelle	no
Weekly closure	Fermeture hebdomadaire	no

Fees main season Tarifs haute saison 18 holes

	Week days Semaine	We/Bank holidays We/Férié
Individual Individuel	£ 25	£ 30
Couple Couple	£ 50	£ 60

£ 15 after 3 p.m. (Saturday & Sunday) -
Ava Course: £ 20

Caddy	Caddy	on request/£ 15-20
Electric Trolley	Chariot électrique	no
Buggy	Voiturette	no
Clubs	Clubs	£ 5

Credit cards Cartes de crédit
VISA - MasterCard - Access

782

Access Accès : Belfast, A20 to Newtownards.
A21 → Bangor.
Map 1 on page 695 Carte 1 Page 695

GOLF COURSE
PARCOURS

15/20

Site	Site	■■■■■
Maintenance	Entretien	■■■■■
Architect	Architecte	W.R. Robinson
Type	Type	inland, copse
Relief	Relief	■■
Water in play	Eau en jeu	■■
Exp. to wind	Exposé au vent	■■■
Trees in play	Arbres en jeu	■■■

Scorecard Carte de score	Chp. Chp.	Mens Mess.	Ladies Da.
Length Long.	5916	5700	5180
Par	71	71	73

Advised golfing ability		0	12	24	36
Niveau de jeu recommandé			■■■■		
Hcp required	Handicap exigé	no			

CLUB HOUSE & AMENITIES
CLUB HOUSE ET ANNEXES

6/10

Pro shop	Pro-shop	■■■
Driving range	Practice	■■■
Sheltered	couvert	no
On grass	sur herbe	yes
Putting-green	putting-green	yes
Pitching-green	pitching green	yes

HOTEL FACILITIES
ENVIRONNEMENT HOTELIER

6/10

HOTELS HÔTELS

Clandeboye Lodge — Bangor
43 rooms, D £ 75 — 6 km
Tel (44) 01247 - 852 500, Fax (44) 01247 - 852 772

Marine Court Hotel — Bangor
51 rooms, D £ 80 — 6 km
Tel (44) 01247 - 451 100, Fax (44) 01247 - 451 200

O'Hara's Royal — Bangor
34 rooms, D £ 70 — 6 km
Tel (44) 01247 - 271 866, Fax (44) 01247 - 467 810

RESTAURANTS RESTAURANT

Shanks — Bangor
Tel (44) 01247 - 853 313 — 6 km

Poachers Arms (Clandeboye Lodge) — Bangor
Tel (44) 01247 - 853 311 — 6 km

With breath-taking views over the Irish Sea, gently contoured landscape and a sandy soil, you can understand why James Braid exclaimed "if only this spot were within 50 miles of London !" Not far from the sea but closer to a lush park-land style than anything else, it does nonetheless have something of the links about it, not to mention the wind, which blows wherever it wants to and magnifies every error and difficulty. The course's bunkering is particularly remarkable, but the green-side bunkers generally leave a way open for bump and run shots, which are just the job for firm greens like these. This pretty course is a high-class design, which is only to be expected from its architect, and offers a refreshing and quaintly old-fashioned alternative to modern layouts splattered with water hazards. Even with a par 69 and low yardage, this friendly course is well worth a visit.

Avec ses vues admirables et imprenables sur la mer d'Irlande, son relief très modéré et un sol sablonneux, on comprend que James Braid en ait dit : "Si seulement ce terrain se trouvait à moins de 50 miles de Londres !" Non loin de la mer, mais plus proche d'un parc que d'un véritable links, il en présente malgré tout certains aspects, sans parler du vent, qui souffle où il veut, mais qui amplifie toutes les erreurs et les difficultés. Le bunkering de ce parcours est particulièrement remarquable, mais les bunkers de greens laissent généralement une ouverture, ce qui permet de jouer les "bump 'n run" bien adaptés à des greens fermes. Ce joli parcours bénéficie d'un dessin de haut niveau, que l'on pouvait attendre de son architecte, et offre une alternative rafraîchissante et un peu surannée aux tracés modernes envahis d'obstacles d'eau. Même avec un par 69 et sa longueur réduite, ce parcours amical mérite une visite.

Kirkistown Castle

142, Main Road, Cloughey
NIR - NEWTOWNARDS, Co Down BT22 1JA

Office	Secrétariat	(44) 012477 - 71 233
Pro shop	Pro-shop	(44) 012477 - 71 004
Fax	Fax	(44) 012477 - 71 699
Situation	Situation	

38 km SE of Bangor - 30 km SE of Newtownards

Annual closure	Fermeture annnuelle	no
Weekly closure	Fermeture hebdomadaire	no

Fees main season
Tarifs haute saison 18 holes

	Week days Semaine	We/Bank holidays We/Férié
Individual Individuel	£ 13	£ 25
Couple Couple	£ 26	£ 50

Restrictions on Week ends

Caddy	Caddy	£ 10/18 holes
Electric Trolley	Chariot électrique	no
Buggy	Voiturette	no
Clubs	Clubs	£ 10

Credit cards Cartes de crédit
VISA - MasterCard - Access (Pro Shop only)

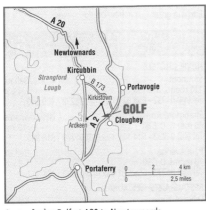

Access Accès : Belfast A20 to Newtownards.
A20 to Kircubbin. B173 to Cloughey
Map 1 on page 695 Carte 1 Page 695

GOLF COURSE
PARCOURS
15/20

Site	Site	■■■■
Maintenance	Entretien	■■■■
Architect	Architecte	James Braid
Type	Type	links, parkland
Relief	Relief	■■
Water in play	Eau en jeu	□
Exp. to wind	Exposé au vent	■■
Trees in play	Arbres en jeu	■■■

Scorecard Carte de score	Chp. Chp.	Mens Mess.	Ladies Da.
Length Long.	5550	5335	5120
Par	70	69	73

Advised golfing ability Niveau de jeu recommandé	0	12	24	36

Hcp required   Handicap exigé   no

CLUB HOUSE & AMENITIES
CLUB HOUSE ET ANNEXES
6/10

Pro shop	Pro-shop	■■■
Driving range	Practice	■■■
Sheltered	couvert	no
On grass	sur herbe	yes
Putting-green	putting-green	yes
Pitching-green	pitching green	yes

HOTEL FACILITIES
ENVIRONNEMENT HOTELIER
5/10

HOTELS HÔTELS

Coastal Lodge Hotel — Cloughey
9 rooms, D £ 25 — 500 m
Tel (44) 012477 - 72 100

Portaferry Hotel — Portaferry
14 rooms, D £ 89 — 7 km
Tel (44) 012477 - 28 231, Fax (44) 012477 - 28 999

Strangford Arms — Newtownards
40 rooms, D £ 80 — 20 km
Tel (44) 01232 - 814 141, Fax (44) 01232 - 818 846

RESTAURANTS RESTAURANT

Portaferry Hotel — Portaferry
Tel (44) 012477 - 28 231 — 7 km

Copeland's — Donaghady
Tel (44) 01247 - 888 189 — 25 km

783

This is a generally flat course with a hill in the middle, which you climb twice, although climb is hardly the word. As with all courses close to Belfast, Knock is very busy on week-ends and the week-days are quieter for green-feers. They will have a lot of fun here, unless their swing is off-colour or they start spraying their drives. If you do go into the woods, a little recovery shot back to the fairway is all you can hope for. Most of the holes are lined with trees, which make for a peaceful setting, but wayward hitters will suffer the consequences. The hazards are clearly visible and you feel confident from the very first visit ; all you need do is avoid the meanders of two streams which come and go over the course. Although not one of the country's most spectacular and original courses, Knock is at the very least extremely pleasant to play, perhaps more so for mid-handicappers than for the more proficient golfers.

C'est un parcours généralement plat, avec une colline en son centre, que l'on grimpe deux fois, mais il ne s'agit certes pas d'une escalade ! Comme tous les golfs à proximité de Belfast, il est très fréquenté en week-end, mais la semaine est plus calme pour les visiteurs. Il s'y amuseront beaucoup, sauf si leur swing est malade ce jour là et qu'ils "arrosent" au drive : il leur faudra bien souvent se contenter de se recentrer s'ils se sont un peu enfoncés dans les bois. La plupart des trous sont bordés d'arbres, ce qui garantit une tranquillité certaine, mais il faut en subir les conséquences. Les obstacles sont ici bien visibles, on se sent en confiance dès la première visite, il suffira d'éviter les méandres de deux cours d'eau qui vont et viennent sur le parcours. S'il ne figure pas parmi les golfs les plus spectaculaires et originaux du pays, Knock est du moins très agréable à jouer, peut-être davantage pour les joueurs moyens que pour les meilleurs.

Knock Golf Club
Summerfield, Dundonald
NIR - BELFAST BT16 0QX

Office	Secrétariat	(44) 01232 - 483 251
Pro shop	Pro-shop	(44) 01232 - 483 825
Fax	Fax	
Situation	Situation	

7 km from Belfast (pop. 279 237)
9 km from Newtownards

Annual closure	Fermeture annnuelle	no
Weekly closure	Fermeture hebdomadaire	no

Fees main season
Tarifs haute saison 18 holes

	Week days Semaine	We/Bank holidays We/Férié
Individual Individuel	£ 20	£ 25
Couple Couple	£ 40	£ 50

Caddy	Caddy	no
Electric Trolley	Chariot électrique	no
Buggy	Voiturette	no
Clubs	Clubs	£ 10/18 holes

Credit cards Cartes de crédit
VISA - Access (Pro Shop only)

Access Accès : Belfast, A20 → Newtownards
Map 1 on page 695 Carte 1 Page 695

784

GOLF COURSE
PARCOURS

15/20

Site	Site	▬▬▬▬▬
Maintenance	Entretien	▬▬▬▬▬
Architect	Architecte	Harry Colt, MacKenzie, Allison
Type	Type	parkland
Relief	Relief	
Water in play	Eau en jeu	▬▬
Exp. to wind	Exposé au vent	▬▬▬
Trees in play	Arbres en jeu	▬▬▬▬

Scorecard Carte de score	Chp. Chp.	Mens Mess.	Ladies Da.
Length Long.	5800	5615	5205
Par	70	70	73

Advised golfing ability	0	12	24	36
Niveau de jeu recommandé		▬▬▬▬		
Hcp required Handicap exigé	no			

CLUB HOUSE & AMENITIES
CLUB HOUSE ET ANNEXES

7/10

Pro shop	Pro-shop	▬▬▬
Driving range	Practice	▬
Sheltered	couvert	no
On grass	sur herbe	yes
Putting-green	putting-green	yes
Pitching-green	pitching green	yes

HOTEL FACILITIES
ENVIRONNEMENT HOTELIER

6/10

HOTELS HÔTELS
Stormont — Belfast
110 rooms, D £ 130 — 4 km
Tel (44) 01232 - 658 621, Fax (44) 01232 - 480 240

Strangford Arms — Newtownards
40 rooms, D £ 80 — 10 km
Tel (44) 01232 - 814 141, Fax (44) 01232 - 818 846

Park Avenue — Belfast
70 rooms, D £ 90 — 8 km
Tel (44) 01232 - 656 520, Fax (44) 01232 - 471 417

RESTAURANTS RESTAURANT
Duke of York — Belfast
Tel (44) 01232 - 241 062 — 9 km

Strand — Belfast
Tel (44) 01232 - 682 266 — 9 km

LISBURN

A beautiful tree-lined drive leads to the Lisburn Golf Club, and sets the mood. Here, you are in the wide open space of park-land and meadows, with the feeling of tranquillity that prevails throughout the Irish countryside. But don't let such bucolic thoughts go to your head, as this course is far-from-easy, especially from the back tees. With that said, the men's yellow and ladies tees are well forward, so most golfers can breathe easily. Created in 1905, Lisburn was overhauled by Fred Hawtree, whose strategic positioning of fairway and green-side bunkers is clear to see, although the latter seldom block the front of the greens. The terrain is rather flat and only one hole could really be called blind, the 17th, a tricky hole before finishing on a spectacular downhill par 3, itself something of a rarity. This very pretty layout is well worth visiting if you are up Belfast way.

Une belle allée bordée d'arbres conduit au Golf de Lisburn, et donne l'ambiance. Nous allons nous trouver dans un espace de grand parc et de prairies, avec le sentiment de tranquillité associé à la campagne irlandaise. Mais il ne faudra pas se laisser endormir par des pensées bucoliques, ce parcours n'est pas des plus faciles, notamment du fond, mais les départs hommes et dames sont assez avancés pour que la majorité des golfeurs s'y trouve à l'aise. Créé en 1905, il a été révisé par Fred Hawtree, dont on peut remarquer le positionnement stratégique des bunkers de fairway et de greens, mais ces derniers masquent rarement l'entrée des greens. Le terrain est assez plat, et un seul green peut être considéré comme aveugle, au 17, un trou délicat, avant de finir par un par 3 spectaculaire en descente : une disposition très rare sur un parcours. Cette très jolie réalisation mérite le détour si vous passez à Belfast.

Lisburn Golf Club

68 Eglantine Road
NIR - LISBURN, Co Antrim

Office	Secrétariat	(44) 01846 - 677 216
Pro shop	Pro-shop	(44) 01846 - 677 217
Fax	Fax	(44) 01846 - 603 608
Situation	Situation	

14 km from Belfast (pop. 279 237)
4 km from Lisburg

Annual closure	Fermeture annnuelle	no
Weekly closure	Fermeture hebdomadaire	no

Fees main season
Tarifs haute saison 18 holes

	Week days Semaine	We/Bank holidays We/Férié
Individual Individuel	£ 25	£ 30
Couple Couple	£ 50	£ 60

Caddy	Caddy	no
Electric Trolley	Chariot électrique	no
Buggy	Voiturette	no
Clubs	Clubs	£ 15/18 holes

Credit cards Cartes de crédit   VISA - MasterCard

BELFAST

M1

A1

LISBURN

Craigavon   Mazetown

M 1

R Lagan   Ravernet

GOLF

Dromore

A1

0   2   4 km
0   2,5 miles

Access Accès : Belfast M1 → Lisburn. Turn left to A1 → Hillsborough. Golf 4 km S of Lisburn
Map 1 on page 695 Carte 1 Page 695

GOLF COURSE
PARCOURS   15/20

Site	Site	
Maintenance	Entretien	
Architect	Architecte	Fred Hawtree
Type	Type	parkland
Relief	Relief	
Water in play	Eau en jeu	
Exp. to wind	Exposé au vent	
Trees in play	Arbres en jeu	

Scorecard Carte de score	Chp. Chp.	Mens Mess.	Ladies Da.
Length Long.	6075	5754	5049
Par	72	72	72

Advised golfing ability	0 12 24 36
Niveau de jeu recommandé	
Hcp required Handicap exigé	24 Men, 36 Ladies

CLUB HOUSE & AMENITIES
CLUB HOUSE ET ANNEXES   7/10

Pro shop	Pro-shop	
Driving range	Practice	
Sheltered	couvert	no
On grass	sur herbe	yes
Putting-green	putting-green	yes
Pitching-green	pitching green	yes

HOTEL FACILITIES
ENVIRONNEMENT HOTELIER   6/10

HOTELS HÔTELS

Whites Gables	Lisburn
31 rooms, D £ 75	4 km
Tel (44) 01846 - 682 755, Fax (44) 01846 - 689 532	
Aldergrove International	Belfast
108 rooms, D £ 80	12 km
Tel (44) 01849 - 422 033	
Forte Posthouse	Belfast
82 rooms, D £ 70	4 km
Tel (44) 01232 - 612 101	

RESTAURANTS RESTAURANT

Tidy Doffer	Hillsborough
Tel (44) 01846 - 689 188	2 km
Ashoka	Belfast
Tel (44) 01232 - 660 362	12 km

785

A course with forty bunkers, both necessary and sufficient, as water hazards also play a significant role on certain holes : the 7th, 15th and 16th, a pretty and short par 3 where the tee-box and green bite into a large lake, and again on the 18th, a superb par 4 where slicers might spend a few nervous moments. Created in 1895, the Malone Golf Club moved to this pleasantly rolling terrain in the early 1960s. It is a typical Fred Hawtree design with well-guarded greens of all different sizes, but with the front door left open for crisply hit rolled shots. The existing natural setting was hardly touched, the course being a frank and finely landscaped layout designed around the trees. Of course, visitors used to the British inland style will hardly notice any particular local character, but if you are in the region, you will find this a challenge of high standard.

On trouve une quarantaine de bunkers ici, à la fois nécessaires et suffisants, car les obstacles d'eau jouent un grand rôle, au 7, au 15, au 16, joli par 3 court où le départ et le green empiètent sur un lac de neuf hectares, et encore au 18, superbe par 4 où les slicers risquent d'éprouver des émotions fortes. Créé en 1895, le club de Malone a émigré sur ce terrain agréablement vallonné au début des années 60, avec un dessin assez typique de Fred Hawtree, avec des greens de dimensions variées, bien défendus, mais laissant souvent la porte ouverte aux approches roulées bien touchées. Il n'a guère modifié la nature existante, mais y a inscrit un tracé bien paysagé en fonction des arbres, et d'une parfaite franchise. Certes, les visiteurs habitués au style britannique "inland" ne trouveront pas ici de caractère local très fort, mais si vous vous trouvez dans la région, vous trouverez ici un challenge de très bonne qualité.

Malone Golf Club

240, Upper Malone Road
NIR - DUNMURRY, Co Belfast BT17 9LB

Office	Secrétariat	(44) 01232 - 612 758
Pro shop	Pro-shop	(44) 01232 - 614 917
Fax	Fax	(44) 01232 - 431 394
Situation	Situation	

8 km S of Belfast (pop. 279 237)

| **Annual closure** | Fermeture annnuelle | no |
| **Weekly closure** | Fermeture hebdomadaire | no |

Fees main season
Tarifs haute saison 18 holes

	Week days Semaine	We/Bank holidays We/Férié
Individual Individuel	£ 33	£ 38
Couple Couple	£ 66	£ 76

Caddy	Caddy	on request/£ 15
Electric Trolley	Chariot électrique	£ 5/18 holes
Buggy	Voiturette	£ 20/18 holes
Clubs	Clubs	£ 10

Credit cards Cartes de crédit
VISA - Eurocard - MasterCard - AMEX

BELFAST

Access Accès : Belfast. B23 (Upper Malone Road)
Map 1 on page 695 Carte 1 Page 695

GOLF COURSE
PARCOURS   13/20

Site	Site	
Maintenance	Entretien	
Architect	Architecte	Fred Hawtree
Type	Type	inland, parkland
Relief	Relief	
Water in play	Eau en jeu	
Exp. to wind	Exposé au vent	
Trees in play	Arbres en jeu	

Scorecard Carte de score	Chp. Chp.	Mens Mess.	Ladies Da.
Length Long.	6084	5680	5213
Par	71	71	72

Advised golfing ability		0	12	24	36
Niveau de jeu recommandé					
Hcp required	Handicap exigé	no			

CLUB HOUSE & AMENITIES
CLUB HOUSE ET ANNEXES   6/10

Pro shop	Pro-shop	
Driving range	Practice	
Sheltered	couvert	no
On grass	sur herbe	yes
Putting-green	putting-green	yes
Pitching-green	pitching green	yes

HOTEL FACILITIES
ENVIRONNEMENT HOTELIER   6/10

HOTELS HÔTELS

Forte Posthouse   Dunmurry
82 rooms, D £ 85   2 km
Tel (44) 01232 - 612 101, Fax (44) 01232 - 626 546

Wellington Park   Belfast
50 rooms, D £ 60   7 km
Tel (44) 01232 - 381 111, Fax (44) 01232 - 665 410

Lansdowne Court   Belfast
25 rooms, D £ 70   7 km
Tel (44) 01232 - 773 317, Fax (44) 01232 - 370 125

RESTAURANTS RESTAURANT

Roscoff   Belfast
Tel (44) 01232 - 331 532   6 km

Nicks Warehouse   Belfast
Tel (44) 01232 - 439 690   7 km

786

The course's location on the banks of Lough Neagh, the largest lake in the British Isles, is a convincing argument in its favour. There are others. Created in 1895, the course was tampered with on several occasions before Fred Hawtree came along in 1961 and brought some order and consistency to the layout. There are any number of trees here, many of which have been planted and are already of an age to come clearly into play (especially on the 17th). The front 9, on clay, can be heavy going in winter, but the back 9 are laid out over sandy soil which drains easily when it rains. There are a lot of hazards, basically bunkers (and water on the 16th), not always very deep but always well-placed and clearly visible. The variety in the size and shape of greens adds to the diversity of holes, and while beginners will unquestionably suffer, good players can test their driving accuracy. A course worth discovering.

Sa situation en bordure du Lough Neagh, le plus grand lac des Iles Britanniques, est un argument de taille (si l'on peut dire). Ce n'est pas le seul. Fondé en 1895, il a été modifié à de multiples reprises, avant que Fred Hawtree vienne mettre un peu d'ordre et de cohérence dans le tracé, en 1961. On trouve de nombreux arbres, dont beaucoup ont été plantés, mais ils ont assez atteint leur maturité pour venir nettement en jeu (spéciale- ment au 17). L'aller, sur un sol argileux, peut être assez mou en hiver, mais le retour bénéficie d'un sol sa- blonneux, et bien drainant en cas de pluie. Les obstacles sont nombreux, essentiellement les bunkers (de l'eau au 16), mais pas très profonds, toujours bien placés et bien visibles. La variété de dimension et de forme des greens contribue à la diversité des trous, et si les débutants souffriront sans doute, les bons joueurs pour- ront y tester la précision de leurs drives. Un parcours à découvrir.

Massereene Golf Club

51 Lough Road
NIR - ANTRIM BT41 4OQ

Office	Secrétariat	(44) 01849 - 428 096
Pro shop	Pro-shop	(44) 01849 - 464 074
Fax	Fax	(44) 01849 - 487 661
Situation	Situation	

1.5 km from Antrim
35 km from Belfast (pop. 279 237)

Annual closure	Fermeture annnuelle	no
Weekly closure	Fermeture hebdomadaire	no

Fees main season
Tarifs haute saison 18 holes

	Week days Semaine	We/Bank holidays We/Férié
Individual Individuel	£ 20	£ 25
Couple Couple	£ 40	£ 50

Caddy	Caddy	on request
Electric Trolley	Chariot électrique	no
Buggy	Voiturette	no
Clubs	Clubs	yes

Credit cards Cartes de crédit	no

Access Accès : A26 S of Antrim. 1 km, right turn at leisure center. Golf 1.5 km along this road
Map 1 on page 695 Carte 1 Page 695

GOLF COURSE / PARCOURS — 14/20

Site	Site	■■■■■■□□
Maintenance	Entretien	■■■■■■□□
Architect	Architecte	Fred Hawtree
Type	Type	inland, parkland
Relief	Relief	
Water in play	Eau en jeu	■□□□□□
Exp. to wind	Exposé au vent	■■□□□□
Trees in play	Arbres en jeu	■■■■■□

Scorecard Carte de score	Chp. Chp.	Mens Mess.	Ladies Da.
Length Long.	5980	5760	0
Par	72	72	0

Advised golfing ability Niveau de jeu recommandé	0	12	24	36
Hcp required Handicap exigé	no			

CLUB HOUSE & AMENITIES / CLUB HOUSE ET ANNEXES — 5/10

Pro shop	Pro-shop	■■■■■□□
Driving range	Practice	■■□□□□
Sheltered	couvert	no
On grass	sur herbe	no
Putting-green	putting-green	yes
Pitching-green	pitching green	yes

787

HOTEL FACILITIES / ENVIRONNEMENT HOTELIER — 6/10

HOTELS HÔTELS

Dunadry Hotel & Country Club — Dunadry
67 rooms, D £ 110 — 6 km
Tel (44) 01849 - 432 474, Fax (44) 01849 - 433 389

Deerpark Hotel — Antrim
19 rooms, D £ 70 — 1.5 km
Tel (44) 01849 - 462 480, Fax (44) 01849 - 467 126

Galgorm Manor — Ballymena
23 rooms, D £ 90 — 15 km
Tel (44) 01266 - 881 001, Fax (44) 01266 - 880 080

RESTAURANTS RESTAURANT

Roscoff — Belfast
Tel (44) 01232 - 331 532 — 30 km

Dunadry Hotel — Dunadry
Tel (44) 01849 - 432 474 — 6 km

PORTSTEWART STRAND COURSE

16	7	7

The seaside resorts of Portrush and Portstewart are very busy, but foreign tourists come here for the golf. Kept in the shadows of its illustrious neighbour for many a year, the Portstewart (Championship) course has been recently restyled and toughened up, and is now a very respectable test of golf which unquestionably deserves a good visit. Seven new holes have been built over an area of what were virgin dunes, and the old holes were used as a base for a 9 holer, which has completed a second 18 hole course (the "Old" course). From the back tees Portstewart is a very competent course with a dangerous collection of bunkers, but you can still play to your handicap... when the wind is just a breeze and the fairways roll well. The most intimidating hole is the first, a par 4, where you probably will have to make do with the bogey. The next holes are spectacular but not quite as fearsome as they look. Make a point of playing here.

Les stations balnéaires de Portrush et Portstewart sont très fréquentées, mais les touristes étrangers viennent pour jouer au golf ! Longtemps à l'ombre de son illustre voisin, le parcours de Portstewart (Championship) a été récemment rajeuni et durci, c'est maintenant devenu un test fort respectable, qui mérite sans discussion le détour. Sept nouveaux trous ont été construits dans un espace de dunes autrefois vierge, et les anciens trous ont servi de base pour un 9 trous, complétant un autre 18 trous (le "Old"). Des départs arrière, c'est devenu un très solide parcours, avec notamment une collection dangereuse de bunkers, mais il reste possible d'y jouer son handicap... quand le vent s'appelle brise, et quand les fairways roulent bien. Le trou le plus intimidant est le 1, un par 4 où il faut savoir se contenter d'un bogey. Les trous sont ensuite très spectaculaires, mais un peu moins terribles qu'ils ne paraissent. A connaître sans faute.

Portstewart Golf Club
117, Strand Road
NIR - PORTSTEWART BT55 7PG

Office	Secrétariat	(44) 01265 - 832 015
Pro shop	Pro-shop	(44) 01265 - 832 601
Fax	Fax	(44) 01265 - 834 077
Situation	Situation	

75 km from Belfast (pop. 279 237)
8 km from Coleraine (pop. 20 721)

Annual closure	Fermeture annnuelle	no
Weekly closure	Fermeture hebdomadaire	no

Fees main season
Tarifs haute saison 18 holes

	Week days Semaine	We/Bank holidays We/Férié
Individual Individuel	£ 30	£ 40
Couple Couple	£ 60	£ 80

Caddy	Caddy	on request/£15
Electric Trolley	Chariot électrique	£ 6.50/18 holes
Buggy	Voiturette	no
Clubs	Clubs	£ 7.50/18 holes
Credit cards Cartes de crédit		no

788

	2	4 km
0	2,5 miles	

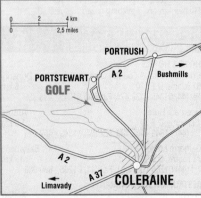

Access Accès : Belfast M2 North to Antrim.
Turn right on A26 to Ballymena and Coleraine.
Coleraine A2 → Portstewart
Map 1 on page 695 Carte 1 Page 695

GOLF COURSE
PARCOURS
16/20

Site	Site	
Maintenance	Entretien	
Architect	Architecte	Willie Park Jr Des Giffin
Type	Type	links
Relief	Relief	
Water in play	Eau en jeu	
Exp. to wind	Exposé au vent	
Trees in play	Arbres en jeu	

Scorecard Carte de score	Chp. Chp.	Mens Mess.	Ladies Da.
Length Long.	6167	5979	5301
Par	72	72	74

Advised golfing ability Niveau de jeu recommandé	0 12 24 36
Hcp required Handicap exigé	28 Men, 36 Ladies

CLUB HOUSE & AMENITIES
CLUB HOUSE ET ANNEXES
7/10

Pro shop	Pro-shop	
Driving range	Practice	
Sheltered	couvert	no
On grass	sur herbe	yes
Putting-green	putting-green	yes
Pitching-green	pitching green	no

HOTEL FACILITIES
ENVIRONNEMENT HOTELIER
7/10

HOTELS HÔTELS
Edgewater   Portstewart
31 rooms, D £ 70   adjancent
Tel (44) 01265 - 832 224, Fax (44) 01265 - 832 224

O'Neills Causeway Coast Hotel   Portrush
101 rooms, D £ 75   5 km
Tel (44) 01265 - 822 435, Fax (44) 01265 - 824 495

Royal Court Hotel   Portrush
18 rooms, D £ 85   8 km
Tel (44) 01265 - 822 236, Fax (44) 01265 - 823 176

RESTAURANTS RESTAURANT
Cromore Halt   Portstewart
Tel (44) 01265 - 836 888   2 km

Some Place Else   Portrush
Tel (44) 01265 - 824 945   4 km

As you might expect from a course with a regal title in a capital city, Royal Belfast is a rather exclusive club, but it is certainly not impossible to play here (especially during the week) if you book a tee-off time. Although you shouldn't expect the warm atmosphere of a vacation club in Florida, it would be a shame not to play the oldest established club in Ireland, not only for historical reasons but also because of the good course, modified slightly in the 1920s by Harry Colt. Although clearly visible, the hazards are genuinely dangerous (there is a total of 61 bunkers) and need extreme precision if they are to be avoided. So this is hardly what you would call a course for beginners. In addition, the greens are well-guarded and should be approached from exactly the right angle to keep your score down. Course upkeep is excellent.

Comme on peut l'attendre d'un golf avec un titre de noblesse et situé dans une capitale, Royal Belfast est un club assez exclusif, mais il n'est certes pas impossible d'y jouer (surtout en semaine) en réservant à l'avance. Bien sûr, il ne faut pas y attendre l'ambiance chaleureuse d'un club de vacances en Floride ! Il serait malgré tout dommage de ne pas visiter le plus ancien club établi en Irlande, non seulement pour raisons historiques, mais aussi parce qu'il dispose d'un bon parcours, auquel Harry Colt a apporté quelques modifications dans les années 20. Bien que les obstacles soient visibles, ils sont effectivement dangereux (il y a 61 bunkers au total), et demandent une grande précision pour être évités. De fait, ce n'est pas exactement un parcours pour débutants ! De plus, les greens sont bien protégés, et il faut les aborder avec un angle d'attaque correct pour préserver un bon score. L'entretien est excellent.

Royal Belfast Golf Club

Station Road, Craigavad
NIR - HOLYWOOD, Co Down BT18 OBP

Office	Secrétariat	(44) 01232 - 428 165
Pro shop	Pro-shop	(44) 01232 - 428 586
Fax	Fax	(44) 01232 - 421 404
Situation	Situation	

13 km from Belfast (pop. 279 237)
9 km from Bangor

Annual closure	Fermeture annnuelle	no
Weekly closure	Fermeture hebdomadaire	no

Fees main season
Tarifs haute saison 18 holes

	Week days Semaine	We/Bank holidays We/Férié
Individual Individuel	£ 30	£ 35
Couple Couple	£ 60	£ 70

Caddy	Caddy	no
Electric Trolley	Chariot électrique	no
Buggy	Voiturette	no
Clubs	Clubs	yes

Credit cards Cartes de crédit	no

Access Accès : Belfast, A2 → Bangor.
Map 1 on page 695 Carte 1 Page 695

GOLF COURSE PARCOURS · 15/20

Site	Site	
Maintenance	Entretien	
Architect	Architecte	Harry S. Colt
Type	Type	parkland
Relief	Relief	
Water in play	Eau en jeu	
Exp. to wind	Exposé au vent	
Trees in play	Arbres en jeu	

Scorecard Carte de score	Chp. Chp.	Mens Mess.	Ladies Da.
Length Long.	5676	5575	5000
Par	71	70	72

Advised golfing ability		0 12 24 36
Niveau de jeu recommandé		
Hcp required	Handicap exigé	24 Men, 36 Ladies

CLUB HOUSE & AMENITIES CLUB HOUSE ET ANNEXES · 7/10

Pro shop	Pro-shop	
Driving range	Practice	
Sheltered	couvert	
On grass	sur herbe	yes
Putting-green	putting-green	yes
Pitching-green	pitching green	no

HOTEL FACILITIES ENVIRONNEMENT HOTELIER · 7/10

HOTELS HÔTELS
Culloden Hotel — Holywood
89 rooms, D £ 140 — 1.5 km
Tel (44) 01232 - 425 223, Fax (44) 01232 - 426 777

Old Inn-Crawfords Burn — Bangor
33 rooms, D £ 90 — 6 km
Tel (44) 01247 - 853 255, Fax (44) 01247 - 852 175

Clandeboye Lodge — Bangor
43 rooms, D £ 75 — 9 km
Tel (44) 01247 - 852 500, Fax (44) 01247 - 852 772

RESTAURANTS RESTAURANT
Sullivans — Holywood
Tel (44) 01232 - 421 000 — 6 km

Shanks — Bangor
Tel (44) 01247 - 853 313 — 9 km

789

Choosing between Ballybunnion, Royal Portrush, Portmarnock and Royal County Down is like trying to give an order of preference to four children. This is a masterly links, with enough blind shots and tricky greens to make a caddie well worthwhile on your first visit. Designed by Old Tom Morris, the course has been modernised with no loss of character or majesty, and without the hazards losing their strategic role : the rough, bushes, bunkers and huge dunes collect poor or over-ambitious shots. For a decent score, your game has to be up to the standard demanded by the course, and a degree of humility will also help you to come to terms with the hazards, without which the game of golf would be boring. If you can, tee off from the 10th ; despite their excellence, the last 9 holes are a little less impressive than the front 9, which wind their way through sand dunes. This is, perhaps, the only hint of a blemish on an otherwise perfect masterpiece.

Choisir entre Ballybunion, Royal Portrush, Portmarnock et Royal County Down, c'est comme classer ses quatre enfants par ordre de préférence. Celui-ci est un links magistral, avec assez de coups aveugles et des greens assez délicats à lire pour inciter à prendre un caddie la première fois. Conçu par Old Tom Morris, ce parcours a été modernisé sans perdre son caractère et sa grandeur, sans que les obstacles perdent leur rôle stratégique : les roughs, les buissons, les bunkers, les immenses dunes accueillent tous les coups médiocres ou trop audacieux. Il faut un jeu à la hauteur du parcours pour y scorer décemment, mais aussi beaucoup d'humilité pour accepter les hasards sans lesquels le golf serait bien ennuyeux. Si l'on peut, on commencera par le retour : en dépit de leur qualité golfique, les derniers trous ne sont pas aussi impressionnnants que les autres, insinués dans les dunes. C'est la seule petite ombre à un tableau de maître.

Royal County Down
NIR - NEWCASTLE, Co Down

Office	Secrétariat	(44) 013967 - 23 314
Pro shop	Pro-shop	(44) 013967 - 22 419
Fax	Fax	(44) 013967 - 26 281
Situation	Situation	

48 km S of Belfast (pop. 279 237)
1 km from Newcastle (pop. 7 214)

Annual closure	Fermeture annnuelle	no
Weekly closure	Fermeture hebdomadaire	no

Fees main season
Tarifs haute saison 18 holes

	Week days Semaine	We/Bank holidays We/Férié
Individual Individuel	£ 60	£ 70
Couple Couple	£ 120	£ 140

No visitors on Sunday

Caddy	Caddy	£ 15/18 holes
Electric Trolley	Chariot électrique	£ 5/18 holes
Buggy	Voiturette	no
Clubs	Clubs	£ 15/18 holes
Credit cards Cartes de crédit		VISA - MasterCard

790

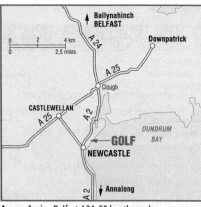

Access Accès : Belfast A24, 50 km through
Newcastle on A2
Map 1 on page 695 Carte 1 Page 695

GOLF COURSE
PARCOURS   **19**/20

Site	Site	▆▆▆▆▆▆▆▆▆▆
Maintenance	Entretien	▆▆▆▆▆▆▆▆▆▆
Architect	Architecte	Old Tom Morris
Type	Type	links
Relief	Relief	▆▆▆▆
Water in play	Eau en jeu	▆▆
Exp. to wind	Exposé au vent	▆▆▆▆
Trees in play	Arbres en jeu	▆▆

Scorecard Carte de score	Chp. Chp.	Mens Mess.	Ladies Da.
Length Long.	6335	6084	5672
Par	71	71	76

Advised golfing ability		0 12 24 36
Niveau de jeu recommandé		▆▆▆▆▆▆▆▆
Hcp required	Handicap exigé	28 Men, 36 Ladies

CLUB HOUSE & AMENITIES
CLUB HOUSE ET ANNEXES   **6**/10

Pro shop	Pro-shop	▆▆▆▆▆▆
Driving range	Practice	▆▆▆▆▆▆
Sheltered	couvert	no
On grass	sur herbe	yes
Putting-green	putting-green	yes
Pitching-green	pitching green	no

HOTEL FACILITIES
ENVIRONNEMENT HOTELIER   **7**/10

HOTELS HÔTELS
Slieve Donard Hotel   Newcastle
130 rooms, D £ 110   500 m
Tel (44) 013967 - 23 681, Fax (44) 013967 - 24 830

Glasdrumman Hotel   Glasdrumman
10 rooms, D £ 115   11 km
Tel (44) 013967 - 68 585, Fax (44) 013967 - 67 041

The Burrendale Hotel   Newcastle
68 rooms, D £ 80   1 km
Tel (44) 013967 - 22 599, Fax (44) 013967 - 22 328

RESTAURANTS RESTAURANT
The Pavillion   Newcastle
Tel (44) 013967 - 26 239   adjacent

Mario's   Newcastle
Tel (44) 013967 - 23 912   1 km

ROYAL PORTRUSH DUNLUCE LINKS

19	7	7

Being so close to the Giant's Causeway effectively brings to mind how a course can dwarf your golf. The Dunluce course is rated as one of Ireland's greatest courses, a fact you can easily check for yourself. Over an area covered with enormous dunes, the course comes and goes in a perfectly nothing-to-hide manner. In fact, it never leaves you alone and not a single hole fails to impress, so woe betide the golfer who drops his guard. You need not only extreme skill with club and ball, but also nerves of steel so as not to shrink from the difficulties you are sure to encounter sooner or later. Even the greens, with some tantalising slopes, demand unfailing concentration. You need a certain level of golfing ability to appreciate the subtler sides to this devilish course, which really snarls when the wind gets up. Harry Colt considered this to be his masterpiece. It is, quite simply, a masterpiece.

La proximité de la "Chaussée des Géants" fait penser que l'on est un nain, golfiquement parlant du moins. Le "Dunluce" de Royal Portrush passe pour être l'un des plus grands parcours d'Irlande, vous le vérifierez aisément. Dans un espace occupé par d'énormes dunes, le parcours va et vient avec une franchise parfaite. Il n'est pas un trou pour vous laisser tranquille ou indifférent, pour vous permettre de baisser la garde. Il faut non seulement une grande maîtrise de ses clubs et du maniement de la balle, mais aussi des nerfs d'acier pour ne pas fléchir devant les difficultés, à un moment ou à un autre. Même les greens exigent une concentration sans faille, avec leurs pentes déconcertantes. Il faut un certain niveau de jeu pour apprécier les subtilités de ce parcours démoniaque, dont les dents sont encore plus acérées avec le vent. Harry Colt le considérait comme "son" chef-d'oeuvre. C'est un chef d'oeuvre, tout simplement.

Royal Portrush Golf Club

Bushmills Road
NIR - PORTRUSH, Co Antrim

Office	Secrétariat	(44) 01265 - 822 311
Pro shop	Pro-shop	(44) 01265 - 823 335
Fax	Fax	(44) 01265 - 823 139
Situation	Situation	

90 km from Belfast (pop. 279 237)
8 km N of Coleraine (pop. 20 721)

Annual closure	Fermeture annuelle	no
Weekly closure	Fermeture hebdomadaire	no

Fees main season
Tarifs haute saison 18 holes

	Week days Semaine	We/Bank holidays We/Férié
Individual Individuel	£ 55	£ 65
Couple Couple	£ 110	£ 130

Additional round: £ 25 (any day)

Caddy	Caddy	on request/£ 20
Electric Trolley	Chariot électrique	£ 7.50/18 holes
Buggy	Voiturette	no
Clubs	Clubs	£ 10/18 holes

Credit cards Cartes de crédit
VISA - MasterCard - AMEX

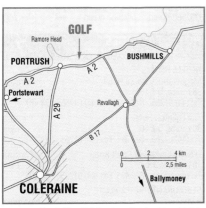

Access Accès : Belfast M2 North → Antrim. Turn right to A26 → Ballymena/Coleraine. Coleraine → Portrush
Map 1 on page 695 Carte 1 Page 695

GOLF COURSE PARCOURS

19/20

Site	Site	▬▬▬▬▬□
Maintenance	Entretien	▬▬▬▬▬□
Architect	Architecte	Harry S. Colt
Type	Type	links
Relief	Relief	
Water in play	Eau en jeu	▬□
Exp. to wind	Exposé au vent	▬▬▬▬□
Trees in play	Arbres en jeu	□

Scorecard Carte de score	Chp. Chp.	Mens Mess.	Ladies Da.
Length Long.	6137	6000	5601
Par	72	72	75

Advised golfing ability		0	12	24	36
Niveau de jeu recommandé			▬▬▬▬	
Hcp required	Handicap exigé	24 Men, 36 Ladies

CLUB HOUSE & AMENITIES
CLUB HOUSE ET ANNEXES

7/10

Pro shop	Pro-shop	▬▬▬▬□
Driving range	Practice	▬▬▬□
Sheltered	couvert	no
On grass	sur herbe	yes
Putting-green	putting-green	yes
Pitching-green	pitching green	yes

HOTEL FACILITIES
ENVIRONNEMENT HOTELIER

7/10

HOTELS HÔTELS

Magherabuoy House Hotel — Portrush
38 rooms, D £ 100 — 2 km
Tel (44) 01265 - 823 907, Fax (44) 01265 - 824 687

The Eglinton Hotel — Portrush
30 rooms, D £ 60 — 1 km
Tel (44) 01265 - 822 371, Fax (44) 01265 - 823 155

O'Neills Causeway Coast Hotel — Portrush
101 rooms, D £ 75 — 1 km
Tel (44) 01265 - 822 435, Fax (44) 01265 - 824 495

RESTAURANTS RESTAURANT

Ramore — Portrush
Tel (44) 01265 - 824 313 — 2 km

Some Place Else — Portrush
Tel (44) 01265 - 824 945 — 2 km

791

How can we assess the "second course" at Portrush ? Would we rate it a very good course if it went by any other name ? The answer is seemingly yes, even though it is some way from the greatness and majesty of Dunluce Links. Located, as its name suggests, in a valley between dunes, there are, strangely enough, no more than twenty bunkers, and the par 3s are particularly devoid of sand. Otherwise, the rolling terrain, rough, bushes and wind are trouble enough to upset most players, especially when the end-targets are as small as they generally are here. The nature of the terrain will also pose a few problems for players who are used to the immaculately prepared fairways of inland courses. As with all links courses, this is a test of ball-play and feeling, and the natural setting only adds to the appeal. Golfers who end up discovering this course by chance are generally surprised at the overall excellence of the layout. A very good practice course.

Comment juger le "second parcours" de Royal Portrush ? S'il portait un autre nom, serait-il considéréé comme un très bon parcours ? A l'évidence oui, même s'il est loin de la grandeur et de la majesté du "Dunluce Links". Situé comme son nom l'indique dans une vallée entre les dunes, il ne compte curieusement qu'une vingtaine de bunkers, particulièrement sur les par 3. Autrement, les ondulations du terrain, les roughs, les buissons et le vent suffisent amplement à troubler les joueurs, surtout quand les cibles finales sont petites, ce qui est généralement le cas. Et la nature du terrain posera forcément des problèmes aux joueurs habitués aux fairways impeccablement garnis des parcours intérieurs. Comme tous les links, celui-ci est un test de toucher de balle, et son aspect naturel ajoute à la séduction. Ceux qui sont amenés à le découvrir par hasard sont généralement surpris de sa qualité générale. Un bon parcours d'entraînement.

Royal Portrush Golf Club
Bushmills Road
NIR - PORTRUSH, Co Antrim

Office	Secrétariat	(44) 01265 - 822 311
Pro shop	Pro-shop	(44) 01265 - 823 335
Fax	Fax	(44) 01265 - 823 139
Situation	Situation	

90 km from Belfast (pop. 279 237)
8 km N of Coleraine (pop. 20 721)

Annual closure	Fermeture annnuelle	no
Weekly closure	Fermeture hebdomadaire	no

Fees main season
Tarifs haute saison 18 holes

	Week days Semaine	We/Bank holidays We/Férié
Individual Individuel	£ 22	£ 30
Couple Couple	£ 44	£ 60
Additional round: £ 10		

Caddy	Caddy	on request/£ 20
Electric Trolley	Chariot électrique	£ 7.50/18 holes
Buggy	Voiturette	no
Clubs	Clubs	£ 10/18 holes

Credit cards Cartes de crédit
VISA - MasterCard - AMEX

792

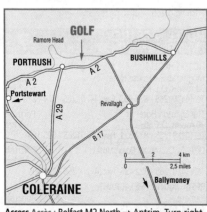

GOLF
Ramore Head
PORTRUSH
A 2
Portstewart
A 29
BUSHMILLS
A 2
Revallagh
B 17
0   2   4 km
0   2,5 miles
Ballymoney
COLERAINE

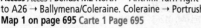

Access Accès : Belfast M2 North → Antrim. Turn right to A26 → Ballymena/Coleraine. Coleraine → Portrush
Map 1 on page 695 Carte 1 Page 695

GOLF COURSE
PARCOURS   **13**/20

Site	Site	
Maintenance	Entretien	
Architect	Architecte	
Type	Type	links
Relief	Relief	
Water in play	Eau en jeu	
Exp. to wind	Exposé au vent	
Trees in play	Arbres en jeu	

Scorecard Carte de score	Chp. Chp.	Mens Mess.	Ladies Da.
Length Long.	5700	5450	4995
Par	70	68	72

Advised golfing ability		0 12 24 36
Niveau de jeu recommandé		
Hcp required	Handicap exigé	no

CLUB HOUSE & AMENITIES
CLUB HOUSE ET ANNEXES   **7**/10

Pro shop	Pro-shop	
Driving range	Practice	
Sheltered	couvert	no
On grass	sur herbe	yes
Putting-green	putting-green	yes
Pitching-green	pitching green	yes

HOTEL FACILITIES
ENVIRONNEMENT HOTELIER   **7**/10

HOTELS HÔTELS

Magherabuoy House Hotel   Portrush
38 rooms, D £ 100   2 km
Tel (44) 01265 - 823 907, Fax (44) 01265 - 824 687

The Eglinton Hotel   Portrush
30 rooms, D £ 60   1 km
Tel (44) 01265 - 822 371, Fax (44) 01265 - 823 155

O'Neills Causeway Coast Hotel   Portrush
101 rooms, D £ 75   1 km
Tel (44) 01265 - 822 435, Fax (44) 01265 - 824 495

RESTAURANTS RESTAURANT

Ramore   Portrush
Tel (44) 01265 - 824 313   2 km

Some Place Else   Portrush
Tel (44) 01265 - 824 945   2 km

The setting for the Warrenpoint course, between mountains and Carringford bay, provides some breath-taking scenery and gives a marvellous sensation of space. To appreciate it fully, though, you will need to disregard the noise of the adjacent road, which is a shame. This is otherwise a very pleasant course, maybe more for mid- to high-handicappers than for the more skilled exponents, who might feel a little frustrated if expecting an adversary measuring up to their ability. But we need courses for every taste and anyway, there is no shortage of tough courses in Ireland. This layout requires no great length off the tee (which is a reserved privilege, anyway) but it does call for a sharp and subtle short game, as some approaches and bunkers around the greens are tricky. But these difficulties are generally on either side of the greens, so you can lay up short and stay out of trouble. A pleasant stop-off on "hard-working" holidays.

La situation du golf de Warrenpoint, entre les montagnes et la baie de Carringford permet des points de vue majestueux, donnant une sensation merveilleuse d'espace, mais il faut, pour en profiter, faire abstraction du bruit de la route adjacente... C'est dommage, car ce parcours est autrement très agréable, peut-être davantage encore pour les handicaps moyens et élevés, alors que les meilleurs joueurs seront un peu frustrés s'ils attendent un adversaire à la mesure de leur talent. Mais il faut des golfs pour tous les goûts, et le pays ne manque pas de parcours difficiles. Celui-ci ne requiert pas une grande longueur (elle n'est pas donnée à tout le monde), mais plutôt de la finesse de petit jeu, car certains abords de greens sont délicats, de même que les bunkers. Mais ces difficultés sont plutôt de part et d'autre des greens, ce qui autorise à jouer court pour ne pas en souffrir. Une halte sympathique pour des vacances studieuses.

Warrenpoint Golf Club

Lower Dromore Road
NIR - WARRENPOINT, Co Down BT34 3LN

Office	Secrétariat	(44) 016937 - 53 695
Pro shop	Pro-shop	(44) 016937 - 52 371
Fax	Fax	(44) 016937 - 52 918
Situation	Situation	

50 km from Belfast (pop. 279 237)
8 km from Newry

Annual closure	Fermeture annnuelle	no
Weekly closure	Fermeture hebdomadaire	no

Fees main season
Tarifs haute saison 18 holes

	Week days Semaine	We/Bank holidays We/Férié
Individual Individuel	£ 18	£ 24
Couple Couple	£ 36	£ 48

Caddy	Caddy	no
Electric Trolley	Chariot électrique	£ 10/18 holes
Buggy	Voiturette	no
Clubs	Clubs	£ 10

Credit cards Cartes de crédit	no

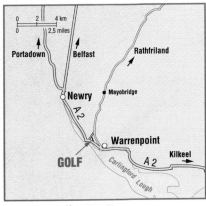

| 0 | 2 | 4 km |
| 0 | | 2,5 miles |

Portadown — Belfast — Rathfriland
Newry • Mayobridge
A2
Warrenpoint
GOLF — A 2 — Kilkeel
Carlingford Lough

Access Accès : Belfast, A1 to Newry.
A2 → Warrenpoint.
Map 1 on page 695 Carte 1 Page 695

GOLF COURSE
PARCOURS

13 /20

Site	Site	▬▬▬
Maintenance	Entretien	▬▬▬
Architect	Architecte	
Type	Type	parkland, hilly
Relief	Relief	▬▬▬
Water in play	Eau en jeu	▬
Exp. to wind	Exposé au vent	▬▬▬
Trees in play	Arbres en jeu	▬▬▬

Scorecard Carte de score	Chp. Chp.	Mens Mess.	Ladies Da.
Length Long.	6161	5778	5377
Par	71	71	72

Advised golfing ability	0	12	24	36
Niveau de jeu recommandé		▬▬		
Hcp required	Handicap exigé	no		

CLUB HOUSE & AMENITIES
CLUB HOUSE ET ANNEXES

6 /10

Pro shop	Pro-shop	▬▬▬
Driving range	Practice	▬▬▬
Sheltered	couvert	no
On grass	sur herbe	yes
Putting-green	putting-green	yes
Pitching-green	pitching green	no

HOTEL FACILITIES
ENVIRONNEMENT HOTELIER

5 /10

HOTELS HÔTELS

Kilmorey Arms Hotel — Kilkeel
50 rooms, D £ 40 — 20 km
Tel (44) 016937 - 62 220
Fax (44) 016937 - 65 399

Carlingford Bay Hotel — Warrenpoint
24 rooms, D £ 50 — 1 km
Tel (44) 016937 - 73 521
Fax (44) 016937 - 74 202

RESTAURANTS RESTAURANT

The Brass Monkey — Newry
Tel (44) 01693 - 63 176 — 8 km

Aylesfort House — Warrenpoint
Tel (44) 016937 -72 255 — 100 m

793

JE VOELT JE LEKKERDER IN EEN PEUGEOT

COUPÉ
406
PEUGEOT

The Netherlands
Nederland

M et meer dan 110.000 spelers behoort Nederland tot de landen van Europa met een sterke groei. Er zijn meer dan 60 18-holes-banen, die logischerwijze vooral rond de grote steden liggen. Wat betekent dat het er vooral in de weekends druk kan zijn. Maar de afstanden van ene naar de andere kant van dit land zijn nooit erg groot en het wegennet is vrij dich, waardoor je een groot gebied rond de verblijfplaats kunt bereiken. Naast de 'grote' banen aan de kust heeft het land golftechnisch nog meer in zijn mars, met banen die vaak goed in het lanschap zijn opgenomen. Het is een weinig bekende bestemming, die vooral en de zomer ontdekt moet worden.

795

The Netherlands, with 110,000 golfers, is one of the countries in Europe where golf is developing fast. There are more than 60 eighteen-hole courses, naturally spread around large cities, thus implying busy week-ends. But here, distances from one end of the country to the other are never too great, and the very dense road system makes for easy travelling round and about your holiday location. Alongside the great seaside courses, the country has a number of solid arguments to attract golf-trotters, with courses that, more often than not, blend in very tastefully with the natural landscape. This is still a little known destination, and one well worth discovering during the warmer months.

797

RANGSCHIKKING VAN DE TERREINEN
CLASSIFICATION OF COURSES

Deze rangschikking houdt eerst en vooral rekening met het cijfer,
dat aan het terrein werd toegekend.

This classification gives priority consideration
to the score awarded to the actual course.

Cijfer van het Club-House & dependances
Club-house and facilities

Cijfer van het terrein
Course score

Cijfer van hotelaccomodatie in de omgeving
Hotel facility score

					Blz
18 8 6	Eindhoven			807	*Page*

Cijfer			Baan	Blz	Cijfer			Baan	Blz
18	8	6	Eindhoven	807	**15**	6	7	Hoge Kleij	816
18	7	8	Haagsche	813	**15**	5	3	Nunspeet North/East	820
18	8	8	Kennemer	817	**15**	7	7	Oosterhout	821
18	7	8	Noordwijk	819	**15**	7	7	Rosendael	824
16	8	5	Cromstrijen	804	**15**	7	5	Sint Nicolaasga	825
16	8	7	De Pan	805	**15**	6	6	Sybrook	826
16	8	5	Efteling	806	**15**	7	6	Wouwse Plantage	828
16	7	6	Herkenbosch	814	**15**	7	6	Anderstein	801
16	7	7	Hilversum	815	**14**	4	5	Gelpenberg	808
16	7	7	Purmerend	822	**14**	7	4	Grevelingenhout	812
15	7	7	Amsterdam	800	**14**	6	7	Lauswolt	818
15	7	3	Batouwe	802	**14**	6	5	Rijk van Nijmegen	
15	7	6	Broekpolder	803				*Nijmeegse Baan*	823
15	7	7	Gendersteyn	809	**14**	7	6	Toxandria	827
15	3	6	Goes	810	**14**	7	7	Zuid Limburgse	829
15	7	6	Graafschap	811					

RANGSCHIKKING VAN DE HOTELACCOMODATIE
CLASSIFICATION OF HOTELS FACILITIES

Cijfer van het Club-House & dependances
Club-house and facilities

Cijfer van het terrein
Course score

Cijfer van hotelaccomodatie in de omgeving
Hotel facility score

					Blz
18 7 **8**	Haagsche			813	*Page*

Cijfer			Baan	Blz	Cijfer			Baan	Blz
18	7	**8**	Haagsche	813	15	7	**7**	Gendersteyn	809
18	8	**8**	Kennemer	817	16	7	**7**	Hilversum	815
18	7	**8**	Noordwijk	819	15	6	**7**	Hoge Kleij	816
15	7	**7**	Amsterdam	800	14	6	**7**	Lauswolt	818
16	8	**7**	De Pan	805	15	7	**7**	Oosterhout	821

RANGSCHIKKING VAN DE TERREINEN

Cijfer			Baan	Blz	Cijfer			Baan	Blz
16	7	**7**	Purmerend	822	15	7	**6**	Wouwse Plantage	828
15	7	**7**	Rosendael	824	16	8	**5**	Cromstrijen	804
14	7	**7**	Zuid Limburgse	829	16	8	**5**	Efteling	806
14	7	**6**	Anderstein	801	14	4	**5**	Gelpenberg	808
15	7	**6**	Broekpolder	803	14	6	**5**	Rijk van Nijmegen	
18	8	**6**	Eindhoven	807				Nijmeegse Baan	823
15	3	**6**	Goes	810	15	7	**5**	Sint Nicolaasga	825
15	7	**6**	Graafschap	811	14	7	**4**	Grevelingenhout	812
16	7	**6**	Herkenbosch	814	15	7	**3**	Batouwe	802
15	6	**6**	Sybrook	826	15	5	**3**	Nunspeet North/East	820
14	7	**6**	Toxandria	827					

AAN TE RADEN VAKANTIEVERBLIJF
RECOMMENDED GOLFING STAY

Cijfer	Baan				Blz	Cijfer	Baan				Blz
	De Pan	16	8	7	805		Hilversum	16	7	7	815
	Eindhoven	18	8	6	807		Kennemer	18	8	8	817
	Haagsche	18	7	8	813		Noordwijk	18	7	8	819

ARCHITECTEN EN TERREINEN
ARCHITECTS AND COURSES

Seizoenen / baan	Cijfer			Blz	Seizoenen / baan	Cijfer			Blz
`1 2 3 4 5 6 7 8 9 10 11 12`					`1 2 3 4 5 6 7 8 9 10 11 12`				
Goes	15	3	6	810	Hoge Kleij	15	6	7	816
Haagsche	18	7	8	813	Kennemer	18	8	8	817
Noordwijk	18	7	8	819	Lauswolt	14	6	7	818
Nunspeet North/East	15	5	3	820	Oosterhout	15	7	7	821
					Purmerend	16	7	7	822
`1 2 3 4 5 6 7 8 9 10 11 12`					Rijk van Nijmegen				
Anderstein	14	7	6	801	Nijmeegse Baan	14	6	5	823
Batouwe	15	7	3	802	Rosendael	15	7	7	824
Broekpolder	15	7	6	803	Sybrook	15	6	6	826
Cromstrijen	16	8	5	804	Toxandria	14	7	6	827
De Pan	16	8	7	805	Wouwse Plantage	15	7	6	828
Efteling	16	8	5	806	Zuid Limburgse	14	7	7	829
Eindhoven	18	8	6	807					
Gelpenberg	14	4	5	808	`1 2 3 4 5 6 7 8 9 10 11 12`				
Gendersteyn	15	7	7	809	Amsterdam	15	7	7	800
Graafschap	15	7	6	811	Herkenbosch	16	7	6	814
Grevelingenhout	14	7	4	812	Sint Nicolaasga	15	7	5	825
Hilversum	16	7	7	815					

799

Toen de oude Amsterdamse de helft van zijn holes aan de Spoorwegen verloor, vertrok de club naar een nieuw, open terrein aan de westkant van de stad (soms een beetje rumoerig door de overvliegende vliegtuigen). Aanvankelijk waren er problemen waardoor alle greens moesten worden gerenoveerd. Die ingreep en het verder groeien van de jonge aanplant, zullen de baan sterk verbeteren. De eerste zeven holes zijn niet om over naar huis te schrijven, met alleen de fairway bunkers en de wind als moeilijkheidsfactor. Dan wordt het spannender met twee par-4 holes en water. Water speelt ook een belangrijke rol op de tweede negen, vooral op de 14e (een par-5 dogleg met twee vijvers) en de 18e waar de green wordt afgeschermd door water. Een prachtige slothole. De baan is niet te druk. Er zijn plannen voor ingrijpende veranderingen aan de fairways.

When the old Amsterdam Golf Club lost half of its holes to the railways, the club moved out into a very open area to the west of the city (sometimes a little noisy because of the airport). Owing to a number of serious problems, the greens have all been re-laid and their maturity should do much to improve the terrain still further; the same goes for the newly planted trees and bushes. The seven first holes are not much to write home about, the only difficulties being the bunker fairways and wind. Then, it gets a little more exciting with two par 4s and water hazards. Water, in fact, is very much to the fore on the way in, especially on the 14th (a par 5 dog-leg with two ponds and two ditches) and the 18th, where the green is again guarded by water to make an excellent final hole. The course is not too crowded and significant improvement work on a number of fairways is planned in the near future.

Amsterdamse Golfclub
Bauduinlaan 35
NL - 1165 NE HALFWEG

Office	Secretariaat	(31) 020 - 497 7866
Pro shop	Pro shop	(31) 020 - 497 4906
Fax	Fax	(31) 020 - 497 5966
Situation	Locatie	

10 km Amsterdam, 724 096 inw.

Annual closure	Jaarlijkse sluiting	neen
Weekly closure	Wekelijkse sluitingsdag	neen

Fees main season
Hoogseizoen tarieven 18 holes

	Week days Weekdagen	We/Bank holidays We/Feestdagen
Individual Individueel	Fl 100,-	Fl 100,-
Couple Paar	Fl 200,-	Fl 200,-

Caddy	Caddy	neen
Electric Trolley	Electrische trolley	Fl 7.50,-
Buggy	Buggy	Fl 25,-
Clubs	Clubs	Fl 25,-
Credit cards Creditkaarten		neen

Access Toegang : Amsterdam N5/A5 → Haarlem.
Exit Spaarnwoude. 1 km → Ruigoord/Houtrak
Map 1 on page 796 Auto kaart 1 Blz 796

GOLF COURSE
BAAN
15/20

Site	Terrein	
Maintenance	Onderhoud	
Architect	Architect	Paul Rolin Gerard Jol (1993)
Type	Type baan	polderbaan
Relief	Reliëf	
Water in play	Waterhazards	
Exp. to wind	Windgevoelig	
Trees in play	Bomen	

Scorecard Scorekaart	Chp. Back tees	Mens Heren	Ladies Damen
Length Lengte	6103	5948	5084
Par	72	72	72

Advised golfing ability Aanbevolen golfvaardigheid	0	12	24	36

Hcp required	Vereiste hcp	ja

CLUB HOUSE & AMENITIES
CLUB HOUSE EN ANNEXEN
7/10

Pro shop	Pro shop	
Driving range	Oefenbaan	
Sheltered	overdekt	5 plaatsen
On grass	op gras	neen
Putting-green	putting-green	ja
Pitching-green	pitching-green	ja

HOTEL FACILITIES
HOTELS IN OMGEVING
7/10

HOTELS HOTELS
Radisson SAS — Amsterdam
246 kamers, D Fl 375,- — 15 km
Tel. (31) 020 - 623 1231
Fax (31) 020 - 520 8200

Canal House — Amsterdam
26 kamers, D Fl 225,- — 15 km
Tel. (31) 020 - 622 5182
Fax (31) 020 - 624 1317

RESTAURANTS RESTAURANT
La Rive — Amsterdam
Tel. (31) 020 - 622 6060 — 10 km

De Bokkedorns — Overveen/Haarlem
Tel.(31) 023 - 526 3600 — 15 km

800

De spoorweg en de A12 op de achtergrond van een aantal holes zouden niet teveel de aandacht van de vele kwaliteiten van deze baan moeten afleiden. Het vroegere familiedomein is omgetoverd in een 18-holes baan, met het clubhuis in de gerestaureerde en onlangs nog eens gerenoveerde boerenstal. Bij de uitbreiding zijn acht van de oorspronkelijke holes intact gebleven. Die zijn vrij smal omdat er in eerste aanleg niet veel ruimte was. Van de tien nieuwe holes liggen er vijf in open land. Het zijn doglegs met brede fairways, twee grote vijvers en strategisch geplaatste fairway bunkers. De overige vijf liggen meer tussen de bomen, zoals de oorspronkelijke holes. Alles bij elkaar is het een aantrekkelijke baan geworden, met allerlei moeilijkheden. Allereerst al de noodzaak om aan de grote variëteit in holes te wennen. Je moet er eigenlijk meerdere keren spelen om de baan te gaan begrijpen. Doe dit vooral door de week, want in de weekenden zijn er veel leden op de been/baan.

The railway line and road that form a backdrop to some holes here should not conceal the many virtues of this course. The erstwhile family property was extended and built into a private 18 hole course, and the old farmhouse, now the clubhouse, has recently been restored. Eight of the first nine holes have been preserved and are very narrow - they were built over a restricted amount of space. Of the ten new holes, five run through wide open land in the form of doglegs with broad fairways, two major water hazards and strategically located fairway bunkers. The other five are in woodland, like the original holes. In all, this has become a very attractive course, offering all sorts of difficulty, the first of which is to get accustomed to the very different nature of each hole. You definitely need to play here several times to understand the course. If you do, make it a week-day, as there are a lot of members at week-ends.

Golfclub Anderstein

Woudenbergseweg 13 A
NL 3953 ME MAARSBERGEN

Office	Secretariaat	(31) 0343 - 431 330
Pro shop	Pro shop	(31) 0343 - 431 560
Fax	Fax	(31) 0343 - 432 062
Situation	Locatie	

20 km Utrecht, 234 106 inw.

Annual closure	Jaarlijkse sluiting	neen
Weekly closure	Wekelijkse sluitingsdag	neen

Fees main season
Hoogseizoen tarieven 18 holes

	Week days Weekdagen	We/Bank holidays We/Feestdagen
Individual Individueel	Fl 80,-	—
Couple Paar	Fl 160,-	—

Caddy	Caddy	neen
Electric Trolley	Electrische trolley	Fl 7,50,-
Buggy	Buggy	neen
Clubs	Clubs	neen

Credit cards Creditkaarten	neen

Access Toegang : A 12 Utrecht-Arnhem.
Exit 22 → Maarsbergen, N226. 500 m links
Map 1 on page 796 Auto kaart 1 Blz 796

GOLF COURSE
BAAN
14/20

Site	Terrein	
Maintenance	Onderhoud	
Architect	Architect	Joan Dudok van Heel Gerard Jol (1989)
Type	Type baan	parkbaan
Relief	Reliëf	
Water in play	Waterhazards	
Exp. to wind	Windgevoelig	
Trees in play	Bomen	

Scorecard Scorekaart	Chp. Back tees	Mens Heren	Ladies Damen
Length Lengte	6015	5719	4910
Par	72	72	72

Advised golfing ability Aanbevolen golfvaardigheid	0	12	24	36
Hcp required	Vereiste hcp	neen		

CLUB HOUSE & AMENITIES
CLUB HOUSE EN ANNEXEN
7/10

Pro shop	Pro shop	
Driving range	Oefenbaan	
Sheltered	overdekt	6 plaatsen
On grass	op gras	neen
Putting-green	putting-green	ja
Pitching-green	pitching-green	ja

HOTEL FACILITIES
HOTELS IN OMGEVING
6/10

HOTELS HOTELS
Motel Maarsbergen   Maarsbergen
38 kamers, D Fl. 95,-   500 m
Tel. (31) 0343 - 431 341
Fax (31) 0343 - 431 379

De Hoefslag   Bosch en Duin
34 kamers, D FL 220,-   15 km
Tel. (31) 030 - 225 1051
Fax (31) 030 - 228 5821

RESTAURANTS RESTAURANT
De Hoefslag   Bosch en Duin
Tel. (31) 030 - 225 1051   15 km

801

Deze nieuwe baan ligt in open terrein, midden tussen de grote rivieren. Bij de aanleg stonden er al een handjevol bomen en die zijn goed in het ontwerp ingepast. Ze staan langs de fairways of beschermen enkele greens, waardoor spelers twee keer moeten denken voordat ze een driver uit de tas halen. Er komen heel wat waterhazards in het spel, zoals op de 15e, een par-3 met een eilandgreen, of de 18e waar water de green beschermd tegen mislukte approaches. De negen andere holes hebben gewoon veel bunkers vooral op de fairways, zeker op twee holes. Honderden jonge bomen zijn aangeplant, maar die zijn nog niet groot genoeg om veel bescherming tegen de wind te bieden. Hoewel de baan vrij kort is, zijn het vooral de elementen, zoals wind en water, die dwingen tot een nauwkeurige clubkeuze. De beste tijd om Batouwe te spelen is in het voorjaar, als de fruitbomen in de Betuwe in bloei staan.

This recent course has been laid out over wide open space between the main rivers in the centre of Holland. There were a handful of trees, and these have been intelligently used by the designer. They line certain fairways and protect a number of greens, forcing players to think twice before taking the driver out of the bag. A lot of water hazards come into play, like on the par 3 15th, with an island green, or the 18th, where water protects the green from mis-hit approach shots. Most of the other holes just have lots of bunkers, especially of the fairway variety, numerous on two holes in particular. Hundreds of other trees have been planted but are no size as yet, so there is precious little protection from the wind - even though the course itself is on the short side, the elements are a key factor here for choosing the right club. The best time to play Batouwe is in the Spring, when the region's fruit trees are in full blossom.

Betuws Golfcentrum de Batouwe

Ost Kanaalweg 1
NL - 4011 LA ZOELEN

Office	Secretariaat	(31) 0344 - 624 370
Pro shop	Pro shop	(31) 0344 - 624 370
Fax	Fax	(31) 0344 - 613 096
Situation	Locatie	

3 km N Tiel, 33 571 inw.

Annual closure	Jaarlijkse sluiting	neen
Weekly closure	Wekelijkse sluitingsdag	neen

Fees main season
Hoogseizoen tarieven 18 holes

	Week days Weekdagen	We/Bank holidays We/Feestdagen
Individual Individueel	Fl 65,-	Fl 80,-
Couple Paar	Fl 130,-	Fl 160,-

Caddy	Caddy	Fl 10,-
Electric Trolley	Electrische trolley	neen
Buggy	Buggy	Fl 10,-
Clubs	Clubs	Fl 5,-

Credit cards Creditkaarten
VISA - Eurocard - MasterCard

Access Toegang : A15 Rotterdam-Arnhem/Nijmegen.
Exit 33 → Maurik, 3,5 km → Echtfeld. Golf 1 km
Map 1 on page 796 Auto kaart 1 Blz 796

GOLF COURSE
BAAN

15/20

Site	Terrein	▆▆▆▆□
Maintenance	Onderhoud	▆▆▆▆□
Architect	Architect	Alan Rijks
Type	Type baan	polderbaan
Relief	Reliëf	▆□□□□
Water in play	Waterhazards	▆▆▆▆□
Exp. to wind	Windgevoelig	▆▆▆▆□
Trees in play	Bomen	▆▆▆□□

Scorecard Scorekaart	Chp. Back tees	Mens Heren	Ladies Damen
Length Lengte	5775	5775	4839
Par	72	72	72

Advised golfing ability Aanbevolen golfvaardigheid		0 12 24 36 ▆▆▆▆
Hcp required Vereiste hcp	neen	

CLUB HOUSE & AMENITIES
CLUB HOUSE EN ANNEXEN

7/10

Pro shop	Pro shop	▆▆▆▆□
Driving range	Oefenbaan	▆▆▆□□
Sheltered	overdekt	6 plaatsen
On grass	op gras	neen
Putting-green	putting-green	ja
Pitching-green	pitching-green	ja

HOTEL FACILITIES
HOTELS IN OMGEVING

3/10

HOTELS HOTELS

't Paviljoen — Rhenen
32 kamers, D Fl 165,- — 20 km
Tel. (31) 0317 - 619 003
Fax (31) 0317 - 617 213

RESTAURANTS RESTAURANT

Gravin van Buren — Buren
Tel. (31) 0344 - 571 663 — 7 km

't Kalkoentje — Rhenen
Tel. (31) 0317 - 612 344 — 20 km

Hier vindt u een voorbeeld van een nog vrij nieuwe baan, waar de oorspronkelijk nogal kale ruimte geleidelijk aan voller en rijker wordt. Na de aanleg in 1983 zijn bomen en struiken nu bijna volgroeid hetgeen zowel bescherming tegen de wind biedt als een visuele verbetering is. De ontwikkeling van de baan wordt versterkt door recente ingrepen die wat oorspronkelijke zwaktes hebben opgeheven. Waterhazards komen op vijf holes in het spel en vormen met de sloten de belangrijkste hindernissen. Ook bunkers spelen een rol in de verdediging van de grote greens. Sommige holes zijn behoorlijk aan de lange kant, maar toch is de baan geschikt voor spelers van alle niveaus. Broekpolder ligt maar een paar meter boven het zeeniveau, maar dat is voldoende om een paar mooie vergezichten over de omliggende polders op te leveren, met de haveninstallatie van Rotterdam op de achtergrond.

Here is an example of a recently built course, where the original barren space is gradually becoming richer, visibly developing and maturing year in year out. Since 1983, the trees and bushes are already almost full grown, bringing greater protection from the wind and visual improvement. The course's evolution has also been marked by recent changes, which have put right some of the flaws exposed by the course's immaturity. The water hazards come into play on four holes, and, with a number of ditches, form the main difficulties. The bunkers, too, provide a firm line of defence for the large greens. We might add that some of the holes are on the long side, but overall the course can be played by golfers of all levels. Broekpolder is only a few metres above sea level, but that's enough to provide some pretty views over the surrounding lakes and fields, with the port of Rotterdam in the background.

Golfclub Broekpolder

Watersportweg 100
NL - 3138 HD VLAARDINGEN

Office	Secretariaat	(31) 010 - 249 5566
Pro shop	Pro shop	(31) 010 - 474 7610
Fax	Fax	(31) 010 - 474 4094
Situation	Locatie	

12 km Rotterdam, 598 521 inw.

| Annual closure | Jaarlijkse sluiting | neen |
| Weekly closure | Wekelijkse sluitingsdag | neen |

Fees main season
Hoogseizoen tarieven 18 holes

	Week days Weekdagen	We/Bank holidays We/Feestdagen
Individual Individueel	Fl 80,-	Fl 100,-
Couple Paar	Fl 160,-	Fl 200,-

Caddy	Caddy	neen
Electric Trolley	Electrische trolley	neen
Buggy	Buggy	neen
Clubs	Clubs	neen

Credit cards Creditkaarten
Eurocard - MasterCard

Access Toegang : A20 Rotterdam → Vlaardingen.
Exit 8 → Broekpolderweg, Golf 3 km
Map 1 on page 796 Auto kaart 1 Blz 796

GOLF COURSE
BAAN 15/20

Site	Terrein	
Maintenance	Onderhoud	
Architect	Architect	Frank Pennink Gerard Jol (1991)
Type	Type baan	polderbaan
Relief	Reliëf	
Water in play	Waterhazards	
Exp. to wind	Windgevoelig	
Trees in play	Bomen	

Scorecard Scorekaart	Chp. Back tees	Mens Heren	Ladies Damen
Length Lengte	6429	6048	5313
Par	72	72	72

Advised golfing ability Aanbevolen golfvaardigheid	0	12	24	36

| Hcp required | Vereiste hcp | 30 |

CLUB HOUSE & AMENITIES
CLUB HOUSE EN ANNEXEN 7/10

Pro shop	Pro shop	
Driving range	Oefenbaan	
Sheltered	overdekt	20 plaatsen
On grass	op gras	neen
Putting-green	putting-green	ja
Pitching-green	pitching-green	ja

HOTEL FACILITIES
HOTELS IN OMGEVING 6/10

HOTELS HOTELS

| Delta | Vlaardingen |
| 78 kamers, D Fl 140,- | 5 km |
Tel. (31) 010 - 434 5477, Fax (31) 010 - 434 9525

| New York | Rotterdam |
| 73 kamers, D Fl 135,- | 20 km |
Tel. (31) 010 - 439 0500, Fax (31) 010 - 484 2701

| Parkhotel | Rotterdam |
| 187 kamers, D Fl 335,- | 15 km |
Tel. (31) 010 - 436 3611, Fax (31) 010 - 436 4212

RESTAURANTS RESTAURANT

| Parkheuvel | Rotterdam |
Tel. (31) 010 - 475 0011 | 15 km

| La Duchesse | Schiedam |
Tel. (31) 010 - 426 4626 | 10 km

803

Deze nog vrij nieuwe baan, niet ver van Rotterdam, ligt in een wijd open gebied. Weliswaar dichtbij een autoweg, maar ook met fraaie vergezichten over de omliggende weidegebieden. De plaatselijke autoriteiten keurden de aanleg van een golfbaan goed op voorwaarde dat die open zou staan voor iedereen. Het resultaat daarvan is een openbare 9-holes baan naast een besloten 18-holes baan. Het meest opvallende natuurlijke element wordt gevormd door vier rijen met hoge bomen. De stukken water daartussen zijn uitgebouwd tot een klein meertje, dat meerdere keren in het spel komt. Een andere moeilijkheidsfactor bestaat uit de 75 strategisch geplaatste bunkers en, natuurlijk, uit de wind. Er is veel jonge aanplant, bedoeld om deze vlakke baan een beetje vorm te geven. De greens zijn groot, goed gevormd, goed ontworpen en sterk bewaakt. De baan is door Tom McAuley ontworpen voor alle type golfers en wordt zeer goed onderhouden baan. Naarmate de baan rijpt, zal het een van de meeste interessante banen van het land worden.

This recent course, situated not far from Rotterdam, is laid out in wide open space, close to a motorway but with scenic views over farmland. The local authorities agreed to building the course as long as it was open to everyone. The result is a public 9-holer next to a private 18-hole course. The most striking natural elements are the four rows of trees. The patches of water have been extended to form a real lake, which comes into play several times. The other hazards are the 75 strategically placed bunkers and, of course, the wind. A great many shrubs have been planted as well, to give this flat course a little relief. The greens are huge, well-contoured, well-designed and very safely-guarded. As it matures, this Tom McAuley course, designed for all golfers and very well upkept, should become one of the most interesting in Holland. The clubhouse already has the majestic allure worthy of such a status.

Golfclub Cromstrijen

Veerweg 26
NL - 3281 LX NUMANSDORP

Office	Secretariaat	(31) 0186 - 655 155
Pro shop	Pro shop	(31) 0186 - 654 630
Fax	Fax	(31) 0186 - 654 681
Situation	Locatie	

20 km Rotterdam, 598 521 inw.
15 km Dordrecht, 113 394 inw.

Annual closure	Jaarlijkse sluiting	neen
Weekly closure	Wekelijkse sluitingsdag	neen

Fees main season
Hoogseizoen tarieven per dag

	Week days Weekdagen	We/Bank holidays We/Feestdagen
Individual Individueel	Fl 70,-	Fl 85,-
Couple Paar	Fl 140,-	Fl 170,-

Caddy	Caddy	neen
Electric Trolley	Electrische trolley	Fl 7,50,-
Buggy	Buggy	neen
Clubs	Clubs 1/2 set	Fl 25,-
Credit cards Creditkaarten		neen

Access Toegang : Rotterdam A29. Exit 22 → Havens Numansdorp, → Veenhaven
Map 1 on page 796 Auto kaart 1 Blz 796

GOLF COURSE
BAAN   16/20

Site	Terrein	
Maintenance	Onderhoud	
Architect	Architect	Tom MacAuley
Type	Type baan	open parkbaan
Relief	Reliëf	
Water in play	Waterhazards	
Exp. to wind	Windgevoelig	
Trees in play	Bomen	

Scorecard Scorekaart	Chp. Back tees	Mens Heren	Ladies Damen
Length Lengte	6128	5934	5039
Par	72	72	72

Advised golfing ability Aanbevolen golfvaardigheid	0	12	24	36
Hcp required Vereiste hcp	neen			

CLUB HOUSE & AMENITIES
CLUB HOUSE EN ANNEXEN   8/10

Pro shop	Pro shop	
Driving range	Oefenbaan	
Sheltered	overdekt	12 plaatsen
On grass	op gras	neen
Putting-green	putting-green	ja
Pitching-green	pitching-green	ja

HOTEL FACILITIES
HOTELS IN OMGEVING   5/10

HOTELS HOTELS
Het Wapen van Willemstad   Willemstad
6 kamers, D Fl. 150,-   8 km
Tel. (31) 0168 - 473 450
Fax (31) 0168 - 473 705

Zuiderparkhotel   Rotterdam
117 kamers, D Fl. 175,-   20 km
Tel. (31) 010 - 485 0055
Fax (31) 010 - 485 6304

RESTAURANTS RESTAURANT
Wapen van Willemstad   Willemstad
Tel. (31) 0168 - 473 450   8 km

Hosman Frères   Schiedam
Tel.(31) 010 - 426 4096   25 km

804

DE PAN

Harry Colt heeft zijn stempel op meerdere banen in Nederland gezet en zijn ontwerpen zijn altijd een plezierige erva-ring. Een korte bootreis was voor hem voldoende om hier naartoe te komen vanuit zijn geboorteland Engeland, waar hij ook een aantal meesterwerken afleverde (Sunningdale, Wentworth en Ganton, bijvoorbeeld). Hij was onder andere een van de eerste grote ontwerpers van banen in het binnenland. De Pan is een van die uitstekende voorbeelden van zijn vermogen net het juiste aantal hazards te op nemen om wat pikants aan het spel toe te voegen. Op heel natuur-lijke wijze werkend met de omgeving en altijd een paar strategische verrassingen toevoegend, zoals een aantal fasci-nerende doglegs en veeleisende par-3 holes. De baan heeft meer glooiing dan je zou verwachten zo midden in Holland. De belangrijkste obstakels om te ontwijken zijn de bomen en een paar goed geplaatste bunkers. Weggestopt in de bossen, ver van alle lawaai, is deze aantrekkelijke baan er een die u echt aan uw collectie moet toevoegen.

For Harry Colt, coming in the Netherlands was a short boat trip from his native England, where he also produ-ced a number of masterpieces (Sunningdale, Wentworth and Ganton, for example). Among other things, he was one of the first great designers of inland courses. This is one excellent example of his skill in placing just the right number of hazards needed to add a little spice to the game, working very naturally with the surroundings and always adding a few strategic surprises, such as a number of compelling dog-legs and tough par 3s. The course undulates a little more than you might expect in this part of Holland, and the major hazards to be avoi-ded are the trees and a few well-located bunkers. Tucked away in the woods far from any noise, this fine course is most definitely one to add to your collection.

Utrechse Golf Club De Pan

Amersfoortseweg 1
NL - 3735 LJ BOSCH EN DUIN

Office	Secretariaat	(31) 030 - 695 6427
Pro shop	Pro shop	(31) 030 - 695 6427
Fax	Fax	(31) 030 - 696 3769
Situation	Locatie	

10 km Utrecht, 234 106 inw.

Annual closure	Jaarlijkse sluiting	neen
Weekly closure	Wekelijkse sluitingsdag	neen

Fees main season
Hoogseizoen tarieven 18 holes

	Week days Weekdagen	We/Bank holidays We/Feestdagen
Individual Individueel	Fl 90,-	Fl 90,-
Couple Paar	Fl 180,-	Fl 180,-

Caddy	Caddy	neen
Electric Trolley	Electrische trolley	neen
Buggy	Buggy	neen
Clubs	Clubs	neen

Credit cards Creditkaarten · neen

Access Toegang : Utrecht A28 → Amersfoort, exit 3 → Den Dolder. 500 m links. 1.7 km parallel road
Map 1 on page 796 Auto kaart 1 Blz 796

GOLF COURSE
BAAN · 16/20

Site	Terrein	
Maintenance	Onderhoud	
Architect	Architect	Harry S. Colt
Type	Type baan	bosbaan
Relief	Reliëf	
Water in play	Waterhazards	
Exp. to wind	Windgevoelig	
Trees in play	Bomen	

Scorecard Scorekaart	Chp. Back tees	Mens Heren	Ladies Damen
Length Lengte	6088	5707	4951
Par	72	72	72

Advised golfing ability		0	12	24	36
Aanbevolen golfvaardigheid					
Hcp required	Vereiste hcp	28			

CLUB HOUSE & AMENITIES
CLUB HOUSE EN ANNEXEN · 8/10

Pro shop	Pro shop	
Driving range	Oefenbaan	
Sheltered	overdekt	6 plaatsen
On grass	op gras	neen
Putting-green	putting-green	ja
Pitching-green	pitching-green	ja

HOTEL FACILITIES
HOTELS IN OMGEVING · 7/10

HOTELS HOTELS
De Hoefslag — Bosch en Duin
34 kamers, D FL 220,- — 1 km
Tel. (31) 030 - 225 1051
Fax (31) 030 - 228 5821

Kerkebosch — Zeist
30 kamers, D Fl 195,- — 5 km
Tel. (31) 030 - 691 4734
Fax (31) 030 - 691 3114

RESTAURANTS RESTAURANT
De Hoefslag — Bosch en Duin
Tel. (31) 030 - 225 1051 — 1 km

Wilhelmina Park — Utrecht
Tel.(31) 030 - 251 0693 — 10 km

805

Deze nieuwe baan is onderdeel van het bekende, gelijknamige attractiepark (ideaal voor de niet-golfers in de familie), waarvan sommige onderdelen vanaf de fairways te zien zijn. De baan ligt in een landelijke omgeving met aan weerszijden een natuurgebied. Veel open ruimtes waardoor de richting en kracht van de wind een grote rol spelen, omdat maar vier holes beschermd liggen. Bij gebrek aan bomen is water de belangrijkste hindernis, in de vorm van grote vijvers langs de baan of voor de green. Op de derde hole kronkelt een kreekje door de fairway, waardoor spelers voor de keuze worden gesteld rechts of links te houden. De greens zijn groot, goed gevormd en beschermd door handig geplaatste bunkers omgeven door heuveltjes en andere vormen van aarden wallen. Met smaak ontworpen door Donald Steel. Een prettige en boeiende baan geschikt voor spelers van alle nivo's. Goed aangelegd en goed onderhouden.

This recent course is part of the celebrated "De Efteling" theme park (ideal for non-golfers in the family), which you can actually see from the fairways. The whole piece is located in a rural spot surrounded by two nature reserves. There is a lot of very open space here, which gives great importance to the direction and strength of the wind, as only four holes are protected. For want of trees, water is the main hazard to cope with, in the shape of large ponds lining the fairways or in front of the greens. At the 3rd, a stretch of water winds its way down the fairway, forcing players to choose from which side of the fairway they want to play the hole. The greens are huge, well-contoured and protected by cleverly placed bunkers surrounded by mounds and other forms of earthwork. Tastefully designed by Donald Steel, this is a very pleasant and entertaining course for golfers of all abilities. Well built and well upkept.

Golfpark de Efteling

Veldstraat 6
NL - 5176 NB KAATSHEUVEL

Office	Secretariaat	(31) 0416 - 288 399
Pro shop	Pro shop	(31) 0416 - 288 399
Fax	Fax	(31) 0416 - 281 095
Situation	Locatie	

10 km N Tilburg, 163 383 inw.

Annual closure	Jaarlijkse sluiting	neen
Weekly closure	Wekelijkse sluitingsdag	neen

Fees main season
Hoogseizoen tarieven 18 holes

	Week days Weekdagen	We/Bank holidays We/Feestdagen
Individual Individueel	Fl 80,-	Fl 80,-
Couple Paar	Fl 160,-	Fl 160,-

Caddy	Caddy	neen
Electric Trolley	Electrische trolley	neen
Buggy	Buggy	Fl 40,-
Clubs	Clubs	Fl 20,-

Credit cards Creditkaarten
VISA - Eurocard - MasterCard - AMEX - DC

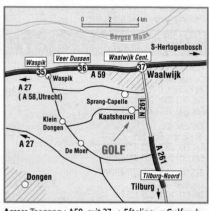

Access Toegang : A59, exit 37 → Efteling → Golfpark
Map 1 on page 796 Auto kaart 1 Blz 796

806

GOLF COURSE
BAAN
16/20

Site	Terrein	▬▬▬
Maintenance	Onderhoud	▬▬▬
Architect	Architect	Donald Steel
Type	Type baan	open parkbaan
Relief	Reliëf	▬
Water in play	Waterhazards	▬▬▬
Exp. to wind	Windgevoelig	▬▬▬
Trees in play	Bomen	▬▬▬

Scorecard Scorekaart	Chp. Back tees	Mens Heren	Ladies Damen
Length Lengte	6258	5960	5072
Par	72	72	72

Advised golfing ability Aanbevolen golfvaardigheid		0 12 24 36
Hcp required Vereiste hcp	neen	

CLUB HOUSE & AMENITIES
CLUB HOUSE EN ANNEXEN
8/10

Pro shop	Pro shop	▬▬▬
Driving range	Oefenbaan	▬▬▬
Sheltered	overdekt	6 plaatsen
On grass	op gras	ja
Putting-green	putting-green	ja
Pitching-green	pitching-green	ja

HOTEL FACILITIES
HOTELS IN OMGEVING
5/10

HOTELS HOTELS

De Efteling
121 kamers, D Fl 200,-
Tel. (31) 0416 - 282 000
Fax (31) 0416 - 281 515

Kaatsheuvel
1 km

De Postelse Hoeve
35 kamers, D Fl 200,-
Tel. (31) 013 - 463 6335
Fax (31) 013 - 463 9390

Tilburg
10 km

RESTAURANTS RESTAURANT

De Pepermolen
Tel. (31) 0416 - 339 308

Waalwijk
8 km

Valentijn
Tel.(31) 013 - 543 3386

Tilburg
10 km

Een van de beste banen in het binnenland met een nivo van onderhoud dat overeenkomt met de hoge kwaliteit van de geboden faciliteiten. De baan ligt midden in een prachtig bos met beekjes en vennetjes. Twee lussen van negen holes omcirkelen grote stukken bos, waardoor spelers een gevoel van afzonde-ring en rust krijgen dat zeer bevorderlijk voor de concentratie is. Hoewel de fairways breed zijn - goed nieuws voor krachtpatsers - is het oppassen geblazen voor de doglegs, die vragen om met effect geslagen ballen, zowel naar links als naar rechts. Dit is een baan voor technisch ervaren spelers, met goed ontworpen greens, bewaakt door grote bunkers. Kenmerkend voor Harry Colt, duidelijk een van de grootste golf-architecten uit de eerste helft van deze eeuw. Zijn ontwerpen zijn veeleisend voor de goede, maar toch ook mild voor de stomme slagen van de gemiddelde speler. Een aardig element is het grote ven voor het clubhuis dat in de zomer als openlucht zwembad fungeert.

One of Holland's best inland courses with a standard upkeep to match the general quality of facilities. The course is laid out in a magnificent forest with streams and ponds. The trees are right in the middle of the two parts of the course, out and in, and this gives players an impression of isolation and tranquillity that can be very useful for concentration. Although the fairways are wide - good news for big-hitters - still watch out for the dog-legs winding left and right and calling for a number of flighted shots in both directions. This is a course for skilled technicians, with well designed putting surfaces and greens well-guarded by large bunkers, another distinctive feature of Harry Colt, definitely one of the greatest course designers from the first half of the century. His layouts demand a great deal from good players but are somehow more lenient on duff shots from the average hacker.

Eindhovensche Golf

Eindhovenseweg 300
NL - 5553 VB VALKENSWAARD

Office	Secretariaat	(31) 040 - 201 4816
Pro shop	Pro shop	(31) 040 - 204 4546
Fax	Fax	(31) 040 - 201 4038
Situation	Locatie	

10 km Eindhoven, 196 130 inw.

Annual closure	Jaarlijkse sluiting	neen
Weekly closure	Wekelijkse sluitingsdag	neen

Fees main season
Hoogseizoen tarieven per dag

	Week days Weekdagen	We/Bank holidays We/Feestdagen
Individual Individueel	Fl 85,-	Fl 110,-
Couple Paar	Fl 170,-	Fl 220,-

NGF members Fl 25,- reduction

Caddy	Caddy	neen
Electric Trolley	Electrische trolley	neen
Buggy	Buggy	neen
Clubs	Clubs	neen

Credit cards Creditkaarten   neen

Access Toegang : Eindhoven A2 → Weert. Exit 33.
N 69 → Valkenswaard. 4 km
Map 1 on page 796 Auto kaart 1 Blz 796

GOLF COURSE
BAAN
18/20

Site	Terrein	
Maintenance	Onderhoud	
Architect	Architect	Harry S. Colt

Type	Type baan	bos
Relief	Reliëf	
Water in play	Waterhazards	
Exp. to wind	Windgevoelig	
Trees in play	Bomen	

Scorecard Scorekaart	Chp. Back tees	Mens Heren	Ladies Damen
Length Lengte	6176	5918	5048
Par	72	72	72

Advised golfing ability Aanbevolen golfvaardigheid	0	12	24	36

Hcp required   Vereiste hcp   36, We 24

CLUB HOUSE & AMENITIES
CLUB HOUSE EN ANNEXEN
8/10

Pro shop	Pro shop	
Driving range	Oefenbaan	
Sheltered	overdekt	5
On grass	op gras	ja
Putting-green	putting-green	ja
Pitching-green	pitching-green	ja

HOTEL FACILITIES
HOTELS IN OMGEVING
6/10

HOTELS HOTELS
Dorint Hotel   Eindhoven
191 kamers, D Fl 190,-   8 km
Tel. (31) 040 - 232 6111
Fax (31) 040 - 244 0148

Holiday Inn Hotel   Eindhoven
201 kamers, D Fl 190,-   8 km
Tel. (31) 040 - 243 3222
Fax (31) 040 - 244 9235

RESTAURANTS RESTAURANT
De Waterkers   Eindhoven
Tel. (31) 040 - 212 4999   7 km

Karpendonkse Hoeve   Eindhoven
Tel.(31) 040 - 281 3663   7 km

807

GELPENBERG

Zoals veel banen in Nederland is de Gelpenberg in twee fasen tot stand gekomen. En zoals vaker liggen negen holes in een bosgebied en de andere in vroeger agrarisch, meer open terrein. Hier zijn de eerste negen holes betrekkelijk smal, met bomen als voornaamste hindernis. Middenin het bos liggen flinke stukken hei, die op vier holes in het spel komen en voldoende problemen geven om het praktisch ontbreken van fairway-bunkers te verklaren. Omdat er zes doglegs bij zijn, is een goede strategie en effectvolle slagen (in de goede richting) een 'must'. De tweede negen zijn veel breder, maar ook meer beïnvloed door de wind. Een klein meertje komt op drie holes in het spel, net als een paar grote fairway bunkers, zoals op de 18e. De bunker die op de slothole de fairway doorkruist moet een van de grootste van Europa zijn. Een baan die het waard is gespeeld te worden, door spelers van elk nivo.

Like several courses in the Netherlands, Gelpenberg was designed in two stages. Like the others, you find nine holes amidst an old forest and the others on former farming land, which is much more open. Here, the front 9 are tight, with trees as the main hazards, so take care to avoid them. In the middle of the forest, there is a huge area of heather, which comes into play on four holes and causes enough difficulty to explain the virtual absence of fairway bunkers. And as there are 6 dog-legs to cope with, choosing the right strategy and flighting the ball (in the right direction) are important. The back 9 are much wider, but also much exposed to the wind. A small lake comes into play on three holes, as do some large fairway bunkers, notably on the 18th. The bunker splitting the fairway on this final hole must be one of the largest in Europe. A course well worth getting to know, for players of all levels.

Drentse Golfclub De Gelpenberg

Gebbeveenweg 1
NL - 7854 TD AALDEN

Office	Secretariaat	(31) 0591 - 371 929
Pro shop	Pro shop	(31) 0591 - 372 174
Fax	Fax	(31) 0591 - 372 422
Situation	Locatie	

15 km Emmen, 93 476 inw.

Annual closure	Jaarlijkse sluiting	neen
Weekly closure	Wekelijkse sluitingsdag	neen

Fees main season
Hoogseizoen tarieven 18 holes

	Week days Weekdagen	We/Bank holidays We/Feestdagen
Individual Individueel	Fl 50,-	Fl 60,-
Couple Paar	Fl 100,-	Fl 120,-

Caddy	Caddy	neen
Electric Trolley	Electrische trolley	neen
Buggy	Buggy	neen
Clubs	Clubs	neen
Credit cards Creditkaarten		neen

808

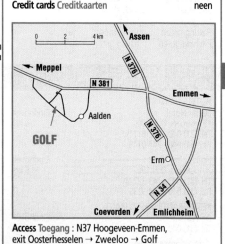

Access Toegang : N37 Hoogeveen-Emmen,
exit Oosterhesselen → Zweeloo → Golf
Map 1 on page 797 Auto kaart 1 Blz 797

GOLF COURSE
BAAN
14/20

Site	Terrein	
Maintenance	Onderhoud	
Architect	Architect	Frank Pennink Donald Steel
Type	Type baan	bosbaan
Relief	Reliëf	
Water in play	Waterhazards	
Exp. to wind	Windgevoelig	
Trees in play	Bomen	

Scorecard Scorekaart	Chp. Back tees	Mens Heren	Ladies Damen
Length Lengte	6031	6031	5093
Par	71	71	71

Advised golfing ability Aanbevolen golfvaardigheid		0 12 24 36
Hcp required	Vereiste hcp	neen

CLUB HOUSE & AMENITIES
CLUB HOUSE EN ANNEXEN
4/10

Pro shop	Pro shop	
Driving range	Oefenbaan	
Sheltered	overdekt	5 plaatsen
On grass	op gras	neen
Putting-green	putting-green	ja
Pitching-green	pitching-green	ja

HOTEL FACILITIES
HOTELS IN OMGEVING
5/10

HOTELS HOTELS
Ten Cate — Emmen
33 kamers, D Fl 125,- — 15 km
Tel. (31) 0591 - 617 600
Fax (31) 0591 - 618 432

Boorland — Emmen
14 kamers, D 135,- — 15 km
Tel. (31 591) 613 746
Fax (31 591) 616 525

RESTAURANTS RESTAURANT
Idylle — Zweeloo
Tel. (31) 0591 - 371 857 — 2 km

Zuudbarge — Emmen
Tel.(31) 0591 - 630 813 — 16 km

Deze baan is aangelegd in een landelijk gebied, tussen een autoweg en wat industrie. Alhoewel ook een aantal holes verborgen ligt in de bossen, waardoor een vredige atmosfeer is geschapen. Hoewel de baan nog jong is, ogen de bomen zeer volwassen. De fairways mogen wat korter gemaaid (er is nauwelijks een semi-rough). Twee vijvers en een paar kleine vennetjes komen op verschillende manieren in het spel, zoals op de 6e, een par-3 waarvan de tee (niet de green) op een eiland ligt. De tweede negen strekken zich uit over een tot 20 meter verhoogd stuk land, zodat spelers worden geconfronteerd met blinde slagen en sterk hellende fairways. Het hoogste punt levert een fraai uitzicht over de omgeving op. Het vormt een welkome onderbreking van het vlakke deel van de baan. De greens kunnen lastig zijn, afhankelijk van de pin-positie en een aantal afslagen zijn veeleisend, maar er is altijd ruimte om een veilige weg te vinden. Geschikt voor alle type golfers.

This course is laid out in a rural zone between a motorway and industrial estate, although several holes are tucked away in a woodland area and help give the site something of a peaceful atmosphere. Although still very young, the trees create an air of maturity, even though the grass is not yet mown short enough (there is no semi-rough). Two lakes and several little ponds come into play in different ways, like on the 6th, a par 3 where the tee is an island (but not the green). The back 9 are built some a plot of fallow land some 20 metres high, where players are confronted with a few blind shots and many sloping lies. This altitude offers some pretty views over the region and breaks up the rather flat nature of the course. The greens can be difficult, depending on the pin positions, and a number of drives can be tricky, but there is always room to play safe. For golfers of all levels.

Golfbaan Gendersteyn

Locht 140
NL - 5504 RP VELDHOVEN

Office	Secretariaat	(31) 040 - 253 4444
Pro shop	Pro shop	(31) 040 - 253 4444
Fax	Fax	(31) 040 - 254 9747
Situation	Locatie	

8 km Eindhoven, 196 130 inw.

Annual closure	Jaarlijkse sluiting	neen
Weekly closure	Wekelijkse sluitingsdag	neen

Fees main season	Hoogseizoen tarieven	18 holes
	Week days	We/Bank holidays
	Weekdagen	We/Feestdagen
Individual Individueel	Fl 65,-	Fl 80,-
Couple Paar	Fl 130,-	Fl 160,-

Caddy	Caddy	neen
Electric Trolley	Electrische trolley	Fl 7,50 /18 holes
Buggy	Buggy	Fl 50,-
Clubs	Clubs	Fl 5,-
Credit cards Creditkaarten		neen

Access Toegang : A2 Eindhoven → Antwerpen.
Exit 32 → Veldhoven → Eersel. Golf 2 km
Map 1 on page 796 Auto kaart 1 Blz 796

GOLF COURSE
BAAN
15 /20

Site	Terrein	
Maintenance	Onderhoud	
Architect	Architect	Alan Rijks
Type	Type baan	parkbaan
Relief	Reliëf	
Water in play	Waterhazards	
Exp. to wind	Windgevoelig	
Trees in play	Bomen	

Scorecard	Chp.	Mens	Ladies
Scorekaart	Back tees	Heren	Damen
Length Lengte	5965	5770	4869
Par	72	72	72

Advised golfing ability	0	12	24	36
Aanbevolen golfvaardigheid				

Hcp required	Vereiste hcp	neen

CLUB HOUSE & AMENITIES
CLUB HOUSE EN ANNEXEN
7 /10

Pro shop	Pro shop	
Driving range	Oefenbaan	
Sheltered	overdekt	10 plaatsen
On grass	op gras	neen
Putting-green	putting-green	ja
Pitching-green	pitching-green	ja

HOTEL FACILITIES
HOTELS IN OMGEVING
7 /10

HOTELS HOTELS
Dorint Hotel		Eindhoven
191 kamers, D Fl 190,-		8 km
Tel. (31) 040 - 232 6111, Fax (31) 040 - 244 0148		
Holiday Inn Hotel		Eindhoven
201 kamers, D Fl 190,-		8 km
Tel. (31) 040 - 243 3222, Fax (31) 040 - 244 9235		
Motel Eindhoven		Eindhoven
175 kamers, D FL 100,-		8 km
Tel. (31) 040 - 212 3435, Fax (31) 040 - 212 0774		

RESTAURANTS RESTAURANT
De Waterkers		Eindhoven
Tel. (31) 040 - 212 4999		7 km
Karpendonkse Hoeve		Eindhoven
Tel.(31) 040 - 281 3663		7 km

809

GOES

15	3	6

Van een afstand lijkt deze baan misschien op een van de vele nieuwe 'polderbanen'. Maar als je op de fairways loopt vallen direct de glooiingen en heuveltjes op, die elke slag een beetje moeilijker dan normaal kunnen maken. Deze heuveltjes zijn gemaakt met de grond die vrijkwam bij het graven van de waterpartijen die op dertien holes in het spel komen. Soms alleen langs de kant van de fairway, maar in veel gevallen vlak voor de green. Water is niet de enige hindernis om rekening mee te houden. Er ligt een flink aantal bunkers op strategische plaatsen. De greens zijn alle wat glooiend, maar zonder de overdreven contouren die je op veel nieuwe banen tegenkomt. Op dit moment is het clubhuis nog wat bescheiden, maar met de bouw van een nieuw onderkomen moet binnenkort worden begonnen.

From a distance, Goes may look like one of the many new courses in the flat Dutch "polderland". But once walking its fairways you will notice the subtle undulations and hills that frequently make your next shot a little more awkward. These slopes result from the clever use of soil dug out to create the many water hazards that come into play, sometimes edging the fairway but on several occasions in front of the greens. And water is not the only hazard to cope with, as a fair number of bunkers are strategically located on the fairways. The greens are rather distinctly contoured but don't have the excessive bumps often seen on today's new courses. The facilities are still rather restricted but a new building is due for completion shortly.

De Goese Golf
Golfpark 1
NL - 4465 AJ GOES

Office	Secretariaat	(31) 0113 - 229 557
Pro shop	Pro shop	(31) 0113 - 229 557
Fax	Fax	(31) 0113 - 229 556
Situation	Locatie	
1 km Goes, 33 300 inw.		
Annual closure	Jaarlijkse sluiting	neen
Weekly closure	Wekelijkse sluitingsdag	neen

Fees main season
Hoogseizoen tarieven per dag

	Week days Weekdagen	We/Bank holidays We/Feestdagen
Individual Individueel	Fl 70,-	Fl 80,-
Couple Paar	Fl 140,-	Fl 160,-

Caddy	Caddy	neen
Electric Trolley	Electrische trolley	Fl 20,-/18 holes
Buggy	Buggy	Fl 40,-/18 holes
Clubs	Clubs	Fl 25,-/18 holes

Credit cards Creditkaarten
VISA - Eurocard - MasterCard - AMEX

Access Toegang : A58 → N256 → Goes Centrum
→ Goese Meer
Map 1 on page 796 Auto kaart 1 Blz 796

GOLF COURSE
BAAN
15/20

Site	Terrein	
Maintenance	Onderhoud	
Architect	Architect	Donald Steel H. Hertzberger
Type	Type baan	polderbaan
Relief	Reliëf	
Water in play	Waterhazards	
Exp. to wind	Windgevoelig	
Trees in play	Bomen	

Scorecard Scorekaart	Chp. Back tees	Mens Heren	Ladies Damen
Length Lengte	6269	6110	5145
Par	72	72	72

Advised golfing ability		0	12	24	36
Aanbevolen golfvaardigheid					
Hcp required	Vereiste hcp	neen			

CLUB HOUSE & AMENITIES
CLUB HOUSE EN ANNEXEN
3/10

Pro shop	Pro shop	
Driving range	Oefenbaan	
Sheltered	overdekt	9 plaatsen
On grass	op gras	neen
Putting-green	putting-green	ja
Pitching-green	pitching-green	ja

HOTEL FACILITIES
HOTELS IN OMGEVING
6/10

HOTELS HOTELS

Bolsjoi	Goes
12 kamers, D Fl 145,-	3 km
Tel. (31) 0113 - 232 323	
Fax (31) 0113 - 251 755	
Le Manoir	Kruiningen
8 kamers, D Fl 300,-	15 km
Tel. (31) 0113 - 381 753	
Fax (31) 0113 - 381 763	

RESTAURANTS RESTAURANT

Inter Scaldes	Kruiningen
Tel. (31) 0113 - 381 753	15 km
Nolet-Reymerswale	Yerseke
Tel.(31) 0113 - 517 642	14 km

810

GRAAFSCHAP

Het specifieke karakter van deze goed ontworpen baan is de afwisseling tussen open en bebost terrein, een typische eigenschap van het hele gebied. Het uit zich hier in het feit dat bijna de helft van de holes begint in een open stuk en eindigt temidden van bomen. Of andersom. In tegenstelling tot veel nieuwe banen is hier weinig grond verzet, zelfs niet voor de waterhazards die klein en heel natuurlijk zijn. De meeste fairways zijn breed en mild voor afgedwaalde ballen, maar enkele losse bomen kunnen voor flinke problemen zorgen. In combinatie met de wind (in de open gedeelten) kunnen zij elke hoop op een goede score de nek omdraaien. Ondanks het ontbreken van reliëf valt er van prachtige vergezichten te genieten, vooral in de herfst. De greens zijn middelgroot, niet moeilijk te lezen en over het algemeen niet spectaculair. Wel afdoende bewaakt door bunkers.

The full character of this competently designed course lies with its alternating forest and open landscape, a frequent feature throughout the region. It is plain to see on almost half the holes, which start under the open sky and end up in the trees, or inversely. As opposed to many recent courses, there has been little artificial moving of earth, even for the water hazards that are small and very natural. Most of the fairways are wide and forgiving for wayward shots, but several isolated trees can spell serious trouble. Combined with the wind (in the more exposed sections), they can dash any hope of playing to your handicap, a feat that otherwise is more than possible. Despite the lack of relief, there are some beautiful views to be had here, especially in the Autumn. The greens are mid-sized, pretty easy to read and generally, but none too imaginatively, well-guarded by a brace of bunkers.

Golf & Country Club De Graafschap

Sluitdijk 4
NL - 7241 RR LOCHEM

Office	Secretariaat	(31) 0573 - 254 323
Pro shop	Pro shop	(31) 0573 - 258 179
Fax	Fax	(31) 0573 - 258 450
Situation	Locatie	

22 km Deventer, 69 079 inw.

Annual closure	Jaarlijkse sluiting	neen
Weekly closure	Wekelijkse sluitingsdag	neen

Fees main season
Hoogseizoen tarieven per dag

	Week days Weekdagen	We/Bank holidays We/Feestdagen
Individual Individueel	Fl 85,-	Fl 95,-
Couple Paar	Fl 170,-	Fl 190,-

Caddy	Caddy	nee
Electric Trolley	Electrische trolley	nee
Buggy	Buggy	nee
Clubs	Clubs	Fl 25,-
Credit cards Creditkaarten		neen

Access Toegang : A1 Amsterdam -Enschede. Exit 23.
N348 → Zutphen. N346 → Lochem. Golf km 11,5
Map 1 on page 797 Auto kaart 1 Blz 797

GOLF COURSE
BAAN
15/20

Site	Terrein	■■■■■
Maintenance	Onderhoud	■■■■■
Architect	Architect	Eschauzier & Thate
Type	Type baan	bosbaan
Relief	Reliëf	■
Water in play	Waterhazards	■■■
Exp. to wind	Windgevoelig	■■■■
Trees in play	Bomen	■■■■

Scorecard Scorekaart	Chp. Back tees	Mens Heren	Ladies Damen
Length Lengte	6306	6059	5277
Par	72	72	72

Advised golfing ability		0	12	24	36
Aanbevolen golfvaardigheid		■■■■			
Hcp required	Vereiste hcp	neen			

CLUB HOUSE & AMENITIES
CLUB HOUSE EN ANNEXEN
7/10

Pro shop	Pro shop	■■■■
Driving range	Oefenbaan	■■■■
Sheltered	overdekt	9 plaatsen
On grass	op gras	neen
Putting-green	putting-green	ja
Pitching-green	pitching-green	ja

HOTEL FACILITIES
HOTELS IN OMGEVING
6/10

HOTELS HOTELS

De Scheperskamp	Lochem
46 kamers, D Fl. 185,-	3 km
Tel. (31) 0573 - 254 051	
Fax (31) 0573 - 257 150	
't Hof van Gelre	Lochem
49 kamers, D Fl. 150,-	3 km
Tel. (31) 0573 - 253 351	
Fax (31) 0573 - 254 245	

RESTAURANTS RESTAURANT

Mondani	Lochem
Tel. (31) 0573 - 257 595	3 km
Galantijn	Zutphen
Tel.(31) 0575 - 525 555	8 km

811

GREVELINGENHOUT

Wat kunt u anders verwachten in de provincie Zeeland dan een straffe wind? Grevelingenhout is ontworpen in een mooi gebied langs de rivierendelta, waar zeilen de traditionele sport is. Het is de eerste golfbaan in Nederland waar ook gewoond kan worden, al zijn de huizen op de vrij kleine stukken grond niet altijd wonderen van architectuur. Zij zijn gescheiden van de baan door vijvertjes en sloten, die op bijna alle holes in het spel komen. We hopen maar dat de aangeplante bomen en struiken de bewoners, en de spelers, geleidelijk wat meer privacy zullen bieden. Dit is een goede golfbaan om spelers aan water te laten wennen. Dat komt op fraaie wijze in het spel op de 12e (een par-3) over een vijver en de 9e en de 18e, die een dubbelgreen delen, bewaakt door water. Het zal niet verbazen dat al die nattigheid het grootste obstakel vormt, samen met de wind. Het zou spelers ertoe kunnen aanzetten juist hier matchplay te spelen.

What else would you expect in the province of Zeeland than persistent wind? Grevelingenhout was designed in a pretty region along the delta, where sailing is the traditional sport. This is Holland's first residential course, although the houses built on small plots of land are hardly wonders of architecture. They are separated from the fairways by ponds and other stretches of water, which come into play on most holes. We can only hope that the newly planted trees and bushes will offer the inhabitants, and players, a little more privacy. This is a good course for accustoming all golfers to the problems posed by water, which is excellently brought into play on the 12th (a par 3 over water) and the 9th and 18th holes, which share a very well-guarded double green. Water is, not surprisingly, the key difficulty here, together with the wind we talked about, and this should incite most golfers to opt for the match-play format.

Golfclub Grevelingenhout
Oudendijk 3
NL - 4311 NA BRUINISSE

Office	Secretariaat	(31) 0111 - 482 650
Pro shop	Pro shop	(31) 0111 - 482 650
Fax	Fax	(31) 0111 - 481 566
Situation	Locatie	

30 km Goes, 33 281 inw.
50 km Rotterdam, 598 521 inw.

Annual closure	Jaarlijkse sluiting	neen
Weekly closure	Wekelijkse sluitingsdag	neen

Fees main season
Hoogseizoen tarieven per dag

	Week days Weekdagen	We/Bank holidays We/Feestdagen
Individual Individueel	Fl 72,50	Fl 92,50
Couple Paar	Fl 145,-	Fl 185,-

Caddy	Caddy	neen
Electric Trolley	Electrische trolley	Fl 40,-/18 holes
Buggy	Buggy	neen
Clubs	Clubs	neen

Credit cards Creditkaarten — neen

GOLF COURSE
BAAN — 14/20

Site	Terrein	▬▬▬
Maintenance	Onderhoud	▬▬▬
Architect	Architect	Donald Harradine
Type	Type baan	parkbaan
Relief	Reliëf	▬
Water in play	Waterhazards	▬▬▬▬
Exp. to wind	Windgevoelig	▬▬▬
Trees in play	Bomen	▬▬▬

Scorecard Scorekaart	Chp. Back tees	Mens Heren	Ladies Damen
Length Lengte	6193	5951	5144
Par	72	72	72

Advised golfing ability Aanbevolen golfvaardigheid	0	12	24	36
Hcp required Vereiste hcp	neen			

CLUB HOUSE & AMENITIES
CLUB HOUSE EN ANNEXEN — 7/10

Pro shop	Pro shop	▬▬▬
Driving range	Oefenbaan	▬▬▬
Sheltered	overdekt	6 plaatsen
On grass	op gras	neen
Putting-green	putting-green	ja
Pitching-green	pitching-green	ja

HOTEL FACILITIES
HOTELS IN OMGEVING — 4/10

HOTELS HOTELS
Mondragon — Zierikzee
8 kamers, D Fl 195,- — 10 km
Tel. (31) 0111 - 413 051
Fax (31) 0111 - 415 997

Schuddebeurs — Schuddebeurs
21 kamers, D Fl 205,- — 15 km
Tel. (31) 0111 - 415 651
Fax (31) 0111 - 413 103

RESTAURANTS RESTAURANT
De drie Morianen — Zierikzee
Tel. (31) 0111 - 412 931 — 10 km

Mondragon — Zierikzee
Tel.(31) 0111 - 412 670 — 10 km

Access Toegang : Rotterdam A29, Exit Middelharnis,
N59 → Zierikzee. Exit Aquadelta
Map 1 on page 796 Auto kaart 1 Blz 796

HAAGSCHE

De Hollandse kust leent zich uitstekend voor de aanleg van prachtige banen en deze is daar een goed voorbeeld van. Naar het ontwerp van de architecten Colt en Alison die borg stonden voor een uitdagend ontwerp. Het is maar goed dat de lengte niet overdreven is, want het komt vaak voor dat je slagen verliest in dichte struiken of in diepe bunkers. Maar als u door de wind en rust gelaten wordt en alle aandacht aan uw swing kunt besteden, dan hebt u een goede kans een mooi resultaat te scoren. Zoals je in de duinen kan verwachten zijn er maar weinig echt vlakke stukken op de fairways. Veel uphill of downhill slagen dus, plus interessante situaties rond de greens. De Haagsche heeft talloze internationale wedstrijden (waaronder het Dutch Open) mogen ontvangen. Het is de moeite waard hier een dag voor uit te trekken. Zowaar een linksbaan zonder het Kanaal te hoeven oversteken.

The Dutch coast is a marvellous site for building great courses, and this is one of the finest. The cachet of designers Colt and Alison speaks volumes for the challenging style of this layout. Although not excessively long, there are more than enough opportunities to drop shots, in the thickets lining the fairways or in the pot bunkers. If the wind leaves you alone, with just your problems of swing to cope with, you will have every chance of returning a good score. As you might expect among sand dunes, there are few really flat lies on the fairways, a lot of shots uphill and down, and some tantalising situations around the greens. Haagsche has hosted a number of international events (including the Dutch Open) and, with its counterparts along the coast, deserves a special golfing holiday. Here is a great links to play without having to ferry across the Channel.

Koninklijke Haagsche Golf & Countryclub

Groot Haesenbroekseweg 22
NL - 2243 EC WASSENAAR

Office	Secretariaat	(31) 070 - 511 9251
Pro shop	Pro shop	(31) 070 - 517 9822
Fax	Fax	(31) 070 - 514 0171
Situation	Locatie	

4 km Den Haag, 445 279 inw.

Annual closure	Jaarlijkse sluiting	neen
Weekly closure	Wekelijkse sluitingsdag	neen

Fees main season
Hoogseizoen tarieven per dag

	Week days Weekdagen	We/Bank holidays We/Feestdagen
Individual Individueel	Fl. 130,-	—
Couple Paar	Fl. 260,-	—

Weekdagen

Caddy	Caddy	neen
Electric Trolley	Electrische trolley	Fl. 20,-
Buggy	Buggy	neen
Clubs	Clubs	Fl. 50,-
Credit cards Creditkaarten		neen

Access Toegang : A44 → Wassenaar
Map 1 on page 796 Auto kaart 1 Blz 796

GOLF COURSE
BAAN — 18/20

Site	Terrein	
Maintenance	Onderhoud	
Architect	Architect	Harry S. Colt Allison
Type	Type baan	links, duinbaan
Relief	Reliëf	
Water in play	Waterhazards	
Exp. to wind	Windgevoelig	
Trees in play	Bomen	

Scorecard Scorekaart	Chp. Back tees	Mens Heren	Ladies Damen
Length Lengte	6142	5674	5006
Par	72	72	72

Advised golfing ability Aanbevolen golfvaardigheid	0	12	24	36
Hcp required Vereiste hcp	26			

CLUB HOUSE & AMENITIES
CLUB HOUSE EN ANNEXEN — 7/10

Pro shop	Pro shop	
Driving range	Oefenbaan	
Sheltered	overdekt	12 Plaatsen
On grass	op gras	ja
Putting-green	putting-green	ja
Pitching-green	pitching-green	ja

813

HOTEL FACILITIES
HOTELS IN OMGEVING — 8/10

HOTELS HOTELS

Des Indes — Den Haag
70 kamers, D Fl. 505,- — 5 km
Tel. (31) 070 - 363 2932, Fax (31) 070 - 356 2863

Kurhaus — Scheveningen
233 kamers, D Fl. 400,- — 5 km
Tel. (31) 070 - 416 2636, Fax (31) 070 - 416 2646

Green Park — Leidschendam
92 kamers, D Fl. 290,- — 7 km
Tel. (31) 070 - 320 9280, Fax (31) 070 - 327 4907

RESTAURANTS RESTAURANT

Auberge de Kievit (23 kamers, D Fl. 350) — Wassenaar
Tel. (31) 070 - 511 9232 — 1 km

't Ganzenest — Den Haag
Tel.(31) 070 - 389 6709 — 5 km

Dit is waarschijnlijk een van de laatste keren dat de aanleg van een baan in zulke bebost terrein werd toegestaan. In dit geval was het verkrijgen van een kapvergunning iets makkelijker, omdat het om mijnhout ging. Er is nog steeds veel daarvan blijven staan, en die bomen zijn de belangrijkste hindernis, vooral op de smallere holes en de vele doglegs. De begroeiing onder de bomen kan heel dicht zijn, hetgeen een extra afstraffing van onnauwkeurige slagen oplevert (neem wat extra ballen mee als u niet zo zuiver slaat). Dit is het enige zwakke punt in wat verder een knappe baan is, waarvan een deel over een heuvel is gedrapeerd, hetgeen resulteert in moeilijke uphill en downhill slagen. Er ligt daarentegen niet zoveel water. Al komt wat er ligt wel duidelijk in het spel, zoals op de fraaie 11e hole. De greens zijn tamelijk groot, goed ontworpen en goed bewaakt.

This is probably one of the last courses that the authorities will allow to be built in such a wooded area. Permission to fell trees was granted because they were lean pines planted for the mining industry. There are a lot of them left and they form the main hazard, especially on a number of tight holes and numerous dog-legs. The undergrowth is thick to say the least and adds an extra and perhaps unwarranted difficulty, given that mis-hit shots are already punished enough (bring a stock of balls if you are wayward off the tee). This is the only real flaw in what is an intelligent course, a part of which hugs a steepish hill, thus giving some tricky holes uphill and down. In contrast, there is little water to bother you, although what there is well in play, as on the very fine 11th hole. The greens are rather large, well-contoured and well-guarded.

Burggolf Herkenbosch
Stationsweg 100
NL - 6075 CD HERKENBOSCH

Office	Secretariaat	(31) 0475 - 531 458
Pro shop	Pro shop	(31) 0475 - 535 804
Fax	Fax	(31) 0475 - 533 580
Situation	Locatie	

5 km Roermond, 43 110 inw.

Annual closure	Jaarlijkse sluiting	neen
Weekly closure	Wekelijkse sluitingsdag	neen

Fees main season
Hoogseizoen tarieven 18 holes

	Week days Weekdagen	We/Bank holidays We/Feestdagen
Individual Individueel	Fl 70,-	Fl 95,-
Couple Paar	Fl 140,-	Fl 190,-

Caddy	Caddy	neen
Electric Trolley	Electrische trolley	Fl 15,-
Buggy	Buggy	neen
Clubs	Clubs	Fl 7,50

Credit cards Creditkaarten
VISA - Eurocard - MasterCard

Access Toegang : A2 Maastricht-Weert-Eindhoven.
Exit 40. N68, A68 → Roermond. N68,
N281 → Herkenbosch → Golf
Map 1 on page 797 Auto kaart 1 Blz 797

GOLF COURSE
BAAN
16/20

Site	Terrein	■■■■■□
Maintenance	Onderhoud	■■■■■□
Architect	Architect	Joan Dudok van Heel B. Steensels
Type	Type baan	bosbaan
Relief	Reliëf	
Water in play	Waterhazards	■■■□□
Exp. to wind	Windgevoelig	■■■□□
Trees in play	Bomen	■■■■□

Scorecard Scorekaart	Chp. Back tees	Mens Heren	Ladies Damen
Length Lengte	5682	5682	4924
Par	71	71	71

Advised golfing ability Aanbevolen golfvaardigheid	0	12	24	36

Hcp required   Vereiste hcp   We: 36

CLUB HOUSE & AMENITIES
CLUB HOUSE EN ANNEXEN
7/10

Pro shop	Pro shop	■■■■□
Driving range	Oefenbaan	■■■□□
Sheltered	overdekt	6 plaatsen
On grass	op gras	neen
Putting-green	putting-green	ja
Pitching-green	pitching-green	ja

HOTEL FACILITIES
HOTELS IN OMGEVING
6/10

HOTELS HOTELS
Kasteeltje Hattem   Roermond
11 kamers, D Fl. 250,-   5 km
Tel. (31) 0475 - 319 222, Fax (31) 0475 - 319 292

Landhotel Cox   Roermond
54 kamers, D Fl. 175,-   5 km
Tel. (31) 0475 - 329 966, Fax (31) 0475 - 325 142

Boshotel   Vlodrop
60 kamers, D Fl. 150,-   3 km
Tel. (31) 0475 - 534 959, Fax (31) 0475 - 534 580

RESTAURANTS RESTAURANT
Kasteel Daelenbroek   Herkenbosch
Tel. (31) 0475 - 532 465   2 km

La Cascade, Tel. (31) 0475 - 319 274   Roermond, 5 km

814

Sinds deze baan aan het begin van de eeuw is aangelegd, heeft hij een aantal ingrijpende wijzigingen onder-gaan. Hoewel sommige van die aanpassingen twijfelachtig zijn, blijft Hilversum wat het altijd is geweest: een verbluffend voorbeeld van een goed ontwerp voor een baan in het binnenland. Door de vele oude bomen zijn de meeste fairways behoorlijk smal, waardoor ze precisie en effectvolle slagen vereisen. De zanderige heuvels, die vaak tot slagen van glooiende hellingen dwingen, verhogen het technisch aspect van het spel. De spaarzame fairway-bunkers zijn goed geplaatst en moeilijk, de middelgrote greens worden goed bewaakt en de heidevelden voegen extra moeilijkheden aan de baan toe. De baan is heel rustig (de enige verstoring kan komen van fietsers of ruiters) en heeft het onderhoudsnivo de laatste tijd sterk verbeterd. Dat zou te maken kunnen hebben met het Dutch Open dat hier vanaf 1994 wordt gespeeld.

Since it was created at the turn of the century, this course has undergone a number of significant changes. Although some of these are questionable, the course is still the strikingly good example of excellent inland design it always has been. Owing to the very many old trees, some fairways are very tight and require precision and flighted shots. The sandy slopes, which often call for shots played from sloping lies, augment the technical aspect of golf here. The few fairway bunkers you come across are still well-placed and tough, the mid-sized greens are well-guarded and the heather adds an extra difficulty to the course. Very quiet (the only disturbance here might come from cyclists or horse-riders), Hilversum has significantly improved its standard of course upkeep: to prove it, the Dutch Open has been played here since 1994.

Hilversumsche Golf Club

Soestdijkerstraatsweg 172
NL - 1213 XJ HILVERSUM

Office	Secretariaat	(31) 035 - 683 8859
Pro shop	Pro shop	(31) 035 - 685 7140
Fax	Fax	(31) 035 - 685 3813
Situation	Locatie	

2 km Hilversum, 84 213 inw.

Annual closure	Jaarlijkse sluiting	neen
Weekly closure	Wekelijkse sluitingsdag	neen

Fees main season
Hoogseizoen tarieven 18 holes

	Week days Weekdagen	We/Bank holidays We/Feestdagen
Individual Individueel	Fl 75,-	Fl 100,-
Couple Paar	Fl 150,-	Fl 200,-

Caddy	Caddy	neen
Electric Trolley	Electrische trolley	Fl 7,50,-
Buggy	Buggy	neen
Clubs	Clubs	Fl 50,-

Credit cards Creditkaarten   neen

Access Toegang : Amsterdam A1 → Hilversum.
A27 → Utrecht. Exit 33 → Hilversum. → Golf
Map 1 on page 796 Auto kaart 1 Blz 796

GOLF COURSE
BAAN   16/20

Site	Terrein	
Maintenance	Onderhoud	
Architect	Architect	Burrows Del C. van Krimpen
Type	Type baan	bosbaan
Relief	Reliëf	
Water in play	Waterhazards	
Exp. to wind	Windgevoelig	
Trees in play	Bomen	

Scorecard Scorekaart	Chp. Back tees	Mens Heren	Ladies Damen
Length Lengte	6098	5859	5102
Par	72	72	72

Advised golfing ability		0	12 24	36
Aanbevolen golfvaardigheid				
Hcp required	Vereiste hcp	26		

CLUB HOUSE & AMENITIES
CLUB HOUSE EN ANNEXEN   7/10

Pro shop	Pro shop	
Driving range	Oefenbaan	
Sheltered	overdekt	6 plaatsen
On grass	op gras	neen
Putting-green	putting-green	ja
Pitching-green	pitching-green	ja

HOTEL FACILITIES
HOTELS IN OMGEVING   7/10

HOTELS HOTELS

Lapershoek	Hilversum
63 kamers, D Fl. 225,-	2 km
Tel. (31) 035 - 623 1341	
Fax (31) 035 - 628 4360	

De Hooge Vuursche	Baarn
20 kamers, D Fl. 300,-	2 km
Tel. (31) 035 - 541 2541	
Fax (31) 035 - 542 3288	

RESTAURANTS RESTAURANT

Joffers	Hilversum
Tel. (31) 035 - 621 4556	2 km

De Kastanjehof	Lage Vuursche
Tel. (31) 035 - 666 8248	3 km

815

Deze opvallende baan, in het midden van het land, was een van de eerste van een serie nieuwe privé banen die begin jaren '80 werden aangelegd. Een groot deel van de baan ligt temidden van bestaande bossen, de rest in meer open terrein. Door dat laatste biedt de Hoge Kleij een groter gevoel van ruimte dan de 'oudere' buren Hilversum en De Pan. Op enkele holes is goed gebruik gemaakt van de hoogteverschillen, terwijl de overige holes vrij vlak zijn. Dat maakt de baan toegankelijk voor elk nivo speler. Het mag dan geen spectaculaire baan zijn, er zitten een paar mooie holes tussen, met een grote variëteit in vormen, maten en moeilijkheden. Maar dat kun je verwachten van ontwerpers en kenners als Steel en Pennink, die zich nooit druk maken om al te subtiele details. De oefenfaciliteiten houden gelijke tred met de kwaliteit van de baan en hetzelfde kan worden gezegd van het clubhuis (met een goed restaurant).

This remarkable course, in the centre of Holland, was one of the first of a series of new private courses built in the first half of the 1980s. A large section was laid out in trees, the rest in wide open spaces, and this gives "Hoge Kleij" a much more definite impression of space than its elder neighbours at Hilversum and De Pan. The differences in level on several holes have been cleverly used, while the rest of the course is flat, making it easier for players of all levels and ages. This is hardly a spectacular course, but there are some competent holes here and a wide variety of shapes, sizes and difficulties. Again, this is only to be expected from designers and fine connoisseurs of golf such as Steel and Pennink, who never care unduly about excessively sophisticated details. Practice facilities are consistent with the standard of the course design, and the same can be said for the clubhouse (with a good restaurant).

Bolfclub De Hoge Kleij

Appelweg 4
NL - 3832 RK LEUSDEN

Office	Secretariaat	(31) 033 - 461 6944
Pro shop	Pro shop	(31) 033 - 463 8221
Fax	Fax	(31) 033 - 465 2921
Situation	Locatie	

2 km Amersfoort, 110 117 inw.
15 km Utrecht, 234 106 inw.

Annual closure	Jaarlijkse sluiting	neen
Weekly closure	Wekelijkse sluitingsdag	neen

Fees main season
Hoogseizoen tarieven 18 holes

	Week days Weekdagen	We/Bank holidays We/Feestdagen
Individual Individueel	Fl. 65,-	Fl. 95,-
Couple Paar	Fl. 130,-	Fl. 190,-

Caddy	Caddy	neen
Electric Trolley	Electrische trolley	neen
Buggy	Buggy	neen
Clubs	Clubs	Fl. 40,-

Credit cards Creditkaarten		neen

Access Toegang : A28 Utrecht-Amersfoort, Exit 5
Map 1 on page 796 Auto kaart 1 Blz 796

GOLF COURSE
BAAN
15/20

Site	Terrein	
Maintenance	Onderhoud	
Architect	Architect	Donald Steel Frank Pennink
Type	Type baan	bosbaan
Relief	Reliëf	
Water in play	Waterhazards	
Exp. to wind	Windgevoelig	
Trees in play	Bomen	

Scorecard Scorekaart	Chp. Back tees	Mens Heren	Ladies Damen
Length Lengte	6244	6046	5243
Par	72	72	72

Advised golfing ability Aanbevolen golfvaardigheid	0	12	24	36
Hcp required Vereiste hcp	We: 29			

CLUB HOUSE & AMENITIES
CLUB HOUSE EN ANNEXEN
6/10

Pro shop	Pro shop	
Driving range	Oefenbaan	
Sheltered	overdekt	6 Plaatsen
On grass	op gras	neen
Putting-green	putting-green	ja
Pitching-green	pitching-green	ja

HOTEL FACILITIES
HOTELS IN OMGEVING
7/10

HOTELS HOTELS

De Klepperman — Hoevelaken
79 kamers, D Fl. 285,- — 5 km
Tel. (31) 033 - 253 4120, Fax (31) 033 - 253 7434

Den Treek — Leusden
18 kamers, D Fl. 125,- — 2 km
Tel. (31) 033 - 286 1425, Fax (31) 033 - 286 3007

Berghotel — Amersfoort
92 kamers, D Fl. 210,- — 3 km
Tel. (31) 033 - 462 0444, Fax (31) 033 - 465 0505

RESTAURANTS RESTAURANT

Mariënhof — Amersfoort
Tel. (31) 033 - 463 2979 — 2 km

Tollius, Tel. (31) 033 - 465 1793 — Amersfoort, 2 km

816

Als Holland een vlak land is, dan liggen hier haar bergen. Duintoppen, wind en sobere vegetatie zijn de kenmerken van een echte linksbaan. De Kennemer is een van de mooiste voorbeeld daarvan in Europa. Je kunt de zee dan wel niet zien van hieruit, het stijlvolle, zeer traditionele clubhuis zal u zeker bekoren. De baan, ontworpen door Harry Colt in 1920, is in 1985 met negen holes uitgebreid, maar het gedeelte waar dit gebeurde had minder natuurlijke aanleg daarvoor. De hoogte-verschillen zijn beperkt (met wat blinde slagen), al zal menige bal uiteindelijk na wat stuiteren en rollen op een interessante plaats tot rust komen. Laat de afwezigheid van water en de schaarste aan bomen (enkele vliegdennen) u niet overmoedig maken. De bunkers zijn talrijk en goed geplaatst, de struiken ontbreken niet. Als u ze weet te ontlopen, kunt u een goede score neerzetten. Op voorwaarde dat de wind niet te hard waait, maar dit spreekt vanzelf op dit type baan.

If Holland is a flat country, then here are her mountains. High dunes, wind and scant vegetation are the unmistakable features of a links course, of which Kennemer is one of the finest examples in Europe. You don't really see the sea, but you will appreciate the stylish and very traditional clubhouse. Designed by Harry Colt in 1920, the original course was supplemented with an additional 9 holes in 1985, but the natural terrain has not quite worked as well for the newer layout. The course is moderately hilly, enough for slightly wayward shots to kick, roll and end up in some pretty interesting positions. Don't feel too confident about the absence of water and the scarcity of trees; there are loads of well placed bunkers, and there is no shortage of gorse, either. Keep out of them and you might hope to sign for a good score, providing the wind doesn't blow too hard. On this type of course, that goes without saying. An absolute must.

Kennemer Golf & Country Club

Kennemerweg 78
NL - 2042 XT ZANDVOORT

Office	Secretariaat	(31) 023 - 571 8456
Pro shop	Pro shop	(31) 023 - 571 4974
Fax	Fax	(31) 023 - 571 9520
Situation	Locatie	
8 km Haarlem, 150 213 inw.		
Annual closure	Jaarlijkse sluiting	neen
Weekly closure	Wekelijkse sluitingsdag	neen

Fees main season
Hoogseizoen tarieven 18 holes

	Week days Weekdagen	We/Bank holidays We/Feestdagen
Individual Individueel	Fl. 100,-	Fl. 100,-
Couple Paar	Fl. 200,-	Fl. 200,-

Caddy	Caddy	neen
Electric Trolley	Electrische trolley	neen
Buggy	Buggy	neen
Clubs	Clubs	Fl. 25,-

Credit cards Creditkaarten   neen

Access Toegang : Haarlem, Aerdenhout → Zandvoort
Map 1 on page 796 Auto kaart 1 Blz 796

GOLF COURSE
BAAN   18 /20

Site	Terrein	▬▬▬▬
Maintenance	Onderhoud	▬▬▬▬
Architect	Architect	Harry S. Colt
Type	Type baan	links, duinbaan
Relief	Reliëf	▬▬▬
Water in play	Waterhazards	▬
Exp. to wind	Windgevoelig	▬▬▬▬▬
Trees in play	Bomen	▬▬

Scorecard Scorekaart	Chp. Back tees	Mens Heren	Ladies Damen
Length Lengte	6045	5738	5006
Par	72	72	72

Advised golfing ability		0	12	24	36
Aanbevolen golfvaardigheid		▬▬▬▬▬			
Hcp required	Vereiste hcp	28			

CLUB HOUSE & AMENITIES
CLUB HOUSE EN ANNEXEN   8 /10

Pro shop	Pro shop	▬▬▬▬
Driving range	Oefenbaan	▬▬▬
Sheltered	overdekt	3 Plaatsen
On grass	op gras	neen
Putting-green	putting-green	ja
Pitching-green	pitching-green	ja

HOTEL FACILITIES
HOTELS IN OMGEVING   8 /10

HOTELS HOTELS
Elysée Beach   Zandvoort
200 kamers, D Fl. 225,-   3 km
Tel. (31) 023 - 571 3234, Fax (31) 023 - 571 9094

Palace, 53 kamers, D Fl. 175,-   Zandvoort, 3 km
Tel. (31) 023 - 571 2911, Fax (31) 023 - 572 0131

Carlton Square   Haarlem
106 kamers, D Fl. 275,-   8 km
Tel. (31) 023 - 531 9091, Fax (31) 023 - 532 9853

Zuiderbad, 27 kamers, D Fl. 180,-   Zandvoort, 3 km
Tel. (31) 023 - 571 2613, Fax (31) 023 - 571 3190

RESTAURANTS RESTAURANT
De Bokkedoorns   Overveen
Tel. (31) 023 - 526 3600   12 km

Landgoed Groenendaal   Heemstede
Tel. (31) 023 - 528 1555   3 km

817

Opnieuw een golfbaan die in twee fasen tot stand is gekomen, maar waar de samenwerking Pennink-Steel, twee ontwerpers met eenzelfde achtergrond, een vrij consistent en gelijkmatig resultaat heeft opgeleverd. Vooral omdat de meeste holes in een bosgebied liggen, met nadruk op eenheid van stijl. Zoals altijd kunnen de bomen het leven zuur maken voor zwierige spelers. Je moet echt recht slaan en je niet teveel om de lengte bekommeren (zeker niet van de medaltees), wat de meeste spelers als muziek in de oren zal klinken. Er zijn maar weinig fairway-bunkers en die er zijn leveren niet al te veel problemen op. Ook bij de greens liggen niet veel bunkers, zodat de meeste greens met een stuiterend schot gehaald kunnen worden. De greens zelf zijn middelgroot, redelijk gevormd en makkelijk te lezen. Zoals je in dit waterrijke gebied mag verwachten komt water regelmatig in het spel, soms onverwachts, zelfs een beetje stiekem. Het gelijknamige hotel voegt extra allure aan de baan toe.

Yet another course built in two parts, but the partnership between Pennink and Steel, two designers of the same culture, has produced a rather consistent and even result, especially since the majority of holes are laid out in a forest to accentuate unity of style. But as always, trees also make life complicated for wayward players. You have to play straight here and not necessarily look for length all the time (not from the front tees, anyway), which is probably good news for most players. There are few fairway bunkers, and the ones there are don't add much to the overall difficulty. Green-side bunkers are scarce, too, meaning that most greens can be approached with bump and run shots. The greens are mid-sized, moderately contoured and easy to read. As you might expect in a province with so many lakes, water comes into play, sometimes surprisingly and even sneakily. The hotel on site adds to the course's overall appeal.

Golf en Country Club Lauswolt

Van Harinxmaweg 8a
NL - 9244 CJ BEESTERZWAAG

Office	Secretariaat	(31) 0512 - 382 594
Pro shop	Pro shop	(31) 0512 - 383 869
Fax	Fax	(31) 0512 - 383 739
Situation	Locatie	

5 km Drachten, 50 440 inw.
40 km Groningen, 170 535 inw.

Annual closure	Jaarlijkse sluiting	neen
Weekly closure	Wekelijkse sluitingsdag	neen

Fees main season
Hoogseizoen tarieven 18 holes

	Week days Weekdagen	We/Bank holidays We/Feestdagen
Individual Individueel	Fl 80,-	Fl 100,-
Couple Paar	Fl 160,-	Fl 200,-

Caddy	Caddy	neen
Electric Trolley	Electrische trolley	Fl 7,50,-
Buggy	Buggy	neen
Clubs	Clubs	Fl 20,-

Credit cards Creditkaarten
VISA - Eurocard - MasterCard - AMEX - DC

Access Toegang : A7 Groningen-Drachten,
exit 28 → Beesterzwaag
Map 1 on page 796 Auto kaart 1 Blz 796

GOLF COURSE BAAN

14/20

Site	Terrein	■■■■■□
Maintenance	Onderhoud	■■■■■□
Architect	Architect	Frank Pennink Donald Steel
Type	Type baan	bosbaan
Relief	Reliëf	■□□□□
Water in play	Waterhazards	■■□□□
Exp. to wind	Windgevoelig	■■□□□
Trees in play	Bomen	■■■■□

Scorecard Scorekaart	Chp. Back tees	Mens Heren	Ladies Damen
Length Lengte	6152	5916	5353
Par	72	72	72

Advised golfing ability Aanbevolen golfvaardigheid	0 12 24 36	
Hcp required Vereiste hcp	36	

CLUB HOUSE & AMENITIES CLUB HOUSE EN ANNEXEN

6/10

Pro shop	Pro shop	■■■■□
Driving range	Oefenbaan	■■■□□
Sheltered	overdekt	4 plaatsen
On grass	op gras	neen
Putting-green	putting-green	ja
Pitching-green	pitching-green	ja

HOTEL FACILITIES HOTELS IN OMGEVING

7/10

HOTELS HOTELS
Landgoed Lauswolt — Golf
58 kamers, D Fl. 250,-
Tel. (31) 0512 - 381 245, Fax (31) 0512 - 381 496

Het Witte Huis — Beesterzwaag
8 kamers, D Fl. 130,- — 1 km
Tel. (31) 0512 - 382 222, Fax (31) 0512 - 382 307

Hotel Drachten — Drachten
48 kamers, D Fl. 155,- — 5 km
Tel. (31) 0512 - 520 705, Fax (31) 0512 - 523 232

RESTAURANTS RESTAURANT
Landgoed Lauswolt — Golf
Tel. (31) 0512 - 381 245

De Wilgenhoeve — Drachten
Tel. (31) 0512 - 512 510 — 5 km

818

| 18 | 7 | 8 |

De derde parel in de trilogie van Nederlandse linksbanen. Met magnifiek uitzicht over de duinen en de bollenvelden in het binnenland. Een klassieke lay-out, waarbij alleen natuurlijke elementen in het spel komen. Met alle moeilijkheden van het golfspel in de duinen, zoals potbunkers, blinde slagen en de wind. Slechts vijf holes liggen in bebost terrein. Ook hier kennen de fairways maar weinig vlakke stukken, dus is een goede techniek nodig voor elke slag. En om de bal laag te houden als het waait. De meeste greens worden omringd door rough of heuveltjes, zonder al te veel bunkers, maar denk niet dat scoren gemakkelijk is. Andere interessante elementen zijn de dichte struiken in de rough, een enkel poeltje en de renovatie van het clubhuis. Een uitdagende baan, die tot de beste van Europa gerekend kan worden (bij voorkeur spelen op een werkdag).

The third absolute gem in the magnificent trilogy of Dutch links, one that offers some magnificent views over the dunes and inland, covered with fields of flowers in the Spring. The layout is a classic, bringing into play only natural elements and the difficulties of golfing amidst sand dunes, including pot bunkers, blind shots and exposure to the wind. Only five holes are laid out over woody terrain. Again, there are few flat lies, so good technique is needed to shape the shot and to hit low balls when the wind blows. As most of the greens are surrounded by rough or rolling mounds, there aren't too many bunkers, but don't ever think scoring is easy. Other interesting features are the thick bushes in the middle of the rough, a single water hazard and the welcome renovation of the clubhouse. A challenging layout that has to be rated amongst the front-running courses in Europe (choose a week-day to play here).

Noordwijkse Golfclub
Randweg 25
NL - 2200 AB NOORDWIJK

Office	Secretariaat	(31) 0252 - 373 763
Pro shop	Pro shop	(31) 0252 - 373 763
Fax	Fax	(31) 0252 - 370 044
Situation	Locatie	

15 km N Leiden, 114 892 inw.

| Annual closure | Jaarlijkse sluiting | neen |
| Weekly closure | Wekelijkse sluitingsdag | neen |

Fees main season
Hoogseizoen tarieven 18 holes

	Week days Weekdagen	We/Bank holidays We/Feestdagen
Individual Individueel	Fl 100,-	—
Couple Paar	Fl 200,-	—

NGF-members: Fl 65,-

Caddy	Caddy	neen
Electric Trolley	Electrische trolley	neen
Buggy	Buggy	neen
Clubs	Clubs	ja

Credit cards Creditkaarten
VISA - Eurocard - MasterCard

Access Toegang : Amsterdam, A4, A44 → Leiden.
Exit 3 → Noordwijk aan Zee. 6 km →
Nordwijkerhout. 1 km → zee
Map 1 on page 796 Auto kaart 1 Blz 796

GOLF COURSE / BAAN — 18/20

Site	Terrein	
Maintenance	Onderhoud	
Architect	Architect	Frank Pennink
Type	Type baan	links
Relief	Reliëf	
Water in play	Waterhazards	
Exp. to wind	Windgevoelig	
Trees in play	Bomen	

Scorecard Scorekaart	Chp. Back tees	Mens Heren	Ladies Damen
Length Lengte	6242	5875	5029
Par	72	72	72

Advised golfing ability Aanbevolen golfvaardigheid	0	12	24	36
Hcp required Vereiste hcp	28			

CLUB HOUSE & AMENITIES / CLUB HOUSE EN ANNEXEN — 7/10

Pro shop	Pro shop	
Driving range	Oefenbaan	
Sheltered	overdekt	5 plaatsen
On grass	op gras	neen
Putting-green	putting-green	ja
Pitching-green	pitching-green	ja

HOTEL FACILITIES / HOTELS IN OMGEVING — 8/10

HOTELS HOTELS

Huis ter Duin — Noordwijk
238 kamers, D Fl. 400,- — 6 km
Tel. (31) 071 - 361 9220, Fax (31) 071 - 361 9401

Noordwijk — Noordwijk
62 kamers, D Fl. 200,- — 6 km
Tel. (31) 071 - 361 8900, Fax (31) 071 - 361 7882

De Witte Raaf — Noordwijk
35 kamers, D Fl. 170,- — 1 km
Tel. (31) 0252 - 375 984, Fax (31) 0252 - 377 578

RESTAURANTS RESTAURANT

Cleyburg — Noordwijk-Binnen
Tel. (31) 071 - 364 8448 — 8 km

De Palmentuin — Noordwijk
Tel. (31) 071 - 361 9340 — 6 km

819

Temidden van oude bospercelen zijn drie lussen van elk negen holes aangelegd. Het levert een aantrekkelijke, maar ook vrij smalle golfbaan op. Misschien is het terrein net iets te klein voor 27 holes en zou een 18-holesbaan meer op zijn plaats zijn geweest. Hoewel, als je geen probleem hebt met holes die soms wat kunstmatig aandoen, blijft er een 'spannende' baan over. Vooral de 'North'-baan, waar op de zesde hole een zandverstuiving voor een soort superbunker zorgt. De 'North' en 'East' baan eindigen beide op een grote dubbelgreen. Het clubhuis en de oefenfaciliteiten zijn groot genoeg om meerdere groepen te huisvesten. Wel vreemd: in de kleedkamers zijn golfschoenen uit den boze. Dus altijd schone sokken meenemen !

Three loops of 9 holes have each been cut out of the existing woodland, making a pretty but somewhat narrow layout. Maybe the total area was just too small for 27 holes and a full-size 18-holer with an additional par-3 course would have been more appropriate. Yet if you accept that some holes are a little artificial, what is left is still an attractive layout, especially the North course, where the 6th hole features a huge natural sandtrap in the form of a drifting dune. Both the North and East courses finish on a large twin green. The clubhouse and practice facilities are good enough to handle groups easily, the only strange phenomenon here being the fact that golf shoes are not allowed in the locker-rooms.

Nunspeetse Golf & Country Club

Plesmalaan 30
NL - 8072 PT NUNSPEET

Office	Secretariaat	(31) 0341 - 250 834
Pro shop	Pro shop	(31) 0341 - 250 834
Fax	Fax	(31) 0341 - 260 526
Situation	Locatie	

25 km Zwolle, 99 139 inw.
40 km Amersfoort, 110 117 inw.

Annual closure	Jaarlijkse sluiting	neen
Weekly closure	Wekelijkse sluitingsdag	neen

Fees main season
Hoogseizoen tarieven 18 holes

	Week days Weekdagen	We/Bank holidays We/Feestdagen
Individual Individueel	Fl 80,-	Fl 90,-
Couple Paar	Fl 160,-	Fl 180,-

Caddy	Caddy	neen
Electric Trolley	Electrische trolley	neen
Buggy	Buggy	Fl 50,-
Clubs	Clubs	Fl 40,-

Credit cards Creditkaarten
VISA - Eurocard - MasterCard - AMEX

820

Access Toegang : A28 exit 14 (Zwolle-Amersfoort)
→ Nunspeet. Rechts
Map 1 on page 797 Auto kaart 1 Blz 797

GOLF COURSE
BAAN
15/20

Site	Terrein	
Maintenance	Onderhoud	
Architect	Architect	Paul Rolin
Type	Type baan	bosbaan
Relief	Reliëf	
Water in play	Waterhazards	
Exp. to wind	Windgevoelig	
Trees in play	Bomen	

Scorecard Scorekaart	Chp. Back tees	Mens Heren	Ladies Damen
Length Lengte	6094	5866	5127
Par	72	72	72

Advised golfing ability		0 12 24 36
Aanbevolen golfvaardigheid		
Hcp required	Vereiste hcp	neen

CLUB HOUSE & AMENITIES
CLUB HOUSE EN ANNEXEN
5/10

Pro shop	Pro shop	
Driving range	Oefenbaan	
Sheltered	overdekt	8 plaatsen
On grass	op gras	neen
Putting-green	putting-green	ja
Pitching-green	pitching-green	ja

HOTEL FACILITIES
HOTELS IN OMGEVING
3/10

HOTELS HOTELS

Het Roode Wold   Nunspeet
14 kamers, D Fl. 155   3 km
Tel. (31) 0341 - 260 134, Fax (31) 0341 - 256 508

Keizerskroon   Apeldoorn
96 kamers, D Fl. 295,-   30 km
Tel. (31) 055 - 521 7744, Fax (31) 055 - 521 4737

Dennenheuvel   Epe
28 kamers, D Fl. 170,-   10 km
Tel. (31) 0578 - 612 326, Fax (31) 0578 - 621 857

RESTAURANTS RESTAURANT

't Soerel, Tel. (31) 0578 - 688 276   Epe, 10 km

De Echoput   Apeldoorn
Tel.(31) 055 - 519 1248   30 km

Het Jachthuis   Apeldoorn
Tel. (31) 055 - 519 1397   30 km

Helaas is een deel van het aangrenzende industrieterrein zichtbaar en is de autoweg continu hoorbaar. Voor het overige waant u zich hier temidden van het buitenleven (weilanden, graanvelden, koeien) op een baan die veel aandacht voor ecologie heeft. Zo wordt de rough lang gehouden om de knaagdieren te huisvesten, die op hun beurt roofvogels aantrekken. Ondanks de relatief jonge leeftijd oogt de baan vrij volwassen. Een paar losse bomen en struiken zijn in het ontwerp opgenomen en vormen zo hindernissen, net als waterpartijen, talloze bunkers en de wind, die altijd aanwezig lijkt. Vier vijvertjes komen in het spel op acht holes, waarbij ze op de 5e en 15e recht voor de green liggen. Twee fraaie par-3 holes, die vooral onervaren spelers ontzag zullen inboezemen. Behalve een paar blinde bunkers heeft de baan een eerlijk karakter. Uitgezonderd misschien de 16e hole, een controversiële dogleg.

Unfortunately, a number of buildings from the nearby industrial estate can still be seen and the noise from the road is never-ending. Otherwise, you are in the country here (meadows, fields of wheat and cows) and the club pays very special attention to the environment. Hence a rough that is left to grow rather tall, attracting rodents, falcons and eagles. Despite its tender age, this course is remarkably mature. A few isolated trees or copses are fully integrated into the course and form one of the difficulties, along with the water hazards, numerous bunkers and the wind, which is always a frequent feature. Four small lakes come into play on eight holes, forming frontal hazards on the 5th and 15th holes, two fine par 3s which could be a real handful for inexperienced players. Despite a few hidden hazards, the course is forthright in style, except the 16th, a very controversial dog-leg.

Oosterhoutse Golf Club

Dukaatstraat 21
NL - 4903 RN OOSTERHOUT

Office	Secretariaat	(31) 0162 - 421 210
Pro shop	Pro shop	(31) 0162 - 436 397
Fax	Fax	(31) 0162 - 433 285
Situation	Locatie	

5 km Breda, 129 125 inw.

Annual closure	Jaarlijkse sluiting	neen
Weekly closure	Wekelijkse sluitingsdag	neen

Fees main season
Hoogseizoen tarieven 18 holes

	Week days Weekdagen	We/Bank holidays We/Feestdagen
Individual Individueel	Fl 70,-	Fl 75,-
Couple Paar	Fl 140,-	Fl 150,-

Caddy	Caddy	neen
Electric Trolley	Electrische trolley	Fl 10,-/18 holes
Buggy	Buggy	neen
Clubs	Clubs	neen

Credit cards Creditkaarten   neen

Access Toegang : A27, exit 17 → Rijen. 200 m, rechts. → Golf
Map 1 on page 796 Auto kaart 1 Blz 796

GOLF COURSE
BAAN   15/20

Site	Terrein	
Maintenance	Onderhoud	
Architect	Architect	Joan Dudok van Heel
Type	Type baan	open parkbaan
Relief	Reliëf	
Water in play	Waterhazards	
Exp. to wind	Windgevoelig	
Trees in play	Bomen	

Scorecard Scorekaart	Chp. Back tees	Mens Heren	Ladies Damen
Length Lengte	6182	5907	5110
Par	71	72	72

Advised golfing ability Aanbevolen golfvaardigheid	0	12	24	36

Hcp required   Vereiste hcp   neen

CLUB HOUSE & AMENITIES
CLUB HOUSE EN ANNEXEN   7/10

Pro shop	Pro shop	
Driving range	Oefenbaan	
Sheltered	overdekt	9 plaatsen
On grass	op gras	neen
Putting-green	putting-green	ja
Pitching-green	pitching-green	ja

HOTEL FACILITIES
HOTELS IN OMGEVING   7/10

HOTELS HOTELS

Golden Tulip   Oosterhout
53 kamers, D Fl. 175,-   3 km
Tel. (31) 0162 - 452 003, Fax (31) 0162 - 435 003

A.C. Hotel   Oosterhout
63 kamers, D Fl. 100,-   3 km
Tel. (31) 0162 - 453 643, Fax (31) 0162 - 434 662

Korenbeurs   Made
54 kamers, D Fl. 165,-   5 km
Tel. (31) 0162 - 682 150, Fax (31) 0162 - 684 647

RESTAURANTS RESTAURANT

Le Bouc   Oosterhout
Tel. (31) 0162 - 450 888   3 km

De Arent   Breda
Tel. (31) 076 - 514 4601   5 km

821

Purmerend is een goed voorbeeld van een golfbaan-ontwerp in een polder, het vlakke boerenland in de loop der eeuwen aan de zee onttrokken. De bodem is rijk en vruchtbaar, maar elke vorm van fysiek reliëf moet kunstmatig worden aangebracht. Zoals op de meeste nieuwe banen zijn er vijvers en sloten gegraven en is de aarde gebruikt om hoogtes en heuveltjes te creëren. Of dat lukt hangt af van het talent van de ontwerper. In dit geval komen we dicht bij het sublieme, en dat zal nog duidelijker worden als de vele nieuw geplante bomen en bosjes tot wasdom zijn gekomen. Voorlopig bepalen de kracht en richting van de wind of de baan moeilijk of makkelijk is. De speler moet vooral het water en de vele bunkers zien te ontlopen. Met zijn redelijke lengte is dit een baan voor alle categoriën spelers. Naast de hier beschreven 18 holes (geel-blauw) is er een iets kortere 9-holes baan (rood).

Purmerend is a good example of golf-course architecture in a polder landscape, i.e. the flat farming land that has been won back from the sea over the centuries. The soil is rich and fertile, but each physical feature has had to be created artificially. As with most modern courses, they have dug ponds and ditches, and shifted earth to design mounds and other hillocks. Success depends on the talent of the designer. In this case, we are close to excellence, and this should become more apparent as the many newly-planted trees and bushes begin to mature. For the time being, the strength and direction of the wind make the course more difficult or easier to play. The player's job is to avoid the water hazards and plentiful bunkers. Very walkable and reasonable in length, this is a layout playable by golfers of all abilities, and also features a smaller 9 hole course.

BurgGolf Purmerend

Westerweg 60
NL - 1445 AD PURMEREND

Office	Secretariaat	(31) 0299 - 481 650
Pro shop	Pro shop	(31) 0299 - 481 650
Fax	Fax	(31) 0299 - 447 081
Situation	Locatie	

15 km Amsterdam, 724 096 inw.

Annual closure	Jaarlijkse sluiting	neen
Weekly closure	Wekelijkse sluitingsdag	neen

Fees main season
Hoogseizoen tarieven 18 holes

	Week days Weekdagen	We/Bank holidays We/Feestdagen
Individual Individueel	Fl. 75,-	Fl. 95,-
Couple Paar	Fl. 150,-	Fl. 190,-

Caddy	Caddy	neen
Electric Trolley	Electrische trolley	Fl. 50,-
Buggy	Buggy	neen
Clubs	Clubs	Fl. 40,-

Credit cards Creditkaarten
VISA - Eurocard - MasterCard - AMEX - DC

Access Toegang : Amsterdam A7 Exit 6 → Purmerend-Noord. Rechts → Volendam
Map 1 on page 796 Auto kaart 1 Blz 796

GOLF COURSE
BAAN

16/20

Site	Terrein	■■■■■
Maintenance	Onderhoud	■■■■■
Architect	Architect	Tom MacAuley
Type	Type baan	polderbaan
Relief	Reliëf	▭
Water in play	Waterhazards	■■■
Exp. to wind	Windgevoelig	■■■■
Trees in play	Bomen	■■

Scorecard Scorekaart	Chp. Back tees	Mens Heren	Ladies Damen
Length Lengte	5781	5781	5148
Par	72	72	72

Advised golfing ability Aanbevolen golfvaardigheid	0	12	24	36
Hcp required Vereiste hcp	neen			

CLUB HOUSE & AMENITIES
CLUB HOUSE EN ANNEXEN

7/10

Pro shop	Pro shop	■■■■■
Driving range	Oefenbaan	■■■■
Sheltered	overdekt	neen
On grass	op gras	neen
Putting-green	putting-green	ja
Pitching-green	pitching-green	ja

HOTEL FACILITIES
HOTELS IN OMGEVING

7/10

HOTELS HOTELS
Purmerend   Purmerend
85 kamers, D Fl. 180,-   3 km
Tel. (31) 0299 - 481 666, Fax (31) 0299 - 644 691

Damhotel   Edam
10 kamers, D Fl. 120,-   3 km
Tel. (31) 0299 - 371 766, Fax (31) 0299 - 373 031

De Fortuna   Edam
26 kamers, D Fl. 152,-   3 km
Tel. (31) 0299 - 371 671, Fax (31) 0299 - 371 469

RESTAURANTS RESTAURANT
La Ciboulette   Zuidoostbeemster
Tel. (31) 0299 - 683 585   4 km

Manno   Neck
Tel. (31) 0299 - 423 949   5 km

822

Deze baan was een van der eerste commerciële projecten in Nederland en als zodanig zeer succesvol. Oorspronkelijk lagen er twee kortere 9-holesbanen en een 18-holes wedstrijdbaan. De 9-holesbanen zijn samengevoegd en uitgebreid tot een volwaardige 18-holesbaan, de Groesbeekse Baan. Nog steeds wat korter, maar ook veel heuvelachtiger dan de andere, de Nijmeegse Baan. Hoewel de vele bosjes die tussen de holes zijn geplant wat bescherming bieden, is de wind een factor om terdege rekening mee te houden. Net als met de vele, soms van de tee niet-zichtbare bunkers. Er zijn meerder holes met blinde slagen naar de green. Alles bij elkaar een prettige baan in een golvend landschap, dat in Nederland niet veel voorkomt.

This course was one of the early commercial golf projects in the Netherlands and a rather successful one, too. It originally consisted of one 18-hole course and two short 9-holers, but the latter have been merged into a second 18-hole course (Groesbeekse Baan). It is a little shorter but also much more hilly than its senior companion, the Nijmeegse Baan. Although the many bushes planted between the holes seem to offer some protection from the wind, it is still a factor to consider. As are the many bunkers, some of which are not easily visible from the tees. There are also several holes with blind shots to the greens. Altogether, this is a pleasant course in rolling countryside not often seen in the Netherlands, with excellent clubhouse and practice facilities.

Golfbaan Rijk van Nijmegen

Postweg 17
NL - 6561 KJ GROESBEEK

Office	Secretariaat	(31) 024 - 397 6644
Pro shop	Pro shop	(31) 024 - 397 6644
Fax	Fax	(31) 024 - 397 6942
Situation	Locatie	

5 km Nijmegen, 147 000 inw.

Annual closure	Jaarlijkse sluiting	neen
Weekly closure	Wekelijkse sluitingsdag	neen

Fees main season
Hoogseizoen tarieven 18 holes

	Week days Weekdagen	We/Bank holidays We/Feestdagen
Individual Individueel	Fl 60,-	Fl 80,-
Couple Paar	Fl 120,-	Fl 160,-

Caddy	Caddy	neen
Electric Trolley	Electrische trolley	neen
Buggy	Buggy	Fl 40,-
Clubs	Clubs	Fl 10,-

Credit cards Creditkaarten
VISA - Eurocard - MasterCard - AMEX - DC

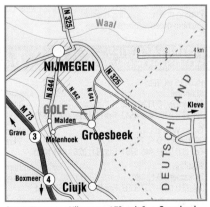

Access Toegang : Nijmegen: A73, exit 3 → Groesbeek → Nijmegen
Map 1 on page 797 Auto kaart 1 Blz 797

GOLF COURSE BAAN   14/20

Site	Terrein	
Maintenance	Onderhoud	
Architect	Architect	Paul Rolin
Type	Type baan	parkbaan
Relief	Reliëf	
Water in play	Waterhazards	
Exp. to wind	Windgevoelig	
Trees in play	Bomen	

Scorecard Scorekaart	Chp. Back tees	Mens Heren	Ladies Damen
Length Lengte	6076	6010	5307
Par	72	72	72

Advised golfing ability Aanbevolen golfvaardigheid	0	12	24	36
Hcp required Vereiste hcp	neen			

CLUB HOUSE & AMENITIES CLUB HOUSE EN ANNEXEN   6/10

Pro shop	Pro shop	
Driving range	Oefenbaan	
Sheltered	overdekt	24 plaatsen
On grass	op gras	neen
Putting-green	putting-green	ja
Pitching-green	pitching-green	ja

HOTEL FACILITIES HOTELS IN OMGEVING   5/10

HOTELS HOTELS
Hotel Erica   Berg en Dal
59 kamers, D Fl. 200,-   2 km
Tel. (31) 024 - 684 3514, Fax (31) 024 - 684 3613

Hotel Val Monte   Berg en Dal
103 kamers, D Fl. 175,-   2 km
Tel. (31) 024 - 684 2000, Fax (31) 024 - 684 3353

Jachtslot Mookerheide   Molenhoek
20 kamers, D Fl. 250,-   6 km
Tel. (31) 024 - 358 3035, Fax (31) 024 - 358 4355

RESTAURANTS RESTAURANT
Jachslot Mookerheide   Molenhoek
Tel. (31) 024 - 358 3035   6 km

Chalet Brakenstein   Nijmegen
Tel. (31) 024 - 355 3949   5 km

Claudius   Nijmegen
Tel. (31) 024 - 322 1456   5 km

823

De enige zwakke schakel hier is de rumoerige nabijheid van twee autowegen, hoewel die niet bestonden aan het eind van de vorige eeuw toen deze baan tussen bos, heide en doornenstruiken werd aangelegd. Dit zijn de oudste holes in Nederland en de eerste negen volgen nog het originele ontwerp. In de loop der tijden zijn ingrijpende veranderingen aangebracht, hoewel het oorspronkelijke plan van Del Court van Krimpen onaangetast is gebleven. We vermoeden dat Harry Colt iets met de latere wijzigingen te maken heeft gehad. Het zou niet verbazen, gegeven de positionering van de hazards en het natuurlijk karakter van de baan, die in licht heuvelachtig terrein ligt. De tweede negen holes zijn in 1977 gereedgekomen in een stijl die aansluit op de eerste negen. Let ook eens op de grappige holes, zoals de 13e, een korte dogleg met een hoger liggende tee en green. En alle par-3 holes, echte juweeltjes. Rosendaal is zonder twijfel een van Neerlands beste banen.

The only weak link here is the noisy proximity of two motorways, although they didn't exist at the turn of the century when this course was created through forest, heather and gorse. This was Holland's very first course, and the front nine are the original layout. Significant changes have been made, although the original design of Del Court van Krimpen remains unspoiled. We suspect that Harry Colt had something to do with these changes, it wouldn't be surprising given the layout of hazards and the natural character of the course over slightly hilly terrain. The back nine were completed in 1977 in a style consistent with the front nine. Make a note of some amusing holes here, like the 13th, a short dog-leg with elevated tee and green, and all the par 3, pure gems. Rosendaal is unquestionably one of Holland's best inland courses.

Rosendaelsche Golfclub

Apeldoornseweg 450
NL - 6816 SN ARNHEM

Office	Secretariaat	(31) 026 - 442 1438
Pro shop	Pro shop	(31) 026 - 443 7283
Fax	Fax	(31) 026 - 351 1196
Situation	Locatie	

2 km Arnhem, 133 670 inw.

Annual closure	Jaarlijkse sluiting	neen
Weekly closure	Wekelijkse sluitingsdag	neen

Fees main season
Hoogseizoen tarieven **per dag**

	Week days Weekdagen	We/Bank holidays We/Feestdagen
Individual Individueel	Fl. 75,-	—
Couple Paar	Fl. 150,-	—

Caddy	Caddy	neen
Electric Trolley	Electrische trolley	neen
Buggy	Buggy	neen
Clubs	Clubs	ja
Credit cards Creditkaarten		neen

Access Toegang : Arnhem A12. Exit 26, links, rechts.
Map 1 on page 797 Auto kaart 1 Blz 797

GOLF COURSE
BAAN

15/20

Site	Terrein	■■■■
Maintenance	Onderhoud	■■■■
Architect	Architect	D.C. van Krimpen F. Pennink
Type	Type baan	bosbaan
Relief	Reliëf	■■
Water in play	Waterhazards	□
Exp. to wind	Windgevoelig	■
Trees in play	Bomen	■■■■

Scorecard Scorekaart	Chp. Back tees	Mens Heren	Ladies Damen
Length Lengte	6324	6057	5159
Par	72	72	72

Advised golfing ability		0 12 24 36
Aanbevolen golfvaardigheid		■■■■
Hcp required	Vereiste hcp	36

CLUB HOUSE & AMENITIES
CLUB HOUSE EN ANNEXEN

7/10

Pro shop	Pro shop	■■■■
Driving range	Oefenbaan	■■■
Sheltered	overdekt	2 Plaatsen
On grass	op gras	neen
Putting-green	putting-green	ja
Pitching-green	pitching-green	ja

HOTEL FACILITIES
HOTELS IN OMGEVING

7/10

HOTELS HOTELS
Rijnhotel — Arnhem
56 kamers, D Fl 205,- — 4 km
Tel. (31) 026 - 443 4642, Fax (31) 026 - 445 4847

Groot Warnsborn — Arnhem
29 kamers, D Fl. 250,- — 5 km
Tel. (31) 026 - 445 5751, Fax (31) 026 - 443 1010

Postiljon — Arnhem
84 kamers, D Fl. 180,- — 1 km
Tel. (31) 026 - 357 3333, Fax (31) 026 - 357 3361

RESTAURANTS RESTAURANT
De Steenen Tafel — Arnhem
Tel. (31) 026 - 443 5313 — 1 km

Chez Arie, Tel. (31) 026 - 445 6191 — Arnhem, 5 km

824

Er is maar weinig reliëf in Friesland, de provincie van de wijde horizon en telkens wisselende luchten. In dit land van meren en weilanden vormen koeien en paarden een deel van het landschap. Er liggen maar weinig golfbanen, maar dit is een van de beste, heel fraai opgenomen in de omgeving. Een vlakke baan, niet erg lang, met brede fairways en weinig bomen, maar des te meer struiken om u dwars te zitten. Long-hitters kunnen zich laten gaan, maar moeten wel rekening houden met de wind, die het leven aardig zuur kan maken. Hetzelfde geldt voor de waterhazards (vijvertjes en sloten) die op zo'n twaalf holes in het spel komen. Deze nog vrij nieuwe baan is snel gerijpt en biedt veel variatie, zowel visueel (er is een hoop grond verplaatst) als golftechnisch. Een minpunt zijn de lange afstanden tussen de holes. Heel bijzonder is de klokkenstoel op het kerkhofje, aan drie zijden door de baan ingesloten.

There is little relief to speak of in the Frise, a region of endless horizons and changing skies. In this land of lakes, pastureland and crops, cows and horses are all part of the landscape. Golf courses are few and far between here, but this is one of the best, blending in very nicely with the surrounding countryside. Very flat, not very long but with wide fairways, it has few trees to bother you but quite a few bushes. Long-hitters will let rip, but will still have to watch out for the wind, which can make life very difficult. The same goes for the water hazards (ponds and ditches), in play on about a dozen holes. This recent course has quickly matured and has considerable variety to it, both visually (a lot of earth was moved) and technically. The one minor flaw are the long walks between holes, and the one peculiarity the little cemetery in front of the clubhouse, overlooked by a bell-tower and surrounded on three sides by the course.

Burggolf Sint Nicolaasga
Legemeersterweg 18
NL - 8527 DS LEGEMEER

Office	Secretariaat	(31) 0513 - 499 466
Pro shop	Pro shop	(31) 0513 - 499 466
Fax	Fax	(31) 0513 - 499 777
Situation	Locatie	

15 km Heerenveen, 38 936 inw.

Annual closure	Jaarlijkse sluiting	neen
Weekly closure	Wekelijkse sluitingsdag	neen

Fees main season
Hoogseizoen tarieven 18 holes

	Week days Weekdagen	We/Bank holidays We/Feestdagen
Individual Individueel	Fl 65,-	Fl 75,-
Couple Paar	Fl 130,-	Fl 150,-

Caddy	Caddy	neen
Electric Trolley	Electrische trolley	neen
Buggy	Buggy	Fl 40,-
Clubs	Clubs	Fl 20,-

Credit cards Creditkaarten
VISA - Eurocard - MasterCard - AMEX - DC - Pinpas

Access Toegang : Amsterdam A6 →
Groningen/Leeuwarden.
Exit 19 → Woudsend. 3,5 km → Golf
Map 1 on page 796 Auto kaart 1 Blz 796

GOLF COURSE
BAAN   15/20

Site	Terrein	
Maintenance	Onderhoud	
Architect	Architect	Paul Rolin Alan Rijks
Type	Type baan	polderbaan
Relief	Reliëf	
Water in play	Waterhazards	
Exp. to wind	Windgevoelig	
Trees in play	Bomen	

Scorecard Scorekaart	Chp. Back tees	Mens Heren	Ladies Damen
Length Lengte	6038	5765	4993
Par	72	72	72

Advised golfing ability Aanbevolen golfvaardigheid	0	12	24	36
Hcp required Vereiste hcp	neen			

CLUB HOUSE & AMENITIES
CLUB HOUSE EN ANNEXEN   7/10

Pro shop	Pro shop	
Driving range	Oefenbaan	
Sheltered	overdekt	10 plaatsen
On grass	op gras	neen
Putting-green	putting-green	ja
Pitching-green	pitching-green	ja

HOTEL FACILITIES
HOTELS IN OMGEVING   5/10

HOTELS HOTELS
Hotel Legemeer   Legemeer
14 kamers, D FL 170,-
Tel. (31) 0513 - 432 999, Fax (31) 0513 - 432 876

Lauswolt   Beetsterzwaag
58 kamers, Fl 195,-   35 km
Tel. (31) 0527 - 291 833, Fax (31) 0527 - 291 836

Postiljon   Heerenveen
55 kamers, D Fl 145,-   15 km
Tel. (31) 0513 - 618 618, Fax (31) 0513 - 629 100

RESTAURANTS RESTAURANT
Kaatje bij de Sluis   Blokzijl
Tel. (31) 0527 - 291 833   20 km

Sir Sebastian   Heerenveen
Tel. (31) 0513 - 650 408   15 km

825

Deze baan ligt buiten de traditionele toeristische routes, in het groene land van Twente, dichtbij Duitsland. Veel water, weilanden, dichte bossen en grote boerderijen, waarvan de architectuur kennelijk de inspiratie vormde toen het clubhuis met binnenplaats werd ontworpen. Sybrook is een van de weinige nieuwe banen die in bosgebied mochten worden aangelegd. Bossen waarin nog volop wild voorkomt. Die ziet u dan ook regelmatig in de vroege ochtend of avond. Er zijn wat waterhazards, maar niet overdreven veel. De aantrekkingskracht van deze baan zit in een aantal doorkijkjes en de bloeiende rhodondendrons. Het is geen ideale baan voor onstuimige spelers, want er wordt om voorzichtigheid en precisie gevraagd. Ondanks de jonge leeftijd, maakt de baan een volwassen indruk. Het is een lange baan, dus voor de meeste spelers zijn de backtees taboe.

This is a course off the traditional tourist track in the very green region of Twente, close to Germany. Water abounds, as do pasture-land, thick forest and large farms, whose architecture obviously inspired that of the Clubhouse, built with an inner courtyard. Sybrook is one of the few new courses laid out in a forest, which is still home to all sorts of wild animals. You will see a lot of furry creatures at dawn or in the early evening. Several small water hazards come into play, but never excessively so. The appeal of this course is all the greater for a number of views over the countryside and the flowering rhododendrons. Sybrook is not the ideal course for the reckless player, as it demands care, a little thought and considerable accuracy. Despite its infancy, there is a clear impression of maturity. This is a long course, so we would advise the front tees for most players.

Golf & Countryclub 't Sybrook
Veendijk 100
NL - 7525 PZ ENSCHEDE

Office	Secretariaat	(31) 0541 - 530 331
Pro shop	Pro shop	(31) 0541 - 530 331
Fax	Fax	(31) 0541 - 531 690
Situation	Locatie	

5 km Enschede, 147 624 inw. 10 km Hengelo.

Annual closure	Jaarlijkse sluiting	neen
Weekly closure	Wekelijkse sluitingsdag	neen

Fees main season
Hoogseizoen tarieven 18 holes

	Week days Weekdagen	We/Bank holidays We/Feestdagen
Individual Individueel	Fl. 70,-	Fl. 70,-
Couple Paar	Fl. 140,-	Fl. 140,-

Caddy	Caddy	neen
Electric Trolley	Electrische trolley	neen
Buggy	Buggy	neen
Clubs	Clubs	ja

Credit cards Creditkaarten
VISA - Eurocard - MasterCard - AMEX

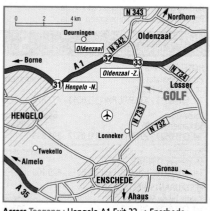

Access Toegang : Hengelo A1 Exit 33 → Enschede.
2,5 km, links
Map 1 on page 797 Auto kaart 1 Blz 797

GOLF COURSE
BAAN — 15/20

Site	Terrein	
Maintenance	Onderhoud	
Architect	Architect	Alan Rijks
		Paul Rolin
Type	Type baan	bosbaan
Relief	Reliëf	
Water in play	Waterhazards	
Exp. to wind	Windgevoelig	
Trees in play	Bomen	

Scorecard	Chp.	Mens	Ladies
Scorekaart	Back tees	Heren	Damen
Length Lengte	6242	5951	5093
Par	72	72	72

Advised golfing ability		0	12	24	36
Aanbevolen golfvaardigheid					
Hcp required	Vereiste hcp	neen			

CLUB HOUSE & AMENITIES
CLUB HOUSE EN ANNEXEN — 6/10

Pro shop	Pro shop	
Driving range	Oefenbaan	
Sheltered	overdekt	ja
On grass	op gras	neen
Putting-green	putting-green	ja
Pitching-green	pitching-green	ja

HOTEL FACILITIES
HOTELS IN OMGEVING — 6/10

HOTELS HOTELS

De Broeierd	Enschede
30 kamers, D Fl. 200,-	5 km
tel. (31) 053 - 435 9882, Fax (31) 053 - 434 0502	
Dish	Enschede
80 kamers, D Fl. 135,-	5 km
Tel. (31) 053 - 486 6666, Fax (31) 053 - 435 3104	
't Lansink	Hengelo
18 kamers, D Fl. 125,-	10 km
Tel. (31) 074 - 291 0066, Fax (31) 074 - 243 5891	

RESTAURANTS RESTAURANT

't Koesthuis	Enschede
Tel. (31) 053 - 432 866	5 km
Mondriaan	Hengelo
Tel. (31) 074 - 291 5321	10 km

Een ontwerp van John S.F. Morrison, die werd geholpen door Harry Colt en Sir Guy Campbell. De baan is in de loop der tijd aangepast en recent met twee holes uitgebreid. Zo midden in een bos laat de baan een indruk van rust achter, als je het lawaai van de weg en de nabij gelegen vliegbasis even wegdenkt. In grote lijnen is het een echte Britse baan, zonder veel verrassingen, met natuurlijk de bomen als belangrijkste hindernis (er zijn veel do-glegs). Vooral vanaf de backtees kan de baan soms erg nauw ogen. De ruwweg twintig natuurlijk aandoende fairway-bunkers spelen een belangrijke rol door hun strategische ligging. De greens zijn middelgroot, goed ontworpen, goed bewaakt en over het algemeen open genoeg om allerlei soorten approaches toe te staan. Aardigheidje: de 150-meter markers bestaan uit nestkastjes in de bomen.

Designed by John S.F. Morrison, who worked with Harry Colt and Sir Guy Campbell, this course has been altered and recently lengthened with two new holes. Laid out in a forest, it exudes an impression of tranquillity, if you can forget the slight traffic noise and the planes from a nearby air base. The general style is rather British and offers no great surprises, while the main difficulties are, naturally, the trees (there are a lot of dog-legs), especially from the back-tees from where the fairways at times look despairingly narrow. The twenty or so very natural-looking fairway bunkers also play an important role through their strategic positioning. The greens are mid-size, slightly contoured, neatly designed, well-guarded and, by and large, open enough to allow all types of approach shots. Interestingly, the 150 yard-to-green markers are nests placed in the trees.

Noord-Brabantsche Golfclub Toxandria

Veenstraat 89
NL - 5124 NC MOLENSCHOT

Office	Secretariaat	(31) 0161 - 411 200
Pro shop	Pro shop	(31) 0161 - 411 200
Fax	Fax	(31) 0161 - 411 715
Situation	Locatie	

5 km Breda, 129 125 inw.

Annual closure	Jaarlijkse sluiting	neen
Weekly closure	Wekelijkse sluitingsdag	neen

Fees main season
Hoogseizoen tarieven 18 holes

	Week days Weekdagen	We/Bank holidays We/Feestdagen
Individual Individueel	Fl. 75,-	Fl. 100,-
Couple Paar	Fl. 150,-	Fl. 200,-

Caddy	Caddy	neen
Electric Trolley	Electrische trolley	neen
Buggy	Buggy	neen
Clubs	Clubs	neen

Credit cards Creditkaarten	neen

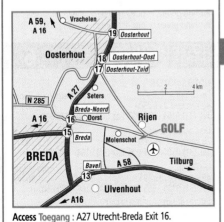

Access Toegang : A27 Utrecht-Breda Exit 16.
N263 → Rijen. 4 km → Molenschot
Map 1 on page 796 Auto kaart 1 Blz 796

GOLF COURSE / BAAN

14/20

Site	Terrein	
Maintenance	Onderhoud	
Architect	Architect	J. Morrison
Type	Type baan	bosbaan
Relief	Reliëf	
Water in play	Waterhazards	
Exp. to wind	Windgevoelig	
Trees in play	Bomen	

Scorecard Scorekaart	Chp. Back tees	Mens Heren	Ladies Damen
Length Lengte	6140	5974	5188
Par	72	72	72

Advised golfing ability		0	12	24	36
Aanbevolen golfvaardigheid					
Hcp required	Vereiste hcp	neen			

CLUB HOUSE & AMENITIES / CLUB HOUSE EN ANNEXEN

7/10

Pro shop	Pro shop	
Driving range	Oefenbaan	
Sheltered	overdekt	8 Plaatsen
On grass	op gras	neen
Putting-green	putting-green	ja
Pitching-green	pitching-green	ja

HOTEL FACILITIES / HOTELS IN OMGEVING

6/10

HOTELS HOTELS

De Herbergh	Rijen
44 kamers, D Fl. 130,-	2 km

Tel. (31) 0161 - 224 318, Fax (31) 0161 - 222 327

Motel Gilze-Rijen	Rijen
134 kamers, D Fl. 100,-	2 km

Tel. (31) 0161 - 454 951, Fax (31) 0161 - 452 171

Mercure Hotel	Breda
40 kamers, D Fl. 225,-	5 km

Tel. (31) 0161 - 522 0200, Fax (31) 0161 - 521 4967

RESTAURANTS RESTAURANT

La Grille d'Or	Breda
Tel. (31) 0161 - 520 4333	5 km

Mirabelle	Breda
Tel. (31) 0161 - 565 6650	5 km

827

De oorspronkelijk aangelegde holes liggen in bebost terrein, waar bomen natuurlijk de belangrijkste hindernis vormen. Zeker op de vier dog-legs en de lange smalle 6e, nu 15e hole. Zo ook op de daaropvolgende schitterende par-3, waar de bomen voor de green weinig ruimte voor fouten laten. Later werden negen nieuwe holes aangelegd, op vroegere landbouwgrond, met vier kleine vijvertjes en een paar sloten, maar ook met bredere fairways. Oude en nieuwe holes zijn door elkaar gemengd, wat variatie in het spel, maar ook behoorlijke afstanden tussen de holes heeft opgeleverd. Een nadeel is dat je tegen de tijd dat je aan de 'oude' greens gewend bent, overstapt naar de nieuwe en omgekeerd. Dat maakt het spel niet eenvoudiger, maar misschien hebben alleen de wat betere spelers hier last van.

The front nine were laid out in woody terrain and trees naturally form the main difficulty, especially on the four dog-legs and the long, narrow 15th. Likewise, on the 16th, a beautiful par 3, the trees in front of the green leave little room for error. They then created nine new holes, over much more open farming land, with four small water hazards and a few ditches, but with much wider fairways. The old and new holes have been intermingled, thus varying the pleasure but sometimes leaving considerable distances between green and next tee. Another obvious drawback is that by the time you get accustomed to the grass and greens on the old holes, you are back to the new ones, and vice versa. This does not make scoring easy, and it just might be that better players are more affected by this subtle difference than their less experienced counterparts.

Wouwse Plantage
Zoomvlietweg 66
NL - 4725 TD WOUWSE PLANTAGE

Office	Secretariaat	(31) 0165 - 379 593
Pro shop	Pro shop	(31) 0165 - 379 547
Fax	Fax	(31) 0165 - 379 888
Situation	Locatie	

10 km Roosendaal, 62 784 inw.
15 km Bergen op Zoom, 47 483 inw.

Annual closure	Jaarlijkse sluiting	neen
Weekly closure	Wekelijkse sluitingsdag	neen

Fees main season
Hoogseizoen tarieven 18 holes

	Week days Weekdagen	We/Bank holidays We/Feestdagen
Individual Individueel	Fl 70,-	Fl 80,-
Couple Paar	Fl 140,-	Fl 160,-

Caddy	Caddy	neen
Electric Trolley	Electrische trolley	Fl 7,50 /18 holes
Buggy	Buggy	neen
Clubs	Clubs	Fl 35,-

Credit cards Creditkaarten — neen

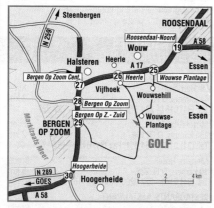

Access Toegang : A58 Breda → Bergen op Zoom.
Exit 26 → Wouwse Plantage. 100 m, rechts, links
(Zoomvlietweg). Golf 3,5 km.
Map 1 on page 796 Auto kaart 1 Blz 796

GOLF COURSE
BAAN
15/20

Site	Terrein	■■■■
Maintenance	Onderhoud	■■■■
Architect	Architect	Donald Steel
		Paul Rolin
Type	Type baan	open parkbaan
Relief	Reliëf	■■
Water in play	Waterhazards	■■■
Exp. to wind	Windgevoelig	■■■■
Trees in play	Bomen	■■■

Scorecard Scorekaart	Chp. Back tees	Mens Heren	Ladies Damen
Length Lengte	5909	5909	5111
Par	72	72	72

Advised golfing ability		0	12	24	36
Aanbevolen golfvaardigheid					
Hcp required	Vereiste hcp	36			

CLUB HOUSE & AMENITIES
CLUB HOUSE EN ANNEXEN
7/10

Pro shop	Pro shop	■■■
Driving range	Oefenbaan	■■■
Sheltered	overdekt	5 plaatsen
On grass	op gras	neen
Putting-green	putting-green	ja
Pitching-green	pitching-green	ja

HOTEL FACILITIES
HOTELS IN OMGEVING
6/10

HOTELS HOTELS
De Draak — Bergen op Zoom
48 kamers, D Fl. 250,- — 8 km
Tel. (31) 0164 - 235 000, Fax (31) 0164 - 236 001

De Gouden Leeuw — Bergen op Zoom
28 kamers, D Fl. 200,- — 8 km
Tel. (31) 0164 - 235 000, Fax (31) 0164 - 236 001

De Draak — Roosendaal
49 kamers, D Fl. 195,- — 10 km
Tel. (31) 0165 - 555 400, Fax (31) 0165 - 560 660

RESTAURANTS RESTAURANT
Mijn Keuken, Tel. (31) 0165 - 530 2208 — Wouw, 5 km

Moerstede, — Bergen op Zoom
Tel. (31) 0164 - 258 800 — 8 km

828

gewonnen zou wel eens meer toeristen naar dit heerlijke gebied kunnen trekken. We zitten hier dicht bij Aken, een van de belangrijkste Duitse steden, waarvan de historische waarde, sinds de grootse plannen van Karel de Grote, nooit in twijfel is getrokken. Dit gebied is ook het hoogste van Nederland... iets onder de 300 meter (elk land heeft zijn bergen, Moeder Natuur bepaalt hoe hoog ze zijn!). De baan werd aangelegd als een 9-holes baan en werd uitgebreid tot 18 holes in 1990. De 'oude' holes lopen door een bos, terwijl acht van de 'nieuwe' holes in een open landschap liggen met sterke hoogteverschillen en prachtige vergezichten. Al met al is de baan goed te bespelen, voor iedereen. Om je handicap te spelen moet je wel de bomen op de eerste negen zien te ontlopen en op de twee negen vooral nauwkeurige teeshots afleveren. Afgedwaalde ballen komen snel op onplezierige plaatsen terecht, op sterk glooiende hellingen.

Maastricht's newly acquired fame, or notoriety, in Europe should attract the tourists to this lovely region. Here, we are very close to Aachen, one of the great German cities whose historical importance, since the great European designs of Charlemagne, has never been questioned. The region is also one of the highest in the Netherlands...a little below 300 metres (each country has its natural mountains, mother nature decides how high!). The course here began as a 9-holer and was extended to 18 holes in 1980. The first holes wind their way through a forest, while 8 of the last 9 are in open countryside with sharp differences in level and some beautiful views. All in all, the course is easily walkable, for everyone. Playing to your handicap demands avoidance of the trees on the way out and carefully placed drives on the way in. Wayward shots can leave your ball in some very tricky positions, with steeply sloping lies.

Zuid Limburgse Golf & Countryclub

Dalbissenweg 22
NL - 6281 NC MECHELEN

Office	Secretariaat	(31) 043 - 455 1254
Pro shop	Pro shop	(31) 043 - 455 1254
Fax	Fax	(31) 043 - 455 1576
Situation	Locatie	

18 km Maastricht, 118 102 inw.
15 km Aachen (Deutschland)

Annual closure	Jaarlijkse sluiting	neen
Weekly closure	Wekelijkse sluitingsdag	neen

Fees main season
Hoogseizoen tarieven per dag

	Week days Weekdagen	We/Bank holidays We/Feestdagen
Individual Individueel	Fl. 60,-	Fl. 90,-
Couple Paar	Fl. 120,-	Fl. 180,-

Caddy	Caddy	neen
Electric Trolley	Electrische trolley	neen
Buggy	Buggy	neen
Clubs	Clubs	ja
Credit cards Creditkaarten		neen

Access Toegang : N278 Maastricht → Aachen.
Gulpen → Landsrade.
Map 1 on page 797 Auto kaart 1 Blz 797

GOLF COURSE
BAAN
14/20

Site	Terrein	▰▰▰▰▱
Maintenance	Onderhoud	▰▰▰▰▱
Architect	Architect	FW Hawtree Rolin/Snelders
Type	Type baan	bosbaan
Relief	Reliëf	▰▰▰▱▱
Water in play	Waterhazards	▰▱▱▱▱
Exp. to wind	Windgevoelig	▰▰▰▱▱
Trees in play	Bomen	▰▰▰▰▱

Scorecard Scorekaart	Chp. Back tees	Mens Heren	Ladies Damen
Length Lengte	5924	5924	5071
Par	71	71	71

Advised golfing ability Aanbevolen golfvaardigheid	0 12 24 36
	▰▰▰▰▱
Hcp required Vereiste hcp	We: 30

CLUB HOUSE & AMENITIES
CLUB HOUSE EN ANNEXEN
7 /10

Pro shop	Pro shop	▰▰▰▰▱
Driving range	Oefenbaan	▰▰▰▱▱
Sheltered	overdekt	2 Plaatsen
On grass	op gras	neen
Putting-green	putting-green	ja
Pitching-green	pitching-green	ja

HOTEL FACILITIES
HOTELS IN OMGEVING
7 /10

HOTELS HOTELS

Kasteel Wittem — Wittem
12 kamers, D Fl. 210,- — 12 km
Tel. (31) 043 - 450 1208, Fax (31) 043 - 450 1260

Landgoed Schoutenhof — Epen
10 kamers, D Fl. 170,- — 8 km
Tel. (31) 043 - 455 2002, Fax (31) 043 - 455 2605

Brull — Mechelen
32 kamers, D Fl. 140,- — 4 km
Tel. (31) 043 - 455 1263, Fax (31) 043 - 455 2300

RESTAURANTS RESTAURANT

De Leuf — Ubachsberg
Tel. (31) 045 - 575 0226 — 4 km

De Bloasbalg — Wahlwiller
Tel. (31) 043 - 451 1364 — 5 km

829

O SEU MELHOR
CLUB HOUSE EM PORTUGAL.

Como se prova nestas páginas, o que não falta
em Portugal são bons campos de Golfe.
Felizmente, a Peugeot Portugal também não quis
que lhe faltasse outro tipo de comodidades
e reuniu na Sucursal de Lisboa alguns serviços
exclusivos: com os **Serviços Imediatos**, pode ter
a certeza de que as assistências rápidas serão
realmente rápidas; com a **Recepção 24 Horas**,
pode deixar o seu Peugeot bem entregue
a qualquer hora do dia ou da noite. Para
além, claro, daquilo que você já espera:
a gama completa de modelos Peugeot
e um atendimento dedicado e profissional, em
modernas e espaçosas instalações. Porque,
feliz ou infelizmente, os buggies e os trolleys
não são os únicos veículos da sua vida.

PEUGEOT
PORTUGAL
SUCURSAL LISBO
Rua Quinta do Paizinho, 5
2795 CARNAXIDE
Telef. 416 66 00 Fax 417 62 59

Portugal

C om um clima privilegiado, Portugal é desde há muito tempo um refúgio de inverno para os turistas do Norte da Europa e em particular golfistas. O País conta com cerca de 6 000 golfistas e 40 percursos de 18 buracos. Todos estão abertos ao público, mas aos fins de semana congestionam-se um pouco com os sócios dos Clubes, sobretudo na regiáó de Lisboa. Assim, é sempre melhor reservar, os tempos de saída, nomeadamente na região do Algarve, ao sul de Portugal, onde os visitantes são em grande número, do Outono à Primavera. O Verão é contudo uma época agradável, onde uma suave brisa maritimal, atenua o calor.

831

With a privileged climate, Portugal has long been a winter refuge for tourists from northern Europe, and especially for golfers. The country has only 6,000 players and around 40 eighteen-hole courses. All are open to the public, but they do tend to get crowded on week-ends with club members, especially in the Lisbon area. It is, therefore, always preferable to book a tee-off time, especially in the Algarve in the south of the country, where visitors abound from Autumn to Spring. Summer is also a pleasant time to play, with a cooling sea breeze to ease the heat.

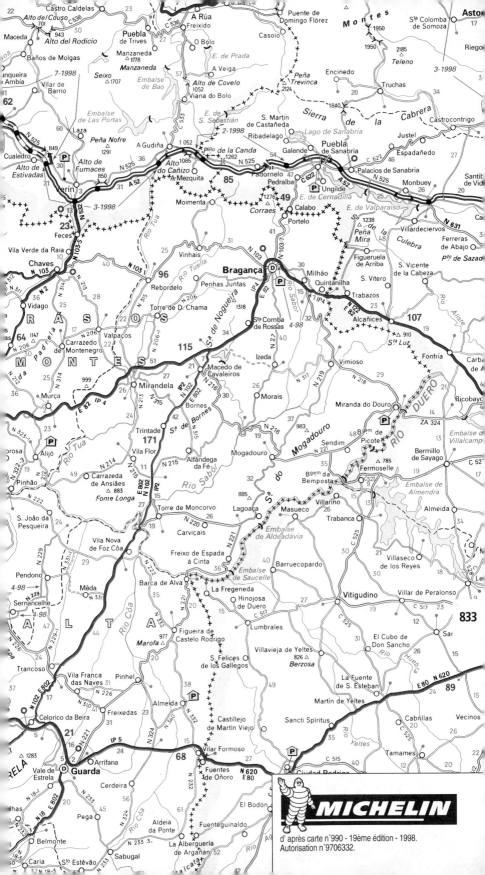

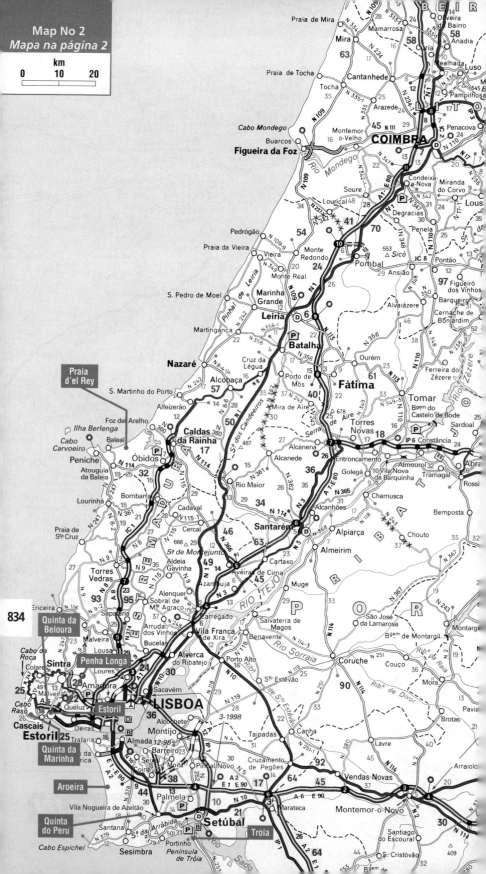

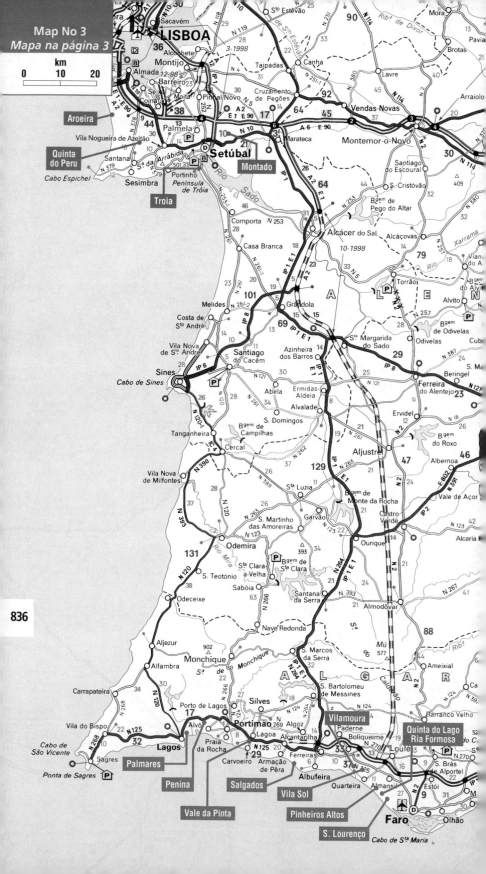

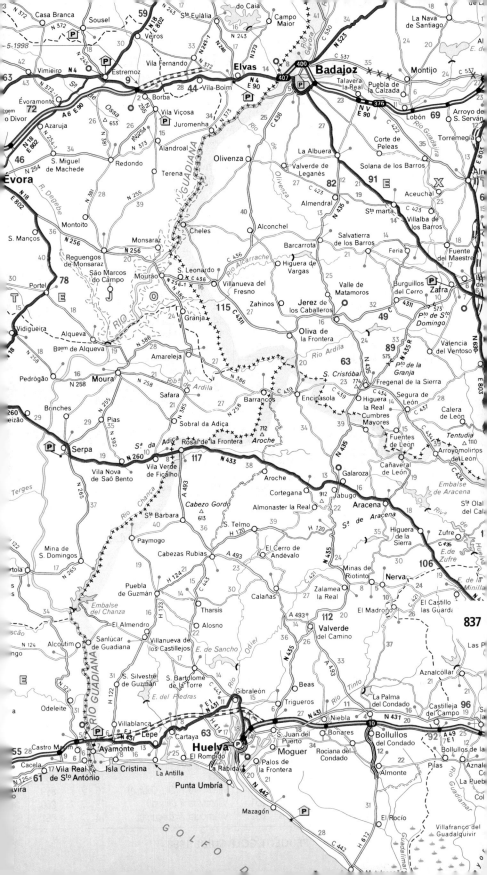

CLASSIFICAÇÃO DOS PERCURSOS
CLASSIFICATION OF COURSES

Nota do Club-House e anexos
Club house and facilities score

Nota do percurso
(Course score)

Nota do envolvimento hoteleiro
Hotel facility score

| 17 7 5 | Praia d'El Rey | 848 |

Página
Page

Nota			Percurso	Página	Nota			Percurso	Página
17	7	5	Praia d'El Rey	848	14	8	8	Pinheiros Altos	847
17	6	8	S. Lourenço	854	14	8	7	Quinta da Beloura	849
16	7	5	Quinta do Peru	853	14	7	7	Salgados	855
16	7	7	Vilamoura I (Old Course)	859	14	6	6	Vale da Pinta	857
15	6	6	Aroeira	840	14	7	7	Vila Sol	858
15	7	8	Penha Longa	845	14	7	7	Vilamoura III (Laguna)	861
15	7	8	Quinta do Lago B/C	851	13	7	7	Estoril	841
15	7	8	Quinta do Lago Ria Formosa	852	13	7	6	Montado	843
15	7	5	Troia	856	13	7	5	Palmares	844
14	7	5	Madeira	842	13	7	7	Quinta da Marinha	850
14	7	8	Penina	846	13	7	7	Vilamoura II (Pinhal)	860

CLASSIFICAÇÃO DO ENVOLVIMENTO HOTELEIRO
CLASSIFICATION OF HOTELS FACILITIES

Nota			Percurso	Página	Nota			Percurso	Página
15	7	8	Penha Longa	845	16	7	7	Vilamoura I (Old Course)	859
14	7	8	Penina	846	13	7	7	Vilamoura II (Pinhal)	860
14	8	8	Pinheiros Altos	847	14	7	7	Vilamoura III (Laguna)	861
15	7	8	Quinta do Lago B/C	851	15	6	6	Aroeira	840
15	7	8	Quinta do Lago Ria Formosa	852	13	7	6	Montado	843
17	6	8	S. Lourenço	854	14	6	6	Vale da Pinta	857
13	7	7	Estoril	841	14	7	5	Madeira	842
14	8	7	Quinta da Beloura	849	13	7	5	Palmares	844
13	7	7	Quinta da Marinha	850	17	7	5	Praia d'El Rey	848
14	7	7	Salgados	855	16	7	5	Quinta do Peru	853
14	7	7	Vila Sol	858	15	7	5	Troia	856

ESTADIA DE GOLF RECOMENDADA
RECOMMENDED GOLFING STAY

Percurso	Nota			Página	Percurso	Nota			Página
Madeira	14	7	5	842	S. Lourenço	17	6	8	854
Penha Longa	15	7	8	845	Troia	15	7	5	856
Praia d'El Rey	17	7	5	848	Vilamoura I (Old Course)	16	7	7	859
Quinta do Lago B/C	15	7	8	851	Vilamoura II (Pinhal)	13	7	7	860
Quinta do Lago Ria Formosa	15	7	8	852	Vilamoura III (Laguna)	14	7	7	861

FÉRIAS RECOMENDADAS
RECOMMENDED GOLFING HOLIDAYS

Percurso	Nota		Página	Percurso	Nota		Página
Estoril	13	7 7	841	Quinta do Lago *Ria Formosa*	15	7 8	852
Madeira	14	7 5	842	Quinta do Peru	16	7 5	853
Palmares	13	7 5	844	S. Lourenço	17	6 8	854
Penha Longa	15	7 8	845	Salgados	14	7 7	855
Penina	14	7 8	846	Vale da Pinta	14	6 6	857
Pinheiros Altos	14	8 8	847	Vila Sol	14	7 7	858
Praia d'El Rey	17	7 5	848	Vilamoura *I (Old Course)*	16	7 7	859
Quinta da Marinha	13	7 7	850	Vilamoura *II (Pinhal)*	13	7 7	860
Quinta do Lago *B/C*	15	7 8	851	Vilamoura *III (Laguna)*	14	7 7	861

ESTAÇOES DO ANOS RECOMENDADAS
RECOMMENDED SEASONS

Estaçoes do anos / Percurso	Nota		Página	Estaçoes do anos / Percurso	Nota		Página
1 2 3 4 5 6 7 8 9 10 11 12				1 2 3 4 5 6 7 8 9 10 11 12			
Aroeira	15	6 6	840	Quinta da Marinha	13	7 7	850
Estoril	13	7 7	841	Quinta do Lago *B/C*	15	7 8	851
Madeira	14	7 5	842	Quinta do Peru	16	7 5	853
Montado	13	7 6	843	S. Lourenço	17	6 8	854
Palmares	13	7 5	844	Salgados	14	7 7	855
Penha Longa	15	7 8	845	Troia	15	7 5	856
Penina	14	7 8	846	Vale da Pinta	14	6 6	857
Pinheiros Altos	14	8 8	847	Vila Sol	14	7 7	858
Praia d'El Rey	17	7 5	848	Vilamoura *I (Old Course)*	16	7 7	859
Quinta da Beloura	14	8 7	849				

RELEVO DOS PERCURSOS
GEOGRAPHICAL RELIEF

Pouco acidentado Rather flat	Relevo médio Averagely hilly	Muito acidentado Very hilly

Percurso	Nota		Página	Percurso	Nota		Página
Penina	14	7 8	846	S. Lourenço	17	6 8	854
Quinta da Marinha	13	7 7	850	Vila Sol	14	7 7	858
Salgados	14	7 7	855				
Troia	15	7 5	856	Quinta do Lago *Ria Formosa*	15	7 8	852
Aroeira	15	6 6	840	Estoril	13	7 7	841
Montado	13	7 6	843	Palmares	13	7 5	844
Quinta da Beloura	14	8 7	849	Pinheiros Altos	14	8 8	847
				Vale da Pinta	14	6 6	857
Praia d'El Rey	17	7 5	848				
Vilamoura *I (Old Course)*	16	7 7	859	Penha Longa	15	7 8	845
Quinta do Peru	16	7 5	853	Madeira	14	7 5	842

AROEIRA ✳ | 15 | 6 | 6 |

A primeira impressão é a de um ambiente muito agradável entre pinheiros e flores silvestres, habitat natural de diversos tipos de aves. Sem interferir com esse quadro o arquitecto Frank Pennink realizou um percurso de uma grande franqueza, e com um traçado muito simples, onde os obstáculos (a excepção das árvores) raramente sao perigosos. Os jogadores médios e os prin-cipiantes sentem-se logo à vontade neste percurso amigável, onde se caminha facilmente e onde os "rough" não são muito penalizantes. Os melhores jogadores, no entanto, podem achá-lo um pouco monotono para jogar muitas vezes, uma vez que lhe faltam verdadeiros desafios, com a excepção do 11, redesenhado por Robert Trent Jones. Em contrapartida a Aroeira é um local ideal para se jogar uma partida em família ou para uma partida entre amigos.

The first impression is one of a very pleasant setting of pine-trees and wild flowers, and the natural habitat for numerous birds. Without spoiling the scenery, architect Frank Penninck has laid out a clear and candid course of rather simple design, where the hazards are seldom too dangerous (except the trees). High-handicappers and beginners will feel immediately at home on this friendly and easily-walkable course, where the rough and undergrowth could never be called penalising. The better players might possibly find it boring to play regularly, given the absence of real challenge. Only the 11th hole, redesigned by Robert Trent Jones, stands out from a pretty colourless picture. By contrast, Aroeira is the ideal spot for a round with all the family and for giving less experienced players welcome practice.

C.G. Aroeira
Herdade da Aroeira - Fonte da Jelha
P - 2825 MONTE DE CAPARICA

Office	Secretariado	(351) 01 - 297 13 14
Pro shop	Pro-shop	(351) 01 - 296 18 02
Fax	Fax	(351) 01 - 297 12 38
Situation	Localização	

11 km Lisboa, 662 782 h.
48 km Setubal, 89 106 h.

Annual closure	Fecho anual	não
Weekly closure	Fecho semanal	não

Fees main season
Tarifas de época alta O percurso

	Week days Semana	We/Bank holidays Fim de sem./Feriad
Individual Individual	5 500 Esc	10 000 Esc
Couple Casal	11 000 Esc	20 000 Esc

Caddy	Caddy	não
Electric Trolley	Trolley eléctrico	2 000 Esc.
Buggy	Buggy	5 500 Esc.
Clubs	Tacos	3 500 Esc.

Credit cards Cartão de crédito
VISA - AMEX - DC

840

Access Acesso : A2 Lisboa → Setubal,
N377 → Caparica, Golf
Map 2 on page 835 Mapa 2 Página 835

GOLF COURSE
PERCURSO **15**/20

Site	Sitio	▰▰▰
Maintenance	Conversa	▰▰▰▰
Architect	Arquitecto	Frank Pennink
Type	Tipo	floresta
Relief	Relevo	▰
Water in play	Lago	▰
Exp. to wind	Exposto ao vento	▰
Trees in play	Arvores	▰▰▰

Scorecard Cartão de resultados	Chp. Camp.	Mens Homens	Ladies Senhoras
Length Compriment	6040	5700	5241
Par	72	72	72

Advised golfing ability	0	12	24	36
Nivel de jogo recomendado				

Hcp required Handicap exigido 28 Hom., 36 Senh.

CLUB HOUSE & AMENITIES
CLUB HOUSE E ANEXOS **6**/10

Pro shop	Pro-shop	▰▰▰
Driving range	Campo de prática	▰
Sheltered	coberto	4 lugares
On grass	om relva	sim
Putting-green	putting-green	sim
Pitching-green	pitching-green	não

HOTEL FACILITIES
INFRAESTRUCTURAS HOTELEIRAS **6**/10

HOTELS HOTELS
Costa da Caparica   Caparica
340 quartos, D 19 500 Esc.   3 km
Tel (351) 01 - 291 03 10, Fax (351) 01 - 291 06 87

Praia do Sol   Caparica
53 quartos, D 8 500 Esc.   3 km
Tel (351) 01 - 290 00 12, Fax (351) 01 - 290 25 41

RESTAURANTS RESTAURANTE
Centyonze   São João da Caparica
Tel (351) 01 - 290 39 68   4 km

Maniés   Caparica
Tel (351) 01 - 290 33 98   3 km

ESTORIL ✳ 13 | 7 | 7

Inaugurado em 1945, é um dos campos mais conhecidos de Portugal. Inserido numa paisagem típica da região, bastante acidentado mas não muito cansativo. Mackenzie Ross desenhou um percurso de estilo britânico de uma grande sobriedade estética. O enquadramento de pinheiros e eucaliptos não só é muito agradável como desenha bem os buracos, os quais não são especialmente perigosos se se evitar utilizar o "drive". Tem de ser direito mas a dimensão curta do percurso permite realizar resultados gratificantes. E porem necessário dominar o jogo curto uma vez que é muito fácil falhar os greenes bastante pequenos. Pode tambem, para facilitar, recorrer aos "caddies" locais, muito experientes e muito uteis para evitar as diversas armadilhas de um percurso do género "tricky". Divertido a atraente, o campo do Estoril merecia uma melhor manutenção da que observámos quando para merecer uma nota melhor.

Opened in 1945, this is one of Portugal's better known courses. In countryside that is typical of this region, i.e. rolling landscape but nothing too steep, Mackenzie Ross has designed a beautifully discreet, British style course. There was hardly any need to enhance this setting of eucalyptus and pine trees, which are not only agreeable to the eye but also neatly outline each hole. And they are none too dangerous if you leave the driver in the bag. You have to play straight here, and the lack of yardage can give some flattering scores, as long as your short game is in good shape. The small greens are easy to miss. The first time out, you can hire an experienced local caddy, who will certainly prove most useful in avoiding the many traps on what is a tricky course. Estoril is fun and appealing, but for a better score it deserves better upkeep than what we saw during our visits.

Estoril Golf Club
Avenida da Republica
P - 2765 ESTORIL

Office	Secretariado	(351) 01 - 468 01 76
Pro shop	Pro-shop	(351) 01 - 468 01 76
Fax	Fax	(351) 01 - 468 27 96
Situation	Localização	

23 km Lisboa, 662 782 h.
5 km Sintra, 20 574 h.

Annual closure	Fecho anual	não
Weekly closure	Fecho semanal	não

Fees main season
Tarifas de época alta O percurso

	Week days Semana	We/Bank holidays Fim de sem./Feriad
Individual Individual	8 250 Esc	11 000 Esc
Couple Casal	16 500 Esc	22 000 Esc

Caddy	Caddy	não
Electric Trolley	Trolley eléctrico	não
Buggy	Buggy	5 500 Esc.
Clubs	Tacos	2 500 Esc.

Credit cards Cartão de crédito
VISA - AMEX

Access Acesso : A5 Lisboa → Cascais, N9 → Estoril, Sintra
Map 2 on page 834 Mapa 2 Página 834

GOLF COURSE
PERCURSO   13 /20

Site	Sitio	▰▰▰
Maintenance	Conversa	▰▰
Architect	Arquitecto	Mackenzie Ross
Type	Tipo	floresta
Relief	Relevo	▰▰▰
Water in play	Lago	▰
Exp. to wind	Exposto ao vento	▰▰
Trees in play	Arvores	▰▰▰

Scorecard Cartão de resultados	Chp. Camp.	Mens Homens	Ladies Senhoras
Length Compriment	5238	5238	4569
Par	69	69	69

Advised golfing ability		0 12 24 36
Nivel de jogo recomendado		
Hcp required	Handicap exigido	

CLUB HOUSE & AMENITIES
CLUB HOUSE E ANEXOS   7 /10

Pro shop	Pro-shop	▰▰
Driving range	Campo de prática	▰▰
Sheltered	coberto	6 lugares
On grass	om relva	sim
Putting-green	putting-green	sim
Pitching-green	pitching-green	não

HOTEL FACILITIES
INFRAESTRUCTURAS HOTELEIRAS   7 /10

HOTELS HOTELS

Palacio   Estoril
162 quartos, D 28 000 Esc   4 km
Tel (351) 01 - 468 04 00, Fax (351) 01 - 468 48 67

Lennox Country Club   Estoril
30 quartos, D 17 600 Esc.   4 km
Tel (351) 01 - 468 04 24, Fax (351) 01 - 467 08 59

Atlantis   Alcabideche
129 quartos, D 12 000 Esc   3 km
Tel (351) 01 - 469 07 21, Fax (351) 01 - 469 07 40

RESTAURANTS RESTAURANTE
English Bar   Estoril
Tel (351) 01 - 468 04 13   4 km

A Choupana   S. Joãn do Estoril
Tel (351) 01 - 468 30 99   6 km

841

A várias centenas de metros de altitude, este percurso oferece panorámicas de uma beleza fántastica, sobre a Ilha da Madeira e o Oceano Atlântico. E um dos percursos mais extraordinários da Europa. O inconveniente da sua situação, em média montanha, é a de que se torna bastante cansativo par jogar a pé, mas a beleza do espectáculo, nomeadamente nos buracos 12 e 13, valem alguns esforços. O Arquitecto Robert Trent Jones jogou com delícia e imaginação sobre um terreno extraordinário e propõe aos jogadores de todos os níveis desafios apaixonantes. Estes terão que estudar bem a estratégia a seguir em cada buraco sem se distraírem demasiado com a paisagem. As dificuldades são múltiplas mas sempre bem visíveis, com uma vegetação muito rica, "roughs" bastante densos, "bunkers" muito em jogo, "greens" bem trabalhados mas tendo um único obstáculo de água. Em contrapardida o seu comprimento mantém-se razoável... se não houver vento. Aconselha-se jogar em "match-play", é um percurso muito divertido.

At several hundred metres above sea-level, this course primarily offers a fantastically beautiful panorama over the island of Madeira and the Atlantic ocean. It has to be one of Europe's most extraordinary golfing venues. The drawback of being half-way up a mountain is the toll it takes on your feet and legs. But the beauty of the site, especially on the 12th and 13th holes is well worth the effort. Designer Robert Trent Jones used a lot of fun and imagination over this remarkable terrain and offers some exciting challenges to players of all abilities, who will need to consider carefully their strategy on each hole, without being distracted by the scenery. The difficulties are many and varied, but always there to be seen: lush vegetation, pretty thick rough, omnipresent bunkers, well-designed greens but just the one water hazard. In contrast, yardage is reasonable... as long as the wind doesn't blow. Try it in match-play, it's great fun.

Golfe da Madeira

Casais Proximos - Sº Antº da Serra
P - 9200 MACHICO / MADEIRA

Office	Secretariado	(351) 091 - 55 23 21
Pro shop	Pro-shop	(351) 091 - 55 23 21
Fax	Fax	(351) 091 - 55 23 67
Situation	Localização	

6 km Machico, 2 142 h.
26 km Funchal, 99 244 h.

| Annual closure | Fecho anual | não |
| Weekly closure | Fecho semanal | não |

Fees main season
Tarifas de época alta O percurso

	Week days Semana	We/Bank holidays Fim de sem./Feriad
Individual Individual	8 000 Esc	8 000 Esc
Couple Casal	16 000 Esc	16 000 Esc

Caddy	Caddy	3 000 Esc.
Electric Trolley	Trolley eléctrico	2 000 Esc.
Buggy	Buggy	6 000 Esc.
Clubs	Tacos	2 800 Esc.

Credit cards Cartão de crédito
VISA - AMEX - DC

Access Acesso : E 101 Funchal → Machico.
N 675 → Sto da Serra

GOLF COURSE
PERCURSO 14/20

Site	Sitio	
Maintenance	Conversa	
Architect	Arquitecto	Robert Trent Jones

Type	Tipo	montanha
Relief	Relevo	
Water in play	Lago	
Exp. to wind	Exposto ao vento	
Trees in play	Arvores	

Scorecard Cartão de resultados	Chp. Camp.	Mens Homens	Ladies Senhoras
Length Comprimento	6039	5496	4511
Par	72	72	72

Advised golfing ability		0 12 24 36
Nivel de jogo recomendado		
Hcp required	Handicap exigido	não

CLUB HOUSE & AMENITIES
CLUB HOUSE E ANEXOS 7/10

Pro shop	Pro-shop	
Driving range	Campo de prática	
Sheltered	coberto	não
On grass	om relva	sim
Putting-green	putting-green	sim
Pitching-green	pitching-green	não

HOTEL FACILITIES
INFRAESTRUCTURAS HOTELEIRAS 5/10

HOTELS HOTELS
Reids — Funchal
148 quartos, D 54 000 Esc — 21 km
Tel (351) 091 - 700 71 7, Fax (351) 091 - 700 71 7

Cliff Bay Resort — Funchal
97 quartos, D 45 000 Esc — 21 km
Tel (351) 091 - 76 18 18, Fax (351) 091 - 76 25 25

Madeira Carlton — Funchal
374 quartos, D 37 000 Esc. — 21 km
Tel (351) 091 - 23 10 31, Fax (351) 091 - 22 33 77

RESTAURANTS RESTAURANTE
Casa Velha — Funchal
Tel (351) 091 - 22 57 49 — 21 km

Trattoria — Funchal
Tel (351) 091 - 76 69 99 — 21 km

MONTADO

Em contrapartida com alguns campos prestigiados mas muitas vezes muito difíceis de jogar para os jogadores médios, o percurso do Montado oferece um desenho muito agradável da autoria de Duarte Sottomayor e que nos dará prazer em jogar muitas vezes sem anfado. Situado num local campestre muito agradável, as suas dificuldades são bem equilibradas, mas poderíamos desejar greens por vezes melhor protegidos, uma vez que temos frequentemente de jogar ferros curtos depois de um bom drive. Poucos jogadores, no entanto, se queixarão. Se vieram aqui de férias poderão jogar confortavelmente os seus handicaps. Trata-se de um percurso sem complicações com obstáculos de água que estão pouco em jogo, situado numa região que tinha necessidade de percursos deste género.

Alongside the prestigious courses in this part of the world, which are often very tough to play for average players, Montado is a very pleasant course designed by Duarte Sottomayor and fun to play several times over. This is a pleasant country setting where difficulties are nearly balanced, but we might have preferred more tightly protected greens, as after a good drive the second shot is often a short iron. Few players will really complain about that if they are here on holiday and they should play to their handicap quite comfortably. An uncomplicated course where water hazards are not too much in the way, and located in a region that was badly in need of this type of layout.

Club de Golf de Montado

Apartado 40 Algeruz
P - 2950 PALMELA

Office	Secretariado	(351) 065 - 70 66 48
Pro shop	Pro-shop	(351) 065 - 70 66 48
Fax	Fax	(351) 065 - 70 67 75
Situation	Localização	

7 km Setubal, 89 106 h.
45 km Lisboa, 662 782 h.

Annual closure	Fecho anual	não
Weekly closure	Fecho semanal	não

Fees main season
Tarifas de época alta O percurso

	Week days Semana	We/Bank holidays Fim de sem./Feriad
Individual Individual	3 500 Esc	5 000 Esc
Couple Casal	7 000 Esc	10 000 Esc

Caddy	Caddy	não
Electric Trolley	Trolley eléctrico	sim
Buggy	Buggy	sim
Clubs	Tacos	sim
Credit cards Cartão de crédito		VISA - AMEX

GOLF COURSE
PERCURSO · 13/20

Site	Sitio	
Maintenance	Conversa	
Architect	Arquitecto	Duarte Sottomayor
Type	Tipo	parque
Relief	Relevo	
Water in play	Lago	
Exp. to wind	Exposto ao vento	
Trees in play	Arvores	

Scorecard Cartão de resultados	Chp. Camp.	Mens Homens	Ladies Senhoras
Length Comprimento	6003	5702	4849
Par	72	72	72

Advised golfing ability · 0 12 24 36
Nível de jogo recomendado

Hcp required · Handicap exigido 24

CLUB HOUSE & AMENITIES
CLUB HOUSE E ANEXOS · 7/10

Pro shop	Pro-shop	
Driving range	Campo de prática	
Sheltered	coberto	4 lugares
On grass	om relva	sim
Putting-green	putting-green	sim
Pitching-green	pitching-green	sim

843

HOTEL FACILITIES
INFRAESTRUCTURAS HOTELEIRAS · 6/10

HOTELS HOTELS

Novotel		Setubal
105 quartos, D 15 000 Esc		8 km
Tel (351) 065 - 52 28 09, (351) 065 - 52 29 12		

Pousada de S. Felipe		Setubal
16 quartos, D 28 000 Esc		15 km
Tel (351) 065 - 52 38 44, (351) 065 - 53 25 38		

Mar e Sol		Setubal
71 quartos, D 10 000 Esc		7 km
Tel (351) 065 - 53 46 03, (351) 065 - 53 20 36		

RESTAURANTS RESTAURANTE

A Roda	Setubal
Tel (351) 065 - 292 64	7 km

O Beco	Setubal
Tel (351) 065 - 52 46 17	7 km

Access : Lisboa, A2 → Palmela, Poceirão, Algeruz.
Map 3 on page 836 3 836

PALMARES

Como muitos dos percursos portugueses foi desenhado por Frank Pennink a partir de dois espaços diferentes: cinco buracos são à beira mar, com uma arquitectura que faz lembrar um "links", os outros desenvolvem-se entre pinheiros, muito mais acidentados e com magníficas vistas sobre o Atlântico. Os buracos de borda de água constituem o encanto e o interesse principal deste percurso que para alem disso tem um desenho muito simples. Alguns "drives" podem causar problemas mas os golfistas de todos os níveis não encontrarão muitas dificuldades para alêm das criadas pelo seu proprio jogo. Os "greens" são muito simples, bastante pequenos e pouco defendidos. Nesta bela paisagem seria de mau gosto estragar o prazer! Se este percurso não dá para maravilhar, não deixa de ser muito agradável para se passar uma tarde em família ou com um grupo de amigos aínda que de níveis diferentes.

Like many courses in Portugal, Palmares was designed by Frank Pennink using two different sorts of space: five holes run along the seashore in true links style, the others are laid out amidst a much hillier pine forest with some magnificent views over the Atlantic. The seaboard holes give the course its basic charm and appeal, as otherwise the design is fairly simple. Some tee-shots can cause problems, but apart from those arising from your own game, there are no real difficulties here, whatever your playing ability. The greens are very simple, smallish and wide open. In such pretty countryside, it would have been in very poor taste to make life too difficult. This course might not be over-exciting, but it is great fun to play with the family or friends, whatever their ability.

Palmares Golf

Apartado 74
P - 8600 LAGOS

Office	Secretariado	(351) 082 - 76 29 53
Pro shop	Pro-shop	(351) 082 - 76 29 53
Fax	Fax	(351) 082 - 76 25 34
Situation	Localização	

6 km Lagos, 11 746 h.
15 km Portimão, 21 196 h.

Annual closure	Fecho anual	não
Weekly closure	Fecho semanal	não

Fees main season
Tarifas de época alta O percurso

	Week days Semana	We/Bank holidays Fim de sem./Feriad
Individual Individual	8 500 Esc	8 500 Esc
Couple Casal	17 000 Esc	17 000 Esc

Caddy	Caddy	não
Electric Trolley	Trolley eléctrico	não
Buggy	Buggy	5 000 Esc.
Clubs	Tacos	3 000 Esc.

Credit cards Cartão de crédito   VISA - AMEX

CABO De São Vicente
Odiáxere   N 125   Portimão
Lagos   FARO
GOLF
PONTA DA PIEDADE

Access Acesso : N125 Portimão → Sagres, → Meia Praia
Map 3 on page 836 Mapa 3 Página 836

GOLF COURSE
PERCURSO   13 /20

Site	Sitio	▰▰▰▱
Maintenance	Conversa	▰▰▰▱
Architect	Arquitecto	Frank Pennink
Type	Tipo	beira-mar, campo
Relief	Relevo	▰▰▰▱
Water in play	Lago	▰▱▱▱
Exp. to wind	Exposto ao vento	▰▰▰▱
Trees in play	Arvores	▰▰▱▱

Scorecard Cartão de resultados	Chp. Camp.	Mens Homens	Ladies Senhoras
Length Compriment	5961	5614	5020
Par	71	71	71

Advised golfing ability   0   12   24   36
Nivel de jogo recomendado   ▰▰▰▰▰▰▱
Hcp required Handicap exigido 28 Hom., 36 Senh.

CLUB HOUSE & AMENITIES
CLUB HOUSE E ANEXOS   7 /10

Pro shop	Pro-shop	▰▰▰▱
Driving range	Campo de prática	▰▰▰▱
Sheltered	coberto	não
On grass	om relva	sim
Putting-green	putting-green	sim
Pitching-green	pitching-green	não

HOTEL FACILITIES
INFRAESTRUCTURAS HOTELEIRAS   5 /10

HOTELS HOTELS
De Lagos   Lagos
317 quartos, D 14 300 Esc.   12 km
Tel (351) 082 - 76 99 67, Fax (351) 082 - 76 99 20

Meia Praia   Meia Praia
65 quartos, D 7 500 Esc.   4 km
Tel (351) 082 - 76 99 80, Fax (351) 082 - 76 99 80

Golfinho   Praia Dona
262 quartos, D 27 000 Esc.   16 km
Tel (351) 082 - 76 99 00, Fax (351) 082 - 76 99 99

RESTAURANTS RESTAURANTE
O Castelo   Lagos
Tel (351) 082 - 76 09 57   6 km

O Galeão   Lagos
Tel (351) 082 - 76 39 09   6 km

PENHA LONGA ✳ ⛳ 15 7 8

Localizado num belo local histórico, semeado de vestigios do passado, é um dos bons exitos dos ultimos anos. O desenho de Robert Trent Jones Junior é muito imaginativo e seduzirá primeiramente os bons jogadores que deverão saber ultrapassar com habilidade os numerosos obstáculos que se lhes deparam, para alem do terreno acidentado que oferece, porem, belas vistas do mar e da serra. O comprimento do percurso e a sua variedade exigem um jogo muito complete desde as saídas até aos "greens" de boa dimensao e bem modelados. Os jogadores menos habilitados podera escolher as saidas mais avançadas para retirar ao jogo um máximo de prazer. E certo que as dificuldades subsistem, mas se não derem demasiada importância ao "score" terão muitas ocasiões de exercer a sua destrêsa, ou mesmo de progredir sobre um percurso exigente depois de terem feito a mão nalgum percurso, mais facil, da região. A manutenção é geralmente muito bom.

In a beautiful historical site, dotted with vestiges from the past, this is one of the best new courses in recent years. The very imaginative design of Robert Trent Jones Jnr. will firstly appeal to very good players, who will need all their skills to negotiate the numerous hazards and the steep hills, which offer some beautiful views over the sea and mountain. The length and variety of the course demand a good, all-round game from tee to green, most of the latter being large and well contoured. Lesser players will play from the front tees to really enjoy themselves. The difficulties are still there, of course, but if they don't pay too much attention to dropped strokes, average golfers will have many opportunities to exercise their skills and even make progress on a demanding course. This is a good test after getting warmed up on some of the easier courses in the region. Upkeep is generally very good.

Penha Longa Golf Club
Quinta da Penha Longa - Linho
P - 2710 SINTRA

Office	Secretariado	(351) 01 - 924 00 14
Pro shop	Pro-shop	(351) 01 - 924 00 14
Fax	Fax	(351) 01 - 924 90 24
Situation	Localização	

25 km Lisboa, 662 782 h.
2 km Sintra, 20 574 h.

Annual closure	Fecho anual	não
Weekly closure	Fecho semanal	não

Fees main season
Tarifas de época alta O percurso

	Week days Semana	We/Bank holidays Fim de sem./Feriad
Individual Individual	11 000 Esc.	16 000 Esc.
Couple Casal	22 000 Esc.	32 000 Esc.

Caddy	Caddy	4 000 Esc.
Electric Trolley	Trolley eléctrico	2 000 Esc.
Buggy	Buggy	7 000 Esc.
Clubs	Tacos	4 000 Esc.

Credit cards Cartão de crédito VISA - AMEX

Access Acesso : N9 Estoril → Sintra, → Lagon Azul

Map 2 on page 834 Mapa 2 Página 834

GOLF COURSE
PERCURSO 15/20

Site	Sitio	▭
Maintenance	Conversa	▭
Architect	Arquitecto	R. Trent Jones Jr
Type	Tipo	montanha, urbano
Relief	Relevo	▭
Water in play	Lago	▭
Exp. to wind	Exposto ao vento	▭
Trees in play	Arvores	▭

Scorecard Cartão de resultados	Chp. Camp.	Mens Homens	Ladies Senhoras
Length Comprimento	6290	5942	5100
Par	72	72	72

Advised golfing ability		0 12 24 36
Nivel de jogo recomendado		▭
Hcp required	Handicap exigido	

CLUB HOUSE & AMENITIES
CLUB HOUSE E ANEXOS 7/10

Pro shop	Pro-shop	▭
Driving range	Campo de prática	▭
Sheltered	coberto	4 lugares
On grass	om relva	sim
Putting-green	putting-green	sim
Pitching-green	pitching-green	sim

HOTEL FACILITIES
INFRAESTRUCTURAS HOTELEIRAS 8/10

HOTELS HOTELS
Caesar Park Penha Longa — Sintra
160 quartos, D 41 000 Esc. — 150 m
Tel (351) 01 - 924 90 11, Fax (351) 01 - 924 90 07

Palacio de Seteais — Sintra
29 quartos, D 40 000 Esc. — 3 km
Tel (351) 01 - 923 32 00, Fax (351) 01 - 923 42 77

Quinta da Capela — Sintra
5 quartos, D 24 000 Esc. — 3 km
Tel (351) 01 - 929 01 70, Fax (351) 01 - 929 34 25

RESTAURANTS RESTAURANTE
Penha Longa — Sintra
Tel (351) 01 - 924 90 11 — 150 m

Tacho Real — Sintra
Tel (351) 01 - 923 52 77 — 3 km

845

Tendo estado fechado para obras durante alguns meses, o primeiro Campo de Golfe do Algarve em termos de antiguade, sofreu alguns melhoramentos mas sem grandes moficações. Continua um percurso longo e dificil dos "Tees" de campeonato, tornando-se mais acessivel dos "Tees" normais. Bastante plano e tendo algumas árvores a dificultar as pancadas não chegam no entanto a ser perigosas. O seu traçado salienta-se por um bom número de "bunkers" com bom desenho mas sem nada de especial a assinalar. A sua colocação sugere um estilo britânico que se torna evidente se nos lembrarmos que foi desenhado por Henry Cotton. A Penina pode por vezes lembrar "Carnoustie" sem no entanto se poder considerar um verdadeiro "links" o que aumentaria ainda a sua dificuldade. Se conseguirmos bater longe e direito, a bola estará sempre em boa posição. Os greens, bastante grandes e razoavelmente planos não causam problemas - embora haja necessidade de os atingir... De salientar os 4 par 5 da 2a volta.

Closed for many months, the Algarve's very first course has been given a fresh look, but with no notable changes. It is still long and tough from the back tees, but mellows the further forward you go. Very flat and covered with a variety of trees which, although in play, are none too dangerous, this layout is marked by the huge number of bunkers, correctly designed but with no real personality. Their positioning testifies to an obvious British style, knowing that the course was in fact designed by Henry Cotton. Besides, Penina is a little reminiscent of Carnoustie in some ways, but without the links features, which would only increase the difficulty here. If you can drive long and straight, you will always find your ball in a good position. The greens, which are pretty large and generally flat, pose no real problem, the trouble is reaching them. A noticeable feature are the four par 5s on the back nine.

Penina Golf & Resort Hotel

ALVOR
P - PORTIMÃO - Algarve

Office	Secretariado	(351) 082 - 41 54 15
Pro shop	Pro-shop	(351) 082 - 41 54 15
Fax	Fax	(351) 082 - 22 059
Situation	Localização	

4 km Portimão, 21 196 h.

Annual closure	Fecho anual	não
Weekly closure	Fecho semanal	não

Fees main season
Tarifas de época alta 18 buracos

	Week days Semana	We/Bank holidays Fim de sem./Feriad
Individual Individual	10 500 Esc.	10 500 Esc.
Couple Casal	21 000 Esc.	21 000 Esc.

Caddy	Caddy	não
Electric Trolley	Trolley eléctrico	2 000 Esc.
Buggy	Buggy	6 500 Esc.
Clubs	Tacos	4 000 Esc.

Credit cards Cartão de crédito
VISA - Eurocard - MasterCard - AMEX - DC

846

Access Acesso : Portimão-Lagos
Map 3 on page 836 Mapa 3 Página 836

GOLF COURSE
PERCURSO 14/20

Site	Sítio	■■■■
Maintenance	Conversa	■■■■
Architect	Arquitecto	Henry Cotton
Type	Tipo	planicie
Relief	Relevo	■
Water in play	Lago	■■
Exp. to wind	Exposto ao vento	■■■
Trees in play	Arvores	■■■

Scorecard Cartão de resultados	Chp. Camp.	Mens Homens	Ladies Senhoras
Length Compriment	6439	6054	5322
Par	73	73	73

Advised golfing ability
Nivel de jogo recomendado

0 12 24 36

Hcp required Handicap exigido não

CLUB HOUSE & AMENITIES
CLUB HOUSE E ANEXOS 7/10

Pro shop	Pro-shop	■■■■
Driving range	Campo de prática	■■■■
Sheltered	coberto	4 lugares
On grass	om relva	sim
Putting-green	putting-green	sim
Pitching-green	pitching-green	sim

HOTEL FACILITIES
INFRAESTRUCTURAS HOTELEIRAS 8/10

HOTELS HOTELS
Penina Hotel   golf
192 quartos, D 30 000 Esc.
Tel (351) 082 - 415 415, Fax (351) 082 - 415 000

Alvor Praia   Praia dos Três Irmãos
217 quartos, D 45 000 Esc.   8 km
Tel (351) 082 - 45 89 00, Fax (351) 082 - 45 89 99

Algarve   Praia da Rocha
220 quartos, D 35 000 Esc.   7 km
Tel (351) 082 - 41 50 01, Fax (351) 082 - 41 59 99

RESTAURANTS RESTAURANTE
Titanic   Praia da Rocha
Tel (351) 082 - 22 371   7 km

Falésia   Praia da Rocha
Tel (351) 082 - 23 524   7 km

Os dois 9 buracos são muito diferentes. Os primeiros, muito acidentados e cansativos, desenvolvem-se entre pinheiros, sempre em jogo. Os segundos são planos, com àgua, practicamente em todos os buracos. Esta falta de unidade pode explicar-se pela intervenção de McEvoy a Howard Swan sobre o desenho original de Ronald Fream. O ritmo de jogo pode ser prejudicado para os jogadores que se deixem perturbar pelo ambiente circundante. A qualidade e o desenho dos "greens", alguns difíceis de lêr, é um dos pontos positivos, para mais por estarem bem defendidos, o que torna os "aproches" muito interessantes. Não e um percurso para se jogar todos os dias, mas merece algumas vistas muito atentas, desde que se jogue das saídas de trás e se esteja em boa forma física. Muito próximo do parque natural da Ria Formosa este golf dispõe de muito boas instalações de treino, nomeadamente para o jogo curto.

The two 9-hole courses are very different. The front nine, hilly and tiring, are laid out in a pine forest, where trees come very much into play. The back nine are flatter, with water on virtually every hole. This lack of unity might be explained by the work made by McEvoy and Howard Swan on Ronald Fream's original design, and it might upset players who are over-attentive to surroundings. Otherwise, the excellence and design of the greens, some of which are tricky to read, are very positive points, all the more so in that their defence makes for some very interesting approach shots. This is not a course you would play every day, but it does deserve some careful visiting, providing you and your game are fit enough for the back-tees. Close to the Ria Formosa Nature Park, the course boasts excellent practice facilities, particularly for the short game.

Pinheiros Campo de Golf

Quinta do Lago
P - 8135 ALMANCIL

Office	Secretariado	(351) 089 - 39 43 40
Pro shop	Pro-shop	(351) 089 - 39 43 40
Fax	Fax	(351) 089 - 39 43 92
Situation	Localização	

15 km Faro, 33 664 h.

Annual closure	Fecho anual	não
Weekly closure	Fecho semanal	não

Fees main season
Tarifas de época alta 18 buracos

	Week days Semana	We/Bank holidays Fim de sem./Feriad
Individual Individual	13 000 Esc	13 000 Esc
Couple Casal	26 000 Esc	26 000 Esc

Caddy	Caddy	não
Electric Trolley	Trolley eléctrico	2 000 Esc.
Buggy	Buggy	7 000 Esc.
Clubs	Tacos	

Credit cards Cartão de crédito
VISA - MasterCard - AMEX - DC

Access Acesso : N 125 Faro → Portimão. Almancil →
Vale do Lobo
Map 3 on page 836 Mapa 3 Página 836

GOLF COURSE
PERCURSO 14/20

Site	Sitio	▬▬▬
Maintenance	Conversa	▬▬▬▬
Architect	Arquitecto	Ronald Fream
Type	Tipo	floresta, planicie
Relief	Relevo	▬▬▬
Water in play	Lago	▬▬
Exp. to wind	Exposto ao vento	▬▬
Trees in play	Arvores	▬▬▬

Scorecard Cartão de resultados	Chp. Camp.	Mens Homens	Ladies Senhoras
Length Compriment	6057	5614	4762
Par	71	71	71

Advised golfing ability   0   12   24   36
Nivel de jogo recomendado
Hcp required   Handicap exigido 28 Hom., 36 Senh.

CLUB HOUSE & AMENITIES
CLUB HOUSE E ANEXOS 8/10

Pro shop	Pro-shop	▬▬▬▬
Driving range	Campo de prática	▬▬▬▬
Sheltered	coberto	não
On grass	om relva	sim
Putting-green	putting-green	sim
Pitching-green	pitching-green	sim

HOTEL FACILITIES
INFRAESTRUCTURAS HOTELEIRAS 8/10

HOTELS HOTELS

Quinta do Lago   Quinta do Lago
132 quartos, D 17 000 Esc.   3 km
Tel (351) 089 - 39 66 66, Fax (351) 089 - 39 63 93

Four Seasons Fairways   Quinta do Lago
0 quartos, D 12 000 Esc   2 km
Tel (351) 089 - 39 80 20, Fax (351) 089 - 39 80 29

Dona Filipa   Vale do Lobo
147 quartos, D 31 500 Esc.   8 km
Tel (351) 089 - 39 41 41, Fax (351) 089 - 39 42 88

RESTAURANTS RESTAURANTE

Casa Velha   2 km
Tel (351) 089 - 39 49 83

Bobby Jones Club   Vilar do Golf
    1 km

847

Durante muito tempo braço direito de Robert Trent Jones, Cabell Robinson impôs-se como um arquitecto imaginativo e muito conhecedor a todos os niveis do golf. Praia D'El Rey é disso a demonstração. Com uma bela localização à beira mar rodeado de pinheiros, por vezes espectaculares, este percurso tem muitos aspectos em que se assemelha a um Links tradicional, obrigando a bem trabalhar a bola. Quando o vento sopra, porem raramente tão violentamente como na Escócia ou Irlanda, isto acrescenta um condimento especial a u prato de grande qualidade. A despeito da sua juventude, Praia d'El Rey promete vir a ser um dos grandes percursos da península Ibérica. Tem ainda a vantagem de permitir tanto partidas de golf de alto nível como jornadas agradáveis em família.

For many years Robert Trent Jones' right-hand man, Cabell Robinson has become established as an imaginative designer and excellent connoisseur of golf played at all levels. Praia d'El Rey is further demonstration of his expertise. Set on a very beautiful and often spectacular sea-side site enhanced with pine-trees on some holes, the course has many facets of a traditional links with the need to work the ball all ways. And while the wind is kinder than in Scotland or Ireland, it can often add a little spice to what is already a savoury dish. Although still in infancy, Praia d'El Rey promises to emerge as one of the great courses on the Iberian peninsula, with the extra pleasure of allowing rounds of golf for highly skilled players and enjoyable days with the family.

Praia d'El Rey
Vale de Janelas, Apartado 2
P - 2510 OBIDOS

Office	Secretariado	(351) 062 - 90 96 26
Pro shop	Pro-shop	(351) 062 - 90 96 26
Fax	Fax	(351) 062 - 90 96 29
Situation	Localização	

5 km Peniche, 15 304 h.

Annual closure	Fecho anual	não
Weekly closure	Fecho semanal	não

Fees main season
Tarifas de época alta O percurso

	Week days Semana	We/Bank holidays Fim de sem./Feriad
Individual Individual	5 000 Esc	7 000 Esc
Couple Casal	10 000 Esc	14 000 Esc

Caddy	Caddy	não
Electric Trolley	Trolley eléctrico	não
Buggy	Buggy	sim
Clubs	Tacos	sim

Credit cards Cartão de crédito
VISA - AMEX

848

GOLF COURSE / PERCURSO 17/20

Site	Sitio	▬▬▬
Maintenance	Conversa	▬▬▬
Architect	Arquitecto	Cabell Robinson
Type	Tipo	beira-mar, links
Relief	Relevo	▬▬▬
Water in play	Lago	▬▬▬
Exp. to wind	Exposto ao vento	▬▬▬▬
Trees in play	Arvores	▬▬▬

Scorecard Cartão de resultados	Chp. Camp.	Mens Homens	Ladies Senhoras
Length Comprimento	6467	5586	5216
Par	72	72	72

Advised golfing ability Nivel de jogo recomendado		0 12 24 36
Hcp required	Handicap exigido	28

CLUB HOUSE & AMENITIES / CLUB HOUSE E ANEXOS 7/10

Pro shop	Pro-shop	▬▬▬
Driving range	Campo de prática	▬▬▬
Sheltered	coberto	6 lugares
On grass	om relva	sim
Putting-green	putting-green	sim
Pitching-green	pitching-green	sim

HOTEL FACILITIES / INFRAESTRUCTURAS HOTELEIRAS 5/10

HOTELS HOTELS

Caldas Internacional 83 , D 8 500 Esc Tel (351) 062 - 83 23 07, (351) 062 - 84 44 82		Caldas da Rainha 15 km
Estal. do Convento 31 , D 13 000 Esc Tel (351) 062 - 95 92 16, (351) 062 - 95 91 59		Obidos 12 km
Dona Leonor 30 , D 6 500 Esc Tel (351) 062 - 84 21 71, (351) 062 - 84 21 72		Caldas de Rainha 15 km

RESTAURANTS RESTAURANTE

Pousada do Castelho Tel (351) 062 - 95 91 05		Obidos 12 km
A Ilustre Casa de Ramiro Tel (351) 062 - 95 91 94		Obido 12 km

GOLF

Peniche · Baleal · Caldas da Rainha · Obidos · Lagoa de Odidos · Atouguia da Baleia · Serra d'El-Rei · N 114 · N 8 · Lisboa

0   3   6 km

Access : Lisboa, A8-IC1 → Obidos, N114 → Peniche.
Map 2 on page 834 2 834

QUINTA DA BELOURA ✴ | 14 | 8 | 7 |

Desenhado por Duarte Sottomayor, secundo a concepção de Rocky Roquemore é o mais recente percurso desta região. O envolvimento imobiliário deverá vir a ser gradualmente escondido pela plantação de pinheiros, carvalhos, palmeiras etc, o que permitirá de melhor defenir os "fairways". Os obstáculos de agua e os "bunkers" estão pouco em jogo, à excepção de alguns lagos perigosos, principalmente nos últimos buracos. Porem, todas as dificuldades estão bem à vista, nada é aqui uma fonte de surpresas, nem mesmo os "greens" bem desenhados e fáceis de lêr. Percebe-se que não hoyuve aqui à intenção de fazer um percurso de campeonato nem para os jogadores muito compridos nem para os mestres do jogo curto que não vão encontrar motivos para saciar as suas emoções. Tem de jogar-se bastante direito mas os jogadores de nível médio ou mesmo os principiantes conseguirão fazer.

This is the region's newest course, designed by Duarte Sottomayor and Rocky Roquemore. The surrounding property development should gradually be blotted out by a plantation programme of new pine, oak and/or palm trees, also designed to outline the fairways. The sand and water hazards are seldom in play, with the exception of a few dangerous lakes, especially over the last holes. But all the difficulties here are clear to see with no surprises, not even on the greens, which are rather well designed and easy to read. Visibly, no-one was aiming to build a course for tournaments, big-hitters or short-game wizards, who will probably find this lay-out a little low on excitement. The key is to play straight, and then high-handicappers and even beginners can card an honourable score.

Quinta da Beloura Golf Club

Estrada de Albarraque
P - 2710 SINTRA

Office	Secretariado	(351) 01 - 924 00 21
Pro shop	Pro-shop	(351) 01 - 924 00 21
Fax	Fax	(351) 01 - 924 00 61
Situation	Localização	

3 km Sintra, 25 574 h.
4 km Estoril, 25 230 h.

Annual closure	Fecho anual	não
Weekly closure	Fecho semanal	não

Fees main season
Tarifas de época alta O percurso

	Week days Semana	We/Bank holidays Fim de sem./Feriad
Individual Individual	6 000 Esc	8 500 Esc
Couple Casal	12 000 Esc	17 000 Esc

Caddy	Caddy	não
Electric Trolley	Trolley eléctrico	não
Buggy	Buggy	5 500 Esc.
Clubs	Tacos	2 000 Esc.
Credit cards Cartão de crédito		VISA - AMEX

Access Acesso : N9 Estoril-Sintra, → Alcabideche
Map 2 on page 834 Mapa 2 Página 834

GOLF COURSE
PERCURSO   **14**/20

Site	Sitio	
Maintenance	Conversa	
Architect	Arquitecto	Duarte Sottomayor
Type	Tipo	urbano
Relief	Relevo	
Water in play	Lago	
Exp. to wind	Exposto ao vento	
Trees in play	Arvores	

Scorecard Cartão de resultados	Chp. Camp.	Mens Homens	Ladies Senhoras
Length Compriment	5917	5474	5092
Par	72	72	73

Advised golfing ability	0	12	24	36
Nivel de jogo recomendado				

Hcp required	Handicap exigido	28 Hom., 36 Senh.

CLUB HOUSE & AMENITIES
CLUB HOUSE E ANEXOS   **8**/10

Pro shop	Pro-shop	
Driving range	Campo de prática	
Sheltered	coberto	não
On grass	om relva	sim
Putting-green	putting-green	sim
Pitching-green	pitching-green	sim

849

HOTEL FACILITIES
INFRAESTRUCTURAS HOTELEIRAS   **7**/10

HOTELS HOTELS

Atlantis   Estoril
129 quartos, D 12 000 Esc   3 km
Tel (351) 01 - 469 07 21, Fax (351) 01 - 469 07 40

Palacio   Estoril
162 quartos, D 28 000 Esc   15 km
Tel (351) 01 - 468 04 00, Fax (351) 01 - 468 48 67

Estoril Eden   Estoril
162 quartos, D 15 000 Esc.   18 km
Tel (351) 01 - 467 05 73, Fax (351) 01 - 467 08 48

RESTAURANTS RESTAURANTE

A. Choupana   S. Joán do Estoril
    8 km

Solar de São Pedro   Sintra
Tel (351) 01 - 923 18 60   3 km

QUINTA DA MARINHA ✳ | 13 | 7 | 7 |

Embora situado numa imensa zona de pinhal, este percurso merecia que lhe tivessem concedido um pouco mais de espaço para permitor a Robert Trent Jones de dar averdadeira medida do seu talento. O seu desenho é de muito boa qualidade, mas para conseguir um par 71, teve de criar 5 pares 5 para contrabalançar os 6 pares 3 (entre os quais os belos 5 e 14) o que provoca um ritmo de jogo pouco habitual. Aqueles que conhecem o estilo do arquitecto não ficam surpreendidos mas terão a impressão que já jogaram aqueles buracos noutro lugar qualquer. Isto não retira muito ao prazer do jogo e do local, donde se pode apreciar algumas lindas vistas do mar, nomeadamente n° 13, o buraco modêlo do percurso. As dificuldades são numerosas, equilibradas e bem visiveis, permitindo jogar o percurso desde a primeira vez sem temer armadilhas escondidas. Em contrapardida náo fica muito por descobrir se o percurso fôr jogado frequentemente. Por pouco, tinha-se obtido um exito total.

Although sited in a huge pine estate, this course would have deserved a little more space to enable Trent Jones to fully express his many talents. This is certainly an excellent layout, but to achieve a par 71, he had to create five par 5s to offset the six par 3s (including the pretty 5th and 14th holes). Hence a rather unusually balanced course. Those of you who know the designer's style will not be surprised, but you will get the impression of having already played some of these holes before. But don't let that detract from the pleasure of golfing on a site that offers some beautiful views over the sea, notably from the 13th, the course's signature hole. Difficulties are manifold but visible, so new-comers need have no fear of hidden hazards. In contrast, you will soon get to the bottom of everything the course has to offer if you play here often. This looks very much like a missed opportunity to create a great golf course.

Club-Golf da Quinta da Marinha
Quinta da Marinha
P - 2750 CASCAIS

Office	Secretariado	(351) 01 - 486 98 81
Pro shop	Pro-shop	(351) 01 - 486 98 81
Fax	Fax	(351) 01 - 486 90 32
Situation	Localização	

6 km Cascais, 29 882 h.
26 km Lisboa, 662 782 h.

Annual closure	Fecho anual	não
Weekly closure	Fecho semanal	não

Fees main season
Tarifas de época alta O percurso

	Week days Semana	We/Bank holidays Fim de sem./Feriad
Individual Individual	8 200 Esc	9 900 Esc
Couple Casal	16 400 Esc	19 800 Esc

Caddy	Caddy	não
Electric Trolley	Trolley eléctrico	não
Buggy	Buggy	6 000 Esc.
Clubs	Tacos	3 000 Esc.
Credit cards Cartão de crédito		VISA - AMEX

850

GOLF COURSE
PERCURSO 13/20

Site	Sitio	▆▆▆
Maintenance	Conversa	▆▆▆
Architect	Arquitecto	Robert Trent Jones
Type	Tipo	floresta, urbano
Relief	Relevo	▆
Water in play	Lago	▆
Exp. to wind	Exposto ao vento	▆▆▆
Trees in play	Arvores	▆▆

Scorecard Cartão de resultados	Chp. Camp.	Mens Homens	Ladies Senhoras
Length Compriment	6014	5606	5081
Par	71	71	71

Advised golfing ability Nível de jogo recomendado	0	12	24	36
Hcp required Handicap exigido	▆▆▆			

CLUB HOUSE & AMENITIES
CLUB HOUSE E ANEXOS 7/10

Pro shop	Pro-shop	▆▆▆
Driving range	Campo de prática	▆▆
Sheltered	coberto	não
On grass	om relva	sim
Putting-green	putting-green	sim
Pitching-green	pitching-green	não

HOTEL FACILITIES
INFRAESTRUCTURAS HOTELEIRAS 7/10

HOTELS HOTELS
Estoril Sol   Cascais
298 quartos, D 27 000 Esc.   3 km
Tel (351) 01 - 483 28 31, Fax (351) 01 - 483 22 80
Atlantic Gardens, 150 quartos, D 22 000 Esc.   Cascais
Tel (351) 01 - 483 37 37, Fax (351) 01 - 483 52 26   8 km
Cidadela   Cascais
106 quartos, D 35 000 Esc.   9 km
Tel (351) 01 - 483 29 21, Fax (351) 01 - 486 72 26
Estalagem Senhora da Guia   Cascais
39 quartos, D 24 000 Esc.   3 km
Tel (351) 01 - 487 92 39, Fax (351) 01 - 486 92 27

RESTAURANTS RESTAURANTE
Fortaleza do Guincho   Cascais
Tel (351) 01 - 487 04 91   3 km
Porto de Santa Maria   Praia do Guincho
Tel (351) 01 - 487 02 40   3 km

Access Acesso : Lisboa A5, → Cascais, N 247 → Praia do Guincho
Map 2 on page 834 Mapa 2 Página 834

A despeito da qualidade dos outros grupos de 9 buracos, a combinaçao dos percursos B e C é a mais satisfatória e a que foi mais utilizada nas grandes competições. O seu comprimento não deve assustar. E razoável a partir das saídas normais. A largura dos "fairways" e o equilibrio do comprimento dos buracos, torna o percurso acessivel a todos os jogadores com alguma experiência. Para mais, anatureza arenosa do terreno permite não so andar com prazer, mas tambem fazer roalr muito a bola. Os obstáculos de àgua entram em jogo em alguns buracos mas a principal dificuldade são os pinheiros que sobresaiem de outros tipos de vegetação. Pelo seu equilibrio, este percurso permite um jogo confortável sem criar problemas inuteis aos golfistas em férias. A Quinta do Lago conquistou uma bela reputação, seria merecida se a manutenção fosse sempre impecável.

Despite the excellence of the two other 9-hole courses, the B & C combination is the most satisfying and the most widely used for top tournaments. The yardage is nothing to be afraid of and is reasonable from the normal tees. And the width of the fairways and nicely balanced length of holes make this a course playable by any golfer with some experience. What's more, the sandy sub-soil makes it a pleasure to walk and gives balls a lot of extra roll. Water hazards are in play only on a few holes, and the main difficulties are the pine-trees looming over the heather, and the broom. A nicely balanced course for a relaxed round of golf, and one that doesn't create needless problems for golfers on holiday. Quinta do Lago has acquired a great reputation, which would be deserved if upkeep were immaculate all the time.

Quinta do Lago Golf Club
P - 8135 ALMANCIL (Algarve)

Office	Secretariado	(351) 089 - 39 45 29
Pro shop	Pro-shop	(351) 089 - 39 60 0
Fax	Fax	(351) 089 - 39 40 13
Situation	Localização	
12 km Faro, 33 664 h.		
Annual closure	Fecho anual	não
Weekly closure	Fecho semanal	não

Fees main season
Tarifas de época alta 18 buracos

	Week days Semana	We/Bank holidays Fim de sem./Feriad
Individual Individual	13 000 Esc	13 000 Esc
Couple Casal	26 000 Esc	26 000 Esc

Caddy	Caddy	não
Electric Trolley	Trolley eléctrico	não
Buggy	Buggy	7 000 Esc.
Clubs	Tacos	4 250 Esc.
Credit cards Cartão de crédito		VISA - AMEX

Access Acesso : N 125 Faro → Portimão, Almancil →
Quinta do Lago
Map 3 on page 836 Mapa 3 Página 836

GOLF COURSE / PERCURSO — 15/20

Site	Sitio	
Maintenance	Conversa	
Architect	Arquitecto	William Mitchell
Type	Tipo	floresta, urbano
Relief	Relevo	
Water in play	Lago	
Exp. to wind	Exposto ao vento	
Trees in play	Arvores	

Scorecard Cartão de resultados	Chp. Camp.	Mens Homens	Ladies Senhoras
Length Compriment	6488	5870	5192
Par	72	72	72

Advised golfing ability	0	12	24	36
Nivel de jogo recomendado				

Hcp required Handicap exigido 28 Hom., 36 Senh.

CLUB HOUSE & AMENITIES / CLUB HOUSE E ANEXOS — 7/10

Pro shop	Pro-shop	
Driving range	Campo de prática	
Sheltered	coberto	não
On grass	om relva	não
Putting-green	putting-green	sim
Pitching-green	pitching-green	sim

HOTEL FACILITIES / INFRAESTRUCTURAS HOTELEIRAS — 8/10

HOTELS HOTELS
Quinta do Lago   Quinta do Lago
132 quartos, D 17 000 Esc.   3 km
Tel (351) 089 - 39 66 66, Fax (351) 089 - 39 63 93

Dona Filipa   Vale do Lobo
147 quartos, D 31 500 Esc.   6 km
Tel (351) 089 - 39 41 41, Fax (351) 089 - 39 42 88

RESTAURANTS RESTAURANTE
Casa Velha   Quinta do Lago
Tel (351) 089 - 39 49 83   3 km

São Gabriel   Almancil
Tel (351) 089 - 39 45 21   5 km

851

QUINTA DO LAGO RIA FORMOSA ✳ ♪ | 15 | 7 | 8 |

Sob o nome de Ria Formosa reuniram-se os percursos A e D da Quinta do Lago, desenhados por dois arquitectos diferentes, William Mitchell e Rocky Roquemore. Resulta num certo desequilibrio visual e golfístico, uma vez que as personalidades dos dois signatários é forçosamente diferente. Este "defeito" contribui, porem, para da muita variedade aos 18 buracos que são, pelo menos, identicos no ponto de vista da vegetação. A estrategia é bastante simples, os "greens" são desenhados com gosto, o desenho geral é bastante imaginativo com uma estética principalmente americana, principalmente pela integração de vários lagos, sobretudo aos primeiros 9 buracos. Em relação ao outro percurso do complexo é aínda mais adequado a todos os níveis de jogo, quer se trate de jogar para o seu próprio resultado ou numa competiçao. Se juntarmos a este vasto complexo o belo e mítico percurso do São Lourenço confirma-se a necessidade de uma visita.

The A & D courses of Quinta do Lago, collectively called Ria Formosa, were designed by two different architects, William Mitchell and Joseph Lee. The result is a slight feeling of visual and golfing imbalance created by two necessarily different personalities and styles. In fact, this "flaw" actually adds a lot of variety to the 18-hole layout, where the vegetation at least is the same. Game strategy is simple to see, the greens have been tastefully designed and the general layout is rather imaginative and mainly American in style with the presence of several lakes, especially on the front nine. Compared to the other course on the same site, the A & D combination is even better suited to all levels, whichever way you play. Add to this huge golf resort the fabulous neighbouring course of San Lorenzo, then a long visit is called for.

Quinta do Lago Golf Club
P - 8135 ALMANCIL (Algarve)

Office	Secretariado	(351) 089 - 39 45 29
Pro shop	Pro-shop	(351) 089 - 39 60 0
Fax	Fax	(351) 089 - 39 40 13
Situation	Localização	

12 km Faro, 33 664 h.

Annual closure	Fecho anual	não
Weekly closure	Fecho semanal	não

Fees main season
Tarifas de época alta 18 buracos

	Week days Semana	We/Bank holidays Fim de sem./Feriad
Individual Individual	13 000 Esc	13 000 Esc
Couple Casal	26 000 Esc	26 000 Esc

Caddy	Caddy	não
Electric Trolley	Trolley eléctrico	não
Buggy	Buggy	7 000 Esc.
Clubs	Tacos	4 250 Esc.

Credit cards Cartão de crédito
VISA - AMEX

852

Access Acesso : N 125 Faro → Portimão,
Almancil → Quinta do Lago
Map 3 on page 836 Mapa 3 Página 836

GOLF COURSE
PERCURSO   15/20

Site	Sitio	▬▬▬
Maintenance	Conversa	▬▬▬
Architect	Arquitecto	William Mitchell Rocky Roquemore
Type	Tipo	floresta, urbano
Relief	Relevo	▬▬
Water in play	Lago	▬▬▬
Exp. to wind	Exposto ao vento	▬▬
Trees in play	Arvores	▬▬▬

Scorecard Cartão de resultados	Chp. Camp.	Mens Homens	Ladies Senhoras
Length Compriment	6205	5804	5031
Par	72	72	72

Advised golfing ability	0 12 24 36
Nivel de jogo recomendado	
Hcp required	Handicap exigido 28 Hom., 36 Senh.

CLUB HOUSE & AMENITIES
CLUB HOUSE E ANEXOS   7/10

Pro shop	Pro-shop	▬▬▬
Driving range	Campo de prática	▬▬
Sheltered	coberto	não
On grass	om relva	não
Putting-green	putting-green	sim
Pitching-green	pitching-green	sim

HOTEL FACILITIES
INFRAESTRUCTURAS HOTELEIRAS   8/10

HOTELS HOTELS

Quinta do Lago   Quinta do Lago
132 quartos, D 17 000 Esc.   3 km
Tel (351) 089 - 39 66 66, Fax (351) 089 - 39 63 93

Dona Filipa   Vale do Lobo
147 quartos, D 31 500 Esc.   6 km
Tel (351) 089 - 39 41 41, Fax (351) 089 - 39 42 88

RESTAURANTS RESTAURANTE

Casa Velha   Quinta do Lago
Tel (351) 089 - 39 49 83   3 km

São Gabriel   Almancil
Tel (351) 089 - 39 45 21   5 km

A visão de algumas realizações imobiliarias é largamente compensada pelos belas paisagens. Esta agradável impressão é confirmada pela qualidade do percurso, muito recente mas já em boa condição. Com aos excepções de 2 pares 3, compridos e bem protegidos por lagos, este desenho de Rocky Roquemore adapta-se muito bem a todo o tipo de jogadores se não escolherem as saídas mais longas. O sentimento dominante é o de um percurso bem equilibrado e de uma grande franqueza com os obstáculos bem visiveis. As dificuldades são bastante numerosas para evitar o aborrecimento sem no entanto se tornar opressivo, tendo "greens" bem desenhados. Construido no meio de um agradável pinhal, com um relêvo moderato está evidentemente destinado a dar prazer e os melhores jogadores tirarão dele o melhor partido a partir das saídas de trás. A qualidade das instalações de treino permitem que se passe uma agradável jornada.

The sight of several property development projects is compensated by some beautiful landscapes, and this pleasant impression is confirmed by the excellence of the course, a very recent layout but one that is already in good condition. With the exception of two par 3s, both long and tightly defended by water, this Rocky Roquemore design is well suited to players of all abilities if they avoid the back-tees. The overall feeling is one of a nicely balanced and candid course, where hazards are clearly there to be seen. Although evenly spaced to give golfers room to breathe, there are enough difficulties to keep you on your toes, and the greens are interesting. Laid out in a flattish and pleasant pine forest, this course is obviously designed for fun, and the better players will be better off playing from the back. The standard of practice facilities makes this a good day's golfing.

Club Quinta do Peru
Vila Nogueira de Azeirão
P - 2950 AZEIRÃO

Office	Secretariado	(351) 01 - 210 61 60
Pro shop	Pro-shop	(351) 01 - 210 61 60
Fax	Fax	(351) 01 - 210 69 60
Situation	Localização	

46 km Lisboa, 662 782 h.
12 km Setubal, 89 106 h.

Annual closure	Fecho anual	não
Weekly closure	Fecho semanal	não

Fees main season
Tarifas de época alta 18 buracos

	Week days Semana	We/Bank holidays Fim de sem./Feriad
Individual Individual	10 000 Esc	12 500 Esc
Couple Casal	20 000 Esc	25 000 Esc

Caddy	Caddy	não
Electric Trolley	Trolley eléctrico	2 000 Esc.
Buggy	Buggy	5 000 Esc.
Clubs	Tacos	3 000 Esc.

Credit cards Cartão de crédito — VISA - AMEX

Access Acesso : A2 Lisboa → Setubal, N10 → Azeitão, Golf

Map 2 on page 834 Mapa 2 Página 834

GOLF COURSE / PERCURSO — 16/20

Site	Sítio	▰▰▰▰▱▱▱
Maintenance	Conversa	▰▰▰▰▱▱▱
Architect	Arquitecto	Rocky Roquemore
Type	Tipo	floresta, urbano
Relief	Relevo	▰▰▱▱▱▱▱
Water in play	Lago	▰▰▰▱▱▱▱
Exp. to wind	Exposto ao vento	▰▰▱▱▱▱▱
Trees in play	Arvores	▰▰▰▰▱▱▱

Scorecard Cartão de resultados	Chp. Camp.	Mens Homens	Ladies Senhoras
Length Compriment	6074	5617	4486
Par	72	72	72

Advised golfing ability
Nivel de jogo recomendado — 0 12 24 36

Hcp required Handicap exigido — 28 Hom., 36 Senh.

CLUB HOUSE & AMENITIES / CLUB HOUSE E ANEXOS — 7/10

Pro shop	Pro-shop	▰▰▰▱▱
Driving range	Campo de prática	▰▰▰▰▱
Sheltered	coberto	4 lugares
On grass	om relva	sim
Putting-green	putting-green	sim
Pitching-green	pitching-green	não

HOTEL FACILITIES / INFRAESTRUCTURAS HOTELEIRAS — 5/10

HOTELS HOTELS

Bonfim — Setubal
100 quartos, D 13 500 Esc. — 12 km
Tel (351) 01 - 53 41 11, Fax (351) 01 - 53 48 58

Estalagem Quinta das Torres — Azeitão
12 quartos, D 10 000 Esc. — 9 km
Tel (351) 01 - 208 00 01, Fax (351) 01 - 219 06 07

RESTAURANTS RESTAURANTE

Quinta das Torres — Azeitão
Tel (351) 01 - 218 00 01 — 9 km

A Roda — Setubal
Tel (351) 065 - 292 64 — 12 km

853

S. LOURENÇO ✳ ♪ | 17 | 6 | 8 |

É incontestávelmente o N° 1 de Portugal, pelo seu traçado pelo seu ambiente e pela sua manutenção. Num belo local rodeado de casas de grande qualidade, Joseph Lee demonstrou uma grande imaginação e uma preocupação de espectaculo visual e golfístico. Aqui é necessário não só utilizar todos os ferros do saco, mas tambem utilizá-los de forma diferente tão importante se torna a colocação das pancadas para se conseguir um bom resultado. Há um encontro de todas as dificuldades: arevores, "bunkers", lagos e largos braços da Ria Formosa. A tranquilidade e a beleza da paisagem incitam a dar o melhor de si próprio e a responder aos desafios técnicos postos pelo arquitecto. E certo que os jogadores inexperientes terão dificuldades, mas para aqueles que tem um handicap razoável será o culminar de uma viagem golfistica. Quanto aos jogadores de bom nível, terão aqui um máximo de prazer ao tentarem enfrentar este percurso.

This is unquestionably Portugal's top course for its design, setting and upkeep. Given a very beautiful site, dotted by some equally attractive villas, Joseph Lee employed heaps of imagination and considerable concern for golf as a visual spectacle. Here, you not only use every club in your bag, you also use clubs in different ways. That's how important positioning the ball can be for a good score. The course has every difficulty in the book: trees, fairway bunkers, lakes and a large arm of the Ria Formosa. The tranquillity and beauty of the landscape prompt the golfer to play above himself and meet the technical challenges laid down by the designer. Inexperienced players will have problems, sure, but with a decent handicap, a day spent here can be the perfect climax to a golfing holiday. The better players will have fun trying to tame a course such as this.

S. Lourenço Golf Club
Quinta do Lago
P - 8135 ALMANCIL

Office	Secretariado	(351) 089 - 39 65 22
Pro shop	Pro-shop	(351) 089 - 39 65 22
Fax	Fax	(351) 089 - 39 69 08
Situation	Localização	

15 km Faro, 33 664 h.

Annual closure	Fecho anual	não
Weekly closure	Fecho semanal	não

Fees main season
Tarifas de época alta O percurso

	Week days Semana	We/Bank holidays Fim de sem./Feriad
Individual Individual	18 000 Esc	18 000 Esc
Couple Casal	36 000 Esc	36 000 Esc

Caddy	Caddy	não
Electric Trolley	Trolley eléctrico	sim
Buggy	Buggy	7 500 Esc.
Clubs	Tacos	4 000 Esc.

Credit cards Cartão de crédito — VISA - AMEX

854

Access Acesso : N125 Faro → Portimão,
Almancil → Quinta do Lago
Map 3 on page 836 Mapa 3 Página 836

GOLF COURSE
PERCURSO — 17/20

Site	Sitio	
Maintenance	Conversa	
Architect	Arquitecto	Joseph Lee
Type	Tipo	beira-mar, floresta
Relief	Relevo	
Water in play	Lago	
Exp. to wind	Exposto ao vento	
Trees in play	Arvores	

Scorecard Cartão de resultados	Chp. Camp.	Mens Homens	Ladies Senhoras
Length Compriment	6238	5837	5171
Par	72	72	72

Advised golfing ability		0	12	24	36
Nivel de jogo recomendado					

Hcp required Handicap exigido 28 Hom., 36 Senh.

CLUB HOUSE & AMENITIES
CLUB HOUSE E ANEXOS — 6/10

Pro shop	Pro-shop	
Driving range	Campo de prática	
Sheltered	coberto	não
On grass	om relva	sim
Putting-green	putting-green	sim
Pitching-green	pitching-green	não

HOTEL FACILITIES
INFRAESTRUCTURAS HOTELEIRAS — 8/10

HOTELS HOTELS

Quinta do Lago — Quinta do Lago
132 quartos, D 17 000 Esc. — 2 km
Tel (351) 089 - 39 66 66, Fax (351) 089 - 39 63 93

Dona Filipa — Vale do Lobo
147 quartos, D 31 500 Esc. — 3 km
Tel (351) 089 - 39 41 41, Fax (351) 089 - 39 42 88

RESTAURANTS RESTAURANTE

Casa Velha — Quinta do Lago
Tel (351) 089 - 39 49 83 — 3 km

São Gabriel — Almancil
Tel (351) 089 - 39 45 21 — 5 km

Aqueles que não gostam de àgua, arriscam-se a passar aqui um mau bocado, uma vez que está presente em jogo em todos os buracos mas é o prêço a pagar para ter uma paisagem marinha muito agradável e desnuda. O comprimento do percurso não é deshumano (tem de se utilizar muitas vezes ferros curtos) e os jogadores direitos estarão à vontade bem como aqueles que controlam bem a bola: a colocação das pancadas de saída é muito importante para se estar bem posicionado para atacar os "greens" bem defendidos. São bastante planos sem terem um desenho escepcional, sendo para alem disso fáceis de lêr. Como a maior parte dos percursos de Portugal este traçado de Pedro de Vasconcellos (revisto por Robert Muir Graves) é acessivel a todos os jogadores. Não podem esperar cumprir fácilmente os seus handicaps mas encontrarão multiplas ocasiões para se habituarem à presença da àgua, muitas vezes intimidatórias para os amadores.

Golfers who are allergic to water might have a tough time here, as just about every hole has its water hazard. This is the price you pay for a very pleasant and bare marine landscape. The course is very reasonable in length (the second shot is often a short iron) and straight-hitters and flighters of the ball will feel at home. Placing the tee-shot is more important than usual to get a better angle at the very well defended greens, which are rather flat, easy to read and pleasantly designed. Like the majority of courses in Portugal, this Pedro de Vasconcelos layout (restyled by Robert Muir Graves) is playable for golfers of all abilities. They won't find it easy to play to their handicap, but they will find numerous opportunities to get used to the sort of water hazard that often intimidates the average golfer.

Salgados Golf Club

Apartado 2266 - Vale do Rabelho
P - 8200 ALBUFEIRA

Office	Secretariado	(351) 089 - 59 11 11
Pro shop	Pro-shop	(351) 089 - 59 11 11
Fax	Fax	(351) 089 - 59 11 12
Situation	Localização	

8 km Armação de Pêra, 2 894 h.
9 km Albufeira, 4 324 h.

Annual closure	Fecho anual	não
Weekly closure	Fecho semanal	não

Fees main season
Tarifas de época alta O percurso

	Week days Semana	We/Bank holidays Fim de sem./Feriad
Individual Individual	7 900 Esc	7 900 Esc
Couple Casal	15 800 Esc	15 800 Esc

Caddy	Caddy	não
Electric Trolley	Trolley eléctrico	2 000 Esc.
Buggy	Buggy	6 000 Esc.
Clubs	Tacos	2 500 Esc.
Credit cards Cartão de crédito		VISA - AMEX

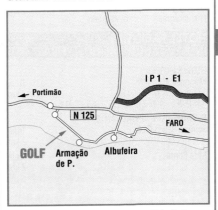

IP 1 - E1

Portimão

N 125

FARO

GOLF   Armação   Albufeira
de P.

Access Acesso : N125 Faro-Portimão, → Vale de Parra
Map 3 on page 836 Mapa 3 Página 836

GOLF COURSE / PERCURSO 14/20

Site	Sítio	
Maintenance	Conversa	
Architect	Arquitecto	Pedro Vasconcelos
Type	Tipo	beira-mar
Relief	Relevo	
Water in play	Lago	
Exp. to wind	Exposto ao vento	
Trees in play	Arvores	

Scorecard Cartão de resultados	Chp. Camp.	Mens Homens	Ladies Senhoras
Length Compriment	6080	5640	5157
Par	72	72	72

Advised golfing ability 0 12 24 36
Nivel de jogo recomendado
Hcp required Handicap exigido 35

CLUB HOUSE & AMENITIES / CLUB HOUSE E ANEXOS 7/10

Pro shop	Pro-shop	
Driving range	Campo de prática	
Sheltered	coberto	não
On grass	om relva	sim
Putting-green	putting-green	sim
Pitching-green	pitching-green	não

855

HOTEL FACILITIES / INFRAESTRUCTURAS HOTELEIRAS 7/10

HOTELS HOTELS

Almansor   Carvoeira
290 quartos, D 28 000 Esc.   14 km
Tel (351) 082 - 35 80 26, Fax (351) 082 - 35 87 70

Alisios   Albufeira
100 quartos, D 20 000 Esc.   18 km
Tel (351) 082 - 58 92 84, Fax (351) 082 - 58 92 88

Vila Galé Praia   Albufeira
40 quartos, D 24 000 Esc.   11 km
Tel (351) 082 - 59 10 50, Fax (351) 082 - 59 14 36

Aparthotel Cristal   Carvoeira
117 quartos, D 24 000 Esc.   14 km
Tel (351) 082 - 35 86 01, Fax (351) 082 - 35 86 48

RESTAURANTS RESTAURANTE

Centianes, Tel (351) 082 - 35 87 24   Carvoeira, 19 km
Vila Joya, Tel (351) 082 - 59 17 95   Albufeira, 3 km

TROIA

Foi durante muito tempo o melhor percurso de Portugal. Mas uma manutenção muito irregular e medíocre, reduziram bastante o seu prestígio. E pena porque a intelligência estratégica de Robert Trent Jones foi magistral. Localizado numa península à beira mar, êle interpretou a tradição dos "links" com a presença constante da areia bem como um envolvimento de pinheiros e plantas silvestres especificas da região. O percurso parece por vezes mais estreito do que é na realidade mas os obstáculos são bem visiveis e estão bem colocados, come por exemplo alguns "bunkers" profundos: defendem vigorosamente "greens" geralmente bastante pequenos e bem modelados. Troia é um grande desafio para os bons jugadores mas tambem é umteste apaixonante para os outros: é sempre muito instrutivo jogar num grande percurso de golf, num quadro atraente e natural.

For many year this was the best course in Portugal, but inadequate and inconsistent upkeep has considerably dulled its prestige. This is a pity, because the strategic intelligence deployed by designer Robert Trent Jones is brilliant. Over a seaboard peninsula, he has given his own interpretation of the links tradition with ubiquitous sand and a setting of maritime pines and wild plants, both typical of this region. The course often looks tighter than it actually is, but the hazards are clear to see and well located, particularly several deep bunkers. They provide stern defence for greens that are generally rather small and well-contoured. Troia is a great challenge for the better player and an exciting test for the rest. There is always something to learn from playing a great golf course in a natural and attractive setting.

Troia Golf

Complexo Turistico de Troia
P - 2900 SETUBAL

Office	Secretariado	(351) 065 - 4 41 12
Pro shop	Pro-shop	(351) 065 - 4 41 12
Fax	Fax	(351) 065 - 4 43 15
Situation	Localização	

2 km Setubal, 89 106 h.
42 km Lisboa, 662 782 h.

Annual closure	Fecho anual	não
Weekly closure	Fecho semanal	não

Fees main season
Tarifas de época alta O dia

	Week days Semana	We/Bank holidays Fim de sem./Feriad
Individual Individual	6 000 Esc	12 000 Esc
Couple Casal	12 000 Esc	24 000 Esc

Caddy	Caddy	não
Electric Trolley	Trolley eléctrico	não
Buggy	Buggy	5 500 Esc.
Clubs	Tacos	3 500 Esc.

Credit cards Cartão de crédito
VISA - Eurocard - MasterCard - AMEX - DC

Access Acesso : Lisboa → Setubal. Ferry-boat.
N 253-1 → Melides
Map 2 on page 834 Mapa 2 Página 834

GOLF COURSE
PERCURSO
15/20

Site	Sitio	
Maintenance	Conversa	
Architect	Arquitecto	Robert Trent Jones
Type	Tipo	beira-mar, links
Relief	Relevo	
Water in play	Lago	
Exp. to wind	Exposto ao vento	
Trees in play	Arvores	

Scorecard Cartão de resultados	Chp. Camp.	Mens Homens	Ladies Senhoras
Length Compriment	6337	5861	5426
Par	72	72	72

Advised golfing ability		0 12 24 36
Nivel de jogo recomendado		
Hcp required	Handicap exigido	não

CLUB HOUSE & AMENITIES
CLUB HOUSE E ANEXOS
7/10

Pro shop	Pro-shop	
Driving range	Campo de prática	
Sheltered	coberto	não
On grass	om relva	sim
Putting-green	putting-green	sim
Pitching-green	pitching-green	sim

HOTEL FACILITIES
INFRAESTRUCTURAS HOTELEIRAS
5/10

HOTELS HOTELS
Magnolia Mar ★★★★ Troia
132 quartos, D 16 000 Esc. 2 km
(351) 065 - 4 42 21, Fax (351) 065 - 4 41 62

RESTAURANTS RESTAURANTE
Soltroia Beach Club Troia
 2 km

Mira Ponte Troia
 2 km

VALE DA PINTA

✻ | 14 | 6 | 6

Muito ondulado, mas não deixa de ser fácil para jogar a pé.. Este percurso foi desenhado pelo Americano Ronald Fream. Os que conhecem o seu estilo poderão julgar que ele aqui não foi tão exigente para os golfistas como em outros locais. Visivelmente manteve o espirito de que são sobretudo turistas de nível de jogo médio que visitam a região. Para mais, quis preservar a natureza do terreno e portanto não abusou dos obstáculos de água. Os "greens" são bastante profundos e requerem uma boa precisão nos "approaches" mas estão razoavelmente defendidos, o que acentua a impressão "amigável" do percurso. As sáidas múltiplas permitem adaptá-lo a todos os níveis de jogo e a distrairse sem ter a sensação de ser um percurso fácil de mais. Os melhores jogadores ficam "aguados". Durante o passeio, poder-se-ão admirar belas oliveiras, algumas com mais de 700 anos; existe um exemplar que se calcula que tenha 1200 anos: se ele pudesse contar-nos a sua vida!

A little hilly but nonetheless easily walkable, this course was designed by the Americn Ronald Fream. Those of you who know his style might consider that he has been less demanding here than elsewhere, and visibly he bore in mind the fact that the region is visited primarily by mid-to-high handicappers on holiday. He also set out to preserve the natural look of the terrain and did not overdo the water hazards. The greens are rather deep and call for accurate approach shots, but they are reasonably defended, a fact that underlines the friendly feeling you get with this course. The many tee-areas adapt the course easily to all players, who can enjoy themselves without feeling that the course is too easy, but the best might want more than this. In passing, a word of admiration for the beautiful olive-trees, some of which are over 700 years old. One is even 1200 years old: its life-story would make interesting reading!.

Vale da Pinta
Quinta de Gramacho
P - 8400 Lagoa

Office	Secretariado	(351) 082 - 34 21 68
Pro shop	Pro-shop	(351) 082 - 34 21 68
Fax	Fax	(351) 082 - 34 21 89
Situation	Localização	

13 km Carvoeiro
42 km Faro, 33 664 h.

Annual closure	Fecho anual	não
Weekly closure	Fecho semanal	não

Fees main season
Tarifas de época alta O percurso

	Week days Semana	We/Bank holidays Fim de sem./Feriad
Individual Individual	9 000 Esc.	9 000 Esc.
Couple Casal	18 000 Esc.	18 000 Esc.

Caddy	Caddy	não
Electric Trolley	Trolley eléctrico	2 500 Esc.
Buggy	Buggy	5 500 Esc.
Clubs	Tacos	2 500 Esc.

Credit cards Cartão de crédito
VISA - AMEX - DC

Portimão
Lagoa
N 125
FARO
Carvoeiro
GOLF

Access Acesso : N125 Lagos-Faro. Lagoa → Carvoeiro
Map 3 on page 836 Mapa 3 Página 836

GOLF COURSE
PERCURSO   14/20

Site	Sitio	▣▣▣▣▢
Maintenance	Conversa	▣▣▣▣▢
Architect	Arquitecto	Ronald Fream
Type	Tipo	campo, urbano
Relief	Relevo	▣▣▢▢▢
Water in play	Lago	▣▣▣▢▢
Exp. to wind	Exposto ao vento	▣▣▢▢▢
Trees in play	Arvores	▣▣▣▢▢

Scorecard Cartão de resultados	Chp. Camp.	Mens Homens	Ladies Senhoras
Length Compriment	5861	5382	4528
Par	71	71	71

Advised golfing ability   0   12   24   36
Nivel de jogo recomendado   ▣▣▣▣▢
Hcp required   Handicap exigido 28 Hom., 36 Senh.

CLUB HOUSE & AMENITIES
CLUB HOUSE E ANEXOS   6/10

Pro shop	Pro-shop	▣▣▣▢▢
Driving range	Campo de prática	▣▣▣▢▢
Sheltered	coberto	6 lugares
On grass	om relva	sim
Putting-green	putting-green	sim
Pitching-green	pitching-green	sim

857

HOTEL FACILITIES
INFRAESTRUCTURAS HOTELEIRAS   6/10

HOTELS HOTELS
Almansor   Carvoeira
290 quartos, D 28 000 Esc.   3 km
Tel (351) 082 - 35 80 26, Fax (351) 082 - 35 87 70

Alisios   Albufeira
100 quartos, D 20 000 Esc.   13 km
Tel (351) 082 - 58 92 84, Fax (351) 082 - 58 92 88

Vila Galé Praia   Albufeira
40 quartos, D 24 000 Esc.   13 km
Tel (351) 082 - 59 10 50, Fax (351) 082 - 59 14 36

Aparthotel Cristal   Carvoeira
117 quartos, D 24 000 Esc.   3 km
Tel (351) 082 - 35 86 01, Fax (351) 082 - 35 86 48

RESTAURANTS RESTAURANTE
Centianes - Tel (351) 082 - 35 87 24   Carvoeira, 3 km
Vila Joya - Tel (351) 082 - 59 17 95   Albufeira, 13 km

Criado em 1991 numa zona de pinhal com alguns sobreiros bem como algumas figueiras a amendoeiras. Vila Sol foi desenhada po Donald Steel que não procurou em renegar o seu espírito britânico. Renunciou a quaisquer movimentos de terra espectaculares, conservando o lado natural do terreno. Pode lastimar-se que não tenha um traçado mais original, mas não dixa de ser um percurso bem adaptado a uma grande variedade de jogadores embora os primeiros buracos sejam um pouco difíceis para amadores. Podem tranquilizar-se, o seguimento é mas tranquilo. Bastante estreito, o percurso pode causar problemas aos jogadores imprecisos. Deverão jogar com cuidado para evitar as árvores e salvar o seu par. Com excepção do "green" do 11, os outros são bastante visíveis pouco defendidos, planos a de dimensão média. Com muito boa manutenção este percurso não é uma obra prima, mas merece o desvio.

Created in 1991 over an estate of pine, cork-oak, fig and almond trees, Vila Sol was laid out by Donald Steel, who worked in a distinctly British style. Preferring to keep the terrain's natural look, there was no spectacular earth-moving. This is an arguable point, as we would have liked a more personal layout. As it is, the course is very honest and playable by all golfers, even though the first holes are a tough test for the average hacker. They can relax, though, because the course tends to ease off later on. This is a rather tight course which can cause problems to wayward hitters. Getting out of the trees to save par requires some well-flighted recovery shots. With the exception of the 11th hole, all the greens are visible, relatively undefended, rather flat and medium-sized. A well upkept course, hardly a masterpiece but well worth the trip.

Golf de Vila Sol

Alto do Semino. Est. Nacional 396, km 24,8
P - 8125 QUARTEIRA

Office	Secretariado	(351) 089 - 30 21 44
Pro shop	Pro-shop	(351) 089 - 30 21 44
Fax	Fax	(351) 089 - 30 21 47
Situation	Localização	
3 km Quarteira, 8 905 h.		
18 km Faro, 33 664 h.		
Annual closure	Fecho anual	não
Weekly closure	Fecho semanal	não

Fees main season
Tarifas de época alta O percurso

	Week days Semana	We/Bank holidays Fim de sem./Feriad
Individual Individual	13 500 Esc.	13 500 Esc.
Couple Casal	27 000 Esc.	27 000 Esc.

Caddy	Caddy	não
Electric Trolley	Trolley eléctrico	2 000 Esc.
Buggy	Buggy	6 500 Esc.
Clubs	Tacos	2 500 Esc.
Credit cards Cartão de crédito		VISA - AMEX

Access Acesso : N1, N125 → Faro, N 396 → Quarteira
Map 3 on page 836 Mapa 3 Página 836

GOLF COURSE
PERCURSO   14/20

Site	Sítio	▰▰▰
Maintenance	Conversa	▰▰▰
Architect	Arquitecto	Donald Steel
Type	Tipo	floresta, urbano
Relief	Relevo	▰▰▰
Water in play	Lago	▰
Exp. to wind	Exposto ao vento	▰▰▰
Trees in play	Arvores	▰▰▰▰

Scorecard Cartão de resultados	Chp. Camp.	Mens Homens	Ladies Senhoras
Length Compriment	6189	5880	5338
Par	72	72	72

Advised golfing ability Nivel de jogo recomendado	0	12	24	36
Hcp required	Handicap exigido	28 Hom., 36 Senh.		

CLUB HOUSE & AMENITIES
CLUB HOUSE E ANEXOS   7/10

Pro shop	Pro-shop	▰▰▰
Driving range	Campo de prática	▰▰▰
Sheltered	coberto	não
On grass	om relva	sim
Putting-green	putting-green	sim
Pitching-green	pitching-green	sim

HOTEL FACILITIES
INFRAESTRUCTURAS HOTELEIRAS   7/10

HOTELS HOTELS
Marinotel   Vilamoura
364 quartos, D 50 000 Esc.   3 km
Tel (351) 89 - 38 99 88, Fax (351) 89 - 38 98 69

Atlantis   Vilamoura
302 quartos, D 40 000 Esc.   4 km
Tel (351) 089 - 38 99 77, Fax (351) 089 - 38 99 62

Ampalius   Vilamoura
357 quartos, D 33 500 Esc.   4 km
Tel (351) 089 - 38 09 10, Fax (351) 089 - 38 09 11

RESTAURANTS RESTAURANTE
Al Garb (Atlantis)   Vilamoura
Tel (351) 089 - 38 99 77   4 km

Gril Sirius   Vilamoura
Tel (351) 089 - 38 99 88   3 km

VILAMOURA I (OLD COURSE) ✳) | 16 | 7 | 7 |

Construídos entre 1973 e 1990, o complexo de três percursos de Vilamoura foi-se pouco a pouco modernizando. O primeiro, Vilamoura I, continua a ser o mais interessante e a sua renovação, em particular, dos greens, acrescenta ao prazer da sua reabertura. O arquitecto Frank Pennink soube preservar a naturalidade de uma paisagem magnífica, servida de uma bela vegetação. O seu percurso lembra muitas vezes a arquitectura dos golfes britânicos de interior, com a vantagem do clima. Embora tenha um par 73, é suficientemente longo para perturbar os jogadores imprecisos, pois as arvores estão muito em jogo. Os pares 3 tambén não são fáceis. E um persurso para técnicistas, expertos na arte de trabalhar a bola, mas os cinco pares 5 podem salvar os resultados de outro modo ameaçados. Um excelente test bem rejuvenescido.

Built between 1973 and 1990, the three-course complex at Vilamoura has gradually been modernised. The oldest, Vilamoura 1, is still the most interesting and its restyling, especially the greens, will make its re-opening all the more enjoyable. Designer Frank Pennink has successfully preserved the natural look of magnificent landscape and vegetation. The layout is often reminiscent of some of the great British parkland courses, with the climate as an added benefit. Although a par 73, it is long enough to upset wayward hitters as the trees are very much in play. The par 3s are no walk-over, either, making this a course for the technically-minded golfer who excels in working the ball. But rest assured, the par 5s can save a card that the other holes might have condemned to the litter-bin. An excellent test of golf, now looking wonderfully younger.

VILAMOURA GOLF CLUB
P - 8125 VILAMOURA

Office	Secretariado	(351) 089 - 32 16 52
Pro shop	Pro-shop	(351) 089 - 32 16 52
Fax	Fax	(351) 089 - 38 07 26
Situation	Localização	

3 km Quarteira, 8 905 h.
20 km Faro, 33 664 h.

Annual closure	Fecho anual	não
Weekly closure	Fecho semanal	não

Fees main season
Tarifas de época alta O percurso

	Week days Semana	We/Bank holidays Fim de sem./Feriad
Individual Individual	18 000 Esc.	18 000 Esc.
Couple Casal	36 000 Esc.	36 000 Esc.

Caddy	Caddy	não
Electric Trolley	Trolley eléctrico	2 000 Esc.
Buggy	Buggy	6 000 Esc.
Clubs	Tacos	5 000 Esc.
Credit cards Cartão de crédito		VISA - AMEX

◄— Portimão
Loulé
E 1 - IP 1
Villamoura
FARO →
N 396
N 125
GOLF
Quarteira
Quinta do Lago

0   2   4 km

Access Acesso : N125 Lagos-Faro. → Vilamoura
Map 3 on page 836 Mapa 3 Página 836

GOLF COURSE
PERCURSO   16/20

Site	Sitio	
Maintenance	Conversa	
Architect	Arquitecto	Frank Pennink
Type	Tipo	floresta
Relief	Relevo	
Water in play	Lago	
Exp. to wind	Exposto ao vento	
Trees in play	Arvores	

Scorecard Cartão de resultados	Chp. Camp.	Mens Homens	Ladies Senhoras
Length Compriment	6254	5988	5789
Par	73	73	73

Advised golfing ability Nivel de jogo recomendado		0 12 24 36
Hcp required	Handicap exigido 28	

CLUB HOUSE & AMENITIES
CLUB HOUSE E ANEXOS   7/10

Pro shop	Pro-shop	
Driving range	Campo de prática	
Sheltered	coberto	3 lugares
On grass	om relva	sim
Putting-green	putting-green	sim
Pitching-green	pitching-green	sim

HOTEL FACILITIES
INFRAESTRUCTURAS HOTELEIRAS   7/10

HOTELS HOTELS

Marinotel   Vilamoura
364 quartos, D 50 000 Esc.   3 km
Tel (351) 89 - 38 99 88, Fax (351) 89 - 38 98 69

Atlantis   Vilamoura
302 quartos, D 40 000 Esc.   4 km
Tel (351) 089 - 38 99 77, Fax (351) 089 - 38 99 62

Ampalius   Vilamoura
357 quartos, D 33 500 Esc.   4 km
Tel (351) 089 - 38 09 10, Fax (351) 089 - 38 09 11

RESTAURANTS RESTAURANTE

Al Garb (Atlantis)   Vilamoura
Tel (351) 089 - 38 99 77   4 km

Gril Sirius   Vilamoura
Tel (351) 089 - 38 99 88   3 km

859

O complexo de Vilamoura, apresenta percursos de interesse diferente, mas é um local muito aprazível para uma estadia, numa região onde a religião dos numeroses visitantes é o culto di Golf. Vilamoura II foi desenhada num vasto pinhal, o que impõe uma grande precisão aos jogadores, para mais sendo os "greens" bastante pequenos e sem grande modulação. Desenhado de inicio por Frank Pennink, foi parcialmente modificado por Robert Trent Jones, o que lhe da um certo toque "Americano", no estilo tradicional do arquitecto, nomeadamente quanto aos obstáculos de água do 5 e do 8. Para os que têm distância, o 17 oferece uma boa oportunidade de correr um risco, cortando o "dog-leg" para tentar chegar ao green em 2 pancadas. Agradável para percorrer, com algumas vistas sobre o Atlántico. Oferece algumas boas sombras, mas as arvores são essencialmente obstáculos, uma vez que os bunkers estão raramente em jogo.

The Vilamoura resort offers courses with differing appeal, but is without a doubt a very pleasant holiday venue in a region where many visitors religiously come along to worship the gods of golf. Vilamoura II was laid out in a huge pine forest, which calls for some precision play compounded by some smallish and uncontoured greens. Getting there is the main problem. Originally designed by Franck Pennink, it has been partly restyled by Robert Trent Jones, who gave the course some American touches along the way in his traditional manner. These include the only water hazards on the 5th and 8th holes. The 17th offers big-hitters an interesting opportunity to risk cutting corners around a dog-leg to hit the green in two. This is a pleasant course to play, with a few viewpoints over the Atlantic, and some welcome shade in summer. But once again, the trees are the main hazard, with bunkers seldom coming into play.

VILAMOURA GOLF CLUB
P - 8125 VILAMOURA

Office	Secretariado	(351) 089 - 32 16 52
Pro shop	Pro-shop	(351) 089 - 32 16 52
Fax	Fax	(351) 089 - 38 07 26
Situation	Localização	

3 km Quarteira, 8 905 h.
20 km Faro, 33 664 h.

| Annual closure | Fecho anual | não |
| Weekly closure | Fecho semanal | não |

Fees main season
Tarifas de época alta O percurso

	Week days Semana	We/Bank holidays Fim de sem./Feriad
Individual Individual	11 000 Esc.	11 000 Esc.
Couple Casal	22 000 Esc.	22 000 Esc.

Caddy	Caddy	não
Electric Trolley	Trolley eléctrico	2 000 Esc.
Buggy	Buggy	6 000 Esc.
Clubs	Tacos	5 000 Esc.

Credit cards Cartão de crédito
VISA - AMEX

Access Acesso : N125 Lagos-Faro. → Vilamoura
Map 3 on page 836 Mapa 3 Página 836

GOLF COURSE
PERCURSO · **13**/20

Site	Sitio	
Maintenance	Conversa	
Architect	Arquitecto	Frank Pennink
Type	Tipo	floresta
Relief	Relevo	
Water in play	Lago	
Exp. to wind	Exposto ao vento	
Trees in play	Arvores	

Scorecard Cartão de resultados	Chp. Camp.	Mens Homens	Ladies Senhoras
Length Compriment	6300	5880	5212
Par	72	72	72

Advised golfing ability	0	12	24	36
Nivel de jogo recomendado				

| Hcp required | Handicap exigido | não |

CLUB HOUSE & AMENITIES
CLUB HOUSE E ANEXOS · **7**/10

Pro shop	Pro-shop	
Driving range	Campo de prática	
Sheltered	coberto	3 lugares
On grass	om relva	sim
Putting-green	putting-green	sim
Pitching-green	pitching-green	sim

HOTEL FACILITIES
INFRAESTRUCTURAS HOTELEIRAS · **7**/10

HOTELS HOTELS
Marinotel — Vilamoura
364 quartos, D 50 000 Esc. — 3 km
Tel (351) 89 - 38 99 88, Fax (351) 89 - 38 98 69

Atlantis — Vilamoura
302 quartos, D 40 000 Esc. — 4 km
Tel (351) 089 - 38 99 77, Fax (351) 089 - 38 99 62

Ampalius — Vilamoura
357 quartos, D 33 500 Esc. — 4 km
Tel (351) 089 - 38 09 10, Fax (351) 089 - 38 09 11

RESTAURANTS RESTAURANTE
Al Garb (Atlantis) — Vilamoura
Tel (351) 089 - 38 99 77 — 4 km

Gril Sirius — Vilamoura
Tel (351) 089 - 38 99 88 — 3 km

VILAMOURA III (LAGUNA) ✳ ❫ | 14 | 7 | 7 |

Em comparação com Vilamoura II, este percurso tem uma estética e uma paisagem muito diferente. De facto, é constituido por 3 grupos de 9 buracos que se combinam (Pinhal, Lago, Marina) próximo do mar. O desenho é do arquitecto Joseph Lee (e Rocky Roquemore) um dos grandes representantes da "Escola da Florida", come se nota sobretudo nos percursos Lago e Marina que são, aliás, os mais interessantes. Como o seu nome indica a água está muito presente: em cerca de metade dos buracos. Mas o aspecto natural do terreno foi mantido. Os jogadores com distância podem exprimir-se ai melhor do que nos outros percursos do complexo, visto terem "fairways" mais largos e o arvoredo ser menos ameaçador, mesmo que visualmente seja mais intimidante do que o é na realidade. Vilamoura III é, apesar de tudo, mais difícil para fazer resultado: é o mais divertido para "match-play". Os greens têm um desenho interessante mas há que cuidar da manutenção, aliás como no resto do complexo que é uma verdadeira fábrica de golfe.

Compared with Vilamoura I and II, this is a course with a different style and landscape. It consists in fact of three combinable 9-holers (Pinhal, Lago and Marina), close to the Atlantic. It was designed by Joseph Lee (and Rocky Roquemore), one of the great representatives of the Florida school, as is clear to see on the "Lago" and "Marina" course, the most interesting of the three, as it happens. As their name suggests, water is in great supply on about half the holes, but the terrain's natural look has been preserved. Big-hitters can hit more freely than on the other courses in this resort, as the fairways are wider and the trees less threatening. Even though it looks more intimidating than it plays, making a good score can be hard going, so match-play is often more fun. The greens are interestingly designed, but upkeep needs watching here and throughout the resort, where golf is non-stop production-business.

VILAMOURA GOLF CLUB
P - 8125 VILAMOURA

Office	Secretariado	(351) 089 - 32 16 52
Pro shop	Pro-shop	(351) 089 - 32 16 52
Fax	Fax	(351) 089 - 38 07 26
Situation	Localização	

3 km Quarteira, 8 905 h.
20 km Faro, 33 664 h.

Annual closure	Fecho anual	não
Weekly closure	Fecho semanal	não

Fees main season
Tarifas de época alta O percurso

	Week days Semana	We/Bank holidays Fim de sem./Feriad
Individual Individual	10 000 Esc.	10 000 Esc.
Couple Casal	20 000 Esc.	20 000 Esc.

Caddy	Caddy	não
Electric Trolley	Trolley eléctrico	2 000 Esc.
Buggy	Buggy	6 000 Esc.
Clubs	Tacos	5 000 Esc.

Credit cards Cartão de crédito
VISA - AMEX

← Portimão

Loulé

E 1 - IP 1

FARO →

Villamoura

N 396   N 125

GOLF   Quarteira

Quinta do Lago

0   2   4 km

Access Acesso : N125 Lagos-Faro. → Vilamoura
Map 3 on page 836 Mapa 3 Página 836

GOLF COURSE
PERCURSO   14/20

Site	Sitio	▰▰▰▱▱
Maintenance	Conversa	▰▰▰▱▱
Architect	Arquitecto	Joseph Lee Rocky Roquemore
Type	Tipo	planicie
Relief	Relevo	▰▰▱▱▱
Water in play	Lago	▰▰▰▰▱
Exp. to wind	Exposto ao vento	▰▰▱▱▱
Trees in play	Arvores	▰▰▰▱▱

Scorecard Cartão de resultados	Chp. Camp.	Mens Homens	Ladies Senhoras
Length Comprimento	6130	5760	4900
Par	72	72	72

Advised golfing ability		0 12 24 36
Nivel de jogo recomendado		▰▰▰▰▰▰▱
Hcp required	Handicap exigido	não

CLUB HOUSE & AMENITIES
CLUB HOUSE E ANEXOS   7/10

Pro shop	Pro-shop	▰▰▰▱▱
Driving range	Campo de prática	▰▰▰▱▱
Sheltered	coberto	3 lugares
On grass	om relva	sim
Putting-green	putting-green	sim
Pitching-green	pitching-green	sim

HOTEL FACILITIES
INFRAESTRUCTURAS HOTELEIRAS   7/10

HOTELS HOTELS
Marinotel   Vilamoura
364 quartos, D 50 000 Esc.   3 km
Tel (351) 89 - 38 99 88, Fax (351) 89 - 38 98 69

Atlantis   Vilamoura
302 quartos, D 40 000 Esc.   4 km
Tel (351) 089 - 38 99 77, Fax (351) 089 - 38 99 62

Ampalius   Vilamoura
357 quartos, D 33 500 Esc.   4 km
Tel (351) 089 - 38 09 10, Fax (351) 089 - 38 09 11

RESTAURANTS RESTAURANTE
Al Garb (Atlantis)   Vilamoura
Tel (351) 089 - 38 99 77   4 km

Gril Sirius   Vilamoura
Tel (351) 089 - 38 99 88   3 km

861

LO IMPORTANTE ERES **TÚ**

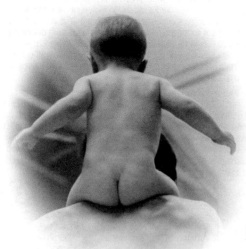

N U E V A
generación

PEUGEOT
306
B R E A K

NUEVO *en* **T**ECNOLOGÍA/NUEVO *en* **D**ISEÑO

DESCUBRIRLES SIEMPRE ALGO *Nuevo*. ENSEÑARLES EL MUNDO. Y OFRECERLES LO MEJOR.
EN EL *Nuevo* PEUGEOT 306 BREAK ENCONTRARÁS TODO LO QUE ESPERAS EN UN COCHE.
UN *Nuevo* ESPACIO. UN *Nuevo* CONCEPTO EN SEGURIDAD. UN *Nuevo* CONFORT.
DISFRUTADLO JUNTOS. DE *Nuevo*. **GAMA 306 BREAK: GASOLINA:** 1.6 CC. / 90 CV.
DIESEL: 1.9 CC. / 70 CV Y 1.9 CC. TURBO DIESEL / 90 CV.

PARA MAYOR INFORMACIÓN, LLAMA A **PEUGEOT DIRECTO 900 106 306.** PEUGEOT EN INTERNET: http://www.peugeot.es

P E U G E O T .   P A R A   D I S F R U T A R   D E L   A U T O M O V I L

NUEVA
generació

306
PEUGEOT

Spain  España

T here are around 120,000 registered golfers in Spain playing more than 130 eighteen-hole courses and over 60 nine-hole layouts. Yet despite the prestige that comes from having a number of international stars, golf is still not a particularly popular sport in Spain. By contrast, the country's geographic location and climate have led to already long-standing investment in tourism with patent success, particularly during the winter months. Golf today represents a blue-chip argument in favour of this development. On the fairways lining the eastern and southern coasts of Spain, you can hear just about every language from Northern Europe. The country's climate has, of course, played a key role in this success, but don't for a minute think that the cooler months are the only time for an agreeable visit to Spain or even for a golfing holiday.

Indeed, Spain is a country for all seasons. Summers are hot but can still be a good time for golf-trotters to come and play a few rounds in the Basque country, on the middle mountain courses of the Pyrenees or even around Madrid, where the heat is often less oppressive than on the coast. What is more, as many of the capital's inhabitants are out of town on holiday, it is much easier to play some of the region's top clubs. This is why we have also included the leading private courses in the guide, even though playing them on a weekend is virtually impossible. Make the most of Spring and Autumn to visit some of the regions inland from the coast, for example Seville, where temperatures rarely drop below fifteen degrees Celsius. Seasoned travellers know that this is also the best time to go and play the top clubs on the Costa Brava or the Costa del Sol while golfers from Northern Europe stay at home.

863

As a general rule, club members have full priority and green fees are high enough to be prohibitive. Excepting the truly commercial courses, it is preferable →

Ejemplo
de dos cosas geniales
que se pueden hacer con un palo y una bol·

simple y sabroso   sofisticado y exquisit·

No es una revista, es un bombón

Alesport, S:A. Gran Via 8-10, 7ª planta 08908 L'Hospitalet (Barcelona). Teléfonos: (93) 431 55 33. Fax: (93) 422 06 93 y 42.
Pº de la Castellana, 268. 7º D, 28046 Madrid. Teléfono: (91) 733 33 11 Fax: (91) 733 37 63
Dirección de Web: http://www.alesport.com, Correo electrónico (e-m ail): sologolf@alesport.com

to carry a letter of introduction from your own club and proof of handicap. Lastly, it is always wise to reserve a tee-off time and to confirm by fax if you book some way ahead of time.

Last but not least, remember that Spain is a country of history and tradition, the first of which is never to eat lunch before 1:30 pm and to sit down for dinner only from 10:30 pm onwards. And while you can play in casual wear (that does not mean jeans, T-shirt and shorts), it might be useful to take a tie and a light jacket with you for after your round.

España cuenta con unos 120.000 golfistas aproximadamente, 130 recorridos de 18 hoyos y más de 60 de 9 hoyos. Sin embargo el golf, a pesar de los numerosos campeones nacionales, no es un deporte muy popular en el país. La situación geográfica y su clima han favorecido las inversiones en el turismo desde hace mucho tiempo con un éxito evidente, sobre todo en los meses de invierno. Y el golf es un elemento de primera categoría en el desarrollo turístico : en los campos de golf de las costas orientales y meridionales se oye hablar en todos los idiomas del norte de Europa. El clima es un factor primordial de este éxito, y no hay que pensar que los meses más fríos sean los únicos aconsejables para hacer turismo o jugar al golf cómodamente.

En realidad el país goza de cuatro estaciones bien variadas. El verano es caluroso y tal vez sea preferible jugar al golf en el País Vasco, en los recorridos de media montaña de los Pireneos o incluso en la region de Madrid, ya que las fuertes temperaturas son menos agobiantes que en la costa. Además muchos habitantes de la capital española la abandonan para irse de vacaciones, lo que facilita el jugar con mayor facilidad en los clubs de la región. Por esta razón hemos incluido en esta Guía los grandes Clubs privados, aunque sea casi imposible poder jugar durante los fines de semana. Hay que aprovechar la primavera y el otoño para visitar las regiones del interior de la costa, como por ejemplo Sevilla donde las temperaturas raramente se sitúan por debajo de los quince grados. Los profesionales del turismo de golf saben perfectamente que son las mejores épocas del año para jugar en los grandes recorridos de la Costa Brava o de la Costa del Sol, ya que en esa época los jugadores del norte de Europa se quedan en sus países.

Por regla general los socios de los clubs gozan de prioridad y el precio de los green-fees son a veces disuasivos por su alto precio. Excepto en los recorridos verdaderamente comerciales, es aconsejable presentarse con una carta de recomendación de su proprio club y un certificado con el handicap. Finalmente, siempre es conveniente reservar las salidas y, si se hace con antelación, confirmarlo por fax.

No hay que olvidar que España es un país con sus propias costumbres. La primera consiste en no almorzar antes de las 13h30 y cenar después de las 22h00. Si bien se puede jugar el golf con una vestimenta cómoda (evitando siempre los vaqueros y camisetas), no está de más llevar consigo una corbata y chaqueta ligera. Enhorabuena !

865

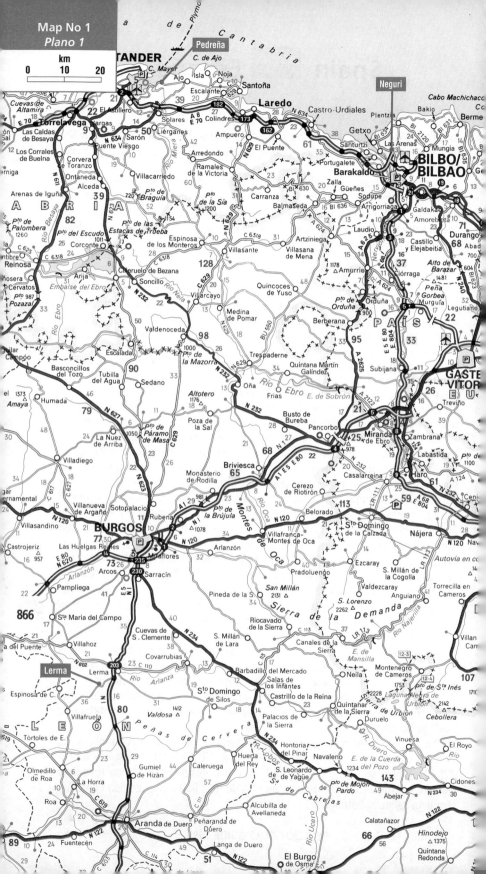

Map No 1
Plano 1

km
0   10   20

867

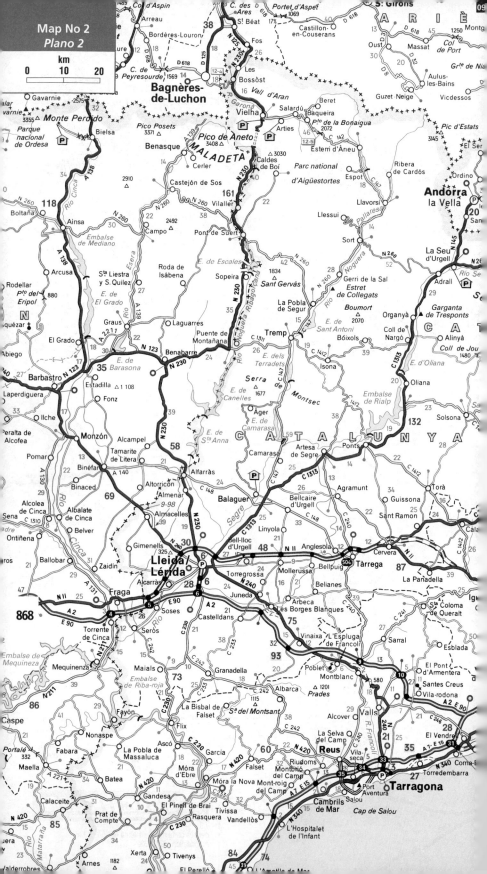

869

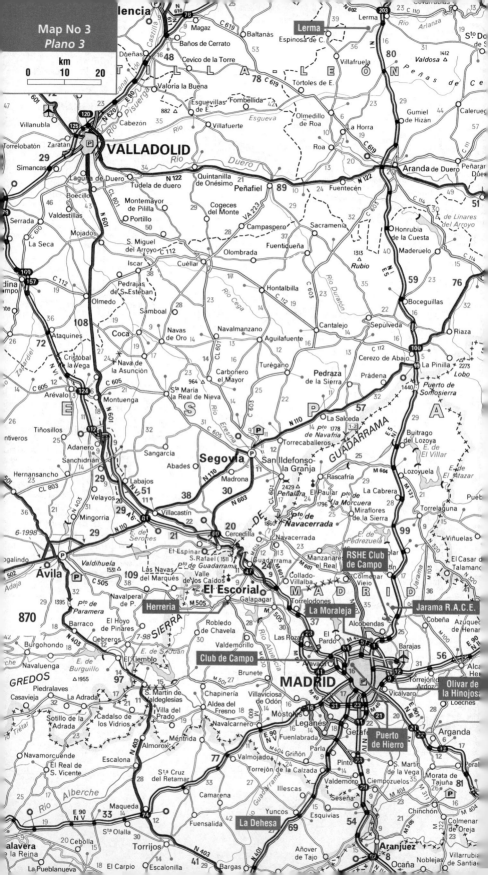

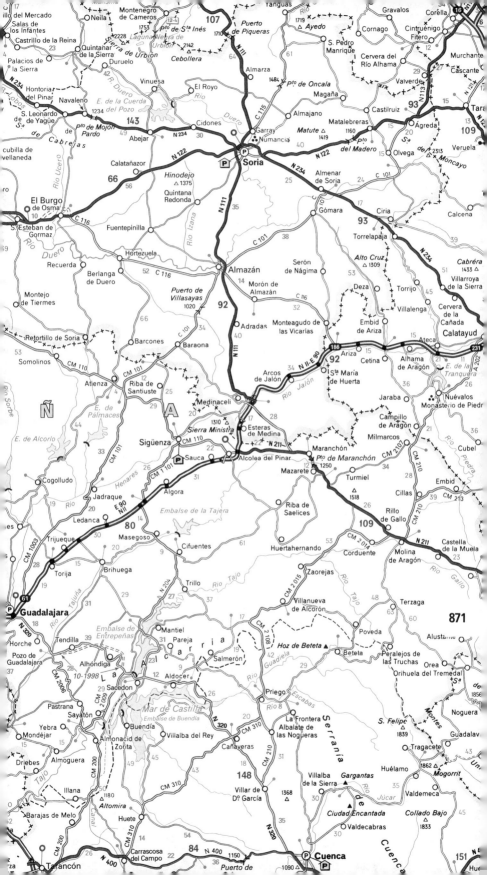

873

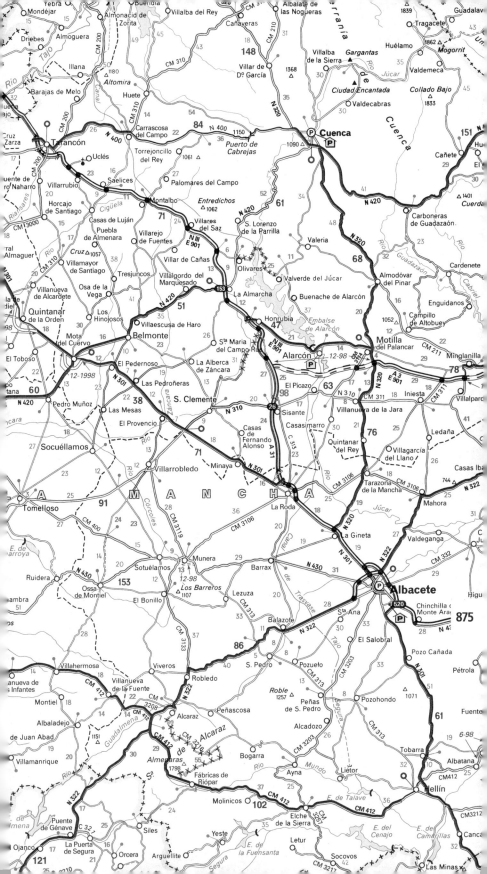

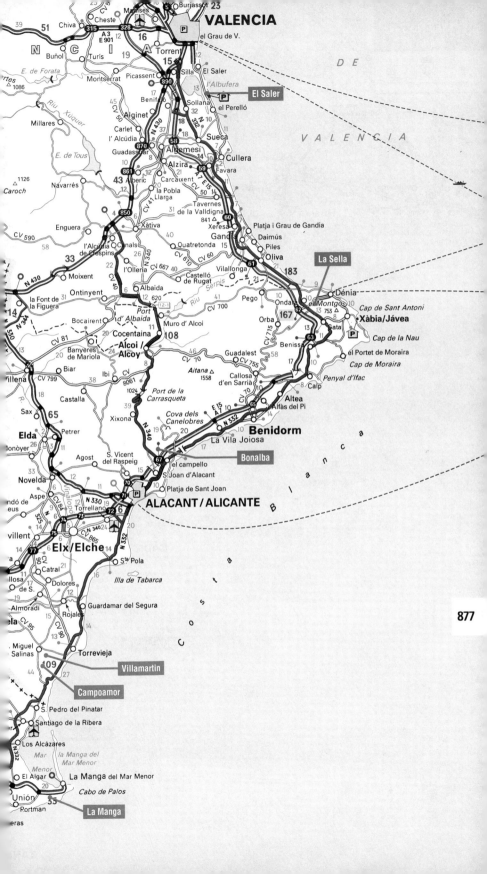

VALENCIA 23

E. de Forata
△ 1086

Buñol
Chiva 51
39
Cheste
Manises
Burjassot
315
E 901
A3
328
16
N
I A
el Grau de V.
Torrent
15
12
Silla
El Saler
P
l'Albufera
El Saler
Turís
19
Picassent
890
Benifaió
Sollana
13
el Perelló
P
Montserrat
45
Alginet
50
CV 32
32
Millares
Carlet
l' Alcúdia
18
Sueca
E. de Tous
870
58
Algemesí
14
Cullera
△ 1126
Caroch
Navarrés
43
Alberic
861
8
12
Alzira
59
Favara
Guadassuar
12
Carcaixent
57
50 14
la Pobla
Llarga
Tavernes
de la Valldigna
841 △
CV 41
E. de Tous
850
CV 590
Enguera
4
Xàtiva
Xeresa
60
Gandia
Platja i Grau de Gandia
33
l'Alcúdia
de Crespins
Canals
26
l'Olleria
Quatretonda
CV 610
Vilallonga
Daimús
Piles
61
Oliva
La Sella
Moixent
22
Ontinyent
CV 40
6
Albaida
Serpis
Pego
Ondara
183
Dénia
la Font de
la Figuera
31
CV 590
58
Port
d'Albaida
12-1
Muro d'Alcoi
Riu
41
CV 700
el Montgó
Cap de Sant Antoni
167
62
9
753 △
13
Xàbia/Jávea
Cap de la Nau
N 430
Bocairent
Cocentaina
108
Orba
CV 715
Gata
63
Benissa
el Portet de Moraira
Cap de Moraira
CV 81
Alcoi /
Alcoy
46
Guadalest
CV 755
58
17
Penyal d'Ifac
Banyeres
de Mariola
20
Aitana △
1558
Callosa
d'en Sarrià
10
Biar
Ibi
CV
8061
Port de la
Carrasqueta
Cova dels
Canelobres
E 15
A7
CV 65
Altea
l'Alfàs del Pi
8
Calp
Villena
CV 799
38
1024
39
N 332
14
Castalla
Xixona
N 340
19
Benidorm
Sax
65
Petrer
S. Vicent
del Raspeig
17
La Vila Joiosa
Elda
Agost
67
el campello
Bonalba
Monòver
26
S. Joan d'Alacant
Novelda
12
70
Platja de Sant Joan
Aspe
11
71
P
Torrellano
ALACANT/ALICANTE
N 330
525
N 84
72
6
N 340
20
villent
24
N 666
Elx/Elche
77
14
Catral
S'ta Pola
Dolores
Illa de Tabarca
llosa
de S.
Almoradí
Guardamar del Segura
CV 95
Rojales
877
Miguel
Salinas
109
Torrevieja
Villamartín
27
Campoamor
S. Pedro del Pinatar
Santiago de la Ribera
Los Alcázares
N 332
Mar
Menor
la Manga del
Mar Menor
El Algar
La Manga del Mar Menor
Unión
55
Cabo de Palos
La Manga
Portman

km
0   10   20

878

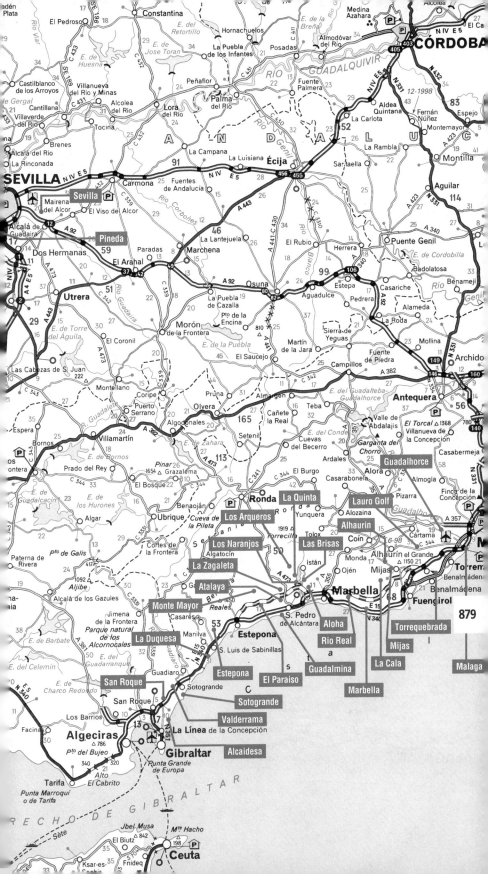

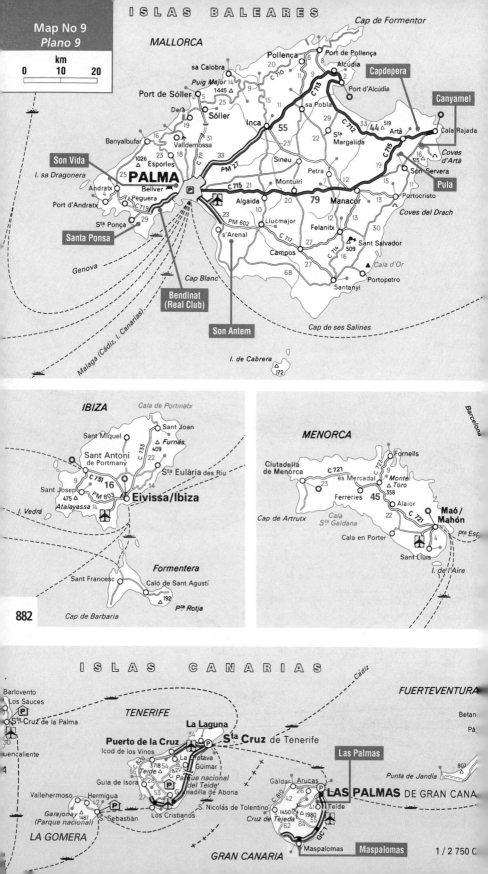

CLASIFICACION DE LOS RECORRIDOS
CLASSIFICATION OF COURSES

Esta clasificación da prioridad a la nota atribuida al recorrido.
This classification gives priority consideration
to the score awarded to the actual course.

Nota del club-house y anejos
Club-house and facilities

Nota del recorrido
Course score

Nota de la infraestructura
hotelera
Hotel facility score

19 8 6   Valderrama   977   Página *Page*

Nota			Recorrido	Página	Nota			Recorrido	Página
19	8	6	Valderrama	977	**16**	8	9	Puerta de Hierro	963
18	7	6	El Saler	913	**16**	6	6	Ulzama	976
18	6	5	Fontanals	917	**16**	7	6	Villamartin	978
18	7	7	Las Brisas	937	**16**	7	6	Zaudin	979
18	7	6	R.S.H.E. Club de Campo	965	**15**	6	6	Canyamel	901
18	7	6	Sotogrande	974	**15**	7	6	Capdepera	902
17	7	7	Aloha	895	**15**	7	7	Club d'Aro (Mas Nou)	905
17	7	7	Castillo de Gorraiz	903	**15**	7	6	El Prat *Amarillo*	911
17	7	6	El Prat *Verde*	912	**15**	6	6	Herreria	922
17	7	6	Emporda	914	**15**	7	7	La Manga *Norte*	929
17	8	6	La Cala *Norte*	925	**15**	7	8	La Moraleja *La Moraleja 1*	932
17	7	4	Lerma	939	**15**	8	7	La Quinta	934
17	8	7	Montecastillo	950	**15**	6	5	La Sella	935
17	7	7	Neguri	952	**15**	7	8	Marbella	943
17	8	6	San Roque	967	**15**	7	6	Masia Bach	944
17	7	8	Sevilla	971	**15**	7	7	Montenmedio	951
16	7	6	Bonmont	899	**15**	7	9	Pineda	960
16	8	8	Club de Campo	906	**14**	6	5	Alcaidesa	892
16	7	4	El Bosque	909	**14**	7	5	Alhaurin	893
16	8	8	Islantilla	923	**14**	6	6	Almerimar	894
16	8	6	La Cala *Sur*	926	**14**	6	6	Bonalba	898
16	7	8	La Moraleja *La Moraleja 2*	933	**14**	6	6	Campoamor	900
16	7	7	La Zagaleta	936	**14**	7	7	Cerdaña	904
16	7	7	Los Naranjos	941	**14**	7	6	Estepona	916
16	7	8	Maspalomas	945	**14**	6	5	Granada	919
16	7	6	Mediterraneo	946	**14**	7	6	Guadalhorce	920
16	6	7	Mijas *Los Lagos*	947	**14**	7	7	Guadalmina *Sur*	921
16	7	7	Novo Sancti Petri	953	**14**	7	4	La Dehesa	927
16	7	6	Pals	956	**14**	7	7	La Manga *Oeste*	930
16	6	5	Peralada	959	**14**	7	7	La Manga *Sur*	931

883

CLASIFICACION DE LOS RECORRIDOS

Nota	Recorrido	Página	Nota	Recorrido	Página
14 6 7	Los Arqueros	940	13 7 5	Girona	918
14 7 4	Osona Montanya	955	13 7 6	Jarama R.A.C.E.	924
14 6 4	Panoramica	957	13 7 6	La Duquesa	928
14 6 5	Pedreña	958	13 7 5	Lauro	938
14 6 6	San Sebastián	968	13 4 6	Malaga	942
14 7 6	Son Antem	972	13 6 7	Mijas Los Olivos	948
14 6 7	Son Vida	973	13 5 5	Monte Mayor	949
14 7 7	Torrequebrada	975	13 7 8	Olivar de la Hinojosa	954
13 6 7	Atalaya Old Course	896	13 6 4	Playa Serena	961
13 6 7	Bendinat	897	13 6 5	Poniente	962
13 7 7	Costa Brava	907	13 6 5	Pula	964
13 6 6	Costa Dorada	908	13 6 7	Rio Real	966
13 6 6	El Paraiso	910	13 6 5	Sant Cugat	969
13 8 4	Escorpion	915	13 6 7	Santa Ponsa	970

CLASIFICACION DE LA INFRAESTRUCTURA HOTELERA
CLASSIFICATION OF HOTELS FACILITIES

Nota del club-house y anejos
Club-house and facilities

Nota del recorrido
Course score

Nota de la infraestructura hotelera
Hotel facility score

15 7 9 Pineda 960

Página
Page

Nota	Recorrido	Página	Nota	Recorrido	Página
15 7 9	Pineda	960	15 7 7	Club d'Aro (Mas Nou)	905
16 8 9	Puerta de Hierro	963	13 7 7	Costa Brava	907
16 8 8	Club de Campo	906	14 7 7	Guadalmina Sur	921
16 8 8	Islantilla	923	15 7 7	La Manga Norte	929
15 7 8	La Moraleja La Moraleja 1	932	14 7 7	La Manga Oeste	930
16 7 8	La Moraleja La Moraleja 2	933	14 7 7	La Manga Sur	931
15 7 8	Marbella	943	15 8 7	La Quinta	934
16 7 8	Maspalomas	945	16 7 7	La Zagaleta	936
13 7 8	Olivar de la Hinojosa	954	18 7 7	Las Brisas	937
17 7 8	Sevilla	971	14 6 7	Los Arqueros	940
17 7 7	Aloha	895	16 7 7	Los Naranjos	941
13 6 7	Atalaya Old Course	896	16 6 7	Mijas Los Lagos	947
13 6 7	Bendinat	897	13 6 7	Mijas Los Olivos	948
17 7 7	Castillo de Gorraiz	903	17 8 7	Montecastillo	950
14 7 7	Cerdaña	904	15 7 7	Montenmedio	951

CLASIFICACION DE LA INFRAESTRUCTURA HOTELERA

Nota			Recorrido	Página	Nota			Recorrido	Página
17	7	**7**	Neguri	952	18	7	**6**	R.S.H.E. Club de Campo	965
16	7	**7**	Novo Sancti Petri	953	17	8	**6**	San Roque	967
13	6	**7**	Rio Real	966	14	6	**6**	San Sebastián	968
13	6	**7**	Santa Ponsa	970	14	7	**6**	Son Antem	972
14	6	**7**	Son Vida	973	18	7	**6**	Sotogrande	974
14	7	**7**	Torrequebrada	975	16	6	**6**	Ulzama	976
14	6	**6**	Almerimar	894	19	8	**6**	Valderrama	977
14	6	**6**	Bonalba	898	16	7	**6**	Villamartin	978
16	7	**6**	Bonmont	899	16	7	**6**	Zaudin	979
14	6	**6**	Campoamor	900	14	6	**5**	Alcaidesa	892
15	6	**6**	Canyamel	901	14	7	**5**	Alhaurin	893
15	7	**6**	Capdepera	902	18	6	**5**	Fontanals	917
13	6	**6**	Costa Dorada	908	13	7	**5**	Girona	918
13	6	**6**	El Paraiso	910	14	6	**5**	Granada	919
15	7	**6**	El Prat *Amarillo*	911	15	6	**5**	La Sella	935
17	7	**6**	El Prat *Verde*	912	13	7	**5**	Lauro	938
18	7	**6**	El Saler	913	13	5	**5**	Monte Mayor	949
17	7	**6**	Emporda	914	14	6	**5**	Pedreña	958
14	7	**6**	Estepona	916	16	6	**5**	Peralada	959
14	7	**6**	Guadalhorce	920	13	6	**5**	Poniente	962
15	6	**6**	Herreria	922	13	6	**5**	Pula	964
13	7	**6**	Jarama R.A.C.E.	924	13	6	**5**	Sant Cugat	969
17	8	**6**	La Cala *Norte*	925	16	7	**4**	El Bosque	909
16	8	**6**	La Cala *Sur*	926	13	8	**4**	Escorpion	915
13	7	**6**	La Duquesa	928	14	7	**4**	La Dehesa	927
13	4	**6**	Malaga	942	17	7	**4**	Lerma	939
15	7	**6**	Masia Bach	944	14	7	**4**	Osona Montanya	955
16	7	**6**	Mediterraneo	946	14	6	**4**	Panoramica	957
16	7	**6**	Pals	956	13	6	**4**	Playa Serena	961

885

VACACIONES RECOMENDADAS
RECOMMENDED GOLFING HOLIDAYS

Recorrido	Nota			Página	Recorrido	Nota			Página
Bonmont	16	7	6	899	Marbella	15	7	8	943
Capdepera	15	7	6	902	Maspalomas	16	7	8	945
Costa Dorada	13	6	6	908	Mediterraneo	16	7	6	946
El Bosque	16	7	4	909	Mijas *Los Lagos*	16	6	7	947
El Saler	18	7	6	913	Mijas *Los Olivos*	13	6	7	948
Emporda	17	7	6	914	Novo Sancti Petri	16	7	7	953
Islantilla	16	8	8	923	Pals	16	7	6	956
La Cala *Norte*	17	8	6	925	Playa Serena	13	6	4	961
La Cala *Sur*	16	8	6	926	Poniente	13	6	5	962
La Manga *Norte*	15	7	7	929	Pula	13	6	5	964
La Manga *Oeste*	14	7	7	930	Son Antem	14	7	6	972
La Manga *Sur*	14	7	7	931	Torrequebrada	14	7	7	975
La Sella	15	6	5	935					

EPOCA DEL AÑO ACONSEJADA
RECOMMENDED SEASONS

Epoca del ano/ Recorrido	Nota			Página	Epoca del ano/ Recorrido	Nota			Página
1 2 3 4 5 6 7 8 9 10 11 12					**1 2 3 4 5 6 7 8 9 10 11 12**				
Bendinat	13	6	7	897	Pula	13	6	5	964
Bonalba	14	6	6	898	San Roque	17	8	6	967
Campoamor	14	6	6	900	Santa Ponsa	13	6	7	970
Canyamel	15	6	6	901	Son Antem	14	7	6	972
Capdepera	15	7	6	902	Son Vida	14	6	7	973
Costa Dorada	13	6	6	908	Sotogrande	18	7	6	974
El Bosque	16	7	4	909	Valderrama	19	8	6	977
El Saler	18	7	6	913	Villamartin	16	7	6	978
Escorpion	13	8	4	915					
La Manga *Norte*	15	7	7	929	**1 2 3 4 5 6 7 8 9 10 11 12**				
La Manga *Oeste*	14	7	7	930	Costa Brava	13	7	7	907
La Manga *Sur*	14	7	7	931	El Prat *Amarillo*	15	7	6	911
La Sella	15	6	5	935	El Prat *Verde*	17	7	6	912
Maspalomas	16	7	8	945	Girona	13	7	5	918
Mediterraneo	16	7	6	946	Novo Sancti Petri	16	7	7	953
Montenmedio	15	7	7	951	Sant Cugat	13	6	5	969
Pals	16	7	6	956					
Peralada	16	6	5	959	**1 2 3 4 5 6 7 8 9 10 11 12**				
Pineda	15	7	9	960	Alhaurin	14	7	5	893
Poniente	13	6	5	962	Almerimar	14	6	6	894

886

EPOCA DEL AÑO ACONSEJADA

Epoca del ano/ Recorrido	Nota	Página	Epoca del ano/ Recorrido	Nota	Página
1 2 3 4 5 6 7 8 9 10 11 12			**1 2 3 4 5 6 7 8 9 10 11 12**		
Aloha	17 7 7	895	Club de Campo	16 8 8	906
Atalaya *Old Course*	13 6 7	896	Emporda	17 7 6	914
El Paraiso	13 6 6	910	San Sebastián	14 6 6	968
Estepona	14 7 6	916			
Guadalmina *Sur*	14 7 7	921	**1 2 3 4 5 6 7 8 9 10 11 12**		
La Cala *Norte*	17 8 6	925	Granada	14 6 5	919
La Cala *Sur*	16 8 6	926			
Malaga	13 4 6	942	**1 2 3 4 5 6 7 8 9 10 11 12**		
Marbella	15 7 8	943	Castillo de Gorraiz	17 7 7	903
Mijas *Los Lagos*	16 6 7	947	Club d'Aro (Mas Nou)	15 7 7	905
Mijas *Los Olivos*	13 6 7	948	Jarama R.A.C.E.	13 7 6	924
Rio Real	13 6 7	966	La Dehesa	14 7 4	927
			La Moraleja *La Moraleja 1*	15 7 8	932
1 2 3 4 5 6 7 8 9 10 11 12			La Moraleja *La Moraleja 2*	16 7 8	933
Alcaidesa	14 6 5	892	Neguri	17 7 7	952
Guadalhorce	14 7 6	920	Olivar de la Hinojosa	13 7 8	954
Islantilla	16 8 8	923	Osona Montanya	14 7 4	955
La Duquesa	13 7 6	928	Pedreña	14 6 5	958
La Quinta	15 8 7	934	Puerta de Hierro	16 8 9	963
La Zagaleta	16 7 7	936			
Las Brisas	18 7 7	937	**1 2 3 4 5 6 7 8 9 10 11 12**		
Lauro	13 7 5	938	Fontanals	18 6 5	917
Los Arqueros	14 6 7	940	Herreria	15 6 6	922
Los Naranjos	16 7 7	941	Lerma	17 7 4	939
Monte Mayor	13 5 5	949	Ulzama	16 6 6	976
Montecastillo	17 8 7	950			
Panoramica	14 6 4	957	**1 2 3 4 5 6 7 8 9 10 11 12**		
Playa Serena	13 6 4	961	Masia Bach	15 7 6	944
Sevilla	17 7 8	971			
Torrequebrada	14 7 7	975	**1 2 3 4 5 6 7 8 9 10 11 12**		
Zaudin	16 7 6	979	R.S.H.E. Club de Campo	18 7 6	965
1 2 3 4 5 6 7 8 9 10 11 12			**1 2 3 4 5 6 7 8 9 10 11 12**		
Bonmont	16 7 6	899	Cerdaña	14 7 7	904

887

ALTITUD DE LOS RECORRIDOS > 500 m
COURSES ALTITUDE

Altitud/ Recorrido	Nota	Página	Altitud/ Recorrido	Nota	Página
500 Castillo de Gorraiz	17 7 7	903	600 Olivar de la Hinojosa	13 7 8	954
500 Ulzama	16 6 6	976	650 Club de Campo	16 8 8	906
600 La Moraleja			680 Granada	14 6 5	919
La Moraleja 2	16 7 8	933	740 R.S.H.E. Club de Campo	18 7 6	965
600 Puerta de Hierro	16 8 9	963	830 Osona Montanya	14 7 4	955
600 La Moraleja			840 Lerma	17 7 4	939
La Moraleja 1	15 7 8	932	950 Herreria	15 6 6	922
600 La Dehesa	14 7 4	927	1100 Fontanals	18 6 5	917
600 Jarama R.A.C.E.	13 7 6	924	1100 Cerdaña	14 7 7	904

RELIEVE DE LOS RECORRIDOS
GEOGRAPHICAL RELIEF

Con poco relieve Rather flat	Medianamente accidentado Averagely hilly	Muy accidentado Very hilly

Ano/ Recorrido	Nota			Página	Ano/ Recorrido	Nota			Página
Almerimar	14	6	6	894	Bonmont	16	7	6	899
Playa Serena	13	6	4	961	Capdepera	15	7	6	902
					Club de Campo	16	8	8	906
					Costa Dorada	13	6	6	908
El Paraiso	13	6	6	910	Guadalhorce	14	7	6	920
El Prat *Amarillo*	15	7	6	911	Lauro	13	7	5	938
El Prat *Verde*	17	7	6	912	Marbella	15	7	8	943
Escorpion	13	8	4	915	Mijas *Los Olivos*	13	6	7	948
Guadalmina *Sur*	14	7	7	921	Montenmedio	15	7	7	951
Malaga	13	4	6	942	Pula	13	6	5	964
Olivar de la Hinojosa	13	7	8	954	Son Vida	14	6	7	973
Pineda	15	7	9	960	Valderrama	19	8	6	977
Santa Ponsa	13	6	7	970	Zaudin	16	7	6	979
Sevilla	17	7	8	971					
Son Antem	14	7	6	972	Aloha	17	7	7	895
					Bonalba	14	6	6	898
Atalaya *Old Course*	13	6	7	896	Costa Brava	13	7	7	907
El Saler	18	7	6	913	Islantilla	16	8	8	923
Emporda	17	7	6	914	Jarama R.A.C.E.	13	7	6	924
Fontanals	18	6	5	917	La Dehesa	14	7	4	927
Granada	14	6	5	919	La Duquesa	13	7	6	928
Lerma	17	7	4	939	La Manga *Norte*	15	7	7	929
Los Naranjos	16	7	7	941	La Manga *Oeste*	14	7	7	930
Maspalomas	16	7	8	945	La Manga *Sur*	14	7	7	931
Mediterraneo	16	7	6	946	Neguri	17	7	7	952
Novo Sancti Petri	16	7	7	953	Puerta de Hierro	16	8	9	963
Panoramica	14	6	4	957	San Roque	17	8	6	967
Poniente	13	6	5	962	Villamartin	16	7	6	978
Rio Real	13	6	7	966					
Sotogrande	18	7	6	974	Alcaidesa	14	6	5	892
					Bendinat	13	6	7	897
La Moraleja *La Moraleja 1*	15	7	8	932	Campoamor	14	6	6	900
La Moraleja *La Moraleja 2*	16	7	8	933	Canyamel	15	6	6	901
Las Brisas	18	7	7	937	Castillo de Gorraiz	17	7	7	903
Mijas *Los Lagos*	16	6	7	947	Cerdaña	14	7	7	904
Pals	16	7	6	956	Club d'Aro (Mas Nou)	15	7	7	905
Peralada	16	6	5	959	Herreria	15	6	6	922

RELIEVE DE LOS RECORRIDOS

Ano/ Recorrido	Nota	Página	Ano/ Recorrido	Nota	Página
La Quinta	15 8 7	934	Girona	13 7 5	918
La Sella	15 6 5	935	La Cala *Norte*	17 8 6	925
Masia Bach	15 7 6	944	Osona Montanya	14 7 4	955
Montecastillo	17 8 7	950	Sant Cugat	13 6 5	969
Pedreña	14 6 5	958	Ulzama	16 6 6	976
R.S.H.E. Club de Campo	18 7 6	965			
San Sebastián	14 6 6	968			
Torrequebrada	14 7 7	975	La Cala *Sur*	16 8 6	926
			La Zagaleta	16 7 7	936
			Los Arqueros	14 6 7	940
Alhaurin	14 7 5	893			
El Bosque	16 7 4	909			
Estepona	14 7 6	916	Monte Mayor	13 5 5	949

TIPO DE RECORRIDOS
TYPE OF COURSE

Tipo/ Recorrido	Nota	Página	Tipo/ Recorrido	Nota	Página
Al borde del mar			Osona Montanya	14 7 4	955
Olivar de la Hinojosa	13 7 8	954	Pals	16 7 6	956
Alcaidesa	14 6 5	892	Pedreña	14 6 5	958
Almerimar	14 6 6	894	R.S.H.E. Club de Campo	18 7 6	965
El Prat *Verde*	17 7 6	912	San Sebastián	14 6 6	968
Guadalmina *Sur*	14 7 7	921	Ulzama	16 6 6	976
Islantilla	16 8 8	923			
Malaga	13 4 6	942	**Campo**		
Novo Sancti Petri	16 7 7	953	Canyamel	15 6 6	901
Pedreña	14 6 5	958	Capdepera	15 7 6	902
Playa Serena	13 6 4	961	El Bosque	16 7 4	909
Sotogrande	18 7 6	974	Escorpion	13 8 4	915
			Guadalhorce	14 7 6	920
Bosque			Jarama R.A.C.E.	13 7 6	924
Club d'Aro (Mas Nou)	15 7 7	905	La Dehesa	14 7 4	927
Club de Campo	16 8 8	906	La Manga *Oeste*	14 7 7	930
El Saler	18 7 6	913	La Moraleja *La Moraleja 1*	15 7 8	932
Emporda	17 7 6	914	La Moraleja *La Moraleja 2*	16 7 8	933
Herreria	15 6 6	922	La Sella	15 6 5	935
Islantilla	16 8 8	923	Lauro	13 7 5	938
Lerma	17 7 4	939	Lerma	17 7 4	939
Maspalomas	16 7 8	945	Mediterraneo	16 7 6	946
Neguri	17 7 7	952	Mijas *Los Lagos*	16 6 7	947

TIPO DE RECORRIDOS

Tipo/ Recorrido	Nota	Página	Tipo/ Recorrido	Nota	Página
Mijas *Los Olivos*	13 6 7	948	**Parque**		
Montecastillo	17 8 7	950	Castillo de Gorraiz	17 7 7	903
Pula	13 6 5	964	Montenmedio	15 7 7	951
Son Antem	14 7 6	972	Pineda	15 7 9	960
Zaudin	16 7 6	979	Puerta de Hierro	16 8 9	963
Campo, bosque			**Urbano**		
Panoramica	14 6 4	957	Aloha	17 7 7	895
			Atalaya *Old Course*	13 6 7	896
llanura			Bendinat	13 6 7	897
Atalaya *Old Course*	13 6 7	896	Bonmont	16 7 6	899
Bonalba	14 6 6	898	Campoamor	14 6 6	900
El Paraiso	13 6 6	910	Castillo de Gorraiz	17 7 7	903
El Prat *Amarillo*	15 7 6	911	Costa Brava	13 7 7	907
Emporda	17 7 6	914	La Manga *Norte*	15 7 7	929
Fontanals	18 6 5	917	La Manga *Sur*	14 7 7	931
Granada	14 6 5	919	La Quinta	15 8 7	934
Guadalhorce	14 7 6	920	La Zagaleta	16 7 7	936
Guadalmina *Sur*	14 7 7	921	Los Naranjos	16 7 7	941
La Duquesa	13 7 6	928	Las Brisas	18 7 7	937
llanura			Panoramica	14 6 4	957
La Manga *Norte*	15 7 7	929	Sant Cugat	13 6 5	969
La Manga *Sur*	14 7 7	931	Santa Ponsa	13 6 7	970
Los Naranjos	16 7 7	941	Son Vida	14 6 7	973
Peralada	16 6 5	959	Zaudin	16 7 6	979
Poniente	13 6 5	962			
Rio Real	13 6 7	966	**Vagüada**		
Santa Ponsa	13 6 7	970	Aloha	17 7 7	895
Sevilla	17 7 8	971	Bendinat	13 6 7	897
Son Antem	14 7 6	972	Bonalba	14 6 6	898
Sotogrande	18 7 6	974	Bonmont	16 7 6	899
Villamartin	16 7 6	978	Campoamor	14 6 6	900
			Capdepera	15 7 6	902
Montaña			Cerdaña	14 7 7	904
Alhaurin	14 7 5	893	Costa Brava	13 7 7	907
Canyamel	15 6 6	901	Costa Dorada	13 6 6	908
Club d'Aro (Mas Nou)	15 7 7	905	El Paraiso	13 6 6	910
Estepona	14 7 6	916	Granada	14 6 5	919
Girona	13 7 5	918	La Duquesa	13 7 6	928
La Cala *Norte*	17 8 6	925	La Quinta	15 8 7	934
La Cala *Sur*	16 8 6	926	La Sella	15 6 5	935
La Zagaleta	16 7 7	936	Las Brisas	18 7 7	937
Los Arqueros	14 6 7	940	Los Arqueros	14 6 7	940
Masia Bach	15 7 6	944	Marbella	15 7 8	943
Monte Mayor	13 5 5	949	Mijas *Los Olivos*	13 6 7	948
			Osona Montanya	14 7 4	955

890

TIPO DE RECORRIDOS

Tipo/ Recorrido	Nota	Página	Tipo/ Recorrido	Nota	Página
Vagüada			Villamartin	16 7 6	978
R.S.H.E. Club de Campo	18 7 6	965			
San Roque	17 8 6	967	**Links**		
San Sebastián	14 6 6	968	El Saler	18 7 6	913
Sant Cugat	13 6 5	969			
Son Vida	14 6 7	973	**Urbano, vagüada**		
Torrequebrada	14 7 7	975	El Bosque	16 7 4	909
Valderrama	19 8 6	977			

ESTANCIA DE GOLF RECOMENDADA
RECOMMENDED GOLFING STAY

Recorrido	Nota	Página	Recorrido	Nota	Página
Almerimar	14 6 6	894	La Manga *Sur*	14 7 7	931
Aloha	17 7 7	895	La Moraleja *La Moraleja 1*	15 7 8	932
Canyamel	15 6 6	901	La Moraleja La Moraleja 2	16 7 8	933
Castillo de Gorraiz	17 7 7	903	La Quinta	15 8 7	934
Club de Campo	16 8 8	906	Las Brisas	18 7 7	937
El Prat *Amarillo*	15 7 6	911	Los Naranjos	16 7 7	941
El Prat *Verde*	17 7 6	912	Mediterraneo	16 7 6	946
El Saler	18 7 6	913	Mijas *Los Lagos*	16 6 7	947
Emporda	17 7 6	914	Mijas *Los Olivos*	13 6 7	948
Fontanals	18 6 5	917	Montecastillo	17 8 7	950
Guadalmina *Sur*	14 7 7	921	Neguri	17 7 7	952
Islantilla	16 8 8	923	Pals	16 7 6	956
La Cala *Norte*	17 8 6	925	San Roque	17 8 6	967
La Cala *Sur*	16 8 6	926	San Sebastián	14 6 6	968
La Dehesa	14 7 4	927	Sotogrande	18 7 6	974
La Manga *Norte*	15 7 7	929	Valderrama	19 8 6	977
La Manga *Oeste*	14 7 7	930	Villamartin	16 7 6	978

891

Es una pena que este recorrido no sea tan excepcional como su vista panorámica sobre el Mediterráneo y el Peñón de Gibraltar. Los arquitectos quisieron darle una fisionomía de links, pero el terreno no se prestaba por ser demasiado accidentado. Las mejoras recientemente realizadas lo han convertido en un poco más fácil para los amateurs, incluso de buen nivel. Es mejor no contar los golpes para pasar un día agradable en este recorrido estrecho y tortuoso, desconcertante a la hora de elegir el palo que hay que jugar con un viento siempre presente. Sin embargo puede resultar muy agradable jugar en match-play: emociones y sobresaltos garantizados, todo puede ocurrir... incluso "birdies". Los greens no son ni inmensos ni excesivamente complicados. Si es usted un jugador que pega largo y derecho, si sabe imprimir efecto a la bola, si posee una buena intuición y un buen juego corto, puede decirse que el golf de Alcaidesa está hecho para usted.

It is a pity that this course does not quite come up to the view it provides over the Mediterranean and the Rock of Gibraltar. The architects certainly tried to give it the physionomy of a links course, but the very broken terrain was only partly suited to such ambitions. The recent improvements made to the course make it only slightly easier, even for the more accomplished golfer. Don't bother counting your score if you want to spend a pleasant day on this narrow, twisting layout, which makes the choice of club a difficult business, especially when the never-abating wind is blowing. However, a round of match-play can be great fun, with excitement and the unexpected guaranteed. Anything can happen, even birdies. The greens are not huge and not too complicated, either. If you play long and straight, if you know how to work the ball both ways, if you have intuition and a good short game, then Alcaidesa is made for you.

Alcaidesa Links Golf Course

CN 340, km 124,6
E - 11315 LA LINEA (CADIZ)

Office	Secretaria	(34) 956 - 79 10 40
Pro shop	Pro-shop	(34) 956 - 79 10 40
Fax	Fax	(34) 956 - 79 10 41
Situation	Situación	

15 km Algeciras, 101 556 h.
10 km Gibraltar, 28 350 h.

Annual closure	Cierre anual	no
Weekly closure	Cierre semanal	no

Fees main season
Precios tempor. alta el campo

	Week days Semana	We/Bank holidays Fin de sem./fiestas
Individual Individual	8 000 Pts	8 000 Pts
Couple Pareja	16 000 Pts	16 000 Pts

Caddy	Caddy	no
Electric Trolley	Carro eléctrico	no
Buggy	Coche	5 000 Pts/18 hoyos
Clubs	Palos	2 000 Pts/18 hoyos

Credit cards Tarjetas de crédito
VISA - MasterCard - AMEX - DC

Access Acceso : Marbella → Estepona, Sotogrande →
Cadiz, Golf a la izquierda (km 124,6)
Map 7 on page 879 Plano 7 Página 879

GOLF COURSE
RECORRIDO

14/20

Site	Emplazamiento	
Maintenance	Mantenimiento	
Architect	Arquitecto	P. Alliss Clive Clark
Type	Tipo	al borde del mar
Relief	Relieve	
Water in play	Agua	
Exp. to wind	Exp. al viento	
Trees in play	Arboles	

Scorecard Tarjeta	Chp. Campeonato	Mens Caballeros	Ladies Damas
Length Longitud	5708	5385	4512
Par	71	71	71

Advised golfing ability	0	12	24	36
Nivel de juego aconsejado				

Hcp required	Handicap exigido	28 Cab., 36 Damas

CLUB HOUSE & AMENITIES
CLUB HOUSE Y DEPENDENCIAS

6/10

Pro shop	Pro-shop	
Driving range	Campo de prácticas	
Sheltered	cubierto	no
On grass	sobre hierba	si
Putting-green	putting-green	si
Pitching-green	pitching-green	si

HOTEL FACILITIES
HOTELES CERCANOS

5/10

HOTELS HOTELES
Soto Grande   Sotogrande
46 habitaciones, D 19 000 Pts   8 km
Tel (34) 956 - 79 43 86, Fax (34) 956 - 79 43 33

San Roque   San Roque
50 habitaciones, D 19 500 Pts   2 km
Tel (34) 956 - 61 30 30, Fax (34) 956 - 61 30 12

La Solana   San Roque
19 habitaciones, D 9 000 Pts   5 km
Tel (34) 956 - 78 02 36, Fax (34) 956 - 78 02 36

RESTAURANTS RESTAURANTE
Los Remos   San Roque
Tel (34) 956 - 69 84 12   5 km

Pedro   San Roque
Tel (34) 956 - 69 84 53   5 km

Al lado de Mijas, este ambicioso proyecto, aún no acabado, es prometedor, sobre todo teniendo en cuenta que la firma de Ballesteros es una excelente publicidad. En un magnífico entorno, con vistas espectaculares hacia la montaña, ha diseñado un recorrido bastante accidentado (a veces demasiado), que exige un juego preciso, aunque sólo sea para evitar algunos barrancos, e incluso el rough, a menudo en la línea de juego y muy osalvaje. Favorece a aquellos que juegan en "fade", por lo que los jugadores con tendencia al "slice" no se sentirán muy perjudicados. Un buen número de tees de salida permite adaptar el recorrido a todos los niveles de juego, pero los jugadores con poca experiencia tendrán problemas. Los obstáculos de agua dan a veces un aspecto americano a este diseño que a pesar de todo está en armonía con el paisaje. Hay que tener muy en cuenta el recorrido anejo de 18 hoyos reservado a los "junior", ... y a los padres si los niños les invitan!

Next door to Mijas, this ambitious and still incomplete resort promises a great deal, all the more so in that the label of Ballesteros is a commercial argument of the highest order. In a magnificent setting with spectacular views over mountains, Seve has designed a very, and sometimes too, hilly course, which demands precision golf, if only to avoid a number of precipices or even the rough, a frequent hazard and growing wild. It is a course for players who fade the ball, allowing the amateur slice more leeway than they might usually find. The many different tees make this a course for all levels, but inexperienced players will have problems. Water hazards sometimes give the layout a very American style, although the general character blends harmoniously with the setting. Worthy of note is the adjoining 18-hole course reserved for juniors, and their parents if invited by the kids!

Alhaurin Golf
Alhaurin El Grande
E - 29650 CTRA DE MIJAS KM 6 (MALAGA)

Office	Secretaria	(34) 95 - 259 59 70
Pro shop	Pro-shop	(34) 95 - 259 59 70
Fax	Fax	(34) 95 - 259 45 86
Situation	Situación	

15 km Fuengirola, 43 048 h., 3 km Alhaurin

Annual closure	Cierre anual	no
Weekly closure	Cierre semanal	no

Fees main season
Precios tempor. alta

	Week days Semana	We/Bank holidays Fin de sem./fiestas
Individual Individual	5 000 Pts	5 000 Pts
Couple Pareja	10 000 Pts	10 000 Pts

2 GF + 2 comidas + golf coche = 15 500 Pts

Caddy	Caddy	no
Electric Trolley	Carro eléctrico	1 700 Pts/18 hoyos
Buggy	Coche	3 200 Pts/18 hoyos
Clubs	Palos no	1 900 Pts/18 hoyos
Credit cards Tarjetas de crédito		VISA - AMEX

Alhaurín el Grande

0 2 4 km

GOLF

Mijas

E 15 N340

MALAGA

FUENGIROLA

Mijas Costa

MARBELLA

Access Acceso : Malaga → Marbella. Salida "Churiana", → Mijas → Alhaurín El Grande
Map 7 on page 879 Plano 7 Página 879

GOLF COURSE
RECORRIDO
14/20

Site	Emplazamiento	
Maintenance	Mantenimiento	
Architect	Arquitecto	Seve Ballesteros
Type	Tipo	montaña
Relief	Relieve	
Water in play	Agua	
Exp. to wind	Exp. al viento	
Trees in play	Arboles	

Scorecard Tarjeta	Chp. Campeonato	Mens Caballeros	Ladies Damas
Length Longitud	6221	5857	4941
Par	72	72	72

Advised golfing ability   0   12   24   36
Nivel de juego aconsejado

Hcp required	Handicap exigido	no

CLUB HOUSE & AMENITIES
CLUB HOUSE Y DEPENDENCIAS
7/10

Pro shop	Pro-shop	
Driving range	Campo de prácticas	
Sheltered	cubierto	
On grass	sobre hierba	si
Putting-green	putting-green	si
Pitching-green	pitching-green	no

HOTEL FACILITIES
HOTELES CERCANOS
5/10

HOTELS HOTELES
Hotel Alhaurin Golf   Alhaurin
38 habitaciones, D 14 800 Pts.
Tel (34) 95 - 259 58 00, Fax (34) 95 - 259 4195

Byblos   Fuengirola
144 habitaciones, D 37 500 Pts   12 km
Tel (34) 95 - 247 30 50, Fax (34) 95 - 247 67 83

Mijas   Mijas
97 habitaciones, D 14 000 Pts   6 km
Tel (34) 95 - 248 58 00, Fax (34) 95 - 248 58 25

RESTAURANTS RESTAURANTE
La Ventilla   Alhaurin
Tel (34) 95 - 259 58 00

Valparaiso   Cta de Fuengirola
Tel (34) 95 - 248 59 96   8 km

893

14	6	6

Situado en un zona urbanizada con toda clase de distracciones, colaboraron en su diseño Ron Kirby y Gary Player. Tiene una vegetación rica que, en contraste con el fondo de montañas áridas, da la impresión de un oasis. Ha sido comprado por una sociedad japonesa con la intención de transformar este complejo en uno de los grandes centros turísticos del sur de Europa. Sus calles anchas, sus bunkers grandes y sus amplios obstáculos de agua en la línea de juego en una media docena de hoyos, dan a este recorrido un incontestable estilo de inspiración americana. Su longitud puede parecer importante desde cualquiera de los tees de salida, pero las bolas por lo general ruedan bastante. El punto álgido del recorrido se encuentra en el hoyo 12, un par 3, más bien largo, con el green en medio de una isla y que intimidará a muchos jugadores !.

Located in a built-up area where there are all sorts of leisure facilities, this course was designed at a period when Ron Kirby and Gary Player were working together. Lush vegetation affords a pleasant, oasis-style contrast with the arid mountains in the background. The course has been taken over by a Japanese group, which is keen to transform the complex into one of the biggest tourist resorts in southern Europe. With wide fairways, large bunkers and huge water hazards in play on half a dozen holes, the course is unquestionably American in style. It may seem a little long, whichever tee you use, but the ball generally rolls a long way here. The highlight of the course is the 12th hole, a rather long par 3 with an island green. A daunting prospect for many a player.

Golf Almerimar S.L.

Urb. Almerimar
E - 04700 EL EJIDO - ALMERIA

Office	Secretaria	(34) 950 - 49 74 54
Pro shop	Pro-shop	(34) 950 - 49 74 54
Fax	Fax	(34) 950 - 49 72 33
Situation	Situación	

10 km El Ejido, 41 700 h.
32 km Almería, 159 587 h.

Annual closure	Cierre anual	no
Weekly closure	Cierre semanal	

Fees main season
Precios tempor. alta El dia

	Week days Semana	We/Bank holidays Fin de sem./fiestas
Individual Individual	5 500 Pts	5 500 Pts
Couple Pareja	11 000 Pts	11 000 Pts

Caddy	Caddy	si, reservar
Electric Trolley	Carro eléctrico	no
Buggy	Coche	3 500 Pts/18 hoyos
Clubs	Palos	2 000 Pts/18 hoyos

Credit cards Tarjetas de crédito
VISA - MasterCard - AMEX

894

El Ejido N 340
ALMERÍA →
Matagorda
GOLF
Roquetas de Mar
Almerimar
Salinas
0 2 4 km

Access Acceso : Almería N340 → El Ejido, Almerimar
Map 8 on page 881 Plano 8 Página 881

GOLF COURSE
RECORRIDO
14/20

Site	Emplazamiento	
Maintenance	Mantenimiento	
Architect	Arquitecto	Gary Player Ron Kirby
Type	Tipo	al borde del mar
Relief	Relieve	
Water in play	Agua	
Exp. to wind	Exp. al viento	
Trees in play	Arboles	

Scorecard Tarjeta	Chp. Campeonato	Mens Caballeros	Ladies Damas
Length Longitud	5981	5892	5101
Par	72	72	72

Advised golfing ability		0 12 24 36
Nivel de juego aconsejado		
Hcp required	Handicap exigido	28 Cab., 36 Damas

CLUB HOUSE & AMENITIES
CLUB HOUSE Y DEPENDENCIAS
6/10

Pro shop	Pro-shop	
Driving range	Campo de prácticas	
Sheltered	cubierto	no
On grass	sobre hierba	si
Putting-green	putting-green	si
Pitching-green	pitching-green	no

HOTEL FACILITIES
HOTELES CERCANOS
6/10

HOTELS HOTELES
Golf Hotel Almerimar — Golf
147 habitaciones, D 10 500 Pts — 400 m
Tel (34) 950 - 49 70 50, Fax (34) 950 - 49 70 19

Porto Magno — Aguadulce
400 habitaciones, D 16 800 Pts. — 35 km
Tel (34) 950 - 34 22 16, Fax (34) 950 - 34 29 65

Costasol Hotel — Almería
55 habitaciones, D 10 000 Pts. — 30 km
Tel (34) 950 - 23 40 11, Fax (34) 950 - 23 40 11

RESTAURANTS RESTAURANTE
El Segoviano — Almerimar
Tel (34) 950 - 48 00 84 — 10 km

El Bello Rincón — Ctra de Almería
Tel (34) 950 - 23 84 27 — 25 km

Ya desde su apertura sedujo este recorrido diseñado por Javier Arana y las recientes obras efectuadas lo han mejorado aún más. Aquí es primordial la precisión de los golpes, sobre todo los de salida: Aloha no es un recorrido muy largo, pero sí a veces estrecho y accidentado. Los árboles son a menudo peligrosos, ciertos greens son ciegos, otros en alto, pero que ruedan siempre bien. Por tanto hay que permanecer constantemente atento, sobre todo para pegar a la bola con efecto en cualquier dirección. Con su original diseño, este recorrido deja una impresión de gran armonía e inteligente utilización golfística del terreno, sobre todo en tres hoyos de gran calidad: el 1, el 12 y el 18. Algunas inclinaciones naturales del campo pueden ser peligrosas, al igual que muchos obstáculos de agua, sobre todo a la vuelta. Agradable y bien decorado, Aloha es una excelente test de golf y un lugar donde no se cansa uno de jugar.

This course, designed by Javier Arana, was an attractive proposition from the first day it opened, and recent work has helped to improve the overall layout. It is important here to place your shots carefully, especially off the tee. Aloha is not a very long course, but it is sometimes tight and hilly; the trees are often dangerous and a number of greens are blind, multi-tiered and very fast. You have to keep your wits about you all the time, especially when trying to work the ball in all directions. Although an original layout, Aloha leaves an impression of harmony and intelligent use of terrain from a golfing point of view, especially on holes 1, 12 and 18, all three excellent. A number of natural banks can cause problems, as can several water hazards, particularly on the back nine. Pleasant to play and well laid out, Aloha is an excellent test of golf which is always a pleasure to play.

Club de Golf Aloha
Nueva Andalucia
E - 29660 MARBELLA (MALAGA)

Office	Secretaria	(34) 95 - 281 37 50
Pro shop	Pro-shop	(34) 95 - 281 47 55
Fax	Fax	(34) 95 - 281 23 89
Situation	Situación	

3 km San Pedro de Alcantara
7 km Marbella, 84 410 h.

Annual closure	Cierre anual	no
Weekly closure	Cierre semanal	no

Fees main season
Precios tempor. alta el campo

	Week days Semana	We/Bank holidays Fin de sem./fiestas
Individual Individual	15 000 Pts	15 000 Pts
Couple Pareja	30 000 Pts	30 000 Pts

Caddy	Caddy	4 000 Pts
Electric Trolley	Carro eléctrico	1 500 Pts
Buggy	Coche	5 000 Pts/18 hoyos
Clubs	Palos	2 000 Pts/18 hoyos

Credit cards Tarjetas de crédito
VISA - Eurocard - MasterCard - AMEX - JCB

Access Acceso : Marbella → Cadiz. Nueva Andalucia km 180, a la derecha → Golf
Map 7 on page 879 Plano 7 Página 879

GOLF COURSE
RECORRIDO — 17 /20

Site	Emplazamiento	
Maintenance	Mantenimiento	
Architect	Arquitecto	Javier Araña
Type	Tipo	urbano, vagüada
Relief	Relieve	
Water in play	Agua	
Exp. to wind	Exp. al viento	
Trees in play	Arboles	

Scorecard Tarjeta	Chp. Campeonato	Mens Caballeros	Ladies Damas
Length Longitud	6242	5936	5167
Par	72	72	72

Advised golfing ability	0	12	24	36
Nivel de juego aconsejado				

Hcp required Handicap exigido 28 Cab., 36 Damas

CLUB HOUSE & AMENITIES
CLUB HOUSE Y DEPENDENCIAS — 7 /10

Pro shop	Pro-shop	
Driving range	Campo de prácticas	
Sheltered	cubierto	no
On grass	sobre hierba	si
Putting-green	putting-green	si
Pitching-green	pitching-green	no

895

HOTEL FACILITIES
HOTELES CERCANOS — 7 /10

HOTELS HOTELES

Andalucia Plaza   Nueva Andalucia
415 habitaciones, D 29 000 Pts   4 km
Tel (34) 95 - 281 20 00, Fax (34) 95 - 281 47 92

Puente Romano   Marbella, Cta de Cádiz
217 habitaciones, D 49 500 Pts.   2 km
Tel (34) 95 - 282 09 00, Fax (34) 95 - 277 57 66

Pyr Hotel   Puerto Banus
319 habitaciones, D 15 000 Pts   2 km
Tel (34) 95 - 281 73 53, Fax (34) 95 - 281 79 07

RESTAURANTS RESTAURANTE

Cypriano   Puerto Banús
Tel (34) 95 - 281 10 77   5 km

Taberna del Alabardero   Puerto Banús
Tel (34) 95 - 281 27 94   5 km

El más que aceptable 18 hoyos «Rosner» es sin duda más difícil que éste, pero es demasiado acidentado y todo el mundo no tiene el presupuesto - o el deseo - para añadir al green-fee el precio de un coche eléctrico casi obligatorio si no se quiere terminar a cuatro patas. Este campo es mucho más plano, y pese a no estar entre las mejores realizaciones de la región, posee suficientes cualidades como para justificar una visita. Tal vez los buenos jugadores encuentren que sus dificultades son escasas, pero el golfista medio, sobre todo si está de vacaciones, pensará que son más que suficientes. Las calles son anchas, los greenes rápidos y bastante ondulados lo que exige mucho a la hora de patear. Como los obstáculos son muy visibles, la estrategia es clara y eso puede conducir a conseguir un buen resultado en la primera visita. Si preferimos divertir nos antes que concentrarnos, el match play es muy agradable. Siendo el terreno muy arcilloso es preferible evitar las épocas de lluvias.

The very fortright "New" 18 hole course is unquestionably tougher than this one, but it is very hilly and not everyone has the budget (or inclination) to supplement their green-fee with the virtually compulsory buggy (if you don't want to end up crawling home on all fours, that is). This layout is much flatter, and without attaining the standard of some other courses in the region, it has enough going for it to warrant a visit. While the experts might find the challenge a little limited, the average hacker will certainly find it quite enough to handle... if they are in the holiday mood. The fairways are wide and the greens rather sharply contoured and quick, so putting requires careful consideration. Since the hazards are clearly visible, game strategy is clear and you might even attempt to card a good score first time out. If you prefer having fun to concentrating, match-play is an enjoyable solution. The terrain contains a lot of clay, so avoid rainy days.

Atalaya Golf & Country Club

Ctra de Benahavis km. 0.7 - San Pedro
E - 29680 ESTEPONA (MALAGA)

Office	Secretaria	(34) 95 - 288 28 12
Pro shop	Pro-shop	(34) 95 - 288 81 42
Fax	Fax	(34) 95 - 288 78 97
Situation	Situación	

12 km Estepona, 36 307 h.
3 km San Pedro de Alcantara

Annual closure	Cierre anual	no
Weekly closure	Cierre semanal	no

Fees main season
Precios tempor. alta el campo

	Week days Semana	We/Bank holidays Fin de sem./fiestas
Individual Individual	7 500 Pts	7 500 Pts
Couple Pareja	15 000 Pts	15 000 Pts

Caddy	Caddy	no
Electric Trolley	Carro eléctrico	no
Buggy	Coche	5 000 Pts/18 hoyos
Clubs	Palos	4 000 Pts/el dia

Credit cards Tarjetas de crédito   VISA - AMEX

Access Acceso : Marbella → Estepona
Map 7 on page 879 Plano 7 Página 879

GOLF COURSE
RECORRIDO

13/20

Site	Emplazamiento	▰▰▰▰
Maintenance	Mantenimiento	▰▰▰▰
Architect	Arquitecto	B. Von Limburger
Type	Tipo	llanura, urbano
Relief	Relieve	
Water in play	Agua	
Exp. to wind	Exp. al viento	▰▰▰
Trees in play	Arboles	▰▰▰

Scorecard Tarjeta	Chp. Campeonato	Mens Caballeros	Ladies Damas
Length Longitud	6142	5856	5188
Par	72	72	72

Advised golfing ability		0	12	24	36
Nivel de juego aconsejado					

Hcp required	Handicap exigido	28 Cab., 36 Damas

CLUB HOUSE & AMENITIES
CLUB HOUSE Y DEPENDENCIAS

6/10

Pro shop	Pro-shop	▰▰▰
Driving range	Campo de prácticas	▰▰▰
Sheltered	cubierto	no
On grass	sobre hierba	si
Putting-green	putting-green	si
Pitching-green	pitching-green	si

HOTEL FACILITIES
HOTELES CERCANOS

7/10

HOTELS HOTELES

Atalaya Park		Estepona
448 habitaciones, D 24 000 Pts		1,5 km
Tel (34) 95 - 288 48 01, Fax (34) 95 - 288 57 35		
El Paraiso		Estepona
182 habitaciones, D 25 725 Pts		3 km
Tel (34) 95 - 288 30 00, Fax (34) 95 - 288 20 19		
Guadalmina		San Pedro
80 habitaciones, D 25 850 Pts		4 km
Tel (34) 95 - 288 22 11, Fax (34) 95 - 288 22 91		

RESTAURANTS RESTAURANTE

El Gamonal	San Pedro de Alcantara	
Tel (34) 95 - 278 99 21	4 km	
Los Nieto	San Pedro de Alcantara	
Tel (34) 95 - 288 34 91	3 km	

896

Agrandado en 1995, Bendinat sigue siendo un recorrido muy corto en el que los desniveles impiden apreciar bien las distancias, especialmente a la hora de atacar unos green a menudo en alto y bien diseñados por el arquitecto Martin Hawtree. Sin embargo el diseño de los bunkers y calles no son muy originales. Conviene ser prudente cuando se juega por primera vez ya que es difícil encontrar las bolas que se salen de calle. En el primer hoyo ya uno se da cuenta que no será fácil obtener un buen resultado. No obstante resulta muy divertido jugar en match-play incluso entre jugadores de diferentes niveles. El relieve del campo aconseja alquilar un coche, sobre todo si hace calor. Bien es verdad que la proximidad del mar refresca un poco, pero el viento puede ser molesto. No es un golf inolvidable, pero merece la pena conocerlo.

Enlarged in 1995, Bendinat is still a very short course, although the steep slopes do tend to confuse appreciation of distance, an important factor here to hit a number of elevated greens, well designed by designer Martin Hawtree. Unfortunately, the bunkers and fairways are not quite in the same class. Your first round will require a cautious approach, as balls that leave the fairway are never easy to find. From the very first hole, you can tell that a good score here is quite some achievement. It is, though, fun to play in match-play, even with players of different abilities. This hilly course calls for a buggy, especially in hot weather, although the sea close-by brings a welcome cooling breeze, and wind that can cause a few upsets on the course. Bendinat is hardly unforgettable, but is worth a visit.

Real Club de Bendinat

Campoamor S/N
E - 07181 CALVIA - MALLORCA

Office	Secretaria	(34) 971- 40 52 00
Pro shop	Pro-shop	(34) 971- 40 54 50
Fax	Fax	(34) 971- 70 07 86
Situation	Situación	

7 km Palma, 308 616 h.

Annual closure	Cierre anual	no
Weekly closure	Cierre semanal	no

Fees main season
Precios tempor. alta el campo

	Week days Semana	We/Bank holidays Fin de sem./fiestas
Individual Individual	7 500 Pts	7 500 Pts
Couple Pareja	15 000 Pts	15 000 Pts

Caddy	Caddy	no
Electric Trolley	Carro eléctrico	no
Buggy	Coche	5 000 Pts/18 hoyos
Clubs	Palos	2 000 Pts/18 hoyos

Credit cards Tarjetas de crédito
VISA - Eurocard - MasterCard - AMEX

Access Acceso : Palma → Bendinat, Golf entre Illetas y Portals Nous
Map 9 on page 883 Plano 9 Página 883

GOLF COURSE
RECORRIDO

13/20

Site	Emplazamiento	
Maintenance	Mantenimiento	
Architect	Arquitecto	Fred Hawtree
Type	Tipo	urbano, vagüada
Relief	Relieve	
Water in play	Agua	
Exp. to wind	Exp. al viento	
Trees in play	Arboles	

Scorecard Tarjeta	Chp. Campeonato	Mens Caballeros	Ladies Damas
Length Longitud	5650	5650	4990
Par	70	70	70

Advised golfing ability Nivel de juego aconsejado	0	12	24	36
Hcp required	Handicap exigido		27 Cab., 35 Damas	

CLUB HOUSE & AMENITIES
CLUB HOUSE Y DEPENDENCIAS

6/10

Pro shop	Pro-shop	
Driving range	Campo de prácticas	
Sheltered	cubierto	no
On grass	sobre hierba	si
Putting-green	putting-green	si
Pitching-green	pitching-green	si

897

HOTEL FACILITIES
HOTELES CERCANOS

7/10

HOTELS HOTELES
Bendinat   Bendinat
32 habitaciones, D 30 000 Pts.   2 km
Tel (34) 971 - 67 57 25, Fax (34) 971 - 67 72 76

Punta Negra   Palmanova
69 habitaciones, D 24 000 Pts.   3 km
Tel (34) 971 - 68 07 62, Fax (34) 971 - 68 39 19

Son Caliu   Palmanova
235 habitaciones, D 22 000 Pts   3 km
Tel (34) 971 - 68 22 00, Fax (34) 971 - 68 37 20

RESTAURANTS RESTAURANTE
Binnacle   Portals Nous
Tel (34) 971 - 67 69 77   5 km

BONALBA

Confirma la clase de Ramón Espinosa. Bonalba a pesar de su corta existencia es un recorrido que hay que conocer. La diversidad de los hoyos y la variedad de golpes que hay que jugar constituye un desafío para los más técnicos que tendrán que evitar numerosos laguitos, en línea de juego en una buena mitad del recorrido, que aparecen después de los primeros hoyos que sirven de precalentamiento. Pero no hay que dejarse impresionar por esas dificultades: con tees de salida adelantados, resultará divertido para cualquier jugador. Sólo los buenos pegadores escogerán las salidas de atrás, donde la longitud y colocación de los obstáculos dan al recorrido su verdadera fisionomía. No obstante, para emitir un juicio más definitivo hay que esperar que la vegetación se desarrolle: se han plantado 3.000 árboles, especialmente palmeras. Pero ya desde ahora es un recorrido que merece la pena conocer.

This is definitely a Ramon Espinosa layout which, despite its tender years, is a course worth knowing. The variety between holes and shots makes this a good challenge for technicans, who like the rest have to negotiate a number of small lakes, in play on half the holes, especially at the beginning. Thereafter the going gets a little easier. But don't be put off by the water; if they play from the front tees, players of all abilities can get along together here. Only the big-hitters will prefer the back-tees, where the length of the layout and position of hazards give the course its true physionomy. To really judge, though, we'll wait until the plants and trees start to grow. Some 3,000 were planted, especially palm trees, but this is already a course well worth knowing about.

Club de Golf Bonalba

Partida de Bonalba S/N
E - 03110 MUCHAMIEL-ALICANTE

Office	Secretaria	(34) 96 - 597 05 11
Pro shop	Pro-shop	(34) 96 - 596 03 31
Fax	Fax	(34) 96 - 596 05 05
Situation	Situación	

15 km Alicante, 275 111 h.

Annual closure	Cierre anual	no
Weekly closure	Cierre semanal	no

Fees main season
Precios tempor. alta El campo

	Week days Semana	We/Bank holidays Fin de sem./fiestas
Individual Individual	4 500 Pts	5 000 Pts
Couple Pareja	9 000 Pts	10 000 Pts

Caddy	Caddy	no
Electric Trolley	Carro eléctrico	1 200 Pts
Buggy	Coche	3 000 Pts/18 hoyos
Clubs	Palos	1 500 Pts/18 hoyos

Credit cards Tarjetas de crédito
VISA - MasterCard - AMEX

898

Access Acceso : A7 → Alicante, salida 67 → Alcoy →
Busot → Golf
Map 6 on page 877 Plano 6 Página 877

GOLF COURSE
RECORRIDO
14/20

Site	Emplazamiento	■■■■■
Maintenance	Mantenimiento	■■■■■
Architect	Arquitecto	Ramón Espinosa
Type	Tipo	llanura, vagüada
Relief	Relieve	■■■■
Water in play	Agua	■■■■
Exp. to wind	Exp. al viento	■■■■
Trees in play	Arboles	■■

Scorecard Tarjeta	Chp. Campeonato	Mens Caballeros	Ladies Damas
Length Longitud	6367	6096	5483
Par	72	72	72

Advised golfing ability		0	12	24	36
Nivel de juego aconsejado					

Hcp required   Handicap exigido   28 Cab., 36 Damas

CLUB HOUSE & AMENITIES
CLUB HOUSE Y DEPENDENCIAS
6/10

Pro shop	Pro-shop	■■■■
Driving range	Campo de prácticas	■■■■
Sheltered	cubierto	no
On grass	sobre hierba	no
Putting-green	putting-green	si
Pitching-green	pitching-green	si

HOTEL FACILITIES
HOTELES CERCANOS
6/10

HOTELS HOTELES
Meliá Alicante   Alicante
540 habitaciones, D 20 400 Pts.   15 km
Tel (34) 96 - 520 50 00, Fax (34) 96 - 520 47 56

San Juan   Campello
29 habitaciones, D 7 500 Pts.   2 km
Tel (34) 96 - 565 23 08, Fax (34) 96 - 565 26 42

Villa San Juan   San Juan de Alicante
40 habitaciones, D 7 500 Pts.   3 km
Tel (34) 96 - 565 23 08, Fax (34) 96 - 565 26 42

RESTAURANTS RESTAURANTE
El Patio de San Juan   San Juan de Alicante
Tel (34) 96 - 565 68 00   3 km

La Maestra   San Juan de Alicante
Tel (34) 96 - 565 85 60   3 km

Las dificultades económicas han frenado la expansión de este golf residencial y si el recorrido estuviese mejor cuidado se le podría atribuir una mejor nota. Robert Trent Jones Jr, siguiendo la tradición de su padre, ha creado un diseño muy estratégico en el que constantemente hay que calcular los riesgos antes de jugar. Lo ha construido con un refinamiento estético muy personal, removiendo grandes cantidades de tierra, tarea indispensable para poder jugar en un terreno tan rocoso. Construido alrededor del "Barranco", una especie de riachuelo omnipresente y protegido por numerosos bunkers, el recorrido presenta dificultades bien diseminadas y permite un buen ritmo de juego, especialmente a los jugadores con experiencia, ya que a los demás les costará bastante jugar su handicap. Los greens son amplios y bien diseñados, algunos tienen múltiples escalones, pero ninguno es ciego. Sin caer en la exageración y teniendo en cuenta las cuestas, se aconseja alquilar un coche.

Financial problems have jeopardised the expansion of this residential course and better green-keeping would certainly have meant a higher score. In the family tradition, Robert Trent Jones Jnr. has designed a highly strategic layout, where risks constantly need calculating before each shot. He has modeled space in his very own tasteful and stylish way, but also with impressive contouring of the land. And this was necessary for this rocky terrain to be at all playable. Revolving around the "Barocco", a sort of omnipresent wadi, and defended by numerous bunkers, the course has an even spread of hazards to provide good golf at a good pace. At least for experienced players, as the less proficient golfer will have a problem playing to his handicap. The greens are huge and very well designed; some have several tiers, but none is blind. Without being too steep, the course is hilly enough to advise taking a buggy.

Bonmont - Terres Noves
E - 43300 MONTROIG DEL CAMP (TARRAGONA)

Office	Secretaria	(34) 977 - 81 81 40
Pro shop	Pro-shop	(34) 977 - 81 81 40
Fax	Fax	(34) 977 - 81 81 46
Situation	Situación	

6 km Hospitalet del Infante, 2 690 h.
15 km Cambrils, 14 903 h.

Annual closure	Cierre anual	no
Weekly closure	Cierre semanal	no

Fees main season
Precios tempor. alta El dia

	Week days Semana	We/Bank holidays Fin de sem./fiestas
Individual Individual	4 800 Pts	6 500 Pts
Couple Pareja	9 600 Pts	13 000 Pts

Caddy	Caddy	no
Electric Trolley	Carro eléctrico	no
Buggy	Coche	4 000 Pts/18 hoyos
Clubs	Palos	3 000 Pts/18 hoyos

Credit cards Tarjetas de crédito
VISA - Eurocard - MasterCard - AMEX - DC

Access Acceso : A7 Barcelona → Valencia, salida 38.
Hospitalet del Infante → Mora, 2 km → Mont Roig,
Golf 4 km
Map 4 on page 873 Plano 4 Página 873

GOLF COURSE
RECORRIDO 16/20

Site	Emplazamiento	
Maintenance	Mantenimiento	
Architect	Arquitecto	R. Trent Jones Jr
Type	Tipo	urbano, vagüada
Relief	Relieve	
Water in play	Agua	
Exp. to wind	Exp. al viento	
Trees in play	Arboles	

Scorecard Tarjeta	Chp. Campeonato	Mens Caballeros	Ladies Damas
Length Longitud	6371	6050	5501
Par	72	72	72

Advised golfing ability   0   12   24   36
Nivel de juego aconsejado
Hcp required   Handicap exigido   28 Cab., 36 Damas

CLUB HOUSE & AMENITIES
CLUB HOUSE Y DEPENDENCIAS 7/10

Pro shop	Pro-shop	
Driving range	Campo de prácticas	
Sheltered	cubierto	no
On grass	sobre hierba	si
Putting-green	putting-green	si
Pitching-green	pitching-green	si

899

HOTEL FACILITIES
HOTELES CERCANOS 6/10

HOTELS HOTELES

Pino Alto	Hospitalet del Infante
137 habitaciones, D 16 400 Pts.	6 km
Tel (34) 977 - 81 10 00, Fax (34) 977 - 81 09 07	

Bonmont	Golf
9 habitaciones, D 16 800 Pts.	500 m
Tel (34) 977 - 81 81 40, Fax (34) 977 - 81 81 46	

Termes Montbrio	Montbrio
133 habitaciones, D 17 900 Pts.	8 km
Tel (34) 977 - 81 40 00, Fax (34) 977 - 82 62 51	

RESTAURANTS RESTAURANTE

Can Bosch	Cambrils
Tel (34) 977 - 36 00 19	15 km

Casa Gatell	Cambrils
Tel (34) 977 - 36 00 57	15 km

La belleza del lugar anuncia una agradable jornada en medio de un paisaje con poco arbolado en el que predomina la vegetación de monte. Es un recorrido no muy accidentado con una longitud que gustará a los pegadores que podrán intentar llegar a green en dos pares 4 muy cortos (el 11 y el 13) y ganar puntos en los pares 5. El diseño de Sanz y García no denota una gran imaginación ya que lo que han intentado ante todo es agradar a todos los jugadores, logrando un recorrido muy funcional. Con greens correctos y poco protegidos se pueden obtener buenos resultados que agradarán a los jugadores. Bien es verdad que se pueden encontrar en la región recorridos más difíciles, pero Campoamor es un buen test para afinar su juego sin demasiadas dificultades. Un verdadero recorrido para las vacaciones.

A very pretty site heralds a pleasant day's golfing in rather open countryside, where the garrigue shrub is the main and most attractive form of vegetation. The course is not hilly, and the length will appeal to big-hitters, who can try and reach two very short par 4s (the 11th and 13th) from the tee and pick up points on the par 5s. The Sanz and Garcia layout has nothing exceptionally imaginative about it, but their aim was to appeal to players, so the course's functional side is a positive point. The greens are good but have few bunkers, and the opportunities are there to card a good score, always a welcome treat for the wounded ego. You can certainly find more challenging courses than this in the region, but Campoamor is a great place to sharpen up your game without too many mishaps. A real holiday course.

Real Club de Golf Campoamor

Ctra de Torrevieja a Cartagena, km 9
E - 03192 DEHESA DE CAMPOAMOR - ORIHUELA
(ALICANTE)

Office	Secretaria	(34) 96 - 532 13 66
Pro shop	Pro-shop	(34) 96 - 532 13 66
Fax	Fax	(34) 96 - 530 24 54
Situation	Situación	

57 km Alicante, 275 111 h.
8 km Torrevieja, 25 891 h.

Annual closure	Cierre anual	no
Weekly closure	Cierre semanal	no

Fees main season
Precios tempor. alta El campo

	Week days Semana	We/Bank holidays Fin de sem./fiestas
Individual Individual	5 000 Pts	5 000 Pts
Couple Pareja	8 000 Pts	8 000 Pts

Damas GF 3500 Pts

Caddy	Caddy	no
Electric Trolley	Carro eléctrico	1 200 Pts
Buggy	Coche	4 000 Pts/el dia
Clubs	Palos	1 500 Pts/el dia

Credit cards Tarjetas de crédito   no

900

Access Acceso : N332 Torrevieja → Dehesa de
Campoamor, Cabo Roig, km 48 → Golf
Map 6 on page 877 Plano 6 Página 877

GOLF COURSE
RECORRIDO   **14**/20

Site	Emplazamiento	
Maintenance	Mantenimiento	
Architect	Arquitecto	Gregorio Sanz Carmelo Garcia
Type	Tipo	urbano, vagüada
Relief	Relieve	
Water in play	Agua	
Exp. to wind	Exp. al viento	
Trees in play	Arboles	

Scorecard Tarjeta	Chp. Campeonato	Mens Caballeros	Ladies Damas
Length Longitud	6203	6056	5094
Par	72	72	72

Advised golfing ability		0 12 24 36
Nivel de juego aconsejado		
Hcp required	Handicap exigido	28 Cab., 36 Damas

CLUB HOUSE & AMENITIES
CLUB HOUSE Y DEPENDENCIAS   **6**/10

Pro shop	Pro-shop	
Driving range	Campo de prácticas	
Sheltered	cubierto	no
On grass	sobre hierba	si
Putting-green	putting-green	si
Pitching-green	pitching-green	si

HOTEL FACILITIES
HOTELES CERCANOS   **6**/10

HOTELS HOTELES

Torrejoven   Torrevieja
105 habitaciones, D 8 400 Pts.   4 km
Tel (34) 96 - 571 40 52, Fax (34) 96 - 571 53 15

Orihuela Costa   La Zenia
15 habitaciones, D 14 000 Pts   8 km
Tel (34) 96 - 676 08 00, Fax (34) 96 - 676 13 26

Meridional   Guardamar del Segura
52 habitaciones, D 12 300 Pts   20 km
Tel (34) 96 - 572 83 40, Fax (34) 96 - 572 83 06

RESTAURANTS RESTAURANTE

Cabo Roig   Torrevieja
Tel (34) 96 - 676 02 90   8 km

Morales   Los Montesinos
Tel (34) 96 - 672 12 93

Emplazado dentro de un paisaje típico de la montaña mallorquina, es un éxito de José Gancedo el haber conseguido realizar algunos hoyos espectaculares en la parte más accidentada (los nueve hoyos de la ida). Se ha preservado la naturaleza, así como algunas tapias e incluso una antigua granja que delimita el ángulo del dog-leg del hoyo 9. Al igual que en otros golfs de la isla hay que reflexionar antes de atacar, logrando muchas veces mejores resultados si se juega la seguridad y se sabe evitar las dificultades. Mejor es preservar sus fuerzas para atacar unos greens a menudo en alto, con escalones y bien protegidos. Su longitud es razonable y hay que juagarlo varias veces para mejor apreciar la progresión de los resultados. No se aburre uno.

In a typical setting of Majorcan countryside and mountains, Canyamel is a pretty little number designed by José Gancedo. The hillier part of the course (the front 9) includes some quite spectacular holes. The land's natural beauty has been preserved, together with some low walls and even an old farmhouse marking the corner of the dog-leg on hole N° 9. As with many other courses on the island, this is not a layout to attack without thinking first. Playing safe often gives better results. If you keep out of trouble, the going is easier and you can save your strength (important here) to negotiate some tricky approach shots to elevated, multi-tiered and well-defended greens. Very human in length, Canyamel is a course you want to play several times, not to understand it (it has little to hide) but to enjoy getting your score down. Good fun all the way.

Canyamel Golf

Carretera de las Cuevas s/n
E - 07589 CAPDEPERA MALLORCA

Office	Secretaria	(34) 971 - 84 13 13
Pro shop	Pro-shop	(34) 971 - 84 13 13
Fax	Fax	(34) 971 - 56 53 80
Situation	Situación	

76 km Palma, 308 616 h.

Annual closure	Cierre anual	no
Weekly closure	Cierre semanal	no

Fees main season
Precios tempor. alta el campo

	Week days Semana	We/Bank holidays Fin de sem./fiestas
Individual Individual	7 500 Pts	7 500 Pts
Couple Pareja	15 000 Pts	15 000 Pts

Caddy	Caddy	no
Electric Trolley	Carro eléctrico	no
Buggy	Coche	5 000 Pts/18 hoyos
Clubs	Palos	2 500 Pts/18 hoyos

Credit cards Tarjetas de crédito
VISA - MasterCard

Access Acceso : C715 Palma → Manacor → Artá → Cala Rajada
Map 9 on page 882 Plano 9 Página 882

GOLF COURSE
RECORRIDO

15/20

Site	Emplazamiento	
Maintenance	Mantenimiento	
Architect	Arquitecto	J. Gancedo
Type	Tipo	campo, montaña
Relief	Relieve	
Water in play	Agua	
Exp. to wind	Exp. al viento	
Trees in play	Arboles	

Scorecard Tarjeta	Chp. Campeonato	Mens Caballeros	Ladies Damas
Length Longitud	6017	5841	5393
Par	73	73	73

Advised golfing ability Nivel de juego aconsejado	0	12	24	36
Hcp required Handicap exigido	27 Cab., 35 Damas			

CLUB HOUSE & AMENITIES
CLUB HOUSE Y DEPENDENCIAS

6/10

Pro shop	Pro-shop	
Driving range	Campo de prácticas	
Sheltered	cubierto	no
On grass	sobre hierba	si
Putting-green	putting-green	si
Pitching-green	pitching-green	si

901

HOTEL FACILITIES
HOTELES CERCANOS

6/10

HOTELS HOTELES
Aguait — Cala Rajada
188 habitaciones, D 14 700 Pts. — 15 km
Tel (34) 971 - 56 34 08, Fax (34) 971 - 56 51 06

Canyamel Park — Capdepera
133 habitaciones, D 14 000 Pts. — 1 km
Tel (34) 971 - 56 55 11, Fax (34) 971 - 56 56 14

S'Entrador Playa — Cala Guya
207 habitaciones, D 12 000 Pts — 8 km
Tel (34) 971 - 56 43 12, Fax (34) 971 - 56 45 17

RESTAURANTS RESTAURANTE
Ses Rotjes — Cala Rajada
Tel (34) 971 - 56 31 08 — 15 km

Los Pablos — Capdepera
Tel (34) 971 - 56 55 43 — 5 km

Es una obra de Dan Maples que ha trabajado mucho en Carolina del Norte y en Florida. De hecho los seis lagos le dan un aire de estilo americano sin desfigurar el paisaje natural. Desde las salidas de atrás es un excelente recorrido de competición que se puede "dulcificar" escogiendo tees de salida más avanzados, logrando así que las calles parezcan menos estrechas. Tiene muchos bunkers y bosques de los que es difícil salir. Hay que saber manejar bien todos los palos, sin olvidar el pat en unos greens bastante grandes y con ondulaciones nada fáciles de apreciar. Si a la belleza de algunas vistas hacia la montaña añadimos la calidad de los cuidados de mantenimiento, comprenderemos mejor por qué Capdepera se sitúa entre los mejores recorridos de Mallorca.

This is one of the few courses in Europe designed by Dan Maples, who has worked extensively in North Carolina and Florida. The American style is evident with the six artificial lakes, which in no way upset the natural look of the landscape and terrain. This is an excellent tournament course from the back-tees and one which gradually mellows as you move further forward. From the front, the course doesn't look as tight, and the many bunkers and tough undergrowth seem less harrowing. You will need every club in the bag, not forgetting the putter on greens which are on the large side, well-shaped and not always easy to read. Add to this some pretty viewpoints over the mountains and good general upkeep and you will understand why we consider this to be a class golf course, one of the very best in Majorca.

Capdepera Golf - Roca Viva
Ctra Arta - Calá Rajada, km. 3,5 - Apdo 39
E - 07570 ARTA (MALLORCA)

Office	Secretaria	(34) 971 - 56 58 75
Pro shop	Pro-shop	(34) 971 - 56 58 75
Fax	Fax	(34) 971 - 56 58 74
Situation	Situación	

70 km Palma, 308 616 h.

Annual closure	Cierre anual	no
Weekly closure	Cierre semanal	no

Fees main season
Precios tempor. alta el campo

	Week days Semana	We/Bank holidays Fin de sem./fiestas
Individual Individual	7 900 Pts	7 900 Pts
Couple Pareja	15 800 Pts	15 800 Pts

Caddy	Caddy	no
Electric Trolley	Carro eléctrico	700 Pts
Buggy	Coche	5 000 Pts/18 hoyos
Clubs	Palos	2 500 Pts/18 hoyos

Credit cards Tarjetas de crédito
VISA - Eurocard - MasterCard - AMEX

902

Access Acceso : C715 Palma → Manacor, → Artá,
→ Cala Rajada
Map 9 on page 882 Plano 9 Página 882

GOLF COURSE
RECORRIDO
15/20

Site	Emplazamiento	
Maintenance	Mantenimiento	
Architect	Arquitecto	Dan Maples
Type	Tipo	campo, vaguada
Relief	Relieve	
Water in play	Agua	
Exp. to wind	Exp. al viento	
Trees in play	Arboles	

Scorecard Tarjeta	Chp. Campeonato	Mens Caballeros	Ladies Damas
Length Longitud	6284	5919	4800
Par	72	72	72

Advised golfing ability Nivel de juego aconsejado		0 12 24 36
Hcp required	Handicap exigido	28 Cab., 36 Damas

CLUB HOUSE & AMENITIES
CLUB HOUSE Y DEPENDENCIAS
7/10

Pro shop	Pro-shop	
Driving range	Campo de prácticas	
Sheltered	cubierto	no
On grass	sobre hierba	si
Putting-green	putting-green	si
Pitching-green	pitching-green	si

HOTEL FACILITIES
HOTELES CERCANOS
6/10

HOTELS HOTELES
Aguait — Cala Rajada
188 habitaciones, D 14 700 Pts. — 3 km
Tel (34) 971 - 56 34 08, Fax (34) 971 - 56 51 06

Serrano Palace — Cala Rajada
150 habitaciones, D 28 600 Pts. — 3 km
Tel (34) 971 - 56 33 50, Fax (34) 971 - 56 36 30

Canyamel Park — Capdepera
133 habitaciones, D 14 000 Pts. — 4 km
Tel (34) 971 - 56 55 11, Fax (34) 971 - 56 56 14

RESTAURANTS RESTAURANTE
Ses Rotjes — Cala Rajada
Tel (34) 971 - 56 31 08 — 15 km

Los Pablos — Capdepera
Tel(34) 971 - 56 55 43 — 5 km

No había muchos golfs en la región de Pamplona y teniendo en cuenta que el de Ulzama ha sido ampliado a 18 hoyos muy recientemente, la creación de Castillo de Gorraiz ha sido muy bien acogida. Las instalaciones son muy completas con un amplísimo campo de prácticas, tenis y piscina. Su creador es Cabell Robinson, autor también de La Cala en la Costa del Sol y de soberbios recorridos en Marruecos. Ha sabido aprovechar el terreno reservando una parte a residencias entre las que serpentean las calles anchas y muy abiertas. Los tees de salida son elevados dominando los hoyos. No siempre es necesario utilizar el drive ya que al peligro de roughs densos recomienda la prudencia si no se tiene mucha precisión. Tres grandes obstáculos de agua se encuentran en la línea de juego, lo que obliga a bien calcular tanto la distancia como la precisión de los golpes. Un golf bien logrado.

Given that the region of Pamplona is not too well off for golf courses and that Ulzama has only recently been up-graded to a full 18-holer, the advent of Castillo de Gorraiz was most welcome. Facilities are excellent, with a huge driving range, tennis courts and a pool. The course is the work of Cabell Robinson, who designed La Cala on the Costa del Sol and some superb courses in Morocco. Here he has worked wonders with the terrain, a part of which is reserved for villas through which the wide and very open fairways wind their way around the course. The tee-boxes are elevated so you are looking down on the holes, and you don't always have to use the driver; danger from the thick rough calls for care if accuracy is not your forte. At the other end of the fairway, the huge, roundly-contoured greens give you the opportunity to show your putting skills. Three large water hazards are also in play, so accuracy as well as accuracy is at a premium. A very fine course.

Club de Golf Castillo de Gorraiz

Urbanizacion Gorraiz
E - 31620 VALLE DE EGUES (Navarra)

Office	Secretaria	(34) 948 - 33 70 73
Pro shop	Pro-shop	(34) 948 - 33 70 73
Fax	Fax	(34) 948 - 33 73 15
Situation	Situación	

5 km Pamplona, 191 197 h.

Annual closure	Cierre anual	no
Weekly closure	Cierre semanal	no

Fees main season
Precios tempor. alta recorrido

	Week days Semana	We/Bank holidays Fin de sem./fiestas
Individual Individual	5 000 Pts	5 000 Pts
Couple Pareja	10 000 Pts	10 000 Pts

Caddy	Caddy	no
Electric Trolley	Carro eléctrico	700 Pts/18 hoyos
Buggy	Coche	3 000 Pts/18 hoyos
Clubs	Palos	1 000 Pts/18 hoyos

Credit cards Tarjetas de crédito   VISA

Access Acceso : Salida de Pamplona → Francia. Desvio a Olaz-Huarte
Map 1 on page 867 Plano 1 Página 867

GOLF COURSE
RECORRIDO   17 /20

Site	Emplazamiento	
Maintenance	Mantenimiento	
Architect	Arquitecto	Cabell Robinson
Type	Tipo	parque, urbano
Relief	Relieve	
Water in play	Agua	
Exp. to wind	Exp. al viento	
Trees in play	Arboles	

Scorecard Tarjeta	Chp. Campeonato	Mens Caballeros	Ladies Damas
Length Longitud	6321	6036	5131
Par	72	72	72

Advised golfing ability Nivel de juego aconsejado		0 12 24 36	
Hcp required	Handicap exigido	no	

CLUB HOUSE & AMENITIES
CLUB HOUSE Y DEPENDENCIAS   7 /10

Pro shop	Pro-shop	
Driving range	Campo de prácticas	
Sheltered	cubierto	12 puestos
On grass	sobre hierba	no
Putting-green	putting-green	si
Pitching-green	pitching-green	si

903

HOTEL FACILITIES
HOTELES CERCANOS   7 /10

HOTELS HOTELES

Iruña Park	Pamplona
225 habitaciones, D 19 400 Pts	7 km
Tel (34) 948 - 17 32 00, Fax (34) 948 - 17 23 87	
Tres Reyes	Pamplona
160 habitaciones, D 20 000 Pts	7 km
Tel (34) 948 - 22 66 00, Fax (34) 948 - 22 29 30	
Aguirre	Pamplona
12 habitaciones, D 5 000 Pts	5 km
Tel (34) 948 - 33 03 75	

RESTAURANTS RESTAURANTE

Hartza	Pamplona
Tel (34) 948 - 22 45 68	5 km
Egües	Egües
Tel (34) 948 - 33 00 81	5 km
Josetxo	Pamplona
Tel(34) 948 - 22 20 97	5 km

Situado en plena naturaleza, este recorrido es algo más que un simple paseo. Era de esperar dada la fama de Javier Arana, cuyos diseños dejan siempre de lado lo que es trivial y son testimonio de un gran conocimiento del golf. Ha sabido adaptarse a un terreno en el que las desnivelaciones ya eran suficientes para no añadir más dificultades. Las calles son claras, sin trampas, lo esencial del juego se desarrolla en las llegadas a green, donde es necesario evitar árboles y algunos bunkers peligrosos. No muy largo, a veces estrecho, este recorrido exige precisión, favorece el placer del golf entre jugadores de diferente nivel o en familia. Robusto y natural, no es un recorrido de campeonato, pero todos los amateurs se sentirán agusto sin que por eso se pueda decir que es un golf fácil. Unicos defectos: aguanta mal la lluvia y los greens normales están cerrados en invierno.

Located out in the country, this course is more than just a pleasant walk. And this is only to be expected from Javier Arana, whose layouts are always out of the ordinary and reveal considerable golfing intelligence. He has played a lot with the terrain and the marked differences in relief in order not to add too many hazards. With the fairways free of traps, the key to playing the course is around the greens, avoiding the trees and the few dangerous bunkers. Not particularly long and sometimes tight, this course places emphasis on accuracy and provides shared golfing pleasure among players of different levels or with the family. Rugged and natural, Cerdaña is definitely not a championship course, but all week-end golfers will feel at home here, without ever finding the course too easy. The only faults are a terrain that doesn't take too well to heavy rain, and the greens that are closed in winter.

Real Club de Golf de Cerdaña

Apartat de correus 63
E - 17520 PUIGCERDA (Girona)

Office	Secretaria	(34) 972 - 14 14 08
Pro shop	Pro-shop	(34) 972 - 14 14 08
Fax	Fax	(34) 972 - 88 13 38
Situation	Situación	

1 km Puigcerdà, 6 414 h.
150 km Barcelona, 1 681 132 h.

Annual closure	Cierre anual	no
Weekly closure	Cierre semanal	no

Fees main season
Precios tempor. alta

	Week days Semana	We/Bank holidays Fin de sem./fiestas
Individual Individual	5 000 Pts	6 000 Pts
Couple Pareja	10 000 Pts	12 000 Pts

Caddy	Caddy	no
Electric Trolley	Carro eléctrico	1 000 Pts
Buggy	Coche	5 000 Pts/18 hoyos
Clubs	Palos	1 000 Pts/18 hoyos

Credit cards Tarjetas de crédito
VISA - Eurocard - MasterCard - AMEX

FONT-ROMEU (FRANCE) →
Puigcerdà
Bolvir
Ger
GOLF
N 260
Prats de Cerdanya
Alp
Bellver de Cerdanya
La Molina
BERGA Túnel del Cadi
0 2 4 km

Access Acceso : Barcelona A18 → Manresa
→ Tunel del Cadi y Puigcerda
Map 2 on page 869 Plano 2 Página 869

GOLF COURSE
RECORRIDO
14/20

Site	Emplazamiento	▰▰▰▰▰▱
Maintenance	Mantenimiento	▰▰▰▰▱▱
Architect	Arquitecto	Javier Araña
Type	Tipo	vagüada
Relief	Relieve	▰▰▰▰▱▱
Water in play	Agua	▰▱▱▱▱▱
Exp. to wind	Exp. al viento	▰▰▱▱▱▱
Trees in play	Arboles	▰▰▰▰▱▱

Scorecard Tarjeta	Chp. Campeonato	Mens Caballeros	Ladies Damas
Length Longitud	5886	5726	5015
Par	71	71	71

Advised golfing ability Nivel de juego aconsejado	0 12 24 36
Hcp required Handicap exigido	28 Cab., 36 Damas

CLUB HOUSE & AMENITIES
CLUB HOUSE Y DEPENDENCIAS
7/10

Pro shop	Pro-shop	▰▰▰▰▰▱
Driving range	Campo de prácticas	▰▰▰▰▱▱
Sheltered	cubierto	7 puestos
On grass	sobre hierba	si
Putting-green	putting-green	si
Pitching-green	pitching-green	si

HOTEL FACILITIES
HOTELES CERCANOS
7/10

HOTELS HOTELES
Torre del Remei — Bolvir de Cerdaña
11 habitaciones, D 38 000 Pts — 1 km
Tel (34) 972 - 14 01 82, Fax (34) 972 - 14 04 49

Chalet del Golf — Puigcerda
11 habitaciones, D 18 000 Pts — 500 m
Tel (34) 972 - 88 09 50, Fax (34) 972 - 88 09 66

Puigcerda — Puigcerda
39 habitaciones, D 9 000 Pts. — 1 km
Tel (34) 972 - 88 21 81, Fax (34) 972 - 88 12 56

RESTAURANTS RESTAURANTE
Torre del Remei — Bolvir de Cerdaña
Tel (34) 972 - 14 01 82 — 1 km

La Tieta — Puigcerda
Tel (34) 972 - 88 01 56 — 2 km

904

Tras pasar bordeando preciosas casas, la llegada a este campo de golf, construido en la cima de una pequeña montaña, augura un recorrido espectacular. Encaramado como un mirador dominando fantásticos paisajes, es además impresionante: Ramón Espinosa ha pensado más en los buenos jugadores que en los que sobrepasan 24 de handicap, los cuales se asustarán ante las hondanadas llenas de matorrales a lo largo de una docena de hoyos (se les considera como obstáculos de agua). Más vale no relajar la concentración y es mejor elegir la precisión que la distancia sobre todo cuando uno se siente inseguro de su propio juego. Es preferible evitar los días de viento. Antes de pensar en el resultado más vale reconocer el terreno una o dos veces, aunque sólo sea para identificar los sitios peligrosos, calcular bien las distancias y... el número de bolas que se van a necesitar. Nada fácil pero interesante.

After running alongside a number of pretty houses, the arrival on the course built atop a small mountain promises some spectacular golfing. Perched liked a mirador overlooking some wonderful landscapes, the course is indeed impressive. Here, Ramon Espinosa thought more about proficient players than about 24+ handicappers, who might often be intimidated by the ravines overrun with scrub bordering at least 12 fairways (they are considered to be water hazards). Any lapses in concentration are out of the question here, and straightness is preferable to distance whenever a player has a feeling of not being quite sure about his game. Also, try and avoid days when the wind gets up. Before thinking about your score, try and play one or two exploratory rounds if only to get the lie of the land, locate hidden dangers and evaluate the distances and numbers of balls you might need. Not easy but definitely interesting.

Club de Golf d'Aro

Urbanització Mas Nou
E - 17250 PLATJA D'ARO (GIRONA)

Office	Secretaria	(34) 972 - 82 69 00
Pro shop	Pro-shop	(34) 972 - 81 76 56
Fax	Fax	(34) 972 - 82 69 06
Situation	Situación	

6 km Platja d'Aro, 4 785 h.
10 km Sant Feliu de Guixols, 16 088 h.

Annual closure	Cierre anual	no
Weekly closure	Cierre semanal	no

Fees main season
Precios tempor. alta el campo

	Week days Semana	We/Bank holidays Fin de sem./fiestas
Individual Individual	7 600 Pts	8 000 Pts
Couple Pareja	15 200 Pts	16 000 Pts

Caddy	Caddy	no
Electric Trolley	Carro eléctrico	2 000 Pts
Buggy	Coche	4 500 Pts/18 hoyos
Clubs	Palos	1 500 Pts/18 hoyos

Credit cards Tarjetas de crédito
VISA - MasterCard - AMEX

Access Acceso : Barcelona, Sant Feliu C253 →
Palafrugell.
La Platja d'Aro, → Golf Mas Nou a la izquierda
Map 2 on page 869 Plano 2 Página 869

GOLF COURSE
RECORRIDO   15/20

Site	Emplazamiento	
Maintenance	Mantenimiento	
Architect	Arquitecto	Ramón Espinosa
Type	Tipo	bosque, montaña
Relief	Relieve	
Water in play	Agua	
Exp. to wind	Exp. al viento	
Trees in play	Arboles	

Scorecard Tarjeta	Chp. Campeonato	Mens Caballeros	Ladies Damas
Length Longitud	6218	6004	5031
Par	72	72	72

Advised golfing ability	0	12	24	36
Nivel de juego aconsejado				

Hcp required   Handicap exigido   28 Cab., 36 Damas

CLUB HOUSE & AMENITIES
CLUB HOUSE Y DEPENDENCIAS   7/10

Pro shop	Pro-shop	
Driving range	Campo de prácticas	
Sheltered	cubierto	no
On grass	sobre hierba	si
Putting-green	putting-green	si
Pitching-green	pitching-green	si

HOTEL FACILITIES
HOTELES CERCANOS   7/10

HOTELS HOTELES
Park Hotel San Jorge   Calonge
104 habitaciones, D 22 800 Pts   13 km
Tel (34) 972 - 65 23 11, Fax (34) 972 - 65 25 76

Golf Costa Brava   Santa Cristina
91 habitaciones, D 15 000 Pts.   9 km
Tel (34) 972 - 83 51 51, Fax (34) 972 - 83 75 88

La Gavina   S'Agaró
74 habitaciones, D 33 000 Pts   10 km
Tel (34) 972 - 32 11 00, Fax (34) 972 - 32 15 73

RESTAURANTS RESTAURANTE
Mas Nou   Platja d'Aro
Tel (34) 972 - 81 78 53   1 km

Carles Camos-Big Rock   Platja d'Aro
Tel (34) 972 - 81 80 12   7 km

905

16 | 8 | 8

Una vez más, Javier Arana demuestra aquí estar entre los mejores arquitéctos del siglo. Es una pena que no haya expresado su talento fuera de las fronteras españolas. A la vez exigente por su longitud así como por la precisión que requiere, éste campo nos proporciona un placer siempre renovado. De mediano relieve, no se deja descubrir tan facilmente y hacen falta muchas veces para llegar a entender todas sus sutilezas. Los árboles y los bunkers de recorrido constituyen sus principales dificultades, y le damos las gracias a Arana de no haber creado demasiados problemas en los accesos a los greenes. Tan sólo el estado de estos nos incita a revisar nuestra opinión, aunque se está llevando a cabo la reconstrucción de todos y cada uno de los greenes lo que servirá a que vuelva a ser uno de los grandes campos en el futuro. Hay que decir que el índice de ocupación del campo es altísimo ya que el Club de Campo es uno de los más grandes de España. Aconsejamos por tanto a los vistantes de evitar los fines de semana.

Here again, Javier Arana gives a further demonstration of why he will go down as one of the century's greatest architects. What a shame his great talent is not on show outside his home country. Demanding both in length and accuracy, this course is a real joy to play everytime. Averagely hilly (but easy to walk), the course is not easy to discover and needs several rounds to grasp the subtler points. The trees and fairway bunkers are the main difficulties, and we should be grateful to Arana for not having created too many difficulties when approaching the greens. The state of the putting surfaces is the only slight blemish on our appreciation, but whole-scale replanting should lead to an improvement in the future. It should also be said that the course is very busy in what is certainly Spain's biggest golf club. So follow our advice and avoid week-ends.

Club de Campo Villa de Madrid

Carretera de Castilla km 2
E - 28040 MADRID

Office	Secretaria	(34) 91 - 357 21 32
Pro shop	Pro-shop	(34) 91 - 357 21 32
Fax	Fax	(34) 91 - 307 06 29
Situation	Situación	

1 km Madrid, 3 084 373 h.

Annual closure	Cierre anual	no
Weekly closure	Cierre semanal	no

Fees main season
Precios tempor. alta 18 hoyos

	Week days Semana	We/Bank holidays Fin de sem./fiestas
Individual Individual	6 500 Pts	12 200 Pts
Couple Pareja	13 000 Pts	24 400 Pts

Acceso al Club: 1 800 Pts (semana), 3 500 Pts (We)

Caddy	Caddy	no
Electric Trolley	Carro eléctrico	1 200 Pts
Buggy	Coche	6 100 Pts/18 hoyos
Clubs	Palos	2 500 Pts/18 hoyos

Credit cards Tarjetas de crédito — no

Access Acceso : Madrid, Carretera de Castilla
→ Segovia
Map 3 on page 870 Plano 3 Página 870

GOLF COURSE
RECORRIDO

16/20

Site	Emplazamiento	
Maintenance	Mantenimiento	
Architect	Arquitecto	Javier Arana
Type	Tipo	bosque
Relief	Relieve	
Water in play	Agua	
Exp. to wind	Exp. al viento	
Trees in play	Arboles	

Scorecard Tarjeta	Chp. Campeonato	Mens Caballeros	Ladies Damas
Length Longitud	6335	6094	5169
Par	72	72	72

Advised golfing ability		0 12 24 36
Nivel de juego aconsejado		
Hcp required	Handicap exigido	28 Cab., 36 Damas

CLUB HOUSE & AMENITIES
CLUB HOUSE Y DEPENDENCIAS

8/10

Pro shop	Pro-shop	
Driving range	Campo de prácticas	
Sheltered	cubierto	112 puestos
On grass	sobre hierba	si
Putting-green	putting-green	si
Pitching-green	pitching-green	si

HOTEL FACILITIES
HOTELES CERCANOS

8/10

HOTELS HOTELES

Princesa 275 habitaciones, D 33 250 Pts Tel (34) 91 - 542 21 00, Fax (34) 91 - 542 73 28	Madrid 3 km
Melia Madrid 276 habitaciones, D 26 500 Pts Tel (34) 91 - 541 82 00, Fax (34) 91 - 541 19 88	Madrid 3 km
Moncloa Garden 121 habitaciones, D 16 500 Pts Tel (34) 91 - 542 45 82, Fax (34) 91 - 542 71 69	Madrid 3 km

RESTAURANTS RESTAURANTE

El Amparo Tel (34) 91 - 431 64 56	Madrid 6 km
Taberna de Alabardero Tel (34) 91 - 547 25 77	Madrid 5 km
La Trainera Tel (34) 91 - 576 05 75	Madrid 5 km

13 | 7 | 7

El gabinete del arquitecto Hamilton Stutt no es de los más conocidos, pero aquí ha construido un recorrido simpático, sin dificultades infranqueables permitiendo que jugadores de todos los niveles y edades pasen un día agradable. El relieve es mesurado, las pendientes suaves, alternando hoyos anchos y estrechos rodeados de pinos a menudo en la línea de juego y alcornoques, lo que obliga a pegar con efecto a la bola para contornearlos, pasar por arriba... o por debajo.Los greens están bien protegidos, correctamente diseñados y la mayor parte de las veces se puede aprochar haciendo rodar la bola. Sólo hay un hoyo ciego, reflejando así la filosofía del recorrido: el golf es para todo el mundo y si hay recorridos exigentes también tiene que haber otros para los golfistas de nivel medio. Este forma parte de esa categoría, pero los buenos jugadores tampoco se aburrirán.

Hamilton Stutt & Co is not the most famous name in golf course design, but here they have produced a pleasant course without insuperable difficulties on which players of all levels and all ages can spend an enjoyable day. The ground relief is moderate, with a few gentle slopes and alternating wide and tight fairways edged by pine and oak trees that are often very much in play. The player will often have to work the ball to get around them, put the ball over the top... or keep low below the branches. The greens are well defended and correctly designed, but most of them can be approached with chip shots. Only one green is blind, which reflects the thinking behind the whole course, namely golf is for everyone, and while there are demanding courses, there should also be courses for average players. This is one such course, but even the best players will have fun.

Club de Golf Costa Brava

Urbanitzacio Golf Costa Brava
E - 17246 SANTA CRISTINA D'ARO (GIRONA)

Office	Secretaria	(34) 972 - 83 71 50
Pro shop	Pro-shop	(34) 972 - 83 70 55
Fax	Fax	(34) 972 - 83 72 72
Situation	Situación	

7 km San Feliu de Guixols, 16 088 h.
30 km Girona, 70 409 h.

Annual closure	Cierre anual	no
Weekly closure	Cierre semanal	no

Fees main season
Precios tempor. alta el campo

	Week days Semana	We/Bank holidays Fin de sem./fiestas
Individual Individual	7 500 Pts	7 500 Pts
Couple Pareja	15 000 Pts	15 000 Pts

Caddy	Caddy	no
Electric Trolley	Carro eléctrico	no
Buggy	Coche	5 000 Pts/18 hoyos
Clubs	Palos	1 500 Pts/18 hoyos

Credit cards Tarjetas de crédito
VISA - Eurocard - MasterCard - AMEX

Access Acceso : C250 Sant Feliu → Girona, Santa Cristina d'Aro → Golf
Map 2 on page 869 Plano 2 Página 869

GOLF COURSE
RECORRIDO
13 /20

Site	Emplazamiento	
Maintenance	Mantenimiento	
Architect	Arquitecto	Hamilton Stutt & Co
Type	Tipo	urbano, vagüada
Relief	Relieve	
Water in play	Agua	
Exp. to wind	Exp. al viento	
Trees in play	Arboles	

Scorecard Tarjeta	Chp. Campeonato	Mens Caballeros	Ladies Damas
Length Longitud	5573	5445	4670
Par	70	70	70

Advised golfing ability	0	12	24	36
Nivel de juego aconsejado				

Hcp required	Handicap exigido	28 Cab., 36 Damas

CLUB HOUSE & AMENITIES
CLUB HOUSE Y DEPENDENCIAS
7 /10

Pro shop	Pro-shop	
Driving range	Campo de prácticas	
Sheltered	cubierto	4 puestos
On grass	sobre hierba	si
Putting-green	putting-green	si
Pitching-green	pitching-green	si

907

HOTEL FACILITIES
HOTELES CERCANOS
7 /10

HOTELS HOTELES
Golf Costa Brava — Santa Cristina
91 habitaciones, D 15 000 Pts. — 50 m
Tel (34) 972 - 83 51 51, Fax (34) 972 - 83 75 88

Hostal de la Gavina — S'Agaró
74 habitaciones, D 33 000 Pts — 7 km
Tel (34) 972 - 32 11 00, Fax (34) 972 - 32 15 73

Park Hotel San Jorge — Calonge
104 habitaciones, D 22 800 Pts — 12 km
Tel (34) 972 - 65 23 11, Fax (34) 972 - 65 25 76

RESTAURANTS RESTAURANTE
Els Tinars — Llagostera
Tel (34) 972 - 83 06 26 — 6 km

Les Panolles — Santa Cristina
Tel (34) 972 - 83 70 11 — 1 km

El lugar es agradable y descansado. A pesar de que el recorrido se sitúa muy a menudo en la falda de la ladera y es muy ondulado, no se necesita alquilar un coche. Las calles con hierba bien tupida sostienen bien la bola, los greens la aguantan bien, sólo algunos olivos aislados o agrupados pueden perturbar la trayectoria de juego: no es un recorrido de gran dificultad y gustará a la mayoría de los jugadores. El recorrido no ofrece emociones fuertes, aunque la vuelta, a partir del 12, es más técnica que la ida, especialmente en los dos pares 5 (el 13 y el 16). Sin embargo, los arquitectos podrían haber tenido un poco más de imaginación colocando dificultades en lugares más amenazadores. En la familia de golfs gratos y agradables para todos los niveles de juego, Costa Dorada ocupa un buen lugar.

The site is pleasant and relaxing after reaching the course set in a little palm grove. Although much of Costa Dorada is laid out on the side of a hill with rolling fairways, it is easily walkable. The lushly-grassed fairways carry the ball well and the greens pitch well, too. Only a few isolated or bunches of olive trees can get in the way of your ball, so this is not too complicated a course to get around. Most players will like its honest style, but they shouldn't expect too much in the way of excitement, even though from the 12th hole onwards the course becomes more technical, especially the two par 5s (especially holes 13 and 16). We might have expected a little more imagination from the architects, with hazards perhaps located in a more threatening manner. But in the family of pleasant and encouraging courses for all levels of play, Costa Dorada is a front-runner.

Club de Golf Costa Dorada Tarragona

Carretera de El Catllar, km. 2,7
E - 43000 TARRAGONA

Office	Secretaria	(34) 977 - 65 33 61
Pro shop	Pro-shop	(34) 977 - 65 33 61
Fax	Fax	(34) 977 - 65 30 28
Situation	Situación	

5 km Tarragona, 112 802 h.

Annual closure	Cierre anual	no
Weekly closure	Cierre semanal	no
		lunes, restaurante

Fees main season
Precios tempor. alta

	Week days Semana	We/Bank holidays Fin de sem./fiestas
Individual Individual	5 000 Pts	10 000 Pts
Couple Pareja	10 000 Pts	20 000 Pts

Caddy	Caddy	si, reservar
Electric Trolley	Carro eléctrico	1000 Pts
Buggy	Coche	4 000 Pts/18 hoyos
Clubs	Palos	2 500 Pts/el dia

Credit cards Tarjetas de crédito
VISA - MasterCard

Access Acceso : A7 Barcelona → Valencia, salida 32,
RN340 → Tarragona, Ctra El Catllar, Golf 2,7 km.
Map 4 on page 873 Plano 4 Página 873

GOLF COURSE
RECORRIDO 13/20

Site	Emplazamiento	
Maintenance	Mantenimiento	
Architect	Arquitecto	José Gancedo
		V. Sardá Saenger
Type	Tipo	vagüada
Relief	Relieve	
Water in play	Agua	
Exp. to wind	Exp. al viento	
Trees in play	Arboles	

Scorecard Tarjeta	Chp. Campeonato	Mens Caballeros	Ladies Damas
Length Longitud	6223	5978	5136
Par	72	72	72

Advised golfing ability			0	12	24	36
Nivel de juego aconsejado						
Hcp required	Handicap exigido	no				

CLUB HOUSE & AMENITIES
CLUB HOUSE Y DEPENDENCIAS 6/10

Pro shop	Pro-shop	
Driving range	Campo de prácticas	
Sheltered	cubierto	6 puestos
On grass	sobre hierba	si
Putting-green	putting-green	si
Pitching-green	pitching-green	no

HOTEL FACILITIES
HOTELES CERCANOS 6/10

HOTELS HOTELES
Imperial Tarraco — Tarragona
155 habitaciones, D 17 800 Pts — 6 km
Tel (34) 977 - 23 30 40, Fax (34) 977 - 21 65 66

Lauria — Tarragona
72 habitaciones, D 10 000 Pts — 6 km
Tel (34) 977 - 23 67 12, Fax (34) 977 - 23 67 00

RESTAURANTS RESTAURANTE
Sol Ric — Tarragona
Tel (34) 977 - 23 20 32 — 6 km

Can Sala (Les Fonts) — N 240, 2 km, Tarragona
Tel (34) 977 - 22 85 75 — 4 km

908

La buena calidad del conjunto inmobiliario no sólo no molesta a los jugadores sino que se adapta muy bien al estilo americano del recorrido. Si añadimos que más vale alquilar un coche, uno podría creerse en Estados Unidos. El Bosque figura entre los buenos éxitos de Robert Trent Jones en España. El relieve es importante, se juega a menudo en pendiente y felizmente la estrategia de juego es clara ya que si los obstáculos son bien visibles, no dejan de ser peligrosos. La primera vez uno se siente acosado (para obtener un buen resultado) por una serie de greens ciegos que requieren trayectorias altas. No hay que dudar tirar a bandera puesto que los greens aguantan bien la bola. Los hoyos están bien integrados en el paisaje cuyo diseño y dificultades son variados, sobre todo cuatro excelentes dog-legs. Hay que hacer mención especial de los pares 3.

The surrounding real estate is a stylish programme and won't bother the players, especially since the properties fit in very well with what is a very American-style course. Add to that the definite advantage of playing with a buggy and you might think you actually were on American soil. El Bosque is one of the great success-stories of Robert Trent Jones in Spain. It is hilly, you are often faced with a sloping lie, but the game strategy is pretty clear. And that's lucky, because although the hazards are visible, they are very dangerous. First time out, players looking for a good score will have trouble only with a series of blind greens which demand high approach shots. Go for the pin, too, because these greens pitch well. The holes blend in well with the landscape, and the design and difficulties vary considerably. In particular there are four beautiful dog-legs. A special mention should go to the quality of the par 3s.

El Bosque Club de Golf
Carretera de Godelleta, km 4,1
E - 46370 CHIVA (VALENCIA)

Office	Secretaria	(34) 96 - 180 80 00
Pro shop	Pro-shop	(34) 96 - 180 80 00
Fax	Fax	(34) 96 - 180 80 01
Situation	Situación	

20 km Valencia, 751 734 h.
5 km Chiva, 7 562 h.

Annual closure	Cierre anual	no
Weekly closure	Cierre semanal	no

Fees main season
Precios tempor. alta el campo

	Week days Semana	We/Bank holidays Fin de sem./fiestas
Individual Individual	8 000 Pts	8 000 Pts
Couple Pareja	16 000 Pts	16 000 Pts

Caddy	Caddy	no
Electric Trolley	Carro eléctrico	no
Buggy	Coche	4 500 Pts/18 hoyos
Clubs	Palos	1 000 Pts/18 hoyos

Credit cards Tarjetas de crédito — VISA - AMEX

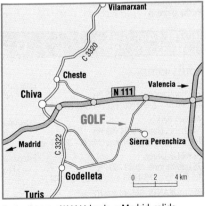

Access Acceso : N111 Valencia → Madrid, salida
Godelleta, km. 324, → Godelleta, Golf km. 4,1
Map 4 on page 873 Plano 4 Página 873

GOLF COURSE
RECORRIDO **16**/20

Site	Emplazamiento	
Maintenance	Mantenimiento	
Architect	Arquitecto	Robert Trent Jones
Type	Tipo	campo, urbano, vagüada
Relief	Relieve	
Water in play	Agua	
Exp. to wind	Exp. al viento	
Trees in play	Arboles	

Scorecard Tarjeta	Chp. Campeonato	Mens Caballeros	Ladies Damas
Length Longitud	6367	5995	5178
Par	72	72	72

Advised golfing ability	0	12	24	36
Nivel de juego aconsejado				
Hcp required	Handicap exigido	28 Cab., 36 Damas		

CLUB HOUSE & AMENITIES
CLUB HOUSE Y DEPENDENCIAS **7**/10

Pro shop	Pro-shop	
Driving range	Campo de prácticas	
Sheltered	cubierto	25 puestos
On grass	sobre hierba	si
Putting-green	putting-green	si
Pitching-green	pitching-green	si

909

HOTEL FACILITIES
HOTELES CERCANOS **4**/10

HOTELS HOTELES
Sidi Saler		El Saler
276 habitaciones, D 22 500 Pts		24 km
Tel (34) 96 - 161 04 11, Fax (34) 96 - 161 08 38		
Melia Valencia Palace		Valencia
199 habitaciones, D 26 500 Pts		30 km
Tel (34) 96 - 337 50 37, Fax (34) 96 - 337 55 32		
Sol Azafata		Manises
126 habitaciones, D 14 800 Pts		10 km
Tel (34) 96 - 154 61 00, Fax (34) 96 - 153 20 19		

RESTAURANTS RESTAURANTE
Azafata		Manises
Tel (34) 96 - 154 61 00		10 km
Albacar		Valencia
Tel (34) 96 - 395 10 05		30 km

EL PARAISO

13	6	6

Gary Player goza hoy de una gran reputación como arquitécto de golf, y dirige una verdadera empresa. En 1974 era más bien su fama como jugador la que le permítia conseguir contratos como diseñador de campos, y su éxito dependía para mucho de quienes ejecutaban sus diseños. El Paraiso pertenece a su «primera época», en la cual su personalidad como creador se afirmada más timidamente que ahora y su estilo británico era muy tradicional. Player no busco dificuldades particulares lo que hace que el campo sea generoso con la mayoría de los jugadores. Los campeones, los amantes de los desafíos tácticos, de los riesgos calculados y de los golpes imposibles tendrán pocas oportunidades de dar rienda suelta a sus aficiones, pero no faltan campos en la región para ellos. Mientras tanto para los jugadores más modestos y menos experimentados el campo ofrece la posibilidad de divertirse sin correr el riesgo de verse humillados. En ese sentido es una realización más util.

Today, Gary Player has forged quite some reputation as an architect and presides over a whole course design business. In 1974, it was his prestige as a player that led to his winning course design contests, and his success depended a great deal on the people who were executing his plans. El Paraiso belongs to this first period when his personality as an architect was less assertive than today, and he stays with the traditional British look. Player didn't look for any special difficulties and this course is friendly enough for most players. The experts and lovers of tactical challenges, calculated risks and the shot of a million will have little opportunity to develop their skills here, but there is a lot of other courses in this part of the country for their ilk. In between time, the less ambitious or less experienced players can have fun here without fear of making a fool of themselves. In this respect, this is a useful course.

El Paraiso Club de Golf
Ctra Cadiz - km. 167
E - 29680 ESTEPONA (MALAGA)

Office	Secretaria	(34) 95 - 288 38 35
Pro shop	Pro-shop	(34) 95 - 288 73 26
Fax	Fax	(34) 95 - 288 58 27
Situation	Situación	

5 km. de San Pedro de Alcantara
10 km. de Estepona, 36 307 h.

Annual closure	Cierre anual	no
Weekly closure	Cierre semanal	no

Fees main season
Precios tempor. alta

	Week days Semana	We/Bank holidays Fin de sem./fiestas
Individual Individual	7 000 Pts	7 000 Pts
Couple Pareja	14 000 Pts	14 000 Pts

Caddy	Caddy	no
Electric Trolley	Carro eléctrico	no
Buggy	Coche	4000 Pts/18 hoyos
Clubs	Palos	1000 Pts/18 hoyos

Credit cards Tarjetas de crédito
VISA - MasterCard - AMEX

910

Access Acceso : Marbella → San Pedro de Alcantara, → Estepona
Map 7 on page 879 Plano 7 Página 879

GOLF COURSE
RECORRIDO
13/20

Site	Emplazamiento	
Maintenance	Mantenimiento	
Architect	Arquitecto	Gary Player
Type	Tipo	llanura, vagüada
Relief	Relieve	
Water in play	Agua	
Exp. to wind	Exp. al viento	
Trees in play	Arboles	

Scorecard Tarjeta	Chp. Campeonato	Mens Caballeros	Ladies Damas
Length Longitud	6116	5729	4998
Par	71	71	71

Advised golfing ability Nivel de juego aconsejado	0	12	24	36
Hcp required Handicap exigido	28 Cab., 36 Damas			

CLUB HOUSE & AMENITIES
CLUB HOUSE Y DEPENDENCIAS
6/10

Pro shop	Pro-shop	
Driving range	Campo de prácticas	
Sheltered	cubierto	15 puestos
On grass	sobre hierba	si
Putting-green	putting-green	si
Pitching-green	pitching-green	si

HOTEL FACILITIES
HOTELES CERCANOS
6/10

HOTELS HOTELES

El Paraiso — Estepona Golf
182 habitaciones, D 25 725 Pts
Tel (34) 95 - 288 30 00, Fax (34) 95 - 288 20 19

Atalaya Park — Estepona 3 km
448 habitaciones, D 24 000 Pts
Tel (34) 95 - 288 48 01, Fax (34) 95 - 288 57 35

Hotel Las Dunas — Estepona 5 km
75 habitaciones, D 39 000 Pts
Tel (34) 95 - 279 43 45, Fax (34) 95 - 279 48 25

RESTAURANTS RESTAURANTE

La Alcaria de Ramos — Estepona 1 km
Tel (34) 95 - 288 61 78

La Alcaria Chica — Estepona 2 km
Tel (34) 95 - 288 46 54

Abierto en 1987, ha quedado un poco eclipsado por la cercanía del recorrido "Verde". Es hora de rehabilitarlo incluso si la proximidad del aeropuerto es más molesta e incluso a veces insoportable. Es una pena , ya que este recorrido enriquecido de pinos, palmeras y numerosos obstáculos de agua, tiene su propia personalidad con inspiración americana de los golfs de Florida o del Sur de California. El arquitecto Dave Thomas ha construido un recorrido franco, sin trampas camufladas: se le puede atacar de entrada y lograr jugar su handicap..., si no hay mucho viento. Adeñás de los obstáculos de agua, los bunkers son numerosos y peligrosos, especialmente los de calle, inteligentemente colocados, bien cuidados y rodeados de montículos. Grandes y bien diseñados, los greens no son ni fáciles ni desconcertantes.

The nearby "Green" course has somewhat eclipsed its "Yellow" neighbour, opened in 1987. So it's time this course was restored to favour, even though the closeness of the airport is much more irksome and sometimes even unbearable. It's a pity, because lined with pines, palm trees and numerous water hazards, it has its own personality, largely inspired by the American style of courses such as those found in Florida or southern California. Architect Dave Thomas has produced an honest course without concealing the traps, so you can get to grips with your game and hope to play to your handicap... if there's not too much wind. Away from the water, there are many dangerous bunkers, especially on the fairways, all of which are cleverly placed, well-designed and edged with mounds. The greens, all large and very well-designed, are not easy but never really disconcerting.

Real Club de Golf "El Prat"

Ap. de Correus 10
E - 08820 EL PRAT DE LLOBREGAT (BARCELONA)

Office	Secretaria	(34) 93 - 379 02 78
Pro shop	Pro-shop	(34) 93 - 379 02 78
Fax	Fax	(34) 93 - 370 51 02
Situation	Situación	

10 km Barcelona, 1 681 132 h. 1 km El Prat

Annual closure	Cierre anual	no
Weekly closure	Cierre semanal	no

Fees main season
Precios tempor. alta El dia

	Week days Semana	We/Bank holidays Fin de sem./fiestas
Individual Individual	11 780 Pts	23 625 Pts
Couple Pareja	23 560 Pts	47 250 Pts

Caddy	Caddy	si, reservar
Electric Trolley	Carro eléctrico	580 Pts
Buggy	Coche	4 035 Pts/18 hoyos
Clubs	Palos	3 000 Pts/el dia

Credit cards Tarjetas de crédito — VISA - MasterCard

BARCELONA

L'Hospitalet de Llobregat

Sant Bol

El Prat de Llobregat

Castelldefels

C 246

GOLF

0   2   4 km

Access Acceso : C246 → Sitges → El Prat de Llobregat, El Prat, Golf 1 km
Map 2 on page 869 Plano 2 Página 869

GOLF COURSE
RECORRIDO   15/20

Site	Emplazamiento	
Maintenance	Mantenimiento	
Architect	Arquitecto	David Thomas
Type	Tipo	llanura
Relief	Relieve	
Water in play	Agua	
Exp. to wind	Exp. al viento	
Trees in play	Arboles	

Scorecard Tarjeta	Chp. Campeonato	Mens Caballeros	Ladies Damas
Length Longitud	6172	5873	5079
Par	72	72	72

Advised golfing ability	0	12	24	36
Nivel de juego aconsejado				

Hcp required	Handicap exigido	28 Cab., 36 Damas

CLUB HOUSE & AMENITIES
CLUB HOUSE Y DEPENDENCIAS   7/10

Pro shop	Pro-shop	
Driving range	Campo de prácticas	
Sheltered	cubierto	8 puestos
On grass	sobre hierba	si
Putting-green	putting-green	si
Pitching-green	pitching-green	si

HOTEL FACILITIES
HOTELES CERCANOS   6/10

HOTELS HOTELES

Alfa Aeropuerto	Mercabarna
99 habitaciones, D 17 950 Pts.	5 km
Tel (34) 93 - 336 25 64, Fax (34) 93 - 335 55 92	
Rallye	Barcelona
107 habitaciones, D 14 000 Pts	10 km
Tel (34) 93 - 339 90 50, Fax (34) 93 - 411 07 90	
Barcelona Plaza Hotel	Barcelona
357 habitaciones, D 22 900 Pts	10 km
Tel (34) 93 - 426 26 00, Fax (34) 93 - 426 23 51	

RESTAURANTS RESTAURANTE

Casa Alcaide	El Prat
Tel (34) 93 - 379 10 12	1 km
Gran Mercat (Hotel Alfa)	Mercabarna
Tel(34) 93 - 336 25 64	5 km
Via Veneto	Barcelona
Tel(34) 93 - 200 72 44	10 km

911

EL PRAT VERDE

Con toda razón, uno de los recorridos más famosos de España. Llano y al borde del mar, despliega algunos de sus hoyos entre pinos, aunque la mayor parte, por haberse secado, han desaparecido del resto del recorrido. En cambio algunas palmeras pueden complicar la vida y trayectoria de los jugadores. Sin que su arquitectura sea la de los tradicionales links, sin embargo presenta un aspecto típicamente briánico, tal vez una forma de homenaje por parte del arquitecto Javier Arana. Si los bunkers son numerosos tanto en calle como alrededor de los greens, en general no están en la línea de juego, lo que permite escoger entre aprochar por alto o hacer rodar la bola y cambiar de juego en función del viento. Los roughs, difíciles a causa de la hierba bermuda, sí que están en la línea de juego. Muy equilibrado, sin artificios, este grande de España pertenece a la mejor nobleza.

One of Spain's most famous courses, and quite rightly so. Flat and by the sea, the first holes wind their way through the pines, but on the rest of the course most of the trees have disappeared because of disease. In contrast, certain palm trees can make life difficult for off-line shots. Without having the typical architecture of a links course, it offers traditional British character, perhaps as a form of tribute from the architect Javier Arana. While bunkers are plentiful on the fairways and around the greens, they are not generally in the line of fire, thus allowing players to choose between pitching and chipping onto the greens, and to vary their play depending on the wind. The rough, however, is very much to the fore, and the Bermuda grass can be a tough proposition. Well-balanced and totally honest, this great little Spanish number is of the very best vintage.

Real Club de Golf "El Prat"

Ap. de Correus 10
E - 08820 EL PRAT DE LLOBREGAT (BARCELONA)

Office	Secretaria	(34) 93 - 379 02 78
Pro shop	Pro-shop	(34) 93 - 379 02 78
Fax	Fax	(34) 93 - 370 51 02
Situation	Situación	

10 km Barcelona, 1 681 132 h. 1 km El Prat

Annual closure	Cierre anual	no
Weekly closure	Cierre semanal	no

Fees main season
Precios tempor. alta El dia

	Week days Semana	We/Bank holidays Fin de sem./fiestas
Individual Individual	11 780 Pts	23 625 Pts
Couple Pareja	23 560 Pts	47 250 Pts

Caddy	Caddy	si, reservar
Electric Trolley	Carro eléctrico	580 Pts/18 hoyos
Buggy	Coche	4 035 Pts/18 hoyos
Clubs	Palos	3 000 Pts/el dia

Credit cards Tarjetas de crédito
VISA - MasterCard

912

Access Acceso : C246 → Sitges → El Prat de Llobregat, El Prat, Golf 1 km
Map 2 on page 869 Plano 2 Página 869

GOLF COURSE
RECORRIDO
17 /20

Site	Emplazamiento	
Maintenance	Mantenimiento	
Architect	Arquitecto	Javier Araña
Type	Tipo	al borde del mar
Relief	Relieve	
Water in play	Agua	
Exp. to wind	Exp. al viento	
Trees in play	Arboles	

Scorecard Tarjeta	Chp. Campeonato	Mens Caballeros	Ladies Damas
Length Longitud	6224	5947	5124
Par	73	73	73

Advised golfing ability
Nivel de juego aconsejado
0   12   24   36

Hcp required   Handicap exigido   28 Cab., 36 Damas

CLUB HOUSE & AMENITIES
CLUB HOUSE Y DEPENDENCIAS
7 /10

Pro shop	Pro-shop	
Driving range	Campo de prácticas	
Sheltered	cubierto	8 puestos
On grass	sobre hierba	si
Putting-green	putting-green	si
Pitching-green	pitching-green	si

HOTEL FACILITIES
HOTELES CERCANOS
6 /10

HOTELS HOTELES
Alfa Aeropuerto   Mercabarna
99 habitaciones, D 17 950 Pts.   5 km
Tel (34) 93 - 336 25 64, Fax (34) 93 - 335 55 92

Rallye   Barcelona
107 habitaciones, D 14 000 Pts   10 km
Tel (34) 93 - 339 90 50, Fax (34) 93 - 411 07 90

Barcelona Plaza Hotel   Barcelona
357 habitaciones, D 22 900 Pts   10 km
Tel (34) 93 - 426 26 00, Fax (34) 93 - 426 23 51

RESTAURANTS RESTAURANTE
Casa Alcaide   El Prat
Tel (34) 93 - 379 10 12   1 km

Gran Mercat (Hotel Alfa)   Mercabarna
Tel(34) 93 - 336 25 64   5 km

Via Veneto   Barcelona
Tel(34) 93 - 200 72 44   10 km

El placer de saborear uno de los mejores recorridos de Europa sólo puede verse alterado por un cuidado mediano. Los hoyos de links (del 5 al 9 y del 16 al 18) pueden compararse a los mejores recorridos del Reino Unido a los que el gran arquitecto Javier Arana ha rendido homenaje. Los demás hoyos presentan la misma estética y sólo el bosque les da un aspecto diferente. Hay muchos greens y obstáculos ciegos, lo que es característico en este tipo de recorridos que se amoldan a las dunas. Los greens son inmensos con caídas y ondulaciones difíciles. Por supuesto, jugar aquí su handicap es problemático, hay que dominar todos los golpes de golf, sobre todo con viento, y es casi una alegría perder ante tal recorrido. Incluso en neto será muy difícil igualar la proeza de Bernhard Langer, que logró aquí un 62 el último día del Open de España en 1984...

Only rather average standards of upkeep might spoil the joys of savouring one of Europe's best courses. The links holes (5 to 9 and 16 to 18) bear comparison with the best courses in the UK, to which architect Javier Arana has paid tribute here. The other holes are equally attractive, but run through a forest. There are a lot of blind greens and hazards here, but this is typical of this kind of course which hugs the dunes. The greens are often huge and the slopes hard to read. Naturally, playing to your handicap on a course of this standard can pose problems, as it takes every shot in the book, especially when the wind is up. But losing to a course like this is almost a pleasure. Even with a net score, you will be hard put to equal the achievement of Bernhard Langer, who carded a 62 here in the last round of the 1984 Spanish Open...

Campo de Golf El Saler
Parador Nacional "Luis Vivès"
E - 46012 EL SALER (VALENCIA)

Office	Secretaria	(34) 96 - 161 03 84
Pro shop	Pro-shop	(34) 96 - 161 03 84
Fax	Fax	(34) 96 - 162 70 16
Situation	Situación	

8 km Valencia, 777 427 h.

Annual closure	Cierre anual	no
Weekly closure	Cierre semanal	no

Fees main season
Precios tempor. alta el campo

	Week days Semana	We/Bank holidays Fin de sem./fiestas
Individual Individual	5 000 Pts	5 000 Pts
Couple Pareja	10 000 Pts	10 000 Pts

Caddy	Caddy	no
Electric Trolley	Carro eléctrico	2 000 Pts/18 hoyos
Buggy	Coche	4500 Pts/18 hoyos
Clubs	Palos	1 500 Pts/18 hoyos

Credit cards Tarjetas de crédito
VISA - Eurocard - AMEX

VALENCIA

Pinedo

Catarroja

Pista de Silla

V 15

A 7

Silla

N 332

El Saler

GOLF

L'Albufera

Hipódromo

N 340

Gandía

Sueca

0 2 4 km

Access Acceso : V15 Valencia → El Saler, Golf 8 km
Map 6 on page 877 Plano 6 Página 877

GOLF COURSE
RECORRIDO 18/20

Site	Emplazamiento	
Maintenance	Mantenimiento	
Architect	Arquitecto	Javier Araña
Type	Tipo	bosque, links
Relief	Relieve	
Water in play	Agua	
Exp. to wind	Exp. al viento	
Trees in play	Arboles	

Scorecard Tarjeta	Chp. Campeonato	Mens Caballeros	Ladies Damas
Length Longitud	6355	6044	5182
Par	72	72	72

Advised golfing ability		0 12 24 36
Nivel de juego aconsejado		
Hcp required	Handicap exigido	no

CLUB HOUSE & AMENITIES
CLUB HOUSE Y DEPENDENCIAS 7/10

Pro shop	Pro-shop	
Driving range	Campo de prácticas	
Sheltered	cubierto	no
On grass	sobre hierba	si
Putting-green	putting-green	si
Pitching-green	pitching-green	si

HOTEL FACILITIES
HOTELES CERCANOS 6/10

HOTELS HOTELES

Parador "Luis Vívés" — El Saler
58 habitaciones, D 18 500 Pts.
Tel (34) 96 - 161 11 86, Fax (34) 96 - 162 70 16

Melia Valencia Palace — Valencia
199 habitaciones, D 26 500 Pts — 10 km
Tel (34) 96 - 337 50 37, Fax (34) 96 - 337 55 32

Sidi Saler — El Saler
276 habitaciones, D 22 500 Pts — 4 km
Tel (34) 96 - 161 04 11, Fax (34) 96 - 161 08 38

RESTAURANTS RESTAURANTE

Oscar Torrijos — Valencia
Tel (34) 96 - 373 29 49 — 10 km

Sidi Saler — El Saler
Tel(34) 96 - 161 04 11 — 5 km

Rias Gallegas — Valencia
Tel(34) 96 - 357 20 07 — 10 km

913

Empordá tendrá en el futuro 36 hoyos. Por el momento y antes de que se haya acabado de construir el club-house, previsto para finales de esta primavera, 18 hoyos ya han alcanzado su madurez (se han abierto otros 9). Los admiradores de von Hagge no se sorprenderán del diseño característico de montículos que separan las calles, sobre todo en los hoyos sin árboles. Fuera de calle, los roughs están cortados a diferentes alturas hasta convertirse en hierbas altas en los montículos. Esta preparación refinada se confirma con unos greens de excelente calidad, bien diseñados y a menudo muy largos, lo que complica la elección del palo en función de la colocación de las banderas. Si se tiene en cuenta los numerosos tees de salida, la longitud del recorrido puede variar al infinito. Espectacular y muy bien concebido, jugar aquí es apasionante y se ha convertido en uno de los grandes recorridos de Cataluña

Eventually, Emporda will feature 36 holes. For the time being, even before the completion of the club-house, scheduled for this spring, 18 holes have reached maturity (and 9 others are now open). Admirers of von Hagge will not be surprised by this layout, with mounds separating fairways, particularly on the holes without trees. Off the fairway there are two levels of rough before the high grass on the mounds. The same refined preparation is to be found on the excellent greens, which are well designed and often very long, another factor to complicate club selection according to pin positions. When looking at the very many tees, the length of this course can vary enormously. A spectacular, very well "crafted" and exciting course to play, whatever your level, this is already one of the great courses in Catalonia.

Emporda Golf Club
Ctra de Palafrugell a Torroella
E - 17257 GUALTA (GIRONA)

Office	Secretaria	(34) 972 - 76 04 50
Pro shop	Pro-shop	(34) 972 - 76 04 50
Fax	Fax	(34) 972 - 75 71 00
Situation	Situación	

17 km Palafrugell, 17 343 h.
40 km Girona, 70 409 h.

Annual closure	Cierre anual	no
Weekly closure	Cierre semanal	no

Fees main season
Precios tempor. alta El dia

	Week days Semana	We/Bank holidays Fin de sem./fiestas
Individual Individual	8 500 Pts	8 500 Pts
Couple Pareja	17 000 Pts	17 000 Pts

Caddy	Caddy	no
Electric Trolley	Carro eléctrico	1 600 Pts/18 hoyos
Buggy	Coche	5 000 Pts/18 hoyos
Clubs	Palos	2 000 Pts/el dia

Credit cards Tarjetas de crédito
VISA - Eurocard - MasterCard - AMEX

914

Access Acceso : A7 Salida 6 → Girona, GE643 →
Parlavà, Torroella, GE650 → Pals y Palafrugell
Map 2 on page 869 Plano 2 Página 869

GOLF COURSE
RECORRIDO   17 /20

Site	Emplazamiento	
Maintenance	Mantenimiento	
Architect	Arquitecto	Robert von Hagge
Type	Tipo	bosque, llanura
Relief	Relieve	
Water in play	Agua	
Exp. to wind	Exp. al viento	
Trees in play	Arboles	

Scorecard Tarjeta	Chp. Campeonato	Mens Caballeros	Ladies Damas
Length Longitud	6160	5855	4969
Par	71	71	71

Advised golfing ability   0   12   24   36
Nivel de juego aconsejado
Hcp required   Handicap exigido   28 Cab., 36 Damas

CLUB HOUSE & AMENITIES
CLUB HOUSE Y DEPENDENCIAS   7 /10

Pro shop	Pro-shop	
Driving range	Campo de prácticas	
Sheltered	cubierto	no
On grass	sobre hierba	si
Putting-green	putting-green	si
Pitching-green	pitching-green	si

HOTEL FACILITIES
HOTELES CERCANOS   6 /10

HOTELS HOTELES
La Costa   Platja de Pals
120 habitaciones, D 24 000 Pts   10 km
Tel (34) 972 - 66 77 40, Fax (34) 972 - 66 77 36

Mas de Torrent   Torrent
30 habitaciones, D 29 000 Pts   13 km
Tel (34) 972 - 30 32 92, Fax (34) 972 - 30 32 93

Hotel Aiguablava   Fornells
90 habitaciones, D 14 900 Pts   15 km
Tel (34) 972 - 62 20 58, Fax (34) 972 - 62 21 12

RESTAURANTS RESTAURANTE
Can Bech   Fontanilles
Tel (34) 972 - 75 93 17   5 km

Sa Punta   Pals
Tel(34) 972 - 66 73 76   17 km

Mas Pou   Palau-Sator
Tel(34) 972 - 63 41 25   6 km

Construido en un antiguo naranjal, Escorpión ofrece una vegetación compuesta de naranjos y también de palmeras y algarrobos. Se puede jugar fácilmente sin coche. Sus excelentes cuidados realzan el interés de un diseño sencillo y no excepcional. Si bien hay que deplorar la semejanza repetitiva de los pares 4 (en dog-leg), debe resaltarse al menos la calidad técnica de los pares 5 y de los pares 3. No obstante, no se puede decir que este recorrido sea muy difícil por lo que se puede jugar fácilmente en familia o entre amigos de diferentes niveles de juego. Los greens son buenos, bien diseñados y los ante-green poco protegidos: se pueden atacar haciendo rodar la bola. Hay agua en la línea de juego de ocho hoyos, sin que ésto pueda asustar al jugador con cierta precisión. Finalmente, hay que resaltar la calidad y belleza del conjunto que alberga el club-house, muy bien restaurado.

Built in a former orange orchard, Escorpion naturally has a lot of orange trees, together with palm trees and carobs. It is easily walkable and the excellent maintenance work enhances the appeal of what is an honest, but never exceptional, layout. The repetitive style of the par 4s (all dog-legs) is a pity, but the par 3s and 5s are high standard, technical holes. With that said, no-one would consider this to be a tough course, and it is fun to play with the family or friends. The greens are grassy and well-designed, and the few frontal and green-side hazards mean you can often roll the ball onto the putting surface. Water is in play on eight of the holes, but should not unduly scare the more accurate players. One last item is the club house, whose splendid buildings have been beautifully renovated.

Club de Golf Escorpion

Apartado de Correos No 1
E - 46117 - BETERA (VALENCIA)

Office	Secretaria	(34) 96 - 160 12 11
Pro shop	Pro-shop	(34) 96 - 160 12 11
Fax	Fax	(34) 96 - 169 01 87
Situation	Situación	

20 km Valencia, 777 427 h.

Annual closure	Cierre anual	no
Weekly closure	Cierre semanal	no

Fees main season
Precios tempor. alta el campo

	Week days Semana	We/Bank holidays Fin de sem./fiestas
Individual Individual	4 000 pts	8 000 Pts
Couple Pareja	8 000 Pts	16 000 Pts

Caddy	Caddy	no
Electric Trolley	Carro eléctrico	1500 Pts
Buggy	Coche	4500 Pts/18 hoyos
Clubs	Palos	1200 Pts/18 hoyos

Credit cards Tarjetas de crédito   no

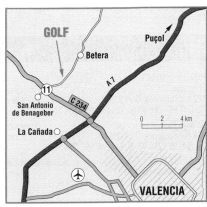

GOLF
Puçol
Betera
A 7
11
C 234
San Antonio
de Benageber
La Cañada
0   2   4 km
VALENCIA

Access Acceso : A7 → Ademús, salida 11,
→ Betera (3,5 km)
Map 4 on page 873 Plano 4 Página 873

GOLF COURSE
RECORRIDO   13/20

Site	Emplazamiento	▬▬▬▬
Maintenance	Mantenimiento	▬▬▬▬▬
Architect	Arquitecto	Ron Kirby
Type	Tipo	campo
Relief	Relieve	▬
Water in play	Agua	▬▬▬
Exp. to wind	Exp. al viento	▬
Trees in play	Arboles	▬▬▬

Scorecard Tarjeta	Chp. Campeonato	Mens Caballeros	Ladies Damas
Length Longitud	6319	6091	5293
Par	72	72	72

Advised golfing ability		0 12 24 36
Nivel de juego aconsejado		▬▬▬▬
Hcp required	Handicap exigido	28 Cab., 36 Damas

CLUB HOUSE & AMENITIES
CLUB HOUSE Y DEPENDENCIAS   8/10

Pro shop	Pro-shop	▬▬▬
Driving range	Campo de prácticas	▬▬▬▬
Sheltered	cubierto	5 puestos
On grass	sobre hierba	si
Putting-green	putting-green	si
Pitching-green	pitching-green	si

HOTEL FACILITIES
HOTELES CERCANOS   4/10

HOTELS HOTELES

Sidi Saler		El Saler
276 habitaciones, D 22 500 Pts		25 km
Tel (34) 96 - 161 04 11, Fax (34) 96 - 161 08 38		
Melia Valencia Palace		Valencia
199 habitaciones, D 26 500 Pts		20 km
Tel (34) 96 - 337 50 37, Fax (34) 96 - 337 55 32		
Feria		Valencia
140 habitaciones, D 10 500 Pts		10 km
Tel (34) 96 - 364 44 11, Fax (34) 96 - 364 54 83		

RESTAURANTS RESTAURANTE

Azafata		Manises
Tel (34) 96 - 154 61 00		15 km
Albacar		Valencia
Tel (34) 96 - 395 10 05		20 km

915

| 14 | 7 | 6 |

Es de esperar que este paisaje de montaña no quede alterado por los proyectos de construcción inmobiliaria, que el recorrido conserve un aspecto natural, en contraste con los grandes recorridos ajardinados, y que la flora y fauna salvajes conserven sus hábitos y su medio ambiente. En una buena mitad del recorrido hay muchas subidas y bajadas por lo que se aconseja alquilar un coche. El arquitecto José Luis López, con inteligencia y buen sentido de golf, ha sabido transformar este terreno difícil. Los greens está¿n bien diseñados,son de buena calidad e interesantes de jugar. Por lo que respecta a las dificultades, hay que evaluar con mucha precisión las ondulaciones del terreno para escoger el buen palo, evitar los roughs poco acogedores. No hay que dejarse impresionar por el hoyo 3, ni por el muy largo par cinco llamado "la pista de esquí", ni tampoco por los lagos del hoyo 10. Si se quiere cambiar del ambiente "chic" de los recorridos de la costa, Estepona es un buen destino.

Hopefully, this mountain landscape will not be spoilt by real estate projects, the course will retain its natural appearance, in contrast with larger, more manicured courses, and the wild flora and fauna will carry on living and growing the way they are. A good half of the course is very hilly, so a buggy is more than recommended. Architect José-Luis Lopez has shaped this difficult terrain intelligently and with a good golfing mind. The well-designed and good quality greens are interesting to play. The course's difficulties involve more often than not assessing the changes in relief to choose the right clubs, avoiding the most unwelcome rough, and not being overwhelmed by the third hole, a very long par 5 called the "ski trail", or by the lakes around the tenth. Estepona is a handy address to make a change from the posher world of the coastal courses.

Estepona Golf

Arroyo Vaquero - CN 340 km 150
E - 29680 ESTEPONA

Office	Secretaria	(34) 95 - 211 30 81
Pro shop	Pro-shop	(34) 95 - 211 30 81
Fax	Fax	(34) 95 - 211 30 80
Situation	Situación	

40 km Gibraltar, 28 339 h.
10 km Estepona, 36 307 h.

| **Annual closure** | Cierre anual | no |
| **Weekly closure** | Cierre semanal | no |

Fees main season
Precios tempor. alta

	Week days Semana	We/Bank holidays Fin de sem./fiestas
Individual Individual	3 500 Pts	3 500 Pts
Couple Pareja	7 000 Pts	7 000 Pts

Caddy	Caddy	no
Electric Trolley	Carro eléctrico	no
Buggy	Coche	3 000 Pts/18 hoyos
Clubs	Palos	1 200 Pts/18 hoyos

Credit cards Tarjetas de crédito — VISA

916

Access Acceso : CN 340 Marbella → Cadiz, Estepona km 150
Map 7 on page 879 Plano 7 Página 879

GOLF COURSE
RECORRIDO **14**/20

Site	Emplazamiento	
Maintenance	Mantenimiento	
Architect	Arquitecto	José Luis Lopez
Type	Tipo	montaña
Relief	Relieve	
Water in play	Agua	
Exp. to wind	Exp. al viento	
Trees in play	Arboles	

Scorecard Tarjeta	Chp. Campeonato	Mens Caballeros	Ladies Damas
Length Longitud	6001	5610	5137
Par	72	72	72

Advised golfing ability
Nivel de juego aconsejado — 0 12 24 36

Hcp required Handicap exigido — no

CLUB HOUSE & AMENITIES
CLUB HOUSE Y DEPENDENCIAS **7**/10

Pro shop	Pro-shop	
Driving range	Campo de prácticas	
Sheltered	cubierto	no
On grass	sobre hierba	si
Putting-green	putting-green	si
Pitching-green	pitching-green	no

HOTEL FACILITIES
HOTELES CERCANOS **6**/10

HOTELS HOTELES
El Paraiso — Estepona
182 habitaciones, D 25 725 Pts — 8 km
Tel (34) 95 - 288 30 00, Fax (34) 95 - 288 20 19

Atalaya Park — Estepona
448 habitaciones, D 24 000 Pts — 8 km
Tel (34) 95 - 288 48 01, Fax (34) 95 - 288 57 35

Andalucia Plaza — Nueva Andalucia
415 habitaciones, D 29 000 Pts — 18 km
Tel (34) 95 - 281 20 00, Fax (34) 95 - 281 47 92

RESTAURANTS RESTAURANTE
De Medici — Estepona
Tel (34) 95 - 288 46 87 — 8 km

El Rocio — Estepona
Tel(34) 95 - 280 00 46 — 8 km

Por supuesto el mejor recorrido de monte en Europa. Rodeado de montañas, aunque llano, con algunas ondulaciones, es un test de primer orden con multitud de obstáculos, encontrándose los más peligrosos en los hoyos más cortos. Numerosos bunkers de calle y de green, con contornos muy elaborados (un poco al estilo de Trent Jones), ponen a prueba el sentido táctico y la virtuosidad del jugador, sin que la suerte intervenga para nada en un buen resultado. Se ha cuidado mucho la estética con muretes o guijarros delimitando los obstáculos de agua. Por momentos impresionante y siempre espectacular, este recorrido de Ramón Espinosa es largo , propicio a los buenos pegadores y en general a los jugadores con experiencia y con un buen juego corto. Difícilmente se le encontrarán defectos a esta obra maestra en la que sólo el club-house está sin acabar.

It's probably the best mountain golf course in Europe. Surrounded by mountains but flat with only a few rolling fairways, this is a test of golf of the highest order with a multitude of hazards, the most dangerous of which are reserved for the short holes. Countless fairway and green-side bunkers, all carefully shaped (a little in the style of Trent Jones), are a great test for the tactical mind and virtuosity of any player, and luck plays no role in a good score. Very special care has been given to the visual side, with the water hazards neatly lined with low walls or pebbles. Often impressive and sometimes quite spectacular, this course by Ramon Espinosa is long and can be recommended to long-hitters and in general to experienced players with a sharp short game. They will be hard pushed to find any faults in this superb achievement, were only the club house remains to be completed.

Golf Fontanals de Cerdanya

E - 17538 SORIGUEROLA,
FONTANALS DE CERDANYA (GIRONA)

Office	Secretaria	(34) 972 - 14 43 74
Pro shop	Pro-shop	(34) 972 - 14 43 74
Fax	Fax	(34) 972 - 89 08 56
Situation	Situación	

12 km Puigcerdà, 6 414 h.

Annual closure	Cierre anual	no
Weekly closure	Cierre semanal	martes
		restaurante

Fees main season
Precios tempor. alta el campo

	Week days Semana	We/Bank holidays Fin de sem./fiestas
Individual Individual	5 000 Pts	14 000 Pts
Couple Pareja	10 000 Pts	28 000 Pts

Caddy	Caddy	no
Electric Trolley	Carro eléctrico	no
Buggy	Coche	5 000 Pts/18 hoyos
Clubs	Palos	1 000 Pts/el dia

Credit cards Tarjetas de crédito
VISA - Eurocard - MasterCard

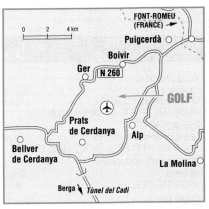

Access Acceso : Barcelona A18 → Manresa y Puigcerdà. Manresa E9 → Puigcerdà, Alp → Golf a la izquierda
Map 2 on page 869 Plano 2 Página 869

GOLF COURSE
RECORRIDO

18/20

Site	Emplazamiento	
Maintenance	Mantenimiento	
Architect	Arquitecto	Ramón Espinosa
Type	Tipo	llanura
Relief	Relieve	
Water in play	Agua	
Exp. to wind	Exp. al viento	
Trees in play	Arboles	

Scorecard Tarjeta	Chp. Campeonato	Mens Caballeros	Ladies Damas
Length Longitud	6454	6159	5256
Par	72	72	72

Advised golfing ability Nivel de juego aconsejado	0	12	24	36
Hcp required Handicap exigido	28 Cab., 36 Damas			

CLUB HOUSE & AMENITIES
CLUB HOUSE Y DEPENDENCIAS

6/10

Pro shop	Pro-shop	
Driving range	Campo de prácticas	
Sheltered	cubierto	14 puestos
On grass	sobre hierba	si
Putting-green	putting-green	si
Pitching-green	pitching-green	si

HOTEL FACILITIES
HOTELES CERCANOS

5/10

HOTELS HOTELES

Torre del Remei		Bolvir de Cerdanya
11 habitaciones, D 38 000 Pts		10 km
Tel (34) 972 - 14 01 82, Fax (34) 972 - 14 04 49		

Chalet del Golf		Puigcerda
11 habitaciones, D 18 000 Pts		9 km
Tel (34) 972 - 88 09 50, Fax (34) 972 - 88 09 66		

RESTAURANTS RESTAURANTE

Torre del Remei		Bolvir de Cerdanya
Tel (34) 972 - 14 01 82		10 km
La Vila		Puigcerdà
Tel (34) 972 - 14 08 04		8 km

917

Un recorrido con bastantes cuestas que requiere estar en buena forma física. Mejor alquilar un coche para concentrarse exclusivamente en el juego. El diseño, aunque no es excepcional, tiene el mérito de valorizar el emplaziamiento del recorrido. Casi todos los hoyos tienen una buena panorámica ya que los tees de salida están generalmente en alto y los obstáculos de agua bien visibles, contrariamente a lo que sucede con algunos bunkers. No es un recorrido que se pueda recomendar a jugadores sin experiencia ya que requiere buena técnica y saber pegar con efecto a la bola: es indispensable jugar estratégicamente pues los obstáculos son peligrosos. Los greens no son muy grandes pero sí bastante ondulados, y no en muy buen estado en el momento de nuestra visita. Un punto de interrogación en caso de intemperie. Bastante largo desde las salidas de atrás, aconsejamos que se juegue desde salidas más adelantadas.

This hilly course calls for fitness and stamina, but in a buggy you will be able to focus more on your game. And you need to, because Girona is full of trees and as a result rather, but nor excessively, tight. There is nothing exceptional about the design, but the layout is good and adds value to the site. The general vision of holes is good, because tees are usually elevated, meaning that hazards are also clearly in view, except for a few bunkers. We wouldn't recommend this course too much to inexperienced players, because it demands sound technique and sometimes the ability to flight the ball both ways. Strategy is important because the hazards are dangerous. The greens are medium-sized with a lot of slopes, but during our visit they were not in perfect condition. This could be a weak point in the event of poor weather. A rather long course from the back tees, so play further forward.

Club de Golf Girona
E - 17481 SANT JULIÀ DE RAMIS (GIRONA)

Office	Secretaria	(34) 972 - 17 16 41
Pro shop	Pro-shop	(34) 972 - 17 16 41
Fax	Fax	(34) 972 - 17 16 82
Situation	Situación	

4 km Girona, 70 500 h.

Annual closure	Cierre anual	no
Weekly closure	Cierre semanal	no

Fees main season
Precios tempor. alta el campo

	Week days Semana	We/Bank holidays Fin de sem./fiestas
Individual Individual	4 500 Pts	6 000 Pts
Couple Pareja	9 000 Pts	12 000 Pts

Caddy	Caddy	no
Electric Trolley	Carro eléctrico	no
Buggy	Coche	5 500 Pts/18 hoyos
Clubs	Palos	1 500 Pts/18 hoyos

Credit cards Tarjetas de crédito
VISA - MasterCard

Access Acceso : A7 salida 6, C150 → Banyoles,
Golf a la izquierda → La Mota
Map 2 on page 869 Plano 2 Página 869

GOLF COURSE
RECORRIDO
13/20

Site	Emplazamiento	
Maintenance	Mantenimiento	
Architect	Arquitecto	Frederic Hawtree
Type	Tipo	montaña
Relief	Relieve	
Water in play	Agua	
Exp. to wind	Exp. al viento	
Trees in play	Arboles	

Scorecard Tarjeta	Chp. Campeonato	Mens Caballeros	Ladies Damas
Length Longitud	6100	6058	5190
Par	72	72	71

Advised golfing ability
Nivel de juego aconsejado
0   12   24   36

Hcp required	Handicap exigido	28 Cab., 36 Damas

CLUB HOUSE & AMENITIES
CLUB HOUSE Y DEPENDENCIAS
7/10

Pro shop	Pro-shop	
Driving range	Campo de prácticas	
Sheltered	cubierto	6 puestos
On grass	sobre hierba	si
Putting-green	putting-green	si
Pitching-green	pitching-green	no

HOTEL FACILITIES
HOTELES CERCANOS
5/10

HOTELS HOTELES

Carlemany	Girona
84 habitaciones, D 13 600 Pts.	10 km
Tel (34) 972 - 21 12 12, Fax (34) 972 - 21 49 94	

Fornells Park	Fornells
50 habitaciones, D 11 400 Pts	10 km
Tel (34) 972 - 47 61 25, Fax (34) 972 - 47 65 79	

RESTAURANTS RESTAURANTE

Albereda	Girona
Tel (34) 972 - 22 60 02	10 km

Quatre Estacions	Banyoles
Tel (34) 972 - 57 33 00	3 km

918

A noventa minutos de la costa, este recorrido no sólo ofrece una buena oportunidad de jugar al golf cuando se va a visitar la soberbia ciudad de Granada, sino que merece la pena por si mismo. Está situado en altura frente a Sierra Nevada, pero sin demasiadas cuestas, su longitud es razonable, salvo en los pares 3 y en los demás hoyos (sobre todo a la vuelta) si se sale de atrás. Las dificultades están colocadas de manera estratégica y peligrosa si no se tiene mucha precisión, especialmente los temibles obsáculos de agua entre los hoyos 15 y 17. Los greens están bien diseñados, son bastante grandes, bien protegidos, con sutiles ondulaciones. En este tipo de recorrido con dificultades bien repartidas, no hay que dudar en atacar en cuanto la ocasión se presente. Se aconsejará jugar con golfistas de mismo nivel para apreciar mejor los desafíos tácticos, pero es un recorrido muy agradable para todo tipo de jugadores.

This course, 90 minutes inland, not only provides a great opportunity to play golf when visiting the superb city of Granada, it is also well worth playing. At altitude, it stands opposite the Sierra Nevada, although the layout is rather flat and the length reasonable, except the par 3s and if you choose to play from the back tees (especially on the back nine). Hazards are strategically placed and often dangerous for wayward shots, especially the formidable water hazards between the 15th and 17th holes. The greens are well-designed, rather large and well defended with tricky slopes. This is a type of course where the difficulties are evenly spread, inviting players to attack whenever the opportunity arises. We recommend playing here with golfers of your own level in order to better appreciate the tactical challenges, but the course is a pleasant day's golfing for everyone.

Granada Club de Golf

Av. Delos Cosarios, 1
E - 18110 LAS GABIAS (GRANADA)

Office	Secretaria	(34) 958 - 58 44 36
Pro shop	Pro-shop	(34) 958 - 58 44 36
Fax	Fax	(34) 958 - 58 40 60
Situation	Situación	

8 km Granada, 287 864 h.

Annual closure	Cierre anual	no
Weekly closure	Cierre semanal	no

Fees main season
Precios tempor. alta el campo

	Week days Semana	We/Bank holidays Fin de sem./fiestas
Individual Individual	4 000 Pts	4 000 Pts
Couple Pareja	8 000 Pts	8 000 Pts

Caddy	Caddy	no
Electric Trolley	Carro eléctrico	no
Buggy	Coche	4500 Pts/18 hoyos
Clubs	Palos	800 Pts/18 hoyos

Credit cards Tarjetas de crédito   no

Access Acceso : Granada N323 → Motril,
Armilla → C340 → Gabia La Grande
Map 8 on page 880 Plano 8 Página 880

GOLF COURSE
RECORRIDO
14/20

Site	Emplazamiento	
Maintenance	Mantenimiento	
Architect	Arquitecto	Ibergolf
Type	Tipo	llanura, vagüada
Relief	Relieve	
Water in play	Agua	
Exp. to wind	Exp. al viento	
Trees in play	Arboles	

Scorecard Tarjeta	Chp. Campeonato	Mens Caballeros	Ladies Damas
Length Longitud	6037	5623	5135
Par	71	71	71

Advised golfing ability	0	12	24	36
Nivel de juego aconsejado				

Hcp required   Handicap exigido   no

CLUB HOUSE & AMENITIES
CLUB HOUSE Y DEPENDENCIAS
6/10

Pro shop	Pro-shop	
Driving range	Campo de prácticas	
Sheltered	cubierto	no
On grass	sobre hierba	si
Putting-green	putting-green	si
Pitching-green	pitching-green	si

919

HOTEL FACILITIES
HOTELES CERCANOS
5/10

HOTELS HOTELES
Melia Granada   Granada
191 habitaciones, D 17 900 Pts   8 km
Tel (34) 958 - 22 74 00, Fax (34) 958 - 22 74 03

Carmen   Granada
283 habitaciones, D 18 000 Pts   8 km
Tel (34) 958 - 25 83 00, Fax (34) 958 - 25 64 62

Princesa Ana   Granada
59 habitaciones, D 16 000 Pts   8 km
Tel (34) 958 - 28 74 47, Fax (34) 958 - 27 39 54

RESTAURANTS RESTAURANTE
Bogavante   Granada
Tel (34) 958 - 25 91 12   8 km

Tavares   Granada
Tel (34) 958 - 22 67 69   8 km

GUADALHORCE

14	7	6

En la campiña al oeste de Málaga, este recorrido diseñado por el finlandés Kosti Kuronen presenta dos caras: los nueve primeros hoyos son bastante clásicos, los nueve últimos más imaginativos con greens en alto, calles y lagos bien cuidados. Los greens son de excelente calidad, a veces dobles (6 y 8, 12 y 16), rápidos y bien protegidos, y aguantan bien la bola. El conjunto no es que sea excepcional, pero es muy agradable y divertido el jugar todas las fórmulas de golf, tanto con jugadores de mismo nivel como de niveles muy diferentes. Sobre todo reserva sus dificultades a los mejores, respondiendo exactamente a la definición de un buen campo de golf, y el hecho de que no sea necesario alquilar un coche hace que sea muy placentero el jugar en familia. Algunas trampas estratégicas le dan un cierto encanto e incitan a jugarlo varias veces.

In the countryside to the west of Malaga, this course, designed by Finnish architect Kosti Kuronen, offers two different faces. The front nine are classical holes, while the back nine are more imaginative with elevated greens, lakes and well laid out fairways. The greens are excellent, sometimes double (6 and 8, 12 and 16), fast and well-defended, but they pitch well. This is probably not an exceptional course, but it is very pleasant and fun to play with players of your own standard or with anyone, for that matter. In fact, the difficulties of Guadalhorce, as with any good course, are reserved for the better players, and being easily playable on foot it is great fun to play with all the family. A few strategic traps add a little spice to the round and make you want to come back and play it again, and again.

Guadalhorce Club de Golf

Apartado de Correos 48
E - 29590 CAMPANILLAS-MALAGA

Office	Secretaria	(34) 95 - 217 93 78
Pro shop	Pro-shop	(34) 95 - 217 94 40
Fax	Fax	(34) 95 - 217 93 72
Situation	Situación	

6 km Málaga, 534 683 h.
15 km Fuengirola, 43 048 h.

Annual closure	Cierre anual	no
Weekly closure	Cierre semanal	no

Fees main season
Precios tempor. alta

	Week days Semana	We/Bank holidays Fin de sem./fiestas
Individual Individual	5 000 Pts	5 000 Pts
Couple Pareja	10 000 Pts	10 000 Pts

Caddy	Caddy	no
Electric Trolley	Carro eléctrico	no
Buggy	Coche	3 000 Pts/18 hoyos
Clubs	Palos	1 500 Pts/18 hoyos

Credit cards Tarjetas de crédito — VISA

920

Access Acceso : Málaga → Parque Tecnologico, Salida "Campanillas", 2 km, Golf.
Map 7 on page 879 Plano 7 Página 879

GOLF COURSE
RECORRIDO — 14/20

Site	Emplazamiento	
Maintenance	Mantenimiento	
Architect	Arquitecto	Kosti Kuronen
Type	Tipo	campo, llanura
Relief	Relieve	
Water in play	Agua	
Exp. to wind	Exp. al viento	
Trees in play	Arboles	

Scorecard Tarjeta	Chp. Campeonato	Mens Caballeros	Ladies Damas
Length Longitud	6194	5860	4992
Par	72	72	72

Advised golfing ability		0	12	24	36
Nivel de juego aconsejado					

Hcp required Handicap exigido — 28 Cab., 36 Damas

CLUB HOUSE & AMENITIES
CLUB HOUSE Y DEPENDENCIAS — 7/10

Pro shop	Pro-shop	
Driving range	Campo de prácticas	
Sheltered	cubierto	4 puestos
On grass	sobre hierba	si
Putting-green	putting-green	si
Pitching-green	pitching-green	si

HOTEL FACILITIES
HOTELES CERCANOS — 6/10

HOTELS HOTELES

Malaga Palacio — Malaga 12 km
221 habitaciones, D 18 600 Pts
Tel (34) 95 - 221 51 85, Fax (34) 95 - 221 51 85

Guadalmar — Malaga 5 km
200 habitaciones, D 16 350 Pts
Tel (34) 95 - 223 17 03, Fax (34) 95 - 224 03 85

Larios — Malaga 12 km
40 habitaciones, D 19 000 Pts
Tel (34) 95 - 222 22 00, Fax (34) 95 - 222 24 07

RESTAURANTS RESTAURANTE

Adolfo — Malaga
Tel (34) 95 - 260 19 14

Cueva del Camborio — Malaga
Tel (34) 95 - 234 78 16

Es el segundo recorrido creado en la Costa del Sol, diseñado por el legendario Javier Arana. Mucho más llano que el "Norte", sin embargo sus calles son más anchas, con árboles a menudo en la línea de juego. Al tener pocas carreteras que lo atraviesen, se juega más tranquilamente, al menos en los hoyos que dan al mar. Más difícil de lo que parece, sobre todo con viento, no se siúa entre los más exigentes de la costa, máxime teniendo en cuenta que sus dificultades son perfectamente visibles y la estrategia de juego evidente. Un riachuelo está en la línea de juego en varios hoyos, pero no es demasiado peligroso. La ida tiene algunos hoyos bastante largos, mientras que a la vuelta hay algunos bastante cortos, especialmente pares 4 cortitos en los que los bienvenidos birdies pueden aliviar la tarjeta , pares 3 de buena calidad (sobre todo el 11) y dos pares 5 de los que en uno al menos (el 17) se puede llegar en dos golpes. Hay que conocerlo.

This is the second course opened on the Costa del Sol designed by the legendary Javier Arana. Much flatter than the "Norte", it also has wider fairways and more trees, which often get in the way. There are fewer roads around, so it is a quieter course, at least for the holes facing the sea. Harder than it looks, especially when the wind is up, it is not the most challenging course on this coast, especially since the hazards are perfectly visible and playing strategy rather obvious. A small river comes into play on several holes but is rarely too dangerous. The front nine include some rather long holes, while the inward half has a number of shortish holes, notably the short part 4s, where a few welcome birdies can do your score-card a world of good, enjoyable par 3s (especially the 11th) and two par 5s, of which at least one (the 17th) is reachable in two. Worth knowing.

Guadalmina Club de Golf

Urb. Guadalmina Alta
E - 29678 SAN PEDRO DE ALCANTARA (MALAGA)

Office	Secretaria	(34) 95 - 288 65 22
Pro shop	Pro-shop	(34) 95 - 288 20 23
Fax	Fax	(34) 95 - 288 34 83
Situation	Situación	

1 km San Pedro de Alcantara
14 km Estepona, 36 307 h.

Annual closure	Cierre anual	no
Weekly closure	Cierre semanal	no

Fees main season
Precios tempor. alta el campo

	Week days Semana	We/Bank holidays Fin de sem./fiestas
Individual Individual	6 500 Pts	6 500 Pts
Couple Pareja	13 000 Pts	13 000 Pts

Caddy	Caddy	no
Electric Trolley	Carro eléctrico	1500 Pts/18 hoyos
Buggy	Coche	4500 Pts/18 hoyos
Clubs	Palos	2000 Pts/18 hoyos

Credit cards Tarjetas de crédito	VISA - AMEX

Access Acceso : N340 Marbella →
San Pedro de Alcantara
Map 7 on page 879 Plano 7 Página 879

GOLF COURSE
RECORRIDO   14/20

Site	Emplazamiento	
Maintenance	Mantenimiento	
Architect	Arquitecto	Javier Araña
Type	Tipo	al borde del mar, llanura
Relief	Relieve	
Water in play	Agua	
Exp. to wind	Exp. al viento	
Trees in play	Arboles	

Scorecard Tarjeta	Chp. Campeonato	Mens Caballeros	Ladies Damas
Length Longitud	6025	5874	5130
Par	72	72	72

Advised golfing ability		0 12 24 36
Nivel de juego aconsejado		
Hcp required	Handicap exigido	28 Cab., 36 Damas

CLUB HOUSE & AMENITIES
CLUB HOUSE Y DEPENDENCIAS   7/10

Pro shop	Pro-shop	
Driving range	Campo de prácticas	
Sheltered	cubierto	no
On grass	sobre hierba	si
Putting-green	putting-green	si
Pitching-green	pitching-green	no

921

HOTEL FACILITIES
HOTELES CERCANOS   7/10

HOTELS HOTELES
Guadalmina   San Pedro
80 habitaciones, D 25 850 Pts   1 km
Tel (34) 95 - 288 22 11, Fax (34) 95 - 288 22 91

El Paraiso   Estepona
182 habitaciones, D 25 725 Pts   3 km
Tel (34) 95 - 288 30 00, Fax (34) 95 - 288 20 19

Atalaya Park   Estepona
448 habitaciones, D 24 000 Pts   2 km
Tel (34) 95 - 288 48 01, Fax (34) 95 - 288 57 35

RESTAURANTS RESTAURANTE
Meridiana   Marbella
Tel (34) 95 - 277 61 90

Bistrot Cristian - Tel(34) 95 - 281 10 06   Puerto Banús

Los Nietos   San Pedro de Alcantara
Tel(34) 95 - 288 34 91   1 km

Es muy raro poder jugar a proximidad de monumentos históricos como el Monasterio de San Lorenzo del Escorial que domina el recorrido. La Herreria es tan espectacular como las vistas que proporciona. En el diseño de Antonio Lucena Gómez los peligros vienen de los árboles y los bunkers, que defienden al mismo las caídas de drive como los greenes, bastante lisos pero a la vez bien moldeados. Estas dificultades no son nunca infranqueables sea cual sea el nivel del jugador ya que son muy visibles para permitir adoptar una estrategia que nos permita eludir las malas sorpresas. Si el 2 es un par 5 muy complicado, las vistas panorámicas de los hoyos 12, 13 y 14 permiten reposar el espíritu antes de abordar el hoyo 18, uno de los mejores pares 4 de España...

It is rare indeed to be able to swing a club so close to historical landmarks such as the Monasterio de San Lorenzo de El Escorial, which overlooks this course. La Herreria is also one of the truly public courses in the Madrid area, even though private courses are beginning to open up to visitors. The site is as spectacular as the vistas from the course, designed by Antonio Lucena Gomez. The main hazards are the trees and bunkers, guarding both the drive landing zone and the greens, the latter being flat but well shaped. These difficulties are never impossible to negotiate, whatever your level of proficiency, and are visible enough to adopt a strategy to avoid unpleasant surprises. While the second hole is a rather complicated par 5, the scenic views from the 12th, 13th and 14 th holes are enough to calm frayed nerves before attacking the 18th, one of the best par 4s in Spain.

La Herreria Club de Golf
Ctra de Robledo S/N
E - 28200 SAN LORENZO DE EL ESCORIAL (MADRID)

Office	Secretaria	(34) 91 - 890 51 11
Pro shop	Pro-shop	(34) 91 - 890 56 17
Fax	Fax	(34) 91 - 890 71 54
Situation	Situación	

2 km San Lorenzo de El Escorial, 8 704 h.
57 km Madrid, 3 084 673 h.

Annual closure	Cierre anual	no
Weekly closure	Cierre semanal	no

Fees main season
Precios tempor. alta El campo

	Week days Semana	We/Bank holidays Fin de sem./fiestas
Individual Individual	5 900 Pts	9 000 Pts
Couple Pareja	11 800 Pts	18 000 Pts

Caddy	Caddy	no
Electric Trolley	Carro eléctrico	1000 Pts/18 hoyos
Buggy	Coche	4000 Pts/18 hoyos
Clubs	Palos	no

Credit cards Tarjetas de crédito — no

Access Acceso : Madrid A6 → Segovia.
Salida El Escorial, M600 → San Lorenzo de El Escorial. → Robledo de Chavela, Golf a la izquierda
Map 3 on page 870 Plano 3 Página 870

GOLF COURSE
RECORRIDO
15/20

Site	Emplazamiento	
Maintenance	Mantenimiento	
Architect	Arquitecto	Antonio Lucena Gomez
Type	Tipo	bosque
Relief	Relieve	
Water in play	Agua	
Exp. to wind	Exp. al viento	
Trees in play	Arboles	

Scorecard Tarjeta	Chp. Campeonato	Mens Caballeros	Ladies Damas
Length Longitud	6050	6050	5121
Par	72	72	72

Advised golfing ability Nivel de juego aconsejado	0	12	24	36
Hcp required Handicap exigido	28 Cab., 36 Damas			

CLUB HOUSE & AMENITIES
CLUB HOUSE Y DEPENDENCIAS
6/10

Pro shop	Pro-shop	
Driving range	Campo de prácticas	
Sheltered	cubierto	no
On grass	sobre hierba	si
Putting-green	putting-green	si
Pitching-green	pitching-green	no

HOTEL FACILITIES
HOTELES CERCANOS
6/10

HOTELS HOTELES

Victoria Palace — San Lorenzo
90 habitaciones, D 17 500 Pts — 2 km
Tel (34) 91 - 890 15 11, Fax (34) 91 - 890 12 48

Cristina — San Lorenzo
16 habitaciones, D 6 000 Pts — 2 km
Tel (34) 91 - 890 19 61, Fax (34) 91 - 890 12 04

Miranda Suizo — San Lorenzo
52 habitaciones, D 11 000 Pts — 2 km
Tel (34) 91 - 890 47 11, Fax (34) 91 - 890 43 52

RESTAURANTS RESTAURANTE

Charolés — San Lorenzo
Tel (34) 91 - 890 59 75 — 2 km

Parilla Principe — San Lorenzo
Tel (34) 91 - 890 16 11 — 2 km

922

Con 27 hoyos y un bonito club-house de estilo andaluz, el conjunto de este ambicioso proyecto domina el Atlántico. Los magníficos árboles de este inmenso parque han sido preservados y constituyen una de las dificultades con bosquecitos que penalizan. Adeñás de los numerosos bunkers bien diseñados y de un cierto número de obstáculos de agua, greens ondulados y a menudo en alto hacen muy técnico un recorrido generalmente utilizado como el principal 18 hoyos. Raramente existen trampas escondidas y se puede afrontar sin miedo. La anchura de las calles pueden dar la impresión de que es un recorrido fácil, pero es una impresión ilusoria, sobre todo desde las salidas de atrás. Si al gusto de jugar se añade el placer de la vista (especialmente el Océano en el 12), Islantilla es una de las buenas sorpresas de estos últimos años y merece la pena conocerlo.

The 27 holes and attractive Andalusian style clubhouse of this ambitious complex overlook the Atlantic Ocean. The fine trees in this huge park have been spared and form some of the difficulties along with penalising undergrowth. In addition to the well-designed bunkers and a number of water hazards, the well-contoured and often elevated greens (some are blind) help make the 18 holes generally used as the main course a rather technical layout. But since the traps are rarely concealed, there is not a great deal to be afraid of. The wide fairways perhaps give the impression of a course that is easy to score on, but this is only an impression, especially when playing from the back tees. If you combine the pleasure of playing and the surrounding view (notably over the ocean on hole N° 12), Islantilla is one of the nicest surprises in recent years and well worth the trip.

Islantilla
Ctra La Antilla - Isla Cristina
E - 21410 HUELVA

Office	Secretaria	(34) 959 - 48 60 39
Pro shop	Pro-shop	(34) 959 - 48 60 39
Fax	Fax	(34) 959 - 48 61 04
Situation	Situación	

147 km Sevilla, 704 857 h.
40 km Huelva, 144 579 h.

Annual closure	Cierre anual	no
Weekly closure	Cierre semanal	no

Fees main season
Precios tempor. alta el campo

	Week days Semana	We/Bank holidays Fin de sem./fiestas
Individual Individual	6 500 Pts	6 500 Pts
Couple Pareja	13 000 Pts	13 000 Pts

Caddy	Caddy	si, reservar
Electric Trolley	Carro eléctrico	1 750 Pts
Buggy	Coche	4 000 Pts/18 hoyos
Clubs	Palos	2000 Pts/18 hoyos

Credit cards Tarjetas de crédito   VISA - AMEX - DC

Access Acceso : Huelva, N431 → Ayamonte,
Lepe → La Antilla, Golf 3 km
Map 7 on page 878 Plano 7 Página 878

GOLF COURSE
RECORRIDO   16/20

Site	Emplazamiento	▮▮▮▮▮▮
Maintenance	Mantenimiento	▮▮▮▮▮▮
Architect	Arquitecto	Enrique Canales Luis Recasens
Type	Tipo	al borde del mar, bosque
Relief	Relieve	▮▮▮
Water in play	Agua	▮▮▮
Exp. to wind	Exp. al viento	▮▮▮
Trees in play	Arboles	▮▮▮▮

Scorecard Tarjeta	Chp. Campeonato	Mens Caballeros	Ladies Damas
Length Longitud	5926	5389	4686
Par	72	72	72

Advised golfing ability Nivel de juego aconsejado	0 12 24 36
Hcp required Handicap exigido	28 Cab., 36 Damas

CLUB HOUSE & AMENITIES
CLUB HOUSE Y DEPENDENCIAS   8/10

Pro shop	Pro-shop	▮▮▮▮▮▮
Driving range	Campo de prácticas	▮▮▮▮▮
Sheltered	cubierto	no
On grass	sobre hierba	si
Putting-green	putting-green	si
Pitching-green	pitching-green	si

HOTEL FACILITIES
HOTELES CERCANOS   8/10

HOTELS HOTELES
Confortel Islantilla   Islantilla
344 habitaciones, D 18 100 Pts   1 km
Tel (34) 959 - 48 60 17, Fax (34) 959 - 48 60 70

Paraiso Playa   Isla Cristina
35 habitaciones, D 8 500 Pts   3 km
Tel (34) 959 - 33 18 73, Fax (34) 959 - 34 37 45

Sol y Mar   Isla Cristina
16 habitaciones, D 8 000 Pts   3 km
Tel (34) 959 - 33 20 50

RESTAURANTS RESTAURANTE
El Coral   La Antilla
Tel (34) 959 - 48 14 06   2 km

Meson La Isla   Isla Cristina
Tel (34) 959 - 34 30 18   5 km

923

El interesante diseño de Arana se ve desgraciadamente alterado por el paso de los años y por una tierra demasiado vieja que provoca problemas de drenaje en tiempo húmedo, problemas que sin embargo el Real Automovil Club de España están tratando remediar. Bien situado, con magníficas vistas, sería un sitio muy tranquilo para jugar si la proximidad del circuito automovilístico no trajese a veces problemas sonoros. Sería una pena sin embargo no aceptar una visita al campo ya que si requiere una cierta longitud (¡sobre todo desde atrás!), es lo suficientemente amplio para permitir cualquier error de dirección muy frecuentes con el driver. Cierto es que los árboles y los bunkers de recorrido constituyen sus principales defensas, pero serán sobre todo los tiros a green que proporcionarán a los jugadores imprecisos los principales problemas. Será más por la precisión que por la longitud que podremos aspirar a jugar nuestro handicap.

Javier Arana's interesting design has unfortunately been badly affected by aging terrain and a few drainage problems in wet weather. We are told that the Royal Automobile Club of Spain (the course's owner) envisage remedying this very shortly. Well located with some wonderful views, this would be a very quiet place to play if it weren't for the racing track close-by (going by the same name of Jarama), which can be noisy at times. It would, though, be a shame to turn down a visit here, because while the course demands length off the tee (especially from the back), it is wide enough to forgive the all too frequent sliced or hooked drive. Although the trees and fairway bunkers form a solid wall of defence, the biggest problems here for wayward hitters are approach shots to greens. Accuracy more than length is called for if you want to hope to play to your handicap.

Club Jarama R.A.C.E.
Carretera de Madrid Burgos km 28,100
E - 28700 S.S. DE LOS REYES-MADRID

Office	Secretaria	(34) 91 - 657 00 11
Pro shop	Pro-shop	(34) 91 - 657 00 11
Fax	Fax	(34) 91 - 657 04 62
Situation	Situación	

28 km Madrid, 3 084 673 h.

Annual closure	Cierre anual	no
Weekly closure	Cierre semanal	no

Fees main season
Precios tempor. alta 18 hoyos

	Week days Semana	We/Bank holidays Fin de sem./fiestas
Individual Individual	5 000 Pts	10 000 Pts
Couple Pareja	10 000 Pts	20 000 Pts

Caddy	Caddy	no
Electric Trolley	Carro eléctrico	1000 Pts/18 hoyos
Buggy	Coche	4000 Pts/18 hoyos
Clubs	Palos	no

Credit cards Tarjetas de crédito — no

924

Access Acceso : Carretera Madrid → Burgos, km 28,100
Map 3 on page 870 Plano 3 Página 870

GOLF COURSE
RECORRIDO — 13/20

Site	Emplazamiento	
Maintenance	Mantenimiento	
Architect	Arquitecto	Javier Arana
Type	Tipo	campo
Relief	Relieve	
Water in play	Agua	
Exp. to wind	Exp. al viento	
Trees in play	Arboles	

Scorecard Tarjeta	Chp. Campeonato	Mens Caballeros	Ladies Damas
Length Longitud	6497	6070	5109
Par	72	72	72

Advised golfing ability		0 12 24 36
Nivel de juego aconsejado		
Hcp required	Handicap exigido	28 Cab., 36 Damas

CLUB HOUSE & AMENITIES
CLUB HOUSE Y DEPENDENCIAS — 7/10

Pro shop	Pro-shop	
Driving range	Campo de prácticas	
Sheltered	cubierto	60 puestos
On grass	sobre hierba	si
Putting-green	putting-green	si
Pitching-green	pitching-green	si

HOTEL FACILITIES
HOTELES CERCANOS — 6/10

HOTELS HOTELES
Chamartin — Madrid
360 habitaciones, D 19 100 Pts — 20 km
Tel (34) 91 - 334 49 00, Fax (34) 91 - 733 02 14

Melia Castilla — Madrid
900 habitaciones, D 32 400 Pts — 20 km
Tel (34) 91 - 567 50 00, Fax (34) 91 - 567 50 51

La Moraleja — Alcobendas
37 habitaciones, D 19 200 Pts — 15 km
Tel (34) 91 - 661 80 55, Fax (34) 91 - 661 21 88

RESTAURANTS RESTAURANTE
Mesón Tejas Verde — S.S. de Los Reyes
Tel (34) 91 - 652 73 07 — 10 km

Vicente — S.S. de Los Reyes
Tel(34) 91 - 651 31 71 — 10 km

Izamar — S.S. de Los Reyes
Tel(34) 91 - 654 38 93 — 10 km

Es un verdadero éxito el haber podido alojar dos recorridos en una región tan montañosa..., ¡ se necesita estar en excelente condición física para prescindir de un coche! . El "Norte" ofrece buenas ocasiones de utilizar el drive, pero en general es tan importante colocar la bola y los roughs tan peligrosos (matorrales), que la madera 3 es más que suficiente. Las ondulaciones del recorrido y las impresiones ópticas exigen reflexión tanto en cada golpe como en la elección del palo, por lo que se aconseja ñás bien a jugadores ya experimentados. Sólo después de haberlo jugado una o dos veces se puede intentar obtener un buen resultado, pero es un recorrido para jugar sobre todo en match-play, apasionante por el diseño de las caídas de los greens, generalmente protegidos por grandes y profundos bunkers. Pequeño consuelo en caso de decepción: sólo hay agua en dos hoyos y la vista panorámica sobre esta región salvaje es magnífica.

Accommodating two courses into such a moutainous region is something of an exploit, but you need to be pretty fit to refuse a buggy. The "Norte" offers some fine opportunities to take the driver out of the bag, but as a general rule, positioning the ball is so important and the rough so dangerous (scrub) that the 3-wood (or long-iron) will suffice. The general relief of this course and the optical illusions call for careful consideration when choosing the club before every shot, which is why we recommend it for experienced players. After one or two reconnaissance rounds they might think about scoring, but this is a course made for match-play, an exciting format on these contoured greens which are generally well-defended by large, deep bunkers. A minor compensation in the event of wayward shot-making is the thought that water only comes into play on two holes and the vista over this wild region is magnificent.

La Cala Resort

La Cala de Mijas
E - 29647 MIJAS COSTA (MALAGA)

Office	Secretaria	(34) 95 - 266 90 00
Pro shop	Pro-shop	(34) 95 - 266 90 00
Fax	Fax	(34) 95 - 266 90 39
Situation	Situación	

20 km Marbella, 84 410 h.
10 km Mijas, 32 835 h.

Annual closure	Cierre anual	no
Weekly closure	Cierre semanal	no

Fees main season
Precios tempor. alta el campo

	Week days Semana	We/Bank holidays Fin de sem./fiestas
Individual Individual	7 500 Pts	7 500 Pts
Couple Pareja	15 000 Pts	15 000 Pts

Caddy	Caddy	no
Electric Trolley	Carro eléctrico	no
Buggy	Coche	4500 Pts/18 hoyos
Clubs	Palos	2 500 Pts/18 hoyos

Credit cards Tarjetas de crédito
VISA - MasterCard - AMEX

Access Acceso : Málaga, N340 → Fuengirola,
Cala de Mijas → Golf
Map 7 on page 879 Plano 7 Página 879

GOLF COURSE
RECORRIDO 17 /20

Site	Emplazamiento	▨▨▨▨▨▨▨□□
Maintenance	Mantenimiento	▨▨▨▨▨▨▨▨□
Architect	Arquitecto	Cabell Robinson
Type	Tipo	montaña
Relief	Relieve	▨▨▨▨▨▨▨▨□
Water in play	Agua	▨▨□□□□□□□
Exp. to wind	Exp. al viento	▨▨▨□□□□□□
Trees in play	Arboles	▨▨▨▨▨▨▨□□

Scorecard Tarjeta	Chp. Campeonato	Mens Caballeros	Ladies Damas
Length Longitud	6160	5723	4690
Par	72	73	73

Advised golfing ability
Nivel de juego aconsejado

0	12	24	36

▨▨▨▨▨▨□□

Hcp required Handicap exigido   28 Cab., 36 Damas

CLUB HOUSE & AMENITIES
CLUB HOUSE Y DEPENDENCIAS 8 /10

Pro shop	Pro-shop	▨▨▨▨▨▨▨□□
Driving range	Campo de prácticas	▨▨▨▨▨▨▨▨□
Sheltered	cubierto	no
On grass	sobre hierba	si
Putting-green	putting-green	si
Pitching-green	pitching-green	si

HOTEL FACILITIES
HOTELES CERCANOS 6 /10

HOTELS HOTELES

La Cala Resort — Golf
73 habitaciones, D 30 000 Pts
Tel (34) 95 - 266 90 00, Fax (34) 95 - 266 90 39

Byblos — Fuengirola
144 habitaciones, D 37 500 Pts — 6 km
Tel (34) 95 - 247 30 50, Fax (34) 95 - 247 67 83

Mijas — Mijas
97 habitaciones, D 14 000 Pts — 20 km
Tel (34) 95 - 248 58 00, Fax (34) 95 - 248 58 25

RESTAURANTS RESTAURANTE

El Olivar — Mijas
Tel (34) 95 - 248 61 96 — 20 km

El Tomate — Fuengirola
Tel (34) 95 - 247 35 99 — 6 km

925

Preferir uno u otro de los dos recorridos de La Cala es una cuestión de gusto. El "Sur" da la impresión de ser un poco más corto, o en todo caso que perdona más lo errores. También aquí los desniveles son engañosos y no hay que fiarse de la longitud teórica de los hoyos. Los drive aterrizan a menudo en zonas en alto y una vegetación densa forma una buena parte de los roughs. Algunas pendientes pronunciadas alrededor de los greens exigen un buen juego corto y mucha intuición. Al igual que en el "Norte", poco importa el resultado cuando se juega por primera vez y para mantener intacto el placer de jugar hay que aceptar las cosas como vienen y con un cierto sentido del humor. Si es mejor que los principiantes se abstengan y prefieran las excelentes instalaciones del campo de prácticas, los jugadores más aguerridos alquilarán un coche para saborear una jornada apasionante.

Preference for one or the other of La Cala courses is a matter of taste. The "Sur" gives the impression of being a little less long, or in any case of being more forgiving for mis-hit shots. Here, too, the terrain's physical contours are misleading and not too much faith should be put in the theoretical lengths of holes. The drive often lands on plateaus which players should not stray too far from, as a large part of rough here is dense vegetation. A number of steep slopes around the greens call for a sharp short game and loads of intuition. As with the "Norte", the score is of little consequence when playing the course for the first time. To really enjoy yourself, take things as they come and never lose your sense of humour. While beginners should refrain from playing the course and stick to the excellent practice facilities, the more proficient players can hop in a buggy and soak up an exciting day's golf.

La Cala Resort

La Cala de Mijas
E - 29647 MIJAS COSTA (MALAGA)

Office	Secretaria	(34) 95 - 266 90 00
Pro shop	Pro-shop	(34) 95 - 266 90 00
Fax	Fax	(34) 95 - 266 90 39
Situation	Situación	

20 km Marbella, 84 410 h.
10 km Mijas, 32 835 h.

Annual closure	Cierre anual	no
Weekly closure	Cierre semanal	no

Fees main season
Precios tempor. alta el campo

	Week days Semana	We/Bank holidays Fin de sem./fiestas
Individual Individual	7 500 Pts	7 500 Pts
Couple Pareja	15 000 Pts	15 000 Pts

Caddy	Caddy	no
Electric Trolley	Carro eléctrico	no
Buggy	Coche	4500 Pts/18 hoyos
Clubs	Palos	2 500 Pts/18 hoyos

Credit cards Tarjetas de crédito
VISA - MasterCard - AMEX

Access Acceso : Málaga, N340 → Fuengirola,
Cala de Mijas → Golf
Map 7 on page 879 Plano 7 Página 879

GOLF COURSE
RECORRIDO 16/20

Site	Emplazamiento	▰▰▰▰▰▱
Maintenance	Mantenimiento	▰▰▰▰▰▱
Architect	Arquitecto	Cabell Robinson
Type	Tipo	montaña
Relief	Relieve	▰▰▰▰▰▰
Water in play	Agua	▰▰▰▱▱▱
Exp. to wind	Exp. al viento	▰▰▰▰▱▱
Trees in play	Arboles	▰▰▰▰▱▱

Scorecard Tarjeta	Chp. Campeonato	Mens Caballeros	Ladies Damas
Length Longitud	5960	5440	4530
Par	71	71	71

Advised golfing ability Nivel de juego aconsejado	0	12	24	36

Hcp required Handicap exigido 28 Cab., 36 Damas

CLUB HOUSE & AMENITIES
CLUB HOUSE Y DEPENDENCIAS 8/10

Pro shop	Pro-shop	▰▰▰▰▰▱
Driving range	Campo de prácticas	▰▰▰▰▰▱
Sheltered	cubierto	no
On grass	sobre hierba	si
Putting-green	putting-green	si
Pitching-green	pitching-green	si

HOTEL FACILITIES
HOTELES CERCANOS 6/10

HOTELS HOTELES
La Cala Resort   Golf
73 habitaciones, D 30 000 Pts
Tel (34) 95 - 266 90 00, Fax (34) 95 - 266 90 39

Byblos   Fuengirola
144 habitaciones, D 37 500 Pts   6 km
Tel (34) 95 - 247 30 50, Fax (34) 95 - 247 67 83

Mijas   Mijas
97 habitaciones, D 14 000 Pts   20 km
Tel (34) 95 - 248 58 00, Fax (34) 95 - 248 58 25

RESTAURANTS RESTAURANTE
El Olivar   Mijas
Tel (34) 95 - 248 61 96   20 km

El Tomate   Fuengirola
Tel (34) 95 - 247 35 99   6 km

926

El recorrido de La Dehesa forma parte de un gran complejo concebido para el ocio familiar, siendo igual de agradable para el golfista como para el no golfista, éste último se ve reducido demasiadas veces a ser un mero acompañante durante las vacaciones de golf. Las instalaciones de entrenamiento les permitirá incluso iniciarse en la práctica del golf. A la hora de diseñar el campo, Manuel Piñero pensó en todos los jugadores: es un campo competitivo, pero existen siempre soluciones para salirse de los peligros que encierra. Estos son numerosos durante los 18 hoyos, pero están los suficientemente a la vista para poder decidir rápidamente atacar a ser prudente. Los greens son suficientemente amplios, bien defendidos, pero agradables de atacar y de jugar. Los espacios muy abiertos, el respeto del entorno existente y las magníficas vistas de la Sierra Madrileña dan al lugar una gran belleza.

The La Dehesa course is part of a large resort designed for family recreation, an equally pleasant spot for golfers and non-golfers alike. On a golfing day, the latter are often left having to accompany their playing partners, but not so here. What's more, the practice facilities might even entice them into having a swing themselves. In designing this course, Manuel Pinero spared a thought for everyone: it is a competitive layout, but there are always solutions for getting around the main difficulties. There is indeed a lot of danger, well spread over the 18 holes, but hazards are visible enough for anyone to decide quickly whether to "go for it" or "lay up". Wide open space, the respect for existing natural beauty and some magnificent views over the Madrid Sierra make this a wonderful spot for golf.

Golf La Dehesa

Avenida de la Universidad S/N
E - 28691 VILLANUEVA DE LA CAÑADA (MADRID)

Office	Secretaria	(34) 91 - 815 70 22
Pro shop	Pro-shop	(34) 91 - 815 70 22
Fax	Fax	(34) 91 - 815 54 68
Situation	Situación	

28 km Madrid, 3 084 673 h.
5 km Brunete, 2 505 h.

Annual closure	Cierre anual	no
Weekly closure	Cierre semanal	no

Fees main season
Precios tempor. alta El campo

	Week days Semana	We/Bank holidays Fin de sem./fiestas
Individual Individual	6 000 Pts	16 000 Pts
Couple Pareja	12 000 Pts	32 000 Pts

Caddy	Caddy	no
Electric Trolley	Carro eléctrico	1 000 Pts
Buggy	Coche	4 000 Pts/18 hoyos
Clubs	Palos	2 000 Pts/el dia

Credit cards Tarjetas de crédito — no

Access Acceso : Madrid O, M511 → Brunete.
M600 a la derecha → Villanueva del Pardillo.
Map 3 on page 870 Plano 3 Página 870

GOLF COURSE
RECORRIDO
14/20

Site	Emplazamiento	
Maintenance	Mantenimiento	
Architect	Arquitecto	Manuel Piñero
Type	Tipo	campo
Relief	Relieve	
Water in play	Agua	
Exp. to wind	Exp. al viento	
Trees in play	Arboles	

Scorecard Tarjeta	Chp. Campeonato	Mens Caballeros	Ladies Damas
Length Longitud	6444	6037	5146
Par	72	72	72

Advised golfing ability Nivel de juego aconsejado	0	12	24	36

Hcp required	Handicap exigido	28 Cab., 36 Damas

CLUB HOUSE & AMENITIES
CLUB HOUSE Y DEPENDENCIAS
7/10

Pro shop	Pro-shop	
Driving range	Campo de prácticas	
Sheltered	cubierto	20 puestos
On grass	sobre hierba	si
Putting-green	putting-green	si
Pitching-green	pitching-green	si

HOTEL FACILITIES
HOTELES CERCANOS
4/10

HOTELS HOTELES

Husa Princesa	Madrid
275 habitaciones, D 33 250 Pts.	30 km
Tel (34) 91 - 542 21 00, Fax (34) 91 - 542 35 01	

Majadahonda	Majadahonda
41 habitaciones, D 18 500 Pts	15 km
Tel (34) 91 - 638 21 22, Fax (34) 91 - 638 21 57	

Victoria Palace	El Escorial
90 habitaciones, D 17 500 Pts	1 km
Tel (34) 91 - 890 15 11, Fax (34) 91 - 890 12 48	

RESTAURANTS RESTAURANTE

Zalacain	Madrid
Tel (34) 91 - 561 48 40	28 km

El Vivero	Brunete
Tel (34) 91 - 815 92 22	5 km

927

Rodeando la colina de El Hacho, verdadero balcón sobre el mar con una magnífica vista sobre Gibraltar, La Duquesa es uno de los múltiples recorridos de Robert Trent Jones en el sur de España. Pero no es el más difícil: los greens están a menudo en alto y algunas veces son ciegos, no con excesivas caídas, hay numerosos bunkers de los que no es difícil salir, las calles a menudo inclinadas pero no con excesivo peligro. Los roughs son tupidos, aunque bien alejados de la calle, los obstáculos de agua poco numerosos (dos lagos), este recorrido permite jugar con toda la familia sin que ningún jugador se sienta "desplazado". A pesar de las numerosas cuestas no es necesario un coche. Gozarán de una cierta ventaja los jugadores con precisión, pero también los buenos pegadores tendrán ocasión de expresarse. El recorrido de La Duquesa forma parte de un club con múltiples instalaciones (especialmente un puerto de recreo).

Running right around the El Hacho hill, which provides a balcony over the Mediterranean and a fine view of Gibraltar, La Duquesa is one of a number of courses designed by Robert Trent Jones in the south of Spain. But it is not the most difficult: the greens are often elevated and sometimes blind, but only gently contoured. There are loads of bunkers but they are not too difficult to escape from, the fairways sometimes have a sideways slope, but this is nothing too dangerous. With thick but generally distant rough and only a few water hazards (two lakes), this is a course for all the family without any one player feeling left behind. Despite the slopes, the course is easily playable on foot. Precision play is rewarded but the long-hitters also have good opportunity to swing the driver. The La Duquesa course is located within a resort which includes a number of other facilities (in particular a marina).

Golf & Country Club La Duquesa

Urb. El Hacho - km. 143,5
E - 29691 MANILVA (MALAGA)

Office	Secretaria	(34) 95 - 289 04 25
Pro shop	Pro-shop	(34) 95 - 289 07 25
Fax	Fax	(34) 95 - 289 04 25
Situation	Situación	

15 km Estepona, 36 307 h.
30 km Gibraltar, 28 339 h.

Annual closure	Cierre anual	no
Weekly closure	Cierre semanal	no

Fees main season
Precios tempor. alta

	Week days Semana	We/Bank holidays Fin de sem./fiestas
Individual Individual	5 000 Pts	5 000 Pts
Couple Pareja	10 000 Pts	10 000 Pts

Caddy	Caddy	no
Electric Trolley	Carro eléctrico	no
Buggy	Coche	5 000 Pts/18 hoyos
Clubs	Palos	2 000 Pts/18 hoyos

Credit cards Tarjetas de crédito
VISA - Eurocard - MasterCard - AMEX

928

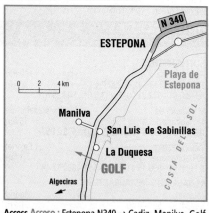

ESTEPONA
N 340
Playa de Estepona
0 2 4 km
Manilva
San Luis de Sabinillas
La Duquesa
GOLF
Algeciras
COSTA DEL SOL

Access Acceso : Estepona N340 → Cadiz, Manilva, Golf
Map 7 on page 879 Plano 7 Página 879

GOLF COURSE
RECORRIDO
13 /20

Site	Emplazamiento	
Maintenance	Mantenimiento	
Architect	Arquitecto	Robert Trent Jones
Type	Tipo	llanura, vagüada
Relief	Relieve	
Water in play	Agua	
Exp. to wind	Exp. al viento	
Trees in play	Arboles	

Scorecard Tarjeta	Chp. Campeonato	Mens Caballeros	Ladies Damas
Length Longitud	6142	5672	4772
Par	72	72	72

Advised golfing ability   0   12   24   36
Nivel de juego aconsejado

Hcp required   Handicap exigido   28 Cab., 36 Damas

CLUB HOUSE & AMENITIES
CLUB HOUSE Y DEPENDENCIAS
7 /10

Pro shop	Pro-shop	
Driving range	Campo de prácticas	
Sheltered	cubierto	3 puestos
On grass	sobre hierba	si
Putting-green	putting-green	si
Pitching-green	pitching-green	si

HOTEL FACILITIES
HOTELES CERCANOS
6 /10

HOTELS HOTELES

La Duquesa   Golf
93 habitaciones, D 16 000 Pts   500 m
Tel (34) 95 - 289 12 11, Fax (34) 95 - 289 16 30

Sotogrande   Sotogrande
46 habitaciones, D 19 000 Pts   10 km
Tel (34) 956 - 79 43 86, Fax (34) 956 - 79 43 33

San Roque   San Roque
50 habitaciones, D 19 500 Pts   10 km
Tel (34) 956 - 61 30 30, Fax (34) 956 - 61 30 12

RESTAURANTS RESTAURANTE

Meson del Castillo   Manilva
Tel (34) 95 - 289 07 66   2 km

Macues   Manilva
Tel (34) 95 - 289 03 39   2 km

Mucha gente lo prefiere a pesar de ser más corto que el "Sur". No se trata de una oposición sino de subrayar la diversidad de los dos recorridos y permitir pasar de uno a otro según se esté más o menos en forma. El "Norte", aunque mucho más corto, no se le puede considerar como un recorrido fácil ya que exige mucha precisión. Tan bien cuidado como su vecino, la longitud de los hoyos es muy variada y con un poco de intuición no es muy difícil evitar las trampas. Los greens no son muy grandes y están poco protegidos, lo que evita la presión a los los jugadores con poca experiencia. El paisaje es agradable, pero mejor evitarlo en los días de mucho calor en pleno verano. La Manga es una "fábrica" de golf, y aunque hay muchas distracciones deportivas, sin embargo los amantes de cultura y turismo pueden quedar un poco defraudados.

Although much shorter than its "South" sister, the "North" does have its supporters. We won't set out to compare the two, only to emphasise the variety they offer, allowing players to switch from one to the other depending on their game. Although much less long, the "North" can still be a handful because of the emphasis on precision. Generally as well upkept as its neighbour, the course offers considerable variety in the length of holes, but with a little intuition, you can get around the traps. The greens are not huge and not well defended, so they take some of the pressure off inexperienced players. The landscape is pleasant, but the course could hardly be recommended at the height of summer. La Manga is a golfing mega-centre, and while there are many other sports and leisure activities in the area, non-golfing lovers of culture and sightseeing might soon wish they were somewhere else.

Hyatt La Manga Club de Golf

Los Belones
E - 30385 CARTAGENA - MURCIA

Office	Secretaria	(34) 968 - 13 72 34
Pro shop	Pro-shop	(34) 968 - 13 72 34
Fax	Fax	(34) 968 - 13 72 72
Situation	Situación	

30 km Cartagena, 173 061 h.
75 km Murcia, 338 250 h.

Annual closure	Cierre anual	no
Weekly closure	Cierre semanal	no

Fees main season
Precios tempor. alta El dia

	Week days Semana	We/Bank holidays Fin de sem./fiestas
Individual Individual	14 000 Pts	14 000 Pts
Couple Pareja	28 000 Pts	28 000 Pts

Caddy	Caddy	si, reservar
Electric Trolley	Carro eléctrico	1500 Pts/18 hoyos
Buggy	Coche	4000 Pts/18 hoyos
Clubs	Palos	3 000 Pts/18 hoyos

Credit cards Tarjetas de crédito
VISA - MasterCard - AMEX - DC

0   4   8 km

Torrevieja
Mar Menor
Murcia
La Manga de Mar Menor
N 301
M U 312   Islas Menores
Los Belones
CARTAGENA   La Unión   GOLF
La Manga
Atamaria

Access Acceso : Murcia → Cartagena, → La Manga
Map 6 on page 877 Plano 6 Página 877

GOLF COURSE
RECORRIDO   15/20

Site	Emplazamiento	▪▪▪▪▪▪▪▫
Maintenance	Mantenimiento	▪▪▪▪▪▪▪▪
Architect	Arquitecto	Thomas/Puttman Arnold Palmer
Type	Tipo	llanura, urbano
Relief	Relieve	▪▪▪▪▪▫▫▫
Water in play	Agua	▪▪▪▪▫▫▫▫
Exp. to wind	Exp. al viento	▪▪▪▪▪▫▫▫
Trees in play	Arboles	▪▪▪▪▫▫▫▫

Scorecard Tarjeta	Chp. Campeonato	Mens Caballeros	Ladies Damas
Length Longitud	5780	5518	5139
Par	71	71	71

Advised golfing ability		0 12 24 36
Nivel de juego aconsejado		▪▪▪▪▪▪▫▫
Hcp required	Handicap exigido	no

CLUB HOUSE & AMENITIES
CLUB HOUSE Y DEPENDENCIAS   7/10

Pro shop	Pro-shop	▪▪▪▪▪▪▫▫
Driving range	Campo de prácticas	▪▪▪▪▪▪▫▫
Sheltered	cubierto	no
On grass	sobre hierba	si
Putting-green	putting-green	si
Pitching-green	pitching-green	si

HOTEL FACILITIES
HOTELES CERCANOS   7/10

HOTELS HOTELES
Hyatt Principe Felipe   Golf
192 habitaciones, D 43 000 Pts.
Tel (34) 968 - 13 72 34, Fax (34) 968 - 13 72 72

Villa La Manga   La Manga
60 habitaciones, D 15 600 Pts.   10 km
Tel (34) 968 - 14 52 22, Fax (34) 968 - 14 53 53

RESTAURANTS RESTAURANTE
Amapola Restaurant   La Manga
Tel (34) 968 - 13 72 34   10 km

Borsalino   La Manga
Tel (34) 968 - 56 31 30   10 km

929

En el complejo golfístico de la Manga, la apertura de un tercer recorrido de 18 hoyos era esperada desde hacía ya mucho tiempo. De hecho se trata de los 9 hoyos existentes desde 1970, rejuvenecidos y completados por Dave Thomas. Los que conocen su trabajo en San Roque encontrarán aquí muchos de los aspectos visuales - sobre todo en la forma de los bunkers - del campo gaditano aunque el conjunto no pretenda igualar ese éxito. La limitacíon del espacio ha influido en ello, lo que ha motivado que el arquitécto haya preferido hacer un campo más corto pero a la voz más técnico. Los nueve últimos hoyos son muy acidentados, más que los primeros, pero caminar por ellos no es complicado. Arboles y arbustos han sido habilmente colocados así como tres lagos. Los pares 3 son bastante largos, y si los pegadores pueden aspirar a tocar los pares 5 de dos, también pueden aspirar al birdie en algunos pares 4 muy cortos. Un tanto difícil para los jugadores poco experimentados, este recorrido es muy divertido para los buenos jugadores.

The opening of a third 18-hole course at La Manga golf resort had been awaited for some time. It is in fact an extension of an existing 9-holer built in 1970, rejuvenated and completed by Dave Thomas. If you know his course at San Roque, you will recognise several of the same visual aspects here, notably in the shape of the bunkers, but the course as a whole is not quite in the same class. There was less space to play with, so the architect preferred to create a rather short, but nonetheless very technical layout. The back 9 are a little hillier than the rest of the course, although walking is never an ordeal. Trees and thickets have been cleverly brought into play, as have three lakes. The par 3s are on the long side, and while long-hitters will attempt to reach the par 5s in two, they can also hope for the elusive birdie on some very short par 4s. A course that is a little difficult for learners, but great fun for the better players.

Hyatt La Manga Club de Golf

Los Belones
E - 30385 CARTAGENA - MURCIA

Office	Secretaria	(34) 968 - 13 72 34
Pro shop	Pro-shop	(34) 968 - 13 72 34
Fax	Fax	(34) 968 - 13 72 72
Situation	Situación	

30 km Cartagena, 173 061 h.
75 km Murcia, 338 250 h.

Annual closure	Cierre anual	no
Weekly closure	Cierre semanal	no

Fees main season
Precios tempor. alta El dia

	Week days Semana	We/Bank holidays Fin de sem./fiestas
Individual Individual	14 000 Pts	14 000 Pts
Couple Pareja	28 000 Pts	28 000 Pts

Caddy	Caddy	si, reservar
Electric Trolley	Carro eléctrico	1500 Pts/18 hoyos
Buggy	Coche	4000 Pts/18 hoyos
Clubs	Palos	3 000 Pts/18 hoyos

Credit cards Tarjetas de crédito
VISA - MasterCard - AMEX - DC

Access Acceso : Murcia → Cartagena, → La Manga
Map 6 on page 877 Plano 6 Página 877

GOLF COURSE
RECORRIDO 14/20

Site	Emplazamiento	▬▬▬▬▬
Maintenance	Mantenimiento	▬▬▬▬▬
Architect	Arquitecto	Dave Thomas
Type	Tipo	campo
Relief	Relieve	▬▬▬▬
Water in play	Agua	▬▬▬
Exp. to wind	Exp. al viento	▬▬▬
Trees in play	Arboles	▬▬▬▬

Scorecard Tarjeta	Chp. Campeonato	Mens Caballeros	Ladies Damas
Length Longitud	5971	5680	4922
Par	73	73	73

Advised golfing ability Nivel de juego aconsejado	0	12	24	36
Hcp required	Handicap exigido	no		

CLUB HOUSE & AMENITIES
CLUB HOUSE Y DEPENDENCIAS 7/10

Pro shop	Pro-shop	▬▬▬▬
Driving range	Campo de prácticas	▬▬▬
Sheltered	cubierto	no
On grass	sobre hierba	si
Putting-green	putting-green	si
Pitching-green	pitching-green	si

HOTEL FACILITIES
HOTELES CERCANOS 7/10

HOTELS HOTELES
Hyatt Principe Felipe — Golf
192 habitaciones, D 43 000 Pts.
Tel (34) 968 - 13 72 34, Fax (34) 968 - 13 72 72

Villa La Manga — La Manga
60 habitaciones, D 15 600 Pts. — 10 km
Tel (34) 968 - 14 52 22, Fax (34) 968 - 14 53 53

RESTAURANTS RESTAURANTE
Amapola Restaurant — La Manga
Tel (34) 968 - 13 72 34 — 10 km

Borsalino — La Manga
Tel (34) 968 - 56 31 30 — 10 km

930

El complejo de La Manga es desde hace mucho tiempo uno de los más famosos de España con construcciones immobiliarias que no todos apreciarán. El recorrido "Sur" es el más largo y sin duda el más franco, aunque sea necesario juagarlo varias veces para impregnarse de sus sutilezas. Arnold Palmer ha modificado, con gran acierto, el diseño original mejorando su aspecto visual y acentuando una estética de carácter americano, aunque bien es verdad que hubiera podido diseñar mejor tanto los bunkers como los greens. Hay muchos obstáculos de agua pequeños, especialmente en el 17 y el 18. La longitud de este recorrido es un excelente test: si logra jugar su handicap querrá decir que posee un juego muy completo. Sin que sea una obra maestra y teniendo en cuenta el lugar, es un recorrido que no se debe ignorar.

La Manga has long been one of Spain's most famous resorts and a site for real estate property development that is not to everyone's taste. The "South" course is the longest and certainly the most open, even though you need several rounds to understand the more subtle sides to it. Arnold Palmer made a few welcome visual changes to the original layout, emphasising the American style design, but the great man's restyling was unable to hide the fact that the bunkers and greens could have been redesigned better. The course is dotted with little water hazards, especially on the 17th and 18th holes. The length of the course makes it a good test, and if you play to your handicap, you will have shown good all-round skills and versatility. This is not your actual masterpiece, but the facilities on site make this a course not to be missed.

Hyatt La Manga Club de Golf

Los Belones
E - 30385 CARTAGENA - MURCIA

Office	Secretaria	(34) 968 - 13 72 34
Pro shop	Pro-shop	(34) 968 - 13 72 34
Fax	Fax	(34) 968 - 13 72 72
Situation	Situación	

30 km Cartagena, 173 061 h.
75 km Murcia, 338 250 h.

Annual closure	Cierre anual	no
Weekly closure	Cierre semanal	no

Fees main season
Precios tempor. alta El dia

	Week days Semana	We/Bank holidays Fin de sem./fiestas
Individual Individual	14 000 Pts	14 000 Pts
Couple Pareja	28 000 Pts	28 000 Pts

Caddy	Caddy	si, reservar
Electric Trolley	Carro eléctrico	1500 Pts/18 hoyos
Buggy	Coche	4000 Pts/18 hoyos
Clubs	Palos	3 000 Pts/18 hoyos

Credit cards Tarjetas de crédito
VISA - MasterCard - AMEX - DC

Torrevieja
Mar Menor
Murcia
La Manga de Mar Menor
M U 312
Islas Menores
Los Belones
CARTAGENA
La Unión
GOLF
Atamaria
N 301

0   4   8 km

Access Acceso : Murcia → Cartagena, → La Manga
Map 6 on page 877 Plano 6 Página 877

GOLF COURSE / RECORRIDO — 14/20

Site	Emplazamiento	
Maintenance	Mantenimiento	
Architect	Arquitecto	Thomas/Puttman Arnold Palmer
Type	Tipo	llanura, urbano
Relief	Relieve	
Water in play	Agua	
Exp. to wind	Exp. al viento	
Trees in play	Arboles	

Scorecard Tarjeta	Chp. Campeonato	Mens Caballeros	Ladies Damas
Length Longitud	6361	6065	5490
Par	72	72	72

Advised golfing ability		0 12 24 36
Nivel de juego aconsejado		
Hcp required	Handicap exigido	28 Cab., 36 Damas

CLUB HOUSE & AMENITIES / CLUB HOUSE Y DEPENDENCIAS — 7/10

Pro shop	Pro-shop	
Driving range	Campo de prácticas	
Sheltered	cubierto	no
On grass	sobre hierba	si
Putting-green	putting-green	si
Pitching-green	pitching-green	si

HOTEL FACILITIES / HOTELES CERCANOS — 7/10

HOTELS HOTELES
Hyatt Principe Felipe — Golf
192 habitaciones, D 43 000 Pts.
Tel (34) 968 - 13 72 34, Fax (34) 968 - 13 72 72

Villa La Manga — La Manga 10 km
60 habitaciones, D 15 600 Pts.
Tel (34) 968 - 14 52 22, Fax (34) 968 - 14 53 53

RESTAURANTS RESTAURANTE
Amapola Restaurant — La Manga 10 km
Tel (34) 968 - 13 72 34

Borsalino — La Manga 10 km
Tel (34) 968 - 56 31 30

931

En la época de la construcción de éste campo (como de Muirfield Village en los Estados Unidos), Jack Nicklaus trabajada con Desmond Muirhead, uno de los arquitéctos más originales de éste siglo, y uno de los menos orientados sobre la longitud a cualquier precio. Si La Moraleja 1 es bastante corto, exige la máxima precisión si se quiere conseguir un buen resultado, sobre todo porque los greenes son bastante pequeños, muy ondulados, rápidos y muy bien defendidos. Si se les quiere atacar en buena posición, es importante colocar correctamente el drive, lo que no siempre es fácil, y mucha lucidez a la hora de seleccionar el palo: sobre los 4 pares 4 cortos será recomendable jugar un hierro de salida. Los pegadores impenitentes podrán intentar los más posible de los greenes, o atacar de dos los pares 5, sobre todo en match-play ya que los peligros son constantes. Un campo muy divertido sin ser por ello una obra maestra inolvidable.

When building this course (the same goes for Muirfield Village in the USA), Jack Nicklaus was working with Desmond Muirhead, one of the most original course designers of our day, and one who doesn't go for length at any price. While La Moraleja 1 is on the short side, it demands extreme accuracy for a good card, especially since the greens are only average in size, steeply contoured, quick and very well guarded. To be in the right position to make your approach, the drive has to be exactly in the right place, a feat that is not always so easy and one that demands clear-headed club selection: on the four very short par 4s, you are best advised to use a long iron. Incorrigible big-hitters can attempt to get as close as possible to the green and also reach the par 5s in two, at least in match-play, the ideal formula given the profusion of dangerous hazards. A very amusing course, but hardly an unforgettable master-piece.

Golf La Moraleja

Avenida Marquesa Viuda de Aldana, 50
E - 28109 LA MORALEJA-MADRID

Office	Secretaria	(34) 91 - 650 07 00
Pro shop	Pro-shop	(34) 91 - 650 07 00
Fax	Fax	(34) 91 - 650 43 31
Situation	Situación	

12 km Madrid, 3 084 673 h.

Annual closure	Cierre anual	no
Weekly closure	Cierre semanal	no

Fees main season
Precios tempor. alta 18 hoyos

	Week days Semana	We/Bank holidays Fin de sem./fiestas
Individual Individual	8 000 Pts	20 000 Pts
Couple Pareja	16 000 Pts	40 000 Pts

solo invitados de socios (member's guests only)

Caddy	Caddy	no
Electric Trolley	Carro eléctrico	700 Pts/18 hoyos
Buggy	Coche	3 700 Pts/18 hoyos
Clubs	Palos	no

Credit cards Tarjetas de crédito   no

932

Access Acceso : Madrid → Burgos
Map 3 on page 870 Plano 3 Página 870

GOLF COURSE
RECORRIDO 15/20

Site	Emplazamiento	
Maintenance	Mantenimiento	
Architect	Arquitecto	Jack Nicklaus Desmond Muirhead
Type	Tipo	campo
Relief	Relieve	
Water in play	Agua	
Exp. to wind	Exp. al viento	
Trees in play	Arboles	

Scorecard Tarjeta	Chp. Campeonato	Mens Caballeros	Ladies Damas
Length Longitud	5989	5689	4930
Par	72	72	72

Advised golfing ability	0 12 24 36	
Nivel de juego aconsejado		
Hcp required	Handicap exigido	28 Cab., 36 Damas

CLUB HOUSE & AMENITIES
CLUB HOUSE Y DEPENDENCIAS 7/10

Pro shop	Pro-shop	
Driving range	Campo de prácticas	
Sheltered	cubierto	no
On grass	sobre hierba	no
Putting-green	putting-green	si
Pitching-green	pitching-green	no

HOTEL FACILITIES
HOTELES CERCANOS 8/10

HOTELS HOTELES
Novotel-Campo de las Naciones   600 m
246 habitaciones, D 18 300 Pts
Tel (34) 91 - 721 18 18, Fax (34) 91 - 721 11 22

Melia Castilla   Madrid
900 habitaciones, D 32 400 Pts   10 km
Tel (34) 91 - 567 50 00, Fax (34) 91 - 567 50 51

Castilla Plaza   Madrid
147 habitaciones, D 20 800 Pts   10 km
Tel (34) 91 - 323 11 86, Fax (34) 91 - 315 54 06

RESTAURANTS RESTAURANTE
Zalacain - Tel (34) 91 - 561 48 40   Madrid, 10 km

Principe de Viana   Madrid
Tel (34) 91 - 457 15 49   10 km

El Olivo - Tel (34) 91 - 359 15 35   Madrid,10 km

Este segundo recorrido del gran club de La Moraleja ha sido diseñado por los arquitéctos asociados a Jack Nicklaus. Este no lo ha firmado, pero su influencia sobre sus colaboradores se deja sentir. Los greenes son de gran tamaño, y los tres putts no son raros, sobre todo si se está alejado de la bandera. Es entonces cuando las numerosas caídas y la rapidez de la superficie exigen una gran concentración en la lectura del green y mucho toque. Están bien protegidos por el agua, por árboles, por unos bunkers muy dibujados, sobre todo en el 9 y 18, cuando protegen éste doble green. La primera mitad es tal vez menos impresionante pero ello no significa ni mucho menos que se deba bajar la guardia. Hay que estar alerta los 18 hoyos puesto que las dificultades surgen cuando uno menos se lo espera. La estrategia de juego en función de la forma del momento juega pues un papel determinante. Tiene que conocerse aunque se deben evitar los fines de semana.

This second golf course on the Club La Moraleja was designed by architects associated with Jack Nicklaus, and although not carrying his signature, the great man evidently had some influence on his partners. The greens are huge and three-putts not an uncommon occurrence, especially if you are nowhere near the pin, as the numerous slopes and speed of the putting surfaces call for careful reading and a delicate touch. They are often well-guarded by water, sometimes by trees and by well-designed bunkers, especially on the 9th and 18th holes, which share a double green. The first half of the course is less intimidating, but that doesn't mean you can take things easy. Stay on your toes the whole time, because the difficulties here crop up when you least expect them. As a result, game strategy, depending on the shape of your game, plays a significant role. Well worth knowing, but avoid week-ends.

Golf La Moraleja

Avenida Marquesa Viuda de Aldana, 50
E - 28109 LA MORALEJA-MADRID

Office	Secretaria	(34) 91 - 650 07 00
Pro shop	Pro-shop	(34) 91 - 650 07 00
Fax	Fax	(34) 91 - 650 43 31
Situation	Situación	

12 km Madrid, 3 084 673 h.

| Annual closure | Cierre anual | no |
| Weekly closure | Cierre semanal | no |

Fees main season
Precios tempor. alta 18 hoyos

	Week days Semana	We/Bank holidays Fin de sem./fiestas
Individual Individual	8 000 Pts	20 000 Pts
Couple Pareja	16 000 Pts	40 000 Pts

solo invitados de socios (member's guests only)

Caddy	Caddy	no
Electric Trolley	Carro eléctrico	700 Pts/18 hoyos
Buggy	Coche	3 700 Pts/18 hoyos
Clubs	Palos	no

Credit cards Tarjetas de crédito	no

Access Acceso : Madrid → Burgos
Map 3 on page 870 Plano 3 Página 870

GOLF COURSE
RECORRIDO

16/20

Site	Emplazamiento	
Maintenance	Mantenimiento	
Architect	Arquitecto	Golden Bear Design Associates
Type	Tipo	campo
Relief	Relieve	
Water in play	Agua	
Exp. to wind	Exp. al viento	
Trees in play	Arboles	

Scorecard Tarjeta	Chp. Campeonato	Mens Caballeros	Ladies Damas
Length Longitud	6451	5888	5014
Par	72	72	72

Advised golfing ability		0 12 24 36
Nivel de juego aconsejado		
Hcp required	Handicap exigido	28 Cab., 36 Damas

CLUB HOUSE & AMENITIES
CLUB HOUSE Y DEPENDENCIAS

7/10

Pro shop	Pro-shop	
Driving range	Campo de prácticas	
Sheltered	cubierto	no
On grass	sobre hierba	no
Putting-green	putting-green	si
Pitching-green	pitching-green	no

933

HOTEL FACILITIES
HOTELES CERCANOS

8/10

HOTELS HOTELES
Novotel-Campo de las Naciones   600 m
246 habitaciones, D 18 300 Pts
Tel (34) 91 - 721 18 18, Fax (34) 91 - 721 11 22

Melia Castilla   Madrid
900 habitaciones, D 32 400 Pts   10 km
Tel (34) 91 - 567 50 00, Fax (34) 91 - 567 50 51

Castilla Plaza   Madrid
147 habitaciones, D 20 800 Pts   10 km
Tel (34) 91 - 323 11 86, Fax (34) 91 - 315 54 06

RESTAURANTS RESTAURANTE
Zalacain - Tel (34) 91 - 561 48 40   Madrid, 10 km

Principe de Viana   Madrid
Tel (34) 91 - 457 15 49   10 km

El Olivo - Tel (34) 91 - 359 15 35   Madrid
Tel (34) 91 - 457 15 49   10 km

Dos grandes campeones, Antonio Garrido y Manuel Piñeiro, han diseñado uno de los recorridos más técnicos de la región , con un total de 27 hoyos, siendo la combinación de "San Pedro" y de "Guadaiza" la más larga. Como las distancias no son excesivas, los jugadores precisos se encontrarán más agusto que los pegadores a pesar de que las zonas de caída del drive sean anchas y los tees de salida a menudo en alto. Hay dificultades de todas clases : árboles, bunkers de green, ríos y lagos no siempre a la vista. El relieve es bastante accidentado, sin que sea exagerado, lo que complica la apreciación de los aproches: conviene tirar a bandera para evitar los putts largos ya que las caídas de green son difíciles de apreciar. No todo el mundo apreciará el entorno inmobiliario (cosa inevitable en la región) escondido parcialmente por la vegetación de este gran jardín.

Two top champions, Antonio Garrido and Manuel Pinero, designed this, one of the region's most technical golf courses comprising 27 holes. The "San Pedro" and "Guadaiza" together form the longest 18-hole combination. Not being over-long, accurate players will probably feel more at home than the big hitters, even though the landing areas for drives are pretty wide and the tees often elevated. There are all kinds of hazards here, from trees to green-side bunkers to rivers and lakes, and they are not always very visible. This is pretty hilly terrain, a factor which complicates the approach shot. It is also important to go for the pin to avoid over-long putts, as the greens are tricky to read. The property development surroundings are not to everyone's liking but are unavoidable in this part of the world and are partly concealed by the trees.

La Quinta Golf & Country Club

Nueva Andalucia
E - 29660 MARBELLA (MALAGA)

Office	Secretaria	(34) 95 - 278 34 62
Pro shop	Pro-shop	(34) 95 - 278 34 62
Fax	Fax	(34) 95 - 278 34 66
Situation	Situación	

3 km San Pedro de Alcantara
16 km Marbella, 84 410 h.

Annual closure	Cierre anual	no
Weekly closure	Cierre semanal	no

Fees main season
Precios tempor. alta el campo

	Week days Semana	We/Bank holidays Fin de sem./fiestas
Individual Individual	7 900 Pts	7 900 Pts
Couple Pareja	15 800 Pts	15 800 Pts

Caddy	Caddy	si, reservar
Electric Trolley	Carro eléctrico	1 500 Pts/18 hoyos
Buggy	Coche	4 600 Pts/18 hoyos
Clubs	Palos	3 000 Pts/18 hoyos

Credit cards Tarjetas de crédito
VISA - MasterCard - AMEX

934

Access Acceso : Marbella N340 → San Pedro de Alcantara, → Ronda, Golf 3 km
Map 7 on page 879 Plano 7 Página 879

GOLF COURSE
RECORRIDO
15/20

Site	Emplazamiento	
Maintenance	Mantenimiento	
Architect	Arquitecto	Manuel Piñero Antonio Garrido
Type	Tipo	urbano, vagüada
Relief	Relieve	
Water in play	Agua	
Exp. to wind	Exp. al viento	
Trees in play	Arboles	

Scorecard Tarjeta	Chp. Campeonato	Mens Caballeros	Ladies Damas
Length Longitud	5597	5517	4810
Par	72	72	72

Advised golfing ability Nivel de juego aconsejado	0	12	24	36

Hcp required	Handicap exigido	28 Cab., 36 Damas

CLUB HOUSE & AMENITIES
CLUB HOUSE Y DEPENDENCIAS
8/10

Pro shop	Pro-shop	
Driving range	Campo de prácticas	
Sheltered	cubierto	10 puestos
On grass	sobre hierba	si
Putting-green	putting-green	si
Pitching-green	pitching-green	si

HOTEL FACILITIES
HOTELES CERCANOS
7/10

HOTELS HOTELES
Puente Romano   Marbella, Cta de Cádiz
217 habitaciones, D 49 500 Pts.   3 km
Tel (34) 95 - 282 09 00, Fax (34) 95 - 277 57 66

Pyr Hotel   Puerto Banus
319 habitaciones, D 15 000 Pts   2 km
Tel (34) 95 - 281 73 53, Fax (34) 95 - 281 79 07

RESTAURANTS RESTAURANTE
Albatros   Golf
Tel (34) 95 - 276 23 33

Cipriano   Puerto Banús
Tel (34) 95 - 281 10 77   5 km

Situado en la falda de una montaña no es un recorrido excesivamente cansado, pero en pleno verano es mejor alquilar un coche. De longitud moderada, si se domina con maestría todos los palos se puede lograr un buen resultado. Pinos, naranjos, olivos y almendros le dan un cierto colorido y suponen muchos problemas para jugadores sin precisión. Con una arquitectura bastante personal, La Sella demuestra que sus creadores conocían muy bien toda la gama de jugadores, adaptando las dificulta¨des a los diferentes tees de salida. Efectivamente, Juan de la Cuadra lo diseñó con la experta ayuda de José María Olazabal. Si se falla la llegada a green, habrá que emplear toda la virtuosidad del campeón español para salvar el par.... La Sella es uno de los buenos golfs de la región.

Although laid out on the side of a mountain, the course can be walked, although a buggy is advisable in mid-summer to get a bit of air. La Sella is not too long, but if all your clubs are in good working order, a good score should not be beyond you. The pine, orange, olive and almond trees bring a touch of colour and relief, and sometimes a number of problems for wayward hitters. A very personal design, La Sella shows how much the architects knew about players of all ability, as difficulties are geared to the different tees. Not surprisingly, the course was laid out by Juan de la Cuadra, expertly assisted by José-Maria Olazabal. If you miss the greens, you will need some of the Spanish champion's virtuosity to save par. La Sella is a good address in the region.

Club de Golf La Sella

Ctra La Jara - Jesus Pobre
E - 03749 JESUS POBRE - DENIA (ALICANTE)

Office	Secretaria	(34) 96 - 645 42 52
Pro shop	Pro-shop	(34) 96 - 645 41 63
Fax	Fax	(34) 96 - 645 42 01
Situation	Situación	

8 km Denia, 25 157 h. 8 km Jávea, 16 603 h.

Annual closure	Cierre anual	no
Weekly closure	Cierre semanal	no

Fees main season
Precios tempor. alta El campo

	Week days	We/Bank holidays
	Semana	Fin de sem./fiestas
Individual Individual	5 500 Pts	5 500 Pts
Couple Pareja	11 000 Pts	11 000 Pts

Caddy	Caddy	no
Electric Trolley	Carro eléctrico	no
Buggy	Coche	4 000 Pts/18 hoyos
Clubs	Palos	2 000 Pts/18 hoyos

Credit cards Tarjetas de crédito
VISA - MasterCard - AMEX

Access Acceso : A7 Valencia - Alicante,
Salida 62 → Denia → Jara → Golf
Map 6 on page 877 Plano 6 Página 877

GOLF COURSE
RECORRIDO

15/20

Site	Emplazamiento	
Maintenance	Mantenimiento	
Architect	Arquitecto	Juan de la Cuadra J.M. Olazabal
Type	Tipo	campo, vagüada
Relief	Relieve	
Water in play	Agua	
Exp. to wind	Exp. al viento	
Trees in play	Arboles	

Scorecard	Chp.	Mens	Ladies
Tarjeta	Campeonato	Caballeros	Damas
Length Longitud	6072	5919	5118
Par	72	72	72

Advised golfing ability		0 12 24 36
Nivel de juego aconsejado		
Hcp required	Handicap exigido	28 Cab., 36 Damas

CLUB HOUSE & AMENITIES
CLUB HOUSE Y DEPENDENCIAS

6/10

Pro shop	Pro-shop	
Driving range	Campo de prácticas	
Sheltered	cubierto	2 puestos
On grass	sobre hierba	si
Putting-green	putting-green	si
Pitching-green	pitching-green	si

935

HOTEL FACILITIES
HOTELES CERCANOS

5/10

HOTELS HOTELES
Romano · Denia
6 habitaciones, D 18 000 Pts · 6 km
Tel (34) 96 - 642 17 89, Fax (34) 96 - 642 29 58

Parador de Jávea · Jávea
65 habitaciones, D 13 000 Pts. · 10 km
Tel (34) 96 - 579 02 00, Fax (34) 96 - 579 03 08

El Rodat · Jávea
25 habitaciones, D 15 000 Pts · 8 km
Tel (34) 96 - 647 07 10, Fax (34) 96 - 647 15 50

RESTAURANTS RESTAURANTE
Romano - Tel (34) 96 - 642 17 89 · Denia, 6 km

El Pegoli · Denia
Tel (34) 96 - 578 01 35 · 6 km

La Casa del Arroz - Tel (34) 96 - 578 10 47 · Denia, 6 km

Es un recorrido muy privado, merece la pena esforzarse en conocer algún socio para que le inviten a jugar. Es aconsejable coger un coche ya que los desnivelaciones son grandes: es casi un recorrido de montaña, situado a menos de diez kilómetros de la Costa del Sol. Hay que jugar sin miedo a perder bolas, evitar los barrancos y sobrevolar bastantes obstáculos de agua. No obstante, cualquier jugador (no los principiantes!) puede adaptarse al recorrido utilizando uno de los muchos tees de salida construidos por el arquitecto. La estética es bastante americana, un poco similar a ciertos recorridos de California del Sur. Las calles son bastante anchas, los greens muy amplios, con caídas y rápidos. El mantenimiento es de muy buena calidad, cosa no muy difícil de obtener dado el limitado número de jugadores.

A very private course but one which is worth the effort involved in getting to know members well enough to be invited. They will certainly recommend a buggy because there is some steep climbing to do on what is almost a mountain style course, less than 7 miles from the Costa del Sol. Here you should not be too afraid of losing balls, just make sure you avoid the ravines and lift the ball over the many water hazards. Despite these obvious pitfalls, players of all levels (but not beginners) can play here because there are so many different tee-boxes. The style is definitely American and rather similar to some of the courses in southern California. The fairways are wide and the greens large, often multi-tiered, slick and fast. An emphatic word, too, for the excellence of green-keeping, perhaps a task made easier when there are so few players out on the course.

Club de Golf La Zagaleta

Carretera de Ronda 38
E - 29679 BENHAVIS (Malaga)

Office	Secretaria	(34) 95 - 285 54 53
Pro shop	Pro-shop	(34) 95 - 285 54 53
Fax	Fax	(34) 95 - 285 54 53
Situation	Situación	

12 km San Pedro de Alcantara

Annual closure	Cierre anual	no
Weekly closure	Cierre semanal	no

Fees main season
Precios tempor. alta recorrido

	Week days Semana	We/Bank holidays Fin de sem./fiestas
Individual Individual	25 000 Pts	25 000 Pts
Couple Pareja	50 000 Pts	50 000 Pts
Club privado		

Caddy	Caddy	no
Electric Trolley	Carro eléctrico	si
Buggy	Coche	5 000 Pts/18 hoyos
Clubs	Palos	si

Credit cards Tarjetas de crédito
VISA - Eurocard - MasterCard - AMEX

936

Access Acceso : San Pedro → Ronda
Map 7 on page 879 Plano 7 Página 879

GOLF COURSE
RECORRIDO   16/20

Site	Emplazamiento	
Maintenance	Mantenimiento	
Architect	Arquitecto	Bradford Benz
Type	Tipo	montaña, urbano
Relief	Relieve	
Water in play	Agua	
Exp. to wind	Exp. al viento	
Trees in play	Arboles	

Scorecard Tarjeta	Chp. Campeonato	Mens Caballeros	Ladies Damas
Length Longitud	6039	5709	5279
Par	72	72	72

Advised golfing ability Nivel de juego aconsejado	0	12	24	36

Hcp required	Handicap exigido	28 Cab / 36 Damas

CLUB HOUSE & AMENITIES
CLUB HOUSE Y DEPENDENCIAS   7/10

Pro shop	Pro-shop	
Driving range	Campo de prácticas	
Sheltered	cubierto	no
On grass	sobre hierba	si
Putting-green	putting-green	si
Pitching-green	pitching-green	si

HOTEL FACILITIES
HOTELES CERCANOS   7/10

HOTELS HOTELES
Atalaya Park   Estepona
448 habitaciones, D 24 000 Pts   8 km
Tel (34) 95 - 288 48 01, Fax (34) 95 - 288 57 35

El Paraiso   Estepona
182 habitaciones, D 25 725 Pts   10 km
Tel (34) 95 - 288 30 00, Fax (34) 95 - 288 20 19

Guadalmina   San Pedro
80 habitaciones, D 25 850 Pts   12 km
Tel (34) 95 - 288 22 11, Fax (34) 95 - 288 22 91

RESTAURANTS RESTAURANTE
El Gamonal   San Pedro
Tel (34) 95 - 288 33 75   12 km

Los Nieto   San Pedro
Tel (34) 95 - 288 34 91   12 km

Uno de los grandes recorridos de la Costa del Sol, aunque conservando una dimensión humana por el gran número de tees de salida que permiten que los jugadores de nivel medio puedan evolucionar sin miedo. Rodeado de bonitos chalés, el terreno es poco accidentado, y numerosos greens en alto complican los aproches. Numerosos bunkers y obsáculos de agua (en la línea de juego en 12 hoyos) protegen los greens. Aquí es necesario poseer un juego preciso y muy completo (hoyos estrechos alternan con otros más anchos), se debe tirar a bandera y saber dar toda clase de golpes para obtener un buen resultado. Ya en el green queda todavía mucho por hacer ya que no es fácil calcular las caídas. Es apasionante jugar en este golf tanto en stroke-play como en match-play, es el más divertido de todos los "monumentos" de la región, aunque sólo sea por su seducción visual añadida a la calidad del desafío.

One of the really great courses on the Costa del Sol but one that has kept a very human dimension through the number of tees, allowing players of average standard to play the course without feeling terrorised. Surrounded by beautiful villas, the terrain is pretty even but the many elevated greens make approach shots a tricky business. The greens are well protected by the many bunkers and water hazards (affecting 12 holes in all). Las Brisas calls for accurate, comprehensive golf (tight holes alternate with wider fairways) and the ability to play most shots in order to card a good score. The emphasis here is on American-style target golf. Although once on the greens, you are still far from home and dry, because none of them are easy to read. An exciting course for stroke-play and match-play, this is the most amusing of the region's golfing landmarks, if only for the view which adds to the amazing challenge of golf.

Real Club de Golf Las Brisas

Nueva Andalucia
E - 29660 MARBELLA (MALAGA)

Office	Secretaria	(34) 95 - 281 08 75
Pro shop	Pro-shop	(34) 95 - 281 12 57
Fax	Fax	(34) 95 - 281 55 18
Situation	Situación	

15 km Marbella, 84 410 h.
6 km San Pedro de Alcantara

Annual closure	Cierre anual	no
Weekly closure	Cierre semanal	no

Fees main season
Precios tempor. alta el campo

	Week days Semana	We/Bank holidays Fin de sem./fiestas
Individual Individual	15 000 Pts	15 000 Pts
Couple Pareja	30 000 Pts	30 000 Pts

Caddy	Caddy	si
Electric Trolley	Carro eléctrico	2 000 Pts/18 hoyos
Buggy	Coche	5 000 Pts/18 hoyos
Clubs	Palos	2 000 Pts/18 hoyos

Credit cards Tarjetas de crédito
VISA - MasterCard - AMEX

Access Acceso : Marbella N340 → San Pedro de Alcantara, Nueva Andalucia (km 180), a la derecha → Golf **Map 7 on page 879** Plano 7 Página 879

GOLF COURSE
RECORRIDO $18_{/20}$

Site	Emplazamiento	
Maintenance	Mantenimiento	
Architect	Arquitecto	Robert Trent Jones
Type	Tipo	urbano, vagüada
Relief	Relieve	
Water in play	Agua	
Exp. to wind	Exp. al viento	
Trees in play	Arboles	

Scorecard Tarjeta	Chp. Campeonato	Mens Caballeros	Ladies Damas
Length Longitud	6163	5893	5096
Par	72	72	72

Advised golfing ability
Nivel de juego aconsejado   0   12   24   36

Hcp required   Handicap exigido   24 Cab., 36 Damas

CLUB HOUSE & AMENITIES
CLUB HOUSE Y DEPENDENCIAS $7_{/10}$

Pro shop	Pro-shop	
Driving range	Campo de prácticas	
Sheltered	cubierto	4 puestos
On grass	sobre hierba	si
Putting-green	putting-green	si
Pitching-green	pitching-green	si

937

HOTEL FACILITIES
HOTELES CERCANOS $7_{/10}$

HOTELS HOTELES
Puente Romano   Marbella
217 habitaciones, D 49 500 Pts   4 km
Tel (34) 95 - 282 09 00, Fax (34) 95 - 277 57 66

Melia Don Pepe   Marbella
200 habitaciones, D 39 400 Pts   8 km
Tel (34) 95 - 277 03 00, Fax (34) 95 - 277 99 54

Pyr Hotel   Puerto Banus
319 habitaciones, D 15 000 Pts   13 km
Tel (34) 95 - 281 73 53, Fax (34) 95 - 281 79 07

RESTAURANTS RESTAURANTE
Cipriano   Puerto Banús
Tel (34) 95 - 281 10 77   4 km

Bistrot Cristian   Puerto Banús
Tel (34) 95 - 281 10 06   4 km

LAURO

13 7 5

Al final de una carretera de montaña, está situado en un lugar muy tranquilo. Cada hoyo lleva el nombre de un célebre torero, pero no por eso se trata de un recorrido agresivo que exija dotes de combate. Al contrario, la belleza de los paisajes inspira calma y el recorrido en sí mismo es más bien acogedor, incluso para los jugadores con poca experiencia. Cantidad de olivos bordean la mayor parte de las calles y algunos obstáculos de agua están situados en plena línea de juego (hoyos 9,14,17 y 18) sin ser temibles. De razonable dificultad, prácticamente sin trampas escondidas (los obstáculos son perfectamente visibles), Lauro Golf es un recorrido muy noble y el sitio ideal para evaluar el nivel de su juego actual y sus propias posibilidades frente a jugadores de nivel equivalente. Los mejores pueden obtener resulta¨dos halagadores para su propio "ego".

This course is a quiet little place at the end of a mountain road. Each hole bears the name of a famous torero but the course itself is far from being aggressive and does not call for any real fighting virtues. On the contrary, the beautiful landscape inspires peace and quiet and the layout is a friendly one, even for inexperienced players. Numerous olive trees line most of the fairways and certain water hazards are very much to the fore (on the 9th, 14th, 17th and 18th holes) but never fearsome. Never too demanding with virtually no hidden traps (all hazards are clearly visible) and benign greens, Lauro Golf is a very honest layout and the ideal spot to assess your current game and potential and to measure up with players of similar ability. The better players can card flattering scores and do their ego a world of good.

Lauro Golf

Los Caracolillos
E - 29130 ALHAURIN DE LA TORRE (MALAGA)

Office	Secretaria	(34) 95 - 241 27 67
Pro shop	Pro-shop	(34) 95 - 241 27 67
Fax	Fax	(34) 95 - 241 47 57
Situation	Situación	

5 km Alhaurin de la Torre
15 km Málaga, 534 683 h.

Annual closure	Cierre anual	no
Weekly closure	Cierre semanal	no

Fees main season
Precios tempor. alta

	Week days Semana	We/Bank holidays Fin de sem./fiestas
Individual Individual	5 000 Pts	5 000 Pts
Couple Pareja	9 000 Pts	9 000 Pts

Caddy	Caddy	no
Electric Trolley	Carro eléctrico	no
Buggy	Coche	4000 Pts/18 hoyos
Clubs	Palos	1000 Pts/18 hoyos

Credit cards Tarjetas de crédito   no

MALAGA

GOLF

C 344

Alhaurìn el Grande

Torremolinos

N 340

COSTA DEL SOL

Marbella

Access Acceso : Málaga, N340 → Torremolinos, salida "Churiana", C344, a la derecha Alhaurín
Map 7 on page 879 Plano 7 Página 879

GOLF COURSE
RECORRIDO

13/20

Site	Emplazamiento	
Maintenance	Mantenimiento	
Architect	Arquitecto	Falco Nardi
Type	Tipo	campo
Relief	Relieve	
Water in play	Agua	
Exp. to wind	Exp. al viento	
Trees in play	Arboles	

Scorecard Tarjeta	Chp. Campeonato	Mens Caballeros	Ladies Damas
Length Longitud	5971	5679	4864
Par	72	72	72

Advised golfing ability		0 12 24 36
Nivel de juego aconsejado		
Hcp required	Handicap exigido	28 Cab., 36 Damas

CLUB HOUSE & AMENITIES
CLUB HOUSE Y DEPENDENCIAS

7/10

Pro shop	Pro-shop	
Driving range	Campo de prácticas	
Sheltered	cubierto	no
On grass	sobre hierba	si
Putting-green	putting-green	si
Pitching-green	pitching-green	no

HOTEL FACILITIES
HOTELES CERCANOS

5/10

HOTELS HOTELES
Larios   Malaga
40 habitaciones, D 19 000 Pts   18 km
Tel (34) 95 - 222 22 00, Fax (34) 95 - 222 24 07

Tryp Costa Golf   Chiclana
195 habitaciones, 19 850 Pts   10 km
Tel (34) 956 - 49 45 35, Fax (34) 956 - 49 46 26

Byblos   Fuengirola
144 habitaciones, D 37 500 Pts   12 km
Tel (34) 95 - 247 30 50, Fax (34) 95 - 247 67 83

RESTAURANTS RESTAURANTE
El Olivar   Mijas
Tel (34) 95 - 248 61 96   5 km

Valparaiso   Mijas → Fuengirola
Tel (34) 95 - 248 59 96   7 km

938

Uno de los arquitéctos más originales de su época, José Gancedo, ha diseñado en un magnífico paraje un campo a la vez espectacular y lleno de encanto. Si se le puede considerar como difícil para los buenos jugadores, sobre todo desde las barras de atrás, se adapta sin embargo perfectamente a los jugadores todos los niveles. Tendrán aún más placer ya que no es imposible cumplir su handicap, siempre y cuando sean conscientes de sua limitaciones. El trazado exige una excelente estrategia y un buen dominio de la bola. Suele recompensar más al jugador técnico que coloca la bola que al pegador que puede encontrar dificultades con los árboles o los obstáculos de agua. Sin embargo en el 18 los pegadores tendrán la oportunidad de jugar a green por encima del lago, sobre todo si juegan en match-play, la fórmula ideal para descubrir el campo. Bien equilibrado en su desarrollo, con un buen diseño, Lerma pertenece sin duda a la categoría de campos «inteligentes».

José Gancedo, one of today's most original architects, has designed a spectacular and truly charming layout over a beautiful site. While considered tough for the better players, especially from the back-tees, it is nonetheless largely suitable for players of all abilities. They will find it all the more pleasing in that playing to their handicap is not impossible, as long as they know their limits. The course demands tight strategy and excellent ball control, and generally will reward the accurate technician more than the long-hitters, who may have problems with the trees and water. But on the 18th, they can try and hit the green over the lake, especially in match-play, the ideal format when discovering this course. Well-balanced and nicely-landscaped, Lerma is undoubtedly one of the more "intelligent" courses.

Club de Golf de Lerma

Autovía Madrid-Burgos Km 195,5
E - 09340 LERMA (BURGOS)

Office	Secretaria	(34) 947 - 17 12 14
Pro shop	Pro-shop	(34) 947 - 17 12 14
Fax	Fax	(34) 947 - 17 12 16
Situation	Situación	

45 km Burgos, 169 111 h.
8 km Lerma, 2 417 h.

Annual closure	Cierre anual	no
Weekly closure	Cierre semanal	lunes

Fees main season
Precios tempor. alta 18 hoyos

	Week days Semana	We/Bank holidays Fin de sem./fiestas
Individual Individual	4 800 Pts	6 900 Pts
Couple Pareja	9 600 Pts	13 800 Pts

Caddy	Caddy	no
Electric Trolley	Carro eléctrico	1500 Pts/18 hoyos
Buggy	Coche	5000 Pts/18 hoyos
Clubs	Palos	2000 Pts/18 hoyos

Credit cards Tarjetas de crédito
VISA - MasterCard

GOLF

Access Acceso : Madrid → Burgos, km 195
Map 3 on page 870 Plano 3 Página 870

GOLF COURSE
RECORRIDO   17 /20

Site	Emplazamiento	▬▬▬▬▬
Maintenance	Mantenimiento	▬▬▬▬
Architect	Arquitecto	José Gancedo
Type	Tipo	campo, bosque
Relief	Relieve	▬▬
Water in play	Agua	▬▬▬
Exp. to wind	Exp. al viento	▬▬
Trees in play	Arboles	▬▬▬▬

Scorecard Tarjeta	Chp. Campeonato	Mens Caballeros	Ladies Damas
Length Longitud	6263	5905	5064
Par	72	72	72

Advised golfing ability Nivel de juego aconsejado	0	12	24	36
Hcp required Handicap exigido	28 Cab., 36 Damas			

CLUB HOUSE & AMENITIES
CLUB HOUSE Y DEPENDENCIAS   7 /10

Pro shop	Pro-shop	▬▬▬▬
Driving range	Campo de prácticas	▬▬▬
Sheltered	cubierto	8 puestos
On grass	sobre hierba	si
Putting-green	putting-green	si
Pitching-green	pitching-green	si

HOTEL FACILITIES
HOTELES CERCANOS   4 /10

HOTELS HOTELES

Alisa 36 habitaciones, D 8 000 Pts Tel (34) 947 - 17 02 50, Fax (34) 947 - 17 11 60	Lerma	8 km
Docar 15 habitaciones, D 5 800 Pts Tel (34) 947 - 17 10 73	Lerma	8 km
Landa Palace 42 habitaciones, D 23 000 Pts Tel (34) 947 - 20 63 43, Fax (34) 947 - 26 46 76	Burgos	42 km
Maria Luisa 44 habitaciones, D 11 000 Pts Tel (34) 947 - 22 80 00, Fax (34) 947 - 22 80 80	Burgos	45 km

RESTAURANTS RESTAURANTE

Lis 2 - Tel (34) 947 - 17 01 26	Lerma, 8 km
Casa Ojeda, Tel (34) 947 - 20 90 52	Burgos, 45 km

939

Desde los paisajes áridos de la carretera que sube a Ronda, da la impresión de ser un golf "extremado". En realidad no lo es, pero sus pronunciadas cuestas aconsejan utilizar un coche para jugar más fácilmente en este recorrido cuya construcción exigió enormes obras para nivelar el terreno. No es muy largo, estrecho en algunos sitios, los obstáculos son peligrosos y situados en la línea de juego, lo que incita a jugar con cierta prudencia. Teniendo en cuenta que el arquitecto es Seve Ballesteros, atraerá más bien a los jugadores de ataque que serán recompensados por sus golpes audaces, sobre todo los que juegan en "fade" o los especialistas de bolas altas cuyo objetivo son unos greens no inmensos, sin grandes trampas, que aguantan bien la bola y su trayectoria a la hora de patear. De gran imaginación y espectacular, se recomienda conocerlo antes de seguir camino hacia la bella ciudad de Ronda.

From the road and arid landscape leading to Ronda,, the impression is one of an extremely hilly golf course. This is not quite the case, but the steep slopes call for the use of a buggy to play a little more easily on a course whose construction demanded very considerable grading work. It is not very long, but sometimes tight, and the hazards are always in play and dangerously placed. The result can sometimes be an over-cautious approach when playing the course. Designed by Seve Ballesteros, Los Arqueros should appeal to attacking players and will reward bold strokes. This is particularly true for players who fade the ball or who are specialists of high shots aimed at the smallish greens, which have little in the way of traps, pitch well and putt true. Imaginative and sometimes quite spectacular, this course is to be recommended before getting back on the road and heading for the beautiful town of Ronda.

Los Arqueros Golf

Ctra Ronda, km. 166,5
E - 29679 BENAHAVIS (MALAGA)

Office	Secretaria	(34) 95 - 278 46 00
Pro shop	Pro-shop	(34) 95 - 278 46 00
Fax	Fax	(34) 95 - 278 67 07
Situation	Situación	

3 km San Pedro de Alcantara
10 km Marbella, 84 410 h.

Annual closure	Cierre anual	no
Weekly closure	Cierre semanal	no

Fees main season
Precios tempor. alta

	Week days Semana	We/Bank holidays Fin de sem./fiestas
Individual Individual	5 500 Pts	5 500 Pts
Couple Pareja	11 000 Pts	11 000 Pts

Caddy	Caddy	no
Electric Trolley	Carro eléctrico	no
Buggy	Coche	4 000 Pts/18 hoyos
Clubs	Palos	2000 Pts/18 hoyos

Credit cards Tarjetas de crédito
VISA - Eurocard - MasterCard - AMEX - DC - JCB

940

Access Acceso : Marbella N340 → Cadiz, San Pedro de Alcantara, C339 → Ronda, Golf 4 km a la izquierda
Map 7 on page 879 Plano 7 Página 879

GOLF COURSE
RECORRIDO   14/20

Site	Emplazamiento	▬▬▬
Maintenance	Mantenimiento	▬▬▬
Architect	Arquitecto	Seve Ballesteros
Type	Tipo	montaña, vagüada
Relief	Relieve	▬▬▬
Water in play	Agua	▬▬
Exp. to wind	Exp. al viento	▬▬
Trees in play	Arboles	▬

Scorecard Tarjeta	Chp. Campeonato	Mens Caballeros	Ladies Damas
Length Longitud	6048	5632	5139
Par	72	72	72

Advised golfing ability		0 12 24 36
Nivel de juego aconsejado		▬▬▬
Hcp required	Handicap exigido	28 Cab., 36 Damas

CLUB HOUSE & AMENITIES
CLUB HOUSE Y DEPENDENCIAS   6/10

Pro shop	Pro-shop	▬▬▬
Driving range	Campo de prácticas	▬▬
Sheltered	cubierto	no
On grass	sobre hierba	si
Putting-green	putting-green	si
Pitching-green	pitching-green	si

HOTEL FACILITIES
HOTELES CERCANOS   7/10

HOTELS HOTELES

Andalucia Plaza	Nueva Andalucia
415 habitaciones, D 29 000 Pts	6 km
Tel (34) 95 - 281 20 00, Fax (34) 95 - 281 47 92	

Coral Beach	Nueva Andalucia
150 habitaciones, D 33 000 Pts	8 km
Tel (34) 95 - 282 45 00, Fax (34) 95 - 282 62 57	

Pyr Hotel	Puerto Banus
319 habitaciones, D 15 000 Pts	10 km
Tel (34) 95 - 281 73 53, Fax (34) 95 - 281 79 07	

RESTAURANTS RESTAURANTE

El Rodeito	Nueva Andalucia
Tel (34) 95 - 281 56 99	6 km

Cipriano	Puerto Banús
Tel (34) 95 - 281 10 77	10 km

En el corazón del "Valle del golf" en Nueva Andalucía, Los Naranjos, sin ser un monstruo, es uno de los más famosos diseños de Robert Trent Jones. Las mejoras en el mantenimiento del recorrido y la construcción de un nuevo club-house han contribuido a restaurar su gloria. Los nueve primeros hoyos, ligeramente accidentados, obligan a reflexionar tanto sobre la elección del palo como sobre la trayectoria de la bola. La vuelta es prácticamente llana, insinuándose entre naranjos, y más favorable a los pegadores que no dudarán en salir de atrás. Los jugadores más razonables encontrarán que este recorrido es ya bastante largo desde los tees de salida "normales". ¿Por qué sufrir si se puede evitar? En cada partido hallarán toda clase de situaciones diferentes de las que podrán gozar. Los greens están bien protegidos, son muy grandes y se ven bien las caídas.

At the heart of "Golf Valley" in Nueva Andalucia, "Los Naranjos" (meaning Orange Trees) is one of Robert Trent Jones' more famous designs but it is no monster. Considerably improved upkeep and the building of a new club house have helped restore its former glory. The front nine, on slightly broken terrain, require careful thought as much for the choice of club as for the trajectory of the ball. The back nine are virtually flat holes winding their way between the orange trees. They will appeal to long hitters who in every case won't think twice about playing the course from the back tees. More reasonable players will find the course long enough from the "normal" tees; after all, why suffer when you don't have to? All sorts of different situations arise every time you play here, so the course is sure-fire enjoyment every time. The greens are well-defended, often huge but never too difficult to read.

Los Naranjos Golf Club

APDO 64
E - 29660 MARBELLA (MALAGA)

Office	Secretaria	(34) 95 - 281 24 28
Pro shop	Pro-shop	(34) 95 - 281 52 06
Fax	Fax	(34) 95 - 281 14 28
Situation	Situación	

15 km Marbella, 84 410 h.
6 km San Pedro de Alcantara

Annual closure	Cierre anual	no
Weekly closure	Cierre semanal	no

Fees main season
Precios tempor. alta el campo

	Week days Semana	We/Bank holidays Fin de sem./fiestas
Individual Individual	8 200 Pts	8 200 Pts
Couple Pareja	16 400 Pts	16 400 Pts

Caddy	Caddy	si
Electric Trolley	Carro eléctrico	1500 Pts/18 hoyos
Buggy	Coche	5000 Pts/18 hoyos
Clubs	Palos	2 500 Pts/el dia

Credit cards Tarjetas de crédito
VISA - Eurocard - MasterCard - AMEX

Access Acceso : Marbella N340 → Cadiz, Nueva Andalucia (km 180), a la derecha → Golf
Map 7 on page 879 Plano 7 Página 879

GOLF COURSE
RECORRIDO
16/20

Site	Emplazamiento	
Maintenance	Mantenimiento	
Architect	Arquitecto	Robert Trent Jones
Type	Tipo	llanura, urbano
Relief	Relieve	
Water in play	Agua	
Exp. to wind	Exp. al viento	
Trees in play	Arboles	

Scorecard Tarjeta	Chp. Campeonato	Mens Caballeros	Ladies Damas
Length Longitud	6457	6038	5143
Par	72	72	72

Advised golfing ability		0	12	24	36
Nivel de juego aconsejado					
Hcp required	Handicap exigido		28 Cab., 36 Damas		

CLUB HOUSE & AMENITIES
CLUB HOUSE Y DEPENDENCIAS
7/10

Pro shop	Pro-shop	
Driving range	Campo de prácticas	
Sheltered	cubierto	no
On grass	sobre hierba	si
Putting-green	putting-green	si
Pitching-green	pitching-green	si

HOTEL FACILITIES
HOTELES CERCANOS
7/10

HOTELS HOTELES

Puente Romano — Marbella
217 habitaciones, D 49 500 Pts — 5 km
Tel (34) 95 - 282 09 00, Fax (34) 95 - 277 57 66

Andalucia Plaza — Nueva Andalucia
415 habitaciones, D 29 000 Pts — 1,5 km
Tel (34) 95 - 281 20 00, Fax (34) 95 - 281 47 92

Pyr Hotel — Puerto Banus
319 habitaciones, D 15 000 Pts — 4 km
Tel (34) 95 - 281 73 53, Fax (34) 95 - 281 79 07

RESTAURANTS RESTAURANTE

Meson El Coto — San Pedro → Ronda
Tel (34) 95 - 278 51 23 — 7 km

El Rodeito — Nueva Andalucia
Tel (34) 95 - 281 56 99 — 6 km

941

Fue el primer recorrido crado en la Costa del Sol, es como un monumento histórico, construido por HS Colt y supervisado por Tom Simpson. Sólo le faltan las dunas para ser un verdadero links, y sería interesante conocer los planos de la época para comprobar lo que sin duda alguna ha sido modificado posteriormente. Las principales dificultades son los árboles y los bosquecillos, los bunkers bien situados y algunos lagos naturales. El secreto de un buen resultado radica en dominar el juego por abajo ya que este recorrido, a la orilla del mar, está muy expuesto al viento y no en muy buen estado, pues el agua salada nunca ha hecho buenas migas con la hierba. Es indiscutible que el sitio tiene su encanto por una mezcla insólita de vegetación mediterránea y de ambiente británico, pero es de desear que una remodelación restaure el estilo específico de los primeros arquitectos.

The Costa del Sol's first course and a sort of historical landmark, designed by H.S. Colt and remodelled by Tom Simpson. The only thing missing to make this a real links course are the dunes, but it would be fun to consult the original plans to see just what exactly was altered. The main hazards are the trees and undergrowth, well-placed bunkers and a few natural lagoons. The secret of a low score here is making low shots on a seaside course which is very exposed to the wind and not in very good condition. Sea-water and grass have never got on too well together. The site has unquestionable charm with an uncommon blend of Mediterranean vegetation and British overtones, but a little remodelling to restore the specific style of the original architects would be most welcome.

Real Club de Campo de Málaga

Apdo 324
E - 29080 MALAGA

Office	Secretaria	(34) 95 - 237 66 77
Pro shop	Pro-shop	(34) 95 - 237 20 72
Fax	Fax	(34) 95 - 237 66 12
Situation	Situación	

4 km Torremolinos, 35 309 h.
10 km Málaga, 534 683 h.

Annual closure	Cierre anual	no
Weekly closure	Cierre semanal	no

Fees main season
Precios tempor. alta el campo

	Week days Semana	We/Bank holidays Fin de sem./fiestas
Individual Individual	5 800 Pts	5 800 Pts
Couple Pareja	11 600 Pts	11 600 Pts

Caddy	Caddy	no
Electric Trolley	Carro eléctrico	no
Buggy	Coche	4500 Pts/18 hoyos
Clubs	Palos	1 700 Pts/18 hoyos

Credit cards Tarjetas de crédito
VISA - Eurocard - MasterCard - AMEX

942

Access Acceso : Málaga → Torremolinos,
a la izquierda → Parador del Golf
Map 7 on page 879 Plano 7 Página 879

GOLF COURSE
RECORRIDO
13 /20

Site	Emplazamiento	▰▰▰
Maintenance	Mantenimiento	▰▰
Architect	Arquitecto	H.S. Colt Tom Simpson
Type	Tipo	al borde del mar
Relief	Relieve	
Water in play	Agua	▰▰▰
Exp. to wind	Exp. al viento	▰▰▰
Trees in play	Arboles	▰▰▰

Scorecard Tarjeta	Chp. Campeonato	Mens Caballeros	Ladies Damas
Length Longitud	6204	6040	5134
Par	72	72	72

Advised golfing ability		0	12	24	36
Nivel de juego aconsejado					

Hcp required Handicap exigido   27 Cab., 36 Damas

CLUB HOUSE & AMENITIES
CLUB HOUSE Y DEPENDENCIAS
4 /10

Pro shop	Pro-shop	▰▰
Driving range	Campo de prácticas	▰▰▰
Sheltered	cubierto	21 puestos
On grass	sobre hierba	si
Putting-green	putting-green	si
Pitching-green	pitching-green	si

HOTEL FACILITIES
HOTELES CERCANOS
6 /10

HOTELS HOTELES
Parador Málaga   Golf
60 habitaciones, D 17 500 Pts   100 m
Tel (34) 95 - 238 12 55, Fax (34) 95 - 238 89 63

Guadalmar   Malaga
200 habitaciones, D 16 350 Pts   3 km
Tel (34) 95 - 223 17 03, Fax (34) 95 - 224 03 85

RESTAURANTS RESTAURANTE
Casa Pedro   Málaga
Tel (34) 95 - 229 00 13   3 km

Calycanto   Málaga
Tel (34) 95 - 221 22 22   3 km

La nueva dirección del club ha vuelto a dar vida a este recorrido con cierta imaginación, aunque por momentos tortuoso, de Robert Trent Jones. Muy en cuesta, es mejor alquilar un coche y a pesar de las dificultades que ello implica habría que actualizarlo. La gran diversidad de hoyos y de golpes que hay que jugar es asombrosa, encontrando los famosos bunkers del arquitecto y algunos obstáculos de agua peligrosos que requieren un serio análisis de su buena forma de juego, antes de tomar una decisión entre el ataque o la prudencia. Teniendo en cuenta que los greenes tienen muchas caídas: hay que atacar resueltamente a bandera. No se trata ni mucho menos de un recorrido imposible, pero los jugadores sin handicap sufrirán más que los otros. Algunas hondonadas y sinuosidades del terreno son una seria amenaza para los drives en algunos hoyos. Bien es verdad que por momentos el maravilloso panorama sobre el mar puede servir de consuelo a ciertos desastres.

A change of management has breathed new life into this imaginative but sometimes tortuous course, designed by Robert Trent Jones. This is rather broken terrain, making walking a little difficult, but the demanding layout is very much back in the modern trend. The variety of holes and the shots they require is remarkable. There are, of course, the architect's hallmark bunkers and a number of dangerous water hazards, which call for serious analysis of current playing form before deciding whether to attack or lay up. All the more so in that the greens are well designed and definitely favour players who go for the pin. It is not an impossible course, far from it, but high-handicappers will suffer, especially with the few ravines and hollows that pose a serious threat to a number of tee-shots. The scenic views over the sea will more than compensate should disaster strike.

Golf Club Marbella

Ctra Cadiz, Km. 188
E - 29002 MARBELLA (MALAGA)

Office	Secretaria	(34) 95 - 283 05 00
Pro shop	Pro-shop	(34) 95 - 283 05 00
Fax	Fax	(34) 95 - 283 43 53
Situation	Situación	

5 km Marbella, 24 410 h.
20 km Fuengirola, 43 048 h.

Annual closure	Cierre anual	no
Weekly closure	Cierre semanal	no

Fees main season
Precios tempor. alta el campo

	Week days Semana	We/Bank holidays Fin de sem./fiestas
Individual Individual	8 000 Pts	8 000 Pts
Couple Pareja	16 000 Pts	16 000 Pts

Caddy	Caddy	no
Electric Trolley	Carro eléctrico	no
Buggy	Coche	5000 Pts/18 hoyos
Clubs	Palos	4 000 Pts/18 hoyos

Credit cards Tarjetas de crédito
VISA - MasterCard - AMEX

Access Acceso : Marbella N340 → Fuengirola,
Golf km 188
Map 7 on page 879 Plano 7 Página 879

GOLF COURSE
RECORRIDO
15/20

Site	Emplazamiento	
Maintenance	Mantenimiento	
Architect	Arquitecto	Robert Trent Jones
Type	Tipo	vagüada
Relief	Relieve	
Water in play	Agua	
Exp. to wind	Exp. al viento	
Trees in play	Arboles	

Scorecard Tarjeta	Chp. Campeonato	Mens Caballeros	Ladies Damas
Length Longitud	5933	5558	4661
Par	71	71	71

Advised golfing ability Nivel de juego aconsejado	0 12 24 36
Hcp required Handicap exigido	28 Cab., 36 Damas

CLUB HOUSE & AMENITIES
CLUB HOUSE Y DEPENDENCIAS
7/10

Pro shop	Pro-shop	
Driving range	Campo de prácticas	
Sheltered	cubierto	no
On grass	sobre hierba	si
Putting-green	putting-green	si
Pitching-green	pitching-green	si

943

HOTEL FACILITIES
HOTELES CERCANOS
8/10

HOTELS HOTELES

Los Monteros — Marbella, 1 km
168 habitaciones, D 35 200 Pts
Tel (34) 95 - 277 17 00, Fax (34) 95 - 282 58 46

Artola — Artola, 7 km
32 habitaciones, D 12 000 Pts
Tel (34) 95 - 283 13 90, Fax (34) 95 - 238 04 50

RESTAURANTS RESTAURANTE

La Fonda — Marbella, 3 km
Tel (34) 95 - 277 25 12

Santiago — Marbella, 3 km
Tel (34) 95 - 277 43 39

Es mejor utilizar un coche sobre todo en los tramos accidentados de un hoyo a otro, a pesar de que el relieve del recorrido en sí mismo sea moderado. José María Olazábal ha sabido sacar provecho de un terreno a primera vista más bien quebrado y peligroso. El relieve impide muy a menudo ver los greens desde los tees de salida de los pares 4 y 5, pero los bunkers de calle indican la línea de juego y acogen las bolas imprecisas. Los pares 3, generalmente con hondanadas en medio, parecen peligrosos pero de longitud razonable. Los greens tienen muchas caídas, son o muy largos o muy anchos y aguantan bien la bola. Incluso cuando la posición de las banderas puede dificultar seriamente el juego ,sobre todo si se ha salido de atrás, Masia Bach es un recorrido menos peligroso de lo que generalmente piensan los jugadores si logran conservar su aplomo y una cierta precisión.

A buggy can come in handy here to cross the broken terrain between holes, but much of the course here is not too hilly. José Maria Olazabal has brought the best out of what, at first sight, looks to be much more rugged and dangerous terrain. Indeed, the relief often obscures any view of the greens from the tees on the par 4s and 5s, but the fairway bunkers show the line of play and often stop mishit balls in their tracks. Generally laid out with large hollows between tee and green, the par 3s look dangerous but their lengths are very reasonable. The greens are very undulating, sometimes very long or very wide, and pitch well. Even though the pin positions can sometimes seriously complicate play when driving from the back-tees, Masia Bach is a friendlier course for players of all levels than people might think. As long as they keep a cool head, and play straight.

Club de Golf Masia Bach
Ctra de Martorell-Capellades - Km 19,5
E - 08781 SANT ESTEVE SESROVIRES (BARCELONA)

Office	Secretaria	(34) 93 - 772 63 10
Pro shop	Pro-shop	(34) 93 - 772 63 10
Fax	Fax	(34) 93 - 772 63 56
Situation	Situación	

7 km Martorell, 16 793 h.
25 km Barcelona, 1 754 900 h.

Annual closure	Cierre anual	no
Weekly closure	Cierre semanal	lunes

Fees main season
Precios tempor. alta el campo

	Week days Semana	We/Bank holidays Fin de sem./fiestas
Individual Individual	6 400 Pts	17 250 Pts
Couple Pareja	12 800 Pts	34 500 Pts

Semana: 2 personas + coche, 10 000 Pts

Caddy	Caddy	no
Electric Trolley	Carro eléctrico	750 Pts/18 hoyos
Buggy	Coche	4 000 Pts/18 hoyos
Clubs	Palos	2 000 Pts/18 hoyos

Credit cards Tarjetas de crédito
VISA - Eurocard - MasterCard - AMEX

944

Access Acceso : Barcelona A2/A7 → Tarragona, salida 25 → Martorell, B224 → Capellades, Golf a la derecha Map 2 on page 869 Plano 2 Página 869

GOLF COURSE
RECORRIDO
15/20

Site	Emplazamiento	▪▪▪▪▪▪▪▪
Maintenance	Mantenimiento	▪▪▪▪▪▪▪
Architect	Arquitecto	José Maria Olazábal
Type	Tipo	montaña
Relief	Relieve	▪▪▪▪▪
Water in play	Agua	▪▪▪▪
Exp. to wind	Exp. al viento	▪▪▪▪
Trees in play	Arboles	▪▪▪▪

Scorecard Tarjeta	Chp. Campeonato	Mens Caballeros	Ladies Damas
Length Longitud	6271	6039	5161
Par	72	72	72

Advised golfing ability		0	12	24	36
Nivel de juego aconsejado		▪▪▪▪▪▪▪▪▪			

| Hcp required | Handicap exigido | 28 Cab., 36 Damas |

CLUB HOUSE & AMENITIES
CLUB HOUSE Y DEPENDENCIAS
7/10

Pro shop	Pro-shop	▪▪▪▪▪
Driving range	Campo de prácticas	▪▪▪▪▪
Sheltered	cubierto	7 puestos
On grass	sobre hierba	si
Putting-green	putting-green	si
Pitching-green	pitching-green	si

HOTEL FACILITIES
HOTELES CERCANOS
6/10

HOTELS HOTELES
Las Torres   Sant Esteve
22 habitaciones, D 6 420 Pts   5 km
Tel (34) 93 - 771 41 81, Fax (34) 93 - 771 34 62

Manel   Martorell
29 habitaciones, D 6 600 Pts   4 km
Tel (34) 93 - 775 23 87, Fax (34) 93 - 775 23 87

RESTAURANTS RESTAURANTE
Las Torres   Sant Esteve
Tel (34) 93 - 771 41 81   5 km

Prácticamente en el borde del mar y cerca de la ciudad, Maspalomas fue construido en un terreno muy llano cerca de las dunas, lo que le da un aspecto de links que uno no se espera encontrar en la Isla de Gran Canaria. La paternidad de Mackenzie Ross (autor de la reconstrucción de Turnberry) ofrece la garantía de autenticidad de estilo. Aunque es un recorrido de competición muy exigente, sin embargo es un buen golf para ir de vacaciones. Es un par 73 de longitud razonable, pero con dificuldades enormes, que invita a los jugadores a proceder sin complejos y según sus posibilidades. No hay que dormirse ni extraviarse en las dunas, donde el rough es muy peligroso. Grandes bunkers con una arena de agradable color amarillo esperan las bolas poco precisas. La flora subtropical compuesta de palmeras, pinos canarios y marítimos, ibiscos, buganvillas, etc., confiere un color muy particular a este diseño bastante británico...

Virtually by the sea and in town, Maspalomas was built on a very flat land. Its layout, close to sand-dunes, gives it a links style which you wouldn't expect to find on Grand Canary island, and the patronage of Mackenzie Ross (who re-designed Turnberry) provides a sure-fire guarantee of authenticity in terms of style. Although this is a rather challenging tournament course, it still makes for very good holiday golfing and so is very "functional" golfing facility in this part of the world. This is a par 73 of reasonable with no insurmountable difficulties, inviting players to "go for it" to the best of their ability. But they'll need to keep on their toes and not stray into the dunes where the rough can make a big dent in your card. Large bunkers filled with pretty yellow sand also wait the mishit ball (and others too). The sub-tropical vegetation of palm-trees, Canary pines, hibiscus-trees and bougainvillaea add special colour to this very British-style layout.

Club de Golf Maspalomas
Auda de Neckerman S/N
E - 35100 MASPALOMAS (Gran Canaria)

Office	Secretaria	(34) 928 - 76 25 81
Pro shop	Pro-shop	(34) 928 - 76 87 51
Fax	Fax	(34) 928 - 76 82 45
Situation	Situación	
30 km Las Palmas, 360 483 h.		
Annual closure	Cierre anual	no
Weekly closure	Cierre semanal	no

Fees main season
Precios tempor. alta recorrido

	Week days Semana	We/Bank holidays Fin de sem./fiestas
Individual Individual	8 500 Pts	8 500 Pts
Couple Pareja	17 000 Pts	17 000 Pts

Caddy	Caddy	no
Electric Trolley	Carro eléctrico	no
Buggy	Coche	5 000 Pts/18 hoyos
Clubs	Palos	si

Credit cards Tarjetas de crédito
VISA - Eurocard - MasterCard

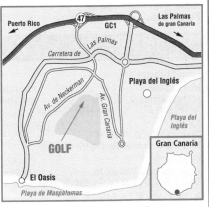

Access Acceso : Autopista Sur, → Maspalomas
Map 9 on page 0 Plano 9 Página 0

GOLF COURSE
RECORRIDO   16/20

Site	Emplazamiento	
Maintenance	Mantenimiento	
Architect	Arquitecto	Mackenzie Ross
Type	Tipo	bosque
Relief	Relieve	
Water in play	Agua	
Exp. to wind	Exp. al viento	
Trees in play	Arboles	

Scorecard Tarjeta	Chp. Campeonato	Mens Caballeros	Ladies Damas
Length Longitud	6189	6037	5210
Par	73	73	73

Advised golfing ability		0 12 24 36
Nivel de juego aconsejado		
Hcp required	Handicap exigido	30

CLUB HOUSE & AMENITIES
CLUB HOUSE Y DEPENDENCIAS   7/10

Pro shop	Pro-shop	
Driving range	Campo de prácticas	
Sheltered	cubierto	12 puestos
On grass	sobre hierba	si
Putting-green	putting-green	si
Pitching-green	pitching-green	si

945

HOTEL FACILITIES
HOTELES CERCANOS   8/10

HOTELS HOTELES
Ifa-Faro   Maspalomas
183 habitaciones, D 39 800 Pts   3 km
Tel (34) 928 - 14 22 14, Fax (34) 928 - 14 19 40

Palm Beach   Maspalomas
347 habitaciones, D 66100 Pts   3 km
Tel (34) 928 - 14 08 06, Fax (34) 928 - 14 18 08

Oasis   Maspalomas
319 habitaciones, D 46 000 Pts   3 km
Tel (34) 928 - 14 14 48, Fax (34) 928 - 14 11 92

RESTAURANTS RESTAURANTE
La Aquarela   Maspalomas
Tel (34) 928 - 14 01 78   1 km

Amaiur   Maspalomas
Tel (34) 928 - 76 14 14   1 km

Orangerie   Maspalomas
Tel (34) 928 - 14 08 06   3 km

Este recorrido ha contribuido a la fama creciente de su arquitecto Ramón Espinosa. Es una joya depositada en un amplio valle, sus sutiles dificultades lo hacen más delicado de lo que a primera vista parece, sin por ello desalentar a los jugadores de nivel medio. Los bunkers de calle y de green están inteligentemente situados y bien visibles e indican la táctica de juego que hay que adoptar. Algunos árboles aislados obligan a pegar la bola con efecto y algunos lagos pequeñitos están en línea de juego en siete hoyos, completando una panoplia de dificultades muy variadas. Los greens, tan tupidos como las calles, son falsamente planos y desconcertantes si no se les examina con mucha atención. Inteligente y franco, es un recorrido para todo el mundo y se puede aconsejar tanto por su armonía como por su cuidadoso mantenimiento: se pasa una óptima jornada.

This course has done much to enhance the growing reputation of architect Ramon Espinosa. This is a gem of a course located in a wide valley, and the subtly placed hazards make it tougher than you might think at first sight, but not to the point of scaring off the lesser players. The fairway and green-side bunkers are cleverly located and visible enough to help your game tactics. A few isolated trees call for elaborate shots, moving the ball both ways, and small ponds are in play on seven holes, thus completing a highly varied panoply of hazards. The greens, as grassy as the fairways, are deceptively flat and disconcerting if not read carefully. An intelligent and honest course, this is a golfing arena for everyone. Being well-balanced and well-cared for, it is a course well worth recommending for spending a great day out.

Club de Campo Mediterraneo

Urbanización "La Coma" S/N
E - 12190 BORRIOL (CASTELLON DE LA PLANA)

Office	Secretaria	(34) 964 - 32 12 27
Pro shop	Pro-shop	(34) 964 - 32 20 80
Fax	Fax	(34) 964 - 32 13 57
Situation	Situación	

5 km Castellón de la Plana, 138 489 h.

Annual closure	Cierre anual	no
Weekly closure	Cierre semanal	no

Fees main season
Precios tempor. alta el campo

	Week days Semana	We/Bank holidays Fin de sem./fiestas
Individual Individual	6 000 Pts	6 000 Pts
Couple Pareja	12 000 Pts	12 000 Pts

Caddy	Caddy	no
Electric Trolley	Carro eléctrico	1500 Pts/18 hoyos
Buggy	Coche	3 500 Pts/18 hoyos
Clubs	Palos	1500 Pts/18 hoyos

Credit cards Tarjetas de crédito   no

Access **Acceso** : A7 Barcelona-Valencia, salida 46 →
Castellón Norte. 700 m a la derecha → "Club de Campo". Golf 2,5 km
Map 4 on page 873 Plano 4 Página 873

GOLF COURSE
RECORRIDO   16 /20

Site	Emplazamiento	▰▰▰▰▱
Maintenance	Mantenimiento	▰▰▰▰▱
Architect	Arquitecto	Ramón Espinosa
Type	Tipo	campo
Relief	Relieve	▰▱▱▱▱
Water in play	Agua	▰▰▱▱▱
Exp. to wind	Exp. al viento	▰▰▰▱▱
Trees in play	Arboles	▰▰▰▱▱

Scorecard Tarjeta	Chp. Campeonato	Mens Caballeros	Ladies Damas
Length Longitud	6239	6038	5266
Par	72	72	72

Advised golfing ability Nivel de juego aconsejado	0	12	24	36

Hcp required   Handicap exigido   28 Cab., 36 Damas

CLUB HOUSE & AMENITIES
CLUB HOUSE Y DEPENDENCIAS   7 /10

Pro shop	Pro-shop	▰▰▰▱▱
Driving range	Campo de prácticas	▰▰▰▱▱
Sheltered	cubierto	no
On grass	sobre hierba	si
Putting-green	putting-green	si
Pitching-green	pitching-green	si

HOTEL FACILITIES
HOTELES CERCANOS   6 /10

HOTELS HOTELES
Intur Castellón   Castellón
123 habitaciones, D 17 000 Pts   5 km
Tel (34) 964 - 22 50 00, Fax (34) 964 - 23 26 06

Turcosa   El Grao/Castellón
70 habitaciones, D 11 600 Pts   7 km
Tel (34) 964 - 28 36 00, Fax (34) 964 - 28 47 37

Mindoro   Castellón
103 habitaciones, D 14 800 Pts   5 km
Tel (34) 964 - 22 23 00, Fax (34) 964 - 23 31 54

RESTAURANTS RESTAURANTE
Mare Nostrum   El Grao/Castellón
Tel (34) 964 - 28 29 29   7 km

Tasca del Puerto   El Grao/Castellón
Tel (34) 964 - 28 44 81   7 km

946

De los dos recorridos de Mijas, éste es para los "pegadores" y el que da mayor sensación de espacio. Bien es verdad que hay ocho lagos en la línea de juego en una decena de hoyos, pero las calles son anchas. Y menos mal, porque Los Lagos es muy largo, sin muchas cuestas, lo que permite jugarlo sin recurrir a un coche. Algo característico de Trent Jones es la disposición de los bunkers, no sólo para defender los greens, sino para dificultar la tarea de quienes intentan cortar en los dog-legs. Además, presenta una cierta variedad visual en hoyos que son muy semejantes entre sí. Los greens son extensos, con bastantes caídas, en muy buen estado, y su rapidez no impide que aguanten bien la bola: cosa muy importante ya que a menudo hay que aprochar con hierros largos. Que los jugadores medianos no se desanimen, pueden acortar el recorrido escogiendo tees de salida más adelantados.

Of the two courses at Mijas, this is the one for the big-hitters and for the greatest impression of open space. Sure, the eight lakes are very much to the fore on ten holes, but the fairways are wide. And so they should be, because "Los Lagos" is very long. But it is a pleasant course to play walking, as the terrain is relatively flat. Typical of Trent Jones, the bunkers are there not only to defend the greens but also to trap players who try and cut corners on the dog-legs. They also add a little variety to holes that are often very similar in style. The greens are huge, undulating and in good condition, and although fast they pitch well. This is important because approach shots often call for a long iron. Average players should not lose heart though, as they can shorten the course considerably by playing off the front-tees.

Mijas Golf International

Apdo de Coreos 145
E - 29640 FUENGIROLA (MALAGA)

Office	Secretaria	(34) 95 - 247 68 43
Pro shop	Pro-shop	(34) 95 - 246 80 38
Fax	Fax	(34) 95 - 246 79 43
Situation	Situación	

25 km Málaga, 534 683 h.

Annual closure	Cierre anual	no
Weekly closure	Cierre semanal	

Fees main season
Precios tempor. alta el campo

	Week days Semana	We/Bank holidays Fin de sem./fiestas
Individual Individual	7 000 Pts	7 000 Pts
Couple Pareja	14 000 Pts	14 000 Pts

Caddy	Caddy	no
Electric Trolley	Carro eléctrico	1 500 Pts
Buggy	Coche	5000 Pts/18 hoyos
Clubs	Palos	1 800 Pts/18 hoyos

Credit cards Tarjetas de crédito   VISA - MasterCard

Alhaurin el Grande

MA 485
Mijas
GOLF
MA 426
N 340
Malaga
FUENGIROLA
COSTA DEL SOL
Mijas Costa
Marbella

0   4   8 km

Access Acceso : Málaga N340 → Cadiz. Salida "Cambio de Sentido", Fuengirola → Mijas, Golf 3 km
Map 7 on page 879 Plano 7 Página 879

GOLF COURSE RECORRIDO
16/20

Site	Emplazamiento	▬▬▬
Maintenance	Mantenimiento	▬▬▬
Architect	Arquitecto	Robert Trent Jones
Type	Tipo	campo
Relief	Relieve	▬▬
Water in play	Agua	▬▬▬
Exp. to wind	Exp. al viento	▬▬▬
Trees in play	Arboles	▬▬

Scorecard Tarjeta	Chp. Campeonato	Mens Caballeros	Ladies Damas
Length Longitud	6367	6007	5148
Par	71	71	71

Advised golfing ability Nivel de juego aconsejado	0	12	24	36

Hcp required   Handicap exigido   28 Cab., 36 Damas

CLUB HOUSE & AMENITIES CLUB HOUSE Y DEPENDENCIAS
6/10

Pro shop	Pro-shop	▬▬
Driving range	Campo de prácticas	▬▬
Sheltered	cubierto	no
On grass	sobre hierba	si
Putting-green	putting-green	si
Pitching-green	pitching-green	no

HOTEL FACILITIES HOTELES CERCANOS
7/10

HOTELS HOTELES

Byblos		Mijas
144 habitaciones, D 37 500 Pts		200 m
Tel (34) 95 - 247 30 50, Fax (34) 95 - 247 67 83		

Florida		Fuengirola
116 habitaciones, D 11 000 Pts		3 km
Tel (34) 95 - 247 61 00, Fax (34) 95 - 258 15 29		

Mijas		Mijas
97 habitaciones, D 14 000 Pts		5 km
Tel (34) 95 - 248 58 00, Fax (34) 95 - 248 58 25		

RESTAURANTS RESTAURANTE

El Olivar		Mijas
Tel (34) 95 - 248 61 96		5 km

El Tomate		Fuengirola
Tel(34) 95 - 247 35 99		3 km

El Mirlo Blanco		Mijas
Tel(34) 95 - 246 02 50		5 km

947

De los dos recorridos de Mijas, Los Olivos conviene más a los jugadores de nivel medio. Por supuesto es estrecho, rodeado de numerosos olivos, algunos lagos pueden perturbar a los jugadores con poca técnica, su relieve es ligeramente más accidentado que el de "Los Lagos", pero encontrarán un trazado más a su medida y al alcance de sus posibilidades. Los greens son más pequeños, algunos ciegos, pero aguantan correctamente la bola y la progresión general del recorrido lo hace más divertido para jugar en familia cuando el resultado es menos importante que el placer. No es un recorrido para atacar y ciertamente no fue diseñado para ello. Da la impresión que Trent Jones quiso poner de relieve en Mijas dos facetas muy diferentes de su buen hacer. En todo caso, este conjunto permite que todos puedan escoger según su forma actual.

When choosing between the two courses at Mijas, average players are perhaps better off playing Los Olivos. The course is certainly tight and bordered by numerous olive trees, there are a few lakes to scare players with limited technique and the relief is in part much more broken than its sister course, Los Lagos. But the layout is probably much more within their scope and ability. The greens are smaller and some are blind, but they pitch pretty well and the general layout makes this course fun for playing with the family when scores are less important than having a good time. It is not a course for attacking players and visibly was not designed to be so. You get the impression that Trent Jones wanted to demonstrate two very different facets of his architectural know-how at Mijas. In any case, this golfing resort allows everyone to choose according to the shape of his or her game.

Mijas Golf International

Apdo de Coreos 145
E - 29640 FUENGIROLA (MALAGA)

Office	Secretaria	(34) 95 - 247 68 43
Pro shop	Pro-shop	(34) 95 - 246 80 38
Fax	Fax	(34) 95 - 246 79 43
Situation	Situación	

25 km Málaga, 534 683 h.

Annual closure	Cierre anual	no
Weekly closure	Cierre semanal	no

Fees main season
Precios tempor. alta el campo

	Week days Semana	We/Bank holidays Fin de sem./fiestas
Individual Individual	7 000 Pts	7 000 Pts
Couple Pareja	14 000 Pts	14 000 Pts

Caddy	Caddy	no
Electric Trolley	Carro eléctrico	1 500 Pts
Buggy	Coche	5000 Pts/18 hoyos
Clubs	Palos	1 800 Pts/18 hoyos

Credit cards Tarjetas de crédito
VISA - MasterCard

GOLF COURSE
RECORRIDO
13/20

Site	Emplazamiento	▐▐▐▐▐▐
Maintenance	Mantenimiento	▐▐▐▐▐▐
Architect	Arquitecto	Robert Trent Jones
Type	Tipo	campo, vagüada
Relief	Relieve	▐▐▐▐
Water in play	Agua	▐▐▐
Exp. to wind	Exp. al viento	▐▐▐
Trees in play	Arboles	▐▐▐▐

Scorecard Tarjeta	**Chp.** Campeonato	**Mens** Caballeros	**Ladies** Damas
Length Longitud	6009	5866	4969
Par	72	72	72

Advised golfing ability			0	12	24	36
Nivel de juego aconsejado						

Hcp required	Handicap exigido	28 Cab., 36 Damas

CLUB HOUSE & AMENITIES
CLUB HOUSE Y DEPENDENCIAS
6/10

Pro shop	Pro-shop	▐▐▐▐
Driving range	Campo de prácticas	▐▐▐▐▐
Sheltered	cubierto	no
On grass	sobre hierba	si
Putting-green	putting-green	si
Pitching-green	pitching-green	no

HOTEL FACILITIES
HOTELES CERCANOS
7/10

HOTELS HOTELES

Byblos — Mijas
144 habitaciones, D 37 500 Pts — 200 m
Tel (34) 95 - 247 30 50, Fax (34) 95 - 247 67 83

Florida — Fuengirola
116 habitaciones, D 11 000 Pts — 3 km
Tel (34) 95 - 247 61 00, Fax (34) 95 - 258 15 29

Mijas — Mijas
97 habitaciones, D 14 000 Pts — 5 km
Tel (34) 95 - 248 58 00, Fax (34) 95 - 248 58 25

RESTAURANTS RESTAURANTE

El Olivar — Mijas
Tel (34) 95 - 248 61 96 — 5 km

El Tomate — Fuengirola
Tel (34) 95 - 247 35 99 — 3 km

El Mirlo Blanco, Tel (34) 95 - 246 02 50 — Mijas, 5 km

948

Access Acceso : Málaga N340 → Cadiz. Salida "Cambio de Sentido", Fuengirola → Mijas, Golf 3 km
Map 7 on page 879 Plano 7 Página 879

El golf más extravagante de toda la región y sin duda de España. Diseñado por Pepe Gancedo, este recorrido o gusta o se detesta. En plena montaña y muy expuesto al viento, reserva toda clase de sorpresas, hasta tal punto que algunos hoyos "normales" parecen insulsos. Sinuoso entre rocas, franqueando quebradas, bajando colinas, en medio de una vegetación salvaje y tupida, hay que conservar el dominio de sí mismo. Si se sale de calle, ¡o desgracia!. Pero las reglas locales son indulgentes: toda bola perdida se considera que reposa en un obstáculo de agua lateral. Uno se encuentra solo ante su propio juego como si estuviese al otro lado del mundo. Que el emblema del recorrido sea un toro no es mera casualidad: hay que luchar contra él, aguantar sus embistes, esquivar sus ataques. Se acaba agotado pero encantado de los magníficos paisajes. Un recorrido barroco, de gran inteligencia e imposible de ignorar.

The most extravagant course in the whole region and certainly in the whole of Spain. Designed by Pepe Gancedo, you either love it or hate it, with no middle ground. Right in the mountains and very exposed to the wind, it reserves every sort of surprise to the extent where certain "normal" holes look positively insipid. Winding its way through rocks, crossing gorges and running down hills amidst wild thick vegetation, the course calls for a cool head. Too bad if you miss the fairways. But the local rules are pretty lenient, as any lost ball is considered to be in a side water hazard. Here you are at the world's end, alone with your game of golf. It is no accident to see that the course's emblem is a bull; you have to fight it, stave off its charges and sidestep its attacks. You leave the 18th green exhausted but delighted with the magnificent landscapes. A baroque course of great intelligence, and one that is impossible to overlook.

Monte Mayor Golf Club

Urbanizacion Los Naranjos - Nueva Andalucia
E - 29660 MARBELLA (MALAGA)

Office	Secretaria	(34) 95 - 211 30 88
Pro shop	Pro-shop	(34) 95 - 211 30 88
Fax	Fax	(34) 95 - 211 30 87
Situation	Situación	

14 km Estepona, 36 307 h.
22 km Marbella, 84 410 h.

Annual closure	Cierre anual	no
Weekly closure	Cierre semanal	no

Fees main season
Precios tempor. alta el campo

	Week days Semana	We/Bank holidays Fin de sem./fiestas
Individual Individual	7 000 Pts	7 000 Pts
Couple Pareja	14 000 PtS	14 000 PTS

Caddy	Caddy	no
Electric Trolley	Carro eléctrico	no
Buggy	Coche	3500 Pts/18 hoyos
Clubs	Palos	2500 Pts/18 hoyos
Credit cards Tarjetas de crédito		no

Access Acceso : Marbella N340 → Estepona. Salida "La Cancelada". Km 163,6 a la derecha → Golf
Map 7 on page 879 Plano 7 Página 879

GOLF COURSE / RECORRIDO   13/20

Site	Emplazamiento	
Maintenance	Mantenimiento	
Architect	Arquitecto	P. Gancedo
Type	Tipo	montaña
Relief	Relieve	
Water in play	Agua	
Exp. to wind	Exp. al viento	
Trees in play	Arboles	

Scorecard Tarjeta	Chp. Campeonato	Mens Caballeros	Ladies Damas
Length Longitud	5652	5354	4800
Par	71	71	71

Advised golfing ability		0 12 24 36
Nivel de juego aconsejado		
Hcp required	Handicap exigido	28 Cab., 36 Damas

CLUB HOUSE & AMENITIES / CLUB HOUSE Y DEPENDENCIAS   5/10

Pro shop	Pro-shop	
Driving range	Campo de prácticas	
Sheltered	cubierto	no
On grass	sobre hierba	no
Putting-green	putting-green	si
Pitching-green	pitching-green	no

HOTEL FACILITIES / HOTELES CERCANOS   5/10

HOTELS HOTELES
Atalaya Park — Estepona
448 habitaciones, D 24 000 Pts — 14 km
Tel (34) 95 - 288 48 01, Fax (34) 95 - 288 57 35

Pyr Hotel — Puerto Banus
319 habitaciones, D 15 000 Pts — 25 km
Tel (34) 95 - 281 73 53, Fax (34) 95 - 281 79 07

RESTAURANTS RESTAURANTE
El Carnicero — La Cancelada
Tel (34) 95 - 288 63 07 — 6 km

El Rocio — Estepona
Tel (34) 95 - 280 00 46 — 14 km

949

Era de esperar encontrarse un día con la firma de Jack Nicklaus en el sur de España. Ha sacado buen partido de un terreno moderadamente accidentado, y si los greens están frecuentemente en alto, no hay hoyos ciegos ni hoyos en subida, lo que confirma su filosofía de que: "hay que ver lo que hay que hacer". Prueba de ello el 18 con el tee de salida allá en alto. En realidad es un recorrido franco y difícil de lidiar, pero su dificultad general no impide el jugarlo en familia (salvo los principiantes), siempre y cuando cada uno se mantenga tranquilo y no se obsesione por el resultado. Todas las dificultades se concentran en la línea de juego (sobre todo los obstáculos de agua), y hay muchos fuera de límites. La variedad de situaciones incita a jugarlo varias veces para comprender mejor sus sutilezas. Espectacular y original (por la región), este recorrido no reniega el espíritu americano de su autor. Los que conocen sus otras realizaciones no quedarán sorprendidos.

It was only to be expected that one day Jack Nicklaus would leave his mark in southern Spain. He has extracted the best out of a moderately hilly terrain, and while the greens are frequently elevated, there are no blind or uphill holes, thus illustrating the great man's philosophy of: "you have to see what you have to do". Witness hole N° 18 with a very elevated tee. As a result, this is a very open but very tricky course to get around, but the general difficulty does not prevent this from being a course for all the family (but not beginners) as long as you don't get obsessed with your score. All the hazards are very much in play, especially the water and even more so the out-of-bounds. The variety of situations will make you want to play here several times to fully understand the more subtle sides to the course. Spectacular and original (for the region, that is), the course does not break with the American spirit of its designer.

Montecastillo Hotel & Golf Resort

Carretera de Arcos, km. 9,6
E - 11406 JEREZ DE LA FRONTERA (Cádiz)

Office	Secretaria	(34) 956 - 15 12 00
Pro shop	Pro-shop	(34) 956 - 15 12 00
Fax	Fax	(34) 956 - 15 12 09
Situation	Situación	

8 km Jerez, 184 364 h.
70 km Sevilla, 704 857 h.

Annual closure	Cierre anual	no
Weekly closure	Cierre semanal	no

Fees main season
Precios tempor. alta el campo

	Week days Semana	We/Bank holidays Fin de sem./fiestas
Individual Individual	7 000 Pts	7 000 Pts
Couple Pareja	14 000 Pts	14 000 Pts

Caddy	Caddy	no
Electric Trolley	Carro eléctrico	no
Buggy	Coche	4 500 Pts/18 hoyos
Clubs	Palos	2 000 Pts/18 hoyos

Credit cards Tarjetas de crédito
VISA - Eurocard - MasterCard - AMEX - DC

950

Jerez de la Frontera
Arcos de la Frontera
N IV
4
N 342
GOLF
A4
EL PUERTO de Sta Maria
0   2   4 km
CADIZ

Access Acceso : Jerez, N342 → Arcos de la Frontera,
9,8 km desvio a la derecha, Golf 1,5 km
Map 7 on page 878 Plano 7 Página 878

GOLF COURSE
RECORRIDO
17 /20

Site	Emplazamiento	
Maintenance	Mantenimiento	
Architect	Arquitecto	Jack Nicklaus
Type	Tipo	campo
Relief	Relieve	
Water in play	Agua	
Exp. to wind	Exp. al viento	
Trees in play	Arboles	

Scorecard Tarjeta	Chp. Campeonato	Mens Caballeros	Ladies Damas
Length Longitud	6424	6043	5230
Par	72	72	72

Advised golfing ability		0 12 24 36
Nivel de juego aconsejado		
Hcp required	Handicap exigido	28 Cab., 36 Damas

CLUB HOUSE & AMENITIES
CLUB HOUSE Y DEPENDENCIAS
8 /10

Pro shop	Pro-shop	
Driving range	Campo de prácticas	
Sheltered	cubierto	18 puestos
On grass	sobre hierba	si
Putting-green	putting-green	si
Pitching-green	pitching-green	si

HOTEL FACILITIES
HOTELES CERCANOS
7 /10

HOTELS HOTELES
Montecastillo   Montecastillo
120 habitaciones, D 23 500 Pts   100 m
Tel (34) 956 - 15 12 00, Fax (34) 956 - 15 12 09

La Cueva Park   Jerez de la Frontera
58 habitaciones, D 12 000 Pts.   3
Tel (34) 956 - 18 91 20, Fax (34) 956 - 18 91 21

Royal Sherry   Jerez de la Frontera
173 habitaciones, D 17 750 Pts   7 km
Tel (34) 956 - 30 30 11, Fax (34) 956 - 31 13 00

RESTAURANTS RESTAURANTE
Tendido 6   Jerez de la Frontera
Tel (34) 956 - 34 48 35   10 km

Mesón La Cueva   Montecastillo
Tel (34) 956 - 18 90 20   1 km

| 15 | 7 | 7 |

La Dehesa de Montenmedio es un recorrido reciente de buena calidad en general, salido del pincel de Alejandro Maldonado y que creemos es, hasta ahora, su realización más prestigiosa. La región está cada día mejor equipada de golfs, y es cada vez más difícil encontrar terrenos entre Málaga, Marbella y Gibraltar. . En este recorrido, por el momento no se aceptan más de 60 jugadores al día, distribuidos en partidas a veinte minutos de intervalo, lo que garantiza una gran comodidad de juego. Las calles y greens son anchos favoreciendo a los jugadores de tipo medio que son la mayor parte de los visitantes de la región. La mayor parte de las veces en los segundos golpes hacia los greens se pueden utilizar hierros medianos. Los pares 3 exigen mucha precisión. No obstante hay que permanecer vigilantes y no atacar de cualquier manera, ya que la configuración natural del terreno ha sido preservada al igual que la vegetación, mientras que el agua es un elemento más bien decorativo que no dificulta el juego.

La Dehesa de Montenmedio is a brand new course of generally excellent standard thanks to the design skills of Alejandro Maldonado, from whom this is the most prestigious achievement to date as far as we know. This region is being given more and more courses as land becomes increasingly scarce between Malaga, Marbella and Gibraltar. For the time being this course admits only 60 players a day teeing at 20 minutes intervals, so you are in for a relaxed round. The fairways and greens are wide, which is good news for the average players who form the core of green-feers visiting the region. Most of their approach shots will be medium-irons, and the par 3s call for an accurate tee-shot. However, they will need to be careful and not go for the greens in any old way, because the designer has kept the terrain's natural contours and vegetation. There is water but it is more decorative than really in play.

Dehesa Montenmedio Golf & Country Club

CN. 340 - Km 42,500
E - 11150 VEJER-BARBATE

Office	Secretaria	(34) 956 - 23 24 40
Pro shop	Pro-shop	(34) 956 - 23 24 40
Fax	Fax	(34) 956 - 45 12 95
Situation	Situación	

42 km Cadiz,157 355 h.

Annual closure	Cierre anual	no
Weekly closure	Cierre semanal	no

Fees main season
Precios tempor. alta recorrido

	Week days Semana	We/Bank holidays Fin de sem./fiestas
Individual Individual	7 000 Pts	7 000 Pts
Couple Pareja	14 000 Pts	14 000 Pts

Solo 60 jugadores al dia

Caddy	Caddy	no
Electric Trolley	Carro eléctrico	1 800 Pts
Buggy	Coche	3 000 Pts/18 hoyos
Clubs	Palos	1 000 Pts/18 hoyos

Credit cards Tarjetas de crédito
VISA - MasterCard - AMEX - DC

Cadiz
Conil de la Frontera
Río Barbate
Vejer de la Frontera
Tarifa
GOLF
El Palmar
Zahora
Parque natural
Los Caños Barbate
Cabo de Trafalgar
COSTA DE LA LUZ
2 km

Access Acceso :
Map 7 on page 879 Plano 7 Página 879

GOLF COURSE / RECORRIDO — 15/20

Site	Emplazamiento	
Maintenance	Mantenimiento	
Architect	Arquitecto	Alejandro Maldonado
Type	Tipo	parque
Relief	Relieve	
Water in play	Agua	
Exp. to wind	Exp. al viento	
Trees in play	Arboles	

Scorecard Tarjeta	Chp. Campeonato	Mens Caballeros	Ladies Damas
Length Longitud	5897	5751	5563
Par	71	71	71

Advised golfing ability
Nivel de juego aconsejado   0   12   24   36

Hcp required   Handicap exigido   26 Cab./32 Damas

CLUB HOUSE & AMENITIES / CLUB HOUSE Y DEPENDENCIAS — 7/10

Pro shop	Pro-shop	
Driving range	Campo de prácticas	
Sheltered	cubierto	no
On grass	sobre hierba	si
Putting-green	putting-green	si
Pitching-green	pitching-green	si

951

HOTEL FACILITIES / HOTELES CERCANOS — 7/10

HOTELS HOTELES
Convento de San Francisco   Vejer
25 habitaciones, D 9 200 Pts
Tel (34) 956 - 45 10 01, Fax (34) 956 - 45 10 04

Royal Andalus Golf   Chiclana de la Frontera
263 habitaciones, D 17 000 Pts
Tel (34) 956 - 49 41 09, Fax (34) 956 - 49 44 90

Flamenco   Conil
114 habitaciones, D 10 000 Pts
Tel (34) 956 - 44 07 11, Fax (34) 956 - 44 05 42

RESTAURANTS RESTAURANTE
Torres   Barbate
Tel (34) 956 - 43 09 85   5 km

Junto a El Saler, El Prat o el Club de Campo, Neguri es uno de los grandes ejemplos del estilo de Javier Arana, a la vez humilde (en su respeto a la tradición), y muy personal (en su interpretación). Considerado como un club privado, abre sus puertas entre semana a los jugadores de fuera nunca muy numerosos ya que Bilbao no es un destino prioritario para el turismo. Campo para los entendidos, Neguri está en perfectos condiciones aunque la tierra éste demasiado cansada. A su trazado clásico y de una rara elegancia, pocos cambios han sido incorporados desde sus orígines aunque numerosos pinos hayan sido plantados para sustituir las especies desaparecidas en primera linea de calle. Ha sido una saludable iniciativa ya que reconstruirán, con el conjunto de bunkers, las principales dificultades de juego. Muy difícil desde las barras de atrás, Neguri es un poco más asequible desde las otras salidas, pero sus sutilezas exigen un cierto nivel de juego para poder ser apreciadas plenamente.

Neguri is one of the great examples of the Javier Arana style, at once humble (in his respect of tradition) and very personal (in his interpretation). Considered to be a private club, Neguri half-opens its doors to green-feers during the week, although visitors can hardly be accused of invading the course given that Bilbao is not yet a major tourist destination. A course for connoisseurs, Neguri is in good condition, although the soil seems to be growing a little weary. Few changes have been made to the original layout, but a large number of pine-trees have been planted to replace the trees that have disappeared from the front-line of the fairway limits. This is a welcome initiative, because with the bunkers the trees form the course's main difficulties. Very tough from the back-tees, Neguri mellows slightly when playing further forward, but the course's subtleties require a certain standard of skill to be fully appreciated.

Real Sociedad de Golf de Neguri

Campo "La Galea", Aptdo de Correos 9
E - 48990 ALGORTA (Vizcaya)

Office	Secretaria	(34) 94 - 491 02 00
Pro shop	Pro-shop	(34) 94 - 491 02 00
Fax	Fax	(34) 94 - 460 56 11
Situation	Situación	

2 km Algorta, 79 517 h.
13 km Bilbao, 372 054 h.

Annual closure	Cierre anual	no
Weekly closure	Cierre semanal	

Fees main season
Precios tempor. alta 18 hoyos

	Week days Semana	We/Bank holidays Fin de sem./fiestas
Individual Individual	15 000 Pts	15 000 Pts
Couple Pareja	30 000 Pts	30 000 Pts

Caddy	Caddy	5 000 Pts/18 holes
Electric Trolley	Carro eléctrico	900 Pts/18 hoyos
Buggy	Coche	4 000 Pts/18 hoyos
Clubs	Palos	no

Credit cards Tarjetas de crédito — VISA

952

Access Acceso : Bilbao → Getxo, → Algorta
Map 1 on page 866 Plano 1 Página 866

GOLF COURSE
RECORRIDO

17 /20

Site	Emplazamiento	
Maintenance	Mantenimiento	
Architect	Arquitecto	Javier Arana
Type	Tipo	bosque
Relief	Relieve	
Water in play	Agua	
Exp. to wind	Exp. al viento	
Trees in play	Arboles	

Scorecard Tarjeta	Chp. Campeonato	Mens Caballeros	Ladies Damas
Length Longitud	6280	6054	5112
Par	72	72	72

Advised golfing ability Nivel de juego aconsejado		0 12 24 36
Hcp required	Handicap exigido	28 Cab., 36 Damas

CLUB HOUSE & AMENITIES
CLUB HOUSE Y DEPENDENCIAS

7 /10

Pro shop	Pro-shop	
Driving range	Campo de prácticas	
Sheltered	cubierto	20 puestos
On grass	sobre hierba	si
Putting-green	putting-green	si
Pitching-green	pitching-green	si

HOTEL FACILITIES
HOTELES CERCANOS

7 /10

HOTELS HOTELES

Los Tamarises 42 habitaciones, D 17 000 Pts Tel (34) 94 - 491 00 05, Fax (34) 94 - 491 13 10		Algorta 4 km
Igeretxe Agustín 21 habitaciones, D 12 800 Pts Tel (34) 94 - 491 00 09, Fax (34) 94 - 460 85 99		Algorta 2 km
Lopez de Aro 53 habitaciones, D 27 250 Pts Tel (34) 94 - 423 55 00, Fax (34) 94 - 423 45 00		Bilbao 13 km

RESTAURANTS RESTAURANTE

Jolastoki Tel (34) 94 - 491 20 31		Neguri
Cubita Tel(34) 94 - 491 17 00		Algorta 2 km
Zortziko Tel(34) 94 - 423 97 43		Bilbao 13 km

Todas las combinaciones de estos tres 9 hoyos dan una longitud mas o menos equivalente, no se puede distinguir un 18 y un 9 hoyos. El rigor del diseño y el reparto de dificultades se añaden a la homogeneidad del lugar. De relieve moderado, este conjunto está desprovisto de trampas, pero no de dificultades. Ballesteros ha diseñado 27 hoyos de estilo mas bien americano, con obstáculos de agua (excepto en el recorrido "Azul"), numerosos bunkers bien hechos, poco profundos, y árboles (muchos recién plantados). Las calles generalmente estrechas requieren una gran precisión para no irse al rough bien tupido o a los bunkers de calle. Favorece a los jugadores con tendencia al "hook", y los aproches hacia los amplios greens han de hacerse por alto ya que están bien protegidos. El club propone muchas otras actividades deportivas.

As every combination of these three 9-hole courses gives an 18 hole course of more or less the same length, you can't say that this is an 18 hole and 9 hole complex. The very thorough layout and the distribution of hazards add further to the site's uniformity. Only moderately hilly, the course is free of traps but not of hazards. Ballesteros designed this complex in a rather American style with water hazards (except on the "Azul" course), numerous well-designed but shallow bunkers, and trees (there are a lot of young plantations). The generally tight fairways call for great accuracy to avoid the very dense rough and the fairway bunkers. It is a course for hook-shots, and the approach shots to the well-defended huge greens often require a high ball. The club features a number of other recreational activities.

Golf Novo Sancti Petri S.A.

Urb. Novo Sancti Petri - Playa de la Barrosa
E - 11130 CHICLANA DE LA FRONTERA - CADIZ

Office	Secretaria	(34) 956 - 49 40 05
Pro shop	Pro-shop	(34) 956 - 49 40 05
Fax	Fax	(34) 956 - 49 43 50
Situation	Situación	

50 km Jerez, 184 364 h.
11 km Chiclana de la Frontera, 46 610 h.

Annual closure	Cierre anual	no
Weekly closure	Cierre semanal	no

Fees main season
Precios tempor. alta el campo

	Week days Semana	We/Bank holidays Fin de sem./fiestas
Individual Individual	7 000 Pts	7 000 Pts
Couple Pareja	14 000 Pts	14 000 Pts

Caddy	Caddy	5 000 Pts/18 hoyos
Electric Trolley	Carro eléctrico	no
Buggy	Coche	4 500 Pts/18 hoyos
Clubs	Palos	2 000 Pts/18 hoyos

Credit cards Tarjetas de crédito
VISA - Eurocard - MasterCard - AMEX - DC

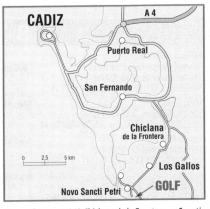

Access Acceso : N340 Chiclana de la Frontera → Sancti Petri
Map 7 on page 878 Plano 7 Página 878

GOLF COURSE
RECORRIDO 16/20

Site	Emplazamiento	
Maintenance	Mantenimiento	
Architect	Arquitecto	Seve Ballesteros
Type	Tipo	al borde del mar
Relief	Relieve	
Water in play	Agua	
Exp. to wind	Exp. al viento	
Trees in play	Arboles	

Scorecard Tarjeta	Chp. Campeonato	Mens Caballeros	Ladies Damas
Length Longitud	6510	6169	5337
Par	72	72	72

Advised golfing ability		0 12 24 36
Nivel de juego aconsejado		
Hcp required	Handicap exigido	28 Cab., 36 Damas

CLUB HOUSE & AMENITIES
CLUB HOUSE Y DEPENDENCIAS 7/10

Pro shop	Pro-shop	
Driving range	Campo de prácticas	
Sheltered	cubierto	no
On grass	sobre hierba	si
Putting-green	putting-green	si
Pitching-green	pitching-green	si

HOTEL FACILITIES
HOTELES CERCANOS 7/10

HOTELS HOTELES
Royal Andalus Golf — Playa de la Barrosa
263 habitaciones, D 22 000 Pts — 100 m
Tel (34) 956 - 49 41 09, Fax (34) 956 - 49 44 90

Tryp Costa Golf — La Barrosa
195 habitaciones, D 19 850 Pts. — 10 km
Tel (34) 956 - 49 45 35, Fax (34) 956 - 49 46 26

Playa La Barrosa — Playa de la Barrosa
264 habitaciones, D 22 400 Pts. — 500 m
Tel (34) 956 - 49 48 24, Fax (34) 956 - 49 48 60

RESTAURANTS RESTAURANTE
Novo Golf Gachito — Chiclana dela Frontera
Tel (34) 956 - 49 52 49 — 9 km

El Faro — Cádiz
Tel(34) 956 - 21 10 68 — 25 km

953

En España al igual que en numerosos páises, los jugadores profesionales sucumben a la tentación del diseño de campos, con suertes diversas. José Rivero no sólo se ha preocupado de sus colegas de alto nivel, ha pensado igualmente en todos los niveles, y éste recorrido (próximo al Campo de las Naciones y al aeropuerto) les convendrá perfectamente. Si un exceso de longitud y suficientemente amplio ofrece al debutante y al jugador experto la posibilidad de pasar una jornada agradable en un sitio esplendido. Sin embargo para conseguir un buen resultado, se necessitará saber jugar todo tipo de golpes, tener una estrategia de juego eficaz, y sacar a relucir sus dotes de buen pateador ya que si las ondulaciones son moderadas, algunas posiciones de banderas pueden ser peligrosas cuando nuestro tiro a green no ha sido muy preciso. Un mejor mantenimiento del rough y de las zonas de salida redundaría en beneficio del placer que procurá el campo.

In Spain as in many other countries, professional golfers fall for the lure of course design, with mixed results. José Rivero not only set out to satisfy his professional colleagues, he also spared many a thought for players of all abilities. This course (close to Campo de Las Naciones and the airport) will suit them just fine. Very wide without being agressively long, it allows beginners and experts alike to spend a great day on a pleasant site. To score well, though, you will need to play the full panoply of shots, decide upon and stick to an effective game strategy and putt your best, because while the greens are reasonably contoured, certain pin positions can be dangerous when the approach shot strays off target. Slightly tidier green-keeping, especially for the rough and around the tee-boxes, could only enhance the pleasure of playing here.

Golf Olivar de la Hinojosa

Avenida de Dublin, Campo de Las Naciones
E - 28042 MADRID

Office	Secretaria	(34) 91 - 721 18 89
Pro shop	Pro-shop	(34) 91 - 721 18 89
Fax	Fax	(34) 91 - 721 06 61
Situation	Situación	

12 km Madrid, 3 084 673 h.

Annual closure	Cierre anual	no
Weekly closure	Cierre semanal	

Fees main season
Precios tempor. alta 18 hoyos

	Week days Semana	We/Bank holidays Fin de sem./fiestas
Individual Individual	5 800 Pts	5 800 Pts
Couple Pareja	11 600 Pts	11 600 Pts

Caddy	Caddy	no
Electric Trolley	Carro eléctrico	800 Pts/18 hoyos
Buggy	Coche	4000 Pts/18 hoyos
Clubs	Palos	1200 Pts/18 hoyos

Credit cards Tarjetas de crédito
VISA - Eurocard - MasterCard - AMEX - 4 B

954

GOLF COURSE
RECORRIDO
13 /20

Site	Emplazamiento	
Maintenance	Mantenimiento	
Architect	Arquitecto	José Rivero
Type	Tipo	
Relief	Relieve	
Water in play	Agua	
Exp. to wind	Exp. al viento	
Trees in play	Arboles	

Scorecard Tarjeta	Chp. Campeonato	Mens Caballeros	Ladies Damas
Length Longitud	6163	6053	5183
Par	72	72	72

Advised golfing ability Nivel de juego aconsejado	0	12	24	36
Hcp required Handicap exigido	28 Cab., 36 Damas			

CLUB HOUSE & AMENITIES
CLUB HOUSE Y DEPENDENCIAS
7 /10

Pro shop	Pro-shop	
Driving range	Campo de prácticas	
Sheltered	cubierto	21 puestos
On grass	sobre hierba	si
Putting-green	putting-green	si
Pitching-green	pitching-green	si

HOTEL FACILITIES
HOTELES CERCANOS
8 /10

HOTELS HOTELES

Novotel-Campo de las Naciones — 600 m
246 habitaciones, D 18 300 Pts
Tel (34) 91 - 721 18 18, Fax (34) 91 - 721 11 22

Melia Castilla — Madrid
900 habitaciones, D 32 400 Pts
Tel (34) 91 - 567 50 00, Fax (34) 91 - 567 50 51

Castilla Plaza — Madrid
147 habitaciones, D 20 800 Pts
Tel (34) 91 - 323 11 86, Fax (34) 91 - 315 54 06

Aristos — Madrid
24 habitaciones, D 19 000 Pts
Tel (34) 91 - 345 04 50, Fax (34) 91 - 345 10 23

RESTAURANTS RESTAURANTE

Zalacain - Tel (34) 91 - 561 48 40 — Madrid

Principe de Viana - Tel(34) 91 - 457 15 49 — Madrid

Access Acceso : Madrid → Aeropuerto → Ifema
Map 3 on page 870 Plano 3 Página 870

Dave Thomas no ha querido añadir demasiadas dificultades técnicas a un recorrido bastante físico por sus cuestas. Naturalmente, hay árboles en la línea de juego, también algunos obstáculos de agua y aunque los bunkers de green están bastante alejados son poco visibles (están como hundidos) al igual que los bunkers de calle. Los greens tienen en general un declive bastante importante y pueden ser peligrosos cuando son rápidos. Todo ello hace que la estrategia de juego sea delicada cuando no se conoce el recorrido. Una vez conocido se pueden cortar los dog-legs con un buen drive, ya sea voleando los árboles o imprimiendo efecto a la bola. Agradable y variado merece la pena jugarlo varias veces, pero dada su situación en altura y en el interior, no se aconseja ir en invierno a no ser que se quiera contemplar el panorama de los Pirineos nevados desde la terraza del precioso club-house.

Dave Thomas did not want to add too many technical difficulties to an already hilly and physically quite demanding course. The trees are there, of course, together with a little water, but while the green-side bunkers are not too close to the greens, they are hard to see (they are sunk into dips). The same goes for the fairway bunkers. There is quite a lot of slope on the greens, which can be difficult when playing fast. All this makes for a tricky choice of game strategy when playing the course for the first time. When you know the course, long drivers can cut corners on the dog-legs either by hitting over the trees or by flighting the ball. Pleasant and varied, this pretty course is well worth a few visits, but the high-altitude location inland is not to be recommended in winter, except perhaps to gaze over the panorama of the snow-covered Pyrenees from the terrace of the very elegant club-house.

Club de Golf Osona Montanya
Masia el Estanyol
E - 08553 EL BRULL (BARCELONA)

Office	Secretaria	(34) 93 - 884 01 70
Pro shop	Pro-shop	(34) 93 - 884 01 70
Fax	Fax	(34) 93 - 884 04 07
Situation	Situación	

60 km Barcelona, 1 754 900 h.
17 km Vic (Vich), 30 060 h.

Annual closure	Cierre anual	no
Weekly closure	Cierre semanal	no

Fees main season
Precios tempor. alta El día

	Week days Semana	We/Bank holidays Fin de sem./fiestas
Individual Individual	4 000 Pts	10 000 Pts
Couple Pareja	8 000 Pts	20 000 Pts

Caddy	Caddy	si, reservar
Electric Trolley	Carro eléctrico	1 300 Pts
Buggy	Coche	5 000 Pts/18 hoyos
Clubs	Palos	2 500 Pts/el dia
Credit cards Tarjetas de crédito		VISA - MasterCard

Access Acceso : Barcelona, N152 → Vic (Vich).
Tona → Seva, El Brull
Map 2 on page 869 Plano 2 Página 869

GOLF COURSE
RECORRIDO **14**/20

Site	Emplazamiento	
Maintenance	Mantenimiento	
Architect	Arquitecto	David Thomas
Type	Tipo	bosque, vagüada
Relief	Relieve	
Water in play	Agua	
Exp. to wind	Exp. al viento	
Trees in play	Arboles	

Scorecard Tarjeta	Chp. Campeonato	Mens Caballeros	Ladies Damas
Length Longitud	6036	5810	5032
Par	72	72	72

Advised golfing ability		0	12	24	36
Nivel de juego aconsejado					

Hcp required	Handicap exigido	28 Cab., 36 Damas

CLUB HOUSE & AMENITIES
CLUB HOUSE Y DEPENDENCIAS **7**/10

Pro shop	Pro-shop	
Driving range	Campo de prácticas	
Sheltered	cubierto	25 puestos
On grass	sobre hierba	si
Putting-green	putting-green	si
Pitching-green	pitching-green	no

HOTEL FACILITIES
HOTELES CERCANOS **4**/10

HOTELS HOTELES
El Montanya — Montanya
120 habitaciones, D 11 000 Pts — 4 km
Tel (34) 93 - 884 06 06, Fax (34) 93 - 884 05 58

Ciutat de Vic — Vic
36 habitaciones, D 10 000 Pts — 20 km
Tel (34) 93 - 889 25 51, Fax (34) 93 - 889 14 47

RESTAURANTS RESTAURANTE
Estanyol — Golf
Tel (34) 93 - 884 03 54

El Montanya — Montanya
Tel (34) 93 - 884 00 04 — 4 km

955

Pals no ha usurpado su reputación. Su situación entre pinos, su tranquilidad, su moderado relieve (algunos greens en alto), la flexibilidad entre diferentes tees de salida, lo convierten en un recorrido atractivo para todos los niveles. Su terreno arenoso aguanta bien la lluvia y ofrece una confortable alfombra a los jugadores. Su diseño clásico (FW Hawtree) pone esencialmente en línea de juego árboles y bunkers que protegen los greens. El bosque no sólo es denso, lo que obliga a pegar un buen drive para evitarlo y buenos golpes para salir de él, sino que además la envergadura de los pinos, en forma de sombrilla, estrecha las calles y alguna que otra vez la bola queda encaramada en las ramas. El arquitecto ha revalorizado este terreno ideal para construir un golf conservando su aspecto natural. Los greens son fáciles de apreciar pero no muy grandes.

The reputation of Pals is rightfully deserved. This is firstly a very appealing course for all levels, laid out in the quiet of pinetrees, with mainly smooth unbroken terrain (only a few elevated greens) and the flexibility afforded by several different tees. The sandy terrain also soaks up any rain very quickly and provides a very comfortable carpet for players to play on. The classic design (F.W. Hawtree) basically brings bunkers into play to defend the greens, and uses trees. The forest is not only pretty thick - requiring good drives to keep out, and very good recovery shots to get out, of the woods - but the span of these parasol pines tends to make the fairways narrower, and the branches sometimes even keep the balls! The architect has successfully developed this ideal terrain for building a golf course while preserving its natural character. The greens are comparatively easy to read and not very large.

Club Golf de Pals

Carretera de Pals
E - 17256 PALS (GIRONA)

Office	Secretaria	(34) 972 - 63 60 06
Pro shop	Pro-shop	(34) 972 - 66 79 64
Fax	Fax	(34) 972 - 63 70 09
Situation	Situación	

12 km Palafrugell, 17 343 h.
4 km Pals, 1 675 h.

Annual closure	Cierre anual	no
Weekly closure	Cierre semanal	martes
		Temporada baja

Fees main season
Precios tempor. alta el campo

	Week days Semana	We/Bank holidays Fin de sem./fiestas
Individual Individual	6 000 Pts	10 000 Pts
Couple Pareja	12 000 Pts	20 000 Pts

Caddy	Caddy	no
Electric Trolley	Carro eléctrico	no
Buggy	Coche	5 000 Pts/18 hoyos
Clubs	Palos	1 900 Pts/18 hoyos

Credit cards Tarjetas de crédito
VISA - Eurocard - MasterCard - AMEX

Access Acceso : A7 Salida 6 → Girona,
C255 → Palafrugell, GE650 → Pals.
Map 2 on page 869 Plano 2 Página 869

GOLF COURSE
RECORRIDO

16/20

Site	Emplazamiento	
Maintenance	Mantenimiento	
Architect	Arquitecto	Fred Hawtree
Type	Tipo	bosque
Relief	Relieve	
Water in play	Agua	
Exp. to wind	Exp. al viento	
Trees in play	Arboles	

Scorecard Tarjeta	Chp. Campeonato	Mens Caballeros	Ladies Damas
Length Longitud	6222	5940	5081
Par	73	73	73

Advised golfing ability   0   12   24   36
Nivel de juego aconsejado
Hcp required   Handicap exigido   27 Cab., 35 Damas

CLUB HOUSE & AMENITIES
CLUB HOUSE Y DEPENDENCIAS

7/10

Pro shop	Pro-shop	
Driving range	Campo de prácticas	
Sheltered	cubierto	12 puestos
On grass	sobre hierba	si
Putting-green	putting-green	si
Pitching-green	pitching-green	si

HOTEL FACILITIES
HOTELES CERCANOS

6/10

HOTELS HOTELES

Mas de Torrent — Torrent
30 habitaciones, D 29 000 Pts — 6 km
Tel (34) 972 - 30 32 92, Fax (34) 972 - 30 32 93

Parador d'Aiguablava — Begur
87 habitaciones, D 19 500 Pts — 10 km
Tel (34) 972 - 62 21 62, Fax (34) 972 - 62 21 66

La Costa — Platja de Pals
120 habitaciones, D 24 000 Pts — 200 m
Tel (34) 972 - 66 77 40, Fax (34) 972 - 66 77 36

RESTAURANTS RESTAURANTE

Alfred — Pals
Tel (34) 972 - 63 62 74 — 5 km

La Xicra — Palafrugell
Tel(34) 972 - 30 56 30 — 12 km

956

No obstante, a pesar de ser muy reciente, la hierba ya está bien tupida y muy bien cuidada. Por falta de remodelación, el recorrido es bastante llano. Su paisaje de palmeras y algarrobos deberá adquirir más densidad, aunque sólo sea para ocultar a los jugadores un enorme complejo inmobiliario que marcará el fuera de límites en una docena de hoyos. La falta de relieve oculta una gran parte de las dificultades y la estrategia de juego sólo se percibe después de haber jugado una o dos veces. A favor de Panorámica, cuyo nombre esconde precisamente la falta de panorama, hay que destacar la progresión de las dificultades según el nivel de juego. Es un recorrido como muchos de los que se pueden ver en Florida, que merece la pena visitarlos pero no suscitan ninguna sensación particular.

Yet despite its young age, the grass is already thick and the green-keeping of a good standard. In the absence of any significant grading, the course is rather flat, and in time the landscape of palm trees and carobs should thicken out, if only to help protect players from a rather imposing property development programme, which will enforce out-of-bounds on at least twelve holes. The course's flatness tends to conceal a good number of the hazards and the game strategy becomes clear only after two or three exploratory rounds. To the credit of Panoramica (whose very name precisely conceals the lack of views) is the scaling of difficulty according to playing ability. This is a course the likes of which are widespread in Florida. Worth a visit but generally lacking in excitement.

Panoramica Golf & Country Club

Urbanización Panoramica
E - 12320 SAN JORGE (CASTELLON)

Office	Secretaria	(34) 964 - 49 30 72
Pro shop	Pro-shop	(34) 964 - 49 30 64
Fax	Fax	(34) 964 - 49 30 63
Situation	Situación	

15 km Vinaròs, 19 202 h.
25 km Peñíscola, 3 077 h.

Annual closure	Cierre anual	no
Weekly closure	Cierre semanal	no
		lunes, restaurante

Fees main season Precios tempor. alta 18 hoyos

	Week days Semana	We/Bank holidays Fin de sem./fiestas
Individual Individual	5 000 Pts	7 000 Pts
Couple Pareja	10 000 Pts	14 000 Pts

Caddy	Caddy	no
Electric Trolley	Carro eléctrico	1 200 Pts
Buggy	Coche	4 000 Pts/18 hoyos
Clubs	Palos	1500 Pts/18 hoyos

Credit cards Tarjetas de crédito
VISA - Eurocard - MasterCard

Access Acceso : A7 Barcelona-Valencia, salida 42 →
Vinaròs. 1 km. → Sant Raphaël a la derecha.
6 km a la izquierda, → Golf
Map 4 on page 873 Plano 4 Página 873

GOLF COURSE
RECORRIDO
14/20

Site	Emplazamiento	
Maintenance	Mantenimiento	
Architect	Arquitecto	Bernhard Langer
Type	Tipo	campo, bosque, urbano
Relief	Relieve	
Water in play	Agua	
Exp. to wind	Exp. al viento	
Trees in play	Arboles	

Scorecard Tarjeta	Chp. Campeonato	Mens Caballeros	Ladies Damas
Length Longitud	6429	6037	5001
Par	72	72	72

Advised golfing ability
Nivel de juego aconsejado

0	12	24	36

Hcp required Handicap exigido — 28 Cab., 36 Damas

CLUB HOUSE & AMENITIES
CLUB HOUSE Y DEPENDENCIAS
6/10

Pro shop	Pro-shop	
Driving range	Campo de prácticas	
Sheltered	cubierto	no
On grass	sobre hierba	si
Putting-green	putting-green	si
Pitching-green	pitching-green	si

957

HOTEL FACILITIES
HOTELES CERCANOS
4/10

HOTELS HOTELES

Parador — Benicarló
108 habitaciones, D 14 500 Pts — 20 km
Tel (34) 964 - 47 01 00, Fax (34) 964 - 47 09 34

Hosteria del Mar — Peñíscola
85 habitaciones, D 15 400 Pts. — 29 km
Tel (34) 964 - 48 06 00, Fax (34) 964 - 48 13 63

RESTAURANTS RESTAURANTE

El Langostino de Oro — Vinaròs
Tel (34) 964 - 45 12 04 — 15 km

El Faro — Vinaròs
Tel (34) 964 - 45 63 62 — 15 km

14	6	5

En éste marco incomparable, con unas vistas magníficas, Severiano Ballesteros hizo su aprendizaje. Y cuando recorremos éste trazado muy británico (con todas las astucias estratégicas de su diseñador Harry Colt), cuando debemos negociar con los árboles, y muchas veces salirnos de ellos, entendemos que el campeón español haya acumulado todos los recursos para salirse de las situaciones más difíciles. Aquí hace falta pegar recto (lo que no es precisamente su fuerte). Bastante accidentado, con roughs a menudo muy densos, el campo tiene algunos greenes ciegos lo que complica todavía más sus aspectos técnicos que compensan ampliamente su falta de longitud. Sin embargo el jugador medio que sepa jugar recto se las arreglará muy bien, sobre todo en match-play, ya que es un campo perfecto para asumir riesgos. En cuanto a los mejores, deberán aplacar sus ansias y adaptar su técnica a la situación.

This impressive site, with some magnificent views, is where Severiano Ballesteros learnt his trade. When you play this classical layout (with all the strategic tricks of architect Harry Colt) and as you cope with all the trees and sometimes struggle to find your way out of them, you realise that the Spanish champion learnt his amazing art of recovery in very tough conditions indeed. Here, you have to drive straight (that was never Seve's forte). Rather hilly, with some often thick rough, this highly-reputed course includes a few blind greens, which complicate a still further the technical aspects of playing here and easily make up for the lack of yardage. With this said, average and straight players should get by just fine, especially in match-play, because this is the ideal terrain for taking risks. As for the wunderkinds, they'll just have to keep a check on their adrenaline flow and adjust their technique to matters at hand.

Real Golf de Pedreña

Apartado, 233
E - 39 080 SANTANDER

Office	Secretaria	(34) 942 - 50 00 01
Pro shop	Pro-shop	(34) 942 - 50 00 01
Fax	Fax	(34) 942 - 50 04 21
Situation	Situación	

24 km Santander, 196 218 h.

Annual closure	Cierre anual	no
Weekly closure	Cierre semanal	no

Fees main season
Precios tempor. alta 18 hoyos

	Week days Semana	We/Bank holidays Fin de sem./fiestas
Individual Individual	10 000 Pts	12 000 Pts
Couple Pareja	20 000 Pts	24 000 Pts

Caddy	Caddy	3 500 Pts/18 hoyos
Electric Trolley	Carro eléctrico	1 000 Pts
Buggy	Coche	5000 Pts/18 hoyos
Clubs	Palos	1500 Pts/18 hoyos

Credit cards Tarjetas de crédito — no

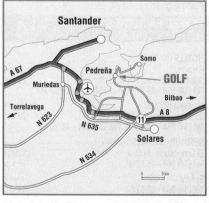

Access Acceso : Bilbao, N 634, N 635 → Santander.
Map 1 on page 866 Plano 1 Página 866

GOLF COURSE
RECORRIDO — 14/20

Site	Emplazamiento	
Maintenance	Mantenimiento	
Architect	Arquitecto	Harry S. Colt
Type	Tipo	al borde del mar, bosque
Relief	Relieve	
Water in play	Agua	
Exp. to wind	Exp. al viento	
Trees in play	Arboles	

Scorecard Tarjeta	Chp. Campeonato	Mens Caballeros	Ladies Damas
Length Longitud	5764	5511	4764
Par	70	70	70

Advised golfing ability
Nivel de juego aconsejado — 0 12 24 36

Hcp required Handicap exigido — 28 Cab., 36 Damas

CLUB HOUSE & AMENITIES
CLUB HOUSE Y DEPENDENCIAS — 6/10

Pro shop	Pro-shop	
Driving range	Campo de prácticas	
Sheltered	cubierto	5 puestos
On grass	sobre hierba	si
Putting-green	putting-green	si
Pitching-green	pitching-green	no

HOTEL FACILITIES
HOTELES CERCANOS — 5/10

HOTELS HOTELES

Real		Santander
123 habitaciones, D 21 750 Pts		24 km
Tel (34) 942 - 27 25 50, Fax (34) 942 - 27 45 73		

NH Ciudad de Santander		Santander
60 habitaciones, D 18 500 Pts		24 km
Tel (34) 942 - 22 79 65, Fax (34) 942 - 21 73 03		

Sardinero		Santander
108 habitaciones, D 17 500 Pts		24 km
Tel (34) 942 - 27 11 00, Fax (34) 942 - 27 16 98		

RESTAURANTS RESTAURANTE

La Sardina		Santander
Tel (34) 942 - 27 10 35		24 km

Mesón Segoviano		Santander
Tel (34) 942 - 31 10 10		24 km

Rhin - Tel (34) 942 - 27 30 34 — Santander, 24 km

Un recorrido táctico. En primer lugar hay que sobrepasar los bunkers, saber evitarlos o quedarse corto: en cada par 4, un bunker de calle acoge las caídas de drive entre 190 y 240 metros desde las salidas de atrás. Después y en cinco hoyos hay que decidir si se puede sobrepasar un río situado a unos treinta metros antes del green. Pero estas dificultades no menguan la franqueza de un recorrido en el que algunos dog-legs y varios fuera de límites ayudan a mantener la concentración. Poniendo empeño se puede jugar su handicap. En todo caso, es un recorrido agradable para jugar en familia dejando que cada uno escoja el tee de salida que más le convenga. Al igual que las calles y los greens (hay 8 con doble escalón), los roughs son densos, sembrados de olivos y es de desear que el proyecto de construcción de casas se lleve a cabo en los espacios vacíos entre algunos hoyos.

This is a tactical course. First of all you have to avoid the sand by either carrying the bunkers or laying up short. Because on each par 4, a fairway bunker lurks close to the drive landing zone, from 190 to 240 metres from the back-tees. Then, on five holes you have to decide whether to carry a widish river located about thirty metres in front of the greens. But these difficulties take absolutely nothing away from the course's openness, where a few gentle dog-legs and out-of-bounds help keep players focused. With a little concentration, you might even play to your handicap at Peralada. But at all events, this is a pleasant course for all the family where everyone can choose the tees that suit them best. Like the fairways and the greens (8 of which have two tiers), the thick rough is dotted with olive trees. Hopefully, the villas under development in the open spaces between certain holes will soon be finished.

Peralada Golf Club

Paraje la Garriga
E - 17491 PERALADA (GIRONA)

Office	Secretaria	(34) 972 - 53 82 87
Pro shop	Pro-shop	(34) 972 - 53 82 87
Fax	Fax	(34) 972 - 53 82 36
Situation	Situación	

6 km Figueras, 35 301 h.

Annual closure	Cierre anual	no
Weekly closure	Cierre semanal	no

Fees main season
Precios tempor. alta el campo

	Week days Semana	We/Bank holidays Fin de sem./fiestas
Individual Individual	6 000 Pts	7 500 Pts
Couple Pareja	12 000 Pts	15 000 Pts

Caddy	Caddy	no
Electric Trolley	Carro eléctrico	no
Buggy	Coche	5 000 Pts/18 hoyos
Clubs	Palos	2 500 Pts/18 hoyos

Credit cards Tarjetas de crédito
VISA - Eurocard - MasterCard - AMEX

Access Acceso : A7 Perpignan-Barcelona, salida 4, N260
→ Llança y Portbou, Golf a la izquierda → Peralada
Map 2 on page 869 Plano 2 Página 869

GOLF COURSE
RECORRIDO

16/20

Site	Emplazamiento	
Maintenance	Mantenimiento	
Architect	Arquitecto	Jorge Soler
Type	Tipo	llanura
Relief	Relieve	
Water in play	Agua	
Exp. to wind	Exp. al viento	
Trees in play	Arboles	

Scorecard Tarjeta	Chp. Campeonato	Mens Caballeros	Ladies Damas
Length Longitud	6128	5886	4947
Par	72	72	72

Advised golfing ability		0 12 24 36
Nivel de juego aconsejado		
Hcp required	Handicap exigido	28 Cab., 36 Damas

CLUB HOUSE & AMENITIES
CLUB HOUSE Y DEPENDENCIAS

6/10

Pro shop	Pro-shop	
Driving range	Campo de prácticas	
Sheltered	cubierto	no
On grass	sobre hierba	si
Putting-green	putting-green	si
Pitching-green	pitching-green	si

HOTEL FACILITIES
HOTELES CERCANOS

5/10

HOTELS HOTELES

Terraza		Roses
98 habitaciones, D 18 400 Pts		15 km
Tel (34) 972 - 25 61 54, Fax (34) 972 - 25 68 66		
Bon Retorn		Figueras
50 habitaciones, D 9 900 Pts		6 km
Tel (34) 972 - 50 46 23, Fax (34) 972 - 67 39 79		
Vista Bella		Roses
35 habitaciones, D 25 000 Pts		18 km
Tel (34) 972 - 25 62 00, Fax (34) 942 - 25 32 13		

RESTAURANTS RESTAURANTE

Mas Pau		Figueras
Tel (34) 972 - 54 61 54		6 km
La Llar		Roses
Tel (34) 972 - 25 53 68		15 km

959

Se trata de un recorrido con todas las características de un Country Club, con actividades sociales y deportivas variadas (tenis, piscina, paddle) al lado de Sevilla, lo que le asegura una fuerte frecuentación. Esencialmente son los invitados de los socios quienes pueden jugar. Creado en 1939, el recorrido sólo tenía 9 hoyos, y ha habido que esperar hasta 1992 para verlo convertido en un 18 hoyos con una longitud respetable. Su estética es la de un verdadero parque con abundante vegetación, cosa bella y apreciable sobre todo en los veranos calurosos. Los hoyos están bien estructurados y el ritmo de juego es excelente. Hay que ser muy precisos en los segundos golpes ya que los greens no son muy grandes. En realidad es un recorridos muy formador que ha facilitado excelentes jugadores a los equipos nacionales españoles.

Pineda is part of a real country-club concept with a wide variety of social and sporting activities (tennis, swimming-pool, paddle-tennis) at the gates of Seville. This makes it a busy course and explains why the majority of visitors are member guests. Created in 1939, Pineda originally had only 9 holes and was extended to 18 holes and a very respectable yardage only in 1992. This is a park-style course with lush vegetation which most will find pretty welcome, particularly on hot summer afternoons. The holes are neatly proportioned and the layout well-balanced, but your approach shots must be accurate to hit the smallish greens. This is in fact a very instructive course, as it has provided many excellent players who have go on to play in the Spanish national teams.

Real Golf Club Pineda de Sevilla

Apartado 1049
E - 41080 SEVILLA

Office	Secretaria	(34) 95 - 461 33 99
Pro shop	Pro-shop	(34) 95 - 461 33 99
Fax	Fax	(34) 95 - 461 77 04
Situation	Situación	

3 km Sevilla, 70 4857 h.

Annual closure	Cierre anual	no
Weekly closure	Cierre semanal	no

Fees main season
Precios tempor. alta recorrido

	Week days Semana	We/Bank holidays Fin de sem./fiestas
Individual Individual	6 500 Pts	12 000 Pts
Couple Pareja	13 000 Pts	24 000 Pts

Club privado - solo con socios (w. members)

Caddy	Caddy	no
Electric Trolley	Carro eléctrico	1 500 Pts
Buggy	Coche	no
Clubs	Palos	si

Credit cards Tarjetas de crédito   no

Access Acceso : CN IV Sevilla → Cadiz, en El Cortijo de Pineda
Map 7 on page 879 Plano 7 Página 879

GOLF COURSE
RECORRIDO   15/20

Site	Emplazamiento	
Maintenance	Mantenimiento	
Architect	Arquitecto	R.& F. M. Benjumea Luis Recasens
Type	Tipo	parque
Relief	Relieve	
Water in play	Agua	
Exp. to wind	Exp. al viento	
Trees in play	Arboles	

Scorecard Tarjeta	Chp. Campeonato	Mens Caballeros	Ladies Damas
Length Longitud	6147	6037	5077
Par	72	72	72

Advised golfing ability Nivel de juego aconsejado		0 12 24 36
Hcp required	Handicap exigido	28 Cab/36 Damas

CLUB HOUSE & AMENITIES
CLUB HOUSE Y DEPENDENCIAS   7/10

Pro shop	Pro-shop	
Driving range	Campo de prácticas	
Sheltered	cubierto	10 puestos
On grass	sobre hierba	si
Putting-green	putting-green	si
Pitching-green	pitching-green	si

HOTEL FACILITIES
HOTELES CERCANOS   9/10

HOTELS HOTELES

Principe de Asturias	Sevilla
288 habitaciones, D 32 000 Pts	4 km
Tel (34) 95 - 446 22 22, Fax (34) 95 - 446 04 28	
Alfonso XIII	Sevilla
124 habitaciones, D 50 000 Pts	3 km
Tel (34) 95 - 422 28 50, Fax (34) 95 - 421 60 33	
Al-Andalus Palace	Sevilla
327 habitaciones, D 16 500 Pts	3 km
Tel (34) 95 - 423 06 00, Fax (34) 95 - 423 02 00	

RESTAURANTS RESTAURANTE

La Dorada	Sevilla, 4 km
Tel (34) 95 - 492 10 66	
La Albahaca - Tel (34) 95 - 422 07 14	Sevilla, 4 km
El Espigon - Tel (34) 95 - 462 68 51	Sevilla, 4 km

Con obstáculos de agua en la línea de juego en 12 hoyos, es un recorrido que no se aborda con tranquilidad, al menos por los golfistas poco acostumbrados a esta caraterística esencial de los golfs "modernos". Con el mar al lado, manifiestan en cierto modo la importancia que tiene el agua en el sur de Europa. La vegetación de pinos, acacias y palmeras adornan un paisaje bastante llano en el que se puede jugar sin necesidad de alquilar un coche. Sin embargo es necesario ser largo y preciso ya que los pares 4 de esta recorrido, diseñado por Gallardo y Aliss, son bastante difíciles desde los tees de salida de atrás (más aún con viento). Con los tees más adelantados se convierte en más humano y divertido para jugar en match-play. Si bien es verdad que los greens son pequeños, en pendiente y bien protegidos, en realidad no es un recorrido tan difícil como parece.

With water hazards on 12 holes, this is not one of the most reassuring layouts in the world, at least for golfers who are unused to this key component of "modern" courses. In their own way, they and the neighbouring sea seem to emphasise the importance of water in southern European society. Pine, acacia and palm trees add an element of landscaping to a course where there is virtually no relief and which is easy to walk. It does nonetheless demand length and precision play, as a number of long par 4s make this Gallardo and Alliss layout a tough proposition from the back tees (especially when the wind blows). Teeing off further foward makes the course more playable and more fun, and even though the smallish and often sloping greens are well-defended, it is easier to play than it looks.

Club de Golf Playa Serena

Urbanización Playa Serena S/N
E - 04740 ROQUETAS DE MAR (ALMERIA)

Office	Secretaria	(34) 950 - 33 30 55
Pro shop	Pro-shop	(34) 950 - 33 30 55
Fax	Fax	(34) 950 - 33 30 55
Situation	Situación	

1 km Roquetas de Mar, 32 361 h.
18 km Almería, 159 587 h.

Annual closure	Cierre anual	no
Weekly closure	Cierre semanal	no

Fees main season
Precios tempor. alta El campo

	Week days Semana	We/Bank holidays Fin de sem./fiestas
Individual Individual	5 800 Pts	5 800 Pts
Couple Pareja	11 600 Pts	11 600 Pts

Caddy	Caddy	no
Electric Trolley	Carro eléctrico	1 500 Pts/18 hoyos
Buggy	Coche	3 000 Pts/18 hoyos
Clubs	Palos	1 000 Pts/18 hoyos

Credit cards Tarjetas de crédito
VISA - Eurocard - MasterCard

Access Acceso : Almería N340, → Roquetas de Mar
Map 8 on page 881 Plano 8 Página 881

GOLF COURSE / RECORRIDO 13/20

Site	Emplazamiento	■■■■
Maintenance	Mantenimiento	■■■■
Architect	Arquitecto	A. Gallardo, Alliss
Type	Tipo	al borde del mar
Relief	Relieve	▭
Water in play	Agua	■■■■
Exp. to wind	Exp. al viento	■■■■
Trees in play	Arboles	■■■

Scorecard Tarjeta	Chp. Campeonato	Mens Caballeros	Ladies Damas
Length Longitud	6301	6070	5174
Par	72	72	72

Advised golfing ability Nivel de juego aconsejado	0	12	24	36
Hcp required	Handicap exigido	no		

CLUB HOUSE & AMENITIES / CLUB HOUSE Y DEPENDENCIAS 6/10

Pro shop	Pro-shop	■■■
Driving range	Campo de prácticas	■■
Sheltered	cubierto	no
On grass	sobre hierba	si
Putting-green	putting-green	si
Pitching-green	pitching-green	si

HOTEL FACILITIES / HOTELES CERCANOS 4/10

HOTELS HOTELES

Playa Capricho — Roquetas
330 habitaciones, D 20 000 Pts — 1 km
Tel (34) 950 - 33 31 00, Fax (34) 950 - 33 38 06

Playa Linda — Roquetas
129 habitaciones, D 18 000 Pts — 1 km
Tel (34) 950 - 33 45 00, Fax (34) 950 - 33 41 10

Playa Azul — Roquetas
211 habitaciones, D 11 000 Pts — 1 km
Tel (34) 950 - 33 33 11, Fax (34) 950 - 33 33 11

RESTAURANTS RESTAURANTE

Al-Baida — Roquetas de Mar
Tel (34) 950 - 33 38 21

La Colmena — Roquetas de Mar
Tel(34) 950 - 33 35 65

Il Teatro — Playa Serena
Tel(34) 950 - 33 37 10 — 2 km

961

Desde las salidas de atrás es un recorrido largo pero bastante llano, por lo que no es necesario alquilar un coche. No es muy difícil ya que la bola rueda bastante, pero hay que ser prudente ya que si bien las dificultades no son enormes ni verdaderamente peligrosas, sin embargo son frecuentes. La falta de concentración puede acarrear la pérdida de puntos (como un saco roto) sin darse apenas cuenta, y en estas condiciones serà bien difícil jugar su handicap!. John Harris ha sabido aprovechar el terreno con inteligencia logrando conservar su aspecto natural en la mayor parte del recorrido, aunque algunos hoyos carezcan de una buena definición de espacio disminuyendo así el placer visual. Afortunadamente acaba el recorrido con una buen impresión en el hoyo 18, un par 5 diseñado en una bajada sinuosa que ofrece magníficas vistas de la isla. Aconsejamos que los jugadores de tipo medio elijan tees de salida avanzados para que el juego sea más divertido.

A long course from the back tees, Poniente is nonetheless flat enough to walk and easy on the legs. The rolling landscape doesn't make this too difficult a course, but it should be approached with care, because while the difficulties are neither too impressive nor really dangerous, they do come thick and fast. One careless moment can lead to a flood of dropped strokes, without the player really realising. John Harris has skilfully used the terrain and taken care to preserve the natural features over most of the course, but some holes are poorly outlined, and this tends to spoil the visual side. Happily, you leave the course with a very positive impression on the 18th, a fine par 5 slotted into twisting downhill terrain, which offers some pretty views over the island's landscape features. In order to enjoy the course to he full, average golfers are advised to play from the front tees.

Golf de Poniente
C/Cala Figuera
E - 07184 CALVIA (MALLORCA)

Office	Secretaria	(34) 971 - 13 01 48
Pro shop	Pro-shop	(34) 971 - 13 00 59
Fax	Fax	(34) 971 - 13 01 76
Situation	Situación	

15 km Palma, 308 616 h.

Annual closure	Cierre anual	no
Weekly closure	Cierre semanal	no

Fees main season
Precios tempor. alta el campo

	Week days Semana	We/Bank holidays Fin de sem./fiestas
Individual Individual	8 200 Pts	8 200 Pts
Couple Pareja	16 400 Pts	16 400 Pts

Caddy	Caddy	no
Electric Trolley	Carro eléctrico	no
Buggy	Coche	5 500 Pts/18 hoyos
Clubs	Palos	2 000 Pts/18 hoyos

Credit cards Tarjetas de crédito   no

GOLF COURSE
RECORRIDO   13/20

Site	Emplazamiento	
Maintenance	Mantenimiento	
Architect	Arquitecto	John Harris
Type	Tipo	llanura
Relief	Relieve	
Water in play	Agua	
Exp. to wind	Exp. al viento	
Trees in play	Arboles	

Scorecard Tarjeta	Chp. Campeonato	Mens Caballeros	Ladies Damas
Length Longitud	6430	6140	5100
Par	72	72	72

Advised golfing ability   0   12   24   36
Nivel de juego aconsejado
Hcp required   Handicap exigido   28 Cab., 36 Damas

CLUB HOUSE & AMENITIES
CLUB HOUSE Y DEPENDENCIAS   6/10

Pro shop	Pro-shop	
Driving range	Campo de prácticas	
Sheltered	cubierto	10 puestos
On grass	sobre hierba	si
Putting-green	putting-green	si
Pitching-green	pitching-green	si

HOTEL FACILITIES
HOTELES CERCANOS   5/10

HOTELS HOTELES

Punta Negra   Palmanova
69 habitaciones, D 24 000 Pts.   5 km
Tel (34) 971 - 68 07 62, Fax (34) 971 - 68 39 19

Son Caliu   Palmanova
235 habitaciones, D 22 000 Pts   6 km
Tel (34) 971 - 68 22 00, Fax (34) 971 - 68 37 20

RESTAURANTS RESTAURANTE

Tristán   Puerto Portals
Tel (34) 971 - 67 55 47

Binnacle   Puerto Portals
Tel (34) 971 - 67 69 77

962

Access Acceso : Palma PM1 → Palmanova,
C719 → Portals Vells
Map 9 on page 882 Plano 9 Página 882

Este recorrido, diseñado por Tom Simpson en 1904, ha sido remodelado en los años 70. Ofrece un aspecto de colinas y bosque con constantes desniveles en harmonía con la naturaleza del terreno. Los greens tienen una superficie de tipo medio, son de muy buena calidad y particularmente rápidos. Es un recorrido de competición muy bueno, no excesivamente ancho, lo que requiere una gran precisión de juego para obtener un buen resultado por parte de los jugadores scratch. Sin embargo, los de handicap de tipo medio tienen siempre la posibilidad de jugar la seguridad en casi todos los hoyos. No hay obstáculos de agua ni otras dificultades que requieran golpes particularmente delicados para hacer el par o el bogey. Este club prestigioso - en el que se entra sólo con invitacion - tiene un segundo recorridos de 18 hoyos, basado en un diseño muy americano de Robert Trent Jones, con numerosos obstáculos de agua. Su apertura está prevista para principios de primavera en 1998.

Designed in 1904 by Tom Simpson, this course was remodelled in the 1970s. The skyline is one of hills and woods with constantly sloping landscape embracing the natural terrain. The greens are generally average in size, of excellent standard, fast and slick. A very good tournament course which is not over-wide, Puerta de Hierro calls for extreme accuracy if you want to card a good score. But even mid-handicappers will not find this too troublesome because you can always play safe on every hole. There are no water hazards, either, or other difficulties that force you to shape those delicate shots to make par or scrape a bogey. This prestigious club - you'll need to be invited to play here - also boasts a second 18-hole course rebuilt over a very American layout by Robert Trent Jones with an array of water hazards. It is due to re-open in early Spring 1998.

Real Club de la Puerta de Hierro

Avda de Miraflores S/N
E - 28035 MADRID

Office	Secretaria	(34) 91 - 316 17 45
Pro shop	Pro-shop	(34) 91 - 316 17 45
Fax	Fax	(34) 91 - 373 81 11
Situation	Situación	

4 km Madrid, 3 084 673 h.

Annual closure	Cierre anual	no
Weekly closure	Cierre semanal	no

Fees main season
Precios tempor. alta recorrido

	Week days Semana	We/Bank holidays Fin de sem./fiestas
Individual Individual	—	—
Couple Pareja	—	—

Solo con socios (with members)

Caddy	Caddy	si
Electric Trolley	Carro eléctrico	si
Buggy	Coche	si
Clubs	Palos	si

Credit cards Tarjetas de crédito	no

Access Acceso : Junto a la Ciudad Universitaria, a las puertas de la urbanización Puerta de Hierro
Map 3 on page 870 Plano 3 Página 870

GOLF COURSE / RECORRIDO — 16/20

Site	Emplazamiento	
Maintenance	Mantenimiento	
Architect	Arquitecto	Tom Simpson John Harris
Type	Tipo	parque
Relief	Relieve	
Water in play	Agua	
Exp. to wind	Exp. al viento	
Trees in play	Arboles	

Scorecard Tarjeta	Chp. Campeonato	Mens Caballeros	Ladies Damas
Length Longitud	6347	5914	4962
Par	72	72	72

Advised golfing ability Nivel de juego aconsejado	0 12 24 36
Hcp required Handicap exigido	si

CLUB HOUSE & AMENITIES / CLUB HOUSE Y DEPENDENCIAS — 8/10

Pro shop	Pro-shop	
Driving range	Campo de prácticas	
Sheltered	cubierto	25 puestos
On grass	sobre hierba	si
Putting-green	putting-green	si
Pitching-green	pitching-green	si

HOTEL FACILITIES / HOTELES CERCANOS — 9/10

HOTELS HOTELES

Palace — Madrid, 4 km
436 habitaciones, D 38 500 Pts
Tel (34) 91 - 429 75 51, Fax (34) 91 - 429 82 66

Tryp Fenix — Madrid, 4 km
213 habitaciones, D 23 000 Pts
Tel (34) 91 - 431 67 00, Fax (34) 91 - 576 06 61

NH Sanvy — Madrid, 4 km
144 habitaciones, D 20 500 Pts
Tel (34) 91 - 576 08 00, Fax (34) 91 - 575 24 43

RESTAURANTS RESTAURANTE

El Amparo — Madrid, 6 km
Tel (34) 91 - 431 64 56

Casa Lucio - Tel(34) 91 - 431 64 56 — Madrid, 4 km

El Pescador — Madrid, 5 km
Tel(34) 91 - 365 32 52

963

Inaugurado en 1.995, es un recorrido prometedor, con espacios ya bien tupidos a pesar de su corta existencia. Dado su relieve no es necesario alquilar un coche. Los greens, bastante en alto, hay que atacarlos elevando bien la bola. La anchura de las calles da sensación de espacio, cosa que agradará a los pegadores, pero no hay que fiarse ya que algunos obstáculos no son muy visibles. El arquitecto Francisco López Segales no ha pretendido realizar cosas espectaculares sino que ha mantenido la tradición británica con inteligencia y buen gusto. Y en todo caso ha logrado un recorrido que hay que seguir de cerca con interés, bien adaptado a los diferentes niveles de juego y bien integrado en un paisaje que ofrece magníficas vistas panorámicas sobre el mar y la montaña.

Opened in 1995, Pula is a promising course with an already well-grassed and pleasant playing surface, despite its early age. Only slightly hilly, the course is easy to walk, but elevated greens call for controlled high approach shots. The width of the fairways gives a pleasant sensation of open space, and will appeal to big-hitters, although they should watch out for a number of hazards that are not always clearly visible. Designer Francisco Lopes Segales has not attempted any sort of exploit in style and has followed a British tradition with intelligence and good taste. At all events, he has succeeded in creating a course whose development deserves to be watched closely. It is well suited to players of all abilities, fits in beautifully with the landscape and offers fine panoramas over the sea and mountains.

Pula Golf

Ctra Son Servera - Capdepera km. 3
E - 07559 SON SERVERA (MALLORCA)

Office	Secretaria	(34) 971 - 56 74 81
Pro shop	Pro-shop	(34) 971 - 56 74 81
Fax	Fax	(34) 971 - 81 70 35
Situation	Situación	

70 km Palma, 308 616 h.

Annual closure	Cierre anual	no
Weekly closure	Cierre semanal	no

Fees main season
Precios tempor. alta el campo

	Week days Semana	We/Bank holidays Fin de sem./fiestas
Individual Individual	8 500 Pts	8 500 Pts
Couple Pareja	17 000 Pts	17 000 Pts

Caddy	Caddy	no
Electric Trolley	Carro eléctrico	no
Buggy	Coche	5 500 Pts/18 hoyos
Clubs	Palos	2 000 Pts/18 hoyos

Credit cards Tarjetas de crédito
VISA - Eurocard - MasterCard - AMEX - DC

964

Access Acceso : Palma C715 → Manacor, → Son Servera, Pula Golf a la izquierda → Capdepera
Map 9 on page 882 Plano 9 Página 882

GOLF COURSE
RECORRIDO   **13**/20

Site	Emplazamiento	▆▆▆▆▆▁▁
Maintenance	Mantenimiento	▆▆▆▆▆▁▁
Architect	Arquitecto	F.L. Segales
Type	Tipo	campo
Relief	Relieve	▆▆▆▁▁▁
Water in play	Agua	▆▆▁▁▁▁
Exp. to wind	Exp. al viento	▆▆▆▆▁▁
Trees in play	Arboles	▆▆▆▁▁▁

Scorecard Tarjeta	Chp. Campeonato	Mens Caballeros	Ladies Damas
Length Longitud	6003	6003	5077
Par	71	71	71

Advised golfing ability   0   12   24   36
Nivel de juego aconsejado
Hcp required   Handicap exigido   28 Cab., 36 Damas

CLUB HOUSE & AMENITIES
CLUB HOUSE Y DEPENDENCIAS   **6**/10

Pro shop	Pro-shop	▆▆▆▆▆▁
Driving range	Campo de prácticas	▆▆▆▆▁▁
Sheltered	cubierto	10 puestos
On grass	sobre hierba	si
Putting-green	putting-green	si
Pitching-green	pitching-green	si

HOTEL FACILITIES
HOTELES CERCANOS   **5**/10

HOTELS HOTELES

Eurotel Golf Punta Rotja   Son Servera
202 habitaciones, D 24 680 Pts.   4 km
Tel (34) 971 - 84 00 00, Fax (34) 971 - 84 01 15

Aguait   Cala Rajada
188 habitaciones, D 14 700 Pts.   10 km
Tel (34) 971 - 56 34 08, Fax (34) 971 - 56 51 06

Petit Hotel Cases de Pula   Golf
10 habitaciones, D 32 000 Pts (suite)
Tel (34) 971 - 56 74 92, Fax (34) 971 - 56 72 71

RESTAURANTS RESTAURANTE

S'Era de Pula   Son Servera
Tel (34) 971 - 56 79 40   7 km

Son Floriana   Son Servera
Tel (34) 971 - 58 60 75   10 km

R.S.H.E. CLUB DE CAMPO

18	7	6

Construido en una pequeña colina, en un terreno muy típico de los alrededores de Madrid, este nuevo recorrido de la Real Sociedad Hípica Española de Club de Campo ofrece una gran variedad de distancias y tipo de hoyos gracias a sus múltiples tees de salida. Nos encontramos con el afán de variedad de Robert von Hagge y su diseño bien característico: roughs espesos, calles muy cuidadas en superficie, greens amplios con múltiples desniveles, constituyendo un recorrido destinado más bien a los buenos jugadores. Pero también los jugadores inteligentes y sagaces técnicos sabrán salvar un buen resultado si son diestros en el juego corto. La ambición del club es clara: organizar grandes competiciones internacionales. Cercano al circuito del Jarama, el golf añade un nuevo elemento a una región bien servida en golfs de calidad (Jarama R.A.C.E., La Moraleja).

Built on a little hill, typical of the type of terrain found around Madrid, the new course belonging to the Real Sociedad Hípica Española de Club de Campo offers an amazing combination of distances and types of hole thanks to the many different tee-boxes. This reflects the emphasis on variety which is the trademark of Robert von Hagge (who also designed Emporda). Other distinctive features are the thick rough, highly contoured fairways and huge, multi-tiered greens which generally tend to make this a course for good players. It is also intended for smart players and fine craftsmen who can save their card if their short game is on song. The club's ambition is clearly to host major international competitions. Close to the Jarama circuit, this layout is a new addition to a region already spoilt for excellent courses (Jarama R.A.C.E., La Moraleja).

Real Sociedad Hípica Española Club de Campo

Ctra de Burgos - Km 26,400
E - 28709 SAN SEBASTIAN DE LOS REYES

Office	Secretaria	(34) 91 - 657 10 18
Pro shop	Pro-shop	(34) 91 - 657 10 18
Fax	Fax	(34) 91 - 657 10 22
Situation	Situación	

26 km Madrid, 3 084 673 h.

Annual closure	Cierre anual	no
Weekly closure	Cierre semanal	no

Fees main season
Precios tempor. alta recorrido

	Week days Semana	We/Bank holidays Fin de sem./fiestas
Individual Individual	6 000 Pts	20 000 Pts
Couple Pareja	12 000 Pts	40 000 Pts

Club privado

Caddy	Caddy	no
Electric Trolley	Carro eléctrico	2 500 Pts
Buggy	Coche	3 500 Pts/18 hoyos
Clubs	Palos	si

Credit cards Tarjetas de crédito   no

Access Acceso : CN I - Km 26,400
Map 3 on page 870 Plano 3 Página 870

GOLF COURSE / RECORRIDO — 18/20

Site	Emplazamiento	▇▇▇▇░
Maintenance	Mantenimiento	▇▇▇▇░
Architect	Arquitecto	Robert von Hagge
Type	Tipo	bosque, vagüada
Relief	Relieve	▇▇▇▇░
Water in play	Agua	▇▇░░░
Exp. to wind	Exp. al viento	▇▇▇░░
Trees in play	Arboles	▇▇▇▇░

Scorecard Tarjeta	Chp. Campeonato	Mens Caballeros	Ladies Damas
Length Longitud	6389	5890	5330
Par	72	72	72

Advised golfing ability		0 12 24 36
Nivel de juego aconsejado		▇▇▇▇░
Hcp required	Handicap exigido	no

CLUB HOUSE & AMENITIES / CLUB HOUSE Y DEPENDENCIAS — 7/10

Pro shop	Pro-shop	▇▇▇▇░
Driving range	Campo de prácticas	▇▇▇░░
Sheltered	cubierto	
On grass	sobre hierba	si
Putting-green	putting-green	si
Pitching-green	pitching-green	si

HOTEL FACILITIES / HOTELES CERCANOS — 6/10

HOTELS HOTELES

Chamartin — Madrid
360 habitaciones, D 19 100 Pts — 20 km
Tel (34) 91 - 334 49 00, Fax (34) 91 - 733 02 14

Melia Castilla — Madrid
900 habitaciones, D 32 400 Pts — 20 km
Tel (34) 91 - 567 50 00, Fax (34) 91 - 567 50 51

RESTAURANTS RESTAURANTE

Mesón Tejas Verde — S.S. de Los Reyes
Tel (34) 91 - 652 73 07 — 10 km

Vicente — S.S. de Los Reyes
Tel (34) 91 - 651 31 71 — 10 km

Izamar — S.S. de Los Reyes
Tel (34) 91 - 654 38 93 — 10 km

965

En un terreno sin un relieve muy pronunciado, adosado a algunas colinas utilizadas para algunos hoyos, este recorrido es uno de los más populares de la región, sobre todo para el jugador medio que sabe apreciar que por una vez el slice no éste demasiado penalizado, así como que la vegetación contribuya a crear zonas de sombras de lo más agradables, pero sobre todo la diversidad del recorrido. Diseñado en un espacio muy reducido, los hoyos están por supuesto demasiado cerca los unos de los otros, lo que resta un poco de intimidad. Incluso cuando los hoyos 4 y 5 nos acercan al mar, lo debemos hacer pasando por un paso subterráneo debajo de la autopista: pintoresco, pero ruidoso! El entorno sin embargo es de gran calidad, los obstáculos muy visibles, no demasiado molestos, y los greenes son más difíciles de leer de lo que parece. En resumen, sin esperar descubrir el campo del siglo, es un campo para las vacaciones que se adapta a todos los niveles y donde se pasan muy bueno ratos.

This is one of the region's best-loved courses, laid out over a terrain with no slopes to speak of, and backed against some low hills, which are used on a few holes. It is particularly popular with average players, who will appreciate that for once, their slice doesn't cost them heavily. Besides, very pleasant vegetation affords some welcome shade and adds to the general variety of the course. Designed over a rather limited space, holes are obviously very close to each other and so adversely affect the intimate feel every course should offer. Likewise, while holes 4 and 5 are close to the sea, you have to walk through a tunnel under a motorway to reach them... picturesque maybe, but noisy too. But the general setting is excellent, the hazards are clearly visible and not too much of a nuisance, and the greens are trickier to read than they seem. In a word or two, this is a good holiday golfing for all players, and a good day out.

Golf Rio Real

Ctra Cádiz, km. 192
E - 29 660 MARBELLA (MALAGA)

Office	Secretaria	(34) 95 - 277 95 09
Pro shop	Pro-shop	(34) 95 - 282 95 29
Fax	Fax	(34) 95 - 277 21 40
Situation	Situación	

5 km Marbella, 84 410 h.
15 km San Pedro de Alcantara

Annual closure	Cierre anual	no
Weekly closure	Cierre semanal	no

Fees main season
Precios tempor. alta

	Week days Semana	We/Bank holidays Fin de sem./fiestas
Individual Individual	7 500 Pts	7 500 Pts
Couple Pareja	15 000 Pts	15 000 Pts

Caddy	Caddy	si
Electric Trolley	Carro eléctrico	no
Buggy	Coche	4 500 Pts/18 hoyos
Clubs	Palos	2 500 Pts/18 hoyos

Credit cards Tarjetas de crédito
VISA - MasterCard - AMEX

Access Acceso : Marbella → Fuengirola
Map 7 on page 879 Plano 7 Página 879

GOLF COURSE
RECORRIDO   13/20

Site	Emplazamiento	
Maintenance	Mantenimiento	
Architect	Arquitecto	Javier Araña
Type	Tipo	llanura
Relief	Relieve	
Water in play	Agua	
Exp. to wind	Exp. al viento	
Trees in play	Arboles	

Scorecard Tarjeta	Chp. Campeonato	Mens Caballeros	Ladies Damas
Length Longitud	6057	5730	5312
Par	72	72	72

Advised golfing ability		0	12	24	36
Nivel de juego aconsejado					
Hcp required	Handicap exigido		28 Cab., 36 Damas		

CLUB HOUSE & AMENITIES
CLUB HOUSE Y DEPENDENCIAS   6/10

Pro shop	Pro-shop	
Driving range	Campo de prácticas	
Sheltered	cubierto	no
On grass	sobre hierba	si
Putting-green	putting-green	si
Pitching-green	pitching-green	no

HOTEL FACILITIES
HOTELES CERCANOS   7/10

HOTELS HOTELES

Don Carlos — Marbella 7 km
238 habitaciones, D 35 500 Pts
Tel (34) 95 - 283 11 40, Fax (34) 95 - 283 34 29

Los Monteros — Marbella 2 km
168 habitaciones, D 35 200 Pts
Tel (34) 95 - 277 17 00, Fax (34) 95 - 282 58 46

El Fuerte **** — Marbella 5 km
244 habitaciones, 15 900 Pts
Tel (34) 95 - 286 15 00, Fax (34) 95 - 282 44 11

Lima Hostal — Marbella 8 km
64 habitaciones,
Tel (34 2) 77 05 00, Fax (34 2) 86 30 91

RESTAURANTS RESTAURANTE

La Hacienda — Marbella (→ Malaga) 7 km
Tel (34) 95 - 283 12 67

Santiago — Marbella 5 km
Tel (34) 95 - 277 43 39

San Roque gustará incluso a los que no les gustan los golfs inmobiliarios. En primer lugar porque las casas y residencias que lo rodean son magníficas, y en segundo lugar porque están apartadas del recorrido. No es necesario alquilar un coche y está bien protegido por los árboles, excepto un tramo expuesto al viento, entre el 13 y el 15, que bordea la colina. Muy largo saliendo desde atrás y con una ida muy estrecha, es más "humano" con los tees de salida adelantados para los jugadores con un handicap superior a 10. Exige ser un jugador completo, con mucho "feeling" para negociar los aproches a greens con muchas caídas y que están perfectamente protegidos, así como una gran finura en el juego corto. Si a ésto añadimos la calidad de las instalaciones y de su mantenimiento, comprenderemos que Tony Jacklin y Dave Thomas han diseñado uno de los grandes recorridos de la Costa. Unico reproche: su dificultad para los jugadores con poca experiencia (difícil para jugar en familia).

Golfers who don't like property development courses will love San Roque. Firstly because the villas and residences are magnificent, secondly because the course is some distance from them. The terrain is easy for walking and well protected by trees, except the 13th and 15th holes, laid out on the side of a hill and exposed to the wind. Very long off the back-tees, compounded by tight fairways on the front nine, the course is more "human" when played from the front-tees for players with handicaps in double figures. It demands an all-round game and a lot of feeling to negotiate the approach shots to greens that are very undulating and perfectly well-defended. Add to these compliments the quality of upkeep and of the facilities and you will understand how Tony Jacklin and Dave Thomas have designed one of the coast's great courses. One minor criticism would be the course's difficulty for inexperienced players.

San Roque

CN. 340 - km 127
E - 11360 SAN ROQUE (CADIZ)

Office	Secretaria	(34) 956 - 61 30 30
Pro shop	Pro-shop	(34) 956 - 61 30 30
Fax	Fax	(34) 956 - 61 30 13
Situation	Situación	

20 km Algeciras, 101 556 h.
6 km San Roque, 23 092 h.

Annual closure	Cierre anual	no
Weekly closure	Cierre semanal	no

Fees main season
Precios tempor. alta El campo

	Week days Semana	We/Bank holidays Fin de sem./fiestas
Individual Individual	8 000 Pts	8 000 Pts
Couple Pareja	16 000 Pts	16 000 Pts

Caddy	Caddy	no
Electric Trolley	Carro eléctrico	no
Buggy	Coche	5 000 Pts/18 hoyos
Clubs	Palos	2 500 Pts/18 hoyos

Credit cards Tarjetas de crédito
VISA - MasterCard - AMEX - DC

Access Acceso : N340 Estepona → Cadiz, km 126,5
a la derecha → Golf
Map 7 on page 879 Plano 7 Página 879

GOLF COURSE
RECORRIDO   **17**/20

Site	Emplazamiento	
Maintenance	Mantenimiento	
Architect	Arquitecto	Tony Jacklin David Thomas
Type	Tipo	vagüada
Relief	Relieve	
Water in play	Agua	
Exp. to wind	Exp. al viento	
Trees in play	Arboles	

Scorecard Tarjeta	Chp. Campeonato	Mens Caballeros	Ladies Damas
Length Longitud	6440	6048	5479
Par	72	72	72

Advised golfing ability   0   12   24   36
Nivel de juego aconsejado
Hcp required   Handicap exigido   28 Cab., 36 Damas

CLUB HOUSE & AMENITIES
CLUB HOUSE Y DEPENDENCIAS   **8**/10

Pro shop	Pro-shop	
Driving range	Campo de prácticas	
Sheltered	cubierto	no
On grass	sobre hierba	si
Putting-green	putting-green	si
Pitching-green	pitching-green	si

967

HOTEL FACILITIES
HOTELES CERCANOS   **6**/10

HOTELS HOTELES
San Roque   San Roque
50 habitaciones, D 19 500 Pts   100 m
Tel (34) 956 - 61 30 30, Fax (34) 956 - 61 30 12

La Solana   San Roque
19 habitaciones, D 9 000 Pts   7 km
Tel (34) 956 - 78 02 36, Fax (34) 956 - 78 02 36

Sotogrande   Sotogrande
46 habitaciones, D 19 000 Pts   7 km
Tel (34) 956 - 79 43 86, Fax (34) 956 - 79 43 33

RESTAURANTS RESTAURANTE
Los Remos   San Roque
Tel (34) 956 - 69 84 12   7 km

Pedro   San Roque
Tel (34) 956 - 69 84 53   7 km

Es la cuna y feudo del gran campeón español José Maria Olazábal, a quien se puede ver muy amenudo en el campo de práticas?. El recorrido fue diseñado por el profesional francés Pierre Hirigoyen en un terreno con muchas cuestas y con una media docena de hoyos en una planicie bastante húmeda con algunos obstáculos de agua. La dificultad esencial, a parte de dejar la pelota en calle, radica en no ponerse nervioso ni desmoralizarse ante los muchos desniveles del terreno. Sin embargo, los obstáculos son visibles y se puede decir que es un recorrido claro con algunos greens en alto dando lugar a situaciones muy variadas alrededor de los mismos, lo que explica la virtuosidad adquirida por Olazábal. Es muy difícil jugar su handicap desde las salidas de atrás, a pesare de que no sea excesivamente largo, por lo que es mejor escoger salidas mas avanzadas. No es un recorrido que guste a todos, pero posee un personalidad incontestable. Las montañas son realmente muy bonitas...

It is the home course and fief of the top Spanish champion Olazábal, who can often be seen on the driving range. The course was designed by the French pro Pierre Hirigoyen over very hilly terrain, although half a dozen holes are flat-tish, dampish and protected by a few hazards. The essential difficulty here, apart from keeping your ball in the fairway, is keeping cool head and not letting the steep slopes get the better of you. Luckily, the hazards are clearly in view and the course hides nothing, apart from a number of elevated greens. There is a variety of interesting situations around the greens, which might explain the virtuosity of Olazábal in this area, developed out on the course. A good score is a tough proposition from the back tees, but a distinct possibility when playing further forward. Not everyone loves this course, but it does have definite personality. And the mountains look beautiful.

Real Golf Club de San Sebastián

Chalet Borda Gain Apartado 6
E - 20 280 HONDARRIBIA - GUIPUZCOA

Office	Secretaria	(34) 943 - 61 68 45
Pro shop	Pro-shop	(34) 943 - 61 68 45
Fax	Fax	(34) 943 - 61 14 91
Situation	Situación	

3 km Irún, 53 861 h.
18 km San Sebastián, 176 019 h.

Annual closure	Cierre anual	no
Weekly closure	Cierre semanal	no

Fees main season
Precios tempor. alta El campo

	Week days Semana	We/Bank holidays Fin de sem./fiestas
Individual Individual	8 000 Pts	8 000 Pts
Couple Pareja	16 000 Pts	16 000 Pts

Caddy	Caddy	si, reservar
Electric Trolley	Carro eléctrico	1 000 Pts
Buggy	Coche	no
Clubs	Palos	500 Pts/18 hoyos

Credit cards Tarjetas de crédito
VISA - Eurocard - MasterCard - AMEX - DC

968

Access Acceso : San Sebastián A8 → Irún, Biarritz.
Salida 4 → Aeropuerto, Golf 3 km
St Jean de Luz → Irún, Golf 3 km → San Sebastián
Map 1 on page 866 Plano 1 Página 866

GOLF COURSE
RECORRIDO 14/20

Site	Emplazamiento	
Maintenance	Mantenimiento	
Architect	Arquitecto	Pierre Hirigoyen
Type	Tipo	bosque, vaguada
Relief	Relieve	
Water in play	Agua	
Exp. to wind	Exp. al viento	
Trees in play	Arboles	

Scorecard Tarjeta	Chp. Campeonato	Mens Caballeros	Ladies Damas
Length Longitud	5962	5790	4883
Par	71	71	71

Advised golfing ability   0   12   24   36
Nivel de juego aconsejado
Hcp required   Handicap exigido   28 Cab., 36 Damas

CLUB HOUSE & AMENITIES
CLUB HOUSE Y DEPENDENCIAS 6/10

Pro shop	Pro-shop	
Driving range	Campo de prácticas	
Sheltered	cubierto	20 puestos
On grass	sobre hierba	si
Putting-green	putting-green	si
Pitching-green	pitching-green	si

HOTEL FACILITIES
HOTELES CERCANOS 6/10

HOTELS HOTELES
Parador de Hondarribia   Hondarribia (Fuenterrabia)
36 habitaciones, D 19 000 Pts.   5 km
Tel (34) 943 - 64 55 00, Fax (34) 943 - 64 21 53

Obispo   Hondarribia (Fuenterrabia)
17 habitaciones, D 15 200 Pts.   5 km
Tel (34) 943 - 64 54 00, Fax (34) 943 - 64 23 86

Tryp Urdanibia   Irún
115 habitaciones, D 14 250 Pts.   1 km
Tel (34) 943 - 63 04 40, Fax (34) 943 - 63 04 10

RESTAURANTS RESTAURANTE
Ramón Roteta   Irún
Tel (34) 943 - 64 16 93   5 km

Ibaiondo   Irún
Tel (34) 943 - 63 28 88   1 km

SANT CUGAT

A pesar de ser un terreno accidentado, es tan fácil jugar caminando en Sant Cugat que sólo tiene un coche para alquilar. No es difícil lograr un buen resultado: las dificultades están a la vista, rara vez en la línea de juego, hasta tal punto que se puede aprochar a green haciendo rodar la bola (evitando sobrepasarlos). Algunos obstáculos de agua, algunos bunkers de green, árboles y bosque, son las mayores dificultades de este recorrido. Su escasa longitud permite no sólo jugar fácilmente su handicap sino que lo hace muy agradable para jugar en match-play: pueden caer muchos birdies. Los buenos jugadores se explayarán agusto y no dudarán en intentar llegar a green con el drive en ciertos pares 4. Los principiantes conseguirán sus primeros pares. Un golf para todos y de buena calidad.

Despite the broken terrain, San Cugat is easy to walk around, which is just as well as there is only one buggy. And it is not too difficult to shoot a good score, either. The hazards are clearly in view and seldom affect your game, to the extent that many greens can be approached with chip shots (but beware overshooting the green!). A few water hazards, certain green-side bunkers, trees and woods form the basic part of the course's difficulties. Being a short course, most players should play to their handicap without too much problem, and it is also fun for match-play, with birdies more common than usual. Very good players will have lots of fun and won't think twice about driving the green on a number of short par 4s, while beginners should easily find their feet. A good quality golf-course, for everyone to enjoy.

Club de Golf Sant Cugat

C/Villa, S/N
E - 08190 SANT CUGAT DEL VALLES (BARCELONA)

Office	Secretaria	(34) 93 - 674 39 08
Pro shop	Pro-shop	(34) 93 - 674 39 08
Fax	Fax	(34) 93 - 675 51 52
Situation	Situación	

20 km Barcelona, 1 681 132 h.

Annual closure	Cierre anual	no
Weekly closure	Cierre semanal	lunes

Fees main season
Precios tempor. alta

	Week days Semana	We/Bank holidays Fin de sem./fiestas
Individual Individual	9 000 Pts	20 000 Pts
Couple Pareja	18 000 Pts	40 000 Pts

Caddy	Caddy	si, reservar
Electric Trolley	Carro eléctrico	1 500 Pts
Buggy	Coche	4 000 Pts/18 hoyos
Clubs	Palos	2 500 Pts/el dia

Credit cards Tarjetas de crédito   no

Access Acceso : Barcelona E9 → Sant Cugat del Vallès
Map 2 on page 869 Plano 2 Página 869

GOLF COURSE
RECORRIDO   13/20

Site	Emplazamiento	
Maintenance	Mantenimiento	
Architect	Arquitecto	
Type	Tipo	urbano, vagüada
Relief	Relieve	
Water in play	Agua	
Exp. to wind	Exp. al viento	
Trees in play	Arboles	

Scorecard Tarjeta	Chp. Campeonato	Mens Caballeros	Ladies Damas
Length Longitud	5214	5214	4578
Par	70	70	70

Advised golfing ability		0	12	24	36
Nivel de juego aconsejado					
Hcp required	Handicap exigido		28 Cab., 36 Damas		

CLUB HOUSE & AMENITIES
CLUB HOUSE Y DEPENDENCIAS   6/10

Pro shop	Pro-shop	
Driving range	Campo de prácticas	
Sheltered	cubierto	15 puestos
On grass	sobre hierba	si
Putting-green	putting-green	si
Pitching-green	pitching-green	si

HOTEL FACILITIES
HOTELES CERCANOS   5/10

HOTELS HOTELES
Novotel   Sant Cugat
150 habitaciones, D 15 700 Pts   2 km
Tel (34) 93 - 589 41 41, Fax (34) 93 - 589 30 31

RESTAURANTS RESTAURANTE
La Fonda   Sant Cugat
Tel (34) 93 - 675 54 26

969

Con dos recorridos (de lo cuales uno es privado) y tres otros en proyecto, Santa Ponsa se está convirtiendo en un conjunto residencial imponente y difícil de ignorar cuando se está jugando: los jugadores no encontrarán ninguna intimidad. El diseño de Folco Nardi es sobrio, aunque convencional, sin inspiración excepcional y curiosamente más difícil con los tees de salida adelantados. La longitud puede intimidar a los jugadores de tipo medio y a las señoras: la primera vez es mucho más divertido jugar en match-play que intentar cumplir su handicap. Los greens, de una superficie normal, son más bien planos y protegidos sólo por los costados, lo que permite llegar haciendo rodar la bola...La mayor dificultad son los obstáculos de agua. Los cuidados de mantenimiento son correctos.

With two courses (one of which is private) and three others on the drawing board, Santa Ponça is an impressive residential resort, a fact that can be hard to forget even when you are on the course. There is very little privacy. Folco Nardi's layout is discreet and rather conventional with nothing exceptional in terms of inspiration. Strangely, the course is harder to play from the front tees than from the back. Owing to the very little difference between tee-positions, the length of the course can be intimidating for high-handicappers and ladies. First time out, match-play will be much more fun than trying to play your handicap. The medium-sized greens are generally flat and are defended on the sides only, so you can roll (or top!) the ball onto the green. The main hazard is the water. Upkeep is good.

Golf Santa Ponsa I

Urb. Nova Santa Ponsa
E - 07180 CALVIA (MALLORCA)

Office	Secretaria	(34) 971 - 69 49 25
Pro shop	Pro-shop	(34) 971 - 69 57 03
Fax	Fax	(34) 971 - 69 33 64
Situation	Situación	

16 km Palma, 308 616 h.

| Annual closure | Cierre anual | no |
| Weekly closure | Cierre semanal | no |

Fees main season
Precios tempor. alta el campo

	Week days Semana	We/Bank holidays Fin de sem./fiestas
Individual Individual	8 200 Pts	8 200 Pts
Couple Pareja	16 400 Pts	16 400 Pts

Caddy	Caddy	no
Electric Trolley	Carro eléctrico	no
Buggy	Coche	5 500 Pts/18 hoyos
Clubs	Palos	2 000 Pts/18 hoyos

Credit cards Tarjetas de crédito   VISA - MasterCard

970

Access Acceso : Palma PM1 → Andraix, Viejo Molino, a la izquierda → Santa Ponsa, → Golf
Map 9 on page 882 Plano 9 Página 882

GOLF COURSE
RECORRIDO

13 /20

Site	Emplazamiento	
Maintenance	Mantenimiento	
Architect	Arquitecto	Falco Nardi
Type	Tipo	llanura, urbano
Relief	Relieve	
Water in play	Agua	
Exp. to wind	Exp. al viento	
Trees in play	Arboles	

Scorecard Tarjeta	Chp. Campeonato	Mens Caballeros	Ladies Damas
Length Longitud	6543	6106	5241
Par	72	72	72

Advised golfing ability   0   12   24   36
Nivel de juego aconsejado
Hcp required   Handicap exigido   28 Cab., 36 Damas

CLUB HOUSE & AMENITIES
CLUB HOUSE Y DEPENDENCIAS

6 /10

Pro shop	Pro-shop	
Driving range	Campo de prácticas	
Sheltered	cubierto	10 puestos
On grass	sobre hierba	si
Putting-green	putting-green	si
Pitching-green	pitching-green	si

HOTEL FACILITIES
HOTELES CERCANOS

7 /10

HOTELS HOTELES
Golf Santa Ponsa   Santa Ponsa
13 habitaciones, D 31 000 Pts   1 km
Tel (34) 971 - 69 02 11, Fax (34) 971 - 69 48 53

Bahia del Sol   Santa Ponsa
161 habitaciones, D 12 000 Pts   3 km
Tel (34) 971 - 69 11 50, Fax (34) 971 - 69 06 50

Casablanca   Santa Ponsa
87 habitaciones, D 7 000 Pts   3 km
Tel (34) 971 - 69 03 61, Fax (34) 971 - 69 05 51

RESTAURANTS RESTAURANTE
Miguel   Santa Ponsa
Tel (34) 971 - 69 09 13   3 km

La Rotonda   Santa Ponsa
Tel (34) 971 - 69 02 19   3 km

Con una gran preocupación por los detalles y la estrategia, José María Olazábal ha "firmado" este recorrido. Al limitar la talla de los greens, ha querido favorecer el juego corto, uno de sus puntos fuertes. Al ser un malabarista con la bola, ha creado un recorrido que necesita dominar perfectamente todos los efectos y trayectorias (altas y bajas). Hay un gran número de bunkers y obstáculos de agua en la línea de juego, completados por 12.000 árboles y matorrales plantados para lograr un recorrido más complejo... y no sólo para protegerse del sol en verano. Equilibrado en su conjunto se adapta bien a los diferentes niveles de juego y se complica a medida que se retroceden los tees de salida. Franco y fácil de jugar sin coche, el Real Golf de Sevilla es una síntesis del estilo americano y de los links. Todo este conjunto de cualidades explican su éxito.

A course carrying the José-Maria Olazabal "label" where a lot of attention has gone into the finest detail and strategy. By restricting the size of the greens, he has highlighted the short game, one of his own fortes. And because Olazabal is a worker of the ball, the course demands skills for every trajectory (high and low) and for fashioning the ball both ways. The course has a large number of bunkers and water hazards, all very much in play, and these will be completed by the 12,000 trees and bushes that have been planted to make the course a little trickier... and not only to provide shade from the sun in summer. This is a finely balanced layout that adapts easily to different levels of skill and becomes more complex from the back-tees. Open and easy to walk, the Real Golf de Seville is a sort of synthesis combining American and links style golf. Might this explain the course's success?

Real Club de Golf de Sevilla

Autovia Sevilla-Utrera, km 3,2
E - 41089 MONTEQUINTO - SEVILLA

Office	Secretaria	(34) 95 - 412 43 01
Pro shop	Pro-shop	(34) 95 - 412 43 01
Fax	Fax	(34) 95 - 412 42 29
Situation	Situación	

10 km Sevilla, 704 857 h.

Annual closure	Cierre anual	no
Weekly closure	Cierre semanal	no

Fees main season
Precios tempor. alta

	Week days Semana	We/Bank holidays Fin de sem./fiestas
Individual Individual	8 000 Pts	15 000 Pts
Couple Pareja	16 000 Pts	30 000 Pts

Caddy	Caddy	no
Electric Trolley	Carro eléctrico	1 100 Pts
Buggy	Coche	4 000 Pts/18 hoyos
Clubs	Palos	2 125 Pts/18 hoyos

Credit cards Tarjetas de crédito
VISA - Eurocard - MasterCard - AMEX

SEVILLA

Access Acceso : Sevilla SE401 → Utrera
Map 7 on page 879 Plano 7 Página 879

GOLF COURSE
RECORRIDO

17 /20

Site	Emplazamiento	
Maintenance	Mantenimiento	
Architect	Arquitecto	José Maria Olazábal
Type	Tipo	llanura
Relief	Relieve	
Water in play	Agua	
Exp. to wind	Exp. al viento	
Trees in play	Arboles	

Scorecard Tarjeta	Chp. Campeonato	Mens Caballeros	Ladies Damas
Length Longitud	6321	6049	5121
Par	73	72	72

Advised golfing ability		0	12	24	36
Nivel de juego aconsejado					
Hcp required	Handicap exigido	28 Cab., 36 Damas			

CLUB HOUSE & AMENITIES
CLUB HOUSE Y DEPENDENCIAS

7 /10

Pro shop	Pro-shop	
Driving range	Campo de prácticas	
Sheltered	cubierto	10 puestos
On grass	sobre hierba	si
Putting-green	putting-green	si
Pitching-green	pitching-green	si

971

HOTEL FACILITIES
HOTELES CERCANOS

8 /10

HOTELS HOTELES

Hotel Ciudad de Sevilla	Sevilla
95 habitaciones, D 13 000 Pts	3 km
Tel (34) 95 - 423 05 05, Fax (34) 95 - 423 85 39	

Principe de Asturias	Sevilla
288 habitaciones, D 32 000 Pts	10 km
Tel (34) 95 - 446 22 22, Fax (34) 95 - 446 04 28	

Puerta de Triana	Sevilla
65 habitaciones, D 9 500 Pts	8 km
Tel (34) 95 - 421 54 04, Fax (34) 95 - 421 54 01	

RESTAURANTS RESTAURANTE

Taberna Alabardero	Sevilla
Tel (34) 95 - 456 06 37	10 km

La Albahaca	Sevilla
Tel (34) 95 - 422 07 14	10 km

Una realización prometedora no sólo por el recorrido sino también por las enormes instalaciones de entrenamiento. Los arquitectos del proyecto, Pepín Rivero y Miguel Angel Martín, gozan de una fama bien merecida como jugadores profesionales y el recorrido refleja las competencias de ambos. El escalonamiento de los tees de salida se adapta perfectamente a todos los niveles y el recorrido va aumentando en dificultad a medida que se retroceden. Las dificultades son muy variadas: hay agua en siete hoyos, ciertos enormes bunkers de calle recogen algunas caídas de drive, la longitud de los hoyos es muy variable obligando a jugar con todos los palos. El tamaño de los greens es normal y están bien diseñados y protegidos: hay que tener muy en cuenta la posición de las banderas para jugar bien cada hoyo. Es un recorrido muy equilibrado por lo que no es necesario alquilar un coche para jugar. Habrá que seguir de cerca los progresos de Son Antem!.

A highly promising project, not only for the course but also for the very extensive practice facilities. Architects Jose Rivero and Miguel Angel Martin are highly-reputed pros and this course tends to reflect their skills. The staggering of tees is remarkably well suited to all levels, and the course gradually and naturally becomes tougher as you move back. There is a variety of hazards, with water in play on seven holes and a few large fairway bunkers to protect drive-landing areas. The length of holes also varies a great deal and calls for every club in the bag. The averagely-sized greens are well designed and defended, and pin-positions are particularly important if you are to keep your score down. We will keep a close eye on Son Antem, but the course is already a nicely balanced layout and easy to walk.

Son Antem - Academia de Golf

C/Llucmajor - Palma de Mallorca. PM 602, km 3,4
E - 07620 LLUCMAJOR (PALMA DE MALLORCA)

Office	Secretaria	(34) 971 - 66 11 24
Pro shop	Pro-shop	(34) 971 - 12 08 88
Fax	Fax	(34) 971 - 66 26 49
Situation	Situación	

18 km Palma, 308 616 h.

Annual closure	Cierre anual	no
Weekly closure	Cierre semanal	no

Fees main season
Precios tempor. alta

	Week days Semana	We/Bank holidays Fin de sem./fiestas
Individual Individual	8 000 Pts	8 000 Pts
Couple Pareja	16 000 Pts	16 000 Pts

Caddy	Caddy	no
Electric Trolley	Carro eléctrico	no
Buggy	Coche	5 000 Pts/18 hoyos
Clubs	Palos	3 000 Pts/18 hoyos

Credit cards Tarjetas de crédito — VISA - MasterCard

972

Access Acceso

← Palma de Mallorca
Aeropuerto de Palma de Mallorca
El Arenal
C 717
PM 19
PM 602
GOLF
Liucmajo

Access Acceso : Palma PM19 → Aeropuerto,
→ Llucmajor PM602, km 3,4 → Golf
Map 9 on page 882 Plano 9 Página 882

GOLF COURSE
RECORRIDO — 14 /20

Site	Emplazamiento	
Maintenance	Mantenimiento	
Architect	Arquitecto	J. Rivero
		M.A. Martin
Type	Tipo	campo, llanura
Relief	Relieve	
Water in play	Agua	
Exp. to wind	Exp. al viento	
Trees in play	Arboles	

Scorecard Tarjeta	Chp. Campeonato	Mens Caballeros	Ladies Damas
Length Longitud	6317	6052	5071
Par	72	72	72

Advised golfing ability Nivel de juego aconsejado	0	12	24	36

Hcp required — Handicap exigido — 28 Cab., 36 Damas

CLUB HOUSE & AMENITIES
CLUB HOUSE Y DEPENDENCIAS — 7 /10

Pro shop	Pro-shop	
Driving range	Campo de prácticas	
Sheltered	cubierto	20 puestos
On grass	sobre hierba	si
Putting-green	putting-green	si
Pitching-green	pitching-green	si

HOTEL FACILITIES
HOTELES CERCANOS — 6 /10

HOTELS HOTELES
Delta — Playa de Palma
288 habitaciones, D 16 000 Pts — 5 km
Tel (34) 971 - 74 10 00, Fax (34) 971 - 74 10 00

Garonda — Playa de Palma
183 habitaciones, D 16 500 Pts — 6 km
Tel (34) 971 - 26 22 00, Fax (34) 971 - 26 21 09

Cristobal Colon — Playa de Palma
158 habitaciones, D 13 600 Pts — 15 km
Tel (34) 971 - 74 40 00, Fax (34) 971 - 74 34 42

RESTAURANTS RESTAURANTE
C'sa Cotxer — Playa de Palma
Tel (34) 971 - 26 20 49 — 5 km

Koldo Royo — Palma
Tel (34) 971 - 73 24 35 — 18 km

Sus numerosos dog-legs ofrecen la oportunidad de arriesgar para acortar aún más este recorrido cuyas principales dificultades son los bunkers (colocados a uno y otro lado de los greens), algún que otro obstáculo de agua (en el 16 y 18) y losárboles: pinos, palmeras, almendros.... Desde las salidas da la impresión de ser un recorrido estrecho y con sorpresas, pero las calles se ensanchan a la caída de los drives. FW Hawtree ha sabido sacar buen partido de un terreno ondulado sin querer mostrar excesivas pretensiones arquitectónicas. Los greens son redondos, sin fantasías, planos, no muy grandes y ligeramente en alto. A pesar del carácter residencial, Son Vida conserva un aspecto muy natural. La calidad de su mantenimiento y su equilibrio nos incitan a aconsejarlo a todos los jugadores, cualquiera que sea su handicap.

The very many dog-legs provide the opportunity to take risks and shorten this course still further. The main hazards are the bunkers (on either side of the green), a few rare water hazards (on the 16th and 18th holes) and the pine, palm and almond trees. The course often looks very tight from the tee, and this can cause surprise, but the fairways open out to reach a fair width at driving length. F.W. Hawtree has made good use of averagely hilly terrain but was obviously not attempting any real architectural exploit. In particular, the greens are round, fancy-free, flat, not very large and slightly elevated. Despite the residential side, Son Vida still has a very natural appearance to it, upkeep is good and the balanced layout makes this a course we would recommend to players of all abilities.

Son Vida Golf S.A.

Urb./Son Vida S/N
E - 07013 PALMA DE MALLORCA

Office	Secretaria	(34) 971 - 79 12 10
Pro shop	Pro-shop	(34) 971 - 79 12 10
Fax	Fax	(34) 971 - 79 11 27
Situation	Situación	

3 km Palma, 308 616 h.

Annual closure	Cierre anual	no
Weekly closure	Cierre semanal	no

Fees main season
Precios tempor. alta el campo

	Week days Semana	We/Bank holidays Fin de sem./fiestas
Individual Individual	8 100 Pts	8 100 Pts
Couple Pareja	16 200 Pts	16 200 Pts

Caddy	Caddy	no
Electric Trolley	Carro eléctrico	no
Buggy	Coche	5 900 Pts/18 hoyos
Clubs	Palos	2 200 Pts/18 hoyos

Credit cards Tarjetas de crédito	VISA - MasterCard

GOLF
Son Vida
○ La Villeta
C 711
Palma de Mallorca
PM 20
Illetas
Bahia de Palma

0   1 km

Access Acceso : Palma, Salida Son Rapinya →
Urbanizacion Son Vida
Map 9 on page 882 Plano 9 Página 882

GOLF COURSE
RECORRIDO
14/20

Site	Emplazamiento	
Maintenance	Mantenimiento	
Architect	Arquitecto	F.W. Hawtree
Type	Tipo	urbano, vagüada
Relief	Relieve	
Water in play	Agua	
Exp. to wind	Exp. al viento	
Trees in play	Arboles	

Scorecard Tarjeta	Chp. Campeonato	Mens Caballeros	Ladies Damas
Length Longitud	5740	5740	4910
Par	72	72	72

Advised golfing ability Nivel de juego aconsejado	0	12	24	36

Hcp required	Handicap exigido	28 Cab., 36 Damas

CLUB HOUSE & AMENITIES
CLUB HOUSE Y DEPENDENCIAS
6/10

Pro shop	Pro-shop	
Driving range	Campo de prácticas	
Sheltered	cubierto	10 puestos
On grass	sobre hierba	si
Putting-green	putting-green	si
Pitching-green	pitching-green	si

973

HOTEL FACILITIES
HOTELES CERCANOS
7/10

HOTELS HOTELES

Son Vida	Son Vida
171 habitaciones, D 37 600 Pts	1 km
Tel (34) 971 - 79 00 00, Fax (34) 971 - 79 00 17	

Arabella Golf	Son Vida
92 habitaciones, D 36 100 Pts	1 km
Tel (34) 971 - 79 99 99, Fax (34) 971 - 79 99 97	

Saratoga	Palma
187 habitaciones, D 16 800 Pts	6 km
Tel (34) 971 - 72 72 40, Fax (34) 971 - 72 73 12	

RESTAURANTS RESTAURANTE

El Pato	Golf
Tel (34) 971 - 79 15 00	

Diplomatic	Palma
Tel (34) 971 - 72 64 82	6 km

Abierto en 1964, es uno de los clubs con más solera de la Costa y uno de los mejores recorridos. La prioridad la tienen los socios, aunque se admiten visitantes (reservar de antemano). En un sitio muy tranquilo, rodeado de casas espléndidas, con variedad de árboles (pinos, olivos, alcornoques, eucaliptus y palmeras), es más duro de lo que uno quisiera y menos de lo que parece. Gracias en parte a la ausencia casi total de rough, lo que permite que los "pegadores" puedan expresarse con todas sus fuerzas sin más preocupación que la de evitar los numerosos obstáculos de agua concentrados sobre todo en los últimos hoyos. Los golfistas de diferentes niveles se deleitarán con esta armoniosa preparación del recorrido, a pesar de que los greens sean extensos, con muchas caídas y a menudo asesinen el resultado. Bien acompasado, con dificultades bien repartidas, Sotogrande es uno de los grandes ejemplos de la arquitectura de Trent Jones.

Opened in 1964, this is one of the coast's poshest golf clubs and one of the best courses. Members have priority but it is open to visitors (book in advance). On a very quiet site, encircled by majestic houses and enhanced with numerous trees (pine, olive, oak, eucalyptus and palm trees), it is at once harder than you would like and easier than it looks. This is partly because of the virtual absence of rough, enabling long-hitters to open their shoulders with no worries other than avoiding the numerous water hazards, concentrated particularly over the last holes. But players of all levels will have fun with this friendly preparation, even though the greens are huge, very undulating and often murderous for the score card. Very well paced with difficulties evenly spread around the course, Sotogrande is one of the great examples of architecture à la Trent Jones.

Real Club de Golf Sotogrande

Paseo del Parque S/N
E - 11310 SOTOGRANDE - CADIZ

Office	Secretaria	(34) 956 - 79 50 50
Pro shop	Pro-shop	(34) 956 - 79 57 22
Fax	Fax	(34) 956 - 79 50 29
Situation	Situación	

30 km Algeciras, 101 556 h.
30 km Estepona, 36 307 h.

Annual closure	Cierre anual	no
Weekly closure	Cierre semanal	no

Fees main season
Precios tempor. alta El campo

	Week days Semana	We/Bank holidays Fin de sem./fiestas
Individual Individual	15 000 Pts	15 000 Pts
Couple Pareja	30 000 Pts	30 000 Pts

Caddy	Caddy	si, reservar
Electric Trolley	Carro eléctrico	1 200 Pts
Buggy	Coche	5 000 Pts/18 hoyos
Clubs	Palos	2 500 Pts/el dia

Credit cards Tarjetas de crédito   VISA - MasterCard

974

Access Acceso : N340 Estepona → Cadiz. Sotogrande, Golf a la izquierda
Map 7 on page 879 Plano 7 Página 879

GOLF COURSE
RECORRIDO

18/20

Site	Emplazamiento	▬▬▬▬▬▬
Maintenance	Mantenimiento	▬▬▬▬▬▬
Architect	Arquitecto	Robert Trent Jones
Type	Tipo	al borde del mar, llanura
Relief	Relieve	▬▬▬
Water in play	Agua	▬▬▬
Exp. to wind	Exp. al viento	▬▬▬▬
Trees in play	Arboles	▬▬▬▬

Scorecard Tarjeta	Chp. Campeonato	Mens Caballeros	Ladies Damas
Length Longitud	6224	5853	5077
Par	72	72	72

Advised golfing ability		0	12	24	36
Nivel de juego aconsejado					
Hcp required	Handicap exigido		25 Cab., 30 Damas		

CLUB HOUSE & AMENITIES
CLUB HOUSE Y DEPENDENCIAS

7/10

Pro shop	Pro-shop	▬▬▬▬▬
Driving range	Campo de prácticas	▬▬▬▬
Sheltered	cubierto	no
On grass	sobre hierba	si
Putting-green	putting-green	si
Pitching-green	pitching-green	si

HOTEL FACILITIES
HOTELES CERCANOS

6/10

HOTELS HOTELES

Sotogrande	Sotogrande
46 habitaciones, D 19 000 Pts	3 km
Tel (34) 956 - 79 43 86, Fax (34) 956 - 79 43 33	

Club Maritimo	Sotogrande
39 habitaciones, D 19 000 Pts	3 km
Tel (34) 956 - 79 02 00, Fax (34) 956 - 79 03 77	

San Roque	San Roque
50 habitaciones, D 19 500 Pts	10 km
Tel (34) 956 - 61 30 30, Fax (34) 956 - 61 30 12	

RESTAURANTS RESTAURANTE

Los Remos	San Roque
Tel (34) 956 - 69 84 12	15 km

Pedro	San Roque
Tel (34) 956 - 69 84 53	15 km

TORREQUEBRADA

Fiel a su filosofía, Pepe Gancedo ha adaptado el recorrido a un terreno cuyo relieve hace que sea muy complejo y difícil el jugar sin coche. La calidad de los golpes de salida es de importancia capital: se puede perder todo de entrada con golpes demasiado desperdigados. No hay que dejarse engañar por su reducida distancia, ya que las múltiples dificultades hacen que hasta los golpes del juego corto sean delicados: árboles, bosque, rough, bunkers y obstáculos de agua se encuentran en la línea de juego. La belleza del panorama es de poco consuelo si se pierde el control de la bola. Al menos las primeras veces hay que jugar en match-play: de esta manera el recorrido es divertido (incluso en los hoyos ciegos) excepto para los jugadores con poca experiencia en quienes aumentará la presión cuando les vayan quedando pocas bolas...

True to his philosophy, Pepe Gancedo has adapted the course to the terrain, whose relief makes it difficult not only to walk but also to play. Here, the tee-shot is of prime importance. A wild drive and all may be lost. And don't be fooled by the short yardage because the numerous hazards make even the shortest irons a tricky business. Trees, woods, rough, bunkers and water are all very much to the fore, and the beauty of the scenery is scant consolation should you lose your grip and your game. For the first couple of rounds, you are better off in match-play, in which case the course can be great fun (even on the few blind holes) except for the less experienced players, who will feel the pressure even more when they start running out of balls...

Golf Torrequebrada

Apt de Correos 120
E - 29630 BENALMADENA COSTA (MALAGA)

Office	Secretaria	(34) 95 - 256 11 02
Pro shop	Pro-shop	(34) 95 - 256 15 44
Fax	Fax	(34) 95 - 256 11 29
Situation	Situación	

8 km Torremolinos, 35 309 h.
5 km Fuengirola, 43 048 h.

Annual closure	Cierre anual	no
Weekly closure	Cierre semanal	no

Fees main season
Precios tempor. alta el campo

	Week days Semana	We/Bank holidays Fin de sem./fiestas
Individual Individual	7 400 Pts	7 400 Pts
Couple Pareja	14 800 Pts	14 800 Pts

Caddy	Caddy	no
Electric Trolley	Carro eléctrico	no
Buggy	Coche	4 500 Pts/18 hoyos
Clubs	Palos	2 650 Pts/18 hoyos
Credit cards Tarjetas de crédito		VISA - AMEX

Access Acceso : Málaga → Marbella. Torremolinos →
Benalmadena Costa.
Map 7 on page 879 Plano 7 Página 879

GOLF COURSE
RECORRIDO
14/20

Site	Emplazamiento	
Maintenance	Mantenimiento	
Architect	Arquitecto	J. Gancedo
Type	Tipo	vagüada
Relief	Relieve	
Water in play	Agua	
Exp. to wind	Exp. al viento	
Trees in play	Arboles	

Scorecard Tarjeta	Chp. Campeonato	Mens Caballeros	Ladies Damas
Length Longitud	5806	5513	4680
Par	72	72	72

Advised golfing ability Nivel de juego aconsejado		0 12 24 36	
Hcp required	Handicap exigido	28 Cab., 36 Damas	

CLUB HOUSE & AMENITIES
CLUB HOUSE Y DEPENDENCIAS
7/10

Pro shop	Pro-shop	
Driving range	Campo de prácticas	
Sheltered	cubierto	no
On grass	sobre hierba	si
Putting-green	putting-green	si
Pitching-green	pitching-green	si

975

HOTEL FACILITIES
HOTELES CERCANOS
7/10

HOTELS HOTELES

Torrequebrada — Benalmadena
350 habitaciones, D 29 000 Pts — 2 km
Tel (34) 95 - 244 60 00, Fax (34) 95 - 244 57 02

Triton — Benalmadena
186 habitaciones, D 21 000 Pts — 2 km
Tel (34) 95 - 244 32 40, Fax (34) 95 - 244 26 49

Sol La Roca — Benalmadena
156 habitaciones, D 15 500 Pts — 2 km
Tel (34) 95 - 244 17 40, Fax (34) 95 - 244 32 55

RESTAURANTS RESTAURANTE

Mar de Alboran — Benalmadena
Tel (34) 95 - 244 64 27 — 2 km

Chef Alonso — Benalmadena
Tel (34) 95 - 244 34 35 — 2 km

Creado en 1965, Ulzama se ha convertido en 18 hoyos en 1990. Situado a 500 metros de altura, discurre en un terreno bastante accidentado en el que los jugadores poco en forma acabarán agotados. La adaptación del recorrido al terreno es extraordinaria: se trata de una de las últimas obras del gran arquitecto Javier Arana. Toda la panorámica transcurre en medio de un inmenso bosque. Aunque las calles no son muy estrechas, el jugador que no logre mantener la bola bien recta será "recompensado" a la altura de sus errores. Es un recorrido natural, con un paisaje análogo al de un parque con unos greens de superficie media y bastante llanos. Felizmente no hay muchos bunkers ya que muchos golpes son ciegos. Hay que conocerlo antes para lograr un buen resultado. Para el jugador de tipo medio es un recorrido de longitud asequible en el que los pares 3 son bastante largos exceptuando el hoyo numero 2.

Opened in 1965, Ulzama was extended to 18 holes only in 1990. At over 1500 ft. above sea-level, it unfolds over hilly terrain where the less fit player will probably feel the strain. But the way the course has been adapted to the lie of the land is quite remarkable, hardly a surprise when you learn that this is one of the latest courses by the great designer Javier Arana. The major visual feature is basically its layout in a majestic oak forest. With this said, the fairways are never too tight, which doesn't mean to say that players who make a mess of their tee-shot and don't hit it straight won't be penalised accordingly. This course is a very natural-looking layout in landscape reminiscent of park-land with average-sized, rather flat greens. Bunkers are limited in number, which is probably a good thing given the number of blind shots, and you need to know the course well before any hope of shooting a good score. For the average player, this is a course of reachable length but the par 3s are on the long side (except hole N° 2)

Club de Golf Ulzama

Valle Ulzama
E - 31799 GUERENDIAIN (Navarra)

Office	Secretaria	(34) 948 - 30 54 71
Pro shop	Pro-shop	(34) 948 - 30 51 62
Fax	Fax	(34) 948 - 30 54 71
Situation	Situación	

22 km Pamplona, 191 197 h.

Annual closure	Cierre anual	no
Weekly closure	Cierre semanal	no

Fees main season
Precios tempor. alta recorrido

	Week days Semana	We/Bank holidays Fin de sem./fiestas
Individual Individual	5 000 Pts	5 000 Pts
Couple Pareja	10 000 Pts	10 000 Pts

Caddy	Caddy	no
Electric Trolley	Carro eléctrico	no
Buggy	Coche	no
Clubs	Palos	si

Credit cards Tarjetas de crédito	VISA

GOLF COURSE
RECORRIDO
16/20

Site	Emplazamiento	
Maintenance	Mantenimiento	
Architect	Arquitecto	Javier Arana
Type	Tipo	bosque
Relief	Relieve	
Water in play	Agua	
Exp. to wind	Exp. al viento	
Trees in play	Arboles	

Scorecard Tarjeta	Chp. Campeonato	Mens Caballeros	Ladies Damas
Length Longitud	6232	6065	5154
Par	73	72	72

Advised golfing ability Nivel de juego aconsejado	0	12	24	36

Hcp required	Handicap exigido	28 Cab / 36 Damas

CLUB HOUSE & AMENITIES
CLUB HOUSE Y DEPENDENCIAS
6/10

Pro shop	Pro-shop	
Driving range	Campo de prácticas	
Sheltered	cubierto	
On grass	sobre hierba	si
Putting-green	putting-green	si
Pitching-green	pitching-green	si

HOTEL FACILITIES
HOTELES CERCANOS
6/10

HOTELS HOTELES

Ventas Ulzama — Puerto Belate
15 habitaciones, D 5 200 Pts — 8 km
Tel (34) 948 - 30 51 38, Fax (34) 948 - 30 51 38

Lorentxo — Olabe
9 habitaciones, D 5 000 Pts — 10 km
Tel (34) 948 - 33 24 86, Fax (34) 948 - 33 26 79

Aguirre — Oricain
12 habitaciones, D 5 000 Pts — 14 km
Tel (34) 948 - 33 03 75

RESTAURANTS RESTAURANTE

Josetxo — Pamplona
Tel (34) 948 - 22 20 97 — 21 km

La Chistera — Pamplona
Tel (34) 948 - 21 05 12 — 21 km

Castillo de Javier, Tel (34) 948 - 22 18 94 — Pamplona

Access Acceso : Pamplona, Ncnal 121 → Irun. Desvio en Ostiz km 15 y → Lizaso (Valle Ulzama) a 6 km.
Map 1 on page 867 Plano 1 Página 867

Valderrama ha adquirido notoriedad internacional bajo la impulsión de su propietario Jaime Ortiz-Patiño, quien impuso no sólo modificaciones del recorrido original (sobre todo el 17) sino que ha exigido un mantenimiento del campo de excepcional calidad (hasta uno teme sacar chuletas). La dificultad estratégica del trazado, la omnipresencia de árboles, la dimensión de los bunkers y algunos obstáculos de agua, le obligan a uno a estudiar muy bien cada golpe. Las caídas de los greens aumentan aún más la presión. Es inútil esperar jugar su handicap, incluso a los grandes campeones les cuesta muchísimo jugar el par. Pero ante la calidad del desafío, debe servir ahora como ejemplo para todos los jugadores despuès de haber asistido à la "Ryder Cup 1997" entre los equipos de Estados Unidos y Europa. Es un golf privado donde se admiten visitantes previa reserva. No hay que perdérselo.

Valderrama has gained international fame through the energy of proprietor Jaime Ortiz-Patiño, who not only insisted on making changes to the original layout (notably to the 17th hole) but also demanded exceptional standards of course upkeep (you hardly dare take a divot!). The strategic difficulty, omnipresent trees, the size of the bunkers and a few water hazards keep the player constantly on his wits for every stroke. And the pressure is made worse when it comes to reading the greens. Don't bother about playing to your handicap, as even the top champions find making par a tough enough task. But the quality of this challenge is enough to make anyone want to walk in footsteps of the professionals in the 1997 "summit" at Valderrama, when the Ryder Cup was staged here. This is a private course but is open to green-feers who book in advance. Not to be missed.

Valderrama

Ctra de Cadíz, km. 132
E - 11310 SOTOGRANDE - CADIZ

Office	Secretaria	(34) 956 - 79 12 00
Pro shop	Pro-shop	(34) 956 - 79 57 75
Fax	Fax	(34) 956 - 79 60 28
Situation	Situación	

30 km Algeciras, 101 556 h. 30 km Estepona, 36 307 h.

Annual closure	Cierre anual	si, 1/06→30/06
Weekly closure	Cierre semanal	no

Fees main season
Precios tempor. alta El campo

	Week days Semana	We/Bank holidays Fin de sem./fiestas
Individual Individual	22 000 Pts	22 000 Pts
Couple Pareja	44 000 Pts	44 000 Pts

Socios e invitados (mostly members & guests, visitors must book in advance)

Caddy	Caddy	5 000 Pts/18 hoyos
Electric Trolley	Carro eléctrico	no
Buggy	Coche	5 000 Pts/18 hoyos
Clubs	Palos	2 500 Pts/18 hoyos

Credit cards Tarjetas de crédito   VISA - AMEX

GOLF
Estepona →
← Castellar
Sotogrande
costa del sol
N 340
San Roque
Gibraltar   0   2   4 km
N 351

Access Acceso : N340 Estepona → Cadiz.
Sotogrande, Golf a la derecha
Map 7 on page 879 Plano 7 Página 879

GOLF COURSE
RECORRIDO   19/20

Site	Emplazamiento	
Maintenance	Mantenimiento	
Architect	Arquitecto	Robert Trent Jones
Type	Tipo	vagüada
Relief	Relieve	
Water in play	Agua	
Exp. to wind	Exp. al viento	
Trees in play	Arboles	

Scorecard Tarjeta	Chp. Campeonato	Mens Caballeros	Ladies Damas
Length Longitud	6311	5983	5091
Par	71	71	71

Advised golfing ability		0 12 24 36
Nivel de juego aconsejado		
Hcp required	Handicap exigido	24 Cab., 36 Damas

CLUB HOUSE & AMENITIES
CLUB HOUSE Y DEPENDENCIAS   8/10

Pro shop	Pro-shop	
Driving range	Campo de prácticas	
Sheltered	cubierto	no
On grass	sobre hierba	si
Putting-green	putting-green	si
Pitching-green	pitching-green	si

977

HOTEL FACILITIES
HOTELES CERCANOS   6/10

HOTELS HOTELES

Sotogrande		Sotogrande
46 habitaciones, D 19 000 Pts		3 km
Tel (34) 956 - 79 43 86, Fax (34) 956 - 79 43 33		

San Roque		San Roque
50 habitaciones, D 19 500 Pts		10 km
Tel (34) 956 - 61 30 30, Fax (34) 956 - 61 30 12		

La Solana		San Roque
19 habitaciones, D 9 000 Pts		15 km
Tel (34) 956 - 78 02 36, Fax (34) 956 - 78 02 36		

RESTAURANTS RESTAURANTE

Los Remos		San Roque
Tel (34) 956 - 69 84 12		15 km

Pedro		San Roque
Tel (34) 956 - 69 84 53		15 km

Aunque todavía no goza de fama internacional, merece la pena ir a Villamartín. Sin que sea un recorrido excesivamente largo, Paul Putman, con mucha imaginación, ha sabido adaptar su diseño al terreno, dándole gran personalidad: se aconseja que sólo los mejores elijan los tees de salida de atrás. Varios pares 4 más bien cortos permiten disfrutar un poquito. El agua, que tan poco gusta a los jugadores de tipo medio, se halla verdaderamente en línea de juego en tres hoyos (sobre todo en el 9), y preferirán admirar los árboles, raramente en línea de juego pero muy presentes. Los greens son de buen tamaño, con ligeras ondulaciones y aguantan bien la bola aún cuando el golpe no sea perfecto. Es un recorrido adaptable fácilmente para jugar en familia y con jugadores de niveles diferentes, y en general muy bien cuidado.

Although yet to forge a great international reputation, Villamartin is well worth going out of your way for. While not a terribly long course, the layout has personality and has been cleverly adopted to the terrain thanks to Paul Putman's keen imagination. In our opinion, the back-tees are for the best players only. A number of short par 4s are fun to play, and water is only really in play on three holes (especially the 9th). High-handicappers, who tend not to like water, can preferably admire the trees, which although rarely in play, are very much a part of the course. The greens are large, rolling and pitch well, even from slightly mishit shots. This is a most versatile and generally well-prepared course, easy to play with the family or with players of all different levels.

Campo de Golf Villamartin

Ctra Alicante - Cartagena km 50
E - 03189 ORIHUELA COSTA (ALICANTE)

Office	Secretaria	(34) 96 - 676 51 27
Pro shop	Pro-shop	(34) 96 - 676 51 70
Fax	Fax	(34) 96 - 676 51 58
Situation	Situación	

7 km Torrevieja, 25 891 h.
50 km Alicante, 275 111 h.

Annual closure	Cierre anual	no
Weekly closure	Cierre semanal	no

Fees main season
Precios tempor. alta El campo

	Week days Semana	We/Bank holidays Fin de sem./fiestas
Individual Individual	6 000 Pts	6 000 Pts
Couple Pareja	10 000 Pts	10 000 Pts

Caddy	Caddy	no
Electric Trolley	Carro eléctrico	1 000 Pts
Buggy	Coche	4 000 Pts/18 hoyos
Clubs	Palos	1 500 Pts/el dia

Credit cards Tarjetas de crédito   no

978

Access Acceso : N332 → Cartagena, 55 km S. de Alicante. Torrevieja → Golf
Map 6 on page 877 Plano 6 Página 877

GOLF COURSE
RECORRIDO   16/20

Site	Emplazamiento	
Maintenance	Mantenimiento	
Architect	Arquitecto	P. Puttman
Type	Tipo	llanura, vagüada
Relief	Relieve	
Water in play	Agua	
Exp. to wind	Exp. al viento	
Trees in play	Arboles	

Scorecard Tarjeta	Chp. Campeonato	Mens Caballeros	Ladies Damas
Length Longitud	6132	6037	5259
Par	72	72	72

Advised golfing ability Nivel de juego aconsejado	0 12 24 36
Hcp required Handicap exigido	28 Cab., 36 Damas

CLUB HOUSE & AMENITIES
CLUB HOUSE Y DEPENDENCIAS   7/10

Pro shop	Pro-shop	
Driving range	Campo de prácticas	
Sheltered	cubierto	no
On grass	sobre hierba	si
Putting-green	putting-green	si
Pitching-green	pitching-green	si

HOTEL FACILITIES
HOTELES CERCANOS   6/10

HOTELS HOTELES
Torrejoven   Torrevieja
105 habitaciones, D 8 400 Pts.   3 km
Tel (34) 96 - 571 40 52, Fax (34) 96 - 571 53 15

Meridional   Guadamar
52 habitaciones, D 12 300 Pts
Tel (34) 96 - 572 83 40, Fax (34) 96 - 572 83 06

Orihuela Costa   La Zenia
15 habitaciones, D 14 000 Pts   1 km
Tel (34) 96 - 676 08 00, Fax (34) 96 - 676 13 26

RESTAURANTS RESTAURANTE
Cabo Roig   Torrevieja
Tel (34) 96 - 676 02 90   4 km

Morales   Torrevieja
Tel(34) 96 - 672 12 93   4 km

En veinte años, el arquitecto Gary Player ha evolucionado. Sus recorridos son más detallistas y las dificultades más variadas. Aparte de unos cuantos hoyos dispuestos en ida y vuelta y la distancia a veces larga de un hoyo a otro, Zaudín figura entre las buenas realizaciones del Sur de España. Palmeras, naranjos y grandes lagos hacen pensar en Florida, pero los olivos están tan presentes como en el panorama de Sevilla. Aquí, el drive de salida en los pares 4 y 5 no plantea grandes problemas pero los aproches son delicados (especialmente en 17 y 18). Una vez en el green, no hay malas sorpresas, no son inmensos ni tortuosos. La distancia razonable del recorrido y la calidad de las instalaciones hacen que sea una realización prometedora.

The architecture of Gary Player has evolved in 20 years: his courses are now much more intricate in the smaller details and offer a greater variety of difficulty. If we exclude the large number of holes running parallel up and down and the sometimes long walk between holes, Zaudin is one of the great golfing achievements in southern Spain. The palm trees, orange trees and large lakes are reminiscent of Florida, but olive groves are as present as the views over Seville. The tee-shots on the par 4s and par 5s pose no real danger but the approach shots are often tricky affairs (especially on the 17th and 18th holes). Once on the greens, there are no unpleasant surprises in store. They are not huge, but they are not too tortuous, either. The reasonable length of this course and the standard of facilities make this a most inviting location.

Zaudin Golf
Ctra Mairena-Tomares Km 1,5
E - 41940 TOMARES (SEVILLA)

Office	Secretaria	(34) 95 - 415 41 59
Pro shop	Pro-shop	(34) 95 - 415 41 59
Fax	Fax	(34) 95 - 415 41 59
Situation	Situación	

10 km Sevilla, 704 857 h.

Annual closure	Cierre anual	no
Weekly closure	Cierre semanal	no

Fees main season
Precios tempor. alta El dia

	Week days Semana	We/Bank holidays Fin de sem./fiestas
Individual Individual	5 000 Pts	7 000 Pts
Couple Pareja	10 000 Pts	14 000 Pts

Caddy	Caddy	no
Electric Trolley	Carro eléctrico	1 000 Pts
Buggy	Coche	3 500 Pts/18 hoyos
Clubs	Palos	2 000 Pts/18 hoyos

Credit cards Tarjetas de crédito
VISA - Eurocard - MasterCard - AMEX

Access Acceso :
Map 7 on page 878 Plano 7 Página 878

GOLF COURSE
RECORRIDO
16/20

Site	Emplazamiento	
Maintenance	Mantenimiento	
Architect	Arquitecto	Gary Player
Type	Tipo	campo, urbano
Relief	Relieve	
Water in play	Agua	
Exp. to wind	Exp. al viento	
Trees in play	Arboles	

Scorecard Tarjeta	Chp. Campeonato	Mens Caballeros	Ladies Damas
Length Longitud	6192	5869	4967
Par	71	71	71

Advised golfing ability		0 12 24 36
Nivel de juego aconsejado		
Hcp required	Handicap exigido	28 Cab., 36 Damas

CLUB HOUSE & AMENITIES
CLUB HOUSE Y DEPENDENCIAS
7/10

Pro shop	Pro-shop	
Driving range	Campo de prácticas	
Sheltered	cubierto	10 puestos
On grass	sobre hierba	si
Putting-green	putting-green	si
Pitching-green	pitching-green	no

HOTEL FACILITIES
HOTELES CERCANOS
6/10

HOTELS HOTELES

Alcora	S. Juan de Aznalfarache
401 habitaciones, D 20 000 Pts	5
Tel (34) 95 - 476 94 00, Fax (34) 95 - 417 01 28	

Melia Sevilla	Sevilla
361 habitaciones, D 19 600 Pts	15 km
Tel (34) 95 - 442 15 11, Fax (34) 95 - 442 29 77	

Sol Macarena	Sevilla
317 habitaciones, D 15 900 Pts	10 km
Tel (34) 95 - 437 57 00, Fax (34) 95 - 438 18 03	

Cervantes	Sevilla
46 habitaciones, D 9 500 Pts	10 km
Tel (34) 95 - 490 02 80, Fax (34) 95 - 490 05 36	

RESTAURANTS RESTAURANTE

Taberna Alabardero	Sevilla
Tel (34) 95 - 456 06 37	15 km

Egaña Oriza - Tel (34) 95 - 422 72 11	Sevilla,15 km

979

Donnez des ailes à vos rêves.

COUPÉ
406
PEUGEOT

Pour que l'automobile soit toujours un plaisir.

Switzerland
Suisse Schweiz
 Svizzera

C omme dans les autres pays d'Europe, la majeure partie des golfs présentés ici sont privés, mais ouverts au public avec quelques restrictions ou difficultés d'accès en week-end. Il convient donc de s'informer et de réserver à l'avance, et une lettre d'introduction de votre club ne sera jamais inutile. Avec 28.500 joueurs, et une quarantaine de 18 trous, la Suisse n'est pas un très grand pays golfique, mais ses parcours sont souvent situés dans des paysages superbes.

Wie auch in anderen europäischen Ländern sind die meisten Golfplätze privat, aber der Öffentlichkeit unter gewissen Vorbehalten oder Einschränkungen an den Wochenenden zugänglich. Es ist daher empfehlenswert, sich vorgängig zu informieren oder zu reservieren, und ein Empfehlungsschreiben Ihres Clubs ist sicher immer nützlich. Mit ihren 28'500 Golfern und ungefähr 40 18-Loch-Bahnen zählt die Schweiz sicherlich nicht zu den bekannten Golfländern, aber dafür befinden sich die Golfplätze in einer landschaftlich reizvollen Umgebung.

981

As in other European countries, the majority of golf courses featured here are private, but open to the general public with a few restrictions or dufficulties for playing on week-ends. The best idea, therefore, is to make enquiries and book in advance, and emember that a letter of introduction from your own club is always a good idea. With 28,500 players and around 40 eighteen-hole courses, Switzerland is not a big golfing country but the courses are often set amidst some fabulous landscapes.

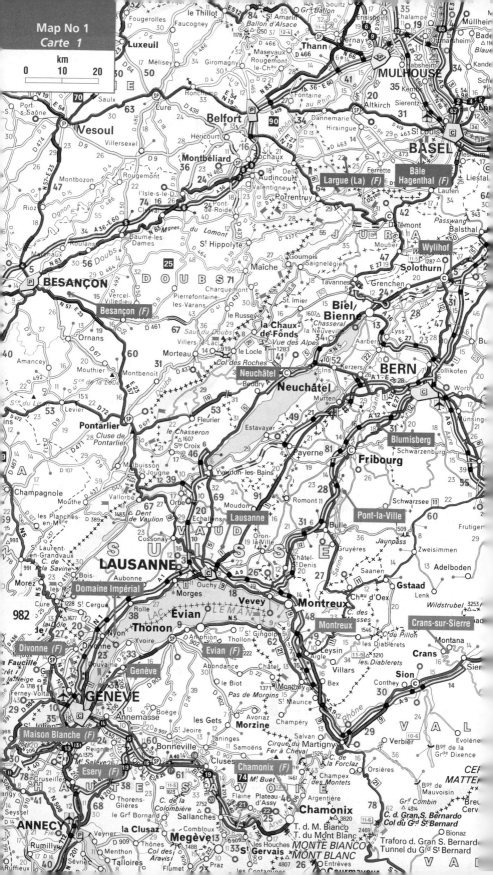

CLASSEMENT DES PARCOURS
EINTEILUNG DER GOLFPLÄTZE
CLASSIFICATION OF COURSES

Note du Club-house et annexes
Note für das Clubhaus und die Einrichtungen
Club-house and facilities

Note du parcours
Note für den Golfplatz
Course score

Note de l'environnement hôtelier
Note für das Hotelangebot der Umgebung
Hotel facility score

18	8	6	Domaine Impérial	990	P. / Seite

Score			Parcours	P.	Score			Parcours	P.
18	8	6	Domaine Impérial	990	**14**	6	6	Interlaken	995
17	7	8	Genève	993	**14**	6	7	Neuchâtel	1000
16	7	7	Lausanne	996	**14**	7	6	Schönenberg	1003
15	7	6	Blumisberg	987	**13**	7	6	Bad Ragaz	986
15	6	6	Engadin	991	**13**	7	6	Breitenloo	988
15	7	8	Lugano	997	**13**	7	6	Ennetsee-Holzhäusern	992
15	7	7	Patriziale Ascona	1002	**13**	6	7	Luzern	998
15	7	6	Zumikon	1005	**13**	6	5	Montreux	999
14	7	8	Crans-sur-Sierre	989	**13**	7	7	Niederbüren	1001
14	7	6	Golf de la Gruyère	994	**13**	6	6	Wylihof	1004

CLASSEMENT DE L'ENVIRONNEMENT HOTELIER
EINTEILUNG DES HOTELANGEBOTS DER UMGEBUNG
CLASSIFICATION OF HOTELS FACILITIES

Note			Parcours	P.	Note			Parcours	P.
14	7	**8**	Crans-sur-Sierre	989	13	7	**6**	Breitenloo	988
17	7	**8**	Genève	993	18	8	**6**	Domaine Impérial	990
15	7	**8**	Lugano	997	15	6	**6**	Engadin	991
16	7	**7**	Lausanne	996	13	7	**6**	Ennetsee-Holzhäusern	992
13	6	**7**	Luzern	998	14	7	**6**	Golf de la Gruyère	994
14	6	**7**	Neuchâtel	1000	14	6	**6**	Interlaken	995
13	7	**7**	Niederbüren	1001	14	7	**6**	Schönenberg	1003
15	7	**7**	Patriziale Ascona	1002	13	6	**6**	Wylihof	1004
13	7	**6**	Bad Ragaz	986	15	7	**6**	Zumikon	1005
15	7	**6**	Blumisberg	987	13	6	**5**	Montreux	999

SEJOUR DE GOLF RECOMMANDÉ	**VACANCES RECOMMANDEES**	
FÜR GOLFFERIEN EMPFOHLEN	**FÜR EINEN FERIENAUFENTHALT EMPFOHLEN**	
RECOMMENDED GOLFING STAY	**RECOMMENDED GOLFING HOLIDAYS**	

Note	Parcours				P.	Note	Parcours				P.
	Domaine Impérial	18	8	6	990		Crans-sur-Sierre	14	7	8	989
	Genève	17	7	8	993		Engadin	15	6	6	991
	Lausanne	16	7	7	996		Lugano	15	7	8	997
							Patriziale Ascona	15	7	7	1002

Wie viele andere Schweizer Plätze stammt auch dieser Parcours aus der Feder Donald Harradines, einem begnadeten Architekten, der die Natur gekonnt in seine Arbeit einbezieht. Das Bergpanorama und die bewaldete Gegend verleihen Bad Ragaz einen besonderen Charme. Gestaltung und Platzcharakter bergen keine Überraschungen, aber der Golfcourse garantiert dank seinen wenig ausgeprägten Geländeformen und seiner vernünftigen Länge für Spielfreude. Zu bedauern wäre höchstens, dass der Fluss, der durch die Anlage führt, das Spiel etwas zu wenig beeinflusst. Die eher schmalen Fairways der ersten neun Loch verlangen präzise Bälle. Longhitter spielen ihre Trümpfe auf der zweiten Platzhälfte aus. In Bad Ragaz bietet sich die Chance für schmeichelhafte Scores. Warum nicht ?

Like many Swiss courses, Bad Ragaz was designed by Donald Harradine, a generally academic architect who willingly lets nature keep the upper hand. Moreover, the setting for Bad Ragaz is a very pleasant site in a forest surrounded by mountains. The course itself has very little in the way of stylish surprises or outstanding personality, but it is pleasant to play for its flattish relief and very reasonable length. It is a pity that the river crossing the course was not brought into play in a more imaginative way. The front nine are rather tight and call for precision play, while the back nine give greater scope to the long-hitters. A round of golf here is perhaps the opportunity to sign for a flattering score, but why not, after all?

Bad Ragaz Golf Club
CH - 7310 BAD RAGAZ

Office	Sekretariat	(41) 081 - 303 37 17
Pro shop	Pro shop	(41) 081 - 303 53 14
Fax	Fax	(41) 081 - 303 37 27
Situation	Lage	

Bad Ragaz, 4 325 Ew. 24 km Chur, 32 868 Ew.

Annual closure	Jährliche Schliessung	ja
		8/12→18/01/99
Weekly closure	Wöchentliche Schliessung	nein

Fees main season
Preisliste hochsaison den ganzen Tag

	Week days Woche	We/Bank holidays We/Feiertag
Individual Individuell	100 CHF	100 CHF
Couple Ehepaar	200 CHF	200 CHF

Caddy	Caddy	nein
Electric Trolley	Elektrokarren	18 CHF/18 Löcher
Buggy	Elektrischer Wagen	nein
Clubs	Clubs	15 CHF/18 Löcher

Credit cards Kreditkarten
VISA - Eurocard - MasterCard - AMEX - DC

986

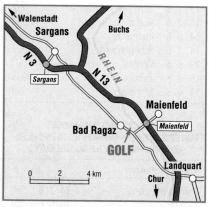

Access Zufahrt : Autobahn N 13 → Maienfeld
→ Bad Ragaz → Golf
Map 2 on page 984 Karte 2 Seite 984

GOLF COURSE
PLATZ
13/20

Site	Lage	
Maintenance	Instandhaltung	
Architect	Architekt	Donald Harradine
Type	Typ	Wald
Relief	Relief	
Water in play	Platz mit Wasser	
Exp. to wind	Wind ausgesetzt	
Trees in play	Platz mit Bäumen	

Scorecard Scorekarte	Chp. Chp.	Mens Herren	Ladies Damen
Length Länge	5750	5494	4860
Par	70	70	70

Advised golfing ability		0	12	24	36
Empfohlene Spielstärke				
Hcp required	Min. Handicap	30		

CLUB HOUSE & AMENITIES
KLUBHAUS UND NEBENGEBÄUDE
7/10

Pro shop	Pro shop	
Driving range	Übungsplatz	
Sheltered	überdacht	12 Plätze
On grass	auf Rasen	nein
Putting-green	Putting-grün	ja
Pitching-green	Pitching-grün	ja

HOTEL FACILITIES
HOTEL BESCHREIBUNG
6/10

HOTELS HOTELS
Grand Hotel Hof Ragaz   Bad Ragaz
133 Zimmer, D 560 CHF
Tel (41) 081 - 303 30 30, Fax (41) 081 - 303 30 33

Bristol   Bad Ragaz
25 Zimmer, D 260 CHF
Tel (41) 081 - 302 82 61, Fax (41) 081 - 302 64 94

Parkhotel Bad Ragaz   Bad Ragaz
60 Zimmer, D 244 CHF
Tel (41) 081 - 302 22 44, Fax (41) 081 - 302 64 39

RESTAURANTS RESTAURANT
Paradies   Bad Ragaz
Tel (41) 081 - 302 14 41

Schloss Wartenstein   Pfäfers
Tel (41) 081 - 302 40 47   2 km

Blumisberg - mit Aussicht auf den Jura und die Alpen - liegt in coupiertem Gelände mit stolzem Baumbestand (vor allem auf den ersten neun Loch). Die Anlage ist aber trotzdem zu Fuss zu bewältigen. Die Mehrheit der Holes bietet gut sichtbare Hindernisse, hauptsächlich Greenbunker. Die Greens sind von mittlerer Grösse, gut verteidigt, relativ wellig und einige Etagengreens eignen sich für interessante Fahnenpositionen. Schon mittlere Handicaps finden zu einem guten Spielrhythmus und geniessen die vernünftige Länge der Holes. Gute Golfer legen ihr Ballkönnen vor allem auf gewissen, schräg abfallenden Fairways in die Waagschale. Der Platz geniesst einen sehr guten Unterhalt.

With the Jura mountains on one side and the Alps on the other, Blumisberg is hilly and woody (especially the front nine), but walkable if you settle for just the 18 holes. Although a few holes require a little explanation, the vast majority hide nothing with clearly visible hazards, basically green-side bunkers. The greens are average in size, well-defended and sloping, with a number of two-tiered surfaces which make for some interesting pin positions. By and large, players can get a good rhythm going and the length of the course is reasonable enough to suit all players of decent ability. The best will be in their element here, working the ball both ways in order to card a good score. This is important, especially to handle some of the sloping fairways. Green-keeping and general upkeep are good.

Golf & Country Club Blumisberg
CH - 3184 WÜNNEWIL

Office	Sekretariat	(41) 026 - 496 34 38
Pro shop	Pro shop	(41) 026 - 496 17 27
Fax	Fax	(41) 026 - 496 35 23
Situation	Lage	

17 km Freiburg, 36 355 Ew. 17 km Bern, 136 338 Ew.

Annual closure	Jährliche Schliessung	ja
		17/11 → 21/03/99
Weekly closure	Wöchentliche Schliessung	nein

Fees main season
Preisliste hochsaison den ganzen Tag

	Week days Woche	We/Bank holidays We/Feiertag
Individual Individuell	80 CHF	—
Couple Ehepaar	160 CHF	—

We/Feiertag: nur in Mitgliederbegleitung (with members)

Caddy	Caddy	nein
Electric Trolley	Elektrokarren	12 CHF/Tag
Buggy	Elektrischer Wagen	nein
Clubs	Clubs	ja
Credit cards Kreditkarten		nein

Access Zufahrt : Autobahn E 25 Freiburg-Bern
→ Flamat, 6 km → Freiburg, → Golf
Map 1 on page 982 Karte 1 Seite 982

GOLF COURSE
PLATZ
15/20

Site	Lage	
Maintenance	Instandhaltung	
Architect	Architekt	B. von Limburger
Type	Typ	Wald, Gebirge
Relief	Relief	
Water in play	Platz mit Wasser	
Exp. to wind	Wind ausgesetzt	
Trees in play	Platz mit Bäumen	

Scorecard Scorekarte	Chp. Chp.	Mens Herren	Ladies Damen
Length Länge	6048	5707	5014
Par	72	72	72

Advised golfing ability	0	12	24	36
Empfohlene Spielstärke				
Hcp required	Min. Handicap	30		

CLUB HOUSE & AMENITIES
KLUBHAUS UND NEBENGEBÄUDE
7/10

Pro shop	Pro shop	
Driving range	Übungsplatz	
Sheltered	überdacht	4 Plätze
On grass	auf Rasen	ja
Putting-green	Putting-grün	ja
Pitching-green	Pitching-grün	ja

HOTEL FACILITIES
HOTEL BESCHREIBUNG
6/10

HOTELS HOTELS
Central — Düdingen
16 Zimmer, D 160 CHF — 8 km
Tel (41) 026 - 493 13 48, Fax (41) 026 - 493 34 88

Belle Epoque — Bern
17 Zimmer, D 285 CHF — 17 km
Tel (41) 031 - 311 43 36, Fax (41) 031 - 311 39 36

Bellevue Palace — Bern
145 Zimmer, D 350 CHF — 17 km
Tel (41) 031 - 320 45 45, Fax (41) 031 - 311 47 43

RESTAURANTS RESTAURANT
Central — Düdingen
Tel (41) 026 - 493 13 48 — 8 km

Le Moléson — Düdingen
Tel (41) 026 - 741 02 40 — 8 km

987

BREITENLOO

Ein kleiner, bewaldeter Flecken auf dem Land mit Aussichten auf die umliegende Gegend. Donald Harradine hat diesen Platz (wie viele Schweizer Golfcourses) in britischem Stil in eine hügelige Landschaft gezeichnet. Das Gelände wird auf den zweiten neun Loch etwas flacher. Mit einigen Out of bounds und kleinen Wasserhindernissen sind die Schwierigkeiten nicht allzu zahlreich, aber der Ball muss auf den Fairways gut plaziert werden, um die Greens leicht angreifen zu können. Präzision im Umgang mit dem kleinen Ball kann sich als nützlich erweisen. In jedem Fall lässt sich dieser gut gepflegte Platz unter Golfern verschiedener Niveaus mit viel Spass spielen - vor allem im Sommer, wenn der Ball gut rollt.

A little patch of remote forest in the countryside, with wide spaces opening onto the surrounding region. Another Harradine course, Breitenloo has a clearly British style to it and is laid out over a gently hilly terrain (even though the back nine are flatter). Despite a number of out-of-bounds and small water hazards, the difficulties are few and far between, are evenly spread and clearly visible. Some of the greens need a carefully placed tee-shot for an easier second shot, and fading or drawing the ball can, as always, prove helpful. At all events, this well-cared for course is easily playable by all the family or with players of varying ability. All good fun, especially in summer when the ball rolls a lot.

Golf Club Breitenloo

Untere Zaüne 9
CH - 8001 ZÜRICH

Office	Sekretariat	(41) 01 - 836 40 80
Pro shop	Pro shop	(41) 01 - 836 40 80
Fax	Fax	(41) 01 - 837 10 85
Situation	Lage	

22 km Zürich, 365 043 Ew.

Annual closure	Jährliche Schliessung	ja
		31/10 → 31/03/99
Weekly closure	Wöchentliche Schliessung	nein

Fees main season
Preisliste hochsaison 18 Löcher

	Week days Woche	We/Bank holidays We/Feiertag
Individual Individuell	100 CHF	—
Couple Ehepaar	200 CHF	—

90 CHF mit ASG Karte - We/Feiertag: nur in Mitgliederbegleitung (with members)

Caddy	Caddy	auf Reservieren
Electric Trolley	Elektrokarren	30 CHF /18 Löcher
Buggy	Elektrischer Wagen	nein
Clubs	Clubs	20 CHF / Tag
Credit cards Kreditkarten		nein

Access Zufahrt : Zürich-Kloten → Kloten → Bassersdorf
→ Birchwil-Oberwil, im Oberwil → Golf
Map 1 on page 983 Karte 1 Seite 983

GOLF COURSE
PLATZ
13/20

Site	Lage	
Maintenance	Instandhaltung	
Architect	Architekt	Donald Harradine
Type	Typ	Park
Relief	Relief	
Water in play	Platz mit Wasser	
Exp. to wind	Wind ausgesetzt	
Trees in play	Platz mit Bäumen	

Scorecard Scorekarte	Chp. Chp.	Mens Herren	Ladies Damen
Length Länge	6125	5750	5045
Par	72	72	72

Advised golfing ability Empfohlene Spielstärke	0	12	24	36
Hcp required Min. Handicap	30			

CLUB HOUSE & AMENITIES
KLUBHAUS UND NEBENGEBÄUDE
7/10

Pro shop	Pro shop	
Driving range	Übungsplatz	
Sheltered	überdacht	2 Plätze
On grass	auf Rasen	ja
Putting-green	Putting-grün	ja
Pitching-green	Pitching-grün	ja

HOTEL FACILITIES
HOTEL BESCHREIBUNG
6/10

HOTELS HOTELS
Renaissance Hôtel ★★★★★ — Glattbrugg
204 Zimmer, D 245 CHF — 14 km
Tel (41) 01 - 810 85 00, Fax (41) 01 - 810 87 55

Zum Bären — Nürensdorf
14 Zimmer, D 215 CHF — 4 km
Tel (41) 01 - 836 42 12, Fax (41) 01 - 836 42 17

RESTAURANTS RESTAURANT
Bruno's — Glattbrugg
Tel (41) 01 - 810 03 01 — 14 km

Tübli — Zürich
Tel (41) 01 - 251 26 26 — 22 km

CRANS-SUR-SIERRE ✳ | 14 | 7 | 8

C'est le plus célèbre parcours de Suisse, grâce aux efforts de son président Gaston Barras pour y accueillir depuis des années le European Masters professionnel. Il n'est jamais vraiment intimidant : ses obstacles sont bien visibles, modérément en jeu, la difficulté principale reste le choix de club en fonction des dénivellations. Assez accidenté, il est d'ailleurs fatigant à jouer à pied. La splendeur du panorama sur les Alpes (Cervin, Mont Blanc, Alpes bernoises) est parfois à couper le souffle, et console des petites désillusions golfiques. En altitude, les balles volant loin, quelques drives peuvent être flatteurs. Un bon parcours de vacances, avec un entretien souvent simplement honnête. On attendait quelques remodelages de ce tracé : Seve Ballesteros a introduit des modifications au 15 et au 17, devenus plus esthétiques et délicats. D'autres interviennent peu à peu.

This is the most famous of Swiss courses thanks to the work put in by club chairman Gaston Barras to stage the European Masters here over the past few years. The course is never really intimidating, the hazards are clearly in view and not always directly in play. The main problem is the choice of club to offset the steep gradients. It is a hilly course which can be tiring to cover on foot. The beautiful scenery of the Alps (Cervin, Mont Blanc) is quite breathtaking and enough to make up for the mishaps that can so easily mess up your card. At altitude, the ball travels further and a number of drives will prove flattering. A good holiday course where green-keeping is often no more than decent. A little restyling work has been awaited here, and Seve Ballesteros has already made a few changes to the 15th and 17th holes, which are now more attractive and trickier. Other alterations will be added step by step.

Golf Club de Crans-sur-Sierre
CH - 3953 CRANS-SUR-SIERRE

Office	Secrétariat	(41) 027 - 481 21 68
Pro shop	Pro-shop	(41) 027 - 481 40 61
Fax	Fax	(41) 027 - 481 95 68
Situation	Situation	

15 km Sierre, 14 551 hab.

Annual closure	Fermeture annnuelle	oui
		31/10→31/05/99
Weekly closure	Fermeture hebdomadaire	

Fees main season
Tarifs haute saison le parcours

	Week days Semaine	We/Bank holidays We/Férié
Individual Individuel	80 CHF	80 CHF
Couple Couple	160 CHF	160 CHF

Caddy	Caddy	sur réservation
Electric Trolley	Chariot électrique	25 CHF / 18 trous
Buggy	Voiturette	65 CHF / 18 trous
Clubs	Clubs	25-35 CHF /jour

Credit cards Cartes de crédit
VISA - Eurocard - MasterCard - AMEX - DC

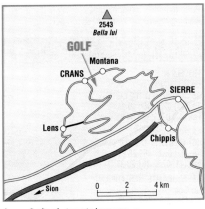

GOLF
2543
Bella lui
Montana
CRANS
SIERRE
Lens
Chippis
Sion
0   2   4 km

Access Accès : Autoroute Lausanne →
Granges → Crans
Map 1 on page 982 Carte 1 Page 982

GOLF COURSE
PARCOURS   **14**/20

Site	Site	▬▬▬
Maintenance	Entretien	▬▬
Architect	Architecte	M. Nicholson
Type	Type	montagne, parc
Relief	Relief	
Water in play	Eau en jeu	▬
Exp. to wind	Exposé au vent	▬▬
Trees in play	Arbres en jeu	▬▬▬

Scorecard Carte de score	Chp. Chp.	Mens Mess.	Ladies Da.
Length Long.	6170	5785	5075
Par	72	72	72

Advised golfing ability		0	12	24	36
Niveau de jeu recommandé				▬▬▬	
Hcp required	Handicap exigé	36			

CLUB HOUSE & AMENITIES
CLUB HOUSE ET ANNEXES   **7**/10

Pro shop	Pro-shop	▬▬▬
Driving range	Practice	▬▬
Sheltered	couvert	9 places
On grass	sur herbe	oui
Putting-green	putting-green	oui
Pitching-green	pitching green	oui

989

➕

HOTEL FACILITIES
ENVIRONNEMENT HOTELIER   **8**/10

HOTELS HÔTELS
Grand Hôtel du Golf   Crans-sur-Sierre
45 chambres, D 500 CHF
Tél (41) 027 - 41 42 42, Fax (41) 027 - 41 97 58

Alpina et Savoy   Crans-sur-Sierre
50 chambres, D 320 CHF
Tél (41) 027 - 481 21 42, Fax (41) 027 - 481 61 75

Alpha   Crans-sur-Sierre
23 chambres, D 260 CHF
Tél (41) 027 - 483 31 13, Fax (41) 027 - 483 31 19

RESTAURANTS RESTAURANT
Rôtisserie de la Reine   Crans-sur-Sierre
Tél (41) 027 - 481 18 85

Restaurant de la Poste   Montana
Tél(41) 027 - 481 27 45

Par son esthétique et la stratégie de jeu, ce parcours est le plus nettement américain des golfs suisses (Pete Dye !). En bordure du Lac Léman, avec de belles perspectives sur le Jura et les Alpes, il se joue sans fatigue physique, mais les fairways bien travaillés, les profonds bunkers, la diversité des obstacles (arbres , obstacles d'eau) et l'intelligence de leur placement en font un défi permanent, constamment renouvelé : on joue ici tous les clubs de son sac, et de multiples façons. On notera en particulier l'excellent rythme du parcours, la subtilité des par 3, de longueur pourtant fort raisonnable, et le modelage de greens très défendus, qu'il faut savoir "rater du bon côté". Techniquement impressionnant, il se laisse apprivoiser si l'on ajoute la réflexion à la maîtrise du jeu. L'entretien a beaucoup progressé depuis quelques années, tous les détails sont soignés, et les greens sont souvent rapides. A la hauteur de l'architecte !

In style and game strategy, this is clearly the most American of all Swiss courses (designed by Pete Dye). On the banks of lake Geneva with fine views over the Jura mountains and the Alps, it is an easily walkable course, but the well-designed fairways, the deep bunkers, the variety of hazards (trees and water) and the intelligence deployed in placing them make this course a permanent challenge which will never lie down. You play every club in the bag, and in different ways. In particular, this is a good course for quick play with subtle but reasonably-lengthed par 3s and well-designed, well-defended greens which, if you are going to miss, should not be missed on the wrong side. Although technically very impressive, you can keep your head above water by playing with skill and brains. Green-keeping is much improved since a few years ; every detail is carefully tended and the greens are fast... matching the standard of the architect.

Domaine Impérial
Villa Prangins
CH - 1196 GLAND

Office	Secrétariat	(41) 022 - 999 06 00
Pro shop	Pro-shop	(41) 022 - 999 06 80
Fax	Fax	(41) 022 - 999 06 06
Situation	Situation	

3 km Nyon, 14 747 hab.

Annual closure	Fermeture annnuelle	oui
		21/12→28/02/99
Weekly closure	Fermeture hebdomadaire	lundi

Fees main season
Tarifs haute saison le parcours

	Week days Semaine	We/Bank holidays We/Férié
Individual Individuel	90 CHF	—
Couple Couple	180 CHF	—

We : membres seulement (only members)

Caddy	Caddy	sur réservation
Electric Trolley	Chariot électrique	20 CHF / 18 trous
Buggy	Voiturette	non
Clubs	Clubs	25 CHF / 18 trous

Credit cards Cartes de crédit
VISA - Eurocard - MasterCard - AMEX

Access Accès : Autoroute Genève-Lausanne → Gland, Route Suisse → Genève, 40O m gauche
Map 1 on page 982 Carte 1 Page 982

GOLF COURSE
PARCOURS
18/20

Site	Site	
Maintenance	Entretien	
Architect	Architecte	Pete Dye
Type	Type	forêt, vallon
Relief	Relief	
Water in play	Eau en jeu	
Exp. to wind	Exposé au vent	
Trees in play	Arbres en jeu	

Scorecard Carte de score	Chp. Chp.	Mens Mess.	Ladies Da.
Length Long.	6297	5903	4993
Par	72	72	72

Advised golfing ability	0	12	24	36
Niveau de jeu recommandé				

Hcp required	Handicap exigé	30

CLUB HOUSE & AMENITIES
CLUB HOUSE ET ANNEXES
8/10

Pro shop	Pro-shop	
Driving range	Practice	
Sheltered	couvert	10 places
On grass	sur herbe	non
Putting-green	putting-green	oui
Pitching-green	pitching green	oui

HOTEL FACILITIES
ENVIRONNEMENT HOTELIER
6/10

HOTELS HÔTELS
de la Plage — Gland
18 chambres, D 100 CHF — 4 km
Tél (41) 022 - 364 10 35
Fax (41) 022 - 364 34 81

Clos-de-Sadex — Nyon
187 chambres, D 200 CHF — 6 km
Tél (41) 022 - 361 28 31
Fax (41) 022 - 361 28 33

RESTAURANTS RESTAURANT
du Golf — sur place
Tél (41) 022 - 364 45 45

Auberge du Soleil — Bursins
Tél(41) 021 - 824 13 44 — 8 km

990

Vor mehr als einem Jahrhundert entstanden, wurde dieser Platz mehrmals und von Mario Verdieri wesentlich verändert, hat aber dabei seinen britischen Touch nicht verloren. Der Kontrast zu den majestätischen Schneegipfeln rundum ist beeindruckend. Wasserläufe und kleine Seen sind die wesentlichen Hindernisse, aber die besten Spieler werden sich davon wenig beeindrucken lassen und richtig loslegen, da auch Bäume nicht zu stark ins Spielgeschehen eingreifen. Dieser sehr natürliche und angenehme Golfcourse würde mit der Neugestaltung gewisser Greens und einigen verteidigenden Hindernissen (man kann den Ball oft rollen lassen) anspruchsvoller werden. Doch er soll vor allem Vergnügen und gutes Scores ermöglichen und nicht Hochleistungen abverlangen.

Opened more than a century ago, this course has undergone many a facelift, essentially by Mario Verdieri, but has retained an evidently British flavour in contrast with the majestic setting of snow-capped mountains. Little lakes and rivers form the main hazards, but these should not over-concern the better players who have the chance here to open their shoulders, since the trees (a lot of very old larch trees) are never too much in play. This is a very natural and deliberately pleasing course which could be made more demanding by redesigning some of the greens and creating hazards to defend them more effectively (you can often chip and roll the ball from fairway to green). But as we said, it was designed more for fun and for producing flattering scores than for any great exploit on the part of the player.

Engadin Golf
CH - 7503 SAMEDAN

Office	Sekretariat	(41) 081 - 852 52 26
Pro shop	Pro shop	(41) 081 - 852 31 81
Fax	Fax	(41) 081 - 852 46 82
Situation	Lage	

5 km St-Moritz, 5 582 Ew.

Annual closure	Jährliche Schliessung	ja
		1/10→30/04/99
Weekly closure	Wöchentliche Schliessung	nein

Fees main season
Preisliste hochsaison Den ganzen Tag

	Week days Woche	We/Bank holidays We/Feiertag
Individual Individuell	90 CHF	90 CHF
Couple Ehepaar	180 CHF	180 CHF

Caddy	Caddy	auf Reservierung
Electric Trolley	Elektrokarren	nein
Buggy	Elektrischer Wagen	50 CHF /18 Löcher
Clubs	Clubs	30 CHF / Tag

Credit cards Kreditkarten
VISA - Eurocard - MasterCard - AMEX - DC

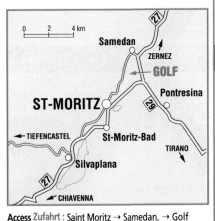

Access Zufahrt : Saint Moritz → Samedan, → Golf
Map 2 on page 984 Karte 2 Seite 984

GOLF COURSE
PLATZ
15/20

Site	Lage	
Maintenance	Instandhaltung	
Architect	Architekt	Mario Verdieri
Type	Typ	campagne, parc
Relief	Relief	
Water in play	Platz mit Wasser	
Exp. to wind	Wind ausgesetzt	
Trees in play	Platz mit Bäumen	

Scorecard Scorekarte	Chp. Chp.	Mens Herren	Ladies Damen
Length Länge	6350	6080	5320
Par	72	72	72

Advised golfing ability Empfohlene Spielstärke	0	12	24	36
Hcp required	Min. Handicap	30		

CLUB HOUSE & AMENITIES
KLUBHAUS UND NEBENGEBÄUDE
6/10

Pro shop	Pro shop	
Driving range	Übungsplatz	
Sheltered	überdacht	nein
On grass	auf Rasen	nein
Putting-green	Putting-grün	ja
Pitching-green	Pitching-grün	ja

HOTEL FACILITIES
HOTEL BESCHREIBUNG
6/10

HOTELS HOTELS

Alpen Golf Hotel	Samedan
42 Zimmer, D 220 CHF	500 m
Tel (41) 081 - 852 52 62	
Fax (41) 081 - 852 33 38	
Bernina	Samedan
59 Zimmer, D 280 CHF	1 km
Tel (41) 081 - 852 12 12	
Fax (41) 081 - 852 36 06	

RESTAURANTS RESTAURANT

Jöhri's Talvo	Champfer
Tel (41) 081 - 852 44 55	8 km
Chesa Veglia	St. Moritz
Tel(41) 081 - 852 35 96	5 km

991
✚

1995 war es soweit: der erste öffentliche Golfplatz der Schweiz wurde eröffnet. Er wurde in einer wenig schmeichelnden Industriezone erbaut, doch dieses Manko könnte mit einem soliden Bepflanzungsprogramm behoben werden. Mit dem Ziel, Golfer auszubilden und eine erschwingliche Alternative zu den Privatclubs zu bieten, wurden keine zusätzlichen golferischen Schwierigkeiten gesucht (kaum Wasserhindernisse im Spiel), was die besten Spieler enttäuschen mag. Es ist schade, dass die Greens und Bunkers nicht vielseitiger gestaltet wurden. Der sonst angenehm zu spielende Platz würde so mehr fürs Auge bieten und dem Stammspieler zu technisch vielseitigeren Herausforderungen verhelfen. Die Anlage offeriert nebst dem Golfplatz grossangelegte Trainingsmöglichkeiten.

This is at last Switzerland's first truly public golf course, opened in 1995. It has been laid out on an industrial site which is still a little unattractive but it could easily grow into something much better with a good plantation programme. The aim here is to coach golfers and offer an economical alternative to the private courses. As a result, there was no deliberate quest for difficulty (for example, there are very few water hazards in play), so the better players might feel disappointed. It is though a shame that the greens and bunkers weren't given more careful thought - they would have added a little more style and pleasure to a course which elsewhere makes for a pleasant round of golf - and that there is not more technical variety for the people who play here regularly. The whole complex also includes huge practice facilities.

Golfpark Holzhäusern
CH - 6343 ROTKREUZ

Office	Sekretariat	(41) 041 - 799 70 10
Pro shop	Pro shop	(41) 041 - 799 06 19
Fax	Fax	(41) 041 - 799 70 15
Situation	Lage	

10 km Zug, 21 705 Ew.
20 km Luzern, 61 034 Ew.

Annual closure	Jährliche Schliessung	ja
		1/01/99→31/01/99
Weekly closure	Wöchentliche Schliessung	nein

Fees main season
Preisliste hochsaison 18 Löcher

	Week days Woche	We/Bank holidays We/Feiertag
Individual Individuell	50 CHF	60 CHF
Couple Ehepaar	100 CHF	120 CHF

Caddy	Caddy	nein
Electric Trolley	Elektrokarren	27 CHF / 18 Löcher
Buggy	Elektrischer Wagen	nein
Clubs	Clubs	25 CHF / 18 Löcher
Credit cards Kreditkarten		nein

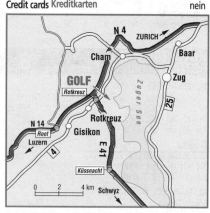

Access Zufahrt : Autobahn N4 oder N14 → Rotkreuz → Industrie Ost → "Golfpark"
Map 1 on page 983 Karte 1 Seite 983

GOLF COURSE
PLATZ 13/20

Site	Lage	■
Maintenance	Instandhaltung	■■
Architect	Architekt	Marco Verdieri
Type	Typ	Fachland
Relief	Relief	
Water in play	Platz mit Wasser	■
Exp. to wind	Wind ausgesetzt	■■
Trees in play	Platz mit Bäumen	■■

Scorecard Scorekarte	Chp. Chp.	Mens Herren	Ladies Damen
Length Länge	6110	6050	5100
Par	73	73	73

Advised golfing ability	0 12 24 36
Empfohlene Spielstärke	
Hcp required	Min. Handicap 35

CLUB HOUSE & AMENITIES
KLUBHAUS UND NEBENGEBÄUDE 7/10

Pro shop	Pro shop	■■■
Driving range	Übungsplatz	■■■
Sheltered	überdacht	40 Plätze
On grass	auf Rasen	ja
Putting-green	Putting-grün	ja
Pitching-green	Pitching-grün	ja

HOTEL FACILITIES
HOTEL BESCHREIBUNG 6/10

HOTELS HOTELS
Waldheim — Risch
34 Zimmer, D 190 CHF — 2 km
Tel (41) 041 - 799 70 70
Fax (41) 041 - 799 70 79

Parkhotel — Zug
112 Zimmer, D 300 CHF — 10 km
Tel (41) 041 - 711 66 11
Fax (41) 041 - 710 66 11

RESTAURANTS RESTAURANT
Rathauskeller — Zug
Tel (41) 041 - 711 00 58 — 10 km

Hecht — Zug
Tel (41) 041 - 711 01 93 — 10 km

992

GENÈVE

	17	7	8

Un des parcours suisses les plus intéressants. Nul n'en sera étonné : Robert Trent Jones en est l'auteur. Dans un site magnifique surplombant le Lac Léman, il a une fois de plus signé un dessin très imaginatif et d'une grande intelligence stratégique. La multiplicité des départs et des positions de drapeaux permet de l'adapter à tous les niveaux, même si les joueurs très moyens auront du mal à y scorer. Les greens sont vastes (un double green aux 9 et 18), très dessinés, ce qui rend essentielle une bonne maîtrise du petit jeu et du putting... même si l'on réussit à bien travailler la balle au grand jeu, notamment sur les nombreux dog-legs. Une consolation pour ceux dont le swing n'est pas exceptionnel : si certains arbres peuvent poser problème, il y a peu d'obstacles d'eau (8, 16 et 17).

One of the most interesting Swiss courses, and, surprise surprise, it was designed by a one Robert Trent Jones. In a magnificent setting overlooking Lake Geneva, Jones has once again come up with a very imaginative layout calling for considerable strategic intelligence. The many different tees and pin positions make this a course for players of all ability, even though your average hacker will find scoring a tough proposition. The greens are huge (the 9th and 18th have a double green) and well designed, thus calling for good putting skills and a sharp short game, even if your long game is on tune with the ball moving both ways, particularly on the very many dog-legs. There is one consolation for high-handicappers, namely that although a few trees may cause problems, there are few water hazards (on the 8th, 16th and 17th holes only).

Golf Club de Genève

70, route de la Capite
CH - 1233 COLOGNY

Office	Secrétariat	(41) 022 - 707 48 00
Pro shop	Pro-shop	(41) 022 - 707 48 15
Fax	Fax	(41) 022 - 707 48 20
Situation	Situation	

5 km Genève, 172 486 hab.

Annual closure	Fermeture annnuelle	oui
		7/12→7/03/99

Weekly closure	Fermeture hebdomadaire	lundi

Fees main season
Tarifs haute saison le parcours

	Week days Semaine	We/Bank holidays We/Férié
Individual Individuel	80 CHF	80 CHF
Couple Couple	160 CHF	160 CHF

Caddy	Caddy	sur réservation
Electric Trolley	Chariot électrique	20 CHF / 18 trous
Buggy	Voiturette	non
Clubs	Clubs	20 CHF / 18 trous

Credit cards Cartes de crédit	non

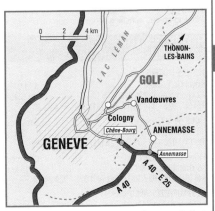

Access Accès : Genève → Evian, → Cologny, → Golf
Map 1 on page 982 Carte 1 Page 982

GOLF COURSE / PARCOURS — 17/20

Site	Site	
Maintenance	Entretien	
Architect	Architecte	Robert Trent Jones
Type	Type	parc
Relief	Relief	
Water in play	Eau en jeu	
Exp. to wind	Exposé au vent	
Trees in play	Arbres en jeu	

Scorecard Carte de score	Chp. Chp.	Mens Mess.	Ladies Da.
Length Long.	6289	5626	5321
Par	72	72	72

Advised golfing ability Niveau de jeu recommandé		0 12 24 36
Hcp required Handicap exigé		24 Mess., 26 Da.

CLUB HOUSE & AMENITIES / CLUB HOUSE ET ANNEXES — 7/10

Pro shop	Pro-shop	
Driving range	Practice	
Sheltered	couvert	12 places
On grass	sur herbe	oui (04 → 10)
Putting-green	putting-green	oui
Pitching-green	pitching green	oui

993

HOTEL FACILITIES / ENVIRONNEMENT HOTELIER — 8/10

HOTELS HÔTELS

La Cigogne — Genève 5 km
42 chambres, D 400 CHF
Tél (41) 022 - 311 42 42
Fax (41) 022 - 311 40 65

Century — Genève 5 km
133 chambres, D 250 CHF
Tél (41) 022 - 736 80 95
Fax (41) 022 - 736 52 74

RESTAURANTS RESTAURANT

Parc des Eaux-Vives — Genève 6 km
Tél (41) 022 - 735 41 40

Lion d'Or — Genève 4 km
Tél (41) 022 - 736 44 32

Il n'est pas très habituel de conseiller des parcours courts, mais celui-ci, avec son par 68, est des plus amusants. Evidemment, les golfeurs du plus haut niveau n'y seront pas à l'aise, mais ils sont une minorité ! En premier lieu, Jeremy Pern a tiré un parti remarquable d'un terrain difficile à adapter au golf, et mis l'accent sur la précision, dans tous les secteurs du jeu. Qu'il s'agisse du drive, du second coup, des approches vers des greens très défendus ou du putting, cet aspect ludique est à la fois intéressant et formateur. Le parcours est assez physique, mais les fairways (étroits) sont assez plats, ce qui ne rend pas la marche trop ardue. L'imagination et l'intelligence de l'architecte en font une réussite, même s'il n'a pas eu l'espace pour s'exprimer pleinement. La qualité de l'entretien et la facilité relative pour y scorer en font une bonne adresse, relevée encore par un environnement magnifique au bord du lac de Gruyère.

It is not every day that we recommend short courses, but this one, a par 68, is most amusing. The most proficient golfers will obviously not feel too excited about it, but they are a minority anyway. Firstly, Jeremy Pern has done a remakable job with terrain that was difficult to harness for golf and has placed emphasis on precision in every department of the game. Whether for the drive, the second shot, approaches to very well-guarded greens or putting, this fun aspect is both interesting and educational. The course is pretty hilly, although the actual fairways are rather flat (and narrow), which means easy walking. The architect's imagination and intelligence have made this a class course, even though space was restricted. The standard of green-keeping and the relative ease of scoring make this a good address, enhanced by a magnificent setting on the banks of Lake Gruyère.

Golf de la Gruyère
Le Château
CH - 1649 PONT-LA-VILLE

Office	Secrétariat	(41) 026 - 414 91 11
Pro shop	Pro-shop	(41) 026 - 414 94 00
Fax	Fax	(41) 026 - 414 92 20
Situation	Situation	
12 km Fribourg, 36 355 hab.		
Annual closure	Fermeture annnuelle	oui
	2/01/99 → 1/03/99	
Weekly closure	Fermeture hebdomadaire	

Fees main season
Tarifs haute saison le parcours

	Week days Semaine	We/Bank holidays We/Férié
Individual Individuel	85 CHF	105 CHF
Couple Couple	170 CHF	210 CHF

Caddy	Caddy	sur réservation
Electric Trolley	Chariot électrique	25 CHF/18 trous
Buggy	Voiturette	50 CHF/18 trous
Clubs	Clubs	35 CHF/18 trous

Credit cards Cartes de crédit
VISA - MasterCard - AMEX - DC

Access Accès : Autoroute E25 Fribourg-Vevey →
Rossens → Pont-la-Ville
Map 1 on page 982 Carte 1 Page 982

GOLF COURSE
PARCOURS 14/20

Site	Site	
Maintenance	Entretien	
Architect	Architecte	Jeremy Pern
Type	Type	campagne
Relief	Relief	
Water in play	Eau en jeu	
Exp. to wind	Exposé au vent	
Trees in play	Arbres en jeu	

Scorecard Carte de score	Chp. Chp.	Mens Mess.	Ladies Da.
Length Long.	5058	4740	4095
Par	68	68	68

Advised golfing ability   0   12   24   36
Niveau de jeu recommandé
Hcp required   Handicap exigé   36

CLUB HOUSE & AMENITIES
CLUB HOUSE ET ANNEXES 7/10

Pro shop	Pro-shop	
Driving range	Practice	
Sheltered	couvert	3 places
On grass	sur herbe	non
Putting-green	putting-green	oui
Pitching-green	pitching green	oui

HOTEL FACILITIES
ENVIRONNEMENT HOTELIER 6/10

HOTELS HÔTELS
Royal Golf Hôtel — Pont-la-Ville
12 chambres, D 120 CHF — sur place
Tél (41) 026 - 414 91 11, Fax (41) 026 - 414 92 20

Hôtel de la Gruyère — Gruyères
36 chambres, D 77 CHF — 8 km
Tél (41) 026 - 915 22 30, Fax (41) 026 - 915 10 28

Hôtel Cailler/Charmey — Charmey
45 chambres, D 90 CHF — 15 km
Tél (41) 026 - 927 10 13, Fax (41) 026 - 927 24 13

RESTAURANTS RESTAURANT
La Fleur de Lys — Fribourg
Tél (41) 026 - 322 79 61 — 12 km

Restaurant de la Tour — Bulle
Tél (41) 026 - 912 74 70 — 15 km

994

INTERLAKEN

Vom Thunerseeufer nur durch eine Naturschutzzone getrennt, bietet der Interlakner Golfplatz je nach Wasserstand des Sees und Regenmenge recht feuchte Bedingungen, doch er gibt ein gutes Beispiel für das Miteinander von Golf und Oekologie ab. Die recht flache Anlage steht in einem faszinierenden Kontrast zu den umliegenden Berner Alpengipfeln. Der Spielrhythmus ist ansprechend, doch die ersten fünf Loch können - bedingt durch ihre beträchtliche Länge - eine gute Scorekarte schon zu allem Anfang gefährden. Die gut und vielseitig gestalteten Greens bieten einige interessante Annäherungen. Moderate Schwierigkeiten bestimmen den Gesamteindruck dieses Golfcourses, der sich zur angenehmen Familienrunde eignet. Einige Fairways mögen vor allem aus Sicht des hintersten Abschlags schmal erscheinen. Einem Abschlag übrigens, den man bei Regen besser ignoriert.

Not far from Lake Thun, from which the course is separated by a protected natural expanse of land, this can be a very wet course when it rains but forms a good example of coexistence with ecological requirements. In contrast with the impressive mountain setting, the course is rather flat and can be played at a good pace, even though the first five holes are a tough proposition in terms of length and can spoil any hope of returning a good card. The greens are well cut out, rather varied and make for some interesting approach shots. The overriding impression is that of a course where difficulties have been kept to a reasonable minimum for a pleasant round of golf with all the family. With this said, some holes can look decidedly tight, especially from the back tees, which should be unashamedly forgotten whenever it rains.

Golf-Club Interlaken-Unterseen

Postfach 110
CH - 3800 INTERLAKEN

Office	Sekretariat	(41) 033 - 823 60 16
Pro shop	Pro shop	(41) 033 - 822 79 70
Fax	Fax	(41) 033 - 823 42 03
Situation	Lage	

2 km Interlaken, 5 176 Ew.

Annual closure	Jährliche Schliessung	ja
		15/11→31/03/99
Weekly closure	Wöchentliche Schliessung	nein

Fees main season
Preisliste hochsaison

	Week days Woche	We/Bank holidays We/Feiertag
Individual Individuell	70 CHF	80 CHF
Couple Ehepaar	140 CHF	160 CHF

Caddy	Caddy	nein
Electric Trolley	Elektrokarren	25 CHF/18 Löcher
Buggy	Elektrischer Wagen	nein
Clubs	Clubs	30 CHF/18 Löcher

Credit cards Kreditkarten
VISA - Eurocard - MasterCard - AMEX

INTERLAKEN
GOLF

Brienz
Thun
Unterseen
Interlaken
BRIENZERSEE
N8
THUNERSEE
wilderswil
Unterseen
N8
Spiez
Därligen

0   2   4 km

Access Zufahrt : Autobahn N8 → Unterseen → Thunersee, Golf
Map 1 on page 983 Karte 1 Seite 983

GOLF COURSE
PLATZ
14/20

Site	Lage	■■■■
Maintenance	Instandhaltung	■■■
Architect	Architekt	

Type	Typ	Park, Fachland
Relief	Relief	■
Water in play	Platz mit Wasser	■■
Exp. to wind	Wind ausgesetzt	■■
Trees in play	Platz mit Bäumen	■■

Scorecard Scorekarte	Chp. Chp.	Mens Herren	Ladies Damen
Length Länge	6274	5875	5298
Par	72	72	72

Advised golfing ability		
Empfohlene Spielstärke	0 36	
Hcp required	Min. Handicap	30

CLUB HOUSE & AMENITIES
KLUBHAUS UND NEBENGEBÄUDE
6/10

Pro shop	Pro shop	■■■
Driving range	Übungsplatz	■■
Sheltered	überdacht	4 Plätze
On grass	auf Rasen	ja (01/03 → 15/11)
Putting-green	Putting-grün	ja
Pitching-green	Pitching-grün	ja

HOTEL FACILITIES
HOTEL BESCHREIBUNG
6/10

HOTELS HOTELS
Landhotel Golf — Golf
26 Zimmer, D 184 CHF
Tel (41) 033 - 823 21 31, Fax (41) 033 - 823 21 91

Victoria Jungfrau — Interlaken
227 Zimmer, D 550 CHF — 2 km
Tel (41) 033 - 827 11 11, Fax (41) 033 - 827 37 37

Lötschberg — Interlaken
19 Zimmer, D 180 CHF — 2 km
Tel (41) 036 - 22 25 45, Fax (41) 036 - 22 25 79

RESTAURANTS RESTAURANT
La Terrasse — Interlaken
Tel (41) 033 - 827 11 11 — 2 km

Hirschen — Interlaken
Tel (41) 033 - 822 15 45 — 2 km

995

Un parcours séduisant et tranquille à première vue, mais dont les nombreuses difficultés se révèlent peu à peu, dans ce site très boisé. Bien rythmé dans son enchaînement, il est souvent étroit, assez vallonné, mais sans vraiment de pièges cachés. Le remodelage des greens par Jeremy Pern a rajeuni ce parcours classique de façon spectaculaire, et oblige plus encore à penser avant de jouer, d'autant que les bunkers de green, également retravaillés, amènent à porter souvent la balle au lieu de la faire rouler. Les joueurs moyens, qui ont souvent du mal à le faire, auront intérêt à jouer des départs avancés. Très agréable à jouer en été quand le terrain est sec, il pouvait s'avérer plus difficile dans des conditions humides, le placement de la balle au drive devenant alors encore plus crucial, mais des travaux ont nettement amélioré cet aspect des choses, tout en maintenant le cachet du parcours. Une véritable réussite où les greens, un instant menacés, ont été bien repris.

At first view, an appealing and quiet golf course, but one where the numerous difficulties gradually emerge in a very woody site. With nicely paced continuity, the fairways are often tight and rather hilly, but with no real hidden traps. Restyling by architect Jeremy Pern has spectacularly rejuvenated this classic course which now requires more careful thought before each shot, especially since the green-side bunkers, which have also been redesigned, often call for a high lob shot instead of the easier chip into the green. Average players, who often have problems with this kind of approach, will be better off playing from the front tees. Very pleasant to play in summer when the terrain is dry, Lausanne can prove to be a tougher proposition in wet conditions, when placing the ball off the tee becomes even more crucial. However, work has been carried out and has distinctly improved this side of things.

Golf Club de Lausanne

3, route du Golf
CH - 1000 Lausanne 25

Office	Secrétariat	(41) 021 - 784 84 84
Pro shop	Pro-shop	(41) 021 - 784 84 74
Fax	Fax	(41) 021 - 784 84 80
Situation	Situation	

5 km N.E. Lausanne, 125 395 hab.

Annual closure	Fermeture annnuelle	oui
		15/12→21/03/99
Weekly closure	Fermeture hebdomadaire	non

Fees main season
Tarifs haute saison le parcours

	Week days Semaine	We/Bank holidays We/Férié
Individual Individuel	80 CHF	100 CHF
Couple Couple	160 CHF	200 CHF

Caddy	Caddy	sur réservation
Electric Trolley	Chariot électrique	15 CHF/18 trous
Buggy	Voiturette	non
Clubs	Clubs	20 CHF

Credit cards Cartes de crédit — VISA - MasterCard

Access Accès : Aurotoute N9, sortie Vennes →
Epalinges. Chalet-à-Gobet, → Le Mont, Golf
Map 1 on page 982 Carte 1 Page 982

GOLF COURSE
PARCOURS
16/20

Site	Site	
Maintenance	Entretien	
Architect	Architecte	Narbel
		Jeremy Pern
Type	Type	parc
Relief	Relief	
Water in play	Eau en jeu	
Exp. to wind	Exposé au vent	
Trees in play	Arbres en jeu	

Scorecard Carte de score	Chp. Chp.	Mens Mess.	Ladies Da.
Length Long.	6295	5900	5170
Par	72	72	72

Advised golfing ability		0 12 24 36
Niveau de jeu recommandé		
Hcp required	Handicap exigé	24 Mess., 28 Da.

CLUB HOUSE & AMENITIES
CLUB HOUSE ET ANNEXES
7/10

Pro shop	Pro-shop	
Driving range	Practice	
Sheltered	couvert	4 places
On grass	sur herbe	oui (05 → 10)
Putting-green	putting-green	oui
Pitching-green	pitching green	oui

HOTEL FACILITIES
ENVIRONNEMENT HOTELIER
7/10

HOTELS HÔTELS

Les Chevreuils — Vers-chez-les-Blancs
30 chambres, D 215 CHF — 5 km
Tél (41) 021 - 784 20 21, Fax (41) 021 - 784 15 45

Beau Rivage Palace ***** — Lausanne
180 chambres, D 390 CHF — 6 km
Tél (41) 021 - 613 33 33, Fax (41) 021 - 613 33 34

Mövenpick Radisson **** — Lausanne
265 chambres, D 240 CHF — 6 km
Tél (41) 021 - 617 21 21, Fax (41) 021 - 616 15 27

RESTAURANTS RESTAURANT

Girardet — Crissier
Tél (41) 021 - 634 05 05 — 10 km

La Grappe d'Or — Lausanne
Tél (41) 021 - 323 07 60 — 6 km

LUGANO

Fondata nel 1925, il percorso é stato rimodellato succesivamente da Donald Harradine e Cabell Robinson che à aggiunto qualche laghetto al corso d'acqua esistente, ma non ha potuto allungarlo per la mancanza dello spazio. I green sono ben difesi, ció che puo ostacolare il desiderio di performance. Molto franco, non ha bisogno di essere giocate dieci volte per essere capito, la vegetazione attenua molto l'impressione di va e vieni suggeriti dal disegno, e obliga i giocatori d'un altro livello, dove possono rifarsi con la precisione, in quanto il percorso non é molto lungo. In un sito ed una piacevole regione, é un buon percorso di vacanze, la sua manutenzione deve essere migliorata per attribuirgli una nota migliore.

Opened in 1925, the course has been successively reshaped by Donald Harradine and Cabell Robinson, who added several lakes to the existing river but were unable to lengthen the course owing to lack of space. The greens are well defended, which may cut short any desire to go for the performance. You don't need to play this very honest course ten times to understand what it is about. The vegetation reduces the impression of up and down holes, suggested by the layout, and forces long-hitters to fade or draw the ball to get a good approach into the green. Good and not so good players can get along well together here, where lack of precision is offset by short yardage. In a pleasant setting and region, this is a good holiday course, but to get a better score, green-keeping and maintenance could still do with a little improvement.

Golf Club Lugano
CH - 6983 MAGLIASO

Office	Segreteria	(41) 091 - 606 15 57
Pro shop	Pro shop	(41) 091 - 606 46 76
Fax	Fax	(41) 091 - 606 65 58
Situation	Localita'	

5 km Lugano, 25 334 ab.

Annual closure	Chiusura annuale	no
Weekly closure	Chiusura settimanale	no

Fees main season
Tariffe alta stagione il percorso

	Week days Settimana	We/Bank holidays Feriale/Festivo
Individual Individuale	85 CHF	110 CHF
Couple Coppia	170 CHF	220 CHF

Caddy	Caddy	no
Electric Trolley	Carello elettrico	no
Buggy	Car	110 CHF/18 buche
Clubs	Bastoni	30 CHF/18 buche

Credit cards Carte di credito — no

Access Itinerario : Lugano, → Ponte Tresa, → Magliaso, Golf
Map 1 on page 983 Carta 1 Pagina 983

GOLF COURSE
PERCORSO

15/20

Site	Paesaggio	▆▆▆▭
Maintenance	Manutenzione	▆▭▭▭
Architect	Architetto	Donald Harradine Cabell B. Robinson
Type	Tipologia	parco
Relief	Relievo terreno	▆▆▭▭
Water in play	Acqua in gioco	▆▆▆▭
Exp. to wind	Esposto al vento	▆▆▭▭
Trees in play	Alberi in gioco	▆▆▆▭

Scorecard Carta-score	Chp. Camp.	Mens Uomini	Ladies Donne
Length Lunghezza	5775	5775	5040
Par	71	71	71

Advised golfing ability		0 12 24 36
Livello di gioco consigliato		▆▆▆▆▆
Hcp required	Handicap richiesto 30	

CLUB HOUSE & AMENITIES
CLUB HOUSE E SERVIZI

7/10

Pro shop	Pro shop	▆▆▆▭
Driving range	Campo pratica	▆▆▆▭
Sheltered	coperto	8 posti
On grass	in erba	no
Putting-green	Putting-green	si
Pitching-green	Green-pratica	si

997

➕

HOTEL FACILITIES
ALBERGHI

8/10

HOTELS ALBERGHI

Villa Magliasina — Magliaso
25 camere, D 270 CHF — 500 m
Tel (41) 091 - 611 29 29, Fax (41) 091 - 611 29 20

Principe Leopoldo — Lugano
39 camere, D 480 CHF — 5 km
Tel (41) 091 - 985 88 55, Fax (41) 091 - 985 88 25

Locanda Esterel — Caslano
9 camere, D 180 CHF — 1 km
Tel (41) 091 - 606 43 13, Fax (41) 091 - 606 62 02

RESTAURANTS RISTORANTE

Locanda Esterel — Caslano
Tel (41) 091 - 606 43 13 — 1 km

Al Portone — Lugano
Tel(41) 091 - 923 55 11 — 5 km

LUZERN

1925 erbaut und seither mehrfach verändert, bietet dieser Golfcourse hübsche und abwechslungsreiche Aussichten auf den Vierwaldstättersee, auf Hügellandschaften und auf verschneite Berge. Bie betonten Geländeformen wurden geschickt einbezogen, denn die grossen Höhenunterschiede liegen meist zwischen den Holes. Doglegs sind wenige zu finden, aber die Bahnen sind oft schmal, verlangen gerade Schläge und den einen oder anderen Flirt mit Baümen. Bei nur einem Wasserhindernis haben gute Spieler Chancen auf tiefe Scores, obwohl Annäherungen auf oft tiefergelegene oder überhöhte Greens solide Schläge verlangen. Ein traditionelles Platzkonzept, dem aber die Schwierigkeiten eines modernen Courses nicht fehlen und die charmante Umgebung machen Luzern zum lohnenden Golfabstecher.

This course has been considerably restyled since its opening in 1925. There are a number of different pretty views over lake Lucerne, the hills and the snow-capped mountains. The terrain is steep and rather hilly but has been well utilised, as the steepest slopes are to be found primarily between holes. There are few dog-legs, as most holes are often straight and require straight shots, skirting the trees. With a single water hazard, skilled players will doubtless find this an easy course to score on, even though care is called for when attacking the greens, which are rarely on the same level as the fairway (elevated or in a hollow). We liked the charm of the site and a certain idea of old-style golf courses, without the difficulties found on many modern courses.

Luzern Golf Club

Dietschiberg
CH - 6006 LUZERN

Office	Sekretariat	(41) 041 - 420 97 87
Pro shop	Pro shop	(41) 041 - 420 97 87
Fax	Fax	(41) 041 - 420 82 48
Situation	Lage	

2 km Luzern, 61 034 Ew.

Annual closure	Jährliche Schliessung	ja
		31/10→1/04/99
Weekly closure	Wöchentliche Schliessung	nein
		Montag, das Restaurant

Fees main season
Preisliste hochsaison 18 Löcher

	Week days Woche	We/Bank holidays We/Feiertag
Individual Individuell	80 CHF	100 CHF
Couple Ehepaar	160 CHF	200 CHF

Caddy	Caddy	nein
Electric Trolley	Elektrokarren	nein
Buggy	Elektrischer Wagen	nein
Clubs	Clubs	15 CHF/Tag

Credit cards Kreditkarten
VISA - Eurocard - MasterCard - AMEX

998

Access Zufahrt : Luzern → Dreilinden, →
Trachtenmuseum, Dietschibergstrasse
Map 1 on page 983 Karte 1 Seite 983

GOLF COURSE
PLATZ
13/20

Site	Lage	■■■■■
Maintenance	Instandhaltung	■■■■
Architect	Architekt	Ruzzo Reuss
Type	Typ	Wald, Gebirge
Relief	Relief	
Water in play	Platz mit Wasser	■
Exp. to wind	Wind ausgesetzt	■
Trees in play	Platz mit Bäumen	■■■■

Scorecard Scorekarte	Chp. Chp.	Mens Herren	Ladies Damen
Length Länge	6082	5760	4931
Par	73	72	72

Advised golfing ability		0 12 24 36
Empfohlene Spielstärke		■■■■
Hcp required	Min. Handicap	30

CLUB HOUSE & AMENITIES
KLUBHAUS UND NEBENGEBÄUDE
6/10

Pro shop	Pro shop	■■■■
Driving range	Übungsplatz	■■■
Sheltered	überdacht	4 Plätze
On grass	auf Rasen	ja (06 → 09)
Putting-green	Putting-grün	ja
Pitching-green	Pitching-grün	ja

HOTEL FACILITIES
HOTEL BESCHREIBUNG
7/10

HOTELS HOTELS

Montana	Luzern
60 Zimmer, D 286 CHF	2 km
Tel (41) 041 - 410 65 65, Fax (41) 041 - 410 66 76	

Grand Hôtel National	Luzern
78 Zimmer, D 400 CHF	2 km
Tel (41) 041 - 50 11 11, Fax (41) 041 - 51 55 39	

Drei Könige, 60 Zimmer, D 150 CHF	Luzern
Tel (41) 041 - 22 88 33, Fax (41) 041 - 22 88 52	2 km

RESTAURANTS RESTAURANT

Zunfthaus zu Pfistern	Luzern
Tel (41) 041 - 51 36 50	2 km

Old Swiss House, Tel (41) 041 - 410 61 71 Luzern, 2 km

Le Manoir, Tel (41) 041 - 23 23 48 Luzern, 2 km

On pourrait souligner la beauté du panorama sur les Alpes , mais cette qualité est commune à la majorité des golfs de Suisse ! Elle contribue au moins à faire apprécier un parcours autrement sans originalité particulière, et sans obstacles d'eau. Eviter les arbres constitue le principal "challenge", car ils sont souvent en jeu, et rompent un peu la monotonie des trous, trop similaires de dessin pour frapper la mémoire. Les difficultés ne sont pas très grandes, ce qui peut réserver des parties plaisantes entre joueurs de niveau différent, mais les meilleurs resteront certainement sur leur faim. Au moment des visites, les greens étaient toujours en état moyen : se renseigner à ce sujet. Si vous passez dans la région...

We could point to the beautiful scenery of the Alps, but such panoramas are common to the majority of Swiss courses. But it does help the player to enjoy a course which otherwise has no particular originality and no water hazards. The main challenge is to avoid the trees, which are often in play and break the monotony of holes which are too similar to really leave an indelible impression. The difficulties are not enormous, which can lead to pleasant rounds with friends of differing ability, but the better players will feel a touch of frustration. When we visited, the greens still were in average condition, so if you are in the neighbourhood, call first to check.

Golf Club Montreux

Route d'Evian
CH - 1860 AIGLE

Office	Secrétariat	(41) 024 - 466 4616
Pro shop	Pro-shop	(41) 024 - 466 14 64
Fax	Fax	(41) 024 - 466 10 47
Situation	Situation	

25 km Montreux, 21 325 hab.

Annual closure	Fermeture annnuelle	non
Weekly closure	Fermeture hebdomadaire	non
	janvier, le restaurant	

Fees main season
Tarifs haute saison le parcours

	Week days Semaine	We/Bank holidays We/Férié
Individual Individuel	70 CHF	90 CHF
Couple Couple	140 CHF	180 CHF

Caddy	Caddy	non
Electric Trolley	Chariot électrique	non
Buggy	Voiturette	non
Clubs	Clubs	15 CHF/jour
Credit cards Cartes de crédit		non

Access Accès : Autoroute N9 Montreux-Martigny, sortie Aigle, → Golf
Map 1 on page 982 Carte 1 Page 982

GOLF COURSE PARCOURS 13/20

Site	Site	
Maintenance	Entretien	
Architect	Architecte	

Type	Type	parc
Relief	Relief	
Water in play	Eau en jeu	
Exp. to wind	Exposé au vent	
Trees in play	Arbres en jeu	

Scorecard Carte de score	Chp. Chp.	Mens Mess.	Ladies Da.
Length Long.	6143	5828	5092
Par	72	72	72

Advised golfing ability Niveau de jeu recommandé	0	12	24	36
Hcp required Handicap exigé	30			

CLUB HOUSE & AMENITIES CLUB-HOUSE ET ANNEXES 6/10

Pro shop	Pro-shop	
Driving range	Practice	
Sheltered	couvert	6 places
On grass	sur herbe	oui
Putting-green	putting-green	oui
Pitching-green	pitching green	oui

HOTEL FACILITIES ENVIRONNEMENT HOTELIER 5/10

HOTELS HÔTELS
Le Montreux Palace — Montreux
250 chambres, D 570 CHF — 25 km
Tél (41) 021 - 962 12 12, Fax (41) 021 - 962 17 17

Bonivard — Montreux/Veytaux
70 chambres, D 240 CHF — 20 km
Tél (41) 021 - 963 43 41, Fax (41) 021 - 963 48 15

Nord — Aigle
19 chambres, D 180 CHF — 20 km
Tél (41) 024 - 466 10 55, Fax (41) 024 - 466 42 48

RESTAURANTS RESTAURANT
Le Pont de Brent — Montreux-Brent
Tél (41) 021 - 964 52 30 — 30 km

L'Ermitage — Montreux
Tél (41) 021 - 964 44 11 — 25 km

999

Ce parcours accidenté, mais sans excès, a été dessiné dans une ancienne zone agricole au pied du Jura. L'absence d'arrosage automatique oblige à le déconseiller en temps de forte sécheresse, mais les précipitations naturelles permettent de le maintenir généralement en bon état. Les obstacles sont rarement très dangereux (quelques hors-limites), et la longueur raisonnable permet d'offrir pas mal d'occasions de birdie (ou de pars pour les joueurs moyens). Pas de pièges ici ni de complications artificielles : ce parcours a été coulé dans la nature, à l'intention évidente des familles, ou de ceux qui ne souhaitent pas trop se compliquer la vie sur un parcours (ils sont nombreux).

This is a hilly course laid out over a former farming region at the foot of the Jura mountains. There being no automatic sprinklers, it is not a course to be recommended during a drought, but natural rainfall generally tends to keep it in good condition. The hazards are rarely very dangerous (a few out-of-bounds) and the reasonable length can produce more than one opportunity to catch an elusive birdie (or the equally elusive par for lesser players). There are no traps or artificial complications here, as this course was cast in natural land, evidently intended for families or golfers who prefer not to make life any more complicated than it often can be on a golf course (and there are a lot of those).

Golf & Country Club Neuchâtel
Voëns
CH - 2072 SAINT-BLAISE

Office	Secrétariat	(41) 032 - 753 55 50
Pro shop	Pro-shop	(41) 032 - 753 70 84
Fax	Fax	(41) 032 - 753 29 40
Situation	Situation	

5 km Neuchâtel, 32 080 hab.

Annual closure	Fermeture annnuelle	oui
		15/11→21/03/99
Weekly closure	Fermeture hebdomadaire	non

Fees main season
Tarifs haute saison le parcours

	Week days Semaine	We/Bank holidays We/Férié
Individual Individuel	70 CHF	90 CHF
Couple Couple	140 CHF	180 CHF

Caddy	Caddy	sur réservation
Electric Trolley	Chariot électrique	non
Buggy	Voiturette	non
Clubs	Clubs	15 CHF/jour
Credit cards Cartes de crédit		non

1000

Access Accès : Neuchâtel sortie St Blaise, → Lignières ou St Blaise Centre, → Chaumont
Map 1 on page 982 Carte 1 Page 982

GOLF COURSE
PARCOURS   14/20

Site	Site	
Maintenance	Entretien	
Architect	Architecte	Donald Harradine
Type	Type	parc
Relief	Relief	
Water in play	Eau en jeu	
Exp. to wind	Exposé au vent	
Trees in play	Arbres en jeu	

Scorecard Carte de score	Chp. Chp.	Mens Mess.	Ladies Da.
Length Long.	5930	5630	4870
Par	71	71	71

Advised golfing ability		0 12 24 36
Niveau de jeu recommandé		
Hcp required	Handicap exigé	30

CLUB HOUSE & AMENITIES
CLUB HOUSE ET ANNEXES   6/10

Pro shop	Pro-shop	
Driving range	Practice	
Sheltered	couvert	8 places
On grass	sur herbe	non
Putting-green	putting-green	oui
Pitching-green	pitching green	oui

HOTEL FACILITIES
ENVIRONNEMENT HOTELIER   7/10

HOTELS HÔTELS
Beaurivage, 65 chambres, D 310 CHF   Neuchâtel
Tél (41) 032 - 724 0024, Fax (41) 032 - 724 7894   9 km

Chaumont et Golf   Chaumont
88 chambres, D 200 CHF   2 km
Tél (41) 032 - 755 21 75, Fax (41) 032 - 753 27 22

Les Vieux Toits   Hauterive
10 chambres, D 175 CHF   2 km
Tél (41) 032 - 753 42 42, Fax (41) 032 - 753 24 52

Cheval Blanc, 11 chambres, D 90 CHF   Saint-Blaise,
Tél (41) 032 - 753 30 07, Fax (41) 032 - 753 30 06   4 km

RESTAURANTS RESTAURANT
Au Boccalino   Saint-Blaise 4 km
Tél (41) 032 - 753 36 80

Auberge du Grand Pin,   Peseux
Tél (41) 032 - 751 77 07   12 km

Niederbüren, entworfen von dem allseits gefragten Donald Harradine, entrollt sich wie ein schmales Band vor den Augen des Spielers, ganz so wie der Old Course von St. Andrews. Nur, dass der Platz an den Flüsschen Thun liegt und nicht am Meer. Einzig der Entwurf entspricht britischer Tradition, der Vergleich lässt sich nicht weiter ausdehnen. Es beginnt damit, dass der Wind hier längst nicht so häufig und so gewaltig weht. Weiterhin bilden die Bunker die haupsächliche Bedrohung der Fairways, jedoch veranlassen deren Profil und Schwierigkeitsgrad zu keinerlei Besorgnis. Die Bahnen sind von Tannen gesäumt, die an ein gerades Spiel appellieren und keinerlei Fehler zulassen, wie etwa die breiten Flächen der richtigen Links. Der Platz ist insgesamt nicht zu lang und die schwierigen Passagen sind gleichmässig verteilt. Es handelt sich um ein angenehmes Areal, ideal für die ganze Familie.

Laid out by the prolific designer Donald Harradine, Niederbüren is peculiar in that it unwinds in a narrow strip, like the Old Course at St Andrews, only alongside the river Thun and not the sea. Despite the British tradition here, the comparison ends there. Firstly the wind is less frequent and more clement, then the basic hazards emerge as bunkers, although their shape and difficulty are anything but fearsome. The fairways here are lined with fir-trees, which call for accuracy and do not leave the room for error you find on real links courses. The layout is moderate in length and difficulties are evenly spread around the course. A pleasant course for all the family.

Ostschweizerischer Golf Club
CH - 9246 NIEDERBÜREN

Office	Sekretariat	(41) 071 - 422 18 56
Pro shop	Pro shop	(41) 071 - 422 18 56
Fax	Fax	(41) 071 - 422 18 25
Situation	Lage	

16 km von St-Gallen, 71 917 Ew.
48 km von Winterthur, 88 812 Ew.

Annual closure	Jährliche Schliessung	ja
		1/12→1/03/99
Weekly closure	Wöchentliche Schliessung	
		Montag, das Restaurant

Fees main season
Preisliste hochsaison den ganzen Tag

	Week days Woche	We/Bank holidays We/Feiertag
Individual Individuell	80 CHF	100 CHF
Couple Ehepaar	160 CHF	200 CHF

Caddy	Caddy	nein
Electric Trolley	Elektrokarren	25 CHF/Tag
Buggy	Elektrischer Wagen	nein
Clubs	Clubs	20 CHF/18 Löcher
Credit cards Kreditkarten		nein

Access Zufahrt : Autobahn 1 → St Gallen, →
Uzwil/Oberbüren, → Niederbüren, → Golf
Map 1 on page 983 Karte 1 Seite 983

GOLF COURSE
PERCORSO
13/20

Site	Lage	▆▆▆▆▆▁
Maintenance	Instandhaltung	▆▆▆▆▁▁
Architect	Architekt	Donald Harradine
Type	Typ	Land
Relief	Relief	▆▁▁▁▁▁
Water in play	Platz mit Wasser	▆▆▆▁▁▁
Exp. to wind	Wind ausgesetzt	▆▆▆▁▁▁
Trees in play	Platz mit Bäumen	▆▆▆▆▁▁

Scorecard Scorekarte	Chp. Chp.	Mens Herren	Ladies Damen
Length Länge	6096	5698	5040
Par	72	72	72

		0 12 24 36
Advised golfing ability		
Empfohlene Spielstärke		▭▬▬▭
Hcp required	Min. Handicap	30

CLUB HOUSE & AMENITIES
CLUB HOUSE E SERVIZI
7/10

Pro shop	Pro shop	▆▆▆▆▁▁
Driving range	Übungsplatz	▆▆▆▆▁▁
Sheltered	überdacht	6 Plätze
On grass	auf Rasen	ja
Putting-green	Putting-grün	ja
Pitching-green	Pitching-grün	ja

HOTEL FACILITIES
ALBERGHI
7/10

HOTELS HOTELS
Alte Herberge — Niederbüren
2 Zimmer, D 75 CHF, Tel (41) 071 - 422 20 91 — 1 km

Hotel Uzwil — Uzwil
38 Zimmer, D 80 CHF — 10 km
Tel (41) 071 - 955 70 70, Fax (41) 071 - 955 35 55

Hotel Sonne — Gossau
8 Zimmer, D 140 CHF — 12 km
Tel (41) 071 - 385 16 51, Fax (41) 071 - 385 90 22

RESTAURANTS RESTAURANT
Linde — Bischofszell
Tel (41) 071 - 422 16 10 — 6 km

Alte Herberge — Niederbüren
Tel (41) 071 - 422 20 91 — 1 km

1001

Sulle rive dello splendido Lago Maggiore, una delle più belle villeggiature della Svizzera, dove il Patriziale aggiunge un'attrazione supplementare alla regione in quanto pianeggiante, e senza trappole. I molti alberi danno in estate un ombra benvenuta, senza che il sottobosco ne sia penalizzato. Lo si puo considerare come un'agreabile percorso di vacanze in famiglia, ma anche come testo di buona fattura, dove i giocatori precisi e regolari, saranno a loro agio, dovranno pero, impiegare tutte le risorse del piccolo gioco, in quanto i green non sono molto grandi ma ben difesi, e sovente in altezza. Il piacere del clima, la natura del terreno, permettono di giocare una gran parte dell'anno, ció che non é freguente in Svizzera.

Alongside the beautiful Lake Maggiore, one of the prettiest Swiss holiday sites, the "Patriziale" adds extra charm to the region, all the more so in that the course is flat with no hidden traps. The very many trees bring welcome shade in summer, and the undergrowth is never too penalising. This is what might be considered to be a very pleasant holiday course, for playing with all the family with little at stake, but also a cleverly worked out test of golf where straight and consistent players will feel at home. They will, nonetheless, need a finely tuned short game, because the greens are not enormous, are well-defended and often come with several tiers. The pleasant climate and the nature of the terrain mean being able to play here most of the year, a feature that is not all that common in Switzerland.

Golf Club Patriziale Ascona
Via al Lido 81
CH - 6612 ASCONA

Office	Segreteria	(41) 091 - 791 21 32
Pro shop	Pro shop	(41) 091 - 791 14 36
Fax	Fax	(41) 091 - 791 07 96
Situation	Localita'	

3 km Locarno, 13 796 ab.

Annual closure	Chiusura annuale	no
Weekly closure	Chiusura settimanale	no

Fees main season
Tariffe alta stagione il percorso

	Week days Settimana	We/Bank holidays Feriale/Festivo
Individual Individuale	80 CHF	80 CHF
Couple Coppia	160 CHF	160 CHF

Caddy	Caddy	no
Electric Trolley	Carello elettrico	20 CHF/la giornata
Buggy	Car	no
Clubs	Bastoni	20 CHF/la giornata

Credit cards Carte di credito — no

Access Itinerario : Locarno → Ascona, → Via Lido, Golf
Map 1 on page 983 Carta 1 Pagina 983

GOLF COURSE
PERCORSO — 15/20

Site	Paesaggio	
Maintenance	Manutenzione	
Architect	Architetto	C.K. Cotton
Type	Tipologia	parco
Relief	Relievo terreno	
Water in play	Acqua in gioco	
Exp. to wind	Esposto al vento	
Trees in play	Alberi in gioco	

Scorecard Carta-score	Chp. Camp.	Mens Uomini	Ladies Donne
Length Lunghezza	5948	5948	5268
Par	71	71	71

Advised golfing ability — 0 12 24 36
Livello di gioco consigliato
Hcp required — Handicap richiesto 30

CLUB HOUSE & AMENITIES
CLUB HOUSE E SERVIZI — 7/10

Pro shop	Pro shop	
Driving range	Campo pratica	
Sheltered	coperto	40 posti
On grass	in erba	si
Putting-green	Putting-green	si
Pitching-green	Green-pratica	si

HOTEL FACILITIES
ALBERGHI — 7/10

HOTELS ALBERGHI
Casa Berno — Ascona
60 camere, D 368 CHF
Tel (41) 091 - 791 32 32, Fax (41) 091 - 792 11 14

Castello del Sole — Ascona
85 camere, D 450 CHF
Tel (41) 091 - 791 02 02, Fax (41) 091 - 791 11 18

Castello — Ascona
45 camere, D 350 CHF
Tel (41) 091 - 791 01 61, Fax (41) 091 - 791 18 04

RESTAURANTS RISTORANTE
Ascolago — Ascona
Tel (41) 091 - 791 20 55

Osteria Giardino — Ascona
Tel(41) 091 - 791 01 01

1002

Die Lage des Platzes auf einem schmalen Terrain entlang des Flüsschens Krebs erklärt die zahlreichen aber nicht allzu spielbestimmenden Out of bounds und auch den feuchten Torfboden. Von der hintersten Abschlägen gespielt, ist der Platz recht lang. Bäume, Bunkers und zahlreiche Wasserflächen scheuen entwichene Bälle nicht und machen die Aufgaben heikel. Die Strategie ist auf jedem Hole wichtig und macht das Spiel vielfältig und interessant. Auch ohne golfarchitektonische Sonderleistungen ist Schönenberg eine ausserordentliche Anlage und dank geschützten Zonen ein gutes Beispiel für das Nebeneinander von Golf und Natur.

A lay-out on a narrow strip of terrain along the river Krebs explains both the many out-of bounds (although not too many in play) and the wetness of the soil, which is basically peat. Reasonable from the normal tees, it gets much longer from the back-tees, especially since the bunkers and many water hazards easily collect balls hit off-target. Each hole requires a definite strategy, but this and especially the variety of holes make it a pleasant course to play. Without displaying any exceptional imagination on the part of the architect, Schönenberg is a very attractive course and again shows a good example of ecology and golf living easily side by side (several areas are natural trust land). This is always a thorny problem in Switzerland.

Golf & Country Club Schönenberg
CH - 8824 SCHÖNENBERG

Office	Sekretariat	(41) 01 - 788 90 40
Pro shop	Pro shop	(41) 01 - 788 90 55
Fax	Fax	(41) 01 - 788 90 45
Situation	Lage	

25 km Zürich, 365 043 Ew.

Annual closure	Jährliche Schliessung	ja
		15/11→20/03
Weekly closure	Wöchentliche Schliessung	nein

Fees main season
Preisliste hochsaison 18 Löcher

	Week days Woche	We/Bank holidays We/Feiertag
Individual Individuell	90 CHF	90 CHF
Couple Ehepaar	180 CHF	180 CHF

Caddy	Caddy	nein
Electric Trolley	Elektrokarren	27 CHF/18 Löcher
Buggy	Elektrischer Wagen	nein
Clubs	Clubs	ja

Credit cards Kreditkarten   nein

Access Zufahrt : Autobahn Zürich-Chur → Horgen oder Wädenswil, → Zug, Hirsel → Schönenberg, Golf 1,5 km. **Map 1 on page 983** Karte 1 Seite 983

GOLF COURSE
PLATZ   **14**/20

Site	Lage	
Maintenance	Instandhaltung	
Architect	Architekt	Donald Harradine
Type	Typ	Land
Relief	Relief	
Water in play	Platz mit Wasser	
Exp. to wind	Wind ausgesetzt	
Trees in play	Platz mit Bäumen	

Scorecard Scorekarte	Chp. Chp.	Mens Herren	Ladies Damen
Length Länge	6135	5672	4864
Par	72	72	72

Advised golfing ability Empfohlene Spielstärke	0	12	24	36
Hcp required Min. Handicap	30			

CLUB HOUSE & AMENITIES
KLUBHAUS UND NEBENGEBÄUDE   **7**/10

Pro shop	Pro shop	
Driving range	Übungsplatz	
Sheltered	überdacht	4 Plätze
On grass	auf Rasen	ja (04 - 10)
Putting-green	Putting-grün	ja
Pitching-green	Pitching-grün	ja

1003

HOTEL FACILITIES
HOTEL BESCHREIBUNG   **6**/10

HOTELS HOTELS

Post   Biberbrugg
13 Zimmer, D 120 CHF   15 km
Tel (41) 055 - 412 27 71
Fax (41) 055 - 412 70 72

Seehotel Meierhof   Horgen
113 Zimmer, D 200 CHF   5 km
Tel (41) 01 - 725 29 61
Fax (41) 01 - 725 55 23

RESTAURANTS RESTAURANT

Golf & Country Club   Schönenberg
Tel (41) 01 - 788 15 74

Eichmühle   Wädenswil
Tel (41) 01 - 780 34 44

13 6 6

Bedingt durch seine Länge und Wasserhindernisse auf sechs Holes ist dieser Platz vor allem von den hinteren Abschlägen schwierig zu meistern. Dies um so mehr, weil Steine und schlechtes Gras in den Roughs bei unserem Besuch dem Gesamtzustand noch abträglich waren. Die Anlage ist aber jung und muss noch bearbeitet werden. Die Umgebung am Ufer der Aare ist nicht von überragender Schönheit, bietet aber einige schöne Blicke auf den Jura. Architektonisch wurde gut gearbeitet, aber die geniale Gestaltung blieb aus. Der Ball kann meist rollender-weise auf die Greens gebracht werden, was Spieler beruhigt, die sich von den Wassergefahren beeindrucken lassen. Der Platz versteckt seine golferischen Tücken kaum und kann mit gesundem Selbstvertrauen angegangen werden. Auch schon beim erstem Mal.

Judging by length and the number of water hazards (on 6 holes), this is a tough course to play from the back-tees, especially since the state of upkeep was pretty rough when we visited, notably because of the stones and weeds in the rough. But this is a young course and further work is still needed. On the banks of the Aar, the setting is hardly outstanding, despite a few pleasant views over the Jura mountains. The architecture has been given careful thought, but without any special flair for landscaping. Most of the time, players can chip the ball onto the green, which will reassure lesser players who are already under stress from the water hazards. At least the course does not have too many hidden traps, meaning that golfers can play here confidently, even the first time out.

Golf Club Wylihof
CH - 4708 LUTERBACH

Office	Sekretariat	(41) 032 - 882 28 28
Pro shop	Pro shop	(41) 032 - 882 28 28
Fax	Fax	(41) 032 - 882 28 24
Situation	Lage	

8 km Solothurn, 15 748 Ew.

Annual closure	Jährliche Schliessung	nein
Weekly closure	Wöchentliche Schliessung	nein
	Restaurant (im Winter)	

Fees main season
Preisliste hochsaison 18 Löcher

	Week days Woche	We/Bank holidays We/Feiertag
Individual Individuell	90 CHF	90 CHF
Couple Ehepaar	180 CHF	180 CHF

Caddy	Caddy	nein
Electric Trolley	Elektrokarren	ja
Buggy	Elektrischer Wagen	80 CHF/18 Löcher
Clubs	Clubs	nein

Credit cards Kreditkarten
VISA - Eurocard - MasterCard

1004

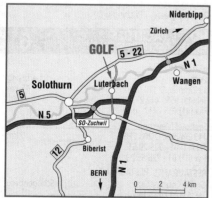

Access Zufahrt : Autobahn N1→ Wangen/Aar, →
Solothurn, → Koppingen, Aarbrücke, links → Golf
Map 1 on page 982 Karte 1 Seite 982

GOLF COURSE
PLATZ
13/20

Site	Lage	■■■□□□
Maintenance	Instandhaltung	■■■□□□
Architect	Architekt	Ruzzo Reuss
Type	Typ	Fachland
Relief	Relief	□□□□□
Water in play	Platz mit Wasser	■■■□□
Exp. to wind	Wind ausgesetzt	■■□□□
Trees in play	Platz mit Bäumen	■■■■□

Scorecard Scorekarte	Chp. Chp.	Mens Herren	Ladies Damen
Length Länge	6581	6105	5274
Par	73	73	73

Advised golfing ability		0 12 24 36
Empfohlene Spielstärke		■■■■
Hcp required	Min. Handicap	30

CLUB HOUSE & AMENITIES
KLUBHAUS UND NEBENGEBÄUDE
6/10

Pro shop	Pro shop	■■■□□
Driving range	Übungsplatz	■■■□□
Sheltered	überdacht	16 Plätze
On grass	auf Rasen	ja
Putting-green	Putting-grün	ja
Pitching-green	Pitching-grün	ja

HOTEL FACILITIES
HOTEL BESCHREIBUNG
6/10

HOTELS HOTELS

Krone — Solothurn 10 km
42 Zimmer, D 195 CHF
Tel (41) 032 - 622 44 12
Fax (41) 032 - 622 37 24

Astoria — Solothurn 10 km
40 Zimmer, D 130 CHF
Tel (41) 032 - 622 75 71
Fax (41) 032 - 623 68 57

RESTAURANTS RESTAURANT

Zunfthaus zu Wirthen — Solothurn 10 km
Tel (41) 032 - 623 33 44

Chutz — Langendorf 8 km
Tel (41) 032 - 622 34 71

Die ersten neun Loch in Zumikon sind recht flach, aber sehr lang. Der Weg zurück ist mit einigen Schräglagen und Hängen wesentlich coupierter und kann Senioren Mühe bereiten. Dieser Nachteil wird aber durch kürzere Spielbahnen kompensiert. Die gut plazierten Hindernisse stören vor allem gute Golfer, beeinflussen aber das Spiel höherer Handicaps wenig. Zumikon ist ein guter Test des golferischen Könnens, lässt aber in seinem durchschnittlichen Design das gewisse Etwas an Originalität und den perfekten Unterhalt der Greens vermissen. Trotzdem langweilt sich hier niemand, und das ist für Golfer jedes Handicaps ein wichtiger Punkt.

The front nine at Zumikon are pretty flat but very long. The back nine are much hillier with a number of dangerous slopes in all directions, often a problem for senior players but one that is offset by the shorter length of holes. The hazards are generally well sited and tend to bother the better players more than the rest. Reassuring for the latter, at least. Zumikon is a very honourable test of golf, but we were sorry to see a little lack of originality and stamina in a very reasonable layout, and greens in a fair condition only, still putting this course a little way behind the best courses in Switzerland. However, there is never a dull moment here, and golfers of all levels will appreciate that.

Golf & Country Club Zurich
CH - 8126 ZUMIKON

Office	Sekretariat	(41) 01 - 918 00 50
Pro shop	Pro shop	(41) 01 - 918 00 52
Fax	Fax	(41) 01 - 918 00 39
Situation	Lage	

Situation Lage
7 km Zurich, 365 043 Ew.

Annual closure	Jährliche Schliessung	ja
		31/10→1/04/99
Weekly closure	Wöchentliche Schliessung	nein
	Montag, das Restaurant	

Fees main season
Preisliste hochsaison 18 Löcher

	Week days Woche	We/Bank holidays We/Feiertag
Individual Individuell	100 CHF	
Couple Ehepaar	200 CHF	

Caddy	Caddy	auf Reservierung
Electric Trolley	Elektrokarren	20 CHF/18 Löcher
Buggy	Elektrischer Wagen	nein
Clubs	Clubs	20 CHF/Tag
Credit cards Kreditkarten		nein

ZÜRICH
GOLF
Dübendorf
N1
Zollikon
ZUMIKON
Küsnacht Foch
Wädenswil
Zug
N3
ZÜRICHSEE
17
0   2   4 km

Access Zufahrt : Zürich → Forch, Zumikon → Dorfplatz → Strubenacher Strasse
Map 1 on page 983 Karte 1 Seite 983

GOLF COURSE
PLATZ
15/20

Site	Lage	▰▰▰▰▱
Maintenance	Instandhaltung	▰▰▰▰▱
Architect	Architekt	Donald Harradine
Type	Typ	Park
Relief	Relief	▰▰▱▱▱
Water in play	Platz mit Wasser	▰▰▰▱▱
Exp. to wind	Wind ausgesetzt	▰▰▱▱▱
Trees in play	Platz mit Bäumen	▰▰▰▰▱

Scorecard Scorekarte	Chp. Chp.	Mens Herren	Ladies Damen
Length Länge	6360	5860	5155
Par	72	72	72

Advised golfing ability Empfohlene Spielstärke	0 12 24 36
Hcp required Min. Handicap	30

CLUB HOUSE & AMENITIES
KLUBHAUS UND NEBENGEBÄUDE
7/10

Pro shop	Pro shop	▰▰▰▰▱
Driving range	Übungsplatz	▰▰▰▱▱
Sheltered	überdacht	4 Plätze
On grass	auf Rasen	ja
Putting-green	Putting-grün	ja
Pitching-green	Pitching-grün	ja

1005

HOTEL FACILITIES
HOTEL BESCHREIBUNG
6/10

HOTELS HOTELS

Wassberg		Forch
17 Zimmer, D 240 CHF		6 km
Tel (41) 01 - 980 43 00		
Fax (41) 01 - 980 43 03		
Ermitage am See		Küsnacht
26 Zimmer, D 244 CHF		5 km
Tel (41) 01 - 910 52 22		
Fax (41) 01 - 910 52 44		

RESTAURANTS RESTAURANT

Golf & Country Club	Zumikon
Tel (41) 01 - 918 00 51	
Petersmann's Kunststuben	Küsnacht
Tel (41) 01 - 910 07 15	2 km

EXCHANGE CROSS RATES
TABLEAU DE CHANGE DES MONNAIES
CAMBIO DE DIVISAS

	BF	DKr	F	DM	IR£	L	Fl
Belgium (BF)	100	18.46	16.24	4.843	1.948	4778	5.459
Denmark (DKr)	54.17	10	8.800	2.624	1.055	2588	2.957
France (F)	61.56	11.36	10	2.982	1.199	2941	3.361
Germany (DM)	20.65	3.811	3.354	1	0.402	986.5	1.127
Ireland (IR£)	51.35	9.478	8.341	2.487	1	2453	2.803
Italy (L)	2.093	0.386	0.340	0.101	0.041	100.	0.114
Netherlands (Fl)	18.32	3.382	2.976	0.887	0.357	875.2	1
Norway (NKr)	49.37	9.114	8.020	2.391	0.962	2359	2.695
Portugal (Esc)	20.17	3.724	3.277	0.977	0.393	963.8	1.101
Spain (Pts)	24.37	4.798	3.958	1.180	0.475	1164	1.330
Sweden (SKr)	46.37	8.559	7.532	2.246	0.903	2215	2.531
Switzerland (CHF)	25.59	4.723	4.156	1.239	0.498	1222	1.397
Un. Kingdom (£)	61.04	11.27	9.915	2.956	1.189	2916	3.332
Canada (C$)	26.09	4.817	4.238	1.264	0.508	1247	1.424
United States ($)	37.14	6.856	6.033	1.799	0.723	1774	2.027
Japan (¥)	29.03	5.359	4.716	1.406	0.565	1387	1.585

1006

Danish Kroner, French Franc, Norwegian Kroner and Swedish Kroner x 10.
Belgian Franc, Yen, Escudo, Lira and Peseta x 100.

Source: Financial Times, February 24, 1998

TABELLE FÜR DIE WÄHRUNGSUMRECHNUNG
TABEL VAN WISSELKOERSEN
QUADRO PARA CAMBIO DE MONEDAS

NKr	Esc	Pts	SKr	CHF	£	C$	$	¥
20.25	495.7	410.4	21.57	3.908	1.638	3.833	2.693	344.5
10.97	268.5	222.3	11.68	2.117	0.888	2.076	1.459	186.6
12.47	305.2	252.6	13.28	2.406	1.009	2.359	1.658	212.1
4.182	102.4	84.73	4.453	0.807	0.338	0.791	0.556	71.13
10.40	254.5	210.7	11.07	2.007	0.841	1.968	1.383	176.9
0.424	10.38	8.589	0.451	0.082	0.034	0.080	0.056	7.210
3.710	90.81	75.18	3.951	0.716	0.300	0.702	0.493	63.11
10	244.7	202.6	10.65	1.930	0.809	1.892	1.329	170.1
4.086	100.	82.78	4.351	0.788	0.331	0.773	0.543	69.49
4.935	120.8	100.	5.255	0.952	0.399	0.934	0.656	83.94
9.391	229.8	190.3	10	1.812	0.760	1.777	1.248	159.7
5.183	126.8	105.0	5.519	1	0.419	0.981	0.689	88.14
12.36	302.6	250.5	13.16	2.385	1	2.339	1.643	210.3
5.285	129.3	107.1	5.627	1.020	0.428	1	0.703	89.88
7.522	184.1	152.4	8.010	1.452	0.609	1.423	1	127.9
5.880	143.9	119.1	6.261	1.135	0.476	1.113	0.782	100.

1007

L'ÉNERGIE DE L'INFORMATION

TECHNIQUES GRAPHIQUES

Berger-Levrault Graphique • ZI de la Croix-de-Metz • ROUTE DE VILLEY-SAINT-ÉTIENNE • 54200 TOUL

Bureaux commerciaux • 34, AVENUE DU ROULE • 92200 NEUILLY-SUR-SEINE

Téléphone • 01.47.22.25.00

ALPHABETIC ORDER
AND CLOSEST AIRPORTS
CLASSEMENT ALPHABÉTIQUE
ET AÉROPORTS
CLASIFICACION ALFABETICA
Y AEROPUERTOS
ALPHABETISCHE EINTEILUNG
UND FLUGHAFEN

GOLF COURSE PARCOURS RECORRIDOS GOLFPLATZ	CLASSIFICATIONS CLASSEMENT LAS CLASIFICACIONES EINTEILUNGEN				PAGE PAGE PÁGINA ZEITE
Abenberg	14	7	6	Nürnberg, 30 km	312
Aberdovey	17	7	7	Cardiff, 140 km	677
Ableiges *Les Etangs*	15	6	4	Charles-de-Gaulle, 48 km	148
Aboyne	14	6	6	Aberdeen, 45 km	586
Adare	15	6	7	Shannon, 20 km	704
Ailette (L')	15	6	5	Charles-de-Gaulle, 109 km	149
Aisses (Les) *Rouge/Blanc*	16	5	4	Orly, 145 km	150
Aix-les-Bains	13	5	7	Chambéry, 13 km	151
Albi	15	6	6	Albi, 4 km - Toulouse, 65 km	152
Alcaidesa	14	6	5	Gibraltar, 10 km	892
Aldeburgh	13	6	7	Stansted, 140 km	439
Alhaurin	14	7	5	Malaga, 30 km	893
Alloa	15	7	6	Edinburgh, 50 km	587
Almerimar	14	6	6	Almería, 48 km	894
Aloha	17	7	7	Malaga, 60 km	895
Alwoodley (The)	18	7	7	Leeds, 7 km	440
Alyth	14	6	6	Edinburgh, 96 km	588
Amirauté (L')	15	7	8	Charles-de-Gaulle, 200 km	153
Amnéville	13	6	5	Metz-Nancy, 35 km	154
Amsterdam	15	7	7	Amsterdam Schiphol, 10 km	800
Anderstein	14	7	6	Amsterdam-Schiphol, 60 km	801
Anjou-Champigné	13	6	6	Nantes-Atlantique, 123 km	155
Annonay-Gourdan	13	6	5	Lyon-Satolas, 90 km	156
Antwerp	16	7	7	Antwerpen, 15 km	76
Apremont	15	8	6	Charles de Gaulle, 34 km	157
Arcachon	13	6	6	Bordeaux, 66 km	158
Arcangues	14	7	8	Biarritz-Parme, 3 km	159
Ardglass	14	6	4	Belfast, 65 km	776
Aroeira	15	6	6	Lisboa, 11 km	840
Ashburnham	17	6	5	Cardiff, 90 km	678
Ashridge	16	7	6	Heathrow, 48 km	441
Atalaya *Old Course*	13	6	7	Malaga, 75 km.	896
Athlone	13	6	6	Dublin, 125 km	705
Augerville	13	5	4	Orly, 70 km	160
Augsburg	15	7	7	München, 90 km	313

Ayr (Belleisle)	16	5	7	Glasgow, 55 km	589
Baberton	14	6	8	Edinburgh, 8 km	590
Bad Griesbach *Brunnwies*	17	9	9	München, 180 km	314
Bad Griesbach-Sagmühle *Sagmühle*	15	9	9	München, 180 km	315
Bad Liebenzell	14	7	7	Stuttgart, 40 km	316
Bad Ragaz	13	7	6	Zürich-Kloten, 100 km	986
Bad Wörishofen	14	6	6	München, 120 km	317
Baden	15	6	5	Lorient, 45 km	161
Badgemore Park	14	7	7	Heathrow, 48 km	442
Bâle-Hagenthal	15	7	7	Bâle-Mulhouse, 8 km	162
Ballater	15	6	7	Dyce, 35 km	591
Ballybunion *Cashen (New Course)*	16	7	7	Shannon, 88 km	706
Ballybunion *Old Course*	19	7	7	Shannon, 88 km	707
Ballykisteen	14	7	6	Shannon, 50 km / Cork, 90 km	708
Ballyliffin *Glashedy Links*	17	6	5	Belfast, 160 km	709
Ballyliffin *Old Course*	15	6	5	Belfast, 160 km	710
Bamberg	15	7	7	Nürnberg, 40 km	318
Bangor	14	6	6	Belfast, 40 km	777
Barbaroux	17	7	6	Toulon-Hyères, 51 km	163
Bath	16	6	9	Bristol, 20 km	443
Batouwe	15	7	3	Amsterdam Schiphol, 80 km	802
Baule (La) *Rouge*	15	7	8	Nantes, 60 km	164
Beau Desert	16	7	7	Birmingham, 30 km	444
Beaufort	14	6	7	Cork, 85 km	711
Belle-Dune	16	6	5	Le Touquet, 25 km	165
Belvoir Park	15	5	6	Belfast, 12 km	778
Bendinat	13	6	7	Palma, 15 km	897
Bercuit	13	7	7	Bruxelles (Brussel), 30 km	77
Berkhamsted	16	7	6	Heathrow, 48 km	445
Berkshire (The) *Blue Course*	17	8	7	Heathrow, 25 km	446
Berkshire (The) *Red Course*	17	8	7	Heathrow, 25 km	447
Berlin-Wannsee	15	6	8	Berlin, 18 km	319
Berwick-upon-Tweed	15	6	5	Newcastle, 60 km	448
Besançon	13	7	5	Bâle-Mulhouse, 170 km	166
Béthemont	14	7	5	Charles-de-Gaulle, 55 km	167
Beuerberg	17	7	6	München, 80 km	320
Biarritz-le-Phare	14	6	8	Biarritz-Parme, 3 km	168
Bitche	14	6	5	Strasbourg, 80 km	169
Blackmoor	17	6	5	Heathrow, 65 km	449
Blainroe	13	6	6	Dublin, 65 km	712
Blairgowrie *Lansdowne*	15	8	6	Edinburgh, 90 km	592
Blairgowrie *Rosemount*	18	8	6	Edinburgh, 90 km	593
Blumisberg	15	7	6	Genève, 135 km, Zürich, 156 km	987
Boat of Garten	14	6	7	Inverness, 45 km	594
Bodensee-Weissensberg	17	7	7	Zürich, 130 km / München, 180 km	321
Bolton Old Links	15	5	7	Manchester, 25 km	450
Bonalba	14	6	6	Alicante, 15 km	898
Bondues *Blanc*	16	7	6	Lille-Lesquin, 20 km	170
Bondues *Jaune*	15	7	6	Lille-Lesquin, 20 km	171
Bonmont	16	7	6	Barcelona, 140 km	899
Bordes (Les)	19	8	6	Orly, 130 km	172
Bowood (Cornwall)	16	7	6	Plymouth, 65 km	451
Bowood G&CC	17	6	6	Bristol, 50 km	452
Brampton	17	7	6	Glasgow, 160 km	453

1010

Brancepeth Castle	14	6	5	Newcastle, 20 km	454
Braunschweig	17	6	7	Hannover, 75 km	322
Breitenloo	13	7	6	Zürich-Kloten, 8 km	988
Bresse (La)	15	6	4	Lyon, 62 km	173
Brest Iroise	14	7	6	Brest, 20 km	174
Bretesche (La)	15	7	7	Nantes, 61 km	175
Brigode	14	7	6	Lille, 15 km	176
Broadstone	17	7	7	Bournemouth, 17 km	455
Broekpolder	15	7	6	Rotterdam, 15 km	803
Brora	15	7	7	Inverness, 92 km	595
Bruntsfield	15	8	9	Edinburgh, 10 km	596
Buchanan Castle	14	6	6	Glasgow, 33 km	597
Buckinghamshire (The)	17	8	7	Heathrow, 16 km	456
Bundoran	13	6	7	Sligo, 45 km/Belfast, 176 km	713
Burnham & Berrow	18	7	6	Bristol, 38 km	457
Buxtehude	15	7	6	Hamburg, 60 km	323
Cairndhu	13	6	5	Belfast, 40 km	779
Campoamor	14	6	6	Alicante, 50 km	900
Cannes Mandelieu Old Course	13	7	8	Nice, 38 km	177
Cannes-Mougins	15	7	8	Nice, 18 km	178
Canyamel	15	6	6	Palma, 68 km	901
Cap d'Agde	15	6	5	Béziers, 25 km	179
Capdepera	15	7	6	Palma, 62 km	902
Carden Park	14	8	8	Manchester, 50 km	458
Carlisle	17	7	7	Glasgow, 160 km	459
Carlow	16	6	6	Dublin, 100 km	714
Carn	16	5	3	Sligo, 115 km	715
Carnoustie Burnside	14	3	4	Edinburgh, 100 km	598
Carnoustie Championship	19	3	4	Edinburgh, 100 km	599
Casteljaloux	15	6	5	Agen, 70 km	180
Castillo de Gorraiz	17	7	7	Pamplona, 8 km	903
Castle Hume	13	7	6	Belfast, 100 km	780
Castlerock	16	6	6	Belfast, 80 km	781
Castletown	18	6	8	Ronaldsway, 4 km	460
Celtic Manor Roman Road	18	9	7	Cardiff, 30 km	679
Cély	15	7	6	Orly, 40 km	181
Cerdaña	14	7	7	Barcelona, 150 km	904
Chailly (Château de)	14	8	6	Dijon-Bourgogne, 66 km	182
Chamonix	15	6	7	Genève-Cointrin, 80 km	183
Champ de Bataille	14	6	3	Charles-de-Gaulle, 145 km	184
Chantaco	14	7	7	Biarritz-Parme, 15 km	185
Chantilly Vineuil	18	7	6	Charles-de-Gaulle, 21 km	186
Charleville	13	4	6	Cork, 60 km	716
Charmeil	16	6	6	Grenoble, 15 km	187
Chart Hills	18	8	6	Gatwick, 50 km	461
Cheverny	14	7	6	Tours-Saint-Symphorien, 70 km	188
Chiberta	16	6	8	Biarritz-Parme, 5 km	189
Clandeboye Dufferin Course	15	6	6	Belfast, 35 km	782
Clitheroe	17	7	7	Manchester, 60 km	462
Club d'Aro (Mas Nou)	15	7	7	Girona, 40 km	905
Club de Campo	16	8	8	Madrid, 20 km	906
Club zur Vahr (Garlstedt)	18	6	5	Bremen, 30 km	324
Cognac	13	7	5	Angoulème, 44 km	190
Collingtree Park	14	8	7	Luton, 45 km	463

Connemara	14	6	6	Galway, 100 km	717
Conwy	17	7	8	Manchester, 120 km	680
Cork GC	15	3	5	Cork, 10 km	718
Costa Brava	13	7	7	Barcelona, 100 km	907
Costa Dorada	13	6	6	Barcelona, 100 km	908
Côte d'Argent (La)	17	6	5	Biarritz-Parme, 50 km	191
County Louth	18	5	6	Dublin, 36 km	719
County Sligo	17	4	3	Sligo, 15 km	720
County Tipperary	15	7	5	Cork, 90 km / Dublin, 156 km	721
Courson Lilas/Orange	15	7	3	Orly, 20 km	192
Courson Vert/Noir	16	7	3	Orly, 20 km	193
Coxmoor	15	6	6	East Midlands, 40 km	464
Crail	15	6	6	Edinburgh, 85 km	600
Crans-sur-Sierre	14	7	8	Sion, 25 km - Genève, 200 km	989
Crieff Ferntower Course	15	7	7	Edinburgh, 70 km	601
Cromstrijen	16	8	5	Rotterdam, 35 km	804
Cruden Bay	18	7	6	Aberdeen, 38 km	602
Cumberwell Park	17	7	7	Bristol, 40 km	465
Dalmahoy East Course	17	8	8	Edinburgh, 5 km	603
Dartmouth	16	9	6	Plymouth, 60 km	466
De Pan	16	8	7	Amsterdam, 65 km	805
Delamere Forest	15	6	7	Manchester, 40 km	467
Denham	15	7	7	Heathrow, 16 km	468
Dieppe-Pourville	14	6	5	Charles-de-Gaulle, 175 km	194
Dinard	14	6	7	Rennes 75 km, Dinard 6 km	195
Dingle (Ceann Sibeal)	16	6	4	Cork, 160 km	722
Disneyland Paris Never Land + Wonderland	16	7	8	Orly, 40 km - Charles-de-Gaulle, 28 km	196
Divonne	14	6	7	Genève-Cointrin, 15 km	197
Domaine Impérial	18	8	6	Genève-Cointrin, 25 km	990
Domont-Montmorency	13	7	4	Charles-de-Gaulle, 20 km	198
Donegal (Murvagh)	16	2	6	Belfast, 160 km / Sligo, 45 km	723
Dooks	15	5	5	Cork, 115 km	724
Downfield	17	6	7	Edinburgh, 80 km	604
Dromoland Castle	14	7	7	Shannon, 15 km	725
Druids Glen	16	9	7	Dublin, 40 km	726
Duddingston	15	7	9	Edinburgh, 12 km	605
Duff House Royal	15	6	6	Aberdeen, 75 km	606
Duke's Course St Andrews	16	7	8	Edinburgh, 80 km	607
Dumfries & County	15	7	5	Edinburgh/Glasgow, 115 km	608
Dunbar	16	5	6	Edinburgh, 48 km	609
Dundalk	15	6	6	Dublin, 80 km	727
Dunfermline	15	7	7	Edinburgh, 25 km	610
Düsseldorf/Hösel	13	6	6	Düsseldorf, 12 km	325
Düsseldorfer	13	7	7	Düsseldorf, 8 km	326
East Renfrewshire	15	6	8	Glasgow, 20 km	611
East Sussex National East Course	17	8	7	Gatwick, 35 km	469
Edzell	14	6	3	Aberdeen, 60 km	612
Efteling	16	8	5	Eindhoven, 40 km	806
Eindhoven	18	8	6	Eindhoven, 12 km	807
El Bosque	16	7	4	Valencia, 5 km	909
El Paraiso	13	6	6	Malaga, 70 km.	910
El Prat Amarillo	15	7	6	Barcelona, 7 km	911
El Prat Verde	17	7	6	Barcelona, 7 km	912
El Saler	18	7	6	Valencia, 16 km	913

1012

Elfrather Mühle	14	7	7	Düsseldorf, 30 km	327
Elgin	15	7	6	Aberdeen, 100 km	613
Elie	15	6	6	Edinburgh, 80 km	614
Emporda	17	7	6	Barcelona 120 km - Perpignan, 90 km	914
Engadin	15	6	6	Zürich, 225 km	991
Ennetsee-Holzhäusern	13	7	6	Zürich-Kloten, 45 km	992
Enniscrone	16	7	6	Sligo, 55 km	728
Eschenried	14	7	7	München, 35 km	328
Escorpion	13	8	4	Valencia-Manises, 10 km	915
Esery	15	7	5	Genève-Cointrin,16 km	199
Estepona	14	7	6	Gibraltar, 40 km	916
Estérel Latitudes	16	6	7	Nice, 60 km	200
Estoril	13	7	7	Lisboa, 25 km	841
Etiolles Les Cerfs	15	6	5	Orly, 15 km	201
Etretat	14	6	5	Le Havre-Octeville, 20 km	202
European (The)	18	6	6	Dublin, 90 km	729
Evian	15	7	9	Genève-Cointrin, 52 km	203
Fairhaven	17	7	8	Manchester, 100 km	470
Faithlegg	13	7	6	Cork, 135 km	730
Falkenstein	18	6	7	Hamburg, 30 km	329
Falnuee	14	7	4	Charleroi, 25 km	78
Feldafing	18	7	6	München, 80 km	330
Felixstowe Ferry Martello Course	15	6	6	Stansted, 120 km	471
Ferndown Old Course	17	7	7	Bournemouth, 7 km	472
Feucherolles	15	7	5	Orly, 30 km	204
Fontainebleau	17	7	7	Orly, 40 km	205
Fontanals	18	6	5	Perpignan, 110 km	917
Fontcaude	14	6	6	Montpellier- Fréjorgues, 15 km	206
Fontenailles Blanc	14	7	6	Orly, 55 km	207
Fontenelles (Les)	14	7	4	Nantes, 70 km	208
Forest of Arden Arden Course	14	8	8	Birmingham, 6 km	473
Forest Pines Forest + Pines	17	6	7	Humberside, 35 km	474
Forfar	14	6	6	Edinburgh, 120 km	615
Formby	18	7	7	Manchester, 80 km	475
Formby Hall	14	8	6	Manchester, 80 km	476
Fortrose & Rosemarkie	16	6	5	Inverness, 40 km	616
Fota Island	15	7	6	Cork, 18 km	731
Frankfurter GC	16	7	8	Frankfurt, 5 km	331
Fränkische Schweiz	14	7	6	Nürnberg, 45 km	332
Frégate	15	7	7	Toulon Hyères, 50 km	209
Fulford	17	7	8	Leeds, 35 km	477
Fürstliches Hofgut Kolnhausen	14	7	6	Frankfurt, 60 km	333
Gainsborough-Karsten Lakes	14	8	6	Humberside, 28 km	478
Galway Bay	14	7	6	Shannon, 65 km	732
Galway GC	13	6	6	Shannon, 80 km	733
Ganton	19	8	5	Leeds, 60 km	479
Garmisch-Partenkirchen	14	6	7	München, 110 km	334
Gelpenberg	14	4	5	Eelde, 50 km	808
Gendersteyn	15	7	7	Eindhoven, 10 km	809
Genève	17	7	8	Genève-Cointrin, 10 km	993
Girona	13	7	5	Barcelona, 120 km	918
Glasson	16	7	7	Dublin, 120 km	734
Glen	14	7	7	Edinburgh, 30 km	617
Gleneagles King's	18	9	7	Edinburgh, 70 km	618

Gleneagles *Monarch's*	17	9	7	Edinburgh, 70 km	619
Gleneagles *Queen's*	15	9	7	Edinburgh, 70 km	620
Goes	15	3	6	Rotterdam, 80 km	810
Gog Magog *Old Course*	15	7	8	Stansted, 48 km	480
Golf de la Gruyère	14	7	6	Genève, 120 km	994
Golspie	14	5	4	Inverness, 90 km	621
Gouverneur (Le) *Le Breuil*	16	7	6	Lyon-Satolas, 40 km	210
Gouverneur (Le) *Montaplan*	14	7	6	Lyon-Satolas, 40 km	211
Graafschap	15	7	6	Amsterdam-Schiphol, 110 km	811
Granada	14	6	5	Granada, 15 km	919
Grand Ducal de Luxembourg	13	6	7	Luxembourg, 1 km	95
Grande Bastide (La)	16	6	6	Nice, 26 km	212
Grande-Motte (La) *Les Flamants Roses*	16	6	4	Montpellier-Fréjorgues, 10 km	213
Grantown on Spey	14	6	7	Inverness, 56 km	622
Granville *Les Dunes*	14	4	4	Bréville, 4 km	214
Grasse	13	7	6	Nice, 37 km	215
Greenore	14	6	5	Dublin, 104 km	735
Grenoble Bresson	17	7	6	Grenoble, 50 km	216
Grevelingenhout	14	7	4	Rotterdam, 65 km	812
Guadalhorce	14	7	6	Málaga, 4 km	920
Guadalmina *Sur*	14	7	7	Málaga, 64 km	921
Guerville	14	7	4	Orly, 75 km	217
Gujan-Mestras	15	7	6	Bordeaux-Mérignac, 50 km	218
Gullane *No 1*	17	8	7	Edinburgh, 50 km	623
Gut Kaden *Platz B + Platz C*	17	7	6	Hamburg, 20 km	335
Gut Ludwigsberg	15	6	6	München, 70 km	336
Gut Rieden	14	7	6	München, 70 km	337
Gut Thailing	16	7	5	München, 65 km	338
Gut Waldhof	17	7	5	Hamburg, 27 km	339
Haagsche	18	7	8	Amsterdam-Schiphol, 45 km	813
Hadley Wood	16	7	7	Heathrow, 48 km	481
Haggs Castle	15	7	9	Glasgow, 9 km	624
Hainaut *Bruyere-Quesnoy*	15	7	5	St-Ghislain, 10 km	79
Hamburg-Ahrensburg	17	8	7	Hamburg, 20 km	340
Hamburg-Holm	15	6	6	Hamburg, 15 km	341
Hanau-Wilhelmsbad	15	6	6	Frankfurt, 25 km	342
Hankley Common	16	6	6	Heathrow, 50 km	482
Hannover	16	7	7	Hannover, 12 km	343
Hardelot *Les Pins*	16	6	6	Lille, 153 km	219
Haut-Poitou	14	6	4	Poitiers-Biart, 25 km	220
Hawkstone Park *Hawkstone*	15	8	7	Manchester, 65 km	483
Hayling	16	7	7	Southampton, 45 km	484
Hechingen-Hohenzollern	14	6	6	Stuttgart, 50 km	344
Henley	14	6	7	Heathrow, 48 km	485
Herkenbosch	16	7	6	Maastricht, 35 km	814
Hermitage	15	6	7	Dublin, 10 km	736
Herreria	15	6	6	Madrid, 60 km	922
Hertfordshire (The)	15	7	7	Heathrow, 55 km	486
Hetzenhof	14	7	6	Stuttgart, 60 km	345
Hever	14	8	8	Gatwick, 25 km	487
High Post	15	6	7	Heathrow, 130 km	488
Hillside	18	7	7	Manchester, 80 km	489
Hilversum	16	7	7	Amsterdam-Schiphol, 40 km	815
Hindhead	16	7	6	Heathrow, 55 km	490

1014

Hof Trages	16	7	5	Frankfurt, 45 km	346
Hoge Kleij	15	6	7	Amsterdam-Schiphol, 50 km	816
Hohenpähl	15	7	6	München, 73 km	347
Hoisdorf	13	6	6	Hamburg, 30 km	348
Holyhead	16	7	5	Manchester, 150 km	681
Hossegor	16	6	6	Biarritz-Parme, 28 km	221
Hubbelrath	17	8	6	Düsseldorf, 18 km	349
Hunstanton	17	7	6	Stansted, 150 km	491
Huntercombe	14	6	7	Heathrow, 65 km	492
Huntly	14	6	6	Aberdeen, 56 km	625
Iffeldorf	16	7	6	München, 70 km	350
Ilkley	18	7	6	Leeds, 15 km	493
Im Chiemgau	14	7	6	München, 100 km	351
Interlaken	14	6	6	Bern, 59 km	995
Ipswich (Purdis Heath)	16	7	7	Stansted, 84 km	494
Isernhagen	15	7	6	Hannover, 17 km	352
Islantilla	16	8	8	Faro (Portugal), 69 km	923
Isle Adam (L')	16	7	4	Charles-de-Gaulle, 23 km	222
Isle of Purbeck	16	7	6	Bournemouth, 16 km	495
Jakobsberg	15	7	6	Frankfurt, 100 km	353
Jarama R.A.C.E.	13	7	6	Madrid, 20 km	924
John O'Gaunt	16	7	6	Luton 28 km/Heathrow, 65 km	496
Joyenval Marly	16	8	7	Orly, 32 km	223
Joyenval Retz	15	8	7	Orly, 32 km	224
K Club	17	8	8	Dublin, 44 km	737
Keerbergen	14	7	6	Brussel (Bruxelles), 15 km	80
Kempferhof (Le)	18	8	6	Strasbourg-Entzheim, 14 km	225
Kennemer	18	8	8	Amsterdam-Schiphol, 20 km	817
Kilkenny	13	7	6	Dublin, 110 km	738
Killarney *Killeen Course*	16	7	8	Cork, 105 km	739
Killarney *Mahony's Point*	15	7	8	Cork, 105 km	740
Killorglin	14	6	5	Cork, 126 km	741
Kilmarnock (Barassie)	17	6	8	Glasgow, 50 km	626
Kingussie	15	4	5	Inverness, 70 km	627
Kirkistown Castle	15	6	5	Belfast, 55 km	783
Knock	15	7	6	Belfast, 21 km	784
Köln	17	6	7	Köln-Bonn, 25 km	354
Königsfeld	13	6	6	Stuttgart, 100 km	355
Krefelder	17	7	7	Düsseldorf, 30 km	356
La Boulie (R.C.F.) *La Vallée*	15	7	8	Orly, 20 km	226
La Cala *Norte*	17	8	6	Málaga, 35 km	925
La Cala *Sur*	16	8	6	Málaga, 35 km	926
La Dehesa	14	7	4	Madrid, 35 km	927
La Duquesa	13	7	6	Gibraltar, 30 km	928
La Manga *Norte*	15	7	7	Alicante, 110 km	929
La Manga *Oeste*	14	7	7	Alicante, 110 km	930
La Manga *Sur*	14	7	7	Alicante, 110 km	931
La Moraleja *La Moraleja 1*	15	7	8	Madrid, 15 km	932
La Moraleja *La Moraleja 2*	16	7	8	Madrid, 15 km	933
La Moye	17	7	8	Jersey, 3 km	497
La Quinta	15	8	7	Málaga, 64 km	934
La Sella	15	6	5	Valencia, 70 km	935
La Zagaleta	16	7	7	Malaga, 65 km	936
Lacanau	14	6	4	Bordeaux-Mérignac, 55 km	227

Ladybank	17	7	5	Edinburgh, 56 km	628
Lahinch	18	6	6	Shannon, 55 km	742
Lanark	16	6	5	Edinburgh, 48 km	629
Largue (La)	15	7	4	Bâle-Mulhouse, 35 km	228
Las Brisas	18	7	7	Málaga, 60 km	937
Lauro	13	7	5	Málaga, 10 km	938
Lausanne	16	7	7	Genève-Cointrin, 60 km	996
Lauswolt	14	6	7	Groningen-Eelde, 50 km	818
Laval-Changé *La Chabossière*	14	7	5	Nantes, 100 km	229
Lee Valley	13	7	6	Cork, 14 km	743
Lerma	17	7	4	Madrid, 200 km	939
Letham Grange *Old Course*	15	7	5	Edinburgh, 110 km	630
Leven	16	6	6	Edinburgh, 56 km	631
Lichtenau-Weickershof	15	7	6	Nürnberg, 40 km	357
Limburg	16	7	4	Brussel (Bruxelles), 75 km	81
Limère	17	6	5	Orly, 130 km	230
Limerick County	15	7	6	Shannon, 40 km	744
Lindau-Bad Schachen	14	7	8	Zürich, 130 km/München, 180 km	358
Linden Hall	17	8	6	Newcastle, 40 km	498
Lindrick	17	6	6	Leeds/Bradford, 40 km	499
Liphook	16	7	6	Gatwick, 48 km	500
Lisburn	15	7	6	Belfast, 14 km	785
Littlestnen	14	6	5	Gatwick, 110 km	501
Los Arqueros	14	6	7	Málaga, 65 km	940
Los Naranjos	16	7	7	Málaga, 62 km	941
Lothianburn	14	6	8	Edinburgh, 12 km	632
Luffness New	16	5	6	Edinburgh, 30 km	633
Lugano	15	7	8	Lugano (Agno), 2 km	997
Lundin	16	6	7	Edinburgh, 55 km	634
Lüneburger Heide	17	7	5	Hamburg, 70 km	359
Luttrellstown	15	7	7	Dublin, 10 km	745
Luzern	13	6	7	Zürich, 70 km	998
Lytham Green Drive	15	7	8	Manchester, 100 km	502
Machrie	17	7	7	Islay Airport, 5 km	635
Machrihanish	18	6	4	Glasgow (+ ferry or air)	636
Madeira	14	7	5	Funchal, 6 km	842
Main-Taunus	13	7	6	Frankfurt, 20 km	360
Maison Blanche	14	7	5	Genève-Cointrin, 10 km	231
Makila Golf Club	14	6	8	Biarritz-Parme, 4 km	232
Malaga	13	4	6	Málaga, 3 km	942
Malahide *Red + Blue + Yellow*	13	7	8	Dublin, 7 km	746
Malone	13	6	6	Belfast, 16 km	786
Manchester	16	7	7	Manchester, 20 km	503
Mannings Heath *Waterfall Course*	14	8	6	Gatwick, 18 km	504
Manor House (Castle Combe)	15	8	7	Bristol, 45 km	505
Marbella	15	7	8	Málaga, 51 km	943
Märkischer Potsdam	14	7	6	Berlin, 45 km	361
Marriott St Pierre *Old Course*	16	8	7	Cardiff, 45 km	682
Masia Bach	15	7	6	Barcelona, 40 km	944
Maspalomas	16	7	8	Las Palmas, 30 km	945
Massereene	14	5	6	Belfast, 7 km	787
Mazamet-La Barouge	13	5	4	Toulouse-Blagnac, 90 km	233
Mediterraneo	16	7	6	Valencia-Manises, 70 km	946
Médoc *Les Châteaux*	17	7	5	Bordeaux-Mérignac, 20 km	234

1016

Médoc *Les Vignes*	15	7	5	Bordeaux-Mérignac, 20 km	235
Memmingen Gut Westerhart	14	6	6	München, 140	362
Mendip	15	5	7	Bristol, 30 km	506
Mere	15	7	7	Manchester, 8 km	507
Mijas *Los Lagos*	16	6	7	Málaga, 20 km	947
Mijas *Los Olivos*	13	6	7	Málaga, 20 km	948
Mittelrheinischer	15	7	7	Frankfurt, 100 km	363
Monifieth	17	7	7	Edinburgh, 96 km	637
Mont-Garni	13	7	6	Bruxelles, 70 km	82
Montado	13	7	6	Lisboa, 50 km	843
Monte Mayor	13	5	5	Málaga, 65 km	949
Montecastillo	17	8	7	Jerez, 7 km	950
Montenmedio	15	7	7	Jerez, 70 km	951
Montpellier-Massane	16	7	5	Montpellier-Fréjorgues, 14 km	236
Montreux	13	6	5	Genève-Cointrin, 85 km	999
Montrose	17	5	6	Aberdeen, 72 km	638
Moor Park *High Course*	17	8	7	Heathrow, 16 km	508
Moortown	18	7	7	Leeds, 10 km	509
Moray	17	5	5	Inverness, 60 km	639
Motzener See	18	8	6	Berlin, 45 km	364
Mount Juliet	18	9	8	Dublin, 136 km	747
Mount Wolsley	13	6	5	Dublin, 93 km	748
Muirfield	19	7	6	Edinburgh, 40 km	640
Mülheim	13	6	7	Düsseldorf, 12 km	365
Mullingar	14	5	5	Dublin, 90 km	749
München-Riedhof	16	7	7	München, 90 km	366
Münchner-Strasslach	14	6	7	München, 80 km	367
Murcar	15	6	6	Aberdeen, 12 km	641
Murrayshall	14	7	8	Edinburgh, 72 km	642
Nahetal	14	7	6	Frankfurt, 75 km	368
Nairn	19	7	8	Inverness, 9 km	643
Nairn Dunbar	15	6	7	Inverness, 15 km	644
National *L'Albatros*	18	6	6	Orly, 32 km	237
Neckartal	16	6	7	Stuttgart, 25 km	369
Nefyn & District - G	16	6	5	Manchester, 180 km	683
Neguri	17	7	7	Bilbao, 12 km	952
Neuchâtel	14	6	7	Genève-Cointrin, 125 km	1000
Neuhof	15	7	7	Frankfurt, 18 km	370
New Golf Deauville *Rouge/Blanc*	15	7	8	Charles-de-Gaulle, 200 km	238
Newbury & Crookham	15	6	7	Heathrow, 80 km	510
Newcastle West	13	7	5	Shannon, 55 km	750
Newport - G	15	6	7	Cardiff, 30 km	684
Niederbüren	13	7	7	Zürich-Kloten, 80 km	1001
Nîmes-Campagne	16	7	6	Nîmes-Garons, 2 km	239
Noordwijk	18	7	8	Amsterdam Schiphol, 35 km	819
North Berwick	18	7	8	Edinburgh, 50 km	645
North Foreland	13	7	7	Gatwick, 140 km	511
North Hants	17	7	6	Heathrow, 40 km	512
Notts (Hollinwell)	18	6	6	East Midlands, 40 km	513
Novo Sancti Petri	16	7	7	Jerez, 50 km	953
Nunspeet *North/East*	15	5	3	Amsterdam-Schiphol, 85 km	820
Obere Alp	14	7	7	Stuttgart, 135 km	371
Oberfranken	17	6	5	Nürnberg, 80 km	372
Oberschwaben Bad Waldsee	15	6	6	Stuttgart, 140 km	373

Old Head	15	7	7	Cork, 20 km	751
Olivar de la Hinojosa	13	7	8	Madrid, 1 km	954
Omaha Beach *La Mer/Le Bocage*	14	7	5	Caen, 40 km	240
Oostende	15	7	7	Brussel (Bruxelles), 115 km	83
Oosterhout	15	7	7	Amsterdam-Schiphol, 100 km	821
Opio Valbonne	13	6	7	Nice Côte d'Azur, 29 km	241
Orchardleigh	17	7	7	Bristol, 32 km	514
Ormskirk	14	6	4	Manchester, 48 km	515
Öschberghof	15	7	7	Stuttgart, 100 km	374
Osona Montanya	14	7	4	Barcelona, 80 km	955
Oudenaarde	14	6	6	Brussel (Bruxelles), 85 km	84
Ozoir-la-Ferrière *Château/Monthéty*	13	7	5	Charles-de-Gaulle, 47 km	242
Palingbeek	13	6	6	Lille, 60 km	85
Palmares	13	7	5	Faro, 75 km	844
Pals	16	7	6	Barcelona, 120 km	956
Panmure	17	6	5	Edinburgh, 100 km	646
Pannal	15	6	7	Leeds, 20 km	516
Panoramica	14	6	4	Barcelona, 200 km - Valencia, 150 km	957
Paris International	16	7	5	Charles-de-Gaulle, 15 km	243
Parkstone	16	7	8	Bournemouth, 12 km	517
Patriziale Ascona	15	7	7	Lugano, 40 km	1002
Patshull Park Hotel	13	8	8	Birmingham, 48 km	518
Pedreña	14	6	5	Santander, 7 km	958
Penha Longa	15	7	8	Lisboa, 25 km	845
Penina	14	7	8	Faro, 60 km	846
Pennard - G	18	6	6	Cardiff, 50 km	685
Peralada	16	6	5	Perpignan (France), 60 km	959
Perranporth	16	6	6	Plymouth, 80 km	519
Pessac	13	7	7	Bordeaux-Mérignac, 10 km	244
Peterhead	15	5	4	Aberdeen, 43 km	647
Pineda	15	7	9	Sevilla, 15 km	960
Pinheiros Altos	14	8	8	Faro, 12 km	847
Pinnau	14	6	6	Hamburg, 25 km	375
Pitlochry	14	6	7	Edinburgh, 105 km	648
Playa Serena	13	6	4	Almería, 33 km	961
Pleasington	16	8	6	Manchester, 45 km	520
Pléneuf-Val-André	17	7	5	Rennes, 80 km	245
Ploemeur Océan	15	7	6	Lorient Lann-Bihoué, 4 km	246
Poniente	13	6	5	Palma, 23 km	962
Pont Royal	16	6	5	Marseille-Marignane, 50 km	247
Porcelaine (La)	14	6	4	Limoges-Bellegarde, 15 km	248
Pornic	15	6	6	Nantes-Atlantique, 41 km	249
Portal *Championship*	15	8	7	Manchester, 30 km	521
Portmarnock	19	8	8	Dublin, 8 km	752
Portmarnock Links	17	7	8	Dublin, 8 km	753
Portpatrick (Dunskey)	15	6	7	Glasgow, 150 km	649
Portsalon	16	5	5	Belfast, 160 km	754
Portstewart *Strand Course*	16	7	7	Belfast, 64 km	788
Powerscourt	15	7	7	Dublin, 20 km	755
Powfoot	16	6	4	Glasgow, 130 km	650
Praia d'El Rey	17	7	5	Lisboa, 75 km	848
Prestbury	17	8	7	Manchester, 15 km	522
Prestwick	18	6	7	Glasgow, 55 km	651
Prestwick St Nicholas	16	6	7	Glasgow, 55 km	652

1018

Prince's *Himalayas-Shore*	13	6	4	Gatwick, 145 km	523
Puerta de Hierro	16	8	9	Madrid, 15 km	963
Pula	13	6	5	Palma, 63 km	964
Purmerend	16	7	7	Amsterdam-Schiphol, 25 km	822
Pyle & Kenfig - G	17	7	5	Cardiff, 25 km	686
Quinta da Beloura	14	8	7	Lisboa, 26 km	849
Quinta da Marinha	13	7	7	Lisboa, 28 km	850
Quinta do Lago *B/C*	15	7	8	Faro, 10 km	851
Quinta do Lago *Ria Formosa*	15	7	8	Faro, 10 km	852
Quinta do Peru	16	7	5	Lisboa, 46 km	853
R.S.H.E. Club de Campo	18	7	6	Madrid, 20 km	965
Raray (Château de) *La Licorne*	14	6	4	Roissy, 34 km	250
Rathsallagh	15	7	6	Dublin, 80 km	756
Ravenstein	17	8	7	Bruxelles, 12 km	86
Rebetz	16	6	4	Charles-de-Gaulle, 67 km	251
Reichsstadt Bad Windsheim	14	6	7	Nürnberg, 50 km	376
Reichswald-Nürnberg	17	7	7	Nürnberg, 2 km	377
Reims-Champagne	13	7	6	Charles-de-Gaulle, 145 km	252
Rigenée	14	7	6	Bruxelles, 35 km	87
Rijk van Nijmegen *Nijmeegse Baan*	14	6	5	Eindhoven, 65 km	823
Rinkven *Red - White*	14	6	5	Antwerpen, 30 km	88
Rio Real	13	6	7	Malaga, 43 km.	966
Riviéra Golf Club	13	7	8	Nice Côte d'Azur, 32 km	253
Rochefort-Chisan	14	6	4	Orly, 35 km	254
Rolls of Monmouth (The) - G	15	6	6	Cardiff, 65 km	687
Roncemay	15	7	4	Orly, 135 km	255
Rosapenna	16	7	6	Sligo, 150 km / Belfast, 160 km	757
Rosendael	15	7	7	Amsterdam-Schiphol, 90 km	824
Ross-on-Wye	15	5	6	Birmingham, 95 km	524
Rosslare	13	5	6	Dublin, 160 km	758
Roxburghe (The)	15	7	7	Edinburgh, 90 km	653
Royal Aberdeen *Balgownie Links*	18	7	8	Aberdeen, 10 km	654
Royal Ashdown Forest	14	7	6	Gatwick, 20 km	525
Royal Belfast	15	7	7	Belfast, 30 km	789
Royal Birkdale (The)	19	9	7	Manchester, 80 km	526
Royal Burgess	16	7	9	Edinburgh, 4 km	655
Royal Cinque Ports	17	6	5	Gatwick, 145 km	527
Royal County Down	19	6	7	Belfast, 48 km	790
Royal Cromer	15	7	6	Stansted, 120 km	528
Royal Dornoch	19	7	7	Inverness, 82 km	656
Royal Dublin	16	7	7	Dublin, 13 km	759
Royal Guernsey	16	7	7	Guernsey, 8 km	529
Royal Jersey	16	7	8	Jersey, 10 km	530
Royal Latem	15	8	6	Brussel, 65 km	89
Royal Liverpool (Hoylake)	18	8	7	Liverpool, 35 km	531
Royal Lytham & St Anne's	19	7	8	Manchester, 100 km	532
Royal Mid-Surrey *Outer*	14	7	8	Heathrow, 17 km	533
Royal Mougins	17	7	8	Nice, 29 km	256
Royal Musselburgh	16	8	7	Edinburgh, 20 km	657
Royal North Devon (Westward Ho!)	18	6	6	Plymouth, 90 km	534
Royal Porthcawl - G	19	7	5	Cardiff, 25 km	688
Royal Portrush *Dunluce Links*	19	7	7	Belfast, 80 km	791
Royal Portrush *Valley*	13	7	7	Belfast, 80 km	792
Royal St David's - G	18	6	5	Manchester, 120 km	689

Royal St George's	19	7	5	Gatwick, 145 km	535
Royal Troon Old Course	19	7	7	Glasgow, 50 km	658
Royal West Norfolk (Brancaster)	17	7	6	Stansted, 150 km	536
Royal Winchester	15	6	8	Heathrow, 90 km	537
Royal Zoute	18	7	7	Brussel (Bruxelles), 108 km	90
Rudding Park	15	8	8	Leeds, 20 km	538
S. Lourenço	17	6	8	Faro, 12 km	854
Sablé-Solesmes *La Forêt/La Rivière*	16	7	4	Orly, 250 km	257
Saint-Cloud *Vert*	14	7	7	Orly, 25 km	258
Saint-Donat	15	7	8	Nice, 37 km	259
Saint-Endréol	15	7	4	Nice, 70 km	260
Saint-Germain	17	7	7	Orly, 30 km	261
Saint-Jean-de-Monts	16	6	5	Nantes, 68 km	262
Saint-Laurent	14	7	5	Lorient Lann-Bihoué, 40 km	263
Saint-Nom-la-Bretèche *Bleu*	15	8	8	Orly, 30 km	264
Saint-Nom-la-Bretèche *Rouge*	16	8	8	Orly, 30 km	265
Saint-Thomas	14	7	5	Béziers-Vias, 15 km	266
Sainte-Baume (La)	13	7	6	Marseille-Marignane, 73 km	267
Sainte-Maxime	13	7	7	Toulon, 55 km	268
Salgados	14	7	7	Faro, 55 km	855
San Roque	17	8	6	Gibraltar, 15 km	967
San Sebastián	14	6	6	Biarritz, 20 km	968
Sand Moor	14	7	7	Leeds, 10 km	539
Sandiway	17	5	7	Manchester, 35 km	540
Sant Cugat	13	6	5	Barcelona, 35 km	969
Santa Ponsa	13	6	7	Palma, 26 km	970
Sart-Tilman	16	7	7	Liège, 20 km	91
Saunton *East Course*	18	7	6	Plymouth, 90 km	541
Savenay	15	6	4	Nantes-Atlantique, 40 km	269
Scharmützelsee *Arnold Palmer*	16	8	7	Berlin, 80 km	378
Scharmützelsee *Nick Faldo*	18	8	7	Berlin, 80 km	379
Scheibenhardt	13	7	7	Frankfurt, 110 km	380
Schloss Braunfels	16	7	7	Frankfurt, 85 km	381
Schloss Egmating	15	7	7	München, 55 km	382
Schloss Klingenburg	14	6	6	München, 150 km	383
Schloss Langenstein	16	8	7	Stuttgart, 150 km	384
Schloss Liebenstein *Gelb + Blau*	16	8	7	Stuttgart, 40 km	385
Schloss Lüdersburg *Old/New*	17	7	6	Hamburg, 50 km	386
Schloss Myllendonk	16	7	7	Düsseldorf, 25 km	387
Schloss Wilkendorf	15	7	5	Berlin, 65 km	388
Schönenberg	14	7	6	Zürich-Kloten, 30 km	1003
Scotscraig	16	6	6	Edinburgh, 95 km	659
Seacroft	17	6	4	Humberside, 80 km	542
Seapoint	15	6	6	Dublin, 48 km	760
Seascale	18	5	4	Manchester, 200 km	543
Seignosse	17	7	7	Biarritz-Parme, 39 km	270
Semlin am See	14	8	7	Berlin, 70 km	389
Servanes	13	7	7	Marseille-Marignane, 57 km	271
Sevilla	17	7	8	Sevilla, 10 km	971
Shanklin & Sandown	15	7	6	Southampton, 65 km	544
Shannon	13	6	6	Shannon, 1 km	761
Sherborne	15	6	7	Bristol, 45 km	545
Sheringham	15	7	6	Stansted, 120 km	546
Sherwood Forest	17	7	6	East Midlands, 40 km	547

1020

Shiskine (Blackwaterfoot)	17	5	5	Glasgow	660
Silloth-on-Solway	18	7	4	Glasgow, 200 km	548
Sint Nicolaasga	15	7	5	Amsterdam Schiphol, 120 km	825
Slaley Hall	17	8	7	Newcastle, 35 km	549
Slieve Russell	15	8	6	Dublin, 128 km	762
Son Antem	14	7	6	Palma, 10 km	972
Son Vida	14	6	7	Palma, 8 km	973
Sonnenalp	16	7	7	München, 190 km	390
Sotogrande	18	7	6	Málaga, 120 km	974
Soufflenheim	16	7	4	Strasbourg, 50 km	272
Southerndown	16	7	7	Cardiff, 36 km	690
Southerness	18	6	5	Glasgow, 155 km	661
Southport & Ainsdale	18	7	7	Manchester, 80 km	550
Spa (Les Fagnes)	17	7	7	Liège, 25 km	92
Spérone	17	7	5	Figari, 27 km	273
Spiegelven	14	7	8	Maastricht, 25 km	93
St Andrews Eden Course	14	8	8	Edinburgh, 80 km	662
St Andrews Jubilee Course	16	8	8	Edinburgh, 80 km	663
St Andrews New Course	17	8	8	Edinburgh, 80 km	664
St Andrews Old Course	18	8	8	Edinburgh, 80 km	665
St Enodoc Church Course	18	7	4	Plymouth, 80 km	551
St George's Hill	17	7	7	Heathrow, 28 km	552
St Helen's Bay	14	6	6	Dublin, 160 km	763
St Margaret's	16	7	7	Dublin, 6 km	764
St Mellion Nicklaus Course	17	9	7	Plymouth, 16 km	553
St. Dionys	17	7	6	Hamburg, 60 km	391
St. Eurach	16	7	6	München, 70 km	392
Stoke Poges	17	8	8	Heathrow, 24 km	554
Stolper Heide	17	7	5	Berlin, 15 km	393
Stoneham	15	7	8	Southampton, 4 km	555
Stonehaven	13	5	5	Aberdeen, 25 km	666
Strasbourg Illkirch Jaune + Rouge	13	7	6	Strasbourg, 12 km	274
Strathaven	15	5	6	Glasgow, 35 km	667
Stuttgarter Solitude	17	5	5	Stuttgart, 25 km	394
Sunningdale New Course	18	8	8	Heathrow, 20 km	556
Sunningdale Old Course	18	8	8	Heathrow, 20 km	557
Sybrook	15	6	6	Enschede Twente, 5 km	826
Tain	17	6	6	Inverness, 65 km	668
Tandridge	14	7	6	Gatwick, 18 km	558
Taulane	15	7	4	Nice, 75 km	275
Tegernseer Bad Wiessee	15	7	8	München, 85 km	395
Tenby - G	18	7	6	Cardiff, 75 km	691
The Island	15	7	7	Dublin, 8 km	765
Thetford	14	7	5	Stansted, 90 km	559
Thorndon Park	14	7	6	Stansted, 37 km	560
Thornhill	15	6	5	Edinburgh, Glasgow, 109 km	669
Thorpeness	14	7	7	Stansted, 145 km	561
Thurlestone	16	6	4	Plymouth, 50 km	562
Torrequebrada	14	7	7	Málaga, 15 km	975
Toulouse Palmola	15	7	4	Toulouse-Blagnac, 40 km	276
Toulouse-Seilh Rouge	15	7	6	Toulouse-Blagnac, 8 km	277
Touquet (Le) La Mer	17	6	7	Lille-Lesquin, 151 km	278
Touraine	13	7	6	Tours-Saint-Symphorien, 25 km	279
Toxandria	14	7	6	Eindhoven, 40 km	827

Tralee	18	7	6	Cork, 120 km	766
Tramore	13	7	6	Cork, 120 km	767
Treudelberg	13	8	7	Hamburg, 6 km	396
Trevose *Championship*	17	7	7	Plymouth, 80 km	563
Troia	15	7	5	Lisboa, 42 km	856
Tullamore	15	6	5	Dublin, 96 km	768
Turnberry *Ailsa Course*	19	9	8	Glasgow, 80 km	670
Turnberry *Arran Course*	16	9	8	Glasgow, 80 km	671
Tutzing	15	7	6	München, 80 km	397
Ulzama	16	6	6	Pamplona, 28 km	976
Val de Sorne	14	7	5	Lyon-Satolas, 134 km	280
Val Queven	15	6	5	Lorient Lann-Bihoué, 3 km	281
Valderrama	19	8	6	Málaga, 120 km	977
Vale da Pinta	14	6	6	Faro, 42 km	857
Vaucouleurs (La) *Les Vallons*	15	7	4	Orly, 71 km	282
Vila Sol	14	7	7	Faro, 22 km	858
Vilamoura I *(Old Course)*	16	7	7	Faro, 22 km	859
Vilamoura II *(Pinhal)*	13	7	7	Faro, 22 km	860
Vilamoura III *(Laguna)*	14	7	7	Faro, 22 km	861
Villamartin	16	7	6	Alicante, 50 km	978
Villette d'Anthon *Les Sangliers*	17	6	4	Lyon-Satolas, 12 km	283
Volcans (Les)	14	6	5	Clermont-Ferrand, 19 km	284
Walddörfer	15	7	6	Hamburg, 20 km	398
Wallasey	17	7	7	Liverpool, 35 km	564
Walton Heath *New Course*	16	7	6	Gatwick, 15 km	565
Walton Heath *Old Course*	18	7	7	Gatwick, 15 km	566
Wantzenau (La)	16	6	6	Strasbourg, 27 km	285
Warrenpoint	13	6	5	Belfast, 75 km	793
Warwickshire (The)	15	7	8	Birmingham, 30 km	567
Waterford	14	6	6	Cork, 130 km / Dublin, 170 km	769
Waterford Castle	14	5	6	Cork, 130 km / Dublin, 170 km	770
Waterloo *La Marache*	16	8	7	Bruxelles, 20 km	94
Waterville	17	6	7	Cork	771
Wendlohe *A-Kurs + B-Kurs*	16	7	6	Hamburg, 10 km	399
Wentorf-Reinbeker	16	7	6	Hamburg, 40 km	400
Wentworth *East Course*	16	8	7	Heathrow, 20 km	568
Wentworth *West Course*	18	8	7	Heathrow, 20 km	569
West Berkshire	15	7	7	Heathrow, 80 km	570
West Cornwall	16	7	6	Plymouth, 120 km	571
West Hill	15	6	6	Heathrow, 44 km	572
West Kilbride	16	7	5	Glasgow, 50 km	672
West Lancashire	17	7	7	Manchester, 80 km	573
West Surrey	15	7	7	Gatwick, 15 km	574
West Sussex	18	7	6	Gatwick, 40 km	575
West Waterford	12	7	6	Cork, 80 km	772
Western Gailes	17	5	7	Glasgow, 50 km	673
Westerwood	14	8	6	Glasgow, 32 km	674
Weston-Super-Mare	16	6	7	Bristol, 25 km	576
Westport	15	7	7	Knock, 50 km	773
Whitekirk	15	7	7	Edinburgh, 50 km	675
Whittington Heath	17	6	7	Birmingham, 20 km	577
Wimereux	15	4	5	Lille-Lesquin, 143 km	286
Wittelsbacher	15	7	6	München, 80 km	401
Woburn *Dukes Course*	18	7	7	Heathrow, 70 km	578

1022

Woking	16	6	6	Heathrow, 38 km	579
Woodbridge	14	7	7	Stansted, 120 km	580
Woodbury Park *The Oaks*	15	9	6	Exeter, 10 km	581
Woodenbridge	16	7	6	Dublin, 88 km	774
Woodhall Spa	18	7	8	Humberside, 90 km	582
Woodstock	13	5	6	Shannon, 25 km	775
Worplesdon	16	7	6	Heathrow, 39 km	583
Wouwse Plantage	15	7	6	Eindhoven, 70 km	828
Wylihof	13	6	6	Zurich-Kloten, 110 km	1004
Yvelines *Les Chênes*	13	7	4	Orly, 48 km	287
Zaudin	16	7	6	Sevilla, 15 km	979
Zuid Limburgse	14	7	7	Maastricht, 25 km	829
Zumikon	15	7	6	Zurich-Kloten, 30 km	1005

1023